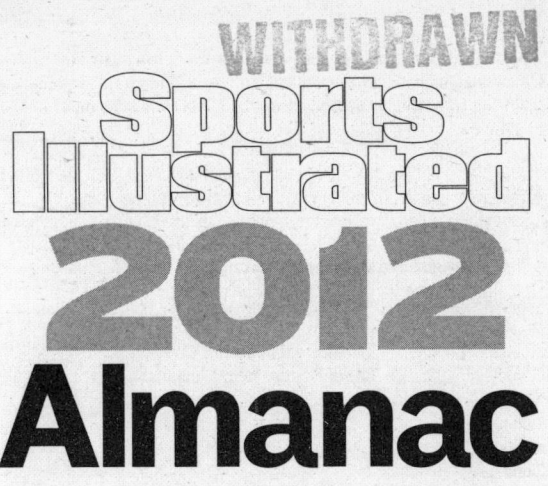

# Sports Illustrated 2012 Almanac

## By the Editors of Sports Illustrated

YEAR IN SPORTS
CALENDAR

BASEBALL

PRO
FOOTBALL

COLLEGE
FOOTBALL

PRO
BASKETBALL

COLLEGE
BASKETBALL

HOCKEY

OLYMPICS

TENNIS

GOLF

SOCCER

MOTOR
SPORTS

First Edition
ISBN10: 1-60320-903-4
ISBN 13: 978-1-60320-903-8

SPORTS ILLUSTRATED is a registered trademark of Time Inc.

*SPORTS ILLUSTRATED 2012 Almanac* was prepared by
Touchpoint Sports Publishing

| | |
|---|---|
| Managing Editor: Reed Richardson | Art Director: Barbara Chilenskas |
| Proofreader: Morin Bishop | Photo Editor: John Blackmar |

Cover photography credits:
AARON RODGERS: Al Tielemans
JUSTIN VERLANDER: Greg Nelson
HOPE SOLO : EPA/Peter Steffen
JIMMER FREDETTE: Kenny Crookston

Back cover photography credits:
ANDREW LUCK: John W. McDonough
MAYA MOORE : Bill Frakes
TIM THOMAS: David E. Klutho

Spine photography credit: DIRK NOWITZKI: Greg Nelson

## TIME INC. HOME ENTERTAINMENT

Publisher . . . . . . . . . . . . . . . . . . . . . . . . . . . . . . . . . . . . . . . . . . . . . . . . . . . . . . . . . . . . . . . . . Richard Fraiman
Vice President, Business Development & Strategy . . . . . . . . . . . . . . . . . . . . . . . . . .Steven Sandonato
Executive Director, Marketing Services . . . . . . . . . . . . . . . . . . . . . . . . . . . . . . . . . . . . . . . . . . Carol Pittard
Executive Director, Retail & Special Sales . . . . . . . . . . . . . . . . . . . . . . . . . . . . . . . . . . . . . . . Tom Mifsud
Executive Director, New Product Development . . . . . . . . . . . . . . . . . . . . . . . . . . . . . . . . . Peter Harper
Director, Bookazine Development & Marketing . . . . . . . . . . . . . . . . . . . . . . . . . . . . . Laura Adam
Publishing Director . . . . . . . . . . . . . . . . . . . . . . . . . . . . . . . . . . . . . . . . . . . . . . . . . . . . . . . . . . . . . .Joy Butts
Finance Director . . . . . . . . . . . . . . . . . . . . . . . . . . . . . . . . . . . . . . . . . . . . . . . . . . . . . . . . .Glenn Buonocore
Assistant General Counsel . . . . . . . . . . . . . . . . . . . . . . . . . . . . . . . . . . . . . . . . . . . . . . . . . . . . . Helen Wan
Assistant Director, Special Sales . . . . . . . . . . . . . . . . . . . . . . . . . . . . . . . . . . . . . . . . . . . . . . Ilene Schreider
Design & Prepress Manager . . . . . . . . . . . . . . . . . . . . . . . . . . . . . . . . . . . . . . . . . . Anne-Michelle Gallero
Book Production Manager . . . . . . . . . . . . . . . . . . . . . . . . . . . . . . . . . . . . . . . . . . .Susan Chodakiewicz
Brand Manager . . . . . . . . . . . . . . . . . . . . . . . . . . . . . . . . . . . . . . . . . . . . . . . . . . . . . . . . . . . Allison Parker
Associate Prepress Manager . . . . . . . . . . . . . . . . . . . . . . . . . . . . . . . . . . . . . . . . . Alex Voznesenskiy
Editorial Director . . . . . . . . . . . . . . . . . . . . . . . . . . . . . . . . . . . . . . . . . . . . . . . . . . . . . . . .Stephen Koepp

Special thanks: Christine Austin, Jeremy Biloon, Jim Childs, Rose Cirrincione, Jacqueline Fitzgerald, Carrie Hertan, Christine Font, Jenna Goldberg, Lauren Hall, Hillary Hirsch, Suzanne Janso, Mona Li, Amy Mangus, Robert Marasco, Kimberly Marshall, Any Migliaccio, Nina Mistry, Dave Rozzelle, Ilene Schreider, Adriana Tierno, Vanessa Wu

We welcome your comments and suggestions about Sports Illustrated. Please write to us at: Sports Illustrated, Attention: Book Editors, P.O. Box 11016, Des Moines, IA 50336-1016
If you would like to order any of our hardcover Collector's Edition books, please call us at 1-800-327-6388. (Monday through Friday, 7:00 a.m.- 8:00 p.m. or Saturday, 7:00 a.m.- 6:00 p.m. Central Time)

# CONTENTS

THE YEAR IN SPORTS   by Hank Hersch ...........................................................................7

BASEBALL   by Merrell Noden .........................................................................................17

PRO FOOTBALL   by Hank Hersch ...............................................................................95

COLLEGE FOOTBALL   by B.J. Schecter.....................................................................183

PRO BASKETBALL   by Chris Mannix .........................................................................249

COLLEGE BASKETBALL   by B.J. Schecter................................................................285

HOCKEY   by Mark Beech ...............................................................................................327

OLYMPICS   by Merrell Noden.......................................................................................369

TENNIS.................................................................................................................................391

GOLF.....................................................................................................................................413

SOCCER...............................................................................................................................441

MOTOR SPORTS...............................................................................................................451

HORSE RACING................................................................................................................469

BOXING................................................................................................................................481

NCAA SPORTS...................................................................................................................495

TRACK AND FIELD..........................................................................................................507

SWIMMING.........................................................................................................................519

MISCELLANEOUS SPORTS...........................................................................................529

AWARDS ..............................................................................................................................551

OBITUARIES.......................................................................................................................555

2012 MAJOR EVENTS.....................................................................................................559

In compiling the *Sports Illustrated 2012 Almanac*, the editors would like to extend their gratitude to Robert Yalen as well as to the following organizations for their help in providing information and materials relating to their sports: Major League Baseball; Elias Sports Bureau, the Canadian Football League; the National Football League, the National Collegiate Athletic Association; the National Basketball Association; the National Hockey League; the Association of Tennis Professionals; the Women's Tennis Association; the U.S. Tennis Association; the U.S. Golf Association; the Ladies Professional Golf Association; the Professional Golfers Association; National Thoroughbred Racing Association; the Breeders' Cup; Churchill Downs; the New York Racing Association, Inc.; the Jockey's Guild, Inc.; the International Motor Sports Association; the National Association for Stock Car Auto Racing; the Professional Bowlers Association; the United Soccer Leagues; Major League Soccer; the Fédération Internationale de Futbol Association; the U.S. Soccer Federation; the U.S. Olympic Committee; USA Track & Field; U.S. Swimming; U.S. Diving; U.S. Skiing; U.S. Figure Skating Association; U.S. Curling; the Iditarod Trail Committee; USA Gymnastics; U.S. Handball Association; the Lacrosse Foundation; the American Power Boat Association; the Unlimited Hydroplane Racing Association; the Professional Rodeo Cowboys Association; U.S. Rowing; the Amateur Softball Association of America; U.S. Speed Skating; U.S. Rugby Football Union; USA Triathlon; the National Archery Association; USA Wrestling; the U.S. Squash Racquets Association; the U.S. Polo Association and the U.S. Volleyball Association.

The following sources were consulted in gathering information:

**Baseball** mlb.com, worldseries.com, baseballhalloffame.org, baseball-reference.com, *Associated Press* (LCS, WS game recaps)

**Pro Football** nfl.com, superbowl.com, profootballhof.com, cfl.ca, greycup.cfl.ca

**College Football** ncaasports.com, heisman.com, *Official 2011 NCAA Division I-A and I-AA Football Records Book, Official 2011 Division II and III Football Records Book*

**Pro Basketball** nba.com, hoophall.com

**College Basketball** ncaasports.com, *Official 2012 NCAA Division I Men's Basketball Records Book, Official 2012 NCAA Division I Women's Basketball Records Book, Official 2012 NCAA Division II and III Men's Basketball Records Book*

**Hockey** nhl.com, hhof.com, ushockeyhall.com

**Tennis** atptennis.com, sonyericssonwtatour.com, usopen.org, australianopen.com, wimbledon.org, rolandgarros.com, masters-cup.com, daviscup.com, fedcup.com, tennisfame.com

**Golf** pgatour.com, masters.org, usopen.org, usga.org, opengolf.com, pga.com, lpga.com, knc.com, ussenioropen.com, usamateur.org, rydercup.com, walkercup.org, curtiscup.org, pinggolf.com

**Boxing** wbaonline.com, wbcboxing.com, ibf-usba-boxing.com, ibhof.com, thering-online.com, usaboxing.org, olympic.org

**Horse Racing** ntra.com, equibase.com, bloodhorse.com, kentuckyderby.com, preakness.com, belmontstakes.nyra.com

**Motor Sports** nascar.com, formula1.com, indycar.com, americanlemans.com, lemans.org, champcarworldseries.com, indy500.com, daytona24hr.com

**Soccer** fifa.com, mlsnet.com, ussoccer.com, soccernet.com, uslsoccer.com,

**NCAA Sports** ncaasports.com

**Olympics** olympic.org, usoc.org

**Track and Field** iaaf.org, usatf.org, usoc.org

**Swimming** fina.org, usaswimming.org, usoc.org

**Miscellaneous Sports** letour.fr, usarchery.org, pba.com, fide.com, worldcurling.org, usacurl.org, usacycling.org, iditarod.com, usfigureskating.org, isu.org, fig-gymnastics.com, usa-gymnastics.org, ushandball.org, uscla.com, nll.com, littleleague.org, us-polo.org, prorodeo.org, usrowing.org, usarugby.org, rugbyworldcup.com, amnrl.com, fis-ski.com, asasoftball.com, us-squash.org, ironmanlive.com, usatriathlon.org, fivb.org, usavolleyball.org, themat.com

**Obituaries** *Associated Press*

EZRA SHAW

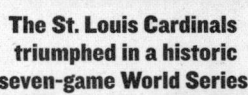

The St. Louis Cardinals triumphed in a historic seven-game World Series

# The Year In Sports

# Quieting the Doubters

## Underdogs, longshots, and dark horses had a very good year in 2011, while dream teams often fell flat

### BY HANK HERSCH

ONE WAS THE BARREL-SHAPED definition of a journeyman when he finally got the starting job, bouncing from nine teams in five leagues and fresh off yet another stint in the minors. Another was an All-Star in 10 of his 13 seasons, once even an MVP, but still panned more than prized, cast as insufficiently tough to ever deliver when it mattered most. A third went unrecruited out of high school by major programs and so spent two years at junior college, then languished on the bench as a pro while a legend strutted and fretted his final hours on the tundra. Dismissed, derided, denied—the stars of 2011 fell from some of the more unexpected corners of the sky.

Not to mention the most shocking bolt from the blue: the indomitable Cardinals. They erased a National League record 10½-game deficit in the month of August, overcame the favored Phillies and Brewers in the playoffs and were twice down to their final strike against the Rangers in Game 6 of the World Series. But third baseman David Freese delivered a two-run triple to tie the game in the ninth, then smacked a walk-off homer to straightaway center in the 11th to lift St. Louis to a 10–9 victory in what will rank as a Fall Classic classic. One

night later at Busch Stadium, the Cards were celebrating the franchise's 11th title after a 6–2 win, and the 28-year-old Freese, who had quit baseball for a year following high school because of burnout, was hoisting the MVP trophy after setting a postseason record with 21 RBIs. "It's been amazing," he said on the confetti-strewn field 45 minutes from his hometown of Wildwood, Mo. "I've had a lot of days in my life where I thought I wouldn't be even close to being a big leaguer."

True, there were other champions whose trajectories seemed more inevitable. Dual threat quarterback Cam Newton's season at Auburn could have easily been sidetracked—an NCAA investigation revealed that his father, Cecil, had requested money from Mississippi State in exchange for Cam's signing a letter of intent—but he plowed through defenses undaunted, leading an epic, 24-point comeback against archrival Alabama, winning the Heisman Trophy and, in Glendale, Ariz., capping an unbeaten season with a 22–19 defeat of Oregon to win the school's second national title. Maya Moore was a four-time All-America guard and two-time Player of the Year who from April 2008 to December 2010 led Connecticut to 90 straight victories, breaking the 36-year-old

championship—Notre Dame knocked the Huskies out in the semifinals, then lost to Texas A&M—she quickly established herself as a WNBA star, earning Rookie of the Year honors and helping the Lynx sweep the Dream in the Finals. (Behind point guard Kemba Walker, UConn did come away with the men's crown.)

The ascent of Novak Djokovic, while steady, was accelerated by a change in diet: He stopped eating gluten, then (more or less) stopped losing. A four-set defeat by Roger Federer in the French Open ended Djokovic's 43-match unbeaten streak, which included the Australian Open title, and prevented his bid for a Grand Slam. In what many called the best season by a male tennis player, the 24-year-old from Serbia went on to win Wimbledon and the U.S. Open and finished the season 64–3, assuming the world No. 1 ranking from Rafael Nadal.

Then there were the surprising stars. The Bruins had not won a Stanley Cup since 1972, then lost two of their top scorers to concussions, dropped three of their four postseason openers and had to survive three postseason Game 7s. But through it all they had Tim Thomas in goal, a 37-year-old fireplug whose idiosyncratic, hardnose style won over Boston

**Despite his inelegant goaltending technique, the Bruins' Thomas won fans and games thanks to a relentless, never-say-die mindset.**

when he finally seized the starter's job in 2006. The onetime member of the ECHL, IHL, SM-Liiga (Finland), AHL and Elitserien (Sweden) set a record with a .938 save percentage during the regular season and led the league with a 2.00 goals-against average. "This is a blue-collar city, and his success took a ton of hard work," says Bruins president Cam Neely. "Our fans are sharp. They respect battlers and see through phonies. They see their best qualities in Timmy."

In the finals, Boston faced the Canucks, the NHL's top-scoring team. Thomas held them to eight goals in seven games, blanking Vancouver 4–0 in the clincher to earn the Conn Smythe Trophy, becoming only the second American-born player to win the award. Along the way he stored up all the memorabilia and clips he could get his hands on. "I never know when this will be over," said Thomas, "and I'll want to look back and be amazed by it."

During the same season Thomas reemerged from the minors and took the starting job in Boston, the NBA's MVP was

JOHN W. MCDONOUGH

torn tendon in his left hand and another win in Game 4 with a 102-degree fever. In the first half of a potentially clinching Game 6, he missed 11 of 12 shots—a huge stumble for a player who would average 27.7 points on 48.5-percent shooting in the postseason. "Remember '06," said Terry, reminding him of the series known as the Meltdown. Nowitzki finished with 21 points in a 105–95 win, and his 62 fourth-quarter points in the Finals matched the total for James and Wade. "He made us raise our game to another level," said Terry. "That's when you have a superstar."

For three years quarterback Aaron Rodgers watched a superstar, and waited. He was used to it. After a prolific career in high school, Rodgers had waited for Division I offers; he settled for two years at Butte Community College in nearby Oroville. After a record-setting career at Cal he had waited for his name to be called at the 2005 NFL draft; the Packers eventually grabbed him with the 24th pick. And when Brett Favre finally left Green Bay in 2008, Rodgers waited to be accepted in Packerland.

The waiting ended—and the unflinching acceptance came—at Super Bowl XLV in Arlington, Texas. Midway throught the fourth quarter, Rodgers faced third-and-10 at his own 25 after the Steelers had cut the lead to 28–25. He zipped a pass to receiver Greg Jennings over the middle for a 31-yard gain, keeping alive a 10-play drive of 5½ minutes that helped seal a 31–25 win and the franchise's 13th NFL championship. Rodgers finished with 24 completions in 39 attempts for 304 yards and three scores. "That one throw was all about the last three years of my career," said Rodgers, referring to the the time since he replaced Favre. "The journey has been special. I'm not vindictive, but I'm blessed with a very good memory. You wait, you keep quiet and you take advantage of an opportunity when it comes."

reemerged from the minors and took the starting job in Boston, the NBA's MVP was having his heart questioned after the Mavericks blew a 2–0 lead in the Finals, bowing to the Heat in six. Dirk Nowitzki, a lean 7-footer from Wurzburg, Germany, with a magnificent shooting touch, did little to dispel that rap over the next four seasons, when Dallas failed to win a playoff series three times. (As sixth man Jason Terry summed up the perception of his team: "Same old Mavericks, one and done, first round and outski.") Despite a season-ending injury to high-scoring Caron Butler, the Mavs blitzed through the Western Conference playoffs, sweeping the defending champion Lakers in the second round and once again drawing Miami in the Finals.

Only this time the Heat were even more formidable: Over the summer of 2010 free agents LeBron James and Chris Bosh had joined Dwyane Wade to form what many (including the three principals) believed to be an instant dynasty. Yet one star proved more reliable than three: Nowitzki, who led Dallas to a win in Game 2 with a freshly

# THE YEAR IN SPORTS CALENDAR

### NOVEMBER 2010

**11/1:** For the first time in five years, Tiger Woods is not the No. 1 golfer in the world, as England's Lee Westwood edges past him in the rankings.

**11/4:** Hall of Fame baseball manager Sparky Anderson, who led the Cincinnati Reds to back-to-back World Series titles in 1974–75 and won one more with the Detroit Tigers in 1984, dies at age 76.

**11/4:** News reports surface that representatives for Auburn QB Cam Newton sought $180,000 in cash during the 2009 season to secure Newton's commitment to transfer to Mississippi State after a stint playing at a junior college.

**11/7:** Edison Pena, who, along with 32 other Chilean miners, had been trapped underground for 69 days, finishes the New York City Marathon in 5 hours and 50 minutes less than a month after being rescued.

**11/9:** Thanks to 20-of-21 field goal shooting, the Indiana Pacers score 54 points in the third quarter of a game against the Denver Nuggets—the highest single-quarter point total in 20 years.

**11/10:** Just six games into his NBA career, rookie guard John Wall posts his first career triple-double, as he leads the Washington Wizards to a 98–91 victory over the Houston Rockets.

**11/13:** Manny Pacquiao wins a unanimous decision over his much heavier opponent, Antonio Margarito, claiming the WBC Super Welterweight title, his eighth career title in eight different weight divisions.

**11/7:** The MLS' Kansas City Wizards announce that their new team name will be Sporting Kansas City.

**11/19:** Big Ten officials announce that the next day's Northwestern-Illinois game at Wrigley Field, both teams will run offensive plays toward the same end zone, due to the close proximity of the ballpark's brick wall to one end of the field.

**11/21:** As the seventh out of eight MLS playoff seeds, the Colorado Rapids complete an improbable run by winning the MLS Cup 2–1 in overtime, thanks to an own goal by FC Dallas' George John.

**11/21:** Oakland Raiders DE Richard Seymour is ejected—and later fined $25,000—for punching Pittsburgh Steelers QB Ben Roethlisberger in the face during Oakland's 35–3 loss to Pittsburgh.

**11/22:** Ending Albert Pujols' two-year reign, Cincinnati slugger Joey Votto is named NL MVP, receiving first-place votes on 31 of 32 ballots.

**11/26:** Boise State kicker Kyle Brotzman misses two short field goals—one at the end of regulation and one in overtime—and the Broncos lose to Nevada 34–31, spoiling their undefeated season and any chance for a BCS title shot.

**11/27:** Both the Denver Broncos and head coach Josh McDaniels are each fined $50,000 by the NFL for failing to report that a Broncos assistant had secretly videotaped an opponent's practice prior to a game earlier in the month. The assistant, later fired by Denver, had been guilty of the same behavior while with the New England Patriots during the 2007 season, an episode known as "Spygate."

### DECEMBER 2010

**12/1:** After investigating possible recruiting violations at Auburn and Mississippi State, the NCAA rules that Tigers QB Cam Newton was not involved in any wrongdoing and is eligible to play.

**12/2:** FIFA announces that Russia and Qatar will host the 2018 and 2022 World Cups, respectively.

**12/4:** After a surprisingly drawn-out negotiation, shortstop Derek Jeter re-signs with the New York Yankees, inking a three-year, $51-million deal.

**12/6:** With four weeks left in the regular season, the Denver Broncos fire head coach Josh McDaniels, who had an 11–17 record during his short tenure.

**12/7:** "Dandy" Don Meredith, the former Dallas Cowboys QB and long-time *Monday Night Football* color analyst, dies at age 72.

**12/7:** The trustee of a compensation fund tasked with repaying victims of Bernie Madoff's Ponzi scheme sues the New York Mets, charging that the team's ownership made a substantial profit thanks to their relationship with Madoff.

**12/11:** Just ten days after being cleared of any NCAA rules violations, Auburn QB Cam Newton wins the Heisman Trophy.

**12/11:** Navy beats Army for the ninth straight season, 31–17, the longest winning streak in the storied college football rivalry's 111 years.

**12/12:** Brett Favre's streak of 297 consecutive NFL starts finally comes to an end when he rides the Minnesota Vikings bench in a Week 14 game due to an injured throwing shoulder.

**12/12:** In a home game against the Miami Dolphins, New York Jets strength coach Sal Alosi sticks out his knee during a punt play and trips a Miami player running along the sideline.

**12/14:** In a surprise move, free agent pitcher Cliff Lee forgoes an extra $30 million from the New York Yankees and instead returns to the Philadelphia Phillies, inking a six-year, $138-million deal.

**12/19:** With time expiring, Philadelphia Eagles punt returner DeSean Jackson scampers 65 yards for the game-winning touchdown against the New York Giants, capping a remarkable 38–31 comeback victory that saw the Eagles overcome a 21-point deficit in the game's final eight minutes.

**12/21:** UConn's women's basketball team earns its 89th consecutive victory, surpassing the Div. I win streak set by the UCLA men's team from 1971–74.

**12/21:** Goalie Martin Brodeur becomes the NHL's all-time shutout leader when he records his 104th career shutout in the New Jersey Devils' 4–0 victory over the Pittsburgh Penguins.

**12/29:** Minnesota Vikings QB Brett Favre is fined $50,000 for being uncooperative with the NFL's investigation into whether or not he sent sexually suggestive text messages to former female employees of the New York Jets.

## JANUARY 2011

**1/1:** At the NHL's annual outdoor Winter Classic game, 68,111 fans sit through on-and-off drizzle to watch the visiting Washington Capitals earn a 3–1 victory over the Pittsburgh Penguins at Heinz Field.

**1/2:** By defeating the St. Louis Rams, 16–6, the Seattle Seahawks win the NFC West and clinch a playoff spot despite their 7–9 record. It's the first time an NFL team with a losing record has earned a postseason trip in a non-strike season.

**1/4:** Michigan fires head football coach Rich Rodriguez after three mediocre seasons during which he compiled a 15–22 record overall and went 6–18 in Big Ten conference play.

**1/5:** Voting results for baseball's 2011 Hall of Fame ballot are released and only Bert Blyleven and Robbie Alomar garner enough votes to be inducted.

**1/10:** Thanks in part to a controversial ruling that Auburn RB Michael Dyer was not downed during an apparent tackle, the Tigers execute a last-minute drive to defeat the Oregon Ducks in the BCS national championship game, 22–19, kicking a game-winning field goal with no time remaining.

**1/11:** BYU basketball phenom Jimmer Fredette scores 47 points, including a first-half buzzer beater from half court, to power the Cougars past their in-state rivals Utah, 104–79.

**1/17:** Thanks to a 2010 race record of 19–1, mare Zenyatta edges out Blame—the only racehorse to beat her all year—to win Horse of the Year.

**1/19:** *Reuters* reports that the NFL, unhappy with a Toyota commercial that features two youth football players in a helmet-to-helmet collision, successfully pressured the carmaker to edit the ad and remove the offending images.

**1/20:** Golfer Padraig Harrington is disqualified from the first round of the HSBC Championship after a TV viewer emails officials that the three-time major winner accidentally moved his ball on the green without penalizing himself two strokes.

**1/24:** *Sports Illustrated* publishes "The Case Against Lance Armstrong," which looks at the evidence suggesting the cyclist used performance-enhancing drugs during his career.

**1/25:** News reports surface that University of Connecticut booster Robert Burton wrote a letter to the school demanding a refund of $3 million of his donations after the school hired a new head football coach that Burton deemed unacceptable.

**1/29:** Li Na, the first Chinese tennis player ever to advance to a Grand Slam final, succumbs to Belgium's Kim Clijsters in three sets, 3–6, 6–3, 6–3, in the Australian Open women's final match.

**1/30:** Novak Djokovic wins his second Grand Slam singles title, defeating England's Andy Murray in straight sets at the Australian Open.

## FEBRUARY

**2/1:** The Minnesota Twins re-sign their catcher, three-time All-Star and 2009 AL MVP Joe Mauer, to a 10-year contract extension.

**2/4:** Snow and ice slides off the roof of Cowboys Stadium and injures six people, just two days before the stadium hosts Super Bowl XLV.

**2/6:** QB Aaron Rodgers throws for three touchdowns and the Green Bay Packers hold off the Pittsburgh Steelers 31–25 to win Super Bowl XLV.

**2/8:** On this day in the NBA, a record eight road teams notch wins, surpassing the previous record for visiting team success that had been set when all seven road teams won on Feb. 3, 1996.

**2/10:** Boston shooting guard Ray Allen breaks the NBA's career three-point field goal record by hitting his 2,561st three-pointer in a 92–86 Celtics' home loss to the Los Angeles Lakers.

**2/11:** Cleveland finally snaps its NBA-record 26-game consecutive losing streak by defeating the Los Angeles Clippers 126–119 in overtime.

**2/12:** Wisconsin's men's basketball team upsets No. 1-ranked Ohio State 71–67, snapping the undefeated Buckeyes' 24-game winning streak.

**2/13:** One game after snapping its 26-game skid, Cleveland loses at home to the Washington Wizards 115–100, allowing the Wizards to end their streak of 25 straight consecutive road losses.

**2/16:** After an earlier positive test for a banned substance, WNBA basketball star Diana Taurasi is cleared of any wrongdoing when the Turkish test lab that performed the test retracts its findings.

**2/17:** Ex-NFL player Dave Duerson dies of a self-inflicted shotgun wound. Subsequent analysis of his brain tissue will find he suffered from a neuro-degenerative disease likely caused by concussions.

**2/20:** Unknown driver Trevor Bayne, starting in only his second Sprint Cup race, wins the 2011 Daytona 500, which featured a record 74 lead changes.

**2/21:** In a blockbuster, three-team, NBA trade-deadline deal involving Denver, Minnesota, and New York, the Nuggets send All-Stars Carmelo Anthony and Chauncey Billups to the Knicks.

**2/23:** In their season finale, Caltech's men's basketball team defeats Occidental College 46–45, snapping a 310-game intra-conference losing streak that stretched back 26 years.

**2/25:** In what news reports call a "player mutiny" against Detroit Pistons head coach John Kuester, more than half the team skips a pre-game shootaround in Philadelphia. In the Pistons 110–94 loss to the 76ers later that same day, Kuester uses only the six players who showed up for practice.

**2/26:** Three weeks after sustaining a concussion during a training run, U.S. skier Lindsey Vonn wins her 40th career FIS World Cup race in Sweden.

**2/26:** UCLA walk-on Tyler Trapani, great grandson of Bruins coach John Wooden, scores the final basket—and the only two points of his collegiate career—in the final game at storied Pauley Pavilion.

### MARCH

**3/1:** Brandon Davies, the sophomore center on BYU's Top 20-ranked men's basketball team, is kicked off the team after admitting to violating the school's honor code by having pre-marital sex.

**3/3:** After making a game-winning layup in overtime to clinch Fennville (Mich.) High's undefeated season, 16-year-old basketball star Wes Leonard collapses on the court and dies shortly thereafter at a nearby hospital.

**3/5:** Croatian tennis player Ivo Karlovic slams a 156-m.p.h. serve in a doubles match of his country's Davis Cup competition, breaking Andy Roddick's seven-year-old speed record.

**3/6:** Duke records its most lopsided defeat ever of basketball archrival North Carolina, 82–50.

**3/9:** Minnesota Timberwolves power forward Kevin Love records his 52nd double-double in a row in a 101–75 victory over the Indiana Pacers, breaking Moses Malone's mark and giving Love the longest such streak since the ABA-NBA merger in 1975.

**3/10:** Down 10 points with just 42 seconds left in a ACC Conference tournament matchup, Miami (Fla.) rallies to tie Virginia and send the game into overtime, where the 'Canes eventually win 69–62.

**3/12:** After both sides fail to reach a negotiated agreement, the NFL begins its first work stoppage in 24 years as the owners lock out the players.

**3/13:** The NCAA Selection Committee announces the first-ever 68-team field for the men's Division I men's basketball tournament.

**3/14:** The International Skating Union postpones the World Figure Skating Championships in Tokyo because of widespread damage resulting from a massive tsunami striking the Japanese coast.

**3/19:** In a wild men's NCAA tournament game marked by two fouls in the final second, No. 8-seed Butler upsets No. 1 seed Pittsburgh, 71–70.

**3/19:** Despite having been born without a right leg,

Arizona State senior wrestler Anthony Robles wins the 125-lb. NCAA wrestling title.

**3/20:** Though widely criticized for its inclusion in March Madness, No. 11-seed Virginia Commonwealth defeats No. 3-seed Purdue for their third tournament victory in five nights and advances to the Sweet Sixteen round.

**3/20:** Duke defeats Michigan 73–71 in the second round of March Madness, giving head coach Mike Krzyzewski his 900th career victory, just two shy of Bobby Knight's all-time win mark.

**3/21:** Out of concern for the high rate of injuries on kickoffs, the NFL Competition Committee decides to move them up five yards—to the 35-yard line—for the 2011–12 season.

**3/21:** Tennessee fires head basketball coach Bruce Pearl upon completion of the season after he admitted to lying to NCAA investigators about recruiting violations by his coaching staff.

**3/26:** After 22 innings, Fresno State finally defeats the Univ. of San Diego 3–2 in the third-longest game in Division III baseball history.

**3/28:** Boxer Bernard Hopkins punches future opponent Jean Pascal in the face during a pre-fight press conference. Hopkins would later win their actual fight in May by unanimous decision.

**3/29:** Fiesta Bowl CEO John Junkard is fired after an internal report finds he grossly misused bowl funds, including spending $1,000 at a strip club.

### APRIL

**4/1:** Following a 2–1 Dodgers victory over the visiting Giants, two men brutally attack Giants fan Bryan Stow in the parking lot of Dodger Stadium. His resulting injuries send him into a coma.

**4/4:** In a brick-laden men's Division I basketball title game, Connecticut defeats Butler 53–41, with the Bulldogs shooting a record-low 18 percent from the field.

**4/8:** After being alerted that he failed a spring training drug test, noted slugger Manny Ramirez abruptly retires from baseball rather than serve a 100-game suspension.

**4/9:** Though he was the only member of his team not to dye his hair blond, Minnesota-Duluth senior forward Kyle Schmidt scored the game-winning overtime goal in the men's Division I Frozen Four final, helping the Bulldogs defeat Michigan 3–2 and secure the school's first NCAA hockey title.

**4/10:** South African golfer Charl Schwartzel birdies the last four holes to shoot a final round 66 at the Masters, winning the tournament by two strokes.

**4/13:** More than seven years after testifying to a grand jury that he never knowingly received steroids, former San Francisco Giants slugger Barry Bonds is convicted in federal court of one count of obstruction of justice.

**4/18:** Kenyan distance runner Geoffrey Mutai runs the fastest marathon in history, finishing the Boston Marathon in 2:03:02, but his time doesn't qualify as a world record because of the race course's layout and the brisk tailwind during the event.

**4/18:** Cincinnati Reds pitcher Aroldis Chapman is clocked by his hometown stadium radar gun throwing a 106-mph fastball in a game against the Pittsburgh Pirates.

**4/20:** The state legislature passes a law requiring the University of North Dakota to retain the name "Fighting Sioux" in the face of the NCAA's efforts to ban what it calls an offensive mascot.

**4/21:** Major League Baseball announces that it will take over the day-to-day operations of the L.A. Dodgers after a messy divorce between the team's owners, Frank and Jamie McCourt, leaves the franchise in questionable financial straits.

**4/28:** In the first overall pick of the 2011 NFL draft, the Carolina Panthers choose 2010 Heisman Trophy winner and Auburn QB Cam Newton. Alabama RB Mark Ingram, the 2009 Heisman winner, goes 28th, to the New Orleans Saints.

**4/29:** Chicago White Sox manager Ozzie Guillen is fined $20,000 and suspended two games by Major League Baseball for posting complaints about umpiring on Twitter during a game.

### MAY

**5/2:** Sacramento Kings co-owner George Maloof announces that the team will stay in place for at least one more year, instead of moving to Anaheim.

**5/3:** Chicago Bulls point guard Derrick Rose is named the NBA's 2010–11 MVP, making the 22-year-old Rose the youngest ever to win the award.

**5/3:** Despite six walks and only two strikeouts, Minnesota Twins pitcher Francisco Liriano tosses a 1–0 no-hit victory over the Chicago White Sox.

**5/3:** Los Angeles Lakers forward Ron Artest, recipient of the NBA's 2010–11 Citizenship Award, is suspended by the league from Game 3 of the Western Conference semifinals for his flagrant clothesline foul on Dallas Mavericks guard Jose Barea in the closing moments of Game 2.

**5/7:** Justin Verlander throws the second no-hitter of his career—and the second no-hitter in four days—as his Detroit Tigers thump the Toronto Blue Jays 9–0.

**5/7:** After Animal Kingdom's regular jockey, Robby Albarado, breaks his nose and is replaced, John Velazquez rides to victory in the Kentucky Derby on the 20–1 longshot.

**5/9:** Belgian cyclist Wouter Weylandt crashes and dies during a mountainous stretch of the Giro D'Italia.

**5/11:** In Game 5 of the NBA Eastern Conference semifinals, Heat forward LeBron James scores the final ten pointsy to defeat the Celtics 97–87 and knock Boston out of the playoffs.

**5/15:** K.J. Choi becomes the first Asian golfer to win The Players Championship when David Toms misses a three-and-a-half-foot putt during a one-hole playoff at the TPC Stadium Course.

**5/18:** Despite having just a 2.8-percent chance of taking the top spot, the Cleveland Cavaliers win the 2011 NBA Draft Lottery.

**5/22:** Shackleford holds off 2–1 favorite Animal Kingdom down the stretch and wins the Preakness Stakes at Pimlico by half a length.

**5/26:** In a wild series of events that features multiple throws across the baseball diamond, the New Britain Rock Cats minor league team turns a 3-2-6-1-5-4-6-8 double play against the Binghamton Mets.

**5/26:** Philadelphia Phillies backup second-baseman Wilson Valdez becomes the first position player since 2000 to record a major league victory when he throws just 10 pitches to finish off the final frame of a 19-inning, 5–4 win over the Cincinnati Reds.

**5/28:** FC Barcelona defeats Manchester United 3–1 in the UEFA Champions League Final in London, England.

**5/29:** In a stunning conclusion to the Indy 500, race leader JR Hildebrand crashes into the wall on the last turn before the finish line, allowing Dan Wheldon to pass him and take the checkered flag for his second career Indy 500 victory.

**5/30:** Ohio State head football coach Jim Tressel resigns over revelations that he failed to notify the school back in April that Buckeye players were involved in improperly selling team merchandise.

**5/31:** Atlanta, former home of the NHL's Flames, again loses a hockey franchise, when the league approves the sale and relocation of its current hockey team, the Thrashers, to Winnipeg, Canada.

### JUNE

**6/1:** Four-time champion and 15-time All-Star Shaquille O'Neal retires from the NBA via Twitter.

**6/3:** Roger Federer defeats Novak Djokovic in the French Open semifinals, ending the latter's 43-match consecutive win streak that began in 2010.

**6/6:** The Bowl Championship Series officially strips USC of its 2004 national championship due to NCAA rules violations by former Trojan player Reggie Bush. The 2004 title will remain vacant.

**6/7:** Battling a 102-degree fever, Dirk Nowitzki scores 21 points and grabs 11 rebounds to help the Dallas Mavericks defeat the Miami Heat 86–83 and even the NBA Finals at two games apiece.

**6/11:** Bumped right out of the gate, Derby winner Animal Kingdom never recovers and Preakness champion Shackleford fades down the stretch, while 24–1 longshot Ruler on Ice charges home to an improbable Belmont Stakes victory.

**6/15:** The Boston Bruins defeat the Vancouver Canucks 4–0 in Game 7 of the Stanley Cup final, the team's third such Game 7 victory of the 2011 playoffs, which sets a new NHL postseason record.

**6/11:** Following the Canucks' Game 7 loss in the Stanley Cup final, rioting breaks out in Vancouver in the early morning hours, prompting riot police to use tear gas to quell the violence and vandalism.

**6/19:** With an incredible wire-to-wire victory at the U.S. Open, Rory McIlroy sets 12 new scoring records, including one for lowest overall tournament score—previously 272, set by Tiger Woods in 2000 at Pebble Beach—which he surpasses by four strokes

**6/23:** At the 2011 NBA Draft, Duke point guard Kyrie Irving goes first overall to the Cleveland Cavs, while twin brothers Markieff and Marcus Morris of Kansas are picked back-to-back by the Phoenix Suns and Houston Rockets, respectively.

**6/23:** Frustrated by his team's refusal to pick up his option for the 2012 season, Washington Nationals manager Jim Riggleman abruptly resigns on the same day the Nationals move over the .500 mark in June for the first time since 2005.

**6/25:** Though the U.S. men's national soccer team jumps out to an early 2–0 lead in the 2011 Gold Cup final, Mexico storms back with four unanswered goals to claim victory.

**6/28:** The U.S. Supreme Court declines to hear Roger Clemens' appeal of his dismissed defamation case against his former trainer.

**6/29:** After having set a new College World Series tournament record with 11 consecutive wins, South Carolina claims its second national title in as many years, defeating Florida 5–2 to sweep the best-of-three CWS final.

## JULY

**7/1:** The NBA officially delares a lockout after contract negotiations with the players break down, marking the league's first work stoppage since the 1998–99 season.

**7/4:** One day after defeating Rafael Nadal in the final at Wimbledon, Serbian tennis star Novak Djokovic surpasses Nadal in the rankings to become the world's new No. 1 player.

**7/8:** Texas Rangers fan Shannon Stone tips over an outfield railing and falls 20 feet to the concrete below at Rangers Ballpark. His injuries prove fatal.

**7/8:** After nine seasons, Chinese basketball star and Houston Rocket Yao Ming retires from the NBA.

**7/9:** New York Yankees shortstop Derek Jeter bashes a home run against the Tampa Bay Rays in the third inning for his 3,000th career hit, making him only the second player in major league history—the other being Wade Boggs—to hit a home run for such a milestone.

**7/10:** Down one player and one goal with just a minute left in stoppage time in a World Cup quarterfinal match, the U.S. women's national soccer team rallies to tie Brazil 2–2 and then win in a thrilling shootout 3–2.

**7/12:** For the first time since 1996, the National League wins consecutive All-Star Games, beating the American League 5–1 at Chase Field in Phoenix.

*****7/14:** English amateur Tom Lewis enters the clubhouse as co-leader after the first round of the British Open, having shot a 5-under 65 in blustery conditions at Royal St. George's.

**7/20:** After 13 years of working together, Tiger Woods fires his longtime caddie Steve Williams via an announcement on his website.

**7/24:** Australian Cadel Evans wins the Tour de France, after having been runner-up in 2009 and 2010.

**7/25:** After 130 days, the NFL lockout officially comes to an end.

**7/25:** The Pittsburgh Pirates sit atop the NL Central (tied with St. Louis) in late July for the first time since 1997.

**7/28:** U.S. swimmer Ryan Lochte sets a new world record in the 200-meter individual medley at the 2011 World Championships, one of five new marks set at the meet. At the 2009 Worlds, when full-body swimsuits were still allowed, 43 world records were broken.

**7/29:** Former German soccer star Jurgen Klinsmann, who is tied for fifth all-time in World Cup goals scored, is named as the new head coach of the U.S. men's national team.

**7/31:** Korean golfer Yani Tseng successfully defends her Women's British Open title.

## AUGUST

**8/6:** The NFL Hall of Fame inducts its 2011 class, consisting of Richard Dent, Marshall Faulk, Chris Hanburger, Les Richter, Ed Sabol, Deion Sanders, and Shannon Sharpe.

**8/14:** Atlanta Braves second-baseman Dan Uggla's hit streak ends at 33 games, when he goes 0-for-3 in a 6–5 loss to the Chicago Cubs.

**8/15:** Down five shots with just three holes to play, Keegan Bradley rallies to tie Jason Dufner after 72 holes and then defeat him in a one-hole playoff at the PGA Championship, claiming his first major title.

**8/18:** Seven former players, including former Chicago Bears QB Jim McMahon, file a class action lawsuit against the NFL, alleging "negligence and intentional misconduct" with regard to brain injury-related illnesses among NFL veterans.

**8/23:** NASCAR's Kyle Busch's has his driver's license suspended for 45 days after he is found guilty of going 128 mph in a 45-mph zone.

**8/24:** During a 22–9 shellacking of the Oakland A's, the New York Yankees hit a new single-game major-league record three grand slams.

**8/28:** The team from Huntington Beach, California scores the winning run with two out in the bottom of the sixth inning to defeat Hamamatsu, Japan 2–1 in the Little League World Series.

**8/31:** Atlanta Braves closer Craig Kimbrel sets a new major league rookie record with his 41st save.

## SEPTEMBER

**9/1:** The *Wall Street Journal* runs a story that counts the number of times New York Mets starting pitcher Mike Pelfrey licked his hand in his most recent six-plus inning outing—89.

**9/7:** The charter airplane carrying the Russian pro hockey team Lokomotiv Yaroslavl crashes just after takeoff, killing 36 of the 37 team members, some of them former NHL players.

**9/8:** Injured Indianapolis Colts QB Peyton Manning, who missed the first start of his 14-year career four days earlier, undergoes neck surgery and will be out for the entire 2011–12 NFL season.

**9/11:** Australian Samantha Stosur upsets Serena Williams 6–2, 6–3 to win the U.S. Open, but not before Williams gets into a verbal altercation with the chair umpire after she calls a hindrance violation on Williams that costs her a game.

**9/11:** In his NFL debut, rookie Carolina Panthers QB Cam Newton throws for 422 yards in a 28–21 loss to the Arizona Cardinals, shattering Peyton Manning's previous first-game record by 102 yards.

**9/12:** The NBA fines Charlotte Bobcats owner Michael Jordan $100,000 for discussing the ongoing lockout with an Australian newspaper.

**9/16:** L.A. Laker forward Ron Artest officially changes his name to Metta World Peace.

**9/17:** Floyd Mayweather Jr. knocks out WBC welterweight champion Victor Ortiz in the fourth round as Ortiz appears to be apologizing to Mayweather for head-butting him moments earlier.

**9/19:** New York Yankees closer Mariano Rivera notches his 602nd career save in a 6–4 win over the Minnesota Twins, moving past Trevor Hoffman to the top of the all-time saves list.

**9/25:** European golfers win the Solheim Cup for the first time in eight years, defeating the U.S. 15–13.

**9/26:** Continuing the college football conference realignment shuffle that began in 2010, Texas A&M leaves the Big 12 and officially joins the SEC.

**9/28:** On the last day of the season, the Boston Red Sox blow a ninth-inning lead and lose the AL wild card spot after the Tampa Bay Rays complete a seven-run comeback against the New York Yankees. Boston ends up 7–20 in the month of September.

**9/30:** High school senior Austin Pacheco kicks a game-winning, 64-yard field goal to help Carson City High (Nevada) defeat Bishop Manogue 27–24.

## OCTOBER

**10/5:** During the fifth-inning of Game 3 of the NLDS between the St. Louis Cardinals and Philadelphia Phillies, a squirrel inexplicably runs onto the field and across home plate.

**10/7:** Twenty-five years after winning Super Bowl XX, the 1985 Chicago Bears, whose initial visit was cancelled after the Space Shuttle Challenger disaster, finally get to visit the White House.

**10/8:** Longtime Oakland Raiders owner and NFL Hall of Famer Al Davis dies at his home in Oakland.

**10/9:** During the final round of the Frys.com golf tournament, a fan is arrested after throwing a hot dog at Tiger Woods.

**10/10:** With labor negotiations at an impasse, the NBA cancels the first two weeks of the 2011–12 season.

**10/12:** After Boston's collapse down the stretch, Red Sox general manager Theo Epstein moves on, signing a five-year deal with the Chicago Cubs.

**10/15:** The Texas Rangers defeat the Detroit Tigers in the ALCS in six games, paced by series MVP Nelson Cruz, who set new postseason series records with his 13 RBIs and six home runs, one of which was an extra-inning, game-winning, grand slam in Game 2.

**10/16:** Two-time Indianapolis 500 winner Dan Wheldon dies in a massive, 15-car wreck at the Las Vegas Motor Speedway.

**10/22:** St. Louis Cardinals slugger Albert Pujols hits three home runs in Game 3 of the World Series, tying a World Series single-game record held by Babe Ruth and Reggie Jackson.

**10/23:** At the 2011 Rugby World Cup in Auckland, New Zealand, the host nation, known as the "All Blacks," defeats France in the final 8–7.

**10/25:** Formula1 racing announces that it will hold a November 2012 grand prix race along the New Jersey waterfront.

**10/27:** Down two with two on and two out in the ninth inning, the St. Louis Cardinals tie Game 6 of the World Series on a David Freese triple. They later win the game 10–9 in the bottom of the 11th on a Freese home run to force a deciding Game 7.

**10/28:** In a somewhat anti-climactic Game 7, the St. Louis Cardinals come back from a early two-run deficit and cruise home to a 6–2 victoy, earning the franchise's 11th championship.

**10/31:** Three days after winning his third World Series, Cardinals manager Tony LaRussa retires.

# Baseball

RON T. ENNIS

Cardinals 3B David Freese
led St. Louis to its
11th championship, earning
MVP honors in the
NLCS and World Series

# One Strike Away

In 2011, an incredibly dramatic end to the regular season foreshadowed a record-breaking postseason that was capped off by an unforgettable, unbelievable World Series

## BY MERRELL NODEN

IT'S HARD TO IMAGINE A WORLD SERIES Game 7 feeling anti-climactic, but this one, between the St. Louis Cardinals and the Texas Rangers, did. Then again, how could it not—so wild and weird and improbable had been Game 6, all 11 incredibly entertaining innings of it?

That game for the ages mixed comic blunders with clutch hitting as great as ever we've seen. There were five errors in the first six innings, six home runs in all, and the unusual sight of pitchers pinch-hitting—twice! As they had all season, the Cardinals kept coming back from the brink of defeat. Twice, in the 9th and 10th innings, the Rangers were up two runs and needed just one more strike to win the franchise's first championship in 51 years. Yet St. Louis always managed to get the hit it needed to stay alive.

Just as sweet for delirious Cardinal fans was the fact that the hero of the team's improbable comeback was local boy David Freese, who, like them, had grown up rooting for St. Louis. In the 9th inning, with two outs and two strikes on him, Freese lined a triple over Nelson Cruz's head and off the right field wall to drive in two runs and tie the game. Then, after Josh Hamilton hit a two-run homer in the top of the 10th, Lance Berkman tied things up once more with a two-out, two-strike single. Freese led off the bottom of the 11th by drilling Mark Lowe's pitch over the center field fence for a walk off homer and a 10–9 win. The Cards had come from behind to win Game 7, too, thanks in part to Freese's two-run double in the first.

The final score was 6–2. Freese won the MVP Award and the Cardinals took the most amazing of their eleven World Series titles.

Has any team ever come from farther back than these Cardinals, who in late August were 10½ games out of a wild card berth? They clinched a postseason spot on the last day of the season—with help from the collapsing Braves—and came from behind in all three playoff series.

Then again, this was a strange season. No, make that three strange seasons: the regular season up until Labor Day, September, and the playoffs. The Phillies, boosted as expected by their killer starting rotation, paced the National League with a franchise record 102 wins, while the Yankees topped the American League with 97. Then came the final month of the regular season, which ended on a night that saw rapid shifts of fortune more improbable than any in the game's long history. On that night when the Cardinals clinched their playoff berth by beating the Astros in Houston, two teams that had seemed to be shoe-ins for at least a wildcard berth before spending September in desperate freefall, were eliminated from the playoffs in extra inning games that defied belief. For Atlanta fans—who saw their playoff-reliable team blow a 8½-game wild card lead by going 11–20 in September—this was something new. But for long-suffering Boston fans, who watched the Sox lose an even bigger cushion—it was further excruciating proof that the laws of the universe are stacked against their beloved Red Sox.

Long before the season reached that memorable finale, it had been dominated by great pitching. Offensive output, which has been declining steadily for the past decade, continued to slide. Jose Bautista of the Blue Jays led the majors with 43 home runs, the lowest total to do so since 1994.

Whether this power outage was due to great pitching or to a drug testing program that is working—or to something else entirely—remains to be seen. But pitchers, paced by Justin Verlander of the Detroit Tigers, dominated as they haven't for years. After pitching a no-hjtter against Toronto on May 7, Verlander won 12 straight starts—from July 21 to September 18—and earned a pitcher's Triple Crown, with a record of 24–5, 250 strikeouts, and an earned run average of 2.40.

Clayton Kershaw was almost as dominant in the National League. Despite pitching for the Dodgers, who were disappointing on the field and troubled in the front office, Kershaw finished the season with a record of 21–5, 248 strikeouts, and an ERA of 2.28.

These were eye-popping numbers. But the rotation that intimidated batters the most belonged to Philadelphia. Already blessed with 2010 National League Cy Young Award winner Roy Halladay, Roy

**Tigers ace Justin Verlander dominated in 2011, racking up the best ERA, strikeout, and win total in the AL and he threw a no-hitter as well.**

Oswalt, and Cole Hamels, the Phillies re-acquired lefty Cliff Lee in the offseason, giving them four starters who could reasonably stand comparison to the greatest rotations of the past. With the Phillies' Mount Rushmore living up to expectations—all but Oswalt made the All Star team—and the front office making a great midseason acquisition in the ungainly form of Houston outfielder Hunter Pence, the Phillies led their division virtually from Opening Day on.

If Philadelphia had an equal, it was Milwaukee. The Brewers had power in the form of Ryan Braun, who batted .332 with 33 homers and 111 RBIs, and Prince Fielder, who hit .299 with 120 RBIs and 38 homers. The last number put him one behind Matt Kemp of the Dodgers for the league lead. (Kemp also led the league with 126 RBIs). Milwaukee had a killer quartet of pitchers, led by Zack Greinke, and the league's top reliever in John Axford, who had 46 saves. The Brewers finished six games up on the Cardinals and were expected to hammer them in the NLCS.

In the American League, it looked as if the

In Game 3, Albert Pujols awoke from his 0-for-World Series batting slump to have a "Mr. October" moment, going 5-for-6 with three home runs, six RBIs, and 14 total bases.

pionship series was Ranger Nelson Cruz, who hit six homers in the ALCS—eight total in the playoffs—including the first-ever walk-off grand 0slam in the eleventh inning of Game 2. In the ACLS the Rangers beat the Tigers four games to two, and under their gyrating, gesticulating rag doll of a manager, Ron Washington, looked like the team to end the Cardinals' dream run.

The Cardinals overcame a first game loss to the Brewers and won the pennant at Miller Park, where the Brewers had the best home record in baseball. They also had a brilliant strategist in manager Tony LaRussa, renowned for his creative use of his bullpen.

The first two games of the Series were one-run squeakers, with Texas scoring twice in the ninth to win Game 2. Albert Pujols had a Game 3 for the ages, tying Babe Ruth and Reggie Jackson by hitting three home runs, as well as two singles, for a Series-record 14 total bases in a 16–7 Cardinals win. The Rangers took Games 4 and 5, boosted by the superb starting pitching of Derek Holland and the all-around brilliance of catcher Mike Napoli; they also benefited from crossed signals between LaRussa and his bullpen.

What came next you already know. It will be savored for years to come as part of the game's most cherished lore. The triumphant Cardinals must now decide how much they want to spend to re-sign Pujols, who is now a free agent, and who will replace retiring manager Tony La Russa. The Rangers probably won't find much consolation in having reached back-to-back World Series. Too bad, because this was a Series to be savored, not only by Cardinals fans of course, but by baseball fans all over.

Yankees and Red Sox would battle each other all season and that the winner would ultimately face the Phillies in the World Series. This Yankees team was a hybrid of old and new, with the trio of Derek Jeter, Jorge Posada, and Mariano Rivera harking back to the Bronx dynasties of the late-90s. We were reminded of just how good that group was when, on July 9, Jeter passed the 3,000-hit plateau and again, on September 19, when Rivera became the alltime saves leader (603 at season's end). To that trio add newer acquisitions like Curtis Granderson, Mark Teixeira, and Robinson Cano, who had 119, 111, and 118 RBIs, respectively, and you had a Yankee team that seemed capable of overcoming its questionable starting rotation.

The Rangers had lost last year's World Series to the Giants. But they'd made themselves considerably stronger this year by acquiring slugger Adrian Beltre and reliever Mike Adams. They had speed at the top of the lineup, as well as a relentless offense that was the only one in the majors with three 30-plus homer hitters. Texas won the AL West by 10 games. That was five games less than the margin Verlander's Detroit Tigers, paced by batting champion (.344) Miguel Cabrera, had finished ahead of the Indians in the Central.

The hitting star of the two league cham-

# FOR THE RECORD•2011

## 2011 Final Regular Season Standings

### National League

#### EASTERN DIVISION

| Team | Won | Lost | Pct | GB | Home | Away |
|------|-----|------|-----|-----|------|------|
| Philadelphia | 102 | 60 | .630 | — | 52–29 | 50–31 |
| Atlanta | 89 | 73 | .549 | 13.0 | 47–34 | 42–39 |
| Washington | 80 | 81 | .497 | 21.5 | 44–36 | 36–45 |
| NY Mets | 77 | 85 | .475 | 25.0 | 34–47 | 43–38 |
| Florida | 72 | 90 | .444 | 30.0 | 31–47 | 41–43 |

#### CENTRAL DIVISION

| Team | Won | Lost | Pct | GB | Home | Away |
|------|-----|------|-----|-----|------|------|
| Milwaukee | 96 | 66 | .593 | — | 57–24 | 39–42 |
| †St. Louis | 90 | 72 | .556 | 6.0 | 45–36 | 45–36 |
| Cincinnati | 79 | 83 | .488 | 17.0 | 42–39 | 37–44 |
| Pittsburgh | 72 | 90 | .444 | 24.0 | 36–45 | 36–45 |
| Chicago | 71 | 91 | .438 | 25.0 | 39–42 | 32–49 |
| Houston | 56 | 106 | .346 | 40.0 | 31–50 | 25–56 |

#### WESTERN DIVISION

| Team | Won | Lost | Pct | GB | Home | Away |
|------|-----|------|-----|-----|------|------|
| Arizona | 94 | 68 | .580 | — | 51–30 | 43–38 |
| San Francisco | 86 | 76 | .531 | 8.0 | 46–35 | 40–41 |
| LA Dodgers | 82 | 79 | .509 | 11.5 | 42–39 | 40–40 |
| Colorado | 73 | 89 | .451 | 21.0 | 38–43 | 35–46 |
| San Diego | 71 | 91 | .438 | 23.0 | 35–46 | 36–45 |

†Wild-card teams.

### American League

#### EASTERN DIVISION

| Team | Won | Lost | Pct | GB | Home | Away |
|------|-----|------|-----|-----|------|------|
| NY Yankees | 97 | 65 | .599 | — | 52–29 | 45–36 |
| †Tampa Bay | 91 | 71 | .562 | 6.0 | 47–34 | 44–37 |
| Boston | 90 | 72 | .556 | 7.0 | 45–36 | 45–36 |
| Toronto | 81 | 81 | .500 | 16.0 | 42–39 | 39–42 |
| Baltimore | 69 | 93 | .426 | 28.0 | 39–42 | 30–51 |

#### CENTRAL DIVISION

| Team | Won | Lost | Pct | GB | Home | Away |
|------|-----|------|-----|-----|------|------|
| Detroit | 95 | 67 | .586 | — | 50–31 | 45–36 |
| Cleveland | 80 | 82 | .494 | 15.0 | 44–37 | 36–45 |
| Chicago | 79 | 83 | .488 | 16.0 | 36–45 | 43–38 |
| Kansas City | 71 | 91 | .438 | 24.0 | 40–41 | 31–50 |
| Minnesota | 63 | 99 | .389 | 32.0 | 33–48 | 30–51 |

#### WESTERN DIVISION

| Team | Won | Lost | Pct | GB | Home | Away |
|------|-----|------|-----|-----|------|------|
| Texas | 96 | 66 | .593 | — | 52–29 | 44–37 |
| LA Angels | 86 | 76 | .531 | 10.0 | 45–36 | 41–40 |
| Oakland | 74 | 88 | .457 | 22.0 | 43–38 | 31–50 |
| Seattle | 67 | 95 | .414 | 29.0 | 39–45 | 28–50 |

## 2011 Playoffs

### National League Division Playoffs

| | | | |
|---|---|---|---|
| Game 1 | St. Louis 6 at Philadelphia 11 | Game 4 | Philadelphia 3 at St. Louis 5 |
| Game 2 | St. Louis 5 at Philadelphia 4 | Game 5 | St. Louis 1 at Philadelphia 0 |
| Game 3 | Philadelphia 3 at St. Louis 2 | | |

(St. Louis won series 3–2)

| | | | |
|---|---|---|---|
| Game 1 | Arizona 1 at Milwaukee 4 | Game 4 | Milwaukee 6 at Arizona 10 |
| Game 2 | Arizona 4 at Milwaukee 9 | Game 5 | Arizona 2 at Milwaukee 3 (10 inn.) |
| Game 3 | Milwaukee 1 at Arizona 3 | | |

(Milwaukee won series 3–2)

### National League Championship Series

| | | | |
|---|---|---|---|
| Game 1 | St. Louis 6 at Milwaukee 9 | Game 4 | Milwaukee 4 at St. Louis 2 |
| Game 2 | St. Louis 12 at Milwaukee 3 | Game 5 | Milwaukee 1 at St. Louis 7 |
| Game 3 | Milwaukee 3 at St. Louis 4 | Game 6 | St. Louis 12 at Milwaukee 6 |

(St. Louis won series 4–2)

#### GAME 1

| | | | | | | | | | | | R | H | E |
|------|---|---|---|---|---|---|---|---|---|---|---|---|---|
| St. Louis | 1 | 0 | 0 | 3 | 1 | 0 | 1 | 0 | 0 | | 6 | 9 | 1 |
| Milwaukee | 2 | 0 | 0 | 0 | 6 | 0 | 1 | 0 | x | | 9 | 11 | 0 |

**W**—Mil: Greinke. **L**—StL: Garcia. **SV**—Mil: Axford. **LOB**—StL: 5; Mil: 8. **2B**—StL: Furcal; Mil: Weeks, Hairston, Braun, Lucroy, Betancourt. **HR**—StL: Freese; Mil: Braun, Fielder, Betancourt. **RBI**—StL: Holliday, Freese (3), Berkman; Mil: Braun (4), Fielder (2), Betancourt (2), Lucroy. **GIDP**—StL: Pujols; Mil: Weeks. **SAC**—Mil: Gomez. **E**—StL: Dotel. **IBB**—Mil: Fielder. **HBP**—Mil: Fielder.
**T**—3:35. **A**—43,613.

**Recap:** (AP) It's one thing for a team to say it won't be beaten by the Milwaukee Brewers' dueling duo of MVP candidates, Ryan Braun and Prince Fielder, as the St. Louis Cardinals found out in Game 1 of the NLCS, actually keeping those two quiet isn't so easy. Back-to-back big hits by Braun and Fielder powered a rapid-fire fifth-inning rally, helping the Brewers come back to beat the Cardinals 9–6 for a 1–0 lead in the series.

#### GAME 2

| | | | | | | | | | | | R | H | E |
|------|---|---|---|---|---|---|---|---|---|---|---|---|---|
| St. Louis | 2 | 0 | 2 | 1 | 2 | 0 | 4 | 0 | 1 | | 12 | 17 | 0 |
| Milwaukee | 0 | 0 | 0 | 2 | 0 | 0 | 1 | 0 | | | 3 | 8 | 1 |

**W**—StL: Lynn. **L**—Mil: Marcum. **LOB**—StL: 6; Mil: 7. **2B**—StL: Pujols (3), Molina, Jay; Mil: Fielder, Braun. **HR**—StL: Pujols, Freese; Mil: Weeks, Fielder. **RBI**—StL: Pujols (5), Punto (2), Holliday, Molina, Freese (2); Mil: Weeks (2), Fielder. **GIDP**—Mil: Weeks. **SAC**—StL: Jackson. **E**—Mil: Weeks. **WP**—Mil: Estrada
**T**—3:36. **A**—43,937.

**Recap:** (AP) Thanks to Albert Pujols' monster night, the St. Louis Cardinals did exactly what they set out to do in the NL championship series: Erase the Milwaukee Brewers' home-field advantage. After a 12–3 victory over the Brewers in Game 2, the Cardinals are tied in the series with their ace Chris Carpenter ready to take the mound in Game 3. This is mostly thanks to Pujols, who spanked the Brewers' pitching in Game 2, going 4 for 5 with a home run, three doubles and five RBIs.

## National League Championship Series (Cont.)

### GAME 3

| | | | | | | | | | | | | |
|---|---|---|---|---|---|---|---|---|---|---|---|---|
| Milwaukee | 0 | 2 | 1 | 0 | 0 | 0 | 0 | 0 | 0 | **3** | **6** | **0** |
| St. Louis | 4 | 0 | 0 | 0 | 0 | 0 | 0 | 0 | x | **4** | **9** | **0** |

**W**—StL: Carpenter. **L**—Mil: Gallardo. **SV**—StL: Motte.
**LOB**—Mil: 5; StL: 9. **2B**—StL: Jay, Pujols, Freese (2).
**HR**—Mil: Kotsay. **RBI**—Mil: Betancourt, Gallardo,
Kotsay; StL: Jay, Pujols, Freese. **SAC**—StL: Furcal.
**SF**—Mil: Gallardo. **GIDP**—Mil: Fielder; StL: Molina, Jay,
Freese. **IBB**—Mil: Fielder; StL: Punto, Pujols (2).
**WP**—Mil: Gallardo (3).
**T**—3:10. **A**—43,584.

**Recap:** (AP) Far from his best performance, Cardinals
ace Chris Carpenter lasted just five innings in a 4–3
victory over the Milwaukee Brewers that gave St.
Louis a 2–1 edge in the NL championship series. The
bullpen that got no work in Carpenter's NLDS-
clinching win over Roy Halladay and the Philadelphia
Phillies came up aces with four relievers retiring the
last 12 Milwaukee batters in order. Albert Pujols had
one of three RBI doubles during a four-run first inning
against Yovani Gallardo for the wild-card Cardinals.

### GAME 4

| | | | | | | | | | | | | |
|---|---|---|---|---|---|---|---|---|---|---|---|---|
| Milwaukee | 0 | 0 | 0 | 2 | 1 | 1 | 0 | 0 | 0 | **4** | **10** | **1** |
| St. Louis | 0 | 1 | 1 | 0 | 0 | 0 | 0 | 0 | 0 | **2** | **8** | **1** |

**W**—Mil: Wolf. **L**—StL: Lohse. **SV**—Mil: Axford. **LOB**—
Mil: 8; StL: 8. **2B**—Mil: Wolf, Fielder, Hairston (2),
Morgan; StL: Molina, Holliday. **HR**—StL: Holliday, Craig.
**RBI**—Mil: Hairston, Betancourt, Braun, Kottaras; StL:
Holliday, Craig. **SAC**—Mil: Wolf. **GIDP**—Mil: Fielder.
**E**—Mil: Weeks; StL: Theriot. **HBP**—Mil: Morgan.
**T**—3:25. **A**—45,606.

**Recap:** (AP) Randy Wolf was more relieved than
elated after his first career postseason win got the
Brewers back to even in the NL championship
series. Prior to his Game 2 win, Wolf's 342 starts
without a postseason victory were the most among
active pitchers. But he ensured that the pennant will
be decided at Miller Park. Ryan Braun had two hits
and an RBI, giving him a .471 average (16 for 34)
with two homers and nine RBIs in the postseason.

### GAME 5

| | | | | | | | | | | | | |
|---|---|---|---|---|---|---|---|---|---|---|---|---|
| Milwaukee | 0 | 0 | 0 | 0 | 1 | 0 | 0 | 0 | 0 | **1** | **9** | **4** |
| St. Louis | 0 | 3 | 0 | 1 | 0 | 1 | 0 | 2 | x | **7** | **10** | **0** |

**W**—StL: Dotel. **L**—Mil: Greinke. **SV**—StL: Motte.
**LOB**—Mil: 7; StL: 11. **2B**—Mil: Braun; StL: Molina,
Furcal, Holliday. **RBI**—Mil: Hart; StL: Molina, Garcia,
Pujols, Holliday (2). **SAC**—StL: Punto; Mil: Greinke.
**SB**—StL: Berkman. **CS**—Mil: Gomez. **PO**—Mil: Gomez.
**GIDP**—Mil: Morgan; StL: Freese. **E**—Mil: Hairston,
Weeks, Betancourt, Estrada. **HBP**—StL: Freese.
**T**—3:09. **A**—46,904.

**Recap:** (AP) Tony La Russa dialed up more bullpen
magic as the St. Louis Cardinals survived a short
start by starter Jaime Garcia. Yet another round of
spotless relief has a team that squeaked into the postseason on the final day one victory away from the
World Series. The Brewers helped out with four errors,
leading to three unearned runs against Zack Greinke.

### GAME 6

| | | | | | | | | | | | | |
|---|---|---|---|---|---|---|---|---|---|---|---|---|
| St. Louis | 4 | 1 | 4 | 0 | 2 | 0 | 0 | 1 | 0 | **12** | **14** | **0** |
| Milwaukee | 1 | 3 | 0 | 1 | 1 | 0 | 0 | 0 | 0 | **6** | **7** | **3** |

**W**—StL: Rzepczynski. **L**—Mil: Marcum. **LOB**—StL: 5;
Mil: 3. **2B**—StL: Freese; Mil: Hairston, Betancourt.
**HR**—StL: Freese, Furcal, Pujols; Mil: Hart, Weeks,
Lucroy. **RBI**—StL: Berkman, Freese (3), Furcal, Punto,
Pujols (2), Craig (2), Chambers; Mil: Hart, Weeks,
Lucroy (2), Betancourt, Braun. **SAC**—StL: Punto.
**SF**—StL: Punto, Chambers. **SB**—StL: Jay. **E**—Mil:
Hart, Hairston (2). **IBB**—StL: Molina. **HBP**—Mil: Gomez.
**WP**—StL: Rzepczynski.
**T**—3:43. **A**—43,926.

**Recap:** (AP) Left behind in the postseason race, the
St. Louis Cardinals decided that they'd focus on
small goals in September. After winning Game 6, the
Cardinals' wild ride is headed to the World Series.
NLCS MVP David Freese hit a three-run homer in the
first inning and manager Tony La Russa again turned
to his brilliant bullpen for seven sturdy innings as St.
Louis captured its 18th pennant with a 12–6 victory.

## American League Division Playoffs

| | |
|---|---|
| Game 1 ...........Tampa Bay 9 at Texas 0 | Game 3 ...........Texas 4 at Tampa Bay 3 |
| Game 2 ...........Tampa Bay 6 at Texas 8 | Game 4 ...........Texas 4 at Tampa Bay 3 |

(Texas won series 3–1)

| | |
|---|---|
| Game 1 ...........Detroit 3 at New York 9 | Game 4 ...........New York 10 at Detroit 1 |
| Game 2 ...........Detroit 5 at New York 3 | Game 5 ...........Detroit 3 at New York 2 |
| Game 3 ...........New York 4 at Detroit 5 | |

(Detroit won series 3–2)

## American League Championship Series

| | |
|---|---|
| Game 1 ...........Detroit 2 at Texas 3 | Game 4 ...........Texas 7 at Detroit 3 (11 inn.) |
| Game 2 ...........Detroit 3 at Texas 7 (11 inn.) | Game 5 ...........Texas 5 at Detroit 7 |
| Game 3 ...........Texas 2 at Detroit 5 | Game 6 ...........Detroit 5 at Texas 15 |

(Texas won series 4–2)

### GAME 1

| | | | | | | | | | | | | |
|---|---|---|---|---|---|---|---|---|---|---|---|---|
| Detroit | 0 | 0 | 0 | 0 | 2 | 0 | 0 | 0 | 0 | **2** | **7** | **1** |
| Texas | 0 | 2 | 1 | 0 | 0 | 0 | 0 | x | | **3** | **6** | **0** |

**W**—Tex: Ogando. **L**—Det: Verlander. **SV**—Tex: Feliz.
**LOB**—Det: 9; Tex: 5. **2B**—Det: Santiago, Jackson.
**3B**—Tex: Murphy. **HR**—Tex: Cruz. **RBI**—Det: Jackson;
Tex: Kinsler, Cruz, Murphy. **CS**—Tex: Kinsler. **GIDP**—
Det: Ordonez, Martinez. **E**—Det: Jackson. **IBB**—Det:
Ordonez. **WP**—Tex: Wilson.
**T**—3:07 (1:50 delay). **A**—50,114.

### GAME 1 (CONT.)

**Recap:** (AP) A few minutes past midnight, the Texas
Rangers had one more victory over Justin Verlander
and the Detroit Tigers lost yet another wet playoff
opener started by their ace. Before the game was
interrupted twice by rain for a total of 1 hour, 50
minutes in the top of the fifth inning, Nelson Cruz
broke a postseason slump with a home run and the
defending AL champions scored all of their runs off
Verlander.

## American League Championship Series (Cont.)

### GAME 2

| | | | | | | | | | | | | | | |
|---|---|---|---|---|---|---|---|---|---|---|---|---|---|---|
| Detroit | 0 0 3 | 0 0 0 | 0 0 0 | 0 0 | **3** | **8** | **0** |
| Texas | 2 0 0 | 0 0 0 | 1 0 0 | 0 4 | **7** | **11** | **1** |

**W**—Tex: Adams. **L**—Det: Perry. **LOB**—Det: 13; Tex: 6. **2B**—Det: Cabrera, Peralta, Kelly; Tex: Hamilton, Beltre (2), Cruz. **HR**—Det: Raburn; Tex: Cruz (2). **RBI**—Det: Raburn (3); Tex: Hamilton, Beltre, Cruz (5). **SAC**—Det: Inge, Peralta. **GIDP**—Tex: Moreland. **E**—Tex: Moreland. **IBB**—Det: Cabrera; Tex: Napoli. **HBP**—Det: Martinez; Tex: Cruz.
**T**—4:25. **A**—51,227.

**Recap:** (AP) Two innings after Nelson Cruz crumbled to the ground writhing in pain, the slugger provided a grand finish for the Texas Rangers. Cruz hit the first game-ending grand slam in postseason history, sending the defending AL champions to Detroit with a 2–0 lead in the American League championship series after a 7–3 victory over the Tigers in 11 innings. The high drive to left off Ryan Perry was the second homer of the game for Cruz, and his third in the ALCS after struggling so badly in the first round of the playoffs (1 for 15 with only a single against Tampa Bay).

### GAME 3

| | | | | | | | | |
|---|---|---|---|---|---|---|---|---|
| Texas | 1 0 0 | 0 0 0 | 0 1 0 | **2** | **8** | **0** |
| Detroit | 0 0 0 | 1 1 2 | 1 0 x | **5** | **11** | **0** |

**W**—Det: Fister. **L**—Tex: Lewis. **SV**—Det: Valverde. **LOB**—Tex: 4; Det: 8. **2B**—Tex: Torrealba, Hamilton; Det: Cabrera, Raburn. **HR**—Det: Martinez, Peralta, Cabrera. **RBI**—Tex: Hamilton, Kinsler; Det: Martinez, Cabrera (2), Peralta, Jackson. **SB**—Det: Dirks. **SAC**—Tex: Andrus. **GIDP**—Tex: Young, Andrus. **HBP**—Tex: Kinsler.
**T**—3:08. **A**—41,905.

**Recap:** (AP) The banged-up Detroit Tigers are teetering but still standing, thanks to Victor Martinez, Miguel Cabrera and another pivotal performance on the mound by Doug Fister, who again delivered a strong start in a game Detroit needed. Cabrera homered and had a tiebreaking double to lead the Tigers past the Texas Rangers 5-2 in Game 3 of the AL championship series. Martinez homered in the fourth to tie the score at 1, hurting his ribcage in the process. He stayed in the game and has every intention of being in the lineup in Game 4 when Detroit will try to even the series.

### GAME 4

| | | | | | | | | |
|---|---|---|---|---|---|---|---|---|
| Texas | 0 0 0 | 0 0 3 | 0 0 0 | 0 4 | **7** | **11** | **0** |
| Detroit | 0 0 2 | 0 0 0 | 1 0 0 | 0 0 | **3** | **5** | **1** |

**W**—Tex: Feldman. **L**—Det: Valverde. **LOB**—Tex: 5; Det: 5. **2B**—Tex: Murphy, Kinsler, Hamilton; Det: Cabrera. **HR**—Tex: Cruz; Det: Inge. **RBI**—Tex: Kinsler, Andrus, Young, Napoli, Cruz (3); Det: Cabrera (2), Inge. **SB**—Tex: Kinsler. **CS**—Tex: Cruz; Det; Jackson. **GIDP**—Tex: Cruz; Det: Porcello. **E**—Det: Porcello. **IBB**—Det: Cabera; Tex: Beltre. **HBP**—Det: Jackson.
**T**—4:00 (2:13 delay). **A**—42,234.

**Recap:** (AP) Nelson Cruz made the throw. Mike Napoli endured the collision. Then this Texas tag team put the game away with their bats. Cruz made a rocket throw to Napoli at the plate to keep the score tied, then hit a crushing three-run homer in the 11th inning off Jose Valverde that helped send Texas over Detroit 7–3 for a 3–1 lead in the AL championship series. Napoli put the Rangers ahead with an RBI single earlier in the 11th, and Cruz—whose grand slam in the 11th inning won Game 2—once again starred in a game delayed at the start for two hours.

### GAME 5

| | | | | | | | | |
|---|---|---|---|---|---|---|---|---|
| Texas | 1 0 0 | 0 1 0 | 0 2 1 | **5** | **10** | **1** |
| Detroit | 0 0 1 | 1 0 4 | 1 0 x | **7** | **10** | **1** |

**W**—Det: Verlander. **L**—Tex: Wilson. **SV**—Det: Coke. **LOB**—Tex: 10; Det: 4. **2B**—Tex: Kinsler, Young, Murphy, Hamilton; Det: Cabrera. **3B**—Det: Martinez. **HR**—Tex: Cruz; Det: Avila, Young, Raburn. **RBI**—Tex: Hamilton (2), Cruz (2), Young; Det: Avila, Young (3), Cabrera, Martinez, Raburn. **SF**—Tex: Hamilton. **SB**—Det: Cabrera. **GIDP**—Tex: Kinsler; Det: Martinez, Avila. **E**—Tex: Andrus; Det: Santiago. **WP**—Det: Verlander.
**T**—3:21. **A**—41,908.

**Recap:** (AP) A loss from elimination, the exhausted Detroit Tigers needed another big start from their determined ace. When Justin Verlander began to struggle, a fluky bounce helped extend their season. Verlander kept Detroit in the game with a gutsy effort, and Miguel Cabrera put the Tigers ahead with a sixth-inning grounder that hit third base before bouncing down the line for a double. Detroit held on for a 7–5 victory over Texas that cut the Rangers' lead to 3–2 in the AL championship series: Cabrera's hit was part of a sudden cycle in the sixth. The Tigers turned a bases-loaded double play to keep the score tied at 2, then opened the bottom of the inning with a single, double, triple and homer—in order—to take a 6–2 lead. It was the first time four consecutive batters on one team hit for a "natural" cycle in a postseason game, according to STATS LLC. After building a five-run cushion, Detroit held on despite Nelson Cruz 's record fifth home run of the series. With closer Jose Valverde unavailable for the Tigers, Texas cut it to 7–5 in the ninth and had Cruz on deck when Phil Coke retired Mike Napoli on a game-ending groundout with two runners on.

### GAME 6

| | | | | | | | | |
|---|---|---|---|---|---|---|---|---|
| Detroit | 1 1 0 | 0 2 0 | 0 1 0 | **5** | **10** | **2** |
| Texas | 0 0 9 | 0 1 2 | 3 0 x | **15** | **17** | **0** |

**W**—Tex: Ogando. **L**—Det: Scherzer. **LOB**—Det: 3 Tex. 11. **2B**—Tex: Cruz, Young (2), Beltre. **HR**—Tex: Young, Cruz; Det: Cabrera, Peralta, Jackson. **RBI**—Det: Cabrera (2), Peralta, Jackson (2); Tex: Young (5), Beltre, Murphy (2), Kinsler (3), Hamilton, Gentry, Cruz (2). **SB**—Tex: Andrus. **CS**—Tex: Andrus. **SF**—Tex: Hamilton. **GIDP**—Det: Raburn (2). **E**—Det: Young, Raburn. **IBB**—Tex: Hamilton, Murphy. **WP**—Det: Penny, Alburquerque.
**T**—3:32. **A**—51,508.

**Recap:** After waiting until their 50th season to reach their first World Series, the Texas Rangers are going right back. Nelson Cruz had one more big blast, Michael Young caught the final out after hitting a pair of doubles in one of the highest-scoring postseason innings ever and the Rangers became the American League's first repeat champion in a decade. The team that lost Cliff Lee in free agency and held onto Young after his offseason trade request finished off the Detroit Tigers with a 15–5 romp to win the AL championship series in six games. Cruz was selected ALCS MVP after his postseason-record sixth home run of the series, and he also had a record 13 RBIs. Young hit a pair of two-run doubles in a nine-run third inning that sent Texas on its way to becoming the AL's first consecutive pennant winner since the New York Yankees won four in a row from 1998-2001.

Game 1 ..........Texas 2 at St. Louis 3
Game 2 ..........Texas 1 at St. Louis 1
Game 3 ..........St. Louis 16 at Texas 7
Game 4 ..........St. Louis 0 at Texas 4

Game 5 ..........St. Louis 2 at Texas 4
Game 6 ..........Texas 9 at St. Louis 10 (11 innings)
Game 7 ..........Texas 2 at St. Louis 6

(St. Louis won series 4–3)

### GAME 1

| | | | | | | | | | | | | |
|---|---|---|---|---|---|---|---|---|---|---|---|---|
| Texas | 0 0 0 | 0 2 0 | 0 0 0 | **2** | **6** | **0** |
| St. Louis | 0 0 0 | 2 0 1 | 0 0 x | **3** | **6** | **0** |

**W**—StL: Carpenter. **L**—Tex: Wilson. **SV**—StL: Motte. **LOB**—Tex: 4; StL: 8. **2B**—Tex: Beltre; StL: Holliday, Freese. **HR**—Tex: Napoli. **RBI**—Tex: Napoli (2); StL: Berkman (2), Craig. **SAC**—Tex: Andrus; StL: Jay, Descalso. **GIDP**—Tex: Napoli; StL: Jay, Holliday. **CS**—Tex: Kinsler. **WP**—Tex: Wilson. **IBB**—StL: Punto, Pujols. **HBP**—StL: Pujols.
**T**—3:06. **A**—46,406.

**Recap:** (AP) St. Louis manager Tony LaRussa used 17 of his 25 players, including five relievers, in Game 1 of the World Series, mixing and matching his way to a 3–2 Cardinals win over the Texas Rangers. Allen Craig pinch-hit for Cardinals ace Chris Carpenter and delivered a go-ahead single in the sixth inning. The slicing drive off reliever Alexi Ogando fell inches from sliding right fielder Nelson Cruz—the opener was that tight throughout a cold, damp evening. The Cardinals even won without their Rally Squirrel. There were no sightings of the elusive critter still roaming Busch Stadium—good thing for the rodent, too, because La Russa probably would've devised a way to catch him. Texas did make some history in Game 1 despite losing. Rangers starter C.J. Wilson became the first pitcher to lose an All-Star game, an ALDS game, an ALCS and a World Series game in the same year.

### GAME 2

| | | | | | | | | | | | | |
|---|---|---|---|---|---|---|---|---|---|---|---|---|
| Texas | 0 0 0 | 0 0 0 | 0 0 2 | **2** | **5** | **1** |
| St. Louis | 0 0 0 | 0 0 0 | 1 0 0 | **1** | **6** | **1** |

**W**—Tex: Adams. **L**—StL: Motte. **SV**—Tex: Feliz. **LOB**—Tex: 3; StL: 9. **2B**—StL: Furcal. **RBI**—Tex: Hamilton, Young; StL: Craig. **SF**—Tex: Hamilton, Young, Andrus. **GIDP**—Tex: Andrus; StL: Holliday **E**—Tex: Kinsler; StL: Pujols.
**T**—3:04. **A**—47,288.

**Recap:** (AP) A little bloop, a daring steal and a couple of fly balls may not sound like much. It was enough, though, for the Texas Rangers to inch their way back into this World Series and it was the first time in Series history that the tying and go-ahead runs scored on sacrifice flies. Looking lost at the plate all game, Josh Hamilton and the Rangers suddenly resembled the team that bashed its way to Busch Stadium. Down to their last three outs, the Rangers kept things interesting—for themselves, and for baseball fans yearning for some October drama when they rallied for two runs against the nearly spotless St. Louis bullpen to beat the Cardinals 2–1.

### GAME 3

| | | | | | | | | | | | | |
|---|---|---|---|---|---|---|---|---|---|---|---|---|
| St. Louis | 1 0 0 | 4 3 4 | 2 1 1 | **16** | **15** | **0** |
| Texas | 0 0 0 | 3 3 0 | 1 0 0 | **7** | **13** | **3** |

**W**—StL: Lynn. **L**—Tex: Harrison. **LOB**—StL: 6; Tex: 8. **2B**—StL: Freese, Molina (2); Tex: Young, Beltre. **HR**—StL: Craig, Pujols (3); Tex: Young, Cruz. **RBI**—StL: Craig, Freese (2), Theriot, Molina (4), Pujols (6); Tex: Young (2), Cruz (2), Beltre, Napoli (2). **SF**—StL: Molina; Tex: Napoli (2). **GIDP**—StL: Furcal; Tex: Hamilton. **CS**—Tex: Jay. **E**—Tex: Kinsler, Napoli, Andrus. **IBB**—StL: Molina.
**T**—4:04. **A**—51,462.

### GAME 3 *(CONT.)*

**Recap:** (AP) Albert Pujols began the game hoping to shake his slump and maybe get a hit. He did that, and a whole lot more: He produced the defining game of his monster career, and perhaps the greatest hitting performance in World Series history. Pujols launched three long homers, drove in six runs and finished with five hits—tying Series records with each accomplishment—as the St. Louis Cardinals romped past the Texas Rangers 16–7 for a two games to one edge. The three-time NL MVP matched Babe Ruth and Reggie Jackson for the most home runs in a game, connecting on fastballs from three different pitchers. Pujols added two singles and set a Series mark with 14 total bases.

### GAME 4

| | | | | | | | | | | | | |
|---|---|---|---|---|---|---|---|---|---|---|---|---|
| St. Louis | 0 0 0 | 0 0 0 | 0 0 0 | **0** | **2** | **0** |
| Texas | 1 0 0 | 0 0 3 | 0 0 x | **4** | **6** | **0** |

**W**—Tex: Holland. **L**—StL: Jackson. **LOB**—StL: 4; Tex: 8. **2B**—StL: Berkman; Tex: Hamilton, Andrus. **HR**—Tex: Napoli. **RBI**—Tex: Hamilton, Napoli (3). **GIDP**—StL: Freese; Tex: Moreland. **CS**—Tex: Kinsler. **PO**—Tex: Kinsler.
**T**—3:07. **A**—51,539.

**Recap:** (AP) Inning by inning, this World Series is getting more intriguing. Derek Holland provided the latest twist, boosted by a pregame pep talk from his manager. The Texas lefty shut down the St. Louis Cardinals on two hits into the ninth inning, and the Rangers won 4–0 Sunday to even things up at two games apiece. A day after the St. Louis Cardinals set a team record by scoring 16 runs in a postseason game, they never got close against Holland. Holland struck out seven and came within two outs of pitching the first complete-game shutout in the World Series since Josh Beckett's gem for Florida to clinch the 2003 title at Yankee Stadium.

### GAME 5

| | | | | | | | | | | | | |
|---|---|---|---|---|---|---|---|---|---|---|---|---|
| St. Louis | 0 2 0 | 0 0 0 | 0 0 0 | **2** | **7** | **1** |
| Texas | 0 0 1 | 0 0 1 | 0 2 x | **4** | **9** | **2** |

**W**—Tex: Oliver. **L**—StL: Dotel. **SV**—Tex: Feliz. **LOB**—StL: 12; Tex: 10. **2B**—Tex: Young, Napoli. **HR**—Tex: Moreland, Beltre. **RBI**—StL: Molina, Schumaker; Tex: Moreland, Beltre, Napoli (2). **GIDP**—StL: Holliday. **CS**—StL: Craig (2). **E**—StL: Carpenter; Tex: Murphy, Wilson. **WP**—Tex: Wilson. **IBB**—StL: Pujols (3), Berkman; Tex: Cruz, Kinsler **HBP**—StL: Craig.
**T**—3:31. **A**—51,459.

**Recap:** (AP) Mike Napoli was dialed in, no matter who he was going to face. A charmed season for Napoli and the Texas Rangers got even better in Game 4, thanks to a most unlikely twist—a bullpen telephone mix-up. La Russa said he called down to the bullpen in the eighth and wanted Marc Rzepczynski and closer Jason Motte to get ready. Instead, bullpen coach Derek Lilliquist heard only Rzepczynski at first. So, the right-handed Napoli ended up facing the left-handed Rzepczynski with the one out and the score tied at two. Napoli delivered a tiebreaking two-run double that beat the St. Louis Cardinals 4–2 and gave Texas a 3–2 edge in the World Series.

### GAME 6

```
Texas      1 1 0 1 1 0 3 0 0  2 0   9 15 2
St. Louis  2 0 0 1 0 1 0 1 2  2 1  10 13 3
```

**W**—StL: Westbrook. **L**—Tex: Lowe. **LOB**—Tex: 12; StL: 11. **2B**—Tex: Kinsler, Young; StL: Pujols. **3B**—StL: Freese. **HR**—Tex: Berkman, Cruz, Hamilton; StL: Berkman, Craig, Freese. **RBI**—Tex: Hamilton (3), Kinsler (2), Naploi, Young, Beltre, Cruz; StL: Berkman (3), Molina (2), Craig, Freese (3), Theriot. **SAC**—StL: Lohse. **PO**—StL: Holliday. **GIDP**—Tex: Lewis, Beltre. **E**—Tex: Young (2), StL: Holliday, Salas, Freese. **WP**—Tex: Ogando; StL: Dotel. **IBB**—Tex: Napoli; StL: Pujols. **T**—4:33. **A**—47,325.

**Recap:** (AP) In one of the greatest thrillers in baseball history, the St. Louis Cardinals twice rallied when they were down to their last strike of the season. First, Freese saved them with a two-run triple in the ninth, then Lance Berkman delivered a tying single in the 10th. "You had to be here to believe it," St. Louis manager Tony La Russa said. And when Freese led off the bottom of the 11th with his solo shot to beat Texas 10–9 and stomped on the plate, this Game 6 had already been stamped forever. "Turned out to be one for the ages," said Daniel Descalso, who keyed a Cardinals comeback. A sloppy game that made for terrible viewing turned terrific in the late innings, Freese added to the Series lore created by the Carlton Fisk homer in Game 6 of the 1975 Series and Bill Buckner's error in Game 6 of the 1986 Series. This was just the third time that a team one out from elimination in the World Series came back to win the game.

### GAME 7

```
Texas      2 0 0 0 0 0 0 0 0  2 6 0
St. Louis  2 0 1 0 2 0 1 0 x  6 7 1
```

**W**—StL: Carpenter. **L**—Tex: Harrison. **LOB**—Tex: 6; StL: 8. **2B**—Tex: Hamilton, Young, Murphy; StL: Freese. **HR**—StL: Craig. **RBI**—Tex: Hamilton, Young; StL: Freese (2), Craig, Molina (2), Furcal. **SAC**—Tex: Harrison, Andrus. **GIDP**—StL: Schumaker. **CS**—Tex: Kinsler. **PO**—Tex: Kinsler. **E**—StL: Pujols. **IBB**—StL: Freese. **HBP**—Tex: Beltre; StL: Pujols, Furcal. **T**—3:17. **A**—47,399.

**Recap:** (AP) Allen Craig drifted back, reached up and made the catch, setting off a stampede from the dugout. The St. Louis Cardinals, the team that wasn't even supposed to be here, had won a most remarkable World Series. A day after twice being down to their last strike, the Cardinals became champions by beating the Texas Rangers 6–2 in Game 7, boosted by another key hit from hometown MVP David Freese and six gutty innings from Chris Carpenter. "It's hard to explain how this happened," Cardinals manager Tony La Russa said. Beyond that final boxscore, that is. Pushed to the brink, the Cardinals kept saving themselves. A frantic rush from 10½ games out in late August to reach the postseason on the final day. A nifty pair of comebacks against Philadelphia and Milwaukee in the playoffs. And then two desperate rallies in Game 6. "This whole ride, this team deserves this," said Freese, who added more hardware to the trophy he won as the NL championship series MVP, making him only the sixth player in history to win both.

## 2011 World Series Composite Box Score

### ST. LOUIS

| BATTING | AB | R | H | HR | RBI | Avg |
|---|---|---|---|---|---|---|
| Furcal | 28 | 1 | 5 | 0 | 1 | .179 |
| Berkman | 26 | 9 | 11 | 1 | 5 | .423 |
| Pujols | 25 | 8 | 6 | 3 | 5 | .240 |
| Molina | 24 | 1 | 8 | 0 | 9 | .333 |
| Freese | 23 | 4 | 8 | 1 | 7 | .348 |
| Craig | 19 | 5 | 5 | 3 | 6 | .263 |
| Holliday | 19 | 5 | 3 | 0 | 0 | .158 |
| Jay | 18 | 1 | 2 | 0 | 0 | .111 |
| Punto | 14 | 0 | 3 | 0 | 0 | .214 |
| Theriot | 13 | 1 | 1 | 0 | 2 | .077 |
| Schumaker | 11 | 1 | 2 | 0 | 1 | .182 |
| Descalso | 3 | 2 | 2 | 0 | 0 | .667 |
| Laird | 2 | 0 | 0 | 0 | 0 | .000 |
| Pitchers | 7 | 0 | 0 | 0 | 0 | .000 |
| **Totals** | **230** | **38** | **56** | **8** | **36** | **.245** |

### TEXAS

| BATTING | AB | R | H | HR | RBI | Avg |
|---|---|---|---|---|---|---|
| Beltre | 30 | 5 | 9 | 2 | 3 | .300 |
| Andrus | 29 | 5 | 8 | 0 | 0 | .276 |
| Hamilton | 29 | 4 | 7 | 1 | 6 | .241 |
| Young | 27 | 3 | 7 | 1 | 5 | .259 |
| Cruz | 25 | 5 | 5 | 2 | 3 | .200 |
| Kinsler | 25 | 2 | 9 | 0 | 2 | .360 |
| Napoli | 20 | 2 | 7 | 2 | 10 | .350 |
| Murphy | 18 | 1 | 4 | 0 | 0 | .222 |
| Moreland | 10 | 1 | 1 | 1 | 1 | .100 |
| Gentry | 5 | 1 | 1 | 0 | 0 | .200 |
| Torrealba | 5 | 0 | 2 | 0 | 0 | .400 |
| German | 3 | 0 | 0 | 0 | 0 | .000 |
| Chavez | 1 | 0 | 0 | 0 | 0 | .000 |
| Pitchers | 9 | 1 | 0 | 0 | 0 | .000 |
| **Totals** | **236** | **30** | **60** | **9** | **30** | **.254** |

### ST. LOUIS PITCHING

| PITCHING | G | IP | H | BB | SO | ERA |
|---|---|---|---|---|---|---|
| Carpenter | 3 | 19.0 | 17 | 5 | 13 | 2.84 |
| Garcia | 2 | 10.0 | 8 | 3 | 10 | 1.80 |
| Lynn | 5 | 5.2 | 7 | 3 | 4 | 6.35 |
| Jackson | 1 | 5.1 | 3 | 7 | 3 | 5.06 |
| Motte | 5 | 4.1 | 4 | 1 | 1 | 6.23 |
| Dotel | 5 | 3.2 | 3 | 1 | 5 | 4.91 |
| Salas | 4 | 3.2 | 7 | 3 | 4 | 7.36 |
| Lohse | 1 | 3.0 | 5 | 2 | 3 | 9.00 |
| Boggs | 2 | 2.2 | 2 | 0 | 4 | 3.38 |
| Rzepczynski | 4 | 2.2 | 2 | 0 | 4 | 0.00 |
| Westbrook | 2 | 2.0 | 2 | 1 | 0 | 0.00 |
| Rhodes | 3 | 1.0 | 0 | 0 | 0 | 0.00 |
| **Totals** | **7** | **63.0** | **60** | **26** | **51** | **3.86** |

### TEXAS PITCHING

| PITCHING | G | IP | H | BB | SO | ERA |
|---|---|---|---|---|---|---|
| Wilson | 3 | 12.1 | 8 | 11 | 9 | 2.92 |
| Lewis | 2 | 12.0 | 7 | 5 | 8 | 2.25 |
| Holland | 2 | 10.1 | 4 | 2 | 7 | 0.87 |
| Harrison | 2 | 7.2 | 11 | 3 | 4 | 7.04 |
| Feldman | 5 | 5.0 | 5 | 6 | 2 | 9.00 |
| Feliz | 4 | 3.2 | 2 | 4 | 7 | 4.91 |
| Gonzalez | 3 | 3.0 | 1 | 1 | 2 | 6.00 |
| Ogando | 6 | 2.2 | 7 | 7 | 3 | 10.12 |
| Oliver | 3 | 2.1 | 3 | 0 | 3 | 11.57 |
| Adams | 3 | 2.0 | 5 | 2 | 1 | 4.50 |
| Lowe | 2 | 1.0 | 3 | 0 | 1 | 18.00 |
| **Totals** | **7** | **62.0** | **56** | **41** | **47** | **4.65** |

## National League Batting

### BATTING AVERAGE

| | |
|---|---|
| Jose Reyes, NY | .337 |
| Ryan Braun, Mil | .332 |
| Matt Kemp, LA | .324 |
| Hunter Pence, Hou/Phi | .314 |
| Joey Votto, Cin | .309 |
| Starlin Castro, Chi | .307 |
| Aramis Ramirez, Chi | .306 |
| Yadier Molina, StL | .305 |
| Michael Morse, Was | .303 |
| Troy Tulowitzki, Col | .302 |

### HITS

| | |
|---|---|
| Starlin Castro, Chi | 207 |
| Matt Kemp, LA | 195 |
| Michael Bourn, Hou/Atl | 193 |
| Hunter Pence, Hou/Phi | 190 |
| Ryan Braun, Mil | 187 |
| Joey Votto, Cin | 185 |
| Brandon Phillips, Cin | 183 |
| Jose Reyes, NY | 181 |
| Aramis Ramirez, Chi | 173 |
| Albert Pujols, StL | 173 |

### DOUBLES

| | |
|---|---|
| Joey Votto, Cin | 40 |
| Carlos Beltran, NY/SF | 39 |
| Justin Upton, Ari | 39 |
| Carlos Lee, Hou | 38 |
| Brandon Phillips, Cin | 38 |
| Chris Young, Ari | 38 |
| Hunter Pence, Hou/Phi | 38 |
| Ryan Braun, Mil | 38 |

### TRIPLES

| | |
|---|---|
| Shane Victorino, Phi | 16 |
| Jose Reyes, NY | 16 |
| Dexter Fowler, Col | 15 |
| Michael Bourn, Hou/Atl | 10 |
| Seth Smith, Col | 9 |
| Starlin Castro, Chi | 9 |

### STOLEN BASES

| | |
|---|---|
| Michael Bourn, Hou/Atl | 61 |
| Cameron Maybin, SD | 40 |
| Matt Kemp, LA | 40 |
| Emilio Bonifacio, Fla | 40 |
| Drew Stubbs, Cin | 40 |
| Jose Reyes, NY | 39 |
| Ryan Braun, Mil | 33 |
| Angel Pagan, NY | 32 |
| Jason Bourgeois, HOU | 31 |
| Jimmy Rollins, Phi | 30 |

### HOME RUNS

| | |
|---|---|
| Matt Kemp, LA | 39 |
| Prince Fielder, Mil | 38 |
| Albert Pujols, StL | 37 |
| Dan Uggla, Atl | 36 |
| Mike Stanton, Fla | 34 |
| Ryan Howard, Phi | 33 |
| Ryan Braun, Mil | 33 |
| Jay Bruce, Cin | 32 |
| Lance Berkman, StL | 31 |
| Michael Morse, Was | 31 |
| Justin Upton, Ari | 31 |
| Troy Tulowitzki, Col | 30 |

### RUNS SCORED

| | |
|---|---|
| Matt Kemp, LA | 115 |
| Ryan Braun, Mil | 109 |
| Albert Pujols, StL | 105 |
| Justin Upton, Ari | 105 |
| Jose Reyes, NY | 101 |
| Joey Votto, Cin | 101 |
| Shane Victorino, Phi | 95 |
| Prince Fielder, Mil | 95 |
| Brandon Phillips, Cin | 94 |
| Michael Bourn, Hou/Atl | 94 |
| Carlos Gonzalez, Col | 92 |
| Drew Stubbs, Cin | 92 |

### RUNS BATTED IN

| | |
|---|---|
| Matt Kemp, LA | 126 |
| Prince Fielder, Mil | 120 |
| Ryan Howard, Phi | 116 |
| Ryan Braun, Mil | 111 |
| Troy Tulowitzki, Col | 105 |
| Joey Votto, Cin | 103 |
| Albert Pujols, StL | 99 |
| Hunter Pence, Hou/Phi | 97 |
| Jay Bruce, Cin | 97 |
| Michael Morse, Was | 95 |
| Carlos Lee, Hou | 94 |
| Lance Berkman, StL | 94 |
| Aramis Ramirez, Chi | 93 |
| Carlos Gonzalez, Col | 92 |
| Andrew McCutchen, Pit | 89 |

### SLUGGING PERCENTAGE

| | |
|---|---|
| Ryan Braun, Mil | .597 |
| Matt Kemp, LA | .586 |
| Prince Fielder, Mil | .566 |
| Michael Morse, Was | .550 |
| Lance Berkman, StL | .547 |

### ON-BASE PERCENTAGE

| | |
|---|---|
| Joey Votto, Cin | .416 |
| Prince Fielder, Mil | .415 |
| Lance Berkman, StL | .412 |
| Matt Kemp, LA | .399 |
| Ryan Braun, Mil | .397 |

### BASES ON BALLS

| | |
|---|---|
| Joey Votto, Cin | 110 |
| Prince Fielder, Mil | 107 |
| Carlos Pena, Chi | 101 |
| Lance Berkman, StL | 92 |
| Andrew McCutchen, Pit | 89 |

## National League Pitching

### EARNED RUN AVERAGE

| | |
|---|---|
| Clayton Kershaw, LA | 2.28 |
| Roy Halladay, Phi | 2.35 |
| Cliff Lee, Phi | 2.40 |
| Ryan Vogelsong, SF | 2.71 |
| Tim Lincecum, SF | 2.74 |
| Cole Hamels, Phi | 2.79 |
| Ian Kennedy, Ari | 2.88 |
| Matt Cain, SF | 2.88 |
| Hiroki Kuroda, LA | 3.07 |

### SAVES

| | |
|---|---|
| John Axford, Mil | 46 |
| Craig Kimbrel, Atl | 46 |
| J.J. Putz, Ari | 45 |
| Heath Bell, SD | 43 |
| Drew Storen, Was | 43 |
| Joel Hanrahan, Pit | 40 |
| Francisco Cordero, Cin | 37 |
| Leo Nunez, Fla | 36 |
| Brian Wilson, SF | 36 |
| Carlos Marmol, Chi | 34 |

### WINS

| | |
|---|---|
| Ian Kennedy, Ari | 21 |
| Clayton Kershaw, LA | 21 |
| Roy Halladay, Phi | 19 |
| Cliff Lee, Phi | 17 |
| Yovani Gallardo, Mil | 17 |

### GAMES PITCHED

| | |
|---|---|
| Jonny Venters, Atl | 85 |
| Bill Bray, Cin | 79 |
| Jose Veras, Pit | 79 |
| Craig Kimbrel, Atl | 79 |
| Sean Marshall, Chi | 78 |
| Eric O'Flaherty, Atl | 78 |
| Jason Motte, StL | 78 |

### INNINGS PITCHED

| | |
|---|---|
| Chris Carpenter, StL | 237.1 |
| Roy Halladay, Phi | 233.2 |
| Clayton Kershaw, LA | 233.1 |
| Cliff Lee, Phi | 232.2 |
| Ian Kennedy, Ari | 222.0 |
| Daniel Hudson, Ari | 222.0 |

### STRIKEOUTS

| | |
|---|---|
| Clayton Kershaw, LA | 248 |
| Cliff Lee, Phi | 238 |
| Roy Halladay, Phi | 220 |
| Tim Lincecum, SF | 220 |
| Yovani Gallardo, Mil | 207 |
| Anibal Sanchez, FLA | 202 |
| Zack Greinke, Mil | 201 |
| Ian Kennedy, Ari | 198 |
| Matt Garza, Chi | 197 |

### COMPLETE GAMES

| | |
|---|---|
| Roy Halladay, Phi | 8 |
| Cliff Lee, Phi | 6 |
| Clayton Kershaw, LA | 5 |
| Chris Carpenter, StL | 4 |
| Four tied with 3. | |

### SHUTOUTS

| | |
|---|---|
| Cliff Lee, Phi | 6 |
| Chris Carpenter, StL | 2 |
| Anibal Sanchez, Fla | 2 |
| Clayton Kershaw, LA | 2 |
| Jaime Garcia, StL | 2 |

## American League Batting

### BATTING AVERAGE

| | |
|---|---|
| Miguel Cabrera, Det | .344 |
| Adrian Gonzalez, Bos | .338 |
| Michael Young, Tex | .338 |
| Victor Martinez, Det | .330 |
| Jacoby Ellsbury, Bos | .321 |
| David Ortiz, Bos | .309 |
| Dustin Pedroia, Bos | .307 |
| Casey Kotchman, TB | .306 |
| Melky Cabrera, KC | .305 |
| Alex Gordon, KC | .303 |

### HITS

| | |
|---|---|
| Michael Young, Tex | 213 |
| Adrian Gonzalez, Bos | 213 |
| Jacoby Ellsbury, Bos | 212 |
| Melky Cabrera, KC | 201 |
| Miguel Cabrera, Det | 197 |
| Dustin Pedroia, Bos | 195 |
| Robinson Cano, NY | 188 |
| Alex Gordon, KC | 185 |
| Ichiro Suzuki, Sea | 184 |
| Nick Markakis, Bal | 182 |

### DOUBLES

| | |
|---|---|
| Miguel Cabera, Det | 48 |
| Jeff Francoeur, KC | 47 |
| Robinson Cano, NY | 46 |
| Ben Zobrist, TB | 46 |
| Jacoby Ellsbury, Bos | 46 |
| Adrian Gonzalez, Bos | 45 |
| Alex Gordon, KC | 45 |

### TRIPLES

| | |
|---|---|
| Peter Bourjos, LA | 11 |
| Austin Jackson, Det | 11 |
| Curtis Granderson, NY | 10 |
| Erick Aybar, LA | 8 |
| Brett Gardner, NY | 8 |
| Alcides Escobar, KC | 8 |
| Jemile Weeks, Oak | 8 |
| Four tied with 7. | |

### STOLEN BASES

| | |
|---|---|
| Coco Crisp, Oak | 49 |
| Brett Gardner, NY | 49 |
| Ichiro Suzuki, Sea | 40 |
| Jacoby Ellsbury, Bos | 39 |
| Elvis Andrus, Tex | 37 |
| B.J. Upton, TB | 36 |
| Rajai Davis, Tor | 34 |
| Ben Revere, Min | 34 |
| Ian Kinsler, Tex | 30 |
| Erick Aybar, LA | 30 |

### HOME RUNS

| | |
|---|---|
| Jose Bautista, Tor | 43 |
| Curtis Granderson, NY | 41 |
| Mark Teixeira, NY | 39 |
| Mark Reynolds, Bal | 37 |
| Adrian Beltre, Tex | 32 |
| Ian Kinsler, Tex | 32 |
| Jacoby Ellsbury, Bos | 32 |
| Paul Konerko, Chi | 31 |
| Evan Longoria, TB | 31 |
| Miguel Cabrera, Det | 30 |
| J.J. Hardy, Bal | 30 |
| Mike Napoli, Tex | 30 |
| David Ortiz, Bos | 29 |
| Josh Willingham, Oak | 29 |
| Nelson Cruz, Tex | 29 |
| Mark Trumbo, LA | 29 |

### RUNS SCORED

| | |
|---|---|
| Curtis Granderson, NY | 136 |
| Ian Kinsler, Tex | 121 |
| Jacoby Ellsbury, Bos | 119 |
| Miguel Cabrera, Det | 111 |
| Adrain Gonzalez, Bos | 108 |
| Jose Bautista, Tor | 105 |
| Robinson Cano, NY | 104 |
| Melky Cabrera, KC | 102 |
| Dustin Pedroia, Bos | 102 |
| Alex Gordon, KC | 101 |
| Ben Zobrist, TB | 99 |

### RUNS BATTED IN

| | |
|---|---|
| Curtis Granderson, NY | 119 |
| Robinson Cano, NYY | 118 |
| Adrian Gonzalez, Bos | 117 |
| Mark Teixeira, NY | 111 |
| Michael Young, Tex | 106 |
| Paul Konerko, Chi | 105 |
| Adrian Beltre, Tex | 105 |
| Miguel Cabrera, Det | 105 |
| Jacoby Ellsbury, Bos | 105 |
| Victor Martinez, Det | 103 |
| Jose Bautista, Tor | 103 |
| Evan Longoria, TB | 99 |
| Josh Willingham, Oak | 98 |
| David Ortiz, Bos | 96 |
| Billy Butler, KC | 95 |
| Josh Hamilton, Tex | 94 |

### SLUGGING PERCENTAGE

| | |
|---|---|
| Jose Bautista, Tor | .608 |
| Miguel Cabrera, Det | .586 |
| Adrian Beltre, Tex | .561 |
| David Ortiz, Bos | .554 |
| Curtis Granderson, NY | .552 |
| Jacoby Ellsbury, Bos | .552 |
| Adrian Gonzalez, Bos | .548 |

### ON-BASE PERCENTAGE

| | |
|---|---|
| Miguel Cabrera, Det | .448 |
| Jose Bautista, Tor | .447 |
| Adrian Gonzalez, Bos | .410 |
| David Ortiz, Bos | .398 |
| Alex Avila, Det | .389 |
| Paul Konerko, Chi | .388 |

### BASES ON BALLS

| | |
|---|---|
| Jose Bautista, Tor | 132 |
| Miguel Cabrera, Det | 108 |
| Carlos Santana, Cle | 97 |
| Nick Swisher, NY | 95 |
| Ian Kinsler, Tex | 89 |
| Dustin Pedroia, Bos | 86 |

## American League Pitching

### EARNED RUN AVERAGE

| | |
|---|---|
| Justin Verlander, Det | 2.40 |
| Jered Weaver, LA | 2.41 |
| James Shields, TB | 2.82 |
| Doug Fister, Sea/Det | 2.83 |
| Josh Beckett, Bos | 2.89 |
| Ricky Romero, Tor | 2.92 |
| C.J. Wilson, Tex | 2.94 |
| Jeremy Hellickson, TB | 2.95 |
| C.C. Sabathia, NY | 3.00 |
| Gio Gonzalez, Oak | 3.12 |

### SAVES

| | |
|---|---|
| Jose Valverde, Det | 49 |
| Mariano Rivera, NY | 44 |
| Brandon League, Sea | 37 |
| Chris Perez, Cle | 36 |
| Jordan Walden, LA | 32 |
| Neftali Feliz, Tex | 32 |
| Jonathan Papelbon, Bos | 31 |
| Sergio Santos, Chi | 30 |
| Joakim Soria, KC | 28 |
| Kyle Farnsworth, TB | 25 |

### WINS

| | |
|---|---|
| Justin Verlander, Det | 24 |
| C.C. Sabathia, NY | 19 |
| Jered Weaver, LA | 18 |
| Dan Haren, LA | 16 |
| C.J. Wilson, Tex | 16 |
| James Shields, TB | 16 |
| Gio Gonzalez, Oak | 16 |
| Derek Holland, Tex | 16 |
| Ivan Nova, NY | 16 |

### GAMES PITCHED

| | |
|---|---|
| Jose Valverde, Det | 75 |
| Joel Peralta, TB | 71 |
| Rafael Perez, Cle | 71 |
| Joe Smith, Cle | 71 |

### INNINGS PITCHED

| | |
|---|---|
| Justin Verlander, Det | 251.0 |
| James Shields, TB | 249.1 |
| Dan Haren, LA | 238.1 |
| C.C. Sabathia, NY | 237.1 |
| Jered Weaver, LA | 235.2 |
| Felix Hernandez, Sea | 233.2 |

### STRIKEOUTS

| | |
|---|---|
| Justin Verlander, Det | 250 |
| C.C. Sabathia, NYY | 230 |
| James Shields, TB | 225 |
| Felix Hernandez, Sea | 222 |
| David Price, TB | 218 |
| C.J. Wilson, Tex | 206 |
| Brandon Morrow, Tor | 203 |
| Jered Weaver, LA | 198 |
| Gio Gonzalez, Oak | 197 |
| Dan Haren, LA | 192 |

### COMPLETE GAMES

| | |
|---|---|
| James Shields, TB | 11 |
| Brandon McCarthy, Oak | 5 |
| Felix Hernandez, Sea | 5 |
| Seven tied with 4. | |

### SHUTOUTS

| | |
|---|---|
| James Shields, TB | 4 |
| Derek Holland, Tex | 4 |
| Dan Haren, LA | 3 |
| Jason Vargas, Sea | 3 |
| Three tied with 2. | |

## National League

| TEAM BATTING | G | AB | R | H | 2B | 3B | HR | TB | RBI | OBP | SLG | OPS | BAVG |
|---|---|---|---|---|---|---|---|---|---|---|---|---|---|
| St. Louis Cardinals | 162 | 5532 | 762 | 1513 | 308 | 22 | 162 | 2351 | 726 | .341 | .425 | .766 | .273 |
| New York Mets | 162 | 5600 | 718 | 1477 | 309 | 39 | 108 | 2188 | 676 | .335 | .391 | .725 | .264 |
| Milwaukee Brewers | 162 | 5447 | 721 | 1422 | 276 | 31 | 185 | 2315 | 693 | .325 | .425 | .750 | .261 |
| Colorado Rockies | 162 | 5544 | 735 | 1429 | 274 | 40 | 163 | 2272 | 697 | .329 | .410 | .739 | .258 |
| Houston Astros | 162 | 5598 | 615 | 1442 | 309 | 28 | 95 | 2092 | 579 | .311 | .374 | .684 | .258 |
| Los Angeles Dodgers | 161 | 5436 | 644 | 1395 | 237 | 28 | 117 | 2039 | 613 | .322 | .375 | .697 | .257 |
| Chicago Cubs | 162 | 5549 | 654 | 1423 | 285 | 36 | 148 | 2224 | 610 | .314 | .401 | .715 | .256 |
| Cincinnati Reds | 162 | 5612 | 735 | 1438 | 264 | 19 | 183 | 2289 | 697 | .326 | .408 | .734 | .256 |
| Philadelphia Phillies | 162 | 5579 | 713 | 1409 | 258 | 38 | 153 | 2202 | 693 | .323 | .395 | .717 | .253 |
| Arizona Diamondbacks | 162 | 5421 | 731 | 1357 | 293 | 37 | 172 | 2240 | 702 | .322 | .413 | .736 | .250 |
| Florida Marlins | 162 | 5508 | 625 | 1358 | 274 | 30 | 149 | 2139 | 596 | .318 | .388 | .706 | .247 |
| Pittsburgh Pirates | 162 | 5421 | 610 | 1325 | 277 | 35 | 107 | 1993 | 580 | .309 | .368 | .676 | .244 |
| Atlanta Braves | 162 | 5528 | 641 | 1345 | 244 | 16 | 173 | 2140 | 606 | .308 | .387 | .695 | .243 |
| Washington Nationals | 161 | 5441 | 624 | 1319 | 257 | 22 | 154 | 2082 | 594 | .309 | .383 | .691 | .242 |
| San Francisco Giants | 162 | 5486 | 570 | 1327 | 282 | 24 | 121 | 2020 | 534 | .303 | .368 | .671 | .242 |
| San Diego Padres | 162 | 5417 | 593 | 1284 | 247 | 42 | 91 | 1888 | 563 | .305 | .349 | .653 | .237 |

| TEAM PITCHING | GP | W | L | SV | SVO | CG | SHO | R | IP | Ks | BB | ERA |
|---|---|---|---|---|---|---|---|---|---|---|---|---|
| Philadelphia Phillies | 162 | 102 | 60 | 47 | 56 | 18 | 21 | 529 | 1477.0 | 1299 | 404 | 3.02 |
| San Francisco Giants | 162 | 86 | 76 | 52 | 66 | 3 | 12 | 578 | 1468.0 | 1316 | 559 | 3.20 |
| San Diego Padres | 162 | 71 | 91 | 44 | 62 | 0 | 10 | 611 | 1449.1 | 1139 | 521 | 3.42 |
| Atlanta Braves | 162 | 89 | 73 | 52 | 77 | 3 | 16 | 605 | 1479.2 | 1332 | 521 | 3.48 |
| Los Angeles Dodgers | 161 | 82 | 79 | 40 | 53 | 7 | 17 | 612 | 1432.0 | 1265 | 507 | 3.54 |
| Washington Nationals | 161 | 80 | 81 | 49 | 77 | 3 | 10 | 643 | 1449.1 | 1049 | 477 | 3.58 |
| Milwaukee Brewers | 162 | 96 | 66 | 47 | 66 | 1 | 13 | 638 | 1441.2 | 1257 | 440 | 3.63 |
| St. Louis Cardinals | 162 | 90 | 72 | 47 | 73 | 7 | 9 | 692 | 1462.0 | 1098 | 448 | 3.74 |
| Arizona Diamondbacks | 162 | 94 | 68 | 58 | 71 | 5 | 12 | 662 | 1443.1 | 1058 | 442 | 3.80 |
| Florida Marlins | 162 | 72 | 90 | 40 | 59 | 7 | 11 | 702 | 1459.2 | 1218 | 500 | 3.95 |
| Pittsburgh Pirates | 162 | 72 | 90 | 43 | 65 | 5 | 11 | 712 | 1449.1 | 1031 | 535 | 4.04 |
| Cincinnati Reds | 162 | 79 | 83 | 39 | 61 | 4 | 5 | 720 | 1467.2 | 1112 | 539 | 4.16 |
| New York Mets | 162 | 77 | 85 | 43 | 67 | 6 | 9 | 742 | 1448.0 | 1126 | 514 | 4.19 |
| Chicago Cubs | 162 | 71 | 91 | 40 | 64 | 4 | 5 | 756 | 1434.1 | 1224 | 580 | 4.33 |
| Colorado Rockies | 162 | 73 | 89 | 41 | 64 | 5 | 7 | 774 | 1447.2 | 1118 | 522 | 4.43 |
| Houston Astros | 162 | 56 | 106 | 25 | 50 | 2 | 6 | 796 | 1435.0 | 1191 | 560 | 4.51 |

## American League

| TEAM BATTING | G | AB | R | H | 2B | 3B | HR | TB | RBI | OBP | SLG | OPS | BAVG |
|---|---|---|---|---|---|---|---|---|---|---|---|---|---|
| Texas Rangers | 162 | 5659 | 855 | 1599 | 310 | 32 | 210 | 2603 | 807 | .340 | .460 | .800 | .283 |
| Boston Red Sox | 162 | 5710 | 875 | 1600 | 352 | 35 | 203 | 2631 | 842 | .349 | .461 | .810 | .280 |
| Detroit Tigers | 162 | 5563 | 787 | 1540 | 297 | 34 | 169 | 2412 | 750 | .340 | .434 | .773 | .277 |
| Kansas City Royals | 162 | 5672 | 730 | 1560 | 325 | 41 | 129 | 2354 | 705 | .329 | .415 | .744 | .275 |
| New York Yankees | 162 | 5518 | 867 | 1452 | 267 | 33 | 222 | 2451 | 836 | .343 | .444 | .788 | .263 |
| Baltimore Orioles | 162 | 5585 | 708 | 1434 | 273 | 13 | 191 | 2306 | 684 | .316 | .413 | .729 | .257 |
| Los Angeles Angels | 162 | 5513 | 667 | 1394 | 289 | 34 | 155 | 2216 | 629 | .313 | .402 | .714 | .253 |
| Chicago White Sox | 162 | 5502 | 654 | 1387 | 252 | 16 | 154 | 2133 | 625 | .319 | .388 | .706 | .252 |
| Cleveland Indians | 162 | 5509 | 704 | 1380 | 290 | 26 | 154 | 2184 | 671 | .317 | .396 | .714 | .250 |
| Toronto Blue Jays | 162 | 5559 | 743 | 1384 | 285 | 34 | 186 | 2295 | 704 | .317 | .413 | .730 | .249 |
| Minnesota Twins | 162 | 5487 | 619 | 1357 | 259 | 25 | 103 | 1975 | 572 | .306 | .360 | .666 | .247 |
| Oakland Athletics | 162 | 5452 | 645 | 1330 | 280 | 29 | 114 | 2010 | 612 | .311 | .369 | .680 | .244 |
| Tampa Bay Rays | 162 | 5436 | 707 | 1324 | 273 | 37 | 172 | 2187 | 674 | .322 | .402 | .724 | .244 |
| Seattle Mariners | 162 | 5421 | 556 | 1263 | 253 | 22 | 109 | 1887 | 534 | .292 | .348 | .640 | .233 |

| TEAM PITCHING | GP | W | L | SV | SVO | CG | SHO | R | IP | Ks | BB | ERA |
|---|---|---|---|---|---|---|---|---|---|---|---|---|
| Los Angeles Angels | 162 | 86 | 76 | 39 | 64 | 12 | 11 | 633 | 1465.0 | 1058 | 476 | 3.57 |
| Tampa Bay Rays | 162 | 91 | 71 | 32 | 44 | 15 | 13 | 614 | 1449.0 | 1143 | 504 | 3.58 |
| Oakland Athletics | 162 | 74 | 88 | 39 | 57 | 6 | 12 | 679 | 1447.2 | 1160 | 519 | 3.71 |
| New York Yankees | 162 | 97 | 65 | 47 | 63 | 5 | 8 | 657 | 1458.1 | 1222 | 507 | 3.73 |
| Texas Rangers | 162 | 96 | 66 | 38 | 57 | 10 | 19 | 677 | 1441.1 | 1179 | 461 | 3.79 |
| Seattle Mariners | 162 | 67 | 95 | 39 | 55 | 12 | 10 | 675 | 1433.0 | 1088 | 436 | 3.90 |
| Detroit Tigers | 162 | 95 | 67 | 52 | 62 | 4 | 14 | 711 | 1440.0 | 1115 | 492 | 4.04 |
| Chicago White Sox | 162 | 79 | 83 | 42 | 62 | 6 | 14 | 706 | 1460.0 | 1220 | 439 | 4.10 |
| Boston Red Sox | 162 | 90 | 72 | 36 | 52 | 2 | 13 | 737 | 1457.1 | 1213 | 540 | 4.20 |
| Cleveland Indians | 162 | 80 | 82 | 38 | 54 | 2 | 4 | 760 | 1453.1 | 1024 | 463 | 4.23 |
| Toronto Blue Jays | 162 | 81 | 81 | 33 | 58 | 7 | 10 | 761 | 1458.2 | 1169 | 540 | 4.32 |
| Kansas City Royals | 162 | 71 | 91 | 37 | 59 | 2 | 6 | 762 | 1451.1 | 1080 | 557 | 4.44 |
| Minnesota Twins | 162 | 63 | 99 | 32 | 52 | 7 | 8 | 804 | 1421.0 | 940 | 480 | 4.58 |
| Baltimore Orioles | 162 | 69 | 93 | 32 | 51 | 3 | 7 | 860 | 1446.2 | 1044 | 535 | 4.89 |

### Arizona Diamondbacks

| BATTING | G | AB | R | H | 2B | 3B | HR | RBI | TB | BB | SO | SB | OBP | SLG | BAVG |
|---|---|---|---|---|---|---|---|---|---|---|---|---|---|---|---|
| Justin Upton | 159 | 592 | 105 | 171 | 39 | 5 | 31 | 88 | 313 | 59 | 126 | 21 | .369 | .529 | .289 |
| Chris Young | 156 | 567 | 89 | 134 | 38 | 3 | 20 | 71 | 238 | 80 | 139 | 22 | .331 | .420 | .236 |
| Miguel Montero | 140 | 493 | 65 | 139 | 36 | 1 | 18 | 86 | 231 | 47 | 97 | 1 | .351 | .469 | .282 |
| Ryan Roberts | 143 | 482 | 86 | 120 | 25 | 2 | 19 | 65 | 206 | 66 | 98 | 18 | .341 | .427 | .249 |
| Gerardo Parra | 141 | 445 | 55 | 130 | 20 | 8 | 8 | 46 | 190 | 43 | 82 | 15 | .357 | .427 | .292 |
| *Kelly Johnson | 114 | 430 | 59 | 90 | 23 | 5 | 18 | 49 | 177 | 44 | 132 | 13 | .287 | .412 | .209 |
| Willie Bloomquist | 97 | 350 | 44 | 93 | 10 | 2 | 4 | 26 | 119 | 23 | 51 | 20 | .317 | .340 | .266 |
| Stephen Drew | 86 | 321 | 44 | 81 | 21 | 5 | 5 | 45 | 127 | 30 | 74 | 4 | .317 | .396 | .252 |
| Xavier Nady | 82 | 206 | 26 | 51 | 11 | 0 | 4 | 35 | 74 | 10 | 46 | 2 | .287 | .359 | .248 |
| Juan Miranda | 65 | 174 | 18 | 37 | 8 | 2 | 7 | 23 | 70 | 23 | 48 | 0 | .315 | .402 | .213 |
| Paul Goldschmidt | 48 | 156 | 28 | 39 | 9 | 1 | 8 | 26 | 74 | 20 | 53 | 4 | .333 | .474 | .250 |
| Melvin Mora | 42 | 127 | 5 | 29 | 6 | 0 | 0 | 16 | 35 | 2 | 24 | 0 | .244 | .276 | .228 |
| *Aaron Hill | 33 | 124 | 23 | 39 | 12 | 2 | 2 | 16 | 61 | 12 | 19 | 5 | .386 | .492 | .315 |
| Sean Burroughs | 78 | 110 | 8 | 30 | 4 | 0 | 1 | 8 | 37 | 3 | 15 | 1 | .289 | .336 | .273 |
| Henry Blanco | 37 | 100 | 12 | 25 | 3 | 1 | 8 | 12 | 54 | 12 | 21 | 0 | .330 | .540 | .250 |

| PITCHING | GP | GS | W–L | SV | SHO | R | ERA | IP | Ks | BB |
|---|---|---|---|---|---|---|---|---|---|---|
| Ian Kennedy | 33 | 33 | 21-4 | 0 | 0 | 98 | 2.88 | 222.0 | 198 | 55 |
| Daniel Hudson | 33 | 33 | 16-12 | 0 | 1 | 73 | 3.49 | 222.0 | 169 | 50 |
| Joe Saunders | 33 | 33 | 12-13 | 0 | 0 | 94 | 3.69 | 212.0 | 108 | 67 |
| Josh Collmenter | 31 | 24 | 10-10 | 0 | 0 | 61 | 3.38 | 154.1 | 100 | 28 |
| Zach Duke | 21 | 9 | 3-4 | 1 | 0 | 42 | 4.93 | 76.2 | 32 | 19 |
| David Hernandez | 74 | 0 | 5-3 | 11 | 0 | 27 | 3.38 | 69.1 | 77 | 30 |
| Micah Owings | 33 | 4 | 8-0 | 0 | 0 | 27 | 3.57 | 63.0 | 44 | 23 |
| J.J. Putz | 60 | 0 | 2-2 | 45 | 0 | 15 | 2.17 | 58.0 | 61 | 12 |
| Armando Galarraga | 8 | 8 | 3-4 | 0 | 0 | 36 | 5.91 | 42.2 | 28 | 22 |
| Wade Miley | 8 | 7 | 4-2 | 0 | 0 | 20 | 4.50 | 40.0 | 25 | 18 |
| Barry Enright | 7 | 7 | 1-4 | 0 | 0 | 31 | 7.41 | 37.2 | 21 | 15 |
| Aaron Heilman | 32 | 0 | 4-1 | 0 | 0 | 28 | 6.88 | 35.1 | 33 | 11 |
| Joe Paterson | 62 | 0 | 0-3 | 1 | 0 | 11 | 2.91 | 34.0 | 28 | 15 |
| Esmerling Vasquez | 31 | 0 | 1-1 | 0 | 0 | 16 | 4.15 | 30.1 | 20 | 13 |

### Atlanta Braves

| BATTING | G | AB | R | H | 2B | 3B | HR | RBI | TB | BB | SO | SB | OBP | SLG | BAVG |
|---|---|---|---|---|---|---|---|---|---|---|---|---|---|---|---|
| Dan Uggla | 161 | 600 | 88 | 140 | 22 | 1 | 36 | 82 | 272 | 62 | 156 | 1 | .311 | .453 | .233 |
| Freddie Freeman | 157 | 571 | 67 | 161 | 32 | 0 | 21 | 76 | 256 | 53 | 142 | 4 | .346 | .448 | .282 |
| Alex Gonzalez | 149 | 564 | 59 | 136 | 27 | 1 | 15 | 56 | 210 | 22 | 126 | 2 | .270 | .372 | .241 |
| Martin Prado | 129 | 551 | 66 | 143 | 26 | 2 | 13 | 57 | 212 | 34 | 52 | 4 | .302 | .385 | .260 |
| Brian McCann | 129 | 466 | 51 | 126 | 19 | 0 | 24 | 71 | 217 | 57 | 89 | 3 | .351 | .466 | .270 |
| Chipper Jones | 126 | 455 | 56 | 125 | 33 | 1 | 18 | 70 | 214 | 51 | 80 | 2 | .344 | .470 | .275 |
| Jason Heyward | 128 | 396 | 50 | 90 | 18 | 2 | 14 | 42 | 154 | 51 | 93 | 9 | .319 | .389 | .227 |
| Nate McLouth | 81 | 267 | 35 | 61 | 12 | 2 | 4 | 16 | 89 | 44 | 52 | 4 | .344 | .333 | .228 |
| Eric Hinske | 117 | 236 | 24 | 55 | 10 | 0 | 10 | 28 | 95 | 26 | 71 | 0 | .311 | .403 | .233 |
| *Michael Bourn | 53 | 227 | 30 | 63 | 8 | 3 | 1 | 18 | 80 | 15 | 50 | 22 | .321 | .352 | .278 |
| *Jordan Schafer | 52 | 196 | 32 | 47 | 6 | 3 | 1 | 7 | 62 | 18 | 42 | 15 | .307 | .316 | .240 |
| David Ross | 52 | 152 | 14 | 40 | 7 | 0 | 6 | 23 | 65 | 16 | 51 | 0 | .333 | .428 | .263 |
| Jose Constanza | 42 | 109 | 21 | 33 | 1 | 1 | 2 | 10 | 42 | 6 | 14 | 7 | .339 | .385 | .303 |
| Brooks Conrad | 92 | 103 | 11 | 23 | 5 | 0 | 4 | 13 | 40 | 15 | 41 | 2 | .325 | .388 | .223 |
| Joe Mather | 36 | 75 | 4 | 16 | 4 | 0 | 1 | 9 | 23 | 6 | 23 | 0 | .272 | .307 | .213 |

| PITCHING | GP | GS | W–L | SV | SHO | R | ERA | IP | Ks | BB |
|---|---|---|---|---|---|---|---|---|---|---|
| Tim Hudson | 33 | 33 | 16-10 | 0 | 1 | 86 | 3.22 | 215.0 | 158 | 56 |
| Derek Lowe | 34 | 34 | 9-17 | 0 | 0 | 110 | 5.05 | 187.0 | 137 | 70 |
| Jair Jurrjens | 23 | 23 | 13-6 | 0 | 1 | 52 | 2.96 | 152.0 | 90 | 44 |
| Brandon Beachy | 25 | 25 | 7-3 | 0 | 0 | 62 | 3.68 | 141.2 | 169 | 46 |
| Tommy Hanson | 22 | 22 | 11-7 | 0 | 0 | 55 | 3.60 | 130.0 | 142 | 46 |
| Jonny Venters | 85 | 0 | 6-2 | 5 | 0 | 19 | 1.84 | 88.0 | 96 | 43 |
| Mike Minor | 15 | 15 | 5-3 | 0 | 0 | 39 | 4.14 | 82.2 | 77 | 30 |
| Cristhian Martinez | 46 | 0 | 1-3 | 0 | 0 | 30 | 3.36 | 77.2 | 58 | 19 |
| Craig Kimbrel | 79 | 0 | 4-3 | 46 | 0 | 19 | 2.10 | 77.0 | 127 | 32 |
| Eric O'Flaherty | 78 | 0 | 2-4 | 0 | 0 | 9 | 0.98 | 73.2 | 67 | 21 |
| Scott Linebrink | 64 | 0 | 4-4 | 1 | 0 | 22 | 3.64 | 54.1 | 42 | 21 |
| George Sherrill | 51 | 0 | 3-1 | 0 | 0 | 12 | 3.00 | 36.0 | 38 | 12 |
| Randall Delgado | 7 | 7 | 1-1 | 0 | 0 | 12 | 2.83 | 35.0 | 18 | 14 |
| *Scott Proctor | 31 | 0 | 2-3 | 0 | 0 | 21 | 6.44 | 29.1 | 18 | 19 |

*Mid-season trade.

### Chicago Cubs

| BATTING | G | AB | R | H | 2B | 3B | HR | RBI | TB | BB | SO | SB | OBP | SLG | BAVG |
|---|---|---|---|---|---|---|---|---|---|---|---|---|---|---|---|
| Starlin Castro | 158 | 674 | 91 | 207 | 36 | 9 | 10 | 66 | 291 | 35 | 96 | 22 | .341 | .432 | .307 |
| Aramis Ramirez | 149 | 565 | 80 | 173 | 35 | 1 | 26 | 93 | 288 | 43 | 69 | 1 | .361 | .510 | .306 |
| Darwin Barney | 143 | 529 | 66 | 146 | 23 | 6 | 2 | 43 | 187 | 22 | 67 | 9 | .313 | .353 | .276 |
| Carlos Pena | 153 | 493 | 72 | 111 | 27 | 3 | 28 | 80 | 228 | 101 | 161 | 2 | .357 | .462 | .225 |
| Alfonso Soriano | 137 | 475 | 50 | 116 | 27 | 1 | 26 | 88 | 223 | 27 | 113 | 2 | .289 | .469 | .244 |
| Marlon Byrd | 119 | 446 | 51 | 123 | 22 | 2 | 9 | 35 | 176 | 25 | 78 | 3 | .324 | .395 | .276 |
| Geovany Soto | 125 | 421 | 46 | 96 | 26 | 0 | 17 | 54 | 173 | 45 | 124 | 0 | .310 | .411 | .228 |
| *Kosuke Fukudome | 87 | 293 | 33 | 80 | 15 | 2 | 3 | 13 | 108 | 46 | 57 | 2 | .374 | .369 | .273 |
| Reed Johnson | 111 | 246 | 33 | 76 | 21 | 1 | 5 | 28 | 115 | 5 | 63 | 2 | .348 | .467 | .309 |
| Blake DeWitt | 121 | 230 | 21 | 61 | 11 | 4 | 5 | 26 | 95 | 12 | 31 | 1 | .305 | .413 | .265 |
| Tyler Colvin | 80 | 206 | 17 | 31 | 8 | 3 | 6 | 20 | 63 | 14 | 58 | 0 | .204 | .306 | .150 |
| Jeff Baker | 81 | 201 | 20 | 54 | 12 | 1 | 3 | 23 | 77 | 10 | 46 | 0 | .302 | .383 | .269 |
| Tony Campana | 95 | 143 | 24 | 37 | 3 | 0 | 1 | 6 | 43 | 8 | 30 | 24 | .303 | .301 | .259 |
| Koyie Hill | 46 | 134 | 15 | 26 | 3 | 1 | 2 | 9 | 37 | 14 | 40 | 1 | .268 | .276 | .194 |

| PITCHING | GP | GS | W-L | SV | SHO | R | ERA | IP | Ks | BB |
|---|---|---|---|---|---|---|---|---|---|---|
| Ryan Dempster | 34 | 34 | 10-14 | 0 | 0 | 111 | 4.80 | 202.1 | 191 | 82 |
| Matt Garza | 31 | 31 | 10-10 | 0 | 0 | 90 | 3.32 | 198.0 | 197 | 63 |
| Carlos Zambrano | 24 | 24 | 9-7 | 0 | 0 | 80 | 4.82 | 145.2 | 101 | 56 |
| Randy Wells | 23 | 23 | 7-6 | 0 | 1 | 76 | 4.99 | 135.1 | 82 | 47 |
| Rodrigo Lopez | 26 | 16 | 6-6 | 0 | 0 | 56 | 4.42 | 97.2 | 54 | 29 |
| Jeff Samardzija | 75 | 0 | 8-4 | 0 | 0 | 35 | 2.97 | 88.0 | 87 | 50 |
| Casey Coleman | 19 | 17 | 3-9 | 0 | 0 | 62 | 6.40 | 84.1 | 75 | 46 |
| Sean Marshall | 78 | 0 | 6-6 | 5 | 0 | 21 | 2.26 | 75.2 | 79 | 17 |
| Carlos Marmol | 75 | 0 | 2-6 | 34 | 0 | 33 | 4.01 | 74.0 | 99 | 48 |
| James Russell | 64 | 5 | 1-6 | 0 | 0 | 37 | 4.12 | 67.2 | 43 | 14 |
| John Grabow | 58 | 0 | 3-1 | 0 | 0 | 39 | 4.76 | 62.1 | 38 | 28 |
| Kerry Wood | 55 | 0 | 3-5 | 1 | 0 | 23 | 3.35 | 51.0 | 57 | 21 |
| Doug Davis | 9 | 9 | 1-7 | 0 | 0 | 38 | 6.50 | 45.2 | 36 | 26 |
| Ramon Ortiz | 22 | 2 | 1-2 | 0 | 0 | 20 | 4.86 | 33.1 | 25 | 11 |

### Cincinnati Reds

| BATTING | G | AB | R | H | 2B | 3B | HR | RBI | TB | BB | SO | SB | OBP | SLG | BAVG |
|---|---|---|---|---|---|---|---|---|---|---|---|---|---|---|---|
| Brandon Phillips | 150 | 610 | 94 | 183 | 38 | 2 | 18 | 82 | 279 | 44 | 85 | 14 | .353 | .457 | .300 |
| Drew Stubbs | 158 | 604 | 92 | 147 | 22 | 3 | 15 | 44 | 220 | 63 | 205 | 40 | .321 | .364 | .243 |
| Joey Votto | 161 | 599 | 101 | 185 | 40 | 3 | 29 | 103 | 318 | 110 | 129 | 8 | .416 | .531 | .309 |
| Jay Bruce | 157 | 585 | 84 | 150 | 27 | 2 | 32 | 97 | 277 | 71 | 158 | 8 | .341 | .474 | .256 |
| Paul Janish | 114 | 336 | 27 | 72 | 14 | 1 | 0 | 23 | 88 | 18 | 46 | 3 | .259 | .262 | .214 |
| Edgar Renteria | 96 | 299 | 34 | 75 | 14 | 0 | 5 | 36 | 104 | 24 | 65 | 4 | .306 | .348 | .251 |
| Ramon Hernandez | 91 | 298 | 28 | 84 | 13 | 0 | 12 | 36 | 133 | 23 | 41 | 0 | .341 | .446 | .282 |
| Chris Heisey | 120 | 279 | 44 | 71 | 9 | 1 | 18 | 50 | 136 | 19 | 78 | 6 | .309 | .487 | .254 |
| Ryan Hanigan | 91 | 266 | 27 | 71 | 6 | 0 | 6 | 31 | 95 | 35 | 32 | 0 | .356 | .357 | .267 |
| Scott Rolen | 65 | 252 | 31 | 61 | 20 | 2 | 5 | 36 | 100 | 10 | 36 | 1 | .279 | .397 | .242 |
| Miguel Cairo | 102 | 245 | 33 | 65 | 8 | 2 | 8 | 33 | 101 | 18 | 36 | 3 | .330 | .412 | .265 |
| *Jonny Gomes | 77 | 218 | 30 | 46 | 8 | 0 | 11 | 31 | 87 | 38 | 74 | 5 | .336 | .399 | .211 |
| Fred Lewis | 81 | 183 | 20 | 42 | 7 | 0 | 3 | 19 | 58 | 22 | 38 | 2 | .321 | .317 | .230 |
| Todd Frazier | 41 | 112 | 17 | 26 | 5 | 0 | 6 | 15 | 49 | 7 | 27 | 1 | .289 | .438 | .232 |
| Dave Sappelt | 38 | 107 | 14 | 26 | 8 | 0 | 0 | 5 | 34 | 7 | 17 | 1 | .289 | .318 | .243 |
| Juan Francisco | 31 | 93 | 10 | 24 | 7 | 1 | 3 | 15 | 42 | 4 | 24 | 1 | .289 | .452 | .258 |
| Yonder Alonso | 47 | 88 | 9 | 29 | 4 | 0 | 5 | 15 | 48 | 10 | 21 | 0 | .398 | .545 | .330 |

| PITCHING | GP | GS | W-L | SV | SHO | R | ERA | IP | Ks | BB |
|---|---|---|---|---|---|---|---|---|---|---|
| Bronson Arroyo | 32 | 32 | 9-12 | 0 | 1 | 119 | 5.07 | 199.0 | 108 | 45 |
| Mike Leake | 29 | 26 | 12-9 | 0 | 0 | 74 | 3.86 | 167.2 | 118 | 38 |
| Johnny Cueto | 24 | 24 | 9-5 | 0 | 1 | 51 | 2.31 | 156.0 | 104 | 47 |
| Homer Bailey | 22 | 22 | 9-7 | 0 | 0 | 68 | 4.43 | 132.0 | 106 | 33 |
| Edinson Volquez | 20 | 20 | 5-7 | 0 | 0 | 72 | 5.71 | 108.2 | 104 | 65 |
| Travis Wood | 22 | 18 | 6-6 | 0 | 0 | 57 | 4.84 | 106.0 | 76 | 40 |
| Sam LeCure | 43 | 4 | 2-1 | 0 | 0 | 33 | 3.71 | 77.2 | 73 | 21 |
| Dontrelle Willis | 13 | 13 | 1-6 | 0 | 0 | 42 | 5.00 | 75.2 | 57 | 37 |
| Nick Masset | 75 | 0 | 3-6 | 1 | 0 | 30 | 3.71 | 70.1 | 62 | 31 |
| Francisco Cordero | 68 | 0 | 5-3 | 37 | 0 | 20 | 2.45 | 69.2 | 42 | 22 |
| Logan Ondrusek | 66 | 0 | 5-5 | 0 | 0 | 25 | 3.23 | 61.1 | 41 | 28 |
| Jose Arredondo | 53 | 0 | 4-4 | 0 | 0 | 21 | 3.23 | 53.0 | 48 | 31 |
| Aroldis Chapman | 54 | 0 | 4-1 | 1 | 0 | 21 | 3.60 | 50.0 | 71 | 41 |
| Bill Bray | 79 | 0 | 5-3 | 0 | 0 | 16 | 2.98 | 48.1 | 44 | 17 |
| Carlos Fisher | 17 | 0 | 0-3 | 0 | 0 | 15 | 4.50 | 24.0 | 17 | 11 |

*Mid-season trade.

### Colorado Rockies

| BATTING | G | AB | R | H | 2B | 3B | HR | RBI | TB | BB | SO | SB | OBP | SLG | BAVG |
|---|---|---|---|---|---|---|---|---|---|---|---|---|---|---|---|
| Troy Tulowitzki | 143 | 537 | 81 | 162 | 36 | 2 | 30 | 105 | 292 | 59 | 79 | 9 | .372 | .544 | .302 |
| Carlos Gonzalez | 127 | 481 | 92 | 142 | 27 | 3 | 26 | 92 | 253 | 48 | 105 | 20 | .363 | .526 | .295 |
| Dexter Fowler | 125 | 481 | 84 | 128 | 35 | 15 | 5 | 45 | 208 | 68 | 130 | 12 | .363 | .432 | .266 |
| Seth Smith | 147 | 476 | 67 | 135 | 32 | 9 | 15 | 59 | 230 | 46 | 93 | 10 | .347 | .483 | .284 |
| Todd Helton | 124 | 421 | 59 | 127 | 27 | 0 | 14 | 69 | 196 | 59 | 71 | 0 | .385 | .466 | .302 |
| Ty Wigginton | 130 | 401 | 52 | 97 | 21 | 2 | 15 | 47 | 167 | 38 | 84 | 8 | .315 | .416 | .242 |
| Chris Iannetta | 112 | 345 | 51 | 82 | 17 | 1 | 14 | 55 | 143 | 70 | 89 | 6 | .370 | .414 | .238 |
| Jonathan Herrera | 104 | 281 | 28 | 68 | 5 | 1 | 3 | 14 | 84 | 28 | 40 | 4 | .313 | .299 | .242 |
| *Mark Ellis | 70 | 263 | 34 | 72 | 13 | 0 | 6 | 25 | 103 | 14 | 43 | 7 | .317 | .392 | .274 |
| Ryan Spilborghs | 98 | 200 | 22 | 42 | 8 | 1 | 3 | 22 | 61 | 19 | 49 | 2 | .283 | .305 | .210 |
| Eric Young Jr. | 77 | 198 | 34 | 49 | 4 | 3 | 0 | 10 | 59 | 26 | 38 | 27 | .342 | .298 | .247 |
| Chris Nelson | 63 | 180 | 20 | 45 | 10 | 1 | 4 | 16 | 69 | 7 | 35 | 3 | .280 | .383 | .250 |
| Jason Giambi | 64 | 131 | 20 | 34 | 6 | 0 | 13 | 32 | 79 | 17 | 45 | 0 | .355 | .603 | .260 |
| *Jose Lopez | 38 | 125 | 10 | 26 | 4 | 0 | 2 | 8 | 36 | 3 | 15 | 2 | .233 | .288 | .208 |
| Ian Stewart | 48 | 122 | 14 | 19 | 6 | 1 | 0 | 6 | 27 | 14 | 37 | 3 | .243 | .221 | .156 |
| *Kevin Kouzmanoff | 27 | 98 | 11 | 25 | 5 | 0 | 3 | 16 | 39 | 4 | 19 | 0 | .315 | .398 | .255 |

| PITCHING | GP | GS | W–L | SV | SHO | R | ERA | IP | Ks | BB |
|---|---|---|---|---|---|---|---|---|---|---|
| Jhoulys Chacin | 31 | 31 | 11-14 | 0 | 1 | 87 | 3.62 | 194.0 | 150 | 87 |
| Jason Hammel | 32 | 27 | 7-13 | 1 | 0 | 100 | 4.76 | 170.1 | 94 | 68 |
| *Ubaldo Jimenez | 21 | 21 | 6-9 | 0 | 1 | 68 | 4.46 | 123.0 | 118 | 51 |
| Aaron Cook | 18 | 17 | 3-10 | 0 | 0 | 67 | 6.03 | 97.0 | 48 | 37 |
| Esmil Rogers | 18 | 13 | 6-6 | 0 | 0 | 65 | 7.05 | 83.0 | 63 | 47 |
| Matt Belisle | 74 | 0 | 10-4 | 0 | 0 | 33 | 3.25 | 72.0 | 58 | 14 |
| Juan Nicasio | 13 | 13 | 4-4 | 0 | 0 | 35 | 4.14 | 71.2 | 58 | 18 |
| Rafael Betancourt | 68 | 0 | 2-0 | 8 | 0 | 21 | 2.89 | 62.1 | 73 | 8 |
| Jorge De La Rosa | 10 | 10 | 5-2 | 0 | 0 | 25 | 3.51 | 59.0 | 52 | 22 |
| Huston Street | 62 | 0 | 1-4 | 29 | 0 | 28 | 3.86 | 58.1 | 55 | 9 |
| Clayton Mortensen | 16 | 6 | 2-4 | 0 | 0 | 30 | 3.86 | 58.1 | 30 | 24 |
| Kevin Millwood | 9 | 9 | 4-3 | 0 | 0 | 26 | 3.98 | 54.1 | 36 | 8 |
| Matt Lindstrom | 63 | 0 | 2-2 | 2 | 0 | 21 | 3.00 | 54.0 | 36 | 14 |
| Matt Reynolds | 73 | 0 | 1-2 | 0 | 0 | 24 | 4.09 | 50.2 | 50 | 18 |

### Florida Marlins

| BATTING | G | AB | R | H | 2B | 3B | HR | RBI | TB | BB | SO | SB | OBP | SLG | BAVG |
|---|---|---|---|---|---|---|---|---|---|---|---|---|---|---|---|
| Omar Infante | 148 | 579 | 55 | 160 | 24 | 8 | 7 | 49 | 221 | 34 | 67 | 4 | .315 | .382 | .276 |
| Gaby Sanchez | 159 | 572 | 72 | 152 | 35 | 0 | 19 | 78 | 244 | 74 | 97 | 3 | .352 | .427 | .266 |
| Emilio Bonifacio | 152 | 565 | 78 | 167 | 26 | 7 | 5 | 36 | 222 | 59 | 129 | 40 | .360 | .393 | .296 |
| Mike Stanton | 150 | 516 | 79 | 135 | 30 | 5 | 34 | 87 | 277 | 70 | 166 | 5 | .356 | .537 | .262 |
| John Buck | 140 | 466 | 41 | 106 | 15 | 1 | 16 | 57 | 171 | 54 | 115 | 0 | .316 | .367 | .227 |
| Logan Morrison | 123 | 462 | 54 | 114 | 25 | 4 | 23 | 72 | 216 | 54 | 99 | 2 | .330 | .468 | .247 |
| Greg Dobbs | 134 | 411 | 38 | 113 | 23 | 0 | 8 | 49 | 160 | 22 | 83 | 0 | .311 | .389 | .275 |
| Hanley Ramirez | 92 | 338 | 55 | 82 | 16 | 0 | 10 | 45 | 128 | 44 | 66 | 20 | .333 | .379 | .243 |
| Chris Coghlan | 65 | 269 | 33 | 62 | 20 | 1 | 5 | 22 | 99 | 22 | 49 | 7 | .296 | .368 | .230 |
| Bryan Petersen | 74 | 204 | 18 | 54 | 13 | 3 | 2 | 10 | 79 | 26 | 49 | 7 | .357 | .387 | .265 |
| *Mike Cameron | 45 | 143 | 18 | 34 | 8 | 0 | 6 | 18 | 60 | 20 | 34 | 1 | .331 | .420 | .238 |
| Brett Hayes | 64 | 130 | 19 | 30 | 9 | 0 | 5 | 16 | 54 | 11 | 39 | 0 | .291 | .415 | .231 |
| Wes Helms | 69 | 110 | 10 | 21 | 5 | 0 | 0 | 6 | 26 | 11 | 35 | 0 | .276 | .236 | .191 |
| *Jose Lopez | 44 | 106 | 13 | 24 | 8 | 0 | 6 | 13 | 50 | 4 | 13 | 0 | .259 | .472 | .226 |
| Donnie Murphy | 36 | 92 | 10 | 17 | 4 | 1 | 2 | 9 | 29 | 4 | 21 | 0 | .240 | .315 | .185 |

| PITCHING | GP | GS | W–L | SV | SHO | R | ERA | IP | Ks | BB |
|---|---|---|---|---|---|---|---|---|---|---|
| Ricky Nolasco | 33 | 33 | 10-12 | 0 | 1 | 117 | 4.67 | 206.0 | 148 | 44 |
| Anibal Sanchez | 32 | 32 | 8-9 | 0 | 2 | 85 | 3.67 | 196.1 | 202 | 64 |
| Javier Vazquez | 32 | 32 | 13-11 | 0 | 1 | 91 | 3.69 | 192.2 | 162 | 50 |
| Chris Volstad | 29 | 29 | 5-13 | 0 | 0 | 96 | 4.89 | 165.2 | 117 | 49 |
| Edward Mujica | 67 | 0 | 9-6 | 0 | 0 | 27 | 2.96 | 76.0 | 63 | 14 |
| Clay Hensley | 37 | 9 | 6-7 | 0 | 0 | 41 | 5.19 | 67.2 | 46 | 30 |
| Leo Nunez | 68 | 0 | 1-4 | 36 | 0 | 30 | 4.06 | 64.1 | 55 | 21 |
| Burke Badenhop | 50 | 0 | 2-3 | 1 | 0 | 29 | 4.10 | 63.2 | 51 | 24 |
| Mike Dunn | 72 | 0 | 5-6 | 0 | 0 | 28 | 3.43 | 63.0 | 68 | 31 |
| Brian Sanches | 39 | 2 | 4-1 | 0 | 0 | 32 | 3.94 | 61.2 | 53 | 36 |
| Josh Johnson | 9 | 9 | 3-1 | 0 | 0 | 13 | 1.64 | 60.1 | 56 | 20 |
| Brad Hand | 12 | 12 | 1-8 | 0 | 0 | 32 | 4.20 | 60.0 | 38 | 35 |
| Steve Cishek | 45 | 0 | 2-1 | 3 | 0 | 18 | 2.63 | 54.2 | 55 | 19 |
| Ryan Webb | 53 | 0 | 2-4 | 0 | 0 | 20 | 3.20 | 50.2 | 31 | 20 |
| Randy Choate | 54 | 0 | 1-1 | 0 | 0 | 7 | 1.82 | 24.2 | 31 | 13 |
| Jose Ceda | 17 | 0 | 0-1 | 0 | 0 | 11 | 4.43 | 20.1 | 21 | 12 |

*Mid-season trade.

### Houston Astros

| BATTING | G | AB | R | H | 2B | 3B | HR | RBI | TB | BB | SO | SB | OBP | SLG | BAVG |
|---|---|---|---|---|---|---|---|---|---|---|---|---|---|---|---|
| *Michael Bourn | 105 | 429 | 64 | 130 | 26 | 7 | 1 | 32 | 173 | 38 | 90 | 39 | .363 | .403 | .303 |
| *Hunter Pence | 100 | 399 | 49 | 123 | 26 | 3 | 11 | 62 | 188 | 30 | 86 | 7 | .356 | .471 | .308 |
| Chris Johnson | 107 | 378 | 32 | 95 | 21 | 3 | 7 | 42 | 143 | 16 | 97 | 2 | .291 | .378 | .251 |
| Brett Wallace | 115 | 336 | 37 | 87 | 22 | 0 | 5 | 29 | 124 | 36 | 91 | 1 | .334 | .369 | .259 |
| Angel Sanchez | 110 | 288 | 35 | 69 | 10 | 0 | 1 | 28 | 82 | 27 | 44 | 3 | .305 | .285 | .240 |
| Humberto Quintero | 79 | 262 | 22 | 63 | 12 | 1 | 2 | 25 | 83 | 6 | 53 | 1 | .258 | .317 | .240 |
| Jason Bourgeois | 93 | 238 | 30 | 70 | 8 | 2 | 1 | 16 | 85 | 10 | 24 | 31 | .323 | .357 | .294 |
| Jose Altuve | 57 | 221 | 26 | 61 | 10 | 1 | 2 | 12 | 79 | 5 | 29 | 7 | .297 | .357 | .276 |
| J.D. Martinez | 53 | 208 | 29 | 57 | 13 | 0 | 6 | 35 | 88 | 13 | 48 | 0 | .319 | .423 | .274 |
| Matt Downs | 106 | 199 | 29 | 55 | 18 | 0 | 10 | 41 | 103 | 17 | 47 | 0 | .347 | .518 | .276 |
| Jimmy Paredes | 46 | 168 | 16 | 48 | 8 | 2 | 2 | 18 | 66 | 9 | 47 | 5 | .320 | .393 | .286 |
| Brian Bogusevic | 87 | 164 | 22 | 47 | 14 | 1 | 4 | 15 | 75 | 15 | 40 | 4 | .348 | .457 | .287 |
| *Jeff Keppinger | 43 | 163 | 22 | 50 | 9 | 0 | 4 | 20 | 71 | 4 | 7 | 0 | .320 | .436 | .307 |
| Jason Michaels | 89 | 156 | 10 | 31 | 9 | 0 | 2 | 10 | 46 | 11 | 31 | 1 | .256 | .295 | .199 |
| Carlos Corporan | 52 | 154 | 9 | 29 | 8 | 1 | 0 | 11 | 39 | 10 | 49 | 0 | .253 | .253 | .188 |
| J.R. Towles | 54 | 147 | 11 | 27 | 7 | 0 | 3 | 11 | 43 | 13 | 26 | 0 | .256 | .293 | .184 |

| PITCHING | GP | GS | W-L | SV | SHO | R | ERA | IP | Ks | BB |
|---|---|---|---|---|---|---|---|---|---|---|
| Brett Myers | 34 | 33 | 7-14 | 0 | 0 | 116 | 4.46 | 216.0 | 160 | 57 |
| Wandy Rodriguez | 30 | 30 | 11-11 | 0 | 0 | 81 | 3.49 | 191.0 | 166 | 69 |
| Bud Norris | 31 | 31 | 6-11 | 0 | 0 | 93 | 3.77 | 186.0 | 176 | 70 |
| J.A. Happ | 28 | 28 | 6-15 | 0 | 0 | 103 | 5.35 | 156.1 | 134 | 83 |
| Jordan Lyles | 20 | 15 | 2-8 | 0 | 0 | 61 | 5.36 | 94.0 | 67 | 26 |
| Aneury Rodriguez | 43 | 8 | 1-6 | 0 | 0 | 57 | 5.27 | 85.1 | 64 | 32 |
| Mark Melancon | 71 | 0 | 8-4 | 20 | 0 | 28 | 2.78 | 74.1 | 66 | 26 |
| Wilton Lopez | 73 | 0 | 2-6 | 0 | 0 | 26 | 2.79 | 71.0 | 56 | 18 |
| Henry Sosa | 10 | 10 | 3-5 | 0 | 0 | 31 | 5.23 | 53.1 | 38 | 23 |
| Enerio Del Rosario | 54 | 0 | 0-3 | 0 | 0 | 30 | 4.58 | 53.0 | 31 | 31 |
| Fernando Rodriguez | 47 | 0 | 2-3 | 0 | 0 | 24 | 3.96 | 52.1 | 57 | 30 |
| *Jeff Fulchino | 36 | 0 | 1-4 | 0 | 0 | 19 | 5.18 | 33.0 | 31 | 18 |
| Nelson Figueroa | 8 | 5 | 0-3 | 0 | 0 | 33 | 8.69 | 29.0 | 17 | 16 |

### Los Angeles Dodgers

| BATTING | G | AB | R | H | 2B | 3B | HR | RBI | TB | BB | SO | SB | OBP | SLG | BAVG |
|---|---|---|---|---|---|---|---|---|---|---|---|---|---|---|---|
| Matt Kemp | 161 | 602 | 115 | 195 | 33 | 4 | 39 | 126 | 353 | 74 | 159 | 40 | .399 | .586 | .324 |
| James Loney | 158 | 531 | 56 | 153 | 30 | 1 | 12 | 65 | 221 | 42 | 67 | 4 | .339 | .416 | .288 |
| Andre Ethier | 135 | 487 | 67 | 142 | 30 | 0 | 11 | 62 | 205 | 58 | 103 | 0 | .368 | .421 | .292 |
| Aaron Miles | 136 | 454 | 49 | 125 | 17 | 3 | 3 | 45 | 157 | 25 | 49 | 4 | .314 | .346 | .275 |
| Jamey Carroll | 146 | 452 | 52 | 131 | 14 | 6 | 0 | 17 | 157 | 47 | 58 | 10 | .359 | .347 | .290 |
| Tony Gwynn | 136 | 312 | 37 | 80 | 12 | 6 | 2 | 22 | 110 | 23 | 61 | 22 | .308 | .353 | .256 |
| Rod Barajas | 98 | 305 | 29 | 70 | 13 | 0 | 16 | 47 | 131 | 22 | 71 | 0 | .287 | .430 | .230 |
| Juan Uribe | 77 | 270 | 21 | 55 | 12 | 0 | 4 | 28 | 79 | 17 | 60 | 2 | .264 | .293 | .204 |
| Dee Gordon | 56 | 224 | 34 | 68 | 9 | 2 | 0 | 11 | 81 | 7 | 27 | 24 | .325 | .362 | .304 |
| *Juan Rivera | 62 | 219 | 24 | 60 | 12 | 1 | 5 | 46 | 89 | 21 | 35 | 2 | .333 | .406 | .274 |
| Casey Blake | 63 | 202 | 32 | 51 | 10 | 1 | 4 | 26 | 75 | 26 | 50 | 1 | .342 | .371 | .252 |
| Jerry Sands | 61 | 198 | 20 | 50 | 15 | 0 | 4 | 26 | 77 | 25 | 51 | 3 | .338 | .389 | .253 |
| Dioner Navarro | 64 | 176 | 13 | 34 | 6 | 1 | 5 | 17 | 57 | 20 | 35 | 0 | .276 | .324 | .193 |
| *Rafael Furcal | 37 | 137 | 15 | 27 | 4 | 0 | 1 | 12 | 34 | 11 | 21 | 5 | .272 | .248 | .197 |
| Justin Sellers | 36 | 123 | 20 | 25 | 9 | 0 | 1 | 13 | 37 | 12 | 21 | 1 | .283 | .301 | .203 |
| A.J. Ellis | 31 | 85 | 8 | 23 | 1 | 1 | 2 | 11 | 32 | 14 | 16 | 0 | .392 | .376 | .271 |

| PITCHING | GP | GS | W-L | SV | SHO | R | ERA | IP | Ks | BB |
|---|---|---|---|---|---|---|---|---|---|---|
| Clayton Kershaw | 33 | 33 | 21-5 | 0 | 2 | 66 | 2.28 | 233.1 | 248 | 54 |
| Hiroki Kuroda | 32 | 32 | 13-16 | 0 | 0 | 77 | 3.07 | 202.0 | 161 | 49 |
| Ted Lilly | 33 | 33 | 12-14 | 0 | 0 | 88 | 3.97 | 192.2 | 158 | 51 |
| Chad Billingsley | 32 | 32 | 11-11 | 0 | 0 | 98 | 4.21 | 188.0 | 152 | 84 |
| Matt Guerrier | 70 | 0 | 4-3 | 1 | 0 | 31 | 4.07 | 66.1 | 50 | 25 |
| Rubby De La Rosa | 13 | 10 | 4-5 | 0 | 0 | 26 | 3.71 | 60.2 | 60 | 31 |
| Mike MacDougal | 69 | 0 | 3-1 | 1 | 0 | 16 | 2.05 | 57.0 | 41 | 29 |
| Jon Garland | 9 | 9 | 1-5 | 0 | 0 | 26 | 4.33 | 54.0 | 28 | 20 |
| Kenley Jansen | 51 | 0 | 2-1 | 5 | 0 | 17 | 2.85 | 53.2 | 96 | 26 |
| Blake Hawksworth | 49 | 0 | 2-5 | 0 | 0 | 29 | 4.08 | 53.0 | 43 | 17 |
| Javy Guerra | 47 | 0 | 2-2 | 21 | 0 | 12 | 2.31 | 46.2 | 38 | 18 |
| Nate Eovaldi | 10 | 6 | 1-2 | 0 | 0 | 14 | 3.63 | 34.2 | 23 | 20 |
| Scott Elbert | 47 | 0 | 0-1 | 2 | 0 | 9 | 2.43 | 33.1 | 34 | 14 |
| Josh Lindblom | 27 | 0 | 1-0 | 0 | 0 | 10 | 2.73 | 29.2 | 28 | 10 |
| Dana Eveland | 5 | 5 | 3-2 | 0 | 0 | 9 | 3.03 | 29.2 | 16 | 6 |

*Mid-season trade.

## Milwaukee Brewers

| BATTING | G | AB | R | H | 2B | 3B | HR | RBI | TB | BB | SO | SB | OBP | SLG | BAVG |
|---|---|---|---|---|---|---|---|---|---|---|---|---|---|---|---|
| Prince Fielder | 162 | 569 | 95 | 170 | 36 | 1 | 38 | 120 | 322 | 107 | 106 | 1 | .415 | .566 | .299 |
| Ryan Braun | 150 | 563 | 109 | 187 | 38 | 6 | 33 | 111 | 336 | 58 | 93 | 33 | .397 | .597 | .332 |
| Yuniesky Betancourt | 152 | 556 | 51 | 140 | 27 | 3 | 13 | 68 | 212 | 16 | 63 | 4 | .271 | .381 | .252 |
| Casey McGehee | 155 | 546 | 46 | 122 | 24 | 2 | 13 | 67 | 189 | 45 | 104 | 0 | .280 | .346 | .223 |
| Corey Hart | 130 | 492 | 80 | 140 | 25 | 4 | 26 | 63 | 251 | 51 | 114 | 7 | .356 | .510 | .285 |
| Rickie Weeks | 118 | 453 | 77 | 122 | 26 | 2 | 20 | 49 | 212 | 50 | 107 | 9 | .350 | .468 | .269 |
| Jonathan Lucroy | 136 | 430 | 45 | 114 | 16 | 1 | 12 | 59 | 168 | 29 | 99 | 2 | .313 | .391 | .265 |
| Nyjer Morgan | 119 | 378 | 61 | 115 | 20 | 6 | 4 | 37 | 159 | 19 | 70 | 13 | .357 | .421 | .304 |
| Mark Kotsay | 104 | 233 | 18 | 63 | 13 | 1 | 3 | 31 | 87 | 21 | 27 | 3 | .329 | .373 | .270 |
| Carlos Gomez | 94 | 231 | 37 | 52 | 11 | 3 | 8 | 24 | 93 | 15 | 64 | 16 | .276 | .403 | .225 |
| Craig Counsell | 107 | 157 | 19 | 28 | 2 | 1 | 1 | 9 | 35 | 20 | 21 | 2 | .280 | .223 | .178 |
| *Jerry Hairston Jr. | 45 | 124 | 18 | 34 | 10 | 0 | 1 | 7 | 47 | 11 | 16 | 1 | .348 | .379 | .274 |
| George Kottaras | 49 | 111 | 15 | 28 | 6 | 1 | 5 | 17 | 51 | 10 | 26 | 0 | .311 | .459 | .252 |
| *Josh Wilson | 54 | 75 | 10 | 17 | 4 | 0 | 2 | 4 | 27 | 4 | 21 | 1 | .266 | .360 | .227 |

| PITCHING | GP | GS | W-L | SV | SHO | R | ERA | IP | Ks | BB |
|---|---|---|---|---|---|---|---|---|---|---|
| Randy Wolf | 33 | 33 | 13-10 | 0 | 0 | 95 | 3.69 | 212.1 | 134 | 66 |
| Yovani Gallardo | 33 | 33 | 17-10 | 0 | 1 | 92 | 3.52 | 207.1 | 207 | 59 |
| Shaun Marcum | 33 | 33 | 13-7 | 0 | 0 | 84 | 3.54 | 200.2 | 158 | 57 |
| Zack Greinke | 28 | 28 | 15-6 | 0 | 0 | 82 | 3.80 | 170.1 | 201 | 45 |
| Chris Narveson | 30 | 28 | 11-8 | 0 | 0 | 82 | 4.45 | 161.2 | 126 | 65 |
| Marco Estrada | 43 | 7 | 4-8 | 0 | 0 | 45 | 4.08 | 92.2 | 88 | 29 |
| John Axford | 73 | 0 | 2-2 | 46 | 0 | 19 | 1.98 | 72.2 | 85 | 25 |
| Kameron Loe | 72 | 0 | 4-7 | 1 | 0 | 30 | 3.50 | 72.0 | 61 | 16 |
| LaTroy Hawkins | 52 | 0 | 3-1 | 0 | 0 | 15 | 2.42 | 48.1 | 28 | 10 |
| *Sergio Mitre | 22 | 0 | 0-1 | 0 | 0 | 14 | 3.27 | 33.0 | 14 | 10 |
| Tim Dillard | 24 | 0 | 1-1 | 0 | 0 | 7 | 4.08 | 28.2 | 27 | 4 |
| *Francisco Rodriguez | 30 | 0 | 4-0 | 0 | 0 | 13 | 1.93 | 28.0 | 32 | 10 |
| Takashi Saito | 29 | 0 | 4-2 | 0 | 0 | 6 | 2.10 | 25.2 | 22 | 9 |
| Zach Braddock | 25 | 0 | 0-1 | 0 | 0 | 15 | 7.27 | 17.1 | 18 | 11 |

## New York Mets

| BATTING | G | AB | R | H | 2B | 3B | HR | RBI | TB | BB | SO | SB | OBP | SLG | BAVG |
|---|---|---|---|---|---|---|---|---|---|---|---|---|---|---|---|
| Jose Reyes | 126 | 537 | 101 | 181 | 31 | 16 | 7 | 44 | 265 | 43 | 41 | 39 | .384 | .493 | .337 |
| Angel Pagan | 123 | 478 | 68 | 125 | 24 | 4 | 7 | 56 | 178 | 44 | 62 | 32 | .322 | .372 | .262 |
| Jason Bay | 123 | 444 | 59 | 109 | 19 | 1 | 12 | 57 | 166 | 56 | 109 | 11 | .329 | .374 | .245 |
| Justin Turner | 117 | 435 | 49 | 113 | 30 | 0 | 4 | 51 | 155 | 39 | 59 | 7 | .334 | .356 | .260 |
| Daniel Murphy | 109 | 391 | 49 | 125 | 28 | 2 | 6 | 49 | 175 | 24 | 42 | 5 | .362 | .448 | .320 |
| David Wright | 102 | 389 | 60 | 99 | 23 | 1 | 14 | 61 | 166 | 52 | 97 | 13 | .345 | .427 | .254 |
| *Carlos Beltran | 98 | 353 | 61 | 102 | 30 | 2 | 15 | 66 | 181 | 60 | 61 | 3 | .391 | .513 | .289 |
| Josh Thole | 114 | 340 | 22 | 91 | 17 | 0 | 3 | 40 | 117 | 38 | 47 | 0 | .345 | .344 | .268 |
| Ruben Tejada | 96 | 328 | 31 | 93 | 15 | 1 | 0 | 36 | 110 | 35 | 50 | 5 | .360 | .335 | .284 |
| Lucas Duda | 100 | 301 | 38 | 88 | 21 | 3 | 10 | 50 | 145 | 33 | 57 | 1 | .370 | .482 | .292 |
| Willie Harris | 126 | 240 | 36 | 59 | 11 | 0 | 2 | 23 | 76 | 36 | 62 | 5 | .351 | .317 | .246 |
| Ronny Paulino | 78 | 228 | 19 | 61 | 13 | 0 | 2 | 19 | 80 | 15 | 38 | 0 | .312 | .351 | .268 |
| Jason Pridie | 101 | 208 | 28 | 48 | 11 | 3 | 4 | 20 | 77 | 24 | 64 | 7 | .309 | .370 | .231 |
| Nick Evans | 59 | 176 | 26 | 45 | 10 | 2 | 4 | 25 | 71 | 15 | 48 | 0 | .314 | .403 | .256 |
| Scott Hairston | 79 | 132 | 20 | 31 | 8 | 1 | 7 | 24 | 62 | 11 | 34 | 1 | .303 | .470 | .235 |
| Ike Davis | 36 | 129 | 20 | 39 | 8 | 1 | 7 | 25 | 70 | 17 | 31 | 0 | .383 | .543 | .302 |

| PITCHING | GP | GS | W-L | SV | SHO | R | ERA | IP | Ks | BB |
|---|---|---|---|---|---|---|---|---|---|---|
| R.A. Dickey | 33 | 32 | 8-13 | 0 | 0 | 85 | 3.28 | 208.2 | 134 | 54 |
| Mike Pelfrey | 34 | 33 | 7-13 | 0 | 0 | 111 | 4.74 | 193.2 | 105 | 65 |
| Chris Capuano | 33 | 31 | 11-12 | 0 | 1 | 99 | 4.55 | 186.0 | 168 | 53 |
| Dillon Gee | 30 | 27 | 13-6 | 0 | 0 | 85 | 4.43 | 160.2 | 114 | 71 |
| Jonathon Niese | 27 | 26 | 11-11 | 0 | 0 | 88 | 4.40 | 157.1 | 138 | 44 |
| Pedro Beato | 60 | 0 | 2-1 | 0 | 0 | 41 | 4.30 | 67.0 | 39 | 27 |
| Bobby Parnell | 60 | 0 | 4-6 | 6 | 0 | 29 | 3.64 | 59.1 | 64 | 27 |
| D.J. Carrasco | 42 | 1 | 1-3 | 0 | 0 | 35 | 6.02 | 49.1 | 27 | 16 |
| Manny Acosta | 44 | 0 | 4-1 | 4 | 0 | 21 | 3.45 | 47.0 | 46 | 15 |
| Jason Isringhausen | 53 | 0 | 3-3 | 7 | 0 | 23 | 4.05 | 46.2 | 44 | 24 |
| *Francisco Rodriguez | 42 | 0 | 2-2 | 23 | 0 | 15 | 3.16 | 42.2 | 46 | 16 |
| Ryota Igarashi | 45 | 0 | 4-1 | 0 | 0 | 20 | 4.66 | 38.2 | 42 | 28 |
| Tim Byrdak | 72 | 0 | 2-1 | 1 | 0 | 20 | 3.82 | 37.2 | 47 | 19 |
| *Miguel Batista | 9 | 4 | 2-0 | 0 | 0 | 9 | 2.64 | 30.2 | 15 | 14 |
| Taylor Buchholz | 23 | 0 | 1-1 | 0 | 0 | 10 | 3.12 | 26.0 | 26 | 7 |
| Chris Young | 4 | 4 | 1-0 | 0 | 0 | 5 | 1.88 | 24.0 | 22 | 11 |
| Chris Schwinden | 4 | 4 | 0-2 | 0 | 0 | 13 | 4.71 | 21.0 | 17 | 6 |

*Mid-season trade.

## Philadelphia Phillies

| BATTING | G | AB | R | H | 2B | 3B | HR | RBI | TB | BB | SO | SB | OBP | SLG | BAVG |
|---|---|---|---|---|---|---|---|---|---|---|---|---|---|---|---|
| Jimmy Rollins | 142 | 567 | 87 | 152 | 22 | 2 | 16 | 63 | 226 | 58 | 59 | 30 | .338 | .399 | .268 |
| Ryan Howard | 152 | 557 | 81 | 141 | 30 | 1 | 33 | 116 | 272 | 75 | 172 | 1 | .346 | .488 | .253 |
| Raul Ibanez | 144 | 535 | 65 | 131 | 31 | 1 | 20 | 84 | 224 | 33 | 106 | 2 | .289 | .419 | .245 |
| Shane Victorino | 132 | 519 | 95 | 145 | 27 | 16 | 17 | 61 | 255 | 55 | 63 | 19 | .355 | .491 | .279 |
| Placido Polanco | 122 | 469 | 46 | 130 | 14 | 0 | 5 | 50 | 159 | 42 | 44 | 3 | .335 | .339 | .277 |
| Carlos Ruiz | 132 | 410 | 49 | 116 | 23 | 0 | 6 | 40 | 157 | 48 | 48 | 1 | .371 | .383 | .283 |
| Chase Utley | 103 | 398 | 54 | 103 | 21 | 6 | 11 | 44 | 169 | 39 | 47 | 14 | .344 | .425 | .259 |
| Wilson Valdez | 99 | 273 | 39 | 68 | 14 | 4 | 1 | 30 | 93 | 18 | 41 | 3 | .294 | .341 | .249 |
| John Mayberry Jr. | 104 | 267 | 37 | 73 | 17 | 1 | 15 | 49 | 137 | 26 | 55 | 8 | .341 | .513 | .273 |
| Ben Francisco | 100 | 250 | 24 | 61 | 10 | 1 | 6 | 34 | 91 | 33 | 42 | 4 | .340 | .364 | .244 |
| Michael Martinez | 88 | 209 | 25 | 41 | 5 | 2 | 3 | 24 | 59 | 18 | 35 | 3 | .258 | .282 | .196 |
| *Hunter Pence | 54 | 207 | 35 | 67 | 12 | 2 | 11 | 35 | 116 | 26 | 38 | 1 | .394 | .560 | .324 |
| Domonic Brown | 56 | 184 | 28 | 45 | 10 | 1 | 5 | 19 | 72 | 25 | 35 | 3 | .333 | .391 | .245 |
| Brian Schneider | 41 | 125 | 11 | 22 | 4 | 0 | 2 | 9 | 32 | 11 | 35 | 0 | .246 | .256 | .176 |
| Ross Gload | 93 | 113 | 3 | 29 | 8 | 0 | 0 | 8 | 37 | 3 | 23 | 0 | .276 | .327 | .257 |

| PITCHING | GP | GS | W-L | SV | SHO | R | ERA | IP | Ks | BB |
|---|---|---|---|---|---|---|---|---|---|---|
| Roy Halladay | 32 | 32 | 19-6 | 0 | 1 | 65 | 2.35 | 233.2 | 220 | 35 |
| Cliff Lee | 32 | 32 | 17-8 | 0 | 6 | 66 | 2.40 | 232.2 | 238 | 42 |
| Cole Hamels | 32 | 31 | 14-9 | 0 | 0 | 68 | 2.79 | 216.0 | 194 | 44 |
| Roy Oswalt | 23 | 23 | 9-10 | 0 | 0 | 60 | 3.69 | 139.0 | 93 | 33 |
| Vance Worley | 25 | 21 | 11-3 | 0 | 0 | 47 | 3.01 | 131.2 | 119 | 46 |
| Kyle Kendrick | 34 | 15 | 8-6 | 0 | 0 | 50 | 3.22 | 114.2 | 59 | 30 |
| Michael Stutes | 57 | 0 | 6-2 | 0 | 0 | 25 | 3.63 | 62.0 | 58 | 28 |
| Ryan Madson | 62 | 0 | 4-2 | 32 | 0 | 16 | 2.37 | 60.2 | 62 | 16 |
| Antonio Bastardo | 64 | 0 | 6-1 | 8 | 0 | 17 | 2.64 | 58.0 | 70 | 26 |
| David Herndon | 45 | 0 | 1-4 | 1 | 0 | 26 | 3.32 | 57.0 | 39 | 24 |
| Joe Blanton | 11 | 8 | 1-2 | 0 | 0 | 23 | 5.01 | 41.1 | 35 | 9 |
| Danys Baez | 29 | 0 | 2-4 | 0 | 0 | 28 | 6.25 | 36.0 | 18 | 13 |
| Brad Lidge | 25 | 0 | 0-2 | 1 | 0 | 3 | 1.40 | 19.1 | 23 | 13 |
| *J.C. Romero | 24 | 0 | 0-0 | 0 | 0 | 7 | 3.86 | 16.1 | 10 | 12 |
| Michael Schwimer | 12 | 0 | 1-1 | 0 | 0 | 8 | 5.02 | 14.1 | 16 | 7 |
| Jose Contreras | 17 | 0 | 0-0 | 5 | 0 | 6 | 3.86 | 14.0 | 13 | 8 |

## Pittsburgh Pirates

| BATTING | G | AB | R | H | 2B | 3B | HR | RBI | TB | BB | SO | SB | OBP | SLG | BAVG |
|---|---|---|---|---|---|---|---|---|---|---|---|---|---|---|---|
| Neil Walker | 159 | 596 | 76 | 163 | 36 | 4 | 12 | 83 | 243 | 54 | 112 | 9 | .334 | .408 | .273 |
| Andrew McCutchen | 158 | 572 | 87 | 148 | 34 | 5 | 23 | 89 | 261 | 89 | 126 | 23 | .364 | .456 | .259 |
| Garrett Jones | 148 | 423 | 51 | 103 | 30 | 1 | 16 | 58 | 183 | 48 | 104 | 6 | .321 | .433 | .243 |
| Ronny Cedeno | 128 | 413 | 43 | 103 | 25 | 3 | 2 | 32 | 140 | 30 | 93 | 2 | .297 | .339 | .249 |
| *Lyle Overbay | 103 | 352 | 40 | 80 | 17 | 1 | 8 | 37 | 123 | 36 | 77 | 1 | .300 | .349 | .227 |
| Jose Tabata | 91 | 334 | 53 | 89 | 18 | 1 | 4 | 21 | 121 | 40 | 61 | 16 | .349 | .362 | .266 |
| *Brandon Wood | 99 | 236 | 25 | 52 | 9 | 0 | 7 | 31 | 82 | 19 | 65 | 0 | .277 | .347 | .220 |
| Pedro Alvarez | 74 | 235 | 18 | 45 | 9 | 1 | 4 | 19 | 68 | 24 | 80 | 1 | .272 | .289 | .191 |
| *Xavier Paul | 121 | 232 | 30 | 59 | 6 | 5 | 2 | 20 | 81 | 13 | 57 | 16 | .293 | .349 | .254 |
| Ryan Doumit | 77 | 218 | 17 | 66 | 12 | 1 | 8 | 30 | 104 | 16 | 35 | 0 | .353 | .477 | .303 |
| *Matt Diaz | 100 | 216 | 14 | 56 | 12 | 1 | 0 | 19 | 70 | 11 | 44 | 4 | .303 | .324 | .259 |
| Alex Presley | 52 | 215 | 27 | 64 | 12 | 6 | 4 | 20 | 100 | 13 | 40 | 9 | .339 | .465 | .298 |
| Josh Harrison | 65 | 193 | 21 | 53 | 13 | 2 | 1 | 16 | 73 | 3 | 24 | 4 | .281 | .374 | .272 |
| Michael McKenry | 58 | 180 | 17 | 40 | 12 | 0 | 2 | 11 | 58 | 14 | 49 | 0 | .306 | .322 | .222 |
| Chase D'Arnaud | 48 | 143 | 17 | 31 | 6 | 2 | 0 | 6 | 41 | 4 | 36 | 12 | .242 | .287 | .217 |
| *Ryan Ludwick | 38 | 112 | 14 | 26 | 5 | 0 | 2 | 11 | 37 | 19 | 37 | 0 | .341 | .330 | .232 |
| *Derrek Lee | 28 | 101 | 16 | 34 | 2 | 1 | 7 | 18 | 59 | 8 | 27 | 0 | .398 | .584 | .337 |

| PITCHING | GP | GS | W-L | SV | SHO | R | ERA | IP | Ks | BB |
|---|---|---|---|---|---|---|---|---|---|---|
| Charlie Morton | 29 | 29 | 10-10 | 0 | 1 | 82 | 3.83 | 171.2 | 110 | 77 |
| James McDonald | 31 | 31 | 9-9 | 0 | 0 | 86 | 4.21 | 171.0 | 142 | 78 |
| Paul Maholm | 26 | 26 | 6-14 | 0 | 1 | 72 | 3.66 | 162.1 | 97 | 50 |
| Jeff Karstens | 30 | 26 | 9-9 | 0 | 1 | 69 | 3.38 | 162.1 | 96 | 33 |
| Kevin Correia | 27 | 26 | 12-11 | 0 | 0 | 90 | 4.79 | 154.0 | 77 | 39 |
| Daniel McCutchen | 73 | 0 | 5-3 | 0 | 0 | 38 | 3.72 | 84.2 | 47 | 33 |
| Jose Veras | 79 | 0 | 2-4 | 1 | 0 | 32 | 3.80 | 71.0 | 79 | 34 |
| Chris Resop | 76 | 0 | 5-4 | 1 | 0 | 34 | 4.39 | 69.2 | 79 | 30 |
| Joel Hanrahan | 70 | 0 | 1-4 | 40 | 0 | 17 | 1.83 | 68.2 | 61 | 16 |
| Brad Lincoln | 12 | 8 | 2-3 | 0 | 0 | 27 | 4.72 | 47.2 | 29 | 16 |
| Tony Watson | 43 | 0 | 2-2 | 0 | 0 | 18 | 3.95 | 41.0 | 37 | 20 |
| Ross Ohlendorf | 9 | 9 | 1-3 | 0 | 0 | 38 | 8.15 | 38.2 | 27 | 15 |
| Jason Grilli | 28 | 0 | 2-1 | 1 | 0 | 10 | 2.48 | 32.2 | 37 | 15 |
| Joe Beimel | 35 | 0 | 1-1 | 0 | 0 | 17 | 5.33 | 25.1 | 17 | 9 |

*Mid-season trade.

## St. Louis Cardinals

| BATTING | G | AB | R | H | 2B | 3B | HR | RBI | TB | BB | SO | SB | OBP | SLG | BAVG |
|---|---|---|---|---|---|---|---|---|---|---|---|---|---|---|---|
| Albert Pujols | 147 | 579 | 105 | 173 | 29 | 0 | 37 | 99 | 313 | 61 | 58 | 9 | .366 | .541 | .299 |
| Lance Berkman | 145 | 488 | 90 | 147 | 23 | 2 | 31 | 94 | 267 | 92 | 93 | 2 | .412 | .547 | .301 |
| Yadier Molina | 139 | 475 | 55 | 145 | 32 | 1 | 14 | 65 | 221 | 33 | 44 | 4 | .349 | .465 | .305 |
| Jon Jay | 159 | 455 | 56 | 135 | 24 | 2 | 10 | 37 | 193 | 28 | 81 | 6 | .344 | .424 | .297 |
| Matt Holliday | 124 | 446 | 83 | 132 | 36 | 0 | 22 | 75 | 234 | 60 | 93 | 2 | .388 | .525 | .296 |
| Ryan Theriot | 132 | 442 | 46 | 120 | 26 | 1 | 1 | 47 | 151 | 29 | 41 | 4 | .321 | .342 | .271 |
| *Colby Rasmus | 94 | 338 | 61 | 83 | 14 | 6 | 11 | 40 | 142 | 45 | 77 | 5 | .332 | .420 | .246 |
| David Freese | 97 | 333 | 41 | 99 | 16 | 1 | 10 | 55 | 147 | 24 | 75 | 1 | .350 | .441 | .297 |
| Daniel Descalso | 148 | 326 | 35 | 86 | 20 | 3 | 1 | 28 | 115 | 33 | 65 | 2 | .334 | .353 | .264 |
| Allen Craig | 75 | 200 | 33 | 63 | 15 | 0 | 11 | 40 | 111 | 15 | 40 | 5 | .362 | .555 | .315 |
| *Rafael Furcal | 50 | 196 | 29 | 50 | 11 | 0 | 7 | 16 | 82 | 17 | 18 | 4 | .316 | .418 | .255 |
| Nick Punto | 63 | 133 | 21 | 37 | 8 | 4 | 1 | 20 | 56 | 25 | 21 | 1 | .388 | .421 | .278 |
| Tyler Greene | 58 | 104 | 22 | 22 | 5 | 0 | 1 | 11 | 30 | 13 | 31 | 11 | .322 | .288 | .212 |
| Gerald Laird | 37 | 95 | 11 | 22 | 7 | 1 | 1 | 12 | 34 | 9 | 19 | 1 | .302 | .358 | .232 |

| PITCHING | GP | GS | W–L | SV | SHO | R | ERA | IP | Ks | BB |
|---|---|---|---|---|---|---|---|---|---|---|
| Chris Carpenter | 34 | 34 | 11-9 | 0 | 2 | 98 | 3.45 | 237.1 | 191 | 55 |
| Jaime Garcia | 32 | 32 | 13-7 | 0 | 2 | 100 | 3.56 | 194.2 | 156 | 50 |
| Kyle Lohse | 30 | 30 | 14-8 | 0 | 1 | 80 | 3.39 | 188.1 | 111 | 42 |
| Jake Westbrook | 33 | 33 | 12-9 | 0 | 0 | 103 | 4.66 | 183.1 | 104 | 73 |
| Kyle McClellan | 43 | 17 | 12-7 | 0 | 0 | 71 | 4.19 | 141.2 | 76 | 43 |
| *Edwin Jackson | 13 | 12 | 5-2 | 0 | 0 | 37 | 3.58 | 78.0 | 51 | 23 |
| Fernando Salas | 68 | 0 | 5-6 | 24 | 0 | 20 | 2.28 | 75.0 | 75 | 21 |
| Jason Motte | 78 | 0 | 5-2 | 9 | 0 | 22 | 2.25 | 68.0 | 63 | 16 |
| Mitchell Boggs | 51 | 0 | 2-3 | 4 | 0 | 27 | 3.56 | 60.2 | 48 | 21 |
| Lance Lynn | 18 | 2 | 1-1 | 1 | 0 | 12 | 3.12 | 34.2 | 40 | 11 |
| Eduardo Sanchez | 26 | 0 | 3-1 | 5 | 0 | 6 | 1.80 | 30.0 | 35 | 16 |
| *Miguel Batista | 26 | 1 | 3-2 | 0 | 0 | 20 | 4.60 | 29.1 | 16 | 19 |
| Ryan Franklin | 21 | 0 | 1-4 | 1 | 0 | 27 | 8.46 | 27.2 | 17 | 7 |
| *Octavio Dotel | 29 | 0 | 3-3 | 2 | 0 | 10 | 3.28 | 24.2 | 32 | 5 |
| *Marc Rzepczynski | 28 | 0 | 0-3 | 0 | 0 | 11 | 3.97 | 22.2 | 28 | 11 |

## San Diego Padres

| BATTING | G | AB | R | H | 2B | 3B | HR | RBI | TB | BB | SO | SB | OBP | SLG | BAVG |
|---|---|---|---|---|---|---|---|---|---|---|---|---|---|---|---|
| Jason Bartlett | 139 | 554 | 61 | 136 | 22 | 3 | 2 | 40 | 170 | 48 | 98 | 23 | .308 | .307 | .245 |
| Cameron Maybin | 137 | 516 | 82 | 136 | 24 | 8 | 9 | 40 | 203 | 44 | 125 | 40 | .323 | .393 | .264 |
| Orlando Hudson | 119 | 398 | 54 | 98 | 15 | 3 | 7 | 43 | 140 | 49 | 84 | 19 | .329 | .352 | .246 |
| Chase Headley | 113 | 381 | 43 | 110 | 28 | 1 | 4 | 44 | 152 | 52 | 92 | 13 | .374 | .399 | .289 |
| *Ryan Ludwick | 101 | 378 | 42 | 90 | 18 | 0 | 11 | 64 | 141 | 32 | 87 | 1 | .301 | .373 | .238 |
| Will Venable | 121 | 370 | 49 | 91 | 14 | 7 | 9 | 44 | 146 | 31 | 92 | 26 | .310 | .395 | .246 |
| Chris Denorfia | 111 | 307 | 38 | 85 | 13 | 2 | 5 | 19 | 117 | 28 | 49 | 11 | .337 | .381 | .277 |
| Nick Hundley | 82 | 281 | 34 | 81 | 16 | 5 | 9 | 29 | 134 | 22 | 74 | 1 | .347 | .477 | .288 |
| Alberto Gonzalez | 102 | 247 | 18 | 53 | 10 | 2 | 1 | 32 | 70 | 13 | 37 | 1 | .256 | .283 | .215 |
| Jesus Guzman | 76 | 247 | 33 | 77 | 22 | 2 | 5 | 44 | 118 | 22 | 43 | 9 | .369 | .478 | .312 |
| Brad Hawpe | 62 | 195 | 19 | 45 | 10 | 0 | 4 | 19 | 67 | 19 | 68 | 0 | .301 | .344 | .231 |
| Rob Johnson | 67 | 179 | 9 | 34 | 6 | 1 | 3 | 16 | 51 | 14 | 58 | 3 | .259 | .285 | .190 |
| Kyle Blanks | 55 | 170 | 21 | 39 | 7 | 1 | 7 | 26 | 69 | 16 | 51 | 2 | .300 | .406 | .229 |
| Logan Forsythe | 62 | 150 | 12 | 32 | 9 | 1 | 0 | 12 | 43 | 12 | 33 | 3 | .281 | .287 | .213 |
| Jorge Cantu | 57 | 144 | 8 | 28 | 4 | 0 | 3 | 16 | 41 | 7 | 28 | 0 | .232 | .285 | .194 |
| Anthony Rizzo | 49 | 128 | 9 | 18 | 8 | 1 | 1 | 9 | 31 | 21 | 46 | 2 | .281 | .242 | .141 |
| Aaron Cunningham | 52 | 90 | 12 | 16 | 6 | 1 | 3 | 9 | 33 | 9 | 17 | 1 | .257 | .367 | .178 |

| PITCHING | GP | GS | W–L | SV | SHO | R | ERA | IP | Ks | BB |
|---|---|---|---|---|---|---|---|---|---|---|
| Mat Latos | 31 | 31 | 9-14 | 0 | 0 | 82 | 3.47 | 194.1 | 185 | 62 |
| Tim Stauffer | 31 | 31 | 9-12 | 0 | 0 | 81 | 3.73 | 185.2 | 128 | 53 |
| Aaron Harang | 28 | 28 | 14-7 | 0 | 0 | 73 | 3.64 | 170.2 | 124 | 58 |
| Cory Luebke | 46 | 17 | 6-10 | 0 | 0 | 54 | 3.29 | 139.2 | 154 | 44 |
| Dustin Moseley | 20 | 20 | 3-10 | 0 | 0 | 59 | 3.30 | 120.0 | 64 | 36 |
| Clayton Richard | 18 | 18 | 5-9 | 0 | 0 | 52 | 3.88 | 99.2 | 53 | 38 |
| Wade LeBlanc | 14 | 14 | 5-6 | 0 | 0 | 42 | 4.63 | 79.2 | 51 | 28 |
| Chad Qualls | 77 | 0 | 6-8 | 0 | 0 | 30 | 3.51 | 74.1 | 43 | 20 |
| Ernesto Frieri | 59 | 0 | 1-2 | 0 | 0 | 21 | 2.71 | 63.0 | 76 | 34 |
| Heath Bell | 64 | 0 | 3-4 | 43 | 0 | 20 | 2.44 | 62.2 | 51 | 19 |
| Luke Gregerson | 61 | 0 | 3-3 | 0 | 0 | 23 | 2.75 | 55.2 | 34 | 19 |
| Anthony Bass | 27 | 3 | 2-0 | 0 | 0 | 9 | 1.68 | 48.1 | 24 | 21 |
| *Mike Adams | 48 | 0 | 3-1 | 1 | 0 | 7 | 1.13 | 48.0 | 49 | 9 |
| Josh Spence | 40 | 0 | 0-2 | 0 | 0 | 6 | 2.73 | 29.2 | 31 | 19 |

*Mid-season trade.

## San Francisco Giants

| BATTING | G | AB | R | H | 2B | 3B | HR | RBI | TB | BB | SO | SB | OBP | SLG | BAVG |
|---|---|---|---|---|---|---|---|---|---|---|---|---|---|---|---|
| Aubrey Huff | 150 | 521 | 45 | 128 | 27 | 1 | 12 | 59 | 193 | 47 | 90 | 5 | .306 | .370 | .246 |
| Pablo Sandoval | 117 | 426 | 55 | 134 | 26 | 3 | 23 | 70 | 235 | 32 | 63 | 2 | .357 | .552 | .315 |
| Cody Ross | 121 | 405 | 54 | 97 | 25 | 0 | 14 | 52 | 164 | 49 | 96 | 5 | .325 | .405 | .240 |
| Andres Torres | 112 | 348 | 50 | 77 | 24 | 1 | 4 | 19 | 115 | 42 | 95 | 19 | .312 | .330 | .221 |
| Nate Schierholtz | 115 | 335 | 42 | 93 | 22 | 1 | 9 | 41 | 144 | 21 | 61 | 7 | .326 | .430 | .278 |
| Aaron Rowand | 108 | 331 | 34 | 77 | 22 | 2 | 4 | 21 | 115 | 10 | 84 | 2 | .274 | .347 | .233 |
| Miguel Tejada | 91 | 322 | 28 | 77 | 16 | 0 | 4 | 26 | 105 | 12 | 35 | 4 | .270 | .326 | .239 |
| Freddy Sanchez | 60 | 239 | 21 | 69 | 15 | 1 | 3 | 24 | 95 | 13 | 35 | 0 | .332 | .397 | .289 |
| Mike Fontenot | 85 | 220 | 22 | 50 | 15 | 3 | 4 | 21 | 83 | 25 | 48 | 5 | .304 | .377 | .227 |
| *Jeff Keppinger | 56 | 216 | 17 | 55 | 11 | 0 | 2 | 15 | 72 | 8 | 17 | 0 | .285 | .333 | .255 |
| Eli Whiteside | 82 | 213 | 14 | 42 | 8 | 2 | 4 | 17 | 66 | 18 | 59 | 2 | .264 | .310 | .197 |
| Brandon Crawford | 66 | 196 | 22 | 40 | 5 | 2 | 3 | 21 | 58 | 23 | 31 | 1 | .288 | .296 | .204 |
| Brandon Belt | 63 | 187 | 21 | 42 | 6 | 1 | 9 | 18 | 77 | 20 | 57 | 3 | .306 | .412 | .225 |
| Pat Burrell | 92 | 183 | 17 | 42 | 9 | 1 | 7 | 21 | 74 | 33 | 67 | 0 | .352 | .404 | .230 |
| *Carlos Beltran | 44 | 167 | 17 | 54 | 9 | 4 | 7 | 18 | 92 | 11 | 27 | 1 | .369 | .551 | .323 |
| Chris Stewart | 67 | 162 | 20 | 33 | 8 | 0 | 3 | 10 | 50 | 16 | 18 | 0 | .283 | .309 | .204 |
| Buster Posey | 45 | 162 | 17 | 46 | 5 | 0 | 4 | 21 | 63 | 18 | 30 | 3 | .368 | .389 | .284 |

| PITCHING | GP | GS | W–L | SV | SHO | R | ERA | IP | Ks | BB |
|---|---|---|---|---|---|---|---|---|---|---|
| Matt Cain | 33 | 33 | 12-11 | 0 | 0 | 82 | 2.88 | 221.2 | 179 | 63 |
| Tim Lincecum | 33 | 33 | 13-14 | 0 | 1 | 74 | 2.74 | 217.0 | 220 | 86 |
| Madison Bumgarner | 33 | 33 | 13-13 | 0 | 0 | 82 | 3.21 | 204.2 | 191 | 46 |
| Ryan Vogelsong | 30 | 28 | 13-7 | 0 | 1 | 62 | 2.71 | 179.2 | 139 | 61 |
| Jonathan Sanchez | 19 | 19 | 4-7 | 0 | 0 | 54 | 4.26 | 101.1 | 102 | 66 |
| Guillermo Mota | 52 | 0 | 2-2 | 1 | 0 | 34 | 3.81 | 80.1 | 77 | 30 |
| Ramon Ramirez | 66 | 0 | 3-3 | 4 | 0 | 24 | 2.62 | 68.2 | 66 | 26 |
| Jeremy Affeldt | 67 | 0 | 3-2 | 3 | 0 | 22 | 2.63 | 61.2 | 54 | 24 |
| Brian Wilson | 57 | 0 | 6-4 | 36 | 0 | 20 | 3.11 | 55.0 | 54 | 31 |
| Barry Zito | 13 | 9 | 3-4 | 0 | 0 | 35 | 5.87 | 53.2 | 32 | 24 |
| Javier Lopez | 70 | 0 | 5-2 | 1 | 0 | 16 | 2.72 | 53.0 | 40 | 26 |
| Santiago Casilla | 49 | 0 | 2-2 | 6 | 0 | 11 | 1.74 | 51.2 | 45 | 25 |
| Sergio Romo | 65 | 0 | 3-1 | 1 | 0 | 8 | 1.50 | 48.0 | 70 | 5 |
| Dan Runzler | 31 | 1 | 1-2 | 0 | 0 | 21 | 6.26 | 27.1 | 25 | 16 |

## Washington Nationals

| BATTING | G | AB | R | H | 2B | 3B | HR | RBI | TB | BB | SO | SB | OBP | SLG | BAVG |
|---|---|---|---|---|---|---|---|---|---|---|---|---|---|---|---|
| Ian Desmond | 154 | 584 | 65 | 148 | 27 | 5 | 8 | 49 | 209 | 35 | 139 | 25 | .298 | .358 | .253 |
| Danny Espinosa | 158 | 573 | 72 | 135 | 29 | 5 | 21 | 66 | 237 | 57 | 166 | 17 | .323 | .414 | .236 |
| Jayson Werth | 150 | 561 | 69 | 130 | 26 | 1 | 20 | 58 | 218 | 74 | 160 | 19 | .330 | .389 | .232 |
| Michael Morse | 146 | 522 | 73 | 158 | 36 | 0 | 31 | 95 | 287 | 36 | 126 | 2 | .360 | .550 | .303 |
| Ryan Zimmerman | 101 | 395 | 52 | 114 | 21 | 2 | 12 | 49 | 175 | 41 | 73 | 3 | .355 | .443 | .289 |
| Wilson Ramos | 113 | 389 | 48 | 104 | 22 | 1 | 15 | 52 | 173 | 38 | 76 | 0 | .334 | .445 | .267 |
| Rick Ankiel | 122 | 380 | 46 | 91 | 20 | 0 | 9 | 37 | 138 | 29 | 96 | 10 | .296 | .363 | .239 |
| Laynce Nix | 124 | 324 | 38 | 81 | 15 | 1 | 16 | 44 | 146 | 23 | 82 | 2 | .299 | .451 | .250 |
| Roger Bernadina | 91 | 309 | 40 | 75 | 12 | 2 | 7 | 27 | 112 | 22 | 63 | 17 | .301 | .362 | .243 |
| *Jerry Hairston Jr. | 75 | 213 | 25 | 57 | 11 | 1 | 4 | 24 | 82 | 22 | 30 | 2 | .342 | .385 | .268 |
| Alex Cora | 91 | 156 | 12 | 35 | 6 | 1 | 0 | 6 | 43 | 12 | 23 | 2 | .287 | .276 | .224 |
| Adam LaRoche | 43 | 151 | 15 | 26 | 4 | 0 | 3 | 15 | 39 | 25 | 37 | 1 | .288 | .258 | .172 |
| Ivan Rodriguez | 44 | 124 | 14 | 27 | 7 | 0 | 2 | 19 | 40 | 10 | 28 | 0 | .281 | .323 | .218 |
| Chris Marrero | 31 | 109 | 6 | 27 | 5 | 0 | 0 | 10 | 32 | 4 | 27 | 0 | .274 | .294 | .248 |
| *Jonny Gomes | 43 | 93 | 11 | 19 | 4 | 1 | 3 | 12 | 34 | 10 | 31 | 2 | .299 | .366 | .204 |

| PITCHING | GP | GS | W–L | SV | SHO | R | ERA | IP | Ks | BB |
|---|---|---|---|---|---|---|---|---|---|---|
| John Lannan | 33 | 33 | 10-13 | 0 | 0 | 90 | 3.70 | 184.2 | 106 | 76 |
| Livan Hernandez | 29 | 29 | 8-13 | 0 | 1 | 98 | 4.47 | 175.1 | 99 | 46 |
| Jordan Zimmermann | 26 | 26 | 8-11 | 0 | 0 | 62 | 3.18 | 161.1 | 124 | 31 |
| *Jason Marquis | 20 | 20 | 8-5 | 0 | 1 | 58 | 3.95 | 120.2 | 71 | 39 |
| Tom Gorzelanny | 30 | 15 | 4-6 | 0 | 0 | 50 | 4.03 | 105.0 | 95 | 33 |
| Tyler Clippard | 72 | 0 | 3-0 | 0 | 0 | 18 | 1.83 | 88.1 | 104 | 26 |
| Drew Storen | 73 | 0 | 6-3 | 43 | 0 | 24 | 2.75 | 75.1 | 74 | 20 |
| Ross Detwiler | 15 | 10 | 4-5 | 0 | 0 | 26 | 3.00 | 66.0 | 41 | 20 |
| Henry Rodriguez | 59 | 0 | 3-3 | 2 | 0 | 30 | 3.56 | 65.2 | 70 | 45 |
| Chien-Ming Wang | 11 | 11 | 4-3 | 0 | 0 | 35 | 4.04 | 62.1 | 25 | 13 |
| Todd Coffey | 69 | 0 | 5-1 | 0 | 0 | 25 | 3.62 | 59.2 | 46 | 20 |
| Sean Burnett | 69 | 0 | 5-5 | 4 | 0 | 24 | 3.81 | 56.2 | 33 | 21 |
| Collin Balester | 23 | 0 | 1-4 | 0 | 0 | 21 | 4.54 | 35.2 | 34 | 14 |
| Yunesky Maya | 10 | 5 | 1-1 | 0 | 0 | 19 | 5.23 | 32.2 | 15 | 10 |
| Ryan Mattheus | 35 | 0 | 2-2 | 0 | 0 | 11 | 2.81 | 32.0 | 12 | 15 |

*Mid-season trade.

# American League Team-by-Team Statistical Leaders

## Baltimore Orioles

| BATTING | G | AB | R | H | 2B | 3B | HR | RBI | TB | BB | SO | SB | OBP | SLG | BAVG |
|---|---|---|---|---|---|---|---|---|---|---|---|---|---|---|---|
| Nick Markakis | 160 | 641 | 72 | 182 | 31 | 1 | 15 | 73 | 260 | 62 | 75 | 12 | .351 | .406 | .284 |
| Adam Jones | 151 | 567 | 68 | 159 | 26 | 2 | 25 | 83 | 264 | 29 | 113 | 12 | .319 | .466 | .280 |
| Vladimir Guerrero | 145 | 562 | 60 | 163 | 30 | 1 | 13 | 63 | 234 | 17 | 56 | 2 | .317 | .416 | .290 |
| Mark Reynolds | 155 | 534 | 84 | 118 | 27 | 1 | 37 | 86 | 258 | 75 | 196 | 6 | .323 | .483 | .221 |
| J.J. Hardy | 129 | 527 | 76 | 142 | 27 | 0 | 30 | 80 | 259 | 31 | 92 | 0 | .310 | .491 | .269 |
| Matt Wieters | 139 | 500 | 72 | 131 | 28 | 0 | 22 | 68 | 225 | 48 | 84 | 1 | .328 | .450 | .262 |
| Robert Andino | 139 | 457 | 63 | 120 | 22 | 0 | 5 | 36 | 157 | 41 | 83 | 13 | .327 | .344 | .263 |
| *Derrek Lee | 85 | 334 | 39 | 82 | 15 | 1 | 12 | 41 | 135 | 25 | 83 | 2 | .302 | .404 | .246 |
| Nolan Reimold | 87 | 267 | 40 | 66 | 10 | 3 | 13 | 45 | 121 | 28 | 57 | 7 | .328 | .453 | .247 |
| Luke Scott | 64 | 209 | 24 | 46 | 11 | 0 | 9 | 22 | 84 | 24 | 54 | 1 | .301 | .402 | .220 |
| Felix Pie | 85 | 164 | 15 | 36 | 8 | 1 | 0 | 7 | 46 | 10 | 32 | 3 | .264 | .280 | .220 |
| Brian Roberts | 39 | 163 | 18 | 36 | 7 | 1 | 3 | 19 | 54 | 12 | 21 | 6 | .273 | .331 | .221 |
| *Chris Davis | 31 | 123 | 16 | 34 | 9 | 0 | 2 | 13 | 49 | 6 | 39 | 1 | .310 | .398 | .276 |
| Ryan Adams | 29 | 89 | 9 | 25 | 4 | 0 | 0 | 7 | 29 | 6 | 25 | 0 | .333 | .326 | .281 |
| Craig Tatum | 31 | 87 | 7 | 17 | 3 | 0 | 0 | 7 | 20 | 6 | 21 | 1 | .245 | .230 | .195 |
| Matt Angle | 31 | 79 | 12 | 14 | 4 | 0 | 1 | 7 | 21 | 12 | 13 | 11 | .293 | .266 | .177 |

| PITCHING | GP | GS | W-L | SV | SHO | R | ERA | IP | Ks | BB |
|---|---|---|---|---|---|---|---|---|---|---|
| Jeremy Guthrie | 34 | 32 | 9-17 | 0 | 0 | 113 | 4.33 | 208.0 | 130 | 66 |
| Zach Britton | 28 | 28 | 11-11 | 0 | 0 | 93 | 4.61 | 154.1 | 97 | 62 |
| Jake Arrieta | 22 | 22 | 10-8 | 0 | 0 | 70 | 5.05 | 119.1 | 93 | 59 |
| Alfredo Simon | 23 | 16 | 4-9 | 0 | 0 | 69 | 4.90 | 115.2 | 83 | 40 |
| Brad Bergesen | 34 | 12 | 2-7 | 0 | 1 | 73 | 5.70 | 101.0 | 61 | 32 |
| Jim Johnson | 69 | 0 | 6-5 | 9 | 0 | 30 | 2.67 | 91.0 | 58 | 21 |
| Chris Jakubauskas | 33 | 6 | 2-2 | 0 | 0 | 46 | 5.72 | 72.1 | 52 | 29 |
| *Tommy Hunter | 12 | 11 | 3-3 | 0 | 0 | 44 | 5.06 | 69.1 | 35 | 10 |
| Chris Tillman | 13 | 13 | 3-5 | 0 | 0 | 41 | 5.52 | 62.0 | 46 | 25 |
| Kevin Gregg | 63 | 0 | 0-3 | 22 | 0 | 35 | 4.37 | 59.2 | 53 | 40 |
| Brian Matusz | 12 | 12 | 1-9 | 0 | 0 | 60 | 10.69 | 49.2 | 38 | 24 |
| *Koji Uehara | 43 | 0 | 1-1 | 0 | 0 | 9 | 1.72 | 47.0 | 62 | 8 |
| Jason Berken | 40 | 0 | 1-2 | 0 | 0 | 29 | 5.36 | 47.0 | 41 | 21 |
| *Mike Gonzalez | 49 | 0 | 2-2 | 1 | 0 | 26 | 4.27 | 46.1 | 46 | 18 |
| Jeremy Accardo | 31 | 0 | 3-3 | 0 | 0 | 24 | 5.73 | 37.2 | 23 | 18 |

## Boston Red Sox

| BATTING | G | AB | R | H | 2B | 3B | HR | RBI | TB | BB | SO | SB | OBP | SLG | BAVG |
|---|---|---|---|---|---|---|---|---|---|---|---|---|---|---|---|
| Jacoby Ellsbury | 158 | 660 | 119 | 212 | 46 | 5 | 32 | 105 | 364 | 52 | 98 | 39 | .376 | .552 | .321 |
| Dustin Pedroia | 159 | 635 | 102 | 195 | 37 | 3 | 21 | 91 | 301 | 86 | 85 | 26 | .387 | .474 | .307 |
| Adrian Gonzalez | 159 | 630 | 108 | 213 | 45 | 3 | 27 | 117 | 345 | 74 | 119 | 1 | .410 | .548 | .338 |
| David Ortiz | 146 | 525 | 84 | 162 | 40 | 1 | 29 | 96 | 291 | 78 | 83 | 1 | .398 | .554 | .309 |
| Carl Crawford | 130 | 506 | 65 | 129 | 29 | 7 | 11 | 56 | 205 | 23 | 104 | 18 | .289 | .405 | .255 |
| Kevin Youkilis | 120 | 431 | 68 | 111 | 32 | 2 | 17 | 80 | 198 | 68 | 100 | 3 | .373 | .459 | .258 |
| Marco Scutaro | 113 | 395 | 59 | 118 | 26 | 1 | 7 | 54 | 167 | 38 | 36 | 4 | .358 | .423 | .299 |
| Jarrod Saltalamacchia | 103 | 358 | 52 | 84 | 23 | 3 | 16 | 56 | 161 | 24 | 119 | 1 | .288 | .450 | .235 |
| Jed Lowrie | 88 | 309 | 40 | 78 | 14 | 4 | 6 | 36 | 118 | 23 | 60 | 1 | .303 | .382 | .252 |
| Josh Reddick | 87 | 254 | 41 | 71 | 18 | 3 | 7 | 28 | 116 | 19 | 50 | 1 | .327 | .457 | .280 |
| J.D. Drew | 81 | 248 | 23 | 55 | 6 | 1 | 4 | 22 | 75 | 33 | 58 | 0 | .315 | .302 | .222 |
| Jason Varitek | 68 | 222 | 32 | 49 | 10 | 1 | 11 | 36 | 94 | 21 | 67 | 0 | .300 | .423 | .221 |
| Darnell McDonald | 79 | 157 | 26 | 37 | 6 | 1 | 6 | 24 | 63 | 14 | 33 | 2 | .303 | .401 | .236 |
| *Mike Aviles | 38 | 101 | 17 | 32 | 6 | 0 | 2 | 8 | 44 | 4 | 17 | 4 | .340 | .436 | .317 |
| *Mike Cameron | 33 | 94 | 9 | 14 | 2 | 0 | 3 | 9 | 25 | 8 | 25 | 0 | .212 | .266 | .149 |
| Drew Sutton | 31 | 54 | 11 | 17 | 7 | 0 | 0 | 7 | 24 | 3 | 13 | 0 | .362 | .444 | .315 |
| Ryan Lavarnway | 17 | 39 | 5 | 9 | 2 | 0 | 2 | 8 | 17 | 4 | 10 | 0 | .302 | .436 | .231 |

| PITCHING | GP | GS | W-L | SV | SHO | R | ERA | IP | Ks | BB |
|---|---|---|---|---|---|---|---|---|---|---|
| Josh Beckett | 30 | 30 | 13-7 | 0 | 1 | 65 | 2.89 | 193.0 | 175 | 52 |
| Jon Lester | 31 | 31 | 15-9 | 0 | 0 | 77 | 3.47 | 191.2 | 182 | 75 |
| John Lackey | 28 | 28 | 12-12 | 0 | 0 | 119 | 6.41 | 160.0 | 108 | 56 |
| Tim Wakefield | 33 | 23 | 7-8 | 0 | 0 | 110 | 5.12 | 154.2 | 93 | 47 |
| Alfredo Aceves | 55 | 4 | 10-2 | 2 | 0 | 37 | 2.61 | 114.0 | 80 | 42 |
| Clay Buchholz | 14 | 14 | 6-3 | 0 | 0 | 34 | 3.48 | 82.2 | 60 | 31 |
| Daniel Bard | 70 | 0 | 2-9 | 1 | 0 | 29 | 3.33 | 73.0 | 74 | 24 |
| Andrew Miller | 17 | 12 | 6-3 | 0 | 0 | 43 | 5.54 | 65.0 | 50 | 41 |
| Matt Albers | 56 | 0 | 4-4 | 0 | 0 | 35 | 4.73 | 64.2 | 68 | 31 |
| Jonathan Papelbon | 63 | 0 | 4-1 | 31 | 0 | 22 | 2.94 | 64.1 | 87 | 10 |
| Dan Wheeler | 47 | 0 | 2-2 | 0 | 0 | 24 | 4.38 | 49.1 | 39 | 8 |
| *Erik Bedard | 8 | 8 | 1-2 | 0 | 0 | 22 | 4.03 | 38.0 | 38 | 18 |
| Daisuke Matsuzaka | 8 | 7 | 3-3 | 0 | 0 | 24 | 5.30 | 37.1 | 26 | 23 |
| *Franklin Morales | 36 | 0 | 1-1 | 0 | 0 | 15 | 3.62 | 32.1 | 31 | 11 |

*Mid-season trade.

## Chicago White Sox

| BATTING | G | AB | R | H | 2B | 3B | HR | RBI | TB | BB | SO | SB | OBP | SLG | BAVG |
|---|---|---|---|---|---|---|---|---|---|---|---|---|---|---|---|
| Juan Pierre | 158 | 639 | 80 | 178 | 17 | 4 | 2 | 50 | 209 | 43 | 41 | 27 | .329 | .327 | .279 |
| Alexei Ramirez | 158 | 614 | 81 | 165 | 31 | 2 | 15 | 70 | 245 | 51 | 84 | 7 | .328 | .399 | .269 |
| Paul Konerko | 149 | 543 | 69 | 163 | 25 | 0 | 31 | 105 | 281 | 77 | 89 | 1 | .388 | .517 | .300 |
| Alex Rios | 145 | 537 | 64 | 122 | 22 | 2 | 13 | 44 | 187 | 27 | 68 | 11 | .265 | .348 | .227 |
| Gordon Beckham | 150 | 499 | 60 | 115 | 23 | 0 | 10 | 44 | 168 | 35 | 111 | 5 | .296 | .337 | .230 |
| A.J. Pierzynski | 129 | 464 | 38 | 133 | 29 | 1 | 8 | 48 | 188 | 23 | 33 | 0 | .323 | .405 | .287 |
| Carlos Quentin | 118 | 421 | 53 | 107 | 31 | 0 | 24 | 77 | 210 | 34 | 84 | 1 | .340 | .499 | .254 |
| Adam Dunn | 122 | 415 | 36 | 66 | 16 | 0 | 11 | 42 | 115 | 75 | 177 | 0 | .292 | .277 | .159 |
| Brent Morel | 126 | 413 | 44 | 101 | 18 | 1 | 10 | 41 | 151 | 22 | 57 | 5 | .287 | .366 | .245 |
| Brent Lillibridge | 97 | 186 | 38 | 48 | 5 | 1 | 13 | 29 | 94 | 17 | 62 | 10 | .340 | .505 | .258 |
| Omar Vizquel | 58 | 167 | 18 | 42 | 7 | 1 | 0 | 8 | 51 | 9 | 18 | 1 | .287 | .305 | .251 |
| Alejandro De Aza | 54 | 152 | 29 | 50 | 11 | 3 | 4 | 23 | 79 | 17 | 34 | 12 | .400 | .520 | .329 |
| *Mark Teahen | 51 | 118 | 11 | 24 | 3 | 0 | 3 | 11 | 36 | 12 | 28 | 0 | .277 | .305 | .203 |
| Tyler Flowers | 38 | 110 | 13 | 23 | 5 | 1 | 5 | 16 | 45 | 14 | 38 | 0 | .310 | .409 | .209 |

| PITCHING | GP | GS | W–L | SV | SHO | R | ERA | IP | Ks | BB |
|---|---|---|---|---|---|---|---|---|---|---|
| Mark Buehrle | 31 | 31 | 13-9 | 0 | 0 | 93 | 3.59 | 205.1 | 109 | 45 |
| Gavin Floyd | 31 | 30 | 12-13 | 0 | 0 | 97 | 4.37 | 193.2 | 151 | 45 |
| John Danks | 27 | 27 | 8-12 | 0 | 1 | 89 | 4.33 | 170.1 | 135 | 46 |
| Philip Humber | 28 | 26 | 9-9 | 0 | 0 | 71 | 3.75 | 163.0 | 116 | 41 |
| *Edwin Jackson | 19 | 19 | 7-7 | 0 | 1 | 55 | 3.92 | 121.2 | 97 | 39 |
| Jake Peavy | 19 | 18 | 7-7 | 0 | 1 | 61 | 4.92 | 111.2 | 95 | 24 |
| Chris Sale | 58 | 0 | 2-2 | 8 | 0 | 22 | 2.79 | 71.0 | 79 | 27 |
| Jesse Crain | 67 | 0 | 8-3 | 1 | 0 | 20 | 2.62 | 65.1 | 70 | 31 |
| Sergio Santos | 63 | 0 | 4-5 | 30 | 0 | 25 | 3.55 | 63.1 | 92 | 29 |
| Matt Thornton | 62 | 0 | 2-5 | 3 | 0 | 34 | 3.32 | 59.2 | 63 | 21 |
| Will Ohman | 59 | 0 | 1-3 | 0 | 0 | 26 | 4.22 | 53.1 | 54 | 17 |
| *Zach Stewart | 10 | 8 | 2-5 | 0 | 0 | 35 | 6.22 | 50.2 | 35 | 13 |
| Tony Pena | 17 | 0 | 1-1 | 0 | 0 | 15 | 6.20 | 20.1 | 17 | 10 |
| Brian Bruney | 23 | 0 | 1-0 | 0 | 0 | 15 | 6.86 | 19.2 | 16 | 12 |
| Dylan Axelrod | 4 | 3 | 1-0 | 0 | 0 | 6 | 2.89 | 18.2 | 19 | 9 |
| *Jason Frasor | 20 | 0 | 1-2 | 0 | 0 | 13 | 5.09 | 17.2 | 20 | 11 |

## Cleveland Indians

| BATTING | G | AB | R | H | 2B | 3B | HR | RBI | TB | BB | SO | SB | OBP | SLG | BAVG |
|---|---|---|---|---|---|---|---|---|---|---|---|---|---|---|---|
| Asdrubal Cabrera | 151 | 604 | 87 | 165 | 32 | 3 | 25 | 92 | 278 | 44 | 119 | 17 | .332 | .460 | .273 |
| Carlos Santana | 155 | 552 | 84 | 132 | 35 | 2 | 27 | 79 | 252 | 97 | 133 | 5 | .351 | .457 | .239 |
| Michael Brantley | 114 | 451 | 63 | 120 | 24 | 4 | 7 | 46 | 173 | 34 | 76 | 13 | .318 | .384 | .266 |
| Matt LaPorta | 107 | 352 | 34 | 87 | 23 | 1 | 11 | 53 | 145 | 23 | 87 | 1 | .299 | .412 | .247 |
| Travis Hafner | 94 | 325 | 41 | 91 | 16 | 0 | 13 | 57 | 146 | 36 | 78 | 0 | .361 | .449 | .280 |
| *Orlando Cabrera | 91 | 324 | 35 | 79 | 13 | 0 | 4 | 38 | 104 | 13 | 40 | 6 | .277 | .321 | .244 |
| Jack Hannahan | 110 | 320 | 38 | 80 | 16 | 2 | 8 | 40 | 124 | 38 | 80 | 2 | .331 | .388 | .250 |
| Shin-Soo Choo | 85 | 313 | 37 | 81 | 11 | 3 | 8 | 36 | 122 | 36 | 78 | 12 | .344 | .390 | .259 |
| Grady Sizemore | 71 | 268 | 34 | 60 | 21 | 1 | 10 | 32 | 113 | 18 | 85 | 0 | .285 | .422 | .224 |
| Lou Marson | 79 | 243 | 26 | 56 | 9 | 2 | 1 | 19 | 72 | 24 | 68 | 4 | .300 | .296 | .230 |
| *Kosuke Fukudome | 59 | 237 | 26 | 59 | 12 | 1 | 5 | 22 | 88 | 15 | 53 | 2 | .300 | .371 | .249 |
| Shelley Duncan | 76 | 223 | 29 | 58 | 17 | 0 | 11 | 47 | 108 | 19 | 56 | 0 | .324 | .484 | .260 |
| Lonnie Chisenhall | 66 | 212 | 27 | 54 | 13 | 0 | 7 | 22 | 88 | 8 | 49 | 1 | .284 | .415 | .255 |
| Ezequiel Carrera | 68 | 202 | 27 | 49 | 8 | 3 | 0 | 14 | 63 | 16 | 35 | 10 | .301 | .312 | .243 |
| Austin Kearns | 57 | 150 | 18 | 30 | 5 | 1 | 2 | 7 | 43 | 18 | 48 | 0 | .302 | .287 | .200 |
| Travis Buck | 50 | 149 | 18 | 34 | 11 | 0 | 2 | 18 | 51 | 8 | 30 | 1 | .275 | .342 | .228 |

| PITCHING | GP | GS | W–L | SV | SHO | R | ERA | IP | Ks | BB |
|---|---|---|---|---|---|---|---|---|---|---|
| Justin Masterson | 34 | 33 | 12-10 | 0 | 0 | 89 | 3.21 | 216.0 | 158 | 65 |
| Fausto Carmona | 32 | 32 | 7-15 | 0 | 0 | 125 | 5.25 | 188.2 | 109 | 60 |
| Josh Tomlin | 26 | 26 | 12-7 | 0 | 0 | 80 | 4.25 | 165.1 | 89 | 21 |
| Carlos Carrasco | 21 | 21 | 8-9 | 0 | 0 | 68 | 4.62 | 124.2 | 85 | 40 |
| Chad Durbin | 56 | 0 | 2-2 | 0 | 0 | 45 | 5.53 | 68.1 | 59 | 26 |
| Joe Smith | 71 | 0 | 3-3 | 0 | 0 | 16 | 2.01 | 67.0 | 45 | 21 |
| *Ubaldo Jimenez | 11 | 11 | 4-4 | 0 | 0 | 43 | 5.10 | 65.1 | 62 | 27 |
| Mitch Talbot | 12 | 12 | 2-6 | 0 | 0 | 47 | 6.64 | 63.2 | 36 | 28 |
| Rafael Perez | 71 | 0 | 5-2 | 0 | 0 | 27 | 3.00 | 63.0 | 33 | 19 |
| Tony Sipp | 69 | 0 | 6-3 | 0 | 0 | 22 | 3.03 | 62.1 | 57 | 24 |
| Vinnie Pestano | 67 | 0 | 1-2 | 2 | 0 | 16 | 2.32 | 62.0 | 84 | 24 |
| Chris Perez | 64 | 0 | 4-7 | 36 | 0 | 24 | 3.32 | 59.2 | 39 | 26 |
| Jeanmar Gomez | 11 | 10 | 5-3 | 0 | 0 | 31 | 4.47 | 58.1 | 31 | 15 |
| Frank Herrmann | 40 | 0 | 4-0 | 0 | 0 | 35 | 5.11 | 56.1 | 34 | 16 |
| David Huff | 11 | 10 | 2-6 | 0 | 0 | 35 | 4.09 | 50.2 | 36 | 17 |

*Mid-season trade.

### Detroit Tigers

| BATTING | G | AB | R | H | 2B | 3B | HR | RBI | TB | BB | SO | SB | OBP | SLG | BAVG |
|---|---|---|---|---|---|---|---|---|---|---|---|---|---|---|---|
| Austin Jackson | 153 | 591 | 90 | 147 | 22 | 11 | 10 | 45 | 221 | 56 | 181 | 22 | .317 | .374 | .249 |
| Miguel Cabrera | 161 | 572 | 111 | 197 | 48 | 0 | 30 | 105 | 335 | 108 | 89 | 2 | .448 | .586 | .344 |
| Victor Martinez | 145 | 540 | 76 | 178 | 40 | 0 | 12 | 103 | 254 | 46 | 51 | 1 | .380 | .470 | .330 |
| Jhonny Peralta | 146 | 525 | 68 | 157 | 25 | 3 | 21 | 86 | 251 | 40 | 95 | 0 | .345 | .478 | .299 |
| Alex Avila | 141 | 464 | 63 | 137 | 33 | 4 | 19 | 82 | 235 | 73 | 131 | 3 | .389 | .506 | .295 |
| Brennan Boesch | 115 | 428 | 75 | 121 | 25 | 1 | 16 | 54 | 196 | 35 | 83 | 5 | .341 | .458 | .283 |
| Ryan Raburn | 121 | 387 | 53 | 99 | 22 | 2 | 14 | 49 | 167 | 21 | 114 | 1 | .297 | .432 | .256 |
| Magglio Ordonez | 92 | 329 | 33 | 84 | 10 | 0 | 5 | 32 | 109 | 23 | 41 | 2 | .303 | .331 | .255 |
| Brandon Inge | 102 | 269 | 29 | 53 | 10 | 2 | 3 | 23 | 76 | 24 | 74 | 1 | .265 | .283 | .197 |
| Ramon Santiago | 101 | 258 | 29 | 67 | 11 | 3 | 5 | 30 | 99 | 17 | 38 | 0 | .311 | .384 | .260 |
| Don Kelly | 113 | 257 | 35 | 63 | 8 | 3 | 7 | 28 | 98 | 14 | 32 | 2 | .291 | .381 | .245 |
| Andy Dirks | 78 | 219 | 34 | 55 | 13 | 0 | 7 | 28 | 89 | 11 | 36 | 5 | .296 | .406 | .251 |
| *Delmon Young | 40 | 168 | 28 | 46 | 5. | 1 | 8 | 32 | 77 | 5 | 30 | 0 | .298 | .458 | .274 |
| *Wilson Betemit | 40 | 120 | 11 | 35 | 7 | 3 | 5 | 19 | 63 | 11 | 47 | 1 | .346 | .525 | .292 |
| *Casper Wells | 64 | 113 | 16 | 29 | 10 | 0 | 4 | 12 | 51 | 9 | 29 | 1 | .323 | .451 | .257 |
| Carlos Guillen | 28 | 95 | 8 | 22 | 2 | 1 | 3 | 13 | 35 | 5 | 16 | 1 | .265 | .368 | .232 |

| PITCHING | GP | GS | W-L | SV | SHO | R | ERA | IP | Ks | BB |
|---|---|---|---|---|---|---|---|---|---|---|
| Justin Verlander | 34 | 34 | 24-5 | 0 | 2 | 73 | 2.40 | 251.0 | 250 | 57 |
| Max Scherzer | 33 | 33 | 15-9 | 0 | 0 | 101 | 4.43 | 195.0 | 174 | 56 |
| Rick Porcello | 31 | 31 | 14-9 | 0 | 0 | 103 | 4.75 | 182.0 | 104 | 46 |
| Brad Penny | 31 | 31 | 11-11 | 0 | 0 | 117 | 5.30 | 181.2 | 74 | 62 |
| Phil Coke | 48 | 14 | 3-9 | 1 | 0 | 64 | 4.47 | 108.2 | 69 | 40 |
| Jose Valverde | 75 | 0 | 2-4 | 49 | 0 | 21 | 2.24 | 72.1 | 69 | 34 |
| *Doug Fister | 11 | 10 | 8-1 | 0 | 0 | 19 | 1.79 | 70.1 | 57 | 5 |
| Joaquin Benoit | 66 | 0 | 4-3 | 2 | 0 | 22 | 2.95 | 61.0 | 63 | 17 |
| Daniel Schlereth | 49 | 0 | 2-2 | 0 | 0 | 20 | 3.49 | 49.0 | 44 | 31 |
| Al Alburquerque | 41 | 0 | 6-1 | 0 | 0 | 9 | 1.87 | 43.1 | 67 | 29 |
| Ryan Perry | 36 | 0 | 2-0 | 0 | 0 | 25 | 5.35 | 37.0 | 24 | 21 |
| *Charlie Furbush | 17 | 2 | 1-3 | 0 | 0 | 18 | 3.62 | 32.1 | 26 | 14 |
| Duane Below | 14 | 2 | 0-2 | 0 | 0 | 16 | 4.34 | 29.0 | 14 | 11 |
| *David Pauley | 14 | 0 | 0-2 | 0 | 0 | 14 | 5.95 | 19.2 | 10 | 6 |

### Kansas City Royals

| BATTING | G | AB | R | H | 2B | 3B | HR | RBI | TB | BB | SO | SB | OBP | SLG | BAVG |
|---|---|---|---|---|---|---|---|---|---|---|---|---|---|---|---|
| Melky Cabrera | 155 | 658 | 102 | 201 | 44 | 5 | 18 | 87 | 309 | 35 | 94 | 20 | .339 | .470 | .305 |
| Alex Gordon | 151 | 611 | 101 | 185 | 45 | 4 | 23 | 87 | 307 | 67 | 139 | 17 | .376 | .502 | .303 |
| Jeff Francoeur | 153 | 601 | 77 | 171 | 47 | 4 | 20 | 87 | 286 | 37 | 123 | 22 | .329 | .476 | .285 |
| Billy Butler | 159 | 597 | 74 | 174 | 44 | 0 | 19 | 95 | 275 | 66 | 95 | 2 | .361 | .461 | .291 |
| Alcides Escobar | 158 | 548 | 69 | 139 | 21 | 8 | 4 | 46 | 188 | 25 | 73 | 26 | .290 | .343 | .254 |
| Eric Hosmer | 128 | 523 | 66 | 153 | 27 | 3 | 19 | 78 | 243 | 34 | 82 | 11 | .334 | .465 | .293 |
| Chris Getz | 118 | 380 | 50 | 97 | 6 | 3 | 0 | 26 | 109 | 30 | 45 | 21 | .313 | .287 | .255 |
| Mike Moustakas | 89 | 338 | 26 | 89 | 18 | 1 | 5 | 30 | 124 | 22 | 51 | 2 | .309 | .367 | .263 |
| Brayan Pena | 72 | 222 | 17 | 55 | 11 | 0 | 3 | 24 | 75 | 12 | 24 | 0 | .288 | .338 | .248 |
| *Wilson Betemit | 57 | 203 | 29 | 57 | 15 | 1 | 3 | 27 | 83 | 20 | 58 | 3 | .341 | .409 | .281 |
| *Matt Treanor | 65 | 186 | 24 | 42 | 6 | 0 | 3 | 21 | 57 | 33 | 49 | 2 | .351 | .306 | .226 |
| *Mike Aviles | 53 | 185 | 14 | 41 | 11 | 3 | 5 | 31 | 73 | 9 | 27 | 10 | .261 | .395 | .222 |
| Johnny Giavotella | 46 | 178 | 20 | 44 | 9 | 4 | 2 | 21 | 67 | 6 | 32 | 5 | .273 | .376 | .247 |
| Salvador Perez | 39 | 148 | 20 | 49 | 8 | 2 | 3 | 21 | 70 | 7 | 20 | 0 | .361 | .473 | .331 |
| Mitch Maier | 45 | 95 | 19 | 22 | 4 | 3 | 0 | 7 | 32 | 16 | 32 | 1 | .345 | .337 | .232 |
| Kila Ka'aihue | 23 | 82 | 6 | 16 | 4 | 0 | 2 | 6 | 26 | 12 | 26 | 0 | .295 | .317 | .195 |
| Jarrod Dyson | 26 | 44 | 8 | 9 | 1 | 0 | 0 | 3 | 10 | 7 | 14 | 11 | .308 | .227 | .205 |

| PITCHING | GP | GS | W-L | SV | SHO | R | ERA | IP | Ks | BB |
|---|---|---|---|---|---|---|---|---|---|---|
| Luke Hochevar | 31 | 31 | 11-11 | 0 | 0 | 110 | 4.68 | 198.0 | 128 | 62 |
| Jeff Francis | 31 | 31 | 6-16 | 0 | 0 | 102 | 4.82 | 183.0 | 91 | 39 |
| Bruce Chen | 25 | 25 | 12-8 | 0 | 0 | 71 | 3.77 | 155.0 | 97 | 50 |
| *Felipe Paulino | 21 | 20 | 4-6 | 0 | 0 | 62 | 4.11 | 124.2 | 119 | 48 |
| Danny Duffy | 20 | 20 | 4-8 | 0 | 0 | 66 | 5.64 | 105.1 | 87 | 51 |
| Blake Wood | 55 | 0 | 5-3 | 1 | 0 | 30 | 3.75 | 69.2 | 62 | 32 |
| Tim Collins | 68 | 0 | 4-4 | 0 | 0 | 28 | 3.63 | 67.0 | 60 | 48 |
| Aaron Crow | 57 | 0 | 4-4 | 0 | 0 | 20 | 2.76 | 62.0 | 65 | 31 |
| Kyle Davies | 13 | 13 | 1-9 | 0 | 0 | 52 | 6.75 | 61.1 | 50 | 26 |
| Joakim Soria | 60 | 0 | 5-5 | 28 | 0 | 29 | 4.03 | 60.1 | 60 | 17 |
| Nate Adcock | 24 | 3 | 1-1 | 1 | 0 | 34 | 4.62 | 60.1 | 36 | 26 |
| Greg Holland | 46 | 0 | 5-1 | 4 | 0 | 13 | 1.80 | 60.0 | 74 | 19 |
| Louis Coleman | 48 | 0 | 1-4 | 1 | 0 | 20 | 2.87 | 59.2 | 64 | 26 |
| Sean O'Sullivan | 12 | 10 | 2-6 | 0 | 0 | 52 | 7.25 | 58.1 | 19 | 26 |

*Mid-season trade.

## Los Angeles Angels of Anaheim

| BATTING | G | AB | R | H | 2B | 3B | HR | RBI | TB | BB | SO | SB | OBP | SLG | BAVG |
|---|---|---|---|---|---|---|---|---|---|---|---|---|---|---|---|
| Torii Hunter | 156 | 580 | 80 | 152 | 24 | 2 | 23 | 82 | 249 | 62 | 125 | 5 | .336 | .429 | .262 |
| Erick Aybar | 143 | 555 | 71 | 155 | 33 | 8 | 10 | 59 | 234 | 30 | 68 | 30 | .322 | .422 | .279 |
| Mark Trumbo | 149 | 539 | 65 | 137 | 31 | 1 | 29 | 87 | 257 | 25 | 120 | 9 | .291 | .477 | .254 |
| Howard Kendrick | 140 | 537 | 86 | 153 | 30 | 6 | 18 | 63 | 249 | 33 | 119 | 14 | .338 | .464 | .285 |
| Vernon Wells | 131 | 503 | 60 | 110 | 15 | 4 | 25 | 66 | 208 | 20 | 86 | 9 | .249 | .414 | .219 |
| Peter Bourjos | 147 | 501 | 72 | 136 | 26 | 11 | 12 | 43 | 220 | 32 | 124 | 22 | .327 | .439 | .271 |
| Bobby Abreu | 141 | 501 | 54 | 127 | 30 | 1 | 8 | 60 | 183 | 78 | 112 | 21 | .353 | .365 | .253 |
| Alberto Callaspo | 141 | 473 | 54 | 137 | 23 | 0 | 6 | 46 | 178 | 58 | 48 | 8 | .367 | .376 | .290 |
| Maicer Izturis | 121 | 448 | 51 | 124 | 35 | 0 | 5 | 38 | 174 | 33 | 64 | 9 | .335 | .388 | .277 |
| Jeff Mathis | 93 | 247 | 18 | 43 | 12 | 0 | 3 | 22 | 64 | 15 | 75 | 1 | .225 | .259 | .174 |
| Hank Conger | 59 | 177 | 14 | 37 | 8 | 0 | 6 | 19 | 63 | 17 | 37 | 0 | .282 | .356 | .209 |
| Mike Trout | 40 | 121 | 20 | 25 | 6 | 0 | 5 | 16 | 46 | 9 | 30 | 4 | .271 | .380 | .207 |
| Bobby Wilson | 57 | 110 | 4 | 21 | 8 | 0 | 1 | 8 | 32 | 10 | 15 | 0 | .254 | .291 | .191 |
| *Russell Branyan | 37 | 65 | 7 | 12 | 2 | 0 | 4 | 12 | 26 | 11 | 21 | 2 | .299 | .400 | .185 |
| Alexi Amarista | 23 | 52 | 2 | 8 | 3 | 1 | 0 | 5 | 13 | 2 | 8 | 0 | .182 | .250 | .154 |

| PITCHING | GP | GS | W-L | SV | SHO | R | ERA | IP | Ks | BB |
|---|---|---|---|---|---|---|---|---|---|---|
| Dan Haren | 35 | 34 | 16-10 | 0 | 3 | 91 | 3.17 | 238.1 | 192 | 33 |
| Jered Weaver | 33 | 33 | 18-8 | 0 | 2 | 65 | 2.41 | 235.2 | 198 | 56 |
| Ervin Santana | 33 | 33 | 11-12 | 0 | 1 | 95 | 3.38 | 228.2 | 178 | 72 |
| Joel Pineiro | 27 | 24 | 7-7 | 0 | 0 | 90 | 5.13 | 145.2 | 62 | 38 |
| Tyler Chatwood | 27 | 25 | 6-11 | 0 | 0 | 81 | 4.75 | 142.0 | 74 | 71 |
| Hisanori Takahashi | 61 | 0 | 4-3 | 2 | 0 | 30 | 3.44 | 68.0 | 52 | 25 |
| Jordan Walden | 62 | 0 | 5-5 | 32 | 0 | 22 | 2.98 | 60.1 | 67 | 26 |
| Rich Thompson | 44 | 0 | 1-3 | 0 | 0 | 18 | 3.00 | 54.0 | 56 | 20 |
| Scott Downs | 60 | 0 | 6-3 | 1 | 0 | 11 | 1.34 | 53.2 | 35 | 15 |
| Jerome Williams | 10 | 6 | 4-0 | 0 | 0 | 20 | 3.68 | 44.0 | 28 | 15 |
| Bobby Cassevah | 30 | 0 | 1-1 | 0 | 0 | 12 | 2.72 | 39.2 | 24 | 19 |
| Trevor Bell | 19 | 0 | 1-1 | 0 | 0 | 14 | 3.41 | 34.1 | 17 | 10 |
| Fernando Rodney | 39 | 0 | 3-5 | 3 | 0 | 18 | 4.50 | 32.0 | 26 | 28 |

## Minnesota Twins

| BATTING | G | AB | R | H | 2B | 3B | HR | RBI | TB | BB | SO | SB | OBP | SLG | BAVG |
|---|---|---|---|---|---|---|---|---|---|---|---|---|---|---|---|
| Danny Valencia | 154 | 564 | 63 | 139 | 28 | 2 | 15 | 72 | 216 | 40 | 102 | 2 | .294 | .383 | .246 |
| Michael Cuddyer | 139 | 529 | 70 | 150 | 29 | 2 | 20 | 70 | 243 | 48 | 95 | 11 | .346 | .459 | .284 |
| Ben Revere | 117 | 450 | 56 | 120 | 9 | 5 | 0 | 30 | 139 | 26 | 41 | 34 | .310 | .309 | .267 |
| Jason Kubel | 99 | 366 | 37 | 100 | 21 | 1 | 12 | 58 | 159 | 32 | 86 | 1 | .332 | .434 | .273 |
| Alexi Casilla | 97 | 323 | 52 | 84 | 21 | 4 | 2 | 21 | 119 | 28 | 45 | 15 | .322 | .368 | .260 |
| *Delmon Young | 84 | 305 | 26 | 81 | 16 | 0 | 4 | 32 | 109 | 18 | 55 | 1 | .305 | .357 | .266 |
| Joe Mauer | 82 | 296 | 38 | 85 | 15 | 0 | 3 | 30 | 109 | 32 | 38 | 0 | .360 | .368 | .287 |
| Luke Hughes | 96 | 287 | 31 | 64 | 12 | 0 | 7 | 30 | 97 | 24 | 79 | 3 | .289 | .338 | .223 |
| Trevor Plouffe | 81 | 286 | 47 | 68 | 18 | 1 | 8 | 31 | 112 | 25 | 71 | 3 | .305 | .392 | .238 |
| Denard Span | 70 | 284 | 37 | 75 | 11 | 5 | 2 | 16 | 102 | 27 | 36 | 6 | .328 | .359 | .264 |
| Justin Morneau | 69 | 264 | 19 | 60 | 16 | 0 | 4 | 30 | 88 | 19 | 44 | 0 | .285 | .333 | .227 |
| Drew Butera | 93 | 234 | 19 | 39 | 9 | 1 | 2 | 23 | 56 | 11 | 42 | 0 | .210 | .239 | .167 |
| Tsuyoshi Nishioka | 68 | 221 | 14 | 50 | 5 | 0 | 0 | 19 | 55 | 15 | 43 | 2 | .278 | .249 | .226 |
| Matt Tolbert | 87 | 207 | 22 | 41 | 10 | 2 | 0 | 11 | 55 | 11 | 31 | 3 | .252 | .266 | .198 |
| *Jim Thome | 71 | 206 | 21 | 50 | 12 | 0 | 12 | 40 | 98 | 35 | 69 | 0 | .351 | .476 | .243 |
| Rene Tosoni | 60 | 172 | 20 | 35 | 7 | 1 | 5 | 22 | 59 | 14 | 42 | 0 | .275 | .343 | .203 |

| PITCHING | GP | GS | W-L | SV | SHO | R | ERA | IP | Ks | BB |
|---|---|---|---|---|---|---|---|---|---|---|
| Carl Pavano | 33 | 33 | 9-13 | 0 | 1 | 123 | 4.30 | 222.0 | 102 | 40 |
| Brian Duensing | 32 | 28 | 9-14 | 0 | 1 | 102 | 5.23 | 161.2 | 115 | 52 |
| Nick Blackburn | 26 | 26 | 7-10 | 0 | 0 | 91 | 4.49 | 148.1 | 76 | 54 |
| Scott Baker | 23 | 21 | 8-6 | 0 | 0 | 50 | 3.14 | 134.2 | 123 | 32 |
| Francisco Liriano | 26 | 24 | 9-10 | 0 | 1 | 81 | 5.09 | 134.1 | 112 | 75 |
| Anthony Swarzak | 27 | 11 | 4-7 | 0 | 0 | 53 | 4.32 | 102.0 | 55 | 26 |
| Matt Capps | 69 | 0 | 4-7 | 15 | 0 | 31 | 4.25 | 65.2 | 34 | 13 |
| Glen Perkins | 65 | 0 | 4-4 | 2 | 0 | 19 | 2.48 | 61.2 | 65 | 21 |
| Kevin Slowey | 14 | 8 | 0-8 | 0 | 0 | 44 | 6.67 | 59.1 | 34 | 5 |
| Alex Burnett | 66 | 0 | 2-5 | 0 | 0 | 32 | 5.51 | 50.2 | 33 | 21 |
| Jose Mijares | 58 | 0 | 0-2 | 0 | 0 | 31 | 4.59 | 49.0 | 30 | 30 |
| Joe Nathan | 48 | 0 | 2-1 | 14 | 0 | 26 | 4.84 | 44.2 | 43 | 14 |
| Phil Dumatrait | 45 | 0 | 1-3 | 1 | 0 | 22 | 3.92 | 41.1 | 29 | 25 |
| Scott Diamond | 7 | 7 | 1-5 | 0 | 0 | 25 | 5.08 | 39.0 | 19 | 17 |
| Jim Hoey | 26 | 0 | 1-2 | 0 | 0 | 20 | 5.47 | 24.2 | 14 | 13 |
| Liam Hendriks | 4 | 4 | 0-2 | 0 | 0 | 16 | 6.17 | 23.1 | 16 | 6 |

*Mid-season trade.

## New York Yankees

### BATTING

| | G | AB | R | H | 2B | 3B | HR | RBI | TB | BB | SO | SB | OBP | SLG | BAVG |
|---|---|---|---|---|---|---|---|---|---|---|---|---|---|---|---|
| Robinson Cano | 159 | 623 | 104 | 188 | 46 | 7 | 28 | 118 | 332 | 38 | 96 | 8 | .349 | .533 | .302 |
| Mark Teixeira | 156 | 589 | 90 | 146 | 26 | 1 | 39 | 111 | 291 | 76 | 110 | 4 | .341 | .494 | .248 |
| Curtis Granderson | 156 | 583 | 136 | 153 | 26 | 10 | 41 | 119 | 322 | 85 | 169 | 25 | .364 | .552 | .262 |
| Derek Jeter | 131 | 546 | 84 | 162 | 24 | 4 | 6 | 61 | 212 | 46 | 81 | 16 | .355 | .388 | .297 |
| Nick Swisher | 150 | 526 | 81 | 137 | 30 | 0 | 23 | 85 | 236 | 95 | 125 | 2 | .374 | .449 | .260 |
| Brett Gardner | 159 | 510 | 87 | 132 | 19 | 8 | 7 | 36 | 188 | 60 | 93 | 49 | .345 | .369 | .259 |
| Russell Martin | 125 | 417 | 57 | 99 | 17 | 0 | 18 | 65 | 170 | 50 | 81 | 8 | .324 | .408 | .237 |
| Alex Rodriguez | 99 | 373 | 67 | 103 | 21 | 0 | 16 | 62 | 172 | 47 | 80 | 4 | .362 | .461 | .276 |
| Jorge Posada | 115 | 344 | 34 | 81 | 14 | 0 | 14 | 44 | 137 | 39 | 76 | 0 | .315 | .398 | .235 |
| Eduardo Nunez | 112 | 309 | 38 | 82 | 18 | 2 | 5 | 30 | 119 | 22 | 37 | 22 | .313 | .385 | .265 |
| Andruw Jones | 77 | 190 | 27 | 47 | 8 | 0 | 13 | 33 | 94 | 29 | 62 | 0 | .356 | .495 | .247 |
| Eric Chavez | 58 | 160 | 16 | 42 | 7 | 1 | 2 | 26 | 57 | 14 | 34 | 0 | .320 | .356 | .263 |
| Francisco Cervelli | 43 | 124 | 17 | 33 | 4 | 0 | 4 | 22 | 49 | 9 | 29 | 4 | .324 | .395 | .266 |
| Jesus Montero | 18 | 61 | 9 | 20 | 4 | 0 | 4 | 12 | 36 | 7 | 17 | 0 | .406 | .590 | .328 |

### PITCHING

| | GP | GS | W–L | SV | SHO | R | ERA | IP | Ks | BB |
|---|---|---|---|---|---|---|---|---|---|---|
| CC Sabathia | 33 | 33 | 19-8 | 0 | 1 | 87 | 3.00 | 237.1 | 230 | 61 |
| A.J. Burnett | 33 | 32 | 11-11 | 0 | 0 | 115 | 5.15 | 190.1 | 173 | 83 |
| Ivan Nova | 28 | 27 | 16-4 | 0 | 0 | 74 | 3.70 | 165.1 | 98 | 57 |
| Bartolo Colon | 29 | 26 | 8-10 | 0 | 1 | 85 | 4.00 | 164.1 | 135 | 40 |
| Freddy Garcia | 26 | 25 | 12-8 | 0 | 0 | 63 | 3.62 | 146.2 | 96 | 45 |
| Phil Hughes | 17 | 14 | 5-5 | 0 | 1 | 48 | 5.79 | 74.2 | 47 | 27 |
| David Robertson | 70 | 0 | 4-0 | 1 | 0 | 9 | 1.08 | 66.2 | 100 | 35 |
| Mariano Rivera | 64 | 0 | 1-2 | 44 | 0 | 13 | 1.91 | 61.1 | 60 | 8 |
| Hector Noesi | 30 | 2 | 2-2 | 0 | 0 | 29 | 4.47 | 56.1 | 45 | 22 |
| Luis Ayala | 52 | 0 | 2-2 | 0 | 0 | 17 | 2.09 | 56.0 | 39 | 20 |
| Boone Logan | 64 | 0 | 5-3 | 0 | 0 | 20 | 3.46 | 41.2 | 46 | 13 |
| Cory Wade | 40 | 0 | 6-1 | 0 | 0 | 10 | 2.04 | 39.2 | 30 | 8 |
| Rafael Soriano | 42 | 0 | 2-3 | 2 | 0 | 18 | 4.12 | 39.1 | 36 | 18 |
| Joba Chamberlain | 27 | 0 | 2-0 | 0 | 0 | 10 | 2.83 | 28.2 | 24 | 7 |
| *Lance Pendleton | 11 | 0 | 0-0 | 0 | 0 | 5 | 3.21 | 14.0 | 8 | 10 |
| *Scott Proctor | 8 | 0 | 0-3 | 0 | 0 | 13 | 9.00 | 11.0 | 11 | 12 |

## Oakland Athletics

### BATTING

| | G | AB | R | H | 2B | 3B | HR | RBI | TB | BB | SO | SB | OBP | SLG | BAVG |
|---|---|---|---|---|---|---|---|---|---|---|---|---|---|---|---|
| Coco Crisp | 136 | 531 | 69 | 140 | 27 | 5 | 8 | 54 | 201 | 41 | 65 | 49 | .314 | .379 | .264 |
| Hideki Matsui | 141 | 517 | 58 | 130 | 28 | 0 | 12 | 72 | 194 | 56 | 84 | 1 | .321 | .375 | .251 |
| Cliff Pennington | 148 | 515 | 57 | 136 | 26 | 2 | 8 | 58 | 190 | 42 | 104 | 14 | .319 | .369 | .264 |
| Josh Willingham | 136 | 488 | 69 | 120 | 26 | 0 | 29 | 98 | 233 | 56 | 150 | 4 | .332 | .477 | .246 |
| Kurt Suzuki | 134 | 460 | 54 | 109 | 26 | 0 | 14 | 44 | 177 | 38 | 64 | 2 | .301 | .385 | .237 |
| David DeJesus | 131 | 442 | 60 | 106 | 20 | 5 | 10 | 46 | 166 | 45 | 86 | 4 | .323 | .376 | .240 |
| Jemile Weeks | 97 | 406 | 50 | 123 | 26 | 8 | 2 | 36 | 171 | 21 | 62 | 22 | .340 | .421 | .303 |
| *Conor Jackson | 102 | 333 | 30 | 83 | 17 | 1 | 4 | 38 | 114 | 30 | 50 | 3 | .315 | .342 | .249 |
| *Scott Sizemore | 93 | 305 | 42 | 76 | 21 | 1 | 11 | 52 | 132 | 43 | 93 | 4 | .345 | .433 | .249 |
| Ryan Sweeney | 108 | 264 | 34 | 70 | 11 | 3 | 1 | 25 | 90 | 33 | 48 | 1 | .346 | .341 | .265 |
| Daric Barton | 67 | 236 | 27 | 50 | 13 | 0 | 0 | 21 | 63 | 39 | 47 | 2 | .325 | .267 | .212 |
| *Mark Ellis | 62 | 217 | 21 | 47 | 11 | 1 | 1 | 16 | 63 | 8 | 32 | 7 | .253 | .290 | .217 |
| *Brandon Allen | 41 | 146 | 18 | 30 | 9 | 2 | 3 | 11 | 52 | 11 | 55 | 2 | .259 | .356 | .205 |
| *Kevin Kouzmanoff | 46 | 136 | 13 | 30 | 6 | 0 | 4 | 17 | 48 | 8 | 27 | 2 | .262 | .353 | .221 |
| Landon Powell | 36 | 111 | 10 | 19 | 3 | 0 | 1 | 4 | 25 | 11 | 32 | 0 | .246 | .225 | .171 |
| Andy LaRoche | 40 | 93 | 10 | 23 | 6 | 1 | 0 | 5 | 31 | 8 | 19 | 0 | .320 | .333 | .247 |

### PITCHING

| | GP | GS | W–L | SV | SHO | R | ERA | IP | Ks | BB |
|---|---|---|---|---|---|---|---|---|---|---|
| Trevor Cahill | 34 | 34 | 12-14 | 0 | 0 | 102 | 4.16 | 207.2 | 147 | 82 |
| Gio Gonzalez | 32 | 32 | 16-12 | 0 | 0 | 81 | 3.12 | 202.0 | 197 | 91 |
| Brandon McCarthy | 25 | 25 | 9-9 | 0 | 1 | 73 | 3.32 | 170.2 | 123 | 25 |
| Guillermo Moscoso | 23 | 21 | 8-10 | 0 | 0 | 59 | 3.38 | 128.0 | 74 | 38 |
| Brett Anderson | 13 | 13 | 3-6 | 0 | 0 | 40 | 4.00 | 83.1 | 61 | 25 |
| Rich Harden | 15 | 15 | 4-4 | 0 | 0 | 48 | 5.12 | 82.2 | 91 | 31 |
| Grant Balfour | 62 | 0 | 5-2 | 2 | 0 | 17 | 2.47 | 62.0 | 59 | 20 |
| Craig Breslow | 67 | 0 | 0-2 | 0 | 0 | 29 | 3.79 | 59.1 | 44 | 21 |
| Brian Fuentes | 67 | 0 | 2-8 | 12 | 0 | 30 | 3.70 | 58.1 | 42 | 20 |
| Josh Outman | 13 | 9 | 3-5 | 0 | 0 | 27 | 3.70 | 58.1 | 35 | 23 |
| Andrew Bailey | 42 | 0 | 0-4 | 24 | 0 | 18 | 3.24 | 41.2 | 41 | 12 |
| *Brad Ziegler | 43 | 0 | 3-2 | 1 | 0 | 14 | 2.39 | 37.2 | 29 | 13 |
| Tyson Ross | 9 | 6 | 3-3 | 0 | 0 | 12 | 2.75 | 36.0 | 24 | 13 |
| Michael Wuertz | 39 | 0 | 0-0 | 0 | 0 | 25 | 6.68 | 33.2 | 32 | 26 |
| Fautino De Los Santos | 34 | 0 | 3-2 | 0 | 0 | 19 | 4.32 | 33.1 | 43 | 17 |

*Mid-season trade.

### Seattle Mariners

| BATTING | G | AB | R | H | 2B | 3B | HR | RBI | TB | BB | SO | SB | OBP | SLG | BAVG |
|---|---|---|---|---|---|---|---|---|---|---|---|---|---|---|---|
| Ichiro Suzuki | 161 | 677 | 80 | 184 | 22 | 3 | 5 | 47 | 227 | 39 | 69 | 40 | .310 | .335 | .272 |
| Miguel Olivo | 130 | 477 | 54 | 107 | 19 | 1 | 19 | 62 | 185 | 20 | 140 | 6 | .253 | .388 | .224 |
| Brendan Ryan | 123 | 436 | 51 | 108 | 19 | 3 | 3 | 39 | 142 | 34 | 87 | 13 | .313 | .326 | .248 |
| Justin Smoak | 123 | 427 | 38 | 100 | 24 | 0 | 15 | 55 | 169 | 55 | 105 | 0 | .323 | .396 | .234 |
| Adam Kennedy | 114 | 380 | 36 | 89 | 23 | 1 | 7 | 38 | 135 | 22 | 67 | 8 | .277 | .355 | .234 |
| Dustin Ackley | 90 | 333 | 39 | 91 | 16 | 7 | 6 | 36 | 139 | 40 | 79 | 6 | .348 | .417 | .273 |
| Franklin Gutierrez | 92 | 322 | 26 | 72 | 13 | 0 | 1 | 19 | 88 | 16 | 56 | 13 | .261 | .273 | .224 |
| Mike Carp | 79 | 290 | 27 | 80 | 17 | 1 | 12 | 46 | 135 | 19 | 81 | 0 | .326 | .466 | .276 |
| Chone Figgins | 81 | 288 | 24 | 54 | 11 | 1 | 1 | 15 | 70 | 21 | 42 | 11 | .241 | .243 | .188 |
| Jack Cust | 67 | 225 | 19 | 48 | 15 | 1 | 3 | 23 | 74 | 44 | 87 | 0 | .344 | .329 | .213 |
| Kyle Seager | 53 | 182 | 22 | 47 | 13 | 0 | 3 | 13 | 69 | 13 | 36 | 3 | .312 | .379 | .258 |
| *Jack Wilson | 62 | 173 | 22 | 43 | 8 | 0 | 0 | 11 | 51 | 9 | 27 | 5 | .283 | .295 | .249 |
| Michael Saunders | 58 | 161 | 16 | 24 | 5 | 0 | 2 | 8 | 35 | 12 | 56 | 6 | .207 | .217 | .149 |
| Carlos Peguero | 46 | 143 | 14 | 28 | 3 | 2 | 6 | 19 | 53 | 8 | 54 | 0 | .252 | .371 | .196 |
| Trayvon Robinson | 44 | 143 | 12 | 30 | 12 | 0 | 2 | 14 | 48 | 8 | 61 | 1 | .250 | .336 | .210 |

| PITCHING | GP | GS | W–L | SV | SHO | R | ERA | IP | Ks | BB |
|---|---|---|---|---|---|---|---|---|---|---|
| Felix Hernandez | 33 | 33 | 14-14 | 0 | 0 | 99 | 3.47 | 233.2 | 222 | 67 |
| Jason Vargas | 32 | 32 | 10-13 | 0 | 3 | 105 | 4.25 | 201.0 | 131 | 59 |
| Michael Pineda | 28 | 28 | 9-10 | 0 | 0 | 76 | 3.74 | 171.0 | 173 | 55 |
| *Doug Fister | 21 | 21 | 3-12 | 0 | 0 | 57 | 3.33 | 146.0 | 89 | 32 |
| Blake Beavan | 15 | 15 | 5-6 | 0 | 0 | 46 | 4.27 | 97.0 | 42 | 15 |
| *Erik Bedard | 16 | 16 | 4-7 | 0 | 0 | 41 | 3.45 | 91.1 | 87 | 30 |
| Jamey Wright | 60 | 0 | 2-3 | 1 | 0 | 26 | 3.16 | 68.1 | 48 | 30 |
| Brandon League | 65 | 0 | 1-5 | 37 | 0 | 25 | 2.79 | 61.1 | 45 | 10 |
| *David Pauley | 39 | 0 | 5-4 | 0 | 0 | 13 | 2.15 | 54.1 | 34 | 16 |
| *Charlie Furbush | 11 | 10 | 3-7 | 0 | 0 | 41 | 6.62 | 53.0 | 41 | 16 |
| *Aaron Laffey | 36 | 0 | 1-1 | 0 | 0 | 20 | 4.01 | 42.2 | 24 | 16 |
| *Jeff Gray | 24 | 0 | 0-1 | 1 | 0 | 19 | 4.89 | 35.0 | 16 | 17 |
| Tom Wilhelmsen | 25 | 0 | 2-0 | 0 | 0 | 18 | 3.31 | 32.2 | 30 | 13 |
| Josh Lueke | 25 | 0 | 1-1 | 0 | 0 | 13 | 6.06 | 32.2 | 29 | 13 |
| Chris Ray | 29 | 0 | 3-2 | 0 | 0 | 22 | 4.68 | 32.2 | 22 | 12 |

### Tampa Bay Rays

| BATTING | G | AB | R | H | 2B | 3B | HR | RBI | TB | BB | SO | SB | OBP | SLG | BAVG |
|---|---|---|---|---|---|---|---|---|---|---|---|---|---|---|---|
| Ben Zobrist | 156 | 588 | 99 | 158 | 46 | 6 | 20 | 91 | 276 | 77 | 128 | 19 | .353 | .469 | .269 |
| Johnny Damon | 150 | 582 | 79 | 152 | 29 | 7 | 16 | 73 | 243 | 51 | 92 | 19 | .326 | .418 | .261 |
| B.J. Upton | 153 | 560 | 82 | 136 | 27 | 4 | 23 | 81 | 240 | 71 | 161 | 36 | .331 | .429 | .243 |
| Casey Kotchman | 146 | 500 | 44 | 153 | 24 | 2 | 10 | 48 | 211 | 48 | 66 | 2 | .378 | .422 | .306 |
| Evan Longoria | 133 | 483 | 78 | 118 | 26 | 1 | 31 | 99 | 239 | 80 | 93 | 3 | .355 | .495 | .244 |
| Matt Joyce | 141 | 462 | 69 | 128 | 32 | 2 | 19 | 75 | 221 | 49 | 106 | 13 | .347 | .478 | .277 |
| Sean Rodriguez | 131 | 373 | 45 | 83 | 20 | 3 | 8 | 36 | 133 | 38 | 87 | 11 | .323 | .357 | .223 |
| Sam Fuld | 105 | 308 | 41 | 74 | 18 | 5 | 3 | 27 | 111 | 32 | 49 | 20 | .313 | .360 | .240 |
| Reid Brignac | 92 | 249 | 18 | 48 | 4 | 0 | 1 | 15 | 55 | 10 | 63 | 3 | .227 | .221 | .193 |
| Desmond Jennings | 63 | 247 | 44 | 64 | 9 | 4 | 10 | 25 | 111 | 31 | 59 | 20 | .356 | .449 | .259 |
| John Jaso | 89 | 246 | 26 | 55 | 15 | 1 | 5 | 27 | 87 | 25 | 36 | 1 | .298 | .354 | .224 |
| Kelly Shoppach | 87 | 221 | 23 | 39 | 3 | 0 | 11 | 22 | 75 | 19 | 79 | 0 | .268 | .339 | .176 |
| Elliot Johnson | 70 | 160 | 20 | 31 | 7 | 2 | 4 | 17 | 54 | 14 | 53 | 6 | .257 | .338 | .194 |
| Justin Ruggiano | 46 | 105 | 11 | 26 | 4 | 0 | 4 | 13 | 42 | 4 | 26 | 1 | .273 | .400 | .248 |
| *Felipe Lopez | 32 | 97 | 8 | 21 | 4 | 0 | 2 | 8 | 31 | 4 | 28 | 1 | .248 | .320 | .216 |
| Dan Johnson | 31 | 84 | 7 | 10 | 1 | 0 | 2 | 4 | 17 | 6 | 18 | 0 | .187 | .202 | .119 |

| PITCHING | GP | GS | W–L | SV | SHO | R | ERA | IP | Ks | BB |
|---|---|---|---|---|---|---|---|---|---|---|
| James Shields | 33 | 33 | 16-12 | 0 | 4 | 83 | 2.82 | 249.1 | 225 | 65 |
| David Price | 34 | 34 | 12-13 | 0 | 0 | 93 | 3.49 | 224.1 | 218 | 63 |
| Jeremy Hellickson | 29 | 29 | 13-10 | 0 | 1 | 64 | 2.95 | 189.0 | 117 | 72 |
| Wade Davis | 29 | 29 | 11-10 | 0 | 0 | 96 | 4.45 | 184.0 | 105 | 63 |
| Jeff Niemann | 23 | 23 | 11-7 | 0 | 0 | 65 | 4.06 | 135.1 | 105 | 37 |
| Joel Peralta | 71 | 0 | 3-4 | 6 | 0 | 23 | 2.93 | 67.2 | 61 | 18 |
| Kyle Farnsworth | 63 | 0 | 5-1 | 25 | 0 | 15 | 2.18 | 57.2 | 51 | 12 |
| Alex Cobb | 9 | 9 | 3-2 | 0 | 0 | 21 | 3.42 | 52.2 | 37 | 21 |
| Juan Cruz | 56 | 0 | 5-0 | 0 | 0 | 21 | 3.88 | 48.2 | 46 | 28 |
| Cesar Ramos | 59 | 0 | 0-1 | 0 | 0 | 22 | 3.92 | 43.2 | 31 | 25 |
| Brandon Gomes | 40 | 0 | 2-1 | 0 | 0 | 15 | 2.92 | 37.0 | 32 | 16 |
| Andy Sonnanstine | 15 | 4 | 0-2 | 0 | 0 | 22 | 5.55 | 35.2 | 12 | 12 |
| Adam Russell | 36 | 0 | 1-2 | 0 | 0 | 13 | 3.03 | 32.2 | 13 | 20 |
| J.P. Howell | 46 | 0 | 2-3 | 1 | 0 | 24 | 6.16 | 30.2 | 26 | 18 |

*Mid-season trade.

### Texas Rangers

| BATTING | G | AB | R | H | 2B | 3B | HR | RBI | TB | BB | SO | SB | OBP | SLG | BAVG |
|---|---|---|---|---|---|---|---|---|---|---|---|---|---|---|---|
| Michael Young | 159 | 631 | 88 | 213 | 41 | 6 | 11 | 106 | 299 | 47 | 78 | 6 | .380 | .474 | .338 |
| Ian Kinsler | 155 | 620 | 121 | 158 | 34 | 4 | 32 | 77 | 296 | 89 | 71 | 30 | .355 | .477 | .255 |
| Elvis Andrus | 150 | 587 | 96 | 164 | 27 | 3 | 5 | 60 | 212 | 56 | 74 | 37 | .347 | .361 | .279 |
| Adrian Beltre | 124 | 487 | 82 | 144 | 33 | 0 | 32 | 105 | 273 | 25 | 53 | 1 | .331 | .561 | .296 |
| Josh Hamilton | 121 | 487 | 80 | 145 | 31 | 5 | 25 | 94 | 261 | 39 | 93 | 8 | .346 | .536 | .298 |
| Nelson Cruz | 124 | 475 | 64 | 125 | 28 | 1 | 29 | 87 | 242 | 33 | 116 | 9 | .312 | .509 | .263 |
| Mitch Moreland | 134 | 464 | 60 | 120 | 22 | 1 | 16 | 51 | 192 | 39 | 92 | 2 | .320 | .414 | .259 |
| David Murphy | 120 | 404 | 46 | 111 | 14 | 2 | 11 | 46 | 162 | 33 | 61 | 11 | .328 | .401 | .275 |
| Yorvit Torrealba | 113 | 396 | 40 | 108 | 27 | 1 | 7 | 37 | 158 | 20 | 65 | 0 | .306 | .399 | .273 |
| Mike Napoli | 113 | 369 | 72 | 118 | 25 | 0 | 30 | 75 | 233 | 58 | 85 | 4 | .414 | .631 | .320 |
| Endy Chavez | 83 | 256 | 37 | 77 | 11 | 3 | 5 | 27 | 109 | 10 | 30 | 10 | .323 | .426 | .301 |
| Craig Gentry | 64 | 133 | 26 | 36 | 5 | 1 | 1 | 13 | 46 | 10 | 27 | 18 | .347 | .346 | .271 |
| Julio Borbon | 32 | 89 | 10 | 24 | 1 | 3 | 0 | 11 | 31 | 3 | 9 | 6 | .305 | .348 | .270 |
| Andres Blanco | 36 | 76 | 9 | 17 | 3 | 0 | 2 | 3 | 26 | 4 | 14 | 0 | .263 | .342 | .224 |
| *Chris Davis | 28 | 76 | 9 | 19 | 3 | 0 | 3 | 6 | 31 | 5 | 24 | 0 | .296 | .408 | .250 |

| PITCHING | GP | GS | W-L | SV | SHO | R | ERA | IP | Ks | BB |
|---|---|---|---|---|---|---|---|---|---|---|
| C.J. Wilson | 34 | 34 | 16-7 | 0 | 1 | 89 | 2.94 | 223.1 | 206 | 74 |
| Colby Lewis | 32 | 32 | 14-10 | 0 | 1 | 103 | 4.40 | 200.1 | 169 | 56 |
| Derek Holland | 32 | 32 | 16-5 | 0 | 4 | 97 | 3.95 | 198.0 | 162 | 67 |
| Matt Harrison | 31 | 30 | 14-9 | 0 | 0 | 79 | 3.39 | 185.2 | 126 | 57 |
| Alexi Ogando | 31 | 29 | 13-8 | 0 | 1 | 73 | 3.51 | 169.0 | 126 | 43 |
| Neftali Feliz | 64 | 0 | 2-3 | 32 | 0 | 22 | 2.74 | 62.1 | 54 | 30 |
| Darren Oliver | 61 | 0 | 5-5 | 2 | 0 | 17 | 2.29 | 51.0 | 44 | 11 |
| Mark Lowe | 52 | 0 | 2-3 | 1 | 0 | 26 | 3.80 | 45.0 | 42 | 19 |
| Yoshinori Tateyama | 39 | 0 | 2-0 | 1 | 0 | 23 | 4.50 | 44.0 | 43 | 11 |
| Dave Bush | 17 | 3 | 0-1 | 0 | 0 | 27 | 5.79 | 37.1 | 23 | 9 |
| Scott Feldman | 11 | 2 | 2-1 | 0 | 0 | 14 | 3.94 | 32.0 | 22 | 10 |
| Michael Kirkman | 15 | 0 | 1-1 | 0 | 0 | 22 | 6.59 | 27.1 | 21 | 12 |
| *Mike Adams | 27 | 0 | 2-3 | 1 | 0 | 6 | 2.10 | 25.2 | 25 | 5 |
| *Arthur Rhodes | 32 | 0 | 3-3 | 1 | 0 | 13 | 4.81 | 24.1 | 15 | 8 |
| *Koji Uehara | 22 | 0 | 1-2 | 0 | 0 | 9 | 4.00 | 18.0 | 23 | 1 |
| Brett Tomko | 8 | 0 | 0-1 | 0 | 0 | 9 | 4.58 | 17.2 | 14 | 10 |

### Toronto Blue Jays

| BATTING | G | AB | R | H | 2B | 3B | HR | RBI | TB | BB | SO | SB | OBP | SLG | BAVG |
|---|---|---|---|---|---|---|---|---|---|---|---|---|---|---|---|
| Jose Bautista | 149 | 513 | 105 | 155 | 24 | 2 | 43 | 103 | 312 | 132 | 111 | 9 | .447 | .608 | .302 |
| Yunel Escobar | 133 | 513 | 77 | 149 | 24 | 3 | 11 | 48 | 212 | 61 | 70 | 3 | .369 | .413 | .290 |
| Adam Lind | 125 | 499 | 56 | 125 | 16 | 0 | 26 | 87 | 219 | 32 | 107 | 1 | .295 | .439 | .251 |
| Edwin Encarnacion | 134 | 481 | 70 | 131 | 36 | 0 | 17 | 55 | 218 | 43 | 77 | 8 | .334 | .453 | .272 |
| J.P. Arencibia | 129 | 443 | 47 | 97 | 20 | 4 | 23 | 78 | 194 | 36 | 133 | 1 | .282 | .438 | .219 |
| *Aaron Hill | 104 | 396 | 38 | 89 | 15 | 1 | 6 | 45 | 124 | 23 | 53 | 16 | .270 | .313 | .225 |
| Eric Thames | 95 | 362 | 58 | 95 | 24 | 5 | 12 | 37 | 165 | 23 | 88 | 2 | .313 | .456 | .262 |
| Rajai Davis | 95 | 320 | 44 | 76 | 21 | 6 | 1 | 29 | 112 | 15 | 63 | 34 | .273 | .350 | .238 |
| *Corey Patterson | 89 | 317 | 44 | 80 | 16 | 3 | 6 | 33 | 120 | 15 | 65 | 13 | .287 | .379 | .252 |
| *Juan Rivera | 70 | 247 | 22 | 60 | 11 | 0 | 6 | 28 | 89 | 22 | 41 | 3 | .305 | .360 | .243 |
| Mike McCoy | 80 | 197 | 26 | 39 | 8 | 0 | 2 | 10 | 53 | 25 | 41 | 12 | .291 | .269 | .198 |
| Travis Snider | 49 | 187 | 23 | 42 | 14 | 0 | 3 | 30 | 65 | 11 | 56 | 9 | .269 | .348 | .225 |
| Jose Molina | 55 | 171 | 19 | 48 | 12 | 1 | 3 | 15 | 71 | 15 | 44 | 2 | .342 | .415 | .281 |
| *John McDonald | 65 | 168 | 19 | 42 | 8 | 1 | 2 | 20 | 58 | 8 | 18 | 2 | .285 | .345 | .250 |
| Brett Lawrie | 43 | 150 | 26 | 44 | 8 | 4 | 9 | 25 | 87 | 16 | 31 | 7 | .373 | .580 | .293 |

| PITCHING | GP | GS | W-L | SV | SHO | R | ERA | IP | Ks | BB |
|---|---|---|---|---|---|---|---|---|---|---|
| Ricky Romero | 32 | 32 | 15-11 | 0 | 2 | 85 | 2.92 | 225.0 | 178 | 80 |
| Brandon Morrow | 30 | 30 | 11-11 | 0 | 0 | 103 | 4.72 | 179.1 | 203 | 69 |
| Brett Cecil | 20 | 20 | 4-11 | 0 | 1 | 68 | 4.73 | 123.2 | 87 | 42 |
| *Jo-Jo Reyes | 20 | 20 | 5-8 | 0 | 0 | 78 | 5.40 | 110.0 | 64 | 35 |
| Carlos Villanueva | 33 | 13 | 6-4 | 0 | 0 | 49 | 4.04 | 107.0 | 68 | 32 |
| Kyle Drabek | 18 | 14 | 4-5 | 0 | 0 | 54 | 6.06 | 78.2 | 51 | 55 |
| Jesse Litsch | 28 | 8 | 6-3 | 1 | 0 | 40 | 4.44 | 75.0 | 66 | 28 |
| Shawn Camp | 67 | 0 | 6-3 | 1 | 0 | 34 | 4.21 | 66.1 | 32 | 22 |
| Luis Perez | 37 | 4 | 3-3 | 0 | 0 | 40 | 5.12 | 65.0 | 54 | 27 |
| Henderson Alvarez | 10 | 10 | 1-3 | 0 | 0 | 26 | 3.53 | 63.2 | 40 | 8 |
| Casey Janssen | 55 | 0 | 6-0 | 2 | 0 | 14 | 2.26 | 55.2 | 53 | 14 |
| Jon Rauch | 53 | 0 | 5-4 | 11 | 0 | 28 | 4.85 | 52.0 | 36 | 14 |
| Frank Francisco | 54 | 0 | 1-4 | 17 | 0 | 21 | 3.55 | 50.2 | 53 | 18 |
| *Jason Frasor | 44 | 0 | 2-1 | 0 | 0 | 15 | 2.98 | 42.1 | 37 | 15 |
| *Marc Rzepczynski | 43 | 0 | 2-3 | 0 | 0 | 16 | 2.97 | 39.1 | 33 | 15 |

*Mid-season trade.

# FOR THE RECORD • Year by Year

## The World Series

### Results

| | |
|---|---|
| 1903...............Boston (A) 5, Pittsburgh (N) 3 | 1958...............New York (A) 4, Milwaukee (N) 3 |
| 1904...............No series | 1959...............Los Angeles (N) 4, Chicago (A) 2 |
| 1905...............New York (N) 4, Philadelphia (A) 1 | 1960...............Pittsburgh (N) 4, New York (A) 3 |
| 1906...............Chicago (A) 4, Chicago (N) 2 | 1961...............New York (A) 4, Cincinnati (N) 1 |
| 1907...............Chicago (N) 4, Detroit (A) 0; 1 tie | 1962...............New York (A) 4, San Francisco (N) 3 |
| 1908...............Chicago (N) 4, Detroit (A) 1 | 1963...............Los Angeles (N) 4, New York (A) 0 |
| 1909...............Pittsburgh (N) 4, Detroit (A) 3 | 1964...............St. Louis (N) 4, New York (A) 3 |
| 1910...............Philadelphia (A) 4, Chicago (N) 1 | 1965...............Los Angeles (N) 4, Minnesota (A) 3 |
| 1911...............Philadelphia (A) 4, New York (N) 2 | 1966...............Baltimore (A) 4, Los Angeles (N) 0 |
| 1912...............Boston (A) 4, New York (N) 3; 1 tie | 1967...............St. Louis (N) 4, Boston (A) 3 |
| 1913...............Philadelphia (A) 4, New York (N) 1 | 1968...............Detroit (A) 4, St. Louis (N) 3 |
| 1914...............Boston (N) 4, Philadelphia (A) 0 | 1969...............New York (N) 4, Baltimore (A) 1 |
| 1915...............Boston (A) 4, Philadelphia (N) 1 | 1970...............Baltimore (A) 4, Cincinnati (N) 1 |
| 1916...............Boston (A) 4, Brooklyn (N) 1 | 1971...............Pittsburgh (N) 4, Baltimore (A) 3 |
| 1917...............Chicago (A) 4, New York (N) 2 | 1972...............Oakland (A) 4, Cincinnati (N) 3 |
| 1918...............Boston (A) 4, Chicago (N) 2 | 1973...............Oakland (A) 4, New York (N) 3 |
| 1919...............Cincinnati (N) 5, Chicago (A) 3 | 1974...............Oakland (A) 4, Los Angeles (N) 1 |
| 1920...............Cleveland (A) 5, Brooklyn (N) 2 | 1975...............Cincinnati (N) 4, Boston (A) 3 |
| 1921...............New York (N) 5, New York (A) 3 | 1976...............Cincinnati (N) 4, New York (A) 0 |
| 1922...............New York (N) 4, New York (A) 0; 1 tie | 1977...............New York (A) 4, Los Angeles (N) 2 |
| 1923...............New York (A) 4, New York (N) 2 | 1978...............New York (A) 4, Los Angeles (N) 2 |
| 1924...............Washington (A) 4, New York (N) 3 | 1979...............Pittsburgh (N) 4, Baltimore (A) 3 |
| 1925...............Pittsburgh (N) 4, Washington (A) 3 | 1980...............Philadelphia (N) 4, Kansas City (A) 2 |
| 1926...............St. Louis (N) 4, New York (A) 3 | 1981...............Los Angeles (N) 4, New York (A) 2 |
| 1927...............New York (A) 4, Pittsburgh (N) 0 | 1982...............St. Louis (N) 4, Milwaukee (A) 3 |
| 1928...............New York (A) 4, St. Louis (N) 0 | 1983...............Baltimore (A) 4, Philadelphia (N) 1 |
| 1929...............Philadelphia (A) 4, Chicago (N) 1 | 1984...............Detroit (A) 4, San Diego (N) 1 |
| 1930...............Philadelphia (A) 4, St. Louis (N) 2 | 1985...............Kansas City (A) 4, St. Louis (N) 3 |
| 1931...............St. Louis (N) 4, Philadelphia (A) 3 | 1986...............New York (N) 4, Boston (A) 3 |
| 1932...............New York (A) 4, Chicago (N) 0 | 1987...............Minnesota (A) 4, St. Louis (N) 3 |
| 1933...............New York (N) 4, Washington (A) 1 | 1988...............Los Angeles (N) 4, Oakland (A) 1 |
| 1934...............St. Louis (N) 4, Detroit (A) 3 | 1989...............Oakland (A) 4, San Francisco (N) 0 |
| 1935...............Detroit (A) 4, Chicago (N) 2 | 1990...............Cincinnati (N) 4, Oakland (A) 0 |
| 1936...............New York (A) 4, New York (N) 2 | 1991...............Minnesota (A) 4, Atlanta (N) 3 |
| 1937...............New York (A) 4, New York (N) 1 | 1992...............Toronto (A) 4, Atlanta (N) 2 |
| 1938...............New York (A) 4, Chicago (N) 0 | 1993...............Toronto (A) 4, Philadelphia (N) 2 |
| 1939...............New York (A) 4, Cincinnati (N) 0 | 1994...............Series canceled due to players' strike. |
| 1940...............Cincinnati (N) 4, Detroit (A) 3 | 1995...............Atlanta (N) 4, Cleveland (A) 2 |
| 1941...............New York (A) 4, Brooklyn (N) 1 | 1996...............New York (A) 4, Atlanta (N) 2 |
| 1942...............St. Louis (N) 4, New York (A) 1 | 1997...............Florida (N) 4, Cleveland (A) 3 |
| 1943...............New York (A) 4, St. Louis (N) 1 | 1998...............New York (A) 4, San Diego (N) 0 |
| 1944...............St. Louis (N) 4, St. Louis (A) 2 | 1999...............New York (A) 4, Atlanta (N) 0 |
| 1945...............Detroit (A) 4, Chicago (N) 3 | 2000...............New York (A) 4 , New York (N) 1 |
| 1946...............St. Louis (N) 4, Boston (A) 3 | 2001...............Arizona (N) 4, New York (A) 3 |
| 1947...............New York (A) 4, Brooklyn (N) 3 | 2002...............Anaheim (A) 4, San Francisco (N) 3 |
| 1948...............Cleveland (A) 4, Boston (N) 2 | 2003...............Florida (N) 4, New York (A) 2 |
| 1949...............New York (A) 4, Brooklyn (N) 1 | 2004...............Boston (A) 4, St. Louis (N) 0 |
| 1950...............New York (A) 4, Philadelphia (N) 0 | 2005...............Chicago (A) 4, Houston (N) 0 |
| 1951...............New York (A) 4, New York (N) 2 | 2006...............St. Louis (N) 4, Detroit (A) 1 |
| 1952...............New York (A) 4, Brooklyn (N) 3 | 2007...............Boston (A) 4, Colorado (N) 0 |
| 1953...............New York (A) 4, Brooklyn (N) 2 | 2008...............Philadelphia (N) 4, Tampa Bay (A) 1 |
| 1954...............New York (N) 4, Cleveland (A) 0 | 2009...............New York (A) 4, Philadelphia (N) 2 |
| 1955...............Brooklyn (N) 4, New York (A) 3 | 2010...............San Francisco (N) 4, Texas (A) 1 |
| 1956...............New York (A) 4, Brooklyn (N) 3 | 2011...............St. Louis (N) 4, Texas (A) 3 |
| 1957...............Milwaukee (N) 4, New York (A) 3 | |

## Most Valuable Players

| | | | |
|---|---|---|---|
| 1955 | Johnny Podres, Bklyn | 1984 | Alan Trammell, Det |
| 1956 | Don Larsen, NY (A) | 1985 | Bret Saberhagen, KC |
| 1957 | Lew Burdette, Mil | 1986 | Ray Knight, NY (N) |
| 1958 | Bob Turley, NY (A) | 1987 | Frank Viola, Minn |
| 1959 | Larry Sherry, LA | 1988 | Orel Hershiser, LA |
| 1960 | Bobby Richardson, NY (A) | 1989 | Dave Stewart, Oak |
| 1961 | Whitey Ford, NY (A) | 1990 | Jose Rijo, Cin |
| 1962 | Ralph Terry, NY (A) | 1991 | Jack Morris, Minn |
| 1963 | Sandy Koufax, LA | 1992 | Pat Borders, Tor |
| 1964 | Bob Gibson, StL | 1993 | Paul Molitor, Tor |
| 1965 | Sandy Koufax, LA | 1994 | Series canceled due to strike. |
| 1966 | Frank Robinson, Balt | 1995 | Tom Glavine, Atl |
| 1967 | Bob Gibson, StL | 1996 | John Wetteland, NY (A) |
| 1968 | Mickey Lolich, Det | 1997 | Livan Hernandez, Fla |
| 1969 | Donn Clendenon, NY (N) | 1998 | Scott Brosius, NY (A) |
| 1970 | Brooks Robinson, Balt | 1999 | Mariano Rivera, NY (A) |
| 1971 | Roberto Clemente, Pitt | 2000 | Derek Jeter, NY (A) |
| 1972 | Gene Tenace, Oak | 2001 | Randy Johnson, Ariz |
| 1973 | Reggie Jackson, Oak | | Curt Schilling, Ariz |
| 1974 | Rollie Fingers, Oak | 2002 | Troy Glaus, Ana |
| 1975 | Pete Rose, Cin | 2003 | Josh Beckett, Fla |
| 1976 | Johnny Bench, Cin | 2004 | Manny Ramirez, Bos |
| 1977 | Reggie Jackson, NY (A) | 2005 | Jermaine Dye, Chi (A) |
| 1978 | Bucky Dent, NY (A) | 2006 | David Eckstein, StL |
| 1979 | Willie Stargell, Pitt | 2007 | Mike Lowell, Bos |
| 1980 | Mike Schmidt, Phil | 2008 | Cole Hamels, Phi |
| 1981 | Ron Cey, LA; Steve Yeager, LA; | 2009 | Hideki Matsui, NY (A) |
| | Pedro Guerrero, LA | 2010 | Edgar Renteria, SF |
| 1982 | Darrell Porter, StL | 2011 | David Freese, StL |
| 1983 | Rick Dempsey, Balt | | |

## Career Batting Leaders (Minimum 40 at bats)

### GAMES

| | |
|---|---|
| Yogi Berra | 75 |
| Mickey Mantle | 65 |
| Elston Howard | 54 |
| Hank Bauer | 53 |
| Gil McDougald | 53 |
| Phil Rizzuto | 52 |
| Joe DiMaggio | 51 |
| Frankie Frisch | 50 |
| Pee Wee Reese | 44 |
| Roger Maris | 41 |
| Babe Ruth | 41 |

### AT BATS

| | |
|---|---|
| Yogi Berra | 259 |
| Mickey Mantle | 230 |
| Joe DiMaggio | 199 |
| Frankie Frisch | 197 |
| Gil McDougald | 190 |
| Hank Bauer | 188 |
| Phil Rizzuto | 183 |
| Elston Howard | 171 |
| Pee Wee Reese | 169 |
| Derek Jeter | 156 |
| Roger Maris | 152 |

### BATTING AVERAGE

| | |
|---|---|
| Bobby Brown | .439 |
| Paul Molitor | .418 |
| Pepper Martin | .418 |
| Hal McRae | .400 |
| Lou Brock | .391 |
| Marquis Grissom | .390 |
| Thurman Munson | .373 |
| George Brett | .373 |
| Pat Borders | .372 |
| Hank Aaron | .364 |

### TOTAL BASES

| | |
|---|---|
| Mickey Mantle | 123 |
| Yogi Berra | 117 |
| Babe Ruth | 96 |
| Lou Gehrig | 87 |
| Joe DiMaggio | 84 |
| Duke Snider | 79 |
| Hank Bauer | 75 |
| Reggie Jackson | 74 |
| Frankie Frisch | 74 |
| Gil McDougald | 72 |

### HOME RUNS

| | |
|---|---|
| Mickey Mantle | 18 |
| Babe Ruth | 15 |
| Yogi Berra | 12 |
| Duke Snider | 11 |
| Reggie Jackson | 10 |
| Lou Gehrig | 10 |
| Frank Robinson | 8 |
| Bill Skowron | 8 |
| Joe DiMaggio | 8 |
| Goose Goslin | 7 |
| Hank Bauer | 7 |
| Gil McDougald | 7 |
| Chase Utley | 7 |

### RUNS

| | |
|---|---|
| Mickey Mantle | 42 |
| Yogi Berra | 41 |
| Babe Ruth | 37 |
| Derek Jeter | 32 |
| Lou Gehrig | 30 |
| Joe DiMaggio | 27 |
| Derek Jeter | 27 |
| Roger Maris | 26 |
| Elston Howard | 25 |
| Gil McDougald | 23 |
| Jackie Robinson | 22 |

### RUNS BATTED IN

| | |
|---|---|
| Mickey Mantle | 40 |
| Yogi Berra | 39 |
| Lou Gehrig | 35 |
| Babe Ruth | 33 |
| Joe DiMaggio | 30 |
| Bill Skowron | 29 |
| Duke Snider | 26 |
| Reggie Jackson | 24 |
| Bill Dickey | 24 |
| Hank Bauer | 24 |
| Gil McDougald | 24 |

### HITS

| | |
|---|---|
| Yogi Berra | 71 |
| Mickey Mantle | 59 |
| Frankie Frisch | 58 |
| Joe DiMaggio | 54 |
| Derek Jeter | 50 |
| Pee Wee Reese | 46 |
| Hank Bauer | 46 |
| Phil Rizzuto | 45 |
| Gil McDougald | 45 |
| Lou Gehrig | 43 |
| Eddie Collins | 42 |
| Babe Ruth | 42 |
| Elston Howard | 42 |

### STOLEN BASES

| | |
|---|---|
| Lou Brock | 14 |
| Eddie Collins | 14 |
| Frank Chance | 10 |
| Davey Lopes | 10 |
| Phil Rizzuto | 10 |
| Honus Wagner | 9 |
| Frankie Frisch | 9 |
| Kenny Lofton | 9 |

## Career Batting Leaders *(Cont.)*

### STOLEN BASES (CONT.)
| | |
|---|---|
| Johnny Evers | 8 |
| Roberto Alomar | 7 |
| Joe Tinker | 7 |
| Pepper Martin | 7 |
| Joe Morgan | 7 |
| Rickey Henderson | 7 |

### SLUGGING AVERAGE
| | |
|---|---|
| Reggie Jackson | .755 |
| Babe Ruth | .744 |
| Lou Gehrig | .731 |
| Bobby Brown | .707 |
| Lenny Dykstra | .700 |
| Al Simmons | .658 |
| Lou Brock | .655 |
| Pepper Martin | .636 |
| Paul Molitor | .636 |
| Joe Harris | .625 |

### STRIKEOUTS
| | |
|---|---|
| Mickey Mantle | 54 |
| Derek Jeter | 39 |
| Elston Howard | 37 |
| Duke Snider | 33 |
| Jorge Posada | 31 |
| Babe Ruth | 30 |
| David Justice | 30 |
| Gil McDougald | 29 |
| Bill Skowron | 26 |
| Bernie Williams | 26 |
| Hank Bauer | 25 |

### GAMES
| | |
|---|---|
| Mariano Rivera | 24 |
| Whitey Ford | 22 |
| Mike Stanton | 19 |
| Jeff Nelson | 16 |
| Rollie Fingers | 16 |
| Allie Reynolds | 15 |
| Bob Turley | 15 |
| Clay Carroll | 14 |
| Clem Labine | 13 |
| Mark Wohlers | 13 |
| Andy Pettitte | 13 |

### INNINGS PITCHED
| | |
|---|---|
| Whitey Ford | 146 |
| Christy Mathewson | 101.2 |
| Red Ruffing | 85.2 |
| Chief Bender | 85 |
| Waite Hoyt | 83.2 |
| Bob Gibson | 81 |
| Art Nehf | 79 |
| Andy Pettitte | 77.2 |
| Allie Reynolds | 77 |

### WINS
| | |
|---|---|
| Whitey Ford | 10 |
| Bob Gibson | 7 |
| Red Ruffing | 7 |
| Allie Reynolds | 7 |
| Lefty Gomez | 6 |
| Chief Bender | 6 |
| Waite Hoyt | 6 |
| Jack Coombs | 5 |
| Three Finger Brown | 5 |
| Herb Pennock | 5 |
| Christy Mathewson | 5 |
| Vic Raschi | 5 |
| Catfish Hunter | 5 |
| Andy Pettitte | 5 |

## Career Pitching Leaders

### LOSSES
| | |
|---|---|
| Whitey Ford | 8 |
| Eddie Plank | 5 |
| Schoolboy Rowe | 5 |
| Joe Bush | 5 |
| Rube Marquard | 5 |
| Christy Mathewson | 5 |

### SAVES
| | |
|---|---|
| Mariano Rivera | 11 |
| Rollie Fingers | 6 |
| Allie Reynolds | 4 |
| Johnny Murphy | 4 |
| John Wetteland | 4 |
| Robb Nen | 4 |

### *EARNED RUN AVERAGE
| | |
|---|---|
| Jack Billingham | 0.36 |
| Harry Brecheen | 0.83 |
| Babe Ruth | 0.87 |
| Sherry Smith | 0.89 |
| Sandy Koufax | 0.95 |
| Mariano Rivera | 0.99 |
| Hippo Vaughn | 1.00 |
| Monte Pearson | 1.01 |
| Christy Mathewson | 1.06 |
| Babe Adams | 1.29 |

### SHUTOUTS
| | |
|---|---|
| Christy Mathewson | 4 |
| Three Finger Brown | 3 |
| Whitey Ford | 3 |
| Bill Hallahan | 2 |
| Lew Burdette | 2 |
| Bill Dinneen | 2 |
| Sandy Koufax | 2 |
| Allie Reynolds | 2 |
| Art Nehf | 2 |
| Bob Gibson | 2 |

### COMPLETE GAMES
| | |
|---|---|
| Christy Mathewson | 10 |
| Chief Bender | 9 |
| Bob Gibson | 8 |
| Red Ruffing | 7 |
| Whitey Ford | 7 |
| George Mullin | 6 |
| Eddie Plank | 6 |
| Art Nehf | 6 |
| Waite Hoyt | 6 |

### STRIKEOUTS
| | |
|---|---|
| Whitey Ford | 94 |
| Bob Gibson | 92 |
| Allie Reynolds | 62 |
| Sandy Koufax | 61 |
| Red Ruffing | 61 |
| Chief Bender | 59 |
| Andy Pettitte | 56 |
| George Earnshaw | 56 |
| John Smoltz | 52 |
| Waite Hoyt | 49 |
| Roger Clemens | 49 |
| Christy Mathewson | 48 |

### BASES ON BALLS
| | |
|---|---|
| Whitey Ford | 34 |
| Allie Reynolds | 32 |
| Art Nehf | 32 |
| Jim Palmer | 31 |
| Bob Turley | 29 |
| Paul Derringer | 27 |
| Red Ruffing | 27 |
| Don Gullett | 26 |
| Burleigh Grimes | 26 |
| Andy Pettitte | 26 |
| Vic Raschi | 25 |

*Minimum 25 innings pitched.

## Alltime Team Rankings, by Championships

| Team | W | L | Appearances | Pct. | Most Recent App. | Last Championship |
|---|---|---|---|---|---|---|
| New York Yankees | 27 | 13 | 40 | .675 | 2009 | 2009 |
| St. Louis Cardinals | 11 | 7 | 18 | .611 | 2011 | 2011 |
| Phila./K.C./Oakland Athletics | 9 | 5 | 14 | .643 | 1990 | 1989 |
| Boston Red Sox | 7 | 5 | 12 | .583 | 2007 | 2007 |
| New York/San Francisco Giants | 6 | 12 | 18 | .333 | 2010 | 2010 |
| Brooklyn/Los Angeles Dodgers | 6 | 12 | 18 | .333 | 1988 | 1988 |
| Pittsburgh Pirates | 5 | 2 | 7 | .714 | 1979 | 1979 |
| Cincinnati Reds | 5 | 4 | 9 | .556 | 1990 | 1990 |
| Detroit Tigers | 4 | 6 | 10 | .400 | 2006 | 1984 |
| Chicago White Sox | 3 | 2 | 5 | .600 | 2005 | 2005 |
| Wash. Senators/Minnesota Twins | 3 | 3 | 6 | .500 | 1991 | 1991 |
| St. Louis Browns/Baltimore Orioles | 3 | 4 | 7 | .429 | 1983 | 1983 |
| Boston/Milwaukee/Atlanta Braves | 3 | 6 | 9 | .333 | 1999 | 1995 |
| Florida Marlins | 2 | 0 | 2 | 1.000 | 2003 | 2003 |

## Alltime Team Rankings, by Championships *(Cont.)*

| Team | W | L | Appearances | Pct. | Most Recent App. | Last Championship |
|------|---|---|-------------|------|------------------|-------------------|
| Toronto Blue Jays | 2 | 0 | 2 | 1.000 | 1993 | 1993 |
| New York Mets | 2 | 2 | 4 | .500 | 2000 | 1986 |
| Cleveland Indians | 2 | 3 | 5 | .400 | 1997 | 1948 |
| Philadelphia Phillies | 2 | 5 | 7 | .286 | 2009 | 2008 |
| Chicago Cubs | 2 | 8 | 10 | .200 | 1945 | 1908 |
| California/Anaheim/L.A. Angels | 1 | 0 | 1 | 1.000 | 2002 | 2002 |
| Arizona Diamondbacks | 1 | 0 | 1 | 1.000 | 2001 | 2001 |
| Kansas City Royals | 1 | 1 | 2 | .500 | 1985 | 1985 |
| Tampa Bay Rays | 0 | 1 | 1 | .000 | 2008 | — |
| Colorado Rockies | 0 | 1 | 1 | .000 | 2007 | — |
| Houston Astros | 0 | 1 | 1 | .000 | 2005 | — |
| Seattle Pilots/Milwaukee Brewers | 0 | 1 | 1 | .000 | 1982 | — |
| Texas Rangers | 0 | 2 | 2 | .000 | 2011 | — |
| San Diego Padres | 0 | 2 | 2 | .000 | 1998 | — |

# League Pennant Winners

## National League

| Year | Team | Manager | W | L | Pct | GA |
|------|------|---------|---|---|-----|-----|
| 1900 | Brooklyn | Ned Hanlon | 82 | 54 | .603 | 4½ |
| 1901 | Pittsburgh | Fred Clarke | 90 | 49 | .647 | 7½ |
| 1902 | Pittsburgh | Fred Clarke | 103 | 36 | .741 | 27½ |
| 1903 | Pittsburgh | Fred Clarke | 91 | 49 | .650 | 6½ |
| 1904 | New York | John McGraw | 106 | 47 | .693 | 13 |
| 1905 | New York | John McGraw | 105 | 48 | .686 | 9 |
| 1906 | Chicago | Frank Chance | 116 | 36 | .763 | 20 |
| 1907 | Chicago | Frank Chance | 107 | 45 | .704 | 17 |
| 1908 | Chicago | Frank Chance | 99 | 55 | .643 | 1 |
| 1909 | Pittsburgh | Fred Clarke | 110 | 42 | .724 | 6½ |
| 1910 | Chicago | Frank Chance | 104 | 50 | .675 | 13 |
| 1911 | New York | John McGraw | 99 | 54 | .647 | 7½ |
| 1912 | New York | John McGraw | 103 | 48 | .682 | 10 |
| 1913 | New York | John McGraw | 101 | 51 | .664 | 12½ |
| 1914 | Boston | George Stallings | 94 | 59 | .614 | 10½ |
| 1915 | Philadelphia | Pat Moran | 90 | 62 | .592 | 7 |
| 1916 | Brooklyn | Wilbert Robinson | 94 | 60 | .610 | 2½ |
| 1917 | New York | John McGraw | 98 | 56 | .636 | 10 |
| 1918 | Chicago | Fred Mitchell | 84 | 45 | .651 | 10½ |
| 1919 | Cincinnati | Pat Moran | 96 | 44 | .686 | 9 |
| 1920 | Brooklyn | Wilbert Robinson | 93 | 61 | .604 | 7 |
| 1921 | New York | John McGraw | 94 | 59 | .614 | 4 |
| 1922 | New York | John McGraw | 93 | 61 | .604 | 7 |
| 1923 | New York | John McGraw | 95 | 58 | .621 | 4½ |
| 1924 | New York | John McGraw | 93 | 60 | .608 | 1½ |
| 1925 | Pittsburgh | Bill McKechnie | 95 | 58 | .621 | 8½ |
| 1926 | St. Louis | Rogers Hornsby | 89 | 65 | .578 | 2 |
| 1927 | Pittsburgh | Donie Bush | 94 | 60 | .610 | 1½ |
| 1928 | St. Louis | Bill McKechnie | 95 | 59 | .617 | 2 |
| 1929 | Chicago | Joe McCarthy | 98 | 54 | .645 | 10½ |
| 1930 | St. Louis | Gabby Street | 92 | 62 | .597 | 2 |
| 1931 | St. Louis | Gabby Street | 101 | 53 | .656 | 13 |
| 1932 | Chicago | Charlie Grimm | 90 | 64 | .584 | 4 |
| 1933 | New York | Bill Terry | 91 | 61 | .599 | 5 |
| 1934 | St. Louis | Frankie Frisch | 95 | 58 | .621 | 2 |
| 1935 | Chicago | Charlie Grimm | 100 | 54 | .649 | 4 |
| 1936 | New York | Bill Terry | 92 | 62 | .597 | 5 |
| 1937 | New York | Bill Terry | 95 | 57 | .625 | 3 |
| 1938 | Chicago | Gabby Hartnett | 89 | 63 | .586 | 2 |
| 1939 | Cincinnati | Bill McKechnie | 97 | 57 | .630 | 4½ |
| 1940 | Cincinnati | Bill McKechnie | 100 | 53 | .654 | 12 |
| 1941 | Brooklyn | Leo Durocher | 100 | 54 | .649 | 2½ |
| 1942 | St. Louis | Billy Southworth | 106 | 48 | .688 | 2 |
| 1943 | St. Louis | Billy Southworth | 105 | 49 | .682 | 18 |
| 1944 | St. Louis | Billy Southworth | 105 | 49 | .682 | 14½ |
| 1945 | Chicago | Charlie Grimm | 98 | 56 | .636 | 3 |
| 1946 | St. Louis* | Eddie Dyer | 98 | 58 | .628 | 2 |
| 1947 | Brooklyn | Burt Shotton | 94 | 60 | .610 | 5 |

## National League (Cont.)

| Year | Team | Manager | W | L | Pct | GA |
|------|------|---------|---|---|-----|-----|
| 1948 | Boston | Billy Southworth | 91 | 62 | .595 | 6½ |
| 1949 | Brooklyn | Burt Shotton | 97 | 57 | .630 | 1 |
| 1950 | Philadelphia | Eddie Sawyer | 91 | 63 | .591 | 2 |
| 1951 | New York† | Leo Durocher | 98 | 59 | .624 | 1 |
| 1952 | Brooklyn | Chuck Dressen | 96 | 57 | .627 | 4½ |
| 1953 | Brooklyn | Chuck Dressen | 105 | 49 | .682 | 13 |
| 1954 | New York | Leo Durocher | 97 | 57 | .630 | 5 |
| 1955 | Brooklyn | Walter Alston | 98 | 55 | .641 | 13½ |
| 1956 | Brooklyn | Walter Alston | 93 | 61 | .604 | 1 |
| 1957 | Milwaukee | Fred Haney | 95 | 59 | .617 | 8 |
| 1958 | Milwaukee | Fred Haney | 92 | 62 | .597 | 8 |
| 1959 | Los Angeles‡ | Walter Alston | 88 | 68 | .564 | 2 |
| 1960 | Pittsburgh | Danny Murtaugh | 95 | 59 | .617 | 7 |
| 1961 | Cincinnati | Fred Hutchinson | 93 | 61 | .604 | 4 |
| 1962 | San Francisco# | Al Dark | 103 | 62 | .624 | 1 |
| 1963 | Los Angeles | Walter Alston | 99 | 63 | .611 | 6 |
| 1964 | St. Louis | Johnny Keane | 93 | 69 | .574 | 1 |
| 1965 | Los Angeles | Walter Alston | 97 | 65 | .599 | 2 |
| 1966 | Los Angeles | Walter Alston | 95 | 67 | .586 | 1½ |
| 1967 | St. Louis | Red Schoendienst | 101 | 60 | .627 | 10½ |
| 1968 | St. Louis | Red Schoendienst | 97 | 65 | .599 | 9 |
| 1969 | New York (E)†† | Gil Hodges | 100 | 62 | .617 | 8 |
| 1970 | Cincinnati (W)†† | Sparky Anderson | 102 | 60 | .630 | 14½ |
| 1971 | Pittsburgh (E)†† | Danny Murtaugh | 97 | 65 | .599 | 7 |
| 1972 | Cincinnati (W)†† | Sparky Anderson | 95 | 59 | .617 | 10½ |
| 1973 | New York (E)†† | Yogi Berra | 82 | 79 | .509 | 1½ |
| 1974 | Los Angeles (W)†† | Walter Alston | 102 | 60 | .630 | 4 |
| 1975 | Cincinnati (W)†† | Sparky Anderson | 108 | 54 | .667 | 20 |
| 1976 | Cincinnati (W)†† | Sparky Anderson | 102 | 60 | .630 | 10 |
| 1977 | Los Angeles (W)†† | Tommy Lasorda | 98 | 64 | .605 | 10 |
| 1978 | Los Angeles (W)†† | Tommy Lasorda | 95 | 67 | .586 | 2½ |
| 1979 | Pittsburgh (E)†† | Chuck Tanner | 98 | 64 | .605 | 2 |
| 1980 | Philadelphia (E)†† | Dallas Green | 91 | 71 | .562 | 1 |
| 1981 | Los Angeles (W)†† | Tommy Lasorda | 63 | 47 | .573 | ** |
| 1982 | St. Louis (E)†† | Whitey Herzog | 92 | 70 | .568 | 3 |
| 1983 | Philadelphia (E)†† | Pat Corrales/ Paul Owens | 90 | 72 | .556 | 6 |
| 1984 | San Diego (W)†† | Dick Williams | 92 | 70 | .568 | 12 |
| 1985 | St. Louis (E)†† | Whitey Herzog | 101 | 61 | .623 | 3 |
| 1986 | New York (E)†† | Davey Johnson | 108 | 54 | .667 | 21½ |
| 1987 | St. Louis (E)†† | Whitey Herzog | 95 | 67 | .586 | 3 |
| 1988 | Los Angeles (W)†† | Tommy Lasorda | 94 | 67 | .584 | 7 |
| 1989 | San Francisco (W)†† | Roger Craig | 92 | 70 | .568 | 3 |
| 1990 | Cincinnati (W)†† | Lou Piniella | 91 | 71 | .562 | 5 |
| 1991 | Atlanta (W)†† | Bobby Cox | 94 | 68 | .580 | 1 |
| 1992 | Atlanta (W)†† | Bobby Cox | 98 | 64 | .605 | 8 |
| 1993 | Philadelphia (E)†† | Jim Fregosi | 97 | 65 | .599 | 3 |
| 1994 | Season ended Aug. 11 due to players' strike. | | | | | |
| 1995 | Atlanta (E)†† | Bobby Cox | 90 | 54 | .625 | 21 |
| 1996 | Atlanta (E)†† | Bobby Cox | 96 | 66 | .593 | 8 |
| 1997 | Florida (wc)†† | Jim Leyland | 92 | 70 | .568 | -9 |
| 1998 | San Diego (W)†† | Bruce Bochy | 98 | 64 | .605 | 9½ |
| 1999 | Atlanta (E)†† | Bobby Cox | 103 | 59 | .636 | 6½ |
| 2000 | New York (wc)†† | Bobby Valentine | 94 | 68 | .580 | -6½ |
| 2001 | Arizona (W)†† | Bob Brenly | 92 | 70 | .568 | 2 |
| 2002 | San Francisco (wc)†† | Dusty Baker | 95 | 66 | .590 | -2½ |
| 2003 | Florida (wc)†† | Jack McKeon | 91 | 71 | .562 | -10 |
| 2004 | St. Louis (C)†† | Tony LaRussa | 105 | 57 | .648 | 13 |
| 2005 | Houston (wc)†† | Phil Garner | 89 | 73 | .549 | -11 |
| 2006 | St. Louis (C)†† | Tony LaRussa | 83 | 78 | .516 | 1½ |
| 2007 | Colorado (wc)††§ | Clint Hurdle | 89 | 73 | .549 | -1 |
| 2008 | Philadelphia (E)†† | Charlie Manuel | 92 | 70 | .568 | 3 |
| 2009 | Philadelphia (E)†† | Charlie Manuel | 93 | 69 | .574 | 6 |
| 2010 | San Francisco (W)†† | Bruce Bochy | 92 | 70 | .568 | 2 |
| 2011 | St. Louis (wc)†† | Tony LaRussa | 90 | 72 | .556 | -6 |

*Defeated Brooklyn, two games to none, in playoff for pennant. †Defeated Brooklyn, two games to one, in playoff for pennant. ‡Defeated Milwaukee, two games to none, in playoff for pennant. #Defeated Los Angeles, two games to one, in playoff for pennant. § Defeated San Diego in one-game playoff for wild card. ††Won Championship Series. **First half 36–21; second half 27–26, in season split by strike; defeated Houston in playoff for Western Division title.

## American League

| Year | Team | Manager | W | L | Pct | GA |
|------|------|---------|---|---|-----|-----|
| 1901 | Chicago | Clark Griffith | 83 | 53 | .610 | 4 |
| 1902 | Philadelphia | Connie Mack | 83 | 53 | .610 | 5 |
| 1903 | Boston | Jimmy Collins | 91 | 47 | .659 | 14½ |
| 1904 | Boston | Jimmy Collins | 95 | 59 | .617 | 1½ |
| 1905 | Philadelphia | Connie Mack | 92 | 56 | .622 | 2 |
| 1906 | Chicago | Fielder Jones | 93 | 58 | .616 | 3 |
| 1907 | Detroit | Hughie Jennings | 92 | 58 | .613 | 1½ |
| 1908 | Detroit | Hughie Jennings | 90 | 63 | .588 | ½ |
| 1909 | Detroit | Hughie Jennings | 98 | 54 | .645 | 3½ |
| 1910 | Philadelphia | Connie Mack | 102 | 48 | .680 | 14½ |
| 1911 | Philadelphia | Connie Mack | 101 | 50 | .669 | 13½ |
| 1912 | Boston | Jake Stahl | 105 | 47 | .691 | 14 |
| 1913 | Philadelphia | Connie Mack | 96 | 57 | .627 | 6½ |
| 1914 | Philadelphia | Connie Mack | 99 | 53 | .651 | 8½ |
| 1915 | Boston | Bill Carrigan | 101 | 50 | .669 | 2½ |
| 1916 | Boston | Bill Carrigan | 91 | 63 | .591 | 2 |
| 1917 | Chicago | Pants Rowland | 100 | 54 | .649 | 9 |
| 1918 | Boston | Ed Barrow | 75 | 51 | .595 | 2½ |
| 1919 | Chicago | Kid Gleason | 88 | 52 | .629 | 3½ |
| 1920 | Cleveland | Tris Speaker | 98 | 56 | .636 | 2 |
| 1921 | New York | Miller Huggins | 98 | 55 | .641 | 4½ |
| 1922 | New York | Miller Huggins | 94 | 60 | .610 | 1 |
| 1923 | New York | Miller Huggins | 98 | 54 | .645 | 16 |
| 1924 | Washington | Bucky Harris | 92 | 62 | .597 | 2 |
| 1925 | Washington | Bucky Harris | 96 | 55 | .636 | 8½ |
| 1926 | New York | Miller Huggins | 91 | 63 | .591 | 3 |
| 1927 | New York | Miller Huggins | 110 | 44 | .714 | 19 |
| 1928 | New York | Miller Huggins | 101 | 53 | .656 | 2½ |
| 1929 | Philadelphia | Connie Mack | 104 | 46 | .693 | 18 |
| 1930 | Philadelphia | Connie Mack | 102 | 52 | .662 | 8 |
| 1931 | Philadelphia | Connie Mack | 107 | 45 | .704 | 13½ |
| 1932 | New York | Joe McCarthy | 107 | 47 | .695 | 13 |
| 1933 | Washington | Joe Cronin | 99 | 53 | .651 | 7 |
| 1934 | Detroit | Mickey Cochrane | 101 | 53 | .656 | 7 |
| 1935 | Detroit | Mickey Cochrane | 93 | 58 | .616 | 3 |
| 1936 | New York | Joe McCarthy | 102 | 51 | .667 | 19½ |
| 1937 | New York | Joe McCarthy | 102 | 52 | .662 | 13 |
| 1938 | New York | Joe McCarthy | 99 | 53 | .651 | 9½ |
| 1939 | New York | Joe McCarthy | 106 | 45 | .702 | 17 |
| 1940 | Detroit | Del Baker | 90 | 64 | .584 | 1 |
| 1941 | New York | Joe McCarthy | 101 | 53 | .656 | 17 |
| 1942 | New York | Joe McCarthy | 103 | 51 | .669 | 9 |
| 1943 | New York | Joe McCarthy | 98 | 56 | .636 | 13½ |
| 1944 | St. Louis | Luke Sewell | 89 | 65 | .578 | 1 |
| 1945 | Detroit | Steve O'Neill | 88 | 65 | .575 | 1½ |
| 1946 | Boston | Joe Cronin | 104 | 50 | .675 | 12 |
| 1947 | New York | Bucky Harris | 97 | 57 | .630 | 12 |
| 1948 | Cleveland† | Lou Boudreau | 97 | 58 | .626 | 1 |
| 1949 | New York | Casey Stengel | 97 | 57 | .630 | 1 |
| 1950 | New York | Casey Stengel | 98 | 56 | .636 | 3 |
| 1951 | New York | Casey Stengel | 98 | 56 | .636 | 5 |
| 1952 | New York | Casey Stengel | 95 | 59 | .617 | 2 |
| 1953 | New York | Casey Stengel | 99 | 52 | .656 | 8½ |
| 1954 | Cleveland | Al Lopez | 111 | 43 | .721 | 8 |
| 1955 | New York | Casey Stengel | 96 | 58 | .623 | 3 |
| 1956 | New York | Casey Stengel | 97 | 57 | .630 | 9 |
| 1957 | New York | Casey Stengel | 98 | 56 | .636 | 8 |
| 1958 | New York | Casey Stengel | 92 | 62 | .597 | 10 |
| 1959 | Chicago | Al Lopez | 94 | 60 | .610 | 5 |
| 1960 | New York | Casey Stengel | 97 | 57 | .630 | 8 |
| 1961 | New York | Ralph Houk | 109 | 53 | .673 | 8 |
| 1962 | New York | Ralph Houk | 96 | 66 | .593 | 5 |
| 1963 | New York | Ralph Houk | 104 | 57 | .646 | 10½ |
| 1964 | New York | Yogi Berra | 99 | 63 | .611 | 1 |
| 1965 | Minnesota | Sam Mele | 102 | 60 | .630 | 7 |
| 1966 | Baltimore | Hank Bauer | 97 | 63 | .606 | 9 |
| 1967 | Boston | Dick Williams | 92 | 70 | .568 | 1 |

†Defeated Boston in one-game playoff.

## American League (Cont.)

| Year | Team | Manager | W | L | Pct | GA |
|------|------|---------|---|---|-----|-----|
| 1968 | Detroit | Mayo Smith | 103 | 59 | .636 | 12 |
| 1969 | Baltimore (E)‡ | Earl Weaver | 109 | 53 | .673 | 19 |
| 1970 | Baltimore (E)‡ | Earl Weaver | 108 | 54 | .667 | 15 |
| 1971 | Baltimore (E)‡ | Earl Weaver | 101 | 57 | .639 | 12 |
| 1972 | Oakland (W)‡ | Dick Williams | 93 | 62 | .600 | 5½ |
| 1973 | Oakland (W)‡ | Dick Williams | 94 | 68 | .580 | 6 |
| 1974 | Oakland (W)‡ | Al Dark | 90 | 72 | .556 | 5 |
| 1975 | Boston (E)‡ | Darrell Johnson | 95 | 65 | .594 | 4½ |
| 1976 | New York (E)‡ | Billy Martin | 97 | 62 | .610 | 10½ |
| 1977 | New York (E)‡ | Billy Martin | 100 | 62 | .617 | 2½ |
| 1978 | New York (E)†‡ | Billy Martin, Bob Lemon | 100 | 63 | .613 | 1 |
| 1979 | Baltimore (E)‡ | Earl Weaver | 102 | 57 | .642 | 8 |
| 1980 | Kansas City (W)‡ | Jim Frey | 97 | 65 | .599 | 14 |
| 1981 | New York (E)‡ | Gene Michael/Bob Lemon | 59 | 48 | .551 | # |
| 1982 | Milwaukee (E)‡ | Buck Rodgers, Harvey Kuenn | 95 | 67 | .586 | 1 |
| 1983 | Baltimore (E)‡ | Joe Altobelli | 98 | 64 | .605 | 6 |
| 1984 | Detroit (E)‡ | Sparky Anderson | 104 | 58 | .642 | 15 |
| 1985 | Kansas City (W)‡ | Dick Howser | 91 | 71 | .562 | 1 |
| 1986 | Boston (E)‡ | John McNamara | 95 | 66 | .590 | 5½ |
| 1987 | Minnesota (W)‡ | Tom Kelly | 85 | 77 | .525 | 2 |
| 1988 | Oakland (W)‡ | Tony LaRussa | 104 | 58 | .642 | 13 |
| 1989 | Oakland (W)‡ | Tony LaRussa | 99 | 63 | .611 | 7 |
| 1990 | Oakland (W)‡ | Tony LaRussa | 103 | 59 | .636 | 9 |
| 1991 | Minnesota (W)‡ | Tom Kelly | 95 | 67 | .586 | 8 |
| 1992 | Toronto‡ | Cito Gaston | 96 | 66 | .593 | 4 |
| 1993 | Toronto‡ | Cito Gaston | 95 | 67 | .586 | 7 |
| 1994 | Season ended Aug. 11 due to players' strike. | | | | | |
| 1995 | Cleveland (C)‡ | Mike Hargrove | 100 | 44 | .694 | 30 |
| 1996 | New York (E)‡ | Joe Torre | 92 | 70 | .568 | 4 |
| 1997 | Cleveland (C)‡ | Mike Hargrove | 86 | 75 | .534 | 6 |
| 1998 | New York (E)‡ | Joe Torre | 114 | 48 | .704 | 22 |
| 1999 | New York (E)‡ | Joe Torre | 98 | 64 | .605 | 4 |
| 2000 | New York (E)‡ | Joe Torre | 87 | 74 | .540 | 2½ |
| 2001 | New York (E)‡ | Joe Torre | 95 | 65 | .594 | 13½ |
| 2002 | Anaheim (wc)‡ | Mike Scioscia | 99 | 63 | .611 | -4 |
| 2003 | New York (E)‡ | Joe Torre | 101 | 61 | .623 | 6 |
| 2004 | Boston (wc)‡ | Terry Francona | 98 | 64 | .605 | -3 |
| 2005 | Chicago (C)‡ | Ozzie Guillen | 99 | 63 | .611 | 6 |
| 2006 | Detroit (wc)‡ | Jim Leyland | 95 | 67 | .586 | -1 |
| 2007 | Boston (E)‡ | Terry Francona | 96 | 66 | .593 | 2 |
| 2008 | Tampa Bay (E)‡ | Joe Maddon | 97 | 65 | .599 | 2 |
| 2009 | New York (E)‡ | Joe Girardi | 103 | 59 | .636 | 8 |
| 2010 | Texas (W)‡ | Ron Washington | 90 | 72 | .556 | 9 |
| 2011 | Texas (W)‡ | Ron Washington | 96 | 66 | .593 | 5 |

‡Won championship series.

## League Championship Series

### National League

1969 ...............New York (E) 3, Atlanta (W) 0
1970 ...............Cincinnati (W) 3, Pittsburgh (E) 0
1971 ...............Pittsburgh (E) 3, San Francisco (W) 1
1972 ...............Cincinnati (W) 3, Pittsburgh (E) 2
1973 ...............New York (E) 3, Cincinnati (W) 2
1974 ...............Los Angeles (W) 3, Pittsburgh (E) 1
1975 ...............Cincinnati (W) 3, Pittsburgh (E) 0
1976 ...............Cincinnati (W) 3, Philadelphia (E) 0
1977 ...............Los Angeles (W) 3, Philadelphia (E) 1
1978 ...............Los Angeles (W) 3, Philadelphia (E) 1
1979 ...............Pittsburgh (E) 3, Cincinnati (W) 0
1980 ...............Philadelphia (E) 3, Houston (W) 2
1981 ...............Los Angeles (W) 3, Montreal (E) 2
1982 ...............St. Louis (E) 3, Atlanta (W) 0
1983 ...............Philadelphia (E) 3, Los Angeles (W) 1
1984 ...............San Diego (W) 3, Chicago (E) 2
1985 ...............St. Louis (E) 4, Los Angeles (W) 2
1986 ...............New York (E) 4, Houston (W) 2
1987 ...............St. Louis (E) 4, San Francisco (W) 3
1988 ...............Los Angeles (W) 4, New York (E) 3
1989 ...............San Francisco (W) 4, Chicago (E) 1
1990 ...............Cincinnati (W) 4, Pittsburgh (E) 2
1991 ...............Atlanta (W) 4, Pittsburgh (E) 3
1992 ...............Atlanta (W) 4, Pittsburgh (E) 3
1993 ...............Philadelphia (E) 4, Atlanta (W) 2
1994 ...............Playoffs canceled due to players' strike.
1995 ...............Atlanta (E) 4, Cincinnati (C) 0
1996 ...............Atlanta (E) 4, St. Louis (C) 3
1997 ...............Florida (wc) 4, Atlanta (E) 2
1998 ...............San Diego (W) 4, Atlanta (E) 2
1999 ...............Atlanta (E) 4, New York (wc) 2
2000 ...............New York (wc) 4, St. Louis (C) 1
2001 ...............Arizona (W) 4, Atlanta (E) 1
2002 ...............San Francisco (wc) 4, St. Louis (C) 1
2003 ...............Florida (wc) 4, Chicago (C) 3
2004 ...............St. Louis (C) 4, Houston (wc) 3
2005 ...............Houston (wc) 4, St. Louis (C) 2
2006 ...............St. Louis (C) 4, New York (E) 3
2007 ...............Colorado (wc) 4, Arizona (W) 0
2008 ...............Philadelphia (E) 4, Los Angeles (W) 1
2009 ...............Philadelphia (E) 4, Los Angeles (W) 1
2010 ...............San Francisco (W) 4, Philadelphia (E) 2
2011 ...............St. Louis (wc) 4, Milwaukee (C) 2

### American League

1969 ...............Baltimore (E) 3, Minnesota (W) 0
1970 ...............Baltimore (E) 3, Minnesota (W) 0
1971 ...............Baltimore (E) 3, Oakland (W) 0
1972 ...............Oakland (W) 3, Detroit (E) 2
1973 ...............Oakland (W) 3, Baltimore (E) 2
1974 ...............Oakland (W) 3, Baltimore (E) 1
1975 ...............Boston (E) 3, Oakland (W) 0
1976 ...............New York (E) 3, Kansas City (W) 2
1977 ...............New York (E) 3, Kansas City (W) 2
1978 ...............New York (E) 3, Kansas City (W) 1
1979 ...............Baltimore (E) 3, California (W) 1
1980 ...............Kansas City (W) 3, New York (E) 0
1981 ...............New York (E) 3, Oakland (W) 0
1982 ...............Milwaukee (E) 3, California (W) 2
1983 ...............Baltimore (E) 3, Chicago (W) 1
1984 ...............Detroit (E) 3, Kansas City (W) 0
1985 ...............Kansas City (W) 4, Toronto (E) 3
1986 ...............Boston (E) 4, California (W) 3
1987 ...............Minnesota (W) 4, Detroit (E) 1
1988 ...............Oakland (W) 4, Boston (E) 0
1989 ...............Oakland (W) 4, Toronto (E) 1
1990 ...............Oakland (W) 4, Boston (E) 0
1991 ...............Minnesota (W) 4, Toronto (E) 1
1992 ...............Toronto (E) 4, Oakland (W) 2
1993 ...............Toronto (E) 4, Chicago (W) 2
1994 ...............Playoffs canceled due to players' strike.
1995 ...............Cleveland (C) 4, Seattle (W) 2
1996 ...............New York (E) 4, Baltimore (wc) 1
1997 ...............Cleveland (C) 4, Baltimore (E) 2
1998 ...............New York (E) 4, Cleveland (C) 2
1999 ...............New York (E) 4, Boston (wc) 1
2000 ...............New York (E) 4, Seattle (wc) 2
2001 ...............New York (E) 4, Seattle (W) 1
2002 ...............Anaheim (wc) 4, Minnesota (C) 1
2003 ...............New York (E) 4, Boston (wc) 3
2004 ...............Boston (wc) 4, New York (E) 3
2005 ...............Chicago (C) 4, Los Angeles (W) 1
2006 ...............Detroit (wc) 4, Oakland (W) 0
2007 ...............Boston (E) 4, Cleveland (C) 3
2008 ...............Tampa Bay (E) 4, Boston (wc) 3
2009 ...............New York (E) 4, Los Angeles (W) 2
2010 ...............Texas (W) 4, New York (E) 2
2011 ...............Texas (W) 4, Detroit (C) 2

### NLCS Most Valuable Player

1977 ........Dusty Baker, LA
1978 ........Steve Garvey, LA
1979 ........Willie Stargell, Pitt
1980 ........Manny Trillo, Phi
1981 ........Burt Hooton, LA
1982 ........Darrell Porter, StL
1983 ........Gary Matthews, Phi
1984 ........Steve Garvey, SD
1985 ........Ozzie Smith, StL
1986 ........Mike Scott, Hou
1987 ........Jeffrey Leonard, SF
1988 ........Orel Hershiser, LA

1989 ........Will Clark, SF
1990 ........R. Myers/R. Dibble, Cin
1991 ........Steve Avery, Atl
1992 ........John Smoltz, Atl
1993 ........Curt Schilling, Phi
1994 ........Playoffs canceled
1995 ........Mike Devereaux, Atl
1996 ........Javier Lopez, Atl
1997 ........Livan Hernandez, Fla
1998 ........Sterling Hitchcock, SD
1999 ........Eddie Perez, Atl
2000 ........Mike Hampton, NY

2001 ........Craig Counsell, Ariz
2002 ........Benito Santiago, SF
2003 ........Ivan Rodriguez, Fla
2004 ........Albert Pujols, StL
2005 ........Roy Oswalt, Hou
2006 ........Jeff Suppan, StL
2007 ........Matt Holliday, Col
2008 ........Cole Hamels, Phi
2009 ........Ryan Howard, Phi
2010 ........Cody Ross, SF
2011 ........David Freese, StL

### ALCS Most Valuable Player

1980 ........Frank White, KC
1981 ........Graig Nettles, NY
1982 ........Fred Lynn, Calif
1983 ........Mike Boddicker, Balt
1984 ........Kirk Gibson, Det
1985 ........George Brett, KC
1986 ........Marty Barrett, Bos
1987 ........Gary Gaetti, Minn
1988 ........Dennis Eckersley, Oak
1989 ........Rickey Henderson, Oak
1990 ........Dave Stewart, Oak

1991 ........Kirby Puckett, Minn
1992 ........Roberto Alomar, Tor
1993 ........Dave Stewart, Tor
1994 ........Playoffs canceled
1995 ........Orel Hershiser, Clev
1996 ........Bernie Williams, NY
1997 ........Marquis Grissom, Clev
1998 ........David Wells, NY
1999 ........Orlando Hernandez, NY
2000 ........David Justice, NY
2001 ........Andy Pettitte, NY

2002 ........Adam Kennedy, Ana
2003 ........Mariano Rivera, NY
2004 ........David Ortiz, Bos
2005 ........Paul Konerko, Chi
2006 ........Placido Polanco, Det
2007 ........Josh Beckett, Bos
2008 ........Matt Garza, TB
2009 ........C.C. Sabathia, NY
2010 ........Josh Hamilton, Tex
2011 ........Nelson Cruz, Tex

## National League

| | |
|---|---|
| 1995 | Atlanta (E) 3, Colorado (wc) 1 |
| | Cincinnati (C) 3, Los Angeles (W) 0 |
| 1996 | St. Louis (C) 3, San Diego (W) 0 |
| | Atlanta (E) 3, Los Angeles (wc) 0 |
| 1997 | Atlanta (E) 3, Houston (C) 0 |
| | Florida (wc) 3, San Francisco (W) 0 |
| 1998 | San Diego (W) 3, Houston (C) 1 |
| | Atlanta (E) 3, Chicago (wc) 0 |
| 1999 | Atlanta (E) 3, Houston (C) 1 |
| | New York (wc) 3, Arizona (W) 1 |
| 2000 | St. Louis (C) 3, Atlanta (E) 0 |
| | New York (wc) 3, San Francisco (W) 1 |
| 2001 | Atlanta (E) 3, Houston (C) 0 |
| | Arizona (W) 3, St. Louis (wc) 2 |
| 2002 | St. Louis (C) 3, Arizona (W) 0 |
| | San Francisco (wc) 3, Atlanta (E) 2 |
| 2003 | Chicago (C) 3, Atlanta (E) 2 |
| | Florida (wc) 3, San Francisco (W) 1 |
| 2004 | St. Louis (C) 3, Los Angeles (W) 1 |
| | Houston (wc) 3, Atlanta (E) 2 |
| 2005 | Houston (wc) 3, Atlanta (E) 1 |
| | St. Louis (C) 3, San Diego (W) 1 |
| 2006 | St. Louis (C) 3, San Diego (W) 1 |
| | New York (E) 3, Los Angeles (wc) 0 |
| 2007 | Colorado (wc) 3, Philadelphia (E) 0 |
| | Arizona (W) 3, Chicago (C) 0 |
| 2008 | Los Angeles (W) 3, Chicago (C) 0 |
| | Philadelphia (E) 3, Milwaukee (wc) 1 |
| 2009 | Los Angeles (W) 3, St. Louis, (C) 0 |
| | Philadelphia (E) 3, Colorado (wc) 1 |
| 2010 | San Francisco (W) 3, Atlanta, (wc) 1 |
| | Philadelphia (E) 3, Cincinnati (C) 0 |
| 2010 | Milwaukee (C) 3, Arizona (W) 2 |
| | St. Louis (wc) 3, Philadelphia (E) 2 |

## American League

| | |
|---|---|
| 1995 | Cleveland (C) 3, Boston (E) 0 |
| | Seattle (W) 3, New York (wc) 2 |
| 1996 | Baltimore (wc) 3, Cleveland (C) 1 |
| | New York (E) 3, Texas (W) 1 |
| 1997 | Baltimore (E) 3, Seattle (W) 1 |
| | Cleveland (C) 3, New York (wc) 2 |
| 1998 | New York (E) 3, Texas (W) 0 |
| | Cleveland (C) 3, Boston (wc) 1 |
| 1999 | New York (E) 3, Texas (W) 1 |
| | Boston (wc) 3, Cleveland (C) 2 |
| 2000 | New York (E) 3, Oakland (W) 2 |
| | Seattle (wc) 3, Chicago (C) 0 |
| 2001 | Seattle (W) 3, Cleveland (wc) 2 |
| | New York (E) 3, Oakland (wc) 2 |
| 2002 | Minnesota (C) 3, Oakland (W) 2 |
| | Anaheim (wc) 3, New York (E) 1 |
| 2003 | New York (E) 3, Minnesota (C) 1 |
| | Boston (wc) 3, Oakland (W) 2 |
| 2004 | New York (E) 3, Minnesota (C) 1 |
| | Boston (wc) 3 Anaheim (W) 0 |
| 2005 | Los Angeles (W) 3, New York (E) 2 |
| | Chicago (C) 3, Boston (wc) 0 |
| 2006 | Oakland (W) 3, Minnesota (C) 0 |
| | Detroit (wc) 3, New York (E) 1 |
| 2007 | Boston (E) 3, Los Angeles (W) 0 |
| | Cleveland (C) 3, New York (wc) 1 |
| 2008 | Boston (wc) 3, Los Angeles (W) 1 |
| | Tampa Bay (E) 3, Chicago (C) 1 |
| 2009 | Los Angeles (W) 3, Boston (wc) 0 |
| | New York (E) 3, Minnesota (C) 0 |
| 2010 | Texas (W) 3, Tampa Bay (E) 2 |
| | New York (wc) 3, Minnesota (C)  0 |
| 2011 | Detroit (C) 3, New York (E) 2 |
| | Texas (W) 3, Tampa Bay (wc) 1 |

# The All-Star Game

| Date | Winner | Score | Site |
|---|---|---|---|
| 7-6-33 | American | 4–2 | Comiskey Park, Chi |
| 7-10-34 | American | 9–7 | Polo Grounds, NY |
| 7-8-35 | American | 4–1 | Municipal Stadium, Clev |
| 7-7-36 | National | 4–3 | Braves Field, Bos |
| 7-7-37 | American | 8–3 | Griffith Stadium, Wash |
| 7-6-38 | National | 4–1 | Crosley Field, Cin |
| 7-11-39 | American | 3–1 | Yankee Stadium, NY |
| 7-10-40 | National | 4–0 | Sportsman's Park, StL |
| 7-8-41 | American | 7–5 | Briggs Stadium, Det |
| 7-6-42 | American | 3–1 | Polo Grounds, NY |
| 7-13-43 | American | 5–3 | Shibe Park, Phi |
| 7-11-44 | National | 7–1 | Forbes Field, Pitt |
| 1945 | No game due to wartime travel restrictions. | | |
| 7-9-46 | American | 12–0 | Fenway Park, Bos |
| 7-8-47 | American | 2–1 | Wrigley Field, Chi |
| 7-13-48 | American | 5–2 | Sportsman's Park, StL |
| 7-12-49 | American | 11–7 | Ebbets Field, Bklyn |
| 7-11-50 | National | 4–3 | Comiskey Park, Chi |
| 7-10-51 | National | 8–3 | Briggs Stadium, Det |
| 7-8-52 | National | 3–2 | Shibe Park, Phi |
| 7-14-53 | National | 5–1 | Crosley Field, Cin |
| 7-13-54 | American | 11–9 | Municipal Stadium, Clev |
| 7-12-55 | National | 6–5 | County Stadium, Mil |
| 7-10-56 | National | 7–3 | Griffith Stadium, Wash |
| 7-9-57 | American | 6–5 | Busch Stadium, StL |
| 7-8-58 | American | 4–3 | Memorial Stadium, Balt |
| 7-7-59 | National | 5–4 | Forbes Field, Pitt |
| 8-3-59 | American | 5–3 | Memorial Coliseum, LA |
| 7-11-60 | National | 5–3 | Municipal Stadium, KC |
| 7-13-60 | National | 6–0 | Yankee Stadium, NY |
| 7-11-61 | National | 5–4 | Candlestick Park, SF |
| 7-31-61 | Tie* | 1–1 | Fenway Park, Bos |
| 7-10-62 | National | 3–1 | D.C. Stadium, Wash |
| 7-30-62 | American | 9–4 | Wrigley Field, Chi |
| 7-9-63 | National | 5–3 | Municipal Stadium, Clev |
| 7-7-64 | National | 7–4 | Shea Stadium, NY |
| 7-13-65 | National | 6–5 | Metro. Stadium, Minn |
| 7-12-66 | National | 2–1 | Busch Stadium, StL |
| 7-11-67 | National | 2–1 | Anaheim Stadium, Cal |
| 7-9-68 | National | 1–0 | Astrodome, Hou |
| 7-23-69 | National | 9–3 | R.F.K. Stadium, Wash. |
| 7-14-70 | National | 5–4 | Riverfront Stadium, Cin |
| 7-13-71 | American | 6–4 | Tiger Stadium, Det |
| 7-25-72 | National | 4–3 | Atlanta Stadium, Atl |
| 7-24-73 | National | 7–1 | Royals Stadium, KC |
| 7-23-74 | National | 7–2 | Three Rivers Stadium, Pitt |
| 7-15-75 | National | 6–3 | County Stadium, Mil |
| 7-13-76 | National | 7–1 | Veterans Stadium, Phi |
| 7-19-77 | National | 7–5 | Yankee Stadium, NY |
| 7-11-78 | National | 7–3 | Jack Murphy Stadium, SD |
| 7-17-79 | National | 7–6 | Kingdome, Sea |
| 7-8-80 | National | 4–2 | Dodger Stadium, LA |
| 8-9-81 | National | 5–4 | Municipal Stadium, Clev |
| 7-13-82 | National | 4–1 | Olympic Stadium, Mtl |
| 7-6-83 | American | 13–3 | Comiskey Park, Chi |
| 7-10-84 | National | 3–1 | Candlestick Park, SF |
| 7-16-85 | National | 6–1 | Metrodome, Minn |
| 7-15-86 | American | 3–2 | Astrodome, Hou |
| 7-14-87 | National | 2–0 | Oakland Coliseum, Oak |
| 7-12-88 | American | 2–1 | Riverfront Stadium, Cin |
| 7-11-89 | American | 5–3 | Anaheim Stadium, Cal |
| 7-10-90 | American | 2–0 | Wrigley Field, Chi |

*Game called because of rain after nine innings.

## Results (Cont.)

| Date | Winner | Score | Site | Date | Winner | Score | Site |
|------|--------|-------|------|------|--------|-------|------|
| 7-9-91 | American | 4–2 | SkyDome, Tor | 7-9-02 | Tie (11 inn) | 7–7 | Miller Park, Mil |
| 7-14-92 | American | 13–6 | Jack Murphy Stadium, SD | 7-15-03 | American | 7–6 | Comiskey Park, Chi |
| 7-13-93 | American | 9–3 | Camden Yards, Balt | 7-13-04 | American | 9–4 | Minute Maid Park, Hou |
| 7-12-94 | National | 8–7 | Three Rivers Stadium, Pitt | 7-12-05 | American | 7–5 | Comerica Park, Det |
| 7-11-95 | National | 3–2 | Ballpark in Arlington, Tex | 7-11-06 | American | 3–2 | PNC Park, Pitt |
| 7-9-96 | National | 6–0 | Veterans Stadium, Phi | 7-10-07 | American | 5–4 | AT&T Park, SF |
| 7-8-97 | American | 3–1 | Jacobs Field, Cle | 7-15-08 | American | 4–3 | Yankee Stadium, NY |
| 7-7-98 | American | 13–8 | Coors Field, Col | 7-14-09 | American | 4–3 | Busch Stadium, StL |
| 7-13-99 | American | 4–1 | Fenway Park, Bos | 7-13-10 | National | 3–1 | Angel Stadium, LA |
| 7-11-00 | American | 6–3 | Turner Field, Atl | 7-12-11 | National | 5–1 | Chase Field, Ari |
| 7-10-01 | American | 4–1 | Safeco Field, Sea | | | | |

## Most Valuable Players

| | | |
|---|---|---|
| 1962...Maury Wills, LA | NL | |
| Leon Wagner, LA | AL | |
| 1963...Willie Mays, SF | NL | |
| 1964...Johnny Callison, Phi | NL | |
| 1965...Juan Marichal, SF | NL | |
| 1966...Brooks Robinson, Balt | AL | |
| 1967...Tony Perez, Cin | NL | |
| 1968...Willie Mays, SF | NL | |
| 1969...Willie McCovey, SF | NL | |
| 1970...Carl Yastrzemski, Bos | AL | |
| 1971...Frank Robinson, Balt | AL | |
| 1972...Joe Morgan, Cin | NL | |
| 1973...Bobby Bonds, SF | NL | |
| 1974...Steve Garvey, LA | NL | |
| 1975...Bill Madlock, Chi | NL | |
| Jon Matlack, NY | NL | |
| 1976...George Foster, Cin | NL | |
| 1977...Don Sutton, LA | NL | |

| | |
|---|---|
| 1978...Steve Garvey, LA | NL |
| 1979...Dave Parker, Pitt | NL |
| 1980...Ken Griffey, Cin | NL |
| 1981...Gary Carter, Mtl | NL |
| 1982...Dave Concepcion, Cin | NL |
| 1983...Fred Lynn, Calif | AL |
| 1984...Gary Carter, Mtl | NL |
| 1985...LaMarr Hoyt, SD | NL |
| 1986...Roger Clemens, Bos | AL |
| 1987...Tim Raines, Mtl | NL |
| 1988...Terry Steinbach, Oak | AL |
| 1989...Bo Jackson, KC | AL |
| 1990...Julio Franco, Tex | AL |
| 1991...Cal Ripken Jr., Balt | AL |
| 1992...Ken Griffey Jr., Sea | AL |
| 1993...Kirby Puckett, Minn | AL |
| 1994...Fred McGriff, Atl | NL |
| 1995...Jeff Conine, Fla | NL |

| | |
|---|---|
| 1996...Mike Piazza, LA | NL |
| 1997...Sandy Alomar, Clev | AL |
| 1998...Roberto Alomar, Balt | AL |
| 1999...Pedro Martinez, Bos | AL |
| 2000...Derek Jeter, NY | AL |
| 2001...Cal Ripken Jr., Balt | AL |
| 2002...None selected | |
| 2003...Garret Anderson, Ana | AL |
| 2004...Alfonso Soriano, Tex | AL |
| 2005...Miguel Tejada, Balt | AL |
| 2006...Michael Young, Tex | AL |
| 2007...Ichiro Suzuki, Sea | AL |
| 2008...J.D. Drew, Bos | AL |
| 2009...Carl Crawford, TB | AL |
| 2010...Brian McCann, Atl | NL |
| 2011...Prince Fielder, Mil | NL |

# The Regular Season

## Most Valuable Players

### NATIONAL LEAGUE

| Year | Name and Team | Position | Noteworthy |
|------|---------------|----------|------------|
| 1911 | Wildfire Schulte, Chi | Outfield | 21 HR†, 121 RBI†, .300 |
| 1912 | *Larry Doyle, NY | Second base | 10 HR, 90 RBI, .330 |
| 1913 | Jake Daubert, Bklyn | First base | 52 RBI, .350† |
| 1914 | *Johnny Evers, Bos | Second base | FA .976†, .279 |
| 1915–23 | No selection | | |
| 1924 | Dazzy Vance, Bklyn | Pitcher | 28†–6, 2.16 ERA†, 262 K† |
| 1925 | Rogers Hornsby, StL | Second base, Manager | 39 HR†, 143 RBI†, .403† |
| 1926 | Bob O'Farrell, StL | Catcher | 7 HR, 68 RBI, .293 |
| 1927 | *Paul Waner, Pitt | Outfield | 237 hits†, 131 RBI†, .380† |
| 1928 | *Jim Bottomley, StL | First base | 31 HR†, 136 RBI†, .325 |
| 1929 | Rogers Hornsby, Chi | Second base | 39 HR, 149 RBI, 156 runs†, .380 |
| 1930 | No selection | | |
| 1931 | *Frankie Frisch, StL | Second base | 4 HR, 82 RBI, 28 SB†, .311 |
| 1932 | Chuck Klein, Phi | Outfield | 38 HR†, 137 RBI, 226 hits†, .348 |
| 1933 | *Carl Hubbell, NY | Pitcher | 23†–12, 1.66 ERA†, 10 SO† |
| 1934 | *Dizzy Dean, StL | Pitcher | 30†–7, 2.66 ERA, 195 K† |
| 1935 | *Gabby Hartnett, Chi | Catcher | 13 HR, 91 RBI, .344 |
| 1936 | *Carl Hubbell, NY | Pitcher | 26†–6, 2.31 ERA† |
| 1937 | Joe Medwick, StL | Outfield | 31 HR‡, 154 RBI†, 111 runs†, .374† |
| 1938 | Ernie Lombardi, Cin | Catcher | 19 HR, 95 RBI, .342† |
| 1939 | *Bucky Walters, Cin | Pitcher | 27†–11, 2.29 ERA†, 137 K‡ |
| 1940 | *Frank McCormick, Cin | First base | 19 HR, 127 RBI, 191 hits†, .309 |
| 1941 | *Dolph Camilli, Bklyn | First base | 34 HR†, 120 RBI†, .285 |
| 1942 | *Mort Cooper, StL | Pitcher | 22†–7, 1.78 ERA†, 10 SO† |
| 1943 | *Stan Musial, StL | Outfield | 13 HR, 81 RBI, 220 hits†, .357† |
| 1944 | *Marty Marion, StL | Shortstop | FA .972†, 63 RBI |
| 1945 | *Phil Cavarretta, Chi | First base | 6 HR, 97 RBI, .355† |
| 1946 | *Stan Musial, StL | First base, Outfield | 103 RBI, 124 runs†, 228 hits†, .365† |

*Played for pennant or, after 1968, division winner. †Led league. ‡Tied for league lead.

## Most Valuable Players (Cont.)
### NATIONAL LEAGUE (Cont.)

| Year | Name and Team | Position | Noteworthy |
|------|---------------|----------|------------|
| 1947 | Bob Elliott, Bos | Third base | 22 HR, 113 RBI, .317 |
| 1948 | Stan Musial, StL | Outfield | 39 HR, 131 RBI†, .376† |
| 1949 | *Jackie Robinson, Bklyn | Second base | 16 HR, 124 RBI, 37 SB†, .342† |
| 1950 | *Jim Konstanty, Phi | Pitcher | 16–7, 22 saves†, 2.66 ERA |
| 1951 | Roy Campanella, Bklyn | Catcher | 33 HR, 108 RBI, .325 |
| 1952 | Hank Sauer, Chi | Outfield | 37 HR‡, 121 RBI†, .270 |
| 1953 | *Roy Campanella, Bklyn | Catcher | 41 HR, 142 RBI†, .312 |
| 1954 | *Willie Mays, NY | Outfield | 41 HR, 110 RBI, 13 3B†, .345† |
| 1955 | *Roy Campanella, Bklyn | Catcher | 32 HR, 107 RBI, .318 |
| 1956 | *Don Newcombe, Bklyn | Pitcher | 27†–7, 3.06 ERA |
| 1957 | *Hank Aaron, Mil | Outfield | 44 HR†, 132 RBI†, .322 |
| 1958 | Ernie Banks, Chi | Shortstop | 47 HR†, 129 RBI†, .313 |
| 1959 | Ernie Banks, Chi | Shortstop | 45 HR, 143 RBI†, .304 |
| 1960 | *Dick Groat, Pitt | Shortstop | 2 HR, 50 RBI, .325† |
| 1961 | *Frank Robinson, Cin | Outfield | 37 HR, 124 RBI, .323 |
| 1962 | Maury Wills, LA | Shortstop | 104 SB†, 208 hits, .299, GG |
| 1963 | *Sandy Koufax, LA | Pitcher | 25‡–5, 1.88 ERA†, 306 K† |
| 1964 | *Ken Boyer, StL | Third Base | 24 HR, 119 RBI†, .295 |
| 1965 | Willie Mays, SF | Outfield | 52 HR†, 112 RBI, .317, GG |
| 1966 | Roberto Clemente, Pitt | Outfield | 29 HR, 119 RBI, 202 hits, .317, GG |
| 1967 | *Orlando Cepeda, StL | First base | 25 HR, 111 RBI†, .325 |
| 1968 | *Bob Gibson, StL | Pitcher | 22–9, 1.12 ERA†, 268 K†, 13 SO†, GG |
| 1969 | Willie McCovey, SF | First base | 45 HR†, 126 RBI†, .320 |
| 1970 | *Johnny Bench, Cin | Catcher | 45 HR†, 148 RBI†, .293, GG |
| 1971 | Joe Torre, StL | Third base | 24 HR, 137 RBI†, .363† |
| 1972 | *Johnny Bench, Cin | Catcher | 40 HR†, 125 RBI†, .270, GG |
| 1973 | *Pete Rose, Cin | Outfield | 5 HR, 64 RBI, .338†, 230 hits† |
| 1974 | *Steve Garvey, LA | First base | 21 HR, 111 RBI, 200 hits, .312, GG |
| 1975 | *Joe Morgan, Cin | Second base | 17 HR, 94 RBI, 67 SB, .327, GG |
| 1976 | *Joe Morgan, Cin | Second base | 27 HR, 111 RBI, 60 SB, .320, GG |
| 1977 | George Foster, Cin | Outfield | 52 HR†, 149 RBI†, .320 |
| 1978 | Dave Parker, Pitt | Outfield | 30 HR, 117 RBI, .334†, GG |
| 1979 | Keith Hernandez, StL | First base | 11 HR, 105 RBI, 210 hits, .344†, GG |
| | *Willie Stargell, Pitt | First base | 32 HR, 82 RBI, .281 |
| 1980 | *Mike Schmidt, Phi | Third base | 48 HR†, 121 RBI†, .286, GG |
| 1981 | Mike Schmidt, Phi | Third base | 31 HR†, 91 RBI†, 78 runs†, .316, GG |
| 1982 | *Dale Murphy, Atl | Outfield | 36 HR, 109 RBI‡, .281, GG |
| 1983 | Dale Murphy, Atl | Outfield | 36 HR, 121 RBI†, .302, GG |
| 1984 | *Ryne Sandberg, Chi | Second base | 19 HR, 84 RBI, 114 runs†, .314, GG |
| 1985 | *Willie McGee, StL | Outfield | 10 HR, 82 RBI, 18 3B†, .353†, GG |
| 1986 | Mike Schmidt, Phi | Third base | 37 HR†, 119 RBI†, .290, GG |
| 1987 | Andre Dawson, Chi | Outfield | 49 HR†, 137 RBI†, .287, GG |
| 1988 | *Kirk Gibson, LA | Outfield | 25 HR, 76 RBI, 106 runs, .290 |
| 1989 | *Kevin Mitchell, SF | Outfield | 47 HR†, 125 RBI†, .291 |
| 1990 | *Barry Bonds, Pitt | Outfield | 33 HR, 114 RBI, .301 |
| 1991 | *Terry Pendleton, Atl | Third base | 23 HR, 86 RBI, .319† |
| 1992 | Barry Bonds, Pitt | Outfield | 34 HR, 103 RBI, .311 |
| 1993 | Barry Bonds, SF | Outfield | 46 HR†, 123 RBI†, .336 |
| 1994 | Jeff Bagwell, Hou | First base | 39 HR, 116 RBI†, .368 |
| 1995 | *Barry Larkin, Cin | Shortstop | 15 HR, 66 RBI, 51 SB, .319 |
| 1996 | *Ken Caminiti, SD | Third base | 40 HR, 130 RBI, .326 |
| 1997 | Larry Walker, Col | Outfield | 49 HR†, 130 RBI, .452 OBA†, .366, GG |
| 1998 | Sammy Sosa, Chi | Outfield | 66 HR, 158 RBI†, 134 runs†, 416 TB†, .308 |
| 1999 | *Chipper Jones, Atl | Third Base | 45 HR, 110 RBI, 116 runs, .319 |
| 2000 | *Jeff Kent, SF | Second Base | 33 HR, 125 RBI, 114 runs, .334 |
| 2001 | Barry Bonds, SF | Outfield | 73 HR†, 137 RBI. 177 BB†, .328, .863 SLG† |
| 2002 | *Barry Bonds, SF | Outfield | 46 HR, 110 RBI, .582 OBP, 198 BB†, .370 |
| 2003 | *Barry Bonds, SF | Outfield | 45 HR, .341, .529 OBP†, .749 SLG† |
| 2004 | Barry Bonds, SF | Outfield | 45HR, 101 RBI, .609 OBP, .812 SLG |
| 2005 | *Albert Pujols, StL | First Base | 41 HR, 117 RBI, .330, .430 OBP†, .609 SLG† |
| 2006 | Ryan Howard, Phi | First Base | 58 HR, 149 RBI†, .313, .425 OBP, .659 SLG |
| 2007 | *Jimmy Rollins, Phi | Shortstop | 30 HR, 94 RBI, .296, 139 runs†, 41 SB, GG |
| 2008 | Albert Pujols, StL | First Base | 37HR, 116RBI, 100 runs, .357, .653 SLG† |
| 2009 | *Albert Pujols, StL | First Base | 47HR†, 135RBI, 124 runs†, .327, .658 SLG† |
| 2010 | *Joey Votto, Cin | First Base | 37HR, 113RBI, 106 runs, .324, .600 SLG† |

*Played for pennant or, after 1968, division winner. †Led league. ‡Tied for league lead.

## Most Valuable Players *(Cont.)*

### AMERICAN LEAGUE

| Year | Name and Team | Position | Noteworthy |
|------|---------------|----------|------------|
| 1911 | Ty Cobb, Det | Outfield | 8 HR, 144 RBI†, 24 3B†, .420† |
| 1912 | *Tris Speaker, Bos | Outfield | 10 HR‡, 98 RBI, 53 2B†, .383 . |
| 1913 | Walter Johnson, Wash | Pitcher | 36†–7, 1.09 ERA†, 11 SO†, 243 K† |
| 1914 | *Eddie Collins, Phi | Second base | 2 HR, 85 RBI, 122 runs†, .344 |
| 1915–21 | No selection | | |
| 1922 | George Sisler, StL | First base | 8 HR, 105 RBI, 246 hits†, .420† |
| 1923 | *Babe Ruth, NY | Outfield | 41 HR†, 131 RBI†, .393 |
| 1924 | *Walter Johnson, Wash | Pitcher | 23†–7, 2.72 ERA†, 158 K† |
| 1925 | *Roger Peckinpaugh, Wash | Shortstop | 4 HR, 64 RBI, .294 |
| 1926 | George Burns, Clev | First base | 114 RBI, 216 hits‡, 64 2B‡, .358 |
| 1927 | *Lou Gehrig, NY | First base | 47 HR, 175 RBI†, 52 2B†, .373 |
| 1928 | Mickey Cochrane, Phi | Catcher | 10 HR, 57 RBI, .293 |
| 1929 | No selection | | |
| 1930 | No selection | | |
| 1931 | *Lefty Grove, Phi | Pitcher | 31†–4, 2.06 ERA†, 175 K† |
| 1932 | Jimmie Foxx, Phi | First base | 58 HR†, 169 RBI†, 151 runs†, .364 |
| 1933 | Jimmie Foxx, Phi | First base | 48 HR†, 163 RBI†, .356† |
| 1934 | *Mickey Cochrane, Det | Catcher | 2 HR, 76 RBI, .320 |
| 1935 | *Hank Greenberg, Det | First base | 36 HR‡, 170 RBI†, 203 hits, .328 |
| 1936 | *Lou Gehrig, NY | First base | 49 HR†, 152 RBI, 167 runs†, .354 |
| 1937 | Charlie Gehringer, Det | Second base | 14 HR, 96 RBI, 133 runs, .371† |
| 1938 | Jimmie Foxx, Bos | First base | 50 HR, 175 RBI†, .349† |
| 1939 | *Joe DiMaggio, NY | Outfield | 30 HR, 126 RBI, .381† |
| 1940 | *Hank Greenberg, Det | Outfield | 41 HR†, 150 RBI†, 50 2B†, .340 |
| 1941 | *Joe DiMaggio, NY | Outfield | 30 HR, 125 RBI†, .357 |
| 1942 | *Joe Gordon, NY | Second base | 18 HR, 103 RBI, .322 |
| 1943 | *Spud Chandler, NY | Pitcher | 20†–4, 1.64 ERA†, 5 SO‡ |
| 1944 | Hal Newhouser, Det | Pitcher | 29†–9, 2.22 ERA†, 187 K† |
| 1945 | *Hal Newhouser, Det | Pitcher | 25†–9, 1.81 ERA†, 8 SO†, 212 K† |
| 1946 | *Ted Williams, Bos | Outfield | 38 HR, 123 RBI, 142 runs†, .342 |
| 1947 | *Joe DiMaggio, NY | Outfield | 20 HR, 97 RBI, .315 |
| 1948 | *Lou Boudreau, Clev | Shortstop | 18 HR, 106 RBI, .355 |
| 1949 | Ted Williams, Bos | Outfield | 43 HR†, 159 RBI‡, 150 runs†, .343 |
| 1950 | *Phil Rizzuto, NY | Shortstop | 125 runs, 200 hits, .324 |
| 1951 | *Yogi Berra, NY | Catcher | 27 HR, 88 RBI, .294 |
| 1952 | Bobby Shantz, Phi | Pitcher | 24†–7, 2.48 ERA |
| 1953 | Al Rosen, Clev | Third base | 43 HR†, 145 RBI†, 115 runs†, .336 |
| 1954 | Yogi Berra, NY | Catcher | 22 HR, 125 RBI, .307 |
| 1955 | *Yogi Berra, NY | Catcher | 27 HR, 108 RBI, .272 |
| 1956 | *Mickey Mantle, NY | Outfield | 52 HR†, 130 RBI†, 132 runs†, .353† |
| 1957 | *Mickey Mantle, NY | Outfield | 34 HR, 94 RBI, 121 runs†, .365 |
| 1958 | Jackie Jensen, Bos | Outfield | 35 HR, 122 RBI†, .286 |
| 1959 | *Nellie Fox, Chi | Second base | 2 HR, 70 RBI, .306, GG |
| 1960 | *Roger Maris, NY | Outfield | 39 HR, 112 RBI†, .283, GG |
| 1961 | *Roger Maris, NY | Outfield | 61 HR†, 142 RBI†, .269 |
| 1962 | *Mickey Mantle, NY | Outfield | 30 HR, 89 RBI, .321, GG |
| 1963 | *Elston Howard, NY | Catcher | 28 HR, 85 RBI, .287, GG |
| 1964 | Brooks Robinson, Balt | Third base | 28 HR, 118 RBI†, .317, GG |
| 1965 | *Zoilo Versalles, Minn | Shortstop | 126 runs†, 45 2B‡, 12 3B‡, GG |
| 1966 | *Frank Robinson, Balt | Outfield | 49 HR†, 122 RBI†, 122 runs†, .316† |
| 1967 | *Carl Yastrzemski, Bos | Outfield | 44 HR†, 121 RBI†, 112 runs†, .326†, GG |
| 1968 | *Denny McLain, Det | Pitcher | 31†–6, 1.96 ERA, 280 K |
| 1969 | *Harmon Killebrew, Minn | Third base, First base | 49 HR†, 140 RBI†, .276 |
| 1970 | *Boog Powell, Balt | First base | 35 HR, 114 RBI, .297 |
| 1971 | *Vida Blue, Oak | Pitcher | 24–8, 1.82 ERA†, 8 SO†, 301 K |
| 1972 | Dick Allen, Chi | First base | 37 HR†, 113 RBI†, .308 |
| 1973 | *Reggie Jackson, Oak | Outfield | 32 HR†, 117 RBI†, 99 runs†, .293 |
| 1974 | Jeff Burroughs, Tex | Outfield | 25 HR, 118 RBI†, .301 |
| 1975 | *Fred Lynn, Bos | Outfield | 21 HR, 105 RBI, 103 runs†, .331, GG |
| 1976 | *Thurman Munson, NY | Catcher | 17 HR, 105 RBI, .302 |
| 1977 | Rod Carew, Minn | First base | 100 RBI, 128 runs†, 239 hits†, .388† |
| 1978 | Jim Rice, Bos | Outfield, DH | 46 HR†, 139 RBI†, 213 hits†, .315 |
| 1979 | *Don Baylor, Calif | Outfield, DH | 36 HR, 139 RBI†, 120 runs†, .296 |
| 1980 | *George Brett, KC | Third base | 24 HR, 118 RBI, .390† |
| 1981 | *Rollie Fingers, Mil | Pitcher | 6–3, 28 saves†, 1.04 ERA |
| 1982 | *Robin Yount, Mil | Shortstop | 29 HR, 114 RBI, 210 hits†, .331, GG |
| 1983 | *Cal Ripken Jr., Balt | Shortstop | 27 HR, 102 RBI, 121 runs†, 211 hits†, .318 |

### Most Valuable Players *(Cont.)*
#### AMERICAN LEAGUE *(Cont.)*

| Year | Name and Team | Position | Noteworthy |
|------|---------------|----------|------------|
| 1984 | *Willie Hernandez, Det | Pitcher | 9–3, 32 saves, 1.92 ERA |
| 1985 | Don Mattingly, NY | First base | 35 HR, 145 RBI†, 48 2B†, .324, GG |
| 1986 | *Roger Clemens, Bos | Pitcher | 24†–4, 2.48 ERA†, 238 K |
| 1987 | George Bell, Tor | Outfield | 47 HR, 134 RBI†, .308 |
| 1988 | *Jose Canseco, Oak | Outfield | 42 HR†, 124 RBI†, 40 SB, .307 |
| 1989 | Robin Yount, Mil | Outfield | 21 HR, 103 RBI, 101 runs, .318 |
| 1990 | *Rickey Henderson, Oak | Outfield | 28 HR, 119 runs†, 65 SB†, .325 |
| 1991 | Cal Ripken Jr., Balt | Shortstop | 34 HR, 114 RBI, .323 |
| 1992 | Dennis Eckersley, Oak | Pitcher | 7–1, 1.91 ERA, 51 saves |
| 1993 | Frank Thomas, Chi | First base | 41 HR, 128 RBI, .317 |
| 1994 | Frank Thomas, Chi | First base | 38 HR, 101 RBI, .353 |
| 1995 | *Mo Vaughn, Bos | First base | 39 HR, 126 RBI, .300 |
| 1996 | *Juan Gonzalez, Tex | Outfield | 47 HR, 144 RBI, .314 |
| 1997 | *Ken Griffey Jr., Sea | Outfield | 56 HR†, 125 runs†, 393 TB†, 147 RBI†, .304 |
| 1998 | *Juan Gonzalez, Tex | Outfield | 45 HR, 157 RBI†, 50 2B†, .318 |
| 1999 | *Ivan Rodriguez, Tex | Catcher | 35 HR, 113 RBI, 116 runs, .332, GG |
| 2000 | *Jason Giambi, Oak | First Base | 43 HR, 137 RBI, .333 |
| 2001 | *Ichiro Suzuki, Sea | Outfield | .350†, 242 H†, 127 runs, 56 SB†, GG |
| 2002 | *Miguel Tejada, Oak | Shortstop | 34 HR, 131 RBI, .308 |
| 2003 | Alex Rodriguez, Tex | Shortstop | 47 HR†, 118 RBI, .600 SLG†, GG |
| 2004 | *Vladimir Guerrero, Ana | Outfield | 39 HR, 126 RBI, .598 SLG |
| 2005 | *Alex Rodriguez, NYY | Third Base | 48 HR†, 130 RBI, .610 SLG† |
| 2006 | *Justin Morneau, Min | First Base | 30 HR, 130 RBI, .321, 190 hits |
| 2007 | Alex Rodriguez, NYY | Third Base | 54 HR, 156 RBI, .314, 183 hits, 24 SB |
| 2008 | Dustin Pedroia, Bos | Second Base | 17 HR, 118 runs, 213 hits, .326, 20 SB, GG |
| 2009 | *Joe Mauer, Min | Catcher | 28 HR, 94 runs, 96 RBIs, 191 hits, .365, GG |
| 2010 | *Josh Hamilton, Tex | Outfield | 32 HR, 100 RBI, 95 runs, .359†, .633 SLG† |

*Played for pennant or, after 1968, division winner. †Led league. ‡Tied for league lead.
Notes: 2B=doubles; 3B=triples; FA=fielding average; GG=won Gold Glove, award begun in 1957;
K=strikeouts; O=shutouts; SB=stolen bases; TB=total bases.

### Rookies of the Year

| | NATIONAL LEAGUE | | AMERICAN LEAGUE |
|------|-----------------|------|-----------------|
| 1947* | Jackie Robinson, Bklyn (1B) | 1949 | Roy Sievers, StL (OF) |
| 1948* | Alvin Dark, Bos (SS) | 1950 | Walt Dropo, Bos (1B) |
| 1949 | Don Newcombe, Bklyn (P) | 1951 | Gil McDougald, NY (3B) |
| 1950 | Sam Jethroe, Bos (OF) | 1952 | Harry Byrd, Phi (P) |
| 1951 | Willie Mays, NY (OF) | 1953 | Harvey Kuenn, Det (SS) |
| 1952 | Joe Black, Bklyn (P) | 1954 | Bob Grim, NY (P) |
| 1953 | Junior Gilliam, Bklyn (2B) | 1955 | Herb Score, Clev (P) |
| 1954 | Wally Moon, StL (OF) | 1956 | Luis Aparicio, Chi (SS) |
| 1955 | Bill Virdon, StL (OF) | 1957 | Tony Kubek, NY (OF, SS) |
| 1956 | Frank Robinson, Cin (OF) | 1958 | Albie Pearson, Wash (OF) |
| 1957 | Jack Sanford, Phi (P) | 1959 | Bob Allison, Wash (OF) |
| 1958 | Orlando Cepeda, SF (1B) | 1960 | Ron Hansen, Balt (SS) |
| 1959 | Willie McCovey, SF (1B) | 1961 | Don Schwall, Bos (P) |
| 1960 | Frank Howard, LA (OF) | 1962 | Tom Tresh, NY (SS) |
| 1961 | Billy Williams, Chi (OF) | 1963 | Gary Peters, Chi (P) |
| 1962 | Ken Hubbs, Chi (2B) | 1964 | Tony Oliva, Minn (OF) |
| 1963 | Pete Rose, Cin (2B) | 1965 | Curt Blefary, Balt (OF) |
| 1964 | Dick Allen, Phi (3B) | 1966 | Tommie Agee, Chi (OF) |
| 1965 | Jim Lefebvre, LA (2B) | 1967 | Rod Carew, Minn (2B) |
| 1966 | Tommy Helms, Cin (2B) | 1968 | Stan Bahnsen, NY (P) |
| 1967 | Tom Seaver, NY (P) | 1969 | Lou Piniella, KC (OF) |
| 1968 | Johnny Bench, Cin (C) | 1970 | Thurman Munson, NY (C) |
| 1969 | Ted Sizemore, LA (2B) | 1971 | Chris Chambliss, Clev (1B) |
| 1970 | Carl Morton, Mtl(P) | 1972 | Carlton Fisk, Bos (C) |
| 1971 | Earl Williams, Atl (C) | 1973 | Al Bumbry, Balt (OF) |
| 1972 | Jon Matlack, NY (P) | 1974 | Mike Hargrove, Tex (1B) |
| 1973 | Gary Matthews, SF (OF) | 1975 | Fred Lynn, Bos (OF) |
| 1974 | Bake McBride, StL (OF) | 1976 | Mark Fidrych, Det (P) |
| 1975 | John Montefusco, SF (P) | 1977 | Eddie Murray, Balt (DH) |
| 1976 | Pat Zachry, Cin (P) | 1978 | Lou Whitaker, Det (2B) |
| | Butch Metzger, SD (P) | 1979 | Alfredo Griffin, Tor (SS) |
| 1977 | Andre Dawson, Mtl (OF) | | John Castino, Minn (3B) |
| 1978 | Bob Horner, Atl (3B) | 1980 | Joe Charboneau, Clev (OF) |

*Just one selection for both leagues.

## Rookies of the Year *(Cont.)*

### NATIONAL LEAGUE *(Cont.)*

| | |
|---|---|
| 1979 | Rick Sutcliffe, LA (P) |
| 1980 | Steve Howe, LA (P) |
| 1981 | Fernando Valenzuela, LA (P) |
| 1982 | Steve Sax, LA (2B) |
| 1983 | Darryl Strawberry, NY (OF) |
| 1984 | Dwight Gooden, NY (P) |
| 1985 | Vince Coleman, StL (OF) |
| 1986 | Todd Worrell, StL (P) |
| 1987 | Benito Santiago, SD (C) |
| 1988 | Chris Sabo, Cin (3B) |
| 1989 | Jerome Walton, Chi (OF) |
| 1990 | Dave Justice, Atl (OF) |
| 1991 | Jeff Bagwell, Hou (3B) |
| 1992 | Eric Karros, LA (1B) |
| 1993 | Mike Piazza, LA (C) |
| 1994 | Raul Mondesi, LA (OF) |
| 1995 | Hideo Nomo, LA (P) |
| 1996 | Todd Hollandsworth, LA (OF) |
| 1997 | Scott Rolen, Phi (3B) |
| 1998 | Kerry Wood, Chi (P) |
| 1999 | Scott Williamson, Cin (P) |
| 2000 | Rafael Furcal, Atl (SS) |
| 2001 | Albert Pujols, StL (OF) |
| 2002 | Jason Jennings, Col (P) |
| 2003 | Dontrelle Willis, Fla (P) |
| 2004 | Jason Bay, Pit (OF) |
| 2005 | Ryan Howard, Phi (1B) |
| 2006 | Hanley Ramirez, Fla (SS) |
| 2007 | Ryan Braun, Mil (OF) |
| 2008 | Geovany Soto, Chi (C) |
| 2009 | Chris Coghlan, Fla (OF) |
| 2010 | Buster Posey, SF (C) |

### AMERICAN LEAGUE *(Cont.)*

| | |
|---|---|
| 1981 | Dave Righetti, NY (P) |
| 1982 | Cal Ripken Jr., Balt (SS) |
| 1983 | Ron Kittle, Chi (OF) |
| 1984 | Alvin Davis, Sea (1B) |
| 1985 | Ozzie Guillen, Chi (SS) |
| 1986 | Jose Canseco, Oak (OF) |
| 1987 | Mark McGwire, Oak (1B) |
| 1988 | Walt Weiss, Oak (SS) |
| 1989 | Gregg Olson, Balt (P) |
| 1990 | Sandy Alomar Jr, Clev (C) |
| 1991 | Chuck Knoblauch, Minn (2B) |
| 1992 | Pat Listach, Mil (SS) |
| 1993 | Tim Salmon, Calif (OF) |
| 1994 | Bob Hamelin, KC (DH) |
| 1995 | Marty Cordova, Minn (OF) |
| 1996 | Derek Jeter, NY (SS) |
| 1997 | Nomar Garciaparra, Bos (SS) |
| 1998 | Ben Grieve, Oak (OF) |
| 1999 | Carlos Beltran, KC (OF) |
| 2000 | Kazuhiro Sasaki, Sea (P) |
| 2001 | Ichiro Suzuki, Sea (OF) |
| 2002 | Eric Hinske, Tor (3B) |
| 2003 | Angel Berroa, KC (SS) |
| 2004 | Bobby Crosby, Oak (SS) |
| 2005 | Huston Street, Oak (P) |
| 2006 | Justin Verlander, Det (P) |
| 2007 | Dustin Pedroia, Bos (2B) |
| 2008 | Evan Longoria, TB (3B) |
| 2009 | Andrew Bailey, Oak (P) |
| 2010 | Neftali Feliz, Tex (P) |

## 2010 Gold Glove winners

### NATIONAL LEAGUE

| | |
|---|---|
| C | Yadier Molina, StL (3) |
| P | Bronson Arroyo, Cin |
| 1B | Albert Pujols (2) |
| 2B | Brandon Phillips, Cin (2) |
| SS | Troy Tulowitzki, Col |
| 3B | Scott Rolen, Cin (8) |
| OF | Carlos Gonzalez, Col |
| OF | Michael Bourn, Hou (2) |
| OF | Shane Victorino, Phi (3) |

### AMERICAN LEAGUE

| | |
|---|---|
| C | Joe Mauer, Min (3) |
| P | Mark Buehrle, Chi (2) |
| 1B | Mark Teixeira, NY (4) |
| 2B | Robinson Cano, NY |
| SS | Derek Jeter, NY (5) |
| 3B | Evan Longoria, TB (2) |
| OF | Ichiro Suzuki, Sea (10) |
| OF | Franklin Gutierrez, Sea |
| OF | Carl Crawford, TB |

Note: Number in parentheses indicates career totals.

## 2010 Silver Slugger winners

### NATIONAL LEAGUE

| | |
|---|---|
| C | Brian McCann, Atl (4) |
| P | Yovani Gallardo, Mil |
| 1B | Albert Pujols, StL (6) |
| 2B | Dan Uggla, Fla |
| SS | Troy Tulowitzki, Col |
| 3B | Ryan Zimmerman, Was (2) |
| OF | Carlos Gonzalez, Col |
| OF | Ryan Braun, Mil (3) |
| OF | Matt Holliday, StL (4) |

### AMERICAN LEAGUE

| | |
|---|---|
| C | Joe Mauer, Min (4) |
| DH | Vladimir Guerrero, Tex (8) |
| 1B | Miguel Cabrera, Det (3) |
| 2B | Robinson Cano, NY (2) |
| SS | Alexei Ramirez, Chi |
| 3B | Adrian Beltre, Bos (2) |
| OF | Carl Crawford, TB |
| OF | Jose Bautista, Tor |
| OF | Josh Hamilton, Tex (2) |

Note: Number in parentheses indicates career totals.

## Cy Young Award

| Year | W–L | Sv | ERA | Year | W–L | Sv | ERA |
|---|---|---|---|---|---|---|---|
| 1956....*Don Newcombe, Bklyn (NL) | 27–7 | 0 | 3.06 | 1962....Don Drysdale, LA (NL) | 25–9 | 1 | 2.83 |
| 1957....Warren Spahn, Mil (NL) | 21–11 | 3 | 2.69 | 1963....*Sandy Koufax, LA (NL) | 25–5 | 0 | 1.88 |
| 1958....Bob Turley, NY (AL) | 21–7 | 1 | 2.97 | 1964....Dean Chance, LA (AL) | 20–9 | 4 | 1.65 |
| 1959....Early Wynn, Chi (AL) | 22–10 | 0 | 3.17 | 1965....Sandy Koufax, LA (NL) | 26–8 | 2 | 2.04 |
| 1960....Vernon Law, Pitt (NL) | 20–9 | 0 | 3.08 | 1966....Sandy Koufax, LA (NL) | 27–9 | 0 | 1.73 |
| 1961....Whitey Ford, NY (AL) | 25–4 | 0 | 3.21 | | | | |

### NATIONAL LEAGUE

| Year | W–L | Sv | ERA |
|---|---|---|---|
| 1967.....Mike McCormick, SF | 22–10 | 0 | 2.85 |
| 1968.....*Bob Gibson, StL | 22–9 | 0 | 1.12 |
| 1969.....Tom Seaver, NY | 25–7 | 0 | 2.21 |
| 1970.....Bob Gibson, StL | 23–7 | 0 | 3.12 |
| 1971.....Ferguson Jenkins, Chi | 24–13 | 0 | 2.77 |
| 1972.....Steve Carlton, Phi | 27–10 | 0 | 1.97 |
| 1973.....Tom Seaver, NY | 19–10 | 0 | 2.08 |
| 1974.....Mike Marshall, LA | 15–12 | 21 | 2.42 |
| 1975.....Tom Seaver, NY | 22–9 | 0 | 2.38 |
| 1976.....Randy Jones, SD | 22–14 | 0 | 2.74 |
| 1977.....Steve Carlton, Phi | 23–10 | 0 | 2.64 |
| 1978.....Gaylord Perry, SD | 21–6 | 0 | 2.72 |
| 1979.....Bruce Sutter, Chi | 6–6 | 37 | 2.23 |
| 1980.....Steve Carlton, Phi | 24–9 | 0 | 2.34 |
| 1981.....Fernando Valenzuela, LA | 13–7 | 0 | 2.48 |
| 1982.....Steve Carlton, Phi | 23–11 | 0 | 3.10 |
| 1983.....John Denny, Phi | 19–6 | 0 | 2.37 |
| 1984.....†Rick Sutcliffe, Chi | 16–1 | 0 | 2.69 |
| 1985.....Dwight Gooden, NY | 24–4 | 0 | 1.53 |
| 1986.....Mike Scott, Hou | 18–10 | 0 | 2.22 |
| 1987.....Steve Bedrosian, Phi | 5–3 | 40 | 2.83 |
| 1988.....Orel Hershiser, LA | 23–8 | 1 | 2.26 |
| 1989.....Mark Davis, SD | 4–3 | 44 | 1.85 |
| 1990.....Doug Drabek, Pitt | 22–6 | 0 | 2.76 |
| 1991.....Tom Glavine, Atl | 20–11 | 0 | 2.55 |
| 1992.....Greg Maddux, Chi | 20–11 | 0 | 2.18 |
| 1993.....Greg Maddux, Atl | 20–10 | 0 | 2.36 |
| 1994.....Greg Maddux, Atl | 16–6 | 0 | 1.56 |
| 1995.....Greg Maddux, Atl | 19–2 | 0 | 1.63 |
| 1996.....John Smoltz, Atl | 24–8 | 0 | 2.94 |
| 1997.....Pedro Martinez, Mtl | 17–8 | 0 | 1.90 |
| 1998.....Tom Glavine, Atl | 20–6 | 0 | 2.47 |
| 1999.....Randy Johnson, Ari | 17–9 | 0 | 2.48 |
| 2000.....Randy Johnson, Ari | 19–7 | 0 | 2.64 |
| 2001.....Randy Johnson, Ari | 21–6 | 0 | 2.49 |
| 2002.....Randy Johnson, Ari | 24–5 | 0 | 2.32 |
| 2003.....Eric Gagne, LA | 2–3 | 55 | 1.20 |
| 2004.....Roger Clemens, Hou | 18–4 | 0 | 2.98 |
| 2005.....Chris Carpenter, StL | 21–5 | 0 | 2.83 |
| 2006.....Brandon Webb, Ari | 16–8 | 0 | 3.10 |
| 2007.....Jake Peavy, SD | 19–6 | 0 | 2.54 |
| 2008.....Tim Lincecum, SF | 18–5 | 0 | 2.62 |
| 2009.....Tim Lincecum, SF | 15–7 | 0 | 2.48 |
| 2010.....Roy Halladay, Phi | 21–10 | 0 | 2.44 |

### AMERICAN LEAGUE

| Year | W–L | Sv | ERA |
|---|---|---|---|
| 1967.....Jim Lonborg, Bos | 22–9 | 0 | 3.16 |
| 1968.....*Denny McLain, Det | 31–6 | 0 | 1.96 |
| 1969.....Denny McLain, Det | 24–9 | 0 | 2.80 |
| | Mike Cuellar, Balt | 23–11 | 0 | 2.38 |
| 1970.....Jim Perry, Minn | 24–12 | 0 | 3.03 |
| 1971.....*Vida Blue, Oak | 24–8 | 0 | 1.82 |
| 1972.....Gaylord Perry, Clev | 24–16 | 1 | 1.92 |
| 1973.....Jim Palmer, Balt | 22–9 | 1 | 2.40 |
| 1974.....Catfish Hunter, Oak | 25–12 | 0 | 2.49 |
| 1975.....Jim Palmer, Balt | 23–11 | 1 | 2.09 |
| 1976.....Jim Palmer, Balt | 22–13 | 0 | 2.51 |
| 1977.....Sparky Lyle, NY | 13–5 | 26 | 2.17 |
| 1978.....Ron Guidry, NY | 25–3 | 0 | 1.74 |
| 1979.....Mike Flanagan, Balt | 23–9 | 0 | 3.08 |
| 1980.....Steve Stone, Balt | 25–7 | 0 | 3.23 |
| 1981.....*Rollie Fingers, Mil | 6–3 | 28 | 1.04 |
| 1982.....Pete Vuckovich, Mil | 18–6 | 0 | 3.34 |
| 1983.....LaMarr Hoyt, Chi | 24–10 | 0 | 3.66 |
| 1984.....*Willie Hernandez, Det | 9–3 | 32 | 1.92 |
| 1985.....Bret Saberhagen, KC | 20–6 | 0 | 2.87 |
| 1986.....*Roger Clemens, Bos | 24–4 | 0 | 2.48 |
| 1987.....Roger Clemens, Bos | 20–9 | 0 | 2.97 |
| 1988.....Frank Viola, Minn | 24–7 | 0 | 2.64 |
| 1989.....Bret Saberhagen, KC | 23–6 | 0 | 2.16 |
| 1990.....Bob Welch, Oak | 27–6 | 0 | 2.95 |
| 1991.....Roger Clemens, Bos | 18–10 | 0 | 2.62 |
| 1992.....*Dennis Eckersley, Oak | 7–1 | 51 | 1.91 |
| 1993.....Jack McDowell, Chi | 22–10 | 0 | 3.37 |
| 1994.....David Cone, KC | 16–4 | 0 | 2.94 |
| 1995.....Randy Johnson, Sea | 18–2 | 0 | 2.48 |
| 1996.....Pat Hentgen, Tor | 20–10 | 0 | 3.22 |
| 1997.....Roger Clemens, Tor | 21–7 | 0 | 2.05 |
| 1998.....Roger Clemens, Tor | 20–6 | 0 | 2.65 |
| 1999.....Pedro Martinez, Bos | 23–4 | 0 | 1.55 |
| 2000.....Pedro Martinez, Bos | 18–6 | 0 | 1.74 |
| 2001.....Roger Clemens, NY | 20–3 | 0 | 3.51 |
| 2002.....Barry Zito, Oak | 23–5 | 0 | 2.75 |
| 2003.....Roy Halladay, Tor | 22–7 | 0 | 3.25 |
| 2004.....Johan Santana, Min | 20–6 | 0 | 2.61 |
| 2005.....Bartolo Colon, LA | 21–8 | 0 | 3.48 |
| 2006.....Johan Santana, Min | 19–6 | 0 | 2.77 |
| 2007.....C.C. Sabathia, Cle | 19–7 | 0 | 3.21 |
| 2008.....Cliff Lee, Cle | 22–3 | 0 | 2.54 |
| 2009.....Zack Greinke, KC | 16–8 | 0 | 2.16 |
| 2010.....Felix Hernandez, Sea | 13–12 | 0 | 2.27 |

*Won the MVP and Cy Young awards in the same season.
†NL games only. Sutcliffe pitched 15 games with Cleveland before being traded to the Cubs.

## Career Individual Batting

### GAMES

| | |
|---|---|
| Pete Rose | 3562 |
| Carl Yastrzemski | 3308 |
| Hank Aaron | 3298 |
| Rickey Henderson | 3081 |
| Ty Cobb | 3034 |
| Eddie Murray | 3026 |
| Stan Musial | 3026 |
| Cal Ripken Jr. | 3001 |
| Willie Mays | 2992 |
| Dave Winfield | 2973 |
| Rusty Staub | 2951 |
| Brooks Robinson | 2896 |
| Robin Yount | 2856 |
| Craig Biggio | 2850 |
| Al Kaline | 2834 |
| Rafael Palmeiro | 2831 |
| Harold Baines | 2830 |
| Eddie Collins | 2826 |
| Reggie Jackson | 2820 |
| Frank Robinson | 2808 |
| Honus Wagner | 2792 |

### AT BATS

| | |
|---|---|
| Pete Rose | 14053 |
| Hank Aaron | 12364 |
| Carl Yastrzemski | 11988 |
| Cal Ripken Jr. | 11551 |
| Ty Cobb | 11434 |
| Eddie Murray | 11336 |
| Robin Yount | 11008 |
| Dave Winfield | 11003 |
| Stan Musial | 10972 |
| Rickey Henderson | 10961 |
| Willie Mays | 10881 |
| Craig Biggio | 10876 |
| Paul Molitor | 10835 |
| Brooks Robinson | 10654 |
| Rafael Palmeiro | 10472 |
| *Omar Vizquel | 10433 |
| Honus Wagner | 10430 |
| George Brett | 10349 |

### RUNS

| | |
|---|---|
| Rickey Henderson | 2295 |
| Ty Cobb | 2246 |
| Barry Bonds | 2227 |
| Hank Aaron | 2174 |
| Babe Ruth | 2174 |
| Pete Rose | 2165 |
| Willie Mays | 2062 |
| Cap Anson | 1996 |
| Stan Musial | 1949 |
| Lou Gehrig | 1888 |
| Tris Speaker | 1882 |
| Mel Ott | 1859 |
| Craig Biggio | 1834 |
| Frank Robinson | 1829 |
| *Alex Rodriguez | 1824 |
| Eddie Collins | 1821 |
| Carl Yastrzemski | 1816 |
| Ted Williams | 1798 |
| Paul Molitor | 1782 |
| Charlie Gehringer | 1774 |
| *Derek Jeter | 1769 |

### BATTING AVERAGE (5,000 AB)

| | |
|---|---|
| Ty Cobb | .367 |
| Rogers Hornsby | .358 |
| Ed Delahanty | .346 |
| Tris Speaker | .345 |
| Billy Hamilton | .344 |
| Ted Williams | .344 |
| Dan Brouthers | .342 |
| Harry Heilmann | .342 |
| Babe Ruth | .342 |
| Willie Keeler | .341 |
| Bill Terry | .341 |
| Lou Gehrig | .340 |
| George Sisler | .340 |
| Jesse Burkett | .338 |
| Tony Gwynn | .338 |
| Nap Lajoie | .338 |
| Al Simmons | .334 |
| Cap Anson | .333 |
| Eddie Collins | .333 |
| Paul Waner | .333 |
| Sam Thompson | .331 |
| Heinie Manush | .330 |
| *Albert Pujols | .328 |
| Wade Boggs | .328 |
| Rod Carew | .328 |
| Honus Wagner | .327 |

### HOME RUNS

| | |
|---|---|
| Barry Bonds | 762 |
| Hank Aaron | 755 |
| Babe Ruth | 714 |
| Willie Mays | 660 |
| Ken Griffey Jr. | 630 |
| *Alex Rodriguez | 629 |
| Sammy Sosa | 609 |
| *Jim Thome | 604 |
| Frank Robinson | 586 |
| Mark McGwire | 583 |
| Harmon Killebrew | 573 |
| Rafael Palmeiro | 569 |
| Reggie Jackson | 563 |
| *Manny Ramirez | 555 |
| Mike Schmidt | 548 |
| Mickey Mantle | 536 |
| Jimmie Foxx | 534 |
| Willie McCovey | 521 |
| Ted Williams | 521 |
| Frank Thomas | 521 |
| Ernie Banks | 512 |
| Eddie Mathews | 512 |
| Mel Ott | 511 |
| Gary Sheffield | 509 |
| Eddie Murray | 504 |
| Lou Gehrig | 493 |
| Fred McGriff | 493 |
| Stan Musial | 475 |
| Willie Stargell | 475 |

### RUNS BATTED IN

| | |
|---|---|
| Hank Aaron | 2297 |
| Babe Ruth | 2213 |
| Cap Anson | 2076 |
| Barry Bonds | 1996 |
| Lou Gehrig | 1995 |
| Stan Musial | 1951 |
| Ty Cobb | 1937 |
| Jimmie Foxx | 1922 |
| Eddie Murray | 1917 |
| Willie Mays | 1903 |
| *Alex Rodriguez | 1893 |
| Mel Ott | 1860 |
| Carl Yastrzemski | 1844 |
| Ted Williams | 1839 |
| Ken Griffey Jr. | 1836 |
| Rafael Palmeiro | 1835 |
| Dave Winfield | 1833 |
| *Manny Ramirez | 1831 |
| Al Simmons | 1827 |
| Frank Robinson | 1812 |
| Honus Wagner | 1732 |
| Frank Thomas | 1704 |
| Reggie Jackson | 1702 |
| Cal Ripken Jr. | 1695 |
| Gary Sheffield | 1676 |
| *Jim Thome | 1674 |

### HITS

| | |
|---|---|
| Pete Rose | 4256 |
| Ty Cobb | 4191 |
| Hank Aaron | 3771 |
| Stan Musial | 3630 |
| Tris Speaker | 3515 |
| Carl Yastrzemski | 3419 |
| Cap Anson | 3418 |
| Honus Wagner | 3415 |
| Paul Molitor | 3319 |
| Eddie Collins | 3313 |
| Willie Mays | 3283 |
| Eddie Murray | 3255 |
| Nap Lajoie | 3251 |
| Cal Ripken Jr. | 3184 |
| George Brett | 3154 |
| Paul Waner | 3152 |
| Robin Yount | 3142 |
| Tony Gwynn | 3141 |
| Dave Winfield | 3110 |
| *Derek Jeter | 3088 |
| Craig Biggio | 3060 |
| Rickey Henderson | 3055 |
| Rod Carew | 3053 |
| Lou Brock | 3023 |
| Rafael Palmeiro | 3020 |
| Wade Boggs | 3010 |
| Al Kaline | 3007 |
| Roberto Clemente | 3000 |

* Active in 2011.

## Career Individual Batting *(Cont.)*

### DOUBLES

| | |
|---|---|
| Tris Speaker | 792 |
| Pete Rose | 746 |
| Stan Musial | 725 |
| Ty Cobb | 724 |
| Craig Biggio | 668 |
| George Brett | 665 |
| Nap Lajoie | 657 |
| Carl Yastrzemski | 646 |
| Honus Wagner | 640 |
| Hank Aaron | 624 |
| Paul Molitor | 605 |
| Paul Waner | 605 |
| Cal Ripken Jr. | 603 |
| Barry Bonds | 601 |
| Luis Gonzalez | 596 |
| Rafael Palmeiro | 585 |
| Robin Yount | 583 |
| Cap Anson | 581 |
| Wade Boggs | 578 |
| Charlie Gehringer | 574 |

### TRIPLES

| | |
|---|---|
| Sam Crawford | 309 |
| Ty Cobb | 295 |
| Honus Wagner | 252 |
| Jake Beckley | 243 |
| Roger Connor | 233 |
| Tris Speaker | 222 |
| Fred Clarke | 220 |
| Dan Brouthers | 205 |
| Joe Kelley | 194 |
| Paul Waner | 191 |
| Bid McPhee | 188 |
| Eddie Collins | 187 |
| Ed Delahanty | 185 |
| Sam Rice | 184 |
| Jesse Burkett | 182 |
| Ed Konetchy | 182 |
| Edd Roush | 182 |
| Buck Ewing | 178 |
| Rabbit Maranville | 177 |
| Stan Musial | 177 |

### BASES ON BALLS

| | |
|---|---|
| Barry Bonds | 2558 |
| Rickey Henderson | 2190 |
| Babe Ruth | 2062 |
| Ted Williams | 2021 |
| Joe Morgan | 1865 |
| Carl Yastrzemski | 1845 |
| Mickey Mantle | 1733 |
| *Jim Thome | 1725 |
| Mel Ott | 1708 |
| Frank Thomas | 1667 |
| Eddie Yost | 1614 |
| Darrell Evans | 1605 |
| Stan Musial | 1599 |
| Pete Rose | 1566 |
| Harmon Killebrew | 1559 |
| Lou Gehrig | 1508 |
| Mike Schmidt | 1507 |
| Eddie Collins | 1499 |
| Gary Sheffield | 1475 |
| Willie Mays | 1464 |
| *Chipper Jones | 1455 |
| Jimmie Foxx | 1452 |
| Eddie Mathews | 1444 |

\* Active in 2011.

### SLUGGING AVERAGE (5,000 AB)

| | |
|---|---|
| Babe Ruth | .690 |
| Ted Williams | .634 |
| Lou Gehrig | .632 |
| *Albert Pujols | .617 |
| Jimmie Foxx | .609 |
| Barry Bonds | .607 |
| Hank Greenberg | .605 |
| Mark McGwire | .588 |
| *Manny Ramirez | .585 |
| Joe Dimaggio | .579 |
| Rogers Hornsby | .577 |
| *Alex Rodriguez | .567 |
| Larry Walker | .565 |
| Albert Belle | .564 |
| Johnny Mize | .562 |
| Juan Gonzalez | .561 |
| Stan Musial | .559 |
| Mickey Mantle | .557 |
| Willie Mays | .557 |
| *Jim Thome | .556 |

### STOLEN BASES

| | |
|---|---|
| Rickey Henderson | 1406 |
| Lou Brock | 938 |
| Billy Hamilton | 912 |
| Ty Cobb | 892 |
| Tim Raines | 808 |
| Vince Coleman | 752 |
| Eddie Collins | 745 |
| Max Carey | 738 |
| Honus Wagner | 722 |
| Joe Morgan | 689 |
| Willie Wilson | 668 |
| Bert Campaneris | 649 |
| Kenny Lofton | 622 |
| Otis Nixon | 620 |
| George Davis | 616 |
| Tom Brown | 615 |
| Dummy Hoy | 594 |
| Maury Wills | 586 |
| George Van Haltren | 583 |
| Ozzie Smith | 580 |

### ON-BASE PERCENTAGE (5,000 AB)

| | |
|---|---|
| Ted Williams | .482 |
| Babe Ruth | .474 |
| Billy Hamilton | .455 |
| Lou Gehrig | .447 |
| Barry Bonds | .444 |
| Rogers Hornsby | .434 |
| Ty Cobb | .433 |
| Jimmie Foxx | .428 |
| Tris Speaker | .428 |
| Eddie Collins | .424 |
| *Todd Helton | .421 |
| Mickey Mantle | .421 |
| *Albert Pujols | .420 |
| Dan Brouthers | .420 |
| Mickey Cochrane | .419 |
| Frank Thomas | .419 |
| Edgar Martinez | .418 |
| Stan Musial | .417 |
| Ed Delahanty | .417 |
| Clarence Childs | .416 |
| Jesse Burkett | .415 |
| Wade Boggs | .415 |
| Mel Ott | .414 |

### TOTAL BASES

| | |
|---|---|
| Hank Aaron | 6856 |
| Stan Musial | 6134 |
| Willie Mays | 6066 |
| Barry Bonds | 5976 |
| Ty Cobb | 5859 |
| Babe Ruth | 5793 |
| Pete Rose | 5752 |
| Carl Yastrzemski | 5539 |
| Eddie Murray | 5397 |
| Rafael Palmeiro | 5388 |
| Frank Robinson | 5373 |
| Ken Griffey Jr. | 5271 |
| Dave Winfield | 5221 |
| *Alex Rodriguez | 5215 |
| Cal Ripken Jr. | 5168 |
| Tris Speaker | 5101 |
| Lou Gehrig | 5060 |
| George Brett | 5044 |
| Mel Ott | 5041 |
| Jimmie Foxx | 4956 |
| Ted Williams | 4884 |

### STRIKEOUTS

| | |
|---|---|
| Reggie Jackson | 2597 |
| *Jim Thome | 2487 |
| Sammy Sosa | 2306 |
| Andres Galarraga | 2003 |
| Jose Canseco | 1942 |
| Willie Stargell | 1936 |
| *Alex Rodriguez | 1916 |
| *Mike Cameron | 1901 |
| Mike Schmidt | 1883 |
| Fred McGriff | 1882 |
| Tony Perez | 1867 |
| Dave Kingman | 1816 |
| *Manny Ramirez | 1813 |
| Ken Griffey Jr. | 1779 |
| Bobby Bonds | 1757 |
| Craig Biggio | 1753 |
| Dale Murphy | 1748 |
| Carlos Delgado | 1745 |
| Lou Brock | 1730 |
| Jim Edmonds | 1729 |
| Mickey Mantle | 1710 |

## The 30–30 Club (minimum of 30 HR and 30 SB in single season)

| Year | | HR | SB | Year | | HR | SB |
|---|---|---|---|---|---|---|---|
| 1922 | Kenny Williams, StL | 39 | 37 | 1997 | Jeff Bagwell, Hou | 43 | 31 |
| 1956 | Willie Mays, NYG | 36 | 40 | 1997 | Raul Mondesi, LA | 30 | 32 |
| 1957 | Willie Mays, NYG | 35 | 38 | 1997 | Barry Bonds, SF | 40 | 37 |
| 1963 | Hank Aaron, Mil | 44 | 31 | 1998 | Alex Rodriguez, Sea | 42 | 46 |
| 1969 | Bobby Bonds, SF | 32 | 45 | 1998 | Shawn Green, Tor | 35 | 35 |
| 1970 | Tommy Harper, Mil | 31 | 38 | 1999 | Jeff Bagwell, Hou | 42 | 30 |
| 1973 | Bobby Bonds, SF | 39 | 43 | 1999 | Raul Mondesi, LA | 33 | 36 |
| 1975 | Bobby Bonds, NYY | 32 | 30 | 2000 | Preston Wilson, Fla | 31 | 36 |
| 1977 | Bobby Bonds, Cal | 37 | 41 | 2001 | Vladimir Guerrero, Mtl | 34 | 37 |
| 1978 | Bobby Bonds, Chi/Tex | 31 | 43 | 2001 | Jose Cruz Jr., Tor | 34 | 32 |
| 1983 | Dale Murphy, Atl | 36 | 30 | 2001 | Bobby Abreu, Phi | 31 | 36 |
| 1987 | Joe Carter, Clev | 32 | 31 | 2002 | Alfonso Soriano, NYY | 39 | 41 |
| 1987 | Eric Davis, Cin | 37 | 50 | 2002 | Vladimir Guerrero, Mtl | 39 | 40 |
| 1987 | Darryl Strawberry, NYM | 39 | 36 | 2003 | Alfonso Soriano, NYY | 38 | 35 |
| 1987 | Howard Johnson, NYM | 36 | 32 | 2004 | Carlos Beltran, KC/Hou | 38 | 42 |
| 1988 | Jose Canseco, Oak | 42 | 40 | 2004 | Bobby Abreu, Phi | 30 | 40 |
| 1989 | Howard Johnson, NYM | 36 | 41 | 2005 | Alfonso Soriano, Tex | 36 | 30 |
| 1990 | Ron Gant, Atl | 32 | 33 | 2006 | Alfonso Soriano, Wash | 46 | 41 |
| 1990 | Barry Bonds, Pitt | 33 | 52 | 2007 | Brandon Phillips, Cin | 30 | 32 |
| 1991 | Ron Gant, Atl | 32 | 34 | 2007 | Jimmy Rollins, Phi | 30 | 41 |
| 1991 | Howard Johnson, NYM | 38 | 30 | 2007 | David Wright, NYM | 30 | 34 |
| 1992 | Barry Bonds, Pitt | 34 | 39 | 2008 | Grady Sizemore, Cle | 33 | 38 |
| 1993 | Sammy Sosa, ChiC | 33 | 36 | 2008 | Hanley Ramirez, Fla | 33 | 35 |
| 1995 | Barry Bonds, SF | 33 | 31 | 2009 | Ian Kinsler, Tex | 31 | 31 |
| 1995 | Sammy Sosa, ChiC | 36 | 34 | 2011 | Matt Kemp, LA | 39 | 40 |
| 1996 | Barry Bonds, SF | 42 | 40 | 2011 | Ryan Bruan, Mil | 33 | 33 |
| 1996 | Ellis Burks, Col | 40 | 32 | 2011 | Jacoby Ellsbury, Bos | 32 | 39 |
| 1996 | Barry Larkin, Cin | 33 | 36 | 2011 | Ian Kinsler, Tex | 32 | 30 |
| 1996 | Dante Bichette, Col | 31 | 31 | | | | |
| 1997 | Larry Walker, Col | 49 | 33 | | | | |

## Career Individual Pitching

### GAMES

| | |
|---|---|
| Jesse Orosco | 1251 |
| Mike Stanton | 1178 |
| John Franco | 1119 |
| Dennis Eckersley | 1071 |
| Hoyt Wilhelm | 1070 |
| Dan Plesac | 1064 |
| Mike Timlin | 1058 |
| Kent Tekulve | 1050 |
| *Mariano Rivera | 1042 |
| Trevor Hoffman | 1035 |
| Jose Mesa | 1022 |
| Lee Smith | 1022 |
| Roberto Hernandez | 1010 |
| Mike Jackson | 1005 |
| Goose Gossage | 1002 |
| Lindy McDaniel | 987 |
| Todd Jones | 982 |
| David Weathers | 964 |
| Rollie Fingers | 944 |
| Gene Garber | 931 |
| Eddie Guardado | 908 |
| Cy Young | 906 |
| *Arthur Rhodes | 900 |
| Sparky Lyle | 899 |
| Jim Kaat | 898 |
| Tom Gordon | 890 |

### INNINGS PITCHED

| | |
|---|---|
| Cy Young | 7356.0 |
| Pud Galvin | 6003.1 |
| Walter Johnson | 5914.1 |
| Phil Niekro | 5404.1 |
| Nolan Ryan | 5386.0 |
| Gaylord Perry | 5350.1 |
| Don Sutton | 5282.1 |
| Warren Spahn | 5243.1 |
| Steve Carlton | 5217.1 |
| Grover Alexander | 5190.0 |
| Kid Nichols | 5056.1 |
| Tim Keefe | 5049.2 |
| Greg Maddux | 5008.1 |
| Bert Blyleven | 4970.0 |
| Bobby Mathews | 4956.0 |
| Roger Clemens | 4916.2 |
| Mickey Welch | 4802.0 |
| Tom Seaver | 4782.2 |
| Christy Mathewson | 4780.2 |
| Tommy John | 4710.1 |
| Robin Roberts | 4688.2 |
| Early Wynn | 4564.0 |
| John Clarkson | 4536.1 |
| Charley Radbourn | 4535.1 |
| Tony Mullane | 4531.1 |
| Jim Kaat | 4530.1 |

### WINS

| | |
|---|---|
| Cy Young | 511 |
| Walter Johnson | 417 |
| Grover Alexander | 373 |
| Christy Mathewson | 373 |
| Pud Galvin | 365 |
| Warren Spahn | 363 |
| Kid Nichols | 361 |
| Greg Maddux | 355 |
| Roger Clemens | 354 |
| Tim Keefe | 342 |
| Steve Carlton | 329 |
| John Clarkson | 328 |
| Eddie Plank | 326 |
| Nolan Ryan | 324 |
| Don Sutton | 324 |
| Phil Niekro | 318 |
| Gaylord Perry | 314 |
| Tom Seaver | 311 |
| Charley Radbourn | 309 |
| Mickey Welch | 307 |
| Tom Glavine | 305 |
| Randy Johnson | 303 |
| Lefty Grove | 300 |
| Early Wynn | 300 |
| Bobby Matthews | 297 |
| Tommy John | 288 |

### LOSSES

| | |
|---|---|
| Cy Young | 316 |
| Pud Galvin | 310 |
| Nolan Ryan | 292 |
| Walter Johnson | 279 |
| Phil Niekro | 274 |
| Gaylord Perry | 265 |
| Don Sutton | 256 |
| Jack Powell | 254 |
| Eppa Rixey | 251 |
| Bert Blyleven | 250 |
| Bobby Mathews | 248 |
| Robin Roberts | 245 |
| Warren Spahn | 245 |
| Steve Carlton | 244 |
| Early Wynn | 244 |
| Jim Kaat | 237 |
| Frank Tanana | 236 |
| Gus Weyhing | 232 |
| Tommy John | 231 |
| Bob Friend | 230 |
| Ted Lyons | 230 |
| Greg Maddux | 227 |
| Ferguson Jenkins | 226 |
| Tim Keefe | 225 |
| Red Ruffing | 225 |
| Bob Newsom | 222 |

### WINNING PERCENTAGE**

| | |
|---|---|
| Al Spalding | .795 |
| Spud Chandler | .717 |
| Whitey Ford | .690 |
| Dave Foutz | .690 |
| Bob Caruthers | .688 |
| Pedro Martinez | .687 |
| Don Gullett | .686 |
| Lefty Grove | .680 |
| Joe Wood | .672 |
| *Roy Halladay | .671 |
| Vic Raschi | .667 |
| Larry Corcoran | .665 |
| Christy Mathewson | .665 |
| Sam Leever | .660 |
| Roger Clemens | .658 |
| *Johan Santana | .658 |
| Sal Maglie | .657 |
| Dick McBride | .656 |
| Sandy Koufax | .655 |
| Johnny Allen | .654 |
| Adam Wainwright | .654 |
| *Justin Verlander | .652 |

### SAVES

| | |
|---|---|
| *Mariano Rivera | 603 |
| Trevor Hoffman | 601 |
| Lee Smith | 478 |
| John Franco | 424 |
| Billy Wagner | 422 |
| Dennis Eckersley | 390 |
| Jeff Reardon | 367 |
| Troy Percival | 358 |
| Randy Myers | 347 |
| Rollie Fingers | 341 |
| John Wetteland | 330 |
| *Francisco Cordero | 327 |
| Roberto Hernandez | 326 |
| Jose Mesa | 321 |
| Todd Jones | 319 |
| Rick Aguilera | 318 |
| Robb Nen | 314 |
| Tom Henke | 311 |
| Goose Gossage | 310 |
| Jeff Montgomery | 304 |
| Doug Jones | 303 |
| *Jason Isringhausen | 300 |
| Bruce Sutter | 300 |
| *Francisco Rodriguez | 291 |
| Armando Benitez | 289 |

* Active in 2011. ** Minumum 100 victories.

## Career Individual Pitching *(Cont.)*

### EARNED RUN AVERAGE (2,000 IP)

| | |
|---|---|
| Ed Walsh | 1.82 |
| Addie Joss | 1.89 |
| Al Spalding | 2.04 |
| Three Finger Brown | 2.06 |
| John Ward | 2.10 |
| Christy Mathewson | 2.13 |
| Tommy Bond | 2.14 |
| Rube Waddell | 2.16 |
| Walter Johnson | 2.17 |
| Ed Reulbach | 2.28 |
| Will White | 2.28 |
| Eddie Plank | 2.35 |
| Larry Corcoran | 2.36 |
| Eddie Cicotte | 2.38 |
| Candy Cummings | 2.39 |
| Doc White | 2.39 |
| Nap Rucker | 2.42 |
| George Bradley | 2.43 |
| Jim McCormick | 2.43 |
| Chief Bender | 2.46 |

### SHUTOUTS

| | |
|---|---|
| Walter Johnson | 110 |
| Grover Alexander | 90 |
| Christy Mathewson | 79 |
| Cy Young | 76 |
| Eddie Plank | 69 |
| Warren Spahn | 63 |
| Nolan Ryan | 61 |
| Tom Seaver | 61 |
| Bert Blyleven | 60 |
| Don Sutton | 58 |
| Pud Galvin | 57 |
| Ed Walsh | 57 |
| Bob Gibson | 56 |
| Three Finger Brown | 55 |
| Steve Carlton | 55 |
| Jim Palmer | 53 |
| Gaylord Perry | 53 |
| Juan Marichal | 52 |
| Rube Waddell | 50 |
| Vic Willis | 50 |

### COMPLETE GAMES

| | |
|---|---|
| Cy Young | 749 |
| Pud Galvin | 639 |
| Tim Keefe | 554 |
| Walter Johnson | 531 |
| Kid Nichols | 531 |
| Mickey Welch | 525 |
| Bobby Mathews | 525 |
| Charley Radbourn | 489 |
| John Clarkson | 485 |
| Tony Mullane | 468 |
| Jim McCormick | 466 |
| Gus Weyhing | 448 |
| Grover Alexander | 437 |
| Christy Mathewson | 434 |
| Jack Powell | 422 |
| Eddie Plank | 410 |
| Will White | 394 |
| Amos Rusie | 392 |
| Vic Willis | 388 |
| Tommy Bond | 386 |

### STRIKEOUTS

| | |
|---|---|
| Nolan Ryan | 5714 |
| Randy Johnson | 4875 |
| Roger Clemens | 4672 |
| Steve Carlton | 4136 |
| Bert Blyleven | 3701 |
| Tom Seaver | 3640 |
| Don Sutton | 3574 |
| Gaylord Perry | 3534 |
| Walter Johnson | 3509 |
| Greg Maddux | 3371 |
| Phil Niekro | 3342 |
| Ferguson Jenkins | 3192 |
| Pedro Martinez | 3154 |
| Bob Gibson | 3117 |
| Curt Schilling | 3116 |
| John Smoltz | 3084 |
| Jim Bunning | 2855 |
| Mickey Lolich | 2832 |
| Mike Mussina | 2813 |
| Cy Young | 2803 |

### BASES ON BALLS

| | |
|---|---|
| Nolan Ryan | 2795 |
| Steve Carlton | 1833 |
| Phil Niekro | 1809 |
| Early Wynn | 1775 |
| Bob Feller | 1764 |
| Bobo Newsom | 1732 |
| Amos Rusie | 1707 |
| Charlie Hough | 1665 |
| Roger Clemens | 1580 |
| Gus Weyhing | 1566 |
| Red Ruffing | 1541 |
| Tom Glavine | 1500 |
| Randy Johnson | 1497 |
| Bump Hadley | 1442 |
| Warren Spahn | 1434 |
| Earl Whitehill | 1431 |
| Tony Mullane | 1408 |
| Sad Sam Jones | 1396 |
| Jack Morris | 1390 |
| Tom Seaver | 1390 |
| Gaylord Perry | 1379 |

* Active in 2011.

## Alltime Winningest Managers

### CAREER

| | W | L | Pct | Yrs | | W | L | Pct | Yrs |
|---|---|---|---|---|---|---|---|---|---|
| Connie Mack | 3755 | 3967 | .486 | 53 | Casey Stengel | 1942 | 1868 | .510 | 25 |
| John McGraw | 2810 | 1987 | .586 | 33 | Gene Mauch | 1907 | 2044 | .483 | 26 |
| *Tony LaRussa | 2796 | 2419 | .536 | 33 | Bill McKechnie | 1904 | 1737 | .523 | 25 |
| Bobby Cox | 2571 | 2068 | .554 | 29 | Lou Piniella | 1858 | 1737 | .517 | 23 |
| Joe Torre | 2406 | 2051 | .540 | 29 | Ralph Houk | 1627 | 1539 | .514 | 20 |
| Sparky Anderson | 2238 | 1855 | .547 | 26 | *Jim Leyland | 1620 | 1613 | .501 | 20 |
| Bucky Harris | 2168 | 2228 | .493 | 29 | Fred Clarke | 1609 | 1189 | .575 | 19 |
| Joe McCarthy | 2155 | 1346 | .616 | 24 | Dick Williams | 1592 | 1474 | .519 | 21 |
| Walter Alston | 2063 | 1634 | .558 | 23 | Tommy Lasorda | 1589 | 1434 | .526 | 20 |
| Leo Durocher | 2015 | 1717 | .540 | 24 | Earl Weaver | 1506 | 1080 | .582 | 17 |

### REGULAR SEASON

| | W | L | Pct | Yrs | | W | L | Pct | Yrs |
|---|---|---|---|---|---|---|---|---|---|
| Connie Mack | 3731 | 3948 | .486 | 53 | Casey Stengel | 1905 | 1842 | .508 | 25 |
| John McGraw | 2784 | 1959 | .587 | 33 | Gene Mauch | 1902 | 2037 | .483 | 26 |
| *Tony LaRussa | 2728 | 2365 | .536 | 33 | Bill McKechnie | 1896 | 1723 | .524 | 25 |
| Bobby Cox | 2504 | 2001 | .556 | 29 | Lou Piniella | 1835 | 1713 | .517 | 23 |
| Joe Torre | 2326 | 1997 | .538 | 29 | Ralph Houk | 1619 | 1531 | .514 | 20 |
| Sparky Anderson | 2194 | 1834 | .545 | 26 | Fred Clarke | 1602 | 1181 | .576 | 19 |
| Bucky Harris | 2157 | 2218 | .493 | 29 | Dick Williams | 1571 | 1451 | .520 | 21 |
| Joe McCarthy | 2125 | 1333 | .615 | 24 | *Jim Leyland | 1588 | 1585 | .500 | 20 |
| Walter Alston | 2040 | 1613 | .558 | 23 | Tommy Lasorda | 1558 | 1404 | .526 | 20 |
| Leo Durocher | 2008 | 1709 | .540 | 24 | Lou Piniella | 1519 | 1420 | .523 | 19 |

### WORLD SERIES

| | W | L | T | Pct | App | WS | | W | L | T | Pct | App | WS |
|---|---|---|---|---|---|---|---|---|---|---|---|---|---|
| Casey Stengel | 37 | 26 | 0 | .587 | 10 | 7 | Bucky Harris | 11 | 10 | 0 | .524 | 3 | 2 |
| Joe McCarthy | 30 | 13 | 0 | .698 | 9 | 7 | Billy Southworth | 11 | 11 | 0 | .500 | 4 | 2 |
| John McGraw | 26 | 28 | 2 | .482 | 9 | 2 | Earl Weaver | 11 | 13 | 0 | .458 | 4 | 1 |
| Connie Mack | 24 | 19 | 0 | .558 | 8 | 5 | Bobby Cox | 11 | 18 | 0 | .379 | 5 | 1 |
| Joe Torre | 21 | 11 | 0 | .657 | 6 | 4 | Whitey Herzog | 10 | 11 | 0 | .476 | 3 | 1 |
| Walter Alston | 20 | 20 | 0 | .500 | 7 | 4 | *Terry Francona | 8 | 0 | 0 | 1.000 | 2 | 2 |
| Miller Huggins | 18 | 15 | 1 | .544 | 6 | 3 | Bill Carrigan | 8 | 2 | 0 | .800 | 2 | 2 |
| Sparky Anderson | 16 | 12 | 0 | .571 | 5 | 3 | Cito Gaston | 8 | 4 | 0 | .667 | 2 | 2 |
| *Tony LaRussa | 13 | 16 | 0 | .448 | 6 | 3 | Danny Murtaugh | 8 | 6 | 0 | .571 | 2 | 2 |
| Tommy Lasorda | 12 | 11 | 0 | .522 | 4 | 2 | Tom Kelly | 8 | 6 | 0 | .571 | 2 | 2 |
| Dick Williams | 12 | 14 | 0 | .462 | 4 | 2 | Ralph Houk | 8 | 8 | 0 | .500 | 3 | 2 |
| Frank Chance | 11 | 9 | 1 | .548 | 4 | 2 | Bill McKechnie | 8 | 14 | 0 | .364 | 4 | 2 |

* Active in 2011.

## Individual Batting Records (Single Season)

### HITS

| | |
|---|---|
| Ichiro Suzuki, 2004 | 262 |
| George Sisler, 1920 | 257 |
| Lefty O'Doul, 1929 | 254 |
| Bill Terry, 1930 | 254 |
| Al Simmons, 1925 | 253 |
| Rogers Hornsby, 1922 | 250 |
| Chuck Klein, 1930 | 250 |
| Ty Cobb, 1911 | 248 |
| George Sisler, 1922 | 246 |
| Ichiro Suzuki, 2001 | 242 |

### BATTING AVERAGE

| | |
|---|---|
| Levi Meyerle, 1871 | .492 |
| Hugh Duffy, 1894 | .440 |
| Tip O'Neill, 1887 | .435 |
| Ross Barnes, 1872 | .432 |
| Cal McVey, 1871 | .431 |
| Ross Barnes, 1876 | .429 |
| Nap Lajoie, 1901 | .426 |
| Ross Barnes, 1873 | .425 |
| Willie Keeler, 1897 | .424 |
| Rogers Hornsby, 1924 | .424 |

### DOUBLES

| | |
|---|---|
| Earl Webb, 1931 | 67 |
| George Burns, 1926 | 64 |
| Joe Medwick, 1936 | 64 |
| Hank Greenberg, 1934 | 63 |
| Paul Waner, 1932 | 62 |
| Charlie Gehringer, 1936 | 60 |
| Tris Speaker, 1923 | 59 |
| Chuck Klein, 1930 | 59 |
| Todd Helton, 2000 | 59 |
| Billy Herman, 1936 | 57 |
| Billy Herman, 1935 | 57 |
| Carlos Delgado, 2000 | 57 |

### TOTAL BASES

| | |
|---|---|
| Babe Ruth, 1921 | 457 |
| Rogers Hornsby, 1922 | 450 |
| Lou Gehrig, 1927 | 447 |
| Chuck Klein, 1930 | 445 |
| Jimmie Foxx, 1932 | 438 |
| Stan Musial, 1948 | 429 |
| Sammy Sosa, 2001 | 425 |
| Hack Wilson, 1930 | 423 |
| Chuck Klein, 1932 | 420 |
| Luis Gonzalez, 2001 | 419 |
| Lou Gehrig, 1930 | 419 |

### TRIPLES

| | |
|---|---|
| Chief Wilson, 1912 | 36 |
| Dave Orr, 1886 | 31 |
| Heinie Reitz, 1894 | 31 |
| Perry Werden, 1893 | 29 |
| Harry Davis, 1897 | 28 |
| George Davis, 1893 | 27 |
| Sam Thompson, 1894 | 27 |
| Jimmy Williams, 1899 | 27 |
| Sam Crawford, 1914 | 26 |
| Kiki Cuyler, 1925 | 26 |
| Joe Jackson, 1912 | 26 |
| John Reilly, 1890 | 26 |
| George Treadway | 26 |

### HOME RUNS

| | |
|---|---|
| Barry Bonds, 2001 | 73 |
| Mark McGwire, 1998 | 70 |
| Sammy Sosa, 1998 | 66 |
| Mark McGwire, 1999 | 65 |
| Sammy Sosa, 2001 | 64 |
| Sammy Sosa, 1999 | 63 |
| Roger Maris, 1961 | 61 |
| Babe Ruth, 1927 | 60 |
| Babe Ruth, 1921 | 59 |
| Jimmie Foxx, 1932 | 58 |
| Hank Greenberg, 1938 | 58 |
| Mark McGwire, 1997 | 58 |
| Ryan Howard, 2006 | 58 |

### RUNS BATTED IN

| | |
|---|---|
| Hack Wilson, 1930 | 191 |
| Lou Gehrig, 1931 | 184 |
| Hank Greenberg, 1937 | 183 |
| Lou Gehrig, 1927 | 175 |
| Jimmie Foxx, 1938 | 175 |
| Lou Gehrig, 1930 | 174 |
| Babe Ruth, 1921 | 171 |
| Chuck Klein, 1930 | 170 |
| Hank Greenberg, 1935 | 170 |
| Jimmie Foxx, 1932 | 169 |

### STRIKEOUTS

| | |
|---|---|
| Mark Reynolds, 2009 | 223 |
| Mark Reynolds, 2010 | 211 |
| Drew Stubbs, 2011 | 205 |
| Mark Reynolds, 2008 | 204 |
| Adam Dunn, 2010 | 199 |
| Ryan Howard, 2008 | 199 |
| Ryan Howard, 2007 | 199 |
| Jack Cust, 2008 | 197 |
| Mark Reynolds, 2011 | 196 |
| Adam Dunn, 2004 | 195 |

### RUNS

| | |
|---|---|
| Billy Hamilton, 1894 | 192 |
| Tom Brown, 1891 | 177 |
| Babe Ruth, 1921 | 177 |
| Lou Gehrig, 1936 | 167 |
| Tip O'Neill, 1887 | 167 |
| Billy Hamilton, 1895 | 166 |
| Willie Keeler, 1894 | 165 |
| Joe Kelley, 1894 | 165 |
| Lou Gehrig, 1931 | 163 |
| Arlie Latham, 1887 | 163 |
| Babe Ruth, 1928 | 163 |

### STOLEN BASES

| | |
|---|---|
| Hugh Nicol, 1887 | 138 |
| Rickey Henderson, 1982 | 130 |
| Arlie Latham, 1887 | 129 |
| Lou Brock, 1974 | 118 |
| Charlie Comiskey, 1887 | 117 |
| Billy Hamilton, 1891 | 111 |
| Billy Hamilton, 1889 | 111 |
| John Ward, 1887 | 111 |
| Vince Coleman, 1985 | 110 |
| Vince Coleman, 1987 | 109 |
| Arlie Latham, 1888 | 109 |

### BASES ON BALLS

| | |
|---|---|
| Barry Bonds, 2004 | 232 |
| Barry Bonds, 2002 | 198 |
| Barry Bonds, 2001 | 177 |
| Babe Ruth, 1923 | 170 |
| Ted Williams, 1947 | 162 |
| Ted Williams, 1949 | 162 |
| Mark McGwire, 1998 | 162 |
| Ted Williams, 1946 | 156 |
| Barry Bonds, 1996 | 151 |
| Eddie Yost, 1956 | 151 |
| Babe Ruth, 1920 | 150 |

### SLUGGING AVERAGE

| | |
|---|---|
| Barry Bonds, 2001 | .863 |
| Babe Ruth, 1920 | .847 |
| Babe Ruth, 1921 | .846 |
| Barry Bonds, 2004 | .812 |
| Barry Bonds, 2002 | .799 |
| Babe Ruth, 1927 | .772 |
| Lou Gehrig, 1927 | .765 |
| Babe Ruth, 1923 | .764 |
| Rogers Hornsby, 1925 | .756 |
| Mark McGwire, 1998 | .752 |

## Individual Pitching Records (Single Season)

### GAME APPEARANCES

| | |
|---|---|
| Mike Marshall, 1974 | 106 |
| Kent Tekulve, 1979 | 94 |
| Salomon Torres, 2006 | 94 |
| Pedro Feliciano, 2010 | 92 |
| Mike Marshall, 1973 | 92 |
| Kent Tekulve, 1978 | 91 |
| Wayne Granger, 1969 | 90 |
| Mike Marshall, 1979 | 90 |
| Kent Tekulve, 1987 | 90 |
| Steve Kline, 2001 | 89 |
| Jim Brower, 2004 | 89 |
| Mark Eichhorn, 1987 | 89 |
| Paul Quantrill, 2003 | 89 |
| Julian Tavarez, 2009 | 89 |

### GAMES STARTED

| | |
|---|---|
| Will White, 1879 | 75 |
| Pud Galvin, 1883 | 75 |
| Jim McCormick, 1880 | 74 |
| Charley Radbourn, 1884 | 73 |
| Guy Hecker, 1884 | 73 |
| Jim Galvin, 1884 | 72 |
| John Clarkson, 1889 | 72 |
| Bill Hutchison, 1892 | 70 |
| John Clarkson, 1885 | 70 |
| Bobby Mathews, 1875 | 70 |

### INNINGS PITCHED

| | |
|---|---|
| Will White, 1878 | 680.0 |
| Charley Radbourn, 1884 | 678.2 |
| Guy Hecker, 1884 | 670.2 |
| Jim McCormick, 1880 | 657.2 |
| Jim Galvin, 1883 | 656.1 |
| Jim Galvin, 1884 | 636.1 |
| Charley Radbourn, 1883 | 632.1 |
| Bill Hutchison, 1892 | 627.0 |
| Bobby Mathews, 1875 | 626.2 |

### WINS

| | |
|---|---|
| Charley Radbourn, 1884 | 59 |
| Al Spalding, 1875 | 55 |
| John Clarkson, 1885 | 53 |
| Guy Hecker, 1884 | 52 |
| Al Spalding, 1874 | 52 |
| John Clarkson, 1889 | 49 |
| Charlie Buffinton, 1884 | 48 |
| Charley Radbourn, 1883 | 48 |
| Al Spalding, 1876 | 47 |
| John Ward, 1879 | 47 |

### LOSSES

| | |
|---|---|
| John Coleman, 1883 | 48 |
| Will White, 1880 | 42 |
| Larry McKeon, 1884 | 41 |
| George Bradley, 1879 | 40 |
| Jim McCormick, 1879 | 40 |
| Bobby Mathews, 1875 | 38 |
| Kid Carsey, 1891 | 37 |
| George Cobb, 1892 | 37 |
| Henry Porter, 1888 | 37 |

### WINNING PERCENTAGE

| | |
|---|---|
| Roy Face, 1959 | .947 |
| Johnny Allen, 1937 | .938 |
| Greg Maddux, 1995 | .905 |
| Randy Johnson, 1995 | .900 |
| Ron Guidry, 1978 | .893 |
| Freddie Fitzsimmons, 1940 | .889 |
| Lefty Grove, 1931 | .886 |
| Bob Stanley, 1978 | .882 |
| Preacher Roe, 1951 | .880 |
| Cliff Lee, 2008 | .880 |
| Fred Goldsmith, 1880 | .875 |
| Tom Seaver, 1981 | .875 |

### SAVES

| | |
|---|---|
| Francisco Rodriguez, 2008 | 62 |
| Bobby Thigpen, 1990 | 57 |
| Eric Gagne, 2003 | 55 |
| John Smoltz, 2002 | 55 |
| Mariano Rivera, 2004 | 53 |
| Randy Myers, 1993 | 53 |
| Trevor Hoffman, 1998 | 53 |
| Eric Gagne, 2002 | 52 |
| Rod Beck, 1998 | 51 |
| Dennis Eckersley, 1992 | 51 |
| Mariano Rivera, 2001 | 50 |

### EARNED RUN AVERAGE

| | |
|---|---|
| Tim Keefe, 1880 | 0.86 |
| Dutch Leonard, 1914 | 0.96 |
| Three Finger Brown, 1906 | 1.04 |
| Bob Gibson, 1968 | 1.12 |
| Christy Mathewson, 1909 | 1.14 |
| Walter Johnson, 1913 | 1.14 |
| Jack Pfiester, 1907 | 1.15 |
| Addie Joss, 1908 | 1.16 |
| Carl Lundgren, 1907 | 1.17 |
| Denny Driscoll, 1882 | 1.21 |

### SHUTOUTS

| | |
|---|---|
| Grover Alexander, 1916 | 16 |
| George Bradley, 1876 | 16 |
| Jack Coombs, 1910 | 13 |
| Bob Gibson, 1968 | 13 |
| Grover Alexander, 1915 | 12 |
| Jim Galvin, 1884 | 12 |
| Ed Morris, 1886 | 12 |
| Tommy Bond, 1879 | 11 |
| Dean Chance, 1964 | 11 |
| Dave Foutz, 1886 | 11 |
| Walter Johnson, 1913 | 11 |
| Sandy Koufax, 1963 | 11 |
| Christy Mathewson, 1908 | 11 |
| Charles Radbourn, 1884 | 11 |
| Ed Walsh, 1908 | 11 |

### COMPLETE GAMES

| | |
|---|---|
| Will White, 1879 | 75 |
| Charley Radbourn, 1884 | 73 |
| Pud Galvin, 1883 | 72 |
| Guy Hecker, 1884 | 72 |
| Jim McCormick, 1880 | 72 |
| Pud Galvin, 1884 | 71 |
| Bobby Mathews, 1875 | 69 |
| John Clarkson, 1885 | 68 |
| John Clarkson, 1889 | 68 |

### STRIKEOUTS

| | |
|---|---|
| Matt Kilroy, 1886 | 513 |
| Toad Ramsey, 1886 | 499 |
| Hugh Daily, 1884 | 483 |
| Dupee Shaw, 1884 | 451 |
| Charley Radbourn, 1884 | 441 |
| Charlie Buffinton, 1884 | 417 |
| Guy Hecker, 1884 | 385 |
| Nolan Ryan, 1973 | 383 |
| Sandy Koufax, 1965 | 382 |

### BASES ON BALLS

| | |
|---|---|
| Amos Rusie, 1890 | 289 |
| Mark Baldwin, 1889 | 274 |
| Amos Rusie, 1892 | 267 |
| Amos Rusie, 1891 | 262 |
| Mark Baldwin, 1890 | 249 |
| Jack Stivetts, 1891 | 232 |
| Mark Baldwin, 1891 | 227 |
| Phil Knell, 1891 | 226 |
| Bob Barr, 1890 | 219 |

## Manager of the Year

### NATIONAL LEAGUE

| | |
|---|---|
| 1983 | Tommy Lasorda, LA |
| 1984 | Jim Frey, Chi |
| 1985 | Whitey Herzog, StL |
| 1986 | Hal Lanier, Hou |
| 1987 | Buck Rodgers, Mtl |
| 1988 | Tommy Lasorda, LA |
| 1989 | Don Zimmer, Chi |
| 1990 | Jim Leyland, Pitt |
| 1991 | Bobby Cox, Atl |
| 1992 | Jim Leyland, Pitt |
| 1993 | Dusty Baker, SF |
| 1994 | Felipe Alou, Mtl |
| 1995 | Don Baylor, Col |
| 1996 | Bruce Bochy, SD |
| 1997 | Dusty Baker, SF |
| 1998 | Larry Dierker, Hou |
| 1999 | Jack McKeon, Cin |

### AMERICAN LEAGUE

| | |
|---|---|
| 1983 | Tony LaRussa, Chi |
| 1984 | Sparky Anderson, Det |
| 1985 | Bobby Cox, Tor |
| 1986 | John McNamara, Bos |
| 1987 | Sparky Anderson, Det |
| 1988 | Tony LaRussa, Oak |
| 1989 | Frank Robinson, Balt |
| 1990 | Jeff Torborg, Chi |
| 1991 | Tom Kelly, Minn |
| 1992 | Tony LaRussa, Oak |
| 1993 | Gene Lamont, Chi |
| 1994 | Buck Showalter, NY |
| 1995 | Lou Piniella, Sea |
| 1996 | Joe Torre, NY/Johnny Oates, Tex |
| 1997 | Davey Johnson, Balt |
| 1998 | Joe Torre, NY |
| 1999 | Jimy Williams, Bos |

## Manager of the Year *(Cont.)*

| NATIONAL LEAGUE | | AMERICAN LEAGUE | |
|---|---|---|---|
| 2000 | Dusty Baker, SF | 2000 | Jerry Manuel, Chi |
| 2001 | Larry Bowa, Phi | 2001 | Lou Piniella, Sea |
| 2002 | Tony LaRussa, StL | 2002 | Mike Scioscia, Ana |
| 2003 | Jack McKeon, Fla | 2003 | Tony Pena, KC |
| 2004 | Bobby Cox, Atl | 2004 | Buck Showalter, Tex |
| 2005 | Bobby Cox, Atl | 2005 | Ozzie Guillen, Chi |
| 2006 | Joe Girardi, Fla | 2006 | Jim Leyland, Det |
| 2007 | Bob Melvin, Ari | 2007 | Eric Wedge, Cle |
| 2008 | Lou Piniella, Chi | 2008 | Joe Maddon, TB |
| 2009 | Jim Tracy, Col | 2009 | Mike Scioscia, LA |
| 2010 | Bud Black, SD | 2010 | Ron Gardenhire, Min |

## Individual Batting Records (Single Game)

### MOST HITS

| | | |
|---|---|---|
| 7 | Wilbert Robinson, Balt | June 10, 1892 |
| | Rennie Stennett, Pitt | Sept 16, 1975 |

### MOST HOME RUNS

| | | |
|---|---|---|
| 4 | Bobby Lowe, Bos (N) | May 30, 1894 |
| | Ed Delahanty, Phi | July 13, 1896 |
| | Lou Gehrig, NY (A) | June 3, 1932 |
| | Chuck Klein, Phi (N) | July 10, 1936 |
| | Pat Seerey, Chi (A) | July 18, 1948 |
| | Gil Hodges, Bklyn | Aug 31, 1950 |
| | Joe Adcock, Mil (N) | July 31, 1954 |
| | Rocky Colavito, Clev | June 10, 1959 |
| | Willie Mays, SF | April 30, 1961 |
| | Mike Schmidt, Phi | April 17, 1976 |
| | Bob Horner, Atl | July 6, 1986 |
| | Mark Whiten, StL | Sept 7, 1993 |
| | Mike Cameron, Sea | May 2, 2002 |
| | Shawn Green, LA | May 23, 2002 |
| | Carlos Delgado, Tor | Sept 25, 2003 |

Note: All single-game hitting records for a nine-inning game.

### MOST GRAND SLAMS

| | | |
|---|---|---|
| 2 | Tony Lazzeri, NY (A) | May 24, 1936 |
| | Jim Tabor, Bos (A) | July 4, 1939 |
| | Rudy York, Bos (A) | July 27, 1946 |
| | Jim Gentile, Balt | May 9, 1961 |
| | Tony Cloninger, Atl | July 3, 1966 |
| | Jim Northrup, Det | June 24, 1968 |
| | Frank Robinson, Balt | June 26, 1970 |
| | Robin Ventura, Chi (A) | Sept 4, 1995 |
| | Chris Hoiles, Balt | Aug 14, 1998 |
| | Fernando Tatis, StL | Apr 23, 1999 |
| | N. Garciaparra, Bos | May 10, 1999 |
| | Bill Mueller, Bos | July 29, 2003 |
| | Josh Willingham, Was | July 27, 2009 |

### MOST RUNS

| | | |
|---|---|---|
| 7 | Guy Hecker, Lou | Aug 15, 1886 |

### MOST RBIs

| | | |
|---|---|---|
| 12 | Jim Bottomley, StL | Sept 16, 1924 |
| | Mark Whiten, StL | Sept 7, 1993 |

## Individual Batting Records (Single Inning)

### MOST RUNS

| | | |
|---|---|---|
| 3 | Tommy Burns, Chi (N) | Sept 6, 1883, 7th inning |
| | Ned Williamson, Chi (N) | Sept 6, 1883, 7th inning |
| | Sammy White, Bos (A) | June 18, 1953, 7th inning |

### MOST HITS

| | | |
|---|---|---|
| 3 | Tommy Burns, Chi (N) | Sept 6, 1883, 7th inning |
| | Fred Pfeiffer, Chi (N) | Sept 6, 1883, 7th inning |
| | Ned Williamson, Chi (N) | Sept 6, 1883, 7th inning |
| | Gene Stephens, Bos (A) | June 18, 1953, 7th inning |
| | Johnny Damon, Bos (A), | June 27, 2003, 1st inning |

### MOST RBIs

| | | |
|---|---|---|
| 8 | Fernando Tatis, StL | Apr 23, 1999, 3rd inning |

## Individual Pitching Records (Single Game)

### MOST INNINGS PITCHED

| | | |
|---|---|---|
| 26 | Leon Cadore, Bklyn | May 1, 1920, tie 1–1 |
| | Joe Oeschger, Bos (N) | May 1, 1920, tie 1–1 |

### MOST RUNS ALLOWED

| | | |
|---|---|---|
| 24 | Al Travers, Det | May 18, 1912 |

### MOST HITS ALLOWED

| | | |
|---|---|---|
| 36 | Jack Wadsworth, Lou | Aug 17, 1894 |

### MOST STRIKEOUTS

| | | |
|---|---|---|
| 20 | Roger Clemens, Bos | April 29, 1986 |
| 20 | Roger Clemens, Bos | Sept 18, 1996 |
| 20 | Kerry Wood, Chi (N) | May 6, 1998 |
| 20 | Randy Johnson, Ariz | May 8, 2001 |

### MOST WALKS ALLOWED

| | | |
|---|---|---|
| 16 | Bill George, NY (N) | May 30, 1887 |
| | George Van Haltren, Chi (N) | June 27, 1887 |
| | Henry Gruber, Clev | Apr 19, 1890 |
| | Bruno Haas, Phi (A) | June 2, 1915 |

### MOST WILD PITCHES

| | | |
|---|---|---|
| 6 | J.R. Richard, Hou | April 10, 1979 |
| | Phil Niekro, Atl | Aug 14, 1979 |
| | Bill Gullickson, Mtl | April 10, 1982 |

## Individual Pitching Records (Single Inning)

### MOST RUNS ALLOWED

13 .....Lefty O'Doul, Bos (A)  July 7, 1923

### MOST WILD PITCHES

| 4 .......Walter Johnson, Wash | Sept 21, 1914 |
| Phil Niekro, Atl | Aug 14, 1979 |
| Kevin Gregg, Ana | July 25, 2004 |
| Ryan Madson, Phi | July 25, 2006 |

### MOST WALKS ALLOWED

8 .......Dolly Gray, Wash  Aug 28, 1909

## Miscellaneous Records

### LONGEST GAME, BY INNINGS

26 .....Brooklyn 1, Boston 1  May 1, 1920

### LONGEST NINE-INNING GAME, BY TIME

4:45...New York (A) 14, Boston 11  Aug 18, 2006

# Baseball Hall of Fame

## Players

| Name | Position | Career | Selected | Name | Position | Career | Selected |
|---|---|---|---|---|---|---|---|
| Hank Aaron | OF | 1954–76 | 1982 | Sam Crawford | OF | 1899–1917 | 1957 |
| Grover Alexander | P | 1911–30 | 1938 | Joe Cronin | SS | 1926–45 | 1956 |
| Roberto Alomar | 2B | 1988–2004 | 2011 | Candy Cummings | P | 1872–77 | 1939 |
| Cap Anson | 1B | 1876–97 | 1939 | Kiki Cuyler | OF | 1921–38 | 1968 |
| Luis Aparicio | SS | 1956–73 | 1984 | Ray Dandridge* | 3B | | 1987 |
| Luke Appling | SS | 1930–50 | 1964 | George Davis | SS | 1890–1909 | 1998 |
| Richie Ashburn | OF | 1948–62 | 1995 | Andre Dawson | OF | 1976–96 | 2010 |
| Earl Averill | OF | 1929–41 | 1975 | Leon Day* | P | | 1995 |
| Jose Mendez Baez* | P | 1908–26 | 2006 | Dizzy Dean | P | 1930–47 | 1953 |
| Frank Baker | 3B | 1908–22 | 1955 | Ed Delahanty | OF | 1888–1903 | 1945 |
| Dave Bancroft | SS | 1915–30 | 1971 | Bill Dickey | C | 1928–46 | 1954 |
| Ernie Banks | SS-1B | 1953–71 | 1977 | Martin Dihigo* | P-OF | | 1977 |
| Jake Beckley | 1B | 1888–1907 | 1971 | Joe DiMaggio | OF | 1936–51 | 1955 |
| Cool Papa Bell* | OF | | 1974 | Larry Doby | OF | 1947–59 | 1998 |
| Johnny Bench | C | 1967–83 | 1989 | Bobby Doerr | 2B | 1937–51 | 1986 |
| Chief Bender | P | 1903–25 | 1953 | Don Drysdale | P | 1956–69 | 1984 |
| Yogi Berra | C | 1946–65 | 1972 | Hugh Duffy | OF | 1888–1906 | 1945 |
| Bert Blyleven | P | 1970–90; '92 | 2011 | Dennis Eckersley | P | 1975–98 | 2004 |
| Wade Boggs | 3B | 1982-99 | 2005 | Johnny Evers | 2B | 1902–29 | 1939 |
| Jim Bottomley | 1B | 1922–37 | 1974 | Buck Ewing | C | 1880–97 | 1946 |
| Lou Boudreau | SS | 1938–52 | 1970 | Red Faber | P | 1914–33 | 1964 |
| Roger Bresnahan | C | 1897–1915 | 1945 | Bob Feller | P | 1936–56 | 1962 |
| George Brett | 3B | 1973–93 | 1999 | Rick Ferrell | C | 1929–47 | 1984 |
| Lou Brock | OF | 1961–79 | 1985 | Rollie Fingers | P | 1968–85 | 1992 |
| Dan Brouthers | 1B | 1879–1904 | 1945 | Carlton Fisk | C | 1969–93 | 2000 |
| Ray Brown* | P | 1930–48 | 2006 | Elmer Flick | OF | 1898–1910 | 1963 |
| Three Finger Brown | P | 1903–16 | 1949 | Whitey Ford | P | 1950–67 | 1974 |
| Willard Jesse Brown* | OF | 1935-58 | 2006 | Bill Foster* | P | | 1996 |
| Jim Bunning | P | 1955–71 | 1996 | Nellie Fox | 2B | 1947–65 | 1997 |
| Jesse Burkett | OF | 1890–1905 | 1946 | Jimmie Foxx | 1B | 1925–45 | 1951 |
| Roy Campanella | C | 1948–57 | 1969 | Frankie Frisch | 2B | 1919–37 | 1947 |
| Rod Carew | 1B-2B | 1967–85 | 1991 | Pud Galvin | P | 1879–92 | 1965 |
| Max Carey | OF | 1910–29 | 1961 | Lou Gehrig | 1B | 1923–39 | 1939 |
| Steve Carlton | P | 1965–88 | 1994 | Charlie Gehringer | 2B | 1924–42 | 1949 |
| Gary Carter | C | 1974–92 | 2003 | Bob Gibson | P | 1959–75 | 1981 |
| Orlando Cepeda | 1B | 1958–74 | 1999 | Josh Gibson* | C | | 1972 |
| Frank Chance | 1B | 1898–1914 | 1946 | Lefty Gomez | P | 1930–43 | 1972 |
| Oscar Charleston* | OF | | 1976 | Joe Gordon | 2B | 1938-43/46-50 | 2009 |
| Jack Chesbro | P | 1899–1909 | 1946 | Goose Goslin | OF | 1921–38 | 1968 |
| Fred Clarke | OF | 1894–1915 | 1945 | Rich "Goose" Gossage | P | 1972-94 | 2008 |
| John Clarkson | P | 1882–94 | 1963 | Ulysses F. Grant* | 2B | 1886–1903 | 2006 |
| Roberto Clemente | OF | 1955–72 | 1973 | Hank Greenberg | 1B | 1930–47 | 1956 |
| Ty Cobb | OF | 1905–28 | 1936 | Burleigh Grimes | P | 1916–34 | 1964 |
| Mickey Cochrane | C | 1925–37 | 1947 | Lefty Grove | P | 1925–41 | 1947 |
| Eddie Collins | 2B | 1906–30 | 1939 | Tony Gwynn | OF | 1982–2001 | 2007 |
| Jimmy Collins | 3B | 1895–1908 | 1945 | Chick Hafey | OF | 1924–37 | 1971 |
| Earle Combs | OF | 1924–35 | 1970 | Jesse Haines | P | 1918–37 | 1970 |
| Roger Connor | 1B | 1880–97 | 1976 | Billy Hamilton | OF | 1888–1901 | 1961 |
| Andrew Cooper* | P | 1920–41 | 2006 | Gabby Hartnett | C | 1922–41 | 1955 |
| Stan Coveleski | P | 1912–28 | 1969 | Harry Heilmann | OF | 1914–32 | 1952 |

Note: Career dates indicate first and last appearances in the majors.
*Elected on the basis of their career in the Negro leagues.

## Players *(Cont.)*

| | Position | Career | Selected | | Position | Career | Selected |
|---|---|---|---|---|---|---|---|
| Rickey Henderson | OF | 1979–2003 | 2009 | Pee Wee Reese | SS | 1940–58 | 1984 |
| Billy Herman | 2B | 1931–47 | 1975 | Jim Rice | OF | 1974–89 | 2009 |
| Joseph Hill* | OF | 1899–1925 | 2006 | Sam Rice | OF | 1915–35 | 1963 |
| Harry Hooper | OF | 1909–25 | 1971 | Cal Ripken Jr. | SS | 1981–2001 | 2007 |
| Rogers Hornsby | 2B | 1915–37 | 1942 | Eppa Rixey | P | 1912–33 | 1963 |
| Waite Hoyt | P | 1918–38 | 1969 | Phil Rizzuto | SS | 1941–56 | 1994 |
| Carl Hubbell | P | 1928–43 | 1947 | Robin Roberts | P | 1948–66 | 1976 |
| Catfish Hunter | P | 1965–79 | 1987 | Brooks Robinson | 3B | 1955–77 | 1983 |
| Monte Irvin* | OF | 1949–56 | 1973 | Frank Robinson | OF | 1956–76 | 1982 |
| Reggie Jackson | OF | 1967–87 | 1993 | Jackie Robinson | 2B | 1947–56 | 1962 |
| Travis Jackson | SS | 1922–36 | 1982 | Joe (Bullet) Rogan* | P | | 1998 |
| Ferguson Jenkins | P | 1965–83 | 1991 | Edd Roush | OF | 1913–31 | 1962 |
| Hugh Jennings | SS | 1891–1918 | 1945 | Red Ruffing | P | 1924–47 | 1967 |
| Judy Johnson* | 3B | | 1975 | Amos Rusie | P | 1889–1901 | 1977 |
| Walter Johnson | P | 1907–27 | 1936 | Babe Ruth | OF | 1914–35 | 1936 |
| Addie Joss | P | 1902–10 | 1978 | Nolan Ryan | P | 1966–93 | 1999 |
| Al Kaline | OF | 1953–74 | 1980 | Ryne Sandberg | 2B | 1981-97 | 2005 |
| Tim Keefe | P | 1880–93 | 1964 | Louis Santop* | C | 1909–26 | 2006 |
| Willie Keeler | OF | 1892–1910 | 1939 | Ray Schalk | C | 1912–29 | 1955 |
| George Kell | 3B | 1943–57 | 1983 | Mike Schmidt | 3B | 1972–89 | 1995 |
| Joe Kelley | OF | 1891–1908 | 1971 | Red Schoendienst | 2B | 1945–63 | 1989 |
| George Kelly | 1B | 1915–32 | 1973 | Tom Seaver | P | 1967–86 | 1992 |
| King Kelly | C | 1878–93 | 1945 | Joe Sewell | SS | 1920–33 | 1977 |
| Harmon Killebrew | 1B-3B | 1954–75 | 1984 | Al Simmons | OF | 1924–44 | 1953 |
| Ralph Kiner | OF | 1946–55 | 1975 | George Sisler | 1B | 1915–30 | 1939 |
| Chuck Klein | OF | 1928–44 | 1980 | Enos Slaughter | OF | 1938–59 | 1985 |
| Sandy Koufax | P | 1955–66 | 1972 | Hilton Smith* | P | | 2001 |
| Nap Lajoie | 2B | 1896–1916 | 1937 | Ozzie Smith | SS | 1978–96 | 2002 |
| Tony Lazzeri | 2B | 1926–39 | 1991 | Duke Snider | OF | 1947–64 | 1980 |
| Bob Lemon | P | 1941–58 | 1976 | Warren Spahn | P | 1942–65 | 1973 |
| Buck Leonard* | 1B | | 1977 | Al Spalding | P | 1871–78 | 1939 |
| Fred Lindstrom | 3B | 1924–36 | 1976 | Tris Speaker | OF | 1907–28 | 1937 |
| Pop Lloyd* | SS-1B | | 1977 | Willie Stargell | OF-1B | 1962–82 | 1988 |
| Ernie Lombardi | C | 1931–47 | 1986 | Turkey Stearns* | CF | | 2000 |
| Ted Lyons | P | 1923–46 | 1955 | Don Sutton | P | 1966–88 | 1998 |
| James Mackey* | C | 1920–47 | 2006 | Bruce Sutter | P | 1976–88 | 2006 |
| Mickey Mantle | OF | 1951–68 | 1974 | George Suttles* | C | 1923–44 | 2006 |
| Heinie Manush | OF | 1923–39 | 1964 | Benjamin Harrison Taylor* | P-1B | 1908–29 | 2006 |
| Rabbit Maranville | SS-2B | 1912–35 | 1954 | Bill Terry | 1B | 1923–36 | 1954 |
| Juan Marichal | P | 1960–75 | 1983 | Sam Thompson | OF | 1885–1906 | 1974 |
| Rube Marquard | P | 1908–25 | 1971 | Joe Tinker | SS | 1902–16 | 1946 |
| Eddie Mathews | 3B | 1952–68 | 1978 | Cristóbal Torriente* | OF | 1913–32 | 2006 |
| Christy Mathewson | P | 1900–16 | 1936 | Pie Traynor | 3B | 1920–37 | 1948 |
| Willie Mays | OF | 1951–73 | 1979 | Dazzy Vance | P | 1915–35 | 1955 |
| Bill Mazeroski | 2B | 1956–72 | 2001 | Arky Vaughan | SS | 1932–48 | 1985 |
| Tommy McCarthy | OF | 1884–96 | 1946 | Rube Waddell | P | 1897–1910 | 1946 |
| Willie McCovey | 1B | 1959–80 | 1986 | Honus Wagner | SS | 1897–1917 | 1936 |
| Joe McGinnity | P | 1899–1908 | 1946 | Bobby Wallace | SS | 1894–1918 | 1953 |
| Bid McPhee | 2B | 1882–99 | 2000 | Ed Walsh | P | 1904–17 | 1946 |
| Joe Medwick | OF | 1932–48 | 1968 | Lloyd Waner | OF | 1927–45 | 1967 |
| Johnny Mize | 1B | 1936–53 | 1981 | Paul Waner | OF | 1926–45 | 1952 |
| Paul Molitor | 3B | 1978–98 | 2004 | John Ward | 2B-P | 1878–94 | 1964 |
| Joe Morgan | 2B | 1963–84 | 1990 | Mickey Welch | P | 1880–92 | 1973 |
| Eddie Murray | 1B | 1977–97 | 2003 | Willie Wells* | SS | 1924–49 | 1997 |
| Stan Musial | OF-1B | 1941–63 | 1969 | Zach Wheat | OF | 1909–27 | 1959 |
| Hal Newhouser | P | 1939–55 | 1992 | Hoyt Wilhelm | P | 1952–72 | 1985 |
| Kid Nichols | P | 1890–1906 | 1949 | Billy Williams | OF | 1959–76 | 1987 |
| Phil Niekro | P | 1964–87 | 1997 | Ted Williams | OF | 1939–60 | 1966 |
| Jim O'Rourke | OF | 1876–1904 | 1945 | Vic Willis | P | 1898–1910 | 1995 |
| Mel Ott | OF | 1926–47 | 1951 | Ernest Judson Wilson* | 3B | 1922–45 | 2006 |
| Satchel Paige* | P | 1948–65 | 1971 | Hack Wilson | OF | 1923–34 | 1979 |
| Jim Palmer | P | 1965–84 | 1990 | Dave Winfield | P | 1973–95 | 2001 |
| Herb Pennock | P | 1912–34 | 1948 | Early Wynn | P | 1939–63 | 1972 |
| Tony Perez | 1B | 1964–86 | 2000 | Carl Yastrzemski | OF | 1961–83 | 1989 |
| Gaylord Perry | P | 1962–83 | 1991 | Cy Young | P | 1890–1911 | 1937 |
| Eddie Plank | P | 1901–17 | 1946 | Ross Youngs | OF | 1917–26 | 1972 |
| Kirby Puckett | OF | 1984–95 | 2001 | Robin Yount | SS | 1974–93 | 1999 |
| Charley Radbourn | P | 1880–91 | 1939 | | | | |

*Elected on the basis of their career in the Negro leagues.

### Pioneers/Executives

| | Selected |
|---|---|
| Ed Barrow (manager-executive) | 1953 |
| Morgan Bulkeley (executive) | 1937 |
| Alexander Cartwright (executive) | 1938 |
| Henry Chadwick (writer-executive) | 1938 |
| Happy Chandler (commissioner) | 1982 |
| Charles Comiskey (manager-executive) | 1939 |
| Barney Dreyfuss (executive) | 2008 |
| Ford Frick (commissioner-executive) | 1970 |
| Warren Giles (executive) | 1979 |
| Pat Gillick (executive) | 2011 |
| Clark Griffith (executive) | 1946 |
| Will Harridge (executive) | 1972 |
| William Hulbert (executive) | 1995 |
| Ban Johnson (executive) | 1937 |
| Bowie Kuhn (commissioner) | 2008 |
| Kenesaw M. Landis (commissioner) | 1944 |
| Larry MacPhail Sr. (executive) | 1978 |
| Lee MacPhail Jr. (executive) | 1998 |
| Effa Manley (executive) | 2006 |
| Walter O'Malley (executive) | 2008 |
| Alex Pompez (executive) | 2006 |
| Cum Posey (player-manager-owner) | 2006 |
| Branch Rickey (manager-executive) | 1967 |
| Al Spalding (player-executive) | 1939 |
| Bill Veeck Jr. (owner) | 1991 |
| George Weiss (executive) | 1971 |
| Sol White (player-manager) | 2006 |
| J.L. Wilkinson (executive) | 2006 |
| George Wright (player-manager) | 1937 |
| Harry Wright (player-manager-executive) | 1953 |
| Tom Yawkey (executive) | 1980 |

### Managers

| | Managed | Selected |
|---|---|---|
| Walter Alston | 1954–76 | 1983 |
| Sparky Anderson | 1970–94 | 2000 |
| Leo Durocher | 1939–73 | 1994 |
| Rube Foster | 1907–26 | 1981 |
| Ned Hanlon | 1899–1907 | 1996 |
| Bucky Harris | 1924–56 | 1975 |
| Miller Huggins | 1913–29 | 1964 |
| Tommy Lasorda | 1977–96 | 1997 |
| Al Lopez | 1951–69 | 1977 |
| Connie Mack | 1894–1950 | 1937 |
| Joe McCarthy | 1926–50 | 1957 |
| John McGraw | 1899–1932 | 1937 |
| Bill McKechnie | 1915–46 | 1962 |
| Wilbert Robinson | 1902–31 | 1945 |
| Frank Selee | 1890–1905 | 1999 |
| Billy Southworth | 1929, 1940–51 | 2008 |
| Casey Stengel | 1934–65 | 1966 |
| Earl Weaver | 1968–82, 85–86 | 1996 |
| Dick Williams | 1967–69, 1971–88 | 2008 |
| Whitey Herzog | 1973–90 | 2010 |

### Umpires

| | Selected |
|---|---|
| Al Barlick | 1989 |
| Nestor Chylak | 1999 |
| Jocko Conlan | 1974 |
| Tom Connolly | 1953 |
| Billy Evans | 1973 |
| Cal Hubbard | 1976 |
| Bill Klem | 1953 |
| Bill McGowan | 1992 |
| Doug Harvey | 2010 |

## Notable Achievements

### No-Hit Games, Nine Innings or More

#### NATIONAL LEAGUE

| Date | | Pitcher and Game |
|---|---|---|
| 1876 | July 15 | George Bradley, StL vs Hart 2–0 |
| 1880 | June 12 | John Richmond, Wor vs Clev 1–0 (perfect game) |
| | June 17 | Monte Ward, Prov vs Buff 5–0 (perfect game) |
| | Aug 19 | Larry Corcoran, Chi vs Bos 6–0 |
| | Aug 20 | Pud Galvin, Buff vs Wor 1–0 |
| 1882 | Sept 20 | Larry Corcoran, Chi vs Wor 5–0 |
| | Sept 22 | Tim Lovett, Bklyn vs NY 4–0 |
| 1883 | July 25 | Hoss Radbourn, Prov vs Clev 8–0 |
| | Sept 13 | Hugh Daily, Clev vs Phi 1–0 |
| 1884 | June 27 | Larry Corcoran, Chi vs Prov 6–0 |
| | Aug 4 | Pud Galvin, Buff vs Det 18–0 |
| 1885 | July 27 | John Clarkson, Chi vs Prov 4–0 |
| | Aug 29 | Charles Ferguson, Phi vs Prov 1–0 |
| 1891 | July 31 | Amos Rusie, NY vs Bklyn 6–0 |
| | June 22 | Tom Lovett, Bklyn vs NY 4–0 |
| 1892 | Aug 6 | Jack Stivetts, Bos vs Bklyn 11–0 |
| | Aug 22 | Alex Sanders, Lou vs Balt 6–2 |
| | Oct 15 | Bumpus Jones, Cin vs Pitt 7–1 (first major league game) |
| 1893 | Aug 16 | Bill Hawke, Balt vs Wash 5–0 |
| 1897 | Sept 18 | Cy Young, Clev vs Cin 6–0 |
| 1898 | Apr 22 | Ted Breitenstein, Cin vs Pitt 11–0 |
| | Apr 22 | Jim Hughes, Balt vs Bos 8–0 |
| | July 8 | Frank Donahue, Phi vs Bos 5–0 |
| | Aug 21 | Walter Thornton, Chi vs Bklyn 2–0 |

| Date | | Pitcher and Game |
|---|---|---|
| 1899 | May 25 | Deacon Phillippe, Lou vs NY 7–0 |
| | Aug 7 | Vic Willis, Bos vs Wash 7–1 |
| 1900 | July 12 | Noodles Hahn, Cin vs Phi 4–0 |
| 1901 | July 15 | Christy Mathewson, NY vs StL 5–0 |
| 1903 | Sept 18 | Chick Fraser, Phi vs Chi 10–0 |
| 1904 | June 11 | Bob Wicker, Chi at NY 1–0 (hit in 10th; won in 12th) |
| 1905 | June 13 | Christy Mathewson, NY vs Chi 1–0 |
| 1906 | May 1 | John Lush, Phi vs Bklyn 6–0 |
| | July 20 | Mal Eason, Bklyn vs StL 2–0 |
| | Aug 1 | Harry McIntire, Bklyn vs Pitt 0–1 (hit in 11th; lost in 13th) |
| 1907 | May 8 | Frank Pfeffer, Bos vs Cin 6–0 |
| | Sept 20 | Nick Maddox, Pitt vs Bklyn 2–1 |
| 1908 | July 4 | George Wiltse, NY vs Phi 1–0 (10 innings) |
| | Sept 5 | Nap Rucker, Bklyn vs Bos 6–0 |
| 1909 | Apr 15 | Leon Ames, NY vs Bklyn 0–3 (hit in 10th; lost in 13th) |
| 1912 | Sept 6 | Jeff Tesreau, NY vs Phi 3–0 |
| 1914 | Sept 9 | George Davis, Bos vs Phi 7–0 |
| 1915 | Apr 15 | Rube Marquard, NY vs Bklyn 2–0 |
| | Aug 31 | Jimmy Lavender, Chi vs NY 2–0 |
| 1916 | June 16 | Tom Hughes, Bos vs Pitt 2–0 |
| 1917 | May 2 | Jim Vaughn, Chi vs Cin 0–1 (hit in 10th; lost in 10th) |
| | May 2 | Fred Toney, Cin vs Chi 1–0 (10 innings) |

### No-Hit Games, Nine Innings or More *(Cont.)*
#### NATIONAL LEAGUE *(Cont.)*

| Date | Pitcher and Game | Date | Pitcher and Game |
|------|------------------|------|------------------|
| 1919......May 11 | Hod Eller, Cin vs StL 6–0 | 1973......Aug 5 | Phil Niekro, Atl vs SD 9–0 |
| 1922......May 7 | Jesse Barnes, NY vs Phi 6–0 | 1975......Aug 24 | Ed Halicki, SF vs NY 6–0 |
| 1924......July 17 | Jesse Haines, StL vs Bos 5–0 | 1976......July 9 | Larry Dierker, Hou vs Mtl 6–0 |
| 1925......Sept 13 | Dazzy Vance, Bklyn vs Phi 10–1 | Aug 9 | John Candelaria, Pitt vs LA 2–0 |
| 1929......May 8 | Carl Hubbell, NY vs Pitt 11–0 | Sept 29 | John Montefusco, SF vs Atl 9–0 |
| 1934......Sept 21 | Paul Dean, StL vs Bklyn 3–0 | 1978......Apr 16 | Bob Forsch, StL vs Phi 5–0 |
| 1938......June 11 | Johnny Vander Meer, Cin vs Bos 3–0 | June 16 | Tom Seaver, Cin vs StL 4–0 |
| June 15 | Johnny Vander Meer, Cin vs Bklyn 6–0 | 1979......Apr 7 | Ken Forsch, Hou vs Atl 6–0 |
| 1940......Apr 30 | Tex Carleton, Bklyn vs Cin, 3–0 | 1980......June 27 | Jerry Reuss, LA vs SF 8–0 |
| 1941......Aug 30 | Lon Warneke, StL vs Cin 2–0 | 1981......May 10 | Charlie Lea, Mtl vs SF 4–0 |
| 1944......Apr 27 | Jim Tobin, Bos vs Bklyn 2–0 | Sept 26 | Nolan Ryan, Hou vs LA 5–0 |
| May 15 | Clyde Shoun, Cin vs Bos 1–0 | 1983......Sept 26 | Bob Forsch, StL vs Mtl 3–0 |
| 1946......Apr 23 | Ed Head, Bklyn vs Bos 5–0 | 1986......Sept 25 | Mike Scott, Hou vs SF 2–0 |
| 1947......June 18 | Ewell Blackwell, Cin vs Bos 6–0 | 1988......Sept 16 | Tom Browning, Cin vs LA 1–0 |
| 1948......Sept 9 | Rex Barney, Bklyn vs NY 2–0 | | (perfect game) |
| 1950......Aug 11 | Vern Bickford, Bos vs Bklyn 7–0 | 1990 ......June 29 | Fernando Valenzuela, LA vs StL 6–0 |
| 1951......May 6 | Cliff Chambers, Pitt vs Bos 3–0 | Aug 15 | Terry Mulholland, Phi vs SF 6–0 |
| 1952......June 19 | Carl Erskine, Bklyn vs Chi 5–0 | 1991......May 23 | Tommy Greene, Phi vs Mtl 2–0 |
| 1954......June 12 | Jim Wilson, Mil vs Phi 2–0 | July 26 | Mark Gardner, Mtl vs LA 0–1 |
| 1955......May 12 | Sam Jones, Chi vs Pitt 4–0 | | (hit in 10th, lost in 10th) |
| 1956......May 12 | Carl Erskine, Bklyn vs NY 3–0 | July 28 | Dennis Martinez, Mtl vs LA 2–0 |
| Sept 25 | Sal Maglie, Bklyn vs Phi 5–0 | | (perfect game) |
| 1959......May 26 | Harvey Haddix, Pitt vs Mil 0–1 | Sept 11 | Kent Mercker (6), Mark Wohlers (2), |
| | (hit in 13th; lost in 13th) | | and Alejandro Pena (1), Atl vs SD 1–0 |
| 1960......May 15 | Don Cardwell, Chi vs StL 4–0 | 1992......Aug 17 | Kevin Gross, LA vs SF 2–0 |
| Aug 18 | Lew Burdette, Mil vs Phi 1–0 | 1993......Sept 8 | Darryl Kile, Hou vs NY 7–1 |
| Sept 16 | Warren Spahn, Mil vs Phi 4–0 | 1994......Apr 8 | Kent Mercker, Atl vs LA 6–0 |
| 1961......Apr 28 | Warren Spahn, Mil vs SF 1–0 | 1995......June 3 | Pedro Martinez, Mtl vs SD 1–0 |
| 1962......June 30 | Sandy Koufax, LA vs NY 5–0 | | (perfect through nine, hit in 10th) |
| 1963......May 11 | Sandy Koufax, LA vs SF 8–0 | July 14 | Ramon Martinez, LA vs Fla 7–0 |
| May 17 | Don Nottebart, Hou vs Phi 4–1 | 1996......May 11 | Al Leiter, Fla vs Col 11–0 |
| June 15 | Juan Marichal, SF vs Hou 1–0 | Sept 17 | Hideo Nomo, LA vs Col 9–0 |
| 1964......Apr 23 | Ken Johnson, Hou vs Cin 0–1 | 1997......June 10 | Kevin Brown, Fla vs SF 9–0 |
| June 4 | Sandy Koufax, LA vs Phi 3–0 | July 12 | Francisco Cordova (9) and |
| June 21 | Jim Bunning, Phi vs NY 6–0 | | Ricardo Rincon (1), Pitt vs Col 3–0 |
| | (perfect game) | 1999......June 25 | Jose Jimenez, StL vs Ariz 1–0 |
| 1965......June 14 | Jim Maloney, Cin vs NY 0–1 | 2001......May 12 | A.J. Burnett, Fla vs SD 3–0 |
| | (hit in 11th; lost in 11th) | Sept 3 | Bud Smith, StL vs SD 4–0 |
| Aug 19 | Jim Maloney, Cin vs Chi 1–0 | 2003......April 27 | Kevin Millwood, Phi vs SF 1–0 |
| | (10 innings) | June 11 | R. Oswalt (1), P. Munro (2.2), K. |
| Sept 9 | Sandy Koufax, LA vs Chi 1–0 | | Saarloos (1.1), B. Lidge (2), O. Dotel |
| | (perfect game) | | (1), B. Wagner (1), Hou vs NYY 8–0 |
| 1967......June 18 | Don Wilson, Hou vs Atl 2–0 | April 27 | Kevin Millwood, Phi vs SF 1–0 |
| 1968......July 29 | George Culver, Cin vs Phi 6–1 | 2004......May 18 | Randy Johnson, Ariz vs Atl 2–0 |
| Sept 18 | Gaylord Perry, SF vs StL 1–0 | | (perfect game) |
| Sept 18 | Ray Washburn, StL vs SF 2–0 | 2006......Sept 6 | Anibal Sanchez, Fla vs Ariz 2–0 |
| 1969......Apr 17 | Bill Stoneman, Mtl vs Phi 7–0 | 2008......Sept 14 | †Carlos Zambrano, Chi vs Hou 5–0 |
| Apr 30 | Jim Maloney, Cin vs Hou 10–0 | 2009......July 10 | Jonathan Sanchez, SF vs SD 8–0 |
| May 1 | Don Wilson, Hou vs Cin 4–0 | 2010......Apr 17 | Ubaldo Jimenez, Col vs Atl 4–0 |
| Aug 19 | Ken Holtzman, Chi vs Atl 3–0 | May 29 | Roy Halladay, Phi vs Fla 1–0 |
| Sept 20 | Bob Moose, Pitt vs NY 4–0 | | (perfect game) |
| 1970......June 12 | Dock Ellis, Pitt vs SD 2–0 | June 26 | ‡Edwin Jackson, Ariz vs TB 1–0 |
| July 20 | Bill Singer, LA vs Phi 5–0 | Oct 6 | Roy Halladay, Phi vs Cin 4–0 |
| 1971......June 3 | Ken Holtzman, Chi vs Cin 1–0 | | (NLDS) |
| June 23 | Rick Wise, Phi vs Cin 4–0 | | |
| Aug 14 | Bob Gibson, StL vs Pitt 11–0 | | |
| 1972......Apr 16 | Burt Hooton, Chi vs Phi 4–0 | | |
| Sept 2 | Milt Pappas, Chi vs SD 8–0 | | |
| Oct 2 | Bill Stoneman, Mtl vs NY 7–0 | | |

Note: Includes the games struck from the official record book on Sept. 4, 1991, when baseball's committee on statistical accuracy voted to define no-hitters as games of nine innings or more that end with a team getting no hits.

†Game played in Milwaukee due to weather-related closure of Houston's home field.

‡Interleague game.

## No-Hit Games, Nine Innings or More *(Cont.)*

### AMERICAN LEAGUE

| Date | Pitcher and Game | Date | Pitcher and Game |
|------|------------------|------|------------------|
| 1901......May 9 | Earl Moore, Clev vs Chi 2–4 (hit in 10th; lost in 10th) | 1957......Aug 20 | Bob Keegan, Chi vs Wash 6–0 |
| 1902......Sept 20 | Jimmy Callahan, Chi vs Det 3–0 | 1958......July 20 | Jim Bunning, Det vs Bos 3–0 |
| 1904......May 5 | Cy Young, Bos vs Phi 3–0 (perfect game) | Sept 20 | Hoyt Wilhelm, Balt vs NY 1–0 |
| Aug 17 | Jesse Tannehill, Bos vs Chi 6–0 | 1962......May 5 | Bo Belinsky, LA vs Balt 2–0 |
| 1905......July 22 | Weldon Henley, Phi vs StL 6–0 | June 26 | Earl Wilson, Bos vs LA 2–0 |
| Sept 6 | Frank Smith, Chi vs Det 15–0 | Aug 1 | Bill Monbouquette, Bos vs Chi 1–0 |
| Sept 27 | Bill Dinneen, Bos vs Chi 2–0 | Aug 26 | Jack Kralick, Minn vs KC 1–0 |
| 1908......June 30 | Cy Young, Bos vs NY 8–0 | 1965......Sept 16 | Dave Morehead, Bos vs Clev 2–0 |
| Sept 18 | Bob Rhoades, Clev vs Bos 2–1 | 1966......June 10 | Sonny Siebert, Clev vs Wash 2–0 |
| Sept 20 | Frank Smith, Chi vs Phi 1–0 | 1967......Apr 30 | Steve Barber (8⅔) and Stu Miller (⅓), Balt vs Det 1–2 |
| Oct 2 | Addie Joss, Clev vs Chi 1–0 (perfect game) | Aug 25 | Dean Chance, Minn vs Clev 2–1 |
| 1910......Apr 20 | Addie Joss, Clev vs Chi 1–0 | Sept 10 | Joel Horlen, Chi vs Det 6–0 |
| May 12 | Chief Bender, Phi vs Clev 4–0 | 1968......Apr 27 | Tom Phoebus, Balt vs Bos 6–0 |
| Aug 30 | Tom Hughes, NY vs Clev 0–5 (hit in 10th; lost in 11th) | May 8 | Catfish Hunter, Oak vs Minn 4–0 (perfect game) |
| 1911......July 29 | Joe Wood, Bos vs StL 5–0 | 1969......Aug 13 | Jim Palmer, Balt vs Oak 8–0 |
| Aug 27 | Ed Walsh, Chi vs Bos 5–0 | 1970......July 3 | Clyde Wright, Cal vs Oak 4–0 |
| 1912......July 4 | George Mullin, Det vs StL 7–0 | Sept 21 | Vida Blue, Oak vs Minn 6–0 |
| Aug 30 | Earl Hamilton, StL vs Det 5–1 | 1973......Apr 27 | Steve Busby, KC vs Det 3–0 |
| 1914......May 14 | Jim Scott, Chi vs Wash 0–1 (hit in 10th; lost in 10th) | May 15 | Nolan Ryan, Cal vs KC 3–0 |
| May 31 | Joe Benz, Chi vs Clev 6–1 | July 15 | Nolan Ryan, Cal vs Det 6–0 |
| 1916......June 21 | George Foster, Bos vs NY 2–0 | July 30 | Jim Bibby, Tex vs Oak 6–0 |
| Aug 26 | Joe Bush, Phi vs Clev 5–0 | 1974......June 19 | Steve Busby, KC vs Mil 2–0 |
| Aug 30 | Dutch Leonard, Bos vs StL 4–0 | July 19 | Dick Bosman, Clev vs Oak 4–0 |
| 1917......Apr 14 | Ed Cicotte, Chi vs StL 11–0 | Sept 28 | Nolan Ryan, Cal vs Minn 4–0 |
| Apr 24 | George Mogridge, NY vs Bos 2–1 | 1975......June 1 | Nolan Ryan, Cal vs Balt 1–0 |
| May 5 | Ernie Koob, StL vs Chi 1–0 | Sept 28 | Vida Blue (5), Glenn Abbott and Paul Lindblad (1), Rollie Fingers (2), Oak vs Cal 5–0 |
| May 6 | Bob Groom, StL vs Chi 3–0 | | |
| June 23 | Ernie Shore, Bos vs Wash 4–0 (perfect game) | 1976......July 28 | John Odom (5) and Francisco Barrios (4), Chi vs Oak 2–1 |
| 1918......June 3 | Dutch Leonard, Bos vs Det 5–0 | 1977......May 14 | Jim Colborn, KC vs Tex 6–0 |
| 1919......Sept 10 | Ray Caldwell, Clev vs NY 3–0 | May 30 | Dennis Eckersley, Clev vs Cal 1–0 |
| 1920......July 1 | Walter Johnson, Wash vs Bos 1–0 | Sept 22 | Bert Blyleven, Tex vs Cal 6–0 |
| 1922......Apr 30 | Charlie Robertson, Chi vs Det 2–0 (perfect game) | 1981......May 15 | Len Barker, Clev vs Tor 3–0 (perfect game) |
| 1923......Sept 4 | Sam Jones, NY vs Phi 2–0 | 1983......July 4 | Dave Righetti, NY vs Bos 4–0 |
| Sept 7 | Howard Ehmke, Bos vs Phi 4–0 | Sept 29 | Mike Warren, Oak vs Chi 3–0 |
| 1926......Aug 21 | Ted Lyons, Chi vs Bos 6–0 | 1984......Apr 7 | Jack Morris, Det vs Chi 4–0 |
| 1931......Apr 29 | Wes Ferrell, Clev vs StL 9–0 | Sept 30 | Mike Witt, Cal vs Tex 1–0 (perfect game) |
| Aug 8 | Bob Burke, Wash vs Bos 5–0 | 1986......Sept 19 | Joe Cowley, Chi vs Cal 7–1 |
| 1934......Sept 18 | Bobo Newsom, StL vs Bos 1–2 (hit in 10th; lost in 10th) | 1987......Apr 15 | Juan Nieves, Mil vs Balt 7–0 |
| 1935......Aug 31 | Vern Kennedy, Chi vs Clev 5–0 | 1990......Apr 11 | Mark Langston (7), Mike Witt (2), Cal vs Sea 1–0 |
| 1937......June 1 | Bill Dietrich, Chi vs StL 8–0 | June 2 | Randy Johnson, Sea vs Det 2–0 |
| 1938......Aug 27 | Mtle Pearson, NY vs Clev 13–0 | June 11 | Nolan Ryan, Tex vs Oak 5–0 |
| 1940......Apr 16 | Bob Feller, Clev vs Chi 1–0 (opening day) | June 29 | Dave Stewart, Oak vs Tor 5–0 |
| 1945......Sept 9 | Dick Fowler, Phi vs StL 1–0 | July 1 | Andy Hawkins, NY vs Chi 0–4 (pitched eight of nine–innning game) |
| 1946......Apr 30 | Bob Feller, Clev vs NY 1–0 | Sept 2 | Dave Stieb, Tor vs Clev 3–0 |
| 1947......July 10 | Don Black, Clev vs Phi 3–0 | 1991......May 1 | Nolan Ryan, Tex vs Tor 3–0 |
| Sep 3 | Bill McCahan, Phi vs Wash 3–0 | July 13 | Bob Milacki (6), Mike Flanagan (1), Mark Williamson (1), and Gregg Olson (1), Balt vs Oak 2–0 |
| 1948......June 30 | Bob Lemon, Clev vs Det 2–0 | | |
| 1951......July 1 | Bob Feller, Clev vs Det 2–1 | Aug 11 | Wilson Alvarez, Chi vs Balt 7–0 |
| July 12 | Allie Reynolds, NY vs Clev 1–0 | Aug 26 | Bret Saberhagen, KC vs Chi 7–0 |
| Sept 28 | Allie Reynolds, NY vs Bos 8–0 | 1993......Apr 22 | Chris Bosio, Sea vs Bos 7–0 |
| 1952......May 15 | Virgil Trucks, Det vs Wash 1–0 | Sept 4 | Jim Abbott, NY vs Clev 4–0 |
| Aug 25 | Virgil Trucks, Det vs NY 1–0 | 1994......Apr 27 | Scott Erickson, Minn vs Mil 6–0 |
| 1953......May 6 | Bobo Holloman, StL vs Phi 6–0 (first major league start) | July 28 | Kenny Rogers, Texas vs Cal 4–0 (perfect game) |
| 1956......July 14 | Mel Parnell, Bos vs Chi 4–0 | 1996......May 14 | Dwight Gooden, NY vs Sea 2–0 |
| Oct 8 | Don Larsen, NY (A) vs Bklyn (N) 2–0 (World Series) (perfect game) | | |

## No-Hit Games, Nine Innings or More *(Cont.)*

### AMERICAN LEAGUE *(Cont.)*

| Date | Pitcher and Game |
|---|---|
| 1998.....May 17 | David Wells, NY vs Minn 4–0 (perfect game) |
| 1999.....July 18 | David Cone, NY vs Mtl 6–0 (perfect game) |
| Sept 11 | Eric Milton, Minn vs Ana 7–0 |
| 2001.....Apr 4 | Hideo Nomo, Bos vs Balt 3–0 |
| 2002.....Apr 27 | Derek Lowe, Bos vs TB 10–0 |
| 2007.....Apr 19 | Mark Buehrle, Chi vs Tex, 6–0 |
| June 12 | Justin Verlander, Det vs Mil 4–0 |
| Sep 1 | Clay Buchholz, Bos vs Balt 10–0 |
| 2008.....May 19 | Jon Lester, Bos vs KC 7–0 |
| 2009.....July 23 | Mark Buehrle, Chi vs TB 5–0 |
| 2010......May 9 | Dallas Braden, Oak vs TB 4–0 (perfect game) |
| July 26 | Matt Garza, TB vs Det 5–0 |
| 2011.....May 3 | Francisco Liriano, Min vs Chi 1–0 |
| May 7 | Justin Verlander, Det vs Tor 9–0 |
| July 27 | Ervin Santana, LAA vs Cle 3–1 |

## Longest Hitting Streaks

### NATIONAL LEAGUE

| Player and Team | Year | G |
|---|---|---|
| Willie Keeler, Balt | 1897 | 44 |
| Pete Rose, Cin | 1978 | 44 |
| Bill Dahlen, Chi | 1894 | 42 |
| Tommy Holmes, Bos | 1945 | 37 |
| Billy Hamilton, Phi | 1894 | 36 |
| Jimmy Rollins, Phi | 2005–06 | 36 |
| Fred Clarke, Lou | 1895 | 35 |
| Luis Castillo, Fla | 2002 | 35 |
| Chase Utley, Phi | 2006 | 35 |
| Benito Santiago, SD | 1987 | 34 |
| George Davis, NY | 1893 | 33 |
| Rogers Hornsby, StL | 1922 | 33 |
| Dan Uggla, Atl | 2011 | 33 |

### AMERICAN LEAGUE

| Player and Team | Year | G |
|---|---|---|
| Joe DiMaggio, NY | 1941 | 56 |
| George Sisler, StL | 1922 | 41 |
| Ty Cobb, Det | 1911 | 40 |
| Paul Molitor, Mil | 1987 | 39 |
| Ty Cobb, Det | 1917 | 35 |
| George Sisler, StL | 1925 | 34 |
| George McQuinn, StL | 1938 | 34 |
| Dom DiMaggio, Bos | 1949 | 34 |
| Hal Chase, NY | 1907 | 33 |
| Heinie Manush, Wash | 1933 | 33 |

## Triple Crown Hitters

### NATIONAL LEAGUE

| Player and Team | Year | HR | RBI | BA |
|---|---|---|---|---|
| Paul Hines, Prov | 1878 | 4 | 50 | .358 |
| Hugh Duffy, Bos | 1894 | 18 | 145 | .438 |
| Heinie Zimmerman*, Chi | 1912 | 14 | 103 | .372 |
| Rogers Hornsby, StL | 1922 | 42 | 152 | .401 |
| | 1925 | 39 | 143 | .403 |
| Chuck Klein, Phi | 1933 | 28 | 120 | .368 |
| Joe Medwick, StL | 1937 | 31 | 154 | .374 |

*Zimmerman ranked first in RBIs as calculated by Ernie Lanigan, but only third as calculated by Information Concepts Inc.

### AMERICAN LEAGUE

| Player and Team | Year | HR | RBI | BA |
|---|---|---|---|---|
| Nap Lajoie, Phi | 1901 | 14 | 125 | .422 |
| Ty Cobb, Det | 1909 | 9 | 115 | .377 |
| Jimmie Foxx, Phi | 1933 | 48 | 163 | .356 |
| Lou Gehrig, NY | 1934 | 49 | 165 | .363 |
| Ted Williams, Bos | 1942 | 36 | 137 | .356 |
| | 1947 | 32 | 114 | .343 |
| Mickey Mantle, NY | 1956 | 52 | 130 | .353 |
| Frank Robinson, Balt | 1966 | 49 | 122 | .316 |
| Carl Yastrzemski, Bos | 1967 | 44 | 121 | .326 |

## Triple Crown Pitchers

### NATIONAL LEAGUE

| Player and Team | Year | W | L | SO | ERA |
|---|---|---|---|---|---|
| Tommy Bond, Bos | 1877 | 40 | 17 | 170 | 2.11 |
| Hoss Radbourn, Prov | 1884 | 60 | 12 | 441 | 1.38 |
| Tim Keefe, NY | 1888 | 35 | 12 | 333 | 1.74 |
| John Clarkson, Bos | 1889 | 49 | 19 | 284 | 2.73 |
| Amos Rusie, NY | 1894 | 36 | 13 | 195 | 2.78 |
| Christy Mathewson, NY | 1905 | 31 | 8 | 206 | 1.27 |
| | 1908 | 37 | 11 | 259 | 1.43 |
| Grover Alexander, Phi | 1915 | 31 | 10 | 241 | 1.22 |
| | 1916 | 33 | 12 | 167 | 1.55 |
| | 1917 | 30 | 13 | 201 | 1.86 |
| Hippo Vaughn, Chi | 1918 | 22 | 10 | 148 | 1.74 |
| Dazzy Vance, Bklyn | 1924 | 28 | 6 | 262 | 2.16 |
| Bucky Walters, Cin | 1939 | 27 | 11 | 137 | 2.29 |
| Sandy Koufax, LA | 1963 | 25 | 5 | 306 | 1.88 |
| | 1965 | 26 | 8 | 382 | 2.04 |
| | 1966 | 27 | 9 | 317 | 1.73 |
| Steve Carlton, Phi | 1972 | 27 | 10 | 310 | 1.97 |
| Dwight Gooden, NY | 1985 | 24 | 4 | 268 | 1.53 |
| Randy Johnson, Ariz | 2002 | 24 | 5 | 334 | 2.32 |
| *Clayton Kershaw, LA | 2011 | 21 | 5 | 248 | 2.28 |

### AMERICAN LEAGUE

| Player and Team | Year | W | L | SO | ERA |
|---|---|---|---|---|---|
| Cy Young, Bos | 1901 | 33 | 10 | 158 | 1.62 |
| Rube Waddell, Phi | 1905 | 26 | 11 | 287 | 1.48 |
| Walter Johnson, Wash | 1913 | 36 | 7 | 303 | 1.09 |
| | 1918 | 23 | 13 | 162 | 1.27 |
| | 1924 | 23 | 7 | 158 | 2.72 |
| Lefty Grove, Phi | 1930 | 28 | 5 | 209 | 2.54 |
| | 1931 | 31 | 4 | 175 | 2.06 |
| Lefty Gomez, NY | 1934 | 26 | 5 | 158 | 2.33 |
| | 1937 | 21 | 11 | 194 | 2.33 |
| Hal Newhouser, Det | 1945 | 25 | 9 | 212 | 1.81 |
| Roger Clemens, Tor | 1997 | 21 | 7 | 292 | 2.05 |
| | 1998 | 20 | 6 | 271 | 2.64 |
| Pedro Martinez, Bos | 1999 | 23 | 4 | 313 | 2.07 |
| *Johan Santana, Minn | 2006 | 19 | 6 | 245 | 2.77 |
| Justin Verlander, Det | 2011 | 24 | 5 | 250 | 2.40 |

*Tied with another pitcher for most wins

### Consecutive Games Played, 500 or More Games

| | | | |
|---|---|---|---|
| Cal Ripken Jr. | 2,632 | Frank McCormick | 652 |
| Lou Gehrig | 2,130 | Sandy Alomar Sr. | 648 |
| Everett Scott | 1,307 | Eddie Brown | 618 |
| Steve Garvey | 1,207 | Roy McMillan | 585 |
| Miguel Tejada | 1,152 | George Pinckney | 577 |
| Billy Williams | 1,117 | Steve Brodie | 574 |
| Joe Sewell | 1,103 | Aaron Ward | 565 |
| Stan Musial | 895 | Alex Rodriguez | 546 |
| Eddie Yost | 829 | Candy LaChance | 540 |
| Gus Suhr | 822 | Buck Freeman | 535 |
| Nellie Fox | 798 | Fred Luderus | 533 |
| Pete Rose | 745 | Hideki Matsui | 518 |
| Dale Murphy | 740 | Clyde Milan | 511 |
| Richie Ashburn | 730 | Charlie Gehringer | 511 |
| Ernie Banks | 717 | Vada Pinson | 508 |
| Pete Rose | 678 | Tony Cuccinello | 504 |
| Earl Averill | 673 | Charlie Gehringer | 504 |

### Unassisted Triple Plays

| Player and Team | Date | Pos | Opp | Opp Batter |
|---|---|---|---|---|
| Neal Ball, Clev | 7-19-09 | SS | Bos | Amby McConnell |
| Bill Wambsganss, Clev | 10-10-20 | 2B | Bklyn | Clarence Mitchell |
| George Burns, Bos | 9-14-23 | 1B | Clev | Frank Brower |
| Ernie Padgett, Bos | 10-6-23 | SS | Phi | Walter Holke |
| Glenn Wright, Pitt | 5-7-25 | SS | StL | Jim Bottomley |
| Jimmy Cooney, Chi | 5-30-27 | SS | Pitt | Paul Waner |
| Johnny Neun, Det | 5-31-27 | 1B | Clev | Homer Summa |
| Ron Hansen, Wash | 7-30-68 | SS | Clev | Joe Azcue |
| Mickey Morandini, Phi | 9-20-92 | 2B | Pitt | Jeff King |
| John Valentin, Bos | 7-15-94 | SS | Minn | Marc Newfield |
| Randy Velarde, Oak | 5-29-00 | 2B | NYY | Shane Spencer |
| Rafael Furcal, Atl | 8-10-03 | SS | StL | Woody Williams |
| Troy Tulowitzki, Col | 4-29-07 | SS | Atl | Chipper Jones |
| Asdrubal Cabrera, Cle | 5-12-08 | 2B | Tor | Lyle Overbay |
| Eric Bruntlett, Phi | 8-23-09 | 2B | NYM | Jeff Francoeur |

## Year-by-Year Leaders

### NATIONAL LEAGUE
#### Leading Batsmen

| Year | Player and Team | BA | Year | Player and Team | BA |
|---|---|---|---|---|---|
| 1900 | Honus Wagner, Pitt | .381 | 1923 | Rogers Hornsby, StL | .384 |
| 1901 | Jesse Burkett, StL | .382 | 1924 | Rogers Hornsby, StL | .424 |
| 1902 | Ginger Beaumtl, Pitt | .357 | 1925 | Rogers Hornsby, StL | .403 |
| 1903 | Honus Wagner, Pitt | .355 | 1926 | Bubbles Hargrave, Cin | .353 |
| 1904 | Honus Wagner, Pitt | .349 | 1927 | Paul Waner, Pitt | .380 |
| 1905 | Cy Seymour, Cin | .377 | 1928 | Rogers Hornsby, Bos | .387 |
| 1906 | Honus Wagner, Pitt | .339 | 1929 | Lefty O'Doul, Phi | .398 |
| 1907 | Honus Wagner, Pitt | .350 | 1930 | Bill Terry, NY | .401 |
| 1908 | Honus Wagner, Pitt | .354 | 1931 | Chick Hafey, StL | .349 |
| 1909 | Honus Wagner, Pitt | .339 | 1932 | Lefty O'Doul, Phi | .368 |
| 1910 | Sherry Magee, Phi | .331 | 1933 | Chuck Klein, Phi | .368 |
| 1911 | Honus Wagner, Pitt | .334 | 1934 | Paul Waner, Pitt | .362 |
| 1912 | Heinie Zimmerman, Chi | .372 | 1935 | Arky Vaughan, Pitt | .385 |
| 1913 | Jake Daubert, Bklyn | .350 | 1936 | Paul Waner, Pitt | .373 |
| 1914 | Jake Daubert, Bklyn | .329 | 1937 | Joe Medwick, StL | .374 |
| 1915 | Larry Doyle, NY | .320 | 1938 | Ernie Lombardi, Cin | .342 |
| 1916 | Hal Chase, Cin | .339 | 1939 | Johnny Mize, StL | .349 |
| 1917 | Edd Roush, Cin | .341 | 1940 | Debs Garms, Pitt | .355 |
| 1918 | Zach Wheat, Bklyn | .335 | 1941 | Pete Reiser, Bklyn | .343 |
| 1919 | Edd Roush, Cin | .321 | 1942 | Ernie Lombardi, Bos | .330 |
| 1920 | Rogers Hornsby, StL | .370 | 1943 | Stan Musial, StL | .357 |
| 1921 | Rogers Hornsby, StL | .397 | 1944 | Dixie Walker, Bklyn | .357 |
| 1922 | Rogers Hornsby, StL | .401 | 1945 | Phil Cavarretta, Chi | .355 |

## NATIONAL LEAGUE
### Leading Batsmen *(Cont.)*

| Year | Player and Team | BA | Year | Player and Team | BA |
|---|---|---|---|---|---|
| 1946 | Stan Musial, St | .365 | 1980 | Bill Buckner, Chi | .324 |
| 1947 | Harry Walker, StL-Phi | .363 | 1981 | Bill Madlock, Pitt | .341 |
| 1948 | Stan Musial, StL | .376 | 1982 | Al Oliver, Mtl | .331 |
| 1949 | Jackie Robinson, Bklyn | .342 | 1983 | Bill Madlock, Pitt | .323 |
| 1950 | Stan Musial, StL | .346 | 1984 | Tony Gwynn, SD | .351 |
| 1951 | Stan Musial, StL | .355 | 1985 | Willie McGee, StL | .353 |
| 1952 | Stan Musial, StL | .336 | 1986 | Tim Raines, Mtl | .334 |
| 1953 | Carl Furillo, Bklyn | .344 | 1987 | Tony Gwynn, SD | .370 |
| 1954 | Willie Mays, NY | .345 | 1988 | Tony Gwynn, SD | .313 |
| 1955 | Richie Ashburn, Phi | .338 | 1989 | Tony Gwynn, SD | .336 |
| 1956 | Hank Aaron, Mil | .328 | 1990 | Willie McGee, StL | .335 |
| 1957 | Stan Musial, StL | .351 | 1991 | Terry Pendleton, Atl | .319 |
| 1958 | Richie Ashburn, Phi | .350 | 1992 | Gary Sheffield, SD | .330 |
| 1959 | Hank Aaron, Mil | .355 | 1993 | Andres Galarraga, Col | .370 |
| 1960 | Dick Groat, Pitt | .325 | 1994 | Tony Gwynn, SD | .394 |
| 1961 | Roberto Clemente, Pitt | .351 | 1995 | Tony Gwynn, SD | .368 |
| 1962 | Tommy Davis, LA | .346 | 1996 | Tony Gwynn, SD | .353 |
| 1963 | Tommy Davis, LA | .326 | 1997 | Tony Gwynn, SD | .372 |
| 1964 | Roberto Clemente, Pitt | .339 | 1998 | Larry Walker, Col | .363 |
| 1965 | Roberto Clemente, Pitt | .329 | 1999 | Larry Walker, Col | .379 |
| 1966 | Matty Alou, Pitt | .342 | 2000 | Todd Helton, Col | .372 |
| 1967 | Roberto Clemente, Pitt | .357 | 2001 | Larry Walker, Col | .350 |
| 1968 | Pete Rose, Cin | .335 | 2002 | Barry Bonds, SF | .370 |
| 1969 | Pete Rose, Cin | .348 | 2003 | Albert Pujols, StL | .359 |
| 1970 | Rico Carty, Atl | .366 | 2004 | Barry Bonds, SF | .362 |
| 1971 | Joe Torre, StL | .363 | 2005 | Derrek Lee, Chi | .335 |
| 1972 | Billy Williams, Chi | .333 | 2006 | Freddy Sanchez, Pitt | .334 |
| 1973 | Pete Rose, Cin | .338 | 2007 | Matt Holliday, Col | .340* |
| 1974 | Ralph Garr, Atl | .353 | 2008 | Chipper Jones, Atl | .364 |
| 1975 | Bill Madlock, Chi | .354 | 2009 | Hanley Ramirez, Fla | .342 |
| 1976 | Bill Madlock, Chi | .339 | 2010 | Carlos Gonzalez, Col | .336 |
| 1977 | Dave Parker, Pitt | .338 | 2011 | Jose Reyes, NY | .337 |
| 1978 | Dave Parker, Pitt | .334 | | | |
| 1979 | Keith Hernandez, StL | .344 | | | |

*Includes one-game NL Wild Card tiebreaker.

## Leaders in Runs Scored

| Year | Player and Team | Runs | Year | Player and Team | Runs |
|---|---|---|---|---|---|
| 1900 | Roy Thomas, Phi | 131 | 1925 | Kiki Cuyler, Pitt | 144 |
| 1901 | Jesse Burkett, StL | 139 | 1926 | Kiki Cuyler, Pitt | 113 |
| 1902 | Honus Wagner, Pitt | 105 | 1927 | Lloyd Waner, Pitt | 133 |
| 1903 | Ginger Beaumont, Pitt | 137 | | Rogers Hornsby, NY | 133 |
| 1904 | George Browne, NY | 99 | 1928 | Paul Waner, Pitt | 142 |
| 1905 | Mike Donlin, NY | 124 | 1929 | Rogers Hornsby, Chi | 156 |
| 1906 | Honus Wagner, Pitt | 103 | 1930 | Chuck Klein, Phi | 158 |
| | Frank Chance, Chi | 103 | 1931 | Bill Terry, NY | 121 |
| 1907 | Spike Shannon, NY | 104 | | Chuck Klein, Phi | 121 |
| 1908 | Fred Tenney, NY | 101 | 1932 | Chuck Klein, Phi | 152 |
| 1909 | Tommy Leach, Pitt | 126 | 1933 | Pepper Martin, StL | 122 |
| 1910 | Sherry Magee, Phi | 110 | 1934 | Paul Waner, Pitt | 122 |
| 1911 | Jimmy Sheckard, Chi | 121 | 1935 | Augie Galan, Chi | 133 |
| 1912 | Bob Bescher, Cin | 120 | 1936 | Arky Vaughan, Pitt | 122 |
| 1913 | Tommy Leach, Chi | 99 | 1937 | Joe Medwick, StL | 111 |
| | Max Carey, Pitt | 99 | 1938 | Mel Ott, NY | 116 |
| 1914 | George Burns, NY | 100 | 1939 | Billy Werber, Cin | 115 |
| 1915 | Gavvy Cravath, Phi | 89 | 1940 | Arky Vaughan, Pitt | 113 |
| 1916 | George Burns, NY | 105 | 1941 | Pete Reiser, Bklyn | 117 |
| 1917 | George Burns, NY | 103 | 1942 | Mel Ott, NY | 118 |
| 1918 | Heinie Groh, Cin | 88 | 1943 | Arky Vaughan, Bklyn | 112 |
| 1919 | George Burns, NY | 86 | 1944 | Bill Nicholson, Chi | 116 |
| 1920 | George Burns, NY | 115 | 1945 | Eddie Stanky, Bklyn | 128 |
| 1921 | Rogers Hornsby, StL | 131 | 1946 | Stan Musial, StL | 124 |
| 1922 | Rogers Hornsby, StL | 141 | 1947 | Johnny Mize, NY | 137 |
| 1923 | Ross Youngs, NY | 121 | 1948 | Stan Musial, StL | 135 |
| 1924 | Frankie Frisch, NY | 121 | 1949 | Pee Wee Reese, Bklyn | 132 |
| | Rogers Hornsby, StL | 121 | 1950 | Earl Torgeson, Bos | 120 |

## NATIONAL LEAGUE
### Leaders in Runs Scored (Cont.)

| Year | Player and Team | Runs | Year | Player and Team | Runs |
|---|---|---|---|---|---|
| 1951 | Stan Musial, StL | 124 | 1981 | Mike Schmidt, Phi | 78 |
|  | Ralph Kiner, Pitt | 124 | 1982 | Lonnie Smith, StL | 120 |
| 1952 | Stan Musial, StL | 105 | 1983 | Tim Raines, Mtl | 133 |
|  | Solly Hemus, StL | 105 | 1984 | Ryne Sandberg, Chi | 114 |
| 1953 | Duke Snider, Bklyn | 132 | 1985 | Dale Murphy, Atl | 118 |
| 1954 | Stan Musial, StL | 120 | 1986 | Von Hayes, Phi | 107 |
|  | Duke Snider, Bklyn | 120 |  | Tony Gwynn, SD | 107 |
| 1955 | Duke Snider, Bklyn | 126 | 1987 | Tim Raines, Mtl | 123 |
| 1956 | Frank Robinson, Cin | 122 | 1988 | Brett Butler, SF | 109 |
| 1957 | Hank Aaron, Mil | 118 | 1989 | Howard Johnson, NY | 104 |
| 1958 | Willie Mays, SF | 121 |  | Will Clark, SF | 104 |
| 1959 | Vada Pinson, Cin | 131 |  | Ryne Sandberg, Chi | 104 |
| 1960 | Bill Bruton, Mil | 112 | 1990 | Ryne Sandberg, Chi | 116 |
| 1961 | Willie Mays, SF | 129 | 1991 | Brett Butler, LA | 112 |
| 1962 | Frank Robinson, Cin | 134 | 1992 | Barry Bonds, Pitt | 109 |
| 1963 | Hank Aaron, Mil | 121 | 1993 | Lenny Dykstra, Phi | 143 |
| 1964 | Dick Allen, Phi | 125 | 1994 | Jeff Bagwell, Hou | 104 |
| 1965 | Tommy Harper, Cin | 126 | 1995 | Craig Biggio, Hou | 123 |
| 1966 | Felipe Alou, Atl | 122 | 1996 | Ellis Burks, Col | 142 |
| 1967 | Hank Aaron, Atl | 113 | 1997 | Craig Biggio, Hou | 146 |
|  | Lou Brock, StL | 113 | 1998 | Sammy Sosa, Chi | 134 |
| 1968 | Glenn Beckert, Chi | 98 | 1999 | Jeff Bagwell, Hou | 143 |
| 1969 | Bobby Bonds, SF | 120 | 2000 | Jeff Bagwell, Hou | 152 |
|  | Pete Rose, Cin | 120 | 2001 | Sammy Sosa, Chi | 146 |
| 1970 | Billy Williams, Chi | 137 | 2002 | Sammy Sosa, Chi | 122 |
| 1971 | Lou Brock, StL | 126 | 2003 | Albert Pujols, StL | 137 |
| 1972 | Joe Morgan, Cin | 122 | 2004 | Albert Pujols, StL | 133 |
| 1973 | Bobby Bonds, SF | 131 | 2005 | Albert Pujols, StL | 129 |
| 1974 | Pete Rose, Cin | 110 | 2006 | Chase Utley, Phi | 131 |
| 1975 | Pete Rose, Cin | 112 | 2007 | Jimmy Rollins, Phi | 139 |
| 1976 | Pete Rose, Cin | 130 | 2008 | Hanley Ramirez, Fla | 125 |
| 1977 | George Foster, Cin | 124 | 2009 | Albert Pujols, StL | 124 |
| 1978 | Ivan DeJesus, Chi | 104 | 2010 | Albert Pujols, StL | 115 |
| 1979 | Keith Hernandez, StL | 116 | 2011 | Matt Kemp, LA | 115 |
| 1980 | Keith Hernandez, StL | 111 |  |  |  |

### Leaders in Hits

| Year | Player and Team | Hits | Year | Player and Team | Hits |
|---|---|---|---|---|---|
| 1900 | Willie Keeler, Bklyn | 208 | 1927 | Paul Waner, Pitt | 237 |
| 1901 | Jesse Burkett, StL | 228 | 1928 | Freddy Lindstrom, NY | 231 |
| 1902 | Ginger Beaumont, Pitt | 194 | 1929 | Lefty O'Doul, Phi | 254 |
| 1903 | Ginger Beaumont, Pitt | 209 | 1930 | Bill Terry, NY | 254 |
| 1904 | Ginger Beaumont, Pitt | 185 | 1931 | Lloyd Waner, Pitt | 214 |
| 1905 | Cy Seymour, Cin | 219 | 1932 | Chuck Klein, Phi | 226 |
| 1906 | Harry Steinfeldt, Chi | 176 | 1933 | Chuck Klein, Phi | 223 |
| 1907 | Ginger Beaumont, Bos | 187 | 1934 | Paul Waner, Pitt | 217 |
| 1908 | Honus Wagner, Pitt | 201 | 1935 | Billy Herman, Chi | 227 |
| 1909 | Larry Doyle, NY | 172 | 1936 | Joe Medwick, StL | 223 |
| 1910 | Bobby Byrne, Pitt | 178 | 1937 | Joe Medwick, StL | 237 |
|  | Honus Wagner, Pitt | 178 | 1938 | Frank McCormick, Cin | 209 |
| 1911 | Doc Miller, Bos | 192 | 1939 | Frank McCormick, Cin | 209 |
| 1912 | Heinie Zimmerman, Chi | 207 | 1940 | Stan Hack, Chi | 191 |
| 1913 | Gavvy Cravath, Phi | 179 |  | Frank McCormick, Cin | 191 |
| 1914 | Sherry Magee, Phi | 171 | 1941 | Stan Hack, Chi | 186 |
| 1915 | Larry Doyle, NY | 189 | 1942 | Enos Slaughter, StL | 188 |
| 1916 | Hal Chase, Cin | 184 | 1943 | Stan Musial, StL | 220 |
| 1917 | Heinie Groh, Cin | 182 | 1944 | Phil Cavarretta, Chi | 197 |
| 1918 | Charlie Hollocher, Chi | 161 |  | Stan Musial, StL | 197 |
| 1919 | Ivy Olson, Bklyn | 164 | 1945 | Tommy Holmes, Bos | 224 |
| 1920 | Rogers Hornsby, StL | 218 | 1946 | Stan Musial, StL | 228 |
| 1921 | Rogers Hornsby, StL | 235 | 1947 | Tommy Holmes, Bos | 191 |
| 1922 | Rogers Hornsby, StL | 250 | 1948 | Stan Musial, StL | 230 |
| 1923 | Frankie Frisch, NY | 223 | 1949 | Stan Musial, StL | 207 |
| 1924 | Rogers Hornsby, StL | 227 | 1950 | Duke Snider, Bklyn | 199 |
| 1925 | Jim Bottomley, StL | 227 | 1951 | Richie Ashburn, Phi | 221 |
| 1926 | Eddie Brown, Bos | 201 | 1952 | Stan Musial, StL | 194 |

## NATIONAL LEAGUE
### Leaders in Hits *(Cont.)*

| Year | Player and Team | Hits | Year | Player and Team | Hits |
|------|-----------------|------|------|-----------------|------|
| 1953 | Riche Ashburn, Phi | 205 | 1984 | Tony Gwynn, SD | 213 |
| 1954 | Don Mueller, NY | 212 | 1985 | Willie McGee, StL | 216 |
| 1955 | Ted Kluszewski, Cin | 192 | 1986 | Tony Gwynn, SD | 211 |
| 1956 | Hank Aaron, Mil | 200 | 1987 | Tony Gwynn, SD | 218 |
| 1957 | Red Schoendienst, NY-Mil | 200 | 1988 | Andres Galarraga, Mtl | 184 |
| 1958 | Richie Ashburn, Phi | 215 | 1989 | Tony Gwynn, SD | 203 |
| 1959 | Hank Aaron, Mil | 223 | 1990 | Brett Butler, SF | 192 |
| 1960 | Willie Mays, SF | 190 | | Lenny Dykstra, Phi | 192 |
| 1961 | Vada Pinson, Cin | 208 | 1991 | Terry Pendleton, Atl | 187 |
| 1962 | Tommy Davis, LA | 230 | 1992 | Terry Pendleton, Atl | 199 |
| 1963 | Vada Pinson, Cin | 204 | | Andy Van Slyke, Pitt | 199 |
| 1964 | Roberto Clemente, Pitt | 211 | 1993 | Lenny Dykstra, Phi | 194 |
| | Curt Flood, StL | 211 | 1994 | Tony Gwynn, SD | 165 |
| 1965 | Pete Rose, Cin | 209 | 1995 | Dante Bichette, Col | 197 |
| 1966 | Felipe Alou, Atl | 218 | | Tony Gwynn, SD | 197 |
| 1967 | Roberto Clemente, Pitt | 209 | 1996 | Lance Johnson, NY | 227 |
| 1968 | Felipe Alou, Atl | 210 | 1997 | Tony Gwynn, SD | 220 |
| | Pete Rose, Cin | 210 | 1998 | Dante Bichette, Col | 219 |
| 1969 | Matty Alou, Pitt | 231 | 1999 | Luis Gonzalez, Ariz | 206 |
| 1970 | Pete Rose, Cin | 205 | 2000 | Todd Helton, Col | 216 |
| | Billy Williams, Chi | 205 | 2001 | Rich Aurilia, SF | 206 |
| 1971 | Joe Torre, StL | 230 | 2002 | Vladimir Guerrero | 206 |
| 1972 | Pete Rose, Cin | 198 | 2003 | Albert Pujols, StL | 212 |
| 1973 | Pete Rose, Cin | 230 | 2004 | Juan Pierre, Fla | 221 |
| 1974 | Ralph Garr, Atl | 214 | 2005 | Derrek Lee, Chi | 199 |
| 1975 | Dave Cash, Phi | 213 | 2006 | Juan Pierre, Chi | 204 |
| 1976 | Pete Rose, Cin | 215 | 2007 | Matt Holliday, Col | 216* |
| 1977 | Dave Parker, Pitt | 215 | 2008 | Jose Reyes, NYM | 204 |
| 1978 | Steve Garvey, LA | 202 | 2009 | Ryan Braun, Mil | 203 |
| 1979 | Garry Templeton, StL | 211 | 2010 | Carlos Gonzalez, Col | 197 |
| 1980 | Steve Garvey, LA | 200 | 2011 | Starlin Castro, Chi | 207 |
| 1981 | Pete Rose, Phi | 140 | | | |
| 1982 | Al Oliver, Mtl | 204 | | | |
| 1983 | Jose Cruz, Hou | 189 | | | |
| | Andre Dawson, Mtl | 189 | | | |

*Includes one-game NL Wild Card tiebreaker.

### Home Run Leaders

| Year | Player and Team | HR | Year | Player and Team | HR |
|------|-----------------|-----|------|-----------------|-----|
| 1900 | Herman Long, Bos | 12 | 1924 | Jack Fournier, Bklyn | 27 |
| 1901 | Sam Crawford, Cin | 16 | 1925 | Rogers Hornsby, StL | 39 |
| 1902 | Tommy Leach, Pitt | 6 | 1926 | Hack Wilson, Chi | 21 |
| 1903 | Jimmy Sheckard, Bklyn | 9 | 1927 | Hack Wilson, Chi | 30 |
| 1904 | Harry Lumley, Bklyn | 9 | | Cy Williams, Phi | 30 |
| 1905 | Fred Odwell, Cin | 9 | 1928 | Jim Bottomley, StL | 31 |
| 1906 | Tim Jordan, Bklyn | 12 | | Hack Wilson, Chi | 31 |
| 1907 | Dave Brain, Bos | 10 | 1929 | Chuck Klein, Phi | 43 |
| 1908 | Tim Jordan, Bklyn | 12 | 1930 | Hack Wilson, Chi | 56 |
| 1909 | Red Murray, NY | 7 | 1931 | Chuck Klein, Phi | 31 |
| 1910 | Fred Beck, Bos | 10 | 1932 | Chuck Klein, Phi | 38 |
| | Wildfire Schulte, Chi | 10 | | Mel Ott, NY | 38 |
| 1911 | Wildfire Schulte, Chi | 21 | 1933 | Chuck Klein, Phi | 28 |
| 1912 | Heinie Zimmerman, Chi | 14 | 1934 | Ripper Collins, StL | 35 |
| 1913 | Gavvy Cravath, Phi | 19 | | Mel Ott, NY | 35 |
| 1914 | Gavvy Cravath, Phi | 19 | 1935 | Wally Berger, Bos | 34 |
| 1915 | Gavvy Cravath, Phi | 24 | 1936 | Mel Ott, NY | 33 |
| 1916 | Dave Robertson, NY | 12 | 1937 | Joe Medwick, StL | 31 |
| | Cy Williams, Chi | 12 | | Mel Ott, NY | 31 |
| 1917 | Gavvy Cravath, Phi | 12 | 1938 | Mel Ott, NY | 36 |
| | Dave Robertson, NY | 12 | 1939 | Johnny Mize, StL | 28 |
| 1918 | Gavvy Cravath, Phi | 8 | 1940 | Johnny Mize, StL | 43 |
| 1919 | Gavvy Cravath, Phi | 12 | 1941 | Dolph Camilli, Bklyn | 34 |
| 1920 | Cy Williams, Phi | 15 | 1942 | Mel Ott, NY | 30 |
| 1921 | George Kelly, NY | 23 | 1943 | Bill Nicholson, Chi | 29 |
| 1922 | Rogers Hornsby, StL | 42 | 1944 | Bill Nicholson, Chi | 33 |
| 1923 | Cy Williams, Phi | 41 | 1945 | Tommy Holmes, Bos | 28 |

## NATIONAL LEAGUE
### Home Run Leaders (Cont.)

| Year | Player and Team | HR | Year | Player and Team | HR |
|------|-----------------|-----|------|-----------------|-----|
| 1946 | Ralph Kiner, Pitt | 23 | 1978 | George Foster, Cin | 40 |
| 1947 | Ralph Kiner, Pitt | 51 | 1979 | Dave Kingman, Chi | 48 |
| | Johnny Mize, NY | 51 | 1980 | Mike Schmidt, Phi | 48 |
| 1948 | Ralph Kiner, Pitt | 40 | 1981 | Mike Schmidt, Phi | 31 |
| | Johnny Mize, NY | 40 | 1982 | Dave Kingman, NY | 37 |
| 1949 | Ralph Kiner, Pitt | 54 | 1983 | Mike Schmidt, Phi | 40 |
| 1950 | Ralph Kiner, Pitt | 47 | 1984 | Dale Murphy, Atl | 36 |
| 1951 | Ralph Kiner, Pitt | 42 | | Mike Schmidt, Phi | 36 |
| 1952 | Ralph Kiner, Pitt | 37 | 1985 | Dale Murphy, Atl | 37 |
| | Hank Sauer, Chi | 37 | 1986 | Mike Schmidt, Phi | 37 |
| 1953 | Eddie Mathews, Mil | 47 | 1987 | Andre Dawson, Chi | 49 |
| 1954 | Ted Kluszewski, Cin | 49 | 1988 | Darryl Strawberry, NY | 39 |
| 1955 | Willie Mays, NY | 51 | 1989 | Kevin Mitchell, SF | 47 |
| 1956 | Duke Snider, Bklyn | 43 | 1990 | Ryne Sandberg, Chi | 40 |
| 1957 | Hank Aaron, Mil | 44 | 1991 | Howard Johnson, NY | 38 |
| 1958 | Ernie Banks, Chi | 47 | 1992 | Fred McGriff, SD | 35 |
| 1959 | Eddie Mathews, Mil | 46 | 1993 | Barry Bonds, SF | 46 |
| 1960 | Ernie Banks, Chi | 41 | 1994 | Matt Williams, SF | 43 |
| 1961 | Orlando Cepeda, SF | 46 | 1995 | Dante Bichette, Col | 40 |
| 1962 | Willie Mays, SF | 49 | 1996 | Andres Galarraga, Col | 47 |
| 1963 | Hank Aaron, Mil | 44 | 1997 | Larry Walker, Col | 49 |
| | Willie McCovey, SF | 44 | 1998 | Mark McGwire, StL | 70 |
| 1964 | Willie Mays, SF | 47 | 1999 | Mark McGwire, StL | 65 |
| 1965 | Willie Mays, SF | 52 | 2000 | Sammy Sosa, Chi | 50 |
| 1966 | Hank Aaron, Atl | 44 | 2001 | Barry Bonds, SF | 73 |
| 1967 | Hank Aaron, Atl | 39 | 2002 | Sammy Sosa, Chi | 49 |
| 1968 | Willie McCovey, SF | 36 | 2003 | Jim Thome, Phi | 47 |
| 1969 | Willie McCovey, SF | 45 | 2004 | Adrian Beltre, LA | 48 |
| 1970 | Johnny Bench, Cin | 45 | 2005 | Andruw Jones, Atl | 51 |
| 1971 | Willie Stargell, Pitt | 48 | 2006 | Ryan Howard, Phi | 58 |
| 1972 | Johnny Bench, Cin | 40 | 2007 | Prince Fielder, Mil | 50 |
| 1973 | Willie Stargell, Pitt | 44 | 2008 | Ryan Howard, Phi | 48 |
| 1974 | Mike Schmidt, Phi | 36 | 2009 | Albert Pujols, StL | 47 |
| 1975 | Mike Schmidt, Phi | 38 | 2010 | Albert Pujols, StL | 42 |
| 1976 | Mike Schmidt, Phi | 38 | 2011 | Matt Kemp, LA | 39 |
| 1977 | George Foster, Cin | 52 | | | |

### Runs Batted In Leaders

| Year | Player and Team | RBI | Year | Player and Team | RBI |
|------|-----------------|-----|------|-----------------|-----|
| 1900 | Elmer Flick, Phi | 110 | 1924 | George Kelly, NY | 136 |
| 1901 | Honus Wagner, Pitt | 126 | 1925 | Rogers Hornsby, StL | 143 |
| 1902 | Honus Wagner, Pitt | 91 | 1926 | Jim Bottomley, StL | 120 |
| 1903 | Sam Mertes, NY | 104 | 1927 | Paul Waner, Pitt | 131 |
| 1904 | Bill Dahlen, NY | 80 | 1928 | Jim Bottomley, StL | 136 |
| 1905 | Cy Seymour, Cin | 121 | 1929 | Hack Wilson, Chi | 159 |
| 1906 | Jim Nealon, Pitt | 83 | 1930 | Hack Wilson, Chi | 190 |
| | Harry Steinfeldt, Chi | 83 | 1931 | Chuck Klein, Phi | 121 |
| 1907 | Sherry Magee, Phi | 85 | 1932 | Don Hurst, Phi | 143 |
| 1908 | Honus Wagner, Pitt | 109 | 1933 | Chuck Klein, Phi | 120 |
| 1909 | Honus Wagner, Pitt | 100 | 1934 | Mel Ott, NY | 135 |
| 1910 | Sherry Magee, Phi | 123 | 1935 | Wally Berger, Bos | 130 |
| 1911 | Wildfire Schulte, Chi | 121 | 1936 | Joe Medwick, StL | 138 |
| 1912 | Heinie Zimmerman, Chi | 103 | 1937 | Joe Medwick, StL | 154 |
| 1913 | Gavvy Cravath, Phi | 128 | 1938 | Joe Medwick, StL | 122 |
| 1914 | Sherry Magee, Phi | 103 | 1939 | Frank McCormick, Cin | 128 |
| 1915 | Gavvy Cravath, Phi | 115 | 1940 | Johnny Mize, StL | 137 |
| 1916 | Heinie Zimmerman, Chi-NY | 83 | 1941 | Dolph Camilli, Bklyn | 120 |
| 1917 | Heinie Zimmerman, NY | 102 | 1942 | Johnny Mize, NY | 110 |
| 1918 | Sherry Magee, Phi | 76 | 1943 | Bill Nicholson, Chi | 128 |
| 1919 | Hi Myers, Bklyn | 73 | 1944 | Bill Nicholson, Chi | 122 |
| 1920 | Rogers Hornsby, StL | 94 | 1945 | Dixie Walker, Bklyn | 124 |
| | George Kelly, NY | 94 | 1946 | Enos Slaughter, StL | 130 |
| 1921 | Rogers Hornsby, StL | 126 | 1947 | Johnny Mize, NY | 138 |
| 1922 | Rogers Hornsby, StL | 152 | 1948 | Stan Musial, StL | 131 |
| 1923 | Irish Meusel, NY | 125 | 1949 | Ralph Kiner, Pitt | 127 |

## NATIONAL LEAGUE
### Runs Batted In Leaders *(Cont.)*

| Year | Player and Team | RBI | Year | Player and Team | RBI |
|---|---|---|---|---|---|
| 1950 | Del Ennis, Phi | 126 | 1983 | Dale Murphy, Atl | 121 |
| 1951 | Monte Irvin, NY | 121 | 1984 | Gary Carter, Mtl | 106 |
| 1952 | Hank Sauer, Chi | 121 | | Mike Schmidt, Phi | 106 |
| 1953 | Roy Campanella, Bklyn | 142 | 1985 | Dave Parker, Cin | 125 |
| 1954 | Ted Kluszewski, Cin | 141 | 1986 | Mike Schmidt, Phi | 119 |
| 1955 | Duke Snider, Bklyn | 136 | 1987 | Andre Dawson, Chi | 137 |
| 1956 | Stan Musial, StL | 109 | 1988 | Will Clark, SF | 109 |
| 1957 | Hank Aaron, Mil | 132 | 1989 | Kevin Mitchell, SF | 125 |
| 1958 | Ernie Banks, Chi | 129 | 1990 | Matt Williams, SF | 122 |
| 1959 | Ernie Banks, Chi | 143 | 1991 | Howard Johnson, NY | 117 |
| 1960 | Hank Aaron, Mil | 126 | 1992 | Darren Daulton, Phi | 109 |
| 1961 | Orlando Cepeda, SF | 142 | 1993 | Barry Bonds, SF | 123 |
| 1962 | Tommy Davis, LA | 153 | 1994 | Jeff Bagwell, Hou | 116 |
| 1963 | Hank Aaron, Mil | 130 | 1995 | Dante Bichette, Col | 128 |
| 1964 | Ken Boyer, StL | 119 | 1996 | Andres Galarraga, Col | 150 |
| 1965 | Deron Johnson, Cin | 130 | 1997 | Andres Galarraga, Col | 140 |
| 1966 | Hank Aaron, Atl | 127 | 1998 | Sammy Sosa, Chi | 158 |
| 1967 | Orlando Cepeda, StL | 111 | 1999 | Mark McGwire, StL | 147 |
| 1968 | Willie McCovey, SF | 105 | 2000 | Todd Helton, Col | 147 |
| 1969 | Willie McCovey, SF | 126 | 2001 | Sammy Sosa, Chi | 160 |
| 1970 | Johnny Bench, Cin | 148 | 2002 | Lance Berkman, Hou | 128 |
| 1971 | Joe Torre, StL | 137 | 2003 | Preston Wilson, Col | 141 |
| 1972 | Johnny Bench, Cin | 125 | 2004 | Vinny Castilla, Col | 131 |
| 1973 | Willie Stargell, Pitt | 119 | 2005 | Andruw Jones, Atl | 128 |
| 1974 | Johnny Bench, Cin | 129 | 2006 | Ryan Howard, Phi | 149 |
| 1975 | Greg Luzinski, Phi | 120 | 2007 | Matt Holliday, Col | 137* |
| 1976 | George Foster, Cin | 121 | 2008 | Ryan Howard, Phi | 146 |
| 1977 | George Foster, Cin | 149 | 2009 | Prince Fielder, Mil | 141 |
| 1978 | George Foster, Cin | 120 | | Ryan Howard, Phi | 141 |
| 1979 | Dave Winfield, SD | 118 | 2010 | Albert Pujols, StL | 118 |
| 1980 | Mike Schmidt, Phi | 121 | 2011 | Matt Kemp, LA | 126 |
| 1981 | Mike Schmidt, Phi | 91 | | | |
| 1982 | Dale Murphy, Atl | 109 | *Includes one-game NL Wild Card tiebreaker. | | |
| | Al Oliver, Mtl | 109 | | | |

## Leading Base Stealers

| Year | Player and Team | SB | Year | Player and Team | SB |
|---|---|---|---|---|---|
| 1900 | George Van Haltren, NY | 45 | 1925 | Max Carey, Pitt | 46 |
| | Patsy Donovan, StL | 45 | 1926 | Kiki Cuyler, Pitt | 35 |
| 1901 | Honus Wagner, Pitt | 48 | 1927 | Frankie Frisch, StL | 48 |
| 1902 | Honus Wagner, Pitt | 43 | 1928 | Kiki Cuyler, Chi | 37 |
| 1903 | Jimmy Sheckard, Bklyn | 67 | 1929 | Kiki Cuyler, Chi | 43 |
| | Frank Chance, Chi | 67 | 1930 | Kiki Cuyler, Chi | 37 |
| 1904 | Honus Wagner, Pitt | 53 | 1931 | Frankie Frisch, StL | 28 |
| 1905 | Billy Maloney, Chi | 59 | 1932 | Chuck Klein, Phi | 20 |
| | Art Devlin, NY | 59 | 1933 | Pepper Martin, StL | 26 |
| 1906 | Frank Chance, Chi | 57 | 1934 | Pepper Martin, StL | 23 |
| 1907 | Honus Wagner, Pitt | 61 | 1935 | Augie Galan, Chi | 22 |
| 1908 | Honus Wagner, Pitt | 53 | 1936 | Pepper Martin, StL | 23 |
| 1909 | Bob Bescher, Cin | 54 | 1937 | Augie Galan, Chi | 23 |
| 1910 | Bob Bescher, Cin | 70 | 1938 | Stan Hack, Chi | 16 |
| 1911 | Bob Bescher, Cin | 80 | 1939 | Stan Hack, Chi | 17 |
| 1912 | Bob Bescher, Cin | 67 | | Lee Handley, Pitt | 17 |
| 1913 | Max Carey, Pitt | 61 | 1940 | Lonny Frey, Cin | 22 |
| 1914 | George Burns, NY | 62 | 1941 | Danny Murtaugh, Phi | 18 |
| 1915 | Max Carey, Pitt | 36 | 1942 | Pete Reiser, Bklyn | 20 |
| 1916 | Max Carey, Pitt | 63 | 1943 | Arky Vaughan, Bklyn | 20 |
| 1917 | Max Carey, Pitt | 46 | 1944 | Johnny Barrett, Pitt | 28 |
| 1918 | Max Carey, Pitt | 58 | 1945 | Red Schoendienst, StL | 26 |
| 1919 | George Burns, NY | 40 | 1946 | Pete Reiser, Bklyn | 34 |
| 1920 | Max Carey, Pitt | 52 | 1947 | Jackie Robinson, Bklyn | 29 |
| 1921 | Frankie Frisch, NY | 49 | 1948 | Richie Ashburn, Phi | 32 |
| 1922 | Max Carey, Pitt | 51 | 1949 | Jackie Robinson, Bklyn | 37 |
| 1923 | Max Carey, Pitt | 51 | 1950 | Sam Jethroe, Bos | 35 |
| 1924 | Max Carey, Pitt | 49 | 1951 | Sam Jethroe, Bos | 35 |

## NATIONAL LEAGUE
### Leading Base Stealers (*Cont.*)

| Year | Player and Team | SB | Year | Player and Team | SB |
|------|-----------------|-----|------|-----------------|-----|
| 1952 | Pee Wee Reese, Bklyn | 30 | 1983 | Tim Raines, Mtl | 90 |
| 1953 | Bill Bruton, Mil | 26 | 1984 | Tim Raines, Mtl | 75 |
| 1954 | Bill Bruton, Mil | 34 | 1985 | Vince Coleman, StL | 110 |
| 1955 | Bill Bruton, Mil | 35 | 1986 | Vince Coleman, StL | 107 |
| 1956 | Willie Mays, NY | 40 | 1987 | Vince Coleman, StL | 109 |
| 1957 | Willie Mays, NY | 38 | 1988 | Vince Coleman, StL | 81 |
| 1958 | Willie Mays, SF | 31 | 1989 | Vince Coleman, StL | 65 |
| 1959 | Willie Mays, SF | 27 | 1990 | Vince Coleman, StL | 77 |
| 1960 | Maury Wills, LA | 50 | 1991 | Marquis Grissom, Mtl | 76 |
| 1961 | Maury Wills, LA | 35 | 1992 | Marquis Grissom, Mtl | 78 |
| 1962 | Maury Wills, LA | 104 | 1993 | Chuck Carr, Fla | 58 |
| 1963 | Maury Wills, LA | 40 | 1994 | Craig Biggio, Hou | 39 |
| 1964 | Maury Wills, LA | 53 | 1995 | Quilvio Veras, Fla | 56 |
| 1965 | Maury Wills, LA | 94 | 1996 | Eric Young, Col | 53 |
| 1966 | Lou Brock, StL | 74 | 1997 | Tony Womack, Pitt | 60 |
| 1967 | Lou Brock, StL | 52 | 1998 | Tony Womack, Pitt | 58 |
| 1968 | Lou Brock, StL | 62 | 1999 | Tony Womack, Ariz | 72 |
| 1969 | Lou Brock, StL | 53 | 2000 | Luis Castillo, Fla | 62 |
| 1970 | Bobby Tolan, Cin | 57 | 2001 | Juan Pierre, Col | 46 |
| 1971 | Lou Brock, StL | 64 | 2002 | Luis Castillo, Fla | 48 |
| 1972 | Lou Brock, StL | 63 | 2003 | Juan Pierre, Fla | 65 |
| 1973 | Lou Brock, StL | 70 | 2004 | Scott Podsednik, Mil | 70 |
| 1974 | Lou Brock, StL | 118 | 2005 | Jose Reyes, NY | 60 |
| 1975 | Davey Lopes, LA | 77 | 2006 | Jose Reyes, NY | 64 |
| 1976 | Davey Lopes, LA | 63 | 2007 | Jose Reyes, NY | 78 |
| 1977 | Frank Taveras, Pitt | 70 | 2008 | Willy Taveras, Hou | 68 |
| 1978 | Omar Moreno, Pitt | 71 | 2009 | Michael Bourn, Hou | 61 |
| 1979 | Omar Moreno, Pitt | 77 | 2010 | Michael Bourn, Hou | 52 |
| 1980 | Ron LeFlore, Mtl | 97 | 2011 | Micheal Bourn, Hou/Atl | 61 |
| 1981 | Tim Raines, Mtl | 71 | | | |
| 1982 | Tim Raines, Mtl | 78 | | | |

## Leading Pitchers—Winning Percentage

| Year | Pitcher and Team | W | L | Pct | Year | Pitcher and Team | W | L | Pct |
|------|------------------|----|----|------|------|------------------|----|----|------|
| 1900 | Jesse Tannehill, Pitt | 20 | 6 | .769 | 1930 | Freddie Fitzsimmons, NY | 19 | 7 | .731 |
| 1901 | Jack Chesbro, Pitt | 21 | 10 | .677 | 1931 | Paul Derringer, StL | 18 | 8 | .692 |
| 1902 | Jack Chesbro, Pitt | 28 | 6 | .824 | 1932 | Lon Warneke, Chi | 22 | 6 | .786 |
| 1903 | Sam Leever, Pitt | 25 | 7 | .781 | 1933 | Ben Cantwell, Bos | 20 | 10 | .667 |
| 1904 | Joe McGinnity, NY | 35 | 8 | .814 | 1934 | Dizzy Dean, StL | 30 | 7 | .811 |
| 1905 | Sam Leever, Pitt | 20 | 5 | .800 | 1935 | Bill Lee, Chi | 20 | 6 | .769 |
| 1906 | Ed Reulbach, Chi | 19 | 4 | .826 | 1936 | Carl Hubbell, NY | 26 | 6 | .813 |
| 1907 | Ed Reulbach, Chi | 17 | 4 | .810 | 1937 | Carl Hubbell, NY | 22 | 8 | .733 |
| 1908 | Ed Reulbach, Chi | 24 | 7 | .774 | 1938 | Bill Lee, Chi | 22 | 9 | .710 |
| 1909 | Howie Camnitz, Pitt | 25 | 6 | .806 | 1939 | Paul Derringer, Cin | 25 | 7 | .781 |
| | Christy Mathewson, NY | 25 | 6 | .806 | 1940 | Freddie Fitzsimmons, Bklyn | 16 | 2 | .889 |
| 1910 | King Cole, Chi | 20 | 4 | .833 | 1941 | Elmer Riddle, Cin | 19 | 4 | .826 |
| 1911 | Rube Marquard, NY | 24 | 7 | .774 | 1942 | Larry French, Bklyn | 15 | 4 | .789 |
| 1912 | Claude Hendrix, Pitt | 24 | 9 | .727 | 1943 | Mort Cooper, StL | 21 | 8 | .724 |
| 1913 | Bert Humphries, Chi | 16 | 4 | .800 | 1944 | Ted Wilks, StL | 17 | 4 | .810 |
| 1914 | Bill James, Bos | 26 | 7 | .788 | 1945 | Harry Brecheen, StL | 15 | 4 | .789 |
| 1915 | Grover Alexander, Phi | 31 | 10 | .756 | 1946 | Murray Dickson, StL | 15 | 6 | .714 |
| 1916 | Tom Hughes, Bos | 16 | 3 | .842 | 1947 | Larry Jansen, NY | 21 | 5 | .808 |
| 1917 | Ferdie Schupp, NY | 21 | 7 | .750 | 1948 | Harry Brecheen, StL | 20 | 7 | .741 |
| 1918 | Claude Hendrix, Chi | 19 | 7 | .731 | 1949 | Preacher Roe, Bklyn | 15 | 6 | .714 |
| 1919 | Dutch Ruether, Cin | 19 | 6 | .760 | 1950 | Sal Maglie, NY | 18 | 4 | .818 |
| 1920 | Burleigh Grimes, Bklyn | 23 | 11 | .676 | 1951 | Preacher Roe, Bklyn | 22 | 3 | .880 |
| 1921 | Bill Doak, StL | 15 | 6 | .714 | 1952 | Hoyt Wilhelm, NY | 15 | 3 | .833 |
| 1922 | Pete Donohue, Cin | 18 | 9 | .667 | 1953 | Carl Erskine, Bklyn | 20 | 6 | .769 |
| 1923 | Dolf Luque, Cin | 27 | 8 | .771 | 1954 | Johnny Antonelli, NY | 21 | 7 | .750 |
| 1924 | Emil Yde, Pitt | 16 | 3 | .842 | 1955 | Don Newcombe, Bklyn | 20 | 5 | .800 |
| 1925 | Bill Sherdel, StL | 15 | 6 | .714 | 1956 | Don Newcombe, Bklyn | 27 | 7 | .794 |
| 1926 | Ray Kremer, Pitt | 20 | 6 | .769 | 1957 | Bob Buhl, Mil | 18 | 7 | .720 |
| 1927 | Larry Benton, Bos-NY | 17 | 7 | .708 | 1958 | Warren Spahn, Mil | 22 | 11 | .667 |
| 1928 | Larry Benton, NY | 25 | 9 | .735 | | Lew Burdette, Mil | 20 | 10 | .667 |
| 1929 | Charlie Root, Chi | 19 | 6 | .760 | 1959 | Roy Face, Pitt | 18 | 1 | .947 |

Note: Percentages based on 15 or more victories.

## NATIONAL LEAGUE
### Leading Pitchers—Winning Percentage (Cont.)

| Year | Pitcher and Team | W | L | Pct | Year | Pitcher and Team | W | L | Pct |
|------|------------------|---|---|-----|------|------------------|---|---|-----|
| 1960 | Ernie Broglio, StL | 21 | 9 | .700 | 1987 | Dwight Gooden, NY | 15 | 7 | .682 |
| 1961 | Johnny Podres, LA | 18 | 5 | .783 | 1988 | David Cone, NY | 20 | 3 | .870 |
| 1962 | Bob Purkey, Cin | 23 | 5 | .821 | 1989 | Mike Bielecki, Chi | 18 | 7 | .720 |
| 1963 | Ron Perranoski, LA | 16 | 3 | .842 | 1990 | Doug Drabeck, Pitt | 22 | 6 | .786 |
| 1964 | Sandy Koufax, LA | 19 | 5 | .792 | 1991 | John Smiley, Pitt | 20 | 8 | .714 |
| 1965 | Sandy Koufax, LA | 26 | 8 | .765 | | Jose Rijo, Cin | 15 | 6 | .714 |
| 1966 | Juan Marichal, SF | 25 | 6 | .806 | 1992 | Bob Tewksbury, StL | 16 | 5 | .762 |
| 1967 | Dick Hughes, StL | 16 | 6 | .727 | 1993 | Tom Glavine, Atl | 22 | 6 | .786 |
| 1968 | Steve Blass, Pitt | 18 | 6 | .750 | 1994 | Ken Hill, Mtl | 16 | 5 | .762 |
| 1969 | Tom Seaver, NY | 25 | 7 | .781 | 1995 | Greg Maddux, Atl | 19 | 2 | .905 |
| 1970 | Bob Gibson, StL | 23 | 7 | .767 | 1996 | John Smoltz, Atl | 24 | 8 | .750 |
| 1971 | Don Gullett, Cin | 16 | 6 | .727 | 1997 | Denny Neagle, Atl | 20 | 5 | .800 |
| 1972 | Gary Nolan, Cin | 15 | 5 | .750 | 1998 | John Smoltz, Atl | 17 | 3 | .850 |
| 1973 | Tommy John, LA | 16 | 7 | .696 | 1999 | Mike Hampton, Hou | 22 | 4 | .846 |
| 1974 | Andy Messersmith, LA | 20 | 6 | .769 | 2000 | Randy Johnson, Ariz | 19 | 7 | .730 |
| 1975 | Don Gullett, Cin | 15 | 4 | .789 | 2001 | Curt Schilling, Ariz | 22 | 6 | .786 |
| 1976 | Steve Carlton, Phi | 20 | 7 | .741 | 2002 | Randy Johnson, Ariz | 24 | 5 | .828 |
| 1977 | John Candelaria, Pitt | 20 | 5 | .800 | 2003 | Jason Schmidt, SF | 17 | 5 | .773 |
| 1978 | Gaylord Perry, SD | 21 | 6 | .778 | 2004 | Roger Clemens, Hou | 18 | 4 | .818 |
| 1979 | Tom Seaver, Cin | 16 | 6 | .727 | 2005 | Chris Carpenter, StL | 21 | 5 | .808 |
| 1980 | Jim Bibby, Pitt | 19 | 6 | .760 | 2006 | Carlos Zambrano, Chi | 16 | 7 | .695 |
| 1981* | Tom Seaver, Cin | 14 | 2 | .875 | 2007 | Brad Penny, LA | 16 | 4 | .800 |
| 1982 | Phil Niekro, Atl | 17 | 4 | .810 | 2008 | Tim Lincecum, SF | 18 | 5 | .783 |
| 1983 | John Denny, Phi | 19 | 6 | .760 | 2009 | Chris Carpenter, StL | 17 | 4 | .810 |
| 1984 | Rick Sutcliffe, Chi | 16 | 1 | .941 | 2010 | Ubaldo Jimenez, Col | 19 | 8 | .704 |
| 1985 | Orel Hershiser, LA | 19 | 3 | .864 | 2011 | Ian Kennedy, Ari | 21 | 4 | .840 |
| 1986 | Bob Ojeda, NY | 18 | 5 | .783 | | | | | |

*1981 percentages based on 10 or more victories. All other years, percentages based on 15 or more victories.

### Leading Pitchers—Earned Run Average

| Year | Player and Team | ERA | Year | Player and Team | ERA |
|------|-----------------|-----|------|-----------------|-----|
| 1900 | Rube Waddell, Pitt | 2.37 | 1932 | Lon Warneke, Chi | 2.37 |
| 1901 | Jesse Tannehill, Pitt | 2.18 | 1933 | Carl Hubbell, NY | 1.66 |
| 1902 | Jack Taylor, Chi | 1.33 | 1934 | Carl Hubbell, NY | 2.30 |
| 1903 | Sam Leever, Pitt | 2.06 | 1935 | Cy Blanton, Pitt | 2.59 |
| 1904 | Joe McGinnity, NY | 1.61 | 1936 | Carl Hubbell, NY | 2.31 |
| 1905 | Christy Mathewson, NY | 1.27 | 1937 | Jim Turner, Bos | 2.38 |
| 1906 | Three Finger Brown, Chi | 1.04 | 1938 | Bill Lee, Chi | 2.66 |
| 1907 | Jack Pfiester, Chi | 1.15 | 1939 | Bucky Walters, Cin | 2.29 |
| 1908 | Christy Mathewson, NY | 1.43 | 1940 | Bucky Walters, Cin | 2.48 |
| 1909 | Christy Mathewson, NY | 1.14 | 1941 | Elmer Riddle, Cin | 2.24 |
| 1910 | George McQuillan, Phi | 1.60 | 1942 | Mort Cooper, StL | 1.77 |
| 1911 | Christy Mathewson, NY | 1.99 | 1943 | Howie Pollet, StL | 1.75 |
| 1912 | Jeff Tesreau, NY | 1.96 | 1944 | Ed Heusser, Cin | 2.38 |
| 1913 | Christy Mathewson, NY | 2.06 | 1945 | Hank Borowy, Chi | 2.14 |
| 1914 | Bill Doak, StL | 1.72 | 1946 | Howie Pollet, StL | 2.10 |
| 1915 | Grover Alexander, Phi | 1.22 | 1947 | Warren Spahn, Bos | 2.33 |
| 1916 | Grover Alexander, Phi | 1.55 | 1948 | Harry Brecheen, StL | 2.24 |
| 1917 | Grover Alexander, Phi | 1.83 | 1949 | Dave Koslo, NY | 2.50 |
| 1918 | Hippo Vaughn, Chi | 1.74 | 1950 | Jim Hearn, StL-NY | 2.49 |
| 1919 | Grover Alexander, Chi | 1.72 | 1951 | Chet Nichols, Bos | 2.88 |
| 1920 | Grover Alexander, Chi | 1.91 | 1952 | Hoyt Wilhelm, NY | 2.43 |
| 1921 | Bill Doak, StL | 2.58 | 1953 | Warren Spahn, Mil | 2.10 |
| 1922 | Rosy Ryan, NY | 3.00 | 1954 | Johnny Antonelli, NY | 2.29 |
| 1923 | Dolf Luque, Cin | 1.93 | 1955 | Bob Friend, Pitt | 2.84 |
| 1924 | Dazzy Vance, Bklyn | 2.16 | 1956 | Lew Burdette, Mil | 2.71 |
| 1925 | Dolf Luque, Cin | 2.63 | 1957 | Johnny Podres, Bklyn | 2.66 |
| 1926 | Ray Kremer, Pitt | 2.61 | 1958 | Stu Miller, SF | 2.47 |
| 1927 | Ray Kremer, Pitt | 2.47 | 1959 | Sam Jones, SF | 2.82 |
| 1928 | Dazzy Vance, Bklyn | 2.09 | 1960 | Mike McCormick, SF | 2.70 |
| 1929 | Bill Walker, NY | 3.08 | 1961 | Warren Spahn, Mil | 3.01 |
| 1930 | Dazzy Vance, Bklyn | 2.61 | 1962 | Sandy Koufax, LA | 2.54 |
| 1931 | Bill Walker, NY | 2.26 | 1963 | Sandy Koufax, LA | 1.88 |

Note: Based on 10 complete games through 1950, then 154 innings until National League expanded in 1962, when it became 162 innings. In strike-shortened 1981, one inning per game required.

## NATIONAL LEAGUE

### Leading Pitchers—Earned Run Average *(Cont.)*

| Year | Player and Team | ERA | Year | Player and Team | ERA |
|------|-----------------|-----|------|-----------------|-----|
| 1964 | Sandy Koufax, LA | 1.74 | 1989 | Scott Garrelts, SF | 2.28 |
| 1965 | Sandy Koufax, LA | 2.04 | 1990 | Danny Darwin, Hou | 2.21 |
| 1966 | Sandy Koufax, LA | 1.73 | 1991 | Dennis Martinez, Mtl | 2.39 |
| 1967 | Phil Niekro, Atl | 1.87 | 1992 | Bill Swift, SF | 2.08 |
| 1968 | Bob Gibson, StL | 1.12 | 1993 | Greg Maddux, Atl | 2.36 |
| 1969 | Juan Marichal, SF | 2.10 | 1994 | Greg Maddux, Atl | 1.56 |
| 1970 | Tom Seaver, NY | 2.81 | 1995 | Greg Maddux, Atl | 1.63 |
| 1971 | Tom Seaver, NY | 1.76 | 1996 | Kevin Brown, Fla | 1.89 |
| 1972 | Steve Carlton, Phi | 1.98 | 1997 | Pedro Martinez, Mtl | 1.90 |
| 1973 | Tom Seaver, NY | 2.08 | 1998 | Greg Maddux, Atl | 1.98 |
| 1974 | Buzz Capra, Atl | 2.28 | 1999 | Randy Johnson, Ariz | 2.48 |
| 1975 | Randy Jones, SD | 2.24 | 2000 | Kevin Brown, LA | 2.58 |
| 1976 | John Denny, StL | 2.52 | 2001 | Randy Johnson, Ariz | 2.49 |
| 1977 | John Candelaria, Pitt | 2.34 | 2002 | Randy Johnson, Ariz | 2.32 |
| 1978 | Craig Swan, NY | 2.43 | 2003 | Jason Schmidt, SF | 2.34 |
| 1979 | J.R. Richard, Hou | 2.71 | 2004 | Jake Peavy, SD | 2.27 |
| 1980 | Don Sutton, LA | 2.21 | 2005 | Roger Clemens, Hou | 1.87 |
| 1981 | Nolan Ryan, Hou | 1.69 | 2006 | Roy Oswalt, Hou | 2.98 |
| 1982 | Steve Rogers, Mtl | 2.40 | 2007 | Jake Peavy, SD | 2.54* |
| 1983 | Atlee Hammaker, SF | 2.25 | 2008 | Johan Santana, NYM | 2.53 |
| 1984 | Alejandro Pena, LA | 2.48 | 2009 | Chris Carpenter, StL | 2.24 |
| 1985 | Dwight Gooden, NY | 1.53 | 2010 | Josh Johnson, Fla | 2.30 |
| 1986 | Mike Scott, Hou | 2.22 | 2011 | Clayton Kershaw, LA | 2.28 |
| 1987 | Nolan Ryan, Hou | 2.76 | | | |
| 1988 | Joe Magrane, StL | 2.18 | *Includes one-game NL Wild Card tiebreaker. | | |

### Leading Pitchers—Strikeouts

| Year | Player and Team | SO | Year | Player and Team | SO |
|------|-----------------|-----|------|-----------------|-----|
| 1900 | Rube Waddell, Pitt | 133 | 1937 | Carl Hubbell, NY | 159 |
| 1901 | Noodles Hahn, Cin | 233 | 1938 | Clay Bryant, Chi | 135 |
| 1902 | Vic Willis, Bos | 226 | 1939 | Claude Passeau, Phi-Chi | 137 |
| 1903 | Christy Mathewson, NY | 267 | | Bucky Walters, Cin | 137 |
| 1904 | Christy Mathewson, NY | 212 | 1940 | Kirby Higbe, Phi | 137 |
| 1905 | Christy Mathewson, NY | 206 | 1941 | Johnny Vander Meer, Cin | 202 |
| 1906 | Fred Beebe, Chi-StL | 171 | 1942 | Johnny Vander Meer, Cin | 186 |
| 1907 | Christy Mathewson, NY | 178 | 1943 | Johnny Vander Meer, Cin | 174 |
| 1908 | Christy Mathewson, NY | 259 | 1944 | Bill Voiselle, NY | 161 |
| 1909 | Orval Overall, Chi | 205 | 1945 | Preacher Roe, Pitt | 148 |
| 1910 | Christy Mathewson, NY | 190 | 1946 | Johnny Schmitz, Chi | 135 |
| 1911 | Rube Marquard, NY | 237 | 1947 | Ewell Blackwell, Cin | 193 |
| 1912 | Grover Alexander, Phi | 195 | 1948 | Harry Brecheen, StL | 149 |
| 1913 | Tom Seaton, Phi | 168 | 1949 | Warren Spahn, Bos | 151 |
| 1914 | Grover Alexander, Phi | 214 | 1950 | Warren Spahn, Bos | 191 |
| 1915 | Grover Alexander, Phi | 241 | 1951 | Warren Spahn, Bos | 164 |
| 1916 | Grover Alexander, Phi | 167 | | Don Newcombe, Bklyn | 164 |
| 1917 | Grover Alexander, Phi | 200 | 1952 | Warren Spahn, Bos | 183 |
| 1918 | Hippo Vaughn, Chi | 148 | 1953 | Robin Roberts, Phi | 198 |
| 1919 | Hippo Vaughn, Chi | 141 | 1954 | Robin Roberts, Phi | 185 |
| 1920 | Grover Alexander, Chi | 173 | 1955 | Sam Jones, Chi | 198 |
| 1921 | Burleigh Grimes, Bklyn | 136 | 1956 | Sam Jones, Chi | 176 |
| 1922 | Dazzy Vance, Bklyn | 134 | 1957 | Jack Sanford, Phi | 188 |
| 1923 | Dazzy Vance, Bklyn | 197 | 1958 | Sam Jones, StL | 225 |
| 1924 | Dazzy Vance, Bklyn | 262 | 1959 | Don Drysdale, LA | 242 |
| 1925 | Dazzy Vance, Bklyn | 221 | 1960 | Don Drysdale, LA | 246 |
| 1926 | Dazzy Vance, Bklyn | 140 | 1961 | Sandy Koufax, LA | 269 |
| 1927 | Dazzy Vance, Bklyn | 184 | 1962 | Don Drysdale, LA | 232 |
| 1928 | Dazzy Vance, Bklyn | 200 | 1963 | Sandy Koufax, LA | 306 |
| 1929 | Pat Malone, Chi | 166 | 1964 | Bob Veale, Pitt | 250 |
| 1930 | Bill Hallahan, StL | 177 | 1965 | Sandy Koufax, LA | 382 |
| 1931 | Bill Hallahan, StL | 159 | 1966 | Sandy Koufax, LA | 317 |
| 1932 | Dizzy Dean, StL | 191 | 1967 | Jim Bunning, Phi | 253 |
| 1933 | Dizzy Dean, StL | 199 | 1968 | Bob Gibson, StL | 268 |
| 1934 | Dizzy Dean, StL | 195 | 1969 | Ferguson Jenkins, Chi | 273 |
| 1935 | Dizzy Dean, StL | 182 | 1970 | Tom Seaver, NY | 283 |
| 1936 | Van Lingle Mungo, Bklyn | 238 | 1971 | Tom Seaver, NY | 289 |

## NATIONAL LEAGUE
### Leading Pitchers—Strikeouts *(Cont.)*

| Year | Player and Team | SO | Year | Player and Team | SO |
|------|-----------------|-----|------|-----------------|-----|
| 1972 | Steve Carlton, Phi | 310 | 1993 | Jose Rijo, Cin | 227 |
| 1973 | Tom Seaver, NY | 251 | 1994 | Andy Benes, SD | 189 |
| 1974 | Steve Carlton, Phi | 240 | 1995 | Hideo Nomo, LA | 236 |
| 1975 | Tom Seaver, NY | 243 | 1996 | John Smoltz, Atl | 276 |
| 1976 | Tom Seaver, NY | 235 | 1997 | Curt Schilling, Phi | 319 |
| 1977 | Phil Niekro, Atl | 262 | 1998 | Curt Schilling, Phi | 300 |
| 1978 | J.R. Richard, Hou | 303 | 1999 | Randy Johnson, Ariz | 364 |
| 1979 | J.R. Richard, Hou | 313 | 2000 | Randy Johnson, Ariz | 347 |
| 1980 | Steve Carlton, Phi | 286 | 2001 | Randy Johnson, Ariz | 372 |
| 1981 | Fernando Valenzuela, LA | 180 | 2002 | Randy Johnson, Ariz | 334 |
| 1982 | Steve Carlton, Phi | 286 | 2003 | Kerry Wood, Chi | 266 |
| 1983 | Steve Carlton, Phi | 275 | 2004 | Randy Johnson, Ariz | 290 |
| 1984 | Dwight Gooden, NY | 276 | 2005 | Jake Peavy, SD | 216 |
| 1985 | Dwight Gooden, NY | 268 | 2006 | Aaron Harang, Cin | 216 |
| 1986 | Mike Scott, Hou | 306 | 2007 | Jake Peavy, SD | 240* |
| 1987 | Nolan Ryan, Hou | 270 | 2008 | Tim Lincecum, SF | 265 |
| 1988 | Nolan Ryan, Hou | 228 | 2009 | Tim Lincecum, SF | 261 |
| 1989 | Jose DeLeon, StL | 201 | 2010 | Tim Lincecum, SF | 231 |
| 1990 | David Cone, NY | 233 | 2011 | Clayton Kershaw, LA | 248 |
| 1991 | David Cone, NY | 241 | | | |
| 1992 | John Smoltz, Atl | 215 | | | |

*Includes one-game NL Wild Card tiebreaker.

### Leading Pitchers—Saves

| Year | Player and Team | SV | Year | Player and Team | SV |
|------|-----------------|-----|------|-----------------|-----|
| 1947 | Hugh Casey, Bklyn | 18 | 1980 | Bruce Sutter, Chi | 28 |
| 1948 | Harry Gumpert, Cin | 17 | 1981 | Bruce Sutter, StL | 25 |
| 1949 | Ted Wilks, StL | 9 | 1982 | Bruce Sutter, StL | 36 |
| 1950 | Jim Konstanty, Phi | 22 | 1983 | Lee Smith, Chi | 29 |
| 1951 | Ted Wilks, StL, Pitt | 13 | 1984 | Bruce Sutter, StL | 45 |
| 1952 | Al Brazle, StL | 16 | 1985 | Jeff Reardon, Mtl | 41 |
| 1953 | Al Brazle, StL | 18 | 1986 | Todd Worrell, StL | 36 |
| 1954 | Jim Hughes, Bklyn | 24 | 1987 | Steve Bedrosian, Phi | 40 |
| 1955 | Jack Meyer, Phi | 16 | 1988 | John Franco, Cin | 39 |
| 1956 | Clem Labine, Bklyn | 19 | 1989 | Mark Davis, SD | 44 |
| 1957 | Clem Labine, Bklyn | 17 | 1990 | John Franco, NY | 33 |
| 1958 | Roy Face, Pitt | 20 | 1991 | Lee Smith, StL | 47 |
| 1959 | Lindy McDaniel, StL | 15 | 1992 | Lee Smith, StL | 42 |
| | Don McMahon, Mil | 15 | 1993 | Randy Myers, Chi | 53 |
| 1960 | Lindy McDaniel, StL | 26 | 1994 | John Franco, NY | 30 |
| 1961 | Roy Face, Pitt | 17 | 1995 | Randy Myers, Chi | 38 |
| | Stu Miller, SF | 17 | 1996 | Jeff Brantley, Cin | 44 |
| 1962 | Roy Face, Pitt | 28 | | Todd Worrell, LA | 44 |
| 1963 | Lindy McDaniel, Chi | 22 | 1997 | Jeff Shaw, Cin | 42 |
| 1964 | Hal Woodeshick, Hou | 23 | 1998 | Trevor Hoffman, SD | 53 |
| 1965 | Ted Abernathy, Chi | 31 | 1999 | Ugueth Urbina, Mtl | 41 |
| 1966 | Phil Regan, LA | 21 | 2000 | Antonio Alfonseca, Fla | 45 |
| 1967 | Ted Abernathy, Cin | 28 | 2001 | Robb Nen, SF | 45 |
| 1968 | Phil Regan, Chi, LA | 25 | 2002 | John Smoltz, Atl | 55 |
| 1969 | Fred Gladding, Hou | 29 | 2003 | Eric Gagne, LA | 55 |
| 1970 | Wayne Granger, Cin | 35 | 2004 | Armando Benitez, Fla | 47 |
| 1971 | Dave Giusti, Pitt | 30 | | Jason Isringhausen, StL | 47 |
| 1972 | Clay Carroll, Cin | 37 | 2005 | Chad Cordero, Wash | 47 |
| 1973 | Mike Marshall, Mtl | 13 | 2006 | Trevor Hoffman, SD | 46 |
| 1974 | Mike Marshall, LA | 21 | 2007 | Jose Valverde, Ariz | 47 |
| 1975 | Rawly Eastwick, Cin | 22 | 2008 | Jose Valverde, Hou | 44 |
| | Al Hrabosky, StL | 22 | 2009 | Heath Bell, SD | 42 |
| 1976 | Rawly Eastwick, Cin | 26 | 2010 | Brian Wilson, SF | 48 |
| 1977 | Rollie Fingers, SD | 35 | 2011 | John Axford, Mil | 46 |
| 1978 | Rollie Fingers, SD | 37 | | Craig Kimbrel, Atl | 46 |
| 1979 | Bruce Sutter, Chi | 37 | | | |

## AMERICAN LEAGUE
### Leading Batsmen

| Year | Player and Team | BA | Year | Player and Team | BA |
|---|---|---|---|---|---|
| 1901 | Nap Lajoie, Phi | .422 | 1957 | Ted Williams, Bos | .388 |
| 1902 | Ed Delahanty, Wash | .376 | 1958 | Ted Williams, Bos | .328 |
| 1903 | Nap Lajoie, Clev | .355 | 1959 | Harvey Kuenn, Det | .353 |
| 1904 | Nap Lajoie, Clev | .381 | 1960 | Pete Runnels, Bos | .320 |
| 1905 | Elmer Flick, Clev | .306 | 1961 | Norm Cash, Det | .361 |
| 1906 | George Stone, StL | .358 | 1962 | Pete Runnels, Bos | .326 |
| 1907 | Ty Cobb, Det | .350 | 1963 | Carl Yastrzemski, Bos | .321 |
| 1908 | Ty Cobb, Det | .324 | 1964 | Tony Oliva, Minn | .323 |
| 1909 | Ty Cobb, Det | .377 | 1965 | Tony Oliva, Minn | .321 |
| 1910 | Nap Lajoie, Clev† | .383 | 1966 | Frank Robinson, Balt | .316 |
| 1911 | Ty Cobb, Det | .420 | 1967 | Carl Yastrzemski, Bos | .326 |
| 1912 | Ty Cobb, Det | .410 | 1968 | Carl Yastrzemski, Bos | .301 |
| 1913 | Ty Cobb, Det | .390 | 1969 | Rod Carew, Minn | .332 |
| 1914 | Ty Cobb, Det | .368 | 1970 | Alex Johnson, Cal | .329 |
| 1915 | Ty Cobb, Det | .369 | 1971 | Tony Oliva, Minn | .337 |
| 1916 | Tris Speaker, Clev | .386 | 1972 | Rod Carew, Minn | .318 |
| 1917 | Ty Cobb, Det | .383 | 1973 | Rod Carew, Minn | .350 |
| 1918 | Ty Cobb, Det | .382 | 1974 | Rod Carew, Minn | .364 |
| 1919 | Ty Cobb, Det | .384 | 1975 | Rod Carew, Minn | .359 |
| 1920 | George Sisler, StL | .407 | 1976 | George Brett, KC | .333 |
| 1921 | Harry Heilmann, Det | .394 | 1977 | Rod Carew, Minn | .388 |
| 1922 | George Sisler, StL | .420 | 1978 | Rod Carew, Minn | .333 |
| 1923 | Harry Heilmann, Det | .403 | 1979 | Fred Lynn, Bos | .333 |
| 1924 | Babe Ruth, NY | .378 | 1980 | George Brett, KC | .390 |
| 1925 | Harry Heilmann, Det | .393 | 1981 | Carney Lansford, Bos | .336 |
| 1926 | Heinie Manush, Det | .378 | 1982 | Willie Wilson, KC | .332 |
| 1927 | Harry Heilmann, Det | .398 | 1983 | Wade Boggs, Bos | .361 |
| 1928 | Goose Goslin, Wash | .379 | 1984 | Don Mattingly, NY | .343 |
| 1929 | Lew Fonseca, Clev | .369 | 1985 | Wade Boggs, Bos | .368 |
| 1930 | Al Simmons, Phi | .381 | 1986 | Wade Boggs, Bos | .357 |
| 1931 | Al Simmons, Phi | .390 | 1987 | Wade Boggs, Bos | .363 |
| 1932 | Dale Alexander, Det-Bos | .367 | 1988 | Wade Boggs, Bos | .366 |
| 1933 | Jimmie Foxx, Phi | .356 | 1989 | Kirby Puckett, Minn | .339 |
| 1934 | Lou Gehrig, NY | .363 | 1990 | George Brett, KC | .329 |
| 1935 | Buddy Myer, Wash | .349 | 1991 | Julio Franco, Tex | .341 |
| 1936 | Luke Appling, Chi | .388 | 1992 | Edgar Martinez, Sea | .343 |
| 1937 | Charlie Gehringer, Det | .371 | 1993 | John Olerud, Tor | .363 |
| 1938 | Jimmie Foxx, Bos | .349 | 1994 | Paul O'Neill, NY | .359 |
| 1939 | Joe DiMaggio, NY | .381 | 1995 | Edgar Martinez, Sea | .356 |
| 1940 | Joe DiMaggio, NY | .352 | 1996 | Alex Rodriguez, Sea | .358 |
| 1941 | Ted Williams, Bos | .406 | 1997 | Frank Thomas, Chi | .347 |
| 1942 | Ted Williams, Bos | .356 | 1998 | Bernie Williams, NY | .339 |
| 1943 | Luke Appling, Chi | .328 | 1999 | Nomar Garciaparra, Bos | .357 |
| 1944 | Lou Boudreau, Clev | .327 | 2000 | Nomar Garciaparra, Bos | .372 |
| 1945 | Snuffy Stirnweiss, NY | .309 | 2001 | Ichiro Suzuki, Sea | .350 |
| 1946 | Mickey Vernon, Wash | .353 | 2002 | Manny Ramirez, Bos | .349 |
| 1947 | Ted Williams, Bos | .343 | 2003 | Bill Mueller, Bos | .326 |
| 1948 | Ted Williams, Bos | .369 | 2004 | Ichiro Suzuki, Sea | .372 |
| 1949 | George Kell, Det | .343 | 2005 | Michael Young, Tex | .331 |
| 1950 | Billy Goodman, Bos | .354 | 2006 | Joe Mauer, Minn | .347 |
| 1951 | Ferris Fain, Phi | .344 | 2007 | Magglio Ordonez, Det | .363 |
| 1952 | Ferris Fain, Phi | .327 | 2008 | Joe Mauer, Minn | .330 |
| 1953 | Mickey Vernon, Wash | .337 | 2009 | Joe Mauer, Minn* | .365 |
| 1954 | Bobby Avila, Clev | .341 | 2010 | Josh Hamilton, Tex | .359 |
| 1955 | Al Kaline, Det | .340 | 2011 | Miguel Cabrera, Det | .344 |
| 1956 | Mickey Mantle, NY | .353 | | | |

†League president Ban Johnson declared Ty Cobb batting champion with a .385 average, beating Lajoie's .384. However, subsequent research has led to the revision of Lajoie's average to .383 and Cobb's to .382.
*Includes one-game AL Central playoff tiebreaker.

## AMERICAN LEAGUE
### Leaders in Runs Scored

| Year | Player and Team | Runs | Year | Player and Team | Runs |
|------|-----------------|------|------|-----------------|------|
| 1901 | Nap Lajoie, Phi | 145 | 1958 | Mickey Mantle, NY | 127 |
| 1902 | Dave Fultz, Phi | 110 | 1959 | Eddie Yost, Det | 115 |
| 1903 | Patsy Dougherty, Bos | 108 | 1960 | Mickey Mantle, NY | 119 |
| 1904 | Patsy Dougherty, Bos-NY | 113 | 1961 | Mickey Mantle, NY | 132 |
| 1905 | Harry Davis, Phi | 92 | | Roger Maris, NY | 132 |
| 1906 | Elmer Flick, Clev | 98 | 1962 | Albie Pearson, LA | 115 |
| 1907 | Sam Crawford, Det | 102 | 1963 | Bob Allison, Minn | 99 |
| 1908 | Matty McIntyre, Det | 105 | 1964 | Tony Oliva, Minn | 109 |
| 1909 | Ty Cobb, Det | 116 | 1965 | Zoilo Versalles, Minn | 126 |
| 1910 | Ty Cobb, Det | 106 | 1966 | Frank Robinson, Balt | 122 |
| 1911 | Ty Cobb, Det | 147 | 1967 | Carl Yastrzemski, Bos | 112 |
| 1912 | Eddie Collins, Phi | 137 | 1968 | Dick McAuliffe, Det | 95 |
| 1913 | Eddie Collins, Phi | 125 | 1969 | Reggie Jackson, Oak | 123 |
| 1914 | Eddie Collins, Phi | 122 | 1970 | Carl Yastrzemski, Bos | 125 |
| 1915 | Ty Cobb, Det | 144 | 1971 | Don Buford, Balt | 99 |
| 1916 | Ty Cobb, Det | 113 | 1972 | Bobby Murcer, NY | 102 |
| 1917 | Donie Bush, Det | 112 | 1973 | Reggie Jackson, Oak | 99 |
| 1918 | Ray Chapman, Clev | 84 | 1974 | Carl Yastrzemski, Bos | 93 |
| 1919 | Babe Ruth, Bos | 103 | 1975 | Fred Lynn, Bos | 103 |
| 1920 | Babe Ruth, NY | 158 | 1976 | Roy White, NY | 104 |
| 1921 | Babe Ruth, NY | 177 | 1977 | Rod Carew, Minn | 128 |
| 1922 | George Sisler, StL | 134 | 1978 | Ron LeFlore, Det | 126 |
| 1923 | Babe Ruth, NY | 151 | 1979 | Don Baylor, Cal | 120 |
| 1924 | Babe Ruth, NY | 143 | 1980 | Willie Wilson, KC | 133 |
| 1925 | Johnny Mostil, Chi | 135 | 1981 | Rickey Henderson, Oak | 89 |
| 1926 | Babe Ruth, NY | 139 | 1982 | Paul Molitor, Mil | 136 |
| 1927 | Babe Ruth, NY | 158 | 1983 | Cal Ripken, Balt | 121 |
| 1928 | Babe Ruth, NY | 163 | 1984 | Dwight Evans, Bos | 121 |
| 1929 | Charlie Gehringer, Det | 131 | 1985 | Rickey Henderson, NY | 146 |
| 1930 | Al Simmons, Phi | 152 | 1986 | Rickey Henderson, NY | 130 |
| 1931 | Lou Gehrig, NY | 163 | 1987 | Paul Molitor, Mil | 114 |
| 1932 | Jimmie Foxx, Phi | 151 | 1988 | Wade Boggs, Bos | 128 |
| 1933 | Lou Gehrig, NY | 138 | 1989 | Wade Boggs, Bos | 113 |
| 1934 | Charlie Gehringer, Det | 134 | | Rickey Henderson, NY-Oak | 113 |
| 1935 | Lou Gehrig, NY | 125 | 1990 | Rickey Henderson, Oak | 119 |
| 1936 | Lou Gehrig, NY | 167 | 1991 | Paul Molitor, Mil | 133 |
| 1937 | Joe DiMaggio, NY | 151 | 1992 | Tony Philips, Det | 114 |
| 1938 | Hank Greenberg, Det | 144 | 1993 | Rafael Palmeiro, Tex | 124 |
| 1939 | Red Rolfe, NY | 139 | 1994 | Frank Thomas, Chi | 106 |
| 1940 | Ted Williams, Bos | 134 | 1995 | Albert Belle, Clev | 121 |
| 1941 | Ted Williams, Bos | 135 | | Edgar Martinez, Sea | 121 |
| 1942 | Ted Williams, Bos | 141 | 1996 | Alex Rodriguez, Sea | 141 |
| 1943 | George Case, Wash | 102 | 1997 | Ken Griffey Jr., Sea | 125 |
| 1944 | Snuffy Stirnweiss, NY | 125 | 1998 | Derek Jeter, NY | 127 |
| 1945 | Snuffy Stirnweiss, NY | 107 | 1999 | Roberto Alomar, Clev | 138 |
| 1946 | Ted Williams, Bos | 142 | 2000 | Johnny Damon, KC | 136 |
| 1947 | Ted Williams, Bos | 125 | 2001 | Alex Rodriguez, Tex | 133 |
| 1948 | Tommy Henrich, NY | 138 | 2002 | Alfonso Soriano, NY | 128 |
| 1949 | Ted Williams, Bos | 150 | 2003 | Alex Rodriguez, Tex | 124 |
| 1950 | Dom DiMaggio, Bos | 131 | 2004 | Vladimir Guerrero, Ana | 124 |
| 1951 | Dom DiMaggio, Bos | 113 | 2005 | Alex Rodriguez, NY | 124 |
| 1952 | Larry Doby, Clev | 104 | 2006 | Grady Sizemore, Clev | 134 |
| 1953 | Al Rosen, Clev | 115 | 2007 | Alex Rodriguez, NY | 143 |
| 1954 | Mickey Mantle, NY | 129 | 2008 | Dustin Pedroia, Bos | 118 |
| 1955 | Al Smith, Clev | 123 | 2009 | Dustin Pedroia, Bos | 115 |
| 1956 | Mickey Mantle, NY | 132 | 2010 | Mark Teixeira, NY | 113 |
| 1957 | Mickey Mantle, NY | 121 | 2011 | Curtis Granderson, NY | 136 |

## AMERICAN LEAGUE
### Leaders in Hits

| Year | Player and Team | Hits | Year | Player and Team | Hits |
|------|-----------------|------|------|-----------------|------|
| 1901 | Nap Lajoie, Phi | 229 | 1955 | Al Kaline, Det | 200 |
| 1902 | Piano Legs Hickman, Bos-Clev | 194 | 1956 | Harvey Kuenn, Det | 196 |
| 1903 | Patsy Dougherty, Bos | 195 | 1957 | Nellie Fox, Chi | 196 |
| 1904 | Nap Lajoie, Clev | 211 | 1958 | Nellie Fox, Chi | 187 |
| 1905 | George Stone, StL | 187 | 1959 | Harvey Kuenn, Det | 198 |
| 1906 | Nap Lajoie, Clev | 214 | 1960 | Minnie Minoso, Chi | 184 |
| 1907 | Ty Cobb, Det | 212 | 1961 | Norm Cash, Det | 193 |
| 1908 | Ty Cobb, Det | 188 | 1962 | Bobby Richardson, NY | 209 |
| 1909 | Ty Cobb, Det | 216 | 1963 | Carl Yastrzemski, Bos | 183 |
| 1910 | Nap Lajoie, Clev | 227 | 1964 | Tony Oliva, Minn | 217 |
| 1911 | Ty Cobb, Det | 248 | 1965 | Tony Oliva, Minn | 185 |
| 1912 | Ty Cobb, Det | 227 | 1966 | Tony Oliva, Minn | 191 |
| 1913 | Joe Jackson, Clev | 197 | 1967 | Carl Yastrzemski, Bos | 189 |
| 1914 | Tris Speaker, Bos | 193 | 1968 | Bert Campaneris, Oak | 177 |
| 1915 | Ty Cobb, Det | 208 | 1969 | Tony Oliva, Minn | 197 |
| 1916 | Tris Speaker, Clev | 211 | 1970 | Tony Oliva, Minn | 204 |
| 1917 | Ty Cobb, Det | 225 | 1971 | Cesar Tovar, Minn | 204 |
| 1918 | George Burns, Phi | 178 | 1972 | Joe Rudi, Oak | 181 |
| 1919 | Ty Cobb, Det | 191 | 1973 | Rod Carew, Minn | 203 |
|      | Bobby Veach, Det | 191 | 1974 | Rod Carew, Minn | 218 |
| 1920 | George Sisler, StL | 257 | 1975 | George Brett, KC | 195 |
| 1921 | Harry Heilmann, Det | 237 | 1976 | George Brett, KC | 215 |
| 1922 | George Sisler, StL | 246 | 1977 | Rod Carew, Minn | 239 |
| 1923 | Charlie Jamieson, Clev | 222 | 1978 | Jim Rice, Bos | 213 |
| 1924 | Sam Rice, Wash | 216 | 1979 | George Brett, KC | 212 |
| 1925 | Al Simmons, Phi | 253 | 1980 | Willie Wilson, KC | 230 |
| 1926 | George Burns, Clev | 216 | 1981 | Rickey Henderson, Oak | 135 |
|      | Sam Rice, Wash | 216 | 1982 | Robin Yount, Mil | 210 |
| 1927 | Earle Combs, NY | 231 | 1983 | Cal Ripken Jr., Balt | 211 |
| 1928 | Heinie Manush, StL | 241 | 1984 | Don Mattingly, NY | 207 |
| 1929 | Dale Alexander, Det | 215 | 1985 | Wade Boggs, Bos | 240 |
|      | Charlie Gehringer, Det | 215 | 1986 | Don Mattingly, NY | 238 |
| 1930 | Johnny Hodapp, Clev | 225 | 1987 | Kirby Puckett, Minn | 207 |
| 1931 | Lou Gehrig, NY | 211 |      | Kevin Seitzer, KC | 207 |
| 1932 | Al Simmons, Phi | 216 | 1988 | Kirby Puckett, Minn | 234 |
| 1933 | Heinie Manush, Wash | 221 | 1989 | Kirby Puckett, Minn | 215 |
| 1934 | Charlie Gehringer, Det | 214 | 1990 | Rafael Palmeiro, Tex | 191 |
| 1935 | Joe Vosmik, Clev | 216 | 1991 | Paul Molitor, Mil | 216 |
| 1936 | Earl Averill, Clev | 232 | 1992 | Kirby Puckett, Minn | 210 |
| 1937 | Beau Bell, StL | 218 | 1993 | Paul Molitor, Tor | 211 |
| 1938 | Joe Vosmik, Bos | 201 | 1994 | Kenny Lofton, Clev | 160 |
| 1939 | Red Rolfe, NY | 213 | 1995 | Lance Johnson, Chi | 186 |
| 1940 | Doc Cramer, Bos | 200 | 1996 | Paul Molitor, Minn | 225 |
|      | Barney McCosky, Det | 200 | 1997 | Nomar Garciaparra, Bos | 209 |
|      | Rip Radcliff, StL | 200 | 1998 | Alex Rodriguez, Sea | 213 |
| 1941 | Cecil Travis, Wash | 218 | 1999 | Derek Jeter, NY | 219 |
| 1942 | Johnny Pesky, Bos | 205 | 2000 | Darin Erstad, Ana | 240 |
| 1943 | Dick Wakefield, Det | 200 | 2001 | Ichiro Suzuki, Sea | 242 |
| 1944 | Snuffy Stirnweiss, NY | 205 | 2002 | Alfonso Soriano, NY | 209 |
| 1945 | Snuffy Stirnweiss, NY | 195 | 2003 | Vernon Wells, Tor | 215 |
| 1946 | Johnny Pesky, Bos | 208 | 2004 | Ichiro Suzuki, Sea | 262 |
| 1947 | Johnny Pesky, Bos | 207 | 2005 | Michael Young, Tex | 221 |
| 1948 | Bob Dillinger, StL | 207 | 2006 | Ichiro Suzuki, Sea | 224 |
| 1949 | Dale Mitchell, Clev | 203 | 2007 | Ichiro Suzuki, Sea | 238 |
| 1950 | George Kell, Det | 218 | 2008 | Dustin Pedroia, Bos | 213 |
| 1951 | George Kell, Det | 191 |      | Ichiro Suzuki, Sea | 213 |
| 1952 | Nellie Fox, Chi | 192 | 2009 | Ichiro Suzuki, Sea | 225 |
| 1953 | Harvey Kuenn, Det | 209 | 2010 | Ichiro Suzuki, Sea | 214 |
| 1954 | Nellie Fox, Chi | 201 | 2011 | Adrian Gonzalez, Bos | 213 |
|      | Harvey Kuenn, Det | 201 |      | Michael Young, Tex | 213 |

## AMERICAN LEAGUE
### Home Run Leaders

| Year | Player and Team | HR | Year | Player and Team | HR |
|---|---|---|---|---|---|
| 1901 | Nap Lajoie, Phi | 13 | 1960 | Mickey Mantle, NY | 40 |
| 1902 | Socks Seybold, Phi | 16 | 1961 | Roger Maris, NY | 61 |
| 1903 | Buck Freeman, Bos | 13 | 1962 | Harmon Killebrew, Minn | 48 |
| 1904 | Harry Davis, Phi | 10 | 1963 | Harmon Killebrew, Minn | 45 |
| 1905 | Harry Davis, Phi | 8 | 1964 | Harmon Killebrew, Minn | 49 |
| 1906 | Harry Davis, Phi | 12 | 1965 | Tony Conigliaro, Bos | 32 |
| 1907 | Harry Davis, Phi | 8 | 1966 | Frank Robinson, Balt | 49 |
| 1908 | Sam Crawford, Det | 7 | 1967 | Harmon Killebrew, Minn | 44 |
| 1909 | Ty Cobb, Det | 9 | | Carl Yastrzemski, Bos | 44 |
| 1910 | Jake Stahl, Bos | 10 | 1968 | Frank Howard, Wash | 44 |
| 1911 | Frank Baker, Phi | 9 | 1969 | Harmon Killebrew, Minn | 49 |
| 1912 | Frank Baker, Phi | 10 | 1970 | Frank Howard, Wash | 44 |
| | Tris Speaker, Bos | 10 | 1971 | Bill Melton, Chi | 33 |
| 1913 | Frank Baker, Phi | 13 | 1972 | Dick Allen, Chi | 37 |
| 1914 | Frank Baker, Phi | 9 | 1973 | Reggie Jackson, Oak | 32 |
| 1915 | Braggo Roth, Chi-Clev | 7 | 1974 | Dick Allen, Chi | 32 |
| 1916 | Wally Pipp, NY | 12 | 1975 | Reggie Jackson, Oak | 36 |
| 1917 | Wally Pipp, NY | 9 | | George Scott, Mil | 36 |
| 1918 | Babe Ruth, Bos | 11 | 1976 | Graig Nettles, NY | 32 |
| | Tilly Walker, Phi | 11 | 1977 | Jim Rice, Bos | 39 |
| 1919 | Babe Ruth, Bos | 29 | 1978 | Jim Rice, Bos | 46 |
| 1920 | Babe Ruth, NY | 54 | 1979 | Gorman Thomas, Mil | 45 |
| 1921 | Babe Ruth, NY | 59 | 1980 | Reggie Jackson, NY | 41 |
| 1922 | Ken Williams, StL | 39 | | Ben Oglivie, Mil | 41 |
| 1923 | Babe Ruth, NY | 41 | 1981 | Tony Armas, Oak | 22 |
| 1924 | Babe Ruth, NY | 46 | 1981 | Dwight Evans, Bos | 22 |
| 1925 | Bob Meusel, NY | 33 | | Bobby Grich, Cal | 22 |
| 1926 | Babe Ruth, NY | 47 | | Eddie Murray, Balt | 22 |
| 1927 | Babe Ruth, NY | 60 | 1982 | Reggie Jackson, Cal | 39 |
| 1928 | Babe Ruth, NY | 54 | | Gorman Thomas, Mil | 39 |
| 1929 | Babe Ruth, NY | 46 | 1983 | Jim Rice, Bos | 39 |
| 1930 | Babe Ruth, NY | 49 | 1984 | Tony Armas, Bos | 43 |
| 1931 | Babe Ruth/ Lou Gehrig NY | 46 | 1985 | Darrell Evans, Det | 40 |
| 1932 | Jimmie Foxx, Phi | 58 | 1986 | Jesse Barfield, Tor | 40 |
| 1933 | Jimmie Foxx, Phi | 48 | 1987 | Mark McGwire, Oak | 49 |
| 1934 | Lou Gehrig, NY | 49 | 1988 | Jose Canseco, Oak | 42 |
| 1935 | Jimmie Foxx, Phi | 36 | 1989 | Fred McGriff, Tor | 36 |
| | Hank Greenberg, Det | 36 | 1990 | Cecil Fielder, Det | 51 |
| 1936 | Lou Gehrig, NY | 49 | 1991 | Jose Canseco, Oak | 44 |
| 1937 | Joe DiMaggio, NY | 46 | | Cecil Fielder, Det | 44 |
| 1938 | Hank Greenberg, Det | 58 | 1992 | Juan Gonzalez, Tex | 43 |
| 1939 | Jimmie Foxx, Bos | 35 | 1993 | Juan Gonzalez, Tex | 46 |
| 1940 | Hank Greenberg, Det | 41 | 1994 | Ken Griffey Jr., Sea | 40 |
| 1941 | Ted Williams, Bos | 37 | 1995 | Albert Belle, Clev | 50 |
| 1942 | Ted Williams, Bos | 36 | 1996 | Mark McGwire, Oak | 52 |
| 1943 | Rudy York, Det | 34 | 1997 | Ken Griffey Jr., Sea | 56 |
| 1944 | Nick Etten, NY | 22 | 1998 | Ken Griffey Jr., Sea | 56 |
| 1945 | Vern Stephens, StL | 24 | 1999 | Ken Griffey Jr., Sea | 48 |
| 1946 | Hank Greenberg, Det | 44 | 2000 | Troy Glaus, Ana | 47 |
| 1947 | Ted Williams, Bos | 32 | 2001 | Alex Rodriguez, Tex | 52 |
| 1948 | Joe DiMaggio, NY | 39 | 2002 | Alex Rodriguez, Tex | 57 |
| 1949 | Ted Williams, Bos | 43 | 2003 | Alex Rodriguez, Tex | 47 |
| 1950 | Al Rosen, Clev | 37 | 2004 | Manny Ramirez, Bos | 43 |
| 1951 | Gus Zernial, Chi-Phi | 33 | 2005 | Alex Rodriguez, NY | 48 |
| 1952 | Larry Doby, Clev | 32 | 2006 | David Ortiz, Bos | 54 |
| 1953 | Al Rosen, Clev | 43 | 2007 | Alex Rodriguez, NY | 54 |
| 1954 | Larry Doby, Clev | 32 | 2008 | Miguel Cabrera, Det | 37 |
| 1955 | Mickey Mantle, NY | 37 | 2009 | Carlos Pena, TB | 39 |
| 1956 | Mickey Mantle, NY | 52 | | Mark Teixeira, NY | 39 |
| 1957 | Roy Sievers, Wash | 42 | 2010 | Jose Bautista, Tor | 54 |
| 1958 | Mickey Mantle, NY | 42 | 2011 | Jose Bautista, Tor | 43 |
| 1959 | Rocky Colavito, Clev | 42 | | | |
| | Harmon Killebrew, Wash | 42 | | | |

### AMERICAN LEAGUE
### Runs Batted In Leaders

| Year | Player and Team | RBI | Year | Player and Team | RBI |
|------|-----------------|-----|------|-----------------|-----|
| 1907 | Ty Cobb, Det | 116 | 1960 | Roger Maris, NY | 112 |
| 1908 | Ty Cobb, Det | 108 | 1961 | Roger Maris, NY | 142 |
| 1909 | Ty Cobb, Det | 107 | 1962 | Harmon Killebrew, Minn | 126 |
| 1910 | Sam Crawford, Det | 120 | 1963 | Dick Stuart, Bos | 118 |
| 1911 | Ty Cobb, Det | 144 | 1964 | Brooks Robinson, Balt | 118 |
| 1912 | Frank Baker, Phi | 133 | 1965 | Rocky Colavito, Clev | 108 |
| 1913 | Frank Baker, Phi | 126 | 1966 | Frank Robinson, Balt | 122 |
| 1914 | Sam Crawford, Det | 104 | 1967 | Carl Yastrzemski, Bos | 121 |
| 1915 | Sam Crawford, Det | 112 | 1968 | Ken Harrelson, Bos | 109 |
|      | Bobby Veach, Det | 112 | 1969 | Harmon Killebrew, Minn | 140 |
| 1916 | Del Pratt, StL | 103 | 1970 | Frank Howard, Wash | 126 |
| 1917 | Bobby Veach, Det | 103 | 1971 | Harmon Killebrew, Minn | 119 |
| 1918 | Bobby Veach, Det | 78 | 1972 | Dick Allen, Chi | 113 |
| 1919 | Babe Ruth, Bos | 114 | 1973 | Reggie Jackson, Oak | 117 |
| 1920 | Babe Ruth, NY | 137 | 1974 | Jeff Burroughs, Tex | 118 |
| 1921 | Babe Ruth, NY | 171 | 1975 | George Scott, Mil | 109 |
| 1922 | Ken Williams, StL | 155 | 1976 | Lee May, Balt | 109 |
| 1923 | Babe Ruth, NY | 131 | 1977 | Larry Hisle, Minn | 119 |
| 1924 | Goose Goslin, Wash | 129 | 1978 | Jim Rice, Bos | 139 |
| 1925 | Bob Meusel, NY | 138 | 1979 | Don Baylor, Cal | 139 |
| 1926 | Babe Ruth, NY | 145 | 1980 | Cecil Cooper, Mil | 122 |
| 1927 | Lou Gehrig, NY | 175 | 1981 | Eddie Murray, Balt | 78 |
| 1928 | Babe Ruth/ Lou Gehrig, NY | 142 | 1982 | Hal McRae, KC | 133 |
| 1929 | Al Simmons, Phi | 157 | 1983 | Cecil Cooper, Mil | 126 |
| 1930 | Lou Gehrig, NY | 174 |      | Jim Rice, Bos | 126 |
| 1931 | Lou Gehrig, NY | 184 | 1984 | Tony Armas, Bos | 123 |
| 1932 | Jimmie Foxx, Phi | 169 | 1985 | Don Mattingly, NY | 145 |
| 1933 | Jimmie Foxx, Phi | 163 | 1986 | Joe Carter, Clev | 121 |
| 1934 | Lou Gehrig, NY | 165 | 1987 | George Bell, Tor | 134 |
| 1935 | Hank Greenberg, Det | 170 | 1988 | Jose Canseco, Oak | 124 |
| 1936 | Hal Trosky, Clev | 162 | 1989 | Ruben Sierra, Tex | 119 |
| 1937 | Hank Greenberg, Det | 183 | 1990 | Cecil Fielder, Det | 132 |
| 1938 | Jimmie Foxx, Bos | 175 | 1991 | Cecil Fielder, Det | 133 |
| 1939 | Ted Williams, Bos | 145 | 1992 | Cecil Fielder, Det | 124 |
| 1940 | Hank Greenberg, Det | 150 | 1993 | Albert Belle, Clev | 129 |
| 1941 | Joe DiMaggio, NY | 125 | 1994 | Kirby Puckett, Minn | 112 |
| 1942 | Ted Williams, Bos | 137 | 1995 | Albert Belle, Clev | 126 |
| 1943 | Rudy York, Det | 118 |      | Mo Vaughn, Bos | 126 |
| 1944 | Vern Stephens, StL | 109 | 1996 | Albert Belle, Clev | 148 |
| 1945 | Nick Etten, NY | 111 | 1997 | Ken Griffey Jr., Sea | 147 |
| 1946 | Hank Greenberg, Det | 127 | 1998 | Juan Gonzales, Tex | 157 |
| 1947 | Ted Williams, Bos | 114 | 1999 | Manny Ramirez, Clev | 165 |
| 1948 | Joe DiMaggio, NY | 155 | 2000 | Edgar Martinez, Sea | 145 |
| 1949 | Vern Stephens, Bos | 159 | 2001 | Bret Boone, Sea | 141 |
|      | Ted Williams, Bos | 159 | 2002 | Alex Rodriguez, Tex | 142 |
| 1950 | Walt Dropo, Bos | 144 | 2003 | Carlos Delgado, Tor | 145 |
|      | Vern Stephens, Bos | 144 | 2004 | Miguel Tejada, Balt | 150 |
| 1951 | Gus Zernial, Chi-Phi | 129 | 2005 | David Ortiz, Bos | 148 |
| 1952 | Al Rosen, Clev | 105 | 2006 | David Ortiz, Bos | 137 |
| 1953 | Al Rosen, Clev | 145 | 2007 | Alex Rodriguez, NY | 156 |
| 1954 | Larry Doby, Clev | 126 | 2008 | Josh Hamilton, Tex | 130 |
| 1955 | Ray Boone, Det | 116 | 2009 | Mark Teixeira, NY | 122 |
|      | Jackie Jensen, Bos | 116 | 2010 | Miguel Cabrera, Det | 126 |
| 1956 | Mickey Mantle, NY | 130 | 2011 | Curtis Granderson, NY | 119 |
| 1957 | Roy Sievers, Wash | 114 |      |  |  |
| 1958 | Jackie Jensen, Bos | 122 |      |  |  |
| 1959 | Jackie Jensen, Bos | 112 |      |  |  |

Note: Runs Batted In not compiled before 1907; officially adopted in 1920.

## AMERICAN LEAGUE
### Leading Base Stealers

| Year | Player and Team | SB | Year | Player and Team | SB |
|---|---|---|---|---|---|
| 1901 | Frank Isbell, Chi | 48 | 1956 | Luis Aparicio, Chi | 21 |
| 1902 | Topsy Hartsel, Phi | 54 | 1957 | Luis Aparicio, Chi | 28 |
| 1903 | Harry Bay, Clev | 46 | 1958 | Luis Aparicio, Chi | 29 |
| 1904 | Harry Bay, Clev | 42 | 1959 | Luis Aparicio, Chi | 56 |
|  | Elmer Flick, Clev | 42 | 1960 | Luis Aparicio, Chi | 51 |
| 1905 | Danny Hoffman, Phi | 46 | 1961 | Luis Aparicio, Chi | 53 |
| 1906 | John Anderson, Wash | 39 | 1962 | Luis Aparicio, Chi | 31 |
|  | Elmer Flick, Clev | 39 | 1963 | Luis Aparicio, Balt | 40 |
| 1907 | Ty Cobb, Det | 49 | 1964 | Luis Aparicio, Balt | 57 |
| 1908 | Patsy Dougherty, Chi | 47 | 1965 | Bert Campaneris, KC | 51 |
| 1909 | Ty Cobb, Det | 76 | 1966 | Bert Campaneris, KC | 52 |
| 1910 | Eddie Collins, Phi | 81 | 1967 | Bert Campaneris, KC | 55 |
| 1911 | Ty Cobb, Det | 83 | 1968 | Bert Campaneris, Oak | 62 |
| 1912 | Clyde Milan, Wash | 88 | 1969 | Tommy Harper, Sea | 73 |
| 1913 | Clyde Milan, Wash | 75 | 1970 | Bert Campaneris, Oak | 42 |
| 1914 | Fritz Maisel, NY | 74 | 1971 | Amos Otis, KC | 52 |
| 1915 | Ty Cobb, Det | 96 | 1972 | Bert Campaneris, Oak | 52 |
| 1916 | Ty Cobb, Det | 68 | 1973 | Tommy Harper, Bos | 54 |
| 1917 | Ty Cobb, Det | 55 | 1974 | Bill North, Oak | 54 |
| 1918 | George Sisler, StL | 45 | 1975 | Mickey Rivers, Cal | 70 |
| 1919 | Eddie Collins, Chi | 33 | 1976 | Bill North, Oak | 75 |
| 1920 | Sam Rice, Wash | 63 | 1977 | Freddie Patek, KC | 53 |
| 1921 | George Sisler, StL | 35 | 1978 | Ron LeFlore, Det | 68 |
| 1922 | George Sisler, StL | 51 | 1979 | Willie Wilson, KC | 83 |
| 1923 | Eddie Collins, Chi | 49 | 1980 | Rickey Henderson, Oak | 100 |
| 1924 | Eddie Collins, Chi | 42 | 1981 | Rickey Henderson, Oak | 56 |
| 1925 | John Mostil, Chi | 43 | 1982 | Rickey Henderson, Oak | 130 |
| 1926 | John Mostil, Chi | 35 | 1983 | Rickey Henderson, Oak | 108 |
| 1927 | George Sisler, StL | 27 | 1984 | Rickey Henderson, Oak | 66 |
| 1928 | Buddy Myer, Bos | 30 | 1985 | Rickey Henderson, NY | 80 |
| 1929 | Charlie Gehringer, Det | 27 | 1986 | Rickey Henderson, NY | 87 |
| 1930 | Marty McManus, Det | 23 | 1987 | Harold Reynolds, Sea | 60 |
| 1931 | Ben Chapman, NY | 61 | 1988 | Rickey Henderson, NY | 93 |
| 1932 | Ben Chapman, NY | 38 | 1989 | Rickey Henderson, NY-Oak | 77 |
| 1933 | Ben Chapman, NY | 27 | 1990 | Rickey Henderson, Oak | 65 |
| 1934 | Bill Werber, Bos | 40 | 1991 | Rickey Henderson, Oak | 58 |
| 1935 | Bill Werber, Bos | 29 | 1992 | Kenny Lofton, Clev | 66 |
| 1936 | Lyn Lary, StL | 37 | 1993 | Kenny Lofton, Clev | 70 |
| 1937 | Ben Chapman, Wash-Bos | 35 | 1994 | Kenny Lofton, Clev | 60 |
|  | Bill Werber, Phi | 35 | 1995 | Kenny Lofton, Clev | 54 |
| 1938 | Frank Crosetti, NY | 27 | 1996 | Kenny Lofton, Clev | 75 |
| 1939 | George Case, Wash | 51 | 1997 | Brian Hunter, Det | 74 |
| 1940 | George Case, Wash | 35 | 1998 | Rickey Henderson, Oak | 66 |
| 1941 | George Case, Wash | 33 | 1999 | Brian Hunter, Sea | 44 |
| 1942 | George Case, Wash | 44 | 2000 | Johnny Damon, KC | 46 |
| 1943 | George Case, Wash | 61 | 2001 | Ichiro Suzuki, Sea | 56 |
| 1944 | Snuffy Stirnweiss, NY | 55 | 2002 | Alfonso Soriano, NY | 41 |
| 1945 | Snuffy Stirnweiss, NY | 33 | 2003 | Carl Crawford, TB | 55 |
| 1946 | George Case, Clev | 28 | 2004 | Carl Crawford, TB | 59 |
| 1947 | Bob Dillinger, StL | 34 | 2005 | Chone Figgins, LA | 62 |
| 1948 | Bob Dillinger, StL | 28 | 2006 | Carl Crawford, TB | 58 |
| 1949 | Bob Dillinger, StL | 20 | 2007 | Carl Crawford, TB | 50 |
| 1950 | Dom DiMaggio, Bos | 15 |  | Brian Roberts, Balt | 50 |
| 1951 | Minnie Minoso, Clev-Chi | 31 | 2008 | Jacoby Ellsbury, Bos | 50 |
| 1952 | Minnie Minoso, Chi | 22 | 2009 | Jacoby Ellsbury, Bos | 70 |
| 1953 | Minnie Minoso, Chi | 25 | 2010 | Juan Pierre, Chi | 68 |
| 1954 | Jackie Jensen, Bos | 22 | 2011 | Coco Crisp, Oak | 49 |
| 1955 | Jim Rivera, Chi | 25 |  | Brett Gardner, NY | 49 |

### AMERICAN LEAGUE

### Leading Pitchers—Winning Percentage

| Year | Pitcher and Team | W | L | Pct | Year | Pitcher and Team | W | L | Pct |
|---|---|---|---|---|---|---|---|---|---|
| 1901 | Clark Griffith, Chi | 24 | 7 | .774 | 1958 | Bob Turley, NY | 21 | 7 | .750 |
| 1902 | Bill Bernhard, Phi-Clev | 18 | 5 | .783 | 1959 | Bob Shaw, Chi | 18 | 6 | .750 |
| 1903 | Earl Moore, Clev | 22 | 7 | .759 | 1960 | Jim Perry, Clev | 18 | 10 | .643 |
| 1904 | Jack Chesbro, NY | 41 | 12 | .774 | 1961 | Whitey Ford, NY | 25 | 4 | .862 |
| 1905 | Jess Tannehill, Bos | 22 | 9 | .710 | 1962 | Ray Herbert, Chi | 20 | 9 | .690 |
| 1906 | Eddie Plank, Phi | 19 | 6 | .760 | 1963 | Whitey Ford, NY | 24 | 7 | .774 |
| 1907 | Wild Bill Donovan, Det | 25 | 4 | .862 | 1964 | Wally Bunker, Balt | 19 | 5 | .792 |
| 1908 | Ed Walsh, Chi | 40 | 15 | .727 | 1965 | Mudcat Grant, Minn | 21 | 7 | .750 |
| 1909 | George Mullin, Det | 29 | 8 | .784 | 1966 | Sonny Siebert, Clev | 16 | 8 | .667 |
| 1910 | Chief Bender, Phi | 23 | 5 | .821 | 1967 | Joel Horlen, Chi | 19 | 7 | .731 |
| 1911 | Chief Bender, Phi | 17 | 5 | .773 | 1968 | Denny McLain, Det | 31 | 6 | .838 |
| 1912 | Smoky Joe Wood, Bos | 34 | 5 | .872 | 1969 | Jim Palmer, Balt | 16 | 4 | .800 |
| 1913 | Walter Johnson, Wash | 36 | 7 | .837 | 1970 | Mike Cuellar, Balt | 24 | 8 | .750 |
| 1914 | Chief Bender, Phi | 17 | 3 | .850 | 1971 | Dave McNally, Balt | 21 | 5 | .808 |
| 1915 | Smoky Joe Wood, Bos | 15 | 5 | .750 | 1972 | Catfish Hunter, Oak | 21 | 7 | .750 |
| 1916 | Eddie Cicotte, Chi | 15 | 7 | .682 | 1973 | Catfish Hunter, Oak | 21 | 5 | .808 |
| 1917 | Reb Russell, Chi | 15 | 5 | .750 | 1974 | Mike Cuellar, Balt | 22 | 10 | .688 |
| 1918 | Sad Sam Jones, Bos | 16 | 5 | .762 | 1975 | Mike Torrez, Balt | 20 | 9 | .690 |
| 1919 | Eddie Cicotte, Chi | 29 | 7 | .806 | 1976 | Bill Campbell, Minn | 17 | 5 | .773 |
| 1920 | Jim Bagby, Clev | 31 | 12 | .721 | 1977 | Paul Splittorff, KC | 16 | 6 | .727 |
| 1921 | Carl Mays, NY | 27 | 9 | .750 | 1978 | Ron Guidry, NY | 25 | 3 | .893 |
| 1922 | Joe Bush, NY | 26 | 7 | .788 | 1979 | Mike Caldwell, Mil | 16 | 6 | .727 |
| 1923 | Herb Pennock, NY | 19 | 6 | .760 | 1980 | Steve Stone, Balt | 25 | 7 | .781 |
| 1924 | Walter Johnson, Wash | 23 | 7 | .767 | 1981* | Pete Vuckovich, Mil | 14 | 4 | .778 |
| 1925 | Stan Coveleski, Wash | 20 | 5 | .800 | 1982 | Pete Vuckovich, Mil | 18 | 6 | .750 |
| 1926 | George Uhle, Clev | 27 | 11 | .711 | | Jim Palmer, Balt | 15 | 5 | .750 |
| 1927 | Waite Hoyt, NY | 22 | 7 | .759 | 1983 | Richard Dotson, Chi | 22 | 7 | .759 |
| 1928 | General Crowder, StL | 21 | 5 | .808 | 1984 | Doyle Alexander, Tor | 17 | 6 | .739 |
| 1929 | Lefty Grove, Phi | 20 | 6 | .769 | 1985 | Ron Guidry, NY | 22 | 6 | .786 |
| 1930 | Lefty Grove, Phi | 28 | 5 | .848 | 1986 | Roger Clemens, Bos | 24 | 4 | .857 |
| 1931 | Lefty Grove, Phi | 31 | 4 | .886 | 1987 | Roger Clemens, Bos | 20 | 9 | .690 |
| 1932 | Johnny Allen, NY | 17 | 4 | .810 | 1988 | Frank Viola, Minn | 24 | 7 | .774 |
| 1933 | Lefty Grove, Phi | 24 | 8 | .750 | 1989 | Bret Saberhagen, KC | 23 | 6 | .793 |
| 1934 | Lefty Gomez, NY | 26 | 5 | .839 | 1990 | Bob Welch, Oak | 27 | 6 | .818 |
| 1935 | Eldon Auker, Det | 18 | 7 | .720 | 1991 | Scott Erickson, Minn | 20 | 8 | .714 |
| 1936 | Monte Pearson, NY | 19 | 7 | .731 | 1992 | Mike Mussina, Balt | 18 | 5 | .783 |
| 1937 | Johnny Allen, Clev | 15 | 1 | .938 | 1993 | Jimmy Key, NY | 18 | 6 | .750 |
| 1938 | Red Ruffing, NY | 21 | 7 | .750 | 1994 | Jimmy Key, NY | 17 | 4 | .810 |
| 1939 | Lefty Grove, Bos | 15 | 4 | .789 | 1995 | Randy Johnson, Sea | 18 | 2 | .900 |
| 1940 | Schoolboy Rowe, Det | 16 | 3 | .842 | 1996 | Charles Nagy, Clev | 17 | 5 | .773 |
| 1941 | Lefty Gomez, NY | 15 | 5 | .750 | 1997 | Randy Johnson, Sea | 20 | 4 | .833 |
| 1942 | Ernie Bonham, NY | 21 | 5 | .808 | 1998 | David Wells, NY | 18 | 4 | .818 |
| 1943 | Spud Chandler, NY | 20 | 4 | .833 | 1999 | Pedro Martinez, Bos | 23 | 4 | .852 |
| 1944 | Tex Hughson, Bos | 18 | 5 | .783 | 2000 | Tim Hudson, Oak | 20 | 6 | .769 |
| 1945 | Hal Newhouser, Det | 25 | 9 | .735 | 2001 | Roger Clemens, NY | 20 | 3 | .870 |
| 1946 | Boo Ferriss, Bos | 25 | 6 | .806 | 2002 | Pedro Martinez, Bos | 20 | 4 | .833 |
| 1947 | Allie Reynolds, NY | 19 | 8 | .704 | 2003 | Roy Halladay, Tor | 22 | 7 | .759 |
| 1948 | Jack Kramer, Bos | 18 | 5 | .783 | 2004 | Curt Schilling, Bos | 21 | 6 | .778 |
| 1949 | Ellis Kinder, Bos | 23 | 6 | .793 | 2005 | Cliff Lee, Cle | 18 | 5 | .783 |
| 1950 | Vic Raschi, NY | 21 | 8 | .724 | 2006 | Roy Halladay, Tor | 16 | 5 | .762 |
| 1951 | Bob Feller, Clev | 22 | 8 | .733 | 2007 | Justin Verlander, Det | 18 | 6 | .750 |
| 1952 | Bobby Shantz, Phi | 24 | 7 | .774 | 2008 | Cliff Lee, Cle | 22 | 3 | .880 |
| 1953 | Ed Lopat, NY | 16 | 4 | .800 | 2009 | Felix Hernandez, Sea | 19 | 5 | .792 |
| 1954 | Sandy Consuegra, Chi | 16 | 3 | .842 | 2010 | David Price, TB | 19 | 6 | .760 |
| 1955 | Tommy Byrne, NY | 16 | 5 | .762 | 2011 | Justin Verlander, Det | 24 | 5 | .828 |
| 1956 | Whitey Ford, NY | 19 | 6 | .760 | | | | | |
| 1957 | Dick Donovan, Chi | 16 | 6 | .727 | | | | | |
| | Tom Sturdivant, NY | 16 | 6 | .727 | | | | | |

*1981 percentages based on 10 or more victories. Note: Percentages based on 15 or more victories in all other years.

## AMERICAN LEAGUE
### Leading Pitchers—Earned Run Average

| Year | Player and Team | ERA | Year | Player and Team | ERA |
|------|-----------------|-----|------|-----------------|-----|
| 1913 | Walter Johnson, Wash | 1.14 | 1963 | Gary Peters, Chi | 2.33 |
| 1914 | Dutch Leonard, Bos | 1.01 | 1964 | Dean Chance, LA | 1.65 |
| 1915 | Smoky Joe Wood, Bos | 1.49 | 1965 | Sam McDowell, Clev | 2.18 |
| 1916 | Babe Ruth, Bos | 1.75 | 1966 | Gary Peters, Chi | 1.98 |
| 1917 | Eddie Cicotte, Chi | 1.53 | 1967 | Joe Horlen, Chi | 2.06 |
| 1918 | Walter Johnson, Wash | 1.27 | 1968 | Luis Tiant, Clev | 1.60 |
| 1919 | Walter Johnson, Wash | 1.49 | 1969 | Dick Bosman, Wash | 2.19 |
| 1920 | Bob Shawkey, NY | 2.46 | 1970 | Diego Segui, Oak | 2.56 |
| 1921 | Red Faber, Chi | 2.47 | 1971 | Vida Blue, Oak | 1.82 |
| 1922 | Red Faber, Chi | 2.80 | 1972 | Luis Tiant, Bos | 1.91 |
| 1923 | Stan Coveleski, Clev | 2.76 | 1973 | Jim Palmer, Balt | 2.40 |
| 1924 | Walter Johnson, Wash | 2.72 | 1974 | Catfish Hunter, Oak | 2.49 |
| 1925 | Stan Coveleski, Wash | 2.84 | 1975 | Jim Palmer, Balt | 2.09 |
| 1926 | Lefty Grove, Phi | 2.51 | 1976 | Mark Fidrych, Det | 2.34 |
| 1927 | Wilcy Moore, NY# | 2.28 | 1977 | Frank Tanana, Cal | 2.54 |
| 1928 | Garland Braxton, Wash | 2.52 | 1978 | Ron Guidry, NY | 1.74 |
| 1929 | Lefty Grove, Phi | 2.81 | 1979 | Ron Guidry, NY | 2.78 |
| 1930 | Lefty Grove, Phi | 2.54 | 1980 | Rudy May, NY | 2.47 |
| 1931 | Lefty Grove, Phi | 2.06 | 1981 | Steve McCatty, Oak | 2.32 |
| 1932 | Lefty Grove, Phi | 2.84 | 1982 | Rick Sutcliffe, Clev | 2.96 |
| 1933 | Monte Pearson, Clev | 2.33 | 1983 | Rick Honeycutt, Tex | 2.42 |
| 1934 | Lefty Gomez, NY | 2.33 | 1984 | Mike Boddicker, Balt | 2.79 |
| 1935 | Lefty Grove, Bos | 2.70 | 1985 | Dave Stieb, Tor | 2.48 |
| 1936 | Lefty Grove, Bos | 2.81 | 1986 | Roger Clemens, Bos | 2.48 |
| 1937 | Lefty Gomez, NY | 2.33 | 1987 | Jimmy Key, Tor | 2.76 |
| 1938 | Lefty Grove, Bos | 3.07 | 1988 | Allan Anderson, Minn | 2.45 |
| 1939 | Lefty Grove, Bos | 2.54 | 1989 | Bret Saberhagen, KC | 2.16 |
| 1940 | Bob Feller, Clev† | 2.62 | 1990 | Roger Clemens, Bos | 1.93 |
| 1941 | Thornton Lee, Chi | 2.37 | 1991 | Roger Clemens, Bos | 2.62 |
| 1942 | Ted Lyons, Chi | 2.10 | 1992 | Roger Clemens, Bos | 2.41 |
| 1943 | Spud Chandler, NY | 1.64 | 1993 | Kevin Appier, KC | 2.56 |
| 1944 | Dizzy Trout, Det | 2.12 | 1994 | Steve Ontiveros, Oak | 2.65 |
| 1945 | Hal Newhouser, Det | 1.81 | 1995 | Randy Johnson, Sea | 2.48 |
| 1946 | Hal Newhouser, Det | 1.94 | 1996 | Juan Guzman, Tor | 2.93 |
| 1947 | Spud Chandler, NY | 2.46 | 1997 | Roger Clemens, Tor | 2.05 |
| 1948 | Gene Bearden, Clev | 2.43 | 1998 | Roger Clemens, Tor | 2.64 |
| 1949 | Mel Parnell, Bos | 2.78 | 1999 | Pedro Martinez, Bos | 2.07 |
| 1950 | Early Wynn, Clev | 3.20 | 2000 | Pedro Martinez, Bos | 1.74 |
| 1951 | Saul Rogovin, Det-Chi | 2.78 | 2001 | Freddy Garcia, Sea | 3.05 |
| 1952 | Allie Reynolds, NY | 2.07 | 2002 | Pedro Martinez, Bos | 2.26 |
| 1953 | Ed Lopat, NY | 2.43 | 2003 | Pedro Martinez, Bos | 2.22 |
| 1954 | Mike Garcia, Clev | 2.64 | 2004 | Johan Santana, Minn | 2.61 |
| 1955 | Billy Pierce, Chi | 1.97 | 2005 | Kevin Millwood, Cle | 2.86 |
| 1956 | Whitey Ford, NY | 2.47 | 2006 | Johan Santana, Minn | 2.77 |
| 1957 | Bobby Shantz, NY | 2.45 | 2007 | John Lackey, LA | 3.01 |
| 1958 | Whitey Ford, NY | 2.01 | 2008 | Cliff Lee, Cle | 2.54 |
| 1959 | Hoyt Wilhelm, Balt | 2.19 | 2009 | Zack Greinke, KC | 2.16 |
| 1960 | Frank Baumann, Chi | 2.68 | 2010 | Felix Hernandez, Sea | 2.27 |
| 1961 | Dick Donovan, Wash | 2.40 | 2011 | Justin Verlander, Det | 2.40 |
| 1962 | Hank Aguirre, Det | 2.21 | | | |

Note: Based on 10 complete games through 1950, then 154 innings until the American League expanded in 1961, when it became 162 innings. In strike-shortened 1981, one inning per game required. Earned runs not tabulated in American League prior to 1913. #Wilcy Moore pitched only six complete games—he started 12—in 1927 but was recognized as leader because of 213 innings pitched. †Ernie Bonham, New York, had 1.91 ERA and 10 complete games in 1940 but appeared in only 12 games and 99 innings, and Bob Feller was recognized as the leader.

## AMERICAN LEAGUE
### Leading Pitchers—Strikeouts

| Year | Player and Team | SO | Year | Player and Team | SO |
|------|-----------------|-----|------|-----------------|-----|
| 1901 | Cy Young, Bos | 159 | 1956 | Herb Score, Clev | 263 |
| 1902 | Rube Waddell, Phi | 210 | 1957 | Early Wynn, Clev | 184 |
| 1903 | Rube Waddell, Phi | 301 | 1958 | Early Wynn, Chi | 179 |
| 1904 | Rube Waddell, Phi | 349 | 1959 | Jim Bunning, Det | 201 |
| 1905 | Rube Waddell, Phi | 286 | 1960 | Jim Bunning, Det | 201 |
| 1906 | Rube Waddell, Phi | 203 | 1961 | Camilo Pascual, Minn | 221 |
| 1907 | Rube Waddell, Phi | 226 | 1962 | Camilo Pascual, Minn | 206 |
| 1908 | Ed Walsh, Chi | 269 | 1963 | Camilo Pascual, Minn | 202 |
| 1909 | Frank Smith, Chi | 177 | 1964 | Al Downing, NY | 217 |
| 1910 | Walter Johnson, Wash | 313 | 1965 | Sam McDowell, Clev | 325 |
| 1911 | Ed Walsh, Chi | 255 | 1966 | Sam McDowell, Clev | 225 |
| 1912 | Walter Johnson, Wash | 303 | 1967 | Jim Lonborg, Bos | 246 |
| 1913 | Walter Johnson, Wash | 243 | 1968 | Sam McDowell, Clev | 283 |
| 1914 | Walter Johnson, Wash | 225 | 1969 | Sam McDowell, Clev | 279 |
| 1915 | Walter Johnson, Wash | 203 | 1970 | Sam McDowell, Clev | 304 |
| 1916 | Walter Johnson, Wash | 228 | 1971 | Mickey Lolich, Det | 308 |
| 1917 | Walter Johnson, Wash | 188 | 1972 | Nolan Ryan, Cal | 329 |
| 1918 | Walter Johnson, Wash | 162 | 1973 | Nolan Ryan, Cal | 383 |
| 1919 | Walter Johnson, Wash | 147 | 1974 | Nolan Ryan, Cal | 367 |
| 1920 | Stan Coveleski, Clev | 133 | 1975 | Frank Tanana, Cal | 269 |
| 1921 | Walter Johnson, Wash | 143 | 1976 | Nolan Ryan, Cal | 327 |
| 1922 | Urban Shocker, StL | 149 | 1977 | Nolan Ryan, Cal | 341 |
| 1923 | Walter Johnson, Wash | 130 | 1978 | Nolan Ryan, Cal | 260 |
| 1924 | Walter Johnson, Wash | 158 | 1979 | Nolan Ryan, Cal | 223 |
| 1925 | Lefty Grove, Phi | 116 | 1980 | Len Barker, Clev | 187 |
| 1926 | Lefty Grove, Phi | 194 | 1981 | Len Barker, Clev | 127 |
| 1927 | Lefty Grove, Phi | 174 | 1982 | Floyd Bannister, Sea | 209 |
| 1928 | Lefty Grove, Phi | 183 | 1983 | Jack Morris, Det | 232 |
| 1929 | Lefty Grove, Phi | 170 | 1984 | Mark Langston, Sea | 204 |
| 1930 | Lefty Grove, Phi | 209 | 1985 | Bert Blyleven, Clev-Minn | 206 |
| 1931 | Lefty Grove, Phi | 175 | 1986 | Mark Langston, Sea | 245 |
| 1932 | Red Ruffing, NY | 190 | 1987 | Mark Langston, Sea | 262 |
| 1933 | Lefty Gomez, NY | 163 | 1988 | Roger Clemens, Bos | 291 |
| 1934 | Lefty Gomez, NY | 158 | 1989 | Nolan Ryan, Tex | 301 |
| 1935 | Tommy Bridges, Det | 163 | 1990 | Nolan Ryan, Tex | 232 |
| 1936 | Tommy Bridges, Det | 175 | 1991 | Roger Clemens, Bos | 241 |
| 1937 | Lefty Gomez, NY | 194 | 1992 | Randy Johnson, Sea | 241 |
| 1938 | Bob Feller, Clev | 240 | 1993 | Randy Johnson, Sea | 308 |
| 1939 | Bob Feller, Clev | 246 | 1994 | Randy Johnson, Sea | 204 |
| 1940 | Bob Feller, Clev | 261 | 1995 | Randy Johnson, Sea | 294 |
| 1941 | Bob Feller, Clev | 260 | 1996 | Roger Clemens, Bos | 257 |
| 1942 | Bobo Newsom, Wash | | 1997 | Roger Clemens, Tor | 292 |
| | Tex Hughson, Bos | 113 | 1998 | Roger Clemens, Tor | 271 |
| 1943 | Allie Reynolds, Clev | 151 | 1999 | Pedro Martinez, Bos | 313 |
| 1944 | Hal Newhouser, Det | 187 | 2000 | Pedro Martinez, Bos | 284 |
| 1945 | Hal Newhouser, Det | 212 | 2001 | Hideo Nomo, Bos | 220 |
| 1946 | Bob Feller, Clev | 348 | 2002 | Pedro Martinez, Bos | 239 |
| 1947 | Bob Feller, Clev | 196 | 2003 | Esteban Loaiza, Chi | 207 |
| 1948 | Bob Feller, Clev | 164 | 2004 | Johan Santana, Minn | 265 |
| 1949 | Virgil Trucks, Det | 153 | 2005 | Johan Santana, Minn | 238 |
| 1950 | Bob Lemon, Clev | 170 | 2006 | Johan Santana, Minn | 245 |
| 1951 | Vic Raschi, NY | 164 | 2007 | Scott Kazmir, TB | 239 |
| 1952 | Allie Reynolds, NY | 160 | 2008 | A.J. Burnett, Tor | 231 |
| 1953 | Billy Pierce, Chi | 186 | 2009 | Justin Verlander, Det | 269 |
| 1954 | Bob Turley, Balt | 185 | 2010 | Jered Weaver, LA | 233 |
| 1955 | Herb Score, Clev | 245 | 2011 | Justin Verlander, Det | 250 |

## AMERICAN LEAGUE
### Leading Pitchers—Saves

| FYear | Player and Team | SV | Year | Player and Team | SV |
|---|---|---|---|---|---|
| 1947 | Joe Page, NY | 17 | 1980 | Dan Quisenberry, KC | 33 |
| 1948 | Russ Christopher, Clev | 17 | 1981 | Rollie Fingers, Mil | 28 |
| 1949 | Joe Page, NY | 29 | 1982 | Dan Quisenberry, KC | 35 |
| 1950 | Mickey Harris, Wash | 15 | 1983 | Dan Quisenberry, KC | 35 |
| 1951 | Ellis Kinder, Bos | 14 | 1984 | Dan Quisenberry, KC | 44 |
| 1952 | Harry Dorish, Chi | 11 | 1985 | Dan Quisenberry, KC | 37 |
| 1953 | Ellis Kinder, Bos | 27 | 1986 | Dave Righetti, NY | 46 |
| 1954 | Johnny Sain, NY | 22 | 1987 | Tom Henke, Tor | 34 |
| 1955 | Ray Narleski, Clev | 19 | 1988 | Dennis Eckersley, Oak | 45 |
| 1956 | George Zuverink, Bal | 16 | 1989 | Jeff Russell, Tex | 38 |
| 1957 | Bob Grim, NY | 19 | 1990 | Bobby Thigpen, Chi | 57 |
| 1958 | Ryne Duren, NY | 20 | 1991 | Bryan Harvey, Cal | 46 |
| 1959 | Turk Lown, Chi | 15 | 1992 | Dennis Eckersley, Oak | 51 |
| 1960 | Mike Fornieles, Bos | 14 | 1993 | Jeff Montgomery, KC | 45 |
|  | Johnny Klippstein, Clev | 14 |  | Duane Ward, Tor | 45 |
| 1961 | Luis Arroyo, NY | 29 | 1994 | Lee Smith, Bal | 33 |
| 1962 | Dick Radatz, Bos | 24 | 1995 | Jose Mesa, Clev | 46 |
| 1963 | Stu Miller, Bal | 27 | 1996 | John Wetteland, NY | 43 |
| 1964 | Dick Radatz, Bos | 29 | 1997 | Randy Myers, Balt | 45 |
| 1965 | Ron Kline, Wash | 29 | 1998 | Tom Gordon, Bos | 46 |
| 1966 | Jack Aker, KC | 32 | 1999 | Mariano Rivera, NY | 45 |
| 1967 | Minnie Rojas, Cal | 27 | 2000 | Todd Jones, Det | 42 |
| 1968 | Al Worthington, Minn | 18 | 2001 | Mariano Rivera, NY | 50 |
| 1969 | Ron Perranoski, Minn | 31 | 2002 | Eddie Guardado, Minn | 45 |
| 1970 | Ron Perranoski, Minn | 34 | 2003 | Keith Foulke, Oak | 43 |
| 1971 | Ken Sanders, Mil | 31 | 2004 | Mariano Rivera, NY | 53 |
| 1972 | Sparky Lyle, NY | 35 | 2005 | Francisco Rodríguez, LA | 45 |
| 1973 | John Hiller, Det | 38 |  | Bob Wickman, Cle | 45 |
| 1974 | Terry Forster, Chi | 24 | 2006 | Francisco Rodriguez, LA | 47 |
| 1975 | Goose Gossage, Chi | 26 | 2007 | Joe Borowski, Cle | 45 |
| 1976 | Sparky Lyle, NY | 23 | 2008 | Francisco Rodriguez, LA | 62 |
| 1977 | Bill Campbell, Bos | 31 | 2009 | Brian Fuentes, LA | 48 |
| 1978 | Goose Gossage, NY | 27 | 2010 | Rafael Soriano, TB | 45 |
| 1979 | Mike Marshall, Minn | 32 | 2011 | Jose Valverde, Det | 49 |

## The Commissioners of Baseball

| | |
|---|---|
| Kenesaw Mountain Landis | Elected Nov. 12, 1920. Served until his death on Nov. 25, 1944. |
| Happy Chandler | Elected April 24, 1945. Served until July 15, 1951. |
| Ford Frick | Elected Sept. 20, 1951. Served until Nov. 16, 1965. |
| William Eckert | Elected Nov. 17, 1965. Served until Dec. 20, 1968. |
| Bowie Kuhn | Elected Feb. 8, 1969. Served until Sept. 30, 1984. |
| Peter Ueberroth | Elected March 3, 1984. Took office Oct. 1, 1984. Served through March 31, 1989. |
| A. Bartlett Giamatti | Elected Sept. 8, 1988. Took office April 1, 1989. Served until his death on Sept. 1, 1989. |
| Francis Vincent Jr. | Appointed Acting Commissioner Sept. 2, 1989. Elected Commissioner Sept. 13, 1989. Served through Sept. 7, 1992. |
| Allan H. (Bud) Selig | Elected chairman of the executive council and given the powers of interim commissioner on Sept. 9, 1992. Unanimously elected Commissioner July 9, 1998. |

# Pro Football

QB Aaron Rodgers
steered the
Green Bay Packers
to victory in
Super Bowl XLV

# Changing Of the Guard

Led by young, strong-armed quarterback Aaron Rodgers, Green Bay overcame a stalwart Pittsburgh defense in Super Bowl XLV to reclaim its nickname of Titletown

## BY HANK HERSCH

FOR TWO DECADES HE WAS the epitome of a certain kind of NFL quarterback, the risk-taking, bomb-slinging, thrill-seeking action hero who took hit after hit after hit yet relentlessly kept defenses on their heels. Since 1992 he had never failed to answer the call as a starter—an unbelievable streak for any NFL player, let alone a QB—and with his unique combination of bravura, skill and enthusiasm he claimed almost every career passing record. Most of those marks came wrapped in green-and-gold: Brett Favre was the face of the Green Bay Packers for 16 years. And his shortcomings there could be effectively reduced to one: the number of Super Bowl victories he earned for the hamlet known as Titletown.

Decades from now, there's a good chance that 2010 will be viewed as a transitional year—with the transition once again embodied by Favre, who retired after a desultory season with the Vikings. Because of the high volume of concussions, increased awareness about their pernicious effects and a greater emphasis on player safety, it seemed unlikely anyone would equal Favre's string of starts, which ended at an astounding 297. Social media took

hold, too: As players like Cincinnati Bengals receiver Chad Ochocinco built huge Twitter followings, Favre faced accusations that he had sent salacious texts to a female New York Jets employee when he was with the team in 2008. (A league investigation found that he hadn't violated workplace conduct policies, but fined him $50,000 for failing to properly cooperate with the investigation.) Nor was it clear how a future franchise player like Favre would be treated and compensated as team owners, unable to reach a new collective bargaining agreement with the union, locked out the players after the season, resulting in the first NFL work stoppage since 1987. After 136 days—the longest work stoppage in league history—players and owners finally agreed to a new, 10-year deal that included a rookie wage scale but that abandoned the idea of a 18-game regular season.

Not least, there was a new leader of the Pack: In just his third season as a starting quarterback, 27-year-old Aaron Rodgers matched Favre's title total with a 31–25 victory over the Steelers in Super Bowl XLV. A pinpoint passer with a demeanor as steady as his gaze, Rodgers had to carry Green Bay's offense almost singlehandedly; against Pittsburgh's league-leading rush defense, he

Thanks to a resurgent performance in 2010, controversial Eagles QB Michael Vick returned to a starting role and won the AP Comeback Player of the Year award.

AL TIELEMANS

completed 24 of 39 passes for 304 yards and three touchdowns, handing off only 11 times. Slugging down a grape soda in the Cowboys Stadium locker room after the game, Rodgers reflected on the time he had to bide in Favre's shadow. "The journey has been special," he said. "I'm not vindictive, but I'm blessed with a very good memory."

Few seasons seemed as wide open as 2010. Witness the Seattle Seahawks: They went 7–9 yet won the NFC West, becoming the first team to qualify for the playoffs with a losing record in a full season. What's more, they then knocked off the defending champion New Orleans Saints 41–36 in the wild card round. Kansas City, behind the rushing of Jamaal Charles and Thomas Jones (a combined average of 147.7 yards per game) and the pass rushing of defensive end Tamba Hali (14.5 sacks, second to the Cowboys' DeMarcus Ware), completed a six-game turnaround and reached the postseason for the first time since 2006. And the Atlanta Falcons, led by the pass-catch combo of Matt Ryan and Roddy White, charged to a 13–3 finish, only to lose to the 10–6 Packers by 27 points in their divisional showdown.

The Philadelphia Eagles returned to the playoffs, but not behind Donovan McNabb, their quarterback of 11 years, who had been traded to the Redskins during the off-sea-

son. Nor did Kevin Kolb, McNabb's designated heir, guide Philadelphia; he lost his grip on the job after suffering, yes, a concussion, on a jaw-cracking hit by Green Bay linebacker Clay Matthews in the opener. Instead, the Eagles' field leader was a 30-year-old who had served a 19-month term in federal prison for running a dogfighting ring and had thrown all of 13 passes after his reinstatement to the league in 2009. Before a 21–16 wild card loss to Green Bay, Michael Vick finished as the league leader in total yards, a return to form that mortified some and enthralled others.

In a 59–28 Monday night win over McNabb's 'Skins, Michael Vick put on one of the

**Patriots QB Tom Brady led his team to the best regular-season record in the NFL and was named the league's first-ever unanimous MVP.**

the Pats set a single-season record for fewest turnovers (10).

But in the divisional playoffs the Jets—who had been embarrassed in a 45–3 loss at New England in Week 13—picked off Brady once, sacked him five times and pulled off an improbable 28–21 upset. New York's run ended in the AFC title game though, when Pittsburgh returned a fumble for a touchdown and made a fourth-quarter goal-line stand in a 24–19 victory. In safety Troy Polamalu, the Steelers had the Defensive Player of the Year—he edged out Green Bay's Matthews—and in Ben Roethlisberger, a quarterback who, like Vick, was trying to overcome his troubled past. Roethlisberger served a four-game suspension to start the year for violating the league's personal conduct policy; he had been accused of sexual assault for the second time in a year. He entered Dallas attempting to win the third championship of his seven-year career.

Trailing 21–10 at halftime of the Super Bowl, Big Ben rallied Pittsburgh to within three points midway through the fourth quarter with a touchdown pass and slick two-point conversion. Then, after a Green Bay field goal pushed the score to 31–25, he got the ball back on his own 13-yard line with one timeout and 1:59 left. But even with Green Bay's star cornerback, Charles Woodson, on the sidelines with a broken left collarbone, Roethlisberger could get no further than his own 33-yard line and the Packers, without hosting a playoff game, had won their 13th league championship and fourth Super Bowl.

And with the victory came vindication for Favre's former understudy. "You wait, you keep quiet," Rodgers said, "and you take advantage of opportunity when it comes."

most magnificent offensive displays in NFL history: 20 of 28 passing for 333 yards and four touchdowns, plus 80 yards rushing and two more TDs. "Guys look at him not as a quarterback; we look at him as an inspiration," said Philly receiver Jason Avant. "A guy who has been through hell and back—and he's conquered it."

The team most closely resembling a favorite was supposed to be in a rebuilding year. The New England Patriots turned over much of their defensive personnel, and in October they dumped their marquee wide receiver of three years, Randy Moss, who had complained about his contract in a postvictory press conference. (Moss, 33, joined Favre in Minnesota, then was inexplicably waived a month later and claimed by the Titans.) What New England had, though, was the resurgent Tom Brady, who became the first unanimous MVP choice in league history. The 33-year-old Brady led the league in passer rating (111.0) and TDs (36), while throwing only four interceptions, helping

# FOR THE RECORD•2010–2011

## 2010 NFL Final Standings

### American Football Conference

#### EAST DIVISION

|  | W | L | T | Pct | Pts | OP |
|---|---|---|---|---|---|---|
| New England | 14 | 2 | 0 | .875 | 518 | 313 |
| *NY Jets | 11 | 5 | 0 | .688 | 367 | 304 |
| Miami | 7 | 9 | 0 | .438 | 273 | 333 |
| Buffalo | 4 | 12 | 0 | .250 | 283 | 425 |

#### NORTH DIVISION

|  | W | L | T | Pct | Pts | OP |
|---|---|---|---|---|---|---|
| Pittsburgh | 12 | 4 | 0 | .750 | 375 | 232 |
| *Baltimore | 12 | 4 | 0 | .750 | 357 | 270 |
| Cleveland | 5 | 11 | 0 | .313 | 271 | 332 |
| Cincinnati | 4 | 12 | 0 | .250 | 322 | 395 |

#### SOUTH DIVISION

|  | W | L | T | Pct | Pts | OP |
|---|---|---|---|---|---|---|
| Indianapolis | 10 | 6 | 0 | .625 | 435 | 388 |
| Jacksonville | 8 | 8 | 0 | .500 | 353 | 419 |
| Houston | 6 | 10 | 0 | .375 | 390 | 427 |
| Tennessee | 6 | 10 | 0 | .375 | 356 | 339 |

#### WEST DIVISION

|  | W | L | T | Pct | Pts | OP |
|---|---|---|---|---|---|---|
| Kansas City | 10 | 6 | 0 | .625 | 366 | 326 |
| San Diego | 9 | 7 | 0 | .563 | 441 | 322 |
| Oakland | 8 | 8 | 0 | .500 | 410 | 371 |
| Denver | 4 | 12 | 0 | .250 | 344 | 471 |

### National Football Conference

#### EAST DIVISION

|  | W | L | T | Pct | Pts | OP |
|---|---|---|---|---|---|---|
| Philadelphia | 10 | 6 | 0 | .625 | 439 | 377 |
| NY Giants | 10 | 6 | 0 | .625 | 394 | 347 |
| Dallas | 6 | 10 | 0 | .375 | 394 | 436 |
| Washington | 6 | 10 | 0 | .375 | 302 | 377 |

#### NORTH DIVISION

|  | W | L | T | Pct | Pts | OP |
|---|---|---|---|---|---|---|
| Chicago | 11 | 5 | 0 | .688 | 334 | 286 |
| *Green Bay | 10 | 6 | 0 | .625 | 388 | 240 |
| Detroit | 6 | 10 | 0 | .375 | 362 | 369 |
| Minnesota | 6 | 10 | 0 | .375 | 281 | 348 |

#### SOUTH DIVISION

|  | W | L | T | Pct | Pts | OP |
|---|---|---|---|---|---|---|
| Atlanta | 13 | 3 | 0 | .813 | 414 | 288 |
| *New Orleans | 11 | 5 | 0 | .688 | 384 | 307 |
| Tampa Bay | 10 | 6 | 0 | .625 | 341 | 318 |
| Carolina | 2 | 14 | 0 | .125 | 196 | 408 |

#### WEST DIVISION

|  | W | L | T | Pct | Pts | OP |
|---|---|---|---|---|---|---|
| Seattle | 7 | 9 | 0 | .438 | 310 | 407 |
| St. Louis | 7 | 9 | 0 | .438 | 289 | 328 |
| San Francisco | 6 | 10 | 0 | .375 | 305 | 346 |
| Arizona | 5 | 11 | 0 | .313 | 289 | 434 |

*: Wild-card team.

## 2010–11 NFL Playoffs

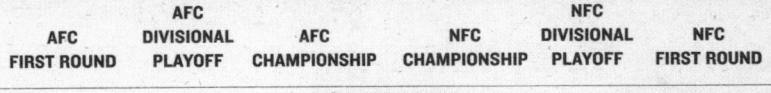

| AFC FIRST ROUND | AFC DIVISIONAL PLAYOFF | AFC CHAMPIONSHIP | NFC CHAMPIONSHIP | NFC DIVISIONAL PLAYOFF | NFC FIRST ROUND |
|---|---|---|---|---|---|

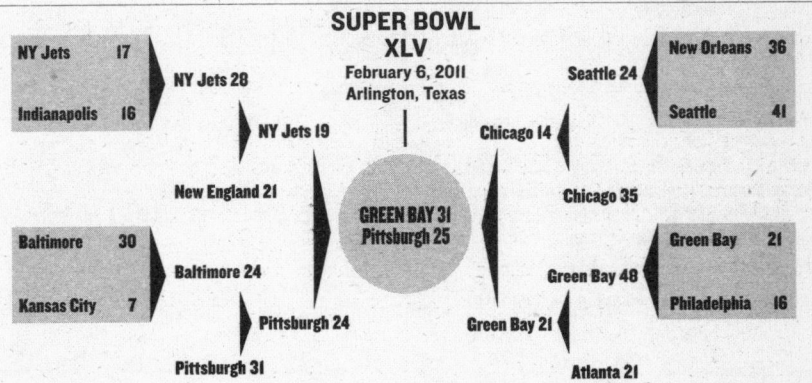

**SUPER BOWL XLV**
February 6, 2011
Arlington, Texas

**GREEN BAY 31**
**Pittsburgh 25**

NY Jets 17
Indianapolis 16
NY Jets 28
NY Jets 19
New England 21
Baltimore 30
Kansas City 7
Baltimore 24
Pittsburgh 24
Pittsburgh 31

New Orleans 36
Seattle 41
Seattle 24
Chicago 14
Chicago 35
Green Bay 21
Philadelphia 16
Green Bay 48
Green Bay 21
Atlanta 21

# NFL Playoff Recaps

## AFC Wild-card Games

| NY Jets | 0 | 0 | 7 | 10—17 |
|---|---|---|---|---|
| Indianapolis | 0 | 7 | 3 | 6—16 |

**SECOND QUARTER:** Indianapolis: TD Garcon 57 pass from Manning (Vinatieri kick), 5:25.

**THIRD QUARTER:** NY Jets: TD Tomlinson 1 run (Folk kick), 9:48.

Indianapolis: FG Vinatieri 47, 4:53.

**FOURTH QUARTER:** NY Jets: TD Tomlinson 1 run (Folk kick), 9:59.

Indianapolis: FG Vinatieri 32, 4:37.

Indianapolis: FG Vinatieri 50, 0:53.

NY Jets: FG Folk 32, 0:00.

A: 65,332.

| Baltimore | 3 | 7 | 13 | 7—30 |
|---|---|---|---|---|
| Kansas City | 7 | 0 | 0 | 0—7 |

**FIRST QUARTER:** Baltimore: FG Cundiff 19, 9:01.

Kansas City: TD Charles 41 run (Succop kick), 2:09.

**SECOND QUARTER:** Baltimore: TD Rice 9 pass from Flacco (Cundiff kick), 0:19.

**THIRD QUARTER:** Baltimore: FG Cundiff 29, 6:36.

Baltimore: FG Cundiff 29, 4:20.

Baltimore: TD Boldin 4 pass from Flacco (Cundiff kick), 0:27.

**FOURTH QUARTER:** Baltimore: TD McGahee 25 run (Cundiff kick), 4:26.

A: 72,190.

## NFC Wild-card Games

| New Orleans | 10 | 10 | 0 | 16—36 |
|---|---|---|---|---|
| Seattle | 7 | 17 | 10 | 7—41 |

**FIRST QUARTER:** New Orleans: FG Hartley 26, 11:43.

New Orleans: TD Evans 1 pass from Brees (Hartley kick), 6:21.

Seattle: TD Carlson 11 pass from Hasselbeck (Mare kick), 3:38.

**SECOND QUARTER:** New Orleans: TD Jones 5 run (Hartley kick), 13:38.

Seattle: TD Carlson 7 pass from Hasselbeck (Mare kick), 11:00.

Seattle: FG Mare 29, 7:03.

Seattle: TD Stokely 45 pass from Hasselbeck (Mare kick), 1:15.

New Orleans: FG Hartley 22, 0:00.

**THIRD QUARTER:** Seattle: TD Williams 38 pass from Hasselbeck (Mare kick), 11:48.
Seattle: FG Mare 39, 5:27.

**FOURTH QUARTER:** New Orleans: TD Jones 4 run (Hartley kick), 13:11.

New Orleans: FG Hartley 21, 9:13.

Seattle: TD Lynch 67 run (Mare kick), 3:22.

New Orleans: TD Henderson 6 pass from Brees (2-pt. conversion failed).

A: 66,336.

| Green Bay | 7 | 7 | 7 | 0—21 |
|---|---|---|---|---|
| Philadelphia | 0 | 3 | 7 | 6—16 |

**FIRST QUARTER:** Green Bay: TD Crabtree 7 pass from Rodgers (Crosby kick), 0:08.

**SECOND QUARTER:** Green Bay: TD Jones 9 pass from Rodgers (Crosby kick), 5:21.

Philadelphia: FG Akers 29, 1:11.

**THIRD QUARTER:** Philadelphia: TD Avant 24 pass from Vick (Akers kick), 13:50.

Green Bay: TD Jackson 16 pass from Rodgers (Crosby kick), 7:33.

**FOURTH QUARTER:** Philadelphia: TD Vick 1 run (2-pt. conversion failed), 4:02.

A: 69,144.

### AFC Divisional Games

| Baltimore | 14 | 7 | 0 | 3—24 |
|---|---|---|---|---|
| Pittsburgh | 7 | 0 | 14 | 10—31 |

**FIRST QUARTER:** Pittsburgh: TD Mendenhall 1 run (Suisham kick), 6:18.

Baltimore: TD Rice 14 run (Cundiff kick), 1:20.

Baltimore: TD Redding 13 fumble return (Cundiff kick), 0:53.

**SECOND QUARTER:** Baltimore: Heap 4 pass from Flacco (Cundiff kick), 5:43.

**THIRD QUARTER:** Pittsburgh: Miller 9 pass from Roethlisberger (Suisham kick), 9:11.

Pittsburgh: Ward 8 pass from Roethlisberger (Suisham kick), 1:21.

**FOURTH QUARTER:** Pittsburgh: FG Suisham 35, 12:15.

Baltimore: FG Cundiff 24, 3:54.

Pittsburgh: TD Mendenhall 2 run (Suisham kick), 1:33.

A: 64,879.

| NY Jets | 0 | 14 | 0 | 14—28 |
|---|---|---|---|---|
| New England | 3 | 0 | 8 | 10—21 |

**FIRST QUARTER:** New England: FG Graham 34, 1:12.

**SECOND QUARTER:** NY Jets: TD Tomlinson 7 pass from Sanchez (Folk kick), 10:24.

NY Jets: TD Edwards 15 pass from Sanchez (Folk kick), 0:33.

**THIRD QUARTER:** New England: TD Crumpler 2 pass from Brady (Morris 2 run for 2-pt. conversion), 0:13.

**FOURTH QUARTER:** NY Jets: TD Holmes 7 pass from Sanchez (Folk kick), 13:00.

New England: FG Graham 35, 1:57.

NY Jets: TD Greene 16 run (Folk kick), 1:41.

New England: TD Branch 13 pass from Brady (Graham kick), 0:24.

A: 68,756.

### NFC Divisional Games

| Seattle | 0 | 0 | 3 | 21—24 |
|---|---|---|---|---|
| Chicago | 14 | 7 | 7 | 7—35 |

**FIRST QUARTER:** Chicago: TD Olsen 58 pass from Cutler (Gould kick), 12:08.

Chicago: TD Taylor 1 run (Gould kick), 1:19.

**SECOND QUARTER:** Chicago: TD Cutler 6 run (Gould kick), 10:01.

**THIRD QUARTER:** Chicago: TD Cutler 9 run (Gould kick), 4:12.

Seattle: FG Mare 30, 1:52.

**FOURTH QUARTER:** Seattle: TD M. Williams 2 pass from Hasselbeck (Mare kick), 11:21.

Chicago: TD Davis 39 pass from Cutler (Gould kick), 4:40.

Seattle: TD M. Williams 3 pass from Hasselbeck (Mare kick), 2:16.

Seattle: TD Stokely 9 pass from Hasselbeck (Mare kick), 1:24.

A: 62,265.

| Green Bay | 0 | 28 | 14 | 6—48 |
|---|---|---|---|---|
| Atlanta | 7 | 7 | 0 | 7—21 |

**FIRST QUARTER:** Atlanta: TD Turner 12 run (Bryant kick), 5:00.

**SECOND QUARTER:** Green Bay: TD Nelson 6 pass from Rodgers (Crosby kick), 12:04.

Atlanta: TD Weems 102 kickoff return (Bryant kick), 11:50.

Green Bay: TD Kuhn 1 run (Crosby kick), 6:06.

Green Bay: TD Jones 20 pass from Rodgers (Crosby kick), 0:42.

Green Bay: TD T. Williams 70 interception return (Crosby kick), 0:00.

**THIRD QUARTER:** Green Bay: TD Rodgers 7 run (Crosby kick), 8:28.

Green Bay: TD Kuhn 7 pass from Rodgers (Crosby kick), 2:41.

**FOURTH QUARTER:** Atlanta: TD White 6 pass from Ryan (Bryant kick), 14:21.

Green Bay: FG Crosby 43, 6:29.

Green Bay: FG Crosby 32, 1:56.

A: 69,210.

## AFC Championship

| | | | |
|---|---|---|---|
| NY Jets.............................0 | 3 | 7 | 9—19 |
| Pittsburgh ....................7 | 17 | 0 | 0—24 |

**FIRST QUARTER:** Pittsburgh: TD Mendenhall 1 run (Suisham kick), 5:54.

**SECOND QUARTER:** Pittsburgh: FG Suisham 20, 6:51.

Pittsburgh: TD Roethlisberger 2 run (Suisham kick), 2:00.

Pittsburgh: TD Gay 19 fumble return (Suisham kick), 1:13.

NY Jets: FG Folk 42, 0:09.

**THIRD QUARTER:** NY Jets: TD Holmes 45 pass from Sanchez (Folk kick), 12:13.

**FOURTH QUARTER:** NY Jets: Safety DeVito tackled Roethlisberger in end zone, 7:38.

NY Jets: TD Cotchery 4 pass from Sanchez (Folk kick), 3:06.

A: 66,662.

## NFC Championship

| | | | |
|---|---|---|---|
| Green Bay......................7 | 7 | 0 | 7—21 |
| Chicago.........................0 | 0 | 0 | 14—14 |

**FIRST QUARTER:** Green Bay: TD Rodgers 1 run (Crosby kick), 10:50.

**SECOND QUARTER:** Green Bay: TD Starks 4 run (Crosby kick), 11:13.

**FOURTH QUARTER:** Chicago: TD Taylor 1 run (Gould kick), 12:02.

Green Bay: TD Raji 18 interception return (Crosby kick), 6:04.

Chicago: TD Bennett 35 pass from Hanie (Gould kick), 4:43.

A: 62,377.

# Super Bowl XLV Recap

| | | | |
|---|---|---|---|
| Pittsburgh ....................0 | 10 | 7 | 8—25 |
| Green Bay ....................14 | 7 | 0 | 10—31 |

**FIRST QUARTER:** Green Bay: TD Nelson 29 pass from Rodgers (Crosby kick), 3:44.
**Green Bay 7–0.**
Green Bay TD Collins 37 interception return (Crosby kick), 3:20.
**Green Bay 14–0.**

**SECOND QUARTER:** Pittsburgh: FG Suisham 33, 11:08.
**Green Bay 14–3.**
Green Bay: TD Jennings 21 pass from Rodgers (Crosby kick), 2:24.
**Green Bay 21–3.**
Pittsburgh: TD Ward 8 pass from Roethlisberger (Suisham kick), 0:39.
**Green Bay 21–10.**

**THIRD QUARTER:** Pittsburgh: TD Mendenhall 8 run (Suisham kick), 10:19.
**Green Bay 21–17.**

**FOURTH QUARTER:** Green Bay: TD Jennings 8 pass from Rodgers (Crosby kick), 11:57.
**Green Bay 28–17.**
Pittsburgh: TD Wallace 25 pass from Roethlisberger (Randle El 2 run for 2-pt. conversion), 7:34.
**Green Bay 28–25.**
Green Bay: FG Crosby 23, 2:07.
**Green Bay 31–25.**

A: 103,219.

## Team Statistics

| | Pittsburgh | Green Bay |
|---|---|---|
| FIRST DOWNS | 19 | 15 |
| Rushing | 8 | 4 |
| Passing | 11 | 11 |
| Penalty | 0 | 0 |
| THIRD DOWN EFF | 7–13 | 6–13 |
| FOURTH DOWN EFF | 0–1 | 0–0 |
| TOTAL NET YARDS | 387 | 338 |
| Total plays | 64 | 55 |
| Avg gain | 6.0 | 6.1 |
| NET YARDS RUSHING | 126 | 50 |
| Rushes | 23 | 13 |
| Avg per rush | 5.5 | 3.8 |
| NET YARDS PASSING | 261 | 288 |
| Completed–Att–Int | 25–40–2 | 24–39–0 |
| Yards per pass | 6.5 | 7.4 |
| Sacked–yards lost | 1–2 | 3–16 |
| Had intercepted | 2 | 0 |
| PUNTS–Avg | 3–51.0 | 6–40.5 |
| PENALTIES–Yds | 6–55 | 7–67 |
| FUMBLES–Lost | 1–1 | 1–0 |
| Time of Possession | 33:25 | 26:35 |

## Passing

### PITTSBURGH

| | Comp | Att | Yds | Int | TD |
|---|---|---|---|---|---|
| Roethlisberger | 25 | 40 | 263 | 2 | 2 |

### GREEN BAY

| | Comp | Att | Yds | Int | TD |
|---|---|---|---|---|---|
| Rodgers | 24 | 39 | 304 | 0 | 3 |

## Rushing

### PITTSBURGH

| | No. | Yds | Lg | TD |
|---|---|---|---|---|
| Mendenhall | 14 | 63 | 17 | 1 |
| Roethlisberger | 4 | 31 | 18 | 0 |
| Redman | 2 | 19 | 16 | 0 |
| Moore | 3 | 13 | 7 | 0 |

### GREEN BAY

| | No. | Yds | Lg | TD |
|---|---|---|---|---|
| Starks | 11 | 52 | 14 | 0 |
| Rodgers | 2 | -2 | -1 | 0 |

## Receiving

### PITTSBURGH

| | No. | Yds | Lg | TD |
|---|---|---|---|---|
| M. Wallace | 9 | 89 | 25 | 1 |
| Ward | 7 | 78 | 17 | 1 |
| Randle El | 2 | 50 | 37 | 0 |
| Sanders | 2 | 17 | 13 | 0 |
| Miller | 2 | 12 | 15 | 0 |
| Spaeth | 1 | 9 | 9 | 0 |
| Mendenhall | 1 | 7 | 7 | 0 |
| Brown | 1 | 1 | 1 | 0 |

### GREEN BAY

| | No. | Yds | Lg | TD |
|---|---|---|---|---|
| Nelson | 9 | 140 | 38 | 1 |
| Jones | 5 | 50 | 21 | 0 |
| Jennings | 4 | 64 | 31 | 2 |
| Driver | 2 | 28 | 24 | 0 |
| Jackson | 1 | 14 | 14 | 0 |
| Quarless | 1 | 5 | 5 | 0 |
| Hall | 1 | 2 | 2 | 0 |
| Crabtree | 1 | 1 | 1 | 0 |

## Defense

### PITTSBURGH

| | Tck | Ast | Int | Sack |
|---|---|---|---|---|
| Clark | 6 | 2 | 0 | 0 |
| Taylor | 4 | 0 | 0 | 0 |
| McFadden | 4 | 0 | 0 | 0 |
| Woodley | 3 | 0 | 0 | 1 |
| Timmons | 3 | 0 | 0 | 0 |
| Polamalu | 3 | 0 | 0 | 0 |
| Keisel | 2 | 1 | 0 | 0 |
| Gay | 2 | 0 | 0 | 0 |
| Farrior | 1 | 1 | 0 | 0 |
| Madison | 1 | 0 | 0 | 0 |
| Harrison | 1 | 0 | 0 | 1 |
| Hood | 1 | 0 | 0 | 1 |
| Hampton | 1 | 0 | 0 | 0 |
| Leqursky | 1 | 0 | 0 | 0 |
| Fox | 1 | 0 | 0 | 0 |
| Wallace | 1 | 0 | 0 | 0 |
| Mundy | 0 | 1 | 0 | 0 |

### GREEN BAY

| | Tck | Ast | Int | Sack |
|---|---|---|---|---|
| Peprah | 9 | 1 | 0 | 0 |
| Bishop | 6 | 2 | 0 | 0 |
| Williams | 3 | 3 | 0 | 0 |
| Zombo | 5 | 0 | 0 | 1 |
| Bush | 2 | 1 | 1 | 0 |
| Hawk | 2 | 3 | 0 | 0 |
| Collins | 4 | 0 | 1 | 0 |
| Matthews | 3 | 0 | 0 | 0 |
| Swain | 3 | 0 | 0 | 0 |
| Woodson | 2 | 1 | 0 | 0 |
| Pickett | 2 | 0 | 0 | 0 |
| Shields | 2 | 0 | 0 | 0 |
| Lee | 1 | 0 | 0 | 0 |
| Hall | 1 | 0 | 0 | 0 |
| Bigby | 1 | 0 | 0 | 0 |
| Wilhelm | 1 | 0 | 0 | 0 |
| Crabtree | 1 | 0 | 0 | 0 |
| Crosby | 1 | 0 | 0 | 0 |
| Briggs | 0 | 1 | 0 | 0 |

### First Team
#### OFFENSE

| | |
|---|---|
| Tom Brady, New England | Quarterback |
| Jamaal Charles, Kansas City | Running Back |
| Arian Foster, Houston | Running Back |
| Vonta Leach, Houston | Fullback |
| Jason Witten, Dallas | Tight End |
| Roddy White, Atlanta | Wide Receiver |
| Reggie Wayne, Indianapolis | Wide Receiver |
| Jake Long, Miami | Tackle |
| Joe Thomas, Cleveland | Tackle |
| Jahri Evans, New Orleans | Guard |
| Logan Mankins, New England | Guard |
| Nick Mangold, NY Jets | Center |

#### DEFENSE

| | |
|---|---|
| Julius Peppers, Chicago | Defensive End |
| John Abraham, Atlanta | Defensive End |
| Ndamukong Suh, Detroit | Defensive Tackle |
| Haloti Ngata, Baltimore | Defensive Tackle |
| Clay Matthews, Green Bay | Linebacker |
| James Harrison, Pittsburgh | Linebacker |
| Jerod Mayo, New England | Linebacker |
| Patrick Willis, San Francisco | Linebacker |
| Nnamdi Asomugha, Oakland | Cornerback |
| Darelle Revis, NY Jets | Cornerback |
| Troy Polamalu, Pittsburgh | Safety |
| Ed Reed, Baltimore | Safety |

#### SPECIALISTS

| | |
|---|---|
| Billy Cundiff, Baltimore | Kicker |
| Devin Hester, Chicago | Kick Returner |
| Shane Lechler, Oakland | Punter |

### Second Team
#### OFFENSE

| | |
|---|---|
| Vacant | Quarterback |
| Michael Turner, Atlanta | Running Back |
| Adrian Peterson, Minnesota | Running Back |
| Ovie Mughelli, Atlanta | Fullback |
| Antonio Gates, San Diego | Tight End |
| Brandon Lloyd, Denver | Wide Receiver |
| Calvin Johnson, Detroit | Wide Receiver (tie) |
| Dwayne Bowe, Kansas City | Wide Receiver (tie) |
| Jason Peters, Philadelphia | Tackle |
| Sebastian Vollmer, New England | Tackle |
| Chris Snee, NY Giants | Guard |
| Carl Nicks, New Orleans | Guard |
| Maurice Pouncey, Pittsburgh | Center |

#### DEFENSE

| | |
|---|---|
| Osi Umenyiora, NY Giants | Defensive End |
| Justin Tuck, NY Giants | Defensive End |
| Vince Wilfork, New England | Defensive Tackle |
| Kyle Williams, Baltimore | Defensive Tackle |
| Cameron Wake, Miami | Linebacker |
| DeMarcus Ware, Dallas | Linebacker |
| Brian Urlacher, Chicago | Linebacker |
| Ray Lewis, Baltimore | Linebacker |
| Devin McCourty, New England | Cornerback |
| Charles Woodson, Green Bay | Cornerback |
| Nick Collins, Green Bay | Safety |
| Antrel Rolle, NY Giants | Safety (tie) |
| Eric Weddle, San Diego | Safety (tie) |
| Malcolm Jenkins, New Orleans | Safety (tie) |
| Darren Sharper, New Orleans | Safety (tie) |
| Quintin Mikell, Philadelphia | Safety (tie) |
| Chris Harris, Chicago | Safety (tie) |
| Michael Huff, Oakland | Safety (tie) |
| Michael Griffin, Tennessee | Safety (tie) |

#### SPECIALISTS

| | |
|---|---|
| David Akers, Philadelphia | Kicker |
| Leon Washington, Seattle | Kick Returner |
| Mat McBriar, Dallas | Punter |

### BALTIMORE RAVENS (12-4)

| | | |
|---|---|---|
| 10 | at NY Jets | 9 |
| 10 | at Cincinnati | 15 |
| 24 | CLEVELAND | 17 |
| 17 | at Pittsburgh | 14 |
| 31 | DENVER | 17 |
| *20 | at New England | 23 |
| *37 | BUFFALO | 34 |
| 26 | MIAMI | 10 |
| 21 | at Atlanta | 26 |
| 37 | at Carolina | 13 |
| 17 | TAMPA BAY | 10 |
| 10 | PITTSBURGH | 13 |
| *34 | at Houston | 28 |
| 30 | NEW ORLEANS | 24 |
| 20 | at Cleveland | 10 |
| 13 | CINCINNATI | 7 |
| 357 | | 270 |

### BUFFALO BILLS (4-12)

| | | |
|---|---|---|
| 10 | MIAMI | 15 |
| 7 | at Green Bay | 34 |
| 30 | at New England | 38 |
| 14 | NY Jets | 38 |
| 26 | JACKSONVILLE | 36 |
| *34 | at Baltimore | 37 |
| *10 | at Kansas City | 13 |
| 19 | CHICAGO | 22 |
| 14 | DETROIT | 12 |
| 49 | at Cincinnati | 31 |
| *16 | PITTSBURGH | 19 |
| 14 | at Minnesota | 38 |
| 13 | CLEVELAND | 6 |
| 17 | at Miami | 14 |
| 3 | NEW ENGLAND | 34 |
| 7 | at NY Jets | 38 |
| 283 | | 425 |

### CINCINNATI BENGALS (4-12)

| | | |
|---|---|---|
| 24 | at New England | 38 |
| 15 | BALTIMORE | 10 |
| 20 | at Carolina | 7 |
| 20 | at Cleveland | 23 |
| 21 | TAMPA BAY | 24 |
| 32 | at Atlanta | 39 |
| 14 | MIAMI | 22 |
| 21 | PITTSBURGH | 27 |
| 17 | at Indianapolis | 23 |
| 31 | BUFFALO | 49 |
| 10 | at NY Jets | 26 |
| 30 | NEW ORLEANS | 34 |
| 7 | at Pittsburgh | 23 |
| 19 | CLEVELAND | 17 |
| 34 | SAN DIEGO | 20 |
| 7 | at Baltimore | 13 |
| 322 | | 395 |

### CLEVELAND BROWNS (5-11)

| | | |
|---|---|---|
| 14 | at Tampa Bay | 17 |
| 14 | KANSAS CITY | 16 |
| 17 | at Baltimore | 24 |
| 23 | CINCINNATI | 20 |
| 10 | ATLANTA | 20 |
| 10 | at Pittsburgh | 28 |
| 30 | at New Orleans | 17 |
| 34 | NEW ENGLAND | 14 |
| *20 | NY JETS | 26 |
| 20 | at Jacksonville | 24 |
| 24 | CAROLINA | 23 |
| 13 | at Miami | 10 |
| 6 | at Buffalo | 13 |
| 17 | at Cincinnati | 19 |
| 10 | BALTIMORE | 20 |
| 9 | PITTSBURGh | 41 |
| 271 | | 332 |

### DENVER BRONCOS (4-12)

| | | |
|---|---|---|
| 17 | at Jacksonville | 24 |
| 31 | SEATTLE | 14 |
| 13 | INDIANAPOLIS | 27 |
| 26 | at Tennessee | 20 |
| 17 | at Baltimore | 31 |
| 20 | NY JETS | 24 |
| 14 | OAKLAND | 59 |
| 16 | at San Francisco | 24 |
| 49 | KANSAS CITY | 29 |
| 14 | at San Diego | 35 |
| 33 | ST. LOUIS | 36 |
| 6 | at Kansas City | 10 |
| 13 | at Arizona | 43 |
| 23 | at Oakland | 39 |
| 24 | HOUSTON | 23 |
| 28 | SAN DIEGO | 33 |
| 344 | | 471 |

### HOUSTON TEXANS (6-10)

| | | |
|---|---|---|
| 34 | INDIANAPOLIS | 24 |
| *30 | at Washington | 27 |
| 13 | DALLAS | 27 |
| 31 | at Oakland | 24 |
| 10 | NY GIANTS | 34 |
| 35 | KANSAS CITY | 31 |
| 17 | at Indianapolis | 30 |
| 23 | SAN DIEGO | 29 |
| 24 | at Jacksonville | 31 |
| 27 | at NY Jets | 30 |
| 20 | TENNESSEE | 0 |
| 24 | at Philadelphia | 34 |
| *28 | BALTIMORE | 34 |
| 17 | at Tennessee | 31 |
| 23 | at Denver | 24 |
| 34 | JACKSONVILLE | 17 |
| 390 | | 427 |

### INDIANAPOLIS COLTS (10-6)

| | | |
|---|---|---|
| 24 | at Houston | 34 |
| 38 | NY GIANTS | 14 |
| 27 | at Denver | 13 |
| 28 | at Jacksonville | 31 |
| 19 | KANSAS CITY | 9 |
| 27 | at Washington | 24 |
| 30 | HOUSTON | 17 |
| 24 | at Philadelphia | 26 |
| 23 | CINCINNATI | 17 |
| 28 | at New England | 31 |
| 14 | SAN DIEGO | 36 |
| *25 | DALLAS | 38 |
| 30 | at Tennessee | 28 |
| 34 | JACKSONVILLE | 24 |
| 31 | at Oakland | 26 |
| 23 | TENNESSEE | 20 |
| 435 | | 388 |

### JACKSONVILLE JAGUARS (8-8)

| | | |
|---|---|---|
| 24 | DENVER | 17 |
| 13 | at San Diego | 38 |
| 3 | PHILADELPHIA | 28 |
| 31 | INDIANAPOLIS | 28 |
| 36 | at Buffalo | 26 |
| 3 | TENNESSEE | 30 |
| 20 | at Kansas City | 42 |
| 35 | at Dallas | 17 |
| 31 | HOUSTON | 24 |
| 24 | CLEVELAND | 20 |
| 20 | at NY Giants | 24 |
| 17 | at Tennessee | 6 |
| 38 | OAKLAND | 31 |
| 24 | at Indianapolis | 34 |
| *17 | WASHINGTON | 20 |
| 17 | at Houston | 34 |
| 353 | | 419 |

### KANSAS CITY CHIEFS (10-6)

| | | |
|---|---|---|
| 21 | SAN DIEGO | 14 |
| 16 | at Cleveland | 14 |
| 31 | SAN FRANCISCO | 10 |
| 9 | at Indianapolis | 19 |
| 31 | at Houston | 35 |
| 42 | JACKSONVILLE | 20 |
| *13 | BUFFALO | 10 |
| *20 | at Oakland | 23 |
| 29 | at Denver | 49 |
| 31 | ARIZONA | 13 |
| 42 | at Seattle | 24 |
| 10 | DENVER | 6 |
| 0 | at San Diego | 31 |
| 27 | at St. Louis | 13 |
| 34 | TENNESSEE | 14 |
| 10 | OAKLAND | 31 |
| 366 | | 326 |

### MIAMI DOLPHINS (7-9)

| | | | | | |
|---|---|---|---|---|---|
| 15 | at Buffalo | 10 | 29 | TENNESSEE | 17 |
| 14 | at Minnesota | 10 | 0 | CHICAGO | 16 |
| 23 | NY JETS | 31 | 33 | at Oakland | 17 |
| 14 | NEW ENGLAND | 41 | 10 | CLEVELAND | 13 |
| *23 | at Green Bay | 20 | 10 | at NY Jets | 6 |
| 22 | PITTSBURGH | 23 | 14 | BUFFALO | 17 |
| 22 | at Cincinnati | 14 | 27 | DETROIT | 34 |
| 10 | at Baltimore | 26 | 7 | at New England | 38 |
| | | | 273 | | 333 |

* overtime

### NEW ENGLAND PATRIOTS (14–2)

| | | |
|---|---|---:|
| 38 | CINCINNATI | 24 |
| 14 | at NY Jets | 28 |
| 38 | BUFFALO | 30 |
| 41 | at Miami | 14 |
| *23 | BALTIMORE | 20 |
| 23 | at San Diego | 20 |
| 28 | MINNESOTA | 18 |
| 14 | at Cleveland | 34 |
| 39 | at Pittsburgh | 26 |
| 31 | INDIANAPOLIS | 28 |
| 45 | at Detroit | 24 |
| 45 | NY JETS | 3 |
| 36 | at Chicago | 7 |
| 31 | GREEN BAY | 27 |
| 34 | at Buffalo | 3 |
| 38 | MIAMI | 7 |
| 518 | | 313 |

### NEW YORK JETS (11–5)

| | | |
|---|---|---:|
| 9 | BALTIMORE | 10 |
| 28 | NEW ENGLAND | 14 |
| 31 | at Miami | 23 |
| 38 | at Buffalo | 14 |
| 29 | MINNESOTA | 20 |
| 24 | at Denver | 20 |
| 0 | GREEN BAY | 9 |
| *23 | at Detroit | 20 |
| *26 | at Cleveland | 20 |
| 30 | HOUSTON | 27 |
| 26 | CINCINNATI | 10 |
| 3 | at New England | 45 |
| 6 | MIAMI | 10 |
| 22 | at Pittsburgh | 17 |
| 34 | at Chicago | 38 |
| 38 | BUFFALO | 7 |
| 367 | | 304 |

### OAKLAND RAIDERS (8–8)

| | | |
|---|---|---:|
| 13 | at Tennessee | 38 |
| 16 | ST. LOUIS | 14 |
| 23 | at Arizona | 24 |
| 24 | HOUSTON | 31 |
| 35 | SAN DIEGO | 27 |
| 9 | at San Francisco | 17 |
| 59 | at Denver | 14 |
| 33 | SEATTLE | 3 |
| *23 | KANSAS CITY | 20 |
| 3 | at Pittsburgh | 35 |
| 17 | MIAMI | 33 |
| 28 | at San Diego | 13 |
| 31 | at Jacksonville | 38 |
| 39 | DENVER | 23 |
| 26 | INDIANAPOLIS | 31 |
| 31 | at Kansas City | 10 |
| 410 | | 371 |

### PITTSBURGH STEELERS (12–4)

| | | |
|---|---|---:|
| *15 | ATLANTA | 9 |
| 19 | at Tennessee | 11 |
| 38 | at Tampa Bay | 13 |
| 14 | BALTIMORE | 17 |
| 28 | CLEVELAND | 10 |
| 23 | at Miami | 22 |
| 10 | at New Orleans | 20 |
| 27 | at Cincinnati | 21 |
| 26 | NEW ENGLAND | 39 |
| 35 | OAKLAND | 3 |
| *19 | at Buffalo | 16 |
| 13 | at Baltimore | 10 |
| 23 | CINCINNATI | 7 |
| 17 | NY JETS | 22 |
| 27 | CAROLINA | 3 |
| 41 | at Cleveland | 9 |
| 375 | | 232 |

### SAN DIEGO CHARGERS (9–7)

| | | |
|---|---|---:|
| 14 | at Kansas City | 21 |
| 38 | JACKSONVILLE | 13 |
| 20 | at Seattle | 27 |
| 41 | ARIZONA | 10 |
| 27 | at Oakland | 35 |
| 17 | at St. Louis | 20 |
| 20 | NEW ENGLAND | 23 |
| 33 | TENNESSEE | 25 |
| 29 | at Houston | 23 |
| 35 | DENVER | 14 |
| 36 | at Indianapolis | 14 |
| 13 | OAKLAND | 28 |
| 31 | KANSAS CITY | 0 |
| 34 | SAN FRANCISCO | 7 |
| 20 | at Cincinnati | 34 |
| 33 | at Denver | 28 |
| 441 | | 322 |

### TENNESSEE TITANS (6–10)

| | | |
|---|---|---:|
| 38 | OAKLAND | 13 |
| 11 | PITTSBURGh | 19 |
| 29 | at NY Giants | 10 |
| 20 | DENVER | 26 |
| 34 | at Dallas | 27 |
| 30 | at Jacksonville | 3 |
| 37 | PHILADELPHIA | 19 |
| 25 | at San Diego | 33 |
| 17 | at Miami | 29 |
| *16 | WASHINGTON | 19 |
| 0 | at Houston | 20 |
| 6 | JACKSONVILLE | 17 |
| 28 | INDIANAPOLIS | 30 |
| 31 | HOUSTON | 17 |
| 14 | at Kansas City | 34 |
| 20 | at Indianapolis | 23 |
| 356 | | 339 |

## 2010 NFC Team-by-Team Results

### ARIZONA CARDINALS (5–11)

| | | |
|---|---|---:|
| 17 | at St. Louis | 13 |
| 7 | at Atlanta | 41 |
| 24 | OAKLAND | 23 |
| 10 | at San Diego | 41 |
| 30 | NEW ORLEANS | 20 |
| 10 | at Seattle | 22 |
| 35 | TAMPA BAY | 38 |
| *24 | at Minnesota | 27 |
| 18 | SEATTLE | 36 |
| 13 | at Kansas City | 31 |
| 6 | SAN FRANCISCO | 27 |
| 6 | ST. LOUIS | 19 |
| 43 | DENVER | 13 |
| 12 | at Carolina | 19 |
| 27 | DALLAS | 26 |
| 7 | at San Francisco | 38 |
| 289 | | 434 |

### ATLANTA FALCONS (13–3)

| | | |
|---|---|---:|
| *9 | at Pittsburgh | 15 |
| 41 | ARIZONA | 7 |
| *27 | at New Orleans | 24 |
| 16 | SAN FRANCISCO | 14 |
| 20 | at Cleveland | 10 |
| 17 | at Philadelphia | 31 |
| 39 | CINCINNATI | 32 |
| 27 | TAMPA BAY | 21 |
| 26 | BALTIMORE | 21 |
| 34 | at St. Louis | 17 |
| 20 | GREEN BAY | 17 |
| 28 | at Tampa Bay | 24 |
| 31 | at Carolina | 10 |
| 34 | at Seattle | 18 |
| 14 | NEW ORLEANS | 17 |
| 31 | CAROLINA | 10 |
| 414 | | 288 |

### CAROLINA PANTHERS (2–14)

| | | |
|---|---|---:|
| 18 | at NY Giants | 31 |
| 7 | TAMPA BAY | 20 |
| 7 | CINCINNATI | 20 |
| 14 | at New Orleans | 16 |
| 6 | CHICAGO | 23 |
| 23 | SAN FRANCISCO | 20 |
| 10 | at St. Louis | 20 |
| 3 | NEW ORLEANS | 34 |
| 16 | at Tampa Bay | 31 |
| 13 | BALTIMORE | 37 |
| 23 | at Cleveland | 24 |
| 14 | at Seattle | 31 |
| 10 | ATLANTA | 31 |
| 19 | ARIZONA | 12 |
| 3 | at Pittsburgh | 27 |
| 10 | at Atlanta | 31 |
| 196 | | 408 |

* overtime

### CHICAGO BEARS (11-5)

| | | |
|---|---|---|
| 19 | DETROIT | 14 |
| 27 | at Dallas | 20 |
| 20 | GREEN BAY | 17 |
| 3 | at NY Giants | 17 |
| 23 | at Carolina | 6 |
| 20 | SEATTLE | 23 |
| 14 | WASHINGTON | 17 |
| 22 | at Buffalo | 19 |
| 27 | MINNESOTA | 13 |
| 16 | at Miami | 0 |
| 31 | PHILADELPHIA | 26 |
| 24 | at Detroit | 20 |
| 7 | NEW ENGLAND | 36 |
| 40 | at Minnesota | 14 |
| 38 | NY JETS | 34 |
| 3 | at Green Bay | 10 |
| 334 | | 286 |

### GREEN BAY PACKERS (10-6)

| | | |
|---|---|---|
| 27 | at Philadelphia | 20 |
| 34 | BUFFALO | 7 |
| 17 | at Chicago | 20 |
| 28 | DETROIT | 26 |
| *13 | at Washington | 16 |
| *20 | MIAMI | 23 |
| 28 | MINNESOTA | 24 |
| 9 | at NY Jets | 0 |
| 45 | DALLAS | 7 |
| 31 | at Minnesota | 3 |
| 17 | at Atlanta | 20 |
| 34 | SAN FRANCISCO | 16 |
| 3 | at Detroit | 7 |
| 27 | at New England | 31 |
| 45 | NY GIANTS | 17 |
| 10 | CHICAGO | 3 |
| 388 | | 240 |

### NEW YORK GIANTS (10-6)

| | | |
|---|---|---|
| 31 | CAROLINA | 18 |
| 14 | at Indianapolis | 38 |
| 10 | TENNESSEE | 29 |
| 17 | CHICAGO | 3 |
| 34 | at Houston | 10 |
| 28 | DETROIT | 20 |
| 41 | at Dallas | 35 |
| 41 | at Seattle | 7 |
| 20 | DALLAS | 33 |
| 17 | at Philadelphia | 27 |
| 24 | JACKSONVILLE | 20 |
| 31 | WASHINGTON | 7 |
| 21 | at Minnesota | 3 |
| 31 | PHILADELPHIA | 38 |
| 17 | at Green Bay | 45 |
| 17 | at Washington | 14 |
| 394 | | 347 |

### DALLAS COWBOYS (6-10)

| | | |
|---|---|---|
| 7 | at Washington | 13 |
| 20 | CHICAGO | 27 |
| 27 | at Houston | 13 |
| 27 | TENNESSEE | 34 |
| 21 | at Minnesota | 24 |
| 35 | NY GIANTS | 41 |
| 17 | JACKSONVILLE | 35 |
| 7 | at Green Bay | 45 |
| 33 | at NY Giants | 20 |
| 35 | DETROIT | 19 |
| 27 | NEW ORLEANS | 30 |
| *38 | at Indianapolis | 35 |
| 27 | PHILADELPHIA | 30 |
| 33 | WASHINGTON | 30 |
| 26 | at Arizona | 27 |
| 14 | at Philadelphia | 13 |
| 394 | | 436 |

### MINNESOTA VIKINGS (6-10)

| | | |
|---|---|---|
| 9 | at New Orleans | 14 |
| 10 | MIAMI | 14 |
| 24 | DETROIT | 10 |
| 20 | at NY Jets | 29 |
| 24 | DALLAS | 21 |
| 24 | at Green Bay | 28 |
| 18 | at New England | 28 |
| *27 | ARIZONA | 24 |
| 13 | at Chicago | 27 |
| 3 | GREEN BAY | 31 |
| 17 | at Washington | 13 |
| 38 | BUFFALO | 14 |
| 3 | NY GIANTS | 21 |
| 14 | CHICAGO | 40 |
| 24 | at Philadelphia | 14 |
| 13 | at Detroit | 20 |
| 281 | | 348 |

### PHILADELPHIA EAGLES (10-6)

| | | |
|---|---|---|
| 20 | GREEN BAY | 27 |
| 35 | at Detroit | 32 |
| 28 | at Jacksonville | 3 |
| 12 | WASHINGTON | 17 |
| 27 | at San Francisco | 24 |
| 31 | ATLANTA | 17 |
| 19 | at Tennessee | 37 |
| 26 | INDIANAPOLIS | 24 |
| 59 | at Washington | 28 |
| 27 | NY GIANTS | 17 |
| 26 | at Chicago | 31 |
| 34 | HOUSTON | 24 |
| 30 | at Dallas | 27 |
| 38 | at NY Giants | 31 |
| 14 | MINNESOTA | 24 |
| 13 | DALLAS | 14 |
| 439 | | 377 |

### DETROIT LIONS (6-10)

| | | |
|---|---|---|
| 14 | at Chicago | 19 |
| 32 | PHILADELPHIA | 35 |
| 10 | at Minnesota | 24 |
| 26 | at Green Bay | 28 |
| 44 | ST. LOUIS | 6 |
| 20 | at NY Giants | 28 |
| 37 | WASHINGTON | 25 |
| *20 | NY JETS | 23 |
| 12 | at Buffalo | 14 |
| 19 | at Dallas | 35 |
| 24 | NEW ENGLAND | 45 |
| 20 | CHICAGO | 24 |
| 7 | GREEN BAY | 3 |
| *23 | at Tampa Bay | 20 |
| 34 | at Miami | 27 |
| 20 | MINNESOTA | 13 |
| 362 | | 369 |

### NEW ORLEANS SAINTS (11-5)

| | | |
|---|---|---|
| 14 | MINNESOTA | 9 |
| 25 | at San Francisco | 22 |
| *24 | ATLANTA | 27 |
| 16 | CAROLINA | 14 |
| 20 | at Arizona | 30 |
| 31 | at Tampa Bay | 6 |
| 17 | CLEVELAND | 30 |
| 20 | PITTSBURGH | 10 |
| 34 | at Carolina | 3 |
| 34 | SEATTLE | 19 |
| 30 | at Dallas | 27 |
| 34 | at Cincinnati | 30 |
| 31 | ST. LOUIS | 13 |
| 24 | at Baltimore | 30 |
| 17 | at Atlanta | 14 |
| 13 | TAMPA BAY | 23 |
| 384 | | 307 |

### SAN FRANCISCO 49ERS (6-10)

| | | |
|---|---|---|
| 6 | at Seattle | 31 |
| 22 | NEW ORLEANS | 25 |
| 10 | at Kansas City | 31 |
| 14 | at Atlanta | 16 |
| 24 | PHILADELPHIA | 27 |
| 17 | OAKLAND | 9 |
| 20 | at Carolina | 23 |
| 24 | DENVER | 16 |
| *23 | ST. LOUIS | 20 |
| 0 | TAMPA BAY | 21 |
| 27 | at Arizona | 6 |
| 16 | at Green Bay | 34 |
| 40 | SEATTLE | 21 |
| 7 | at San Diego | 34 |
| 17 | at St. Louis | 25 |
| 38 | ARIZONA | 7 |
| 305 | | 346 |

* overtime

| **SEATTLE SEAHAWKS (7-9)** | | |
|---|---|---|
| 31 | SAN FRANCISCO | 6 |
| 14 | at Denver | 31 |
| 27 | SAN DIEGO | 20 |
| 3 | at St. Louis | 20 |
| 23 | at Chicago | 20 |
| 22 | ARIZONA | 10 |
| 3 | at Oakland | 33 |
| 7 | NY GIANTS | 41 |
| 36 | at Arizona | 18 |
| 19 | at New Orleans | 34 |
| 24 | KANSAS CITY | 42 |
| 31 | CAROLINA | 14 |
| 21 | at San Francisco | 40 |
| 18 | ATLANTA | 34 |
| 15 | at Tampa Bay | 38 |
| 16 | ST. LOUIS | 6 |
| 310 | | 407 |

| **ST. LOUIS RAMS (7-9)** | | |
|---|---|---|
| 13 | ARIZONA | 17 |
| 14 | at Oakland | 16 |
| 30 | WASHINGTON | 16 |
| 20 | SEATTLE | 3 |
| 6 | at Detroit | 44 |
| 20 | SAN DIEGO | 17 |
| 17 | at Tampa Bay | 18 |
| 20 | CAROLINA | 10 |
| *20 | at San Francisco | 23 |
| 17 | ATLANTA | 34 |
| 36 | at Denver | 33 |
| 19 | at Arizona | 6 |
| 13 | at New Orleans | 31 |
| 13 | KANSAS CITY | 27 |
| 25 | SAN FRANCISCO | 17 |
| 6 | at Seattle | 16 |
| 289 | | 328 |

| **TAMPA BAY BUCCANEERS (10-6)** | | |
|---|---|---|
| 17 | CLEVELAND | 14 |
| 20 | at Carolina | 7 |
| 13 | PITTSBURGH | 38 |
| 24 | at Cincinnati | 21 |
| 6 | NEW ORLEANS | 31 |
| 18 | ST. LOUIS | 17 |
| 38 | at Arizona | 35 |
| 21 | at Atlanta | 27 |
| 31 | CAROLINA | 16 |
| 21 | at San Francisco | 0 |
| 10 | at Baltimore | 17 |
| 24 | ATLANTA | 28 |
| 17 | at Washington | 16 |
| *20 | DETROIT | 23 |
| 38 | SEATTLE | 15 |
| 23 | at New Orleans | 13 |
| 341 | | 318 |

| **WASHINGTON REDSKINS (6-10)** | | | | | |
|---|---|---|---|---|---|
| 13 | DALLAS | 7 | 28 | PHILADELPHIA | 59 |
| *27 | HOUSTON | 30 | *19 | at Tennessee | 16 |
| 16 | at St. Louis | 30 | 13 | MINNESOTA | 17 |
| 17 | at Philadelphia | 12 | 7 | at NY Giants | 31 |
| *16 | GREEN BAY | 13 | 16 | TAMPA BAY | 17 |
| 24 | INDIANAPOLIS | 27 | 30 | at Dallas | 33 |
| 17 | at Chicago | 14 | *20 | at Jacksonville | 17 |
| 25 | at Detroit | 37 | 14 | NY GIANTS | 17 |
| | | | 302 | | 377 |

* overtime

## American Football Conference

### Scoring

| TOUCHDOWNS | TD | Rush | Rec | Ret | 2PT | Pts |
|---|---|---|---|---|---|---|
| A. Foster, Hou | 18 | 16 | 2 | 0 | 0 | 108 |
| D. Bowe, KC | 15 | 0 | 15 | 0 | 0 | 90 |
| B. Green-Ellis, NE | 13 | 13 | 0 | 0 | 0 | 78 |
| P. Hillis, Cle | 13 | 11 | 2 | 0 | 0 | 78 |
| R. Mendenhall, Pit | 13 | 13 | 0 | 0 | 0 | 78 |
| C. Johnson, Ten | 12 | 11 | 1 | 0 | 0 | 72 |
| M. Tolbert, SD | 11 | 11 | 0 | 0 | 1 | 68 |
| B. Lloyd, Den | 11 | 0 | 11 | 0 | 0 | 66 |
| A. Gates, SD | 10 | 0 | 10 | 0 | 0 | 60 |
| R. Gronkowski, NE | 10 | 0 | 10 | 0 | 0 | 60 |
| S. Johnson, Buf | 10 | 0 | 10 | 0 | 0 | 60 |
| M. Lewis, Jax | 10 | 0 | 10 | 0 | 0 | 60 |
| D. McFadden, Oak | 10 | 7 | 3 | 0 | 0 | 60 |
| M. Wallace, Pit | 10 | 0 | 10 | 0 | 0 | 60 |

| KICKING | PAT | FG | Pts |
|---|---|---|---|
| S. Janikowski, Oak | 43 | 33 | 142 |
| A. Vinatieri, Ind | 51 | 26 | 129 |
| N. Folk, NY Jets | 37 | 30 | 127 |
| N. Rackers, Hou | 43 | 27 | 124 |
| B. Cundiff, Bal | 39 | 26 | 117 |
| D. Carpenter, Mia | 25 | 30 | 115 |
| R. Bironas, Ten | 38 | 24 | 110 |
| N. Kaeding, SD | 40 | 23 | 109 |
| J. Scobee, Jax | 41 | 22 | 107 |
| R. Succop, KC | 42 | 20 | 102 |

### Passing

| | Att | Comp | Yds | TD | Int | Lg | Rating Pts |
|---|---|---|---|---|---|---|---|
| T. Brady, NE | 492 | 324 | 3900 | 36 | 4 | 79 | 111.0 |
| P. Rivers, SD | 541 | 357 | 4710 | 30 | 13 | 59 | 101.8 |
| B. Roethlisberger, Pit | 389 | 240 | 3200 | 17 | 5 | 56 | 97.0 |
| J. Flacco, Bal | 489 | 306 | 3622 | 25 | 10 | 67 | 93.6 |
| M. Cassel, KC | 450 | 262 | 3116 | 27 | 7 | 75 | 93.0 |
| M. Schaub, Hou | 574 | 365 | 4370 | 24 | 12 | 60 | 92.0 |
| P. Manning, Ind | 679 | 450 | 4700 | 33 | 17 | 73 | 91.9 |
| J. Garrard, Jax | 366 | 236 | 2734 | 23 | 15 | 75 | 90.8 |
| K. Orton, Den | 498 | 293 | 3653 | 20 | 9 | 71 | 87.5 |
| J. Campbell, Oak | 329 | 194 | 2387 | 13 | 8 | 73 | 84.5 |

## American Football Conference (Cont.)

### Pass Receiving

| RECEPTIONS | No. | Yds | Avg | Lg | TD |
|---|---|---|---|---|---|
| R. Wayne, Ind | 111 | 1355 | 12.2 | 50 | 6 |
| A. Johnson, Hou | 86 | 1216 | 14.1 | 60 | 8 |
| B. Marshall, Mia | 86 | 1014 | 11.8 | 46 | 3 |
| W. Welker, NE | 86 | 848 | 9.9 | 35 | 7 |
| S. Johnson, Buf | 82 | 1073 | 13.1 | 45 | 10 |
| D. Bess, Mia | 79 | 820 | 10.4 | 29 | 5 |
| B. Lloyd, Den | 77 | 1448 | 18.8 | 71 | 11 |
| D. Bowe, KC | 72 | 1162 | 16.1 | 75 | 15 |
| T. Owens, Cin | 72 | 983 | 13.7 | 78 | 9 |
| B. Watson, Cle | 68 | 763 | 11.2 | 44 | 3 |

| YARDS | Yds | No. | Avg | Lg | TD |
|---|---|---|---|---|---|
| B. Lloyd, Den | 1448 | 77 | 18.8 | 71 | 11 |
| R. Wayne, Ind | 1355 | 111 | 12.2 | 50 | 6 |
| M. Wallace, Pit | 1257 | 60 | 21.0 | 56 | 10 |
| A. Johnson, Hou | 1216 | 86 | 14.1 | 60 | 8 |
| D. Bowe, KC | 1162 | 72 | 16.1 | 75 | 15 |
| S. Johnson, Buf | 1073 | 82 | 13.1 | 45 | 10 |
| B. Marshall, Mia | 1014 | 86 | 11.8 | 46 | 3 |
| T. Owens, Cin | 983 | 72 | 13.7 | 78 | 9 |
| B. Edwards, NYJ | 904 | 53 | 17.1 | 74 | 7 |
| J. Gaffney, Den | 875 | 65 | 13.5 | 50 | 2 |

### Rushing

| | Att | Yds | Avg | Lg | TD |
|---|---|---|---|---|---|
| A. Foster, Hou | 327 | 1616 | 4.9 | 74 | 16 |
| J. Charles, KC | 230 | 1467 | 6.4 | 80 | 5 |
| C. Johnson, Ten | 316 | 1364 | 4.3 | 76 | 11 |
| M. Jones-Drew, Jax | 299 | 1324 | 4.4 | 37 | 5 |
| R. Mendenhall, Pit | 324 | 1273 | 3.9 | 50 | 13 |
| R. Rice, Bal | 307 | 1220 | 4.0 | 50 | 5 |
| P. Hillis, Cle | 270 | 1177 | 4.4 | 48 | 11 |
| D. McFadden, Oak | 223 | 1157 | 5.2 | 57 | 7 |
| C. Benson, Cin | 321 | 1111 | 3.5 | 26 | 7 |
| B. Green-Ellis, NE | 229 | 1008 | 4.4 | 33 | 13 |
| F. Jackson, Buf | 222 | 927 | 4.2 | 39 | 5 |
| L. Tomlinson, NYJ | 219 | 914 | 4.2 | 31 | 6 |
| T. Jones, KC | 245 | 896 | 3.7 | 70 | 6 |
| K. Moreno, Den | 182 | 779 | 4.3 | 35 | 5 |
| S. Greene, NYJ | 185 | 766 | 4.1 | 23 | 2 |

### Interceptions

| | No. | Yds | Lg | TD |
|---|---|---|---|---|
| E. Reed, Bal | 8 | 183 | 44 | 0 |
| D. McCourty, NE | 7 | 110 | 50 | 0 |
| T. Polamalu, Pit | 7 | 101 | 45 | 1 |
| J. Allen, Mia/Hou | 6 | 18 | 17 | 0 |
| J. Haden, Cle | 6 | 101 | 62 | 0 |

### Sacks

| | |
|---|---|
| T. Hali, KC | 14.5 |
| C. Wake, Mia | 14.0 |
| J. Babin, Ten | 12.5 |
| R. Mathis, Ind | 11.0 |
| S. Phillips, SD | 11.0 |
| T. Suggs, Bal | 11.0 |

### Punting

| | No. | Yds | Avg | Net Avg | TB | In 20 | Lg | Blk | Ret | Ret Avg |
|---|---|---|---|---|---|---|---|---|---|---|
| S. Lechler, Oak | 77 | 3618 | 47.0 | 40.8 | 4 | 27 | 68 | 0 | 45 | 8.9 |
| M. Scifres, SD | 52 | 2430 | 46.7 | 30.8 | 9 | 13 | 67 | 4 | 28 | 18.8 |
| B. Fields, Mia | 73 | 3369 | 46.2 | 37.8 | 4 | 31 | 69 | 2 | 43 | 10.6 |
| D. Sepulveda, Pit | 56 | 2550 | 45.5 | 39.1 | 8 | 16 | 62 | 0 | 23 | 8.6 |
| B. Colquitt, Den | 86 | 3835 | 44.6 | 36.6 | 7 | 19 | 63 | 0 | 50 | 11.0 |

### Punt Returns

| | No. | Yds | Avg | Lg | TD |
|---|---|---|---|---|---|
| J. Edelman, NE | 21 | 321 | 15.3 | 94 | 1 |
| M. Mariani, Ten | 27 | 329 | 12.2 | 87 | 1 |
| E. Royal, Den | 25 | 298 | 11.9 | 33 | 0 |
| D. Bess, Mia | 25 | 284 | 11.4 | 47 | 0 |
| J. Leonhard, NYJ | 21 | 238 | 11.3 | 32 | 0 |

### Kickoff Returns

| | No. | Yds | Avg | Lg | TD |
|---|---|---|---|---|---|
| D. Reed, Bal | 21 | 616 | 29.3 | 103 | 1 |
| B. Smith, NYJ | 50 | 1432 | 28.6 | 97 | 2 |
| B. Tate, NE | 41 | 1057 | 25.8 | 103 | 2 |
| M. Mariani, Ten | 60 | 1530 | 25.5 | 98 | 1 |
| E. Decker, Den | 22 | 556 | 25.3 | 51 | 0 |

## National Football Conference

### Scoring

| TOUCHDOWNS | TD | Rush | Rec | Ret | 2PT | Pts |
|---|---|---|---|---|---|---|
| A. Peterson, Min | 13 | 12 | 1 | 0 | 0 | 78 |
| C. Johnson, Det | 12 | 0 | 12 | 0 | 1 | 74 |
| G. Jennings, GB | 12 | 0 | 12 | 0 | 0 | 72 |
| M. Turner, Atl | 12 | 12 | 0 | 0 | 0 | 72 |
| H. Nicks, NYG | 11 | 0 | 11 | 0 | 0 | 66 |
| M. Williams, TB | 11 | 0 | 11 | 0 | 0 | 66 |
| R. White, Atl | 10 | 0 | 10 | 0 | 2 | 64 |
| J. Maclin, Phi | 10 | 0 | 10 | 0 | 0 | 60 |
| M. Forte, Chi | 9 | 6 | 3 | 0 | 1 | 56 |
| J. Witten, Dal | 9 | 0 | 9 | 0 | 1 | 56 |
| B. Jacobs, NYG | 9 | 9 | 0 | 0 | 0 | 54 |
| M. Manningham, NYG | 9 | 0 | 9 | 0 | 0 | 54 |
| L. McCoy, Phi | 9 | 7 | 2 | 0 | 0 | 54 |
| M. Vick, Phi | 9 | 9 | 0 | 0 | 0 | 54 |

| KICKING | PAT | FG | Pts |
|---|---|---|---|
| D. Akers, Phi | 47 | 32 | 143 |
| M. Bryant, Atl | 44 | 28 | 128 |
| J. Brown, StL | 26 | 33 | 125 |
| D. Buehler, Dal | 42 | 24 | 114 |
| M. Crosby, GB | 46 | 22 | 112 |
| R. Gould, Chi | 35 | 25 | 110 |
| J. Feely, Ari | 29 | 24 | 107 |
| O. Mare, Sea | 31 | 25 | 106 |
| C. Barth, TB | 36 | 23 | 105 |
| G. Gano, Was | 28 | 24 | 100 |
| G. Hartley, NO | 40 | 20 | 100 |
| L. Tynes, NYG | 43 | 19 | 100 |

### National Football Conference (Cont.)

#### Passing

| | Att | Comp | Yds | TD | Int | Lg | Rating Pts |
|---|---|---|---|---|---|---|---|
| A. Rodgers, GB | 475 | 312 | 3922 | 28 | 11 | 86 | 101.2 |
| M. Vick, Phi | 372 | 233 | 3018 | 21 | 6 | 91 | 100.2 |
| J. Freeman, TB | 474 | 291 | 3451 | 25 | 6 | 64 | 95.9 |
| M. Ryan, Atl | 571 | 357 | 3705 | 28 | 9 | 46 | 91.0 |
| D. Brees, NO | 658 | 448 | 4620 | 33 | 22 | 80 | 90.9 |
| J. Kitna, Dal | 318 | 209 | 2365 | 16 | 12 | 71 | 88.9 |
| J. Cutler, Chi | 432 | 261 | 3274 | 23 | 16 | 89 | 86.3 |
| E. Manning, NYG | 539 | 339 | 4002 | 31 | 25 | 92 | 85.3 |
| A. Smith, SF | 342 | 204 | 2370 | 14 | 10 | 62 | 82.1 |
| S. Hill, Det | 416 | 257 | 2686 | 16 | 12 | 75 | 81.3 |

#### Pass Receiving

| RECEPTIONS | No. | Yds | Avg | Lg | TD | YARDS | Yds | No. | Avg | Lg | TD |
|---|---|---|---|---|---|---|---|---|---|---|---|
| R. White, Atl | 115 | 1389 | 12.1 | 46 | 10 | R. White, Atl | 1389 | 115 | 12.1 | 46 | 10 |
| J. Witten, Dal | 94 | 1002 | 10.7 | 33 | 9 | G. Jennings, GB | 1265 | 76 | 16.6 | 86 | 12 |
| S. Moss, Was | 93 | 1115 | 12.0 | 56 | 6 | L. Fitzgerald, Ari | 1137 | 90 | 12.6 | 41 | 6 |
| L. Fitzgerald, Ari | 90 | 1137 | 12.6 | 41 | 6 | C. Johnson, Det | 1120 | 77 | 14.5 | 87 | 12 |
| D. Amendola, StL | 85 | 689 | 8.1 | 36 | 3 | S. Moss, Was | 1115 | 93 | 12.0 | 56 | 6 |
| M. Colston, NO | 84 | 1023 | 12.2 | 43 | 7 | D. Jackson, Phi | 1056 | 47 | 22.5 | 91 | 6 |
| H. Nicks, NYG | 79 | 1052 | 13.3 | 46 | 11 | H. Nicks, NYG | 1052 | 79 | 13.3 | 46 | 11 |
| L. McCoy, Phi | 78 | 592 | 7.6 | 40 | 2 | M. Austin, Dal | 1041 | 69 | 15.1 | 69 | 7 |
| C. Cooley, Was | 77 | 849 | 11.0 | 35 | 3 | M. Colston, NO | 1023 | 84 | 12.2 | 43 | 7 |
| C. Johnson, Det | 77 | 1120 | 14.5 | 87 | 12 | J. Witten, Dal | 1002 | 94 | 10.7 | 33 | 9 |

#### Rushing

| | Att | Yds | Avg | Lg | TD |
|---|---|---|---|---|---|
| M. Turner, Atl | 334 | 1371 | 4.1 | 55 | 12 |
| A. Peterson, Min | 283 | 1298 | 4.6 | 80 | 12 |
| S. Jackson, StL | 330 | 1241 | 3.8 | 42 | 6 |
| A. Bradshaw, NYG | 276 | 1235 | 4.5 | 48 | 8 |
| L. McCoy, Phi | 207 | 1080 | 5.2 | 62 | 7 |
| M. Forte, Chi | 237 | 1069 | 4.5 | 68 | 6 |
| L. Blount, TB | 201 | 1007 | 5.0 | 53 | 6 |
| F. Gore, SF | 203 | 853 | 4.2 | 64 | 3 |
| B. Jacobs, NYG | 147 | 823 | 5.6 | 73 | 9 |
| F. Jones, Dal | 185 | 800 | 4.3 | 34 | 1 |
| J. Stewart, Car | 178 | 770 | 4.3 | 48 | 2 |
| R. Torain, Was | 164 | 742 | 4.5 | 54 | 4 |
| T. Hightower, Ari | 153 | 736 | 4.8 | 80 | 5 |
| C. Ivory, NO | 137 | 716 | 5.2 | 55 | 5 |
| B. Jackson, GB | 190 | 703 | 3.7 | 71 | 3 |

#### Interceptions

| | No. | Yds | Lg | TD |
|---|---|---|---|---|
| A. Samuel, Phi | 7 | 70 | 33 | 0 |
| D. Hall, Was | 6 | 92 | 92 | 1 |
| A. Talib, TB | 6 | 91 | 45 | 1 |
| T. Williams, GB | 6 | 87 | 64 | 0 |
| Ten tied with 5. | | | | |

#### Sacks

| | |
|---|---|
| D. Ware, Dal | 15.5 |
| C. Matthews, GB | 13.5 |
| J. Abraham, Atl | 13.0 |
| C. Johnson, Car | 11.5 |
| J. Tuck, NYG | 11.5 |
| O. Umenyiora, NYG | 11.5 |
| J. Allen, Min | 11.0 |
| C. Clemons, Sea | 11.0 |

#### Punting

| | No. | Yds | Avg | Net Avg | TB | In 20 | Lg | Blk | Ret | Ret Avg |
|---|---|---|---|---|---|---|---|---|---|---|
| M. McBriar, Dal | 65 | 3115 | 47.9 | 41.7 | 8 | 22 | 65 | 1 | 33 | 6.2 |
| A. Lee, SF | 91 | 4203 | 46.2 | 38.2 | 12 | 34 | 64 | 0 | 54 | 8.9 |
| T. Morstead, NO | 57 | 2618 | 45.9 | 38.4 | 6 | 21 | 64 | 0 | 26 | 11.9 |
| D. Jones, StL | 94 | 4276 | 45.5 | 40.0 | 4 | 32 | 63 | 0 | 45 | 9.7 |
| M. Dodge, NYG | 72 | 3222 | 44.8 | 34.3 | 9 | 20 | 69 | 1 | 36 | 14.9 |

#### Punt Returns

| | No. | Yds | Avg | Lg | TD |
|---|---|---|---|---|---|
| D. Hester, Chi | 33 | 564 | 17.1 | 89 | 3 |
| T. Ginn, SF | 24 | 321 | 13.4 | 78 | 1 |
| S. Logan, Det | 30 | 362 | 12.1 | 71 | 0 |
| D. Jackson, Phi | 20 | 231 | 11.6 | 65 | 1 |
| D. Amendola, StL | 40 | 452 | 11.3 | 42 | 0 |
| B. Banks, Was | 38 | 431 | 11.3 | 53 | 0 |
| L. Washington, Sea | 22 | 249 | 11.3 | 84 | 0 |

#### Kickoff Returns

| | No. | Yds | Avg | Lg | TD |
|---|---|---|---|---|---|
| E. Weems, Atl | 40 | 1100 | 27.5 | 102 | 1 |
| L. Stephens-Howling, Ari | 57 | 1548 | 27.2 | 102 | 2 |
| S. Logan, Det | 55 | 1448 | 26.3 | 105 | 1 |
| M. Spurlock, TB | 44 | 1129 | 25.7 | 89 | 1 |
| L. Washington, Sea | 57 | 1461 | 25.6 | 101 | 3 |
| B. Banks, Was | 46 | 1155 | 25.1 | 96 | 1 |
| D. Manning, Chi | 33 | 816 | 24.7 | 62 | 0 |

## AFC Total Offense

| | Total Plays | Yds/Game | Pts/Game | 1st Dwns/Game | Time of Poss |
|---|---|---|---|---|---|
| San Diego | 1039 | 395.6 | 27.6 | 22.3 | 33:03 |
| Houston | 1029 | 386.6 | 24.4 | 22.5 | 29:26 |
| Indianapolis | 1088 | 380.8 | 27.2 | 22.9 | 29:55 |
| New England | 986 | 363.8 | 32.4 | 20.9 | 29:24 |
| Oakland | 1039 | 354.6 | 25.6 | 19.1 | 31:12 |
| NY Jets | 1087 | 351.0 | 22.9 | 19.2 | 32:37 |
| Kansas City | 1063 | 349.7 | 22.9 | 19.9 | 31:39 |
| Denver | 1018 | 348.9 | 21.5 | 19.3 | 28:09 |
| Pittsburgh | 993 | 345.3 | 23.4 | 18.4 | 32:24 |
| Jacksonville | 1019 | 341.2 | 22.1 | 20.6 | 31:48 |
| Cincinnati | 1046 | 330.6 | 20.1 | 19.8 | 31:14 |
| Miami | 1040 | 323.1 | 17.1 | 18.8 | 30:54 |
| Baltimore | 1018 | 322.9 | 22.3 | 18.9 | 31:20 |
| Buffalo | 954 | 304.9 | 17.7 | 16.4 | 28:36 |
| Tennessee | 907 | 302.1 | 22.2 | 15.8 | 26:02 |
| Cleveland | 927 | 289.7 | 16.9 | 16.6 | 28:21 |

## AFC Total Defense

| | Opp Total Plays | Opp Yds/Game | Opp Yds/Play | Opp Pts/Game |
|---|---|---|---|---|
| San Diego | 939 | 271.6 | 4.6 | 20.1 |
| Pittsburgh | 974 | 276.8 | 4.5 | 14.5 |
| NY Jets | 979 | 291.5 | 4.8 | 19.0 |
| Miami | 988 | 309.3 | 5.0 | 20.8 |
| Baltimore | 1007 | 318.9 | 5.1 | 16.9 |
| Oakland | 991 | 322.8 | 5.2 | 23.2 |
| Kansas City | 1028 | 330.2 | 5.1 | 20.4 |
| Cincinnati | 957 | 332.0 | 5.6 | 24.7 |
| Indianapolis | 1010 | 341.6 | 5.4 | 24.2 |
| Cleveland | 1041 | 350.1 | 5.4 | 20.8 |
| Buffalo | 1071 | 361.6 | 5.4 | 26.6 |
| New England | 1056 | 366.5 | 5.6 | 19.6 |
| Tennessee | 1139 | 367.7 | 5.2 | 21.2 |
| Jacksonville | 948 | 371.8 | 6.3 | 26.2 |
| Houston | 1010 | 376.9 | 6.0 | 26.7 |
| Denver | 1056 | 390.8 | 5.9 | 29.4 |

## NFC Total Offense

| | Total Plays | Yds/Game | Pts/Game | 1st Dwns/Game | Time of Poss |
|---|---|---|---|---|---|
| Philadelphia | 1038 | 389.4 | 27.4 | 20.1 | 31:15 |
| NY Giants | 1035 | 380.3 | 24.6 | 20.7 | 32:32 |
| New Orleans | 1067 | 372.5 | 24.0 | 21.9 | 32:05 |
| Dallas | 1035 | 364.2 | 24.6 | 20.4 | 31:25 |
| Green Bay | 1000 | 358.1 | 24.2 | 19.5 | 32:01 |
| Atlanta | 1097 | 341.1 | 25.9 | 22.1 | 32:47 |
| Detroit | 1064 | 338.9 | 22.6 | 19.0 | 29:48 |
| Washington | 1002 | 335.9 | 18.9 | 18.4 | 28:50 |
| Tampa Bay | 955 | 335.1 | 21.3 | 18.0 | 30:49 |
| Minnesota | 982 | 314.9 | 17.6 | 18.1 | 30:25 |
| San Francisco | 945 | 313.3 | 19.1 | 15.7 | 28:47 |
| St. Louis | 1053 | 302.9 | 18.1 | 18.2 | 31:01 |
| Seattle | 964 | 297.8 | 19.4 | 16.2 | 27:33 |
| Chicago | 936 | 289.4 | 20.9 | 16.4 | 29:31 |
| Arizona | 931 | 269.3 | 18.1 | 15.1 | 26:23 |
| Carolina | 962 | 258.4 | 12.2 | 14.1 | 27:24 |

## NFC Total Defense

| | Opp Total Plays | Opp Yds/Game | Opp Yds/Play | Opp Pts/Game |
|---|---|---|---|---|
| New Orleans | 948 | 306.2 | 5.2 | 19.2 |
| Green Bay | 969 | 309.1 | 5.1 | 15.0 |
| NY Giants | 974 | 310.8 | 5.1 | 21.7 |
| Minnesota | 977 | 312.6 | 5.1 | 21.8 |
| Chicago | 1002 | 314.3 | 5.0 | 17.9 |
| Philadelphia | 998 | 327.2 | 5.2 | 23.6 |
| San Francisco | 1033 | 327.8 | 5.1 | 21.6 |
| Atlanta | 957 | 332.4 | 5.6 | 18.0 |
| Tampa Bay | 991 | 332.7 | 5.4 | 19.9 |
| Carolina | 1060 | 335.9 | 5.1 | 25.5 |
| St. Louis | 1017 | 336.8 | 5.3 | 20.5 |
| Detroit | 1005 | 343.6 | 5.5 | 23.1 |
| Dallas | 977 | 351.8 | 5.8 | 27.2 |
| Seattle | 1074 | 368.6 | 5.5 | 25.4 |
| Arizona | 1092 | 373.6 | 5.5 | 27.1 |
| Washington | 1051 | 389.2 | 5.9 | 23.6 |

## Takeaways/Giveaways

### American Football Conference

| | Takeaways | | | Giveaways | | | Net Diff |
|---|---|---|---|---|---|---|---|
| | Int | Fum | Total | Int | Fum | Total | |
| New England | 25 | 13 | 38 | 5 | 5 | 10 | 28 |
| Pittsburgh | 21 | 14 | 35 | 9 | 9 | 18 | 17 |
| Kansas City | 14 | 9 | 23 | 8 | 6 | 14 | 9 |
| NY Jets | 12 | 18 | 30 | 14 | 7 | 21 | 9 |
| Baltimore | 19 | 8 | 27 | 10 | 10 | 20 | 7 |
| Houston | 13 | 5 | 18 | 12 | 6 | 18 | 0 |
| Cleveland | 19 | 9 | 28 | 18 | 11 | 29 | -1 |
| Oakland | 12 | 12 | 24 | 16 | 10 | 26 | -2 |
| Indianapolis | 10 | 11 | 21 | 17 | 8 | 25 | -4 |
| Tennessee | 17 | 8 | 25 | 15 | 14 | 29 | -4 |
| San Diego | 16 | 7 | 23 | 13 | 16 | 29 | -6 |
| Cincinnati | 16 | 10 | 26 | 20 | 14 | 34 | -8 |
| Denver | 10 | 8 | 18 | 12 | 15 | 27 | -9 |
| Miami | 11 | 8 | 19 | 21 | 10 | 31 | -12 |
| Jacksonville | 13 | 5 | 18 | 21 | 12 | 33 | -15 |
| Buffalo | 11 | 11 | 22 | 21 | 18 | 39 | -17 |

### National Football Conference

| | Takeaways | | | Giveaways | | | Net Diff |
|---|---|---|---|---|---|---|---|
| | Int | Fum | Total | Int | Fum | Total | |
| Atlanta | 22 | 9 | 31 | 9 | 8 | 17 | 14 |
| Green Bay | 24 | 8 | 32 | 13 | 9 | 22 | 10 |
| Philadelphia | 23 | 11 | 34 | 13 | 12 | 25 | 9 |
| Tampa Bay | 19 | 9 | 28 | 6 | 13 | 19 | 9 |
| St. Louis | 14 | 12 | 26 | 15 | 6 | 21 | 5 |
| Detroit | 14 | 15 | 29 | 16 | 9 | 25 | 4 |
| Chicago | 21 | 14 | 35 | 21 | 10 | 31 | 4 |
| Dallas | 20 | 10 | 30 | 19 | 11 | 30 | 0 |
| San Francisco | 15 | 7 | 22 | 15 | 8 | 23 | -1 |
| NY Giants | 16 | 23 | 39 | 25 | 17 | 42 | -3 |
| Washington | 14 | 13 | 27 | 19 | 12 | 31 | -4 |
| Arizona | 17 | 13 | 30 | 19 | 16 | 35 | -5 |
| New Orleans | 9 | 16 | 25 | 22 | 9 | 31 | -6 |
| Carolina | 17 | 12 | 29 | 21 | 16 | 37 | -8 |
| Seattle | 12 | 10 | 22 | 20 | 11 | 31 | -9 |
| Minnesota | 15 | 11 | 26 | 26 | 11 | 37 | -11 |

## Baltimore Ravens

| SCORING | Rush | TD Rec | Ret | PAT | FG | 2PT | Pts |
|---|---|---|---|---|---|---|---|
| Cundiff | 0 | 0 | 0 | 39 | 26 | 0 | 117 |
| Mason | 0 | 7 | 0 | 0 | 0 | 0 | 42 |
| Boldin | 0 | 7 | 0 | 0 | 0 | 0 | 42 |
| McGahee | 5 | 1 | 0 | 0 | 0 | 0 | 36 |
| Rice | 5 | 1 | 0 | 0 | 0 | 0 | 36 |
| Heap | 0 | 5 | 0 | 0 | 0 | 0 | 30 |
| Houshmandzadeh | 0 | 3 | 0 | 0 | 0 | 0 | 18 |

| RUSHING | No. | Yds | Avg | Lg | TD |
|---|---|---|---|---|---|
| Rice | 307 | 1220 | 4.0 | 50 | 5 |
| McGahee | 100 | 380 | 3.8 | 30 | 5 |

| PASSING | Att | Comp | Pct Comp | Yds | Avg Gain | TD | Int | Rating Pts |
|---|---|---|---|---|---|---|---|---|
| Flacco | 489 | 306 | 62.6 | 3622 | 7.4 | 25 | 10 | 93.6 |

| RECEIVING | No. | Yds | Avg | Lg | TD |
|---|---|---|---|---|---|
| Boldin | 64 | 837 | 13.1 | 61 | 7 |
| Mason | 61 | 802 | 13.1 | 42 | 7 |
| Heap | 40 | 599 | 15.0 | 65 | 5 |
| Rice | 63 | 556 | 8.8 | 34 | 1 |
| Houshmandzadeh | 30 | 398 | 13.3 | 56 | 3 |
| Dickson | 11 | 152 | 13.8 | 58 | 1 |

**INTERCEPTIONS:** Reed, 8

| PUNTING | No. | Yds | Avg | Net Avg | TB | In 20 | Lg | Blk |
|---|---|---|---|---|---|---|---|---|
| Koch | 81 | 3530 | 43.6 | 39.2 | 4 | 39 | 60 | 0 |

**SACKS:** Suggs, 11

## Cincinnati Bengals

| SCORING | Rush | TD Rec | Ret | PAT | FG | 2PT | Pts |
|---|---|---|---|---|---|---|---|
| Nugent | 0 | 0 | 0 | 17 | 15 | 0 | 62 |
| Owens | 0 | 9 | 0 | 0 | 0 | 0 | 54 |
| Benson | 7 | 1 | 0 | 0 | 0 | 1 | 50 |
| Stitser | 0 | 0 | 0 | 8 | 7 | 0 | 29 |
| Gresham | 0 | 4 | 0 | 0 | 0 | 1 | 26 |
| Ochocinco | 0 | 4 | 0 | 0 | 0 | 0 | 24 |
| J. Simpson | 0 | 3 | 0 | 0 | 0 | 0 | 18 |
| Shipley | 0 | 3 | 0 | 0 | 0 | 0 | 18 |

| RUSHING | No. | Yds | Avg | Lg | TD |
|---|---|---|---|---|---|
| Benson | 321 | 1111 | 3.5 | 26 | 7 |
| Scott | 61 | 299 | 4.9 | 18 | 1 |

| PASSING | Att | Comp | Pct Comp | Yds | Avg Gain | TD | Int | Rating Pts |
|---|---|---|---|---|---|---|---|---|
| Palmer | 586 | 362 | 61.8 | 3970 | 6.8 | 26 | 20 | 82.4 |

| RECEIVING | No. | Yds | Avg | Lg | TD |
|---|---|---|---|---|---|
| Owens | 72 | 983 | 13.7 | 78 | 9 |
| Ochocinco | 67 | 831 | 12.4 | 42 | 4 |
| Shipley | 52 | 600 | 11.5 | 64 | 3 |
| Gresham | 52 | 471 | 9.1 | 27 | 4 |
| Caldwell | 25 | 345 | 13.8 | 53 | 0 |
| J. Simpson | 20 | 277 | 13.9 | 59 | 3 |

**INTERCEPTIONS:** Hall, 4

| PUNTING | No. | Yds | Avg | Net Avg | TB | In 20 | Lg | Blk |
|---|---|---|---|---|---|---|---|---|
| Huber | 71 | 2992 | 42.1 | 38.7 | 6 | 28 | 72 | 1 |

**SACKS:** Dunlap, 9.5

## Buffalo Bills

| SCORING | Rush | TD Rec | Ret | PAT | FG | 2PT | Pts |
|---|---|---|---|---|---|---|---|
| Lindell | 0 | 0 | 0 | 31 | 16 | 0 | 79 |
| S. Johnson | 0 | 10 | 0 | 0 | 0 | 0 | 60 |
| F. Jackson | 5 | 2 | 0 | 0 | 0 | 0 | 42 |
| Evans | 0 | 4 | 0 | 0 | 0 | 0 | 24 |
| D. Nelson | 0 | 3 | 0 | 0 | 0 | 0 | 18 |
| Florence | 0 | 0 | 2 | 0 | 0 | 0 | 12 |
| Parrish | 0 | 2 | 0 | 0 | 0 | 0 | 12 |
| Spiller | 0 | 1 | 1 | 0 | 0 | 0 | 12 |

| RUSHING | No. | Yds | Avg | Lg | TD |
|---|---|---|---|---|---|
| F. Jackson | 222 | 927 | 4.2 | 39 | 5 |
| Spiller | 74 | 283 | 3.8 | 20 | 0 |

| PASSING | Att | Comp | Pct Comp | Yds | Avg Gain | TD | Int | Rating Pts |
|---|---|---|---|---|---|---|---|---|
| Fitzpatrick | 441 | 255 | 57.8 | 3000 | 6.8 | 23 | 15 | 81.8 |
| Edwards | 52 | 29 | 55.8 | 241 | 4.6 | 1 | 2 | 58.3 |

| RECEIVING | No. | Yds | Avg | Lg | TD |
|---|---|---|---|---|---|
| S. Johnson | 82 | 1073 | 13.1 | 45 | 10 |
| Evans | 37 | 578 | 15.6 | 54 | 4 |
| Parrish | 33 | 400 | 12.1 | 37 | 2 |
| D. Nelson | 31 | 353 | 11.4 | 37 | 3 |
| F. Jackson | 31 | 215 | 6.9 | 65 | 2 |
| D. Jones | 18 | 213 | 11.8 | 40 | 1 |

**INTERCEPTIONS:** Florence, 3

| PUNTING | No. | Yds | Avg | Net Avg | TB | In 20 | Lg | Blk |
|---|---|---|---|---|---|---|---|---|
| Moorman | 75 | 3181 | 42.4 | 36.6 | 7 | 17 | 61 | 0 |

**SACKS:** K. Williams, 5.5

## Cleveland Browns

| SCORING | Rush | TD Rec | Ret | PAT | FG | 2PT | Pts |
|---|---|---|---|---|---|---|---|
| Dawson | 0 | 0 | 0 | 28 | 23 | 0 | 97 |
| Hillis | 11 | 2 | 0 | 0 | 0 | 0 | 78 |
| Watson | 0 | 3 | 0 | 0 | 0 | 0 | 18 |
| Robiskie | 0 | 3 | 0 | 0 | 0 | 0 | 18 |
| Bowens | 0 | 0 | 2 | 0 | 0 | 0 | 12 |
| Massaquoi | 0 | 2 | 0 | 0 | 0 | 0 | 12 |

| RUSHING | No. | Yds | Avg | Lg | TD |
|---|---|---|---|---|---|
| Hillis | 270 | 1177 | 4.4 | 48 | 11 |

| PASSING | Att | Comp | Pct Comp | Yds | Avg Gain | TD | Int | Rating Pts |
|---|---|---|---|---|---|---|---|---|
| McCoy | 222 | 135 | 60.8 | 1576 | 7.1 | 6 | 9 | 74.5 |
| Delhomme | 149 | 93 | 62.4 | 872 | 5.9 | 2 | 7 | 63.4 |
| Wallace | 101 | 64 | 63.4 | 694 | 6.9 | 4 | 2 | 88.5 |

| RECEIVING | No. | Yds | Avg | Lg | TD |
|---|---|---|---|---|---|
| Watson | 68 | 763 | 11.2 | 44 | 3 |
| Massaquoi | 36 | 483 | 13.4 | 41 | 2 |
| Hillis | 61 | 477 | 7.8 | 47 | 2 |
| Stuckey | 40 | 346 | 8.7 | 25 | 0 |
| E. Moore | 16 | 322 | 20.1 | 49 | 1 |
| Robiskie | 29 | 310 | 10.7 | 46 | 3 |
| Cribbs | 23 | 292 | 12.7 | 65 | 1 |

**INTERCEPTIONS:** Haden, 6

| PUNTING | No. | Yds | Avg | Net Avg | TB | In 20 | Lg | Blk |
|---|---|---|---|---|---|---|---|---|
| Hodges | 78 | 3424 | 43.9 | 39.0 | 5 | 29 | 59 | 0 |

**SACKS:** Benard, 7.5

## Denver Broncos

### SCORING

| | | TD | | | | | |
|---|---|---|---|---|---|---|---|
| | Rush | Rec | Ret | PAT | FG | 2PT | Pts |
| Prater | 0 | 0 | 0 | 28 | 16 | 0 | 76 |
| Lloyd | 0 | 11 | 0 | 0 | 0 | 0 | 66 |
| Moreno | 5 | 3 | 0 | 0 | 0 | 0 | 48 |
| Tebow | 6 | 0 | 0 | 0 | 0 | 0 | 36 |
| Hauschka | 0 | 2 | 0 | 10 | 6 | 0 | 28 |
| Buckhalter | 2 | 2 | 0 | 0 | 0 | 0 | 24 |
| Royal | 0 | 3 | 0 | 0 | 0 | 0 | 18 |

### RUSHING

| | No. | Yds | Avg | Lg | TD |
|---|---|---|---|---|---|
| Moreno | 182 | 779 | 4.3 | 35 | 5 |
| Tebow | 43 | 227 | 5.3 | 40 | 6 |

### PASSING

| | Att | Comp | Pct Comp | Yds | Avg Gain | TD | Int | Rating Pts |
|---|---|---|---|---|---|---|---|---|
| Orton | 498 | 293 | 58.8 | 3653 | 7.3 | 20 | 9 | 87.5 |
| Tebow | 82 | 41 | 50.0 | 654 | 8.0 | 5 | 3 | 82.1 |

### RECEIVING

| | No. | Yds | Avg | Lg | TD |
|---|---|---|---|---|---|
| Lloyd | 77 | 1448 | 18.8 | 71 | 11 |
| Gaffney | 65 | 875 | 13.5 | 50 | 2 |
| Royal | 59 | 627 | 10.6 | 41 | 3 |
| Moreno | 37 | 372 | 10.1 | 45 | 3 |
| D. Thomas | 22 | 283 | 12.9 | 31 | 2 |

**INTERCEPTIONS:** Bailey, R. Hill, S. Thompson, 2

### PUNTING

| | No. | Yds | Avg | Net Avg | TB | In 20 | Lg | Blk |
|---|---|---|---|---|---|---|---|---|
| B. Colquitt | 86 | 3835 | 44.6 | 36.6 | 7 | 19 | 63 | 0 |

**SACKS:** D.J. Williams, 5.5

## Houston Texans

### SCORING

| | | TD | | | | | |
|---|---|---|---|---|---|---|---|
| | Rush | Rec | Ret | PAT | FG | 2PT | Pts |
| Rackers | 0 | 0 | 0 | 43 | 27 | 0 | 124 |
| Foster | 16 | 2 | 0 | 0 | 0 | 0 | 108 |
| A. Johnson | 0 | 8 | 0 | 0 | 0 | 0 | 48 |
| Walter | 0 | 5 | 0 | 0 | 0 | 0 | 30 |
| Ward | 4 | 0 | 0 | 0 | 0 | 0 | 24 |
| Dreessen | 0 | 4 | 0 | 0 | 0 | 0 | 24 |
| J. Jones | 0 | 3 | 0 | 0 | 0 | 1 | 20 |
| Daniels | 0 | 2 | 0 | 0 | 0 | 0 | 12 |

### RUSHING

| | No. | Yds | Avg | Lg | TD |
|---|---|---|---|---|---|
| Foster | 327 | 1616 | 4.9 | 74 | 16 |
| Ward | 50 | 315 | 6.3 | 38 | 4 |

### PASSING

| | Att | Comp | Pct Comp | Yds | Avg Gain | TD | Int | Rating Pts |
|---|---|---|---|---|---|---|---|---|
| Schaub | 574 | 365 | 63.6 | 4370 | 7.6 | 24 | 12 | 92.0 |

### RECEIVING

| | No. | Yds | Avg | Lg | TD |
|---|---|---|---|---|---|
| A. Johnson | 86 | 1216 | 14.1 | 60 | 8 |
| Walter | 51 | 621 | 12.2 | 35 | 5 |
| Foster | 66 | 604 | 9.2 | 50 | 2 |
| J. Jones | 51 | 562 | 11.0 | 47 | 3 |
| Dreessen | 36 | 518 | 14.4 | 43 | 4 |
| Daniels | 38 | 471 | 12.4 | 31 | 2 |

**INTERCEPTIONS:** J. Allen, Nolan, Quin, 3

### PUNTING

| | No. | Yds | Avg | Net Avg | TB | In 20 | Lg | Blk |
|---|---|---|---|---|---|---|---|---|
| Turk | 63 | 2650 | 42.1 | 36.8 | 5 | 19 | 60 | 0 |

**SACKS:** M. Williams, 8.5

## Indianapolis Colts

### SCORING

| | | TD | | | | | |
|---|---|---|---|---|---|---|---|
| | Rush | Rec | Ret | PAT | FG | 2PT | Pts |
| Vinatieri | 0 | 0 | 0 | 51 | 26 | 0 | 129 |
| Collie | 0 | 8 | 0 | 0 | 0 | 0 | 48 |
| Wayne | 0 | 6 | 0 | 0 | 0 | 0 | 36 |
| Garcon | 0 | 6 | 0 | 0 | 0 | 0 | 36 |
| Ja. James | 6 | 0 | 0 | 0 | 0 | 0 | 36 |
| White | 0 | 5 | 0 | 0 | 0 | 0 | 30 |
| Addai | 4 | 0 | 0 | 0 | 0 | 0 | 24 |
| Tamme | 0 | 4 | 0 | 0 | 0 | 0 | 24 |
| D. Clark | 0 | 3 | 0 | 0 | 0 | 0 | 18 |

### RUSHING

| | No. | Yds | Avg | Lg | TD |
|---|---|---|---|---|---|
| D. Brown | 129 | 497 | 3.9 | 49 | 2 |
| Addai | 116 | 495 | 4.3 | 46 | 4 |

### PASSING

| | Att | Comp | Pct Comp | Yds | Avg Gain | TD | Int | Rating Pts |
|---|---|---|---|---|---|---|---|---|
| Manning | 679 | 450 | 66.3 | 4700 | 6.9 | 33 | 17 | 91.9 |

### RECEIVING

| | No. | Yds | Avg | Lg | TD |
|---|---|---|---|---|---|
| Wayne | 111 | 1355 | 12.2 | 50 | 6 |
| Garcon | 67 | 784 | 11.7 | 57 | 6 |
| Collie | 58 | 649 | 11.2 | 73 | 8 |
| Tamme | 67 | 631 | 9.4 | 30 | 4 |
| White | 36 | 355 | 9.9 | 33 | 5 |
| D. Clark | 37 | 347 | 9.4 | 50 | 3 |

**INTERCEPTIONS:** Francisco, Hayden, Powers, 2

### PUNTING

| | No. | Yds | Avg | Net Avg | TB | In 20 | Lg | Blk |
|---|---|---|---|---|---|---|---|---|
| McAfee | 65 | 2731 | 42.0 | 35.4 | 7 | 21 | 66 | 0 |

**SACKS:** Mathis, 11.0

## Jacksonville Jaguars

### SCORING

| | | TD | | | | | |
|---|---|---|---|---|---|---|---|
| | Rush | Rec | Ret | PAT | FG | 2PT | Pts |
| Scobee | 0 | 0 | 0 | 41 | 22 | 0 | 107 |
| M. Lewis | 0 | 10 | 0 | 0 | 0 | 0 | 60 |
| Jones-Drew | 5 | 2 | 0 | 0 | 0 | 0 | 42 |
| Sims-Walker | 0 | 7 | 0 | 0 | 0 | 0 | 42 |
| Garrard | 5 | 0 | 0 | 0 | 0 | 0 | 30 |
| M. Thomas | 0 | 4 | 1 | 0 | 0 | 0 | 30 |
| R. Jennings | 4 | 0 | 0 | 0 | 0 | 0 | 24 |

### RUSHING

| | No. | Yds | Avg | Lg | TD |
|---|---|---|---|---|---|
| Jones-Drew | 299 | 1324 | 4.4 | 37 | 5 |
| R. Jennings | 84 | 459 | 5.5 | 74 | 4 |
| Garrard | 66 | 279 | 4.2 | 25 | 5 |

### PASSING

| | Att | Comp | Pct Comp | Yds | Avg Gain | TD | Int | Rating Pts |
|---|---|---|---|---|---|---|---|---|
| Garrard | 366 | 236 | 64.5 | 2734 | 7.5 | 23 | 15 | 90.8 |

### RECEIVING

| | No. | Yds | Avg | Lg | TD |
|---|---|---|---|---|---|
| M. Thomas | 66 | 820 | 12.4 | 50 | 4 |
| M. Lewis | 58 | 700 | 12.1 | 42 | 10 |
| Sims-Walker | 43 | 562 | 13.1 | 39 | 7 |
| Jones-Drew | 34 | 317 | 9.3 | 75 | 2 |
| J. Hill | 11 | 248 | 22.5 | 48 | 1 |
| R. Jennings | 26 | 223 | 8.6 | 25 | 0 |
| Z. Miller | 20 | 216 | 10.8 | 52 | 1 |

**INTERCEPTIONS:** Cox, 4

### PUNTING

| | No. | Yds | Avg | Net Avg | TB | In 20 | Lg | Blk |
|---|---|---|---|---|---|---|---|---|
| Podlesh | 57 | 2496 | 43.8 | 39.2 | 7 | 26 | 63 | 0 |

**SACKS:** Mincey, 5.0

### Kansas City Chiefs

| SCORING | Rush | Rec | Ret | PAT | FG | 2PT | Pts |
|---|---|---|---|---|---|---|---|
| Succop | 0 | 0 | 0 | 42 | 20 | 0 | 102 |
| Bowe | 0 | 15 | 0 | 0 | 0 | 0 | 90 |
| J. Charles | 5 | 3 | 0 | 0 | 0 | 0 | 48 |
| T. Jones | 6 | 0 | 0 | 0 | 0 | 0 | 36 |
| Moeaki | 0 | 3 | 0 | 0 | 0 | 0 | 18 |
| Pope | 0 | 2 | 0 | 0 | 0 | 0 | 12 |
| McCluster | 0 | 1 | 1 | 0 | 0 | 0 | 12 |

| RUSHING | No. | Yds | Avg | Lg | TD |
|---|---|---|---|---|---|
| J. Charles | 230 | 1467 | 6.4 | 80 | 5 |
| T. Jones | 245 | 896 | 3.7 | 70 | 6 |

| PASSING | Att | Comp | Pct Comp | Yds | Avg Gain | TD | Int | Rating Pts |
|---|---|---|---|---|---|---|---|---|
| Cassel | 450 | 262 | 58.2 | 3116 | 6.9 | 27 | 7 | 93.0 |

| RECEIVING | No. | Yds | Avg | Lg | TD |
|---|---|---|---|---|---|
| Bowe | 72 | 1162 | 16.1 | 75 | 15 |
| Moeaki | 47 | 556 | 11.8 | 34 | 3 |
| J. Charles | 45 | 468 | 10.4 | 31 | 3 |
| Chambers | 22 | 213 | 9.7 | 26 | 1 |
| McCluster | 21 | 209 | 10.0 | 31 | 1 |
| Copper | 18 | 157 | 8.7 | 20 | 0 |

INTERCEPTIONS: Berry, 4

| PUNTING | No. | Yds | Avg | Net Avg | TB | In 20 | Lg | Blk |
|---|---|---|---|---|---|---|---|---|
| D. Colquitt | 88 | 3908 | 44.4 | 38.0 | 10 | 33 | 72 | 1 |

SACKS: Hali, 14.5

### Miami Dolphins

| SCORING | Rush | Rec | Ret | PAT | FG | 2PT | Pts |
|---|---|---|---|---|---|---|---|
| Carpenter | 0 | 0 | 0 | 25 | 30 | 0 | 115 |
| R. Brown | 5 | 0 | 0 | 0 | 0 | 0 | 30 |
| Bess | 0 | 5 | 0 | 0 | 0 | 0 | 30 |
| Fasano | 0 | 4 | 0 | 0 | 0 | 0 | 24 |
| R. Williams | 2 | 1 | 0 | 0 | 0 | 0 | 18 |
| Marshall | 0 | 3 | 0 | 0 | 0 | 0 | 18 |
| Cobbs | 0 | 2 | 0 | 0 | 0 | 0 | 12 |

| RUSHING | No. | Yds | Avg | Lg | TD |
|---|---|---|---|---|---|
| R. Brown | 200 | 734 | 3.7 | 51 | 5 |
| R. Williams | 159 | 637 | 4.2 | 45 | 2 |

| PASSING | Att | Comp | Pct Comp | Yds | Avg Gain | TD | Int | Rating Pts |
|---|---|---|---|---|---|---|---|---|
| Henne | 490 | 301 | 61.4 | 3301 | 6.7 | 15 | 19 | 75.4 |
| Thigpen | 62 | 33 | 53.2 | 435 | 7.0 | 2 | 2 | 73.0 |

| RECEIVING | No. | Yds | Avg | Lg | TD |
|---|---|---|---|---|---|
| Marshall | 86 | 1014 | 11.8 | 46 | 3 |
| Bess | 79 | 820 | 10.4 | 29 | 5 |
| Hartline | 43 | 615 | 14.3 | 54 | 1 |
| Fasano | 39 | 528 | 13.5 | 31 | 4 |
| R. Brown | 33 | 242 | 7.3 | 24 | 0 |
| R. Williams | 19 | 141 | 7.4 | 28 | 1 |

INTERCEPTIONS: Allen, 3

| PUNTING | No. | Yds | Avg | Net Avg | TB | In 20 | Lg | Blk |
|---|---|---|---|---|---|---|---|---|
| Fields | 73 | 3369 | 46.2 | 38.8 | 4 | 31 | 69 | 2 |

SACKS: Wake, 14.0

### New England Patriots

| SCORING | Rush | Rec | Ret | PAT | FG | 2PT | Pts |
|---|---|---|---|---|---|---|---|
| Green-Ellis | 13 | 0 | 0 | 0 | 0 | 0 | 78 |
| Graham | 0 | 0 | 0 | 35 | 12 | 0 | 71 |
| Gronkowski | 0 | 10 | 0 | 0 | 0 | 0 | 60 |
| Gostkowski | 0 | 0 | 0 | 26 | 10 | 0 | 56 |
| Welker | 0 | 7 | 0 | 1 | 0 | 0 | 43 |
| Woodhead | 5 | 1 | 0 | 0 | 0 | 0 | 36 |
| Hernandez | 0 | 6 | 0 | 0 | 0 | 0 | 36 |
| Branch | 0 | 5 | 0 | 0 | 0 | 0 | 30 |
| Tate | 0 | 3 | 2 | 0 | 0 | 0 | 30 |
| Moss | 0 | 3 | 0 | 0 | 0 | 0 | 18 |

| RUSHING | No. | Yds | Avg | Lg | TD |
|---|---|---|---|---|---|
| Green-Ellis | 229 | 1008 | 4.4 | 33 | 13 |
| Woodhead | 97 | 547 | 5.6 | 36 | 5 |

| PASSING | Att | Comp | Pct Comp | Yds | Avg Gain | TD | Int | Rating Pts |
|---|---|---|---|---|---|---|---|---|
| Brady | 492 | 324 | 65.9 | 3900 | 7.9 | 36 | 4 | 111.0 |

| RECEIVING | No. | Yds | Avg | Lg | TD |
|---|---|---|---|---|---|
| Welker | 86 | 848 | 9.9 | 35 | 7 |
| Branch | 48 | 706 | 14.7 | 79 | 5 |
| Hernandez | 45 | 563 | 12.5 | 46 | 6 |
| Gronkowski | 42 | 546 | 13.0 | 28 | 10 |
| Tate | 24 | 432 | 18.0 | 65 | 3 |
| Woodhead | 34 | 379 | 11.1 | 50 | 1 |
| Moss | 9 | 139 | 15.4 | 35 | 3 |

INTERCEPTIONS: McCourty, 7

| PUNTING | No. | Yds | Avg | Net Avg | TB | In 20 | Lg | Blk |
|---|---|---|---|---|---|---|---|---|
| Mesko | 58 | 2505 | 43.2 | 38.4 | 5 | 19 | 65 | 0 |

SACKS: Wright, 5.5

### New York Jets

| SCORING | Rush | Rec | Ret | PAT | FG | 2PT | Pts |
|---|---|---|---|---|---|---|---|
| Folk | 0 | 0 | 0 | 37 | 30 | 0 | 127 |
| Edwards | 0 | 7 | 0 | 0 | 0 | 1 | 44 |
| Tomlinson | 6 | 0 | 0 | 0 | 0 | 0 | 36 |
| Holmes | 0 | 6 | 0 | 0 | 0 | 0 | 36 |
| Keller | 0 | 5 | 0 | 0 | 0 | 0 | 30 |
| B. Smith | 1 | 0 | 2 | 0 | 0 | 0 | 18 |
| Sanchez | 3 | 0 | 0 | 0 | 0 | 0 | 18 |
| Cotchery | 0 | 2 | 0 | 0 | 0 | 0 | 12 |
| Lowery | 0 | 0 | 2 | 0 | 0 | 0 | 12 |
| Greene | 2 | 0 | 0 | 0 | 0 | 0 | 12 |

| RUSHING | No. | Yds | Avg | Lg | TD |
|---|---|---|---|---|---|
| Tomlinson | 219 | 914 | 4.2 | 31 | 6 |
| Greene | 185 | 766 | 4.1 | 23 | 2 |
| B. Smith | 38 | 299 | 7.9 | 53 | 1 |

| PASSING | Att | Comp | Pct Comp | Yds | Avg Gain | TD | Int | Rating Pts |
|---|---|---|---|---|---|---|---|---|
| Sanchez | 507 | 278 | 54.8 | 3291 | 6.5 | 17 | 13 | 75.3 |

| RECEIVING | No. | Yds | Avg | Lg | TD |
|---|---|---|---|---|---|
| Edwards | 53 | 904 | 17.1 | 74 | 7 |
| Holmes | 52 | 746 | 14.3 | 52 | 6 |
| Keller | 55 | 687 | 12.5 | 41 | 5 |
| Cotchery | 41 | 433 | 10.6 | 49 | 2 |
| Tomlinson | 52 | 368 | 7.1 | 21 | 0 |

INTERCEPTIONS: Cromartie, Lowery, 3

| PUNTING | No. | Yds | Avg | Net Avg | TB | In 20 | Lg | Blk |
|---|---|---|---|---|---|---|---|---|
| Weatherford | 84 | 3581 | 42.6 | 38.1 | 4 | 42 | 61 | 0 |

SACKS: Thomas, 6.0

## Oakland Raiders

| SCORING | Rush | Rec | Ret | PAT | FG | 2PT | Pts |
|---|---|---|---|---|---|---|---|
| Janikowski | 0 | 0 | 0 | 43 | 33 | 0 | 142 |
| McFadden | 7 | 3 | 0 | 0 | 0 | 0 | 60 |
| M. Bush | 8 | 0 | 0 | 0 | 0 | 0 | 48 |
| Ford | 2 | 2 | 3 | 0 | 0 | 0 | 42 |
| Z. Miller | 0 | 5 | 0 | 0 | 0 | 0 | 30 |
| Reece | 1 | 3 | 0 | 0 | 0 | 0 | 24 |
| Murphy | 0 | 2 | 0 | 0 | 0 | 0 | 12 |

| RUSHING | No. | Yds | Avg | Lg | TD |
|---|---|---|---|---|---|
| McFadden | 223 | 1157 | 5.2 | 57 | 7 |
| M. Bush | 158 | 655 | 4.1 | 30 | 8 |
| Campbell | 47 | 222 | 4.7 | 24 | 1 |

| PASSING | Att | Comp | Pct Comp | Yds | Avg Gain | TD | Int | Rating Pts |
|---|---|---|---|---|---|---|---|---|
| Campbell | 329 | 194 | 59.0 | 2387 | 7.3 | 13 | 8 | 84.5 |
| Gradkowski | 157 | 83 | 52.9 | 1059 | 6.7 | 5 | 7 | 66.3 |

| RECEIVING | No. | Yds | Avg | Lg | TD |
|---|---|---|---|---|---|
| Z. Miller | 60 | 685 | 11.4 | 43 | 5 |
| Murphy | 41 | 609 | 14.9 | 70 | 2 |
| McFadden | 47 | 507 | 10.8 | 67 | 3 |
| Ford | 25 | 470 | 18.8 | 52 | 2 |
| Heyward-Bey | 26 | 366 | 14.1 | 69 | 1 |
| Reece | 25 | 333 | 13.3 | 73 | 3 |

**INTERCEPTIONS:** Huff, 3

| PUNTING | No. | Yds | Avg | Net Avg | TB | In 20 | Lg | Blk |
|---|---|---|---|---|---|---|---|---|
| Lechler | 77 | 3618 | 47.0 | 40.8 | 4 | 27 | 68 | 0 |

**SACKS:** Wimbley, 9.0

## San Diego Chargers

| SCORING | Rush | Rec | Ret | PAT | FG | 2PT | Pts |
|---|---|---|---|---|---|---|---|
| Kaeding | 0 | 0 | 0 | 40 | 23 | 0 | 109 |
| Tolbert | 11 | 0 | 0 | 0 | 0 | 1 | 68 |
| Gates | 0 | 10 | 0 | 0 | 0 | 0 | 60 |
| Mathews | 7 | 0 | 0 | 0 | 0 | 0 | 42 |
| Floyd | 0 | 6 | 0 | 0 | 0 | 0 | 36 |
| K. Brown | 0 | 0 | 0 | 8 | 4 | 0 | 20 |

| RUSHING | No. | Yds | Avg | Lg | TD |
|---|---|---|---|---|---|
| Tolbert | 182 | 735 | 4.0 | 36 | 11 |
| Mathews | 158 | 678 | 4.3 | 31 | 7 |
| Sproles | 50 | 267 | 5.3 | 34 | 0 |

| PASSING | Att | Comp | Pct Comp | Yds | Avg Gain | TD | Int | Rating Pts |
|---|---|---|---|---|---|---|---|---|
| Rivers | 541 | 357 | 66.0 | 4710 | 8.7 | 30 | 13 | 101.8 |

| RECEIVING | No. | Yds | Avg | Lg | TD |
|---|---|---|---|---|---|
| Gates | 50 | 782 | 15.6 | 48 | 10 |
| Floyd | 37 | 717 | 19.4 | 55 | 6 |
| Sproles | 59 | 520 | 8.8 | 57 | 2 |
| Crayton | 28 | 514 | 18.4 | 49 | 1 |
| Naanee | 23 | 371 | 16.1 | 59 | 1 |
| Ajirotutu | 13 | 262 | 20.2 | 55 | 2 |
| B. Davis | 21 | 259 | 12.3 | 49 | 1 |
| V. Jackson | 14 | 248 | 17.7 | 58 | 3 |
| McMichael | 20 | 221 | 11.1 | 28 | 2 |

**INTERCEPTIONS:** Cason, 4

| PUNTING | No. | Yds | Avg | Net Avg | TB | In 20 | Lg | Blk |
|---|---|---|---|---|---|---|---|---|
| Scifres | 52 | 2430 | 46.7 | 33.1 | 9 | 13 | 67 | 4 |

**SACKS:** Phillips, 11.0

## Pittsburgh Steelers

| SCORING | Rush | Rec | Ret | PAT | FG | 2PT | Pts |
|---|---|---|---|---|---|---|---|
| Mendenhall | 13 | 0 | 0 | 0 | 0 | 0 | 78 |
| Reed | 0 | 0 | 0 | 19 | 15 | 0 | 64 |
| Suisham | 0 | 0 | 0 | 19 | 14 | 0 | 61 |
| M. Wallace | 0 | 10 | 0 | 0 | 0 | 0 | 60 |
| Ward | 0 | 5 | 0 | 0 | 0 | 0 | 30 |

| RUSHING | No. | Yds | Avg | Lg | TD |
|---|---|---|---|---|---|
| Mendenhall | 324 | 1273 | 3.9 | 50 | 13 |
| Redman | 52 | 247 | 4.8 | 23 | 0 |
| Roethlisberger | 34 | 176 | 5.2 | 31 | 2 |

| PASSING | Att | Comp | Pct Comp | Yds | Avg Gain | TD | Int | Rating Pts |
|---|---|---|---|---|---|---|---|---|
| Roethlisberger | 389 | 240 | 61.7 | 3200 | 8.2 | 17 | 5 | 97.0 |
| Batch | 49 | 29 | 59.2 | 352 | 7.2 | 3 | 3 | 76.2 |
| Dixon | 32 | 22 | 68.8 | 254 | 7.9 | 0 | 1 | 79.4 |

| RECEIVING | No. | Yds | Avg | Lg | TD |
|---|---|---|---|---|---|
| M. Wallace | 60 | 1257 | 21.0 | 56 | 10 |
| Ward | 59 | 755 | 12.8 | 43 | 5 |
| H. Miller | 42 | 512 | 12.2 | 36 | 2 |
| Sanders | 28 | 376 | 13.4 | 35 | 2 |
| Randle El | 22 | 253 | 11.5 | 34 | 0 |
| Moore | 26 | 205 | 7.9 | 29 | 0 |

**INTERCEPTIONS:** Polamalu, 7

| PUNTING | No. | Yds | Avg | Net Avg | TB | In 20 | Lg | Blk |
|---|---|---|---|---|---|---|---|---|
| Sepulveda | 56 | 2550 | 45.5 | 39.1 | 8 | 16 | 62 | 0 |
| Kapinos | 14 | 576 | 41.1 | 32.3 | 2 | 5 | 59 | 0 |

**SACKS:** Harrison, 10.5

## Tennessee Titans

| SCORING | Rush | Rec | Ret | PAT | FG | 2PT | Pts |
|---|---|---|---|---|---|---|---|
| Bironas | 0 | 0 | 0 | 38 | 24 | 0 | 110 |
| C. Johnson | 11 | 1 | 0 | 0 | 0 | 0 | 72 |
| Britt | 0 | 9 | 0 | 0 | 0 | 1 | 56 |
| N. Washington | 0 | 6 | 0 | 0 | 0 | 0 | 36 |
| Scaife | 0 | 4 | 0 | 0 | 0 | 0 | 24 |
| Stevens | 0 | 2 | 0 | 0 | 0 | 0 | 12 |
| Ringer | 2 | 0 | 0 | 0 | 0 | 0 | 12 |
| Mariani | 0 | 0 | 2 | 0 | 0 | 0 | 12 |

| RUSHING | No. | Yds | Avg | Lg | TD |
|---|---|---|---|---|---|
| C. Johnson | 316 | 1364 | 4.3 | 76 | 11 |
| Ringer | 51 | 239 | 4.7 | 54 | 2 |
| V. Young | 25 | 125 | 5.0 | 20 | 0 |

| PASSING | Att | Comp | Pct Comp | Yds | Avg Gain | TD | Int | Rating Pts |
|---|---|---|---|---|---|---|---|---|
| Collins | 278 | 160 | 57.6 | 1823 | 6.6 | 14 | 8 | 82.2 |
| V. Young | 156 | 93 | 59.6 | 1255 | 8.0 | 10 | 3 | 98.6 |

| RECEIVING | No. | Yds | Avg | Lg | TD |
|---|---|---|---|---|---|
| Britt | 42 | 775 | 18.5 | 80 | 9 |
| N. Washington | 42 | 687 | 16.4 | 71 | 6 |
| Cook | 29 | 361 | 12.4 | 36 | 1 |
| Scaife | 36 | 318 | 8.8 | 30 | 4 |
| Gage | 20 | 266 | 13.3 | 30 | 1 |
| C. Johnson | 44 | 245 | 5.6 | 25 | 1 |
| D. Williams | 16 | 219 | 13.7 | 39 | 0 |

**INTERCEPTIONS:** Griffin, 4

| PUNTING | No. | Yds | Avg | Net Avg | TB | In 20 | Lg | Blk |
|---|---|---|---|---|---|---|---|---|
| Kern | 77 | 3302 | 42.9 | 39.1 | 4 | 24 | 68 | 0 |

**SACKS:** Babin, 12.5

## Arizona Cardinals

| SCORING | Rush | TD Rec | Ret | PAT | FG | 2PT | Pts |
|---|---|---|---|---|---|---|---|
| Feely | 1 | 0 | 0 | 29 | 24 | 0 | 107 |
| Fitzgerald | 0 | 6 | 0 | 0 | 0 | 1 | 38 |
| Hightower | 5 | 0 | 0 | 0 | 0 | 0 | 30 |
| Stephens-Howling | 1 | 0 | 2 | 0 | 0 | 0 | 18 |
| Rhodes | 0 | 0 | 2 | 0 | 0 | 0 | 12 |
| Breaston | 0 | 1 | 1 | 0 | 0 | 0 | 12 |
| Rodgers-Cromartie | 0 | 0 | 2 | 0 | 0 | 0 | 12 |
| Wells | 2 | 0 | 0 | 0 | 0 | 0 | 12 |
| A. Roberts | 0 | 2 | 0 | 0 | 0 | 0 | 12 |

| RUSHING | No. | Yds | Avg | Lg | TD |
|---|---|---|---|---|---|
| Hightower | 153 | 736 | 4.8 | 80 | 5 |
| Wells | 116 | 397 | 3.4 | 24 | 2 |

| PASSING | Att | Comp | Pct Comp | Yds | Avg Gain | TD | Int | Rating Pts |
|---|---|---|---|---|---|---|---|---|
| Anderson | 327 | 169 | 51.7 | 2065 | 6.3 | 7 | 10 | 65.9 |
| Skelton | 126 | 60 | 47.6 | 662 | 5.3 | 2 | 2 | 62.3 |
| Hall | 78 | 39 | 50.0 | 370 | 4.7 | 1 | 6 | 35.7 |

| RECEIVING | No. | Yds | Avg | Lg | TD |
|---|---|---|---|---|---|
| Fitzgerald | 90 | 1137 | 12.6 | 41 | 6 |
| Breaston | 47 | 718 | 15.3 | 37 | 1 |
| A. Roberts | 24 | 307 | 12.8 | 74 | 2 |
| Doucet | 26 | 291 | 11.2 | 36 | 1 |

INTERCEPTIONS: Rhodes, 4

| PUNTING | No. | Yds | Avg | Net Avg | TB | In 20 | Lg | Blk |
|---|---|---|---|---|---|---|---|---|
| Graham | 94 | 4080 | 43.4 | 36.6 | 9 | 29 | 65 | 0 |

SACKS: Campbell, 6.0

## Atlanta Falcons

| SCORING | Rush | TD Rec | Ret | PAT | FG | 2PT | Pts |
|---|---|---|---|---|---|---|---|
| Bryant | 0 | 0 | 0 | 44 | 28 | 0 | 128 |
| Turner | 12 | 0 | 0 | 0 | 0 | 0 | 72 |
| R. White | 0 | 10 | 0 | 0 | 0 | 2 | 64 |
| Gonzalez | 0 | 6 | 0 | 0 | 0 | 0 | 36 |
| Snelling | 2 | 3 | 0 | 0 | 0 | 0 | 30 |
| Finneran | 0 | 3 | 0 | 0 | 0 | 0 | 18 |
| Jenkins | 0 | 2 | 0 | 0 | 0 | 0 | 12 |
| Weems | 0 | 0 | 2 | 0 | 0 | 0 | 12 |

| RUSHING | No. | Yds | Avg | Lg | TD |
|---|---|---|---|---|---|
| Turner | 334 | 1371 | 4.1 | 55 | 12 |
| Snelling | 87 | 324 | 3.7 | 30 | 2 |

| PASSING | Att | Comp | Pct Comp | Yds | Avg Gain | TD | Int | Rating Pts |
|---|---|---|---|---|---|---|---|---|
| Ryan | 571 | 357 | 62.5 | 3705 | 6.5 | 28 | 9 | 91.0 |

| RECEIVING | No. | Yds | Avg | Lg | TD |
|---|---|---|---|---|---|
| R. White | 115 | 1389 | 12.1 | 46 | 10 |
| Gonzalez | 70 | 656 | 9.4 | 34 | 6 |
| Jenkins | 41 | 505 | 12.3 | 43 | 2 |
| Snelling | 44 | 303 | 6.9 | 28 | 3 |
| Douglas | 22 | 294 | 13.4 | 46 | 1 |
| Finneran | 19 | 166 | 8.7 | 21 | 3 |

INTERCEPTIONS: Grimes, W. Moore, 5

| PUNTING | No. | Yds | Avg | Net Avg | TB | In 20 | Lg | Blk |
|---|---|---|---|---|---|---|---|---|
| Koenen | 74 | 3014 | 40.7 | 36.1 | 5 | 29 | 61 | 1 |

SACKS: Abraham, 13.0

## Carolina Panthers

| SCORING | Rush | TD Rec | Ret | PAT | FG | 2PT | Pts |
|---|---|---|---|---|---|---|---|
| Kasay | 0 | 0 | 0 | 17 | 25 | 0 | 92 |
| Stewart | 2 | 1 | 0 | 0 | 0 | 0 | 18 |
| Goodson | 3 | 0 | 0 | 0 | 0 | 0 | 18 |
| Gettis | 0 | 3 | 0 | 0 | 0 | 0 | 18 |
| S. Smith | 0 | 2 | 0 | 0 | 0 | 0 | 12 |
| King | 0 | 2 | 0 | 0 | 0 | 0 | 12 |

| RUSHING | No. | Yds | Avg | Lg | TD |
|---|---|---|---|---|---|
| Stewart | 178 | 770 | 4.3 | 48 | 2 |
| Goodson | 103 | 452 | 4.4 | 45 | 3 |
| DeA. Williams | 87 | 361 | 4.1 | 39 | 1 |

| PASSING | Att | Comp | Pct Comp | Yds | Avg Gain | TD | Int | Rating Pts |
|---|---|---|---|---|---|---|---|---|
| Clausen | 299 | 157 | 52.5 | 1558 | 5.2 | 3 | 9 | 58.4 |
| Moore | 143 | 79 | 55.2 | 857 | 6.0 | 5 | 10 | 55.6 |

| RECEIVING | No. | Yds | Avg | Lg | TD |
|---|---|---|---|---|---|
| S. Smith | 46 | 554 | 12.0 | 39 | 2 |
| Gettis | 37 | 508 | 13.7 | 88 | 3 |
| LaFell | 38 | 468 | 12.3 | 44 | 1 |
| Goodson | 40 | 310 | 7.8 | 32 | 0 |
| Rosario | 32 | 264 | 8.3 | 26 | 0 |
| King | 19 | 121 | 6.4 | 16 | 2 |

INTERCEPTIONS: Godfrey, 5

| PUNTING | No. | Yds | Avg | Net Avg | TB | In 20 | Lg | Blk |
|---|---|---|---|---|---|---|---|---|
| Baker | 95 | 4097 | 43.1 | 36.5 | 7 | 22 | 60 | 0 |

SACKS: C. Johnson, 11.5

## Chicago Bears

| SCORING | Rush | TD Rec | Ret | PAT | FG | 2PT | Pts |
|---|---|---|---|---|---|---|---|
| Gould | 0 | 0 | 0 | 35 | 25 | 0 | 110 |
| Forte | 6 | 3 | 0 | 0 | 0 | 1 | 56 |
| Hester | 0 | 4 | 3 | 0 | 0 | 0 | 42 |
| Olsen | 0 | 5 | 0 | 0 | 0 | 0 | 30 |
| Knox | 0 | 5 | 0 | 0 | 0 | 0 | 30 |
| C. Taylor | 3 | 0 | 0 | 0 | 0 | 0 | 18 |
| Bennett | 0 | 3 | 0 | 0 | 0 | 0 | 18 |

| RUSHING | No. | Yds | Avg | Lg | TD |
|---|---|---|---|---|---|
| Forte | 237 | 1069 | 4.5 | 68 | 6 |
| C. Taylor | 117 | 267 | 2.4 | 24 | 3 |
| Cutler | 50 | 232 | 4.6 | 25 | 1 |

| PASSING | Att | Comp | Pct Comp | Yds | Avg Gain | TD | Int | Rating Pts |
|---|---|---|---|---|---|---|---|---|
| Cutler | 432 | 261 | 60.4 | 3274 | 7.6 | 23 | 16 | 86.3 |

| RECEIVING | No. | Yds | Avg | Lg | TD |
|---|---|---|---|---|---|
| Knox | 51 | 960 | 18.8 | 67 | 5 |
| Bennett | 46 | 561 | 12.2 | 48 | 3 |
| Forte | 51 | 547 | 10.7 | 89 | 3 |
| Hester | 40 | 475 | 11.9 | 39 | 4 |
| Olsen | 41 | 404 | 9.9 | 39 | 5 |

INTERCEPTIONS: C. Harris, Tillman, 5

| PUNTING | No. | Yds | Avg | Net Avg | TB | In 20 | Lg | Blk |
|---|---|---|---|---|---|---|---|---|
| Maynard | 83 | 3326 | 40.1 | 35.2 | 5 | 24 | 56 | 0 |

SACKS: Idonije, Peppers, 8.0

## Dallas Cowboys

### SCORING

| SCORING | Rush | TD Rec | Ret | PAT | FG | 2PT | Pts |
|---|---|---|---|---|---|---|---|
| Buehler | 0 | 0 | 0 | 42 | 24 | 0 | 114 |
| Witten | 0 | 9 | 0 | 0 | 0 | 1 | 56 |
| Austin | 1 | 7 | 0 | 0 | 0 | 0 | 48 |
| Bryant | 0 | 6 | 2 | 0 | 0 | 0 | 48 |
| Roy E. Williams | 0 | 5 | 0 | 0 | 0 | 1 | 32 |
| Barber | 4 | 0 | 0 | 0 | 0 | 0 | 24 |
| Choice | 3 | 0 | 0 | 0 | 0 | 0 | 18 |

### RUSHING

| RUSHING | No. | Yds | Avg | Lg | TD |
|---|---|---|---|---|---|
| F. Jones | 185 | 800 | 4.3 | 34 | 1 |
| Barber | 113 | 374 | 3.3 | 25 | 4 |
| Choice | 66 | 243 | 3.7 | 26 | 3 |

### PASSING

| PASSING | Att | Comp | Pct Comp | Yds | Avg Gain | TD | Int | Rating Pts |
|---|---|---|---|---|---|---|---|---|
| Kitna | 318 | 209 | 65.7 | 2365 | 7.4 | 16 | 12 | 88.9 |
| Romo | 213 | 148 | 69.5 | 1605 | 7.5 | 11 | 7 | 94.9 |

### RECEIVING

| RECEIVING | No. | Yds | Avg | Lg | TD |
|---|---|---|---|---|---|
| Austin | 69 | 1041 | 15.1 | 69 | 7 |
| Witten | 94 | 1002 | 10.7 | 33 | 9 |
| Bryant | 45 | 561 | 12.5 | 46 | 6 |
| Roy E. Williams | 37 | 530 | 14.3 | 63 | 5 |
| F. Jones | 48 | 450 | 9.4 | 71 | 1 |

**INTERCEPTIONS:** Newman, Sensabaugh, 5

| PUNTING | No. | Yds | Avg | Net Avg | TB | In 20 | Lg | Blk |
|---|---|---|---|---|---|---|---|---|
| McBriar | 65 | 3115 | 47.9 | 42.3 | 8 | 22 | 65 | 1 |

**SACKS:** Ware, 15.5

## Green Bay Packers

### SCORING

| SCORING | Rush | TD Rec | Ret | PAT | FG | 2PT | Pts |
|---|---|---|---|---|---|---|---|
| Crosby | 0 | 0 | 0 | 46 | 22 | 0 | 112 |
| Jennings | 0 | 12 | 0 | 0 | 0 | 0 | 72 |
| Kuhn | 4 | 2 | 0 | 0 | 0 | 0 | 36 |
| J. Jones | 0 | 5 | 0 | 0 | 0 | 0 | 30 |
| Driver | 0 | 4 | 0 | 0 | 0 | 0 | 24 |
| Rodgers | 4 | 0 | 0 | 0 | 0 | 0 | 24 |
| B. Jackson | 3 | 1 | 0 | 0 | 0 | 0 | 24 |

### RUSHING

| RUSHING | No. | Yds | Avg | Lg | TD |
|---|---|---|---|---|---|
| B. Jackson | 190 | 703 | 3.7 | 71 | 3 |
| Rodgers | 64 | 356 | 5.6 | 27 | 4 |
| Kuhn | 84 | 281 | 3.3 | 18 | 4 |

### PASSING

| PASSING | Att | Comp | Pct Comp | Yds | Avg Gain | TD | Int | Rating Pts |
|---|---|---|---|---|---|---|---|---|
| Rodgers | 475 | 312 | 65.7 | 3922 | 8.3 | 28 | 11 | 101.2 |
| Flynn | 66 | 40 | 60.6 | 433 | 6.6 | 3 | 2 | 82.5 |

### RECEIVING

| RECEIVING | No. | Yds | Avg | Lg | TD |
|---|---|---|---|---|---|
| Jennings | 76 | 1265 | 16.6 | 86 | 12 |
| J. Jones | 50 | 679 | 13.6 | 66 | 5 |
| Nelson | 45 | 582 | 12.9 | 80 | 2 |
| Driver | 51 | 565 | 11.1 | 61 | 4 |
| B. Jackson | 43 | 342 | 8.0 | 37 | 1 |
| Finley | 21 | 301 | 14.3 | 34 | 1 |
| Quarless | 21 | 238 | 11.3 | 23 | 1 |

**INTERCEPTIONS:** T. Williams, 6

| PUNTING | No. | Yds | Avg | Net Avg | TB | In 20 | Lg | Blk |
|---|---|---|---|---|---|---|---|---|
| Masthay | 71 | 3114 | 43.9 | 37.6 | 5 | 25 | 62 | 0 |

**SACKS:** Matthews, 13.5

## Detroit Lions

### SCORING

| SCORING | Rush | TD Rec | Ret | PAT | FG | 2PT | Pts |
|---|---|---|---|---|---|---|---|
| C. Johnson | 0 | 12 | 0 | 0 | 0 | 1 | 74 |
| Hanson | 0 | 0 | 0 | 19 | 12 | 0 | 55 |
| Rayner | 0 | 0 | 0 | 16 | 13 | 0 | 55 |
| Burleson | 0 | 6 | 0 | 0 | 0 | 0 | 36 |
| Best | 4 | 2 | 0 | 0 | 0 | 0 | 36 |
| Morris | 5 | 0 | 0 | 0 | 0 | 1 | 30 |
| Pettigrew | 0 | 4 | 0 | 0 | 0 | 0 | 24 |

### RUSHING

| RUSHING | No. | Yds | Avg | Lg | TD |
|---|---|---|---|---|---|
| Best | 171 | 555 | 3.2 | 45 | 4 |
| Morris | 90 | 336 | 3.7 | 26 | 5 |

### PASSING

| PASSING | Att | Comp | Pct Comp | Yds | Avg Gain | TD | Int | Rating Pts |
|---|---|---|---|---|---|---|---|---|
| Hill | 416 | 257 | 61.8 | 2686 | 6.6 | 16 | 12 | 81.3 |
| Stanton | 119 | 69 | 58.0 | 780 | 6.6 | 4 | 3 | 78.4 |
| Stafford | 96 | 57 | 59.4 | 535 | 5.6 | 6 | 1 | 91.3 |

### RECEIVING

| RECEIVING | No. | Yds | Avg | Lg | TD |
|---|---|---|---|---|---|
| C. Johnson | 77 | 1120 | 14.5 | 87 | 12 |
| Pettigrew | 71 | 722 | 10.2 | 35 | 4 |
| Burleson | 55 | 625 | 11.4 | 58 | 6 |
| Best | 58 | 487 | 8.4 | 75 | 2 |
| Scheffler | 45 | 378 | 8.4 | 25 | 1 |

**INTERCEPTIONS:** A. Smith, 5

| PUNTING | No. | Yds | Avg | Net Avg | TB | In 20 | Lg | Blk |
|---|---|---|---|---|---|---|---|---|
| Harris | 90 | 4018 | 44.6 | 35.8 | 8 | 24 | 66 | 0 |

**SACKS:** Suh, 10.0

## Minnesota Vikings

### SCORING

| SCORING | Rush | TD Rec | Ret | PAT | FG | 2PT | Pts |
|---|---|---|---|---|---|---|---|
| Longwell | 0 | 0 | 0 | 30 | 17 | 0 | 81 |
| Peterson | 12 | 1 | 0 | 0 | 0 | 0 | 78 |
| Harvin | 1 | 5 | 1 | 0 | 0 | 1 | 44 |
| Moss | 0 | 2 | 0 | 0 | 0 | 0 | 12 |
| Shiancoe | 0 | 2 | 0 | 0 | 0 | 0 | 12 |
| Rice | 0 | 2 | 0 | 0 | 0 | 0 | 12 |
| Webb | 2 | 0 | 0 | 0 | 0 | 0 | 12 |

### RUSHING

| RUSHING | No. | Yds | Avg | Lg | TD |
|---|---|---|---|---|---|
| Peterson | 283 | 1298 | 4.6 | 80 | 12 |
| Gerhart | 81 | 322 | 4.0 | 21 | 1 |

### PASSING

| PASSING | Att | Comp | Pct Comp | Yds | Avg Gain | TD | Int | Rating Pts |
|---|---|---|---|---|---|---|---|---|
| Favre | 358 | 217 | 60.6 | 2509 | 7.0 | 11 | 19 | 69.9 |
| Webb | 89 | 54 | 60.7 | 477 | 5.4 | 0 | 3 | 60.9 |
| T. Jackson | 58 | 34 | 58.6 | 341 | 5.9 | 3 | 4 | 63.9 |

### RECEIVING

| RECEIVING | No. | Yds | Avg | Lg | TD |
|---|---|---|---|---|---|
| Harvin | 71 | 868 | 12.2 | 53 | 5 |
| Shiancoe | 47 | 530 | 11.3 | 33 | 2 |
| Peterson | 36 | 341 | 9.5 | 34 | 1 |
| Rice | 17 | 280 | 16.5 | 46 | 2 |
| Berrian | 28 | 252 | 9.0 | 30 | 0 |
| Camarillo | 20 | 240 | 12.0 | 31 | 1 |

**INTERCEPTIONS:** Abdullah, E.J. Henderson, 3

| PUNTING | No. | Yds | Avg | Net Avg | TB | In 20 | Lg | Blk |
|---|---|---|---|---|---|---|---|---|
| Kluwe | 83 | 3569 | 43.0 | 38.9 | 5 | 32 | 59 | 0 |

**SACKS:** J. Allen, 11.0

### New Orleans Saints

| SCORING | Rush | TD Rec | Ret | PAT | FG | 2PT | Pts |
|---|---|---|---|---|---|---|---|
| Hartley | 0 | 0 | 0 | 40 | 20 | 0 | 100 |
| Moore | 0 | 8 | 0 | 0 | 0 | 0 | 48 |
| Colston | 0 | 7 | 0 | 0 | 0 | 0 | 42 |
| Meachem | 0 | 5 | 0 | 0 | 0 | 0 | 30 |
| J. Graham | 0 | 5 | 0 | 0 | 0 | 0 | 30 |
| Ivory | 5 | 0 | 0 | 0 | 0 | 0 | 30 |
| Carney | 0 | 0 | 3 | 0 | 5 | 0 | 18 |
| Shockey | 0 | 3 | 0 | 0 | 0 | 0 | 18 |

| RUSHING | No. | Yds | Avg | Lg | TD |
|---|---|---|---|---|---|
| Ivory | 137 | 716 | 5.2 | 55 | 5 |
| P. Thomas | 183 | 269 | 3.2 | 16 | 2 |

| PASSING | Att | Comp | Pct Comp | Yds | Avg Gain | TD | Int | Rating Pts |
|---|---|---|---|---|---|---|---|---|
| Brees | 658 | 448 | 68.1 | 4620 | 7.0 | 33 | 22 | 90.9 |

| RECEIVING | No. | Yds | Avg | Lg | TD |
|---|---|---|---|---|---|
| Colston | 84 | 1023 | 12.2 | 43 | 7 |
| Moore | 66 | 763 | 11.6 | 80 | 8 |
| Meachem | 44 | 638 | 14.5 | 55 | 5 |
| Henderson | 34 | 464 | 13.6 | 57 | 1 |
| Shockey | 41 | 408 | 10.0 | 31 | 3 |
| J. Graham | 31 | 356 | 11.5 | 52 | 5 |
| D. Thomas | 30 | 219 | 7.3 | 22 | 2 |
| Bush | 34 | 208 | 6.1 | 20 | 1 |

**INTERCEPTIONS:** Greer, Jenkins, 2

| PUNTING | No. | Yds | Avg | Net Avg | TB | In 20 | Lg | Blk |
|---|---|---|---|---|---|---|---|---|
| Morstead | 57 | 2618 | 45.9 | 38.4 | 6 | 21 | 64 | 0 |

**SACKS:** Ellis, 6.0

### Philadelphia Eagles

| SCORING | Rush | TD Rec | Ret | PAT | FG | 2PT | Pts |
|---|---|---|---|---|---|---|---|
| Akers | 0 | 0 | 0 | 47 | 32 | 0 | 143 |
| Maclin | 0 | 10 | 0 | 0 | 0 | 0 | 60 |
| Vick | 9 | 0 | 0 | 0 | 0 | 0 | 54 |
| McCoy | 7 | 2 | 0 | 0 | 0 | 0 | 54 |
| D. Jackson | 1 | 6 | 1 | 0 | 0 | 0 | 48 |
| Celek | 0 | 4 | 0 | 0 | 0 | 0 | 24 |

| RUSHING | No. | Yds | Avg | Lg | TD |
|---|---|---|---|---|---|
| McCoy | 207 | 1080 | 5.2 | 62 | 7 |
| Vick | 100 | 676 | 6.8 | 35 | 9 |
| Harrison | 40 | 239 | 6.0 | 50 | 1 |

| PASSING | Att | Comp | Pct Comp | Yds | Avg Gain | TD | Int | Rating Pts |
|---|---|---|---|---|---|---|---|---|
| Vick | 372 | 233 | 62.6 | 3018 | 8.1 | 21 | 6 | 100.2 |
| Kolb | 189 | 115 | 60.8 | 1197 | 6.3 | 7 | 7 | 76.1 |

| RECEIVING | No. | Yds | Avg | Lg | TD |
|---|---|---|---|---|---|
| D. Jackson | 47 | 1056 | 22.5 | 91 | 6 |
| Maclin | 70 | 964 | 13.8 | 83 | 10 |
| McCoy | 78 | 592 | 7.6 | 40 | 2 |
| Avant | 51 | 573 | 11.2 | 34 | 1 |
| Celek | 42 | 511 | 12.2 | 65 | 4 |

**INTERCEPTIONS:** Samuel, 7

| PUNTING | No. | Yds | Avg | Net Avg | TB | In 20 | Lg | Blk |
|---|---|---|---|---|---|---|---|---|
| Rocca | 73 | 3195 | 43.8 | 39.0 | 1 | 28 | 63 | 0 |

**SACKS:** Cole, 10.0

### New York Giants

| SCORING | Rush | TD Rec | Ret | PAT | FG | 2PT | Pts |
|---|---|---|---|---|---|---|---|
| Tynes | 0 | 0 | 0 | 43 | 19 | 0 | 100 |
| Nicks | 0 | 11 | 0 | 0 | 0 | 0 | 66 |
| Jacobs | 9 | 0 | 0 | 0 | 0 | 0 | 54 |
| Manningham | 0 | 9 | 0 | 0 | 0 | 0 | 54 |
| Bradshaw | 8 | 0 | 0 | 0 | 0 | 1 | 50 |
| Boss | 0 | 5 | 0 | 0 | 0 | 0 | 30 |
| S. Smith | 0 | 3 | 0 | 0 | 0 | 0 | 18 |
| Beckum | 0 | 2 | 0 | 0 | 0 | 0 | 12 |

| RUSHING | No. | Yds | Avg | Lg | TD |
|---|---|---|---|---|---|
| Bradshaw | 276 | 1235 | 4.5 | 48 | 8 |
| Jacobs | 147 | 823 | 5.6 | 73 | 9 |

| PASSING | Att | Comp | Pct Comp | Yds | Avg Gain | TD | Int | Rating Pts |
|---|---|---|---|---|---|---|---|---|
| Manning | 539 | 339 | 62.9 | 4002 | 7.4 | 31 | 25 | 85.3 |

| RECEIVING | No. | Yds | Avg | Lg | TD |
|---|---|---|---|---|---|
| Nicks | 79 | 1052 | 13.3 | 46 | 11 |
| Manningham | 60 | 944 | 15.7 | 92 | 9 |
| Boss | 35 | 531 | 15.2 | 54 | 5 |
| S. Smith | 48 | 529 | 11.0 | 45 | 3 |
| Bradshaw | 47 | 314 | 6.7 | 18 | 0 |
| Hagan | 24 | 223 | 9.3 | 17 | 1 |
| Beckum | 13 | 116 | 8.9 | 29 | 2 |

**INTERCEPTIONS:** Thomas, 5

| PUNTING | No. | Yds | Avg | Net Avg | TB | In 20 | Lg | Blk |
|---|---|---|---|---|---|---|---|---|
| Dodge | 72 | 3222 | 44.8 | 34.8 | 9 | 20 | 69 | 1 |

**SACKS:** Tuck, Umenyiora, 11.5

### St. Louis Rams

| SCORING | Rush | TD Rec | Ret | PAT | FG | 2PT | Pts |
|---|---|---|---|---|---|---|---|
| J. Brown | 0 | 0 | 0 | 26 | 33 | 0 | 125 |
| S. Jackson | 6 | 0 | 0 | 0 | 0 | 0 | 36 |
| Darby | 2 | 1 | 0 | 0 | 0 | 0 | 18 |
| Amendola | 0 | 3 | 0 | 0 | 0 | 0 | 18 |
| Hoomanawanui | 0 | 3 | 0 | 0 | 0 | 0 | 18 |

| RUSHING | No. | Yds | Avg | Lg | TD |
|---|---|---|---|---|---|
| S. Jackson | 330 | 1241 | 3.8 | 42 | 6 |

| PASSING | Att | Comp | Pct Comp | Yds | Avg Gain | TD | Int | Rating Pts |
|---|---|---|---|---|---|---|---|---|
| Bradford | 590 | 354 | 60.0 | 3512 | 6.0 | 18 | 15 | 76.5 |

| RECEIVING | No. | Yds | Avg | Lg | TD |
|---|---|---|---|---|---|
| Amendola | 85 | 689 | 8.1 | 36 | 3 |
| Gibson | 53 | 620 | 11.7 | 41 | 2 |
| Fells | 41 | 391 | 9.5 | 36 | 2 |
| S. Jackson | 46 | 383 | 8.3 | 49 | 0 |
| Robinson | 34 | 344 | 10.1 | 32 | 2 |
| Clayton | 23 | 306 | 13.3 | 39 | 2 |
| Alexander | 20 | 306 | 15.3 | 46 | 1 |
| Hoomanawanui | 13 | 146 | 11.2 | 36 | 3 |

**INTERCEPTIONS:** Fletcher, 4

| PUNTING | No. | Yds | Avg | Net Avg | TB | In 20 | Lg | Blk |
|---|---|---|---|---|---|---|---|---|
| Jones | 94 | 4276 | 45.5 | 40.0 | 4 | 32 | 63 | 0 |

**SACKS:** J. Hall, 10.5

## San Francisco 49ers

| SCORING | TD Rush | Rec | Ret | PAT | FG | 2PT | Pts |
|---|---|---|---|---|---|---|---|
| Nedney | 0 | 0 | 0 | 17 | 11 | 0 | 50 |
| V. Davis | 0 | 7 | 0 | 0 | 0 | 1 | 44 |
| Reed | 0 | 0 | 0 | 13 | 9 | 0 | 40 |
| Crabtree | 0 | 6 | 0 | 0 | 0 | 0 | 36 |
| Westbrook | 4 | 1 | 0 | 0 | 0 | 0 | 30 |
| Gore | 3 | 2 | 0 | 0 | 0 | 0 | 30 |

| RUSHING | No. | Yds | Avg | Lg | TD |
|---|---|---|---|---|---|
| Gore | 203 | 853 | 4.2 | 64 | 3 |
| Westbrook | 77 | 340 | 4.4 | 30 | 4 |
| Dixon | 70 | 237 | 3.4 | 34 | 2 |

| PASSING | Att | Comp | Pct Comp | Yds | Avg Gain | TD | Int | Rating Pts |
|---|---|---|---|---|---|---|---|---|
| A. Smith | 342 | 204 | 59.6 | 2370 | 6.9 | 14 | 10 | 82.1 |
| T. Smith | 145 | 73 | 50.3 | 1176 | 8.1 | 5 | 4 | 77.8 |

| RECEIVING | No. | Yds | Avg | Lg | TD |
|---|---|---|---|---|---|
| V. Davis | 56 | 914 | 16.3 | 66 | 7 |
| Crabtree | 55 | 741 | 13.5 | 60 | 6 |
| Morgan | 44 | 698 | 15.9 | 65 | 2 |
| Gore | 46 | 452 | 9.8 | 41 | 2 |
| Walker | 29 | 331 | 11.4 | 38 | 0 |

**INTERCEPTIONS:** Clements, Spencer, Spikes, 3

| PUNTING | No. | Yds | Avg | Net Avg | TB | In 20 | Lg | Blk |
|---|---|---|---|---|---|---|---|---|
| Lee | 91 | 4203 | 46.2 | 38.2 | 12 | 34 | 64 | 0 |

**SACKS:** J. Smith, 8.5

## Tampa Bay Buccaneers

| SCORING | TD Rush | Rec | Ret | PAT | FG | 2PT | Pts |
|---|---|---|---|---|---|---|---|
| Barth | 0 | 0 | 0 | 36 | 23 | 0 | 105 |
| M. Williams | 0 | 11 | 0 | 0 | 0 | 0 | 66 |
| Blount | 6 | 0 | 0 | 0 | 0 | 0 | 36 |
| Winslow | 0 | 5 | 0 | 0 | 0 | 0 | 30 |
| C. Williams | 2 | 1 | 0 | 0 | 0 | 0 | 18 |
| Spurlock | 0 | 2 | 1 | 0 | 0 | 0 | 18 |
| E. Graham | 1 | 1 | 0 | 0 | 0 | 0 | 12 |
| Benn | 0 | 2 | 0 | 0 | 0 | 0 | 12 |

| RUSHING | No. | Yds | Avg | Lg | TD |
|---|---|---|---|---|---|
| Blount | 201 | 1007 | 5.0 | 53 | 6 |
| C. Williams | 125 | 437 | 3.5 | 45 | 2 |
| Freeman | 68 | 364 | 5.4 | 33 | 0 |

| PASSING | Att | Comp | Pct Comp | Yds | Avg Gain | TD | Int | Rating Pts |
|---|---|---|---|---|---|---|---|---|
| Freeman | 474 | 291 | 61.4 | 3451 | 7.3 | 25 | 6 | 95.9 |

| RECEIVING | No. | Yds | Avg | Lg | TD |
|---|---|---|---|---|---|
| M. Williams | 65 | 964 | 14.8 | 58 | 11 |
| Winslow | 66 | 730 | 11.1 | 41 | 5 |
| Benn | 25 | 395 | 15.8 | 64 | 2 |
| C. Williams | 46 | 355 | 7.7 | 20 | 1 |
| Spurlock | 17 | 250 | 14.7 | 43 | 2 |
| Stroughter | 24 | 239 | 10.0 | 27 | 0 |

**INTERCEPTIONS:** Talib, 6

| PUNTING | No. | Yds | Avg | Net Avg | TB | In 20 | Lg | Blk |
|---|---|---|---|---|---|---|---|---|
| Malone | 52 | 2160 | 41.5 | 36.5 | 5 | 17 | 64 | 0 |
| Bryan | 23 | 860 | 37.4 | 34.3 | 0 | 7 | 57 | 0 |

**SACKS:** S. White, 4.5

## Seattle Seahawks

| SCORING | TD Rush | Rec | Ret | PAT | FG | 2PT | Pts |
|---|---|---|---|---|---|---|---|
| Mare | 0 | 0 | 0 | 31 | 25 | 0 | 106 |
| Lynch | 6 | 0 | 0 | 0 | 0 | 0 | 36 |
| Obomanu | 0 | 4 | 0 | 0 | 0 | 2 | 28 |
| L. Washington | 1 | 0 | 3 | 0 | 0 | 0 | 24 |
| Butler | 0 | 4 | 0 | 0 | 0 | 0 | 24 |
| Hasselbeck | 3 | 0 | 0 | 0 | 0 | 0 | 18 |

| RUSHING | No. | Yds | Avg | Lg | TD |
|---|---|---|---|---|---|
| Lynch | 165 | 573 | 3.5 | 39 | 6 |
| Forsett | 118 | 523 | 4.4 | 52 | 2 |

| PASSING | Att | Comp | Pct Comp | Yds | Avg Gain | TD | Int | Rating Pts |
|---|---|---|---|---|---|---|---|---|
| Hasselbeck | 444 | 266 | 59.9 | 3001 | 6.8 | 12 | 17 | 73.2 |
| Whitehurst | 99 | 57 | 57.6 | 507 | 5.1 | 2 | 3 | 65.5 |

| RECEIVING | No. | Yds | Avg | Lg | TD |
|---|---|---|---|---|---|
| M. Williams | 65 | 751 | 11.6 | 68 | 2 |
| Obomanu | 30 | 494 | 16.5 | 87 | 4 |
| Butler | 36 | 385 | 10.7 | 63 | 4 |
| Stokley | 31 | 354 | 11.4 | 36 | 0 |
| Carlson | 31 | 318 | 10.3 | 37 | 1 |
| Forsett | 33 | 252 | 7.6 | 21 | 0 |
| Tate | 21 | 227 | 10.8 | 52 | 0 |

**INTERCEPTIONS:** E. Thomas, 5

| PUNTING | No. | Yds | Avg | Net Avg | TB | In 20 | Lg | Blk |
|---|---|---|---|---|---|---|---|---|
| Ryan | 78 | 3254 | 41.7 | 37.3 | 1 | 27 | 63 | 0 |

**SACKS:** Clemons, 11.0

## Washington Redskins

| SCORING | TD Rush | Rec | Ret | PAT | FG | 2PT | Pts |
|---|---|---|---|---|---|---|---|
| Gano | 0 | 0 | 0 | 28 | 24 | 0 | 100 |
| Moss | 0 | 6 | 0 | 0 | 0 | 0 | 36 |
| Torain | 4 | 2 | 0 | 0 | 0 | 0 | 36 |
| K. Williams | 3 | 2 | 0 | 0 | 0 | 0 | 30 |
| Cooley | 0 | 3 | 0 | 0 | 0 | 1 | 20 |
| F. Davis | 0 | 3 | 0 | 0 | 0 | 0 | 18 |
| Armstrong | 0 | 3 | 0 | 0 | 0 | 0 | 18 |

| RUSHING | No. | Yds | Avg | Lg | TD |
|---|---|---|---|---|---|
| Torain | 164 | 742 | 4.5 | 54 | 4 |
| K. Williams | 65 | 261 | 4.0 | 32 | 3 |

| PASSING | Att | Comp | Pct Comp | Yds | Avg Gain | TD | Int | Rating Pts |
|---|---|---|---|---|---|---|---|---|
| McNabb | 472 | 275 | 58.3 | 3377 | 7.2 | 14 | 15 | 77.1 |
| Grossman | 133 | 74 | 55.6 | 884 | 6.6 | 7 | 4 | 81.2 |

| RECEIVING | No. | Yds | Avg | Lg | TD |
|---|---|---|---|---|---|
| Moss | 93 | 1115 | 12.0 | 56 | 6 |
| Armstrong | 44 | 871 | 19.8 | 76 | 3 |
| Cooley | 77 | 849 | 11.0 | 35 | 3 |
| F. Davis | 21 | 316 | 15.0 | 71 | 3 |
| K. Williams | 39 | 309 | 7.9 | 36 | 2 |
| Sellers | 20 | 224 | 11.2 | 28 | 0 |

**INTERCEPTIONS:** Hall, 6

| PUNTING | No. | Yds | Avg | Net Avg | TB | In 20 | Lg | Blk |
|---|---|---|---|---|---|---|---|---|
| H. Smith | 57 | 2310 | 40.5 | 33.7 | 1 | 17 | 56 | 0 |
| Paulescu | 17 | 700 | 41.2 | 33.1 | 1 | 2 | 52 | 0 |
| Bidwell | 15 | 625 | 41.7 | 37.7 | 0 | 3 | 52 | 0 |

**SACKS:** Orakpo, 8.5

First two rounds of the 75th annual NFL Draft, held April 28, 2011 in New York City.

## First Round

| Team | Selection | Position |
|------|-----------|----------|
| 1. ...............Carolina | Cam Newton, Auburn | QB |
| 2. ...............Denver | Von Miller, Texas A&M | LB |
| 3. ...............Buffalo | Marcell, Dareus, Alabama | DT |
| 4. ...............Cincinnati | A.J. Green, Georgia | WR |
| 5. ...............Arizona | Patrick Peterson, LSU | DB |
| 6. ...............Atlanta (from Cleveland) | Julio Jones, Alabama | WR |
| 7. ...............San Francisco | Aldon Smith, Missouri | DE |
| 8. ...............Tennessee | Jake Locker, Washington | QB |
| 9. ...............Dallas | Tyron Smith, USC | OT |
| 10. ............Jacksonville (from Washington) | Blaine Gabbert, Missouri | QB |
| 11. ............Houston | J.J. Watt, Wisconsin | DE |
| 12. ............Minnesota | Christian Ponder, Florida St | QB |
| 13. ............Detroit | Nick Fairley, Aubrun | DT |
| 14. ............St. Louis | Robert Quinn, North Carolina | DE |
| 15. ............Miami | Mike Pouncey, Florida | OL |
| 16. ............Washington (from Jacksonville) | Ryan Kerrigan, Purdue | DE |
| 17. ............New England (from Oakland) | Nate Solder, Colorado | OL |
| 18. ............San Diego | Corey Liuget, Illinois | DT |
| 19. ............NY Giants | Prince Amukamara, Nebraska | DB |
| 20. ............Tampa Bay | Adrian Clayborn, Iowa | DL |
| 21. ............Cleveland (from Kansas City) | Phil Taylor, Baylor | DL |
| 22. ............Indianapolis | Anthony Castonzo, Boston College | OL |
| 23. ............Philadelphia | Danny Watkins, Baylor | OL |
| 24. ............New Orleans | Cameron Jordan, California | DE |
| 25. ............Seattle | James Carpenter, Alabama | OL |
| 26. ............Kansas City (from Atlanta through Cleveland) | Jonathan Baldwin, Pittsburgh | WR |
| 27. ............Baltimore | Jimmy Smith, Colorado | DB |
| 28. ............New Orleans (from New England) | Mark Ingram, Alabama | RB |
| 29. ............Chicago | Gabe Carimi, Wisconsin | OL |
| 30. ............NY Jets | Muhammad Wilkerson, Temple | DT |
| 31. ............Pittsburgh | Cam Heyward, Ohio St | DT |
| 32. ............Green Bay | Derek Sherrod, Mississippi | OL |

## Second Round

| Team | Selection | Position |
|------|-----------|----------|
| 33. ...........New England (from Carolina) | Ras-I Dowling, Virginia | DB |
| 34. ...........Buffalo | Aaron Williams, Texas | DB |
| 35. ...........Cincinnati | Andy Dalton, TCU | QB |
| 36. ...........San Francisco (from Denver) | Colin Kaepernick, Nevada | RB |
| 37. ...........Cleveland | Jabaal Sheard, Pittsburgh | DL |
| 38. ...........Arizona | Ryan Williams, Virginia Tech | RB |
| 39. ...........Tennessee | Akeem Ayers, UCLA | LB |
| 40. ...........Dallas | Bruce Carter, North Carolina | LB |
| 41. ...........Washington | Jarvis Jenkins, Clemson | DL |
| 42. ...........Houston | Brooks Reed, Arizona | DL |
| 43. ...........Minnesota | Kyle Rudolph, Notre Dame | TE |
| 44. ...........Detroit | Titus Young, Boise St | WR |
| 45. ...........Denver (from San Francisco) | Rahim Moore, UCLA | DB |
| 46. ...........Denver (from Miami) | Orlando Franklin, Miami (Fla.) | OL |
| 47. ...........St. Louis | Lance Kendricks, Wisconsin | TE |
| 48. ...........Oakland | Stefen Wisniewski, Penn St | OL |
| 49. ...........Indianapolis (from Jacksonville through Washington) | Ben Ijalana, Villanova | OL |
| 50. ...........San Diego | Marcus Gilchrist, Clemson | DB |
| 51. ...........Tampa Bay | Da'Quan Bowers, Clemson | DE |
| 52. ...........NY Giants | Marvin Austin, North Carolina | DL |
| 53. ...........Chicago (from Indianapolis through Washington) | Stephen Paea, Oregon St | DT |
| 54. ...........Philadelphia | Jaiquawn Jarrett, Temple | DB |
| 55. ...........Kansas City | Rodney Hudson, Florida St | OL |
| 56. ...........New England (from New Orleans) | Shane Vereen, California | RB |
| 57. ...........Detroit (from Seattle) | Mikel Leshoure, Illinois | RB |
| 58. ...........Baltimore | Torrey Smith, Maryland | WR |
| 59. ...........Cleveland (from Atlanta) | Greg Little, North Carolina | WR |
| 60. ...........Houston (from New England) | Brandon Harris, Miami (Fla.) | DB |
| 61. ...........San Diego (NY Jets) | Jonas Mouton, Michigan | LB |
| 62. ...........Miami (from Chicago through Washington) | Daniel Thomas, Kansas St | RB |
| 63. ...........Pittsburgh | Marcus Gilbert, Florida | OL |
| 64. ...........Green Bay | Randall Cobb, Kentucky | WR |

## Regular Season Results

**WEST DIVISION**

| | W | L | T | Pts | PF | PA |
|---|---|---|---|---|---|---|
| †Calgary | 13 | 5 | 0 | 26 | 626 | 459 |
| *Saskatchewan | 10 | 8 | 0 | 20 | 497 | 488 |
| *British Columbia | 8 | 10 | 0 | 16 | 466 | 466 |
| Edmonton | 7 | 11 | 0 | 14 | 382 | 545 |

**EAST DIVISION**

| | W | L | T | Pts | PF | PA |
|---|---|---|---|---|---|---|
| †Montreal | 12 | 6 | 0 | 24 | 521 | 475 |
| *Hamilton | 9 | 9 | 0 | 18 | 481 | 450 |
| *Toronto | 9 | 9 | 0 | 18 | 373 | 442 |
| Winnipeg | 4 | 14 | 0 | 8 | 464 | 485 |

†Clinched division title.

*Clinched playoff berth.

## Playoff Results

### DIVISION SEMI-FINALS

Nov. 14, 2010

Toronto 16, HAMILTON 13
SASKATCHEWAN 41, B.C 38 (OT)

### DIVISION FINALS

Nov. 21, 2010

MONTREAL 48, Toronto 17
Saskatchewan 20, CALGARY 16
Home team in caps.

## 2010 Grey Cup Championship

**Nov. 28, 2010, Edmonton, Alberta**

| | | | | | |
|---|---|---|---|---|---|
| **Montreal Alouettes** | 8 | 0 | 3 | 10 | 21 |
| **Sask. Roughriders** | 7 | 4 | 0 | 7 | 18 |

**FIRST QUARTER:** Montreal: TD Cobourne 3 run (Duval kick), 9:52. **Montreal 7–0.**

Montreal: FG Single Duval 31, 4:06. **Montreal 8–0.**

Saskatchewan: TD Cates 1 run (Kean kick), 0:01. **Montreal 8–7.**

**SECOND QUARTER:** Saskatchewan: FG Kean 27, 12:07. **Saskatchewan 10–8.**

Saskatchwean: Punt Single Johnson 53, 1:25. **Saskatchewan 11–8.**

**THIRD QUARTER:** Montreal: FG Duval 22, 5:53. **11–11.**

**FOURTH QUARTER:** Montreal: FG Duval 43, 13:43. **Montreal 14–11.**

Montreal: TD Cobourne 2 run (Duval kick), 8:25. **Montreal 21–11.**

Saskatchewan: TD Parenteau 1 pass from Durant (Kean kick), 4:00. **Montreal 21–18.**

A: 63,317.

## Season-by-Season NFL Final Standings

### 1920*

| | W | L | T | Pct | Pts | OP |
|---|---|---|---|---|---|---|
| Akron Pros | 8 | 0 | 3 | 1.000 | 151 | 7 |
| Decatur Staleys | 10 | 1 | 2 | .909 | 164 | 21 |
| Buffalo All-Americans | 9 | 1 | 1 | .900 | 258 | 32 |
| Chicago Cardinals | 6 | 2 | 1 | .750 | 101 | 29 |
| Rock Island Independents | 6 | 2 | 2 | .750 | 201 | 49 |
| Dayton Triangles | 5 | 2 | 2 | .714 | 150 | 54 |
| Rochester Jeffersons | 6 | 3 | 2 | .667 | 156 | 57 |
| Canton Bulldogs | 7 | 4 | 2 | .636 | 208 | 57 |
| Detroit Heralds | 2 | 3 | 4 | .400 | 53 | 82 |
| Cleveland Tigers | 2 | 4 | 2 | .333 | 28 | 46 |
| Chicago Tigers | 2 | 5 | 1 | .286 | 49 | 63 |
| Hammond Pros | 2 | 5 | 0 | .286 | 41 | 154 |
| Columbus Panhandles | 2 | 6 | 2 | .250 | 41 | 121 |
| Muncie Flyers | 0 | 1 | 0 | .000 | 0 | 45 |

*no official standings kept

### 1921

| | W | L | T | Pct | Pts | OP |
|---|---|---|---|---|---|---|
| Buffalo All-Americans | 9 | 1 | 2 | .900 | 211 | 29 |
| Chicago Staleys | 9 | 1 | 1 | .900 | 128 | 53 |
| Akron Pros | 8 | 3 | 1 | .727 | 148 | 31 |
| Canton Bulldogs | 5 | 2 | 3 | .714 | 106 | 55 |
| Rock Island Independents | 4 | 2 | 1 | .667 | 65 | 30 |
| Evansville Crimson Giants | 3 | 2 | 0 | .600 | 89 | 46 |
| Green Bay Packers | 3 | 2 | 1 | .600 | 70 | 55 |
| Chicago Cardinals | 3 | 3 | 2 | .500 | 54 | 53 |
| Dayton Triangles | 4 | 4 | 1 | .500 | 96 | 67 |
| Rochester Jeffersons | 2 | 3 | 0 | .400 | 85 | 76 |
| Cleveland Tigers | 3 | 5 | 0 | .375 | 95 | 58 |
| Washington Senators | 1 | 2 | 0 | .333 | 21 | 43 |
| Cincinnati Celts | 1 | 3 | 0 | .250 | 14 | 117 |
| Hammond Pros | 1 | 3 | 1 | .250 | 17 | 45 |
| Minneapolis Marines | 1 | 3 | 0 | .250 | 37 | 41 |
| Detroit Tigers | 1 | 5 | 1 | .167 | 19 | 109 |
| Columbus Panhandles | 1 | 8 | 0 | .111 | 47 | 222 |
| Muncie Flyers | 0 | 2 | 0 | .000 | 0 | 28 |
| Louisville Brecks | 0 | 2 | 0 | .000 | 0 | 27 |
| New York Giants | 0 | 2 | 0 | .000 | 0 | 72 |
| Tonawanda Kardex | 0 | 1 | 0 | .000 | 0 | 45 |

### 1922

| | W | L | T | Pct | Pts | OP |
|---|---|---|---|---|---|---|
| Canton Bulldogs | 10 | 0 | 2 | 1.000 | 184 | 15 |
| Chicago Bears | 9 | 3 | 0 | .750 | 123 | 44 |
| Chicago Cardinals | 8 | 3 | 0 | .727 | 96 | 50 |
| Toledo Maroons | 5 | 2 | 2 | .714 | 94 | 59 |
| Rock Island Independents | 4 | 2 | 1 | .667 | 154 | 27 |
| Racine Legion | 6 | 4 | 1 | .600 | 122 | 56 |
| Dayton Triangles | 4 | 3 | 1 | .571 | 80 | 62 |
| Green Bay Packers | 4 | 3 | 3 | .571 | 70 | 54 |
| Buffalo All-Americans | 5 | 4 | 1 | .556 | 87 | 41 |
| Akron Pros | 3 | 5 | 2 | .375 | 146 | 95 |
| Milwaukee Badgers | 2 | 4 | 3 | .333 | 51 | 71 |
| Oorang Indians | 3 | 6 | 0 | .333 | 69 | 190 |
| Minneapolis Marines | 1 | 3 | 0 | .250 | 19 | 40 |
| Louisville Brecks | 1 | 3 | 0 | .250 | 13 | 140 |
| Evansville Crimson Giants | 0 | 3 | 0 | .000 | 6 | 88 |
| Rochester Jeffersons | 0 | 4 | 1 | .000 | 13 | 76 |
| Hammond Pros | 0 | 5 | 1 | .000 | 0 | 69 |
| Columbus Panhandles | 0 | 8 | 0 | .000 | 24 | 174 |

### 1923

| | W | L | T | Pct | Pts | OP |
|---|---|---|---|---|---|---|
| Canton Bulldogs | 11 | 0 | 1 | 1.000 | 246 | 19 |
| Chicago Bears | 9 | 2 | 1 | .818 | 123 | 35 |
| Green Bay Packers | 7 | 2 | 1 | .778 | 85 | 34 |
| Milwaukee Badgers | 7 | 2 | 3 | .778 | 100 | 49 |
| Cleveland Indians | 3 | 1 | 3 | .750 | 52 | 49 |
| Chicago Cardinals | 8 | 4 | 0 | .667 | 139 | 37 |
| Duluth Kelleys | 4 | 3 | 0 | .571 | 35 | 33 |
| Buffalo All-Americans | 5 | 4 | 3 | .556 | 94 | 43 |
| Columbus Tigers | 5 | 4 | 1 | .556 | 119 | 35 |
| Racine Legion | 4 | 4 | 2 | .500 | 86 | 76 |
| Toledo Maroons | 3 | 3 | 2 | .500 | 35 | 66 |
| Rock Island Independents | 2 | 3 | 2 | .400 | 83 | 62 |
| Minneapolis Marines | 2 | 5 | 1 | .286 | 48 | 80 |
| St. Louis All-Stars | 1 | 4 | 2 | .200 | 14 | 32 |
| Hammond Pros | 1 | 5 | 1 | .167 | 14 | 59 |
| Dayton Triangles | 1 | 6 | 1 | .143 | 16 | 95 |
| Akron Pros | 1 | 6 | 0 | .143 | 25 | 74 |
| Oorang Indians | 1 | 10 | 0 | .091 | 24 | 235 |
| Louisville Brecks | 0 | 3 | 0 | .000 | 0 | 90 |
| Rochester Jeffersons | 0 | 4 | 0 | .000 | 6 | 141 |

### 1924

| | W | L | T | Pct | Pts | OP |
|---|---|---|---|---|---|---|
| Cleveland Bulldogs | 7 | 1 | 1 | .875 | 229 | 60 |
| Chicago Bears | 6 | 1 | 4 | .857 | 136 | 55 |
| Frankfort Yellow Jackets | 11 | 2 | 1 | .846 | 326 | 109 |
| Duluth Kelleys | 5 | 1 | 0 | .833 | 56 | 16 |
| Rock Island Independents | 5 | 2 | 2 | .714 | 81 | 15 |
| Green Bay Packers | 7 | 4 | 0 | .636 | 108 | 38 |
| Racine Legion | 4 | 3 | 3 | .571 | 69 | 47 |
| Chicago Cardinals | 5 | 4 | 1 | .556 | 90 | 67 |
| Buffalo Bisons | 6 | 5 | 0 | .545 | 120 | 140 |
| Columbus Tigers | 4 | 4 | 0 | .500 | 91 | 68 |
| Hammond Pros | 2 | 2 | 1 | .500 | 18 | 45 |
| Milwaukee Badgers | 5 | 8 | 0 | .385 | 142 | 188 |
| Akron Pros | 2 | 6 | 0 | .250 | 59 | 132 |
| Dayton Triangles | 2 | 6 | 0 | .250 | 45 | 148 |
| Kansas City Blues | 2 | 7 | 0 | .222 | 46 | 124 |
| Kenosha Maroons | 0 | 4 | 1 | .000 | 12 | 117 |
| Minneapolis Marines | 0 | 6 | 0 | .000 | 14 | 108 |
| Rochester Jeffersons | 0 | 7 | 0 | .000 | 14 | 179 |

### 1925

| | W | L | T | Pct | Pts | OP |
|---|---|---|---|---|---|---|
| Chicago Cardinals | 11 | 2 | 1 | .846 | 230 | 65 |
| Pottsville Maroons | 10 | 2 | 0 | .833 | 280 | 45 |
| Detroit Panthers | 8 | 2 | 2 | .800 | 118 | 42 |
| New York Giants | 8 | 4 | 0 | .667 | 122 | 67 |
| Akron Pros | 4 | 2 | 2 | .650 | 65 | 51 |
| Frankfort Yellow Jackets | 13 | 7 | 0 | .643 | 196 | 189 |
| Chicago Bears | 9 | 5 | 3 | .625 | 158 | 96 |
| Rock Island Independents | 5 | 3 | 3 | .615 | 99 | 58 |
| Green Bay Packers | 8 | 5 | 0 | .545 | 151 | 120 |
| Providence Steam Roller | 6 | 5 | 1 | .500 | 131 | 108 |
| Canton Bulldogs | 4 | 4 | 0 | .385 | 50 | 73 |
| Cleveland Bulldogs | 5 | 8 | 1 | .286 | 75 | 134 |
| Kansas City Cowboys | 2 | 5 | 1 | .200 | 68 | 106 |
| Hammond Pros | 1 | 4 | 0 | .143 | 23 | 87 |

## 1925 (Cont.)

|  | W | L | T | Pct | Pts | OP |
|---|---|---|---|---|---|---|
| Buffalo Bisons | 1 | 6 | 2 | .143 | 33 | 113 |
| Duluth Kelleys | 0 | 3 | 0 | .000 | 6 | 25 |
| Rochester Jeffersons | 0 | 6 | 1 | .000 | 26 | 91 |
| Milwaukee Badgers | 0 | 6 | 0 | .000 | 7 | 191 |
| Dayton Triangles | 0 | 7 | 1 | .000 | 3 | 84 |
| Columbus Tigers | 0 | 9 | 0 | .000 | 28 | 124 |

## 1926

|  | W | L | T | Pct | Pts | OP |
|---|---|---|---|---|---|---|
| Frankfort Yellow Jackets | 14 | 1 | 2 | .765 | 223 | 43 |
| Chicago Bears | 12 | 1 | 3 | .844 | 216 | 63 |
| Pottsville Maroons | 10 | 2 | 2 | .714 | 155 | 29 |
| Kansas City Cowboys | 8 | 3 | 0 | .727 | 76 | 54 |
| Green Bay Packers | 7 | 3 | 3 | .462 | 144 | 68 |
| Los Angeles Buccaneers | 6 | 3 | 1 | .600 | 67 | 57 |
| NY Giants | 8 | 4 | 1 | .583 | 140 | 45 |
| Duluth Eskimos | 6 | 5 | 3 | .429 | 114 | 81 |
| Buffalo Rangers | 4 | 4 | 2 | .400 | 53 | 62 |
| Chicago Cardinals | 5 | 6 | 1 | .417 | 67 | 86 |
| Providence Steam Roller | 5 | 7 | 1 | .417 | 94 | 96 |
| Detroit Panthers | 4 | 6 | 2 | .500 | 115 | 52 |
| Hartford Blues | 3 | 7 | 0 | .300 | 57 | 99 |
| Brooklyn Lions | 3 | 8 | 0 | .273 | 60 | 150 |
| Milwaukee Badgers | 2 | 7 | 0 | .222 | 41 | 66 |
| Akron Indians | 1 | 4 | 3 | .125 | 23 | 89 |
| Dayton Triangles | 1 | 4 | 1 | .167 | 15 | 82 |
| Racine Tornadoes | 1 | 4 | 0 | .200 | 8 | 92 |
| Columbus Tigers | 1 | 6 | 0 | .143 | 26 | 93 |
| Canton Bulldogs | 1 | 9 | 3 | .077 | 46 | 172 |
| Hammond Pros | 0 | 4 | 0 | .000 | 3 | 56 |
| Louisville Colonels | 0 | 4 | 0 | .000 | 0 | 108 |

## 1927

|  | W | L | T | Pct | Pts | OP |
|---|---|---|---|---|---|---|
| NY Giants | 11 | 1 | 1 | .917 | 197 | 20 |
| Green Bay Packers | 7 | 2 | 1 | .778 | 113 | 43 |
| Chicago Bears | 9 | 3 | 2 | .750 | 149 | 98 |
| Cleveland Bulldogs | 8 | 4 | 1 | .667 | 209 | 107 |
| Providence Steam Roller | 8 | 5 | 1 | .615 | 105 | 88 |
| New York Yankees | 7 | 8 | 1 | .467 | 142 | 174 |
| Frankfort Yellow Jackets | 6 | 9 | 3 | .400 | 152 | 166 |
| Pottsville Maroons | 5 | 8 | 0 | .385 | 80 | 163 |
| Chicago Cardinals | 3 | 7 | 1 | .300 | 69 | 134 |
| Dayton Triangles | 1 | 6 | 1 | .143 | 15 | 57 |
| Duluth Eskimos | 1 | 8 | 0 | .111 | 68 | 134 |
| Buffalo Bisons | 0 | 5 | 0 | .000 | 8 | 123 |

## 1928

|  | W | L | T | Pct | Pts | OP |
|---|---|---|---|---|---|---|
| Providence Steam Roller | 8 | 1 | 1 | .889 | 128 | 36 |
| Frankfort Yellow Jackets | 11 | 3 | 1 | .786 | 169 | 84 |
| Detroit Wolverines | 7 | 2 | 1 | .778 | 189 | 76 |
| Green Bay Packers | 6 | 4 | 3 | .600 | 120 | 92 |
| Chicago Bears | 7 | 5 | 1 | .583 | 182 | 85 |
| NY Giants | 4 | 7 | 2 | .364 | 79 | 137 |
| NY Yankees | 4 | 8 | 1 | .333 | 104 | 179 |
| Pottsville Maroons | 2 | 8 | 0 | .200 | 74 | 134 |
| Chicago Cardinals | 1 | 5 | 0 | .167 | 7 | 107 |
| Dayton Triangles | 0 | 7 | 0 | .000 | 9 | 131 |

## 1929

|  | W | L | T | Pct | Pts | OP |
|---|---|---|---|---|---|---|
| Green Bay Packers | 12 | 0 | 1 | 1.000 | 198 | 22 |
| NY Giants | 13 | 1 | 1 | .929 | 312 | 86 |
| Frankfort Yellow Jackets | 10 | 4 | 5 | .714 | 139 | 128 |
| Chicago Cardinals | 6 | 6 | 1 | .500 | 154 | 83 |
| Boston Bulldogs | 4 | 4 | 0 | .500 | 98 | 73 |
| Staten Island Stapletons | 3 | 6 | 3 | .429 | 89 | 62 |
| Providence Steam Roller | 4 | 5 | 2 | .400 | 107 | 117 |
| Orange Tornadoes | 3 | 6 | 4 | .375 | 32 | 90 |
| Chicago Bears | 4 | 9 | 2 | .308 | 119 | 227 |
| Buffalo Bisons | 1 | 7 | 1 | .125 | 48 | 142 |
| Minneapolis Red Jackets | 1 | 9 | 0 | .100 | 48 | 185 |
| Dayton Triangles | 0 | 6 | 0 | .000 | 7 | 136 |

## 1930

|  | W | L | T | Pct | Pts | OP |
|---|---|---|---|---|---|---|
| Green Bay Packers | 10 | 3 | 1 | .769 | 234 | 111 |
| NY Giants | 13 | 4 | 0 | .765 | 308 | 98 |
| Chicago Bears | 9 | 4 | 1 | .692 | 169 | 71 |
| Brooklyn Dodgers | 7 | 4 | 1 | .636 | 154 | 59 |
| Providence Steam Roller | 6 | 4 | 1 | .600 | 90 | 125 |
| Staten Island Stapletons | 5 | 5 | 2 | .500 | 95 | 112 |
| Chicago Cardinals | 5 | 6 | 2 | .455 | 128 | 132 |
| Portsmouth Spartans | 5 | 6 | 3 | .455 | 176 | 161 |
| Frankfort Yellow Jackets | 4 | 13 | 1 | .222 | 113 | 321 |
| Minneapolis Red Jackets | 1 | 7 | 1 | .125 | 27 | 165 |
| Newark Tornadoes | 1 | 10 | 1 | .091 | 51 | 190 |

## 1931

|  | W | L | T | Pct | Pts | OP |
|---|---|---|---|---|---|---|
| Green Bay Packers | 12 | 2 | 0 | .857 | 318 | 94 |
| Portsmouth Spartans | 11 | 3 | 0 | .786 | 161 | 77 |
| Chicago Bears | 8 | 5 | 0 | .615 | 145 | 92 |
| Chicago Cardinals | 5 | 4 | 0 | .556 | 120 | 128 |
| NY Giants | 7 | 6 | 1 | .538 | 161 | 127 |
| Providence Steam Roller | 4 | 4 | 3 | .500 | 78 | 127 |
| Staten Island Stapletons | 4 | 6 | 1 | .400 | 79 | 118 |
| Cleveland Indians | 2 | 8 | 0 | .200 | 45 | 137 |
| Brooklyn Dodgers | 2 | 12 | 0 | .143 | 64 | 199 |
| Frankfort Yellow Jackets | 1 | 6 | 1 | .143 | 13 | 85 |

## 1932

|  | W | L | T | Pct | Pts | OP |
|---|---|---|---|---|---|---|
| Chicago Bears | 7 | 1 | 6 | .875 | 160 | 44 |
| Green Bay Packers | 10 | 3 | 1 | .769 | 152 | 63 |
| Portsmouth Spartans | 6 | 2 | 4 | .750 | 116 | 71 |
| Boston Braves | 4 | 4 | 2 | .500 | 55 | 79 |
| NY Giants | 4 | 6 | 2 | .400 | 93 | 113 |
| Brooklyn Dodgers | 3 | 9 | 0 | .250 | 63 | 131 |
| Chiago Cardinals | 2 | 6 | 2 | .250 | 72 | 114 |
| Staten Island Stapletons | 2 | 7 | 3 | .222 | 77 | 173 |

## 1933

| EAST | W | L | T | Pct | Pts | OP |
|---|---|---|---|---|---|---|
| NY Giants | 11 | 3 | 0 | .786 | 244 | 101 |
| Brooklyn Dodgers | 5 | 4 | 1 | .556 | 93 | 54 |
| Boston Redskins | 5 | 5 | 2 | .500 | 103 | 97 |
| Philadelphia Eagles | 3 | 5 | 1 | .375 | 77 | 158 |
| Pittsburgh Pirates | 3 | 6 | 2 | .333 | 67 | 208 |

## 1933 *(Cont.)*

| WEST | W | L | T | Pct | Pts | OP |
|---|---|---|---|---|---|---|
| Chicago Bears | 10 | 2 | 1 | .833 | 133 | 82 |
| Portsmouth Spartans | 6 | 5 | 0 | .545 | 128 | 87 |
| Green Bay Packers | 5 | 7 | 1 | .417 | 170 | 107 |
| Cincinnati Reds | 3 | 6 | 1 | .333 | 38 | 110 |
| Chicago Cardinals | 1 | 9 | 1 | .100 | 52 | 101 |

## 1934

| EAST | W | L | T | Pct | Pts | OP |
|---|---|---|---|---|---|---|
| NY Giants | 8 | 5 | 0 | .615 | 147 | 107 |
| Boston Redskins | 6 | 6 | 0 | .500 | 107 | 94 |
| Brooklyn Dodgers | 4 | 7 | 0 | .364 | 60 | 153 |
| Philadelphia Eagles | 4 | 7 | 0 | .364 | 127 | 85 |
| Pittsburgh Pirates | 2 | 10 | 0 | .167 | 51 | 206 |

| WEST | W | L | T | Pct | Pts | OP |
|---|---|---|---|---|---|---|
| Chicago Bears | 13 | 0 | 0 | 1.000 | 286 | 86 |
| Detroit Lions | 10 | 3 | 0 | .769 | 238 | 59 |
| Green Bay Packers | 7 | 6 | 0 | .538 | 156 | 112 |
| Chicago Cardinals | 5 | 6 | 0 | .455 | 80 | 84 |
| St. Louis Gunners | 1 | 2 | 0 | .333 | 27 | 61 |
| Cincinnati Reds | 0 | 8 | 0 | .000 | 10 | 243 |

## 1935

| EAST | W | L | T | Pct | Pts | OP |
|---|---|---|---|---|---|---|
| NY Giants | 9 | 3 | 0 | .750 | 180 | 96 |
| Brooklyn Dodgers | 5 | 6 | 1 | .455 | 90 | 141 |
| Pittsburgh Pirates | 4 | 8 | 0 | .333 | 99 | 209 |
| Boston Redskins | 2 | 8 | 1 | .200 | 65 | 122 |
| Philadelphia Eagles | 2 | 9 | 0 | .182 | 60 | 179 |

| WEST | W | L | T | Pct | Pts | OP |
|---|---|---|---|---|---|---|
| Detroit Lions | 7 | 3 | 2 | .700 | 191 | 111 |
| Green Bay Packers | 8 | 4 | 0 | .667 | 181 | 96 |
| Chicago Bears | 6 | 4 | 2 | .600 | 192 | 106 |
| Chicago Cardinals | 6 | 4 | 2 | .600 | 99 | 97 |

## 1936

| EAST | W | L | T | Pct | Pts | OP |
|---|---|---|---|---|---|---|
| Boston Redskins | 7 | 5 | 0 | .583 | 149 | 110 |
| Pittsburgh Pirates | 6 | 6 | 0 | .500 | 98 | 187 |
| NY Giants | 5 | 6 | 1 | .455 | 115 | 163 |
| Brooklyn Dodgers | 3 | 8 | 1 | .273 | 92 | 161 |
| Philadelphia Eagles | 1 | 11 | 0 | .083 | 51 | 206 |

| WEST | W | L | T | Pct | Pts | OP |
|---|---|---|---|---|---|---|
| Green Bay | 10 | 1 | 1 | .909 | 248 | 118 |
| Chicago Bears | 9 | 3 | 0 | .750 | 222 | 94 |
| Detroit Lions | 8 | 4 | 0 | .667 | 235 | 102 |
| Chicago Cardinals | 3 | 8 | 1 | .273 | 74 | 143 |

## 1937

| EAST | W | L | T | Pct | Pts | OP |
|---|---|---|---|---|---|---|
| Washington Redskins | 8 | 3 | 0 | .727 | 195 | 120 |
| NY Giants | 6 | 3 | 2 | .667 | 128 | 109 |
| Pittsburgh Pirates | 4 | 7 | 0 | .364 | 122 | 145 |
| Brooklyn Dodgers | 3 | 7 | 1 | .300 | 82 | 174 |
| Philadelphia Eagles | 2 | 8 | 1 | .200 | 86 | 177 |

| WEST | W | L | T | Pct | Pts | OP |
|---|---|---|---|---|---|---|
| Chicago Bears | 9 | 1 | 1 | .900 | 201 | 100 |
| Green Bay Packers | 7 | 4 | 0 | .636 | 220 | 122 |
| Detroit Lions | 7 | 4 | 0 | .636 | 180 | 105 |
| Chicago Cardinals | 5 | 5 | 1 | .500 | 135 | 165 |
| Cleveland Rams | 1 | 10 | 0 | .091 | 75 | 207 |

## 1938

| EAST | W | L | T | Pct | Pts | OP |
|---|---|---|---|---|---|---|
| NY Giants | 8 | 2 | 1 | .800 | 194 | 79 |
| Washington Redskins | 6 | 3 | 2 | .667 | 148 | 154 |
| Brooklyn Dodgers | 4 | 4 | 3 | .500 | 131 | 161 |
| Philadelphia Eagles | 5 | 6 | 0 | .455 | 154 | 164 |
| Pittsburgh Pirates | 2 | 9 | 0 | .182 | 79 | 169 |

| WEST | W | L | T | Pct | Pts | OP |
|---|---|---|---|---|---|---|
| Green Bay Packers | 8 | 3 | 0 | .727 | 223 | 118 |
| Detroit Lions | 7 | 4 | 0 | .636 | 119 | 108 |
| Chicago Bears | 6 | 5 | 0 | .545 | 194 | 148 |
| Cleveland Rams | 4 | 7 | 0 | .364 | 131 | 215 |
| Chicago Cardinals | 2 | 9 | 0 | .182 | 111 | 168 |

## 1939

| EAST | W | L | T | Pct | Pts | OP |
|---|---|---|---|---|---|---|
| NY Giants | 9 | 1 | 1 | .168 | 168 | 85 |
| Washington Redskins | 8 | 2 | 1 | .242 | 242 | 94 |
| Brooklyn Dodgers | 4 | 6 | 1 | .108 | 108 | 219 |
| Philadelphia Eagles | 1 | 9 | 1 | .105 | 105 | 200 |
| Pittsburgh Pirates | 1 | 9 | 1 | .114 | 114 | 216 |

| WEST | W | L | T | Pct | Pts | OP |
|---|---|---|---|---|---|---|
| Green Bay Packers | 9 | 2 | 0 | .818 | 233 | 153 |
| Chicago Bears | 8 | 3 | 0 | .727 | 298 | 157 |
| Detroit Lions | 6 | 5 | 0 | .545 | 145 | 150 |
| Cleveland Rams | 5 | 5 | 1 | .195 | 195 | 164 |
| Chicago Cardinals | 1 | 10 | 0 | .091 | 84 | 254 |

## 1940

| EAST | W | L | T | Pct | Pts | OP |
|---|---|---|---|---|---|---|
| Washington Redskins | 9 | 2 | 0 | .818 | 245 | 142 |
| Brooklyn Dodgers | 8 | 2 | 0 | .800 | 179 | 110 |
| NY Giants | 6 | 4 | 1 | .545 | 131 | 133 |
| Pittsburgh Pirates | 2 | 7 | 2 | .182 | 67 | 174 |
| Philadelphia Eagles | 1 | 10 | 0 | .091 | 121 | 200 |

| WEST | W | L | T | Pct | Pts | OP |
|---|---|---|---|---|---|---|
| Chicago Bears | 8 | 3 | 0 | .727 | 238 | 152 |
| Green Bay Packers | 6 | 4 | 0 | .600 | 238 | 155 |
| Detroit Lions | 5 | 5 | 1 | .500 | 120 | 177 |
| Cleveland Rams | 4 | 6 | 1 | .400 | 181 | 191 |
| Chicago Cardinals | 2 | 7 | 2 | .222 | 139 | 222 |

## 1941

| EAST | W | L | T | Pct | Pts | OP |
|---|---|---|---|---|---|---|
| NY Giants | 8 | 3 | 0 | .727 | 238 | 114 |
| Brooklyn Dodgers | 7 | 4 | 0 | .636 | 158 | 127 |
| Washington | 6 | 5 | 0 | .545 | 176 | 174 |
| Philadelphia | 2 | 8 | 1 | .200 | 119 | 218 |
| Pittsburgh Steelers | 1 | 9 | 1 | .100 | 103 | 276 |

| WEST | W | L | T | Pct | Pts | OP |
|---|---|---|---|---|---|---|
| Green Bay | 10 | 1 | 0 | .909 | 258 | 120 |
| Chicago Bears | 10 | 1 | 0 | .909 | 396 | 147 |
| Detroit | 4 | 6 | 1 | .400 | 121 | 195 |
| Chicago Cardinals | 3 | 7 | 1 | .300 | 127 | 197 |
| Cleveland Rams | 2 | 9 | 0 | .182 | 116 | 244 |

## 1942

| EAST | W | L | T | Pct | Pts | OP |
|---|---|---|---|---|---|---|
| Washington | 10 | 1 | 0 | .909 | 227 | 102 |
| Pittsburgh Steelers | 7 | 4 | 0 | .636 | 167 | 119 |
| NY Giants | 5 | 5 | 1 | .500 | 155 | 139 |
| Brooklyn Dodgers | 3 | 8 | 0 | .273 | 100 | 168 |
| Philadelphia | 2 | 9 | 0 | .182 | 134 | 239 |

| WEST | W | L | T | Pct | Pts | OP |
|---|---|---|---|---|---|---|
| Chicago Bears | 11 | 0 | 0 | 1.000 | 376 | 84 |
| Green Bay | 8 | 2 | 1 | .800 | 300 | 215 |
| Cleveland Rams | 5 | 6 | 0 | .455 | 150 | 207 |
| Chicago Cardinals | 3 | 8 | 0 | .273 | 98 | 209 |
| Detroit | 0 | 11 | 0 | .000 | 38 | 263 |

## 1943

| EAST | W | L | T | Pct | Pts | OP |
|---|---|---|---|---|---|---|
| Washington | 6 | 3 | 1 | .667 | 229 | 137 |
| NY Giants | 6 | 3 | 1 | .667 | 197 | 170 |
| Phi/Pitt Eagles/Steelers | 5 | 4 | 1 | .556 | 225 | 230 |
| Brooklyn Dodgers | 2 | 8 | 0 | .200 | 65 | 234 |

| WEST | W | L | T | Pct | Pts | OP |
|---|---|---|---|---|---|---|
| Chicago Bears | 8 | 1 | 1 | .889 | 303 | 157 |
| Green Bay | 7 | 2 | 1 | .778 | 264 | 172 |
| Detroit | 3 | 6 | 1 | .333 | 178 | 218 |
| Chicago Cardinals | 0 | 10 | 0 | .000 | 95 | 238 |

## 1944

| EAST | W | L | T | Pct | Pts | OP |
|---|---|---|---|---|---|---|
| NY Giants | 8 | 1 | 1 | .889 | 206 | 75 |
| Philadelphia | 7 | 1 | 2 | .875 | 267 | 131 |
| Washington | 6 | 3 | 1 | .667 | 169 | 180 |
| Boston Yanks | 2 | 8 | 0 | .200 | 82 | 233 |
| Brooklyn Tigers | 0 | 10 | 0 | .000 | 69 | 166 |

| WEST | W | L | T | Pct | Pts | OP |
|---|---|---|---|---|---|---|
| Green Bay | 8 | 2 | 0 | .800 | 238 | 141 |
| Chicago Bears | 6 | 3 | 1 | .667 | 258 | 172 |
| Detroit | 6 | 3 | 1 | .667 | 216 | 151 |
| Cleveland Rams | 4 | 6 | 0 | .400 | 188 | 224 |
| Chi/Pitt Cards/Steelers | 0 | 10 | 0 | .000 | 116 | 336 |

## 1945

| EAST | W | L | T | Pct | Pts | OP |
|---|---|---|---|---|---|---|
| Washington | 8 | 2 | 0 | .800 | 209 | 121 |
| Philadelphia | 7 | 3 | 0 | .700 | 272 | 133 |
| NY Giants | 3 | 6 | 1 | .333 | 179 | 198 |
| Bos/Bkn Yanks/Tigers | 3 | 6 | 1 | .333 | 123 | 211 |
| Pittsburgh | 2 | 8 | 0 | .200 | 79 | 220 |

| WEST | W | L | T | Pct | Pts | OP |
|---|---|---|---|---|---|---|
| Cleveland Rams | 9 | 1 | 0 | .900 | 244 | 136 |
| Detroit | 7 | 3 | 0 | .700 | 195 | 194 |
| Green Bay | 6 | 4 | 0 | .600 | 258 | 173 |
| Chicago Bears | 3 | 7 | 0 | .300 | 192 | 235 |
| Chicago Cardinals | 1 | 9 | 0 | .100 | 98 | 228 |

## 1946

| EAST | W | L | T | Pct | Pts | OP |
|---|---|---|---|---|---|---|
| NY Giants | 7 | 3 | 1 | .700 | 236 | 162 |
| Philadelphia | 6 | 5 | 0 | .545 | 231 | 220 |
| Washington | 5 | 5 | 1 | .500 | 171 | 191 |
| Pittsburgh | 5 | 5 | 1 | .500 | 136 | 117 |
| Boston Yanks | 2 | 8 | 1 | .200 | 189 | 273 |

| WEST | W | L | T | Pct | Pts | OP |
|---|---|---|---|---|---|---|
| Chicago Bears | 8 | 2 | 1 | .800 | 289 | 193 |
| LA Rams | 6 | 4 | 1 | .600 | 277 | 257 |
| Chicago Cardinals | 6 | 5 | 0 | .545 | 260 | 198 |
| Green Bay | 6 | 5 | 0 | .545 | 148 | 158 |
| Detroit | 1 | 10 | 0 | .091 | 142 | 310 |

## 1947

| EAST | W | L | T | Pct | Pts | OP |
|---|---|---|---|---|---|---|
| Pittsburgh | 8 | 4 | 0 | .667 | 240 | 259 |
| Philadelphia | 8 | 4 | 0 | .667 | 308 | 242 |
| Boston Yanks | 4 | 7 | 1 | .364 | 168 | 256 |
| Washington | 4 | 8 | 0 | .333 | 295 | 367 |
| NY Giants | 2 | 8 | 2 | .200 | 190 | 309 |

| WEST | W | L | T | Pct | Pts | OP |
|---|---|---|---|---|---|---|
| Chicago Cardinals | 9 | 3 | 0 | .750 | 306 | 231 |
| Chicago Bears | 8 | 4 | 0 | .667 | 363 | 241 |
| Green Bay | 6 | 5 | 1 | .542 | 274 | 210 |
| LA Rams | 6 | 6 | 0 | .500 | 259 | 214 |
| Detroit Lions | 3 | 9 | 0 | .250 | 231 | 305 |

## 1948

| EAST | W | L | T | Pct | Pts | OP |
|---|---|---|---|---|---|---|
| Philadelphia | 9 | 2 | 1 | .818 | 376 | 156 |
| Washington | 7 | 5 | 0 | .583 | 291 | 287 |
| Pittsburgh | 4 | 8 | 0 | .333 | 200 | 243 |
| NY Giants | 4 | 8 | 0 | .333 | 297 | 388 |
| Boston Yanks | 3 | 9 | 0 | .250 | 174 | 372 |

| WEST | W | L | T | Pct | Pts | OP |
|---|---|---|---|---|---|---|
| Chicago Cardinals | 11 | 1 | 0 | .917 | 395 | 226 |
| Chicago Bears | 10 | 2 | 0 | .833 | 375 | 151 |
| LA Rams | 6 | 5 | 1 | .545 | 327 | 269 |
| Green Bay | 3 | 9 | 0 | .250 | 154 | 290 |
| Detroit Lions | 2 | 10 | 0 | .167 | 200 | 407 |

## 1949

| EAST | W | L | T | Pct | Pts | OP |
|---|---|---|---|---|---|---|
| Philadelphia | 11 | 1 | 0 | .917 | 364 | 134 |
| Pittsburgh | 6 | 5 | 1 | .545 | 224 | 214 |
| NY Giants | 6 | 6 | 0 | .500 | 287 | 298 |
| Washington | 4 | 7 | 1 | .364 | 268 | 339 |
| NY Bulldogs | 1 | 10 | 1 | .091 | 153 | 368 |

| WEST | W | L | T | Pct | Pts | OP |
|---|---|---|---|---|---|---|
| LA Rams | 8 | 2 | 2 | .800 | 360 | 239 |
| Chicago Bears | 9 | 3 | 0 | .750 | 332 | 218 |
| Chicago Cardinals | 6 | 5 | 1 | .545 | 360 | 301 |
| Detroit Lions | 4 | 8 | 0 | .333 | 237 | 259 |
| Green Bay | 2 | 10 | 0 | .167 | 114 | 329 |

## 1950

| EAST | W | L | T | Pct | Pts | OP |
|---|---|---|---|---|---|---|
| Cleveland Browns | 10 | 2 | 0 | .833 | 310 | 144 |
| NY Giants | 10 | 2 | 0 | .833 | 268 | 150 |
| Philadelphia | 6 | 6 | 0 | .500 | 254 | 141 |
| Pittsburgh | 6 | 6 | 0 | .500 | 180 | 195 |
| Chicago Cardinals | 5 | 7 | 0 | .417 | 233 | 287 |
| Washington | 3 | 9 | 0 | .250 | 232 | 326 |

| WEST | W | L | T | Pct | Pts | OP |
|---|---|---|---|---|---|---|
| Chicago Bears | 9 | 3 | 0 | .750 | 279 | 207 |
| LA Rams | 9 | 3 | 0 | .750 | 466 | 309 |
| New York Yanks | 7 | 5 | 0 | .583 | 366 | 367 |
| Detroit | 6 | 6 | 0 | .500 | 321 | 285 |
| San Francisco 49ers | 3 | 9 | 0 | .250 | 213 | 300 |
| Green Bay | 3 | 9 | 0 | .250 | 244 | 406 |
| Baltimore Colts | 1 | 11 | 0 | .067 | 213 | 462 |

## 1951

| AMERICAN | W | L | T | Pct | Pts | OP |
|---|---|---|---|---|---|---|
| Cleveland | 11 | 1 | 0 | .917 | 331 | 152 |
| NY Giants | 9 | 2 | 1 | .818 | 254 | 161 |
| Washington | 5 | 7 | 0 | .417 | 183 | 296 |
| Pittsburgh | 4 | 7 | 1 | .364 | 183 | 235 |
| Philadelphia | 4 | 8 | 0 | .333 | 234 | 264 |
| Chicago Cardinals | 3 | 9 | 0 | .250 | 210 | 287 |

| NATIONAL | W | L | T | Pct | Pts | OP |
|---|---|---|---|---|---|---|
| LA Rams | 8 | 4 | 0 | .667 | 392 | 261 |
| Detroit Lions | 7 | 4 | 1 | .636 | 336 | 259 |
| San Francisco 49ers | 7 | 4 | 1 | .636 | 255 | 205 |
| Chicago Bears | 7 | 5 | 0 | .583 | 286 | 282 |
| Green Bay | 3 | 9 | 0 | .250 | 254 | 375 |
| New York Yanks | 1 | 9 | 2 | .100 | 241 | 382 |

## 1952

| AMERICAN | W | L | T | Pct | Pts | OP |
|---|---|---|---|---|---|---|
| Cleveland | 8 | 4 | 0 | .667 | 310 | 213 |
| Philadelphia | 7 | 5 | 0 | .583 | 252 | 271 |
| NY Giants | 7 | 5 | 0 | .583 | 234 | 231 |
| Pittsburgh | 5 | 7 | 0 | .417 | 300 | 273 |
| Washington | 4 | 8 | 0 | .333 | 240 | 287 |
| Chicago Cardinals | 4 | 8 | 0 | .333 | 172 | 221 |

| NATIONAL | W | L | T | Pct | Pts | OP |
|---|---|---|---|---|---|---|
| Detroit | 9 | 3 | 0 | .750 | 344 | 192 |
| LA Rams | 9 | 3 | 0 | .750 | 349 | 234 |
| San Francisco | 7 | 5 | 0 | .583 | 285 | 221 |
| Green Bay | 6 | 6 | 0 | .500 | 295 | 312 |
| Chicago Bears | 5 | 7 | 0 | .417 | 245 | 326 |
| Dallas Texans | 1 | 11 | 0 | .083 | 182 | 427 |

## 1953

| EAST | W | L | T | Pct | Pts | OP |
|---|---|---|---|---|---|---|
| Cleveland | 11 | 1 | 0 | .917 | 348 | 162 |
| Philadelphia | 7 | 4 | 1 | .636 | 352 | 215 |
| Washington | 6 | 5 | 1 | .545 | 208 | 215 |
| Pittsburgh | 5 | 7 | 0 | .417 | 211 | 272 |
| NY Giants | 4 | 8 | 0 | .333 | 188 | 277 |
| Chicago Cardinals | 1 | 10 | 1 | .091 | 190 | 337 |

| WEST | W | L | T | Pct | Pts | OP |
|---|---|---|---|---|---|---|
| Detroit | 10 | 2 | 0 | .833 | 271 | 205 |
| San Francisco | 9 | 3 | 0 | .750 | 372 | 237 |
| LA Rams | 8 | 3 | 1 | .727 | 366 | 236 |
| Chicago Bears | 3 | 8 | 1 | .273 | 218 | 262 |
| Baltimore Colts | 3 | 9 | 0 | .250 | 182 | 350 |
| Green Bay | 2 | 9 | 1 | .182 | 200 | 338 |

## 1954

| EAST | W | L | T | Pct | Pts | OP |
|---|---|---|---|---|---|---|
| Cleveland | 9 | 3 | 0 | .750 | 336 | 162 |
| Philadelphia | 7 | 4 | 1 | .636 | 284 | 230 |
| NY Giants | 7 | 5 | 0 | .583 | 293 | 184 |
| Pittsburgh | 5 | 7 | 0 | .417 | 219 | 263 |
| Washington | 3 | 9 | 0 | .250 | 207 | 432 |
| Chicago Cardinals | 2 | 10 | 0 | .167 | 183 | 347 |

| WEST | W | L | T | Pct | Pts | OP |
|---|---|---|---|---|---|---|
| Detroit | 9 | 2 | 1 | .818 | 337 | 189 |
| Chicago Bears | 8 | 4 | 0 | .667 | 301 | 279 |
| San Francisco | 7 | 4 | 1 | .636 | 313 | 251 |
| LA Rams | 6 | 5 | 1 | .545 | 314 | 285 |
| Green Bay | 4 | 8 | 0 | .333 | 234 | 251 |
| Baltimore | 3 | 9 | 0 | .250 | 131 | 279 |

## 1955

| EAST | W | L | T | Pct | Pts | OP |
|---|---|---|---|---|---|---|
| Cleveland | 9 | 2 | 1 | .818 | 349 | 218 |
| Washington | 8 | 4 | 0 | .667 | 246 | 222 |
| NY Giants | 6 | 5 | 1 | .545 | 267 | 223 |
| Philadelphia | 4 | 7 | 1 | .364 | 248 | 231 |
| Chicago Cardinals | 4 | 7 | 1 | .364 | 224 | 252 |
| Pittsburgh | 4 | 8 | 0 | .333 | 195 | 285 |

| WEST | W | L | T | Pct | Pts | OP |
|---|---|---|---|---|---|---|
| LA Rams | 8 | 3 | 1 | .727 | 260 | 231 |
| Chicago Bears | 8 | 4 | 0 | .667 | 294 | 251 |
| Green Bay | 6 | 6 | 0 | .500 | 258 | 276 |
| Baltimore | 5 | 6 | 1 | .455 | 214 | 239 |
| San Francisco | 4 | 8 | 0 | .333 | 216 | 298 |
| Detroit | 3 | 9 | 0 | .250 | 230 | 275 |

## 1956

| EAST | W | L | T | Pct | Pts | OP |
|---|---|---|---|---|---|---|
| NY Giants | 8 | 3 | 1 | .727 | 264 | 197 |
| Chicago Cardinals | 7 | 5 | 0 | .583 | 240 | 182 |
| Washington | 6 | 6 | 0 | .500 | 183 | 225 |
| Pittsburgh | 5 | 7 | 0 | .417 | 217 | 250 |
| Cleveland | 5 | 7 | 0 | .417 | 167 | 177 |
| Philadelphia | 3 | 8 | 1 | .273 | 143 | 215 |

| WEST | W | L | T | Pct | Pts | OP |
|---|---|---|---|---|---|---|
| Chicago Bears | 9 | 2 | 1 | .818 | 269 | 169 |
| Detroit | 9 | 3 | 0 | .750 | 300 | 188 |
| San Francisco | 5 | 6 | 1 | .455 | 233 | 284 |
| Baltimore | 5 | 7 | 0 | .417 | 270 | 322 |
| Green Bay | 4 | 8 | 0 | .333 | 264 | 342 |
| LA Rams | 4 | 8 | 0 | .333 | 291 | 307 |

## 1957

| EAST | W | L | T | Pct | Pts | OP |
|---|---|---|---|---|---|---|
| Cleveland | 9 | 2 | 1 | .818 | 269 | 169 |
| NY Giants | 7 | 5 | 0 | .583 | 251 | 211 |
| Pittsburgh | 6 | 6 | 0 | .500 | 155 | 178 |
| Washington | 5 | 6 | 1 | .455 | 251 | 230 |
| Philadelphia | 4 | 8 | 0 | .333 | 173 | 224 |
| Chicago Cardinals | 3 | 9 | 0 | .250 | 200 | 299 |

| WEST | W | L | T | Pct | Pts | OP |
|---|---|---|---|---|---|---|
| San Francisco | 8 | 4 | 0 | .667 | 260 | 264 |
| Detroit | 8 | 4 | 0 | .667 | 251 | 231 |
| Baltimore | 7 | 5 | 0 | .583 | 303 | 235 |
| LA Rams | 6 | 6 | 0 | .500 | 307 | 278 |
| Chicago Bears | 5 | 7 | 0 | .417 | 203 | 211 |
| Green Bay | 3 | 9 | 0 | .250 | 218 | 311 |

## 1958

| EAST | W | L | T | Pct | Pts | OP |
|---|---|---|---|---|---|---|
| Cleveland | 9 | 3 | 0 | .750 | 302 | 217 |
| NY Giants | 9 | 3 | 0 | .750 | 246 | 183 |
| Pittsburgh | 7 | 4 | 1 | .636 | 261 | 230 |
| Washington | 4 | 7 | 1 | .364 | 214 | 268 |
| Chicago Cardinals | 2 | 9 | 1 | .182 | 261 | 356 |
| Philadelphia | 2 | 9 | 1 | .182 | 235 | 306 |

| WEST | W | L | T | Pct | Pts | OP |
|---|---|---|---|---|---|---|
| Baltimore | 9 | 3 | 0 | .750 | 381 | 203 |
| LA Rams | 8 | 4 | 0 | .667 | 344 | 278 |
| Chicago Bears | 8 | 4 | 0 | .667 | 298 | 230 |
| San Francisco | 6 | 6 | 0 | .500 | 257 | 324 |
| Detroit | 4 | 7 | 1 | .364 | 261 | 276 |
| Green Bay | 1 | 10 | 1 | .091 | 193 | 382 |

## 1959

| EAST | W | L | T | Pct | Pts | OP |
|---|---|---|---|---|---|---|
| NY Giants | 10 | 2 | 0 | .833 | 284 | 167 |
| Philadelphia | 7 | 5 | 0 | .583 | 268 | 278 |
| Cleveland | 7 | 5 | 0 | .583 | 270 | 214 |
| Pittsburgh | 6 | 5 | 1 | .545 | 257 | 216 |
| Washington | 3 | 9 | 0 | .250 | 185 | 350 |
| Chicago Cardinals | 2 | 10 | 0 | .167 | 231 | 324 |

| WEST | W | L | T | Pct | Pts | OP |
|---|---|---|---|---|---|---|
| Baltimore | 9 | 3 | 0 | .750 | 374 | 251 |
| Chicago Bears | 8 | 4 | 0 | .667 | 246 | 196 |
| Green Bay | 7 | 5 | 0 | .583 | 248 | 240 |
| San Francisco | 7 | 5 | 0 | .583 | 255 | 237 |
| Detroit | 3 | 8 | 1 | .273 | 203 | 275 |
| LA Rams | 2 | 10 | 0 | .167 | 242 | 315 |

## 1960

| NFL EAST | W | L | T | Pct | Pts | OP |
|---|---|---|---|---|---|---|
| Philadelphia | 10 | 2 | 0 | .833 | 321 | 246 |
| Cleveland | 8 | 3 | 1 | .727 | 362 | 217 |
| NY Giants | 6 | 4 | 2 | .600 | 271 | 261 |
| St. Louis Cardinals | 6 | 5 | 1 | .545 | 288 | 230 |
| Pittsburgh | 5 | 6 | 1 | .455 | 240 | 275 |
| Washington | 1 | 9 | 2 | .100 | 178 | 309 |

| NFL WEST | W | L | T | Pct | Pts | OP |
|---|---|---|---|---|---|---|
| Green Bay | 8 | 4 | 0 | .667 | 332 | 209 |
| Detroit | 7 | 5 | 0 | .583 | 239 | 212 |
| San Francisco | 7 | 5 | 0 | .583 | 208 | 205 |
| Baltimore | 6 | 6 | 0 | .500 | 288 | 234 |
| Chicago Bears | 5 | 6 | 1 | .455 | 194 | 299 |
| LA Rams | 4 | 7 | 1 | .364 | 265 | 297 |
| Dallas Cowboys | 0 | 11 | 1 | .000 | 177 | 369 |

| AFL EAST | W | L | T | Pct | Pts | OP |
|---|---|---|---|---|---|---|
| Houston Oilers | 10 | 4 | 0 | .714 | 379 | 285 |
| NY Titans | 7 | 7 | 0 | .500 | 382 | 399 |
| Buffalo Bills | 5 | 8 | 1 | .385 | 296 | 303 |
| Boston Patriots | 5 | 9 | 0 | .357 | 286 | 349 |

| AFL WEST | W | L | T | Pct | Pts | OP |
|---|---|---|---|---|---|---|
| Los Angeles Chargers | 10 | 4 | 0 | .714 | 373 | 336 |
| Dallas Texans | 8 | 6 | 0 | .571 | 361 | 253 |
| Oakland Raiders | 6 | 8 | 0 | .429 | 319 | 388 |
| Denver Broncos | 4 | 9 | 1 | .308 | 309 | 393 |

## 1961

| NFL EAST | W | L | T | Pct | Pts | OP |
|---|---|---|---|---|---|---|
| NY Giants | 10 | 3 | 1 | .769 | 368 | 220 |
| Philadelphia | 10 | 4 | 0 | .714 | 361 | 297 |
| Cleveland | 8 | 5 | 1 | .615 | 319 | 270 |
| St. Louis Cardinals | 7 | 7 | 0 | .500 | 279 | 267 |
| Pittsburgh | 6 | 8 | 0 | .429 | 295 | 287 |
| Dallas Cowboys | 4 | 9 | 1 | .308 | 236 | 380 |
| Washington | 1 | 12 | 1 | .077 | 174 | 392 |

| NFL WEST | W | L | T | Pct | Pts | OP |
|---|---|---|---|---|---|---|
| Green Bay | 11 | 3 | 0 | .786 | 391 | 223 |
| Detroit | 8 | 5 | 1 | .615 | 270 | 258 |
| Baltimore | 8 | 6 | 0 | .571 | 302 | 307 |
| Chicago | 8 | 6 | 0 | .571 | 326 | 302 |
| San Francisco | 7 | 6 | 1 | .538 | 346 | 272 |
| LA Rams | 4 | 10 | 0 | .286 | 263 | 407 |
| Minnesota Vikings | 3 | 11 | 0 | .214 | 285 | 407 |

| AFL EAST | W | L | T | Pct | Pts | OP |
|---|---|---|---|---|---|---|
| Houston Oilers | 10 | 3 | 1 | .769 | 513 | 242 |
| Boston Patriots | 9 | 4 | 1 | .692 | 413 | 313 |
| New York Titans | 7 | 7 | 0 | .500 | 301 | 390 |
| Buffalo Bills | 6 | 8 | 0 | .429 | 294 | 342 |

| AFL WEST | W | L | T | Pct | Pts | OP |
|---|---|---|---|---|---|---|
| San Diego Chargers | 12 | 2 | 0 | .857 | 396 | 219 |
| Dallas Texans | 6 | 8 | 0 | .429 | 334 | 343 |
| Denver | 3 | 11 | 0 | .214 | 251 | 432 |
| Oakland | 2 | 12 | 0 | .143 | 237 | 458 |

### 1962

**NFL EAST**

| | W | L | T | Pct | Pts | OP |
|---|---|---|---|---|---|---|
| NY Giants | 12 | 2 | 0 | .857 | 398 | 283 |
| Pittsburgh | 9 | 5 | 0 | .642 | 312 | 363 |
| Cleveland | 7 | 6 | 1 | .538 | 291 | 257 |
| Washington | 5 | 7 | 2 | .417 | 305 | 376 |
| Dallas Cowboys | 5 | 8 | 1 | .385 | 398 | 402 |
| St. Louis Cardinals | 4 | 9 | 1 | .308 | 287 | 361 |
| Philadelphia | 3 | 10 | 1 | .231 | 282 | 356 |

**NFL WEST**

| | W | L | T | Pct | Pts | OP |
|---|---|---|---|---|---|---|
| Green Bay | 13 | 1 | 0 | .929 | 415 | 148 |
| Detroit | 11 | 3 | 0 | .786 | 315 | 177 |
| Chicago | 9 | 5 | 0 | .643 | 321 | 287 |
| Baltimore | 7 | 7 | 0 | .500 | 293 | 288 |
| San Francisco | 6 | 8 | 0 | .429 | 282 | 331 |
| Minnesota | 2 | 11 | 1 | .154 | 254 | 410 |
| LA Rams | 1 | 12 | 1 | .077 | 220 | 334 |

**AFL EAST**

| | W | L | T | Pct | Pts | OP |
|---|---|---|---|---|---|---|
| Houston | 11 | 3 | 0 | .786 | 387 | 270 |
| Boston | 9 | 4 | 1 | .692 | 346 | 295 |
| Buffalo | 7 | 6 | 1 | .538 | 309 | 272 |
| NY Titans | 5 | 9 | 0 | .357 | 278 | 423 |

**AFL WEST**

| | W | L | T | Pct | Pts | OP |
|---|---|---|---|---|---|---|
| Dallas Texans | 11 | 3 | 0 | .786 | 389 | 233 |
| Denver | 6 | 7 | 0 | .462 | 323 | 313 |
| San Diego | 4 | 9 | 0 | .308 | 293 | 362 |
| Oakland | 1 | 13 | 0 | .071 | 213 | 370 |

### 1963

**NFL EAST**

| | W | L | T | Pct | Pts | OP |
|---|---|---|---|---|---|---|
| NY Giants | 11 | 3 | 0 | .786 | 448 | 280 |
| Cleveland | 10 | 4 | 0 | .714 | 343 | 262 |
| St. Louis | 9 | 5 | 0 | .643 | 341 | 283 |
| Pittsburgh | 7 | 4 | 3 | .636 | 321 | 295 |
| Dallas Cowboys | 4 | 10 | 0 | .286 | 305 | 378 |
| Washington | 3 | 11 | 0 | .214 | 279 | 398 |
| Philadelphia | 2 | 10 | 2 | .214 | 242 | 381 |

**NFL WEST**

| | W | L | T | Pct | Pts | OP |
|---|---|---|---|---|---|---|
| Chicago | 11 | 1 | 2 | .917 | 301 | 144 |
| Green Bay | 11 | 2 | 1 | .846 | 369 | 206 |
| Baltimore | 8 | 6 | 0 | .571 | 316 | 285 |
| Minnesota | 5 | 8 | 1 | .385 | 309 | 390 |
| Detroit | 5 | 8 | 1 | .385 | 32 | 265 |
| LA Rams | 5 | 9 | 0 | .357 | 210 | 350 |
| San Francisco | 2 | 12 | 0 | .143 | 198 | 391 |

**AFL EAST**

| | W | L | T | Pct | Pts | OP |
|---|---|---|---|---|---|---|
| Boston | 7 | 6 | 1 | .538 | 327 | 257 |
| Buffalo | 7 | 6 | 1 | .538 | 304 | 291 |
| Houston | 6 | 8 | 0 | .429 | 302 | 372 |
| NY Jets | 5 | 8 | 1 | .385 | 249 | 399 |

**AFL WEST**

| | W | L | T | Pct | Pts | OP |
|---|---|---|---|---|---|---|
| San Diego | 11 | 3 | 0 | .786 | 399 | 255 |
| Oakland | 10 | 4 | 0 | .714 | 363 | 282 |
| Kansas City Chiefs | 5 | 7 | 2 | .417 | 347 | 263 |
| Denver | 2 | 11 | 1 | .154 | 301 | 473 |

### 1964

**NFL EAST**

| | W | L | T | Pct | Pts | OP |
|---|---|---|---|---|---|---|
| Cleveland | 10 | 3 | 1 | .769 | 415 | 293 |
| St. Louis | 9 | 3 | 2 | .750 | 357 | 331 |
| Philadelphia | 6 | 8 | 0 | .429 | 312 | 313 |
| Washington | 6 | 8 | 0 | .429 | 307 | 305 |
| Dallas | 5 | 8 | 1 | .385 | 250 | 289 |
| Pittsburgh | 5 | 9 | 0 | .357 | 253 | 315 |
| NY Giants | 2 | 10 | 2 | .167 | 241 | 399 |

**NFL WEST**

| | W | L | T | Pct | Pts | OP |
|---|---|---|---|---|---|---|
| Baltimore | 12 | 2 | 0 | .857 | 428 | 225 |
| Green Bay | 8 | 5 | 1 | .615 | 342 | 245 |
| Minnesota | 8 | 5 | 1 | .615 | 355 | 296 |
| Detroit | 7 | 5 | 2 | .583 | 280 | 260 |
| LA Rams | 5 | 7 | 2 | .417 | 283 | 339 |
| Chicago | 5 | 9 | 0 | .357 | 260 | 379 |
| San Francisco | 4 | 10 | 0 | .286 | 236 | 330 |

**AFL EAST**

| | W | L | T | Pct | Pts | OP |
|---|---|---|---|---|---|---|
| Buffalo | 12 | 2 | 0 | .857 | 400 | 242 |
| Boston | 10 | 3 | 1 | .769 | 365 | 297 |
| NY Jets | 5 | 8 | 1 | .385 | 278 | 315 |
| Houston | 4 | 10 | 0 | .286 | 310 | 355 |

**AFL WEST**

| | W | L | T | Pct | Pts | OP |
|---|---|---|---|---|---|---|
| San Diego | 8 | 5 | 1 | .615 | 341 | 300 |
| Kansas City Chiefs | 7 | 7 | 0 | .500 | 366 | 306 |
| Oakland | 5 | 7 | 2 | .417 | 303 | 350 |
| Denver | 2 | 11 | 1 | .154 | 240 | 438 |

### 1965

**NFL EAST**

| | W | L | T | Pct | Pts | OP |
|---|---|---|---|---|---|---|
| Cleveland | 11 | 3 | 0 | .786 | 363 | 325 |
| NY Giants | 7 | 7 | 0 | .500 | 270 | 338 |
| Dallas | 7 | 7 | 0 | .500 | 325 | 280 |
| Washington | 6 | 8 | 0 | .429 | 257 | 301 |
| St. Louis | 5 | 9 | 0 | .357 | 296 | 309 |
| Philadelphia | 5 | 9 | 0 | .357 | 363 | 359 |
| Pittsburgh | 2 | 12 | 0 | .143 | 202 | 397 |

**NFL WEST**

| | W | L | T | Pct | Pts | OP |
|---|---|---|---|---|---|---|
| Green Bay | 10 | 3 | 1 | .769 | 316 | 224 |
| Baltimore | 9 | 3 | 1 | .769 | 389 | 263 |
| Chicago | 9 | 5 | 0 | .643 | 409 | 275 |
| San Francisco | 7 | 6 | 1 | .538 | 421 | 402 |
| Minnesota | 7 | 6 | 0 | .500 | 383 | 362 |
| Detroit | 6 | 7 | 1 | .462 | 257 | 295 |
| LA Rams | 4 | 10 | 0 | .286 | 269 | 328 |

**AFL EAST**

| | W | L | T | Pct | Pts | OP |
|---|---|---|---|---|---|---|
| Buffalo | 10 | 3 | 1 | .769 | 313 | 226 |
| NY Jets | 5 | 8 | 1 | .385 | 285 | 303 |
| Boston | 4 | 8 | 2 | .333 | 244 | 302 |
| Houston | 4 | 10 | 0 | .286 | 298 | 429 |

**AFL WEST**

| | W | L | T | Pct | Pts | OP |
|---|---|---|---|---|---|---|
| San Diego | 9 | 2 | 3 | .818 | 340 | 227 |
| Oakland | 8 | 5 | 1 | .615 | 298 | 239 |
| Kansas City | 7 | 5 | 2 | .583 | 322 | 285 |
| Denver | 4 | 10 | 0 | .286 | 303 | 392 |

### 1966

**NFL EAST**

| | W | L | T | Pct | Pts | OP |
|---|---|---|---|---|---|---|
| Dallas | 10 | 3 | 1 | .769 | 445 | 239 |
| Cleveland | 9 | 5 | 0 | .643 | 403 | 259 |
| Philadelphia | 9 | 5 | 0 | .643 | 326 | 340 |
| St. Louis | 8 | 5 | 1 | .625 | 264 | 265 |
| Washington | 7 | 7 | 0 | .500 | 351 | 355 |
| Pittsburgh | 5 | 8 | 1 | .385 | 316 | 347 |
| Atlanta Falcons | 3 | 11 | 0 | .214 | 204 | 437 |
| NY Giants | 1 | 12 | 1 | .077 | 263 | 501 |

**NFL WEST**

| | W | L | T | Pct | Pts | OP |
|---|---|---|---|---|---|---|
| Green Bay | 12 | 2 | 0 | .857 | 335 | 163 |
| Baltimore | 9 | 5 | 0 | .643 | 314 | 226 |
| LA Rams | 8 | 6 | 0 | .571 | 289 | 212 |
| San Francisco | 6 | 6 | 2 | .500 | 320 | 325 |
| Chicago | 5 | 7 | 2 | .417 | 234 | 272 |
| Detroit | 4 | 9 | 1 | .308 | 206 | 317 |
| Minnesota | 4 | 9 | 1 | .308 | 292 | 304 |

**AFL EAST**

| | W | L | T | Pct | Pts | OP |
|---|---|---|---|---|---|---|
| Buffalo | 9 | 4 | 1 | .692 | 358 | 255 |
| Boston | 8 | 4 | 2 | .677 | 315 | 283 |
| NY Jets | 6 | 6 | 2 | .500 | 322 | 312 |
| Houston | 3 | 11 | 0 | .214 | 335 | 396 |
| Miami Dolphins | 3 | 11 | 0 | .214 | 213 | 362 |

**AFL WEST**

| | W | L | T | Pct | Pts | OP |
|---|---|---|---|---|---|---|
| Kansas City | 11 | 2 | 1 | .846 | 448 | 276 |
| Oakland | 8 | 5 | 1 | .615 | 315 | 288 |
| San Diego | 7 | 6 | 1 | .538 | 335 | 284 |
| Denver | 4 | 10 | 0 | .286 | 196 | 381 |

---

### 1967

**NFL CAPITOL**

| | W | L | T | Pct | Pts | OP |
|---|---|---|---|---|---|---|
| Dallas | 9 | 5 | 0 | .643 | 342 | 268 |
| Philadelphia | 6 | 7 | 1 | .462 | 351 | 409 |
| Washington | 5 | 6 | 3 | .455 | 347 | 353 |
| New Orleans Saints | 3 | 11 | 0 | .214 | 233 | 379 |

**NFL CENTURY**

| | W | L | T | Pct | Pts | OP |
|---|---|---|---|---|---|---|
| Cleveland | 9 | 5 | 0 | .643 | 334 | 297 |
| NY Giants | 7 | 7 | 0 | .500 | 369 | 379 |
| St. Louis | 6 | 7 | 1 | .462 | 333 | 356 |
| Pittsburgh | 4 | 9 | 1 | .308 | 281 | 320 |

**NFL COASTAL**

| | W | L | T | Pct | Pts | OP |
|---|---|---|---|---|---|---|
| LA Rams | 11 | 1 | 2 | .917 | 398 | 196 |
| Baltimore | 11 | 1 | 2 | .917 | 394 | 198 |
| San Francisco | 7 | 7 | 0 | .500 | 273 | 337 |
| Atlanta | 1 | 12 | 1 | .077 | 175 | 422 |

**NFL CENTRAL**

| | W | L | T | Pct | Pts | OP |
|---|---|---|---|---|---|---|
| Green Bay | 9 | 4 | 1 | .692 | 332 | 209 |
| Chicago | 7 | 6 | 1 | .538 | 239 | 218 |
| Detroit | 5 | 7 | 2 | .417 | 260 | 259 |
| Minnesota | 3 | 8 | 3 | .273 | 233 | 294 |

**AFL EAST**

| | W | L | T | Pct | Pts | OP |
|---|---|---|---|---|---|---|
| Houston | 9 | 4 | 1 | .692 | 258 | 199 |
| NY Jets | 8 | 5 | 1 | .615 | 371 | 329 |
| Buffalo | 4 | 10 | 0 | .286 | 237 | 285 |
| Miami | 4 | 10 | 0 | .286 | 219 | 407 |
| Boston | 3 | 10 | 1 | .231 | 280 | 389 |

### 1967 *(Cont.)*

**AFL WEST**

| | W | L | T | Pct | Pts | OP |
|---|---|---|---|---|---|---|
| Oakland | 13 | 1 | 0 | .929 | 468 | 233 |
| Kansas City | 9 | 5 | 0 | .643 | 408 | 254 |
| San Diego | 8 | 5 | 1 | .615 | 360 | 352 |
| Denver | 3 | 11 | 0 | .214 | 256 | 409 |

---

### 1968

**NFL CAPITOL**

| | W | L | T | Pct | Pts | OP |
|---|---|---|---|---|---|---|
| Dallas | 12 | 2 | 0 | .857 | 431 | 186 |
| NY Giants | 7 | 7 | 0 | .500 | 294 | 325 |
| Washington | 5 | 9 | 0 | .357 | 249 | 358 |
| Philadelphia | 2 | 12 | 0 | .143 | 202 | 351 |

**NFL CENTURY**

| | W | L | T | Pct | Pts | OP |
|---|---|---|---|---|---|---|
| Cleveland | 10 | 4 | 0 | .714 | 394 | 273 |
| St. Louis | 9 | 4 | 1 | .692 | 325 | 289 |
| New Orleans | 4 | 9 | 1 | .308 | 246 | 327 |
| Pittsburgh | 2 | 11 | 1 | .154 | 244 | 397 |

**NFL COASTAL**

| | W | L | T | Pct | Pts | OP |
|---|---|---|---|---|---|---|
| Baltimore | 13 | 1 | 0 | .929 | 402 | 144 |
| LA Rams | 10 | 3 | 1 | .769 | 312 | 200 |
| San Francisco | 7 | 6 | 1 | .538 | 303 | 310 |
| Atlanta | 2 | 12 | 0 | .143 | 202 | 351 |

**NFL CENTRAL**

| | W | L | T | Pct | Pts | OP |
|---|---|---|---|---|---|---|
| Minnesota | 8 | 6 | 0 | .571 | 282 | 242 |
| Chicago | 7 | 7 | 0 | .500 | 250 | 333 |
| Green Bay | 6 | 7 | 1 | .462 | 281 | 227 |
| Detroit | 4 | 8 | 2 | .333 | 207 | 241 |

**AFL EAST**

| | W | L | T | Pct | Pts | OP |
|---|---|---|---|---|---|---|
| NY Jets | 11 | 3 | 0 | .786 | 419 | 280 |
| Houston | 7 | 7 | 0 | .500 | 303 | 248 |
| Miami | 5 | 8 | 1 | .385 | 276 | 355 |
| Boston | 4 | 10 | 0 | .286 | 229 | 406 |
| Buffalo | 1 | 12 | 1 | .077 | 199 | 367 |

**AFL WEST**

| | W | L | T | Pct | Pts | OP |
|---|---|---|---|---|---|---|
| Oakland | 12 | 2 | 0 | .857 | 453 | 233 |
| Kansas City | 12 | 2 | 0 | .857 | 371 | 170 |
| San Diego | 9 | 5 | 0 | .643 | 382 | 310 |
| Denver | 5 | 9 | 0 | .357 | 255 | 404 |
| Cincinnati Bengals | 3 | 11 | 0 | .214 | 215 | 329 |

---

### 1969

**NFL CAPITOL**

| | W | L | T | Pct | Pts | OP |
|---|---|---|---|---|---|---|
| Dallas | 11 | 2 | 1 | .846 | 369 | 223 |
| Washington | 7 | 5 | 2 | .583 | 307 | 319 |
| New Orleans | 5 | 9 | 0 | .357 | 311 | 393 |
| Philadelphia | 4 | 9 | 1 | .308 | 279 | 377 |

**NFL CENTURY**

| | W | L | T | Pct | Pts | OP |
|---|---|---|---|---|---|---|
| Cleveland | 10 | 3 | 1 | .769 | 351 | 300 |
| NY Giants | 6 | 8 | 0 | .429 | 264 | 298 |
| St. Louis | 4 | 9 | 1 | .308 | 314 | 389 |
| Pittsburgh | 1 | 13 | 0 | .071 | 218 | 404 |

**NFL COASTAL**

| | W | L | T | Pct | Pts | OP |
|---|---|---|---|---|---|---|
| LA Rams | 11 | 3 | 0 | .786 | 320 | 243 |
| Baltimore | 7 | 5 | 2 | .615 | 307 | 319 |
| Atlanta | 6 | 8 | 0 | .429 | 276 | 268 |
| San Francisco | 4 | 8 | 2 | .333 | 277 | 319 |

## 1969 *(Cont.)*

### NFL CENTRAL

| | W | L | T | Pct | Pts | OP |
|---|---|---|---|---|---|---|
| Minnesota | 12 | 2 | 0 | .857 | 379 | 133 |
| Detroit | 9 | 4 | 1 | .692 | 259 | 188 |
| Green Bay | 8 | 6 | 0 | .571 | 269 | 221 |
| Chicago | 1 | 13 | 0 | .071 | 210 | 339 |

### AFL EAST

| | W | L | T | Pct | Pts | OP |
|---|---|---|---|---|---|---|
| NY Jets | 10 | 4 | 0 | .714 | 353 | 269 |
| Houston | 6 | 6 | 2 | .500 | 278 | 279 |
| Buffalo | 4 | 10 | 0 | .286 | 230 | 359 |
| Boston | 4 | 10 | 0 | .286 | 266 | 316 |
| Miami | 3 | 10 | 1 | .231 | 233 | 332 |

### AFL WEST

| | W | L | T | Pct | Pts | OP |
|---|---|---|---|---|---|---|
| Oakland | 12 | 1 | 1 | .923 | 377 | 242 |
| Kansas City | 11 | 3 | 0 | .786 | 359 | 177 |
| San Diego | 8 | 6 | 0 | .571 | 288 | 276 |
| Denver | 5 | 8 | 1 | .385 | 297 | 344 |
| Cincinnati | 4 | 9 | 1 | .308 | 280 | 367 |

## 1970

### AFC EAST

| | W | L | T | Pct | Pts | OP |
|---|---|---|---|---|---|---|
| Baltimore | 11 | 2 | 1 | .846 | 321 | 234 |
| Miami | 10 | 4 | 0 | .714 | 297 | 228 |
| NY Jets | 4 | 10 | 0 | .286 | 255 | 286 |
| Buffalo | 3 | 10 | 1 | .231 | 204 | 337 |
| Boston | 2 | 12 | 0 | .143 | 149 | 361 |

### AFC CENTRAL

| | W | L | T | Pct | Pts | OP |
|---|---|---|---|---|---|---|
| Cincinnati | 8 | 6 | 0 | .571 | 312 | 255 |
| Cleveland | 7 | 7 | 0 | .500 | 286 | 265 |
| Pittsburgh | 5 | 9 | 0 | .357 | 210 | 272 |
| Houston | 3 | 10 | 1 | .231 | 217 | 352 |

### AFC WEST

| | W | L | T | Pct | Pts | OP |
|---|---|---|---|---|---|---|
| Oakland | 8 | 4 | 2 | .667 | 300 | 293 |
| Kansas City | 7 | 5 | 2 | .583 | 272 | 244 |
| San Diego | 5 | 6 | 3 | .455 | 282 | 278 |
| Denver | 5 | 8 | 1 | .385 | 253 | 264 |

### NFC EAST

| | W | L | T | Pct | Pts | OP |
|---|---|---|---|---|---|---|
| Dallas | 10 | 4 | 0 | .714 | 299 | 221 |
| NY Giants | 9 | 5 | 0 | .643 | 301 | 270 |
| St. Louis | 8 | 5 | 1 | .615 | 325 | 228 |
| Washington | 6 | 8 | 0 | .429 | 297 | 314 |
| Philadelphia | 3 | 10 | 1 | .231 | 241 | 332 |

### NFC CENTRAL

| | W | L | T | Pct | Pts | OP |
|---|---|---|---|---|---|---|
| Minnesota | 12 | 2 | 0 | .857 | 335 | 143 |
| Detroit | 10 | 4 | 0 | .714 | 347 | 202 |
| Green Bay | 6 | 8 | 0 | .429 | 196 | 293 |
| Chicago | 6 | 8 | 0 | .429 | 256 | 261 |

### NFC WEST

| | W | L | T | Pct | Pts | OP |
|---|---|---|---|---|---|---|
| San Francisco | 10 | 3 | 1 | .769 | 352 | 267 |
| LA Rams | 9 | 4 | 1 | .692 | 325 | 202 |
| Atlanta | 4 | 8 | 2 | .333 | 206 | 261 |
| New Orleans | 2 | 11 | 1 | .154 | 172 | 347 |

## 1971

### AFC EAST

| | W | L | T | Pct | Pts | OP |
|---|---|---|---|---|---|---|
| Miami | 10 | 3 | 1 | .769 | 315 | 174 |
| Baltimore | 10 | 4 | 0 | .714 | 313 | 140 |
| New England Patriots | 6 | 8 | 0 | .429 | 238 | 325 |
| NY Jets | 6 | 8 | 0 | .429 | 212 | 299 |
| Buffalo | 1 | 13 | 0 | .071 | 184 | 394 |

### AFC CENTRAL

| | W | L | T | Pct | Pts | OP |
|---|---|---|---|---|---|---|
| Cleveland | 9 | 5 | 0 | .643 | 285 | 273 |
| Pittsburgh | 6 | 8 | 0 | .429 | 246 | 292 |
| Houston | 4 | 9 | 1 | .308 | 251 | 330 |
| Cincinnati | 4 | 10 | 0 | .286 | 284 | 265 |

### AFC WEST

| | W | L | T | Pct | Pts | OP |
|---|---|---|---|---|---|---|
| Kansas City | 10 | 3 | 1 | .769 | 302 | 208 |
| Oakland | 8 | 4 | 2 | .667 | 344 | 278 |
| San Diego | 6 | 8 | 0 | .429 | 311 | 341 |
| Denver | 4 | 9 | 1 | .308 | 203 | 275 |

### NFC EAST

| | W | L | T | Pct | Pts | OP |
|---|---|---|---|---|---|---|
| Dallas | 11 | 3 | 0 | .786 | 406 | 222 |
| Washington | 9 | 4 | 1 | .692 | 276 | 190 |
| Philadelphia | 6 | 7 | 1 | .462 | 221 | 302 |
| St. Louis | 4 | 9 | 1 | .308 | 231 | 279 |
| NY Giants | 4 | 10 | 0 | .286 | 228 | 362 |

### NFC CENTRAL

| | W | L | T | Pct | Pts | OP |
|---|---|---|---|---|---|---|
| Minnesota | 11 | 3 | 0 | .786 | 245 | 139 |
| Detroit | 7 | 6 | 1 | .538 | 341 | 286 |
| Chicago | 6 | 8 | 0 | .429 | 185 | 276 |
| Green Bay | 4 | 8 | 2 | .333 | 274 | 298 |

### NFC WEST

| | W | L | T | Pct | Pts | OP |
|---|---|---|---|---|---|---|
| San Francisco | 9 | 5 | 0 | .643 | 300 | 216 |
| LA Rams | 8 | 5 | 1 | .615 | 313 | 260 |
| Atlanta | 7 | 6 | 1 | .538 | 274 | 277 |
| New Orleans | 4 | 8 | 2 | .333 | 266 | 347 |

## 1972

### AFC EAST

| | W | L | T | Pct | Pts | OP |
|---|---|---|---|---|---|---|
| Miami | 14 | 0 | 0 | 1.000 | 385 | 171 |
| NY Jets | 7 | 7 | 0 | .500 | 367 | 324 |
| Baltimore | 5 | 9 | 0 | .357 | 235 | 252 |
| Buffalo | 4 | 9 | 1 | .321 | 257 | 377 |
| New England | 3 | 11 | 0 | .214 | 192 | 446 |

### AFC CENTRAL

| | W | L | T | Pct | Pts | OP |
|---|---|---|---|---|---|---|
| Pittsburgh | 11 | 3 | 0 | .786 | 343 | 175 |
| Cleveland | 10 | 4 | 0 | .714 | 268 | 249 |
| Cincinnati | 8 | 6 | 0 | .571 | 299 | 229 |
| Houston | 1 | 13 | 0 | .071 | 164 | 380 |

### AFC WEST

| | W | L | T | Pct | Pts | OP |
|---|---|---|---|---|---|---|
| Oakland | 10 | 3 | 1 | .750 | 365 | 248 |
| Kansas City | 8 | 6 | 0 | .571 | 287 | 254 |
| Denver | 5 | 9 | 0 | .357 | 325 | 350 |
| San Diego | 4 | 9 | 1 | .321 | 264 | 344 |

### NFC EAST

| | W | L | T | Pct | Pts | OP |
|---|---|---|---|---|---|---|
| Washington | 11 | 3 | 0 | .786 | 336 | 218 |
| Dallas | 10 | 4 | 0 | .286 | 319 | 240 |
| NY Giants | 8 | 6 | 0 | .571 | 331 | 247 |
| St. Louis | 4 | 9 | 1 | .321 | 193 | 303 |
| Philadelphia | 2 | 11 | 1 | .179 | 145 | 352 |

## 1972 *(Cont.)*

### NFC CENTRAL

| | W | L | T | Pct | Pts | OP |
|---|---|---|---|---|---|---|
| Green Bay | 10 | 4 | 0 | .714 | 304 | 226 |
| Detroit | 8 | 5 | 1 | .607 | 339 | 290 |
| Minnesota | 7 | 7 | 0 | .500 | 301 | 252 |
| Chicago | 4 | 9 | 1 | .321 | 225 | 275 |

### NFC WEST

| | W | L | T | Pct | Pts | OP |
|---|---|---|---|---|---|---|
| San Francisco | 8 | 5 | 1 | .607 | 353 | 249 |
| Atlanta | 7 | 7 | 0 | .500 | 269 | 274 |
| LA Rams | 6 | 7 | 1 | .464 | 291 | 286 |
| New Orleans | 2 | 11 | 1 | .179 | 215 | 361 |

## 1973

### AFC EAST

| | W | L | T | Pct | Pts | OP |
|---|---|---|---|---|---|---|
| Miami | 12 | 2 | 0 | .857 | 343 | 150 |
| Buffalo | 9 | 5 | 0 | .643 | 259 | 230 |
| New England | 5 | 9 | 0 | .357 | 258 | 300 |
| Baltimore | 4 | 10 | 0 | .286 | 226 | 341 |
| NY Jets | 4 | 10 | 0 | .286 | 240 | 306 |

### AFC CENTRAL

| | W | L | T | Pct | Pts | OP |
|---|---|---|---|---|---|---|
| Pittsburgh | 10 | 4 | 0 | .714 | 347 | 210 |
| Cincinnati | 10 | 4 | 0 | .714 | 286 | 231 |
| Cleveland | 7 | 5 | 2 | .571 | 234 | 255 |
| Houston | 1 | 13 | 0 | .071 | 199 | 447 |

### AFC WEST

| | W | L | T | Pct | Pts | OP |
|---|---|---|---|---|---|---|
| Oakland | 9 | 4 | 1 | .679 | 292 | 175 |
| Kansas City | 7 | 5 | 2 | .571 | 231 | 192 |
| Denver | 7 | 5 | 2 | .571 | 354 | 296 |
| San Diego | 2 | 11 | 1 | .179 | 188 | 386 |

### NFC EAST

| | W | L | T | Pct | Pts | OP |
|---|---|---|---|---|---|---|
| Washington | 10 | 4 | 0 | .714 | 325 | 198 |
| Dallas | 10 | 4 | 0 | .714 | 325 | 198 |
| Philadelphia | 5 | 8 | 1 | .393 | 310 | 393 |
| St. Louis | 4 | 9 | 1 | .321 | 286 | 365 |
| NY Giants | 2 | 11 | 1 | .179 | 226 | 362 |

### NFC CENTRAL

| | W | L | T | Pct | Pts | OP |
|---|---|---|---|---|---|---|
| Minnesota | 12 | 2 | 0 | .857 | 296 | 168 |
| Detroit | 6 | 7 | 1 | .464 | 271 | 247 |
| Green Bay | 5 | 7 | 2 | .429 | 202 | 259 |
| Chicago | 3 | 11 | 0 | .214 | 195 | 334 |

### NFC WEST

| | W | L | T | Pct | Pts | OP |
|---|---|---|---|---|---|---|
| LA Rams | 12 | 2 | 0 | .857 | 388 | 178 |
| Atlanta | 9 | 5 | 0 | .643 | 318 | 224 |
| New Orleans | 5 | 9 | 0 | .357 | 163 | 312 |
| San Francisco | 5 | 9 | 0 | .357 | 262 | 319 |

## 1974

### AFC EAST

| | W | L | T | Pct | Pts | OP |
|---|---|---|---|---|---|---|
| Miami | 11 | 3 | 0 | .786 | 327 | 216 |
| Buffalo | 9 | 5 | 0 | .643 | 264 | 244 |
| NY Jets | 7 | 7 | 0 | .500 | 279 | 300 |
| New England | 7 | 7 | 0 | .500 | 348 | 289 |
| Baltimore | 2 | 12 | 0 | .143 | 190 | 329 |

### AFC CENTRAL

| | W | L | T | Pct | Pts | OP |
|---|---|---|---|---|---|---|
| Pittsburgh | 10 | 3 | 1 | .750 | 305 | 189 |
| Houston | 7 | 7 | 0 | .500 | 236 | 282 |
| Cincinnati | 7 | 7 | 0 | .500 | 283 | 259 |
| Cleveland | 4 | 10 | 0 | .283 | 251 | 344 |

### AFC WEST

| | W | L | T | Pct | Pts | OP |
|---|---|---|---|---|---|---|
| Oakland | 12 | 2 | 0 | .857 | 355 | 228 |
| Denver | 7 | 6 | 1 | .536 | 302 | 294 |
| Kansas City | 5 | 9 | 0 | .357 | 233 | 293 |
| San Diego | 5 | 9 | 0 | .357 | 212 | 285 |

### NFC EAST

| | W | L | T | Pct | Pts | OP |
|---|---|---|---|---|---|---|
| Washington | 10 | 4 | 0 | .714 | 320 | 196 |
| St. Louis | 10 | 4 | 0 | .714 | 285 | 218 |
| Dallas | 8 | 6 | 0 | .571 | 297 | 235 |
| Philadelphia | 7 | 7 | 0 | .500 | 242 | 217 |
| NY Giants | 2 | 12 | 0 | .143 | 195 | 299 |

### NFC CENTRAL

| | W | L | T | Pct | Pts | OP |
|---|---|---|---|---|---|---|
| Minnesota | 10 | 4 | 0 | .714 | 310 | 195 |
| Detroit | 7 | 7 | 0 | .500 | 256 | 270 |
| Green Bay | 6 | 8 | 0 | .429 | 210 | 206 |
| Chicago | 4 | 10 | 0 | .286 | 152 | 279 |

### NFC WEST

| | W | L | T | Pct | Pts | OP |
|---|---|---|---|---|---|---|
| LA Rams | 10 | 4 | 0 | .714 | 263 | 181 |
| San Francisco | 6 | 8 | 0 | .429 | 226 | 236 |
| New Orleans | 5 | 9 | 0 | .357 | 166 | 263 |
| Atlanta | 3 | 11 | 0 | .214 | 111 | 271 |

## 1975

### AFC EAST

| | W | L | T | Pct | Pts | OP |
|---|---|---|---|---|---|---|
| Miami | 10 | 4 | 0 | .714 | 357 | 222 |
| Baltimore | 10 | 4 | 0 | .714 | 395 | 269 |
| Buffalo | 8 | 6 | 0 | .571 | 420 | 355 |
| NY Jets | 3 | 11 | 0 | .214 | 258 | 433 |
| New England | 3 | 11 | 0 | .214 | 258 | 358 |

### AFC CENTRAL

| | W | L | T | Pct | Pts | OP |
|---|---|---|---|---|---|---|
| Pittsburgh | 12 | 2 | 0 | .857 | 373 | 162 |
| Cincinnati | 11 | 3 | 0 | .786 | 340 | 246 |
| Houston | 10 | 4 | 0 | .714 | 293 | 226 |
| Cleveland | 3 | 11 | 0 | .214 | 218 | 372 |

### AFC WEST

| | W | L | T | Pct | Pts | OP |
|---|---|---|---|---|---|---|
| Oakland | 11 | 3 | 0 | .786 | 375 | 255 |
| Denver | 6 | 8 | 0 | .429 | 254 | 307 |
| Kansas City | 5 | 9 | 0 | .357 | 282 | 341 |
| San Diego | 2 | 12 | 0 | .143 | 189 | 345 |

### NFC EAST

| | W | L | T | Pct | Pts | OP |
|---|---|---|---|---|---|---|
| St. Louis | 11 | 3 | 0 | .786 | 356 | 276 |
| Dallas | 10 | 4 | 0 | .714 | 350 | 268 |
| Washington | 8 | 6 | 0 | .571 | 325 | 276 |
| NY Giants | 5 | 9 | 0 | .357 | 216 | 306 |
| Philadelphia | 4 | 10 | 0 | .286 | 225 | 302 |

### NFC CENTRAL

| | W | L | T | Pct | Pts | OP |
|---|---|---|---|---|---|---|
| Minnesota | 12 | 2 | 0 | .857 | 377 | 180 |
| Detroit | 7 | 7 | 0 | .500 | 245 | 262 |
| Green Bay | 4 | 10 | 0 | .286 | 226 | 285 |
| Chicago | 4 | 10 | 0 | .286 | 191 | 379 |

### NFC WEST

| | W | L | T | Pct | Pts | OP |
|---|---|---|---|---|---|---|
| LA Rams | 12 | 2 | 0 | .857 | 312 | 135 |
| San Francisco | 5 | 9 | 0 | .357 | 255 | 286 |
| Atlanta | 4 | 10 | 0 | .286 | 240 | 289 |
| New Orleans | 2 | 12 | 0 | .143 | 165 | 360 |

## 1976

### AFC EAST
| | W | L | T | Pct | Pts | OP |
|---|---|---|---|---|---|---|
| Baltimore | 11 | 3 | 0 | .786 | 417 | 246 |
| New England | 11 | 3 | 0 | .786 | 376 | 236 |
| Miami | 6 | 8 | 0 | .429 | 263 | 264 |
| NY Jets | 3 | 11 | 0 | .214 | 169 | 383 |
| Buffalo | 2 | 12 | 0 | .143 | 246 | 363 |

### AFC CENTRAL
| | W | L | T | Pct | Pts | OP |
|---|---|---|---|---|---|---|
| Cincinnati | 10 | 4 | 0 | .714 | 335 | 210 |
| Pittsburgh | 10 | 4 | 0 | .714 | 342 | 138 |
| Cleveland | 9 | 5 | 0 | .643 | 267 | 287 |
| Houston | 5 | 9 | 0 | .357 | 222 | 273 |

### AFC WEST
| | W | L | T | Pct | Pts | OP |
|---|---|---|---|---|---|---|
| Oakland | 13 | 1 | 0 | .929 | 350 | 237 |
| Denver | 9 | 5 | 0 | .643 | 315 | 206 |
| San Diego | 6 | 8 | 0 | .429 | 248 | 285 |
| Kansas City | 5 | 9 | 0 | .357 | 290 | 376 |
| Tampa Bay Buccaneers | 0 | 14 | 0 | .000 | 125 | 412 |

### NFC EAST
| | W | L | T | Pct | Pts | OP |
|---|---|---|---|---|---|---|
| Dallas | 11 | 3 | 0 | .786 | 296 | 194 |
| Washington | 10 | 4 | 0 | .714 | 291 | 217 |
| St. Louis | 10 | 4 | 0 | .714 | 309 | 267 |
| Philadelphia | 4 | 10 | 0 | .286 | 165 | 286 |
| NY Giants | 3 | 11 | 0 | .214 | 170 | 250 |

### NFC CENTRAL
| | W | L | T | Pct | Pts | OP |
|---|---|---|---|---|---|---|
| Minnesota | 11 | 2 | 1 | .821 | 305 | 176 |
| Chicago | 7 | 7 | 0 | .500 | 253 | 216 |
| Detroit | 6 | 8 | 0 | .429 | 218 | 299 |
| Green Bay | 5 | 9 | 0 | .357 | 218 | 299 |

### NFC WEST
| | W | L | T | Pct | Pts | OP |
|---|---|---|---|---|---|---|
| LA Rams | 10 | 3 | 1 | .750 | 351 | 190 |
| San Francisco | 8 | 6 | 0 | .571 | 270 | 190 |
| Atlanta | 4 | 10 | 0 | .286 | 172 | 312 |
| New Orleans | 4 | 10 | 0 | .286 | 253 | 346 |
| Seattle Seahawks | 2 | 12 | 0 | .143 | 229 | 429 |

## 1977

### AFC EAST
| | W | L | T | Pct | Pts | OP |
|---|---|---|---|---|---|---|
| Miami | 10 | 4 | 0 | .714 | 313 | 197 |
| Baltimore | 10 | 4 | 0 | .714 | 295 | 221 |
| New England | 9 | 5 | 0 | .643 | 279 | 217 |
| Buffalo | 3 | 11 | 0 | .214 | 160 | 313 |
| NY Jets | 3 | 11 | 0 | .214 | 191 | 313 |

### AFC CENTRAL
| | W | L | T | Pct | Pts | OP |
|---|---|---|---|---|---|---|
| Pittsburgh | 9 | 5 | 0 | .643 | 283 | 243 |
| Houston | 8 | 6 | 0 | .571 | 299 | 230 |
| Cincinnati | 8 | 6 | 0 | .571 | 238 | 235 |
| Cleveland | 6 | 8 | 0 | .429 | 269 | 267 |

### AFC WEST
| | W | L | T | Pct | Pts | OP |
|---|---|---|---|---|---|---|
| Denver | 12 | 2 | 0 | .857 | 274 | 148 |
| Oakland | 11 | 3 | 0 | .786 | 351 | 230 |
| San Diego | 7 | 7 | 0 | .500 | 222 | 205 |
| Seattle | 5 | 9 | 0 | .357 | 282 | 373 |
| Kansas City | 2 | 12 | 0 | .143 | 225 | 349 |

## 1977 (Cont.)

### NFC EAST
| | W | L | T | Pct | Pts | OP |
|---|---|---|---|---|---|---|
| Dallas | 12 | 2 | 0 | .857 | 345 | 212 |
| Washington | 9 | 5 | 0 | .643 | 196 | 189 |
| St. Louis | 7 | 7 | 0 | .500 | 272 | 287 |
| NY Giants | 5 | 9 | 0 | .357 | 181 | 265 |
| Philadelphia | 5 | 9 | 0 | .357 | 220 | 207 |

### NFC CENTRAL
| | W | L | T | Pct | Pts | OP |
|---|---|---|---|---|---|---|
| Chicago | 9 | 5 | 0 | .643 | 255 | 253 |
| Minnesota | 9 | 5 | 0 | .643 | 231 | 227 |
| Detroit | 6 | 8 | 0 | .429 | 183 | 252 |
| Green Bay | 4 | 10 | 0 | .286 | 134 | 219 |
| Tampa Bay | 2 | 12 | 0 | .143 | 103 | 223 |

### NFC WEST
| | W | L | T | Pct | Pts | OP |
|---|---|---|---|---|---|---|
| LA Rams | 10 | 4 | 0 | .714 | 302 | 146 |
| Atlanta | 7 | 7 | 0 | .500 | 179 | 129 |
| San Francisco | 5 | 9 | 0 | .357 | 220 | 260 |
| New Orleans | 3 | 11 | 0 | .214 | 232 | 336 |

## 1978

### AFC EAST
| | W | L | T | Pct | Pts | OP |
|---|---|---|---|---|---|---|
| New England | 11 | 5 | 0 | .688 | 358 | 286 |
| Miami | 11 | 5 | 0 | .688 | 372 | 254 |
| NY Jets | 8 | 8 | 0 | .500 | 359 | 364 |
| Buffalo | 5 | 11 | 0 | .313 | 302 | 354 |
| Baltimore | 5 | 11 | 0 | .313 | 239 | 421 |

### AFC CENTRAL
| | W | L | T | Pct | Pts | OP |
|---|---|---|---|---|---|---|
| Pittsburgh | 14 | 2 | 0 | .875 | 356 | 195 |
| Houston | 10 | 6 | 0 | .625 | 283 | 298 |
| Cleveland | 8 | 8 | 0 | .500 | 334 | 356 |
| Cincinnati | 4 | 12 | 0 | .250 | 252 | 284 |

### AFC WEST
| | W | L | T | Pct | Pts | OP |
|---|---|---|---|---|---|---|
| Denver | 10 | 6 | 0 | .625 | 282 | 198 |
| Seattle | 9 | 7 | 0 | .563 | 345 | 358 |
| Oakland | 9 | 7 | 0 | .563 | 311 | 283 |
| San Diego | 9 | 7 | 0 | .563 | 355 | 309 |
| Kansas City | 4 | 12 | 0 | .250 | 243 | 327 |

### NFC EAST
| | W | L | T | Pct | Pts | OP |
|---|---|---|---|---|---|---|
| Dallas | 12 | 4 | 0 | .750 | 384 | 208 |
| Philadelphia | 9 | 7 | 0 | .563 | 270 | 250 |
| Washington | 8 | 8 | 0 | .500 | 273 | 283 |
| St. Louis | 6 | 10 | 0 | .375 | 248 | 296 |
| NY Giants | 6 | 10 | 0 | .375 | 264 | 298 |

### NFC CENTRAL
| | W | L | T | Pct | Pts | OP |
|---|---|---|---|---|---|---|
| Green Bay | 8 | 7 | 1 | .531 | 249 | 269 |
| Minnesota | 8 | 7 | 1 | .531 | 294 | 306 |
| Detroit | 7 | 9 | 0 | .438 | 290 | 300 |
| Chicago | 7 | 9 | 0 | .438 | 253 | 274 |
| Tampa Bay | 5 | 11 | 0 | .313 | 241 | 259 |

### NFC WEST
| | W | L | T | Pct | Pts | OP |
|---|---|---|---|---|---|---|
| LA Rams | 12 | 4 | 0 | .750 | 316 | 245 |
| Atlanta | 9 | 7 | 0 | .563 | 240 | 290 |
| New Orleans | 7 | 9 | 0 | .438 | 281 | 298 |
| San Francisco | 2 | 14 | 0 | .125 | 219 | 350 |

### 1979

**AFC EAST**

| | W | L | T | Pct | Pts | OP |
|---|---|---|---|---|---|---|
| Miami | 10 | 6 | 0 | .625 | 341 | 257 |
| New England | 9 | 7 | 0 | .563 | 411 | 326 |
| NY Jets | 8 | 8 | 0 | .500 | 337 | 383 |
| Buffalo | 7 | 9 | 0 | .438 | 268 | 279 |
| Baltimore | 5 | 11 | 0 | .313 | 271 | 351 |

**AFC CENTRAL**

| | W | L | T | Pct | Pts | OP |
|---|---|---|---|---|---|---|
| Pittsburgh | 12 | 4 | 0 | .750 | 416 | 262 |
| Houston | 11 | 5 | 0 | .688 | 362 | 331 |
| Cleveland | 9 | 7 | 0 | .563 | 359 | 352 |
| Cincinnati | 4 | 12 | 0 | .250 | 337 | 421 |

**AFC WEST**

| | W | L | T | Pct | Pts | OP |
|---|---|---|---|---|---|---|
| San Diego | 12 | 4 | 0 | .750 | 411 | 246 |
| Denver | 10 | 6 | 0 | .625 | 289 | 262 |
| Seattle | 9 | 7 | 0 | .563 | 378 | 372 |
| Oakland | 9 | 7 | 0 | .563 | 365 | 337 |
| Kansas City | 7 | 9 | 0 | .438 | 238 | 262 |

**NFC EAST**

| | W | L | T | Pct | Pts | OP |
|---|---|---|---|---|---|---|
| Dallas | 11 | 5 | 0 | .688 | 371 | 313 |
| Philadelphia | 11 | 5 | 0 | .688 | 339 | 282 |
| Washington | 10 | 6 | 0 | .625 | 348 | 295 |
| NY Giants | 6 | 10 | 0 | .375 | 237 | 323 |
| St. Louis | 5 | 11 | 0 | .313 | 307 | 358 |

**NFC CENTRAL**

| | W | L | T | Pct | Pts | OP |
|---|---|---|---|---|---|---|
| Chicago | 10 | 6 | 0 | .625 | 306 | 249 |
| Tampa Bay | 10 | 6 | 0 | .625 | 273 | 237 |
| Minnesota | 7 | 9 | 0 | .438 | 259 | 337 |
| Green Bay | 5 | 11 | 0 | .313 | 246 | 316 |
| Detroit | 2 | 14 | 0 | .125 | 219 | 365 |

**NFC WEST**

| | W | L | T | Pct | Pts | OP |
|---|---|---|---|---|---|---|
| LA Rams | 9 | 7 | 0 | .563 | 323 | 309 |
| New Orleans | 8 | 8 | 0 | .500 | 370 | 360 |
| Atlanta | 6 | 10 | 0 | .375 | 300 | 388 |
| San Francisco | 2 | 14 | 0 | .125 | 308 | 416 |

### 1980

**AFC EAST**

| | W | L | T | Pct | Pts | OP |
|---|---|---|---|---|---|---|
| Buffalo | 11 | 5 | 0 | .688 | 320 | 260 |
| New England | 10 | 6 | 0 | .625 | 441 | 325 |
| Miami | 8 | 8 | 0 | .500 | 266 | 305 |
| Baltimore | 7 | 9 | 0 | .438 | 355 | 387 |
| NY Jets | 4 | 12 | 0 | .250 | 302 | 395 |

**AFC CENTRAL**

| | W | L | T | Pct | Pts | OP |
|---|---|---|---|---|---|---|
| Cleveland | 11 | 5 | 0 | .688 | 357 | 310 |
| Houston | 11 | 5 | 0 | .688 | 295 | 251 |
| Pittsburgh | 9 | 7 | 0 | .563 | 352 | 313 |
| Cincinnati | 6 | 10 | 0 | .375 | 244 | 312 |

**AFC WEST**

| | W | L | T | Pct | Pts | OP |
|---|---|---|---|---|---|---|
| San Diego | 11 | 5 | 0 | .688 | 418 | 327 |
| Oakland | 11 | 5 | 0 | .688 | 364 | 306 |
| Denver | 8 | 8 | 0 | .500 | 310 | 323 |
| Kansas City | 8 | 8 | 0 | .500 | 319 | 336 |
| Seattle | 4 | 12 | 0 | .250 | 291 | 408 |

**NFC EAST**

| | W | L | T | Pct | Pts | OP |
|---|---|---|---|---|---|---|
| Dallas | 12 | 4 | 0 | .750 | 454 | 311 |
| Philadelphia | 12 | 4 | 0 | .750 | 384 | 222 |
| Washington | 6 | 10 | 0 | .375 | 261 | 293 |
| St. Louis | 5 | 11 | 0 | .313 | 299 | 350 |
| NY Giants | 4 | 12 | 0 | .250 | 249 | 425 |

### 1980 *(Cont.)*

**NFC CENTRAL**

| | W | L | T | Pct | Pts | OP |
|---|---|---|---|---|---|---|
| Detroit | 9 | 7 | 0 | .563 | 334 | 272 |
| Minnesota | 9 | 7 | 0 | .563 | 317 | 308 |
| Chicago | 7 | 9 | 0 | .438 | 304 | 264 |
| Tampa Bay | 5 | 10 | 1 | .344 | 271 | 341 |
| Green Bay | 5 | 10 | 1 | .344 | 231 | 371 |

**NFC WEST**

| | W | L | T | Pct | Pts | OP |
|---|---|---|---|---|---|---|
| Atlanta | 12 | 4 | 0 | .750 | 405 | 272 |
| LA Rams | 11 | 5 | 0 | .688 | 424 | 289 |
| San Francisco | 6 | 10 | 0 | .375 | 320 | 415 |
| New Orleans | 1 | 15 | 0 | .063 | 291 | 487 |

### 1981

**AFC EAST**

| | W | L | T | Pct | Pts | OP |
|---|---|---|---|---|---|---|
| Miami | 11 | 4 | 1 | .719 | 345 | 275 |
| NY Jets | 10 | 5 | 1 | .656 | 355 | 287 |
| Buffalo | 10 | 6 | 0 | .625 | 311 | 276 |
| Baltimore | 2 | 14 | 0 | .125 | 259 | 533 |
| New England | 2 | 14 | 0 | .125 | 322 | 370 |

**AFC CENTRAL**

| | W | L | T | Pct | Pts | OP |
|---|---|---|---|---|---|---|
| Cincinnati | 12 | 4 | 0 | .750 | 421 | 304 |
| Pittsburgh | 8 | 8 | 0 | .500 | 356 | 297 |
| Houston | 7 | 9 | 0 | .438 | 281 | 355 |
| Cleveland | 5 | 11 | 0 | .313 | 276 | 375 |

**AFC WEST**

| | W | L | T | Pct | Pts | OP |
|---|---|---|---|---|---|---|
| Denver | 10 | 6 | 0 | .625 | 321 | 289 |
| San Diego | 10 | 6 | 0 | .625 | 478 | 390 |
| Kansas City | 9 | 7 | 0 | .563 | 343 | 290 |
| Oakland | 7 | 9 | 0 | .438 | 273 | 343 |
| Seattle | 6 | 10 | 0 | .375 | 322 | 388 |

**NFC EAST**

| | W | L | T | Pct | Pts | OP |
|---|---|---|---|---|---|---|
| Dallas | 12 | 4 | 0 | .750 | 367 | 277 |
| Philadelphia | 10 | 6 | 0 | .625 | 368 | 221 |
| NY Giants | 9 | 7 | 0 | .563 | 295 | 257 |
| Washington | 8 | 8 | 0 | .500 | 347 | 349 |
| St. Louis | 7 | 9 | 0 | .438 | 315 | 407 |

**NFC CENTRAL**

| | W | L | T | Pct | Pts | OP |
|---|---|---|---|---|---|---|
| Tampa Bay | 9 | 7 | 0 | .563 | 315 | 268 |
| Detroit | 8 | 8 | 0 | .500 | 397 | 322 |
| Green Bay | 8 | 8 | 0 | .500 | 324 | 361 |
| Minnesota | 7 | 9 | 0 | .438 | 325 | 369 |
| Chicago | 6 | 10 | 0 | .375 | 253 | 324 |

**NFC WEST**

| | W | L | T | Pct | Pts | OP |
|---|---|---|---|---|---|---|
| San Francisco | 13 | 3 | 0 | .813 | 357 | 250 |
| Atlanta | 7 | 9 | 0 | .438 | 426 | 355 |
| LA Rams | 6 | 10 | 0 | .375 | 303 | 351 |
| New Orleans | 4 | 12 | 0 | .250 | 207 | 378 |

### 1982

| AFC EAST | W | L | T | Pct | Pts | OP |
|---|---|---|---|---|---|---|
| Miami | 7 | 2 | 0 | .778 | 198 | 131 |
| NY Jets | 6 | 3 | 0 | .667 | 245 | 166 |
| New England | 5 | 4 | 0 | .556 | 143 | 157 |
| Buffalo | 4 | 5 | 0 | .444 | 150 | 154 |
| Baltimore | 0 | 8 | 1 | .056 | 113 | 236 |

| AFC CENTRAL | W | L | T | Pct | Pts | OP |
|---|---|---|---|---|---|---|
| Cincinnati | 7 | 2 | 0 | .778 | 232 | 177 |
| Pittsburgh | 6 | 3 | 0 | .667 | 204 | 146 |
| Cleveland | 4 | 5 | 0 | .444 | 140 | 182 |
| Houston | 1 | 8 | 0 | .111 | 136 | 245 |

| AFC WEST | W | L | T | Pct | Pts | OP |
|---|---|---|---|---|---|---|
| Los Angeles Raiders | 8 | 1 | 0 | .889 | 260 | 200 |
| San Diego | 6 | 3 | 0 | .667 | 288 | 221 |
| Seattle | 4 | 5 | 0 | .444 | 127 | 147 |
| Kansas City | 3 | 6 | 0 | .333 | 176 | 184 |
| Denver | 2 | 7 | 0 | .222 | 148 | 226 |

| NFC EAST | W | L | T | Pct | Pts | OP |
|---|---|---|---|---|---|---|
| Washington | 8 | 1 | 0 | .889 | 190 | 128 |
| Dallas | 6 | 3 | 0 | .667 | 226 | 145 |
| St. Louis | 5 | 4 | 0 | .556 | 135 | 170 |
| NY Giants | 4 | 5 | 0 | .444 | 164 | 160 |
| Philadelphia | 3 | 6 | 0 | .333 | 191 | 195 |

| NFC CENTRAL | W | L | T | Pct | Pts | OP |
|---|---|---|---|---|---|---|
| Green Bay | 5 | 3 | 1 | .611 | 226 | 169 |
| Tampa Bay | 5 | 4 | 0 | .556 | 158 | 178 |
| Minnesota | 5 | 4 | 0 | .556 | 187 | 198 |
| Detroit | 4 | 5 | 0 | .444 | 181 | 176 |
| Chicago | 3 | 6 | 0 | .333 | 141 | 174 |

| NFC WEST | W | L | T | Pct | Pts | OP |
|---|---|---|---|---|---|---|
| Atlanta | 5 | 4 | 0 | .556 | 183 | 199 |
| New Orleans | 4 | 5 | 0 | .444 | 129 | 160 |
| San Francisco | 3 | 6 | 0 | .333 | 209 | 206 |
| Los Angeles Rams | 2 | 7 | 0 | .222 | 200 | 250 |

### 1983

| AFC EAST | W | L | T | Pct | Pts | OP |
|---|---|---|---|---|---|---|
| Miami | 12 | 4 | 0 | .750 | 389 | 250 |
| Buffalo | 8 | 8 | 0 | .500 | 283 | 351 |
| New England | 8 | 8 | 0 | .500 | 274 | 289 |
| Baltimore | 7 | 9 | 0 | .438 | 264 | 354 |
| NY Jets | 7 | 9 | 0 | .438 | 313 | 331 |

| AFC CENTRAL | W | L | T | Pct | Pts | OP |
|---|---|---|---|---|---|---|
| Pittsburgh | 10 | 6 | 0 | .625 | 355 | 303 |
| Cleveland | 9 | 7 | 0 | .563 | 356 | 342 |
| Cincinnati | 7 | 9 | 0 | .438 | 346 | 302 |
| Houston | 2 | 14 | 0 | .125 | 288 | 460 |

| AFC WEST | W | L | T | Pct | Pts | OP |
|---|---|---|---|---|---|---|
| LA Raiders | 12 | 4 | 0 | .750 | 442 | 338 |
| Seattle | 9 | 7 | 0 | .563 | 403 | 397 |
| Denver | 9 | 7 | 0 | .563 | 302 | 327 |
| San Diego | 6 | 10 | 0 | .375 | 358 | 462 |
| Kansas City | 6 | 10 | 0 | .375 | 386 | 367 |

| NFC EAST | W | L | T | Pct | Pts | OP |
|---|---|---|---|---|---|---|
| Washington | 14 | 2 | 0 | .875 | 541 | 332 |
| Dallas | 12 | 4 | 0 | .750 | 479 | 360 |
| St. Louis | 8 | 7 | 1 | .531 | 374 | 428 |
| Philadelphia | 5 | 11 | 0 | .313 | 233 | 322 |
| NY Giants | 3 | 12 | 1 | .219 | 267 | 347 |

### 1983 *(Cont.)*

| NFC CENTRAL | W | L | T | Pct | Pts | OP |
|---|---|---|---|---|---|---|
| Detroit | 9 | 7 | 0 | .563 | 47 | 286 |
| Minnesota | 8 | 8 | 0 | .500 | 316 | 348 |
| Chicago | 8 | 8 | 0 | .500 | 311 | 301 |
| Green Bay | 8 | 8 | 0 | .500 | 429 | 439 |
| Tampa Bay | 2 | 14 | 0 | .125 | 241 | 380 |

| NFC WEST | W | L | T | Pct | Pts | OP |
|---|---|---|---|---|---|---|
| San Francisco | 10 | 6 | 0 | .625 | 432 | 293 |
| LA Rams | 9 | 7 | 0 | .563 | 361 | 344 |
| New Orleans | 8 | 8 | 0 | .500 | 319 | 337 |
| Atlanta | 7 | 9 | 0 | .438 | 370 | 389 |

### 1984

| AFC EAST | W | L | T | Pct | Pts | OP |
|---|---|---|---|---|---|---|
| Miami | 14 | 2 | 0 | .875 | 513 | 298 |
| New England | 9 | 7 | 0 | .563 | 362 | 352 |
| NY Jets | 7 | 9 | 0 | .438 | 332 | 364 |
| Indianapolis Colts | 4 | 12 | 0 | .250 | 239 | 414 |
| Buffalo | 2 | 14 | 0 | .125 | 250 | 454 |

| AFC CENTRAL | W | L | T | Pct | Pts | OP |
|---|---|---|---|---|---|---|
| Pittsburgh | 9 | 7 | 0 | .563 | 387 | 310 |
| Cincinnati | 8 | 8 | 0 | .500 | 339 | 339 |
| Cleveland | 5 | 11 | 0 | .313 | 250 | 297 |
| Houston | 3 | 13 | 0 | .188 | 240 | 437 |

| AFC WEST | W | L | T | Pct | Pts | OP |
|---|---|---|---|---|---|---|
| Denver | 13 | 3 | 0 | .813 | 353 | 241 |
| Seattle | 12 | 4 | 0 | .750 | 418 | 282 |
| LA Raiders | 11 | 5 | 0 | .313 | 368 | 278 |
| Kansas City | 8 | 8 | 0 | .500 | 314 | 324 |
| San Diego | 7 | 9 | 0 | .438 | 394 | 413 |

| NFC EAST | W | L | T | Pct | Pts | OP |
|---|---|---|---|---|---|---|
| Washington | 11 | 5 | 0 | .688 | 426 | 310 |
| NY Giants | 9 | 7 | 0 | .563 | 299 | 301 |
| Dallas | 9 | 7 | 0 | .563 | 308 | 308 |
| St. Louis | 9 | 7 | 0 | .563 | 423 | 345 |
| Philadelphia | 6 | 9 | 1 | .406 | 278 | 320 |

| NFC CENTRAL | W | L | T | Pct | Pts | OP |
|---|---|---|---|---|---|---|
| Chicago | 10 | 6 | 0 | .625 | 325 | 248 |
| Green Bay | 8 | 8 | 0 | .500 | 390 | 309 |
| Tampa Bay | 6 | 10 | 0 | .375 | 335 | 380 |
| Detroit | 4 | 11 | 1 | .281 | 283 | 408 |
| Minnesota | 3 | 13 | 0 | .188 | 276 | 484 |

| NFC WEST | W | L | T | Pct | Pts | OP |
|---|---|---|---|---|---|---|
| San Francisco | 15 | 1 | 0 | .938 | 475 | 227 |
| LA Rams | 10 | 6 | 0 | .625 | 346 | 316 |
| New Orleans | 7 | 9 | 0 | .438 | 298 | 361 |
| Atlanta | 4 | 12 | 0 | .250 | 281 | 382 |

### 1985

**AFC EAST**

| | W | L | T | Pct | Pts | OP |
|---|---|---|---|---|---|---|
| Miami | 12 | 4 | 0 | .750 | 428 | 320 |
| New England | 11 | 5 | 0 | .688 | 362 | 290 |
| NY Jets | 11 | 5 | 0 | .688 | 393 | 264 |
| Indianapolis | 5 | 11 | 0 | .313 | 320 | 386 |
| Buffalo | 2 | 14 | 0 | .125 | 200 | 381 |

**AFC CENTRAL**

| | W | L | T | Pct | Pts | OP |
|---|---|---|---|---|---|---|
| Cleveland | 8 | 8 | 0 | .500 | 287 | 294 |
| Cincinnati | 7 | 9 | 0 | .438 | 441 | 437 |
| Pittsburgh | 7 | 9 | 0 | .438 | 379 | 355 |
| Houston | 5 | 11 | 0 | .313 | 284 | 412 |

**AFC WEST**

| | W | L | T | Pct | Pts | OP |
|---|---|---|---|---|---|---|
| LA Raiders | 12 | 4 | 0 | .750 | 354 | 308 |
| Denver | 11 | 5 | 0 | .688 | 380 | 329 |
| Seattle | 8 | 8 | 0 | .500 | 349 | 303 |
| San Diego | 8 | 8 | 0 | .500 | 467 | 435 |
| Kansas City | 6 | 10 | 0 | .375 | 317 | 360 |

**NFC EAST**

| | W | L | T | Pct | Pts | OP |
|---|---|---|---|---|---|---|
| Washington | 10 | 6 | 0 | .625 | 297 | 312 |
| NY Giants | 10 | 6 | 0 | .625 | 399 | 283 |
| Dallas | 10 | 6 | 0 | .625 | 357 | 333 |
| Philadelphia | 7 | 9 | 0 | .438 | 286 | 310 |
| St. Louis | 5 | 11 | 0 | .313 | 278 | 414 |

**NFC CENTRAL**

| | W | L | T | Pct | Pts | OP |
|---|---|---|---|---|---|---|
| Chicago | 15 | 1 | 0 | .938 | 456 | 198 |
| Green Bay | 8 | 8 | 0 | .500 | 337 | 355 |
| Detroit | 7 | 9 | 0 | .438 | 307 | 366 |
| Minnesota | 7 | 9 | 0 | .438 | 346 | 359 |
| Tampa Bay | 2 | 14 | 0 | .125 | 294 | 448 |

**NFC WEST**

| | W | L | T | Pct | Pts | OP |
|---|---|---|---|---|---|---|
| LA Rams | 11 | 5 | 0 | .688 | 340 | 277 |
| San Francisco | 10 | 6 | 0 | .625 | 411 | 263 |
| New Orleans | 5 | 11 | 0 | .313 | 294 | 401 |
| Atlanta | 4 | 12 | 0 | .250 | 282 | 452 |

### 1986

**AFC EAST**

| | W | L | T | Pct | Pts | OP |
|---|---|---|---|---|---|---|
| New England | 11 | 5 | 0 | .688 | 412 | 307 |
| NY Jets | 10 | 6 | 0 | .625 | 364 | 386 |
| Miami | 8 | 8 | 0 | .500 | 430 | 405 |
| Buffalo | 4 | 12 | 0 | .250 | 287 | 348 |
| Indianapolis | 3 | 13 | 0 | .188 | 299 | 400 |

**AFC CENTRAL**

| | W | L | T | Pct | Pts | OP |
|---|---|---|---|---|---|---|
| Cleveland | 12 | 4 | 0 | .750 | 391 | 310 |
| Cincinnati | 10 | 6 | 0 | .625 | 409 | 394 |
| Pittsburgh | 6 | 10 | 0 | .375 | 307 | 336 |
| Houston | 5 | 11 | 0 | .313 | 274 | 329 |

**AFC WEST**

| | W | L | T | Pct | Pts | OP |
|---|---|---|---|---|---|---|
| Denver | 11 | 5 | 0 | .688 | 378 | 327 |
| Kansas City | 10 | 6 | 0 | .625 | 358 | 326 |
| Seattle | 10 | 6 | 0 | .625 | 366 | 293 |
| LA Raiders | 8 | 8 | 0 | .500 | 323 | 346 |
| San Diego | 4 | 12 | 0 | .250 | 335 | 396 |

**NFC EAST**

| | W | L | T | Pct | Pts | OP |
|---|---|---|---|---|---|---|
| NY Giants | 14 | 2 | 0 | .875 | 371 | 236 |
| Washington | 12 | 4 | 0 | .750 | 368 | 296 |
| Dallas | 7 | 9 | 0 | .438 | 346 | 337 |
| Philadelphia | 5 | 10 | 1 | .344 | 256 | 312 |
| St. Louis | 4 | 11 | 1 | .281 | 518 | 351 |

### 1986 *(Cont.)*

**NFC CENTRAL**

| | W | L | T | Pct | Pts | OP |
|---|---|---|---|---|---|---|
| Chicago | 14 | 2 | 0 | .875 | 352 | 187 |
| Minnesota | 9 | 7 | 0 | .563 | 398 | 271 |
| Detroit | 5 | 11 | 0 | .313 | 277 | 326 |
| Green Bay | 4 | 12 | 0 | .250 | 254 | 418 |
| Tampa Bay | 2 | 14 | 0 | .125 | 239 | 473 |

**NFC WEST**

| | W | L | T | Pct | Pts | OP |
|---|---|---|---|---|---|---|
| San Francisco | 10 | 5 | 1 | .656 | 374 | 247 |
| LA Rams | 10 | 6 | 0 | .625 | 309 | 267 |
| Atlanta | 7 | 8 | 1 | .469 | 280 | 280 |
| New Orleans | 7 | 9 | 0 | .438 | 288 | 287 |

### 1987

**AFC EAST**

| | W | L | T | Pct | Pts | OP |
|---|---|---|---|---|---|---|
| Indianapolis | 9 | 6 | 0 | .643 | 300 | 238 |
| Miami | 8 | 7 | 0 | .533 | 362 | 335 |
| New England | 8 | 7 | 0 | .533 | 320 | 293 |
| Buffalo | 7 | 8 | 0 | .467 | 320 | 293 |
| NY Jets | 6 | 9 | 0 | .400 | 334 | 360 |

**AFC CENTRAL**

| | W | L | T | Pct | Pts | OP |
|---|---|---|---|---|---|---|
| Cleveland | 10 | 5 | 0 | .700 | 390 | 239 |
| Houston | 9 | 6 | 0 | .600 | 345 | 349 |
| Pittsburgh | 8 | 7 | 0 | .533 | 285 | 299 |
| Cincinnati | 4 | 11 | 0 | .267 | 285 | 370 |

**AFC WEST**

| | W | L | T | Pct | Pts | OP |
|---|---|---|---|---|---|---|
| Denver | 10 | 4 | 1 | .667 | 379 | 288 |
| Seattle | 9 | 6 | 0 | .600 | 371 | 314 |
| San Diego | 8 | 7 | 0 | .563 | 253 | 317 |
| LA Raiders | 5 | 10 | 0 | .333 | 301 | 289 |
| Kansas City | 4 | 11 | 0 | .267 | 276 | 388 |

**NFC EAST**

| | W | L | T | Pct | Pts | OP |
|---|---|---|---|---|---|---|
| Washington | 11 | 4 | 0 | .733 | 379 | 285 |
| Dallas | 7 | 8 | 0 | .467 | 340 | 348 |
| St. Louis | 7 | 8 | 0 | .467 | 362 | 368 |
| Philadelphia | 7 | 8 | 0 | .467 | 337 | 380 |
| NY Giants | 6 | 9 | 0 | .400 | 280 | 312 |

**NFC CENTRAL**

| | W | L | T | Pct | Pts | OP |
|---|---|---|---|---|---|---|
| Chicago | 11 | 4 | 0 | .733 | 356 | 282 |
| Minnesota | 8 | 7 | 0 | .533 | 336 | 335 |
| Green Bay | 5 | 9 | 1 | .367 | 255 | 300 |
| Tampa Bay | 4 | 11 | 0 | .267 | 286 | 360 |
| Detroit | 4 | 11 | 0 | .267 | 269 | 384 |

**NFC WEST**

| | W | L | T | Pct | Pts | OP |
|---|---|---|---|---|---|---|
| San Francisco | 13 | 2 | 0 | .867 | 459 | 253 |
| New Orleans | 12 | 3 | 0 | .800 | 422 | 283 |
| LA Rams | 6 | 9 | 0 | .400 | 317 | 361 |
| Atlanta | 3 | 12 | 0 | .200 | 205 | 436 |

## 1988

### AFC EAST

| | W | L | T | Pct | Pts | OP |
|---|---|---|---|---|---|---|
| Buffalo | 12 | 4 | 0 | .750 | 329 | 237 |
| New England | 9 | 7 | 0 | .563 | 250 | 284 |
| Indianapolis | 9 | 7 | 0 | .563 | 354 | 315 |
| NY Jets | 8 | 7 | 1 | .531 | 372 | 354 |
| Miami | 6 | 10 | 0 | .375 | 319 | 380 |

### AFC CENTRAL

| | W | L | T | Pct | Pts | OP |
|---|---|---|---|---|---|---|
| Cincinnati | 12 | 4 | 0 | .750 | 448 | 329 |
| Cleveland | 10 | 6 | 0 | .625 | 304 | 288 |
| Houston | 10 | 6 | 0 | .625 | 424 | 365 |
| Pittsburgh | 5 | 1 | 0 | .313 | 336 | 421 |

### AFC WEST

| | W | L | T | Pct | Pts | OP |
|---|---|---|---|---|---|---|
| Seattle | 9 | 7 | 0 | .563 | 339 | 329 |
| Denver | 8 | 8 | 0 | .500 | 327 | 352 |
| LA Raiders | 7 | 9 | 0 | .438 | 325 | 369 |
| San Diego | 6 | 10 | 0 | .375 | 231 | 332 |
| Kansas City | 4 | 11 | 1 | .281 | 254 | 320 |

### NFC EAST

| | W | L | T | Pct | Pts | OP |
|---|---|---|---|---|---|---|
| NY Giants | 10 | 6 | 0 | .625 | 359 | 304 |
| Philadelphia | 10 | 6 | 0 | .625 | 379 | 319 |
| Phoenix Cardinals | 7 | 9 | 0 | .438 | 344 | 398 |
| Washington | 7 | 9 | 0 | .438 | 345 | 387 |
| Dallas | 3 | 13 | 0 | .188 | 265 | 381 |

### NFC CENTRAL

| | W | L | T | Pct | Pts | OP |
|---|---|---|---|---|---|---|
| Chicago | 12 | 4 | 0 | .750 | 312 | 215 |
| Minnesota | 11 | 5 | 0 | .688 | 406 | 233 |
| Tampa Bay | 5 | 11 | 0 | .313 | 261 | 350 |
| Detroit | 4 | 12 | 0 | .250 | 220 | 313 |
| Green Bay | 4 | 12 | 0 | .250 | 240 | 315 |

### NFC WEST

| | W | L | T | Pct | Pts | OP |
|---|---|---|---|---|---|---|
| New Orleans | 10 | 6 | 0 | .625 | 312 | 283 |
| San Francisco | 10 | 6 | 0 | .625 | 369 | 294 |
| LA Rams | 10 | 6 | 0 | .625 | 407 | 293 |
| Atlanta | 5 | 11 | 0 | .313 | 244 | 315 |

## 1989

### AFC EAST

| | W | L | T | Pct | Pts | OP |
|---|---|---|---|---|---|---|
| Buffalo | 9 | 7 | 0 | .563 | 407 | 317 |
| Miami | 8 | 8 | 0 | .500 | 331 | 379 |
| Indianapolis | 8 | 8 | 0 | .500 | 298 | 301 |
| New England | 5 | 11 | 0 | .313 | 297 | 391 |
| NY Jets | 4 | 12 | 0 | .250 | 253 | 411 |

### AFC CENTRAL

| | W | L | T | Pct | Pts | OP |
|---|---|---|---|---|---|---|
| Cleveland | 9 | 6 | 1 | .594 | 334 | 254 |
| Houston | 9 | 7 | 0 | .563 | 365 | 412 |
| Pittsburgh | 9 | 7 | 0 | .563 | 265 | 326 |
| Cincinnati | 8 | 8 | 0 | .500 | 404 | 285 |

### AFC WEST

| | W | L | T | Pct | Pts | OP |
|---|---|---|---|---|---|---|
| Denver | 11 | 5 | 0 | .688 | 362 | 226 |
| Kansas City | 8 | 7 | 1 | .531 | 318 | 286 |
| LA Raiders | 8 | 8 | 0 | .500 | 315 | 297 |
| Seattle | 7 | 9 | 0 | .438 | 241 | 327 |
| San Diego | 6 | 10 | 0 | .375 | 266 | 290 |

## 1989 (*Cont.*)

### NFC EAST

| | W | L | T | Pct | Pts | OP |
|---|---|---|---|---|---|---|
| NY Giants | 12 | 4 | 0 | .750 | 348 | 252 |
| Philadelphia | 11 | 5 | 0 | .688 | 342 | 274 |
| Washington | 10 | 6 | 0 | .625 | 386 | 308 |
| Phoenix | 5 | 11 | 0 | .313 | 258 | 377 |
| Dallas | 1 | 15 | 0 | .063 | 204 | 393 |

### NFC CENTRAL

| | W | L | T | Pct | Pts | OP |
|---|---|---|---|---|---|---|
| Green Bay | 10 | 6 | 0 | .625 | 362 | 356 |
| Minnesota | 10 | 6 | 0 | .625 | 351 | 275 |
| Detroit | 7 | 9 | 0 | .438 | 312 | 364 |
| Chicago | 6 | 10 | 0 | .375 | 358 | 377 |
| Tampa Bay | 5 | 11 | 0 | .313 | 320 | 419 |

### NFC WEST

| | W | L | T | Pct | Pts | OP |
|---|---|---|---|---|---|---|
| San Francisco | 14 | 2 | 0 | .875 | 442 | 253 |
| LA Rams | 11 | 5 | 0 | .688 | 426 | 344 |
| New Orleans | 9 | 7 | 0 | .563 | 386 | 301 |
| Atlanta | 3 | 13 | 0 | .188 | 279 | 437 |

## 1990

### AFC EAST

| | W | L | T | Pct | Pts | OP |
|---|---|---|---|---|---|---|
| Buffalo | 13 | 3 | 0 | .813 | 428 | 263 |
| Miami | 12 | 4 | 0 | .750 | 336 | 242 |
| Indianapolis | 7 | 9 | 0 | .438 | 281 | 353 |
| NY Jets | 6 | 10 | 0 | .375 | 295 | 345 |
| New England | 1 | 15 | 0 | .063 | 181 | 446 |

### AFC CENTRAL

| | W | L | T | Pct | Pts | OP |
|---|---|---|---|---|---|---|
| Pittsburgh | 9 | 7 | 0 | .563 | 292 | 240 |
| Cincinnati | 9 | 7 | 0 | .563 | 360 | 352 |
| Houston | 9 | 7 | 0 | .563 | 405 | 307 |
| Cleveland | 3 | 13 | 0 | .188 | 228 | 462 |

### AFC WEST

| | W | L | T | Pct | Pts | OP |
|---|---|---|---|---|---|---|
| LA Raiders | 12 | 4 | 0 | .750 | 337 | 268 |
| Kansas City | 11 | 5 | 0 | .688 | 369 | 257 |
| Seattle | 9 | 7 | 0 | .563 | 306 | 286 |
| San Diego | 6 | 10 | 0 | .375 | 315 | 281 |
| Denver | 5 | 11 | 0 | .313 | 331 | 374 |

### NFC EAST

| | W | L | T | Pct | Pts | OP |
|---|---|---|---|---|---|---|
| NY Giants | 13 | 3 | 0 | .813 | 335 | 211 |
| Washington | 10 | 6 | 0 | .625 | 381 | 301 |
| Philadelphia | 10 | 6 | 0 | .625 | 396 | 299 |
| Dallas | 7 | 9 | 0 | .438 | 244 | 308 |
| Phoenix | 5 | 11 | 0 | .313 | 268 | 396 |

### NFC CENTRAL

| | W | L | T | Pct | Pts | OP |
|---|---|---|---|---|---|---|
| Chicago | 11 | 5 | 0 | .688 | 348 | 280 |
| Green Bay | 6 | 10 | 0 | .375 | 271 | 347 |
| Minnesota | 6 | 10 | 0 | .375 | 351 | 326 |
| Detroit | 6 | 10 | 0 | .375 | 373 | 413 |
| Tampa Bay | 6 | 10 | 0 | .375 | 264 | 367 |

### NFC WEST

| | W | L | T | Pct | Pts | OP |
|---|---|---|---|---|---|---|
| San Francisco | 14 | 2 | 0 | .875 | 353 | 239 |
| New Orleans | 8 | 8 | 0 | .500 | 274 | 275 |
| LA Rams | 5 | 11 | 0 | .313 | 345 | 412 |
| Atlanta | 5 | 11 | 0 | .313 | 348 | 365 |

## 1991

### AFC EAST

| | W | L | T | Pct | Pts | OP |
|---|---|---|---|---|---|---|
| Buffalo | 13 | 3 | 0 | .813 | 458 | 318 |
| Miami | 8 | 8 | 0 | .500 | 343 | 349 |
| NY Jets | 8 | 8 | 0 | .500 | 314 | 293 |
| New England | 6 | 10 | 0 | .375 | 211 | 305 |
| Indianapolis | 1 | 15 | 0 | .063 | 143 | 381 |

### AFC CENTRAL

| | W | L | T | Pct | Pts | OP |
|---|---|---|---|---|---|---|
| Houston | 11 | 5 | 0 | .688 | 386 | 251 |
| Pittsburgh | 7 | 9 | 0 | .438 | 292 | 344 |
| Cleveland | 6 | 10 | 0 | .375 | 293 | 298 |
| Cincinnati | 3 | 13 | 0 | .188 | 263 | 435 |

### AFC WEST

| | W | L | T | Pct | Pts | OP |
|---|---|---|---|---|---|---|
| Denver | 12 | 4 | 0 | .750 | 304 | 235 |
| Kansas City | 10 | 6 | 0 | .625 | 322 | 252 |
| LA Raiders | 9 | 7 | 0 | .563 | 298 | 297 |
| Seattle | 7 | 9 | 0 | .438 | 276 | 261 |
| San Diego | 4 | 12 | 0 | .250 | 274 | 342 |

### NFC EAST

| | W | L | T | Pct | Pts | OP |
|---|---|---|---|---|---|---|
| Washington | 14 | 2 | 0 | .875 | 485 | 224 |
| Dallas | 11 | 5 | 0 | .688 | 342 | 310 |
| Philadelphia | 10 | 6 | 0 | .625 | 285 | 244 |
| NY Giants | 8 | 8 | 0 | .500 | 281 | 297 |
| Phoenix | 4 | 12 | 0 | .250 | 196 | 344 |

### NFC CENTRAL

| | W | L | T | Pct | Pts | OP |
|---|---|---|---|---|---|---|
| Detroit | 12 | 4 | 0 | .750 | 339 | 295 |
| Chicago | 11 | 5 | 0 | .688 | 299 | 269 |
| Minnesota | 8 | 8 | 0 | .500 | 301 | 306 |
| Green Bay | 4 | 12 | 0 | .250 | 273 | 313 |
| Tampa Bay | 3 | 13 | 0 | .188 | 199 | 365 |

### NFC WEST

| | W | L | T | Pct | Pts | OP |
|---|---|---|---|---|---|---|
| New Orleans | 11 | 5 | 0 | .688 | 341 | 211 |
| Atlanta | 10 | 6 | 0 | .625 | 361 | 338 |
| San Francisco | 10 | 6 | 0 | .625 | 393 | 239 |
| LA Rams | 3 | 13 | 0 | .188 | 234 | 390 |

## 1992

### AFC EAST

| | W | L | T | Pct | Pts | OP |
|---|---|---|---|---|---|---|
| Buffalo | 11 | 5 | 0 | .688 | 381 | 283 |
| Miami | 11 | 5 | 0 | .688 | 340 | 281 |
| Indianapolis | 9 | 7 | 0 | .563 | 216 | 302 |
| NY Jets | 4 | 12 | 0 | .250 | 220 | 315 |
| New England | 2 | 14 | 0 | .125 | 205 | 363 |

### AFC CENTRAL

| | W | L | T | Pct | Pts | OP |
|---|---|---|---|---|---|---|
| Pittsburgh | 11 | 5 | 0 | .688 | 299 | 225 |
| Houston | 10 | 6 | 0 | .625 | 352 | 258 |
| Cleveland | 7 | 9 | 0 | .438 | 272 | 275 |
| Cincinnati | 5 | 11 | 0 | .313 | 274 | 364 |

### AFC WEST

| | W | L | T | Pct | Pts | OP |
|---|---|---|---|---|---|---|
| San Diego | 11 | 5 | 0 | .688 | 335 | 241 |
| Kansas City | 10 | 6 | 0 | .625 | 348 | 282 |
| Denver | 8 | 8 | 0 | .500 | 262 | 329 |
| LA Raiders | 7 | 9 | 0 | .438 | 249 | 281 |
| Seattle | 2 | 14 | 0 | .125 | 140 | 312 |

## 1992 *(Cont.)*

### NFC EAST

| | W | L | T | Pct | Pts | OP |
|---|---|---|---|---|---|---|
| Dallas | 13 | 3 | 0 | .813 | 409 | 243 |
| Philadelphia | 11 | 5 | 0 | .688 | 354 | 245 |
| Washington | 9 | 7 | 0 | .563 | 300 | 255 |
| NY Giants | 6 | 10 | 0 | .375 | 306 | 367 |
| Phoenix | 4 | 12 | 0 | .250 | 243 | 332 |

### NFC CENTRAL

| | W | L | T | Pct | Pts | OP |
|---|---|---|---|---|---|---|
| Minnesota | 11 | 5 | 0 | .688 | 374 | 249 |
| Green Bay | 9 | 7 | 0 | .563 | 276 | 296 |
| Tampa Bay | 5 | 11 | 0 | .313 | 267 | 365 |
| Detroit | 5 | 11 | 0 | .313 | 273 | 332 |
| Chicago | 5 | 11 | 0 | .313 | 295 | 361 |

### NFC WEST

| | W | L | T | Pct | Pts | OP |
|---|---|---|---|---|---|---|
| San Francisco | 14 | 2 | 0 | .875 | 431 | 236 |
| New Orleans | 12 | 4 | 0 | .750 | 330 | 202 |
| Atlanta | 6 | 10 | 0 | .375 | 327 | 414 |
| LA Rams | 6 | 10 | 0 | .375 | 313 | 383 |

## 1993

### AFC EAST

| | W | L | T | Pct | Pts | OP |
|---|---|---|---|---|---|---|
| Buffalo | 12 | 4 | 0 | .750 | 329 | 242 |
| Miami | 9 | 7 | 0 | .563 | 349 | 351 |
| NY Jets | 8 | 8 | 0 | .500 | 270 | 247 |
| New England | 5 | 11 | 0 | .313 | 238 | 286 |
| Indianapolis | 4 | 12 | 0 | .250 | 189 | 378 |

### AFC CENTRAL

| | W | L | T | Pct | Pts | OP |
|---|---|---|---|---|---|---|
| Houston | 12 | 4 | 0 | .750 | 368 | 238 |
| Pittsburgh | 9 | 7 | 0 | .563 | 308 | 281 |
| Cleveland | 7 | 9 | 0 | .438 | 304 | 307 |
| Cincinnati | 3 | 13 | 0 | .188 | 187 | 319 |

### AFC WEST

| | W | L | T | Pct | Pts | OP |
|---|---|---|---|---|---|---|
| Kansas City | 11 | 5 | 0 | .688 | 328 | 291 |
| LA Raiders | 10 | 6 | 0 | .625 | 306 | 326 |
| Denver | 9 | 7 | 0 | .563 | 373 | 284 |
| San Diego | 8 | 8 | 0 | .500 | 322 | 290 |
| Seattle | 6 | 10 | 0 | .375 | 280 | 314 |

### NFC EAST

| | W | L | T | Pct | Pts | OP |
|---|---|---|---|---|---|---|
| Dallas | 12 | 4 | 0 | .750 | 376 | 229 |
| NY Giants | 11 | 5 | 0 | .688 | 288 | 205 |
| Philadelphia | 8 | 8 | 0 | .500 | 293 | 315 |
| Phoenix | 7 | 9 | 0 | .438 | 326 | 269 |
| Washington | 4 | 12 | 0 | .250 | 230 | 345 |

### NFC CENTRAL

| | W | L | T | Pct | Pts | OP |
|---|---|---|---|---|---|---|
| Detroit | 10 | 6 | 0 | .625 | 298 | 292 |
| Green Bay | 9 | 7 | 0 | .563 | 340 | 282 |
| Minnesota | 9 | 7 | 0 | .563 | 277 | 290 |
| Chicago | 7 | 9 | 0 | .438 | 234 | 230 |
| Tampa Bay | 5 | 11 | 0 | .313 | 237 | 375 |

### NFC WEST

| | W | L | T | Pct | Pts | OP |
|---|---|---|---|---|---|---|
| San Francisco | 10 | 6 | 0 | .625 | 473 | 295 |
| New Orleans | 8 | 8 | 0 | .500 | 317 | 343 |
| Atlanta | 6 | 10 | 0 | .375 | 316 | 385 |
| LA Rams | 5 | 11 | 0 | .313 | 221 | 367 |

### 1994

| AFC EAST | W | L | T | Pct | Pts | OP |
|---|---|---|---|---|---|---|
| Miami | 10 | 6 | 0 | .625 | 389 | 327 |
| New England | 10 | 6 | 0 | .625 | 351 | 312 |
| Indianapolis | 8 | 8 | 0 | .500 | 307 | 320 |
| Buffalo | 7 | 9 | 0 | .438 | 340 | 356 |
| NY Jets | 6 | 10 | 0 | .375 | 264 | 320 |

| AFC CENTRAL | W | L | T | Pct | Pts | OP |
|---|---|---|---|---|---|---|
| Pittsburgh | 12 | 4 | 0 | .750 | 316 | 234 |
| Cleveland | 11 | 5 | 0 | .688 | 340 | 204 |
| Cincinnati | 3 | 13 | 0 | .188 | 276 | 406 |
| Houston | 2 | 14 | 0 | .125 | 226 | 352 |

| AFC WEST | W | L | T | Pct | Pts | OP |
|---|---|---|---|---|---|---|
| San Diego | 11 | 5 | 0 | .688 | 384 | 306 |
| LA Raiders | 9 | 7 | 0 | .563 | 303 | 327 |
| Kansas City | 9 | 7 | 0 | .563 | 319 | 298 |
| Denver | 7 | 9 | 0 | .438 | 347 | 396 |
| Seattle | 6 | 10 | 0 | .375 | 287 | 323 |

| NFC EAST | W | L | T | Pct | Pts | OP |
|---|---|---|---|---|---|---|
| Dallas | 12 | 4 | 0 | .750 | 414 | 248 |
| NY Giants | 9 | 7 | 0 | .563 | 279 | 305 |
| Arizona Cardinals | 8 | 8 | 0 | .500 | 235 | 267 |
| Philadelphia | 7 | 9 | 0 | .438 | 308 | 308 |
| Washington | 3 | 13 | 0 | .188 | 320 | 412 |

| NFC CENTRAL | W | L | T | Pct | Pts | OP |
|---|---|---|---|---|---|---|
| Minnesota | 10 | 6 | 0 | .625 | 356 | 314 |
| Green Bay | 9 | 7 | 0 | .563 | 382 | 287 |
| Detroit | 9 | 7 | 0 | .563 | 357 | 342 |
| Chicago | 9 | 7 | 0 | .563 | 271 | 307 |
| Tampa Bay | 6 | 10 | 0 | .375 | 251 | 351 |

| NFC WEST | W | L | T | Pct | Pts | OP |
|---|---|---|---|---|---|---|
| San Francisco | 13 | 3 | 0 | .813 | 505 | 296 |
| New Orleans | 7 | 9 | 0 | .438 | 348 | 407 |
| Atlanta | 7 | 9 | 0 | .438 | 317 | 385 |
| LA Rams | 4 | 12 | 0 | .250 | 286 | 365 |

### 1995

| AFC EAST | W | L | T | Pct | Pts | OP |
|---|---|---|---|---|---|---|
| Buffalo | 10 | 6 | 0 | .625 | 350 | 335 |
| Miami | 9 | 7 | 0 | .563 | 398 | 332 |
| Indianapolis | 9 | 7 | 0 | .563 | 331 | 316 |
| New England | 6 | 10 | 0 | .375 | 294 | 377 |
| NY Jets | 3 | 13 | 0 | .188 | 233 | 384 |

| AFC CENTRAL | W | L | T | Pct | Pts | OP |
|---|---|---|---|---|---|---|
| Pittsburgh | 11 | 5 | 0 | .688 | 407 | 327 |
| Houston | 7 | 9 | 0 | .438 | 348 | 324 |
| Cincinnati | 7 | 9 | 0 | .438 | 349 | 374 |
| Cleveland | 5 | 11 | 0 | .313 | 289 | 356 |
| Jacksonville Jaguars | 4 | 12 | 0 | .250 | 275 | 404 |

| AFC WEST | W | L | T | Pct | Pts | OP |
|---|---|---|---|---|---|---|
| Kansas City | 13 | 3 | 0 | .813 | 358 | 241 |
| San Diego | 9 | 7 | 0 | .563 | 321 | 323 |
| Oakland Raiders | 8 | 8 | 0 | .500 | 348 | 332 |
| Denver | 8 | 8 | 0 | .500 | 388 | 345 |
| Seattle | 8 | 8 | 0 | .500 | 363 | 366 |

### 1995 *(Cont.)*

| NFC EAST | W | L | T | Pct | Pts | OP |
|---|---|---|---|---|---|---|
| Dallas | 12 | 4 | 0 | .750 | 435 | 291 |
| Philadelphia | 10 | 6 | 0 | .625 | 318 | 338 |
| Washington | 6 | 10 | 0 | .375 | 326 | 359 |
| NY Giants | 5 | 11 | 0 | .313 | 290 | 340 |
| Arizona | 4 | 12 | 0 | .250 | 275 | 422 |

| NFC CENTRAL | W | L | T | Pct | Pts | OP |
|---|---|---|---|---|---|---|
| Green Bay | 11 | 5 | 0 | .688 | 404 | 314 |
| Detroit | 10 | 6 | 0 | .625 | 436 | 336 |
| Chicago | 9 | 7 | 0 | .563 | 392 | 360 |
| Minnesota | 8 | 8 | 0 | .500 | 412 | 385 |
| Tampa Bay | 7 | 9 | 0 | .438 | 238 | 335 |

| NFC WEST | W | L | T | Pct | Pts | OP |
|---|---|---|---|---|---|---|
| San Francisco | 11 | 5 | 0 | .688 | 457 | 258 |
| Atlanta | 9 | 7 | 0 | .563 | 362 | 349 |
| St. Louis Rams | 7 | 9 | 0 | .438 | 309 | 418 |
| Carolina Panthers | 7 | 9 | 0 | .438 | 289 | 325 |
| New Orleans | 7 | 9 | 0 | .438 | 319 | 348 |

### 1996

| AFC EAST | W | L | T | Pct | Pts | OP |
|---|---|---|---|---|---|---|
| New England | 11 | 5 | 0 | .688 | 418 | 313 |
| Buffalo | 10 | 6 | 0 | .625 | 319 | 266 |
| Indianapolis | 9 | 7 | 0 | .563 | 317 | 334 |
| Miami | 8 | 8 | 0 | .500 | 339 | 325 |
| NY Jets | 1 | 15 | 0 | .063 | 279 | 454 |

| AFC CENTRAL | W | L | T | Pct | Pts | OP |
|---|---|---|---|---|---|---|
| Pittsburgh | 10 | 6 | 0 | .625 | 344 | 257 |
| Jacksonville | 9 | 7 | 0 | .563 | 325 | 334 |
| Houston | 8 | 8 | 0 | .500 | 345 | 319 |
| Cincinnati | 8 | 8 | 0 | .500 | 372 | 369 |
| Baltimore Ravens | 4 | 12 | 0 | .250 | 371 | 441 |

| AFC WEST | W | L | T | Pct | Pts | OP |
|---|---|---|---|---|---|---|
| Denver | 13 | 3 | 0 | .813 | 391 | 275 |
| Kansas City | 9 | 7 | 0 | .563 | 297 | 300 |
| San Diego | 8 | 8 | 0 | .500 | 310 | 376 |
| Seattle | 7 | 9 | 0 | .438 | 317 | 375 |
| Oakland | 7 | 9 | 0 | .438 | 340 | 293 |

| NFC EAST | W | L | T | Pct | Pts | OP |
|---|---|---|---|---|---|---|
| Dallas | 10 | 6 | 0 | .625 | 286 | 250 |
| Philadelphia | 10 | 6 | 0 | .625 | 363 | 341 |
| Washington | 9 | 7 | 0 | .563 | 364 | 312 |
| Arizona | 7 | 9 | 0 | .438 | 300 | 397 |
| NY Giants | 6 | 10 | 0 | .375 | 242 | 297 |

| NFC CENTRAL | W | L | T | Pct | Pts | OP |
|---|---|---|---|---|---|---|
| Green Bay | 13 | 3 | 0 | .813 | 456 | 210 |
| Minnesota | 9 | 7 | 0 | .563 | 298 | 315 |
| Chicago | 7 | 9 | 0 | .438 | 283 | 305 |
| Tampa Bay | 6 | 10 | 0 | .375 | 221 | 293 |
| Detroit | 5 | 11 | 0 | .313 | 302 | 368 |

| NFC WEST | W | L | T | Pct | Pts | OP |
|---|---|---|---|---|---|---|
| San Francisco | 12 | 4 | 0 | .750 | 398 | 257 |
| Carolina | 12 | 4 | 0 | .750 | 367 | 218 |
| St. Louis | 6 | 10 | 0 | .375 | 303 | 409 |
| New Orleans | 3 | 13 | 0 | .188 | 229 | 339 |
| Atlanta | 3 | 13 | 0 | .188 | 309 | 461 |

## 1997

### AFC EAST
| | W | L | T | Pct | Pts | OP |
|---|---|---|---|---|---|---|
| New England | 10 | 6 | 0 | .625 | 369 | 289 |
| Miami | 9 | 7 | 0 | .563 | 339 | 327 |
| NY Jets | 9 | 7 | 0 | .563 | 348 | 287 |
| Buffalo | 6 | 10 | 0 | .375 | 255 | 367 |
| Indianapolis | 3 | 13 | 0 | .188 | 313 | 401 |

### AFC CENTRAL
| | W | L | T | Pct | Pts | OP |
|---|---|---|---|---|---|---|
| Jacksonville | 11 | 5 | 0 | .688 | 394 | 318 |
| Pittsburgh | 11 | 5 | 0 | .688 | 372 | 307 |
| Tennessee Oilers | 8 | 8 | 0 | .500 | 333 | 310 |
| Cincinnati | 7 | 9 | 0 | .438 | 355 | 405 |
| Baltimore | 6 | 9 | 1 | .375 | 326 | 345 |

### AFC WEST
| | W | L | T | Pct | Pts | OP |
|---|---|---|---|---|---|---|
| Kansas City | 13 | 3 | 0 | .813 | 375 | 232 |
| Denver | 12 | 4 | 0 | .750 | 472 | 287 |
| Seattle | 8 | 8 | 0 | .500 | 365 | 362 |
| Oakland | 4 | 12 | 0 | .250 | 324 | 419 |
| San Diego | 4 | 12 | 0 | .250 | 266 | 425 |

### NFC EAST
| | W | L | T | Pct | Pts | OP |
|---|---|---|---|---|---|---|
| NY Giants | 10 | 5 | 1 | .656 | 307 | 265 |
| Washington | 8 | 7 | 1 | .531 | 327 | 289 |
| Philadelphia | 6 | 9 | 1 | .406 | 317 | 372 |
| Dallas | 6 | 10 | 0 | .375 | 304 | 314 |
| Arizona | 4 | 12 | 0 | .250 | 283 | 379 |

### NFC CENTRAL
| | W | L | T | Pct | Pts | OP |
|---|---|---|---|---|---|---|
| Green Bay | 13 | 3 | 0 | .813 | 422 | 282 |
| Tampa Bay | 10 | 6 | 0 | .625 | 299 | 263 |
| Detroit | 9 | 7 | 0 | .563 | 379 | 306 |
| Minnesota | 9 | 7 | 0 | .563 | 354 | 359 |
| Chicago | 4 | 12 | 0 | .250 | 263 | 421 |

### NFC WEST
| | W | L | T | Pct | Pts | OP |
|---|---|---|---|---|---|---|
| San Francisco | 13 | 3 | 0 | .813 | 375 | 265 |
| Carolina | 7 | 9 | 0 | .438 | 265 | 314 |
| Atlanta | 7 | 9 | 0 | .438 | 320 | 361 |
| New Orleans | 6 | 10 | 0 | .375 | 237 | 327 |
| St. Louis | 5 | 11 | 0 | .313 | 299 | 359 |

## 1998

### AFC EAST
| | W | L | T | Pct | Pts | OP |
|---|---|---|---|---|---|---|
| NY Jets | 12 | 4 | 0 | .750 | 416 | 266 |
| Miami | 10 | 6 | 0 | .625 | 321 | 265 |
| Buffalo | 10 | 6 | 0 | .625 | 400 | 333 |
| New England | 9 | 7 | 0 | .563 | 337 | 329 |
| Indianapolis | 3 | 13 | 0 | .188 | 310 | 444 |

### AFC CENTRAL
| | W | L | T | Pct | Pts | OP |
|---|---|---|---|---|---|---|
| Jacksonville | 11 | 5 | 0 | .688 | 392 | 338 |
| Tennessee | 8 | 8 | 0 | .500 | 330 | 320 |
| Pittsburgh | 7 | 9 | 0 | .438 | 263 | 303 |
| Baltimore | 6 | 10 | 0 | .375 | 269 | 335 |
| Cincinnati | 3 | 13 | 0 | .188 | 268 | 452 |

### AFC WEST
| | W | L | T | Pct | Pts | OP |
|---|---|---|---|---|---|---|
| Denver | 14 | 2 | 0 | .875 | 501 | 309 |
| Oakland | 8 | 8 | 0 | .500 | 288 | 356 |
| Seattle | 8 | 8 | 0 | .500 | 372 | 310 |
| Kansas City | 7 | 9 | 0 | .438 | 327 | 363 |
| San Diego | 5 | 11 | 0 | .313 | 241 | 342 |

## 1998 *(Cont.)*

### NFC EAST
| | W | L | T | Pct | Pts | OP |
|---|---|---|---|---|---|---|
| Dallas | 10 | 6 | 0 | .625 | 381 | 275 |
| Arizona | 9 | 7 | 0 | .563 | 325 | 378 |
| NY Giants | 8 | 8 | 0 | .500 | 287 | 309 |
| Washington | 6 | 10 | 0 | .375 | 319 | 421 |
| Philadelphia | 3 | 13 | 0 | .188 | 161 | 344 |

### NFC CENTRAL
| | W | L | T | Pct | Pts | OP |
|---|---|---|---|---|---|---|
| Minnesota | 15 | 1 | 0 | .938 | 556 | 296 |
| Green Bay | 11 | 5 | 0 | .688 | 408 | 319 |
| Tampa Bay | 8 | 8 | 0 | .500 | 314 | 295 |
| Detroit | 5 | 11 | 0 | .313 | 306 | 378 |
| Chicago | 4 | 12 | 0 | .250 | 276 | 368 |

### NFC WEST
| | W | L | T | Pct | Pts | OP |
|---|---|---|---|---|---|---|
| Atlanta | 14 | 2 | 0 | .875 | 442 | 289 |
| San Francisco | 12 | 4 | 0 | .750 | 479 | 328 |
| New Orleans | 6 | 10 | 0 | .375 | 305 | 359 |
| Carolina | 4 | 12 | 0 | .250 | 336 | 413 |
| St. Louis | 4 | 12 | 0 | .250 | 285 | 378 |

## 1999

### AFC EAST
| | W | L | T | Pct | Pts | OP |
|---|---|---|---|---|---|---|
| Indianapolis | 13 | 3 | 0 | .813 | 423 | 333 |
| Buffalo | 11 | 5 | 0 | .688 | 320 | 229 |
| Miami | 9 | 7 | 0 | .563 | 326 | 336 |
| NY Jets | 8 | 8 | 0 | .500 | 309 | 309 |
| New England | 8 | 8 | 0 | .500 | 299 | 284 |

### AFC CENTRAL
| | W | L | T | Pct | Pts | OP |
|---|---|---|---|---|---|---|
| Jacksonville | 14 | 2 | 0 | .875 | 396 | 217 |
| Tennessee Titans | 13 | 3 | 0 | .813 | 392 | 324 |
| Baltimore | 8 | 8 | 0 | .500 | 324 | 277 |
| Pittsburgh | 6 | 10 | 0 | .375 | 317 | 320 |
| Cincinnati | 4 | 12 | 0 | .250 | 283 | 460 |
| Cleveland Browns | 2 | 14 | 0 | .125 | 217 | 437 |

### AFC WEST
| | W | L | T | Pct | Pts | OP |
|---|---|---|---|---|---|---|
| Seattle | 9 | 7 | 0 | .563 | 338 | 298 |
| Kansas City | 9 | 7 | 0 | .563 | 390 | 322 |
| Oakland | 8 | 8 | 0 | .500 | 390 | 329 |
| San Diego | 8 | 8 | 0 | .500 | 269 | 316 |
| Denver | 6 | 10 | 0 | .375 | 314 | 318 |

### NFC EAST
| | W | L | T | Pct | Pts | OP |
|---|---|---|---|---|---|---|
| Washington | 10 | 6 | 0 | .625 | 443 | 377 |
| Dallas | 8 | 8 | 0 | .500 | 352 | 276 |
| NY Giants | 7 | 9 | 0 | .438 | 299 | 358 |
| Arizona | 6 | 10 | 0 | .375 | 245 | 382 |
| Philadelphia | 5 | 11 | 0 | .313 | 272 | 357 |

### NFC CENTRAL
| | W | L | T | Pct | Pts | OP |
|---|---|---|---|---|---|---|
| Tampa Bay | 11 | 5 | 0 | .688 | 270 | 235 |
| Minnesota | 10 | 6 | 0 | .625 | 399 | 335 |
| Green Bay | 8 | 8 | 0 | .500 | 357 | 341 |
| Detroit | 8 | 8 | 0 | .500 | 322 | 323 |
| Chicago | 6 | 10 | 0 | .375 | 272 | 341 |

### NFC WEST
| | W | L | T | Pct | Pts | OP |
|---|---|---|---|---|---|---|
| St. Louis | 13 | 3 | 0 | .813 | 526 | 242 |
| Carolina | 8 | 8 | 0 | .500 | 421 | 381 |
| Atlanta | 5 | 11 | 0 | .313 | 285 | 380 |
| San Francisco | 4 | 12 | 0 | .250 | 295 | 453 |
| New Orleans | 3 | 13 | 0 | .188 | 260 | 434 |

### 2000

**AFC EAST**

| | W | L | T | Pct | Pts | OP |
|---|---|---|---|---|---|---|
| Miami | 11 | 5 | 0 | .688 | 323 | 226 |
| Indianapolis | 10 | 6 | 0 | .625 | 429 | 326 |
| NY Jets | 9 | 7 | 0 | .563 | 321 | 321 |
| Buffalo | 8 | 8 | 0 | .500 | 315 | 350 |
| New England | 5 | 11 | 0 | .313 | 276 | 338 |

**AFC CENTRAL**

| | W | L | T | Pct | Pts | OP |
|---|---|---|---|---|---|---|
| Tennessee | 13 | 3 | 0 | .813 | 346 | 191 |
| Baltimore | 12 | 4 | 0 | .750 | 333 | 165 |
| Pittsburgh | 9 | 7 | 0 | .563 | 321 | 255 |
| Jacksonville | 7 | 9 | 0 | .438 | 367 | 327 |
| Cincinnati | 4 | 12 | 0 | .250 | 185 | 359 |
| Cleveland | 3 | 13 | 0 | .188 | 161 | 419 |

**AFC WEST**

| | W | L | T | Pct | Pts | OP |
|---|---|---|---|---|---|---|
| Oakland | 12 | 4 | 0 | .750 | 479 | 299 |
| Denver | 11 | 5 | 0 | .688 | 485 | 369 |
| Kansas City | 7 | 9 | 0 | .438 | 355 | 354 |
| Seattle | 6 | 10 | 0 | .375 | 320 | 405 |
| San Diego | 1 | 15 | 0 | .063 | 269 | 440 |

**NFC EAST**

| | W | L | T | Pct | Pts | OP |
|---|---|---|---|---|---|---|
| NY Giants | 12 | 4 | 0 | .750 | 328 | 246 |
| Philadelphia | 11 | 5 | 0 | .688 | 351 | 245 |
| Washington | 8 | 8 | 0 | .500 | 281 | 269 |
| Dallas | 5 | 11 | 0 | .313 | 294 | 361 |
| Arizona | 3 | 13 | 0 | .188 | 210 | 443 |

**NFC CENTRAL**

| | W | L | T | Pct | Pts | OP |
|---|---|---|---|---|---|---|
| Minnesota | 11 | 5 | 0 | .688 | 397 | 371 |
| Tampa Bay | 10 | 6 | 0 | .625 | 388 | 269 |
| Green Bay | 9 | 7 | 0 | .563 | 353 | 323 |
| Detroit | 9 | 7 | 0 | .563 | 307 | 307 |
| Chicago | 5 | 11 | 0 | .313 | 216 | 355 |

**NFC WEST**

| | W | L | T | Pct | Pts | OP |
|---|---|---|---|---|---|---|
| New Orleans | 10 | 6 | 0 | .625 | 354 | 306 |
| St. Louis | 10 | 6 | 0 | .625 | 540 | 471 |
| Carolina | 7 | 9 | 0 | .438 | 310 | 310 |
| San Francisco | 6 | 10 | 0 | .375 | 388 | 422 |
| Atlanta | 4 | 12 | 0 | .250 | 252 | 413 |

### 2001

**AFC EAST**

| | W | L | T | Pct | Pts | OP |
|---|---|---|---|---|---|---|
| New England | 11 | 5 | 0 | .688 | 371 | 272 |
| Miami | 11 | 5 | 0 | .688 | 344 | 290 |
| NY Jets | 10 | 6 | 0 | .625 | 413 | 486 |
| Indianapolis | 6 | 10 | 0 | .375 | 413 | 486 |
| Buffalo | 3 | 13 | 0 | .188 | 265 | 420 |

**AFC CENTRAL**

| | W | L | T | Pct | Pts | OP |
|---|---|---|---|---|---|---|
| Pittsburgh | 13 | 3 | 0 | .813 | 352 | 212 |
| Baltimore | 10 | 6 | 0 | .625 | 303 | 265 |
| Cleveland | 7 | 9 | 0 | .438 | 285 | 319 |
| Tennessee | 7 | 9 | 0 | .438 | 336 | 388 |
| Jacksonville | 6 | 10 | 0 | .375 | 294 | 286 |
| Cincinnati | 6 | 10 | 0 | .375 | 226 | 309 |

**AFC WEST**

| | W | L | T | Pct | Pts | OP |
|---|---|---|---|---|---|---|
| Oakland | 10 | 6 | 0 | .625 | 399 | 327 |
| Seattle | 9 | 7 | 0 | .563 | 301 | 324 |
| Denver | 8 | 8 | 0 | .500 | 340 | 339 |
| Kansas City | 6 | 10 | 0 | .375 | 320 | 344 |
| San Diego | 5 | 11 | 0 | .313 | 332 | 321 |

### 2001 *(Cont.)*

**NFC EAST**

| | W | L | T | Pct | Pts | OP |
|---|---|---|---|---|---|---|
| Philadelphia | 11 | 5 | 0 | .688 | 343 | 208 |
| Washington | 8 | 8 | 0 | .500 | 256 | 303 |
| NY Giants | 7 | 9 | 0 | .438 | 294 | 321 |
| Arizona | 7 | 9 | 0 | .438 | 295 | 343 |
| Dallas | 5 | 11 | 0 | .313 | 246 | 338 |

**NFC CENTRAL**

| | W | L | T | Pct | Pts | OP |
|---|---|---|---|---|---|---|
| Chicago | 13 | 3 | 0 | .813 | 338 | 203 |
| Green Bay | 12 | 4 | 0 | .750 | 390 | 266 |
| Tampa Bay | 9 | 7 | 0 | .563 | 324 | 280 |
| Minnesota | 5 | 11 | 0 | .313 | 290 | 390 |
| Detroit | 2 | 14 | 0 | .125 | 270 | 424 |

**NFC WEST**

| | W | L | T | Pct | Pts | OP |
|---|---|---|---|---|---|---|
| St. Louis | 14 | 2 | 0 | .875 | 503 | 273 |
| San Francisco | 12 | 4 | 0 | .750 | 409 | 282 |
| Atlanta | 7 | 9 | 0 | .438 | 291 | 377 |
| New Orleans | 7 | 9 | 0 | .438 | 333 | 409 |
| Carolina | 1 | 15 | 0 | .938 | 253 | 410 |

### 2002

**AFC EAST**

| | W | L | T | Pct | Pts | OP |
|---|---|---|---|---|---|---|
| New England | 9 | 7 | 0 | .563 | 384 | 346 |
| Miami | 9 | 7 | 0 | .563 | 378 | 301 |
| NY Jets | 9 | 7 | 0 | .563 | 359 | 336 |
| Buffalo | 8 | 8 | 0 | .500 | 379 | 397 |

**AFC NORTH**

| | W | L | T | Pct | Pts | OP |
|---|---|---|---|---|---|---|
| Pittsburgh | 10 | 5 | 1 | .656 | 390 | 345 |
| Cleveland | 9 | 7 | 0 | .563 | 344 | 320 |
| Baltimore | 7 | 9 | 0 | .438 | 316 | 354 |
| Cincinnati | 2 | 14 | 0 | .125 | 279 | 456 |

**AFC SOUTH**

| | W | L | T | Pct | Pts | OP |
|---|---|---|---|---|---|---|
| Tennessee | 11 | 5 | 0 | .688 | 367 | 324 |
| Indianapolis | 10 | 6 | 0 | .625 | 349 | 313 |
| Jacksonville | 6 | 10 | 0 | .375 | 328 | 315 |
| Houston Texans | 4 | 12 | 0 | .250 | 213 | 356 |

**AFC WEST**

| | W | L | T | Pct | Pts | OP |
|---|---|---|---|---|---|---|
| Oakland | 11 | 5 | 0 | .688 | 450 | 304 |
| Denver | 9 | 7 | 0 | .563 | 392 | 344 |
| Kansas City | 8 | 8 | 0 | .500 | 467 | 399 |
| San Diego | 8 | 8 | 0 | .500 | 333 | 367 |

**NFC EAST**

| | W | L | T | Pct | Pts | OP |
|---|---|---|---|---|---|---|
| Philadelphia | 12 | 4 | 0 | .750 | 415 | 241 |
| NY Giants | 10 | 6 | 0 | .625 | 320 | 279 |
| Washington | 7 | 9 | 0 | .438 | 307 | 365 |
| Dallas | 5 | 11 | 0 | .313 | 217 | 329 |

**NFC NORTH**

| | W | L | T | Pct | Pts | OP |
|---|---|---|---|---|---|---|
| Green Bay | 12 | 4 | 0 | .750 | 398 | 328 |
| Minnesota | 6 | 10 | 0 | .375 | 390 | 442 |
| Chicago | 4 | 12 | 0 | .250 | 281 | 379 |
| Detroit | 3 | 13 | 0 | .188 | 306 | 451 |

### 2002 (*Cont.*)

**NFC SOUTH**

| | W | L | T | Pct | Pts | OP |
|---|---|---|---|---|---|---|
| Tampa Bay | 12 | 4 | 0 | .750 | 346 | 196 |
| Atlanta | 9 | 6 | 1 | .594 | 402 | 314 |
| New Orleans | 9 | 7 | 0 | .563 | 432 | 388 |
| Carolina | 7 | 9 | 0 | .438 | 258 | 302 |

**NFC WEST**

| | W | L | T | Pct | Pts | OP |
|---|---|---|---|---|---|---|
| San Francisco | 10 | 6 | 0 | .625 | 367 | 351 |
| St. Louis | 7 | 9 | 0 | .438 | 316 | 367 |
| Seattle | 7 | 9 | 0 | .438 | 355 | 369 |
| Arizona | 5 | 11 | 0 | .313 | 262 | 417 |

### 2003

**AFC EAST**

| | W | L | T | Pct | Pts | OP |
|---|---|---|---|---|---|---|
| New England | 14 | 2 | 0 | .875 | 348 | 238 |
| Miami | 10 | 6 | 0 | .625 | 311 | 261 |
| Buffalo | 6 | 10 | 0 | .375 | 243 | 279 |
| NY Jets | 6 | 10 | 0 | .375 | 283 | 299 |

**AFC NORTH**

| | W | L | T | Pct | Pts | OP |
|---|---|---|---|---|---|---|
| Baltimore | 10 | 6 | 0 | .625 | 391 | 281 |
| Cincinnati | 8 | 8 | 0 | .500 | 346 | 384 |
| Pittsburgh | 6 | 10 | 0 | .375 | 300 | 327 |
| Cleveland | 5 | 11 | 0 | .313 | 254 | 322 |

**AFC SOUTH**

| | W | L | T | Pct | Pts | OP |
|---|---|---|---|---|---|---|
| Indianapolis | 12 | 4 | 0 | .750 | 447 | 336 |
| Tennessee | 12 | 4 | 0 | .750 | 435 | 324 |
| Houston | 5 | 11 | 0 | .313 | 255 | 380 |
| Jacksonville | 5 | 11 | 0 | .313 | 276 | 331 |

**AFC WEST**

| | W | L | T | Pct | Pts | OP |
|---|---|---|---|---|---|---|
| Kansas City | 13 | 3 | 0 | .813 | 484 | 332 |
| Denver | 10 | 6 | 0 | .625 | 381 | 301 |
| Oakland | 4 | 12 | 0 | .250 | 270 | 379 |
| San Diego | 4 | 12 | 0 | .250 | 313 | 441 |

**NFC EAST**

| | W | L | T | Pct | Pts | OP |
|---|---|---|---|---|---|---|
| Philadelphia | 12 | 4 | 0 | .750 | 374 | 287 |
| Dallas | 10 | 6 | 0 | .625 | 289 | 260 |
| Washington | 5 | 11 | 0 | .313 | 287 | 372 |
| NY Giants | 4 | 12 | 0 | .250 | 243 | 387 |

**NFC NORTH**

| | W | L | T | Pct | Pts | OP |
|---|---|---|---|---|---|---|
| Green Bay | 10 | 6 | 0 | .625 | 442 | 307 |
| Minnesota | 9 | 7 | 0 | .563 | 416 | 353 |
| Chicago | 7 | 9 | 0 | .438 | 283 | 346 |
| Detroit | 5 | 11 | 0 | .313 | 270 | 379 |

**NFC SOUTH**

| | W | L | T | Pct | Pts | OP |
|---|---|---|---|---|---|---|
| Carolina | 11 | 5 | 0 | .688 | 325 | 304 |
| New Orleans | 8 | 8 | 0 | .500 | 340 | 326 |
| Tampa Bay | 7 | 9 | 0 | .438 | 301 | 264 |
| Atlanta | 5 | 11 | 0 | .313 | 299 | 422 |

**NFC WEST**

| | W | L | T | Pct | Pts | OP |
|---|---|---|---|---|---|---|
| St. Louis | 12 | 4 | 0 | .750 | 447 | 328 |
| Seattle | 10 | 6 | 0 | .625 | 404 | 327 |
| San Francisco | 7 | 9 | 0 | .438 | 384 | 337 |
| Arizona | 4 | 12 | 0 | .250 | 225 | 452 |

### 2004

**AFC EAST**

| | W | L | T | Pct | Pts | OP |
|---|---|---|---|---|---|---|
| New England | 14 | 2 | 0 | .875 | 437 | 260 |
| NY Jets | 10 | 6 | 0 | .625 | 333 | 261 |
| Buffalo | 9 | 7 | 0 | .562 | 395 | 284 |
| Miami | 4 | 12 | 0 | .250 | 275 | 354 |

### 2004 (*Cont.*)

**AFC NORTH**

| | W | L | T | Pct | Pts | OP |
|---|---|---|---|---|---|---|
| Pittsburgh | 15 | 1 | 0 | .938 | 372 | 251 |
| Baltimore | 9 | 7 | 0 | .562 | 317 | 268 |
| Cincinnati | 8 | 8 | 0 | .500 | 374 | 372 |
| Cleveland | 4 | 12 | 0 | .250 | 275 | 354 |

**AFC SOUTH**

| | W | L | T | Pct | Pts | OP |
|---|---|---|---|---|---|---|
| Indianapolis | 12 | 4 | 0 | .750 | 522 | 351 |
| Jacksonville | 9 | 7 | 0 | .562 | 261 | 280 |
| Houston | 7 | 9 | 0 | .438 | 309 | 339 |
| Tennessee | 5 | 11 | 0 | .312 | 344 | 439 |

**AFC WEST**

| | W | L | T | Pct | Pts | OP |
|---|---|---|---|---|---|---|
| San Diego | 12 | 4 | 0 | .750 | 446 | 313 |
| Denver | 10 | 6 | 0 | .625 | 381 | 304 |
| Kansas City | 7 | 9 | 0 | .438 | 483 | 435 |
| Oakland | 5 | 11 | 0 | .312 | 320 | 442 |

**NFC EAST**

| | W | L | T | Pct | Pts | OP |
|---|---|---|---|---|---|---|
| Philadelphia | 13 | 3 | 0 | .812 | 386 | 260 |
| NY Giants | 6 | 10 | 0 | .375 | 303 | 347 |
| Dallas | 6 | 10 | 0 | .375 | 293 | 405 |
| Washington | 6 | 10 | 0 | .375 | 240 | 265 |

**NFC NORTH**

| | W | L | T | Pct | Pts | OP |
|---|---|---|---|---|---|---|
| Green Bay | 10 | 6 | 0 | .625 | 424 | 380 |
| Minnesota | 8 | 8 | 0 | .500 | 405 | 395 |
| Detroit | 6 | 10 | 0 | .375 | 296 | 350 |
| Chicago | 5 | 11 | 0 | .312 | 231 | 331 |

**NFC SOUTH**

| | W | L | T | Pct | Pts | OP |
|---|---|---|---|---|---|---|
| Atlanta | 11 | 5 | 0 | .688 | 340 | 337 |
| New Orleans | 8 | 8 | 0 | .500 | 348 | 405 |
| Carolina | 7 | 9 | 0 | .438 | 355 | 339 |
| Tampa Bay | 5 | 11 | 0 | .312 | 301 | 304 |

**NFC WEST**

| | W | L | T | Pct | Pts | OP |
|---|---|---|---|---|---|---|
| Seattle | 9 | 7 | 0 | .562 | 371 | 373 |
| St. Louis | 8 | 8 | 0 | .500 | 319 | 392 |
| Arizona | 6 | 10 | 0 | .375 | 284 | 322 |
| San Francisco | 2 | 14 | 0 | .125 | 259 | 452 |

### 2005

**AFC EAST**

| | W | L | T | Pct | Pts | OP |
|---|---|---|---|---|---|---|
| New England | 10 | 6 | 0 | .625 | 379 | 338 |
| Miami | 9 | 7 | 0 | .562 | 318 | 317 |
| Buffalo | 5 | 11 | 0 | .312 | 271 | 367 |
| NY Jets | 4 | 12 | 0 | .250 | 240 | 355 |

**AFC NORTH**

| | W | L | T | Pct | Pts | OP |
|---|---|---|---|---|---|---|
| Cincinnati | 11 | 5 | 0 | .688 | 421 | 350 |
| Pittsburgh | 11 | 5 | 0 | .688 | 389 | 258 |
| Cleveland | 6 | 10 | 0 | .375 | 232 | 301 |
| Baltimore | 6 | 10 | 0 | .375 | 265 | 299 |

**AFC SOUTH**

| | W | L | T | Pct | Pts | OP |
|---|---|---|---|---|---|---|
| Indianapolis | 14 | 2 | 0 | .875 | 439 | 247 |
| Jacksonville | 12 | 4 | 0 | .750 | 361 | 269 |
| Tennessee | 4 | 12 | 0 | .250 | 299 | 421 |
| Houston | 2 | 14 | 0 | .125 | 260 | 431 |

**AFC WEST**

| | W | L | T | Pct | Pts | OP |
|---|---|---|---|---|---|---|
| Denver | 13 | 3 | 0 | .812 | 395 | 258 |
| Kansas City | 10 | 6 | 0 | .625 | 403 | 325 |
| San Diego | 9 | 7 | 0 | .562 | 418 | 312 |
| Oakland | 4 | 12 | 0 | .250 | 290 | 383 |

### 2005 *(Cont.)*

**NFC EAST**

| | W | L | T | Pct | Pts | OP |
|---|---|---|---|---|---|---|
| NY Giants | 11 | 5 | 0 | .688 | 422 | 314 |
| Washington | 10 | 6 | 0 | .625 | 359 | 293 |
| Dallas | 9 | 7 | 0 | .562 | 325 | 308 |
| Philadelphia | 6 | 10 | 0 | .375 | 310 | 388 |

**NFC NORTH**

| | W | L | T | Pct | Pts | OP |
|---|---|---|---|---|---|---|
| Chicago | 11 | 5 | 0 | .688 | 260 | 202 |
| Minnesota | 9 | 7 | 0 | .562 | 306 | 344 |
| Detroit | 5 | 11 | 0 | .312 | 254 | 345 |
| Green Bay | 4 | 12 | 0 | .250 | 298 | 344 |

**NFC SOUTH**

| | W | L | T | Pct | Pts | OP |
|---|---|---|---|---|---|---|
| Carolina | 11 | 5 | 0 | .688 | 391 | 259 |
| Tampa Bay | 11 | 5 | 0 | .688 | 300 | 274 |
| Atlanta | 8 | 8 | 0 | .500 | 351 | 341 |
| New Orleans | 3 | 13 | 0 | .188 | 235 | 398 |

**NFC WEST**

| | W | L | T | Pct | Pts | OP |
|---|---|---|---|---|---|---|
| Seattle | 13 | 3 | 0 | .812 | 452 | 271 |
| St. Louis | 6 | 10 | 0 | .375 | 363 | 429 |
| Arizona | 5 | 11 | 0 | .312 | 311 | 387 |
| San Francisco | 4 | 12 | 0 | .250 | 239 | 428 |

### 2006

**AFC EAST**

| | W | L | T | Pct | Pts | OP |
|---|---|---|---|---|---|---|
| New England | 12 | 4 | 0 | .750 | 385 | 237 |
| NY Jets | 10 | 6 | 0 | .625 | 316 | 295 |
| Buffalo | 7 | 9 | 0 | .438 | 300 | 311 |
| Miami | 6 | 10 | 0 | .375 | 260 | 283 |

**AFC NORTH**

| | W | L | T | Pct | Pts | OP |
|---|---|---|---|---|---|---|
| Baltimore | 13 | 3 | 0 | .812 | 353 | 201 |
| Cincinnati | 8 | 8 | 0 | .500 | 373 | 331 |
| Pittsburgh | 8 | 8 | 0 | .500 | 353 | 315 |
| Cleveland | 4 | 12 | 0 | .250 | 238 | 356 |

**AFC SOUTH**

| | W | L | T | Pct | Pts | OP |
|---|---|---|---|---|---|---|
| Indianapolis | 12 | 4 | 0 | .750 | 427 | 360 |
| Tennessee | 8 | 8 | 0 | .500 | 324 | 400 |
| Jacksonville | 8 | 8 | 0 | .500 | 371 | 274 |
| Houston | 6 | 10 | 0 | .375 | 267 | 366 |

**AFC WEST**

| | W | L | T | Pct | Pts | OP |
|---|---|---|---|---|---|---|
| San Diego | 14 | 2 | 0 | .875 | 492 | 303 |
| Kansas City | 9 | 7 | 0 | .562 | 331 | 315 |
| Denver | 9 | 7 | 0 | .562 | 319 | 305 |
| Oakland | 2 | 14 | 0 | .125 | 168 | 332 |

**NFC EAST**

| | W | L | T | Pct | Pts | OP |
|---|---|---|---|---|---|---|
| Philadelphia | 10 | 6 | 0 | .625 | 398 | 328 |
| Dallas | 9 | 7 | 0 | .562 | 425 | 350 |
| NY Giants | 8 | 8 | 0 | .500 | 355 | 362 |
| Washington | 5 | 11 | 0 | .312 | 307 | 376 |

**NFC NORTH**

| | W | L | T | Pct | Pts | OP |
|---|---|---|---|---|---|---|
| Chicago | 13 | 3 | 0 | .812 | 427 | 255 |
| Green Bay | 8 | 8 | 0 | .500 | 301 | 366 |
| Minnesota | 6 | 10 | 0 | .375 | 282 | 327 |
| Detroit | 3 | 13 | 0 | .188 | 305 | 398 |

**NFC SOUTH**

| | W | L | T | Pct | Pts | OP |
|---|---|---|---|---|---|---|
| New Orleans | 10 | 6 | 0 | .625 | 413 | 322 |
| Carolina | 8 | 8 | 0 | .500 | 270 | 305 |
| Atlanta | 7 | 9 | 0 | .438 | 292 | 328 |
| Tampa Bay | 4 | 12 | 0 | .250 | 211 | 353 |

**NFC WEST**

| | W | L | T | Pct | Pts | OP |
|---|---|---|---|---|---|---|
| Seattle | 9 | 7 | 0 | .562 | 335 | 341 |
| St. Louis | 8 | 8 | 0 | .500 | 367 | 381 |
| San Francisco | 7 | 9 | 0 | .438 | 298 | 412 |
| Arizona | 5 | 11 | 0 | .312 | 314 | 389 |

### 2007

**AFC EAST**

| | W | L | T | Pct | Pts | OP |
|---|---|---|---|---|---|---|
| New England | 16 | 0 | 0 | 1.000 | 589 | 274 |
| Buffalo | 7 | 9 | 0 | .438 | 252 | 354 |
| NY Jets | 4 | 12 | 0 | .250 | 268 | 355 |
| Miami | 1 | 15 | 0 | .063 | 267 | 437 |

**AFC NORTH**

| | W | L | T | Pct | Pts | OP |
|---|---|---|---|---|---|---|
| Pittsburgh | 10 | 6 | 0 | .625 | 393 | 269 |
| Cleveland | 10 | 6 | 0 | .625 | 402 | 382 |
| Cincinnati | 7 | 9 | 0 | .438 | 380 | 385 |
| Baltimore | 5 | 11 | 0 | .313 | 275 | 384 |

**AFC SOUTH**

| | W | L | T | Pct | Pts | OP |
|---|---|---|---|---|---|---|
| Indianapolis | 13 | 3 | 0 | .813 | 450 | 262 |
| Jacksonville | 11 | 5 | 0 | .688 | 411 | 304 |
| Tennessee | 10 | 6 | 0 | .625 | 301 | 297 |
| Houston | 8 | 8 | 0 | .500 | 379 | 384 |

**AFC WEST**

| | W | L | T | Pct | Pts | OP |
|---|---|---|---|---|---|---|
| San Diego | 11 | 5 | 0 | .688 | 412 | 284 |
| Denver | 7 | 9 | 0 | .438 | 320 | 409 |
| Kansas City | 4 | 12 | 0 | .250 | 226 | 335 |
| Oakland | 4 | 12 | 0 | .250 | 286 | 398 |

**NFC EAST**

| | W | L | T | Pct | Pts | OP |
|---|---|---|---|---|---|---|
| Dallas | 13 | 3 | 0 | .813 | 455 | 325 |
| NY Giants | 10 | 6 | 0 | .625 | 373 | 351 |
| Washington | 9 | 7 | 0 | .563 | 334 | 310 |
| Philadelphia | 8 | 8 | 0 | .500 | 336 | 300 |

**NFC NORTH**

| | W | L | T | Pct | Pts | OP |
|---|---|---|---|---|---|---|
| Green Bay | 13 | 3 | 0 | .813 | 435 | 291 |
| Minnesota | 8 | 8 | 0 | .500 | 365 | 311 |
| Detroit | 7 | 9 | 0 | .438 | 346 | 444 |
| Chicago | 7 | 9 | 0 | .438 | 334 | 348 |

**NFC SOUTH**

| | W | L | T | Pct | Pts | OP |
|---|---|---|---|---|---|---|
| Tampa Bay | 9 | 7 | 0 | .563 | 334 | 270 |
| Carolina | 7 | 9 | 0 | .438 | 267 | 347 |
| New Orleans | 7 | 9 | 0 | .438 | 379 | 388 |
| Atlanta | 4 | 12 | 0 | .250 | 259 | 414 |

**NFC WEST**

| | W | L | T | Pct | Pts | OP |
|---|---|---|---|---|---|---|
| Seattle | 10 | 6 | 0 | .625 | 393 | 291 |
| Arizona | 8 | 8 | 0 | .500 | 404 | 399 |
| San Francisco | 5 | 11 | 0 | .313 | 219 | 364 |
| St. Louis | 3 | 13 | 0 | .188 | 263 | 438 |

### 2008

**AFC EAST**

| | W | L | T | Pct | Pts | OP |
|---|---|---|---|---|---|---|
| Miami | 11 | 5 | 0 | .688 | 345 | 317 |
| New England | 11 | 5 | 0 | .688 | 410 | 309 |
| NY Jets | 9 | 7 | 0 | .563 | 405 | 356 |
| Buffalo | 7 | 9 | 0 | .438 | 336 | 342 |

**AFC NORTH**

| | W | L | T | Pct | Pts | OP |
|---|---|---|---|---|---|---|
| Pittsburgh | 12 | 4 | 0 | .750 | 347 | 223 |
| *Baltimore | 11 | 5 | 0 | .688 | 385 | 244 |
| Cincinnati | 4 | 11 | 1 | .281 | 204 | 364 |
| Cleveland | 4 | 12 | 0 | .250 | 232 | 350 |

## 2008 *(Cont.)*

### AFC SOUTH
| | W | L | T | Pct | Pts | OP |
|---|---|---|---|---|---|---|
| Tennessee | 13 | 3 | 0 | .813 | 375 | 234 |
| Indianapolis | 12 | 4 | 0 | .750 | 377 | 298 |
| Houston | 8 | 8 | 0 | .500 | 366 | 394 |
| Jacksonville | 5 | 11 | 0 | .313 | 302 | 367 |

### AFC WEST
| | W | L | T | Pct | Pts | OP |
|---|---|---|---|---|---|---|
| San Diego | 8 | 8 | 0 | .500 | 439 | 347 |
| Denver | 8 | 8 | 0 | .500 | 370 | 448 |
| Oakland | 5 | 11 | 0 | .313 | 263 | 388 |
| Kansas City | 2 | 14 | 0 | .125 | 291 | 440 |

### NFC EAST
| | W | L | T | Pct | Pts | OP |
|---|---|---|---|---|---|---|
| NY Giants | 12 | 4 | 0 | .750 | 427 | 294 |
| Philadelphia | 9 | 6 | 1 | .594 | 416 | 289 |
| Dallas | 9 | 7 | 0 | .563 | 362 | 365 |
| Washington | 8 | 8 | 0 | .500 | 265 | 296 |

### NFC NORTH
| | W | L | T | Pct | Pts | OP |
|---|---|---|---|---|---|---|
| Minnesota | 10 | 6 | 0 | .625 | 379 | 333 |
| Chicago | 9 | 7 | 0 | .563 | 375 | 350 |
| Green Bay | 6 | 10 | 0 | .375 | 419 | 380 |
| Detroit | 0 | 16 | 0 | .000 | 268 | 517 |

### NFC SOUTH
| | W | L | T | Pct | Pts | OP |
|---|---|---|---|---|---|---|
| Carolina | 12 | 4 | 0 | .750 | 414 | 329 |
| Atlanta | 11 | 5 | 0 | .688 | 391 | 325 |
| Tampa Bay | 9 | 7 | 0 | .563 | 361 | 323 |
| New Orleans | 8 | 8 | 0 | .500 | 463 | 393 |

### NFC WEST
| | W | L | T | Pct | Pts | OP |
|---|---|---|---|---|---|---|
| Arizona | 9 | 7 | 0 | .563 | 427 | 426 |
| San Francisco | 7 | 9 | 0 | .438 | 339 | 381 |
| Seattle | 4 | 12 | 0 | .250 | 294 | 392 |
| St. Louis | 2 | 14 | 0 | .125 | 232 | 465 |

## 2009

### AFC EAST
| | W | L | T | Pct | Pts | OP |
|---|---|---|---|---|---|---|
| New England | 10 | 6 | 0 | .625 | 427 | 285 |
| NY Jets | 9 | 7 | 0 | .563 | 348 | 236 |
| Miami | 7 | 9 | 0 | .438 | 360 | 390 |
| Buffalo | 6 | 10 | 0 | .375 | 258 | 326 |

### AFC NORTH
| | W | L | T | Pct | Pts | OP |
|---|---|---|---|---|---|---|
| Cincinnati | 10 | 6 | 0 | .625 | 305 | 291 |
| Baltimore | 9 | 7 | 0 | .563 | 391 | 261 |
| Pittsburgh | 9 | 7 | 0 | .563 | 368 | 324 |
| Cleveland | 5 | 11 | 0 | .313 | 245 | 375 |

### AFC SOUTH
| | W | L | T | Pct | Pts | OP |
|---|---|---|---|---|---|---|
| Indianapolis | 14 | 2 | 0 | .875 | 416 | 307 |
| Houston | 9 | 7 | 0 | .563 | 388 | 333 |
| Tennessee | 8 | 8 | 0 | .500 | 354 | 402 |
| Jacksonville | 7 | 9 | 0 | .438 | 290 | 380 |

### AFC WEST
| | W | L | T | Pct | Pts | OP |
|---|---|---|---|---|---|---|
| San Diego | 13 | 3 | 0 | .813 | 454 | 320 |
| Denver | 8 | 8 | 0 | .500 | 326 | 324 |
| Oakland | 5 | 11 | 0 | .313 | 379 | 379 |
| Kansas City | 4 | 12 | 0 | .250 | 424 | 424 |

### NFC EAST
| | W | L | T | Pct | Pts | OP |
|---|---|---|---|---|---|---|
| Dallas | 11 | 5 | 0 | .688 | 361 | 250 |
| Philadelphia | 11 | 5 | 0 | .688 | 429 | 337 |
| NY Giants | 8 | 8 | 0 | .500 | 402 | 427 |
| Washington | 4 | 12 | 0 | .250 | 266 | 336 |

## 2009 *(Cont.)*

### NFC NORTH
| | W | L | T | Pct | Pts | OP |
|---|---|---|---|---|---|---|
| Minnesota | 12 | 4 | 0 | .750 | 470 | 312 |
| Green Bay | 11 | 5 | 0 | .688 | 461 | 297 |
| Chicago | 7 | 9 | 0 | .438 | 327 | 375 |
| Detroit | 2 | 14 | 0 | .125 | 262 | 494 |

### NFC SOUTH
| | W | L | T | Pct | Pts | OP |
|---|---|---|---|---|---|---|
| New Orleans | 13 | 3 | 0 | .813 | 510 | 341 |
| Atlanta | 9 | 7 | 0 | .563 | 363 | 325 |
| Carolina | 8 | 8 | 0 | .500 | 315 | 308 |
| Tampa Bay | 3 | 13 | 0 | .188 | 244 | 400 |

### NFC WEST
| | W | L | T | Pct | Pts | OP |
|---|---|---|---|---|---|---|
| Arizona | 10 | 6 | 0 | .625 | 375 | 325 |
| San Francisco | 8 | 8 | 0 | .500 | 330 | 281 |
| Seattle | 5 | 11 | 0 | .313 | 280 | 390 |
| St. Louis | 1 | 15 | 0 | .063 | 175 | 436 |

## 2010

### AFC EAST
| | W | L | T | Pct | Pts | OP |
|---|---|---|---|---|---|---|
| New England | 14 | 2 | 0 | .875 | 518 | 313 |
| NY Jets | 11 | 5 | 0 | .688 | 367 | 304 |
| Miami | 7 | 9 | 0 | .438 | 273 | 333 |
| Buffalo | 4 | 12 | 0 | .250 | 283 | 425 |

### AFC NORTH
| | W | L | T | Pct | Pts | OP |
|---|---|---|---|---|---|---|
| Pittsburgh | 12 | 4 | 0 | .750 | 375 | 232 |
| Baltimore | 12 | 4 | 0 | .750 | 357 | 270 |
| Cincinnati | 5 | 11 | 0 | .313 | 271 | 332 |
| Cleveland | 4 | 12 | 0 | .250 | 322 | 395 |

### AFC SOUTH
| | W | L | T | Pct | Pts | OP |
|---|---|---|---|---|---|---|
| Indianapolis | 10 | 6 | 0 | .625 | 435 | 388 |
| Jacksonville | 8 | 8 | 0 | .500 | 353 | 419 |
| Houston | 6 | 10 | 0 | .375 | 390 | 427 |
| Tennessee | 6 | 10 | 0 | .375 | 356 | 336 |

### AFC WEST
| | W | L | T | Pct | Pts | OP |
|---|---|---|---|---|---|---|
| Kansas City | 10 | 6 | 0 | .625 | 366 | 326 |
| San Diego | 9 | 7 | 0 | .563 | 441 | 322 |
| Oakland | 8 | 8 | 0 | .500 | 410 | 371 |
| Denver | 4 | 12 | 0 | .250 | 344 | 471 |

### NFC EAST
| | W | L | T | Pct | Pts | OP |
|---|---|---|---|---|---|---|
| Philadelphia | 10 | 6 | 0 | .625 | 439 | 377 |
| NY Giants | 10 | 6 | 0 | .625 | 394 | 347 |
| Dallas | 6 | 10 | 0 | .375 | 394 | 436 |
| Washington | 6 | 10 | 0 | .375 | 302 | 377 |

### NFC NORTH
| | W | L | T | Pct | Pts | OP |
|---|---|---|---|---|---|---|
| Chicago | 11 | 5 | 0 | .688 | 334 | 286 |
| Green Bay | 10 | 6 | 0 | .625 | 388 | 240 |
| Detroit | 6 | 10 | 0 | .375 | 362 | 369 |
| Minnesota | 6 | 10 | 0 | .375 | 281 | 348 |

### NFC SOUTH
| | W | L | T | Pct | Pts | OP |
|---|---|---|---|---|---|---|
| Atlanta | 13 | 3 | 0 | .813 | 414 | 288 |
| *New Orleans | 11 | 5 | 0 | .688 | 384 | 307 |
| Tampa Bay | 10 | 6 | 0 | .625 | 341 | 318 |
| Carolina | 2 | 14 | 0 | .125 | 196 | 408 |

### NFC WEST
| | W | L | T | Pct | Pts | OP |
|---|---|---|---|---|---|---|
| Seattle | 7 | 9 | 0 | .438 | 310 | 407 |
| St. Louis | 7 | 9 | 0 | .438 | 289 | 328 |
| San Francisco | 6 | 10 | 0 | .375 | 305 | 346 |
| Arizona | 5 | 11 | 0 | .313 | 289 | 434 |

### Results

| | Date | Winner (Share) | Loser (Share) | Score | Site (Attendance) |
|---|---|---|---|---|---|
| I | 1-15-67 | Green Bay ($15,000) | Kansas City ($7,500) | 35–10 | Los Angeles (61,946) |
| II | 1-14-68 | Green Bay ($15,000) | Oakland ($7,500) | 33–14 | Miami (75,546) |
| III | 1-12-69 | NY Jets ($15,000) | Baltimore ($7,500) | 16–7 | Miami (75,389) |
| IV | 1-11-70 | Kansas City ($15,000) | Minnesota ($7,500) | 23–7 | New Orleans (80,562) |
| V | 1-17-71 | Baltimore ($15,000) | Dallas ($7,500) | 16–13 | Miami (79,204) |
| VI | 1-16-72 | Dallas ($15,000) | Miami ($7,500) | 24–3 | New Orleans (81,023) |
| VII | 1-14-73 | Miami ($15,000) | Washington ($7,500) | 14–7 | Los Angeles (90,182) |
| VIII | 1-13-74 | Miami ($15,000) | Minnesota ($7,500) | 24–7 | Houston (71,882) |
| IX | 1-12-75 | Pittsburgh ($15,000) | Minnesota ($7,500) | 16–6 | New Orleans (80,997) |
| X | 1-18-76 | Pittsburgh ($15,000) | Dallas ($7,500) | 21–17 | Miami (80,187) |
| XI | 1-9-77 | Oakland ($15,000) | Minnesota ($7,500) | 32–14 | Pasadena (103,438) |
| XII | 1-15-78 | Dallas ($18,000) | Denver ($9,000) | 27–10 | New Orleans (76,400) |
| XIII | 1-21-79 | Pittsburgh ($18,000) | Dallas ($9,000) | 35–31 | Miami (79,484) |
| XIV | 1-20-80 | Pittsburgh ($18,000) | Los Angeles ($9,000) | 31–19 | Pasadena (103,985) |
| XV | 1-25-81 | Oakland ($18,000) | Philadelphia ($9,000) | 27–10 | New Orleans (76,135) |
| XVI | 1-24-82 | San Francisco ($18,000) | Cincinnati ($9,000) | 26–21 | Pontiac, Mich. (81,270) |
| XVII | 1-30-83 | Washington ($36,000) | Miami ($18,000) | 27–17 | Pasadena (103,667) |
| XVIII | 1-22-84 | LA Raiders ($36,000) | Washington ($18,000) | 38–9 | Tampa (72,920) |
| XIX | 1-20-85 | San Francisco ($36,000) | Miami ($18,000) | 38–16 | Stanford, Calif. (84,059) |
| XX | 1-26-86 | Chicago ($36,000) | New England ($18,000) | 46–10 | New Orleans (73,818) |
| XXI | 1-25-87 | NY Giants ($36,000) | Denver ($18,000) | 39–20 | Pasadena (101,063) |
| XXII | 1-31-88 | Washington ($36,000) | Denver ($18,000) | 42–10 | San Diego (73,302) |
| XXIII | 1-22-89 | San Francisco ($36,000) | Cincinnati ($18,000) | 20–16 | Miami (75,129) |
| XXIV | 1-28-90 | San Francisco ($36,000) | Denver ($18,000) | 55–10 | New Orleans (72,919) |
| XXV | 1-27-91 | NY Giants ($36,000) | Buffalo ($18,000) | 20–19 | Tampa (73,813) |
| XXVI | 1-26-92 | Washington ($36,000) | Buffalo ($18,000) | 37–24 | Minneapolis (63,130) |
| XXVII | 1-31-93 | Dallas ($36,000) | Buffalo ($18,000) | 52–17 | Pasadena (98,374) |
| XXVIII | 1-30-94 | Dallas ($38,000) | Buffalo ($23,500) | 30–13 | Atlanta (72,817) |
| XXIX | 1-29-95 | San Francisco ($42,000) | San Diego ($26,000) | 49–26 | Miami (74,107) |
| XXX | 1-28-96 | Dallas ($42,000) | Pittsburgh ($27,000) | 27–17 | Tempe, Ariz. (76,347) |
| XXXI | 1-26-97 | Green Bay ($48,000) | New England ($29,000) | 35–21 | New Orleans (72,301) |
| XXXII | 1-25-98 | Denver ($48,000) | Green Bay ($27,500) | 31–24 | San Diego (68,912) |
| XXXIII | 1-31-99 | Denver ($53,000) | Atlanta ($32,500) | 34–19 | Miami (74,803) |
| XXXIV | 1-30-00 | St. Louis ($58,000) | Tennessee ($33,000) | 23–16 | Atlanta (72,625) |
| XXXV | 1-28-01 | Baltimore ($58,000) | NY Giants ($34,500) | 34–7 | Tampa (71,921) |
| XXXVI | 2-3-02 | New England ($63,000) | St. Louis ($34,500) | 20–17 | New Orleans (72,922) |
| XXXVII | 1-26-03 | Tampa Bay ($64,000) | Oakland ($35,000) | 48–21 | San Diego (67,603) |
| XXXVIII | 2-1-04 | New England ($64,000) | Carolina ($35,000) | 32–29 | Houston (71,525) |
| XXXIX | 2-6-05 | New England ($68,000) | Philadelphia ($36,500) | 24–21 | Jacksonville (78,125) |
| XL | 2-5-06 | Pittsburgh ($73,000) | Seattle ($38,000) | 21–10 | Detroit (68,206) |
| XLI | 2-4-07 | Indianapolis ($78,000) | Chicago ($40,000) | 29–17 | Miami (74,512) |
| XLII | 2-3-08 | NY Giants ($78,000) | New England ($40,000) | 17–14 | Glendale, Ariz. (71,101) |
| XLIII | 2-1-09 | Pittsburgh ($78,000) | Arizona ($40,000) | 27–23 | Tampa (70,774) |
| XLIV | 2-7-10 | New Orleans ($83,000) | Indianapolis ($42,000) | 31–17 | Miami (74,059) |
| XLV | 2-6-11 | Green Bay ($83,000) | Pittsburgh ($42,000) | 31–25 | Arlington, Tex. (103,219) |

### Most Valuable Players

| Super Bowl | Player/ Team | Position | Super Bowl | Player/ Team | Position |
|---|---|---|---|---|---|
| I | Bart Starr, GB | QB | XXIV | Joe Montana, SF | QB |
| II | Bart Starr, GB | QB | XXV | Ottis Anderson, NYG | RB |
| III | Joe Namath, NYJ | QB | XXVI | Mark Rypien, Wash | QB |
| IV | Len Dawson, KC | QB | XXVII | Troy Aikman, Dal | QB |
| V | Chuck Howley, Dal | LB | XXVIII | Emmitt Smith, Dal | RB |
| VI | Roger Staubach, Dal | QB | XXIX | Steve Young, SF | QB |
| VII | Jake Scott, Mia | S | XXX | Larry Brown, Dal | CB |
| VIII | Larry Csonka, Mia | RB | XXXI | Desmond Howard, GB | KR |
| IX | Franco Harris, Pit | RB | XXXII | Terrell Davis, Den | RB |
| X | Lynn Swann, Pit | WR | XXXIII | John Elway, Den | QB |
| XI | Fred Biletnikoff, Oak | WR | XXXIV | Kurt Warner, StL | QB |
| XII | Randy White/Harvey Martin, Dal | DT/DE | XXXV | Ray Lewis, Balt | LB |
| XIII, XIV | Terry Bradshaw, Pit | QB | XXXVI | Tom Brady, NE | QB |
| XV | Jim Plunkett, Oak | QB | XXXVII | Dexter Jackson, TB | S |
| XVI | Joe Montana, SF | QB | XXXVIII | Tom Brady, NE | QB |
| XVII | John Riggins, Wash | RB | XXXIX | Deion Branch, NE | WR |
| XVIII | Marcus Allen, LA Rai | RB | XL | Hines Ward, Pit | WR |
| XIX | Joe Montana, SF | QB | XLI | Peyton Manning, Ind | QB |
| XX | Richard Dent, Chi | DE | XLII | Eli Manning, NYG | QB |
| XXI | Phil Simms, NYG | QB | XLIII | Santonio Holmes, Pit | WR |
| XXII | Doug Williams, Wash | QB | XLIV | Drew Brees, NO | QB |
| XXIII | Jerry Rice, SF | WR | XLV | Aaron Rodgers, GB | QB |

### Composite Standings, by Win Percentage

| | W | L | Pct | Pts | Opp Pts |
|---|---|---|---|---|---|
| San Francisco 49ers | 5 | 0 | 1.000 | 188 | 89 |
| Tampa Bay Buccaneers | 1 | 0 | 1.000 | 48 | 21 |
| Baltimore Ravens | 1 | 0 | 1.000 | 34 | 7 |
| New Orleans Saints | 1 | 0 | 1.000 | 34 | 17 |
| New York Jets | 1 | 0 | 1.000 | 16 | 7 |
| Green Bay Packers | 4 | 1 | .800 | 158 | 101 |
| Pittsburgh Steelers | 6 | 2 | .750 | 193 | 164 |
| New York Giants | 3 | 1 | .750 | 83 | 87 |
| Dallas Cowboys | 5 | 3 | .625 | 221 | 132 |
| Oakland/LA Raiders | 3 | 2 | .600 | 132 | 114 |
| Washington Redskins | 3 | 2 | .600 | 122 | 103 |
| New England Patriots | 3 | 3 | .500 | 121 | 165 |
| Baltimore/Indianapolis Colts | 2 | 2 | .500 | 69 | 77 |
| Chicago Bears | 1 | 1 | .500 | 63 | 39 |
| Kansas City Chiefs | 1 | 1 | .500 | 33 | 42 |
| Miami Dolphins | 2 | 3 | .400 | 74 | 103 |
| Denver Broncos | 2 | 4 | .333 | 115 | 206 |
| Los Angeles/St. Louis Rams | 1 | 2 | .333 | 59 | 67 |
| Carolina Panthers | 0 | 1 | .000 | 29 | 32 |
| San Diego Chargers | 0 | 1 | .000 | 26 | 49 |
| Arizona Cardinals | 0 | 1 | .000 | 23 | 27 |
| Atlanta Falcons | 0 | 1 | .000 | 19 | 34 |
| Tennessee Titans | 0 | 1 | .000 | 16 | 23 |
| Seattle Seahawks | 0 | 1 | .000 | 10 | 21 |
| Cincinnati Bengals | 0 | 2 | .000 | 37 | 46 |
| Philadelphia Eagles | 0 | 2 | .000 | 31 | 51 |
| Buffalo Bills | 0 | 4 | .000 | 73 | 139 |
| Minnesota Vikings | 0 | 4 | .000 | 34 | 95 |

### Career Leaders

#### Passing

| | GP | Att | Comp | Pct Comp | Yds | Avg Gain/ Att | TD | Pct TD | Int | Pct Int | Lg | Rating Pts |
|---|---|---|---|---|---|---|---|---|---|---|---|---|
| Joe Montana, SF | 4 | 122 | 83 | 68.0 | 1142 | 9.36 | 11 | 9.0 | 0 | 0.0 | 44 | 127.8 |
| Jim Plunkett, Oak/LA Rai | 2 | 46 | 29 | 63.0 | 433 | 9.41 | 4 | 8.7 | 0 | 0.0 | t80 | 122.8 |
| Terry Bradshaw, Pit | 4 | 84 | 49 | 58.3 | 932 | 11.10 | 9 | 10.7 | 4 | 4.8 | t75 | 112.8 |
| Troy Aikman, Dal | 3 | 80 | 56 | 70.0 | 689 | 8.61 | 5 | 6.3 | 1 | 1.3 | t56 | 111.9 |
| Bart Starr, GB | 2 | 47 | 29 | 61.7 | 452 | 9.62 | 3 | 6.4 | 1 | 2.1 | t62 | 106.0 |
| Brett Favre, GB | 2 | 69 | 39 | 56.5 | 502 | 7.28 | 5 | 7.2 | 1 | 1.4 | t81 | 97.7 |
| Kurt Warner, StL, Ari | 3 | 132 | 83 | 62.9 | 1156 | 8.76 | 6 | 4.5 | 3 | 2.3 | t73 | 96.7 |
| Roger Staubach, Dal | 4 | 98 | 61 | 62.2 | 734 | 7.49 | 8 | 8.2 | 4 | 4.1 | t45 | 95.4 |
| Tom Brady, NE | 4 | 156 | 100 | 64.1 | 1001 | 6.42 | 7 | 4.5 | 1 | 0.1 | 52 | 94.5 |
| Peyton Manning, Ind | 2 | 83 | 58 | 67.5 | 580 | 6.99 | 2 | 2.4 | 2 | 2.4 | t53 | 85.4 |
| Len Dawson, KC | 2 | 44 | 28 | 63.6 | 353 | 8.02 | 2 | 4.5 | 2 | 4.5 | t46 | 84.8 |

Note: Minimum 40 attempts.

#### Rushing Yards

| | GP | Yds | Att | Avg | Lg | TD |
|---|---|---|---|---|---|---|
| Franco Harris, Pit | 4 | 354 | 101 | 3.5 | 25 | 4 |
| Larry Csonka, Mia | 3 | 297 | 57 | 5.2 | 49 | 2 |
| Emmitt Smith, Dal | 3 | 289 | 70 | 4.1 | 38 | 5 |
| Terrell Davis, Den | 2 | 259 | 55 | 4.7 | 27 | 3 |
| John Riggins, Was | 2 | 230 | 64 | 3.6 | 43 | 2 |
| Timmy Smith, Was | 1 | 204 | 22 | 9.3 | 58 | 2 |
| Thurman Thomas, Buf | 4 | 204 | 52 | 3.9 | 31 | 4 |
| Roger Craig, SF | 3 | 217 | 44 | 4.9 | 20 | 3 |
| Marcus Allen, LA Rai | 1 | 191 | 20 | 9.6 | t74 | 2 |
| Antowain Smith, NE | 2 | 175 | 44 | 4.0 | 17 | 1 |

t-scored touchdown

#### Receptions

| | GP | No. | Yds | Avg | Lg | TD |
|---|---|---|---|---|---|---|
| Jerry Rice, SF | 4 | 33 | 589 | 17.9 | t48 | 8 |
| Andre Reed, Buf | 4 | 27 | 323 | 12.0 | 40 | 0 |
| Roger Craig, SF | 3 | 20 | 212 | 10.6 | 40 | 2 |
| Deion Branch, NE | 2 | 21 | 276 | 13.1 | 52 | 1 |
| Thurman Thomas, Buf | 4 | 20 | 144 | 7.2 | 24 | 0 |
| Jay Novacek, Dal | 3 | 17 | 148 | 8.7 | 23 | 2 |
| Joseph Addai, Ind | 2 | 17 | 124 | 7.3 | 17 | 0 |
| Lynn Swann, Pit | 4 | 16 | 364 | 22.8 | t74 | 3 |
| Michael Irvin, Dal | 3 | 16 | 256 | 16.0 | 25 | 2 |
| Troy Brown, NE | 3 | 16 | 182 | 11.4 | 23 | 0 |

## Single-Game Leaders

### Scoring

Pts

Roger Craig: XIX, San Francisco vs Miami
(1 rush, 2 rec) ............................................................18
Jerry Rice: XXIV, San Francisco vs Denver
(3 rec); XXIX, SF vs San Diego (3 rec) ....................18
Ricky Watters: XXIX, San Francisco vs San Diego
(1 rush, 2 rec) ............................................................18
Terrell Davis: XXXII, Denver vs Green Bay (3 rec)...18

### Rushing Yards

Yds

Timmy Smith: XXII, Washington vs Denver...........204
Marcus Allen: XVIII, LA Raiders vs Washington ....191
John Riggins: XVII, Washington vs Miami ..............166
Franco Harris: IX, Pittsburgh vs Minnesota .,........158
Terrell Davis: XXXII, Denver vs Green Bay ...........157
Larry Csonka: VIII, Miami vs Minnesota ................145
Clarence Davis: XI, Oakland vs Minnesota ...........137
Thurman Thomas: XXV, Buffalo vs NY Giants........135
Emmitt Smith: XXVIII, Dallas vs Buffalo.................132
Michael Pittman: XXXVII, Tampa Bay vs Oakland.....124

### Receptions

No.

Wes Welker: XLII, New England vs NY Giants ........11
Deion Branch: XXXIX, New England vs Phila...........11
Jerry Rice: XXIII, San Francisco vs Cincinnati .......11
Dan Ross: XVI, Cincinnati vs San Francisco ...........11
Joseph Addai: XLI, Indianapolis vs Chicago...........10
Deion Branch: XXXVIII, New England vs Carolina ...10
Andre Hastings: XXX, Pittsburgh vs Dallas .............10
Jerry Rice: XXIX, San Francisco vs San Diego ........10
Tony Nathan: XIX, Miami vs San Francisco .............10
Jordy Nelson: XLV, Green Bay vs Pittsburgh............9
Mike Wallace: XLV, Pittsburgh vs Green Bay............9
Santonio Holmes: XLIII, Pittsburgh vs Arizona .........9
Terrell Owens: XXXIX, Philadelphia vs New England ...9
Antonio Freeman: XXXII, Green Bay vs Denver ........9
Ricky Sanders: XXII, Washington vs Denver .............9

### Touchdown Passes

No.

Steve Young: XXIX, San Francisco vs San Diego......6
Joe Montana: XXIV, San Francisco vs Denver..........5
Troy Aikman: XXVII, Dallas vs Buffalo.......................4
Doug Williams: XXII, Washington vs Denver .............4
Terry Bradshaw: XIII, Pittsburgh vs Dallas................4
Nine tied with three.

### Passing Yards

Yds

Kurt Warner: XXXIV, St. Louis vs Tennessee.........414
Kurt Warner: XLIII, Arizona vs Pittsburgh ..............377
Kurt Warner: XXXVI, St. Louis vs New England.....365
Joe Montana: XXIII, San Francisco vs Cincinnati ..357
Donovan McNabb, XXXIX, Phila. vs New England..357
Tom Brady: XXXVIII, New England vs Carolina .....354
Doug Williams: XXII, Washington vs Denver ..........340
John Elway: XXXIII, Denver vs Atlanta....................336
Peyton Manning: XLIV, Indianapolis vs New Orl'ns..333
Joe Montana: XIX, San Francisco vs Miami ...........331
Steve Young: XXIX, San Francisco vs San Diego..325
Jake Delhomme: XXXVIII Carolina vs New England..323
Terry Bradshaw: XIII, Pittsburgh vs Dallas.............318
Dan Marino: XIX, Miami vs San Francisco.............318

### Receiving Yards

Yds

Jerry Rice: XXIII, San Francisco vs Cincinnati ......215
Ricky Sanders: XXII, Washington vs Denver .........193
Isaac Bruce: XXXIV, St. Louis vs Tennessee .........162
Lynn Swann: X, Pittsburgh vs Dallas ....................:161
Andre Reed: XXVII, Buffalo vs Dallas ....................152
Rod Smith: XXXIII, Denver vs Atlanta.....................152
Jerry Rice: XXIX, San Francisco vs San Diego .....149
Jerry Rice: XXIV, San Francisco vs Denver ...........148
Deion Branch: XXXVIII, New England vs Carolina ..143

## Super Bowl History Recaps*

### I - 1967

| Green Bay | 7 | 7 | 14 | 7—35 |
|-----------|---|---|----|----|
| Kansas City | 0 | 10 | 0 | 0—10 |

**FIRST QUARTER:** GB: McGee 37 pass from Starr (Chandler kick), 8:56. **Green Bay 7-0.**

**SECOND QUARTER:** KC: McClinton 7 pass from Dawson (Mercer kick), 4:20. **7-7.**
GB: Taylor 14 run (Chandler kick), 10:23. **Green Bay 14-7.**
KC: FG Mercer 31, 14:06. **Green Bay 14-10.**

**THIRD QUARTER:** GB: Pitts 5 run (Chandler kick), 2:27. **Green Bay 21-10.**
GB: McGee 13 pass from Starr (Chandler kick), 14:09. **Green Bay 28-10.**

**FOURTH QUARTER:** GB: Pitts 1 run (Chandler kick), 8:25. **Green Bay 35-10.**

A: 61,946.

### II - 1968

| Green Bay | 3 | 13 | 10 | 7—33 |
|-----------|---|----|----|----|
| Oakland | 0 | 7 | 0 | 7—14 |

**FIRST QUARTER:** GB: FG Chandler 39 5:07. **Green Bay 3-0.**

**SECOND QUARTER:** GB: FG Chandler, 20, 3:08. **Green Bay 6-0.**
GB: Dowler 62 pass from Starr (Chandler kick), 4:10. **Green Bay 13-0.**

**SECOND QUARTER (*CONT.*):** Oak: Miller 23 pass from Lamonica (Blanda kick), 8:45. **Green Bay 13-7.**
GB: FG Chandler 43, 14:59. **Green Bay 16-7.**

**THIRD QUARTER:** GB: Anderson 2 run (Chandler kick), 9:06. **Green Bay 23-7.**
GB: FG Chandler 31, 14:58. **Green Bay 26-7.**

**FOURTH QUARTER:**
GB: Adderley 60 int return (Chandler kick), 3:57. **Green Bay 33-7.**
Oak: Miller 23 pass from Lamonica (Blanda kick), 5:47. **Green Bay 33-14.**

A: 75,546.

*From 1967 to 1999, Super Bowl scoring times indicate the time elapsed in each quarter. Starting in 2000, times listed give the time remaining in each quarter.

### III - 1969

| | | | | |
|---|---|---|---|---|
| NY Jets | 0 | 7 | 6 | 3—16 |
| Baltimore | 0 | 0 | 0 | 7—7 |

**SECOND QUARTER:** Jets: Snell 4 run (Turner kick), 5:57. **Jets: 7-0.**

**THIRD QUARTER:** Jets: FG Turner 32, 4:52. **Jets: 10-0.** Jets: FG Turner 30, 11:02. **Jets: 13-0.**

**FOURTH QUARTER:** Jets: FG Turner 9, 1:34. **Jets: 16-0.** Balt: Hill 1 run (Michaels kick), 11:41. **Jets: 16-7.** A: 75,389.

### IV - 1970

| | | | | |
|---|---|---|---|---|
| Kansas City | 3 | 13 | 7 | 0—23 |
| Minnesota | 0 | 0 | 7 | 0—7 |

**FIRST QUARTER:** KC: FG Stenerud 48, 8:08. **Kansas City 3-0.**

**SECOND QUARTER:** KC: FG Stenerud 32, 1:40. **Kansas City 6-0.** KC: FG Stenerud 25, 7:08. **Kansas City 9-0.** KC: Garrett 5 run (Stenerud kick), 9:26. **Kansas City 16-0.**

**THIRD QUARTER:** Minn: Osborn 4 run (Cox kick), 10:28. **Kansas City 16-7.** KC: Taylor 46 pass from Dawson (Stenerud kick), 13:38. **Kansas City 23-7.** A: 80,562.

### V - 1971

| | | | | |
|---|---|---|---|---|
| Baltimore | 0 | 6 | 0 | 10—16 |
| Dallas | 3 | 10 | 0 | 0—13 |

**FIRST QUARTER:** Dal (9:28): FG Clark 14, 9:28. **Dallas 3-0.**

**SECOND QUARTER:** Dal: FG Clark 30, 0:08. **Dallas 6-0.** Balt: Mackey 75 pass from Unitas (kick blocked). 0:50. **6-6.** Dal: Thomas 7 pass from Morton (Clark kick), 7:07. **Dallas 13-6.**

**FOURTH QUARTER:** Balt: Nowatzke 2 run (O'Brien kick), 7:25. **13-13.** Balt: FG O'Brien 32, 14:55. **Baltimore 16-13.** A: 79,204.

### VI - 1972

| | | | | |
|---|---|---|---|---|
| Dallas | 3 | 7 | 7 | 7—24 |
| Miami | 0 | 3 | 0 | 0—3 |

**FIRST QUARTER:** Dal: FG Clark 9, 13:37. **Dallas 3-0.**

**SECOND QUARTER:** Dal: Alworth 7 pass from Staubach (Clark kick), 13:45. **Dallas 10-0.** Mia: FG Yepremian, 31, 14:56. **Dallas 10-3.**

**THIRD QUARTER:** Dal: D. Thomas 3 run (Clark kick), 5:17. **Dallas 17-3.**

**FOURTH QUARTER:** Dal: Ditka 7 pass from Staubach (Clark kick), 3:18. **Dallas 24-3.** A: 81,023.

### VII - 1973

| | | | | |
|---|---|---|---|---|
| Miami | 7 | 7 | 0 | 0—14 |
| Washington | 0 | 0 | 0 | 7—7 |

**FIRST QUARTER:** Mia: Twilley 28 pass from Griese (Yepremian kick), 14:59. **Miami 7-0.**

**SECOND QUARTER:** Mia: Kiick 1 run (Yepremian kick), 14:42. **Miami 14-0.**

**FOURTH QUARTER:** Wash: Bass 49 fumble recovery return (Knight kick), 12:53. **Miami 14-7.** A: 90,182.

### VIII - 1974

| | | | | |
|---|---|---|---|---|
| Miami | 14 | 3 | 7 | 0—24 |
| Minnesota | 0 | 0 | 0 | 7—7 |

**FIRST QUARTER:** Mia: Csonka 5 run (Yepremian kick), 5:27. Mia: Kiick 1 run (Yepremian kick), 13:38. **Miami 14-0.**

**SECOND QUARTER:** Mia: FG Yepremian 28, 8:58. **Miami 17-0.**

**THIRD QUARTER:** Mia: Csonka 2 run (Yepremian kick), 6:16. **Miami 24-0.**

**FOURTH QUARTER:** Minn: Tarkenton 4 run (Cox kick), 1:35. **Miami 24-7.** A: 71,882.

### IX - 1975

| | | | | |
|---|---|---|---|---|
| Pittsburgh | 0 | 2 | 7 | 7—16 |
| Minnesota | 0 | 0 | 0 | 6—6 |

**SECOND QUARTER:** Pit: White tackled Tarkenton for safety, 7:49. **Pittsburgh 2-0.**

**THIRD QUARTER:** Pit: Harris 9 run (Gerela kick), 1:35. **Pittsburgh 9-0.**

**FOURTH QUARTER:** Minn: T. Brown recovered blocked punt in end zone (kick failed), 4:27. **Pittsburgh 9-6.** Pit: L. Brown 4 pass from Bradshaw (Gerela kick), 11:29. **Pittsburgh 16-6.** A: 80,997.

### X - 1976

| | | | | |
|---|---|---|---|---|
| Pittsburgh | 7 | 0 | 0 | 14—21 |
| Dallas | 7 | 3 | 0 | 7—17 |

**FIRST QUARTER:** Dal: D. Pearson 29 pass from Staubach (Fritsch kick), 4:36. **Dallas 7-0.** Pit: Grossman 7 pass from Bradshaw (Gerela kick), 9:03. **7-7.**

**SECOND QUARTER:** Dal: FG Fritsch 36, 0:15. **Dallas 10-7.**

**FOURTH QUARTER:** Pit: Harrison blocked Hoopes's punt for safety, 3:32. **Dallas 10-9.** Pit: FG Gerela 36, 6:19. **Pittsburgh 12-10.** Pit: FG Gerela 18, 8:32. **Pittsburgh 15-10.** Pit: Swann 64 pass from Bradshaw (kick failed), 11:58. **Pittsburgh 21-10.** Dal: P. Howard 34 pass from Staubach (Fritsch kick), 13:12. **Pittsburgh 21-17.** A: 80,187.

### XI - 1977

| | | | | |
|---|---|---|---|---|
| Oakland | 0 | 16 | 3 | 13—32 |
| Minnesota | 0 | 0 | 7 | 7—14 |

**SECOND QUARTER:** Oak: FG Mann, 24, 0:48. **Oakland 3-0.** Oak: Casper 1 pass from Stabler (Mann kick), 7:50. **Oakland 10-0.** Oak: Banaszak 1 run (kick failed), 11:27. **Oakland 16-0.**

**THIRD QUARTER:** Oak: FG Mann, 40, 9:44. **Oakland 19-0.** Min: S. White 8 pass from Tarkenton (Cox kick), 14:13. **Oakland 19-7.**

**FOURTH QUARTER:** Oak: Banaszak 2 run (Mann kick), 7:21. **Oakland 26-7.** Oak: Brown 75 int return (kick failed), 9:17. **Oakland 32-7.** Min: Voigt 13 pass from Lee (Cox kick), 14:35. **Oakland 32-14.** A: 103,438.

### XII - 1978

| Dallas | 10 | 3 | 7 | 7—27 |
|--------|----|----|----|------|
| Denver | 0 | 0 | 10 | 0—10 |

**FIRST QUARTER: FIRST QUARTER:** Dal: Dorsett 3 run (Herrera kick), 10:31. **Dallas 7-0.**
Dal: FG Herrera 35, 13:29. **Dallas 10-0.**

**SECOND QUARTER:** Dal: FG Herrera 43, 3:44. **Dallas 13-0.**

**THIRD QUARTER:** Den: FG Turner 47, 2:28. **Dallas 13-3.**
Dal: Johnson 45 pass from Staubach (Herrera kick), 8:01. **Dallas 20-3.**
Den: Lytle 1 run (Turner kick), 9:21. **Dallas 20-10.**

**FOURTH QUARTER:** Dal: Richards 29 pass from Newhouse (Herrera kick), 7:56. **Dallas 27-10.**

A: 76,400.

### XIII - 1979

| Pittsburgh | 7 | 14 | 0 | 14—35 |
|------------|----|----|----|------|
| Dallas | 7 | 7 | 3 | 14—31 |

**FIRST QUARTER:** Pit: Stallworth 28 pass from Bradshaw (Gerela kick), 5:13. **Pittsburgh 7-0.**
Dal: Hill 39 pass from Staubach (Septien kick), 15:00. **7-7.**

**SECOND QUARTER:** Dal: Hegman 37 fumble recovery return (Septien kick), 2:52. **Dallas 14-7.**
Pit: Stallworth 75 pass from Bradshaw (Gerela kick), 4:35. **14-14.**
Pit: Bleier 7 pass from Bradshaw (Gerela kick), 14:34. **Pittsburgh 21-14.**

**THIRD QUARTER:** Dal: FG Septien 27, 12:24. **Pittsburgh 21-17.**

**FOURTH QUARTER:** Pit: Harris 22 run (Gerela kick), 7:50. **Pittsburgh 28-17.**
Pit: Swann 18 pass from Bradshaw (Gerela kick), 8:09. **Pittsburgh 35-17.**
Dal: DuPree 7 pass from Staubach (Septien kick), 12:33. **Pittsburgh 35-24.**
Dal: B. Johnson 4 pass from Staubach (Septien kick), 14:38. **Pittsburgh 35-31.**

A: 79,484.

### XIV - 1980

| Pittsburgh | 3 | 7 | 7 | 14—31 |
|------------|----|----|----|------|
| LA Rams | 7 | 6 | 6 | 0—19 |

**FIRST QUARTER:** Pit: FG Bahr, 41, 7:29. **Pittsburgh 3-0.**
LA: Bryant 1 run (Corral kick), 12:16. **LA Rams 7-3.**

**SECOND QUARTER:** Pit: Harris 1 run (Bahr kick), 2:08. **Pittsburgh 10-7.**
LA: FG Corral 31, 7:39. **10-10.**
LA: FG Corral 45, 14:46. **LA Rams 13-10.**

**THIRD QUARTER:** Pit: Swann 47 pass from Bradshaw (Bahr kick), 2:48. **Pittsburgh 17-13.**
LA: Smith 24 pass from McCutcheon (kick failed), 4:45. **LA Rams 19-17.**

**FOURTH QUARTER:** Pit: Stallworth 73 pass from Bradshaw (Bahr kick), 2:56. **Pittsburgh 24-19.**
Pit: Harris 1 run (Bahr kick), 13:11. **Pittsburgh 31-19.**

A: 103,985.

### XV - 1981

| Oakland | 14 | 0 | 10 | 3—27 |
|---------|----|----|----|------|
| Philadelphia | 0 | 3 | 0 | 7—10 |

**FIRST QUARTER:** Oak: Branch 2 pass from Plunkett (Bahr kick), 6:04. **Oakland 7-0.**
Oak: King 80 pass from Plunkett (Bahr kick), 14:51. **Oakland 14-0.**

**SECOND QUARTER:** Phi: FG Franklin 30, 4:32. **Oakland 14-3.**

**THIRD QUARTER:** Oak: Branch 29 pass from Plunkett (Bahr kick), 2:36. **Oakland 21-3.**
Oak: FG Bahr 46, 10:25. **Oakland 24-3.**

**FOURTH QUARTER:** Phi: Krepfle 8 pass from Jaworski (Franklin kick), 1:01. **Oakland 24-10.**
Oak: FG Bahr, 35, 6:31. **Oakland 27-10.**

A: 76,135.

### XVI - 1982

| San Francisco | 7 | 13 | 0 | 6—26 |
|---------------|----|----|----|------|
| Cincinnati | 0 | 0 | 7 | 14—21 |

**FIRST QUARTER:** SF: Montana 1 run (Wersching kick), 9:08. **San Francisco 7-0.**

**SECOND QUARTER:** SF: E. Cooper 11 pass from Montana (Wersching kick), 8:07. **San Francisco 14-0.**
SF: FG Wersching 22, 14:45. **San Francisco 17-0.**
SF: FG Wersching 26, 14:58. **San Francisco 20-0.**

**THIRD QUARTER:** Cin: Anderson 5 run (Breech kick), 3:35. **San Francisco 20-7.**

**FOURTH QUARTER:** Cin: Ross 4 pass from Anderson (Breech kick), 4:54. **San Francisco 20-14.**
SF: FG Wersching 40, 9:35. **San Francisco 23-14.**
SF: FG Wersching 23, 13:03. **San Francisco 26-14.**
Cin: Ross 3 pass from Anderson (Breech kick), 14:44. **San Francisco 26-21.**

A: 81,270.

### XVII - 1983

| Washington | 0 | 10 | 3 | 14—27 |
|------------|----|----|----|------|
| Miami | 7 | 10 | 0 | 0—17 |

**FIRST QUARTER:** Mia: Cefalo 76 pass from Woodley (Von Schamann kick), 6:49. **Miami 7-0.**

**SECOND QUARTER:** Wash: FG Moseley 31, 0:21. **Miami 7-3.**
Mia: FG Von Schamann 20, 9:00. **Miami 10-3.**
Wash: Garrett 4 pass from Theismann (Moseley kick), 13:09. **10-10.**
Mia: Walker 98 kick return (Von Schamann kick), 13:22. **Miami 17-10.**

**THIRD QUARTER:** Wash: FG Moseley 20, 6:51. **Miami 17-13.**

**FOURTH QUARTER:** Wash: Riggins 43 run (Moseley kick), 4:59. **Washington 20-17.**
Wash: Brown 6 pass from Theismann (Moseley kick), 13:05. **Washington 27-17.**

A: 103,667.

### XVIII - 1984

| | | | | |
|---|---|---|---|---|
| LA Raiders | 7 | 14 | 14 | 3—38 |
| Washington | 0 | 3 | 6 | 0—9 |

**FIRST QUARTER:** LA: Jensen 0 blocked punt return (Bahr kick), 4:52. **LA Raiders 7-0.**

**SECOND QUARTER:** LA: Branch 12 pass from Plunkett (Bahr kick), 5:46. **LA Raiders 14-0.** Wash: FG Moseley 24, 11:55. **LA Raiders 14-3.** LA: Squirek 5 int return (Bahr kick), 14:53. **LA Raiders 21-3.**

**THIRD QUARTER:** Wash: Riggins 1 run (kick blocked), 4:08. LA: Allen 5 run (Bahr kick), 7:54. **LA Raiders 28-9.** LA: Allen 74 run (Bahr kick), 15:00. **LA Raiders 35-9.**

**FOURTH QUARTER:** LA: FG Bahr 21, 12:36. **LA Raiders 38-9.** A: 72,920.

### XIX - 1985

| | | | | |
|---|---|---|---|---|
| San Francisco | 7 | 21 | 10 | 0—38 |
| Miami | 10 | 6 | 0 | 0—16 |

**FIRST QUARTER:** Mia: FG Von Schamann 37, 7:36. **Miami 3-0.** SF: Monroe 33 pass from Montana (Wersching kick), 11:48. **San Francisco 7-3.** Mia: D. Johnson 2 pass from Marino (Von Schamann kick), 14:15. **Miami 10-7.**

**SECOND QUARTER:** SF: Craig 8 pass from Montana (Wersching kick), 3:26. **San Francisco 14-10.** SF: Montana 6 run (Wersching kick), 8:02. **San Francisco 21-10.** SF: Craig 2 run (Wersching kick), 12:55. **San Francisco 28-10.** Mia: FG Von Schamann 31, 14:48. **San Francisco 28-13.** Mia: FG Von Schamann 30, 15:00. **San Francisco 28-16.**

**THIRD QUARTER:** SF: FG Wersching 27, 4:48. **San Francisco 31-16.** SF: Craig 16 pass from Montana (Wershing kick), 8:42. **San Francisco 38-16.** A: 84,059.

### XX - 1986

| | | | | |
|---|---|---|---|---|
| Chicago | 13 | 10 | 21 | 2—46 |
| New England | 3 | 0 | 0 | 7—10 |

**FIRST QUARTER:** NE: FG Franklin 36, 1:19. **New England 3-0.** Chi: FG Butler 28, 5:40. **3-3.** Chi: FG Butler 24, 13:34. **Chicago 6-3.** Chi: Suhey 11 run (Butler kick), 14:37. **Chicago 13-3.**

**SECOND QUARTER:** Chi: McMahon 2 run (Butler kick), 7:36. **Chicago 20-3.** Chi: FG Butler 24, 15:00. **Chicago 23-3.**

**THIRD QUARTER:** Chi: McMahon 1 run (Butler kick), 7:38. **Chicago 30-3.** Chi: Phillips 28 int return (Butler kick), 8:44. **Chicago 37-3.** Chi: Perry 1 run (Butler kick), 11:38. **Chicago 44-3.**

**FOURTH QUARTER:** NE: Fryar 8 pass from Grogan (Franklin kick), 1:46. **Chicago 44-10.** Chi: Waechter safety, 9:24. **Chicago 46-10.** A: 73,818.

### XXI - 1987

| | | | | |
|---|---|---|---|---|
| NY Giants | 7 | 2 | 17 | 13—39 |
| Denver | 10 | 0 | 0 | 10—20 |

**FIRST QUARTER:** Den: FG Karlis 48, 4:09. **Denver 3-0.** NYG: Mowatt 6 pass from Simms (Allegre kick), 9:33. **NY Giants 7-3.** Den: Elway 4 run (Karlis kick), 12:54. **Denver 10-7.**

**SECOND QUARTER:** NYG: Martin safety, 12:14. **Denver 10-9.**

**THIRD QUARTER:** NYG: Bavaro 13 pass from Simms (Allegre kick), 4:52. **NY Giants 16-10.** NYG: FG Allegre 21, 11:06. **NY Giants 19-10.** NYG: Morris 1 run (Allegre kick), 14:36. **NY Giants 26-10.**

**FOURTH QUARTER:** NYG: McConkey 6 pass from Simms (Allegre kick), 4:04. **NY Giants 33-10.** Den: FG Karlis 28, 8:59. **NY Giants 33-13.** NYG: Anderson 2 run (kick failed), 11:42. **NY Giants 39-13.** Den: Johnson 47 pass from Elway (Karlis kick), 12:54. **NY Giants 39-20.**

A: 101,063.

### XXII - 1988

| | | | | |
|---|---|---|---|---|
| Washington | 0 | 35 | 0 | 7—42 |
| Denver | 10 | 0 | 0 | 0—10 |

**FIRST QUARTER:** Den: Nattiel 56 pass from Elway (Karlis kick), 1:57. **Denver 7-0.** Den: FG Karlis 24, 5:51. **Denver 10-0.**

**SECOND QUARTER:** Wash: Sanders 80 pass from D. Williams (Haji-Sheikh kick), 0:53. **Denver 10-7.** Wash: Clark 27 pass from D. Williams (Haji-Sheikh kick), 4:45. **Washington 14-10.** Wash: Smith 58 run (Haji-Sheikh kick), 8:33. **Washington 21-10.** Wash: Sanders 50 pass from D. Williams (Haji-Sheikh kick), 11:18. **Washington 28-10.** Wash: Didier 8 pass from D. Williams (Haji-Sheikh kick), 13:56. **Washington 35-10.**

**FOURTH QUARTER:** Wash: Smith 4 run (Haji-Sheikh kick), 1:51. **Washington 42-10.**

A: 73,302.

### XXIII - 1989

| | | | | |
|---|---|---|---|---|
| San Francisco | 3 | 0 | 3 | 14—20 |
| Cincinnati | 0 | 3 | 10 | 3—16 |

**FIRST QUARTER:** SF: FG Cofer 41, 11:46. **San Francisco 3-0.**

**SECOND QUARTER:** Cin: FG Breech 34, 13:41. **3-3.**

**THIRD QUARTER:** Cin: FG Breech 43, 9:15. **Cincinnati 6-3.** SF: FG Cofer 32, 14:10. **6-6.** Cin: Jennings 93 kick return (Breech kick), 14:26. **Cincinnati 13-6.**

**FOURTH QUARTER:** SF: Rice 14 pass from Montana (Cofer kick), 0:57. **13-13.** Cin: FG Breech 40, 11:40. **Cincinnati 16-13.** SF: Taylor 10 pass from Montana (Cofer kick), 14:26. **San Francisco 20-16.**

A: 75,129.

## XXIV - 1990

| | | | | |
|---|---|---|---|---|
| San Francisco | 13 | 14 | 14 | 14—55 |
| Denver | 3 | 0 | 7 | 0—10 |

**FIRST QUARTER:** SF: Rice 20 pass from Montana (Cofer kick), 4:54. **San Francisco 7-0.**
Den: FG Treadwell 42, 8:13. **San Francisco 7-3.**
SF: Jones 7 pass from Montana (kick failed), 14:57. **San Francisco 13-3.**

**SECOND QUARTER:** SF: Rathman 1 run (Cofer kick), 7:45. **San Francisco 20-3.**
SF: Rice 38 pass from Montana (Cofer kick), 14:26. **San Francisco 27-3.**

**THIRD QUARTER:** SF: Rice 28 pass from Montana (Cofer kick), 2:12. **San Francisco 34-3.**
SF: Taylor 35 pass from Montana (Cofer kick), 5:16. **San Francisco 41-3.**
Den: Elway 3 run (Treadwell kick), 8:07. **San Francisco 41-10.**

**FOURTH QUARTER:** SF: Rathman 3 run (Cofer kick), 0:03. **San Francisco 48-10.**
SF: Craig 1 run (Cofer kick), 1:13. **San Francisco 55-10.**
A: 72,919.

## XXV - 1991

| | | | | |
|---|---|---|---|---|
| NY Giants | 3 | 7 | 7 | 3—20 |
| Buffalo | 3 | 9 | 0 | 7—19 |

**FIRST QUARTER:** NYG: FG Bahr 28, 7:46. **NY Giants 3-0.**
Buff: FG Norwood 23, 9:09. **3-3.**

**SECOND QUARTER:** Buff: D. Smith 1 run (Norwood kick), 2:30. **Buffalo 10-3.**
Buff: B. Smith safety 0, 6:33. **Buffalo 12-3.**
NYG: Baker 14 pass from Hostetler (Bahr kick), 14:35. **Buffalo 12-10.**

**THIRD QUARTER:** NYG: Anderson 1 run (Bahr kick), 9:29. **NY Giants 17-12.**

**FOURTH QUARTER:** Buff: Thomas 31 run (Norwood kick), 0:08. **Buffalo 19-17.**
NYG: FG Bahr 21, 7:40. **NY Giants 20-19.**
A: 73,813.

## XXVI - 1992

| | | | | |
|---|---|---|---|---|
| Washington | 0 | 17 | 14 | 6—37 |
| Buffalo | 0 | 0 | 10 | 14—24 |

**SECOND QUARTER:** Wash: FG Lohmiller 34, 1:58. **Washington 3-0.**
Wash: Byner 10 pass from Rypien (Lohmiller kick), 5:06. **Washington 10-0.**
Wash: Riggs 1 run (Lohmiller kick), 7:43. **Washington 17-0.**

**THIRD QUARTER:** Wash: Riggs 2 run (Lohmiller kick), 0:16. **Washington 24-0.**
Buff: FG Norwood 21, 3:01. **Washington 24-3.**
Buff: Thomas 1 run (Norwood kick), 9:02. **Washington 24-10.**
Wash: Clark 30 pass from Rypien (Lohmiller kick), 13:36. **Washington 31-10.**

**FOURTH QUARTER:** Wash: FG Lohmiller 25, 0:06. **Washington 34-10.**
Wash: FG Lohmiller 39, 3:24. **Washington 37-10.**
Buff: Metzelaars 2 pass from Kelly (Norwood kick), 9:01. **Washington 37-17.**
Buff: Beebe 4 pass from Kelly (Norwood kick), 11:05. **Washington 37-24.**
A: 63,130.

## XXVII - 1993

| | | | | |
|---|---|---|---|---|
| Dallas | 14 | 14 | 3 | 21—52 |
| Buffalo | 7 | 3 | 7 | 0—17 |

**FIRST QUARTER:** Buff: Thomas 2 run (Christie kick), 5:00. **Buffalo 7-0.**
Dal: Novacek 23 pass from Aikman (Elliott kick), 13:24. **7-7.**
Dal: J.Jones 2 fumble return (Elliott kick), 13:39. **Dallas 14-7.**

**SECOND QUARTER:** Buff: FG Christie 21, 11:36. **Dallas 14-10.**
Dal: Irvin 19 pass from Aikman (Elliott kick)13:06. **Dallas 21-10.**
Dal: Irvin 18 pass from Aikman (Elliott kick), 13:24. **Dallas 28-10.**

**THIRD QUARTER:** Dal: FG Elliott 20, 6:39. **Dallas 31-10.**
Buff: Beebe 40 pass from Reich (Christie kick), 15:00. **Dallas 31-17.**

**FOURTH QUARTER:** Dal: Harper 45 pass from Aikman (Elliott kick), 4:56. **Dallas 38-17.**
Dal: E. Smith 10 run (Elliott kick), 6:48. **Dallas 45-17.**
Dal: Norton 9 fumble return (Elliott kick), 7:29. **Dallas 52-17.**
A: 98,374.

## XXVIII - 1994

| | | | | |
|---|---|---|---|---|
| Dallas | 6 | 0 | 14 | 10—30 |
| Buffalo | 3 | 10 | 0 | 0—13 |

**FIRST QUARTER:** Dal: FG Murray 41, 2:19. **Dallas 3-0.**
Buff: FG Christie 54: 4:41. **3-3.**
Dal: FG Murray 24, 11:05. **Dallas 6-3.**

**SECOND QUARTER:** Buff: Thomas 4 run (Christie kick), 2:34. **Buffalo 10-6.**
Buff: FG Christie 28, 15:00. **Buffalo 13-6.**

**THIRD QUARTER:** Dal: Washington fumble return (Murray kick), 0:55. **13-13.**
Dal: Smith15 run (Murray kick), 0:55. **Dallas 20-13.**

**FOURTH QUARTER:** Dal: Smith1 run (Murray kick), 5:10. **Dallas 27-13.**
Dal: FG Murray 20, 12:10. **Dallas 30-13.**
A: 72,817.

## XXIX - 1995

| | | | | |
|---|---|---|---|---|
| San Francisco | 14 | 14 | 14 | 7—49 |
| San Diego | 7 | 3 | 8 | 8—26 |

**FIRST QUARTER:** SF: Rice 44 pass from Young (Brien kick), 1:24. **San Francisco 7-0.**
SF: Watters 51 pass from Young (Brien kick, 4:55. **San Francisco 14-0.**
SD: Means 1 run (Carney kick), 12:16. **San Francisco 14-7.**

**SECOND QUARTER:** SF: Floyd 5 pass from Young (Brien kick), 1:58. **San Francisco 21-7.**
SF: Watters 8 pass from Young (Brien kick), 10:16. **San Francisco 28-7.**
SD: FG Carney 31, 13:16. **San Francisco 28-10.**

**THIRD QUARTER:** SF: Watters 9 run (Brien kick), 5:25. **San Francisco 35-10.**
SF: Rice 15 pass from Young (Brien kick), 11:42. **San Francisco 42-10.**

### XXIX - 1995 *(Cont.)*

**THIRD QUARTER** *(CONT.)*:SD: Coleman 98 kickoff return (Humphries 2-pt conv pass to Seay), 11:59. **San Francisco 42–18.**

**FOURTH QUARTER:** SF: Rice 7 pass from Young (Brien kick), 1:11.
**San Francisco 49–18.**
SD: Martin 30 pass from Humphries (Humphries 2 pt-conv pass to Pupunu), 12:35. **San Francisco 49–26.**
A: 74,107.

### XXX - 1996

| | | | | |
|---|---|---|---|---|
| Dallas | 10 | 3 | 7 | 7—27 |
| Pittsburgh | 0 | 7 | 0 | 10—17 |

**FIRST QUARTER:** Dal: FG Boniol 42, 2:55. **Dallas 3–0.**
Dal: Novacek 3 pass from Aikman (Boniol kick), 9:37. **Dallas 10–0.**

**SECOND QUARTER:** Dal: FG Boniol 35, 8:57. **Dallas 13–0.**
Pitt: Thigpen 6 pass from O'Donnell (N. Johnson kick), 14:47. **Dallas 13–7.**

**THIRD QUARTER:** Dal: E. Smith 1 run (Boniol kick), 8:18. **Dallas 20–7.**

**FOURTH QUARTER:** Pitt: FG N. Johnson 46, 3:40. **Dallas 20–10.**
Pitt: Morris 1 run (N. Johnson kick), 8:24. **Dallas 20–17.**
Dal: E. Smith 4 run (Boniol kick), 11:17. **Dallas 27–17.**
A: 76,347.

### XXXI - 1997

| | | | | |
|---|---|---|---|---|
| Green Bay | 10 | 17 | 8 | 0—35 |
| New England | 14 | 0 | 7 | 0—21 |

**FIRST QUARTER:** GB: Rison 54 pass from Favre (Jacke kick), 3:32. **Green Bay 7–0.**
GB: FG Jacke 37, 6:18. **Green Bay 10–0.**
NE: Byars 1 pass from Bledsoe (Vinatieri kick), 8:25. **Green Bay 10–7.**
NE: Coates 4 pass from Bledsoe (Vinatieri kick), 12:27. **New England 14–10.**

**SECOND QUARTER:** GB: Freeman 81 pass from Favre (Jacke kick), 0:56. **Green Bay 17–14.**
GB: FG Jacke 31, 6:45. **Green Bay 20–14.**
GB: Favre 2 run (Jacke kick), 13:49. **Green Bay 27–14.**

**THIRD QUARTER:** NE: Martin 18 run (Vinatieri kick), 11:33. **Green Bay 27–21.**
GB: Howard 99 kickoff return (Favre 2 pt conv pass to Chmura), 11:50. **Green Bay 35–21.**

A: 72,301.

### XXXII - 1998

| | | | | |
|---|---|---|---|---|
| Denver | 7 | 10 | 7 | 7—31 |
| Green Bay | 7 | 7 | 3 | 7—24 |

**FIRST QUARTER:** GB: Freeman 22 pass from Favre (Longwell kick), 4:02. **Green Bay 7–0.**
Den: Davis 1 run (Elam kick), 9:21. **7–7.**

**SECOND QUARTER:** Den: Elway 1 run (Elam kick), 0:05. **Denver 14–7.**
Den: FG Elam 51, 2:39. **Denver 17–7.**
GB: Chmura 6 pass from Favre (Longwell kick), 14:48. **Denver 17–14.**

### XXXII - 1998 *(Cont.)*

**THIRD QUARTER:** GB: FG Longwell 27, 3:01. **17–17.**
Den: Davis 1 run (Elam kick), 14:26. **Denver 24–17.**

**FOURTH QUARTER:** GB: Freeman 13 pass from Favre (Longwell kick), 1:28. **24–24.**
Den: Davis 1 run (Elam kick), 13:15. **Denver 31–24.**
A: 68,912.

### XXXIII - 1999

| | | | | |
|---|---|---|---|---|
| Denver | 7 | 10 | 0 | 17—34 |
| Atlanta | 3 | 3 | 0 | 13—19 |

**FIRST QUARTER:** Atl: FG Andersen 32, 5:25. **Atlanta 3–0.**
Den: Griffith 1 run (Elam kick), 11:05. **Denver 7–3.**

**SECOND QUARTER:** Den: FG Elam 26, 5:43. **Denver 10–3.**
Den: Smith 80 pass from Elway (Elam kick), 10:06. **Denver 17–3.**
Atl: FG Andersen 28, 12:35. **Denver 17–6.**

**FOURTH QUARTER:** Den: Griffith 1 run (Elam kick), 0:04. **Denver 24–6.**
Den: Elway 3 run (Elam kick), 3:40. **Denver 31–6.**
Atl: Dwight 94 kickoff return (Andersen kick), 3:59. **Denver 31–13.**
Den: FG Elam 37, 7:52. **Denver 34–13.**
Atl: Mathis 3 pass from Chandler (2-pt conv failed), 12:56. **Denver 34–19.**
A: 74,803.

### XXXIV - 2000

| | | | | |
|---|---|---|---|---|
| St. Louis | 3 | 6 | 7 | 7—23 |
| Tennessee | 0 | 0 | 6 | 10—16 |

**FIRST QUARTER:** StL: FG Wilkins 27, 3:00. **St. Louis 3–0.**

**SECOND QUARTER:** StL: FG Wilkins 29, 4:16. **St. Louis 6–0.**
StL: FG Wilkins 28, 0:15. **St. Louis 9–0.**

**THIRD QUARTER:** StL: Holt 9 pass from Warner (Wilkins kick), 7:20. **St. Louis 16–0.**
Tenn: George 1 run (2-pt conv failed), 0:14. **St. Louis 16–6.**

**FOURTH QUARTER:** Tenn: George 2 run (Del Greco kick), 7:21. **St. Louis 16–13.**
Tenn: FG Del Greco 43, 2:15. **16–16.**
StL: Bruce 73 pass from Warner, 1:54. **St. Louis 23–16.**
A: 72,265.

### XXXV - 2001

| | | | | |
|---|---|---|---|---|
| Baltimore | 7 | 3 | 14 | 10—34 |
| NY Giants | 0 | 0 | 7 | 0—7 |

**FIRST QUARTER:** Balt: Stokely 38 pass from Dilfer (Stover kick), 6:50. **Baltimore 7–0.**

**SECOND QUARTER:** Balt: FG Stover 47, 1:41. **Baltimore 10–0.**

**THIRD QUARTER:** Balt: Starks 49 int return (Stover kick), 3:49. **Baltimore 17–0.**
NYG: Dixon 97 kickoff return (Daluiso kick), 3:31. **Baltimore 17–7.**
Balt: Je. Lewis 84 kickoff return (Stover kick), 3:13. **Baltimore 24–7.**

### XXXV - 2001 *(Cont.)*

**FOURTH QUARTER:** Balt: Ja. Lewis 3 run (Stover kick), 8:45. **Baltimore 31-7.**
Balt: FG Stover 34, 5:28. **Baltimore 34-7.**
A: 71,921.

### XXXVI - 2002

| | | | | |
|---|---|---|---|---|
| New England | 0 | 14 | 3 | 3—20 |
| St. Louis | 3 | 0 | 0 | 14—17 |

**FIRST QUARTER:** StL: FG Wilkins 50, 3:50. **St. Louis 3-0.**

**SECOND QUARTER:** NE: Law 47 int return (Vinatieri kick), 8:49. **New England 7-3.**
NE: Patten 8 pass from Brady (Vinatieri kick), 0:31. **New England 14-3.**

**THIRD QUARTER:** NE: FG Vinatieri 37, 1:18. **New Eng. 17-3.**

**FOURTH QUARTER:** StL: Warner 2 run (Wilkins kick), 9:31. **New England 17-10.**
StL: Proehl 26 pass from Warner (Wilkins kick), 1:30. **17-17.**
NE: FG Vinatieri 48, 0:00. **New England 20-17.**
A: 72,922.

### XXXVII - 2003

| | | | | |
|---|---|---|---|---|
| Tampa Bay | 3 | 17 | 14 | 14—48 |
| Oakland | 3 | 0 | 6 | 12—21 |

**FIRST QUARTER:** Oak: FG Janikowski 40, 10:20. **Oakland 3-0.**
TB: FG Gramatica 31, 7:51. **3-3.**

**SECOND QUARTER:** TB: FG Gramatica 43, 11:16. **Tampa Bay 6-3.**
TB: Alstott 2 run (Gramatica kick), 6:24. **Tampa Bay 13-3.**
TB: McCardell 5 pass from B. Johnson (Gramatica kick), 0:30. **Tampa Bay 20-3.**

**THIRD QUARTER:** TB: McCardell 8 pass from B. Johnson (Gramatica kick), 5:30. **Tampa Bay 27-3.**
TB: Smith 44 int. return (Gramatica kick), 4:47. **Tampa Bay 34-3.**
Oak: Porter 39 pass from Gannon (2-pt conv failed), 2:14. **Tampa Bay 34-9.**

**FOURTH QUARTER:** Oak: Johnson 13 return of blocked punt (two-pt. conversion failed), 14:14. **Tampa Bay 34-15.**
Oak: Rice 48 pass from Gannon (2-pt conv failed), 6:06. **Tampa Bay 34-21.**
TB: Brooks 44 int. return (Gramatica kick), 1:18. **Tampa Bay 41-21.**
TB: Smith 50 int. return (Gramatica kick), 0:02. **Tampa Bay 48-21.**
A: 67,603.

### XXXVIII - 2004

| | | | | |
|---|---|---|---|---|
| New England | 0 | 14 | 0 | 18—32 |
| Carolina | 0 | 10 | 0 | 19—29 |

**SECOND QUARTER:** NE: Branch 5 pass from Brady (Vinatieri kick), 3:11. **New England 7-0.**
Car: Smith 39 pass from Delhomme (Kasay kick), 1:17. **7-7.**
NE: Givens 5 pass from Brady (Vinatieri kick), 0:28. **New England 14-7.**
Car: FG Kasay 50, 0:00. **New England 14-10.**

### XXXVIII - 2004 *(Cont.)*

**FOURTH QUARTER:** NE: Smith 2 run (Vinatieri kick), 14:49. **New England 21-10.**
Car: Foster 33 run (2-pt conv failed), 12:49. **New England 21-16.**
Car: Muhammad 85 pass from Delhomme (2-pt conv failed), 7:13. **Carolina 22-21.**
NE: Vrabel 1 pass from Brady (Faulk ran for 2-pt conv), 2:51. **New England 29-22.**
Car: Proehl 12 pass from Delhomme (Kasay kick), 1:18. **29-29.**
NE: FG Vinatieri 41, 0:04. **New England 32-29.**

A: 71,525.

### XXXIX - 2005

| | | | | |
|---|---|---|---|---|
| New England | 0 | 7 | 7 | 10—24 |
| Philadelphia | 0 | 7 | 7 | 7—21 |

**SECOND QUARTER:** Phil: Smith 6 pass from McNabb (Akers kick), 10:05. **Philadelphia 7-0.**
NE: Givens 4 pass from Brady (Vinatieri kick), 1:10. **7-7.**

**THIRD QUARTER:** NE: Vrabel 2 pass from Brady (Vinatieri kick), 11:04. **New England 14-7.**
Phil: Westbrook 10 pass from McNabb (Akers kick), 3:45. **14-14.**

**FOURTH QUARTER:** NE: Dillon 2 run (Vinatieri kick), 1:16. **New England 21-14.**
NE: FG Vinatieri 22, 6:20. **New England 24-14.**
Phil: Lewis 30 pass from McNabb (Akers kick), 13:12. **New England 24-21.**

A: 78,125.

### XL - 2006

| | | | | |
|---|---|---|---|---|
| Pittsburgh | 0 | 7 | 7 | 7—21 |
| Seattle | 3 | 0 | 7 | 0—10 |

**FIRST QUARTER:** Sea: FG Brown 47, 0:22. **Seattle 3-0.**

**SECOND QUARTER:** Pit: Roethlisberger 1 run (Reed kick), 1:55. **Pittsburgh 7-3.**

**THIRD QUARTER:** Pit: Parker 75 run (Reed kick) , 14:38. **Pittsburgh 14-3.**
Sea: Stevens 16 pass from Hasselbeck (Brown kick), 6:45. **Pittsburgh 14-10.**

**FOURTH QUARTER:** Pit: Ward 43 pass from Randle El (Reed kick), 8:56. **Pittsburgh 21-10.**

A: 68,206.

### XLI - 2007

| | | | | |
|---|---|---|---|---|
| Indianapolis | 6 | 10 | 6 | 7—29 |
| Chicago | 14 | 0 | 3 | 0—17 |

**FIRST QUARTER:** Chicago: TD Hester 92 kick return (Gould kick)14:46. **Chicago 7-0.**
Indianapolis: TD Wayne 53 pass from Manning, 6:50 (Vinatieri kick failed). **Chicago 7-6.**
Chicago: TD Muhammad 4 pass from Grossman (Gould kick), 4:34. **Chicago 14-6.**

**SECOND QUARTER:** Indianapolis: FG Vinatieri 29, 11:17. **Chicago 14-9.**
Indianapolis: TD Rhodes 1 run (Vinatieri kick), 6:09. **Indianapolis 16-14.**

## XLI - 2007 *(Cont.)*

**THIRD QUARTER:** Indianapolis: FG Vinatieri 24, 7:26. **Indianapolis 19-14.**
Indianapolis: FG Vinatieri 20, 3:16. **Indianapolis 22-14.**
Chicago: FG Gould 44, 1:14. **Indianapolis 22-17.**

**FOURTH QUARTER:** Indianapolis: TD Hayden 56 interception return (Vinatieri kick) 11:44.
**Indianapolis 29-17.**

A: 74,512.

## XLII - 2008

| | | | | |
|---|---|---|---|---|
| **NY Giants** | 3 | 0 | 0 | 14—17 |
| **New England** | 0 | 7 | 0 | 7—14 |

**FIRST QUARTER:** NY Giants: FG Tynes 32, 5:01.
**NY Giants 3-0.**

**SECOND QUARTER:** New England: TD Maroney 1 run (Gostkowski kick), 14:57.
**New England 7-3.**

**FOURTH QUARTER:** NY Giants: TD Tyree 5 pass from Manning (Tynes kick), 11:05. **NY Giants 10-7.**
New England: TD Moss 6 pass from Brady (Gostkowski kick), 02:42. **New England 14-10.**
NY Giants: TD Burress 13 pass from Manning (Tynes kick), 00:35. **NY Giants 17-14.**

A: 71,101.

## XLIII - 2009

| | | | | |
|---|---|---|---|---|
| **Pittsburgh** | 3 | 14 | 3 | 7—27 |
| **Arizona** | 0 | 7 | 0 | 16—23 |

**FIRST QUARTER:** Pittsburgh: FG Reed 18, 9:45.
**Pittsburgh 3-0.**

**SECOND QUARTER:** Pittsburgh: Russell 1 run (Reed kick), 14:01. **Pittsburgh 10-0.**
Arizona: Patrick 1 pass from Warner (Rackers kick), 8:34. **Pittsburgh 10-7.**
Pittsburgh: Harrison 100 Int return (Rackers kick), 0:00. **Pittsburgh 17-7.**

**THIRD QUARTER:** Pittsburgh: FG Reed 21, 2:11.
**Pittsburgh 20-7.**

**FOURTH QUARTER:** Arizona: Fitzgerald 1 pass from Warner (Rackers kick), 7:33. **Pittsburgh 20-14.**
Arizona: Safety (Hartwig offensive holding penalty in end zone), 2:58. **Pittsburgh 20-16.**
Arizona: Fitzgerald 64 pass from Warner (Rackers kick), 2:37. **Arizona 23-20.**
Pittsburgh: Holmes 6 pass from Roethlisberger (Reed kick), 0:35. **Pittsburgh 27-23.**

A: 70,774.

## XLIV - 2010

| | | | | |
|---|---|---|---|---|
| **New Orleans** | 0 | 6 | 10 | 15—31 |
| **Indianapolis** | 10 | 0 | 7 | 0—17 |

**FIRST QUARTER:** Indianapolis: FG Stover 38, 7:29.
**Indianapolis 3-0.**
Indianapolis: TD Garcon 19 pass from Manning (Stover kick), 0:36. **Indianapolis 10-0.**

**SECOND QUARTER:** New Orleans: FG Hartley 46, 9:34.
**Indianapolis 10-3.**
New Orleans: FG Hartley 44, 0:00.
**Indianapolis 10-6.**

## XLIV - 2010 *(Cont.)*

**THIRD QUARTER:** New Orleans: TD Thomas 16 pass from Brees (Hartley kick), 11:41.
**New Orleans 13-10.**
Indianapolis: TD Addai 4 run (Stover kick), 6:15.
**Indianapolis 17-13.**
New Orleans: FG Hartley 47, 2:01.
**Indianapolis 17-16.**

**FOURTH QUARTER:** New Orleans: TD Shockey 2 pass from Brees (Moore 2 pass from Brees for 2-pt. conversion), 5:42.
**New Orleans 24-17.**
New Orleans: TD Porter 74 interception return (Hartley kick), 3:12.
**New Orleans 31-17.**

A: 74,059.

## XLV - 2011

| | | | | |
|---|---|---|---|---|
| **Pittsburgh** | 0 | 10 | 7 | 8—25 |
| **Green Bay** | 14 | 7 | 0 | 10—31 |

**FIRST QUARTER:** Green Bay: TD Nelson 29 pass from Rodgers (Crosby kick), 3:44.
**Green Bay 7-0.**
Green Bay TD Collins 37 interception return (Crosby kick), 3:20. **Green Bay 14-0.**

**SECOND QUARTER:** Pittsburgh: FG Suisham 33, 11:08.
**Green Bay 14-3.**
Green Bay: TD Jennings 21 pass from Rodgers (Crosby kick), 2:24. **Green Bay 21-3.**
Pittsburgh: TD Ward 8 pass from Roethlisberger (Suisham kick), 0:39.
**Green Bay 21-10.**

**THIRD QUARTER:** Pittsburgh: TD Mendenhall 8 run (Suisham kick), 10:19.
**Green Bay 21-17.**

**FOURTH QUARTER:** Green Bay: TD Jennings 8 pass from Rodgers (Crosby kick), 11:57.
**Green Bay 28-17.**
Pittsburgh: TD Wallace 25 pass from Roethlisberger (Randle El 2 run for 2-pt. conversion), 7:34.
**Green Bay 28-25.**
Green Bay: FG Crosby 23, 2:07.
**Green Bay 31-25.**

A: 103,219.

### 1933
NFL championship  Chicago Bears 23, NY Giants 21

### 1934
NFL championship  NY Giants 30, Chicago Bears 13

### 1935
NFL championship  Detroit 26, NY Giants 7

### 1936
NFL championship  Green Bay 21, Boston 6

### 1937
NFL championship  Washington 28, Chicago Bears 21

### 1938
NFL championship  NY Giants 23, Green Bay 17

### 1939
NFL championship  Green Bay 27, NY Giants 0

### 1940
NFL championship  Chicago Bears 73, Washington 0

### 1941
W. div. playoff  Chicago Bears 33, Green Bay 14
NFL championship  Chicago Bears 37, NY Giants 9

### 1942
NFL championship  Washington 14, Chicago Bears 6

### 1943
E. div. playoff  Washington 28, NY Giants 0
NFL championship  Chicago Bears 41, Washington 21

### 1944
NFL championship  Green Bay 14, NY Giants 7

### 1945
NFL championship  Cleveland 15, Washington 14

### 1946
NFL championship  Chicago Bears 24, NY Giants 14

### 1947
E. div. playoff  Philadelphia 21, Pittsburgh 0
NFL championship  Chi Cardinals 28, Philadelphia 21

### 1948
NFL championship  Philadelphia 7, Chi Cardinals 0

### 1949
NFL championship  Philadelphia 14, Los Angeles 0

### 1950
Am. Conf. playoff  Cleveland 8, NY Giants 3
Nat. Conf. playoff  Los Angeles 24, Chicago Bears 14
NFL championship  Cleveland 30, Los Angeles 28

### 1951
NFL championship  Los Angeles 24, Cleveland 17

### 1952
Nat. Conf. playoff  Detroit 31, Los Angeles 21
NFL championship  Detroit 17, Cleveland 7

### 1953
NFL championship  Detroit 17, Cleveland 16

### 1954
NFL championship  Cleveland 56, Detroit 10

### 1955
NFL championship  Cleveland 38, Los Angeles 14

### 1956
NFL championship  NY Giants 47, Chicago Bears 7

### 1957
W. Conf. playoff  Detroit 31, San Francisco 27
NFL championship  Detroit 59, Cleveland 14

### 1958
E. Conf. playoff  NY Giants 10, Cleveland 0
NFL championship  Baltimore 23, NY Giants 17

### 1959
NFL championship  Baltimore 31, NY Giants 16

### 1960
NFL championship  Philadelphia 17, Green Bay 13
AFL championship  Houston 24, LA Chargers 16

### 1961
NFL championship  Green Bay 37, NY Giants 0
AFL championship  Houston 10, San Diego 3

### 1962
NFL championship  Green Bay 16, NY Giants 7
AFL championship  Dallas Texans 20, Houston 17

### 1963
NFL championship  Chicago 14, NY Giants 10
AFL E. div. playoff  Boston 26, Buffalo 8
AFL championship  San Diego 51, Boston 10

### 1964
NFL championship  Cleveland 27, Baltimore 0
AFL championship  Buffalo 20, San Diego 7

### 1965
NFL W. Conf. playoff  Green Bay 13, Baltimore 10
NFL championship  Green Bay 23, Cleveland 12
AFL championship  Buffalo 23, San Diego 0

### 1966
NFL championship  Green Bay 34, Dallas 27
AFL championship  Kansas City 31, Buffalo 7

### 1967
NFL E. Conf. championship  Dallas 52, Cleveland 14
NFL W. Conf. championship  Green Bay 28, Los Angeles 7
NFL championship  Green Bay 21, Dallas 17
AFL championship  Oakland 40, Houston 7

### 1968
NFL E. Conf. championship  Cleveland 31, Dallas 20
NFL W. Conf. championship  Baltimore 24, Minnesota 14
NFL championship  Baltimore 34, Cleveland 0
AFL W. div. playoff  Oakland 41, Kansas City 6
AFL championship  NY Jets 27, Oakland 23

### 1969
NFL E. Conf. championship  Cleveland 38, Dallas 14
NFL W. Conf. championship  Minnesota 23, Los Angeles 20
NFL championship  Minnesota 27, Cleveland 7
AFL div. playoffs  Kansas City 13, NY Jets 6
Oakland 56, Houston 7
AFL championship  Kansas City 17, Oakland 7

**1970**

| | |
|---|---|
| AFC div. playoffs | Baltimore 17, Cincinnati 0 |
| | Oakland 21, Miami 14 |
| AFC championship | Baltimore 27, Oakland 17 |
| NFC div. playoffs | Dallas 5, Detroit 0 |
| | San Francisco 17, Minnesota 14 |
| NFC championship | Dallas 17, San Francisco 10 |

**1971**

| | |
|---|---|
| AFC div. playoffs | Miami 27, Kansas City 24 |
| | Baltimore 20, Cleveland 3 |
| AFC championship | Miami 21, Baltimore 0 |
| NFC div. playoffs | Dallas 20, Minnesota 12 |
| | San Francisco 24, Washington 20 |
| NFC championship | Dallas 14, San Francisco 3 |

**1972**

| | |
|---|---|
| AFC div. playoffs | Pittsburgh 13, Oakland 7 |
| | Miami 20, Cleveland 14 |
| AFC championship | Miami 21, Pittsburgh 17 |
| NFC div. playoffs | Dallas 30, San Francisco 28 |
| | Washington 16, Green Bay 3 |
| NFC championship | Washington 26, Dallas 3 |

**1973**

| | |
|---|---|
| AFC div. playoffs | Oakland 33, Pittsburgh 14 |
| | Miami 34, Cincinnati 16 |
| AFC championship | Miami 27, Oakland 10 |
| NFC div. playoffs | Minnesota 27, Washington 20 |
| | Dallas 27, Los Angeles 16 |
| NFC championship | Minnesota 27, Dallas 10 |

**1974**

| | |
|---|---|
| AFC div. playoffs | Oakland 28, Miami 26 |
| | Pittsburgh 32, Buffalo 14 |
| AFC championship | Pittsburgh 24, Oakland 13 |
| NFC div. playoffs | Minnesota 30, St Louis 14 |
| | Los Angeles 19, Washington 10 |
| NFC championship | Minnesota 14, Los Angeles 10 |

**1975**

| | |
|---|---|
| AFC div. playoffs | Pittsburgh 28, Baltimore 10 |
| | Oakland 31, Cincinnati 28 |
| AFC championship | Pittsburgh 16, Oakland 10 |
| NFC div. playoffs | Los Angeles 35, St Louis 23 |
| | Dallas 17, Minnesota 14 |
| NFC championship | Dallas 37, Los Angeles 7 |

**1976**

| | |
|---|---|
| AFC div. playoffs | Oakland 24, New England 21 |
| | Pittsburgh 40, Baltimore 14 |
| AFC championship | Oakland 24, Pittsburgh 7 |
| NFC div. playoffs | Minnesota 35, Washington 20 |
| | Los Angeles 14, Dallas 12 |
| NFC championship | Minnesota 24, Los Angeles 13 |

**1977**

| | |
|---|---|
| AFC div. playoffs | Denver 34, Pittsburgh 21 |
| | Oakland 37, Baltimore 31 |
| AFC championship | Denver 20, Oakland 17 |
| NFC div. playoffs | Dallas 37, Chicago 7 |
| | Minnesota 14, Los Angeles 7 |
| NFC championship | Dallas 23, Minnesota 6 |

**1978**

| | |
|---|---|
| AFC 1st-rd. playoff | Houston 17, Miami 9 |
| AFC div. playoffs | Houston 31, New England 14 |
| | Pittsburgh 33, Denver 10 |
| AFC championship | Pittsburgh 34, Houston 5 |
| NFC 1st-rd. playoff | Atlanta 14, Philadelphia 13 |
| NFC div. playoffs | Dallas 27, Atlanta 20 |
| | Los Angeles 34, Minnesota 10 |
| NFC championship | Dallas 28, Los Angeles 0 |

**1979**

| | |
|---|---|
| AFC 1st-rd. playoff | Houston 13, Denver 7 |
| AFC div. playoffs | Houston 17, San Diego 14 |
| | Pittsburgh 34, Miami 14 |
| AFC championship | Pittsburgh 27, Houston 13 |
| NFC 1st-rd. playoff | Philadelphia 27, Chicago 17 |
| NFC div. playoffs | Tampa Bay 24, Philadelphia 17 |
| | Los Angeles 21, Dallas 19 |
| NFC championship | Los Angeles 9, Tampa Bay 0 |

**1980**

| | |
|---|---|
| AFC 1st-rd. playoff | Oakland 27, Houston 7 |
| AFC div. playoffs | San Diego 20, Buffalo 14 |
| | Oakland 14, Cleveland 12 |
| AFC championship | Oakland 34, San Diego 27 |
| NFC 1st-rd. playoff | Dallas 34, Los Angeles 13 |
| NFC div. playoffs | Philadelphia 31, Minnesota 16 |
| | Dallas 30, Atlanta 27 |
| NFC championship | Philadelphia 20, Dallas 7 |

**1981**

| | |
|---|---|
| AFC 1st-rd. playoff | Buffalo 31, NY Jets 27 |
| AFC div. playoffs | San Diego 41, Miami 38 |
| | Cincinnati 28, Buffalo 21 |
| AFC championship | Cincinnati 27, San Diego 7 |
| NFC 1st-rd. playoff | NY Giants 27, Philadelphia 21 |
| NFC div. playoffs | Dallas 38, Tampa Bay 0 |
| | San Francisco 38, NY Giants 24 |
| NFC championship | San Francisco 28, Dallas 27 |

**1982**

| | |
|---|---|
| AFC 1st-rd. playoffs | Miami 28, New England 13 |
| | LA Raiders 27, Cleveland 10 |
| | NY Jets 44, Cincinnati 17 |
| | San Diego 31, Pittsburgh 28 |
| AFC div. playoffs | NY Jets 17, LA Raiders 14 |
| | Miami 34, San Diego 13 |
| AFC championship | Miami 14, NY Jets 0 |
| NFC 1st-rd. playoffs | Washington 31, Detroit 7 |
| | Green Bay 41, St Louis 16 |
| | Minnesota 30, Atlanta 24 |
| | Dallas 30, Tampa Bay 17 |
| NFC div. playoffs | Washington 21, Minnesota 7 |
| | Dallas 37, Green Bay 26 |
| NFC championship | Washington 31, Dallas 17 |

**1983**

| | |
|---|---|
| AFC 1st-rd. playoff | Seattle 31, Denver 7 |
| AFC div. playoffs | Seattle 27, Miami 20 |
| | LA Raiders 38, Pittsburgh 10 |
| AFC championship | LA Raiders 30, Seattle 14 |
| NFC 1st-rd. playoff | LA Rams 24, Dallas 17 |
| NFC div. playoffs | San Francisco 24, Detroit 23 |
| | Washington 51, LA Rams 7 |
| NFC championship | Washington 24, San Francisco 21 |

**1984**

| | |
|---|---|
| AFC 1st-rd. playoff | Seattle 13, LA Raiders 7 |
| AFC div. playoffs | Miami 31, Seattle 10 |
| | Pittsburgh 24, Denver 17 |
| AFC championship | Miami 45, Pittsburgh 28 |
| NFC 1st-rd. playoff | NY Giants 16, LA Rams 13 |
| NFC div. playoffs | San Francisco 21, NY Giants 10 |
| | Chicago 23, Washington 19 |
| NFC championship | San Francisco 23, Chicago 0 |

**1985**

| | |
|---|---|
| AFC 1st-rd. playoff | New England 26, NY Jets 14 |
| AFC div. playoffs | Miami 24, Cleveland 21 |
| | New England 27, LA Raiders 20 |
| AFC championship | New England 31, Miami 14 |
| NFC 1st-rd. playoff | NY Giants 17, San Francisco 3 |
| NFC div. playoffs | LA Rams 20, Dallas 0 |
| | Chicago 21, NY Giants 0 |
| NFC championship | Chicago 24, LA Rams 0 |

## 1986

| | |
|---|---|
| AFC 1st-rd. playoff | NY Jets 35, Kansas City 15 |
| AFC div. playoffs | Cleveland 23, NY Jets 20 |
| | Denver 22, New England 17 |
| AFC championship | Denver 23, Cleveland 20 |
| NFC 1st-rd. playoff | Washington 19, LA Rams 7 |
| NFC div playoffs | Washington 27, Chicago 13 |
| | NY Giants 49, San Francisco 3 |
| NFC championship | NY Giants 17, Washington 0 |

## 1987

| | |
|---|---|
| AFC 1st-rd. playoff | Houston 23, Seattle 20 |
| AFC div. playoffs | Cleveland 38, Indianapolis 21 |
| | Denver 34, Houston 10 |
| AFC championship | Denver 38, Cleveland 33 |
| NFC 1st-rd. playoff | Minnesota 44, New Orleans 10 |
| NFC div playoffs | Minnesota 36, San Francisco 24 |
| | Washington 21, Chicago 17 |
| NFC championship | Washington 17, Minnesota 10 |

## 1988

| | |
|---|---|
| AFC 1st-rd. playoff | Houston 24, Cleveland 23 |
| AFC div. playoffs | Cincinnati 21, Seattle 13 |
| | Buffalo 17, Houston 10 |
| AFC championship | Cincinnati 21, Buffalo 10 |
| NFC 1st-rd. playoff | Minnesota 28, LA Rams 17 |
| NFC div. playoffs | Chicago 20, Philadelphia 12 |
| | San Francisco 34, Minnesota 9 |
| NFC championship | San Francisco 28, Chicago 3 |

## 1989

| | |
|---|---|
| AFC 1st-rd. playoff | Pittsburgh 26, Houston 23 |
| AFC div. playoffs | Cleveland 34, Buffalo 30 |
| | Denver 24, Pittsburgh 23 |
| AFC championship | Denver 37, Cleveland 21 |
| NFC 1st-rd. playoff | LA Rams 21, Philadelphia 7 |
| NFC div. playoffs | LA Rams 19, NY Giants 13 |
| | San Francisco 41, Minnesota 13 |
| NFC championship | San Francisco 30, LA Rams 3 |

## 1990

| | |
|---|---|
| AFC 1st-rd. playoffs | Miami 17, Kansas City 16 |
| | Cincinnati 41, Houston 14 |
| AFC div. playoffs | Buffalo 44, Miami 34 |
| | LA Raiders 20, Cincinnati 10 |
| AFC championship | Buffalo 51, LA Raiders 3 |
| NFC 1st-rd. playoffs | Chicago 16, New Orleans 6 |
| | Washington 20, Philadelphia 6 |
| NFC div. playoffs | NY Giants 31, Chicago 3 |
| | San Francisco 28, Washington 10 |
| NFC championship | NY Giants 15, San Francisco 13 |

## 1991

| | |
|---|---|
| AFC 1st-rd. playoffs | Houston 17, NY Jets 10 |
| | Kansas City 10, LA Raiders 6 |
| AFC div. playoffs | Denver 26, Houston 24 |
| | Buffalo 37, Kansas City 14 |
| AFC championship | Buffalo 10, Denver 7 |
| NFC 1st-rd. playoffs | Atlanta 27, New Orleans 20 |
| | Dallas 17, Chicago 13 |
| NFC div. playoffs | Washington 24, Atlanta 7 |
| | Detroit 38, Dallas 6 |
| NFC championship | Washington 41, Detroit 10 |

## 1992

| | |
|---|---|
| AFC 1st-rd. playoffs | San Diego 17, Kansas City 0 |
| | Buffalo 41, Houston 38 (OT) |
| AFC div. playoffs | Buffalo 24, Pittsburgh 3 |
| | Miami 31, San Diego 0 |
| AFC championship | Buffalo 29, Miami 10 |
| NFC 1st-rd. playoffs | Washington 24, Minnesota 7 |
| | Philadelphia 36, New Orleans 20 |
| NFC div. playoffs | San Francisco 20, Washington 13 |
| | Dallas 34, Philadelphia 10 |
| NFC championship | Dallas 30, San Francisco 20 |

## 1993

| | |
|---|---|
| AFC 1st-rd. playoffs | LA Raiders 42, Denver 24 |
| | Kansas City 27, Pittsburgh 24 (OT) |
| AFC div. playoffs | Buffalo 29, LA Raiders 23 |
| | Kansas City 28, Houston 20 |
| AFC championship | Buffalo 30, Kansas City 13 |
| NFC 1st-rd. playoffs | NY Giants 17, Minnesota 10 |
| | Green Bay 28, Detroit 24 |
| NFC div. playoffs | San Francisco 44, NY Giants 3 |
| | Dallas 27, Green Bay 17 |
| NFC championship | Dallas 38, San Francisco 21 |

## 1994

| | |
|---|---|
| AFC 1st-rd. playoffs | Miami 27, Kansas City 17 |
| | Cleveland 20, New England 13 |
| AFC div. playoffs | San Diego 22, Miami 21 |
| | Pittsburgh 29, Cleveland 9 |
| AFC championship | San Diego 17, Pittsburgh 13 |
| NFC 1st-rd. playoffs | Green Bay 16, Detroit 12 |
| | Chicago 35, Minnesota 18 |
| NFC div. playoffs | Dallas 35, Green Bay 9 |
| | San Francisco 44, Chicago 15 |
| NFC championship | San Francisco 38, Dallas 28 |

## 1995

| | |
|---|---|
| AFC 1st-rd. playoffs | Buffalo 37, Miami 22 |
| | Indianapolis 35, San Diego 20 |
| AFC div. playoffs | Pittsburgh 40, Buffalo 21 |
| | Indianapolis 10, Kansas City 7 |
| AFC championship | Pittsburgh 20, Indianapolis 16 |
| NFC 1st-rd. playoffs | Philadelphia 58, Detroit 37 |
| | Green Bay 37, Atlanta 20 |
| NFC div. playoffs | Dallas 30, Philadelphia 11 |
| | Green Bay 27, San Francisco 17 |
| NFC championship | Dallas 38, Green Bay 27 |

## 1996

| | |
|---|---|
| AFC 1st-rd. playoffs | Jacksonville 30, Buffalo 27 |
| | Pittsburgh 42, Indianapolis 14 |
| AFC div. playoffs | Jacksonville 30, Denver 27 |
| | New England 28, Pittsburgh 3 |
| AFC championship | New England 20, Jacksonville 6 |
| NFC 1st-rd. playoffs | Dallas 40, Minnesota 15 |
| | San Francisco 14, Philadelphia 0 |
| NFC div. playoffs | Green Bay 35, San Francisco 14 |
| | Carolina 26, Dallas 17 |
| NFC championship | Green Bay 30, Carolina 13 |

## 1997

| | |
|---|---|
| AFC 1st-rd. playoffs | Denver 42, Jacksonville 17 |
| | New England 17, Miami 3 |
| AFC div. playoffs | Denver 14, Kansas City 10 |
| | Pittsburgh 7, New England 6 |
| AFC championship | Denver 24, Pittsburgh 21 |
| NFC 1st-rd. playoffs | Minnesota 23, NY Giants 22 |
| | Tampa Bay 20, Detroit 10 |
| NFC div. playoffs | Green Bay 21, Tampa Bay 7 |
| | San Francisco 38, Minnesota 22 |
| NFC championship | Green Bay 23, San Francisco 10 |

## 1998

| | |
|---|---|
| AFC 1st-rd. playoffs | Miami 24, Buffalo 17 |
| | Jacksonville 25, New England 10 |
| AFC div. playoffs | Denver 38, Miami 3 |
| | NY Jets 34, Jacksonville 24 |
| AFC championship | Denver 23, NY Jets 10 |
| NFC 1st-rd. playoffs | Arizona 20, Dallas 7 |
| | San Francisco 30, Green Bay 27 |
| NFC div. playoffs | Atlanta 20, San Francisco 18 |
| | Minnesota 41, Arizona 21 |
| NFC championship | Atlanta 30, Minnesota 27 (OT) |

## 1999

| | |
|---|---|
| AFC 1st-rd. playoffs | Tennessee 22, Buffalo 16 |
| | Miami 20, Seattle 17 |
| AFC div. playoffs | Jacksonville 62, Miami 7 |
| | Tennessee 19, Indianapolis 16 |
| AFC championship | Tennessee 33, Jacksonville 14 |
| NFC 1st-rd. playoffs | Washington 27, Detroit 13 |
| | Minnesota 27, Dallas 10 |
| NFC div. playoffs | Tampa Bay 14, Washington 13 |
| | St Louis 49, Minnesota 37 |
| NFC championship | St Louis 11, Tampa Bay 6 |

## 2000

| | |
|---|---|
| AFC 1st-rd. playoffs | Baltimore 21, Denver 3 |
| | Miami 23, Indianapolis 17 (OT) |
| AFC div. playoffs | Baltimore 24, Tennessee 10 |
| | Oakland 27, Miami 0 |
| AFC championship | Baltimore 16, Oakland 3 |
| NFC 1st-rd. playoffs | New Orleans 31, St. Louis 28 |
| | Philadelphia 21, Tampa Bay 3 |
| NFC div. playoffs | NY Giants 20, Philadelphia 10 |
| | Minnesota 34, New Orleans 16 |
| NFC championship | NY Giants 41, Minnesota 0 |

## 2001

| | |
|---|---|
| AFC 1st-rd. playoffs | Oakland 38, NY Jets 24 |
| | Baltimore 20, Miami 3 |
| AFC div. playoffs | New England 16, Oakland 13 (OT) |
| | Pittsburgh 27, Baltimore 10 |
| AFC championship | New England 24, Pittsburgh 17 |
| NFC 1st-rd. playoffs | Philadelphia 31, Tampa Bay 9 |
| | Green Bay 25, San Francisco 15 |
| NFC div. playoffs | Philadelphia 33, Chicago 19 |
| | St. Louis 45, Green Bay 17 |
| NFC championship | St. Louis 29, Philadelphia 24 |

## 2002

| | |
|---|---|
| AFC 1st-rd. playoffs | NY Jets 41, Indianapolis 0 |
| | Pittsburgh 36, Cleveland 33 |
| AFC div. playoffs | Tennessee 34, Pittsburgh 31 (OT) |
| | Oakland 30, NY Jets 10 |
| AFC championship | Oakland 41, Tennessee 24 |
| NFC 1st-rd. playoffs | Atlanta 27, Green Bay 7 |
| | San Francisco 39, NY Giants 38 |
| NFC div. playoffs | Philadelphia 20, Atlanta 6 |
| | Tampa Bay 31, San Francisco 6 |
| NFC championship | Tampa Bay 27, Philadelphia 10 |

## 2003

| | |
|---|---|
| AFC 1st-rd. playoffs | Tennessee 20, Baltimore 17 |
| | Indianapolis 41, Denver 10 |
| AFC div. playoffs | New England 17, Tennessee 14 |
| | Indianapolis 38, Kansas City 31 |
| AFC championship | New England 24, Indianapolis 14 |
| NFC 1st-rd. playoffs | Carolina 29, Dallas 10 |
| | Green Bay 37, Seattle 31 (OT) |
| NFC div. playoffs | Carolina 29, St. Louis 23 |
| | Philadelphia 20, Green Bay 17 (OT) |
| NFC championship | Carolina 14, Philadelphia 3 |

## 2004

| | |
|---|---|
| AFC 1st-rd. playoffs | Indianapolis 49, Denver 24 |
| | NY Jets 20, San Diego 17 |
| AFC div. playoffs | New England 20, Indianapolis 3 |
| | Pittsburgh 20, NY Jets 17 |
| AFC championship | New England 41, Pittsburgh 27 |
| NFC 1st-rd. playoffs | Minnesota 31, Green Bay 17 |
| | St. Louis 27, Seattle 20 |
| NFC div. playoffs | Atlanta 47, St. Louis 17 |
| | Philadelphia 27, Minnesota 14 |
| NFC championship | Philadelphia 27, Atlanta 10 |

## 2005

| | |
|---|---|
| AFC 1st-rd. playoffs | Pittsburgh 31, Cincinnati 17 |
| | New England 28, Jacksonville 3 |
| AFC div. playoffs | Pittsburgh 21, Indianapolis 18 |
| | Denver 27, New England 13 |
| AFC championship | Pittsburgh 34, Denver 17 |
| NFC 1st-rd. playoffs | Washington 17, Tampa Bay 10 |
| | Carolina 23, NY Giants 0 |
| NFC div. playoffs | Seattle 20, Washington 10 |
| | Carolina 29, Chicago 21 |
| NFC championship | Seattle 34, Carolina 14 |

## 2006

| | |
|---|---|
| AFC 1st-rd. playoffs | Indianapolis 23, Kansas City 8 |
| | New England 37, NY Jets 16 |
| AFC div. playoffs | Indianapolis 15, Baltimore 6 |
| | New England 24, San Diego 21 |
| AFC championship | Indianapolis 38, New England 34 |
| NFC 1st-rd. playoffs | Seattle 21, Dallas 20 |
| | Philadelphia 23, NY Giants 20 |
| NFC div. playoffs | Chicago 27, Seattle 24 |
| | New Orleans 27, Philadelphia 24 |
| NFC championship | Chicago 39, New Orleans 14 |

## 2007

| | |
|---|---|
| AFC 1st-rd. playoffs | Jacksonville 31, Pittsburgh 29 |
| | San Diego 17, Tennessee 6 |
| AFC Div. Playoffs | New England 31, Jacksonville 20 |
| | San Diego 28, Indianapolis 24 |
| AFC Championship | New England 21, San Diego 12 |
| NFC 1st-rd. playoffs | Seattle 35, Washington 14 |
| | NY Giants 24, Tampa Bay 14 |
| NFC Div. Playoffs | NY Giants 21, Dallas 17 |
| | Green Bay 42, Seattle 20 |
| NFC Championship | NY Giants 23, Green Bay 20 (OT) |

## 2008

| | |
|---|---|
| AFC 1st-rd. playoffs | Baltimore 27, Miami 9 |
| | San Diego 23, Indianapolis 17 (OT) |
| AFC Div. Playoffs | Baltimore 13, Tennessee 10 |
| | Pittsburgh 35, San Diego 24 |
| AFC Championship | Pittsburgh 23, Baltimore 14 |
| NFC 1st-rd. playoffs | Philadelphia 26, Minnesota 14 |
| | Arizona 30, Atlanta 24 |
| NFC Div. Playoffs | Philadelphia 23, NY Giants 11 |
| | Arizona 33, Carolina 13 |
| NFC Championship | Arizona 32, Philadelphia 25 |

## 2009

| | |
|---|---|
| AFC 1st-rd. playoffs | NY Jets 24, Cincinnati 14 |
| | Baltimore 33, New England 14 |
| AFC Div. Playoffs | NY Jets 17, San Diego 14 |
| | Indianapolis 20, Baltimore 3 |
| AFC Championship | Indianapolis 30, NY Jets 17 |
| NFC 1st-rd. playoffs | Dallas 34, Philadelphia 14 |
| | Arizona 51, Green Bay 45 (OT) |
| NFC Div. Playoffs | Minnesota 34, Dallas 3 |
| | New Orleans 45, Arizona 14 |
| NFC Championship | New Orleans 31, Minnesota 28 (OT) |

## 2010

| | |
|---|---|
| AFC 1st-rd. playoffs | NY Jets 17, Indianapolis 16 |
| | Baltimore 30, Kansas City 17 |
| AFC Div. Playoffs | NY Jets 28, New England 21 |
| | Pittsburgh 31, Baltimore 24 |
| AFC Championship | Pittsburgh 24, NY Jets 19 |
| NFC 1st-rd. playoffs | Seattle 41, New Orleans 36 |
| | Green Bay 21, Philadelphia 16 |
| NFC Div. Playoffs | Chicago 35, Seattle 24 |
| | Green Bay 48, Atlanta 21 |
| NFC Championship | Green Bay 21, Chicago 14 |

## Career Leaders

### Scoring

| | Yrs | TD | FG | PAT | Pts |
|---|---|---|---|---|---|
| Morten Andersen | 25 | 0 | 565 | 849 | 2,544 |
| Gary Anderson | 23 | 0 | 538 | 820 | 2,434 |
| †John Carney | 23 | 0 | 478 | 628 | 2,062 |
| Matt Stover | 20 | 0 | 471 | 591 | 2,004 |
| George Blanda | 26 | 9 | 335 | 943 | 2,002 |
| Jason Elam | 17 | 0 | 436 | 675 | 1,983 |
| †Jason Hanson | 19 | 0 | 439 | 573 | 1,890 |
| †John Kasay | 20 | 0 | 433 | 524 | 1,823 |
| Norm Johnson | 18 | 0 | 366 | 638 | 1,736 |
| Nick Lowery | 18 | 0 | 383 | 562 | 1,711 |
| Jan Stenerud | 19 | 0 | 373 | 580 | 1,699 |
| †Adam Vinatieri | 15 | 0 | 364 | 565 | 1,659 |
| Lou Groza | 21 | 1 | 264 | 810 | 1,608 |
| Eddie Murray | 19 | 0 | 352 | 538 | 1,594 |
| Al Del Greco | 17 | 0 | 347 | 543 | 1,584 |
| †Ryan Longwell | 14 | 0 | 339 | 566 | 1,583 |
| Steve Christie | 15 | 0 | 336 | 468 | 1,476 |
| Pat Leahy | 18 | 0 | 304 | 558 | 1,470 |
| Jim Turner | 16 | 0 | 304 | 521 | 1,439 |
| Matt Bahr | 17 | 0 | 300 | 522 | 1,422 |

### Rushing

| | Yrs | Att | Yds | Avg | Lg | TD |
|---|---|---|---|---|---|---|
| Emmitt Smith | 15 | 4,409 | 18,355 | 4.2 | 75 | 164 |
| Walter Payton | 13 | 3,838 | 16,726 | 4.4 | 76 | 110 |
| Barry Sanders | 10 | 3,062 | 15,269 | 5.0 | 85 | 99 |
| Curtis Martin | 11 | 3,518 | 14,101 | 4.0 | 70 | 90 |
| Jerome Bettis | 13 | 3,479 | 13,662 | 3.9 | 71 | 91 |
| †LaD. Tomlinson | 10 | 3,099 | 13,404 | 4.3 | 85 | 144 |
| Eric Dickerson | 11 | 2,996 | 13,259 | 4.4 | 85 | 90 |
| Tony Dorsett | 12 | 2,936 | 12,739 | 4.3 | 99 | 77 |
| Jim Brown | 9 | 2,359 | 12,312 | 5.2 | 80 | 106 |
| Marshall Faulk | 12 | 2,836 | 12,279 | 4.3 | 71 | 100 |
| Edgerrin James | 11 | 3,028 | 12,246 | 4.0 | 72 | 80 |
| Marcus Allen | 16 | 3,022 | 12,243 | 4.1 | 61 | 123 |
| Franco Harris | 13 | 2,949 | 12,120 | 4.1 | 75 | 91 |
| Thurman Thomas | 13 | 2,877 | 12,074 | 4.2 | 80 | 66 |
| †Fred Taylor | 13 | 2,534 | 11,695 | 4.6 | 80 | 66 |
| John Riggins | 14 | 2,916 | 11,352 | 3.9 | 66 | 104 |
| Corey Dillon | 10 | 2,618 | 11,241 | 4.3 | 96 | 82 |
| O.J. Simpson | 11 | 2,404 | 11,236 | 4.7 | 94 | 61 |
| Warrick Dunn | 12 | 2,669 | 10,967 | 4.1 | 90 | 49 |
| Ricky Watters | 10 | 2,622 | 10,643 | 4.1 | 57 | 78 |

## Touchdowns

| | Yrs | Rush | Rec | Ret | Total TD |
|---|---|---|---|---|---|
| Jerry Rice | 20 | 10 | 197 | 1 | 208 |
| Emmitt Smith | 15 | 164 | 11 | 0 | 175 |
| †LaDainian Tomlinson | 10 | 144 | 15 | 0 | 159 |
| †Terrell Owens | 15 | 3 | 153 | 0 | 156 |
| †Randy Moss | 13 | 0 | 153 | 1 | 154 |
| Marcus Allen | 16 | 123 | 21 | 1 | 145 |
| Marshall Faulk | 12 | 100 | 36 | 0 | 136 |
| Cris Carter | 16 | 0 | 130 | 1 | 131 |
| Marvin Harrison | 13 | 0 | 128 | 0 | 128 |
| Jim Brown | 9 | 106 | 20 | 0 | 126 |

| | Yrs | Rush | Rec | Ret | Total TD |
|---|---|---|---|---|---|
| Walter Payton | 13 | 110 | 15 | 0 | 125 |
| John Riggins | 14 | 104 | 12 | 0 | 116 |
| Lenny Moore | 12 | 63 | 48 | 2 | 113 |
| Shaun Alexander | 9 | 100 | 12 | 0 | 112 |
| Barry Sanders | 10 | 99 | 10 | 0 | 109 |
| Tim Brown | 17 | 1 | 100 | 4 | 105 |
| Don Hutson | 11 | 3 | 99 | 3 | 105 |
| Steve Largent | 14 | 1 | 100 | 0 | 101 |
| Curtis Martin | 12 | 90 | 10 | 0 | 100 |
| Franco Harris | 13 | 91 | 9 | 0 | 100 |

## Combined Yards Gained

| | Yrs | Total | Rush | Rec | Int Ret | Punt Ret | Kickoff Ret | Fum Ret |
|---|---|---|---|---|---|---|---|---|
| Jerry Rice | 20 | 23,546 | 645 | 22,895 | 0 | 0 | 6 | 0 |
| Brian Mitchell | 14 | 23,330 | 1,967 | 2,336 | 0 | 4,999 | 14,014 | 14 |
| Walter Payton | 13 | 21,803 | 16,726 | 4,538 | 0 | 0 | 539 | 0 |
| Emmitt Smith | 15 | 21,583 | 18,355 | 3,224 | 0 | 0 | 0 | 4 |
| Tim Brown | 17 | 19,682 | 190 | 14,934 | 0 | 3,320 | 1,235 | 3 |
| Marshall Faulk | 12 | 19,154 | 12,279 | 6,875 | 0 | 0 | 18 | 18 |
| Barry Sanders | 10 | 18,308 | 15,269 | 2,921 | 0 | 0 | 118 | 0 |
| Herschel Walker | 12 | 18,168 | 8,225 | 4,859 | 0 | 0 | 5,084 | 0 |
| †LaDainian Tomlinson | 10 | 17,727 | 13,404 | 4,323 | 0 | 0 | 0 | 0 |
| Marcus Allen | 16 | 17,654 | 12,243 | 5,411 | 0 | 0 | 0 | 0 |
| Curtis Martin | 11 | 17,430 | 14,101 | 3,329 | 0 | 0 | 0 | 0 |
| Tiki Barber | 10 | 17,359 | 10,449 | 5,183 | 0 | 1,181 | 544 | 2 |
| Eric Metcalf | 13 | 17,230 | 2,392 | 5,572 | 0 | 3,453 | 5,813 | 0 |
| †Derrick Mason | 14 | 16,980 | 3 | 11,891 | 0 | 1,590 | 3,496 | 0 |
| Thurman Thomas | 13 | 16,532 | 12,074 | 4,458 | 0 | 0 | 0 | 0 |
| Tony Dorsett | 12 | 16,293 | 12,739 | 3,554 | 0 | 0 | 0 | 0 |
| †Terrell Owens | 15 | 16,263 | 251 | 15,934 | 0 | 0 | 78 | 0 |
| Henry Ellard | 16 | 15,718 | 50 | 13,777 | 0 | 1,527 | 364 | 0 |
| Edgerrin James | 11 | 15,610 | 12,246 | 3,364 | 0 | 0 | 0 | 0 |
| Irving Fryar | 17 | 15,587 | 242 | 12,785 | 0 | 2,055 | 505 | 0 |

†–Active in 2010.

## Career Leaders (Cont.)
### Passing
### PASSER RATING*

| | Yrs | Att | Comp | Pct Comp | Yds | Avg Gain | TD | Pct TD | Int | Pct Int | Rating Pts |
|---|---|---|---|---|---|---|---|---|---|---|---|
| †Aaron Rodgers | 6 | 1,611 | 1,038 | 64.4 | 12,723 | 7.9 | 87 | 5.4 | 32 | 2.0 | 98.4 |
| †Philip Rivers | 7 | 2,455 | 1,564 | 63.7 | 19,661 | 8.0 | 136 | 5.5 | 58 | 2.4 | 97.2 |
| Steve Young | 15 | 4,149 | 2,667 | 64.3 | 33,124 | 8.0 | 232 | 5.6 | 107 | 2.6 | 96.8 |
| †Tony Romo | 7 | 2,070 | 1,326 | 64.1 | 16,650 | 8.0 | 118 | 5.7 | 62 | 3.0 | 95.5 |
| †Tom Brady | 11 | 4,710 | 2,996 | 63.6 | 34,744 | 7.4 | 261 | 5.5 | 103 | 2.2 | 95.2 |
| †Peyton Manning | 13 | 7,210 | 4,682 | 64.9 | 54,828 | 7.6 | 399 | 5.5 | 198 | 2.7 | 94.9 |
| Kurt Warner | 12 | 4,070 | 2,666 | 65.5 | 32,344 | 7.9 | 208 | 5.1 | 128 | 3.1 | 93.7 |
| †Ben Roethlisberger | 7 | 2,800 | 1,766 | 63.1 | 22,502 | 8.0 | 144 | 5.1 | 86 | 3.1 | 92.5 |
| Joe Montana | 15 | 5,391 | 3,409 | 63.2 | 40,551 | 7.5 | 273 | 5.2 | 139 | 2.6 | 92.3 |
| †Drew Brees | 10 | 4,822 | 3,145 | 65.2 | 35,266 | 7.3 | 235 | 4.9 | 132 | 2.7 | 91.7 |
| †Matt Schaub | 7 | 1,987 | 1,288 | 64.8 | 15,457 | 7.8 | 83 | 4.2 | 52 | 2.6 | 91.5 |
| †Chad Pennington | 11 | 2,471 | 1,632 | 66.0 | 17,823 | 7.2 | 102 | 4.1 | 64 | 2.6 | 90.1 |
| Daunte Culpepper | 11 | 3,199 | 2,016 | 63.0 | 24,123 | 7.6 | 149 | 4.7 | 106 | 3.3 | 87.8 |
| Jeff Garcia | 11 | 3,676 | 2,264 | 61.6 | 25,537 | 6.9 | 161 | 4.4 | 83 | 2.3 | 87.5 |
| †Carson Palmer | 7 | 3,217 | 2,024 | 62.9 | 22,694 | 7.1 | 154 | 4.8 | 100 | 3.1 | 86.9 |
| Otto Graham | 10 | 2,626 | 1,464 | 55.8 | 23,584 | 9.0 | 174 | 6.6 | 135 | 5.1 | 86.6 |
| Dan Marino | 17 | 8,358 | 4,967 | 59.4 | 61,361 | 7.3 | 420 | 5.0 | 252 | 3.0 | 86.4 |
| †Brett Favre | 20 | 10,169 | 6,300 | 62.0 | 71,838 | 7.1 | 508 | 5.0 | 336 | 3.3 | 86.0 |
| Trent Green | 11 | 3,740 | 2,266 | 60.6 | 28,475 | 7.6 | 162 | 4.3 | 114 | 3.0 | 86.0 |
| †David Garrard | 9 | 2,281 | 1,406 | 61.6 | 16,003 | 7.0 | 89 | 3.9 | 54 | 2.4 | 85.8 |
| †Donovan McNabb | 12 | 5,218 | 3,076 | 58.9 | 36,250 | 6.9 | 230 | 4.4 | 115 | 2.2 | 85.7 |
| Rich Gannon | 18 | 4,206 | 2,533 | 60.2 | 28,743 | 6.8 | 180 | 4.3 | 104 | 2.3 | 84.7 |
| Marc Bulger | 9 | 3,171 | 1,969 | 62.1 | 22,814 | 7.2 | 122 | 3.8 | 93 | 2.9 | 84.4 |
| Jim Kelly | 11 | 4,779 | 2,874 | 60.1 | 35,467 | 7.4 | 237 | 5.0 | 175 | 3.7 | 84.4 |

*1,500 or more attempts. The passer ratings are based on performance standards established for completion percentage, interception percentage, touchdown percentage and average gain. Passers are allocated points according to how their marks compare with those standards.

### PASSING YARDS

| | Yrs | Att | Comp | Pct Comp | Yds |
|---|---|---|---|---|---|
| †Brett Favre | 20 | 10,169 | 6,300 | 62.0 | 71,838 |
| Dan Marino | 17 | 8,358 | 4,967 | 59.4 | 61,361 |
| †Peyton Manning | 13 | 7,210 | 4,682 | 64.9 | 54,828 |
| John Elway | 16 | 7,250 | 4,123 | 56.9 | 51,475 |
| Warren Moon | 17 | 6,823 | 3,988 | 58.5 | 49,325 |
| Fran Tarkenton | 18 | 6,467 | 3,686 | 57.0 | 47,003 |
| Vinny Testaverde | 21 | 6,701 | 3,787 | 56.5 | 46,233 |
| Drew Bledsoe | 14 | 6,717 | 3,839 | 57.2 | 44,611 |
| Dan Fouts | 15 | 5,604 | 3,297 | 58.8 | 43,040 |
| Joe Montana | 15 | 5,391 | 3,409 | 63.2 | 40,551 |
| †Kerry Collins | 16 | 6,163 | 3,439 | 55.8 | 40,441 |
| Johnny Unitas | 18 | 5,186 | 2,830 | 54.6 | 40,239 |

| | Yrs | Att | Comp | Pct Comp | Yds |
|---|---|---|---|---|---|
| Dave Krieg | 19 | 5,311 | 3,105 | 58.5 | 38,147 |
| Boomer Esiason | 14 | 5,205 | 2,969 | 57.0 | 37,920 |
| †Donovan McNabb | 12 | 5,218 | 3,076 | 58.9 | 36,250 |
| Jim Kelly | 11 | 4,779 | 2,874 | 60.1 | 35,467 |
| †Drew Brees | 10 | 4,822 | 3,145 | 65.2 | 35,266 |
| Jim Everett | 12 | 4,923 | 2,841 | 57.7 | 34,837 |
| †Tom Brady | 11 | 4,710 | 2,996 | 63.6 | 34,744 |
| Jim Hart | 19 | 5,076 | 2,593 | 51.1 | 34,665 |
| Steve DeBerg | 17 | 4,746 | 2,924 | 61.6 | 34,241 |
| John Hadl | 16 | 4,687 | 2,363 | 50.4 | 33,503 |
| Phil Simms | 14 | 4,647 | 2,576 | 55.4 | 33,462 |
| Steve Young | 15 | 4,149 | 2,667 | 64.3 | 33,124 |

### PASSING TOUCHDOWNS

| | No. |
|---|---|
| †Brett Favre | 508 |
| Dan Marino | 420 |
| †Peyton Manning | 399 |
| Fran Tarkenton | 342 |
| John Elway | 300 |
| Warren Moon | 291 |
| Johnny Unitas | 290 |
| Vinny Testaverde | 275 |
| Joe Montana | 273 |
| †Tom Brady | 261 |
| Dave Krieg | 261 |

| | No. |
|---|---|
| Sonny Jurgensen | 255 |
| Dan Fouts | 254 |
| Drew Bledsoe | 251 |
| Boomer Esiason | 247 |
| John Hadl | 244 |
| *Y.A. Tittle | 242 |
| Len Dawson | 239 |
| Jim Kelly | 237 |
| George Blanda | 236 |
| †Drew Brees | 235 |
| Steve Young | 232 |

| | No. |
|---|---|
| †Donovan McNabb | 230 |
| John Brodie | 214 |
| Terry Bradshaw | 212 |
| Jim Hart | 209 |
| Kurt Warner | 208 |
| Randall Cunningham | 207 |
| †Kerry Collins | 206 |
| Jim Everett | 203 |
| Roman Gabriel | 201 |
| Phil Simms | 199 |
| Ken Anderson | 197 |

* Includes 30TDs with Baltimore Colts (1948–49) in All-American Football Conference.

† Active in 2010.

## Career Leaders *(Cont.)*

### Receiving

#### RECEPTIONS

| | Yrs | No. | Yds | Avg | Lg | TD | | Yrs | No. | Yds | Avg | Lg | TD |
|---|---|---|---|---|---|---|---|---|---|---|---|---|---|
| Jerry Rice | 20 | 1,549 | 22,895 | 14.8 | 96 | 197 | Muhsin Muhammad | 14 | 860 | 11,438 | 13.3 | 72 | 62 |
| Marvin Harrison | 12 | 1,102 | 14,580 | 13.2 | 80 | 128 | Irving Fryar | 17 | 851 | 12,785 | 15.0 | 80 | 84 |
| Cris Carter | 16 | 1,101 | 13,899 | 12.6 | 80 | 130 | Rod Smith | 12 | 849 | 11,389 | 13.4 | 85 | 68 |
| Tim Brown | 17 | 1,094 | 14,934 | 13.7 | 80 | 100 | Larry Centers | 14 | 827 | 6,797 | 8.2 | 54 | 28 |
| †Terrell Owens | 15 | 1,078 | 15,934 | 14.8 | 98 | 153 | Steve Largent | 14 | 819 | 13,089 | 16.0 | 74 | 100 |
| †Tony Gonzalez | 14 | 1,069 | 12,463 | 11.7 | 73 | 88 | Shannon Sharpe | 15 | 815 | 10,060 | 12.3 | 82 | 62 |
| Isaac Bruce | 16 | 1,024 | 15,208 | 14.9 | 80 | 91 | Henry Ellard | 16 | 814 | 13,777 | 16.9 | 81 | 65 |
| †Randy Moss | 13 | 954 | 14,858 | 15.6 | 82 | 153 | Keyshawn Johnson | 11 | 814 | 10,571 | 13.0 | 76 | 64 |
| †Hines Ward | 13 | 954 | 11,702 | 12.3 | 85 | 83 | †Reggie Wayne | 10 | 787 | 10,748 | 13.7 | 71 | 69 |
| Andre Reed | 16 | 951 | 13,198 | 13.9 | 83 | 87 | Marshall Faulk | 11 | 767 | 6,875 | 9.0 | 85 | 36 |
| Art Monk | 16 | 940 | 12,721 | 13.5 | 79 | 68 | James Lofton | 16 | 764 | 14,004 | 18.3 | 80 | 75 |
| †Derrick Mason | 14 | 924 | 11,891 | 12.9 | 79 | 66 | Eric Moulds | 12 | 764 | 9,995 | 13.1 | 84 | 49 |
| Torry Holt | 11 | 920 | 13,382 | 14.5 | 85 | 74 | †Chad Ochocinco | 10 | 751 | 10,783 | 14.4 | 82 | 66 |
| Keenan McCardell | 17 | 883 | 11,373 | 12.9 | 76 | 63 | Michael Irvin | 12 | 750 | 11,904 | 15.9 | 87 | 65 |
| Jimmy Smith | 13 | 862 | 12,287 | 14.3 | 75 | 67 | Charlie Joiner | 18 | 750 | 12,146 | 16.2 | 87 | 65 |

#### YARDS

| | | | |
|---|---|---|---|
| Jerry Rice | 22,895 | Henry Ellard | 13,777 | Charlie Joiner | 12,146 |
| †Terrell Owens | 15,934 | Torry Holt | 13,382 | Michael Irvin | 11,904 |
| Isaac Bruce | 15,208 | Andre Reed | 13,198 | †Derrick Mason | 11,891 |
| Tim Brown | 14,934 | Steve Largent | 13,089 | Don Maynard | 11,834 |
| †Randy Moss | 14,858 | Irving Fryar | 12,785 | †Hines Ward | 11,702 |
| Marvin Harrison | 14,580 | Art Monk | 12,721 | Muhsin Muhammad | 11,438 |
| James Lofton | 14,004 | †Tony Gonzalez | 12,463 | Rod Smith | 11,389 |
| Cris Carter | 13,899 | Jimmy Smith | 12,287 | Keenan McCardell | 11,373 |

### Sacks

| | | | |
|---|---|---|---|
| Bruce Smith | 200.0 | John Randle | 137.5 |
| Reggie White | 198.0 | Richard Dent | 137.5 |
| Kevin Greene | 160.0 | Leslie O'Neal | 132.5 |
| Chris Doleman | 150.5 | †Jason Taylor | 132.5 |
| Michael Strahan | 141.5 | Lawrence Taylor | 132.5 |

Note: Stat officially compiled since 1982.

### Interceptions

| | Yrs | No. | Yds | Avg | Lg | TD |
|---|---|---|---|---|---|---|
| Paul Krause | 16 | 81 | 1,185 | 14.6 | 81 | 3 |
| Emlen Tunnell | 14 | 79 | 1,282 | 16.2 | 55 | 4 |
| Rod Woodson | 17 | 71 | 1,483 | 20.9 | 98 | 12 |
| Dick (Night Train) Lane | 14 | 68 | 1,207 | 17.8 | 80 | 5 |
| Ken Riley | 15 | 65 | 596 | 9.2 | 66 | 5 |
| Ronnie Lott | 14 | 63 | 730 | 8.5 | 63 | 5 |
| †Darren Sharper | 14 | 63 | 1,412 | 22.4 | 99 | 11 |
| Dick LeBeau | 14 | 62 | 762 | 12.3 | 70 | 3 |
| Dave Brown | 15 | 62 | 698 | 11.3 | 90 | 5 |
| Emmitt Thomas | 13 | 58 | 937 | 16.2 | 73 | 5 |

### Punting

| | Yrs | No. | Yds | Avg | Lg | Blk |
|---|---|---|---|---|---|---|
| †Shane Lechler | 11 | 855 | 40,429 | 47.3 | 73 | 3 |
| †Donnie Jones | 7 | 543 | 24,727 | 45.5 | 80 | 2 |
| †Mat McBriar | 7 | 436 | 19,827 | 45.5 | 75 | 2 |
| Sammy Baugh | 16 | 338 | 15,245 | 45.1 | 85 | 9 |
| †Andy Lee | 7 | 645 | 29,099 | 45.1 | 82 | 2 |
| †Brandon Fields | 4 | 299 | 13,417 | 44.9 | 71 | 2 |
| Tommy Davis | 11 | 511 | 22,833 | 44.7 | 82 | 2 |
| †Jon Ryan | 5 | 388 | 17,282 | 44.5 | 72 | 3 |
| †Mike Scifres | 8 | 445 | 19,810 | 44.5 | 71 | 5 |
| Yale Lary | 11 | 503 | 22,279 | 44.3 | 73 | 4 |

Note: 250 or more punts.

† Active in 2010.

### Punt Returns

| | Yrs | No. | Yds | Avg | Lg | TD |
|---|---|---|---|---|---|---|
| George McAfee | 8 | 112 | 1,431 | 12.8 | 74 | 2 |
| Jack Christiansen | 8 | 85 | 1,084 | 12.8 | 89 | 8 |
| Claude Gibson | 5 | 110 | 1,381 | 12.6 | 85 | 3 |
| †Devin Hester | 5 | 178 | 2,200 | 12.4 | 89 | 10 |
| Bill Dudley | 9 | 124 | 1,515 | 12.2 | 96 | 3 |
| Rick Upchurch | 9 | 248 | 3,008 | 12.1 | 92 | 8 |
| †Roscoe Parrish | 6 | 130 | 1,576 | 12.1 | 82 | 3 |
| Desmond Howard | 11 | 244 | 2,895 | 11.9 | 95 | 8 |
| Billy Johnson | 14 | 282 | 3,317 | 11.8 | 87 | 6 |
| Mack Herron | 3 | 84 | 982 | 11.7 | 66 | 0 |

Note: 75 or more returns.

### Kickoff Returns

| | Yrs | No. | Yds | Avg | Lg | TD |
|---|---|---|---|---|---|---|
| Gale Sayers | 7 | 91 | 2,781 | 30.6 | 103 | 6 |
| Lynn Chandnois | 7 | 92 | 2,720 | 29.6 | 93 | 3 |
| Abe Woodson | 9 | 193 | 5,538 | 28.7 | 105 | 5 |
| Claude (Buddy) Young | 6 | 90 | 2,514 | 27.9 | 104 | 2 |
| Travis Williams | 5 | 102 | 2,801 | 27.5 | 105 | 6 |
| Joe Arenas | 7 | 139 | 3,798 | 27.3 | 96 | 1 |
| †Clifton Smith | 3 | 75 | 2,038 | 27.2 | 97 | 1 |
| Clarence Davis | 7 | 79 | 2,140 | 27.1 | 76 | 0 |
| †Danieal Manning | 5 | 101 | 2,711 | 26.8 | 83 | 1 |
| Steve Van Buren | 7 | 76 | 2,030 | 26.7 | 98 | 3 |
| Lenny Lyles | 12 | 81 | 2,161 | 26.7 | 103 | 3 |

Note: 75 or more returns.

## Single-Season Leaders

### Scoring

#### POINTS

| | Year | TD | PAT | FG | Pts |
|---|---|---|---|---|---|
| †LaDainian Tomlinson,SD | 2006 | 31 | 0 | 0 | 186 |
| Paul Hornung, GB | 1960 | 15 | 41 | 15 | 176 |
| Shaun Alexander, Sea | 2005 | 28 | 0 | 0 | 168 |
| Gary Anderson, Min | 1998 | 0 | 59 | 35 | 164 |
| Jeff Wilkins, StL | 2003 | 0 | 46 | 39 | 163 |
| Priest Holmes, KC | 2003 | 27 | 0 | 0 | 162 |
| Mark Moseley, Was | 1983 | 0 | 62 | 33 | 161 |
| Marshall Faulk, StL | 2000 | 26 | 2 | 0 | 160 |
| Mike Vanderjagt, Ind | 2003 | 0 | 46 | 37 | 157 |
| Gino Cappelletti, Bos | 1964 | 7 | 37 | 25 | 155 |
| Emmitt Smith, Dal | 1995 | 25 | 0 | 0 | 150 |
| Chip Lohmiller, Was | 1991 | 0 | 56 | 31 | 149 |
| †Stephen Gostkowski, NE | 2008 | 0 | 40 | 36 | 148 |
| †Jay Feely, NYG | 2005 | 0 | 43 | 35 | 148 |
| Gino Cappelletti, Bos | 1961 | 8 | 48 | 17 | 147 |

Note: Faulk's and Cappelletti's totals include two-point conversions.

#### TOUCHDOWNS

| | Year | Rush | Rec | Ret | Total |
|---|---|---|---|---|---|
| †LaDainian Tomlinson, SD | 2006 | 28 | 3 | 0 | 31 |
| Shaun Alexander, Sea | 2005 | 27 | 1 | 0 | 28 |
| Priest Holmes, KC | 2003 | 27 | 0 | 0 | 27 |
| Marshall Faulk, StL | 2000 | 18 | 8 | 0 | 26 |
| Emmitt Smith, Dal | 1995 | 25 | 0 | 0 | 25 |
| Priest Holmes, KC | 2002 | 21 | 3 | 0 | 24 |
| John Riggins, Was | 1983 | 24 | 0 | 0 | 24 |
| †Randy Moss, NE | 2007 | 0 | 0 | 23 | 23 |
| Terrell Davis, Den | 1998 | 21 | 2 | 0 | 23 |
| Jerry Rice, SF | 1987 | 1 | 22 | 0 | 23 |
| O.J. Simpson, Buf | 1975 | 16 | 7 | 0 | 23 |

#### FIELD GOALS

| | Year | FGA | FGM |
|---|---|---|---|
| †Neil Rackers, Ari | 2005 | 42 | 40 |
| Jeff Wilkins, StL | 2003 | 42 | 39 |
| †Olindo Mare, Mia | 1999 | 46 | 39 |
| Mike Vanderjagt, Ind | 2003 | 37 | 37 |
| †John Kasay, Car | 1996 | 45 | 37 |
| †Stephen Gostkowski, NE | 2008 | 40 | 36 |
| Al Del Greco, Ten | 1998 | 39 | 36 |
| Cary Blanchard, Ind | 1996 | 40 | 36 |

### Rushing

#### YARDS GAINED

| | Year | Att | Yds | Avg |
|---|---|---|---|---|
| Eric Dickerson, LA Rams | 1984 | 379 | 2,105 | 5.6 |
| Jamal Lewis, Bal | 2003 | 387 | 2,066 | 5.3 |
| Barry Sanders, Det | 1997 | 335 | 2,053 | 6.1 |
| Terrell Davis, Den | 1998 | 392 | 2,008 | 5.1 |
| †Chris Johnson, Ten | 2009 | 358 | 2,006 | 5.6 |
| O.J. Simpson, Buf | 1973 | 332 | 2,003 | 6.0 |
| Earl Campbell, Hou | 1980 | 373 | 1,934 | 5.2 |
| Ahman Green, GB | 2003 | 355 | 1,883 | 5.3 |
| Barry Sanders, Det | 1994 | 331 | 1,883 | 5.7 |
| Shaun Alexander, Sea | 2005 | 370 | 1,880 | 5.1 |
| Jim Brown, Cle | 1963 | 291 | 1,863 | 6.4 |
| Tiki Barber, NYG | 2005 | 357 | 1,860 | 5.2 |
| †Ricky Williams, Mia | 2002 | 383 | 1,853 | 4.8 |
| Walter Payton, Chi | 1977 | 339 | 1,852 | 5.5 |
| Jamal Anderson, Atl | 1998 | 410 | 1,846 | 4.5 |
| Eric Dickerson, LA Rams | 1986 | 404 | 1,821 | 4.5 |
| O.J. Simpson, Buf | 1975 | 329 | 1,817 | 5.5 |
| †LaDainian Tomlinson, SD | 2006 | 348 | 1,815 | 5.2 |
| Eric Dickerson, LA Rams | 1983 | 390 | 1,808 | 4.6 |

#### AVERAGE GAIN

| | Year | Avg |
|---|---|---|
| †Michael Vick, Atl | 2006 | 8.45 |
| Beattie Feathers, Chi | 1934 | 8.44 |
| Randall Cunningham, Phi | 1990 | 7.98 |
| †Michael Vick, Atl | 2004 | 7.50 |
| †Michael Vick, Atl | 2002 | 6.88 |

Minimum 100 attempts.

#### TOUCHDOWNS

| | Year | No. |
|---|---|---|
| †LaDainian Tomlinson, SD | 2006 | 28 |
| Shaun Alexander, Sea | 2005 | 27 |
| Priest Holmes, KC | 2003 | 27 |
| Emmitt Smith, Dal | 1995 | 25 |
| John Riggins, Was | 1983 | 24 |
| Priest Holmes, KC | 2002 | 21 |
| Terrell Davis, Den | 1998 | 21 |
| Terry Allen, Wash | 1996 | 21 |
| Emmitt Smith, Dal | 1994 | 21 |
| Joe Morris, NYG | 1985 | 21 |

### Passing

#### YARDS GAINED

| | Year | Att | Comp | Pct | Yds |
|---|---|---|---|---|---|
| Dan Marino, Mia | 1984 | 564 | 362 | 64.2 | 5,084 |
| †Drew Brees, NO | 2008 | 635 | 413 | 65.0 | 5,069 |
| Kurt Warner, StL Rams | 2001 | 546 | 375 | 68.7 | 4,830 |
| †Tom Brady, NE | 2007 | 578 | 398 | 68.9 | 4,806 |
| Dan Fouts, SD | 1981 | 609 | 360 | 59.1 | 4,802 |
| †Matt Schaub, Hou | 2009 | 583 | 396 | 67.9 | 4,770 |
| Dan Marino, Mia | 1986 | 623 | 378 | 60.7 | 4,746 |
| D. Culpepper, Min | 2004 | 548 | 379 | 69.2 | 4,717 |
| Dan Fouts, SD | 1980 | 589 | 348 | 59.1 | 4,715 |
| †Philip Rivers, SD | 2010 | 541 | 357 | 66.0 | 4,710 |
| †Peyton Manning, Ind. | 2010 | 679 | 450 | 66.3 | 4,700 |
| Warren Moon, Hou | 1991 | 655 | 404 | 61.7 | 4,690 |
| Rich Gannon, Oak | 2002 | 618 | 418 | 67.6 | 4,689 |
| Warren Moon, Hou | 1990 | 584 | 362 | 62.0 | 4,689 |
| †Drew Brees, NO | 2010 | 658 | 448 | 68.1 | 4,620 |
| Neil Lomax, StL Cards | 1984 | 560 | 345 | 61.6 | 4,614 |
| Trent Green, StL Rams | 2004 | 556 | 369 | 66.4 | 4,591 |

† Active in 2010.

#### PASSER RATING

| | Year | Rat. |
|---|---|---|
| †Peyton Manning, Ind | 2004 | 121.1 |
| †Tom Brady, NE | 2007 | 117.2 |
| Steve Young, SF | 1994 | 112.8 |
| Joe Montana, SF | 1989 | 112.4 |
| †Tom Brady, NE | 2010 | 111.0 |
| Daunte Culpepper, Min | 2004 | 110.9 |

#### TOUCHDOWNS

| | Year | No. |
|---|---|---|
| †Tom Brady, NE | 2007 | 50 |
| †Peyton Manning, Ind | 2004 | 49 |
| Dan Marino, Mia | 1984 | 48 |
| Dan Marino, Mia | 1986 | 44 |
| Kurt Warner, StL Rams | 1999 | 41 |
| Daunte Culpepper, Min | 2004 | 39 |
| †Brett Favre, GB | 1996 | 39 |
| †Brett Favre, GB | 1995 | 38 |

Seven tied with 36.

## Single-Season Leaders (*Cont.*)

### Receiving

#### RECEPTIONS

| | Year | No. | Yds |
|---|---|---|---|
| Marvin Harrison, Ind | 2002 | 143 | 1,722 |
| Herman Moore, Det | 1995 | 123 | 1,686 |
| †Wes Welker, NE | 2009 | 123 | 1,348 |
| Cris Carter, Min | 1994 | 122 | 1,256 |
| Jerry Rice, SF | 1995 | 122 | 1,848 |
| Cris Carter, Min | 1995 | 122 | 1,371 |
| Isaac Bruce, StL | 1995 | 119 | 1,781 |
| Torry Holt, StL | 2003 | 117 | 1,696 |
| Jimmy Smith, Jac | 1999 | 116 | 1,636 |
| Marvin Harrison, Ind | 1999 | 115 | 1,663 |
| †Roddy White, Atl | 2010 | 115 | 1,389 |
| †Andre Johnson, Hou | 2008 | 115 | 1,575 |
| Rod Smith, Den | 2001 | 113 | 1,343 |

#### YARDS GAINED

| | Year | Yds |
|---|---|---|
| Jerry Rice, SF | 1995 | 1,848 |
| Isaac Bruce, StL | 1995 | 1,781 |
| Charley Hennigan, Hou | 1961 | 1,746 |
| Marvin Harrison, Ind | 2002 | 1,722 |
| Torry Holt, StL | 2003 | 1,696 |

#### TOUCHDOWNS

| | Year | No. |
|---|---|---|
| †Randy Moss, NE | 2007 | 23 |
| Jerry Rice, SF | 1987 | 22 |
| Mark Clayton, Mia | 1984 | 18 |
| Sterling Sharpe, GB | 1994 | 18 |

Seven players tied with 17.

#### All-Purpose Yards

| | Year | Run | Rec | Ret | Ttl |
|---|---|---|---|---|---|
| Yds | | | | | |
| †Derrick Mason, Ten | 2000 | 1 | 895 | 1794 | 2690 |
| Michael Lewis, NO | 2002 | 15 | 200 | 2432 | 2647 |
| †Fred Jackson, Buf | 2009 | 1062 | 371 | 1083 | 2516 |
| †Josh Cribbs, Cle | 2009 | 381 | 135 | 1994 | 2510 |
| †Chris Johnson, Ten | 2009 2006 | 503 | | 0 | 2509 |
| Lionel James, SD | 1985 | 516 | 1027 | 992 | 2535 |
| Brian Mitchell, Was | 1994 | 311 | 236 | 1930 | 2477 |
| Dante Hall, KC | 2003 | 73 | 423 | 1950 | 2446 |
| Mack Herron, NE | 1974 | 824 | 474 | 1146 | 2444 |
| Gale Sayers, Chi | 1966 | 1231 | 447 | 762 | 2440 |
| Terry Metcalf, StL Cards | 1975 | 816 | 378 | 1245 | 2439 |
| Marshall Faulk, StL Rams | 1999 | 1381 | 1048 | 0 | 2429 |
| Timmy Brown, Phi | 1963 | 841 | 487 | 1097 | 2425 |
| MarTay Jenkins, Ari | 2000 | -4 | 219 | 2187 | 2402 |
| Tiki Barber, NYG | 2005 | 1860 | 530 | 0 | 2390 |
| †LaD. Tomlinson, SD | 2003 | 1645 | 725 | 0 | 2370 |

#### Minimum of 15 returns.

#### Punting

| | Year | No. | Yds | Avg |
|---|---|---|---|---|
| Sammy Baugh, Was | 1940 | 35 | 1,799 | 51.4 |
| †Shane Lechler, Oak | 2009 | 96 | 4,909 | 51.1 |
| †Donnie Jones, StL | 2008 | 82 | 4,100 | 50.0 |
| †Shane Lechler, Oak | 2007 | 73 | 3,585 | 49.1 |
| †Mat McBriar, Dal | 2008 | 24 | 1,175 | 49.0 |
| Yale Lary, Det | 1963 | 35 | 1,713 | 48.9 |
| †Shane Lechler, Oak | 2008 | 90 | 4,391 | 48.8 |
| Sammy Baugh, Was | 1941 | 30 | 1,462 | 48.7 |
| Yale Lary, Det | 1961 | 52 | 2,519 | 48.4 |

#### Interceptions

| | Year | No. |
|---|---|---|
| Dick (Night Train) Lane, LA Rams | 1952 | 14 |
| Lester Hayes, Oak | 1980 | 13 |
| Spec Sanders, NY Yanks | 1950 | 13 |
| Dan Sandifer, Was | 1948 | 13 |

Nine tied with 12.

#### Sacks

| | Year | No. |
|---|---|---|
| Michael Strahan, NYG | 2001 | 22.5 |
| Mark Gastineau, NYJ | 1984 | 22.0 |
| Chris Doleman, Min | 1989 | 21.0 |
| Reggie White, Phi | 1987 | 21.0 |
| Lawrence Taylor, NYG | 1986 | 20.5 |
| †DeMarcus Ware, Dal | 2008 | 20.0 |
| Derrick Thomas, KC | 1990 | 20.0 |
| Tim Harris, GB | 1989 | 19.5 |

Three tied with 19.0.

#### Punt Returns

| | Year | Avg |
|---|---|---|
| Jack Christiansen, Det | 1952 | 21.5 |
| Red Cochran, Chi Cards | 1949 | 20.9 |
| Jerry Davis, Chi Cards | 1948 | 20.9 |

#### Kickoff Returns

| | Year | Avg |
|---|---|---|
| Travis Williams, GB | 1967 | 41.1 |
| Gale Sayers, Chi | 1967 | 37.7 |
| Ollie Matson, Chi Cards | 1958 | 35.5 |
| Jim Duncan, Balt Colts | 1970 | 35.4 |
| Lynn Chandnois, Pit | 1952 | 35.2 |

## Single-Game Leaders

### Scoring

#### POINTS

| | Date | Pts |
|---|---|---|
| Ernie Nevers, Chi Cards vs Chi | 11-28-29 | 40 |
| Gale Sayers, Chi vs SF | 12-12-65 | 36 |
| Dub Jones, Clev vs Chi | 11-25-51 | 36 |
| Paul Hornung, GB vs Balt Colts | 10-8-61 | 33 |

On Thanksgiving Day, 1929, Nevers scored all the Cardinals' points on six rushing TDs and four PATs. The Cards defeated Red Grange and the Bears, 40–6. Jones and Sayers each rushed for four touchdowns and scored two more on returns in their teams' victories. Hornung scored four touchdowns and kicked 6 PATs and a field goal in a 45-7 win over the Colts.

#### FIELD GOALS

| | Date | No. |
|---|---|---|
| †Rob Bironas, Ten vs Hou | 10-21-07 | 8 |
| †Shayne Graham, Cin vs Balt | 11-11-07 | 7 |
| †Billy Cundiff, Dal vs NYG (OT) | 9-15-03 | 7 |
| Chris Boniol, Dal vs GB | 11-18-96 | 7 |
| Rich Karlis, Min vs LA Rams (OT) | 11-5-89 | 7 |
| Jim Bakken, StL Cards vs Pit | 9-24-67 | 7 |

Bironas was 8 for 8.

Bakken was 7 for 9; Cundiff was 7 for 8; and Karlis, Boniol, and Graham went 7 for 7.

† Active in 2010.

## Single-Game Leaders (Cont.)
### Scoring (Cont.)
#### TOUCHDOWNS

| | Date | No. |
|---|---|---|
| Gale Sayers, Chi vs SF | 12-12-65 | 6 |
| Dub Jones, Clev vs Chi | 11-25-51 | 6 |
| Ernie Nevers, Chi Cards vs Chi | 11-28-29 | 6 |
| †Clinton Portis, Den vs KC | 12-07-03 | 5 |
| Shaun Alexander, Sea vs Min | 9-29-02 | 5 |
| James Stewart, Jac vs Phil | 10-12-97 | 5 |
| Jerry Rice, SF vs Atl | 10-14-90 | 5 |
| Kellen Winslow, SD vs Oak | 11-22-81 | 5 |
| Paul Hornung, GB vs Balt Colts | 12-12-65 | 5 |
| Cookie Gilchrist, Buf vs NYJ | 12-8-63 | 5 |
| Billy Cannon, Hou vs NY Titans | 12-10-61 | 5 |
| Abner Haynes, Dal Texans vs Oak | 11-26-61 | 5 |
| Jim Brown, Clev vs Balt Colts | 11-1-59 | 5 |
| Bob Shaw, Chi Cards vs Balt Colts | 10-2-50 | 5 |

### Rushing
#### YARDS GAINED

| | Date | Yds |
|---|---|---|
| †Adrian Peterson, Min vs SD | 11-4-07 | 296 |
| Jamal Lewis, Balt vs Cle | 9-14-03 | 295 |
| Jerome Harrison, Cle vs KC | 12-20-09 | 286 |
| Corey Dillon, Cin vs Den | 10-22-00 | 278 |
| Walter Payton, Chi vs Min | 11-20-77 | 275 |
| O.J. Simpson, Buf vs Det | 11-25-76 | 273 |

#### CARRIES

| | Date | No. |
|---|---|---|
| Jamie Morris, Wash vs Cin | 12-17-88 | 45 |
| Rudi Johnson, Cin vs Hou | 11-9-03 | 43 |
| James Wilder, TB vs GB | 9-30-84 | 43 |
| Butch Woolfolk, NYG vs Phil | 11-20-83 | 43 |
| †Ricky Williams, Mia vs Buf | 9-21-03 | 42 |
| Terrell Davis, Den vs Buf (OT) | 10-26-97 | 42 |
| James Wilder, TB vs Pit | 10-30-83 | 42 |

#### TOUCHDOWNS

| | Date | No. |
|---|---|---|
| Ernie Nevers, Chi Cards vs Chi | 11-28-29 | 6 |
| †Clinton Portis, Den vs KC | 12-7-03 | 5 |
| James Stewart, Jac vs Phil | 10-12-97 | 5 |
| Cookie Gilchrist, Buf vs NYJ | 12-8-63 | 5 |
| Jim Brown, Clev vs Balt Colts | 11-1-59 | 5 |
| Jimmie Conzelman, RI vs Evansville | 10-15-22 | 5 |

### Passing
#### YARDS GAINED

| | Date | Yds |
|---|---|---|
| N. Van Brocklin, Rams vs NY Yanks | 9-28-51 | 554 |
| Warren Moon, Hou vs KC | 12-16-90 | 527 |
| Boomer Esiason, Ariz vs Wash | 11-10-96 | 522 |
| Dan Marino, Mia vs NYJ | 10-23-88 | 521 |
| Phil Simms, NYG vs Cin | 10-13-85 | 513 |

#### COMPLETIONS

| | Date | No. |
|---|---|---|
| Drew Bledsoe, NE vs Min | 11-13-94 | 45 |
| Rich Gannon, Oak vs Pit | 9-15-02 | 43 |
| Vinny Testaverde, NYJ vs Sea | 12-6-98 | 42 |
| Richard Todd, NYJ vs SF | 9-21-80 | 42 |
| †Tony Romo, Dal vs NYG | 12-06-09 | 41 |
| Warren Moon, Hou vs Dal | 11-10-91 | 41 |
| †Peyton Manning, Ind vs Hou | 9-12-10 | 40 |
| Kurt Warner, Ari vs NYJ | 9-28-08 | 40 |
| †Marc Bulger, StL Rams vs NYG | 10-02-05 | 40 |
| Brad Johnson, TB vs Chi | 11-18-01 | 40 |
| Phil Simms, NYG vs Cin | 10-13-85 | 40 |
| Ken Anderson, Cin vs SD | 12-20-82 | 40 |

#### TOUCHDOWNS

| | Date | No. |
|---|---|---|
| Joe Kapp, Min vs Balt Colts | 9-28-69 | 7 |
| Y. A. Tittle, NYG vs Wash | 10-28-62 | 7 |
| George Blanda, Hou vs NY Titans | 11-19-61 | 7 |
| Adrian Burk, Phil vs Wash | 10-17-54 | 7 |
| Sid Luckman, Chi vs NYG | 11-14-43 | 7 |

### Receiving
#### YARDS GAINED

| | Date | Yds |
|---|---|---|
| Flipper Anderson, LA Rams vs NO | 11-26-89 | 336 |
| Stephone Paige, KC vs SD | 12-22-85 | 309 |
| Jim Benton, Clev vs Det | 11-22-45 | 303 |
| Cloyce Box, Det vs Balt Colts | 12-3-50 | 302 |
| Jimmy Smith, Jax vs Balt Ravens | 9-10-00 | 291 |

#### RECEPTIONS

| | Date | No. |
|---|---|---|
| †Brandon Marshall, Den vs Ind | 12-13-09 | 21 |
| †Terrell Owens, SF vs Chi | 12-17-00 | 20 |
| Tom Fears, Rams vs GB | 12-3-50 | 18 |
| †Brandon Marshall, Den vs SD | 9-14-08 | 18 |
| Clark Gaines, NYJ vs SF | 9-21-80 | 17 |
| Troy Brown, NE vs KC | 9-22-02 | 16 |
| Keenan McCardell, Jax vs Rams | 10-20-96 | 16 |
| Jerry Rice, SF vs Rams | 11-20-94 | 16 |
| Sonny Randle, StL Cards vs NYG | 11-4-62 | 16 |

† Active in 2010.

## Single-Game Leaders *(Cont.)*

### Receiving *(Cont.)*
#### TOUCHDOWNS

| | Date | No. |
|---|---|---|
| Jerry Rice, SF vs Atl | 10-14-90 | 5 |
| Kellen Winslow, SD vs Oak | 11-22-81 | 5 |
| Bob Shaw, Chi Cards vs Balt Colts | 10-2-50 | 5 |

### All-Purpose Yards

| | Date | Yds |
|---|---|---|
| Glyn Milburn, Den vs Sea | 12-10-95 | 404 |
| Billy Cannon, Hou vs NY Titans | 12-10-61 | 373 |
| Tyrone Hughes, NO vs LA Rams | 10-23-94 | 347 |
| Lionel James, SD vs LA Rai | 11-10-85 | 345 |
| Timmy Brown, Phi vs StL Cards | 12-16-62 | 341 |

## Longest Plays

| RUSHING | Opponent | Year | Yds |
|---|---|---|---|
| Tony Dorsett, Dal | Min | 1983 | 99 |
| Ahman Green, GB | Den | 2003 | 98 |
| Bob Gage, Pit | Chi | 1949 | 97 |
| Andy Uram, GB | Chi Cards | 1939 | 97 |
| Corey Dillon, Cin | Det | 2001 | 96 |
| Garrison Hearst, SF | NYJ | 1998 | 96 |
| Jim Spavital, Balt Colts | GB | 1950 | 96 |
| Bob Hoernschemeyer, Det | NY Yanks | 1950 | 96 |

| PASSING | Opponent | Year | Yds |
|---|---|---|---|
| Gus Frerotte to Bernard Berrian, Min | Chi | 2008 | 99 |
| Jeff Garcia to Andre Davis, Clev | Cin | 2004 | 99 |
| Trent Green to Marc Boerigter, KC | SD | 2002 | 99 |
| †Brett Favre to Robert Brooks, GB | Chi | 1995 | 99 |
| Stan Humphries to Tony Martin, SD | Sea | 1994 | 99 |
| Ron Jaworski to Mike Quick, Phil | Atl | 1985 | 99 |
| Jim Plunkett to Cliff Branch, LA Rai | Wash | 1983 | 99 |
| Sonny Jurgensen to Gerry Allen, Wash | Chi | 1968 | 99 |
| Karl Sweetan to Pat Studstill, Det | Balt Colts | 1966 | 99 |
| George Izo to Bobby Mitchell, Wash | Clev | 1963 | 99 |
| Frank Filchock to Andy Farkas, Wash | Pit | 1939 | 99 |

| FIELD GOALS | Opponent | Year | Yds |
|---|---|---|---|
| Tom Dempsey, NO | Det | 1970 | 63 |
| †Jason Elam, Den | Jac | 1998 | 63 |
| †Matt Bryant, TB | Phi | 2006 | 62 |
| †Sebastian Janikowski | Oak | 2009 | 61 |

| PUNTS | Opponent | Year | Yds |
|---|---|---|---|
| Steve O'Neal, NYJ | Den | 1969 | 98 |
| Joe Lintzenich, Chi | NYG | 1931 | 94 |
| Shawn McCarthy, NE | Buf | 1991 | 93 |
| Randall Cunningham, Phil | NYG | 1989 | 91 |

| INTERCEPTION RETURNS | Opponent | Year | Yds |
|---|---|---|---|
| †Ed Reed, Balt | Phi | 2008 | 107 |
| †Ed Reed, Balt | Clev | 2004 | 106 |
| Louis Oliver, Mia | Buf | 1992 | 103 |
| Vencie Glenn, SD | Den | 1987 | 103 |

| FUMBLE RETURNS | Opponent | Year | Yds |
|---|---|---|---|
| Aeneas Williams, Ari | Was | 2000 | 104 |
| Jack Tatum, Oak | GB | 1972 | 104 |
| Travis Davis, Pit | Car | 1999 | 102 |
| Chris Martin, KC | Mia | 1991 | 100 |

| KICKOFF RETURNS | Opponent | Year | Yds |
|---|---|---|---|
| †Ellis Hobbs, NE | NYJ | 2007 | 108 |
| †Brad Smith, NYJ | Ind | 2009 | 106 |
| Roy Green, StL Cards | Dal | 1979 | 106 |
| Noland Smith, NYJ | Den | 1967 | 106 |
| Al Carmichael, GB | Chi | 1956 | 106 |
| Eight players tied at 105. | | | |

| PUNT RETURNS | Opponent | Year | Yds |
|---|---|---|---|
| Robert Bailey, LA Rams | NO | 1994 | 103 |
| Gil LeFebvre, Cin | Brooklyn | 1933 | 98 |
| Charlie West, Min | Wash | 1968 | 98 |
| Dennis Morgan, Dal | StL Cards | 1974 | 98 |
| Terance Mathis, NYJ | Dal | 1990 | 98 |
| Greg Pruitt, LA Rai | Wash | 1983 | 97 |
| Bryan McCann, Dal | Det | 2010 | 97 |

| MISSED FIELD GOAL RETURNS | Opponent | Year | Yds |
|---|---|---|---|
| †Antonio Cromartie, SD | Min | 2007 | 109 |
| †Devin Hester, Chi | NYG | 2006 | 108 |
| †Nathan Vasher, Chi | SF | 2005 | 108 |
| Chris McAlister, Balt | Den | 2002 | 107 |
| Aaron Glenn, NYJ | Ind | 1998 | 104 |

† Active in 2010.

## Rushing

| Year | Player, Team | Att | Yards | Avg | TD |
|------|--------------|-----|-------|-----|-----|
| 1932 | Cliff Battles, Bos | 148 | 576 | 3.9 | 3 |
| 1933 | Jim Musick, Bos | 173 | 809 | 4.7 | 5 |
| 1934 | Beattie Feathers, Chi | 119 | 1,004 | 8.4 | 8 |
| 1935 | Doug Russell, Chi Cards | 140 | 499 | 3.6 | 0 |
| 1936 | Alphonse Leemans, NY | 206 | 830 | 4.0 | 2 |
| 1937 | Cliff Battles, Wash | 216 | 874 | 4.0 | 5 |
| 1938 | Byron White, Pit | 152 | 567 | 3.7 | 4 |
| 1939 | Bill Osmanski, Chi | 121 | 699 | 5.8 | 7 |
| 1940 | Byron White, Det | 146 | 514 | 3.5 | 5 |
| 1941 | Clarence Manders, Bklyn | 111 | 486 | 4.4 | 5 |
| 1942 | Bill Dudley, Pit | 162 | 696 | 4.3 | 5 |
| 1943 | Bill Paschal, NY | 147 | 572 | 3.9 | 10 |
| 1944 | Bill Paschal, NY | 196 | 737 | 3.8 | 9 |
| 1945 | Steve Van Buren, Phil | 143 | 832 | 5.8 | 15 |
| 1946 | Bill Dudley, Pit | 146 | 604 | 4.1 | 3 |
| 1947 | Steve Van Buren, Phil | 217 | 1,008 | 4.6 | 13 |
| 1948 | Steve Van Buren, Phil | 201 | 945 | 4.7 | 10 |
| 1949 | Steve Van Buren, Phil | 263 | 1,146 | 4.4 | 11 |
| 1950 | Marion Motley, Clev | 140 | 810 | 5.8 | 3 |
| 1951 | Eddie Price, NY | 271 | 971 | 3.6 | 7 |
| 1952 | Dan Towler, LA | 156 | 894 | 5.7 | 10 |
| 1953 | Joe Perry, SF | 192 | 1,018 | 5.3 | 10 |
| 1954 | Joe Perry, SF | 173 | 1,049 | 6.1 | 8 |
| 1955 | Alan Ameche, Balt | 213 | 961 | 4.5 | 9 |
| 1956 | Rick Casares, Chi | 234 | 1,126 | 4.8 | 12 |
| 1957 | Jim Brown, Clev | 202 | 942 | 4.7 | 9 |
| 1958 | Jim Brown, Clev | 257 | 1,527 | 5.9 | 17 |
| 1959 | Jim Brown, Clev | 290 | 1,329 | 4.6 | 14 |
| 1960 | Jim Brown, Clev, NFL | 215 | 1,257 | 5.8 | 9 |
|      | Abner Haynes, Dallas Texans, AFL | 156 | 875 | 5.6 | 9 |
| 1961 | Jim Brown, Clev, NFL | 305 | 1,408 | 4.6 | 8 |
|      | Billy Cannon, Hou, AFL | 200 | 948 | 4.7 | 6 |
| 1962 | Jim Taylor, GB, NFL | 272 | 1,474 | 5.4 | 19 |
|      | Cookie Gilchrist, Buf, AFL | 214 | 1,096 | 5.1 | 13 |
| 1963 | Jim Brown, Clev, NFL | 291 | 1,863 | 6.4 | 12 |
|      | Clem Daniels, Oak, AFL | 215 | 1,099 | 5.1 | 3 |
| 1964 | Jim Brown, Clev, NFL | 280 | 1,446 | 5.2 | 7 |
|      | Cookie Gilchrist, Buf, AFL | 230 | 981 | 4.3 | 6 |
| 1965 | Jim Brown, Clev, NFL | 289 | 1,544 | 5.3 | 17 |
|      | Paul Lowe, SD, AFL | 222 | 1,121 | 5.0 | 7 |
| 1966 | Jim Nance, Bos, AFL | 299 | 1,458 | 4.9 | 11 |
|      | Gale Sayers, Chi, NFL | 229 | 1,231 | 5.4 | 8 |
| 1967 | Jim Nance, Bos, AFL | 269 | 1,216 | 4.5 | 7 |
|      | Leroy Kelly, Clev, NFL | 235 | 1,205 | 5.1 | 11 |
| 1968 | Leroy Kelly, Clev, NFL | 248 | 1,239 | 5.0 | 16 |
|      | Paul Robinson, Cin, AFL | 238 | 1,023 | 4.3 | 8 |
| 1969 | Gale Sayers, Chi, NFL | 236 | 1,032 | 4.4 | 8 |
|      | Dickie Post, SD, AFL | 182 | 873 | 4.8 | 6 |
| 1970 | Larry Brown, Wash, NFC | 237 | 1,125 | 4.7 | 5 |
|      | Floyd Little, Den, AFC | 209 | 901 | 4.3 | 3 |
| 1971 | Floyd Little, Den, AFC | 284 | 1,133 | 4.0 | 6 |
|      | John Brockington, GB, NFC | 216 | 1,105 | 5.1 | 4 |
| 1972 | O.J. Simpson, Buf, AFC | 292 | 1,251 | 4.3 | 6 |
|      | Larry Brown, Wash, NFC | 285 | 1,216 | 4.3 | 8 |
| 1973 | O.J. Simpson, Buf, AFC | 332 | 2,003 | 6.0 | 12 |
|      | John Brockington, GB, NFC | 265 | 1,144 | 4.3 | 3 |
| 1974 | Otis Armstrong, Den, AFC | 263 | 1,407 | 5.3 | 9 |
|      | Lawrence McCutcheon, LA, NFC | 236 | 1,109 | 4.7 | 3 |
| 1975 | O.J. Simpson, Buf, AFC | 329 | 1,817 | 5.5 | 16 |
|      | Jim Otis, StL, NFC | 269 | 1,076 | 4.0 | 5 |
| 1976 | O.J. Simpson, Buf, AFC | 290 | 1,503 | 5.2 | 8 |
|      | Walter Payton, Chi, NFC | 311 | 1,390 | 4.5 | 13 |
| 1977 | Walter Payton, Chi, NFC | 339 | 1,852 | 5.5 | 14 |
|      | Mark van Eeghen, Oak, AFC | 324 | 1,273 | 3.9 | 7 |
| 1978 | Earl Campbell, Hou, AFC | 302 | 1,450 | 4.8 | 13 |
|      | Walter Payton, Chi, NFC | 333 | 1,395 | 4.2 | 11 |
| 1979 | Earl Campbell, Hou, AFC | 368 | 1,697 | 4.6 | 19 |
|      | Walter Payton, Chi, NFC | 369 | 1,610 | 4.4 | 14 |
| 1980 | Earl Campbell, Hou, AFC | 373 | 1,934 | 5.2 | 13 |
|      | Walter Payton, Chi, NFC | 317 | 1,460 | 4.6 | 6 |
| 1981 | George Rogers, NO, NFC | 378 | 1,674 | 4.4 | 13 |
|      | Earl Campbell, Hou, AFC | 361 | 1,376 | 3.8 | 10 |
| 1982 | Freeman McNeil, NYJ, AFC | 151 | 786 | 5.2 | 6 |
|      | Tony Dorsett, Dal, NFC | 177 | 745 | 4.2 | 5 |
| 1983 | Eric Dickerson, LA, NFC | 390 | 1,808 | 4.6 | 18 |
|      | Curt Warner, Sea, AFC | 335 | 1,449 | 4.3 | 13 |
| 1984 | Eric Dickerson, LA, NFC | 379 | 2,105 | 5.6 | 14 |
|      | Earnest Jackson, SD, AFC | 296 | 1,179 | 4.0 | 8 |
| 1985 | Marcus Allen, LA, AFC | 380 | 1,759 | 4.6 | 11 |
|      | Gerald Riggs, Atl, NFC | 397 | 1,719 | 4.3 | 10 |
| 1986 | Eric Dickerson, LA, NFC | 404 | 1,821 | 4.5 | 11 |
|      | Curt Warner, Sea, AFC | 319 | 1,481 | 4.6 | 13 |
| 1987 | Charles White, LA, NFC | 324 | 1,374 | 4.2 | 11 |
|      | Eric Dickerson, Ind, AFC | 223 | 1,011 | 4.5 | 5 |
| 1988 | Eric Dickerson, Ind, AFC | 388 | 1,659 | 4.3 | 14 |
|      | Herschel Walker, Dal, NFC | 361 | 1,514 | 4.2 | 5 |
| 1989 | Christian Okoye, KC, AFC | 370 | 1,480 | 4.0 | 12 |
|      | Barry Sanders, Det, NFC | 280 | 1,470 | 5.3 | 14 |
| 1990 | Barry Sanders, Det, NFC | 255 | 1,304 | 5.1 | 13 |
|      | Thurman Thomas, Buf, AFC | 271 | 1,297 | 4.8 | 11 |
| 1991 | Emmitt Smith, Dal, NFC | 365 | 1,563 | 4.3 | 12 |
|      | Thurman Thomas, Buf, AFC | 288 | 1,407 | 4.9 | 7 |
| 1992 | Emmitt Smith, Dal, NFC | 373 | 1,713 | 4.6 | 18 |
|      | Barry Foster, Pit, AFC | 390 | 1,690 | 4.3 | 11 |
| 1993 | Emmitt Smith, Dal, NFC | 283 | 1,486 | 5.3 | 9 |
|      | Thurman Thomas, Buf, AFC | 355 | 1,315 | 3.7 | 6 |

### Rushing *(Cont.)*

| Year | Player, Team | Att | Yards | Avg | TD |
|---|---|---|---|---|---|
| 1994 | Barry Sanders, Det, NFC | .331 | 1,883 | 5.7 | 7 |
| | Chris Warren, Sea, AFC | .333 | 1,545 | 4.6 | 9 |
| 1995 | Emmitt Smith, Dal, NFC | .377 | 1,773 | 4.7 | 25 |
| | Curtis Martin, NE, AFC | .368 | 1,487 | 4.0 | 14 |
| 1996 | Barry Sanders, Det, NFC | .307 | 1,553 | 5.1 | 11 |
| | Terrell Davis, Den, AFC | .345 | 1,538 | 4.5 | 13 |
| 1997 | Barry Sanders, Det, NFC | .335 | 2,053 | 6.1 | 11 |
| | Terrell Davis, Den, AFC | .369 | 1,750 | 4.7 | 15 |
| 1998 | Terrell Davis, Den, AFC | .392 | 2,008 | 5.1 | 21 |
| | Jamal Anderson, Atl, NFC | .410 | 1,846 | 4.5 | 14 |
| 1999 | Edgerrin James, Ind, AFC | .369 | 1,553 | 4.2 | 13 |
| | Stephen Davis, Wash, NFC | .290 | 1,405 | 4.8 | 17 |
| 2000 | Edgerrin James, Ind, AFC | .387 | 1,709 | 4.4 | 13 |
| | Robert Smith, Min, NFC | .295 | 1,521 | 5.2 | 7 |
| 2001 | Priest Holmes, Kan, AFC | .327 | 1,555 | 4.8 | 8 |
| | Stephen Davis, Wash, NFC | .356 | 1,432 | 4.0 | 5 |
| 2002 | Ricky Williams, Mia, AFC | .383 | 1,853 | 4.8 | 16 |
| | Deuce McAllister, NO, NFC | | 325 | 1,388 | 4.3 | 13 |
| 2003 | Jamal Lewis, Balt, AFC | .387 | 2,066 | 5.3 | 14 |
| | Ahman Green, GB, NFC | .355 | 1,883 | 5.3 | 15 |
| 2004 | Curtis Martin, NY Jets, AFC | | 371 | 1,697 | 4.6 | 12 |

| Year | Player, Team | Att | Yards | Avg | TD |
|---|---|---|---|---|---|
| 2004 | Shaun Alexander, Sea, NFC | 353 | 1,696 | 4.8 | 16 |
| 2005 | Shaun Alexander, Sea, NFC | 370 | 1,880 | 5.1 | 27 |
| | Larry Johnson, KC, AFC | .336 | 1,750 | 5.2 | 20 |
| 2006 | LaDainian Tomlinson, SD, AFC | 348 | 1,815 | 5.2 | 28 |
| | Frank Gore, SF, NFC | 312 | 1,695 | 5.4 | 8 |
| 2007 | LaDainian Tomlinson, SD, AFC | 315 | 1,474 | 4.7 | 15 |
| | Adrian Peterson, Min, NFC | 238 | 1,341 | 5.6 | 12 |
| 2008 | Adrian Peterson, Min, NFC | 363 | 1,760 | 4.8 | 10 |
| | Thomas Jones, NYJ, AFC | .290 | 1,312 | 4.5 | 13 |
| 2009 | Chris Johnson, Ten, AFC | .358 | 2,006 | 5.6 | 14 |
| | Steven Jackson, StL, NFC | 324 | 1,416 | 4.4 | 4 |
| 2010 | Arian Foster, Hou, AFC | 327 | 1,616 | 4.9 | 16 |
| | Michael Turner, Atl, NFC | 334 | 1,371 | 4.1 | 12 |

### Passing

| Year | Player, Team | Att | Comp | Yards | TD | Int |
|---|---|---|---|---|---|---|
| 1932 | Arnie Herber, GB | 101 | 37 | 639 | 9 | 9 |
| 1933 | Harry Newman, NYG | 136 | 53 | 973 | 11 | 17 |
| 1934 | Arnie Herber, GB | 115 | 42 | 799 | 8 | 12 |
| 1935 | Ed Danowski, NYG | 113 | 57 | 794 | 10 | 9 |
| 1936 | Arnie Herber, GB | 173 | 77 | 1,239 | 11 | 13 |
| 1937 | Sammy Baugh, Wash | 171 | 81 | 1,127 | 8 | 14 |
| 1938 | Ed Danowski, NYG | 129 | 70 | 848 | 7 | 8 |
| 1939 | Parker Hall, Clev | 208 | 106 | 1,227 | 9 | 13 |
| 1940 | Sammy Baugh, Wash | 177 | 111 | 1,367 | 12 | 10 |
| 1941 | Cecil Isbell, GB | 206 | 117 | 1,479 | 15 | 11 |
| 1942 | Cecil Isbell, GB | 268 | 146 | 2,021 | 24 | 14 |
| 1943 | Sammy Baugh, Wash | 239 | 133 | 1,754 | 23 | 19 |
| 1944 | Frank Filchock, Wash | 147 | 84 | 1,139 | 13 | 9 |
| 1945 | Sid Luckman, Chi | 217 | 117 | 1,725 | 14 | 10 |
| 1946 | Bob Waterfield, LA | 251 | 127 | 1,747 | 18 | 17 |
| 1947 | Sammy Baugh, Wash | 354 | 210 | 2,938 | 25 | 15 |
| 1948 | Tommy Thompson, Phil | 246 | 141 | 1,965 | 25 | 11 |
| 1949 | Sammy Baugh, Wash | 255 | 145 | 1,903 | 18 | 14 |
| 1950 | Norm Van Brocklin, LA | 233 | 127 | 2,061 | 18 | 14 |
| 1951 | Bob Waterfield, LA | 176 | 88 | 1,566 | 13 | 10 |
| 1952 | Norm Van Brocklin, LA | 205 | 113 | 1,736 | 14 | 17 |
| 1953 | Otto Graham, Clev | 258 | 167 | 2,722 | 11 | 9 |
| 1954 | Norm Van Brocklin, LA | 260 | 139 | 2,637 | 13 | 21 |
| 1955 | Otto Graham, Clev | 185 | 98 | 1,721 | 15 | 8 |
| 1956 | Ed Brown, Chi | 168 | 96 | 1,667 | 11 | 12 |
| 1957 | Tommy O'Connell, Clev | 110 | 63 | 1,229 | 9 | 8 |
| 1958 | Eddie LeBaron, Wash | 145 | 79 | 1,365 | 11 | 10 |
| 1959 | Charlie Conerly, NYG | 194 | 113 | 1,706 | 14 | 4 |

| Year | Player, Team | Att | Comp | Yards | TD | Int |
|---|---|---|---|---|---|---|
| 1960 | Milt Plum, Clev, NFL | 250 | 151 | 2,297 | 21 | 5 |
| | Jack Kemp, LA, AFL | 406 | 211 | 3,018 | 20 | 25 |
| 1961 | George Blanda, Hou, AFL | 362 | 187 | 3,330 | 36 | 22 |
| | Milt Plum, Clev, NFL | 302 | 177 | 2,416 | 18 | 10 |
| 1962 | Len Dawson, Dal, AFL | 310 | 189 | 2,759 | 29 | 17 |
| | Bart Starr, GB, NFL | 285 | 178 | 2,438 | 12 | 9 |
| 1963 | Y.A. Tittle, NY, NFL | 367 | 221 | 3,145 | 36 | 14 |
| | Tobin Rote, SD, AFL | 286 | 170 | 2,510 | 20 | 17 |
| 1964 | Len Dawson, KC, AFL | 354 | 199 | 2,879 | 30 | 18 |
| | Bart Starr, GB, NFL | 272 | 163 | 2,144 | 15 | 4 |
| 1965 | Rudy Bukich, Chi, NFL | 312 | 176 | 2,641 | 20 | 9 |
| | John Hadl, SD, AFL | 348 | 174 | 2,798 | 20 | 21 |
| 1966 | Bart Starr, GB, NFL | 251 | 156 | 2,257 | 14 | 3 |
| | Len Dawson, KC, AFL | 284 | 159 | 2,527 | 26 | 10 |
| 1967 | Sonny Jurgensen, Wash, NFL | 508 | 288 | 3,747 | 31 | 16 |
| | Daryle Lamonica, Oak, AFL | 425 | 220 | 3,228 | 30 | 20 |
| 1968 | Len Dawson, KC, AFL | 224 | 131 | 2,109 | 17 | 9 |
| | Earl Morrall, Balt, NFL | 317 | 182 | 2,909 | 26 | 17 |
| 1969 | S. Jurgensen, Wash, NFL | 442 | 274 | 3,102 | 22 | 15 |
| | Greg Cook, Cin, AFL | 197 | 106 | 1,854 | 15 | 11 |
| 1970 | John Brodie, SF, NFC | 378 | 223 | 2,941 | 24 | 10 |
| | Daryle Lamonica, Oak, AFC | 356 | 179 | 2,516 | 22 | 15 |
| 1971 | Roger Staubach, Dal, NFC | 211 | 126 | 1,882 | 15 | 4 |
| | Bob Griese, Mia, AFC | 263 | 145 | 2,089 | 19 | 9 |
| 1972 | Norm Snead, NY, NFC | 325 | 196 | 2,307 | 17 | 12 |
| | Earl Morrall, Mia, AFC | 150 | 83 | 1,360 | 11 | 7 |

## Passing* *(Cont.)*

*Since 1973, the annual passing NFL leaders have been determined by a passer rating system that compares individual performances to a fixed performance standard. Before 1973, total passing yards gained was used.

| Year | Player, Team | Comp% | Yds | TD | Int | Rating |
|------|--------------|-------|-----|-----|-----|--------|
| 1973 | Roger Staubach, Dal, NFC | 62.6 | 2,428 | 23 | 15 | 94.6 |
|  | Ken Stabler, Oak, AFC | 62.7 | 1,997 | 14 | 10 | 88.3 |
| 1974 | Ken Anderson, Cin, AFC | 64.9 | 2,667 | 18 | 10 | 95.7 |
|  | Sonny Jurgensen, Wash, NFC | 64.1 | 1,185 | 11 | 5 | 94.5 |
| 1975 | Ken Anderson, Cin, AFC | 60.5 | 3,169 | 21 | 11 | 93.9 |
|  | Fran Tarkenton, Min, NFC | 64.2 | 2,994 | 25 | 13 | 91.8 |
| 1976 | Ken Stabler, Oak, AFC | 66.7 | 2,737 | 27 | 17 | 103.4 |
|  | James Harris, LA, NFC | 57.6 | 1,460 | 8 | 6 | 89.6 |
| 1977 | Bob Griese, Mia, AFC | 58.6 | 2,252 | 22 | 13 | 87.8 |
|  | Roger Staubach, Dal, NFC | 58.2 | 2,620 | 18 | 9 | 87.0 |
| 1978 | Roger Staubach, Dal, NFC | 55.9 | 3,190 | 25 | 16 | 84.9 |
|  | Terry Bradshaw, Pit, AFC | 56.3 | 2,915 | 28 | 20 | 84.7 |
| 1979 | Roger Staubach, Dal, NFC | 57.9 | 3,586 | 27 | 11 | 92.3 |
|  | Dan Fouts, SD, AFC | 62.6 | 4,082 | 24 | 24 | 82.6 |
| 1980 | Brian Sipe, Clev, AFC | 60.8 | 4,132 | 30 | 14 | 91.4 |
|  | Ron Jaworski, Phi, NFC | 57.0 | 3,529 | 27 | 12 | 91.0 |
| 1981 | Ken Anderson, Cin, AFC | 62.6 | 3,754 | 29 | 10 | 98.4 |
|  | Joe Montana, SF, NFC | 63.7 | 3,565 | 19 | 12 | 88.4 |
| 1982 | Ken Anderson, Cin, AFC | 70.6 | 2,495 | 12 | 9 | 95.3 |
|  | Joe Theismann, Wash, NFC | 63.9 | 2,033 | 13 | 9 | 91.3 |
| 1983 | Steve Bartkowski, Atl, NFC | 63.4 | 3,167 | 22 | 5 | 97.6 |
|  | Dan Marino, Mia AFC | 58.4 | 2,210 | 20 | 6 | 96.0 |
| 1984 | Dan Marino, Mia, AFC | 64.2 | 5,084 | 48 | 17 | 108.9 |
|  | Joe Montana, SF, NFC | 64.6 | 3,630 | 28 | 10 | 102.9 |
| 1985 | Ken O'Brien, NY, AFC | 60.9 | 3,888 | 25 | 8 | 96.2 |
|  | Joe Montana, SF, NFC | 61.3 | 3,653 | 27 | 13 | 91.3 |
| 1986 | Tommy Kramer, Min, NFC | 55.9 | 3,000 | 24 | 10 | 92.6 |
|  | Dan Marino, Mia, AFC | 60.7 | 4,746 | 44 | 23 | 92.5 |
| 1987 | Joe Montana, SF, NFC | 66.8 | 3,054 | 31 | 13 | 102.1 |
|  | Bernie Kosar, Clev, AFC | 61.9 | 3,033 | 22 | 9 | 95.4 |
| 1988 | Boomer Esiason, Cin, AFC | 57.5 | 3,572 | 28 | 14 | 97.4 |
|  | Wade Wilson, Min, NFC | 61.4 | 2,746 | 15 | 9 | 91.5 |
| 1989 | Joe Montana, SF, NFC | 70.2 | 3,521 | 26 | 8 | 112.4 |
|  | Boomer Esiason, Cin, AFC | 56.7 | 3,525 | 28 | 11 | 92.1 |
| 1990 | Jim Kelly, Buf, AFC | 63.3 | 2,829 | 24 | 9 | 101.2 |
|  | Phil Simms, NY, NFC | 59.2 | 2,284 | 15 | 4 | 92.7 |
| 1991 | Steve Young, SF, NFC | 64.5 | 2,517 | 17 | 8 | 101.8 |
|  | Jim Kelly, Buf, AFC | 64.1 | 3,844 | 33 | 17 | 97.6 |
| 1992 | Steve Young, SF, NFC | 66.7 | 3,465 | 25 | 7 | 107.0 |
|  | Warren Moon, Hou, AFC | 64.7 | 2,521 | 18 | 12 | 89.3 |
| 1993 | Steve Young, SF, NFC | 68.0 | 4,023 | 29 | 16 | 101.5 |
|  | John Elway, Den, AFC | 63.2 | 4,030 | 25 | 10 | 92.8 |
| 1994 | Steve Young, SF, NFC | 70.3 | 3,969 | 35 | 10 | 112.8 |
|  | Dan Marino, Mia, AFC | 62.0 | 4,453 | 30 | 17 | 89.2 |
| 1995 | Brett Favre, GB, NFC | 62.9 | 4,413 | 38 | 13 | 99.5 |
|  | Jim Harbaugh, Ind, AFC | 61.2 | 2,575 | 17 | 5 | 100.7 |
| 1996 | John Elway, Den, AFC | 61.6 | 3,328 | 26 | 14 | 89.2 |
|  | Steve Young, SF, NFC | 67.7 | 2,410 | 14 | 6 | 97.2 |
| 1997 | Steve Young, SF, NFC | 67.7 | 3,029 | 19 | 6 | 104.7 |
|  | Mark Brunell, Jax, AFC | 60.7 | 3,281 | 18 | 7 | 91.2 |
| 1998 | Randall Cunningham, Min, NFC | 60.9 | 3,704 | 34 | 10 | 106.0 |
|  | Vinny Testaverde, NYJ, AFC | 61.5 | 3,256 | 29 | 7 | 101.6 |
| 1999 | Kurt Warner, StL, NFC | 65.1 | 4,353 | 41 | 13 | 109.2 |
|  | Peyton Manning, Ind, AFC | 62.1 | 4,135 | 26 | 15 | 90.7 |
| 2000 | Trent Green, StL, NFC | 60.4 | 2,063 | 16 | 5 | 101.8 |
|  | Brian Griese, Den, AFC | 64.3 | 2,688 | 19 | 4 | 102.9 |
| 2001 | Kurt Warner, StL, NFC | 68.7 | 4,830 | 36 | 22 | 101.4 |
|  | Rich Gannon, Oak, AFC | 65.8 | 3,828 | 27 | 9 | 95.5 |
| 2002 | Brad Johnson, TB, NFC | 62.3 | 3,049 | 22 | 6 | 92.9 |
|  | Chad Pennington, NY, AFC | 68.9 | 3,120 | 22 | 6 | 104.2 |

## Passing *(Cont.)*

| Year | Player, Team | Comp% | Yds | TD | Int | Rating |
|------|-------------|-------|-----|----|----|--------|
| 2003 | Steve McNair, Ten, AFC | 62.5 | 3,215 | 24 | 7 | 100.4 |
| | Daunte Culpepper, Min, NFC | 65.0 | 3,479 | 25 | 11 | 96.4 |
| 2004 | Peyton Manning, Ind, AFC | 67.6 | 4,557 | 49 | 10 | 121.1 |
| | Daunte Culpepper, Min, NFC | 69.2 | 4,717 | 39 | 11 | 110.9 |
| 2005 | Peyton Manning, Ind, AFC | 67.3 | 3,747 | 28 | 10 | 104.1 |
| | Matt Hasselbeck, GB, NFC | 65.5 | 3,459 | 24 | 9 | 98.2 |
| 2006 | Peyton Manning, Ind, AFC | 65.0 | 4,397 | 31 | 9 | 101.0 |
| | Drew Brees, NO, NFC | 64.3 | 4,418 | 26 | 11 | 96.2 |

| Year | Player, Team | Comp% | Yds | TD | Int | Rating |
|------|-------------|-------|-----|----|----|--------|
| 2007 | Tom Brady, NE, AFC | 68.9 | 4,806 | 50 | 8 | 117.2 |
| | Tony Romo, Dal, NFC | 64.4 | 4,211 | 36 | 19 | 97.4 |
| 2008 | Philip Rivers, SD, AFC | 65.3 | 4,009 | 34 | 11 | 105.5 |
| | Kurt Warner, Ari, NFC | 67.1 | 4,583 | 30 | 14 | 96.9 |
| 2009 | Drew Brees, NO, NFC | 70.6 | 4,388 | 34 | 11 | 109.6 |
| | Philip Rivers, SD, AFC | 65.2 | 4,254 | 28 | 9 | 104.4 |
| 2010 | Tom Brady, NE, AFC | 65.9 | 3,900 | 36 | 4 | 111.0 |
| | Aaron Rodgers, GB, NFC | 65.7 | 3,922 | 28 | 11 | 101.5 |

## Pass Receiving†

| Year | Player, Team | No. | Yds | Avg | TD |
|------|-------------|-----|-----|-----|----|
| 1932 | Ray Flaherty, NY | 21 | 350 | 16.7 | 3 |
| 1933 | John Kelly, Brooklyn | 22 | 246 | 11.2 | 3 |
| 1934 | Joe Carter, Phil | 16 | 238 | 14.9 | 4 |
| | Morris Badgro, NY | 16 | 206 | 12.9 | 1 |
| 1935 | Tod Goodwin, NY | 26 | 432 | 16.6 | 4 |
| 1936 | Don Hutson, GB | 34 | 536 | 15.8 | 8 |
| 1937 | Don Hutson, GB | 41 | 552 | 13.5 | 7 |
| 1938 | Gaynell Tinsley, Chi Cards | 41 | 516 | 12.6 | 1 |
| 1939 | Don Hutson, GB | 34 | 846 | 24.9 | 6 |
| 1940 | Don Looney, Phil | 58 | 707 | 12.2 | 4 |
| 1941 | Don Hutson, GB | 58 | 738 | 12.7 | 10 |
| 1942 | Don Hutson, GB | 74 | 1,211 | 16.4 | 17 |
| 1943 | Don Hutson, GB | 47 | 776 | 16.5 | 11 |
| 1944 | Don Hutson, GB | 58 | 866 | 14.9 | 9 |
| 1945 | Don Hutson, GB | 47 | 834 | 17.7 | 9 |
| 1946 | Jim Benton, LA | 63 | 981 | 15.6 | 6 |
| 1947 | Jim Keane, Chi | 64 | 910 | 14.2 | 10 |
| 1948 | Tom Fears, LA | 51 | 698 | 13.7 | 4 |
| 1949 | Tom Fears, LA | 77 | 1,013 | 13.2 | 9 |
| 1950 | Tom Fears, LA | 84 | 1,116 | 13.3 | 7 |
| 1951 | Elroy Hirsch, LA | 66 | 1,495 | 22.7 | 17 |
| 1952 | Mac Speedie, Clev | 62 | 911 | 14.7 | 5 |
| 1953 | Pete Pihos, Phil | 63 | 1,049 | 16.7 | 10 |
| 1954 | Pete Pihos, Phil | 60 | 872 | 14.5 | 10 |
| | Billy Wilson, SF | 60 | 830 | 13.8 | 5 |
| 1955 | Pete Pihos, Phil | 62 | 864 | 13.9 | 7 |
| 1956 | Billy Wilson, SF | 60 | 889 | 14.8 | 5 |
| 1957 | Billy Wilson, SF | 52 | 757 | 14.6 | 6 |
| 1958 | Raymond Berry, Balt | 56 | 794 | 14.2 | 9 |
| | Pete Retzlaff, Phil | 56 | 766 | 13.7 | 2 |
| 1959 | Raymond Berry, Balt | 66 | 959 | 14.5 | 14 |
| 1960 | Lionel Taylor, Den, AFL | 92 | 1,235 | 13.4 | 12 |
| | Raymond Berry, Balt, NFL | 74 | 1,298 | 17.5 | 10 |
| 1961 | Lionel Taylor, Den, AFL | 100 | 1,176 | 11.8 | 4 |
| | Jim Phillips, LA, NFL | 78 | 1,092 | 14.0 | 5 |
| 1962 | Lionel Taylor, Den, AFL | 77 | 908 | 11.8 | 4 |
| | Bobby Mitchell, Wash, NFL | 72 | 1,384 | 19.2 | 11 |

| Year | Player, Team | No. | Yds | Avg | TD |
|------|-------------|-----|-----|-----|----|
| 1963 | Lionel Taylor, Den, AFL | 78 | 1,101 | 14.1 | 10 |
| | Bobby Joe Conrad, St. Louis, NFL | 73 | 967 | 13.2 | 10 |
| 1964 | Charley Hennigan, Houston, AFL | 101 | 1,546 | 15.3 | 8 |
| | Johnny Morris, Chi, NFL | 93 | 1,200 | 12.9 | 10 |
| 1965 | Lionel Taylor, Den, AFL | 85 | 1,131 | 13.3 | 6 |
| | Dave Parks, SF, NFL | 80 | 1,344 | 16.8 | 12 |
| 1966 | Lance Alworth, SD, AFL | 73 | 1,383 | 18.9 | 13 |
| | Charley Taylor, Wash, NFL | 72 | 1,119 | 15.5 | 12 |
| 1967 | George Sauer, NY, AFL | 75 | 1,189 | 15.9 | 6 |
| | Charley Taylor, Wash, NFL | 70 | 990 | 14.1 | 9 |
| 1968 | Clifton McNeil, SF, NFL | 71 | 994 | 14.0 | 7 |
| | Lance Alworth, SD, AFL | 68 | 1,312 | 19.3 | 10 |
| 1969 | Dan Abramowicz, NO, NFL | 73 | 1,015 | 13.9 | 7 |
| | Lance Alworth, SD, AFL | 64 | 1,003 | 15.7 | 4 |
| 1970 | Dick Gordon, Chi, NFC | 71 | 1,026 | 14.5 | 13 |
| | Marlin Briscoe, Buf, AFC | 57 | 1,036 | 18.2 | 8 |
| 1971 | Fred Biletnikoff, Oak, AFC | 61 | 929 | 15.2 | 9 |
| | Bob Tucker, NY, NFC | 59 | 791 | 13.4 | 4 |
| 1972 | Harold Jackson, Phil, NFC | 62 | 1,048 | 16.9 | 4 |
| | Fred Biletnikoff, Oak, AFC | 58 | 802 | 13.8 | 7 |
| 1973 | Harold Carmichael, Phil, NFC | 67 | 1,116 | 16.7 | 9 |
| | Fred Willis, Hou, AFC | 57 | 371 | 6.5 | 1 |
| 1974 | Lydell Mitchell, Balt, AFC | 72 | 544 | 7.6 | 2 |
| | Charles Young, Phil, NFC | 63 | 696 | 11.0 | 3 |
| 1975 | Chuck Foreman, Min, NFC | 73 | 691 | 9.5 | 9 |
| | Reggie Rucker, Clev, AFC | 60 | 770 | 12.8 | 3 |
| | Lydell Mitchell, Balt, AFC | 60 | 544 | 9.1 | 4 |
| 1976 | MacArthur Lane, KC, AFC | 66 | 686 | 10.4 | 1 |
| | Drew Pearson, Dal, NFC | 58 | 806 | 13.9 | 6 |
| 1977 | Lydell Mitchell, Balt, AFC | 71 | 620 | 8.7 | 4 |
| | Ahmad Rashad, Min, NFC | 51 | 681 | 13.4 | 2 |
| 1978 | Rickey Young, Min, NFC | 88 | 704 | 8.0 | 5 |
| | Steve Largent, Sea, AFC | 71 | 1,168 | 16.5 | 8 |

†Most catches.

## Pass Receiving† *(Cont.)*

| Year | Player, Team | No. | Yds | Avg | TD |
|------|--------------|-----|-----|-----|-----|
| 1979 | Joe Washington, Balt, AFC | 82 | 750 | 9.1 | 3 |
| | Ahmad Rashad, Min, NFC | 80 | 1,156 | 14.5 | 9 |
| 1980 | Kellen Winslow, SD, AFC | 89 | 1,290 | 14.5 | 9 |
| | Earl Cooper, SF, NFC | 83 | 567 | 6.8 | 4 |
| 1981 | Kellen Winslow, SD, AFC | 88 | 1,075 | 12.2 | 10 |
| | Dwight Clark, SF, NFC | 85 | 1,105 | 13.0 | 4 |
| 1982 | Dwight Clark, SF, NFC | 60 | 913 | 15.2 | 5 |
| | Kellen Winslow, SD, AFC | 54 | 721 | 13.4 | 6 |
| 1983 | Todd Christensen, LA, AFC | 92 | 1,247 | 13.6 | 12 |
| | Roy Green, StL, NFC | 78 | 1,227 | 15.7 | 14 |
| | Charlie Brown, Wash, NFC | 78 | 1,225 | 15.7 | 8 |
| | Earnest Gray, NY, NFC | 78 | 1,139 | 14.6 | 5 |
| 1984 | Art Monk, Wash, NFC | 106 | 1,372 | 12.9 | 7 |
| | Ozzie Newsome, Clev, AFC | 89 | 1,001 | 11.2 | 5 |
| 1985 | Roger Craig, SF, NFC | 92 | 1,016 | 11.0 | 6 |
| | Lionel James, SD, AFC | 86 | 1,027 | 11.9 | 6 |
| 1986 | Todd Christensen, LA, AFC | 95 | 1,153 | 12.1 | 8 |
| | Jerry Rice, SF, NFC | 86 | 1,570 | 18.3 | 15 |
| 1987 | J.T. Smith, StL Card, NFC | 91 | 1,117 | 12.3 | 8 |
| | Al Toon, NY, AFC | 68 | 976 | 14.4 | 5 |
| 1988 | Al Toon, NY, AFC | 93 | 1,067 | 11.5 | 5 |
| | Henry Ellard, LA, NFC | 86 | 1,414 | 16.4 | 10 |
| 1989 | Sterling Sharpe, GB, NFC | 90 | 1,423 | 15.8 | 12 |
| | Andre Reed, Buf, AFC | 88 | 1,312 | 14.9 | 9 |
| 1990 | Jerry Rice, SF, NFC | 100 | 1,502 | 15.0 | 13 |
| | Haywood Jeffires, Hou, AFC | 74 | 1,048 | 14.2 | 8 |
| | Drew Hill, Hou, AFC | 74 | 1,019 | 13.8 | 5 |
| 1991 | Haywood Jeffires, Hou, AFC | 100 | 1,181 | 11.8 | 7 |
| | Michael Irvin, Dal, NFC | 93 | 1,523 | 16.4 | 8 |
| 1992 | Sterling Sharpe, GB, NFC | 108 | 1,461 | 13.5 | 13 |
| | Haywood Jeffires, Hou, AFC | 90 | 913 | 10.1 | 9 |
| 1993 | Sterling Sharpe, GB, NFC | 112 | 1,274 | 11.4 | 11 |
| | Reggie Langhorne, Ind, AFC | 85 | 1,038 | 12.2 | 3 |

| Year | Player, Team | No. | Yds | Avg | TD |
|------|--------------|-----|-----|-----|-----|
| 1994 | Cris Carter, Min, NFC | 122 | 1,256 | 10.3 | 7 |
| | Ben Coates, NE, AFC | 96 | 1,174 | 12.2 | 7 |
| 1995 | Herman Moore, Det, NFC | 123 | 1,686 | 13.7 | 14 |
| | Carl Pickens, Cin, AFC | 99 | 1,234 | 12.5 | 17 |
| 1996 | Jerry Rice, SF, NFC | 108 | 1,254 | 11.6 | 8 |
| | Carl Pickens, Cin, AFC | 100 | 1,180 | 11.8 | 12 |
| 1997 | Herman Moore, Det, NFC | 104 | 1,293 | 12.4 | 8 |
| | Tim Brown, Oak, AFC | 104 | 1,408 | 13.5 | 5 |
| 1998 | Frank Sanders, Ariz, NFC | 89 | 1,145 | 12.9 | 3 |
| | O.J. McDuffie, Mia, AFC | 90 | 1,050 | 11.7 | 7 |
| 1999 | Muhsin Muhammad, Car, NFC | 96 | 1,253 | 13.1 | 8 |
| | Jimmy Smith, Jax, AFC | 116 | 1,636 | 14.1 | 6 |
| 2000 | Muhsin Muhammad, Car, NFC | 102 | 1,183 | 11.6 | 6 |
| | Marvin Harrison, Ind, AFC | 102 | 1,413 | 13.9 | 14 |
| 2001 | Rod Smith, Den, AFC | 113 | 1,343 | 11.9 | 11 |
| | Keyshawn Johnson, TB, NFC | 106 | 1,266 | 11.9 | 1 |
| 2002 | Marvin Harrison, Ind, AFC | 143 | 1,722 | 12.0 | 11 |
| | Randy Moss, Min, NFC | 106 | 1,347 | 12.7 | 7 |
| 2003 | LaDainian Tomlinson, SD, AFC | 100 | 725 | 7.3 | 4 |
| | Torry Holt, StL, NFC | 117 | 1,696 | 14.5 | 12 |
| 2004 | Tony Gonzalez, KC, AFC | 102 | 1,258 | 12.3 | 7 |
| | Joe Horn, NO, NFC | 94 | 1,399 | 14.9 | 11 |
| 2005 | Chad Johnson, Cin, AFC | 97 | 1,432 | 14.8 | 9 |
| | Steve Smith, Car, NFC | 103 | 1,563 | 15.2 | 12 |
| 2006 | Chad Johnson, Cin, AFC | 87 | 1,369 | 15.7 | 7 |
| | Roy Williams, Det, NFC | 82 | 1,310 | 16.0 | 7 |
| 2007 | Reggie Wayne, Ind, AFC | 104 | 1,510 | 14.5 | 10 |
| | Larry Fitzgerald, Ari, NFC | 100 | 1,409 | 14.1 | 10 |
| 2008 | Andre Johnson, Hou, AFC | 115 | 1,575 | 13.7 | 8 |
| | Larry Fitzgerald, Ari, NFC | 96 | 1,431 | 14.9 | 12 |
| 2009 | Wes Welker, NE, AFC | 123 | 1,348 | 11.0 | 4 |
| | Steve Smith, NYG, NFC | 107 | 1,220 | 11.4 | 7 |
| 2010 | Roddy White, Atl, NFC | 115 | 1,389 | 12.1 | 10 |
| | Reggie Wayne, Ind, AFC | 111 | 1,355 | 12.2 | 6 |

†Most catches.

## Scoring

| Year | Player, Team | TD | FG | PAT | TP |
|------|--------------|-----|-----|-----|-----|
| 1932 | Earl Clark, Portsmouth | 6 | 3 | 10 | 55 |
| 1933 | Ken Strong, NY | 6 | 5 | 13 | 64 |
| | Glenn Presnell, Ports | 6 | 6 | 10 | 64 |
| 1934 | Jack Manders, Chi | 3 | 10 | 31 | 79 |
| 1935 | Earl Clark, Det | 6 | 1 | 16 | 55 |
| 1936 | Earl Clark, Det | 7 | 4 | 19 | 73 |
| 1937 | Jack Manders, Chi | 5 | 18 | 15 | 69 |
| 1938 | Clarke Hinkle, GB | 7 | 3 | 7 | 58 |
| 1939 | Andy Farkas, Wash | 11 | 0 | 2 | 68 |
| 1940 | Don Hutson, GB | 7 | 0 | 15 | 57 |
| 1941 | Don Hutson, GB | 12 | 1 | 20 | 95 |
| 1942 | Don Hutson, GB | 17 | 1 | 33 | 138 |

| Year | Player, Team | TD | FG | PAT | TP |
|------|--------------|-----|-----|-----|-----|
| 1943 | Don Hutson, GB | 12 | 3 | 36 | 117 |
| 1944 | Don Hutson, GB | 9 | 0 | 31 | 85 |
| 1945 | Steve Van Buren, Phil | 18 | 0 | 2 | 110 |
| 1946 | Ted Fritsch, GB | 10 | 9 | 13 | 100 |
| 1947 | Pat Harder, Chicago Cards | 7 | 7 | 39 | 102 |
| 1948 | Pat Harder, Chicago Cards | 6 | 7 | 53 | 110 |
| 1949 | Pat Harder, Chicago Cards | 8 | 3 | 45 | 102 |
| | Gene Roberts, NY | 17 | 0 | 0 | 102 |
| 1950 | Doak Walker, Det | 11 | 8 | 38 | 128 |
| 1951 | Elroy Hirsch, LA | 17 | 0 | 0 | 102 |
| 1952 | Gordy Soltau, SF | 7 | 6 | 34 | 94 |
| 1953 | Gordy Soltau, SF | 6 | 10 | 48 | 114 |

## Scoring *(Cont.)*

| Year | Player, Team | TD | FG | PAT | TP |
|------|--------------|-----|-----|-----|-----|
| 1954 | Bobby Walston, Phi | 11 | 4 | 36 | 114 |
| 1955 | Doak Walker, Det | 7 | 9 | 27 | 96 |
| 1956 | Bobby Layne, Det | 5 | 12 | 33 | 99 |
| 1957 | Sam Baker, Was | 1 | 14 | 29 | 77 |
|      | Lou Groza, Cle | 0 | 15 | 32 | 77 |
| 1958 | Jim Brown, Cle | 18 | 0 | 0 | 108 |
| 1959 | Paul Hornung, GB | 7 | 7 | 31 | 94 |
| 1960 | Paul Hornung, GB, NFL | 15 | 15 | 41 | 176 |
|      | Gene Mingo, Den, AFL | 6 | 18 | 33 | 123 |
| 1961 | Gino Cappelletti, Bos, AFL | 8 | 17 | 48 | 147 |
|      | Paul Hornung, GB, NFL | 10 | 15 | 41 | 146 |
| 1962 | Gene Mingo, Den, AFL | 4 | 27 | 32 | 137 |
|      | Jim Taylor, GB, NFL | 19 | 0 | 0 | 114 |
| 1963 | Gino Cappelletti, Bos, AFL | 2 | 22 | 35 | 113 |
|      | Don Chandler, NY, NFL | 0 | 18 | 52 | 106 |
| 1964 | Gino Cappelletti, Bos, AFL | 7 | 25 | 36 | 155 |
|      | Lenny Moore, Balt, NFL | 20 | 0 | 0 | 120 |
| 1965 | Gale Sayers, Chi, NFL | 22 | 0 | 0 | 132 |
|      | Gino Cappelletti, Bos, AFL | 9 | 17 | 27 | 132 |
| 1966 | Gino Cappelletti, Bos, AFL | 6 | 16 | 35 | 119 |
|      | Bruce Gossett, LA, NFL | 0 | 28 | 29 | 113 |
| 1967 | Jim Bakken, StL, NFL | 0 | 27 | 36 | 117 |
|      | George Blanda, Oak, AFL | 0 | 20 | 56 | 116 |
| 1968 | Jim Turner, NY, AFL | 0 | 34 | 43 | 145 |
|      | Leroy Kelly, Clev, NFL | 20 | 0 | 0 | 120 |
| 1969 | Jim Turner, NY, AFL | 0 | 32 | 33 | 129 |
|      | Fred Cox, Min, NFL | 0 | 26 | 43 | 121 |
| 1970 | Fred Cox, Min, NFC | 0 | 30 | 35 | 125 |
|      | Jan Stenerud, KC, AFC | 0 | 30 | 26 | 116 |
| 1971 | Garo Yepremian, Mia, AFC | 0 | 28 | 33 | 117 |
|      | Curt Knight, Was, NFC | 0 | 29 | 27 | 114 |
| 1972 | Chester Marcol, GB, NFC | 0 | 33 | 29 | 128 |
|      | Bobby Howfield, NY AFC | 0 | 27 | 40 | 121 |
| 1973 | David Ray, LA, NFC | 0 | 30 | 40 | 130 |
|      | Roy Gerela, Pit, AFC | 0 | 29 | 36 | 123 |
| 1974 | Chester Marcol, GB, NFC | 0 | 25 | 19 | 94 |
|      | Roy Gerela, Pit, AFC | 0 | 20 | 33 | 93 |
| 1975 | O.J. Simpson, Buf, AFC | 23 | 0 | 0 | 138 |
|      | Chuck Foreman, Min, NFC | 22 | 0 | 0 | 132 |
| 1976 | Toni Linhart, Balt, AFC | 0 | 20 | 49 | 109 |
|      | Mark Moseley, Wash, NFC | 0 | 22 | 31 | 97 |
| 1977 | Errol Mann, Oak, AFC | 0 | 20 | 39 | 99 |
|      | Walter Payton, Chi, NFC | 16 | 0 | 0 | 96 |
| 1978 | Frank Corral, LA, NFC | 0 | 29 | 31 | 118 |
|      | Pat Leahy, NY, AFC | 0 | 22 | 41 | 107 |
| 1979 | John Smith, NE, AFC | 0 | 23 | 46 | 115 |
|      | Mark Moseley, Was, NFC | 0 | 25 | 39 | 114 |
| 1980 | John Smith, NE, AFC | 0 | 26 | 51 | 129 |
|      | Ed Murray, Det, NFC | 0 | 27 | 35 | 116 |
| 1981 | Ed Murray, Det, NFC | 0 | 25 | 46 | 121 |
|      | Rafael Septien, Dal, NFC | 0 | 27 | 40 | 121 |
|      | Jim Breech, Cin, AFC | 0 | 22 | 49 | 115 |
|      | Nick Lowery, KC, AFC | 0 | 26 | 37 | 115 |
| 1982 | Marcus Allen, LA, AFC | 14 | 0 | 0 | 84 |
|      | Wendell Tyler, LA, NFC | 13 | 0 | 0 | 78 |
| 1983 | Mark Moseley, Was, NFC | 0 | 33 | 62 | 161 |
|      | Gary Anderson, Pit, AFC | 0 | 27 | 38 | 119 |
| 1984 | Ray Wersching, SF, NFC | 0 | 25 | 56 | 131 |
| | Gary Anderson, Pit, AFC | 0 | 24 | 45 | 117 |
| 1985 | Kevin Butler, Chi, NFC | 0 | 31 | 51 | 144 |
|      | Gary Anderson, Pit, AFC | 0 | 33 | 40 | 139 |
| 1986 | Tony Franklin, NE, AFC | 0 | 32 | 44 | 140 |
|      | Kevin Butler, Chi, NFC | 0 | 28 | 36 | 120 |
| 1987 | Jerry Rice, SF, NFC | 23 | 0 | 0 | 138 |
|      | Jim Breech, Cin, AFC | 0 | 24 | 25 | 97 |
| 1988 | Scott Norwood, Buf, AFC | 0 | 32 | 33 | 129 |
|      | Mike Cofer, SF, NFC | 0 | 27 | 40 | 121 |
| 1989 | Mike Cofer, SF, NFC | 0 | 29 | 49 | 136 |
|      | David Treadwell, Den, AFC | 0 | 27 | 39 | 120 |
| 1990 | Nick Lowery, KC, AFC | 0 | 34 | 37 | 139 |
|      | Chip Lohmiller, Was, NFC | 0 | 30 | 41 | 131 |
| 1991 | Chip Lohmiller, Was, NFC | 0 | 31 | 56 | 149 |
|      | Pete Stoyanovich, Mia, AFC | 0 | 31 | 28 | 121 |
| 1992 | Pete Stoyanovich, Mia, AFC | 0 | 30 | 34 | 124 |
|      | Morten Anderson, NO, NFC | 0 | 29 | 33 | 120 |
|      | Chip Lohmiller, Was, NFC | 0 | 30 | 30 | 120 |
| 1993 | Jeff Jaeger, Rai, AFC | 0 | 35 | 27 | 132 |
|      | Jason Hanson, Det, NFC | 0 | 34 | 28 | 130 |
| 1994 | John Carney, SD, AFC | 0 | 34 | 33 | 135 |
|      | Fuad Reveiz, Min, NFC | 0 | 34 | 30 | 132 |
|      | Emmitt Smith, Dal, NFC | 22 | 0 | 0 | 132 |
| 1995 | Emmitt Smith, Dal, NFC | 25 | 0 | 0 | 150 |
|      | Norm Johnson, Pit, AFC | 0 | 34 | 39 | 141 |
| 1996 | John Kasay, Car, NFC | 0 | 37 | 34 | 145 |
|      | Cary Blanchard, Ind, AFC | 0 | 36 | 27 | 135 |
| 1997 | Richie Cunningham, Dal, NFC | 0 | 34 | 24 | 126 |
|      | Mike Hollis, Jax, AFC | 0 | 41 | 31 | 134 |
| 1998 | Gary Anderson, Min, NFC | 0 | 35 | 59 | 164 |
|      | Steve Christie, Buf, AFC | 0 | 33 | 41 | 140 |
| 1999 | Jeff Wilkins, StL, NFC | 0 | 20 | 64 | 124 |
|      | Mike Vanderjagt, Ind, AFC | 0 | 34 | 43 | 145 |
| 2000 | Marshall Faulk, StL, NFC | 26 | 0 | 0 | 160 |
|      | Matt Stover, Balt, AFC | 0 | 35 | 30 | 135 |
| 2001 | Marshall Faulk, StL, NFC | 21 | 0 | 0 | 128 |
|      | Mike Vanderjagt, Ind, AFC | 0 | 28 | 41 | 125 |
| 2002 | Jay Feely. Atl, NFC | 0 | 32 | 42 | 138 |
|      | Priest Holmes, KC, AFC | 24 | 0 | 0 | 144 |
| 2003 | Jeff Wilkins StL, NFC | 0 | 39 | 46 | 163 |
|      | Priest Holmes, KC, AFC | 27 | 0 | 0 | 162 |
| 2004 | Adam Vinatieri, NE, AFC | 0 | 31 | 48 | 141 |
|      | David Akers, Phi, NFC | 0 | 27 | 41 | 122 |
| 2005 | Shayne Graham, Cin, AFC | 0 | 28 | 47 | 131 |
|      | Shaun Alexander, Sea, NFC | 28 | 0 | 0 | 168 |
| 2006 | LaDainian Tomlinson, SD, AFC | 31 | 0 | 0 | 186 |
|      | Robbie Gould, Chi, NFC | 0 | 32 | 47 | 143 |
| 2007 | Randy Moss, NE, AFC | 23 | 0 | 0 | 138 |
|      | Mason Crosby, GB, NFC | 0 | 31 | 48 | 141 |
| 2008 | Stephen Gostkowski, NE, AFC | 0 | 36 | 40 | 148 |
|      | David Akers, Phi, NFC | 0 | 33 | 45 | 144 |
| 2009 | Nate Kaeding, SD, AFC | 0 | 32 | 50 | 146 |
|      | David Akers, Phi, NFC | 0 | 32 | 43 | 139 |
| 2010 | David Akers, Phi, NFC | 0 | 32 | 47 | 143 |
|      | Sebastian Janikowski, Oak, AFC | 0 | 33 | 43 | 142 |

## Interceptions

| Year | Player, Team | Int | Yds | Year | Player, Team | Int | Yds |
|---|---|---|---|---|---|---|---|
| 1940 | Clarence Parker, Brooklyn | 6 | 146 | 1972 | Bill Bradley, Phil, NFC | 9 | 73 |
| | Kent Ryan, Det | 6 | 65 | | Mike Sensibaugh, KC, AFC | 8 | 65 |
| | Don Hutson, GB | 6 | 24 | 1973 | Dick Anderson, Mia, AFC | 8 | 163 |
| 1941 | Marshall Goldberg, Chicago Card | 7 | 54 | | Mike Wagner, Pit, AFC | 8 | 134 |
| | Art Jones, Pit | 7 | 35 | | Bobby Bryant, Min, NFC | 7 | 105 |
| 1942 | Clyde Turner, Chicago Bears | 8 | 96 | 1974 | Emmitt Thomas, KC, AFC | 12 | 214 |
| 1943 | Sammy Baugh, Wash | 11 | 112 | | Ray Brown, Atl, NFC | 8 | 164 |
| 1944 | Howard Livingston, NYG | 9 | 172 | 1975 | Mel Blount, Pit, AFC | 11 | 121 |
| 1945 | Ray Zimmerman, Phil | 7 | 90 | | Paul Krause, Min, NFC | 10 | 201 |
| 1946 | Bill Dudley, Pittsburgh | 10 | 242 | 1976 | Monte Jackson, LA, NFC | 10 | 173 |
| 1947 | Frank Reagan, NYG | 10 | 203 | | Ken Riley, Cin, AFC | 9 | 141 |
| | Frank Seno, Bos | 10 | 100 | 1977 | Lyle Blackwood, Balt, AFC | 10 | 163 |
| 1948 | Dan Sandifier, Wash | 13 | 258 | | Rolland Lawrence, Atl, NFC | 7 | 138 |
| 1949 | Bob Nussbaumer, Chicago Car | 12 | 157 | 1978 | Thom Darden, Clev, AFC | 10 | 200 |
| 1950 | Orban Sanders, NY Yanks | 13 | 199 | | Ken Stone, StL, AFC | 9 | 139 |
| 1951 | Otto Schnellbacher, NYG | 11 | 194 | | Willie Buchanon, GB, NFC | 9 | 93 |
| 1952 | Dick Lane, LA | 14 | 298 | 1979 | Mike Reinfeldt, Hou, AFC | 12 | 205 |
| 1953 | Jack Christiansen, Det | 12 | 238 | | Lemar Parrish, Wash, NFC | 9 | 65 |
| 1954 | Dick Lane, Chicago Card | 10 | 181 | 1980 | Lester Hayes, Oak, AFC | 13 | 273 |
| 1955 | Will Sherman, LA | 11 | 101 | | Nolan Cromwell, LA, NFC | 8 | 140 |
| 1956 | Lindon Crow, Chicago Card | 11 | 170 | 1981 | Everson Walls, Dal, NFC | 11 | 133 |
| 1957 | Milt Davis, Balt | 10 | 219 | | John Harris, Sea, AFC | 10 | 155 |
| | Jack Christiansen, Det | 10 | 137 | 1982 | Everson Walls, Dal, NFC | 7 | 61 |
| | Jack Butler, Pit | 10 | 85 | | Ken Riley, Cin, AFC | 5 | 88 |
| 1958 | Jim Patton, NYG | 11 | 183 | | Bobby Jackson, NYJ, AFC | 5 | 84 |
| 1959 | Dean Derby, Pit | 7 | 127 | | Dwayne Woodruff, Pit, AFC | 5 | 53 |
| | Milt Davis, Balt | 7 | 119 | | Donnie Shell, Pit, AFC | 5 | 27 |
| | Don Shinnick, Balt | 7 | 70 | 1983 | Mark Murphy, Wash, NFC | 9 | 127 |
| 1960 | Goose Gonsoulin, Den, AFL | 11 | 98 | | Ken Riley, Cin, AFC | 8 | 89 |
| | Dave Baker, SF, NFL | 10 | 96 | | Vann McElroy, LA, AFC | 8 | 68 |
| | Jerry Norton, StL, NFL | 10 | 96 | 1984 | Ken Easley, Sea, AFC | 10 | 126 |
| 1961 | Billy Atkins, Buf, AFL | 10 | 158 | | Tom Flynn, GB, NFC | 9 | 106 |
| | Dick Lynch, NYG, NFL | 9 | 60 | 1985 | Everson Walls, Dal, NFC | 9 | 31 |
| 1962 | Lee Riley, NY Titans, AFL | 11 | 122 | | Albert Lewis, KC, AFC | 8 | 59 |
| | Willie Wood, GB, NFL | 9 | 132 | | Eugene Daniel, Ind, AFC | 8 | 53 |
| 1963 | Fred Glick, Hous, AFL | 12 | 180 | 1986 | Ronnie Lott, SF, NFC | 10 | 134 |
| | Dick Lynch, NYG, NFL | 9 | 251 | | Deron Cherry, KC, AFC | 9 | 150 |
| | Roosevelt Taylor, Chi, NFL | 9 | 172 | 1987 | Barry Wilburn, Wash, NFC | 9 | 135 |
| 1964 | Dainard Paulson, NYJ, AFL | 12 | 157 | | Mike Prior, Ind, AFC | 6 | 57 |
| | Paul Krause, Wash, NFL | 12 | 140 | | Mark Kelso, Buf, AFC | 6 | 25 |
| 1965 | W. K. Hicks, Hous, AFL | 9 | 156 | | Keith Bostic, Hou, AFC | 6 | -14 |
| | Bobby Boyd, Balt, NFL | 9 | 78 | 1988 | Scott Case, Atl, NFC | 10 | 47 |
| 1966 | Larry Wilson, StL, NFL | 10 | 180 | | Erik McMillan, NYJ, AFC | 8 | 168 |
| | Johnny Robinson, KC, AFL | 10 | 136 | 1989 | Felix Wright, Clev, AFC | 9 | 91 |
| | Bobby Hunt, KC, AFL | 10 | 113 | | Eric Allen, Phil, NFC | 8 | 38 |
| 1967 | Lem Barney, Det, NFL | 10 | 232 | 1990 | Mark Carrier, Chi, NFC | 10 | 39 |
| | Dave Whitsell, NO, NFL | 10 | 178 | | Richard Johnson, Hou, AFC | 8 | 100 |
| | Miller Farr, Hous, AFL | 10 | 264 | 1991 | Ronnie Lott, LA, AFC | 8 | 52 |
| | Tom Janik, Buf, AFL | 10 | 222 | | Ray Crockett, Det, NFC | 6 | 141 |
| | Dick Westmoreland, Mia, AFL | 10 | 127 | | Deion Sanders, Atl, NFC | 6 | 119 |
| 1968 | Dave Grayson, Oak, AFL | 10 | 195 | | Aeneas Williams, Phoenix, NFC | 6 | 60 |
| | Willie Williams, NYG, NFL | 10 | 103 | | Tim McKyer, Atl, NFC | 6 | 24 |
| 1969 | Mel Renfro, Dal, NFL | 10 | 118 | 1992 | Henry Jones, Buf, AFC | 8 | 263 |
| | Emmitt Thomas, KC, AFL | 9 | 146 | | Audray McMillian, Min, NFC | 8 | 157 |
| 1970 | Johnny Robinson, KC, AFC | 10 | 155 | 1993 | Eugene Robinson, Sea, AFC | 9 | 80 |
| | Dick LeBeau, Det, NFC | 9 | 96 | | Nate Odomes, Buf, AFC | 9 | 65 |
| 1971 | Bill Bradley, Phil, NFC | 11 | 248 | | Deion Sanders, Atl, NFC | 7 | 91 |
| | Ken Houston, Hou, AFC | 9 | 220 | 1994 | Eric Turner, Clev, AFC | 9 | 199 |
| | | | | | Aeneas Williams, Ariz, NFC | 9 | 89 |

## Interceptions *(Cont.)*

| Year | Player, Team | Int | Yds |
|------|-------------|-----|-----|
| 1995 | Orlando Thomas, Min, NFC | 9 | 108 |
|      | Willie Williams, Pit, AFC | 7 | 122 |
| 1996 | Tyrone Braxton, Den, AFC | 9 | 128 |
|      | Keith Lyle, StL, NFC | 9 | 152 |
| 1997 | Ryan McNeil, StL, NFC | 9 | 127 |
|      | Mark McMillian, KC, AFC | 8 | 274 |
|      | Darryl Williams, Sea, AFC | 8 | 172 |
| 1998 | Ty Law, NE, AFC | 9 | 133 |
|      | Kwamie Lassiter, Ariz, NFC | 8 | 80 |
| 1999 | Rod Woodson, Balt, AFC | 7 | 195 |
|      | Sam Madison, Mia, AFC | 7 | 164 |
|      | James Hasty, KC, AFC | 7 | 98 |
|      | Donnie Abraham, TB, NFC | 7 | 115 |
|      | Troy Vincent, Phil, NFC | 7 | 91 |
| 2000 | Darren Sharper, GB, NFC | 9 | 109 |
|      | Samari Rolle, Ten, AFC | 7 | 140 |
|      | Brian Walker, Mia, AFC | 7 | 80 |
| 2001 | Ronde Barber, TB, NFC | 10 | 86 |
|      | Anthony Henry, Clev, AFC | 10 | 177 |
| 2002 | Rod Woodson, Oak, AFC | 8 | 225 |
|      | Brian Kelly, TB, NFC | 8 | 68 |
| 2003 | Brian Russell, Min, NFC | 9 | 185 |
|      | Tony Parrish, SFo, NFC | 9 | 202 |
|      | Patrick Surtain, Mia, AFC | 7 | 59 |
|      | Ed Reed, Balt, AFC | 7 | 132 |
|      | Marcus Coleman, Hou, AFC | 7 | 95 |
| 2004 | Ed Reed, Balt, AFC | 9 | 358 |
|      | Chris Gamble, Car, NFC | 6 | 15 |
|      | Ken Lucas, Sea, NFC | 6 | 46 |
| 2005 | Ty Law, NYJ, AFC | 10 | 195 |
|      | Deltha O'Neal, Cin, AFC | 10 | 103 |
|      | Darren Sharper, Min, NFC | 9 | 276 |
| 2006 | Champ Bailey, Den, AFC | 10 | 162 |
|      | Asante Samuel, NE, AFC | 10 | 120 |
|      | Walt Harris, SF, NFC | 8 | 84 |
|      | Charles Woodson, GB, NFC | 8 | 61 |
| 2007 | Antonio Cromartie, SD, AFC | 10 | 144 |
|      | O. J. Atogwe, StL, NFC | 8 | 125 |
| 2008 | Ed Reed, Balt, AFC | 9 | 264 |
|      | Nick Collins, GB, NFC | 7 | 295 |
|      | Charles Woodson, GB, NFC | 7 | 169 |
| 2009 | Darren Sharper, NO, NFC | 9 | 376 |
|      | Charles Woodson, GB, NFC | 9 | 179 |
|      | Asante Samuel, Phi, NFC | 9 | 117 |
|      | Jairus Byrd, Buf, AFC | 9 | 118 |
| 2010 | Ed Reed, Bal, AFC | 8 | 183 |
|      | Asante Samuel, Phi, NFC | 7 | 70 |

## Sacks*

| Year | Player, Team | Sacks |
|------|-------------|-------|
| 1982 | Doug Martin, Min, NFC | 11.5 |
|      | Jesse Baker, Hou, AFC | 7.5 |
| 1983 | Mark Gastineau, NYJ, AFC | 19.0 |
|      | Fred Dean, SF, NFC | 17.5 |
| 1984 | Mark Gastineau, NYJ, AFC | 22.0 |
|      | Richard Dent, Chi, NFC | 17.5 |
| 1985 | Richard Dent, Chi, NFC | 17.0 |
|      | Andre Tippett, NE, AFC | 16.5 |
| 1986 | Lawrence Taylor, NYG, NFC | 20.5 |
|      | Sean Jones, LA, AFC | 15.5 |
| 1987 | Reggie White, Phil, NFC | 21.0 |
|      | Andre Tippett, NE, AFC | 12.5 |
| 1988 | Reggie White, Phil, NFC | 18.0 |
|      | G. Townsend, LA, AFC | 11.5 |
| 1989 | Chris Doleman, Min, NFC | 21.0 |
|      | Lee Williams, SD, AFC | 14.0 |
| 1990 | Derrick Thomas, KC, AFC | 20.0 |
|      | Charles Haley, SF, NFC | 16.0 |
| 1991 | Pat Swilling, NO, NFC | 17.0 |
|      | William Fuller, Hou, AFC | 15.0 |
| 1992 | Clyde Simmons, Phil, NFC | 19.0 |
|      | Leslie O'Neal, SD, AFC | 17.0 |
| 1993 | Neil Smith, KC, AFC | 15.0 |
|      | Renaldo Turnbull, NO, NFC | 13.0 |
|      | Reggie White, GB, NFC | 13.0 |
| 1994 | Kevin Greene, Pit, AFC | 14.0 |
|      | Ken Harvey, Wash, NFC | 13.5 |
|      | John Randle, Min, NFC | 13.5 |
| 1995 | Bryce Paup, Buf, AFC | 17.5 |
|      | William Fuller, Phil, NFC | 13.0 |
|      | Wayne Martin, NO, NFC | 13.0 |

| Year | Player, Team | Int | Yds |
|------|-------------|-----|-----|
| 1996 | Kevin Greene, Car, NFC | | 14.5 |
|      | Michael McCrary, Sea, AFC | | 13.5 |
|      | Bruce Smith, Buf, AFC | | 13.5 |
| 1997 | John Randle, Min, NFC | | 15.5 |
|      | Bruce Smith, Buf, AFC | | 14.0 |
| 1998 | Michael Sinclair, Sea, AFC | | 16.5 |
|      | Reggie White, GB, NFC | | 16.0 |
| 1999 | Kevin Carter, StL, NFC | | 17.0 |
|      | Jevon Kearse, Ten, AFC | | 14.5 |
| 2000 | La'Roi Glover, NO, NFC | | 17.0 |
|      | Trace Armstrong, Mia, AFC | | 16.5 |
| 2001 | Michael Strahan, NYG, NFC | | 22.5 |
|      | Peter Boulware, Balt, AFC | | 15.0 |
| 2002 | Jason Taylor, Mia, AFC | | 18.5 |
|      | Simeon Rice, TB, NFC | | 15.5 |
| 2003 | Michael Strahan, NYG, NFC | | 18.5 |
|      | Adewale Ogunleye, Mia, AFC | | 15.0 |
| 2004 | Dwight Freeney, Ind, AFC | | 16.0 |
|      | Bertrand Berry, Ariz, NFC | | 14.5 |
| 2005 | Derrick Burgess, Oak, AFC | | 16.0 |
|      | Osi Umenyiora, NYG, NFC | | 14.5 |
| 2006 | Shawne Merriman, SD, AFC | | 17.0 |
|      | Aaron Kampman, GB, NFC | | 15.5 |
| 2007 | Jared Allen, KC, AFC | | 15.5 |
|      | Patrick Kerney, Sea, NFC | | 14.5 |
| 2008 | DeMarcus Ware, Dal, NFC | | 20.0 |
|      | Joey Porter, Mia, AFC | | 17.5 |
| 2009 | Elvis Dumervil, Den, AFC | | 17.0 |
|      | Jared Allen, Min, NFC | | 14.5 |
| 2010 | DeMarcus Ware, Dal, NFC | | 15.5 |
|      | Tamba Hali, KC, AFC | | 14.5 |

*Sacks were not kept as an official NFL statistic until 1982.

# Pro Bowl Alltime Results

| Date | Result |
|------|--------|
| 1-15-39 | NY Giants 13, Pro All-Stars 10 |
| 1-14-40 | Green Bay 16, NFL All-Stars 7 |
| 12-29-40 | Chi Bears 28, NFL All-Stars 14 |
| 1-4-42 | Chi Bears 35, NFL All-Stars 24 |
| 12-27-42 | NFL All-Stars 17, Washington 14 |
| 1-14-51 | A. Conf. 28, N. Conf. 27 |
| 1-12-52 | N. Conf. 30, A. Conf. 13 |
| 1-10-53 | N. Conf. 27, A. Conf. 7 |
| 1-17-54 | East 20, West 9 |
| 1-16-55 | West 26, East 19 |
| 1-15-56 | East 31, West 30 |
| 1-13-57 | West 19, East 10 |
| 1-12-58 | West 26, East 7 |
| 1-11-59 | East 28, West 21 |
| 1-17-60 | West 38, East 21 |
| 1-15-61 | West 35, East 31 |
| 1-7-62 | AFL West 47, East 27 |
| 1-14-62 | NFL West 31, East 30 |
| 1-13-63 | AFL West 21, East 14 |
| 1-13-63 | NFL East 30, West 20 |
| 1-12-64 | NFL West 31, East 17 |
| 1-19-64 | AFL West 27, East 24 |

| Date | Result |
|------|--------|
| 1-10-65 | NFL West 34, East 14 |
| 1-16-65 | AFL West 38, East 14 |
| 1-15-66 | AFL All-Stars 30, Buffalo 19 |
| 1-15-66 | NFL East 36, West 7 |
| 1-21-67 | AFL East 30, West 23 |
| 1-22-67 | NFL East 20, West 10 |
| 1-21-68 | AFL East 25, West 24 |
| 1-21-68 | NFL West 38, East 20 |
| 1-19-69 | AFL West 38, East 25 |
| 1-19-69 | NFL West 10, East 7 |
| 1-17-70 | AFL West 26, East 3 |
| 1-18-70 | NFL West 16, East 13 |
| 1-24-71 | NFC 27, AFC 6 |
| 1-23-72 | AFC 26, NFC 13 |
| 1-21-73 | AFC 33, NFC 28 |
| 1-20-74 | AFC 15, NFC 13 |
| 1-20-75 | NFC 17, AFC 10 |
| 1-26-76 | NFC 23, AFC 20 |
| 1-17-77 | AFC 24, NFC 14 |
| 1-23-78 | NFC 14, AFC 13 |
| 1-29-79 | NFC 13, AFC 7 |
| 1-27-80 | NFC 37, AFC 27 |
| 2-1-81 | NFC 21, AFC 7 |
| 1-31-82 | AFC 16, NFC 13 |
| 2-6-83 | NFC 20, AFC 19 |
| 1-29-84 | NFC 45, AFC 3 |

| Date | Result |
|------|--------|
| 1-27-85 | AFC 22, NFC 14 |
| 2-2-86 | NFC 28, AFC 24 |
| 2-1-87 | AFC 10, NFC 6 |
| 2-7-88 | AFC 15, NFC 6 |
| 1-29-89 | NFC 34, AFC 3 |
| 2-4-90 | NFC 27, AFC 21 |
| 2-3-91 | AFC 23, NFC 21 |
| 2-2-92 | NFC 21, AFC 15 |
| 2-7-93 | AFC 23, NFC 20 |
| 2-6-94 | NFC 17, AFC 3 |
| 2-5-95 | AFC 41, NFC 13 |
| 2-4-96 | NFC 20, AFC 13 |
| 2-2-97 | AFC 26, NFC 23 |
| 2-1-98 | AFC 29, NFC 24 |
| 2-7-99 | AFC 23, NFC 10 |
| 2-6-00 | NFC 51, AFC 31 |
| 2-4-01 | AFC 38, NFC 17 |
| 2-10-02 | AFC 38, NFC 30 |
| 2-2-03 | AFC 45, NFC 20 |
| 2-8-04 | NFC 55, AFC 52 |
| 2-13-05 | AFC 38, NFC 27 |
| 2-12-06 | NFC 23, AFC 17 |
| 2-10-07 | AFC 31, NFC 28 |
| 2-10-08 | NFC 42, AFC 30 |
| 2-8-09 | NFC 30, AFC 21 |
| 1-31-10 | AFC 41, NFC 34 |
| 1-30-11 | NFC 55, AFC 41 |

# Chicago All-Star Game* Results

| Date | Result (Attendance) |
|------|---------------------|
| 8-31-34 | Chi Bears 0, All-Stars 0 (79,432) |
| 8-29-35 | Chi Bears 5, All-Stars 0 (77,450) |
| 9-2-36 | All-Stars 7, Detroit 7 (76,000) |
| 9-1-37 | All-Stars 6, Green Bay 0 (84,560) |
| 8-31-38 | All-Stars 28, Washington 16 (74,250) |
| 8-30-39 | NY Giants 9, All-Stars 0 (81,456) |
| 8-29-40 | Green Bay 45, All-Stars 28 (84,567) |
| 8-28-41 | Chi Bears 37, All-Stars 13 (98,203) |
| 8-28-42 | Chi Bears 21, All-Stars 0 (101,100) |
| 8-25-43 | All-Stars 27, Washington 7 (48,471) |
| 8-30-44 | Chi Bears 24, All-Stars 21 (48,769) |
| 8-30-45 | Green Bay 19, All-Stars 7 (92,753) |
| 8-23-46 | All-Stars 16, Los Angeles 0 (97,380) |
| 8-22-47 | All-Stars 16, Chi Bears 0 (105,840) |
| 8-20-48 | Chi Cardinals 28, All-Stars 0 (101,220) |
| 8-12-49 | Philadelphia 38, All-Stars 0 (93,780) |
| 8-11-50 | All-Stars 17, Philadelphia 7 (88,885) |
| 8-17-51 | Cleveland 33, All-Stars 0 (92,180) |
| 8-15-52 | Los Angeles 10, All-Stars 7 (88,316) |
| 8-14-53 | Detroit 24, All-Stars 10 (93,818) |
| 8-13-54 | Detroit 31, All-Stars 6 (93,470) |
| 8-12-55 | All-Stars 30, Cleveland 27 (75,000) |

| Date | Result (Attendance) |
|------|---------------------|
| 8-10-56 | Cleveland 26, All-Stars 0 (75,000) |
| 8-9-57 | NY Giants 22, All-Stars 12 (75,000) |
| 8-15-58 | All-Stars 35, Detroit 19 (70,000) |
| 8-14-59 | Baltimore 29, All-Stars 0 (70,000) |
| 8-12-60 | Baltimore 32, All-Stars 7 (70,000) |
| 8-4-61 | Philadelphia 28, All-Stars 14 (66,000) |
| 8-3-62 | Green Bay 42, All-Stars 20 (65,000) |
| 8-2-63 | All-Stars 20, Green Bay 17 (65,000) |
| 8-7-64 | Chicago 28, All-Stars 17 (65,000) |
| 8-6-65 | Cleveland 24, All-Stars 16 (68,000) |
| 8-5-66 | Green Bay 38, All-Stars 0 (72,000) |
| 8-4-67 | Green Bay 27, All-Stars 0 (70,934) |
| 8-2-68 | Green Bay 34, All-Stars 17 (69,917) |
| 8-1-69 | NY Jets 26, All-Stars 24 (74,208) |
| 7-31-70 | Kansas City 24, All-Stars 3 (69,940) |
| 7-30-71 | Baltimore 24, All-Stars 17 (52,289) |
| 7-28-72 | Dallas 20, All-Stars 7 (54,162) |
| 7-27-73 | Miami 14, All-Stars 3 (54,103) |
| 1974 | No game |
| 8-1-75 | Pittsburgh 21, All-Stars 14 (54,562) |
| 7-23-76 | Pittsburgh 24, All-Stars 0 (52,895) |

*Discontinued.

### Most Career Wins

| Coach | Yrs | Teams | Regular Season | | | | Career | | | |
|---|---|---|---|---|---|---|---|---|---|---|
| | | | W | L | T | Pct | W | L | T | Pct |
| Don Shula | 33 | Balt Colts, Dolphins | 328 | 156 | 6 | .676 | 347 | 173 | 6 | .665 |
| George Halas | 40 | Bears | 318 | 148 | 31 | .671 | 324 | 151 | 31 | .671 |
| Tom Landry | 29 | Cowboys | 250 | 162 | 6 | .605 | 270 | 178 | 6 | .601 |
| Curly Lambeau | 33 | Packers, Chi Cards, Redskins | 226 | 132 | 22 | .624 | 229 | 134 | 22 | .623 |
| *Paul Brown | 25 | Browns, Bengals | 213 | 104 | 9 | .672 | 222 | 116 | 9 | .668 |
| Chuck Noll | 23 | Steelers | 193 | 148 | 1 | .566 | 209 | 156 | 1 | .572 |
| M. Schottenheimer | 20 | Browns, Chiefs, Redskins, Chargers | 200 | 126 | 1 | .613 | 205 | 139 | 1 | .596 |
| Dan Reeves | 23 | Broncos, NY Giants, Falcons | 190 | 165 | 2 | .535 | 201 | 174 | 2 | .536 |
| Chuck Knox | 22 | LA Rams, Bills, Seahawks | 186 | 147 | 1 | .558 | 193 | 158 | 1 | .550 |
| Bill Parcells | 18 | NY Giants, Patriots, NY Jets, Cowboys | 172 | 130 | 1 | .569 | 183 | 138 | 1 | .570 |
| †Bill Belichick | 16 | Browns, Patriots | 162 | 94 | 0 | .633 | 177 | 100 | 0 | .639 |
| Mike Holmgren | 17 | Packers, Seahawks | 161 | 111 | 0 | .592 | 174 | 122 | 0 | .588 |
| Joe Gibbs | 15 | Redskins | 154 | 94 | 0 | .621 | 171 | 101 | 0 | .629 |
| Bud Grant | 18 | Vikings | 158 | 96 | 5 | .620 | 168 | 108 | 5 | .607 |
| Bill Cowher | 14 | Steelers | 149 | 90 | 1 | .623 | 161 | 99 | 1 | .619 |
| †Mike Shanahan | 17 | LA Raiders, Broncos, Redskins | 152 | 108 | 0 | .585 | 160 | 113 | 0 | .586 |
| Marv Levy | 17 | Chiefs, Bills | 143 | 112 | 0 | .561 | 154 | 120 | 0 | .562 |
| Steve Owen | 23 | NY Giants | 151 | 100 | 17 | .595 | 153 | 108 | 17 | .581 |
| Tony Dungy | 13 | Buccaneers, Ind Colts | 139 | 69 | 0 | .668 | 148 | 79 | 0 | .652 |
| †Jeff Fisher | 17 | Hou/Tenn Oilers, Tenn Titans | 142 | 120 | 0 | .542 | 147 | 126 | 0 | .563 |
| †Tom Coughlin | 15 | Jaguars, NY Giants | 133 | 107 | 0 | .554 | 141 | 114 | 0 | .553 |
| Hank Stram | 17 | Chiefs, Saints | 131 | 97 | 10 | .571 | 136 | 100 | 10 | .573 |

### Top Winning Percentages

| | W | L | T | Pct | | W | L | T | Pct |
|---|---|---|---|---|---|---|---|---|---|
| Vince Lombardi | 105 | 35 | 6 | .740 | *Paul Brown | 222 | 112 | 9 | .660 |
| John Madden | 112 | 39 | 7 | .731 | Tony Dungy | 148 | 79 | 0 | .652 |
| George Allen | 118 | 54 | 5 | .681 | George Seifert | 124 | 67 | 0 | .650 |
| George Halas | 324 | 151 | 31 | .671 | †Bill Belichick | 177 | 100 | 0 | .639 |
| Don Shula | 347 | 173 | 6 | .665 | Joe Gibbs | 171 | 101 | 0 | .629 |

Note: Minimum 100 victories.

†Active in 2010. *Includes a 52–4–3 (5–0 playoff) record with Browns in AAFC and a 7–20–1 record with Bengals in AFL.

| Year | Player/ Team | Position |
|---|---|---|
| 1938 | Mel Hein, NYG (NFL) | C |
| 1939 | Parker Hall, Clev (NFL) | HB |
| 1940 | Ace Parker, Brooklyn (NFL) | QB |
| 1941 | Don Hutson, GB (NFL) | E |
| 1942 | Don Hutson, GB (NFL) | E |
| 1943 | Sid Luckman, Chi Bears (NFL) | QB |
| 1944 | Frank Sinkwich, Det (NFL) | HB |
| 1945 | Bob Waterfield, Clev (NFL) | QB |
| 1946 | Bill Dudley, Pit (NFL) | HB |
| | Glenn Dobbs, Brooklyn (AAFC) | HB |
| 1947 | No Selection (NFL) | |
| | Otto Graham, Clev (AAFC) | QB |
| 1948 | No Selection (NFL) | |
| | Otto Graham, Clev (AAFC-tie) | QB |
| | Frankie Albert, SF (AAFC-tie) | QB |
| 1949 | No Selection (NFL) | |
| 1950 | No Selection (NFL) | |
| 1951 | Otto Graham, Clev (UP) | QB |
| 1952 | No Selection (NFL) | |
| 1953 | Otto Graham, Clev (UP) | QB |
| 1954 | Joe Perry, SF (UP) | FB |
| | Lou Groza, Clev (TSN) | OT/K |

| Year | Player/ Team | Position |
|---|---|---|
| 1955 | Otto Graham, Clev (UP, TSN) | QB |
| | Harlon Hill, Chi Bears (NEA) | E |
| 1956 | Frank Gifford, NYG (UP, NEA, TSN) | HB |
| 1957 | Y.A. Tittle, SF (UP) | QB |
| | Jim Brown, Clev (AP, TSN) | FB |
| | John Unitas, Balt (NEA) | QB |
| 1958 | Jim Brown, Clev (UP, AP, NEA, TSN) | FB |
| 1959 | John Unitas, Balt (UP, MCP, TSN) | QB |
| | Charley Conerly, NYG (AP, NEA) | QB |
| 1960 | Norm Van Brocklin, Phil, NFL (UP, AP, NEA, TSN, MCP) | QB |
| | Joe Schmidt, Det, NFL (UP- tie) | LB |
| | Abner Haynes, Dal Texans, AFL (UP, TSN) | HB |
| 1961 | Paul Hornung, GB, NFL (UP, AP, TSN, MCP) | HB |
| | Y.A. Tittle, NYG, NFL (NEA) | QB |
| | George Blanda, Hous, AFL (UP, TSN) | QB |
| 1962 | Y.A. Tittle, NYG, NFL (UP, TSN) | QB |
| | Jim Taylor, GB, NFL (AP, NEA) | FB |
| | Andy Robustelli, NYG, NFL (MCP) | DE |
| | Cookie Gilchrist, Buf, AFL (UP) | FB |
| | Len Dawson, Dal Texans, AFL (TSN) | QB |
| 1963 | Jim Brown, Clev, NFL (UP, NEA, tie, MCP) | FB |
| | Y.A. Tittle, NYG, NFL (AP, NEA, tie), TSN) | QB |
| | Lance Alworth, SD, AFL (UP) | WR |
| | Clem Daniels, Oak, AFL (TSN) | HB |

| Year | Player/Team | Position |
|------|-------------|----------|
| 1964 | Johnny Unitas, Balt, NFL (UP, AP, TSN, MCP) | QB |
| | Lenny Moore, Balt, NFL (NEA) | HB |
| | Gino Cappelletti, Boston, AFL (UP, TSN) | WR |
| 1965 | Jim Brown, Clev, NFL (UP, AP, TSN, NEA) | FB |
| | Pete Retzlaff, Phil, NFL (MCP) | TE |
| | Jack Kemp, Buf, AFL (UP) | QB |
| | Paul Lowe, SD, AFL (TSN) | RB |
| 1966 | Bart Starr, GB, NFL (UP, AP, NEA, TSN) | QB |
| | Don Meredith, Dal, NFL (MCP) | QB |
| | Jim Nance, Boston, AFL (UP, AP, TSN) | FB |
| 1967 | Johnny Unitas, Balt, NFL (UP, AP, NEA, TSN, MCP) | QB |
| | Daryl Lamonica, Oak, AFL (UP, AP, TSN) | QB |
| 1968 | Earl Morrall, Balt, NFL (UP, AP, NEA, TSN, PFW) | QB |
| | Leroy Kelly, Clev, AFL (MCP) | HB |
| | Joe Namath, NY Jets, AFL (UP, TSN, PFW) | QB |
| 1969 | Roman Gabriel, LA Rams, NFL (UP, AP, NEA, MCP, TSN, PFW) | QB |
| | Daryle Lamonica, Oak, AFL (UP, TSN, PFW) | QB |
| | Joe Namath, NY Jets, AFL (AP) | QB |
| 1970 | John Brodie, SF (AP, NEA) | QB |
| | George Blanda, Oak (MCP) | QB/K |
| 1971 | Alan Page, Min (AP) | DT |
| | Bob Griese, Miami (NEA) | QB |
| | Roger Staubach, Dal (MCP) | QB |
| 1972 | Larry Brown, Washington (AP, NEA, MCP) | RB |
| 1973 | O.J. Simpson, Buf (AP, NEA, MCP) | RB |
| 1974 | Ken Stabler, Oak (AP, NEA) | QB |
| | Merlin Olsen, LA Rams (MCP) | DT |
| 1975 | Fran Tarkenton, Min (PFWA, AP, NEA, MCP) | QB |
| 1976 | Bert Jones, Balt (PFWA, AP, NEA) | QB |
| | Ken Stabler, Oak (MCP) | QB |
| 1977 | Walter Payton, Chi (PFWA, AP, NEA) | RB |
| | Bob Griese, Miami (MCP) | QB |
| 1978 | Earl Campbell, Hous (PFWA, NEA) | RB |
| | Terry Bradshaw, Pit (AP, MCP) | QB |
| 1979 | Earl Campbell, Hous (PFWA, AP, NEA, MCP) | RB |
| 1980 | Brian Sipe, Clev (PFWA, AP, TSN) | QB |
| | Earl Campbell, Hous (NEA) | RB |
| | Ron Jaworski, Phil (MCP) | QB |
| 1981 | Ken Anderson, Cin (PFWA, AP, NEA, TSN, MCP) | QB |
| 1982 | Dan Fouts, SD (PFWA, NEA) | QB |
| | Mark Moseley, Washington (AP, TSN) | K |
| | Joe Theismann, Washington (MCP) | QB |
| 1983 | Joe Theismann, Washington (PFWAA, AP, NEA) | QB |

| Year | Player/Team | Position |
|------|-------------|----------|
| | Eric Dickerson, LA Rams (TSN) | RB |
| | John Riggins, Washington (MCP) | RB |
| 1984 | Dan Marino, Miami (PFWAA, AP, NEA, MCP, TSN) | QB |
| 1985 | Marcus Allen, LA Raiders (PFWAA, AP, TSN) | RB |
| | Walter Payton, Chi Bears (NEA, MCP) | RB |
| 1986 | Lawrence Taylor, NYG (PFWAA, AP, MCP, TSN) | LB |
| | Phil Simms, NYG (NEA) | QB |
| 1987 | Jerry Rice, SF (PFWAA, NEA, MCP, TSN) | WR |
| | John Elway, Den (AP) | QB |
| 1988 | Boomer Esiason, Cin (PFWAA, AP, TSN) | QB |
| | Roger Craig, SF (NEA) | RB |
| | Randall Cunningham, Phil (MCP) | QB |
| 1989 | Joe Montana, SF (PFWAA, AP, NEA, MCP, TSN) | QB |
| 1990 | Randall Cunningham, Phil (PFWAA) | QB |
| | Joe Montana, SF (AP) | QB |
| | Jerry Rice, SF (TSN) | WR |
| 1991 | Thurman Thomas, Buf (PFWAA, AP, TSN) | RB |
| | Barry Sanders, Det (MCP) | RB |
| 1992 | Steve Young, SF (PFWAA, AP, MCP, TSN) | QB |
| 1993 | Emmitt Smith, Dal (PFWAA, AP, MCP, TSN) | RB |
| 1994 | Steve Young, SF (PFWAA, AP, MCP, TSN) | QB |
| 1995 | Brett Favre, GB (PFWAA, AP, MCP, TSN) | QB |
| 1996 | Brett Favre, GB (PFWAA, AP, MCP, TSN) | QB |
| 1997 | Brett Favre, GB (AP – tie) | QB |
| | Barry Sanders, Det (PFWAA, AP (tie), MCP, TSN) | RB |
| 1998 | Terrell Davis, Den (PFWAA, AP, TSN) | RB |
| | Randall Cunningham, Min (MCP) | QB |
| 1999 | Kurt Warner, StL (AP, PFWAA, MCP) | QB |
| 2000 | Marshall Faulk, StL (AP, PFWAA) | RB |
| | Rich Gannon, Oak (MCP) | QB |
| 2001 | Kurt Warner, StL (AP) | QB |
| | Marshall Faulk, StL (PFWAA, MCP, TSN) | RB |
| 2002 | Rich Gannon, Oak (AP) | QB |
| 2003 | Peyton Manning, Ind (AP - tie) | QB |
| | Steve McNair, Ten (AP - tie) | QB |
| 2004 | Peyton Manning, Ind (AP) | QB |
| 2005 | Shaun Alexander, Sea (AP) | RB |
| 2006 | LaDainian Tomlinson, SD (AP) | RB |
| 2007 | Tom Brady, NE (AP) | QB |
| 2008 | Peyton Manning, Ind (AP) | QB |
| 2009 | Peyton Manning, Ind (AP) | QB |
| 2010 | Tom Brady, NE (AP) | QB |

NOTE: AP-Associated Press, UP-United Press, PFW-*Pro Football Weekly*, TSN-*The Sporting News*, PFWAA-Pro Football Writers Association of America, PFWA-Pro Football Writers of America, MCP-Maxwell Club of Philadelphia, NEA-Newspaper Enterprise Association.

The NFL began awarding its MVP award, the Joe F. Carr Trophy (Carr was league president from 1921-39), in 1938, and continued to do so until 1946. Since that time, the NFL's Most Valuable Players and Players of the Year have been named by a variety of sources, among them, the United Press, the Associated Press, the Maxwell Club of Philadelphia, and the Pro Football Writers Association of America as well as magazines such as *Pro Football Weekly* and *The Sporting News.*

| Year | Player/ Team | Position |
|------|-------------|----------|
| 1955 | Alan Ameche, Balt (UP, TSN) | FB |
| 1956 | Lenny Moore, Balt (UP) | HB |
| | J.C. Caroline, Chi Bears (TSN) | DB |
| 1957 | Jim Brown, Clev (UP, AP, TSN) | FB |
| 1958 | Jimmy Orr, Pit (UP, AP) | OE |
| | Bobby Mitchell, Cleveland (TSN) | HB |
| 1959 | Nick Pietrosante, Det (AP, TSN) | FB |
| | Boyd Dowler, GB (UP) | OE |
| 1960 | Gail Cogdill, Det, NFL (AP, UP, TSN) | OE |
| | Abner Haynes, Dal Texans, AFL (UP, TSN) | HB |
| 1961 | Mike Ditka, Chi Bears, NFL (AP, UP, TSN) | OE |
| | Earl Faison, SD, AFL (UP, TSN) | DE |
| 1962 | Ronnie Bull, Chi Bears, NFL (AP, UP, TSN) | HB |
| | Curtis McClinton, Dal (AP, TSN) | FB |
| 1963 | Paul Flatley, Min, NFL (AP, UP, TSN) | OE |
| | Billy Joe, Den, AFL (UP, TSN) | FB |
| 1964 | Charley Taylor, Wash, NFL (AP, UP, TSN, NEA) | HB |
| | Matt Snell, NYJ, AFL (UP, TSN) | FB |
| 1965 | Gale Sayers, Chi, NFL (AP, UP, TSN, NEA) | HB |
| | Joe Namath, NYJ, AFL (UP, TSN) | QB |
| 1966 | Johnny Roland, StL, NFL (UP) | HB |
| | Tommy Nobis, Atl, NFL (AP, TSN, NEA) | LB |
| | Bobby Burnett, Buf, AFL (UP, TSN) | HB |
| 1967 | Mel Farr, Det, NFL (AP-Off, UP, TSN, NEA) | HB |
| | Lem Barney, Det NFL (AP-Def) | CB |
| | George Webster, Hous, AFL (UP) | LB |
| | Dickie Post, SD, AFL (TSN) | HB |
| 1968 | Earl McCullouch, Det, NFL (AP-Off, UP, TSN, NEA) | OE |
| | Claude Humphrey NFL (AP-Def) | DE |
| | Paul Robinson, Cin, AFL (UP, TSN) | HB |
| 1969 | Calvin Hill, Dal, NFL (AP-Off, UP, TSN, NEA) | HB |
| | Joe Greene NFL (AP-Def) | DT |
| | Greg Cook, Cin, AFL (UP) | QB |
| | Carl Garrett, Boston, AFL (TSN) | HB |
| 1970 | Raymond Chester, Oak (NEA) | TE |
| | Dennis Shaw Buf (AP-Off, UP-AFC) | QB |
| | Bruce Taylor, DB SF (AP-Def, UP-NFC) | DB |
| 1971 | Jim Plunkett NE (UP-AFC) | QB |
| | John Brockington GB (AP-Off, UP-NFC) | RB |
| | Isiah Robertson, SF (AP-Def) | LB |
| 1972 | Franco Harris, Pit (AP-Off, PFW, UP-AFC) | RB |
| | Chester Marcol, GB (UP-NFC) | PK |
| | Willie Buchanan, GB (AP-Def) | CB |
| 1973 | Chuck Foreman, Min (AP-Off, PFW) | RB |
| | Wally Chambers, Chi (AP-Def) | DT |
| | Bobbie Clark, Cin (UP-AFC) | RB |
| | Charle Young Phil (UP-NFC) | TE |
| 1974 | Don Woods, SD (AP-Off, PFW, UP-AFC) | RB |
| | John Hicks, NYG (UP-NFC) | G |
| | Jack Lambert, Pit (AP-Def) | LB |
| 1975 | Steve Bartkowski, Atl (PFW) | QB |
| | Robert Brazile, Hous (AP-Def, UP-AFC) | LB |
| | Mike Thomas, Wash (AP-Off, UP-NFC) | RB |
| 1976 | Mike Haynes, DB NE (AP-Def, UP-AFC) | DB |
| | Sammy White, Min (AP-Off, UP-NFC) | WR |
| 1977 | Tony Dorsett, Dal (NEA, AP-Off, UP-NFC) | RB |
| | A.J. Duhe, Mia (AP-Def, UP-AFC) | DE |
| 1978 | Earl Campbell, Hous Oilers (NEA, PFWA, AP-Off, UP-AFC) | RB |
| | Al "Bubba" Baker, Det (AP-Def, UP-NFC) | DE |

| Year | Player/ Team | Position |
|------|-------------|----------|
| 1979 | Ottis Anderson, StL Card (NEA, PFWA, AP-Off, UP-NFC) | RB |
| | Jerry Butler, Buf (UP-AFC) | WR |
| | Jim Haslett, Buf (AP-Def | LB |
| 1980 | Billy Sims, Det (NEA, TSN, PFWA, AP-Off, UP-NFC) | RB |
| | Joe Cribbs Buf (UP-AFC) | RB |
| | Buddy Curry, Atl (AP-Def tie) | LB |
| | Al Richardson, Atl (AP-Def tie) | LB |
| 1981 | Lawrence Taylor, NYG (NEA, AP-Def) | LB |
| | George Rogers, NO (TSN, PFWA, AP-Off, UP-NFC) | RB |
| | Joe Delaney, KC (UP-AFC) | RB |
| 1982 | Marcus Allen, LA Raiders (NEA, TSN, PFWA, AP-Off, UP-AFC) | RB |
| | Jim McMahon, Chi (UP-NFC) | QB |
| | Chip Banks, Cle (AP-Def) | LB |
| 1983 | Eric Dickerson, LA Rams (NEA, PFWA, AP-Off, UP-NFC) | RB |
| | Dan Marino, Mia (TSN) | QB |
| | Curt Warner, Sea (UP-AFC) | RB |
| | Vernon Maxwell, Balt (AP-Def) | LB |
| 1984 | Louis Lipps, Pit (NEA, TSN, PFWA, AP-Off, UP-AFC) | WR |
| | Paul McFadden, Phil (UP-NFC) | PK |
| | Bill Maas, KC (AP-Def) | DT |
| 1985 | Eddie Brown, Cin (NEA, TSN, AP-Off, PFWA) | WR |
| | Kevin Mack, Clev (UP-AFC) | RB |
| | Jerry Rice, SF (UP-NFC) | WR |
| | Duane Bickett, Ind (AP-Def) | LB |
| 1986 | Reuben Mayes, NO (NEA, TSN, PFWA, AP-Off, UP-NFC) | RB |
| | Leslie O'Neal, SD (AP-Def, UP-AFC) | DE |
| 1987 | Shane Conlan, Buf (PFWA, AP-Def, UP-AFC) | LB |
| | Bo Jackson, LA Raiders (NEA) | RB |
| | Robert Awalt, StL Card (TSN, UP-NFC) | TE |
| | Troy Stradford, Mia (AP-Off) | RB |
| 1988 | John Stephens, NE (NEA, AP-Off, PFWA) | RB |
| | Keith Jackson, Phil (TSN, UP-NFC) | TE |
| | Eric McMillan, NYJ (AP-Def) | S |
| 1989 | Barry Sanders, Det (NEA, TSN, PFWA, AP-Off, UP-NFC) | RB |
| | Derrick Thomas KC (AP-Def, UP-AFC) | LB |
| 1990 | Mark Carrier, Chi (PFWA, UP-NFC, AP-Def) | S |
| | Emmitt Smith, Dal (AP-Off) | RB |
| | Richmond Webb, Mia (TSN, UP-AFC) | OT |
| 1991 | Mike Croel, Den (PFWA, TSN, AP-Def, UP-AFC) | LB |
| | Lawrence Dawsey TB (UP-NFC) | WR |
| | Leonard Russell, NE (AP-Off) | RB |
| 1992 | Dale Carter, KC (PFWA, AP-Def, UP-AFC) | CB |
| | Carl Pickens, Cin (AP-Off) | WR |
| | Santana Dotson, TB (TSN) | DE |
| | Robert Jones, Dal (UP-NFC) | LB |
| 1993 | Jerome Bettis, LA Rams (PFWA, TSN, AP-Off, UP-NFC) | RB |
| | Rick Mirer, Sea (UP-AFC) | QB |
| | Dana Stubblefield, SF (AP-Def) | DT |
| 1994 | Marshall Faulk, Ind (PFWA, TSN, AP-Off, UP-AFC) | RB |
| | Bryant Young, SF (UP-NFC) | DT |
| | Tim Bowens, Mia (AP-Def) | DT |
| 1995 | Curtis Martin, NE (PFWA, TSN, AP-Off, UP-AFC) | RB |
| | Rashaan Salaam Chi (UP-NFC) | RB |
| | Hugh Douglas, NYJ (AP-Def) | DE |

| Year | Player/ Team | Position | Year | Player/ Team | Position |
|------|------|------|------|------|------|
| 1996 | Eddie George, Ten (AP, PFWA, AP-Off, TSN) | RB | 2004 | Ben Roethlisberger, Pit (AP-Off) | QB |
|  | Terry Glenn, NE (UP-AFC) | WR |  | Jonathan Vilma, NYJ (AP-Def) | LB |
|  | Simeon Rice, Ariz (AP-Def, UP-NFC) | DE | 2005 | Carnell Williams, TB (AP-Off) | RB |
| 1997 | Warrick Dunn, TB (PFWA, AP-Off, TSN) | RB |  | Shawne Merriman, SD (AP-Def) | LB |
|  | Peter Boulware, Balt (AP-Def) | LB | 2006 | Vince Young, Ten (AP-Off) | QB |
| 1998 | Randy Moss, Min (PFWA, AP-Off, TSN) | WR |  | DeMeco Ryans, Hou (AP-Def) | LB |
|  | Charles Woodson LA Raiders (AP-Def) | CB | 2007 | Adrian Peterson, Min (AP-Off) | RB |
| 1999 | Edgerrin James, Ind (AP-Off, TSN) | RB |  | Patrick Willis, SF (AP-Def) | LB |
|  | Jevon Kearse, Ten (AP-Def) | DE | 2008 | Matt Ryan, Atl (AP-Off) | QB |
| 2000 | Mike Anderson, Den (AP-Off, TSN) | RB |  | Jerod Mayo, NE (AP-Def) | LB |
|  | Brian Urlacher, Chi (AP-Def) | LB | 2009 | Percy Harvin, Min (AP-Off) | WR |
| 2001 | Anthony Thomas, Chi (AP-Off) | RB |  | Brian Cushing, Hou (AP-Def) | LB |
|  | Kendrell Bell, Pit (AP-Def) | LB | 2010 | Sam Bradford, StL (AP-Off) | QB |
| 2002 | Clinton Ports, Den (AP-Off) | RB |  | Ndamukong Suh, Det (AP-Def) | DT |
|  | Julius Peppers, Car (AP-Def) | DE |  |  |  |
| 2003 | Anquan Boldin, Ariz (AP-Off) | WR |  |  |  |
|  | Terrell Suggs, Bal (AP-Def) | LB |  |  |  |

NOTE: AP-Associated Press, UP-United Press, PFW-*Pro Football Weekly*, TSN-*The Sporting News*, PFWAA-Pro Football Writers Association of America, PFWA-Pro Football Writers of America, MCP-Maxwell Club of Philadelphia, NEA-Newspaper Enterprise Association

Starting in1960, the United Press annually awarded two Rookie of the Year awards, one to an AFL player and one to a NFL player. After the AFL-NFL merger, the UP kept the two-award format for the AFC and NFC. The UP stopped awarding RoY awards after the 1996 season.

Starting in 1967, the Associated Press began announcing two annual Rookie of the Year awards, as well. One went to the best offensive rookie in the NFL, the other to the best defensive rookie.

## Alltime Number-One Draft Choices

| Year | Team | Selection | Position |
|------|------|------|------|
| 1936 | Philadelphia | Jay Berwanger, Chicago | HB |
| 1937 | Philadelphia | Sam Francis, Nebraska | FB |
| 1938 | Cleveland | Corbett Davis, Indiana | FB |
| 1939 | Chicago Cardinals | Ki Aldrich, Texas Christian | C |
| 1940 | Chicago Cardinals | George Cafego, Tennessee | HB |
| 1941 | Chicago Bears | Tom Harmon, Michigan | HB |
| 1942 | Pittsburgh | Bill Dudley, Virginia | HB |
| 1943 | Detroit | Frank Sinkwich, Georgia | HB |
| 1944 | Boston | Angelo Bertelli, Notre Dame | QB |
| 1945 | Chicago Cardinals | Charley Trippi, Georgia | HB |
| 1946 | Boston | Frank Dancewicz, Notre Dame | QB |
| 1947 | Chicago Bears | Bob Fenimore, Oklahoma A&M | HB |
| 1948 | Washington | Harry Gilmer, Alabama | QB |
| 1949 | Philadelphia | Chuck Bednarik, Pennsylvania | C |
| 1950 | Detroit | Leon Hart, Notre Dame | E |
| 1951 | New York Giants | Kyle Rote, SMU | HB |
| 1952 | Los Angeles | Bill Wade, Vanderbilt | QB |
| 1953 | San Francisco | Harry Babcock, Georgia | E |
| 1954 | Cleveland | Bobby Garrett, Stanford | QB |
| 1955 | Baltimore | George Shaw, Oregon | QB |
| 1956 | Pittsburgh | Gary Glick, Colorado A&M | DB |
| 1957 | Green Bay | Paul Hornung, Notre Dame | HB |
| 1958 | Chicago Cardinals | King Hill, Rice | QB |
| 1959 | Green Bay | Randy Duncan, Iowa | QB |
| 1960 | Los Angeles | Billy Cannon, LSU | RB |
| 1961 | Minnesota | Tommy Mason, Tulane | RB |
|  | Buffalo (AFL) | Ken Rice, Auburn | G |
| 1962 | Washington | Ernie Davis, Syracuse | RB |
|  | Oakland (AFL) | Roman Gabriel, North Carolina St | QB |
| 1963 | LA Rams | Terry Baker, Oregon St | QB |
|  | Kansas City (AFL) | Buck Buchanan, Grambling | DT |
| 1964 | San Francisco | Dave Parks, Texas Tech | E |
|  | Boston (AFL) | Jack Concannon, Boston College | QB |
| 1965 | NY Giants | Tucker Frederickson, Auburn | RB |
|  | Houston (AFL) | Lawrence Elkins, Baylor | E |
| 1966 | Atlanta | Tommy Nobis, Texas | LB |
|  | Miami (AFL) | Jim Grabowski, Illinois | RB |

| Year | Team | Selection | Position |
|------|------|-----------|----------|
| 1967 | Baltimore | Bubba Smith, Michigan St | DT |
| 1968 | Minnesota | Ron Yary, USC | T |
| 1969 | Buffalo (AFL) | O.J. Simpson, USC | RB |
| 1970 | Pittsburgh | Terry Bradshaw, Louisiana Tech | QB |
| 1971 | New England | Jim Plunkett, Stanford | QB |
| 1972 | Buffalo | Walt Patulski, Notre Dame | DE |
| 1973 | Houston | John Matuszak, Tampa | DE |
| 1974 | Dallas | Ed Jones, Tennessee St | DE |
| 1975 | Atlanta | Steve Bartkowski, California | QB |
| 1976 | Tampa Bay | Lee Roy Selmon, Oklahoma | DE |
| 1977 | Tampa Bay | Ricky Bell, USC | RB |
| 1978 | Houston | Earl Campbell, Texas | RB |
| 1979 | Buffalo | Tom Cousineau, Ohio St | LB |
| 1980 | Detroit | Billy Sims, Oklahoma | RB |
| 1981 | New Orleans | George Rogers, South Carolina | RB |
| 1982 | New England | Kenneth Sims, Texas | DT |
| 1983 | Baltimore | John Elway, Stanford | QB |
| 1984 | New England | Irving Fryar, Nebraska | WR |
| 1985 | Buffalo | Bruce Smith, Virginia Tech | DE |
| 1986 | Tampa Bay | Bo Jackson, Auburn | RB |
| 1987 | Tampa Bay | Vinny Testaverde, Miami (Fla.) | QB |
| 1988 | Atlanta | Aundray Bruce, Auburn | LB |
| 1989 | Dallas | Troy Aikman, UCLA | QB |
| 1990 | Indianapolis | Jeff George, Illinois | QB |
| 1991 | Dallas | Russell Maryland, Miami (Fla.) | DT |
| 1992 | Indianapolis | Steve Emtman, Washington | DT |
| 1993 | New England | Drew Bledsoe, Washington St | QB |
| 1994 | Cincinnati | Dan Wilkinson, Ohio St | DT |
| 1995 | Cincinnati | Ki-Jana Carter, Penn St | RB |
| 1996 | New York Jets | Keyshawn Johnson, USC | WR |
| 1997 | St Louis | Orlando Pace, Ohio St | OT |
| 1998 | Indianapolis | Peyton Manning, Tennessee | QB |
| 1999 | Cleveland | Tim Couch, Kentucky | QB |
| 2000 | Cleveland | Courtney Brown, Penn St | DE |
| 2001 | Atlanta | Michael Vick, Virginia Tech | QB |
| 2002 | Houston | David Carr, Fresno St | QB |
| 2003 | Cincinnati | Carson Palmer, USC | QB |
| 2004 | San Diego | Eli Manning, Mississippi | QB |
| 2005 | San Francisco | Alex Smith, Utah | QB |
| 2006 | Houston | Mario Williams, North Carolina St | DE |
| 2007 | Oakland | JaMarcus Russell, LSU | QB |
| 2008 | Miami | Jake Long, Michigan | OT |
| 2009 | Detroit | Matthew Stafford, Georgia | QB |
| 2010 | St. Louis | Sam Bradford, Oklahoma | QB |
| 2011 | Carolina | Cam Newton, Auburn | QB |

From 1947 through 1958, the first selection in the draft was a bonus pick, awarded to the winner of a random draw. That club, in turn, forfeited its last-round draft choice. The winner of the bonus choice was eliminated from future draws. The system was abolished after 1958, by which time all clubs had received a bonus choice.

# Members of the Pro Football Hall of Fame

| | | | |
|---|---|---|---|
| Herb Adderley | Elvin Bethea | Earl Campbell | Len Dawson |
| Troy Aikman | Charles W. Bidwill Sr. | Tony Canadeo | Fred Dean |
| George Allen | Fred Biletnikoff | Joe Carr | Joe DeLamielleure |
| Marcus Allen | George Blanda | Harry Carson | Richard Dent |
| Lance Alworth | Mel Blount | Dave Casper | Eric Dickerson |
| Doug Atkins | Terry Bradshaw | Guy Chamberlin | Dan Dierdorf |
| Morris (Red) Badgro | Bob (the Boomer) Brown | Jack Christiansen | Mike Ditka |
| Lem Barney | Jim Brown | Earl (Dutch) Clark | Art Donovan |
| Cliff Battles | Paul Brown | George Connor | Tony Dorsett |
| Sammy Baugh | Roosevelt Brown | Jimmy Conzelman | John (Paddy) Driscoll |
| Chuck Bednarik | Willie Brown | Lou Creekmur | Bill Dudley |
| Bert Bell | Junios (Buck) Buchanan | Larry Csonka | Albert Glen (Turk) Edwards |
| Bobby Bell | Nick Buoniconti | Al Davis | Carl Eller |
| Raymond Berry | Dick Butkus | Willie Davis | John Elway |

Weeb Ewbank
Marshall Faulk
Tom Fears
Jim Finks
Ray Flaherty
Len Ford
Dan Fortmann
Dan Fouts
Benny Friedman
Frank Gatski
Bill George
Joe Gibbs
Frank Gifford
Sid Gillman
Otto Graham
Harold (Red) Grange
Bud Grant
Darrell Green
Joe Greene
Forrest Gregg
Bob Griese
Russ Grimm
Lou Groza
Joe Guyon
George Halas
Jack Ham
Dan Hampton
Chris Hanburger
John Hannah
Franco Harris
Bob Hayes
Mike Haynes
Ed Healey
Mel Hein
Ted Hendricks
Wilbur (Pete) Henry
Arnie Herber
Bill Hewitt
Gene Hickerson
Clarke Hinkle
Elroy (Crazylegs) Hirsch
Paul Hornung
Ken Houston
Robert (Cal) Hubbard
Sam Huff
Lamar Hunt
Don Hutson
Michael Irvin
Rickey Jackson
Jimmy Johnson
John Henry Johnson
Charlie Joiner
David (Deacon) Jones
Stan Jones
Henry Jordan
Sonny Jurgensen
Jim Kelly
Leroy Kelly
Walt Kiesling
Frank (Bruiser) Kinard
Paul Krause
Earl (Curly) Lambeau
Jack Lambert
Tom Landry
Dick (Night Train) Lane

Jim Langer
Willie Lanier
Steve Largent
Yale Lary
Dante Lavelli
Bobby Layne
Dick LeBeau
Alphonse (Tuffy) Leemans
Marv Levy
Bob Lilly
Floyd Little
Larry Little
James Lofton
Vince Lombardi
Howie Long
Ronnie Lott
Sid Luckman
William Roy (Link) Lyman
Tom Mack
John Mackey
John Madden
Tim Mara
Wellington Mara
Gino Marchetti
Dan Marino
George Preston Marshall
Ollie Matson
Bruce Matthews
Don Maynard
George McAfee
Mike McCormack
Randall McDaniel
Tommy McDonald
Hugh McElhenny
John (Blood) McNally
Mike Michalske
Wayne Millner
Bobby Mitchell
Ron Mix
Art Monk
Joe Montana
Warren Moon
Lenny Moore
Marion Motley
Mike Munchak
Anthony Munoz
George Musso
Bronko Nagurski
Joe Namath
Earle (Greasy) Neale
Ernie Nevers
Ozzie Newsome
Ray Nitschke
Chuck Noll
Leo Nomellini
Merlin Olsen
Jim Otto
Steve Owen
Alan Page
Clarence (Ace) Parker
Jim Parker
Walter Payton
Joe Perry
Pete Pihos
Fritz Pollard

John Randle
Hugh (Shorty) Ray
Dan Reeves
Mel Renfro
Jerry Rice
Les Richter
John Riggins
Jim Ringo
Andy Robustelli
Art Rooney
Dan Rooney
Pete Rozelle
Bob St. Clair
Ed Sabol
Barry Sanders
Deion Sanders
Charlie Sanders
Gale Sayers
Joe Schmidt
Tex Schramm
Lee Roy Selmon
Shannon Sharpe
Billy Shaw
Art Shell
Don Shula
O.J. Simpson
Mike Singletary
Jackie Slater
Bruce Smith
Emmitt Smith
Jackie Smith
John Stallworth
Bart Starr
Roger Staubach
Ernie Stautner
Jan Stenerud
Dwight Stephenson
Hank Stram
Ken Strong
Joe Stydahar
Lynn Swann
Fran Tarkenton
Charley Taylor
Jim Taylor
Lawrence Taylor
Derrick Thomas
Emmitt Thomas
Thurman Thomas
Jim Thorpe
Andre Tippett
Y.A. Tittle
George Trafton
Charley Trippi
Emlen Tunnell
Clyde (Bulldog) Turner
Johnny Unitas
Gene Upshaw
Norm Van Brocklin
Steve Van Buren
Doak Walker
Bill Walsh
Paul Warfield
Bob Waterfield
Mike Webster
Roger Wehrli

Arnie Weinmeister
Randy White
Reggie White
Dave Wilcox
Bill Willis
Larry Wilson
Ralph Wilson
Kellen Winslow
Alex Wojciechowicz
Willie Wood
Rod Woodson
Rayfield Wright
Ron Yary
Steve Young
Jack Youngblood
Gary Zimmerman

## Canadian Football League Grey Cup

| Year | Results | Site | Attendance |
|------|---------|------|-----------|
| 1909 | U of Toronto 26, Parkdale 6 | Toronto | 3,807 |
| 1910 | U of Toronto 16, Hamilton Tigers 7 | Hamilton | 12,000 |
| 1911 | U of Toronto 14, Toronto 7 | Toronto | 13,687 |
| 1912 | Hamilton Alerts 11, Toronto 4 | Hamilton | 5,337 |
| 1913 | Hamilton Tigers 44, Parkdale 2 | Hamilton | 2,100 |
| 1914 | Toronto 14, U of Toronto 2 | Toronto | 10,500 |
| 1915 | Hamilton Tigers 13, Toronto RAA 7 | Toronto | 2,808 |
| 1916–19 | No game | — | — |
| 1920 | U of Toronto 16, Toronto 3 | Toronto | 10,088 |
| 1921 | Toronto 23, Edmonton 0 | Toronto | 9,558 |
| 1922 | Queen's U 13, Edmonton 1 | Kingston | 4,700 |
| 1923 | Queen's U 54, Regina 0 | Toronto | 8,629 |
| 1924 | Queen's U 11, Balmy Beach 3 | Toronto | 5,978 |
| 1925 | Ottawa Senators 24, Winnipeg 1 | Ottawa | 6,900 |
| 1926 | Ottawa Senators 10, Toronto U 7 | Toronto | 8,276 |
| 1927 | Balmy Beach 9, Hamilton Tigers 6 | Toronto | 13,676 |
| 1928 | Hamilton Tigers 30, Regina 0 | Hamilton | 4,767 |
| 1929 | Hamilton Tigers 14, Regina 3 | Hamilton | 1,906 |
| 1930 | Balmy Beach 11, Regina 6 | Toronto | 3,914 |
| 1931 | Montreal AAA 22, Regina 0 | Montreal | 5,112 |
| 1932 | Hamilton Tigers 25, Regina 6 | Hamilton | 4,806 |
| 1933 | Toronto 4, Sarnia 3 | Sarnia | 2,751 |
| 1934 | Sarnia 20, Regina 12 | Toronto | 8,900 |
| 1935 | Winnipeg 18, Hamilton Tigers 12 | Hamilton | 6,405 |
| 1936 | Sarnia 26, Ottawa RR 20 | Toronto | 5,883 |
| 1937 | Toronto 4, Winnipeg 3 | Toronto | 11,522 |
| 1938 | Toronto 30, Winnipeg 7 | Toronto | 18,778 |
| 1939 | Winnipeg 8, Ottawa 7 | Ottawa | 11,738 |
| 1940 | Ottawa 8, Balmy Beach 2 | Toronto | 4,998 |
| 1940 | Ottawa 12, Balmy Beach 5 | Ottawa | 1,700 |
| 1941 | Winnipeg 18, Ottawa 16 | Toronto | 19,065 |
| 1942 | Toronto RCAF 8, Winnipeg RCAF 5 | Toronto | 12,455 |
| 1943 | Hamilton F Wild 23, Winnipeg RCAF 14 | Toronto | 16,423 |
| 1944 | Montreal St H-D Navy 7, Hamilton F Wild 6 | Hamilton | 3,871 |
| 1945 | Toronto 35, Winnipeg 0 | Toronto | 18,660 |
| 1946 | Toronto 28, Winnipeg 6 | Toronto | 18,960 |
| 1947 | Toronto 10, Winnipeg 9 | Toronto | 18,885 |
| 1948 | Calgary 12, Ottawa 7 | Toronto | 20,013 |
| 1949 | Montreal Als 28, Calgary 15 | Toronto | 20,087 |
| 1950 | Toronto 13, Winnipeg 0 | Toronto | 27,101 |
| 1951 | Ottawa 21, Saskatchewan 14 | Toronto | 27,341 |
| 1952 | Toronto 21, Edmonton 11 | Toronto | 27,391 |
| 1953 | Hamilton Ticats 12, Winnipeg 6 | Toronto | 27,313 |
| 1954 | Edmonton 26, Montreal 25 | Toronto | 27,321 |
| 1955 | Edmonton 34, Montreal 19 | Vancouver | 39,417 |
| 1956 | Edmonton 50, Montreal 27 | Toronto | 27,425 |
| 1957 | Hamilton 32, Winnipeg 7 | Toronto | 27,051 |
| 1958 | Winnipeg 35, Hamilton 28 | Vancouver | 36,567 |
| 1959 | Winnipeg 21, Hamilton 7 | Toronto | 33,133 |
| 1960 | Ottawa 16, Edmonton 6 | Vancouver | 38,102 |
| 1961 | Winnipeg 21, Hamilton 14 | Toronto | 32,651 |
| 1962 | Winnipeg 28, Hamilton 27 | Toronto | 32,655 |
| 1963 | Hamilton 21, British Columbia 10 | Vancouver | 36,545 |
| 1964 | British Columbia 34, Hamilton 24 | Toronto | 32,655 |
| 1965 | Hamilton 22, Winnipeg 16 | Toronto | 32,655 |
| 1966 | Saskatchewan 29, Ottawa 14 | Vancouver | 36,553 |
| 1967 | Hamilton 24, Saskatchewan 1 | Ottawa | 31,358 |
| 1968 | Ottawa 24, Calgary 21 | Toronto | 32,655 |
| 1969 | Ottawa 29, Saskatchewan 11 | Montreal | 33,172 |
| 1970 | Montreal 23, Calgary 10 | Toronto | 32,669 |
| 1971 | Calgary 14, Toronto 11 | Vancouver | 34,484 |
| 1972 | Hamilton 13, Saskatchewan 10 | Hamilton | 33,993 |
| 1973 | Ottawa 22, Edmonton 18 | Toronto | 36,653 |
| 1974 | Montreal 20, Edmonton 7 | Vancouver | 34,450 |
| 1975 | Edmonton 9, Montreal 8 | Calgary | 32,454 |
| 1976 | Ottawa 23, Saskatchewan 20 | Toronto | 53,467 |
| 1977 | Montreal 41, Edmonton 6 | Montreal | 68,318 |
| 1978 | Edmonton 20, Montreal 13 | Toronto | 54,695 |

### Canadian Football League Grey Cup

| Year | Results | Site | Attendance |
|------|---------|------|-----------|
| 1979 | Edmonton 17, Montreal 9 | Montreal | 65,113 |
| 1980 | Edmonton 48, Hamilton 10 | Toronto | 54,661 |
| 1981 | Edmonton 26, Ottawa 23 | Montreal | 52,478 |
| 1982 | Edmonton 32, Toronto 16 | Toronto | 54,741 |
| 1983 | Toronto 18, British Columbia 17 | Vancouver | 59,345 |
| 1984 | Winnipeg 47, Hamilton 17 | Edmonton | 60,081 |
| 1985 | British Columbia 37, Hamilton 24 | Montreal | 56,723 |
| 1986 | Hamilton 39, Edmonton 15 | Vancouver | 59,621 |
| 1987 | Edmonton 38, Toronto 36 | Vancouver | 59,478 |
| 1988 | Winnipeg 22, British Columbia 21 | Ottawa | 50,604 |
| 1989 | Saskatchewan 43, Hamilton 40 | Toronto | 54,088 |
| 1990 | Winnipeg 50, Edmonton 11 | Vancouver | 46,968 |
| 1991 | Toronto 36, Calgary 21 | Winnipeg | 51,985 |
| 1992 | Calgary 24, Winnipeg 10 | Toronto | 45,863 |
| 1993 | Edmonton 33, Winnipeg 23 | Calgary | 50,035 |
| 1994 | British Columbia 26, Baltimore 23 | Vancouver | 55,097 |
| 1995 | Baltimore 37, Calgary 20 | Regina, Saskatchewan | 52,564 |
| 1996 | Toronto 43, Edmonton 37 | Hamilton, Ontario | 38,595 |
| 1997 | Toronto 47, Saskatchewan 23 | Edmonton | 60,431 |
| 1998 | Calgary 26, Hamilton 24 | Winnipeg | 34,157 |
| 1999 | Hamilton 32, Calgary 21 | Vancouver | 45,118 |
| 2000 | British Columbia 28, Montreal 26 | Calgary | 43,822 |
| 2001 | Calgary 27, Winnipeg 19 | Montreal | 65,255 |
| 2002 | Montreal 25, Edmonton 16 | Edmonton | 62,531 |
| 2003 | Edmonton 34, Montreal 22 | Regina, Saskatchewan | 50,909 |
| 2004 | Toronto 27, British Columbia 19 | Ottawa | 51,242 |
| 2005 | Edmonton 38, Montreal 35 (OT) | Vancouver | 59,157 |
| 2006 | British Columbia 25, Montreal 14 | Winnipeg | 44,786 |
| 2007 | Saskatchewan 23, Winnipeg 19 | Toronto | 52,230 |
| 2008 | Calgary 22, Montreal 14 | Montreal | 66,308 |
| 2009 | Montreal 28, Saskatchewan 27 | Calgary | 46,020 |
| 2010 | Montreal 21, Saskatchewan 18 | Edmonton | 63,317 |

In 1909, Earl Grey, the Governor-General of Canada, donated a trophy for the Rugby Football Championship of Canada. The trophy, which subsequently became known as the Grey Cup, was originally open only to teams registered with the Canada Rugby Union. Since 1954, it has been awarded to the winner of the Canadian Football League's championship game.

### AMERICAN FOOTBALL LEAGUE I

| Year | Champion | Record |
|------|----------|--------|
| 1926 | Philadelphia Quakers | 7-2 |

### AMERICAN FOOTBALL LEAGUE II

| Year | Champion | Record |
|------|----------|--------|
| 1936 | Boston Shamrocks | 8-3 |
| 1937 | LA Bulldogs | 8-0 |

### AMERICAN FOOTBALL LEAGUE III

| Year | Champion | Record |
|------|----------|--------|
| 1940 | Columbus Bullies | 8-1-1 |
| 1941 | Columbus Bullies | 5-1-2 |

### ALL-AMERICAN FOOTBALL CONFERENCE

| Year | Championship Game |
|------|-------------------|
| 1946 | Cleveland 14, NY Yankees 9 |
| 1947 | Cleveland 14, NY Yankees 3 |
| 1948 | Cleveland 49, Buffalo 7 |
| 1949 | Cleveland 21, San Francisco 7 |

### WORLD FOOTBALL LEAGUE

| Year | World Bowl Championship |
|------|-------------------------|
| 1974 | Birmingham 22, Florida 21 |
| 1975 | Disbanded midseason |

### UNITED STATES FOOTBALL LEAGUE

| Year | Championship Game |
|------|-------------------|
| 1983 | Michigan 24, Philadelphia 22 |
| 1984 | Philadelphia 23, Arizona 3 |
| 1985 | Baltimore 28, Oakland 24 |

### X FOOTBALL LEAGUE

| Year | Championship Game |
|------|-------------------|
| 2001 | Los Angeles 38, San Francisco 6 |

### NFL EUROPE*

| Year Record | Champion | |
|------|----------|--|
| 1991 | London | 9-1-0 |
| 1992 | Sacramento | 8-2-0 |
| 1995 | Frankfurt | 6-4-0 |
| 1996 | Scotland | 7-3-0 |
| 1997 | Barcelona | 5-5-0 |
| 1998 | Rhein | 7-3-0 |
| 1999 | Frankfurt | 6-4-0 |
| 2000 | Rhein | 7-3-0 |
| 2001 | Berlin | 6-4-0 |
| 2002 | Berlin | 6-4-0 |
| 2003 | Frankfurt | 6-4-0 |
| 2004 | Berlin | 9-1-0 |
| 2005 | Amsterdam | 6-4-0 |
| 2006 | Frankfurt | 7-3-0 |
| 2007 | Hamburg | 7-3-0 |

*Known as World League of American Football until 1998. League folded after the 2007 season.

### UNITED FOOTBALL LEAGUE

| Year | Championship Game |
|------|-------------------|
| 2009 | Las Vegas 20, Florida 17 |
| 2010 | Las Vegas 23, Florida 20 |

# College Football

Heisman Trophy winner Cam Newton led the Auburn Tigers to the BCS national title

# Big Newton

Conquering a controversial past, QB Cam Newton led the Auburn Tigers to their first national title in 53 years

## B.J. SCHECTER

O N THE FIELD, HE WAS A man among boys. He looked more imposing than a defensive lineman, was shaped like Adonis at a sculpted 6' 6", 250 pounds, and was faster than most running backs. With a rifle arm and freakish running ability, Auburn's Cam Newton put up video game-like numbers, but he played the game like a little kid loving every second. Newton's passion and smile were infectious and his play was simply jaw-dropping.

"You give and you get," said Newton. "You feed the crowd, and the crowd gives you this type of energy that [makes you] feel like you can do anything."

And Newton did. Entering the season, Auburn and Newton were way off the radar. The Tigers were coming off an 8–5 season and Newton had spent 2009 in exile at Blinn Junior College in Texas after transferring from Florida following an arrest for possessing a stolen laptop. After making his mistake in Gainesville, Newton came back to the SEC with a purpose. He arrived on campus ready to outwork everyone and prove he belonged. Newton could often be spotted around The Plains running or lifting weights by himself. He quickly earned the respect of his coaches and teammates, and when the games began, he quickly gained the attention of the nation.

Newton garnered headlines with his stellar play as Auburn marched through the minefield of the SEC undefeated, and off the field as he became embroiled in controversy. As reporters began looking into Newton's past, beginning with his trouble at Florida, word leaked out that Newton's father, Cecil, tried to broker a deal with a Mississippi State booster for $180,000 to gain his son's commitment to play for the Bulldogs. As Auburn and the NCAA looked into the allegations, Auburn officials continued to maintain that Newton was eligible. Then before the SEC title game against South Carolina, Auburn declared Newton ineligible—for 24 hours. The following day the NCAA came back with its quickest ruling in history, declaring it lacked "sufficient evidence" that Cam knew of the scheme and that his father acted alone and in the end no money changed hands.

Newton dealt with the controversy with his trademark smile and let his game do the talking. Second in the nation in pass efficiency, he accounted for 51 touchdowns (30 passing, 20 rushing, one receiving) and toyed with defenders in the nation's toughest conference (perhaps his signature moment—and there were many to choose from—was leading a 24–0 comeback at Alabama to give the Tigers a 28–27 victory in the Iron Bowl). Controversy aside, he ran away with the Heisman Trophy and more importantly led Auburn to its first BCS title game, where the Tigers would face Oregon and coach Chip Kelly's high-powered offense.

JED JACOBSOHN

The annual flogging of the BCS usually dominates the second half of the season (and 2010 was no different), but no one could argue with an Auburn-Oregon title game. Yes, TCU finished the regular season 12–0, but a trip to the Rose Bowl was a good reward for the Mountain West champs. In the BCS title game, most expected a wild, high-scoring shootout, but what they got instead was a defensive slugfest.

Both teams had trouble moving the ball and sustaining drives, and Newton was uncharacteristically off his game. He rushed for just 64 yards on 22 carries, missed open receivers and gave up a costly fumble with Auburn leading 19–11 and less than five minutes remaining. Oregon marched down the field and scored and Darron Thomas's two-point conversion pass to Jeff Maehl tied it at 19–19 with 2:33 remaining and gave the Ducks the momentum.

With time winding down, Auburn had

**Though Auburn's Newton easily defeated runner-up and fellow QB Andrew Luck of Stanford (above) in the 2010 Heisman balloting, Luck skipped the NFL draft and became an early favorite for the 2011 Trophy.**

the ball first-and-10 from its own 40 when freshman running back Michael Dyer took a handoff and appeared to be stopped for a loss. Players on both teams stopped and thought the play was over, but Dyer heard Tigers coaches screaming, "Go! Go! Go!" from the sideline so he took off for a 37-yard gain. Replays confirmed that Dyer's knees or wrist had never hit the ground, and five plays later Wes Byrum kicked a 19-yard field goal as time expired to give Auburn a 22–19 victory. It was Auburn's first national title since 1957 and the fifth straight for the SEC.

The game was a bizarre finale to a wild season, especially for Newton who was asked more about the NCAA controversy

ROBERT BECK

the nation in scoring offense (47.0 points per game) and in total offense (530.7 yards per game). Oregon operated at such a fever pitch that some opposing players even faked injuries to catch a breath.

TCU was one of the best stories of the season and capped its perfect season with a fantastic finish to beat Wisconsin 21–19 in the Rose Bowl. For nearly 60 minutes the teams slugged it out with the Horned Frogs going toe-to-toe with the Big Ten champs. After Wisconsin scored to go down by two with two minutes remaining, TCU linebacker Tank Carder came up with the play of the game when he deflected a Scott Tolzien pass on the two-point conversion attempt to preserve the victory. "I don't really care about the national championship right now," said TCU defensive end Wayne Daniels. "I'm livin' in the moment."

Ohio State's season was filled with many ups and downs. A preseason national championship contender, Ohio State lost in late October, turned things around and then beat Arkansas in the Sugar Bowl. The victory was shrouded in controversy as five starters, including quarterback Terrelle Pryor, were suspended for five games for selling their jerseys and other memorabilia. But they were allowed to play in the bowl game and serve their suspensions in 2011. Five months later, Buckeyes coach Jim Tressel was forced to resign after acknowledging that he lied to the NCAA about knowledge of the incident.

One year after resigning, then changing his mind, Florida coach Urban Meyer stepped away for good, citing health concerns. The Gators' disappointing 8–5 season was a factor as was "the 24/7 sacrifices" of the profession. While Meyer will be away from coaching for at least a year, he'll very likely be back. As Auburn's Cam Newton proved, in college football there's always an opportunity for another act.

than his play and didn't have his typically dominating performance in the title game. But Newton, who would declare himself eligible for the NFL draft a few days later, got his redemption and went out on top.

"I don't want anybody to feel sorry for me," Newton said after the game. "Throughout this year nobody [felt] sorry for Auburn. And we got the last laugh."

Nobody felt sorry for Oregon when the Ducks had a tumultuous offseason in which Kelly suspended and then subsequently booted starting quarterback Jeremiah Masoli off the team. Oregon starting running back LaMichael James was also suspended for the season opener after he pleaded guilty to a misdemeanor harassment charge involving his girlfriend. The Ducks found the perfect trigger to their offense in Thomas—who was actually better suited to the scheme than Masoli—and led

## Final Polls

### Associated Press

| | | Record | Pts | Head Coach | SI Preseason Rank |
|---|---|---|---|---|---|
| 1. | Auburn (56) | 14–0 | 1472 | Gene Chizik | * |
| 2. | TCU (3) | 13–0 | 1392 | Gary Patterson | 5 |
| 3. | Oregon | 12–1 | 1379 | Chip Kelly | 8 |
| 4. | Stanford | 12–1 | 1300 | Jim Harbaugh | 24 |
| 5. | Ohio St | 12–1 | 1220 | Jim Tressel | 2 |
| 6. | Oklahoma | 12–2 | 1108 | Bob Stoops | 12 |
| 7. | Wisconsin | 11–2 | 1055 | Bret Bielema | 11 |
| 8. | LSU | 11–2 | 1051 | Les Miles | 21 |
| 9. | Boise St | 12–1 | 1031 | Chris Petersen | 3 |
| 10. | Alabama | 10–3 | 961 | Nick Saban | 1 |
| 11. | Nevada | 13–1 | 866 | Chris Ault | * |
| 12. | Arkansas | 10–3 | 863 | Bobby Petrino | 23 |
| 13. | Oklahoma St | 11–2 | 833 | Mike Gundy | * |
| 14. | Michigan St | 11–2 | 696 | Mark Dantonio | * |
| 15. | Mississippi St | 9–4 | 578 | Dan Mullen | * |
| 16. | Virginia Tech | 11–3 | 577 | Frank Beamer | 10 |
| 17. | Florida St | 10–4 | 502 | Jimbo Fisher | 25 |
| 18. | Missouri | 10–3 | 477 | Gary Pinkel | * |
| 19. | Texas A&M | 9–4 | 359 | Mike Sherman | * |
| 20. | Nebraska | 10–4 | 334 | Bo Pelini | 9 |
| 21. | Central Florida | 11–3 | 225 | George O'Leary | * |
| 22. | South Carolina | 9–5 | 169 | Steve Spurrier | * |
| 23. | Maryland | 9–4 | 144 | Ralph Friedgen | * |
| 24. | Tulsa | 10–3 | 128 | Todd Graham | * |
| 25. | North Carolina St | 9–4 | 119 | Tom O'Brien | * |

Note: As voted by a panel of 59 sportswriters and broadcasters following bowl games (first place votes in parentheses).
*Not ranked in preseason top 25.

### USA Today/Coaches

| | | Pts | SI Preseason Rank | | | Pts | SI Preseason Rank |
|---|---|---|---|---|---|---|---|
| 1. | Auburn (56) | 1424 | * | 14. | Michigan St | 676 | * |
| 2. | TCU (1) | 1336 | 5 | 15. | Virginia Tech | 636 | 10 |
| 3. | Oregon | 1333 | 8 | 16. | Florida St | 506 | 25 |
| 4. | Stanford | 1254 | 24 | 17. | Mississippi St | 505 | * |
| 5. | Ohio St | 1197 | 2 | 18. | Missouri | 473 | * |
| 6. | Oklahoma | 1096 | 12 | 19. | Nebraska | 354 | 9 |
| 7. | Boise St | 1012 | 3 | 20. | Central Florida | 328 | * |
| 8. | LSU | 1007 | 21 | 21. | Texas A&M | 277 | * |
| 8. | Wisconsin | 1007 | 11 | 22. | South Carolina | 181 | * |
| 10. | Oklahoma St | 883 | * | 23. | Utah | 156 | 22 |
| 11. | Alabama | 860 | 1 | 24. | Maryland | 111 | * |
| 12. | Arkansas | 818 | 23 | 25. | North Carolina St | 94 | * |
| 13. | Nevada | 734 | * | | | | |

Note: Voted by a panel of 57 FBS (I-A) head coaches; 25 points for 1st, 24 for 2nd, etc. (First place votes in parentheses).
*Not ranked in preseason top 25.

## Bowls and Playoffs

### NCAA Football Bowl Subdivision (I-A) Bowl Results

| Date | Bowl | Result | Payout/Team ($) | Attendance |
|---|---|---|---|---|
| 12-18-10 | New Mexico | BYU 52, UTEP 24 | 750,000 | 32,424 |
| 12-18-10 | Humanitarian | Northern Illinois 40, Fresno St 17 | 750,000 | 25,449 |
| 12-18-10 | New Orleans | Troy 48, Ohio 21 | 325,000 | 29,159 |
| 12-21-10 | St. Petersburg | Louisville 31, Southern Miss 28 | 1 million | 20,017 |
| 12-22-10 | Las Vegas | Boise St 26, Utah 3 | 1 million | 41,923 |
| 12-23-10 | Poinsettia | San Diego St 35, Navy 14 | 750,000 | 48,049 |
| 12-24-10 | Hawaii | Tulsa 62, Hawaii 35 | 750,000 | 43,673 |
| 12-26-10 | Little Caesars | Florida International 34, Toledo 32 | 750,000 | 32,431 |
| 12-27-10 | Independence | Air Force 14, Georgia Tech 7 | 1.1 million | 39,362 |
| 12-28-10 | Champs Sports | North Carolina St 23, West Virginia 7 | 2.13 million | 48,962 |
| 12-28-10 | Insight | Iowa 27, Missouri 24 | 1.25 million | 53,453 |
| 12-29-10 | Military | Maryland 51, East Carolina 20 | 1 million | 38,062 |
| 12-29-10 | Texas | Illinois 38, Baylor 14 | 1.25 million | 68,211 |

### NCAA Football Bowl Subdivision (I-A) Bowl Results (Cont.)

| Date | Bowl | Result | Payout/Team($) | Attendance |
|------|------|--------|----------------|------------|
| 12-29-10 | Alamo | Oklahoma St 36, Arizona 10 | 2.25 million | 57,593 |
| 12-30-10 | Armed Forces | Army 16, SMU 14 | 750,000 | 36,742 |
| 12-30-10 | Pinstripe | Syracuse 36, Kansas St 34 | 2 million | 38,274 |
| 12-30-10 | Music City | North Carolina 30, Tennessee 27 | 3.3 million | 69,143 |
| 12-30-10 | Holiday | Washington 19, Nebraska 7 | 2.2 million | 57,921 |
| 12-31-10 | Meineke Car Care | South Florida 31, Clemson 26 | 1 million | 41,122 |
| 12-31-10 | Sun | Notre Dame 33, Miami (Fla.) 17 | 1.9 million | 54,021 |
| 12-31-10 | Liberty | Central Florida 10, Georgia 6 | 1.7 million | 51,231 |
| 12-31-10 | Chick-fil-A | Florida St 26, South Carolina 17 | 3.3 million (ACC) 2.5 million (SEC) | 72,217 |
| 01-01-11 | Outback | Florida 37, Penn St 24 | 3.1 million | 60,574 |
| 01-01-11 | TicketCity | Texas Tech 45, Northwestern 38 | 1.2 million | 40,121 |
| 01-01-11 | Capital One | Alabama 49, Michigan St 7 | 4.25 million | 61,519 |
| 01-01-11 | Gator | Mississippi St 52, Michigan 14 | 2.75 million | 77,497 |
| 01-01-11 | Rose | TCU 21, Wisconsin 19 | 17 million | 94,118 |
| 01-01-11 | Fiesta | Oklahoma 48, Connecticut 20 | 17 million | 67,232 |
| 01-03-11 | Orange | Stanford 40, Virginia Tech 12 | 17 million | 65,453 |
| 01-04-11 | Sugar | Ohio St 31, Arkansas 26 | 17 million | 73,879 |
| 01-06-11 | GoDaddy.com | Miami (Ohio) 35, Middle Tennessee St 21 | 750,000 | 38,168 |
| 01-07-11 | Cotton | LSU 41, Texas A&M 24 | 3.575 million | 83,514 |
| 01-08-11 | Compass | Pitt 27, Kentucky 10 | 900,000 (SEC) 600,000 (Big East) | 41,207 |
| 01-09-11 | Fight Hunger | Nevada 20, Boston College 13 | 1.65 million | 41,063 |
| 01-10-11 | BCS Championship | Auburn 22, Oregon 19 | 17 million | 78.603 |

## NCAA FCS (I-AA) Championship Box Score

| | | | |
|---|---|---|---|
| Delaware .................6 | 6 | 7 | 0—19 |
| Eastern Washington .........0 | 0 | 6 | 14—20 |

### FIRST QUARTER
Delaware: TD Pierce 2 run (Perry kick blocked), 5:14.

### SECOND QUARTER
Delaware: FG Perry 21, 12:29.
Delaware: FG Perry 33, 6:46.

### THIRD QUARTER
Delaware: TD Hayes 1 run (Perry kick), 7:12.
E. Washington: TD Kaufman 22 pass from Mitchell (2-pt. conversion failied), 1:48.

### FOURTH QUARTER
E. Washington: TD Edwards 9 pass from Mitchell (Jarrett kick), 8:16.
E. Washington: TD Kaufman 11 pass from Mitchell (Jarrett kick), 2:47.

| | DELAWARE | E. WASHINGTON |
|---|---|---|
| First downs | 26 | 20 |
| Rushes-net yards | 46-197 | 21-25 |
| Net passing yards | 220 | 302 |
| Comp/Att/Int | 22-34-1 | 29-43-1 |
| Punts/total yards | 4-152 | 5-227 |
| Fumbles-lost | 0-0 | 1-0 |
| Penalties-yards | 1-5 | 3-25 |
| Time of possession | 33:41 | 26:19 |

1-7-11, Frisco, Texas; Att: 13,027.

## Small College Championship Summaries

### NCAA DIVISION II

**First round**: Bloomsburg 28, California (Pa.) 26; Shepherd 40, Shaw 6; North Alabama 43, Valdosta St 20; Wingate 63, Morehouse 41; NW Missouri St 28, Missouri Western 24; Central Missouri St 55, West Texas A&M 35; Grand Valley St 35, Colorado Mines 13; St. Cloud St 42, Hillsdale 28.
**Second Round**: Mercyhurst 28, Bloomsburg 14; Shepherd 41, Kutztown 34; Delta St 47, North Alabama 24; Albany St 30, Wingate 28; NW Missouri St 35, Texas A&M-Kingsville 31; Central Missouri St 55, Abilene Christian 41; Augustana 38, Grand Valley St 6; Minnesota-Duluth 20, St. Cloud St 17.
**Quarterfinals**: Shepherd 49, Mercyhurst 14; Delta St 28, Albany St 7; NW Missouri St 37, Central Missouri St 20; Minnesota-Duluth 24, Augustana 13.
**Semifinals**: Delta St 29, Shepherd 17; Minnesota-Duluth 17, NW Missouri St 13.

### NCAA DIVISION II

**Championship**: 12-18-10, Florence, Ala., Att: 4,027.

| | | | | |
|---|---|---|---|---|
| Delta St.............7 | 7 | 0 | 3—17 |
| Minnesota-Duluth ..........10 | 0 | 0 | 10—20 |

### NCAA DIVISION III

**First round**: Wesley 53, Muhlenberg 14; Monclair St 16, Hampden-Sydney 14; Thomas More 42, Washington and Lee 14; Mary Hardin-Baylor 59, Chris. Newport 7; North Central 57, St. Norbert 7; Ohio Northern 37, Wittenberg 14; Trine 45, DePauw 35; UW-Whitewater 52, Franklin 21; Mount Union 49, St. Lawrence 0; Delaware Valley 23, Salisbury 12; Alfred 60, SUNY-Maritime 0; Cortland St 49, Endicott 35; St. Thomas 57, Benedictine 10; Linfield 42, Cal Luthern 26; Bethel 28, Wartburg 20; Wheaton (Ill.) 31, Coe 21.

### NCAA DIVISION III *(CONT.)*

**Second Round**: Wesley 44, Montclair St 7; Mary Hardin-Baylor 69, Thomas More 7; North Central 28, Ohio Northern 9; UW-Whitewater 45, Trine 31; Mount Union 31, Delaware Valley 3; Alfred 34, Cortland St 20; St. Thomas 24, Linfield 17 (2 OT); Bethel 15, Wheaton 10.
**Quarterfinals**: Wesley 19, Mary Hardin-Baylor 9; UW-Whitewater 20, North Central 10; Mount Union 37, Alfred 7; Bethel 12, St. Thomas 7.
**Semifinals**: UW-Whitewater 27, Wesley 7; Mount Union 34, Bethel 14.

### NCAA DIVISION III

**Championship**: 12-18-10, Salem, Virginia, Att: 4,598

| | | | | |
|---|---|---|---|---|
| UW-Whitewater | 7 | 17 | 0 | 7—31 |
| Mount Union | 0 | 21 | 0 | 0—21 |

### NAIA CHAMPIONSHIP

**Championship**: 12-18-10, Rome, Georgia, Att: 6,000

| | | | | |
|---|---|---|---|---|
| Carroll (Mont.) | 0 | 7 | 0 | 3—10 |
| Sioux Falls (S.D.) | 0 | 7 | 0 | 0—7 |

## Awards

### Heisman Memorial Trophy

| Player, School | Class | Pos | 1st | 2nd | 3rd | Total |
|---|---|---|---|---|---|---|
| Cam Newton, Auburn | Jr. | QB | 729 | 24 | 28 | 2,263 |
| Andrew Luck, Stanford | So. | QB | 78 | 309 | 227 | 1,079 |
| LaMichael James, Oregon | So. | RB | 22 | 313 | 224 | 916 |
| Kellen Moore, Boise St | Jr. | QB | 40 | 165 | 185 | 635 |

Note: Former Heisman winners and the media vote, with ballots allowing for three names (3 points for 1st, 2 for 2nd, 1 for 3rd).

### Other Awards

| | |
|---|---|
| Maxwell Award (Player) | Cam Newton, Auburn, QB |
| *Sporting News* Player of the Year | Cam Newton, Auburn, QB |
| Walter Camp Player of the Year | Cam Newton, Auburn, QB |
| Chuck Bednarik Award (Defense) | Patrick Peterson, LSU, CB |
| Vince Lombardi/Rotary Award (Lineman/LB) | Nick Fairley, Auburn, DT |
| Outland Trophy (Interior Lineman) | Gabe Carimi, Wisconsin, OT |
| Davey O'Brien Award (QB) | Cam Newton, Auburn, QB |
| Unitas Golden Arm Award (Senior QB) | Scott Tolzien, Wisconsin, QB |
| Doak Walker Award (RB) | LaMichael James, Oregon, RB |
| Biletnikoff Award (WR) | Justin Blackmon, Oklahoma St, WR |
| Butkus Award (Linebacker) | Von Miller, Texas A&M, LB |
| Jim Thorpe Award (Defensive Back) | Patrick Peterson, LSU, CB |
| Associated Press Player of the Year | Cam Newton, Auburn, QB |
| Walter Payton Award (FCS Player) | Jeremy Moses, Stephen F. Austin, QB |
| Harlon Hill Trophy (Div. II Player) | Eric Czerniewski, Central Missouri, QB |
| Gagliardi Trophy (Div. III Player) | Eric Watt, Trine, QB |

### Coaches' Awards

| | |
|---|---|
| Walter Camp Award | Chip Kelly, Oregon |
| Eddie Robinson Award (FCS) | Tony Samuel, Southeast Missouri St |
| Bobby Dodd Award | Chris Petersen, Boise St |
| Bear Bryant Award | Gene Chizik, Auburn |

#### AFCA COACHES OF THE YEAR

| | |
|---|---|
| FBS (Division I-A) | Chip Kelly, Oregon |
| FCS (Division I-AA) | K.C. Keeler, Delaware |
| Division II | Bob Nielson, Minn.-Duluth |
| Division III | Lance Leipold, UW-Whitewater |
| NAIA | Mike Van Diest, Carroll (Mont.) |

### Associated Press First Team All-America

| OFFENSE | DEFENSE |
|---|---|
| QB........Cam Newton, Auburn, Jr. | DT........Nick Fairley, Auburn, Jr. |
| RB ........LaMichael James, Oregon, So. | DT........Stephen Paea, Oregon St, Sr. |
| RB ........Kendall Hunter, Oklahoma St, Jr. | DE........Da'Quan Bowers, Clemson, Jr. |
| WR ........Justin Blackmon, Oklahoma St, So. | DE........Ryan Kerrigan, Purdue, Sr. |
| WR ......Ryan Broyles, Oklahoma, Jr. | LB ........Luke Kuechly, Boston College, So. |
| TE ........Michael Egnew, Missouri, Jr. | LB ........Greg Jones, Michigan St, Sr. |
| OG ......Rodney Hudson, Florida St, Sr. | LB ........Von Miller, Texas A&M, Sr. |
| OG ......John Moffitt, Wisconsin, Jr. | CB........Patrick Peterson, LSU, Jr. |
| OT ........Gabe Carimi, Wisconsin, Sr. | CB........Prince Amukamara, Nebraska, Sr. |
| OT ........Nate Solder, Colorado, Sr. | S ..........Tejay Johnson, TCU, Sr. |
| C ..........Chase Beeler, Stanford, Sr. | S ..........Quinton Carter, Oklahoma, Sr. |
| K ..........Alex Henery, Nebraska, Sr. | P............Chas Henry, Florida, Jr. |
| RS ........Randall Cobb, Kentucky, Jr. | |

## Football Bowl Subdivision (I-A)

### ATLANTIC COAST CONFERENCE

| ATLANTIC | Conference W | L | Full Season W | L | Pct |
|---|---|---|---|---|---|
| Florida St | 6 | 2 | 10 | 4 | .714 |
| Maryland | 5 | 3 | 9 | 4 | .692 |
| North Carolina St | 5 | 3 | 9 | 4 | .692 |
| Boston College | 4 | 4 | 7 | 6 | .538 |
| Clemson | 4 | 4 | 6 | 7 | .462 |
| Wake Forest | 1 | 7 | 3 | 9 | .250 |
| **COASTAL** | | | | | |
| Virginia Tech | 8 | 0 | 11 | 3 | .786 |
| Miami (Fla.) | 5 | 3 | 7 | 6 | .538 |
| Georgia Tech | 4 | 4 | 6 | 7 | .462 |
| North Carolina | 4 | 4 | 8 | 5 | .615 |
| Duke | 1 | 7 | 3 | 9 | .250 |
| Virginia | 1 | 7 | 4 | 8 | .333 |

### BIG EAST CONFERENCE

| | Conference W | L | Full Season W | L | Pct |
|---|---|---|---|---|---|
| Connecticut | 5 | 2 | 8 | 5 | .615 |
| West Virginia | 5 | 2 | 9 | 4 | .692 |
| Pittsburgh | 5 | 2 | 8 | 5 | .615 |
| Syracuse | 4 | 3 | 8 | 5 | .615 |
| South Florida | 3 | 4 | 8 | 5 | .615 |
| Louisville | 3 | 4 | 7 | 6 | .538 |
| Cincinnati | 2 | 5 | 4 | 8 | .333 |
| Rutgers | 1 | 6 | 4 | 8 | .333 |

### BIG TEN CONFERENCE

| | Conference W | L | Full Season W | L | Pct |
|---|---|---|---|---|---|
| Ohio St | 7 | 1 | 12 | 1 | .923 |
| Michigan St | 7 | 1 | 11 | 2 | .846 |
| Wisconsin | 7 | 1 | 11 | 2 | .846 |
| Iowa | 4 | 4 | 8 | 5 | .615 |
| Illinois | 4 | 4 | 7 | 6 | .538 |
| Penn St | 4 | 4 | 7 | 6 | .538 |
| Michigan | 3 | 5 | 7 | 6 | .538 |
| Northwestern | 3 | 5 | 7 | 6 | .538 |
| Purdue | 2 | 6 | 4 | 8 | .333 |
| Minnesota | 2 | 6 | 3 | 9 | .250 |
| Indiana | 1 | 7 | 5 | 7 | .417 |

### BIG 12 CONFERENCE

| NORTH | Conference W | L | Full Season W | L | Pct |
|---|---|---|---|---|---|
| Nebraska | 6 | 2 | 10 | 4 | .714 |
| Missouri | 6 | 2 | 10 | 3 | .769 |
| Kansas St | 3 | 5 | 7 | 6 | .538 |
| Iowa St | 3 | 5 | 5 | 7 | .417 |
| Colorado | 2 | 6 | 5 | 7 | .417 |
| Kansas | 1 | 7 | 3 | 9 | .250 |
| **SOUTH** | | | | | |
| Oklahoma | 6 | 2 | 12 | 2 | .857 |
| Oklahoma St | 6 | 2 | 11 | 2 | .846 |
| Texas A&M | 6 | 2 | 9 | 4 | .692 |
| Baylor | 4 | 4 | 7 | 6 | .538 |
| Texas Tech | 3 | 5 | 8 | 5 | .615 |
| Texas | 2 | 3 | 5 | 7 | .417 |

## Football Bowl Subdivision (I-A) *(Cont.)*

### CONFERENCE USA

| EAST | Conference W | L | Full Season W | L | Pct |
|---|---|---|---|---|---|
| Central Florida | 7 | 1 | 11 | 3 | .786 |
| East Carolina | 5 | 3 | 6 | 7 | .462 |
| Southern Miss | 5 | 3 | 8 | 5 | .615 |
| Marshall | 4 | 4 | 5 | 7 | .417 |
| UAB | 3 | 5 | 4 | 8 | .333 |
| Memphis | 0 | 8 | 1 | 11 | .083 |
| **WEST** | | | | | |
| SMU | 6 | 2 | 7 | 7 | .500 |
| Tulsa | 6 | 2 | 10 | 3 | .769 |
| Houston | 4 | 4 | 5 | 7 | .417 |
| UTEP | 3 | 5 | 6 | 7 | .462 |
| Rice | 3 | 5 | 4 | 8 | .333 |
| Tulane | 2 | 6 | 4 | 8 | .333 |

### MID-AMERICAN ATHLETIC CONFERENCE

| EAST | Conference W | L | Full Season W | L | Pct |
|---|---|---|---|---|---|
| Miami (Ohio) | 7 | 1 | 10 | 4 | .714 |
| Ohio | 6 | 2 | 8 | 5 | .615 |
| Temple | 5 | 3 | 8 | 4 | .667 |
| Kent St | 4 | 4 | 5 | 7 | .417 |
| Bowling Green | 1 | 7 | 2 | 10 | .167 |
| Buffalo | 1 | 7 | 2 | 10 | .167 |
| Akron | 1 | 7 | 1 | 11 | .083 |
| **WEST** | | | | | |
| Northern Illinois | 8 | 0 | 11 | 3 | .786 |
| Toledo | 7 | 1 | 8 | 5 | .615 |
| Western Michigan | 5 | 3 | 6 | 6 | .500 |
| Ball St | 3 | 5 | 4 | 8 | .333 |
| Central Michigan | 2 | 6 | 3 | 9 | .250 |
| Eastern Michigan | 2 | 6 | 2 | 10 | .167 |

### MOUNTAIN WEST CONFERENCE

| | Conference W | L | Full Season W | L | Pct |
|---|---|---|---|---|---|
| TCU | 8 | 0 | 13 | 0 | 1.000 |
| Utah | 7 | 1 | 10 | 3 | .769 |
| Air Force | 5 | 3 | 9 | 4 | .692 |
| San Diego St | 5 | 3 | 9 | 4 | .692 |
| BYU | 5 | 3 | 7 | 6 | .538 |
| Colorado St | 2 | 6 | 3 | 9 | .250 |
| UNLV | 2 | 6 | 2 | 11 | .154 |
| New Mexico | 1 | 7 | 1 | 11 | .083 |
| Wyoming | 1 | 7 | 3 | 9 | .250 |

### PACIFIC 10 CONFERENCE

| | Conference W | L | Full Season W | L | Pct |
|---|---|---|---|---|---|
| Oregon | 9 | 0 | 12 | 1 | .923 |
| Stanford | 8 | 1 | 12 | 1 | .923 |
| Washington | 5 | 4 | 7 | 6 | .538 |
| *USC | 5 | 4 | 8 | 5 | .615 |
| Oregon St | 4 | 5 | 5 | 7 | .417 |
| Arizona St | 4 | 5 | 6 | 6 | .500 |
| Arizona | 4 | 5 | 7 | 6 | .538 |
| California | 3 | 6 | 5 | 7 | .417 |
| UCLA | 2 | 7 | 4 | 8 | .333 |
| Washington St | 1 | 8 | 2 | 10 | .167 |

*Barred from bowl eligibility by the NCAA for rules violations.

## Football Bowl Subdivision (I-A) *(Cont.)*

### SOUTHEASTERN CONFERENCE

| EAST | Conference | | Full Season | | |
|---|---|---|---|---|---|
| | W | L | W | L | Pct |
| South Carolina | 5 | 3 | 9 | 5 | .692 |
| Florida | 4 | 4 | 8 | 5 | .615 |
| Georgia | 3 | 5 | 6 | 7 | .462 |
| Tennessee | 3 | 5 | 6 | 7 | .462 |
| Kentucky | 2 | 6 | 6 | 7 | .462 |
| Vanderbilt | 1 | 7 | 2 | 10 | .167 |
| **WEST** | | | | | |
| Auburn | 8 | 0 | 14 | 0 | 1.000 |
| Arkansas | 6 | 2 | 10 | 3 | .769 |
| LSU | 6 | 2 | 11 | 2 | .846 |
| Alabama | 5 | 3 | 10 | 3 | .769 |
| Mississippi St | 4 | 4 | 9 | 4 | .692 |
| Mississippi | 1 | 7 | 4 | 8 | .333 |

### SUN BELT CONFERENCE

| | Conference | | Full Season | | |
|---|---|---|---|---|---|
| | W | L | W | L | Pct |
| Florida International | 6 | 2 | 7 | 6 | .538 |
| Troy | 6 | 2 | 8 | 5 | .615 |
| Middle Tennessee St | 5 | 3 | 6 | 7 | .462 |
| Arkansas St | 4 | 4 | 4 | 8 | .333 |
| La.-Monroe | 4 | 4 | 5 | 7 | .417 |
| Florida Atlantic | 3 | 5 | 4 | 8 | .333 |
| La.-Lafayette | 3 | 5 | 3 | 9 | .250 |
| North Texas | 3 | 5 | 3 | 9 | .250 |
| Western Kentucky | 2 | 6 | 2 | 10 | .167 |

### WESTERN ATHLETIC CONFERENCE

| | Conference | | Full Season | | |
|---|---|---|---|---|---|
| | W | L | W | L | Pct |
| Nevada | 7 | 1 | 13 | 1 | .929 |
| Boise St | 7 | 1 | 12 | 1 | .923 |
| Hawaii | 7 | 1 | 10 | 4 | .714 |
| Fresno St | 5 | 3 | 8 | 5 | .615 |
| Louisiana Tech | 4 | 4 | 5 | 7 | .417 |
| Idaho | 3 | 5 | 6 | 7 | .462 |
| Utah St | 2 | 6 | 4 | 8 | .333 |
| New Mexico St | 1 | 7 | 2 | 10 | .167 |
| San Jose St | 0 | 8 | 1 | 12 | .077 |

### INDEPENDENTS

| | Full Season | | |
|---|---|---|---|
| | W | L | Pct |
| Navy | 9 | 4 | .692 |
| Notre Dame | 8 | 5 | .615 |
| Army | 7 | 6 | .538 |

## Football Championship Subdivision (I-AA)

### BIG SKY CONFERENCE

| | Conference | | Full Season | | |
|---|---|---|---|---|---|
| | W | L | W | L | Pct |
| Montana St | 7 | 1 | 9 | 3 | .750 |
| Eastern Washington | 7 | 1 | 13 | 2 | .867 |
| Montana | 5 | 3 | 7 | 4 | .636 |
| Sacramento St | 5 | 3 | 6 | 5 | .545 |
| Weber St | 5 | 3 | 6 | 5 | .545 |
| Northern Arizona | 4 | 4 | 6 | 5 | .545 |
| Northern Colorado | 2 | 6 | 3 | 8 | .273 |
| Portland St | 1 | 7 | 2 | 9 | .182 |
| Idaho St | 0 | 8 | 1 | 10 | .091 |

### BIG SOUTH CONFERENCE

| | Conference | | Full Season | | |
|---|---|---|---|---|---|
| | W | L | W | L | Pct |
| Liberty | 5 | 1 | 8 | 3 | .727 |
| Stony Brook | 5 | 1 | 6 | 5 | .545 |
| Coastal Carolina | 5 | 1 | 6 | 6 | .500 |
| Gardner-Webb | 2 | 4 | 4 | 7 | .364 |
| Virginia Military Inst. | 2 | 4 | 3 | 8 | .273 |
| Charleston Southern | 1 | 5 | 3 | 8 | .273 |
| Presbyterian | 1 | 5 | 2 | 9 | .182 |

### COLONIAL CONFERENCE

| | Conference | | Full Season | | |
|---|---|---|---|---|---|
| | W | L | W | L | Pct |
| William & Mary | 6 | 2 | 8 | 4 | .667 |
| Delaware | 6 | 2 | 12 | 3 | .800 |
| Villanova | 5 | 3 | 9 | 5 | .643 |
| New Hampshire | 5 | 3 | 8 | 5 | .655 |
| Richmond | 4 | 4 | 6 | 5 | .545 |
| Massachusetts | 4 | 4 | 6 | 5 | .545 |
| Rhode Island | 4 | 4 | 5 | 6 | .455 |
| James Madison | 3 | 5 | 6 | 5 | .545 |
| Maine | 3 | 5 | 4 | 7 | .364 |
| Towson | 0 | 8 | 1 | 10 | .091 |

### GREAT WEST

| | Conference | | Full Season | | |
|---|---|---|---|---|---|
| | W | L | W | L | Pct |
| Southern Utah | 4 | 0 | 6 | 5 | .545 |
| UC-Davis | 3 | 1 | 6 | 5 | .545 |
| Cal Poly | 2 | 2 | 7 | 4 | .636 |
| South Dakota | 1 | 3 | 4 | 7 | .364 |
| North Dakota | 0 | 4 | 3 | 8 | .273 |

### IVY LEAGUE

| | Conference | | Full Season | | |
|---|---|---|---|---|---|
| | W | L | W | L | Pct |
| Pennsylvania | 7 | 0 | 9 | 1 | .900 |
| Harvard | 5 | 2 | 7 | 3 | .700 |
| Yale | 5 | 2 | 7 | 3 | .700 |
| Brown | 5 | 2 | 6 | 4 | .600 |
| Dartmouth | 3 | 4 | 6 | 4 | .600 |
| Columbia | 2 | 5 | 4 | 6 | .400 |
| Cornell | 1 | 6 | 2 | 8 | .200 |
| Princeton | 0 | 7 | 1 | 9 | .100 |

## Football Champ. Subdivision (I-AA) *(Cont.)*

### MID-EASTERN ATHLETIC CONFERENCE

| | Conference | | Full Season | | |
|---|---|---|---|---|---|
| | W | L | W | L | Pct |
| Bethune-Cookman | 7 | 1 | 10 | 2 | .833 |
| South Carolina St | 7 | 1 | 9 | 3 | .750 |
| Florida A&M | 7 | 1 | 8 | 3 | .727 |
| Hampton | 7 | 1 | 6 | 5 | .545 |
| Norfolk St | 4 | 4 | 6 | 5 | .545 |
| *Savannah St | 1 | 1 | 1 | 10 | .091 |
| Morgan St | 3 | 5 | 4 | 7 | .364 |
| Delaware St | 2 | 6 | 3 | 8 | .273 |
| North Carolina A&T | 1 | 8 | 1 | 10 | .091 |
| *North Carolina Central | 0 | 2 | 3 | 8 | .273 |
| Howard | 0 | 8 | 1 | 10 | .091 |

### MISSOURI VALLEY CONFERENCE

| | Conference | | Full Season | | |
|---|---|---|---|---|---|
| | W | L | W | L | Pct |
| Northern Iowa | 6 | 2 | 7 | 5 | .583 |
| Western Illinois | 5 | 3 | 8 | 5 | .615 |
| North Dakota St | 4 | 4 | 9 | 5 | .643 |
| Illinois St | 4 | 4 | 6 | 5 | .545 |
| Indiana St | 4 | 4 | 6 | 5 | .545 |
| Missouri St | 4 | 4 | 5 | 6 | .455 |
| South Dakota St | 4 | 4 | 5 | 6 | .455 |
| Southern Illinois | 4 | 4 | 5 | 6 | .455 |
| Youngstown St | 1 | 7 | 3 | 8 | .273 |

### NORTHEAST CONFERENCE

| | Conference | | Full Season | | |
|---|---|---|---|---|---|
| | W | L | W | L | Pct |
| Central Connecticut St | 7 | 1 | 8 | 3 | .727 |
| Robert Morris | 7 | 1 | 8 | 3 | .727 |
| Duquesne | 5 | 3 | 7 | 4 | .636 |
| Bryant | 4 | 4 | 7 | 4 | .636 |
| Albany | 4 | 4 | 6 | 5 | .545 |
| Wagner | 3 | 5 | 5 | 6 | .455 |
| Monmouth (N.J.) | 3 | 5 | 3 | 8 | .273 |
| Sacred Heart | 2 | 6 | 4 | 7 | .364 |
| St. Francis (Pa.) | 1 | 7 | 1 | 10 | .091 |

### OHIO VALLEY CONFERENCE

| | Conference | | Full Season | | |
|---|---|---|---|---|---|
| | W | L | W | L | Pct |
| SE Missouri St | 7 | 1 | 9 | 3 | .750 |
| Eastern Kentucky | 5 | 2 | 6 | 5 | .538 |
| Jacksonville St | 6 | 3 | 9 | 3 | .750 |
| Murray St | 5 | 3 | 6 | 5 | .545 |
| Tenn.-Martin | 5 | 3 | 6 | 5 | .545 |
| Tennessee Tech | 4 | 4 | 5 | 6 | .455 |
| Eastern Illinois | 2 | 6 | 2 | 9 | .182 |
| Austin Peay | 1 | 7 | 2 | 9 | .182 |
| Tennessee St | 0 | 7 | 3 | 8 | .273 |

### PATRIOT LEAGUE

| | Conference | | Full Season | | |
|---|---|---|---|---|---|
| | W | L | W | L | Pct |
| Lehigh | 5 | 0 | 10 | 3 | .769 |
| Colgate | 3 | 2 | 7 | 4 | .636 |
| Holy Cross | 3 | 2 | 6 | 5 | .545 |
| Georgetown | 2 | 3 | 4 | 7 | .364 |
| Lafayette | 1 | 4 | 2 | 9 | .182 |
| Bucknell | 1 | 4 | 1 | 10 | .091 |
| Fordham | 0 | 5 | 5 | 6 | .455 |

## Football Champ. Subdivision (I-AA) *(Cont.)*

### PIONEER LEAGUE

| | Conference | | Full Season | | |
|---|---|---|---|---|---|
| | W | L | W | L | Pct |
| Dayton | 8 | 0 | 10 | 1 | .909 |
| Jacksonville | 8 | 0 | 10 | 1 | .909 |
| Drake | 6 | 2 | 7 | 4 | .727 |
| San Diego | 5 | 3 | 5 | 6 | .455 |
| Morehead St | 4 | 4 | 5 | 6 | .455 |
| Davidson | 3 | 5 | 3 | 8 | .273 |
| Butler | 2 | 6 | 4 | 7 | .364 |
| Campbell | 2 | 6 | 3 | 8 | .273 |
| Marist | 2 | 6 | 3 | 8 | .273 |
| Valparaiso | 0 | 8 | 0 | 11 | .000 |

### SOUTHERN CONFERENCE

| | Conference | | Full Season | | |
|---|---|---|---|---|---|
| | W | L | W | L | Pct |
| Wofford | 8 | 1 | 10 | 3 | .769 |
| Appalachian St | 7 | 1 | 10 | 3 | .769 |
| Georgia Southern | 5 | 3 | 10 | 5 | .667 |
| Chattanooga | 5 | 3 | 6 | 5 | .545 |
| Elon | 5 | 3 | 6 | 5 | .545 |
| Furman | 3 | 5 | 5 | 6 | .455 |
| Samford | 2 | 6 | 4 | 7 | .364 |
| Western Carolina | 1 | 7 | 2 | 9 | .182 |
| Citadel | 1 | 7 | 3 | 8 | .273 |

### SOUTHLAND CONFERENCE

| | Conference | | Full Season | | |
|---|---|---|---|---|---|
| | W | L | W | L | Pct |
| Stephen F. Austin | 6 | 1 | 9 | 3 | .750 |
| McNeese St | 5 | 2 | 6 | 5 | .545 |
| Central Arkansas | 4 | 3 | 7 | 4 | .636 |
| Sam Houston St | 4 | 3 | 6 | 5 | .545 |
| Northwestern St | 4 | 3 | 5 | 6 | .455 |
| Nicholls St | 3 | 4 | 4 | 7 | .364 |
| Texas St | 1 | 6 | 4 | 7 | .364 |
| SE Louisiana | 1 | 6 | 2 | 9 | .182 |
| †Lamar | 0 | 0 | 5 | 6 | .455 |

### SOUTHWESTERN ATHLETIC CONFERENCE

| | Conference | | Full Season | | |
|---|---|---|---|---|---|
| EAST | W | L | W | L | Pct |
| Jackson St | 6 | 3 | 8 | 3 | .727 |
| Alabama St | 6 | 3 | 7 | 5 | .583 |
| Alcorn St | 4 | 5 | 5 | 6 | .455 |
| Alabama A&M | 2 | 7 | 3 | 8 | .273 |
| Mississippi Valley St | 0 | 9 | 0 | 10 | .000 |
| **WEST** | | | | | |
| Grambling St | 8 | 1 | 9 | 2 | .818 |
| Texas Southern | 8 | 1 | 9 | 3 | .750 |
| Prairie View A&M | 6 | 3 | 7 | 4 | .636 |
| Ark.-Pine Bluff | 4 | 5 | 5 | 6 | .455 |
| Southern Univ. | 1 | 8 | 2 | 9 | .182 |

### INDEPENDENTS

| | Full Season | | |
|---|---|---|---|
| | W | L | Pct |
| Old Dominion | 8 | 3 | .727 |
| Georgia St | 6 | 5 | .545 |

†Lamar played four Southland Conference opponents in 2010 and went 1–3 in those games, but it won't officially join the conference for football until the 2011 season.

*Due to their having just joined the MEAC in the summer of 2010, Savannah State and North Carolina Central played only two conference games during the 2010 season.

### Football Bowl Subdivision (I-A)

#### SCORING

| | Class | GP | TD | XP | FG | Pts | Pts/Game |
|---|---|---|---|---|---|---|---|
| LaMichael James, Oregon | So. | 12 | 24 | 0 | 0 | 144 | 12.00 |
| Dan Bailey, Oklahoma St | Sr. | 13 | 0 | 68 | 27 | 149 | 11.46 |
| Justin Blackmon, Oklahoma St | So. | 12 | 22 | 0 | 0 | 132 | 11.00 |
| Danny Hrapmann, Southern Miss | Jr. | 13 | 0 | 55 | 26 | 133 | 10.23 |
| Vai Taua, Nevada | Sr. | 13 | 22 | 0 | 0 | 132 | 10.15 |
| Vick Ballard, Mississippi St | Jr. | 12 | 20 | 0 | 0 | 120 | 10.00 |
| Chad Spann, Northern Illinois | Sr. | 14 | 22 | 0 | 0 | 132 | 9.43 |
| Devin Barclay, Ohio St | Sr. | 13 | 0 | 62 | 20 | 122 | 9.38 |
| Mikel Leshoure, Illinois | Jr. | 13 | 20 | 0 | 0 | 122 | 9.38 |
| Josh Jasper, LSU | Sr. | 13 | 0 | 36 | 28 | 120 | 9.23 |
| Jimmy Stevens, Oklahoma | Jr. | 12 | 0 | 53 | 19 | 110 | 9.17 |
| Philip Welch, Wisconsin | Jr. | 13 | 0 | 67 | 17 | 118 | 9.08 |
| Cam Newton, Auburn | Jr. | 14 | 21 | 0 | 0 | 126 | 9.00 |
| Montee Ball, Wisconsin | So. | 12 | 18 | 0 | 0 | 108 | 9.00 |
| Daniel Thomas, Kansas St | Sr. | 13 | 19 | 0 | 0 | 116 | 8.92 |

#### FIELD GOALS

| | Class | GP | FGA | FG | Pct | FG/Game |
|---|---|---|---|---|---|---|
| Josh Jasper, LSU | Sr. | 13 | 34 | 28 | .824 | 2.15 |
| Dan Bailey, Oklahoma St | Sr. | 13 | 31 | 27 | .871 | 2.08 |
| Danny Hrapmann, Southern Miss | Jr. | 13 | 31 | 26 | .839 | 2.00 |
| Dave Teggart, Connecticut | Jr. | 13 | 31 | 25 | .806 | 1.92 |
| Justin Tucker, Texas | Jr. | 12 | 27 | 23 | .852 | 1.92 |

#### TOTAL OFFENSE

| | | | Rushing | | Passing | | | Total Offense | |
|---|---|---|---|---|---|---|---|---|---|
| | Class | GP | Car | Net | Att | Yds | Yds | Yds/Play | Yds/Game |
| Bryant Moniz, Hawaii | Jr. | 14 | 81 | 102 | 555 | 5040 | 5142 | 8.08 | 367.3 |
| Denard Robinson, Michigan | So. | 13 | 256 | 1702 | 291 | 2570 | 4272 | 7.81 | 328.6 |
| Landry Jones, Oklahoma | So. | 14 | 51 | -128 | 617 | 4718 | 4590 | 6.87 | 327.9 |
| G.J. Kinne, Tulsa | Jr. | 13 | 158 | 561 | 460 | 3650 | 4211 | 6.81 | 323.9 |
| Brandon Weeden, Oklahoma St | Jr. | 13 | 17 | -68 | 511 | 4277 | 4209 | 7.97 | 323.8 |
| Robert Griffin III, Baylor | So. | 13 | 149 | 635 | 454 | 3501 | 4136 | 6.86 | 318.2 |
| Dominique Davis, East Carolina | Jr. | 13 | 79 | 141 | 609 | 3967 | 4108 | 5.97 | 316.0 |
| Dan Persa, Northwestern | Jr. | 10 | 164 | 519 | 302 | 2581 | 3100 | 6.65 | 310.0 |
| Cam Newton, Auburn | Jr. | 14 | 264 | 1473 | 280 | 2854 | 4327 | 7.95 | 309.1 |
| Russell Wilson, North Carolina St | Jr. | 13 | 143 | 435 | 527 | 3563 | 3998 | 5.97 | 307.5 |

#### RUSHING

| | Class | GP | Car | Yds | TD | Avg | Yds/Game |
|---|---|---|---|---|---|---|---|
| LaMichael James, Oregon | So. | 12 | 294 | 1731 | 21 | 5.89 | 144.3 |
| Jordan Todman, Connecticut | Jr. | 12 | 334 | 1695 | 14 | 5.07 | 141.3 |
| Bobby Rainey, Western Kentucky | Jr. | 12 | 340 | 1649 | 15 | 4.85 | 137.4 |
| Denard Robinson, Michigan | So. | 13 | 256 | 1702 | 14 | 6.65 | 130.9 |
| Mikel Leshoure, Illinois | Jr. | 13 | 281 | 1697 | 17 | 6.04 | 130.5 |
| Lance Dunbar, North Texas | Jr. | 12 | 274 | 1553 | 13 | 5.67 | 129.4 |
| Vai Taua, Nevada | Sr. | 13 | 284 | 1610 | 19 | 5.67 | 123.9 |
| Daniel Thomas, Kansas St | Sr. | 13 | 298 | 1585 | 19 | 5.32 | 121.9 |
| Kendall Hunter, Oklahoma St | Sr. | 13 | 271 | 1548 | 16 | 5.71 | 119.1 |
| Ronnie Hillman, San Diego St | Fr. | 13 | 262 | 1532 | 17 | 5.85 | 117.9 |

#### PASSING EFFICIENCY

| | Class | GP | Att | Comp | Pct Comp | Yds | Yds/Att | TD | Int | Rating Pts |
|---|---|---|---|---|---|---|---|---|---|---|
| Kellen Moore, Boise St | Jr. | 13 | 383 | 273 | 71.3 | 3845 | 10.0 | 35 | 6 | 182.63 |
| Cam Newton, Auburn | Jr. | 14 | 280 | 185 | 66.1 | 2854 | 10.2 | 30 | 7 | 182.05 |
| Andrew Luck, Stanford | So. | 13 | 372 | 263 | 70.7 | 3338 | 9.0 | 32 | 8 | 170.16 |
| Greg McElroy, Alabama | Sr. | 13 | 313 | 222 | 70.9 | 2987 | 9.5 | 20 | 5 | 168.98 |
| Andy Dalton, TCU | Sr. | 13 | 316 | 209 | 66.1 | 2857 | 9.0 | 27 | 6 | 166.48 |
| Scott Tolzien, Wisconsin | Sr. | 13 | 266 | 194 | 72.9 | 2459 | 9.2 | 16 | 6 | 165.92 |
| Ryan Mallett, Arkansas | Jr. | 13 | 411 | 266 | 64.7 | 3869 | 9.4 | 32 | 12 | 163.65 |
| Bryant Moniz, Hawaii | Jr. | 14 | 555 | 361 | 65.1 | 5040 | 9.1 | 39 | 15 | 159.11 |
| Dan Persa, Northwestern | Jr. | 10 | 302 | 222 | 73.5 | 2581 | 8.6 | 15 | 4 | 159.04 |
| Terrelle Pryor, Ohio St | Jr. | 13 | 323 | 210 | 65.0 | 2772 | 8.6 | 27 | 11 | 157.88 |

Note: Minimum 15 attempts per game.

## Football Bowl Subdivision (I-A) *(Cont.)*

### RECEPTIONS PER GAME

| | Class | GP | No. | Yds | TD | R/Game |
|---|---|---|---|---|---|---|
| Ryan Broyles, Oklahoma | Jr. | 14 | 131 | 1622 | 14 | 9.36 |
| Justin Blackmon, Oklahoma St. | So. | 12 | 111 | 1782 | 20 | 9.25 |
| Greg Salas, Hawaii | Sr. | 14 | 119 | 1889 | 14 | 8.50 |
| Kamar Jorden, Bowling Green | Jr. | 12 | 96 | 1109 | 4 | 8.00 |
| Jordan White, Western Michigan | Sr. | 12 | 94 | 1378 | 10 | 7.83 |

### RECEIVING YARDS PER GAME

| | Class | GP | No. | Yds | TD | Yds/Game |
|---|---|---|---|---|---|---|
| Justin Blackmon, Oklahoma St | So. | 12 | 111 | 1782 | 20 | 148.5 |
| Greg Salas, Hawaii | Sr. | 14 | 119 | 1889 | 14 | 134.9 |
| Ryan Broyles, Oklahoma | Jr. | 14 | 131 | 1622 | 14 | 115.9 |
| Jordan White, Western Michigan | Sr. | 12 | 94 | 1378 | 10 | 114.8 |
| Alshon Jeffery, South Carolina | So. | 14 | 88 | 1517 | 9 | 108.4 |

### ALL-PURPOSE RUNNING

| | Class | GP | Rush | Rec | PR | KOR | Total Yds | Yds/Game |
|---|---|---|---|---|---|---|---|---|
| Damaris Johnson, Tulsa | Jr. | 13 | 560 | 872 | 292 | 904 | 2628 | 202.2 |
| Randall Cobb, Kentucky | Jr. | 13 | 424 | 1017 | 219 | 736 | 2396 | 184.3 |
| Pat Shed, UAB | Jr. | 12 | 847 | 471 | 69 | 738 | 2125 | 177.1 |
| Dwayne Harris, East Carolina | Sr. | 13 | 104 | 1123 | 222 | 839 | 2288 | 176.0 |
| Tandon Doss, Indiana | Jr. | 11 | 163 | 706 | 49 | 1016 | 1934 | 175.8 |

### INTERCEPTIONS

| | Class | GP | No. | Int/Game |
|---|---|---|---|---|
| Jayron Hosley, Virginia Tech | So. | 13 | 9 | .69 |
| Robert Lester, Alabama | So. | 13 | 8 | .62 |
| Mana Silva, Hawaii | Sr. | 14 | 8 | .57 |
| Harrison Smith, Notre Dame | Sr. | 13 | 7 | .54 |

Note: Five tied with .50.

### PUNT RETURNS

| | Class | No. | Yds | TD | Avg |
|---|---|---|---|---|---|
| Shaky Smithson, Utah | Sr. | 30 | 572 | 2 | 19.1 |
| Cliff Harris, Oregon | So. | 29 | 546 | 4 | 18.8 |
| Tony Logan, Maryland | Jr. | 31 | 560 | 2 | 18.1 |
| Patrick Peterson, LSU | Jr. | 26 | 418 | 2 | 16.1 |
| Joe Adams, Arkansas | Jr. | 16 | 249 | 1 | 15.6 |

Note: Minimum 1.2 punt returns per game.

### PUNTING

| | Class | No. | Avg Y/Pt |
|---|---|---|---|
| Tyler Campbell, Mississippi | So. | 60 | 46.37 |
| Quinn Sharp, Oklahoma St | So. | 46 | 46.24 |
| Kyle Martens, Rice | Jr. | 52 | 45.98 |
| Jeff Locke, UCLA | So. | 64 | 45.84 |
| Mickey Groody, Fla. Atlantic | Jr. | 71 | 45.80 |

Note: Minimum of 3.6 punts per game.

### KICKOFF RETURNS

| | Class | No. | Yds | TD | Avg |
|---|---|---|---|---|---|
| Nick Williams, Connecticut | So. | 17 | 600 | 2 | 35.3 |
| Quincy McDuffie, Central Fla. | So. | 27 | 869 | 2 | 32.2 |
| Eric Page, Toledo | So. | 28 | 871 | 3 | 31.1 |
| Marlon McClure, UTEP | So. | 30 | 930 | 2 | 31.0 |
| Jeremy Wright, Lousiville | Fr. | 16 | 489 | 1 | 30.6 |

Note: Minimum of 1.2 kickoff returns per game.

## Football Bowl Subdivision (I-A) Single-Game Highs

### RUSHING AND PASSING

Rushing and passing yards: 581—Bryant Moniz, Hawaii, QB, Oct. 2, 2010 (vs Louisiana Tech)
Rushing and passing plays: 79—Alex Carder, Western Michigan, QB, Sept. 18, 2010 (vs Toledo)
Rushing plays: 45—Bobby Rainey, Western Kentucky, RB, Nov. 20, 2010 (vs Middle Tennessee St)
Net rushing yards: 330—Mikel Leshoure, Illinois, RB, Nov. 20, 2010 (vs Northwestern)
Passes attempted: 65—Dominique Davis, East Carolina, QB, Nov. 6, 2010 (vs Navy)
Passes completed: 45—Ben Chappell, Indiana QB, Oct. 2, 2010 (vs Michigan)
Net passing yards: 560—Bryant Moniz, Hawaii, QB, Nov. 20, 2010 (vs San Jose St)

### RECEIVING AND RETURNS

Passes caught: 18—Kealoha Pilares, Hawaii, WR, Oct. 2, 2010 (vs Louisiana Tech)
Receiving yards: 246—Roy Roundtree, Michigan, WR, Nov. 6, 2010 (vs Illinois)
Punt return Yards: 157—Patrick Peterson, LSU, CB, Sept. 4, 2010 (vs North Carolina)
Kickoff return yards: 273—Venric Mark, Northwestern, WR, Nov. 27, 2010 (vs Wisconsin)

### Football Championship Subdivision (I-AA)

#### SCORING

| | Class | GP | TD | XP | FG | Pts | Pts/Game |
|---|---|---|---|---|---|---|---|
| Nate Eachus, Colgate | Jr. | 11 | 22 | 0 | 0 | 132 | 12.00 |
| Darrius Gates, Indiana St. | Sr. | 11 | 19 | 0 | 0 | 116 | 10.55 |
| Frank Warren, Grambling St. | Sr. | 11 | 19 | 0 | 0 | 114 | 10.36 |
| Eric Breitenstein, Wofford | Jr. | 13 | 22 | 0 | 0 | 132 | 10.15 |
| Matt Bevins, Liberty | Jr. | 11 | 0 | 45 | 20 | 105 | 9.55 |

#### FIELD GOALS

| | Class | GP | FGA | FG | Pct | FG/Game |
|---|---|---|---|---|---|---|
| Matt Bevins, Liberty | Jr. | 11 | 27 | 20 | .741 | 1.82 |
| Jason Cunningham, Montana St | Sr. | 12 | 24 | 20 | .833 | 1.67 |
| Kemar Scarlett, Morgan St | Sr. | 11 | 24 | 18 | .750 | 1.64 |
| Zach Brown, Portland St | So. | 11 | 26 | 18 | .692 | 1.64 |
| Cameron Yaw, Samford | So. | 11 | 23 | 17 | .739 | 1.55 |

#### TOTAL OFFENSE

| | | | Rushing | | Passing | | | Total Offense | |
|---|---|---|---|---|---|---|---|---|---|
| | Class | GP | Car | Net | Att | Yds | Total Yds | Yds/Play | Yds/Game |
| Mike Brown, Liberty | Jr. | 11 | 160 | 854 | 351 | 2956 | 3810 | 7.5 | 346.4 |
| Jeremy Moses, Stephen F. Austin | Sr. | 12 | 16 | -68 | 550 | 3998 | 3930 | 6.9 | 327.5 |
| Casey Therriault, Jackson St | Jr. | 11 | 101 | 164 | 437 | 3436 | 3600 | 6.7 | 327.3 |
| Scott Riddle, Elon | Sr. | 10 | 41 | -43 | 405 | 3231 | 3188 | 7.1 | 318.8 |
| Casey Brockman, Murray St | So. | 9 | 79 | 292 | 320 | 2442 | 2734 | 6.9 | 303.8 |

#### RUSHING

| | Class | GP | Car | Yds | Avg | TD | Yds/Game |
|---|---|---|---|---|---|---|---|
| Nate Eachus, Colgate | Jr. | 11 | 317 | 1871 | 5.9 | 21 | 170.1 |
| Taiwan Jones, Eastern Washington | Jr. | 12 | 221 | 1742 | 7.9 | 14 | 145.2 |
| Henry Harris, Southeast Missouri St | Sr. | 12 | 305 | 1735 | 5.7 | 18 | 144.6 |
| Frank Warren, Grambling St. | Sr. | 11 | 232 | 1537 | 6.6 | 18 | 139.7 |
| Eric Breitenstein, Wofford | Jr. | 13 | 267 | 1639 | 6.1 | 22 | 126.1 |

#### PASSING EFFICIENCY

| | | | | | Pct | | | | | Rating |
|---|---|---|---|---|---|---|---|---|---|---|
| | Class | GP | Att | Comp | Comp | Yds | Yds/Att | TD | Int | Pts |
| Josh McGregor, Jacksonville | Jr. | 11 | 326 | 205 | 62.9 | 3049 | 9.4 | 32 | 7 | 169.54 |
| Matthew Johnson, Bethune-Cookman | Sr. | 11 | 231 | 151 | 65.4 | 2053 | 8.9 | 14 | 5 | 155.69 |
| Scott Riddle, Elon | Sr. | 10 | 405 | 274 | 67.7 | 3231 | 8.0 | 28 | 6 | 154.52 |
| Denarius McGhee, Montana St | Fr. | 12 | 362 | 227 | 62.7 | 3163 | 8.7 | 23 | 6 | 153.75 |
| Pat Devlin, Delaware | Sr. | 14 | 384 | 261 | 68.0 | 3032 | 7.9 | 22 | 3 | 151.64 |

Note: Minimum 15 attempts per game.

#### RECEPTIONS PER GAME

| | Class | GP | No. | Yds | TD | R/G |
|---|---|---|---|---|---|---|
| Marcus Harris, Murray St | Sr. | 9 | 84 | 1057 | 9 | 9.3 |
| Raymond Webber, Arkansas-Pine Bluff | Sr. | 11 | 101 | 1429 | 10 | 9.2 |
| Aaron Mellette, Elon | So. | 11 | 86 | 1100 | 12 | 7.8 |
| Tysson Poots, Southern Utah | Sr. | 11 | 85 | 1230 | 11 | 7.7 |
| Chris Summers, Liberty | Jr. | 10 | 76 | 1081 | 15 | 7.6 |

#### RECEIVING YARDS PER GAME

| | Class | GP | No. | Yds | TD | Yds/G |
|---|---|---|---|---|---|---|
| Raymond Webber, Arkansas-Pine Bluff | Sr. | 11 | 101 | 1429 | 10 | 129.9 |
| Marcus Harris, Murray St | Sr. | 9 | 84 | 1057 | 9 | 117.4 |
| Joel Bradford, Chattanooga | Jr. | 11 | 81 | 1284 | 8 | 116.7 |
| Tysson Poots, Southern Utah | Sr. | 11 | 85 | 1230 | 11 | 111.8 |
| Chris Summers, Liberty | Jr. | 10 | 76 | 1081 | 15 | 108.1 |

#### INTERCEPTIONS

| | Class | GP | No. | Yds | TD | Int/G |
|---|---|---|---|---|---|---|
| Moses Ellis, Prairie View A&M | Sr. | 11 | 8 | 112 | 0 | .73 |
| Torez Jones, W. Carolina | Jr | 10 | 7 | 54 | 0 | .70 |
| Charles James, Charleston So. | So. | 9 | 6 | 0 | 0 | .67 |
| D'Vonte Graham, N.C. A&T | So. | 11 | 7 | 33 | 0 | .64 |
| E.J. Jones, Illinois St. | Sr. | 11 | 7 | 28 | 0 | .64 |

#### PUNTING

| | Class | No. | Avg |
|---|---|---|---|
| David Harrington, Idaho St | Jr. | 69 | 44.3 |
| Jonathan Plisco, Old Dominion | So. | 43 | 44.3 |
| Greg Wood, Valparaiso | So. | 67 | 43.6 |
| Patrick Dolan, Nicholls St. | Sr. | 63 | 43.2 |
| Dominic Scarnecchia, Villanova | Jr. | 53 | 43.2 |

### Football Championship Subdivision (I-AA) *(Cont.)*

#### ALL-PURPOSE RUNNING

| | Class | GP | Rush | Rec | PR | KOR | Total Yds | Yds/Game |
|---|---|---|---|---|---|---|---|---|
| Henry Harris, Southeast Missouri St | Sr. | 12 | 1735 | 183 | 0 | 691 | 2609 | 217.4 |
| Taiwan Jones, Eastern Washington | Jr. | 12 | 1742 | 342 | 28 | 309 | 2421 | 201.8 |
| Terrence Holt, Austin Peay | Sr. | 11 | 793 | 90 | 66 | 1100 | 2049 | 186.3 |
| Nate Eachus, Colgate | Jr. | 11 | 1871 | 168 | 0 | 0 | 2039 | 185.4 |
| Tavoy Moore, Idaho St | Jr. | 11 | 252 | 421 | 275 | 1086 | 2034 | 184.9 |

### Division II

#### SCORING

| | Class | GP | TD | XP | FG | Pts | Pts/Game |
|---|---|---|---|---|---|---|---|
| Kevon Calhoun, West Liberty | Sr. | 8 | 18 | 0 | 0 | 108 | 13.50 |
| Akeem Satterfield, Slippery Rock | So. | 10 | 20 | 0 | 0 | 120 | 12.00 |
| Josh Birmingham, Central Oklahoma | Fr. | 11 | 21 | 0 | 0 | 126 | 11.45 |
| Nykeem Barton, Tuskegee Inst. | Sr. | 11 | 19 | 0 | 0 | 118 | 10.73 |
| Franklyn Quiteh, Bloomsburg | Fr. | 13 | 22 | 0 | 0 | 134 | 10.31 |

#### FIELD GOALS

| | Class | GP | FGA | FG | Pct | FG/Game |
|---|---|---|---|---|---|---|
| Gareth Rowlands, Tusculum | Sr. | 11 | 26 | 21 | .808 | 1.91 |
| Morgan Lineberry, Abilene Christian | So. | 11 | 30 | 21 | .700 | 1.91 |
| Sean Davis, Central Washington | So. | 9 | 28 | 17 | .607 | 1.89 |
| Michael Ziola, Chadron St | Fr. | 11 | 22 | 18 | .818 | 1.64 |
| Dan Fisher, Bloomsburg | Fr. | 13 | 24 | 20 | .833 | 1.54 |

#### TOTAL OFFENSE

| | | | Rushing | | Passing | | Total Offense | | |
|---|---|---|---|---|---|---|---|---|---|
| | Class | GP | Car | Net | Att | Yds | Total Yds | Yds/Play | Yds/Game |
| Bo Cordell, Tusculum | So. | 11 | 97 | 23 | 605 | 4657 | 4680 | 6.7 | 425.5 |
| Zach Amedro, West Liberty | Sr. | 10 | 38 | 38 | 485 | 4058 | 4096 | 7.8 | 409.6 |
| Taylor Harris, West Texas A&M | Sr. | 12 | 31 | -77 | 595 | 4806 | 4729 | 7.6 | 394.1 |
| Nick Hardesty, Henderson St. | Sr. | 11 | 74 | 180 | 507 | 4007 | 4187 | 7.2 | 380.6 |
| Eric Czerniewski, Central Missouri | Sr. | 14 | 49 | -4 | 670 | 5207 | 5203 | 7.2 | 371.6 |

#### RUSHING

| | Class | GP | Car | Yds | TD | Yds/Game |
|---|---|---|---|---|---|---|
| Franklyn Quiteh, Bloomsburg. | Fr. | 13 | 309 | 2015 | 22 | 155.0 |
| Phil Milbrath, Michigan Tech | Sr. | 10 | 203 | 1412 | 10 | 141.2 |
| Jesse Lewis, Colorado St-Pueblo | Jr. | 10 | 176 | 1391 | 14 | 139.1 |
| Walter Sanders, St. Augustine's | Sr. | 10 | 277 | 1377 | 15 | 137.7 |
| Kevon Calhoun, West Liberty | Sr. | 8 | 156 | 1088 | 17 | 136.0 |

#### PASSING EFFICIENCY

| | | | | Pct | | | | | Rating |
|---|---|---|---|---|---|---|---|---|---|
| | Class | GP | Att | Comp | Comp | Yds | TD | Int | Pts |
| Troy Weatherhead, Hillsdale | Sr. | 12 | 363 | 279 | 76.9 | 3215 | 26 | 6 | 171.59 |
| Taylor Housewright, Ashland | So. | 11 | 266 | 179 | 67.3 | 2378 | 24 | 9 | 165.40 |
| Mitchell Gale, Abilene Christian | So. | 12 | 425 | 276 | 64.9 | 3595 | 38 | 3 | 164.09 |
| Phillip Klaphake, St. Cloud St | Fr. | 13 | 320 | 210 | 65.6 | 2918 | 24 | 6 | 163.22 |
| John Teigland, Nebraska-Omaha | Jr. | 11 | 198 | 129 | 65.2 | 1870 | 16 | 8 | 163.07 |

Note: Minimum 15 attempts per game.

#### RECEPTIONS PER GAME

| | Class | GP | No. | Yds | TD | R/G |
|---|---|---|---|---|---|---|
| Ryan Travis, West Liberty | Sr. | 10 | 126 | 1402 | 15 | 12.6 |
| David Canney, Assumption | Sr. | 9 | 86 | 1036 | 5 | 9.6 |
| Justin Johnson, Fort Lewis | Sr. | 10 | 89 | 1242 | 7 | 8.9 |
| Tyson Williams, West Texas A&M | Jr. | 11 | 96 | 1321 | 8 | 8.7 |
| Deonte' Gist, Tusculum | Jr. | 11 | 96 | 1183 | 8 | 8.7 |
| Andre Holmes, Hillsdale | Sr. | 12 | 104 | 1368 | 11 | 8.7 |

#### RECEIVING YARDS PER GAME

| | Class | GP | No. | Yds | TD | Yds/G |
|---|---|---|---|---|---|---|
| Ryan Travis, West Liberty | Sr. | 10 | 126 | 1402 | 15 | 140.2 |
| Joe Hastings, Washburn | Sr. | 12 | 87 | 1546 | 15 | 128.8 |
| Fred Williams, St. Cloud St | Sr. | 13 | 95 | 1616 | 17 | 124.3 |
| Justin Johnson, Fort Lewis | Sr. | 10 | 89 | 1242 | 7 | 124.2 |
| Tyson Williams, West Texas A&M. | Jr. | 11 | 96 | 1321 | 8 | 120.1 |

## Division II *(Cont.)*

### INTERCEPTIONS

| | Class | GP | No. | Yds | Int/Game |
|---|---|---|---|---|---|
| Desmond Anderson, New Haven | Jr. | 9 | 7 | 126 | .78 |
| Stevie Harden, Valdosta St | Sr. | 11 | 8 | 229 | .73 |
| Logan Kerr, Ashland | Jr. | 11 | 8 | 51 | .73 |
| Keon Robinson, Shepherd | So. | 14 | 10 | 222 | .71 |
| Don Hopkins, Bentley | Jr. | 9 | 6 | -4 | .67 |

### PUNTING

| | Class | No. | Avg |
|---|---|---|---|
| Ronnie Partridge, Stillman | Jr. | 65 | 45.5 |
| Taylor Accardi, Colorado Mines | So. | 57 | 45.4 |
| Derek Jambon, Arkansas-Monticello | Jr. | 52 | 44.4 |
| Kevin Berg, Chadron St | Sr. | 48 | 43.6 |
| George Shamblen, Angelo St | Jr. | 44 | 43.4 |
| Randy Weich, Wayne St (Neb.) | So. | 59 | 43.4 |

Note: Minimum 3.6 per game.

## Division III

### SCORING

| | Class | GP | TD | XP | FG | Pts | Pts/Game |
|---|---|---|---|---|---|---|---|
| James McCarthy, Framingham St | Jr. | 9 | 22 | 0 | 0 | 132 | 14.67 |
| Khyree Copeland, Concordia Chicago | Sr. | 10 | 21 | 0 | 0 | 126 | 12.60 |
| Jim Bower, Maine Maritime | Sr. | 11 | 20 | 0 | 0 | 132 | 12.00 |
| Jake Marshall, Ripon | Sr. | 10 | 19 | 0 | 0 | 114 | 11.40 |
| Adam Kniffin, Puget Sound | So. | 9 | 17 | 0 | 0 | 102 | 11.33 |

### FIELD GOALS

| | Class | GP | FGA | FG | Pct | FG/Game |
|---|---|---|---|---|---|---|
| Tyler Funk, Carthage | Jr. | 10 | 18 | 15 | .833 | 1.50 |
| Travis Braun, Kalamazoo | So. | 10 | 19 | 15 | .789 | 1.50 |
| Jered Fohrman, UW-Stevens Point | Jr. | 10 | 21 | 15 | .714 | 1.50 |
| Scott Roche Wheaton (Ill.) | Jr. | 12 | 28 | 18 | .643 | 1.50 |
| Luis Diaz, Greenville | Fr. | 10 | 21 | 14 | .667 | 1.40 |

### TOTAL OFFENSE

| | | Rushing | | Passing | | Total Offense | | |
|---|---|---|---|---|---|---|---|---|
| | Class | GP | Car | Net | Att | Yds | Total Yds | Yds/Play | Yds/Game |
| Ben McLaughlin, Louisiana Coll. | Sr. | 10 | 28 | 10 | 446 | 3770 | 3780 | 8.0 | 378.0 |
| Shane Brozowski, Castleton | So. | 9 | 116 | 185 | 367 | 3052 | 3237 | 6.7 | 359.7 |
| Jake Mullin, McMurry | Jr. | 8 | 71 | -1 | 330 | 2859 | 2858 | 7.1 | 357.3 |
| Donald McKillop, Middlebury | Sr. | 8 | 46 | 83 | 413 | 2556 | 2639 | 5.7 | 329.9 |
| Tim Bailey, St. John Fisher | Sr. | 11 | 85 | 378 | 360 | 3196 | 3574 | 8.0 | 324.9 |

### RUSHING

| | Class | GP | Car | Yds | TD | Yds/Game |
|---|---|---|---|---|---|---|
| Jim Bower, Maine Maritime | Sr. | 11 | 247 | 1916 | 20 | 174.2 |
| Anthony Ambers, Greenville | Sr. | 10 | 213 | 1573 | 18 | 157.3 |
| Khyree Copeland, Concordia Chicago | Sr. | 10 | 237 | 1566 | 18 | 156.6 |
| Shea Dwyer, Wesleyan (Conn.) | Sr. | 8 | 218 | 1242 | 11 | 155.3 |
| Dion Wilson, Millikin | Sr. | 9 | 238 | 1361 | 11 | 151.2 |

### PASSING EFFICIENCY

| | | | | Pct | | | | Rating |
|---|---|---|---|---|---|---|---|---|
| | Class | GP | Att | Comp | Comp | Yds | TD | Int | Pts |
| Eric Watt, Trine | Sr. | 12 | 294 | 197 | 67.0 | 2873 | 33 | 6 | 182.05 |
| Kyle Ray, Franklin | Sr. | 11 | 340 | 237 | 69.7 | 3104 | 35 | 10 | 174.48 |
| Ryan Lehotsky, Buffalo St | So. | 10 | 208 | 119 | 57.2 | 2100 | 23 | 7 | 171.78 |
| Pat Moffitt, Williams | Sr. | 8 | 247 | 161 | 65.2 | 2386 | 25 | 10 | 171.63 |
| Joe Boyle, St. John's (Minn.) | Sr. | 10 | 253 | 173 | 68.4 | 2502 | 18 | 7 | 169.39 |

Note: Minimum 15 attempts per game.

### RECEPTIONS PER GAME

| | Class | GP | No. | Yds | TD | Rec/Game |
|---|---|---|---|---|---|---|
| R. J. Maki, Pomona-Pitzer | Sr. | 9 | 93 | 938 | 7 | 10.3 |
| Adam Kniffin, Puget Sound | So. | 9 | 92 | 911 | 17 | 10.2 |
| Glenn Campbell, Hiram | Sr. | 10 | 91 | 1095 | 7 | 9.1 |
| Daniel Passafiume, Hanover | Jr. | 10 | 91 | 958 | 11 | 9.1 |
| Zach Homyk, Case | Sr. | 10 | 90 | 1165 | 12 | 9.0 |

### RECEIVING YARDS PER GAME

| | Class | GP | No. | Yds | TD | Yds/Game |
|---|---|---|---|---|---|---|
| Tyler Beiler, Bridgewater (Va.) | Sr. | 10 | 61 | 1342 | 16 | 134.2 |
| ZaVious Robbins, Hardin-Simmons | Sr. | 10 | 89 | 1271 | 12 | 127.1 |
| Josh McKee, Wittenberg | Jr. | 11 | 67 | 1386 | 16 | 126.0 |
| James McCarthy, Framingham St | Jr. | 9 | 62 | 1100 | 22 | 122.2 |
| Mike Preston, Heidelberg | Sr. | 10 | 76 | 1213 | 15 | 121.3 |

### Division III *(Cont.)*

#### INTERCEPTIONS

| | Class | GP | No. | Yds | Int/G |
|---|---|---|---|---|---|
| Harry Melendez, Trinity (Conn.) | Sr. | 8 | 9 | 100 | 1.1 |
| Jared Millikan, Anderson (Ind.) | Jr. | 10 | 11 | 86 | 1.1 |
| Brian Hipchen, Carthage | Jr. | 10 | 10 | 187 | 1.0 |
| Mike Langhurst, Aurora | Sr. | 10 | 10 | 81 | 1.0 |
| Brecken Kennedy, Manchester | Jr. | 10 | 9 | 100 | .9 |
| Eric Fisher, Illinois College | Jr. | 9 | 8 | 143 | .9 |

#### PUNTING

| | Class | No. | Avg |
|---|---|---|---|
| Ethan Hunke, Nebraska Wesleyan | Sr. | 54 | 42.9 |
| Robbie Salmon, Wartburg | Jr. | 62 | 42.7 |
| Brik Wedekind, Monmouth (Ill.) | Fr. | 38 | 42.6 |
| TJ Grzesikowski, Ferrum | Sr. | 49 | 42.4 |
| Jeff Sauer, Chicago | So. | 40 | 42.4 |
| Andrew Dejong, Allegheny | Jr. | 48 | 42.4 |

Note: Minimum 3.6 per game.

## 2010 NCAA FBS (I-A) Team Leaders

### Offense

#### SCORING

| | GP | Pts | Avg |
|---|---|---|---|
| Oregon | 13 | 611 | 47.00 |
| Boise St | 13 | 586 | 45.08 |
| Oklahoma St | 13 | 575 | 44.23 |
| TCU | 13 | 541 | 41.62 |
| Wisconsin | 13 | 539 | 41.46 |
| Tulsa | 13 | 538 | 41.38 |
| Auburn | 14 | 577 | 41.21 |
| Nevada | 14 | 574 | 41.00 |
| Stanford | 13 | 524 | 40.31 |
| Hawaii | 14 | 554 | 39.57 |

#### RUSHING

| | GP | Car | Yds | Avg | TD | Yds/Game |
|---|---|---|---|---|---|---|
| Georgia Tech | 13 | 753 | 4203 | 5.58 | 31 | 323.31 |
| Air Force | 13 | 748 | 3985 | 5.33 | 41 | 306.54 |
| Nevada | 14 | 669 | 4091 | 6.12 | 52 | 292.21 |
| Oregon | 13 | 629 | 3721 | 5.92 | 42 | 286.23 |
| Auburn | 14 | 652 | 3987 | 6.12 | 41 | 284.79 |
| Navy | 13 | 692 | 3702 | 5.35 | 37 | 284.77 |
| Northern Illinois | 14 | 581 | 3645 | 6.27 | 42 | 260.36 |
| Army | 13 | 728 | 3271 | 4.49 | 34 | 251.62 |
| Nebraska | 14 | 634 | 3466 | 5.47 | 32 | 247.57 |
| TCU | 13 | 600 | 3216 | 5.36 | 41 | 247.38 |

#### TOTAL OFFENSE

| | GP | Plays | Yds | Avg | TD | Yds/Game |
|---|---|---|---|---|---|---|
| Oregon | 13 | 1024 | 6899 | 6.74 | 81 | 530.69 |
| Boise St | 13 | 910 | 6777 | 7.45 | 77 | 521.31 |
| Oklahoma St | 13 | 982 | 6763 | 6.89 | 71 | 520.23 |
| Nevada | 14 | 1044 | 7268 | 6.96 | 77 | 519.14 |
| Tulsa | 13 | 1006 | 6573 | 6.53 | 70 | 505.62 |
| Hawaii | 14 | 926 | 7009 | 7.57 | 72 | 500.64 |
| Auburn | 14 | 948 | 6989 | 7.37 | 75 | 499.21 |
| Michigan | 13 | 941 | 6353 | 6.75 | 59 | 488.69 |
| Arkansas | 13 | 886 | 6273 | 7.08 | 60 | 482.54 |
| Oklahoma | 14 | 1211 | 6739 | 5.56 | 64 | 481.36 |

#### PASSING

| | GP | Att | Comp | Int | Pct-Comp | Yds | Yds/Gm | TD |
|---|---|---|---|---|---|---|---|---|
| Hawaii | 14 | 618 | 394 | 17 | 63.8 | 5520 | 394.3 | 42 |
| Oklahoma St | 13 | 532 | 357 | 14 | 67.1 | 4496 | 345.8 | 36 |
| Oklahoma | 14 | 633 | 414 | 12 | 65.4 | 4807 | 343.4 | 38 |
| Arkansas | 13 | 465 | 301 | 15 | 64.7 | 4338 | 333.7 | 36 |
| Houston | 12 | 484 | 298 | 20 | 61.6 | 3927 | 327.3 | 34 |
| Boise St | 13 | 424 | 299 | 6 | 70.5 | 4174 | 321.1 | 38 |
| Texas Tech | 13 | 617 | 406 | 11 | 65.8 | 4146 | 318.9 | 39 |
| East Carolina | 13 | 632 | 408 | 16 | 64.6 | 4143 | 318.7 | 39 |
| Arizona | 13 | 524 | 357 | 12 | 68.1 | 4000 | 307.7 | 25 |
| Idaho | 13 | 549 | 313 | 17 | 57.0 | 3882 | 298.6 | 27 |

### Single-Game Highs

Points Scored: 83—Wisconsin, Nov. 13, 2010 (vs Indiana)
Net Rushing Yards: 544—Northern Illinois, Nov. 26, 2010 (vs Eastern Michigan)
Net Passing Yards: 593—Hawaii, Nov. 20, 2010 (vs San Jose St)
Rushing and Passing Yards: 844—Nevada, Nov. 6, 2010 (vs Idaho)
Fewest Rushing and Passing Yards Allowed: 80—Boise St, Oct. 16, 2010
(vs San Jose St)

## Defense

### OPPONENTS' SCORING

| | GP | Pts | Avg |
|---|---|---|---|
| TCU | 13 | 156 | 12.0 |
| Boise St | 13 | 166 | 12.8 |
| Alabama | 13 | 176 | 13.5 |
| West Virginia | 13 | 176 | 13.5 |
| Ohio St. | 13 | 186 | 14.3 |
| Missouri | 13 | 209 | 16.1 |
| Iowa | 13 | 221 | 17.0 |
| Central Florida | 14 | 240 | 17.1 |
| Nebraska | 14 | 243 | 17.4 |
| Stanford | 13 | 226 | 17.4 |

### TOTAL DEFENSE

| | GP | Plays | Yds | Avg Y/Play | Avg Y/G |
|---|---|---|---|---|---|
| TCU | 13 | 714 | 2970 | 4.16 | 228.46 |
| Boise St | 13 | 832 | 3311 | 3.98 | 254.69 |
| West Virginia | 13 | 803 | 3394 | 4.23 | 261.08 |
| Ohio St | 13 | 789 | 3409 | 4.32 | 262.23 |
| Alabama | 13 | 802 | 3723 | 4.64 | 286.38 |
| Texas | 12 | 783 | 3602 | 4.60 | 300.17 |
| Syracuse | 13 | 856 | 3919 | 4.58 | 301.46 |
| Pittsburgh | 13 | 837 | 3966 | 4.74 | 305.08 |
| Florida | 13 | 853 | 3985 | 4.67 | 306.54 |
| Kent St | 12 | 839 | 3680 | 4.39 | 306.67 |

### OPPONENTS' RUSHING

| | GP | Car | Yds | Avg | TD | Yds/Game |
|---|---|---|---|---|---|---|
| Boston College | 13 | 402 | 1076 | 2.68 | 7 | 82.8 |
| West Virginia | 13 | 410 | 1124 | 2.74 | 3 | 86.5 |
| Ohio St | 13 | 404 | 1257 | 3.11 | 9 | 96.7 |
| Kent St | 12 | 434 | 1166 | 2.69 | 21 | 97.2 |
| TCU | 13 | 391 | 1296 | 3.31 | 9 | 99.7 |
| Iowa | 13 | 407 | 1320 | 3.24 | 13 | 101.5 |
| Boise St | 13 | 461 | 1349 | 2.93 | 12 | 103.8 |
| Central Florida | 14 | 451 | 1517 | 3.36 | 9 | 108.4 |
| Auburn | 14 | 448 | 1527 | 3.41 | 16 | 109.1 |
| Alabama | 13 | 435 | 1432 | 3.29 | 6 | 110.2 |

### TURNOVER MARGIN

| | | Turnovers Gained | | | Turnovers Lost | | | |
|---|---|---|---|---|---|---|---|---|
| | GP | Fum | Int | Total | Fum | Int | Total | Mar/Gm |
| Virginia Tech | 14 | 9 | 23 | 32 | 8 | 5 | 13 | 1.36 |
| Tulsa | 13 | 12 | 24 | 36 | 8 | 11 | 19 | 1.31 |
| Army | 13 | 16 | 14 | 30 | 11 | 3 | 14 | 1.23 |
| Maryland | 13 | 10 | 19 | 29 | 4 | 10 | 14 | 1.15 |
| Ohio St | 13 | 11 | 19 | 30 | 2 | 13 | 15 | 1.15 |
| Wisconsin | 13 | 9 | 14 | 23 | 3 | 6 | 9 | 1.08 |
| Iowa | 13 | 5 | 19 | 24 | 5 | 6 | 11 | 1.00 |
| Oklahoma | 14 | 13 | 19 | 32 | 6 | 12 | 18 | 1.00 |
| Oregon | 13 | 16 | 21 | 37 | 15 | 9 | 24 | 1.00 |
| Stanford | 13 | 12 | 18 | 30 | 9 | 8 | 17 | 1.00 |

### OPPONENTS' PASSING EFFICIENCY

| | GP | Att | Comp | Pct Comp | Int | Pct Int | Yds | Yds/Att | TD | Pct TD | Rating Pts |
|---|---|---|---|---|---|---|---|---|---|---|---|
| TCU | 13 | 323 | 157 | 48.6 | 12 | 3.72 | 1674 | 5.18 | 10 | 3.10 | 94.92 |
| Boise St | 13 | 371 | 190 | 51.2 | 14 | 3.77 | 1962 | 5.29 | 8 | 2.16 | 95.19 |
| Nebraska | 14 | 390 | 190 | 48.7 | 19 | 4.87 | 2151 | 5.52 | 13 | 3.33 | 96.29 |
| Ohio St | 13 | 385 | 207 | 53.8 | 19 | 4.94 | 2152 | 5.59 | 9 | 2.34 | 98.60 |
| Miami (Fla.) | 13 | 328 | 163 | 49.7 | 16 | 4.88 | 1957 | 5.97 | 9 | 2.74 | 99.12 |
| Alabama | 13 | 367 | 192 | 52.3 | 22 | 5.99 | 2291 | 6.24 | 12 | 3.27 | 103.54 |
| Oregon | 13 | 489 | 263 | 53.8 | 21 | 4.29 | 2833 | 5.79 | 15 | 3.07 | 104.00 |
| Oklahoma | 14 | 496 | 271 | 54.6 | 19 | 3.83 | 2981 | 6.01 | 15 | 3.02 | 107.40 |
| Maryland | 13 | 499 | 270 | 54.1 | 19 | 3.81 | 2962 | 5.94 | 17 | 3.41 | 107.59 |
| Air Force | 13 | 321 | 176 | 54.8 | 12 | 3.74 | 1921 | 5.98 | 10 | 3.12 | 107.87 |

## NCAA Football Bowl Subdivision* National Champions

| Year | Champion | Record | Bowl Game | Head Coach |
|------|----------|--------|-----------|------------|
| 1883 | Yale | 8-0-0 | No bowl | Ray Tompkins (Captain) |
| 1884 | Yale | 9-0-0 | No bowl | Eugene L. Richards (Captain) |
| 1885 | Princeton | 9-0-0 | No bowl | Charles DeCamp (Captain) |
| 1886 | Yale | 9-0-1 | No bowl | Robert N. Corwin (Captain) |
| 1887 | Yale | 9-0-0 | No bowl | Harry W. Beecher (Captain) |
| 1888 | Yale | 13-0-0 | No bowl | Walter Camp |
| 1889 | Princeton | 10-0-0 | No bowl | Edgar Poe (Captain) |
| 1890 | Harvard | 11-0-0 | No bowl | George A. Stewart/George C. Adams |
| 1891 | Yale | 13-0-0 | No bowl | Walter Camp |
| 1892 | Yale | 13-0-0 | No bowl | Walter Camp |
| 1893 | Princeton | 11-0-0 | No bowl | Tom Trenchard (Captain) |
| 1894 | Yale | 16-0-0 | No bowl | William C. Rhodes |
| 1895 | Pennsylvania | 14-0-0 | No bowl | George Woodruff |
| 1896 | Princeton | 10-0-1 | No bowl | Garrett Cochran |
| 1897 | Pennsylvania | 15-0-0 | No bowl | George Woodruff |
| 1898 | Harvard | 11-0-0 | No bowl | W. Cameron Forbes |
| 1899 | Harvard | 10-0-1 | No bowl | Benjamin H. Dibblee |
| 1900 | Yale | 12-0-0 | No bowl | Malcolm McBride |
| 1901 | Michigan | 11-0-0 | Won Rose | Fielding Yost |
| 1902 | Michigan | 11-0-0 | No bowl | Fielding Yost |
| 1903 | Princeton | 11-0-0 | No bowl | Art Hillebrand |
| 1904 | Pennsylvania | 12-0-0 | No bowl | Carl Williams |
| 1905 | Chicago | 11-0-0 | No bowl | Amos Alonzo Stagg |
| 1906 | Princeton | 9-0-1 | No bowl | Bill Roper |
| 1907 | Yale | 9-0-1 | No bowl | Bill Knox |
| 1908 | Pennsylvania | 11-0-1 | No bowl | Sol Metzger |
| 1909 | Yale | 10-0-0 | No bowl | Howard Jones |
| 1910 | Harvard | 8-0-1 | No bowl | Percy Houghton |
| 1911 | Princeton | 8-0-2 | No bowl | Bill Roper |
| 1912 | Harvard | 9-0-0 | No bowl | Percy Houghton |
| 1913 | Harvard | 9-0-0 | No bowl | Percy Houghton |
| 1914 | Army | 9-0-0 | No bowl | Charley Daly |
| 1915 | Cornell | 9-0-0 | No bowl | Al Sharpe |
| 1916 | Pittsburgh | 8-0-0 | No bowl | Pop Warner |
| 1917 | Georgia Tech | 9-0-0 | No bowl | John Heisman |
| 1918 | Pittsburgh | 4-1-0 | No bowl | Pop Warner |
| 1919 | Harvard | 9-0-1 | Won Rose | Bob Fisher |
| 1920 | California | 9-0-0 | Won Rose | Andy Smith |
| 1921 | Cornell | 8-0-0 | No bowl | Gil Dobie |
| 1922 | Cornell | 8-0-0 | No bowl | Gil Dobie |
| 1923 | Illinois | 8-0-0 | No bowl | Bob Zuppke |
| 1924 | Notre Dame | 10-0-0 | Won Rose | Knute Rockne |
| 1925 | Alabama (H) | 10-0-0 | Won Rose | Wallace Wade |
|  | Dartmouth (D) | 8-0-0 | No bowl | Jesse Hawley |
| 1926 | Alabama (H) | 9-0-1 | Tied Rose | Wallace Wade |
|  | Stanford (D)(H) | 10-0-1 | Tied Rose | Pop Warner |
| 1927 | Illinois | 7-0-1 | No bowl | Bob Zuppke |
| 1928 | Georgia Tech (H) | 10-0-0 | Won Rose | Bill Alexander |
|  | USC (D) | 9-0-1 | No bowl | Howard Jones |
| 1929 | Notre Dame | 9-0-0 | No bowl | Knute Rockne |
| 1930 | Notre Dame | 10-0-0 | No bowl | Knute Rockne |
| 1931 | USC | 10-1-0 | Won Rose | Howard Jones |
| 1932 | USC (H) | 10-0-0 | Won Rose | Howard Jones |
|  | Michigan (D) | 8-0-0 | No bowl | Harry Kipke |
| 1933 | Michigan | 7-0-1 | No bowl | Harry Kipke |
| 1934 | Minnesota | 8-0-0 | No bowl | Bernie Bierman |
| 1935 | Minnesota (H) | 8-0-0 | No bowl | Bernie Bierman |
|  | SMU (D) | 12-1-0 | Lost Rose | Matty Bell |
| 1936 | Minnesota | 7-1-0 | No bowl | Bernie Bierman |
| 1937 | Pittsburgh | 9-0-1 | No bowl | Jock Sutherland |
| 1938 | TCU (AP) | 11-0-0 | Won Sugar | Dutch Meyer |
|  | Notre Dame (D) | 8-1-0 | No bowl | Elmer Layden |
| 1939 | USC (D) | 8-0-2 | Won Rose | Howard Jones |
|  | Texas A&M (AP) | 11-0-0 | Won Sugar | Homer Norton |

*In 2007, the NCAA renamed Division I-A as the "Football Bowl Subdivision" and Division I-AA as the "Football Championship Subdivision."

| Year | Champion | Record | Bowl Game | Head Coach |
|---|---|---|---|---|
| 1940 | Minnesota | 8-0-0 | No bowl | Bernie Bierman |
| 1941 | Minnesota | 8-0-0 | No bowl | Bernie Bierman |
| 1942 | Ohio St | 9-1-0 | No bowl | Paul Brown |
| 1943 | Notre Dame | 9-1-0 | No bowl | Frank Leahy |
| 1944 | Army | 9-0-0 | No bowl | Red Blaik |
| 1945 | Army | 9-0-0 | No bowl | Red Blaik |
| 1946 | Notre Dame | 8-0-1 | No bowl | Frank Leahy |
| 1947 | Notre Dame | 9-0-0 | No bowl | Frank Leahy |
|  | Michigan* | 10-0-0 | Won Rose | Fritz Crisler |
| 1948 | Michigan | 9-0-0 | No bowl | Bennie Oosterbaan |
| 1949 | Notre Dame | 10-0-0 | No bowl | Frank Leahy |
| 1950 | Oklahoma | 10-1-0 | Lost Sugar | Bud Wilkinson |
| 1951 | Tennessee | 10-1-0 | Lost Sugar | Bob Neyland |
| 1952 | Michigan St | 9-0-0 | No bowl | Biggie Munn |
| 1953 | Maryland | 10-1-0 | Lost Orange | Jim Tatum |
| 1954 | Ohio St | 10-0-0 | Won Rose | Woody Hayes |
|  | UCLA (UPI) | 9-0-0 | No bowl | Red Sanders |
| 1955 | Oklahoma | 11-0-0 | Won Orange | Bud Wilkinson |
| 1956 | Oklahoma | 10-0-0 | No bowl | Bud Wilkinson |
| 1957 | Auburn | 10-0-0 | No bowl | Shug Jordan |
|  | Ohio St (UPI) | 9-1-0 | Won Rose | Woody Hayes |
| 1958 | LSU | 11-0-0 | Won Sugar | Paul Dietzel |
| 1959 | Syracuse | 11-0-0 | Won Cotton | Ben Schwartzwalder |
| 1960 | Minnesota | 8-2-0 | Lost Rose | Murray Warmath |
| 1961 | Alabama | 11-0-0 | Won Sugar | Bear Bryant |
| 1962 | USC | 11-0-0 | Won Rose | John McKay |
| 1963 | Texas | 11-0-0 | Won Cotton | Darrell Royal |
| 1964 | Alabama | 10-1-0 | Lost Orange | Bear Bryant |
| 1965 | Alabama | 9-1-1 | Won Orange | Bear Bryant |
|  | Michigan St (UPI) | 10-1-0 | Lost Rose | Duffy Daugherty |
| 1966 | Notre Dame | 9-0-1 | No bowl | Ara Parseghian |
| 1967 | USC | 10-1-0 | Won Rose | John McKay |
| 1968 | Ohio St | 10-0-0 | Won Rose | Woody Hayes |
| 1969 | Texas | 11-0-0 | Won Cotton | Darrell Royal |
| 1970 | Nebraska | 11-0-1 | Won Orange | Bob Devaney |
|  | Texas (UPI) | 10-1-0 | Lost Cotton | Darrell Royal |
| 1971 | Nebraska | 13-0-0 | Won Orange | Bob Devaney |
| 1972 | USC | 12-0-0 | Won Rose | John McKay |
| 1973 | Notre Dame | 11-0-0 | Won Sugar | Ara Parseghian |
|  | Alabama (UPI) | 11-1-0 | Lost Sugar | Bear Bryant |
| 1974 | Oklahoma | 11-0-0 | No bowl | Barry Switzer |
|  | USC (UPI) | 10-1-1 | Won Rose | John McKay |
| 1975 | Oklahoma | 11-1-0 | Won Orange | Barry Switzer |
| 1976 | Pittsburgh | 12-0-0 | Won Sugar | Johnny Majors |
| 1977 | Notre Dame | 11-1-0 | Won Cotton | Dan Devine |
| 1978 | Alabama | 11-1-0 | Won Sugar | Bear Bryant |
|  | USC (UPI) | 12-1-0 | Won Rose | John Robinson |
| 1979 | Alabama | 12-0-0 | Won Sugar | Bear Bryant |
| 1980 | Georgia | 12-0-0 | Won Sugar | Vince Dooley |
| 1981 | Clemson | 12-0-0 | Won Orange | Danny Ford |
| 1982 | Penn St | 11-1-0 | Won Sugar | Joe Paterno |
| 1983 | Miami (Fla.) | 11-1-0 | Won Orange | Howard Schnellenberger |
| 1984 | BYU | 13-0-0 | Won Holiday | LaVell Edwards |
| 1985 | Oklahoma | 11-1-0 | Won Orange | Barry Switzer |
| 1986 | Penn St | 12-0-0 | Won Fiesta | Joe Paterno |
| 1987 | Miami (Fla.) | 12-0-0 | Won Orange | Jimmy Johnson |
| 1988 | Notre Dame | 12-0-0 | Won Fiesta | Lou Holtz |
| 1989 | Miami (Fla.) | 11-1-0 | Won Sugar | Dennis Erickson |
| 1990 | Colorado | 11-1-1 | Won Orange | Bill McCartney |
|  | Georgia Tech (UPI) | 11-0-1 | Won Citrus | Bobby Ross |
| 1991 | Miami (Fla.) | 12-0-0 | Won Orange | Dennis Erickson |
|  | Washington (CNN) | 12-0-0 | Won Rose | Don James |
| 1992 | Alabama | 13-0-0 | Won Sugar | Gene Stallings |
| 1993 | Florida St | 12-1-0 | Won Orange | Bobby Bowden |
| 1994 | Nebraska | 13-0-0 | Won Orange | Tom Osborne |
| 1995 | Nebraska | 12-0-0 | Won Fiesta | Tom Osborne |
| †1996 | Florida | 12–1 | Won Sugar | Steve Spurrier |
| 1997 | Michigan | 12–0 | Won Rose | Lloyd Carr |
|  | Nebraska (ESPN) | 13–0 | Won Orange | Tom Osborne |

| Year | Champion | Record | Bowl Game | Head Coach |
|---|---|---|---|---|
| 1998 | Tennessee | 13–0 | Won Fiesta | Phillip Fulmer |
| 1999 | Florida St | 12–0 | Won Sugar | Bobby Bowden |
| 2000 | Oklahoma | 13–0 | Won Orange | Bob Stoops |
| 2001 | Miami (Fla.) | 12–0 | Won Rose | Larry Coker |
| 2002 | Ohio St | 14–0 | Won Fiesta | Jim Tressel |
| 2003 | LSU | 13–1 | Won Sugar | Nick Saban |
|  | USC | 12–1 | Won Rose | Pete Carroll |
| §2004 | Vacated |  |  |  |
| 2005 | Texas | 13–0 | Won Rose | Mack Brown |
| ‡2006 | Florida | 13–1 | Won BCS Nat'l Championship | Urban Meyer |
| 2007 | LSU | 12–2 | Won BCS Nat'l Championship | Les Miles |
| 2008 | Florida | 13–1 | Won BCS Nat'l Championship | Urban Meyer |
| 2009 | Alabama | 14–0 | Won BCS Nat'l Championship | Nick Saban |
| 2010 | Auburn | 14–0 | Won BCS Nat'l Championship | Gene Chizik |

*The AP, which had voted Notre Dame No. 1, took a second vote, giving the national title to Michigan after its 49–0 win over USC in the Rose Bowl. Note: Selectors: Helms Athletic Foundation (H) 1883–1935, The Dickinson System (D) 1924–40, The Associated Press (AP) 1936–present, United Press International (UPI) 1958–90, *USA Today*/CNN (CNN) 1991–96, and *USA Today*/ESPN (ESPN) 1997–present. †In 1996 the NCAA introduced overtime to break ties.
‡In 2006, the BCS established a separate national championship game in addition to its existing four-bowl structure.
§USC's 2005 Orange Bowl victory and 2004 national championship were vacated in 2010 due to rules violations.

## Results of Major Bowl Games

### Rose Bowl

| | |
|---|---|
| 1-1-02 Michigan 49, Stanford 0 | 1-1-53 USC 7, Wisconsin 0 |
| 1-1-16 Washington St 14, Brown 0 | 1-1-54 Michigan St 28, UCLA 20 |
| 1-1-17 Oregon 14, Pennsylvania 0 | 1-1-55 Ohio St 20, USC 7 |
| 1-1-18 Mare Island 19, Camp Lewis 7 | 1-2-56 Michigan St 17, UCLA 14 |
| 1-1-19 Great Lakes 17, Mare Island 0 | 1-1-57 Iowa 35, Oregon St 19 |
| 1-1-20 Harvard 7, Oregon 6 | 1-1-58 Ohio St 10, Oregon 7 |
| 1-1-21 California 28, Ohio St 0 | 1-1-59 Iowa 38, California 12 |
| 1-2-22 Washington & Jefferson 0, California 0 | 1-1-60 Washington 44, Wisconsin 8 |
| 1-1-23 USC 14, Penn St 3 | 1-2-61 Washington 17, Minnesota 7 |
| 1-1-24 Navy 14, Washington 14 | 1-1-62 Minnesota 21, UCLA 3 |
| 1-1-25 Notre Dame 27, Stanford 10 | 1-1-63 USC 42, Wisconsin 37 |
| 1-1-26 Alabama 20, Washington 19 | 1-1-64 Illinois 17, Washington 7 |
| 1-1-27 Alabama 7, Stanford 7 | 1-1-65 Michigan 34, Oregon St 7 |
| 1-2-28 Stanford 7, Pittsburgh 6 | 1-1-66 UCLA 14, Michigan St 12 |
| 1-1-29 Georgia Tech 8, California 7 | 1-2-67 Purdue 14, USC 13 |
| 1-1-30 USC47, Pittsburgh 14 | 1-1-68 USC 14, Indiana 3 |
| 1-1-31 Alabama 24, Washington St 0 | 1-1-69 Ohio St 27, USC16 |
| 1-1-32 USC 21, Tulane 12 | 1-1-70 USC 10, Michigan 3 |
| 1-2-33 USC 35, Pittsburgh 0 | 1-1-71 Stanford 27, Ohio St 17 |
| 1-1-34 Columbia 7, Stanford 0 | 1-1-72 Stanford 13, Michigan 12 |
| 1-1-35 Alabama 29, Stanford 13 | 1-1-73 USC 42, Ohio St 17 |
| 1-1-36 Stanford 7, Southern Methodist 0 | 1-1-74 Ohio St 42, USC 21 |
| 1-1-37 Pittsburgh 21, Washington 0 | 1-1-75 USC 18, Ohio St 17 |
| 1-1-38 California 13, Alabama 0 | 1-1-76 UCLA 23, Ohio St 10 |
| 1-2-39 USC 7, Duke 3 | 1-1-77 USC 14, Michigan 6 |
| 1-1-40 USC 14, Tennessee 0 | 1-2-78 Washington 27, Michigan 20 |
| 1-1-41 Stanford 21, Nebraska 13 | 1-1-79 USC 17, Michigan 10 |
| 1-1-42 Oregon St 20, Duke 16 | 1-1-80 USC 17, Ohio St 16 |
| 1-1-43 Georgia 9, UCLA 0 | 1-1-81 Michigan 23, Washington 6 |
| 1-1-44 USC 29, Washington 0 | 1-1-82 Washington 28, Iowa 0 |
| 1-1-45 USC 25, Tennessee 0 | 1-1-83 UCLA 24, Michigan 14 |
| 1-1-46 Alabama 34, USC 14 | 1-2-84 UCLA 45, Illinois 9 |
| 1-1-47 Illinois 45, UCLA 14 | 1-1-85 USC 20, Ohio St 17 |
| 1-1-48 Michigan 49, USC 0 | 1-1-86 UCLA 45, Iowa 28 |
| 1-1-49 Northwestern 20, California 14 | 1-1-87 Arizona St 22, Michigan 15 |
| 1-2-50 Ohio St 17, California 14 | 1-1-88 Michigan St 20, USC 17 |
| 1-1-51 Michigan 14, California 6 | 1-2-89 Michigan 22, USC 14 |
| 1-1-52 Illinois 40, Stanford 7 | 1-1-90 USC 17, Michigan 10 |

Note: The Fiesta, Orange, Rose and Sugar Bowls constitute the Bowl Alliance, formed in 1995 and running through the 2009 regular season and 2010 bowl season. Starting in January 2007, it has included a separate BCS National Championship game as well. The four other BCS Bowls will host the following conference champions with consideration for the following conference tie-ins: the ACC or Big East champion in the FedEx Orange Bowl, the SEC champion in the Allstate Sugar Bowl, the Big Ten and the Pac-10 champions in the Rose Bowl and the Big 12 champion in the Tostitos Fiesta Bowl. There are also four at-large positions in the BCS that are open to any Division I-A team. This allows any Division I-A school in the nation the opportunity to play in a BCS bowl game.

### Rose Bowl *(Cont.)*

1-1-91 ..............Washington 46, Iowa 34
1-1-92 ..............Washington 34, Michigan 14
1-1-93 ..............Michigan 38, Washington 31
1-1-94 ..............Wisconsin 21, UCLA 16
1-2-95 ..............Penn St 38, Oregon 20
1-1-96 ..............USC 41, Northwestern 32
1-1-97 ..............Ohio St 20, Arizona St 17
1-1-98 ..............Michigan 21, Washington St 16
1-1-99 ..............Wisconsin 38, UCLA 31
1-1-00 ..............Wisconsin 17, Stanford 9
1-1-01 ..............Washington 34, Purdue 24
1-3-02 ..............Miami 38, Nebraska 14
1-1-03 ..............Oklahoma 34, Washington St 14
1-1-04 ..............USC 28, Michigan 14
1-1-05 ..............Texas 38, Michigan 37
1-4-06 ..............Texas 41, USC 38
1-1-07 ..............USC 32, Michigan 18
1-1-08 ..............USC 49, Illinois 17
1-1-09 ..............USC 38, Penn St 24
1-1-10 ..............Ohio St 26, Oregon 17
1-1-11 ..............TCU 21, Wisconsin 19
City: Pasadena. Stadium: Rose Bowl, capacity 96,576.
Playing Sites: Tournament Park (1902, 1916–22), Rose Bowl
(1923–41, since 1943), Duke Stadium, Durham, NC (1942).

### Orange Bowl

1-1-35 ..............Bucknell 26, Miami (Fla.) 0
1-1-36 ..............Catholic 20, Mississippi 19
1-1-37 ..............Duquesne 13, Mississippi St 12
1-1-38 ..............Auburn 6, Michigan St 0
1-2-39 ..............Tennessee 17, Oklahoma 0
1-1-40 ..............Georgia Tech 21, Missouri 7
1-1-41 ..............Mississippi St 14, Georgetown 7
1-1-42 ..............Georgia 40, TCU 26
1-1-43 ..............Alabama 37, Boston College 21
1-1-44 ..............LSU 19, Texas A&M 14
1-1-45 ..............Tulsa 26, Georgia Tech 12
1-1-46 ..............Miami (Fla.) 13, Holy Cross 6
1-1-47 ..............Rice 8, Tennessee 0
1-1-48 ..............Georgia Tech 20, Kansas 14
1-1-49 ..............Texas 41, Georgia 28
1-2-50 ..............Santa Clara 21, Kentucky 13
1-1-51 ..............Clemson 15, Miami (Fla.) 14
1-1-52 ..............Georgia Tech 17, Baylor 14
1-1-53 ..............Alabama 61, Syracuse 6
1-1-54 ..............Oklahoma 7, Maryland 0
1-1-55 ..............Duke 34, Nebraska 7
1-2-56 ..............Oklahoma 20, Maryland 6
1-1-57 ..............Colorado 27, Clemson 21
1-1-58 ..............Oklahoma 48, Duke 21
1-1-59 ..............Oklahoma 21, Syracuse 6
1-1-60 ..............Georgia 14, Missouri 0
1-2-61 ..............Missouri 21, Navy 14
1-1-62 ..............LSU 25, Colorado 7
1-1-63 ..............Alabama 17, Oklahoma 0
1-1-64 ..............Nebraska 13, Auburn 7
1-1-65 ..............Texas 21, Alabama 17
1-1-66 ..............Alabama 39, Nebraska 28
1-2-67 ..............Florida 27, Georgia Tech 12
1-1-68 ..............Oklahoma 26, Tennessee 24
1-1-69 ..............Penn St 15, Kansas 14
1-1-70 ..............Penn St 10, Missouri 3
1-1-71 ..............Nebraska 17, LSU 12
1-1-72 ..............Nebraska 38, Alabama 6
1-1-73 ..............Nebraska 40, Notre Dame 6
1-1-74 ..............Penn St 16, LSU 9
1-1-75 ..............Notre Dame 13, Alabama 11
1-1-76 ..............Oklahoma 14, Michigan 6

### Orange Bowl *(Cont.)*

1-1-77 ..............Ohio St 27, Colorado 10
1-2-78 ..............Arkansas 31, Oklahoma 6
1-1-79 ..............Oklahoma 31, Nebraska 24
1-1-80 ..............Oklahoma 24, Florida St 7
1-1-81 ..............Oklahoma 18, Florida St 17
1-1-82 ..............Clemson 22, Nebraska 15
1-1-83 ..............Nebraska 21, LSU 20
1-2-84 ..............Miami (Fla.) 31, Nebraska 30
1-1-85 ..............Washington 28, Oklahoma 17
1-1-86 ..............Oklahoma 25, Penn St 10
1-1-87 ..............Oklahoma 42, Arkansas 8
1-1-88 ..............Miami (Fla.) 20, Oklahoma 14
1-2-89 ..............Miami (Fla.) 23, Nebraska 3
1-1-90 ..............Notre Dame 21, Colorado 6
1-1-91 ..............Colorado 10, Notre Dame 9
1-1-92 ..............Miami (Fla.) 22, Nebraska 0
1-1-93 ..............Florida St 27, Nebraska 14
1-1-94 ..............Florida St 18, Nebraska 16
1-1-95 ..............Nebraska 24, Miami (Fla.) 17
1-1-96 ..............Florida St 31, Notre Dame 26
12-31-96 ..............Nebraska 41, Virginia Tech 21
1-2-98 ..............Nebraska 42, Tennessee 17
1-2-99 ..............Florida 31, Syracuse 10
1-1-00 ..............Michigan 35, Alabama 34 (ot)
1-3-01 ..............Oklahoma 13, Florida St 2
1-2-02 ..............Florida 56, Maryland 23
1-2-03 ..............USC 38, Iowa 17
1-1-04 ..............Miami (Fla.) 16, Florida St 15
1-4-05 ..............*Vacated
1-3-06 ..............Penn State 26, Florida State 23 (3OT)
1-2-07 ..............Louisville 24, Wake Forest 13
1-3-08 ..............Kansas 24, Virginia Tech 21
1-1-09 ..............Virginia Tech 20, Cincinnati 7
1-5-10 ..............Iowa 24, Georgia Tech 14
1-3-11 ..............Stanford 40, Virginia Tech 12
City: Miami. Stadium: Pro Player Stadium, capacity 75,192.
Playing Sites: Orange Bowl (1935–96), Pro Player Stadium
(1996–2005), Dolphin(s) Stadium (2005–09), Land Shark
Stadium (2010). *USC's 2005 Orange Bowl victory was
vacated in 2010 due to rules violations.

### Sugar Bowl

1-1-35 ..............Tulane 20, Temple 14
1-1-36 ..............TCU 3, LSU 2
1-1-37 ..............Santa Clara 21, LSU 14
1-1-38 ..............Santa Clara 6, LSU 0
1-2-39 ..............TCU 15, Carnegie Tech 7
1-1-40 ..............Texas A&M 14, Tulane 13
1-1-41 ..............Boston Col 19, Tennessee 13
1-1-42 ..............Fordham 2, Missouri 0
1-1-43 ..............Tennessee 14, Tulsa 7
1-1-44 ..............Georgia Tech 20, Tulsa 18
1-1-45 ..............Duke 29, Alabama 26
1-1-46 ..............Oklahoma St 33, St. Mary's (Ca.) 13
1-1-47 ..............Georgia 20, North Carolina 10
1-1-48 ..............Texas 27, Alabama 7
1-1-49 ..............Oklahoma 14, North Carolina 6
1-2-50 ..............Oklahoma 35, LSU 0
1-1-51 ..............Kentucky 13, Oklahoma 7
1-1-52 ..............Maryland 28, Tennessee 13
1-1-53 ..............Georgia Tech 24, Mississippi 7
1-1-54 ..............Georgia Tech 42, W Virginia 19
1-1-55 ..............Navy 21, Mississippi 0
1-2-56 ..............Georgia Tech 7, Pittsburgh 0
1-1-57 ..............Baylor 13, Tennessee 7
1-1-58 ..............Mississippi 39, Texas 7
1-1-59 ..............LSU 7, Clemson 0
1-1-60 ..............Mississippi 21, LSU 0

## Sugar Bowl (*Cont.*)

1-2-61 ..............Mississippi 14, Rice 6
1-1-62 ..............Alabama 10, Arkansas 3
1-1-63 ..............Mississippi 17, Arkansas 13
1-1-64 ..............Alabama 12, Mississippi 7
1-1-65 ..............LSU 13, Syracuse 10
1-1-66 ..............Missouri 20, Florida 18
1-2-67 ..............Alabama 34, Nebraska 7
1-1-68 ..............LSU 20, Wyoming 13
1-1-69 ..............Arkansas 16, Georgia 2
1-1-70 ..............Mississippi 27, Arkansas 22
1-1-71 ..............Tennessee 34, Air Force 13
1-1-72 ..............Oklahoma 40, Auburn 22
12-31-72 ..........Oklahoma 14, Penn St 0
12-31-73 ..........Notre Dame 24, Alabama 23
12-31-74 ..........Nebraska 13, Florida 10
12-31-75 ..........Alabama 13, Penn St 6
1-1-77 ..............Pittsburgh 27, Georgia 3
1-2-78 ..............Alabama 35, Ohio St 6
1-1-79 ..............Alabama 14, Penn St 7
1-1-80 ..............Alabama 24, Arkansas 9
1-1-81 ..............Georgia 17, Notre Dame 10
1-1-82 ..............Pittsburgh 24, Georgia 20
1-1-83 ..............Penn St 27, Georgia 23
1-2-84 ..............Auburn 9, Michigan 7
1-1-85 ..............Nebraska 28, LSU 10
1-1-86 ..............Tennessee 35, Miami (Fla.) 7
1-1-87 ..............Nebraska 30, LSU 15
1-1-88 ..............Syracuse 16, Auburn 16
1-2-89 ..............Florida St 13, Auburn 7
1-1-90 ..............Miami (Fla.) 33, Alabama 25
1-1-91 ..............Tennessee 23, Virginia 22
1-1-92 ..............Notre Dame 39, Florida 28
1-1-93 ..............Alabama 34, Miami (Fla.) 13
1-1-94 ..............Florida 41, West Virginia 7
1-2-95 ..............Florida St 23, Florida 17
12-31-95 ..........Virginia Tech 28, Texas 10
1-2-97 ..............Florida 52, Florida St 20
1-1-98 ..............Florida St 31, Ohio St 14
1-1-99 ..............Ohio St 24, Texas A&M 14
1-4-00 ..............Florida St 46, Virginia Tech 29
1-2-01 ..............Miami (Fla.) 37, Florida 20
1-1-02 ..............LSU 47, Illinois 34
1-1-03 ..............Georgia 26, Florida St 13
1-4-04 ..............LSU 21, Oklahoma 14
1-3-05 ..............Auburn 16, Virginia Tech 13
1-2-06 ..............West Virginia 38, Georgia 35
1-3-07 ..............LSU 41, Notre Dame 14
1-1-08 ..............Georgia 41, Hawaii 10
1-2-09 ..............Utah 31, Alabama 17
1-1-10 ..............Florida 51, Cincinnati 24
1-4-11 ..............Vacated

City: New Orleans. Stadium: Louisiana Superdome, capacity 76,791. Playing Sites: Tulane Stadium (1935–74), Louisiana Superdome (since 1975). Due to Hurricane Katrina, 2006 Sugar Bowl played in Atlanta's Georgia Dome.

## Cotton Bowl

1-1-37 ..............TCU 16, Marquette 6
1-1-38 ..............Rice 28, Colorado 14
1-2-39 ..............St. Mary's (Ca.) 20, Texas Tech 13
1-1-40 ..............Clemson 6, Boston Col 3
1-1-41 ..............Texas A&M 13, Fordham 12
1-1-42 ..............Alabama 29, Texas A&M 21
1-1-43 ..............Texas 14, Georgia Tech 7
1-1-44 ..............Texas 7, Randolph Field 7
1-1-45 ..............Oklahoma St 34, TCU 0
1-1-46 ..............Texas 40, Missouri 27
1-1-47 ..............Arkansas 0, LSU 0

## Cotton Bowl (*Cont.*)

1-1-48 ..............Southern Methodist 13, Penn St 13
1-1-49 ..............Southern Methodist 21, Oregon 13
1-2-50 ..............Rice 27, North Carolina 13
1-1-51 ..............Tennessee 20, Texas 14
1-1-52 ..............Kentucky 20, TCU 7
1-1-53 ..............Texas 16, Tennessee 0
1-1-54 ..............Rice 28, Alabama 6
1-1-55 ..............Georgia Tech 14, Arkansas 6
1-2-56 ..............Mississippi 14, TCU 13
1-1-57 ..............TCU 28, Syracuse 27
1-1-58 ..............Navy 20, Rice 7
1-1-59 ..............TCU 0, Air Force 0
1-1-60 ..............Syracuse 23, Texas 14
1-2-61 ..............Duke 7, Arkansas 6
1-1-62 ..............Texas 12, Mississippi 7
1-1-63 ..............LSU 13, Texas 0
1-1-64 ..............Texas 28, Navy 6
1-1-65 ..............Arkansas 10, Nebraska 7
1-1-66 ..............LSU 14, Arkansas 7
12-31-66 ..........Georgia 24, Southern Methodist 9
1-1-68 ..............Texas A&M 20, Alabama 16
1-1-69 ..............Texas 36, Tennessee 13
1-1-70 ..............Texas 21, Notre Dame 17
1-1-71 ..............Notre Dame 24, Texas 11
1-1-72 ..............Penn St 30, Texas 6
1-1-73 ..............Texas 17, Alabama 13
1-1-74 ..............Nebraska 19, Texas 3
1-1-75 ..............Penn St 41, Baylor 20
1-1-76 ..............Arkansas 31, Georgia 10
1-1-77 ..............Houston 30, Maryland 21
1-2-78 ..............Notre Dame 38, Texas 10
1-1-79 ..............Notre Dame 35, Houston 34
1-1-80 ..............Houston 17, Nebraska 14
1-1-81 ..............Alabama 30, Baylor 2
1-1-82 ..............Texas 14, Alabama 12
1-1-83 ..............SMU 7, Pittsburgh 3
1-2-84 ..............Georgia 10, Texas 9
1-1-85 ..............Boston Col 45, Houston 28
1-1-86 ..............Texas A&M 36, Auburn 16
1-1-87 ..............Ohio St 28, Texas A&M 12
1-1-88 ..............Texas A&M 35, Notre Dame 10
1-2-89 ..............UCLA 17, Arkansas 3
1-1-90 ..............Tennessee 31, Arkansas 27
1-1-91 ..............Miami (Fla.) 46, Texas 3
1-1-92 ..............Florida St 10, Texas A&M 2
1-1-93 ..............Notre Dame 28, Texas A&M 3
1-1-94 ..............Notre Dame 24, Texas A&M 21
1-2-95 ..............USC 55, Texas Tech 14
1-1-96 ..............Colorado 38, Oregon 6
1-1-97 ..............BYU 19, Kansas St 15
1-1-98 ..............UCLA 29, Texas A&M 23
1-1-99 ..............Texas 38, Mississippi St 11
1-1-00 ..............Arkansas 27, Texas 6
1-1-01 ..............Kansas St 35, Tennessee 21
1-1-02 ..............Oklahoma 10, Arkansas 3
1-1-03 ..............Texas 35, LSU 20
1-2-04 ..............Mississippi 31, Oklahoma St 28
1-1-05 ..............Tennessee 38, Texas A&M 7
1-2-06 ..............Alabama 13, Texas Tech 10
1-1-07 ..............Auburn 17, Nebraska 14
1-1-08 ..............Missouri 38, Arkansas 7
1-2-09 ..............Mississippi 47, Texas Tech 34
1-2-10 ..............Mississippi 21, Oklahoma St 7
1-7-11 ..............LSU 41, Texas A&M 24

City: Dallas. Stadium: Cotton Bowl (1937–2009), capacity 88,175. Cowboys Stadium (2010–), capacity 71,167.

### Sun Bowl

1-1-36..............Hardin-Simmons 14, New Mexico St 14
1-1-37..............Hardin-Simmons 34, UTEP 6
1-1-38..............W Virginia 7, Texas Tech 6
1-2-39..............Utah 26, New Mexico 0
1-1-40..............Catholic 0, Arizona St 0
1-1-41..............Case Reserve 26, Arizona St 13
1-1-42..............Tulsa 6, Texas Tech 0
1-1-43..............2nd Air Force 13, Hardin-Simmons 7
1-1-44..............Southwestern (Tex.) 7, New Mexico 0
1-1-45..............Southwestern (Tex.) 35, New Mexico 0
1-1-46..............New Mexico 34, Denver 24
1-1-47..............Cincinnati 18, Virginia Tech 6
1-1-48..............Miami (OH) 13, Texas Tech 12
1-1-49..............W Virginia 21, UTEP 12
1-2-50..............UTEP 33, Georgetown 20
1-1-51..............W Texas St 14, Cincinnati 13
1-1-52..............Texas Tech 25, Pacific 14
1-1-53..............Pacific 26, Southern Miss 7
1-1-54..............UTEP 37, Southern Miss 14
1-1-55..............UTEP 47, Florida St 20
1-2-56..............Wyoming 21, Texas Tech 14
1-1-57..............George Washington 13, UTEP 0
1-1-58..............Louisville 34, Drake 20
12-31-58..........Wyoming 14, Hardin-Simmons 6
12-31-59..........New Mexico St 28, N Texas 8
12-31-60..........New Mexico St 20, Utah St 13
12-30-61..........Villanova 17, Wichita St 9
12-31-62..........W Texas St 15, Ohio 14
12-31-63..........Oregon 21, Southern Methodist 14
12-26-64..........Georgia 7, Texas Tech 0
12-31-65..........UTEP 13, TCU 12
12-24-66..........Wyoming 28, Florida St 20
12-30-67..........UTEP 14, Mississippi 7
12-28-68..........Auburn 34, Arizona 10
12-20-69..........Nebraska 45, Georgia 6
12-19-70..........Georgia Tech 17, Texas Tech 9
12-18-71..........LSU 33, Iowa St 15
12-30-72..........North Carolina 32, Texas Tech 28
12-29-73..........Missouri 34, Auburn 17
12-28-74..........Mississippi St 26, North Carolina 24
12-26-75..........Pittsburgh 33, Kansas 19
1-2-77..............Texas A&M 37, Florida 14
12-31-77..........Stanford 24, LSU 14
12-23-78..........Texas 42, Maryland 0
12-22-79..........Washington 14, Texas 7
12-27-80..........Nebraska 31, Mississippi St 17
12-26-81..........Oklahoma 40, Houston 14
12-25-82..........North Carolina 26, Texas 10
12-24-83..........Alabama 28, Southern Methodist 7
12-22-84..........Maryland 28, Tennessee 27
12-28-85..........Georgia 13, Arizona 13
12-25-86..........Alabama 28, Washington 6
12-25-87..........Oklahoma St 35, W Virginia 33
12-24-88..........Alabama 29, Army 28
12-30-89..........Pittsburgh 31, Texas A&M 28
12-31-90..........Michigan 17, USC 16
12-31-91..........UCLA 6, Illinois 3
12-31-92..........Baylor 20, Arizona 15
12-24-93..........Oklahoma 41, Texas Tech 10
12-30-94..........Texas 35, North Carolina 31
12-29-95..........Iowa 38, Washington 18
12-31-96..........Stanford 38, Michigan St 0
12-31-97..........Arizona St 17, Iowa 7
12-31-98..........TCU 28, USC 19
12-31-99..........Oregon 24, Minnesota 20
12-29-00..........Wisconsin 21, UCLA 20
12-31-01..........Washington St 33, Purdue 27
12-31-02..........Purdue 34, Washington 24

### Sun Bowl

12-31-03..........Minnesota 31, Oregon 30
12-31-04..........Arizona State 27, Purdue 23
12-30-05..........UCLA 50, Northwestern 39
12-29-06..........Oregon State 39, Missouri 38
12-31-07..........Oregon 56, South Florida 21
12-31-08..........Oregon St 3, Pittsburgh 0
12-31-09..........Oklahoma 31, Stanford 27
12-31-10..........Notre Dame 33, Miami (Fla.) 17

City: El Paso. Stadium: Sun Bowl, capacity 51,270.
Name Changes: Sun Bowl (1936–86; 94–), John Hancock
Sun Bowl (1987–88), John Hancock Bowl (1989–93).
Playing Sites: Kidd Field (1936–62), Sun Bowl (since 1963).

### Gator Bowl

1-1-46..............Wake Forest 26, South Carolina 14
1-1-47..............Oklahoma 34, North Carolina St 13
1-1-48..............Maryland 20, Georgia 20
1-1-49..............Clemson 24, Missouri 23
1-2-50..............Maryland 20, Missouri 7
1-1-51..............Wyoming 20, Washington & Lee 7
1-1-52..............Miami (Fla.) 14, Clemson 0
1-1-53..............Florida 14, Tulsa 13
1-1-54..............Texas Tech 35, Auburn 13
12-31-54..........Auburn 33, Baylor 13
12-31-55..........Vanderbilt 25, Auburn 13
12-29-56..........Georgia Tech 21, Pittsburgh 14
12-28-57..........Tennessee 3, Texas A&M 0
12-27-58..........Mississippi 7, Florida 3
1-2-60..............Arkansas 14, Georgia Tech 7
12-31-60..........Florida 13, Baylor 12
12-30-61..........Penn St 30, Georgia Tech 15
12-29-62..........Florida 17, Penn St 7
12-28-63..........North Carolina 35, Air Force 0
1-2-65..............Florida St 36, Oklahoma 19
12-31-65..........Georgia Tech 31, Texas Tech 21
12-31-66..........Tennessee 18, Syracuse 12
12-30-67..........Penn St 17, Florida St 17
12-28-68..........Missouri 35, Alabama 10
12-27-69..........Florida 14, Tennessee 13
1-2-71..............Auburn 35, Mississippi 28
12-31-71..........Georgia 7, North Carolina 3
12-30-72..........Auburn 24, Colorado 3
12-29-73..........Texas Tech 28, Tennessee 19
12-30-74..........Auburn 27, Texas 3
12-29-75..........Maryland 13, Florida 0
12-27-76..........Notre Dame 20, Penn St 9
12-30-77..........Pittsburgh 34, Clemson 3
12-29-78..........Clemson 17, Ohio St 15
12-28-79..........North Carolina 17, Michigan 15
12-29-80..........Pittsburgh 37, South Carolina 9
12-28-81..........North Carolina 31, Arkansas 27
12-30-82..........Florida St 31, W Virginia 12
12-30-83..........Florida 14, Iowa 6
12-28-84..........Oklahoma St 21, South Carolina 14
12-30-85..........Florida St 34, Oklahoma St 23
12-27-86..........Clemson 27, Stanford 21
12-31-87..........LSU 30, South Carolina 13
1-1-89..............Georgia 34, Michigan St 27
12-30-89..........Clemson 27, W Virginia 7
1-1-91..............Michigan 35, Mississippi 3
12-29-91..........Oklahoma 48, Virginia 14
12-31-92..........Florida 27, North Carolina St 10
12-31-93..........Alabama 24, North Carolina 10
12-30-94..........Tennessee 45, Virginia Tech 23
1-1-96..............Syracuse 41, Clemson 0
1-1-97..............North Carolina 20, W Virginia 13
1-1-98..............North Carolina 42, Viginia Tech 13
1-1-99..............Georgia Tech 35, Notre Dame 28

## Gator Bowl *(Cont.)*

1-1-00 .............Miami 27, Georgia Tech 13
1-1-01 .............Virginia Tech 41, Clemson 20
1-1-02 .............Florida St 30, Virginia Tech 17
1-1-03 .............North Carolina St 28, Notre Dame 6
1-1-04 .............Maryland 41, W Virginia 7
1-1-05 .............Florida State 30, West Virginia 18
1-2-06 .............Virginia Tech 35, Louisville 24
1-1-07 .............West Virginia 38, Georgia Tech 35
1-1-08 .............Texas Tech 31, Virginia 28
1-1-09 .............Nebraska 26, Clemson 21
1-1-10 .............Florida St 33, West Virginia 21
1-1-11 .............Mississippi St 52, Michigan 14
City: Jacksonville, FL. Stadium: Gator Bowl Stadium (1946-1993); Ben Hill Griffin Stadium (1994); Alltel Stadium (1997–2007, capacity 76,976. Jacksonville Municipal Stadium (1995–95, 2007–)

## Capital One Bowl

1-1-47 .............Catawba 31, Maryville (Tenn.) 6
1-1-48 .............Catawba 7, Marshall 0
1-1-49 .............Murray St 21, Sul Ross St 21
1-2-50 .............St. Vincent 7, Emory & Henry 6
1-1-51 .............Morris Harvey 35, Emory & Henry 14
1-1-52 .............Stetson 35, Arkansas St 20
1-1-53 .............E Texas St 33, Tennessee Tech 0
1-1-54 .............E Texas St 7, Arkansas St 7
1-1-55 .............NE-Omaha 7, Eastern Kentucky 6
1-2-56 .............Juniata 6, Missouri Valley 6
1-1-57 .............W Texas St 20, Southern Miss 13
1-1-58 .............E Texas St 10, Southern Miss 9
12-27-58 .........E Texas St 26, Missouri Valley 7
1-1-60 .............Middle Tennessee St 21, Presbyterian 12
12-30-60 .........Citadel 27, Tennessee Tech 0
12-29-61 .........Lamar 21, Middle Tennessee St 14
12-22-62 .........Houston 49, Miami (Ohio) 21
12-28-63 .........Western Kentucky 27, Coast Guard 0
12-12-64 .........E Carolina 14, Massachusetts 13
12-11-65 .........E Carolina 31, Maine 0
12-10-66 .........Morgan St 14, W Chester 6
12-16-67 .........TN-Martin 25, W Chester 8
12-27-68 .........Richmond 49, Ohio 42
12-26-69 .........Toledo 56, Davidson 33
12-28-70 .........Toledo 40, William & Mary 12
12-28-71 .........Toledo 28, Richmond 3
12-29-72 .........Tampa 21, Kent St 18
12-22-73 .........Miami (Ohio) 16, Florida 7
12-21-74 .........Miami (Ohio) 21, Georgia 10
12-20-75 .........Miami (Ohio) 20, South Carolina 7
12-18-76 .........Oklahoma St 49, BYU 21
12-23-77 .........Florida St 40, Texas Tech 17
12-23-78 .........North Carolina St 30, Pittsburgh 17
12-22-79 .........LSU 34, Wake Forest 10
12-20-80 .........Florida 35, Maryland 20
12-19-81 .........Missouri 19, Southern Miss 17
12-18-82 .........Auburn 33, Boston Col 26
12-17-83 .........Tennessee 30, Maryland 23
12-22-84 .........Georgia 17, Florida St 17
12-28-85 .........Ohio St 10, BYU 7
1-1-87 .............Auburn 16, USC 7
1-1-88 .............Clemson 35, Penn St 10
1-2-89 .............Clemson 13, Oklahoma 6
1-1-90 .............Illinois 31, Virginia 21
1-1-91 .............Georgia Tech 45, Nebraska 21
1-1-92 .............California 37, Clemson 13
1-1-93 .............Georgia 21, Ohio State 14
1-1-94 .............Penn State 31, Tennessee 13
1-2-95 .............Alabama 24, Ohio St 17
1-1-96 .............Tennessee 20, Ohio St 14
1-1-97 .............Tennessee 48, Northwestern 28

## Captial One Bowl *(Cont.)*

1-1-98 .............Florida 21, Penn St 6
1-1-99 .............Michigan 45, Arkansas 31
1-1-00 .............Michigan St 37, Florida 34
1-1-01 .............Michigan 31, Auburn 28
1-1-02 .............Tennessee 45, Michigan 17
1-1-03 .............Auburn 13, Penn St 9
1-1-04 .............Georgia 34, Purdue 27 (OT)
1-1-05 .............Iowa 30, LSU 25
1-2-06 .............Wisconsin 24, Auburn 10
1-1-07 .............Wisconsin 17, Arkansas 14
1-1-08 .............Michigan 41, Florida 35
1-1-09 .............Georgia 24, Michigan St 12
1-1-10 .............Penn St 19, LSU 17
1-1-11 .............Alabama 49, Michigan St 7
City: Orlando, FL. Stadium: Florida Citrus Bowl, capacity 70,000. Name Change: Tangerine Bowl (1947–82). Florida Citrus Bowl (1983–2007). Playing Sites: Tangerine Bowl (1947–72, 1974–82); Florida Field, Gainesville (1973); Orlando Stadium/Florida Citrus Bowl-Orlando (1983–2007).

## Liberty Bowl

12-19-59 .........Penn St 7, Alabama 0
12-17-60 .........Penn St 41, Oregon 12
12-16-61 .........Syracuse 15, Miami (Fla.) 14
12-15-62 .........Oregon St 6, Villanova 0
12-21-63 .........Mississippi St 16, North Carolina St 12
12-19-64 .........Utah 32, W Virginia 6
12-18-65 .........Mississippi 13, Auburn 7
12-10-66 .........Miami (Fla.) 14, Virginia Tech 7
12-16-67 .........North Carolina St 14, Georgia 7
12-14-68 .........Mississippi 34, Virginia Tech 17
12-13-69 .........Colorado 47, Alabama 33
12-12-70 .........Tulane 17, Colorado 3
12-20-71 .........Tennessee 14, Arkansas 13
12-18-72 .........Georgia Tech 31, Iowa St 30
12-17-73 .........North Carolina St 31, Kansas 18
12-16-74 .........Tennessee 7, Maryland 3
12-22-75 .........USC 20, Texas A&M 0
12-20-76 .........Alabama 36, UCLA 6
12-19-77 .........Nebraska 21, North Carolina 17
12-23-78 .........Missouri 20, LSU 15
12-22-79 .........Penn St 9, Tulane 6
12-27-80 .........Purdue 28, Missouri 25
12-30-81 .........Ohio St 31, Navy 28
12-29-82 .........Alabama 21, Illinois 15
12-29-83 .........Notre Dame 19, Boston Col 18
12-27-84 .........Auburn 21, Arkansas 15
12-27-85 .........Baylor 21, LSU 7
12-29-86 .........Tennessee 21, Minnesota 14
12-29-87 .........Georgia 20, Arkansas 17
12-28-88 .........Indiana 34, South Carolina 10
12-28-89 .........Mississippi 42, Air Force 29
12-27-90 .........Air Force 23, Ohio St 11
12-29-91 .........Air Force 38, Mississippi St 15
12-31-92 .........Mississippi 13, Air Force 0
12-28-93 .........Louisville 18, Michigan St 7
12-31-94 .........Illinois 30, E Carolina 0
12-30-95 .........East Carolina 19, Stanford 13
12-27-96 .........Syracuse 30, Houston 17
12-31-97 .........Southern Miss 41, Pittsburgh 7
12-31-98 .........Tulane 41, BYU 27
12-31-99 .........Southern Miss 23, Colorado St 17
12-29-01 .........Colorado St 22, Louisville 17
12-31-01 .........Louisville 28, BYU 10
12-31-02 .........TCU 17, Colorado St 3
12-31-03 .........Utah 17, Southern Mississippi 0
12-31-04 .........Louisville 44, Boise State 40
12-31-05 .........Tulsa 31, Fresno State 24

## Liberty Bowl *(Cont.)*

12-29-06..........South Carolina 44, Houston 36
12-29-07..........Mississippi St 10, Central Florida 3
1-2-09..............Kentucky 25, East Carolina 19
1-2-10..............Arkansas 20, East Carolina 17
12-31-10..........Central Florida 10, Georgia 6
City: Memphis (since 1965). Stadium: Liberty Bowl Memorial Stadium, capacity 62,921.
Playing Sites: Philadelphia (Municipal Stadium, 1959–63), Atlantic City (Convention Center, 1964).

## Bluebonnet Bowl

12-19-59..........Clemson 23, TCU 7
12-17-60..........Texas 3, Alabama 3
12-16-61..........Kansas 33, Rice 7
12-22-62..........Missouri 14, Georgia Tech 10
12-21-63..........Baylor 14, LSU 7
12-19-64..........Tulsa 14, Mississippi 7
12-18-65..........Tennessee 27, Tulsa 6
12-17-66..........Texas 19, Mississippi 0
12-23-67..........Colorado 31, Miami (Fla.) 21
12-31-68..........Southern Methodist 28, Oklahoma 27
12-31-69..........Houston 36, Auburn 7
12-31-70..........Alabama 24, Oklahoma 24
12-31-71..........Colorado 29, Houston 17
12-30-72..........Tennessee 24, LSU 17
12-29-73..........Houston 47, Tulane 7
12-23-74..........North Carolina St 31, Houston 31
12-27-75..........Texas 38, Colorado 21
12-31-76..........Nebraska 27, Texas Tech 24
12-31-77..........USC 47, Texas A&M 28
12-31-78..........Stanford 25, Georgia 22
12-31-79..........Purdue 27, Tennessee 22
12-31-80..........North Carolina 16, Texas 7
12-31-81..........Michigan 33, UCLA 14
12-31-82..........Arkansas 28, Florida 24
12-31-83..........Oklahoma St 24, Baylor 14
12-31-84..........West Virginia 31, TCU 14
12-31-85..........Air Force 24, Texas 16
12-31-86..........Baylor 21, Colorado 9
12-31-87..........Texas 32, Pittsburgh 27
City: Houston. Playing sites: Rice Stadium (1959–67; 1985–86), Astrodome (1968–84, 1987).
Name change: Astro-Bluebonnet Bowl (1968–76). Bowl was discontinued after 1987.

## Chick-fil-A Bowl

12-3-68............LSU 31, Florida St 27
12-30-69..........W Virginia 14, South Carolina 3
12-30-70..........Arizona St 48, North Carolina 26
12-30-71..........Mississippi 41, Georgia Tech 18
12-29-72..........North Carolina St 49, W Virginia 13
12-28-73..........Georgia 17, Maryland 16
12-28-74..........Vanderbilt 6, Texas Tech 6
12-31-75..........W Virginia 13, North Carolina St 10
12-31-76..........Kentucky 21, North Carolina 0
12-31-77..........North Carolina St 24, Iowa St 14
12-25-78..........Purdue 41, Georgia Tech 21
12-31-79..........Baylor 24, Clemson 18
1-2-81..............Miami (Fla.) 20, Virginia Tech 10
12-31-81..........West Virginia 26, Florida 6
12-31-82..........Iowa 28, Tennessee 22
12-30-83..........Florida St 28, North Carolina 3
12-31-84..........Virginia 27, Purdue 24
12-31-85..........Army 31, Illinois 29
12-31-86..........Virginia Tech 25, North Carolina St 24
1-2-88..............Tennessee 27, Indiana 22
12-31-88..........North Carolina St 28, Iowa 23
12-30-89..........Syracuse 19, Georgia 18
12-29-90..........Auburn 27, Indiana 23

## Chick-fil-A Bowl *(Cont.)*

1-1-92..............E. Carolina 37, North Carolina St 34
1-2-93..............North Carolina 21, Mississippi St 17
12-31-93..........Clemson 14, Kentucky 13
1-1-95..............North Carolina St 28, Mississippi St 24
12-30-95..........Virginia 34, Georgia 27
12-28-96..........LSU 10, Clemson 7
1-2-98..............Auburn 21, Clemson 17
12-31-98..........Georgia 35, Virginia 33
12-30-99..........Mississippi St 17, Clemson 7
12-29-00..........LSU 28, Georgia Tech 14
12-31-01..........North Carolina 16, Auburn 10
12-31-02..........Maryland 30, Tennessee 3
1-2-04..............Clemson 27, Tennessee 14
12-31-04..........Miami (Fla.) 27, Florida 10
12-30-05..........LSU 40, Miami (Fla.) 3
12-30-06..........Georgia 31, Virginia Tech 24
12-31-07..........Auburn 23, Clemson 20 (OT)
12-31-08..........LSU 38, Georgia Tech 3
12-31-09..........Virginia Tech 37, Tennessee 14
12-31-10..........Florida St 26, South Carolina 17
City: Atlanta. Stadium: Georgia Dome, capacity 71,500.
Name change: Peach Bowl (1968–2005). Playing Sites: Grant Field (1968–70), Atlanta–Fulton County Stadium (1971–92), Georgia Dome (since 1993).

## Fiesta Bowl

12-27-71..........Arizona St 45, Florida St 38
12-23-72..........Arizona St 49, Missouri 35
12-21-73..........Arizona St 28, Pittsburgh 7
12-28-74..........Oklahoma St 16, BYU 6
12-26-75..........Arizona St 17, Nebraska 14
12-25-76..........Oklahoma 41, Wyoming 7
12-25-77..........Penn St 42, Arizona St 30
12-25-78..........Arkansas 10, UCLA 10
12-25-79..........Pittsburgh 16, Arizona 10
12-26-80..........Penn St 31, Ohio St 19
1-1-82..............Penn St 26, USC 10
1-1-83..............Arizona St 32, Oklahoma 21
1-2-84..............Ohio St 28, Pittsburgh 23
1-1-85..............UCLA 39, Miami (Fla.) 37
1-1-86..............Michigan 27, Nebraska 23
1-2-87..............Penn St 14, Miami (Fla.) 10
1-1-88..............Florida St 31, Nebraska 28
1-2-89..............Notre Dame 34, W Virginia 21
1-1-90..............Florida St 41, Nebraska 17
1-1-91..............Louisville 34, Alabama 7
1-1-92..............Penn St 42, Tennessee 17
1-1-93..............Syracuse 26, Colorado 22
1-1-94..............Arizona 29, Miami (Fla.) 0
1-2-95..............Colorado 41, Notre Dame 24
1-2-96..............Nebraska 62, Florida 24
1-1-97..............Penn St 38, Texas 15
12-31-97..........Kansas St 35, Syracuse 18
1-4-99..............Tennessee 23, Florida St 16
1-2-00..............Nebraska 31, Tennessee 21
1-1-01..............Oregon St 41, Notre Dame 9
1-1-02..............Oregon 38, Colorado 16
1-3-03..............Ohio St 31, Miami (Fla.) 24 [2 OT]
1-2-04..............Ohio St 35, Kansas St 28
1-1-05..............Utah 35, Pittsburgh 7
1-2-06..............Ohio St 34, Notre Dame 20
1-1-07..............Boise St 43, Oklahoma 42
1-2-08..............West Virginia 48, Oklahoma 28
1-5-09..............Texas 24, Ohio St 21
1-4-10..............Boise St 17, TCU 10
1-1-11..............Oklahoma 48, Connecticut 20

Stadium: Sun Devil Stadium, Tempe, Ariz. (1971–2006), capacity 73,471. University of Phoenix Stadium, Glendale, Ariz. (2006–), capacity 72,200.

### Independence Bowl

12-13-76..........McNeese St 20, Tulsa 16
12-17-77..........Louisiana Tech 24, Louisville 14
12-16-78..........E Carolina 35, Louisiana Tech 13
12-15-79..........Syracuse 31, McNeese St 7
12-13-80..........Southern Miss 16, McNeese St 14
12-12-81..........Texas A&M 33, Oklahoma St 16
12-11-82..........Wisconsin 14, Kansas St 3
12-10-83..........Air Force 9, Mississippi 3
12-15-84..........Air Force 23, Virginia Tech 7
12-21-85..........Minnesota 20, Clemson 13
12-20-86..........Mississippi 20, Texas Tech 17
12-19-87..........Washington 24, Tulane 12
12-23-88..........Southern Miss 38, UTEP 18
12-16-89..........Oregon 27, Tulsa 24
12-15-90..........Louisiana Tech 34, Maryland 34
12-29-91..........Georgia 24, Arkansas 15
12-31-92..........Wake Forest 39, Oregon 35
12-31-93..........Virginia Tech 45, Indiana 20
12-28-94..........Virginia 20, TCU 10
12-29-95..........LSU 45, Michigan St 26
12-31-96..........Auburn 32, Army 29
12-28-97..........LSU 27, Notre Dame 9
12-31-98..........Mississippi 35, Texas Tech 18
12-31-99..........Mississippi 27, Oklahoma 25
12-31-00..........Mississippi St 43, Texas A&M 41
12-27-01..........Alabama 14, Iowa St 13
12-27-02..........Mississippi 27, Nebraska 23
12-31-03..........Arkansas 27, Missouri 14
12-28-04..........Iowa State 17, Miami (Ohio) 13
12-30-05..........Missouri 38, South Carolina 31
12-28-06..........Oklahoma State 34, Alabama 31
12-30-07..........Alabama 30, Colorado 24
12-28-08..........Louisiana Tech 17, Northern Ill. 10
12-28-09..........Georgia 44, Texas A&M 20
12-27-10..........Air Force 14, Georgia Tech 7

City: Shreveport, LA. Stadium: Independence Stadium, capacity 50,459.

### All-American Bowl

12-22-77..........Maryland 17, Minnesota 7
12-20-78..........Texas A&M 28, Iowa St 12
12-29-79..........Missouri 24, South Carolina 14
12-27-80..........Arkansas 34, Tulane 15
12-31-81..........Mississippi St 10, Kansas 0
12-31-82..........Air Force 36, Vanderbilt 28
12-22-83..........W Virginia 20, Kentucky 16
12-29-84..........Kentucky 20, Wisconsin 19
12-31-85..........Georgia Tech 17, Michigan St 14
12-31-86..........Florida St 27, Indiana 13
12-22-87..........Virginia 22, BYU 16
12-29-88..........Florida 14, Illinois 10
12-28-89..........Texas Tech 49, Duke 21
12-28-90..........North Carolina St 31, Southern Miss 27

City: Birmingham, AL. Stadium: Legion Field.
Name Change: Hall of Fame Classic (1977–84). Bowl was discontinued after 1990.

### Holiday Bowl

12-22-78..........Navy 23, BYU 16
12-21-79..........Indiana 38, BYU 37
12-19-80..........BYU 46, SMU 45
12-18-81..........BYU 38, Washington St 36
12-17-82..........Ohio St 47, BYU 17
12-23-83..........BYU 21, Missouri 17
12-21-84..........BYU 24, Michigan 17
12-22-85..........Arkansas 18, Arizona St 17
12-30-86..........Iowa 39, San Diego St 38
12-30-87..........Iowa 20, Wyoming 19

### Holiday Bowl (Cont.)

12-30-88..........Oklahoma St 62, Wyoming 14
12-29-89..........Penn St 50, BYU 39
12-29-90..........Texas A&M 65, BYU 14
12-30-91..........Iowa 13, BYU 13
12-30-92..........Hawaii 27, Illinois 17
12-30-93..........Ohio St 28, BYU 21
12-30-94..........Michigan 24, Colorado St 14
12-29-95..........Kansas St 54, Colorado St 21
12-30-96..........Colorado 33, Washington 21
12-29-97..........Colorado St 35, Missouri 24
12-30-98..........Arizona 23, Nebraska 20
12-29-99..........Kansas St 24, Washington 20
12-29-00..........Oregon 35, Texas 30
12-28-01..........Texas 47, Washington 43
12-27-02..........Kansas St 34, Arizona St 27
12-30-03..........Washington St 28, Texas 20
12-30-04..........Texas Tech 45, California 31
12-29-05..........Oklahoma 17, Oregon 14
12-28-06..........California 45, Texas A&M 10
12-27-07..........Texas 52, Arizona St 34
12-30-08..........Oregon 42, Oklahoma St 31
12-30-09..........Nebraska 33, Arizona 0
12-30-11..........Washington 19, Nebraska 7

City: San Diego. Stadium: Qualcomm Stadium, capacity 70,000.

### Las Vegas Bowl

12-19-81..........Toledo 27, San Jose St 25
12-18-82..........Fresno St 29, Bowling Green 28
12-17-83..........Northern Illinois 20, Cal St-Fullerton 13
12-15-84..........UNLV 30, Toledo 13*
12-14-85..........Fresno St 51, Bowling Green 7
12-13-86..........San Jose St 37, Miami (Ohio) 7
12-12-87..........Eastern Michigan 30, San Jose St 27
12-10-88..........Fresno St 35, Western Michigan 30
12-9-89............Fresno St 27, Ball St 6
12-8-90............San Jose St 48, Central Michigan 24
12-14-91..........Bowling Green 28, Fresno St 21
12-18-92..........Bowling Green 35, Nevada 34
12-17-93..........Utah St 42, Ball St 33
12-15-94..........UNLV 52, Central Michigan 24
12-14-95..........Toledo 40, Nevada 37
12-19-96..........Nevada 18, Ball St 15
12-19-97..........Oregon 41, Air Force 13
12-19-98..........North Carolina 20, San Diego St 13
12-18-99..........Utah 17, Fresno St 16
12-21-00..........UNLV 31, Arkansas 14
12-25-01..........Utah 10, USC 6
12-25-02..........UCLA 27, New Mexico 13
12-24-03..........Oregon St 55, New Mexico 14
12-23-04..........Wyoming 24, UCLA, 21
12-22-05..........California 35, BYU 28
12-21-06..........BYU 38, Oregon 8
12-22-07..........BYU 17, UCLA 16
12-20-08..........Arizona 31, BYU 21
12-22-09..........BYU 44, Oregon St 20
12-22-10..........Boise St 26, Utah 3

* Toledo won later by forfeit. City: Las Vegas (since 1992). Stadium: Sam Boyd Silver Bowl Stadium, capacity 40,000. Name change: California Bowl (1981–91). Playing sites: Fresno, CA (Bulldog Stadium, 1981–91), Las Vegas.

### Aloha Bowl

12-25-82..........Washington 21, Maryland 20
12-26-83..........Penn St 13, Washington 10
12-29-84..........Southern Methodist 27, Notre Dame 20

### Aloha Bowl *(Cont.)*

12-28-85.........Alabama 24, USC 3
12-27-86.........Arizona 30, North Carolina 21
12-25-87.........UCLA 20, Florida 16
12-25-88.........Washington St 24, Houston 22
12-25-89.........Michigan St 33, Hawaii 13
12-25-90.........Syracuse 28, Arizona 0
12-25-91.........Georgia Tech 18, Stanford 17
12-25-92.........Kansas 23, BYU 20
12-25-93.........Colorado 41, Fresno St 30
12-25-94.........Boston College 12, Kansas St 7
12-25-95.........Kansas 51, UCLA 30
12-25-96.........Navy 42, California 38
12-25-97.........Washington 51, Michigan St 23
12-25-98.........Colorado 51, Oregon 43
12-25-99.........Wake Forest 23, Arizona St 3
12-25-00.........Boston College 31, Arizona St 17

City: Honolulu. Stadium: Aloha Stadium. Bowl was discontinued after 2000.

### Freedom Bowl

12-16-84.........Iowa 55, Texas 17
12-30-85.........Washington 20, Colorado 17
12-30-86.........UCLA 31, BYU 10
12-30-87.........Arizona St 33, Air Force 28
12-29-88.........BYU 20, Colorado 17
12-30-89.........Washington 34, Florida 7
12-29-90.........Colorado St 32, Oregon 31
12-30-91.........Tulsa 28, San Diego St 17
12-29-92.........Fresno St 24, USC 7
12-30-93.........USC 28, Utah 21
12-29-94.........Utah 16, Arizona 13

City: Anaheim. Stadium: Anaheim Stadium. Bowl was discontinued after 1994.

### Outback Bowl

12-23-86.........Boston College 27, Georgia 24
1-2-88.............Michigan 28, Alabama 24
1-2-89.............Syracuse 23, LSU 10
1-1-90.............Auburn 31, Ohio St 14
1-1-91.............Clemson 30, Illinois 0
1-1-92.............Syracuse 24, Ohio St 17
1-1-93.............Tennessee 38, Boston College 23
1-1-94.............Michigan 42, North Carolina St 7
1-2-95.............Wisconsin 34, Duke 20
1-1-96.............Penn St 43, Auburn 14
1-1-97.............Alabama 17, Michigan 14
1-1-98.............Georgia 33, Wisconsin 6
1-1-99.............Penn St 26, Kentucky 14
1-1-00.............Georgia 28, Purdue 25
1-1-01.............South Carolina 24, Ohio St 7
1-1-02.............South Carolina 31, Ohio St 28
1-1-03.............Michigan 38, Florida 30
1-1-04.............Iowa 37, Florida 17
1-1-05.............Georgia 24, Wisconsin 21
1-2-06.............Florida 31, Iowa 24
1-1-07.............Penn State 20, Tennessee 10
1-1-08.............Tennessee 21, Wisconsin 17
1-1-09.............Iowa 31, South Carolina 10
1-1-10.............Auburn 38, Northwestern 35
1-1-11.............Florida 37, Penn St 24

City: Tampa. Stadium: Raymond James Stadium, capacity 75,000. Name change: Hall of Fame Bowl (1986–95).

### Insight Bowl

12-31-89.........Arizona 17, North Carolina St 10
12-31-90.........California 17, Wyoming 15

### Insight Bowl *(Cont.)*

12-31-91.........Indiana 24, Baylor 0
12-29-92.........Washington St 31, Utah 28
12-29-93.........Kansas St 52, Wyoming 17
12-29-94.........BYU 31, Oklahoma 6
12-27-95.........Texas Tech 55, Air Force 41
12-27-96.........Wisconsin 38, Utah 10
12-27-97.........Arizona 20, New Mexico 14
12-26-98.........Missouri 34, W Virginia 31
12-31-99.........Colorado 62, Boston College 28
12-28-00.........Iowa St 37, Pittsburgh 29
12-29-01.........Syracuse 26, Kansas St 3
12-26-02.........Pittsburgh 38, Oregon St 13
12-26-03.........California 52, Virginia Tech 49
12-28-04.........Oregon State 38, Notre Dame 21
12-27-05.........Arizona State 45, Rutgers 40
12-29-06.........Texas Tech 44, Minnesota 41
12-31-07.........Oklahoma St 49, Indiana 33
12-31-08.........Kansas 42, Minnesota 21
12-31-09.........Iowa St 14, Minnesota 13
12-28-10.........Iowa 27, Missouri 24

City: Tucson. Stadium: Arizona Stadium, capacity 55,883. Name change: Copper Bowl (1989–97), Insight.com Bowl (1998–2000).

### Tangerine Bowl

12-28-90.........Florida St 24, Penn St 17
12-28-91.........Alabama 30, Colorado 25
1-1-93.............Stanford 24, Penn St 3
1-1-94.............Boston College 31, Virginia 13
1-2-95.............South Carolina 24, W Virginia 21
12-30-95.........North Carolina 20, Arkansas 10
12-27-96.........Miami (Fla.) 31, Virginia 21
12-29-97.........Georgia Tech 35, W Virginia 30
12-29-98.........Miami (Fla.) 46, North Carolina St 23
12-30-99.........Illinois 62, Virginia 21
12-28-00.........North Carolina St 38, Minnesota 30
12-20-01.........Pittsburgh 34, North Carolina St 19
12-23-02.........Texas Tech 55, Clemson 15
12-22-03.........North Carolina St 56, Kansas 26

City: Miami. Stadium: Pro Player Stadium, capacity 75,192. Name change: Blockbuster Bowl (1990–93), Carquest Bowl (1994–97), Micron PC Bowl (1998–2001). Discontinued after 2003.

### Alamo Bowl

12-31-93.........California 37, Iowa 3
12-31-94.........Washington St 10, Baylor 3
12-28-95.........Texas A&M 22, Michigan 20
12-29-96.........Iowa 27, Texas Tech 0
12-30-97.........Purdue 33, Oklahoma St 20
12-29-98.........Purdue 37, Kansas St 34
12-28-99.........Penn St 24, Texas A&M 0
12-30-00.........Nebraska 66, Northwestern 17
12-29-01.........Iowa 16, Texas Tech 3
12-28-02.........Wisconsin 31, Colorado 28 (OT)
12-29-03.........Nebraska 17, Michigan St 3
12-29-04.........Ohio State 33, Oklahoma State 7
12-28-05.........Nebraska 32, Michigan 28
12-30-06.........Texas 26, Iowa 24
12-29-07.........Penn St 24, Texas A&M 17
12-29-08.........Missouri 30, Northwestern 23
1-2-10.............Texas Tech 41, Michigan St 31
12-29-10.........Oklahoma St 36, Arizona 10

City: San Antonio, TX. Stadium: Alamodome, capaciity 67,000.

## 1936

| | | Record | Coach |
|---|---|---|---|
| 1. | Minnesota | 7-1-0 | Bernie Bierman |
| 2. | LSU | 9-0-1 | Bernie Moore |
| 3. | Pittsburgh | 7-1-1 | Jock Sutherland |
| 4. | Alabama | 8-0-1 | Frank Thomas |
| 5. | Washington | 7-1-1 | Jimmy Phelan |
| 6. | Santa Clara | 7-1-0 | Buck Shaw |
| 7. | Northwestern | 7-1-0 | Pappy Waldorf |
| 8. | Notre Dame | 6-2-1 | Elmer Layden |
| 9. | Nebraska | 7-2-0 | Dana X. Bible |
| 10. | Pennsylvania | 7-1-0 | Harvey Harman |
| 11. | Duke | 9-1-0 | Wallace Wade |
| 12. | Yale | 7-1-0 | Ducky Pond |
| 13. | Dartmouth | 7-1-1 | Red Blaik |
| 14. | Duquesne | 7-2-0 | John Smith |
| 15. | Fordham | 5-1-2 | Jim Crowley |
| 16. | TCU | 8-2-2 | Dutch Meyer |
| 17. | Tennessee | 6-2-2 | Bob Neyland |
| 18. | Arkansas | 7-3-0 | Fred Thomsen |
| 19. | Navy | 6-3-0 | Tom Hamilton |
| 20. | Marquette | 7-1-0 | Frank Murray |

## 1937

| | | Record | Coach |
|---|---|---|---|
| 1. | Pittsburgh | 9-0-1 | Jock Sutherland |
| 2. | California | 9-0-1 | Stub Allison |
| 3. | Fordham | 7-0-1 | Jim Crowley |
| 4. | Alabama | 9-0-0 | Frank Thomas |
| 5. | Minnesota | 6-2-0 | Bernie Bierman |
| 6. | Villanova | 8-0-1 | Clipper Smith |
| 7. | Dartmouth | 7-0-2 | Red Blaik |
| 8. | LSU | 9-1-0 | Bernie Moore |
| 9. | Notre Dame | 6-2-1 | Elmer Layden |
| | Santa Clara | 8-0-0 | Buck Shaw |
| 11. | Nebraska | 6-1-2 | Biff Jones |
| 12. | Yale | 6-1-1 | Ducky Pond |
| 13. | Ohio St | 6-2-0 | Francis Schmidt |
| 14. | Holy Cross | 8-0-2 | Eddie Anderson |
| | Arkansas | 6-2-2 | Fred Thomsen |
| 16. | TCU | 4-2-2 | Dutch Meyer |
| 17. | Colorado | 8-0-0 | Bunnie Oakes |
| 18. | Rice | 5-3-2 | Jimmy Kitts |
| 19. | North Carolina | 7-1-1 | Ray Wolf |
| 20. | Duke | 7-2-1 | Wallace Wade |

## 1938

| | | Record | Coach |
|---|---|---|---|
| 1. | TCU | 10-0-0 | Dutch Meyer |
| 2. | Tennessee | 10-0-0 | Bob Neyland |
| 3. | Duke | 9-0-0 | Wallace Wade |
| 4. | Oklahoma | 10-0-0 | Tom Stidham |
| 5. | #Notre Dame | 8-1-0 | Elmer Layden |
| 6. | Carnegie Tech | 7-1-0 | Bill Kern |
| 7. | USC | 8-2-0 | Howard Jones |
| 8. | Pittsburgh | 8-2-0 | Jock Sutherland |
| 9. | Holy Cross | 8-1-0 | Eddie Anderson |
| 10. | Minnesota | 6-2-0 | Bernie Bierman |
| 11. | Texas Tech | 10-0-0 | Pete Cawthon |
| 12. | Cornell | 5-1-1 | Carl Snavely |
| 13. | Alabama | 7-1-1 | Frank Thomas |
| 14. | California | 10-1-0 | Stub Allison |
| 15. | Fordham | 6-1-2 | Jim Crowley |
| 16. | Michigan | 6-1-1 | Fritz Crisler |
| 17. | Northwestern | 4-2-2 | Pappy Waldorf |

## 1938 (Cont.)

| | | Record | Coach |
|---|---|---|---|
| 18. | Villanova | 8-0-1 | Clipper Smith |
| 19. | Tulane | 7-2-1 | Red Dawson |
| 20. | Dartmouth | 7-2-0 | Red Blaik |

#Selected No. 1 by the Dickinson System.

## 1939

| | | Record | Coach |
|---|---|---|---|
| 1. | Texas A&M | 10-0-0 | Homer Norton |
| 2. | Tennessee | 10-0-0 | Bob Neyland |
| 3. | #USC | 7-0-2 | Howard Jones |
| 4. | Cornell | 8-0-0 | Carl Snavely |
| 5. | Tulane | 8-0-1 | Red Dawson |
| 6. | Missouri | 8-1-0 | Don Faurot |
| 7. | UCLA | 6-0-4 | Babe Horrell |
| 8. | Duke | 8-1-0 | Wallace Wade |
| 9. | Iowa | 6-1-1 | Eddie Anderson |
| 10. | Duquesne | 8-0-1 | Buff Donelli |
| 11. | Boston College | 9-1-0 | Frank Leahy |
| 12. | Clemson | 8-1-0 | Jess Neely |
| 13. | Notre Dame | 7-2-0 | Elmer Layden |
| 14. | Santa Clara | 5-1-3 | Buck Shaw |
| 15. | Ohio St | 6-2-0 | Francis Schmidt |
| 16. | Georgia Tech | 7-2-0 | Bill Alexander |
| 17. | Fordham | 6-2-0 | Jim Crowley |
| 18. | Nebraska | 7-1-1 | Biff Jones |
| 19. | Oklahoma | 6-2-1 | Tom Stidham |
| 20. | Michigan | 6-2-0 | Fritz Crisler |

#Selected No. 1 by the Dickinson System.

## 1940

| | | Record | Coach |
|---|---|---|---|
| 1. | Minnesota | 8-0-0 | Bernie Bierman |
| 2. | Stanford | 9-0-0 | C. Shaughnessy |
| 3. | Michigan | 7-1-0 | Fritz Crisler |
| 4. | Tennessee | 10-0-0 | Bob Neyland |
| 5. | Boston College | 10-0-0 | Frank Leahy |
| 6. | Texas A&M | 8-1-0 | Homer Norton |
| 7. | Nebraska | 8-1-0 | Biff Jones |
| 8. | Northwestern | 6-2-0 | Pappy Waldorf |
| 9. | Mississippi St | 9-0-1 | Allyn McKeen |
| 10. | Washington | 7-2-0 | Jimmy Phelan |
| 11. | Santa Clara | 6-1-1 | Buck Shaw |
| 12. | Fordham | 7-1-0 | Jim Crowley |
| 13. | Georgetown | 8-1-0 | Jack Hagerty |
| 14. | Pennsylvania | 6-1-1 | George Munger |
| 15. | Cornell | 6-2-0 | Carl Snavely |
| 16. | SMU | 8-1-1 | Matty Bell |
| 17. | Hard.-Simmons | 9-0-0 | Abe Woodson |
| 18. | Duke | 7-2-0 | Wallace Wade |
| 19. | Lafayette | 9-0-0 | Hooks Mylin |
| 20. | — | | |

Only 19 teams selected.

## 1941

| | | Record | Coach |
|---|---|---|---|
| 1. | Minnesota | 8-0-0 | Bernie Bierman |
| 2. | Duke | 9-0-0 | Wallace Wade |
| 3. | Notre Dame | 8-0-1 | Frank Leahy |
| 4. | Texas | 8-1-1 | Dana X. Bible |
| 5. | Michigan | 6-1-1 | Fritz Crisler |

Note: Except where indicated with an asterisk, the polls from 1936 through 1964 were taken before the bowl games and those from 1965 through the present were taken after the bowl games.

### 1941 (Cont.)

| | | Record | Coach |
|---|---|---|---|
| 6. | Fordham | 7-1-0 | Jim Crowley |
| 7. | Missouri | 8-1-0 | Don Faurot |
| 8. | Duquesne | 8-0-0 | Buff Donelli |
| 9. | Texas A&M | 9-1-0 | Homer Norton |
| 10. | Navy | 7-1-1 | Swede Larson |
| 11. | Northwestern | 5-3-0 | Pappy Waldorf |
| 12. | Oregon St. | 7-2-0 | Lon Stiner |
| 13. | Ohio St | 6-1-1 | Paul Brown |
| 14. | Georgia | 8-1-1 | Wally Butts |
| 15. | Pennsylvania | 7-1-1 | George Munger |
| 16. | Mississippi St | 8-1-1 | Allyn McKeen |
| 17. | Mississippi | 6-2-1 | Harry Mehre |
| 18. | Tennessee | 8-2-0 | John Barnhill |
| 19. | Washington St | 6-4-0 | Babe Hollingbery |
| 20. | Alabama | 8-2-0 | Frank Thomas |

### 1942

| | | Record | Coach |
|---|---|---|---|
| 1. | Ohio St | 9-1-0 | Paul Brown |
| 2. | Georgia | 10-1-0 | Wally Butts |
| 3. | Wisconsin | 8-1-1 | H. Stuhldreher |
| 4. | Tulsa | 10-0-0 | Henry Frnka |
| 5. | Georgia Tech | 9-1-0 | Bill Alexander |
| 6. | Notre Dame | 7-2-2 | Frank Leahy |
| 7. | Tennessee | 8-1-1 | John Barnhill |
| 8. | Boston College | 8-1-0 | Denny Myers |
| 9. | Michigan | 7-3-0 | Fritz Crisler |
| 10. | Alabama | 7-3-0 | Frank Thomas |
| 11. | Texas | 8-2-0 | Dana X. Bible |
| 12. | Stanford | 6-4-0 | Marchie Schwartz |
| 13. | UCLA | 7-3-0 | Babe Horrell |
| 14. | William & Mary | 9-1-1 | Carl Voyles |
| 15. | Santa Clara | 7-2-0 | Buck Shaw |
| 16. | Auburn | 6-4-1 | Jack Meagher |
| 17. | Washington St | 6-2-2 | Babe Hollingbery |
| 18. | Mississippi St | 8-2-0 | Allyn McKeen |
| 19. | Minnesota | 5-4-0 | George Hauser |
| | Holy Cross | 5-4-1 | Ank Scanlon |
| | Penn St | 6-1-1 | Bob Higgins |

### 1943

| | | Record | Coach |
|---|---|---|---|
| 1. | Notre Dame | 9-1-0 | Frank Leahy |
| 2. | Iowa Pre-Flight | 9-1-0 | Don Faurot |
| 3. | Michigan | 8-1-0 | Fritz Crisler |
| 4. | Navy | 8-1-0 | Billick Whelchel |
| 5. | Purdue | 9-0-0 | Elmer Burnham |
| 6. | Great Lakes | 10-2-0 | Tony Hinkle |
| 7. | Duke | 8-1-0 | Eddie Cameron |
| 8. | Del Monte P-F | 7-1-0 | Bill Kern |
| 9. | Northwestern | 6-2-0 | Pappy Waldorf |
| 10. | March Field | 9-1-0 | Paul Schissler |
| 11. | Army | 7-2-1 | Red Blaik |
| 12. | Washington | 4-0-0 | Ralph Welch |
| 13. | Georgia Tech | 7-3-0 | Bill Alexander |
| 14. | Texas | 7-1-0 | Dana X. Bible |
| 15. | Tulsa | 6-0-1 | Henry Frnka |
| 16. | Dartmouth | 6-1-0 | Earl Brown |
| 17. | Bainbridge NTS | 7-0-0 | Joe Maniaci |
| 18. | Colorado College | 7-0-0 | Hal White |
| 19. | Pacific | 7-2-0 | Amos A. Stagg |
| 20. | Pennsylvania | 6-2-1 | George Munger |

### 1944

| | | Record | Coach |
|---|---|---|---|
| 1. | Army | 9-0-0 | Red Blaik |
| 2. | Ohio St | 9-0-0 | Carroll Widdoes |
| 3. | Randolph Field | 11-0-0 | Frank Tritico |
| 4. | Navy | 6-3-0 | Oscar Hagberg |
| 5. | Bainbridge NTS | 9-0-0 | Joe Maniaci |
| 6. | Iowa Pre-Flight | 10-1-0 | Jack Meagher |
| 7. | USC | 7-0-2 | Jeff Cravath |
| 8. | Michigan | 8-2-0 | Fritz Crisler |
| 9. | Notre Dame | 8-2-0 | Ed McKeever |
| 10. | March Field | 7-1-2 | Paul Schissler |
| 11. | Duke | 5-4-0 | Eddie Cameron |
| 12. | Tennessee | 8-0-1 | John Barnhill |
| 13. | Georgia Tech | 8-2-0 | Bill Alexander |
| | Norman P-F | 6-0-0 | John Gregg |
| 15. | Illinois | 5-4-1 | Ray Eliot |
| 16. | El Toro Marines | 8-1-0 | Dick Hanley |
| 17. | Great Lakes | 9-2-1 | Paul Brown |
| 18. | Fort Pierce | 9-0-0 | Hamp Pool |
| 19. | St. Mary's P-F | 4-4-0 | Jules Sikes |
| 20. | 2nd Air Force | 7-2-1 | Bill Reese |

### 1945

| | | Record | Coach |
|---|---|---|---|
| 1. | Army | 9-0-0 | Red Blaik |
| 2. | Alabama | 9-0-0 | Frank Thomas |
| 3. | Navy | 7-1-1 | Oscar Hagberg |
| 4. | Indiana | 9-0-1 | Bo McMillan |
| 5. | Oklahoma A&M | 8-0-0 | Jim Lookabaugh |
| 6. | Michigan | 7-3-0 | Fritz Crisler |
| 7. | St. Mary's (CA) | 7-1-0 | Jimmy Phelan |
| 8. | Pennsylvania | 6-2-0 | George Munger |
| 9. | Notre Dame | 7-2-1 | Hugh Devore |
| 10. | Texas | 9-1-0 | Dana X. Bible |
| 11. | USC | 7-3-0 | Jeff Cravath |
| 12. | Ohio St | 7-2-0 | Carroll Widdoes |
| 13. | Duke | 6-2-0 | Eddie Cameron |
| 14. | Tennessee | 8-1-0 | John Barnhill |
| 15. | LSU | 7-2-0 | Bernie Moore |
| 16. | Holy Cross | 8-1-0 | John DeGrosa |
| 17. | Tulsa | 8-2-0 | Henry Frnka |
| 18. | Georgia | 8-2-0 | Wally Butts |
| 19. | Wake Forest | 4-3-1 | Peahead Walker |
| 20. | Columbia | 8-1-0 | Lou Little |

### 1946

| | | Record | Coach |
|---|---|---|---|
| 1. | Notre Dame | 8-0-1 | Frank Leahy |
| 2. | Army | 9-0-1 | Red Blaik |
| 3. | Georgia | 10-0-0 | Wally Butts |
| 4. | UCLA | 10-0-0 | B. LaBrucherie |
| 5. | Illinois | 7-2-0 | Ray Eliot |
| 6. | Michigan | 6-2-1 | Fritz Crisler |
| 7. | Tennessee | 9-1-0 | Bob Neyland |
| 8. | LSU | 9-1-0 | Bernie Moore |
| 9. | North Carolina | 8-1-1 | Carl Snavely |
| 10. | Rice | 8-2-0 | Jess Neely |
| 11. | Georgia Tech | 8-2-0 | Bobby Dodd |
| 12. | Yale | 7-1-1 | Howard Odell |
| 13. | Pennsylvania | 6-2-0 | George Munger |
| 14. | Oklahoma | 7-3-0 | Jim Tatum |
| 15. | Texas | 8-2-0 | Dana X. Bible |
| 16. | Arkansas | 6-3-1 | John Barnhill |
| 17. | Tulsa | 9-1-0 | J.O. Brothers |
| 18. | North Carolina St | 8-2-0 | Beattie Feathers |
| 19. | Delaware | 9-0-0 | Bill Murray |
| 20. | Indiana | 6-3-0 | Bo McMillan |

### 1947

| | | Record | Coach |
|---|---|---|---|
| 1. | Notre Dame | 9-0-0 | Frank Leahy |
| 2. | #Michigan | 9-0-0 | Fritz Crisler |
| 3. | SMU | 9-0-1 | Matty Bell |
| 4. | Penn St | 9-0-0 | Bob Higgins |
| 5. | Texas | 9-1-0 | Blair Cherry |
| 6. | Alabama | 8-2-0 | Red Drew |
| 7. | Pennsylvania | 7-0-1 | George Munger |
| 8. | USC | 7-1-1 | Jeff Cravath |
| 9. | North Carolina | 8-2-0 | Carl Snavely |
| 10. | Georgia Tech | 9-1-0 | Bobby Dodd |
| 11. | Army | 5-2-2 | Red Blaik |
| 12. | Kansas | 8-0-2 | George Sauer |
| 13. | Mississippi | 8-2-0 | Johnny Vaught |
| 14. | William & Mary | 9-1-0 | Rube McCray |
| 15. | California | 9-1-0 | Pappy Waldorf |
| 16. | Oklahoma | 7-2-1 | Bud Wilkinson |
| 17. | North Carolina St | 5-3-1 | Beattie Feathers |
| 18. | Rice | 6-3-1 | Jess Neely |
| 19. | Duke | 4-3-2 | Wallace Wade |
| 20. | Columbia | 7-2-0 | Lou Little |

#The AP, which had voted Notre Dame No. 1 before the bowl games, took a second vote, giving the title to Michigan after its 49–0 win over USC in the Rose Bowl.

### 1948

| | | Record | Coach |
|---|---|---|---|
| 1. | Michigan | 9-0-0 | Bennie Oosterbaan |
| 2. | Notre Dame | 9-0-1 | Frank Leahy |
| 3. | North Carolina | 9-0-1 | Carl Snavely |
| 4. | California | 10-0-0 | Pappy Waldorf |
| 5. | Oklahoma | 9-1-0 | Bud Wilkinson |
| 6. | Army | 8-0-1 | Red Blaik |
| 7. | Northwestern | 7-2-0 | Bob Voigts |
| 8. | Georgia | 9-1-0 | Wally Butts |
| 9. | Oregon | 9-1-0 | Jim Aiken |
| 10. | SMU | 8-1-1 | Matty Bell |
| 11. | Clemson | 10-0-0 | Frank Howard |
| 12. | Vanderbilt | 8-2-1 | Red Sanders |
| 13. | Tulane | 9-1-0 | Henry Frnka |
| 14. | Michigan St | 6-2-2 | Biggie Munn |
| 15. | Mississippi | 8-1-0 | Johnny Vaught |
| 16. | Minnesota | 7-2-0 | Bernie Bierman |
| 17. | William & Mary | 6-2-2 | Rube McCray |
| 18. | Penn St | 7-1-1 | Bob Higgins |
| 19. | Cornell | 8-1-0 | Lefty James |
| 20. | Wake Forest | 6-3-C | Peahead Walker |

### 1949

| | | Record | Coach |
|---|---|---|---|
| 1. | Notre Dame | 10-0-0 | Frank Leahy |
| 2. | Oklahoma | 10-0-0 | Bud Wilkinson |
| 3. | California | 10-0-0 | Pappy Waldorf |
| 4. | Army | 9-0-0 | Red Blaik |
| 5. | Rice | 9-1-0 | Jess Neely |
| 6. | Ohio St | 6-1-2 | Wes Fesler |
| 7. | Michigan | 6-2-1 | Bennie Oosterbaan |
| 8. | Minnesota | 7-2-0 | Bernie Bierman |
| 9. | LSU | 8-2-0 | Gaynell Tinsley |
| 10. | Pacific | 11-0-0 | Larry Siemering |
| 11. | Kentucky | 9-2-0 | Bear Bryant |
| 12. | Cornell | 8-1-0 | Lefty James |
| 13. | Villanova | 8-1-0 | Jim Leonard |
| 14. | Maryland | 8-1-0 | Jim Tatum |

### 1949 *(Cont.)*

| | | Record | Coach |
|---|---|---|---|
| 15. | Santa Clara | 7-2-1 | Len Casanova |
| 16. | North Carolina | 7-3-0 | Carl Snavely |
| 17. | Tennessee | 7-2-1 | Bob Neyland |
| 18. | Princeton | 6-3-0 | Charlie Caldwell |
| 19. | Michigan St | 6-3-0 | Biggie Munn |
| 20. | Missouri | 7-3-0 | Don Faurot |
| | Baylor | 8-2-0 | Bob Woodruff |

### 1950

| | | Record | Coach |
|---|---|---|---|
| 1. | Oklahoma | 10-0-0 | Bud Wilkinson |
| 2. | Army | 8-1-0 | Red Blaik |
| 3. | Texas | 9-1-0 | Blair Cherry |
| 4. | Tennessee | 10-1-0 | Bob Neyland |
| 5. | California | 9-0-1 | Pappy Waldorf |
| 6. | Princeton | 9-0-0 | Charlie Caldwell |
| 7. | Kentucky | 10-1-0 | Bear Bryant |
| 8. | Michigan St | 8-1-0 | Biggie Munn |
| 9. | Michigan | 5-3-1 | Bennie Oosterbaan |
| 10. | Clemson | 8-0-1 | Frank Howard |
| 11. | Washington | 8-2-0 | Howard Odell |
| 12. | Wyoming | 9-0-0 | Bowden Wyatt |
| 13. | Illinois | 7-2-0 | Ray Eliot |
| 14. | Ohio St | 6-3-0 | Wes Fesler |
| 15. | Miami (FL) | 9-0-1 | Andy Gustafson |
| 16. | Alabama | 9-2-0 | Red Drew |
| 17. | Nebraska | 6-2-1 | Bill Glassford |
| 18. | Washington & Lee | 8-2-0 | George Barclay |
| 19. | Tulsa | 9-1-1 | J.O. Brothers |
| 20. | Tulane | 6-2-1 | Henry Frnka |

### 1951

| | | Record | Coach |
|---|---|---|---|
| 1. | Tennessee | 10-0-0 | Bob Neyland |
| 2. | Michigan St | 9-0-0 | Biggie Munn |
| 3. | Maryland | 9-0-0 | Jim Tatum |
| 4. | Illinois | 8-0-1 | Ray Eliot |
| 5. | Georgia Tech | 10-0-1 | Bobby Dodd |
| 6. | Princeton | 9-0-0 | Charlie Caldwell |
| 7. | Stanford | 9-1-0 | Chuck Taylor |
| 8. | Wisconsin | 7-1-1 | Ivy Williamson |
| 9. | Baylor | 8-1-1 | George Sauer |
| 10. | Oklahoma | 8-2-0 | Bud Wilkinson |
| 11. | TCU | 6-4-0 | Dutch Meyer |
| 12. | California | 8-2-0 | Pappy Waldorf |
| 13. | Virginia | 8-1-0 | Art Guepe |
| 14. | San Francisco | 9-0-0 | Joe Kuharich |
| 15. | Kentucky | 7-4-0 | Bear Bryant |
| 16. | Boston University | 6-4-0 | Buff Donelli |
| 17. | UCLA | 5-3-1 | Red Sanders |
| 18. | Washington St | 7-3-0 | Forest Evashevski |
| 19. | Holy Cross | 8-2-0 | Eddie Anderson |
| 20. | Clemson | 7-2-0 | Frank Howard |

### 1952

| | | Record | Coach |
|---|---|---|---|
| 1. | Michigan St | 9-0-0 | Biggie Munn |
| 2. | Georgia Tech | 11-0-0 | Bobby Dodd |
| 3. | Notre Dame | 7-2-1 | Frank Leahy |
| 4. | Oklahoma | 8-1-1 | Bud Wilkinson |
| 5. | USC | 9-1-0 | Jess Hill |
| 6. | UCLA | 8-1-0 | Red Sanders |
| 7. | Mississippi | 8-0-2 | Johnny Vaught |

## 1952 *(Cont.)*

| | | Record | Coach |
|---|---|---|---|
| 8. | Tennessee | 8-1-1 | Bob Neyland |
| 9. | Alabama | 9-2-0 | Red Drew |
| 10. | Texas | 8-2-0 | Ed Price |
| 11. | Wisconsin | 6-2-1 | Ivy Williamson |
| 12. | Tulsa | 8-1-1 | J.O. Brothers |
| 13. | Maryland | 7-2-0 | Jim Tatum |
| 14. | Syracuse | 7-2-0 | Ben Schwartzwalder |
| 15. | Florida | 7-3-0 | Bob Woodruff |
| 16. | Duke | 8-2-0 | Bill Murray |
| 17. | Ohio St | 6-3-0 | Woody Hayes |
| 18. | Purdue | 4-3-2 | Stu Holcomb |
| 19. | Princeton | 8-1-0 | Charlie Caldwell |
| 20. | Kentucky | 5-4-2 | Bear Bryant |

## 1953

| | | Record | Coach |
|---|---|---|---|
| 1. | Maryland | 10-0-0 | Jim Tatum |
| 2. | Notre Dame | 9-0-1 | Frank Leahy |
| 3. | Michigan St | 8-1-0 | Biggie Munn |
| 4. | Oklahoma | 8-1-1 | Bud Wilkinson |
| 5. | UCLA | 8-1-0 | Red Sanders |
| 6. | Rice | 8-2-0 | Jess Neely |
| 7. | Illinois | 7-1-1 | Ray Eliot |
| 8. | Georgia Tech | 8-2-1 | Bobby Dodd |
| 9. | Iowa | 5-3-1 | Forest Evashevski |
| 10. | W Virginia | 8-1-0 | Art Lewis |
| 11. | Texas | 7-3-0 | Ed Price |
| 12. | Texas Tech | 10-1-0 | DeWitt Weaver |
| 13. | Alabama | 6-2-3 | Red Drew |
| 14. | Army | 7-1-1 | Red Blaik |
| 15. | Wisconsin | 6-2-1 | Ivy Williamson |
| 16. | Kentucky | 7-2-1 | Bear Bryant |
| 17. | Auburn | 7-2-1 | Shug Jordan |
| 18. | Duke | 7-2-1 | Bill Murray |
| 19. | Stanford | 6-3-1 | Chuck Taylor |
| 20. | Michigan | 6-3-0 | Bennie Oosterbaan |

## 1954

| | | Record | Coach |
|---|---|---|---|
| 1. | Ohio St | 9-0-0 | Woody Hayes |
| 2. | #UCLA | 9-0-0 | Red Sanders |
| 3. | Oklahoma | 10-0-0 | Bud Wilkinson |
| 4. | Notre Dame | 9-1-0 | Terry Brennan |
| 5. | Navy | 7-2-0 | Eddie Erdelatz |
| 6. | Mississippi | 9-1-0 | Johnny Vaught |
| 7. | Army | 7-2-0 | Red Blaik |
| 8. | Maryland | 7-2-1 | Jim Tatum |
| 9. | Wisconsin | 7-2-0 | Ivy Williamson |
| 10. | Arkansas | 8-2-0 | Bowden Wyatt |
| 11. | Miami (FL) | 8-1-0 | Andy Gustafson |
| 12. | W Virginia | 8-1-0 | Art Lewis |
| 13. | Auburn | 7-3-0 | Shug Jordan |
| 14. | Duke | 7-2-1 | Bill Murray |
| 15. | Michigan | 6-3-0 | Bennie Oosterbaan |
| 16. | Virginia Tech | 8-0-1 | Frank Moseley |
| 17. | USC | 8-3-0 | Jess Hill |
| 18. | Baylor | 7-3-0 | George Sauer |
| 19. | Rice | 7-3-0 | Jess Neely |
| 20. | Penn St | 7-2-0 | Rip Engle |

#Selected No. 1 by UP.

## 1955

| | | Record | Coach |
|---|---|---|---|
| 1. | Oklahoma | 10-0-0 | Bud Wilkinson |
| 2. | Michigan St | 8-1-0 | Duffy Daugherty |
| 3. | Maryland | 10-0-0 | Jim Tatum |
| 4. | UCLA | 9-1-0 | Red Sanders |
| 5. | Ohio St | 7-2-0 | Woody Hayes |
| 6. | TCU | 9-1-0 | Abe Martin |
| 7. | Georgia Tech | 8-1-1 | Bobby Dodd |
| 8. | Auburn | 8-1-1 | Shug Jordan |
| 9. | Notre Dame | 8-2-0 | Terry Brennan |
| 10. | Mississippi | 9-1-0 | Johnny Vaught |
| 11. | Pittsburgh | 7-3-0 | John Michelosen |
| 12. | Michigan | 7-2-0 | Bennie Oosterbaan |
| 13. | USC | 6-4-0 | Jess Hill |
| 14. | Miami (FL) | 6-3-0 | Andy Gustafson |
| 15. | Miami (OH) | 9-0-0 | Ara Parseghian |
| 16. | Stanford | 6-3-1 | Chuck Taylor |
| 17. | Texas A&M | 7-2-1 | Bear Bryant |
| 18. | Navy | 6-2-1 | Eddie Erdelatz |
| 19. | W Virginia | 8-2-0 | Art Lewis |
| 20. | Army | 6-3-0 | Red Blaik |

## 1956

| | | Record | Coach |
|---|---|---|---|
| 1. | Oklahoma | 10-0-0 | Bud Wilkinson |
| 2. | Tennessee | 10-0-0 | Bowden Wyatt |
| 3. | Iowa | 8-1-0 | Forest Evashevski |
| 4. | Georgia Tech | 9-1-0 | Bobby Dodd |
| 5. | Texas A&M | 9-0-1 | Bear Bryant |
| 6. | Miami (FL) | 8-1-1 | Andy Gustafson |
| 7. | Michigan | 7-2-0 | Bennie Oosterbaan |
| 8. | Syracuse | 7-1-0 | Ben Schwartzwalder |
| 9. | Michigan St | 7-2-0 | Duffy Daugherty |
| 10. | Oregon St | 7-2-1 | Tommy Prothro |
| 11. | Baylor | 8-2-0 | Sam Boyd |
| 12. | Minnesota | 6-1-2 | Murray Warmath |
| 13. | Pittsburgh | 7-2-1 | John Michelosen |
| 14. | TCU | 7-3-0 | Abe Martin |
| 15. | Ohio St | 6-3-0 | Woody Hayes |
| 16. | Navy | 6-1-2 | Eddie Erdelatz |
| 17. | Geo Washington | 7-1-1 | Gene Sherman |
| 18. | USC | 8-2-0 | Jess Hill |
| 19. | Clemson | 7-1-2 | Frank Howard |
| 20. | Colorado | 7-2-1 | Dallas Ward |
| | Penn St | 6-2-1 | Rip Engle |

## 1957

| | | Record | Coach |
|---|---|---|---|
| 1. | Auburn | 10-0-0 | Shug Jordan |
| 2. | #Ohio St | 8-1-0 | Woody Hayes |
| 3. | Michigan St | 8-1-0 | Duffy Daugherty |
| 4. | Oklahoma | 9-1-0 | Bud Wilkinson |
| 5. | Navy | 8-1-1 | Eddie Erdelatz |
| 6. | Iowa | 7-1-1 | Forest Evashevski |
| 7. | Mississippi | 8-1-1 | Johnny Vaught |
| 8. | Rice | 7-3-0 | Jess Neely |
| 9. | Texas A&M | 8-2-0 | Bear Bryant |
| 10. | Notre Dame | 7-3-0 | Terry Brennan |
| 11. | Texas | 6-3-1 | Darrell Royal |
| 12. | Arizona St | 10-0-0 | Dan Devine |
| 13. | Tennessee | 7-3-0 | Bowden Wyatt |
| 14. | Mississippi St | 6-2-1 | Wade Walker |
| 15. | North Carolina St | 7-1-2 | Earle Edwards |
| 16. | Duke | 6-2-2 | Bill Murray |

### 1957 *(Cont.)*

| | | Record | Coach |
|---|---|---|---|
| 17. | Florida | 6-2-1 | Bob Woodruff |
| 18. | Army | 7-2-0 | Red Blaik |
| 19. | Wisconsin | 6-3-0 | Milt Brunt |
| 20. | VMI | 9-0-1 | John McKenna |

#Selected No. 1 by UP.

### 1958

| | | Record | Coach |
|---|---|---|---|
| 1. | LSU | 10-0-0 | Paul Dietzel |
| 2. | Iowa | 7-1-1 | Forest Evashevski |
| 3. | Army | 8-0-1 | Red Blaik |
| 4. | Auburn | 9-0-1 | Shug Jordan |
| 5. | Oklahoma | 9-1-0 | Bud Wilkinson |
| 6. | Air Force | 9-0-1 | Ben Martin |
| 7. | Wisconsin | 7-1-1 | Milt Bruhn |
| 8. | Ohio St | 6-1-2 | Woody Hayes |
| 9. | Syracuse | 8-1-0 | Ben Schwartzwalder |
| 10. | TCU | 8-2-0 | Abe Martin |
| 11. | Mississippi | 8-2-0 | Johnny Vaught |
| 12. | Clemson | 8-2-0 | Frank Howard |
| 13. | Purdue | 6-1-2 | Jack Mollenkopf |
| 14. | Florida | 6-3-1 | Bob Woodruff |
| 15. | South Carolina | 7-3-0 | Warren Giese |
| 16. | California | 7-3-0 | Pete Elliott |
| 17. | Notre Dame | 6-4-0 | Terry Brennan |
| 18. | SMU | 6-4-0 | Bill Meek |
| 19. | Oklahoma St | 7-3-0 | Cliff Speegle |
| 20. | Rutgers | 8-1-0 | John Stiegman |

### 1959

| | | Record | Coach |
|---|---|---|---|
| 1. | Syracuse | 10-0-0 | Ben Schwartzwalder |
| 2. | Mississippi | 9-1-0 | Johnny Vaught |
| 3. | LSU | 9-1-0 | Paul Dietzel |
| 4. | Texas | 9-1-0 | Darrell Royal |
| 5. | Georgia | 9-1-0 | Wally Butts |
| 6. | Wisconsin | 7-2-0 | Milt Bruhn |
| 7. | TCU | 8-2-0 | Abe Martin |
| 8. | Washington | 9-1-0 | Jim Owens |
| 9. | Arkansas | 8-2-0 | Frank Broyles |
| 10. | Alabama | 7-1-2 | Bear Bryant |
| 11. | Clemson | 8-2-0 | Frank Howard |
| 12. | Penn St | 8-2-0 | Rip Engle |
| 13. | Illinois | 5-3-1 | Ray Eliot |
| 14. | USC | 8-2-0 | Don Clark |
| 15. | Oklahoma | 7-3-0 | Bud Wilkinson |
| 16. | Wyoming | 9-1-0 | Bob Devaney |
| 17. | Notre Dame | 5-5-0 | Joe Kuharich |
| 18. | Missouri | 6-4-0 | Dan Devine |
| 19. | Florida | 5-4-1 | Bob Woodruff |
| 20. | Pittsburgh | 6-4-0 | John Michelosen |

### 1960

| | | Record | Coach |
|---|---|---|---|
| 1. | Minnesota | 8-1-0 | Murray Warmath |
| 2. | Mississippi | 9-0-1 | Johnny Vaught |
| 3. | Iowa | 8-1-0 | Forest Evashevski |
| 4. | Navy | 9-1-0 | Wayne Hardin |
| 5. | Missouri | 9-1-0 | Dan Devine |
| 6. | Washington | 9-1-0 | Jim Owens |
| 7. | Arkansas | 8-2-0 | Frank Broyles |
| 8. | Ohio St | 7-2-0 | Woody Hayes |
| 9. | Alabama | 8-1-1 | Bear Bryant |

### 1960 *(Cont.)*

| | | Record | Coach |
|---|---|---|---|
| 10. | Duke | 7-3-0 | Bill Murray |
| 11. | Kansas | 7-2-1 | Jack Mitchell |
| 12. | Baylor | 8-2-0 | John Bridgers |
| 13. | Auburn | 8-2-0 | Shug Jordan |
| 14. | Yale | 9-0-0 | Jordan Oliver |
| 15. | Michigan St | 6-2-1 | Duffy Daugherty |
| 16. | Penn St | 6-3-0 | Rip Engle |
| 17. | New Mexico St | 10-0-0 | Warren Woodson |
| 18. | Florida | 8-2-0 | Ray Graves |
| 19. | Syracuse | 7-2-0 | Ben Schwartzwalder |
| | Purdue | 4-4-1 | Jack Mollenkopf |

### 1961

| | | Record | Coach |
|---|---|---|---|
| 1. | Alabama | 10-0-0 | Bear Bryant |
| 2. | Ohio St | 8-0-1 | Woody Hayes |
| 3. | Texas | 9-1-0 | Darrell Royal |
| 4. | LSU | 9-1-0 | Paul Dietzel |
| 5. | Mississippi | 9-1-0 | Johnny Vaught |
| 6. | Minnesota | 7-2-0 | Murray Warmath |
| 7. | Colorado | 9-1-0 | Sonny Grandelius |
| 8. | Michigan St | 7-2-0 | Duffy Daugherty |
| 9. | Arkansas | 8-2-0 | Frank Broyles |
| 10. | Utah St | 9-0-1 | John Ralston |
| 11. | Missouri | 7-2-1 | Dan Devine |
| 12. | Purdue | 6-3-0 | Jack Mollenkopf |
| 13. | Georgia Tech | 7-3-0 | Bobby Dodd |
| 14. | Syracuse | 7-3-0 | Ben Schwartzwalder |
| 15. | Rutgers | 9-0-0 | John Bateman |
| 16. | UCLA | 7-3-0 | Bill Barnes |
| 17. | Rice | 7-3-0 | Jess Neely |
| | Penn St | 7-3-0 | Rip Engle |
| | Arizona | 8-1-1 | Jim LaRue |
| 20. | Duke | 7-3-0 | Bill Murray |

### 1962

| | | Record | Coach |
|---|---|---|---|
| 1. | USC | 10-0-0 | John McKay |
| 2. | Wisconsin | 8-1-0 | Milt Bruhn |
| 3. | Mississippi | 9-0-0 | Johnny Vaught |
| 4. | Texas | 9-0-1 | Darrell Royal |
| 5. | Alabama | 9-1-0 | Bear Bryant |
| 6. | Arkansas | 9-1-0 | Frank Broyles |
| 7. | LSU | 8-1-1 | Charlie McClendon |
| 8. | Oklahoma | 8-2-0 | Bud Wilkinson |
| 9. | Penn St | 9-1-0 | Rip Engle |
| 10. | Minnesota | 6-2-1 | Murray Warmath |
| 11–20: UPI | | | |
| 11. | Georgia Tech | 7-2-1 | Bobby Dodd |
| 12. | Missouri | 7-1-2 | Dan Devine |
| 13. | Ohio St | 6-3-0 | Woody Hayes |
| 14. | Duke | 8-2-0 | Bill Murray |
| | Washington | 7-1-2 | Jim Owens |
| 16. | Northwestern | 7-2-0 | Ara Parseghian |
| | Oregon St | 8-2-0 | Tommy Prothro |
| 18. | Arizona St | 7-2-1 | Frank Kush |
| | Miami (FL) | 7-3-0 | Andy Gustafson |
| | Illinois | 2-7-0 | Pete Elliott |

### 1963

| | | Record | Coach |
|---|---|---|---|
| 1. | Texas | 10-0-0 | Darrell Royal |
| 2. | Navy | 9-1-0 | Wayne Hardin |
| 3. | Illinois | 7-1-1 | Pete Elliott |
| 4. | Pittsburgh | 9-1-0 | John Michelosen |
| 5. | Auburn | 9-1-0 | Shug Jordan |
| 6. | Nebraska | 9-1-0 | Bob Devaney |
| 7. | Mississippi | 7-0-2 | Johnny Vaught |
| 8. | Alabama | 8-2-0 | Bear Bryant |
| 9. | Oklahoma | 8-2-0 | Bud Wilkinson |
| 10. | Michigan St | 6-2-1 | Duffy Daugherty |
| 11–20: UPI | | | |
| 11. | Mississippi St | 6-2-2 | Paul Davis |
| 12. | Syracuse | 8-2-0 | Ben Schwartzwalder |
| 13. | Arizona St | 8-1-0 | Frank Kush |
| 14. | Memphis St | 9-0-1 | Billy J. Murphy |
| 15. | Washington | 6-4-0 | Jim Owens |
| 16. | Penn St | 7-3-0 | Rip Engle |
| | USC | 7-3-0 | John McKay |
| | Missouri | 7-3-0 | Dan Devine |
| 19. | North Carolina | 8-2-0 | Jim Hickey |
| 20. | Baylor | 7-3-0 | John Bridgers |

### 1964

| | | Record | Coach |
|---|---|---|---|
| 1. | Alabama | 10-0-0 | Bear Bryant |
| 2. | Arkansas | 10-0-0 | Frank Broyles |
| 3. | Notre Dame | 9-1-0 | Ara Parseghian |
| 4. | Michigan | 8-1-0 | Bump Elliott |
| 5. | Texas | 9-1-0 | Darrell Royal |
| 6. | Nebraska | 9-1-0 | Bob Devaney |
| 7. | LSU | 7-2-1 | Charlie McClendon |
| 8. | Oregon St | 8-2-0 | Tommy Prothro |
| 9. | Ohio St | 7-2-0 | Woody Hayes |
| 10. | USC | 7-3-0 | John McKay |
| 11–20: UPI | | | |
| 11. | Florida St | 8-1-1 | Bill Peterson |
| 12. | Syracuse | 7-3-0 | Ben Schwartzwalder |
| 13. | Princeton | 9-0-0 | Dick Colman |
| 14. | Penn St | 6-4-0 | Rip Engle |
| | Utah | 8-2-0 | Ray Nagel |
| 16. | Illinois | 6-3-0 | Pete Elliott |
| | New Mexico | 9-2-0 | Bill Weeks |
| 18. | Tulsa | 8-2-0 | Glenn Dobbs |
| 19. | Missouri | 6-3-1 | Dan Devine |
| 20. | Mississippi | 5-4-1 | Johnny Vaught |
| | Michigan St | 4-5-1 | Duffy Daugherty |

### 1965

| | | Record | Coach |
|---|---|---|---|
| 1. | Alabama | 9-1-1 | Bear Bryant |
| 2. | #Michigan St | 10-1-0 | Duffy Daugherty |
| 3. | Arkansas | 10-1-0 | Frank Broyles |
| 4. | UCLA | 8-2-1 | Tommy Prothro |
| 5. | Nebraska | 10-1-0 | Bob Devaney |
| 6. | Missouri | 8-2-1 | Dan Devine |
| 7. | Tennessee | 8-1-2 | Doug Dickey |
| 8. | LSU | 8-3-0 | Charlie McClendon |
| 9. | Notre Dame | 7-2-1 | Ara Parseghian |
| 10. | USC | 7-2-1 | John McKay |
| 11–20: UPI | | | |
| 11. | Texas Tech | 8-2-0 | J.T. King |
| 12. | Ohio St | 7-2-0 | Woody Hayes |

### 1965 *(Cont.)*

| | | Record | Coach |
|---|---|---|---|
| 13. | Florida | 7-3-0 | Ray Graves |
| 14. | Purdue | 7-2-1 | Jack Mollenkopf |
| 15. | Georgia | 6-4-0 | Vince Dooley |
| 16. | Tulsa | 8-2-0 | Glenn Dobbs |
| 17. | Mississippi | 6-4-0 | Johnny Vaught |
| 18. | Kentucky | 6-4-0 | Charlie Bradshaw |
| 19. | Syracuse | 7-3-0 | Ben Schwartzwalder |
| 20. | Colorado | 6-2-2 | Eddie Crowder |

#Selected No. 1 by UPI.

### 1966

| | | Record | Coach |
|---|---|---|---|
| 1. | Notre Dame | 9-0-1 | Ara Parseghian |
| 2. | Michigan St | 9-0-1 | Duffy Daugherty |
| 3. | Alabama | 10-0-0 | Bear Bryant |
| 4. | Georgia | 9-1-0 | Vince Dooley |
| 5. | UCLA | 9-1-0 | Tommy Prothro |
| 6. | Nebraska | 9-1-0 | Bob Devaney |
| 7. | Purdue | 8-2-0 | Jack Mollenkopf |
| 8. | Georgia Tech | 9-1-0 | Bobby Dodd |
| 9. | Miami (FL) | 7-2-1 | Charlie Tate |
| 10. | SMU | 8-2-0 | Hayden Fry |
| 11–20: UPI | | | |
| 11. | Florida | 8-2-0 | Ray Graves |
| 12. | Mississippi | 8-2-0 | Johnny Vaught |
| 13. | Arkansas | 8-2-0 | Frank Broyles |
| 14. | Tennessee | 7-3-0 | Doug Dickey |
| 15. | Wyoming | 9-1-0 | Lloyd Eaton |
| 16. | Syracuse | 8-2-0 | Ben Schwartzwalder |
| 17. | Houston | 8-2-0 | Bill Yeoman |
| 18. | USC | 7-3-0 | John McKay |
| 19. | Oregon St | 7-3-0 | Dee Andros |
| 20. | Virginia Tech | 8-1-1 | Jerry Claiborne |

### 1967

| | | Record | Coach |
|---|---|---|---|
| 1. | USC | 9-1-0 | John McKay |
| 2. | Tennessee | 9-1-0 | Doug Dickey |
| 3. | Oklahoma | 9-1-0 | Chuck Fairbanks |
| 4. | Indiana | 9-1-0 | John Pont |
| 5. | Notre Dame | 8-2-0 | Ara Parseghian |
| 6. | Wyoming | 10-0-0 | Lloyd Eaton |
| 7. | Oregon St | 7-2-1 | Dee Andros |
| 8. | Alabama | 8-1-1 | Bear Bryant |
| 9. | Purdue | 8-2-0 | Jack Mollenkopf |
| 10. | Penn St | 8-2-0 | Joe Paterno |
| 11–20: UPI† | | | |
| 11. | UCLA | 7-2-1 | Tommy Prothro |
| 12. | Syracuse | 8-2-0 | Ben Schwartzwalder |
| 13. | Colorado | 8-2-0 | Eddie Crowder |
| 14. | Minnesota | 8-2-0 | Murray Warmath |
| 15. | Florida St | 7-2-1 | Bill Peterson |
| 16. | Miami (FL) | 7-3-0 | Charlie Tate |
| 17. | North Carolina St | 8-2-0 | Earle Edwards |
| 18. | Georgia | 7-3-0 | Vince Dooley |
| 19. | Houston | 9-2-0 | Bill Yeoman |
| 20. | Arizona St | 8-2-0 | Frank Kush |

†UPI ranked Penn St 11th and did not rank Alabama, which was on probation.

### 1968

| | | Record | Coach |
|---|---|---|---|
| 1. | Ohio St | 10-0-0 | Woody Hayes |
| 2. | Penn St | 11-0-0 | Joe Paterno |
| 3. | Texas | 9-1-1 | Darrell Royal |
| 4. | USC | 9-1-1 | John McKay |
| 5. | Notre Dame | 7-2-1 | Ara Parseghian |
| 6. | Arkansas | 10-1-0 | Frank Broyles |
| 7. | Kansas | 9-2-0 | Pepper Rodgers |
| 8. | Georgia | 8-1-2 | Vince Dooley |
| 9. | Missouri | 8-3-0 | Dan Devine |
| 10. | Purdue | 8-2-0 | Jack Mollenkopf |
| 11. | Oklahoma | 7-4-0 | Chuck Fairbanks |
| 12. | Michigan | 8-2-0 | Bump Elliott |
| 13. | Tennessee | 8-2-1 | Doug Dickey |
| 14. | SMU | 8-3-0 | Hayden Fry |
| 15. | Oregon St | 7-3-0 | Dee Andros |
| 16. | Auburn | 7-4-0 | Shug Jordan |
| 17. | Alabama | 8-3-0 | Bear Bryant |
| 18. | Houston | 6-2-2 | Bill Yeoman |
| 19. | LSU | 8-3-0 | Charlie McClendon |
| 20. | Ohio | 10-1-0 | Bill Hess |

### 1969

| | | Record | Coach |
|---|---|---|---|
| 1. | Texas | 11-0-0 | Darrell Royal |
| 2. | Penn St | 11-0-0 | Joe Paterno |
| 3. | USC | 10-0-1 | John McKay |
| 4. | Ohio St | 8-1-0 | Woody Hayes |
| 5. | Notre Dame | 8-2-1 | Ara Parseghian |
| 6. | Missouri | 9-2-0 | Dan Devine |
| 7. | Arkansas | 9-2-0 | Frank Broyles |
| 8. | Mississippi | 8-3-0 | Johnny Vaught |
| 9. | Michigan | 8-3-0 | Bo Schembechler |
| 10. | LSU | 9-1-0 | Charlie McClendon |
| 11. | Nebraska | 9-2-0 | Bob Devaney |
| 12. | Houston | 9-2-0 | Bill Yeoman |
| 13. | UCLA | 8-1-1 | Tommy Prothro |
| 14. | Florida | 9-1-1 | Ray Graves |
| 15. | Tennessee | 9-2-0 | Doug Dickey |
| 16. | Colorado | 8-3-0 | Eddie Crowder |
| 17. | W Virginia | 10-0-1 | Jim Carlen |
| 18. | Purdue | 8-2-0 | Jack Mollenkopf |
| 19. | Stanford | 7-2-1 | John Ralston |
| 20. | Auburn | 8-3-0 | Shug Jordan |

### 1970

| | | Record | Coach |
|---|---|---|---|
| 1. | Nebraska | 11-0-1 | Bob Devaney |
| 2. | Notre Dame | 10-1-0 | Ara Parseghian |
| 3. | #Texas | 10-1-0 | Darrell Royal |
| 4. | Tennessee | 11-0-1 | Bill Battle |
| 5. | Ohio St | 9-1-0 | Woody Hayes |
| 6. | Arizona St | 11-0-0 | Frank Kush |
| 7. | LSU | 9-3-0 | Charlie McClendon |
| 8. | Stanford | 9-3-0 | John Ralston |
| 9. | Michigan | 9-1-0 | Bo Schembechler |
| 10. | Auburn | 9-2-0 | Shug Jordan |
| 11. | Arkansas | 9-2-0 | Frank Broyles |
| 12. | Toledo | 12-0-0 | Frank Lauterbur |
| 13. | Georgia Tech | 9-3-0 | Bud Carson |
| 14. | Dartmouth | 9-0-0 | Bob Blackman |
| 15. | USC | 6-4-1 | John McKay |

### 1970 *(Cont.)*

| | | Record | Coach |
|---|---|---|---|
| 16. | Air Force | 9-3-0 | Ben Martin |
| 17. | Tulane | 8-4-0 | Jim Pittman |
| 18. | Penn St | 7-3-0 | Joe Paterno |
| 19. | Houston | 8-3-0 | Bill Yeoman |
| 20. | Oklahoma | 7-4-1 | Chuck Fairbanks |
| | Mississippi | 7-4-0 | Johnny Vaught |

#Selected No. 1 by UPI.

### 1971

| | | Record | Coach |
|---|---|---|---|
| 1. | Nebraska | 13-0-0 | Bob Devaney |
| 2. | Oklahoma | 11-1-0 | Chuck Fairbanks |
| 3. | Colorado | 10-2-0 | Eddie Crowder |
| 4. | Alabama | 11-1-0 | Bear Bryant |
| 5. | Penn St | 11-1-0 | Joe Paterno |
| 6. | Michigan | 11-1-0 | Bo Schembechler |
| 7. | Georgia | 11-1-0 | Vince Dooley |
| 8. | Arizona St | 11-1-0 | Frank Kush |
| 9. | Tennessee | 10-2-0 | Bill Battle |
| 10. | Stanford | 9-3-0 | John Ralston |
| 11. | LSU | 9-3-0 | Charlie McClendon |
| 12. | Auburn | 9-2-0 | Shug Jordan |
| 13. | Notre Dame | 8-2-0 | Ara Parseghian |
| 14. | Toledo | 12-0-0 | John Murphy |
| 15. | Mississippi | 10-2-0 | Billy Kinard |
| 16. | Arkansas | 8-3-1 | Frank Broyles |
| 17. | Houston | 9-3-0 | Bill Yeoman |
| 18. | Texas | 8-3-0 | Darrell Royal |
| 19. | Washington | 8-3-0 | Jim Owens |
| 20. | USC | 6-4-1 | John McKay |

### 1972

| | | Record | Coach |
|---|---|---|---|
| 1. | USC | 12-0-0 | John McKay |
| 2. | Oklahoma | 11-1-0 | Chuck Fairbanks |
| 3. | Texas | 10-1-0 | Darrell Royal |
| 4. | Nebraska | 9-2-1 | Bob Devaney |
| 5. | Auburn | 10-1-0 | Shug Jordan |
| 6. | Michigan | 10-1-0 | Bo Schembechler |
| 7. | Alabama | 10-2-0 | Bear Bryant |
| 8. | Tennessee | 10-2-0 | Bill Battle |
| 9. | Ohio St | 9-2-0 | Woody Hayes |
| 10. | Penn St | 10-2-0 | Joe Paterno |
| 11. | LSU | 9-2-1 | Charlie McClendon |
| 12. | North Carolina | 11-1-0 | Bill Dooley |
| 13. | Arizona St | 10-2-0 | Frank Kush |
| 14. | Notre Dame | 8-3-0 | Ara Parseghian |
| 15. | UCLA | 8-3-0 | Pepper Rodgers |
| 16. | Colorado | 8-4-0 | Eddie Crowder |
| 17. | North Carolina St | 8-3-1 | Lou Holtz |
| 18. | Louisville | 9-1-0 | Lee Corso |
| 19. | Washington St | 7-4-0 | Jim Sweeney |
| 20. | Georgia Tech | 7-4-1 | Bill Fulch |

### 1973

| | | Record | Coach |
|---|---|---|---|
| 1. | Notre Dame | 11-0-0 | Ara Parseghian |
| 2. | Ohio St | 10-0-1 | Woody Hayes |
| 3. | Oklahoma | 10-0-1 | Barry Switzer |
| 4. | #Alabama | 11-1-0 | Bear Bryant |
| 5. | Penn St | 12-0-0 | Joe Paterno |
| 6. | Michigan | 10-0-1 | Bo Schembechler |

## 1973 (Cont.)

| | | Record | Coach |
|---|---|---|---|
| 7. | Nebraska | 9-2-1 | Tom Osborne |
| 8. | USC | 9-2-1 | John McKay |
| 9. | Arizona St | 11-1-0 | Frank Kush |
| | Houston | 11-1-0 | Bill Yeoman |
| 11. | Texas Tech | 11-1-0 | Jim Carlen |
| 12. | UCLA | 9-2-0 | Pepper Rodgers |
| 13. | LSU | 9-3-0 | Charlie McClendon |
| 14. | Texas | 8-3-0 | Darrell Royal |
| 15. | Miami (OH) | 11-0-0 | Bill Mallory |
| 16. | North Carolina St | 9-3-0 | Lou Holtz |
| 17. | Missouri | 8-4-0 | Al Onofrio |
| 18. | Kansas | 7-4-1 | Don Fambrough |
| 19. | Tennessee | 8-4-0 | Bill Battle |
| 20. | Maryland | 8-4-0 | Jerry Claiborne |
| | Tulane | 9-3-0 | Bennie Ellender |

#Selected No. 1 by UPI.

## 1974

| | | Record | Coach |
|---|---|---|---|
| 1. | Oklahoma | 11-0-0 | Barry Switzer |
| 2. | #USC | 10-1-1 | John McKay |
| 3. | Michigan | 10-1-0 | Bo Schembechler |
| 4. | Ohio St | 10-2-0 | Woody Hayes |
| 5. | Alabama | 11-1-0 | Bear Bryant |
| 6. | Notre Dame | 10-2-0 | Ara Parseghian |
| 7. | Penn St | 10-2-0 | Joe Paterno |
| 8. | Auburn | 10-2-0 | Shug Jordan |
| 9. | Nebraska | 9-3-0 | Tom Osborne |
| 10. | Miami (Ohio) | 10-0-1 | Dick Crum |
| 11. | North Carolina St | 9-2-1 | Lou Holtz |
| 12. | Michigan St | 7-3-1 | Denny Stolz |
| 13. | Maryland | 8-4-0 | Jerry Claiborne |
| 14. | Baylor | 8-4-0 | Grant Teaff |
| 15. | Florida | 8-4-0 | Doug Dickey |
| 16. | Texas A&M | 8-3-0 | Emory Ballard |
| 17. | Mississippi St | 9-3-0 | Bob Tyler |
| | Texas | 8-4-0 | Darrell Royal |
| 19. | Houston | 8-3-1 | Bill Yeoman |
| 20. | Tennessee | 7-3-2 | Bill Battle |

#Selected No. 1 by UPI

## 1975

| | | Record | Coach |
|---|---|---|---|
| 1. | Oklahoma | 11-1-0 | Barry Switzer |
| 2. | Arizona St | 12-0-0 | Frank Kush |
| 3. | Alabama | 11-1-0 | Bear Bryant |
| 4. | Ohio St | 11-1-0 | Woody Hayes |
| 5. | UCLA | 9-2-1 | Dick Vermeil |
| 6. | Texas | 10-2-0 | Darrell Royal |
| 7. | Arkansas | 10-2-0 | Frank Broyles |
| 8. | Michigan | 8-2-2 | Bo Schembechler |
| 9. | Nebraska | 10-2-0 | Tom Osborne |
| 10. | Penn St | 9-3-0 | Joe Paterno |
| 11. | Texas A&M | 10-2-0 | Emory Bellard |
| 12. | Miami (OH) | 11-1-0 | Dick Crum |
| 13. | Maryland | 9-2-1 | Jerry Claiborne |
| 14. | California | 8-3-0 | Mike White |
| 15. | Pittsburgh | 8-4-0 | Johnny Majors |
| 16. | Colorado | 9-3-0 | Bill Mallory |
| 17. | USC | 8-4-0 | John McKay |
| 18. | Arizona | 9-2-0 | Jim Young |
| 19. | Georgia | 9-3-0 | Vince Dooley |
| 20. | W Virginia | 9-3-0 | Bobby Bowden |

## 1976

| | | Record | Coach |
|---|---|---|---|
| 1. | Pittsburgh | 12-0-0 | Johnny Majors |
| 2. | USC | 11-1-0 | John Robinson |
| 3. | Michigan | 10-2-0 | Bo Schembechler |
| 4. | Houston | 10-2-0 | Bill Yeoman |
| 5. | Oklahoma | 9-2-1 | Barry Switzer |
| 6. | Ohio St | 9-2-1 | Woody Hayes |
| 7. | Texas A&M | 10-2-0 | Emory Bellard |
| 8. | Maryland | 11-1-0 | Jerry Claiborne |
| 9. | Nebraska | 9-3-1 | Tom Osborne |
| 10. | Georgia | 10-2-0 | Vince Dooley |
| 11. | Alabama | 9-3-0 | Bear Bryant |
| 12. | Notre Dame | 9-3-0 | Dan Devine |
| 13. | Texas Tech | 10-2-0 | Steve Sloan |
| 14. | Oklahoma St | 9-3-0 | Jim Stanley |
| 15. | UCLA | 9-2-1 | Terry Donahue |
| 16. | Colorado | 8-4-0 | Bill Mallory |
| 17. | Rutgers | 11-0-0 | Frank Burns |
| 18. | Kentucky | 9-3-0 | Fran Curci |
| 19. | Iowa St | 8-3-0 | Earle Bruce |
| 20. | Mississippi St | 9-2-0 | Bob Tyler |

## 1977

| | | Record | Coach |
|---|---|---|---|
| 1. | Notre Dame | 11-1-0 | Dan Devine |
| 2. | Alabama | 11-1-0 | Bear Bryant |
| 3. | Arkansas | 11-1-0 | Lou Holtz |
| 4. | Texas | 11-1-0 | Fred Akers |
| 5. | Penn St | 11-1-0 | Joe Paterno |
| 6. | Kentucky | 10-1-0 | Fran Curci |
| 7. | Oklahoma | 10-2-0 | Barry Switzer |
| 8. | Pittsburgh | 9-2-1 | Jackie Sherrill |
| 9. | Michigan | 10-2-0 | Bo Schembechler |
| 10. | Washington | 10-2-0 | Don James |
| 11. | Ohio St | 9-3-0 | Woody Hayes |
| 12. | Nebraska | 9-3-0 | Tom Osborne |
| 13. | USC | 8-4-0 | John Robinson |
| 14. | Florida St | 10-2-0 | Bobby Bowden |
| 15. | Stanford | 9-3-0 | Bill Walsh |
| 16. | San Diego St | 10-1-0 | Claude Gilbert |
| 17. | North Carolina | 8-3-1 | Bill Dooley |
| 18. | Arizona St | 9-3-0 | Frank Kush |
| 19. | Clemson | 8-3-1 | Charley Pell |
| 20. | BYU | 9-2-0 | LaVell Edwards |

## 1978

| | | Record | Coach |
|---|---|---|---|
| 1. | Alabama | 11-1-0 | Bear Bryant |
| 2. | #USC | 12-1-0 | John Robinson |
| 3. | Oklahoma | 11-1-0 | Barry Switzer |
| 4. | Penn St | 11-1-0 | Joe Paterno |
| 5. | Michigan | 10-2-0 | Bo Schembechler |
| 6. | Clemson | 11-1-0 | Charley Pell |
| 7. | Notre Dame | 9-3-0 | Dan Devine |
| 8. | Nebraska | 9-3-0 | Tom Osborne |
| 9. | Texas | 9-3-0 | Fred Akers |
| 10. | Houston | 9-3-0 | Bill Yeoman |
| 11. | Arkansas | 9-2-1 | Lou Holtz |
| 12. | Michigan St | 8-3-0 | Darryl Rogers |
| 13. | Purdue | 9-2-1 | Jim Young |
| 14. | UCLA | 8-3-1 | Terry Donahue |
| 15. | Missouri | 8-4-0 | Warren Powers |
| 16. | Georgia | 9-2-1 | Vince Dooley |
| 17. | Stanford | 8-4-0 | Bill Walsh |
| 18. | North Carolina St | 9-3-0 | Bo Rein |
| 19. | Texas A&M | 8-4-0 | Emory Bellard (4–2) |
| | | | Tom Wilson (4–2) |
| 20. | Maryland | 9-3-0 | Jerry Claiborne |

#Selected No. 1 by UPI.

## 1979

| | | Record | Coach |
|---|---|---|---|
| 1. | Alabama | 12-0-0 | Bear Bryant |
| 2. | USC | 11-0-1 | John Robinson |
| 3. | Oklahoma | 11-1-0 | Barry Switzer |
| 4. | Ohio St | 11-1-0 | Earle Bruce |
| 5. | Houston | 11-1-0 | Bill Yeoman |
| 6. | Florida St | 11-1-0 | Bobby Bowden |
| 7. | Pittsburgh | 11-1-0 | Jackie Sherrill |
| 8. | Arkansas | 10-2-0 | Lou Holtz |
| 9. | Nebraska | 10-2-0 | Tom Osborne |
| 10. | Purdue | 10-2-0 | Jim Young |
| 11. | Washington | 10-1-0 | Don James |
| 12. | Texas | 9-3-0 | Fred Akers |
| 13. | BYU | 11-1-0 | LaVell Edwards |
| 14. | Baylor | 8-4-0 | Grant Teaff |
| 15. | North Carolina | 8-3-1 | Dick Crum |
| 16. | Auburn | 8-3-0 | Doug Barfield |
| 17. | Temple | 10-2-0 | Wayne Hardin |
| 18. | Michigan | 8-4-0 | Bo Schembechler |
| 19. | Indiana | 8-4-0 | Lee Corso |
| 20. | Penn St | 8-4-0 | Joe Paterno |

## 1980

| | | Record | Coach |
|---|---|---|---|
| 1. | Georgia | 12-0-0 | Vince Dooley |
| 2. | Pittsburgh | 11-1-0 | Jackie Sherrill |
| 3. | Oklahoma | 10-2-0 | Barry Switzer |
| 4. | Michigan | 10-2-0 | Bo Schembechler |
| 5. | Florida St | 10-2-0 | Bobby Bowden |
| 6. | Alabama | 10-2-0 | Bear Bryant |
| 7. | Nebraska | 10-2-0 | Tom Osborne |
| 8. | Penn St | 10-2-0 | Joe Paterno |
| 9. | Notre Dame | 9-2-1 | Dan Devine |
| 10. | North Carolina | 11-1-0 | Dick Crum |
| 11. | USC | 8-2-1 | John Robinson |
| 12. | BYU | 12-1-0 | LaVell Edwards |
| 13. | UCLA | 9-2-0 | Terry Donahue |
| 14. | Baylor | 10-2-0 | Grant Teaff |
| 15. | Ohio St | 9-3-0 | Earle Bruce |
| 16. | Washington | 9-3-0 | Don James |
| 17. | Purdue | 9-3-0 | Jim Young |
| 18. | Miami (FL) | 9-3-0 | H. Schnellenberger |
| 19. | Mississippi St | 9-3-0 | Emory Bellard |
| 20. | SMU | 8-4-0 | Ron Meyer |

## 1981

| | | Record | Coach |
|---|---|---|---|
| 1. | Clemson | 12-0-0 | Danny Ford |
| 2. | Texas | 10-1-1 | Fred Akers |
| 3. | Penn St | 10-2-0 | Joe Paterno |
| 4. | Pittsburgh | 11-1-0 | Jackie Sherrill |
| 5. | SMU | 10-1-0 | Ron Meyer |
| 6. | Georgia | 10-2-0 | Vince Dooley |
| 7. | Alabama | 9-2-1 | Bear Bryant |
| 8. | Miami (FL) | 9-2-0 | H. Schnellenberger |
| 9. | North Carolina | 10-2-0 | Dick Crum |
| 10. | Washington | 10-2-0 | Don James |
| 11. | Nebraska | 9-3-0 | Tom Osborne |
| 12. | Michigan | 9-3-0 | Bo Schembechler |
| 13. | BYU | 11-2-0 | LaVell Edwards |
| 14. | USC | 9-3-0 | John Robinson |

## 1981 (Cont.)

| | | Record | Coach |
|---|---|---|---|
| 15. | Ohio St | 9-3-0 | Earle Bruce |
| 16. | Arizona St | 9-2-0 | Darryl Rogers |
| 17. | W Virginia | 9-3-0 | Don Nehlen |
| 18. | Iowa | 8-4-0 | Hayden Fry |
| 19. | Missouri | 8-4-0 | Warren Powers |
| 20. | Oklahoma | 7-4-1 | Barry Switzer |

## 1982

| | | Record | Coach |
|---|---|---|---|
| 1. | Penn St | 11-1-0 | Joe Paterno |
| 2. | SMU | 11-0-1 | Bobby Collins |
| 3. | Nebraska | 12-1-0 | Tom Osborne |
| 4. | Georgia | 11-1-0 | Vince Dooley |
| 5. | UCLA | 10-1-1 | Terry Donahue |
| 6. | Arizona St | 10-2-0 | Darryl Rogers |
| 7. | Washington | 10-2-0 | Don James |
| 8. | Clemson | 9-1-1 | Danny Ford |
| 9. | Arkansas | 9-2-1 | Lou Holtz |
| 10. | Pittsburgh | 9-3-0 | Foge Fazio |
| 11. | LSU | 8-3-1 | Jerry Stovall |
| 12. | Ohio St | 9-3-0 | Earle Bruce |
| 13. | Florida St | 9-3-0 | Bobby Bowden |
| 14. | Auburn | 9-3-0 | Pat Dye |
| 15. | USC | 8-3-0 | John Robinson |
| 16. | Oklahoma | 8-4-0 | Barry Switzer |
| 17. | Texas | 9-3-0 | Fred Akers |
| 18. | North Carolina | 8-4-0 | Dick Crum |
| 19. | W Virginia | 9-3-0 | Don Nehlen |
| 20. | Maryland | 8-4-0 | Bobby Ross |

## 1983

| | | Record | Coach |
|---|---|---|---|
| 1. | Miami (Fla.) | 11-1-0 | H. Schnellenberger |
| 2. | Nebraska | 12-1-0 | Tom Osborne |
| 3. | Auburn | 11-1-0 | Pat Dye |
| 4. | Georgia | 10-1-1 | Vince Dooley |
| 5. | Texas | 11-1-0 | Fred Akers |
| 6. | Florida | 9-2-1 | Charlie Pell |
| 7. | BYU | 11-1-0 | LaVell Edwards |
| 8. | Michigan | 9-3-0 | Bo Schembechler |
| 9. | Ohio St | 9-3-0 | Earle Bruce |
| 10. | Illinois | 10-2-0 | Mike White |
| 11. | Clemson | 9-1-1 | Danny Ford |
| 12. | SMU | 10-2-0 | Bobby Collins |
| 13. | Air Force | 10-2-0 | Ken Hatfield |
| 14. | Iowa | 9-3-0 | Hayden Fry |
| 15. | Alabama | 8-4-0 | Ray Perkins |
| 16. | W Virginia | 9-3-0 | Don Nehlen |
| 17. | UCLA | 7-4-1 | Terry Donahue |
| 18. | Pittsburgh | 8-3-1 | Foge Fazio |
| 19. | Boston College | 9-3-0 | Jack Bicknell |
| 20. | E Carolina | 8-3-0 | Ed Emory |

## 1984

| | | Record | Coach |
|---|---|---|---|
| 1. | BYU | 13-0-0 | LaVell Edwards |
| 2. | Washington | 11-1-0 | Don James |
| 3. | Florida | 9-1-1 | Chas Pell (0-1-1) Galen Hall (9-0) |

## 1984 *(Cont.)*

| | | Record | Coach |
|---|---|---|---|
| 4. | Nebraska | 10-2-0 | Tom Osborne |
| 5. | Boston College | 10-2-0 | Jack Bicknell |
| 6. | Oklahoma | 9-2-1 | Barry Switzer |
| 7. | Oklahoma St | 10-2-0 | Pat Jones |
| 8. | SMU | 10-2-0 | Bobby Collins |
| 9. | UCLA | 9-3-0 | Terry Donahue |
| 10. | USC | 10-3-0 | Ted Tollner |
| 11. | South Carolina | 10-2-0 | Joe Morrison |
| 12. | Maryland | 9-3-0 | Bobby Ross |
| 13. | Ohio St | 9-3-0 | Earle Bruce |
| 14. | Auburn | 9-4-0 | Pat Dye |
| 15. | LSU | 8-3-1 | Bill Arnsparger |
| 16. | Iowa | 8-4-1 | Hayden Fry |
| 17. | Florida St | 7-3-2 | Bobby Bowden |
| 18. | Miami (Fla.) | 8-5-0 | Jimmy Johnson |
| 19. | Kentucky | 9-3-0 | Jerry Claiborne |
| 20. | Virginia | 8-2-2 | George Welsh |

## 1985

| | | Record | Coach |
|---|---|---|---|
| 1. | Oklahoma | 11-1-0 | Barry Switzer |
| 2. | Michigan | 10-1-1 | Bo Schembechler |
| 3. | Penn St | 11-1-0 | Joe Paterno |
| 4. | Tennessee | 9-1-2 | Johnny Majors |
| 5. | Florida | 9-1-1 | Galen Hall |
| 6. | Texas A&M | 10-2-0 | Jackie Sherrill |
| 7. | UCLA | 9-2-1 | Terry Donahue |
| 8. | Air Force | 12-1-0 | Fisher DeBerry |
| 9. | Miami (Fla.) | 10-2-0 | Jimmy Johnson |
| 10. | Iowa | 10-2-0 | Hayden Fry |
| 11. | Nebraska | 9-3-0 | Tom Osborne |
| 12. | Arkansas | 10-2-0 | Ken Hatfield |
| 13. | Alabama | 9-2-1 | Ray Perkins |
| 14. | Ohio St | 9-3-0 | Earle Bruce |
| 15. | Florida St | 9-3-0 | Bobby Bowden |
| 16. | BYU | 11-3-0 | LaVell Edwards |
| 17. | Baylor | 9-3-0 | Grant Teaff |
| 18. | Maryland | 9-3-0 | Bobby Ross |
| 19. | Georgia Tech. | 9-2-1 | Bill Curry |
| 20. | LSU | 9-2-1 | Bill Arnsparger |

## 1986

| | | Record | Coach |
|---|---|---|---|
| 1. | Penn St | 12-0-0 | Joe Paterno |
| 2. | Miami (Fla.) | 11-1-0 | Jimmy Johnson |
| 3. | Oklahoma | 11-1-0 | Barry Switzer |
| 4. | Arizona St | 10-1-1 | John Cooper |
| 5. | Nebraska | 10-2-0 | Tom Osborne |
| 6. | Auburn | 10-2-0 | Pat Dye |
| 7. | Ohio St | 10-3-0 | Earle Bruce |
| 8. | Michigan | 11-2-0 | Bo Schembechler |
| 9. | Alabama | 10-3-0 | Ray Perkins |
| 10. | LSU | 9-3-0 | Bill Arnsparger |
| 11. | Arizona | 9-3-0 | Larry Smith |
| 12. | Baylor | 9-3-0 | Grant Teaff |
| 13. | Texas A&M | 9-3-0 | Jackie Sherrill |
| 14. | UCLA | 8-3-1 | Terry Donahue |
| 15. | Arkansas | 9-3-0 | Ken Hatfield |
| 16. | Iowa | 9-3-0 | Hayden Fry |
| 17. | Clemson | 8-2-2 | Danny Ford |

## 1986 *(Cont.)*

| | | Record | Coach |
|---|---|---|---|
| 18. | Washington | 8-3-1 | Don James |
| 19. | Boston College | 9-3-0 | Jack Bicknell |
| 20. | Virginia Tech. | 9-2-1 | Bill Dooley |

## 1987

| | | Record | Coach |
|---|---|---|---|
| 1. | Miami (Fla.) | 12-0-0 | Jimmy Johnson |
| 2. | Florida St | 11-1-0 | Bobby Bowden |
| 3. | Oklahoma | 11-1-0 | Barry Switzer |
| 4. | Syracuse | 11-0-1 | Dick MacPherson |
| 5. | LSU | 10-1-1 | Mike Archer |
| 6. | Nebraska | 10-2-0 | Tom Osborne |
| 7. | Auburn | 9-1-2 | Pat Dye |
| 8. | Michigan St | 9-2-1 | George Perles |
| 9. | UCLA | 10-2-0 | Terry Donahue |
| 10. | Texas A&M | 10-2-0 | Jackie Sherrill |
| 11. | Oklahoma St | 10-2-0 | Pat Jones |
| 12. | Clemson | 10-2-0 | Danny Ford |
| 13. | Georgia | 9-3-0 | Vince Dooley |
| 14. | Tennessee | 10-2-1 | Johnny Majors |
| 15. | South Carolina | 8-4-0 | Joe Morrison |
| 16. | Iowa | 10-3-0 | Hayden Fry |
| 17. | Notre Dame | 8-4-0 | Lou Holtz |
| 18. | USC | 8-4-0 | Larry Smith |
| 19. | Michigan | 8-4-0 | Bo Schembechler |
| 20. | Arizona St | 7-4-1 | John Cooper |

## 1988

| | | Record | Coach |
|---|---|---|---|
| 1. | Notre Dame | 12-0-0 | Lou Holtz |
| 2. | Miami (Fla.) | 11-1-0 | Jimmy Johnson |
| 3. | Florida St | 11-1-0 | Bobby Bowden |
| 4. | Michigan | 9-2-1 | Bo Schembechler |
| 5. | West Virginia | 11-1-0 | Don Nehlen |
| 6. | UCLA | 10-2-0 | Terry Donahue |
| 7. | USC | 10-2-0 | Larry Smith |
| 8. | Auburn | 10-2-0 | Pat Dye |
| 9. | Clemson | 10-2-0 | Danny Ford |
| 10. | Nebraska | 11-2-0 | Tom Osborne |
| 11. | Oklahoma St | 10-2-0 | Pat Jones |
| 12. | Arkansas | 10-2-0 | Ken Hatfield |
| 13. | Syracuse | 10-2-0 | Dick MacPherson |
| 14. | Oklahoma | 9-3-0 | Barry Switzer |
| 15. | Georgia | 9-3-0 | Vince Dooley |
| 16. | Washington St | 9-3-0 | Dennis Erickson |
| 17. | Alabama | 9-3-0 | Bill Curry |
| 18. | Houston | 9-3-0 | Jack Pardee |
| 19. | LSU | 8-4-0 | Mike Archer |
| 20. | Indiana | 8-3-1 | Bill Mallory |

## †1989

| | | Record | Coach |
|---|---|---|---|
| 1. | Miami (Fla.) | 11-1-0 | Dennis Erickson |
| 2. | Notre Dame | 12-1-0 | Lou Holtz |
| 3. | Florida St | 10-2-0 | Bobby Bowden |
| 4. | Colorado | 11-1-0 | Bill McCartney |
| 5. | Tennessee | 11-1-0 | Johnny Majors |
| 6. | Auburn | 10-2-0 | Pat Dye |
| 7. | Michigan | 10-2-0 | Bo Schembechler |
| 8. | USC | 9-2-1 | Larry Smith |
| 9. | Alabama | 10-2-0 | Bill Curry |

†In 1989 the AP expanded its final poll to 25 teams.

### †1989 *(Cont.)*

| | | Record | Coach |
|---|---|---|---|
| 10. | Illinois | 10-2-0 | John Mackovic |
| 11. | Nebraska | 10-2-0 | Tom Osborne |
| 12. | Clemson | 10-2-0 | Danny Ford |
| 13. | Arkansas | 10-2-0 | Ken Hatfield |
| 14. | Houston | 9-2-0 | Jack Pardee |
| 15. | Penn St | 8-3-1 | Joe Paterno |
| 16. | Michigan St | 8-4-0 | George Perles |
| 17. | Pittsburgh | 8-3-1 | Mike Gottfried |
| 18. | Virginia | 10-3-0 | George Welsh |
| 19. | Texas Tech | 9-3-0 | Spike Dykes |
| 20. | Texas A&M | 8-4-0 | R.C. Slocum |
| 21. | W Virginia | 8-3-1 | Don Nehlen |
| 22. | BYU | 10-3-0 | LaVell Edwards |
| 23. | Washington | 8-4-0 | Don James |
| 24. | Ohio St | 8-4-0 | John Cooper |
| 25. | Arizona | 8-4-0 | Dick Tomey |

### 1990

| | | Record | Coach |
|---|---|---|---|
| 1. | Colorado | 11-1-1 | Bill McCartney |
| 2. | #Ga. Tech (UPI) | 11-0-1 | Bobby Ross |
| 3. | Miami (Fla.) | 10-2-0 | Dennis Erickson |
| 4. | Florida St | 10-2-0 | Bobby Bowden |
| 5. | Washington | 10-2-0 | Don James |
| 6. | Notre Dame | 9-3-0 | Lou Holtz |
| 7. | Michigan | 9-3-0 | Gary Moeller |
| 8. | Tennessee | 9-2-2 | Johnny Majors |
| 9. | Clemson | 10-2-0 | Ken Hatfield |
| 10. | Houston | 10-1-0 | John Jenkins |
| 11. | Penn St | 9-3-0 | Joe Paterno |
| 12. | Texas | 10-2-0 | David McWilliams |
| 13. | Florida | 9-2-0 | Steve Spurrier |
| 14. | Louisville | 10-1-1 | H. Schnellenberger |
| 15. | Texas A&M | 9-3-1 | R.C. Slocum |
| 16. | Michigan St | 8-3-1 | George Perles |
| 17. | Oklahoma | 8-3-0 | Gary Gibbs |
| 18. | Iowa | 8-4-0 | Hayden Fry |
| 19. | Auburn | 8-3-1 | Pat Dye |
| 20. | USC | 8-4-1 | Larry Smith |
| 21. | Mississippi | 9-3-0 | Billy Brewer |
| 22. | BYU | 10-3-0 | LaVell Edwards |
| 23. | Virginia | 8-4-0 | George Wells |
| 24. | Nebraska | 9-3-0 | Tom Osborne |
| 25. | Illinois | 8-4-0 | John Mackovic |

### 1991

| | | Record | Coach |
|---|---|---|---|
| 1. | Miami (Fla.) | 12-0-0 | Dennis Erickson |
| 2. | #Washington | 12-0-0 | Don James |
| 3. | Penn St | 11-2-0 | Joe Paterno |
| 4. | Florida St | 11-2-0 | Bobby Bowden |
| 5. | Alabama | 11-1-0 | Gene Stallings |
| 6. | Michigan | 10-2-0 | Gary Moeller |
| 7. | Florida | 10-2-0 | Steve Spurrier |
| 8. | California | 10-2-0 | Bruce Snyder |
| 9. | E Carolina | 11-1-0 | Bill Lewis |
| 10. | Iowa | 10-1-1 | Hayden Fry |
| 11. | Syracuse | 10-2-0 | Paul Pasqualoni |
| 12. | Texas A&M | 10-2-0 | R.C. Slocum |
| 13. | Notre Dame | 10-3-0 | Lou Holtz |

### 1991 *(Cont.)*

| | | Record | Coach |
|---|---|---|---|
| 14. | Tennessee | 9-3-0 | Johnny Majors |
| 15. | Nebraska | 9-2-1 | Tom Osborne |
| 16. | Oklahoma | 9-3-0 | Gary Gibbs |
| 17. | Georgia | 9-3-0 | Ray Goff |
| 18. | Clemson | 9-2-1 | Ken Hatfield |
| 19. | UCLA | 9-3-0 | Terry Donahue |
| 20. | Colorado | 8-3-1 | Bill McCartney |
| 21. | Tulsa | 10-2-0 | David Rader |
| 22. | Stanford | 8-4-0 | Dennis Green |
| 23. | BYU | 8-3-2 | LaVell Edwards |
| 24. | North Carolina St | 9-3-0 | Dick Sheridan |
| 25. | Air Force | 10-3-0 | Fisher DeBerry |

#Selected No. 1 by *USA Today*/CNN.

### 1992

| | | Record | Coach |
|---|---|---|---|
| 1. | Alabama | 13-0-0 | Gene Stallings |
| 2. | Florida St | 11-1-0 | Bobby Bowden |
| 3. | Miami | 11-1-0 | Dennis Erickson |
| 4. | Notre Dame | 10-1-1 | Lou Holtz |
| 5. | Michigan | 9-0-3 | Gary Moeller |
| 6. | Syracuse | 10-2-0 | Paul Pasqualoni |
| 7. | Texas A&M | 12-1-0 | R.C. Slocum |
| 8. | Georgia | 10-2-0 | Ray Goff |
| 9. | Stanford | 10-3-0 | Bill Walsh |
| 10. | Florida | 9-4-0 | Steve Spurrier |
| 11. | Washington | 9-3-0 | Don James |
| 12. | Tennessee | 9-3-0 | Johnny Majors |
| 13. | Colorado | 9-2-1 | Bill McCartney |
| 14. | Nebraska | 9-3-0 | Tom Osborne |
| 15. | Washington St | 9-3-0 | Mike Price |
| 16. | Mississippi | 9-3-0 | Billy Brewer |
| 17. | North Carolina St | 9-3-1 | Dick Sheridan |
| 18. | Ohio St | 8-3-1 | John Cooper |
| 19. | North Carolina | 9-3-0 | Mack Brown |
| 20. | Hawaii | 11-2-0 | Bob Wagner |
| 21. | Boston College | 8-3-1 | Tom Coughlin |
| 22. | Kansas | 8-4-0 | Glen Mason |
| 23. | Mississippi St | 7-5-0 | Jackie Sherrill |
| 24. | Fresno St | 9-4-0 | Jim Sweeney |
| 25. | Wake Forest | 8-4-0 | Bill Dooley |

### 1993

| | | Record | Coach |
|---|---|---|---|
| 1. | Florida St | 12-1-0 | Bobby Bowden |
| 2. | Notre Dame | 11-1-0 | Lou Holtz |
| 3. | Nebraska | 11-1-0 | Tom Osborne |
| 4. | Auburn | 11-0-0 | Terry Bowden |
| 5. | Florida | 11-2-0 | Steve Spurrier |
| 6. | Wisconsin | 10-1-1 | Barry Alvarez |
| 7. | W Virginia | 11-1-0 | Don Nehlen |
| 8. | Penn St | 10-2-0 | Joe Paterno |
| 9. | Texas A&M | 10-2-0 | R.C. Slocum |
| 10. | Arizona | 10-2-0 | Dick Tomey |
| 11. | Ohio St | 10-1-1 | John Cooper |
| 12. | Tennessee | 9-2-1 | Phil Fulmer |
| 13. | Boston College | 9-3-0 | Tom Coughlin |
| 14. | Alabama | 9-3-1 | Gene Stallings |
| 15. | Miami | 9-3-0 | Dennis Erickson |
| 16. | Colorado | 8-3-1 | Bill McCartney |

†In 1989 the AP expanded its final poll to 25 teams.

### 1993 *(Cont.)*

| | | Record | Coach |
|---|---|---|---|
| 17. | Oklahoma | 9-3-0 | Gary Gibbs |
| 18. | UCLA | 8-4-0 | Terry Donahue |
| 19. | North Carolina | 10-3-0 | Mack Brown |
| 20. | Kansas St | 9-2-1 | Bill Snyder |
| 21. | Michigan | 8-4-0 | Gary Moeller |
| 22. | Virginia Tech | 9-3-0 | Frank Beamer |
| 23. | Clemson | 9-3-0 | Ken Hatfield |
| 24. | Louisville | 9-3-0 | H. Schnellenberger |
| 25. | California | 9-4-0 | Keith Gilbertson |

### 1994

| | | Record | Coach |
|---|---|---|---|
| 1. | Nebraska | 13-0-0 | Tom Osborne |
| 2. | Penn St | 12-0-0 | Joe Paterno |
| 3. | Colorado | 11-1-0 | Bill McCartney |
| 4. | Florida St | 10-1-1 | Bobby Bowden |
| 5. | Alabama | 12-1-0 | Gene Stallings |
| 6. | Miami (Fla.) | 10-2-0 | Dennis Erickson |
| 7. | Florida | 10-2-1 | Steve Spurrier |
| 8. | Texas A&M | 10-0-1 | R.C. Slocum |
| 9. | Auburn | 9-1-1 | Terry Bowden |
| 10. | Utah | 10-2-0 | Ron McBride |
| 11. | Oregon | 9-4-0 | Rich Brooks |
| 12. | Michigan | 8-4-0 | Gary Moeller |
| 13. | USC | 8-3-1 | John Robinson |
| 14. | Ohio St | 9-4-0 | John Cooper |
| 15. | Virginia | 9-3-0 | George Welsh |
| 16. | Colorado St | 10-2-0 | Sonny Lubick |
| 17. | North Carolina St | 9-3-0 | Mike O'Cain |
| 18. | BYU | 10-3-0 | LaVell Edwards |
| 19. | Kansas St | 9-3-0 | Bill Snyder |
| 20. | Arizona | 8-4-0 | Dick Tomey |
| 21. | Washington St | 8-4-0 | Mike Price |
| 22. | Tennessee | 8-4-0 | Phillip Fulmer |
| 23. | Boston College | 7-4-1 | Dan Henning |
| 24. | Mississippi St | 8-4-0 | Jackie Sherrill |
| 25. | Texas | 8-4-0 | John Mackovic |

### 1995

| | | Record | Coach |
|---|---|---|---|
| 1. | Nebraska | 12-0-0 | Tom Osborne |
| 2. | Florida | 12-1-0 | Steve Spurrier |
| 3. | Tennessee | 11-1-0 | Phillip Fulmer |
| 4. | Florida St | 10-2-0 | Bobby Bowden |
| 5. | Colorado | 10-2-0 | Rick Neuheisel |
| 6. | Ohio St | 11-2-0 | John Cooper |
| 7. | Kansas St | 10-2-0 | Bill Snyder |
| 8. | Northwestern | 10-2-0 | Gary Barnett |
| 9. | Kansas | 10-2-0 | Glen Mason |
| 10. | Virginia Tech | 10-2-0 | Frank Beamer |
| 11. | Notre Dame | 9-3-0 | Lou Holtz |
| 12. | USC | 9-2-1 | John Robinson |
| 13. | Penn St | 9-3-0 | Joe Paterno |
| 14. | Texas | 10-2-1 | John Mackovic |
| 15. | Texas A&M | 9-3-0 | S.C. Slocum |
| 16. | Virginia | 9-4-0 | George Welsh |
| 17. | Michigan | 9-4-0 | Lloyd Carr |
| 18. | Oregon | 9-3-0 | Mike Bellotti |
| 19. | Syracuse | 9-3-0 | Paul Pasqualoni |
| 20. | Miami (Fla.) | 8-3-0 | Butch Davis |
| 21. | Alabama | 8-3-0 | Gene Stallings |

*In 1996 the NCAA introduced overtime to break ties.

### 1995 *(Cont.)*

| | | Record | Coach |
|---|---|---|---|
| 22. | Auburn | 8-4-0 | Terry Bowden |
| 23. | Texas Tech | 9-3-0 | Spike Dykes |
| 24. | Toledo | 11-0-1 | Gary Pinkel |
| 25. | Iowa | 8-4-0 | Hayden Fry |

### 1996

| | | Record* | Coach |
|---|---|---|---|
| 1. | Florida | 12–1 | Steve Spurrier |
| 2. | Ohio St | 11–1 | John Cooper |
| 3. | Florida St | 11–1 | Bobby Bowden |
| 4. | Arizona St | 11–1 | Bruce Snyder |
| 5. | BYU | 14–1 | LaVell Edwards |
| 6. | Nebraska | 11–2 | Tom Osborne |
| 7. | Penn St | 11–2 | Joe Paterno |
| 8. | Colorado | 10–2 | Rick Neuheisel |
| 9. | Tennessee | 10–2 | Phillip Fulmer |
| 10. | North Carolina | 10–2 | Mack Brown |
| 11. | Alabama | 10–3 | Gene Stallings |
| 12. | LSU | 10–2 | Gerry DiNardo |
| 13. | Virginia Tech | 10–2 | Frank Beamer |
| 14. | Miami (Fla.) | 9–3 | Butch Davis |
| 15. | Northwestern | 9–3 | Gary Barnett |
| 16. | Washington | 9–3 | Jim Lambright |
| 17. | Kansas St | 9–3 | Bill Snyder |
| 18. | Iowa | 9–3 | Hayden Fry |
| 19. | Notre Dame | 8–3 | Lou Holtz |
| 20. | Michigan | 8–4 | Lloyd Carr |
| 21. | Syracuse | 9–3 | Paul Pasqualoni |
| 22. | Wyoming | 10–2 | Joe Tiller |
| 23. | Texas | 8–5 | John Mackovic |
| 24. | Auburn | 8–4 | Terry Bowden |
| 25. | Army | 10–2 | Bob Sutton |

### 1997

| | | Record | Coach |
|---|---|---|---|
| 1. | Michigan | 12–0 | Lloyd Carr |
| #2. | Nebraska | 13–0 | Tom Osborne |
| 3. | Florida St | 11–1 | Bobby Bowden |
| 4. | Florida | 10–2 | Steve Spurrier |
| 5. | UCLA | 10–2 | Bob Toledo |
| 6. | North Carolina | 11–1 | Mack Brown |
| 7. | Tennessee | 11–2 | Phillip Fulmer |
| 8. | Kansas St | 11–1 | Bill Snyder |
| 9. | Washington St | 10–2 | Mike Price |
| 10. | Georgia | 10–2 | Jim Donnan |
| 11. | Auburn | 10–3 | Terry Bowden |
| 12. | Ohio St | 10–3 | John Cooper |
| 13. | LSU | 9–3 | Gerry DiNardo |
| 14. | Arizona St | 8–3 | Bruce Snyder |
| 15. | Purdue | 9–3 | Joe Tiller |
| 16. | Penn St | 9–3 | Joe Paterno |
| 17. | Colorado St | 11–2 | Sonny Lubick |
| 18. | Washington | 8–4 | Jim Lambright |
| 19. | Southern Mississippi | 9–3 | Jeff Bower |
| 20. | Texas A&M | 9–4 | R. C. Slocum |
| 21. | Syracuse | 9–4 | Paul Pasqualoni |
| 22. | Mississippi | 8–4 | Tommy Tuberville |
| 23. | Missouri | 7–5 | Larry Smith |
| 24. | Oklahoma St | 8–4 | Bob Simmons |
| 25. | Georgia Tech | 7–5 | George O'Leary |

#Selected No. 1 by *USA Today*/CNN.

### 1998

| | | Record | Coach |
|---|---|---|---|
| 1. | Tennessee | 13–0 | Phillip Fulmer |
| 2. | Ohio St. | 11–1 | John Cooper |
| 3. | Florida St | 11–2 | Bobby Bowden |
| 4. | Arizona | 12–1 | Dick Tomey |
| 5. | Florida | 10–2 | Steve Spurrier |
| 6. | Wisconsin | 11–1 | Barry Alvarez |
| 7. | Tulane | 12–0 | Tommy Bowden |
| 8. | UCLA | 10–2 | Bob Toledo |
| 9. | Georgia Tech | 10–2 | George O'Leary |
| 10. | Kansas St | 11–2 | Bill Snyder |
| 11. | Texas A&M | 11–3 | R.C. Slocum |
| 12. | Michigan | 10–3 | Lloyd Carr |
| 13. | Air Force | 12–1 | Fisher DeBerry |
| 14. | Georgia | 9–3 | Jim Donnan |
| 15. | Texas | 9–3 | Mack Brown |
| 16. | Arkansas | 9–3 | Houston Nutt |
| 17. | Penn St | 9–3 | Joe Paterno |
| 18. | Virginia | 9–3 | George Welsh |
| 19. | Nebraska | 9–4 | Frank Solich |
| 20. | Miami (Fla.) | 9–3 | Butch Davis |
| 21. | Missouri | 8–4 | Larry Smith |
| 22. | Notre Dame | 9–3 | Bob Davie |
| 23. | Virginia Tech | 9–3 | Frank Beamer |
| 24. | Purdue | 9–4 | Joe Tiller |
| 25. | Syracuse | 8–4 | Paul Pasqualoni |

### 1999

| | | Record | Coach |
|---|---|---|---|
| 1. | Florida St | 12–0 | Bobby Bowden |
| 2. | Virginia Tech | 11–1 | Frank Beamer |
| 3. | Nebraska | 12–1 | Frank Solich |
| 4. | Wisconsin | 10–2 | Barry Alvarez |
| 5. | Michigan | 10–2 | Lloyd Carr |
| 6. | Kansas St | 11–1 | Bill Snyder |
| 7. | Michigan St | 10–2 | Nick Saban |
| 8. | Alabama | 10–3 | Mike DuBose |
| 9. | Tennessee | 9–3 | Phillip Fulmer |
| 10. | Marshall | 13–0 | Bob Pruett |
| 11. | Penn St | 10–3 | Joe Paterno |
| 12. | Florida | 9–4 | Steve Spurrier |
| 13. | Mississippi St | 10–2 | Jackie Sherrill |
| 14. | Southern Miss | 9–3 | Jeff Bower |
| 15. | Miami (Fla.) | 9–4 | Butch Davis |
| 16. | Georgia | 8–4 | Jim Donnan |
| 17. | Arkansas | 8–4 | Houston Nutt |
| 18. | Minnesota | 8–4 | Glen Mason |
| 19. | Oregon | 9–3 | Mike Bellotti |
| 20. | Georgia Tech | 8–4 | Goerge O'Leary |
| 21. | Texas | 9–5 | Mack Brown |
| 22. | Mississippi | 8–4 | David Cutcliffe |
| 23. | Texas A&M | 8–4 | R.C. Slocum |
| 24. | Illinois | 8–4 | Ron Turner |
| 25. | Purdue | 7–5 | Joe Tiller |

### 2000

| | | Record | Coach |
|---|---|---|---|
| 1. | Oklahoma | 13–0 | Bob Stoops |
| 2. | Miami (Fla.) | 11–1 | Butch Davis |
| 3. | Washington | 11–1 | Rick Neuheisel |
| 4. | Oregon St | 11–1 | Dennis Erickson |
| 5. | Florida St | 11–2 | Bobby Bowden |
| 6. | Virginia Tech | 11–1 | Frank Beamer |
| 7. | Oregon | 10–2 | Mike Belotti |

### 2000 *(Cont.)*

| | | Record | Coach |
|---|---|---|---|
| 8. | Nebraska | 10–2 | Frank Solich |
| 9. | Kansas St | 11–3 | Bill Snyder |
| 10. | Florida | 10–3 | Steve Spurrier |
| 11. | Michigan | 9–3 | Lloyd Carr |
| 12. | Texas | 9–3 | Mack Brown |
| 13. | Purdue | 8–4 | Joe Tiller |
| 14. | Colorado St | 10–2 | Sonny Lubeck |
| 15. | Notre Dame | 9–3 | Bob Davie |
| 16. | Clemson | 9–3 | Tommy Bowden |
| 17. | Georgia Tech | 9–3 | George O'Leary |
| 18. | Auburn | 9–4 | Tommy Tuberville |
| 19. | South Carolina | 8–4 | Lou Holtz |
| 20. | Georgia | 8–4 | Jim Donnan |
| 21. | TCU | 10–2 | Dennis Franchione |
| 22. | LSU | 8–4 | Nick Saban |
| 23. | Wisconsin | 9–4 | Barry Alvarez |
| 24. | Mississippi St | 8–4 | Jackie Sherrill |
| 25. | Iowa St | 9–3 | Dan McCarney |

### 2001

| | | Record | Coach |
|---|---|---|---|
| 1. | Miami (Fla.) | 12–0 | Larry Coker |
| 2. | Oregon | 11–1 | Mike Belotti |
| 3. | Florida | 10–2 | Steve Spurrier |
| 4. | Tennessee | 11–2 | Phillip Fulmer |
| 5. | Texas | 11–2 | Mack Brown |
| 6. | Oklahoma | 11–2 | Bob Stoops |
| 7. | LSU | 10–3 | Nick Saban |
| 8. | Nebraska | 11–2 | Frank Solich |
| 9. | Colorado | 10–3 | Gary Barnett |
| 10. | Washington St | 10–2 | Mike Price |
| 11. | Maryland | 10–2 | Ralph Friedgen |
| 12. | Illinois | 10–2 | Ron Turner |
| 13. | South Carolina | 9–3 | Lou Holtz |
| 14. | Syracuse | 10–3 | Paul Pasqualoni |
| 15. | Florida St | 8–4 | Bobby Bowden |
| 16. | Stanford | 9–3 | Tyrone Willingham |
| 17. | Louisville | 11–2 | John Smith |
| 18. | Virginia Tech | 8–4 | Frank Beamer |
| 19. | Washington | 8–4 | Rick Neuheisel |
| 20. | Michigan | 8–4 | Lloyd Carr |
| 21. | Boston College | 8–4 | Tom O'Brien |
| 22. | Georgia | 8–4 | Mark Richt |
| 23. | Toledo | 10–2 | Tom Amstutz |
| 24. | Georgia Tech | 8–5 | George O'Leary |
| 25. | BYU | 12–2 | Gary Crowton |

### 2002

| | | Record | Coach |
|---|---|---|---|
| 1. | Ohio St | 14–0 | Jim Tressel |
| 2. | Miami (Fla.) | 12–1 | Larry Coker |
| 3. | Georgia | 13–1 | Mark Richt |
| 4. | USC | 11–2 | Pete Carroll |
| 5. | Oklahoma | 12–2 | Bob Stoops |
| 6. | Texas | 11–2 | Mack Brown |
| 7. | Kansas St | 11–2 | Bill Snyder |
| 8. | Iowa | 11–2 | Kirk Ferentz |
| 9. | Michigan | 10–3 | Lloyd Carr |
| 10. | Washington St | 10–3 | Mike Price |
| 11. | Alabama | 10–3 | Dennis Franchione |
| 12. | North Carolina St | 11–3 | Chuck Amato |
| 13. | Maryland | 11–3 | Ralph Friedgen |

### 2002 *(Cont.)*

| | | Record | Coach |
|---|---|---|---|
| 14. | Auburn | 9–4 | Tommy Tuberville |
| 15. | Boise St | 12–1 | Dan Hawkins |
| 16. | Penn St | 9–4 | Joe Paterno |
| 17. | Notre Dame | 10–3 | Tyrone Willingham |
| 18. | Virginia Tech | 10–4 | Frank Beamer |
| 19. | Pittsburgh | 9–4 | Walt Harris |
| 20. | Colorado | 9–5 | Gary Barnett |
| 21. | Florida St | 9–5 | Bobby Bowden |
| 22. | Virginia | 9–5 | Al Groh |
| 23. | TCU | 10–2 | Gary Patterson |
| 24. | Marshall | 11–2 | Bob Pruett |
| 25. | W Virginia | 9–4 | Rich Rodriguez |

### 2003

| | | Record | Coach |
|---|---|---|---|
| 1. | USC | 12–1 | Pete Carroll |
| #2. | LSU | 13–1 | Nick Saban |
| 3. | Oklahoma | 12–2 | Bob Stoops |
| 4. | Ohio St | 11–2 | Jim Tressel |
| 5. | Miami (Fla.) | 11–2 | Larry Coker |
| 6. | Michigan | 10–3 | Lloyd Carr |
| 7. | Georgia | 11–3 | Mark Richt |
| 8. | Iowa | 10–3 | Kirk Ferentz |
| 9. | Washington St | 10–3 | Bill Doba |
| 10. | Miami (Ohio) | 13–1 | Terry Hoeppner |
| 11. | Florida St | 10–3 | Bobby Bowden |
| 12. | Texas | 10–3 | Mack Brown |
| 13. | Kansas St | 11–4 | Bill Snyder |
| | Mississippi | 10–3 | David Cutcliffe |
| 15. | Tennessee | 10–3 | Phillip Fulmer |
| 16. | Boise St | 13–1 | Dan Hawkins |
| 17. | Maryland | 10–3 | Ralph Friedgen |
| 18. | Nebraska | 10–3 | Frank Solich/Bo Pelini |
| | Purdue | 9–4 | Joe Tiller |
| 20. | Minnesota | 10–3 | Glen Mason |
| 21. | Utah | 10–2 | Urban Meyer |
| 22. | Clemson | 9–4 | Tommy Bowden |
| 23. | Bowling Green | 11–3 | Gregg Brandon |
| 24. | Florida | 8–5 | Ron Zook |
| 25. | TCU | 11–2 | Gary Patterson |

#Selected No. 1 by *USA Today*/CNN.

### 2004

| | | Record | Coach |
|---|---|---|---|
| 1. | *Vacated | | |
| 2. | Auburn | 13–0 | Tommy Tuberville |
| 3. | Oklahoma | 12–1 | Bob Stoops |
| 4. | Utah | 12–0 | Kyle Whittingham |
| 5. | Texas | 11–1 | Mack Brown |
| 6. | Louisville | 11–1 | Bobby Petrino |
| 7. | Georgia | 10–2 | Mark Richt |
| 8. | Iowa | 10–2 | Kirk Ferentz |
| 9. | California | 10–2 | Jeff Tedford |
| 10. | Virginia Tech | 10–3 | Frank Beamer |
| 11. | Miami (Fla.) | 9–3 | Larry Coker |
| 12. | Boise St | 11–1 | Dan Hawkins |
| 13. | Tennessee | 10–3 | Phillip Fulmer |
| 14. | Michigan | 9–3 | Lloyd Carr |
| 15. | Florida St | 8–5 | Bobby Bowden |
| 16. | LSU | 9–3 | Les Miles |
| 17. | Wisconsin | 9–3 | Barry Alvarez |
| 18. | Texas Tech | 8–4 | Mike Leach |
| 19. | Arizona St | 9–3 | Dirk Koetter |

### 2004 *(Cont.)*

| | | Record | Coach |
|---|---|---|---|
| 20. | Ohio St | 8–4 | Jim Tressel |
| 21. | Boston College | 9–3 | Tom O'Brien |
| 22. | Fresno St | 9–3 | Pat Hill |
| 23. | Virginia | 8–4 | Al Groh |
| 24. | Navy | 10–2 | Paul Johnson |
| 25. | Pittsburgh | 8–4 | Walt Harris |

*USC was stripped of its 2004 BCS victory in 2010.

### 2005

| | | Record | Coach |
|---|---|---|---|
| 1. | Texas | 13–0 | Mack Brown |
| 2. | *Vacated | | |
| 3. | Penn St | 11–1 | Joe Paterno |
| 4. | Ohio St | 10–2 | Jim Tressel |
| 5. | Texas | 11–1 | Mack Brown |
| 6. | LSU | 11–2 | Les Miles |
| 7. | Virginia Tech | 10–3 | Frank Beamer |
| 8. | Alabama | 10–2 | Mike Shula |
| 9. | Notre Dame | 9–3 | Charlie Weis |
| 10. | Georgia | 10–3 | Mark Richt |
| 11. | TCU | 11–1 | Gary Patterson |
| 12. | Florida | 9–3 | Urban Meyer |
| 12. | Oregon | 10–2 | Mike Bellotti |
| 14. | Auburn | 9–3 | Tommy Tuberville |
| 14. | Wisconsin | 9–3 | Barry Alvarez |
| 15. | Michigan | 9–3 | Lloyd Carr |
| 16. | UCLA | 10–2 | Karl Dorrell |
| 17. | Miami (Fla.) | 9–3 | Larry Coker |
| 18. | Boston College | 9–3 | Tom O'Brien |
| 19. | Louisville | 9–3 | Bobby Petrino |
| 20. | Texas Tech | 9–3 | Mike Leach |
| 21. | Clemson | 8–4 | Tommy Bowden |
| 22. | Oklahoma | 8–4 | Bob Stoops |
| 23. | Florida St | 8–5 | Bobby Bowden |
| 24. | Nebraska | 8–4 | Bill Callahan |
| 25. | California | 8–4 | Jeff Tedford |

*USC was stripped of its 2005 season victories in 2010.

### 2006

| | | Record | Coach |
|---|---|---|---|
| 1. | Florida | 13–1 | Urban Meyer |
| 2. | Ohio St | 12–1 | Jim Tressel |
| 3. | LSU | 11–2 | Les Miles |
| 4. | USC | 11–2 | Pete Carroll |
| 5. | Boise St | 13–0 | Chris Petersen |
| 6. | Louisville | 12–1 | Steve Kragthorpe |
| 7. | Wisconsin | 12–1 | Bret Bielema |
| 8. | Michigan | 11–2 | Lloyd Carr |
| 9. | Auburn | 11–2 | Tommy Tuberville |
| 10. | West Virginia | 11–2 | Rich Rodriguez |
| 11. | Oklahoma | 11–3 | Bob Stoops |
| 12. | Rutgers | 11–2 | Greg Schiano |
| 13. | Texas | 10–3 | Mack Brown |
| 14. | California | 10–3 | Jeff Tedford |
| 15. | Arkansas | 10–4 | Houston Nutt |
| 16. | BYU | 11–2 | Bronco Mendenhall |
| 17. | Notre Dame | 10–3 | Charlie Weis |
| 18. | Wake Forest | 11–3 | Jim Grobe |
| 19. | Virginia Tech | 10–3 | Frank Beamer |
| 20. | Boston College | 10–3 | Jeff Jagodzinski |
| 21. | Oregon St | 10–4 | Mike Riley |
| 22. | TCU | 11–2 | Gary Patterson |
| 23. | Georgia | 9–4 | Mark Richt |
| 24. | Penn St | 9–4 | Joe Paterno |
| 25. | Tennessee | 9–4 | Phillip Fulmer |

## 2007

| | | Record | Coach |
|---|---|---|---|
| 1. | LSU | 12-2 | Les Miles |
| 2. | Georgia | 11-2 | Mark Richt |
| 3. | USC | 11-2 | Pete Carroll |
| 4. | Missouri | 12-2 | Gary Pinkell |
| 5. | Ohio St | 11-2 | Jim Tressel |
| 6. | West Virginia | 11-2 | Rich Rodriguez |
| 7. | Kansas | 12-1 | Mark Mangino |
| 8. | Oklahoma | 11-3 | Bob Stoops |
| 9. | Virginia Tech | 11-3 | Frank Beamer |
| 10. | Texas | 10-3 | Mack Brown |
| 10. | Boston College | 11-3 | Jeff Jagodzinski |
| 12. | Tennessee | 10-4 | Philip Fulmer |
| 13. | Florida | 9-4 | Urban Meyer |
| 14. | BYU | 11-2 | Bronco Mendenhall |
| 15. | Auburn | 9-4 | Tommy Tuberville |
| 16. | Arizona St | 10-3 | Dennis Erickson |
| 17. | Cincinnati | 10-3 | Brian Kelly |
| 18. | Michigan | 9-4 | Lloyd Carr |
| 19. | Hawaii | 12-1 | June Jones |
| 20. | Illinois | 9-4 | Ron Zook |
| 21. | Clemson | 9-4 | Tommy Bowden |
| 22. | Texas A&M | 9-4 | Mike Leach |
| 23. | Oregon | 9-4 | Mike Bellotti |
| 24. | Wisconsin | 9-4 | Bret Bielema |
| 25. | Oregon St | 9-4 | Mike Riley |

## 2008

| | | Record | Coach |
|---|---|---|---|
| 1. | Florida | 13-1 | Urban Meyer |
| 2. | Ohio St | 12-1 | Jim Tressel |
| 3. | LSU | 11-2 | Les Miles |
| 4. | USC | 11-2 | Pete Carroll |
| 5. | Boise St | 13-0 | Chris Petersen |
| 6. | Louisville | 12-1 | Steve Kragthorpe |
| 7. | Wisconsin | 12-1 | Bret Bielema |
| 8. | Michigan | 11-2 | Lloyd Carr |
| 9. | Auburn | 11-2 | Tommy Tuberville |
| 10. | West Virginia | 11-2 | Rich Rodriguez |
| 11. | Oklahoma | 11-3 | Bob Stoops |
| 12. | Rutgers | 11-2 | Greg Schiano |
| 13. | Texas | 10-3 | Mack Brown |
| 14. | California | 10-3 | Jeff Tedford |
| 15. | Arkansas | 10-4 | Houston Nutt |
| 16. | BYU | 11-2 | Bronco Mendenhall |
| 17. | Notre Dame | 10-3 | Charlie Weis |
| 18. | Wake Forest | 11-3 | Jim Grobe |
| 19. | Virginia Tech | 10-3 | Frank Beamer |
| 20. | Boston College | 10-3 | Jeff Jagodzinski |
| 21. | Oregon St | 10-4 | Mike Riley |
| 22. | TCU | 11-2 | Gary Patterson |
| 23. | Georgia | 9-4 | Mark Richt |
| 24. | Penn St | 9-4 | Joe Paterno |
| 25. | Tennessee | 9-4 | Phillip Fulmer |

## 2009

| | | Record | Coach |
|---|---|---|---|
| 1. | Alabama | 14-0 | Nick Saban |
| 2. | Texas | 13-1 | Mack Brown |
| 3. | Florida | 13-1 | Urban Meyer |
| 4. | Boise St | 14-0 | Chris Petersen |
| 5. | Ohio St | 11-2 | Jim Tressel |
| 6. | TCU | 12-1 | Gary Patterson |
| 7. | Iowa | 11-2 | Mark Mangino |
| 8. | Cincinnati | 12-1 | Brian Kelly |
| 9. | Penn St | 11-2 | Joe Paterno |
| 10. | Virginia Tech | 10-3 | Frank Beamer |
| 11. | Oregon | 10-3 | Chip Kelly |
| 12. | BYU | 11-2 | Bronco Mendenhall |
| 13. | Georgia Tech | 11-3 | Paul Johnson |
| 14. | Nebraska | 10-4 | Bo Pelini |
| 15. | Pittsburgh | 10-3 | Dave Wannstedt |
| 16. | Wisconsin | 10-3 | Bret Bielema |
| 17. | LSU | 9-4 | Les Miles |
| 18. | Utah | 10-3 | Kyle Whittingham |
| 19. | Miami (Fla.) | 9-4 | Randy Shannon |
| 20. | Mississippi | 9-4 | Houston Nutt |
| 21. | Texas Tech | 9-4 | Mike Leach |
| 22. | USC | 9-4 | Pete Carroll |
| 23. | Central Michigan | 12-2 | Butch Jones |
| 24. | Clemson | 9-5 | Dabo Swinney |
| 25. | West Virginia | 9-4 | Bill Stewart |

## 2010

| | | Record | Coach |
|---|---|---|---|
| 1. | Auburn | 14-0 | Gene Chizik |
| 2. | TCU | 13-0 | Gary Patterson |
| 3. | Oregon | 12-1 | Chip Kelly |
| 4. | Stanford | 12-1 | Jim Harbaugh |
| 5. | Ohio St | 12-1 | Jim Tressel |
| 6. | Oklahoma | 12-2 | Bob Stoops |
| 7. | Wisconsin | 11-2 | Bret Bielema |
| 8. | LSU | 11-2 | Les Miles |
| 9. | Boise St | 12-1 | Chris Petersen |
| 10. | Alabama | 10-3 | Nick Saban |
| 11. | Nevada | 13-1 | Chris Ault |
| 12. | Arkansas | 10-3 | Bobby Petrino |
| 13. | Oklahoma St | 11-2 | Mike Gundy |
| 14. | Michigan St | 11-2 | Mark Dantonio |
| 15. | Mississippi St | 9-4 | Dan Mullen |
| 16. | Virginia Tech | 11-3 | Frank Beamer |
| 17. | Florida St | 10-4 | Jimbo Fisher |
| 18. | Missouri | 10-3 | Gary Pinkel |
| 19. | Texas A&M | 9-4 | Mike Sherman |
| 20. | Nebraska | 10-4 | Bo Pelini |
| 21. | Central Florida | 11-3 | George O'Leary |
| 22. | South Carolina | 9-5 | Steve Spurrier |
| 23. | Maryland | 9-4 | Ralph Friedgen |
| 24. | Tulsa | 10-3 | Todd Graham |
| 25. | North Carolina St | 9-4 | Todd O'Brien |

# NCAA Divisional Championships

## Football Championship Subdivision (Div. I-AA)

| Year | Winner | Runner-Up | Score |
|---|---|---|---|
| 1978 | Florida A&M | Massachusetts | 35–28 |
| 1979 | Eastern Kentucky | Lehigh | 30–7 |
| 1980 | Boise St | Eastern Kentucky | 31–29 |
| 1981 | Idaho St | Eastern Kentucky | 34–23 |
| 1982 | Eastern Kentucky | Delaware | 17–14 |
| 1983 | Southern Illinois | Western Carolina | 43–7 |
| 1984 | Montana St | Louisiana Tech | 19–6 |
| 1985 | Georgia Southern | Furman | 44–42 |
| 1986 | Georgia Southern | Arkansas St | 48–21 |
| 1987 | NE Louisiana | Marshall | 43–42 |
| 1988 | Furman | Georgia Southern | 17–12 |
| 1989 | Georgia Southern | Stephen F. Austin St | 37–34 |
| 1990 | Georgia Southern | Nevada-Reno | 36–13 |
| 1991 | Youngstown St | Marshall | 25–17 |
| 1992 | Marshall | Youngstown St | 31–28 |
| 1993 | Youngstown St | Marshall | 17–5 |
| 1994 | Youngstown St | Boise St | 28–14 |
| 1995 | Montana | Marshall | 22–20 |
| 1996 | Marshall | Montana | 49–29 |
| 1997 | Youngstown St | McNesse St | 10–9 |
| 1998 | Massachusetts | Georgia Southern | 55–43 |
| 1999 | Georgia Southern | Youngstown St | 59–24 |
| 2000 | Georgia Southern | Montana | 27–25 |
| 2001 | Montana | Furman | 13–6 |
| 2002 | Western Kentucky | McNeese St | 34–14 |
| 2003 | Delaware | Colgate | 40–0 |
| 2004 | James Madison | Montana | 31–21 |
| 2005 | Appalachian St | Northern Iowa | 21–16 |
| 2006 | Appalachian St | Massachusetts | 28–17 |
| 2007 | Appalachian St | Delaware | 49–21 |
| 2008 | Richmond | Montana | 24–7 |
| 2009 | Villanova | Montana | 23–21 |
| 2010 | Eastern Washington | Delaware | 20–19 |

## Division II

| Year | Winner | Runner-Up | Score |
|---|---|---|---|
| 1973 | Louisiana Tech | Western Kentucky | 34–0 |
| 1974 | Central Michigan | Delaware | 54–14 |
| 1975 | Northern Michigan | Western Kentucky | 16–14 |
| 1976 | Montana St | Akron | 24–13 |
| 1977 | Lehigh | Jacksonville St | 33–0 |
| 1978 | Eastern Illinois | Delaware | 10–9 |
| 1979 | Delaware | Youngstown St | 38–21 |
| 1980 | Cal Poly SLO | Eastern Illinois | 21–13 |
| 1981 | SW Texas St | North Dakota St | 42–13 |
| 1982 | SW Texas St | UC–Davis | 34–9 |
| 1983 | North Dakota St | Central St (Ohio) | 41–21 |
| 1984 | Troy St | North Dakota St | 18–17 |
| 1985 | North Dakota St | North Alabama | 35–7 |
| 1986 | North Dakota St | South Dakota | 27–7 |
| 1987 | Troy St | Portland St | 31–17 |
| 1988 | North Dakota St | Portland St | 35–21 |
| 1989 | Mississippi College | Jacksonville St | 3–0 |
| 1990 | N Dakota St | Indiana (Pa.) | 51–11 |
| 1991 | Pittsburg St | Jacksonville St | 23–6 |
| 1992 | Jacksonville St | Pittsburg St | 17–13 |
| 1993 | North Alabama | Indiana (Pa.) | 41–34 |
| 1994 | North Alabama | Texas A&M–Kingsville | 16–10 |
| 1995 | North Alabama | Pittsburg St | 27–7 |
| 1996 | Northern Colorado | Carson-Newman | 23–14 |
| 1997 | Northern Colorado | New Haven | 51–0 |
| 1998 | NW Missouri St | Carson-Newman | 24–6 |
| 1999 | NW Missouri St | Carson-Newman | 58–52 (OT) |
| 2000 | Delta St | Bloomsburg | 63–34 |
| 2001 | Grand Valley St | North Dakota | 17–14 |
| 2002 | Grand Valley St | Valdosta St | 31–24 |
| 2003 | Grand Valley St | North Dakota | 10–3 |

## Division II *(Cont.)*

| Year | Winner | Runner-Up | Score |
|------|--------|-----------|-------|
| 2004 | Valdosta State | Pittsburg State | 36–31 |
| 2005 | Grand Valley St | NW Missouri St | 21–17 |
| 2006 | Grand Valley St | NW Missouri St | 17–14 |
| 2007 | Valdosta St | NW Missouri St | 25-20 |
| 2008 | Minnesota-Duluth | NW Missouri St | 21–14 |
| 2009 | NW Missouri St | Grand Valley St | 30–23 |
| 2010 | Minnesota-Duluth | Delta St | 20–17 |

## Division III

| Year | Winner | Runner-Up | Score |
|------|--------|-----------|-------|
| 1973 | Wittenberg | Juniata | 41–0 |
| 1974 | Central (Iowa) | Ithaca | 10–8 |
| 1975 | Wittenberg | Ithaca | 28–0 |
| 1976 | St. John's (Minn.) | Towson St | 31–28 |
| 1977 | Widener | Wabash | 39–36 |
| 1978 | Baldwin-Wallace | Wittenberg | 24–10 |
| 1979 | Ithaca | Wittenberg | 14–10 |
| 1980 | Dayton | Ithaca | 63–0 |
| 1981 | Widener | Dayton | 17–10 |
| 1982 | West Georgia | Augustana (Ill.) | 14–0 |
| 1983 | Augustana (Ill.) | Union (N.Y.) | 21–17 |
| 1984 | Augustana (Ill.) | Central (Iowa) | 21–12 |
| 1985 | Augustana (Ill.) | Ithaca | 20–7 |
| 1986 | Augustana (Ill.) | Salisbury St | 31–3 |
| 1987 | Wagner | Dayton | 19–3 |
| 1988 | Ithaca | Central (Iowa) | 39–24 |
| 1989 | Dayton | Union (N.Y.) | 17–7 |
| 1990 | Allegheny | Lycoming | 21–14 (OT) |
| 1991 | Ithaca | Dayton | 34–20 |
| 1992 | UW-LaCrosse | Washington & Jefferson | 16–12 |
| 1993 | Mount Union | Rowan | 34–24 |
| 1994 | Albion | Washington & Jefferson | 38–15 |
| 1995 | UW-LaCrosse | Rowan | 36–7 |
| 1996 | Mount Union | Rowan | 56–24 |
| 1997 | Mount Union | Lycoming | 61–12 |
| 1998 | Mount Union | Rowan | 44–24 |
| 1999 | Pacific Lutheran | Rowan | 42–13 |
| 2000 | Mount Union | St. John's (Minn.) | 10–7 |
| 2001 | Mount Union | Bridgewater | 30–27 |
| 2002 | Mount Union | Trinity (Tex.) | 48–7 |
| 2003 | St. John's (Minn.) | Mount Union | 24–6 |
| 2004 | Linfield | Mary Hardin-Baylor | 28–21 |
| 2005 | Mount Union | UW-Whitewater | 35–28 |
| 2006 | Mount Union | UW-Whitewater | 35–16 |
| 2007 | UW-Whitewater | Mount Union | 31–21 |
| 2008 | Mount Union | UW-Whitewater | 31–26 |
| 2009 | UW-Whitewater | Mount Union | 38–28 |
| 2010 | UW-Whitewater | Mount Union | 31–21 |

## Division I

| Year | Winner | Runner-Up | Score |
|------|--------|-----------|-------|
| 1956 | St. Joseph's (Ind.)/Montana St | | 0–0 |
| 1957 | Pittsburg St (Kan.) | Hillsdale | 27–26 |
| 1958 | NE Oklahoma | Northern Arizona | 19–13 |
| 1959 | Texas A&I | Lenoir-Rhyne | 20–7 |
| 1960 | Lenoir-Rhyne | Humboldt St | 15–14 |
| 1961 | Pittsburg St (Kan.) | Linfield | 12–7 |
| 1962 | Central St (Okla.) | Lenoir-Rhyne | 28–13 |
| 1963 | St. John's (Minn.) | Prairie View | 33–27 |
| 1964 | Concordia-Moorhead/ Sam Houston St | | 7–7 |
| 1965 | St. John's (Minn.) | Linfield | 33–0 |
| 1966 | Waynesburg | UW-Whitewater | 42–21 |
| 1967 | Fairmont St | Eastern Washington | 28–21 |
| 1968 | Troy St (Mich.) | Texas A&I | 43–35 |
| 1969 | Texas A&I | Concordia-Moorhead (Minn.) | 32–7 |
| 1970 | Texas A&I | Wofford | 48–7 |
| 1971 | Livingston (Ala.) | Arkansas Tech | 14–12 |
| 1972 | E Texas St | Carson-Newman | 21–18 |
| 1973 | Abilene Christian | Elon | 42–14 |
| 1974 | Texas A&I | Henderson St | 34–23 |
| 1975 | Texas A&I | Salem (W.V.) | 37–0 |
| 1976 | Texas A&I | Central Arkansas | 26–0 |
| 1977 | Abilene Christian | SW Oklahoma | 24–7 |
| 1978 | Angelo St | Elon | 34–14 |
| 1979 | Texas A&I | Central St (Okla.) | 20–14 |
| 1980 | Elon | NE Oklahoma | 17–10 |
| 1981 | Elon | Pittsburg St | 3–0 |
| 1982 | Central St (Okla.) | Mesa | 14–11 |
| 1983 | Carson-Newman | Mesa | 36–28 |
| 1984 | Carson-Newman/Central Arkansas | | 19–19 |
| 1985 | Central Arkansas/Hillsdale | | 10–10 |
| 1986 | Carson-Newman | Cameron | 17–0 |
| 1987 | Cameron | Carson-Newman | 30–2 |
| 1988 | Carson-Newman | Adams St (Col.) | 56–21 |
| 1989 | Carson-Newman | Emporia St | 34–20 |
| 1990 | Central St (Ohio) | Mesa St | 38–16 |
| 1991 | Central Arkansas | Central St (Ohio) | 19–16 |
| 1992 | Central St (Ohio) | Gardner-Webb | 19–16 |
| 1993 | East Central (Okla.) | Glenville St | 49–35 |
| 1994 | Northeastern St (Okla.) | Arkansas–Pine Bluff | 13–12 |
| 1995 | Central St (Ohio) | Northeastern St (Okla.) | 37–7 |
| 1996 | SW Oklahoma St | Montana Tech | 33–31 |
| 1997 | Findlay | Willamette | 14–7 |
| 1998 | Azusa Pacific | Olivet Nazarene | 17–14 |
| 1999 | Northwestern Oklahoma St | Georgetown (Ky.) | 34–26 |
| 2000 | Georgetown (Ky.) | Northwestern Oklahoma St | 20–0 |
| 2001 | Georgetown (Ky.) | Sioux Falls (S.D.) | 49–27 |
| 2002 | Carroll (Mont.) | Georgetown (Ky.) | 28–7 |
| 2003 | Carroll (Mont.) | Northwestern Oklahoma St | 41–28 |
| 2004 | Carroll (Mont.) | St. Francis (Ind.) | 15–13 |
| 2005 | Carroll (Mont.) | St. Francis (Ind.) | 27–10 |
| 2006 | Sioux Falls (S.D.) | St. Francis (Ind.) | 23–19 |
| 2007 | Carroll (Mont.) | Sioux Falls (S.D.) | 17–9 |
| 2008 | Sioux Falls (S.D.) | Carroll (Mont.) | 23–7 |
| 2009 | Sioux Falls (S.D.) | Lindenwood | 25–22 |
| 2010 | Carroll (Mont.) | Sioux Falls (S.D.) | 10–7 |

## Division II†

| Year | Winner | Runner-Up | Score |
|------|--------|-----------|-------|
| 1970 | Westminster (Pa.) | Anderson | 21–16 |
| 1971 | California Lutheran | Westminster (Pa.) | 30–14 |
| 1972 | Missouri Southern | Northwestern (Iowa) | 21–14 |
| 1973 | Northwestern (Iowa) | Glenville St | 10–3 |
| 1974 | Texas Lutheran | Missouri Valley | 42–0 |
| 1975 | Texas Lutheran | California Lutheran | 34–8 |
| 1976 | Westminster (Pa.) | Redlands | 20–13 |
| 1977 | Westminster (Pa.) | California Lutheran | 17–9 |

†In 1997 the NAIA consolidated its two divisions into one.

## †Division II *(Cont.)*

| Year | Winner | Runner-Up | Score |
|------|--------|-----------|-------|
| 1978 | Concordia-Moorhead (Minn.) | Findlay | 7–0 |
| 1979 | Findlay | Northwestern (Iowa) | 51–6 |
| 1980 | Pacific Lutheran | Wilmington (Ohio) | 38–10 |
| 1981 | Austin Coll./Conc.-Moorhead (Minn.) | | 24–24 |
| 1982 | Linfield | William Jewell | 33–15 |
| 1983 | Northwestern (Iowa) | Pacific Lutheran | 25–21 |
| 1984 | Linfield | Northwestern (Iowa) | 33–22 |
| 1985 | UW-La Crosse | Pacific Lutheran | 24–7 |
| 1986 | Linfield | Baker | 17–0 |
| 1987 | Pacific Lutheran | UW-Stevens Point* | 16–16 |
| 1988 | Westminster (Pa.) | UW-La Crosse | 21–14 |
| 1989 | Westminster (Pa.) | UW-La Crosse | 51–30 |
| 1990 | Peru St | Westminster (Pa.) | 17–7 |
| 1991 | Georgetown (Ky.) | Pacific Lutheran | 28–20 |
| 1992 | Findlay | Linfield | 26–13 |
| 1993 | Pacific Lutheran | Westminster (Pa.) | 50–20 |
| 1994 | Westminster (Pa.) | Pacific Lutheran | 27–7 |
| 1995 | Findlay | Central Washington | 21–21 |
| 1996 | Sioux Falls (S.D.) | Western Washington | 47–25 |

*Forfeited 1987 season due to use of an ineligible player. †In 1997 the NAIA consolidated its two divisions into one.

# Awards

### Heisman Memorial Trophy

Awarded to the best college player by the Downtown Athletic Club of New York City. The trophy is named after John W. Heisman, who coached Georgia Tech to the national championship in 1917 and later served as DAC athletic director.

| Year | Winner, College, Position | Winner's Season Statistics | Runner-Up, College |
|------|---------------------------|----------------------------|---------------------|
| 1935 | Jay Berwanger, Chicago, HB | Rush: 119 Yds: 577 TD: 6 | Monk Meyer, Army |
| 1936 | Larry Kelley, Yale, E | Rec: 17 Yds: 372 TD: 6 | Sam Francis, Nebraska |
| 1937 | Clint Frank, Yale, HB | Rush: 157 Yds: 667 TD: 11 | Byron White, Colorado |
| 1938 | †Davey O'Brien, TCU, QB | Att/Comp: 194/110 Yds: 1733 TD: 19 | Marshall Goldberg, Pittsburgh |
| 1939 | Nile Kinnick, Iowa, HB | Rush: 106 Yds: 374 TD: 5 | Tom Harmon, Michigan |
| 1940 | Tom Harmon, Michigan, HB | Rush: 191 Yds: 852 TD: 16 | John Kimbrough, Texas A&M |
| 1941 | †Bruce Smith, Minnesota, HB | Rush: 98 Yds: 480 TD: 6 | Angelo Bertelli, Notre Dame |
| 1942 | Frank Sinkwich, Georgia, HB | Att/Comp: 166/84 Yds: 1392 TD: 10 | Paul Governali, Columbia |
| 1943 | Angelo Bertelli, Notre Dame, QB | Att/Comp: 36/25 Yds: 511 TD: 10 | Bob Odell, Pennsylvania |
| 1944 | Les Horvath, Ohio State, QB | Rush: 163 Yds: 924 TD: 12 | Glenn Davis, Army |
| 1945 | *†Doc Blanchard, Army, FB | Rush: 101 Yds: 718 TD: 13 | Glenn Davis, Army |
| 1946 | Glenn Davis, Army, HB | Rush: 123 Yds: 712 TD: 7 | Charley Trippi, Georgia |
| 1947 | †John Lujack, Notre Dame, QB | Att/Comp: 109/61 Yds: 777 TD: 9 | Bob Chappius, Michigan |
| 1948 | *Doak Walker, SMU, HB | Rush: 108 Yds: 532 TD: 8 | Charlie Justice, North Carolina |
| 1949 | †Leon Hart, Notre Dame, E | Rec: 19 Yds: 257 TD: 5 | Charlie Justice, North Carolina |
| 1950 | *Vic Janowicz, Ohio St, HB | Att/Comp: 77/32 Yds: 561 TD: 12 | Kyle Rote, SMU |
| 1951 | Dick Kazmaier, Princeton, HB | Rush: 149 Yds: 861 TD: 9 | Hank Lauricella, Tennessee |
| 1952 | Billy Vessels, Oklahoma, HB | Rush: 167 Yds: 1072 TD: 17 | Jack Scarbath, Maryland |
| 1953 | John Lattner, Notre Dame, HB | Rush: 134 Yds: 651 TD: 6 | Paul Giel, Minnesota |
| 1954 | Alan Ameche, Wisconsin, FB | Rush: 146 Yds: 641 TD: 9 | Kurt Burris, Oklahoma |
| 1955 | Howard Cassady, Ohio St, HB | Rush: 161 Yds: 958 TD: 15 | Jim Swink, TCU |
| 1956 | Paul Hornung, Notre Dame, QB | Att/Comp: 111/59 Yds: 917 TD: 3 | Johnny Majors, Tennessee |
| 1957 | John David Crow, Texas A&M, HB | Rush: 129 Yds: 562 TD: 10 | Alex Karras, Iowa |
| 1958 | Pete Dawkins, Army, HB | Rush: 78 Yds: 428 TD: 6 | Randy Duncan, Iowa |
| 1959 | Billy Cannon, LSU, HB | Rush: 139 Yds: 598 TD: 6 | Rich Lucas, Penn St |
| 1960 | Joe Bellino, Navy, HB | Rush: 168 Yds: 834 TD: 18 | Tom Brown, Minnesota |
| 1961 | Ernie Davis, Syracuse, HB | Rush: 150 Yds: 823 TD: 15 | Bob Ferguson, Ohio St |
| 1962 | Terry Baker, Oregon St, QB | Att/Comp: 203/112 Yds: 1738 TD: 15 | Jerry Stovall, LSU |
| 1963 | *Roger Staubach, Navy, QB | Att/Comp: 161/107 Yds: 1474 TD: 7 | Billy Lothridge, Georgia Tech |
| 1964 | John Huarte, Notre Dame, QB | Att/Comp: 205/114 Yds: 2062 TD: 16 | Jerry Rhome, Tulsa |

## Heisman Memorial Trophy (Cont.)

| Year | Winner, College, Position | Winner's Season Statistics | Runner-Up, College |
|---|---|---|---|
| 1965 | Mike Garrett, USC, HB | Rush: 267 Yds: 1440 TD: 16 | Howard Twilley, Tulsa |
| 1966 | Steve Spurrier, Florida, QB | Att/Comp: 291/179 Yds: 2012 TD: 1 | Bob Griese, Purdue |
| 1967 | Gary Beban, UCLA, QB | Att/Comp: 156/87 Yds: 1359 TD: 8 | O.J. Simpson, USC |
| 1968 | O.J. Simpson, USC, HB | Rush: 383 Yds: 1880 TD: 23 | Leroy Keyes, Purdue |
| 1969 | Steve Owens, Oklahoma, FB | Rush: 358 Yds: 1523 TD: 23 | Mike Phipps, Purdue |
| 1970 | Jim Plunkett, Stanford, QB | Att/Comp: 358/191 Yds: 2715 TD: 18 | Joe Theismann, Notre Dame |
| 1971 | Pat Sullivan, Auburn, QB | Att/Comp: 281/162 Yds: 2012; 20 TD | Ed Marinaro, Cornell |
| 1972 | Johnny Rodgers, Nebraska, FL | Rec: 55 Yds: 942 TD: 17 | Greg Pruitt, Oklahoma |
| 1973 | John Cappelletti, Penn St, HB | Rush: 286 Yds: 1522 TD: 17 | John Hicks, Ohio St |
| 1974 | *Archie Griffin, Ohio St, HB | Rush: 256 Yds: 1695 TD: 12 | Anthony Davis, USC |
| 1975 | Archie Griffin, Ohio St, HB | Rush: 262 Yds: 1450 TD: 4 | Chuck Muncie, California |
| 1976 | †Tony Dorsett, Pittsburgh, HB | Rush: 370 Yds: 2150 TD: 23 | Ricky Bell, USC |
| 1977 | Earl Campbell, Texas, FB | Rush: 267 Yds: 1744 TD: 19 | Terry Miller, Oklahoma St |
| 1978 | *Billy Sims, Oklahoma, HB | Rush: 231 Yds: 1762 TD: 20 | Chuck Fusina, Penn St |
| 1979 | Charles White, USC, HB | Rush: 332 Yds: 1803 TD: 19 | Billy Sims, Oklahoma |
| 1980 | George Rogers, South Carolina, HB | Rush: 324 Yds: 1894 TD: 14 | Hugh Green, Pittsburgh |
| 1981 | Marcus Allen, USC, HB | Rush: 433 Yds: 2427 TD: 23 | Herschel Walker, Georgia |
| 1982 | *Herschel Walker, Georgia, HB | Rush: 335 Yds: 1752 TD: 17 | John Elway, Stanford |
| 1983 | Mike Rozier, Nebraska, HB | Rush: 275 Yds: 2148 TD: 29 | Steve Young, BYU |
| 1984 | Doug Flutie, Boston College, QB | Att/Comp: 396/233 Yds: 3454 TD: 27 | Keith Byars, Ohio St |
| 1985 | Bo Jackson, Auburn, HB | Rush: 278 Yds: 1786 TD: 17 | Chuck Long, Iowa |
| 1986 | Vinny Testaverde, Miami (Fla.), QB | Att/Comp: 276/175 Yds: 2557 TD: 26 | Paul Palmer, Temple |
| 1987 | Tim Brown, Notre Dame, WR | Rec: 39 Yds: 846 TD: 7 | Don McPherson, Syracuse |
| 1988 | *Barry Sanders, Oklahoma St, RB | Rush: 344 Yds: 2628 TD: 39 | Rodney Peete, USC |
| 1989 | *Andre Ware, Houston, QB | Att/Comp: 578/365 Yds: 4699 TD: 46 | Anthony Thompson, Indiana |
| 1990 | *Ty Detmer, BYU, QB | Att/Comp: 562/361 Yds: 5188 TD: 41 | Raghib Ismail, Notre Dame |
| 1991 | *Desmond Howard, Michigan, WR | Rec: 61 Yds: 950 TD: 23 | Casey Weldon, Florida St |
| 1992 | Gino Torretta, Miami (FL), QB | Att/Comp: 402/228 Yds: 3060 TD: 19 | Marshall Faulk, San Diego St |
| 1993 | †Charlie Ward, Florida St, QB | Att/Comp: 380/264 Yds: 3032 TD: 27 | Heath Shuler, Tennessee |
| 1994 | Rashaan Salaam, Colorado, RB | Rush: 298 Yds: 2055 TD: 24 | Ki-Jana Carter, Penn St |
| 1995 | Eddie George, Ohio State, RB | Rush: 303 Yds: 1826 TD: 23 | Tommie Frazier, Nebraska |
| 1996 | †Danny Wuerffel, Florida, QB | Att/Comp: 360/207 Yds: 3625 TD: 39 | Troy Davis, Iowa St |
| 1997 | †Charles Woodson, Michigan, CB/ WR | 7 interceptions; Rec: 11 Yds: 231 TD: 4 | Peyton Manning, Tennessee |
| 1998 | Ricky Williams, Texas, RB | Rush: 361 Yds: 2124 TD: 28 | Michael Bishop, Kansas St |
| 1999 | Ron Dayne, Wisconsin, RB | Rush: 303 Yds: 1834 TD: 19 | Joe Hamilton, Georgia Tech |
| 2000 | Chris Weinke, Florida St, QB | Att/Comp: 431/266 Yds: 4167 TD: 33 | Josh Heupel, Oklahoma |
| 2001 | Eric Crouch, Nebraska, QB | Att/Comp: 189/105 Yds: 1510 TD: 7; Rush: 1115 Yds, 18 TD | Rex Grossman, Florida |
| 2002 | Carson Palmer, USC, QB | Att/Comp: 450/228 Yds: 3639 TD: 32 | Brad Banks, Iowa |
| 2003 | Jason White, Oklahoma, QB | Pct. Comp: 64; 3744 Yds; TD: 40 | Larry Fitzgerald, Pittsburgh |
| 2004 | *†Matt Leinart, USC, QB | Att/Comp: 269/412 Yds: 2990 TD: 28 | Adrian Peterson, Oklahoma |
| 2005 | **Vacated | | Vince Young, Texas |
| 2006 | Troy Smith, Ohio State, QB | Att/Comp: 311/203 Yds: 2542 TD: 30 | Darren McFadden, Arkansas |
| 2007 | ^Tim Tebow, Florida, QB | Att/Comp: 350/234 Yds: 3286 TD: 32 | Darren McFadden, Arkansas |
| 2008 | ^Sam Bradford, Oklahoma, QB | Att/Comp: 483/328 Yds: 4720 TD: 50 | Colt McCoy, Texas |
| 2009 | ^†Mark Ingram, Alabama, RB | Rush: 249 Yds:1,542 TD: 15 | Toby Gerhart, Stanford |
| 2010 | *†Cam Newton, Auburn, QB | Att/Comp: 280/185 Yds: 2854 TD: 30 Rush:1473 Yds TD:20 | Andrew Luck, Stanford |

*Juniors; ^Sophomore; (all others seniors). †Winners who played for national championship teams the same year. Note: Former Heisman winners and national media cast votes, with ballots allowing for three names (3 points for first, 2 for second and 1 for third). **In September 2010, Reggie Bush forfeited the 2005 Heisman Trophy he won while at USC.

## Maxwell Award

Given to the outstanding college player of the year by the Maxwell Club of Philadelphia.

| Year | Player, College, Position | Year | Player, College, Position |
|---|---|---|---|
| 1937 | Clint Frank, Yale, HB | 1974 | Steve Joachim, Temple, QB |
| 1938 | Davey O'Brien, TCU, QB | 1975 | Archie Griffin, Ohio St, RB |
| 1939 | Nile Kinnick, Iowa, HB | 1976 | Tony Dorsett, Pittsburgh, RB |
| 1940 | Tom Harmon, Michigan, HB | 1977 | Ross Browner, Notre Dame, DE |
| 1941 | Bill Dudley, Virginia, HB | 1978 | Chuck Fusina, Penn St, QB |
| 1942 | Paul Governali, Columbia, QB | 1979 | Charles White, USC, RB |
| 1943 | Bob Odell, Pennsylvania, HB | 1980 | Hugh Green, Pittsburgh, DE |
| 1944 | Glenn Davis, Army, HB | 1981 | Marcus Allen, USC, RB |
| 1945 | Doc Blanchard, Army, FB | 1982 | Herschel Walker, Georgia, RB |
| 1946 | Charley Trippi, Georgia, HB | 1983 | Mike Rozier, Nebraska, RB |
| 1947 | Doak Walker, SMU, HB | 1984 | Doug Flutie, Boston College, QB |
| 1948 | Chuck Bednarik, Pennsylvania, C | 1985 | Chuck Long, Iowa, QB |
| 1949 | Leon Hart, Notre Dame, E | 1986 | Vinny Testaverde, Miami (Fla.), QB |
| 1950 | Reds Bagnell, Pennsylvania, HB | 1987 | Don McPherson, Syracuse, QB |
| 1951 | Dick Kazmaier, Princeton, HB | 1988 | Barry Sanders, Oklahoma St, RB |
| 1952 | John Lattner, Notre Dame, HB | 1989 | Anthony Thompson, Indiana, RB |
| 1953 | John Lattner, Notre Dame, HB | 1990 | Ty Detmer, BYU, QB |
| 1954 | Ron Beagle, Navy, E | 1991 | Desmond Howard, Michigan, WR |
| 1955 | Howard Cassady, Ohio St, HB | 1992 | Gino Torretta, Miami (Fla.), QB |
| 1956 | Tommy McDonald, Oklahoma, HB | 1993 | Charlie Ward, Florida St, QB |
| 1957 | Bob Reifsnyder, Navy, T | 1994 | Kerry Collins, Penn St, QB |
| 1958 | Pete Dawkins, Army, HB | 1995 | Eddie George, Ohio St, RB |
| 1959 | Rich Lucas, Penn St, QB | 1996 | Danny Wuerffel, Florida, QB |
| 1960 | Joe Bellino, Navy, HB | 1997 | Peyton Manning, Tennessee, QB |
| 1961 | Bob Ferguson, Ohio St, FB | 1998 | Ricky Williams, Texas, RB |
| 1962 | Terry Baker, Oregon St, QB | 1999 | Ron Dayne, Wisconsin, RB |
| 1963 | Roger Staubach, Navy, QB | 2000 | Drew Brees, Purdue, QB |
| 1964 | Glenn Ressler, Penn St, C | 2001 | Ken Dorsey, Miami (Fla.), QB |
| 1965 | Tommy Nobis, Texas, LB | 2002 | Larry Johnson, Penn St, RB |
| 1966 | Jim Lynch, Notre Dame, LB | 2003 | Eli Manning, Mississippi, QB |
| 1967 | Gary Beban, UCLA, QB | 2004 | Jason White, Oklahoma, QB |
| 1968 | O.J. Simpson, USC, RB | 2005 | Vince Young, Texas, QB |
| 1969 | Mike Reid, Penn St, DT | 2006 | Brady Quinn, Notre Dame, QB |
| 1970 | Jim Plunkett, Stanford, QB | 2007 | Tim Tebow, Florida, QB |
| 1971 | Ed Marinaro, Cornell, RB | 2008 | Tim Tebow, Florida, QB |
| 1972 | Brad Van Pelt, Michigan St, DB | 2009 | Colt McCoy, Texas, QB |
| 1973 | John Cappelletti, Penn St, RB | 2010 | Cam Newton, Auburn, QB |

## Davey O'Brien National Quarterback Award

Given to the top quarterback in the nation by the Davey O'Brien Educational and Charitable Trust of Fort Worth. Named for TCU Hall of Fame quarterback Davey O'Brien (1936–38).

| Year | Player, College | Year | Player, College |
|---|---|---|---|
| 1981 | Jim McMahon, BYU | 1996 | Danny Wuerffel, Florida |
| 1982 | Todd Blackledge, Penn St | 1997 | Peyton Manning, Tennessee |
| 1983 | Steve Young, BYU | 1998 | Michael Bishop, Kansas St |
| 1984 | Doug Flutie, Boston College | 1999 | Joe Hamilton, Georgia Tech |
| 1985 | Chuck Long, Iowa | 2000 | Chris Weinke, Florida St |
| 1986 | Vinny Testaverde, Miami (Fla.) | 2001 | Eric Crouch, Nebraska |
| 1987 | Don McPherson, Syracuse | 2002 | Brad Banks, Iowa |
| 1988 | Troy Aikman, UCLA | 2003 | Jason White, Oklahoma |
| 1989 | Andre Ware, Houston | 2004 | Jason White, Oklahoma |
| 1990 | Ty Detmer, BYU | 2005 | Vince Young, Texas |
| 1991 | Ty Detmer, BYU | 2006 | Troy Smith, Ohio St |
| 1992 | Gino Torretta, Miami (Fla.) | 2007 | Tim Tebow, Florida |
| 1993 | Charlie Ward, Florida St | 2008 | Sam Bradford, Oklahoma |
| 1994 | Kerry Collins, Penn St | 2009 | Colt McCoy, Texas |
| 1995 | Danny Wuerffel, Florida | 2010 | Cam Newton, Auburn |

Note: Originally honored the outstanding football player in the Southwest as follows: 1977—Earl Campbell, Texas, RB; 1978—Billy Sims, Oklahoma, RB; 1979—Mike Singletary, Baylor, LB; 1980—Mike Singletary, Baylor, LB.

### Vince Lombardi/Rotary Award

Given to the outstanding college lineman of the year, the award is sponsored by the Rotary Club of Houston.

| Year | Player, College, Position | Year | Player, College, Position |
|------|---------------------------|------|---------------------------|
| 1970 | Jim Stillwagon, Ohio St, MG | 1991 | Steve Emtman, Washington, DT |
| 1971 | Walt Patulski, Notre Dame, DE | 1992 | Marvin Jones, Florida St, LB |
| 1972 | Rich Glover, Nebraska, MG | 1993 | Aaron Taylor, Notre Dame, OT |
| 1973 | John Hicks, Ohio St, OT | 1994 | Warren Sapp, Miami, DT |
| 1974 | Randy White, Maryland, DT | 1995 | Orlando Pace, Ohio St, OT |
| 1975 | Lee Roy Selmon, Oklahoma, DT | 1996 | Orlando Pace, Ohio St, OT |
| 1976 | Wilson Whitley, Houston, DT | 1997 | Grant Wistrom, Nebraska, DE |
| 1977 | Ross Browner, Notre Dame, DE | 1998 | Dat Nguyen, Texas A&M, LB |
| 1978 | Bruce Clark, Penn St, DT | 1999 | Corey Moore, Virginia Tech, DE |
| 1979 | Brad Budde, USC, G | 2000 | Jamal Reynolds, Florida St, DE |
| 1980 | Hugh Green, Pittsburgh, DE | 2001 | Julius Peppers, North Carolina, DE |
| 1981 | Kenneth Sims, Texas, DT | 2002 | Terrell Suggs, Arizona St, DL |
| 1982 | Dave Rimington, Nebraska, C | 2003 | Tommie Harris, Oklahoma, DT |
| 1983 | Dean Steinkuhler, Nebraska, G | 2004 | David Pollack, Georgia, DE |
| 1984 | Tony Degrate, Texas, DT | 2005 | A.J. Hawk, Ohio St, LB |
| 1985 | Tony Casillas, Oklahoma, NG | 2006 | LaMarr Woodley, Michigan, DE |
| 1986 | Cornelius Bennett, Alabama, LB | 2007 | Glenn Dorsey, LSU, DT |
| 1987 | Chris Spielman, Ohio St, LB | 2008 | Brian Orakpo, Texas, DE |
| 1988 | Tracy Rocker, Auburn, DT | 2009 | Ndamukong Suh, Nebraska, DT |
| 1989 | Percy Snow, Michigan St, LB | 2010 | Nick Fairley, Auburn, DT |
| 1990 | Chris Zorich, Notre Dame, NG | | |

### Outland Trophy

Given to the outstanding interior lineman, selected by the Football Writers Association of America.

| Year | Player, College, Position | Year | Player, College, Position |
|------|---------------------------|------|---------------------------|
| 1946 | George Connor, Notre Dame, T | 1979 | Jim Ritcher, North Carolina St, C |
| 1947 | Joe Steffy, Army, G | 1980 | Mark May, Pittsburgh, OT |
| 1948 | Bill Fischer, Notre Dame, G | 1981 | Dave Rimington, Nebraska, C |
| 1949 | Ed Bagdon, Michigan St, G | 1982 | Dave Rimington, Nebraska, C |
| 1950 | Bob Gain, Kentucky, T | 1983 | Dean Steinkuhler, Nebraska, G |
| 1951 | Jim Weatherall, Oklahoma, T | 1984 | Bruce Smith, Virginia Tech, DT |
| 1952 | Dick Modzelewski, Maryland, T | 1985 | Mike Ruth, Boston College, NG |
| 1953 | J.D. Roberts, Oklahoma, G | 1986 | Jason Buck, BYU, DT |
| 1954 | Bill Brooks, Arkansas, G | 1987 | Chad Hennings, Air Force, DT |
| 1955 | Calvin Jones, Iowa, G | 1988 | Tracy Rocker, Auburn, DT |
| 1956 | Jim Parker, Ohio St, G | 1989 | Mohammed Elewonibi, BYU, G |
| 1957 | Alex Karras, Iowa, T | 1990 | Russell Maryland, Miami (Fla.), DT |
| 1958 | Zeke Smith, Auburn, G | 1991 | Steve Emtman, Washington, DT |
| 1959 | Mike McGee, Duke, T | 1992 | Will Shields, Nebraska, G |
| 1960 | Tom Brown, Minnesota, G | 1993 | Rob Waldrop, Arizona, NG |
| 1961 | Merlin Olsen, Utah St, T | 1994 | Zach Wiegert, Nebraska, G |
| 1962 | Bobby Bell, Minnesota, T | 1995 | Jonathan Ogden, UCLA, OT |
| 1963 | Scott Appleton, Texas, T | 1996 | Orlando Pace, Ohio St, OT |
| 1964 | Steve DeLong, Tennessee, T | 1997 | Aaron Taylor, Nebraska, G |
| 1965 | Tommy Nobis, Texas, G | 1998 | Kris Farris, UCLA, OL |
| 1966 | Loyd Phillips, Arkansas, T | 1999 | Chris Samuels, Alabama, OL |
| 1967 | Ron Yary, USC, T | 2000 | John Henderson, Tennessee, DT |
| 1968 | Bill Stanfill, Georgia, T | 2001 | Bryant McKinnie, Miami (Fla.), OT |
| 1969 | Mike Reid, Penn St, DT | 2002 | Rien Long, Washington St, DL |
| 1970 | Jim Stillwagon, Ohio St, MG | 2003 | Robert Gallery, Iowa, OT |
| 1971 | Larry Jacobson, Nebraska, DT | 2004 | Jammal Brown, Oklahoma, OT |
| 1972 | Rich Glover, Nebraska, MG | 2005 | Greg Eslinger, Minnesota, LB |
| 1973 | John Hicks, Ohio St, OT | 2006 | Joe Thomas, Wisconsin, OT |
| 1974 | Randy White, Maryland, DE | 2007 | Glenn Dorsey, LSU, DT |
| 1975 | Lee Roy Selmon, Oklahoma, DT | 2008 | Andre Smith, Alabama, OT |
| 1976 | Ross Browner, Notre Dame, DE | 2009 | Ndamukong Suh, Nebraska, DT |
| 1977 | Brad Shearer, Texas, DT | 2010 | Gabe Carimi, Wisconsin, OT |
| 1978 | Greg Roberts, Oklahoma, G | | |

### Butkus Award

Given to the top collegiate linebacker, the award was established by the Downtown Athletic Club of Orlando and named for college Hall of Famer Dick Butkus of Illinois.

| Year | Player, College | Year | Player, College |
|------|-----------------|------|-----------------|
| 1985 | Brian Bosworth, Oklahoma | 1998 | Chris Claiborne, USC |
| 1986 | Brian Bosworth, Oklahoma | 1999 | LaVar Arrington, Penn St |
| 1987 | Paul McGowan, Florida St | 2000 | Dan Morgan, Miami (Fla.) |
| 1988 | Derrick Thomas, Alabama | 2001 | Rocky Calmus, Oklahoma |
| 1989 | Percy Snow, Michigan St | 2002 | E.J. Henderson, Maryland |
| 1990 | Alfred Williams, Colorado | 2003 | Teddy Lehman, Oklahoma |
| 1991 | Erick Anderson, Michigan | 2004 | Derrick Johnson, Texas |
| 1992 | Marvin Jones, Florida St | 2005 | Paul Posluszny, Penn State |
| 1993 | Trev Alberts, Nebraska | 2006 | Patrick Willis, Mississippi |
| 1994 | Dana Howard, Illinois | 2007 | James Laurinaitis, Ohio St |
| 1995 | Kevin Hardy, Illinois | 2008 | Aaron Curry, Wake Forest |
| 1996 | Matt Russell, Colorado | 2009 | Rolando McClain, Alabama |
| 1997 | Andy Katzenmoyer, Ohio St | 2010 | Von Miller, Texas A&M |

### Jim Thorpe Award

Given to the best defensive back of the year, the award is presented by the Jim Thorpe Athletic Club of Oklahoma City.

| Year | Player, College | Year | Player, College |
|------|-----------------|------|-----------------|
| 1986 | Thomas Everett, Baylor | 1998 | Antoine Winfield, Ohio St |
| 1987 | Bennie Blades, Miami (Fla.) | 1999 | Tyrone Carter, Minnesota |
|      | Rickey Dixon, Oklahoma | 2000 | Jamar Fletcher, Wisconsin |
| 1988 | Deion Sanders, Florida St | 2001 | Roy Williams, Oklahoma |
| 1989 | Mark Carrier, USC | 2002 | Terence Newman, Kansas St |
| 1990 | Darryl Lewis, Arizona | 2003 | Derrick Strait, Oklahoma |
| 1991 | Terrell Buckley, Florida St | 2004 | Carlos Rogers, Auburn |
| 1992 | Deon Figures, Colorado | 2005 | Michael Huff, Texas |
| 1993 | Antonio Langham, Alabama | 2006 | Aaron Ross, Texas |
| 1994 | Chris Hudson, Colorado | 2007 | Antoine Cason, Arizona |
| 1995 | Greg Myers, Colorado St | 2008 | Malcolm Jenkins, Ohio St |
| 1996 | Lawrence Wright, Florida | 2009 | Eric Berry, Tennessee |
| 1997 | Charles Woodson, Michigan | 2010 | Patrick Peterson, LSU |

### Walter Payton Player of the Year Award

Given to the top FCS (I-AA) player, voted by Div. I-AA sports information directors.

| Year | Player, College, Position | Year | Player, College, Position |
|------|---------------------------|------|---------------------------|
| 1987 | Kenny Gamble, Colgate, RB | 1999 | Adrian Peterson, Georgia Southern, RB |
| 1988 | Dave Meggett, Towson St, RB | 2000 | Louis Ivory, Furman, RB |
| 1989 | John Friesz, Idaho, QB | 2001 | Brian Westbrook, Villanova, RB |
| 1990 | Walter Dean, Grambling, RB | 2002 | Tony Romo, Eastern Ilinois, QB |
| 1991 | Jamie Martin, Weber St, QB | 2003 | Jamaal Branch, Colgate, RB |
| 1992 | Michael Payton, Marshall, QB | 2004 | Lang Campbell, William & Mary, QB |
| 1993 | Doug Nussmeier, Idaho, QB | 2005 | Erik Meyer, Eastern Washington, QB |
| 1994 | Steve McNair, Alcorn St, QB | 2006 | Ricky Santos, New Hampshire, QB |
| 1995 | Dave Dickenson, Montana, QB | 2007 | Jayson Foster, Georgia Southern, QB |
| 1996 | Archie Amerson, Northern Arizona, RB | 2008 | Armanti Edwards, Appalachian St, QB |
| 1997 | Brian Finneran, Villanova, WR | 2009 | Armanti Edwards, Appalachian St, QB |
| 1998 | Jerry Azumah, New Hampshire, RB | 2010 | Jeremy Moses, Stephen F. Austin, QB |

## Career

### SCORING

**Most Points Scored:** 468—Travis Prentice, Miami (Ohio), 1996–99
**Most Points Scored per Game:** 12.1—Marshall Faulk, San Diego St, 1991–93
**Most Touchdowns Scored:** 78—Travis Prentice, Miami (Ohio), 1996–99 (73 rushing, 5 receiving)
**Most Touchdowns Scored per Game:** 2.0—Marshall Faulk, San Diego St, 1991–93
**Most Touchdowns Scored, Rushing:** 73—Travis Prentice, Miami (Ohio), 1996–99
**Most Touchdowns Scored, Passing**: 134—Graham Harrell, Texas Tech, 2005–08 (4 years); 131—Colt Brennan, Hawaii, 2005–07 (3 years)
**Most Touchdowns Scored, Receiving:** 60—Jarrett Dillard, Rice, 2005–08
**Most Touchdowns Scored, Interception Returns:** 5—Ken Thomas, San Jose St, 1979–82; Jackie Walker, Tennessee, 1969–71; Deltha O'Neal, California, 1996–99; Darrent Williams, Okla St, 2001–04
**Most Touchdowns Scored, Punt Returns:** 8—Wes Welker, Texas Tech, 2000–03; Antonio Perkins, Oklahoma, 2001–04
**Most Touchdowns Scored, Kickoff Returns:** 7—C.J. Spiller, Clemson, 2006–09

### TOTAL OFFENSE

**Most Plays:** 2,587—Timmy Chang, Hawaii, 2000–04
**Most Plays per Game:** 50.1—Kliff Kingsbury, Texas Tech, 1999–2002
**Most Yards Gained:** 16,910—Timmy Chang, Hawaii, 2000–04 (17,072 passing, -162 rushing)
**Most Yards Gained per Game:** 387.9—Colt Brennan, Hawaii, 2005–07
**Most 300+ Yard Games:** 33 —Ty Detmer, BYU, 1988–91

### RUSHING

**Most Rushes:** 1,215—Steve Bartalo, Colorado St, 1983–86 (4,813 yds)
**Most Rushes per Game:** 34.0—Ed Marinaro, Cornell, 1969–71
**Most Yards Gained:** 6,397—Ron Dayne, Wisconsin, 1996–99
**Most Yards Gained per Game:** 174.6—Ed Marinaro, Cornell, 1969–71
**Most 100+ Yard Games:** 34—DeAngelo Williams, Memphis, 2002–05
**Most 200+ Yard Games:** 11—Marcus Allen, USC, 1978–81; Ricky Williams, Texas, 1995–98; Ron Dayne, Wisconsin, 1996–99

### SPECIAL TEAMS

**Highest Punt Return Average:** 23.6—Jack Mitchell, Oklahoma, 1946–48
**Highest Kickoff Return Average:** 36.2—Forrest Hall, San Francisco, 1946–47
**Highest Average Yards per Punt:** 46.3—Todd Sauerbrun, West Virginia, 1991–93 (150–199 punts). 45.3—Ryan Plackemeier, Wake Forest, 2002–05 (200-250 punts). 45.2—Daniel Sepulveda, Baylor, 2003–06 (250+ punts).

*Minimum 1,000 attempts.
†Minimum 200 receptions.
‡Minimum 275 plays.
§Active player.

### PASSING

**Highest Passing Efficiency Rating:** 175.6—Sam Bradford, Oklahoma, 2007–09 (min. 325 comp.)
**Most Passes Attempted:** 2,436—Timmy Chang, Hawaii, 2000–04
**Most Passes Attempted per Game:** 47.0—Tim Rattay, Louisiana Tech, 1997–99
**Most Passes Completed:** 1,403—Graham Harrell, Texas Tech, 2005–08
**Most Passes Completed per Game:** 31.2—Graham Harrell, Texas Tech, 2005–08
**\*Highest Completion Percentage:** 70.4—Colt Brennan, Hawaii, 2005–07
**Most Yards Gained:** 17,072—Timmy Chang, Hawaii, 2000–04
**Most Yards Gained per Game:** 386.2—Tim Rattay, Louisiana Tech, 1997–99 (3 years); 351.0—Graham Harrell, Texas Tech, 2005–08 (4 years)

### RECEIVING

**Most Passes Caught:** 316—Taylor Stubblefield, Purdue, 2001–04
**Most Passes Caught per Game:** 10.5—Emmanuel Hazard, Houston, 1989–90
**Most Yards Gained:** 5,005—Trevor Insley, Nevada, 1996–99
**Most Yards Gained per Game:** 140.9—Alex Van Dyke, Nevada, 1994–95
**†Highest Average Gain per Reception:** 19.0—Ryan Yarborough, Wyoming, 1990–93

### ALL-PURPOSE RUNNING

**Most Plays:** 1,347—Steve Bartalo, Colorado St, 1983-86 (1,215 rushes, 132 receptions)
**Most Yards Gained:** 7,796—§Damaris Johnson, Tulsa, 2008– (1,062 rushing, 2,746 receiving, 3,417 KO returns)
**Most Yards Gained per Game:** 237.8—Ryan Benjamin, Pacific, 1990–92
**‡Highest Average Gain per Play:** †7.4—Anthony Carter, Michigan, 1979–82

### INTERCEPTIONS

**Most Passes Intercepted:** 29—Al Brosky, Illinois, 1950–52
**Most Passes Intercepted per Game:** 1.1—Al Brosky, Illinois, 1950–52
**Most Yards on Interception Returns**: 501—Terrell Buckley, Florida St, 1989–91
**Highest Average Gain per Interception:** 26.5—Tom Pridemore, West Virginia, 1975–77

## Single Season

### SCORING

**Most Points Scored:** 234—Barry Sanders, Oklahoma St, 1988
**Most Points Scored per Game:** 21.3—Barry Sanders, Oklahoma St, 1988
**Most Touchdowns Scored:** 39—Barry Sanders, Oklahoma St, 1988
**Most Touchdowns Scored, Rushing:** 37—Barry Sanders, Oklahoma St, 1988
**Most Touchdowns Scored, Passing:** 58—Colt Brennan, Hawaii, 2006
**Most Touchdowns Scored, Receiving:** 27—Troy Edwards, Louisiana Tech, 1998
**Most Touchdowns Scored, Interception Returns:** 4—Deltha O'Neal, California, 1999
**Most Touchdowns Scored, Punt Returns:** 5—Chad Owens, Hawaii, 2004
**Most Touchdowns Scored, Kickoff Returns:** 5—Ashlan Davis, Tulsa, 2004

### TOTAL OFFENSE

**Most Plays:** 814—Kliff Kingsbury, Texas Tech, 2002
**Most Yards Gained**: 5,976—B.J. Symons, Texas Tech, 2003
**Most Yards Gained per Game:** 474.6—David Klingler, Houston, 1990
**Most 300+ Yard Games:** 14—Colt Brennan, Hawaii, 2006; Paul Smith, Tulsa, 2007

### RUSHING

**Most Rushes:** 450—Kevin Smith, Central Florida, 2007
**Most Rushes per Game:** 39.6—Ed Marinaro, Cornell, 1971
**Most Yards Gained:** 2,628—Barry Sanders, Oklahoma St, 1988
**Most Yards Gained per Game:** 238.9—Barry Sanders, Oklahoma St, 1988
**Most 100+ Yard Games:** 13—Shonn Greene, Iowa, 2008

### PASSING

**Highest Passing Efficiency Rating:** 186.0—Colt Brennan, Hawaii, 2006
**Most Passes Attempted:** 719—B.J. Symons, Texas Tech, 2003
**Most Passes Attempted per Game:** 58.5—David Klingler, Houston, 1990
**Most Passes Completed:** 512—Graham Harrell, Texas Tech, 2007

### PASSING *(Cont.)*

**Most Passes Completed per Game:** 39.4—Graham Harrell, Texas Tech, 2007
**Highest Completion Percentage:** 76.7—Colt McCoy, Texas, 2008
**Most Yards Gained:** 5,140—David Klingler, Houston, 1990 (11 games); 5,336—B.J. Symons, Texas Tech, 2003 (12 games); 5,833—B.J. Symons, Texas Tech, 2003 (13-plus games); 5,671
**Most Yards Gained per Game:** 467.3—David Klingler, Houston, 1990

### RECEIVING

**Most Passes Caught:** 155—Freddie Barnes, Bowling Green, 2009
**Most Passes Caught per Game:** 13.4—Howard Twilley, Tulsa, 1965
**Most Yards Gained:** 2,060—Trevor Insley, Nevada, 1999
**Most Yards Gained per Game:** 187.3—Trevor Insley, Nevada, 1999
**Highest Average Gain per Reception:** 31.9—Brennan Marion, Tulsa, 2007 (min. 30 receptions)

### ALL-PURPOSE RUNNING

**Most Plays:** 432—Marcus Allen, USC, 1981
**Most Yards Gained:** 3,250—Barry Sanders, Oklahoma St, 1988
**Most Yards Gained per Game:** 295.5—Barry Sanders, Oklahoma St, 1988
**Highest Average Gain per Play:** 19.8—T.Y. Hilton, Florida International, 2008 (min.100 plays)

### INTERCEPTIONS

**Most Passes Intercepted:** 14—Al Worley, Washington, 1968
**Most Yards on Interception Returns:** 302 —Charles Phillips, USC, 1974
**Highest Average Gain per Interception:** 51.8 —Norm Thompson, Utah, 1969

### SPECIAL TEAMS

**Highest Punt Return Average:** 28.5—Maurice Drew, UCLA, 2005
**Highest Kickoff Return Average:** 40.1 — Paul Allen, BYU, 1961
**Highest Average Yards per Punt:** 50.3 — Chad Kessler, LSU, 1997 (min. 36 punts)

## Single Game

### SCORING

**Most Points Scored:** 48—Howard Griffith, Illinois, 1990 (vs Southern Illinois)
**Most Field Goals:** 7—Dale Klein, Nebraska, 1985 (vs Missouri); Mike Prindle, Western Michigan, 1984 (vs Marshall)
**Most Extra Points (Kick):** 13—Derek Mahoney, Fresno St, 1991 (vs New Mexico); Terry Leiweke, Houston, 1968 (vs Tulsa)
**Most Extra Points (2-Pts):** 6—Jim Pilot, New Mexico St, 1961 (vs Hardin-Simmons), all 6 rush

### PASSING

**Most Passes Completed:** 58—Andy Schmitt, Eastern Michigan, 2008 (vs Central Michigan)
**Most Yards Gained:** 716—David Klingler, Houston, 1990 (vs Arizona St)
**Most Touchdown Passes:** 11—David Klingler, Houston, 1990 [vs Eastern Washington (I-AA)]

### TOTAL OFFENSE

**Most Yards Gained:** 732—David Klingler, Houston, 1990 (vs Arizona St); (716 pass, 16 rush)

### RUSHING

**Most Yards Gained:** 406—LaDainian Tomlinson, TCU, 1999 (vs UTEP)
**Most Touchdowns Rushed:** 8—Howard Griffith, Illinois, 1990 (vs Southern Illinois)

### RECEIVING

**Most Passes Caught:** 23—Randy Gatewood, UNLV, 1994 (vs Idaho); Tyler Jones, Eastern Michigan, 2008 (vs Central Michigan)
**Most Yards Gained:** 405—Troy Edwards, Louisiana Tech, 1998 (vs Nebraska)
**Most Touchdown Catches:** 7—Rashaun Woods, Oklahoma St, 2003 (vs SMU)

*Minimum 1,000 attempts.

## Career

### SCORING

**Most Points Scored:** 544—Brian Westbrook, Villanova, 1997–98, 2000-01
**Most Touchdowns Scored:** 89—Brian Westbrook, Villanova, 1997–98, 2000-01
**Most Touchdowns Scored, Rushing:** 84—Adrian Peterson, Georgia Southern, 1998–2001
**Most Touchdowns Scored, Passing:** 140—Bruce Eugene, Grambling St, 2001–05
**Most Touchdowns Scored, Receiving:** 58—David Ball, New Hampshire, 2003–06

### RUSHING

**Most Rushes:** 1,240—Jordan Scott, Colgate, 2005–08
**Most Rushes per Game:** 38.2—Arnold Mickens, Butler, 1994–95
**Most Yards Gained:** 6,559—Adrian Peterson, Georgia Southern, 1998–2001
**Most Yards Gained per Game:** 190.7—Arnold Mickens, Butler, 1994–95 (2 years); 164.5—Adrian Peterson, Georgia Southern, 1998–2000 (3 years); 156.2—Adrian Peterson, Georgia Southern, 1998–2001 (4 years)

### PASSING

**Highest Passing Efficiency Rating:** 176.7—Josh Johnson, San Diego, 2004–07
**Most Passes Attempted:** 1,893—Jeremy Moses, Stephen F. Austin, 2007–10
**Most Passes Completed:** 1,184—Jeremy Moses, Stephen F. Austin, 2007–10
**Most Passes Completed per Game:** 26.9—Jeremy Moses, Stephen F. Austin, 2007–10
**Highest Completion Percentage:** 69.6—Eric Sanders, Northern Iowa, 2004–07
**Most Yards Gained:** 14,496—Steve McNair, Alcorn St, 1991–94
**Most Yards Gained per Game:** 350.0—Neil Lomax, Portland St, 1978–80

### RECEIVING

**Most Passes Caught:** 395—Terrell Hudgins, Elon, 2006–09
**Most Yards Gained:** 5,250—Terrell Hudgins, Elon, 2006–09
**Most Yards Gained per Game:** 116.7—Terrell Hudgins, Elon, 2006–09 (min. 3,000 yds)
**Highest Average Gain per Reception:** 22.0—Dedric Ward, Northern Iowa, 1993–96 (min. 125 rec.)

## Single Season

### SCORING

**Most Points Scored:** 234—Omar Cuff, Delaware, 2007
**Most Touchdowns Scored:** 39—Omar Cuff, Delaware, 2007 (15 games)
**Most Touchdowns Scored, Rushing:** 35—Omar Cuff, Delaware, 2007
**Most Touchdowns Scored, Passing:** 56—Willie Totten, Mississippi Valley St, 1984; Bruce Eugene, Grambling St, 2005
**Most Touchdowns Scored, Receiving:** 27—Jerry Rice, Mississippi Valley St, 1984

### PASSING

**Highest Passing Efficiency Rating:** 204.6—Shawn Knight, William & Mary, 1993
**Most Passes Attempted:** 598—Jeremy Moses, Stephen F. Austin, 2008
**Most Passes Completed:** 385—Brett Gordon, Villanova, 2002; Jeremy Moses, Stephen F. Austin, 2009
**Most Passes Completed per Game:** 32.4—Willie Totten, Mississippi Valley St, 1984
**Highest Completion Percentage:** 75.2—Eric Sanders, Northern Iowa, 2007
**Most Yards Gained:** 4,863—Steve McNair, Alcorn St, 1994
**Most Yards Gained per Game:** 455.7—Willie Totten, Mississippi Valley St, 1984

### RUSHING

**Most Rushes:** 450—Jamaal Branch, Colgate, 2003
**Most Rushes per Game:** 40.9—Arnold Mickens, Butler, 1994
**Most Yards Gained:** 2,326—Jamaal Branch, Colgate, 2003
**Most Yards Gained per Game:** 225.5—Arnold Mickens, Butler, 1994

### RECEIVING

**Most Passes Caught:** 123—Terrell Hudgins, Elon, 2009
**Most Yards Gained:** 1,712—Eddie Conti, Delaware, 1998
**Most Yards Gained per Game:** 168.2—Jerry Rice, Mississippi Valley St, 1984
**Highest Average Gain per Reception:** 28.9—Mikhael Ricks, Stephen F. Austin, 1997; (min. 35 receptions); 20.7—Golden Tate, Tennessee St, 1983 (min 60 receptions)

## Single Game

### SCORING

**Most Points Scored:** 42—Omar Cuff, Delaware, 2007 (vs William & Mary); Jesse Burton, McNeese St, 1998 (vs Southern Utah); Archie Amerson, Northern Arizona, 1996 (vs Weber St)
**Most Field Goals:** 8—Goran Lingmerth, Northern Arizona, 1986 (vs Idaho)

### RUSHING

**Most Yards Gained:** 437—Maurice Hicks, North Carolina A&T, 2001 (vs Morgan St)
**Most Touchdowns Rushed:** 7—Archie Amerson, Northern Arizona, 1996 (vs Weber St)

### PASSING

**Most Passes Completed:** 57—Jeremy Moses, Stephen F. Austin, 2008, (vs. Sam Houston St)
**Most Yards Gained:** 624—Jamie Martin, Weber St, 1991 (vs Idaho St)
**Most Touchdown Passes:** 9—Willie Totten, Mississippi Valley St, 1984 (vs Kentucky St); Drew Hubel, Portland St, 2007 (vs Weber St)

### RECEIVING

**Most Passes Caught:** 24—Chas Gessner, Brown, 2002, (vs Rhode Island); Jerry Rice, Mississippi Valley St, 1983 (vs Southern–Birmingham)
**Most Yards Gained:** 376—Kassim Osgood, Cal Poly, 2000 (vs Northern Iowa)
**Most Touchdown Catches:** 6—Cos DeMatteo, Chattanooga, 2000 (vs Mississippi Valley St)

# NCAA Division II Individual Records

## Career

### SCORING

**Most Points Scored:** 656—Germaine Rice, Pittsburg St, 2003–06
**Most Touchdowns Scored:** 109—Germaine Rice, Pittsburg St, 2003–06; Danny Woodhead, Chadron St 2004–07
**Most Touchdowns Scored, Rushing:** 107—Germaine Rice, Pittsburg St, 2003–06
**Most Touchdowns Scored, Passing:** 148—Jimmy Terwilliger, East Stroudsburg, 2003–06
**Most Touchdowns Scored, Receiving:** 78—Dallas Mall, Bentley, 2001–04

### RUSHING

**Most Rushes:** 1,271—Xavier Omon, NW Missouri St, 2004–07
**Most Rushes per Game:** 29.8—Bernie Peeters, Luther, 1968–71
**Most Yards Gained:** 7,962—Danny Woodhead, Chadron St, 2004–07
**Most Yards Gained per Game:** 183.4—Anthony Gray, Western New Mexico, 1997–98

### PASSING

**Highest Passing Efficiency Rating:** 170.7—Jimmy Terwilliger, East Stroudsburg, 2003–06 (Min. 750 comps.)
**Most Passes Attempted:** 1,898—Andrew Webb, Fort Lewis, 2000–03

### PASSING *(Cont.)*

**Most Passes Completed:** 1,119—Steven Gachette, Southwest Baptist, 2007–10
**Most Passes Completed per Game:** 25.9—Evan Gray, Missouri S&T*, 2003–05
**Highest Completion Percentage:** 70.2—Troy Weatherhead, Hillsdale, 2006–10 (min. 1,000 att.)
**Most Yards Gained:** 14,733—Zach Amedro, West Liberty, 2007–10
**Most Yards Gained per Game:** 334.8—Zach Amedro, West Liberty, 2007–10

### RECEIVING

**Most Passes Caught:** 323—Clarence Coleman, Ferris St, 1998–2001
**Most Yards Gained:** 4,983—Clarence Coleman, Ferris St, 1998–2001
**Most Yards Gained per Game:** 160.8—Chris George, Glenville St, 1993–94
**Highest Average Gain per Reception:** 23.2—Romar Crenshaw, SE Oklahoma, 2000–03 (min. 135 receptions)

*Missouri S&T was formerly known as Missouri-Rolla.

### Single Season

#### SCORING

**Most Points Scored:** 228—Xavier Odom, Northwest Missouri St, 2007; Danny Woodhead, Chadron St, 2006

**Most Touchdowns Scored:** 38—Xavier Omon, NW Missouri St, 2007; Danny Woodhead, Chadron St, 2006

**Most Touchdowns Scored, Rushing:** 37—Xavier Omon, NW Missouri St, 2007

**Most Touchdowns Scored, Passing:** 54—Dusty Bonner, Valdosta St, 2000

**Most Touchdowns Scored, Receiving:** 35—David Kircus, Grand Valley St, 2002

#### RUSHING

**Most Rushes:** 385—Joe Gough, Wayne St (Mich.), 1994

**Most Rushes per Game:** 38.6—Mark Perkins, Hobart, 1968

**Most Yards Gained:** 2,756—Danny Woodhead, Chadron St, 2006

**Most Yards Gained per Game:** 222.0—Anthony Gray, Western New Mexico, 1997

#### PASSING

**Highest Passing Efficiency Rating:** 221.6—Curt Anes, Grand Valley St, 2001 (min. 100 comp.); 196.5—Dusty Bonner, Valdosta St, 2001 (min. 200 comp.)

**Most Passes Attempted:** 670—Eric Czerniewski, Central Missouri, 2010

**Most Passes Completed:** 447—Eric Czerniewski, Central Missouri, 2010

**Most Passes Completed per Game:** 40.4—J.J. Harp, Eastern New Mexico, 2009

**Highest Completion Percentage:** 76.9—Troy Weatherhead, Hillsdale, 2010 (min. 250 att.)

**Most Yards Gained:** 5,207—Eric Czerniewski, Central Missouri, 2010

**Most Yards Gained per Game:** 437.3—J.J. Harp, Eastern New Mexico, 2009

#### RECEIVING

**Most Passes Caught:** 143—Nick Smart, Southwest Baptist, 2007

**Most Yards Gained:** 1,876—Chris George, Glenville St, 1993

**Most Yards Gained per Game:** 187.6—Chris George, Glenville St, 1993

**Highest Average Gain per Reception:** 32.5—Tyrone Johnson, Western St, 1991 (min. 30 receptions)

### Single Game

#### SCORING

**Most Points Scored:** 48—Paul Zaeske, North Park, 1968 (vs North Central [Ill.]); Junior Wolf, Okla. Panhandle St, 1958 (vs St. Mary [Ks.])

**Most Field Goals:** 6—Steve Huff, Central Missouri St, 1985 (vs SE Missouri St); Austin Wellock, Ashland, 2002 (vs. Wayne St)

#### RUSHING

**Most Yards Gained:** 418—Jarom Freeman, Southern Connecticut St, 2007 (vs Bryant)

**Most Touchdowns Rushed:** 8—Junior Wolf, Okla. Panhandle St, 1958 (vs St. Mary [Ks.])

#### PASSING

**Most Passes Completed:** 64—J.J. Harp, Eastern New Mexico, 2009 (vs SE Oklahoma)

**Most Yards Gained:** 695—J.J. Harp, Eastern New Mexico, 2009 (vs SE Oklahoma)

**Most Touchdowns Passed:** 10—Bruce Swanson, North Park, 1968 (vs North Central [Ill.])

#### RECEIVING

**Most Passes Caught:** 23—Chris George, Glenville St, 1994 (vs W.V. Wesleyan); Barry Wagner, Alabama A&M, 1989 (vs Clark Atlanta)

**Most Yards Gained:** 401—Kevin Ingram, West Chester, 1998 (vs Clarion)

**Most Touchdown Catches:** 8—Paul Zaeske, North Park, 1968 (vs North Central [Ill.])

## NCAA Division III Individual Records

### Career

#### SCORING

**Most Points Scored:** 780—Nate Kmic, Mount Union, 2005–08

**Most Touchdowns Scored:** 130—Nate Kmic, Mount Union, 2005–08

**Most Touchdowns Scored, Rushing:** 125—Nate Kmic, Mount Union, 2005–08

**Most Touchdowns Scored, Passing:** 148—Justin Peery, Westminster (Mo.), 1996–99

**Most Touchdowns Scored, Receiving:** 75—Scott Pingel, Westminster (Mo.), 1996–99

#### RUSHING

**Most Rushes:** 1,190—Steve Tardif, Maine Maritime, 1996–99

**Most Rushes per Game:** 32.7—Chris Sizemore, Bridgewater (Va.), 1972–74

#### RUSHING *(Cont.)*

**Most Yards Gained:** 8,074—Nate Kmic, Mount Union, 2005–08

**Most Yards Gained per Game:** 187.1—Tony Sutton, Wooster, 2002–04

#### PASSING

**Highest Passing Efficiency Rating:** 194.2—Greg Micheli, Mount Union, 2005–08 (min. 325 comps.)

**Most Passes Attempted:** 1,982—Josh Vogelbach, Guilford, 2005–08

**Most Passes Completed:** 1,189—Josh Vogelbach, Guilford, 2005–08

**Most Passes Completed per Game:** 29.7—Josh Vogelbach, Guilford, 2005–08

**Highest Completion Percentage:** 74.1—Greg Micheli, Mount Union, 2005–08 (min. 750 att.)

## Career *(Cont.)*

### PASSING *(Cont.)*

**Most Yards Gained:** 13,605—Josh Vogelbach, Guilford, 2005–08
**Most Yards Gained per Game:** 358.9—Brett Elliott, Linfield, 2004–05

### RECEIVING

**Most Passes Caught:** 436—Scott Pingel, Westminster (Mo.), 1996–99
**Most Yards Gained:** 6,108—Scott Pingel, Westminster (Mo.), 1996–99
**Most Yards Gained per Game:** 156.6—Scott Pingel, Westminster (Mo.), 1996–99
**Highest Average Gain per Reception:** 23.4—Michael Coleman, Widener, 1998–2001

## Single Season

### SCORING

**Most Points Scored:** 264—Nate Kmic, Mount Union, 2008
**Most Points Scored per Game:** 20.8—James Regan, Pomona-Pitzer, 1997
**Most Touchdowns Scored:** 44—Nate Kmic, Mount Union, 2008
**Most Touchdowns Scored, Rushing:** 43—Nate Kmic, Mount Union, 2008
**Most Touchdowns Scored, Passing:** 61—Brett Elliott, Linfield, 2004
**Most Touchdowns Scored, Receiving:** 26—Scott Pingel, Westminster (Mo.), 1998; Jack Phelan, Hartwick, 2008

### RUSHING

**Most Rushes:** 463—Dante Washington, Carthage, 2004
**Most Rushes per Game:** 38.0—Mike Birosak, Dickinson, 1989
**Most Yards Gained:** 2,790—Nate Kmic, Mount Union, 2008
**Most Yards Gained per Game:** 238.5—Dante Brown, Marietta, 1996

### PASSING

**Highest Passing Efficiency Rating:** 225.0—Mike Simpson, Eureka, 1994
**Most Passes Attempted:** 575—Brett Dietz, Hanover, 2003
**Most Passes Completed:** 360—Brett Dietz, Hanover, 2003
**Most Passes Completed per Game:** 32.9—Justin Peery, Westminster (Mo.), 1999
**Highest Completion Percentage:** 75.0—Greg Micheli, Mount Union, 2008
**Most Yards Gained:** 4,595—Brett Elliott, Linfield, 2004
**Most Yards Gained per Game:** 450.1—Justin Peery, Westminster (Mo.), 1998

### RECEIVING

**Most Passes Caught:** 136—Scott Pingel, Westminster (Mo.), 1999
**Most Yards Gained:** 2,157—Scott Pingel, Westminster, (Mo.), 1998
**Most Yards Gained per Game:** 215.7—Scott Pingel, Westminster (Mo.), 1998
**Highest Average Gain per Reception:** 26.9—Marty Redlawsk, Concordia (Ill.), 1985 (min. 35 receptions)

## Single Game

### SCORING

**Most Points Scored:** 48—Carey Bender, Coe, 1994 (vs Beloit)
**Most Field Goals:** 6—Jim Hever, Rhodes, 1984 (vs Millsaps)

### PASSING

**Most Passes Completed:** 56—Brandon Luczak, Kalamazoo, 2009 (vs Hope)
**Most Yards Gained:** 731—Zamir Amin, Menlo, 2000 (vs California Lutheran)
**Most Touchdown Passes:** 9—Joe Zarlinga, Ohio Northern, 1998 (vs Capital)

### RUSHING

**Most Yards Gained:** 441—Dante Brown, Marietta, 1996 (vs Baldwin-Wallace)
**Most Touchdowns Rushed:** 8—Carey Bender, Coe, 1994 (vs Beloit)

### RECEIVING

**Most Passes Caught:** 25—Daniel Passafiume, Hanover, 2009 (vs Franklin)
**Most Yards Gained:** 418—Lewis Howes, Principia, 2002 (vs Martin Luther)
**Most Touchdown Catches:** 7—Matt Perceval, Wesleyan (Conn.), 1998 (vs Middlebury)

## Career

### Scoring

**POINTS (KICKERS)**

| | Years | Pts |
|---|---|---|
| Kyle Brotzman, Boise St | 2007–10 | 439 |
| Art Carmody, Louisville | 2004–07 | 433 |
| ‡Kevin Kelly, Penn St | 2005–08 | 425 |
| Roman Anderson, Houston | 1988–91 | 423 |
| Billy Bennett, Georgia | 2000–03 | 409 |

‡includes one TD and one 2-pt. conversion (rush)

**POINTS (NON-KICKERS)**

| | Years | Pts |
|---|---|---|
| Travis Prentice, Miami (Ohio) | 1996–99 | 468 |
| Ricky Williams, Texas | 1995–98 | 452 |
| Taurean Henderson, Texas Tech | 2002–05 | 414 |
| Brock Forsey, Boise St | 1999–02 | 408 |
| Cedric Benson, Texas | 2001–04 | 404 |

**POINTS PER GAME (NON-KICKERS)**

| | Years | Pts/Game |
|---|---|---|
| Marshall Faulk, San Diego St | 1991–93 | 12.1 |
| Ed Marinaro, Cornell | 1969–71 | 11.8 |
| Bill Burnett, Arkansas | 1968–70 | 11.3 |
| Steve Owens, Oklahoma | 1967–69 | 11.2 |
| Eddie Talboom, Wyoming | 1948–50 | 10.8 |

### Total Offense

**YARDS GAINED**

| | Years | Yds |
|---|---|---|
| Timmy Chang, Hawaii | 2000–04 | 16,910 |
| Dan LeFevour, Central Michigan | 2006–09 | 15,853 |
| Graham Harrell, Texas Tech | 2005–08 | 15,599 |
| Colt McCoy, Texas | 2006–09 | 14,824 |
| Colt Brennan, Hawaii | 2005–07 | 14,740 |

**YARDS PER GAME**

| | Years | Yds/Game |
|---|---|---|
| Colt Brennan, Hawaii | 2005–07 | 387.9 |
| Tim Rattay, Louisiana Tech | 1997–99 | 382.4 |
| Graham Harrell, Texas Tech | 2005–08 | 346.6 |
| Chase Holbrook, New Mexico St | 2005–08 | 321.4 |
| Chris Vargas, Nevada | 1992–93 | 320.9 |

### Rushing

**YARDS GAINED**

| | Years | Yds |
|---|---|---|
| Ron Dayne, Wisconsin | 1996–99 | 6,397 |
| Ricky Williams, Texas | 1995–98 | 6,279 |
| Tony Dorsett, Pittsburgh | 1973–76 | 6,082 |
| DeAngelo Williams, Memphis | 2002–05 | 6,026 |
| Charles White, USC | 1976–79 | 5,598 |
| Travis Prentice, Miami (Ohio) | 1996–99 | 5,596 |

**YARDS PER GAME**

| | Years | Yds/Game |
|---|---|---|
| Ed Marinaro, Cornell | 1969–71 | 174.6 |
| O.J. Simpson, USC | 1967–68 | 164.4 |
| Herschel Walker, Georgia | 1980–82 | 159.4 |
| Garrett Wolfe, Northern Illinois | 2004-06 | 156.5 |
| LeShon Johnson, Northern Illinois | 1992–93 | 150.6 |

**TOUCHDOWNS RUSHING**

| | Years | TD |
|---|---|---|
| Travis Prentice, Miami (Ohio) | 1996–99 | 73 |
| Ricky Williams, Texas | 1995–98 | 72 |
| Anthony Thompson, Indiana | 1986–89 | 64 |
| Cedric Benson, Texas | 2001–04 | 64 |
| Ron Dayne, Wisconsin | 1996–99 | 63 |

### Passing

**PASSING EFFICIENCY**

| | Years | Rating |
|---|---|---|
| Sam Bradford, Oklahoma | 2007–09 | 175.6 |
| Tim Tebow, Florida | 2006–09 | 170.8 |
| Ryan Dinwiddie, Boise St | 2000–03 | 168.9 |
| Colt Brennan, Hawaii | 2005–07 | 167.7 |
| Danny Wuerffel, Florida | 1993–96 | 163.6 |

Note: Minimum 500 completions.

**YARDS GAINED**

| | Years | Yds |
|---|---|---|
| Timmy Chang, Hawaii | 2000–04 | 17,072 |
| Graham Harrell, Texas Tech | 2005–08 | 15,793 |
| Ty Detmer, BYU | 1988–91 | 15,031 |
| Colt Brennan, Hawaii | 2005–07 | 14,193 |
| *Case Keenum, Houston | 2007–11 | 13,586 |

**COMPLETIONS**

| | Years | Comp |
|---|---|---|
| Graham Harrell, Texas Tech | 2005–08 | 1,403 |
| Timmy Chang, Hawaii | 2000–04 | 1,388 |
| Kliff Kingsbury, Texas Tech | 1999–02 | 1,231 |
| Dan LeFevour, Central Michigan | 2006–09 | 1,171 |
| Colt McCoy, Texas | 2007–10 | 1,157 |

**TOUCHDOWNS PASSING**

| | Years | TD |
|---|---|---|
| Graham Harrell, Texas Tech | 2005–08 | 134 |
| Colt Brennan, Hawaii | 2005–07 | 131 |
| Ty Detmer, BYU | 1988–91 | 121 |
| Timmy Chang, Hawaii | 2000–04 | 117 |
| Tim Rattay, Louisiana Tech | 1997–99 | 115 |

### Receiving

**CATCHES**

| | Years | No. |
|---|---|---|
| Taylor Stubblefield, Purdue | 2001–04 | 316 |
| Josh Davis, Marshall | 2001–04 | 306 |
| Antonion Brown, Central Michigan | 2007–09 | 305 |
| Taurean Henderson, Texas Tech | 2002–05 | 303 |
| Arnold Jackson, Louisville | 1997–00 | 300 |

**CATCHES PER GAME**

| | Years | No./Game |
|---|---|---|
| Emmanuel Hazard, Houston | 1989–90 | 10.5 |
| Alex Van Dyke, Nevada | 1994–95 | 10.3 |
| Howard Twilley, Tulsa | 1963–65 | 10.0 |
| Jason Phillips, Houston | 1987–88 | 9.4 |
| Michael Crabtree, Texas Tech | 2007–08 | 8.9 |

**YARDS GAINED**

| | Years | Yds |
|---|---|---|
| Trevor Insley, Nevada | 1996–99 | 5,005 |
| Marcus Harris, Wyoming | 1993–96 | 4,518 |
| Rashaun Woods, Oklahoma St | 2000–03 | 4,412 |
| Ryan Yarborough, Wyoming | 1990–93 | 4,357 |
| Troy Edwards, Louisiana Tech | 1996–98 | 4,352 |

**TOUCHDOWN CATCHES**

| | Years | TD |
|---|---|---|
| Jarrett Dillard, Rice | 2005–08 | 60 |
| Troy Edwards, Louisiana Tech | 1996–98 | 50 |
| Darius Watts, Marshall | 2000–03 | 47 |
| Aaron Turner, Pacific | 1989–92 | 43 |
| Ryan Yarborough, Wyoming | 1990–93 | 42 |
| Rashaun Woods, Oklahoma St | 2000–03 | 42 |

*Active player.

## Career *(Cont.)*

### All-Purpose Running

| YARDS GAINED | Years | Yds |
|---|---|---|
| *Damaris Johnson, Tulsa | 2008–10 | 7,796 |
| Brandon West, Western Michigan | 2006–09 | 7,764 |
| C.J. Spiller, Clemson | 2006–09 | 7,588 |
| DeAngelo Williams, Memphis | 2002–05 | 7,573 |
| Ricky Williams, Texas | 1996–98 | 7,206 |

| YARDS PER GAME | Years | Yds/Game |
|---|---|---|
| Ryan Benjamin, Pacific | 1990–92 | 237.8 |
| Sheldon Canley, San Jose St | 1988–90 | 205.8 |
| Jeremy Maclin, Missouri | 2007–08 | 200.3 |
| Howard Stevens, Louisville | 1971–72 | 193.7 |
| O.J. Simpson, USC | 1967–68 | 192.9 |

### Interceptions

| PLAYER/SCHOOL | Years | Int |
|---|---|---|
| Al Brosky, Illinois | 1950–52 | 29 |
| John Provost, Holy Cross | 1972–74 | 27 |
| Martin Bayless, Bowling Green | 1980–83 | 27 |
| Tom Curtis, Michigan | 1967–69 | 25 |
| Tony Thurman, Boston College | 1981–84 | 25 |
| Tracy Saul, Texas Tech | 1989–92 | 25 |

### Punting Average

| PLAYER/SCHOOL | Years | Avg |
|---|---|---|
| Daniel Sepulveda, Baylor | 2003–06 | 45.2 |
| Shane Lechler, Texas A&M | 1996–99 | 44.7 |
| Bill Smith, Mississippi | 1983–86 | 44.3 |
| Jim Arnold, Vanderbilt | 1979–82 | 43.9 |
| Ralf Mojsiejenko, Michigan St | 1981–84 | 43.6 |

Note: Minimum 250 punts.

### Punt Return Average

| PLAYER/SCHOOL | Years | Avg |
|---|---|---|
| Jack Mitchell, Oklahoma | 1946–48 | 23.6 |
| Gene Gibson, Cincinnati | 1949–50 | 20.5 |
| Eddie Macon, Pacific | 1949–51 | 18.9 |
| Jackie Robinson, UCLA | 1939–40 | 18.8 |
| Dan Shelton, Illinois | 2001–04 | 17.9 |

Note: Minimum 30 returns.

### Kickoff Return Average

| PLAYER/SCHOOL | Years | Avg |
|---|---|---|
| Anthony Davis, USC | 1972–74 | 35.1 |
| Eric Booth, Southern Miss | 1994–97 | 32.4 |
| Overton Curtis, Utah St | 1957–58 | 31.0 |
| Fred Montgomery, New Mexico St | 1991–92 | 30.5 |
| Bryan Williams, Akron | 2005–08 | 30.5 |

Note: Minimum 30 returns.

## Single Season

### Scoring

| POINTS | Year | Pts |
|---|---|---|
| Barry Sanders, Oklahoma St | 1988 | 234 |
| Brock Forsey, Boise St | 2002 | 192 |
| Troy Edwards, Louisiana Tech | 1998 | 186 |
| Kevin Smith, Central Florida | 2007 | 180 |
| Lydell Mitchell, Penn St | 1971 | 174 |
| Mike Rozier, Nebraska | 1983 | 174 |

| FIELD GOALS | Year | FG |
|---|---|---|
| Billy Bennett, Georgia | 2003 | 31 |
| Leigh Tiffin, Alabama | 2009 | 30 |
| John Lee, UCLA | 1984 | 29 |
| John Sullivan, New Mexico | 2007 | 29 |
| Paul Woodside, West Virginia | 1982 | 28 |
| Luis Zendejas, Arizona St | 1983 | 28 |
| Nick Browne, TCU | 2003 | 28 |
| Justin Medlock, UCLA | 2006 | 28 |
| Kai Forbath, UCLA | 2009 | 28 |
| John Jasper, LSU | 2010 | 28 |

### All-Purpose Running

| YARDS GAINED | Year | Yds |
|---|---|---|
| Barry Sanders, Oklahoma St | 1988 | 3,250 |
| Ryan Benjamin, Pacific | 1991 | 2,995 |
| Chris Johnson, East Carolina | 2007 | 2,960 |
| Jeremy Maclin, Missouri | 2008 | 2,833 |
| Kevin Smith, Central Florida | 2007 | 2,809 |

| YARDS PER GAME | Year | Yds/Game |
|---|---|---|
| Barry Sanders, Oklahoma St | 1988 | 295.5 |
| Ryan Benjamin, Pacific | 1991 | 249.6 |
| Byron (Whizzer) White, Colorado | 1937 | 246.3 |
| Mike Pringle, Fullerton St | 1989 | 244.6 |
| Paul Palmer, Temple | 1986 | 239.4 |

### Total Offense

| YARDS GAINED | Year | Yds |
|---|---|---|
| B.J. Symons, Texas Tech | 2003 | 5,976 |
| Colt Brennan, Hawaii | 2006 | 5,915 |
| Case Keenum, Houston | 2009 | 5,829 |
| Graham Harrell, Texas Tech | 2007 | 5,614 |
| Case Keenum, Houston | 2008 | 5,241 |

| YARDS PER GAME | Year | Yds/Game |
|---|---|---|
| David Klingler, Houston | 1990 | 474.6 |
| B.J. Symons, Texas Tech | 2003 | 459.7 |
| Graham Harrell, Texas Tech | 2007 | 431.8 |
| Andre Ware, Houston | 1989 | 423.7 |
| Colt Brennan, Hawaii | 2006 | 422.5 |

### Rushing

| YARDS GAINED | Year | Yds |
|---|---|---|
| Barry Sanders, Oklahoma St | 1988 | 2,628 |
| Kevin Smith, Central Florida | 2007 | 2,567 |
| Marcus Allen, USC | 1981 | 2,342 |
| Troy Davis, Iowa St | 1996 | 2,185 |
| LaDainian Tomlinson, TCU | 2000 | 2,158 |

| YARDS PER GAME | Year | Yds/Game |
|---|---|---|
| Barry Sanders, Oklahoma St | 1988 | 238.9 |
| Marcus Allen, USC | 1981 | 212.9 |
| Ed Marinaro, Cornell | 1971 | 209.0 |
| Troy Davis, Iowa St | 1996 | 198.6 |
| LaDainian Tomlinson, TCU | 2000 | 196.2 |

| TOUCHDOWNS RUSHING | Year | TD |
|---|---|---|
| Barry Sanders, Oklahoma St | 1988 | 37 |
| Mike Rozier, Nebraska | 1983 | 29 |
| Kevin Smith, Central Florida | 2007 | 29 |
| Willis McGahee, Miami (Fla.) | 2002 | 28 |
| Toby Gerhart, Stanford | 2009 | 28 |
| Ricky Williams, Texas | 1998 | 27 |
| Lee Suggs, Virginia Tech | 2000 | 27 |
| Ricky Dobbs, Navy [QB] | 2009 | 27 |

*Active player.

## Single Season *(Cont.)*

### Passing

| PASSING EFFICIENCY | Year | Rating |
|---|---|---|
| Colt Brennan, Hawaii | 2006 | 186.0 |
| Shaun King, Tulane | 1998 | 183.3 |
| Kellen Moore, Boise St. | 2010 | 182.6 |
| Cam Newton, Auburn | 2010 | 182.1 |
| Stefan LeFors, Louisville | 2004 | 181.7 |

| YARDS GAINED | Year | Yds |
|---|---|---|
| B.J. Symons, Texas Tech | 2003 | 5,833 |
| Graham Harrell, Texas Tech | 2007 | 5,705 |
| Case Keenum, Houston | 2009 | 5,671 |
| Colt Brennan, Hawaii | 2006 | 5,549 |
| B.J. Symons, Texas Tech | 2003 | 5,336 |

| COMPLETIONS | Year | Att | Comp |
|---|---|---|---|
| Graham Harrell, Texas Tech | 2007 | 713 | 512 |
| Case Keenum, Houston | 2009 | 700 | 492 |
| Kliff Kingsbury, Texas Tech | 2002 | 712 | 479 |
| B.J. Symons, Texas Tech | 2003 | 719 | 470 |
| Graham Harrell, Texas Tech | 2008 | 626 | 442 |

| TOUCHDOWNS PASSING | Year | TD |
|---|---|---|
| Colt Brennan, Hawaii | 2006 | 58 |
| David Klingler, Houston | 1990 | 54 |
| B.J. Symons, Texas Tech | 2003 | 52 |
| Sam Bradford, Oklahoma | 2008 | 50 |
| Graham Harrell, Texas Tech | 2007 | 48 |

### Receiving

| CATCHES | Year | GP | No. |
|---|---|---|---|
| Freddie Barnes, Bowling Green | 2009 | 13 | 155 |
| Emmanuel Hazard, Houston | 1989 | 11 | 142 |
| Troy Edwards, Louisiana Tech | 1998 | 12 | 140 |
| Nate Burleson, Nevada | 2002 | 12 | 138 |
| Howard Twilley, Tulsa | 1965 | 10 | 134 |
| Trevor Insley, Nevada | 1999 | 11 | 134 |
| Michael Crabtree, Texas Tech | 2008 | 13 | 134 |

| CATCHES PER GAME | Year | No. | No./Game |
|---|---|---|---|
| Howard Twilley, Tulsa | 1965 | 134 | 13.4 |
| Emmanuel Hazard, Houston | 1989 | 142 | 12.9 |
| Trevor Insley, Nevada | 1999 | 134 | 12.2 |
| Freddie Barnes, Bowling Green | 2009 | 155 | 11.9 |
| Alex Van Dyke, Nevada | 1995 | 129 | 11.7 |
| Troy Edwards, Louisiana Tech | 1998 | 140 | 11.7 |

| YARDS GAINED | Year | Yds |
|---|---|---|
| Trevor Insley, Nevada | 1999 | 2,060 |
| Troy Edwards, Louisiana Tech | 1998 | 1,996 |
| Michael Crabtree, Texas Tech | 2007 | 1,962 |
| Greg Salas, Hawaii | 2010 | 1,889 |
| Alex Van Dyke, Nevada | 1995 | 1,854 |

| TOUCHDOWN CATCHES | Year | TD |
|---|---|---|
| Troy Edwards, Louisiana Tech | 1998 | 27 |
| Randy Moss, Marshall | 1997 | 25 |
| Emmanuel Hazard, Houston | 1989 | 22 |
| Larry Fitzgerald, Pittsburgh | 2003 | 22 |
| Michael Crabtree, Texas Tech | 2007 | 22 |

## Single Game

### Scoring

| POINTS | Opponent | Year | Pts |
|---|---|---|---|
| Howard Griffith, Illinois | Southern Illinois | 1990 | 48 |
| Marshall Faulk, San Diego St. | Pacific | 1991 | 44 |
| Jim Brown, Syracuse | Colgate | 1956 | 43 |
| Fred Wendt, UTEP* | New Mexico St | 1948 | 42 |
| Arnold Boykin, Mississippi | Mississippi St | 1951 | 42 |
| Rashaun Woods, Okla. St | SMU | 2003 | 42 |

*UTEP was Texas Mines in 1948.

| FIELD GOALS | Opponent | Year | FG |
|---|---|---|---|
| Dale Klein, Nebraska | Missouri | 1985 | 7 |
| Mike Prindle, Western Michigan | Marshall | 1984 | 7 |

Note: 15 tied with 6.

Klein's distances were 32-22-43-44-29-43-43.
Prindle's distances were 32-44-42-23-48-41-27.

### Total Offense

| YARDS GAINED | Opponent | Year | Yds |
|---|---|---|---|
| David Klingler, Houston | Arizona St | 1990 | 732 |
| Matt Vogler, TCU | Houston | 1990 | 696 |
| B.J. Symons, Texas Tech | Mississippi | 2003 | 681 |
| Brian Lindgren, Idaho | Middle Tenn St | 2001 | 657 |
| Graham Harrell, Texas Tech | Oklahoma St | 2007 | 643 |
| David Klingler, Houston | TCU | 1990 | 625 |
| Scott Mitchell, Utah | Air Force | 1988 | 625 |

### Passing

| YARDS GAINED | Opponent | Year | Yds |
|---|---|---|---|
| David Klingler, Houston | Arizona St | 1990 | 716 |
| Matt Vogler, TCU | Houston | 1990 | 690 |
| B.J. Symons, Texas Tech | Mississippi | 2003 | 661 |
| Graham Harrell, Texas Tech | Oklahoma St | 2007 | 646 |
| Cody Hodges, Texas Tech | Kansas St | 2005 | 643 |

### Passing *(Cont.)*

| COMPLETIONS | Opponent | Year | Comp |
|---|---|---|---|
| Andy Schmitt, E. Michigan | Central Mich. | 2008 | 58 |
| Case Keenum, Houston | East Carolina | 2009 | 56 |
| Drew Brees, Purdue | Wisconsin | 1998 | 55 |
| Rusty LaRue, Wake Forest | Duke | 1995 | 55 |
| Case Keenum, Houston | UTEP | 2009 | 51 |
| Andy Schmitt, E. Michigan | Temple | 2008 | 50 |
| Rusty LaRue, Wake Forest | No. Carolina St | 1995 | 50 |

Note: Five tied with 49.

| TOUCHDOWNS PASSING | Opponent | Year | TD |
|---|---|---|---|
| David Klingler, Houston | E. Wash | 1990 | 11 |

Note: Klingler's TD passes were for 5-48-29-7-3-7-40-10-7-8-51 yards, respectively.

### Rushing

| YARDS GAINED | Opponent | Year | Yds |
|---|---|---|---|
| LaDainian Tomlinson, TCU | UTEP | 1999 | 406 |
| Tony Sands, Kansas | Missouri | 1991 | 396 |
| Marshall Faulk, San Diego St. | Pacific | 1991 | 386 |
| Troy Davis, Iowa St | Missouri | 1996 | 378 |
| Anthony Thompson, Indiana | Wisconsin | 1989 | 377 |
| Robbie Mixon, Cent. Mich. | Eastern Mich | 2002 | 377 |

| TOUCHDOWNS RUSHING | Opponent | Year | TD |
|---|---|---|---|
| Howard Griffith, Illinois | Southern Illinois | 1990 | 8 |

Note: Griffith's TD runs were for 5-51-7-41-5-18-5-3 yards, respectively.

## Single Game *(Cont.)*

### Receiving

**CATCHES**

| CATCHES | Opponent | Year | No. |
|---|---|---|---|
| Tyler Jones, E. Michigan.....Central Mich. | | 2008 | 23 |
| Randy Gatewood, UNLV.....Idaho | | 1994 | 23 |
| Freddie Barnes, Bowl. Green..Kent St | | 2009 | 22 |
| Jay Miller, BYU ....................New Mexico | | 1973 | 22 |
| Troy Edwards, La. Tech ......Nebraska | | 1998 | 21 |
| Chris Daniels, Purdue .........Michigan St | | 1999 | 21 |

Note: Three tied with 20.

### Receiving (Cont.)

| YARDS GAINED | Opponent | Year | Yds |
|---|---|---|---|
| Troy Edwards, Louisiana Tech...Nebraska | | 1998 | 405 |
| Randy Gatewood, UNLV .........Idaho | | 1994 | 363 |
| Chuck Hughes, UTEP*............North Texas | | 1965 | 349 |
| Donnie Avery, Houston ...........Rice | | 2007 | 346 |
| Casey Fitzgerald, North Texas..SMU | | 2007 | 327 |

*UTEP was Texas Western in 1965.

| TOUCHDOWN CATCHES | Opponent | Year | TD |
|---|---|---|---|
| Rashaun Woods, Okla. St .....SMU | | 2003 | 7 |
| Tim Delaney, San Diego St....New Mex. St | | 1969 | 6 |

## Longest Plays (since 1941)

| PASSING | Opponent | Year | Yds |
|---|---|---|---|
| Fred Owens to Jack Ford, Portland.................St. Mary's (Ca.) | | 1947 | 99 |
| Bo Burris to Warren McVea, Houston...............Washington St | | 1966 | 99 |
| Colin Clapton to Eddie Jenkins, Holy Cross .............Boston Univ. | | 1970 | 99 |
| Terry Peel to Robert Ford, Houston...............Syracuse | | 1970 | 99 |
| Terry Peel to Robert Ford, Houston...............San Diego St | | 1972 | 99 |
| Cris Collinsworth to Derrick Gaffney, Florida.................Rice | | 1977 | 99 |
| Scott Ankrom to James Maness, TCU......................Rice | | 1984 | 99 |
| Gino Toretta to Horace Copeland, Miami (Fla.) ...........Arkansas | | 1991 | 99 |
| John Paci to Thomas Lewis, Indiana.................Penn St | | 1993 | 99 |
| Troy DeGar to Wes Caswell Tulsa....................Oklahoma | | 1996 | 99 |
| Drew Brees to Vinny Sutherland, Purdue ...........Northwestern | | 1999 | 99 |
| Dan Urban to Justin McCariens, Northern Illinois............Ball St | | 2000 | 99 |
| Jason Johnson to Brandon Marshall, Arizona................Idaho | | 2001 | 99 |
| Dondrial Pinkins to Troy Williamson, South Carolina ............Virginia | | 2003 | 99 |
| Jim Sorgi to Lee Evans, Wisconsin.............Akron | | 2003 | 99 |
| Giovanni Vizza to Casey Fitzgerald, North Texas............La.-Monroe | | 2007 | 99 |
| Jeff Tuel to Johnny Forzani, Washington St.............Arizona St | | 2009 | 99 |

| RUSHING | Opponent | Year | Yd |
|---|---|---|---|
| Gale Sayers, Kansas ............Nebraska | | 1963 | 99 |
| Max Anderson, Arizona St...Wyoming | | 1967 | 99 |
| Ralph Thompson, West Texas St ......................Wichita St | | 1970 | 99 |
| Kelsey Finch, Tennessee ......Florida | | 1977 | 99 |
| Eric Vann, Kansas................Oklahoma | | 1997 | 99 |
| Terry Caulley, Connecticut....Army | | 2006 | 99 |
| Broderick Green, Arkansas ..E. Michigan | | 2009 | 99 |

Eleven tied at 98 yards.

| FIELD GOALS | Opponent | Year | Yds |
|---|---|---|---|
| Steve Little, Arkansas ............Texas | | 1977 | 67 |
| Russell Erxleben, Texas ........Rice | | 1977 | 67 |
| Joe Williams, Wichita St........Southern Ill. | | 1978 | 67 |
| Martin Gramatica, Kansas St...Northern Ill. | | 1998 | 65 |
| Tony Franklin, Texas A&M ......Baylor | | 1976 | 65 |

| PUNTS | Opponent | Year | Yds |
|---|---|---|---|
| Pat Brady, Nevada*................Loyola (Ca.) | | 1950 | 99 |
| George O'Brien, Wisconsin ...Iowa | | 1952 | 96 |
| John Hadl, Kansas................Oklahoma | | 1959 | 94 |
| Carl Knox, TCU ....................Oklahoma St | | 1947 | 94 |
| Preston Johnson, SMU..........Pittsburgh | | 1940 | 94 |

*Nevada was Nevada-Reno in 1950.

## FOOTBALL BOWL SUBDIVISION (I-A) WINNINGEST TEAMS

### Alltime Winning Percentage

| | Yrs | W | L | T | Pct | GP | Bowl Record |
|---|---|---|---|---|---|---|---|
| Michigan | 131 | 884 | 308 | 36 | .735 | 1,228 | 19-21-0 |
| Notre Dame | 122 | 845 | 295 | 42 | .733 | 1,182 | 15-15-0 |
| Ohio St. | 121 | 831 | 309 | 53 | .719 | 1,193 | 20-22-0 |
| Texas | 118 | 850 | 325 | 33 | .717 | 1,208 | 25-22-2 |
| Oklahoma | 116 | 811 | 304 | 53 | .717 | 1,168 | 26-17-1 |
| Boise St. | 43 | 365 | 145 | 2 | .715 | 512 | 7-4-0 |
| Alabama | 116 | 802 | 319 | 43 | .707 | 1,164 | 32-22-3 |
| USC | 118 | 769 | 312 | 54 | .701 | 1,135 | 31-15-0 |
| Nebraska | 121 | 837 | 345 | 40 | .701 | 1,222 | 24-23-0 |
| Tennessee | 114 | 789 | 340 | 53 | .690 | 1,182 | 25-24-0 |
| Penn St. | 124 | 818 | 357 | 41 | .690 | 1,216 | 27-14-2 |
| Florida St. | 64 | 464 | 231 | 17 | .664 | 712 | 21-14-2 |
| Georgia | 117 | 737 | 396 | 54 | .644 | 1,187 | 26-17-3 |
| LSU | 117 | 720 | 389 | 47 | .643 | 1,156 | 22-19-1 |
| Miami (Fla.) | 85 | 568 | 320 | 19 | .637 | 907 | 18-16-0 |
| Auburn | 118 | 703 | 400 | 47 | .632 | 1,150 | 21-13-2 |
| Florida | 104 | 662 | 379 | 40 | .631 | 1,081 | 19-19-0 |
| South Florida | 14 | 103 | 62 | 0 | .624 | 165 | 4-2-0 |
| Miami (Ohio) | 122 | 660 | 394 | 44 | .621 | 1,098 | 7-3-0 |
| Washington | 121 | 663 | 412 | 50 | .612 | 1,125 | 15-14-1 |
| Arizona St. | 98 | 555 | 349 | 24 | .611 | 928 | 12-11-1 |
| Virginia Tech | 117 | 678 | 432 | 46 | .606 | 1,156 | 9-15-0 |
| Central Michigan | 110 | 573 | 366 | 36 | .606 | 975 | 2-4-0 |
| Colorado | 121 | 671 | 442 | 36 | .600 | 1,159 | 12-16-0 |
| West Virginia | 118 | 691 | 454 | 45 | .600 | 1,190 | 13-17-0 |

Note: Includes bowl games.

### Alltime Victories

| | | | | | |
|---|---|---|---|---|---|
| Michigan | 884 | Georgia | 737 | Arkansas | 669 |
| Texas | 850 | LSU | 720 | Washington | 663 |
| Notre Dame | 845 | Auburn | 703 | Florida | 662 |
| Nebraska | 837 | West Virginia | 691 | Miami (Ohio) | 660 |
| Ohio St. | 831 | Syracuse | 686 | North Carolina | 655 |
| Penn St. | 818 | Georgia Tech | 679 | Navy | 651 |
| Oklahoma | 811 | Virginia Tech | 678 | Army | 649 |
| Alabama | 802 | Texas A&M | 674 | California | 648 |
| Tennessee | 789 | Colorado | 671 | Clemson | 647 |
| USC | 769 | Pittsburgh | 671 | Minnesota | 643 |

## NUMBER ONE VS NUMBER TWO

The No. 1 and No. 2 teams, according to the Associated Press Poll, have met 33 times, including 13 bowl games, since the poll's inception in 1936. The No. 1 teams have a 20-11-2 record in these matchups. Notre Dame (4-3-2) has played in nine of the games.

| Date | Results | Stadium |
|---|---|---|
| 10-9-43 | No. 1 Notre Dame 35, No. 2 Michigan 12 | Michigan (Ann Arbor) |
| 11-20-43 | No. 1 Notre Dame 14, No. 2 Iowa Pre-Flight 13 | Notre Dame (South Bend) |
| 12-2-44 | No. 1 Army 23, No. 2 Navy 7 | Municipal (Baltimore) |
| 11-10-45 | No. 1 Army 48, No. 2 Notre Dame 0 | Yankee (New York) |
| 12-1-45 | No. 1 Army 32, No. 2 Navy 13 | Municipal (Philadelphia) |
| 11-9-46 | No. 1 Army 0, No. 2 Notre Dame 0 | Yankee (New York) |
| 1-1-63 | No. 1 USC 42, No. 2 Wisconsin 37 (Rose Bowl) | Rose Bowl (Pasadena) |
| 10-12-63 | No. 2 Texas 28, No. 1 Oklahoma 7 | Cotton Bowl (Dallas) |
| 1-1-64 | No. 1 Texas 28, No. 2 Navy 6 (Cotton Bowl) | Cotton Bowl (Dallas) |
| 11-19-66 | No. 1 Notre Dame 10, No. 2 Michigan St 10 | Spartan (East Lansing) |
| 9-28-68 | No. 1 Purdue 37, No. 2 Notre Dame 22 | Notre Dame (South Bend) |
| 1-1-69 | No. 1 Ohio St. 27, No. 2 USC 16 (Rose Bowl) | Rose Bowl (Pasadena) |
| 12-6-69 | No. 1 Texas 15, No. 2 Arkansas 14 | Razorback (Fayetteville) |
| 11-25-71 | No. 1 Nebraska 35, No. 2 Oklahoma 31 | Owen Field (Norman) |
| 1-1-72 | No. 1 Nebraska 38, No. 2 Alabama 6 (Orange Bowl) | Orange Bowl (Miami) |
| 1-1-79 | No. 2 Alabama 14, No. 1 Penn St 7 (Sugar Bowl) | Sugar Bowl (New Orleans) |
| 9-26-81 | No. 1 USC 28, No. 2 Oklahoma 24 | Coliseum (Los Angeles) |
| 1-1-83 | No. 2 Penn St 27, No. 1 Georgia 23 (Sugar Bowl) | Sugar Bowl (New Orleans) |
| 10-19-85 | No. 1 Iowa 12, No. 2 Michigan 10 | Kinnick (Iowa City) |
| 9-27-86 | No. 2 Miami (Fla.) 28, No. 1 Oklahoma 16 | Orange Bowl (Miami) |
| 1-2-87 | No. 2 Penn St 14, No. 1 Miami (Fla.) 10 (Fiesta Bowl) | Sun Devil (Tempe) |
| 11-21-87 | No. 2 Oklahoma 17, No. 1 Nebraska 7 | Memorial (Lincoln) |

### NUMBER ONE VS NUMBER TWO *(Cont.)*

| Date | Results | Stadium |
|---|---|---|
| 1-1-88 | No. 2 Miami (Fla.) 20, No. 1 Oklahoma 14 (Orange Bowl) | Orange Bowl (Miami) |
| 11-26-88 | No. 1 Notre Dame 27, No. 2 USC 10 | Coliseum (Los Angeles) |
| 9-16-89 | No. 1 Notre Dame 24, No. 2 Michigan 19 | Michigan (Ann Arbor) |
| 11-16-91 | No. 2 Miami (Fla.) 17, No. 1 Florida St 16 | Doak Campbell (Tallahassee) |
| 1-1-93 | No. 2 Alabama 34, No. 1 Miami (Fla.) 13 (Sugar Bowl) | Superdome (New Orleans) |
| 11-13-93 | No. 2 Notre Dame 31, No. 1 Florida St 24 | Notre Dame (South Bend) |
| 1-1-94 | No. 1 Florida St 18, No. 2 Nebraska 16 (Orange Bowl) | Orange Bowl (Miami) |
| 1-2-96 | No. 1 Nebraska 62, No. 2 Florida 24 (Fiesta Bowl) | Sun Devil (Tempe) |
| 11-30-96 | No. 2 Florida St 24, No. 1 Florida 21 | Doak Campbell (Tallahassee) |
| 1-4-99 | No. 1 Tennessee 23, No. 2 Florida St 16 (Fiesta Bowl) | Sun Devil (Tempe) |
| 1-4-00 | No. 1 Florida St 46, No. 2 Virginia Tech 29 (Sugar Bowl) | Superdome (New Orleans) |
| 1-3-03 | No. 2 Ohio St 31, No. 1 Miami (Fla.) 24 [2OT] (Fiesta Bowl) | Sun Devil (Tempe) |
| 1-5-06 | No. 2 Texas 41, No. 1 USC 38 (Rose Bowl) | Rose Bowl (Pasadena) |
| 9-9-06 | No. 1 Ohio St 24, No. 2 Texas 7 | Texas Memorial (Austin) |
| 11-18-06 | No. 1 Ohio St 42, No. 2 Michigan 39 | Ohio (Columbus) |
| 1-8-07 | No. 2 Florida 41, No. 1 Ohio St 14 (BCS Championship) | Univ. of Phoenix (Glendale) |
| 1-7-08 | No. 2 LSU 38, No. 1 Ohio St. 24 (BCS Championship) | Superdome (New Orleans) |
| 12-6-08 | No. 2 Florida 31, No. 1 Alabama 20 (SEC Championship) | Georgia Dome (Atlanta) |
| 1-8-09 | No. 1 Florida 24, No. 2 Oklahoma 14 (BCS Championship) | Dolphins Stadium (Miami) |
| 12-5-09 | No. 1 Florida 13, No. 2 Alabama 32 (SEC Championship) | Georgia Dome (Atlanta) |
| 1-7-10 | No. 1 Alabama 37, No. 2 Texas 21 (BCS Championship) | Rose Bowl (Pasadena) |
| 1-10-11 | No. 1 Auburn 22, No. 2 Oregon 19 (BCS Championship) | Univ. of Phoenix (Glendale) |

Note: #1 USC's Orange Bowl victory over #2 Oklahoma on Jan. 4, 2005 was vacated in 2010 for rules violations.

### LONGEST FBS (I-A) WINNING STREAKS

| Wins | Team | Yrs | Ended by | Score |
|---|---|---|---|---|
| 47 | Oklahoma | 1953–57 | Notre Dame | 7–0 |
| 39 | Washington | 1908–14 | Oregon St | 0–0 |
| 37 | Yale | 1890–93 | Princeton | 6–0 |
| 37 | Yale | 1887–89 | Princeton | 10–0 |
| 35 | Toledo | 1969–71 | Tampa | 21–0 |
| 34 | Miami | 2000–03 | Ohio St | 31–24 (2 OT) |
| 34 | Pennsylvania | 1894–96 | Lafayette | 6–4 |
| 31 | Oklahoma | 1948–50 | Kentucky | 13–7 |
| 31 | Pittsburgh | 1914–18 | Cleveland Naval Reserve | 10–9 |
| 31 | Pennsylvania | 1896–98 | Harvard | 10–0 |
| 30 | Texas | 1968–70 | Notre Dame | 24–11 |

### LONGEST FBS (I-A) UNBEATEN STREAKS

| No. | W | T | Team | Yrs | Ended by | Score |
|---|---|---|---|---|---|---|
| 63 | 59 | 4 | Washington | 1907–17 | California | 27–0 |
| 56 | 55 | 1 | Michigan | 1901–05 | Chicago | 2–0 |
| 50 | 46 | 4 | California | 1920–25 | Olympic Club | 15–0 |
| 48 | 47 | 1 | Oklahoma | 1953–57 | Notre Dame | 7–0 |
| 48 | 47 | 1 | Yale | 1885–89 | Princeton | 10–0 |
| 47 | 42 | 5 | Yale | 1879–85 | Princeton | 6–5 |
| 44 | 42 | 2 | Yale | 1894–96 | Princeton | 24–6 |
| 42 | 39 | 3 | Yale | 1904–08 | Harvard | 4–0 |
| 39 | 37 | 2 | Notre Dame | 1946–50 | Purdue | 28–14 |
| 37 | 36 | 1 | Oklahoma | 1972–75 | Kansas | 23–3 |
| 37 | 37 | 0 | Yale | 1890–93 | Princeton | 6–0 |
| 35 | 35 | 0 | Toledo | 1969–71 | Tampa | 21–0 |
| 35 | 34 | 1 | Minnesota | 1903–05 | Wisconsin | 16–12 |
| 34 | 34 | 0 | Miami (Fla.) | 2000–03 | Ohio St | 31–24 (2 OT) |
| 34 | 33 | 1 | Nebraska | 1912–16 | Kansas | 7–3 |
| 34 | 34 | 0 | Pennsylvania | 1894–96 | Lafayette | 6–4 |
| 34 | 32 | 2 | Princeton | 1884–87 | Harvard | 12–0 |
| 34 | 29 | 5 | Princeton | 1877–82 | Harvard | 1–0 |
| 33 | 30 | 3 | Tennessee | 1926–30 | Alabama | 18–6 |
| 33 | 31 | 2 | Georgia Tech | 1914–18 | Pittsburgh | 32–0 |
| 33 | 30 | 3 | Harvard | 1911–15 | Cornell | 10–0 |
| 32 | 31 | 1 | Nebraska | 1969–71 | UCLA | 20–17 |
| 32 | 30 | 2 | Army | 1944–47 | Columbia | 21–20 |
| 32 | 31 | 1 | Harvard | 1898–1900 | Yale | 28–0 |

Note: Includes bowl games.

### LONGEST FBS (I-A) LOSING STREAKS

| Losses | | Seasons | Ended Against | Score |
|---|---|---|---|---|
| 34 | Northwestern | 1979–82 | Northern Illinois | 31–6 |
| 28 | Virginia | 1958–61 | William & Mary | 21–6 |
| 28 | Kansas St | 1945–48 | Arkansas St | 37–6 |
| 27 | New Mexico St | 1988–90 | Cal St–Fullerton | 43–9 |
| 27 | Eastern Michigan | 1980–82 | Kent St | 9–7 |

### MOST-PLAYED FBS (I-A) RIVALRIES

| GP | Opponents (Series Leader Listed First) | Record | First Game | GP | Opponents (Series Leader Listed First) | Record | First Game |
|---|---|---|---|---|---|---|---|
| 120 | Minnesota–Wisconsin | 59-53-8 | 1890 | 108 | Kansas–Kansas St | 65-38-5 | 1902 |
| 119 | Kansas–Missouri | 55-55-9 | 1891 | 107 | Michigan–Ohio St | 57-44-6 | 1897 |
| 117 | Nebraska–Kansas | 91-23-3 | 1892 | 107 | Mississippi–Mississippi St | 60-41-6 | 1901 |
| 117 | Texas–Texas A&M | 75-37-5 | 1894 | 106 | Baylor–TCU | 50-49-7 | 1899 |
| 115 | Miami (Ohio)–Cincinnati | 59-49-7 | 1888 | 106 | Tennessee–Kentucky | 74-23-9 | 1893 |
| 115 | North Carolina–Virginia | †58-53-4 | 1892 | 105 | Georgia–Georgia Tech | 61-39-5 | 1893 |
| 114 | Auburn–Georgia | 54-52-8 | 1892 | 105 | Nebraska–Iowa St | 86-17-2 | 1896 |
| 114 | Oregon–Oregon St | 58-46-10 | 1894 | 105 | Texas–Oklahoma | 59-41-5 | 1900 |
| 113 | Purdue–Indiana | 70-37-6 | 1891 | 105 | Oklahoma–Oklahoma St | 82-16-7 | 1904 |
| 113 | Stanford–California | 56-46-11 | 1892 | †104 | Tennessee–Vanderbilt | 72-27-2 | 1888 |
| 111 | Navy–Army | 55-49-7 | 1890 | | | | |
| 109 | Utah–Utah St | 77-28-4 | 1892 | | | | |
| 108 | Clemson–South Carolina | 65-39-4 | 1896 | | | | |

†Disputed series records: Virginia claims North Carolina leads series 55-51-4 based on a forfeited game in 1956. Vandy claims Tennessee has 72–28–5 series lead.

## NCAA Coaches' Records

### ALLTIME WINNINGEST FBS (I-A) COACHES

#### By Percentage

| Coach (Alma Mater) | Colleges Coached | Yrs | W | L | T | Pct |
|---|---|---|---|---|---|---|
| Knute Rockne (Notre Dame '14)† | Notre Dame 1918–30 | 13 | 105 | 12 | 5 | .881 |
| Frank W. Leahy (Notre Dame '31)† | Boston College 1939–40; Notre Dame 1941–43, 1946–53 | 13 | 107 | 13 | 9 | .864 |
| George W. Woodruff (Yale 1889)† | Pennsylvania 1892–01; Illinois 1903; Carlisle 1905 | 12 | 142 | 25 | 2 | .846 |
| Barry Switzer (Arkansas '60) | Oklahoma 1973–88 | 16 | 157 | 29 | 4 | .837 |
| Tom Osborne (Hastings '59)† | Nebraska 1973–97 | 25 | 255 | 49 | 3 | .836 |
| Fielding Yost (West Virginia 1895)† | Ohio Wesleyan 1897; Nebraska 1898; Kansas 1899; Stanford 1900; Michigan 1901–23, 1925–26 | 30 | 198 | 35 | 12 | .833 |
| Percy D. Haughton (Harvard 1899)† | Cornell 1899–1900; Harvard 1908–16; Columbia 1923–24 | 13 | 96 | 17 | 6 | .832 |
| Bob Neyland (Army '16)† | Tennessee 1926–34, 1936–40, 1946–52 | 21 | 173 | 31 | 12 | .829 |
| Bud Wilkinson (Minnesota '37)† | Oklahoma 1947–63 | 17 | 145 | 29 | 4 | .826 |
| *Urban Meyer (Cincinnati '86) | Bowling Green 2001–02; Utah 2003–04; Florida 2005– | 10 | 104 | 23 | 0 | .819 |
| Jock Sutherland (Pittsburgh '18)† | Lafayette 1919–23; Pittsburgh 1924–38 | 20 | 144 | 28 | 14 | .812 |
| Bob Devaney (Alma [Mich] '39)† | Wyoming 1957–61; Nebraska 1962–72 | 16 | 136 | 30 | 7 | .806 |
| *Bob Stoops (Iowa '83) | Oklahoma 1999– | 12 | 129 | 31 | 0 | .806 |
| Frank W. Thomas (Notre Dame '23)† | Tenn.-Chattanooga 1925–28; Alabama 1931–42, 1944–46 | 19 | 141 | 33 | 9 | .795 |
| Henry L. Williams (Yale 1891)† | Army 1891; Minnesota 1900–21 | 23 | 141 | 34 | 12 | .786 |
| Gil Dobie (Minnesota '02)† | North Dakota St 1906–07; Washington 1908-16; Navy 1917–19; Cornell 1920–35; Boston College 1936–38 | 33 | 180 | 45 | 15 | .781 |
| Fred Folsom (Dartmouth 1895) | Colorado 1895–99, 1901–02; Dartmouth 1903–06; Colorado 1908–15 | 19 | 107 | 28 | 6 | .780 |
| Paul "Bear" Bryant (Alabama '36)† | Maryland 1945; Kentucky 1946–53, | 38 | 323 | 85 | 17 | .780 |
| *Gary Patterson (Kansas St '83) | TCU 2000– | 11 | 98 | 28 | 0 | .778 |
| Bo Schembechler (Miami [Ohio] '51) | Miami (Ohio) 1963–68; Michigan 1969–89 | 27 | 234 | 65 | 8 | .775 |

*Active in 2010. †Hall of Fame member.

Note: Minimum 10 years as head coach at Division I institutions; record at four-year colleges only; bowl games included; ties computed as half won, half lost

## ALLTIME WINNINGEST FBS (I-A) COACHES *(Cont.)*

### By Victories

| | Yrs | W | L | T | Pct | | Yrs | W | L | T | Pct |
|---|---|---|---|---|---|---|---|---|---|---|---|
| *Joe Paterno | 45 | 401 | 135 | 3 | .747 | Bo Schembechler | 27 | 234 | 65 | 8 | .775 |
| Bobby Bowden | 44 | 377 | 129 | 4 | .743 | Hayden Fry | 37 | 232 | 178 | 10 | .564 |
| Paul (Bear) Bryant | 38 | 323 | 85 | 17 | .780 | *Chris Ault | 26 | 219 | 97 | 1 | .692 |
| Glenn (Pop) Warner | 44 | 319 | 106 | 32 | .733 | *Mack Brown | 27 | 219 | 108 | 1 | .669 |
| Amos Alonzo Stagg | 57 | 314 | 199 | 35 | .605 | Jess Neely | 40 | 207 | 176 | 19 | .539 |
| LaVell Edwards | 29 | 257 | 100 | 3 | .718 | Warren Woodson | 31 | 203 | 95 | 14 | .673 |
| Tom Osborne | 25 | 255 | 49 | 3 | .836 | Don Nehlen | 30 | 202 | 128 | 8 | .609 |
| Lou Holtz | 33 | 249 | 132 | 7 | .651 | Vince Dooley | 25 | 201 | 77 | 10 | .715 |
| *Jim Tressel | 25 | 241 | 79 | 2 | .752 | Eddie Anderson | 39 | 201 | 128 | 15 | .606 |
| *Frank Beamer | 30 | 240 | 118 | 4 | .669 | Jim Sweeney | 27 | 200 | 154 | 4 | .564 |
| Woody Hayes | 33 | 238 | 72 | 10 | .759 | | | | | | |

*Active in 2010. Record at four-year colleges only.

### Most Bowl Victories

| | W | L | T | | W | L | T |
|---|---|---|---|---|---|---|---|
| *Joe Paterno | 24 | 12 | 1 | Philip Fulmer | 8 | 7 | 0 |
| Bobby Bowden | 21 | 10 | 1 | Darrell Royal | 8 | 7 | 1 |
| Paul (Bear) Bryant | 15 | 12 | 2 | Vince Dooley | 8 | 10 | 2 |
| Lou Holtz | 12 | 8 | 2 | *Frank Beamer | 8 | 10 | 0 |
| Tom Osborne | 12 | 13 | 0 | *Urban Meyer | 7 | 1 | 0 |
| *Mack Brown | 11 | 7 | 0 | *Tom O'Brien | 7 | 2 | 0 |
| Don James | 10 | 5 | 0 | Pat Dye | 7 | 2 | 1 |
| John Vaught | 10 | 8 | 0 | Bob Devaney | 7 | 3 | 0 |
| Bobby Dodd | 9 | 4 | 0 | Dan Devine | 7 | 3 | 0 |
| Johnny Majors | 9 | 7 | 0 | *Mark Richt | 7 | 3 | 0 |
| John Robinson | 8 | 1 | 0 | Earle Bruce | 7 | 5 | 0 |
| Barry Alvarez | 8 | 3 | 0 | Charlie McClendon | 7 | 6 | 0 |
| *Tommy Tuberville | 8 | 3 | 0 | Hayden Fry | 7 | 9 | 1 |
| Terry Donahue | 8 | 4 | 1 | *Steve Spurrier | 7 | 10 | 0 |
| Barry Switzer | 8 | 5 | 0 | LaVell Edwards | 7 | 14 | 1 |
| Jackie Sherrill | 8 | 6 | 0 | | | | |

## WINNINGEST ACTIVE* FBS (I-A) COACHES

### By Percentage

| Coach, College | Yrs | W | L | T | Pct. | Bowls W | L | T |
|---|---|---|---|---|---|---|---|---|
| Chris Petersen, Boise St. | 5 | 61 | 5 | 0 | .924 | 3 | 2 | 0 |
| Urban Meyer, Florida | 10 | 104 | 23 | 0 | .826 | 7 | 1 | 0 |
| Bob Stoops, Oklahoma | 12 | 129 | 31 | 0 | .806 | 6 | 6 | 0 |
| Gary Patterson, TCU | 11 | 98 | 28 | 0 | .778 | 6 | 4 | 0 |
| Bret Bielema, Wisconsin | 5 | 49 | 16 | 0 | .754 | 2 | 3 | 0 |
| Jim Tressel, Ohio St | 25 | 241 | 79 | 2 | .752 | 6 | 4 | 0 |
| Joe Paterno, Penn St | 45 | 401 | 135 | 3 | .747 | 24 | 12 | 1 |
| Kyle Whittingham, Utah | 7 | 58 | 20 | 0 | .744 | 5 | 1 | 0 |
| Brian Kelly, Cincinnati | 21 | 179 | 62 | 2 | .741 | 3 | 1 | 0 |
| Mark Richt, Georgia | 10 | 96 | 34 | 0 | .738 | 7 | 3 | 0 |
| Bronco Mendenhall, BYU | 6 | 56 | 21 | 0 | .727 | 4 | 2 | 0 |
| Bobby Petrino, Arkansas | 7 | 64 | 24 | 0 | .727 | 3 | 3 | 0 |
| Steve Spurrier, South Carolina | 21 | 186 | 73 | 2 | .716 | 7 | 10 | 0 |
| Paul Johnson, Georgia Tech | 14 | 133 | 53 | 0 | .715 | 2 | 5 | 0 |
| Nick Saban, Alabama | 15 | 129 | 53 | 1 | .708 | 6 | 6 | 0 |
| Les Miles, LSU | 10 | 90 | 38 | 0 | .703 | 6 | 3 | 0 |
| Chris Ault, Nevada | 26 | 219 | 97 | 1 | .692 | 2 | 6 | 0 |
| Mack Brown, Texas | 27 | 219 | 108 | 1 | .669 | 11 | 7 | 0 |
| Frank Beamer, Virginia Tech | 30 | 240 | 118 | 4 | .669 | 8 | 10 | 0 |

#Bowl games included. Ties computed as half win, half loss. Note: Min. five years as Div. I-A head coach at four-year collges only. †One bowl win and 14 regular-season victories from Carroll's totals were vacated in 2010.

### By Victories

| | | | |
|---|---|---|---|
| Joe Paterno, Penn St | 401 | Mike Price, UTEP | 169 |
| Jim Tressel, Ohio St | 241 | Larry Blakeney, Troy | 160 |
| Frank Beamer, Viginia Tech | 240 | Howard Schellenberger, Fla. Atlantic | 157 |
| Chris Ault, Nevada | 219 | Gary Pinkel, Missouri | 150 |
| Mack Brown, Texas | 219 | Bill Snyder, Kansas St | 149 |
| Steve Spurrier, South Carolina | 186 | Paul Pasqualoni, Connecticut | 141 |
| Brian Kelly, Cincinnati | 179 | Paul Johnson, Georgia Tech | 133 |
| Dennis Erickson, Arizona St | 173 | Houston Nutt, Mississippi | 132 |

*Active in 2010.

## WINNINGEST ACTIVE* FCS (I-AA) COACHES
### By Percentage

| Coach, College | Yrs | W | L | T | Pct |
|---|---|---|---|---|---|
| Al Bagnoli, Pennsylvania | 29 | 222 | 71 | 0 | .758 |
| Buddy Pough, South Carolina St | 9 | 76 | 29 | 0 | .724 |
| Matt Viator, McNeese St | 5 | 39 | 15 | 0 | .722 |
| Joe Taylor, Florida A&M | 28 | 222 | 85 | 4 | .720 |
| K.C. Keeler, Delaware | 18 | 162 | 63 | 1 | .719 |
| Danny Rocco, Liberty | 5 | 40 | 16 | 0 | .714 |
| Mark Farley, Northern Iowa | 10 | 89 | 37 | 0 | .706 |
| David Bennett, Coastal Carolina | 15 | 119 | 52 | 0 | .696 |
| Dick Biddle, Colgate | 15 | 120 | 55 | 0 | .686 |
| Doug Williams, Grambling | 7 | 55 | 26 | 0 | .679 |
| Pete Lembo, Elon | 9 | 73 | 31 | 0 | .702 |
| Jeff McInerney, Central Connecticut St | 5 | 38 | 18 | 0 | .679 |
| Rick Comegy, Jackson St | 19 | 140 | 75 | 0 | .651 |

Ties computed as half win, half loss. Playoff games included.
Note: Minimum five years as a FBS and/or FCS head coach; record at four-year colleges only.

### By Victories

| | | | |
|---|---|---|---|
| Bob Ford, Albany St (N.Y.) | 247 | Mike Ayers, Wofford | 165 |
| Jerry Moore, Appalachian St | 226 | K.C. Keeler, Delaware | 162 |
| Joe Taylor, Florida A&M | 222 | Tim Murphy, Harvard | 143 |
| Al Bagnoli, Pennsylvania | 222 | Bob Spoo, Eastern Ilinois | 142 |
| Andy Talley, Villanova | 215 | Rick Comegy, Jackson St | 140 |
| Jimmye Laycock, William & Mary | 208 | Matt Ballard, Morehead St | 129 |
| Rob Ash, Montana St | 205 | Tim Walsh, Cal Poly | 128 |
| Walt Hameline, Wagner | 200 | | |

## WINNINGEST ACTIVE* DIVISION II COACHES
### By Percentage

| Coach, College | Yrs | W | L | T | Pct |
|---|---|---|---|---|---|
| Willie Slater, Tuskegee | 5 | 49 | 7 | 0 | .875 |
| Ken Sparks, Carson-Newman | 31 | 294 | 74 | 2 | .797 |
| John Luckhardt, California (Pa.) | 26 | 215 | 67 | 2 | .761 |
| Bill O'Boyle, Chadron St | 6 | 54 | 17 | 0 | .761 |
| Danny Hale, Bloomsburg | 23 | 194 | 65 | 1 | .748 |
| Bob Nielson, Minn.-Duluth | 18 | 149 | 54 | 1 | .733 |
| Bill Zwaan, West Chester | 14 | 119 | 46 | 0 | .721 |
| Tom Sawyer, Winona St | 15 | 123 | 50 | 0 | .711 |
| Chris Thomsen, Abilene Christian | 6 | 43 | 18 | 0 | .705 |
| Mike White, Albany St (Ga.) | 11 | 85 | 36 | 0 | .702 |
| Bryan Collins, LIU-C.W. Post | 13 | 100 | 43 | 0 | .699 |
| Darrell Morris, Nebraska-Kearney | 11 | 82 | 37 | 0 | .689 |

Ties computed as half win, half loss. Playoff games included.
Note: Minimum five years as a college head coach; record at four-year colleges only.

### By Victories

| | | | |
|---|---|---|---|
| Ken Sparks, Carson-Newman | 294 | Terry Bowden, North Alabama | 131 |
| Dennis Douds, East Stroudsburg | 229 | Rob Smith, Humboldt St | 124 |
| John Luckhardt, California (Pa.) | 215 | Tom Sawyer, Winona St | 123 |
| Monte Cater, Shepherd | 202 | Bill Zwaan, West Chester | 119 |
| Danny Hale, Bloomsburg | 194 | Keith Otterbein, Hillsdale | 116 |
| Richard Cavanagh, Southern Connecticut St | 156 | Bernie Anderson, Northern Michigan | 111 |
| George Mihalik, Slippery Rock | 153 | Art Wilkins, American International | 106 |
| Bob Nielson, Minnesota-Duluth | 149 | | |

*Active in 2010.

### WINNINGEST ACTIVE* DIVISION III COACHES
#### By Percentage

| Coach, College | Yrs | W | L | T | Pct |
|---|---|---|---|---|---|
| Larry Kehres, Mount Union | 25 | 303 | 23 | 3 | .926 |
| Jeff Devanney, Trinity (Conn.) | 5 | 34 | 6 | 0 | .850 |
| Mike Sirianni, Washington and Jefferson | 8 | 79 | 14 | 0 | .849 |
| Joe Fincham, Wittenberg | 15 | 136 | 31 | 0 | .814 |
| Skip Bandini, Curry | 5 | 47 | 11 | 0 | .810 |
| Rick Willis, Wartburg | 12 | 105 | 25 | 0 | .808 |
| Jeff McMartin, Central (Iowa) | 7 | 61 | 15 | 0 | .803 |
| Pete Fredenberg, Mary Hardin-Baylor | 13 | 121 | 32 | 0 | .791 |
| John Gagliardi, St. John's (Minn.) | 62 | 478 | 129 | 11 | .782 |
| John Thorne, North Central (Ill.) | 9 | 78 | 22 | 0 | .780 |
| Jim Purtill, St. Norbert | 13 | 107 | 30 | 1 | .779 |
| Mike Drass, Wesley | 18 | 154 | 45 | 1 | .773 |

Ties computed as half won, half lost. Playoff games included.
Note: Minimum five years as a college head coach; record at four-year colleges only.

#### By Victories

| | | | |
|---|---|---|---|
| John Gagliardi, St John's (Minn.) | 478 | Larry Kindbom, Wash U.-St. Louis | 165 |
| Larry Kehres, Mount Union | 303 | Steve Mohr, Trinity (Texas) | 164 |
| Rick Giancola, Montclair St | 201 | Barry Streeter, Gettysburg | 161 |
| Eric Hamilton, The College of New Jersey | 201 | Steve Johnson, Bethel (Minn.) | 156 |
| Vic Wallace, Rockford | 174 | Mike Drass, Wesley | 154 |
| Dale Widolff, Occidental | 173 | John Miech, UW-Stevens Point | 152 |
| Michael DeLong, Springfield | 171 | Norm Eash, Illinois Wesleyan | 149 |
| Rich Lackner, Carnegie Mellon | 170 | | |

## NAIA Coaches' Records

### WINNINGEST ACTIVE* NAIA COACHES
#### By Percentage

| Coach, College | Yrs | W | L | T | Pct |
|---|---|---|---|---|---|
| Mike Van Diest, Carroll (Mont.) | 12 | 144 | 20 | 0 | .878 |
| Bill Cronin, Georgetown (Ky.) | 14 | 133 | 34 | 0 | .796 |
| Steve Ryan, Morningside (Ia.) | 9 | 76 | 28 | 0 | .731 |
| John Bland, Cumberlands (Ky.) | 5 | 40 | 15 | 0 | .727 |
| Hank Biesiot, Dickinson St (N.D.) | 35 | 251 | 96 | 1 | .723 |
| Mike Feminis, St. Xavier (Ill.) | 12 | 102 | 40 | 0 | .718 |
| Paul Troth, Missouri Valley | 14 | 106 | 49 | 0 | .684 |
| Kevin Donley, St. Francis (Ind.) | 33 | 246 | 114 | 1 | .683 |
| Monty Lewis, Friends (Ks.) | 18 | 118 | 55 | 0 | .682 |
| Mike Cochran, Southern Nazarene (Okla.) | 10 | 75 | 36 | 0 | .676 |
| Keith Barefield, Northwestern Oklahoma St. | 14 | 96 | 47 | 2 | .669 |
| Mike Gardner, Malone (Ohio) | 7 | 49 | 27 | 0 | .645 |
| Larry Wilcox, Benedictine (Ks.) | 32 | 220 | 123 | 0 | .641 |
| Kent Kessinger, Ottawa (Ks.) | 7 | 41 | 32 | 0 | .562 |
| Phil Jones, Shorter (Ga.) | 6 | 37 | 29 | 0 | .561 |

Playoff games included.
Note: Minimum five years as a collegiate head coach and includes record against
four-year institutions only.

#### By Victories

| | | | |
|---|---|---|---|
| Hank Biesiot, Dickinson St (N.D.) | 251 | Mike Feminis, St. Xavier (Ill.) | 102 |
| Kevin Donley, St. Francis (Ind.) | 246 | Keith Barefield, Northwestern Oklahoma St | 96 |
| Larry Wilcox, Benedictine (Ks.) | 220 | Brian Keller, Nebraska Wesleyan | 83 |
| Mike Van Diest, Carroll (Mont.) | 144 | Dennis McCulloch, Valley City State (N.D.) | 78 |
| Bill Cronin, Georgetown (Ky.) | 133 | Steve Ryan, Morningside (Iowa) | 76 |
| Monty Lewis, Friends (Ks.) | 118 | Andy Lambert, Sterling (Ks.) | 75 |
| Dave Dallas, Kansas Wesleyan | 117 | Mike Cochran, MidAmerica Nazarene (Ks.) | 75 |
| Paul Troth, Kansas Wesleyan | 106 | | |

*Active in 2010.

# Pro Basketball

NBA Finals MVP
Dirk Nowitzki led the
Dallas Mavericks to
their first championship

# Vindication in Big D

## Five years after falling to the Heat in the NBA Finals, Dirk Nowitzki and the Dallas Mavericks got their revenge, upsetting star-studded Miami to win their first title

**BY CHRIS MANNIX**

TWO TEAMS, TWO GROUPS OF players, two very different paths. That was the story of the 2011 NBA Finals, where the Miami Heat and its constellation of stars, its myriad endorsements from deep pocketed companies like State Farm to T-Mobile, its record-setting national TV audience and NBA-best road crowds met the Dallas Mavericks and its collection of geriatric 30-somethings led by Dirk Nowitzki, whose most notable endorsement deal is a German bank few have ever heard of. Indeed, Miami and Dallas were the NBA's odd couple, two teams that had taken very different roads to the mountaintop.

The 2010–11 season began, unofficially, over the summer, when Miami welcomed LeBron James and Chris Bosh to South Beach in a televised, smoke-filled ceremony at American Airlines Arena. The unprecedented free agent haul—James, a two-time MVP, and Bosh, a five-time All-Star, joining forces with Dwyane Wade, a former Finals MVP with six All-Star appearances on his resume—created unprecedented hype that exploded when James declared this new Big Three would win "not one, not two, not three" championships. A 70-plus win season was thought to be within reach with many experts pre-

dicting the Heat would cruise to an NBA championship.

Miami's march, however, wouldn't be quite so smooth. Chemistry issues and controversy dogged the Heat all season. There was the 9–8 start highlighted by the infamous shoulder-to-shoulder bump between James and head coach Erik Spoelstra (one million-plus YouTube hits and counting) and an emotional players-only meeting after a double-digit loss to Dallas; there was a stretch of 21 wins in 22 games where the Heat looked like a juggernaut; there was a five-game losing streak in March where James's ability to deliver in critical situations was questioned; there was the four-game winning streak—highlighted by a 23-point pasting of Boston—to close the season. Miami's year rose and fell like an EKG with a fascinated audience tuning in to watch the drama in enormous numbers. "This year has been a big growth process for us," Wade said before the playoffs. "We've seen it all. We've heard everything."

While the country quickly caught Miami fever, the rest of the Eastern Conference was not similarly impressed. Not in Chicago, where the Bulls quiet superstar, Derrick Rose, showed up at training camp declaring himself to be an MVP candidate and then went out and played like one, averaging

ROBERT SULLIVAN

25.0 points and 7.7 assists while leading Chicago to a 62-win season. Not in Boston, where the defending conference champs added a pair of veteran big men—Shaquille O'Neal and Jermaine O'Neal—to its lineup. The Heat won 58 games during the regular season, but come playoff time were far from considered a favorite.

Neither was Dallas, which began the season with an aging roster—Nowitzki (32), Jason Kidd (37) and Jason Terry (33), in particular—and a pair of formidable foes lurking in the Western Conference. Buoyed by a 50-win 2009–10 season and a surprisingly competitive first round series against the eventual champion Lakers, the Oklahoma City Thunder looked poised to join the NBA's elite. Kevin Durant led the NBA in scoring (27.7 points per game) for the second season in a row while Russell Westbrook established himself as one of the game's premier playmakers, averaging 21.9 points and 8.2 assists in a second-team All-NBA season. Further west the Lakers didn't have a typically strong year, slipping out of the top spot in the conference for the first time in four seasons. But the

**Miami's new Big Three—Chris Bosh (l.), LeBron James (c.), and Dwyane Wade—will have to wait for that first title together, as they fell to Dallas in six games in the Finals.**

core of the two-time title team—Kobe Bryant, Pau Gasol, Andrew Bynum and Ron Artest—was intact and ready to make one more run.

After outlasting Portland in a narrow, six-game series the Mavericks slipped back into the underdog role against the Lakers. It was the first postseason meeting between Bryant and Nowitzki, and it was a memorable one. Well, for Nowitzki anyway. Dallas stormed back from a 16-point deficit to steal Game 1 in L.A. They took the next two before sweeping the Lakers out of the playoffs—and ending Phil Jackson's storied coaching career—with a 36-point drubbing in a Game 4. Said Jackson, "I don't think I've seen a team play to that level in a series."

The Mavs roll continued in the conference finals against Oklahoma City. After jumping out to a 2–1 series lead, Dallas fell behind by 15 points with five minutes to go in Game 4. Instead of folding and heading home, the Mav-

JOHN W. MCDONOUGH

**Bulls point guard Derrick Rose had a breakout season in 2011, averaging 25 points, eight assists, and four rebounds per game, good enough to win the 22-year-old the NBA's regular season MVP award.**

against Chicago but rallied to win the next four behind superb two-way play from LeBron James. Matched up with Derrick Rose, James used his size and speed to force the newly crowned MVP to tough perimeter shots. Offensively, James sparked an 18–3 rally in the fourth quarter of Game 5 to send the Heat to the Finals. "We had to go through a lot of adversity," Spoelstra said. "That struggle that we went through in March, where we lost five straight—all of them close games, where we didn't execute down the stretch and weren't able to close games out— that helped us. As painful as that was, we had to go through that fire together to be able to gain the confidence where we could be successful now in the postseason."

The suddenly clicking Heat were a heavy favorite entering the Finals—a rematch of the '06 series—and a comfortable eight-point win in Game 1 suggested the Miami dynasty was ready to claim its first title. But Dallas rallied to squeeze out a two-point win in Game 2. After dropping Game 3 at home, the Mavs won Game 4, with Nowitzki fighting off a 101-degree fever to score 10 of his 21 points in a critical fourth quarter surge. The momentum continued in Game 5 with Nowitzki (29 points) raining jump shots and Dallas's late-game zone defense flummoxing Miami's prolific offensive attack. And with the memory of that 2006 failure still fresh, Nowitzki and Jason Terry—the lone holdovers from the '06 team—combined for 48 points to close the series and claim their first NBA title with an emphatic 105–95 win. "Tonight," said Terry, "we got vindication."

A season that began with smoke and smiles in Miami ended with tears and a broken down Bosh needing teammates to help him to the locker room. There will be many more opportunities for the Heat to live up to the heightened expectations but in this series, it was the old, sage underdogs who came out on top.

ericks went on a 17–2 run in the final five minutes—paced by 12 points from Nowitzki—to force overtime and eventually steal a 112–105 win. A win in Game 5 propelled Dallas back to the Finals for the first time since 2006.

The Mavs opponent would be Miami, which, surprisingly, after a tumultuous regular season made the conference playoffs look easy. The Heat eased past a spirited—but overmatched—Philadelphia team in five games. They took the first two games against Boston and caught a break (literally) when Rajon Rondo dislocated his elbow in Game 3. With Rondo limited, Miami took Game 4 and closed out the series with a ten-point win in Game 5. The Heat stumbled in Game 1

## NBA Final Standings

### Western Conference
#### NORTHWEST DIVISION

| Team | W | L | Pct | GB |
|---|---|---|---|---|
| †Oklahoma City | 55 | 27 | .671 | — |
| *Denver | 50 | 32 | .610 | 5 |
| *Portland | 48 | 34 | .585 | 7 |
| Utah | 39 | 43 | .476 | 16 |
| Minnesota | 17 | 65 | .207 | 38 |

#### PACIFIC DIVISION

| Team | W | L | Pct | GB |
|---|---|---|---|---|
| †LA Lakers | 57 | 25 | .695 | — |
| Phoenix | 40 | 42 | .488 | 17 |
| Golden State | 36 | 46 | .439 | 21 |
| LA Clippers | 32 | 50 | .390 | 25 |
| Sacramento | 24 | 58 | .293 | 33 |

#### SOUTHWEST DIVISION

| Team | W | L | Pct | GB |
|---|---|---|---|---|
| ‡San Antonio | 61 | 21 | .744 | — |
| *Dallas | 57 | 25 | .695 | 4 |
| *New Orleans | 46 | 36 | .561 | 15 |
| *Memphis | 46 | 36 | .561 | 15 |
| Houston | 43 | 39 | .524 | 18 |

### Eastern Conference
#### ATLANTIC DIVISION

| Team | W | L | Pct | GB |
|---|---|---|---|---|
| †Boston | 56 | 26 | .683 | — |
| *New York | 42 | 40 | .512 | 14 |
| *Philadelphia | 41 | 41 | .500 | 15 |
| New Jersey | 24 | 58 | .293 | 32 |
| Toronto | 22 | 60 | .268 | 34 |

#### CENTRAL DIVISION

| Team | W | L | Pct | GB |
|---|---|---|---|---|
| ‡Chicago | 62 | 20 | .756 | — |
| *Indiana | 37 | 45 | .451 | 25 |
| Milwaukee | 35 | 47 | .427 | 27 |
| Detroit | 30 | 52 | .366 | 32 |
| Cleveland | 19 | 63 | .232 | 43 |

#### SOUTHEAST DIVISION

| Team | W | L | Pct | GB |
|---|---|---|---|---|
| †Miami | 58 | 24 | .707 | — |
| *Orlando | 52 | 30 | .634 | 6 |
| *Atlanta | 44 | 38 | .537 | 14 |
| Charlotte | 34 | 48 | .415 | 24 |
| Washington | 23 | 59 | .280 | 35 |

†Clinched division title.   *Clinched playoff berth.   ‡Clinched conference title.

## 2011 NBA Playoffs

**WESTERN CONFERENCE**

| 1st ROUND | SEMIFINALS | FINALS |
|---|---|---|

1-San Antonio
8-Memphis
4-Okla. City
5-Denver
3-Dallas
6-Portland
2-LA Lakers
7-New Orleans

Memphis (4-2)
Okla. City (4-1)
Dallas (4-1)
Dallas (4-2)
Dallas (4-0)
LA Lakers (4-2)

Okla. City (4-3)
Dallas (4-1)

**NBA FINALS**

**DALLAS (4-2)**

**EASTERN CONFERENCE**

| FINALS | SEMIFINALS | 1st ROUND |
|---|---|---|

Chicago-1
Indiana-8
Orlando-4
Atlanta-5
Boston-3
New York-6
Miami-2
Philadelphia-7

Chicago (4-1)
Atlanta (4-2)
Boston (4-0)
Miami (4-1)
Miami (4-1)

Chicago (4-2)
Miami (4-1)

### Eastern Conference First Round

| | | | | |
|---|---|---|---|---|
| Game 1......Indiana | 99 | at Chicago | 104 |
| Game 2......Indiana | 90 | at Chicago | 96 |
| Game 3......Chicago | 88 | at Indiana | 84 |
| Game 4......Chicago | 84 | at Indiana | 89 |
| Game 5......Indiana | 89 | at Chicago | 116 |

Chicago won series 4–1.

| | | | | |
|---|---|---|---|---|
| Game 1......Philadelphia | 89 | at Miami | 97 |
| Game 2......Philadelphia | 73 | at Miami | 94 |
| Game 3......Miami | 100 | at Philadelphia | 94 |
| Game 4......Miami | 82 | at Philadelphia | 86 |
| Game 5......Philadelphia | 91 | at Miami | 97 |

Miami won series 4–1.

| | | | | |
|---|---|---|---|---|
| Game 1......Atlanta | 103 | at Orlando | 93 |
| Game 2......Atlanta | 82 | at Orlando | 88 |
| Game 3......Orlando | 84 | at Atlanta | 88 |
| Game 4......Orlando | 85 | at Atlanta | 88 |
| Game 5......Atlanta | 76 | at Orlando | 101 |
| Game 6......Orlando | 81 | at Atlanta | 84 |

Atlanta won series 4–2.

| | | | | |
|---|---|---|---|---|
| Game 1......New York | 85 | at Boston | 87 |
| Game 2......New York | 93 | at Boston | 96 |
| Game 3......Boston | 113 | at New York | 96 |
| Game 4......Boston | 101 | at New York | 89 |

Boston won series 4–0.

### Western Conference First Round

| | | | | |
|---|---|---|---|---|
| Game 1......Memphis | 101 | at San Antonio | 98 |
| Game 2......Memphis | 87 | at San Antonio | 93 |
| Game 3......San Antonio | 88 | at Memphis | 91 |
| Game 4......San Antonio | 86 | at Memphis | 104 |
| Game 5......Memphis | 103 | at San Antonio | 110* |
| Game 6......San Antonio | 91 | at Memphis | 99 |

Memphis won series 4–2.

| | | | | |
|---|---|---|---|---|
| Game 1......Portland | 81 | at Dallas | 89 |
| Game 2......Portland | 89 | at Dallas | 101 |
| Game 3......Dallas | 92 | at Portland | 97 |
| Game 4......Dallas | 82 | at Portland | 84 |
| Game 5......Portland | 82 | at Dallas | 93 |
| Game 6......Dallas | 103 | at Portland | 96 |

Dallas won series 4–2.

| | | | | |
|---|---|---|---|---|
| Game 1......New Orleans | 109 | at LA Lakers | 100 |
| Game 2......New Orleans | 78 | at LA Lakers | 87 |
| Game 3......LA Lakers | 100 | at New Orleans | 86 |
| Game 4......LA Lakers | 88 | at New Orleans | 93 |
| Game 5......New Orleans | 90 | at LA Lakers | 106 |
| Game 6......LA Lakers | 98 | at New Orleans | 80 |

LA Lakers won series 4–2.

| | | | | |
|---|---|---|---|---|
| Game 1......Denver | 103 | at Okla. City | 107 |
| Game 2......Denver | 89 | at Okla. City | 106 |
| Game 3......Okla. City | 97 | at Denver | 94 |
| Game 4......Okla. City | 101 | at Denver | 104 |
| Game 5......Denver | 97 | at Okla. City | 100 |

Oklahoma City won series 4–1.

### Eastern Conference Semifinals

| | | | | |
|---|---|---|---|---|
| Game 1......Atlanta | 103 | at Chicago | 95 |
| Game 2......Atlanta | 73 | at Chicago | 86 |
| Game 3......Chicago | 99 | at Atlanta | 82 |
| Game 4......Chicago | 88 | at Atlanta | 100 |
| Game 5......Atlanta | 83 | at Chicago | 95 |
| Game 6......Chicago | 93 | at Atlanta | 73 |

Chicago won series 4–2.

| | | | | |
|---|---|---|---|---|
| Game 1......Boston | 90 | at Miami | 99 |
| Game 2......Boston | 91 | at Miami | 102 |
| Game 3......Miami | 81 | at Boston | 97 |
| Game 4......Miami | 98 | at Boston | 90* |
| Game 5......Boston | 87 | at Miami | 97 |

Miami won series 4–1.

### Western Conference Semifinals

| | | | | |
|---|---|---|---|---|
| Game 1......Dallas | 96 | at LA Lakers | 94 |
| Game 2......Dallas | 93 | at LA Lakers | 81 |
| Game 3......LA Lakers | 92 | at Dallas | 98 |
| Game 4......LA Lakers | 86 | at Dallas | 122 |

Dallas won series 4–0.

| | | | | |
|---|---|---|---|---|
| Game 1......Memphis | 114 | at Okla. City | 101 |
| Game 2......Memphis | 102 | at Okla. City | 111 |
| Game 3......Okla. City | 93 | at Memphis | 101* |
| Game 4......Okla. City | 133 | at Memphis | 123† |
| Game 5......Memphis | 72 | at Okla. City | 99 |
| Game 6......Okla. City | 83 | at Memphis | 95 |
| Game 7......Memphis | 90 | at Okla. City | 105 |

Oklahoma City won series 4–3.

### Eastern Conference Finals

| | | | | |
|---|---|---|---|---|
| Game 1......Miami | 82 | at Chicago | 103 |
| Game 2......Miami | 85 | at Chicago | 75 |
| Game 3......Chicago | 85 | at Miami | 96 |
| Game 4......Chicago | 93 | at Miami | 101* |
| Game 5......Miami | 83 | at Chicago | 80 |

Miami won series 4–1.

### Western Conference Finals

| | | | | |
|---|---|---|---|---|
| Game 1......Okla. City | 112 | at Dallas | 121 |
| Game 2......Okla. City | 106 | at Dallas | 100 |
| Game 3......Dallas | 93 | at Okla. City | 87 |
| Game 4......Dallas | 112 | at Okla. City | 105* |
| Game 5......Okla. City | 96 | at Dallas | 100 |

Dallas won series 4–1.

### NBA Finals

| | | | | |
|---|---|---|---|---|
| Game 1......Dallas | 84 | at Miami | 92 |
| Game 2......Dallas | 95 | at Miami | 93 |
| Game 3......Miami | 88 | at Dallas | 86 |
| Game 4......Miami | 83 | at Dallas | 86 |
| Game 5......Miami | 103 | at Dallas | 112 |
| Game 6......Dallas | 105 | at Miami | 95 |

Dallas won series 4–2.

*Overtime game. †Triple overtime game.

# NBA Finals Composite Box Score

## MIAMI HEAT

| Player | GP | Mpg | FG% | 3FG% | FT% | Off. | Total | Apg | Spg | Bpg | TOpg | Ppg |
|---|---|---|---|---|---|---|---|---|---|---|---|---|
| Dwyane Wade | 6 | 39.0 | .546 | .304 | .694 | 2.5 | 7.0 | 5.2 | 1.5 | 1.5 | 2.5 | 26.5 |
| Chris Bosh | 6 | 39.5 | .413 | .000 | .778 | 2.5 | 7.3 | 1.0 | 0.3 | 0.5 | 2.2 | 18.5 |
| LeBron James | 6 | 43.6 | .478 | .321 | .600 | 1.0 | 7.2 | 6.8 | 1.7 | 0.5 | 4.0 | 17.8 |
| Mario Chalmers | 6 | 29.0 | .426 | .400 | .739 | 0.3 | 2.7 | 3.5 | 1.5 | 0.0 | 1.7 | 11.8 |
| Udonis Haslem | 6 | 29.3 | .450 | .000 | .800 | 1.2 | 5.2 | 0.7 | 0.5 | 0.5 | 0.8 | 6.7 |
| Eddie House | 2 | 12.5 | .333 | .375 | .000 | 0.0 | 2.0 | 0.5 | 1.0 | 0.0 | 0.5 | 4.5 |
| Mlke Bibby | 5 | 17.4 | .350 | .294 | .000 | 0.2 | 1.4 | 1.0 | 1.4 | 0.2 | 0.6 | 3.8 |
| Mike Miller | 6 | 15.7 | .304 | .389 | .000 | 0.5 | 2.8 | 0.8 | 0.8 | 0.2 | 0.7 | 3.5 |
| Juwan Howard | 5 | 5.8 | .600 | .000 | .500 | 0.6 | 1.2 | 0.2 | 0.0 | 0.0 | 0.2 | 1.8 |
| Joel Anthony | 6 | 20.5 | .286 | .000 | .000 | 2.0 | 3.5 | 0.3 | 0.2 | 1.2 | 0.2 | 1.3 |
| **Avg/Total** | **6** | **288.0** | **.451** | **.346** | **.709** | **10.7** | **38.5** | **19.5** | **8.0** | **4.5** | **12.9** | **92.3** |

## DALLAS MAVERICKS

| Player | GP | Mpg | FG% | 3FG% | FT% | Off. | Total | Apg | Spg | Bpg | TOpg | Ppg |
|---|---|---|---|---|---|---|---|---|---|---|---|---|
| Dirk Nowitzki | 6 | 40.3 | .416 | .368 | .978 | 0.3 | 9.7 | 2.0 | 0.7 | 0.7 | 2.8 | 26.0 |
| Jason Terry | 6 | 32.5 | .494 | .393 | .750 | 0.5 | 2.0 | 3.2 | 1.3 | 0.0 | 1.3 | 18.0 |
| Shawn Marion | 6 | 35.7 | .479 | .000 | .824 | 2.3 | 6.3 | 2.3 | 0.8 | 0.7 | 2.3 | 13.7 |
| Tyson Chandler | 6 | 37.3 | .594 | .000 | .625 | 4.0 | 8.8 | 0.7 | 1.2 | 1.2 | 0.5 | 9.7 |
| Jose Barea | 6 | 21.3 | .382 | .333 | .714 | 0.7 | 2.2 | 3.2 | 0.5 | 0.0 | 1.5 | 8.8 |
| Jason Kidd | 6 | 37.5 | .389 | .429 | .750 | 0.3 | 4.5 | 6.3 | 1.2 | 0.8 | 3.5 | 7.7 |
| DeShawn Stevenson | 6 | 17.2 | .542 | .565 | .750 | 0.2 | 1.5 | 0.3 | 0.7 | 0.2 | 0.2 | 7.0 |
| Ian Mahinmi | 3 | 9.0 | .600 | .000 | .600 | 1.0 | 1.7 | 0.0 | 0.3 | 0.0 | 0.3 | 3.0 |
| Brendan Haywood | 3 | 8.3 | .333 | .000 | .500 | 0.7 | 2.3 | 0.0 | 0.3 | 1.0 | 0.3 | 1.7 |
| Brian Cardinal | 5 | 6.0 | .667 | .667 | .500 | 0.0 | 0.2 | 0.2 | 0.2 | 0.0 | 0.6 | 1.4 |
| Peja Stojakovic | 4 | 6.5 | .200 | .000 | .000 | 0.0 | 0.8 | 0.0 | 0.5 | 0.0 | 0.5 | 0.5 |
| **Avg/Total** | **6** | **288.0** | **.454** | **.411** | **.781** | **9.2** | **37.7** | **18.2** | **7.2** | **4.0** | **13.3** | **94.7** |

# NBA Finals Game Box Scores

## Game I

### DALLAS 84

| Player | Min | FG M-A | FT M-A | Reb O-T | A | PF | S | TO | TP |
|---|---|---|---|---|---|---|---|---|---|
| S. Marion | 35 | 6-12 | 4-5 | 3-10 | 4 | 1 | 1 | 3 | 16 |
| T. Chandler | 34 | 3-4 | 3-5 | 0-4 | 2 | 5 | 1 | 2 | 9 |
| D. Nowitzki | 40 | 7-18 | 12-12 | 0-8 | 2 | 4 | 0 | 2 | 27 |
| J. Kidd | 36 | 3-8 | 0-0 | 0-4 | 6 | 0 | 0 | 3 | 9 |
| D. Stevenson | 14 | 2-3 | 0-0 | 0-2 | 0 | 2 | 0 | 0 | 6 |
| J. Terry | 33 | 3-10 | 3-4 | 1-1 | 1 | 2 | 0 | 1 | 12 |
| J.J. Barea | 18 | 1-8 | 0-0 | 0-0 | 3 | 2 | 1 | 0 | 2 |
| P. Stojakovic | 15 | 0-3 | 0-0 | 0-0 | 0 | 3 | 2 | 0 | 0 |
| B. Haywood | 14 | 0-1 | 3-6 | 2-7 | 0 | 3 | 1 | 0 | 3 |
| Totals | 240 | 25-67 | 25-32 | 6-36 | 18 | 22 | 6 | 11 | 84 |

Percentages: FG—.373, FT—.781. 3-pt goals: 9–22, .409 (Nonwitzki 1–2, Kidd 3–7, Stevenson 2–3, Terry 3–7, Stojakovic 0–3). Blocked shots: 8 (Haywood 3, Chandler 2, Kidd, Marion, Stevenson ).

### MIAMI 92

| Player | Min | FG M-A | FT M-A | Reb O-T | A | PF | S | TO | TP |
|---|---|---|---|---|---|---|---|---|---|
| C. Bosh | 39 | 5-18 | 9-12 | 5-9 | 3 | 3 | 0 | 0 | 19 |
| L. James | 45 | 9-16 | 2-2 | 0-9 | 5 | 4 | 1 | 1 | 24 |
| J. Anthony | 18 | 0-1 | 0-0 | 1-3 | 0 | 2 | 0 | 1 | 0 |
| M. Bibby | 14 | 0-4 | 0-0 | 0-0 | 3 | 1 | 2 | 0 | 0 |
| D. Wade | 38 | 9-19 | 2-5 | 3-10 | 6 | 1 | 0 | 3 | 22 |
| J. Howard | 8 | 0-1 | 2-2 | 3-3 | 0 | 0 | 0 | 0 | 2 |
| M. Miller | 20 | 2-5 | 0-0 | 2-5 | 1 | 4 | 0 | 1 | 6 |
| U. Haslem | 30 | 3-8 | 1-1 | 1-6 | 1 | 5 | 1 | 2 | 7 |
| M. Chalmers | 28 | 3-8 | 3-4 | 1-1 | 1 | 1 | 1 | 2 | 12 |
| Totals | 240 | 31-80 | 19-26 | 16-46 | 20 | 21 | 5 | 10 | 92 |

Percentages: FG—.388, FT—.731. 3-pt goals: 11–24, .458 (James 4–5, Bibby 0–4, Wade 2–4, Miller 2–4, Chalmers 3–7). Blocked shots: 4 (Wade 2, Bosh, Anthony).

A: 20,003. Officials: S. Javie, M. Callahan, B. Kennedy.

### Game 2

#### DALLAS 95

| Player | Min | FG M-A | FT M-A | Reb O-T | A | PF | S | TO | TP |
|---|---|---|---|---|---|---|---|---|---|
| S. Marion | 41 | 9-14 | 2-2 | 3-8 | 3 | 2 | 1 | 3 | 20 |
| D. Nowitzki | 42 | 10-22 | 3-3 | 1-11 | 4 | 2 | 0 | 5 | 24 |
| T. Chandler | 38 | 4-6 | 5-8 | 4-7 | 0 | 5 | 1 | 0 | 13 |
| J. Kidd | 38 | 2-7 | 0-0 | 1-8 | 5 | 1 | 1 | 5 | 6 |
| D. Stevenson | 22 | 3-6 | 0-0 | 1-3 | 0 | 2 | 3 | 1 | 9 |
| P. Stojakovic | 5 | 0-0 | 0-0 | 0-0 | 0 | 0 | 0 | 1 | 0 |
| J. Terry | 31 | 5-11 | 6-6 | 1-1 | 5 | 4 | 2 | 2 | 16 |
| B. Cardinal | 1 | 0-0 | 0-0 | 0-0 | 0 | 1 | 0 | 0 | 0 |
| B. Haywood | 8 | 1-2 | 0-0 | 0-0 | 0 | 2 | 0 | 1 | 2 |
| J.J. Barea | 14 | 2-7 | 1-2 | 0-3 | 1 | 1 | 0 | 0 | 5 |
| Totals | 240 | 36-75 | 17-21 | 11-41 | 18 | 20 | 8 | 18 | 95 |

Percentages: FG—.480, FT—.810. 3-pt goals: 6-17, .353 (Nowitzki 1-2, Kidd 2-5, Stevenson 3-5, Terry 0-2, Barea 0-3 ). Technical Fouls: 1 (Carlisle-coach). Blocked shots: 2 (Marion, Nowtizki).

#### MIAMI 93

| Player | Min | FG M-A | FT M-A | Reb O-T | A | PF | S | TO | TP |
|---|---|---|---|---|---|---|---|---|---|
| C. Bosh | 40 | 4-16 | 4-4 | 2-8 | 0 | 3 | 1 | 2 | 12 |
| L. James | 40 | 8-15 | 2-4 | 1-8 | 4 | 4 | 4 | 5 | 20 |
| J. Anthony | 27 | 0-0 | 0-0 | 0-1 | 0 | 3 | 0 | 0 | 0 |
| M. Bibby | 22 | 5-8 | 0-0 | 0-1 | 0 | 0 | 4 | 1 | 14 |
| D. Wade | 42 | 13-20 | 8-12 | 2-5 | 6 | 2 | 3 | 1 | 36 |
| M. Miller | 15 | 0-3 | 0-0 | 0-4 | 0 | 2 | 1 | 0 | 0 |
| U. Haslem | 29 | 1-3 | 0-0 | 1-3 | 0 | 2 | 1 | 2 | 2 |
| M. Chalmers | 25 | 3-8 | 2-4 | 0-0 | 3 | 1 | 1 | 1 | 9 |
| Totals | 240 | 34-73 | 16-24 | 6-30 | 13 | 17 | 15 | 12 | 93 |

Percentages: FG—.466, FT—.667. 3-pt goals: 9-30, .300 (James 2-7, Bibby 4-7, Wade 2-7, Miller 0-3, Chalmers 1-6). Technical Fouls: 1 (Miller). Blocked shots: 7 (Anthony 3, Wade 2, James, Miller).

A: 20,003. Officials: J. Crawford, K. Mauer, E. Malloy.

### Game 3

#### MIAMI 88

| Player | Min | FG M-A | FT M-A | Reb O-T | A | PF | S | TO | TP |
|---|---|---|---|---|---|---|---|---|---|
| C. Bosh | 37 | 7-18 | 4-5 | 1-3 | 1 | 4 | 0 | 2 | 18 |
| L. James | 45 | 6-14 | 4-4 | 0-3 | 9 | 3 | 2 | 4 | 17 |
| J. Anthony | 23 | 1-4 | 0-0 | 4-6 | 1 | 2 | 1 | 0 | 2 |
| M. Bibby | 19 | 1-5 | 0-0 | 0-2 | 1 | 4 | 1 | 1 | 3 |
| D. Wade | 39 | 12-21 | 3-4 | 3-11 | 3 | 3 | 1 | 0 | 29 |
| J. Howard | 6 | 0-0 | 1-2 | 0-1 | 1 | 1 | 0 | 0 | 1 |
| M. Miller | 12 | 0-1 | 0-0 | 0-2 | 1 | 3 | 2 | 1 | 0 |
| U. Haslem | 29 | 1-3 | 0-0 | 1-4 | 1 | 4 | 1 | 1 | 6 |
| M. Chalmers | 29 | 4-8 | 0-0 | 0-4 | 2 | 3 | 0 | 1 | 12 |
| Totals | 240 | 34-78 | 12-15 | 9-36 | 20 | 27 | 8 | 10 | 88 |

Percentages: FG—.436, FT—.800. 3-pt goals: 8-19, .421 (James 1-4, Bibby 1-4, Wade 2-4, Miller 0-1, Chalmers 4-6). Blocked shots: 5 (Anthony 2, Bibby, Wade, Haslem).

#### DALLAS 86

| Player | Min | FG M-A | FT M-A | Reb O-T | A | PF | S | TO | TP |
|---|---|---|---|---|---|---|---|---|---|
| S. Marion | 43 | 4-12 | 2-2 | 2-4 | 3 | 2 | 0 | 2 | 10 |
| D. Nowitzki | 42 | 11-21 | 9-9 | 1-11 | 1 | 1 | 1 | 3 | 34 |
| T. Chandler | 40 | 1-4 | 3-4 | 7-11 | 0 | 2 | 1 | 0 | 5 |
| J. Kidd | 35 | 3-8 | 1-2 | 1-6 | 10 | 2 | 0 | 4 | 9 |
| D. Stevenson | 14 | 1-1 | 0-0 | 0-1 | 1 | 0 | 0 | 0 | 3 |
| P. Stojakovic | 6 | 1-2 | 0-0 | 0-3 | 0 | 1 | 0 | 1 | 2 |
| J. Terry | 32 | 5-13 | 4-6 | 0-3 | 2 | 0 | 1 | 0 | 15 |
| B. Cardinal | 0 | 0-0 | 0-0 | 0-0 | 0 | 0 | 0 | 0 | 0 |
| J.J. Barea | 22 | 2-8 | 1-2 | 0-2 | 1 | 1 | 0 | 4 | 6 |
| I. Mahinmi | 8 | 0-1 | 2-2 | 1-1 | 0 | 5 | 0 | 0 | 2 |
| Totals | 240 | 28-70 | 22-27 | 12-42 | 18 | 14 | 3 | 14 | 86 |

Percentages: FG—.400, FT—.815. 3-pt goals: 8-21, .381 (Marion 0-1, Nowitzki 3-5, Kidd 2-5, Stevenson 1-1, Stojakovic 0-1, Terry 1-3, Barea 1-5). Blocked shots: 8 (Nowitzki 3, Chandler 3, Kidd, Marion).

A: 20,340. Officials: D. Stafford, S. Foster, D. Crawford.

### Game 4

#### MIAMI 83

| Player | Min | FG M-A | FT M-A | Reb O-T | A | PF | S | TO | TP |
|---|---|---|---|---|---|---|---|---|---|
| L. James | 46 | 3-11 | 2-4 | 3-9 | 7 | 4 | 2 | 4 | 8 |
| C. Bosh | 42 | 9-19 | 6-8 | 1-6 | 1 | 1 | 0 | 4 | 24 |
| J. Anthony | 28 | 2-6 | 0-0 | 5-8 | 1 | 4 | 0 | 0 | 4 |
| D. Wade | 39 | 13-20 | 6-9 | 4-6 | 2 | 3 | 2 | 2 | 32 |
| M. Bibby | 16 | 0-1 | 0-0 | 1-2 | 1 | 3 | 0 | 0 | 0 |
| J. Howard | 0 | 0-0 | 0-0 | 0-2 | 0 | 1 | 0 | 0 | 0 |
| M. Miller | 15 | 2-8 | 0-0 | 1-3 | 1 | 2 | 1 | 1 | 6 |
| U. Haslem | 21 | 2-5 | 0-0 | 0-4 | 0 | 3 | 0 | 0 | 4 |
| M. Chalmers | 29 | 1-5 | 3-3 | 0-4 | 6 | 2 | 3 | 2 | 5 |
| Totals | 240 | 32-75 | 17-24 | 15-44 | 19 | 23 | 8 | 13 | 83 |

Percentages: FG—.427, FT—.708. 3-pt goals: 2-14, .143. (James 0-3, Wade 0-2, Bibby 0-1, Miller 2-5, Chalmers 0-3). Blocked shots: 5 (Wade 2, Bosh, Anthony, Haslem)

#### DALLAS 86

| Player | Min | FG M-A | FT M-A | Reb O-T | A | PF | S | TO | TP |
|---|---|---|---|---|---|---|---|---|---|
| S. Marion | 26 | 7-12 | 2-2 | 2-4 | 0 | 2 | 0 | 2 | 16 |
| D. Nowitzki | 39 | 6-19 | 9-10 | 0-11 | 1 | 2 | 0 | 3 | 21 |
| T. Chandler | 43 | 4-7 | 5-8 | 9-16 | 3 | 1 | 0 |  | 13 |
| J. Kidd | 39 | 0-3 | 0-0 | 0-3 | 3 | 1 | 3 | 4 | 0 |
| J.J. Barea | 22 | 3-9 | 2-2 | 1-3 | 4 | 2 | 0 | 1 | 8 |
| B. Haywood | 3 | 0-0 | 0-0 | 0-0 | 0 | 1 | 0 | 0 | 0 |
| D. Stevenson | 26 | 3-7 | 2-2 | 0-3 | 1 | 3 | 0 | 0 | 11 |
| B. Cardinal | 7 | 0-0 | 0-0 | 0-1 | 0 | 2 | 0 | 1 | 0 |
| J. Terry | 35 | 6-15 | 4-6 | 0-3 | 0 | 3 | 2 | 3 | 17 |
| P. Stojakovic | 0 | 0-0 | 0-0 | 0-0 | 0 | 0 | 0 | 0 | 0 |
| Totals | 240 | 29-73 | 24-30 | 12-41 | 13 | 18 | 7 | 11 | 86 |

Percentages: FG—.397, FT—.800. 3-pt goals: 4-19, .211 (Nowitzki 0-2, Kidd 0-3, Barea 0-2, Stevenson 3-7, Cardinal 0-1, Terry 1-4). Technical Fouls: 1 (Carlisle-coach). Blocked shots: 2 (Marion, Kidd).

A: 20,430. Officials: G. Willard, M. McCutchen, M. Davis.

## Game 5

### MIAMI 103

| Player | Min | FG M-A | FT M-A | Reb O-T | A | PF | S | TO | TP |
|---|---|---|---|---|---|---|---|---|---|
| C. Bosh | 39 | 6-12 | 7-9 | 6-10 | 1 | 3 | 0 | 4 | 19 |
| L. James | 46 | 8-19 | 1-2 | 1-10 | 10 | 3 | 0 | 4 | 17 |
| J. Anthony | 16 | 1-1 | 0-0 | 0-0 | 0 | 3 | 0 | 0 | 2 |
| M. Bibby | 15 | 1-2 | 0-0 | 0-2 | 0 | 1 | 0 | 1 | 2 |
| D. Wade | 34 | 6-12 | 10-12 | 0-2 | 8 | 2 | 2 | 4 | 23 |
| J. Howard | 6 | 3-3 | 0-0 | 0-0 | 0 | 3 | 0 | 0 | 6 |
| E. House | 3 | 0-2 | 0-0 | 0-1 | 0 | 1 | 1 | 1 | 0 |
| M. Miller | 23 | 3-5 | 0-0 | 0-2 | 2 | 4 | 1 | 1 | 9 |
| U. Haslem | 33 | 5-8 | 0-0 | 1-5 | 2 | 2 | 0 | 0 | 10 |
| M. Chalmers | 23 | 4-6 | 3-3 | 1-4 | 2 | 4 | 1 | 1 | 15 |
| Totals | 240 | 37-70 | 21-26 | 9-36 | 25 | 26 | 5 | 16 | 103 |

Percentages: FG—.529, FT—.808. 3-pt goals: 8-20, .400 (Bosh 0-1, James 0-4, Bibby 0-1, Wade 1-2, House 0-2, Miller 3-4, Chalmers 4-6). Blocked shots: 4 (Bosh, James, Wade, Haslem).

### DALLAS 112

| Player | Min | FG M-A | FT M-A | Reb O-T | A | PF | S | TO | TP |
|---|---|---|---|---|---|---|---|---|---|
| S. Marion | 34 | 4-11 | 0-0 | 1-4 | 3 | 3 | 2 | 2 | 8 |
| D. Nowitzki | 40 | 9-18 | 10-10 | 0-6 | 3 | 2 | 1 | 2 | 29 |
| T. Chandler | 39 | 5-7 | 3-5 | 2-7 | 0 | 4 | 1 | 0 | 13 |
| J. Kidd | 40 | 4-6 | 2-2 | 0-2 | 6 | 1 | 3 | 3 | 13 |
| J.J. Barea | 26 | 6-11 | 1-1 | 1-2 | 5 | 1 | 0 | 1 | 17 |
| J. Terry | 30 | 8-12 | 2-2 | 0-4 | 6 | 1 | 0 | 2 | 21 |
| B. Cardinal | 10 | 1-1 | 1-2 | 0-0 | 0 | 3 | 1 | 1 | 4 |
| D. Stevenson | 14 | 1-2 | 1-2 | 0-0 | 0 | 2 | 0 | 0 | 4 |
| I. Mahinmi | 8 | 1-1 | 1-3 | 0-1 | 0 | 3 | 0 | 0 | 3 |
| Totals | 240 | 39-69 | 21-27 | 4-26 | 23 | 20 | 8 | 11 | 112 |

Percentages: FG—.565, FT—.778. 3-pt goals: 13-19, .684 (Nowitzki 1-1, Kidd 3-5, Barea 4-5, Terry 3-5, Cardinal 1-1, Stevenson 1-2). Technical Fouls: 1 (Marion). Blocked shots: 3 (Chandler 2, Kidd).

A: 20,433. Officials: J. Crawford, M. Callahan, B. Kennedy.

## Game 6

### DALLAS 105

| Player | Min | FG M-A | FT M-A | Reb O-T | A | PF | S | TO | TP |
|---|---|---|---|---|---|---|---|---|---|
| S. Marion | 35 | 4-10 | 4-6 | 3-8 | 1 | 3 | 1 | 2 | 12 |
| D. Nowitzki | 39 | 9-27 | 2-2 | 0-11 | 1 | 4 | 2 | 2 | 21 |
| T. Chandler | 30 | 2-4 | 1-2 | 2-8 | 1 | 5 | 2 | 1 | 5 |
| J. Kidd | 36 | 2-4 | 3-4 | 0-4 | 8 | 1 | 0 | 2 | 9 |
| J.J. Barea | 30 | 7-12 | 0-0 | 2-3 | 5 | 3 | 2 | 3 | 15 |
| J. Terry | 34 | 11-16 | 2-4 | 1-3 | 2 | 1 | 2 | 3 | 27 |
| B. Cardinal | 12 | 1-1 | 0-0 | 0-0 | 1 | 2 | 0 | 1 | 3 |
| D. Stevenson | 13 | 3-5 | 0-0 | 0-0 | 0 | 0 | 1 | 0 | 9 |
| I. Mahinmi | 11 | 2-3 | 0-0 | 2-3 | 0 | 5 | 1 | 0 | 4 |
| Totals | 240 | 41-82 | 12-18 | 10-40 | 19 | 24 | 11 | 14 | 105 |

Percentages: FG—.500, FT—.667. 3-pt goals: 11-26, .423 (Nowitzki 1-7, Kidd 2-3, Barea 1-3, Terry 3-7, Stevenson 3-5, Cardinal 1-1, ). Technical Fouls: 1 (Stevenson). Blocked shots: 1 (Kidd).

### MIAMI 95

| Player | Min | FG M-A | FT M-A | Reb O-T | A | PF | S | TO | TP |
|---|---|---|---|---|---|---|---|---|---|
| C. Bosh | 39 | 7-9 | 5-7 | 0-8 | 0 | 1 | 1 | 1 | 19 |
| L. James | 40 | 9-15 | 1-4 | 1-4 | 6 | 2 | 1 | 6 | 21 |
| J. Anthony | 11 | 0-2 | 0-0 | 2-3 | 0 | 0 | 0 | 0 | 0 |
| D. Wade | 41 | 6-16 | 5-7 | 3-8 | 6 | 3 | 1 | 5 | 17 |
| M. Chalmers | 39 | 5-12 | 6-9 | 0-3 | 7 | 2 | 3 | 3 | 18 |
| J. Howard | 7 | 0-1 | 0-2 | 0-0 | 0 | 0 | 0 | 1 | 0 |
| E. House | 21 | 3-7 | 3-6 | 0-3 | 1 | 3 | 1 | 0 | 9 |
| M. Miller | 8 | 0-1 | 0-0 | 0-1 | 0 | 0 | 0 | 0 | 0 |
| U. Haslem | 34 | 4-9 | 3-4 | 3-9 | 0 | 3 | 0 | 0 | 11 |
| Totals | 240 | 34-72 | 20-33 | 9-39 | 20 | 14 | 7 | 16 | 95 |

Percentages: FG—.472, FT—.606. 3-pt goals: 7-23, .304 (James 2-5, Wade 0-4, Chalmers 2-7, House 3-6, Miller 0-1). Technical Fouls 3 (Haslem, Chalmers, Wade). Blocked shots: 3 (Wade 2, James).

A: 20,003. Officials: S. Javie, D. Stafford, S. Foster.

## 2010–11 All-NBA Teams

### FIRST TEAM
F LeBron James, Mia
F Kevin Durant, OKC
C Dwight Howard, Orl
G Kobe Bryant, LAL
G Derrick Rose, Chi

### SECOND TEAM
F Pau Gasol, LAL
F Dirk Nowitzki, Dal
C Amare Stoudemire, NYK
G Russell Westbrook, OKC
G Dwyane Wade, Mia

### THIRD TEAM
F LaMarcus Aldridge, Por
F Zach Randolph, Mem
C Al Horford, Atl
G Manu Ginobli, SA
G Chris Paul, NO

## All-Rookie Teams

### FIRST TEAM
Blake Griffin, LAC
John Wall, Was
Landry Fields, NY
DeMarcus Cousins, Sac
Gary Neal, SA

### SECOND TEAM
Greg Monroe, Det
Wesley Johnson, Min
Eric Bledsoe, LAC
Derrick Favors, Utah
Paul George, Ind

## All-Defensive Team

### FIRST TEAM
F LeBron James, Mia
F Kevin Garnett, Bos
C Dwight Howard, Orl
G Kobe Bryant, LAL
G Rajon Rondo, Bos

### SECOND TEAM
F Joakim Noah, Chi
F Andre Iguodala, Phi
C Tyson Chandler, Dal
G Tony Allen, Mem
G Chris Paul, NO

## 2010–11 NBA Regular Season Individual Leaders

### Scoring

| | GP | Pts | Avg |
|---|---|---|---|
| Kevin Durant, OKC | 78 | 2,161 | 27.7 |
| LeBron James, Mia | 79 | 2,111 | 26.7 |
| Carmelo Anthony, Den/NY | 77 | 1,970 | 25.6 |
| Dwyane Wade, Mia | 76 | 1,941 | 25.5 |
| Kobe Bryant, LAL | 82 | 2,078 | 25.3 |
| Amare Stoudemire, NY | 78 | 1,971 | 25.3 |
| Derrick Rose, Chi | 81 | 2,026 | 25.0 |
| Monta Ellis, GS | 80 | 1,929 | 24.1 |
| Kevin Martin, Hou | 80 | 1,876 | 23.5 |
| Dirk Nowitzki, Dal | 73 | 1,681 | 23.0 |

### Rebounds

| | GP | Reb | Avg |
|---|---|---|---|
| Kevin Love, Min | 73 | 1,112 | 15.2 |
| Dwight Howard, Orl | 78 | 1,098 | 14.1 |
| Zach Randolph, Mem | 75 | 914 | 12.2 |
| Blake Griffin, LAC | 82 | 989 | 12.1 |
| Kris Humphries, NJ | 74 | 771 | 10.4 |
| Pau Gasol, LAL | 82 | 836 | 10.2 |
| David Lee, GS | 73 | 714 | 9.8 |
| Al Jefferson, Utah | 82 | 794 | 9.7 |
| Emeka Okafor, NO | 72 | 684 | 9.5 |
| Tyson Chandler, Dal | 74 | 692 | 9.4 |

### Assists

| | GP | Ast | Avg |
|---|---|---|---|
| Steve Nash, Phx | 75 | 855 | 11.4 |
| Rajon Rondo, Bos | 68 | 760 | 11.2 |
| Deron Williams, Utah/NJ | 65 | 667 | 10.3 |
| Chris Paul, NO | 80 | 782 | 9.8 |
| Jose Calderon, Tor | 68 | 605 | 8.9 |
| Raymond Felton, NY/Den | 75 | 625 | 8.3 |
| John Wall, Was | 69 | 574 | 8.3 |
| Jason Kidd, Dal | 80 | 655 | 8.2 |
| Russell Westbrook, OKC | 82 | 670 | 8.2 |
| Derrick Rose, Chi | 81 | 623 | 7.7 |

### Field-Goal Percentage

| | FGA | FGM | Pct |
|---|---|---|---|
| Nene Hilario, Den | 654 | 402 | .615 |
| Dwight Howard, Orl | 1,044 | 619 | .593 |
| Emeka Okafor, NO | 524 | 300 | .573 |
| Marcin Gortat, Orl/Phx | 603 | 338 | .561 |
| Al Horford, Atl | 921 | 513 | .557 |
| Greg Monroe, Det | 550 | 303 | .551 |
| JaVale McGee, Was | 604 | 332 | .550 |
| Serge Ibaka, OKC | 617 | 335 | .543 |
| Thaddeus Young, Phi | 847 | 458 | .541 |
| Paul Millsap, Utah | 988 | 525 | .531 |

### Free-Throw Percentage

| | FTA | FTM | Pct |
|---|---|---|---|
| Stephen Curry, GS | 227 | 212 | .934 |
| Chauncey Billups, Den/NY | 419 | 384 | .916 |
| Steve Nash, Phx | 249 | 227 | .912 |
| D.J. Augustin, Cha | 297 | 269 | .906 |
| Jodie Meeks, Phi | 170 | 152 | .894 |
| Randy Foye, LAC | 149 | 133 | .893 |
| Dirk Nowitzki, Dal | 443 | 395 | .892 |
| Kevin Martin, Hou | 669 | 594 | .888 |
| Ray Allen, Bos | 219 | 193 | .881 |
| Kevin Durant, OKC | 675 | 594 | .880 |

### Three-Point Field-Goal Percentage

| | 3FGA | 3FGM | Pct |
|---|---|---|---|
| Matt Bonner, SA | 230 | 105 | .457 |
| Ray Allen, Bos | 378 | 168 | .444 |
| Stephen Curry, GS | 342 | 151 | .442 |
| Luke Ridnour, Min | 184 | 81 | .440 |
| Richard Jefferson, SA | 307 | 135 | .440 |
| Mike Bibby, Atl/Mia/Was | 348 | 153 | .440 |
| James Jones, Mia | 287 | 123 | .429 |
| Arron Afflalo, Den | 248 | 105 | .423 |
| Reggie Williams, GS | 241 | 102 | .423 |
| Anthony Morrow, NJ | 260 | 110 | .423 |

### Steals

| | GP | Steals | Avg |
|---|---|---|---|
| Chris Paul, NO | 80 | 188 | 2.35 |
| Rajon Rondo, Bos | 68 | 153 | 2.25 |
| Monta Ellis, GS | 80 | 168 | 2.10 |
| Russell Westbrook, OKC | 82 | 155 | 1.89 |
| Tony Allen, Mem | 72 | 129 | 1.79 |
| Mike Conley, Mem | 81 | 144 | 1.78 |
| Jason Kidd, Dal | 80 | 134 | 1.68 |
| Raymond Felton, Den/NY | 75 | 125 | 1.67 |
| Trevor Ariza, NO | 75 | 120 | 1.60 |
| LeBron James, Mia | 79 | 124 | 1.57 |

### Blocked Shots

| | GP | BS | Avg |
|---|---|---|---|
| Andrew Bogut, Mil | 65 | 168 | 2.58 |
| JaVale McGee, Was | 79 | 193 | 2.44 |
| Serge Ibaka, OKC | 82 | 198 | 2.41 |
| Dwight Howard, Orl | 78 | 186 | 2.38 |
| Darko Milicic, Min | 69 | 140 | 2.03 |
| Andrew Bynum, LAL | 54 | 106 | 1.96 |
| Amare Stoudemire, NY | 78 | 150 | 1.92 |
| Tim Duncan, SA | 76 | 146 | 1.92 |
| Al Jefferson, Utah | 82 | 153 | 1.87 |
| DeAndre Jordan, LAC | 80 | 142 | 1.78 |

## Offense

| Team | FG Pct | 3FG Pct | FT Pct | Rebound Avg Off | Total | A | TO | Stl | Scoring Avg |
|------|--------|---------|--------|-----|-------|---|----|-----|-----|
| Denver | 47.6 | 38.8 | 76.5 | 9.6 | 42.0 | 22.1 | 14.1 | 7.4 | 107.5 |
| New York | 45.7 | 36.8 | 80.9 | 10.3 | 40.5 | 21.4 | 13.7 | 7.6 | 106.5 |
| Houston | 45.4 | 36.7 | 80.1 | 11.7 | 42.8 | 23.8 | 13.5 | 7.1 | 105.9 |
| Phoenix | 47.0 | 37.7 | 75.9 | 10.0 | 42.8 | 23.7 | 14.3 | 6.6 | 105.0 |
| Oklahoma City | 46.4 | 34.7 | 82.3 | 11.0 | 40.2 | 20.4 | 14.3 | 8.0 | 104.8 |
| San Antonio | 47.5 | 39.7 | 76.7 | 10.1 | 42.8 | 22.4 | 13.4 | 7.3 | 103.7 |
| Golden State | 46.1 | 39.2 | 76.1 | 11.6 | 40.5 | 22.5 | 14.6 | 9.0 | 103.4 |
| Miami | 48.1 | 37.0 | 76.9 | 9.6 | 42.1 | 20.0 | 13.9 | 6.6 | 102.1 |
| LA Lakers | 46.3 | 35.2 | 77.9 | 12.1 | 44.0 | 22.0 | 13.1 | 7.3 | 101.5 |
| Minnesota | 44.1 | 37.6 | 76.8 | 13.2 | 44.4 | 20.1 | 17.0 | 7.2 | 101.1 |
| Dallas | 47.5 | 36.5 | 77.7 | 9.5 | 41.4 | 23.8 | 14.0 | 6.8 | 100.2 |
| Memphis | 47.1 | 33.4 | 75.0 | 11.8 | 41.0 | 20.6 | 14.0 | 9.4 | 99.9 |
| Indiana | 44.2 | 35.4 | 78.2 | 11.1 | 43.5 | 19.6 | 15.4 | 7.1 | 99.8 |
| Utah | 46.5 | 34.6 | 77.1 | 11.0 | 39.5 | 23.4 | 14.3 | 7.7 | 99.4 |
| Sacramento | 44.9 | 33.5 | 73.4 | 13.1 | 43.9 | 20.4 | 16.1 | 7.4 | 99.4 |
| Orlando | 46.1 | 36.6 | 69.2 | 10.5 | 43.2 | 20.0 | 14.9 | 6.7 | 99.2 |
| Toronto | 46.5 | 31.6 | 75.5 | 11.7 | 40.3 | 21.9 | 14.7 | 7.1 | 99.1 |
| Philadelphia | 46.1 | 35.5 | 77.0 | 10.4 | 41.8 | 22.7 | 13.0 | 7.6 | 99.0 |
| LA Clippers | 45.7 | 33.8 | 70.7 | 11.6 | 42.1 | 22.1 | 16.4 | 7.1 | 98.6 |
| Chicago | 46.2 | 36.1 | 74.3 | 11.8 | 44.2 | 22.3 | 14.2 | 7.2 | 98.6 |
| Washington | 44.3 | 33.2 | 74.5 | 12.4 | 41.3 | 19.4 | 15.3 | 8.1 | 97.3 |
| Detroit | 46.0 | 37.6 | 73.7 | 11.4 | 38.6 | 21.1 | 13.0 | 7.3 | 97.0 |
| Boston | 48.6 | 36.5 | 77.0 | 7.8 | 38.8 | 23.4 | 14.6 | 8.2 | 96.5 |
| Portland | 44.7 | 34.5 | 80.4 | 12.1 | 39.3 | 21.2 | 13.0 | 8.0 | 96.3 |
| Cleveland | 43.4 | 34.2 | 74.5 | 10.4 | 40.3 | 21.0 | 14.2 | 6.6 | 95.5 |
| Atlanta | 46.2 | 35.2 | 77.9 | 9.3 | 39.3 | 22.0 | 13.6 | 6.1 | 95.0 |
| New Orleans | 45.9 | 36.0 | 76.5 | 10.0 | 40.1 | 20.6 | 13.0 | 7.6 | 94.9 |
| New Jersey | 44.0 | 34.3 | 75.9 | 11.1 | 40.8 | 21.0 | 14.0 | 5.6 | 94.2 |
| Charlotte | 45.1 | 32.7 | 75.6 | 10.3 | 40.1 | 21.1 | 14.5 | 6.4 | 93.3 |
| Milwaukee | 43.0 | 34.2 | 75.7 | 10.5 | 40.8 | 18.8 | 13.5 | 7.5 | 91.9 |

## Defense (Opponents' Statistics)

| Team | FG Pct | 3FG Pct | FT Pct | Rebound Avg. Off | Total | A | TO | Stl | Scoring Avg |
|------|--------|---------|--------|-----|-------|---|----|-----|-----|
| Boston | 43.4 | 34.0 | 75.6 | 10.5 | 38.8 | 18.7 | 15.4 | 7.0 | 91.1 |
| Chicago | 43.0 | 32.6 | 76.4 | 10.1 | 38.4 | 19.0 | 14.1 | 6.9 | 91.3 |
| Milwaukee | 44.7 | 33.4 | 77.0 | 10.2 | 42.3 | 20.2 | 15.2 | 6.2 | 92.7 |
| Orlando | 43.6 | 35.0 | 74.3 | 9.8 | 39.7 | 20.1 | 13.9 | 7.4 | 93.7 |
| New Orleans | 45.7 | 35.7 | 77.0 | 9.4 | 39.3 | 21.2 | 14.5 | 6.1 | 94.0 |
| Miami | 43.4 | 34.5 | 74.4 | 10.5 | 39.2 | 20.1 | 13.2 | 7.0 | 94.6 |
| Portland | 46.7 | 36.7 | 76.7 | 10.6 | 39.7 | 19.2 | 15.7 | 6.9 | 94.8 |
| LA Lakers | 43.7 | 33.5 | 76.5 | 12.2 | 41.5 | 22.3 | 13.6 | 7.1 | 95.4 |
| Atlanta | 46.0 | 33.8 | 77.4 | 10.2 | 40.6 | 21.4 | 12.5 | 6.7 | 95.8 |
| Dallas | 45.0 | 34.3 | 75.0 | 10.7 | 40.7 | 20.6 | 13.6 | 7.6 | 96.0 |
| Charlotte | 45.5 | 35.9 | 78.0 | 9.8 | 39.6 | 21.7 | 13.2 | 7.3 | 97.3 |
| Philadelphia | 45.1 | 34.0 | 77.3 | 10.7 | 42.5 | 21.5 | 14.2 | 7.1 | 97.5 |
| Memphis | 44.7 | 36.9 | 76.1 | 11.0 | 40.1 | 21.0 | 16.7 | 7.5 | 97.6 |
| San Antonio | 45.6 | 36.7 | 76.6 | 10.8 | 41.2 | 20.5 | 13.4 | 6.9 | 98.0 |
| New Jersey | 46.5 | 36.4 | 75.1 | 10.4 | 41.8 | 22.2 | 12.3 | 6.8 | 100.4 |
| Detroit | 48.6 | 35.8 | 76.6 | 10.6 | 38.6 | 23.3 | 14.1 | 6.9 | 100.6 |
| Indiana | 44.9 | 35.9 | 75.0 | 11.4 | 43.3 | 20.4 | 13.9 | 7.5 | 100.9 |
| Oklahoma City | 45.8 | 36.1 | 74.4 | 11.4 | 40.6 | 20.9 | 14.0 | 7.2 | 101.0 |
| Utah | 45.9 | 37.6 | 77.8 | 11.3 | 40.9 | 20.7 | 14.6 | 7.4 | 101.3 |
| LA Clippers | 45.5 | 36.5 | 77.1 | 11.1 | 40.5 | 22.3 | 13.7 | 8.0 | 101.8 |
| Denver | 45.9 | 34.4 | 75.6 | 10.5 | 41.3 | 22.2 | 13.7 | 7.5 | 102.7 |
| Houston | 46.8 | 35.8 | 78.1 | 11.6 | 42.8 | 20.8 | 13.7 | 7.2 | 103.7 |
| Cleveland | 47.5 | 41.1 | 75.9 | 10.9 | 43.5 | 24.2 | 13.5 | 7.5 | 104.5 |
| Washington | 47.1 | 37.3 | 76.1 | 12.1 | 43.9 | 23.1 | 15.8 | 7.6 | 104.7 |
| Sacramento | 47.8 | 35.5 | 76.2 | 10.6 | 41.2 | 21.7 | 14.7 | 8.1 | 104.7 |
| Toronto | 48.2 | 37.6 | 76.9 | 11.1 | 41.1 | 22.6 | 13.9 | 7.6 | 105.4 |
| Golden State | 46.7 | 35.8 | 77.6 | 12.8 | 44.8 | 24.7 | 16.1 | 8.2 | 105.7 |
| New York | 47.2 | 37.2 | 76.2 | 11.8 | 44.0 | 20.5 | 15.2 | 7.1 | 105.7 |
| Phoenix | 47.2 | 36.7 | 75.4 | 12.0 | 44.3 | 23.0 | 14.5 | 7.9 | 105.9 |
| Minnesota | 46.8 | 37.4 | 77.8 | 11.1 | 42.6 | 24.8 | 14.4 | 9.5 | 107.7 |

# NBA Team-by-Team Statistical Leaders

## Atlanta Hawks

| Player | GP | MPG | FG% | 3Pt% | FT% | OFF | DEF | Total | APG | SPG | BPG | TO | PF | PPG |
|--------|----|----|----|------|-----|-----|-----|-------|-----|-----|-----|----|----|----|
| Joe Johnson | 72 | 35.5 | 44.3 | 29.7 | 80.2 | 0.8 | 3.2 | 4.0 | 4.7 | 0.7 | 0.1 | 2.0 | 1.8 | 18.2 |
| Josh Smith | 77 | 34.4 | 47.7 | 33.1 | 72.5 | 1.7 | 6.8 | 8.5 | 3.3 | 1.3 | 1.6 | 2.6 | 2.8 | 16.5 |
| Al Horford | 77 | 35.1 | 55.7 | 50.0 | 79.8 | 2.4 | 7.0 | 9.3 | 3.5 | 0.8 | 1.0 | 1.5 | 2.5 | 15.3 |
| Jamal Crawford | 76 | 30.2 | 42.1 | 34.1 | 85.4 | 0.3 | 1.4 | 1.7 | 3.2 | 0.8 | 0.2 | 1.9 | 1.3 | 14.2 |
| Marvin Williams | 65 | 28.7 | 45.8 | 33.6 | 84.5 | 1.0 | 3.8 | 4.8 | 1.4 | 0.5 | 0.4 | 1.0 | 1.6 | 10.4 |
| *Mike Bibby | 56 | 29.9 | 43.5 | 44.1 | 63.0 | 0.3 | 2.3 | 2.6 | 3.6 | 0.7 | 0.1 | 1.2 | 2.2 | 9.4 |
| *Kirk Hinrich | 24 | 28.6 | 43.2 | 42.1 | 66.7 | 0.3 | 1.9 | 2.2 | 3.3 | 0.8 | 0.3 | 1.5 | 2.8 | 8.6 |
| Jeff Teague | 70 | 13.8 | 43.8 | 37.5 | 79.4 | 0.2 | 1.3 | 1.5 | 2.0 | 0.6 | 0.4 | 0.9 | 1.2 | 5.2 |
| *Maurice Evans | 47 | 17.8 | 39.3 | 31.5 | 85.7 | 0.5 | 1.3 | 1.8 | 0.6 | 0.3 | 0.1 | 0.3 | 1.6 | 4.5 |
| Zaza Pachulia | 79 | 15.7 | 46.1 | 0.0 | 75.4 | 1.5 | 2.7 | 4.2 | 0.7 | 0.4 | 0.3 | 0.9 | 2.3 | 4.4 |
| *Jordan Crawford | 16 | 10 | 35.1 | 33.3 | 66.7 | 0.6 | 1.2 | 1.8 | 0.9 | 0.2 | 0.0 | 0.9 | 0.8 | 4.2 |
| Josh Powell | 54 | 12.1 | 45.2 | 0.0 | 80.0 | 0.9 | 1.6 | 2.5 | 0.4 | 0.1 | 0.1 | 1.0 | 1.4 | 4.1 |
| Damien Wilkins | 52 | 13 | 50.4 | 20.0 | 71.4 | 0.4 | 1.3 | 1.7 | 0.8 | 0.5 | 0.2 | 0.4 | 1.4 | 3.5 |
| Etan Thomas | 13 | 6.3 | 47.6 | 0.0 | 80.0 | 0.5 | 1.3 | 1.8 | 0.2 | 0.1 | 0.3 | 0.4 | 0.8 | 2.5 |
| Jason Collins | 49 | 12.1 | 47.9 | 100.0 | 65.9 | 0.6 | 1.5 | 2.1 | 0.4 | 0.2 | 0.5 | 0.5 | 2.0 | 2.0 |
| *Hilton Armstrong | 12 | 6.3 | 50.0 | 100.0 | 20.0 | 0.3 | 1.2 | 1.4 | 0.3 | 0.3 | 0.4 | 0.3 | 0.8 | 1.3 |
| **Hawks** | 82 | 240.6 | 46.2 | 35.2 | 77.9 | 9.3 | 30.0 | 39.3 | 22.0 | 6.1 | 4.2 | 13.6 | 19.0 | 95.0 |
| **Opponents** | 82 | 240.6 | 46.0 | 33.8 | 77.4 | 10.2 | 30.3 | 40.6 | 21.4 | 6.7 | 4.2 | 12.5 | 18.5 | 95.8 |

## Boston Celtics

| Player | GP | MPG | FG% | 3Pt% | FT% | OFF | DEF | Total | APG | SPG | BPG | TO | PF | PPG |
|--------|----|----|----|------|-----|-----|-----|-------|-----|-----|-----|----|----|----|
| Paul Pierce | 80 | 34.7 | 49.7 | 37.4 | 86.0 | 0.4 | 5.0 | 5.4 | 3.3 | 1.0 | 0.6 | 2.1 | 2.9 | 18.9 |
| Ray Allen | 80 | 36.1 | 49.1 | 44.4 | 88.1 | 0.6 | 2.8 | 3.4 | 2.7 | 1.0 | 0.2 | 1.5 | 1.8 | 16.5 |
| Kevin Garnett | 71 | 31.3 | 52.8 | 20.0 | 86.2 | 1.2 | 7.7 | 8.9 | 2.4 | 1.3 | 0.8 | 1.6 | 2.1 | 14.9 |
| Glen Davis | 78 | 29.5 | 44.8 | 13.3 | 73.6 | 1.3 | 4.2 | 5.4 | 1.2 | 1.0 | 0.4 | 1.1 | 3.0 | 11.7 |
| Rajon Rondo | 68 | 37.2 | 47.5 | 23.3 | 56.8 | 1.3 | 3.1 | 4.4 | 11.2 | 2.3 | 0.2 | 3.4 | 1.8 | 10.6 |
| *Jeff Green | 26 | 23.5 | 48.5 | 29.6 | 79.4 | 0.6 | 2.7 | 3.3 | 0.7 | 0.5 | 0.6 | 0.9 | 2.6 | 9.8 |
| Shaquille O'Neal | 37 | 20.3 | 66.7 | 0.0 | 55.7 | 1.3 | 3.5 | 4.8 | 0.7 | 0.4 | 1.1 | 1.5 | 3.2 | 9.2 |
| *Nenad Krstic | 24 | 23 | 53.7 | 0.0 | 75.0 | 2.0 | 3.4 | 5.3 | 0.3 | 0.3 | 0.3 | 1.0 | 3.2 | 9.1 |
| *Kendrick Perkins | 12 | 26.1 | 54.2 | 0.0 | 57.5 | 1.9 | 6.2 | 8.1 | 0.8 | 0.2 | 0.8 | 2.1 | 3.1 | 7.3 |
| *Nate Robinson | 55 | 17.9 | 40.4 | 32.8 | 82.5 | 0.3 | 1.3 | 1.6 | 1.9 | 0.5 | 0.1 | 1.2 | 1.9 | 7.1 |
| Delonte West | 24 | 18.9 | 45.8 | 36.4 | 86.7 | 0.3 | 1.3 | 1.5 | 2.7 | 0.8 | 0.4 | 1.3 | 1.2 | 5.6 |
| Marquis Daniels | 49 | 19.1 | 49.1 | 19.0 | 68.4 | 0.5 | 1.8 | 2.3 | 1.3 | 0.8 | 0.4 | 0.8 | 1.3 | 5.5 |
| Jermaine O'Neal | 24 | 18 | 45.9 | 0.0 | 67.4 | 1.0 | 2.6 | 3.7 | 0.5 | 0.1 | 1.3 | 1.1 | 2.7 | 5.4 |
| *Semih Erden | 37 | 14.4 | 59.8 | 0.0 | 63.0 | 0.8 | 2.1 | 2.9 | 0.5 | 0.4 | 0.6 | 0.9 | 2.5 | 4.1 |
| Von Wafer | 58 | 9.5 | 42.1 | 26.9 | 84.2 | 0.1 | 0.7 | 0.8 | 0.6 | 0.3 | 0.1 | 0.3 | 0.7 | 3.2 |
| *Troy Murphy | 17 | 10.5 | 42.1 | 10.0 | 84.6 | 0.6 | 1.6 | 2.2 | 0.4 | 0.5 | 0.1 | 0.4 | 1.1 | 2.6 |
| *Carlos Arroyo | 15 | 12.7 | 31.4 | 60.0 | 91.7 | 0.5 | 1.1 | 1.5 | 1.7 | 0.5 | 0.0 | 1.1 | 0.7 | 2.4 |
| *Luke Harangody | 28 | 8.6 | 39.4 | 20.0 | 62.5 | 0.6 | 1.4 | 2.0 | 0.4 | 0.1 | 0.3 | 0.2 | 1.3 | 2.3 |
| *Sasha Pavlovic | 17 | 8.8 | 46.2 | 50.0 | 40.0 | 0.1 | 0.8 | 0.8 | 0.2 | 0.3 | 0.0 | 0.4 | 0.9 | 1.8 |
| **Celtics** | 82 | 241.2 | 48.6 | 36.5 | 77.0 | 7.8 | 31.0 | 38.8 | 23.4 | 8.2 | 4.2 | 14.6 | 20.5 | 96.5 |
| **Opponents** | 82 | 241.2 | 43.4 | 34.0 | 75.6 | 10.5 | 29.1 | 39.6 | 18.7 | 7.0 | 4.4 | 15.4 | 20.2 | 91.1 |

## Charlotte Bobcats

| Player | GP | MPG | FG% | 3Pt% | FT% | OFF | DEF | Total | APG | SPG | BPG | TO | PF | PPG |
|--------|----|----|----|------|-----|-----|-----|-------|-----|-----|-----|----|----|----|
| Stephen Jackson | 67 | 35.9 | 41.1 | 33.7 | 81.6 | 0.8 | 3.7 | 4.5 | 3.6 | 1.2 | 0.4 | 3.1 | 2.4 | 18.5 |
| *Gerald Wallace | 48 | 39 | 43.3 | 33.0 | 73.9 | 1.5 | 6.7 | 8.2 | 2.4 | 1.2 | 1.0 | 2.1 | 2.5 | 15.6 |
| D.J. Augustin | 82 | 33.6 | 41.6 | 33.3 | 90.6 | 0.5 | 2.3 | 2.7 | 6.1 | 0.7 | 0.0 | 1.9 | 1.9 | 14.4 |
| Boris Diaw | 82 | 33.9 | 49.2 | 34.5 | 68.3 | 1.3 | 3.8 | 5.0 | 4.1 | 0.9 | 0.6 | 2.0 | 2.3 | 11.3 |
| Tyrus Thomas | 41 | 21 | 47.1 | 0.0 | 78.7 | 1.6 | 3.9 | 5.5 | 0.7 | 0.7 | 1.6 | 1.6 | 2.8 | 10.2 |
| Gerald Henderson | 68 | 24.4 | 45.4 | 19.4 | 78.5 | 0.7 | 2.3 | 3.0 | 1.5 | 0.7 | 0.5 | 0.9 | 1.7 | 9.6 |
| *Dante Cunningham | 22 | 24 | 50.8 | 11.1 | 76.5 | 1.0 | 3.0 | 4.0 | 0.6 | 0.7 | 0.5 | 0.8 | 1.7 | 9.0 |
| *D.J. White | 24 | 19.4 | 52.6 | 0.0 | 75.9 | 1.3 | 3.1 | 4.4 | 0.6 | 0.3 | 0.5 | 0.3 | 1.9 | 8.5 |
| Kwame Brown | 66 | 26 | 51.7 | 0.0 | 58.9 | 2.2 | 4.6 | 6.8 | 0.7 | 0.4 | 0.6 | 1.0 | 2.6 | 7.9 |
| *Nazr Mohammed | 51 | 16.7 | 50.2 | 0.0 | 59.1 | 1.8 | 3.1 | 4.9 | 0.3 | 0.3 | 0.9 | 1.0 | 2.4 | 7.3 |
| Shaun Livingston | 73 | 17.3 | 46.6 | 25.0 | 86.4 | 0.4 | 1.6 | 2.0 | 2.2 | 0.6 | 0.4 | 1.2 | 1.5 | 6.6 |
| Matt Carroll | 54 | 10.8 | 44.7 | 37.0 | 76.9 | 0.2 | 1.0 | 1.3 | 0.4 | 0.3 | 0.1 | 0.4 | 0.8 | 4.4 |
| *Derrick Brown | 41 | 11.9 | 54.9 | 33.3 | 53.2 | 0.8 | 1.3 | 2.0 | 0.7 | 0.4 | 0.2 | 0.7 | 1.2 | 3.7 |
| Dominic McGuire | 52 | 14.6 | 39.6 | 0.0 | 76.9 | 1.2 | 2.6 | 3.8 | 0.8 | 0.2 | 0.6 | 0.5 | 1.8 | 3.3 |
| *Garrett Temple | 12 | 10.5 | 28.6 | 26.9 | 63.6 | 0.0 | 1.3 | 1.3 | 2.0 | 0.8 | 0.3 | 1.7 | 1.2 | 3.2 |
| Eduardo Najera | 31 | 12 | 36.1 | 32.4 | 54.5 | 0.5 | 1.0 | 1.4 | 0.6 | 0.4 | 0.2 | 0.4 | 1.7 | 2.2 |
| *Joel Przybilla | 5 | 14.8 | 40.0 | 0.0 | 25.0 | 1.8 | 3.0 | 4.8 | 0.0 | 0.0 | 0.2 | 1.4 | 3.2 | 1.8 |
| DeSagana Diop | 46 | 11.3 | 33.3 | 0.0 | 10.0 | 1.3 | 1.8 | 2.5 | 0.4 | 0.3 | 0.9 | 0.7 | 1.6 | 1.3 |
| **Bobcats** | 82 | 241.5 | 45.1 | 32.7 | 75.6 | 10.3 | 29.8 | 40.1 | 21.1 | 6.4 | 5.3 | 14.5 | 20.0 | 93.3 |
| **Opponents** | 82 | 241.5 | 45.5 | 35.9 | 78.0 | 9.8 | 29.8 | 39.6 | 21.7 | 7.3 | 6.0 | 13.2 | 21.1 | 97.3 |

* mid-season trade

## Chicago Bulls

| Player | GP | MPG | FG% | 3Pt% | FT% | OFF | DEF | Total | APG | SPG | BPG | TO | PF | PPG |
|---|---|---|---|---|---|---|---|---|---|---|---|---|---|---|
| | | | **Field Goals** | | | **Rebounds** | | | | | | | | |
| Derrick Rose | 81 | 37.4 | 44.5 | 33.2 | 85.8 | 1.0 | 3.1 | 4.1 | 7.7 | 1.0 | 0.6 | 3.4 | 1.7 | 25.0 |
| Carlos Boozer | 59 | 31.9 | 51.0 | 0.0 | 70.1 | 2.2 | 7.4 | 9.6 | 2.5 | 0.8 | 0.3 | 2.5 | 3.2 | 17.5 |
| Luol Deng | 82 | 39.1 | 46.0 | 34.5 | 75.3 | 1.4 | 4.4 | 5.8 | 2.8 | 1.0 | 0.6 | 1.9 | 2.0 | 17.4 |
| Joakim Noah | 48 | 32.8 | 52.5 | 0.0 | 73.9 | 3.8 | 6.6 | 10.4 | 2.2 | 1.0 | 1.5 | 1.9 | 3.3 | 11.7 |
| Kyle Korver | 82 | 20.1 | 43.4 | 41.5 | 88.5 | 0.1 | 1.7 | 1.8 | 1.5 | 0.4 | 0.2 | 0.7 | 1.9 | 8.3 |
| Taj Gibson | 80 | 21.8 | 46.6 | 12.5 | 67.6 | 2.0 | 3.7 | 5.7 | 0.7 | 0.5 | 1.3 | 0.9 | 2.5 | 7.1 |
| Ronnie Brewer | 81 | 22 | 48.0 | 22.2 | 65.4 | 0.7 | 2.6 | 3.2 | 1.7 | 1.3 | 0.3 | 0.7 | 1.0 | 6.2 |
| C.J. Watson | 82 | 13.3 | 37.1 | 39.3 | 74.2 | 0.2 | 1.0 | 1.1 | 2.3 | 0.7 | 0.1 | 0.9 | 1.0 | 4.9 |
| Keith Bogans | 82 | 17.8 | 40.4 | 38.0 | 65.6 | 0.2 | 1.6 | 1.8 | 1.2 | 0.5 | 0.1 | 0.5 | 1.4 | 4.4 |
| Kurt Thomas | 52 | 22.7 | 51.1 | 100.0 | 62.5 | 1.4 | 4.3 | 5.8 | 1.2 | 0.6 | 0.8 | 0.8 | 3.2 | 4.1 |
| *James Johnson | 13 | 9.5 | 41.5 | 22.2 | 46.2 | 0.5 | 1.4 | 1.8 | 1.1 | 0.6 | 0.7 | 1.4 | 1.9 | 4.1 |
| Omer Asik | 82 | 12.1 | 55.3 | 0.0 | 50.3 | 1.4 | 2.4 | 3.7 | 0.4 | 0.2 | 0.7 | 0.8 | 1.9 | 2.8 |
| *Rasual Butler | 6 | 4.3 | 54.5 | 57.1 | 0.0 | 0.0 | 0.2 | 0.2 | 0.0 | 0.0 | 0.0 | 0.3 | 0.5 | 2.7 |
| Brian Scalabrine | 18 | 4.9 | 52.6 | 0.0 | 0.0 | 0.1 | 0.4 | 0.4 | 0.3 | 0.2 | 0.2 | 0.3 | 1.0 | 1.1 |
| John Lucas | 2 | 5 | 33.3 | 0.0 | 0.0 | 0.0 | 0.0 | 0.0 | 0.5 | 0.0 | 0.0 | 0.0 | 0.0 | 1.0 |
| **Bulls** | 82 | 241.8 | 46.2 | 36.1 | 74.3 | 11.8 | 32.4 | 44.2 | 22.3 | 7.2 | 5.7 | 14.2 | 20.0 | 98.6 |
| **Opponents** | 82 | 241.8 | 43.0 | 32.6 | 76.4 | 10.1 | 28.3 | 38.4 | 19.0 | 6.9 | 5.8 | 14.1 | 20.1 | 91.3 |

## Cleveland Cavaliers

| Player | GP | MPG | FG% | 3Pt% | FT% | OFF | DEF | Total | APG | SPG | BPG | TO | PF | PPG |
|---|---|---|---|---|---|---|---|---|---|---|---|---|---|---|
| | | | **Field Goals** | | | **Rebounds** | | | | | | | | |
| Antawn Jamison | 56 | 32.9 | 42.7 | 34.6 | 73.1 | 1.5 | 5.2 | 6.7 | 1.7 | 0.9 | 0.5 | 1.4 | 2.4 | 18.0 |
| *Baron Davis | 15 | 25.3 | 42.1 | 41.4 | 81.5 | 0.4 | 2.0 | 2.4 | 6.1 | 1.1 | 0.4 | 2.6 | 1.9 | 13.9 |
| J.J. Hickson | 80 | 28.2 | 45.8 | 0.0 | 67.3 | 2.7 | 6.0 | 8.7 | 1.1 | 0.6 | 0.7 | 2.2 | 2.7 | 13.8 |
| *Mo Williams | 36 | 29.6 | 38.5 | 26.5 | 83.3 | 0.4 | 2.3 | 2.7 | 7.1 | 0.9 | 0.3 | 2.9 | 2.5 | 13.3 |
| Ramon Sessions | 81 | 26.3 | 46.6 | 20.0 | 82.3 | 0.6 | 2.6 | 3.1 | 5.2 | 0.7 | 0.1 | 2.2 | 1.1 | 13.3 |
| Daniel Gibson | 67 | 27.8 | 40.0 | 40.3 | 82.2 | 0.4 | 2.3 | 2.6 | 3.0 | 0.7 | 0.3 | 1.2 | 2.3 | 11.6 |
| Anderson Varejao | 31 | 32.1 | 52.8 | 0.0 | 66.7 | 3.2 | 6.5 | 9.7 | 1.5 | 0.9 | 1.2 | 1.3 | 2.8 | 9.1 |
| Anthony Parker | 72 | 29 | 39.9 | 37.9 | 77.9 | 0.5 | 2.6 | 3.0 | 3.0 | 0.9 | 0.1 | 1.1 | 1.5 | 8.3 |
| Samardo Samuels | 37 | 18.9 | 45.6 | 0.0 | 61.8 | 2.0 | 2.2 | 4.3 | 0.5 | 0.4 | 0.5 | 1.4 | 2.4 | 7.8 |
| *Alonzo Gee | 40 | 24.3 | 46.2 | 34.7 | 80.0 | 1.2 | 2.7 | 3.9 | 0.8 | 0.8 | 0.4 | 1.1 | 2.0 | 7.4 |
| Christian Eyenga | 44 | 21.5 | 42.5 | 27.5 | 64.3 | 0.6 | 2.2 | 2.8 | 0.8 | 0.8 | 0.6 | 1.1 | 1.8 | 6.9 |
| *Luke Harangody | 21 | 19 | 37.8 | 25.0 | 77.8 | 1.1 | 3.1 | 4.2 | 1.0 | 0.5 | 0.5 | 0.5 | 2.1 | 6.2 |
| Manny Harris | 54 | 17.3 | 37.4 | 37.0 | 76.3 | 0.7 | 1.9 | 2.6 | 1.6 | 0.6 | 0.1 | 1.2 | 1.2 | 5.9 |
| Ryan Hollins | 70 | 16.9 | 59.8 | 0.0 | 68.1 | 1.0 | 1.7 | 2.7 | 0.4 | 0.3 | 0.6 | 1.0 | 2.8 | 5.3 |
| Joey Graham | 39 | 15 | 45.8 | 30.0 | 80.6 | 0.2 | 1.9 | 2.2 | 0.5 | 0.2 | 0.2 | 0.7 | 1.9 | 5.2 |
| *Leon Powe | 14 | 13.4 | 49.2 | 0.0 | 46.2 | 1.1 | 1.6 | 2.7 | 0.1 | 0.5 | 0.2 | 0.4 | 1.4 | 5.0 |
| *Jamario Moon | 40 | 19.1 | 40.2 | 28.4 | 90.9 | 0.4 | 2.6 | 3.0 | 1.1 | 0.6 | 0.7 | 0.4 | 1.0 | 4.7 |
| Jawad Williams | 26 | 15 | 32.5 | 28.9 | 75.0 | 0.3 | 1.6 | 1.8 | 0.8 | 0.3 | 0.1 | 0.6 | 1.3 | 4.0 |
| *Semih Erden | 4 | 16 | 28.6 | 0.0 | 83.3 | 1.5 | 1.3 | 2.8 | 0.3 | 0.5 | 0.8 | 0.5 | 3.0 | 3.3 |
| **Cavaliers** | 82 | 240.9 | 43.4 | 34.2 | 74.5 | 10.4 | 29.9 | 40.3 | 21.0 | 6.6 | 4.2 | 14.2 | 20.1 | 95.5 |
| **Opponents** | 82 | 240.9 | 47.5 | 41.1 | 75.9 | 10.9 | 32.6 | 43.5 | 24.2 | 7.5 | 6.0 | 13.5 | 21.3 | 104.5 |

## Dallas Mavericks

| Player | GP | MPG | FG% | 3Pt% | FT% | OFF | DEF | Total | APG | SPG | BPG | TO | PF | PPG |
|---|---|---|---|---|---|---|---|---|---|---|---|---|---|---|
| | | | **Field Goals** | | | **Rebounds** | | | | | | | | |
| Dirk Nowitzki | 73 | 34.3 | 51.7 | 39.3 | 89.2 | 0.7 | 6.3 | 7.0 | 2.6 | 0.5 | 0.6 | 1.9 | 2.4 | 23.0 |
| Jason Terry | 82 | 31.3 | 45.1 | 36.2 | 85.0 | 0.3 | 1.6 | 1.9 | 4.1 | 1.1 | 0.2 | 2.0 | 1.7 | 15.8 |
| Caron Butler | 29 | 29.9 | 45.0 | 43.1 | 77.3 | 0.8 | 3.3 | 4.1 | 1.6 | 1.0 | 0.3 | 1.7 | 2.0 | 15.0 |
| Shawn Marion | 80 | 28.2 | 52.0 | 15.2 | 76.8 | 2.1 | 4.8 | 6.9 | 1.4 | 0.9 | 0.6 | 1.6 | 1.8 | 12.5 |
| Tyson Chandler | 74 | 27.8 | 65.4 | 0.0 | 73.2 | 2.8 | 6.6 | 9.4 | 0.4 | 0.5 | 1.1 | 1.2 | 3.2 | 10.1 |
| J.J. Barea | 81 | 20.6 | 43.9 | 34.9 | 84.7 | 0.4 | 1.6 | 2.0 | 3.9 | 0.4 | 0.0 | 1.7 | 1.7 | 9.5 |
| *Peja Stojakovic | 25 | 20.2 | 42.9 | 40.0 | 93.8 | 0.6 | 2.1 | 2.6 | 0.9 | 0.4 | 0.1 | 0.4 | 0.9 | 8.6 |
| Rod. Beaubois | 28 | 17.7 | 42.2 | 30.1 | 76.7 | 0.3 | 1.6 | 1.9 | 2.3 | 0.7 | 0.3 | 1.7 | 2.7 | 8.4 |
| Jason Kidd | 80 | 33.2 | 36.1 | 34.0 | 87.0 | 0.4 | 4.0 | 4.4 | 8.2 | 1.7 | 0.4 | 2.2 | 1.5 | 7.9 |
| DeS. Stevenson | 72 | 16.1 | 38.8 | 37.8 | 76.7 | 0.3 | 1.2 | 1.5 | 1.1 | 0.3 | 0.1 | 0.6 | 1.0 | 5.3 |
| *Corey Brewer | 13 | 11.4 | 49.0 | 30.8 | 71.4 | 0.9 | 0.8 | 1.8 | 0.9 | 0.8 | 0.2 | 0.8 | 1.9 | 5.3 |
| Bren. Haywood | 72 | 18.5 | 57.4 | 0.0 | 36.2 | 1.8 | 3.4 | 5.2 | 0.3 | 0.2 | 1.0 | 0.7 | 2.0 | 4.4 |
| *Sasha Pavlovic | 10 | 16.3 | 42.9 | 43.8 | 80.0 | 0.0 | 1.2 | 1.2 | 0.7 | 0.5 | 0.3 | 0.5 | 1.5 | 4.1 |
| Ian Mahinmi | 55 | 8.7 | 56.1 | 0.0 | 70.8 | 0.8 | 1.4 | 2.1 | 0.1 | 0.3 | 0.3 | 0.4 | 1.9 | 3.1 |
| *Alexis Ajinca | 10 | 7.5 | 37.5 | 42.9 | 66.7 | 0.5 | 1.2 | 1.7 | 0.2 | 0.3 | 0.5 | 0.1 | 1.3 | 2.9 |
| Brian Cardinal | 56 | 11 | 43.0 | 48.3 | 94.4 | 0.2 | 0.9 | 1.1 | 0.7 | 0.4 | 0.1 | 0.3 | 1.5 | 2.6 |
| Dominique Jones | 18 | 7.5 | 31.1 | 0.0 | 82.4 | 0.3 | 1.1 | 1.4 | 1.1 | 0.3 | 0.2 | 0.6 | 0.4 | 2.3 |
| *Steve Novak | 7 | 2.6 | 50.0 | 75.0 | 0.0 | 0.0 | 0.7 | 0.7 | 0.0 | 0.0 | 0.0 | 0.0 | 0.4 | 1.6 |
| **Mavericks** | 82 | 240.3 | 47.5 | 36.5 | 77.7 | 9.5 | 31.9 | 41.4 | 23.8 | 6.8 | 4.3 | 14.0 | 19.2 | 100.2 |
| **Opponents** | 82 | 240.3 | 45.0 | 34.3 | 75.0 | 10.7 | 30.0 | 40.7 | 20.6 | 7.6 | 3.7 | 13.6 | 20.1 | 96.0 |

* mid-season trade

### Denver Nuggets

| Player | GP | MPG | FG% | 3Pt% | FT% | OFF | DEF | Total | APG | SPG | BPG | TO | PF | PPG |
|---|---|---|---|---|---|---|---|---|---|---|---|---|---|---|
| *Carmelo Anthony..50 | | 35.5 | 45.2 | 33.3 | 82.3 | 1.5 | 6.1 | 7.6 | 2.8 | 0.9 | 0.6 | 2.8 | 2.7 | 25.2 |
| *Chauncey Billups..51 | | 32.3 | 43.8 | 44.1 | 92.3 | 0.2 | 2.2 | 2.5 | 5.3 | 1.0 | 0.2 | 2.5 | 1.8 | 16.5 |
| *Danilo Gallinari ...14 | | 30.9 | 41.2 | 37.0 | 77.2 | 0.8 | 4.6 | 5.4 | 1.6 | 0.9 | 0.6 | 1.8 | 1.9 | 14.7 |
| Nene Hilario .........75 | | 30.5 | 61.5 | 20.0 | 71.1 | 1.9 | 5.7 | 7.6 | 2.0 | 1.1 | 1.0 | 1.8 | 3.2 | 14.5 |
| Arron Afflalo .........69 | | 33.7 | 49.8 | 42.3 | 84.7 | 0.7 | 3.0 | 3.6 | 2.4 | 0.5 | 0.4 | 1.0 | 2.2 | 12.6 |
| *Wilson Chandler .21 | | 30.6 | 41.9 | 34.7 | 81.0 | 0.6 | 4.4 | 5.0 | 1.6 | 0.7 | 1.1 | 1.8 | 2.2 | 12.5 |
| J.R. Smith ............79 | | 24.9 | 43.5 | 39.0 | 73.8 | 0.6 | 3.5 | 4.1 | 2.2 | 1.2 | 0.2 | 1.3 | 2.2 | 12.3 |
| Ty Lawson ............80 | | 26.3 | 50.3 | 40.4 | 76.4 | 0.8 | 1.8 | 2.6 | 4.7 | 1.0 | 0.1 | 1.7 | 1.7 | 11.7 |
| *Raymond Felton ..21 | | 31.6 | 43.1 | 45.9 | 61.7 | 0.4 | 3.2 | 3.6 | 6.5 | 1.3 | 0.0 | 2.1 | 1.8 | 11.5 |
| Al Harrington ........73 | | 22.8 | 41.6 | 35.7 | 73.5 | 1.0 | 3.5 | 4.5 | 1.4 | 0.5 | 0.1 | 1.5 | 2.8 | 10.5 |
| Kenyon Martin ......48 | | 25.7 | 51.1 | 22.2 | 58.3 | 1.4 | 4.8 | 6.2 | 2.3 | 0.9 | 0.7 | 1.2 | 2.8 | 8.6 |
| Chris Andersen ....45 | | 16.3 | 59.9 | 0.0 | 63.7 | 1.7 | 3.2 | 4.9 | 0.4 | 0.5 | 1.3 | 0.6 | 1.8 | 5.6 |
| Gary Forbes .........63 | | 12.6 | 45.4 | 32.8 | 67.8 | 0.4 | 1.4 | 1.8 | 0.8 | 0.4 | 0.1 | 0.7 | 1.2 | 5.2 |
| *Kosta Koufos ......11 | | 8.9 | 50.0 | 0.0 | 63.2 | 1.4 | 1.6 | 3.0 | 0.0 | 0.2 | 0.5 | 0.5 | 0.8 | 4.9 |
| *Shelden Williams..42 | | 17 | 45.3 | 0.0 | 73.9 | 1.8 | 3.5 | 5.3 | 0.5 | 0.4 | 0.5 | 0.9 | 2.2 | 4.7 |
| *Renaldo Balkman..5 | | 8.8 | 55.6 | 0.0 | 75.0 | 0.2 | 0.6 | 0.8 | 0.4 | 0.6 | 0.4 | 0.0 | 2.2 | 2.6 |
| Melvin Ely ............30 | | 12.2 | 54.9 | 0.0 | 61.9 | 0.9 | 1.6 | 2.5 | 0.5 | 0.1 | 0.4 | 0.5 | 1.7 | 2.3 |
| *Anthony Carter ...14 | | 10.9 | 33.3 | 33.3 | 100.0 | 0.0 | 0.9 | 0.9 | 1.9 | 0.6 | 0.1 | 1.0 | 1.4 | 1.9 |
| **Nuggets .....................82** | | 240.3 | 47.6 | 38.8 | 76.5 | 9.6 | 32.3 | 42.0 | 22.1 | 7.4 | 4.3 | 14.1 | 21.0 | 107.5 |
| **Opponents................82** | | 240.3 | 45.9 | 34.4 | 75.6 | 10.5 | 30.8 | 41.3 | 22.2 | 7.5 | 6.0 | 13.7 | 22.7 | 102.7 |

### Detroit Pistons

| Player | GP | MPG | FG% | 3Pt% | FT% | OFF | DEF | Total | APG | SPG | BPG | TO | PF | PPG |
|---|---|---|---|---|---|---|---|---|---|---|---|---|---|---|
| Rodney Stuckey ....70 | | 31.2 | 43.9 | 28.9 | 86.6 | 1.0 | 2.1 | 3.1 | 5.2 | 1.1 | 0.1 | 2.2 | 2.5 | 15.5 |
| Richard Hamilton...55 | | 27.2 | 42.9 | 38.2 | 84.9 | 0.4 | 1.9 | 2.3 | 3.1 | 0.7 | 0.1 | 1.6 | 1.7 | 14.1 |
| Tayshaun Prince ....78 | | 32.8 | 47.3 | 34.7 | 70.2 | 1.0 | 3.2 | 4.2 | 2.8 | 0.4 | 0.5 | 1.1 | 1.2 | 14.1 |
| Ben Gordon ..........82 | | 26 | 44.0 | 40.2 | 85.0 | 0.5 | 1.9 | 2.4 | 2.1 | 0.6 | 0.2 | 1.7 | 2.2 | 11.2 |
| Charlie Villanueva..76 | | 21.9 | 44.2 | 38.7 | 76.7 | 0.7 | 3.2 | 3.9 | 0.6 | 0.6 | 0.6 | 0.9 | 2.3 | 11.1 |
| Greg Monroe..........80 | | 27.8 | 55.1 | 0.0 | 62.2 | 3.1 | 4.4 | 7.5 | 1.3 | 1.2 | 0.6 | 1.0 | 2.5 | 9.4 |
| Tracy McGrady......72 | | 23.4 | 44.2 | 34.1 | 69.8 | 0.7 | 2.8 | 3.5 | 3.5 | 0.9 | 0.5 | 1.4 | 1.4 | 8.0 |
| Will Bynum ............61 | | 18.4 | 44.8 | 32.0 | 83.6 | 0.2 | 1.0 | 1.2 | 3.2 | 0.9 | 0.1 | 1.4 | 1.9 | 7.9 |
| Austin Daye ..........72 | | 20.1 | 41.0 | 40.1 | 75.9 | 0.9 | 2.9 | 3.8 | 1.1 | 0.5 | 0.5 | 0.8 | 2.3 | 7.5 |
| Chris Wilcox .........57 | | 17.5 | 58.1 | 0.0 | 56.2 | 1.7 | 3.1 | 4.8 | 0.8 | 0.5 | 0.3 | 0.8 | 2.5 | 7.4 |
| Jason Maxiell ........57 | | 16.3 | 49.2 | 0.0 | 51.5 | 1.2 | 1.9 | 3.0 | 0.3 | 0.4 | 0.4 | 0.8 | 1.6 | 4.2 |
| DaJuan Summers..22 | | 9 | 40.6 | 42.9 | 45.0 | 0.1 | 0.5 | 0.5 | 0.1 | 0.1 | 0.0 | 0.6 | 1.0 | 3.4 |
| Ben Wallace ..........54 | | 22.9 | 45.0 | 50.0 | 33.3 | 2.4 | 4.1 | 6.5 | 1.3 | 1.0 | 1.0 | 0.8 | 1.5 | 2.9 |
| **Pistons..........................82** | | 242.4 | 46.0 | 37.6 | 73.7 | 11.4 | 27.3 | 38.6 | 21.1 | 7.3 | 4.0 | 13.0 | 19.9 | 97.0 |
| **Opponents.................82** | | 242.4 | 48.6 | 35.8 | 76.6 | 10.6 | 30.1 | 40.7 | 23.3 | 6.9 | 4.6 | 14.1 | 18.8 | 100.6 |

### Golden State Warriors

| Player | GP | MPG | FG% | 3Pt% | FT% | OFF | DEF | Total | APG | SPG | BPG | TO | PF | PPG |
|---|---|---|---|---|---|---|---|---|---|---|---|---|---|---|
| Monta Ellis............80 | | 40.3 | 45.1 | 36.1 | 78.9 | 0.6 | 3.0 | 3.5 | 5.6 | 2.1 | 0.3 | 3.2 | 2.5 | 24.1 |
| Stephen Curry.......74 | | 33.6 | 48.0 | 44.2 | 93.4 | 0.7 | 3.2 | 3.9 | 5.8 | 1.5 | 0.3 | 3.1 | 3.1 | 18.6 |
| David Lee .............73 | | 36.1 | 50.7 | 33.3 | 78.7 | 3.0 | 6.8 | 9.8 | 3.2 | 1.0 | 0.4 | 2.3 | 2.9 | 16.5 |
| Dorell Wright.........82 | | 38.4 | 42.3 | 37.6 | 78.9 | 1.1 | 4.2 | 5.3 | 3.0 | 1.5 | 0.8 | 1.6 | 2.1 | 16.4 |
| Reggie Williams ...80 | | 20.3 | 46.9 | 42.3 | 74.6 | 0.6 | 2.1 | 2.7 | 1.5 | 0.4 | 0.0 | 0.7 | 1.6 | 9.2 |
| *Al Thornton ..........22 | | 14.3 | 49.0 | 0.0 | 82.9 | 0.5 | 2.1 | 2.6 | 0.5 | 0.3 | 0.1 | 0.9 | 1.8 | 6.0 |
| *Acie Law .............40 | | 15.8 | 46.7 | 20.0 | 75.9 | 0.2 | 1.1 | 1.3 | 1.8 | 0.7 | 0.0 | 0.8 | 1.3 | 5.1 |
| Vlad. Radmanovic..74 | | 15.8 | 43.1 | 40.5 | 88.2 | 0.9 | 2.0 | 2.9 | 1.1 | 0.6 | 0.6 | 0.8 | 2.1 | 5.1 |
| Andris Biedrins .....59 | | 23.7 | 53.4 | 0.0 | 32.3 | 2.5 | 4.8 | 7.2 | 1.0 | 0.9 | 0.9 | 1.0 | 3.4 | 5.0 |
| *Rodney Carney ....25 | | 13.2 | 42.1 | 45.9 | 66.7 | 0.5 | 1.4 | 1.9 | 0.4 | 0.4 | 0.2 | 0.6 | 1.3 | 5.0 |
| Louis Amundson ...46 | | 15 | 45.4 | 0.0 | 39.1 | 1.8 | 2.3 | 4.0 | 0.4 | 0.3 | 0.7 | 0.5 | 1.9 | 4.3 |
| Ekpe Udoh ...........58 | | 17.8 | 43.7 | 0.0 | 65.6 | 1.4 | 1.7 | 3.1 | 0.7 | 0.4 | 1.5 | 0.8 | 2.5 | 4.1 |
| *Brandan Wright ...21 | | 9.3 | 60.3 | 0.0 | 50.0 | 0.7 | 1.3 | 2.0 | 0.2 | 0.1 | 0.5 | 0.5 | 0.9 | 4.0 |
| *Dan Gadzuric ......28 | | 10.6 | 42.0 | 0.0 | 35.7 | 1.9 | 1.2 | 3.1 | 0.4 | 0.4 | 0.6 | 0.8 | 2.3 | 2.8 |
| Jeremy Lin ...........29 | | 9.8 | 38.9 | 20.0 | 76.0 | 0.4 | 0.8 | 1.2 | 1.4 | 1.1 | 0.3 | 0.6 | 1.1 | 2.6 |
| Jeff Adrien.............23 | | 8.5 | 42.6 | 0.0 | 57.9 | 1.0 | 1.5 | 2.5 | 0.4 | 0.2 | 0.2 | 0.4 | 1.2 | 2.5 |
| Charlie Bell...........19 | | 9 | 27.9 | 28.6 | 50.0 | 0.3 | 0.6 | 0.9 | 0.7 | 0.3 | 0.1 | 0.3 | 0.7 | 1.7 |
| **Warriors.....................82** | | 241.8 | 46.1 | 39.2 | 76.1 | 11.6 | 28.9 | 40.5 | 22.5 | 9.0 | 5.0 | 14.6 | 22.0 | 103.4 |
| **Opponents .................82** | | 241.8 | 46.7 | 35.8 | 77.6 | 12.8 | 32.0 | 44.8 | 24.7 | 8.2 | 4.3 | 16.1 | 18.4 | 105.7 |

* mid-season trade

## Houston Rockets

| Player | GP | MPG | FG% | 3Pt% | FT% | OFF | DEF | Total | APG | SPG | BPG | TO | PF | PPG |
|---|---|---|---|---|---|---|---|---|---|---|---|---|---|---|
| Kevin Martin | 80 | 32.5 | 43.6 | 38.3 | 88.8 | 0.4 | 2.9 | 3.2 | 2.5 | 1.0 | 0.2 | 2.3 | 1.9 | 23.5 |
| Luis Scola | 74 | 32.6 | 50.4 | 0.0 | 73.8 | 2.0 | 6.2 | 8.2 | 2.5 | 0.6 | 0.6 | 2.0 | 3.1 | 18.3 |
| Kyle Lowry | 75 | 34.2 | 42.6 | 37.6 | 76.5 | 1.2 | 2.9 | 4.1 | 6.7 | 1.4 | 0.3 | 2.1 | 2.8 | 13.5 |
| *Aaron Brooks | 34 | 23.9 | 34.6 | 28.4 | 94.0 | 0.3 | 1.2 | 1.5 | 3.8 | 0.6 | 0.1 | 1.6 | 2.0 | 11.6 |
| Yao Ming | 5 | 18.2 | 48.6 | 0.0 | 93.8 | 1.4 | 4.0 | 5.4 | 0.8 | 0.0 | 1.6 | 1.4 | 2.6 | 10.2 |
| Chase Budinger | 78 | 22.3 | 42.5 | 32.5 | 85.5 | 0.7 | 2.9 | 3.6 | 1.6 | 0.5 | 0.2 | 0.9 | 1.5 | 9.8 |
| *Shane Battier | 59 | 30.8 | 45.6 | 39.1 | 64.5 | 1.0 | 3.8 | 4.8 | 2.6 | 0.9 | 1.2 | 1.1 | 2.2 | 8.6 |
| Courtney Lee | 81 | 21.3 | 43.9 | 40.8 | 79.2 | 0.6 | 2.0 | 2.6 | 1.2 | 0.7 | 0.2 | 0.8 | 1.3 | 8.3 |
| Chuck Hayes | 74 | 28.1 | 52.7 | 0.0 | 66.2 | 3.0 | 5.1 | 8.1 | 2.7 | 1.1 | 0.7 | 1.2 | 2.7 | 7.9 |
| *Goran Dragic | 22 | 17.2 | 47.2 | 51.9 | 66.7 | 0.5 | 2.0 | 2.5 | 2.5 | 0.6 | 0.2 | 1.0 | 1.6 | 7.7 |
| Brad Miller | 60 | 16.9 | 44.6 | 37.4 | 83.0 | 0.7 | 3.0 | 3.7 | 2.4 | 0.5 | 0.4 | 0.9 | 1.6 | 6.4 |
| Patrick Patterson | 52 | 16.7 | 55.8 | 0.0 | 71.4 | 1.7 | 2.2 | 3.8 | 0.8 | 0.3 | 0.7 | 0.6 | 1.5 | 6.3 |
| Jordan Hill | 72 | 15.6 | 49.1 | 0.0 | 70.6 | 1.8 | 2.5 | 4.3 | 0.4 | 0.2 | 0.7 | 0.9 | 2.2 | 5.6 |
| *Jermaine Taylor | 8 | 9.6 | 50.0 | 40.0 | 83.3 | 0.1 | 1.0 | 1.1 | 0.3 | 0.3 | 0.3 | 0.8 | 0.5 | 4.9 |
| *Terrence Williams | 11 | 7.6 | 33.3 | 20.0 | 81.8 | 0.1 | 1.3 | 1.4 | 0.6 | 0.4 | 0.0 | 0.7 | 0.4 | 3.5 |
| *Ishmael Smith | 28 | 11.8 | 38.6 | 37.5 | 70.0 | 0.2 | 1.3 | 1.5 | 2.3 | 0.5 | 0.1 | 0.9 | 0.9 | 2.6 |
| Mike Harris | 4 | 4 | 50.0 | 0.0 | 50.0 | 0.5 | 0.8 | 1.3 | 0.3 | 0.0 | 0.3 | 0.3 | 0.5 | 2.0 |
| *Jared Jeffries | 18 | 7.7 | 30.6 | 16.7 | 40.0 | 1.1 | 0.8 | 1.9 | 0.6 | 0.4 | 0.2 | 0.2 | 1.2 | 1.5 |
| *DeMarre Carroll | 5 | 2.2 | 0.0 | 0.0 | 0.0 | 0.0 | 0.0 | 0.0 | 0.4 | 0.0 | 0.0 | 0.0 | 0.0 | 0.0 |
| *Hasheem Thabeet | 2 | 2 | 0.0 | 0.0 | 0.0 | 0.0 | 0.0 | 0.0 | 0.0 | 0.0 | 0.5 | 0.0 | 1.5 | 0.0 |
| **Rockets** | 82 | 242.4 | 45.4 | 36.7 | 80.1 | 11.7 | 31.1 | 42.8 | 23.8 | 7.1 | 4.5 | 13.5 | 20.0 | 105.9 |
| **Opponents** | 82 | 242.4 | 46.8 | 35.8 | 78.1 | 11.6 | 31.1 | 42.8 | 20.8 | 7.2 | 5.5 | 13.7 | 21.4 | 103.7 |

## Indiana Pacers

| Player | GP | MPG | FG% | 3Pt% | FT% | OFF | DEF | Total | APG | SPG | BPG | TO | PF | PPG |
|---|---|---|---|---|---|---|---|---|---|---|---|---|---|---|
| Danny Granger | 79 | 35 | 42.5 | 38.6 | 84.8 | 1.1 | 4.3 | 5.4 | 2.6 | 1.1 | 0.8 | 2.6 | 2.7 | 20.5 |
| Darren Collison | 79 | 29.9 | 45.7 | 33.1 | 87.1 | 0.5 | 2.3 | 2.8 | 5.1 | 1.1 | 0.2 | 2.5 | 1.4 | 13.2 |
| Roy Hibbert | 81 | 27.7 | 46.1 | 0.0 | 74.5 | 2.2 | 5.3 | 7.5 | 2.0 | 0.4 | 1.8 | 2.3 | 3.2 | 12.7 |
| Mike Dunleavy | 61 | 27.6 | 46.2 | 40.2 | 80.0 | 0.5 | 4.1 | 4.5 | 1.7 | 0.7 | 0.5 | 1.1 | 1.8 | 11.2 |
| Tyler Hansbrough | 70 | 21.9 | 46.5 | 0.0 | 77.9 | 2.1 | 3.2 | 5.2 | 0.6 | 0.5 | 0.2 | 1.1 | 2.3 | 11.0 |
| Brandon Rush | 67 | 26.2 | 42.1 | 41.7 | 75.5 | 0.5 | 2.7 | 3.2 | 0.9 | 0.6 | 0.5 | 1.0 | 1.6 | 9.1 |
| Paul George | 61 | 20.7 | 45.3 | 29.7 | 76.2 | 0.6 | 3.1 | 3.7 | 1.1 | 1.0 | 0.4 | 1.1 | 2.1 | 7.8 |
| Josh McRoberts | 72 | 22.2 | 54.7 | 38.3 | 73.9 | 1.5 | 3.8 | 5.3 | 2.1 | 0.7 | 0.8 | 1.3 | 2.3 | 7.4 |
| A.J. Price | 50 | 15.9 | 35.6 | 27.5 | 66.7 | 0.3 | 1.1 | 1.4 | 2.2 | 0.6 | 0.0 | 1.1 | 1.2 | 6.5 |
| Dahntay Jones | 45 | 13.1 | 46.7 | 35.9 | 76.7 | 0.1 | 1.4 | 1.4 | 0.7 | 0.4 | 0.2 | 0.7 | 1.6 | 6.3 |
| T.J. Ford | 41 | 18.9 | 38.6 | 18.8 | 72.9 | 0.4 | 1.6 | 2.0 | 3.4 | 0.9 | 0.2 | 1.5 | 1.7 | 5.4 |
| James Posey | 49 | 17.1 | 33.6 | 31.6 | 73.3 | 0.2 | 2.8 | 3.0 | 0.7 | 0.5 | 0.1 | 0.5 | 2.1 | 4.9 |
| Solomon Jones | 39 | 13.5 | 40.5 | 0.0 | 66.1 | 1.2 | 1.7 | 2.9 | 0.8 | 0.3 | 0.6 | 0.9 | 2.4 | 3.6 |
| Jeff Foster | 56 | 16.8 | 47.9 | 0.0 | 56.3 | 2.9 | 3.4 | 6.3 | 0.8 | 0.4 | 0.6 | 0.5 | 2.3 | 3.3 |
| Lance Stephenson | 12 | 9.6 | 33.3 | 0.0 | 78.6 | 0.1 | 1.4 | 1.5 | 1.8 | 0.3 | 0.0 | 1.3 | 1.2 | 3.1 |
| **Pacers** | 82 | 241.2 | 44.2 | 35.4 | 78.2 | 11.1 | 32.4 | 43.5 | 19.6 | 7.1 | 5.6 | 15.4 | 21.7 | 99.8 |
| **Opponents** | 82 | 241.2 | 44.9 | 35.9 | 76.0 | 11.4 | 31.9 | 43.3 | 20.4 | 7.5 | 5.7 | 13.9 | 21.4 | 100.9 |

## Los Angeles Clippers

| Player | GP | MPG | FG% | 3Pt% | FT% | OFF | DEF | Total | APG | SPG | BPG | TO | PF | PPG |
|---|---|---|---|---|---|---|---|---|---|---|---|---|---|---|
| Blake Griffin | 82 | 38 | 50.6 | 29.2 | 64.2 | 3.3 | 8.8 | 12.1 | 3.8 | 0.8 | 0.5 | 2.7 | 3.1 | 22.5 |
| Eric Gordon | 56 | 37.7 | 45.0 | 36.4 | 82.5 | 0.8 | 2.1 | 2.9 | 4.4 | 1.3 | 0.3 | 2.7 | 2.1 | 22.3 |
| *Mo Williams | 22 | 32.9 | 42.2 | 39.8 | 88.0 | 0.3 | 2.3 | 2.5 | 5.6 | 0.9 | 0.0 | 3.0 | 2.7 | 15.2 |
| *Baron Davis | 43 | 29.5 | 41.6 | 29.6 | 76.0 | 0.7 | 2.1 | 2.8 | 7.0 | 1.4 | 0.5 | 2.5 | 2.7 | 12.8 |
| Chris Kaman | 32 | 26.2 | 47.1 | 0.0 | 75.4 | 1.6 | 5.4 | 7.0 | 1.4 | 0.5 | 1.5 | 1.8 | 2.3 | 12.4 |
| Randy Foye | 63 | 24.6 | 38.2 | 32.7 | 89.3 | 0.2 | 1.4 | 1.6 | 2.7 | 0.7 | 0.3 | 1.5 | 1.9 | 9.8 |
| Ryan Gomes | 76 | 27.6 | 41.0 | 34.1 | 71.8 | 0.8 | 2.5 | 3.3 | 1.6 | 0.8 | 0.2 | 0.7 | 2.1 | 7.2 |
| DeAndre Jordan | 80 | 25.6 | 68.6 | 0.0 | 45.2 | 2.6 | 4.6 | 7.2 | 0.5 | 0.5 | 1.8 | 1.3 | 3.2 | 7.1 |
| Eric Bledsoe | 81 | 22.7 | 42.4 | 27.6 | 74.4 | 0.8 | 1.9 | 2.8 | 3.6 | 1.1 | 0.3 | 2.4 | 1.6 | 6.7 |
| Ike Diogu | 36 | 13.1 | 56.1 | 0.0 | 66.1 | 1.1 | 2.1 | 3.2 | 0.1 | 0.1 | 0.1 | 0.6 | 2.0 | 5.8 |
| Al-Farouq Aminu | 81 | 17.9 | 39.4 | 31.5 | 77.3 | 0.9 | 2.4 | 3.3 | 0.7 | 0.7 | 0.3 | 1.3 | 1.5 | 5.6 |
| Craig Smith | 48 | 12.2 | 55.3 | 0.0 | 73.5 | 0.9 | 1.5 | 2.4 | 0.6 | 0.3 | 0.1 | 0.7 | 1.8 | 5.4 |
| *Rasual Butler | 41 | 18.1 | 32.3 | 32.6 | 66.7 | 0.2 | 1.6 | 1.9 | 0.7 | 0.2 | 0.4 | 0.5 | 0.9 | 5.0 |
| Brian Cook | 40 | 11.2 | 42.4 | 43.0 | 62.5 | 0.5 | 1.9 | 2.4 | 0.4 | 0.3 | 0.3 | 0.6 | 1.9 | 4.8 |
| *Jamario Moon | 19 | 14.6 | 42.4 | 39.3 | 83.3 | 0.5 | 2.0 | 2.5 | 0.4 | 0.2 | 0.3 | 0.3 | 1.4 | 3.5 |
| Willie Warren | 19 | 7.1 | 37.1 | 33.3 | 75.0 | 0.1 | 0.6 | 0.6 | 1.4 | 0.3 | 0.0 | 0.4 | 0.9 | 1.9 |
| *Jarron Collins | 23 | 6.8 | 33.3 | 0.0 | 70.0 | 0.3 | 0.4 | 0.7 | 0.2 | 0.0 | 0.2 | | 1.0 | 0.7 |
| **Clippers** | 82 | 242.1 | 45.7 | 33.8 | 70.7 | 11.6 | 30.5 | 42.1 | 22.1 | 7.1 | 4.9 | 16.4 | 21.1 | 98.6 |
| **Opponents** | 82 | 242.1 | 45.5 | 36.5 | 77.1 | 11.1 | 29.4 | 40.5 | 22.3 | 8.0 | 4.9 | 13.7 | 22.1 | 101.8 |

* mid-season trade

## Los Angeles Lakers

| Player | GP | MPG | FG% | 3Pt% | FT% | OFF | DEF | Total | APG | SPG | BPG | TO | PF | PPG |
|---|---|---|---|---|---|---|---|---|---|---|---|---|---|---|
| | | | Field Goals | | | Rebounds | | | | | | | | |
| Kobe Bryant | 82 | 33.9 | 45.1 | 32.3 | 82.8 | 1.0 | 4.1 | 5.1 | 4.7 | 1.2 | 0.1 | 3.0 | 2.1 | 25.3 |
| Pau Gasol | 82 | 37 | 52.9 | 33.3 | 82.3 | 3.3 | 6.9 | 10.2 | 3.3 | 0.6 | 1.6 | 1.7 | 2.5 | 18.8 |
| Lamar Odom | 82 | 32.2 | 53.0 | 38.2 | 67.5 | 2.1 | 6.5 | 8.7 | 3.0 | 0.6 | 0.7 | 1.7 | 2.4 | 14.4 |
| Andrew Bynum | 54 | 27.8 | 57.4 | 0.0 | 66.0 | 3.1 | 6.3 | 9.4 | 1.4 | 0.4 | 2.0 | 1.4 | 2.6 | 11.3 |
| Shannon Brown | 82 | 19.1 | 42.5 | 34.9 | 91.1 | 0.4 | 1.5 | 1.9 | 1.2 | 0.8 | 0.2 | 0.9 | 1.5 | 8.7 |
| Ron Artest | 82 | 29.4 | 39.7 | 35.6 | 67.6 | 1.2 | 2.0 | 3.3 | 2.1 | 1.5 | 0.4 | 1.1 | 2.2 | 8.5 |
| Derek Fisher | 82 | 28 | 38.9 | 39.6 | 80.6 | 0.2 | 1.7 | 1.9 | 2.7 | 1.2 | 0.1 | 0.9 | 2.3 | 6.8 |
| Matt Barnes | 53 | 19.2 | 47.0 | 31.8 | 77.9 | 1.4 | 2.9 | 4.3 | 1.3 | 0.7 | 0.4 | 1.1 | 2.4 | 6.7 |
| *Trey Johnson | 1 | 13 | 66.7 | 0.0 | 100.0 | 0.0 | 0.0 | 0.0 | 0.0 | 0.0 | 0.0 | 0.0 | 1.0 | 6.0 |
| Steve Blake | 79 | 20 | 35.9 | 37.8 | 86.7 | 0.2 | 1.7 | 2.0 | 2.2 | 0.5 | 0.0 | 0.9 | 1.3 | 4.0 |
| Devin Ebanks | 20 | 5.9 | 41.2 | 40.0 | 78.3 | 0.8 | 0.6 | 1.4 | 0.1 | 0.2 | 0.3 | 0.3 | 0.4 | 3.1 |
| Derrick Caracter | 41 | 5.2 | 48.5 | 0.0 | 73.9 | 0.5 | 0.6 | 1.0 | 0.2 | 0.1 | 0.2 | 0.5 | 1.1 | 2.0 |
| *Sasha Vujacic | 11 | 4.9 | 34.8 | 42.9 | 50.0 | 0.1 | 0.3 | 0.4 | 0.5 | 0.1 | 0.0 | 0.5 | 0.6 | 1.8 |
| Luke Walton | 54 | 9 | 32.8 | 23.5 | 70.0 | 0.2 | 1.1 | 1.2 | 1.1 | 0.2 | 0.1 | 0.6 | 0.7 | 1.7 |
| *Joe Smith | 12 | 3.7 | 16.7 | 0.0 | 100.0 | 0.2 | 1.3 | 1.5 | 0.3 | 0.0 | 0.3 | 0.3 | 0.8 | 0.5 |
| Theo Ratliff | 10 | 7.1 | 16.7 | 0.0 | 0.0 | 0.6 | 0.7 | 1.3 | 0.3 | 0.2 | 0.5 | 0.3 | 0.7 | 0.2 |
| **Lakers** | **82** | **241.8** | **46.3** | **35.2** | **77.9** | **12.1** | **31.9** | **44.0** | **22.0** | **7.3** | **5.1** | **13.1** | **19.0** | **101.5** |
| **Opponents** | **82** | **241.8** | **43.7** | **33.5** | **76.5** | **12.2** | **29.3** | **41.5** | **22.3** | **7.1** | **4.5** | **13.6** | **20.7** | **95.4** |

## Memphis Grizzlies

| Player | GP | MPG | FG% | 3Pt% | FT% | OFF | DEF | Total | APG | SPG | BPG | TO | PF | PPG |
|---|---|---|---|---|---|---|---|---|---|---|---|---|---|---|
| | | | Field Goals | | | Rebounds | | | | | | | | |
| Zach Randolph | 75 | 36.3 | 50.3 | 18.6 | 75.8 | 4.3 | 7.8 | 12.2 | 2.2 | 0.8 | 0.3 | 2.0 | 2.3 | 20.1 |
| Rudy Gay | 54 | 39.9 | 47.1 | 39.6 | 80.5 | 1.5 | 4.7 | 6.2 | 2.8 | 1.7 | 1.1 | 2.5 | 2.4 | 19.8 |
| Mike Conley | 81 | 35.5 | 44.4 | 36.9 | 73.3 | 0.4 | 2.7 | 3.0 | 6.5 | 1.8 | 0.2 | 2.2 | 2.2 | 13.7 |
| Marc Gasol | 81 | 31.9 | 52.7 | 42.9 | 74.8 | 1.9 | 5.1 | 7.0 | 2.5 | 0.9 | 1.7 | 1.8 | 3.3 | 11.7 |
| O.J. Mayo | 71 | 26.3 | 40.7 | 36.4 | 75.6 | 0.5 | 1.9 | 2.4 | 2.0 | 1.0 | 0.4 | 1.4 | 1.8 | 11.3 |
| Darrell Arthur | 80 | 20.1 | 49.7 | 0.0 | 81.3 | 1.4 | 2.8 | 4.3 | 0.7 | 0.7 | 0.8 | 1.1 | 2.9 | 9.1 |
| Tony Allen | 72 | 20.8 | 51.0 | 17.4 | 75.3 | 1.0 | 1.7 | 2.7 | 1.4 | 1.8 | 0.6 | 1.2 | 2.2 | 8.9 |
| Sam Young | 78 | 20.2 | 47.2 | 34.0 | 76.7 | 0.5 | 1.9 | 2.4 | 0.9 | 0.9 | 0.3 | 0.8 | 1.5 | 7.3 |
| *Leon Powe | 16 | 8.8 | 50.0 | 0.0 | 60.9 | 0.5 | 1.1 | 1.6 | 0.3 | 0.2 | 0.1 | 0.4 | 1.5 | 5.5 |
| *Shane Battier | 23 | 24.2 | 42.6 | 33.3 | 88.2 | 1.4 | 2.6 | 4.0 | 1.4 | 0.7 | 0.4 | 0.7 | 1.3 | 5.0 |
| Xavier Henry | 38 | 13.9 | 40.6 | 11.8 | 63.5 | 0.2 | 0.7 | 1.0 | 0.5 | 0.3 | 0.1 | 0.3 | 1.3 | 4.3 |
| Greivis Vasquez | 70 | 12.3 | 40.8 | 29.1 | 77.3 | 0.2 | 0.9 | 1.0 | 2.2 | 0.3 | 0.1 | 1.0 | 1.2 | 3.6 |
| Hamed Haddadi | 31 | 5.4 | 51.7 | 0.0 | 65.2 | 0.8 | 1.4 | 2.2 | 0.2 | 0.1 | 0.4 | 0.4 | 0.9 | 2.4 |
| *Jason Williams | 11 | 11.3 | 31.0 | 20.0 | 0.0 | 0.0 | 0.7 | 0.7 | 2.5 | 0.3 | 0.1 | 0.6 | 0.2 | 1.9 |
| *Ishmael Smith | 15 | 7.5 | 34.4 | 0.0 | 45.5 | 0.1 | 0.3 | 0.3 | 1.0 | 0.3 | 0.0 | 0.5 | 0.7 | 1.8 |
| *DeMarre Carroll | 7 | 5.6 | 44.4 | 0.0 | 100.0 | 0.3 | 0.9 | 1.1 | 0.3 | 0.1 | 0.1 | 0.0 | 0.7 | 1.4 |
| *Hasheem Thabeet | 45 | 8.2 | 43.6 | 0.0 | 54.3 | 0.5 | 1.1 | 1.7 | 0.1 | 0.2 | 0.3 | 0.4 | 1.6 | 1.2 |
| *Acie Law | 11 | 8.5 | 15.8 | 0.0 | 60.0 | 0.3 | 0.7 | 1.0 | 1.3 | 0.4 | 0.0 | 0.9 | 0.9 | 1.0 |
| **Grizzlies** | **82** | **242.4** | **47.1** | **33.4** | **75.0** | **11.8** | **29.2** | **41.0** | **20.6** | **9.4** | **5.4** | **14.0** | **20.8** | **99.9** |
| **Opponents** | **82** | **242.4** | **45.7** | **36.9** | **76.1** | **11.0** | **29.1** | **40.1** | **21.0** | **7.5** | **6.2** | **16.7** | **21.4** | **97.6** |

## Miami Heat

| Player | GP | MPG | FG% | 3Pt% | FT% | OFF | DEF | Total | APG | SPG | BPG | TO | PF | PPG |
|---|---|---|---|---|---|---|---|---|---|---|---|---|---|---|
| | | | Field Goals | | | Rebounds | | | | | | | | |
| LeBron James | 79 | 38.8 | 51.0 | 33.0 | 75.9 | 1.0 | 6.5 | 7.5 | 7.0 | 1.6 | 0.6 | 3.6 | 2.1 | 26.7 |
| Dwyane Wade | 76 | 37.2 | 50.0 | 30.6 | 75.8 | 1.6 | 4.8 | 6.4 | 4.6 | 1.5 | 1.1 | 3.1 | 2.6 | 25.5 |
| Chris Bosh | 77 | 36.3 | 49.6 | 24.0 | 81.5 | 1.8 | 6.5 | 8.3 | 1.9 | 0.8 | 0.6 | 1.8 | 2.2 | 18.7 |
| Udonis Haslem | 13 | 26.5 | 51.2 | 0.0 | 80.0 | 2.2 | 5.9 | 8.2 | 0.5 | 0.5 | 0.2 | 1.1 | 3.0 | 8.0 |
| *Mike Bibby | 22 | 26.5 | 43.7 | 45.5 | 62.5 | 0.1 | 2.1 | 2.2 | 2.5 | 0.5 | 0.1 | 1.5 | 2.1 | 7.3 |
| Eddie House | 56 | 17.5 | 39.9 | 38.9 | 95.0 | 0.2 | 1.5 | 1.6 | 1.1 | 0.6 | 0.1 | 0.5 | 1.2 | 6.5 |
| Mario Chalmers | 70 | 22.5 | 39.9 | 35.9 | 87.1 | 0.2 | 1.9 | 2.1 | 2.5 | 1.1 | 0.1 | 1.3 | 2.3 | 6.4 |
| James Jones | 81 | 19.1 | 42.2 | 42.9 | 83.3 | 0.3 | 1.7 | 2.0 | 0.5 | 0.4 | 0.2 | 0.3 | 1.6 | 5.9 |
| *Carlos Arroyo | 49 | 20.3 | 45.8 | 43.8 | 80.0 | 0.3 | 1.4 | 1.6 | 2.0 | 0.6 | 0.0 | 0.9 | 1.2 | 5.6 |
| Mike Miller | 41 | 20.4 | 40.1 | 36.4 | 67.6 | 0.9 | 3.6 | 4.5 | 1.2 | 0.5 | 0.0 | 1.0 | 2.1 | 5.6 |
| Zydrunas Ilgauskas | 72 | 15.9 | 50.8 | 0.0 | 78.3 | 1.5 | 2.5 | 4.0 | 0.4 | 0.3 | 0.8 | 0.7 | 2.6 | 5.0 |
| Erick Dampier | 51 | 16 | 58.4 | 0.0 | 54.5 | 1.0 | 2.4 | 3.5 | 0.4 | 0.3 | 0.9 | 0.6 | 1.6 | 2.5 |
| Juwan Howard | 57 | 10.4 | 44.0 | 0.0 | 82.9 | 0.6 | 1.5 | 2.1 | 0.4 | 0.2 | 0.1 | 0.4 | 1.1 | 2.4 |
| Joel Anthony | 75 | 19.5 | 53.5 | 0.0 | 64.4 | 1.4 | 2.1 | 3.5 | 0.3 | 0.1 | 1.2 | 0.5 | 2.6 | 2.0 |
| Jamaal Magloire | 18 | 8.8 | 59.1 | 0.0 | 50.0 | 0.9 | 2.4 | 3.4 | 0.2 | 0.2 | 0.1 | 0.3 | 1.4 | 1.9 |
| Jerry Stackhouse | 7 | 7.1 | 25.0 | 25.0 | 71.4 | 0.1 | 0.9 | 1.0 | 0.4 | 0.3 | 0.3 | 0.4 |  | 1.7 |
| Dexter Pittman | 2 | 5.5 | 33.3 | 0.0 | 0.0 | 0.5 | 1.0 | 1.5 | 0.0 | 0.0 | 0.0 | 1.0 | 1.0 | 1.0 |
| **Heat** | **82** | **241.2** | **48.1** | **37.0** | **76.9** | **9.6** | **32.5** | **42.1** | **20.0** | **6.6** | **5.2** | **13.9** | **20.4** | **102.1** |
| **Opponents** | **82** | **241.2** | **43.4** | **34.5** | **74.4** | **10.5** | **28.6** | **39.2** | **20.1** | **7.0** | **3.0** | **13.2** | **21.8** | **94.6** |

* mid-season trade

## Milwaukee Bucks

| Player | GP | MPG | FG% | 3Pt% | FT% | OFF | DEF | Total | APG | SPG | BPG | TO | PF | PPG |
|---|---|---|---|---|---|---|---|---|---|---|---|---|---|---|
| Brandon Jennings..63 | | 34.4 | 39.0 | 32.3 | 80.9 | 0.7 | 3.0 | 3.7 | 4.8 | 1.5 | 0.3 | 2.3 | 2.1 | 16.2 |
| John Salmons ......73 | | 35 | 41.5 | 37.9 | 81.3 | 0.4 | 3.3 | 3.6 | 3.5 | 1.0 | 0.4 | 1.9 | 2.2 | 14.0 |
| Andrew Bogut ......65 | | 35.3 | 49.5 | 0.0 | 44.2 | 3.1 | 8.0 | 11.1 | 2.0 | 0.7 | 2.6 | 1.9 | 3.3 | 12.8 |
| Corey Maggette ...67 | | 20.9 | 45.3 | 35.9 | 83.4 | 0.7 | 2.9 | 3.6 | 1.3 | 0.3 | 0.1 | 1.9 | 2.6 | 12.0 |
| Carlos Delfino .....49 | | 32.4 | 39.0 | 37.0 | 80.0 | 0.5 | 3.6 | 4.1 | 2.3 | 1.6 | 0.2 | 1.2 | 1.5 | 11.5 |
| Drew Gooden.......35 | | 24.6 | 43.1 | 15.0 | 79.4 | 2.1 | 4.7 | 6.8 | 1.3 | 0.6 | 0.5 | 1.3 | 2.8 | 11.3 |
| Ersan Ilyasova ....60 | | 25.1 | 43.6 | 29.8 | 89.4 | 1.8 | 4.3 | 6.1 | 0.9 | 0.9 | 0.4 | 1.1 | 2.7 | 9.5 |
| C. Douglas-Roberts..44 | | 20.1 | 42.9 | 32.6 | 83.1 | 0.2 | 1.8 | 2.0 | 1.1 | 0.7 | 0.3 | 0.8 | 1.7 | 7.3 |
| Earl Boykins .........57 | | 15.1 | 44.3 | 38.0 | 84.1 | 0.3 | 0.7 | 1.0 | 2.5 | 0.7 | 0.1 | 0.9 | 0.8 | 7.2 |
| Keyon Dooling ......80 | | 22 | 39.7 | 34.6 | 83.0 | 0.2 | 1.3 | 1.5 | 3.0 | 0.7 | 0.1 | 1.1 | 1.5 | 7.1 |
| L.-R. Mbah a Moute..79 | | 26.5 | 46.3 | 0.0 | 70.7 | 2.1 | 3.2 | 5.3 | 0.9 | 0.9 | 0.4 | 1.0 | 2.3 | 6.7 |
| *Earl Barron...........7 | | 12.1 | 45.9 | 0.0 | 100.0 | 1.7 | 1.4 | 3.1 | 0.6 | 0.3 | 0.3 | 0.3 | 1.4 | 5.1 |
| Michael Redd........10 | | 13.4 | 40.0 | 23.5 | 100.0 | 0.0 | 0.8 | 0.8 | 1.2 | 0.2 | 0.1 | 0.4 | 0.4 | 4.4 |
| Larry Sanders ......60 | | 14.5 | 43.3 | 0.0 | 56.0 | 1.0 | 2.0 | 3.0 | 0.3 | 0.4 | 1.2 | 0.6 | 2.0 | 4.3 |
| Jon Brockman ......63 | | 10.7 | 51.1 | 0.0 | 67.8 | 1.2 | 1.7 | 2.9 | 0.3 | 0.2 | 0.0 | 0.4 | 1.9 | 2.2 |
| *Garrett Temple ......9 | | 9.2 | 33.3 | 30.0 | 0.0 | 0.0 | 0.7 | 0.7 | 0.7 | 0.1 | 0.1 | 0.2 | 0.9 | 1.9 |
| Brian Skinner .......2 | | 3 | 0.0 | 0.0 | 0.0 | 0.0 | 0.0 | 0.0 | 0.0 | 0.0 | 0.0 | 0.0 | 0.0 | 0.0 |
| Bucks.....................82 | | 241.8 | 43.0 | 34.2 | 75.7 | 10.5 | 30.2 | 40.8 | 18.8 | 7.5 | 4.9 | 13.5 | 20.5 | 91.9 |
| Opponents..............82 | | 241.8 | 44.7 | 33.4 | 77.0 | 10.2 | 32.1 | 42.3 | 20.2 | 6.2 | 4.8 | 15.2 | 20.7 | 92.7 |

## Minnesota Timberwolves

| Player | GP | MPG | FG% | 3Pt% | FT% | OFF | DEF | Total | APG | SPG | BPG | TO | PF | PPG |
|---|---|---|---|---|---|---|---|---|---|---|---|---|---|---|
| Kevin Love............73 | | 35.8 | 47.0 | 41.7 | 85.0 | 4.5 | 10.7 | 15.2 | 2.5 | 0.6 | 0.4 | 2.1 | 2.0 | 20.2 |
| Michael Beasley ...73 | | 32.3 | 45.0 | 36.6 | 75.3 | 1.6 | 4.0 | 5.6 | 2.2 | 0.7 | 0.7 | 2.7 | 3.0 | 19.2 |
| Luke Ridnour .......71 | | 30.4 | 46.8 | 44.0 | 88.3 | 0.5 | 2.3 | 2.8 | 5.4 | 1.3 | 0.1 | 2.2 | 2.1 | 11.8 |
| *Anthony Randolph...23 | | 20.1 | 49.8 | 0.0 | 70.3 | 1.4 | 3.8 | 5.2 | 1.1 | 0.8 | 0.7 | 1.9 | 2.0 | 11.7 |
| Martell Webster ....46 | | 23.8 | 44.7 | 41.7 | 77.0 | 0.8 | 2.4 | 3.2 | 1.2 | 0.6 | 0.2 | 1.3 | 2.2 | 9.8 |
| Wesley Johnson ...79 | | 26.2 | 39.7 | 35.6 | 69.6 | 0.6 | 2.4 | 3.0 | 1.9 | 0.7 | 0.7 | 1.2 | 2.1 | 9.0 |
| Darko Milicic........69 | | 24.4 | 46.9 | 0.0 | 55.7 | 1.9 | 3.3 | 5.2 | 1.5 | 0.8 | 2.0 | 2.2 | 3.3 | 8.8 |
| *Corey Brewer .......56 | | 24.3 | 38.4 | 26.3 | 70.8 | 0.8 | 1.9 | 2.7 | 1.4 | 1.6 | 0.3 | 1.4 | 2.4 | 8.6 |
| Sebastian Telfair ...37 | | 19.2 | 40.2 | 35.9 | 73.3 | 0.5 | 1.0 | 1.5 | 3.0 | 0.7 | 0.1 | 1.7 | 1.7 | 7.2 |
| Anthony Tolliver ...65 | | 21 | 45.0 | 40.9 | 80.2 | 1.4 | 3.1 | 4.5 | 1.3 | 0.4 | 0.4 | 0.8 | 2.2 | 6.7 |
| Wayne Ellington ...62 | | 19 | 40.3 | 39.7 | 79.2 | 0.4 | 1.3 | 1.7 | 1.2 | 0.5 | 0.0 | 0.9 | 1.4 | 6.6 |
| Nikola Pekovic ......65 | | 13.6 | 51.7 | 0.0 | 76.3 | 1.4 | 1.6 | 3.0 | 0.4 | 0.3 | 0.5 | 1.4 | 2.8 | 5.5 |
| Jonny Flynn ..........53 | | 18.5 | 36.5 | 31.0 | 76.2 | 0.2 | 1.2 | 1.5 | 3.4 | 0.6 | 0.1 | 2.1 | 1.1 | 5.3 |
| Lazar Hayward ......42 | | 10 | 35.7 | 28.3 | 78.6 | 0.5 | 1.1 | 1.7 | 0.7 | 0.3 | 0.2 | 0.5 | 1.0 | 3.8 |
| Maurice Ager.........4 | | 7.3 | 54.5 | 75.0 | 0.0 | 0.0 | 0.5 | 0.5 | 0.3 | 0.3 | 0.0 | 1.0 | 1.0 | 3.8 |
| *Kosta Koufos.......39 | | 8.6 | 43.5 | 0.0 | 50.0 | 1.1 | 1.4 | 2.5 | 0.2 | 0.2 | 0.5 | 0.6 | 1.3 | 2.7 |
| *Sundiata Gaines....8 | | 8.1 | 31.8 | 33.3 | 50.0 | 0.1 | 0.6 | 0.8 | 0.8 | 0.4 | 0.0 | 0.8 | 0.5 | 2.6 |
| Timberwolves............82 | | 241.2 | 44.1 | 37.6 | 76.8 | 13.2 | 31.2 | 44.4 | 20.1 | 7.2 | 5.1 | 17.0 | 22.3 | 101.1 |
| Opponents ................82 | | 241.2 | 46.8 | 37.4 | 77.8 | 11.1 | 31.4 | 42.6 | 24.8 | 9.5 | 5.5 | 14.4 | 20.9 | 107.7 |

## New Jersey Nets

| Player | GP | MPG | FG% | 3Pt% | FT% | OFF | DEF | Total | APG | SPG | BPG | TO | PF | PPG |
|---|---|---|---|---|---|---|---|---|---|---|---|---|---|---|
| Brook Lopez ..........82 | | 35.2 | 49.2 | 0.0 | 78.7 | 2.4 | 3.5 | 6.0 | 1.6 | 0.6 | 1.5 | 2.1 | 2.9 | 20.4 |
| *Devin Harris .......54 | | 31.9 | 42.5 | 30.0 | 84.0 | 0.2 | 2.2 | 2.4 | 7.6 | 1.1 | 0.1 | 2.9 | 2.4 | 15.0 |
| *Deron Williams ....12 | | 38 | 34.9 | 27.1 | 79.3 | 0.7 | 3.9 | 4.6 | 12.8 | 1.3 | 0.3 | 3.6 | 3.2 | 15.0 |
| Anthony Morrow ....58 | | 32 | 45.0 | 42.3 | 89.7 | 0.6 | 2.3 | 3.0 | 1.2 | 0.3 | 0.1 | 0.9 | 2.3 | 13.2 |
| *Sasha Vujacic .....56 | | 28.5 | 40.4 | 36.9 | 85.1 | 0.5 | 2.7 | 3.3 | 2.3 | 0.9 | 0.1 | 1.1 | 2.3 | 11.4 |
| Kris Humphries ......74 | | 27.9 | 52.7 | 0.0 | 66.5 | 3.0 | 7.4 | 10.4 | 1.1 | 0.4 | 1.1 | 1.4 | 2.3 | 10.0 |
| Jordan Farmar .......73 | | 24.6 | 39.2 | 35.9 | 82.0 | 0.3 | 2.0 | 2.4 | 5.0 | 0.8 | 0.1 | 1.9 | 1.8 | 9.6 |
| Travis Outlaw........82 | | 28.8 | 37.5 | 30.2 | 77.2 | 0.7 | 3.3 | 4.0 | 1.0 | 0.4 | 0.9 | 1.8 | 3.3 | 9.2 |
| *Terrence Williams .10 | | 20.6 | 39.7 | 33.3 | 50.0 | 0.3 | 3.3 | 3.6 | 3.1 | 0.5 | 0.0 | 2.5 | 2.1 | 6.7 |
| *Derrick Favors.....56 | | 19.5 | 51.1 | 0.0 | 61.2 | 2.3 | 3.1 | 5.3 | 0.4 | 0.3 | 1.0 | 1.0 | 3.3 | 6.3 |
| *Sundiata Gaines ..10 | | 14.6 | 41.7 | 23.5 | 55.0 | 1.0 | 1.4 | 2.4 | 2.5 | 0.9 | 0.0 | 1.3 | 1.1 | 5.5 |
| Damion James ......25 | | 16.1 | 44.7 | 0.0 | 64.3 | 0.7 | 2.7 | 3.4 | 0.8 | 0.6 | 0.5 | 1.0 | 1.4 | 4.4 |
| Ben Uzoh..............42 | | 10.4 | 42.4 | 37.5 | 58.9 | 0.7 | 0.7 | 1.5 | 1.6 | 0.3 | 0.2 | 0.6 | 0.7 | 3.8 |
| Mario West............6 | | 19.3 | 42.9 | 25.0 | 60.0 | 0.3 | 1.5 | 1.8 | 1.7 | 1.2 | 0.0 | 0.3 | 2.2 | 3.7 |
| *Brandan Wright....16 | | 11.5 | 40.7 | 0.0 | 82.4 | 1.1 | 1.9 | 3.0 | 0.4 | 0.5 | 0.4 | 0.3 | 0.9 | 3.6 |
| *Troy Murphy ........18 | | 16 | 34.2 | 17.4 | 52.9 | 0.6 | 3.6 | 4.2 | 0.9 | 0.4 | 0.1 | 0.7 | 1.6 | 3.6 |
| Johan Petro ..........17 | | 11.6 | 44.5 | 0.0 | 53.6 | 0.8 | 1.9 | 2.8 | 0.6 | 0.4 | 0.4 | 0.6 | 2.3 | 3.5 |
| Stephen Graham ...59 | | 16.2 | 40.5 | 23.8 | 81.6 | 0.3 | 1.8 | 2.1 | 0.7 | 0.2 | 0.0 | 0.6 | 1.8 | 3.4 |
| *Dan Gadzuric.......14 | | 11.8 | 41.5 | 0.0 | 38.5 | 1.3 | 2.2 | 3.5 | 0.2 | 0.2 | 0.8 | 0.6 | 2.0 | 2.8 |
| Nets.......................82 | | 244.0 | 44.0 | 34.3 | 75.9 | 11.1 | 29.8 | 40.8 | 21.0 | 5.6 | 4.7 | 14.0 | 22.0 | 94.2 |
| Opponents..............82 | | 244.0 | 46.5 | 36.4 | 75.1 | 10.4 | 31.4 | 41.8 | 22.2 | 6.8 | 4.6 | 12.3 | 20.0 | 100.4 |

* mid-season trade

## New Orleans Hornets

| Player | GP | MPG | FG% | 3Pt% | FT% | OFF | DEF | Total | APG | SPG | BPG | TO | PF | PPG |
|---|---|---|---|---|---|---|---|---|---|---|---|---|---|---|
| | | | **Field Goals** | | | **Rebounds** | | | | | | | | |
| David West | 70 | 35 | 50.8 | 22.2 | 80.7 | 2.2 | 5.3 | 7.6 | 2.3 | 1.0 | 0.9 | 2.0 | 2.9 | 18.9 |
| Chris Paul | 80 | 36 | 46.3 | 38.8 | 87.8 | 0.5 | 3.6 | 4.1 | 9.8 | 2.4 | 0.1 | 2.2 | 2.5 | 15.9 |
| *Carl Landry | 23 | 26.2 | 52.7 | 0.0 | 79.5 | 1.7 | 2.4 | 4.1 | 0.6 | 0.4 | 0.5 | 1.2 | 3.1 | 11.8 |
| Trevor Ariza | 75 | 34.7 | 39.8 | 30.3 | 70.1 | 0.8 | 4.6 | 5.4 | 2.2 | 1.6 | 0.4 | 1.6 | 2.4 | 11.0 |
| Marco Belinelli | 80 | 24.5 | 43.7 | 41.4 | 78.4 | 0.2 | 1.7 | 1.9 | 1.2 | 0.5 | 0.1 | 1.0 | 1.8 | 10.5 |
| Emeka Okafor | 72 | 31.8 | 57.3 | 0.0 | 56.2 | 3.2 | 6.3 | 9.5 | 0.6 | 0.6 | 1.8 | 1.7 | 3.2 | 10.3 |
| Willie Green | 77 | 21.7 | 44.3 | 34.8 | 78.0 | 0.3 | 1.8 | 2.1 | 1.0 | 0.5 | 0.2 | 0.9 | 1.9 | 8.7 |
| *Jarrett Jack | 70 | 19.6 | 41.2 | 34.5 | 84.5 | 0.2 | 1.7 | 1.9 | 2.6 | 0.6 | 0.1 | 1.1 | 1.1 | 8.5 |
| *Marcus Thornton | 46 | 16.2 | 41.0 | 37.6 | 75.8 | 0.5 | 2.3 | 2.8 | 0.9 | 0.4 | 0.1 | 0.8 | 1.1 | 7.8 |
| *Peja Stojakovic | 6 | 14.8 | 42.4 | 44.0 | 85.7 | 0.0 | 1.0 | 1.0 | 1.0 | 0.3 | 0.0 | 0.7 | 0.3 | 7.5 |
| *Jerryd Bayless | 11 | 13.5 | 34.7 | 21.4 | 76.5 | 0.2 | 1.2 | 1.4 | 2.5 | 0.2 | 0.1 | 1.5 | 1.5 | 4.5 |
| Jason Smith | 77 | 14.3 | 44.3 | 0.0 | 84.3 | 1.2 | 2.0 | 3.1 | 0.5 | 0.3 | 0.4 | 0.7 | 1.9 | 4.3 |
| Aaron Gray | 41 | 13 | 56.6 | 0.0 | 50.0 | 1.4 | 2.7 | 4.2 | 0.4 | 0.3 | 0.3 | 0.8 | 2.3 | 3.1 |
| Quincy Pondexter | 66 | 11.1 | 40.6 | 36.0 | 70.6 | 0.3 | 1.0 | 1.3 | 0.4 | 0.3 | 0.2 | 0.2 | 1.0 | 2.8 |
| *David Andersen | 29 | 7.7 | 44.6 | 38.5 | 46.7 | 0.4 | 1.3 | 1.7 | 0.2 | 0.1 | 0.2 | 0.5 | 1.0 | 2.7 |
| D. Ilunga-Mbenga | 41 | 8 | 46.9 | 0.0 | 72.2 | 0.9 | 1.2 | 2.1 | 0.1 | 0.1 | 0.7 | 0.5 | 1.3 | 1.4 |
| *Sasha Pavlovic | 4 | 12.5 | 18.2 | 0.0 | 0.0 | 0.0 | 1.5 | 1.5 | 1.5 | 0.0 | 1.0 | 0.3 | 1.0 | 1.0 |
| Patrick Ewing | 7 | 2.7 | 0.0 | 0.0 | 75.0 | 0.1 | 0.1 | 0.3 | 0.3 | 0.0 | 0.1 | 0.1 | 0.1 | 0.4 |
| **Hornets** | 82 | 241.8 | 45.9 | 36.0 | 76.5 | 10.0 | 30.1 | 40.1 | 20.6 | 7.6 | 4.4 | 13.0 | 21.0 | 94.9 |
| **Opponents** | 82 | 241.8 | 45.7 | 35.7 | 77.0 | 9.4 | 30.0 | 39.3 | 21.2 | 6.1 | 4.8 | 14.5 | 20.4 | 94.0 |

## New York Knicks

| Player | GP | MPG | FG% | 3Pt% | FT% | OFF | DEF | Total | APG | SPG | BPG | TO | PF | PPG |
|---|---|---|---|---|---|---|---|---|---|---|---|---|---|---|
| | | | **Field Goals** | | | **Rebounds** | | | | | | | | |
| *Carmelo Anthony | 27 | 36.2 | 46.1 | 42.4 | 87.2 | 1.5 | 5.2 | 6.7 | 3.0 | 0.9 | 0.6 | 2.4 | 3.3 | 26.3 |
| Amare Stoudemire | 78 | 36.8 | 50.2 | 43.5 | 79.2 | 2.5 | 5.6 | 8.2 | 2.6 | 0.9 | 1.9 | 3.2 | 3.5 | 25.3 |
| *Chauncey Billups | 21 | 31.6 | 40.3 | 32.8 | 90.2 | 0.6 | 2.5 | 3.1 | 5.5 | 0.9 | 0.1 | 2.3 | 2.5 | 17.5 |
| *Raymond Felton | 54 | 38.4 | 42.3 | 32.8 | 86.7 | 0.7 | 2.9 | 3.6 | 9.0 | 1.8 | 0.2 | 3.3 | 2.1 | 17.1 |
| *Wilson Chandler | 51 | 34.5 | 46.1 | 35.1 | 80.7 | 1.2 | 4.7 | 5.9 | 1.7 | 0.7 | 1.4 | 1.3 | 3.0 | 16.4 |
| *Danilo Gallinari | 48 | 34.8 | 41.5 | 34.7 | 89.3 | 1.0 | 3.8 | 4.8 | 1.7 | 0.8 | 0.4 | 1.2 | 2.4 | 15.9 |
| Toney Douglas | 81 | 24.3 | 41.6 | 37.3 | 79.4 | 0.8 | 2.2 | 3.0 | 3.0 | 1.1 | 0.0 | 1.1 | 2.2 | 10.6 |
| Landry Fields | 82 | 31 | 49.7 | 39.3 | 76.9 | 1.3 | 5.1 | 6.4 | 1.9 | 1.0 | 0.2 | 1.3 | 1.4 | 9.7 |
| Shawne Williams | 64 | 20.7 | 42.6 | 40.1 | 83.7 | 0.9 | 2.8 | 3.7 | 0.7 | 0.6 | 0.8 | 0.7 | 2.6 | 7.1 |
| Bill Walker | 61 | 12.9 | 44.1 | 38.6 | 70.5 | 0.3 | 1.7 | 2.0 | 0.6 | 0.3 | 0.1 | 0.6 | 1.3 | 4.9 |
| *Anthony Carter | 19 | 16.3 | 46.1 | 28.6 | 100.0 | 0.4 | 1.7 | 2.1 | 2.3 | 0.9 | 0.3 | 1.3 | 1.6 | 4.4 |
| *Derrick Brown | 8 | 11 | 66.7 | 75.0 | 53.8 | 1.1 | 0.8 | 1.9 | 0.5 | 0.5 | 0.3 | 0.9 | 1.4 | 4.3 |
| Ronny Turiaf | 64 | 17.8 | 63.2 | 0.0 | 62.2 | 1.0 | 2.2 | 3.2 | 1.4 | 0.5 | 1.1 | 0.6 | 2.5 | 4.2 |
| *Timofey Mozgov | 34 | 13.5 | 46.4 | 0.0 | 70.5 | 1.2 | 1.9 | 3.1 | 0.4 | 0.4 | 0.7 | 0.9 | 2.2 | 4.0 |
| *Shelden Williams | 17 | 11.6 | 53.8 | 0.0 | 82.8 | 1.1 | 1.8 | 2.9 | 0.8 | 0.3 | 0.2 | 0.4 | 2.0 | 3.9 |
| Roger Mason | 26 | 12.3 | 33.8 | 36.4 | 70.0 | 0.2 | 1.5 | 1.7 | 0.8 | 0.2 | 0.1 | 0.2 | 1.0 | 2.9 |
| *Anthony Randolph | 17 | 7.5 | 31.1 | 25.0 | 50.0 | 0.6 | 1.7 | 2.4 | 0.4 | 0.2 | 0.5 | 0.6 | 0.9 | 2.1 |
| *Jared Jeffries | 24 | 19.3 | 38.0 | 33.3 | 42.1 | 1.8 | 1.6 | 3.4 | 1.0 | 1.0 | 0.6 | 0.7 | 2.3 | 2.0 |
| **Knicks** | 82 | 241.2 | 45.7 | 36.8 | 80.9 | 10.3 | 30.1 | 40.5 | 21.4 | 7.6 | 5.8 | 13.7 | 21.3 | 106.5 |
| **Opponents** | 82 | 241.2 | 47.2 | 37.2 | 76.2 | 11.8 | 32.3 | 44.0 | 20.5 | 7.1 | 4.4 | 15.2 | 20.8 | 105.7 |

## Oklahoma City Thunder

| Player | GP | MPG | FG% | 3Pt% | FT% | OFF | DEF | Total | APG | SPG | BPG | TO | PF | PPG |
|---|---|---|---|---|---|---|---|---|---|---|---|---|---|---|
| | | | **Field Goals** | | | **Rebounds** | | | | | | | | |
| Kevin Durant | 78 | 38.9 | 46.2 | 35.0 | 88.0 | 0.7 | 6.1 | 6.8 | 2.7 | 1.1 | 1.0 | 2.8 | 2.0 | 27.7 |
| Russell Westbrook | 82 | 34.7 | 44.2 | 33.0 | 84.2 | 1.5 | 3.1 | 4.6 | 8.2 | 1.9 | 0.4 | 3.9 | 2.5 | 21.9 |
| *Jeff Green | 49 | 37 | 43.7 | 30.4 | 81.8 | 1.2 | 4.4 | 5.6 | 1.8 | 0.8 | 0.4 | 1.6 | 2.9 | 15.2 |
| James Harden | 82 | 26.7 | 43.6 | 34.9 | 84.3 | 0.5 | 2.6 | 3.1 | 2.1 | 1.1 | 0.3 | 1.3 | 2.5 | 12.2 |
| Serge Ibaka | 82 | 27 | 54.3 | 0.0 | 75.0 | 2.6 | 5.0 | 7.6 | 0.3 | 0.4 | 2.4 | 0.9 | 3.3 | 9.9 |
| *Nenad Krstic | 47 | 21.7 | 49.8 | 0.0 | 83.0 | 1.6 | 2.8 | 4.4 | 0.4 | 0.4 | 0.4 | 0.7 | 2.3 | 7.6 |
| *Nazr Mohammed | 24 | 17.9 | 57.3 | 0.0 | 62.5 | 1.9 | 2.9 | 4.8 | 0.3 | 0.7 | 0.4 | 0.8 | 2.6 | 6.9 |
| Daequan Cook | 43 | 13.9 | 43.6 | 42.2 | 80.0 | 0.2 | 1.5 | 1.7 | 0.5 | 0.3 | 0.0 | 0.4 | 1.2 | 5.6 |
| *Kendrick Perkins | 17 | 25.2 | 49.3 | 0.0 | 53.1 | 2.3 | 5.6 | 7.9 | 0.9 | 0.4 | 0.9 | 1.8 | 3.2 | 5.1 |
| Thabo Sefolosha | 79 | 25.9 | 47.1 | 27.5 | 74.7 | 0.8 | 3.6 | 4.4 | 1.4 | 1.2 | 0.5 | 0.7 | 2.2 | 5.1 |
| Nick Collison | 71 | 21.5 | 56.6 | 0.0 | 75.3 | 1.7 | 2.8 | 4.5 | 1.0 | 0.6 | 0.4 | 0.8 | 3.0 | 4.6 |
| Eric Maynor | 82 | 14.6 | 40.2 | 38.5 | 72.9 | 0.3 | 1.2 | 1.5 | 2.9 | 0.4 | 0.1 | 0.9 | 1.2 | 4.2 |
| *Nate Robinson | 4 | 7.5 | 26.7 | 25.0 | 75.0 | 0.0 | 0.3 | 0.3 | 1.5 | 0.0 | 0.0 | 0.5 | 2.0 | 3.3 |
| *D.J. White | 23 | 9.5 | 46.2 | 0.0 | 50.0 | 1.0 | 1.7 | 2.3 | 0.2 | 0.3 | 0.3 | 0.3 | 1.3 | 2.8 |
| Byron Mullens | 13 | 6.5 | 32.1 | 0.0 | 50.0 | 0.5 | 1.4 | 1.8 | 0.0 | 0.2 | 0.2 | 0.6 | 0.8 | 1.9 |
| Royal Ivey | 25 | 6.2 | 42.1 | 43.8 | 100.0 | 0.1 | 0.6 | 0.6 | 0.3 | 0.2 | 0.0 | 0.2 | 0.7 | 1.6 |
| Cole Aldrich | 18 | 7.8 | 53.3 | 0.0 | 50.0 | 0.7 | 1.2 | 1.9 | 0.2 | 0.3 | 0.4 | 0.4 | 1.7 | 1.0 |
| **Thunder** | 82 | 244.0 | 46.4 | 34.7 | 82.3 | 11.0 | 31.8 | 42.8 | 20.4 | 8.0 | 5.9 | 14.1 | 22.4 | 104.8 |
| **Opponents** | 82 | 244.0 | 45.8 | 36.1 | 74.4 | 11.4 | 29.2 | 40.6 | 20.9 | 7.2 | 4.3 | 14.0 | 21.5 | 101.0 |

* mid-season trade

## Orlando Magic

| Player | GP | MPG | FG% | 3Pt% | FT% | OFF | DEF | Total | APG | SPG | BPG | TO | PF | PPG |
|---|---|---|---|---|---|---|---|---|---|---|---|---|---|---|
| Dwight Howard ....78 | | 37.6 | 59.3 | 0.0 | 59.6 | 4.0 | 10.1 | 14.1 | 1.4 | 1.4 | 2.4 | 3.6 | 3.3 | 22.9 |
| *Vince Carter........22 | | 30.2 | 47.0 | 34.6 | 74.7 | 0.5 | 3.6 | 4.1 | 2.9 | 0.9 | 0.1 | 1.6 | 3.2 | 15.1 |
| *Jason Richardson..55 | | 34.9 | 43.3 | 38.4 | 70.1 | 0.6 | 3.4 | 4.0 | 2.0 | 1.2 | 0.2 | 1.2 | 2.1 | 13.9 |
| Jameer Nelson.....76 | | 30.5 | 44.6 | 40.1 | 80.2 | 0.5 | 2.5 | 3.0 | 6.0 | 1.0 | 0.0 | 2.6 | 2.8 | 13.1 |
| *Rashard Lewis ....25 | | 32.4 | 41.9 | 36.7 | 75.6 | 0.9 | 3.3 | 4.2 | 1.2 | 0.9 | 0.4 | 1.4 | 2.5 | 12.2 |
| *Hedo Turkoglu ....56 | | 34.1 | 44.8 | 40.4 | 66.7 | 0.4 | 4.1 | 4.6 | 5.1 | 1.0 | 0.4 | 1.8 | 3.0 | 11.4 |
| Brandon Bass ......76 | | 26.1 | 51.5 | 0.0 | 81.5 | 1.8 | 3.8 | 5.6 | 0.8 | 0.4 | 0.7 | 1.3 | 2.1 | 11.2 |
| Ryan Anderson ....64 | | 22.3 | 43.0 | 39.3 | 81.2 | 2.0 | 3.5 | 5.5 | 0.8 | 0.5 | 0.6 | 0.8 | 2.1 | 10.6 |
| J.J. Redick .........59 | | 25.6 | 44.1 | 39.7 | 87.5 | 0.1 | 1.8 | 1.9 | 1.7 | 0.5 | 0.1 | 0.9 | 1.4 | 10.1 |
| *Gilbert Arenas ....49 | | 21.8 | 34.4 | 27.5 | 74.4 | 0.3 | 2.1 | 2.4 | 3.2 | 0.9 | 0.2 | 2.2 | 2.3 | 8.0 |
| *Mickael Pietrus ...19 | | 22 | 39.1 | 39.1 | 50.0 | 0.3 | 2.3 | 2.6 | 0.5 | 0.5 | 0.2 | 0.7 | 1.8 | 6.7 |
| Quentin Richardson.57 | | 16.8 | 34.1 | 28.8 | 75.0 | 0.7 | 2.4 | 3.1 | 0.7 | 0.4 | 0.1 | 0.6 | 1.3 | 4.4 |
| *Earl Clark ..........33 | | 11.9 | 44.1 | 0.0 | 59.5 | 1.0 | 1.5 | 2.5 | 0.2 | 0.2 | 0.5 | 0.8 | 1.2 | 4.1 |
| *Marcin Gortat .....25 | | 15.8 | 54.3 | 0.0 | 66.7 | 1.5 | 3.2 | 4.7 | 0.7 | 0.3 | 0.8 | 0.7 | 2.1 | 4.0 |
| Chris Duhon ........51 | | 15.2 | 38.0 | 25.0 | 56.0 | 0.2 | 0.8 | 1.0 | 2.3 | 0.3 | 0.0 | 1.2 | 0.6 | 2.5 |
| *Jason Williams....16 | | 10.7 | 34.2 | 30.4 | 0.0 | 0.2 | 1.2 | 1.4 | 1.5 | 0.5 | 0.0 | 0.7 | 0.4 | 2.1 |
| Malik Allen ........18 | | 9.9 | 35.5 | 0.0 | 50.0 | 0.7 | 1.1 | 1.8 | 0.2 | 0.1 | 0.2 | 0.2 | 1.7 | 1.3 |
| **Magic** ............82 | | 241.8 | 46.1 | 36.6 | 69.2 | 10.5 | 32.7 | 43.2 | 20.0 | 6.7 | 4.7 | 14.9 | 20.0 | 99.2 |
| **Opponents**.............82 | | 241.8 | 43.6 | 35.0 | 74.3 | 9.8 | 29.9 | 39.7 | 20.1 | 7.4 | 3.8 | 14.0 | 21.8 | 93.7 |

## Philadelphia 76ers

| Player | GP | MPG | FG% | 3Pt% | FT% | OFF | DEF | Total | APG | SPG | BPG | TO | PF | PPG |
|---|---|---|---|---|---|---|---|---|---|---|---|---|---|---|
| Elton Brand .........81 | | 34.7 | 51.2 | 0.0 | 78.0 | 2.9 | 5.4 | 8.3 | 1.5 | 1.1 | 1.3 | 1.2 | 3.0 | 15.0 |
| Andre Iguodala ....67 | | 36.9 | 44.5 | 33.7 | 69.3 | 0.9 | 4.9 | 5.8 | 6.3 | 1.5 | 0.6 | 2.1 | 1.6 | 14.1 |
| Jrue Holiday........82 | | 35.4 | 44.6 | 36.5 | 82.3 | 0.8 | 3.2 | 4.0 | 6.5 | 1.5 | 0.4 | 2.7 | 2.5 | 14.0 |
| Louis Williams ......75 | | 23.3 | 40.6 | 34.8 | 82.3 | 0.4 | 1.6 | 2.0 | 3.4 | 0.6 | 0.2 | 1.4 | 1.7 | 13.7 |
| Thaddeus Young ...82 | | 26 | 54.1 | 27.3 | 70.7 | 1.9 | 3.4 | 5.3 | 1.0 | 1.1 | 0.3 | 1.2 | 2.1 | 12.7 |
| Jodie Meeks.......74 | | 27.9 | 42.5 | 39.7 | 89.4 | 0.3 | 2.0 | 2.3 | 1.1 | 0.9 | 0.1 | 0.8 | 1.3 | 10.5 |
| Spencer Hawes ...81 | | 21.2 | 46.5 | 24.3 | 53.4 | 1.6 | 4.1 | 5.7 | 1.5 | 0.4 | 0.9 | 1.2 | 2.5 | 7.2 |
| Evan Turner ........78 | | 23 | 42.5 | 31.8 | 80.8 | 0.5 | 3.4 | 3.9 | 2.0 | 0.6 | 0.2 | 1.0 | 1.8 | 7.2 |
| Andres Nocioni ....54 | | 17.2 | 42.6 | 35.6 | 80.3 | 0.4 | 2.8 | 3.1 | 0.8 | 0.3 | 0.3 | 0.9 | 1.9 | 6.1 |
| Marreese Speights..64 | | 11.5 | 49.5 | 25.0 | 75.3 | 1.0 | 2.3 | 3.3 | 0.5 | 0.1 | 0.3 | 0.6 | 1.9 | 5.4 |
| Craig Brackins .......3 | | 11 | 25.0 | 0.0 | 0.0 | 0.7 | 0.7 | 1.3 | 0.3 | 0.3 | 0.0 | 0.0 | 1.0 | 2.7 |
| Tony Battie .........38 | | 9.9 | 46.9 | 66.7 | 57.1 | 0.4 | 2.2 | 2.6 | 0.3 | 0.1 | 0.4 | 0.3 | 1.6 | 2.6 |
| Darius Songaila....10 | | 7.1 | 46.7 | 0.0 | 50.0 | 0.2 | 0.8 | 1.0 | 0.2 | 0.0 | 0.0 | 0.4 | 1.6 | 1.6 |
| Antonio Daniels ....4 | | 8.8 | 40.0 | 0.0 | 100.0 | 0.0 | 1.3 | 1.3 | 0.5 | 0.0 | 0.0 | 0.3 | 0.0 | 1.5 |
| Jason Kapono....24 | | 4.6 | 25.0 | 12.5 | 50.0 | 0.1 | 0.3 | 0.5 | 0.2 | 0.1 | 0.0 | 0.1 | 0.2 | 0.7 |
| **76ers** .........82 | | 243.0 | 46.1 | 35.5 | 77.0 | 10.4 | 31.4 | 41.8 | 22.7 | 7.6 | 4.3 | 13.0 | 19.4 | 99.0 |
| **Opponents**.............82 | | 243.0 | 45.1 | 34.0 | 77.3 | 10.7 | 31.8 | 42.5 | 21.5 | 7.1 | 4.6 | 14.2 | 18.8 | 97.5 |

## Phoenix Suns

| Player | GP | MPG | FG% | 3Pt% | FT% | OFF | DEF | Total | APG | SPG | BPG | TO | PF | PPG |
|---|---|---|---|---|---|---|---|---|---|---|---|---|---|---|
| *Jason Richardson..25 | | 31.8 | 47.0 | 41.9 | 76.4 | 1.3 | 3.1 | 4.4 | 1.4 | 1.1 | 0.1 | 1.2 | 1.8 | 19.3 |
| Steve Nash.............75 | | 33.3 | 49.2 | 39.5 | 91.2 | 0.5 | 2.9 | 3.5 | 11.4 | 0.6 | 0.1 | 3.5 | 1.2 | 14.7 |
| *Vince Carter........51 | | 27.2 | 42.2 | 36.6 | 73.5 | 0.8 | 2.8 | 3.6 | 1.6 | 0.9 | 0.3 | 1.1 | 2.4 | 13.5 |
| Grant Hill ............80 | | 30.1 | 48.4 | 39.5 | 82.9 | 1.0 | 3.3 | 4.2 | 2.5 | 0.8 | 0.4 | 1.7 | 2.3 | 13.2 |
| *Marcin Gortat.........55 | | 29.7 | 56.3 | 25.0 | 73.1 | 2.0 | 7.3 | 9.3 | 1.0 | 0.5 | 1.3 | 1.2 | 2.5 | 13.0 |
| Channing Frye .......77 | | 33 | 43.2 | 39.0 | 83.2 | 0.8 | 5.8 | 6.7 | 1.2 | 0.6 | 1.0 | 0.9 | 3.5 | 12.7 |
| Jared Dudley.......82 | | 26.1 | 47.7 | 41.5 | 74.3 | 1.4 | 2.5 | 3.9 | 1.3 | 1.1 | 0.2 | 0.9 | 1.7 | 10.6 |
| *Aaron Brooks........25 | | 18.9 | 43.0 | 32.8 | 80.7 | 0.4 | 0.7 | 1.1 | 4.2 | 0.5 | 0.0 | 1.8 | 1.8 | 9.6 |
| *Hedo Turkoglu....25 | | 25.2 | 44.0 | 42.3 | 72.2 | 0.8 | 3.2 | 4.0 | 2.3 | 0.7 | 0.6 | 1.2 | 3.1 | 9.5 |
| Hakim Warrick.....80 | | 17.7 | 51.1 | 9.1 | 72.1 | 1.1 | 2.6 | 3.7 | 0.9 | 0.4 | 0.1 | 1.0 | 1.3 | 8.4 |
| *Goran Dragic.........48 | | 17.8 | 42.1 | 27.7 | 60.8 | 0.5 | 1.3 | 1.8 | 3.1 | 0.8 | 0.1 | 2.0 | 1.9 | 7.4 |
| *Mickael Pietrus.....38 | | 18.1 | 39.2 | 34.2 | 70.6 | 0.2 | 1.8 | 2.0 | 0.6 | 0.5 | 0.5 | 0.7 | 1.7 | 7.4 |
| Robin Lopez........67 | | 14.8 | 50.1 | 0.0 | 74.0 | 1.2 | 2.0 | 3.2 | 0.1 | 0.3 | 0.7 | 0.7 | 2.1 | 6.4 |
| Zabian Dowdell.....24 | | 12.2 | 40.8 | 30.0 | 94.1 | 0.2 | 0.6 | 0.8 | 2.1 | 0.8 | 0.1 | 1.2 | 1.3 | 5.0 |
| Josh Childress.....54 | | 16.6 | 56.5 | 6.3 | 49.2 | 1.3 | 1.6 | 2.9 | 0.8 | 0.6 | 0.4 | 0.8 | 1.3 | 5.0 |
| *Earl Clark ..........9 | | 8 | 38.7 | 0.0 | 50.0 | 0.4 | 1.4 | 1.9 | 0.4 | 0.1 | 0.3 | 0.2 | 0.7 | 3.2 |
| *Earl Barron .........12 | | 15.3 | 23.5 | 0.0 | 60.0 | 1.3 | 2.0 | 3.3 | 0.3 | 0.5 | 0.3 | 0.9 | 2.7 | 3.0 |
| Garret Siler.........21 | | 4.8 | 54.8 | 0.0 | 50.0 | 0.8 | 0.6 | 1.3 | 0.1 | 0.0 | 0.2 | 0.5 | 1.0 | 2.1 |
| **Suns**.............82 | | 244.0 | 47.0 | 37.7 | 75.9 | 10.0 | 30.2 | 40.2 | 23.7 | 6.6 | 4.4 | 14.3 | 20.3 | 105.0 |
| **Opponents**.............82 | | 244.0 | 47.2 | 36.7 | 75.4 | 12.0 | 32.3 | 44.3 | 23.0 | 7.9 | 4.3 | 14.5 | 21.2 | 105.9 |

* mid-season trade

### Portland Trail Blazers

| Player | GP | MPG | Field Goals | | FT% | Rebounds | | Total | APG | SPG | BPG | TO | PF | PPG |
|---|---|---|---|---|---|---|---|---|---|---|---|---|---|---|
| | | | FG% | 3Pt% | | OFF | DEF | | | | | | | |
| LaMarcus Aldridge..81 | | 39.6 | 50.0 | 17.4 | 79.1 | 3.4 | 5.3 | 8.8 | 2.1 | 1.0 | 1.2 | 1.9 | 2.7 | 21.8 |
| Wesley Matthews..82 | | 33.6 | 44.9 | 40.7 | 84.4 | 0.6 | 2.6 | 3.1 | 2.0 | 1.2 | 0.1 | 1.7 | 2.4 | 15.9 |
| *Gerald Wallace ...23 | | 35.7 | 49.8 | 33.8 | 76.7 | 1.7 | 5.9 | 7.6 | 2.5 | 2.0 | 0.7 | 2.3 | 2.7 | 15.8 |
| Andre Miller .........81 | | 32.7 | 46.0 | 10.8 | 85.3 | 1.2 | 2.5 | 3.7 | 7.0 | 1.4 | 0.1 | 2.4 | 2.1 | 12.7 |
| Nicolas Batum ......80 | | 31.5 | 45.5 | 34.5 | 84.1 | 1.4 | 3.2 | 4.5 | 1.5 | 0.9 | 0.6 | 1.0 | 2.4 | 12.4 |
| Brandon Roy .......47 | | 27.9 | 40.0 | 33.3 | 84.8 | 0.6 | 2.0 | 2.6 | 2.7 | 0.8 | 0.3 | 1.2 | 1.6 | 12.2 |
| Rudy Fernandez ..78 | | 23.3 | 37.0 | 32.1 | 86.3 | 0.5 | 1.7 | 2.2 | 2.5 | 1.1 | 0.2 | 1.1 | 1.7 | 8.6 |
| Patrick Mills .......64 | | 12.2 | 41.2 | 35.3 | 76.6 | 0.3 | 0.5 | 0.8 | 1.7 | 0.4 | 0.0 | 1.0 | 1.0 | 5.5 |
| *Dante Cunningham..56 | | 19.8 | 43.3 | 0.0 | 71.1 | 1.3 | 2.1 | 3.4 | 0.5 | 0.7 | 0.6 | 0.6 | 2.5 | 5.1 |
| Marcus Camby.....59 | | 26.1 | 39.8 | 0.0 | 61.4 | 3.1 | 7.2 | 10.3 | 2.1 | 0.7 | 1.6 | 1.1 | 2.4 | 4.7 |
| *Earl Barron ..........2 | | 18.5 | 27.3 | 0.0 | 50.0 | 2.0 | 5.0 | 7.0 | 1.5 | 0.0 | 0.0 | 1.5 | 2.0 | 3.5 |
| Armon Johnson ...38 | | 7.3 | 45.5 | 41.7 | 59.1 | 0.3 | 0.7 | 0.9 | 1.2 | 0.1 | 0.0 | 1.0 | 0.8 | 2.9 |
| *Chris Johnson.....10 | | 10.6 | 38.9 | 0.0 | 72.2 | 1.1 | 1.6 | 2.7 | 0.2 | 0.3 | 0.6 | 0.8 | 1.8 | 2.7 |
| *Joel Przybilla ......31 | | 14.4 | 61.8 | 0.0 | 56.5 | 0.9 | 3.0 | 3.9 | 0.4 | 0.2 | 0.5 | 0.7 | 2.0 | 1.8 |
| Sean Marks .........29 | | 7.2 | 43.2 | 100.0 | 62.5 | 0.6 | 0.8 | 1.4 | 0.1 | 0.1 | 0.2 | 0.4 | 1.5 | 1.6 |
| Luke Babbitt.........24 | | 5.7 | 27.3 | 18.8 | 33.3 | 0.3 | 1.0 | 1.3 | 0.3 | 0.1 | 0.1 | 0.3 | 0.6 | 1.5 |
| Fabricio Oberto......5 | | 9 | 60.0 | 0.0 | 50.0 | 0.6 | 0.8 | 1.4 | 0.0 | 0.0 | 0.0 | 0.6 | 2.0 | 1.4 |
| *Jarron Collins......5 | | 4.8 | 16.7 | 0.0 | 0.0 | 1.4 | 0.0 | 1.4 | 0.2 | 0.0 | 0.0 | 0.4 | 1.0 | 0.4 |
| **Trail Blazers.............82** | | **241.5** | **44.7** | **34.5** | **80.4** | **12.1** | **27.2** | **39.3** | **21.2** | **8.0** | **4.4** | **13.0** | **19.3** | **96.3** |
| **Opponents.................82** | | **241.5** | **46.7** | **36.7** | **76.7** | **10.6** | **29.1** | **39.7** | **19.2** | **6.9** | **4.1** | **15.7** | **21.3** | **94.8** |

### Sacramento Kings

| Player | GP | MPG | Field Goals | | FT% | Rebounds | | Total | APG | SPG | BPG | TO | PF | PPG |
|---|---|---|---|---|---|---|---|---|---|---|---|---|---|---|
| | | | FG% | 3Pt% | | OFF | DEF | | | | | | | |
| *Marcus Thornton..27 | | 38.1 | 45.0 | 36.1 | 80.5 | 1.3 | 3.4 | 4.7 | 3.4 | 1.7 | 0.2 | 2.1 | 2.2 | 21.3 |
| Tyreke Evans ........57 | | 37 | 40.9 | 29.1 | 77.1 | 0.8 | 4.0 | 4.8 | 5.6 | 1.5 | 0.5 | 3.2 | 2.5 | 17.8 |
| DeMarcus Cousins..81 | | 28.5 | 43.0 | 16.7 | 68.7 | 2.7 | 6.0 | 8.6 | 2.5 | 1.0 | 0.8 | 3.3 | 4.1 | 14.1 |
| Beno Udrih ..........79 | | 34.6 | 50.0 | 35.7 | 86.4 | 0.5 | 2.8 | 3.4 | 4.9 | 1.2 | 0.1 | 1.8 | 2.3 | 13.7 |
| *Carl Landry.........53 | | 26.5 | 49.2 | 0.0 | 72.1 | 2.4 | 2.4 | 4.8 | 0.9 | 0.6 | 0.4 | 1.5 | 2.4 | 11.9 |
| Francisco Garcia..58 | | 23.9 | 43.6 | 36.2 | 85.5 | 0.4 | 1.9 | 2.3 | 1.2 | 0.9 | 0.8 | 0.8 | 2.2 | 9.7 |
| Jason Thompson..75 | | 23.3 | 50.7 | 0.0 | 60.5 | 1.9 | 4.1 | 6.1 | 1.2 | 0.4 | 0.6 | 1.3 | 2.8 | 8.8 |
| Omri Casspi ........71 | | 24 | 41.2 | 37.2 | 67.3 | 1.0 | 3.3 | 4.3 | 1.0 | 0.8 | 0.2 | 1.0 | 1.6 | 8.6 |
| Samuel Dalembert..80 | | 24.2 | 47.3 | 0.0 | 73.0 | 2.7 | 5.6 | 8.2 | 0.8 | 0.5 | 1.5 | 1.7 | 2.8 | 8.1 |
| *Jermaine Taylor ..26 | | 15.6 | 47.6 | 30.0 | 72.7 | 1.0 | 1.1 | 2.0 | 1.2 | 0.5 | 0.1 | 1.5 | 1.3 | 7.1 |
| Donte Greene.......69 | | 16.3 | 40.4 | 29.2 | 66.2 | 0.7 | 1.4 | 2.1 | 0.7 | 0.5 | 0.3 | 0.9 | 1.3 | 5.8 |
| Luther Head .........36 | | 16.3 | 41.5 | 39.1 | 78.0 | 0.4 | 1.2 | 1.7 | 1.9 | 0.3 | 0.3 | 0.9 | 1.2 | 5.6 |
| Eugene Jeter........62 | | 13.8 | 40.9 | 20.0 | 90.2 | 0.1 | 1.0 | 1.1 | 2.6 | 0.5 | 0.0 | 0.8 | 0.9 | 4.1 |
| Darnell Jackson ...59 | | 8.2 | 48.7 | 27.3 | 61.2 | 0.8 | 0.8 | 1.6 | 0.2 | 0.2 | 0.1 | 0.4 | 1.0 | 3.2 |
| Antoine Wright......7 | | 4.4 | 12.5 | 0.0 | 0.0 | 0.3 | 0.1 | 0.4 | 0.0 | 0.1 | 0.0 | 0.1 | 0.4 | 0.3 |
| Hassan Whiteside ..1 | | 2 | 0.0 | 0.0 | 0.0 | 0.0 | 0.0 | 0.0 | 0.0 | 0.0 | 0.0 | 0.0 | 2.0 | 0.0 |
| **Kings........................82** | | **242.1** | **44.9** | **33.5** | **73.4** | **13.1** | **30.8** | **43.9** | **20.4** | **7.4** | **4.8** | **16.1** | **22.0** | **99.4** |
| **Opponents.................82** | | **242.1** | **47.8** | **35.5** | **76.2** | **10.6** | **30.6** | **41.2** | **21.7** | **8.1** | **5.7** | **14.7** | **21.0** | **104.7** |

### San Antonio Spurs

| Player | GP | MPG | Field Goals | | FT% | Rebounds | | Total | APG | SPG | BPG | TO | PF | PPG |
|---|---|---|---|---|---|---|---|---|---|---|---|---|---|---|
| | | | FG% | 3Pt% | | OFF | DEF | | | | | | | |
| Tony Parker ..........78 | | 32.4 | 51.9 | 35.7 | 76.9 | 0.4 | 2.7 | 3.1 | 6.6 | 1.2 | 0.0 | 2.6 | 1.7 | 17.5 |
| Manu Ginobili ......80 | | 30.3 | 43.3 | 34.9 | 87.1 | 0.5 | 3.2 | 3.7 | 4.9 | 1.5 | 0.4 | 2.2 | 2.0 | 17.4 |
| Tim Duncan..........76 | | 28.4 | 50.0 | 0.0 | 71.6 | 2.2 | 6.7 | 8.9 | 2.7 | 0.7 | 1.9 | 1.6 | 1.6 | 13.4 |
| George Hill ..........76 | | 28.3 | 45.3 | 37.7 | 86.3 | 0.3 | 2.3 | 2.6 | 2.5 | 0.9 | 0.3 | 1.3 | 2.0 | 11.6 |
| Richard Jefferson..81 | | 30.4 | 47.4 | 44.0 | 75.9 | 0.7 | 3.2 | 3.8 | 1.3 | 0.5 | 0.4 | 1.1 | 2.0 | 11.0 |
| Gary Neal ............80 | | 21.1 | 45.1 | 41.9 | 80.8 | 0.3 | 2.2 | 2.5 | 1.2 | 0.3 | 0.1 | 1.0 | 1.9 | 9.8 |
| DeJuan Blair ........81 | | 21.4 | 50.1 | 0.0 | 65.7 | 2.7 | 4.3 | 7.0 | 1.0 | 1.2 | 0.5 | 1.4 | 2.6 | 8.3 |
| Matt Bonner ........66 | | 21.7 | 46.4 | 45.7 | 74.4 | 0.9 | 2.7 | 3.6 | 0.9 | 0.4 | 0.3 | 0.4 | 1.7 | 7.3 |
| Antonio McDyess...73 | | 19 | 49.1 | 0.0 | 67.5 | 1.7 | 3.7 | 5.4 | 1.2 | 0.5 | 0.5 | 1.0 | 2.2 | 5.3 |
| Danny Green.........8 | | 11.5 | 48.6 | 36.8 | 0.0 | 0.4 | 1.5 | 1.9 | 0.3 | 0.3 | 0.1 | 0.6 | 0.9 | 5.1 |
| Tiago Splitter.......60 | | 12.3 | 52.9 | 0.0 | 54.3 | 1.2 | 2.2 | 3.4 | 0.4 | 0.5 | 0.3 | 0.5 | 1.5 | 4.6 |
| *Steve Novak .......23 | | 8.6 | 52.5 | 54.8 | 100.0 | 0.2 | 0.8 | 1.0 | 0.1 | 0.0 | 0.2 | 0.2 | 0.5 | 4.0 |
| James Anderson ..26 | | 11 | 38.3 | 39.1 | 77.8 | 0.1 | 0.8 | 0.9 | 0.7 | 0.1 | 0.2 | 0.5 | 0.9 | 3.6 |
| Chris Quinn ........41 | | 7.1 | 36.3 | 29.7 | 50.0 | 0.1 | 0.5 | 0.6 | 1.0 | 0.1 | 0.0 | 0.3 | 0.7 | 2.0 |
| *Larry Owens ........7 | | 4.4 | 50.0 | 33.3 | 50.0 | 0.1 | 0.6 | 0.6 | 0.7 | 0.3 | 0.0 | 0.0 | 0.6 | 1.3 |
| *Garrett Temple......3 | | 7 | 20.0 | 0.0 | 0.0 | 0.3 | 0.3 | 0.7 | 0.7 | 0.3 | 0.3 | 0.3 | 0.7 | 0.7 |
| Ime Udoka ...........20 | | 6.5 | 23.8 | 0.0 | 50.0 | 0.3 | 0.7 | 1.0 | 0.7 | 0.4 | 0.1 | 0.3 | 0.7 | 0.7 |
| *Alonzo Gee...........5 | | 3.6 | 33.3 | 0.0 | 0.0 | 0.4 | 0.2 | 0.6 | 0.0 | 0.4 | 0.0 | 0.6 | 0.6 | 0.4 |
| **Spurs ........................82** | | **241.2** | **47.5** | **39.7** | **76.7** | **10.1** | **31.7** | **41.9** | **22.4** | **7.3** | **4.5** | **13.4** | **19.0** | **103.7** |
| **Opponents.................82** | | **241.2** | **45.6** | **36.7** | **76.6** | **10.8** | **30.4** | **41.2** | **20.5** | **6.9** | **4.6** | **13.4** | **20.7** | **98.0** |

* mid-season trade

## Toronto Raptors

| Player | GP | MPG | FG% | 3Pt% | FT% | OFF | DEF | Total | APG | SPG | BPG | TO | PF | PPG |
|---|---|---|---|---|---|---|---|---|---|---|---|---|---|---|
| Andrea Bargnani | 66 | 35.7 | 44.8 | 34.5 | 82.0 | 1.1 | 4.1 | 5.2 | 1.8 | 0.5 | 0.7 | 2.3 | 2.4 | 21.4 |
| DeMar DeRozan | 82 | 34.8 | 46.7 | 9.6 | 81.3 | 0.9 | 2.9 | 3.8 | 1.8 | 1.0 | 0.4 | 1.8 | 2.6 | 17.2 |
| Leandro Barbosa | 58 | 24.1 | 45.0 | 33.8 | 79.6 | 0.2 | 1.5 | 1.7 | 2.1 | 0.9 | 0.1 | 1.4 | 1.9 | 13.3 |
| Linas Kleiza | 39 | 26.5 | 43.8 | 29.8 | 63.1 | 0.9 | 3.6 | 4.5 | 1.0 | 0.5 | 0.2 | 1.7 | 2.5 | 11.2 |
| *Jarrett Jack | 13 | 26.7 | 39.3 | 16.7 | 87.0 | 0.5 | 2.8 | 3.2 | 4.5 | 1.1 | 0.0 | 2.6 | 1.9 | 10.8 |
| *Jerryd Bayless | 60 | 22.5 | 42.9 | 34.8 | 81.0 | 0.4 | 2.1 | 2.5 | 4.0 | 0.6 | 0.1 | 1.8 | 2.2 | 10.0 |
| *Peja Stojakovic | 2 | 11 | 70.0 | 66.7 | 100.0 | 0.0 | 1.5 | 1.5 | 0.5 | 0.0 | 0.0 | 1.0 | 0.0 | 10.0 |
| Jose Calderon | 68 | 30.9 | 44.0 | 36.5 | 85.4 | 0.4 | 2.5 | 3.0 | 8.9 | 1.2 | 0.1 | 2.2 | 2.1 | 9.8 |
| Amir Johnson | 72 | 25.7 | 56.8 | 0.0 | 78.8 | 2.6 | 3.8 | 6.4 | 1.1 | 0.7 | 1.2 | 1.0 | 3.7 | 9.6 |
| *James Johnson | 25 | 28 | 46.4 | 24.0 | 70.7 | 1.2 | 3.5 | 4.7 | 3.0 | 1.0 | 1.1 | 1.8 | 2.8 | 9.2 |
| Sonny Weems | 59 | 23.9 | 44.4 | 27.9 | 76.6 | 0.7 | 1.9 | 2.6 | 1.8 | 0.6 | 0.3 | 1.5 | 1.5 | 9.2 |
| Ed Davis | 65 | 24.6 | 57.6 | 0.0 | 55.5 | 2.6 | 4.5 | 7.1 | 0.6 | 0.6 | 1.0 | 0.7 | 2.8 | 7.7 |
| *Sundiata Gaines | 6 | 14.8 | 42.9 | 20.0 | 33.3 | 0.3 | 1.0 | 1.3 | 1.8 | 0.7 | 0.2 | 1.3 | 1.7 | 5.8 |
| *David Andersen | 11 | 13.6 | 48.9 | 30.0 | 100.0 | 0.7 | 2.4 | 3.1 | 0.6 | 0.3 | 0.3 | 0.7 | 1.0 | 5.1 |
| *Alexis Ajinca | 24 | 11 | 46.5 | 33.3 | 73.3 | 0.5 | 2.0 | 2.5 | 0.3 | 0.3 | 0.6 | 0.7 | 2.5 | 4.8 |
| Reggie Evans | 30 | 26.6 | 40.8 | 0.0 | 54.5 | 4.0 | 7.5 | 11.5 | 1.3 | 1.0 | 0.2 | 1.3 | 3.0 | 4.4 |
| *Trey Johnson | 7 | 11.6 | 33.3 | 33.3 | 87.5 | 0.3 | 0.7 | 1.0 | 1.6 | 0.1 | 0.1 | 0.7 | 1.6 | 4.0 |
| Julian Wright | 52 | 14.7 | 51.3 | 20.0 | 51.2 | 0.9 | 1.4 | 2.3 | 1.1 | 0.8 | 0.4 | 0.8 | 0.9 | 3.6 |
| Joey Dorsey | 43 | 12.5 | 52.5 | 0.0 | 47.7 | 1.8 | 2.6 | 4.4 | 0.6 | 0.6 | 0.4 | 0.9 | 1.8 | 3.1 |
| **Raptors** | 82 | 241.2 | 46.5 | 31.6 | 75.5 | 11.7 | 28.6 | 40.3 | 21.9 | 7.1 | 4.3 | 14.7 | 22.0 | 99.1 |
| **Opponents** | 82 | 241.2 | 48.2 | 37.6 | 76.9 | 11.1 | 30.0 | 41.1 | 22.6 | 7.6 | 5.6 | 14.1 | 19.8 | 105.4 |

## Utah Jazz

| Player | GP | MPG | FG% | 3Pt% | FT% | OFF | DEF | Total | APG | SPG | BPG | TO | PF | PPG |
|---|---|---|---|---|---|---|---|---|---|---|---|---|---|---|
| *Deron Williams | 53 | 37.9 | 45.8 | 34.5 | 85.3 | 0.6 | 3.3 | 3.9 | 9.7 | 1.2 | 0.2 | 3.5 | 2.9 | 21.3 |
| Al Jefferson | 82 | 35.9 | 49.6 | 0.0 | 76.1 | 2.9 | 6.8 | 9.7 | 1.8 | 0.6 | 1.9 | 1.3 | 2.9 | 18.6 |
| Paul Millsap | 76 | 34.3 | 53.1 | 39.1 | 75.7 | 2.2 | 5.5 | 7.6 | 2.5 | 1.4 | 0.9 | 1.9 | 3.6 | 17.3 |
| *Devin Harris | 17 | 31.2 | 41.3 | 35.7 | 81.1 | 0.4 | 2.0 | 2.4 | 5.4 | 0.8 | 0.1 | 2.9 | 1.9 | 15.8 |
| C.J. Miles | 78 | 25.2 | 40.7 | 32.2 | 81.1 | 0.7 | 2.6 | 3.3 | 1.7 | 0.9 | 0.5 | 1.2 | 2.8 | 12.8 |
| Andrei Kirilenko | 64 | 31.2 | 46.7 | 36.7 | 77.0 | 1.6 | 3.5 | 5.1 | 3.0 | 1.3 | 1.2 | 1.8 | 1.8 | 11.7 |
| *Derrick Favors | 22 | 20.2 | 52.9 | 0.0 | 56.1 | 2.0 | 3.2 | 5.2 | 0.8 | 0.5 | 1.2 | 1.0 | 2.9 | 8.2 |
| Raja Bell | 68 | 30.8 | 40.9 | 35.2 | 89.2 | 0.5 | 2.1 | 2.6 | 1.7 | 0.8 | 0.2 | 0.9 | 2.5 | 8.0 |
| Gordon Hayward | 72 | 16.9 | 48.5 | 47.3 | 71.1 | 0.6 | 1.4 | 1.9 | 1.1 | 0.4 | 0.3 | 1.0 | 1.5 | 5.4 |
| Mehmet Okur | 13 | 12.9 | 35.5 | 31.3 | 75.0 | 0.7 | 1.6 | 2.3 | 1.5 | 0.3 | 0.3 | 0.5 | 1.4 | 4.9 |
| Earl Watson | 80 | 19.6 | 41.0 | 33.6 | 67.1 | 0.7 | 1.6 | 2.3 | 3.5 | 0.8 | 0.2 | 1.5 | 1.8 | 4.3 |
| Jeremy Evans | 49 | 9.4 | 66.1 | 0.0 | 70.3 | 0.7 | 1.2 | 2.0 | 0.5 | 0.3 | 0.6 | 0.4 | 1.0 | 3.6 |
| Ronnie Price | 59 | 12.2 | 35.2 | 29.0 | 74.4 | 0.4 | 0.7 | 1.0 | 0.9 | 0.7 | 0.1 | 0.9 | 1.8 | 3.3 |
| Francisco Elson | 62 | 9.8 | 47.8 | 0.0 | 83.9 | 0.6 | 1.3 | 1.9 | 0.5 | 0.3 | 0.2 | 0.5 | 1.4 | 2.2 |
| Kyrylo Fesenko | 53 | 8.6 | 44.0 | 0.0 | 39.1 | 0.6 | 1.4 | 2.0 | 0.3 | 0.1 | 0.3 | 0.5 | 1.7 | 2.0 |
| **Jazz** | 82 | 242.4 | 46.5 | 34.6 | 77.1 | 11.0 | 28.5 | 39.5 | 23.4 | 7.7 | 5.9 | 14.3 | 22.7 | 99.4 |
| **Opponents** | 82 | 242.4 | 45.9 | 37.6 | 77.8 | 11.3 | 29.6 | 40.9 | 20.7 | 7.4 | 5.0 | 14.6 | 22.0 | 101.3 |

## Washington Wizards

| Player | GP | MPG | FG% | 3Pt% | FT% | OFF | DEF | Total | APG | SPG | BPG | TO | PF | PPG |
|---|---|---|---|---|---|---|---|---|---|---|---|---|---|---|
| Nick Young | 64 | 31.8 | 44.1 | 38.7 | 81.6 | 0.4 | 2.3 | 2.7 | 1.2 | 0.7 | 0.3 | 1.4 | 2.3 | 17.4 |
| *Gilbert Arenas | 21 | 34.6 | 39.4 | 32.4 | 83.6 | 0.3 | 3.0 | 3.3 | 5.6 | 1.4 | 0.6 | 3.4 | 3.6 | 17.3 |
| Andray Blatche | 64 | 33.9 | 44.5 | 22.2 | 77.7 | 2.9 | 5.4 | 8.2 | 2.3 | 1.5 | 0.8 | 2.7 | 2.8 | 16.8 |
| John Wall | 69 | 37.8 | 40.9 | 29.6 | 76.6 | 0.5 | 4.1 | 4.6 | 8.3 | 1.8 | 0.5 | 3.8 | 2.5 | 16.4 |
| *Jordan Crawford | 26 | 33.3 | 39.0 | 23.8 | 88.5 | 0.8 | 2.1 | 3.0 | 3.9 | 1.4 | 0.1 | 2.6 | 1.9 | 16.3 |
| *Rashard Lewis | 32 | 31.7 | 44.6 | 34.7 | 84.3 | 1.5 | 4.3 | 5.8 | 2.0 | 0.9 | 0.6 | 1.6 | 3.0 | 11.4 |
| *Kirk Hinrich | 48 | 36.0 | 45.2 | 38.4 | 87.6 | 0.3 | 2.4 | 2.7 | 4.4 | 1.2 | 0.2 | 1.8 | 2.5 | 11.1 |
| JaVale McGee | 79 | 27.8 | 55.0 | 0.0 | 58.3 | 2.8 | 5.2 | 8.0 | 0.5 | 0.5 | 2.4 | 1.3 | 2.9 | 10.1 |
| *Maurice Evans | 26 | 27.4 | 43.9 | 34.6 | 93.3 | 1.1 | 1.7 | 2.8 | 0.6 | 0.7 | 0.3 | 0.7 | 2.1 | 9.7 |
| Josh Howard | 18 | 22.7 | 35.8 | 24.1 | 61.7 | 1.0 | 3.1 | 4.1 | 1.3 | 0.7 | 0.3 | 1.1 | 1.9 | 8.4 |
| *Al Thornton | 49 | 21.8 | 47.1 | 16.0 | 75.7 | 0.9 | 2.2 | 3.2 | 1.0 | 0.6 | 0.2 | 0.9 | 2.1 | 8.0 |
| *Othyus Jeffers | 16 | 19.6 | 48.4 | 25.0 | 65.2 | 1.6 | 2.5 | 4.1 | 1.2 | 1.1 | 0.2 | 0.8 | 1.9 | 5.7 |
| Yi Jianlian | 63 | 17.7 | 41.8 | 23.1 | 68.1 | 1.3 | 2.7 | 3.9 | 0.4 | 0.4 | 0.5 | 0.8 | 1.8 | 5.6 |
| Trevor Booker | 65 | 16.4 | 54.9 | 0.0 | 67.3 | 1.5 | 2.4 | 3.9 | 0.5 | 0.4 | 0.6 | 0.6 | 1.8 | 5.3 |
| Cartier Martin | 52 | 10.4 | 39.0 | 39.4 | 70.0 | 0.4 | 1.0 | 1.4 | 0.3 | 0.3 | 0.1 | 0.3 | 1.0 | 4.0 |
| Kevin Seraphin | 58 | 10.9 | 44.9 | 0.0 | 71.0 | 1.4 | 1.2 | 2.6 | 0.2 | 0.3 | 0.5 | 0.7 | 2.2 | 2.7 |
| Mustafa Shakur | 22 | 7.2 | 35.6 | 10.0 | 53.3 | 0.3 | 0.7 | 1.0 | 1.1 | 0.2 | 0.1 | 0.8 | 0.7 | 2.3 |
| *Hilton Armstrong | 41 | 10 | 48.4 | 33.3 | 60.9 | 1.0 | 1.8 | 2.8 | 0.2 | 0.4 | 0.4 | 0.6 | 1.8 | 1.9 |
| **Wizards** | 82 | 243.0 | 44.3 | 33.2 | 74.5 | 12.4 | 29.0 | 41.3 | 19.4 | 8.1 | 6.1 | 15.3 | 22.6 | 97.3 |
| **Opponents** | 82 | 243.0 | 47.1 | 37.3 | 76.1 | 12.1 | 31.8 | 43.9 | 23.1 | 7.6 | 5.0 | 15.8 | 20.3 | 104.7 |

* mid-season trade

# 2011 NBA Draft

The 2011 NBA Draft was held on June 23, 2011 in Newark, New Jersey.

### First Round

1. CLE—Kyrie Irving, Duke (from LAC)
2. MIN—Derrick Williams, Arizona
3. UTAH—Enes Kanter, Turkey
4. CLE—Tristan Thompson, Texas
5. TOR—Jonas Valanciunas, Lithuania
6. WAS—Jan Vesely, Serbia
7. SAC—Bismack Biyombo, Spain (traded to CHA)
8. DET—Brandon Knight, Kentucky
9. CHA—Kemba Walker, Connecticut
10. MIL—Jimmer Fredette, BYU (traded to SAC)
11. GSW—Klay Thompson, Wash. St
12. UTAH—Alec Burks, Colorado
13. PHX—Markieff Morris, Kansas
14. HOU—Marcus Morris, Kansas
15. IND—Kawhi Leonard, San Diego St (traded to SAS)
16. PHI—Nikola Vucevic, USC
17. NYK—Iman Shumpert, Ga. Tech
18. WAS—Chris Singleton, Florida St (from ATL)
19. CHA—Tobias Harris, Tennessee (from NO via POR, traded to MIL)
20. MIN—Donatas Motiejunas, Italy (from MEM via UTAH, traded to HOU)
21. POR—Nolan Smith, Duke
22. DEN—Kenneth Faried, More. St
23. HOU—Nikola Mirotic, Spain (from ORL via PHX, traded to CHI via MIN)

### First Round (Cont.)

24. OKC—Reggie Jackson, B.C.
25. BOS—Marshon Brooks, Prov.
26. DAL—Jordan Hamilton, Texas
27. NJN—JaJuan Jackson, Purdue
28. CHI—Norris Cole, Cleveland St (from MIA via TOR, traded to MIA via MIN)
29. SAS—Cory Joseph, Texas
30. CHI—Jimmy Butler, Marquette

### Second Round

31. MIA—Bojan Bogdanovic, Croatia (from MIN, traded to NJN via MIN)
32. CLE—Justin Harper, Richmond (traded to ORL)
33. DET—Kyle Singler, Duke (from TOR)
34. WAS—Shelvin Mack, Butler (from GSW)
35. SAC—Tyler Honeycutt, UCLA
36. NJN—Jordan Williams, Maryland
37. LAC—Trey Thompkins, Georgia (from DET)
38. HOU—Chandler Parsons, Florida (from LAC)
39. CHA—Jeremy Tyler, Japan
40. MIL—Jon Leuer, Wisconsin
41. LAL—Darius Morris, Michigan (from GSW via NJN)
42. IND—Davis Bertans, Slovenia (traded to SAS)

### Second Round (Cont.)

43. CHI—Malcolm Lee, UCLA (from UTAH, traded to MIN)
44. GSW—Charles Jenkins, Hofstra (from PHX via CHI)
45. NO—Josh Harrellson, Kentucky (from PHI, traded to NYK)
46. LAL—Andrew Goudelock, Coll. (from NYK)        of Charleston
47. LAC—Travis Leslie, Georgia (from HOU)
48. ATL—Keith Benson, Oakland
49. MEM—Josh Selby, Kansas
50. PHI—Lavoy Allen, Temple (from NO)
51. POR—Jon Diebler, Ohio St
52. DET—Vernon Macklin, Florida (from DEN)
53. ORL—DeAndre Liggins, Ken.
54. CLE—Milan Macvan, Israel (from OKC via MIA)
55. BOS—E'Twaun Moore, Purdue
56. LAL—Chuk. Maduabum, Bakersfield Jam (D-League) (traded to DEN)
57. DAL—Tanguy Ngombo, Qatar (traded to POR)
58. LAL—Ater Majok, Australia (from MIA)
59. SAS—Adam Hanga, Hungary
60. SAC—Isaiah Thomas, Wash. (from CHI via MIL)

# Women's National Basketball Association

## 2011 Final Regular Season Standings

### WESTERN CONFERENCE

| Team | W | L | Pct | GB |
|---|---|---|---|---|
| †Minnesota | 27 | 7 | .794 | — |
| *Seattle | 21 | 13 | .618 | 6.0 |
| *Phoenix | 19 | 15 | .559 | 8.0 |
| *San Antonio | 18 | 16 | .529 | 9.0 |
| Los Angeles | 15 | 19 | .441 | 12.0 |
| Tulsa | 3 | 31 | .088 | 24.0 |

### EASTERN CONFERENCE

| Team | W | L | Pct | GB |
|---|---|---|---|---|
| †Indiana | 21 | 13 | .618 | — |
| *Connecticut | 21 | 13 | .618 | — |
| *Atlanta | 20 | 14 | .588 | 1.0 |
| *New York | 19 | 15 | .559 | 2.0 |
| Chicago | 14 | 20 | .412 | 7.0 |
| Washington | 6 | 28 | .176 | 15.0 |

†Clinched conference title.    *Clinched playoff berth.

## 2011 Playoffs

### WESTERN CONFERENCE SEMI-FINALS

Game 1......Phoenix 61        at Seattle 80
Game 2......Seattle 83        at Phoenix 92
Game 3......Phoenix 77        at Seattle 75
Phoenix won series 2–1.

Game 1......San Antonio 65    at Minnesota 66
Game 2......Minnesota 75      at San Antonio 84
Game 3......San Antonio 67    at Minnesota 85
Minnesota won series 2–1.

### WESTERN CONFERENCE FINALS

Game 1......Phoenix 67        at Minnesota 95
Game 2......Minnesota 103     at Phoenix 86
Minnesota won series 2–0.

### EASTERN CONFERENCE SEMI-FINALS

Game 1......Atlanta 89        at Connecticut 84
Game 2......Connecticut 64    at Atlanta 69
Atlanta won series 2–0.

Game 1......New York 72       at Indiana 74
Game 2......Indiana 72        at New York 87
Game 3......New York 62       at Indiana 72
Indiana won series 2–1.

### EASTERN CONFERENCE FINALS

Game 1......Atlanta 74        at Indiana 82
Game 2......Indiana 77        at Atlanta 94
Game 1......Atlanta 83        at Indiana 67
Atlanta won series 2–1.

### WNBA FINALS

Game 1 ..........Atlanta 74       at Minnesota 88
Game 2 ..........Atlanta 95       at Minnesota 101
Game 3 ..........Minnesota 73     at Atlanta 67
Minnesota won series 3–0.

**2011 WNBA Finals MVP:** Seimone Augustus, Minnesota

## NBA Champions

| Season | Winner | Series | Runner-Up | Winning Coach | Finals MVP |
|---|---|---|---|---|---|
| 1946–47 | Philadelphia | 4–1 | Chicago | Eddie Gottlieb | — |
| 1947–48 | Baltimore | 4–2 | Philadelphia | Buddy Jeannette | — |
| 1948–49 | Minneapolis | 4–2 | Washington | John Kundla | — |
| 1949–50 | Minneapolis | 4–2 | Syracuse | John Kundla | — |
| 1950–51 | Rochester | 4–3 | New York | Les Harrison | — |
| 1951–52 | Minneapolis | 4–3 | New York | John Kundla | — |
| 1952–53 | Minneapolis | 4–1 | New York | John Kundla | — |
| 1953–54 | Minneapolis | 4–3 | Syracuse | John Kundla | — |
| 1954–55 | Syracuse | 4–3 | Ft Wayne | Al Cervi | — |
| 1955–56 | Philadelphia | 4–1 | Ft Wayne | George Senesky | — |
| 1956–57 | Boston | 4–3 | St Louis | Red Auerbach | — |
| 1957–58 | St Louis | 4–2 | Boston | Alex Hannum | — |
| 1958–59 | Boston | 4–0 | Minneapolis | Red Auerbach | — |
| 1959–60 | Boston | 4–3 | St Louis | Red Auerbach | — |
| 1960–61 | Boston | 4–1 | St Louis | Red Auerbach | — |
| 1961–62 | Boston | 4–3 | LA Lakers | Red Auerbach | — |
| 1962–63 | Boston | 4–2 | LA Lakers | Red Auerbach | — |
| 1963–64 | Boston | 4–1 | San Francisco | Red Auerbach | — |
| 1964–65 | Boston | 4–1 | LA Lakers | Red Auerbach | — |
| 1965–66 | Boston | 4–3 | LA Lakers | Red Auerbach | — |
| 1966–67 | Philadelphia | 4–2 | San Francisco | Alex Hannum | — |
| 1967–68 | Boston | 4–2 | LA Lakers | Bill Russell | — |
| 1968–69 | Boston | 4–3 | LA Lakers | Bill Russell | Jerry West, LA |
| 1969–70 | New York | 4–3 | LA Lakers | Red Holzman | Willis Reed, NY |
| 1970–71 | Milwaukee | 4–0 | Baltimore | Larry Costello | Kareem Abdul-Jabbar, Mil |
| 1971–72 | LA Lakers | 4–1 | New York | Bill Sharman | Wilt Chamberlain, LA |
| 1972–73 | New York | 4–1 | LA Lakers | Red Holzman | Willis Reed, NY |
| 1973–74 | Boston | 4–3 | Milwaukee | Tommy Heinsohn | John Havlicek, Bos |
| 1974–75 | Golden State | 4–0 | Washington | Al Attles | Rick Barry, GS |
| 1975–76 | Boston | 4–2 | Phoenix | Tommy Heinsohn | JoJo White, Bos |
| 1976–77 | Portland | 4–2 | Philadelphia | Jack Ramsay | Bill Walton, Port |
| 1977–78 | Washington | 4–3 | Seattle | Dick Motta | Wes Unseld, Wash |
| 1978–79 | Seattle | 4–1 | Washington | Lenny Wilkens | Dennis Johnson, Sea |
| 1979–80 | LA Lakers | 4–2 | Philadelphia | Paul Westhead | Magic Johnson, LA |
| 1980–81 | Boston | 4–2 | Houston | Bill Fitch | Cedric Maxwell, Bos |
| 1981–82 | LA Lakers | 4–2 | Philadelphia | Pat Riley | Magic Johnson, LA |
| 1982–83 | Philadelphia | 4–0 | LA Lakers | Billy Cunningham | Moses Malone, Phil |
| 1983–84 | Boston | 4–3 | LA Lakers | K.C. Jones | Larry Bird, Bos |
| 1984–85 | LA Lakers | 4–2 | Boston | Pat Riley | Kareem Abdul-Jabbar, LA |
| 1985–86 | Boston | 4–2 | Houston | K.C. Jones | Larry Bird, Bos |
| 1986–87 | LA Lakers | 4–2 | Boston | Pat Riley | Magic Johnson, LA |
| 1987–88 | LA Lakers | 4–3 | Detroit | Pat Riley | James Worthy, LA |
| 1988–89 | Detroit | 4–0 | LA Lakers | Chuck Daly | Joe Dumars, Det |
| 1989–90 | Detroit | 4–1 | Portland | Chuck Daly | Isiah Thomas, Det |
| 1990–91 | Chicago | 4–1 | LA Lakers | Phil Jackson | Michael Jordan, Chi |
| 1991–92 | Chicago | 4–2 | Portland | Phil Jackson | Michael Jordan, Chi |
| 1992–93 | Chicago | 4–2 | Phoenix | Phil Jackson | Michael Jordan, Chi |
| 1993–94 | Houston | 4–3 | New York | Rudy Tomjanovich | Hakeem Olajuwon, Hou |
| 1994–95 | Houston | 4–0 | Orlando | Rudy Tomjanovich | Hakeem Olajuwon, Hou |
| 1995–96 | Chicago | 4–2 | Seattle | Phil Jackson | Michael Jordan, Chi |
| 1996–97 | Chicago | 4–2 | Utah | Phil Jackson | Michael Jordan, Chi |
| 1997–98 | Chicago | 4–2 | Utah | Phil Jackson | Michael Jordan, Chi |
| 1998–99 | San Antonio | 4–1 | New York | Gregg Popovich | Tim Duncan, SA |
| 1999–00 | LA Lakers | 4–2 | Indiana | Phil Jackson | Shaquille O'Neal, LA |
| 2000–01 | LA Lakers | 4–1 | Philadelphia | Phil Jackson | Shaquille O'Neal, LA |
| 2001–02 | LA Lakers | 4–0 | New Jersey | Phil Jackson | Shaquille O'Neal, LA |
| 2002–03 | San Antonio | 4–2 | New Jersey | Gregg Popovich | Tim Duncan, SA |
| 2003–04 | Detroit | 4–1 | LA Lakers | Larry Brown | Chauncey Billups, Det |
| 2004–05 | San Antonio | 4–3 | Detroit | Gregg Popovich | Tim Duncan, SA |
| 2005–06 | Miami | 4–2 | Dallas | Pat Riley | Dwyane Wade, Mia |
| 2006–07 | San Antonio | 4–0 | Cleveland | Gregg Popovich | Tony Parker, SA |
| 2007–08 | Boston | 4–2 | LA Lakers | Doc Rivers | Paul Pierce, Bos |
| 2008–09 | LA Lakers | 4–2 | Orlando | Phil Jackson | Kobe Bryant, LA |
| 2009–10 | LA Lakers | 4–3 | Boston | Phil Jackson | Kobe Bryant, LA |
| 2010–11 | Dallas | 4–2 | Miami | Rick Carlisle | Dirk Nowitzki, Dal |

### Regular Season Most Valuable Player: Maurice Podoloff Trophy

| Season | Player, Team | GP | Field Goals | | 3-Pt FG | | Free Throws | | Rebounds | | A | Stl | BS | Avg |
|---|---|---|---|---|---|---|---|---|---|---|---|---|---|---|
| | | | FGM | Pct | FGM | Pct | FTM | Pct | Off | Total | | | | |
| 1955–56 | Bob Pettit, StL | 72 | 646 | 42.9 | – | – | 557 | 73.6 | – | 1,164 | 189 | – | – | 25.7 |
| 1956–57 | Bob Cousy, Bos | 64 | 478 | 37.8 | – | – | 363 | 82.1 | – | 309 | 478 | – | – | 20.6 |
| 1957–58 | Bill Russell, Bos | 69 | 456 | 44.2 | – | – | 230 | 51.9 | – | 1,564 | 202 | – | – | 16.6 |
| 1958–59 | Bob Pettit, StL | 72 | 719 | 43.8 | – | – | 667 | 75.9 | – | 1,182 | 221 | – | – | 29.2 |
| 1959–60 | Wilt Chamberlain, Phil | 72 | 1,065 | 46.1 | – | – | 577 | 58.2 | – | 1,941 | 168 | – | – | 37.6 |
| 1960–61 | Bill Russell, Bos | 78 | 532 | 42.6 | – | – | 258 | 55.0 | – | 1,868 | 264 | – | – | 16.9 |
| 1961–62 | Bill Russell, Bos | 76 | 575 | 45.7 | – | – | 286 | 59.5 | – | 1,891 | 341 | – | – | 18.9 |
| 1962–63 | Bill Russell, Bos | 78 | 511 | 43.2 | – | – | 287 | 55.5 | – | 1,843 | 348 | – | – | 16.8 |
| 1963–64 | Oscar Robertson, Cin | 79 | 840 | 48.3 | – | – | 800 | 85.3 | – | 783 | 868 | – | – | 31.4 |
| 1964–65 | Bill Russell, Bos | 78 | 429 | 43.8 | – | – | 244 | 57.3 | – | 1,878 | 410 | – | – | 14.1 |
| 1965–66 | Wilt Chamberlain, Phil | 79 | 1,074 | 54.0 | – | – | 501 | 51.3 | – | 1,943 | 414 | – | – | 33.5 |
| 1966–67 | Wilt Chamberlain, Phil | 81 | 785 | 68.3 | – | – | 386 | 44.1 | – | 1,957 | 630 | – | – | 24.1 |
| 1967–68 | Wilt Chamberlain, Phil | 82 | 819 | 59.5 | – | – | 354 | 38.0 | – | 1,952 | 702 | – | – | 24.3 |
| 1968–69 | Wes Unseld, Balt | 82 | 427 | 47.6 | – | – | 277 | 60.5 | – | 1,491 | 213 | – | – | 13.8 |
| 1969–70 | Willis Reed, NY | 81 | 702 | 50.7 | – | – | 351 | 75.6 | – | 1,126 | 161 | – | – | 21.7 |
| 1970–71 | Lew Alcindor*, Mil | 82 | 1,063 | 57.7 | – | – | 470 | 69.0 | – | 1,311 | 272 | – | – | 31.7 |
| 1971–72 | Kareem Abdul-Jabbar, Mil | 81 | 1,159 | 57.4 | – | – | 504 | 68.9 | – | 1,346 | 370 | – | – | 34.8 |
| 1972–73 | Dave Cowens, Bos | 82 | 740 | 45.2 | – | – | 204 | 77.9 | – | 1,329 | 333 | – | – | 20.5 |
| 1973–74 | Kareem Abdul-Jabbar, Mil | 81 | 948 | 53.9 | – | – | 295 | 70.2 | 287 | 1,178 | 386 | 112 | 283 | 27.0 |
| 1974–75 | Bob McAdoo, Buff | 82 | 1,095 | 51.2 | – | – | 641 | 80.5 | 307 | 1,155 | 179 | 92 | 174 | 34.5 |
| 1975–76 | Kareem Abdul-Jabbar, LAL | 82 | 914 | 52.9 | – | – | 447 | 70.3 | 272 | 1,383 | 413 | 119 | 338 | 27.7 |
| 1976–77 | Kareem Abdul-Jabbar, LAL | 82 | 888 | 57.9 | – | – | 376 | 70.1 | 266 | 1,090 | 319 | 101 | 261 | 26.2 |
| 1977–78 | Bill Walton, Port | 58 | 460 | 52.2 | – | – | 177 | 72.0 | 118 | 766 | 291 | 60 | 146 | 18.9 |
| 1978–79 | Moses Malone, Hou | 82 | 716 | 54.0 | – | – | 599 | 73.9 | 587 | 1,444 | 147 | 79 | 119 | 24.8 |
| 1979–80 | Kareem Abdul-Jabbar, LAL | 82 | 835 | 60.4 | 0 | 00.0 | 364 | 76.5 | 190 | 886 | 371 | 81 | 280 | 24.8 |
| 1980–81 | Julius Erving, Phil | 82 | 794 | 52.1 | 4 | 22.2 | 422 | 78.7 | 244 | 657 | 364 | 173 | 147 | 24.6 |
| 1981–82 | Moses Malone, Hou | 81 | 945 | 51.9 | 0 | 00.0 | 630 | 76.2 | 558 | 1,188 | 142 | 76 | 125 | 31.1 |
| 1982–83 | Moses Malone, Phil | 78 | 654 | 50.1 | 0 | 00.0 | 600 | 76.1 | 445 | 1,194 | 101 | 89 | 157 | 24.5 |
| 1983–84 | Larry Bird, Bos | 79 | 758 | 49.2 | 18 | 24.7 | 374 | 88.8 | 181 | 796 | 520 | 144 | 69 | 24.2 |
| 1984–85 | Larry Bird, Bos | 80 | 918 | 52.2 | 56 | 42.7 | 403 | 88.2 | 164 | 842 | 531 | 129 | 98 | 28.7 |
| 1985–86 | Larry Bird, Bos | 82 | 796 | 49.6 | 82 | 42.3 | 441 | 89.6 | 190 | 805 | 557 | 166 | 51 | 25.8 |
| 1986–87 | Magic Johnson, LAL | 80 | 683 | 52.2 | 8 | 20.5 | 535 | 84.8 | 122 | 504 | 977 | 138 | 36 | 23.9 |
| 1987–88 | Michael Jordan, Chi | 82 | 1,069 | 53.5 | 7 | 13.2 | 723 | 84.1 | 139 | 449 | 485 | 259 | 131 | 35.0 |
| 1988–89 | Magic Johnson, LAL | 77 | 579 | 50.9 | 59 | 31.4 | 513 | 91.1 | 111 | 607 | 988 | 138 | 22 | 22.5 |
| 1989–90 | Magic Johnson, LAL | 79 | 546 | 48.0 | 106 | 38.4 | 567 | 89.0 | 128 | 522 | 907 | 132 | 34 | 22.3 |
| 1990–91 | Michael Jordan, Chi | 82 | 990 | 53.9 | 29 | 31.2 | 571 | 85.1 | 118 | 492 | 453 | 223 | 83 | 31.5 |
| 1991–92 | Michael Jordan, Chi | 80 | 943 | 51.9 | 27 | 27.0 | 491 | 83.2 | 91 | 511 | 489 | 182 | 75 | 30.1 |
| 1992–93 | Charles Barkley, Phx | 76 | 716 | 52.0 | 67 | 30.5 | 445 | 76.5 | 237 | 928 | 385 | 119 | 74 | 25.6 |
| 1993–94 | Hakeem Olajuwon, Hou | 80 | 894 | 52.8 | 8 | 42.1 | 388 | 71.6 | 229 | 955 | 287 | 128 | 297 | 27.3 |
| 1994–95 | David Robinson, SA | 81 | 788 | 53.0 | 6 | 30.0 | 656 | 77.4 | 234 | 877 | 236 | 134 | 262 | 27.6 |
| 1995–96 | Michael Jordan, Chi | 82 | 916 | 49.5 | 111 | 42.7 | 548 | 83.4 | 148 | 543 | 352 | 180 | 42 | 30.4 |
| 1996–97 | Karl Malone, Utah | 82 | 864 | 55.0 | 0 | 00.0 | 521 | 75.5 | 193 | 809 | 368 | 113 | 48 | 27.4 |
| 1997–98 | Michael Jordan, Chi | 82 | 881 | 46.5 | 30 | 23.8 | 565 | 78.4 | 130 | 475 | 283 | 141 | 45 | 28.7 |
| 1998–99 | Karl Malone, Utah | 49 | 393 | 49.3 | 0 | 00.0 | 378 | 78.8 | 107 | 463 | 201 | 62 | 28 | 23.8 |
| 1999–00 | Shaquille O'Neal, LAL | 79 | 956 | 57.4 | 0 | 00.0 | 432 | 52.4 | 336 | 1078 | 299 | 36 | 239 | 29.7 |
| 2000–01 | Allen Iverson, Phil | 71 | 762 | 42.0 | 98 | 32.0 | 585 | 81.4 | 50 | 273 | 325 | 78 | 20 | 31.1 |
| 2001–02 | Tim Duncan, SA | 82 | 764 | 50.8 | 1 | 10.0 | 560 | 79.9 | 268 | 1042 | 307 | 61 | 203 | 25.5 |
| 2002–03 | Tim Duncan, SA | 81 | 714 | 51.3 | 6 | 27.3 | 450 | 71.0 | 260 | 1045 | 316 | 55 | 237 | 23.3 |
| 2003–04 | Kevin Garnett, Minn | 82 | 804 | 49.9 | 11 | 25.6 | 368 | 79.1 | 245 | 1139 | 409 | 120 | 178 | 24.2 |
| 2004–05 | Steve Nash, Phx | 75 | 430 | 50.2 | 94 | 43.1 | 211 | 88.7 | 80 | 330 | 861 | 74 | 6 | 26.0 |
| 2005–06 | Steve Nash, Phx | 79 | 541 | 51.2 | 150 | 43.9 | 257 | 92.1 | 47 | 333 | 826 | 61 | 12 | 18.8 |
| 2006–07 | Dirk Nowitzki, Dal | 78 | 673 | 50.2 | 72 | 41.6 | 498 | 90.4 | 122 | 693 | 263 | 52 | 62 | 24.6 |
| 2007–08 | Kobe Bryant, LAL | 82 | 775 | 45.9 | 150 | 36.1 | 623 | 84.0 | 94 | 517 | 441 | 151 | 40 | 28.3 |
| 2008–09 | LeBron James, Cle | 81 | 789 | 48.9 | 132 | 34.4 | 594 | 78.0 | 106 | 613 | 587 | 137 | 93 | 28.4 |
| 2009–10 | LeBron James, Cle | 76 | 768 | 50.3 | 129 | 33.3 | 756 | 76.7 | 71 | 554 | 651 | 125 | 77 | 29.7 |
| 2010–11 | Derrick Rose, Chi | 81 | 711 | 44.5 | 128 | 33.2 | 476 | 85.8 | 81 | 330 | 623 | 85 | 51 | 25.0 |

*Alcindor changed his name to Kareem Abdul-Jabbar after the 1970–71 season.

## Coach of the Year: Arnold (Red) Auerbach Trophy

1962–63...Harry Gallatin, StL
1963–64...Alex Hannum, SF
1964–65...Red Auerbach, Bos
1965–66...Dolph Schayes, Phil
1966–67...Johnny Kerr, Chi
1967–68...Richie Guerin, StL
1968–69...Gene Shue, Balt
1969–70...Red Holzman, NY
1970–71...Dick Motta, Chi
1971–72...Bill Sharman, LA
1972–73...Tom Heinsohn, Bos
1973–74...Ray Scott, Det
1974–75...Phil Johnson, KC-Oma
1975–76...Bill Fitch, Clev
1976–77...Tom Nissalke, Hou
1977–78...Hubie Brown, Atl
1978–79...Cotton Fitzsimmons, KC

1979–80...Bill Fitch, Bos
1980–81...Jack McKinney, Ind
1981–82...Gene Shue, Wash
1982–83...Don Nelson, Mil
1983–84...Frank Layden, Utah
1984–85...Don Nelson, Mil
1985–86...Mike Fratello, Atl
1986–87...Mike Schuler, Port
1987–88...Doug Moe, Den
1988–89...Cotton Fitzsimmons, Phx
1989–90...Pat Riley, LAL
1990–91...Don Chaney, Hou
1991–92...Don Nelson, GS
1992–93...Pat Riley, NY
1993–94...Lenny Wilkens, Atl
1994–95...Del Harris, LAL
1995–96...Phil Jackson, Chi

1996–97...Pat Riley, Mia
1997–98...Larry Bird, Ind
1998–99...Mike Dunleavy, Port
1999–00...Glenn (Doc) Rivers, Orl
2000–01...Larry Brown, Phil
2001–02...Rick Carlisle, Det
2002–03...Gregg Popovich, SA
2003–04...Hubie Brown, Mem
2004–05...Mike D'Antoni, Phx
2005–06...Avery Johnson, Dal
2006–07...Sam Mitchell, Tor
2007–08...Byron Scott, NO
2008–09...Mike Brown, Cle
2009–10...Scott Brooks, OKC
2010–11...Tom Thibodeau, Chi

Note: Award named after Auerbach in 1986.

## Rookie of the Year: Eddie Gottlieb Trophy

1952–53...Don Meineke, FW
1953–54...Ray Felix, Balt
1954–55...Bob Pettit, Mil
1955–56...Maurice Stokes, Roch
1956–57...Tom Heinsohn, Bos
1957–58...Woody Sauldsberry, Phil
1958–59...Elgin Baylor, Minn
1959–60...Wilt Chamberlain, Phil
1960–61...Oscar Robertson, Cin
1961–62...Walt Bellamy, Chi
1962–63...Terry Dischinger, Chi
1963–64...Jerry Lucas, Cin
1964–65...Willis Reed, NY
1965–66...Rick Barry, SF
1966–67...Dave Bing, Det
1967–68...Earl Monroe, Balt
1968–69...Wes Unseld, Balt
1969–70...K. Abdul-Jabbar, Mil
1970–71...Dave Cowens, Bos
　　　　　Geoff Petrie, Port
1971–72...Sidney Wicks, Port

1972–73...Bob McAdoo, Buff
1973–74...Ernie DiGregorio, Buf
1974–75...Keith Wilkes, GS
1975–76...Alvan Adams, Phx
1976–77...Adrian Dantley, Buf
1977–78...Walter Davis, Phx
1978–79...Phil Ford, KC
1979–80...Larry Bird, Bos
1980–81...Darrell Griffith, Utah
1981–82...Buck Williams, NJ
1982–83...Terry Cummings, SD
1983–84...Ralph Sampson, Hou
1984–85...Michael Jordan, Chi
1985–86...Patrick Ewing, NY
1986–87...Chuck Person, Ind
1987–88...Mark Jackson, NY
1988–89...Mitch Richmond, GS
1989–90...David Robinson, SA
1990–91...Derrick Coleman, NJ
1991–92...Larry Johnson, Cha
1992–93...Shaquille O'Neal, Orl

1993–94...Chris Webber, GS
1994–95...Grant Hill, Det
　　　　　Jason Kidd, Dal
1995–96...Damon Stoudamire, Tor
1996–97...Allen Iverson, Phil
1997–98...Tim Duncan, SA
1998–99...Vince Carter, Tor
1999–00...Elton Brand, Chi
　　　　　Steve Francis, Hou
2000–01..Mike Miller, Orl
2001–02..Pau Gasol, Mem
2002–03..Amare Stoudemire, Phx
2003–04..LeBron James, Clev
2004–05..Emeka Okafor, Cha
2005–06..Chris Paul, NO
2006–07..Brandon Roy, Port
2007–08..Kevin Durant, Sea
2008–09..Derrick Rose, Chi
2009–10..Tyreke Evans, Sac
2010–11..Blake Griffin, LAC

## Defensive Player of the Year

1982–83...Sidney Moncrief, Mil
1983–84...Sidney Moncrief, Mil
1984–85...Mark Eaton, Utah
1985–86...Alvin Robertson, SA
1986–87...Michael Cooper, LAL
1987–88...Michael Jordan, Chi
1988–89...Mark Eaton, Utah
1989–90...Dennis Rodman, Det
1990–91...Dennis Rodman, Det
1991–92...David Robinson, SA

1992–93...Hakeem Olajuwon, Hou
1993–94...Hakeem Olajuwon, Hou
1994–95...Dikembe Mutombo, Den
1995–96...Gary Payton, Sea
1996–97...Dikembe Mutombo, Atl
1997–98...Dikembe Mutombo, Atl
1998–99...Alonzo Mourning, Mia
1999–00...Alonzo Mourning, Mia
2000–01...Dikembe Mutombo, Phil/Atl
2001–02...Ben Wallace, Det

2002–03...Ben Wallace, Det
2003–04...Ron Artest, Ind
2004–05...Ben Wallace, Det
2005–06...Ben Wallace, Det
2006–07...Marcus Camby, Den
2007–08...Kevin Garnett, Bos
2008–09...Dwight Howard, Orl
2009–10...Dwight Howard, Orl
2010–11...Dwight Howard, Orl

## Sixth Man Award

1982–83...Bobby Jones, Phil
1983–84...Kevin McHale, Bos
1984–85...Kevin McHale, Bos
1985–86...Bill Walton, Bos
1986–87...Ricky Pierce, Mil
1987–88...Roy Tarpley, Dal
1988–89...Eddie Johnson, Phx
1989–90...Ricky Pierce, Mil
1990–91...Detlef Schrempf, Ind
1991–92...Detlef Schrempf, Ind

1992–93...Cliff Robinson, Port
1993–94...Dell Curry, Cha
1994–95...Anthony Mason, NY
1995–96...Tony Kukoc, Chi
1996–97...John Starks, NY
1997–98...Danny Manning, Phx
1998–99...Darrell Armstrong, Orl
1999–00...Rodney Rogers, Phx
2000–01...Aaron McKie, Phil
2001–02...Corliss Williamson, Det

2002–03...Bobby Jackson, Sac
2003–04...Antawn Jamison, Dal
2004–05...Ben Gordon, Chi
2005–06...Mike Miller, Mem
2006–07...Leandro Barbosa, Phx
2007–08...Manu Ginobli, SA
2008–09...Jason Terry, Dal
2009–10...Jamal Crawford, Atl
2010–11...Lamar Odom, LAL

### J. Walter Kennedy Citizenship Award

| | | |
|---|---|---|
| 1974–75...Wes Unseld, Wash | 1986–87...Isiah Thomas, Det | 1998–99...Brian Grant, Port |
| 1975–76...Slick Watts, Sea | 1987–88...Alex English, Den | 1999–00...Vlade Divac, Sac |
| 1976–77...Dave Bing, Wash | 1988–89...Thurl Bailey, Utah | 2000–01...Dikembe Mutombo, Phi |
| 1977–78...Bob Lanier, Det | 1989–90...Glenn (Doc) Rivers, Atl | 2001–02...Alonzo Mourning, Mia |
| 1978–79...Calvin Murphy, Hou | 1990–91...Kevin Johnson, Phx | 2002–03...David Robinson, SA |
| 1979–80...Austin Carr, Cle | 1991–92...Magic Johnson, LAL | 2003–04...Reggie Miller, Ind |
| 1980–81...Mike Glenn, NY | 1992–93...Terry Porter, Port | 2004–05...Eric Snow, Clev |
| 1981–82...Kent Benson, Det | 1993–94...Joe Dumars, Det | 2005–06...Kevin Garnett, Min |
| 1982–83...Julius Erving, Phi | 1994–95...Joe O'Toole, Atl | 2006–07...Luol Deng, Chi |
| 1983–84...Frank Layden, Utah | 1995–96...Chris Dudley, Port | 2007–08...Grant Hill, Phx |
| 1984–85...Dan Issel, Den | 1996–97...P.J. Brown, Mia | 2008–09...Dikembe Mutombo, Hou |
| 1985–86...Michael Cooper, LAL | 1997–98...Steve Smith, Atl | 2009–10...Samuel Dalembert, Phi |
| Rory Sparrow, NY | | 2010–11...Ron Artest, LAL |

### Most Improved Player

| | | |
|---|---|---|
| 1985–86...Alvin Robertson, SA | 1994–95...Dana Barros, Phil | 2003–04...Zach Randolph, Port |
| 1986–87...Dale Ellis, Sea | 1995–96.....Gheorghe Muresan, Wash | 2004–05...Bobby Simmons, LAC |
| 1987–88...Kevin Duckworth, Port | 1996–97...Isaac Austin, Mia | 2005–06...Boris Diaw, Phx |
| 1988–89...Kevin Johnson, Phx | 1997–98...Alan Henderson, Atl | 2006–07...Monta Ellis, GS |
| 1989–90...Rony Seikaly, Mia | 1998–99...Darrell Armstrong, Orl | 2007–08...Hedo Turkoglu, Orl |
| 1990–91...Scott Skiles, Orl | 1999–00...Jalen Rose, Ind | 2008–09...Danny Granger, Ind |
| 1991–92...Pervis Ellison, Wash | 2000–01...Tracy McGrady, Orl | 2009–10...Aaron Brooks, Hou |
| 1992–93...Mahmoud Abdul-Rauf, Den | 2001–02...Jermaine O'Neal, Ind | 2010–11...Kevin Love, Min |
| 1993–94...Don MacLean, Wash | 2002–03...Gilbert Arenas, GS | |

### Executive of the Year

| | | |
|---|---|---|
| 1972–73...Joe Axelson, KC-Oma | 1986–87...Stan Kasten, Atl | 2000–01...Geoff Petrie, Sac |
| 1973–74...Eddie Donovan, Buf | 1987–88...Jerry Krause, Chi | 2001–02...Rod Thorn, NJ |
| 1974–75...Dick Vertlieb, GS | 1988–89...Jerry Colangelo, Phx | 2002–03...Joe Dumars, Det |
| 1975–76...Jerry Colangelo, Phx | 1989–90...Bob Bass, SA | 2003–04...Jerry West, Mem |
| 1976–77...Ray Patterson, Hou | 1990–91...Bucky Buckwalter, Port | 2004–05...Bryan Colangelo, Phx |
| 1977–78...Angelo Drossos, SA | 1991–92...Wayne Embry, Clev | 2005–06...Elgin Baylor, LAC |
| 1978–79...Bob Ferry, Wash | 1992–93...Jerry Colangelo, Phx | 2006–07...Bryan Colangelo, Tor |
| 1979–80...Red Auerbach, Bos | 1993–94...Bob Whitsitt, Sea | 2007–08...Danny Ainge, Bos |
| 1980–81...Jerry Colangelo, Phx | 1994–95...Jerry West, LAL | 2008–09...Mark Warkentien, Den |
| 1981–82...Bob Ferry, Wash | 1995–96...Jerry Krause, Chi | 2009–10...John Hammond, Mil |
| 1982–83...Zollie Volchok, Sea | 1996–97...Bob Bass, Cha | 2010–11...Gar Forman, Chi |
| 1983–84...Frank Layden, Utah | 1997–98...Wayne Embry, Clev | Pat Riley, Mia |
| 1984–85...Vince Boryla, Den | 1998–99...Geoff Petrie, Sac | |
| 1985–86...Stan Kasten, Atl | 1999–00...John Gabriel, Orl | |

## NBA Alltime Individual Leaders

### Scoring

**MOST POINTS, CAREER**

| | Pts | Avg |
|---|---|---|
| Kareem Abdul-Jabbar | 38,387 | 24.6 |
| Karl Malone | 36,928 | 25.0 |
| Michael Jordan | 32,292 | 30.1 |
| Wilt Chamberlain | 31,419 | 30.1 |
| *Shaquille O'Neal | 28,596 | 23.7 |
| *Kobe Bryant | 27,868 | 25.3 |
| Moses Malone | 27,409 | 20.6 |
| Elvin Hayes | 27,313 | 21.0 |
| Hakeem Olajuwon | 26,946 | 21.8 |
| Oscar Robertson | 26,710 | 25.7 |

*Active in 2010–11.

**HIGHEST SCORING AVERAGE, CAREER**

| | | |
|---|---|---|
| Michael Jordan | 30.1 | 1,072 games |
| Wilt Chamberlain | 30.1 | 1,045 games |
| *LeBron James | 27.7 | 627 games |
| Elgin Baylor | 27.4 | 846 games |
| Jerry West | 27.0 | 932 games |
| Allen Iverson | 26.7 | 914 games |
| Bob Pettit | 26.4 | 792 games |
| George Gervin | 26.2 | 791 games |
| Oscar Robertson | 25.7 | 1,040 games |
| *Dwyane Wade | 25.4 | 547 games |

*Acitve in 2010–11. Note: Minimum 400 games.

**MOST POINTS, SEASON**

| | | |
|---|---|---|
| Wilt Chamberlain, Phil | 4,029 | 1961–62 |
| Wilt Chamberlain, SF | 3,586 | 1962–63 |
| Michael Jordan, Chi | 3,041 | 1986–87 |
| Wilt Chamberlain, Phil | 3,033 | 1960–61 |
| Wilt Chamberlain, SF | 2,948 | 1963–64 |
| Michael Jordan, Chi | 2,868 | 1987–88 |
| Kobe Bryant, LA | 2,832 | 2005–06 |
| Bob McAdoo, Buff | 2,831 | 1974–75 |
| Kareem Abdul-Jabbar, Mil | 2,822 | 1971–72 |
| Rick Barry, SF | 2,775 | 1966–67 |
| Michael Jordan, Chi | 2,753 | 1989–90 |

**HIGHEST SCORING AVERAGE, SEASON**

| | | |
|---|---|---|
| Wilt Chamberlain, Phil | 50.4 | 1961–62 |
| Wilt Chamberlain, SF | 44.8 | 1962–63 |
| Wilt Chamberlain, Phil | 38.4 | 1960–61 |
| Wilt Chamberlain, Phil | 37.6 | 1959–60 |
| Michael Jordan, Chi | 37.1 | 1986–87 |
| Wilt Chamberlain, SF | 36.9 | 1963–64 |
| Rick Barry, SF | 35.6 | 1966–67 |
| Kobe Bryant, LA | 35.4 | 2005–06 |
| Michael Jordan, Chi | 35.0 | 1987–88 |
| Kareem Abdul Jabbar, LA | 34.8 | 1971–72 |
| Elgin Baylor, LA | 34.8 | 1960–61 |

Note: Minimum 70 games.

## Scoring (Cont.)

### MOST POINTS, SINGLE GAME

| | Player, Team | Opp | Date |
|---|---|---|---|
| 100 | Wilt Chamberlain, Phil | NY | 3/2/62 |
| 81 | Kobe Bryant, LAL | Tor | 1/22/06 |
| 78 | Wilt Chamberlain, Phil | LAL | 12/8/61 |
| 73 | Wilt Chamberlain, Phil | Chi | 1/13/62 |
| 73 | Wilt Chamberlain, SF | NY | 11/16/62 |
| 73 | David Thompson, Den | Det | 4/9/78 |
| 72 | Wilt Chamberlain, SF | LAL | 11/3/62 |
| 71 | David Robinson, SA | LAC | 4/24/94 |
| 71 | Elgin Baylor, LAL | NY | 11/15/60 |
| 70 | Wilt Chamberlain, SF | Syr | 3/10/63 |

## Field-Goal Percentage

Highest FG Percentage, Career: .599—Artis Gilmore

Highest FG Percentage, Season: .727—Wilt Chamberlain, LA Lakers, 1972–73 (426/586)

## Free Throws

### HIGHEST FREE-THROW PERCENTAGE, CAREER

| | |
|---|---|
| Mark Price | .904 |
| *Steve Nash | .904 |
| Rick Barry | .900 |
| *Peja Stojakovic | .895 |
| *Chauncey Billups | .894 |
| *Ray Allen | .893 |

Note: Minimum 1200 free throws made. *Active 2010–11.

### HIGHEST FREE-THROW PERCENTAGE, SEASON

| | | |
|---|---|---|
| Jose Calderon, Tor | .981 | 2008–09 |
| Calvin Murphy, Hou | .958 | 1980–81 |
| Mahmoud Abdul-Rauf, Den | .956 | 1993–94 |
| Ray Allen, Bos | .952 | 2008–09 |
| Jeff Hornacek, Utah | .950 | 1999–00 |

### MOST FREE THROWS MADE, CAREER

| | No. | Yrs | Pct |
|---|---|---|---|
| Karl Malone | 9,787 | 19 | .742 |
| Moses Malone | 8,531 | 19 | .769 |
| Oscar Robertson | 7,694 | 14 | .838 |
| Michael Jordan | 7,327 | 15 | .835 |
| Jerry West | 7,160 | 14 | .814 |

## Three-Point Field Goals

Most Three-Point Field-Goals, Career: 2,612—Ray Allen

Highest Three-Point Field-Goal Percentage, Career: .454—Steve Kerr

Most Three-Point Field Goals, Season: 269—Ray Allen, Sea, 2005–06

Highest Three-Point Field-Goal Percentage, Season: .536—Kyle Korver, Utah, 2009–10

Most Three-Point Field Goals, Game: 12—Kobe Bryant, LA Lakers vs Seattle, 1/7/03; Donyell Marshall, Toronto vs. Philadelphia, 3/13/05

Note: First season of three-point field goal: 1979–80. *Active 2010–11.

## Steals

Most Steals, Career: 3,265—John Stockton

Most Steals, Season: 301—Alvin Robertson, San Antonio, 1985–86

Most Steals, Game: 11—Kendall Gill, New Jersey vs Miami, 4/3/99; Larry Kenon, San Antonio vs Kansas City, 12/26/76

## Rebounds

### MOST REBOUNDS, CAREER

| | No. | Yrs | Avg |
|---|---|---|---|
| Wilt Chamberlain | 23,924 | 14 | 22.9 |
| Bill Russell | 21,620 | 13 | 22.5 |
| Kareem Abdul-Jabbar | 17,440 | 20 | 11.2 |
| Elvin Hayes | 16,279 | 16 | 12.5 |
| Moses Malone | 16,212 | 19 | 12.2 |
| Karl Malone | 14,968 | 19 | 10.1 |
| Robert Parish | 14,715 | 21 | 9.1 |
| Nate Thurmond | 14,464 | 14 | 15.0 |
| Walt Bellamy | 14,241 | 14 | 13.7 |
| Wes Unseld | 13,769 | 13 | 14.0 |

### MOST REBOUNDS, SEASON

| | No. | |
|---|---|---|
| Wilt Chamberlain, Phil | 2,149 | 1960–61 |
| Wilt Chamberlain, Phil | 2,052 | 1961–62 |
| Wilt Chamberlain, Phil | 1,957 | 1966–67 |
| Wilt Chamberlain, Phil | 1,952 | 1967–68 |
| Wilt Chamberlain, SF | 1,946 | 1962–63 |
| Wilt Chamberlain, Phil | 1,943 | 1965–66 |
| Wilt Chamberlain, Phil | 1,941 | 1959–60 |
| Bill Russell, Bos | 1,930 | 1963–64 |
| Bill Russell, Bos | 1,878 | 1964–65 |
| Bill Russell, Bos | 1,868 | 1960–61 |

### MOST REBOUNDS, GAME

| | Player, Team | Opp | Date |
|---|---|---|---|
| 55 | Wilt Chamberlain, Phil | Bos | 11/24/60 |
| 51 | Bill Russell, Bos | Syr | 02/05/60 |
| 49 | Bill Russell, Bos | Phil | 11/16/57 |
| 49 | Bill Russell, Bos | Det | 03/11/65 |
| 45 | Wilt Chamberlain, Phil | Syr | 02/06/60 |
| 45 | Wilt Chamberlain, Phil | LA | 01/21/61 |

## Assists

### MOST ASSISTS, CAREER

| | |
|---|---|
| John Stockton | 15,806 |
| *Jason Kidd | 11,578 |
| Mark Jackson | 10,334 |
| Magic Johnson | 10,141 |
| Oscar Robertson | 9,887 |

*Active in 2010–11.

### MOST ASSISTS, SEASON

| | | |
|---|---|---|
| John Stockton, Utah | 1,164 | 1990–91 |
| John Stockton, Utah | 1,134 | 1989–90 |
| John Stockton, Utah | 1,128 | 1987–88 |
| John Stockton, Utah | 1,126 | 1991–92 |
| Isiah Thomas, Det | 1,123 | 1984–85 |

**MOST ASSISTS, GAME:** 30—Scott Skiles, Orlando vs Denver, 12/30/90

## Blocked Shots

### MOST BLOCKED SHOTS, CAREER

| | |
|---|---|
| Hakeem Olajuwon | 3,830 |
| Dikembe Mutombo | 3,289 |
| Kareem Abdul-Jabbar | 3,189 |
| Mark Eaton | 3,064 |
| David Robinson | 2,954 |

### MOST BLOCKED SHOTS, SEASON

| | | |
|---|---|---|
| Mark Eaton, Utah | 456 | 1984–85 |
| Manute Bol, Wash | 397 | 1985–86 |
| Elmore Smith, LAL | 393 | 1973–74 |
| Hakeem Olajuown, Hou | 376 | 1989–90 |
| Mark Eaton, Utah | 369 | 1985–86 |

**MOST BLOCKED SHOTS, GAME:** 17—Elmore Smith, LA Lakers vs Portland, 10/28/73

## Scoring

### MOST POINTS, CAREER

| | Pts | App. | Avg |
|---|---|---|---|
| Michael Jordan | 5,987 | 13 | 33.4 |
| Kareem Abdul-Jabbar | 5,762 | 18 | 24.3 |
| *Kobe Bryant | 5,280 | 14 | 25.4 |
| *Shaquille O'Neal | 5,250 | 17 | 24.3 |
| Karl Malone | 4,761 | 19 | 24.7 |
| Jerry West | 4,457 | 13 | 29.1 |
| *Tim Duncan | 3,990 | 13 | 22.7 |
| Larry Bird | 3,897 | 12 | 23.8 |
| John Havlicek | 3,776 | 13 | 22.0 |
| Hakeem Olajuwon | 3,755 | 15 | 25.9 |
| Magic Johnson | 3,701 | 13 | 19.5 |
| Scottie Pippen | 3,642 | 16 | 17.5 |
| Elgin Baylor | 3,623 | 12 | 27.0 |
| Wilt Chamberlain | 3,607 | 13 | 22.5 |
| *Dirk Nowitzki | 3,214 | 11 | 25.9 |

*Active 2010–11.

### †HIGHEST SCORING AVERAGE, CAREER

| | Avg | Games |
|---|---|---|
| Michael Jordan | 33.4 | 179 |
| Allen Iverson | 29.7 | 71 |
| Jerry West | 29.1 | 153 |
| *Tracy McGrady | 28.5 | 38 |
| *LeBron James | 28.0 | 92 |
| Elgin Baylor | 27.0 | 134 |
| George Gervin | 27.0 | 59 |
| *Dirk Nowitzki | 25.9 | 124 |
| Hakeem Olajuwon | 25.9 | 145 |
| *Dwyane Wade | 25.9 | 87 |
| Bob Pettit | 25.5 | 88 |
| Dominique Wilkins | 25.4 | 55 |
| *Kobe Bryant | 25.4 | 208 |
| Rick Barry | 24.8 | 74 |
| Karl Malone | 24.7 | 193 |

†Minimum of 25 games. *Active 2010–11.

### MOST POINTS, GAME

| | Player, Team | Opp | Date |
|---|---|---|---|
| †63 | Michael Jordan, Chi | Bos | 4/20/86 |
| 61 | Elgin Baylor, LAL | Bos | 4/14/62 |
| 56 | Wilt Chamberlain, Phil | Syr | 3/22/62 |
| 56 | Michael Jordan, Chi | Mia | 4/29/92 |
| 56 | Charles Barkley, Phx | GS | 5/4/94 |
| 55 | Rick Barry, SF | Phil | 4/18/67 |
| 55 | Michael Jordan, Chi | Cle | 5/1/88 |
| 55 | Michael Jordan, Chi | Phx | 6/16/93 |
| 55 | Michael Jordan, Chi | Was | 4/27/97 |
| 55 | Allen Iverson, Phi | NO | 4/20/03 |

†Double overtime game.

## Rebounds

### MOST REBOUNDS, CAREER

| | No. | App. | Avg |
|---|---|---|---|
| Bill Russell | 4,104 | 13 | 24.9 |
| Wilt Chamberlain | 3,913 | 13 | 24.5 |
| *Shaquille O'Neal | 2,508 | 17 | 11.6 |
| Kareem Abdul-Jabbar | 2,481 | 18 | 10.5 |
| *Tim Duncan | 2,177 | 13 | 12.4 |
| Karl Malone | 2,062 | 19 | 10.7 |

*Active 2010–11.

### MOST REBOUNDS, GAME

| | Player, Team | Opp | Date |
|---|---|---|---|
| 41 | Wilt Chamberlain, Phil | Bos | 4/5/67 |
| 40 | Bill Russell, Bos | Phil | 3/23/58 |
| 40 | Bill Russell, Bos | StL | 3/29/60 |
| †40 | Bill Russell, Bos | LA | 4/18/62 |

†Overtime game. Three tied at 39.

## Assists

### MOST ASSISTS, CAREER

| | No. | Games |
|---|---|---|
| Magic Johnson | 2,346 | 190 |
| John Stockton | 1,839 | 182 |
| *Jason Kidd | 1,215 | 142 |
| Larry Bird | 1,062 | 164 |
| *Steve Nash | 1,052 | 118 |
| Scottie Pippen | 1,048 | 208 |
| Michael Jordan | 1,022 | 179 |

*Active 2010–11.

### MOST ASSISTS, GAME

| | Player, Team | Opp | Date |
|---|---|---|---|
| 24 | Magic Johnson, LAL | Phx | 5/15/84 |
| 24 | John Stockton, Utah | LAL | 5/17/88 |
| 23 | Magic Johnson, LAL | Port | 5/3/85 |
| 23 | John Stockton, Utah | Port | 4/25/96 |
| 23 | Steve Nash, Phx | LAL | 4/24/07 |

## Games played

| | |
|---|---|
| Robert Horry | 244 |
| Kareem Abdul-Jabbar | 237 |
| *Shaquille O'Neal | 216 |
| *Derek Fisher | 209 |
| *Kobe Bryant | 208 |
| Scottie Pippen | 208 |
| Danny Ainge | 193 |
| Karl Malone | 193 |
| Magic Johnson | 190 |
| Robert Parish | 184 |

## Appearances

| | | | |
|---|---|---|---|
| John Stockton | 19 | Dolph Schayes | 15 |
| Karl Malone | 19 | Clyde Drexler | 15 |
| Kareem Abdul-Jabbar | 18 | Jerome Kersey | 15 |
| *Shaquille O'Neal | 17 | Hakeem Olajuwon | 15 |
| Robert Horry | 16 | Tree Rollins | 15 |
| Robert Parish | 16 | | |
| Scottie Pippen | 16 | | |
| Terry Porter | 16 | | |

*Active 2010–11.

## Scoring

| Season | Player | Pts | | Season | Player | Avg |
|---|---|---|---|---|---|---|
| 1946–47 | Joe Fulks, Phil | 1389 | | 1979–80 | George Gervin, SA | 33.1 |
| 1947–48 | Max Zaslofsky, Chi | 1007 | | 1980–81 | Adrian Dantley, Utah | 30.7 |
| 1948–49 | George Mikan, Min | 1698 | | 1981–82 | George Gervin, SA | 32.3 |
| 1949–50 | George Mikan, Min | 1865 | | 1982–83 | Alex English, Den | 28.4 |
| 1950–51 | George Mikan, Min | 1932 | | 1983–84 | Adrian Dantley, Utah | 30.6 |
| 1951–52 | Paul Arizin, Phil | 1674 | | 1984–85 | Bernard King, NY | 32.9 |
| 1952–53 | Neil Johnston, Phil | 1564 | | 1985–86 | Dominique Wilkins, Atl | 30.3 |
| 1953–54 | Neil Johnston, Phil | 1759 | | 1986–87 | Michael Jordan, Chi | 37.1 |
| 1954–55 | Neil Johnston, Phil | 1631 | | 1987–88 | Michael Jordan, Chi | 35.0 |
| 1955–56 | Bob Pettit, StL | 1849 | | 1988–89 | Michael Jordan, Chi | 32.5 |
| 1956–57 | Paul Arizin, Phil | 1817 | | 1989–90 | Michael Jordan, Chi | 33.6 |
| 1957–58 | George Yardley, Det | 2001 | | 1990–91 | Michael Jordan, Chi | 31.5 |
| 1958–59 | Bob Pettit, StL | 2105 | | 1991–92 | Michael Jordan, Chi | 30.1 |
| 1959–60 | Wilt Chamberlain, Phil | 2707 | | 1992–93 | Michael Jordan, Chi | 32.6 |
| 1960–61 | Wilt Chamberlain, Phil | 3033 | | 1993–94 | David Robinson, SA | 29.8 |
| 1961–62 | Wilt Chamberlain, Phil | 4029 | | 1994–95 | Shaquille O'Neal, Orl | 29.3 |
| 1962–63 | Wilt Chamberlain, SF | 3586 | | 1995–96 | Michael Jordan, Chi | 30.4 |
| 1963–64 | Wilt Chamberlain, SF | 2948 | | 1996–97 | Michael Jordan, Chi | 29.6 |
| 1964–65 | Wilt Chamberlain, SF-Phil | 2534 | | 1997–98 | Michael Jordan, Chi | 28.7 |
| 1965–66 | Wilt Chamberlain, Phil | 2649 | | 1998–99 | Allen Iverson, Phil | 26.8 |
| 1966–67 | Rick Barry, SF | 2775 | | 1999–00 | Shaquille O'Neal, LAL | 29.7 |
| 1967–68 | Dave Bing, Det | 2142 | | 2000–01 | Allen Iverson, Phil | 31.1 |
| 1968–69 | Elvin Hayes, SD | 2327 | | 2001–02 | Allen Iverson, Phil | 31.4 |
| 1969–70 | Jerry West, LAL | *31.2 | | 2002–03 | Tracy McGrady, Orl | 32.1 |
| 1970–71 | Kareem Abdul-Jabbar, Mil | 31.7 | | 2003–04 | Tracy McGrady, Orl | 28.0 |
| 1971–72 | Kareem Abdul-Jabbar, Mil | 34.8 | | 2004–05 | Allen Iverson, Phil | 30.7 |
| 1972–73 | Nate Archibald, KC-Oma | 34.0 | | 2005–06 | Kobe Bryant, LAL | 35.4 |
| 1973–74 | Bob McAdoo, Buff | 30.6 | | 2006–07 | Kobe Bryant, LAL | 31.6 |
| 1974–75 | Bob McAdoo, Buff | 34.5 | | 2007–08 | LeBron James, Cle | 30.0 |
| 1975–76 | Bob McAdoo, Buff | 31.1 | | 2008–09 | Dwyane Wade, Mia | 30.2 |
| 1976–77 | Pete Maravich, NO | 31.1 | | 2009–10 | Kevin Durant, OKC | 30.1 |
| 1977–78 | George Gervin, SA | 27.2 | | 2010–11 | Kevin Durant, OKC | 27.7 |
| 1978–79 | George Gervin, SA | 29.6 | | | | |

*Based on per game average since 1969–70.

## Rebounding

| Season | Player | No. | | Season | Player | Avg |
|---|---|---|---|---|---|---|
| 1950–51 | Dolph Schayes, Syr | 1080 | | 1981–82 | Moses Malone, Hou | 14.7 |
| 1951–52 | Larry Foust, FW | 880 | | 1982–83 | Moses Malone, Phil | 15.3 |
| | Mel Hutchins, Mil | 880 | | 1983–84 | Moses Malone, Phil | 13.4 |
| 1952–53 | George Mikan, Min | 1007 | | 1984–85 | Moses Malone, Phil | 13.1 |
| 1953–54 | Harry Gallatin, NY | 1098 | | 1985–86 | Bill Laimbeer, Det | 13.1 |
| 1954–55 | Neil Johnston, Phil | 1085 | | 1986–87 | Charles Barkley, Phil | 14.6 |
| 1955–56 | Bob Pettit, StL | 1164 | | 1987–88 | Michael Cage, LAC | 13.0 |
| 1956–57 | Maurice Stokes, Roch | 1256 | | 1988–89 | Hakeem Olajuwon, Hou | 13.5 |
| 1957–58 | Bill Russell, Bos | 1564 | | 1989–90 | Hakeem Olajuwon, Hou | 14.0 |
| 1958–59 | Bill Russell, Bos | 1612 | | 1990–91 | David Robinson, SA | 13.0 |
| 1959–60 | Wilt Chamberlain, Phil | 1941 | | 1991–92 | Dennis Rodman, Det | 18.7 |
| 1960–61 | Wilt Chamberlain, Phil | 2149 | | 1992–93 | Dennis Rodman, Det | 18.3 |
| 1961–62 | Wilt Chamberlain, Phil | 2052 | | 1993–94 | Dennis Rodman, SA | 17.3 |
| 1962–63 | Wilt Chamberlain, SF | 1946 | | 1994–95 | Dennis Rodman, SA | 16.8 |
| 1963–64 | Bill Russell, Bos | 1930 | | 1995–96 | Dennis Rodman, Chi | 14.9 |
| 1964–65 | Bill Russell, Bos | 1878 | | 1996–97 | Dennis Rodman, Chi | 16.1 |
| 1965–66 | Wilt Chamberlain, Phil | 1943 | | 1997–98 | Dennis Rodman, Chi | 15.0 |
| 1966–67 | Wilt Chamberlain, Phil | 1957 | | 1998–99 | Chris Webber, Sac | 13.0 |
| 1967–68 | Wilt Chamberlain, Phil | 1952 | | 1999–00 | Dikembe Mutombo, Atl | 14.1 |
| 1968–69 | Wilt Chamberlain, LAL | 1712 | | 2000–01 | Dikembe Mutombo, Atl | 13.5 |
| 1969–70 | Elvin Hayes, SD | *16.9 | | 2001–02 | Ben Wallace, Det | 13.0 |
| 1970–71 | Wilt Chamberlain, LAL | 18.2 | | 2002–03 | Ben Wallace, Det | 15.4 |
| 1971–72 | Wilt Chamberlain, LAL | 19.2 | | 2003–04 | Kevin Garnett, Min | 13.9 |
| 1972–73 | Wilt Chamberlain, LAL | 18.6 | | 2004–05 | Kevin Garnett, Min | 13.5 |
| 1973–74 | Elvin Hayes, Capital (Wash.) | 18.1 | | 2005–06 | Kevin Garnett, Min | 12.7 |
| 1974–75 | Wes Unseld, Wash | 14.8 | | 2006–07 | Kevin Garnett, Min | 12.8 |
| 1975–76 | Kareem Abdul-Jabbar, LAL | 16.9 | | 2007–08 | Dwight Howard, Orl | 14.2 |
| 1976–77 | Bill Walton, Port | 14.4 | | 2008–09 | Dwight Howard, Orl | 13.8 |
| 1977–78 | Len Robinson, NO | 15.7 | | 2009–10 | Dwight Howard, Orl | 12.7 |
| 1978–79 | Moses Malone, Hou | 17.6 | | 2010–11 | Kevin Love, Min | 15.2 |
| 1979–80 | Swen Nater, SD | 15.0 | | | | |
| 1980–81 | Moses Malone, Hou | 14.8 | | | | |

*Based on per game average since 1969–70.

## Assists

| | | |
|---|---|---|
| 1946–47 | Ernie Calverly, Prov | 202 |
| 1947–48 | Howie Dallmar, Phil | 120 |
| 1948–49 | Bob Davies, Roch | 321 |
| 1949–50 | Dick McGuire, NY | 386 |
| 1950–51 | Andy Phillip, Phil | 414 |
| 1951–52 | Andy Phillip, Phil | 539 |
| 1952–53 | Bob Cousy, Bos | 547 |
| 1953–54 | Bob Cousy, Bos | 518 |
| 1954–55 | Bob Cousy, Bos | 557 |
| 1955–56 | Bob Cousy, Bos | 642 |
| 1956–57 | Bob Cousy, Bos | 478 |
| 1957–58 | Bob Cousy, Bos | 463 |
| 1958–59 | Bob Cousy, Bos | 557 |
| 1959–60 | Bob Cousy, Bos | 715 |
| 1960–61 | Oscar Robertson, Cin | 690 |
| 1961–62 | Oscar Robertson, Cin | 899 |
| 1962–63 | Guy Rodgers, SF | 825 |
| 1963–64 | Oscar Robertson, Cin | 868 |
| 1964–65 | Oscar Robertson, Cin | 861 |
| 1965–66 | Oscar Robertson, Cin | 847 |
| 1966–67 | Guy Rodgers, Chi | 908 |
| 1967–68 | Wilt Chamberlain, Phil | 702 |
| 1968–69 | Oscar Robertson, Cin | 772 |
| 1969–70 | Lenny Wilkens, Sea | *9.1 |
| 1970–71 | Norm Van Lier, Cin | 10.1 |
| 1971–72 | Jerry West, LAL | 9.7 |
| 1972–73 | Nate Archibald, KC-Oma | 11.4 |
| 1973–74 | Ernie DiGregorio, Buf | 8.2 |
| 1974–75 | Kevin Porter, Wash | 8.0 |
| 1975–76 | Don Watts, Sea | 8.1 |
| 1976–77 | Don Buse, Ind | 8.5 |
| 1977–78 | Kevin Porter, NJ-Det | 10.2 |
| 1978–79 | Kevin Porter, Det | 13.4 |
| 1979–80 | Micheal Ray Richardson, NY | 10.1 |
| 1980–81 | Kevin Porter, Wash | 9.1 |
| 1981–82 | Johnny Moore, SA | 9.6 |
| 1982–83 | Magic Johnson, LAL | 10.5 |
| 1983–84 | Magic Johnson, LAL | 13.1 |
| 1984–85 | Isiah Thomas, Det | 13.9 |
| 1985–86 | Magic Johnson, LAL | 12.6 |
| 1986–87 | Magic Johnson, LAL | 12.2 |
| 1987–88 | John Stockton, Utah | 13.8 |
| 1988–89 | John Stockton, Utah | 13.6 |
| 1989–90 | John Stockton, Utah | 14.5 |
| 1990–91 | John Stockton, Utah | 14.2 |
| 1991–92 | John Stockton, Utah | 13.7 |
| 1992–93 | John Stockton, Utah | 12.0 |
| 1993–94 | John Stockton, Utah | 12.6 |
| 1994–95 | John Stockton, Utah | 12.3 |
| 1995–96 | John Stockton, Utah | 11.2 |
| 1996–97 | Mark Jackson, Ind | 11.4 |
| 1997–98 | Rod Strickland, Wash | 10.5 |
| 1998–99 | Jason Kidd, Phx | 10.8 |
| 1999–00 | Jason Kidd, Phx | 10.1 |
| 2000–01 | Jason Kidd, Phx | 9.8 |
| 2001–02 | Andre Miller, Cle | 10.9 |
| 2002–03 | Jason Kidd, NJ | 8.9 |
| 2003–04 | Jason Kidd, NJ | 9.2 |
| 2004–05 | Steve Nash, Phx | 11.5 |
| 2005–06 | Steve Nash, Phx | 10.5 |
| 2006–07 | Steve Nash, Phx | 11.6 |
| 2007–08 | Chris Paul, NO | 11.6 |
| 2008–09 | Chris Paul, NO | 11.0 |
| 2009–10 | Steve Nash, Phx | 11.0 |
| 2010–11 | Steve Nash, Phx | 11.4 |

*Based on per game average since 1969–70.

## Free-Throw Percentage

| | | |
|---|---|---|
| 1946–47 | Fred Scolari, Wash | 81.1 |
| 1947–48 | Bob Feerick, Wash | 78.8 |
| 1948–49 | Bob Feerick, Wash | 85.9 |
| 1949–50 | Max Zaslofsky, Chi | 84.3 |
| 1950–51 | Joe Fulks, Phil | 85.5 |
| 1951–52 | Bob Wanzer, Roch | 90.4 |
| 1952–53 | Bill Sharman, Bos | 85.0 |
| 1953–54 | Bill Sharman, Bos | 84.4 |
| 1954–55 | Bill Sharman, Bos | 89.7 |
| 1955–56 | Bill Sharman, Bos | 86.7 |
| 1956–57 | Bill Sharman, Bos | 90.5 |
| 1957–58 | Dolph Schayes, Syr | 90.4 |
| 1958–59 | Bill Sharman, Bos | 93.2 |
| 1959–60 | Dolph Schayes, Syr | 89.3 |
| 1960–61 | Bill Sharman, Bos | 92.1 |
| 1961–62 | Dolph Schayes, Syr | 89.7 |
| 1962–63 | Larry Costello, Syr | 88.1 |
| 1963–64 | Oscar Robertson, Cin | 85.3 |
| 1964–65 | Larry Costello, Phil | 87.7 |
| 1965–66 | Larry Siegfried, Bos | 88.1 |
| 1966–67 | Adrian Smith, Cin | 90.3 |
| 1967–68 | Oscar Robertson, Cin | 87.3 |
| 1968–69 | Larry Siegfried, Bos | 86.4 |
| 1969–70 | Flynn Robinson, Mil | 89.8 |
| 1970–71 | Chet Walker, Chi | 85.9 |
| 1971–72 | Jack Marin, Balt | 89.4 |
| 1972–73 | Rick Barry, GS | 90.2 |
| 1973–74 | Ernie DiGregorio, Buf | 90.2 |
| 1974–75 | Rick Barry, GS | 90.4 |
| 1975–76 | Rick Barry, GS | 92.3 |
| 1976–77 | Ernie DiGregorio, Buf | 94.5 |
| 1977–78 | Rick Barry, GS | 92.4 |
| 1978–79 | Rick Barry, Hou | 94.7 |
| 1979–80 | Rick Barry, Hou | 93.5 |
| 1980–81 | Calvin Murphy, Hou | 95.8 |
| 1981–82 | Kyle Macy, Phx | 89.9 |
| 1982–83 | Calvin Murphy, Hou | 92.0 |
| 1983–84 | Larry Bird, Bos | 88.8 |
| 1984–85 | Kyle Macy, Phx | 90.7 |
| 1985–86 | Larry Bird, Bos | 89.6 |
| 1986–87 | Larry Bird, Bos | 91.0 |
| 1987–88 | Jack Sikma, Mil | 92.2 |
| 1988–89 | Magic Johnson, LAL | 91.1 |
| 1989–90 | Larry Bird, Bos | 93.0 |
| 1990–91 | Reggie Miller, Ind | 91.8 |
| 1991–92 | Mark Price, Clev | 94.7 |
| 1992–93 | Mark Price, Clev | 94.8 |
| 1993–94 | Mahmoud Abdul-Rauf, Den | 95.6 |
| 1994–95 | Spud Webb, Sac | 93.4 |
| 1995–96 | Mahmoud Abdul-Rauf, Den | 93.0 |
| 1996–97 | Mark Price, GS | 90.6 |
| 1997–98 | Chris Mullin, Ind | 93.9 |
| 1998–99 | Reggie Miller, Ind | 91.5 |
| 1999–00 | Jeff Hornacek, Utah | 95.0 |
| 2000–01 | Reggie Miller, Ind | 92.8 |
| 2001–02 | Reggie Miller, Ind | 91.1 |
| 2002–03 | Allan Houston, NY | 91.9 |
| 2003–04 | Peja Stojakovic, Sac | 92.7 |
| 2004–05 | Reggie Miller, Ind | 93.3 |
| 2005–06 | Steve Nash, Phx | 92.1 |
| 2006–07 | Kyle Korver, Phil | 91.4 |
| 2007–08 | Peja Stojakovic, NO | 92.9 |
| 2008–09 | Jose Calderon, Tor | 98.1 |
| 2009–10 | Steve Nash, Phx | 93.8 |
| 2010–11 | Stephen Curry, GSW | 93.4 |

## Field-Goal Percentage

| | | | | | |
|---|---|---|---|---|---|
| 1946–47 | Bob Feerick, Wash | 40.1 | 1979–80 | Cedric Maxwell, Bos | 60.9 |
| 1947–48 | Bob Feerick, Wash | 34.0 | 1980–81 | Artis Gilmore, Chi | 67.0 |
| 1948–49 | Arnie Risen, Roch | 42.3 | 1981–82 | Artis Gilmore, Chi | 65.2 |
| 1949–50 | Alex Groza, Ind | 47.8 | 1982–83 | Artis Gilmore, SA | 62.6 |
| 1950–51 | Alex Groza, Ind | 47.0 | 1983–84 | Artis Gilmore, SA | 63.1 |
| 1951–52 | Paul Arizin, Phil | 44.8 | 1984–85 | James Donaldson, LAC | 63.7 |
| 1952–53 | Neil Johnston, Phil | 45.2 | 1985–86 | Steve Johnson, SA | 63.2 |
| 1953–54 | Ed Macauley, Bos | 48.6 | 1986–87 | Kevin McHale, Bos | 60.4 |
| 1954–55 | Larry Foust, FW | 48.7 | 1987–88 | Kevin McHale, Bos | 60.4 |
| 1955–56 | Neil Johnston, Phil | 45.7 | 1988–89 | Dennis Rodman, Det | 59.5 |
| 1956–57 | Neil Johnston, Phil | 44.7 | 1989–90 | Mark West, Phx | 62.5 |
| 1957–58 | Jack Twyman, Cin | 45.2 | 1990–91 | Buck Williams, Port | 60.2 |
| 1958–59 | Ken Sears, NY | 49.0 | 1991–92 | Buck Williams, Port | 60.4 |
| 1959–60 | Ken Sears, NY | 47.7 | 1992–93 | Cedric Ceballos, Phx | 57.6 |
| 1960–61 | Wilt Chamberlain, Phil | 50.9 | 1993–94 | Shaquille O'Neal, Orl | 59.9 |
| 1961–62 | Walt Bellamy, Chi | 51.9 | 1994–95 | Chris Gatling, GS | 63.3 |
| 1962–63 | Wilt Chamberlain, SF | 52.8 | 1995–96 | Gheorghe Muresan, Wash | 58.4 |
| 1963–64 | Jerry Lucas, Cin | 52.7 | 1996–97 | Gheorghe Muresan, Wash | 60.4 |
| 1964–65 | Wilt Chamberlain, SF-Phil | 51.0 | 1997–98 | Shaquille O'Neal, LAL | 58.4 |
| 1965–66 | Wilt Chamberlain, Phil | 54.0 | 1998–99 | Shaquille O'Neal, LAL | 57.6 |
| 1966–67 | Wilt Chamberlain, Phil | 68.3 | 1999–00 | Shaquille O'Neal, LAL | 57.4 |
| 1967–68 | Wilt Chamberlain, Phil | 59.5 | 2000–01 | Shaquille O'Neal, LAL | 57.2 |
| 1968–69 | Wilt Chamberlain, LAL | 58.3 | 2001–02 | Shaquille O'Neal, LAL | 57.9 |
| 1969–70 | Johnny Green, Cin | 55.9 | 2002–03 | Eddy Curry, Chi | 58.5 |
| 1970–71 | Johnny Green, Cin | 58.7 | 2003–04 | Shaquille O'Neal, LAL | 58.4 |
| 1971–72 | Wilt Chamberlain, LAL | 64.9 | 2004–05 | Shaquille O'Neal, Mia | 60.1 |
| 1972–73 | Wilt Chamberlain, LAL | 72.7 | 2005–06 | Shaquille O'Neal, Mia | 60.0 |
| 1973–74 | Bob McAdoo, Buf | 54.7 | 2006–07 | Mikki Moore, NJ | 60.9 |
| 1974–75 | Don Nelson, Bos | 53.9 | 2007–08 | Andris Biedrins, GS | 62.6 |
| 1975–76 | Wes Unseld, Wash | 56.1 | 2008–09 | Erick Dampier, Dal | 65.0 |
| 1976–77 | Kareem Abdul-Jabbar, LAL | 57.9 | 2009–10 | Erick Dampier, Dal | 62.4 |
| 1977–78 | Bobby Jones, Den | 57.8 | 2010–11 | Nene Hilario, Den | 61.5 |
| 1978–79 | Cedric Maxwell, Bos | 58.4 | | | |

## Three-Point Field-Goal Percentage

| | | | | | |
|---|---|---|---|---|---|
| 1979–80 | Fred Brown, Sea | 44.3 | 1995–96 | Tim Legler, Wash | 52.2 |
| 1980–81 | Brian Taylor, SD | 38.3 | 1996–97 | Glen Rice, Cha | 47.0 |
| 1981–82 | Campy Russell, NY | 43.9 | 1997–98 | Dale Ellis, Sea | 46.0 |
| 1982–83 | Mike Dunleavy, SA | 34.5 | 1998–99 | Dell Curry, Cha | 47.6 |
| 1983–84 | Darrell Griffith, Utah | 36.1 | 1999–00 | Hubert Davis, Dal | 49.1 |
| 1984–85 | Byron Scott, LAL | 43.3 | 2000–01 | Brent Barry, Sea | 47.6 |
| 1985–86 | Craig Hodges, Mil | 45.1 | 2001–02 | Steve Smith, SA | 47.2 |
| 1986–87 | Kiki Vandeweghe, Por | 48.1 | 2002–03 | Bruce Bowen, SA | 44.1 |
| 1987–88 | Craig Hodges, Mil-Phx | 49.1 | 2003–04 | Anthony Peeler, Sac | 48.2 |
| 1988–89 | Jon Sundvold, Mia | 52.2 | 2004–05 | Fred Hoiberg, Min | 48.3 |
| 1989–90 | Steve Kerr, Clev | 50.7 | 2005–06 | Richard Hamilton, Det | 45.8 |
| 1990–91 | Jim Les, Sac | 46.1 | 2006–07 | Jason Kapono, Mia | 51.4 |
| 1991–92 | Dana Barros, Sea | 44.6 | 2007–08 | Jason Kapono, Tor | 48.3 |
| 1992–93 | Chris Mullin, GS | 45.1 | 2008–09 | Anthony Morrow, GS | 46.7 |
| 1993–94 | Tracy Murray, Por | 45.9 | 2009–10 | Mike Miller, Wash | 48.0 |
| 1994–95 | Steve Kerr, Chi | 52.4 | 2010–11 | Matt Bonner, SA | 45.7 |

## Steals

| | | | | | |
|---|---|---|---|---|---|
| 1973–74 | Larry Steele, Por | 2.68 | 1985–86 | Alvin Robertson, SA | 3.67 |
| 1974–75 | Rick Barry, GS | 2.85 | 1986–87 | Alvin Robertson, SA | 3.21 |
| 1975–76 | Don Watts, Sea | 3.18 | 1987–88 | Michael Jordan, Chi | 3.16 |
| 1976–77 | Don Buse, Ind | 3.47 | 1988–89 | John Stockton, Utah | 3.21 |
| 1977–78 | Ron Lee, Phx | 2.74 | 1989–90 | Michael Jordan, Chi | 2.77 |
| 1978–79 | M.L. Carr, Det | 2.46 | 1990–91 | Alvin Robertson, Mil | 3.04 |
| 1979–80 | Micheal Ray Richardson, NY | 3.23 | 1991–92 | John Stockton, Utah | 2.98 |
| 1980–81 | Magic Johnson, LAL | 3.43 | 1992–93 | Michael Jordan, Chi | 2.83 |
| 1981–82 | Magic Johnson, LAL | 2.67 | 1993–94 | Nate McMillan, Sea | 2.96 |
| 1982–83 | Micheal Ray Richardson, GS-NJ | 2.84 | 1994–95 | Scottie Pippen, Chi | 2.94 |
| 1983–84 | Rickey Green, Utah | 2.65 | 1995–96 | Gary Payton, Sea | 2.85 |
| 1984–85 | Micheal Ray Richardson, NJ | 2.96 | 1996–97 | Mookie Blaylock, Atl | 2.72 |

### Steals *(Cont.)*

| | | | | | |
|---|---|---|---|---|---|
| 1997–98 | Mookie Blaylock, Atl | 2.61 | 2004–05 | Larry Hughes, Wash | 2.89 |
| 1998–99 | Kendall Gill, NJ | 2.68 | 2005–06 | Gerald Wallace, Cha | 2.51 |
| 1999–00 | Eddie Jones, Cha | 2.67 | 2006–07 | Baron Davis, GS | 2.14 |
| 2000–01 | Allen Iverson, Phil | 2.51 | 2007–08 | Chris Paul, NO | 2.71 |
| 2001–02 | Allen Iverson, Phil | 2.80 | 2008–09 | Chris Paul, NO | 2.77 |
| 2002–03 | Allen Iverson, Phil | 2.74 | 2009–10 | Rajon Rondo, Bos | 2.33 |
| 2003–04 | Baron Davis, NO | 2.36 | 2010–11 | Chris Paul, NO | 2.35 |

### Blocked Shots

| | | | | | |
|---|---|---|---|---|---|
| 1973–74 | Elmore Smith, LAL | 4.85 | 1992–93 | Hakeem Olajuwon, Hou | 4.17 |
| 1974–75 | Kareem Abdul-Jabbar, Mil | 3.26 | 1993–94 | Dikembe Mutombo, Den | 4.10 |
| 1975–76 | Kareem Abdul-Jabbar, LAL | 4.12 | 1994–95 | Dikembe Mutombo, Den | 3.91 |
| 1976–77 | Bill Walton, Port | 3.25 | 1995–96 | Dikembe Mutombo, Den | 4.49 |
| 1977–78 | George Johnson, NJ | 3.38 | 1996–97 | Shawn Bradley, NJ | 3.40 |
| 1978–79 | Kareem Abdul-Jabbar, LAL | 3.95 | 1997–98 | Marcus Camby, Tor | 3.65 |
| 1979–80 | Kareem Abdul-Jabbar, LAL | 3.41 | 1998–99 | Alonzo Mourning, Mia | 3.91 |
| 1980–81 | George Johnson, SA | 3.39 | 1999–00 | Alonzo Mourning, Mia | 3.72 |
| 1981–82 | George Johnson, SA | 3.12 | 2000–01 | Theo Ratliff, Phil/Atl | 3.74 |
| 1982–83 | Wayne Rollins, Atl | 4.29 | 2001–02 | Ben Wallace, Det | 3.48 |
| 1983–84 | Mark Eaton, Utah | 4.28 | 2002–03 | Theo Ratliff, Atl | 3.23 |
| 1984–85 | Mark Eaton, Utah | 5.56 | 2003–04 | Theo Ratliff, Port | 3.61 |
| 1985–86 | Manute Bol, Wash | 4.96 | 2004–05 | Andrei Kirilenko, Utah | 3.32 |
| 1986–87 | Mark Eaton, Utah | 4.06 | 2005–06 | Marcus Camby, Den | 3.29 |
| 1987–88 | Mark Eaton, Utah | 3.71 | 2006–07 | Marcus Camby, Den | 3.30 |
| 1988–89 | Manute Bol, GS | 4.31 | 2007–08 | Marcus Camby, Den | 3.61 |
| 1989–90 | Hakeem Olajuwon, Hou | 4.59 | 2008–09 | Dwight Howard, Orl | 2.92 |
| 1990–91 | Hakeem Olajuwon, Hou | 3.95 | 2009–10 | Dwight Howard, Orl | 2.78 |
| 1991–92 | David Robinson, SA | 4.49 | 2010–11 | Andrew Bogut, Mil | 2.58 |

## NBA All-Star Game Results

| Year | Result | Site | Winning Coach | Most Valuable Player |
|---|---|---|---|---|
| 1951 | East 111, West 94 | Boston | Joe Lapchick | Ed Macauley, Bos |
| 1952 | East 108, West 91 | Boston | Al Cervi | Paul Arizin, Phil |
| 1953 | West 79, East 75 | Ft Wayne | John Kundla | George Mikan, Min |
| 1954 | East 98, West 93 (OT) | New York | Joe Lapchick | Bob Cousy, Bos |
| 1955 | East 100, West 91 | New York | Al Cervi | Bill Sharman, Bos |
| 1956 | West 108, East 94 | Rochester | Charley Eckman | Bob Pettit, StL |
| 1957 | East 109, West 97 | Boston | Red Auerbach | Bob Cousy, Bos |
| 1958 | East 130, West 118 | St Louis | Red Auerbach | Bob Pettit, StL |
| 1959 | West 124, East 108 | Detroit | Ed Macauley | B. Pettit, StL/ E. Baylor, Min |
| 1960 | East 125, West 115 | Philadelphia | Red Auerbach | Wilt Chamberlain, Phil |
| 1961 | West 153, East 131 | Syracuse | Paul Seymour | Oscar Robertson, Cin |
| 1962 | West 150, East 130 | St Louis | Fred Schaus | Bob Pettit, StL |
| 1963 | East 115, West 108 | Los Angeles | Red Auerbach | Bill Russell, Bos |
| 1964 | East 111, West 107 | Boston | Red Auerbach | Oscar Robertson, Cin |
| 1965 | East 124, West 123 | St Louis | Red Auerbach | Jerry Lucas, Cin |
| 1966 | East 137, West 94 | Cincinnati | Red Auerbach | Adrian Smith, Cin |
| 1967 | West 135, East 120 | San Francisco | Fred Schaus | Rick Barry, SF |
| 1968 | East 144, West 124 | New York | Alex Hannum | Hal Greer, Phil |
| 1969 | East 123, West 112 | Baltimore | Gene Shue | Oscar Robertson, Cin |
| 1970 | East 142, West 135 | Philadelphia | Red Holzman | Willis Reed, NY |
| 1971 | West 108, East 107 | San Diego | Larry Costello | Lenny Wilkens, Sea |
| 1972 | West 112, East 110 | Los Angeles | Bill Sharman | Jerry West, LA |
| 1973 | East 104, West 84 | Chicago | Tom Heinsohn | Dave Cowens, Bos |
| 1974 | West 134, East 123 | Seattle | Larry Costello | Bob Lanier, Det |
| 1975 | East 108, West 102 | Phxnix | K.C. Jones | Walt Frazier, NY |
| 1976 | East 123, West 109 | Philadelphia | Tom Heinsohn | Dave Bing, Wash |
| 1977 | West 125, East 124 | Milwaukee | Larry Brown | Julius Erving, Phil |
| 1978 | East 133, West 125 | Atlanta | Billy Cunningham | Randy Smith, Buff |
| 1979 | West 134, East 129 | Detroit | Lenny Wilkens | David Thompson, Den |
| 1980 | East 144, West 135 (OT) | Washington | Billy Cunningham | George Gervin, SA |
| 1981 | East 123, West 120 | Cleveland | Billy Cunningham | Nate Archibald, Bos |
| 1982 | East 120, West 118 | New Jersey | Bill Fitch | Larry Bird, Bos |
| 1983 | East 132, West 123 | Los Angeles | Billy Cunningham | Julius Erving, Phil |
| 1984 | East 154, West 145 (OT) | Denver | K.C. Jones | Isiah Thomas, Det |
| 1985 | West 140, East 129 | Indiana | Pat Riley | Ralph Sampson, Hou |

| Year | Result | Site | Winning Coach | Most Valuable Player |
|------|--------|------|---------------|----------------------|
| 1986 | East 139, West 132 | Dallas | K.C. Jones | Isiah Thomas, Det |
| 1987 | West 154, East 149 (OT) | Seattle | Pat Riley | Tom Chambers, Sea |
| 1988 | East 138, West 133 | Chicago | Mike Fratello | Michael Jordan, Chi |
| 1989 | West 143, East 134 | Houston | Pat Riley | Karl Malone, Utah |
| 1990 | East 130, West 113 | Miami | Chuck Daly | Magic Johnson, LAL |
| 1991 | East 116, West 114 | Charlotte | Chris Ford | Charles Barkley, Phil |
| 1992 | West 153, East 113 | Orlando | Don Nelson | Magic Johnson, LAL |
| 1993 | West 135, East 132 | Salt Lake City | Paul Westphal | K. Malone/J. Stockton, Utah |
| 1994 | East 127, West 118 | Minneapolis | Lenny Wilkens | Scottie Pippen, Chi |
| 1995 | West 139, East 112 | Phoenix | Paul Westphal | Mitch Richmond, Sac |
| 1996 | East 129, West 118 | San Antonio | Phil Jackson | Michael Jordan, Chi |
| 1997 | East 132, West 120 | Cleveland | Doug Collins | Glen Rice, Cha |
| 1998 | East 135, West 114 | New York | Larry Bird | Michael Jordan, Chi |
| 1999 | Cancelled due to lockout. | | | |
| 2000 | West 137, East 126 | Oakland | Phil Jackson | S. O'Neal, LAL/T. Duncan, SA |
| 2001 | East 111, West 110 | Washington | Larry Brown | Allen Iverson, Phill |
| 2002 | West 135, East 120 | Philadelphia | Don Nelson | Kobe Bryant, LAL |
| 2003 | West 155, East 145 (2OT) | Atlanta | Rick Adelman | Kevin Garnett, Min |
| 2004 | West 136, East 132 | Los Angeles | Flip Saunders | Shaquille O'Neal, LAL |
| 2005 | East 125, West 115 | Denver | Stan Van Gundy | Allen Iverson, Phil |
| 2006 | East 122, West 120 | Houston | Flip Saunders | LeBron James, Cle |
| 2007 | West 153, East 132 | Las Vegas | Mike D'Antoni | Kobe Bryant, LAL |
| 2008 | East 134, West 128 | New Orleans | Doc Rivers | LeBron James, Cle |
| 2009 | West 146, East 119 | Phoenix | Phil Jackson | K. Bryant, LAL/S. O'Neal, Phx |
| 2010 | East 141, West 139 | Dallas | Stan Van Gundy | Dwyane Wade, Mia |
| 2011 | West 148, East 143 | Los Angeles | Gregg Popovich | Kobe Bryant, LAL |

# Members of the Basketball Hall of Fame

## Contributors

Senda Abbott (1984)
Clair F. Bee (1967)
Danny Biasone (2000)
Hubie Brown (2005)
Walter A. Brown (1965)
John W. Bunn (1964)
Jerry Buss (2010)
Jerry Colangelo (2004)
William Davidson (2008)
Bob Douglas (1971)
Al Duer (1981)
Wayne Embry (1999)
Clifford Fagan (1983)
Harry A. Fisher (1973)
Larry Fleisher (1991)
Dave Gavitt (2006)
Edward Gottlieb (1971)
Luther H. Gulick (1959)
Lester Harrison (1979)

Chick Hearn (2003)
Ferenc Hepp (1980)
Edward J. Hickox (1959)
Paul D. (Tony) Hinkle (1965)
Ned Irish (1964)
R. William Jones (1964)
J. Walter Kennedy (1980)
Meadowlark Lemon (2003)
Emil S. Liston (1974)
Earl Lloyd (2003)
Bill Mokray (1965)
Ralph Morgan (1959)
Frank Morgenweck (1962)
James Naismith (1959)
C.M. Newton (2000)
John J. O'Brien (1961)
Larry O'Brien (1991)
Harold G. Olsen (1959)
Maurice Podoloff (1973)

H. V. Porter (1960)
William A. Reid (1963)
Elmer Ripley (1972)
Tom (Satch) Sanders (2011)
Lynn W. St. John (1962)
Abe Saperstein (1970)
Arthur A. Schabinger (1961)
Amos Alonzo Stagg (1959)
Boris Stankovic (1991)
Edward Steitz (1983)
Chuck Taylor (1968)
Bertha F. Teague (1984)
Oswald Tower (1959)
Arthur L. Trester (1961)
Dick Vitale (2008)
Clifford Wells (1971)
Lou Wilke (1982)
Fred Zollner (1999)

## Players

Kareem Abdul-Jabbar (1995)
Nate (Tiny) Archibald (1991)
Paul J. Arizin (1977)
Charles Barkley (2006)
Thomas B. Barlow (1980)
Rick Barry (1987)
Elgin Baylor (1976)
John Beckman (1972)
Walt Bellamy (1993)
Sergei Belov (1992)
Dave Bing (1990)
Larry Bird (1998)
Carol Blazejowski (1994)
Bennie Borgmann (1961)
Bill Bradley (1982)
Joseph Brennan (1974)

Al Cervi (1984)
Wilt Chamberlain (1978)
Charles (Tarzan) Cooper (1976)
Cynthia Cooper (20100
Kresimir Cosic (1996)
Bob Cousy (1970)
Dave Cowens (1991)
Joan Crawford (1997)
Billy Cunningham (1986)
Denise Curry (1997)
Drazen Dalipagic (2004)
Adrian Dantley (2008)
Bob Davies (1969)
Forrest S. DeBernardi (1961)
Dave DeBusschere (1982)
H.G. (Dutch) Dehnert (1968)

Anne Donovan (1995)
Clyde Drexler (2004)
Joe Dumars (2006)
Teresa Edwards (2011)
Paul Endacott (1971)
Alex English (1997)
Julius Erving (1993)
Patrick Ewing (2008)
Harold (Bud) Foster (1964)
Walter (Clyde) Frazier (1987)
Max (Marty) Friedman (1971)
Joe Fulks (1977)
Lauren (Laddie) Gale (1976)
Harry (the Horse) Gallatin (1991)
William Gates (1989)
George Gervin (1996)

## Players *(Cont.)*

Artis Gilmore (2011)
Tom Gola (1975)
Gail Goodrich (1996)
Hal Greer (1981)
Robert (Ace) Gruenig (1963)
Clifford O. Hagan (1977)
Victor Hanson (1960)
Lusia Harris-Stewart (1992)
John Havlicek (1983)
Connie Hawkins (1992)
Elvin Hayes (1990)
Marques Haynes (1998)
Tom Heinsohn (1986)
Nat Holman (1964)
Robert J. Houbregs (1987)
Bailey Howell (1997)
Chuck Hyatt (1959)
Dan Issel (1993)
Harry (Buddy) Jeannette (1994)
Dennis Johnson (2010)
Earvin (Magic) Johnson (2002)
Gus Johnson (2010)
William C. Johnson (1976)
D. Neil Johnston (1990)
K.C. Jones (1989)
Sam Jones (1983)
Michael Jordan (2009)
Edward (Moose) Krause (1975)
Bob Kurland (1961)
Bob Lanier (1992)
Joe Lapchick (1966)
Nancy Lieberman-Cline (1996)
Clyde Lovellette (1988)
Jerry Lucas (1979)
Angelo (Hank) Luisetti (1959)

C. Edward Macauley (1960)
Karl Malone (2010)
Moses Malone (2001)
Peter P. Maravich (1987)
Hortencia Marcari (2005)
Slater Martin (1981)
Bob McAdoo (2000)
Branch McCracken (1960)
Jack McCracken (1962)
Bobby McDermott (1988)
Dick McGuire (1993)
Kevin McHale (1999)
Dino Meneghin (2003)
Ann Meyers (1993)
George L. Mikan (1959)
Vern Mikkelsen (1995)
Cheryl Miller (1995)
Earl Monroe (1990)
Chris Mullin (2011)
Calvin Murphy (1993)
Charles (Stretch) Murphy (1960)
Hakeem Olajuwon (2008)
H. O. (Pat) Page (1962)
Robert Parish (2003)
Maciel (Ubiratan) Pereira (2010)
Drazen Petrovic (2002)
Bob Pettit (1970)
Andy Phillip (1961)
Scottie Pippen (2010)
Jim Pollard (1977)
Frank Ramsey (1981)
Willis Reed (1981)
Arnie Risen (1998)
Oscar Robertson (1979)
David Robinson (2009)

Dennis Rodman (2011)
John S. Roosma (1961)
Bill Russell (1974)
John (Honey) Russell (1964)
Arvydas Sabonis (2011)
Adolph Schayes (1972)
Ernest J. Schmidt (1973)
John J. Schommer (1959)
Barney Sedran (1962)
Uljana Semjonova (1993)
Bill Sharman (1975)
Christian Steinmetz (1961)
Lusia Harris Stewart (1992)
John Stockton (2009)
Maurice Stokes (2004)
Reece (Goose) Tatum (2011)
Isiah Thomas (2000)
David Thompson (1996)
John A. (Cat) Thompson (1962)
Nate Thurmond (1984)
Jack Twyman (1982)
Wes Unseld (1988)
Robert (Fuzzy) Vandivier (1974)
Edward A. Wachter (1961)
Bill Walton (1993)
Robert F. Wanzer (1987)
Jerry West (1979)
Nera White (1992)
Lenny Wilkens (1989)
Dominique Wilkins (2006)
Lynette Woodard (2004)
John R. Wooden (1960)
James Worthy (2003)
George (Bird) Yardley (1996)

## Coaches

Forest C. (Phog) Allen (1959)
Harold Anderson (1984)
Red Auerbach (1968)
Geno Auriemma (2006)
Leon Barmore (2003)
Sam Barry (1978)
Ernest A. Blood (1960)
Jim Boeheim (2005)
Larry Brown (2002)
Jim Calhoun (2005)
Howard G. Cann (1967)
H. Clifford Carlson (1959)
Lou Carnesecca (1992)
Ben Carnevale (1969)
Pete Carril (1997)
Everett Case (1981)
Van Chancellor (2007)
John Chaney (2001)
Jody Conradt (1998)
Denny Crum (1994)
Chuck Daly (1994)
Everett S. Dean (1966)
Antonio Diaz-Miguel (1997)
Edgar A. Diddle (1971)
Bruce Drake (1972)
Pedro Ferrandiz (2007)
Sandro Gamba (2006)
Clarence Gaines (1981)

Jack Gardner (1983)
Amory T. (Slats) Gill (1967)
Aleksandr Gomelsky (1995)
Sue Gunter (2005)
Alex Hannum (1998)
Marv Harshman (1984)
Don Haskins (1997)
Edgar S. Hickey (1978)
Howard A. Hobson (1965)
Red Holzman (1986)
Bob Hurley Sr. (2010)
Hank Iba (1968)
Phil Jackson (2007)
Alvin F. (Doggie) Julian (1967)
Frank W. Keaney (1960)
George E. Keogan (1961)
Bob Knight (1991)
Mike Krzyzewski (2001)
John Kundla (1995)
Ward L. Lambert (1960)
Harry Litwack (1975)
Kenneth D. Loeffler (1964)
A.C. (Dutch) Lonborg (1972)
John B. McLendon (1978)
Arad A. McCutchan (1980)
Herb Magee (2011)
Al McGuire (1992)
Frank McGuire (1976)
Walter E. Meanwell (1959)
Raymond J. Meyer (1978)

Ralph Miller (1988)
Billie Moore (1999)
Peter F. Newell (1978)
Aleksandar Nikolic (1998)
Mirko Novosel (2007)
Lute Olson (2002)
Jack Ramsay (1992)
Pat Riley (2008)
Cesare Rubini (1994)
Adolph F. Rupp (1968)
Cathy Rush (2008)
Leonard D. Sachs (1961)
Bill Sharman (2004)
Everett F. Shelton (1979)
Jerry Sloan (2009)
Dean Smith (1982)
C. Vivian Stringer (2009)
Pat Summitt (2000)
Fred R. Taylor (1985)
John Thompson (1999)
Tara VanDerveer (2011)
Margaret Wade (1984)
Stanley H. Watts (1985)
Lenny Wilkens (1998)
Roy Williams (2007)
Tex Winter (2011)
John R. Wooden (1972)
Morgan Wooten (2000)
Phil Woolpert (1992)
Kay Yow (2002)

Note: Year of election in parentheses.

## Referees

James E. Enright (1978)
George T. Hepbron (1960)
George Hoyt (1961)
Matthew P. Kennedy (1959)
Lloyd Leith (1982)
Zigmund J. Mihalik (1985)
John P. Nucatola (1977)

Ernest C. Quigley (1961)
Marvin Rudolph (2007)
J. Dallas Shirley (1979)
Earl Strom (1995)
David Tobey (1961)
David H. Walsh (1961)

## Teams

Buffalo Germans (1961)
First Team (1959)
Harlem Globetrotters (2002)
Original Celtics (1959)
Renaissance (1963)
1960 USA Olympic Team (2010)
1966 Texas Western (2007)
1992 USA Olympic "Dream" Team (2010)

Note: Year of election in parentheses.

# American Basketball Association

## Champions

| Year | Champion | Series | Runner-up | Winning Coach |
|---|---|---|---|---|
| 1968 | Pittsburgh Pipers | 4–3 | New Orleans Bucs | Vince Cazetta |
| 1969 | Oakland Oaks | 4–1 | Indiana Pacers | Alex Hannum |
| 1970 | Indiana Pacers | 4–2 | Los Angeles Stars | Bob Leonard |
| 1971 | Utah Stars | 4–3 | Kentucky Colonels | Bill Sharman |
| 1972 | Indiana Pacers | 4–2 | New York Nets | Bob Leonard |
| 1973 | Indiana Pacers | 4–3 | Kentucky Colonels | Bob Leonard |
| 1974 | New York Nets | 4–1 | Utah Stars | Kevin Loughery |
| 1975 | Kentucky Colonels | 4–1 | Indiana Pacers | Hubie Brown |
| 1976 | New York Nets | 4–2 | Denver Nuggets | Kevin Loughery |

# ABA Postseason Awards

## Most Valuable Player

| | |
|---|---|
| 1967–68 | Connie Hawkins, Pitt |
| 1968–69 | Mel Daniels, Ind |
| 1969–70 | Spencer Haywood, Den |
| 1970–71 | Mel Daniels, Ind |
| 1971–72 | Artis Gilmore, Ken |
| 1972–73 | Billy Cunningham, Car |
| 1973–74 | Julius Erving, NY |
| 1974–75 | Julius Erving, NY |
| | George McGinnis, Ind |
| 1975–76 | Julius Erving, NY |

## Rookie of the Year

| | |
|---|---|
| 1967–68 | Mel Daniels, Minn |
| 1968–69 | Warren Armstrong, Oak |
| 1969–70 | Spencer Haywood, Den |
| 1970–71 | Dan Issel, Ken |
| | Charlie Scott, Vir |
| 1971–72 | Artis Gilmore, Ken |
| 1972–73 | Brian Taylor, NY |
| 1973–74 | Swen Nater, SA |
| 1974–75 | Marvin Barnes, StL |
| 1975–76 | David Thompson, Den |

## Coach of the Year

| | |
|---|---|
| 1967–68 | Vince Cazetta, Pitt |
| 1968–69 | Alex Hannum, Oak |
| 1969–70 | Joe Belmont, Den |
| | Bill Sharman, LA |
| 1970–71 | Al Bianchi, Vir |
| 1971–72 | Tom Nissalke, Dal |
| 1972–73 | Larry Brown, Car |
| 1973–74 | Babe McCarthy, Ken |
| | Joe Mullaney, Utah |
| 1974–75 | Larry Brown, Den |
| 1975–76 | Larry Brown, Den |

### Scoring

| | GP | Pts | Avg |
|---|---|---|---|
| 1967–68...Connie Hawkins, Pitt | 70 | 1875 | 26.8 |
| 1968–69...Rick Barry, Oak | 35 | 1190 | 34.0 |
| 1969–70...Spencer Haywood, Den | 84 | 2519 | 30.0 |
| 1970–71...Dan Issel, Ken | 83 | 2480 | 29.9 |
| 1971–72...Charlie Scott, Vir | 79 | 2637 | 33.4 |
| 1972–73...Julius Erving, Vir | 71 | 2268 | 31.9 |
| 1973–74...Julius Erving, NY | 84 | 2299 | 27.4 |
| 1974–75...George McGinnis, Ind | 79 | 2353 | 29.8 |
| 1975–76...Julius Erving, NY | 84 | 2462 | 29.3 |

### Rebounds

| | |
|---|---|
| 1967–68...............Mel Daniels, Minn | 15.6 |
| 1968–69...............Mel Daniels, Ind | 16.5 |
| 1969–70...............Spencer Haywood, Den | 19.5 |
| 1970–71...............Mel Daniels, Ind | 18.0 |
| 1971–72...............Artis Gilmore, Ken | 17.8 |
| 1972–73...............Artis Gilmore, Ken | 17.6 |
| 1973–74...............Artis Gilmore, Ken | 18.3 |
| 1974–75...............Swen Nater, SA | 16.4 |
| 1975–76...............Artis Gilmore, Ken | 15.5 |

### Assists

| | |
|---|---|
| 1967–68...............Larry Brown, NO | 6.5 |
| 1968–69...............Larry Brown, Oak | 7.1 |
| 1969–70...............Larry Brown, Wash | 7.1 |
| 1970–71...............Bill Melchionni, NY | 8.3 |
| 1971–72...............Bill Melchionni, NY | 8.4 |
| 1972–73...............Bill Melchionni, NY | 7.4 |
| 1973–74...............Al Smith, Den | 8.2 |
| 1974–75...............Mack Calvin, Den | 7.7 |
| 1975–76...............Don Buse, Ind | 8.2 |

### Steals

| | |
|---|---|
| 1973–74...............Ted McClain, Car | 2.98 |
| 1974–75...............Brian Taylor, NY | 2.80 |
| 1975–76...............Don Buse, Ind | 4.12 |

### Blocked Shots

| | |
|---|---|
| 1973–74...............Caldwell Jones, SD | 4.00 |
| 1974–75...............Caldwell Jones, SD | 3.24 |
| 1975–76...............Billy Paultz, SA | 3.05 |

## World Championship of Basketball

| Year | Winner | Runner-Up | Score | Site |
|---|---|---|---|---|
| 1950 | Argentina | United States | † | Buenos Aires |
| 1954 | United States | Brazil | † | Rio de Janeiro |
| 1959 | Brazil | United States | † | Santiago, Chile |
| 1963 | Brazil | Yugoslavia | † | Rio de Janeiro |
| 1967 | Soviet Union | Yugoslavia | † | Montevideo, Uruguay |
| 1970 | Yugoslavia | Brazil | † | Ljubljana, Yugoslavia |
| 1974 | Soviet Union | Yugoslavia | † | San Juan |
| 1978 | Yugoslavia | Soviet Union | 82–81 (OT) | Manila |
| 1982 | Soviet Union | United States | 95–94 | Cali, Colombia |
| 1986 | United States | Soviet Union | 87–85 | Madrid |
| 1990 | Yugoslavia | Soviet Union | 92–75 | Buenos Aires |
| *1994 | United States | Russia | 137–91 | Toronto |
| †1998 | Yugoslavia | Russia | 64–62 | Athens |
| 2002 | Yugoslavia | Argentina | 84–77 (OT) | Indianapolis |
| 2006 | Spain | Greece | 70–47 | Saitama, Japan |
| 2010 | United States | Turkey | 81–64 | Turkey |

*U.S. professionals began competing in 1994.†In 1998, a labor dispute resulted in a boycott of the World Championship by NBA stars; the U.S. roster was filled by members of the CBA and European professional leagues and college players.
†Result determined by overall record in final round of competition.

College Basketball

UConn won its third national title in 13 years thanks to Kemba Walker, the Final Four's Most Outstanding Player

# Expect the Unexpected

UConn's unheralded men's team beat mid-major bracket buster Butler to be crowned champion of the men's tourney, while UConn's record-breaking women's team fell short and watched Texas A&M defeat Notre Dame for the title

**BY B.J. SCHECTER**

UCONN COACH JIM CALHOUN took his usual post on the sideline, crouching on one knee in front of the Huskies' bench as the final seconds ticked off the clock. The game was in hand, but Calhoun didn't look like a man about to win his third national title. With sweat dripping from his brow and large bags as heavy as boulders under his eyes, Calhoun looked like he had just survived a 15-round fight. And in a way in had. In what was one of the most trying seasons in his illustrious 39-year career, Calhoun managed to guide his team to the top, and as the buzzer sounded he raised his hands in the air and let out a deep breath.

Connecticut did the near impossible. The Huskies finished ninth in the Big East, then went on a miraculous five-wins-in-five-days run to capture the Big East tournament title. Most teams would have run out of gas by then, but led by wonderguard Kemba Walker the Huskies kept going and won six straight NCAA tournament games—an incredible 28-day stretch—to win the national title. It wasn't pretty—the championship game, a hard-fought 53–41 victory

over Butler was particularly brutal and brick-laden—but it didn't matter. Calhoun couldn't care less about style points. His Huskies were the last team standing and as he left Houston's Reliant Stadium with the clock approaching midnight, a wry smile crossed his faced when he was asked about the ugliness of the game.

"To me," he said. "This was beauty."

Connecticut was far from a favorite entering the season. The Huskies were unranked, young, coming off a season in which they didn't make the NCAA tournament, and were in the shadows of a major NCAA investigation. After a terrific start, UConn lost seven of its final 11 regular season games and it looked like a first-round exit was possible. As like he's done his entire career, Calhoun found the right buttons to push and had the ultimate weapon in Walker, who carried the team on his back and established himself as one of the best players in the Huskies' storied history.

Afterward, Calhoun talked about how this title was the most satisfying of his three, perhaps because it was his least expected and occurred during one of the most difficult years of his life. In February,

BYU's dynamic shooting guard Jimmer Fredette led the nation in scoring (28.9 points per game) and was ranked third in total number of three-point field goals made (124).

ROBERT BECK

the NCAA formally announced sanctions against Connecticut, which included a suspension of Calhoun for the first three Big East games of the following season. Ten days later, Calhoun lost his sister-in-law to cancer just a few months after losing a close friend to melanoma. Then on the eve of the Final Four, the *New York Times* tracked down Nate Miles, the central figure in the NCAA violations, and Miles suggested Calhoun knew more than he was letting on. Calhoun called the charges "as low a blow as anybody has ever put on me."

In the end, Calhoun got the last laugh and came out on top as he contemplated retirement. On the floor after beating Butler, surrounded by his team and family, Calhoun finally found peace. "If this is the end," Calhoun's wife, Pat, said, "what a beautiful way to finish."

While Calhoun may be in the final stages of his career, Butler's Brad Stevens is just beginning his. In 2010, the then 33-year-old Stevens led the Bulldogs to the title game and came within one last-second half-court heave of shocking Duke and winning the national title. Many expected Butler to be a one-year wonder, especially when star Gordon Hayward left school early to go to the NBA. And after starting the season 14–9, Butler was in serious danger of not even making the NCAA tournament. But Stevens showed why he's quickly earned the reputation as one of the best coaches in the country by engineering an unthinkable turnaround.

Butler rode its skill, perseverance, meticulous preparation and a little luck to its sec-ond straight Final Four. The reserved and unflappable Stevens refused to cash in and leave for a bigger job after his first Final Four appearance and now most people can understand why: Butler has become a better coaching job than some fledgling major-conference posts. And Stevens, a master tactician, has earned universal respect.

Said Calhoun, "If Brad Stevens represents the future of our profession, then we're in pretty good shape."

BILL FRAKES

Nevertheless, led by high-energy coach Shaka Smart, VCU played like it belonged and one by one knocked off major conference teams: USC, Georgetown, Purdue, Florida State and then top-seeded Kansas, a game VCU led by as many as 18 points. In less than two weeks, VCU became the hottest team in the nation, and like Stevens Smart refused to make the knee-jerk jump to a more high-profile school and chose to remain at VCU.

The women's Final Four experienced a huge jump in excitement and competitiveness as a pair of traditional powers were upset in the semifinals. In late December, Stanford ended UConn's remarkable 90-game winning streak (the Huskies broke the UCLA men's record of 88 games earlier in the season) with a 71–59 victory and the two teams were on a collision course to meet for the national championship in Indianapolis.

Stevens wasn't the only young coach to vault up the latter, and Butler wasn't the only mid-major in the Final Four. Even more improbable than Butler's return was VCU's march to Houston. VCU was horrible at the end of the regular season, losing five of its final eight and when it unexpectedly made the field (the team didn't gather to watch the Selection Show because they didn't want to be disappointed) the Rams were lambasted by pundits as undeserving of a bid. What's more, this was the first year the NCAA expanded the tournament to 68 teams and VCU was placed into one of the First Four preliminary games (the NCAA calls them first-round but they're not), which took place early in the week. The bottom line is if the field hadn't expanded VCU wouldn't have been in.

But No. 2 seeds Notre Dame and Texas A&M had other ideas as the Irish and Aggies knocked off UConn and Stanford, respectively. In a final that was as well-played and entertaining as the men's championship was sloppy and wearisome, Texas A&M's Danielle Adams (30 points) outdueled Notre Dame star Skylar Diggins for a hard-fought 76–70 victory.

It was quite a season in college basketball. Who would have thought the UConn men would rise to the top, while the Huskies women would fall short? Or that Kentucky would get to the Final four a year after losing its famous one-and-done freshmen stars? In an improbable season, a coach chose to stay at Harvard rather than take a job at school in the Big East. In college basketball, we have come to learn to expect the unexpected.

## NCAA Men's Championship Game Box Score

### Connecticut 53

| | Min | FG M-A | FT M-A | Reb O-T | A | PF | TP |
|---|---|---|---|---|---|---|---|
| T. Olander | 7 | 1-3 | 0-0 | 2-3 | 1 | 1 | 2 |
| R. Smith | 22 | 0-2 | 0-0 | 1-4 | 0 | 4 | 0 |
| A. Oriakhi | 25 | 5-6 | 1-1 | 2-11 | 0 | 2 | 11 |
| K. Walker | 37 | 5-19 | 6-7 | 1-9 | 0 | 2 | 16 |
| J. Lamb | 31 | 4-8 | 3-4 | 1-7 | 2 | 2 | 12 |
| D. Beverly | 8 | 1-2 | 0-0 | 0-0 | 1 | 0 | 2 |
| J. C.-McDaniel | 6 | 0-3 | 0-0 | 1-2 | 0 | 0 | 0 |
| N. Giffey | 24 | 1-3 | 2-2 | 3-6 | 0 | 1 | 4 |
| S. Napier | 27 | 1-6 | 2-2 | 0-4 | 2 | 1 | 4 |
| C. Okwandu | 13 | 1-3 | 0-0 | 4-5 | 0 | 2 | 2 |
| **Totals** | | **19-55** | **14-16** | **15-51** | **6** | **15** | **53** |

Percentages: FG-.345, FT-.875. 3-Point Goals: 1–11, .091 (R. Smith 0–1, K. Walker 0–4, J. Lamb, 1–2, J. Coombs-McDaniel 0–1, N. Giffey 0–1, S. Napier 0–2). Team Rebounds: 0. Blocked Shots: 10 (R. Smith 4, A. Oriakhi 4, J. Lamb 1, C. Okwandu 1). Turnovers: 11 (R. Smith 2, K. Walker 2, J. Lamb 1, D. Beverly 1, N. Giffey 2, S. Napier 3). Steals: 4 (K. Walker 1, J. Lamb 1, S. Napier 2). Technical Fouls: None.

**Halftime: Butler 22, Connecticut 19.**
**Final Four Most Outstanding Player: Kemba Walker, Connecticut.**

### Butler 41

| | Min | FG M-A | FT M-A | Reb O-T | A | PF | TP |
|---|---|---|---|---|---|---|---|
| M. Howard | 37 | 1-13 | 4-4 | 2-6 | 0 | 2 | 7 |
| A. Smith | 29 | 2-9 | 1-2 | 6-9 | 1 | 3 | 5 |
| S. Vanzant | 36 | 2-10 | 0-0 | 2-8 | 2 | 1 | 5 |
| S. Mack | 36 | 4-15 | 1-2 | 4-9 | 1 | 1 | 13 |
| C. Stigall | 16 | 3-11 | 0-0 | 1-2 | 1 | 1 | 9 |
| Z. Hahn | 7 | 0-2 | 0-0 | 0-0 | 0 | 2 | 0 |
| R. Nored | 26 | 0-2 | 2-4 | 3-4 | 0 | 4 | 2 |
| C. Hopkins | 4 | 0-0 | 0-0 | 0-0 | 0 | 1 | 0 |
| K. Marshall | 8 | 0-2 | 0-2 | 1-2 | 0 | 2 | 0 |
| G. Butcher | 1 | 0-0 | 0-0 | 0-0 | 0 | 0 | 0 |
| **Totals** | | **12-64** | **8-14** | **19-40** | **5** | **17** | **41** |

Percentages: FG-.188, FT-.571. 3-Point Goals: 9–33, .273 (M. Howard 1–6, S. Vanzant 1–5, S. Mack 4–11, C. Stigall 3–9, Z. Hahn 0–1, R. Nored 0–1). Team Rebounds: 0. Blocked Shots: 2 (A. Smith 1, S. Mack 1). Turnovers: 6 (A. Smith 1, S. Vanzant 2, S. Mack 3). Steals: 8 (M. Howard 1, A. Smith 1, S. Vanzant 3, C. Stigall 1, R. Nored 2). Technical Fouls: None.

Officials: John Cahill, Verne Harris, Doug Shows.
A: 70,376

## Final ESPN/USA Today Top 25 Coaches Poll

| 1. Connecticut (30) | 30–9 |
|---|---|
| 2. Butler | 27–9 |
| 3. Kentucky | 29–8 |
| 4. Kansas | 35–3 |
| 5. Ohio St (1) | 34–3 |
| 6. VCU | 28–11 |
| 7. Duke | 32–5 |
| 8. North Carolina | 29–8 |
| 9. Arizona | 30–8 |
| 10. Florida | 29–8 |
| 11. San Diego St | 34–3 |
| 12. Pittsburgh | 28–6 |
| 13. BYU | 32–5 |

| 14. Notre Dame | 27–7 |
|---|---|
| 15. Wisconsin | 25–9 |
| 16. Texas | 28–8 |
| 17. Purdue | 26–8 |
| 18. Syracuse | 27–8 |
| 19. Florida St | 23–11 |
| 20. Marquette | 22–15 |
| 21. Richmond | 29–8 |
| 22. Louisville | 25–10 |
| 23. Washington | 24–11 |
| 24. Kansas St | 23–11 |
| 25. Utah St | 30–4 |

## National Invitation Tournament Scores

**First round:** Alabama 68, Coastal Carolina 44; New Mexico 69, UTEP 57; Missouri St 89, Murray St 76; Miami (Fla.) 85, Florida Atlantic 62; Colorado 88, Texas Southern 74, California 77, Mississippi 74; Fairfield 62, Colorado St 60; Kent St 71, St. Mary's (Calif.) 70; Boston College 82, McNeese St 64; Northwestern 70, UW-Milwaukee 61; Oklahoma St 71, Harvard 54; Washington St 85, Long Beach St 74, Virginia Tech 79, Bethune-Cookman 54; Wichita St 76, Nebraska 49; Coll. of Charleston 94, Dayton 84; Cleveland St 63, Vermont 60.
**Second round:** Alabama 74, New Mexico 67; Miami (Fla.) 81, Missouri St 72; Colorado 89, California 72; Kent St 72, Fairfield 68; Northwestern 85, Boston College 67; Washington St 74, Oklahoma St 64; Wichita St 79, Virginia Tech 78 (OT); Coll. of Charleston 64, Cleveland St 56.
**Quarterfinals:** Alabama 79, Miami (Fla.) 64; Colorado 81, Kent St 74; Washington St 69, Northwestern 66 (OT); Wichita St 82, Coll. of Charleston 75.
**Semifinals:** Alabama 62, Colorado 61; Wichita St 75, Washington St 44.
**Championship Game:** Wichita St 66, Alabama 57.

## 2nd ROUND · 3rd ROUND · REGIONALS · NATIONAL CHAMPIONSHIP · REGIONALS · 3rd ROUND · 2nd ROUND

### WEST — Anaheim

2nd ROUND:
- 1 Duke (30-4)
- 16 Hampton (24-8)
- 8 Michigan (20-13)
- 9 Tennessee (19-14)
- 5 Arizona (27-7)
- 12 Memphis (25-9)
- 4 Texas (27-7)
- 13 Oakland (25-8)
- 6 Cincinnati (25-8)
- 11 Missouri (23-10)
- 3 Connecticut (26-9)
- 14 Bucknell (25-8)
- 7 Temple (25-7)
- 10 Penn St (19-14)
- 2 San Diego St (32-2)
- 15 Northern Colo. (21-10)

3rd ROUND: Duke 87-45 · Michigan 75-45 · Arizona 77-75 · Texas 85-81 · Cincinnati 78-63 · Connecticut 81-52 · Temple 66-64 · San Diego St 68-50

Regionals: Duke 73-71 · Arizona 70-69 · Connecticut 69-58 · San Diego St 71-64

Arizona 93-77 · Connecticut 74-67

Connecticut 65-63

### EAST — Newark

2nd ROUND:
- 1 Ohio St (32-2)
- 16 Tex.-San Antonio (20-13) *
- 8 George Mason (26-6)
- 9 Villanova (21-11)
- 5 West Virginia (20-11)
- 12 Clemson (22-11)
- 4 Kentucky (25-8)
- 13 Princeton (25-6)
- 6 Xavier (24-7)
- 11 Marquette (20-14)
- 3 Syracuse (26-7)
- 14 Indiana St (20-13)
- 7 Washington (23-10)
- 10 Georgia (21-11)
- 2 North Carolina (26-7)
- 15 Long Island Univ. (27-5)

3rd ROUND: Ohio St 75-46 · George Mason 61-57 · West Virginia 64-76 · Kentucky 59-57 · Marquette 66-55 · Syracuse 77-60 · Washington 68-65 · North Carolina 102-87

Regionals: Ohio St 98-66 · Kentucky 71-63 · Marquette 66-62 · North Carolina 86-83

Kentucky 62-60 · North Carolina 81-63

Kentucky 78-69

Connecticut 56-55

### NATIONAL CHAMPIONSHIP — Houston

CONNECTICUT 53
Butler 41

VCU 71-61

Butler 70-62

Butler 74-71

### SOUTHWEST — San Antonio

3rd ROUND: Kansas 72-53 · Illinois 73-62 · Richmond 69-66 · Morehead St 62-61 · VCU 74-56 · Purdue 65-43 · Florida St 57-50 · Notre Dame 69-56

Regionals: Kansas 73-59 · Richmond 65-48 · VCU 94-76 · Florida St 71-57

Kansas 77-57 · VCU 72-71

2nd ROUND:
- 1 Kansas (32-2)
- 16 Boston Univ. (21-13)
- 8 UNLV (24-8)
- 9 Illinois (19-13)
- 5 Vanderbilt (23-10)
- 12 Richmond (27-7)
- 4 Louisville (25-9)
- 13 Morehead St (24-9)
- 6 Georgetown (21-10)
- 11 VCU (24-1) *
- 3 Purdue (25-7)
- 14 St. Peter's (20-13)
- 7 Texas A&M (24-8)
- 10 Florida St (21-10)
- 2 Notre Dame (26-6)
- 15 Akron (23-12)

### SOUTHEAST — New Orleans

3rd ROUND: Pittsburgh 74-71 · Butler 60-58 · Kansas St 73-68 · Wisconsin 72-58 · Gonzaga 86-71 · BYU 74-66 · UCLA 78-76 · Florida 79-51

Regionals: Pittsburgh 71-70 · Butler 71-70 · Wisconsin 70-65 · BYU 89-67

Butler 61-54 · Florida 83-74

2nd ROUND:
- 1 Pittsburgh (27-6)
- 16 N.C.-Asheville (20-13) *
- 8 Butler (23-9)
- 9 Old Dominion (27-6)
- 5 Kansas St (22-10)
- 12 Utah St (30-3)
- 4 Wisconsin (23-8)
- 13 Belmont (30-4)
- 6 St. John's (21-11)
- 11 Gonzaga (24-9)
- 3 BYU (30-4)
- 14 Wofford (21-12)
- 7 UCLA (22-10)
- 10 Michigan St (19-14)
- 2 Florida (26-7)
- 15 UC-Santa Barbara (18-13)

### *1st ROUND — Dayton, Ohio

| | | |
|---|---|---|
| 11 USC (19-14) | 52 | 70 |
| 11 VCU (23-10) | 70 | 59 |
| 12 UAB (22-8) | 46 | |
| 12 Clemson (21-11) | 59 | |
| 16 N.C.-Asheville (19-13) | 81 | |
| 16 Ark-Little Rock (9-16) | 77 | |
| 16 Tex.-San Antonio (17-17) | 70 | |
| 16 Alabama St (17-17) | 61 | |

## America East

| | Conference | | | All Games | | |
|---|---|---|---|---|---|---|
| | W | L | Pct | W | L | Pct |
| Vermont | 13 | 3 | .813 | 23 | 9 | .719 |
| *Boston Univ. | 12 | 4 | .750 | 21 | 14 | .600 |
| SUNY-Albany | 9 | 7 | .563 | 16 | 16 | .500 |
| Maine | 9 | 7 | .563 | 15 | 15 | .500 |
| SUNY-Stony Brook | 8 | 8 | .500 | 15 | 17 | .469 |
| Hartford | 7 | 9 | .438 | 11 | 20 | .355 |
| New Hampshire | 6 | 10 | .375 | 12 | 18 | .400 |
| SUNY-Binghamton | 4 | 12 | .250 | 8 | 23 | .258 |
| Md.-Baltimore Cty. | 4 | 12 | .250 | 5 | 25 | .167 |

## Atlantic Coast

| | Conference | | | All Games | | |
|---|---|---|---|---|---|---|
| | W | L | Pct | W | L | Pct |
| North Carolina | 14 | 2 | .875 | 29 | 8 | .784 |
| *Duke | 13 | 3 | .813 | 32 | 5 | .865 |
| Florida St | 11 | 5 | .688 | 23 | 11 | .676 |
| Virginia Tech | 9 | 7 | .563 | 22 | 12 | .647 |
| Clemson | 9 | 7 | .563 | 22 | 12 | .647 |
| Boston College | 9 | 7 | .563 | 21 | 13 | .618 |
| Maryland | 7 | 9 | .438 | 19 | 14 | .576 |
| Virginia | 7 | 9 | .438 | 16 | 15 | .516 |
| Miami (Fla.) | 6 | 10 | .375 | 21 | 15 | .583 |
| North Carolina St | 5 | 11 | .313 | 15 | 16 | .484 |
| Georgia Tech | 5 | 11 | .313 | 13 | 18 | .419 |
| Wake Forest | 1 | 15 | .063 | 8 | 24 | .250 |

## Atlantic Sun

| | Conference | | | All Games | | |
|---|---|---|---|---|---|---|
| | W | L | Pct | W | L | Pct |
| *Belmont | 19 | 1 | .950 | 30 | 5 | .857 |
| East Tennessee St | 16 | 4 | .800 | 24 | 12 | .667 |
| Jacksonville | 13 | 7 | .650 | 20 | 12 | .625 |
| Lipscomb | 12 | 8 | .600 | 17 | 13 | .567 |
| Mercer | 11 | 9 | .550 | 15 | 18 | .455 |
| North Florida | 10 | 10 | .500 | 15 | 19 | .441 |
| Florida Gulf Coast | 7 | 13 | .350 | 10 | 20 | .333 |
| Campbell | 6 | 14 | .300 | 12 | 19 | .387 |
| Kennesaw St. | 6 | 14 | .300 | 8 | 23 | .258 |
| Stetson | 6 | 14 | .300 | 8 | 23 | .258 |
| S.C.-Upstate | 4 | 16 | .200 | 5 | 25 | .167 |

## Atlantic 10

| | Conference | | | All Games | | |
|---|---|---|---|---|---|---|
| | W | L | Pct | W | L | Pct |
| Xavier | 15 | 1 | .938 | 24 | 8 | .750 |
| Temple | 14 | 2 | .875 | 26 | 8 | .765 |
| *Richmond | 13 | 3 | .813 | 29 | 8 | .784 |
| Duquesne | 10 | 6 | .625 | 19 | 13 | .594 |
| George Washington | 10 | 6 | .625 | 17 | 14 | .548 |
| Rhode Island | 9 | 7 | .563 | 20 | 14 | .588 |
| St. Bonaventure | 8 | 8 | .500 | 16 | 15 | .516 |
| Dayton | 7 | 9 | .438 | 22 | 14 | .611 |
| Massachusetts | 7 | 9 | .438 | 15 | 15 | .500 |
| La Salle | 6 | 10 | .375 | 15 | 18 | .455 |
| St. Louis | 6 | 10 | .375 | 12 | 19 | .387 |
| St. Joseph's | 4 | 12 | .250 | 11 | 22 | .333 |
| Charlotte | 2 | 14 | .125 | 10 | 20 | .333 |
| Fordham | 1 | 15 | .063 | 7 | 21 | .250 |

## Big East

| | Conference | | | All Games | | |
|---|---|---|---|---|---|---|
| | W | L | Pct | W | L | Pct |
| Pittsburgh | 15 | 3 | .833 | 28 | 6 | .824 |
| Notre Dame | 14 | 4 | .778 | 27 | 7 | .794 |
| Syracuse | 12 | 6 | .667 | 27 | 8 | .771 |
| Louisville | 12 | 6 | .667 | 25 | 10 | .714 |
| St. John's | 12 | 6 | .667 | 21 | 12 | .636 |
| Cincinnati | 11 | 7 | .611 | 26 | 9 | .743 |
| West Virginia | 11 | 7 | .611 | 21 | 12 | .636 |
| Georgetown | 10 | 8 | .556 | 21 | 11 | .656 |
| *Connecticut | 9 | 9 | .500 | 32 | 9 | .780 |
| Villanova | 9 | 9 | .500 | 21 | 12 | .636 |
| Marquette | 9 | 9 | .500 | 22 | 15 | .595 |
| Seton Hall | 7 | 11 | .389 | 13 | 18 | .419 |
| Rutgers | 5 | 13 | .278 | 15 | 17 | .469 |
| Providence | 4 | 14 | .222 | 15 | 17 | .469 |
| South Florida | 3 | 15 | .167 | 10 | 23 | .303 |
| DePaul | 1 | 17 | .056 | 7 | 24 | .226 |

## Big Sky

| | Conference | | | All Games | | |
|---|---|---|---|---|---|---|
| | W | L | Pct | W | L | Pct |
| *Northern Colorado | 13 | 3 | .813 | 21 | 11 | .656 |
| Montana | 12 | 4 | .750 | 21 | 11 | .656 |
| Weber St | 11 | 5 | .688 | 18 | 14 | .563 |
| Northern Arizona | 9 | 7 | .563 | 19 | 13 | .594 |
| Montana St | 7 | 9 | .438 | 13 | 18 | 419 |
| Eastern Washington | 7 | 9 | .438 | 10 | 20 | .333 |
| Portland St | 5 | 11 | .313 | 14 | 16 | .467 |
| Idaho St | 4 | 12 | .250 | 9 | 20 | .310 |
| Sacramento St | 4 | 12 | .250 | 7 | 21 | 250 |

## Big South

| | Conference | | | All Games | | |
|---|---|---|---|---|---|---|
| | W | L | Pct | W | L | Pct |
| Coastal Carolina | 16 | 2 | .889 | 28 | 6 | .824 |
| Liberty | 13 | 5 | .722 | 19 | 13 | .594 |
| *UNC-Asheville | 11 | 7 | .611 | 20 | 14 | .588 |
| Virginia Military Inst. | 10 | 8 | .556 | 18 | 13 | .581 |
| Charleston Southern | 9 | 9 | .500 | 16 | 16 | .500 |
| Winthrop | 9 | 9 | .500 | 13 | 17 | .433 |
| High Point | 7 | 11 | .389 | 12 | 19 | .387 |
| Presbyterian | 7 | 11 | .389 | 13 | 18 | .419 |
| Gardner-Webb | 6 | 12 | .333 | 11 | 21 | .344 |
| Radford | 2 | 16 | .111 | 5 | 24 | .172 |

## Big 10

| | Conference | | | All Games | | |
|---|---|---|---|---|---|---|
| | W | L | Pct | W | L | Pct |
| *Ohio St | 16 | 2 | .889 | 34 | 3 | .919 |
| Purdue | 14 | 4 | .778 | 26 | 8 | .765 |
| Wisconsin | 13 | 5 | .722 | 25 | 9 | .735 |
| Michigan | 9 | 9 | .500 | 21 | 14 | .600 |
| Illinois | 9 | 9 | .500 | 20 | 14 | .588 |
| Penn St | 9 | 9 | .500 | 19 | 15 | .559 |
| Michigan St | 9 | 9 | .500 | 19 | 15 | .559 |
| Northwestern | 7 | 11 | .389 | 20 | 14 | .588 |
| Minnesota | 6 | 12 | .333 | 17 | 14 | .548 |
| Iowa | 4 | 14 | .222 | 11 | 20 | .355 |
| Indiana | 3 | 15 | .167 | 12 | 20 | .375 |

Note: Standings based on regular-season conference play only; overall records include all tournament play.
*Conference tournament winner.

## Big 12

| | Conference | | | All Games | | |
|---|---|---|---|---|---|---|
| | W | L | Pct | W | L | Pct |
| *Kansas | 14 | 2 | .875 | 35 | 3 | .921 |
| Texas | 13 | 3 | .813 | 28 | 8 | .778 |
| Texas A&M | 10 | 6 | .625 | 24 | 9 | .727 |
| Kansas St | 10 | 6 | .625 | 23 | 11 | .676 |
| Missouri | 8 | 8 | .500 | 23 | 11 | .676 |
| Colorado | 8 | 8 | .500 | 24 | 14 | .632 |
| Nebraska | 7 | 9 | .438 | 19 | 13 | .594 |
| Baylor | 7 | 9 | .438 | 18 | 13 | .581 |
| Oklahoma St | 6 | 10 | .375 | 20 | 14 | .588 |
| Oklahoma | 5 | 11 | .313 | 14 | 18 | .438 |
| Texas Tech | 5 | 11 | .313 | 13 | 19 | .406 |
| Iowa St | 3 | 13 | .188 | 16 | 16 | .500 |

## Big West

| | Conference | | | All Games | | |
|---|---|---|---|---|---|---|
| | W | L | Pct | W | L | Pct |
| Long Beach St | 14 | 2 | .875 | 22 | 12 | .647 |
| Cal Poly | 10 | 6 | .625 | 15 | 15 | .500 |
| CSU-Northridge | 9 | 7 | .563 | 14 | 18 | .438 |
| *UC-Santa Barbara | 8 | 8 | .500 | 18 | 14 | .563 |
| Pacific | 8 | 8 | .500 | 16 | 15 | .516 |
| CSU-Fullerton | 7 | 9 | .438 | 11 | 20 | .355 |
| UC-Irvine | 6 | 10 | .375 | 13 | 19 | .406 |
| UC-Riverside | 6 | 10 | .375 | 12 | 19 | .387 |
| UC-Davis | 4 | 12 | .250 | 10 | 20 | .333 |

## Colonial

| | Conference | | | All Games | | |
|---|---|---|---|---|---|---|
| | W | L | Pct | W | L | Pct |
| George Mason | 16 | 2 | .889 | 27 | 7 | .794 |
| *Old Dominion | 14 | 4 | .778 | 27 | 7 | .794 |
| Hofstra | 14 | 4 | .778 | 21 | 12 | .636 |
| VCU | 12 | 6 | .667 | 28 | 12 | .700 |
| Drexel | 11 | 7 | .611 | 21 | 10 | .677 |
| James Madison | 10 | 8 | .556 | 21 | 12 | .636 |
| Delaware | 8 | 10 | .444 | 14 | 17 | .452 |
| UNC-Wilmington | 7 | 11 | .389 | 13 | 18 | .419 |
| Georgia St | 6 | 12 | .333 | 12 | 19 | .387 |
| Northeastern | 6 | 12 | .333 | 11 | 20 | .355 |
| William & Mary | 4 | 14 | .222 | 10 | 22 | .313 |
| Towson | 0 | 18 | .000 | 4 | 26 | .133 |

## Conference USA

| | Conference | | | All Games | | |
|---|---|---|---|---|---|---|
| | W | L | Pct | W | L | Pct |
| UAB | 12 | 4 | .750 | 22 | 9 | .710 |
| UTEP | 11 | 5 | .688 | 25 | 10 | .714 |
| Tulsa | 11 | 5 | .688 | 19 | 13 | .594 |
| *Memphis | 10 | 6 | .625 | 25 | 10 | .714 |
| Southern Miss | 9 | 7 | .563 | 22 | 10 | .688 |
| Marshall | 9 | 7 | .563 | 22 | 12 | .647 |
| SMU | 8 | 8 | .500 | 20 | 15 | .571 |
| East Carolina | 8 | 8 | .500 | 18 | 16 | .529 |
| Central Florida | 6 | 10 | .375 | 21 | 12 | .636 |
| Rice | 5 | 11 | .313 | 14 | 18 | .438 |
| Houston | 4 | 12 | .250 | 12 | 18 | .400 |
| Tulane | 3 | 13 | .188 | 13 | 17 | .433 |

## Great West**

| | Conference | | | All Games | | |
|---|---|---|---|---|---|---|
| | W | L | Pct | W | L | Pct |
| Utah Valley | 11 | 1 | .917 | 19 | 11 | .633 |
| NJIT | 9 | 3 | .750 | 15 | 15 | .500 |
| *North Dakota | 8 | 4 | .667 | 19 | 15 | .559 |
| South Dakota | 7 | 5 | .583 | 18 | 15 | .545 |
| Chicago St | 3 | 9 | .250 | 6 | 26 | .188 |
| UT-Pan American | 2 | 10 | .167 | 6 | 25 | .194 |
| Houston Baptist | 2 | 10 | .167 | 5 | 26 | .161 |

## Horizon League

| | Conference | | | All Games | | |
|---|---|---|---|---|---|---|
| | W | L | Pct | W | L | Pct |
| Cleveland St | 13 | 5 | .722 | 27 | 9 | .750 |
| *Butler | 13 | 5 | .722 | 28 | 10 | .737 |
| UW-Milwaukee | 13 | 5 | .722 | 19 | 14 | .576 |
| Valparaiso | 12 | 6 | .667 | 23 | 12 | .657 |
| Wright St | 10 | 8 | .556 | 19 | 14 | .576 |
| Detroit-Mercy | 10 | 8 | .556 | 17 | 16 | .515 |
| UW-Green Bay | 8 | 10 | .444 | 14 | 18 | .438 |
| Loyola (Ill.) | 7 | 11 | .389 | 16 | 15 | .516 |
| Youngstown St | 2 | 16 | .111 | 9 | 21 | .300 |
| Ill.-Chicago | 2 | 16 | .111 | 7 | 24 | .226 |

## Ivy League†

| | Conference | | | All Games | | |
|---|---|---|---|---|---|---|
| | W | L | Pct | W | L | Pct |
| Princeton | 13 | 2 | .857 | 25 | 7 | .781 |
| Harvard | 12 | 3 | .800 | 23 | 7 | .767 |
| Yale | 8 | 6 | .571 | 15 | 13 | .536 |
| Pennsylvania | 7 | 7 | .500 | 13 | 15 | .464 |
| Columbia | 6 | 8 | .429 | 15 | 13 | .536 |
| Cornell | 6 | 8 | .429 | 10 | 18 | .357 |
| Brown | 4 | 10 | .286 | 11 | 17 | .393 |
| Dartmouth | 1 | 13 | .071 | 5 | 23 | .179 |

## Metro Atlantic

| | Conference | | | All Games | | |
|---|---|---|---|---|---|---|
| | W | L | Pct | W | L | Pct |
| Fairfield | 15 | 3 | .833 | 25 | 8 | .758 |
| Iona | 13 | 5 | .722 | 25 | 12 | .676 |
| Rider | 13 | 5 | .722 | 23 | 11 | .676 |
| *St. Peter's | 11 | 7 | .611 | 20 | 14 | .588 |
| Loyola (Md.) | 10 | 8 | .556 | 15 | 15 | .500 |
| Canisius | 9 | 9 | .500 | 15 | 15 | .500 |
| Siena | 8 | 10 | .444 | 13 | 18 | .419 |
| Niagara | 5 | 13 | .278 | 9 | 23 | .281 |
| Manhattan | 3 | 15 | .167 | 6 | 25 | .194 |
| Marist | 3 | 15 | .167 | 6 | 27 | .182 |

## Mid-American

| | Conference | | | All Games | | |
|---|---|---|---|---|---|---|
| | W | L | Pct | W | L | Pct |
| **EAST** | | | | | | |
| Kent St | 12 | 4 | .750 | 25 | 12 | .676 |
| Miami (Ohio) | 11 | 5 | .688 | 16 | 17 | .485 |
| *Akron | 9 | 7 | .563 | 23 | 13 | .639 |
| Ohio | 9 | 7 | .563 | 19 | 16 | .543 |
| Buffalo | 8 | 8 | .500 | 20 | 14 | .588 |
| Bowling Green | 8 | 8 | .500 | 14 | 19 | .424 |
| **WEST** | | | | | | |
| Western Michigan | 11 | 5 | .688 | 21 | 13 | .618 |
| Ball St | 10 | 6 | .625 | 19 | 13 | .594 |
| Central Michigan | 7 | 9 | .438 | 10 | 21 | .323 |
| Northern Illinois | 5 | 11 | .313 | 9 | 21 | .300 |
| Eastern Michigan | 5 | 11 | .313 | 9 | 22 | .290 |
| Toledo | 1 | 15 | .063 | 4 | 28 | .125 |

*Conference tournament winner.
**No automatic bid for conference tournament winner.
†Does not hold end-of-season conference tournament.

### Mid-Eastern Athletic

| | Conference | | | All Games | | |
|---|---|---|---|---|---|---|
| | W | L | Pct | W | L | Pct |
| Bethune-Cookman | 13 | 3 | .813 | 21 | 13 | .618 |
| *Hampton | 11 | 5 | .688 | 24 | 9 | .727 |
| Coppin St | 11 | 5 | .688 | 16 | 14 | .533 |
| Morgan St | 10 | 6 | .625 | 17 | 14 | .548 |
| North Carolina A&T | 9 | 7 | .563 | 15 | 17 | .469 |
| Norfolk St | 8 | 8 | .500 | 12 | 20 | .375 |
| Florida A&M | 7 | 9 | .438 | 12 | 20 | .375 |
| South Carolina St | 5 | 11 | .313 | 10 | 22 | .313 |
| Delaware St | 5 | 11 | .313 | 9 | 21 | .300 |
| Md.-Eastern Shore | 5 | 11 | .313 | 9 | 22 | .290 |
| Howard | 4 | 12 | .250 | 6 | 24 | .200 |

### Missouri Valley

| | Conference | | | All Games | | |
|---|---|---|---|---|---|---|
| | W | L | Pct | W | L | Pct |
| Missouri St | 15 | 3 | .833 | 26 | 9 | .743 |
| Wichita St | 14 | 4 | .778 | 29 | 8 | .784 |
| *Indiana St | 12 | 6 | .667 | 20 | 14 | .588 |
| Creighton | 10 | 8 | .556 | 23 | 16 | .590 |
| Northern Iowa | 10 | 8 | .556 | 20 | 14 | .588 |
| Evansville | 9 | 9 | .500 | 16 | 16 | .500 |
| Drake | 7 | 11 | .389 | 13 | 18 | .419 |
| Southern Illinois | 5 | 13 | .278 | 13 | 19 | .406 |
| Illinois St | 4 | 14 | .222 | 12 | 19 | .387 |
| Bradley | 4 | 14 | .222 | 12 | 20 | .375 |

### Mountain West

| | Conference | | | All Games | | |
|---|---|---|---|---|---|---|
| | W | L | Pct | W | L | Pct |
| *San Diego St | 14 | 2 | .875 | 34 | 3 | .919 |
| BYU | 14 | 2 | .875 | 32 | 5 | .865 |
| UNLV | 11 | 5 | .688 | 24 | 9 | .727 |
| Colorado St | 9 | 7 | .563 | 19 | 13 | .594 |
| New Mexico | 8 | 8 | .500 | 22 | 13 | .629 |
| Air Force | 6 | 10 | .375 | 16 | 16 | .500 |
| Utah | 6 | 10 | .375 | 13 | 18 | .419 |
| Wyoming | 3 | 13 | .188 | 10 | 21 | .323 |
| TCU | 1 | 15 | .063 | 11 | 22 | .333 |

### Northeast

| | Conference | | | All Games | | |
|---|---|---|---|---|---|---|
| | W | L | Pct | W | L | Pct |
| *Long Island | 16 | 2 | .889 | 27 | 6 | .818 |
| Quinnipiac | 13 | 5 | .722 | 22 | 10 | .688 |
| Robert Morris | 12 | 6 | .667 | 18 | 14 | .563 |
| Central Conn. St | 11 | 7 | .611 | 19 | 12 | .613 |
| St. Francis (N.Y.) | 10 | 8 | .556 | 15 | 15 | .500 |
| Wagner | 9 | 9 | .500 | 13 | 17 | .433 |
| Mount St. Mary's | 9 | 9 | .500 | 11 | 21 | .344 |
| Bryant | 7 | 11 | .389 | 9 | 21 | .300 |
| St. Francis (Pa.) | 7 | 11 | .389 | 9 | 21 | .300 |
| Sacred Heart | 6 | 12 | .333 | 11 | 18 | .379 |
| Monmouth | 5 | 13 | .278 | 9 | 21 | .300 |
| Fairleigh Dickinson | 3 | 15 | .167 | 5 | 24 | .172 |

### Ohio Valley

| | Conference | | | All Games | | |
|---|---|---|---|---|---|---|
| | W | L | Pct | W | L | Pct |
| Murray St | 14 | 4 | .778 | 23 | 9 | .719 |
| *Morehead St | 13 | 5 | .722 | 25 | 10 | .714 |
| Austin Peay | 13 | 5 | .722 | 20 | 14 | .588 |
| Tennessee Tech | 12 | 6 | .667 | 20 | 13 | .606 |
| Tennessee St | 10 | 8 | .556 | 14 | 16 | .467 |
| Eastern Kentucky | 9 | 9 | .500 | 15 | 16 | .484 |
| Tenn.-Martin | 6 | 12 | .333 | 12 | 21 | .364 |
| SE Missouri St | 6 | 12 | .333 | 10 | 22 | .313 |
| Eastern Illinois | 4 | 14 | .222 | 9 | 20 | .310 |
| Jacksonville St | 3 | 15 | .167 | 5 | 25 | .167 |

### Pac 10

| | Conference | | | All Games | | |
|---|---|---|---|---|---|---|
| | W | L | Pct | W | L | Pct |
| Arizona | 14 | 4 | .778 | 30 | 8 | .789 |
| UCLA | 13 | 5 | .722 | 23 | 11 | .676 |
| *Washington | 11 | 7 | .611 | 24 | 11 | .686 |
| USC | 10 | 8 | .556 | 19 | 15 | .559 |
| California | 10 | 8 | .556 | 18 | 15 | .545 |
| Washington St | 9 | 9 | .500 | 22 | 13 | .629 |
| Oregon | 7 | 11 | .389 | 21 | 18 | .538 |
| Stanford | 7 | 11 | .389 | 15 | 16 | .484 |
| Oregon St | 5 | 13 | .278 | 11 | 20 | .355 |
| Arizona St | 4 | 14 | .222 | 12 | 19 | .387 |

### Patriot League

| | Conference | | | All Games | | |
|---|---|---|---|---|---|---|
| | W | L | Pct | W | L | Pct |
| *Bucknell | 13 | 1 | .929 | 25 | 9 | .735 |
| American | 11 | 3 | .786 | 22 | 9 | .710 |
| Holy Cross | 7 | 7 | .500 | 8 | 21 | .276 |
| Lehigh | 6 | 8 | .429 | 16 | 15 | .516 |
| Lafayette | 6 | 8 | .429 | 13 | 19 | .406 |
| Navy | 6 | 8 | .429 | 11 | 20 | .355 |
| Colgate | 4 | 10 | .286 | 7 | 23 | .233 |
| Army | 3 | 11 | .214 | 11 | 19 | .367 |

### Southeastern

| | Conference | | | All Games | | |
|---|---|---|---|---|---|---|
| **EAST** | W | L | Pct | W | L | Pct |
| Florida | 13 | 3 | .813 | 29 | 8 | .784 |
| *Kentucky | 10 | 6 | .625 | 29 | 9 | .763 |
| Vanderbilt | 9 | 7 | .563 | 23 | 11 | .676 |
| Georgia | 9 | 7 | .563 | 21 | 12 | .636 |
| Tennessee | 8 | 8 | .500 | 19 | 15 | .559 |
| South Carolina | 5 | 11 | .313 | 14 | 16 | .467 |
| **WEST** | | | | | | |
| Alabama | 12 | 4 | .750 | 25 | 12 | .676 |
| Mississippi St | 9 | 7 | .563 | 17 | 14 | .548 |
| Mississippi | 7 | 9 | .438 | 20 | 14 | .588 |
| Arkansas | 7 | 9 | .438 | 18 | 13 | .581 |
| Auburn | 4 | 12 | .250 | 11 | 20 | .355 |
| LSU | 3 | 13 | .188 | 11 | 21 | .344 |

*Conference tournament winner.

### Southern

| NORTH | Conference | | | All Games | | |
|---|---|---|---|---|---|---|
| | W | L | Pct | W | L | Pct |
| Western Carolina | 12 | 6 | .667 | 18 | 15 | .545 |
| Chattanooga | 12 | 6 | .667 | 16 | 16 | .500 |
| Appalachian St | 10 | 8 | .556 | 16 | 15 | .516 |
| Elon | 7 | 11 | .389 | 14 | 17 | .452 |
| UNC-Greensboro | 6 | 12 | .333 | 7 | 24 | .226 |
| Samford | 4 | 14 | .222 | 12 | 19 | .387 |
| **SOUTH** | | | | | | |
| Coll. of Charleston | 14 | 4 | .778 | 26 | 11 | .703 |
| *Wofford | 14 | 4 | .778 | 21 | 13 | .618 |
| Furman | 12 | 6 | .667 | 22 | 11 | .667 |
| Davidson | 10 | 8 | .556 | 18 | 15 | .545 |
| Citadel | 6 | 12 | .333 | 10 | 22 | .313 |
| Georgia Southern | 1 | 17 | .056 | 5 | 27 | .156 |

### Southland

| EAST | Conference | | | All Games | | |
|---|---|---|---|---|---|---|
| | W | L | Pct | W | L | Pct |
| McNeese St | 11 | 5 | .688 | 21 | 12 | .636 |
| Northwestern St | 10 | 6 | .625 | 18 | 14 | .563 |
| SE Louisiana | 9 | 7 | .563 | 15 | 14 | .517 |
| Nicholls St | 8 | 8 | .500 | 14 | 14 | .500 |
| Lamar | 7 | 9 | .438 | 13 | 17 | .433 |
| Central Arkansas | 1 | 15 | .063 | 5 | 24 | .172 |
| **WEST** | | | | | | |
| Sam Houston St | 10 | 6 | .625 | 18 | 13 | .581 |
| Texas St | 10 | 6 | .625 | 16 | 16 | .500 |
| *Tex.-San Antonio | 9 | 7 | .563 | 20 | 14 | .588 |
| Stephen F. Austin | 9 | 7 | .563 | 18 | 11 | .621 |
| Tex.-Arlington | 7 | 9 | .438 | 13 | 16 | .448 |
| Tex. A&M-Corp. Chris. | 5 | 11 | .313 | 10 | 21 | .323 |

### Southwestern Athletic

| | Conference | | | All Games | | |
|---|---|---|---|---|---|---|
| | W | L | Pct | W | L | Pct |
| Texas Southern | 16 | 2 | .889 | 19 | 13 | .594 |
| Jackson St | 12 | 6 | .667 | 17 | 15 | .531 |
| Mississippi Valley St | 12 | 6 | .667 | 13 | 19 | .406 |
| *Alabama St | 11 | 7 | .611 | 17 | 18 | .486 |
| Alabama A&M | 10 | 8 | .556 | 13 | 15 | .464 |
| Grambling St | 8 | 10 | .444 | 12 | 21 | .364 |
| Prairie View A&M | 7 | 11 | .389 | 10 | 22 | .313 |
| Ark.-Pine Bluff | 7 | 11 | .389 | 7 | 24 | .226 |
| Alcorn St | 4 | 14 | .222 | 4 | 24 | .143 |
| Southern Univ. | 3 | 15 | .167 | 4 | 26 | .133 |

### Summit League

| | Conference | | | All Games | | |
|---|---|---|---|---|---|---|
| | W | L | Pct | W | L | Pct |
| *Oakland | 17 | 1 | .944 | 25 | 10 | .714 |
| Oral Roberts | 13 | 5 | .722 | 19 | 16 | .543 |
| IUPUI | 12 | 6 | .667 | 19 | 14 | .576 |
| IPFW | 11 | 7 | .611 | 18 | 12 | .600 |
| South Dakota St | 10 | 8 | .556 | 19 | 12 | .613 |
| Mo.-Kansas City | 9 | 9 | .500 | 16 | 14 | .533 |
| North Dakota St | 8 | 10 | .444 | 14 | 15 | .483 |
| Southern Utah | 7 | 11 | .389 | 11 | 19 | .367 |
| Western Illinois | 2 | 16 | .111 | 7 | 23 | .233 |
| Centenary (La.) | 1 | 17 | .056 | 1 | 29 | .033 |

### Sun Belt

| EAST | Conference | | | All Games | | |
|---|---|---|---|---|---|---|
| | W | L | Pct | W | L | Pct |
| Florida Atlantic | 13 | 3 | .813 | 21 | 11 | .656 |
| Middle Tenn. St | 10 | 6 | .625 | 16 | 16 | .500 |
| Western Kentucky | 8 | 8 | .500 | 16 | 16 | .500 |
| South Alabama | 6 | 10 | .375 | 12 | 16 | .429 |
| Troy | 6 | 10 | .375 | 8 | 21 | .276 |
| Florida Int'l | 5 | 11 | .313 | 11 | 19 | .367 |
| **WEST** | | | | | | |
| Arkansas St | 11 | 5 | .688 | 17 | 15 | .531 |
| La.-Lafayette | 11 | 5 | .688 | 14 | 15 | .483 |
| Denver | 9 | 7 | .563 | 13 | 17 | .433 |
| North Texas | 8 | 8 | .500 | 22 | 11 | .667 |
| *Ark.-Little Rock | 7 | 9 | .438 | 19 | 17 | .528 |
| La.-Monroe | 2 | 14 | .125 | 7 | 24 | .226 |

### West Coast

| | Conference | | | All Games | | |
|---|---|---|---|---|---|---|
| | W | L | Pct | W | L | Pct |
| St. Mary's (Calif.) | 11 | 3 | .786 | 25 | 9 | .735 |
| *Gonzaga | 11 | 3 | .786 | 25 | 10 | .714 |
| San Francisco | 10 | 4 | .714 | 19 | 15 | .559 |
| Santa Clara | 8 | 6 | .571 | 24 | 14 | .632 |
| Portland | 7 | 7 | .500 | 20 | 12 | .625 |
| Pepperdine | 5 | 9 | .357 | 12 | 21 | .364 |
| Loyola Marymount | 2 | 12 | .143 | 11 | 21 | .344 |
| San Diego | 2 | 11 | .143 | 6 | 21 | .200 |

### Western Athletic

| | Conference | | | All Games | | |
|---|---|---|---|---|---|---|
| | W | L | Pct | W | L | Pct |
| *Utah St | 15 | 1 | .938 | 30 | 4 | .882 |
| Boise St | 10 | 6 | .625 | 22 | 13 | .629 |
| Idaho | 9 | 7 | .563 | 18 | 14 | .563 |
| New Mexico St | 9 | 7 | .563 | 16 | 17 | .485 |
| Hawaii | 8 | 8 | .500 | 19 | 13 | .594 |
| Nevada | 8 | 8 | .500 | 13 | 19 | .406 |
| Fresno St | 6 | 10 | .375 | 14 | 17 | .452 |
| San Jose St | 5 | 11 | .313 | 17 | 16 | .515 |
| Louisiana Tech | 2 | 14 | .125 | 12 | 20 | .375 |

### Independents

| | All Games | | |
|---|---|---|---|
| | W | L | Pct |
| New Orleans | 16 | 6 | .727 |
| North Carolina Central | 15 | 15 | .500 |
| Savannah St | 12 | 18 | .400 |
| Longwood | 12 | 19 | .387 |
| Seattle | 11 | 20 | .355 |
| CSU-Bakersfield | 9 | 19 | .321 |
| SIU-Edwardsville | 8 | 21 | .276 |

*Conference tournament winner.

### Scoring

| | Class | GP | FG | 3FG | FT | Pts | Avg |
|---|---|---|---|---|---|---|---|
| Jimmer Fredette, BYU | Sr. | 37 | 346 | 124 | 252 | 1068 | 28.9 |
| Marshon Brooks, Providence | Sr. | 32 | 276 | 67 | 169 | 788 | 24.6 |
| Adrian Oliver, San Jose St | Sr. | 31 | 246 | 70 | 181 | 743 | 24.0 |
| Andrew Goudelock, Coll. of Charleston | Sr. | 37 | 318 | 131 | 110 | 877 | 23.7 |
| Kemba Walker, Connecticut | Jr. | 41 | 316 | 75 | 258 | 965 | 23.5 |
| Charles Jenkins, Hofstra | Sr. | 33 | 249 | 66 | 182 | 746 | 22.6 |
| Xavier Silas, Northern Illinois | Sr. | 26 | 178 | 52 | 171 | 579 | 22.3 |
| Anatoly Bose, Nicholls St. | Sr. | 28 | 178 | 67 | 195 | 618 | 22.1 |
| C.J. McCollum, Lehigh | So. | 31 | 214 | 52 | 197 | 677 | 21.8 |
| Norris Cole, Cleveland St | Sr. | 36 | 251 | 51 | 227 | 780 | 21.7 |
| Klay Thompson, Washington St | Jr. | 34 | 240 | 98 | 155 | 733 | 21.6 |
| Devon Beitzel, Northern Colorado | Sr. | 32 | 201 | 87 | 198 | 687 | 21.5 |
| Orlando Johnson, UC-Santa Barbara | Jr. | 32 | 222 | 66 | 164 | 674 | 21.1 |
| Donald Sims, Appalachian St | Sr. | 31 | 198 | 78 | 178 | 652 | 21.0 |
| Andrew Nicholson, St. Bonaventure | Jr. | 31 | 237 | 6 | 165 | 645 | 20.8 |
| Nolan Smith, Duke | Sr. | 37 | 260 | 57 | 187 | 764 | 20.6 |
| JaJuan Johnson, Purdue | Sr. | 34 | 257 | 15 | 169 | 698 | 20.5 |
| Alec Burks, Colorado | So. | 38 | 251 | 28 | 249 | 779 | 20.5 |
| Vlad Moldoveanu, American | Sr. | 30 | 197 | 60 | 159 | 613 | 20.4 |
| Talor Battle, Penn St. | Sr. | 34 | 225 | 106 | 131 | 687 | 20.2 |
| Jacob Pullen, Kansas St. | Sr. | 31 | 191 | 74 | 170 | 626 | 20.2 |
| Kevin Foster, Santa Clara | So. | 38 | 229 | 140 | 168 | 766 | 20.2 |
| Noah Dahlman, Wofford | Sr. | 34 | 255 | 0 | 172 | 682 | 20.1 |
| Justin Hurtt, Tulsa | Sr. | 32 | 206 | 86 | 142 | 640 | 20.0 |
| Cameron Jones, Northern Arizona | Sr. | 32 | 249 | 36 | 106 | 640 | 20.0 |

#### FIELD-GOAL PERCENTAGE

| | Class | GP | FG | FGA | Pct |
|---|---|---|---|---|---|
| Leon Powell, SE Missouri St | Jr. | 32 | 172 | 273 | 63.0 |
| Brian Qvale, Montana | Sr. | 32 | 189 | 302 | 62.6 |
| Kenneth Faried, Morehead St | Sr. | 35 | 233 | 374 | 62.3 |
| Thomas Coleman, N.C. A&T | Sr. | 31 | 200 | 323 | 61.9 |
| Noah Dahlman, Wofford | Sr. | 34 | 255 | 417 | 61.2 |
| Mike Glover, Iona | Sr. | 37 | 260 | 426 | 61.0 |
| Jereal Scott, Stephen F. Austin | Jr. | 28 | 144 | 240 | 60.0 |
| Tai Wesley, Utah St | Sr. | 34 | 176 | 294 | 59.9 |
| Derrick Williams, Arizona | So. | 38 | 226 | 380 | 59.5 |
| Vernon Macklin, Florida | Sr. | 37 | 191 | 322 | 59.3 |

Note: Minimum 5 made per game.

#### FREE-THROW PERCENTAGE

| | Class | GP | FT | FTA | Pct |
|---|---|---|---|---|---|
| Chris Warren, Mississippi | Sr. | 34 | 168 | 181 | 92.8 |
| Oliver McNally, Harvard | Jr. | 30 | 100 | 108 | 92.6 |
| Zamal Nixon, Houston | Sr. | 30 | 94 | 102 | 92.2 |
| Brian Barbour, Columbia | So. | 28 | 122 | 133 | 91.7 |
| Justin Robinson, Rider | Sr. | 34 | 100 | 110 | 90.9 |
| B.J. Jenkins, Murray St | Sr. | 32 | 86 | 95 | 90.5 |
| Devon Beitzel, Northern Colo. | Sr. | 32 | 198 | 219 | 90.4 |
| Jeremy Granger, Eastern Ill. | Jr. | 29 | 103 | 114 | 90.4 |
| Connor Frizzelle, Rice | Jr. | 32 | 82 | 91 | 90.1 |
| Devon Peltier, CSU-Fullerton | Sr. | 31 | 89 | 99 | 89.9 |

Note: Minimum 2.5 made per game.

#### REBOUNDS

| | Class | GP | Reb | Avg |
|---|---|---|---|---|
| Kenneth Faried, Morehead St | Sr. | 35 | 508 | 14.5 |
| Ryan Rossiter, Siena | Sr. | 31 | 408 | 13.2 |
| Jordan Williams, Maryland | So. | 33 | 388 | 11.8 |
| Chris Gaston, Fordham | So. | 28 | 316 | 11.3 |
| Kyle O'Quinn, Norfolk St | Jr. | 32 | 355 | 11.1 |
| Augustine Rubit, South Alabama | Fr. | 28 | 308 | 11.0 |
| Arsalan Kazemi, Rice | So. | 32 | 351 | 11.0 |
| John Brown, Liberty | Jr. | 32 | 344 | 10.8 |
| Kawhi Leonard, San Diego St | So. | 36 | 380 | 10.6 |
| Trevor Mbakwe, Minnesota | Sr. | 31 | 327 | 10.5 |
| Sam Willard, Pacific | Sr. | 31 | 327 | 10.5 |
| Luke Sikma, Portland | Sr. | 32 | 336 | 10.5 |
| Thomas Coleman, N.C. A&T | Sr. | 31 | 325 | 10.5 |

#### ASSISTS

| | Class | GP | Ast | Avg |
|---|---|---|---|---|
| Aaron Johnson, UAB | Sr. | 31 | 239 | 7.7 |
| Scott Machado, Iona | Jr. | 37 | 281 | 7.6 |
| D.J. Cooper, Ohio | So. | 35 | 263 | 7.5 |
| Hank Thorns, TCU | Jr. | 32 | 225 | 7.0 |
| Darius Morris, Michigan | So. | 35 | 235 | 6.7 |
| Will Weathers, Troy | So. | 27 | 178 | 6.6 |
| Zac Swansey, Tennessee Tech | Sr. | 33 | 211 | 6.4 |
| Kevin Galloway, Texas Southern | Sr. | 32 | 201 | 6.3 |
| Kendall Marshall, North Carolina | Fr. | 37 | 230 | 6.2 |
| Demetri McCamey, Illinois | Sr. | 34 | 208 | 6.1 |
| Diante Garrett, Iowa St | Sr. | 32 | 195 | 6.1 |
| Isaiah Thomas, Washington | Jr. | 35 | 213 | 6.1 |
| Nate Wolters, South Dakota St | So. | 31 | 188 | 6.1 |
| Mickey McConnell, St. Mary's (Ca.) | Sr. | 34 | 206 | 6.1 |

*Includes games played in tournaments.

## THREE-POINT FIELD-GOAL PERCENTAGE

| | Class | GP | 3FG | 3FGA | Avg |
|---|---|---|---|---|---|
| Jon Diebler, Ohio St. | Sr. | 37 | 114 | 227 | 50.2 |
| Robert Nyakundi, SMU | Jr. | 35 | 97 | 195 | 49.7 |
| Ashton Gibbs, Pittsburgh | Jr. | 31 | 102 | 208 | 49.0 |
| Scott Bamforth, Weber St. | So. | 31 | 78 | 160 | 48.8 |
| Gabe Rogers, Northern Arizona | So. | 32 | 81 | 173 | 46.8 |
| Nemanja Mitrovic, Portland | Jr. | 32 | 93 | 201 | 46.3 |
| Bryson Johnson, Bucknell | So. | 34 | 99 | 217 | 45.6 |
| Jeff Ledbetter, Idaho | Sr. | 32 | 99 | 218 | 45.4 |
| Travis Bader, Oakland | Fr. | 35 | 94 | 212 | 44.3 |
| Brandon Provost, Tex.-Pan Am. | So. | 31 | 79 | 179 | 44.1 |
| Scott Christopherson, Iowa St. | Jr. | 31 | 86 | 195 | 44.1 |

Note: Minimum 2.5 made per game

## THREE-POINT FIELD GOALS MADE PER GAME

| | Class | GP | 3FG | Avg |
|---|---|---|---|---|
| Kevin Foster, Santa Clara | So. | 38 | 140 | 3.7 |
| Andrew Goudelock, Coll. of Char. | Sr. | 37 | 131 | 3.5 |
| Jimmer Fredette, BYU | Sr. | 37 | 124 | 3.4 |
| Austin Kenon, Virg. Mil. Inst. | Sr. | 28 | 93 | 3.3 |
| Ashton Gibbs, Pittsburgh | Jr. | 31 | 102 | 3.3 |
| Zach Filzen, Buffalo | Jr. | 34 | 110 | 3.2 |
| LaceDarius Dunn, Baylor | Sr. | 28 | 89 | 3.2 |
| Zane Johnson, Hawaii | Jr. | 31 | 98 | 3.2 |
| John Jenkins, Vanderbilt | So. | 32 | 100 | 3.1 |
| Talor Battle, Penn St. | Sr. | 34 | 106 | 3.1 |
| Jeff Ledbetter, Idaho | Sr. | 32 | 99 | 3.1 |
| Jon Diebler, Ohio St. | Sr. | 37 | 114 | 3.1 |
| Corey Stokes, Villanova | Sr. | 29 | 89 | 3.1 |

## BLOCKED SHOTS

| | Class | GP | BS | Avg |
|---|---|---|---|---|
| William Mosley, Northwestern St. | Jr. | 32 | 156 | 4.9 |
| Keith Benson, Oakland | Sr. | 35 | 127 | 3.6 |
| C.J. Aiken, St. Joseph's | Fr. | 33 | 117 | 3.5 |
| Kyle O'Quinn, Norfolk St. | Jr. | 32 | 110 | 3.4 |
| Sam Muldrow, South Carolina | Sr. | 30 | 103 | 3.4 |
| David Foster, Utah | Jr. | 31 | 99 | 3.2 |
| John Henson, North Carolina | So. | 37 | 118 | 3.2 |
| Danny Agbelese, Hampton | Jr. | 33 | 101 | 3.1 |
| Greg Mangano, Yale | Jr. | 28 | 85 | 3.0 |
| Damian Eargle, Youngstown St. | So. | 30 | 91 | 3.0 |
| Brett Royster, Florida Atlantic | Sr. | 32 | 97 | 3.0 |
| Jamelle Hagins, Delaware | So. | 29 | 87 | 3.0 |
| Brain Qvale, Montana | Sr. | 32 | 95 | 3.0 |

## STEALS

| | Class | GP | Stl | Avg |
|---|---|---|---|---|
| Anthony Nelson, Niagara | Sr. | 29 | 98 | 3.4 |
| Josh Slater, Lipscomb | Sr. | 30 | 93 | 3.1 |
| Jay Threatt, Delaware St. | Jr. | 30 | 93 | 3.1 |
| T. J. McConnell, Duquesne | Fr. | 32 | 91 | 2.8 |
| Jared Cunningham, Oregon St. | So. | 30 | 85 | 2.8 |
| Iman Shumpert, Georgia Tech | Jr. | 31 | 85 | 2.7 |
| Jackson Emery, BYU | Sr. | 37 | 101 | 2.7 |
| Devin Gibson, Tex.-San Antonio | Sr. | 34 | 91 | 2.7 |
| Will Cherry, Montana | So. | 30 | 79 | 2.6 |
| Akeem Bennett, St. Francis (N.Y.) | Sr. | 29 | 76 | 2.6 |

## Single-Game Highs

### POINTS

52.........Jimmer Fredette, BYU, March 11, 2011 (vs New Mexico)
52.........Marshon Brooks, Providence, February 23, 2011 (vs Notre Dame)
52.........Mike James, Lamar, January 4, 2011 (vs Louisiana College)
47.........Jimmer Fredette, BYU, January 11, 2011 (vs Utah)
44.........Andrew Nicholson, St. Bonaventure, December 18, 2010 (vs Ohio)

### REBOUNDS

23.........Drew Gordon, New Mexico, February 19, 2011 (vs Utah)
23.........Kenneth Faried, Morehead St, January 27, 2011 (vs Tennessee St)
22.........Brian Benson, New Hampshire, January 15, 2011 (vs Stony Brook)
22.........Keith Benson, Oakland, November 27, 2010 (vs Austin Peay)
22.........Rick Jackson, Syracuse, November 16, 2010 (vs Detroit)

### ASSISTS

17.........Joey Rodriguez, VCU, November 12, 2010 (vs UNC-Greensboro)
16.........Kendall Marshall, North Carolina, February 6, 2011 (vs Florida St)
16.........Vincent Council, Providence, December 6, 2010 (vs Brown)
Six tied with15.

### THREE-POINT FIELD GOALS

11 ........Mike James, Lamar, January 4, 2011 (vs Louisiana College)
10.........Jon Diebler, Ohio St, March 1, 2011 (vs Penn St)
10 ........LaceDarius Dunn, Baylor, January 4, 2011 (vs Morgan St)
10 ........Kevin Winford, Eastern Washington, December 4, 2010 (vs New Hope Christian)
Eight tied with 9.

### STEALS

10.........Josh Slater, Lipscomb, February 17, 2011 (vs S.C. Upstate)
10.........Chris Singleton, Florida St, November 14, 2010 (vs UNC-Greensboro)

### BLOCKED SHOTS

11.........William Mosley, Northwestern St, January 4, 2011 (vs LSU-Shreveport)
11.........William Mosley, Northwestern St, November 30, 2010 (vs Centenary)
11.........Ty Walker, Wake Forest, November 23, 2010 (vs Marist)

## SCORING OFFENSE

| | GP | W | L | Pts | Avg |
|---|---|---|---|---|---|
| Virginia Military Institute | 31 | 18 | 13 | 2726 | 87.9 |
| Oakland | 35 | 25 | 10 | 2992 | 85.5 |
| Washington | 35 | 24 | 11 | 2907 | 83.1 |
| Long Island | 33 | 27 | 6 | 2730 | 82.7 |
| Lamar | 30 | 13 | 17 | 2463 | 82.1 |
| South Dakota St | 31 | 19 | 12 | 2533 | 81.7 |
| BYU | 37 | 32 | 5 | 3012 | 81.4 |
| Kansas | 38 | 35 | 3 | 3084 | 81.2 |
| Duke | 37 | 32 | 5 | 2993 | 80.9 |
| Missouri | 34 | 23 | 11 | 2748 | 80.8 |

## SCORING DEFENSE

| | GP | W | L | Pts | Avg |
|---|---|---|---|---|---|
| Stephen F. Austin | 29 | 18 | 11 | 1643 | 56.7 |
| Fairfield | 33 | 25 | 8 | 1924 | 58.3 |
| Old Dominion | 34 | 27 | 7 | 1984 | 58.4 |
| Wisconsin | 34 | 25 | 9 | 1992 | 58.6 |
| Utah St | 34 | 30 | 4 | 1995 | 58.7 |
| Cal Poly | 30 | 15 | 15 | 1766 | 58.9 |
| San Diego St | 37 | 34 | 3 | 2192 | 59.2 |
| Alabama | 37 | 25 | 12 | 2198 | 59.4 |
| Cincinnati | 35 | 26 | 9 | 2086 | 59.6 |
| Ohio St | 37 | 34 | 3 | 2208 | 59.7 |
| Drexel | 31 | 21 | 10 | 1850 | 59.7 |

## SCORING MARGIN

| | Off | Def | Mar |
|---|---|---|---|
| Belmont | 79.7 | 62.2 | 17.5 |
| Ohio St. | 77.1 | 59.7 | 17.5 |
| Kansas | 81.2 | 64.7 | 16.5 |
| Duke | 80.9 | 64.7 | 16.2 |
| BYU | 81.4 | 67.9 | 13.5 |
| Utah St. | 72.0 | 58.7 | 13.4 |
| Pittsburgh | 73.9 | 61.0 | 13.0 |
| Texas | 75.0 | 62.2 | 12.9 |
| St. Mary's (Calif.) | 78.9 | 66.3 | 12.7 |
| San Diego St | 71.9 | 59.2 | 12.6 |

## FIELD-GOAL PERCENTAGE

| | FGM | FGA | Pct |
|---|---|---|---|
| Kansas | 1114 | 2193 | 50.8 |
| Ohio St. | 1017 | 2059 | 49.4 |
| Oakland | 1052 | 2137 | 49.2 |
| Northern Arizona | 850 | 1747 | 48.7 |
| Coastal Carolina | 930 | 1915 | 48.6 |
| St. Mary's (Calif.) | 946 | 1951 | 48.5 |
| SMU | 788 | 1634 | 48.2 |
| North Texas | 831 | 1735 | 47.9 |
| Tennessee Tech | 890 | 1859 | 47.9 |
| Gonzaga | 932 | 1947 | 47.9 |

## FIELD-GOAL PERCENTAGE DEFENSE

| | Opp FG | Opp FGA | Opp Pct |
|---|---|---|---|
| Florida St. | 696 | 1918 | 36.3 |
| St. Peter's | 683 | 1818 | 37.6 |
| Utah St | 696 | 1815 | 38.3 |
| Hampton | 719 | 1874 | 38.4 |
| Alabama | 758 | 1965 | 38.6 |
| Texas | 816 | 2109 | 38.7 |
| Nebraska | 657 | 1691 | 38.9 |
| Hawaii | 733 | 1883 | 38.9 |
| Stony Brook | 664 | 1704 | 39.0 |
| Vermont | 711 | 1812 | 39.2 |

## FREE-THROW PERCENTAGE

| | FT | FTA | Pct |
|---|---|---|---|
| Wisconsin | 436 | 533 | 81.8 |
| Harvard | 523 | 647 | 80.8 |
| Bucknell | 499 | 633 | 78.8 |
| IUPUI | 458 | 586 | 78.2 |
| Colorado | 679 | 873 | 77.8 |
| IPFW | 458 | 593 | 77.2 |
| Wagner | 491 | 636 | 77.2 |
| Northern Colorado | 571 | 742 | 77.0 |
| Central Connecticut St | 486 | 634 | 76.7 |
| BYU | 662 | 865 | 76.5 |

## THREE-POINT FIELD GOALS MADE PER GAME

| | GP | 3FG | Avg |
|---|---|---|---|
| Virginia Military Institute | 31 | 351 | 11.3 |
| Northwestern | 34 | 319 | 9.4 |
| Belmont | 35 | 327 | 9.3 |
| Elon | 31 | 285 | 9.2 |
| Boston College | 34 | 306 | 9.0 |
| Cornell | 28 | 251 | 9.0 |
| South Dakota St | 31 | 276 | 8.9 |
| Samford | 31 | 275 | 8.9 |
| Louisville | 35 | 309 | 8.8 |
| Army | 30 | 264 | 8.8 |
| Troy | 29 | 255 | 8.8 |

## REBOUNDING MARGIN

| | GP | Reb | Opp Reb | Margin Avg |
|---|---|---|---|---|
| Old Dominion | 34 | 1355 | 957 | 11.7 |
| Pittsburgh | 34 | 1359 | 992 | 10.8 |
| Drexel | 31 | 1249 | 956 | 9.5 |
| Quinnipiac | 32 | 1360 | 1063 | 9.3 |
| Morehead St | 35 | 1311 | 992 | 9.1 |
| Wichita St | 37 | 1389 | 1078 | 8.4 |
| Kansas | 38 | 1475 | 1172 | 8.0 |
| Utah St | 34 | 1266 | 1007 | 7.6 |
| Southern Miss | 32 | 1228 | 985 | 7.6 |
| Stephen F. Austin | 29 | 1029 | 816 | 7.3 |

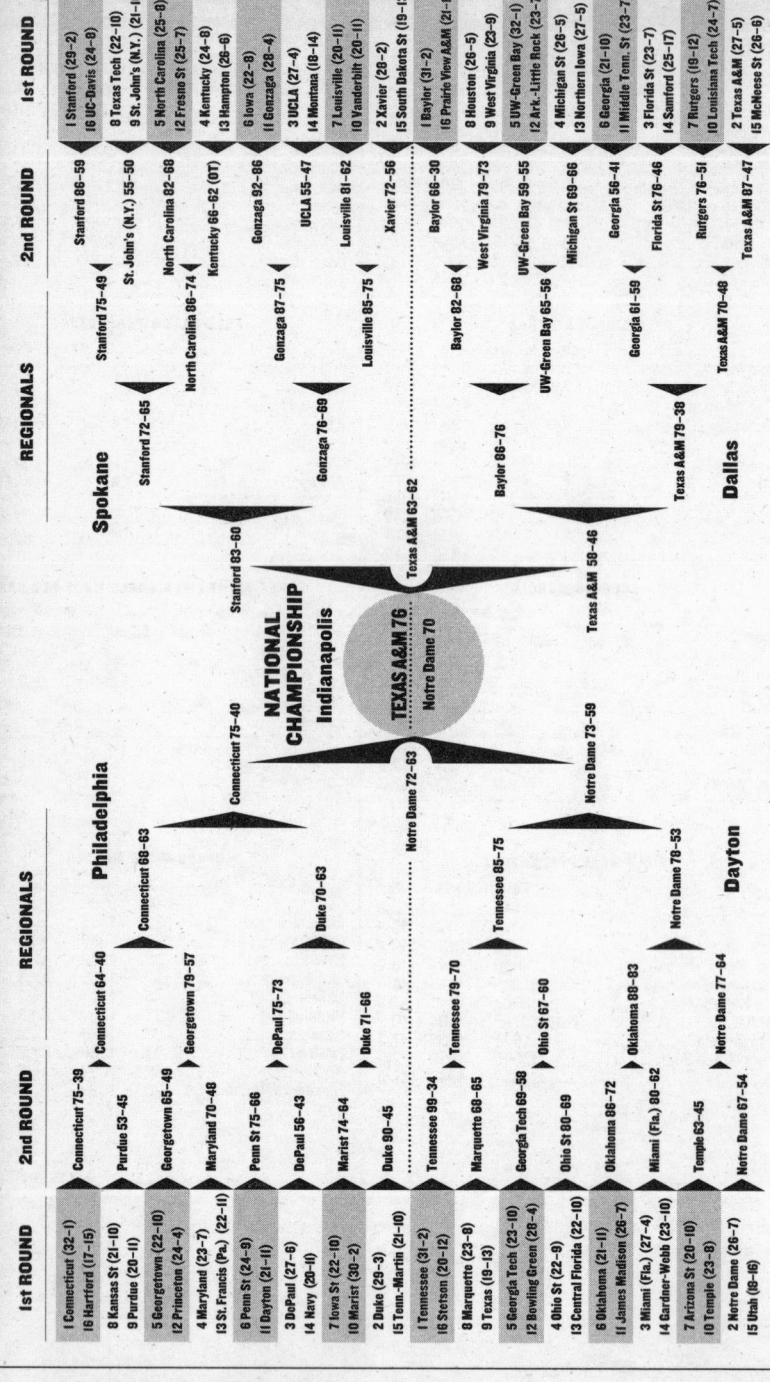

### Texas A&M 76

| | Min | FG M-A | FT M-A | Reb O-T | A | PF | TP |
|---|---|---|---|---|---|---|---|
| A. Elonu | 33 | 4-10 | 1-3 | 3-5 | 1 | 3 | 9 |
| D. Adams | 39 | 13-22 | 4-7 | 4-9 | 0 | 3 | 30 |
| T. White | 40 | 7-9 | 3-5 | 1-5 | 4 | 3 | 18 |
| S. Colson | 30 | 2-4 | 6-6 | 0-0 | 5 | 4 | 10 |
| S. Carter | 38 | 2-6 | 0-0 | 1-5 | 4 | 5 | 5 |
| M. Baker | 9 | 1-2 | 0-0 | 0-1 | 0 | 1 | 2 |
| K. Assarian | 1 | 0-0 | 0-0 | 0-0 | 0 | 1 | 0 |
| A. Pratcher | 1 | 0-0 | 0-0 | 0-0 | 0 | 0 | 0 |
| K. Gilbert | 5 | 0-0 | 2-2 | 0-1 | 0 | 1 | 2 |
| C. Snow | 1 | 0-0 | 0-0 | 0-0 | 0 | 0 | 0 |
| C. Windham | 1 | 0-0 | 0-0 | 0-0 | 0 | 0 | 0 |
| K. Grant | 1 | 0-0 | 0-0 | 0-0 | 0 | 0 | 0 |
| S. Collins | 1 | 0-0 | 0-0 | 0-0 | 0 | 0 | 0 |
| Totals | | 29-53 | 16-23 | 9-28 | 14 | 21 | 76 |

Percentages: FG-.547, FT-.696, 3-pt goals: 2-7, .286 (D. Adams 0-2, T. White 1-1, S. Colson 0-2, S. Carter 1-2.). Blocked shots: 4 (A. Elonu 1, D. Adams 1, S. Carter 2). Turnovers: 18 (A. Elonu 2, D. Adams 5, T. White 2, S. Colson 4, S. Carter 3, A. Pratcher 1, K. Gilbert 1). Steals: 8 (A. Elonu 1, D. Adams 1, T. White 2, S. Colson 3, K. Gilbert 1). Technical Fouls: None.

**Halftime: Notre Dame 35, Texas A&M 33.**

### Notre Dame 70

| | Min | FG M-A | FT M-A | Reb O-T | A | PF | TP |
|---|---|---|---|---|---|---|---|
| B. Bruszewski | 35 | 3-4 | 0-0 | 0-2 | 0 | 1 | 6 |
| D. Peters | 36 | 8-10 | 5-8 | 5-11 | 1 | 4 | 21 |
| B. Mallory | 37 | 1-6 | 1-2 | 0-1 | 3 | 2 | 4 |
| N. Novosel | 27 | 5-10 | 4-4 | 1-4 | 0 | 4 | 14 |
| S. Diggins | 39 | 7-19 | 8-9 | 1-3 | 3 | 0 | 23 |
| F. Miller | 10 | 0-1 | 0-1 | 1-4 | 2 | 3 | 0 |
| K. Turner | 6 | 0-1 | 2-2 | 0-0 | 1 | 0 | 2 |
| N. Achonwa | 10 | 0-1 | 0-0 | 1-5 | 0 | 5 | 0 |
| Totals | | 24-52 | 20-26 | 9-26 | 10 | 19 | 70 |

Percentages: FG-.462, FT-.769, 3-pt goals: 2-10, .200 (B. Mallory 1-4, N. Novosel 0-1, S. Diggins 1-5). Blocked shots: 3 (B. Bruszewski 2, D. Peters 1). Turnovers: 16 (B. Bruszewski 2, D. Peters 1, B. Mallory 3, N. Novosel 4, S. Diggins 6). Steals: 10 (B. Bruszewski 2, B. Mallory 2, S. Diggins 4, F. Miller 1, N. Achonwa 1). Technical Fouls: None.

**Final Four Most Outstanding Player: Danielle Adams, Texas A&M.**

Officials: Dee Kantner, Michael Price, Tina Napier. A: 17,473

### SCORING

| Player and Team | Class | GP | TFG | 3FG | FT | Pts | Avg |
|---|---|---|---|---|---|---|---|
| Kevi Luper, Oral Roberts | So. | 34 | 283 | 63 | 177 | 806 | 23.7 |
| Courtney Hurt, VCU | Jr. | 31 | 253 | 21 | 193 | 720 | 23.2 |
| Dawn Evans, James Madison | Sr. | 33 | 239 | 98 | 185 | 761 | 23.1 |
| Brittney Griner, Baylor | So. | 37 | 302 | 1 | 247 | 852 | 23.0 |
| Maya Moore, Connecticut | Sr. | 38 | 333 | 68 | 134 | 868 | 22.8 |
| Jantel Lavender, Ohio St | Sr. | 34 | 316 | 0 | 142 | 774 | 22.8 |
| Danielle Adams, Texas A&M | Sr. | 38 | 316 | 42 | 173 | 847 | 22.3 |
| Kourtney Brown, Buffalo | Sr. | 32 | 287 | 0 | 134 | 708 | 22.1 |
| Tahnee Robinson, Nevada | Sr. | 31 | 229 | 88 | 139 | 685 | 22.1 |
| Adrienne Johnson, Louisiana Tech | Sr. | 32 | 256 | 14 | 176 | 702 | 21.9 |
| Riquna Williams, Miami (Fla.) | Jr. | 33 | 251 | 75 | 140 | 717 | 21.7 |
| Amy Jaeschke, Northwestern | Sr. | 33 | 274 | 16 | 141 | 705 | 21.4 |
| Chynna Bozeman, Morehead St | Sr. | 31 | 215 | 104 | 128 | 662 | 21.4 |
| Kristin Turk, Drake | Sr. | 30 | 214 | 63 | 109 | 600 | 20.0 |
| Brandi Brown, Youngstown St | So. | 30 | 223 | 37 | 114 | 597 | 19.9 |
| Courtney Vandersloot, Gonzaga | Sr. | 36 | 254 | 42 | 162 | 712 | 19.8 |
| Shenise Johnson, Miami (Fla.) | Jr. | 33 | 236 | 44 | 132 | 648 | 19.6 |
| Chastity Reed, Arkansas-Little Rock | Sr. | 29 | 249 | 9 | 61 | 568 | 19.6 |
| Jori Davis, Indiana | Sr. | 29 | 177 | 32 | 179 | 565 | 19.5 |
| Brittany Spears, Colorado | Sr. | 34 | 239 | 81 | 93 | 652 | 19.2 |
| Brittani Shells, Richmond | Sr. | 30 | 230 | 45 | 70 | 575 | 19.2 |
| Carolyn Davis, Kansas | So. | 34 | 235 | 0 | 176 | 646 | 19.0 |
| Heather Butler, Tennessee-Martin | Fr. | 31 | 199 | 84 | 107 | 589 | 19.0 |
| Aubrey Vandiver, Wyoming | Sr. | 33 | 230 | 67 | 98 | 625 | 18.9 |
| Megan Shoniker, Rhode Island | Sr. | 28 | 159 | 53 | 159 | 530 | 18.9 |

### FIELD-GOAL PERCENTAGE

| Player and Team | Class | GP | FG | FGA | Pct |
|---|---|---|---|---|---|
| Carolyn Swords, Boston College | Sr. | 33 | 240 | 336 | 71.4 |
| Carolyn Davis, Kansas | So. | 34 | 235 | 356 | 66.0 |
| Ta'Shia Phillips, Xavier | Sr. | 32 | 211 | 349 | 60.5 |
| Chloe Hamilton, Butler | Sr. | 34 | 186 | 313 | 59.4 |
| Devereaux Peters, Notre Dame | Jr. | 39 | 195 | 329 | 59.3 |
| Kaetlyn Murdoch, Denver | Jr. | 31 | 203 | 343 | 59.2 |
| Kourtney Brown, Buffalo | Sr. | 32 | 287 | 487 | 58.9 |
| Nnemkadi Ogwumike, Stanford | Jr. | 33 | 231 | 394 | 58.6 |
| Ebony Rowe, Middle Tenn. St | Fr. | 31 | 208 | 356 | 58.4 |
| Jordan Pyle, Oral Roberts | Jr. | 33 | 205 | 359 | 57.1 |

Note: Minimum 5 FG per game.

### REBOUNDS

| Player and Team | Class | GP | Reb | Avg |
|---|---|---|---|---|
| Courtney Hurt, VCU | Jr. | 31 | 385 | 12.4 |
| Ta'Shia Phillips, Xavier | Sr. | 32 | 396 | 12.4 |
| Ashar Harris, Morehead St | So. | 30 | 368 | 12.3 |
| Kamilah Jackson, Hawaii | Fr. | 28 | 333 | 11.9 |
| Kourtney Brown, Buffalo | Sr. | 32 | 372 | 11.6 |
| Tanika Jackson, Alabama St | Sr. | 30 | 338 | 11.3 |
| Lena Gipson, Santa Clara | Sr. | 30 | 336 | 11.2 |
| Mekia Valentine, UC-Santa Barbara | Sr. | 31 | 347 | 11.2 |
| Courtney Taylor, Houston | Sr. | 29 | 322 | 11.1 |
| Kirsten Olowinksi, Miami (Ohio) | So. | 30 | 332 | 11.1 |
| Kaihla Szunko, Central Michigan | Sr. | 31 | 343 | 11.1 |

### FREE-THROW PERCENTAGE

| Player and Team | Class | GP | FT | FTA | Pct |
|---|---|---|---|---|---|
| Emily London, Samford | Sr. | 33 | 117 | 125 | 93.6 |
| Lindsay Laur, UW-Milwaukee | Sr. | 30 | 128 | 138 | 92.8 |
| Lauren Prochaska, Bowl. Green. | Sr. | 33 | 204 | 224 | 91.1 |
| Jacqui Kalin, Northern Iowa | Jr. | 33 | 121 | 133 | 91.0 |
| Casey Garrison, Missouri St | Jr. | 35 | 168 | 187 | 89.8 |
| Michelle Kurowski, Md-Balt. Cnty. | Jr. | 32 | 118 | 132 | 89.4 |
| Brittany Rayburn, Purdue | Jr. | 33 | 168 | 188 | 89.4 |
| Kathleen Nash, Texas | Sr. | 33 | 84 | 94 | 89.4 |
| Tre'Shonti Nottingham, UC-Riv. | So. | 31 | 139 | 156 | 89.1 |
| Kelsey Bolte, Iowa St | Sr. | 33 | 87 | 98 | 88.8 |

Note: Minimum 2.5 made per game.

### ASSISTS

| Player and Team | Class | GP | Ast | Avg |
|---|---|---|---|---|
| Courtney Vandersloot, Gonzaga | Sr. | 36 | 367 | 10.2 |
| Jericka Jenkins, Hampton | Jr. | 28 | 201 | 7.2 |
| Samantha Prahalis, Ohio St | Jr. | 31 | 215 | 6.9 |
| Amy McNear, Western Kentucky | Sr. | 29 | 196 | 6.8 |
| Coco Davis, San Diego St | Sr. | 27 | 171 | 6.3 |
| Angel Goodrich, Kansas | So. | 27 | 170 | 6.3 |
| Erin Lewis, Tex.-Pan American | Jr. | 31 | 194 | 6.3 |
| Ashley Zuber, Buffalo | Sr. | 32 | 198 | 6.2 |
| Sydney Colson, Texas A&M | Sr. | 36 | 221 | 6.1 |
| Cassie Schrock, Eastern Michigan | Sr. | 37 | 220 | 5.9 |
| Jamierra Faulkner, Southern Miss | Fr. | 30 | 178 | 5.9 |
| D'Frantz Smart, Rice | Jr. | 32 | 189 | 5.9 |
| Lindsey Moore, Nebraska | So. | 31 | 183 | 5.9 |
| Dominique Hudson, Gardner-Webb | Sr. | 33 | 194 | 5.9 |

### THREE-POINT FIELD-GOAL PERCENTAGE

| Player and Team | Class | GP | 3FG | 3FGA | Pct |
|---|---|---|---|---|---|
| Cerie Mosgrove, Massachusetts | Sr. | 30 | 78 | 157 | 49.7 |
| Emily London, Samford | Sr. | 33 | 84 | 174 | 48.3 |
| Kamile Nacickaite, Drexel | Jr. | 32 | 75 | 157 | 47.8 |
| Addie Micir, Princeton | Sr. | 29 | 77 | 167 | 46.1 |
| Angie Bjorklund, Tennessee | Sr. | 31 | 73 | 162 | 45.1 |
| Brittany Johnson, Ohio St | Sr. | 34 | 85 | 189 | 45.0 |
| Britteni Rice, Denver | Sr. | 31 | 71 | 158 | 44.9 |
| Iwalani Rodrigues, Utah | So. | 35 | 110 | 245 | 44.9 |
| Eryn Jones, Portland St | Jr. | 32 | 73 | 168 | 43.5 |
| Ali Heller, Rider | Jr. | 29 | 58 | 134 | 43.3 |

Note: Minimum 2.0 made per game.

### BLOCKED SHOTS

| Player and Team | Class | GP | BS | Avg |
|---|---|---|---|---|
| Louella Tomlinson, St. Mary's (Ca.) | Sr. | 32 | 151 | 4.7 |
| Brittany Griner, Baylor | So. | 37 | 170 | 4.6 |
| Mekia Valentine, UC-Santa Barbara | Sr. | 31 | 115 | 3.7 |
| Ashley Gayle, Texas | Jr. | 33 | 117 | 3.5 |
| Kourtney Brown, Buffalo | Sr. | 32 | 104 | 3.3 |
| Amy Jaeschke, Northwestern | Sr. | 33 | 104 | 3.2 |
| Mackenzie Maier, High Point | Sr. | 27 | 84 | 3.1 |
| El Sara Greer, Oregon St | Sr. | 30 | 92 | 3.1 |
| Sophia Aleksandravicius, Davidson | So. | 31 | 95 | 3.1 |
| Tia Mays, Missouri St | So. | 35 | 107 | 3.1 |

## NCAA Men's Division II Individual Leaders

### SCORING

| Player and Team | Class | GP | TFG | 3FG | FT | Pts | Avg |
|---|---|---|---|---|---|---|---|
| Parrish West, Alaska-Fairbanks | Sr. | 25 | 241 | 29 | 170 | 681 | 27.2 |
| Eric Salley, Claflin | Sr. | 22 | 142 | 52 | 198 | 534 | 24.3 |
| Chris Woods, Pfeiffer | Sr. | 27 | 229 | 1 | 196 | 655 | 24.3 |
| Gage Daye, Bloomfield | Sr. | 33 | 242 | 72 | 239 | 795 | 24.1 |
| Davion Berry, CSU-Monterey Bay | So. | 26 | 164 | 50 | 237 | 615 | 23.7 |
| Justin Caldwell, Glenville St | Sr. | 26 | 198 | 48 | 171 | 615 | 23.7 |
| Darius Adams, Indianapolis | Sr. | 27 | 205 | 73 | 143 | 626 | 23.2 |
| Thomas Baudinet, St. Anselm | Sr. | 28 | 223 | 85 | 87 | 618 | 22.1 |
| Gerald Fulton, Missouri-St. Louis | Jr. | 26 | 190 | 71 | 122 | 573 | 22.0 |
| Thomas Manzano, New Mexico Highlands | Jr. | 27 | 206 | 43 | 138 | 593 | 22.0 |
| Marquis Weddle, West Virginia Wesleyan | Sr. | 30 | 228 | 88 | 113 | 657 | 21.9 |
| Josh Miller, West Virginia St | Sr. | 29 | 215 | 54 | 145 | 629 | 21.7 |
| Sharif Bray, Cheyney | Sr. | 28 | 182 | 66 | 175 | 605 | 21.6 |
| Denzel Mooney, Lincoln (Pa.) | Jr. | 26 | 173 | 45 | 170 | 561 | 21.6 |
| Justin Keenan, Ferris St | Sr. | 32 | 225 | 5 | 235 | 690 | 21.6 |

## REBOUNDS

| Player and Team | Class | GP | Reb | Avg |
|---|---|---|---|---|
| Marcus Goode, Benedict | So. | 24 | 284 | 11.8 |
| Blake Poole, St. Martin's | Sr. | 29 | 336 | 11.6 |
| Marques Whippy, BYU-Hawaii | Sr. | 31 | 357 | 11.5 |
| Keon Williams, Pace | So. | 27 | 295 | 10.9 |
| Phillip Brown Georgia Southwestern | Jr. | 29 | 316 | 10.9 |
| Alex Novak, Minn. St-Moorhead | So. | 27 | 288 | 10.7 |
| Willie Whitfield, Barry | Sr. | 27 | 287 | 10.6 |
| Mike Kernan, Stonehill | Sr. | 30 | 318 | 10.6 |
| Quintus Bud Teer, Clarion | Jr. | 26 | 272 | 10.5 |
| Maron Brown, Slippery Rock | Sr. | 32 | 326 | 10.2 |
| L.J. Dunn, Barton | Sr. | 28 | 285 | 10.2 |
| Scott Roehl, Southwest Minnesota St | Sr. | 26 | 264 | 10.2 |

## ASSISTS

| Player and Team | Class | GP | Ast | Avg |
|---|---|---|---|---|
| D.J. Ferguson, Flagler | Sr. | 26 | 240 | 9.2 |
| Josh Magette, Alabama-Huntsville | Jr. | 34 | 272 | 8.0 |
| Braydon Hobbs, Bellarmine | Jr. | 35 | 228 | 6.5 |
| Bradley Turner, Carson-Newman | Jr. | 26 | 164 | 6.3 |
| Dominique Jones, Fort Hays St | Sr. | 33 | 207 | 6.3 |
| Corey Pelle, West Liberty | Sr. | 34 | 211 | 6.2 |
| Gilbert Montalvo, C.W. Post | Sr. | 31 | 191 | 6.2 |
| Gerald Boston, Barton | So. | 21 | 127 | 6.0 |
| Bryce Tesdahl, Bemidji St | Jr. | 26 | 156 | 6.0 |
| Nate Birr, St. Michael's | Sr. | 28 | 166 | 5.9 |

## FIELD-GOAL PERCENTAGE

| Player and Team | Class | GP | FG | FGA | Pct |
|---|---|---|---|---|---|
| Roderick Williams, Morehouse | Sr. | 28 | 144 | 205 | 70.2 |
| Larry Webster, Bloomsburg | Jr. | 25 | 132 | 190 | 69.5 |
| Kevin Kotzur, St. Mary's (Tex.) | So. | 27 | 203 | 299 | 67.9 |
| Patrick Grubbs, Pitt.-Johnstown | Jr. | 28 | 214 | 317 | 67.5 |
| Wilbur O'Neal, Indianapolis | Jr. | 25 | 126 | 187 | 67.4 |
| Brian Barkdoll, NW Nazarene | Sr. | 27 | 158 | 238 | 66.4 |
| Logan Stutz, Washburn | Sr. | 27 | 190 | 290 | 65.5 |
| Aaron Strothers, Merrimack | Jr. | 26 | 148 | 229 | 64.6 |
| Neven Zeravica, W.V. Wesleyan | Sr. | 30 | 178 | 280 | 63.6 |
| Willie Whitfield, Barry | Sr. | 27 | 152 | 240 | 63.3 |

Note: Minimum 5 made per game.

## FREE-THROW PERCENTAGE

| Player and Team | Class | GP | FT | FTA | Pct |
|---|---|---|---|---|---|
| Nathan Hyde, Findlay | Sr. | 28 | 138 | 150 | 92.0 |
| John Allen, Western Washington | So. | 26 | 65 | 71 | 91.5 |
| Justin Caldwell, Glenville St | Sr. | 26 | 171 | 187 | 91.4 |
| Nick Novak, Pitt.-Johnstown | So. | 28 | 128 | 141 | 90.8 |
| Richard Byrd, Adelphi | Sr. | 31 | 144 | 159 | 90.6 |
| Marquis Weddle, W.V. Wesleyan | Sr. | 30 | 113 | 125 | 90.4 |
| Kinard Dozier, Franklin Pierce | Sr. | 27 | 139 | 154 | 90.3 |
| Evrik Gary, Francis Marion | Fr. | 27 | 73 | 81 | 90.1 |
| Curtis Mitchell, Regis (Colo.) | Sr. | 23 | 63 | 70 | 90.0 |
| Jim Connolly, Philadelphia Univ. | So. | 27 | 103 | 115 | 89.6 |

Note: Minimum 2.5 made per game.

# NCAA Women's Division II Individual Leaders

## SCORING

| Player and Team | Class | GP | TFG | 3FG | FT | Pts | Avg |
|---|---|---|---|---|---|---|---|
| Samantha Murphy, Grand Canyon | Sr. | 32 | 233 | 86 | 234 | 786 | 24.6 |
| Chimere Jordan, Georgia College | Sr. | 29 | 229 | 51 | 122 | 631 | 21.8 |
| Tori Hansen, West Liberty | Sr. | 32 | 268 | 17 | 129 | 682 | 21.3 |
| Reyana Colson, Cal Poly-Pomona | Sr. | 32 | 233 | 27 | 188 | 681 | 21.3 |
| Mystee Dale, West Alabama | Sr. | 27 | 208 | 26 | 130 | 572 | 21.2 |
| Amanda Bartlett, Queens (N.Y.) | Sr. | 26 | 156 | 73 | 141 | 526 | 20.2 |
| Conisha Hicks, Clark Atlanta | Fr. | 27 | 203 | 67 | 68 | 541 | 20.0 |
| Caitlin Shaw, Univ. of Sciences Philadelphia | Sr. | 25 | 167 | 0 | 157 | 491 | 19.6 |
| Shannon Singleton-Bates, Francis Marion | Sr. | 27 | 197 | 32 | 102 | 528 | 19.6 |
| Kaitlin Snyder, Fairmont St | So. | 27 | 187 | 56 | 97 | 527 | 19.5 |
| Maria Young, Limestone | So. | 27 | 172 | 80 | 102 | 526 | 19.5 |
| Ashley Beckley, Central Oklahoma | Sr. | 32 | 211 | 2 | 199 | 623 | 19.5 |
| Andrea Dalton, Pittsburgh-Johnstown | Sr. | 28 | 208 | 48 | 80 | 544 | 19.4 |
| Jewel White, Franklin Pierce | Jr. | 32 | 225 | 0 | 170 | 620 | 19.4 |
| Angie Jetvig, Minnesota St-Moorhead | Jr. | 27 | 190 | 33 | 109 | 522 | 19.3 |

## REBOUNDS

| Player and Team | Class | GP | Reb | Avg |
|---|---|---|---|---|
| Aurielle Mosley, Millersville | So. | 29 | 366 | 12.6 |
| Alli Volkens, Emporia St | Sr. | 29 | 365 | 12.6 |
| Kayla Smith, California (Pa.) | Sr. | 30 | 373 | 12.4 |
| Cierra Baker, NYIT | Jr. | 26 | 322 | 12.4 |
| Emma Cannon, Florida Southern | Sr. | 31 | 375 | 12.1 |
| Jewel White, Franklin Pierce | Jr. | 32 | 382 | 11.9 |
| Rachel Murray, Fairmont St | Sr. | 27 | 322 | 11.9 |
| Sumiya Darden, Southwestern Okla. | Jr. | 26 | 308 | 11.8 |
| Dominique Hunter, San Fran. St | Sr. | 26 | 308 | 11.8 |
| Chanessa Blakemore, Concordia (N.Y.) | Jr. | 26 | 306 | 11.8 |

## ASSISTS

| Player and Team | Class | GP | Ast | Avg |
|---|---|---|---|---|
| Bug Cooper, Delta St | Sr. | 32 | 279 | 8.7 |
| Lynsey Timbrouck, St. Rose | Sr. | 29 | 205 | 7.1 |
| Abbie Tepe, Nova Southeastern | Sr. | 27 | 170 | 6.3 |
| Lynisha Nelson, Florida Tech | Sr. | 33 | 192 | 5.8 |
| Jenni Robbins, West Liberty | So. | 31 | 180 | 5.8 |
| Dara Tompkison, BYU-Hawaii | Jr. | 23 | 132 | 5.7 |
| Laura Beth Anderson, Arkansas Tech | Sr. | 33 | 188 | 5.7 |
| Kara Fleming, Central Missouri | Sr. | 28 | 158 | 5.6 |
| Chelsea Carlisle, UC-San Diego | Jr. | 31 | 174 | 5.6 |
| Jamilla Johnson, Barton | Sr. | 31 | 172 | 5.5 |
| Megan Stewart, West Chester | Sr. | 27 | 148 | 5.5 |

### FIELD-GOAL PERCENTAGE

| Player and Team | Class | GP | FG | FGA | Pct |
|---|---|---|---|---|---|
| Shannon McKever, Lander | Sr. | 31 | 225 | 363 | 62.0 |
| Veronica Walker, Delta St | Jr. | 32 | 231 | 374 | 61.8 |
| Jamie Kauffman, W.V. Wesleyan | Jr. | 27 | 193 | 318 | 60.7 |
| Lisa Staehlin, Michigan Tech | Sr. | 34 | 172 | 288 | 59.7 |
| Jewel White, Franklin Pierce | Jr. | 32 | 225 | 377 | 59.7 |
| Michelle McDonald, Winona St | Jr. | 30 | 177 | 297 | 59.6 |
| Amy Achesinski, Mercyhurst | Sr. | 30 | 204 | 343 | 59.5 |
| Michaela Hawley, Fla. Southern | Jr. | 30 | 160 | 271 | 59.0 |
| Dana Schreibvogel, Fort Lewis | Jr. | 31 | 225 | 393 | 57.3 |
| Hillary Hurley, Hawaii Hilo | Jr. | 21 | 115 | 202 | 56.9 |

Note: Minimum 5 FG per game.

### FREE-THROW PERCENTAGE

| Player and Team | Class | GP | FT | FTA | Pct |
|---|---|---|---|---|---|
| Samantha Murphy, Grand Canyon | Sr. | 32 | 234 | 256 | 91.4 |
| Traci Keyser, Fort Hays St | So. | 25 | 80 | 88 | 90.9 |
| Ashley Abed, Anderson (S.C.) | Sr. | 27 | 89 | 100 | 89.0 |
| Ashton McClairen, Florida Tech | Jr. | 33 | 87 | 98 | 88.8 |
| Kelsey Gallagher, Bloomsburg | Jr. | 28 | 83 | 94 | 88.3 |
| Bethanie Funderburk, Drury | Fr. | 30 | 98 | 112 | 87.5 |
| Lacey Claar, Indiana (Pa.) | Sr. | 27 | 70 | 80 | 87.5 |
| Mystee Dale, West Alabama | Sr. | 27 | 130 | 149 | 87.2 |
| Josie Stewart, Cameron | Sr. | 28 | 131 | 151 | 86.8 |
| Angie Jetvig, Minn. St-Moorhead | Jr. | 27 | 109 | 126 | 86.5 |

Note: Minimum 2.5 made per game.

## NCAA Men's Division III Individual Leaders

### SCORING

| Player and Team | Class | GP | TFG | 3FG | FT | Pts | Avg |
|---|---|---|---|---|---|---|---|
| Lamonte Thomas, Johnson & Wales | Jr. | 30 | 289 | 73 | 270 | 921 | 30.7 |
| Michael McClary, Olivet | Sr. | 26 | 269 | 2 | 136 | 676 | 26.0 |
| Tony Mane, UW-LaCrosse | Sr. | 26 | 241 | 82 | 102 | 666 | 25.6 |
| Robert Malone, Rockford | Sr. | 25 | 228 | 41 | 128 | 625 | 25.0 |
| Dave Golembiowski, SUNY-IT | Sr. | 21 | 200 | 45 | 72 | 517 | 24.6 |
| Matt Addison, Hardin-Simmons | Jr. | 22 | 178 | 48 | 136 | 540 | 24.5 |
| Eryk Watson, Maryville (Tenn.) | Sr. | 26 | 191 | 94 | 151 | 627 | 24.1 |
| Jonathan Jones, Kean | Sr. | 26 | 233 | 3 | 153 | 622 | 23.9 |
| Javon Williams, Lasell | Jr. | 25 | 211 | 8 | 166 | 596 | 23.8 |
| Nathaniel Young, City Tech | Sr. | 23 | 186 | 33 | 138 | 543 | 23.6 |
| K.C. Wiser, Linfield | Sr. | 23 | 200 | 36 | 96 | 532 | 23.1 |
| Conley Taylor, Christopher Newport | Jr. | 25 | 185 | 25 | 181 | 576 | 23.0 |
| Asmar Capers, Drew | Sr. | 25 | 179 | 65 | 128 | 551 | 22.0 |
| Wes Smith, Wabash | Sr. | 26 | 201 | 32 | 137 | 571 | 22.0 |
| Steve Djurickovic, Carthage | Sr. | 25 | 164 | 31 | 186 | 545 | 21.8 |
| DaQuan Brooks, Western Connecticut St | Jr. | 27 | 191 | 83 | 123 | 588 | 21.8 |

### REBOUNDS

| Player and Team | Class | GP | Reb | Avg |
|---|---|---|---|---|
| Marcel Esonwune, York (N.Y.) | Sr. | 26 | 364 | 14.0 |
| Jonathan Jones, Kean | Sr. | 26 | 355 | 13.7 |
| Derek Mitchell, Ferrum | Sr. | 27 | 357 | 13.2 |
| Lester Prosper, Old Westbury | Sr. | 26 | 339 | 13.0 |
| Michael Russell, Colby | Sr. | 24 | 303 | 12.6 |
| Matt Pepdjonovic, Suffolk | So. | 26 | 324 | 12.5 |
| Simon Smith, Stevens Inst. | Jr. | 29 | 361 | 12.4 |
| Jon Greenberg, Mass. Liberal Arts | Sr. | 23 | 281 | 12.2 |
| Josh Stein, Maranatha Baptist | Sr. | 27 | 325 | 12.0 |
| Cameron Snelling, Benedictine (Ill.) | Sr. | 29 | 345 | 11.9 |

### ASSISTS

| Player and Team | Class | GP | Ast | Avg |
|---|---|---|---|---|
| Sean Rossi, Ithaca | So. | 27 | 263 | 9.7 |
| Scott Gillespie, Ripon | Sr. | 24 | 182 | 7.6 |
| Austin Claunch, Emory | Jr. | 25 | 186 | 7.4 |
| Jerald Williams, Lycoming | So. | 25 | 182 | 7.3 |
| Steve Kjurickovic, Carthage | Sr. | 25 | 165 | 6.6 |
| Corey Lemons, Cabrini | So. | 29 | 189 | 6.5 |
| Al'Don Muhammad, Rutgers-Newark | So. | 27 | 173 | 6.4 |
| Ryan Birrell, Salve Regina | Sr. | 28 | 177 | 6.3 |
| Todd Zimmerman, Principia | Sr. | 22 | 138 | 6.3 |
| Paul Meredith, Chris. Newport | So. | 21 | 130 | 6.2 |
| Nate Green, Benedictine (Ill.) | Jr. | 29 | 179 | 6.2 |
| Brian Hunter, DeSales | Sr. | 29 | 179 | 6.2 |

### FIELD-GOAL PERCENTAGE

| Player and Team | Class | GP | FG | FGA | Pct |
|---|---|---|---|---|---|
| Troy Whittington, Williams | Sr. | 28 | 168 | 237 | 70.9 |
| Sean Dart, Willamette | So. | 20 | 112 | 168 | 66.7 |
| Phil Barera, Ithaca | Sr. | 27 | 202 | 309 | 65.4 |
| Mike Case, Hanover | Jr. | 27 | 169 | 262 | 64.5 |
| Travis Clark, Lake Forest | Jr. | 23 | 146 | 227 | 64.3 |
| Scott Robertson, Capital | Sr. | 27 | 147 | 230 | 63.9 |
| Chris McGrew, Salisbury | Sr. | 27 | 167 | 262 | 63.7 |
| Jeff Barczak, Edgewood | Sr. | 26 | 135 | 213 | 63.4 |
| John Ward, Ursinus | So. | 25 | 154 | 243 | 63.4 |
| Derek Mitchell, Ferrum | Sr. | 27 | 207 | 327 | 63.3 |

Note: Minimum 5 made per game.

### FREE-THROW PERCENTAGE

| Player and Team | Class | GP | FT | FTA | Pct |
|---|---|---|---|---|---|
| Ryan Martin, Keene St | Fr. | 28 | 99 | 103 | 96.1 |
| Geo. Johnson, East. Mennonite | Sr. | 27 | 91 | 99 | 91.9 |
| Chris DeRojas, Wilkes | Sr. | 25 | 85 | 93 | 91.4 |
| James Jones, Delaware Valley | Sr. | 28 | 189 | 208 | 90.9 |
| Keith Fogel, Elizabethtown | Sr. | 24 | 89 | 98 | 90.8 |
| Nick Rose, Colorado College | Sr. | 24 | 92 | 102 | 90.2 |
| Layton Seeber, Gallaudet | Jr. | 28 | 101 | 112 | 90.2 |
| Matt Hilton, Ursinus | Sr. | 25 | 100 | 111 | 90.1 |
| Matt Addison, Hardin-Simmons | Jr. | 22 | 136 | 151 | 90.1 |
| Stephen Simoneau, Marymount (Va.) | Sr. | 23 | 63 | 70 | 90.0 |

Note: Minimum 2.5 made per game.

## SCORING

| Player and Team | Class | GP | TFG | 3FG | FT | Pts | Avg |
|---|---|---|---|---|---|---|---|
| Chelsie Schweers, Christopher Newport | Sr. | 34 | 301 | 133 | 135 | 870 | 25.6 |
| Lee Jennings, John Carroll | Sr. | 26 | 241 | 6 | 163 | 651 | 25.0 |
| Louvinia Hayes, Lehman | Sr. | 28 | 209 | 90 | 141 | 649 | 23.2 |
| Katie Dewitt, Northwestern (Minn.) | Sr. | 23 | 195 | 38 | 89 | 517 | 22.5 |
| Shante Jones, Eastern | Jr. | 24 | 203 | 13 | 119 | 538 | 22.4 |
| Rachel Williams, New England College | Jr. | 25 | 194 | 12 | 160 | 560 | 22.4 |
| Marche Smith, Concordia Chicago | Sr. | 25 | 204 | 50 | 98 | 556 | 22.2 |
| Ashley Roser, Wells | Fr. | 25 | 191 | 3 | 162 | 547 | 21.9 |
| Danielle Duncan, Greensboro | Jr. | 30 | 215 | 1 | 223 | 654 | 21.8 |
| Jessica Berry, Utica | Sr. | 26 | 229 | 19 | 85 | 562 | 21.6 |
| Mary Wilkowski, Hamline | Sr. | 25 | 218 | 1 | 95 | 532 | 21.3 |
| Easter Faafiti, Gallaudet | Sr. | 28 | 214 | 0 | 145 | 573 | 20.5 |
| Kim Weathers, Old Westbury | Fr. | 28 | 207 | 53 | 106 | 573 | 20.5 |
| Brittany Parks, Vassar | Jr. | 28 | 180 | 46 | 162 | 568 | 20.3 |
| Karin Bird, Thomas (Me.) | Jr. | 21 | 130 | 25 | 140 | 425 | 20.2 |

## REBOUNDS

| Player and Team | Class | GP | Reb | Avg |
|---|---|---|---|---|
| Elizabeth Sunderhaus, Cedar Crest | Jr. | 24 | 374 | 15.6 |
| Maame Amponsah, Marymount (Va.) | Sr. | 23 | 358 | 15.6 |
| Catherine O'Connell, Newbury | So. | 26 | 392 | 15.1 |
| Christine Daniels, Norwich | Sr. | 26 | 379 | 14.6 |
| Lindey Newcombe, Hardin-Simmons | Sr. | 26 | 378 | 14.5 |
| Margaux Pickell, Polytechnic (N.Y.) | Jr. | 27 | 391 | 14.5 |
| Casey Stanton, Pitt.-Greensburg | Sr. | 25 | 362 | 14.5 |
| Jen Wehner, Mass. Coll. of Lib. Arts | Jr. | 27 | 385 | 14.3 |
| Yvanna Jack, Medgar Evers | Jr. | 19 | 262 | 13.8 |
| Ashley Roser, Wells | Fr. | 25 | 343 | 13.7 |

## ASSISTS

| Player and Team | Class | GP | Ast | Avg |
|---|---|---|---|---|
| Monique Salmon, Baruch | Sr. | 29 | 214 | 7.4 |
| Carey Hickey, Manhattanville | Sr. | 26 | 177 | 6.8 |
| Lee Jennings, John Carroll | Sr. | 26 | 177 | 6.8 |
| Cailin Bullett, Colby-Sawyer | So. | 25 | 160 | 6.4 |
| Annie Burns, Bates | Jr. | 25 | 159 | 6.4 |
| Allison Anderson, Oberlin | So. | 24 | 150 | 6.3 |
| Brittany Cohen, SUNY-Cortland | Jr. | 25 | 153 | 6.1 |
| Cory Boyd, Wesley | Sr. | 27 | 165 | 6.1 |
| Kerri Confrey, Catholic | Sr. | 29 | 172 | 5.9 |
| Andrea Hoover, Lebanon Valley | Sr. | 31 | 183 | 5.9 |
| Serafina Nuzzo, Denison | So. | 28 | 165 | 5.9 |

## FIELD-GOAL PERCENTAGE

| Player and Team | Class | GP | FG | FGA | Pct |
|---|---|---|---|---|---|
| Megan Lawler, Rockford | Sr. | 26 | 132 | 207 | 63.8 |
| Stacey Arlis, Illinois Wesleyan | Sr. | 33 | 198 | 315 | 62.9 |
| Melissa Teel, Western Conn. St. | Sr. | 28 | 211 | 349 | 60.5 |
| Dana Thompson, UW-Whitewater | Sr. | 28 | 156 | 260 | 60.0 |
| Carissa Verkaik, Calvin | So. | 30 | 242 | 406 | 59.6 |
| LaTonya Oliver, Richard Stockton | Jr. | 27 | 149 | 250 | 59.6 |
| Jaclyn Daigneault, Amherst | Sr. | 33 | 202 | 343 | 58.9 |
| Rachel Macon, Illinois College | Sr. | 24 | 165 | 284 | 58.1 |
| Britta Petersen, UW-Stevens Point | Sr. | 29 | 188 | 324 | 58.0 |
| Meghan Fiore, Utica | So. | 26 | 186 | 323 | 57.6 |

Note: Minimum 5 made per game.

## THREE-POINT FIELD-GOAL PERCENTAGE

| Player and Team | Class | GP | 3FG | 3FGA | Pct |
|---|---|---|---|---|---|
| Chelsie Schweers, Chris. Newport | Sr. | 34 | 133 | 270 | 49.3 |
| Alex Wilson, LaGrange | Fr. | 25 | 63 | 134 | 47.0 |
| Allie Long, Washington & Lee | Sr. | 27 | 66 | 144 | 45.8 |
| Cydni Matsuoka, Vassar | Fr. | 28 | 78 | 171 | 45.6 |
| Laura Karsten, Wheaton (Ill.) | So. | 22 | 46 | 102 | 45.1 |
| Pui Sham, St. Mary's (Md.) | So. | 25 | 59 | 131 | 45.0 |
| Olivia Lett, Illinois Wesleyan | Jr. | 33 | 67 | 150 | 44.7 |
| Emily Pelletier, Me.-Presque Isle | So. | 23 | 71 | 160 | 44.4 |
| Melissa Eltzroth, Manchester | So. | 22 | 55 | 124 | 44.4 |
| Shelly Kilcup, Pacific Lutheran | So. | 24 | 49 | 111 | 44.1 |

Note: Minimum 2.5 made per game.

## NCAA Men's Division I Championship Results

### NCAA Final Four Results

| Year | Winner | Score | Runner-up | Third Place | Fourth Place | Winning Coach |
|------|--------|-------|-----------|-------------|--------------|---------------|
| 1939 | Oregon | 46–33 | Ohio St | *Oklahoma | *Villanova | Howard Hobson |
| 1940 | Indiana | 60–42 | Kansas | *Duquesne | *USC | Branch McCracken |
| 1941 | Wisconsin | 39–34 | Washington St | *Pittsburgh | *Arkansas | Harold Foster |
| 1942 | Stanford | 53–38 | Dartmouth | *Colorado | *Kentucky | Everett Dean |
| 1943 | Wyoming | 46–34 | Georgetown | *Texas | *DePaul | Everett Shelton |
| 1944 | Utah | 42–40 (OT) | Dartmouth | *Iowa St | *Ohio St | Vadal Peterson |
| 1945 | Oklahoma St | 49–45 | NYU | *Arkansas | *Ohio St | Hank Iba |
| 1946 | Oklahoma St | 43–40 | North Carolina | Ohio St | California | Hank Iba |
| 1947 | Holy Cross | 58–47 | Oklahoma | Texas | CCNY | Alvin Julian |
| 1948 | Kentucky | 58–42 | Baylor | Holy Cross | Kansas St | Adolph Rupp |
| 1949 | Kentucky | 46–36 | Oklahoma St | Illinois | Oregon St | Adolph Rupp |
| 1950 | CCNY | 71–68 | Bradley | North Carolina St | Baylor | Nat Holman |
| 1951 | Kentucky | 68–58 | Kansas St | Illinois | Oklahoma St | Adolph Rupp |
| 1952 | Kansas | 80–63 | St. John's (N.Y.) | Illinois | Santa Clara | Forrest Allen |
| 1953 | Indiana | 69–68 | Kansas | Washington | LSU | Branch McCracken |
| 1954 | La Salle | 92–76 | Bradley | Penn St | USC | Kenneth Loeffler |
| 1955 | San Francisco | 77–63 | La Salle | Colorado | Iowa | Phil Woolpert |
| 1956 | San Francisco | 83–71 | Iowa | Temple | SMU | Phil Woolpert |
| 1957 | North Carolina | 54–53 (3OT) | Kansas | San Francisco | Michigan St | Frank McGuire |
| 1958 | Kentucky | 84–72 | Seattle | Temple | Kansas St | Adolph Rupp |
| 1959 | California | 71–70 | West Virginia | Cincinnati | Louisville | Pete Newell |
| 1960 | Ohio St | 75–55 | California | Cincinnati | NYU | Fred Taylor |
| 1961 | Cincinnati | 70–65 (OT) | Ohio St | Vacated‡ | Utah | Edwin Jucker |
| 1962 | Cincinnati | 71–59 | Ohio St | Wake Forest | UCLA | Edwin Jucker |
| 1963 | Loyola (Ill.) | 60–58 (OT) | Cincinnati | Duke | Oregon St | George Ireland |
| 1964 | UCLA | 98–83 | Duke | Michigan | Kansas St | John Wooden |
| 1965 | UCLA | 91–80 | Michigan | Princeton | Wichita St | John Wooden |
| 1966 | UTEP | 72–65 | Kentucky | Duke | Utah | Don Haskins |
| 1967 | UCLA | 79–64 | Dayton | Houston | North Carolina | John Wooden |
| 1968 | UCLA | 78–55 | North Carolina | Ohio St | Houston | John Wooden |
| 1969 | UCLA | 92–72 | Purdue | Drake | North Carolina | John Wooden |
| 1970 | UCLA | 80–69 | Jacksonville | New Mexico St | St. Bonaventure | John Wooden |
| 1971 | UCLA | 68–62 | Vacated‡ | Vacated‡ | Kansas | John Wooden |
| 1972 | UCLA | 81–76 | Florida St | North Carolina | Louisville | John Wooden |
| 1973 | UCLA | 87–66 | Memphis St | Indiana | Providence | John Wooden |
| 1974 | North Carolina St | 76–64 | Marquette | UCLA | Kansas | Norm Sloan |
| 1975 | UCLA | 92–85 | Kentucky | Louisville | Syracuse | John Wooden |
| 1976 | Indiana | 86–68 | Michigan | UCLA | Rutgers | Bob Knight |
| 1977 | Marquette | 67–59 | North Carolina | UNLV | UNC-Charlotte | Al McGuire |
| 1978 | Kentucky | 94–88 | Duke | Arkansas | Notre Dame | Joe Hall |
| 1979 | Michigan St | 75–64 | Indiana St | DePaul | Penn | Jud Heathcote |
| 1980 | Louisville | 59–54 | Vacated‡ | Purdue | Iowa | Denny Crum |
| 1981 | Indiana | 63–50 | North Carolina | Virginia | LSU | Bob Knight |
| 1982 | North Carolina | 63–62 | Georgetown | *Houston | *Louisville | Dean Smith |
| 1983 | North Carolina St | 54–52 | Houston | *Georgia | *Louisville | Jim Valvano |
| 1984 | Georgetown | 84–75 | Houston | *Kentucky | *Virginia | John Thompson |
| 1985 | Villanova | 66–64 | Georgetown | St. John's (N.Y.) | Vacated‡ | Rollie Massimino |
| 1986 | Louisville | 72–69 | Duke | *Kansas | *LSU | Denny Crum |
| 1987 | Indiana | 74–73 | Syracuse | *UNLV | *Providence | Bob Knight |
| 1988 | Kansas | 83–79 | Oklahoma | *Arizona | *Duke | Larry Brown |
| 1989 | Michigan | 80–79 (OT) | Seton Hall | *Duke | *Illinois | Steve Fisher |
| 1990 | UNLV | 103–73 | Duke | *Arkansas | *Georgia Tech | Jerry Tarkanian |
| 1991 | Duke | 72–65 | Kansas | *UNLV | *North Carolina | Mike Krzyzewski |
| 1992 | Duke | 71–51 | Michigan | *Cincinnati | *Indiana | Mike Krzyzewski |
| 1993 | North Carolina | 77–71 | Michigan | *Kansas | *Kentucky | Dean Smith |
| 1994 | Arkansas | 76–72 | Duke | *Arizona | *Florida | Nolan Richardson |
| 1995 | UCLA | 89–78 | Arkansas | *North Carolina | *Oklahoma St | Jim Harrick |
| 1996 | Kentucky | 76–67 | Syracuse | Vacated‡ | Mississippi St | Rick Pitino |
| 1997 | Arizona | 84–79 (OT) | Kentucky | *Minnesota | *North Carolina | Lute Olson |
| 1998 | Kentucky | 78–69 | Utah | *Stanford | *North Carolina | Tubby Smith |
| 1999 | Connecticut | 77–74 | Duke | *Michigan St | *Ohio St | Jim Calhoun |
| 2000 | Michigan St | 89–76 | Florida | *Wisconsin | *North Carolina | Tom Izzo |
| 2001 | Duke | 82–72 | Arizona | *Maryland | *Michigan St | Mike Krzyzewski |

## NCAA Final Four Results (Cont.)

| Year | Winner | Score | Runner-up | Third Place | Fourth Place | Winning Coach |
|------|--------|-------|-----------|-------------|--------------|---------------|
| 2002 | Maryland | 64–52 | Indiana | *Kansas | *Oklahoma | Gary Williams |
| 2003 | Syracuse | 81–78 | Kansas | *Marquette | *Texas | Jim Boeheim |
| 2004 | Connecticut | 82–73 | Georgia Tech | *Oklahoma St | *Duke | Jim Calhoun |
| 2005 | North Carolina | 75–70 | Illinois | *Louisville | *Michigan St | Roy Williams |
| 2006 | Florida | 73–57 | UCLA | *George Mason | *LSU | Billy Donovan |
| 2007 | Florida | 84–75 | Ohio St | *UCLA | *Georgetown | Billy Donovan |
| 2008 | Kansas | 75–68 (OT) | Vacated‡ | *UCLA | *North Carolina | Bill Self |
| 2009 | North Carolina | 89–72 | Michigan St | *Villanova | *Connecticut | Roy Williams |
| 2010 | Duke | 61–59 | Butler | *West Virginia | *Michigan St | Mike Krzyzewski |
| 2011 | Connecticut | 53–41 | Butler | *Kentucky | *VCU | Jim Calhoun |

*Tied for third place. ‡Student-athletes representing St. Joseph's (Pa.) in 1961, Villanova in 1971, Western Kentucky in 1971, UCLA in 1980, Memphis State in 1985, Massachusetts in 1996, and Memphis in 2008 were declared ineligible subsequent to the tournament. Under NCAA rules, the teams' and ineligible student-athletes' records were deleted, and the teams' places in the tandings were vacated.

## NCAA Final Four Most Outstanding Players

| Year | Winner, School | GP | Field Goals | | 3-Pt FG | | Free Throws | | Reb | Asst | Stl | BS | Avg |
|------|----------------|-----|------|------|-----|-----|-----|------|-----|------|-----|-----|------|
| | | | FGM | Pct | FGA | FGM | FTM | Pct | | | | | |
| 1939 | None selected | | | | | | | | | | | | |
| 1940 | Marv Huffman, Indiana | 2 | 7 | — | — | — | 4 | — | — | — | — | — | 9.0 |
| 1941 | John Kotz, Wisconsin | 2 | 8 | — | — | — | 6 | — | — | — | — | — | 11.0 |
| 1942 | Howard Dallmar, Stanford | 2 | 8 | — | — | — | 4 | 66.7 | — | — | — | — | 10.0 |
| 1943 | Ken Sailors, Wyoming | 2 | 10 | — | — | — | 8 | 72.7 | — | — | — | — | 14.0 |
| 1944 | Arnie Ferrin, Utah | 2 | 11 | — | — | — | 6 | — | — | — | — | — | 14.0 |
| 1945 | Bob Kurland, Oklahoma St | 2 | 16 | — | — | — | 5 | — | — | — | — | — | 18.5 |
| 1946 | Bob Kurland, Oklahoma St | 2 | 21 | — | — | — | 10 | 66.7 | — | — | — | — | 26.0 |
| 1947 | George Kaftan, Holy Cross | 2 | 18 | — | — | — | 12 | 70.6 | — | — | — | — | 24.0 |
| 1948 | Alex Groza, Kentucky | 2 | 16 | — | — | — | 5 | — | — | — | — | — | 18.5 |
| 1949 | Alex Groza, Kentucky | 2 | 19 | — | — | — | 14 | — | — | — | — | — | 26.0 |
| 1950 | Irwin Dambrot, CCNY | 2 | 12 | 42.9 | — | — | 4 | 50.0 | — | — | — | — | 14.0 |
| 1951 | None selected | | | | | | | | | | | | |
| 1952 | Clyde Lovellette, Kansas | 2 | 24 | — | — | — | 18 | — | — | — | — | — | 33.0 |
| 1953 | *B.H. Horn, Kansas | 2 | 17 | — | — | — | 17 | — | — | — | — | — | 25.5 |
| 1954 | Tom Gola, La Salle | 2 | 12 | — | — | — | 14 | — | — | — | — | — | 19.0 |
| 1955 | Bill Russell, San Francisco | 2 | 19 | — | — | — | 9 | — | — | — | — | — | 23.5 |
| 1956 | *Hal Lear, Temple | 2 | 32 | — | — | — | 16 | — | — | — | — | — | 40.0 |
| 1957 | *Wilt Chamberlain, Kansas | 2 | 18 | 51.4 | — | — | 19 | 70.4 | 25 | — | — | — | 32.5 |
| 1958 | *Elgin Baylor, Seattle | 2 | 18 | 34.0 | — | — | 12 | 75.0 | 41 | — | — | — | 24.0 |
| 1959 | *Jerry West, West Virginia | 2 | 22 | 66.7 | — | — | 22 | 68.8 | 25 | — | — | — | 33.0 |
| 1960 | Jerry Lucas, Ohio St | 2 | 16 | 66.7 | — | — | 3 | 100.0 | 23 | — | — | — | 17.5 |
| 1961 | *Jerry Lucas, Ohio St | 2 | 20 | 71.4 | — | — | 16 | 94.1 | 25 | — | — | — | 28.0 |
| 1962 | Paul Hogue, Cincinnati | 2 | 23 | 63.9 | — | — | 12 | 63.2 | 38 | — | — | — | 29.0 |
| 1963 | Art Heyman, Duke | 2 | 18 | 41.0 | — | — | 15 | 68.2 | 19 | — | — | — | 25.5 |
| 1964 | Walt Hazzard, UCLA | 2 | 11 | 55.0 | — | — | 8 | 66.7 | 10 | — | — | — | 15.0 |
| 1965 | *Bill Bradley, Princeton | 2 | 34 | 63.0 | — | — | 19 | 95.0 | 24 | — | — | — | 43.5 |
| 1966 | *Jerry Chambers, Utah | 2 | 25 | 53.2 | — | — | 20 | 83.3 | 35 | — | — | — | 35.0 |
| 1967 | Lew Alcindor, UCLA | 2 | 14 | 60.9 | — | — | 11 | 45.8 | 38 | — | — | — | 19.5 |
| 1968 | Lew Alcindor, UCLA | 2 | 22 | 62.9 | — | — | 9 | 90.0 | 34 | — | — | — | 26.5 |
| 1969 | Lew Alcindor, UCLA | 2 | 23 | 67.7 | — | — | 16 | 64.0 | 41 | — | — | — | 31.0 |
| 1970 | Sidney Wicks, UCLA | 2 | 15 | 71.4 | — | — | 9 | 60.0 | 34 | — | — | — | 19.5 |
| 1971 | *†Howard Porter, Villanova | 2 | 20 | 48.8 | — | — | 7 | 77.8 | 24 | — | — | — | 23.5 |
| 1972 | Bill Walton, UCLA | 2 | 20 | 69.0 | — | — | 17 | 73.9 | 41 | — | — | — | 28.5 |
| 1973 | Bill Walton, UCLA | 2 | 28 | 82.4 | — | — | 2 | 40.0 | 30 | — | — | — | 29.0 |
| 1974 | David Thompson, N.C. St | 2 | 19 | 51.4 | — | — | 11 | 78.6 | 17 | — | — | — | 24.5 |
| 1975 | Richard Washington, UCLA | 2 | 23 | 54.8 | — | — | 8 | 72.7 | 20 | — | — | — | 27.0 |
| 1976 | Kent Benson, Indiana | 2 | 17 | 50.0 | — | — | 7 | 63.6 | 18 | — | — | — | 20.5 |
| 1977 | Butch Lee, Marquette | 2 | 11 | 34.4 | — | — | 8 | 100.0 | 6 | 2 | 1 | 1 | 15.0 |
| 1978 | Jack Givens, Kentucky | 2 | 28 | 65.1 | — | — | 8 | 66.7 | 17 | 4 | 1 | 3 | 32.0 |
| 1979 | Earvin Johnson, Michigan St | 2 | 17 | 68.0 | — | — | 19 | 86.4 | 17 | 3 | 0 | 2 | 26.5 |
| 1980 | Darrell Griffith, Louisville | 2 | 23 | 62.2 | — | — | 11 | 68.8 | 7 | 15 | 0 | 2 | 28.5 |
| 1981 | Isiah Thomas, Indiana | 2 | 14 | 56.0 | — | — | 9 | 81.8 | 4 | 9 | 3 | 4 | 18.5 |
| 1982 | James Worthy, North Carolina | 2 | 20 | 74.1 | — | — | 2 | 28.6 | 8 | 9 | 0 | 4 | 21.0 |
| 1983 | *Akeem Olajuwon, Houston | 2 | 16 | 55.2 | — | — | 9 | 64.3 | 40 | 3 | 2 | 5 | 20.5 |
| 1984 | Patrick Ewing, Georgetown | 2 | 8 | 57.1 | — | — | 2 | 100.0 | 18 | 1 | 1 | 15 | 9.0 |
| 1985 | Ed Pinckney, Villanova | 2 | 8 | 57.1 | — | — | 12 | 75.0 | 15 | 6 | 3 | 0 | 14.0 |
| 1986 | Pervis Ellison, Louisville | 2 | 15 | 60.0 | — | — | 6 | 75.0 | 24 | 2 | 3 | 1 | 18.0 |

*Not a member of the championship-winning team.  †Record later vacated.

## NCAA Final Four MOPs *(Cont.)*

| Year | Winner, School | GP | Field Goals | | 3-Pt FG | | Free Throws | | Reb | Ast | Stl | BS | Avg |
|------|----------------|-----|------|------|------|------|------|------|------|-----|-----|-----|------|
| | | | FGM | Pct | FGA | FGM | FTM | Pct | | | | | |
| 1987 | Keith Smart, Indiana | 2 | 14 | 63.6 | 1 | 0 | 7 | 77.8 | 7 | 7 | 0 | 2 | 17.5 |
| 1988 | Danny Manning, Kansas | 2 | 25 | 55.6 | 1 | 0 | 6 | 66.7 | 17 | 4 | 8 | 9 | 28.0 |
| 1989 | Glen Rice, Michigan | 2 | 24 | 49.0 | 16 | 7 | 4 | 100.0 | 16 | 1 | 0 | 3 | 29.5 |
| 1990 | Anderson Hunt, UNLV | 2 | 19 | 61.3 | 16 | 9 | 2 | 50.0 | 4 | 9 | 1 | 1 | 24.5 |
| 1991 | Christian Laettner, Duke | 2 | 12 | 54.5 | 1 | 1 | 21 | 91.3 | 17 | 2 | 1 | 2 | 23.0 |
| 1992 | Bobby Hurley, Duke | 2 | 10 | 41.7 | 12 | 7 | 8 | 80.0 | 3 | 11 | 0 | 3 | 17.5 |
| 1993 | Donald Williams, North Carolina | 2 | 15 | 65.2 | 14 | 10 | 10 | 100.0 | 4 | 2 | 2 | 0 | 25.0 |
| 1994 | Corliss Williamson, Arkansas | 2 | 21 | 50.0 | 0 | 0 | 10 | 71.4 | 21 | 8 | 4 | 3 | 26.0 |
| 1995 | Ed O'Bannon, UCLA | 2 | 16 | 45.7 | 8 | 3 | 10 | 76.9 | 25 | 3 | 7 | 1 | 22.5 |
| 1996 | Tony Delk, Kentucky | 2 | 15 | 41.7 | 16 | 8 | 6 | 54.6 | 9 | 2 | 3 | 2 | 22.0 |
| 1997 | Miles Simon, Arizona | 2 | 17 | 45.9 | 10 | 3 | 17 | 77.3 | 8 | 6 | 0 | 1 | 27.0 |
| 1998 | Jeff Sheppard, Kentucky | 2 | 16 | 55.2 | 10 | 4 | 7 | 77.8 | 10 | 7 | 4 | 0 | 21.5 |
| 1999 | Richard Hamilton, Connecticut | 2 | 20 | 51.3 | 7 | 3 | 8 | 72.7 | 12 | 4 | 2 | 1 | 25.5 |
| 2000 | Mateen Cleaves, Michigan St | 2 | 8 | 44.4 | 4 | 3 | 10 | 83.3 | 6 | 5 | 2 | 0 | 14.5 |
| 2001 | Shane Battier, Duke | 2 | 13 | 50.0 | 12 | 5 | 12 | 70.6 | 19 | 8 | 2 | 6 | 21.5 |
| 2002 | Juan Dixon, Maryland | 2 | 16 | 59.3 | 15 | 7 | 12 | 80.0 | 8 | 5 | 7 | 0 | 25.5 |
| 2003 | Carmelo Anthony, Syracuse | 2 | 19 | 54.3 | 6 | 9 | 9 | 81.1 | 24 | 8 | 4 | 0 | 26.5 |
| 2004 | Emeka Okafor, Connecticut | 2 | 17 | 65.4 | 0 | 0 | 8 | 53.3 | 22 | 2 | 1 | 4 | 21.0 |
| 2005 | Sean May, North Carolina | 2 | 19 | 65.5 | 0 | 0 | 10 | 71.4 | 17 | 5 | 1 | 2 | 24.0 |
| 2006 | Joakim Noah, Florida | 2 | 12 | 60.0 | 1 | 0 | 4 | 100.0 | 17 | 5 | 2 | 10 | 14.0 |
| 2007 | Corey Brewer, Florida | 2 | 9 | 47.3 | 13 | 7 | 7 | 87.5 | 10 | 2 | 3 | 5 | 16.0 |
| 2008 | Mario Chalmers, Kansas | 2 | 10 | 43.5 | 9 | 3 | 6 | 75.0 | 7 | 6 | 7 | 0 | 14.5 |
| 2009 | Wayne Ellington, North Carolina | 2 | 14 | 53.8 | 11 | 8 | 3 | 75.0 | 13 | 4 | 0 | 0 | 19.5 |
| 2010 | Kyle Singler, Duke | 2 | 15 | 34.1 | 10 | 6 | 4 | 100.0 | 18 | 7 | 3 | 2 | 20.0 |
| 2011 | Kemba Walker, Connecticut | 2 | 11 | 32.4 | 9 | 1 | 11 | 84.6 | 15 | 7 | 3 | 1 | 17.0 |

## Best NCAA Tournament Single-Game Scoring Performances

| Player and Team | Year | Round | FG | 3FG | FT | TP |
|-----------------|------|-------|-----|-----|-----|-----|
| Austin Carr, Notre Dame vs Ohio | 1970 | 1st | 25 | — | 11 | 61 |
| Bill Bradley, Princeton vs Wichita St | 1965 | C* | 22 | — | 14 | 58 |
| Oscar Robertson, Cincinnati vs Arkansas | 1958 | C | 21 | — | 14 | 56 |
| Austin Carr, Notre Dame vs Kentucky | 1970 | 2nd | 22 | — | 8 | 52 |
| Austin Carr, Notre Dame vs TCU | 1971 | 1st | 20 | — | 12 | 52 |
| David Robinson, Navy vs Michigan | 1987 | 1st | 22 | 0 | 6 | 50 |
| Elvin Hayes, Houston vs Loyola (Ill.) | 1968 | 1st | 20 | — | 9 | 49 |
| Hal Lear, Temple vs SMU | 1956 | C* | 17 | — | 14 | 48 |
| Austin Carr, Notre Dame vs Houston | 1971 | C | 17 | — | 13 | 47 |
| Dave Corzine, DePaul vs Louisville | 1978 | 2nd | 18 | — | 10 | 46 |

C=regional third place; C*=third-place game.

## NIT Championship Results

| Year | Winner | Score | Runner-up | Year | Winner | Score | Runner-up |
|------|--------|-------|-----------|------|--------|-------|-----------|
| 1938 | Temple | 60–36 | Colorado | 1958 | Xavier (Ohio) | 78–74 (OT) | Dayton |
| 1939 | Long Island U. | 44–32 | Loyola (Ill.) | 1959 | St. John's (N.Y.) | 76–71 (OT) | Bradley |
| 1940 | Colorado | 51–40 | Duquesne | 1960 | Bradley | 88–72 | Providence |
| 1941 | Long Island U. | 56–42 | Ohio U | 1961 | Providence | 62–59 | St. Louis |
| 1942 | West Virginia | 47–45 | W. Kentucky | 1962 | Dayton | 73–67 | St. John's (N.Y.) |
| 1943 | St. John's (N.Y.) | 48–27 | Toledo | 1963 | Providence | 81–66 | Canisius |
| 1944 | St. John's (N.Y.) | 47–39 | DePaul | 1964 | Bradley | 86–54 | New Mexico |
| 1945 | DePaul | 71–54 | Bowling Green | 1965 | St. John's (N.Y.) | 55–51 | Villanova |
| 1946 | Kentucky | 46–45 | Rhode Island | 1966 | BYU | 97–84 | NYU |
| 1947 | Utah | 49–45 | Kentucky | 1967 | Southern Illinois | 71–56 | Marquette |
| 1948 | St. Louis | 65–52 | NYU | 1968 | Dayton | 61–48 | Kansas |
| 1949 | San Francisco | 48–47 | Loyola (Ill.) | 1969 | Temple | 89–76 | Boston College |
| 1950 | CCNY | 69–61 | Bradley | 1970 | Marquette | 65–53 | St. John's (N.Y.) |
| 1951 | BYU | 62–43 | Dayton | 1971 | North Carolina | 84–66 | Georgia Tech |
| 1952 | La Salle | 75–64 | Dayton | 1972 | Maryland | 100–69 | Niagara |
| 1953 | Seton Hall | 58–46 | St. John's (N.Y.) | 1973 | Virginia Tech | 92–91 (OT) | Notre Dame |
| 1954 | Holy Cross | 71–62 | Duquesne | 1974 | Purdue | 97–81 | Utah |
| 1955 | Duquesne | 70–58 | Dayton | 1975 | Princeton | 80–69 | Providence |
| 1956 | Louisville | 93–80 | Dayton | 1976 | Kentucky | 71–67 | UNC-Charlotte |
| 1957 | Bradley | 84–83 | Memphis St | 1977 | St. Bonaventure | 94–91 | Houston |

## NIT Championship Results *(Cont.)*

| Year | Winner | Score | Runner-up | Year | Winner | Score | Runner-up |
|------|--------|-------|-----------|------|--------|-------|-----------|
| 1978 | Texas | 101–93 | North Carolina St | 1995 | Virginia Tech | 65–64 (OT) | Marquette |
| 1979 | Indiana | 53–52 | Purdue | 1996 | Nebraska | 60–56 | St. Joseph's |
| 1980 | Virginia | 58–55 | Minnesota | 1997 | Michigan | 82–73 | Florida St |
| 1981 | Tulsa | 86–84 (OT) | Syracuse | 1998 | Minnesota | 79–72 | Penn St |
| 1982 | Bradley | 67–58 | Purdue | 1999 | California | 61–60 | Clemson |
| 1983 | Fresno St | 69–60 | DePaul | 2000 | Wake Forest | 71–61 | Notre Dame |
| 1984 | Michigan | 83–63 | Notre Dame | 2001 | Tulsa | 79–60 | Alabama |
| 1985 | UCLA | 65–62 | Indiana | 2002 | Memphis | 72–62 | South Carolina |
| 1986 | Ohio St | 73–63 | Wyoming | 2003 | St. John's | 70–67 | Georgetown |
| 1987 | Southern Miss | 84–80 | La Salle | 2004 | Michigan | 62–55 | Rutgers |
| 1988 | Connecticut | 72–67 | Ohio St | 2005 | South Carolina | 60–57 | Saint Joseph's |
| 1989 | St. John's (N.Y.) | 73–65 | St. Louis | 2006 | South Carolina | 76–64 | Michigan |
| 1990 | Vanderbilt | 74–72 | St. Louis | 2007 | West Virginia | 78–73 | Clemson |
| 1991 | Stanford | 78–72 | Oklahoma | 2008 | Ohio St | 92–85 | Massachusetts |
| 1992 | Virginia | 81–76 | Notre Dame | 2009 | Penn St | 69–63 | Baylor |
| 1993 | Minnesota | 62–61 | Georgetown | 2010 | Dayton | 79–68 | North Carolina |
| 1994 | Villanova | 80–73 | Vanderbilt | 2011 | Wichita St | 66–57 | Alabama |

# NCAA Men's Division I Season Leaders

## Scoring Average

| Year | Player and Team | Ht | Class | GP | FG | 3FG | FT | Pts | Avg |
|------|-----------------|-----|-------|----|----|-----|----|----|-----|
| 1949 | Murray Wier, Iowa | 5-9 | Sr. | 19 | 152 | — | 95 | 399 | 21.0 |
| 1950 | Tony Lavelli, Yale | 6-3 | Sr. | 30 | 228 | — | 215 | 671 | 22.4 |
| 1951 | Paul Arizin, Villanova | 6-3 | Sr. | 29 | 260 | — | 215 | 735 | 25.3 |
| 1952 | Bill Mlkvy, Temple | 6-4 | Sr. | 25 | 303 | — | 125 | 731 | 29.2 |
| 1953 | Clyde Lovellette, Kansas | 6-9 | Sr. | 28 | 315 | — | 165 | 795 | 28.4 |
| 1954 | Frank Selvy, Furman | 6-3 | Jr. | 25 | 272 | — | 194 | 738 | 29.5 |
| 1955 | Frank Selvy, Furman | 6-3 | Sr. | 29 | 427 | — | 355 | 1209 | 41.7 |
| 1956 | Darrell Floyd, Furman | 6-1 | Jr. | 25 | 344 | — | 209 | 897 | 35.9 |
| 1957 | Darrell Floyd, Furman | 6-1 | Sr. | 28 | 339 | — | 268 | 946 | 33.8 |
| 1958 | Grady Wallace, South Carolina | 6-4 | Sr. | 29 | 336 | — | 234 | 906 | 31.2 |
| 1959 | Oscar Robertson, Cincinnati | 6-5 | So. | 28 | 352 | — | 280 | 984 | 35.1 |
| 1960 | Oscar Robertson, Cincinnati | 6-5 | Jr. | 30 | 331 | — | 316 | 978 | 32.6 |
| 1961 | Oscar Robertson, Cincinnati | 6-5 | Sr. | 30 | 369 | — | 273 | 1011 | 33.7 |
| 1962 | Frank Burgess, Gonzaga | 6-1 | Sr. | 26 | 304 | — | 234 | 842 | 32.4 |
| 1963 | Billy McGill, Utah | 6-9 | Sr. | 26 | 394 | — | 221 | 1009 | 38.8 |
| 1964 | Nick Werkman, Seton Hall | 6-3 | Jr. | 22 | 221 | — | 208 | 650 | 29.5 |
| 1965 | Howard Komives, Bowling Green | 6-1 | Sr. | 23 | 292 | — | 260 | 844 | 36.7 |
| 1966 | Rick Barry, Miami (Fla.) | 6-7 | Sr. | 26 | 340 | — | 293 | 973 | 37.4 |
| 1967 | Dave Schellhase, Purdue | 6-4 | Sr. | 24 | 284 | — | 213 | 781 | 32.5 |
| 1968 | Jim Walker, Providence | 6-3 | Sr. | 28 | 323 | — | 205 | 851 | 30.4 |
| 1969 | Pete Maravich, LSU | 6-5 | So. | 26 | 432 | — | 274 | 1138 | 43.8 |
| 1970 | Pete Maravich, LSU | 6-5 | Jr. | 26 | 433 | — | 282 | 1148 | 44.2 |
| 1971 | Pete Maravich, LSU | 6-5 | Sr. | 31 | 522 | — | 337 | 1381 | 44.5 |
| 1972 | Johnny Neumann, Mississippi | 6-6 | So. | 23 | 366 | — | 191 | 923 | 40.1 |
| 1973 | Dwight Lamar, SW Louisiana | 6-1 | Jr. | 29 | 429 | — | 196 | 1054 | 36.3 |
| 1974 | William Averitt, Pepperdine | 6-1 | Sr. | 25 | 352 | — | 144 | 848 | 33.9 |
| 1975 | Larry Fogle, Canisius | 6-5 | So. | 25 | 326 | — | 183 | 835 | 33.4 |
| 1976 | Bob McCurdy, Richmond | 6-7 | Sr. | 26 | 321 | — | 213 | 855 | 32.9 |
| 1977 | Marshall Rodgers, Tex.-Pan American | 6-2 | Sr. | 25 | 361 | — | 197 | 919 | 36.8 |
| 1978 | Freeman Williams, Portland St | 6-4 | Jr. | 26 | 417 | — | 176 | 1010 | 38.8 |
| 1979 | Freeman Williams, Portland St | 6-4 | Sr. | 27 | 410 | — | 149 | 969 | 35.9 |
| 1990 | Lawrence Butler, Idaho St | 6-3 | Sr. | 27 | 310 | — | 192 | 812 | 30.1 |
| 1981 | Tony Murphy, Southern-Birmingham | 6-3 | Sr. | 29 | 377 | — | 178 | 932 | 32.1 |
| 1982 | Zam Fredrick, South Carolina | 6-2 | Sr. | 27 | 300 | — | 181 | 781 | 28.9 |
| 1983 | Harry Kelly, Texas Southern | 6-7 | Jr. | 29 | 336 | — | 190 | 862 | 29.7 |
| 1984 | Harry Kelly, Texas Southern | 6-7 | Sr. | 29 | 333 | — | 169 | 835 | 28.8 |
| 1985 | Joe Jakubick, Akron | 6-5 | Sr. | 27 | 304 | — | 206 | 814 | 30.1 |
| 1986 | Xavier McDaniel, Wichita St | 6-8 | Sr. | 31 | 351 | — | 142 | 844 | 27.2 |
| 1987 | Terrance Bailey, Wagner | 6-2 | Jr. | 29 | 321 | — | 212 | 854 | 29.4 |
| 1988 | Kevin Houston, Army | 5-11 | Sr. | 29 | 311 | 63 | 268 | 953 | 32.9 |
| 1989 | Hersey Hawkins, Bradley | 6-3 | Sr. | 31 | 377 | 87 | 284 | 1125 | 36.3 |
| 1990 | Hank Gathers, Loyola Marymount | 6-7 | Jr. | 31 | 419 | 0 | 177 | 1015 | 32.7 |
| 1991 | Bo Kimble, Loyola Marymount | 6-5 | Sr. | 32 | 404 | 92 | 231 | 1131 | 35.3 |

## Scoring Average *(Cont.)*

| Year | Player and Team | Ht | Class | GP | FG | 3FG | FT | Pts | Avg |
|------|-----------------|-----|-------|-----|-----|-----|-----|-----|-----|
| 1992 | Kevin Bradshaw, U.S. Int'l | 6-6 | Sr. | 28 | 358 | 60 | 278 | 1054 | 37.6 |
| 1993 | Brett Roberts, Morehead St | 6-8 | Sr. | 29 | 278 | 66 | 193 | 815 | 28.1 |
| 1994 | Greg Guy, Tex.-Pan American | 6-1 | Jr. | 19 | 189 | 67 | 111 | 556 | 29.3 |
| 1995 | Glenn Robinson, Purdue | 6-8 | Jr. | 34 | 368 | 79 | 215 | 1030 | 30.3 |
| 1996 | Kurt Thomas, TCU | 6-9 | Sr. | 27 | 288 | 3 | 202 | 781 | 28.9 |
| 1997 | Kevin Granger, Texas Southern | 6-3 | Sr. | 24 | 194 | 30 | 230 | 648 | 27.0 |
| 1998 | Charles Jones, LIU-Brooklyn | 6-3 | Jr. | 30 | 338 | 109 | 118 | 903 | 30.1 |
| 1999 | Charles Jones, LIU-Brooklyn | 6-3 | Sr. | 30 | 326 | 116 | 101 | 869 | 29.0 |
| 2000 | Alvin Young, Niagara | 6-3 | Sr. | 29 | 253 | 65 | 157 | 728 | 25.1 |
| 2001 | Courtney Alexander, Fresno St | 6-6 | Sr. | 27 | 252 | 58 | 107 | 669 | 24.8 |
| 2002 | Ronnie McCollum, Centenary | 6-4 | Sr. | 27 | 244 | 85 | 214 | 787 | 29.1 |
| 2003 | Jason Conley, Virginia Military | 6-5 | Fr. | 28 | 285 | 79 | 171 | 820 | 29.3 |
| 2004 | Ruben Douglas, New Mexico | 6-5 | Sr. | 28 | 218 | 94 | 253 | 783 | 28.0 |
| 2005 | Keydren Clark, St. Peter's | 5-8 | So. | 29 | 233 | 112 | 197 | 775 | 26.7 |
| 2006 | Keydren Clark, St. Peter's | 5-9 | Jr. | 28 | 230 | 109 | 152 | 721 | 25.8 |
| 2007 | Adam Morrison, Gonzaga | 6-8 | Jr. | 33 | 306 | 74 | 240 | 926 | 28.1 |
| 2008 | Reggie Williams, Virginia Military Institute | 6-5 | Jr. | 33 | 338 | 76 | 176 | 928 | 28.1 |
| 2009 | Stephen Curry, Davidson | 6-3 | Jr. | 34 | 312 | 130 | 220 | 974 | 28.6 |
| 2010 | Aubrey Coleman, Houston | 6-4 | Sr. | 35 | 305 | 51 | 235 | 896 | 25.6 |
| 2011 | Jimmer Fredette, BYU | 6-2 | Sr. | 37 | 346 | 124 | 252 | 1068 | 28.9 |

## Rebounds

| Year | Player and Team | Ht | Class | GP | Reb | Avg |
|------|-----------------|-----|-------|-----|-----|-----|
| 1952 | Ernie Beck, Pennsylvania | 6-4 | So. | 27 | 556 | 20.6 |
| 1953 | Bill Hannon, Army | 6-3 | So. | 17 | 355 | 20.9 |
| 1954 | Ed Conlin, Fordham | 6-5 | So. | 26 | 612 | 23.5 |
| 1955 | Art Quimby, Connecticut | 6-5 | Jr. | 26 | 588 | 22.6 |
| 1956 | Charlie Slack, Marshall | 6-5 | Jr. | 21 | 538 | 25.6 |
| 1957 | Joe Holup, George Washington | 6-6 | Sr. | 26 | 604 | †.256 |
| 1958 | Elgin Baylor, Seattle | 6-6 | Jr. | 25 | 508 | †.235 |
| 1959 | Alex Ellis, Niagara | 6-5 | Sr. | 25 | 536 | †.262 |
| 1960 | Leroy Wright, Pacific | 6-8 | Jr. | 26 | 652 | †.238 |
| 1961 | Leroy Wright, Pacific | 6-8 | Sr. | 17 | 380 | †.234 |
| 1961 | Jerry Lucas, Ohio St | 6-8 | Jr. | 27 | 470 | †.198 |
| 1963 | Jerry Lucas, Ohio St | 6-8 | Sr. | 28 | 499 | †.211 |
| 1964 | Paul Silas, Creighton | 6-7 | Sr. | 27 | 557 | 20.6 |
| 1965 | Bob Pelkington, Xavier (Ohio) | 6-7 | Sr. | 26 | 567 | 21.8 |
| 1966 | Toby Kimball, Connecticut | 6-8 | Sr. | 23 | 483 | 21.0 |
| 1967 | Jim Ware, Oklahoma City | 6-8 | Sr. | 29 | 607 | 20.9 |
| 1968 | Dick Cunningham, Murray St | 6-10 | Jr. | 22 | 479 | 21.8 |
| 1969 | Neal Walk, Florida | 6-10 | Jr. | 25 | 494 | 19.8 |
| 1970 | Spencer Haywood, Detroit | 6-8 | So. | 22 | 472 | 21.5 |
| 1971 | Artis Gilmore, Jacksonville | 7-2 | Jr. | 28 | 621 | 22.2 |
| 1972 | Artis Gilmore, Jacksonville | 7-2 | Sr. | 26 | 603 | 23.2 |
| 1973 | Kermit Washington, American | 6-8 | Jr. | 23 | 455 | 19.8 |
| 1974 | Kermit Washington, American | 6-8 | Sr. | 22 | 439 | 20.0 |
| 1975 | Marvin Barnes, Providence | 6-9 | Sr. | 32 | 597 | 18.7 |
| 1976 | John Irving, Hofstra | 6-9 | So. | 21 | 323 | 15.4 |
| 1977 | Sam Pellom, Buffalo | 6-8 | So. | 26 | 420 | 16.2 |
| 1978 | Glenn Mosley, Seton Hall | 6-8 | Sr. | 29 | 473 | 16.3 |
| 1979 | Ken Williams, North Texas St | 6-7 | Sr. | 28 | 411 | 14.7 |
| 1980 | Monti Davis, Tennessee St | 6-7 | Jr. | 26 | 421 | 16.2 |
| 1981 | Larry Smith, Alcorn St | 6-8 | Sr. | 26 | 392 | 15.1 |
| 1982 | Darryl Watson, Miss. Valley St | 6-7 | Sr. | 27 | 379 | 14.0 |
| 1983 | LaSalle Thompson, Texas | 6-10 | Jr. | 27 | 365 | 13.5 |
| 1984 | Xavier McDaniel, Wichita St | 6-7 | So. | 28 | 403 | 14.4 |
| 1985 | Akeem Olajuwon, Houston | 7-0 | Jr. | 37 | 500 | 13.5 |
| 1986 | Xavier McDaniel, Wichita St | 6-8 | Sr | 31 | 460 | 14.8 |
| 1987 | David Robinson, Navy | 6-11 | Jr. | 35 | 455 | 13.0 |
| 1988 | Jerome Lane, Pittsburgh | 6-6 | So. | 33 | 444 | 13.5 |
| 1989 | Kenny Miller, Loyola (Ill.) | 6-9 | Fr. | 29 | 395 | 13.6 |
| 1990 | Hank Gathers, Loyola (Calif.) | 6-7 | Jr. | 31 | 426 | 13.7 |
| 1991 | Anthony Bonner, St. Louis | 6-8 | Sr. | 33 | 456 | 13.8 |
| 1992 | Shaquille O'Neal, LSU | 7-1 | So. | 28 | 411 | 14.7 |
| 1993 | Popeye Jones, Murray St | 6-8 | Sr. | 30 | 431 | 14.4 |

## Rebounds *(Cont.)*

| Year | Player and Team | Ht | Class | GP | Reb | Avg |
|---|---|---|---|---|---|---|
| 1994 | Warren Kidd, Middle Tenn. St | 6-9 | Sr. | 26 | 386 | 14.8 |
| 1995 | Jerome Lambert, Baylor | 6-8 | Jr. | 24 | 355 | 14.8 |
| 1996 | Kurt Thomas, TCU | 6-9 | Sr. | 27 | 393 | 14.6 |
| 1997 | Marcus Mann, Miss. Valley St | 6-8 | Sr. | 29 | 394 | 13.6 |
| 1998 | Tim Duncan, Wake Forest | 6-11 | Sr. | 31 | 457 | 14.7 |
| 1999 | Ryan Perryman, Dayton | 6-7 | Sr. | 33 | 412 | 12.5 |
| 2000 | Ian McGinnis, Dartmouth | 6-8 | So. | 26 | 317 | 12.2 |
| 2001 | Darren Phillips, Fairfield | 6-7 | Sr. | 29 | 405 | 14.0 |
| 2002 | Chris Marcus, Western Kentucky | 7-1 | Jr. | 31 | 374 | 12.1 |
| 2003 | Jeremy Bishop, Quinnipiac | 6-6 | J.. | 29 | 347 | 12.0 |
| 2004 | Brandon Hunter, Ohio | 6-7 | Sr. | 30 | 378 | 12.6 |
| 2005 | Paul Millsap, Louisiana Tech | 6-7 | Fr. | 30 | 374 | 12.5 |
| 2006 | Paul Millsap, Louisiana Tech | 6-8 | So. | 29 | 360 | 12.4 |
| 2007 | Paul Millsap, Louisiana Tech | 6-8 | Jr. | 33 | 438 | 13.3 |
| 2008 | Rashad Jones-Jennings, Ark-Little Rock | 6-8 | Sr. | 30 | 392 | 13.3 |
| 2009 | Blake Griffin, Oklahoma | 6-10 | So. | 35 | 504 | 14.4 |
| 2010 | Artsiom Parakhouski, Radford | 6-11 | Sr. | 31 | 414 | 13.4 |
| 2011 | Kenneth Faried, Morehead St | 6-8 | Sr. | 35 | 508 | 14.5 |

†From 1956–1962, title was based on highest individual recoveries out of total by both teams in all games.

## Assists

| Year | Player and Team | Class | GP | Ast | Avg |
|---|---|---|---|---|---|
| 1985 | Craig Lathen, Ill.-Chicago | Jr. | 29 | 274 | 9.45 |
| 1986 | Rob Weingard, Hofstra | Sr. | 24 | 228 | 9.50 |
| 1987 | Mark Jackson, St. John's (N.Y.) | Jr. | 36 | 328 | 9.11 |
| 1988 | Avery Johnson, Southern-Birm. | Jr. | 31 | 333 | 10.74 |
| 1989 | Avery Johnson, Southern-Birm. | Sr. | 30 | 399 | 13.30 |
| 1990 | Glenn Williams, Holy Cross | Sr. | 28 | 278 | 9.93 |
| 1991 | Todd Lehmann, Drexel | Sr. | 28 | 260 | 9.29 |
| 1992 | Chris Corchiani, North Carolina St | Sr. | 31 | 299 | 9.65 |
| 1993 | Van Usher, Tennessee Tech | Sr. | 29 | 254 | 8.76 |
| 1994 | Sam Crawford, New Mex. St | Sr. | 34 | 310 | 9.12 |
| 1995 | Jason Kidd, California | So. | 30 | 272 | 9.06 |
| 1996 | Nelson Haggerty, Baylor | Sr. | 28 | 284 | 10.10 |
| 1997 | Raimonds Miglinieks, UC-Irvine | Sr. | 27 | 230 | 8.52 |
| 1998 | Kenny Mitchell, Dartmouth | Sr. | 26 | 203 | 7.81 |
| 1999 | Ahlon Lewis, Arizona St | Sr. | 32 | 294 | 9.19 |
| 2000 | Doug Gottlieb, Oklahoma St | Jr. | 34 | 299 | 8.79 |
| 2001 | Mark Dickel, UNLV | Sr. | 31 | 280 | 9.03 |
| 2002 | Markus Carr, CSU–Northridge | Jr. | 32 | 286 | 8.94 |
| 2003 | T.J. Ford, Texas | Fr. | 33 | 273 | 8.27 |
| 2004 | Martell Bailey, Ill.-Chicago | Jr. | 30 | 244 | 8.13 |
| 2005 | Greg Davis, Troy St | Sr. | 31 | 256 | 8.26 |
| 2006 | Damitrius Coleman, Mercer | Jr. | 28 | 224 | 8.00 |
| | Will Funn, Portland St | Sr. | 28 | 224 | 8.00 |
| 2007 | Jared Jordan, Marist | Jr. | 29 | 247 | 8.52 |
| 2008 | Jared Jordan, Marist | Sr. | 31 | 274 | 8.83 |
| 2009 | Johnathon Jones, Oakland | Jr. | 36 | 290 | 8.06 |
| 2010 | Ronald Moore, Siena | Sr. | 34 | 261 | 7.68 |
| 2011 | Aaron Johnson, UAB | Sr. | 31 | 239 | 7.71 |

## Blocked Shots

| Year | Player and Team | Class | GP | BS | Avg |
|------|-----------------|-------|-----|-----|-----|
| 1987 | David Robinson, Navy | Jr. | 35 | 207 | 5.91 |
| 1988 | David Robinson, Navy | Sr. | 32 | 144 | 4.50 |
| 1989 | Rodney Blake, St. Joseph's (Pa.) | Sr. | 29 | 116 | 4.00 |
| 1990 | Alonzo Mourning, Georgetown | Fr. | 34 | 169 | 4.97 |
| 1991 | Kenny Green, Rhode Island | Sr. | 26 | 124 | 4.77 |
| 1992 | Shawn Bradley, BYU | Fr. | 34 | 177 | 5.21 |
| 1993 | Shaquille O'Neal, LSU | Jr. | 30 | 157 | 5.23 |
| 1994 | Theo Ratliff, Wyoming | Jr. | 28 | 124 | 4.43 |
| 1995 | Grady Livingston, Howard | Jr. | 26 | 115 | 4.42 |
| 1996 | Keith Closs, Central Conn. St | Fr. | 26 | 139 | 5.35 |
| 1997 | Keith Closs, Central Conn. St | So. | 28 | 178 | 6.36 |
| 1998 | Adonal Foyle, Colgate | Jr. | 28 | 180 | 6.43 |
| 1999 | Jerome James, Florida A&M | Sr. | 27 | 125 | 4.63 |
| 2000 | Tarvis Williams, Hampton | Jr. | 27 | 135 | 5.00 |
| 2001 | Ken Johnson, Ohio St | Sr. | 30 | 161 | 5.37 |
| 2002 | Tarvis Williams, Hampton | Sr | 32 | 147 | 4.59 |
| 2003 | Wojciech Myrda, La.-Monroe | Sr. | 32 | 172 | 5.38 |
| 2004 | Emeka Okafor, Connecticut | So. | 33 | 156 | 4.73 |
| 2005 | Anwar Ferguson, Houston | Sr. | 27 | 111 | 4.11 |
| 2006 | Deng Gai, Fairfield | Sr. | 30 | 165 | 5.50 |
| 2007 | Shawn James, Northeastern | So. | 30 | 196 | 6.53 |
| 2008 | Mickell Gladness, Ala.-A&M | Jr. | 30 | 188 | 6.26 |
| 2009 | Jarvis Varnado, Mississippi St | Jr. | 36 | 170 | 4.72 |
| 2010 | Hassan Whiteside, Marshall | Fr. | 34 | 182 | 5.35 |
| 2011 | William Mosley, Northwestern St | Jr. | 32 | 156 | 4.88 |

## Steals

| Year | Player and Team | Class | GP | Stl | Avg |
|------|-----------------|-------|-----|-----|-----|
| 1987 | Darron Brittman, Chicago St | Sr. | 28 | 139 | 4.96 |
| 1988 | Tony Fairley, Charleston South. | Sr. | 28 | 114 | 4.07 |
| 1989 | Aldwin Ware, Florida A&M | Sr. | 29 | 142 | 4.90 |
| 1990 | Kenny Robertson, Cleveland St | Jr. | 28 | 111 | 3.96 |
| 1991 | Ronn McMahon, E. Washington | Sr. | 29 | 130 | 4.48 |
| 1992 | Van Usher, Tennessee Tech | Jr. | 28 | 104 | 3.71 |
| 1993 | Victor Snipes, NE Illinois | So. | 25 | 86 | 3.44 |
| 1994 | Jason Kidd, California | Fr. | 29 | 110 | 3.80 |
| 1995 | Shawn Griggs, SW Louisiana | Sr. | 30 | 120 | 4.00 |
| 1996 | Roderick Anderson, Texas | Sr. | 30 | 101 | 3.37 |
| 1997 | Pointer Williams, McNeese St | Sr. | 27 | 118 | 4.37 |
| 1998 | Joel Hoover, Md.-Eastern Shore | Fr. | 28 | 90 | 3.21 |
| 1999 | Bonzi Wells, Ball St | Sr. | 29 | 103 | 3.55 |
| 2000 | Shawnta Rogers, George Wash. | Sr. | 29 | 103 | 3.55 |
| 2001 | Carl Williams, Liberty | Sr. | 28 | 107 | 3.82 |
| 2002 | Greedy Daniels, TCU | Jr. | 25 | 108 | 4.32 |
| 2003 | Desmond Cambridge, Ala. A&M | Sr. | 29 | 160 | 5.52 |
| 2004 | Alexis McMillan, Stetson | Sr. | 22 | 87 | 3.95 |
| 2005 | Marques Green, St. Bonaventure | Sr. | 27 | 107 | 3.96 |
| 2006 | Obie Trotter, Alabama A&M | Jr. | 32 | 125 | 3.91 |
| 2007 | Tim Smith, East Tennessee St | Sr. | 28 | 95 | 3.39 |
| 2008 | Travis Holmes, Virg. Mil. Inst. | So. | 33 | 111 | 3.36 |
| 2009 | Chavis Holmes, Virg. Mil. Inst. | Sr. | 31 | 105 | 3.39 |
| 2010 | Jay Threatt, Delaware St | So. | 29 | 82 | 2.83 |
| 2011 | Anthony Nelson, Niagara | Sr. | 29 | 98 | 3.38 |

## Single Game Records

### SCORING HIGHS VS DIVISION I OPPONENT

| Pts | Player and Team vs Opponent | Date |
|---|---|---|
| 72 | Kevin Bradshaw, U.S. Int'l vs Loyola Marymount | 1-5-91 |
| 69 | Pete Maravich, LSU vs Alabama | 2-7-70 |
| 68 | Calvin Murphy, Niagara vs Syracuse | 12-7-68 |
| 66 | Jay Handlan, Washington & Lee vs Furman | 2-17-51 |
| 66 | Pete Maravich, LSU vs Tulane | 2-10-69 |
| 66 | Anthony Roberts, Oral Roberts vs North Carolina A&T | 2-19-77 |
| 65 | Anthony Roberts, Oral Roberts vs Oregon | 3-9-77 |
| 65 | Scott Haffner, Evansville vs Dayton | 2-18-89 |
| 64 | Pete Maravich, LSU vs Kentucky | 2-21-70 |
| 63 | Johnny Neumann, Mississippi vs LSU | 1-30-71 |
| 63 | Hersey Hawkins, Bradley vs Detroit | 2-22-88 |

### SCORING HIGHS VS NON-DIVISION I OPPONENT

| Pts | Player and Team vs Opponent | Date |
|---|---|---|
| 100 | Frank Selvy, Furman vs Newberry | 2-13-54 |
| 85 | Paul Arizin, Villanova vs Philadelphia NAMC | 2-12-49 |
| 81 | Freeman Williams, Portland St vs Rocky Mountain | 2-3-78 |
| 73 | Bill Mlkvy, Temple vs Wilkes | 3-3-51 |
| 71 | Freeman Williams, Portland St vs S. Oregon | 2-9-77 |

### REBOUNDING HIGHS ALL-TIME

| Reb | Player and Team vs Opponent | Date |
|---|---|---|
| 51 | Bill Chambers, William & Mary vs Virginia | 2-14-53 |
| 43 | Charlie Slack, Marshall vs Morris Harvey | 1-12-54 |
| 42 | Tom Heinsohn, Holy Cross vs Boston College | 3-1-55 |
| 40 | Art Quimby, Connecticut vs Boston University | 1-11-55 |
| 39 | Maurice Stokes, St. Francis (Pa.) vs John Carroll | 1-28-55 |
| 39 | Dave DeBusschere, Detroit vs C. Michigan | 1-30-60 |
| 39 | Keith Swagerty, Pacific vs UC-Santa Barbara | 3-5-65 |

### REBOUNDING HIGHS SINCE 1973*

| Reb | Player and Team vs Opponent | Date |
|---|---|---|
| 35 | Larry Abney, Fresno St vs SMU | 2-17-00 |
| 34 | David Vaughn, Oral Roberts vs Brandeis | 1-8-73 |
| 32 | Jervaughn Scales, Southern-Birm. vs Grambling | 2-7-94 |
| 32 | Durand Macklin, LSU vs Tulane | 11-26-76 |
| 31 | Jim Bradley, Northern Illinois vs UW-Milwaukee | 2-19-73 |
| 31 | Calvin Natt, NE Louisiana vs Georgia Southern | 12-29-76 |

### ASSISTS

| Asst | Player and Team vs Opponent | Date |
|---|---|---|
| 22 | Tony Fairley, Baptist vs Armstrong St | 2-9-87 |
| 22 | Avery Johnson, Southern-Birm. vs Texas Southern | 1-25-88 |
| 22 | Sherman Douglas, Syracuse vs Providence | 1-28-89 |
| 21 | Kelvin Scarborough, New Mexico vs Hawaii | 2-13-87 |
| 21 | Anthony Manuel, Bradley vs UC-Irvine | 12-19-87 |
| 21 | Avery Johnson, Southern-Birm. vs Alabama St | 1-16-88 |

### STEALS

| Stl | Player and Team vs Opponent | Date |
|---|---|---|
| 13 | Mookie Blaylock, Oklahoma vs Centenary | 12-12-87 |
| 13 | Mookie Blaylock, Oklahoma vs Loyola Marymount | 12-17-88 |
| 12 | Kenny Robertson, Cleveland St vs Wagner | 12-3-88 |
| 12 | Terry Evans, Oklahoma vs Florida A&M | 1-27-93 |
| 12 | Richard Duncan, Middle Tenn. St vs Eastern Kentucky | 2-20-99 |
| 12 | Greedy Daniels, Texas Christian vs Ark.-Pine Bluff | 12-30-00 |
| 12 | Jehiel Lewis, Navy vs Bucknell | 1-12-02 |
| 12 | Carldell Johnson, Ala.-Birmingham vs. South Carolina St | 11-27-05 |

### BLOCKED SHOTS

| BS | Player and Team vs Opponent | Date |
|---|---|---|
| 16 | Mickell Gladness, Alabama A&M vs Texas Southern | 2-24-07 |
| 14 | David Robinson, Navy vs UNC–Wilmington | 1-4-86 |
| 14 | Shawn Bradley, BYU vs Eastern Kentucky | 12-7-90 |
| 14 | Roy Rogers, Alabama vs Georgia | 2-10-96 |
| 14 | Loren Woods, Arizona vs Oregon | 2-3-00 |
| 14 | Darrius Garrett, Richmond vs Massachusetts | 1-13-10 |

Eleven players tied with 13

## Single Season Records

### POINTS

| Player and Team | Year | GP | FG | 3FG | FT | Pts |
|---|---|---|---|---|---|---|
| Pete Maravich, LSU | 1970 | 31 | 522 | — | 337 | 1381 |
| Elvin Hayes, Houston | 1968 | 33 | 519 | — | 176 | 1214 |
| Frank Selvy, Furman | 1954 | 29 | 427 | — | 355 | 1209 |
| Pete Maravich, LSU | 1969 | 26 | 433 | — | 282 | 1148 |
| Pete Maravich, LSU | 1968 | 26 | 432 | — | 274 | 1138 |
| Bo Kimble, Loyola Marymount | 1990 | 32 | 404 | 92 | 231 | 1131 |
| Hersey Hawkins, Bradley | 1988 | 31 | 377 | 87 | 284 | 1125 |
| Austin Carr, Notre Dame | 1970 | 29 | 444 | — | 218 | 1106 |
| Austin Carr, Notre Dame | 1971 | 29 | 430 | — | 241 | 1101 |
| Otis Birdsong, Houston | 1977 | 36 | 452 | — | 186 | 1090 |

### SCORING AVERAGE

| Player and Team | Year | GP | FG | 3FG | FT | Pts |
|---|---|---|---|---|---|---|
| Pete Maravich, LSU | 1970 | 31 | 522 | 337 | 1381 | 44.5 |
| Pete Maravich, LSU | 1969 | 26 | 433 | 282 | 1148 | 44.2 |
| Pete Maravich, LSU | 1968 | 26 | 432 | 274 | 1138 | 43.8 |
| Frank Selvy, Furman | 1954 | 29 | 427 | 355 | 1209 | 41.7 |
| Johnny Neumann, Mississippi | 1971 | 23 | 366 | 191 | 923 | 40.1 |
| Freeman Williams, Portland St | 1977 | 26 | 417 | 176 | 1010 | 38.8 |
| Billy McGill, Utah | 1962 | 26 | 394 | 221 | 1009 | 38.8 |
| Calvin Murphy, Niagara | 1968 | 24 | 337 | 242 | 916 | 38.2 |
| Austin Carr, Notre Dame | 1970 | 29 | 444 | 218 | 1106 | 38.1 |
| Austin Carr, Notre Dame | 1971 | 29 | 430 | 241 | 1101 | 38.0 |

### REBOUNDS

| Player and Team | Year | GP | Reb | Player and Team | Year | GP | Reb |
|---|---|---|---|---|---|---|---|
| Walt Dukes, Seton Hall | 1953 | 33 | 734 | Artis Gilmore, Jacksonville | 1970 | 28 | 621 |
| Leroy Wright, Pacific | 1959 | 26 | 652 | Tom Gola, La Salle | 1955 | 31 | 618 |
| Tom Gola, La Salle | 1954 | 30 | 652 | Ed Conlin, Fordham | 1953 | 26 | 612 |
| Charlie Tyra, Louisville | 1956 | 29 | 645 | Art Quimby, Connecticut | 1955 | 25 | 611 |
| Paul Silas, Creighton | 1964 | 29 | 631 | Bill Russell, San Francisco | 1956 | 29 | 609 |
| Elvin Hayes, Houston | 1968 | 33 | 624 | Jim Ware, Oklahoma City | 1966 | 29 | 607 |

### REBOUND AVERAGE ALL-TIME

| Player and Team | Year | GP | Reb | Avg |
|---|---|---|---|---|
| Charlie Slack, Marshall | 1955 | 21 | 538 | 25.6 |
| Leroy Wright, Pacific | 1959 | 26 | 652 | 25.1 |
| Art Quimby, Connecticut | 1955 | 25 | 611 | 24.4 |
| Charlie Slack, Marshall | 1956 | 22 | 520 | 23.6 |
| Ed Conlin, Fordham | 1953 | 26 | 612 | 23.5 |

### REBOUND AVERAGE SINCE 1973*

| Player and Team | Year | GP | Reb | Avg |
|---|---|---|---|---|
| Kermit Washington, American | 1973 | 22 | 439 | 20.0 |
| Marvin Barnes, Providence | 1973 | 30 | 571 | 19.0 |
| Marvin Barnes, Providence | 1974 | 32 | 597 | 18.7 |
| Pete Padgett, Nev.-Reno | 1973 | 26 | 462 | 17.8 |
| Jim Bradley, Northern Illinois | 1973 | 24 | 426 | 17.8 |

### ASSISTS

| Player and Team | Year | GP | Asst | Player and Team | Year | GP | Asst |
|---|---|---|---|---|---|---|---|
| Mark Wade, UNLV | 1987 | 38 | 406 | Sherman Douglas, Syracuse | 1989 | 38 | 326 |
| Avery Johnson, Southern-Birm. | 1988 | 30 | 399 | Sam Crawford, New Mex. St | 1993 | 34 | 310 |
| Anthony Manuel, Bradley | 1988 | 31 | 373 | Greg Anthony, UNLV | 1991 | 35 | 310 |
| Avery Johnson, Southern-Birm. | 1987 | 31 | 333 | Reid Gettys, Houston | 1984 | 37 | 309 |
| Mark Jackson, St. John's (N.Y.) | 1986 | 32 | 328 | Carl Golston, Loyola (Ill.) | 1985 | 33 | 305 |

### ASSIST AVERAGE

| Player and Team | Year | GP | Asst | Avg | Player and Team | Year | GP | Asst | Avg |
|---|---|---|---|---|---|---|---|---|---|
| Avery Johnson, Southern-Birm. | 1988 | 30 | 399 | 13.3 | Chris Corchiani, North Carolina St | 1991 | 31 | 299 | 9.6 |
| Anthony Manuel, Bradley | 1988 | 31 | 373 | 12.0 | Tony Fairley, Charleston South.† | 1987 | 28 | 270 | 9.6 |
| Avery Johnson, Southern-Birm. | 1987 | 31 | 333 | 10.7 | Tyrone Bogues, Wake Forest | 1987 | 29 | 276 | 9.5 |
| Mark Wade, UNLV | 1987 | 38 | 406 | 10.7 | Ron Weingard, Hofstra | 1985 | 24 | 228 | 9.5 |
| Nelson Haggerty, Baylor | 1995 | 28 | 284 | 10.1 | Craig Neal, Georgia Tech | 1988 | 32 | 303 | 9.5 |
| Glenn Williams, Holy Cross | 1989 | 28 | 278 | 9.9 | | | | | |

*Freshmen became eligible for varsity play in 1973. †Formerly Baptist College.

## Single Season Records *(Cont.)*

### FIELD-GOAL PERCENTAGE

| Player and Team | Year | GP | FG | FGA | Pct |
|---|---|---|---|---|---|
| Steve Johnson, Oregon St | 1981 | 28 | 235 | 315 | 74.6 |
| Dwayne Davis, Florida | 1989 | 33 | 179 | 248 | 72.2 |
| Keith Walker, Utica | 1985 | 27 | 154 | 216 | 71.3 |
| Steve Johnson, Oregon St | 1980 | 30 | 211 | 297 | 71.0 |
| Adam Mark, Belmont | 2002 | 26 | 150 | 212 | 70.8 |
| Oliver Miller, Arkansas | 1991 | 38 | 254 | 361 | 70.4 |
| Alan Williams, Princeton | 1987 | 25 | 163 | 232 | 70.3 |
| Mark McNamara, California | 1982 | 27 | 231 | 329 | 70.2 |
| Warren Kidd, Middle Tennessee St | 1991 | 30 | 173 | 247 | 70.0 |
| Pete Freeman, Akron | 1991 | 28 | 175 | 250 | 70.0 |

Based on qualifiers for annual championship.

### FREE-THROW PERCENTAGE

| Player and Team | Year | GP | FT | FTA | Pct |
|---|---|---|---|---|---|
| Blake Ahearn SW Missouri St† | 2004 | 33 | 117 | 120 | 97.5 |
| Ryan Toolson, Utah Valley St | 2006 | 29 | 96 | 99 | 97.0 |
| Derek Raivio, Gonzaga | 2006 | 33 | 146 | 152 | 96.1 |
| Craig Collins, Penn St | 1985 | 27 | 94 | 98 | 95.9 |
| A.J. Graves, Butler | 2006 | 32 | 137 | 143 | 95.8 |
| J.J. Redick, Duke | 2004 | 37 | 143 | 150 | 95.3 |
| Steve Drabyn, Belmont | 2003 | 29 | 78 | 82 | 95.1 |
| Donald Sims, Appalachian St | 2009 | 37 | 175 | 184 | 95.1 |
| Rod Foster, UCLA | 1982 | 27 | 95 | 100 | 95.0 |
| Clay McKnight, Pacific | 2000 | 24 | 74 | 78 | 94.9 |
| Matt Logie, Lehigh | 2003 | 28 | 91 | 96 | 94.8 |

### THREE-POINT FIELD-GOAL PERCENTAGE

| Player and Team | Year | GP | 3FG | 3FGA | Pct |
|---|---|---|---|---|---|
| Glenn Tropf, Holy Cross | 1988 | 29 | 52 | 82 | 63.4 |
| Sean Wightman, Western Michigan | 1992 | 30 | 48 | 76 | 63.2 |
| Keith Jennings, East Tennessee St | 1991 | 33 | 84 | 142 | 59.2 |
| Dave Calloway, Monmouth (N.J.) | 1989 | 28 | 48 | 82 | 58.5 |
| Steve Kerr, Arizona | 1988 | 38 | 114 | 199 | 57.3 |
| Reginald Jones, Prairie View | 1987 | 28 | 64 | 112 | 57.1 |
| Jim Cantamessa, Siena | 1998 | 29 | 66 | 117 | 56.4 |
| Joel Tribelhorn, Colorado St | 1989 | 33 | 76 | 135 | 56.3 |
| Mike Joseph, Bucknell | 1988 | 28 | 65 | 116 | 56.0 |
| Brian Jackson, Evansville | 1995 | 27 | 53 | 95 | 55.8 |

Based on qualifiers for annual championship.

### STEALS

| Player and Team | Year | GP | Stl |
|---|---|---|---|
| Desmond Cambridge, Alabama A&M | 2002 | 29 | 160 |
| Mookie Blaylock, Oklahoma | 1988 | 39 | 150 |
| Aldwin Ware, Florida A&M | 1988 | 29 | 142 |
| Darron Brittman, Chicago St | 1986 | 28 | 139 |
| John Linehan, Providence | 2002 | 31 | 139 |

### STEAL AVERAGE

| Player and Team | Year | GP | Stl | Avg |
|---|---|---|---|---|
| D. Cambridge, Alabama A&M | 2002 | 29 | 160 | 5.52 |
| Darron Brittman, Chicago St | 1986 | 28 | 139 | 4.96 |
| Aldwin Ware, Florida A&M | 1988 | 29 | 142 | 4.90 |
| John Linehan, Providence | 2002 | 31 | 139 | 4.48 |
| Ronn McMahon, E. Washington | 1990 | 29 | 130 | 4.48 |

### BLOCKED SHOTS

| Player and Team | Year | GP | BS |
|---|---|---|---|
| David Robinson, Navy | 1986 | 35 | 207 |
| Shawn James, Northeastern | 2005 | 30 | 196 |
| Mickell Gladness, Alabama A&M | 2006 | 30 | 188 |
| Hassan Whiteside, Marshall | 2010 | 34 | 182 |
| Adonal Foyle, Colgate | 1997 | 28 | 180 |

### BLOCKED-SHOT AVERAGE

| Player and Team | Year | GP | BS | Avg |
|---|---|---|---|---|
| Shawn James, Northeastern | 2005 | 30 | 196 | 6.53 |
| Adonal Foyle, Colgate | 1997 | 28 | 180 | 6.43 |
| Keith Closs, Central Conn. St | 1996 | 28 | 178 | 6.36 |
| Mickell Gladness, Alabama A&M | 2006 | 30 | 188 | 6.26 |
| David Robinson, Navy | 1986 | 35 | 207 | 5.91 |

†Southwest Missouri State changed name to Missouri State after 2004–05 season
Based on qualifiers for annual championship.

### Career Records

#### POINTS

| Player and Team | Ht | Final Year | GP | FG | 3FG* | FT | Pts |
|---|---|---|---|---|---|---|---|
| Pete Maravich, LSU | 6-5 | 1970 | 83 | 1387 | — | 893 | 3667 |
| Freeman Williams, Portland St. | 6-4 | 1978 | 106 | 1369 | — | 511 | 3249 |
| Lionel Simmons, La Salle | 6-7 | 1990 | 131 | 1244 | 56 | 673 | 3217 |
| Alphonso Ford, Mississippi Valley St. | 6-2 | 1993 | 109 | 1121 | 333 | 590 | 3165 |
| Harry Kelly, Texas Southern | 6-7 | 1983 | 110 | 1234 | — | 598 | 3066 |
| Keydren Clark, St. Peter's | 5-9 | 2006 | 118 | 967 | 435 | 689 | 3058 |
| Hersey Hawkins, Bradley | 6-3 | 1988 | 125 | 1100 | 118 | 690 | 3008 |
| Oscar Robertson, Cincinnati | 6-5 | 1960 | 88 | 1052 | — | 869 | 2973 |
| Danny Manning, Kansas | 6-10 | 1988 | 147 | 1216 | 10 | 509 | 2951 |
| Alfredrick Hughes, Loyola (Ill.) | 6-5 | 1985 | 120 | 1226 | — | 462 | 2914 |
| Elvin Hayes, Houston | 6-8 | 1968 | 93 | 1215 | — | 454 | 2884 |
| Tyler Hansbrough, North Carolina | 6-9 | 2009 | 142 | 939 | 12 | 982 | 2872 |
| Larry Bird, Indiana St. | 6-9 | 1979 | 94 | 1154 | — | 542 | 2850 |
| Otis Birdsong, Houston | 6-4 | 1977 | 116 | 1176 | — | 480 | 2832 |
| Kevin Bradshaw, Bethune-Cookman, U.S. Int'l | 6-6 | 1991 | 111 | 1027 | 132 | 618 | 2804 |
| Allan Houston, Tennessee | 6-6 | 1993 | 128 | 902 | 346 | 651 | 2801 |
| J.J. Redick, Duke | 6-4 | 2006 | 139 | 825 | 457 | 662 | 2769 |
| Hank Gathers, USC, Loyola Marymount | 6-7 | 1990 | 117 | 1127 | 0 | 469 | 2723 |
| Reggie Lewis, Northeastern | 6-7 | 1987 | 122 | 1043 | 30 (1) | 592 | 2708 |
| Daren Queenan, Lehigh | 6-5 | 1988 | 118 | 1024 | 29 | 626 | 2703 |

*Listed is the number of three-pointers scored since it became the national rule in 1987; the number in the parentheses is number scored prior to 1987—these counted as three points in the game but counted as two-pointers in the national rankings. The three-pointers in the parentheses are not included in total points.

#### SCORING AVERAGE

| Player and Team | Final Year | GP | FG | FT | Pts | Avg |
|---|---|---|---|---|---|---|
| Pete Maravich, LSU | 1968 | 83 | 1387 | 893 | 3667 | 44.2 |
| Austin Carr, Notre Dame | 1971 | 74 | 1017 | 526 | 2560 | 34.6 |
| Oscar Robertson, Cincinnati | 1960 | 88 | 1052 | 869 | 2973 | 33.8 |
| Calvin Murphy, Niagara | 1970 | 77 | 947 | 654 | 2548 | 33.1 |
| Dwight Lamar, SW Louisiana | 1973 | 57 | 768 | 326 | 1862 | 32.7 |
| Frank Selvy, Furman | 1954 | 78 | 922 | 694 | 2538 | 32.5 |
| Rick Mount, Purdue | 1970 | 72 | 910 | 503 | 2323 | 32.3 |
| Darrell Floyd, Furman | 1956 | 71 | 868 | 545 | 2281 | 32.1 |
| Nick Werkman, Seton Hall | 1964 | 71 | 812 | 649 | 2273 | 32.0 |
| Willie Humes, Idaho St. | 1971 | 48 | 565 | 380 | 1510 | 31.5 |
| William Averitt, Pepperdine | 1973 | 49 | 615 | 311 | 1541 | 31.4 |
| Elgin Baylor, Coll. of Idaho; Seattle | 1958 | 80 | 956 | 588 | 2500 | 31.3 |
| Elvin Hayes, Houston | 1968 | 93 | 1215 | 454 | 2884 | 31.0 |
| Freeman Williams, Portland St. | 1978 | 106 | 1369 | 511 | 3249 | 30.7 |
| Larry Bird, Indiana St. | 1979 | 94 | 1154 | 542 | 2850 | 30.3 |

## Career Records *(Cont.)*

### REBOUNDS ALL-TIME

| Player and Team | Final Year | GP | Reb |
|---|---|---|---|
| Tom Gola, La Salle | 1955 | 118 | 2201 |
| Joe Holup, George Washington | 1956 | 104 | 2030 |
| Charlie Slack, Marshall | 1956 | 88 | 1916 |
| Ed Conlin, Fordham | 1955 | 102 | 1884 |
| Dickie Hemric, Wake Forest | 1955 | 104 | 1802 |

### REBOUNDS SINCE 1973*

| Player and Team | Final Year | GP | Reb |
|---|---|---|---|
| Kenneth Faried, Morehead St | 2011 | 136 | 1673 |
| Tim Duncan, Wake Forest | 1997 | 128 | 1570 |
| Derrick Coleman, Syracuse | 1990 | 143 | 1537 |
| Malik Rose, Drexel | 1996 | 120 | 1514 |
| Ralph Sampson, Virginia | 1983 | 132 | 1511 |

### ASSISTS

| Player and Team | Final Year | GP | Asst |
|---|---|---|---|
| Bobby Hurley, Duke | 1993 | 140 | 1076 |
| Chris Corchiani, North Carolina St | 1991 | 124 | 1038 |
| Ed Cota, North Carolina | 2000 | 138 | 1030 |
| Keith Jennings, East Tennessee St | 1991 | 127 | 983 |
| Steve Blake, Maryland | 2003 | 138 | 972 |

### FIELD-GOAL PERCENTAGE

| Player and Team | Final Year | FG | FGA | Pct |
|---|---|---|---|---|
| Steve Johnson, Oregon St | 1981 | 828 | 1222 | 67.8 |
| Michael Bradley, Kentucky/Villanova | 2001 | 441 | 651 | 67.7 |
| Murray Brown, Florida St | 1980 | 566 | 847 | 66.8 |
| Lee Campbell, SW Missouri St | 1990 | 411 | 618 | 66.5 |
| Warren Kidd, Middle Tennessee St | 1993 | 496 | 747 | 66.4 |

Note: Minimum 400 field goals and 4 FG made per game.

### FREE-THROW PERCENTAGE

| Player and Team | Final Year | FT | FTA | Pct |
|---|---|---|---|---|
| Blake Ahearn, Missouri St | 2007 | 435 | 460 | 94.6 |
| Derek Raivio, Gonzaga | 2007 | 343 | 370 | 92.7 |
| Gary Buchanan, Villanova | 2003 | 324 | 355 | 91.3 |
| J.J. Redick, Duke | 2006 | 662 | 726 | 91.2 |
| Greg Starrick, Kentucky/Southern Illinois | 1972 | 341 | 375 | 90.9 |

Note: Minimum 300 free throws made.

*Freshmen became eligible for varsity play in 1973.

## Career Records *(Cont.)*

### THREE-POINT FIELD GOALS MADE

| Player and Team | Final Year | GP | 3FG |
|---|---|---|---|
| J.J. Redick, Duke | 2006 | 139 | 457 |
| David Holston, Chicago St | 2009 | 119 | 450 |
| Keydren Clark, St. Peter's | 2006 | 118 | 435 |
| Chris Lofton, Tennessee | 2008 | 128 | 431 |
| Stephen Curry, Davidson | 2009 | 104 | 414 |

### THREE-POINT FIELD-GOAL PERCENTAGE

| Player and Team | Final Year | 3FG | 3FGA | Pct |
|---|---|---|---|---|
| Tony Bennett, UW–Green Bay | 1992 | 290 | 584 | 49.7 |
| Stephen Sir, San Diego St/Northern Ariz | 2007 | 323 | 689 | 46.9 |
| David Olson, Eastern Illinois | 1992 | 262 | 562 | 46.6 |
| Jaycee Carroll, Utah St | 2008 | 369 | 793 | 46.5 |
| Ross Land, Northern Arizona | 2000 | 308 | 664 | 46.4 |

Note: Minimum 200 3-point field goals and 2.0 3FG/G.

### STEALS

| Player and Team | Final Year | GP | Stl |
|---|---|---|---|
| John Linehan, Providence | 2002 | 122 | 385 |
| Eric Murdock, Providence | 1991 | 117 | 376 |
| Pepe Sanchez, Temple | 2000 | 116 | 365 |
| Cookie Belcher, Nebraska | 2001 | 131 | 353 |
| Kevin Braswell, Georgetown | 2002 | 128 | 349 |

### BLOCKED SHOTS

| Player and Team | Final Year | GP | BS |
|---|---|---|---|
| Jarvis Varnado, Mississipi St | 2010 | 141 | 564 |
| Wojciech Myrda, La.-Monroe | 2002 | 115 | 535 |
| Adonal Foyle, Colgate | 1997 | 87 | 492 |
| Tim Duncan, Wake Forest | 1997 | 128 | 481 |
| Alonzo Mourning, Georgetown | 1992 | 120 | 453 |

# NCAA Men's Division I Team Leaders

## Division I Team Alltime Wins

| Team | First Year | Yrs | W | L | T |
|---|---|---|---|---|---|
| Kentucky | 1903 | 107 | 2023 | 638 | 1 |
| North Carolina | 1911 | 100 | 2004 | 720 | 0 |
| Kansas | 1899 | 112 | 2003 | 796 | 0 |
| Duke | 1906 | 105 | 1912 | 822 | 0 |
| Syracuse | 1901 | 109 | 1783 | 811 | 0 |
| Temple | 1895 | 114 | 1740 | 966 | 0 |
| St. John's (N.Y.) | 1908 | 103 | 1703 | 884 | 0 |
| UCLA | 1920 | 91 | 1686 | 744 | 0 |
| Notre Dame | 1898 | 105 | 1674 | 920 | 1 |
| Pennsylvania | 1897 | 110 | 1664 | 971 | 2 |
| Indiana | 1901 | 110 | 1651 | 930 | 0 |
| Utah | 1909 | 102 | 1651 | 875 | 0 |
| Illinois | 1906 | 105 | 1630 | 868 | 0 |
| Western Kentucky | 1915 | 91 | 1623 | 793 | 0 |
| Washington | 1896 | 108 | 1617 | 1057 | 0 |

Note: Minimum of 25 years in Division I.

## Division I Alltime Winning Percentage

| Team | First Year | Yrs | W | L | T | Pct |
|---|---|---|---|---|---|---|
| Kentucky | 1903 | 107 | 2023 | 638 | 1 | .760 |
| North Carolina | 1911 | 100 | 2004 | 720 | 0 | .736 |
| Kansas | 1899 | 112 | 2003 | 796 | 0 | .716 |
| UNLV | 1959 | 52 | 1083 | 438 | 0 | .712 |
| Duke | 1906 | 105 | 1912 | 822 | 0 | .699 |
| UCLA | 1920 | 91 | 1686 | 744 | 0 | .694 |
| Syracuse | 1901 | 109 | 1783 | 811 | 0 | .687 |
| Western Kentucky | 1915 | 91 | 1623 | 793 | 0 | .672 |
| St. John's (N.Y.) | 1908 | 103 | 1703 | 884 | 0 | .658 |
| Louisville | 1912 | 96 | 1607 | 844 | 0 | .656 |
| Utah | 1909 | 102 | 1651 | 875 | 0 | .654 |
| Illinois | 1906 | 105 | 1630 | 868 | 0 | .653 |
| Notre Dame | 1898 | 105 | 1674 | 920 | 1 | .645 |
| Temple | 1895 | 114 | 1740 | 966 | 0 | .643 |
| Missouri St | 1909 | 98 | 1522 | 845 | 0 | .643 |

# NCAA Men's Division I Winning Streaks

## Longest—Full Season

| Team | Games | Years | Ended by |
|---|---|---|---|
| UCLA | 88 | 1971–74 | Notre Dame (71–70) |
| San Francisco | 60 | 1955–57 | Illinois (62–33) |
| UCLA | 47 | 1966–68 | Houston (71–69) |
| UNLV | 45 | 1990–91 | Duke (79–77) |
| Texas | 44 | 1913–17 | Rice (24–18) |
| Seton Hall | 43 | 1939–41 | LIU-Brooklyn (49–26) |
| LIU-Brooklyn | 43 | 1935–37 | Stanford (45–31) |
| UCLA | 41 | 1968–69 | USC (46–44) |
| Marquette | 39 | 1970–71 | Ohio St (60–59) |
| Cincinnati | 37 | 1962–63 | Wichita St (65–64) |
| North Carolina | 37 | 1957–58 | West Virginia (75–64) |

## Longest—Regular Season

| Team | Games | Years | Ended by |
|---|---|---|---|
| UCLA | 76 | 1971–74 | Notre Dame (71–70) |
| Indiana | 57 | 1975–77 | Toledo (59–57) |
| Marquette | 56 | 1970–72 | Detroit (70–49) |
| Kentucky | 54 | 1952–55 | Georgia Tech (59–58) |
| San Francisco | 51 | 1955–57 | Illinois (62–33) |
| Pennsylvania | 48 | 1970–72 | Temple (57–52) |
| Ohio State | 47 | 1960–62 | Wisconsin (86–67) |
| Texas | 44 | 1913–17 | Rice (24–18) |
| UCLA | 43 | 1966–68 | Houston (71–69) |
| LIU-Brooklyn | 43 | 1935–37 | Stanford (45–31) |
| Seton Hall | 42 | 1939–41 | LIU-Brooklyn (49–26) |

## Longest—Home Court

| Team | Games | Years | Team | Games | Years |
|---|---|---|---|---|---|
| Kentucky | 129 | 1943–55 | Lamar | 80 | 1978–84 |
| St. Bonaventure | 99 | 1948–61 | Long Beach St | 75 | 1968–74 |
| UCLA | 98 | 1970–76 | UNLV | 72 | 1974–78 |
| Cincinnati | 86 | 1957–64 | Arizona | 71 | 1987–92 |
| Marquette | 81 | 1967–73 | Cincinnati | 68 | 1972–78 |
| Arizona | 81 | 1945–51 | Western Kentucky | 67 | 1949–55 |

# NCAA Men's Division I Winningest Coaches

## Active Coaches*

### WINS

| Coach and Team | W |
|---|---|
| Mike Krzyzewski, Duke | 900 |
| Jim Boeheim, Syracuse | 856 |
| Jim Calhoun, Connecticut | 855 |
| Bob Huggins, West Virginia | 691 |
| Gary Williams, Maryland | 668 |
| Roy Williams, North Carolina | 643 |
| Homer Drew, Valparaiso | 640 |
| Bo Ryan, Wisconsin | 625 |
| Cliff Ellis, Coastal Carolina | 614 |
| Mike Montgomery, California | 611 |

Note: Minimum 5 years as a Division I head coach; includes record at 4-year colleges only.

### WINNING PERCENTAGE

| Coach and Team | Yrs | W | L | Pct |
|---|---|---|---|---|
| Roy Williams, North Carolina | 23 | 643 | 163 | .798 |
| Mark Few, Gonzaga | 12 | 316 | 83 | .792 |
| Jamie Dixon, Pittsburgh | 8 | 216 | 60 | .783 |
| Dave Rose, BYU | 6 | 159 | 45 | .779 |
| Thad Matta, Ohio St | 11 | 292 | 88 | .768 |
| Bo Ryan, Wisconsin | 27 | 625 | 194 | .763 |
| Bruce Pearl, Tennessee | 19 | 462 | 145 | .761 |
| Mike Krzyzewski, Duke | 36 | 900 | 284 | .760 |
| John Calipari, Kentucky | 19 | 467 | 151 | .756 |
| Jim Boeheim, Syracuse | 35 | 856 | 301 | .740 |

Note: Minimum 5 years as a Division I head coach; includes record at 4-year colleges only.

## Alltime Winningest Men's Division I Coaches

| | W |
|---|---|
| Bob Knight (Army, Indiana, Texas Tech) | 902 |
| *Mike Krzyzewski (Army, Duke) | 900 |
| Dean Smith (North Carolina) | 879 |
| Adolph Rupp (Kentucky) | 876 |
| *Jim Boeheim (Syracuse) | 856 |
| *Jim Calhoun (Northeastern, Connecticut) | 855 |
| Jim Phelan (Mt. St. Mary's) | 830 |
| Eddie Sutton (Creighton, Arkansas, Kentucky, Oklahoma St) | 804 |
| Lefty Driesell (Davidson, Maryland, James Madison, Georgia St) | 786 |
| Lute Olson (Long Beach St, Iowa, Arizona) | 780 |
| Lou Henson (Hardin-Simmons, New Mexico St, Illinois, New Mexico St) | 779 |
| Henry Iba (NW Missouri St, Colorado, Oklahoma St) | 764 |
| Ed Diddle (Western Kentucky) | 759 |
| Phog Allen (Baker, Kansas, Haskell, Central Missouri St, Kansas) | 746 |
| John Chaney (Cheyney St, Temple) | 741 |
| Jerry Tarkanian (Long Beach St, UNLV, Fresno St) | 729 |
| Norm Stewart (Northern Iowa, Missouri) | 728 |
| Ray Meyer (DePaul) | 724 |
| Don Haskins (Oklahoma St, UTEP) | 719 |
| *Bob Huggins (Walsh, Akron, Cincinnati, Kansas St, West Virginia) | 691 |
| Denny Crum (UCLA, Louisville) | 675 |
| *Gary Williams (American, Boston College, Ohio St, Maryland) | 668 |
| John Wooden (Purdue, Indiana St, UCLA) | 664 |
| Ralph Miller (Wichita St, Iowa, Oregon St) | 657 |
| Tom Penders (Tufts, Columbia, Fordham, URI, Texas, George Wash., Houston) | 648 |
| Gene Bartow (C. Missouri St, Valparaiso, Memphis, Illinois, UCLA, UAB) | 647 |
| *Roy Williams (Kansas, North Carolina) | 643 |
| Billy Tubbs (Lamar, Southwestern [Tex.], Oklahoma, TCU) | 641 |
| *Homer Drew (Bethel Coll. Indiana-South Bend, Valparaiso) | 640 |
| Marv Harshman (Pacific Lutheran, Washington St, Washington) | 637 |

Note: Minimum 10 head coaching seasons in Division I.

*Active in 2010–11.

### Alltime Winningest Men's Division I Coaches (Cont.)
#### WINNING PERCENTAGE

| Coach (Team, Years) | Yrs | W | L | Pct |
|---|---|---|---|---|
| Clair Bee (Rider 1929–31, LIU-Brooklyn 1932–45, 1946–51) | 21 | 412 | 87 | .826 |
| Adolph Rupp (Kentucky 1931–72) | 41 | 876 | 190 | .822 |
| John Wooden (Indiana St 1947–48, UCLA 1949–75) | 29 | 664 | 162 | .804 |
| *Roy Williams (Kansas 1989–2003, North Carolina 2003–) | 23 | 643 | 163 | .798 |
| John Kresse (College of Charleston 1980–2002) | 23 | 560 | 143 | .797 |
| *Mark Few (Gonzaga 1999–) | 12 | 316 | 83 | .792 |
| Jerry Tarkanian (Long Beach St 1969–73, UNLV 1974–92, Fresno St 1995–2002) | 31 | 729 | 201 | .784 |
| Francis Schmidt (Tulsa 1916–17, Arkansas 1924–29, TCU 1930–34) | 17 | 258 | 72 | .782 |
| Dean Smith (North Carolina 1962–97) | 36 | 879 | 254 | .776 |
| *Thad Matta (Butler 2001, Xavier 2002–04, Ohio St 2005–) | 11 | 292 | 88 | .768 |
| Jack Ramsay (St. Joseph's [Pa.] 1956–66) | 11 | 231 | 71 | .765 |
| Frank Keaney (Rhode Island 1921–48) | 28 | 401 | 124 | .764 |
| George Keogan (St. Louis 1916, Allegheny 1919, Valparaiso 1920–21, Notre Dame 1924–43) | 27 | 414 | 127 | .764 |
| *Bo Ryan (UW-Milwaukee 1999–2001, Wisconsin 2001–) | 27 | 625 | 194 | .763 |
| *Bruce Pearl (UW-Milwaukee 2001–05, Tennessee 2005–11) | 19 | 462 | 145 | .761 |
| Vic Bubas (Duke 1960–69) | 10 | 213 | 67 | .761 |
| Harry Fisher (Columbia 1907–16, Army 1922–23, 1925) | 16 | 189 | 60 | .759 |
| *Mike Krzyzewski (Army 1976–80, Duke 1981–) | 36 | 900 | 284 | .760 |
| *John Calipari (Massachusetts 1989–96, Memphis 2001–09, Kentucky 2009–) | 19 | 467 | 151 | .756 |
| Fred Bennion (Brigham Young 1909–10, Utah 1911-14, Montana St 1915-19) | 11 | 95 | 31 | .756 |
| Charles (Chick) Davies (Duquesne 1925–43, 1947–48) | 21 | 314 | 106 | .748 |
| Ray Mears (Wittenberg 1957–62, Tennessee 1963–77) | 21 | 399 | 135 | .747 |
| Edward McNichol (Penn 1921-30) | 10 | 186 | 63 | .747 |
| Al McGuire (Belmont Abbey 1958–64, Marquette 1965–77) | 20 | 406 | 142 | .741 |
| *Jim Boeheim (Syracuse 1977–) | 35 | 856 | 301 | .740 |
| Phog Allen (Baker 1906–08, Haskell 1909, Cent. Mo. St 1913–19, Kansas 1908–09, 1920–56) | 50 | 746 | 264 | .739 |
| Everett Case (North Carolina St 1947–65) | 19 | 377 | 134 | .738 |
| Lute Olson (Long Beach St 1973–74, Iowa 1974–83, Arizona 1983–) | 34 | 780 | 280 | .736 |
| Arthur Schabinger (Ottawa 1917–20, Emporia St 1921–22, Creighton 1924–25) | 19 | 245 | 88 | .736 |

*Active in 2010–11. Note: Minimum 10 years head coaching in Division I.

## NCAA Women's Division I Winningest Coaches

### Alltime Winningest Women's Division I Coaches
#### WINNING PERCENTAGE

| Coach (Team, Years) | Yrs | W | L | Pct |
|---|---|---|---|---|
| Leon Barmore (Louisiana Tech 1983–02) | 20 | 576 | 87 | .869 |
| *Geno Auriemma (Connecticut 1986–) | 26 | 771 | 124 | .861 |
| *Pat Summitt (Tennessee 1975–) | 37 | 1071 | 199 | .843 |
| *Tara VanDerveer (Idaho 1979-80, Ohio St 1981–85, Stanford 1986–95, 1997–) | 32 | 826 | 198 | .807 |
| *Kim Mulkey (Baylor 2001–) | 11 | 298 | 79 | .790 |
| Bill Sheahan (Mt. St. Mary's 1982–98) | 17 | 372 | 104 | .782 |
| *Wes Moore (Maryville 1988–93, Francis Marion 1996–98, Chattanooga 1999–) | 22 | 507 | 155 | .766 |
| *Robin Selvig (Montana 1979–) | 33 | 758 | 233 | .765 |
| *Gail Goestenkors (Duke 1993–07, Texas 2007–) | 19 | 479 | 148 | .764 |
| *Carey Green (Liberty 1999–) | 12 | 286 | 94 | .753 |

Note: Minimum 10 head coaching seasons in Division I.

*Active in 2010–11.

### Alltime Winningest Women's Division I Coaches

| | W |
|---|---|
| *Pat Summitt (Tennessee) | 1,071 |
| Jody Conradt (Sam Houston St, Tex.-Arlington, Texas) | 900 |
| *C. Vivian Stringer (Cheyney St, Iowa, Rutgers) | 863 |
| *Sylvia Hatchell (Francis Marion, North Carolina) | 859 |
| *Tara VanDerveer (Idaho, Ohio St, Stanford) | 826 |
| *Andy Landers (Georgia) | 773 |
| *Geno Auriemma (Connecticut) | 771 |
| *Robin Selvig (Montana) | 758 |
| *Jim Foster (St. Joseph's, Vanderbilt, Ohio St) | 740 |
| *Debbie Ryan (Virginia) | 739 |
| Kay Yow (Elon, North Carolina St) | 737 |

Note: Minimum 10 head coaching seasons in Division I.

*Active in 2010–11.

| Year | Winner | Score | Runner-up | Winning Coach |
|------|--------|-------|-----------|---------------|
| 1982 | Louisiana Tech | 76–62 | Cheyney | Sonja Hogg/Leon Barmore |
| 1983 | USC | 69–67 | Louisiana Tech | Linda Sharp |
| 1984 | USC | 72–61 | Tennessee | Linda Sharp |
| 1985 | Old Dominion | 70–65 | Georgia | Marianne Stanley |
| 1986 | Texas | 97–81 | USC | Jody Conradt |
| 1987 | Tennessee | 67–44 | Louisiana Tech | Pat Summitt |
| 1988 | Louisiana Tech | 56–54 | Auburn | Leon Barmore |
| 1989 | Tennessee | 76–60 | Auburn | Pat Summitt |
| 1990 | Stanford | 88–81 | Auburn | Tara VanDerveer |
| 1991 | Tennessee | 70–67 (OT) | Virginia | Pat Summitt |
| 1992 | Stanford | 78–62 | Western Kentucky | Tara VanDerveer |
| 1993 | Texas Tech | 84–82 | Ohio State | Marsha Sharp |
| 1994 | North Carolina | 60–59 | Louisiana Tech | Sylvia Hatchell |
| 1995 | Connecticut | 70–64 | Tennessee | Geno Auriemma |
| 1996 | Tennessee | 83–65 | Georgia | Pat Summitt |
| 1997 | Tennessee | 68–59 | Old Dominion | Pat Summitt |
| 1998 | Tennessee | 93–75 | Louisiana Tech | Pat Summitt |
| 1999 | Purdue | 62–45 | Duke | Carolyn Peck |
| 2000 | Connecticut | 71–52 | Tennessee | Geno Auriemma |
| 2001 | Notre Dame | 68–66 | Purdue | Muffet McGraw |
| 2002 | Connecticut | 82–70 | Oklahoma | Geno Auriemma |
| 2003 | Connecticut | 73–68 | Tennessee | Geno Auriemma |
| 2004 | Connecticut | 70–61 | Tennessee | Geno Auriemma |
| 2005 | Baylor | 84–62 | Michigan St | Kim Mulkey-Robinson |
| 2006 | Maryland | 78–75 | Duke | Brenda Frese |
| 2007 | Tennessee | 59–46 | Rutgers | Pat Summitt |
| 2008 | Tennessee | 64–48 | Stanford | Pat Summitt |
| 2009 | Connecticut | 76–54 | Louisville | Geno Auriemma |
| 2010 | Connecticut | 53–47 | Stanford | Geno Auriemma |
| 2011 | Texas A&M | 76–70 | Notre Dame | Gary Blair |

## NCAA Women's Division I Alltime Individual Leaders

### Single-Game Records

#### SCORING HIGHS

| Pts | Player and Team vs Opponent | Year |
|-----|------------------------------|------|
| 60 | Cindy Brown, Long Beach St vs San Jose St | 1987 |
| 58 | Kim Perrot, SW Louisiana vs SE Louisiana | 1990 |
| 58 | Lorri Bauman, Drake vs SW Missouri St* | 1984 |
| 56 | Jackie Stiles, SW Missouri St vs Evansville | 2000 |
| 55 | Patricia Hoskins, Mississippi Valley St vs Southern-Birm. | 1989 |
| 55 | Patricia Hoskins, Mississippi Valley St vs Alabama St | 1989 |
| 54 | Anjinea Hopson, Grambling vs Jackson St | 1994 |
| 54 | Mary Lowry, Baylor vs Texas | 1994 |
| 54 | Wanda Ford, Drake vs SW Missouri St* | 1986 |
| 54 | Elena Delle Donne, Delaware vs James Madison | 2010 |

Three tied with 53.

#### REBOUNDS

| Reb | Player and Team vs Opponent | Year |
|-----|------------------------------|------|
| 40 | Deborah Temple, Delta St vs UAB | 1983 |
| 37 | Rosina Pearson, Bethune-Cookman vs Florida Memorial | 1985 |
| 33 | Maureen Formico, Pepperdine vs Loyola (Calif.) | 1985 |
| 32 | Lachelle Lyles, Southeast Mo. St. vs Tennessee St. | 2006 |
| 31 | Darlene Beale, Howard vs South Carolina St | 1987 |
| 30 | Cindy Bonforte, Wagner vs Queens (N.Y.) | 1983 |
| 30 | Kayone Hankins, New Orleans vs. Nicholls St | 1994 |
| 30 | Wanda Ford, Drake vs Eastern Illinois | 1985 |
| 30 | Jennifer Butler, Massachusetts vs Florida | 2003 |

Three tied with 29.

*School changed name to Missouri State after 2004–05 season.

## Single Game Records *(Cont.)*
### ASSISTS

| Asst | Player and Team vs Opponent | Year |
|------|------------------------------|------|
| 23 | Michelle Burden, Kent St vs Ball St | 1991 |
| 22 | Shawn Monday, Tennessee Tech vs Morehead St | 1988 |
| 22 | Veronica Pettry, Loyola (Ill.) vs Detroit | 1989 |
| 22 | Tine Freil, Pacific vs Wichita St | 1991 |
| 21 | Tine Freil, Pacific vs Fresno St | 1992 |
| 21 | Amy Bauer, Wisconsin vs Detroit | 1989 |
| 21 | Neacole Hall, Alabama St vs Southern-Birm. | 1989 |

Six tied with 20.

## Single Season Records
### POINTS

| Player and Team | Year | GP | FG | 3FG | FT | Pts |
|-----------------|------|----|----|-----|----|----|
| Jackie Stiles, SW Missouri St* | 2001 | 35 | 365 | 65 | 267 | 1062 |
| Cindy Brown, Long Beach St | 1987 | 35 | 362 | — | 250 | 974 |
| Genia Miller, CSU-Fullerton | 1991 | 33 | 376 | 0 | 217 | 969 |
| Sheryl Swoopes, Texas Tech | 1993 | 34 | 356 | 32 | 211 | 955 |
| Alysha Clark, Middle Tennessee St | 2008 | 34 | 343 | 12 | 237 | 935 |
| Andrea Congreaves, Mercer | 1992 | 28 | 353 | 77 | 142 | 925 |
| Wanda Ford, Drake | 1986 | 30 | 390 | — | 139 | 919 |
| Chamique Holdsclaw, Tennessee | 1998 | 39 | 370 | 9 | 166 | 915 |
| Andrea Riley, Oklahoma St | 2010 | 34 | 296 | 78 | 239 | 909 |
| Barbara Kennedy, Clemson | 1982 | 31 | 392 | — | 124 | 908 |
| Patricia Hoskins, Mississippi Valley St | 1989 | 27 | 345 | 13 | 205 | 908 |

### SEASON SCORING AVERAGE

| Player and Team | Year | GP | FG | 3FG | FT | Pts | Avg |
|-----------------|------|----|----|-----|----|----|-----|
| Patricia Hoskins, Mississippi Valley St | 1989 | 27 | 345 | 13 | 205 | 908 | 33.6 |
| Andrea Congreaves, Mercer | 1992 | 28 | 353 | 77 | 142 | 925 | 33.0 |
| Deborah Temple, Delta St | 1984 | 28 | 373 | — | 127 | 873 | 31.2 |
| Andrea Congreaves, Mercer | 1993 | 26 | 302 | 51 | 150 | 805 | 31.0 |
| Wanda Ford, Drake | 1986 | 30 | 390 | — | 139 | 919 | 30.6 |
| Anucha Browne, Northwestern | 1985 | 28 | 341 | — | 173 | 855 | 30.5 |
| LeChandra LeDay, Grambling | 1988 | 28 | 334 | 36 | 146 | 850 | 30.4 |
| Jackie Stiles, SW Missouri St* | 2001 | 35 | 365 | 65 | 267 | 1062 | 30.3 |
| Kim Perrot, SW Louisiana | 1990 | 28 | 308 | 95 | 128 | 839 | 30.0 |
| Tina Hutchinson, San Diego St | 1984 | 30 | 383 | — | 132 | 898 | 29.9 |
| Jan Jensen, Drake | 1991 | 30 | 358 | 6 | 166 | 888 | 29.6 |
| Genia Miller, CSU-Fullerton | 1991 | 33 | 376 | 0 | 217 | 969 | 29.4 |
| Barbara Kennedy, Clemson | 1982 | 31 | 392 | — | 124 | 908 | 29.3 |
| LaTaunya Pollard, Long Beach St | 1983 | 31 | 376 | — | 155 | 907 | 29.3 |
| Lisa McMullen, Alabama St | 1991 | 28 | 285 | 126 | 119 | 815 | 29.1 |

### REBOUNDS

| Player and Team | Year | GP | Reb | Player and Team | Year | GP | Reb |
|-----------------|------|----|-----|-----------------|------|----|-----|
| Courtney Paris, Oklahoma | 2006 | 36 | 539 | Darlene Jones, Miss Valley St | 1983 | 31 | 487 |
| Wanda Ford, Drake | 1985 | 30 | 534 | Melanie Simpson, Okla. City | 1982 | 37 | 481 |
| Lachelle Lyles, SE Missouri St | 2006 | 30 | 517 | R. Pearson, Beth.-Cookman | 1985 | 26 | 480 |
| Wanda Ford, Drake | 1986 | 30 | 506 | Patricia Hoskins, Miss. Valley St | 1987 | 28 | 476 |
| Anne Donovan, Old Dominion | 1983 | 35 | 504 | Cheryl Miller, USC | 1985 | 30 | 474 |

### REBOUND AVERAGE

| Player and Team | Year | GP | Reb | Avg |
|-----------------|------|----|-----|-----|
| Rosina Pearson, Bethune-Cookman | 1985 | 26 | 480 | 18.5 |
| Wanda Ford, Drake | 1985 | 30 | 534 | 17.8 |
| Katie Beck, East Tennessee St | 1988 | 25 | 441 | 17.6 |
| DeShawne Blocker, East Tennessee St | 1994 | 26 | 450 | 17.3 |
| Lachelle Lyles, SE Missouri St. | 2006 | 30 | 517 | 17.2 |
| Patricia Hoskins, Mississippi Valley St | 1987 | 28 | 476 | 17.0 |
| Wanda Ford, Drake | 1986 | 30 | 506 | 16.9 |
| Patricia Hoskins, Mississippi Valley St | 1989 | 27 | 440 | 16.3 |
| Joy Kellogg, Oklahoma City | 1984 | 23 | 373 | 16.2 |
| Courtney Paris, Oklahoma | 2006 | 30 | 485 | 16.2 |
| Deborah Mitchell, Mississippi Coll. | 1983 | 28 | 447 | 16.0 |
| Cheryl Miller, USC | 1985 | 30 | 474 | 15.8 |

*School changed name to Missouri State after 2004–05 season

### Single Season Records *(Cont.)*

#### FIELD-GOAL PERCENTAGE

| Player and Team | Year | GP | FG | FGA | Pct |
|---|---|---|---|---|---|
| Myndee Larsen, Southern Utah | 1998 | 28 | 249 | 344 | 72.4 |
| Chantelle Anderson, Vanderbilt | 2001 | 34 | 292 | 404 | 72.3 |
| Deneka Knowles, SE Louisiana | 1996 | 26 | 199 | 276 | 72.1 |
| Crystal Langhorne, Maryland | 2006 | 32 | 202 | 280 | 72.1 |
| Barbara Farris, Tulane | 1998 | 27 | 151 | 210 | 71.9 |
| Renay Adams, Tennessee Tech | 1991 | 30 | 185 | 258 | 71.7 |
| Carolyn Swords, Boston College | 2011 | 33 | 240 | 336 | 71.4 |
| Regina Days, Georgia Southern | 1986 | 27 | 234 | 332 | 70.5 |
| Kim Wood, UW-Green Bay | 1994 | 27 | 188 | 271 | 69.4 |
| Kelly Lyons, Old Dominion | 1990 | 31 | 308 | 444 | 69.4 |

Based on qualifiers for annual championship.

#### FREE-THROW PERCENTAGE

| Player and Team | Year | GP | FT | FTA | Pct |
|---|---|---|---|---|---|
| Adrienne Squire, Penn St | 2006 | 29 | 80 | 83 | 96.4 |
| Shanna Zolman, Tennessee | 2004 | 35 | 88 | 92 | 95.7 |
| Ginny Doyle, Richmond | 1992 | 29 | 96 | 101 | 95.0 |
| Jill Marano, La Salle | 2003 | 29 | 88 | 93 | 94.6 |
| Sue Bird, Connecticut | 2002 | 39 | 98 | 104 | 94.2 |
| Paula Corder-King, SE Missouri St | 1999 | 28 | 111 | 118 | 94.1 |
| Kandi Brown, Morehead St | 2003 | 28 | 104 | 111 | 93.7 |
| Linda Cyborski, Delaware | 1991 | 29 | 74 | 79 | 93.7 |
| Kandi Brown, Morehead St | 2002 | 29 | 74 | 79 | 93.7 |
| Emily London, Samford | 2011 | 33 | 117 | 125 | 93.6 |

Based on qualifiers for annual championship.

### Career Records

#### POINTS

| Player and Team | Yrs | GP | Pts |
|---|---|---|---|
| Jackie Stiles, SW Missouri St* | 1997–01 | 129 | 3393 |
| Patricia Hoskins, Mississippi Valley St | 1985–89 | 110 | 3122 |
| Lorri Bauman, Drake | 1981–84 | 120 | 3115 |
| Maya Moore, Connecticut | 2007–11 | 154 | 3036 |
| Chamique Holdsclaw, Tennessee | 1995–99 | 148 | 3025 |
| Cheryl Miller, USC | 1983–86 | 128 | 3018 |
| Cindy Blodgett, Maine | 1994–98 | 118 | 3005 |
| LaToya Thomas, Mississippi St | 1999–2003 | 125 | 2981 |
| Valorie Whiteside, Appalachian St | 1984–88 | 116 | 2944 |
| Kelly Mazzante, Penn St | 2000–04 | 133 | 2919 |

#### SCORING AVERAGE

| Player and Team | Yrs | GP | FG | 3FG | FT | Pts | Avg |
|---|---|---|---|---|---|---|---|
| Patricia Hoskins, Mississippi Valley St | 1985–89 | 110 | 1196 | 24 | 706 | 3122 | 28.4 |
| Sandra Hodge, New Orleans | 1981–84 | 107 | 1194 | — | 472 | 2860 | 26.7 |
| Jackie Stiles, SW Missouri St* | 1997–01 | 129 | 1160 | 221 | 852 | 3393 | 26.3 |
| Lorri Bauman, Drake | 1981–84 | 120 | 1104 | — | 907 | 3115 | 26.0 |
| Andrea Congreaves, Mercer | 1989–93 | 108 | 1107 | 153 | 429 | 2796 | 25.9 |
| Cindy Blodgett, Maine | 1994–98 | 118 | 1055 | 219 | 676 | 3005 | 25.5 |
| Valorie Whiteside, Appalachian St | 1984–88 | 116 | 1153 | 0 | 638 | 2944 | 25.4 |
| Joyce Walker, LSU | 1981–84 | 117 | 1259 | — | 388 | 2906 | 24.8 |
| Tarcha Hollis, Grambling | 1989–91 | 84 | 891 | 3 | 246 | 2031 | 24.2 |
| Korie Hlede, Duquesne | 1994–98 | 109 | 1045 | 162 | 379 | 2631 | 24.1 |
| Karen Pelphrey, Marshall | 1983–86 | 114 | 1175 | — | 396 | 2746 | 24.1 |
| Erma Jones, Bethune-Cookman | 1982–84 | 87 | 961 | — | 173 | 2095 | 24.1 |

*School changed name to Missouri State after 2004–05 season

| Year | Winner | Score | Runner-up | Third Place | Fourth Place |
|------|--------|-------|-----------|-------------|--------------|
| 1957 | Wheaton (Ill.) | 89–65 | Kentucky Wesleyan | Mt. St. Mary's (Md.) | CSU-Los Angeles |
| 1958 | South Dakota | 75–53 | St. Michael's | Evansville | Wheaton (Ill.) |
| 1959 | Evansville | 83–67 | SW Missouri St | North Carolina A&T | CSU-Los Angeles |
| 1960 | Evansville | 90–69 | Chapman | Kentucky Wesleyan | Cornell College |
| 1961 | Wittenberg | 42–38 | SE Missouri St | South Dakota St | Mt. St. Mary's (Md.) |
| 1962 | Mt. St. Mary's (Md.) | 58–57 (OT) | CSU-Sacramento | Southern Illinois | Nebraska Wesleyan |
| 1963 | South Dakota St | 44–42 | Wittenberg | Oglethorpe | Southern Illinois |
| 1964 | Evansville | 72–59 | Akron | North Carolina A&T | Northern Iowa |
| 1965 | Evansville | 85–82 (OT) | Southern Illinois | North Dakota | St. Michael's |
| 1966 | Kentucky Wesleyan | 54–51 | Southern Illinois | Akron | North Dakota |
| 1967 | Winston-Salem | 77–74 | SW Missouri St | Kentucky Wesleyan | Illinois St |
| 1968 | Kentucky Wesleyan | 63–52 | Indiana St | Trinity (Tex.) | Ashland |
| 1969 | Kentucky Wesleyan | 75–71 | SW Missouri St | †Vacated | Ashland |
| 1970 | Philadelphia Textile | 76–65 | Tennessee St | UC-Riverside | Buffalo St |
| 1971 | Evansville | 97–82 | Old Dominion | †Vacated | Kentucky Wesleyan |
| 1972 | Roanoke | 84–72 | Akron | Tennessee St | Eastern Mich |
| 1973 | Kentucky Wesleyan | 78–76 (OT) | Tennessee St | Assumption | Brockport St |
| 1974 | Morgan St | 67–52 | SW Missouri St | Assumption | New Orleans |
| 1975 | Old Dominion | 76–74 | New Orleans | Assumption | Tenn.-Chattanooga |
| 1976 | Puget Sound | 83–74 | Tenn.-Chattanooga | Eastern Illinois | Old Dominion |
| 1977 | Tenn.-Chattanooga | 71–62 | Randolph-Macon | North Alabama | Sacred Heart |
| 1978 | Cheyney | 47–40 | UW-Green Bay | Eastern Illinois | Central Florida |
| 1979 | North Alabama | 64–50 | UW-Green Bay | Cheyney | Bridgeport |
| 1980 | Virginia Union | 80–74 | New York Tech | Florida Southern | North Alabama |
| 1981 | Florida Southern | 73–68 | Mt. St. Mary's (Md.) | Cal Poly-SLO | UW-Green Bay |
| 1982 | District of Columbia | 73–63 | Florida Southern | Kentucky Wesleyan | CSU-Bakersfield |
| 1983 | Wright St | 92–73 | District of Columbia | *CSU-Bakersfield | *Morningside |
| 1984 | Central Missouri St | 81–77 | St. Augustine's | *Kentucky Wesleyan | *N Alabama |
| 1985 | Jacksonville St | 74–73 | South Dakota St | *Kentucky Wesleyan | *Mt. St. Mary's (Md.) |
| 1986 | Sacred Heart | 93–87 | SE Missouri St | *Cheyney | *Florida Southern |
| 1987 | Kentucky Wesleyan | 92–74 | Gannon | *Delta St | *Eastern Montana |
| 1988 | Lowell | 75–72 | Ak.-Anchorage | Florida Southern | Troy St |
| 1989 | North Carolina Central | 73–46 | SE Missouri St | UC-Riverside | Jacksonville St |
| 1990 | Kentucky Wesleyan | 93–79 | CSU-Bakersfield | North Dakota | Morehouse |
| 1991 | North Alabama | 79–72 | Bridgeport (Conn.) | *CSU-Bakersfield | *Virginia Union |
| 1992 | Virginia Union | 100–75 | Bridgeport (Conn.) | *CSU-Bakersfield | *California (Pa.) |
| 1993 | CSU-Bakersfield | 85–72 | Troy St (Ala.) | *New Hampshire Coll | *Wayne St (Mich.) |
| 1994 | CSU-Bakersfield | 92–86 | Southern Indiana | *New Hampshire Coll | *Washburn |
| 1995 | Southern Indiana | 71–63 | UC–Riverside | *Norfolk St | *Indiana (Pa.) |
| 1996 | Fort Hays St | 70–63 | Northern Kentucky | *California (Pa.) | *Virginia Union |
| 1997 | CSU-Bakersfield | 57–56 | Northern Kentucky | *Lynn | *Salem-Teikyo |
| 1998 | UC-Davis | 83–77 | Kentucky Wesleyan | *St. Rose | *Virginia Union |
| 1999 | Kentucky Wesleyan | 75–60 | Metropolitan St | *Truman St | *Florida Southern |
| 2000 | Metropolitan St | 97–79 | Kentucky Wesleyan | *Missouri Southern | *Seattle Pacific |
| 2001 | Kentucky Wesleyan | 72–63 | Washburn | *Western Washington | *Tampa |
| 2002 | Metropolitan St | 80–72 | Kentucky Wesleyan | *Shaw | *Indiana (Pa.) |
| 2003 | Northeastern St (Okla.) | 75–64 | †Vacated | *Bowie St | *Queens (N.Y.) |
| 2004 | Kennesaw St | 84–59 | Southern Indiana | *Humboldt St | *Metropolitan St |
| 2005 | Virginia Union | 63–58 | Bryant | *Lynn | *Tarleton St |
| 2006 | Winona St (Minn.) | 73–61 | Virginia Union | *Seattle Pacific | *Stonehill |
| 2007 | Barton | 77–75 | Winona St (Minn.) | *CSU-San Bernardino | *Central Missouri |
| 2008 | Winona St (Minn.) | 87–76 | Augusta St | *Bentley | *Ak.-Anchorage |
| 2009 | Findlay | 56–53 (OT) | Cal Poly.-Pomona | *Augusta St | *Central Missouri |
| 2010 | Cal Poly | 65–53 | Indiana Univ. (Pa.) | *Bentley | *St. Cloud St |
| 2011 | Bellarmine | 71–68 | BYU-Hawaii | *Minnesota St-Mankato | *West Liberty |

*Indicates tied for third. †Student-athletes representing American International in 1969, Southwestern Louisiana in 1971, and Kentucky Wesleyan in 2003 were declared ineligible subsequent to the tournament. Under NCAA rules, the teams' and ineligible student-athletes' records were deleted, and the teams' places in the final standings were vacated.

## SINGLE-GAME SCORING HIGHS

| Pts | Player and Team vs Opponent | Date |
|---|---|---|
| 113 | Bevo Francis, Rio Grande vs Hillsdale | 1954 |
| 84 | Bevo Francis, Rio Grande vs Alliance | 1954 |
| 82 | Bevo Francis, Rio Grande vs Bluffton | 1954 |
| 80 | Paul Crissman, USC vs Pacific Christian | 1966 |
| 77 | William English, Winston-Salem vs Fayetteville St | 1968 |

## Single Season Records

### SCORING AVERAGE

| Player and Team | Year | GP | FG | FT | Pts | Avg |
|---|---|---|---|---|---|---|
| Bevo Francis, Rio Grande | 1954 | 27 | 444 | 367 | 1255 | 46.5 |
| Earl Glass, Mississippi Industrial | 1963 | 19 | 322 | 171 | 815 | 42.9 |
| Earl Monroe, Winston-Salem | 1967 | 32 | 509 | 311 | 1329 | 41.5 |
| John Rinka, Kenyon | 1970 | 23 | 354 | 234 | 942 | 41.0 |
| Willie Shaw, Lane | 1964 | 18 | 303 | 121 | 727 | 40.4 |

### REBOUND AVERAGE

| Player and Team | Year | GP | Reb | Avg |
|---|---|---|---|---|
| Tom Hart, Middlebury | 1955 | 22 | 649 | 29.5 |
| Tom Hart, Middlebury | 1956 | 21 | 620 | 29.5 |
| Frank Stronczek, American Int'l | 1966 | 26 | 717 | 27.6 |
| R.C. Owens, College of Idaho | 1954 | 25 | 677 | 27.1 |
| Maurice Stokes, St. Francis (Pa.) | 1954 | 26 | 689 | 26.5 |

### ASSISTS

| Player and Team | Year | GP | Asst |
|---|---|---|---|
| Steve Ray, Bridgeport | 1989 | 32 | 400 |
| Steve Ray, Bridgeport | 1990 | 33 | 385 |
| Tony Smith, Pfeiffer | 1992 | 35 | 349 |
| Jim Ferrer, Bentley | 1989 | 31 | 309 |
| Rob Paternostro, New Hamp. Coll. | 1995 | 33 | 309 |

### ASSIST AVERAGE

| Player and Team | Year | GP | Asst | Avg |
|---|---|---|---|---|
| Steve Ray, Bridgeport | 1989 | 32 | 400 | 12.5 |
| Steve Ray, Bridgeport | 1990 | 33 | 385 | 11.7 |
| Demetri Beekman, Assumption | 1993 | 23 | 264 | 11.5 |
| Ernest Jenkins, N.M.-Highlands | 1995 | 27 | 291 | 10.8 |
| Brian Gregory, Oakland | 1989 | 28 | 300 | 10.7 |

### FIELD-GOAL PERCENTAGE

| Player and Team | Year | Pct |
|---|---|---|
| Garret Siler, Augusta St | 2008 | 78.9 |
| Todd Linder, Tampa | 1987 | 75.2 |
| Maurice Stafford, North Alabama | 1984 | 75.0 |
| Matthew Cornegay, Tuskegee | 1982 | 74.8 |
| Callistus Eziukwu, Grand Valley St | 2005 | 73.7 |

### FREE-THROW PERCENTAGE

| Player and Team | Year | Pct |
|---|---|---|
| Paul Cluxton, Northern Kentucky | 1997 | 100.0 |
| Tomas Rimkus, Pace | 1997 | 95.6 |
| C.J. Cowgill, Chaminade | 2001 | 95.0 |
| Kent Andrews, McNeese St | 1968 | 94.4 |
| Billy Newton, Morgan St | 1976 | 94.4 |

## Career Records

### POINTS

| Player and Team | Yrs | Pts |
|---|---|---|
| Travis Grant, Kentucky St | 1969–72 | 4045 |
| Bob Hopkins, Grambling | 1953–56 | 3759 |
| Tony Smith, Pfeiffer | 1989–92 | 3350 |
| Earnest Lee, Clark Atlanta | 1984–87 | 3298 |
| Joe Miller, Alderson-Broaddus | 1954–57 | 3294 |

### CAREER SCORING AVERAGE

| Player and Team | Yrs | GP | Pts | Avg |
|---|---|---|---|---|
| Travis Grant, Kentucky St | 1969–72 | 121 | 4045 | 33.4 |
| John Rinka, Kenyon | 1967–70 | 99 | 3251 | 32.8 |
| Florindo Vieira, Quinnipiac | 1954–57 | 69 | 2263 | 32.8 |
| Willie Shaw, Lane | 1961–64 | 76 | 2379 | 31.3 |
| Mike Davis, Virginia Union | 1966–69 | 89 | 2758 | 31.0 |

### REBOUND AVERAGE

| Player and Team | Yrs | GP | Reb | Avg |
|---|---|---|---|---|
| Tom Hart, Middlebury | 1953, 55–56 | 63 | 1738 | 27.6 |
| Maurice Stokes, St. Francis (Pa.) | 1953–55 | 72 | 1812 | 25.2 |
| Frank Stronczek, American Int'l | 1965–67 | 62 | 1549 | 25.0 |
| Bill Thieben, Hofstra | 1954–56 | 76 | 1837 | 24.2 |
| Hank Brown, Lowell Tech | 1965–67 | 49 | 1129 | 23.0 |

### Career Records *(Cont.)*

#### ASSISTS

| Player and Team | Yrs | Asst |
|---|---|---|
| Demetri Beekman, Assumption | 1990–93 | 1044 |
| Adam Kaufman, Edinboro | 1998–01 | 936 |
| Rob Paternostro, New Hamp. Coll. | 1992–95 | 919 |
| Luke Cooper, Alaska-Anchorage | 2005–08 | 880 |
| Tony Smith, Pfeiffer | 1989–92 | 828 |

#### ASSIST AVERAGE

| Player and Team | Yrs | GP | Asst | Avg |
|---|---|---|---|---|
| Steve Ray, Bridgeport | 1989–90 | 65 | 785 | 12.1 |
| Demetri Beekman, Assumption | 1990–93 | 119 | 1044 | 8.8 |
| D.J. Ferguson, Flagler | 2009–11 | 79 | 679 | 8.6 |
| Ernest Jenkins, N.M.-Highlands | 1992–95 | 84 | 699 | 8.3 |
| Zack Whiting, Chaminade | 2004–07 | 86 | 703 | 8.2 |

Note: Minimum 550 Assists.

#### FIELD-GOAL PERCENTAGE

| Player and Team | Yrs | Pct |
|---|---|---|
| Garrett Siler, Augusta St. | 2006–09 | 74.5 |
| Todd Linder, Tampa | 1984–87 | 70.8 |
| Tom Schurfranz, Bellarmine | 1989–92 | 70.2 |
| Chad Scott, California (Pa.) | 1991–94 | 70.0 |
| Ed Phillips, Alabama A&M | 1968–71 | 68.9 |

Note: Minimum 400 FGM.

#### FREE-THROW PERCENTAGE

| Player and Team | Yrs | Pct |
|---|---|---|
| Paul Cluxton, Northern Kentucky | 1994–97 | 93.5 |
| Jake Linton, St. Martin's | 2006–09 | 92.4 |
| Kent Andrews, McNeese St. | 1967–69 | 91.6 |
| Chris Brunson, Southern Ind. | 2002–05 | 90.1 |
| Nathan Hyde, Findlay | 2008–11 | 90.1 |

Note: Minimum 250 FTM.

## NCAA Men's Division III Championship Results

| Year | Winner | Score | Runner-up | Third Place | Fourth Place |
|---|---|---|---|---|---|
| 1975 | LeMoyne-Owen | 57–54 | Glassboro St | Augustana (Ill.) | Brockport St |
| 1976 | Scranton | 60–57 | Wittenberg | Augustana (Ill.) | Plattsburgh St |
| 1977 | Wittenberg | 79–66 | Oneonta St | Scranton | Hamline |
| 1978 | North Park | 69–57 | Widener | Albion | Stony Brook |
| 1979 | North Park | 66–62 | Potsdam St | Franklin & Marshall | Centre |
| 1980 | North Park | 83–76 | Upsala | Wittenberg | Longwood |
| 1981 | Potsdam St | 67–65 (OT) | Augustana (Ill.) | Ursinus | Otterbein |
| 1982 | Wabash | 83–62 | Potsdam St | Brooklyn | CSU-Stanislaus |
| 1983 | Scranton | 64–63 | Wittenberg | Roanoke | UW–Whitewater |
| 1984 | UW–Whitewater | 103–86 | Clark (Mass.) | DePauw | Upsala |
| 1985 | North Park | 72–71 | Potsdam St | Nebraska Wesleyan | Widener |
| 1986 | Potsdam St | 76–73 | LeMoyne-Owen | Nebraska Wesleyan | Jersey City St |
| 1987 | North Park | 106–100 | Clark (Mass.) | Wittenberg | Stockton St |
| 1988 | Ohio Wesleyan | 92–70 | Scranton | Nebraska Wesleyan | Hartwick |
| 1989 | UW–Whitewater | 94–86 | Trenton St | Southern Maine | Centre |
| 1990 | Rochester | 43–42 | DePauw | Washington (Md.) | Calvin |
| 1991 | UW–Platteville | 81–74 | Franklin & Marshall | Otterbein | Ramapo (N.J.) |
| 1992 | Calvin | 62–49 | Rochester | UW–Platteville | Jersey City St |
| 1993 | Ohio Northern | 71–68 | Augustana | Mass.–Dartmouth | Rowan |
| 1994 | Lebanon Valley Coll | 66–59 (OT) | NYU | Wittenberg | St Thomas (Minn.) |
| 1995 | UW–Platteville | 69–55 | Manchester | Rowan | Trinity (Conn.) |
| 1996 | Rowan | 100–93 | Hope (Mich.) | Illinois Wesleyan | Franklin & Marshall |
| 1997 | Illinois Wesleyan | 89–86 | Nebraska Wesleyan | Williams | Alvernia |
| 1998 | UW–Platteville | 69–56 | Hope (Mich.) | Williams | Wilkes |
| 1999 | UW–Platteville | 76–75 (2 OT) | Hampden-Sydney | William Paterson | Connecticut Coll. |
| 2000 | Calvin | 79–74 | UW–Eau Claire | Salem St | Franklin & Marshall |
| 2001 | Catholic | 76–62 | William Paterson | Illinois Wesleyan | Ohio Northern |
| 2002 | Otterbein | 102–83 | Elizabethtown | Carthage | Rochester |
| 2003 | Williams | 67–65 | Gustavus Adolphus | Wooster | Hampden Sydney |
| 2004 | UW–Stevens Point | 84–82 | Williams | John Carroll | Amherst |
| 2005 | UW–Stevens Point | 73–49 | Rochester | Calvin | York |
| 2006 | Virginia Wesleyan | 59–56 | Wittenberg | Illinois Wesleyan | Amherst |
| 2007 | Amherst | 80–67 | Virginia Wesleyan | Washington (Mo.) | Wooster |
| 2008 | Washington-St. Louis | 90–86 | Amherst | Hope | Ursinus |
| 2009 | Washington-St. Louis | 61–52 | Richard Stockton | Guilford | Franklin & Marshall |
| 2010 | UW–Stevens Point | 78–73 | Williams | *Guilford | *Randolph Macon |
| 2011 | St. Thomas (Minn.) | 78–54 | Wooster | *Middlebury | *Williams |

*Indicates tied for third. In 2010, the NCAA eliminated the consolation game to determine third place.

## SINGLE-GAME SCORING HIGHS

| Pts | Player and Team vs Opponent | Year |
|---|---|---|
| 77 | Jeff Clement, Grinnell vs Illinois College | 1998 |
| 69 | Sami Wylie, Lincoln (Pa.) vs Ohio St-Marion | 2007 |
| 69 | Steve Diekmann, Grinnell vs Simpson | 1995 |
| 64 | Tim Russell, Albertus Magnus | 2005 |
| 63 | Ryan Hodges, Cal-Lutheran | 2005 |
| 63 | Joe DeRoche, Thomas vs St. Joseph's (Me.) | 1988 |
| 62 | Shannon Lilly, Bishop vs Southwest Assembly of God | 1983 |
| 62 | Nick Pelotte, Plymouth St | 2005 |
| 62 | Kyle Myrick, Lincoln (Pa.) vs. Penn St.-Abington | 2006 |

Three tied at 61.

## Single Season Records

### SCORING AVERAGE

| Player and Team | Year | GP | FG | FT | Pts | Avg |
|---|---|---|---|---|---|---|
| Steve Diekmann, Grinnell | 1995 | 20 | 223 | 162 | 745 | 37.3 |
| Rickey Sutton, Lyndon St | 1976 | 14 | 207 | 93 | 507 | 36.2 |
| Shannon Lilly, Bishop | 1983 | 26 | 345 | 218 | 908 | 34.9 |
| Dana Wilson, Husson | 1974 | 20 | 288 | 122 | 698 | 34.9 |
| Rickey Sutton, Lyndon St | 1977 | 16 | 223 | 112 | 558 | 34.9 |

### REBOUND AVERAGE

| Player and Team | Year | GP | Reb | Avg |
|---|---|---|---|---|
| Joe Manley, Bowie St | 1976 | 29 | 579 | 20.0 |
| Fred Petty, New Hampshire Coll. | 1974 | 22 | 436 | 19.8 |
| Larry Williams, Pratt | 1977 | 24 | 457 | 19.0 |
| Larry Parker, Plattsburgh St | 1975 | 23 | 430 | 18.7 |
| harles Greer, Thomas | 1977 | 17 | 318 | 18.7 |

### ASSISTS

| Player and Team | Year | GP | Asst |
|---|---|---|---|
| Robert James, Kean | 1989 | 29 | 391 |
| Tennyson Whitted, Ramapo | 2002 | 29 | 319 |
| Ricky Spicer, UW-Whitewater | 1989 | 31 | 295 |
| Joe Marcotte, New Jersey Tech | 1995 | 30 | 292 |
| Andre Bolton, Chris. Newport | 1996 | 30 | 289 |

### ASSIST AVERAGE

| Player and Team | Year | GP | Asst | Avg |
|---|---|---|---|---|
| Robert James, Kean | 1989 | 29 | 391 | 13.5 |
| Albert Kirchner, Mt. St. Vincent | 1990 | 24 | 267 | 11.1 |
| Tennyson Whitted, Ramapo | 2002 | 29 | 319 | 11.0 |
| Ron Torgalski, Hamilton | 1989 | 26 | 275 | 10.6 |
| Louis Adams, Rust | 1989 | 22 | 227 | 10.3 |

### FIELD-GOAL PERCENTAGE

| Player and Team | Year | Pct |
|---|---|---|
| Travis Weiss, St. John's (Minn.) | 1994 | 76.6 |
| Brian Schmitting, Ripon | 2006 | 76.3 |
| Pete Metzelaars, Wabash | 1982 | 75.3 |
| Tony Rychlec, Mass. Maritime | 1981 | 74.9 |
| Tony Rychlec, Mass. Maritime | 1982 | 73.1 |

### FREE-THROW PERCENTAGE

| Player and Team | Year | Pct |
|---|---|---|
| Korey Coon, Illinois Wesleyan | 2000 | 96.3 |
| Ryan Martin, Keene St | 2011 | 96.1 |
| Ryan Junghans, Hood | 2008 | 95.9 |
| Nick Wilkins, Coe | 2003 | 95.7 |
| Chanse Young, Manchester | 1998 | 95.6 |

## Career Records

### POINTS

| Player and Team | Yrs | Pts |
|---|---|---|
| Andre Foreman, Salisbury St | 1989–92 | 2940 |
| Willie Chandler, Misericordia | 2000–03 | 2898 |
| John Grotberg, Grinnell | 2006–09 | 2848 |
| Lamont Strothers, Chris. Newport | 1988–91 | 2709 |
| Matt Hancock, Colby | 1987–90 | 2678 |

### SCORING AVERAGE

| Player and Team | Yrs | GP | Avg |
|---|---|---|---|
| Dwain Govan, Bishop | 1974–75 | 55 | 32.8 |
| Dave Russell, Shepherd | 1974–75 | 60 | 30.6 |
| Kyle Myrick, Lincoln (Pa.) | 2005–06 | 57 | 30.2 |
| Rickey Sutton, Lyndon St | 1976–79 | 80 | 29.7 |
| John Grotberg, Grinnell | 2006–09 | 96 | 29.7 |

### REBOUND AVERAGE

| Player and Team | Yrs | GP | Reb | Avg |
|---|---|---|---|---|
| Larry Parker, Plattsburgh St | 1975–78 | 85 | 1482 | 17.4 |
| Charles Greer, Thomas | 1975–77 | 58 | 926 | 16.0 |
| Willie Parr, LeMoyne-Owen | 1974–76 | 76 | 1182 | 15.6 |
| Michael Smith, Hamilton | 1989–92 | 107 | 1632 | 15.2 |
| Dave Kufeld, Yeshiva | 1977–80 | 81 | 1222 | 15.1 |

### ASSIST AVERAGE

| Player and Team | Yrs | Avg |
|---|---|---|
| David Arsenault, Grinnell | 2006–09 | 9.4 |
| Phil Dixon, Shenandoah | 1993–96 | 8.6 |
| Tennyson Whitted, Ramapo | 2000–03 | 8.5 |
| Steve Artis, Chris. Newport | 1990–93 | 8.1 |
| David Genovese, Mt. St. Vincent | 1992–95 | 7.5 |

# Hockey

Bruins goalie
Tim Thomas
led Boston to its
first Stanley Cup
in 39 years

# Bruin up a Cup

## Scrappy Bruins goalie Tim Thomas became a veritable stone wall in the Finals, guiding an unsung Boston team over high-scoring Vancouver to the Cup title

**BY MARK BEECH**

HOW DID THE BRUINS DO it? How did they rebound from the ignominy of blowing a three-games-to-none lead over the Flyers in the second round of last year's playoffs—only the third team in NHL history ever to do so—to win the 2011 Stanley Cup? How did they become the biggest Cinderella of a wild and unpredictable postseason, twice rebounding from 0–2 series holes and prevailing in no fewer than three Game 7s? And how in the world did they ever beat the Vancouver Canucks, the league's highest scoring team, with their potent mix of American, Canadian and International stars, and their Mariana Trench-deep corps of blueliners.

For the answer, look no further than the man behind the mask, Tim Thomas. Boston's 37-year-old goalie finished off his historically great season by thoroughly shutting down high-powered Vancouver when it counted most. And he did it with a working-class style that helped inspire his teammates. Better than any other player, Thomas embodies the style of the Bruins, themselves a reincarnation of Boston's Cup-winning Lunchpail A.C. outfits of the early 1970s. The Bruins weren't the most talented team on the ice at the end, but there was no way they were going to be denied. "This is a blue-collar city, and his success took a ton of hard work," says club president Cam Neely. "Our fans are sharp.

They respect battlers and see through phonies. They see their best qualities in Timmy."

They also see the best goalie in the NHL. Thomas had won the 2009 Vezina Trophy as the league's best netminder, but a torn left labrum and bone chips in his left hip cost him his starting job. He watched from the bench as rookie Tuukka Rask backstopped Boston in the 2010 playoffs. When this season began, Thomas was Rask's backup, but he quickly wrested the starting job away with a string of dominant games. Thomas is not a textbook goaltender, eschewing classic technique for a more aggressive and pugnacious, whatever-works style. "You can't really scout him," says one rival NHL goalie coach, "because he has no pattern."

But he does have success. Thomas led the NHL with a 2.00 goals-against average and set a league record with his .938 save percentage. And he outdid himself in the playoffs, making the most saves ever (798) while facing a record number of shots (849). In the finals, Thomas held the Canucks to a paltry eight goals in seven games. Not bad for a former collegiate star at Vermont who bounced around Europe and the minors for nearly a decade before becoming an NHL rookie at 31. "Everything about Tim speaks to his work ethic and his integrity," says Bruins defenseman Andrew Ference. "His game isn't fancy; it's honest."

**Thanks to his 50 goals, Anaheim's Corey Perry edged out Vancouver's Daniel Sedin to win the league's Hart Trophy.**

ROBERT BECK

Thomas wasn't the only player to raise his game in 2010–11, a season that fit the scrappy, pugnacious tone of the Stanley Cup finals. There were a host of indelible moments and characters, interspersed with the league's efforts to deal with the violent nature of its game.

First the good: a two-way battle for the goal-scoring title between the Tampa Bay Lightning's Steven Stamkos and the Anaheim Ducks' Corey Perry went down to the season's final weeks. Perry prevailed with a career-high 50 goals, which helped push Anaheim into the playoffs and was enough to earn him his first Hart Trophy as league MVP. And in Tampa Bay, 39-year-old rookie coach Guy Boucher introduced the league to his innovative 1-3-1 forecheck, which he used to carry the Lightning to within a game of the Cup finals.

As for hockey's most intense rivals, the Capitals and the Penguins, the 2010–11 campaign was an up-and-down affair. In Washington, scoring dynamo Alex Ovechkin put up modest numbers by his own standards (32 goals), but the Capitals, struggling to learn a more patient, defensive style of play, suffered another early postseason exit. In Pittsburgh, Sidney Crosby led the Penguins to a torrid start. But while playing the Capitals in the Winter Classic on New Year's Day, Crosby took a shot to the head. He played again four nights later, and was hit again. The Penguins lost him for the rest of the season to a concussion. One month later, they also lost Evgeni Malkin to a torn ACL and MCL.

The loss of Crosby threw a spotlight on head injuries, a problem the league made halting attempts to address this year. Last summer, the NHL instituted Rule 48, which banned blind-side or lateral hits to the head. But the need to take the rule a step further became clear on March 8, when the Bruins' Zdeno Chara ran the Canadiens' Max Pacioretty into a rink-side stanchion, a hit that resulted in another severe concussion. In June, the league moved to outlaw all hits that endanger the head. "I think it's good that they [tweak the rules], so that we can get the head shots out of the game, and, if it happens, you have to pay for it," said Red Wings captain Nicklas Lidstrom.

But hockey is a rough game, and it was almost impossible to keep the Stanley Cup finals from getting scrappy. After Vancouver won Game 1 at home 1–0 forward Alexandre Burrows led them to 3–2 overtime victory in Game 2, chipping in one assist and scoring twice, including the game-winner just 11 seconds into the extra period. But the winger's impact on the game wasn't all positive. Television cameras had caught him biting the finger of the Bruins' Patrice Bergeron during an after-the-whistle scrum in the series opener. In the eyes of many, including most Bruins

DAVID E. KLUTHO

**Canucks left winger Daniel Sedin (l.) led the NHL in points (104) during the regular season, but couldn't get his team past the feisty Bruins in the Stanley Cup final.**

fans, Burrows should have been forced by the NHL to take a seat for at least one game, but the league, citing inconclusive evidence of intent, refused to suspend him.

As the Bruins returned home, coach Claude Julien was still searching for a way to galvanize his team. He got it early in the first period, when Canucks defenseman Aaron Rome leveled the Bruins' Nathan Horton to the ice headfirst. As the forward lay motionless on the ice—he suffered a severe concussion—his teammates watched in stunned silence. When they returned to the locker room for the first intermission, Julien told his club to "win it for Horty." When they returned, they played with a single-minded ferocity that stunned Vancouver. They rolled to successive 8–1 and 4–0 victories in the Games 3 and 4. "Any nerves we had," said Ference, "kind of disappeared."

Boston now had all the momentum, despite a 1–0 loss in Vancouver in Game 5. Thomas had given up the lone, winning goal when he

was caught ranging too far outside his crease. Vancouver goalie Roberto Luongo had begun the series well, but his meltdowns in Boston had become too big to ignore. Luongo, a shaky butterfly specialist, saw fit to tell reporters the next day that Thomas's slip was "an easy save for me." Ouch.

The Bruins were incensed. Thomas had been a mainstay as they battled back in the series, and he showed plenty of fight, moving players out of his crease and trading jabs with Burrows. They won Game 6 in Boston 5–2, then stomped the Canucks 4–0 in Vancouver to win it all, touching off a shameful riot by incensed Vancouver fans. Thomas rightfully won the Conn Smythe Trophy as playoff MVP.

Three days later, Thomas stood on a riser of a Boston duck boat during the Bruins victory parade. As he looked over the crowd, a reporter asked him why, unlike most players, he had taken to clipping magazine stories and keeping souvenirs of his magical season. "I never know when this will be over," he said. "And I'll want to look back and be amazed by it."

The way Thomas is playing, all this might not be over for at least another year.

## 2010−11 NHL Final Regular Season Standings

### Western Conference

#### CENTRAL DIVISION

|  | GP | W | L | OTL | Pts | GF | GA |
|---|---|---|---|---|---|---|---|
| †Detroit | 82 | 47 | 25 | 10 | 104 | 261 | 241 |
| *Nashville | 82 | 44 | 27 | 11 | 99 | 219 | 194 |
| *Chicago | 82 | 44 | 29 | 9 | 97 | 258 | 225 |
| St. Louis | 82 | 38 | 33 | 11 | 87 | 244 | 234 |
| Columbus | 82 | 34 | 35 | 13 | 81 | 215 | 258 |

#### NORTHWEST DIVISION

|  | GP | W | L | OTL | Pts | GF | GA |
|---|---|---|---|---|---|---|---|
| ‡Vancouver | 82 | 54 | 19 | 9 | 117 | 262 | 185 |
| Calgary | 82 | 41 | 29 | 12 | 94 | 250 | 237 |
| Minnesota | 82 | 39 | 35 | 8 | 86 | 206 | 233 |
| Colorado | 82 | 30 | 44 | 8 | 68 | 227 | 288 |
| Edmonton | 82 | 25 | 45 | 12 | 62 | 193 | 269 |

#### PACIFIC DIVISION

|  | GP | W | L | OTL | Pts | GF | GA |
|---|---|---|---|---|---|---|---|
| †San Jose | 82 | 48 | 25 | 9 | 105 | 248 | 213 |
| *Anaheim | 82 | 47 | 30 | 5 | 99 | 239 | 235 |
| *Phoenix | 82 | 43 | 26 | 13 | 99 | 231 | 226 |
| *Los Angeles | 82 | 46 | 30 | 6 | 98 | 219 | 198 |
| Dallas | 82 | 42 | 29 | 11 | 95 | 227 | 233 |

OTL=overtime loss; worth 1 pt.

### Eastern Conference

#### NORTHEAST DIVISION

|  | GP | W | L | OTL | Pts | GF | GA |
|---|---|---|---|---|---|---|---|
| †Boston | 82 | 46 | 25 | 11 | 103 | 246 | 195 |
| *Montreal | 82 | 44 | 30 | 8 | 96 | 216 | 209 |
| *Buffalo | 82 | 43 | 29 | 10 | 96 | 245 | 229 |
| Toronto | 82 | 37 | 34 | 11 | 85 | 218 | 251 |
| Ottawa | 82 | 32 | 40 | 10 | 74 | 192 | 250 |

#### ATLANTIC DIVISION

|  | GP | W | L | OTL | Pts | GF | GA |
|---|---|---|---|---|---|---|---|
| †Philadelphia | 82 | 47 | 23 | 12 | 106 | 259 | 223 |
| *Pittsburgh | 82 | 49 | 25 | 8 | 106 | 238 | 199 |
| *NY Rangers | 82 | 44 | 33 | 5 | 93 | 233 | 198 |
| New Jersey | 82 | 38 | 39 | 5 | 81 | 174 | 209 |
| NY Islanders | 82 | 30 | 39 | 13 | 73 | 229 | 264 |

#### SOUTHEAST DIVISION

|  | GP | W | L | OTL | Pts | GF | GA |
|---|---|---|---|---|---|---|---|
| ‡Washington | 82 | 48 | 23 | 11 | 107 | 224 | 197 |
| *Tampa Bay | 82 | 46 | 25 | 11 | 103 | 247 | 240 |
| Carolina | 82 | 40 | 31 | 11 | 91 | 236 | 239 |
| Atlanta | 82 | 34 | 36 | 12 | 80 | 223 | 269 |
| Florida | 82 | 30 | 40 | 12 | 72 | 195 | 229 |

‡Conference winner. †Division winner. *Playoff team.

## 2011 Stanley Cup Playoffs

### WESTERN CONFERENCE

QUARTERFINALS   SEMIFINALS   CONFERENCE FINAL

### EASTERN CONFERENCE

CONFERENCE FINAL   SEMIFINALS   QUARTERFINALS

STANLEY CUP

1-Vancouver
8-Chicago — Vancouver (4-3)
Vancouver (4-2)
4-Anaheim
5-Nashville — Nashville (4-2)
Vancouver (4-1)
3-Detroit
6-Phoenix — Detroit (4-0)
San Jose (4-3)
2-San Jose
7-Los Angeles — San Jose (4-2)

BOSTON (4-3)

Washington-1
NY Rangers-8 — Washington (4-1)
Tampa Bay (4-0)
Pittsburgh-4
Tampa Bay-5 — Tampa Bay (4-3)
Boston (4-3)
Boston-3
Montreal-6 — Boston (4-3)
Boston (4-0)
Philadelphia-2
Buffalo-7 — Philadelphia (4-3)

Note: Playoff teams are re-seeded after quarterfinals

## Stanley Cup Playoff Results

### Conference Quarterfinals

#### EASTERN CONFERENCE

| Game 1 | Montreal | 2 | at Boston | 0 |
|---|---|---|---|---|
| Game 2 | Montreal | 3 | at Boston | 1 |
| Game 3 | Boston | 4 | at Montreal | 2 |
| Game 4 | Boston | 5 | at Montreal | 4* |

*Overtime game.

| Game 5 | Montreal | 1 | at Boston | 2* |
|---|---|---|---|---|
| Game 6 | Boston | 1 | at Montreal | 2 |
| Game 7 | Montreal | 3 | at Boston | 4* |

Boston won series 4–3.

## Conference Quarterfinals *(Cont.)*

### EASTERN CONFERENCE *(CONT.)*

| | | | | |
|---|---|---|---|---|
| Game 1 | Buffalo | 1 | at Philadelphia | 0 |
| Game 2 | Buffalo | 4 | at Philadelphia | 5 |
| Game 3 | Philadelphia | 4 | at Buffalo | 2 |
| Game 4 | Philadelphia | 0 | at Buffalo | 1 |
| Game 5 | Buffalo | 4 | at Philadelphia | 3* |
| Game 6 | Philadelphia | 5 | at Buffalo | 4* |
| Game 7 | Buffalo | 2 | at Philadelphia | 5 |

Philadelphia won series 4–3.

| | | | | |
|---|---|---|---|---|
| Game 1 | Tampa Bay | 0 | at Pittsburgh | 3 |
| Game 2 | Tampa Bay | 5 | at Pittsburgh | 1 |
| Game 3 | Pittsburgh | 3 | at Tampa Bay | 2 |

| | | | | |
|---|---|---|---|---|
| Game 4 | Pittsburgh | 3 | at Tampa Bay | 2** |
| Game 5 | Tampa Bay | 8 | at Pittsburgh | 2 |
| Game 6 | Pittsburgh | 2 | at Tampa Bay | 4 |
| Game 7 | Tampa Bay | 1 | at Pittsburgh | 0 |

Tampa Bay won series 4–3.

| | | | | |
|---|---|---|---|---|
| Game 1 | NY Rangers | 1 | at Washington | 2* |
| Game 2 | NY Rangers | 0 | at Washington | 2 |
| Game 3 | Washington | 2 | at NY Rangers | 3 |
| Game 4 | Washington | 4 | at NY Rangers | 3** |
| Game 5 | NY Rangers | 1 | at Washington | 3 |

Washington won series 4–1.

### WESTERN CONFERENCE

| | | | | |
|---|---|---|---|---|
| Game 1 | Chicago | 0 | at Vancouver | 2 |
| Game 2 | Chicago | 3 | at Vancouver | 4 |
| Game 3 | Vancouver | 3 | at Chicago | 2 |
| Game 4 | Vancouver | 2 | at Chicago | 7 |
| Game 5 | Chicago | 5 | at Vancouver | 0 |
| Game 6 | Vancouver | 3 | at Chicago | 4* |
| Game 7 | Chicago | 1 | at Vancouver | 2* |

Vancouver won series 4–3.

| | | | | |
|---|---|---|---|---|
| Game 1 | Phoenix | 2 | at Detroit | 4 |
| Game 2 | Phoenix | 3 | at Detroit | 4 |
| Game 3 | Detroit | 4 | at Phoenix | 2 |
| Game 4 | Detroit | 6 | at Phoenix | 2 |

Detroit won series 4–0.

| | | | | |
|---|---|---|---|---|
| Game 1 | Los Angeles | 2 | at San Jose | 3* |
| Game 2 | Los Angeles | 4 | at San Jose | 0 |
| Game 3 | San Jose | 6 | at Los Angeles | 5* |
| Game 4 | San Jose | 6 | at Los Angeles | 3 |
| Game 5 | Los Angeles | 3 | at San Jose | 1 |
| Game 6 | San Jose | 4 | at Los Angeles | 3* |

San Jose won series 4–2.

| | | | | |
|---|---|---|---|---|
| Game 1 | Nashville | 4 | at Anaheim | 1 |
| Game 2 | Nashville | 3 | at Anaheim | 5 |
| Game 3 | Anaheim | 3 | at Nashville | 4 |
| Game 4 | Anaheim | 6 | at Nashville | 3 |
| Game 5 | Nashville | 4 | at Anaheim | 3* |
| Game 6 | Anaheim | 2 | at Nashville | 4 |

Nashville won series 4–2.

## Conference Semifinals

### EASTERN CONFERENCE

| | | | | |
|---|---|---|---|---|
| Game 1 | Boston | 7 | at Philadelphia | 3 |
| Game 2 | Boston | 3 | at Philadelphia | 2* |
| Game 3 | Philadelphia | 1 | at Boston | 5 |
| Game 4 | Philadelphia | 1 | at Boston | 5 |

Boston won series 4–0.

| | | | | |
|---|---|---|---|---|
| Game 1 | Tampa Bay | 4 | at Washington | 2 |
| Game 2 | Tampa Bay | 3 | at Washington | 2* |
| Game 3 | Washington | 3 | at Tampa Bay | 4 |
| Game 4 | Washington | 3 | at Tampa Bay | 5 |

Tampa Bay won series 4–0.

### WESTERN CONFERENCE

| | | | | |
|---|---|---|---|---|
| Game 1 | Detroit | 1 | at San Jose | 2* |
| Game 2 | Detroit | 1 | at San Jose | 2 |
| Game 3 | San Jose | 4 | at Detroit | 3* |
| Game 4 | San Jose | 3 | at Detroit | 4 |
| Game 5 | Detroit | 4 | at San Jose | 3 |
| Game 6 | San Jose | 1 | at Detroit | 3 |
| Game 7 | Detroit | 2 | at San Jose | 3 |

San Jose won series 4–3.

| | | | | |
|---|---|---|---|---|
| Game 1 | Nashville | 0 | at Vancouver | 1 |
| Game 2 | Nashville | 2 | at Vancouver | 1** |
| Game 3 | Vancouver | 3 | at Nashville | 2* |
| Game 4 | Vancouver | 4 | at Nashville | 2 |
| Game 5 | Nashville | 4 | at Vancouver | 3 |
| Game 6 | Vancouver | 2 | at Nashville | 1 |

Vancouver won series 4–2.

## Eastern Conference Finals

| | | | | |
|---|---|---|---|---|
| Game 1 | Tampa Bay | 5 | at Boston | 2 |
| Game 2 | Tampa Bay | 5 | at Boston | 6 |
| Game 3 | Boston | 2 | at Tampa Bay | 0 |
| Game 4 | Boston | 3 | at Tampa Bay | 5 |
| Game 5 | Tampa Bay | 1 | at Boston | 3 |
| Game 6 | Boston | 4 | at Tampa Bay | 5 |
| Game 7 | Tampa Bay | 0 | at Boston | 1 |

Boston won series 4–3.

## Western Conference Finals

| | | | | |
|---|---|---|---|---|
| Game 1 | San Jose | 2 | at Vancouver | 3 |
| Game 2 | San Jose | 3 | at Vancouver | 7 |
| Game 3 | Vancouver | 3 | at San Jose | 4 |
| Game 4 | Vancouver | 4 | at San Jose | 2 |
| Game 5 | San Jose | 2 | at Vancouver | 3** |

Vancouver won series 4–1.

## Stanley Cup Final

| | | | | |
|---|---|---|---|---|
| Game 1 | Boston | 0 | at Vancouver | 1 |
| Game 2 | Boston | 2 | at Vancouver | 3* |
| Game 3 | Vancouver | 1 | at Boston | 8 |
| Game 4 | Vancouver | 0 | at Boston | 4 |

| | | | | |
|---|---|---|---|---|
| Game 5 | Boston | 0 | at Vancouver | 1 |
| Game 6 | Vancouver | 2 | at Boston | 5 |
| Game 7 | Boston | 4 | at Vancouver | 0 |

Boston won series 4–3.

*Overtime game. **Double overtime game.

# Stanley Cup Final Box Scores

## Game 1

| | | | |
|---|---|---|---|
| Boston | 0 | 0 | 0 — 0 |
| Vancouver | 0 | 0 | 1 — 1 |

### FIRST PERIOD
Penalties: Boston, 3, Kelly (high-sticking), 8:47, Marchand (holding), 13:25, Bergeron (roughing), 20:00; Vancouver, 4, D. Sedin (high-sticking), 4:03, Burrows (holding), 10:18, Burrows (roughing, served by Torres), 20:00, Burrows (roughing), 20:00.

### SECOND PERIOD
Penalties: Boston, 4, Krejci (cross checking), 4:00, Seidenberg (kneeing), 9:28, Peverley (hooking), 9:54, Bergeron (tripping), 17:50. Vancouver, 2, Bieksa (high-sticking), 0:28, Burrows (tripping), 10:02.

### THIRD PERIOD
Scoring: Vancouver, 1, Torres (Hansen, Kesler), 19:41.

Shots on goal: BOS 17–9–10—36; VAN 12–8–14—34.

Power-play opportunities: BOS 0–6, VAN 0–6.

Goalies: Bos, Thomas (34 shots, 33 saves); Van, Luongo (36 shots, 36 saves).

Referees: Walkom, O'Rourke. Linesmen: Miller, Racicot.

A: 18,860.

## Game 2

| | | | |
|---|---|---|---|
| Boston | 0 | 2 | 0 0 — 2 |
| Vancouver | 1 | 0 | 1 1 — 3 |

### FIRST PERIOD
Scoring: Vancouver, 1, Burrows (PP-Higgins, Salo), 12:12. Penalties: Boston, 1, Chara (interference), 10:24.

### SECOND PERIOD
Scoring: Boston, 2, Lucic (Boychuk, Krejci), 9:00, Recchi (PP-Chara, Bergeron), 11:35. Penalties: Vancouver, 3, Bieksa (delay of game), 1:03, Rome (holding), 10:26, Rome (inteference), 18:59.

### THIRD PERIOD
Scoring: Vancouver, 1, Sedin (Burrows, Edler), 9:37. Penalties: Boston, 1, Seidenberg (tripping), 00:52.

### OVERTIME
Scoring: Vancouver, 1, Burrows (D. Sedin, Edler), 0:11.

Shots on goal: BOS 11–14–5–0—30; VAN 11–10–11–1—33.

Power-play opportunities: BOS 1–3, VAN 1–2.

Goalies: Bos, Thomas (33 shots, 30 saves); Van, Luongo (30 shots, 28 saves).

Referees: O'Halloran, Sutherland. Linesmen: Sharrers, Morin.

A: 18,860.

## Game 3

| | | | |
|---|---|---|---|
| Vancouver | 0 | 0 | 1 — 1 |
| Boston | 0 | 4 | 4 — 8 |

### FIRST PERIOD
Penalties: Vancouver, 2, Rome (interference, served by Torres), 5:07, Rome (game misconduct), 5:07; Boston, 1, McQuaid (delay of game), 11:41.

### SECOND PERIOD
Scoring: Boston, 4, Ference (Peverley, Krejci), 0:11, Recchi (PP-Ryder, Ference), 4:22, Marchand (SH), 11:30, Krejci (Ryder, Chara), 15:47. Penalites: Vancouver, 1, Tambellini (hooking), 2:42; Boston, 3, Ference (tripping), 6:22, Lucic (slashing), 10:30, Boychuk (high-sticking), 17:36.

### THIRD PERIOD
Scoring: Vancouver, 1, Hansen (Torres, Lapierre), 13:53; Boston, 4, Paille (SH-Boychuk), 11:38, Recchi (Marchand, Bergeron), 17:39, Kelly (Paille, Chara), 18:06, Ryder (PP-Kaberle), 19:29. Penalties: Vancouver, 9, Burrows (unsportsmanlike conduct), 3:33, D. Sedin (misconduct), 6:59, Kesler (boarding), 9:11,

### THIRD PERIOD (CONT.)
Burrows (slashing), 11:16, Burrows (misconduct), 11:16, Kesler (fighting), 11:16, Kesler (misconduct), 11:16, Bieksa (misconduct), 17:51, Torres (charging), 18:53; Boston, 11, Ryder (roughing), 2:50, Chara (unsportsmanlike conduct), 3:33, Ference (misconduct), 6:59, Thornton (roughing, served by Ryder), 7:58, Thornton (misconduct), 7:58, Lucic (slashing, served by Ryder), 11:16, Lucic (roughing), 11:16, Lucic (misconduct), 11:16, Seidenberg (fighting), 11:16, Seidenberg (misconduct), 11:16, Ference (misconduct), 17:51.

Shots on goal: VAN 12–16–13—41; BOS 7–14–17—38.

Power-play opportunities: VAN 0–8, BOS 2–4.

Goalies: Van, Luongo (38 shots, 30 saves). Bos, Thomas (41 shots, 40 saves).

Referees: Walkom, O'Rourke. Linesmen: Miller, Racicot.

A: 17,565.

## Game 4

| Vancouver | 0 | 0 | 0——0 |
| Boston | 1 | 2 | 1——4 |

### FIRST PERIOD

Scoring: Boston, 1, Peverley (Krejci, Chara), 11:59.
Penalties: Boston, 2, Ryder (tripping), 6:58, Marchand (cross checking), 16:10.

### SECOND PERIOD

Scoring: Boston, 2, Ryder (Seguin, Kelly), 11:11, Marchand (Bergeron), 13:29; Penalties: Vancouver, 2, Raymond (high-sticking), 7:41, Alberts (slashing), 12:05; Boston, 2, Peverley (cross checking), 12:05, Boychuk (delay of game), 18:49.

### THIRD PERIOD

Scoring: Boston, 1, Perverley (Lucic, Krejci), 3:39. Penalties: Vancouver, 7, H. Sedin (slashing), 0:52, Kesler (slashing), 10:25, Lapierre (slashing), 14:35,

### THIRD PERIOD *(CONT.)*

Ballard (roughing), 17:33, Burrows (cross checking), 18:09, Kesler (roughing), 18:09, Kesler (misconduct), 18:09; Boston, 8, Recchi (high-sticking), 9:14, Marchand (roughing, served by Seguin), 17:33, Marchand, (holding), 17:33, Marchand (tripping), 17:33, McQuaid (misconduct), 17:33, Chara (roughing), 18:09, Chara (misconduct), 18:09, Thomas (slashing, served by Thornton), 18:09.

Shots on goal: VAN 12–13–13—38; BOS 6–12–11—29.

Power-play opportunities: VAN 0–6, BOS 0–4.

Goalies: Van, Luongo (20 shots, 16 saves), Schneider (9 shots, 9 saves); Bos, Thomas (38 shots, 38 saves).

Referees: O'Halloran, Sutherland. Linesmen: Sharrers, Morin.

A: 17,565.

## Game 5

| Boston | 0 | 0 | 0——0 |
| Vancouver | 0 | 0 | 1——1 |

### FIRST PERIOD

Penalties: Boston, 1, Lucic (tripping), 19:27; Vancouver, 4, Torres (tripping), 1:39, H. Sedin (interference), 6:54, Alberts (roughing), 14:13, Burrows (unsportsmanlike conduct), 19:27.

### SECOND PERIOD

Penalties: Boston, 2, McQuaid (holding), 7:22, Bergeron (holding), 15:56; Vancouver, 1, Kesler (goalie interference), 4:28.

### THIRD PERIOD

Scoring: Vancouver, 1, Lapierre (Bieksa, Torres), 4:35. Penalties: Boston, 1, Peverley (tripping), 12:09.

Shots on goal: BOS 12–9–10—31; VAN 6–12–7—25.

Power-play opportunities: BOS 0–4, VAN 0–3.

Goalies: Bos, Thomas (25 shots, 24 saves). Van, Luongo (31 shots, 31 saves).

Referees: Walkom, O'Rourke. Linesmen: Racicot, Miller.

A: 18,860.

## Game 6

| Vancouver | 0 | 0 | 2——2 |
| Boston | 4 | 0 | 1——5 |

### FIRST PERIOD

Scoring: Boston, 4, Marchand (Recchi, Seidenberg), 5:31, Lucic (Peverley, Boychuk), 6:06, Ference (PP-Ryder, Recchi), 8:35, Ryder (Kaberle) 9:45. Penalties: Vancouver, 4, H. Sedin (unsportsmanlike conduct), 0:56, Edler (boarding), 7:55, Kesler (holding), 10:35, Torres (bench-too many men on ice), 17:09; Boston, 1, Chara (interference), 0:56.

### SECOND PERIOD

Penalties: Boston, 3, Bergeron (goalie int.), 0:28, Bergeron (interference), 12:15, Bergeron (elbowing), 19:08.

### THIRD PERIOD

Scoring: Vancouver, 2, H. Sedin (PP-D. Sedin, Ehrhoff), 0:22, Lapierre (D. Sedin, Hansen), 17:34.; Boston, 1, Krejci (PP-Recchi, Kaberle), 6:59.

### THIRD PERIOD *(CONT.)*

Penalties: Vancouver, 5, Torres (tripping), 5:23, Alberts (cross checking), 6:11, Burrows (slashing), 6:59, D. Sedin (misconduct), 18:29, Lapierre (misconduct), 18:29; Boston, 6, Bergeron (cross checking), 6:59, Recchi (tripping), 11:32, Marchand (roughing, served by Krejci), 18:29, Marchand (misconduct), 18:29, Thornton (misconduct), 18:29, Seidenberg (cross checking), 19:03.

Shots on goal: VAN 11–11–16—38; BOS 19–8–13–40.

Power-play opportunities: VAN 1–6, BOS 2–5.

Goalies : Van, Luongo (8 shots, 5 saves), Schneider (32 shots, 30 saves); Bos, Thomas (38 shots, 36 saves).

Referees: O'Halloran, Sutherland. Linesmen: Sharrers, Morin.

A: 17,565.

## Game 7

| Boston | 1 | 2 | 1——4 |
| Vancouver | 0 | 0 | 0——0 |

### FIRST PERIOD

Scoring: Boston, 1, Bergeron (Marchand), 14:37.

### SECOND PERIOD

Scoring: Boston, 2, Marchand (Seidenberg, Recchi), 12:13, Bergeron (SH-Seidenberg, Campbell), 17:35. Penalties: Boston, 1, Chara (interference), 16:07.

### THIRD PERIOD

Scoring: Boston, 1, Marchand (EN), 17:16. Penalties: Boston, 1, Lucic (hooking), 11:34; Vancouver, 1, Hansen (interference), 5:33.

Shots on goal: BOS 5–8–8—21; VAN 8–13–16—37.

Power-play opportunities: BOS 0–1, VAN 0–2.

Goalies : Bos, Thomas (37 shots, 37 saves). Van, Luongo (20 shots, 17 saves).

Referees: Walkom, O'Halloran. Linesmen: Sharrers, Morin.

A: 18,860.

## Scoring
### POINTS

| Player and Team | GP | G | Ast | Pts | +/− | PM | Player and Team | GP | G | Ast | Pts | +/− | PM |
|---|---|---|---|---|---|---|---|---|---|---|---|---|---|
| David Krejci, Bos | 25 | 12 | 11 | 23 | 8 | 10 | Teddy Purcell, TB | 18 | 6 | 11 | 17 | 4 | 2 |
| Henrik Sedin, Van | 25 | 3 | 19 | 22 | -11 | 16 | Joe Thornton, SJ | 18 | 3 | 14 | 17 | -5 | 16 |
| Martin St. Louis, TB | 18 | 10 | 10 | 20 | -8 | 4 | Dan Boyle, SJ | 18 | 4 | 12 | 16 | -7 | 8 |
| Daniel Sedin, Van | 25 | 9 | 11 | 20 | -9 | 32 | Ryane Clowe, SJ | 17 | 6 | 9 | 15 | 5 | 32 |
| Patrice Bergeron, Bos | 23 | 6 | 14 | 20 | 15 | 28 | Pavel Datsyuk, Det | 11 | 4 | 11 | 15 | 10 | 8 |
| Brad Marchand, Bos | 25 | 11 | 8 | 19 | 12 | 40 | Logan Couture, SJ | 18 | 7 | 7 | 14 | 2 | 2 |
| Ryan Kesler, Van | 25 | 7 | 12 | 19 | 0 | 47 | Mark Recchi, Bos | 25 | 5 | 9 | 14 | 7 | 8 |
| Vincent Lecavalier, TB | 18 | 6 | 13 | 19 | 6 | 16 | Steve Downie, TB | 17 | 2 | 12 | 14 | 7 | 40 |
| Alexandre Burrows, Van | 25 | 9 | 8 | 17 | 0 | 34 | | | | | | | |
| Nathan Horton, Bos | 21 | 8 | 9 | 17 | 11 | 35 | Four tied at 13 points. | | | | | | |
| Michael Ryder, Bos | 25 | 8 | 9 | 17 | 8 | 8 | | | | | | | |

### GOALS

| Player and Team | GP | G |
|---|---|---|
| David Krejci, Bos | 25 | 12 |
| Brad Marchand, Bos | 25 | 11 |
| Martin St. Louis, TB | 18 | 10 |
| Daniel Sedin, Van | 25 | 9 |
| Alexandre Burrows, Van | 25 | 9 |
| Sean Bergenheim, TB | 16 | 9 |
| Nathan Horton, Bos | 21 | 8 |
| Michael Ryder, Bos | 25 | 8 |
| Seven tied at 7 goals. | | |

### SHORT-HANDED GOALS

| Player and Team | GP | SH |
|---|---|---|
| Patrice Bergeron, Bos | 23 | 2 |
| David Legwand, Nsh | 12 | 2 |

### POWER PLAY GOALS

| Player and Team | GP | PP |
|---|---|---|
| Daniel Sedin, Van | 25 | 5 |
| Martin St. Louis, TB | 18 | 4 |
| Thomas Vanek, Buf | 7 | 4 |
| Ryan Kesler, Van | 25 | 4 |
| Teemu Selanne, Ana | 6 | 4 |

### ASSISTS

| Player and Team | GP | A |
|---|---|---|
| Henrik Sedin, Van | 25 | 19 |
| Patrice Bergeron, Bos | 23 | 14 |
| Joe Thornton, SJ | 18 | 14 |
| Vincent Lecavalier, TB | 18 | 13 |
| Three tied at 12 assists. | | |

### PLUS/MINUS

| Player and Team | GP | +/− |
|---|---|---|
| Zdeno Chara, Bos | 24 | 16 |
| Patrice Bergeron, Bos | 23 | 15 |
| Dennis Seidenberg, Bos | 25 | 12 |
| Johnny Boychuk, Bos | 25 | 12 |
| Brad Marchand, Bos | 25 | 12 |
| Milan Lucic, Bos | 25 | 11 |
| Chris Kelly, Bos | 25 | 11 |
| Nathan Horton, Bos | 21 | 11 |
| Pavel Datsyuk, Det | 11 | 10 |
| Andrew Ference, Bos | 25 | 10 |
| Five players tied at 8. | | |

## Goaltending*

### GOALS AGAINST AVERAGE

| Player and Team | GP | W-L | Avg |
|---|---|---|---|
| Tim Thomas, Bos | 25 | 16–9 | 1.98 |
| Carey Price, Mtl | 7 | 3–4 | 2.11 |
| Corey Crawford, Chi | 7 | 3–4 | 2.21 |
| Michal Neuvirth, Was | 9 | 4–5 | 2.34 |
| Jimmy Howard, Det | 11 | 7–4 | 2.50 |
| Dwayne Roloson, TB | 17 | 10–6 | 2.51 |
| *minimum of 420 minutes | | | |

### SAVE PERCENTAGE

| Player and Team | GP | W-L | GAA | GA | SV | SV% | SA |
|---|---|---|---|---|---|---|---|
| Tim Thomas, Bos | 25 | 16–9 | 1.98 | 51 | 798 | .940 | 849 |
| Carey Price, Mtl | 7 | 3–4 | 2.11 | 16 | 226 | .934 | 242 |
| Corey Crawford, Chi | 7 | 3–4 | 2.21 | 16 | 202 | .927 | 218 |
| Dwayne Roloson, TB | 17 | 10–6 | 2.51 | 41 | 500 | .924 | 541 |
| Jimmy Howard, Det | 11 | 7–4 | 2.50 | 28 | 336 | .923 | 364 |
| Rob. Luongo, Van | 25 | 15–10 | 2.56 | 61 | 650 | .914 | 711 |
| Michal Neuvirth, Wsh | 9 | 4–5 | 2.34 | 23 | 238 | .912 | 261 |

# NHL Awards

| Award | Player and Team | Award | Player and Team |
|---|---|---|---|
| Hart Trophy (MVP) | Corey Perry, Ana | Adams Award (top coach) | Dan Bylsma, Pit |
| Lindsay Award (NHLPA MOP) | Daniel Sedin, Van | Selke Trophy (top def. forward) | Ryan Kesler, Van |
| Calder Trophy (top rookie) | Jeff Skinner, Car | Jennings Trophy (goaltender/s on | Robert Luongo/ |
| Vezina Trophy (top goaltender) | Tim Thomas, Bos | club allowing fewest goals) | Cory Schneider, Van |
| Norris Trophy (top defenseman) | Nicklas Lidstrom, Det | Art Ross Trophy (most points) | Daniel Sedin, Van |
| Lady Byng Trophy | | Conn Smythe Trophy | |
| (for gentlemanly play) | Martin St. Louis, TB | (playoff MVP) | Tim Thomas, Bos |

# Individual 2010–11 Regular Season Leaders

## Scoring
### POINTS

| Player and Team | GP | G | Ast | Pts | +/− | PIM | Player and Team | GP | G | Ast | Pts | +/− | PIM |
|---|---|---|---|---|---|---|---|---|---|---|---|---|---|
| Daniel Sedin, Van | 82 | 41 | 63 | 104 | 30 | 32 | Jonathan Toews, Chi | 80 | 32 | 44 | 76 | 25 | 26 |
| Martin St. Louis, TB | 82 | 31 | 68 | 99 | 0 | 12 | Claude Giroux, Phi | 82 | 25 | 51 | 76 | 20 | 47 |
| Corey Perry, Ana | 82 | 50 | 48 | 98 | 9 | 104 | Ryan Getzlaf, Ana | 67 | 19 | 57 | 76 | 14 | 35 |
| Henrik Sedin, Van | 82 | 19 | 75 | 94 | 26 | 40 | Ryan Kesler, Van | 82 | 41 | 32 | 73 | 24 | 66 |
| Steven Stamkos, TB | 82 | 45 | 46 | 91 | 3 | 74 | Patrick Marleau, SJ | 82 | 37 | 36 | 73 | -3 | 16 |
| Jarome Iginla, Cgy | 82 | 43 | 43 | 86 | 0 | 40 | Thomas Vanek, Buf | 80 | 32 | 41 | 73 | 2 | 24 |
| Alex Ovechkin, Wsh | 79 | 32 | 53 | 85 | 24 | 41 | Patrick Kane, Chi | 73 | 27 | 46 | 73 | 7 | 28 |
| Teemu Selanne, Ana | 73 | 31 | 49 | 80 | 6 | 49 | Loui Eriksson, Dal | 79 | 27 | 46 | 73 | 10 | 8 |
| Henrik Zetterberg, Det | 80 | 24 | 56 | 80 | -1 | 40 | Anze Kopitar, LA | 75 | 25 | 48 | 73 | 25 | 20 |
| Brad Richards, Dal | 72 | 28 | 49 | 77 | 1 | 24 | Three tied at 71 points. | | | | | | |
| Eric Staal, Car | 81 | 33 | 43 | 76 | -10 | 72 | | | | | | | |

## Scoring *(Cont.)*

### GOALS

| Player and Team | GP | G |
|---|---|---|
| Corey Perry, Ana | 82 | 50 |
| Steven Stamkos, TB | 82 | 45 |
| Jarome Iginla, Cgy | 82 | 43 |
| Daniel Sedin, Van | 82 | 41 |
| Ryan Kesler, Van | 82 | 41 |
| Patrick Marleau, SJ | 82 | 37 |
| Jeff Carter, Phi | 80 | 36 |
| Patrick Sharp, Chi | 74 | 34 |
| Bobby Ryan, Ana | 82 | 34 |
| Danny Briere, Phi | 77 | 34 |
| Michael Grabner, NYI | 76 | 34 |
| Eric Staal, Car | 81 | 33 |
| Brenden Morrow, Dal | 82 | 33 |

### POWER PLAY GOALS

| Player and Team | GP | PP |
|---|---|---|
| Daniel Sedin, Van | 82 | 18 |
| Steven Stamkos, TB | 82 | 17 |
| Teemu Selanne, Ana | 73 | 16 |
| Ryan Kesler, Van | 82 | 15 |

Two tied with 14 goals.

### SHORT-HANDED GOALS

| Player and Team | GP | SHG |
|---|---|---|
| Frans Nielsen, NYI | 71 | 7 |
| Michael Grabner, NYI | 76 | 6 |
| Brad Marchand, Bos | 77 | 5 |
| Brandon Prust, NYR | 82 | 5 |

Five tied with four goals.

### ASSISTS

| Player and Team | GP | Ast |
|---|---|---|
| Henrik Sedin, Van | 82 | 75 |
| Martin St. Louis, TB | 82 | 68 |
| Daniel Sedin, Van | 82 | 63 |
| Ryan Getzlaf, Ana | 67 | 57 |
| Henrik Zetterberg, Det | 80 | 56 |
| Alex Ovechkin, Wsh | 79 | 53 |
| Mike Ribeiro, Dal | 82 | 52 |
| Claude Giroux, Phi | 82 | 51 |
| Lubomir Visnovsky, Ana | 81 | 50 |

Four tied with 49 assists.

### GAME-WINNING GOALS

| Player and Team | GP | GW |
|---|---|---|
| Alex Ovechkin, Wsh | 79 | 11 |
| Corey Perry, Ana | 82 | 11 |
| Daniel Sedin, Van | 82 | 10 |

Three tied with nine goals.

### PLUS/MINUS

| Player and Team | GP | +/- |
|---|---|---|
| Zdeno Chara, Bos | 81 | 33 |
| David Backes, StL | 82 | 32 |
| Kevin Bieksa, Van | 66 | 32 |
| Toni Lydman, Ana | 78 | 32 |
| Andrej Meszaros, Phi | 81 | 30 |
| Daniel Sedin, Van | 82 | 30 |
| Matt Carle, Phi | 82 | 30 |
| Adam McQuaid, Bos | 67 | 30 |
| Dan Hamhuis, Van | 64 | 29 |
| Nathan Horton, Bos | 80 | 29 |
| Brian Campbell, Chi | 65 | 28 |
| Milan Lucic, Bos | 79 | 28 |
| Jeff Carter, Phi | 80 | 27 |

## Goaltending
### (Minimum 25 games)

### GOALS AGAINST AVERAGE

| Player and Team | GP | W–L | GAA | GA |
|---|---|---|---|---|
| Tim Thomas, Bos | 57 | 35–11 | 2.00 | 112 |
| Roberto Luongo, Van | 60 | 38–15 | 2.11 | 126 |
| Pekka Rinne, Nsh | 64 | 33–22 | 2.12 | 134 |
| Cory Schneider, Van | 25 | 16–4 | 2.23 | 51 |
| Semyon Varlamov, Wsh | 27 | 11–9 | 2.23 | 58 |
| Jonathan Quick, LA | 61 | 35–22 | 2.24 | 134 |
| Henrik Lundqvist, NYR | 68 | 36–27 | 2.28 | 152 |

### WINS

| Player and Team | GP | GAA | W | L |
|---|---|---|---|---|
| Roberto Luongo, Van | 60 | 2.11 | 38 | 15 |
| Carey Price, Mtl | 72 | 2.35 | 38 | 28 |
| Cam Ward, Car | 74 | 2.56 | 37 | 26 |
| Miikka Kiprusoff, Cgy | 71 | 2.63 | 37 | 24 |
| Jimmy Howard, Det | 63 | 2.79 | 37 | 17 |
| Henrik Lundqvist, NYR | 68 | 2.28 | 36 | 27 |
| Marc-Andre Fleury, Pit | 65 | 2.32 | 36 | 20 |
| Ilya Bryzgalov, Phx | 68 | 2.48 | 36 | 20 |

### SAVE PERCENTAGE

| Player and Team | GP | W–L | GA | SV | SV% |
|---|---|---|---|---|---|
| Tim Thomas, Bos | 57 | 35–11 | 112 | 1699 | .938 |
| Pekka Rinne, Nsh | 64 | 33–22 | 134 | 1771 | .930 |
| Cory Schneider, Van | 25 | 16–4 | 51 | 663 | .929 |
| Roberto Luongo, Van | 60 | 38–15 | 126 | 1627 | .928 |
| Semyon Varlamov, Wsh | 27 | 11–9 | 58 | 701 | .924 |
| Jonas Hiller, Ana | 49 | 26–16 | 114 | 1379 | .924 |
| Henrik Lundqvist, NYR | 68 | 36–27 | 152 | 1813 | .923 |
| Carey Price, Mtl | 72 | 38–28 | 165 | 1982 | .923 |

### SHUTOUTS

| Player and Team | GP | W | L | SO |
|---|---|---|---|---|
| Henrik Lundqvist, NYR | 68 | 36 | 27 | 11 |
| Tim Thomas, Bos | 57 | 35 | 11 | 9 |
| Carey Price, Mtl | 72 | 38 | 28 | 8 |
| Ilya Bryzgalov, Phx | 68 | 36 | 20 | 7 |
| Jaroslav Halak, StL | 57 | 27 | 21 | 7 |

Six tied with six shutouts.

# NHL Team-by-Team Statistical Leaders

## Anaheim Ducks

### SCORING

| Player | GP | G | Ast | Pts | +/- | PM |
|---|---|---|---|---|---|---|
| Corey Perry, RW | 82 | 50 | 48 | 98 | 9 | 104 |
| Teemu Selanne, RW | 73 | 31 | 49 | 80 | 6 | 49 |
| Ryan Getzlaf, C | 67 | 19 | 57 | 76 | 14 | 35 |
| Bobby Ryan, RW | 82 | 34 | 37 | 71 | 15 | 61 |
| Lubomir Visnovsky, D | 81 | 18 | 50 | 68 | 18 | 24 |
| Saku Koivu, C | 75 | 15 | 30 | 45 | -8 | 36 |
| Cam Fowler, D | 76 | 10 | 30 | 40 | -25 | 20 |
| Jason Blake, LW | 76 | 16 | 32 | -5 | 41 | |
| Toni Lydman, D | 78 | 3 | 22 | 25 | 32 | 42 |
| Brandon McMillan, C | 60 | 11 | 10 | 21 | -5 | 18 |
| Joffrey Lupul, RW | 26 | 5 | 8 | 13 | -4 | 14 |
| Dan Sexton, RW | 47 | 4 | 9 | 13 | -6 | 4 |
| Luca Sbisa, D | 68 | 2 | 9 | 11 | -11 | 43 |
| Matt Beleskey, LW | 35 | 3 | 7 | 10 | -10 | 36 |
| Todd Marchant, C | 79 | 1 | 7 | 8 | -18 | 26 |
| Andreas Lilja, D | 52 | 1 | 6 | 7 | -15 | 28 |
| Fran. Beauchemin, D | 27 | 3 | 2 | 5 | -4 | 16 |

### SCORING *(CONT.)*

| Player | GP | G | Ast | Pts | +/- | PM |
|---|---|---|---|---|---|---|
| Andy Sutton, D | 39 | 0 | 4 | 4 | 1 | 87 |
| George Parros, RW | 78 | 3 | 1 | 4 | -4 | 171 |
| Maxim Lapierre, C | 21 | 0 | 3 | 3 | -6 | 9 |
| Ryan Carter, C | 18 | 1 | 2 | 3 | -4 | 22 |
| Paul Mara, D | 33 | 1 | 1 | 2 | -1 | 40 |
| Jarkko Ruutu, LW | 23 | 1 | 1 | 2 | 0 | 38 |
| Brad Winchester, LW | 19 | 1 | 1 | 2 | -9 | 28 |
| Kyle Chipchura, C | 40 | 0 | 2 | 2 | 1 | 32 |
| Sheldon Brookbank, D | 40 | 0 | 0 | 0 | -8 | 63 |
| Nick Bonino, C | 26 | 0 | 0 | 0 | -3 | 4 |

### GOALTENDING

| Player | GP | Mins | W | L | TGA | GAA | SO |
|---|---|---|---|---|---|---|---|
| Jonas Hiller | 49 | 2672 | 26 | 16 | 114 | 2.56 | 5 |
| Curtis McElhinney | 21 | 996 | 6 | 9 | 57 | 3.43 | 2 |
| Dan Ellis | 13 | 729 | 8 | 3 | 29 | 2.39 | 0 |
| Ray Emery | 10 | 527 | 7 | 2 | 20 | 2.28 | 0 |

## Atlanta Thrashers

### SCORING

| Player | GP | G | Ast | Pts | +/– | PM |
|---|---|---|---|---|---|---|
| Andrew Ladd, LW | 81 | 29 | 30 | 59 | -10 | 39 |
| Dustin Byfuglien, D | 81 | 20 | 33 | 53 | -2 | 93 |
| Tobias Enstrom, D | 72 | 10 | 41 | 51 | -10 | 54 |
| Bryan Little, C | 76 | 18 | 30 | 48 | 11 | 33 |
| Evander Kane, LW | 73 | 19 | 24 | 43 | -12 | 68 |
| Nik Antropov, C | 76 | 16 | 25 | 41 | -17 | 42 |
| Anthony Stewart, RW | 80 | 14 | 25 | 39 | -10 | 55 |
| Rich Peverley, C | 59 | 14 | 20 | 34 | -16 | 35 |
| Niclas Bergfors, RW | 52 | 11 | 18 | 29 | -11 | 6 |
| Alexander Burmistrov, C | 74 | 6 | 14 | 20 | -12 | 27 |
| Ron Hainsey, D | 82 | 3 | 16 | 19 | 3 | 24 |
| Chris Thorburn, RW | 82 | 9 | 10 | 19 | -4 | 77 |
| Johnny Oduya, D | 82 | 2 | 15 | 17 | -15 | 22 |
| Blake Wheeler, RW | 23 | 7 | 10 | 17 | 2 | 14 |
| Zach Bogosian, D | 71 | 5 | 12 | 17 | -27 | 29 |
| Jim Slater, C | 36 | 5 | 7 | 12 | 4 | 19 |
| Freddy Modin, LW | 36 | 7 | 3 | 10 | -11 | 12 |
| Eric Boulton, LW | 69 | 6 | 4 | 10 | 1 | 87 |
| Ben Eager, LW | 34 | 3 | 7 | 10 | 4 | 77 |
| Brent Sopel, D | 59 | 2 | 5 | 7 | 7 | 16 |
| Tim Stapleton, C | 45 | 5 | 2 | 7 | -10 | 12 |
| Rob Schremp, C | 18 | 3 | 1 | 4 | -1 | 4 |
| Freddy Meyer, D | 15 | 1 | 1 | 2 | -7 | 8 |
| Ben Maxwell, C | 12 | 1 | 1 | 2 | -7 | 9 |
| Patrice Cormier, C | 21 | 1 | 1 | 2 | -5 | 4 |
| Radek Dvorak, RW | 13 | 0 | 1 | 1 | 0 | 4 |
| Mark Stuart, D | 23 | 1 | 0 | 1 | -8 | 24 |
| Nigel Dawes, RW | 9 | 0 | 1 | 1 | -6 | 0 |

### GOALTENDING

| Player | GP | Mins | W | L | TGA | GAA | SO |
|---|---|---|---|---|---|---|---|
| Ondrej Pavelec | 58 | 3225 | 21 | 23 | 147 | 2.73 | 4 |
| Chris Mason | 33 | 1682 | 13 | 13 | 95 | 3.39 | 1 |
| Peter Mannino | 2 | 73 | 0 | 0 | 5 | 4.11 | 0 |

## Boston Bruins

### SCORING

| Player | GP | G | Ast | Pts | +/– | PM |
|---|---|---|---|---|---|---|
| David Krejci, C | 75 | 13 | 49 | 62 | 23 | 28 |
| Milan Lucic, LW | 79 | 30 | 32 | 62 | 28 | 121 |
| Patrice Bergeron, C | 80 | 22 | 35 | 57 | 20 | 26 |
| Nathan Horton, RW | 80 | 26 | 27 | 53 | 29 | 85 |
| Mark Recchi, RW | 81 | 14 | 34 | 48 | 13 | 35 |
| Zdeno Chara, D | 81 | 14 | 30 | 44 | 33 | 88 |
| Michael Ryder, RW | 79 | 18 | 23 | 41 | -1 | 26 |
| Brad Marchand, C | 77 | 21 | 20 | 41 | 25 | 51 |
| Dennis Seidenberg, D | 81 | 7 | 25 | 32 | 3 | 41 |
| Gregory Campbell, C | 80 | 13 | 16 | 29 | 11 | 93 |
| Blake Wheeler, RW | 58 | 11 | 16 | 27 | 8 | 32 |
| Tyler Seguin, C | 74 | 11 | 11 | 22 | -4 | 18 |
| Shawn Thornton, LW | 79 | 10 | 10 | 20 | 8 | 122 |
| Johnny Boychuk, D | 69 | 3 | 13 | 16 | 15 | 45 |
| Andrew Ference, D | 70 | 3 | 12 | 15 | 22 | 60 |
| Adam McQuaid, D | 67 | 3 | 12 | 15 | 30 | 96 |
| Daniel Paille, LW | 43 | 6 | 7 | 13 | 3 | 28 |
| Marc Savard, C | 25 | 2 | 8 | 10 | -7 | 29 |
| Steven Kampfer, D | 38 | 5 | 5 | 10 | 9 | 12 |
| Tomas Kaberle, D | 24 | 1 | 8 | 9 | 6 | 2 |
| Rich Peverley, C | 23 | 4 | 3 | 7 | -1 | 2 |
| Jordan Caron, RW | 23 | 3 | 4 | 7 | 3 | 6 |
| Chris Kelly, C | 24 | 2 | 3 | 5 | -1 | 6 |
| Mark Stuart, D | 31 | 1 | 4 | 5 | 8 | 23 |
| Matt Hunwick, D | 22 | 1 | 2 | 3 | 4 | 9 |
| Zach Hamill, C | 3 | 0 | 1 | 1 | 1 | 0 |
| Shane Hnidy, D | 3 | 0 | 0 | 0 | -2 | 2 |
| Jamie Arniel, C | 1 | 0 | 0 | 0 | -1 | 0 |
| Matt Bartkowski, D | 6 | 0 | 0 | 0 | -1 | 4 |

### GOALTENDING

| Player | GP | Mins | W | L | TGA | GAA | SO |
|---|---|---|---|---|---|---|---|
| Tim Thomas | 57 | 3364 | 35 | 11 | 112 | 2.00 | 9 |
| Tuukka Rask | 29 | 1594 | 11 | 14 | 71 | 2.67 | 2 |

## Buffalo Sabres

### SCORING

| Player | GP | G | Ast | Pts | +/– | PM |
|---|---|---|---|---|---|---|
| Thomas Vanek, LW | 80 | 32 | 41 | 73 | 2 | 24 |
| Jason Pominville, RW | 73 | 22 | 30 | 52 | 1 | 15 |
| Drew Stafford, RW | 62 | 31 | 21 | 52 | 13 | 34 |
| Tyler Ennis, LW | 82 | 20 | 29 | 49 | 0 | 30 |
| Tim Connolly, C | 68 | 13 | 29 | 42 | -10 | 20 |
| Tyler Myers, D | 80 | 10 | 27 | 37 | 0 | 40 |
| Jordan Leopold, D | 71 | 13 | 22 | 35 | -11 | 36 |
| Derek Roy, C | 35 | 10 | 25 | 35 | -1 | 16 |
| Paul Gaustad, C | 81 | 12 | 19 | 31 | 7 | 101 |
| Nathan Gerbe, C | 64 | 16 | 15 | 31 | 11 | 34 |
| Jochen Hecht, C | 67 | 12 | 17 | 29 | 4 | 40 |
| Andrej Sekera, D | 76 | 3 | 26 | 29 | 11 | 34 |
| Steve Montador, D | 73 | 5 | 21 | 26 | 16 | 83 |
| Cody McCormick, C | 81 | 8 | 12 | 20 | 2 | 142 |
| Rob Niedermayer, C | 71 | 5 | 14 | 19 | -8 | 22 |
| Mike Weber, D | 58 | 4 | 13 | 17 | 13 | 69 |
| Michael Grier, RW | 73 | 5 | 11 | 16 | 0 | 12 |
| Brad Boyes, RW | 21 | 5 | 9 | 14 | 2 | 6 |

### SCORING *(CONT.)*

| Player | GP | G | Ast | Pts | +/– | PM |
|---|---|---|---|---|---|---|
| Patrick Kaleta, RW | 51 | 4 | 5 | 9 | -4 | 78 |
| Chris Butler, D | 49 | 2 | 7 | 9 | 8 | 26 |
| Mark Mancari, RW | 20 | 1 | 7 | 8 | -1 | 12 |
| Shaone Morrisonn, D | 62 | 1 | 4 | 5 | -2 | 32 |
| Luke Adam, LW | 19 | 3 | 1 | 4 | -6 | 12 |
| Craig Rivet, D | 23 | 1 | 2 | 3 | -5 | 12 |
| Marc-Andre Gragnani, D | 9 | 1 | 2 | 3 | 0 | 2 |
| Paul Byron, C | 8 | 1 | 1 | 2 | 0 | 2 |
| Mark Parrish, RW | 2 | 0 | 0 | 0 | -2 | 0 |
| Colin Stuart, LW | 3 | 0 | 0 | 0 | 1 | 2 |
| Matt Ellis, LW | 14 | 0 | 0 | 0 | -4 | 0 |

### GOALTENDING

| Player | GP | Mins | W | L | TGA | GAA | SO |
|---|---|---|---|---|---|---|---|
| Ryan Miller | 66 | 3829 | 34 | 22 | 165 | 2.59 | 5 |
| Jhonas Enroth | 14 | 769 | 9 | 2 | 35 | 2.73 | 1 |
| Patrick Lalime | 7 | 365 | 0 | 5 | 18 | 2.96 | 0 |

## Calgary Flames

### SCORING

| Player | GP | G | Ast | Pts | +/- | PM |
|---|---|---|---|---|---|---|
| Jarome Iginla, RW .......82 | 43 | 43 | 86 | 0 | 40 |
| Alex Tanguay, LW ......79 | 22 | 47 | 69 | 0 | 24 |
| Olli Jokinen, C ..........79 | 17 | 37 | 54 | -17 | 44 |
| Rene Bourque, LW ......80 | 27 | 23 | 50 | -17 | 42 |
| Brendan Morrison, C ...66 | 9 | 34 | 43 | 13 | 16 |
| Mark Giordano, D.........82 | 8 | 35 | 43 | -8 | 67 |
| Curtis Glencross, LW...79 | 24 | 19 | 43 | 6 | 59 |
| Matt Stajan, C ..........76 | 6 | 25 | 31 | 1 | 32 |
| David Moss, RW .........58 | 17 | 13 | 30 | 9 | 18 |
| Niklas Hagman, LW.....71 | 11 | 16 | 27 | -2 | 24 |
| Anton Babchuk, D.......65 | 8 | 19 | 27 | 18 | 20 |
| Mikael Backlund, C.....73 | 10 | 15 | 25 | 4 | 18 |
| Jay Bouwmeester, D...82 | 4 | 20 | 24 | -2 | 44 |
| Tim Jackman, RW .......82 | 10 | 13 | 23 | 4 | 86 |
| Cory Sarich, D..........76 | 4 | 13 | 17 | 11 | 75 |
| Robyn Regehr, D.........79 | 2 | 15 | 17 | 2 | 58 |
| Tom Kostopoulos, RW..59 | 7 | 7 | 14 | -3 | 44 |
| Steve Staios, D..........39 | 3 | 7 | 10 | 6 | 24 |
| Adam Pardy, D............30 | 1 | 6 | 7 | 3 | 24 |
| Ales Kotalik, RW ........26 | 4 | 2 | 6 | -7 | 8 |
| Ian White, D...............16 | 2 | 4 | 6 | -10 | 6 |
| Craig Conroy, C..........18 | 2 | 0 | 2 | -1 | 8 |
| Stefan Meyer, LW .......16 | 0 | 2 | 2 | 0 | 17 |
| Daymond Langkow, C...4 | 0 | 1 | 1 | 3 | 0 |
| Brendan Mikkelson, D..19 | 0 | 1 | 1 | -5 | 2 |
| Brett Sutter, C .............4 | 0 | 1 | 1 | -1 | 5 |
| Greg Nemisz, C............6 | 0 | 1 | 1 | -1 | 0 |
| Lance Bouma, C ..........16 | 0 | 1 | 1 | -1 | 2 |
| Freddy Modin, LW .........4 | 0 | 0 | 0 | -3 | 2 |
| Raitis Ivanans, LW.........1 | 0 | 0 | 0 | -1 | 5 |
| Brett Carson, D.............6 | 0 | 0 | 0 | 2 | 0 |
| T.J. Brodie, D...............3 | 0 | 0 | 0 | -3 | 2 |

### GOALTENDING

| Player | GP | Mins | W | L | TGA | GAA | SO |
|---|---|---|---|---|---|---|---|
| Miikka Kiprusoff ......71 | 4156 | 37 | 24 | 182 | 2.63 | 6 |
| Henrik Karlsson.......17 | 838 | 4 | 5 | 36 | 2.58 | 0 |

## Carolina Hurricanes

### SCORING

| Player | GP | G | Ast | Pts | +/- | PM |
|---|---|---|---|---|---|---|
| Eric Staal, C.................81 | 33 | 43 | 76 | -10 | 72 |
| Jeff Skinner, C .............82 | 31 | 32 | 63 | 3 | 46 |
| Tuomo Ruutu, C............82 | 19 | 38 | 57 | 1 | 54 |
| Erik Cole, RW ...............82 | 26 | 26 | 52 | -1 | 49 |
| Jussi Jokinen, LW.........70 | 19 | 33 | 52 | 3 | 24 |
| Joe Corvo, D .................82 | 11 | 29 | 40 | -14 | 18 |
| Joni Pitkanen, D ...........72 | 5 | 30 | 35 | -2 | 60 |
| Chad Larose, RW .........82 | 16 | 15 | 31 | -21 | 59 |
| Jamie McBain, D...........76 | 7 | 23 | 30 | -8 | 32 |
| Brandon Sutter, C.........82 | 14 | 15 | 29 | 13 | 25 |
| Sergei Samsonov, LW..58 | 10 | 16 | 26 | 0 | 12 |
| Patrick Dwyer, RW........80 | 8 | 10 | 18 | -6 | 12 |
| Cory Stillman, LW.........21 | 5 | 11 | 16 | 2 | 4 |
| Tim Gleason, D.............82 | 2 | 14 | 16 | -11 | 85 |
| Jiri Tlusty, C.................57 | 6 | 6 | 12 | 1 | 14 |
| Jay Harrison, D.............72 | 3 | 7 | 10 | 5 | 72 |
| Ian White, D.................39 | 0 | 10 | 10 | 4 | 12 |
| Anton Babchuk, D.........17 | 3 | 5 | 8 | -4 | 12 |
| Zach Boychuk, LW ........23 | 4 | 3 | 7 | -2 | 4 |
| Bryan Allen, D...............19 | 0 | 5 | 5 | 4 | 19 |
| Derek Joslin, D..............17 | 1 | 4 | 5 | 7 | 2 |
| Tom Kostopoulos, RW...17 | 1 | 3 | 4 | -1 | 30 |
| Zac Dalpe, C ................15 | 3 | 1 | 4 | 0 | 0 |
| Troy Bodie, RW.............50 | 1 | 2 | 3 | -4 | 54 |
| Ryan Carter, C..............32 | 0 | 3 | 3 | 0 | 22 |
| Jon Matsumoto, C ........13 | 2 | 0 | 2 | -4 | 4 |
| Jerome Samson, RW.....23 | 0 | 2 | 2 | 0 | 0 |
| Patrick O'Sullivan, C....10 | 1 | 0 | 1 | -1 | 2 |
| Drayson Bowman, LW...23 | 0 | 1 | 1 | 0 | 12 |
| Bryan Rodney, D............3 | 0 | 0 | 0 | 2 | 4 |
| Brett Carson, D.............13 | 0 | 0 | 0 | 7 | 4 |
| Brett Sutter, LW..............1 | 0 | 0 | 0 | 0 | 0 |

### GOALTENDING

| Player | GP | Mins | W | L | TGA | GAA | SO |
|---|---|---|---|---|---|---|---|
| Cam Ward................74 | 4318 | 37 | 26 | 184 | 2.56 | 4 |
| Justin Peters ..........12 | 648 | 3 | 5 | 43 | 3.98 | 0 |

## Chicago Blackhawks

### SCORING

| Player | GP | G | Ast | Pts | +/- | PM |
|---|---|---|---|---|---|---|
| Jonathan Toews, C .......80 | 32 | 44 | 76 | 25 | 26 |
| Patrick Kane, RW ........73 | 27 | 46 | 73 | 7 | 28 |
| Patrick Sharp, C .........74 | 34 | 37 | 71 | -1 | 38 |
| Marian Hossa, RW .......65 | 25 | 32 | 57 | 9 | 32 |
| Brent Seabrook, D........82 | 9 | 39 | 48 | 0 | 47 |
| Duncan Keith, D .........82 | 7 | 38 | 45 | -1 | 22 |
| Tomas Kopecky, RW......81 | 15 | 27 | 42 | -13 | 60 |
| Dave Bolland, C ..........61 | 15 | 22 | 37 | 11 | 34 |
| Bryan Bickell, LW........78 | 17 | 20 | 37 | 6 | 40 |
| Troy Brouwer, LW ........79 | 17 | 19 | 36 | -2 | 38 |
| Brian Campbell, D........65 | 5 | 22 | 27 | 28 | 6 |
| Viktor Stalberg, LW ......77 | 12 | 12 | 24 | 2 | 43 |
| Jake Dowell, C............79 | 6 | 15 | 21 | 5 | 63 |
| Jack Skille, RW ...........49 | 7 | 10 | 17 | 3 | 25 |
| Fernando Pisani, RW...60 | 7 | 9 | 16 | 0 | 10 |
| Niklas Hjalmarsson, D..80 | 3 | 7 | 10 | 13 | 39 |
| Michael Frolik, LW .......28 | 3 | 6 | 9 | 0 | 14 |
| Jassen Cullimore, D ....36 | 0 | 8 | 8 | 4 | 8 |

### SCORING *(CONT.)*

| Player | GP | G | Ast | Pts | +/- | PM |
|---|---|---|---|---|---|---|
| Nick Boynton, D...........41 | 1 | 7 | 8 | 2 | 36 |
| Chris Campoli, D..........19 | 1 | 6 | 7 | 3 | 2 |
| Nick Leddy, D..............46 | 4 | 3 | 7 | -3 | 4 |
| Ryan Johnson, C..........34 | 1 | 5 | 6 | -2 | 8 |
| Jeremy Morin, LW.........9 | 2 | 1 | 3 | 2 | 9 |
| Jordan Hendry, D ........37 | 1 | 0 | 1 | -2 | 4 |
| John Scott, D...............40 | 0 | 1 | 1 | 0 | 72 |
| Ben Smith, RW.............6 | 1 | 0 | 1 | 1 | 0 |
| Jeff Taffe, C..................1 | 0 | 0 | 0 | 0 | 0 |
| Ryan Potulny, C.............9 | 0 | 0 | 0 | -1 | 0 |
| Evan Brophey, C...........1 | 0 | 0 | 0 | 0 | 0 |
| Rob Klinkhammer, LW...1 | 0 | 0 | 0 | 1 | 0 |
| Brandon Pirri, C.............1 | 0 | 0 | 0 | -1 | 0 |
| Marcus Kruger, C.........7 | 0 | 0 | 0 | -4 | 4 |

### GOALTENDING

| Player | GP | Mins | W | L | TGA | GAA | SO |
|---|---|---|---|---|---|---|---|
| Corey Crawford.......57 | 3337 | 33 | 18 | 128 | 2.30 | 4 |
| Marty Turco .............29 | 1631 | 11 | 11 | 82 | 3.02 | 1 |

## Colorado Avalanche

### SCORING

| Player | GP | G | Ast | Pts | +/– | PM |
|---|---|---|---|---|---|---|
| Matt Duchene, C | 80 | 27 | 40 | 67 | -8 | 33 |
| Paul Stastny, C | 74 | 22 | 35 | 57 | -7 | 56 |
| Milan Hejduk, RW | 71 | 22 | 34 | 56 | -23 | 18 |
| John-Michael Liles, D | 76 | 6 | 40 | 46 | -9 | 35 |
| David Jones, RW | 77 | 27 | 18 | 45 | -2 | 28 |
| Chris Stewart, RW | 36 | 13 | 17 | 30 | -10 | 38 |
| Daniel Winnik, LW | 80 | 11 | 15 | 26 | -2 | 35 |
| Kevin Shattenkirk, D | 46 | 7 | 19 | 26 | -11 | 20 |
| Ryan O'Reilly, C | 74 | 13 | 13 | 26 | -7 | 16 |
| Kevin Porter, C | 74 | 14 | 11 | 25 | -11 | 27 |
| Brandon Yip, RW | 71 | 12 | 10 | 22 | -22 | 54 |
| Tomas Fleischmann, LW | 22 | 8 | 13 | 21 | -1 | 8 |
| Philippe Dupuis, C | 74 | 6 | 11 | 17 | -4 | 40 |
| Ryan Wilson, D | 67 | 3 | 13 | 16 | -8 | 68 |
| T.J. Galiardi, LW | 35 | 7 | 8 | 15 | -6 | 12 |
| Greg Mauldin, LW | 29 | 5 | 5 | 10 | 5 | 8 |
| Ryan O'Byrne, D | 64 | 0 | 10 | 10 | -7 | 71 |
| Matt Hunwick, D | 51 | 0 | 10 | 10 | -19 | 16 |
| Erik Johnson, D | 22 | 3 | 7 | 10 | -5 | 19 |
| Mark Olver, C | 18 | 2 | 7 | 9 | -2 | 18 |
| Adam Foote, D | 47 | 0 | 8 | 8 | -9 | 33 |
| Cody McLeod, LW | 71 | 5 | 3 | 8 | -7 | 189 |
| Kyle Cumiskey, D | 18 | 1 | 7 | 8 | -3 | 10 |
| Scott Hannan, D | 23 | 0 | 6 | 6 | 1 | 6 |
| Jonas Holos, D | 39 | 0 | 6 | 6 | -3 | 10 |
| Jay McClement, C | 24 | 1 | 3 | 4 | -8 | 12 |
| Ryan Stoa, C | 25 | 2 | 2 | 4 | -4 | 20 |

### GOALTENDING

| Player | GP | Mins | W | L | TGA | GAA | SO |
|---|---|---|---|---|---|---|---|
| Peter Budaj | 45 | 2439 | 15 | 21 | 130 | 3.20 | 1 |
| Craig Anderson | 33 | 1810 | 13 | 15 | 99 | 3.28 | 0 |
| Brian Elliott | 12 | 690 | 2 | 8 | 44 | 3.83 | 0 |

## Columbus Blue Jackets

### SCORING

| Player | GP | G | Ast | Pts | +/– | PM |
|---|---|---|---|---|---|---|
| Rick Nash, RW | 75 | 32 | 34 | 66 | 2 | 34 |
| RJ Umberger, LW | 82 | 25 | 32 | 57 | 3 | 38 |
| Antoine Vermette, C | 82 | 19 | 28 | 47 | 0 | 60 |
| Derick Brassard, C | 74 | 17 | 30 | 47 | -11 | 55 |
| Jakub Voracek, RW | 80 | 14 | 32 | 46 | -3 | 26 |
| Fedor Tyutin, D | 80 | 7 | 20 | 27 | -12 | 32 |
| Kristian Huselius, LW | 39 | 14 | 9 | 23 | -17 | 10 |
| Derek MacKenzie, C | 63 | 9 | 14 | 23 | 14 | 22 |
| Kris Russell, D | 73 | 5 | 18 | 23 | -9 | 37 |
| Samuel Pahlsson, C | 82 | 7 | 13 | 20 | -13 | 30 |
| Jan Hejda, D | 77 | 5 | 15 | 20 | -6 | 28 |
| Matt Calvert, LW | 42 | 11 | 9 | 20 | 3 | 12 |
| Grant Clitsome, D | 31 | 4 | 15 | 19 | 2 | 16 |
| Anton Stralman, D | 51 | 1 | 17 | 18 | -11 | 22 |
| Derek Dorsett, RW | 76 | 4 | 13 | 17 | -15 | 184 |
| Chris Clark, RW | 53 | 5 | 10 | 15 | -3 | 38 |
| Marc Methot, D | 74 | 0 | 15 | 15 | 2 | 58 |
| Jared Boll, RW | 73 | 7 | 5 | 12 | -2 | 182 |
| Kyle Wilson, C | 32 | 4 | 7 | 11 | -3 | 12 |
| Rostislav Klesla, D | 45 | 3 | 7 | 10 | 10 | 26 |
| Andrew Murray, C | 29 | 4 | 4 | 8 | 2 | 4 |
| Scottie Upshall, RW | 21 | 6 | 1 | 7 | -12 | 10 |
| Nikita Filatov, LW | 23 | 0 | 7 | 7 | 3 | 8 |
| Ethan Moreau, LW | 37 | 1 | 5 | 6 | -9 | 24 |
| Mike Commodore, D | 20 | 2 | 4 | 6 | -8 | 44 |
| Sami Lepisto, D | 19 | 0 | 5 | 5 | 3 | 18 |
| Tom Sestito, LW | 9 | 2 | 2 | 4 | -4 | 40 |

### GOALTENDING

| Player | GP | Mins | W | L | TGA | GAA | SO |
|---|---|---|---|---|---|---|---|
| Steve Mason | 54 | 3027 | 24 | 21 | 153 | 3.03 | 3 |
| Mathieu Garon | 36 | 1938 | 10 | 14 | 88 | 2.72 | 3 |
| David Leneveu | 1 | 20 | 0 | 0 | 2 | 6.00 | 0 |

## Dallas Stars

### SCORING

| Player | GP | G | Ast | Pts | +/– | PM |
|---|---|---|---|---|---|---|
| Brad Richards, C | 72 | 28 | 49 | 77 | 1 | 24 |
| Loui Eriksson, LW | 79 | 27 | 46 | 73 | 10 | 8 |
| Mike Ribeiro, C | 82 | 19 | 52 | 71 | -4 | 28 |
| Brenden Morrow, LW | 82 | 33 | 23 | 56 | -3 | 76 |
| Jamie Benn, LW | 69 | 22 | 34 | 56 | -5 | 52 |
| James Neal, LW | 59 | 21 | 18 | 39 | 8 | 60 |
| Steve Ott, LW | 82 | 12 | 20 | 32 | -9 | 183 |
| Stephane Robidas, D | 81 | 5 | 25 | 30 | -7 | 67 |
| Trevor Daley, D | 82 | 8 | 19 | 27 | 7 | 34 |
| J. Langenbrunner, RW | 39 | 5 | 13 | 18 | -3 | 29 |
| Alex Goligoski, D | 23 | 5 | 10 | 15 | 0 | 12 |
| Adam Burish, RW | 63 | 8 | 6 | 14 | 2 | 91 |
| Jeff Woywitka, D | 63 | 2 | 9 | 11 | 5 | 24 |
| Brandon Segal, RW | 46 | 5 | 5 | 10 | 0 | 41 |
| Nicklas Grossman, D | 59 | 1 | 9 | 10 | 7 | 35 |
| Tom Wandell, C | 75 | 7 | 2 | 9 | -5 | 14 |
| Karlis Skrastins, D | 74 | 3 | 5 | 8 | -1 | 38 |
| Toby Petersen, C | 60 | 2 | 4 | 6 | -7 | 8 |
| Matt Niskanen, D | 45 | 0 | 6 | 6 | -1 | 30 |
| Jason Williams, C | 27 | 2 | 3 | 5 | -2 | 6 |
| Mark Fistric, D | 57 | 2 | 3 | 5 | -10 | 44 |
| Brian Sutherby, C | 51 | 2 | 2 | 4 | -10 | 58 |
| Krystofer Barch, RW | 44 | 2 | 1 | 3 | -7 | 80 |
| Tomas Vincour, C | 24 | 1 | 1 | 2 | -5 | 4 |

### GOALTENDING

| Player | GP | Mins | W | L | TGA | GAA | SO |
|---|---|---|---|---|---|---|---|
| Kari Lehtonen | 69 | 4119 | 34 | 24 | 175 | 2.55 | 3 |
| Andrew Raycroft | 19 | 847 | 8 | 5 | 40 | 2.83 | 2 |
| Richard Bachman | 1 | 10 | 0 | 0 | 0 | 0.00 | 0 |

## Detroit Red Wings

### SCORING

| Player | GP | G | Ast | Pts | +/– | PM |
|---|---|---|---|---|---|---|
| Henrik Zetterberg, LW | 80 | 24 | 56 | 80 | -1 | 40 |
| Nicklas Lidstrom, D | 82 | 16 | 46 | 62 | -2 | 20 |
| Pavel Datsyuk, C | 56 | 23 | 36 | 59 | 11 | 15 |
| Johan Franzen, RW | 76 | 28 | 27 | 55 | 5 | 58 |
| Brian Rafalski, D | 63 | 4 | 44 | 48 | 11 | 22 |
| Danny Cleary, RW | 68 | 26 | 20 | 46 | -1 | 20 |
| Todd Bertuzzi, RW | 81 | 16 | 29 | 45 | -7 | 71 |
| Valtteri Filppula, C | 71 | 16 | 23 | 39 | -1 | 22 |
| Tomas Holmstrom, LW | 73 | 18 | 19 | 37 | -6 | 62 |
| Niklas Kronwall, D | 77 | 11 | 26 | 37 | 5 | 36 |
| Jiri Hudler, C | 73 | 10 | 27 | 37 | -7 | 28 |
| Darren Helm, C | 82 | 12 | 20 | 32 | 9 | 16 |
| Brad Stuart, D | 67 | 3 | 17 | 20 | 4 | 40 |
| Patrick Eaves, RW | 63 | 13 | 7 | 20 | -2 | 14 |
| Justin Abdelkader, LW | 74 | 7 | 12 | 19 | 15 | 61 |
| Drew Miller, LW | 67 | 10 | 8 | 18 | -2 | 13 |
| Mike Modano, C | 40 | 4 | 11 | 15 | -4 | 8 |
| Jonathan Ericsson, D | 74 | 3 | 12 | 15 | 8 | 87 |
| Kris Draper, C | 47 | 6 | 5 | 11 | 1 | 12 |
| Ruslan Salei, D | 75 | 2 | 8 | 10 | 0 | 48 |
| Jakub Kindl, D | 48 | 2 | 2 | 4 | -6 | 36 |
| Jan Mursak, LW | 19 | 1 | 0 | 1 | -3 | 4 |
| Tomas Tatar, C | 9 | 1 | 0 | 1 | 0 | 0 |

### GOALTENDING

| Player | GP | Mins | W | L | TGA | GAA | SO |
|---|---|---|---|---|---|---|---|
| Jimmy Howard | 63 | 3615 | 37 | 17 | 168 | 2.79 | 2 |
| Joey MacDonald | 15 | 721 | 5 | 5 | 31 | 2.58 | 1 |
| Chris Osgood | 11 | 629 | 5 | 3 | 29 | 2.77 | 0 |

## Edmonton Oilers

### SCORING

| Player | GP | G | Ast | Pts | +/- | PM |
|---|---|---|---|---|---|---|
| Jordan Eberle, RW | 69 | 18 | 25 | 43 | -12 | 22 |
| Ales Hemsky, RW | 47 | 14 | 28 | 42 | 3 | 18 |
| Sam Gagner, C | 68 | 15 | 27 | 42 | -17 | 37 |
| Taylor Hall, LW | 65 | 22 | 20 | 42 | -9 | 27 |
| Dustin Penner, RW | 62 | 21 | 18 | 39 | -12 | 45 |
| Andrew Cogliano, C | 82 | 11 | 24 | 35 | -12 | 64 |
| Magnus Paajarvi, LW | 80 | 15 | 19 | 34 | -13 | 16 |
| Shawn Horcoff, C | 47 | 9 | 18 | 27 | -1 | 46 |
| Ryan Whitney, D | 35 | 2 | 25 | 27 | 13 | 33 |
| Linus Omark, LW | 51 | 5 | 22 | 27 | -16 | 26 |
| Tom Gilbert, D | 79 | 6 | 20 | 26 | -14 | 32 |
| Ryan Jones, LW | 81 | 18 | 7 | 25 | -5 | 34 |
| Kurtis Foster, D | 74 | 8 | 14 | 22 | -12 | 45 |
| Jim Vandermeer, D | 62 | 2 | 12 | 14 | -15 | 74 |
| Theo Peckham, D | 71 | 3 | 10 | 13 | -5 | 198 |
| Ladislav Smid, D | 78 | 0 | 10 | 10 | -10 | 85 |
| Liam Reddox, LW | 44 | 1 | 9 | 10 | -8 | 20 |
| Gilbert Brule, C | 41 | 7 | 2 | 9 | -7 | 41 |
| Jean-Franc. Jacques, LW | 51 | 4 | 1 | 5 | -6 | 63 |
| Colin Fraser, C | 67 | 3 | 2 | 5 | -2 | 60 |
| Ryan O'Marra, C | 21 | 1 | 4 | 5 | -2 | 13 |
| Jeff Petry, D | 35 | 1 | 4 | 5 | -12 | 10 |
| Teemu Hartikainen, LW | 12 | 3 | 2 | 5 | -3 | 4 |
| Zack Stortini, RW | 32 | 0 | 4 | 4 | -2 | 76 |
| Taylor Chorney, D | 12 | 1 | 3 | 4 | -5 | 4 |
| Jason Strudwick, D | 43 | 0 | 2 | 2 | -16 | 23 |
| Alexandre Giroux, LW | 8 | 1 | 1 | 2 | -2 | 2 |
| Chris Vandevelde, C | 12 | 0 | 2 | 2 | -6 | 12 |
| Steve MacIntyre, LW | 34 | 0 | 1 | 1 | -1 | 93 |

### GOALTENDING

| Player | GP | Mins | W | L | TGA | GAA | SO |
|---|---|---|---|---|---|---|---|
| Nikolai Khabibulin | 47 | 2701 | 10 | 32 | 153 | 3.40 | 2 |
| Devan Dubnyk | 35 | 2061 | 12 | 13 | 93 | 2.71 | 2 |
| Martin Gerber | 3 | 185 | 3 | 0 | 4 | 1.30 | 0 |

## Florida Panthers

### SCORING

| Player | GP | G | Ast | Pts | +/- | PM |
|---|---|---|---|---|---|---|
| Stephen Weiss, C | 76 | 21 | 28 | 49 | -9 | 49 |
| Mike Santorelli, C | 82 | 20 | 21 | 41 | -17 | 20 |
| David Booth, LW | 82 | 23 | 17 | 40 | -31 | 26 |
| Dennis Wideman, D | 61 | 9 | 24 | 33 | -26 | 33 |
| Marty Reasoner, C | 82 | 14 | 18 | 32 | 2 | 22 |
| Michael Frolik, C | 52 | 8 | 21 | 29 | 2 | 16 |
| Dmitry Kulikov, D | 72 | 6 | 20 | 26 | -5 | 45 |
| Cory Stillman, LW | 44 | 7 | 16 | 23 | 3 | 20 |
| Chris Higgins, LW | 48 | 11 | 12 | 23 | 5 | 10 |
| Bryan McCabe, D | 48 | 5 | 17 | 22 | 3 | 28 |
| Radek Dvorak, RW | 53 | 7 | 14 | 21 | 2 | 20 |
| Jason Garrison, D | 73 | 5 | 13 | 18 | -2 | 26 |
| Rostislav Olesz, LW | 44 | 6 | 11 | 17 | -1 | 8 |
| Evgeny Dadonov, RW | 36 | 8 | 9 | 17 | 0 | 14 |
| Shawn Matthias, C | 51 | 6 | 10 | 16 | 0 | 16 |
| Steve Bernier, RW | 68 | 5 | 10 | 15 | -14 | 21 |
| Sergei Samsonov, LW | 20 | 3 | 11 | 14 | -2 | 2 |
| Mike Weaver, D | 82 | 2 | 11 | 13 | 1 | 34 |
| Bryan Allen, D | 53 | 4 | 8 | 12 | -5 | 63 |
| Keaton Ellerby, D | 54 | 2 | 10 | 12 | -15 | 22 |
| Steve Reinprecht, C | 29 | 4 | 6 | 10 | -2 | 6 |
| Michal Repik, RW | 31 | 2 | 6 | 8 | -6 | 22 |
| Niclas Bergfors, RW | 20 | 1 | 6 | 7 | 2 | 2 |
| Bill Thomas, RW | 24 | 3 | 4 | 7 | 1 | 6 |
| Darcy Hordichuk, LW | 64 | 1 | 4 | 5 | -1 | 76 |
| Clay Wilson, D | 15 | 3 | 2 | 5 | 4 | 6 |
| Ryan Carter, C | 12 | 2 | 1 | 3 | 3 | 22 |
| Jack Skille, RW | 13 | 1 | 1 | 2 | -12 | 4 |
| Joe Callahan, D | 27 | 0 | 1 | 1 | -1 | 12 |

### GOALTENDING

| Player | GP | Mins | W | L | TGA | GAA | SO |
|---|---|---|---|---|---|---|---|
| Tomas Vokoun | 57 | 3224 | 22 | 28 | 137 | 2.55 | 6 |
| Scott Clemmensen | 31 | 1696 | 8 | 11 | 74 | 2.62 | 1 |
| Jacob Markstrom | 1 | 40 | 0 | 1 | 2 | 3.00 | 0 |

## Los Angeles Kings

### SCORING

| Player | GP | G | Ast | Pts | +/- | PM |
|---|---|---|---|---|---|---|
| Anze Kopitar, C | 75 | 25 | 48 | 73 | 25 | 20 |
| Justin Williams, RW | 73 | 22 | 35 | 57 | 14 | 59 |
| Dustin Brown, RW | 82 | 28 | 29 | 57 | 17 | 67 |
| Ryan Smyth, LW | 82 | 23 | 24 | 47 | -1 | 35 |
| Jarret Stoll, C | 82 | 20 | 23 | 43 | -6 | 42 |
| Jack Johnson, D | 82 | 5 | 37 | 42 | -21 | 44 |
| Drew Doughty, D | 76 | 11 | 29 | 40 | 13 | 68 |
| Michal Handzus, C | 82 | 12 | 18 | 30 | -5 | 20 |
| Wayne Simmonds, RW | 80 | 14 | 16 | 30 | -2 | 75 |
| Brad Richardson, C | 68 | 7 | 12 | 19 | -13 | 47 |
| Alec Martinez, D | 60 | 5 | 11 | 16 | 11 | 18 |
| Alexei Ponikarovsky, LW | 61 | 5 | 10 | 15 | 1 | 36 |
| Rob Scuderi, D | 82 | 2 | 13 | 15 | 1 | 16 |
| Kyle Clifford, LW | 76 | 7 | 7 | 14 | -10 | 141 |
| Trevor Lewis, C | 72 | 3 | 10 | 13 | -11 | 6 |
| Matt Greene, D | 71 | 2 | 9 | 11 | 3 | 70 |
| Willie Mitchell, D | 57 | 5 | 5 | 10 | 4 | 21 |
| Marco Sturm, LW | 17 | 4 | 5 | 9 | 6 | 17 |

### SCORING (CONT.)

| Player | GP | G | Ast | Pts | +/- | PM |
|---|---|---|---|---|---|---|
| Andrei Loktionov, C | 19 | 4 | 3 | 7 | 2 | 2 |
| Dustin Penner, LW | 19 | 2 | 4 | 6 | 0 | 2 |
| Davis Drewiske, D | 38 | 0 | 5 | 5 | -1 | 19 |
| Scott Parse, LW | 5 | 1 | 3 | 4 | 5 | 0 |
| Peter Harrold, D | 19 | 1 | 3 | 4 | 3 | 4 |
| Oscar Moller, RW | 13 | 1 | 3 | 4 | -1 | 2 |
| Kevin Westgarth, C | 56 | 0 | 3 | 3 | -6 | 105 |
| Brayden Schenn, C | 8 | 0 | 2 | 2 | -1 | 0 |
| Jake Muzzin, D | 11 | 0 | 1 | 1 | -2 | 0 |
| John Zeiler, RW | 4 | 0 | 0 | 0 | -1 | 0 |
| Dwight King, LW | 6 | 0 | 0 | 0 | -2 | 2 |

### GOALTENDING

| Player | GP | Mins | W | L | TGA | GAA | SO |
|---|---|---|---|---|---|---|---|
| Jonathan Quick | 61 | 3591 | 35 | 22 | 134 | 2.24 | 6 |
| Jonathan Bernier | 25 | 1378 | 11 | 8 | 57 | 2.48 | 3 |

## Minnesota Wild

### SCORING

| Player | GP | G | Ast | Pts | +/- | PM |
|---|---|---|---|---|---|---|
| Martin Havlat, RW | 78 | 22 | 40 | 62 | -10 | 52 |
| Mikko Koivu, C | 71 | 17 | 45 | 62 | 4 | 50 |
| Andrew Brunette, LW | 82 | 18 | 28 | 46 | -7 | 16 |
| Brent Burns, D | 80 | 17 | 29 | 46 | -10 | 98 |
| Matt Cullen, C | 78 | 12 | 27 | 39 | -14 | 34 |
| Pierre-Marc Bouchard, C | 59 | 12 | 26 | 38 | -3 | 14 |
| Kyle Brodziak, C | 80 | 16 | 21 | 37 | -4 | 56 |
| Antti Miettinen, RW | 73 | 16 | 19 | 35 | -3 | 38 |
| Cal Clutterbuck, RW | 76 | 19 | 15 | 34 | -5 | 79 |
| John Madden, C | 76 | 12 | 13 | 25 | -9 | 10 |
| Marek Zidlicky, D | 46 | 7 | 17 | 24 | -6 | 30 |
| Nick Schultz, D | 74 | 3 | 14 | 17 | -4 | 38 |
| Chuck Kobasew, RW | 63 | 9 | 7 | 16 | -6 | 19 |
| Eric Nystrom, LW | 82 | 4 | 8 | 12 | -16 | 30 |
| Jared Spurgeon, D | 53 | 4 | 8 | 12 | -1 | 2 |
| Clayton Stoner, D | 57 | 2 | 7 | 9 | 5 | 96 |
| Brad Staubitz, RW | 71 | 4 | 5 | 9 | -5 | 173 |
| Greg Zanon, D | 82 | 0 | 7 | 7 | -5 | 48 |
| Patrick O'Sullivan, C | 21 | 1 | 6 | 7 | -1 | 2 |
| Guil. Latendresse, LW | 11 | 3 | 3 | 6 | 2 | 8 |
| Cam Barker, D | 52 | 1 | 4 | 5 | -10 | 34 |
| Justin Falk, D | 22 | 0 | 3 | 3 | -4 | 6 |

### GOALTENDING

| Player | GP | Mins | W | L | TGA | GAA | SO |
|---|---|---|---|---|---|---|---|
| Niklas Backstrom | 51 | 2978 | 22 | 23 | 132 | 2.66 | 3 |
| Jose Theodore | 32 | 1793 | 15 | 11 | 81 | 2.71 | 1 |
| Anton Khudobin | 4 | 189 | 2 | 1 | 5 | 1.59 | 1 |

## Nashville Predators

### SCORING

| Player | GP | G | Ast | Pts | +/- | PM |
|---|---|---|---|---|---|---|
| Martin Erat, RW | 64 | 17 | 33 | 50 | 14 | 22 |
| Sergei Kostitsyn, LW | 77 | 23 | 27 | 50 | 10 | 20 |
| Shea Weber, D | 82 | 16 | 32 | 48 | 7 | 56 |
| Patric Hornqvist, RW | 79 | 21 | 27 | 48 | 11 | 47 |
| David Legwand, C | 64 | 17 | 24 | 41 | 13 | 24 |
| Ryan Suter, D | 70 | 4 | 35 | 39 | 20 | 54 |
| Colin Wilson, C | 82 | 16 | 18 | 34 | 9 | 17 |
| Joel Ward, RW | 80 | 10 | 19 | 29 | -1 | 42 |
| Cody Franson, D | 80 | 8 | 21 | 29 | 10 | 30 |
| Marcel Goc, C | 51 | 9 | 15 | 24 | 10 | 6 |
| Steve Sullivan, LW | 44 | 10 | 12 | 22 | 4 | 28 |
| J.P. Dumont, RW | 70 | 10 | 9 | 19 | 2 | 16 |
| Jordin Tootoo, RW | 54 | 8 | 10 | 18 | 8 | 61 |
| Kevin Klein, D | 81 | 2 | 16 | 18 | 9 | 24 |
| Cal O'Reilly, C | 38 | 6 | 12 | 18 | 4 | 2 |
| Nick Spaling, LW | 74 | 8 | 6 | 14 | -10 | 20 |
| Jerred Smithson, C | 82 | 5 | 8 | 13 | -6 | 34 |
| Mike Fisher, C | 27 | 5 | 7 | 12 | 2 | 10 |
| Matt Halischuk, RW | 27 | 4 | 8 | 12 | 5 | 2 |
| Francis Bouillon, D | 44 | 1 | 9 | 10 | -3 | 27 |
| Shane O'Brien, D | 80 | 2 | 7 | 9 | 1 | 83 |
| Blake Geoffrion, LW | 20 | 6 | 2 | 8 | 3 | 7 |
| Jonathon Blum, D | 23 | 3 | 5 | 8 | 8 | 4 |
| Alexander Sulzer, D | 31 | 1 | 3 | 4 | -5 | 14 |
| Marek Svatos, RW | 9 | 1 | 2 | 3 | 1 | 2 |
| Chris Mueller, C | 15 | 0 | 3 | 3 | 0 | 2 |
| Wade Belak, RW | 15 | 0 | 0 | 0 | -1 | 18 |
| Steve Begin, LW | 2 | 0 | 0 | 0 | -2 | 4 |
| Matthew Lombardi, C | 2 | 0 | 0 | 0 | -1 | 0 |

### GOALTENDING

| Player | GP | Mins | W | L | TGA | GAA | SO |
|---|---|---|---|---|---|---|---|
| Pekka Rinne | 64 | 3789 | 33 | 22 | 134 | 2.12 | 6 |
| Anders Lindback | 22 | 1131 | 11 | 5 | 49 | 2.60 | 2 |
| Mark Dekanich | 1 | 50 | 0 | 0 | 3 | 3.60 | 0 |

## Montreal Canadiens

### SCORING

| Player | GP | G | Ast | Pts | +/- | PM |
|---|---|---|---|---|---|---|
| Tomas Plekanec, C | 77 | 22 | 35 | 57 | 8 | 60 |
| Michael Cammalleri, LW | 67 | 19 | 28 | 47 | 2 | 33 |
| Brian Gionta, RW | 82 | 29 | 17 | 46 | 3 | 24 |
| Andrei Kostitsyn, LW | 81 | 20 | 25 | 45 | 3 | 36 |
| Scott Gomez, C | 80 | 7 | 31 | 38 | -15 | 48 |
| P.K. Subban, D | 77 | 14 | 24 | 38 | -8 | 124 |
| Roman Hamrlik, D | 79 | 5 | 29 | 34 | 6 | 81 |
| James Wisniewski, D | 43 | 7 | 23 | 30 | 4 | 20 |
| Benoit Pouliot, LW | 79 | 13 | 17 | 30 | 2 | 87 |
| Jeff Halpern, C | 72 | 11 | 15 | 26 | 6 | 29 |
| Mathieu Darche, LW | 59 | 12 | 14 | 26 | 7 | 10 |
| Max Pacioretty, LW | 37 | 14 | 10 | 24 | -1 | 39 |
| David Desharnais, C | 43 | 8 | 14 | 22 | -3 | 12 |
| Lars Eller, C | 77 | 7 | 10 | 17 | -4 | 48 |
| Jaroslav Spacek, D | 59 | 1 | 15 | 16 | 9 | 45 |
| Travis Moen, LW | 79 | 6 | 10 | 16 | -4 | 96 |
| Yannick Weber, D | 41 | 1 | 10 | 11 | 0 | 14 |
| Hal Gill, D | 75 | 2 | 7 | 9 | -9 | 43 |
| Maxim Lapierre, C | 38 | 5 | 3 | 8 | -7 | 63 |
| Alexandre Picard, D | 43 | 3 | 5 | 8 | 0 | 17 |
| Josh Gorges, D | 36 | 1 | 6 | 7 | -3 | 18 |
| Tom Pyatt, C | 61 | 2 | 5 | 7 | -1 | 9 |
| Ryan White, C | 27 | 2 | 3 | 5 | 5 | 38 |
| Paul Mara, D | 20 | 0 | 4 | 4 | 2 | 48 |

### GOALTENDING

| Player | GP | Mins | W | L | TGA | GAA | SO |
|---|---|---|---|---|---|---|---|
| Carey Price | 72 | 4206 | 38 | 28 | 165 | 2.35 | 8 |
| Alex Auld | 16 | 749 | 6 | 2 | 33 | 2.64 | 1 |

## New Jersey Devils

### SCORING

| Player | GP | G | Ast | Pts | +/- | PM |
|---|---|---|---|---|---|---|
| Patrik Elias, LW | 81 | 21 | 41 | 62 | -4 | 16 |
| Ilya Kovalchuk, LW | 81 | 31 | 29 | 60 | -26 | 28 |
| Travis Zajac, C | 82 | 13 | 31 | 44 | -6 | 24 |
| Brian Rolston, LW | 65 | 14 | 20 | 34 | -6 | 34 |
| Dainius Zubrus, C | 79 | 13 | 17 | 30 | -11 | 53 |
| Jason Arnott, C | 62 | 13 | 11 | 24 | -9 | 32 |
| Andy Greene, D | 82 | 4 | 19 | 23 | -23 | 22 |
| Mattias Tedenby, RW | 58 | 8 | 14 | 22 | 3 | 14 |
| David Clarkson, RW | 82 | 12 | 6 | 18 | -20 | 116 |
| Nick Palmieri, RW | 43 | 9 | 8 | 17 | 9 | 6 |
| Henrik Tallinder, D | 82 | 5 | 11 | 16 | -6 | 40 |
| J. Langenbrunner, RW | 31 | 4 | 10 | 14 | -15 | 16 |
| Mark Fayne, D | 57 | 4 | 10 | 14 | 10 | 27 |
| Rod Pelley, C | 74 | 3 | 7 | 10 | -9 | 27 |
| Jacob Josefson, C | 28 | 3 | 7 | 10 | 5 | 6 |
| Anton Volchenkov, D | 57 | 0 | 8 | 8 | 3 | 36 |
| Anssi Salmela, D | 48 | 1 | 6 | 7 | -11 | 14 |
| Colin White, D | 69 | 0 | 6 | 6 | -2 | 48 |
| Zach Parise, LW | 13 | 3 | 3 | 6 | -1 | 6 |
| Matthew Corrente, D | 22 | 0 | 6 | 6 | -5 | 44 |
| Alexander Vasyunov, LW | 18 | 1 | 4 | 5 | 0 | 0 |
| Matt Taormina, D | 17 | 3 | 2 | 5 | -2 | 2 |
| Adam Mair, C | 65 | 1 | 3 | 4 | -16 | 45 |
| Vladimir Zharkov, RW | 38 | 2 | 2 | 4 | 3 | 2 |
| Tim Sestito, C | 36 | 0 | 2 | 2 | -5 | 9 |
| Mark Fraser, D | 26 | 0 | 2 | 2 | 2 | 29 |
| David Steckel, C | 18 | 1 | 0 | 1 | -3 | 2 |

### GOALTENDING

| Player | GP | Mins | W | L | TGA | GAA | SO |
|---|---|---|---|---|---|---|---|
| Martin Brodeur | 56 | 3116 | 23 | 26 | 127 | 2.45 | 6 |
| Johan Hedberg | 34 | 1717 | 15 | 12 | 68 | 2.38 | 3 |
| Mike McKenna | 2 | 118 | 0 | 1 | 6 | 3.05 | 0 |

## New York Islanders

### SCORING

| Player | GP | G | Ast | Pts | +/- | PM |
|---|---|---|---|---|---|---|
| John Tavares, C | 79 | 29 | 38 | 67 | -16 | 53 |
| P. Parenteau, RW | 81 | 20 | 33 | 53 | -8 | 46 |
| Matt Moulson, LW | 82 | 31 | 22 | 53 | -10 | 24 |
| Michael Grabner, RW | 76 | 34 | 18 | 52 | 13 | 10 |
| Blake Comeau, LW | 77 | 24 | 22 | 46 | -17 | 43 |
| Frans Nielsen, C | 71 | 13 | 31 | 44 | 13 | 38 |
| Josh Bailey, C | 70 | 11 | 17 | 28 | -13 | 37 |
| Andrew MacDonald, D | 60 | 4 | 23 | 27 | 9 | 37 |
| Travis Hamonic, D | 62 | 5 | 21 | 26 | 4 | 103 |
| Rob Schremp, C | 45 | 10 | 12 | 22 | -19 | 12 |
| Jack Hillen, D | 64 | 4 | 18 | 22 | -5 | 45 |
| James Wisniewski, D | 32 | 3 | 18 | 21 | -18 | 18 |
| Kyle Okposo, RW | 38 | 5 | 15 | 20 | 3 | 40 |
| Milan Jurcina, D | 46 | 4 | 13 | 17 | -4 | 30 |
| Radek Martinek, D | 64 | 3 | 13 | 16 | -5 | 35 |
| Matt Martin, LW | 68 | 5 | 9 | 14 | -13 | 147 |
| Doug Weight, C | 18 | 2 | 7 | 9 | -3 | 10 |
| Zenon Konopka, C | 82 | 2 | 7 | 9 | -14 | 307 |
| Jesse Joensuu, LW | 42 | 6 | 3 | 9 | -6 | 33 |
| Bruno Gervais, D | 53 | 0 | 6 | 6 | -14 | 30 |
| Dylan Reese, D | 27 | 0 | 6 | 6 | -12 | 15 |
| Ty Wishart, D | 20 | 1 | 4 | 5 | 5 | 10 |
| Jon Sim, LW | 34 | 1 | 3 | 4 | -10 | 22 |

### GOALTENDING

| Player | GP | Mins | W | L | TGA | GAA | SO |
|---|---|---|---|---|---|---|---|
| Rick Dipietro | 26 | 1533 | 8 | 14 | 88 | 3.44 | 1 |
| Dwayne Roloson | 20 | 1206 | 6 | 13 | 53 | 2.64 | 0 |
| Al Montoya | 20 | 1154 | 9 | 5 | 46 | 2.39 | 1 |
| Kevin Poulin | 10 | 491 | 4 | 2 | 20 | 2.44 | 0 |
| Nathan Lawson | 10 | 384 | 1 | 4 | 26 | 4.06 | 0 |
| Mikko Koskinen | 4 | 208 | 2 | 1 | 15 | 4.33 | 0 |

## New York Rangers

### SCORING

| Player | GP | G | Ast | Pts | +/- | PM |
|---|---|---|---|---|---|---|
| Brandon Dubinsky, C | 77 | 24 | 30 | 54 | -3 | 100 |
| Marian Gaborik, RW | 62 | 22 | 26 | 48 | 8 | 18 |
| Ryan Callahan, RW | 60 | 23 | 25 | 48 | -7 | 46 |
| Derek Stepan, C | 82 | 21 | 24 | 45 | 8 | 20 |
| Artem Anisimov, C | 82 | 18 | 26 | 44 | 3 | 20 |
| Brian Boyle, C | 82 | 21 | 14 | 35 | 2 | 74 |
| Dan Girardi, D | 80 | 4 | 27 | 31 | 7 | 37 |
| Brandon Prust, LW | 82 | 13 | 16 | 29 | 2 | 160 |
| Marc Staal, D | 77 | 7 | 22 | 29 | 8 | 50 |
| Erik Christensen, C | 63 | 11 | 16 | 27 | 3 | 18 |
| Ruslan Fedotenko, LW | 66 | 10 | 15 | 25 | 9 | 25 |
| Sean Avery, LW | 76 | 3 | 21 | 24 | -4 | 174 |
| Vinny Prospal, C | 29 | 9 | 14 | 23 | 4 | 8 |
| Mats Zuccarello, LW | 42 | 6 | 17 | 23 | 3 | 4 |
| Wojtek Wolski, LW | 37 | 6 | 13 | 19 | 12 | 8 |
| Alex Frolov, LW | 43 | 7 | 9 | 16 | 4 | 8 |
| Michal Rozsival, D | 32 | 3 | 12 | 15 | 3 | 22 |
| Michael Sauer, D | 76 | 3 | 12 | 15 | 20 | 75 |
| Michael Del Zotto, D | 47 | 2 | 9 | 11 | -5 | 20 |
| Matt Gilroy, D | 58 | 3 | 8 | 11 | 5 | 14 |
| Ryan McDonagh, D | 40 | 1 | 8 | 9 | 16 | 14 |
| Bryan McCabe, D | 19 | 2 | 4 | 6 | -1 | 6 |
| Steve Eminger, D | 65 | 2 | 4 | 6 | -5 | 22 |
| Chris Drury, C | 24 | 1 | 4 | 5 | 2 | 8 |
| Todd White, C | 18 | 1 | 1 | 2 | -2 | 2 |

### GOALTENDING

| Player | GP | Mins | W | L | TGA | GAA | SO |
|---|---|---|---|---|---|---|---|
| Henrik Lundqvist | 68 | 4007 | 36 | 27 | 152 | 2.28 | 11 |
| Martin Biron | 17 | 928 | 8 | 6 | 33 | 2.13 | 0 |
| Chad Johnson | 1 | 20 | 0 | 0 | 2 | 6.00 | 0 |

## Ottawa Senators

### SCORING

| Player | GP | G | Ast | Pts | +/- | PM |
|---|---|---|---|---|---|---|
| Jason Spezza, C | 62 | 21 | 36 | 57 | -7 | 28 |
| Erik Karlsson, D | 75 | 13 | 32 | 45 | -30 | 50 |
| Nick Foligno, LW | 82 | 14 | 20 | 34 | -19 | 43 |
| Milan Michalek, LW | 66 | 18 | 15 | 33 | -12 | 49 |
| Daniel Alfredsson, RW | 54 | 14 | 17 | 31 | -19 | 18 |
| Alex Kovalev, RW | 54 | 14 | 13 | 27 | -9 | 28 |
| Sergei Gonchar, D | 67 | 7 | 20 | 27 | -15 | 20 |
| Ryan Shannon, RW | 79 | 11 | 16 | 27 | 3 | 24 |
| Mike Fisher, C | 55 | 14 | 10 | 24 | -19 | 33 |
| Chris Kelly, C | 57 | 12 | 11 | 23 | -12 | 27 |
| Bobby Butler, RW | 36 | 10 | 11 | 21 | -16 | 10 |
| Peter Regin, C | 55 | 3 | 14 | 17 | -4 | 12 |
| Filip Kuba, D | 64 | 2 | 14 | 16 | -26 | 16 |
| Chris Neil, RW | 80 | 6 | 10 | 16 | -14 | 210 |
| Chris Campoli, D | 58 | 3 | 11 | 14 | -3 | 34 |
| Colin Greening, C | 24 | 6 | 7 | 13 | 2 | 12 |
| Jesse Winchester, C | 72 | 4 | 9 | 13 | -9 | 42 |
| Erik Condra, RW | 26 | 6 | 5 | 11 | -1 | 12 |
| Jarkko Ruutu, LW | 50 | 1 | 9 | 10 | -2 | 59 |
| Chris Phillips, D | 82 | 1 | 8 | 9 | -35 | 32 |
| Zack Smith, C | 55 | 4 | 5 | 9 | -11 | 120 |
| Matt Carkner, D | 50 | 1 | 6 | 7 | 0 | 136 |
| David Hale, D | 25 | 1 | 4 | 5 | 7 | 6 |

### GOALTENDING

| Player | GP | Mins | W | L | TGA | GAA | SO |
|---|---|---|---|---|---|---|---|
| Brian Elliott | 43 | 2293 | 13 | 19 | 122 | 3.19 | 3 |
| Craig Anderson | 18 | 1055 | 11 | 5 | 36 | 2.05 | 2 |
| Pascal Leclaire | 14 | 763 | 4 | 7 | 36 | 2.83 | 0 |
| Curtis McElhinney | 7 | 399 | 3 | 4 | 17 | 2.56 | 0 |
| Robin Lehner | 8 | 341 | 1 | 4 | 20 | 3.52 | 0 |

## Philadelphia Flyers

### SCORING

| Player | GP | G | Ast | Pts | +/- | PM |
|---|---|---|---|---|---|---|
| Claude Giroux, RW | 82 | 25 | 51 | 76 | 20 | 47 |
| Danny Briere, RW | 77 | 34 | 34 | 68 | 20 | 87 |
| Jeff Carter, C | 80 | 36 | 30 | 66 | 27 | 39 |
| Mike Richards, C | 81 | 23 | 43 | 66 | 11 | 62 |
| Ville Leino, LW | 81 | 19 | 34 | 53 | 14 | 22 |
| Scott Hartnell, LW | 82 | 24 | 25 | 49 | 14 | 142 |
| Matt Carle, D | 82 | 1 | 39 | 40 | 30 | 23 |
| J. Van Riemsdyk, LW | 75 | 21 | 19 | 40 | 15 | 35 |
| Kimmo Timonen, D | 82 | 6 | 31 | 37 | 11 | 36 |
| Andrej Meszaros, D | 81 | 8 | 24 | 32 | 30 | 42 |
| Chris Pronger, D | 50 | 4 | 21 | 25 | 7 | 44 |
| Nikolay Zherdev, RW | 56 | 16 | 6 | 22 | 5 | 22 |
| Andreas Nodl, RW | 67 | 11 | 11 | 22 | 14 | 16 |
| Sean O'Donnell, D | 81 | 1 | 17 | 18 | 8 | 87 |
| Darroll Powe, C | 81 | 7 | 10 | 17 | -6 | 41 |
| Braydon Coburn, D | 82 | 2 | 14 | 16 | 15 | 53 |
| Blair Betts, C | 75 | 5 | 7 | 12 | -3 | 8 |
| Kris Versteeg, RW | 27 | 7 | 4 | 11 | 4 | 24 |
| Daniel Carcillo, LW | 57 | 4 | 2 | 6 | -14 | 127 |
| Jody Shelley, LW | 58 | 2 | 2 | 4 | 0 | 127 |
| Eric Wellwood, LW | 3 | 0 | 1 | 1 | 1 | 2 |
| Nick Boynton, D | 10 | 0 | 0 | 0 | -3 | 4 |
| Matt Walker, D | 4 | 0 | 0 | 0 | 0 | 4 |
| Danny Syvret, D | 4 | 0 | 0 | 0 | 0 | 2 |
| Oskars Bartulis, D | 13 | 0 | 0 | 0 | -4 | 4 |

### GOALTENDING

| Player | GP | Mins | W | L | TGA | GAA | SO |
|---|---|---|---|---|---|---|---|
| Sergei Bobrovsky | 54 | 3017 | 28 | 13 | 130 | 2.59 | 0 |
| Brian Boucher | 34 | 1885 | 18 | 10 | 76 | 2.42 | 0 |
| Michael Leighton | 1 | 60 | 1 | 0 | 4 | 4.00 | 0 |

## Phoenix Coyotes

### SCORING

| Player | GP | G | Ast | Pts | +/- | PM |
|---|---|---|---|---|---|---|
| Shane Doan, RW | 72 | 20 | 40 | 60 | 5 | 67 |
| Keith Yandle, D | 82 | 11 | 48 | 59 | 12 | 68 |
| Ray Whitney, LW | 75 | 17 | 40 | 57 | 0 | 24 |
| Radim Vrbata, RW | 79 | 19 | 29 | 48 | 5 | 20 |
| Eric Belanger, C | 82 | 13 | 27 | 40 | 11 | 36 |
| Lauri Korpikoski, LW | 79 | 19 | 21 | 40 | 17 | 20 |
| Lee Stempniak, RW | 82 | 19 | 19 | 38 | 4 | 19 |
| Taylor Pyatt, LW | 76 | 18 | 13 | 31 | 11 | 27 |
| Scottie Upshall, LW | 61 | 16 | 11 | 27 | 5 | 42 |
| Martin Hanzal, C | 61 | 16 | 10 | 26 | 4 | 54 |
| Kyle Turris, C | 65 | 11 | 14 | 25 | 0 | 16 |
| Adrian Aucoin, D | 75 | 3 | 19 | 22 | 18 | 52 |
| Vernon Fiddler, C | 71 | 6 | 16 | 22 | 3 | 46 |
| Derek Morris, D | 77 | 5 | 11 | 16 | -2 | 10 |
| Wojtek Wolski, LW | 36 | 6 | 10 | 16 | -6 | 10 |
| Ed Jovanovski, D | 50 | 5 | 9 | 14 | 4 | 39 |
| David Schlemko, D | 43 | 4 | 10 | 14 | 8 | 24 |
| Mikkel Boedker, RW | 34 | 4 | 10 | 14 | 11 | 8 |
| Sami Lepisto, D | 51 | 4 | 7 | 11 | 7 | 37 |
| Oliver Ekman-Larsson, D. | 48 | 1 | 10 | 11 | 3 | 24 |
| Michal Rozsival, D | 33 | 3 | 3 | 6 | 3 | 20 |
| Andrew Ebbett, C | 33 | 2 | 3 | 5 | -1 | 4 |
| Brett MacLean, LW | 13 | 2 | 1 | 3 | 0 | 2 |
| Nolan Yonkman, D | 16 | 0 | 1 | 1 | 5 | 39 |
| Rostislav Klesla, D | 16 | 1 | 0 | 1 | -6 | 12 |
| Petr Prucha, RW | 11 | 0 | 1 | 1 | 0 | 4 |
| Paul Bissonnette, LW | 48 | 1 | 0 | 1 | 6 | 71 |

### GOALTENDING

| Player | GP | Mins | W | L | TGA | GAA | SO |
|---|---|---|---|---|---|---|---|
| Ilya Bryzgalov | 68 | 4060 | 36 | 20 | 168 | 2.48 | 7 |
| Jason Labarbera | 17 | 883 | 7 | 6 | 48 | 3.26 | 2 |
| Matt Climie | 1 | 32 | 0 | 0 | 1 | 1.88 | 0 |

## Pittsburgh Penguins

### SCORING

| Player | GP | G | Ast | Pts | +/- | PM |
|---|---|---|---|---|---|---|
| Sidney Crosby, C | 41 | 32 | 34 | 66 | 20 | 31 |
| Kris Letang, D | 82 | 8 | 42 | 50 | 15 | 101 |
| Chris Kunitz, LW | 66 | 23 | 25 | 48 | 18 | 47 |
| Tyler Kennedy, C | 80 | 21 | 24 | 45 | 1 | 37 |
| Pascal Dupuis, RW | 81 | 17 | 20 | 37 | 16 | 59 |
| Evgeni Malkin, C | 43 | 15 | 22 | 37 | -4 | 18 |
| Alex Goligoski, D | 60 | 9 | 22 | 31 | 20 | 28 |
| Matt Cooke, LW | 67 | 12 | 18 | 30 | 14 | 129 |
| Jordan Staal, C | 42 | 11 | 19 | 30 | 7 | 24 |
| Mark Letestu, C | 64 | 14 | 13 | 27 | 4 | 13 |
| Paul Martin, D | 77 | 3 | 21 | 24 | 9 | 16 |
| Maxime Talbot, C | 82 | 8 | 13 | 21 | -3 | 66 |
| Zbynek Michalek, D | 73 | 5 | 14 | 19 | 0 | 30 |
| Mike Rupp, C | 81 | 9 | 8 | 17 | -4 | 124 |
| Ben Lovejoy, D | 47 | 3 | 14 | 17 | 11 | 48 |
| Chris Conner, RW | 60 | 7 | 9 | 16 | 5 | 10 |
| Craig Adams, RW | 80 | 4 | 11 | 15 | -5 | 76 |
| Brooks Orpik, D | 63 | 1 | 12 | 13 | 12 | 66 |
| Dustin Jeffrey, LW | 25 | 7 | 5 | 12 | 5 | 4 |
| Arron Asham, RW | 44 | 5 | 6 | 11 | 0 | 46 |
| Deryk Engelland, D | 63 | 3 | 7 | 10 | -5 | 123 |
| Alex Kovalev, RW | 20 | 2 | 5 | 7 | 3 | 16 |
| Mike Comrie, C | 21 | 1 | 5 | 6 | -4 | 18 |
| James Neal, LW | 20 | 1 | 5 | 6 | -1 | 6 |
| Brett Sterling, LW | 7 | 3 | 2 | 5 | 1 | 16 |
| Matt Niskanen, D | 18 | 1 | 3 | 4 | -2 | 20 |
| Eric Godard, RW | 19 | 0 | 3 | 3 | 4 | 105 |
| Eric Tangradi, LW | 15 | 1 | 2 | 3 | -4 | 10 |

### GOALTENDING

| Player | GP | Mins | W | L | TGA | GAA | SO |
|---|---|---|---|---|---|---|---|
| Marc-Andre Fleury | 65 | 3695 | 36 | 20 | 143 | 2.32 | 3 |
| Brent Johnson | 23 | 1297 | 13 | 5 | 47 | 2.17 | 1 |

## San Jose Sharks

### SCORING

| Player | GP | G | Ast | Pts | +/- | PM |
|---|---|---|---|---|---|---|
| Patrick Marleau, LW | 82 | 37 | 36 | 73 | -3 | 16 |
| Joe Thornton, C | 80 | 21 | 49 | 70 | 4 | 47 |
| Joe Pavelski, C | 74 | 20 | 46 | 66 | 10 | 24 |
| Dany Heatley, RW | 80 | 26 | 38 | 64 | 8 | 56 |
| Ryane Clowe, LW | 75 | 24 | 38 | 62 | 13 | 100 |
| Logan Couture, C | 79 | 32 | 24 | 56 | 18 | 41 |
| Dan Boyle, D | 76 | 9 | 41 | 50 | 2 | 67 |
| Devin Setoguchi, RW | 72 | 22 | 19 | 41 | -2 | 37 |
| Jason Demers, D | 75 | 2 | 22 | 24 | 19 | 28 |
| Torrey Mitchell, C | 66 | 9 | 14 | 23 | 10 | 46 |
| Marc-Ed. Vlasic, D | 80 | 4 | 14 | 18 | 14 | 18 |
| Jamal Mayers, RW | 78 | 3 | 11 | 14 | 3 | 124 |
| Douglas Murray, D | 73 | 1 | 13 | 14 | 5 | 44 |
| Kyle Wellwood, C | 35 | 5 | 8 | 13 | 10 | 0 |
| Justin Braun, D | 28 | 2 | 9 | 11 | -1 | 2 |
| Kent Huskins, D | 50 | 2 | 8 | 10 | 8 | 12 |
| Ian White, D | 23 | 2 | 8 | 10 | 9 | 8 |
| Benn Ferriero, C | 33 | 5 | 4 | 9 | 8 | 9 |

### SCORING *(CONT.)*

| Player | GP | G | Ast | Pts | +/- | PM |
|---|---|---|---|---|---|---|
| Niclas Wallin, D | 74 | 3 | 5 | 8 | 0 | 46 |
| Scott Nichol, C | 56 | 4 | 3 | 7 | -3 | 50 |
| Ben Eager, LW | 34 | 4 | 3 | 7 | 0 | 43 |
| Jamie McGinn, LW | 49 | 1 | 5 | 6 | -6 | 33 |
| Derek Joslin, D | 17 | 1 | 3 | 4 | -2 | 8 |
| John McCarthy, LW | 37 | 2 | 2 | 4 | -8 | 8 |
| Andrew Desjardins, C. | 17 | 1 | 2 | 3 | -1 | 4 |
| Mike Moore, D | 6 | 1 | 0 | 1 | -1 | 7 |
| Frazer McLaren, LW | 9 | 0 | 0 | 0 | -1 | 22 |
| Tommy Wingels, C | 5 | 0 | 0 | 0 | -1 | 0 |
| Brandon Mashinter, C. | 13 | 0 | 0 | 0 | -2 | 17 |

### GOALTENDING

| Player | GP | Mins | W | L | TGA | GAA | SO |
|---|---|---|---|---|---|---|---|
| Antti Niemi | 60 | 3524 | 35 | 18 | 140 | 2.38 | 6 |
| Antero Niittymaki | 24 | 1414 | 12 | 7 | 64 | 2.72 | 0 |
| Alex Stalock | 1 | 30 | 1 | 0 | 0 | 0.00 | 0 |

## St. Louis Blues

### SCORING

| Player | GP | G | Ast | Pts | +/- | PM |
|---|---|---|---|---|---|---|
| David Backes, RW | 82 | 31 | 31 | 62 | 32 | 93 |
| Patrik Berglund, C | 81 | 22 | 30 | 52 | -3 | 26 |
| Alexander Steen, C | 72 | 20 | 31 | 51 | -3 | 26 |
| Andy McDonald, C | 58 | 20 | 30 | 50 | 18 | 26 |
| Matt D'Agostini, RW | 82 | 21 | 25 | 46 | 8 | 40 |
| Alex Pietrangelo, D | 79 | 11 | 32 | 43 | 18 | 19 |
| Brad Boyes, C | 62 | 12 | 29 | 41 | 11 | 30 |
| T.J. Oshie, C | 49 | 12 | 22 | 34 | 10 | 15 |
| Vladimir Sobotka, C | 65 | 7 | 22 | 29 | -4 | 69 |
| Carlo Colaiacovo, D | 65 | 6 | 20 | 26 | -4 | 23 |
| Chris Stewart, RW | 26 | 15 | 8 | 23 | 4 | 15 |
| Erik Johnson, D | 55 | 5 | 14 | 19 | -8 | 37 |
| Kevin Shattenkirk, D | 26 | 2 | 15 | 17 | 7 | 16 |
| Jay McClement, C | 56 | 6 | 10 | 16 | -13 | 18 |
| Eric Brewer, D | 54 | 8 | 6 | 14 | 1 | 57 |
| Brad Winchester, LW | 57 | 9 | 5 | 14 | -9 | 86 |
| B.J. Crombeen, RW | 80 | 7 | 7 | 14 | -18 | 154 |
| Barret Jackman, D | 60 | 0 | 13 | 13 | 3 | 57 |
| Roman Polak, D | 55 | 3 | 9 | 12 | -4 | 33 |
| Nikita Nikitin, D | 41 | 1 | 8 | 9 | 1 | 10 |
| Chris Porter, C | 45 | 3 | 4 | 7 | -4 | 16 |
| Adam Cracknell, RW | 24 | 3 | 4 | 7 | 1 | 8 |
| David Perron, LW | 10 | 5 | 2 | 7 | 7 | 12 |
| Cam Janssen, RW | 54 | 1 | 3 | 4 | -6 | 131 |
| Ryan Reaves, RW | 28 | 2 | 2 | 4 | -1 | 78 |
| Ian Cole, D | 26 | 1 | 3 | 4 | 6 | 35 |
| Nathan Oystrick, D | 9 | 1 | 2 | 3 | 1 | 9 |
| T.J. Hensick, C | 13 | 1 | 2 | 3 | -5 | 2 |
| Philip McRae, C | 15 | 1 | 2 | 3 | -10 | 2 |

### GOALTENDING

| Player | GP | Mins | W | L | TGA | GAA | SO |
|---|---|---|---|---|---|---|---|
| Jaroslav Halak | 57 | 3294 | 27 | 21 | 136 | 2.48 | 7 |
| Ty Conklin | 25 | 1285 | 8 | 8 | 69 | 3.22 | 2 |
| Ben Bishop | 7 | 369 | 3 | 4 | 17 | 2.76 | 1 |

## Tampa Bay Lightning

### SCORING

| Player | GP | G | Ast | Pts | +/- | PM |
|---|---|---|---|---|---|---|
| Martin St Louis, RW | 82 | 31 | 68 | 99 | 0 | 12 |
| Steven Stamkos, C | 82 | 45 | 46 | 91 | 3 | 74 |
| Vincent Lecavalier, C | 65 | 25 | 29 | 54 | -5 | 43 |
| Teddy Purcell, RW | 81 | 17 | 34 | 51 | 5 | 10 |
| Simon Gagne, LW | 63 | 17 | 23 | 40 | -12 | 20 |
| Ryan Malone, LW | 54 | 14 | 24 | 38 | -3 | 51 |
| Dominic Moore, C | 77 | 18 | 14 | 32 | -12 | 52 |
| Steve Downie, RW | 57 | 10 | 22 | 32 | 8 | 171 |
| Brett Clark, D | 82 | 9 | 22 | 31 | 2 | 14 |
| Sean Bergenheim, LW | 80 | 14 | 15 | 29 | 0 | 56 |
| Victor Hedman, D | 79 | 3 | 23 | 26 | 3 | 70 |
| Nate Thompson, C | 79 | 10 | 15 | 25 | -6 | 29 |
| Pavel Kubina, D | 79 | 4 | 19 | 23 | 2 | 62 |
| Adam Hall, RW | 82 | 7 | 11 | 18 | -12 | 32 |
| Dana Tyrell, C | 78 | 6 | 9 | 15 | -5 | 12 |
| Randy Jones, D | 61 | 1 | 12 | 13 | -4 | 15 |
| Mike Lundin, D | 69 | 1 | 11 | 12 | -3 | 12 |
| Marc-Andre Bergeron, D | 23 | 2 | 6 | 8 | -10 | 8 |
| Mattias Ritola, C | 31 | 4 | 4 | 8 | -5 | 11 |
| Mattias Ohlund, D | 72 | 0 | 5 | 5 | -7 | 70 |
| Blair Jones, C | 18 | 1 | 2 | 3 | -2 | 2 |
| Johan Harju, LW | 10 | 1 | 2 | 3 | -2 | 2 |
| Eric Brewer, D | 22 | 1 | 1 | 2 | 5 | 24 |
| Michael Vernace, D | 10 | 0 | 1 | 1 | -2 | 2 |
| Marc-Antoine Pouliot, C | 3 | 0 | 0 | 0 | -2 | 0 |
| Matt Smaby, D | 32 | 0 | 0 | 0 | 2 | 17 |
| Mathieu Roy, D | 4 | 0 | 0 | 0 | -2 | 2 |
| James Wright, C | 1 | 0 | 0 | 0 | -2 | 0 |

### GOALTENDING

| Player | GP | Mins | W | L | TGA | GAA | SO |
|---|---|---|---|---|---|---|---|
| Dwayne Roloson | 34 | 1993 | 18 | 12 | 85 | 2.56 | 4 |
| Dan Ellis | 31 | 1679 | 13 | 7 | 82 | 2.93 | 2 |
| Mike Smith | 22 | 1202 | 13 | 6 | 58 | 2.90 | 1 |
| Cedrick Desjardins | 2 | 120 | 2 | 0 | 2 | 1.00 | 0 |

## Toronto Maple Leafs

### SCORING

| Player | GP | G | Ast | Pts | +/- | PM |
|---|---|---|---|---|---|---|
| Phil Kessel, RW | 82 | 32 | 32 | 64 | -20 | 24 |
| Clarke MacArthur, LW | 82 | 21 | 41 | 62 | -3 | 37 |
| Mikhail Grabovski, C | 81 | 29 | 29 | 58 | 14 | 60 |
| Nikolai Kulemin, LW | 82 | 30 | 27 | 57 | 7 | 26 |
| Tomas Kaberle, D | 58 | 3 | 35 | 38 | -2 | 16 |
| Kris Versteeg, RW | 53 | 14 | 21 | 35 | -13 | 29 |
| Tyler Bozak, C | 82 | 15 | 17 | 32 | -29 | 14 |
| Dion Phaneuf, D | 66 | 8 | 22 | 30 | -2 | 88 |
| Colby Armstrong, RW | 50 | 8 | 15 | 23 | -1 | 38 |
| Luke Schenn, D | 82 | 5 | 17 | 22 | -7 | 34 |
| Tim Brent, C | 79 | 8 | 12 | 20 | -4 | 33 |
| Carl Gunnarsson, D | 68 | 4 | 16 | 20 | -2 | 14 |
| Joffrey Lupul, RW | 28 | 9 | 9 | 18 | -7 | 19 |
| Joey Crabb, RW | 48 | 3 | 12 | 15 | -1 | 24 |
| Darryl Boyce, LW | 46 | 5 | 8 | 13 | 8 | 33 |
| Francois Beauchemin, D | 54 | 2 | 10 | 12 | -4 | 16 |
| Nazem Kadri, C | 29 | 3 | 9 | 12 | -3 | 8 |
| Mike Komisarek, D | 75 | 1 | 9 | 10 | -8 | 86 |
| Mike Brown, RW | 50 | 3 | 5 | 8 | 1 | 69 |
| Fredrik Sjostrom, LW | 66 | 2 | 3 | 5 | -5 | 14 |

### SCORING *(CONT.)*

| Player | GP | G | Ast | Pts | +/- | PM |
|---|---|---|---|---|---|---|
| Brett Lebda, D | 41 | 1 | 3 | 4 | -14 | 14 |
| John Mitchell, C | 23 | 2 | 1 | 3 | -7 | 12 |
| Jay Rosehill, LW | 26 | 1 | 2 | 3 | -6 | 71 |
| Colton Orr, RW | 46 | 2 | 0 | 2 | -1 | 128 |
| Keith Aulie, D | 40 | 2 | 0 | 2 | -1 | 32 |
| Michael Zigomanis, C | 8 | 0 | 1 | 1 | 0 | 4 |
| Matt Lashoff, D | 11 | 0 | 1 | 1 | 1 | 6 |
| Joe Colborne, C | 1 | 0 | 1 | 1 | 1 | 0 |
| Korbinian Holzer, D | 2 | 0 | 0 | 0 | -1 | 2 |
| Luca Caputi, LW | 7 | 0 | 0 | 0 | -2 | 4 |
| Matt Frattin, RW | 1 | 0 | 0 | 0 | -1 | 0 |
| Christian Hanson, C | 6 | 0 | 0 | 0 | 0 | 4 |
| Marcel Mueller, C | 3 | 0 | 0 | 0 | 0 | 2 |

### GOALTENDING

| Player | GP | Mins | W | L | TGA | GAA | SO |
|---|---|---|---|---|---|---|---|
| James Reimer | 37 | 2080 | 20 | 10 | 90 | 2.60 | 3 |
| Jean-Seb. Giguere | 33 | 1633 | 11 | 11 | 78 | 2.87 | 0 |
| Jonas Gustavsson | 23 | 1242 | 6 | 13 | 68 | 3.29 | 0 |

## Vancouver Canucks

### SCORING

| Player | GP | G | Ast | Pts | +/- | PM |
|---|---|---|---|---|---|---|
| Daniel Sedin, LW | 82 | 41 | 63 | 104 | 30 | 32 |
| Henrik Sedin, C | 82 | 19 | 75 | 94 | 26 | 40 |
| Ryan Kesler, C | 82 | 41 | 32 | 73 | 24 | 66 |
| Mikael Samuelsson, RW | 75 | 18 | 32 | 50 | 8 | 36 |
| Christian Ehrhoff, D | 79 | 14 | 36 | 50 | 19 | 52 |
| Alexandre Burrows, LW | 72 | 26 | 22 | 48 | 26 | 77 |
| Mason Raymond, LW | 70 | 15 | 24 | 39 | 8 | 10 |
| Alexander Edler, D | 51 | 8 | 25 | 33 | 13 | 24 |
| Manny Malhotra, C | 72 | 11 | 19 | 30 | 9 | 22 |
| Raffi Torres, LW | 80 | 14 | 15 | 29 | 4 | 78 |
| Jannik Hansen, RW | 82 | 9 | 20 | 29 | 13 | 32 |
| Dan Hamhuis, D | 64 | 6 | 17 | 23 | 29 | 34 |
| Kevin Bieksa, D | 66 | 6 | 16 | 22 | 32 | 73 |
| Jeff Tambellini, LW | 62 | 9 | 8 | 17 | 10 | 18 |
| Tanner Glass, LW | 73 | 3 | 7 | 10 | -5 | 72 |
| Sami Salo, D | 27 | 3 | 4 | 7 | -3 | 14 |
| Andrew Alberts, D | 42 | 1 | 6 | 7 | 0 | 41 |
| Keith Ballard, D | 65 | 2 | 5 | 7 | 10 | 53 |

### SCORING

| Player | GP | G | Ast | Pts | +/- | PM |
|---|---|---|---|---|---|---|
| Chris Higgins, LW | 14 | 2 | 3 | 5 | 0 | 6 |
| Aaron Rome, D | 56 | 1 | 4 | 5 | 1 | 53 |
| Alexandre Bolduc, C | 24 | 2 | 2 | 4 | 1 | 21 |
| Victor Oreskovich, RW | 16 | 0 | 3 | 3 | 1 | 8 |
| Peter Schaefer, LW | 16 | 1 | 1 | 2 | -3 | 2 |
| Lee Sweatt, D | 3 | 1 | 1 | 2 | 4 | 2 |
| Cody Hodgson, C | 8 | 1 | 1 | 2 | 1 | 0 |
| Aaron Volpatti, LW | 15 | 1 | 1 | 2 | -1 | 16 |
| Maxim Lapierre, C | 19 | 1 | 0 | 1 | -1 | 8 |
| Rick Rypien, C | 9 | 0 | 1 | 1 | -5 | 31 |
| Mario Bliznak, C | 4 | 1 | 0 | 1 | 1 | 0 |
| Sergei Shirokov, RW | 2 | 1 | 0 | 1 | 1 | 0 |
| Christopher Tanev, D | 29 | 0 | 1 | 1 | 0 | 0 |

### GOALTENDING

| Player | GP | Mins | W | L | TGA | GAA | SO |
|---|---|---|---|---|---|---|---|
| Roberto Luongo | 60 | 3590 | 38 | 15 | 126 | 2.11 | 4 |
| Cory Schneider | 25 | 1372 | 16 | 4 | 51 | 2.23 | 1 |

## Washington Capitals

### SCORING

| Player | GP | G | Ast | Pts | +/- | PM |
|---|---|---|---|---|---|---|
| Alex Ovechkin, LW | 79 | 32 | 53 | 85 | 24 | 41 |
| Nicklas Backstrom, C | 77 | 18 | 47 | 65 | 24 | 40 |
| Alexander Semin, LW | 65 | 28 | 26 | 54 | 22 | 71 |
| Brooks Laich, C | 82 | 16 | 32 | 48 | 14 | 46 |
| Mike Knuble, RW | 79 | 24 | 16 | 40 | 10 | 36 |
| John Carlson, D | 82 | 7 | 30 | 37 | 21 | 44 |
| Marcus Johansson, C | 69 | 13 | 14 | 27 | 2 | 10 |
| Jason Chimera, LW | 81 | 10 | 16 | 26 | -10 | 64 |
| Matt Hendricks, C | 77 | 9 | 16 | 25 | -2 | 110 |
| Mike Green, D | 49 | 8 | 16 | 24 | 6 | 48 |
| Eric Fehr, RW | 52 | 10 | 10 | 20 | 0 | 16 |
| Mathieu Perreault, C | 35 | 7 | 7 | 14 | -3 | 20 |
| Karl Alzner, D | 82 | 2 | 10 | 12 | 14 | 24 |
| Matt Bradley, RW | 61 | 4 | 7 | 11 | -3 | 68 |
| John Erskine, D | 73 | 4 | 7 | 11 | 1 | 94 |
| David Steckel, LW | 57 | 5 | 6 | 11 | -3 | 24 |
| Tomas Fleischmann, C | 23 | 4 | 6 | 10 | 3 | 10 |
| Jeff Schultz, D | 72 | 1 | 9 | 10 | 6 | 12 |
| Boyd Gordon, RW | 60 | 3 | 6 | 9 | -5 | 16 |

### SCORING

| Player | GP | G | Ast | Pts | +/- | PM |
|---|---|---|---|---|---|---|
| Jason Arnott, C | 11 | 4 | 3 | 7 | 3 | 8 |
| Marco Sturm, LW | 18 | 1 | 6 | 7 | 0 | 6 |
| Tom Poti, D | 21 | 2 | 5 | 7 | -4 | 8 |
| Dennis Wideman, D | 14 | 1 | 6 | 7 | 7 | 6 |
| Tyler Sloan, D | 33 | 1 | 5 | 6 | -6 | 14 |
| Scott Hannan, D | 55 | 1 | 4 | 5 | 3 | 28 |
| Jay Beagle, RW | 31 | 2 | 1 | 3 | -2 | 8 |
| D.J. King, LW | 16 | 0 | 2 | 2 | -3 | 30 |
| Andrew Gordon, RW | 9 | 1 | 1 | 2 | -2 | 0 |
| Brian Willsie, RW | 1 | 0 | 1 | 1 | 0 | 0 |
| Brian Fahey, D | 7 | 0 | 1 | 1 | -1 | 2 |
| Sean Collins, D | 4 | 1 | 0 | 1 | 2 | 0 |
| Keith Aucoin, RW | 1 | 0 | 0 | 0 | 0 | 0 |

### GOALTENDING

| Player | GP | Mins | W | L | TGA | GAA | SO |
|---|---|---|---|---|---|---|---|
| Michal Neuvirth | 48 | 2689 | 27 | 12 | 110 | 2.45 | 4 |
| Semyon Varlamov | 27 | 1560 | 11 | 9 | 58 | 2.23 | 2 |
| Braden Holtby | 14 | 736 | 10 | 2 | 22 | 1.79 | 2 |

# 2011 NHL Draft

## First Round

The opening round of the 2011 NHL entry draft was held on June 24 in Minneapolis, Minnesota.

| Team | Selection | Position |
|---|---|---|
| 1. Edmonton | Ryan Nugent-Hopkins | C |
| 2. Colorado | Gabriel Landeskog | LW |
| 3. Florida | Jonathan Huberdeau | C |
| 4. New Jersey | Adam Larsson | D |
| 5. NY Islanders | Ryan Strome | C |
| 6. Ottawa | Mika Zibanejad | C |
| 7. Winnipeg | Mark Scheifele | C |
| 8. Philadelphia | Sean Couturier | C |
| 9. Boston | Dougie Hamilton | D |
| 10. Minnesota | Jonas Brodin | D |
| 11. Colorado | Duncan Siemens | D |
| 12. Carolina | Ryan Murphy | D |
| 13. Calgary | Sven Baertschi | LW |
| 14. Dallas | Jamie Oleksiak | D |
| 15. NY Rangers | J.T. Miller | C |

| Team | Selection | Position |
|---|---|---|
| 16. Buffalo | Joel Armia | RW |
| 17. Montreal | Nathan Beaulieu | D |
| 18. Chicago | Mark McNeill | C |
| 19. Edmonton | Oscar Klefbom | D |
| 20. Phoenix | Connor Murphy | D |
| 21. Ottawa | Stefan Noesen | RW |
| 22. Toronto | Tyler Biggs | RW |
| 23. Pittsburgh | Joseph Morrow | D |
| 24. Ottawa | Matt Puempel | LW |
| 25. Toronot | Stuart Percy | D |
| 26. Chicago | Phillip Danault | LW |
| 27. Tampa Bay | Vladislav Namestnikov | C |
| 28. Minnesota | Zack Phillips | C |
| 29. Vancouver | Nicklas Jensen | L/RW |
| 30. Anaheim | Rickard Rakell | RW |

## The Stanley Cup

Awarded annually to the team that wins the NHL's best-of-seven final-round playoffs. The Stanley Cup is the oldest trophy competed for by professional athletes in North America. It was donated in 1893 by Frederick Arthur, Lord Stanley of Preston.

### Results

| | |
|---|---|
| 1892–93 | Montreal A.A.A. |
| 1893–94 | Montreal A.A.A. |
| 1894–95 | Montreal Victorias |
| 1895–96 | Winnipeg Victorias (Feb) |
| 1895–96 | Montreal Victorias (Dec) |
| 1896–97 | Montreal Victorias |
| 1897–98 | Montreal Victorias |
| 1898–99 | Montreal Victorias (Feb) |
| 1898–99 | Montreal Shamrocks (Mar) |
| 1899–1900 | Montreal Shamrocks |
| 1900–01 | Winnipeg Victorias |
| 1901–02 | Winnipeg Victorias (Jan) |
| 1901–02 | Montreal A.A.A. (Mar) |
| 1902–03 | Montreal A.A.A. (Feb) |
| 1902–03 | Ottawa Silver Seven (Mar) |
| 1903–04 | Ottawa Silver Seven |
| 1904–05 | Ottawa Silver Seven |
| 1905–06 | Ottawa Silver Seven (Feb) |
| 1905–06 | Montreal Wanderers (Mar) |
| 1906–07 | Kenora Thistles (Jan) |
| 1906–07 | Montreal Wanderers (Mar) |
| 1907–08 | Montreal Wanderers |
| 1908–09 | Ottawa Senators |
| 1909–10 | Montreal Wanderers |
| 1910–11 | Ottawa Senators |
| 1911–12 | Quebec Bulldogs |
| 1912–13 | Quebec Bulldogs |
| 1913–14 | Toronto Blueshirts |
| 1914–15 | Vancouver Millionaires |
| 1915–16 | Montreal Canadiens |
| 1916–17 | Seattle Metropolitans |

### NHL WINNERS AND FINALISTS

| Season | Champion | Finalist | GP in Final |
|---|---|---|---|
| 1917–18 | Toronto Arenas | Vancouver Millionaires | 5 |
| 1918–19 | No decision* | No decision* | 5 |
| 1919–20 | Ottawa Senators | Seattle Metropolitans | 5 |
| 1920–21 | Ottawa Senators | Vancouver Millionaires | 5 |
| 1921–22 | Toronto St. Pats | Vancouver Millionaires | 5 |
| 1922–23 | Ottawa Senators | Vancouver Maroons, Edmonton Eskimos | 2, 4 |
| 1923–24 | Montreal Canadiens | Vancouver Maroons, Calgary Tigers | 2, 2 |
| 1924–25 | Victoria Cougars | Montreal Canadiens | 4 |
| 1925–26 | Montreal Maroons | Victoria Cougars | 4 |
| 1926–27 | Ottawa Senators | Boston Bruins | 4 |
| 1927–28 | New York Rangers | Montreal Maroons | 5 |
| 1928–29 | Boston Bruins | New York Rangers | 2 |
| 1929–30 | Montreal Canadiens | Boston Bruins | 2 |
| 1930–31 | Montreal Canadiens | Chicago Black Hawks | 5 |
| 1931–32 | Toronto Maple Leafs | New York Rangers | 3 |
| 1932–33 | New York Rangers | Toronto Maple Leafs | 4 |
| 1933–34 | Chicago Black Hawks | Detroit Red Wings | 4 |
| 1934–35 | Montreal Maroons | Toronto Maple Leafs | 3 |
| 1935–36 | Detroit Red Wings | Toronto Maple Leafs | 4 |
| 1936–37 | Detroit Red Wings | New York Rangers | 5 |
| 1937–38 | Chicago Black Hawks | Toronto Maple Leafs | 4 |
| 1938–39 | Boston Bruins | Toronto Maple Leafs | 5 |
| 1939–40 | New York Rangers | Toronto Maple Leafs | 6 |
| 1940–41 | Boston Bruins | Detroit Red Wings | 4 |
| 1941–42 | Toronto Maple Leafs | Detroit Red Wings | 7 |
| 1942–43 | Detroit Red Wings | Boston Bruins | 4 |
| 1943–44 | Montreal Canadiens | Chicago Black Hawks | 4 |
| 1944–45 | Toronto Maple Leafs | Detroit Red Wings | 7 |
| 1945–46 | Montreal Canadiens | Boston Bruins | 5 |
| 1946–47 | Toronto Maple Leafs | Montreal Canadiens | 6 |
| 1947–48 | Toronto Maple Leafs | Detroit Red Wings | 4 |
| 1948–49 | Toronto Maple Leafs | Detroit Red Wings | 4 |
| 1949–50 | Detroit Red Wings | New York Rangers | 7 |
| 1950–51 | Toronto Maple Leafs | Montreal Canadiens | 5 |
| 1951–52 | Detroit Red Wings | Montreal Canadiens | 4 |
| 1952–53 | Montreal Canadiens | Boston Bruins | 5 |
| 1953–54 | Detroit Red Wings | Montreal Canadiens | 7 |
| 1954–55 | Detroit Red Wings | Montreal Canadiens | 7 |

## NHL WINNERS AND FINALISTS

| Season | Champion | Finalist | GP in Final |
|---|---|---|---|
| 1955–56 | Montreal Canadiens | Detroit Red Wings | 5 |
| 1956–57 | Montreal Canadiens | Boston Bruins | 5 |
| 1957–58 | Montreal Canadiens | Boston Bruins | 6 |
| 1958–59 | Montreal Canadiens | Toronto Maple Leafs | 5 |
| 1959–60 | Montreal Canadiens | Toronto Maple Leafs | 4 |
| 1960–61 | Chicago Blackhawks | Detroit Red Wings | 6 |
| 1961–62 | Toronto Maple Leafs | Chicago Blackhawks | 6 |
| 1962–63 | Toronto Maple Leafs | Detroit Red Wings | 5 |
| 1963–64 | Toronto Maple Leafs | Detroit Red Wings | 7 |
| 1964–65 | Montreal Canadiens | Chicago Blackhawks | 7 |
| 1965–66 | Montreal Canadiens | Detroit Red Wings | 6 |
| 1966–67 | Toronto Maple Leafs | Montreal Canadiens | 6 |
| 1967–68 | Montreal Canadiens | St. Louis Blues | 4 |
| 1968–69 | Montreal Canadiens | St. Louis Blues | 4 |
| 1969–70 | Boston Bruins | St. Louis Blues | 4 |
| 1970–71 | Montreal Canadiens | Chicago Blackhawks | 7 |
| 1971–72 | Boston Bruins | New York Rangers | 6 |
| 1972–73 | Montreal Canadiens | Chicago Blackhawks | 6 |
| 1973–74 | Philadelphia Flyers | Boston Bruins | 6 |
| 1974–75 | Philadelphia Flyers | Buffalo Sabres | 6 |
| 1975–76 | Montreal Canadiens | Philadelphia Flyers | 4 |
| 1976–77 | Montreal Canadiens | Boston Bruins | 4 |
| 1977–78 | Montreal Canadiens | Boston Bruins | 6 |
| 1978–79 | Montreal Canadiens | New York Rangers | 5 |
| 1979–80 | New York Islanders | Philadelphia Flyers | 6 |
| 1980–81 | New York Islanders | Minnesota North Stars | 5 |
| 1981–82 | New York Islanders | Vancouver Canucks | 4 |
| 1982–83 | New York Islanders | Edmonton Oilers | 4 |
| 1983–84 | Edmonton Oilers | New York Islanders | 5 |
| 1984–85 | Edmonton Oilers | Philadelphia Flyers | 5 |
| 1985–86 | Montreal Canadiens | Calgary Flames | 5 |
| 1986–87 | Edmonton Oilers | Philadelphia Flyers | 7 |
| 1987–88 | Edmonton Oilers | Boston Bruins | 4 |
| 1988–89 | Calgary Flames | Montreal Canadiens | 6 |
| 1989–90 | Edmonton Oilers | Boston Bruins | 5 |
| 1990–91 | Pittsburgh Penguins | Minnesota North Stars | 6 |
| 1991–92 | Pittsburgh Penguins | Chicago Blackhawks | 4 |
| 1992–93 | Montreal Canadiens | Los Angeles Kings | 5 |
| 1993–94 | New York Rangers | Vancouver Canucks | 7 |
| 1994–95 | New Jersey Devils | Detroit Red Wings | 4 |
| 1995–96 | Colorado Avalanche | Florida Panthers | 4 |
| 1996–97 | Detroit Red Wings | Philadelphia Flyers | 4 |
| 1997–98 | Detroit Red Wings | Washington Capitals | 4 |
| 1998–99 | Dallas Stars | Buffalo Sabres | 6 |
| 1999–2000 | New Jersey Devils | Dallas Stars | 6 |
| 2000–01 | Colorado Avalanche | New Jersey Devils | 7 |
| 2001–02 | Detroit Red Wings | Carolina Hurricanes | 5 |
| 2002–03 | New Jersey Devils | Anaheim Mighty Ducks | 7 |
| 2003–04 | Tampa Bay Lightning | Calgary Flames | 7 |
| 2004–05 | No Stanley Cup due to season lockout | | |
| 2005–06 | Carolina Hurricanes | Edmonton Oilers | 7 |
| 2006–07 | Anaheim Ducks | Ottawa Senators | 5 |
| 2007–08 | Detroit Red Wings | Pittsburgh Penguins | 6 |
| 2008–09 | Pittsburgh Penguins | Detroit Red Wings | 7 |
| 2009–10 | Chicago Blackhawks | Philadelphia Flyers | 6 |
| 2010–11 | Boston Bruins | Vancouver Canucks | 7 |

*In 1919 the Montreal Canadiens traveled to meet Seattle, the PCHL champions. After five games had been played—the teams were tied at two wins and one tie—the series was called off by the local Department of Health because of the influenza epidemic and the death of Canadiens defenseman Joe Hall from influenza.

## Conn Smythe Trophy

Awarded to the Most Valuable Player of the Stanley Cup playoffs, as selected by the Professional Hockey Writers Association. The trophy is named after the former coach, general manager, president and owner of the Toronto Maple Leafs.

| | | | |
|---|---|---|---|
| 1965 | Jean Beliveau, Mtl | 1989 | Al MacInnis, Cgy |
| 1966 | Roger Crozier, Det | 1990 | Bill Ranford, Edm |
| 1967 | Dave Keon, Tor | 1991 | Mario Lemieux, Pit |
| 1968 | Glenn Hall, StL | 1992 | Mario Lemieux, Pit |
| 1969 | Serge Savard, Mtl | 1993 | Patrick Roy, Mtl |
| 1970 | Bobby Orr, Bos | 1994 | Brian Leetch, NYR |
| 1971 | Ken Dryden, Mtl | 1995 | Claude Lemieux, NJ |
| 1972 | Bobby Orr, Bos | 1996 | Joe Sakic, Col |
| 1973 | Yvan Cournoyer, Mtl | 1997 | Mike Vernon, Det |
| 1974 | Bernie Parent, Phi | 1998 | Steve Yzerman, Det |
| 1975 | Bernie Parent, Phi | 1999 | Joe Nieuwendyk, Dal |
| 1976 | Reggie Leach, Phi | 2000 | Scott Stevens, NJ |
| 1977 | Guy Lafleur, Mtl | 2001 | Patrick Roy, Col |
| 1978 | Larry Robinson, Mtl | 2002 | Nicklas Lidstrom, Det |
| 1979 | Bob Gainey, Mtl | 2003 | J.-S. Giguere, Ana |
| 1980 | Bryan Trottier, NYI | 2004 | Brad Richards, TB |
| 1981 | Butch Goring, NYI | 2005 | No Award–No Season |
| 1982 | Mike Bossy, NYI | 2006 | Cam Ward, Car |
| 1983 | Bill Smith, NYI | 2007 | Scott Niedermayer, Ana |
| 1984 | Mark Messier, Edm | 2008 | Henrik Zetterberg, Det |
| 1985 | Wayne Gretzky, Edm | 2009 | Evgeni Malkin, Pit |
| 1986 | Patrick Roy, Mtl | 2010 | Jonathan Toews, Chi |
| 1987 | Ron Hextall, Phi | 2011 | Tim Thomas, Bos |
| 1988 | Wayne Gretzky, Edm | | |

## Alltime Stanley Cup Playoff Leaders

### Points

| Playoff Seasons | GP | G | Ast | Pts | Playoff Seasons | GP | G | Ast | Pts |
|---|---|---|---|---|---|---|---|---|---|
| Wayne Gretzky, four teams .......16 | 208 | 122 | 260 | 382 | Jean Beliveau, Mtl .................17 | 162 | 79 | 97 | 176 |
| Mark Messier, Edm, Van, NYR...18 | 236 | 109 | 186 | 295 | Sergei Fedorov, Det, Wsh.......15 | 183 | 52 | 124 | 176 |
| Jari Kurri, four teams ...........15 | 200 | 106 | 127 | 233 | Denis Savard, Chi, Mtl............16 | 169 | 66 | 109 | 175 |
| Glenn Anderson, four teams.....15 | 225 | 93 | 121 | 214 | Mario Lemieux, Pit ..................8 | 107 | 76 | 96 | 172 |
| Paul Coffey, six teams ...........16 | 194 | 59 | 137 | 196 | Peter Forsberg, Que,Col,Phi...13 | 151 | 64 | 107 | 171 |
| Brett Hull, four teams ............19 | 202 | 103 | 87 | 190 | Denis Potvin, NYI....................14 | 185 | 56 | 108 | 164 |
| Doug Gilmour, seven teams.....18 | 182 | 60 | 128 | 188 | Mike Bossy, NYI.....................10 | 129 | 85 | 75 | 160 |
| Joe Sakic, Que, Col...............13 | 172 | 84 | 104 | 188 | Gordie Howe, Det, Hfd ...........20 | 157 | 68 | 92 | 160 |
| Steve Yzerman, Det...............20 | 196 | 70 | 115 | 185 | Bobby Smith, Min, Mtl............13 | 184 | 64 | 96 | 160 |
| Bryan Trottier, NYI, Pit..........17 | 221 | 71 | 113 | 184 | Al MacInnis, Cgy, StL ............19 | 177 | 39 | 121 | 160 |
| *Nicklas Lidstrom, Det...........19 | 258 | 54 | 129 | 183 | Claude Lemieux, six teams......18 | 234 | 80 | 77 | 157 |
| Jaromir Jagr, Pit, Wsh, NYR ...15 | 169 | 77 | 104 | 181 | Adam Oates, six teams .........15 | 163 | 42 | 114 | 156 |
| Ray Bourque, Bos, Col ..........21 | 214 | 41 | 139 | 180 | | | | | |

### Goals

| Playoff Seasons | GP | G |
|---|---|---|
| Wayne Gretzky, four teams ..........16 | 208 | 122 |
| Mark Messier, Edm, NYR .............18 | 236 | 109 |
| Jari Kurri, five teams ......................15 | 200 | 106 |
| Brett Hull, Cgy, StL, Dal, Det.........19 | 202 | 103 |
| Glenn Anderson, four teams..........15 | 225 | 93 |
| Mike Bossy, NYI ...........................10 | 129 | 85 |
| Joe Sakic, Que, Col......................13 | 172 | 84 |
| Maurice Richard, Mtl.....................15 | 133 | 82 |
| Claude Lemieux, six teams............18 | 234 | 80 |
| Jean Beliveau, Mtl.........................17 | 162 | 79 |
| Jaromir Jagr, Pit, Wsh, NYR..........15 | 169 | 77 |
| Mario Lemieux, Pitt .......................8 | 107 | 76 |
| Dino Ciccarelli, Min, Wsh, Det .....14 | 141 | 73 |
| Esa Tikkanen, five teams ..............13 | 186 | 72 |
| Bryan Trottier, NYI, Pit .................17 | 221 | 71 |
| Steve Yzerman, Det......................20 | 196 | 70 |
| Gordie Howe, Det, Hfd .................20 | 157 | 68 |
| Denis Savard, Chi Mtl ..................16 | 169 | 66 |
| Joe Nieuwendyk, Cgy, Dal, NJ, Tor...16 | 158 | 66 |
| Four tied with 64. | | |
| *Active in 2010–11. | | |

### Assists

| Playoff Seasons | GP | Ast |
|---|---|---|
| Wayne Gretzky, four teams ..........16 | 208 | 260 |
| Mark Messier, Edm, NYR .............18 | 236 | 186 |
| Ray Bourque, Bos, Col .................21 | 214 | 139 |
| Paul Coffey, six teams...................16 | 194 | 137 |
| *Nicklas Lidstrom, Det..................19 | 258 | 129 |
| Doug Gilmour, seven teams ..........18 | 182 | 128 |
| Jari Kurri, five teams .....................15 | 200 | 127 |
| Sergei Fedorov, Det, Wsh ............15 | 183 | 124 |
| Glenn Anderson, four teams..........15 | 225 | 121 |
| Al MacInnis, Cgy, StL....................19 | 177 | 121 |
| Larry Robinson, Mtl, LA ................20 | 227 | 116 |
| Steve Yzerman, Det......................20 | 196 | 115 |
| Lawrence Murphy, six teams.........20 | 215 | 115 |
| Adam Oates, six teams ................15 | 163 | 114 |
| Bryan Trottier, NYI, Pit .................17 | 221 | 113 |
| Chris Chelios, Mtl, Chi, Det...........24 | 266 | 113 |
| Denis Savard, Chi, Mtl ..................16 | 169 | 109 |
| Denis Potvin, NYI..........................14 | 185 | 108 |
| Peter Forsberg, Que, Col, Phi.......13 | 151 | 107 |
| Joe Sakic, Que, Col ......................13 | 172 | 104 |
| Jaromir Jagr, Pit, Wsh, NYR..........15 | 169 | 104 |

## Alltime Stanley Cup Playoff Goaltending Leaders

| WINS | W | L | Pct |
|---|---|---|---|
| Patrick Roy, Mtl, Col | 151 | 94 | .616 |
| *Martin Brodeur, NJ | 99 | 82 | .547 |
| Grant Fuhr, five teams | 92 | 50 | .648 |
| Billy Smith, LA, NYI | 88 | 36 | .710 |
| Ed Belfour, five teams | 88 | 68 | .564 |
| Ken Dryden, Mtl | 80 | 32 | .714 |
| Mike Vernon, four teams | 77 | 56 | .579 |
| *Chris Osgood, NYI, StL, Det | 74 | 49 | .602 |
| Jacques Plante, five teams | 71 | 36 | .663 |
| Andy Moog, four teams | 68 | 57 | .544 |
| Dominik Hasek, Chi, Buf, Det | 65 | 49 | .570 |
| Curtis Joseph, four teams | 63 | 66 | .488 |
| Tom Barrasso, Buf, Pit, Ott | 61 | 54 | .530 |
| Turk Broda, Tor | 60 | 39 | .606 |

*Active in 2010–11.

| SHUTOUTS | GP | W | SO |
|---|---|---|---|
| Patrick Roy, Mtl, Col | 247 | 151 | 23 |
| *Martin Brodeur, NJ | 181 | 99 | 23 |
| Curtis Joseph, four teams | 133 | 63 | 16 |
| *Chris Osgood, NYI, StL, Det | 129 | 74 | 15 |

| GOALS AGAINST AVG | Avg |
|---|---|
| George Hainsworth, Mtl, Tor | 1.93 |
| Turk Broda, Tor | 1.98 |
| *Martin Brodeur, NJ | 2.01 |
| Dominik Hasek, Chi, Buf, Det | 2.02 |
| *Jean-Sebastien Giguere, Ana | 2.08 |
| *Chris Osgood, NYI, StL, Det | 2.09 |
| Jacques Plante, Mtl, StL, Tor, Bos | 2.14 |

Note: At least 50 games played.
*Active in 2010–11.

## Alltime Stanley Cup Team Playoff Record, by Wins

| TEAM | W | L | Pct | TEAM | W | L | Pct |
|---|---|---|---|---|---|---|---|
| Montreal | 410 | 291 | .585 | Vancouver | 98 | 116 | .458 |
| Detroit | 312 | 273 | .533 | Calgary* | 94 | 114 | .452 |
| Boston | 273 | 290 | .485 | Washington | 86 | 105 | .450 |
| Toronto | 251 | 269 | .483 | San Jose | 76 | 82 | .481 |
| Pittsburgh | 221 | 195 | .531 | Los Angeles | 69 | 113 | .379 |
| Chicago | 216 | 236 | .478 | Carolina§ | 59 | 68 | .465 |
| Philadelphia | 209 | 193 | .520 | Anaheim | 55 | 43 | .561 |
| NY Rangers | 198 | 216 | .478 | Ottawa | 51 | 58 | .468 |
| Edmonton | 152 | 99 | .606 | Tampa Bay | 37 | 32 | .536 |
| Dallas# | 148 | 149 | .498 | Phoenix†† | 32 | 71 | .311 |
| St. Louis | 138 | 169 | .450 | Florida | 13 | 18 | .419 |
| Colorado** | 132 | 117 | .530 | Nashville | 13 | 22 | .371 |
| NY Islanders | 131 | 102 | .562 | Minnesota | 10 | 14 | .417 |
| Buffalo | 124 | 132 | .484 | Columbus | 0 | 4 | .000 |
| New Jersey† | 122 | 108 | .530 | | | | |

*Atlanta Flames 1972–80. †Colorado Rockies 1976–82, Kansas City Scouts 1974–76. #Minnesota North Stars 1967–93.
**Quebec Nordiques 1979–95. ††Winnipeg Jets 1979–96. §Hartford Whalers 1979–97.

## Stanley Cup Playoff Coaching Records

| Coach | Team | Plf Seas. | Series W | Series L | Games | W | L | T | Cups | Pct |
|---|---|---|---|---|---|---|---|---|---|---|
| Glen Sather | Edm | 10 | 27 | 21 | 6 | †126 | 89 | 37 | 0 | 4 | .706 |
| Toe Blake | Mtl | 13 | 23 | 18 | 5 | 119 | 82 | 37 | 0 | 8 | .689 |
| Scott Bowman | Five teams | 28 | 68 | 49 | 19 | 353 | 223 | 130 | 0 | 9 | .632 |
| *Mike Babcock | Ana, Det | 7 | 21 | 14 | 7 | 112 | 70 | 42 | 0 | 1 | .625 |
| Hap Day | Tor | 9 | 14 | 10 | 4 | 80 | 49 | 31 | 0 | 5 | .613 |
| Al Arbour | StL, NYI | 16 | 42 | 30 | 12 | 209 | 123 | 86 | 0 | 4 | .589 |
| Bob Hartley | Col, Atl | 5 | 14 | 10 | 4 | 84 | 49 | 35 | 0 | 1 | .583 |
| Fred Shero | Phi, NYR | 8 | 21 | 15 | 6 | 110 | 63 | 47 | 0 | 2 | .573 |
| *Lindy Ruff | Buf | 8 | 18 | 10 | 8 | 101 | 57 | 44 | 0 | 0 | .564 |
| Jacques Demers | StL, Det, Mtl | 8 | 18 | 11 | 7 | 98 | 55 | 43 | 0 | 1 | .561 |
| Mike Keenan | five teams | 13 | 30 | 18 | 12 | 173 | 96 | 77 | 0 | 1 | .555 |

*The column headers above: Coach, Team, Plf Seas., Series (W, L), Games (total), W, L, T, Cups, Pct*

†Does not include suspended game, May 24, 1988. *Active in 2010–11.
Note: Coaches ranked by winning percentage. Minimum: 65 games.

## The 10 Longest Overtime Games

| Date | Result | OT | Scorer | Series | Series Winner |
|---|---|---|---|---|---|
| 3-24-36 | Det 1 vs Mtl M 0 | 116:30 | Mud Bruneteau | SF | Det |
| 4-3-33 | Tor 1 vs Bos 0 | 104:46 | Ken Doraty | SF | Tor |
| 5-4-00 | Phi 2 vs Pit 1 | 92:01 | Keith Primeau | CSF | Phi |
| 4-24-03 | Ana 4 vs Dal 3 | 80:48 | Petr Sykora | CSF | Ana |
| 4-24-96 | Pit 3 vs Wsh 2 | 79:15 | Petr Nedved | CQF | Pit |
| 4-11-07 | Van 5 vs Dal 4 | 78:06 | Henrik Sedin | CQF | Van |
| 3-23-43 | Tor 3 vs Det 2 | 70:18 | Jack McLean | SF | Det |
| 5-4-08 | Dal 2 vs SJ 1 | 69:03 | Brenden Morrow | CSF | Dal |
| 3-28-30 | Mtl 2 vs NYR 1 | 68:52 | Gus Rivers | SF | Mtl |
| 4-18-87 | NYI 3 vs Wsh 2 | 68:47 | Pat LaFontaine | DSF | NYI |

### Hart Memorial Trophy

Awarded annually "to the player adjudged to be the most valuable to his team." The original trophy was donated by Dr. David A. Hart, father of Cecil Hart, former manager-coach of the Montreal Canadiens. In the 1980s Wayne Gretzky won the award nine times.

| Year | Winner | Key Statistics | Runner-Up |
|------|--------|----------------|-----------|
| 1924 | Frank Nighbor, Ott | 10 goals, 3 assists in 20 games | Sprague Cleghorn, Mtl |
| 1925 | Billy Burch, Ham | 20 goals, 4 assists in 27 games | Howie Morenz, Mtl |
| 1926 | Nels Stewart, Mtl M | 42 points in 36 games | Sprague Cleghorn, Mtl |
| 1927 | Herb Gardiner, Mtl | 12 points in 44 games as defenseman | Bill Cook, NYR |
| 1928 | Howie Morenz, Mtl | 33 goals, 18 assists | Roy Worters, Pitt |
| 1929 | Roy Worters, NYA | 1.21 goals against, 13 shutouts | Ace Bailey, Tor |
| 1930 | Nels Stewart, Mtl M | 39 goals, 16 assists | Lionel Hitchman, Bos |
| 1931 | Howie Morenz, Mtl | 28 goals, 23 assists | Eddie Shore, Bos |
| 1932 | Howie Morenz, Mtl | 24 goals, 25 assists | Ching Johnson, NYR |
| 1933 | Eddie Shore, Bos | 27 assists in 48 games as defenseman | Bill Cook, NYR |
| 1934 | Aurel Joliat, Mtl | 27 points | Lionel Conacher, Chi |
| 1935 | Eddie Shore, Bos | 26 assists in 48 games as defenseman | Charlie Conacher, Tor |
| 1936 | Eddie Shore, Bos | 16 assists in 46 games as defenseman | Hooley Smith, Mtl M |
| 1937 | Babe Siebert, Mtl | 28 points | Lionel Conacher, Mtl M |
| 1938 | Eddie Shore, Bos | 17 points in 47 games as defenseman | Paul Thompson, Chi |
| 1939 | Toe Blake, Mtl | led NHL in points (47) | Syl Apps, Tor |
| 1940 | Ebbie Goodfellow, Det | 28 points | Syl Apps, Tor |
| 1941 | Bill Cowley, Bos | led NHL in assists (45) and points (62) | Dit Clapper, Bos |
| 1942 | Tom Anderson, Bos | 41 points | Syl Apps, Tor |
| 1943 | Bill Cowley, Bos | led NHL in assists (45) | Doug Bentley, Chi |
| 1944 | Babe Pratt, Tor | 57 points in 50 games | Bill Cowley, Bos |
| 1945 | Elmer Lach, Mtl | led NHL in assists (54) and points (80) | Maurice Richard, Mtl |
| 1946 | Max Bentley, Chi | 61 points in 47 games | Gaye Stewart, Tor |
| 1947 | Maurice Richard, Mtl | led NHL in goals (45); 26 assists | Milt Schmidt, Bos |
| 1948 | Buddy O'Connor, NYR | 60 points in 60 games | Frank Brimsek, Bos |
| 1949 | Sid Abel, Det | 28 goals, 26 assists | Bill Durnan, Mtl |
| 1950 | Charlie Rayner, NYR | 6 shutouts | Ted Kennedy, Tor |
| 1951 | Milt Schmidt, Bos | 61 points in 62 games | Maurice Richard, Mtl |
| 1952 | Gordie Howe, Det | led NHL in goals (47) and points (86) | Elmer Lach, Mtl |
| 1953 | Gordie Howe, Det | led NHL in goals (49) and points (95) | Al Rollins, Chi |
| 1954 | Al Rollins, Chi | 5 shutouts | Red Kelly, Det |
| 1955 | Ted Kennedy, Tor | 52 points | Harry Lumley, Tor |
| 1956 | Jean Beliveau, Mtl | led NHL in goals (47) and points (88) | Tod Sloan, Tor |
| 1957 | Gordie Howe, Det | led NHL in goals (44) and points (89) | Jean Beliveau, Mtl |
| 1959 | Andy Bathgate, NYR | 74 points in 70 games | Gordie Howe, Det |
| 1960 | Gordie Howe, Det | 45 assists, 73 points | Bobby Hull, Chi |
| 1961 | Bernie Geoffrion, Mtl | 50 goals, 95 points | Johnny Bower, Tor |
| 1962 | Jacques Plante, Mtl | 42 wins, 2.37 goals against avg. | Doug Harvey, NYR |
| 1963 | Gordie Howe, Det | 47 assists, 73 points | Stan Mikita, Chi |
| 1964 | Jean Beliveau, Mtl | 50 assists, 78 points | Bobby Hull, Chi |
| 1965 | Bobby Hull, Chi | 39 goals, 32 assists | Norm Ullman, Det |
| 1966 | Bobby Hull, Chi | led NHL in goals (54) and points (97) | Jean Beliveau, Mtl |
| 1967 | Stan Mikita, Chi | led NHL in assists (62) and points (97) | Ed Giacomin, NYR |
| 1968 | Stan Mikita, Chi | 40 goals, 47 assists | Jean Beliveau, Mtl |
| 1969 | Phil Esposito, Bos | led NHL in assists (77) and points (126) | Jean Beliveau, Mtl |
| 1970 | Bobby Orr, Bos | led NHL in assists (87) and points (120) | Tony Esposito, Chi |
| 1971 | Bobby Orr, Bos | 102 assists, 139 points | Phil Esposito, Bos |
| 1972 | Bobby Orr, Bos | 80 assists, 117 points | Ken Dryden, Mtl |
| 1973 | Bobby Clarke, Phi | 67 assists, 104 points | Phil Esposito, Bos |
| 1974 | Phil Esposito, Bos | led NHL in goals (68) and points (145) | Bernie Parent, Phi |
| 1975 | Bobby Clarke, Phi | 89 assists, 116 points | Rogatien Vachon, LA |
| 1976 | Bobby Clarke, Phi | 89 assists, 119 points | Denis Potvin, NYI |
| 1977 | Guy Lafleur, Mtl | led NHL in assists (80) and points (136) | Bobby Clarke, Phi |
| 1978 | Guy Lafleur, Mtl | led NHL in goals (60) and points (132) | Bryan Trottier, NYI |
| 1979 | Bryan Trottier, NYI | led NHL in assists (87) and points (134) | Guy Lafleur, Mtl |
| 1980 | Wayne Gretzky, Edm | 51 goals, 86 assists | Marcel Dionne, LA |
| 1981 | Wayne Gretzky, Edm | led NHL in assists (109) and points (164) | Mike Liut, StL |
| 1982 | Wayne Gretzky, Edm | NHL-record 92 goals and 212 points | Bryan Trottier, NYI |
| 1983 | Wayne Gretzky, Edm | led NHL in goals (71) and points (196) | Pete Peeters, Bos |
| 1984 | Wayne Gretzky, Edm | led NHL in goals (87) and points (205) | Rod Langway, Wsh |
| 1985 | Wayne Gretzky, Edm | led NHL in goals (73) and points (208) | Dale Hawerchuk, Win |
| 1986 | Wayne Gretzky, Edm | NHL-record 163 assists and 215 points | Mario Lemieux, Pit |
| 1987 | Wayne Gretzky, Edm | led NHL in assists (121) and points (183) | Ray Bourque, Bos |
| 1988 | Mario Lemieux, Pit | led NHL in goals (70) and points (168) | Grant Fuhr, Edm |

## Hart Memorial Trophy *(Cont.)*

| Year | Winner | Key Statistics | Runner-Up |
|------|--------|----------------|-----------|
| 1989 | Wayne Gretzky, LA | 114 assists, 168 points | Mario Lemieux, Pit |
| 1990 | Mark Messier, Edm | 84 assists, 129 points | Ray Bourque, Bos |
| 1991 | Brett Hull, StL | led NHL in goals (86); 131 points | Wayne Gretzky, LA |
| 1992 | Mark Messier, NYR | 72 assists, 107 points | Patrick Roy, Mtl |
| 1993 | Mario Lemieux, Pit | 69 goals, 91 assists in 60 games | Doug Gilmour, Tor |
| 1994 | Sergei Fedorov, Det | 56 goals, 64 assists | Dominik Hasek, Buf |
| 1995 | Eric Lindros, Phi | 29 goals, 41 assists in 46 games | Jaromir Jagr, Pit |
| 1996 | Mario Lemieux, Pit | led NHL in goals (69) and points (161) | Mark Messier, NYR |
| 1997 | Dominik Hasek, Buf | 5 shutouts, 2.27 goals against avg. | Paul Kariya, Ana |
| 1998 | Dominik Hasek, Buf | 13 shutouts, 2.09 goals against avg. | Jaromir Jagr, Pit |
| 1999 | Jaromir Jagr, Pit | 44 goals, 127 points | Alexei Yashin, Ott |
| 2000 | Chris Pronger, StL | 62 points, +52 plus/minus rating | Jaromir Jagr, Pit |
| 2001 | Joe Sakic, Col | 118 points, +45 plus/minus rating | Mario Lemieux, Pit |
| 2002 | Jose Theodore, Mtl | 2.11 goals against avg./7 shutouts | Jarome Iginla, Cal |
| 2003 | Peter Forsberg, Col | 77 assists, +52 plus/minus rating | Markus Naslund, Van |
| 2004 | Martin St. Louis, TB | 94 points, +35 plus/minus rating | Jarome Iginla, Cal |
| 2005 | No Award–No Season. | | |
| 2006 | Joe Thornton, Bos/SJ | 29 goals, 96 assists; 125 points | Jaromir Jagr, NYR |
| 2007 | Sidney Crosby, Pit | 36 goals, 84 assists; 120 points | Roberto Luongo, Van |
| 2008 | Alexander Ovechkin, Wsh | 65 goals, 47 assists; 112 points | Evgeni Malkin, Pit |
| 2009 | Alexander Ovechkin, Wsh | 56 goals, 54 assists; 110 points | Evgeni Malkin, Pit |
| 2010 | Henrik Sedin, Van | 29 goals, 83 assists; 112 points | Sidney Crosby, Pit |
| 2011 | Corey Perry, Ana | 50 goals, 48 assists; 98 points | Daniel Sedin, Van |

## Art Ross Trophy

Awarded annually "to the player who leads the league in scoring points at the end of the regular season." The trophy was presented to the NHL in 1947 by Arthur Howie Ross, former manager-coach of the Boston Bruins. The tie-breakers, in order, are: (1) most goals, (2) fewer games played, (3) first goal of the season. Bobby Orr is the only defenseman in NHL history to win this trophy, and he won it twice (1970 and 1975).

| Year | Winner | Pts | Year | Winner | Pts |
|------|--------|-----|------|--------|-----|
| 1919 | Newsy Lalonde, Mtl | 44 | 1957 | Gordie Howe, Det | 89 |
| 1920 | Joe Malone, Que | 30 | 1958 | Dickie Moore, Mtl | 84 |
| 1921 | Newsy Lalonde, Mtl | 48 | 1959 | Dickie Moore, Mtl | 96 |
| 1922 | Punch Broadbent, Ott | 41 | 1960 | Bobby Hull, Chi | 81 |
| 1923 | Babe Dye, Tor | 46 | 1961 | Bernie Geoffrion, Mtl | 95 |
| 1924 | Cy Denneny, Ott | 37 | 1962 | Bobby Hull, Chi | 84 |
| 1925 | Babe Dye, Tor | 23 | 1963 | Gordie Howe, Det | 86 |
| 1926 | Nels Stewart, Mtl M | 44 | 1964 | Stan Mikita, Chi | 89 |
| 1927 | Bill Cook, NYR | 42 | 1965 | Stan Mikita, Chi | 87 |
| 1928 | Howie Morenz, Mtl | 37 | 1966 | Bobby Hull, Chi | 97 |
| 1929 | Ace Bailey, Tor | 51 | 1967 | Stan Mikita, Chi | 97 |
| 1930 | Cooney Weiland, Bos | 32 | 1968 | Stan Mikita, Chi | 87 |
| 1931 | Howie Morenz, Mtl | 73 | 1969 | Phil Esposito, Bos | 126 |
| 1932 | Harvey Jackson, Tor | 51 | 1970 | Bobby Orr, Bos | 120 |
| 1933 | Bill Cook, NYR | 53 | 1971 | Phil Esposito, Bos | 152 |
| 1934 | Charlie Conacher, Tor | 50 | 1972 | Phil Esposito, Bos | 133 |
| 1935 | Charlie Conacher, Tor | 57 | 1973 | Phil Esposito, Bos | 130 |
| 1936 | Sweeney Schriner, NYA | 45 | 1974 | Phil Esposito, Bos | 145 |
| 1937 | Sweeney Schriner, NYA | 46 | 1975 | Bobby Orr, Bos | 135 |
| 1938 | Gordie Drillon, Tor | 52 | 1976 | Guy Lafleur, Mtl | 125 |
| 1939 | Toe Blake, Mtl | 47 | 1977 | Guy Lafleur, Mtl | 136 |
| 1940 | Milt Schmidt, Bos | 52 | 1978 | Guy Lafleur, Mtl | 132 |
| 1941 | Bill Cowley, Bos | 62 | 1979 | Bryan Trottier, NYI | 134 |
| 1942 | Bryan Hextall, NYR | 56 | 1980 | Marcel Dionne, LA | 137 |
| 1943 | Doug Bentley, Chi | 73 | 1981 | Wayne Gretzky, Edm | 164 |
| 1944 | Herb Cain, Bos | 82 | 1982 | Wayne Gretzky, Edm | 212 |
| 1945 | Elmer Lach, Mtl | 80 | 1983 | Wayne Gretzky, Edm | 196 |
| 1946 | Max Bentley, Chi | 61 | 1984 | Wayne Gretzky, Edm | 205 |
| 1947 | *Max Bentley, Chi | 72 | 1985 | Wayne Gretzky, Edm | 208 |
| 1948 | Elmer Lach, Mtl | 61 | 1986 | Wayne Gretzky, Edm | 215 |
| 1949 | Roy Conacher, Chi | 68 | 1987 | Wayne Gretzky, Edm | 183 |
| 1950 | Ted Lindsay, Det | 78 | 1988 | Mario Lemieux, Pit | 168 |
| 1951 | Gordie Howe, Det | 86 | 1989 | Mario Lemieux, Pit | 199 |
| 1952 | Gordie Howe, Det | 86 | 1990 | Wayne Gretzky, LA | 142 |
| 1953 | Gordie Howe, Det | 95 | 1991 | Wayne Gretzky, LA | 163 |
| 1954 | Gordie Howe, Det | 81 | 1992 | Mario Lemieux, Pit | 131 |
| 1955 | Bernie Geoffrion, Mtl | 75 | 1993 | Mario Lemieux, Pit | 160 |
| 1956 | Jean Beliveau, Mtl | 88 | 1994 | Wayne Gretzky, LA | 130 |

### Art Ross Trophy *(Cont.)*

| Year | Winner | Pts | Year | Winner | Pts |
|------|--------|-----|------|--------|-----|
| 1995 | Jaromir Jagr, Pit | 70 | 2004 | Martin St. Louis, TB | 94 |
| 1996 | Mario Lemieux, Pit | 161 | 2005 | No award/no season | |
| 1997 | Mario Lemieux, Pit | 122 | 2006 | Joe Thornton, Bos/SJ | 125 |
| 1998 | Jaromir Jagr, Pit | 102 | 2007 | Sidney Crosby, Pit | 120 |
| 1999 | Jaromir Jagr, Pit | 127 | 2008 | Alexander Ovechkin, Wsh | 112 |
| 2000 | Jaromir Jagr, Pit | 96 | 2009 | Evgeni Malkin, Pit | 113 |
| 2001 | Jaromir Jagr, Pit | 121 | 2010 | Henrik Sedin, Van | 112 |
| 2002 | Jarome Iginla, Cgy | 96 | 2011 | Daniel Sedin, Van | 104 |
| 2003 | Peter Forsberg, Col | 106 | | | |

Note: Listing includes scoring leaders prior to inception of Art Ross Trophy in 1947–48.

### Lady Byng Memorial Trophy

Awarded annually "to the player adjudged to have exhibited the best type of sportsmanship and gentlemanly conduct combined with a high standard of playing ability." Lady Byng, who first presented the trophy in 1925, was the wife of Canada's Governor-General. She donated a second trophy in 1936 after the first was given permanently to Frank Boucher of the New York Rangers, who won it seven times in eight seasons. Stan Mikita, one of the league's most penalized players during his early years in the NHL, won the trophy twice late in his career (1967 and 1968).

| | | |
|---|---|---|
| 1925 Frank Nighbor, Ott | 1954 Red Kelly, Det | 1983 Mike Bossy, NYI |
| 1926 Frank Nighbor, Ott | 1955 Sid Smith, Tor | 1984 Mike Bossy, NYI |
| 1927 Billy Burch, NYA | 1956 Earl Reibel, Det | 1985 Jari Kurri, Edm |
| 1928 Frank Boucher, NYR | 1957 Andy Hebenton, NYR | 1986 Mike Bossy, NYI |
| 1929 Frank Boucher, NYR | 1958 Camille Henry, NYR | 1987 Joe Mullen, Cgy |
| 1930 Frank Boucher, NYR | 1959 Alex Delvecchio, Det | 1988 Mats Naslund, Mtl |
| 1931 Frank Boucher, NYR | 1960 Don McKenney, Bos | 1989 Joe Mullen, Cgy |
| 1932 Joe Primeau, Tor | 1961 Red Kelly, Tor | 1990 Brett Hull, StL |
| 1933 Frank Boucher, NYR | 1962 Dave Keon, Tor | 1991 Wayne Gretzky, LA |
| 1934 Frank Boucher, NYR | 1963 Dave Keon, Tor | 1992 Wayne Gretzky, LA |
| 1935 Frank Boucher, NYR | 1964 Ken Wharram, Chi | 1993 Pierre Turgeon, NYI |
| 1936 Doc Romnes, Chi | 1965 Bobby Hull, Chi | 1994 Wayne Gretzky, LA |
| 1937 Marty Barry, Det | 1966 Alex Delvecchio, Det | 1995 Ron Francis, Pit |
| 1938 Gordie Drillon, Tor | 1967 Stan Mikita, Chi | 1996 Paul Kariya, Ana |
| 1939 Clint Smith, NYR | 1968 Stan Mikita, Chi | 1997 Paul Kariya, Ana |
| 1940 Bobby Bauer, Bos | 1969 Alex Delvecchio, Det | 1998 Ron Francis, Pit |
| 1941 Bobby Bauer, Bos | 1970 Phil Goyette, StL | 1999 Wayne Gretzky, NYR |
| 1942 Syl Apps, Tor | 1971 John Bucyk, Bos | 2000 Pavol Demitra, StL |
| 1943 Max Bentley, Chi | 1972 Jean Ratelle, NYR | 2001 Joe Sakic, Col |
| 1944 Clint Smith, Chi | 1973 Gilbert Perreault, Buf | 2002 Ron Francis, Car |
| 1945 Billy Mosienko, Chi | 1974 John Bucyk, Bos | 2003 Alexander Mogilny, Det |
| 1946 Toe Blake, Mtl | 1975 Marcel Dionne, Det | 2004 Brad Richards, TB |
| 1947 Bobby Bauer, Bos | 1976 Jean Ratelle, NYR-Bos | 2005 No Award |
| 1948 Buddy O'Connor, NYR | 1977 Marcel Dionne, LA | 2006 Pavel Datsyuk, Det |
| 1949 Bill Quackenbush, Det | 1978 Butch Goring, LA | 2007 Pavel Datsyuk, Det |
| 1950 Edgar Laprade, NYR | 1979 Bob MacMillan, Atl | 2008 Pavel Datsyuk, Det |
| 1951 Red Kelly, Det | 1980 Wayne Gretzky, Edm | 2009 Pavel Datsyuk, Det |
| 1952 Sid Smith, Tor | 1981 Rick Kehoe, Pit | 2010 Martin St. Louis, TB |
| 1953 Red Kelly, Det | 1982 Rick Middleton, Bos | 2011 Martin St. Louis, TB |

### James Norris Memorial Trophy

Awarded annually "to the defense player who demonstrates throughout the season the greatest all-around ability in the position." James Norris was the former owner-president of the Detroit Red Wings. Bobby Orr holds the record for most consecutive times winning the award (eight, 1968–1975).

| | | |
|---|---|---|
| 1954 Red Kelly, Det | 1969 Bobby Orr, Bos | 1984 Rod Langway, Wsh |
| 1955 Doug Harvey, Mtl | 1970 Bobby Orr, Bos | 1985 Paul Coffey, Edm |
| 1956 Doug Harvey, Mtl | 1971 Bobby Orr, Bos | 1986 Paul Coffey, Edm |
| 1957 Doug Harvey, Mtl | 1972 Bobby Orr, Bos | 1987 Ray Bourque, Bos |
| 1958 Doug Harvey, Mtl | 1973 Bobby Orr, Bos | 1988 Ray Bourque, Bos |
| 1959 Tom Johnson, Mtl | 1974 Bobby Orr, Bos | 1989 Chris Chelios, Mtl |
| 1960 Doug Harvey, Mtl | 1975 Bobby Orr, Bos | 1990 Ray Bourque, Bos |
| 1961 Doug Harvey, Mtl | 1976 Denis Potvin, NYI | 1991 Ray Bourque, Bos |
| 1962 Doug Harvey, NYR | 1977 Larry Robinson, Mtl | 1992 Brian Leetch, NYR |
| 1963 Pierre Pilote, Chi | 1978 Denis Potvin, NYI | 1993 Chris Chelios, Chi |
| 1964 Pierre Pilote, Chi | 1979 Denis Potvin, NYI | 1994 Ray Bourque, Bos |
| 1965 Pierre Pilote, Chi | 1980 Larry Robinson, Mtl | 1995 Paul Coffey, Det |
| 1966 Jacques Laperriere, Mtl | 1981 Randy Carlyle, Pit | 1996 Chris Chelios, Chi |
| 1967 Harry Howell, NYR | 1982 Doug Wilson, Chi | 1997 Brian Leetch, NYR |
| 1968 Bobby Orr, Bos | 1983 Rod Langway, Wsh | 1998 Rob Blake, LA |

### James Norris Memorial Trophy *(Cont.)*

| | | |
|---|---|---|
| 1999 .......Al MacInnis, StL | 2004 ......Scott Niedermayer, NJ | 2009 .......Zdeno Chara, Bos |
| 2000 .......Chris Pronger, StL | 2005 ......No Award | 2010 .......Duncan Keith, Chi |
| 2001 .......Nicklas Lidstrom, Det | 2006 ......Nicklas Lidstrom, Det | 2011 .......Nicklas Lidstrom, Det |
| 2002 .......Nicklas Lidstrom, Det | 2007 ......Nicklas Lidstrom, Det | |
| 2003 .......Nicklas Lidstrom, Det | 2008 ......Nicklas Lidstrom, Det | |

### Calder Memorial Trophy

Awarded annually "to the player selected as the most proficient in his first year of competition in the National Hockey League." Frank Calder was a former NHL president. Sergei Makarov, who won the award in 1989–90, was the oldest recipient of the trophy, at 31. Players are no longer eligible for the award if they are 26 or older as of September 15th of the season in question.

| | | |
|---|---|---|
| 1933 .......Carl Voss, Det | 1960 .......Bill Hay, Chi | 1987 .......Luc Robitaille, LA |
| 1934 .......Russ Blinko, Mtl M | 1961 .......Dave Keon, Tor | 1988 ........Joe Nieuwendyk, Cgy |
| 1935 .......Dave Schriner, NYA | 1962 .......Bobby Rousseau, Mtl | 1989 .......Brian Leetch, NYR |
| 1936 .......Mike Karakas, Chi | 1963 .......Kent Douglas, Tor | 1990 .......Sergei Makarov, Cgy |
| 1937 .......Syl Apps, Tor | 1964 ........Jacques Laperriere, Mtl | 1991 .......Ed Belfour, Chi |
| 1938 .......Cully Dahlstrom, Chi | 1965 .......Roger Crozier, Det | 1992 .......Pavel Bure, Van |
| 1939 .......Frank Brimsek, Bos | 1966 .......Brit Selby, Tor | 1993 .......Teemu Selanne, Win |
| 1940 .......Kilby MacDonald, NYR | 1967 .......Bobby Orr, Bos | 1994 .......Martin Brodeur, NJ |
| 1941 .......Johnny Quilty, Mtl | 1968 .......Derek Sanderson, Bos | 1995 .......Peter Forsberg, Que |
| 1942 .......Grant Warwick, NYR | 1969 .......Danny Grant, Min | 1996 .......Daniel Alfredsson, Ott |
| 1943 .......Gaye Stewart, Tor | 1970 .......Tony Esposito, Chi | 1997 .......Bryan Berard, NYI |
| 1944 .......Gus Bodnar, Tor | 1971 .......Gilbert Perreault, Buf | 1998 .......Sergei Samsonov, Bos |
| 1945 .......Frank McCool, Tor | 1972 .......Ken Dryden, Mtl | 1999 .......Chris Drury, Col |
| 1946 .......Edgar Laprade, NYR | 1973 .......Steve Vickers, NYR | 2000 .......Scott Gomez, NJ |
| 1947 .......Howie Meeker, Tor | 1974 .......Denis Potvin, NYI | 2001 .......Evgeni Nabokov, SJ |
| 1948 .......Jim McFadden, Det | 1975 .......Eric Vail, Atl | 2002 .......Dany Heatley, Atl |
| 1949 .......Pentti Lund, NYR | 1976 .......Bryan Trottier, NYI | 2003 .......Barret Jackman, StL |
| 1950 .......Jack Gelineau, Bos | 1977 .......Willi Plett, Atl | 2004 .......Andrew Raycroft, Bos |
| 1951 .......Terry Sawchuk, Det | 1978 .......Mike Bossy, NYI | 2005 .......No Award |
| 1952 .......Bernie Geoffrion, Mtl | 1979 .......Bobby Smith, Min | 2006........Alexander Ovechkin, Wsh |
| 1953 .......Gump Worsley, NYR | 1980 .......Ray Bourque, Bos | 2007........Evgeni Malkin, Pit |
| 1954 .......Camille Henry, NYR | 1981 .......Peter Stastny, Que | 2008........Patrick Kane, Chi |
| 1955 .......Ed Litzenberger, Chi | 1982 .......Dale Hawerchuk, Win | 2009........Steve Mason, CBJ |
| 1956 .......Glenn Hall, Det | 1983 .......Steve Larmer, Chi | 2010........Tyler Myers, Buf |
| 1957 .......Larry Regan, Bos | 1984 .......Tom Barrasso, Buf | 2011........Jeff Skinner, Car |
| 1958 .......Frank Mahovlich, Tor | 1985 .......Mario Lemieux, Pit | |
| 1959 .......Ralph Backstrom, Mtl | 1986 .......Gary Suter, Cgy | |

### Vezina Trophy

Awarded annually "to the goalkeeper adjudged to be the best at his position." The trophy is named after Georges Vezina, an outstanding goalie for the Montreal Canadiens who collapsed during a game on November 28, 1925, and died four months later of tuberculosis. The general managers of the NHL teams vote on the award.

| | | |
|---|---|---|
| 1927 .......George Hainsworth, Mtl | 1953 .......Terry Sawchuk, Det | 1973 ........Ken Dryden, Mtl |
| 1928 .......George Hainsworth, Mtl | 1954 .......Harry Lumley, Tor | 1974 ........Bernie Parent, Phi |
| 1929 .......George Hainsworth, Mtl | 1955 .......Terry Sawchuk, Det | Tony Esposito, Chi |
| 1930 .......Tiny Thompson, Bos | 1956 .......Jacques Plante, Mtl | 1975 ........Bernie Parent, Phi |
| 1931 .......Roy Worters, NYA | 1957 .......Jacques Plante, Mtl | 1976 ........Ken Dryden, Mtl |
| 1932 .......Charlie Gardiner, Chi | 1958 .......Jacques Plante, Mtl | 1977 ........Ken Dryden, Mtl |
| 1933 .......Tiny Thompson, Bos | 1959 .......Jacques Plante, Mtl | Michel Larocque, Mtl |
| 1934 .......Charlie Gardiner, Chi | 1960 .......Jacques Plante, Mtl | 1978 ........Ken Dryden, Mtl |
| 1935 .......Lorne Chabot, Chi | 1961 .......Johnny Bower, Tor | Michel Larocque, Mtl |
| 1936 .......Tiny Thompson, Bos | 1962 .......Jacques Plante, Mtl | 1979 ........Ken Dryden, Mtl |
| 1937 .......Normie Smith, Det | 1963 ........Glenn Hall, Chi | Michel Larocque, Mtl |
| 1938 .......Tiny Thompson, Bos | 1964 .......Charlie Hodge, Mtl | 1980 ........Bob Sauve, Buf |
| 1939 .......Frank Brimsek, Bos | 1965 ........Terry Sawchuk, Tor | Don Edwards, Buf |
| 1940 .......Dave Kerr, NYR | Johnny Bower, Tor | 1981 ........Richard Sevigny, Mtl |
| 1941 .......Turk Broda, Tor | 1966 .......Gump Worsley, Mtl | Michel Larocque, Mtl |
| 1942 .......Frank Brimsek, Bos | Charlie Hodge, Mtl | 1982 ........Billy Smith, NYI |
| 1943 .......Johnny Mowers, Det | 1967 .......Glenn Hall, Chi | Denis Herron, Mtl |
| 1944 .......Bill Durnan, Mtl | Denis DeJordy, Chi | 1983 ........Pete Peeters, Bos |
| 1945 .......Bill Durnan, Mtl | 1968 ........Lorne Worsley, Mtl | 1984 ........Tom Barrasso, Buf |
| 1946 .......Bill Durnan, Mtl | 1969 ........Jacques Plante, StL | 1985 ........Pelle Lindbergh, Phi |
| 1947 .......Bill Durnan, Mtl | Glenn Hall, StL | 1986 ........John Vanbiesbrouck, NYR |
| 1948 .......Turk Broda, Tor | 1970 ........Tony Esposito, Chi | 1987 ........Ron Hextall, Phi |
| 1949 .......Bill Durnan, Mtl | 1971 ........Ed Giacomin, NYR | 1988 ........Grant Fuhr, Edm |
| 1950 .......Bill Durnan, Mtl | Gilles Villemure, NYR | 1989 ........Patrick Roy, Mtl |
| 1951 .......Al Rollins, Tor | 1972 ........Tony Esposito, Chi | 1990 ........Patrick Roy, Mtl |
| 1952 .......Terry Sawchuk, Det | Gary Smith, Chi | 1991 ........Ed Belfour, Chi |

### Vezina Trophy *(Cont.)*

| | | |
|---|---|---|
| 1992 ........Patrick Roy, Mtl | 1999 .......Dominik Hasek, Buf | 2006 ........Miikka Kiprusoff, Cgy |
| 1993 ........Ed Belfour, Chi | 2000 ........Olaf Kolzig, Wash | 2007 ........Martin Brodeur, NJ |
| 1994 .......Dominik Hasek, Buf | 2001 .......Dominik Hasek, Buf | 2008 ........Martin Brodeur, NJ |
| 1995 .......Dominik Hasek, Buf | 2002 ........Jose Theodore, Mtl | 2009 ........Tim Thomas, Bos |
| 1996 ........Jim Carey, Wsh | 2003 ........Martin Brodeur, NJ | 2010 ........Ryan Miller, Buf |
| 1997 .......Dominik Hasek, Buf | 2004 ........Martin Brodeur, NJ | 2011 ........Tim Thomas, Bos |
| 1998 ........Dominik Hasek, Buf | 2005 ........No Award | |

### Selke Trophy

Awarded annually "to the forward who best excels in the defensive aspects of the game." The trophy is named after Frank J. Selke, the architect of the Montreal Canadians dynasty that won five consecutive Stanley Cups in the late '50s. The winner is selected by a vote of the Professional Hockey Writers Association.

| | | |
|---|---|---|
| 1978........Bob Gainey, Mtl | 1990........Rick Meagher, StL | 2002........Michael Peca, NYI |
| 1979........Bob Gainey, Mtl | 1991........Dirk Graham, Chi | 2003........Jere Lehtinen, Dal |
| 1980........Bob Gainey, Mtl | 1992........Guy Carbonneau, Mtl | 2004........Kris Draper, Det |
| 1981........Bob Gainey, Mtl | 1993........Doug Gilmour, Tor | 2005........No Award |
| 1982........Steve Kasper, Bos | 1994........Sergei Fedorov, Det | 2006........Rod Brind'Amour, Car |
| 1983........Bobby Clarke, Phi | 1995........Ron Francis, Pit | 2007........Rod Brind'Amour, Car |
| 1984........Doug Jarvis, Wsh | 1996........Sergei Fedorov, Det | 2008........Pavel Datsyuk, Det |
| 1985........Craig Ramsay, Buf | 1997........Michael Peca, Buf | 2009........Pavel Datsyuk, Det |
| 1986........Troy Murray, Chi | 1998........Jere Lehtinen, Dal | 2010........Pavel Datsyuk, Det |
| 1987........Dave Poulin, Phi | 1999........Jere Lehtinen, Dal | 2011........Ryan Kesler, Van |
| 1988........Guy Carbonneau, Mtl | 2000........Steve Yzerman, Det | |
| 1989........Guy Carbonneau, Mtl | 2001........John Madden, NJ | |

### Adams Award

Awarded annually "to the NHL coach adjudged to have contributed the most to his team's success." The trophy is named in honor of Jack Adams, longtime coach and general manager of the Detroit Red Wings. The winner is selected by a vote of the National Hockey League Broadcasters' Association.

| | | |
|---|---|---|
| 1974 .....Fred Shero, Phi | 1987 .....Jacques Demers, Det | 2000 .....Joel Quenneville, StL |
| 1975 .....Bob Pulford, LA | 1988 .....Jacques Demers, Det | 2001 .....Bill Barber, Phi |
| 1976 .....Don Cherry, Bos | 1989 .....Pat Burns, Mtl | 2002 .....Bob Francis, Phx |
| 1977 .....Scott Bowman, Mtl | 1990 .....Bob Murdoch, Win | 2003 .....Jacques Lemaire, Min |
| 1978 .....Bobby Kromm, Det | 1991 .....Brian Sutter, StL | 2004 .....John Tortorella, TB |
| 1979 .....Al Arbour, NYI | 1992 .....Pat Quinn, Van | 2005 .....No Award |
| 1980 .....Pat Quinn, Phi | 1993 .....Pat Burns, Tor | 2006 .....Lindy Ruff, Buf |
| 1981 .....Red Berenson, StL | 1994 .....Jacques Lemaire, NJ | 2007 .....Alain Vigneault, Van |
| 1982 .....Tom Watt, Win | 1995 .....Marc Crawford, Que | 2008 .....Bruce Boudreau, Wsh |
| 1983 .....Orval Tessier, Chi | 1996 .....Scotty Bowman, Det | 2009 .....Claude Julien, Bos |
| 1984 .....Bryan Murray, Wsh | 1997 .....Ted Nolan, Buf | 2010 .....Dave Tippett, Phx |
| 1985 .....Mike Keenan, Phi | 1998 .....Pat Burns, Bos | 2011 .....Dan Bylsma, Pit |
| 1986 .....Glen Sather, Edm | 1999 .....Jacques Martin, Ott | |

## Career Records

### Alltime Point Leaders

| Player | Yrs | GP | G | A | Pts | Pts/game |
|---|---|---|---|---|---|---|
| Wayne Gretzky, Edm, LA, StL, NYR...............20 | | 1487 | 894 | 1963 | 2857 | 1.921 |
| Mark Messier, Edm, NYR, Van.......................25 | | 1756 | 694 | 1193 | 1887 | 1.074 |
| Gordie Howe, Det, Hfd ...................................26 | | 1767 | 801 | 1049 | 1850 | 1.047 |
| Ron Francis, Hfd, Pit, Car, Tor.......................23 | | 1731 | 549 | 1249 | 1798 | 1.039 |
| Marcel Dionne, Det, LA, NYR .......................18 | | 1348 | 731 | 1040 | 1771 | 1.314 |
| Steve Yzerman, Det ......................................22 | | 1514 | 692 | 1063 | 1755 | 1.159 |
| Mario Lemieux, Pit ........................................17 | | 915 | 690 | 1033 | 1723 | 1.883 |
| Joe Sakic, Que, Col ......................................20 | | 1378 | 625 | 1016 | 1641 | 1.191 |
| Jaromir Jagr, Pit, Wsh, NYR .........................17 | | 1273 | 646 | 953 | 1599 | 1.256 |
| Phil Esposito, Chi, Bos, NYR .......................18 | | 1282 | 717 | 873 | 1590 | 1.240 |
| Ray Bourque, Bos, Col .................................22 | | 1612 | 410 | 1169 | 1579 | .980 |
| *Mark Recchi, seven teams ..........................23 | | 1652 | 577 | 956 | 1533 | .928 |
| Paul Coffey, eight teams ..............................21 | | 1409 | 396 | 1135 | 1531 | 1.087 |
| Stan Mikita, Chi ............................................22 | | 1394 | 541 | 926 | 1467 | 1.052 |
| Bryan Trottier, NYI, Pit .................................18 | | 1279 | 524 | 901 | 1425 | 1.114 |

*Active in 2010–11.

## Alltime Goal-Scoring Leaders

| Player | Yrs | GP | G | G/game |
|---|---|---|---|---|
| Wayne Gretzky, Edm, LA, StL, NYR | 20 | 1487 | 894 | .601 |
| Gordie Howe, Det, Hfd | 26 | 1767 | 801 | .453 |
| Brett Hull, Cgy, StL, Dal, Det | 19 | 1269 | 741 | .584 |
| Marcel Dionne, Det, LA, NYR | 18 | 1348 | 731 | .542 |
| Phil Esposito, Chi, Bos, NYR | 18 | 1282 | 717 | .559 |
| Mike Gartner, Wsh, Min, NYR, Tor, Phx | 19 | 1432 | 708 | .494 |
| Mark Messier, Edm, NYR, Van | 25 | 1756 | 694 | .395 |
| Steve Yzerman, Det | 22 | 1514 | 692 | .457 |
| Mario Lemieux, Pit | 17 | 915 | 690 | .754 |
| Luc Robitaille, LA, Pit, NYR, Det | 19 | 1431 | 668 | .467 |
| Brendan Shanahan, NJ, StL, Hfd, Det, NYR | 21 | 1524 | 656 | .430 |

## Alltime Assist Leaders

| Player | Yrs | GP | A | A/game |
|---|---|---|---|---|
| Wayne Gretzky, Edm, LA, StL, NYR | 20 | 1487 | 1963 | 1.320 |
| Ron Francis, Hfd, Pit, Car | 23 | 1731 | 1249 | .722 |
| Mark Messier, Edm, NYR, Van | 25 | 1756 | 1193 | .679 |
| Ray Bourque, Bos, Col | 22 | 1612 | 1169 | .725 |
| Paul Coffey, eight teams | 21 | 1409 | 1135 | .806 |
| Adam Oates, seven teams | 22 | 1337 | 1079 | .807 |
| Steve Yzerman, Det | 22 | 1514 | 1063 | .702 |
| Gordie Howe, Det, Hfd | 26 | 1767 | 1049 | .594 |
| Marcel Dionne, Det, LA, NYR | 18 | 1348 | 1040 | .772 |
| Mario Lemieux, Pit | 17 | 915 | 1033 | 1.129 |
| Joe Sakic, Que, Col | 20 | 1378 | 1016 | .737 |

## Alltime Penalty Minutes Leaders

| Player | Yrs | GP | PIM | Min/game |
|---|---|---|---|---|
| Dave Williams, Tor, Van, Det, LA, Hfd | 14 | 962 | 3966 | 4.12 |
| Dale Hunter, Que, Wsh, Col | 19 | 1407 | 3565 | 2.53 |
| Tie Domi, Tor, NYR, Win | 16 | 1020 | 3515 | 3.45 |
| Marty McSorley, Pit, Edm, LA, NYR, SJ, Bos | 17 | 961 | 3381 | 3.52 |
| Bob Probert, Det, Chi | 16 | 935 | 3300 | 3.53 |
| Rob Ray, Buf, Ott | 15 | 900 | 3207 | 3.56 |
| Craig Berube, Phi, Tor, Cgy, Wsh, NYI | 17 | 1054 | 3149 | 2.99 |
| Tim Hunter, Cgy, Que, Van, SJ | 16 | 815 | 3146 | 3.86 |
| Chris Nilan, Mtl, NYR, Bos | 13 | 688 | 3043 | 4.42 |
| Rick Tocchet, Phi, Pit, LA, Bos, Wsh, Phx | 18 | 1144 | 2972 | 2.60 |

## Goaltending Records

### ALLTIME GOALTENDING LEADERS, BY WINS

| Goaltender | W | L | T/OTL | Pct |
|---|---|---|---|---|
| *Martin Brodeur, NJ | 625 | 350 | 137 | .624 |
| Patrick Roy, Mtl, Col | 551 | 315 | 131 | .618 |
| Ed Belfour, five teams | 484 | 320 | 125 | .588 |
| Curtis Joseph, five teams | 454 | 352 | 96 | .557 |
| Terry Sawchuk, five teams | 447 | 330 | 172 | .562 |
| Jacques Plante, five teams | 437 | 246 | 145 | .615 |
| Tony Esposito, Mtl, Chi | 423 | 306 | 151 | .566 |
| Glenn Hall, Det, Chi, StL | 407 | 326 | 163 | .545 |
| Grant Fuhr, six teams | 403 | 295 | 114 | .567 |
| *Chris Osgood, Det, NYI, StL, Det | 401 | 216 | 95 | .630 |
| Dominik Hasek, Chi, Buf, Ott, Det | 389 | 223 | 95 | .617 |

*Active in 2010–11.

### ACTIVE GOALTENDING LEADERS, BY WIN PERCENTAGE

| Goaltender | W | L | T/OTL | Pct |
|---|---|---|---|---|
| Chris Osgood, Det, NYI, StL, Det | 401 | 216 | 95 | .630 |
| Martin Brodeur, NJ | 625 | 350 | 137 | .624 |
| Ryan Miller, Buf | 221 | 126 | 42 | .622 |
| Marty Turco, Dal | 273 | 165 | 66 | .607 |
| Miikka Kiprusoff, SJ, Cgy | 276 | 177 | 58 | .597 |
| Tim Thomas, Bos | 161 | 102 | 44 | .596 |
| Henrik Lundqvist, NYR | 213 | 137 | 49 | .595 |
| Niklas Backstrom, Min | 141 | 91 | 35 | .594 |
| Marc-Andre Fleury, Pit | 184 | 126 | 37 | .584 |
| Cam Ward, Car | 175 | 126 | 33 | .573 |
| Ilya Bryzgalov, Ana, Phx | 156 | 116 | 35 | .565 |

Note: Minimum 250 games played.

### ALLTIME SHUTOUT LEADERS

| Goaltender | Team | Yrs | GP | SO |
|---|---|---|---|---|
| *Martin Brodeur | NJ | 18 | 1132 | 116 |
| Terry Sawchuk | Det, Bos, Tor, LA, NYR | 21 | 971 | 103 |
| George Hainsworth | Mtl, Tor | 11 | 465 | 94 |
| Glenn Hall | Det, Chi, StL | 18 | 906 | 84 |
| Jacques Plante | Mtl, NYR, StL, Tor, Bos | 18 | 837 | 82 |
| Tiny Thompson | Bos, Det | 12 | 553 | 81 |
| Alex Connell | Ott, Det, NYA, Mtl M | 12 | 417 | 81 |
| Dominik Hasek | Chi, Buf, Ott, Det | 16 | 735 | 81 |
| Tony Esposito | Mtl, Chi | 16 | 886 | 76 |
| Ed Belfour | Chi, SJ, Dal, Tor | 17 | 963 | 76 |

### ALLTIME GOALS AGAINST AVERAGE LEADERS (PRE-1950)

| Goaltender | Team | Yrs | GP | GA | GAA |
|---|---|---|---|---|---|
| Alec Connell | Ott, Det, NYA, Mtl M | 12 | 417 | 830 | 1.91 |
| George Hainsworth | Mtl, Tor | 11 | 465 | 937 | 1.93 |
| Chuck Gardiner | Chi | 7 | 316 | 664 | 2.02 |
| Lorne Chabot | NYR, Tor, Mtl, Chi, Mtl M, NYA | 11 | 411 | 860 | 2.04 |
| Tiny Thompson | Bos, Det | 12 | 553 | 1183 | 2.08 |

### ALLTIME GOALS AGAINST AVERAGE LEADERS (POST-1950)

| Goaltender | Team | Yrs | GP | GA | GAA |
|---|---|---|---|---|---|
| Dominik Hasek | Chi, Buf, Det, Ott | 16 | 735 | 1572 | 2.20 |
| *Martin Brodeur | NJ | 18 | 1132 | 2467 | 2.22 |
| Ken Dryden | Mtl | 8 | 397 | 870 | 2.24 |
| Roman Turek | Dal, StL, Cgy | 8 | 328 | 734 | 2.31 |
| *Henrik Lundqvist | NYR | 6 | 406 | 923 | 2.32 |
| *Marty Turco | Dal | 11 | 538 | 1200 | 2.35 |

*Active in 2010–11. Note: Minimum 250 games played. GAA equals goals against per 60 minutes played.

## Alltime Coaching Leaders, by Win Percentage

| Coach | Team | Seasons | W | L | T | OTL | Pct |
|---|---|---|---|---|---|---|---|
| Scotty Bowman | StL, Mtl, Buf, Pit, Det | 1967–87, 91–2002 | 1244 | 584 | 313 | 0 | .654 |
| *Mike Babcock | Ana, Det | 2002– | 373 | 188 | 19 | 76 | .641 |
| Toe Blake | Mtl | 1955–68 | 500 | 255 | 159 | 0 | .634 |
| *Dave Tippett | Dal, Phx | 2002– | 364 | 207 | 28 | 57 | .620 |
| Fred Shero | Phi, NYR | 1971–81 | 390 | 225 | 119 | 0 | .612 |
| *Joel Quenneville | StL, Col, Chi | 1996– | 579 | 356 | 77 | 69 | .603 |
| Glen Sather | Edm, NYR | 1979-89, 93-94, 2003–04 | 497 | 314 | 121 | 0 | .598 |
| Ken Hitchcock | Dal, Phi, CBJ | 1995–2010 | 534 | 350 | 88 | 70 | .588 |
| Emile Francis | NYR, StL | 1965–77, 81–83 | 388 | 273 | 117 | 0 | .574 |
| Billy Reay | Tor, Chi | 1957–59, 63–77 | 542 | 385 | 175 | 0 | .571 |
| *Peter Laviolette | NYI, Car, Phi | 2001– | 319 | 231 | 25 | 51 | .570 |
| *Alain Vigneault | Mtl, Van | 1997–2001, 2006– | 345 | 251 | 35 | 45 | .570 |
| Pat Burns | Mtl, Tor, Bos, NJ | 1988–2001, 2002–05 | 501 | 367 | 151 | 0 | .566 |

*Active in 2010–11. Note: Minimum 600 regular-season games. Ranked by win percentage. Overtime losses up through 2004 are counted as losses. After 2004, ties were eliminated and overtime losses were awarded one point and so are listed in separate OTL column (and counted like ties).

## Single-Season Records

### Goals

| Player | Season | GP | G | Player | Season | GP | G |
|---|---|---|---|---|---|---|---|
| Wayne Gretzky, Edm | 1981–82 | 80 | 92 | Wayne Gretzky, Edm | 1982–83 | 80 | 71 |
| Wayne Gretzky, Edm | 1983–84 | 74 | 87 | Brett Hull, StL | 1991–92 | 73 | 70 |
| Brett Hull, StL | 1990–91 | 78* | 86 | Mario Lemieux, Pit | 1987–88 | 77 | 70 |
| Mario Lemieux, Pit | 1988–89 | 76 | 85 | Bernie Nicholls, LA | 1988–89 | 79 | 70 |
| Alexander Mogilny, Buf | 1992–93 | 77 | 76 | Mario Lemieux, Pit | 1992–93 | 60 | 69 |
| Phil Esposito, Bos | 1970–71 | 78 | 76 | Mario Lemieux, Pit | 1995–96 | 70 | 69 |
| Teemu Selanne, Win | 1992–93 | 84 | 76 | Mike Bossy, NYI | 1978–79 | 80 | 69 |
| Wayne Gretzky, Edm | 1984–85 | 80 | 73 | Phil Esposito, Bos | 1973–74 | 78 | 68 |
| Brett Hull, StL | 1989–90 | 80 | 72 | Jari Kurri, Edm | 1985–86 | 78 | 68 |
| Jari Kurri, Edm | 1984–85 | 73 | 71 | Mike Bossy, NYI | 1980–81 | 79 | 68 |

### Assists

| Player | Season | GP | Asst | Player | Season | GP | Asst |
|---|---|---|---|---|---|---|---|
| Wayne Gretzky, Edm | 1985–86 | 80 | 163 | Bobby Orr, Bos | 1970–71 | 78 | 102 |
| Wayne Gretzky, Edm | 1984–85 | 80 | 135 | Mario Lemieux, Pit | 1987–88 | 77 | 98 |
| Wayne Gretzky, Edm | 1982–83 | 80 | 125 | Adam Oates, Bos | 1992–93 | 84 | 97 |
| Wayne Gretzky, LA | 1990–91 | 78 | 122 | Joe Thornton, SJ | 2005–06 | 81 | 96 |
| Wayne Gretzky, Edm | 1986–87 | 79 | 121 | Doug Gilmour, Tor | 1992–93 | 83 | 95 |
| Wayne Gretzky, Edm | 1981–82 | 80 | 120 | Pat LaFontaine, Buf | 1992–93 | 84 | 95 |
| Wayne Gretzky, Edm | 1983–84 | 74 | 118 | Mario Lemieux, Pit | 1985–86 | 79 | 93 |
| Mario Lemieux, Pit | 1988–89 | 76 | 114 | Peter Stastny, Que | 1981–82 | 80 | 93 |
| Wayne Gretzky, LA | 1988–89 | 78 | 114 | Wayne Gretzky, LA | 1993–94 | 81 | 92 |
| Wayne Gretzky, Edm | 1987–88 | 64 | 109 | Mario Lemieux, Pit | 1995–96 | 70 | 92 |
| Wayne Gretzky, Edm | 1980–81 | 80 | 109 | Ron Francis, Pit | 1995–96 | 77 | 92 |
| Wayne Gretzky, LA | 1989–90 | 73 | 102 | Joe Thornton, SJ | 2006–07 | 82 | 92 |

## Points

| Player | Season | G | Asst | Pts | Player | Season | G | Asst | Pts |
|---|---|---|---|---|---|---|---|---|---|
| Wayne Gretzky, Edm | 1985–86 | 52 | 163 | 215 | Wayne Gretzky, LA | 1990–91 | 41 | 122 | 163 |
| Wayne Gretzky, Edm | 1981–82 | 92 | 120 | 212 | Mario Lemieux, Pit | 1995–96 | 69 | 92 | 161 |
| Wayne Gretzky, Edm | 1984–85 | 73 | 135 | 208 | Mario Lemieux, Pit | 1992–93 | 69 | 91 | 160 |
| Wayne Gretzky, Edm | 1983–84 | 87 | 118 | 205 | Steve Yzerman, Det | 1988–89 | 65 | 90 | 155 |
| Mario Lemieux, Pit | 1988–89 | 85 | 114 | 199 | Phil Esposito, Bos | 1970–71 | 76 | 76 | 152 |
| Wayne Gretzky, Edm | 1982–83 | 71 | 125 | 196 | Bernie Nicholls, LA | 1988–89 | 70 | 80 | 150 |
| Wayne Gretzky, Edm | 1986–87 | 62 | 121 | 183 | Wayne Gretzky, Edm | 1987–88 | 40 | 109 | 149 |
| Mario Lemieux, Pit | 1987–88 | 70 | 98 | 168 | Jaromir Jagr, Pit | 1995–96 | 82 | 62 | 149 |
| Wayne Gretzky, LA | 1988–89 | 54 | 114 | 168 | Pat LaFontaine, Buf | 1992–93 | 53 | 95 | 148 |
| Wayne Gretzky, Edm | 1980–81 | 55 | 109 | 164 | Mike Bossy, NYI | 1981–82 | 64 | 83 | 147 |

## Points per Game

| Player | Season | GP | Pts | Avg | Player | Season | GP | Pts | Avg |
|---|---|---|---|---|---|---|---|---|---|
| Wayne Gretzky, Edm | 1983–84 | 74 | 205 | 2.77 | Mario Lemieux, Pit | 1987–88 | 77 | 168 | 2.18 |
| Wayne Gretzky, Edm | 1985–86 | 80 | 215 | 2.69 | Wayne Gretzky, LA | 1988–89 | 78 | 168 | 2.15 |
| Mario Lemieux, Pit | 1992–93 | 60 | 160 | 2.67 | Wayne Gretzky, LA | 1990–91 | 78 | 163 | 2.09 |
| Wayne Gretzky, Edm | 1981–82 | 80 | 212 | 2.65 | Mario Lemieux, Pit | 1989–90 | 59 | 123 | 2.08 |
| Mario Lemieux, Pit | 1988–89 | 76 | 199 | 2.62 | Wayne Gretzky, Edm | 1980–81 | 80 | 164 | 2.05 |
| Wayne Gretzky, Edm | 1984–85 | 80 | 208 | 2.60 | Mario Lemieux, Pit | 1991–92 | 64 | 131 | 2.05 |
| Wayne Gretzky, Edm | 1982–83 | 80 | 196 | 2.45 | Bill Cowley, Bos | 1943–44 | 36 | 71 | 1.97 |
| Wayne Gretzky, Edm | 1987–88 | 64 | 149 | 2.33 | Phil Esposito, Bos | 1970–71 | 78 | 152 | 1.95 |
| Wayne Gretzky, Edm | 1986–87 | 79 | 183 | 2.32 | Wayne Gretzky, LA | 1989–90 | 73 | 142 | 1.95 |
| Mario Lemieux, Pitt | 1995–96 | 70 | 161 | 2.30 | Steve Yzerman, Det | 1988–89 | 80 | 155 | 1.94 |

Note: Minimum 50 points in one season.

## Goals per Game

| Player | Season | GP | G | Avg |
|---|---|---|---|---|
| Joe Malone, Mtl | 1917–18 | 20 | 44 | 2.20 |
| Cy Denneny, Ott | 1917–18 | 20 | 36 | 1.80 |
| Newsy Lalonde, Mtl | 1917–18 | 14 | 23 | 1.64 |
| Joe Malone, Que | 1919–20 | 24 | 39 | 1.63 |
| Newsy Lalonde, Mtl | 1919–20 | 23 | 36 | 1.57 |
| Reg Noble, Tor | 1917–18 | 20 | 30 | 1.50 |
| Babe Dye, Ham-Tor | 1920–21 | 24 | 35 | 1.46 |
| Cy Denneny, Ott | 1920–21 | 24 | 34 | 1.42 |
| Joe Malone, Ham | 1920–21 | 20 | 28 | 1.40 |
| Newsy Lalonde, Mtl | 1920–21 | 24 | 33 | 1.38 |

Note: Minimum 20 goals in one season.

## Assists per Game

| Player | Season | GP | Asst | Avg |
|---|---|---|---|---|
| Wayne Gretzky, Edm | 1985–86 | 80 | 163 | 2.04 |
| Wayne Gretzky, Edm | 1987–88 | 64 | 109 | 1.70 |
| Wayne Gretzky, Edm | 1984–85 | 80 | 135 | 1.69 |
| Wayne Gretzky, Edm | 1983–84 | 74 | 118 | 1.59 |
| Wayne Gretzky, Edm | 1982–83 | 80 | 125 | 1.56 |
| Wayne Gretzky, LA | 1990–91 | 78 | 122 | 1.56 |
| Wayne Gretzky, Edm | 1986–87 | 79 | 121 | 1.53 |
| Mario Lemieux, Pit | 1992–93 | 60 | 91 | 1.52 |
| Wayne Gretzky, Edm | 1981–82 | 80 | 120 | 1.50 |
| Mario Lemieux, Pit | 1988–89 | 76 | 114 | 1.50 |

Note: Minimum 35 assists in one season.

## Shutout Leaders

| Player | Season | SO | Length of Schedule | Player | Season | SO | Length of Schedule |
|---|---|---|---|---|---|---|---|
| George Hainsworth, Mtl | 1928–29 | 22 | 44 | Chuck Gardiner, Chi | 1930–31 | 12 | 44 |
| Alec Connell, Ott | 1925–26 | 15 | 36 | Terry Sawchuk, Det | 1951–52 | 12 | 70 |
| Alec Connell, Ott | 1927–28 | 15 | 44 | Terry Sawchuk, Det | 1953–54 | 12 | 70 |
| Hal Winkler, Bos | 1927–28 | 15 | 44 | Terry Sawchuk, Det | 1954–55 | 12 | 70 |
| Tony Esposito, Chi | 1969–70 | 15 | 76 | Glenn Hall, Det | 1955–56 | 12 | 70 |
| George Hainsworth, Mtl | 1926–27 | 14 | 44 | Bernie Parent, Phi | 1973–74 | 12 | 78 |
| Clint Benedict, Mtl M | 1926–27 | 13 | 44 | Bernie Parent, Phi | 1974–75 | 12 | 80 |
| Alec Connell, Ott | 1926–27 | 13 | 44 | Martin Brodeur, NJ | 2006–07 | 12 | 82 |
| George Hainsworth, Mtl | 1927–28 | 13 | 44 | Lorne Chabot, NYR | 1927–28 | 11 | 44 |
| John Roach, NYR | 1928–29 | 13 | 44 | Harry Holmes, Det | 1927–28 | 11 | 44 |
| Roy Worters, NYA | 1928–29 | 13 | 44 | Roy Worters, Pit Pirates | 1927–28 | 11 | 44 |
| Harry Lumley, Tor | 1953–54 | 13 | 70 | Lorne Chabot, Tor | 1928–29 | 11 | 44 |
| Dominik Hasek, Buf | 1997–98 | 13 | 82 | Clint Benedict, Mtl M | 1928–29 | 11 | 44 |
| Tiny Thompson, Bos | 1928–29 | 12 | 44 | Joe Miller, Pit Pirates | 1928–29 | 11 | 44 |

## Shutout Leaders *(Cont.)*

| | Season | SO | Length of Schedule | | Season | SO | Length of Schedule |
|---|---|---|---|---|---|---|---|
| Tiny Thompson, Bos | 1932–33 | 11 | 48 | Harry Lumley, Tor | 1952–53 | 10 | 70 |
| Terry Sawchuck, Det | 1950–51 | 11 | 70 | Tony Esposito, Chi | 1973–74 | 10 | 78 |
| Dominik Hasek, Buf | 2000–01 | 11 | 82 | Ken Dryden, Mtl | 1976–77 | 10 | 80 |
| Martin Brodeur, NJ | 2003–04 | 11 | 82 | Martin Brodeur, NJ | 1996–97 | 10 | 82 |
| Henrik Lundqvist, NYR | 2010–11 | 11 | 82 | Martin Brodeur, NJ | 1997–98 | 10 | 82 |
| Lorne Chabot, NYR | 1926–27 | 10 | 44 | Roman Cechmanek, Phi | 2000–01 | 10 | 82 |
| Clarence Dolson, Det | 1928–29 | 10 | 44 | Byron Dafoe, Bos | 1998–99 | 10 | 82 |
| John Roach, Det | 1932–33 | 10 | 48 | Ed Belfour, Tor | 2003–04 | 10 | 82 |
| Chuck Gardiner, Chi | 1933–34 | 10 | 48 | Miikka Kiprusoff, Cgy | 2005–06 | 10 | 82 |
| Tiny Thompson, Bos | 1935–36 | 10 | 48 | Henrik Lundqvist, NYR | 2007–08 | 10 | 82 |
| Frank Brimsek, Bos | 1938–39 | 10 | 48 | Steve Mason, CBJ | 2008–09 | 10 | 82 |
| Bill Durnan, Mtl | 1948–49 | 10 | 60 | | | | |
| Gerry McNeil, Mtl | 1952–53 | 10 | 70 | | | | |

## Wins

| | Season | Record* | | Season | Record* |
|---|---|---|---|---|---|
| Martin Brodeur, NJ | 2006–07 | 48–23 | Martin Brodeur, NJ | 1997–98 | 43–17–8 |
| Roberto Luongo, Van | 2006–07 | 47–22 | Martin Brodeur, NJ | 1999–00 | 43–20–8 |
| Bernie Parent, Phi | 1973–74 | 47–13–12 | Martin Brodeur, NJ | 2005-06 | 43–23 |
| Evgeni Nabokov, SJ | 2007–08 | 46–21 | Ken Dryden, Mtl | 1975–76 | 42–10–8 |
| Miikka Kiprusoff, Cgy | 2008–09 | 45–24 | Mike Richter, NYR | 1993–94 | 42–12–6 |
| Martin Brodeur, NJ | 2009–10 | 45–25 | Jacques Plante, Mtl | 1955–56 | 42–12–10 |
| Terry Sawchuk, Det | 1950–51 | 44–13–13 | Jacques Plante, Mtl | 1961–62 | 42–14–14 |
| Bernie Parent, Phi | 1974–75 | 44–14–9 | Roman Turek, StL | 1999–00 | 42–15–9 |
| Terry Sawchuk, Det | 1951–52 | 44–14–12 | Martin Brodeur, NJ | 2000–01 | 42–17–11 |
| Evgeni Nabokov, SJ | 2009–10 | 44–16 | Miikka Kiprusoff, Cgy | 2005–06 | 42–20 |
| Martin Brodeur, NJ | 2007–08 | 44–27 | Ilya Bryzgalov, Phx | 2009–10 | 42–20 |
| Tom Barrasso, Pit | 1992–93 | 43–14–5 | | | |
| Ed Belfour, Chi | 1990–91 | 43–19–7 | | | |

*Starting with the 2005–06 season, ties were eliminated.

## Goals Against Average

| (PRE-1950) | Season | GP | GAA | (POST-1950) | Season | GP | GAA |
|---|---|---|---|---|---|---|---|
| George Hainsworth, Mtl | 1928–29 | 44 | 0.92 | Miika Kiprusoff, Cal | 2003–04 | 38 | 1.69 |
| George Hainsworth, Mtl | 1927–28 | 44 | 1.05 | Marty Turco, Dal | 2002–03 | 55 | 1.73 |
| Alec Connell, Ott | 1925–26 | 36 | 1.12 | Tony Esposito, Chi | 1971–72 | 48 | 1.770 |
| Tiny Thompson, Bos | 1928–29 | 44 | 1.15 | Al Rollins, Tor | 1950–51 | 40 | 1.774 |
| Roy Worters, NYA | 1928–29 | 38 | 1.15 | Ron Tugnutt, Ott | 1998–99 | 43 | 1.79 |

# Single-Game Records

## Goals

| | Date | G |
|---|---|---|
| Joe Malone, Que vs Tor | 1-31-20 | 7 |
| Newsy Lalonde, Mtl vs Tor | 1-10-20 | 6 |
| Joe Malone, Que vs Ott | 3-10-20 | 6 |
| Corb Denneny, Tor vs Ham | 1-26-21 | 6 |
| Cy Denneny, Ott vs Ham | 3-7-21 | 6 |
| Syd Howe, Det vs NYR | 2-3-44 | 6 |
| Red Berenson, StL vs Phi | 11-7-68 | 6 |
| Darryl Sittler, Tor vs Bos | 2-7-76 | 6 |

## Assists

| | Date | A |
|---|---|---|
| Billy Taylor, Det vs Chi | 3-16-47 | 7 |
| Wayne Gretzky, Edm vs Wsh | 2-15-80 | 7 |
| Wayne Gretzky, Edm vs Chi | 12-11-85 | 7 |
| Wayne Gretzky, Edm vs Que | 2-14-86 | 7 |

Note: 24 tied with 6.

## Points

| | Date | G | A | Pts |
|---|---|---|---|---|
| Darryl Sittler, Tor vs Bos | 2-7-76 | 6 | 4 | 10 |
| Maurice Richard, Mtl vs Det | 12-28-44 | 5 | 3 | 8 |
| Bert Olmstead, Mtl vs Chi | 1-9-54 | 4 | 4 | 8 |
| Tom Bladon, Phi vs Clev | 12-11-77 | 4 | 4 | 8 |
| Bryan Trottier, NYI vs NYR | 12-23-78 | 5 | 3 | 8 |
| Peter Stastny, Que vs Wsh | 2-22-81 | 4 | 4 | 8 |
| Anton Stastny, Que vs Wsh | 2-22-81 | 3 | 5 | 8 |
| Wayne Gretzky, Edm vs NJ | 11-19-83 | 3 | 5 | 8 |
| Wayne Gretzky, Edm vs Min | 1-4-84 | 4 | 4 | 8 |
| Paul Coffey, Edm vs Det | 3-14-86 | 2 | 6 | 8 |
| Mario Lemieux, Pit vs StL | 10-15-88 | 2 | 6 | 8 |
| Bernie Nicholls, LA vs Tor | 12-1-88 | 2 | 6 | 8 |
| Mario Lemieux, Pit vs NJ | 12-31-88 | 5 | 3 | 8 |

## Points

| Season | Player and Club | Pts | Season | Player and Club | Pts |
|--------|-----------------|-----|--------|-----------------|-----|
| 1917–18 | Joe Malone, Mtl | 44 | 1965–66 | Bobby Hull, Chi | 97 |
| 1918–19 | Newsy Lalonde, Mtl | 30 | 1966–67 | Stan Mikita, Chi | 97 |
| 1919–20 | Joe Malone, Que | 48 | 1967–68 | Stan Mikita, Chi | 87 |
| 1920–21 | Newsy Lalonde, Mtl | 41 | 1968–69 | Phil Esposito, Bos | 126 |
| 1921–22 | Punch Broadbent, Ott | 46 | 1969–70 | Bobby Orr, Bos | 120 |
| 1922–23 | Babe Dye, Tor | 37 | 1970–71 | Phil Esposito, Bos | 152 |
| 1923–24 | Cy Denneny, Ott | 23 | 1971–72 | Phil Esposito, Bos | 133 |
| 1924–25 | Babe Dye, Tor | 44 | 1972–73 | Phil Esposito, Bos | 130 |
| 1925–26 | Nels Stewart, Mtl M | 42 | 1973–74 | Phil Esposito, Bos | 145 |
| 1926–27 | Bill Cook, NY | 37 | 1974–75 | Bobby Orr, Bos | 135 |
| 1927–28 | Howie Morenz, Mtl | 51 | 1975–76 | Guy Lafleur, Mtl | 125 |
| 1928–29 | Ace Bailey, Tor | 32 | 1976–77 | Guy Lafleur, Mtl | 136 |
| 1929–30 | Cooney Weiland, Bos | 73 | 1977–78 | Guy Lafleur, Mtl | 132 |
| 1930–31 | Howie Morenz, Mtl | 51 | 1978–79 | Bryan Trottier, NYI | 134 |
| 1931–32 | Harvey Jackson, Tor | 53 | 1979–80 | Marcel Dionne, LA | 137 |
| 1932–33 | Bill Cook, NY | 50 | | Wayne Gretzky, Edm | 137 |
| 1933–34 | Charlie Conacher, Tor | 52 | 1980–81 | Wayne Gretzky, Edm | 164 |
| 1934–35 | Charlie Conacher, Tor | 57 | 1981–82 | Wayne Gretzky, Edm | 212 |
| 1935–36 | Sweeney Schriner, NYA | 45 | 1982–83 | Wayne Gretzky, Edm | 196 |
| 1936–37 | Sweeney Schriner, NYA | 46 | 1983–84 | Wayne Gretzky, Edm | 205 |
| 1937–38 | Gord Drillon, Tor | 52 | 1984–85 | Wayne Gretzky, Edm | 208 |
| 1938–39 | Hector Blake, Mtl | 47 | 1985–86 | Wayne Gretzky, Edm | 215 |
| 1939–40 | Milt Schmidt, Bos | 52 | 1986–87 | Wayne Gretzky, Edm | 183 |
| 1940–41 | Bill Cowley, Bos | 62 | 1987–88 | Mario Lemieux, Pit | 168 |
| 1941–42 | Bryan Hextall, NY | 54 | 1988–89 | Mario Lemieux, Pit | 199 |
| 1942–43 | Doug Bentley, Chi | 73 | 1989–90 | Wayne Gretzky, LA | 142 |
| 1943–44 | Herb Cain, Bos | 82 | 1990–91 | Wayne Gretzky, LA | 163 |
| 1944–45 | Elmer Lach, Mtl | 80 | 1991–92 | Mario Lemieux, Pit | 131 |
| 1945–46 | Max Bentley, Chi | 61 | 1992–93 | Mario Lemieux, Pit | 160 |
| 1946–47 | Max Bentley, Chi | 72 | 1993–94 | Wayne Gretzky, LA | 130 |
| 1947–48 | Elmer Lach, Mtl | 61 | 1994–95 | Jaromir Jagr, Pit | 70 |
| 1948–49 | Roy Conacher, Chi | 68 | 1995–96 | Mario Lemieux, Pit | 161 |
| 1949–50 | Ted Lindsay, Det | 78 | 1996–97 | Mario Lemieux, Pit | 122 |
| 1950–51 | Gordie Howe, Det | 86 | 1997–98 | Jaromir Jagr, Pit | 102 |
| 1951–52 | Gordie Howe, Det | 86 | 1998–99 | Jaromir Jagr, Pit | 127 |
| 1952–53 | Gordie Howe, Det | 95 | 1999–00 | Jaromir Jagr, Pit | 96 |
| 1953–54 | Gordie Howe, Det | 81 | 2000–01 | Jaromir Jagr, Pit | 121 |
| 1954–55 | Bernie Geoffrion, Mtl | 75 | 2001–02 | Jarome Iginla, Cgy | 96 |
| 1955–56 | Jean Beliveau, Mtl | 88 | 2002–03 | Peter Forsberg, Col | 106 |
| 1956–57 | Gordie Howe, Det | 89 | 2003–04 | Martin St. Louis, TB | 94 |
| 1957–58 | Dickie Moore, Mtl | 84 | 2004–05 | No season | |
| 1958–59 | Dickie Moore, Mtl | 96 | 2005–06 | Joe Thornton, Bos/SJ | 125 |
| 1959–60 | Bobby Hull, Chi | 81 | 2006–07 | Sidney Crosby, Pit | 120 |
| 1960–61 | Bernie Geoffrion, Mtl | 95 | 2007–08 | Alexander Ovechkin, Wsh | 112 |
| 1961–62 | Andy Bathgate, NY | 84 | 2008–09 | Evgeni Malkin, Pit | 113 |
| | Bobby Hull, Chi | 84 | 2009–10 | Henrik Sedin, Van | 112 |
| 1962–63 | Gordie Howe, Det | 86 | 2010–11 | Daniel Sedin, Van | 104 |
| 1963–64 | Stan Mikita, Chi | 89 | | | |
| 1964–65 | Stan Mikita, Chi | 87 | | | |

## Goals

| Season | Player and Club | G | Season | Player and Club | G |
|--------|-----------------|---|--------|-----------------|---|
| 1917–18 | Joe Malone, Mtl | 44 | 1930–31 | Charlie Lonacher, Tor | 31 |
| 1918–19 | Odie Cleghorn, Mtl | 23 | 1931–32 | Charlie Conacher, Tor | 34 |
| 1919–20 | Joe Malone, Que | 39 | | Bill Cook, NY | 34 |
| 1920–21 | Babe Dye, Ham-Tor | 35 | 1932–33 | Bill Cook, NY | 28 |
| 1921–22 | Punch Broadbent, Ott | 32 | 1933–34 | Charlie Conacher, Tor | 32 |
| 1922–23 | Babe Dye, Tor | 26 | 1934–35 | Charlie Conacher, Tor | 36 |
| 1923–24 | Cy Denneny, Ott | 22 | 1935–36 | Charlie Conacher, Tor | 23 |
| 1924–25 | Babe Dye, Tor | 38 | | Bill Thoms, Tor | 23 |
| 1925–26 | Nels Stewart, Mtl | 34 | 1936–37 | Larry Aurie, Det | 23 |
| 1926–27 | Bill Cook, NY | 33 | | Nels Stewart, Bos-NYA | 23 |
| 1927–28 | Howie Morenz, Mtl | 33 | 1937–38 | Gord Drillon, Tor | 26 |
| 1928–29 | Ace Bailey, Tor | 22 | 1938–39 | Roy Conacher, Bos | 26 |
| 1929–30 | Cooney Weiland, Bos | 43 | 1939–40 | Bryan Hextall, NY | 24 |

## Goals *(Cont.)*

| Season | Player and Club | G | Season | Player and Club | G |
|---|---|---|---|---|---|
| 1940–41 | Bryan Hextall, NY | 26 | 1978–79 | Mike Bossy, NYI | 69 |
| 1941–42 | Lynn Patrick, NY | 32 | 1979–80 | Charlie Simmer, LA | 56 |
| 1942–43 | Doug Bentley, Chi | 33 | | Blaine Stoughton, Hart | 56 |
| 1943–44 | Doug Bentley, Chi | 38 | 1980–81 | Mike Bossy, NYI | 68 |
| 1944–45 | Maurice Richard, Mtl | 50 | 1981–82 | Wayne Gretzky, Edm | 92 |
| 1945–46 | Gaye Stewart, Tor | 37 | 1982–83 | Wayne Gretzky, Edm | 71 |
| 1946–47 | Maurice Richard, Mtl | 45 | 1983–84 | Wayne Gretzky, Edm | 87 |
| 1947–48 | Ted Lindsay, Det | 33 | 1984–85 | Wayne Gretzky, Edm | 73 |
| 1948–49 | Sid Abel, Det | 28 | 1985–86 | Jari Kurri, Edm | 68 |
| 1949–50 | Maurice Richard, Mtl | 43 | 1986–87 | Wayne Gretzky, Edm | 62 |
| 1950–51 | Gordie Howe, Det | 43 | 1987–88 | Mario Lemieux, Pit | 70 |
| 1951–52 | Gordie Howe, Det | 47 | 1988–89 | Mario Lemieux, Pit | 85 |
| 1952–53 | Gordie Howe, Det | 49 | 1989–90 | Brett Hull, StL | 72 |
| 1953–54 | Maurice Richard, Mtl | 37 | 1990–91 | Brett Hull, StL | 86 |
| 1954–55 | Bernie Geoffrion, Mtl | 38 | 1991–92 | Brett Hull, StL | 70 |
| | Maurice Richard, Mtl | 38 | 1992–93 | Alexander Mogilny, Buf | 76 |
| 1955–56 | Jean Beliveau, Mtl | 47 | | Teemu Selanne, Win | 76 |
| 1956–57 | Gordie Howe, Det | 44 | 1993–94 | Pavel Bure, Van | 60 |
| 1957–58 | Dickie Moore, Mtl | 36 | 1994–95 | Peter Bondra, Wsh | 34 |
| 1958–59 | Jean Beliveau, Mtl | 45 | 1995–96 | Mario Lemieux, Pit | 69 |
| 1959–60 | Bronco Horvath, Bos | 39 | 1996–97 | Keith Tkachuk, Phx | 52 |
| | Bobby Hull, Chi | 39 | 1997–98 | Peter Bondra, Wsh | 52 |
| 1960–61 | Bernie Geoffrion, Mtl | 50 | | Teemu Selanne, Ana | 52 |
| 1961–62 | Bobby Hull, Chi | 50 | 1998–99 | Teemu Selanne, Ana | 47 |
| 1962–63 | Gordie Howe, Det | 38 | 1999–00 | Pavel Bure, Fla | 58 |
| 1963–64 | Bobby Hull, Chi | 43 | 2000–01 | Pavel Bure, Fla | 59 |
| 1964–65 | Norm Ullman, Det | 42 | 2001–02 | Jarome Iginla, Cgy | 52 |
| 1965–66 | Bobby Hull, Chi | 54 | 2002–03 | Milan Hejduk, Col | 50 |
| 1966–67 | Bobby Hull, Chi | 52 | 2003–04 | Jarome Iginla, Cgy | 41 |
| 1967–68 | Bobby Hull, Chi | 44 | | Ilya Kovalchuk, Atl | 41 |
| 1968–69 | Bobby Hull, Chi | 58 | | Rick Nash, CBJ | 41 |
| 1969–70 | Phil Esposito, Bos | 43 | 2004–05 | No season | |
| 1970–71 | Phil Esposito, Bos | 76 | 2005–06 | Jonathan Cheechoo, SJ | 56 |
| 1971–72 | Phil Esposito, Bos | 66 | 2006–07 | Vincent Lecavalier, TB | 52 |
| 1972–73 | Phil Esposito, Bos | 55 | 2007–08 | Alexander Ovechkin, Wsh | 65 |
| 1973–74 | Phil Esposito, Bos | 68 | 2008–09 | Alexander Ovechkin, Wsh | 56 |
| 1974–75 | Phil Esposito, Bos | 61 | 2009–10 | Sidney Crosby, Pit | 51 |
| 1975–76 | Guy Lafleur, Mtl | 56 | | Steven Stamkos, TB | 51 |
| 1976–77 | Steve Shutt, Mtl | 60 | 2010–11 | Corey Perry, Ana | 50 |
| 1977–78 | Guy Lafleur, Mtl | 60 | | | |

## Assists

| Season | Player and Club | Asst | Season | Player and Club | Asst |
|---|---|---|---|---|---|
| 1917–18 | statistic not kept | | 1940–41 | Bill Cowley, Bos | 45 |
| 1918–19 | Newsy Lalonde, Mtl | 9 | 1941–42 | Phil Watson, NY | 37 |
| 1919–20 | Corbett Denneny, Tor | 12 | 1942–43 | Bill Cowley, Bos | 45 |
| 1920–21 | Louis Berlinquette, Mtl | 9 | 1943–44 | Clint Smith, Chi | 49 |
| 1921–22 | Punch Broadbench, Ott | 14 | 1944–45 | Elmer Lach, Mtl | 54 |
| 1922–23 | Babe Dye, Tor | 11 | 1945–46 | Elmer Lach, Mtl | 34 |
| 1923–24 | Billy Boucher, Mtl | 6 | 1946–47 | Billy Taylor, Det | 46 |
| 1924–25 | Cy Denneny, Ott | 15 | 1947–48 | Doug Bentley, Chi | 37 |
| 1925–26 | Frank Nighbor, Ott | 13 | 1948–49 | Doug Bentley, Chi | 43 |
| 1926–27 | Dick Irvin, Chi | 18 | 1949–50 | Ted Lindsay, Det | 55 |
| 1927–28 | Howie Morenz, Mtl | 18 | 1950–51 | Gordie Howe, Det | 43 |
| 1928–29 | Frank Boucher, NY | 16 | | Ted Kennedy, Tor | 43 |
| 1929–30 | Frank Boucher, NY | 36 | 1951–52 | Elmer Lach, Mtl | 50 |
| 1930–31 | Joe Primeau, Tor | 32 | 1952–53 | Gordie Howe, Det | 46 |
| 1931–32 | Joe Primeau, Tor | 37 | 1953–54 | Gordie Howe, Det | 48 |
| 1932–33 | Frank Boucher, NY | 28 | 1954–55 | Bert Olmstead, Mtl | 48 |
| 1933–34 | Joe Primeau, Tor | 32 | 1955–56 | Bert Olmstead, Mtl | 56 |
| 1934–35 | Art Chapman, NYA | 34 | 1956–57 | Ted Lindsay, Det | 55 |
| 1935–36 | Art Chapman, NYA | 28 | 1957–58 | Henri Richard, Mtl | 52 |
| 1936–37 | Syl Apps, Tor | 29 | 1958–59 | Dickie Moore, Mtl | 55 |
| 1937–38 | Syl Apps, Tor | 29 | 1959–60 | Bobby Hull, Chi | 42 |
| 1938–39 | Bill Cowley, Bos | 34 | 1960–61 | Jean Beliveau, Mtl | 58 |
| 1939–40 | Milt Schmidt, Bos | 30 | 1961–62 | Andy Bathgate, NY | 56 |

## Assists (Cont.)

| Season | Player and Club | Asst | Season | Player and Club | Asst |
|---|---|---|---|---|---|
| 1962–63 | Henri Richard, Mtl | 50 | 1988–89 | Wayne Gretzky, LA | 114 |
| 1963–64 | Andy Bathgate, NY-Tor | 58 | | Mario Lemieux, Pit | 114 |
| 1964–65 | Stan Mikita, Chi | 59 | 1989–90 | Wayne Gretzky, LA | 102 |
| 1965–66 | Jean Beliveau, Mtl | 48 | 1990–91 | Wayne Gretzky, LA | 122 |
| | Bobby Rousseau, Mtl | 48 | 1991–92 | Wayne Gretzky, LA | 90 |
| | Stan Mikita, Chi | 48 | 1992–93 | Adam Oates, Bos | 97 |
| 1966–67 | Stan Mikita, Chi | 62 | 1993–94 | Wayne Gretzky, LA | 92 |
| 1967–68 | Phil Esposito, Bos | 49 | 1994–95 | Ron Francis, Pit | 48 |
| 1968–69 | Phil Esposito, Bos | 77 | 1995–96 | Ron Francis, Pit | 92 |
| 1969–70 | Bobby Orr, Bos | 87 | | Mario Lemieux, Pit | 92 |
| 1970–71 | Bobby Orr, Bos | 102 | 1996–97 | Mario Lemieux, Pit | 72 |
| 1971–72 | Bobby Orr, Bos | 80 | 1997–98 | Wayne Gretzky, NYR | 67 |
| 1972–73 | Phil Esposito, Bos | 75 | | Jaromir Jagr, Pit | 67 |
| 1973–74 | Bobby Orr, Bos | 90 | 1998–99 | Jaromir Jagr, Pit | 83 |
| 1974–75 | Bobby Clarke, Phi | 89 | 1999–00 | Mark Recchi, Phi | 63 |
| | Bobby Orr, Bos | 89 | 2000–01 | Jaromir Jagr, Pit | 69 |
| 1975–76 | Bobby Clarke, Phi | 89 | | Adam Oates, Wsh | 69 |
| 1976–77 | Guy Lafleur, Mtl | 80 | 2001–02 | Adam Oates, Wsh | 64 |
| 1977–78 | Bryan Trottier, NYI | 77 | 2002–03 | Peter Forsberg, Col | 77 |
| 1978–79 | Bryan Trottier, NYI | 87 | 2003–04 | Scott Gomez, NJ | 56 |
| 1979–80 | Wayne Gretzky, Edm | 86 | | Martin St. Louis, TB | 56 |
| 1980–81 | Wayne Gretzky, Edm | 109 | 2004–05 | No season | |
| 1981–82 | Wayne Gretzky, Edm | 120 | 2005–06 | Joe Thornton, Bos/SJ | 96 |
| 1982–83 | Wayne Gretzky, Edm | 125 | 2006–07 | Joe Thornton, SJ | 92 |
| 1983–84 | Wayne Gretzky, Edm | 118 | 2007–08 | Joe Thornton, SJ | 67 |
| 1984–85 | Wayne Gretzky, Edm | 135 | 2008–09 | Evgeni Malkin, Pit | 78 |
| 1985–86 | Wayne Gretzky, Edm | 163 | 2009–10 | Henrik Sedin, Van | 83 |
| 1986–87 | Wayne Gretzky, Edm | 121 | 2010–11 | Henrik Sedin, Van | 75 |
| 1987–88 | Wayne Gretzky, Edm | 109 | | | |

## Goals Against Average

| Season | Goaltender and Club | GP | Min | GA | SO | Avg |
|---|---|---|---|---|---|---|
| 1917–18 | Georges Vezina, Mtl | 21 | 1282 | 84 | 1 | 3.93 |
| 1918–19 | Clint Benedict, Ott | 18 | 1113 | 53 | 2 | 2.86 |
| 1919–20 | Clint Benedict, Ott | 24 | 1444 | 64 | 5 | 2.66 |
| 1920–21 | Clint Benedict, Ott | 24 | 1457 | 75 | 2 | 3.09 |
| 1921–22 | Clint Benedict, Ott | 24 | 1508 | 84 | 2 | 3.34 |
| 1922–23 | Clint Benedict, Ott | 24 | 1478 | 54 | 4 | 2.18 |
| 1923–24 | Georges Vezina, Mtl | 24 | 1459 | 48 | 3 | 1.97 |
| 1924–25 | Georges Vezina, Mtl | 30 | 1860 | 56 | 5 | 1.81 |
| 1925–26 | Alec Connell, Ott | 36 | 2251 | 42 | 15 | 1.12 |
| 1926–27 | Clint Benedict, Mtl M | 43 | 2748 | 65 | 13 | 1.42 |
| 1927–28 | George Hainsworth, Mtl | 44 | 2730 | 48 | 13 | 1.05 |
| 1928–29 | George Hainsworth, Mtl | 44 | 2800 | 43 | 22 | 0.92 |
| 1929–30 | Tiny Thompson, Bos | 44 | 2680 | 98 | 3 | 2.19 |
| 1930–31 | Roy Worters, NYA | 44 | 2760 | 74 | 8 | 1.61 |
| 1931–32 | Chuck Gardiner, Chi | 48 | 2989 | 92 | 4 | 1.85 |
| 1932–33 | Tiny Thompson, Bos | 48 | 3000 | 88 | 11 | 1.76 |
| 1933–34 | Wilf Cude, Det-Mtl | 30 | 1920 | 47 | 5 | 1.47 |
| 1934–35 | Lorne Chabot, Chi | 48 | 2940 | 88 | 8 | 1.80 |
| 1935–36 | Tiny Thompson, Bos | 48 | 2930 | 82 | 10 | 1.68 |
| 1936–37 | Normie Smith, Det | 48 | 2980 | 102 | 6 | 2.05 |
| 1937–38 | Tiny Thompson, Bos | 48 | 2970 | 89 | 7 | 1.80 |
| 1938–39 | Frank Brimsek, Bos | 43 | 2610 | 68 | 10 | 1.56 |
| 1939–40 | Dave Kerr, NYR | 48 | 3000 | 77 | 8 | 1.54 |
| 1940–41 | Turk Broda, Tor | 48 | 2970 | 99 | 5 | 2.00 |
| 1941–42 | Frank Brimsek, Bos | 47 | 2930 | 115 | 3 | 2.35 |
| 1942–43 | Johnny Mowers, Det | 50 | 3010 | 124 | 6 | 2.47 |
| 1943–44 | Bill Durnan, Mtl | 50 | 3000 | 109 | 2 | 2.18 |
| 1944–45 | Bill Durnan, Mtl | 50 | 3000 | 121 | 1 | 2.42 |
| 1945–46 | Bill Durnan, Mtl | 40 | 2400 | 104 | 4 | 2.60 |
| 1946–47 | Bill Durnan, Mtl | 60 | 3600 | 138 | 4 | 2.30 |
| 1947–48 | Turk Broda, Tor | 60 | 3600 | 143 | 5 | 2.38 |
| 1948–49 | Bill Durnan, Mtl | 60 | 3600 | 126 | 10 | 2.10 |

## Goals Against Average *(Cont.)*

| Season | Goaltender and Club | GP | Min | GA | SO | Avg |
|---|---|---|---|---|---|---|
| 1949–50 | Bill Durnan, Mtl | 64 | 3840 | 141 | 8 | 2.20 |
| 1950–51 | Al Rollins, Tor | 40 | 2367 | 70 | 5 | 1.77 |
| 1951–52 | Terry Sawchuk, Det | 70 | 4200 | 133 | 12 | 1.90 |
| 1952–53 | Terry Sawchuk, Det | 63 | 3780 | 120 | 9 | 1.90 |
| 1953–54 | Harry Lumley, Tor | 69 | 4140 | 128 | 13 | 1.86 |
| 1954–55 | Harry Lumley, Tor | 69 | 4140 | 134 | 8 | 1.94 |
| 1955–56 | Jacques Plante, Mtl | 64 | 3840 | 119 | 7 | 1.86 |
| 1956–57 | Jacques Plante, Mtl | 61 | 3660 | 122 | 9 | 2.00 |
| 1957–58 | Jacques Plante, Mtl | 57 | 3386 | 119 | 9 | 2.11 |
| 1958–59 | Jacques Plante, Mtl | 67 | 4000 | 144 | 9 | 2.16 |
| 1959–60 | Jacques Plante, Mtl | 69 | 4140 | 175 | 3 | 2.54 |
| 1960–61 | Charlie Hodge, Mtl | 30 | 1800 | 74 | 4 | 2.47 |
| 1961–62 | Jacques Plante, Mtl | 70 | 4200 | 166 | 4 | 2.37 |
| 1962–63 | Don Simmons, Tor | 28 | 1680 | 69 | 1 | 2.46 |
| 1963–64 | Johnny Bower, Tor | 51 | 3009 | 106 | 5 | 2.11 |
| 1964–65 | Johnny Bower, Tor | 34 | 2040 | 81 | 3 | 2.38 |
| 1965–66 | Johnny Bower, Tor | 35 | 1998 | 75 | 3 | 2.25 |
| 1966–67 | Glenn Hall, Chi | 32 | 1664 | 66 | 2 | 2.38 |
| 1967–68 | Gump Worsley, Mtl | 40 | 2213 | 73 | 6 | 1.98 |
| 1968–69 | Jacques Plante, StL | 37 | 2139 | 70 | 5 | 1.96 |
| 1969–70 | Ernie Wakely, StL | 30 | 1651 | 58 | 4 | 2.11 |
| 1970–71 | Jacques Plante, Tor | 40 | 2329 | 73 | 4 | 1.88 |
| 1971–72 | Tony Esposito, Chi | 48 | 2780 | 82 | 9 | 1.77 |
| 1972–73 | Ken Dryden, Mtl | 54 | 3165 | 119 | 6 | 2.26 |
| 1973–74 | Bernie Parent, Phi | 73 | 4314 | 136 | 12 | 1.89 |
| 1974–75 | Bernie Parent, Phi | 68 | 4041 | 137 | 12 | 2.03 |
| 1975–76 | Ken Dryden, Mtl | 62 | 3580 | 121 | 8 | 2.03 |
| 1976–77 | Michel Larocque, Mtl | 26 | 1525 | 53 | 4 | 2.09 |
| 1977–78 | Ken Dryden, Mtl | 52 | 3071 | 105 | 5 | 2.05 |
| 1978–79 | Ken Dryden, Mtl | 47 | 2814 | 108 | 5 | 2.30 |
| 1979–80 | Bob Sauve, Buff | 32 | 1880 | 74 | 4 | 2.36 |
| 1980–81 | Richard Sevigny, Mtl | 33 | 1777 | 71 | 2 | 2.40 |
| 1981–82 | Denis Herron, Mtl | 27 | 1547 | 68 | 3 | 2.64 |
| 1982–83 | Pete Peeters, Bos | 62 | 3611 | 142 | 8 | 2.36 |
| 1983–84 | Pat Riggin, Wsh | 41 | 2299 | 102 | 4 | 2.66 |
| 1984–85 | Tom Barrasso, Buf | 54 | 3248 | 144 | 5 | 2.66 |
| 1985–86 | Bob Froese, Phi | 51 | 2728 | 116 | 5 | 2.55 |
| 1986–87 | Brian Hayward, Mtl | 37 | 2178 | 102 | 1 | 2.81 |
| 1987–88 | Pete Peeters, Wsh | 35 | 1896 | 88 | 2 | 2.78 |
| 1988–89 | Patrick Roy, Mtl | 48 | 2744 | 113 | 4 | 2.47 |
| 1989–90 | Mike Liut, Hfd-Wsh | 37 | 2161 | 91 | 4 | 2.53 |
|  | Patrick Roy, Mtl | 54 | 3173 | 134 | 3 | 2.53 |
| 1990–91 | Ed Belfour, Chi | 74 | 4127 | 170 | 4 | 2.47 |
| 1991–92 | Patrick Roy, Mtl | 67 | 3935 | 155 | 5 | 2.36 |
| 1992–93 | Felix Potvin, Tor | 48 | 2781 | 116 | 2 | 2.50 |
| 1993–94 | Dominik Hasek, Buf | 58 | 3358 | 109 | 7 | 1.95 |
| 1994–95 | Dominik Hasek, Buf | 41 | 2416 | 85 | 5 | 2.11 |
| 1995–96 | Ron Hextall, Phi | 53 | 3102 | 112 | 4 | 2.17 |
|  | Chris Osgood, Det | 50 | 2932 | 106 | 5 | 2.17 |
| 1996–97 | Martin Brodeur, NJ | 67 | 3838 | 120 | 10 | 1.88 |
| 1997–98 | Ed Belfour, Dal | 61 | 3581 | 112 | 9 | 1.88 |
| 1998–99 | Ron Tugnutt, Ott | 43 | 2508 | 75 | 3 | 1.79 |
| 1999–00 | Brian Boucher, Phi | 35 | 2038 | 65 | 4 | 1.91 |
| 2000–01 | Marty Turco, Dal | 26 | 1266 | 40 | 3 | 1.90 |
| 2001–02 | Patrick Roy, Col | 63 | 3773 | 122 | 9 | 1.94 |
| 2002–03 | Marty Turco, Dal | 55 | 3202 | 92 | 7 | 1.72 |
| 2003–04 | Miikka Kiprusoff, Cgy | 38 | 2301 | 65 | 4 | 1.69 |
| 2004–05 | No season |  |  |  |  |  |
| 2005–06 | Miikka Kiprusoff, Cgy | 74 | 4379 | 151 | 10 | 2.07 |
| 2006–07 | Niklas Backstrom, Min | 41 | 2226 | 73 | 5 | 1.97 |
| 2007–08 | Chris Osgood, Det | 43 | 2409 | 84 | 4 | 2.09 |
| 2008–09 | Tim Thomas, Bos | 54 | 3259 | 114 | 5 | 2.10 |
| 2009–10 | Tuukka Rask, Bos | 45 | 2562 | 84 | 5 | 1.97 |
| 2011–11 | Tim Thomas, Bos | 57 | 3364 | 112 | 9 | 2.00 |

## Penalty Minutes

| Season | Player and Club | GP | PIM | Season | Player and Club | GP | PIM |
|---|---|---|---|---|---|---|---|
| 1918–19 | Joe Hall, Mtl | 17 | 135 | 1965–66 | Reggie Fleming, Bos-NYR | 69 | 166 |
| 1919–20 | Cully Wilson, Tor | 23 | 79 | 1966–67 | John Ferguson, Mtl | 67 | 177 |
| 1920–21 | Bert Corbeau, Mtl | 24 | 86 | 1967–68 | Barclay Plager, StL | 49 | 153 |
| 1921–22 | Sprague Cleghorn, Mtl | 24 | 63 | 1968–69 | Forbes Kennedy, Phi-Tor | 77 | 219 |
| 1922–23 | Billy Boucher, Mtl | 24 | 55 | 1969–70 | Keith Magnuson, Chi | 76 | 213 |
| 1923–24 | Bert Corbeau, Tor | 24 | 55 | 1970–71 | Keith Magnuson, Chi | 76 | 291 |
| 1924–25 | Billy Boucher, Mtl | 30 | 92 | 1971–72 | Brian Watson, Pit | 75 | 212 |
| 1925–26 | Bert Corbeau, Tor | 36 | 121 | 1972–73 | Dave Schultz, Phi | 76 | 259 |
| 1926–27 | Nels Stewart, Mtl M | 44 | 133 | 1973–74 | Dave Schultz, Phi | 73 | 348 |
| 1927–28 | Eddie Shore, Bos | 44 | 165 | 1974–75 | Dave Schultz, Phi | 76 | 472 |
| 1928–29 | Red Dutton, Mtl M | 44 | 139 | 1975–76 | Steve Durbano, Pit-KC | 69 | 370 |
| 1929–30 | Joe Lamb, Ott | 44 | 119 | 1976–77 | Dave Williams, Tor | 77 | 338 |
| 1930–31 | Harvey Rockburn, Det | 42 | 118 | 1977–78 | Dave Schultz, LA-Pit | 74 | 405 |
| 1931–32 | Red Dutton, NYA | 47 | 107 | 1978–79 | Dave Williams, Tor | 77 | 298 |
| 1932–33 | Red Horner, Tor | 48 | 144 | 1979–80 | Jimmy Mann, Win | 72 | 287 |
| 1933–34 | Red Horner, Tor | 42 | 126 | 1980–81 | Dave Williams, Van | 77 | 343 |
| 1934–35 | Red Horner, Tor | 46 | 125 | 1981–82 | Paul Baxter, Pit | 76 | 409 |
| 1935–36 | Red Horner, Tor | 43 | 167 | 1982–83 | Randy Holt, Wsh | 70 | 275 |
| 1936–37 | Red Horner, Tor | 48 | 124 | 1983–84 | Chris Nilan, Mtl | 76 | 338 |
| 1937–38 | Red Horner, Tor | 47 | 82 | 1984–85 | Chris Nilan, Mtl | 77 | 358 |
| 1938–39 | Red Horner, Tor | 48 | 85 | 1985–86 | Joey Kocur, Det | 59 | 377 |
| 1939–40 | Red Horner, Tor | 30 | 87 | 1986–87 | Tim Hunter, Cgy | 73 | 361 |
| 1940–41 | Jimmy Orlando, Det | 48 | 99 | 1987–88 | Bob Probert, Det | 74 | 398 |
| 1941–42 | Pat Egan, Bklyn | 48 | 124 | 1988–89 | Tim Hunter, Cgy | 75 | 375 |
| 1942–43 | Jimmy Orlando, Det | 40 | 89 | 1989–90 | Basil McRae, Min | 66 | 351 |
| 1943–44 | Mike McMahon, Mtl | 42 | 98 | 1990–91 | Rob Ray, Buf | 66 | 350 |
| 1944–45 | Pat Egan, Bos | 48 | 86 | 1991–92 | Mike Peluso, Chi | 63 | 408 |
| 1945–46 | Jack Stewart, Det | 47 | 73 | 1992–93 | Marty McSorley, LA | 81 | 399 |
| 1946–47 | Gus Mortson, Tor | 60 | 133 | 1993–94 | Tie Domi, Win | 81 | 347 |
| 1947–48 | Bill Barilko, Tor | 57 | 147 | 1994–95 | Enrico Ciccone, TB | 41 | 225 |
| 1948–49 | Bill Ezinicki, Tor | 52 | 145 | 1995–96 | Matthew Barnaby, Buf | 73 | 335 |
| 1949–50 | Bill Ezinicki, Tor | 67 | 144 | 1996–97 | Gino Odjick, Van | 70 | 371 |
| 1950–51 | Gus Mortson, Tor | 60 | 142 | 1997–98 | Donald Brashear, Van | 77 | 372 |
| 1951–52 | Gus Kyle, Bos | 69 | 127 | 1998–99 | Rob Ray, Buf | 76 | 261 |
| 1952–53 | Maurice Richard, Mtl | 70 | 112 | 1999–00 | Denny Lambert, Atl | 73 | 219 |
| 1953–54 | Gus Mortson, Chi | 68 | 132 | 2000–01 | Matthew Barnaby, TB | 76 | 265 |
| 1954–55 | Fern Flaman, Bos | 70 | 150 | 2001–02 | Peter Worrell, Fla | 79 | 354 |
| 1955–56 | Lou Fontinato, NYR | 70 | 202 | 2002–03 | Jody Shelley, CBJ | 68 | 249 |
| 1956–57 | Gus Mortson, Chi | 70 | 147 | 2003–04 | Sean Avery, LA | 76 | 261 |
| 1957–58 | Lou Fontinato, NYR | 70 | 152 | 2004–05 | No season | | |
| 1958–59 | Ted Lindsay, Chi | 70 | 184 | 2005–06 | Sean Avery, LA | 75 | 257 |
| 1959–60 | Carl Brewer, Tor | 67 | 150 | 2006–07 | Ben Eager, Phi | 63 | 233 |
| 1960–61 | Pierre Pilote, Chi | 70 | 165 | 2007–08 | Daniel Carcillo, Phx | 57 | 324 |
| 1961–62 | Lou Fontinato, Mtl | 54 | 167 | 2008–09 | Daniel Carcillo, Phi | 74 | 254 |
| 1962–63 | Howie Young, Det | 64 | 273 | 2009–10 | Zenon Konopka, TB | 74 | 265 |
| 1963–64 | Vic Hadfield, NYR | 69 | 151 | 2010–11 | Zenon Konopka, NYI | 82 | 307 |
| 1964–65 | Carl Brewer, Tor | 70 | 177 | | | | |

# NHL All-Star Game

First played in 1947, this game started before the regular season and was used to match the defending Stanley Cup champions against the league All-Stars from other teams. In 1966 the game was moved to midseason, although there was no game that year. The format changed to a inter-conference showdown in 1969. The Challenge Cup, a series between the NHL All-Stars and the Soviet Union, was played instead of the All-Star Game in 1979. Eight years later, Rendez-Vous '87, a two-game series matching the Soviet Union and the NHL All-Stars, replaced the All-Star Game. The 1995 NHL All-Star game was cancelled due to a labor dispute. The 1998 NHL All-Star game, billed as a preview to the 1998 Winter Olympics in Nagano, Japan, matched North Amercian–born All-Stars and All-Stars born elsewhere.

## Results

| Year | Site | Score | MVP | Attendance |
|---|---|---|---|---|
| 1947 | Toronto | All-Stars 4, Toronto 3 | None named | 14,169 |
| 1948 | Chicago | All-Stars 3, Toronto 1 | None named | 12,794 |
| 1949 | Toronto | All-Stars 3, Toronto 1 | None named | 13,541 |
| 1950 | Detroit | Detroit 7, All-Stars 1 | None named | 9,166 |
| 1951 | Toronto | 1st team 2, 2nd team 2 | None named | 11,469 |
| 1952 | Detroit | 1st team 1, 2nd team 1 | None named | 10,680 |
| 1953 | Montreal | All-Stars 3, Montreal 1 | None named | 14,153 |
| 1954 | Detroit | All-Stars 2, Detroit 2 | None named | 10,689 |
| 1955 | Detroit | Detroit 3, All-Stars 1 | None named | 10,111 |
| 1956 | Montreal | All-Stars 1, Montreal 1 | None named | 13,095 |
| 1957 | Montreal | All-Stars 5, Montreal 3 | None named | 13,003 |
| 1958 | Montreal | Montreal 6, All-Stars 3 | None named | 13,989 |
| 1959 | Montreal | Montreal 6, All-Stars 1 | None named | 13,818 |
| 1960 | Montreal | All-Stars 2, Montreal 1 | None named | 13,949 |
| 1961 | Chicago | All-Stars 3, Chicago 1 | None named | 14,534 |
| 1962 | Toronto | Toronto 4, All-Stars 1 | Eddie Shack, Tor | 14,236 |
| 1963 | Toronto | All-Stars 3, Toronto 3 | Frank Mahovlich, Tor | 14,034 |
| 1964 | Toronto | All-Stars 3, Toronto 2 | Jean Beliveau, Mtl | 14,232 |
| 1965 | Montreal | All-Stars 5, Montreal 2 | Gordie Howe, Det | 13,529 |
| 1967 | Montreal | Montreal 3, All-Stars 0 | Henri Richard, Mtl | 14,284 |
| 1968 | Toronto | Toronto 4, All-Stars 3 | Bruce Gamble, Tor | 15,753 |
| 1969 | Montreal | East 3, West 3 | Frank Mahovlich, Det | 16,260 |
| 1970 | St. Louis | East 4, West 1 | Bobby Hull, Chi | 16,587 |
| 1971 | Boston | West 2, East 1 | Bobby Hull, Chi | 14,790 |
| 1972 | Minnesota | East 3, West 2 | Bobby Orr, Bos | 15,423 |
| 1973 | NY Rangers | East 5, West 4 | Greg Polis, Pit | 16,986 |
| 1974 | Chicago | West 6, East 4 | Garry Unger, StL | 16,426 |
| 1975 | Montreal | Wales 7, Campbell 1 | Syl Apps Jr, Pit | 16,080 |
| 1976 | Philadelphia | Wales 7, Campbell 5 | Pete Mahovlich, Mtl | 16,436 |
| 1977 | Vancouver | Wales 4, Campbell 3 | Rick Martin, Buf | 15,607 |
| 1978 | Buffalo | Wales 3, Campbell 2 (OT) | Billy Smith, NYI | 16,433 |
| 1980 | Detroit | Wales 6, Campbell 3 | Reg Leach, Phi | 21,002 |
| 1981 | Los Angeles | Campbell 4, Wales 1 | Mike Liut, StL | 15,761 |
| 1982 | Washington | Wales 4, Campbell 2 | Mike Bossy, NYI | 18,130 |
| 1983 | NY Islanders | Campbell 9, Wales 3 | Wayne Gretzky, Edm | 15,230 |
| 1984 | New Jersey | Wales 7, Campbell 6 | Don Maloney, NYR | 18,939 |
| 1985 | Calgary | Wales 6, Campbell 4 | Mario Lemieux, Pit | 16,825 |
| 1986 | Hartford | Wales 4, Campbell 3 (OT) | Grant Fuhr, Edm | 15,100 |
| 1988 | St. Louis | Wales 6, Campbell 5 (OT) | Mario Lemieux, Pit | 17,878 |
| 1989 | Edmonton | Campbell 9, Wales 5 | Wayne Gretzky, LA | 17,503 |
| 1990 | Pittsburgh | Wales 12, Campbell 7 | Mario Lemieux, Pit | 16,236 |
| 1991 | Chicago | Campbell 11, Wales 5 | Vince Damphousse, Tor | 18,472 |
| 1992 | Philadelphia | Campbell 10, Wales 6 | Brett Hull, StL | 17,380 |
| 1993 | Montreal | Wales 16, Campbell 6 | Mike Gartner, NYR | 17,137 |
| 1994 | NY Rangers | East 9, West 8 | Mike Richter, NYR | 18,200 |
| 1996 | Boston | East 5, West 4 | Ray Bourque, Bos | 17,565 |
| 1997 | San Jose | East 11, West 7 | Mark Recchi, Mtl | 17,422 |
| 1998 | Vancouver | North America 8, World 7 | Teemu Selanne, Ana (World) | 18,422 |
| 1999 | Tampa Bay | North America 8, World 6 | Wayne Gretzky, NYR (N. America) | 19,758 |
| 2000 | Toronto | World 9, North America 4 | Pavel Bure, Fla (World) | 19,300 |
| 2001 | Denver | North America 14, World 12 | Bill Guerin, Bos (North America) | 18,646 |
| 2002 | Los Angeles | World 8, North America 5 | Eric Daze, Chi (North America) | 18,118 |
| 2003 | Sunrise, Fla. | West 6, East 5 (shootout) | Dany Heatley, Atl (East) | 19,250 |
| 2004 | St. Paul, Minn. | East 6, West 4 | Joe Sakic, Col (West) | 19,434 |
| 2005 | No game played (season lockout) | | | |
| 2006 | No game played (2006 Winter Olympics) | | | |
| 2007 | Dallas | West 12, East 9 | Daniel Briere, Buf (East) | 18,532 |

### Results *(Cont.)*

| Year | Site | Score | MVP | Attendance |
|---|---|---|---|---|
| 2008 | Atlanta | East 8, West 7 | Eric Staal, Car (East) | 18,644 |
| 2009 | Montreal | East 12, West 11 | Alexei Kovalev, Mtl (East) | 21,273 |
| 2010 | No game played (2010 Winter Olympics) | | | |
| 2011 | Raleigh | Team Lidstrom 11, Team Staal 10 | Patrick Sharp, Chi (Team Staal) | 18,680 |

## Hockey Hall of Fame

Located in Toronto, the Hockey Hall of Fame was officially opened on August 26, 1961. The current chairman is William C. Hay. There are, at present, 306 members of the Hockey Hall of Fame—209 players, 84 "builders," and 14 on-ice officials. (One member, Alan Eagleson, resigned from the Hall March 25, 1998.) To be eligible, player and referee/linesman candidates should have been out of the game for three years, but the Hall's Board of Directors can make exceptions.

### Players

Sid Abel (1969)
Jack Adams (1959)
Glenn Anderson (2008)
Charles (Syl) Apps (1961)
George Armstrong (1975)
Irvine (Ace) Bailey (1975)
Donald H. (Dan) Bain (1945)
Hobey Baker (1945)
Bill Barber (1990)
Marty Barry (1965)
Andy Bathgate (1978)
Bobby Bauer (1996)
Ed Belfour (2011)
Jean Beliveau (1972)
Clint Benedict (1965)
Douglas Bentley (1964)
Max Bentley (1966)
Hector (Toe) Blake (1966)
Leo Boivin (1986)
Dickie Boon (1952)
Mike Bossy (1991)
Emile (Butch) Bouchard (1966)
Frank Boucher (1958)
George (Buck) Boucher (1960)
Ray Bourque (2004)
Johnny Bower (1976)
Russell Bowie (1945)
Frank Brimsek (1966)
Harry L. (Punch) Broadbent (1962)
Walter (Turk) Broda (1967)
John Bucyk (1981)
Billy Burch (1974)
Harry Cameron (1962)
Gerry Cheevers (1985)
Dino Ciccarelli (2010)
Francis (King) Clancy (1958)
Aubrey (Dit) Clapper (1947)
Bobby Clarke (1987)
Sprague Cleghorn (1958)
Paul Coffey (2004)
Neil Colville (1967)
Charlie Conacher (1961)

Lionel Conacher (1994)
Roy Conacher (1998)
Alex Connell (1958)
Bill Cook (1952)
Fred (Bun) Cook (1995)
Arthur Coulter (1974)
Yvan Cournoyer (1982)
Bill Cowley (1968)
Samuel (Rusty) Crawford (1962)
Jack Darragh (1962)
Allan M. (Scotty) Davidson (1950)
Clarence (Hap) Day (1961)
Alex Delvecchio (1977)
Cy Denneny (1959)
Marcel Dionne (1992)
Gordie Drillon (1975)
Charles Drinkwater (1950)
Ken Dryden (1983)
Terrance (Dick) Duff (2006)
Woody Dumart (1992)
Thomas Dunderdale (1974)
Bill Durnan (1964)
Mervyn A. (Red) Dutton (1958)
Cecil (Babe) Dye (1970)
Phil Esposito (1984)
Tony Esposito (1988)
Arthur F. Farrell (1965)
Bernie Federko (2002)
Viacheslav Fetisov (2001)
Ferdinand (Fern) Flaman (1990)
Frank Foyston (1958)
Ron Francis (2007)
Frank Frederickson (1958)
Grant Fuhr (2003)
Bill Gadsby (1970)
Bob Gainey (1992)
Chuck Gardiner (1945)
Herb Gardiner (1958)
Jimmy Gardner (1962)
Mike Gartner (2001)
Bernie (Boom Boom) Geoffrion (1972)
Eddie Gerard (1945)

Note: Year of election to the Hall of Fame is in parentheses after the member's name.

## Players *(Cont.)*

Ed Giacomin (1987)
Rod Gilbert (1982)
Clark Gillies (2002)
Doug Gilmour (2011)
Hamilton (Billy) Gilmour (1962)
Frank (Moose) Goheen (1952)
Ebenezer R. (Ebbie)
  Goodfellow (1963)
Michel Goulet (1998)
Cammi Granato (2010)
Mike Grant (1950)
Wilfred (Shorty) Green (1962)
Jim Gregory (2007)
Wayne Gretzky (1999)
Si Griffis (1950)
George Hainsworth (1961)
Glenn Hall (1975)
Joe Hall (1961)
Doug Harvey (1973)
Dale Hawerchuk (2001)
George Hay (1958)
William (Riley) Hern (1962)
Bryan Hextall (1969)
Harry (Hap) Holmes (1972)
Tom Hooper (1962)
George (Red) Horner (1965)
Miles (Tim) Horton (1977)
Gordie Howe (1972)
Mark Howe (2011)
Syd Howe (1965)
Harry Howell (1979)
Bobby Hull (1983)
Brett Hull (2009)
John (Bouse) Hutton (1962)
Harry M. Hyland (1962)
James (Dick) Irvin (1958)
Angela James (2010)
Harvey (Busher) Jackson (1971)
Ernest (Moose) Johnson (1952)
Ivan (Ching) Johnson (1958)
Tom Johnson (1970)
Aurel Joliat (1947)
Gordon (Duke) Keats (1958)
Leonard (Red) Kelly (1969)
Ted (Teeder) Kennedy (1966)
Dave Keon (1986)
Valeri Kharlamov (2005)
Jari Kurri (2001)
Elmer Lach (1966)
Guy Lafleur (1988)
Pat LaFontaine (2003)
Edouard (Newsy) Lalonde (1950)
Rod Langway (2002)
Jacques Laperriere (1987)
Guy Lapointe (1993)
Edgar Laprade (1993)
Igor Larionov (2008)
Jean (Jack) Laviolette (1962)
Brian Leetch (2009)
Hugh Lehman (1958)
Jacques Lemaire (1984)
Mario Lemieux (1997)
Percy LeSueur (1961)

Herbert A. Lewis (1989)
Ted Lindsay (1966)
Harry Lumley (1980)
Lanny McDonald (1992)
Frank McGee (1945)
Billy McGimsie (1962)
George McNamara (1958)
Al MacInnis (2007)
Duncan (Mickey) MacKay (1952)
Frank Mahovlich (1981)
Joe Malone (1950)
Sylvio Mantha (1960)
Jack Marshall (1965)
Fred G. (Steamer) Maxwell (1962)
Mark Messier (2007)
Stan Mikita (1983)
Dicky Moore (1974)
Patrick (Paddy) Moran (1958)
Howie Morenz (1945)
Billy Mosienko (1965)
Joe Mullen (2000)
Larry Murphy (2004)
Cam Neely (2005)
Joe Nieuwendyk (2011)
Frank Nighbor (1947)
Reg Noble (1962)
Herbert (Buddy) O'Connor (1988)
Harry Oliver (1967)
Bert Olmstead (1985)
Bobby Orr (1979)
Bernie Parent (1984)
Brad Park (1988)
Lester Patrick (1947)
Lynn Patrick (1980)
Gilbert Perreault (1990)
Tommy Phillips (1945)
Pierre Pilote (1975)
Didier (Pit) Pitre (1962)
Jacques Plante (1978)
Denis Potvin (1991)
Walter (Babe) Pratt (1966)
Joe Primeau (1963)
Marcel Pronovost (1978)
Bob Pulford (1991)
Harvey Pulford (1945)
Hubert (Bill) Quackenbush (1976)
Frank Rankin (1961)
Jean Ratelle (1985)
Claude (Chuck) Rayner (1973)
Kenneth Reardon (1966)
Henri Richard (1979)
Maurice (Rocket) Richard (1961)
George Richardson (1950)
Gordon Roberts (1971)
Larry Robinson (1995)
Luc Robitaille (2009)
Art Ross (1945)
Patrick Roy (2006)
Blair Russel (1965)
Ernest Russell (1965)
Jack Ruttan (1962)
Borje Salming (1996)

Note: Year of election to the Hall of Fame is in parentheses after the member's name.

### Players *(Cont.)*

Denis Savard (2000)
Serge Savard (1986)
Terry Sawchuk (1971)
Fred Scanlan (1965)
Milt Schmidt (1961)
Dave (Sweeney) Schriner (1962)
Earl Seibert (1963)
Oliver Seibert (1961)
Eddie Shore (1947)
Steve Shutt (1993)
Albert C. (Babe) Siebert (1964)
Harold (Bullet Joe) Simpson (1962)
Daryl Sittler (1989)
Alfred E. Smith (1962)
Billy Smith (1993)
Clint Smith (1991)
Reginald (Hooley) Smith (1972)
Thomas Smith (1973)
Allan Stanley (1981)
Russell (Barney) Stanley (1962)
Peter Stastny (1998)
Scott Stevens (2007)
John (Black Jack) Stewart (1964)

Nels Stewart (1962)
Bruce Stuart (1961)
Hod Stuart (1945)
Frederic (Cyclone) Taylor (O.B.E.) (1947)
Cecil R. (Tiny) Thompson (1959)
Vladislav Tretiak (1989)
Harry J. Trihey (1950)
Bryan Trottier (1997)
Norm Ullman (1982)
Georges Vezina (1945)
Jack Walker (1960)
Marty Walsh (1962)
Harry Watson (1994)
Harry E. Watson (1962)
Ralph (Cooney) Weiland (1971)
Harry Westwick (1962)
Fred Whitcroft (1962)
Gordon (Phat) Wilson (1962)
Lorne (Gump) Worsley (1980)
Roy Worters (1969)
Steve Yzerman (2009)

### Builders

@nCharles Adams (1960)
Weston W. Adams (1972)
Thomas (Frank) Ahearn (1962)
John (Bunny) Ahearne (1977)
Montagu Allan (C.V.O.) (1945)
Keith Allen (1992)
Al Arbour (1996)
Harold Ballard (1977)
David Bauer (1989)
John Bickell (1978)
Scott Bowman (1991)
Herb Brooks (2006)
George V. Brown (1961)
Walter A. Brown (1962)
Frank Buckland (1975)
Walter L. Bush (2000)
Jack Butterfield (1980)
Frank Calder (1947)
Angus D. Campbell (1964)
Clarence Campbell (1966)
Joe Cattarinich (1977)
Ed Chynoweth (2008)
Bob Cole (1996, Media)
Murray Costello (2005)
Joseph (Leo) Dandurand (1963)
Jimmy Devellano (2010)
Francis Dilio (1964)
George S. Dudley (1958)
James A. Dunn (1968)
*Robert Alan Eagleson (1989–98)
Cliff Fletcher (2004)
Emile Francis (1982)
Jack Gibson (1976)
Tommy Gorman (1963)
Frank Griffiths (1993)

William Hanley (1986)
Charles Hay (1974)
James C. Hendy (1968)
Foster Hewitt (1965)
William Hewitt (1947)
Harley Hotchkiss (2006)
Fred J. Hume (1962)
Mike Ilitch (2003)
George (Punch) Imlach (1984)
Tommy Ivan (1974)
William M. Jennings (1975)
Bob Johnson (1992)
Gordon W. Juckes (1979)
John Kilpatrick (1960)
Brian Kilrea (2003)
Seymour Knox III (1993)
Lou Lamoriello (2009)
George Leader (1969)
Robert LeBel (1970)
Thomas F. Lockhart (1965)
Paul Loicq (1961)
Frederic McLaughlin (1963)
John Mariucci (1985)
Frank Mathers (1992)
John (Jake) Milford (1984)
Hartland Molson (1973)
Scotty Morrison (1999)
Msgr. Athol (Pere) Murray (1998)
Roger Neilson (2002)
Francis Nelson (1947)
Bruce A. Norris (1969)
James Norris, Sr. (1958)
James D. Norris (1962)
William M. Northey (1947)
John O'Brien (1962)

*Eagleson resigned from Hall March 25, 1998.
Note: Year of election to the Hall of Fame is in parentheses after the member's name.

## Builders *(Cont.)*

Brian O'Neill (1994)
Fred Page (1993)
Craig Patrick (1996)
Frank Patrick (1958)
Allan W. Pickard (1958)
Rudy Pilous (1985)
Norman (Bud) Poile (1990)
Samuel Pollock (1978)
Donat Raymond (1958)
John Robertson (1947)
Claude C. Robinson (1947)
Philip D. Ross (1976)
Gunther Sabetzki (1995)
Glen Sather (1997)
Daryl "Doc" Seaman (2010)
Frank J. Selke (1960)

Harry Sinden (1983)
Frank D. Smith (1962)
Conn Smythe (1958)
Edward M. Snider (1988)
Lord Stanley of Preston (1945)
James T. Sutherland (1947)
Anatoli V. Tarasov (1974)
Bill Torrey (1995)
Lloyd Turner (1958)
William Tutt (1978)
Carl Potter Voss (1974)
Fred C. Waghorn (1961)
Arthur Wirtz (1971)
Bill Wirtz (1976)
John A. Ziegler, Jr. (1987)

## Referees/Linesmen

Neil Armstrong (1991)
John Ashley (1981)
William L. Chadwick (1964)
John D'Amico (1993)
Chaucer Elliott (1961)
George Hayes (1988)
Robert W. Hewitson (1963)
Fred J. (Mickey) Ion (1961)

Matt Pavelich (1987)
Mike Rodden (1962)
Ray Scapinello (2008)
J. Cooper Smeaton (1961)
Roy (Red) Storey (1967)
Frank Udvari (1973)
Andy Van Hellemond (1999)

Note: Year of election to the Hall of Fame is in parentheses after the member's name.

# Olympics

PyeongChang 2018
CANDIDATE CITY

PYEONGCHANG
new horizons

**Pyeongchang,
South Korea was chosen
as the host site for the
2018 Winter Olympics**

# FOR THE RECORD

## BIATHLON

### Men

#### 10 KILOMETERS SPRINT
| | | |
|---|---|---|
| 1. | Vincent Jay, France | 24:07.8 |
| 2. | Emil Hegle Svendsen, Norway | 24:20.0 |
| 3. | Jakov Fak, Croatia | 24:21.8 |

#### 12.5 KILOMETERS PURSUIT
| | | |
|---|---|---|
| 1. | Bjorn Ferry, Sweden | 33:38.4 |
| 2. | Christoph Sumann, Austria | 33:54.9 |
| 3. | Vincent Jay, France | 34:06.6 |

#### 15 KILOMETERS MASS START
| | | |
|---|---|---|
| 1. | Evgeny Ustyugov, Russia | 35:35.7 |
| 2. | Martin Fourcade, France | 35:46.2 |
| 3. | Pavol Hurajt, Slovakia | 35:52.3 |

#### 20 KILOMETERS INDIVIDUAL
| | | |
|---|---|---|
| 1. | Emil Hegle Svendsen, Norway | 48:22.3 |
| 2. | Ole Einar Bjoerndalen, Norway | 48:32.0 |
| 2. | Sergey Novikov, Belarus | 48:32.0 |

#### 4 X 7.5-KILOMETER RELAY
| | | |
|---|---|---|
| 1. | Norway | 1:21:38.1 |
| 2. | Austria | 1:22:16.7 |
| 3. | Russia | 1:22:16.9 |

### Women

#### 7.5 KILOMETERS SPRINT
| | | |
|---|---|---|
| 1. | Anastazia Kuzmina, Slovakia | 19:55.6 |
| 2. | Magdalena Neuner, Germany | 19:57.1 |
| 3. | Marie Dorin, France | 20:06.5 |

#### 10 KILOMETERS PURSUIT
| | | |
|---|---|---|
| 1. | Magdalena Neuner, Germany | 30:16.0 |
| 2. | Anastazia Kuzmina, Slovakia | 30:28.3 |
| 3. | Marie Laure Brunet, France | 30:44.3 |

#### 12.5 KILOMETERS MASS START
| | | |
|---|---|---|
| 1. | Magdalena Neuner, Germany | 35:19.6 |
| 2. | Olga Zaitseva, Russia | 35:25.1 |
| 3. | Simone Hauswald, Germany | 35:26.9 |

#### 15 KILOMETERS INDIVIDUAL
| | | |
|---|---|---|
| 1. | Tora Berger, Norway | 40:52.8 |
| 2. | Elena Khrustaleva, Kazakhstan | 41:13.5 |
| 3. | Darya Domracheva, Belarus | 41:21.0 |

#### 4 X 6-KILOMETER RELAY
| | | |
|---|---|---|
| 1. | Russia | 1:09:36.3 |
| 2. | France | 1:10:09.1 |
| 3. | Germany | 1:10:13.4 |

## BOBSLED

### Men
#### TWO
| | | |
|---|---|---|
| 1. | A. Lange/ K. Kuske, Germany I | 3:26.65 |
| 2. | T. Florschuetz, R. Adjei, Germany II | 3:26.87 |
| 3. | A. Zubkov/ A. Voevoda, Russia I | 3:27.51 |

#### FOUR
| | | |
|---|---|---|
| 1. | USA I | 3:24.46 |
| 2. | Germany I | 3:24.84 |
| 3. | Canada I | 3:24.85 |

### Women
#### TWO
| | | |
|---|---|---|
| 1. | K. Humphries/H. Moyse, Canada I | 3:32.28 |
| 2. | H. Upperton/S. Brown, Canada II | 3:33.13 |
| 3. | E. Pac/E. Meyers, USA II | 3:33.40 |

## CURLING

### Men
| | |
|---|---|
| 1. | Canada |
| 2. | Norway |
| 3. | Switzerland |

### Women
| | |
|---|---|
| 1. | Sweden |
| 2. | Canada |
| 3. | China |

## FIGURE SKATING

### Men
| | | Pts |
|---|---|---|
| 1. | Evan Lysacek, United States | 257.67 |
| 2. | Evgeni Plushenko, Russia | 256.36 |
| 3. | Daisuke Takahashi, Japan | 247.23 |

### Women
| | | Pts |
|---|---|---|
| 1. | Kim Yu-Na, South Korea | 228.56 |
| 2. | Mao Asada, Japan | 205.50 |
| 3. | Joannie Rochette, Canada | 202.64 |

### Pairs
| | | Pts |
|---|---|---|
| 1. | Xue Shen/Hongbo Zhao, China | 216.57 |
| 2. | Qing Pang/Jian Tong, China | 213.31 |
| 3. | Aliona Savchenko/Robin Szolkowy, Germany | 210.60 |

### Ice Dancing
| | | Pts |
|---|---|---|
| 1. | Tessa Virtue/Scott Moir, Canada | 221.57 |
| 2. | Meryl Davis/Charlie White, United States | 215.74 |
| 3. | Oksana Domnina/Maxim Shabalin, Russia | 207.64 |

## ICE HOCKEY

### Men
| | |
|---|---|
| 1. | Canada |
| 2. | United States |
| 3. | Finland |

### Women
| | |
|---|---|
| 1. | Canada |
| 2. | United States |
| 3. | Finland |

# LUGE

| Men | | Women | |
|---|---|---|---|
| **SINGLES** | | **SINGLES** | |
| 1....Felix Loch, Germany | 3:13.085 | 1....Tatjana Huefner, Germany | 2:46.524 |
| 2....David Moeller, Germany | 3:13.764 | 2....Nina Reithmayer, Austria | 2:47.014 |
| 3....Armin Zoeggeler, Italy | 3:14.375 | 3....Natalie Geisenberger, Germany | 2:47.101 |

**DOUBLES**

| | |
|---|---|
| 1....Andreas Linger/Wolfgang Linger, Austria | 1:22.705 |
| 2....Andre Sics/Juris Sics, Latvia | 1:22.969 |
| 3....Patric Leitner/Alexander Resch, Germany | 1:23.040 |

# SKELETON

| Men | | Women | |
|---|---|---|---|
| 1. Jon Montgomery, Canada | 3:29.73 | 1. Amy Williams, United Kingdom | 3:35.64 |
| 2. Martins Dukurs, Latvia | 3:29.80 | 2. Kerstin Szymkowiak, Germany | 3:36.20 |
| 3. Alexander Tretyakov, Russia | 3:30.75 | 3. Anja Huber, Germany | 3:36.36 |

# SPEED SKATING

## Men

| 500 METERS* | | TEAM PURSUIT | |
|---|---|---|---|
| 1....Tae-Bum Mo, South Korea | 1:09.82 | 1....Canada | 3:41.37 |
| 2....Keiichiro Nagashima, Japan | 1:09.98 | 2....United States | 3:41.58 |
| 3....Joji Kato, Japan | 1:10.01 | 3....Netherlands | 3:39.95 OR |
| **1,000 METERS** | | **500 METERS SHORT TRACK** | |
| 1....Shani Davis, United States | 1:08.94 | 1....Charles Hamelin, Canada | 40.770 |
| 2....Tae-Bum Mo, South Korea | 1:09.12 | 2....Si-Bak Sung, South Korea | 40.821 |
| 3....Chad Hedrick, United States | 1:09.32 | 3....Francois-Louis Tremblay, Canada | 41.326 |
| **1,500 METERS** | | **1,000 METERS SHORT TRACK** | |
| 1....Mark Tuitert, Netherlands | 1:45.57 | 1....Jung-Su Lee, South Korea | 1:23.747 OR |
| 2....Shani Davis, United States | 1:46.10 | 2....Ho-Suk Lee, South Korea | 1:23.801 |
| 3....Havard Bokko, Norway | 1:46.13 | 3....Apolo Anton Ohno, United States | 1:24.128 |
| **5,000 METERS** | | **1,500 METERS SHORT TRACK** | |
| 1....Sven Kramer, Netherlands | 6:14.60 OR | 1....Jung-Su Lee, South Korea | 2:10.949 |
| 2....Lee Seung-Hoon, South Korea | 6:16.95 | 2....Apolo Anton Ohno, United States | 2:11.072 |
| 3....Ivan Skobrev, Russia | 6:18.05 | 3....J.R. Celski, United States | 2:12.460 |
| **10,000 METERS** | | **5,000-METER SHORT TRACK RELAY** | |
| 1....Seung-Hoon Lee, South Korea | 12:58.55 OR | 1....Canada | 6:43.610 |
| 2....Ivan Skobrev, Russia | 13:02.07 | 2....South Korea | 6:43.845 |
| 3....Bob de Jong, Netherlands | 13:06.73 | 3....United States | 6:44.498 |

## Women

| 500 METERS* | | TEAM PURSUIT | |
|---|---|---|---|
| 1....Sang-Hwa Lee, South Korea | 1:16.09 | 1....Germany | 3:02.82 |
| 2....Jenny Wolf, Germany | 1:16.14 | 2....Japan | 3:02.84 |
| 3....Beixing Wang, China | 1:16.63 | 3....Poland | 3:03.73 |
| **1,000 METERS** | | **500 METERS SHORT TRACK** | |
| 1....Christine Nesbitt, Canada | 1:16.56 | 1....Meng Wang, China | 42.985 |
| 2....Annette Gerritsen, Netherlands | 1:16.58 | 2....Marianne St-Gelais, Canada | 43.241 |
| 3....Laurine van Riessen, Netherlands | 1:16.72 | 3....Arianna Fontana, Italy | 43.804 |
| **1,500 METERS** | | **1,000 METERS SHORT TRACK** | |
| 1....Ireen Wust, Netherlands | 1:56.89 | 1....Meng Wang, China | 1:29.213 |
| 2....Kristina Groves, Canada | 1:57.14 | 2....Katherine Reutter, United States | 1:29.324 |
| 3....Martina Sablikova, Czech Republic | 1:57.96 | 3....Seung-Hi Park, South Korea | 1:29.379 |
| **3,000 METERS** | | **1,500 METERS SHORT TRACK** | |
| 1....Martina Sablikova, Czech Republic | 4:02.53 | 1....Yang Zhou, China | 2:16.993 |
| 2....Stephanie Beckert, Germany | 4:04.62 | 2....Eun-Byul Lee, South Korea | 2:17.849 |
| 3....Kristina Groves, Canada | 4:04.84 | 3....Seung-Hi Park, South Korea | 2:17.927 |
| **5,000 METERS** | | **3,000-METER SHORT TRACK RELAY** | |
| 1....Martina Sablikova, Czech Republic | 6:50.91 | 1....China | 4:06.610 WR |
| 2....Stephanie Beckert, Germany | 6:51.39 | 2....Canada | 4:09.137 |
| 3....Clara Hughes, Canada | 6:55.73 | 3....United States | 4:14.081 |

*Combined time.
Note: OR=Olympic Record; WR=World Record; EOR=Equals Olympic Record; EWR=Equals World Record; WB=World Best.

# FREESTYLE SKIING

## Men

### MOGULS
| | Pts |
|---|---|
| 1. ...Alexandre Bilodeau, Canada | 26.75 |
| 2. ...Dale Begg-Smith, Australia | 26.58 |
| 3. ...Byron Wilson, United States | 26.08 |

### AERIALS
| | Pts |
|---|---|
| 1. ...Alexei Grishin, Belarus | 248.41 |
| 2. ...Jeret Peterson, United States | 247.21 |
| 3. ...Zhongqing Liu, China | 242.53 |

## Women

### MOGULS
| | Pts |
|---|---|
| 1. ...Hannah Kearney, United States | 26.63 |
| 2. ...Jennifer Heil, Canada | 25.69 |
| 3. ...Shannon Bahrke, United States | 25.43 |

### AERIALS
| | Pts |
|---|---|
| 1. ...Lydia Lassila, Australia | 214.74 |
| 2. ...Nina Li, China | 207.23 |
| 3. ...Xinxin Guo, China | 205.22 |

# ALPINE SKIING

## Men

### DOWNHILL
| | |
|---|---|
| 1. ...Didier Defago, Switzerland | 1:54.31 |
| 2. ...Aksel Lund Svindal, Norway | 1:54.38 |
| 3. ...Bode Miller, United States | 1:54.40 |

### SLALOM
| | |
|---|---|
| 1. ...Giuliano Razzoli, Italy | 1:39.32 |
| 2. ...Ivica Kostelic, Croatia | 1:39.48 |
| 3. ...Andre Myhrer, Sweden | 1:39.76 |

### GIANT SLALOM
| | |
|---|---|
| 1. ...Carlo Janka, Switzerland | 2:37.83 |
| 2. ...Kjetil Jansrud, Norway | 2:38.22 |
| 3. ...Aksel Lund Svindal, Norway | 2:38.44 |

### SUPER GIANT SLALOM
| | |
|---|---|
| 1. ...Aksel Lund Svindal, Norway | 1:30.34 |
| 2. ...Bode Miller, United States | 1:30.62 |
| 3. ...Andrew Weibrecht, United States | 1:30.65 |

### SUPER COMBINED
| | |
|---|---|
| 1. ...Bode Miller, United States | 2:44.92 |
| 2. ...Ivica Kostelic, Croatia | 2:44.25 |
| 3. ...Silvan Zurbriggen, Switzerland | 2:45.32 |

## Women

### DOWNHILL
| | |
|---|---|
| 1. ...Lindsey Vonn, United States | 1:44.19 |
| 2. ...Julia Mancuso, United States | 1:44.75 |
| 3. ...Elisabeth Goergl, Austria | 1:45.65 |

### SLALOM
| | |
|---|---|
| 1. ...Maria Riesch, Germany | 1:42.89 |
| 2. ...Marlies Schild, Austria | 1:43.32 |
| 3. ...Sarka Zahrobska, Czech Republic | 1:43.90 |

### GIANT SLALOM
| | |
|---|---|
| 1. ...Viktoria Rebensburg, Germany | 2:27.11 |
| 2. ...Tina Maze, Slovenia | 2:27.15 |
| 3. ...Elisabeth Goergl, Austria | 2:27.25 |

### SUPER GIANT SLALOM
| | |
|---|---|
| 1. ...Andrea Fischbacher, Austria | 1:20.14 |
| 2. ...Tina Maze, Slovenia | 1:20.63 |
| 3. ...Lindsey Vonn, United States | 1:20.88 |

### SUPER COMBINED
| | |
|---|---|
| 1. ...Maria Riesch, Germany | 2:09.14 |
| 2. ...Julia Mancuso, United States | 2:10.08 |
| 3. ...Anja Paerson, Sweden | 2:10.19 |

# NORDIC SKIING

## Men

### INDIVIDUAL SPRINT CLASSIC
| | |
|---|---|
| 1 ...Nikita Kriukov, Russia | 3:36.3 |
| 2. ...Alexander Panzhinsky, Russia | 3:36.3 |
| 3. ...Petter Northug, Norway | 3:45.5 |

### TEAM SPRINT
| | |
|---|---|
| 1. ...Norway | 19:01.0 |
| 2. ...Germany | 19:02.3 |
| 2. ...Russia | 19:02.5 |

### 15 KILOMETERS FREESTYLE
| | |
|---|---|
| 1. ...Dario Cologna, Switzerland | 33:36.3 |
| 2. ...Pietro Piller Cottrer, Italy | 34:00.9 |
| 3. ...Lukas Bauer, Czech Republic | 34:12.0 |

### 30 KILOMETERS PURSUIT (15K FREE + 15K CLASSIC)
| | |
|---|---|
| 1. ...Marcus Hellner, Sweden | 1:15:11.4 |
| 2. ...Tobias Angerer, Germany | 1:15:13.5 |
| 3. ...Johan Olsson, Sweden | 1:15:14.2 |

### 50 KILOMETERS CLASSIC MASS START
| | |
|---|---|
| 1. ...Petter Northug, Norway | 2:05:35.5 |
| 2. ...Axel Teichmann, Germany | 2:05:35.8 |
| 3. ...Johan Olsson, Sweden | 2:05:36.5 |

### 4 X 10-KILOMETER RELAY MIXED
| | |
|---|---|
| 1. ...Sweden | 1:45:05.4 |
| 2. ...Norway | 1:45:21.3 |
| 3. ...Czech Republic | 1:45:21.9 |

### NORMAL (90-M) HILL SKI JUMPING
| | Pts |
|---|---|
| 1. ...Simon Ammann, Switzerland | 276.5 |
| 2. ...Adam Malysz, Poland | 269.5 |
| 3. ...Gregor Schlierenzauer, Austria | 268.0 |

### LARGE (120-M) HILL SKI JUMPING
| | Pts |
|---|---|
| 1. ...Simon Ammann, Switzerland | 283.6 |
| 2. ...Adam Malysz, Poland | 269.4 |
| 3. ...Gregor Schlierenzauer, Austria | 262.2 |

### LARGE (120-M) HILL TEAM SKI JUMPING
| | Pts |
|---|---|
| 1. ...Austria | 1107.9 |
| 2. ...Germany | 1035.8 |
| 3. ...Norway | 1030.3 |

### 90-METER JUMP/10 KM CC NORDIC COMBINED
| | |
|---|---|
| 1. ...Jason Chappuis Lamy, France | 25:47.1 |
| 2. ...Johnny Spillane, United States | 25:47.5 |
| 3. ...Alessandro Pittin, Italy | 25:47.9 |

### 120-METER JUMP/10 KM CC NORDIC COMBINED
| | |
|---|---|
| 1. ...Bill Demong, United States | 25:32.9 |
| 2. ...Johnny Spillane, United States | 25:36.9 |
| 3. ...Bernhard Gruber, Austria | 25:41.7 |

### 4 X 5-KILOMETER TEAM RELAY
| | |
|---|---|
| 1. ...Austria | 49:31.6 |
| 2. ...United States | 49:36.8 |
| 3. ...Germany | 49:51.1 |

### NORDIC SKIING *(Cont.)*
#### Women

**INDIVIDUAL SPRINT CLASSIC**
1. ...Marit Bjoergen, Norway — 3:39.2
2. ...Justyna Kowalczyk, Poland — 3:40.3
3. ...Petra Majdic, Slovenia — 3:41.0

**TEAM SPRINT**
1. ...Germany — 18:03.7
2. ...Sweden — 18:04.3
3. ...Russia — 18:07.7

**10 KILOMETERS FREESTYLE**
1. ...Charlotte Kalla, Sweden — 24:58.4
2. ...Kristina Smigun-Vaehi, Estonia — 25:05.0
3. ...Marit Bjoergen, Norway — 25:14.3

**15 KILOMETERS PURSUIT (7.5K FREE + 7.5K CLASSIC)**
1. ...Marit Bjoergen, Norway — 39:58.1
2. ...Anna Haag, Sweden — 40:07.0
3. ...Justyna Kowalczyk, Poland — 40:07.4

**30 KILOMETERS CLASSIC MASS START**
1. ...Justyna Kowalczyk, Poland — 1:30:33.7
2. ...Marit Bjoergen, Norway — 1:30:34.0
3. ...Aino-Kaisa Saarinen, Finland — 1:31:38.7

**4 X 5-KILOMETER RELAY MIXED**
1. ...Norway — 55:19.5
2. ...Germany — 55:44.1
3. ...Finland — 55:49.9

## SKI CROSS

### Men
1. ...Michael Schmid, Switzerland
2. ...Andreas Matt, Austria
3. ...Audun Groenvold, Norway

### Women
1. ...Ashleigh McIvor, Canada
2. ...Hedda Berntsen, Norway
3. ...Marion Josserand, France

## SNOWBOARDING

### Men

#### PARALLEL GIANT SLALOM
1. ...Jasey Jay Anderson, Canada
2. ...Benjamin Karl, Austria
3. ...Mathieu Bozzetto, France

| HALF-PIPE | Pts |
|---|---|
| 1. ...Shaun White, United States | 48.4 |
| 2. ...Peetu Piiroinen, Finland | 45.0 |
| 3. ...Scott Lago, United States | 42.8 |

#### SNOWBOARD CROSS
1. ...Seth Wescott, United States
2. ...Mike Robertson, Canada
3. ...Tony Ramoin, France

### Women

#### PARALLEL GIANT SLALOM
1. ...Nicolien Sauerbreij, Netherlands
2. ...Ekaterina Ilyukhina, Russia
3. ...Marion Kreiner, Austria

| HALF-PIPE | Pts |
|---|---|
| 1. ...Torah Bright, Australia | 45.0 |
| 2. ...Hannah Teter, United States | 42.4 |
| 3. ...Kelly Clark, United States | 42.2 |

#### SNOWBOARD CROSS
1. ...Maelle Ricker, Canada
2. ...Deborah Anthonioz, France
3. ...Olivia Nobs, Switzerland

# FOR THE RECORD • Year by Year

## Olympic Games Locations and Dates

### Summer

| | Year | Site | Dates | COMPETITORS | | | Most Medals | US Medals |
| | | | | Men | Women | Nations | | |
|---|---|---|---|---|---|---|---|---|
| I | 1896 | Athens, Greece | Apr 6–15 | 311 | 0 | 13 | Greece (10-19-18—47) | 11-6-2—19 (2nd) |
| II | 1900 | Paris, France | May 20–Oct 28 | 1319 | 11 | 22 | France (29-41-32—102) | 20-14-19—53 (2nd) |
| III | 1904 | St Louis, United States | July 1–Nov 23 | 681 | 6 | 12 | United States (80-86-72—238) | — |
| — | 1906 | Athens, Greece | Apr 22–May 28 | 77 | 7 | 20 | France (15-9-16—40) | 12-6-5—23 (4th) |
| IV | 1908 | London, Great Britain | Apr 27–Oct 31 | 1999 | 36 | 23 | Britain (56-50-39—145) | 23-12-12—47 (2nd) |
| V | 1912 | Stockholm, Sweden | May 5–July 22 | 2490 | 57 | 28 | Sweden (24-24-17—65) | 23-19-19—61 (2nd) |
| VI | 1916 | Berlin, Germany | Canceled because of war | | | | | |
| VII | 1920 | Antwerp, Belgium | Apr 20–Sep 12 | 2543 | 64 | 29 | United States (41-27-28—96) | — |
| VIII | 1924 | Paris, France | May 4–July 27 | 2956 | 136 | 44 | United States (45-27-27—99) | — |
| IX | 1928 | Amsterdam, Netherlands | May 17–Aug 12 | 2724 | 290 | 46 | United States (22-18-16—56) | — |
| X | 1932 | Los Angeles, United States | July 30–Aug 14 | 1281 | 127 | 37 | United States (41-32-31—104) | — |
| XI | 1936 | Berlin, Germany | Aug 1–16 | 3738 | 328 | 49 | Germany (33-26-30—89) | 24-20-12—56 (2nd) |
| XII | 1940 | Tokyo, Japan | Canceled because of war | | | | | |
| XIII | 1944 | London, Great Britain | Canceled because of war | | | | | |
| XIV | 1948 | London, Great Britain | July 29–Aug 14 | 3714 | 385 | 59 | United States (38-27-19—84) | — |
| XV | 1952 | Helsinki, Finland | July 19–Aug 3 | 4407 | 518 | 69 | United States (40-19-17—76) | — |
| XVI | 1956 | Melbourne, Australia* | Nov 22–Dec 8 | 2958 | 384 | 67 | USSR (37-29-32—98) | 32-25-17—74 (2nd) |
| XVII | 1960 | Rome, Italy | Aug 25–Sep 11 | 4738 | 610 | 83 | USSR (43-29-31—103) | 34-21-16—71 (2nd) |
| XVIII | 1964 | Tokyo, Japan | Oct 10–24 | 4457 | 683 | 93 | United States (36-26-28—90) | — |
| XIX | 1968 | Mexico City, Mexico | Oct 12–27 | 4750 | 781 | 112 | United States (45-28-34—107) | — |
| XX | 1972 | Munich, West Germany | Aug 26–Sep 10 | 5848 | 1299 | 122 | USSR (50-27-22—99) | 33-31-30—94 (2nd) |
| XXI | 1976 | Montreal, Canada | July 17–Aug 1 | 4834 | 1251 | 92† | USSR (49-41-35—125) | 34-35-25—94 (3rd) |
| XXII | 1980 | Moscow, USSR | July 19–Aug 3 | 4265 | 1088 | 81‡ | USSR (80-69-46—195) | Did not compete |

## Summer (Cont.)

| | Year | Site | Dates | COMPETITORS | | | Most Medals | US Medals |
|---|---|---|---|---|---|---|---|---|
| | | | | Men | Women | Nations | | |
| XXIII | 1984 | Los Angeles, United States | July 28–Aug 12 | 5458 | 1620 | 141# | United States (83-61-30—174) | — |
| XXIV | 1988 | Seoul, South Korea | Sep 17–Oct 2 | 7105 | 2476 | 160 | USSR (55-31-46—132) | 36-31-27—94 (3rd) |
| XXV | 1992 | Barcelona, Spain | July 25–Aug. 9 | 7555 | 3008 | 172 | Unified Team (45-38-29—112) | 37-34-37—108 (2nd) |
| XXVI | 1996 | Atlanta, United States | July 19–Aug 4 | 6984 | 3766 | 197 | United States (44-32-25—101) | |
| XXVII | 2000 | Sydney, Australia | Sept 15–Oct 1 | 6862 | 4254 | 199 | United States (39-25-33—97) | |
| XXVIII | 2004 | Athens, Greece | Aug 11–Aug 29 | 11099 total | | 202 | United States (35-39-29—103) | |
| XXIX | 2008 | Beijing, China | Aug 8–Aug 24 | 11028 total | | 204 | United States (36-38-36—110) | — |

*The equestrian events were held in Stockholm, Sweden, June 10–17, 1956.
†This figure includes Cameroon, Egypt, Morocco, and Tunisia, countries that boycotted the 1976 Olympics after some of their athletes had already competed.
‡The U.S. was among 65 countries that did not participate in the 1980 Summer Games in Moscow.
#The USSR, East Germany, and 14 other countries did not participate in the 1984 Summer Games in Los Angeles.

## Winter

| | Year | Site | Dates | Competitors | | | Most Medals | US Medals |
|---|---|---|---|---|---|---|---|---|
| | | | | Men | Women | Nations | | |
| I | 1924 | Chamonix, France | Jan 25–Feb 4 | 281 | 13 | 16 | Norway (4-7-6—17) | 1-2-1—4 (3rd) |
| II | 1928 | St. Moritz, Switzerland | Feb 11–19 | 366 | 27 | 25 | Norway (6-4-5—15) | 2-2-2—6 (2nd) |
| III | 1932 | Lake Placid, United States | Feb 4–13 | 277 | 30 | 17 | United States (6-4-2—12) | |
| IV | 1936 | Garmisch-Partenkirchen, Germany | Feb 6–16 | 680 | 76 | 28 | Norway (7-5-3—15) | 1-0-3—4 (T-5th) |
| — | 1940 | Garmisch-Partenkirchen, Germany | Canceled because of war | | | | | |
| — | 1944 | Cortina d'Ampezzo, Italy | Canceled because of war | | | | | |
| V | 1948 | St. Moritz, Switzerland | Jan 30–Feb 8 | 636 | 77 | 28 | Norway (4-3-3—10) Sweden (4-3-3—10) Switzerland (3-4-3—10) | 3-4-2—9 (4th) |
| VI | 1952 | Oslo, Norway | Feb 14–25 | 624 | 108 | 30 | Norway (7-3-6—16) | 4-6-1—11 (2nd) |
| VII | 1956 | Cortina d'Ampezzo, Italy | Jan 26–Feb 5 | 687 | 132 | 32 | USSR (7-3-6—16) | 2-3-2—7 (T-4th) |
| VIII | 1960 | Squaw Valley, United States | Feb 18–28 | 502 | 146 | 30 | USSR (7-5-9—21) | 3-4-3—10 (2nd) |
| IX | 1964 | Innsbruck, Austria | Jan 29–Feb 9 | 758 | 175 | 36 | USSR (11-8-6—25) | 1-2-3—6 (7th) |

## Winter *(Cont.)*

| | Year | Site | Dates | Competitors Men | Women | Nations | Most Medals | US Medals |
|---|---|---|---|---|---|---|---|---|
| X | 1968 | Grenoble, France | Feb 6–18 | 1063 | 230 | 37 | Norway (6-6-2—14) | 1-5-1—7 (T-7th) |
| XI | 1972 | Sapporo, Japan | Feb 3–13 | 927 | 218 | 35 | USSR (8-5-3—16) | 3-2-3—8 (6th) |
| XII | 1976 | Innsbruck, Austria | Feb 4–15 | 1013 | 248 | 37 | USSR (13-6-8—27) | 3-3-4—10 (T-3rd) |
| XIII | 1980 | Lake Placid, United States | Feb 13–24 | 1012 | 271 | 37 | East Germany (9-7-7—23) | 6-4-2—12 (3rd) |
| XIV | 1984 | Sarajevo, Yugoslavia | Feb 8–19 | 1127 | 283 | 49 | USSR (6-10-9—25) | 4-4-0—8 (T-5th) |
| XV | 1988 | Calgary, Canada | Feb 13–28 | 1270 | 364 | 57 | USSR (11-9-9—29) | 2-1-3—6 (T-8th) |
| XVI | 1992 | Albertville, France | Feb 8–23 | 1313 | 488 | 65 | Germany (10-10-6—26) | 5-4-2—11 (6th) |
| XVII | 1994 | Lillehammer, Norway | Feb 12–27 | 1302 | 542 | 67 | Norway (10-11-5—26) | 6-5-2—13 (T-5th) |
| XVIII | 1998 | Nagano, Japan Sweden | Feb 7–22 | 2302 total | | 72 | Germany (12-9-8—29) | 6-3-4—13 (6th) |
| XIX | 2002 | Salt Lake City, United States | Feb 8–24 | 1513 | 886 | 77 | Germany (12-16-7—35) | 10-13-11—34 (2nd) |
| XX | 2006 | Turin, Italy | Feb 10–26 | 1627 | 1006 | 80 | Germany (11-12-6—29) | 9-9-7—25 (2nd) |
| XXI | 2010 | Vancouver, Canada | Feb 12–28 | 2622 total | | 92 | United States (9-15-13—37) | — |

## Summary

### NATIONS

| Nation | Gold | Silver | Bronze | Total | Nation | Gold | Silver | Bronze | Total |
|---|---|---|---|---|---|---|---|---|---|
| United States | 934 | 730 | 643 | 2307 | Japan | 123 | 112 | 125 | 360 |
| USSR (1952–88) | 395 | 319 | 296 | 1010 | Russia | 109 | 101 | 112 | 322 |
| Great Britain | 209 | 259 | 258 | 725 | Finland | 103 | 80 | 113 | 296 |
| Germany | 196 | 222 | 241 | 659 | Romania | 86 | 89 | 117 | 292 |
| (1896–1936, 1992– ) | | | | | Poland | 62 | 80 | 119 | 261 |
| France | 191 | 208 | 241 | 640 | Canada | 57 | 95 | 106 | 258 |
| Italy | 190 | 158 | 173 | 523 | The Netherlands | 72 | 80 | 96 | 248 |
| Sweden | 142 | 160 | 173 | 475 | South Korea | 68 | 74 | 73 | 215 |
| Hungary | 159 | 141 | 160 | 460 | Bulgaria | 51 | 84 | 77 | 212 |
| Australia | 134 | 141 | 169 | 444 | West Germany (1952–88) | 56 | 67 | 81 | 204 |
| East Germany (1956–88) | 153 | 129 | 127 | 409 | Cuba | 67 | 62 | 60 | 189 |
| China | 163 | 117 | 106 | 386 | Switzerland | 45 | 69 | 65 | 179 |

### INDIVIDUALS — OVERALL

#### Men

| Athlete, Nation | Sport | G | S | B | Tot |
|---|---|---|---|---|---|
| Michael Phelps, United States | Swim | 14 | 0 | 2 | 16 |
| Nikolai Andrianov, USSR | Gym | 7 | 5 | 3 | 15 |
| Boris Shakhlin, USSR | Gym | 7 | 4 | 2 | 13 |
| Edoardo Mangiarotti, Italy | Fenc | 6 | 5 | 2 | 13 |
| Takashi Ono, Japan | Gym | 5 | 4 | 4 | 13 |
| Paavo Nurmi, Finland | Track | 9 | 3 | 0 | 12 |
| Sawao Kato, Japan | Gym | 8 | 3 | 1 | 12 |
| Alexei Nemov, Russia | Gym | 4 | 2 | 6 | 12 |
| Mark Spitz, United States | Swim | 9 | 1 | 1 | 11 |
| Matt Biondi, United States | Swim | 8 | 2 | 1 | 11 |
| Viktor Chukarin, USSR | Gym | 7 | 3 | 1 | 11 |
| Carl Osburn, United States | Shoot | 5 | 4 | 2 | 11 |
| Ray Ewry, United States | Track | 10 | 0 | 0 | 10 |
| Carl Lewis, United States | Track | 9 | 1 | 0 | 10 |
| Aladár Gerevich, Hungary | Fen | 7 | 1 | 2 | 10 |
| Akinori Nakayama, Japan | Gym | 6 | 2 | 2 | 10 |
| Vitaly Scherbo, UT/Belarus | Gym | 6 | 0 | 4 | 10 |
| Aleksandr Dityatin, USSR | Gym | 3 | 6 | 1 | 10 |

#### Women

| Athlete, Nation | Sport | G | S | B | Tot |
|---|---|---|---|---|---|
| Larissa Latynina, USSR | Gym | 9 | 5 | 4 | 18 |
| Jenny Thompson, United States | Swim | 8 | 3 | 1 | 12 |
| Vera Cáslavská, Czech | Gym | 7 | 4 | 0 | 11 |
| Agnes Keleti, Hungary | Gym | 5 | 3 | 2 | 10 |
| Polina Astaknova, USSR | Gym | 5 | 2 | 3 | 10 |
| Dara Torres, United States | Swim | 4 | 1 | 4 | 9 |
| Nadia Comaneci, Romania | Gym | 5 | 3 | 1 | 9 |
| Lyudmila Tourischeva, USSR | Gym | 4 | 3 | 2 | 9 |
| Kornelia Ender, E Germany | Swim | 4 | 4 | 0 | 8 |
| Dawn Fraser, Australia | Swim | 4 | 4 | 0 | 8 |
| Shirley Babashoff, United States | Swim | 2 | 6 | 0 | 8 |
| Sofia Muratova, USSR | Gym | 2 | 2 | 4 | 8 |
| Inge de Bruijn, Netherlands | Swim | 4 | 2 | 2 | 8 |

Eight tied with seven.

### Summer *(Cont.)*

#### INDIVIDUALS — GOLD

#### Men

Micheal Phelps, United States .........................14
Ray Ewry, United States ...................................10
Paavo Nurmi, Finland ......................................9
Carl Lewis, United States ................................9
Mark Spitz, United States ................................9
Sawao Kato, Japan...........................................8
Matt Biondi, United States................................8
Nikolai Andrianov, USSR ..................................7
Boris Shakhlin, USSR........................................7
Viktor Chukarin, USSR ......................................7
Aladár Gerevich, Hungary.................................7

#### Women

Larissa Latynina, USSR ....................................9
Jenny Thompson, United States ........................8
Vera Cáslavská, Czech......................................7
Kristin Otto, E Germany.....................................6
Agnes Keleti, Hungary ......................................5
Nadia Comaneci, Romania................................5
Polina Astaknova, USSR....................................5
Krisztina Egerszegi, Hungary ...........................5
Kornelia Ender, E Germany ..............................4
Dawn Fraser, Australia......................................4
Lyudmila Tourischeva, USSR.............................4
Evelyn Ashford, United States...........................4
Janet Evans, United States ..............................4
Fanny Blankers-Koen, Neth..............................4
Betty Cuthbert, Australia ..................................4
Pat McCormick, United States ..........................4
Bärbel Eckert Wöckel, E Ger............................4
Amy Van Dyken, United States..........................4
Inge de Bruijn, Netherlands .............................4
Yana Klochkova, Ukraine...................................4
Dara Torres, United States ...............................4

## Winter

### NATIONS

| Nation | Gold | Silver | Bronze | Total |
|---|---|---|---|---|
| Norway | 107 | 106 | 90 | 303 |
| United States | 87 | 95 | 71 | 253 |
| Germany | 78 | 78 | 53 | 209 |
| Austria | 55 | 70 | 76 | 201 |
| USSR (1956–88) | 78 | 57 | 59 | 194 |
| Finland | 42 | 58 | 56 | 156 |
| Canada | 52 | 45 | 48 | 145 |
| Sweden | 48 | 32 | 48 | 128 |
| Switzerland | 43 | 37 | 46 | 126 |
| East Germany (1956-88) | 39 | 36 | 35 | 110 |
| Italy | 37 | 32 | 37 | 106 |
| France | 27 | 27 | 38 | 92 |
| Russia | 36 | 29 | 26 | 91 |
| Netherlands | 29 | 31 | 26 | 86 |
| South Korea | 23 | 14 | 8 | 45 |
| China | 9 | 18 | 17 | 44 |
| West Germany (1956–88) | 11 | 15 | 13 | 39 |
| Japan | 9 | 13 | 15 | 37 |
| Czechoslovakia (1924–92) | 2 | 8 | 15 | 25 |
| United Kingdom | 8 | 3 | 10 | 21 |

### INDIVIDUALS — OVERALL

#### Men

| Athlete, Nation | Sport | G | S | B | Tot |
|---|---|---|---|---|---|
| Bjørn Dæhlie, Norway | N Ski | 8 | 4 | 0 | 12 |
| Sixten Jernberg, Sweden | N Ski | 4 | 3 | 2 | 9 |
| Apolo Anton Ohno, U.S. | Shrt Trk | 2 | 2 | 4 | 8 |

Seven tied with 7.

#### Women

| Athlete, Nation | Sport | G | S | B | Tot |
|---|---|---|---|---|---|
| Raisa Smetanina, USSR/UT | N Ski | 4 | 5 | 1 | 10 |
| Lyubov Egorova, UT/Russia | N Ski | 6 | 3 | 0 | 9 |
| Larissa Lazutina, UT/Russia | N Ski | 5 | 3 | 1 | 9 |
| Stefania Belmondo, Italy | N Ski | 2 | 3 | 4 | 9 |

Four tied with 8.

### INDIVIDUALS — GOLD

#### Men

| | |
|---|---|
| Bjørn Dæhlie, Norway | 8 |
| A. Clas Thunberg, Finland | 5 |
| O. Bjoerndalen, Norway | 5 |
| Eric Heiden, United States | 5 |

Nine tied with 4.

#### Women

| | |
|---|---|
| Lyubov Egorova, UT/Russia | 6 |
| Lydia Skoblikova, USSR | 6 |
| Larissa Lazutina, UT/Russia | 5 |
| Bonnie Blair, United States | 5 |

Four tied with 4.

## BIATHLON

### Men

#### 10 KILOMETERS SPRINT

1980 ....Frank Ullrich, East Germany 32:10.69
1984 ....Eirik Kvalfoss, Norway 30:53.8
1988 ....Frank-Peter Rötsch, West Germany 25:08.1
1992 ....Mark Kirchner, Germany 26:02.3
1994 ....Sergei Tchepikov, Russia 28:07.0
1998 ....Ole Einar Bjorndalen, Norway 27:16.2
2002 ....Ole Einar Bjorndalen, Norway 24:51.3
2006 ....Sven Fischer, Germany 24:11.6
2010 ....Vincent Jay, France 24:07.8

#### 12.5 KILOMETERS PURSUIT

2002 ....Ole Einar Bjorndalen, Norway 24:51.3
2006 ....Vincent Defrasne, France 35:20.2
2010 ....Bjorn Ferry, Sweden 33:38.4

#### 15 KILOMETERS MASS START

2006 ....Michael Greis, Germany 47:20.0
2010 ....Evgeny Ustyugov, Russia 35:35.7

#### 20 KILOMETERS INDIVIDUAL

1960 ....Klas Lestander, Sweden 1:33:21.6
1964 ....Vladimir Melyanin, USSR 1:20:26.8
1968 ....Magnar Solberg, Norway 1:13:45.9
1972 ....Magnar Solberg, Norway 1:15:55.5
1976 ....Nikolay Kruglov, USSR 1:14:12.26
1980 ....Anatoliy Alyabiev, USSR 1:08:16.31
1984 ....Peter Angerer, West Germany 1:11:52.7
1988 ....Frank-Peter Rötsch, W. Germany 56:33.3
1992 ....Evgueni Redkine, Unified Team 57:34.4
1994 ....Sergei Tarasov, Russia 57:25.3
1998 ....Halvard Hanevold, Norway 56:16.4
2002 ....Ole Einar Bjorndalen, Norway 51:03.3
2006 ....Michael Greis, Germany 54:23.0
2010 ....Emil Hegle Svendsen, Norway 48:22.3

#### 4 X 7.5-KILOMETER RELAY

1968 ...............USSR 2:13:02.4
1972 ...............USSR 1:51:44.92
1976 ...............USSR 1:57:55.64
1980 ...............USSR 1:34:03.27
1984 ...............USSR 1:38:51.7
1988 ...............USSR 1:22:30.0
1992 ...............Germany 1:24:43.5
1994 ...............Germany 1:30:22.1
1998 ...............Germany 1:19:43.3
2002 ...............Norway 1:23:42.3
2006 ...............Germany 1:21:51.5
2010 ...............Norway 1:21:38.1

## Women

### 7.5 KILOMETERS SPRINT

| | | |
|---|---|---|
| 1992 | Antissa Restzova, Unified Team | 24:29.2 |
| 1994 | Myriam Bedard, Canada | 26:08.8 |
| 1998 | Galina Koukleva, Russia | 23:08.0 |
| 2002 | Kati Wilhemn, Germany | 20:41.4 |
| 2006 | Florence Baverel-Robert, France | 22:31.4 |
| 2010 | Anastazia Kuzmina, Slovakia | 19:55.6 |

### 10 KILOMETERS PURSUIT

| | | |
|---|---|---|
| 2002 | Olga Pyleva, Russia | 31:07.7 |
| 2006 | Kati Wilhemn, Germany | 36:43.6 |
| 2010 | Magdalena Neuner, Germany | 30:16.0 |

### 12.5 KILOMETERS MASS START

| | | |
|---|---|---|
| 2006 | Anna Carin Olofsson, Sweden | 40:36.5 |
| 2010 | Magdalena Neuner, Germany | 35:19.6 |

### 15 KILOMETERS INDIVIDUAL

| | | |
|---|---|---|
| 1992 | Antje Misersky, Germany | 51:47.2 |
| 1994 | Myriam Bedard, Canada | 52:06.6 |
| 1998 | Ekaterina Dofovska, Bulgaria | 54:52.0 |
| 2002 | Andrea Henkel, Germany | 47:29.1 |
| 2006 | Svetlana Ishmouratova, Russia | 49:24.1 |
| 2010 | Tora Berger, Norway | 40:52.8 |

### 3 X 7.5-KILOMETER RELAY

| | | |
|---|---|---|
| 1992 | France | 1:15:55.6 |
| 1994 | Russia | 1:47:19.5 |
| 1998 | Germany | 1:40:13.6 |
| 2002 | Germany | 1:27:55.0 |

### 4 X 6-KILOMETER RELAY

| | | |
|---|---|---|
| 2006 | Russia | 1:16:12.5 |
| 2010 | Russia | 1:09:36.3 |

## BOBSLED

### Men

#### FOURS

| | | |
|---|---|---|
| 1924 | Switzerland (Eduard Scherrer) | 5:45.54 |
| 1928 | United States (William Fiske) (5-man) | 3:20.50 |
| 1932 | United States (William Fiske) | 7:53.68 |
| 1936 | Switzerland (Pierre Musy) | 5:19.85 |
| 1948 | United States (Francis Tyler) | 5:20.10 |
| 1952 | Germany (Andreas Ostler) | 5:07.84 |
| 1956 | Switzerland (Franz Kapus) | 5:10.44 |
| 1960 | Not held | |
| 1964 | Canada (Victor Emery) | 4:14.46 |
| 1968 | Italy (Eugenio Monti) (2 runs) | 2:17.39 |
| 1972 | Switzerland (Jean Wicki) | 4:43.07 |
| 1976 | E Germany (Meinhard Nehmer) | 3:40.43 |
| 1980 | E Germany (Meinhard Nehmer) | 3:59.92 |
| 1984 | E Germany (Wolfgang Hoppe) | 3:20.22 |
| 1988 | Switzerland (Ekkehard Fasser) | 3:47.51 |
| 1992 | Austria (Ingo Appelt) | 3:53.90 |
| 1994 | Germany (Harold Czudaj) | 3:27.78 |
| 1998 | Germany (Christoph Langen) | 2:39.41 |
| 2002 | Germany (Andre Lange) | 3:10.11 |
| 2006 | Germany (Andre Lange) | 3:40.42 |
| 2010 | United States (Steven Holcomb) | 3:24.46 |

Note: Driver in parentheses.

#### DOUBLES

| | | |
|---|---|---|
| 1932 | United States (Hubert Stevens) | 8:14.74 |
| 1936 | United States (Ivan Brown) | 5:29.29 |
| 1948 | Switzerland (Felix Endrich) | 5:29.20 |
| 1952 | Germany (Andreas Ostler) | 5:24.54 |
| 1956 | Italy (Lamberto Dalla Costa) | 5:30.14 |
| 1960 | Not held | |
| 1964 | Great Britain (Anthony Nash) | 4:21.90 |
| 1968 | Italy (Eugenio Monti) | 4:41.54 |
| 1972 | West Germany (Wolfgang Zimmerer) | 4:57.07 |
| 1976 | East Germany (Meinhard Nehmer) | 3:44.42 |
| 1980 | Switzerland (Erich Schärer) | 4:09.36 |
| 1984 | East Germany (Wolfgang Hoppe) | 3:25.56 |
| 1988 | USSR (Janis Kipours) | 3:53.48 |
| 1992 | Switzerland (Gustav Weder) | 4:03.26 |
| 1994 | Switzerland (Gustav Weder) | 3:30.81 |
| 1998 | Canada (Pierre Lueders) | 3:37.24 |
| | Italy (Guenther Huber) | 3:37.24 |
| 2002 | Germany (Martin Langen) | 3:10:11 |
| 2006 | Germany (Andre Lange) | 3:43.38 |
| 2010 | Germany (Andre Lange) | 3:26.65 |

Note: Driver in parentheses.

### Women

#### DOUBLES

| | | |
|---|---|---|
| 2002 | United States (Jill Bakken) | 1:37:76 |
| 2006 | Germany (Sandra Kiriasis) | 3:49.98 |
| 2010 | Canada (Kaillie Humphries) | 3:32.28 |

Note: Driver in parentheses.

## CURLING

### Men

1998 .....Switzerland, Canada, Norway
2002 .....Norway, Canada, Switzerland
2006 .....Canada, Finland, United States
2010 .....Canada, Norway, Switzerland
Note: In order: gold, silver, and bronze medals.

### Women

1998 .....Canada, Denmark, Sweden
2002 .....Britain, Switzerland, Canada
2006 .....Sweden, Switzerland, Canada
2010 .....Sweden, Canada, China
Note: In order: gold, silver, and bronze medals.

## ICE HOCKEY

### Men

1920* ....Canada, United States, Czechoslovakia
1924 .....Canada, United States, Great Britain
1928 .....Canada, Sweden, Switzerland
1932 .....Canada, United States, Germany
1936 .....Great Britain, Canada, United States
1948 .....Canada, Czechoslovakia, Switzerland
1952 .....Canada, United States, Sweden
1956 .....USSR, United States, Canada
1960 .....United States, Canada, USSR
1964 .....USSR, Sweden, Czechoslovakia
1968 .....USSR, Czechoslovakia, Canada
1972 .....USSR, United States, Czechoslovakia

1976 .....USSR, Czechoslovakia, West Germany
1980 .....United States, USSR, Sweden
1984 .....USSR, Czechoslovakia, Sweden
1988 .....USSR, Finland, Sweden
1992 .....Unified Team, Canada, Czechoslovakia
1994 .....Sweden, Canada, Finland
1998 .....Czech Republic, Russia, Finland
2002 .....Canada, United States, Russia
2006 .....Sweden, Finland, Czech Republic
2010 .....Canada, United States, Finland
*Competition held at Summer Games in Antwerp.
Note: In order: gold, silver, and bronze medals.

### Women

1998 .....United States, Canada, Finland
2002 .....Canada, United States, Sweden

2006 .....Canada, Sweden, United States
2010 .....Canada, United States, Finland
Note: In order: gold, silver, and bronze medals.

## LUGE

### Men

| | | |
|---|---|---|
| **SINGLES** | | |
| 1964 .....Thomas Köhler, East Germany | 3:26.77 |
| 1968 .....Manfred Schmid, Austria | 2:52.48 |
| 1972 .....Wolfgang Scheidel, West Germany | 3:27.58 |
| 1976 .....Detlef Guenther, West Germany | 3:27.688 |
| 1980 .....Bernhard Glass, West Germany | 2:54.796 |
| 1984 .....Paul Hildgartner, Italy | 3:04.258 |
| 1988 .....Jens Müller, West Germany | 3:05.548 |
| 1992 .....Georg Hackl, Germany | 3:02.363 |
| 1994 .....Georg Hackl, Germany | 3:21.571 |
| 1998 .....Georg Hackl, Germany | 3:18.44 |
| 2002 .....Armin Zoeggeler, Italy | 2:57.941 |
| 2006 .....Armin Zoeggeler, Italy | 3:26.088 |
| 2010 .....Felix Loch, Germany | 3:13.085 |

| | |
|---|---|
| **DOUBLES** | |
| 1964 ...............Austria | 1:41.62 |
| 1968 ...............East Germany | 1:35.85 |
| 1972 ...............East Germany | 1:28.35 |
| 1976 ...............East Germany | 1:25.604 |
| 1980 ...............East Germany | 1:19.331 |
| 1984 ...............West Germany | 1:23.620 |
| 1988 ...............East Germany | 1:31.940 |
| 1992 ...............Germany | 1:32.053 |
| 1994 ...............Italy | 1:36.720 |
| 1998 ...............Germany | 1:41.105 |
| 2002 ...............Germany | 1:26.082 |
| 2006 ...............Austria | 1:34.497 |
| 2010 ...............Austria | 1:22.705 |

### Women

| | |
|---|---|
| **SINGLES** | |
| 1964 .....Ortrun Enderlein, Germany | 3:24.67 |
| 1968 .....Erica Lechner, Italy | 2:28.66 |
| 1972 .....Anna-Maria Müller, East Germany | 2:59.18 |
| 1976 .....Margit Schumann, East Germany | 2:50.621 |
| 1980 .....Vera Zozulya, USSR | 2:36.537 |
| 1984 .....Steffi Martin, East Germany | 2:46.570 |
| 1988 .....Steffi Walter (Martin), East Germany | 3:03.973 |

| | |
|---|---|
| **SINGLES** *(CONT.)* | |
| 1992 .....Doris Neuner, Austria | 3:06.696 |
| 1994 .....Gerda Weissensteiner, Italy | 3:15.517 |
| 1998 .....Silke Kraushaar, Germany | 3:23.779 |
| 2002 .....Sylke Otto, Germany | 2:52.464 |
| 2006 .....Sylke Otto, Germany | 3:07.979 |
| 2010 .....Tatjana Huefner, Germany | 2:46.524 |

## FIGURE SKATING

| **Men** | PTS |
|---|---|
| 1908* ............Ulrich Salchow, Sweden | |
| 1920† ............Gillis Grafström, Sweden | |
| 1924 ............Gillis Grafström, Sweden | |
| 1928 ............Gillis Grafström, Sweden | |
| 1932 ............Karl Schäfer, Austria | |
| 1936 ............Karl Schäfer, Austria | |
| 1948 ............Dick Button, United States | |
| 1952 ............Dick Button, United States | |
| 1956 ............Hayes Alan Jenkins, United States | |
| 1960 ............David Jenkins, United States | |
| 1964 ............Manfred Schnelldorfer, W Germany | |
| 1968 ............Wolfgang Schwarz, Austria | |
| 1972 ............Ondrej Nepela, Czechoslovakia | |
| 1976 ............John Curry, Great Britain | |
| 1980 ............Robin Cousins, Great Britain | |
| 1984 ............Scott Hamilton, United States | |
| 1988 ............Brian Boitano, United States | |
| 1992 ............Victor Petrenko, Unified Team | |
| 1994 ............Alexei Urmanov, Russia | |
| 1998 ............Ilia Kulik, Russia | |
| 2002 ............Alexei Yagudin, Russia | |
| 2006‡ ..........Evgeni Plushenko, Russia | 258.33 |
| 2010 ............Evan Lysacek, United States | 257.67 |

| **Women** | PTS |
|---|---|
| 1908* .............Madge Syers, Great Britain | |
| 1920† .............Magda Julin, Sweden | |
| 1924 .............Herma Szabo-Planck, Austria | |
| 1928 .............Sonja Henie, Norway | |
| 1932 .............Sonja Henie, Norway | |
| 1936 .............Sonja Henie, Norway | |
| 1948 .............Barbara Ann Scott, Canada | |
| 1952 .............Jeanette Altwegg, Great Britain | |
| 1956 .............Tenley Albright, United States | |
| 1960 .............Carol Heiss, United States | |
| 1964 .............Sjoukje Dijkstra, Netherlands | |
| 1968 .............Peggy Fleming, United States | |
| 1972 .............Beatrix Schuba, Austria | |
| 1976 .............Dorothy Hamill, United States | |
| 1980 .............Anett Pötzsch, E Germany | |
| 1984 .............Katarina Witt, E Germany | |
| 1988 .............Katarina Witt, E Germany | |
| 1992 .............Kristi Yamaguchi, United States | |
| 1994 .............Oksana Baiul, Ukraine | |
| 1998 .............Tara Lipinski, United States | |
| 2002 .............Sarah Hughes, United States | |
| 2006‡ ............Shizuka Arakawa, Japan | 191.34 |
| 2010 .............Kim Yu-Na, South Korea | 228.56 |

\*Competition held at Summer Games in London.
†Competition held at Summer Games in Antwerp.
‡In 2004, the ISU adopted a new overall scoring system.

\*Competition held at Summer Games in London.
†Competition held at Summer Games in Antwerp.
‡In 2004, the ISU adopted a new overall scoring system.

## FIGURE SKATING *(Cont.)*

### Mixed

#### PAIRS

| | |
|---|---|
| 1908* | ....Anna Hübler, Heinrich Burger, Germany |
| 1920† | ...Ludowika, Walter Jakobsson-Eilers, Finland |
| 1924 | .....Helene Engelmann, Alfred Berger, Austria |
| 1928 | .....Andree Joly, Pierre Brunet, France |
| 1932 | .....Andree Brunet (Joly), Pierre Brunet, France |
| 1936 | .....Maxi Herber, Ernst Baier, Germany |
| 1948 | .....Micheline Lannoy, Pierre Baugniet, Belgium |
| 1952 | .....Ria Falk and Paul Falk, W Germany |
| 1956 | .....Elisabeth Schwartz, Kurt Oppelt, Austria |
| 1960 | .....Barbara Wagner, Robert Paul, Canada |
| 1964 | .....Lyudmila Beloussova, Oleg Protopopov, USSR |
| 1968 | .....Lyudmila Beloussova, Oleg Protopopov, USSR |
| 1972 | .....Irina Rodnina, Alexei Ulanov, USSR |
| 1976 | .....Irina Rodnina, Aleksandr Zaitzev, USSR |
| 1980 | .....Irina Rodnina, Aleksandr Zaitzev, USSR |
| 1984 | .....Elena Valova, Oleg Vasiliev, USSR |
| 1988 | .....Ekaterina Gordeeva, Sergei Grinkov, USSR |
| 1992 | .....Natalia Michkouteniok, Artour Dmitriev, Unified Team |
| 1994 | ....Ekaterina Gordeeva, Sergei Grinkov, Russia |

#### PAIRS *(CONT.)*

| | | Pts |
|---|---|---|
| 1998 | .....Oksana Kazakova, Artur Dmitriev, Russia | |
| 2002 | .....E. Berezhnaya, A. Sikharulidze, Russia | |
| | J. Sales, D. Pelletier, Canada | |
| 2006‡ | ...T. Totmianina, M. Marinin, Russia | 204.48 |
| 2010 | .....Xue Shen/Hongbo Zhao, China | 216.57 |

#### ICE DANCING

| | | Pts |
|---|---|---|
| 1976 | .....L. Pakhomova, A. Gorshkov, USSR | |
| 1980 | .....N. Linichuk, G. Karponosov, USSR | |
| 1984 | ....Jayne Torvill, Christopher Dean, UK | |
| 1988 | .....N. Bestemianova, A. Bukin, USSR | |
| 1992 | ....M. Klimova, S. Ponomarenko, Unified Team | |
| 1994 | .....Oksana Grishuk, Evgeny Platov, Russia | |
| 1998 | .....Pasha Grishuk, Evgeny Platov, Russia | |
| 2002 | ....Marina Anissina, Gwendal Peizerat, France | |
| 2006‡ | ...T. Navka, R. Kostomarov, Russia | 200.64 |
| 2010 | .....Tessa Virtue/Scott Moir, Canada | 221.57 |

*Competition held at Summer Games in London.
†Competition held at Summer Games in Antwerp.
‡In 2004, the ISU adopted a new overall point-scoring system

## SKELETON

### Men

| | | |
|---|---|---|
| 1928 | .....Jennison Heaton, United States | 3:01.8 |
| 1948 | .....Nino Bibbia, Italy | 5:23.2 |
| 2002 | .....Jim Shea Jr., United States | 1:41.96 |
| 2006 | .....Duff Gibson, Canada | 1:55.88 |
| 2010 | .....Jon Montgomery, Canada | 3:29.73 |

### Women

| | | |
|---|---|---|
| 2002 | .....Tristan Gale, United States | 1:45.11 |
| 2006 | .....Maya Pedersen, Switzerland | 1:59.83 |
| 2010 | .....Amy Williams, United Kingdom | 3:35.64 |

## SPEED SKATING

### Men

#### 500 METERS

| | | |
|---|---|---|
| 1924 | ....Charles Jewtraw, United States | 44.0 |
| 1928 | ....Clas Thunberg, Finland | 43.4 OR |
| | Bernt Evensen, Norway | 43.4 OR |
| 1932 | ....John Shea, United States | 43.4 EOR |
| 1936 | ....Ivar Ballangrud, Norway | 43.4 EOR |
| 1948 | ....Finn Helgesen, Norway | 43.1 OR |
| 1952 | ....Kenneth Henry, United States | 43.2 |
| 1956 | ....Yevgeny Grishin, USSR | 40.2 EWR |
| 1960 | ....Yevgeny Grishin, USSR | 40.2 EWR |
| 1964 | ....Terry McDermott, United States | 40.1 OR |
| 1968 | ....Erhard Keller, West Germany | 40.3 |
| 1972 | ....Erhard Keller, West Germany | 39.44 OR |
| 1976 | ....Yevgeny Kulikov, USSR | 39.17 OR |
| 1980 | ....Eric Heiden, United States | 38.03 OR |
| 1984 | ....Sergei Fokichev, USSR | 38.19 |
| 1988 | ....Uwe-Jens Mey, East Germany | 36.45 WR |
| 1992 | ....Uwe-Jens Mey, East Germany | 37.14 |
| 1994 | ....Aleksandr Golubev, Russia | 36.33 |
| 1998 | ....Hiroyasu Shimizu, Japan (second run) | 35.59 OR |
| 2002 | ....Casey FitzRandolph, United States | 1:09.23* |
| 2006 | ....Joey Cheek, United States | 1:09.76* |
| 2010 | ....Tae-Bum Mo, South Korea | 1:09.82* |

*Combined time.

#### 1,000 METERS

| | | |
|---|---|---|
| 1976 | ....Peter Mueller, United States | 1:19.32 |
| 1980 | ....Eric Heiden, United States | 1:15.18 OR |
| 1984 | ....Gaetan Boucher, Canada | 1:15.80 |
| 1988 | ....Nikolai Gulyaev, USSR | 1:13.03 OR |
| 1992 | ....Olaf Zinke, Germany | 1:14.85 |
| 1994 | ....Dan Jansen, United States | 1:12.43 WR |
| 1998 | ....Ids Postma, Netherlands | 1:10.64 OR |
| 2002 | ....Gerard van Velde, Netherlands | 1:07.18 |
| 2006 | ....Shani Davis, United States | 1:08.89 |
| 2010 | ....Shani Davis, United States | 1:08.94 |

#### 1,500 METERS

| | | |
|---|---|---|
| 1924 | ....Clas Thunberg, Finland | 2:20.8 |
| 1928 | ....Clas Thunberg, Finland | 2:21.1 |
| 1932 | ....John Shea, United States | 2:57.5 |
| 1936 | ....Charles Mathisen, Norway | 2:19.2 OR |
| 1948 | ....Sverre Farstad, Norway | 2:17.6 OR |
| 1952 | ....Hjalmar Andersen, Norway | 2:20.4 |
| 1956 | ....Yevgeny Grishin, USSR | 2:08.6 WR |
| | Yuri Mikhailov, USSR | 2:08.6 WR |
| 1960 | ....Roald Aas, Norway | 2:10.4 |
| | Yevgeny Grishin, USSR | 2:10.4 |
| 1964 | ....Ants Anston, USSR | 2:10.3 |
| 1968 | ....Cornelis Verkerk, Netherlands | 2:03.4 OR |
| 1972 | ....Ard Schenk, Netherlands | 2:02.96 OR |
| 1976 | ....Jan Egil Storholt, Norway | 1:59.38 OR |

Note: OR=Olympic Record; WR=World Record; EOR=Equals Olympic Record; EWR=Equals World Record; WB=World Best.

### SPEED SKATING (Cont.)
### Men (Cont.)

#### 1,500 METERS (CONT.)

| | | |
|---|---|---|
| 1980 | Eric Heiden, United States | 1:55.44 OR |
| 1984 | Gaetan Boucher, Canada | 1:58.36 |
| 1988 | Andre Hoffmann, E Germany | 1:52.06 WR |
| 1992 | Johann Olav Koss, Norway | 1:54.81 |
| 1994 | Johann Olav Koss, Norway | 1:51.29 WR |
| 1998 | Aadne Sondral, Norway | 1:47.87 WR |
| 2002 | Derek Parra, United States | 1:43.95 |
| 2006 | Enrico Fabris, Italy | 1:45.97 |
| 2010 | Mark Tuitert, Netherlands | 1:45.57 |

#### 5,000 METERS

| | | |
|---|---|---|
| 1924 | Clas Thunberg, Finland | 8:39.0 |
| 1928 | Ivar Ballangrud, Norway | 8:50.5 |
| 1932 | Irving Jaffee, United States | 9:40.8 |
| 1936 | Ivar Ballangrud, Norway | 8:19.6 OR |
| 1948 | Reidar Liaklev, Norway | 8:29.4 |
| 1952 | Hjalmar Andersen, Norway | 8:10.6 OR |
| 1956 | Boris Shilkov, USSR | 7:48.7 OR |
| 1960 | Viktor Kosichkin, USSR | 7:51.3 |
| 1964 | Knut Johannesen, Norway | 7:38.4 OR |
| 1968 | Fred Anton Maier, Norway | 7:22.4 WR |
| 1972 | Ard Schenk, Netherlands | 7:23.61 |
| 1976 | Sten Stensen, Norway | 7:24.48 |
| 1980 | Eric Heiden, United States | 7:02.29 OR |
| 1984 | Sven Tomas Gustafson, Sweden | 7:12.28 |
| 1988 | Tomas Gustafson, Sweden | 6:44.63 WR |
| 1992 | Geir Karlstad, Norway | 6:59.97 |
| 1994 | Johann Olav Koss, Norway | 6:34.96 WR |
| 1998 | Gianni Romme, Netherlands | 6:22.20 WR |
| 2002 | Jo. Uytdehaage, Netherlands | 6:41.66 |
| 2006 | Chad Hedrick, United States | 6:14.68 |
| 2010 | Sven Kramer, Netherlands | 6:14.60 OR |

#### 10,000 METERS

| | | |
|---|---|---|
| 1924 | Julius Skutnabb, Finland | 18:04.8 |
| 1928 | Not held due to thawing of ice | |
| 1932 | Irving Jaffee, United States | 19:13.6 |
| 1936 | Ivar Ballangrud, Norway | 17:24.3 OR |
| 1948 | Ake Seyffarth, Sweden | 17:26.3 |
| 1952 | Hjalmar Andersen, Norway | 16:45.8 OR |
| 1956 | Sigvard Ericsson, Sweden | 16:35.9 OR |
| 1960 | Knut Johannesen, Norway | 15:46.6 WR |
| 1964 | Jonny Nilsson, Sweden | 15:50.1 |
| 1968 | Johnny Höglin, Sweden | 15:23.6 OR |
| 1972 | Ard Schenk, Netherlands | 15:01.35 OR |
| 1976 | Piet Kleine, Netherlands | 14:50.59 OR |
| 1980 | Eric Heiden, United States | 14:28.13 WR |
| 1984 | Igor Malkov, USSR | 14:39.90 |
| 1988 | Tomas Gustafson, Sweden | 13:48.20 WR |
| 1992 | Bart Veldkamp, Netherlands | 14:12.12 |
| 1994 | Johann Olav Koss, Norway | 13:30.55 WR |
| 1998 | Gianni Romme, Netherlands | 13:15.33 WR |
| 2002 | Jochem Uytdehaage, Netherlands | 12:58.92 WR |
| 2006 | Bob de Jong, Netherlands | 13:01.57 |
| 2010 | Seung-Hoon Lee, South Korea | 12:58.55 OR |

#### TEAM PURSUIT

| | |
|---|---|
| 2006 | Italy |
| 2010 | Canada |

### Women

#### 500 METERS

| | | |
|---|---|---|
| 1960 | Helga Haase, East Germany | 45.9 |
| 1964 | Lydia Skoblikova, USSR | 45.0 OR |
| 1968 | Lyudmila Titova, USSR | 46.1 |
| 1972 | Anne Henning, United States | 43.33 OR |
| 1976 | Sheila Young, United States | 42.76 OR |
| 1980 | Karin Enke, East Germany | 41.78 OR |
| 1984 | Christa Rothenburger, E Germany | 41.02 OR |
| 1988 | Bonnie Blair, United States | 39.10 WR |
| 1992 | Bonnie Blair, United States | 40.33 |
| 1994 | Bonnie Blair, United States | 39.25 |
| 1998 | Catriona LeMay Doan, Canada (second run) | 38.21 OR |
| 2002 | Catriona LeMay, Canada | 1:14.75* |
| 2006 | Svetlana Zhurova, Russia | 1:16.57* |
| 2010 | Sang-Hwa Lee, South Korea | 1:06.09* |

#### 1,000 METERS

| | | |
|---|---|---|
| 1960 | Klara Guseva, USSR | 1:34.1 |
| 1964 | Lydia Skoblikova, USSR | 1:33.2 OR |
| 1968 | Carolina Geijssen, Netherlands | 1:32.6 OR |
| 1972 | Monika Pflug, West Germany | 1:31.40 OR |
| 1976 | Tatiana Averina, USSR | 1:28.43 OR |
| 1980 | Natalya Petruseva, USSR | 1:24.10 OR |
| 1984 | Karin Enke, East Germany | 1:21.61 OR |

#### 1,000 METERS (CONT.)

| | | |
|---|---|---|
| 1988 | Christa Rothenburger, East Germany | 1:17.65 WR |
| 1992 | Bonnie Blair, United States | 1:21.90 |
| 1994 | Bonnie Blair, United States | 1:18.74 |
| 1998 | Marianne Timmer, Netherlands | 1:16.51 OR |
| 2002 | Chris Witty, United States | 1:13.83 |
| 2006 | Marianne Timmer, Netherlands | 1:16.05 |
| 2010 | Christine Nesbitt, Canada | 1:16.56 |

#### 1,500 METERS

| | | |
|---|---|---|
| 1960 | Lydia Skoblikova, USSR | 2:25.2 WR |
| 1964 | Lydia Skoblikova, USSR | 2:22.6 OR |
| 1968 | Kaija Mustonen, Finland | 2:22.4 OR |
| 1972 | Dianne Holum, United States | 2:20.85 OR |
| 1976 | Galina Stepanskaya, USSR | 2:16.58 OR |
| 1980 | Anne Borckink, Netherlands | 2:10.95 OR |
| 1984 | Karin Enke, East Germany | 2:03.42 WR |
| 1988 | Yvonne van Gennip, Netherlands | 2:00.68 OR |
| 1992 | Jacqueline Boerner, Germany | 2:05.87 |
| 1994 | Emese Hunyady, Austria | 2:02.19 |
| 1998 | Marianne Timmer, Netherlands | 1:57.58 WR |
| 2002 | Anni Friesinger, Germany | 1:54.02 |
| 2006 | Cindy Klassen, Canada | 1:55.27 |
| 2010 | Ireen Wust, Netherlands | 1:56.89 |

*Combined time.
Note: OR=Olympic Record; WR=World Record; EOR=Equals Olympic Record; EWR=Equals World Record; WB=World Best.

## SPEED SKATING *(Cont.)*
### Women *(Cont.)*

#### 3,000 METERS

| | | |
|---|---|---|
| 1960 | Lydia Skoblikova, USSR | 5:14.3 |
| 1964 | Lydia Skoblikova, USSR | 5:14.9 |
| 1968 | Johanna Schut, Netherlands | 4:56.2 OR |
| 1972 | Christina Baas-Kaiser, Netherlands | 4:52.14 OR |
| 1976 | Tatiana Averina, USSR | 4:45.19 OR |
| 1980 | Bjorg Eva Jensen, Norway | 4:32.13 OR |
| 1984 | Andrea Schöne, East Germany | 4:24.79 OR |
| 1988 | Yvonne van Gennip, Netherlands | 4:11.94 WR |
| 1992 | Gunda Niemann, Germany | 4:19.90 |
| 1994 | Svetlana Bazhanova, Russia | 4:17.43 |
| 1998 | G. Niemann-Stirnemann, Germany | 4:07.29 OR |
| 2002 | Claudia Pechstein, Germany | 3:57.70 |

#### 3,000 METERS *(CONT.)*

| | | |
|---|---|---|
| 2006 | Ireen Wust, Netherlands | 4:02.43 |
| 2010 | Martina Sablikova, Czech Republic | 4:02.53 |

#### 5,000 METERS

| | | |
|---|---|---|
| 1988 | Yvonne van Gennip, Netherlands | 7:14.13 WR |
| 1992 | Gunda Niemann, Germany | 7:31.57 |
| 1994 | Claudia Pechstein, Germany | 7:14.37 |
| 1998 | Claudia Pechstein, Germany | 6:59.61 WR |
| 2002 | Claudia Pechstein, Germany | 6:46.91 WR |
| 2006 | Clara Hughes, Canada | 6:59.07 |
| 2010 | Martina Sablikova, Czech Republic | 6:50.91 |

#### TEAM PURSUIT

| | |
|---|---|
| 2006 | Germany |
| 2010 | Germany |

## SHORT TRACK SPEED SKATING

### Men

#### 500 METERS

| | | |
|---|---|---|
| 1994 | Chae Ji-Hoon, South Korea | 43.54 |
| 1998 | Takafumi Nishitani, Japan | 42.862 |
| 2002 | Marc Gagnon, Canada | 41.802 OR |
| 2006 | Apolo Anton Ohno, United States | 41.935 |
| 2010 | Charles Hamelin, Canada | 40.770 |

#### 1,000 METERS

| | | |
|---|---|---|
| 1992 | Kim Ki-Hoon, South Korea | 1:30.76 |
| 1994 | Kim Ki-Hoon, South Korea | 1:34.57 |
| 1998 | Kim Dong Sung, South Korea | 1:32.375 |
| 2002 | Steve Bradbury, Austrailia | 1:29.109 |
| 2006 | Hyun-Soo Ahn, South Korea | 1:26.739 OR |
| 2010 | Jung-Su Lee, South Korea | 1:23.747 OR |

#### 1,500 METERS

| | | |
|---|---|---|
| 2002 | Apolo Anton Ohno, United States | 2:18.541 |
| 2006 | Hyun-Soo Ahn, South Korea | 2:25.341 |
| 2010 | Jung-Su Lee, South Korea | 2:10.949 |

#### 5,000-METER RELAY

| | | |
|---|---|---|
| 1992 | South Korea | 7:14.02 |
| 1994 | Italy | 7:11.74 |
| 1998 | Canada | 7:06.075 |
| 2002 | Canada | 6:51.579 |
| 2006 | South Korea | 6:43.376 OR |
| 2010 | Canada | 6:43.610 |

### Women

#### 500 METERS

| | | |
|---|---|---|
| 1992 | Cathy Turner, United States | 47.04 |
| 1994 | Cathy Turner, United States | 45.98 |
| 1998 | Annie Perreault, Canada | 46.568 |
| 2002 | Yang Yang, China | 44.187 |
| 2006 | Meng Wang, China | 44.345 |
| 2010 | Meng Wang, China | 42.985 |

#### 1,000 METERS

| | | |
|---|---|---|
| 1994 | Chun Lee Kyung, South Korea | 1:36.87 |
| 1998 | Chun Lee Kyung, South Korea | 1:42.776 |
| 2002 | Yang A. Yang, China | 1:36.391 |
| 2006 | Sun-Yu Jin, South Korea | 1:32.859 |
| 2010 | Meng Wang, China | 1:29.213 |

#### 1,500 METERS

| | | |
|---|---|---|
| 2002 | Ko Gi-Hyun, South Korea | 2:31.581 |
| 2006 | Sun-Yu Jin, China | 2:23.494 |
| 2010 | Yang Zhou, China | 2:16.993 |

#### 3,000-METER RELAY

| | | |
|---|---|---|
| 1992 | Canada | 4:36.62 |
| 1994 | South Korea | 4:26.64 |
| 1998 | South Korea | 4:16.260 |
| 2002 | South Korea | 4:12.793 |
| 2006 | South Korea | 4:17.040 |
| 2010 | China | 4:06.610 WR |

## ALPINE SKIING

### Men

#### DOWNHILL

| | | |
|---|---|---|
| 1948 | Henri Oreiller, France | 2:55.0 |
| 1952 | Zeno Colo, Italy | 2:30.8 |
| 1956 | Anton Sailer, Austria | 2:52.2 |
| 1960 | Jean Vuarnet, France | 2:06.0 |
| 1964 | Egon Zimmermann, Austria | 2:18.16 |
| 1968 | Jean-Claude Killy, France | 1:59.85 |
| 1972 | Bernhard Russi, Switzerland | 1:51.43 |
| 1976 | Franz Klammer, Austria | 1:45.73 |
| 1980 | Leonhard Stock, Austria | 1:45.50 |
| 1984 | Bill Johnson, United States | 1:45.59 |
| 1988 | Pirmin Zurbriggen, Switzerland | 1:59.63 |
| 1992 | Patrick Ortlieb, Austria | 1:50.37 |
| 1994 | Tommy Moe, United States | 1:45.75 |
| 1998 | Jean-Luc Crétier, France | 1:50.11 |
| 2002 | Fritz Strobl, Austria | 1:39.13 |
| 2006 | Antoine Deneriaz, France | 1:48.80 |
| 2010 | Didier Defago, Switzerland | 1:54.31 |

#### SLALOM*

| | | |
|---|---|---|
| 1948 | Edi Reinalter, Switzerland | 2:10.3 |
| 1952 | Othmar Schneider, Austria | 2:00.0 |
| 1956 | Anton Sailer, Austria | 3:14.7 |
| 1960 | Ernst Hinterseer, Austria | 2:08.9 |
| 1964 | Josef Stiegler, Austria | 2:11.13 |
| 1968 | Jean-Claude Killy, France | 1:39.73 |
| 1972 | F. Fernandez Ochoa, Spain | 1:49.27 |
| 1976 | Piero Gros, Italy | 2:03.29 |
| 1980 | Ingemar Stenmark, Sweden | 1:44.26 |
| 1984 | Phil Mahre, United States | 1:39.41 |
| 1988 | Alberto Tomba, Italy | 1:39.47 |
| 1992 | Finn Christian Jagge, Norway | 1:44.39 |
| 1994 | Thomas Stangassinger, Austria | 2:02.02 |
| 1998 | Hans-Petter Buraas, Norway | 1:49.31 |
| 2002 | Jean-Pierre Vidal, France | 1:41.06 |
| 2006 | Benjamin Raich, Austria | 1:43.14 |
| 2010 | Giuliano Razzoli, Italy | 1:39.32 |

*Combined time.

Note: OR=Olympic Record; WR=World Record; EOR=Equals Olympic Record; EWR=Equals World Record; WB=World Best.

### ALPINE SKIING *(Cont.)*
### Men *(Cont.)*

#### GIANT SLALOM*

| | | |
|---|---|---|
| 1952 | Stein Eriksen, Norway | 2:25.0 |
| 1956 | Anton Sailer, Austria | 3:00.1 |
| 1960 | Roger Staub, Switzerland | 1:48.3 |
| 1964 | Francois Bonlieu, France | 1:46.71 |
| 1968 | Jean-Claude Killy, France | 3:29.28 |
| 1972 | Gustav Thöni, Italy | 3:09.62 |
| 1976 | Heini Hemmi, Switzerland | 3:26.97 |
| 1980 | Ingemar Stenmark, Sweden | 2:40.74 |
| 1984 | Max Julen, Switzerland | 2:41.18 |
| 1988 | Alberto Tomba, Italy | 2:06.37 |
| 1992 | Alberto Tomba, Italy | 2:06.98 |
| 1994 | Markus Wasmeier, Germany | 2:52.46 |
| 1998 | Hermann Maier, Austria | 2:38.51 |
| 2002 | Stephan Eberharter, Austria | 2:23.28 |
| 2006 | Benjamin Raich, Austria | 2:35.00 |
| 2010 | Carlo Janka, Switzerland | 2:37.83 |

#### SUPER COMBINED (SLALOM + DOWNHILL)†

| | | |
|---|---|---|
| 1936 | Franz Pfnür, Germany | 99.25 |
| 1948 | Henri Oreiller, France | 3.2 |
| 1988 | Hubert Strolz, Austria | 36.55 |
| 1992 | Josef Polig, Italy | 14.58 |
| 1994 | Lasse Kjus, Norway | 3:17.53 |
| 1998 | Mario Reiter, Austria | 3:08.06 |
| 2002 | Kjetil André Aamodt, Norway | 3:17.56 |
| 2006 | Ted Ligety, United States | 3:09.35 |
| 2010 | Bode Miller, United States | 2:44.92 |

#### SUPER GIANT SLALOM

| | | |
|---|---|---|
| 1988 | Franck Piccard, France | 1:39.66 |
| 1992 | Kjetil André Aamodt, Norway | 1:13.04 |
| 1994 | Markus Wasmeier, Germany | 1:32.53 |
| 1998 | Hermann Maier, Austria | 1:34.82 |
| 2002 | Kjetil André Aamodt, Norway | 1:21.58 |
| 2006 | Kjetil André Aamodt, Norway | 1:30.65 |
| 2010 | Aksel Lund Svindal, Norway | 1:30.34 |

### Women

#### DOWNHILL

| | | |
|---|---|---|
| 1948 | Hedy Schlunegger, Switzerland | 2:28.3 |
| 1952 | Trude Jochum-Beiser, Austria | 1:47.1 |
| 1956 | Madeleine Berthod, Switzerland | 1:40.7 |
| 1960 | Heidi Biebl, West Germany | 1:37.6 |
| 1964 | Christl Haas, Austria | 1:55.39 |
| 1968 | Olga Pall, Austria | 1:40.87 |
| 1972 | Marie-Theres Nadig, Switzerland | 1:36.68 |
| 1976 | Rosi Mittermaier, West Germany | 1:46.16 |
| 1980 | Annemarie Moser-Pröll, Austria | 1:37.52 |
| 1984 | Michela Figini, Switzerland | 1:13.36 |
| 1988 | Marina Kiehl, West Germany | 1:25.86 |
| 1992 | Kerrin Lee-Gartner, Canada | 1:52.55 |
| 1994 | Katja Seizinger, Germany | 1:35.93 |
| 1998 | Katja Seizinger, Germany | 1:28.89 |
| 2002 | Carole Montillet, France | 1:39.56 |
| 2006 | Michaela Dorfmeister, Austria | 1:56.49 |
| 2010 | Lindsey Vonn, United States | 1:44.19 |

#### SLALOM*

| | | |
|---|---|---|
| 1948 | Gretchen Fraser, United States | 1:57.2 |
| 1952 | Andrea Mead Lawrence, United States | 2:10.6 |
| 1956 | Renee Colliard, Switzerland | 1:52.3 |
| 1960 | Anne Heggtveigt, Canada | 1:49.6 |
| 1964 | Christine Goitschel, France | 1:29.86 |
| 1968 | Marielle Goitschel, France | 1:25.86 |
| 1972 | Barbara Cochran, United States | 1:31.24 |
| 1976 | Rosi Mittermaier, West Germany | 1:30.54 |
| 1980 | Hanni Wenzel, Liechtenstein | 1:25.09 |
| 1984 | Paoletta Magoni, Italy | 1:36.47 |
| 1988 | Vreni Schneider, Switzerland | 1:36.69 |
| 1992 | Petra Kronberger, Austria | 1:32.68 |
| 1994 | Vreni Schneider, Switzerland | 1:56.01 |
| 1998 | Hilde Gerg, Germany | 1:32.40 |
| 2002 | Janica Kostelic, Croatia | 1:46.10 |
| 2006 | Anja Paerson, Sweden | 1:29.04 |
| 2010 | Maria Riesch, Germany | 1:42.89 |

#### GIANT SLALOM*

| | | |
|---|---|---|
| 1952 | Andrea Mead Lawrence, U.S. | 2:06.8 |
| 1956 | Ossi Reichert, West Germany | 1:56.5 |
| 1960 | Yvonne Rüegg, Switzerland | 1:39.9 |
| 1964 | Marielle Goitschel, France | 1:52.24 |
| 1968 | Nancy Greene, Canada | 1:51.97 |
| 1972 | Marie-Theres Nadig, Switzerland | 1:29.90 |
| 1976 | Kathy Kreiner, Canada | 1:29.13 |
| 1980 | Hanni Wenzel, Liechtenstein (2 runs) | 2:41.66 |
| 1984 | Debbie Armstrong, United States | 2:20.98 |
| 1988 | Vreni Schneider, Switzerland | 2:06.49 |
| 1992 | Pernilla Wiberg, Sweden | 2:12.74 |
| 1994 | Deborah Compagnoni, Italy | 2:30.97 |
| 1998 | Deborah Compagnoni, Italy | 2:50.59 |
| 2002 | Janica Kostelic, Croatia | 2:30.01 |
| 2006 | Julia Mancuso, United States | 2:09.19 |
| 2010 | Viktoria Rebensburg, Germany | 2:27.11 |

#### SUPER COMBINED (SLALOM + DOWNHILL)†

| | | |
|---|---|---|
| 1988 | Anita Wachter, Austria | 29.25 |
| 1992 | Petra Kronberger, Austria | 2.55 |
| 1994 | Pernilla Wiberg, Sweden | 3:05.16 |
| 1998 | Katja Seizinger, Germany | 2:40.74 |
| 2002 | Janica Kostelic, Croatia | 2:43.28 |
| 2006 | Janica Kostelic, Croatia | 2:51.08 |
| 2010 | Maria Riesch, Germany | 2:09.14 |

#### SUPER GIANT SLALOM

| | | |
|---|---|---|
| 1988 | Sigrid Wolf, Austria | 1:19.03 |
| 1992 | Deborah Compagnoni, Italy | 1:21.22 |
| 1994 | Diann Roffe-Steinrotter, U.S. | 1:22.15 |
| 1998 | Picabo Street, United States | 1:18.02 |
| 2002 | Daniela Ceccarelli, Italy | 1:13.59 |
| 2006 | Michaela Dorfmeister, Austria | 1:32.47 |
| 2010 | Andrea Fischbacher, Austria | 1:20.14 |

*Combined time. †Beginning in 1994, Super Combined race scoring based on time.

## FREESTYLE SKIING

### Men

| MOGULS | Pts |
|---|---|
| 1992 ....Edgar Grospiron, France | 25.81 |
| 1994 ....Jean-Luc Brassard, Canada | 27.24 |
| 1998 ....Jonny Moseley, United States | 26.93 |
| 2002 ....Janne Lahtela, Finland | 27.97 |
| 2006 ....Dale Begg-Smith, Australia | 26.77 |
| 2010 ....Alexandre Bilodeau, Canada | 26.75 |

| AERIALS | Pts |
|---|---|
| 1994 ....Andreas Schoenbaechler, Switz. | 234.67 |
| 1998 ....Eric Bergoust, United States | 255.64 |
| 2002 ....Ales Valenta, Czech Republic | 257.02 |
| 2006 ....Han Xiaopeng, China | 250.77 |
| 2010 ....Alexei Grishin, Belarus | 248.41 |

| SKI CROSS | |
|---|---|
| 2010 ....Michael Schmid, Switzerland | |

### Women

| MOGULS | Pts |
|---|---|
| 1992 ....Donna Weinbrecht, United States | 23.69 |
| 1994 ....Stine Lise Hattestad, Norway | 25.97 |
| 1998 ....Tae Satoya, Japan | 25.06 |
| 2002 ....Kari Traa, Norway | 25.94 |
| 2006 ....Jennifer Heil, Canada | 26.50 |
| 2010 ....Hannah Kearney, United States | 26.63 |

| AERIALS | Pts |
|---|---|
| 1994 ....Lina Cherjazova, Uzbekistan | 166.84 |
| 1998 ....Nikki Stone, United States | 193.00 |
| 2002 ....Alisa Camplin, Australia | 193.47 |
| 2006 ....Evelyne Leu, Switzerland | 202.55 |
| 2010 ....Lydia Lassila, Australia | 214.74 |

| SKI CROSS | |
|---|---|
| 2010 ....Ashleigh McIvor, Canada | |

## NORDIC SKIING

### Men

#### 10 KILOMETERS CLASSICAL

| 1992 | Vegard Ulvang, Norway | 27:36.0 |
|---|---|---|
| 1994 | Bjørn Dæhlie, Norway | 24:20.1 |
| 1998 | Bjørn Dæhlie, Norway | 27:24.5 |
| 1976 | Nikolay Bajukov, Unified Team | 43:58.47 |
| 1980 | Thomas Wassberg, Sweden | 41:57.63 |
| 1984 | Gunde Swan, Sweden | 41:25.6 |
| 1988 | Michael Deviatyarov, USSR | 41:18.9 |
| 2002 | Andrus Veerpalu, Estonia | 37:07.4 |
| 2006 | Andrus Veerpalu, Estonia | 38:01.3 |

#### 15 KILOMETERS FREESTYLE

| 2010 | Dario Cologna, Switzerland | 33:36.3 |
|---|---|---|

#### 15 KILOMETERS PURSUIT FREESTYLE

| 1992 | Bjørn Dæhlie, Norway | 1:05:37.9 |
|---|---|---|
| 1994 | Bjørn Dæhlie, Norway | 1:00:08.8 |
| 1998 | Thomas Alsgaard, Norway | 1:07:01.7 |

#### 30 KILOMETERS CLASSICAL

| 1956 | Veikko Hakulinen, Finland | 1:44:06.0 |
|---|---|---|
| 1960 | Sixten Jernberg, Sweden | 1:51:03.9 |
| 1964 | Eero Mantyränta, Finland | 1:30:50.7 |
| 1968 | Franco Nones, Italy | 1:35:39.2 |
| 1972 | Viaceslav Vedenine, USSR | 1:36:31.2 |
| 1976 | Sergei Savelyev, USSR | 1:30:29.38 |
| 1980 | Nikolai Simyatov, USSR | 1:27:02.80 |
| 1984 | Nikolai Simyatov, USSR | 1:28:56.3 |
| 1988 | Alexey Prokororov, USSR | 1:24:26.3 |
| 1992 | Vegard Ulvang, Norway | 1:22:27.8 |
| 1994 | Thomas Alsgaard, Norway | 1:12:26.4 |
| 1998 | Mika Myllylae, Finland | 1:33:55.8 |

#### 30 KILOMETERS PURSUIT

| 2006 | Eugeni Dementiev, Russia | 1:17:00.8 |
|---|---|---|
| 2010 | Marcus Hellner, Sweden | 1:15:11.4 |

#### 50 KILOMETERS CLASSIC MASS START

| 2010 | Petter Northug, Norway | 2:05:35.5 |
|---|---|---|

#### 50 KILOMETERS FREESTYLE

| 1924 | Thorleif Haug, Norway | 3:44:32.0 |
|---|---|---|
| 1928 | Per Erik Hedlund, Sweden | 4:52:03.0 |
| 1932 | Veli Saarinen, Finland | 4:28:00.0 |

#### 50 KILOMETERS FREESTYLE (*CONT.*)

| 1936 | Elis Wiklund, Sweden | 3:30:11.0 |
|---|---|---|
| 1948 | Nils Karlsson, Sweden | 3:47:48.0 |
| 1952 | Veikko Hakulinen, Finland | 3:33:33.0 |
| 1956 | Sixten Jernberg, Sweden | 2:50:27.0 |
| 1960 | Kalevi Hämäläinen, Finland | 2:59:06.3 |
| 1964 | Sixten Jernberg, Sweden | 2:43:52.6 |
| 1968 | Olle Ellefsaeter, Norway | 2:28:45.8 |
| 1972 | Paal Tyldrum, Norway | 2:43:14.75 |
| 1976 | Ivar Formo, Norway | 2:37:30.50 |
| 1980 | Nikolai Simyatov, USSR | 2:27:24.60 |
| 1984 | Thomas Wassberg, Sweden | 2:15:55.8 |
| 1988 | Gunde Svan, Sweden | 2:04:30.9 |
| 1992 | Bjørn Dæhlie, Norway | 2:03:41.5 |
| 1994 | Vladimir Smirnov, Kazakhstan | 2:07:20.3 |
| 1998 | Bjørn Dæhlie, Norway | 2:05:08.2 |
| 2002 | Mikhail Ivanov, Russia | 2:06:20.8 |
| 2006 | Giorgio di Centa, Italy | 2:06:11.8 |

#### 4 X 10-KILOMETER RELAY MIXED

| 1936 | Finland | 2:41:33.0 |
|---|---|---|
| 1948 | Sweden | 2:32:80.0 |
| 1952 | Finland | 2:20:16.0 |
| 1956 | USSR | 2:15:30.0 |
| 1960 | Finland | 2:18:45.6 |
| 1964 | Sweden | 2:18:34.6 |
| 1968 | Norway | 2:08:33.5 |
| 1972 | USSR | 2:04:47.94 |
| 1976 | Finland | 2:07:59.72 |
| 1980 | USSR | 1:57:03.46 |
| 1984 | Sweden | 1:55:06.3 |
| 1988 | Sweden | 1:43:58.6 |
| 1992 | Norway | 1:39:26.0 |
| 1994 | Italy | 1:41:15.0 |
| 1998 | Norway | 1:40:55.7 |
| 2002 | Norway | 1:32:45.5 |
| 2006 | Italy | 1:43:45.7 |
| 2010 | Sweden | 1:45:05.4 |

#### TEAM SPRINT

| 2006 | Sweden | 17:02.9 |
|---|---|---|
| 2010 | Norway | 19:01.0 |

#### INDIVIDUAL SPRINT

| 2006 | Bjoern Lind, Sweden | 2:26.5 |
|---|---|---|
| 2010 | Nikita Kriukov, Russia | 3:36.3 |

\* Different scoring system; 1924–1952 distance was 18 km; 1952–present, 15 km.

† Times in the cross-country race were not converted into points. According to the Gundersen Method, used since 1988, starting times in the race are staggered in proportion to points earned in the ski jumping segment of the event.

## NORDIC SKIING (Cont.)
### Men (Cont.)

| SKI JUMPING, NORMAL (90-M) HILL | | Pts |
|---|---|---|
| 1964 | Veikko Kankkonen, Finland | 229.90 |
| 1968 | Jiri Raska, Czechoslovakia | 216.5 |
| 1972 | Yukio Kasaya, Japan | 244.2 |
| 1976 | Hans-Georg Aschenbach, East Germany | 252.0 |
| 1980 | Toni Innauer, Austria | 266.3 |
| 1984 | Jens Weissflog, East Germany | 215.2 |
| 1988 | Matti Nykänen, Finland | 229.1 |
| 1992 | Ernst Vettori, Austria | 222.8 |
| 1994 | Espen Bredesen, Norway | 282.0 |
| 1998 | Jani Soininen, Finland | 234.5 |
| 2002 | Simon Ammann, Switzerland | 269.0 |
| 2006 | Lars Bystoel, Norway | 266.5 |
| 2010 | Simon Ammann, Switzerland | 276.5 |

| SKI JUMPING, LARGE (120-M) HIL | | Pts |
|---|---|---|
| 1924 | Jacob Tullin Thams, Norway | 18.960 |
| 1928 | Alf Andersen, Norway | 19.208 |
| 1932 | Birger Ruud, Norway | 228.1 |
| 1936 | Birger Ruud, Norway | 232.0 |
| 1948 | Petter Hugsted, Norway | 228.1 |
| 1952 | Arnfinn Bergmann, Norway | 226.0 |
| 1956 | Antti Hyvärinen, Finland | 227.0 |
| 1960 | Helmut Recknagel, East Germany | 227.2 |
| 1964 | Toralf Engan, Norway | 230.70 |
| 1968 | Vladimir Beloussov, USSR | 231.3 |
| 1972 | Wojciech Fortuna, Poland | 219.9 |
| 1976 | Karl Schnabl, Austria | 234.8 |
| 1980 | Jouko Tormanen, Finland | 271.0 |
| 1984 | Matti Nykänen, Finland | 231.2 |
| 1988 | Matti Nykänen, Finland | 224.0 |
| 1992 | Toni Nieminen, Finland | 239.5 |
| 1994 | Jens Weissflog, Germany | 274.5 |
| 1998 | Kazuyoshi Funaki, Japan | 272.3 |
| 2002 | Simon Amman, Switzerland | 281.4 |
| 2006 | Thomas Morgenstern, Austria | 276.9 |
| 2010 | Simon Ammann, Switzerland | 283.6 |

| TEAM SKI JUMPING, LARGE (120-M) HILL | | Pts |
|---|---|---|
| 1988 | Finland | 634.4 |
| 1992 | Finland | 644.4 |
| 1994 | Germany | 970.1 |

| TEAM SKI JUMPING, LARGE (120-M) HILL (CONT.) | | Pts |
|---|---|---|
| 1998 | Japan | 933.0 |
| 2002 | Germany | 974.1 |
| 2006 | Austria | 984.0 |
| 2010 | Austria | 1107.9 |

| NORDIC COMBINED | | Pts |
|---|---|---|
| 1924 | Thorleif Haug, Norway | 18.906 |
| 1928 | Johan Gröttumsbraaten, Norway | 17.833 |
| 1932 | Johan Gröttumsbraaten, Norway | 446.0 |
| 1936 | Oddbjörn Hagen, Norway | 430.30 |
| 1948 | Heikki Hasu, Finland | 448.80 |
| 1952 | Simon Slattvik, Norway | 451.621 |
| 1956 | Sverre Stenersen, Norway | 455.0 |
| 1960 | Georg Thoma, West Germany | 457.952 |
| 1964 | Tormod Knutsen, Norway | 469.28 |
| 1968 | Frantz Keller, West Germany | 449.04 |
| 1972 | Ulrich Wehling, East Germany | 413.34 |
| 1976 | Ulrich Wehling, East Germany | 423.39 |
| 1980 | Ulrich Wehling, East Germany | 432.20 |
| 1984 | Tom Sandberg, Norway | 422.595 |
| 1988 | Hippolyt Kempf, Switzerland | 432.230 |
| 1992 | Fabrice Guy, France | 426.47 |
| 1994 | Fred B. Lundberg, Norway | 457.970 |
| 1998 | Bjarte Engen Vik, Norway | 41:21.1† |
| 2002 | Samppa Lajunen, Finland | 38:18.7† |
| 2006 | Georg Hettich, Norway | 39:44.6† |
| 2010 | Jason Chappuis Lamy, France | 25:47.1† |

| SPRINT NORDIC COMBINED | | |
|---|---|---|
| 2002 | Samppa Lajunen, Finland | 123.8 |
| 2006 | Felix Gottwald, Austria | 17:35.0† |
| 2010 | Bill Demong, United States | 25:32.9† |

| TEAM NORDIC COMBINED RELAY | |
|---|---|
| 1988 | West Germany |
| 1992 | Japan |
| 1994 | Japan |
| 1998 | Norway |
| 2002 | Finland |
| 2006 | Austria |
| 2010 | Austria |

## Women

| INDIVIDUAL SPRINT | | |
|---|---|---|
| 2002 | Julija Tchepalova, Russia | 3:10.6 |
| 2006 | Chandra Crawford, Canada | 2:12.3 |
| 2010 | Marit Bjoergen, Norway | 3:39.2 |

| 5 KILOMETERS PURSUIT | | |
|---|---|---|
| 2002 | Olga Danilova, Russia | 24:52.1 |

| 5 KILOMETERS CLASSIC | | |
|---|---|---|
| 1964 | Klaudia Boyarskikh, USSR | 17:50.5 |
| 1968 | Toini Gustafsson, Sweden | 16:45.2 |
| 1972 | Galina Kulakova, USSR | 17:00.50 |
| 1976 | Helena Takalo, Finland | 15:48.69 |
| 1980 | Raisa Smetanina, USSR | 15:06.92 |
| 1984 | Marja-Liisa Hamalainen, Finland | 17:04.0 |
| 1988 | Marjo Matikainen, Finland | 15:04.0 |
| 1992 | Marjut Lukkarinen, Finland | 14:13.8 |
| 1994 | Lyubova Egorova, Russia | 14:08.8 |
| 1998 | Larissa Lazhutina, Russia | 17:37.9 |

| 10 KILOMETERS CLASSIC | | |
|---|---|---|
| 1952 | Lydia Widemen, Finland | 41:40.0 |
| 1956 | Lyubov Kosyryeva, USSR | 38:11.0 |

| 10 KILOMETERS CLASSIC (CONT.) | | |
|---|---|---|
| 1960 | Maria Gusakova, USSR | 39:46.6 |
| 1964 | Klaudia Boyarskikh, USSR | 40:24.3 |
| 1968 | Toini Gustafsson, Sweden | 36:46.5 |
| 1972 | Galina Kulakova, USSR | 34:17.8 |
| 1976 | Raisa Smetanina, USSR | 30:13.41 |
| 1980 | Barbara Petzold, East Germany | 30:31.54 |
| 1984 | Marja-Lissa Hamalainen, Finland | 31:44.2 |
| 1988 | Vida Ventsene, USSR | 30:08.3 |
| 2002 | Bante Skari, Norway | 28:05.6 |
| 2006 | Kristina Smigun, Estonia | 27:51.4 |

| 10 KILOMETERS FREESTYLE | | |
|---|---|---|
| 2010 | Charlotte Kalla, Sweden | 24:58.4 |

| 10 KILOMETERS PURSUIT FREESTYLE | | |
|---|---|---|
| 1992 | Lyubov Egorova, Unified Team | 40:07.7 |
| 1994 | Lyubov Egorova, Russia | 41:38.1 |
| 1998 | Larissa Lazhutina, Russia | 46:06.9 |

| 15 KILOMETERS CLASSIC | | |
|---|---|---|
| 1992 | Lyubov Egorova, Unified Team | 42:20.8 |
| 1994 | Manuela Di Centa, Italy | 39:44.5 |
| 1998 | Olga Danilova, Russia | 46:55.04 |

†Beginning in 1998, Nordic combined races based on time.

## NORDIC SKIING *(Cont.)*
### Women *(Cont.)*

**15 KILOMETERS FREESTYLE**
2002....Stefania Belmondo, Italy — 39:54.4

**15 KILOMETERS PURSUIT FREESTYLE**
2006....Kristina Smigun, Estonia — 42:48.7
2010....Marit Bjoergen, Norway — 39:58.1

**20 KILOMETERS FREESTYLE**
1984....Marja-Liisa Hamalainen, Finland — 1:01:45.0
1988....Tamara Tikhonova, USSR — 55:53.6

**30 KILOMETERS CLASSIC MASS START**
2010....Justyna Kowalczyk, Poland — 1:30:33.7

**30 KILOMETERS FREESTYLE**
1992....Stefania Belmondo, Italy — 1:22:30.1
1994....Manuela Di Centa, Italy — 1:25:41.6
1998....Julija Tchepalova, Russia — 1:22:01.5
2002....Gabriela Paruzzi, Italy — 1:30:57.1
2006....Katerina Neumannova, Czech Rep. — 1:22:25.4

**TEAM SPRINT**
2006....Sweden — 16:36.9
2010....Germany — 18:03.7

**4 X 5-KILOMETER RELAY MIXED**
1956....Finland — 1:9:01.0
1960....Sweden — 1:4:21.4
1964....USSR — 59:20.0
1968....Norway — 57:30.0
1972....USSR — 48:46.15
1976....USSR — 1:07:49.75
1980....E Germany — 1:02:11.10
1984....Norway — 1:06:49.7
1988....USSR — 59:51.1
1992....Unified Team — 59:34.8
1994....Russia — 57:12.5
1998....Russia — 55:13.5
2002....Germany — 49:30.6
2006....Russia — 54:47.7
2010....Norway — 55:19.5

## SNOWBOARDING

### Men

**GIANT SLALOM**
1998.....Ross Rebagliati, Canada — 2:03.96

**PARALLEL GIANT SLALOM**
2002.....Philipp Schoch, Switzerland
2006.....Philipp Schoch, Switzerland
2010.....Jasey Jay Anderson, Canada

**HALF-PIPE** — Pts
1998.....Gian Simmen, Switzerland — 85.2
2002.....Ross Powers, United States — 46.1
2006.....Shaun White, United States — 46.8
2010.....Shaun White, United States — 48.4

**SNOWBOARD CROSS**
2006.....Seth Wescott, United States
2010.....Seth Wescott, United States

### Women

**GIANT SLALOM**
1998.....Karine Ruby, France — 2:17.34

**PARALLEL GIANT SLALOM**
2002.....Isabella Blanc, France
2006.....Daniela Meuli, Switzerland
2010.....Nicolien Sauerbreij, Netherlands

**HALF-PIPE** — Pts
1998.....Nicola Thost, Germany — 74.6
2002.....Kelly Clark, United States — 47.9
2006.....Hannah Teter, United States — 46.4
2010.....Torah Bright, Australia — 45.0

**SNOWBOARD CROSS**
2006.....Tanja Frieden, Switzerland
2010.....Maelle Ricker, Canada

# Tennis

Novak Djokovic claimed three Grand Slam singles titles and the World No. 1-ranking in 2011

## 2011 Grand Slam Champions

## Australian Open

### Men's Singles

| | Winner | Runner-up | Score |
|---|---|---|---|
| Quarterfinals | David Ferrer | Rafael Nadal | 6–4, 6–2, 6–3 |
| | Andy Murray | Alexandr Dolgopolov | 7–5, 6–3, 6–7 (3–7), 6–3 |
| | Roger Federer | Stanislas Wawrinka | 6–1, 6–3, 6–3 |
| | Novak Djokovic | Tomas Berdych | 6–1, 7–6 (7–5), 6–1 |
| Semifinals | Andy Murray | David Ferrer | 4–6, 7–6 (7–2), 6–1, 7–6 (7–2) |
| | Novak Djokovic | Roger Federer | 7–6 (7–3), 7–5, 6–4 |
| Final | Novak Djokovic | Andy Murray | 6–4, 6–2, 6–3 |

### Women's Singles

| | Winner | Runner-up | Score |
|---|---|---|---|
| Quarterfinals | Caroline Wozniacki | Francesca Schiavone | 3–6, 6–3, 6–3 |
| | Li Na | Andrea Petkovic | 6–2, 6–4 |
| | Vera Zvonareva | Petra Kvitova | 6–2, 6–4 |
| | Kim Clijsters | Agnieszka Radwanska | 6–3, 7–6 (7–4) |
| Semifinals | Li Na | Caroline Wozniacki | 3–6, 7–5, 6–3 |
| | Kim Clijsters | Vera Zvonareva | 6–3, 6–3 |
| Final | Kim Clijsters | Li Na | 3–6, 6–3, 6–3 |

### Doubles

| | Winner | Runner-up | Score |
|---|---|---|---|
| Men's Final | Bob Bryan/ Mike Bryan | Mahesh Bhupathi/ Leander Paes | 6–3, 6–4 |
| Women's Final | Gisela Dulko/ Flavia Pennetta | Victoria Azarenka/ Maria Kirilenko | 2–6, 7–5, 6–1 |
| Mixed Final | Katarina Srebotnik/ Daniel Nestor | Yung-Jan Chan/ Paul Hanley | 6–3, 3–6, 10–7 |

## French Open

### Men's Singles

| | Winner | Runner-up | Score |
|---|---|---|---|
| Quarterfinals | Novak Djokovic† | Fabio Fognini | — |
| | Roger Federer | Gael Monfils | 6–4, 6–3, 7–6 (7–3) |
| | Andy Murray | Juan Ignacio Chela | 7–6 (7–2), 7–5, 6–2 |
| | Rafael Nadal | Robin Soderling | 6–4, 6–1, 7–6 (7–3) |
| Semifinals | Roger Federer | Novak Djokovic | 7–6 (7–5), 6–3, 3–6, 7–6 (7–5) |
| | Rafael Nadal | Andy Murray | 6–4, 7–5, 6–4 |
| Final | Rafael Nadal | Roger Federer | 7–5, 7–6 (7–3), 5–7, 6–1 |

†Won due to an injury walkover (retirement) by opponent prior to start of match.

### Women's Singles

| | Winner | Runner-up | Score |
|---|---|---|---|
| Quarterfinals | Marion Bartoli | Svetlana Kuznetsova | 7–6 (7–4), 6–4 |
| | Francesca Schiavone | Anastasia Pavlyuchenkova | 1–6, 7–5, 7–5 |
| | Maria Sharapova | Andrea Petkovic | 6–0, 6–3 |
| | Li Na | Victoria Azarenka | 7–5, 6–2 |
| Semifinals | Francesca Schiavone | Marion Bartoli | 6–3, 6–3 |
| | Li Na | Maria Sharapova | 6–4, 7–5 |
| Final | Li Na | Francesca Schiavone | 6–4, 7–6 (7–0) |

### Doubles

| | Winner | Runner-Up | Score |
|---|---|---|---|
| Men's Final | Max Mirnyi/ Daniel Nestor | Juan Sebastian Cabal/ Eduardo Schwank | 7–6 (7–3), 3–6, 6–4 |
| Women's Final | Andrea Hlavackova/ Lucie Hradecka | Sania Mirza/ Elena Vesnina | 6–4, 6–3 |
| Mixed Final | Casey Dellacqua/ Scott Lipsky | Katarina Srebotnik/ Nenad Zimonjic | 7–6 (8–6), 4–6, 10–7 |

## Wimbledon

### Men's Singles

| | Winner | Runner-Up | Score |
|---|---|---|---|
| Quarterfinals | Andy Murray | Feliciano Lopez | 6–3, 6–4, 6–4 |
| | Rafael Nadal | Mardy Fish | 6–3, 6–3, 5–7, 6–4 |
| | Jo-Wilfried Tsonga | Roger Federer | 3–6, 6–7 (3–7), 6–4, 6–4, 6–4 |
| | Novak Djokovic | Bernard Tomic | 6–2, 3–6, 6–3, 7–5 |
| Semifinals | Rafael Nadal | Andy Murray | 5–7, 6–2, 6–2, 6–4 |
| | Novak Djokovic | Jo-Wilfried Tsonga | 7–6 (7–4), 6–2, 6–7 (9–11), 6–3 |
| Final | Novak Djokovic | Rafael Nadal | 6–4, 6–1, 1–6, 6–3 |

### Women's Singles

| | Winner | Runner-Up | Score |
|---|---|---|---|
| Quarterfinals | Sabine Lisicki | Marion Bartoli | 6–4, 6–7 (4–7), 6–1 |
| | Maria Sharapova | Dominika Cibulkova | 6–1, 6–1 |
| | Victoria Azarenka | Tamira Paszek | 6–3, 6–1 |
| | Petra Kvitova | Tsvetana Pironkova | 6–3, 6–7 (5–7), 6–2 |
| Semifinals | Maria Sharapova | Sabine Lisicki | 6–4, 6–3 |
| | Petra Kvitova | Victoria Azarenka | 6–1, 3–6, 6–2 |
| Final | Petra Kvitova | Maria Sharapova | 6–3, 6–4 |

### Doubles

| | Winner | Runner-Up | Score |
|---|---|---|---|
| Men's Final | Bob Bryan/ Mike Bryan | Robert Lindstedt Horia Tecau | 6–3, 6–4, 7–6 (7–2) |
| Women's Final | Kveta Peschke/ Katarina Srebotnik | Sabine Lisicki/ Samantha Stosur | 6–3, 6–1 |
| Mixed Final | Iveta Benesova/ Jurgen Melzer | Elena Vesnina/ Mahesh Bhupathi | 6–3, 6–2 |

## U.S. Open

### Men's Singles

| | Winner | Runner-Up | Score |
|---|---|---|---|
| Quarterfinals | Andy Murray | John Isner | 7–5, 6–4, 3–6, 7–6 (7–2) |
| | Rafael Nadal | Andy Roddick | 6–2, 6–1, 6–3 |
| | Roger Federer | Jo-Wilfried Tsonga | 6–4, 6–3, 6–3 |
| | Novak Djokovic | Janko Tipsarevic | 7–6 (7–2), 6–7 (3–7), 6–0, 3–0† |
| Semifinals | Rafael Nadal | Andy Murray | 6–4, 6–2, 3–6, 6–2 |
| | Novak Djokovic | Roger Federer | 6–7 (7–9), 4–6, 6–3, 6–2, 7–5 |
| Final | Novak Djokovic | Rafael Nadal | 6–2, 6–4, 6–7 (3–7), 6–1 |

†Match ended after Tipsarevic retired due to leg injury.

### Women's Singles

| | Winner | Runner-Up | Score |
|---|---|---|---|
| Quarterfinals | Angelique Kerber | Flavia Pennetta | 6–4, 4–6, 6–3 |
| | Serena Williams | Anastasia Pavlyuchenkova | 7–5, 6–1 |
| | Caroline Wozniacki | Andrea Petkovic | 6–1, 7–6 (7–5) |
| | Samantha Stosur | Vera Zvonareva | 6–3, 6–3 |
| Semifinals | Serena Williams | Caroline Wozniacki | 6–2, 6–4 |
| | Samantha Stosur | Angelique Kerber | 6–3, 2–6, 6–2 |
| Final | Samantha Stosur | Serena Williams | 6–2, 6–3 |

### Doubles

| | Winner | Runner-Up | Score |
|---|---|---|---|
| Men's Final | Jurgen Melzer/ Philipp Petzschner | Maruisz Fyrstenberg/ Marcin Matkowski | 6–2, 6–2 |
| Women's Final | Liezel Huber/ Lisa Raymond | Vania King/ Yaroslava Shvedova | 4–6, 7–6 (7–5), 7–6 (7–3) |
| Mixed Final | Melanie Oudin/ Jack Sock | Gisela Dulko/ Eduardo Schwank | 7–6 (7–4), 4–6, 10–8 |

# Major Tournament Results

## ATP-Men's Tour (Late 2010 through Summer 2011)

| Date | Tournament | Site | Singles Winner | Surface | Total Purse |
|---|---|---|---|---|---|
| Oct 4 | Japan Open | Tokyo, Japan | Rafael Nadal | Outdoor Hard | $1,100,000 |
| Oct 4 | China Open | Beijing, China | Novak Djokovic | Outdoor Hard | €$2,100,000 |
| Oct 10 | Shanghai Masters | Shanghai, China | Andy Murray | Outdoor Hard | $3,240,000 |
| Oct 18 | Stockholm Open | Stockholm, Sweden | Roger Federer | Indoor Hard | €531,000 |
| Oct 18 | Kremlin Cup | Moscow, Russia | Victor Troicki | Indoor Hard | $1,100,000 |
| Oct 25 | Austria Trophy | Vienna, Austria | Jurgen Melzer | Indoor Hard | €575,250 |
| Oct 25 | French Grand Prix | Montpellier, France | Gael Monfils | Indoor Hard | €575,250 |
| Oct 25 | St. Petersburg Open | St. Petersburg, Russia | Mikhail Kukushkin | Indoor Hard | €663,750 |
| Oct 31 | Valencia Open | Valencia, Spain | David Ferrer | Indoor Hard | €1,357,000 |
| Nov 1 | Swiss Indoor | Basel, Switzerland | Roger Federer | Indoor Hard | €1,225,000 |
| Nov 7 | Paris Masters | Paris, France | Robin Soderling | Indoor Hard | €2,227,500 |
| Nov 21 | ATP World Tour Finals | London, England | Roger Federer | Indoor Hard | $5,070,000 |
| Jan 2 | Brisbane International | Brisbane, Australia | Robin Soderling | Outdoor Hard | $372,500 |
| Jan 3 | Qatar Open | Doha, Qatar | Roger Federer | Outdoor Hard | $1,024,000 |
| Jan 3 | Chennai Open | Chennai, India | Stanislas Wawrinka | Outdoor Hard | $398,250 |
| Jan 10 | Heineken Open | Auckland, New Zealand | David Ferrer | Outdoor Hard | $355,500 |
| Jan 10 | Sydney International | Sydney, Australia | Gilles Simon | Outdoor Hard | $372,500 |
| Jan 17 | Australian Open | Melbourne, Australia | Novak Djokovic | Outdoor Hard | A$8,900,000 |
| Jan 31 | SA Open | Johannesburg, S. Africa | Kevin Anderson | Outdoor Hard | $442,500 |
| Jan 31 | Zagreb Indoors | Zagreb, Croatia | Ivan Dodig | Indoor Hard | €398,250 |
| Jan 31 | Movistar Open | Santiago, Chile | Tommy Robredo | Outdoor Clay | $398,250 |
| Feb 7 | Brasil Open | Sao Paulo, Brazil | Nicolas Almagro | Indoor Clay | $442,500 |
| Feb 7 | SAP Open | San Jose, California | Milos Raonic | Indoor Hard | $531,000 |
| Feb 7 | ABM/Amro | Rotterdam, Neth. | Robin Soderling | Indoor Hard | €1,150,000 |
| Feb 14 | Regions Championships | Memphis, Tennessee | Andy Roddick | Indoor Hard | $1,100,000 |
| Feb 14 | Copa Claro | Buenos Aires, Argentina | Nicolas Almagro | Outdoor Clay | $475,300 |
| Feb 14 | Open 13 | Marseille, France | Robin Soderling | Indoor Hard | €512,750 |
| Feb 21 | Dubai Championships | Dubai, U.A.E. | Novak Djokovic | Outdoor Hard | $1,619,500 |
| Feb 21 | Mexican Open | Acapulco, Mexico | David Ferrer | Outdoor Clay | $955,000 |
| Feb 21 | Delray Beach Int'l | Delray Beach, Fla. | Juan Martin del Potro | Outdoor Hard | $442,500 |
| Mar 5 | BNP Paribas Open | Indian Wells, Calif. | Novak Djokovic | Outdoor Hard | $3,645,000 |
| Mar 23 | Sony Ericsson Open | Miami, Fla. | Novak Djokovic | Outdoor Hard | $3,645,000 |
| Apr 4 | Grand Prix Hassan II | Casablanca, Morocco | Pablo Andujar | Outdoor Clay | €398,250 |
| Apr 4 | U.S. Clay Champ'ship | Houston, Texas | Ryan Sweeting | Outdoor Clay | $442,500 |
| Apr 10 | Monte Carlo Masters | Monte Carlo, Monaco | Rafael Nadal | Outdoor Clay | €2,227,500 |
| Apr 18 | Barcelona Open | Barcelona, Spain | Rafael Nadal | Outdoor Clay | €1,550,000 |
| Apr 24 | BMW Open | Munich, Germany | Nikolay Davydenko | Outdoor Clay | €398,250 |
| Apr 25 | Serbia Open | Belgrade, Serbia | Novak Djokovic | Outdoor Clay | €373,200 |
| Apr 25 | Estoril Open | Estoril, Portugal | Juan Martin del Potro | Outdoor Clay | €398,250 |
| May 1 | Madrid Open | Madrid, Spain | Novak Djokovic | Outdoor Clay | €2,835,000 |
| May 8 | Italia International | Rome, Italy | Novak Djokovic | Outdoor Clay | €2,227,500 |
| May 15 | Nice Open | Nice, France | Nicolas Almagro | Outdoor Clay | €398,250 |
| May 22 | French Open | Paris, France | Rafael Nadal | Outdoor Clay | €7,884,000 |
| June 6 | Gerry Weber Open | Halle, Germany | Philipp Kohlschreiber | Outdoor Grass | €663,750 |
| June 6 | AEGON Championships | London, England | Andy Murray | Outdoor Grass | €627,700 |
| June 12 | AEGON International | Eastbourne, England | Andreas Seppi | Outdoor Grass | £410,925 |
| June 12 | UNICEF Open | 's-Hertogenbosch, Netherlands | Dmitry Tursunov | Outdoor Grass | €398,250 |
| June 20 | Wimbledon | Wimbledon, England | Novak Djokovic | Outdoor Grass | £7,300,000 |
| July 4 | Hall of Fame Champ's | Newport, R.I. | John Isner | Outdoor Grass | $442,500 |
| July 11 | Swedish Open | Bastad, Sweden | Robin Soderling | Outdoor Clay | €398,250 |
| July 11 | Mercedes Cup | Stuttgart, Germany | Juan Carlos Ferrero | Outdoor Clay | €398,250 |
| July 18 | Atlanta Champ's | Atlanta, Georgia | Mardy Fish | Outdoor Hard | $531,000 |
| July 18 | German Open | Hamburg, Germany | Gilles Simon | Outdoor Clay | €1,000,000 |
| July 25 | Swiss Open | Gstaad, Switzerland | Marcel Granoliers | Outdoor Clay | €398,250 |
| July 25 | Farmer's Classic | Los Angeles | Ernests Gulbis | Outdoor Hard | $619,500 |
| July 25 | Croatia Open | Umag, Croatia | Alexandr Dolgopolov | Outdoor Clay | €398,250 |

### ATP-Men's Tour (Summer 2011 through Fall 2011)

| Date | Tournament | Site | Singles Winner | Surface | Total Purse |
|------|-----------|------|----------------|---------|-------------|
| July 31 | Legg Mason Classic | Washington, D.C. | Radek Stepanek | Oudoor Hard | $1,165,500 |
| July 31 | Kitzbuhel Cup | Kitzbuhel, Austria | Robin Haase | Outdoor Clay | €398,250 |
| Aug 8 | Rogers Cup | Montreal, Canada | Novak Djokovic | Outdoor Hard | $2,430,000 |
| Aug 14 | Western & Southern | Cincinnati, Ohio | Andy Murray | Outdoor Hard | $2,430,000 |
| Aug 21 | Winston-Salem Open | Winston-Salem, N.C. | John Isner | Outdoor Hard | $553,125 |
| Aug 29 | U.S. Open | New York City | Novak Djokovic | Outdoor Hard | $8,468,000 |
| Sept 19 | Moselle Open | Metz, France | Jo-Wilfried Tsonga | Indoor Hard | €398,250 |
| Sept 19 | Nastase Tiriac Trophy | Bucharest, Romania | Florian Mayer | Outdoor Clay | €371,200 |
| Sept 26 | Thailand Open | Bangkok, Thailand | Andy Murray | Outdoor Hard | $551,000 |
| Sept 26 | Malaysian Open | Kuala Lumpur, Malaysia | Janko Tipsarevic | Indoor Hard | $850,000 |

### WTA-Women's Tour (Late 2010 through Spring 2011)

| Date | Tournament | Site | Winner | Runner-Up | Total Purse |
|------|-----------|------|--------|-----------|-------------|
| Oct 2 | China Open | Bejing, China | Caroline Wozniacki | Vera Zvonareva | $4,500,000 |
| Oct 11 | HP Open | Osaka, Japan | Tama. Tanasugarn | Kimiko Date Krumm | $220,000 |
| Oct 11 | Generali Ladies Open | Linz, Austria | Ana Ivanovic | Patty Schnyder | $220,000 |
| Oct 18 | BNP Luxembourg Open | Luxembourg, Lux. | Roberta Vinci | Julia Goerges | $220,000 |
| Oct 18 | Ladies Kremlin Cup | Moscow, Russia | Victoria Azarenka | Maria Kirilenko | $1,000,000 |
| Oct 26 | WTA Tour Championships | Doha, Qatar | Kim Clijsters | Caroline Wozniacki | $4,550,000 |
| Nov 4 | Tour'm't of Champions | Bali, Indonesia | Ana Ivanovic | Alisa Kleybanova | $600,000 |
| Jan 2 | Brisbane Int'l | Brisbane, Australia | Petra Kvitova | Andrea Petkovic | $220,000 |
| Jan 3 | ASB Classic | Auckland, N.Z. | Greta Arn | Yanina Wickmayer | $220,000 |
| Jan 9 | Medibank Int'l | Sydney, Australia | Li Na | Kim Clijsters | $618,000 |
| Jan 9 | Hobart Int'l | Hobart, Australia | Jarmila Groth | Bethanie Mattek-Sands | $220,000 |
| Jan 17 | Australian Open | Melbourne, Australia | Kim Clijsters | Li Na | $9,264,098 |
| Feb 7 | GDF Suez Open | Paris, France | Petra Kvitova | Kim Clijsters | $618,000 |
| Feb 7 | Pattaya Open | Patttaya, Thailand | Dan'la Hantuchova | Sara Errani | $220,000 |
| Feb 13 | Cellular South Cup | Memphis, Tenn. | Magda. Rybarikova | Rebecca Marino | $220,000 |
| Feb 14 | Dubai Championships | Dubai, U.A.E. | Caroline Wozniacki | Svetlana Kuznetsova | $2,050,000 |
| Feb 14 | Copa Colsanitas | Bogota, Colombia | Lourdes Dom.-Lino | Mathilde Johansson | $220,000 |
| Feb 21 | Mexicano Open | Acapulco, Mexico | Gisela Dulko | Arantxa Santonja | $220,000 |
| Feb 21 | Qatar Open | Doha, Qatar | Vera Zvonareva | Caroline Wozniacki | $721,000 |
| Feb 28 | Malaysian Open | Kuala Lumpur, Mal. | Jelena Dokic | Lucie Safarova | $220,000 |
| Feb 28 | Monterrey Open | Monterrey, Mexico | A. Pavlyuchenkova | Jelena Jankovic | $220,000 |
| Mar 9 | BNP Paribas Open | Indian Wells, Calif. | Caroline Wozniacki | Marion Bartoli | $4,500,000 |
| Mar 22 | Sony Ericsson Open | Miami, Florida | Victoria Azarenka | Maria Sharapova | $4,500,000 |
| Apr 4 | Family Circle Cup | Charleston, S.C. | Caroline Wozniacki | Elena Vesnina | $721,000 |
| Apr 4 | Andalucia Int'l | Marbella, Spain | Victoria Azarenka | Irina Begu | $220,000 |
| Apr 18 | Porsche Grand Prix | Stuttgart, Germany | Julia Goerges | Caroline Wozniacki | $721,000 |
| Apr 18 | Morocco Grand Prix | Fez, Morocco | Alberta Brianti | Simona Halep | $220,000 |
| Apr 25 | Barcelona Open | Barcelona, Spain | Roberta Vinci | Lucie Hradecka | $220,000 |
| Apr 25 | Estoril Open | Estoril, Portugal | Anabel Garrigues | Kristina Barrois | $220,000 |
| Apr 30 | Madrid Open | Madrid, Spain | Petra Kvitova | Victoria Azarenka | $4,500,000 |
| May 9 | d'Italia International | Rome, Italy | Maria Sharapova | Samantha Stosur | $2,050,000 |
| May 16 | Brussles Open | Brussels, Belguim | Caroline Wozniacki | Shuai Peng | $618,000 |
| May 16 | Strasbourg Int'l | Strasbourg, France | Andrea Petkovic | Marion Bartoli | $220,000 |

### WTA-Women's Tour (Spring 2011 through Summer 2011)

| Date | Tournament | Site | Winner | Runner-Up | Total Purse |
|------|-----------|------|--------|-----------|-------------|
| May 22 | French Open | Paris, France | Li Na | Francesca Schiavone | $9,938,926 |
| June 6 | AEGON Classic | Birmingham, England | Sabine Lisicki | Daniela Hantuchova | $220,000 |
| June 6 | Copenhagen Open | Copenhagen, Den. | Caroline Wozniacki | Lucie Safarova | $220,000 |
| June 12 | UNICEF Open | 's-Hertogenbosch, Neth. | Roberta Vinci | Jelena Dokic | $220,000 |
| June 13 | AEGON Int'l | Eastbourne, England | Marion Bartoli | Petra Kvitova | $618,000 |
| June 20 | Wimbledon | Wimbledon, England | Petra Kvitova | Maria Sharapova | $9,781,631 |
| July 4 | Swedish Open | Bastad, Sweden | Polona Hercog | Johanna Larsson | $220,000 |
| July 4 | Budapest Grand Prix | Budapest, Hungary | Roberta Vinci | Irina Begu | $220,000 |
| July 11 | Palermo International | Palermo, Italy | Anabel Garrigues | Polona Hercog | $220,000 |
| July 11 | Gastein International | Bad Gastein, Austria | Maria Jose Sanchez | Pat. Mayr-Achleitner | $220,000 |
| July 18 | Baku Cup | Baku, Azerbaijan | Vera Zvonareva | Ksenia Pervak | $220,000 |
| July 25 | Bank of the West Classic | Stanford, California | Serena Williams | Marino Bartoli | $721,000 |
| July 25 | Citi Open | College Park, Md. | Nadia Petrova | Shahar Peer | $220,000 |
| Aug 1 | Mercury Insurance Open | Carlsbad, Calif. | Ag. Radwanska | Vera Zvonareva | $721,000 |
| Aug 8 | Rogers Cup | Toronto, Canada | Serena Williams | Samantha Stosur | $2,050,000 |
| Aug 15 | Western & Southern Open | Cincinnati, Ohio | Maria Sharapova | Jelena Jankovic | $2,050,000 |
| Aug 21 | New Haven Open | New Haven, Conn. | Caroline Wozniacki | Petra Cetkovska | $618,000 |
| Aug 21 | Texas Open | Dallas, Texas | Sabine Lisicki | Aravane Rezai | $220,000 |
| Aug 29 | U.S. Open | New York City | Samantha Stosur | Serena Williams | $11,018,000 |
| Sept 12 | Tashkent Open | Tashkent, Uzbekistan | Ksenia Pervak | Eva Birnerova | $220,000 |
| Sept 12 | Bell Challenge | Quebec City, Canada | Barbora Strycova | Marina Erakovic | $220,000 |
| Sept 19 | Guangzhou Open | Guangzhou, China | Chanelle Scheepers | Magda. Ribarikova | $220,000 |
| Sept 19 | Hansol Korea Open | Seoul, South Korea | Maria Jose Sanchez | Galina Voskoboeva | $220,000 |
| Sept 25 | Pan Pacific Open | Tokyo, Japan | Ag. Radwanska | Vera Zvonareva | $2,050,000 |

## 2010 Final Season Singles Points Leaders

### Men

| Rank | Player | Country | Points | Events |
|------|--------|---------|--------|--------|
| 1. | Rafael Nadal | ESP | 12450 | 20 |
| 2. | Roger Federer | SUI | 9145 | 21 |
| 3. | Novak Djokovic | SRB | 6240 | 21 |
| 4. | Andy Murray | GBR | 5760 | 19 |
| 5. | Robin Soderling | SWE | 5580 | 24 |
| 6. | Tomas Berdych | CZE | 3955 | 26 |
| 7. | David Ferrer | ESP | 3735 | 24 |
| 8. | Andy Roddick | USA | 3665 | 21 |
| 9. | Fernando Verdasco | ESP | 3240 | 25 |
| 10. | Mikhail Youzhny | RUS | 2920 | 24 |

Note: Compiled by the ATP Tour, through the end of the 2010 season.

### Women

| Rank | Player | Country | Points |
|------|--------|---------|--------|
| 1. | Caroline Wozniacki | DEN | 8035 |
| 2. | Vera Zvonareva | RUS | 6785 |
| 3. | Kim Clijsters | BEL | 6635 |
| 4. | Serena Williams | USA | 5355 |
| 5. | Venus Williams | USA | 4985 |
| 6. | Samantha Stosur | AUS | 4982 |
| 7. | Francesca Schiavone | ITA | 4935 |
| 8. | Jelena Jankovic | SRB | 4445 |
| 9. | Elena Dementieva | RUS | 4335 |
| 10. | Victoria Azarenka | BLR | 4235 |

Note: Compiled by the WTA, through the end of the 2010 season.

## Grand Slam Tournaments

### MEN

### Australian Open Championships

| Year | Winner | Finalist | Score |
|------|--------|----------|-------|
| 1905 | Rodney Heath | A. H. Curtis | 4–6, 6–3, 6–4, 6–4 |
| 1906 | Tony Wilding | H. A. Parker | 6–0, 6–4, 6–4 |
| 1907 | Horace M. Rice | H. A. Parker | 6–3, 6–4, 6–4 |
| 1908 | Fred Alexander | A. W. Dunlop | 3–6, 3–6, 6–0, 6–2, 6–3 |
| 1909 | Tony Wilding | E. F. Parker | 6–1, 7–5, 6–2 |
| 1910 | Rodney Heath | Horace M. Rice | 6–4, 6–3, 6–2 |
| 1911 | Norman Brookes | Horace M. Rice | 6–1, 6–2, 6–3 |
| 1912 | J. Cecil Parke | A. E. Beamish | 3–6, 6–3, 1–6, 6–1, 7–5 |
| 1913 | E. F. Parker | H. A. Parker | 2–6, 6–1, 6–2, 6–3 |
| 1914 | Pat O'Hara Wood | G. L. Patterson | 6–4, 6–3, 5–7, 6–1 |
| 1915 | Francis G. Lowe | Horace M. Rice | 4–6, 6–1, 6–1, 6–4 |
| 1916–18 | No tournament | | |
| 1919 | A. R. F. Kingscote | E. O. Pockley | 6–4, 6–0, 6–3 |
| 1920 | Pat O'Hara Wood | Ron Thomas | 6–3, 4–6, 6–8, 6–1, 6–3 |
| 1921 | Rhys H. Gemmell | A. Hedeman | 7–5, 6–1, 6–4 |
| 1922 | Pat O'Hara Wood | Gerald Patterson | 6–0, 3–6, 3–6, 6–3, 6–2 |
| 1923 | Pat O'Hara Wood | C. B. St John | 6–1, 6–1, 6–3 |
| 1924 | James Anderson | R. E. Schlesinger | 6–3, 6–4, 3–6, 5–7, 6–3 |
| 1925 | James Anderson | Gerald Patterson | 11–9, 2–6, 6–2, 6–3 |
| 1926 | John Hawkes | J. Willard | 6–1, 6–3, 6–1 |
| 1927 | Gerald Patterson | John Hawkes | 3–6, 6–4, 3–6, 18–16, 6–3 |
| 1928 | Jean Borotra | R. O. Cummings | 6–4, 6–1, 4–6, 5–7, 6–3 |
| 1929 | John C. Gregory | R. E. Schlesinger | 6–2, 6–2, 5–7, 7–5 |
| 1930 | Gar Moon | Harry C. Hopman | 6–3, 6–1, 6–3 |
| 1931 | Jack Crawford | Harry C. Hopman | 6–4, 6–2, 2–6, 6–1 |
| 1932 | Jack Crawford | Harry C. Hopman | 4–6, 6–3, 3–6, 6–3, 6–1 |
| 1933 | Jack Crawford | Keith Gledhill | 2–6, 7–5, 6–3, 6–2 |
| 1934 | Fred Perry | Jack Crawford | 6–3, 7–5, 6–1 |
| 1935 | Jack Crawford | Fred Perry | 2–6, 6–4, 6–4, 6–4 |
| 1936 | Adrian Quist | Jack Crawford | 6–2, 6–3, 4–6, 3–6, 9–7 |
| 1937 | Vivian B. McGrath | John Bromwich | 6–3, 1–6, 6–0, 2–6, 6–1 |
| 1938 | Don Budge | John Bromwich | 6–4, 6–2, 6–1 |
| 1939 | John Bromwich | Adrian Quist | 6–4, 6–1, 6–3 |
| 1940 | Adrian Quist | Jack Crawford | 6–3, 6–1, 6–2 |
| 1941–45 | No tournament | | |
| 1946 | John Bromwich | Dinny Pails | 5–7, 6–3, 7–5, 3–6, 6–2 |
| 1947 | Dinny Pails | John Bromwich | 4–6, 6–4, 3–6, 7–5, 8–6 |
| 1948 | Adrian Quist | John Bromwich | 6–4, 3–6, 6–3, 2–6, 6–3 |
| 1949 | Frank Sedgman | Ken McGregor | 6–3, 6–3, 6–2 |
| 1950 | Frank Sedgman | Ken McGregor | 6–3, 6–4, 4–6, 6–1 |
| 1951 | Richard Savitt | Ken McGregor | 6–3, 2–6, 6–3, 6–1 |
| 1952 | Ken McGregor | Frank Sedgman | 7–5, 12–10, 2–6, 6–2 |
| 1953 | Ken Rosewall | Mervyn Rose | 6–0, 6–3, 6–4 |
| 1954 | Mervyn Rose | Rex Hartwig | 6–2, 0–6, 6–4, 6–2 |
| 1955 | Ken Rosewall | Lew Hoad | 9–7, 6–4, 6–4 |
| 1956 | Lew Hoad | Ken Rosewall | 6–4, 3–6, 6–4, 7–5 |
| 1957 | Ashley Cooper | Neale Fraser | 6–3, 9–11, 6–4, 6–2 |
| 1958 | Ashley Cooper | Mal Anderson | 7–5, 6–3, 6–4 |
| 1959 | Alex Olmedo | Neale Fraser | 6–1, 6–2, 3–6, 6–3 |
| 1960 | Rod Laver | Neale Fraser | 5–7, 3–6, 6–3, 8–6, 8–6 |
| 1961 | Roy Emerson | Rod Laver | 1–6, 6–3, 7–5, 6–4 |
| 1962 | Rod Laver | Roy Emerson | 8–6, 0–6, 6–4, 6–4 |
| 1963 | Roy Emerson | Ken Fletcher | 6–3, 6–3, 6–1 |
| 1964 | Roy Emerson | Fred Stolle | 6–3, 6–4, 6–2 |
| 1965 | Roy Emerson | Fred Stolle | 7–9, 2–6, 6–4, 7–5, 6–1 |
| 1966 | Roy Emerson | Arthur Ashe | 6–4, 6–8, 6–2, 6–3 |
| 1967 | Roy Emerson | Arthur Ashe | 6–4, 6–1, 6–1 |
| 1968 | Bill Bowrey | Juan Gisbert | 7–5, 2–6, 9–7, 6–4 |
| 1969* | Rod Laver | Andres Gimeno | 6–3, 6–4, 7–5 |

## MEN (Cont.)
### Australian Open Championships (Cont.)

| Year | Winner | Finalist | Score |
|------|--------|----------|-------|
| 1970 | Arthur Ashe | Dick Crealy | 6–4, 9–7, 6–2 |
| 1971 | Ken Rosewall | Arthur Ashe | 6–1, 7–5, 6–3 |
| 1972 | Ken Rosewall | Mal Anderson | 7–6, 6–3, 7–5 |
| 1973 | John Newcombe | Onny Parun | 6–3, 6–7, 7–5, 6–1 |
| 1974 | Jimmy Connors | Phil Dent | 7–6, 6–4, 4–6, 6–3 |
| 1975 | John Newcombe | Jimmy Connors | 7–5, 3–6, 6–4, 7–5 |
| 1976 | Mark Edmondson | John Newcombe | 6–7, 6–3, 7–6, 6–1 |
| 1977 (Jan) | Roscoe Tanner | Guillermo Vilas | 6–3, 6–3, 6–3 |
| 1977 (Dec) | Vitas Gerulaitis | John Lloyd | 6–3, 7–6, 5–7, 3–6, 6–2 |
| 1978 | Guillermo Vilas | John Marks | 6–4, 6–4, 3–6, 6–3 |
| 1979 | Guillermo Vilas | John Sadri | 7–6, 6–3, 6–2 |
| 1980 | Brian Teacher | Kim Warwick | 7–5, 7–6, 6–3 |
| 1981 | Johan Kriek | Steve Denton | 6–2, 7–6, 6–7, 6–4 |
| 1982 | Johan Kriek | Steve Denton | 6–3, 6–3, 6–2 |
| 1983 | Mats Wilander | Ivan Lendl | 6–1, 6–4, 6–4 |
| 1984 | Mats Wilander | Kevin Curren | 6–7, 6–4, 7–6, 6–2 |
| 1985 (Dec) | Stefan Edberg | Mats Wilander | 6–4, 6–3, 6–3 |
| 1987 (Jan) | Stefan Edberg | Pat Cash | 6–3, 6–4, 3–6, 5–7, 6–3 |
| 1988 | Mats Wilander | Pat Cash | 6–3, 6–7, 3–6, 6–1, 8–6 |
| 1989 | Ivan Lendl | Miloslav Mecir | 6–2, 6–2, 6–2 |
| 1990 | Ivan Lendl | Stefan Edberg | 4–6, 7–6, 5–2, ret. |
| 1991 | Boris Becker | Ivan Lendl | 1–6, 6–4, 6–4, 6–4 |
| 1992 | Jim Courier | Stefan Edberg | 6–3, 3–6, 6–4, 6–2 |
| 1993 | Jim Courier | Stefan Edberg | 6–2, 6–1, 2–6, 7–5 |
| 1994 | Pete Sampras | Todd Martin | 7–6, 6–4, 6–4 |
| 1995 | Andre Agassi | Pete Sampras | 4–6, 6–1, 7–6, 6–4 |
| 1996 | Boris Becker | Michael Chang | 6–2, 6–4, 2–6, 6–2 |
| 1997 | Pete Sampras | Carlos Moya | 6–2, 6–3, 6–3 |
| 1998 | Petr Korda | Marcelo Rios | 6–2, 6–2, 6–2 |
| 1999 | Yevgeny Kafelnikov | Thomas Enqvist | 4–6, 6–0, 6–3, 7–6 |
| 2000 | Andre Agassi | Yevgeny Kafelnikov | 3–6, 6–3, 6–2, 6–4 |
| 2001 | Andre Agassi | Arnaud Clement | 6–4, 6–2, 6–2 |
| 2002 | Thomas Johansson | Marat Safin | 3–6, 6–4, 6–4, 7–6 (7–4) |
| 2003 | Andre Agassi | Rainer Schuettler | 6–2, 6–2, 6–1 |
| 2004 | Roger Federer | Marat Safin | 7–6 (7–3), 6–4, 6–2 |
| 2005 | Marat Safin | Lleyton Hewitt | 1–6, 6–3, 6–4, 6–4 |
| 2006 | Roger Federer | Marcos Baghdatis | 5–7, 7–5, 6–0, 6–2 |
| 2007 | Roger Federer | Fernando Gonzalez | 7–6 (7–2), 6–4, 6–4 |
| 2008 | Novak Djokovic | Jo-Wilfried Tsonga | 4–6, 6–4, 6–3, 7–6 (7–2) |
| 2009 | Rafael Nadal | Roger Federer | 7–5, 3–6, 7–6 (7–3), 3–6, 6–2 |
| 2010 | Roger Federer | Andy Murray | 6–3, 6–4, 7–6 (13–11) |
| 2011 | Novak Djokovic | Andy Murray | 6–4, 6–2, 6–3 |

*Became Open (amateur and professional) in 1969.

## MEN *(Cont.)*

### French Championships

| Year | Winner | Finalist | Score |
|------|--------|----------|-------|
| 1925† | Rene Lacoste | Jean Borotra | 7–5, 6–1, 6–4 |
| 1926 | Henri Cochet | Rene Lacoste | 6–2, 6–4, 6–3 |
| 1927 | Rene Lacoste | Bill Tilden | 6–4, 4–6, 5–7, 6–3, 11–9 |
| 1928 | Henri Cochet | Rene Lacoste | 5–7, 6–3, 6–1, 6–3 |
| 1929 | Rene Lacoste | Jean Borotra | 6–3, 2–6, 6–0, 2–6, 8–6 |
| 1930 | Henri Cochet | Bill Tilden | 3–6, 8–6, 6–3, 6–1 |
| 1931 | Jean Borotra | Claude Boussus | 2–6, 6–4, 7–5, 6–4 |
| 1932 | Henri Cochet | Giorgio de Stefani | 6–0, 6–4, 4–6, 6–3 |
| 1933 | Jack Crawford | Henri Cochet | 8–6, 6–1, 6–3 |
| 1934 | Gottfried von Cramm | Jack Crawford | 6–4, 7–9, 3–6, 7–5, 6–3 |
| 1935 | Fred Perry | Gottfried von Cramm | 6–3, 3–6, 6–1, 6–3 |
| 1936 | Gottfried von Cramm | Fred Perry | 6–0, 2–6, 6–2, 2–6, 6–0 |
| 1937 | Henner Henkel | Henry Austin | 6–1, 6–4, 6–3 |
| 1938 | Don Budge | Roderick Menzel | 6–3, 6–2, 6–4 |
| 1939 | Don McNeill | Bobby Riggs | 7–5, 6–0, 6–3 |
| 1940 | No tournament | | |
| 1941‡ | Bernard Destremau | n/a | n/a |
| 1942‡ | Bernard Destremau | n/a | n/a |
| 1943‡ | Yvon Petra | n/a | n/a |
| 1944‡ | Yvon Petra | n/a | n/a |
| 1945‡ | Yvon Petra | Bernard Destremau | 7–5, 6–4, 6–2 |
| 1946 | Marcel Bernard | Jaroslav Drobny | 3–6, 2–6, 6–1, 6–4, 6–3 |
| 1947 | Joseph Asboth | Eric Sturgess | 8–6, 7–5, 6–4 |
| 1948 | Frank Parker | Jaroslav Drobny | 6–4, 7–5, 5–7, 8–6 |
| 1949 | Frank Parker | Budge Patty | 6–3, 1–6, 6–1, 6–4 |
| 1950 | Budge Patty | Jaroslav Drobny | 6–1, 6–2, 3–6, 5–7, 7–5 |
| 1951 | Jaroslav Drobny | Eric Sturgess | 6–3, 6–3, 6–3 |
| 1952 | Jaroslav Drobny | Frank Sedgman | 6–2, 6–0, 3–6, 6–4 |
| 1953 | Ken Rosewall | Vic Seixas | 6–3, 6–4, 1–6, 6–2 |
| 1954 | Tony Trabert | Arthur Larsen | 6–4, 7–5, 6–1 |
| 1955 | Tony Trabert | Sven Davidson | 2–6, 6–1, 6–4, 6–2 |
| 1956 | Lew Hoad | Sven Davidson | 6–4, 8–6, 6–3 |
| 1957 | Sven Davidson | Herbie Flam | 6–3, 6–4, 6–4 |
| 1958 | Mervyn Rose | Luis Ayala | 6–3, 6–4, 6–4 |
| 1959 | Nicola Pietrangeli | Ian Vermaak | 3–6, 6–3, 6–4, 6–1 |
| 1960 | Nicola Pietrangeli | Luis Ayala | 3–6, 6–3, 6–4, 4–6, 6–3 |
| 1961 | Manuel Santana | Nicola Pietrangeli | 4–6, 6–1, 3–6, 6–0, 6–2 |
| 1962 | Rod Laver | Roy Emerson | 3–6, 2–6, 6–3, 9–7, 6–2 |
| 1963 | Roy Emerson | Pierre Darmon | 3–6, 6–1, 6–4, 6–4 |
| 1964 | Manuel Santana | Nicola Pietrangeli | 6–3, 6–1, 4–6, 7–5 |
| 1965 | Fred Stolle | Tony Roche | 3–6, 6–0, 6–2, 6–3 |
| 1966 | Tony Roche | Istvan Gulyas | 6–1, 6–4, 7–5 |
| 1967 | Roy Emerson | Tony Roche | 6–1, 6–4, 2–6, 6–2 |
| 1968* | Ken Rosewall | Rod Laver | 6–3, 6–1, 2–6, 6–2 |
| 1969 | Rod Laver | Ken Rosewall | 6–4, 6–3, 6–4 |
| 1970 | Jan Kodes | Zeljko Franulovic | 6–2, 6–4, 6–0 |
| 1971 | Jan Kodes | Ilie Nastase | 8–6, 6–2, 2–6, 7–5 |
| 1972 | Andres Gimeno | Patrick Proisy | 4–6, 6–3, 6–1, 6–1 |
| 1973 | Ilie Nastase | Nikki Pilic | 6–3, 6–3, 6–0 |
| 1974 | Bjorn Borg | Manuel Orantes | 6–7, 6–0, 6–1, 6–1 |
| 1975 | Bjorn Borg | Guillermo Vilas | 6–2, 6–3, 6–4 |
| 1976 | Adriano Panatta | Harold Solomon | 6–1, 6–4, 4–6, 7–6 |
| 1977 | Guillermo Vilas | Brian Gottfried | 6–0, 6–3, 6–0 |
| 1978 | Bjorn Borg | Guillermo Vilas | 6–1, 6–1, 6–3 |
| 1979 | Bjorn Borg | Victor Pecci | 6–3, 6–1, 6–7, 6–4 |
| 1980 | Bjorn Borg | Vitas Gerulaitis | 6–4, 6–1, 6–2 |
| 1981 | Bjorn Borg | Ivan Lendl | 6–1, 4–6, 6–2, 3–6, 6–1 |
| 1982 | Mats Wilander | Guillermo Vilas | 1–6, 7–6, 6–0, 6–4 |
| 1983 | Yannick Noah | Mats Wilander | 6–2, 7–5, 7–6 |
| 1984 | Ivan Lendl | John McEnroe | 3–6, 2–6, 6–4, 7–5, 7–5 |
| 1985 | Mats Wilander | Ivan Lendl | 3–6, 6–4, 6–2, 6–2 |
| 1986 | Ivan Lendl | Mikael Pernfors | 6–3, 6–2, 6–4 |
| 1987 | Ivan Lendl | Mats Wilander | 7–5, 6–2, 3–6, 7–6 |

†1925 was the first year that entries were accepted from all countries.
‡From 1941 to 1945 the event was called Tournoi de France and was closed to all foreigners.

### MEN *(Cont.)*

#### French Championships *(Cont.)*

| Year | Winner | Finalist | Score |
|---|---|---|---|
| 1988 | Mats Wilander | Henri Leconte | 7–5, 6–2, 6–1 |
| 1989 | Michael Chang | Stefan Edberg | 6–1, 3–6, 4–6, 6–4, 6–2 |
| 1990 | Andres Gomez | Andre Agassi | 6–3, 2–6, 6–4, 6–4 |
| 1991 | Jim Courier | Andre Agassi | 3–6, 6–4, 2–6, 6–1, 6–4 |
| 1992 | Jim Courier | Petr Korda | 7–5, 6–2, 6–1 |
| 1993 | Sergi Bruguera | Jim Courier | 6–4, 2–6, 6–2, 3–6, 6–3 |
| 1994 | Sergi Bruguera | Alberto Berasategui | 6–3, 7–5, 2–6, 6–1 |
| 1995 | Thomas Muster | Michael Chang | 7–5, 6–2, 6–4 |
| 1996 | Yevgeny Kafelnikov | Michael Stich | 7–6, 7–5, 7–6 |
| 1997 | Gustavo Kuerten | Sergi Bruguera | 6–3, 6–4, 6–2 |
| 1998 | Carlos Moya | Alex Corretja | 6–3, 7–5, 6–3 |
| 1999 | Andre Agassi | Andrei Medvedev | 1–6, 2–6, 6–4, 6–3, 6–4 |
| 2000 | Gustavo Kuerten | Magnus Norman | 6–2, 6–3, 2–6, 7–6 |
| 2001 | Gustavo Kuerten | Alex Corretja | 6–7, 7–5, 6–2, 6–0 |
| 2002 | Albert Costa | Juan Carlos Ferrero | 6–1, 6–0, 4–6, 6–3 |
| 2003 | Juan Carlos Ferrero | Martin Verkerk | 6–1, 6–3, 6–2 |
| 2004 | Gaston Gaudio | Guillermo Coria | 0–6, 3–6, 6–4, 6–1, 8–6 |
| 2005 | Rafael Nadal | Mariano Puerta | 6–7, 6–3, 6–1, 7–5 |
| 2006 | Rafael Nadal | Roger Federer | 1–6, 6–1, 6–4, 7–6 |
| 2007 | Rafael Nadal | Roger Federer | 6–3, 4–6, 6–3, 6–4 |
| 2008 | Rafael Nadal | Roger Federer | 6–1, 6–3, 6–0 |
| 2009 | Roger Federer | Robin Soderling | 6–1, 7–6 (7–1), 6–4 |
| 2010 | Rafael Nadal | Robin Soderling | 6–4, 6–2, 6–4 |
| 2011 | Rafael Nadal | Roger Federer | 7–5, 7–6 (7–3), 5–7, 6–1 |

*Became Open (amateur and professional) in 1968, but restricted to only contract professionals in 1972.

#### Wimbledon Championships

| Year | Winner | Finalist | Score |
|---|---|---|---|
| 1877 | Spencer W. Gore | William C. Marshall | 6–1, 6–2, 6–4 |
| 1878 | P. Frank Hadow | Spencer W. Gore | 7–5, 6–1, 9–7 |
| 1879 | John T. Hartley | V. St Leger Gould | 6–2, 6–4, 6–2 |
| 1880 | John T. Hartley | Herbert F. Lawford | 6–0, 6–2, 2–6, 6–3 |
| 1881 | William Renshaw | John T. Hartley | 6–0, 6–2, 6–1 |
| 1882 | William Renshaw | Ernest Renshaw | 6–1, 2–6, 4–6, 6–2, 6–2 |
| 1883 | William Renshaw | Ernest Renshaw | 2–6, 6–3, 6–3, 4–6, 6–3 |
| 1884 | William Renshaw | Herbert F. Lawford | 6–0, 6–4, 9–7 |
| 1885 | William Renshaw | Herbert F. Lawford | 7–5, 6–2, 4–6, 7–5 |
| 1886 | William Renshaw | Herbert F. Lawford | 6–0, 5–7, 6–3, 6–4 |
| 1887 | Herbert F. Lawford | Ernest Renshaw | 1–6, 6–3, 3–6, 6–4, 6–4 |
| 1888 | Ernest Renshaw | Herbert F. Lawford | 6–3, 7–5, 6–0 |
| 1889 | William Renshaw | Ernest Renshaw | 6–4, 6–1, 3–6, 6–0 |
| 1890 | William J. Hamilton | William Renshaw | 6–8, 6–2, 3–6, 6–1, 6–1 |
| 1891 | Wilfred Baddeley | Joshua Pim | 6–4, 1–6, 7–5, 6–0 |
| 1892 | Wilfred Baddeley | Joshua Pim | 4–6, 6–3, 6–3, 6–2 |
| 1893 | Joshua Pim | Wilfred Baddeley | 3–6, 6–1, 6–3, 6–2 |
| 1894 | Joshua Pim | Wilfred Baddeley | 10–8, 6–2, 8–6 |
| 1895 | Wilfred Baddeley | Wilberforce V. Eaves | 4–6, 2–6, 8–6, 6–2, 6–3 |
| 1896 | Harold S. Mahoney | Wilfred Baddeley | 6–2, 6–8, 5–7, 8–6, 6–3 |
| 1897 | Reggie F. Doherty | Harold S. Mahoney | 6–4, 6–4, 6–3 |
| 1898 | Reggie F. Doherty | H. Laurie Doherty | 6–3, 6–3, 2–6, 5–7, 6–1 |
| 1899 | Reggie F. Doherty | Arthur W. Gore | 1–6, 4–6, 6–2, 6–3, 6–3 |
| 1900 | Reggie F. Doherty | Sidney H. Smith | 6–8, 6–3, 6–1, 6–2 |
| 1901 | Arthur W. Gore | Reggie F. Doherty | 4–6, 7–5, 6–4, 6–4 |
| 1902 | H. Laurie Doherty | Arthur W. Gore | 6–4, 6–3, 3–6, 6–0 |
| 1903 | H. Laurie Doherty | Frank L. Riseley | 7–5, 6–3, 6–0 |
| 1904 | H. Laurie Doherty | Frank L. Riseley | 6–1, 7–5, 8–6 |
| 1905 | H. Laurie Doherty | Norman E. Brookes | 8–6, 6–2, 6–4 |
| 1906 | H. Laurie Doherty | Frank L. Riseley | 6–4, 4–6, 6–2, 6–3 |
| 1907 | Norman E. Brookes | Arthur W. Gore | 6–4, 6–2, 6–2 |
| 1908 | Arthur W. Gore | H. Roper Barrett | 6–3, 6–2, 4–6, 3–6, 6–4 |
| 1909 | Arthur W. Gore | M. J. G. Ritchie | 6–8, 1–6, 6–2, 6–2, 6–2 |
| 1910 | Anthony F. Wilding | Arthur W. Gore | 6–4, 7–5, 4–6, 6–2 |
| 1911 | Anthony F. Wilding | H. Roper Barrett | 6–4, 4–6, 2–6, 6–2, ret. |

Note: Prior to 1922 the tournament was run on a challenge-round system. The previous year's winner "stood out" of an All Comers event, which produced a challenger to play him for the title.

## MEN *(Cont.)*

### Wimbledon Championships

| Year | Winner | Finalist | Score |
|------|--------|----------|-------|
| 1912 | Anthony F. Wilding | Arthur W. Gore | 6–4, 6–4, 4–6, 6–4 |
| 1913 | Anthony F. Wilding | Maurice E. McLoughlin | 8–6, 6–3, 10–8 |
| 1914 | Norman E. Brookes | Anthony F. Wilding | 6–4, 6–4, 7–5 |
| 1915–18 | No tournament | | |
| 1919 | Gerald L. Patterson | Norman E. Brookes | 6–3, 7–5, 6–2 |
| 1920 | Bill Tilden | Gerald L. Patterson | 2–6, 6–3, 6–2, 6–4 |
| 1921 | Bill Tilden | Brian I. C. Norton | 4–6, 2–6, 6–1, 6–0, 7–5 |
| 1922 | Gerald L. Patterson | Randolph Lycett | 6–3, 6–4, 6–2 |
| 1923 | Bill Johnston | Francis T. Hunter | 6–0, 6–3, 6–1 |
| 1924 | Jean Borotra | Rene Lacoste | 6–1, 3–6, 6–1, 3–6, 6–4 |
| 1925 | Rene Lacoste | Jean Borotra | 6–3, 6–3, 4–6, 8–6 |
| 1926 | Jean Borotra | Howard Kinsey | 8–6, 6–1, 6–3 |
| 1927 | Henri Cochet | Jean Borotra | 4–6, 4–6, 6–3, 6–4, 7–5 |
| 1928 | Rene Lacoste | Henri Cochet | 6–1, 4–6, 6–4, 6–2 |
| 1929 | Henri Cochet | Jean Borotra | 6–4, 6–3, 6–4 |
| 1930 | Bill Tilden | Wilmer Allison | 6–3, 9–7, 6–4 |
| 1931 | Sidney B. Wood Jr | Francis X. Shields | walkover |
| 1932 | Ellsworth Vines | Henry Austin | 6–4, 6–2, 6–0 |
| 1933 | Jack Crawford | Ellsworth Vines | 4–6, 11–9, 6–2, 2–6, 6–4 |
| 1934 | Fred Perry | Jack Crawford | 6–3, 6–0, 7–5 |
| 1935 | Fred Perry | Gottfried von Cramm | 6–2, 6–4, 6–4 |
| 1936 | Fred Perry | Gottfried von Cramm | 6–1, 6–1, 6–0 |
| 1937 | Don Budge | Gottfried von Cramm | 6–3, 6–4, 6–2 |
| 1938 | Don Budge | Henry Austin | 6–1, 6–0, 6–3 |
| 1939 | Bobby Riggs | Elwood Cooke | 2–6, 8–6, 3–6, 6–3, 6–2 |
| 1940–45 | No tournament | | |
| 1946 | Yvon Petra | Geoff E. Brown | 6–2, 6–4, 6–7 (7–9), 5–7, 6–4 |
| 1947 | Jack Kramer | Tom P. Brown | 6–1, 6–3, 6–2 |
| 1948 | Bob Falkenburg | John Bromwich | 7–5, 0–6, 6–2, 3–6, 7–5 |
| 1949 | Ted Schroeder | Jaroslav Drobny | 3–6, 6–0, 6–3, 4–6, 6–4 |
| 1950 | Budge Patty | Frank Sedgman | 6–1, 6–7 (8–10), 6–2, 6–3 |
| 1951 | Dick Savitt | Ken McGregor | 6–4, 6–4, 6–4 |
| 1952 | Frank Sedgman | Jaroslav Drobny | 4–6, 6–3, 6–2, 6–3 |
| 1953 | Vic Seixas | Kurt Nielsen | 9–7, 6–3, 6–4 |
| 1954 | Jaroslav Drobny | Ken Rosewall | 13–11, 4–6, 6–2, 9–7 |
| 1955 | Tony Trabert | Kurt Nielsen | 6–3, 7–5, 6–1 |
| 1956 | Lew Hoad | Ken Rosewall | 6–2, 4–6, 7–5, 6–4 |
| 1957 | Lew Hoad | Ashley Cooper | 6–2, 6–1, 6–2 |
| 1958 | Ashley Cooper | Neale Fraser | 3–6, 6–3, 6–4, 13–11 |
| 1959 | Alex Olmedo | Rod Laver | 6–4, 6–3, 6–4 |
| 1960 | Neale Fraser | Rod Laver | 6–4, 3–6, 9–7, 7–5 |
| 1961 | Rod Laver | Chuck McKinley | 6–3, 6–1, 6–4 |
| 1962 | Rod Laver | Martin Mulligan | 6–2, 6–2, 6–1 |
| 1963 | Chuck McKinley | Fred Stolle | 9–7, 6–1, 6–4 |
| 1964 | Roy Emerson | Fred Stolle | 6–4, 12–10, 4–6, 6–3 |
| 1965 | Roy Emerson | Fred Stolle | 6–2, 6–4, 6–4 |
| 1966 | Manuel Santana | Dennis Ralston | 6–4, 11–9, 6–4 |
| 1967 | John Newcombe | Wilhelm Bungert | 6–3, 6–1, 6–1 |
| 1968* | Rod Laver | Tony Roche | 6–3, 6–4, 6–2 |
| 1969 | Rod Laver | John Newcombe | 6–4, 5–7, 6–4, 6–4 |
| 1970 | John Newcombe | Ken Rosewall | 5–7, 6–3, 6–2, 3–6, 6–1 |
| 1971 | John Newcombe | Stan Smith | 6–3, 5–7, 2–6, 6–4, 6–4 |
| 1972 | Stan Smith | Ilie Nastase | 4–6, 6–3, 6–3, 4–6, 7–5 |
| 1973 | Jan Kodes | Alex Metreveli | 6–1, 9–8, 6–3 |
| 1974 | Jimmy Connors | Ken Rosewall | 6–1, 6–1, 6–4 |
| 1975 | Arthur Ashe | Jimmy Connors | 6–1, 6–1, 5–7, 6–4 |
| 1976 | Bjorn Borg | Ilie Nastase | 6–4, 6–2, 9–7 |
| 1977 | Bjorn Borg | Jimmy Connors | 3–6, 6–2, 6–1, 5–7, 6–4 |
| 1978 | Bjorn Borg | Jimmy Connors | 6–2, 6–2, 6–3 |
| 1979 | Bjorn Borg | Roscoe Tanner | 6–7, 6–1, 3–6, 6–3, 6–4 |
| 1980 | Bjorn Borg | John McEnroe | 1–6, 7–5, 6–3, 6–7, 8–6 |
| 1981 | John McEnroe | Bjorn Borg | 4–6, 7–6, 7–6, 6–4 |
| 1982 | Jimmy Connors | John McEnroe | 3–6, 6–3, 6–7, 7–6, 6–4 |
| 1983 | John McEnroe | Chris Lewis | 6–2, 6–2, 6–2 |

Note: Prior to 1922 the tournament was run on a challenge-round system. The previous year's winner "stood out" of an All Comers event, which produced a challenger to play him for the title.

*Became Open (amateur and professional) in 1968, but restricted to only contract professionals in 1972.

## MEN (Cont.)
### Wimbledon Championships (Cont.)

| Year | Winner | Finalist | Score |
|------|--------|----------|-------|
| 1984 | John McEnroe | Jimmy Connors | 6–1, 6–1, 6–2 |
| 1985 | Boris Becker | Kevin Curren | 6–3, 6–7, 7–6, 6–4 |
| 1986 | Boris Becker | Ivan Lendl | 6–4, 6–3, 7–5 |
| 1987 | Pat Cash | Ivan Lendl | 7–6, 6–2, 7–5 |
| 1988 | Stefan Edberg | Boris Becker | 4–6, 7–6, 6–4, 6–2 |
| 1989 | Boris Becker | Stefan Edberg | 6–0, 7–6, 6–4 |
| 1990 | Stefan Edberg | Boris Becker | 6–2, 6–2, 3–6, 3–6, 6–4 |
| 1991 | Michael Stich | Boris Becker | 6–4, 7–6, 6–4 |
| 1992 | Andre Agassi | Goran Ivanisevic | 6–7, 6–4, 6–4, 1–6, 6–4 |
| 1993 | Pete Sampras | Jim Courier | 7–6, 7–6, 3–6, 6–3 |
| 1994 | Pete Sampras | Goran Ivanisevic | 7–6, 7–6, 6–0 |
| 1995 | Pete Sampras | Boris Becker | 6–7, 6–2, 6–4, 6–2 |
| 1996 | Richard Krajicek | MaliVai Washington | 6–3, 6–4, 6–3 |
| 1997 | Pete Sampras | Cedric Pioline | 6–4, 6–2, 6–4 |
| 1998 | Pete Sampras | Goran Ivanisevic | 6–7, 7–6, 6–4, 3–6, 6–2 |
| 1999 | Pete Sampras | Andre Agassi | 6–3, 6–4, 7–5 |
| 2000 | Pete Sampras | Patrick Rafter | 6–7, 7–6, 6–4, 6–2 |
| 2001 | Goran Ivanisevic | Patrick Rafter | 6–3, 3–6, 6–3, 2–6, 9–7 |
| 2002 | Lleyton Hewitt | David Nalbandian | 6–1, 6–3, 6–2 |
| 2003 | Roger Federer | Mark Philippoussis | 7–6 (7–5), 6–2, 7–6 (7–3) |
| 2004 | Roger Federer | Andy Roddick | 4–6, 7–5, 7–6 (7–3), 6–4 |
| 2005 | Roger Federer | Andy Roddick | 6–2, 7–6 (7–2), 6–4 |
| 2006 | Roger Federer | Rafael Nadal | 6–0, 7–6, (7–5), 6–7 (2–7), 6–3 |
| 2007 | Roger Federer | Rafael Nadal | 7–6 (9–7), 4–6, 7–6 (7–3), 2–6, 6–2 |
| 2008 | Rafael Nadal | Roger Federer | 6–4, 6–4, 6–7 (5–7), 6–7 (8–10) 9–7 |
| 2009 | Roger Federer | Andy Roddick | 5–7, 7–6 (8–6), 7–6 (7–5), 3–6, 16–14 |
| 2010 | Rafael Nadal | Tomas Berdych | 6–3, 7–5, 6–4 |
| 2011 | Novak Djokovic | Rafael Nadal | 6–4, 6–1, 1–6, 6–3 |

### United States Championships

| Year | Winner | Finalist | Score |
|------|--------|----------|-------|
| 1881 | Richard D. Sears | W.E. Glyn | 6–0, 6–3, 6–2 |
| 1882 | Richard D. Sears | C.M. Clark | 6–1, 6–4, 6–0 |
| 1883 | Richard D. Sears | James Dwight | 6–2, 6–0, 9–7 |
| 1884 | Richard D. Sears | H.A. Taylor | 6–0, 1–6, 6–0, 6–2 |
| 1885 | Richard D. Sears | G.M. Brinley | 6–3, 4–6, 6–0, 6–3 |
| 1886 | Richard D. Sears | R.L. Beeckman | 4–6, 6–1, 6–3, 6–4 |
| 1887 | Richard D. Sears | H.W. Slocum Jr | 6–1, 6–3, 6–2 |
| 1888† | H. W. Slocum Jr | H.A. Taylor | 6–4, 6–1, 6–0 |
| 1889 | H. W. Slocum Jr | Q.A. Shaw | 6–3, 6–1, 4–6, 6–2 |
| 1890 | Oliver S. Campbell | H.W. Slocum Jr | 6–2, 4–6, 6–3, 6–1 |
| 1891 | Oliver S. Campbell | Clarence Hobart | 2–6, 7–5, 7–9, 6–1, 6–2 |
| 1892 | Oliver S. Campbell | Frederick H. Hovey | 7–5, 3–6, 6–3, 7–5 |
| 1893† | Robert D. Wrenn | Frederick H. Hovey | 6–4, 3–6, 6–4, 6–4 |
| 1894 | Robert D. Wrenn | M.F. Goodbody | 6–8, 6–1, 6–4, 6–4 |
| 1895 | Frederick H. Hovey | Robert D. Wrenn | 6–3, 6–2, 6–4 |
| 1896 | Robert D. Wrenn | Frederick H. Hovey | 7–5, 3–6, 6–0, 1–6, 6–1 |
| 1897 | Robert D. Wrenn | Wilberforce V. Eaves | 4–6, 8–6, 6–3, 2–6, 6–2 |
| 1898† | Malcolm D. Whitman | Dwight F. Davis | 3–6, 6–2, 6–2, 6–1 |
| 1899 | Malcolm D. Whitman | J. Parmly Paret | 6–1, 6–2, 3–6, 7–5 |
| 1900 | Malcolm D. Whitman | William A. Larned | 6–4, 1–6, 6–2, 6–2 |
| 1901† | William A. Larned | Beals C. Wright | 6–2, 6–8, 6–4, 6–4 |
| 1902 | William A. Larned | Reggie F. Doherty | 4–6, 6–2, 6–4, 8–6 |
| 1903 | H. Laurie Doherty | William A. Larned | 6–0, 6–3, 10–8 |
| 1904† | Holcombe Ward | William J. Clothier | 10–8, 6–4, 9–7 |
| 1905 | Beals C. Wright | Holcombe Ward | 6–2, 6–1, 11–9 |
| 1906 | William J. Clothier | Beals C. Wright | 6–3, 6–0, 6–4 |
| 1907† | William A. Larned | Robert LeRoy | 6–2, 6–2, 6–4 |
| 1908 | William A. Larned | Beals C. Wright | 6–1, 6–2, 8–6 |
| 1909 | William A. Larned | William J. Clothier | 6–1, 6–2, 5–7, 1–6, 6–1 |
| 1910 | William A. Larned | Thomas C. Bundy | 6–1, 5–7, 6–0, 6–8, 6–1 |
| 1911 | William A. Larned | Maurice E. McLoughlin | 6–4, 6–4, 6–2 |
| 1912‡ | Maurice E. McLoughlin | Bill Johnson | 3–6, 2–6, 6–2, 6–4, 6–2 |

†No challenge round played. ‡Challenge round abolished.

## MEN *(Cont.)*
### United States Championships

| Year | Winner | Finalist | Score |
|------|--------|----------|-------|
| 1913 | Maurice E. McLoughlin | Richard N. Williams | 6–4, 5–7, 6–3, 6–1 |
| 1914 | Richard N. Williams | Maurice E. McLoughlin | 6–3, 8–6, 10–8 |
| 1915 | Bill Johnston | Maurice E. McLoughlin | 1–6, 6–0, 7–5, 10–8 |
| 1916 | Richard N. Williams | Bill Johnston | 4–6, 6–4, 0–6, 6–2, 6–4 |
| 1917# | R.L. Murray | N. W. Niles | 5–7, 8–6, 6–3, 6–3 |
| 1918 | R.L. Murray | Bill Tilden | 6–3, 6–1, 7–5 |
| 1919 | Bill Johnston | Bill Tilden | 6–4, 6–4, 6–3 |
| 1920 | Bill Tilden | Bill Johnston | 6–1, 1–6, 7–5, 5–7, 6–3 |
| 1921 | Bill Tilden | Wallace F. Johnson | 6–1, 6–3, 6–1 |
| 1922 | Bill Tilden | Bill Johnston | 4–6, 3–6, 6–2, 6–3, 6–4 |
| 1923 | Bill Tilden | Bill Johnston | 6–4, 6–1, 6–4 |
| 1924 | Bill Tilden | Bill Johnston | 6–1, 9–7, 6–2 |
| 1925 | Bill Tilden | Bill Johnston | 4–6, 11–9, 6–3, 4–6, 6–3 |
| 1926 | Rene Lacoste | Jean Borotra | 6–4, 6–0, 6–4 |
| 1927 | Rene Lacoste | Bill Tilden | 11–9, 6–3, 11–9 |
| 1928 | Henri Cochet | Francis T. Hunter | 4–6, 6–4, 3–6, 7–5, 6–3 |
| 1929 | Bill Tilden | Francis T. Hunter | 3–6, 6–3, 4–6, 6–2, 6–4 |
| 1930 | John H. Doeg | Francis X. Shields | 10–8, 1–6, 6–4, 16–14 |
| 1931 | Ellsworth Vines | George M. Lott Jr | 7–9, 6–3, 9–7, 7–5 |
| 1932 | Ellsworth Vines | Henri Cochet | 6–4, 6–4, 6–4 |
| 1933 | Fred Perry | Jack Crawford | 6–3, 11–13, 4–6, 6–0, 6–1 |
| 1934 | Fred Perry | Wilmer L. Allison | 6–4, 6–3, 1–6, 8–6 |
| 1935 | Wilmer L. Allison | Sidney B. Wood Jr | 6–2, 6–2, 6–3 |
| 1936 | Fred Perry | Don Budge | 2–6, 6–2, 8–6, 1–6, 10–8 |
| 1937 | Don Budge | Gottfried von Cramm | 6–1, 7–9, 6–1, 3–6, 6–1 |
| 1938 | Don Budge | Gene Mako | 6–3, 6–8, 6–2, 6–1 |
| 1939 | Bobby Riggs | Welby Van Horn | 6–4, 6–2, 6–4 |
| 1940 | Don McNeill | Bobby Riggs | 4–6, 6–8, 6–3, 6–3, 7–5 |
| 1941 | Bobby Riggs | Francis Kovacs II | 5–7, 6–1, 6–3, 6–3 |
| 1942 | Ted Schroeder | Frank Parker | 8–6, 7–5, 3–6, 4–6, 6–2 |
| 1943 | Joseph R. Hunt | Jack Kramer | 6–3, 6–8, 10–8, 6–0 |
| 1944 | Frank Parker | William F. Talbert | 6–4, 3–6, 6–3, 6–3 |
| 1945 | Frank Parker | William F. Talbert | 14–12, 6–1, 6–2 |
| 1946 | Jack Kramer | Tom P. Brown | 9–7, 6–3, 6–0 |
| 1947 | Jack Kramer | Frank Parker | 4–6, 2–6, 6–1, 6–0, 6–3 |
| 1948 | Pancho Gonzales | Eric W. Sturgess | 6–2, 6–3, 14–12 |
| 1949 | Pancho Gonzales | Ted Schroeder | 16–18, 2–6, 6–1, 6–2, 6–4 |
| 1950 | Arthur Larsen | Herbie Flam | 6–3, 4–6, 5–7, 6–4, 6–3 |
| 1951 | Frank Sedgman | Vic Seixas | 6–4, 6–1, 6–1 |
| 1952 | Frank Sedgman | Gardnar Mulloy | 6–1, 6–2, 6–3 |
| 1953 | Tony Trabert | Vic Seixas | 6–3, 6–2, 6–3 |
| 1954 | Vic Seixas | Rex Hartwig | 3–6, 6–2, 6–4, 6–4 |
| 1955 | Tony Trabert | Ken Rosewall | 9–7, 6–3, 6–3 |
| 1956 | Ken Rosewall | Lew Hoad | 4–6, 6–2, 6–3, 6–3 |
| 1957 | Mal Anderson | Ashley J. Cooper | 10–8, 7–5, 6–4 |
| 1958 | Ashley J. Cooper | Mal Anderson | 6–2, 3–6, 4–6, 10–8, 8–6 |
| 1959 | Neale Fraser | Alex Olmedo | 6–3, 5–7, 6–2, 6–4 |
| 1960 | Neale Fraser | Rod Laver | 6–4, 6–4, 9–7 |
| 1961 | Roy Emerson | Rod Laver | 7–5, 6–3, 6–2 |
| 1962 | Rod Laver | Roy Emerson | 6–2, 6–4, 5–7, 6–4 |
| 1963 | Rafael Osuna | Frank Froehling III | 7–5, 6–4, 6–2 |
| 1964 | Roy Emerson | Fred Stolle | 6–4, 6–2, 6–4 |
| 1965 | Manuel Santana | Cliff Drysdale | 6–2, 7–9, 7–5, 6–1 |
| 1966 | Fred Stolle | John Newcombe | 4–6, 12–10, 6–3, 6–4 |
| 1967 | John Newcombe | Clark Graebner | 6–4, 6–4, 8–6 |
| 1968* | Arthur Ashe | Tom Okker | 14–12, 5–7, 6–3, 3–6, 6–3 |
| 1968** | Arthur Ashe | Bob Lutz | 4–6, 6–3, 8–10, 6–0, 6–4 |
| 1969 | Rod Laver | Tony Roche | 7–9, 6–1, 6–3, 6–2 |
| 1969** | Stan Smith | Bob Lutz | 9–7, 6–3, 6–1 |
| 1970 | Ken Rosewall | Tony Roche | 2–6, 6–4, 7–6, 6–3 |
| 1971 | Stan Smith | Jan Kodes | 3–6, 6–3, 6–2, 7–6 |
| 1972 | Ilie Nastase | Arthur Ashe | 3–6, 6–3, 6–7, 6–4, 6–3 |
| 1973 | John Newcombe | Jan Kodes | 6–4, 1–6, 4–6, 6–2, 6–3 |
| 1974 | Jimmy Connors | Ken Rosewall | 6–1, 6–0, 6–1 |
| 1975 | Manuel Orantes | Jimmy Connors | 6–4, 6–3, 6–3 |
| 1976 | Jimmy Connors | Bjorn Borg | 6–4, 3–6, 7–6, 6–4 |

#National Patriotic Tournament. *Became Open (amateur and professional) in 1968. **Amateur event held.

## MEN *(Cont.)*
### United States Championships *(Cont.)*

| Year | Winner | Finalist | Score |
|------|--------|----------|-------|
| 1977 | Guillermo Vilas | Jimmy Connors | 2–6, 6–3, 7–6, 6–0 |
| 1978 | Jimmy Connors | Bjorn Borg | 6–4, 6–2, 6–2 |
| 1979 | John McEnroe | Vitas Gerulaitis | 7–5, 6–3, 6–3 |
| 1980 | John McEnroe | Bjorn Borg | 7–6, 6–1, 6–7, 5–7, 6–4 |
| 1981 | John McEnroe | Bjorn Borg | 4–6, 6–2, 6–4, 6–3 |
| 1982 | Jimmy Connors | Ivan Lendl | 6–3, 6–2, 4–6, 6–4 |
| 1983 | Jimmy Connors | Ivan Lendl | 6–3, 6–7, 7–5, 6–0 |
| 1984 | John McEnroe | Ivan Lendl | 6–3, 6–4, 6–1 |
| 1985 | Ivan Lendl | John McEnroe | 7–6, 6–3, 6–4 |
| 1986 | Ivan Lendl | Miloslav Mecir | 6–4, 6–2, 6–0 |
| 1987 | Ivan Lendl | Mats Wilander | 6–7, 6–0, 7–6, 6–4 |
| 1988 | Mats Wilander | Ivan Lendl | 6–4, 4–6, 6–3, 5–7, 6–4 |
| 1989 | Boris Becker | Ivan Lendl | 7–6, 1–6, 6–3, 7–6 |
| 1990 | Pete Sampras | Andre Agassi | 6–4, 6–3, 6–2 |
| 1991 | Stefan Edberg | Jim Courier | 6–2, 6–4, 6–0 |
| 1992 | Stefan Edberg | Pete Sampras | 3–6, 6–4, 7–6, 6–2 |
| 1993 | Pete Sampras | Cedric Pioline | 6–4, 6–4, 6–3 |
| 1994 | Andre Agassi | Michael Stich | 6–1, 7–6, 7–5 |
| 1995 | Pete Sampras | Andre Agassi | 6–4, 6–3, 4–6, 7–5 |
| 1996 | Pete Sampras | Michael Chang | 6–1, 6–4, 7–6 |
| 1997 | Patrick Rafter | Greg Rusedski | 6–3, 6–2, 4–6, 7–5 |
| 1998 | Patrick Rafter | Mark Philippoussis | 6–3, 3–6, 6–2, 6–0 |
| 1999 | Andre Agassi | Todd Martin | 6–4, 6–7, 6–7, 6–3, 6–2 |
| 2000 | Marat Safin | Pete Sampras | 6–4, 6–3, 6–3 |
| 2001 | Lleyton Hewitt | Pete Sampras | 7–6, 6–1, 6–1 |
| 2002 | Pete Sampras | Andre Agassi | 6–3, 6–4, 5–7, 6–4 |
| 2003 | Andy Roddick | Juan Carlos Ferrero | 6–3, 7–6 (7-2), 6–3 |
| 2004 | Roger Federer | Lleyton Hewitt | 6–0, 7–6 (7-3), 6–0 |
| 2005 | Roger Federer | Andre Agassi | 6–3, 2–6, 7–6 (7–1), 6–1 |
| 2006 | Roger Federer | Andy Roddick | 6–2, 4–6, 7–5, 6–1 |
| 2007 | Roger Federer | Novak Djokovic | 7–6 (7–4), 7–6 (7–2), 6–4 |
| 2008 | Roger Federer | Andy Murray | 6–2, 7–5, 6–2 |
| 2009 | Juan Martin del Potro | Roger Federer | 3–6, 7–6 (7–5), 4–6, 7–6 (7–4), 6–2 |
| 2010 | Rafael Nadal | Novak Djokovic | 6–4, 5–7, 6–4, 6–2 |
| 2011 | Novak Djokovic | Rafael Nadal | 6–2, 6–4, 6–7 (3–7), 6–1 |

# WOMEN
## Australian Open Championships

| Year | Winner | Finalist | Score |
|------|--------|----------|-------|
| 1922 | Margaret Molesworth | Esna Boyd | 6–3, 10–8 |
| 1923 | Margaret Molesworth | Esna Boyd | 6–1, 7–5 |
| 1924 | Sylvia Lance | Esna Boyd | 6–3, 3–6, 6–4 |
| 1925 | Daphne Akhurst | Esna Boyd | 1–6, 8–6, 6–4 |
| 1926 | Daphne Akhurst | Esna Boyd | 6–1, 6–3 |
| 1927 | Esna Boyd | Sylvia Harper | 5–7, 6–1, 6–2 |
| 1928 | Daphne Akhurst | Esna Boyd | 7–5, 6–2 |
| 1929 | Daphne Akhurst | Louise Bickerton | 6–1, 5–7, 6–2 |
| 1930 | Daphne Akhurst | Sylvia Harper | 10–8, 2–6, 7–5 |
| 1931 | Coral Buttsworth | Margorie Crawford | 1–6, 6–3, 6–4 |
| 1932 | Coral Buttsworth | Kathrine Le Messurier | 9–7, 6–4 |
| 1933 | Joan Hartigan | Coral Buttsworth | 6–4, 6–3 |
| 1934 | Joan Hartigan | Margaret Molesworth | 6–1, 6–4 |
| 1935 | Dorothy Round | Nancye Wynne Bolton | 1–6, 6–1, 6–3 |
| 1936 | Joan Hartigan | Nancye Wynne Bolton | 6–4, 6–4 |
| 1937 | Nancye Wynne Bolton | Emily Westacott | 6–3, 5–7, 6–4 |
| 1938 | Dorothy Bundy | D. Stevenson | 6–3, 6–2 |
| 1939 | Emily Westacott | Nell Hopman | 6–1, 6–2 |
| 1940 | Nancye Wynne Bolton | Thelma Coyne | 5–7, 6–4, 6–0 |
| 1941–45 | No tournament | | |
| 1946 | Nancye Wynne Bolton | Joyce Fitch | 6–4, 6–4 |
| 1947 | Nancye Wynne Bolton | Nell Hopman | 6–3, 6–2 |
| 1948 | Nancye Wynne Bolton | Marie Toomey | 6–3, 6–1 |
| 1949 | Doris Hart | Nancye Wynne Bolton | 6–3, 6–4 |
| 1950 | Louise Brough | Doris Hart | 6–4, 3–6, 6–4 |
| 1951 | Nancye Wynne Bolton | Thelma Long | 6–1, 7–5 |
| 1952 | Thelma Long | H. Angwin | 6–2, 6–3 |
| 1953 | Maureen Connolly | Julia Sampson | 6–3, 6–2 |
| 1954 | Thelma Long | J. Staley | 6–3, 6–4 |
| 1955 | Beryl Penrose | Thelma Long | 6–4, 6–3 |
| 1956 | Mary Carter | Thelma Long | 3–6, 6–2, 9–7 |
| 1957 | Shirley Fry | Althea Gibson | 6–3, 6–4 |
| 1958 | Angela Mortimer | Lorraine Coghlan | 6–3, 6–4 |
| 1959 | Mary Carter-Reitano | Renee Schuurman | 6–2, 6–3 |
| 1960 | Margaret Smith | Jan Lehane | 7–5, 6–2 |
| 1961 | Margaret Smith | Jan Lehane | 6–1, 6–4 |
| 1962 | Margaret Smith | Jan Lehane | 6–0, 6–2 |
| 1963 | Margaret Smith | Jan Lehane | 6–2, 6–2 |
| 1964 | Margaret Smith | Lesley Turner | 6–3, 6–2 |
| 1965 | Margaret Smith | Maria Bueno | 5–7, 6–4, 5–2, ret. |
| 1966 | Margaret Smith | Nancy Richey | Default |
| 1967 | Nancy Richey | Lesley Turner | 6–1, 6–4 |
| 1968 | Billie Jean King | Margaret Smith | 6–1, 6–2 |
| 1969* | Margaret Smith Court | Billie Jean King | 6–4, 6–1 |
| 1970 | Margaret Smith Court | Kerry Melville Reid | 6–3, 6–1 |
| 1971 | Margaret Smith Court | Evonne Goolagong | 2–6, 7–6, 7–5 |
| 1972 | Virginia Wade | Evonne Goolagong | 6–4, 6–4 |
| 1973 | Margaret Smith Court | Evonne Goolagong | 6–4, 7–5 |
| 1974 | Evonne Goolagong | Chris Evert | 7–6, 4–6, 6–0 |
| 1975 | Evonne Goolagong | Martina Navratilova | 6–3, 6–2 |
| 1976 | Evonne Goolagong Cawley | Renata Tomanova | 6–2, 6–2 |
| 1977 (Jan) | Kerry Melville Reid | Dianne Balestrat | 7–5, 6–2 |
| 1977 (Dec) | Evonne Goolagong Cawley | Helen Gourlay | 6–3, 6–0 |
| 1978 | Chris O'Neil | Betsy Nagelsen | 6–3, 7–6 |
| 1979 | Barbara Jordan | Sharon Walsh | 6–3, 6–3 |
| 1980 | Hana Mandlikova | Wendy Turnbull | 6–0, 7–5 |
| 1981 | Martina Navratilova | Chris Evert Lloyd | 6–7, 6–4, 7–5 |
| 1982 | Chris Evert Lloyd | Martina Navratilova | 6–3, 2–6, 6–3 |
| 1983 | Martina Navratilova | Kathy Jordan | 6–2, 7–6 |
| 1984 | Chris Evert Lloyd | Helena Sukova | 6–7, 6–1, 6–3 |
| 1985 (Dec) | Martina Navratilova | Chris Evert Lloyd | 6–2, 4–6, 6–2 |
| 1987 (Jan) | Hana Mandlikova | Martina Navratilova | 7–5, 7–6 |
| 1988 | Steffi Graf | Chris Evert | 6–1, 7–6 |
| 1989 | Steffi Graf | Helena Sukova | 6–4, 6–4 |
| 1990 | Steffi Graf | Mary Joe Fernandez | 6–3, 6–4 |
| 1991 | Monica Seles | Jana Novotna | 5–7, 6–3, 6–1 |

*Became Open (amateur and professional) in 1969.

## WOMEN *(Cont.)*
### Australian Championships *(Cont.)*

| Year | Winner | Finalist | Score |
|---|---|---|---|
| 1992 | Monica Seles | Mary Joe Fernandez | 6–2, 6–3 |
| 1993 | Monica Seles | Steffi Graf | 4–6, 6–3, 6–2 |
| 1994 | Steffi Graf | Arantxa Sánchez Vicario | 6–0, 6–2 |
| 1995 | Mary Pierce | Arantxa Sánchez Vicario | 6–3, 6–2 |
| 1996 | Monica Seles | Anke Huber | 6–4, 6–1 |
| 1997 | Martina Hingis | Mary Pierce | 6–2, 6–2 |
| 1998 | Martina Hingis | Conchita Martinez | 6–3, 6–3 |
| 1999 | Martina Hingis | Amelie Mauresmo | 6–2, 6–3 |
| 2000 | Lindsay Davenport | Martina Hingis | 6–1, 7–5 |
| 2001 | Jennifer Capriati | Martina Hingis | 6–4, 6–3 |
| 2002 | Jennifer Capriati | Martina Hingis | 4–6, 7–6 (9–7), 6–2 |
| 2003 | Serena Williams | Venus Williams | 7–6 (7-4), 3–6, 6–4 |
| 2004 | Justine Henin-Hardenne | Kim Clijsters | 6–3, 4–6, 6–3 |
| 2005 | Serena Williams | Lindsay Davenport | 2–6, 6–3, 6–0 |
| 2006 | Amelie Mauresmo | Justine Henin-Hardenne | 6–1, 2–0, ret. |
| 2007 | Serena Williams | Maria Sharapova | 6–1, 6–2 |
| 2008 | Maria Sharapova | Ana Ivanovic | 7–5, 6–3 |
| 2009 | Serena Williams | Dinara Safina | 6–0, 6–3 |
| 2010 | Serena Williams | Justine Henin | 6–4, 3–6, 6–2 |
| 2011 | Kim Clijsters | Li Na | 3–6, 6–3, 6–3 |

### French Championships

| Year | Winner | Finalist | Score |
|---|---|---|---|
| 1925† | Suzanne Lenglen | Kathleen McKane | 6–1, 6–2 |
| 1926 | Suzanne Lenglen | Mary K. Browne | 6–1, 6–0 |
| 1927 | Kea Bouman | Irene Peacock | 6–2, 6–4 |
| 1928 | Helen Wills | Eileen Bennett | 6–1, 6–2 |
| 1929 | Helen Wills | Simone Mathieu | 6–3, 6–4 |
| 1930 | Helen Wills Moody | Helen Jacobs | 6–2, 6–1 |
| 1931 | Cilly Aussem | Betty Nuthall | 8–6, 6–1 |
| 1932 | Helen Wills Moody | Simone Mathieu | 7–5, 6–1 |
| 1933 | Margaret Scriven | Simone Mathieu | 6–2, 4–6, 6–4 |
| 1934 | Margaret Scriven | Helen Jacobs | 7–5, 4–6, 6–1 |
| 1935 | Hilde Sperling | Simone Mathieu | 6–2, 6–1 |
| 1936 | Hilde Sperling | Simone Mathieu | 6–3, 6–4 |
| 1937 | Hilde Sperling | Simone Mathieu | 6–2, 6–4 |
| 1938 | Simone Mathieu | Nelly Landry | 6–0, 6–3 |
| 1939 | Simone Mathieu | Jadwiga Jedrzejowska | 6–3, 8–6 |
| 1940–45 | No tournament | | |
| 1946 | Margaret Osborne | Pauline Betz | 1–6, 8–6, 7–5 |
| 1947 | Patricia Todd | Doris Hart | 6–3, 3–6, 6–4 |
| 1948 | Nelly Landry | Shirley Fry | 6–2, 0–6, 6–0 |
| 1949 | Margaret Osborne duPont | Nelly Adamson | 7–5, 6–2 |
| 1950 | Doris Hart | Patricia Todd | 6–4, 4–6, 6–2 |
| 1951 | Shirley Fry | Doris Hart | 6–3, 3–6, 6–3 |
| 1952 | Doris Hart | Shirley Fry | 6–4, 6–4 |
| 1953 | Maureen Connolly | Doris Hart | 6–2, 6–4 |
| 1954 | Maureen Connolly | Ginette Bucaille | 6–4, 6–1 |
| 1955 | Angela Mortimer | Dorothy Knode | 2–6, 7–5, 10–8 |
| 1956 | Althea Gibson | Angela Mortimer | 6–0, 12–10 |
| 1957 | Shirley Bloomer | Dorothy Knode | 6–1, 6–3 |
| 1958 | Zsuzsi Kormoczi | Shirley Bloomer | 6–4, 1–6, 6–2 |
| 1959 | Christine Truman | Zsuzsi Kormoczi | 6–4, 7–5 |
| 1960 | Darlene Hard | Yola Ramirez | 6–3, 6–4 |
| 1961 | Ann Haydon | Yola Ramirez | 6–2, 6–1 |
| 1962 | Margaret Smith | Lesley Turner | 6–3, 3–6, 7–5 |
| 1963 | Lesley Turner | Ann Haydon Jones | 2–6, 6–3, 7–5 |
| 1964 | Margaret Smith | Maria Bueno | 5–7, 6–1, 6–2 |
| 1965 | Lesley Turner | Margaret Smith | 6–3, 6–4 |
| 1966 | Ann Jones | Nancy Richey | 6–3, 6–1 |
| 1967 | Francoise Durr | Lesley Turner | 4–6, 6–3, 6–4 |
| 1968* | Nancy Richey | Ann Jones | 5–7, 6–4, 6–1 |

†1925 was the first year that entries were accepted from all countries. *Became Open (amateur and professional) in 1968, but restricted to only contract professionals in 1972.

## WOMEN (Cont.)
### French Championships (Cont.)

| Year | Winner | Finalist | Score |
|------|--------|----------|-------|
| 1969 | Margaret Smith Court | Ann Jones | 6–1, 4–6, 6–3 |
| 1970 | Margaret Smith Court | Helga Niessen | 6–2, 6–4 |
| 1971 | Evonne Goolagong | Helen Gourlay | 6–3, 7–5 |
| 1972 | Billie Jean King | Evonne Goolagong | 6–3, 6–3 |
| 1973 | Margaret Smith Court | Chris Evert | 6–7, 7–6, 6–4 |
| 1974 | Chris Evert | Olga Morozova | 6–1, 6–2 |
| 1975 | Chris Evert | Martina Navratilova | 2–6, 6–2, 6–1 |
| 1976 | Sue Barker | Renata Tomanova | 6–2, 0–6, 6–2 |
| 1977 | Mima Jausovec | Florenza Mihai | 6–2, 6–7, 6–1 |
| 1978 | Virginia Ruzici | Mima Jausovec | 6–2, 6–2 |
| 1979 | Chris Evert Lloyd | Wendy Turnbull | 6–2, 6–0 |
| 1980 | Chris Evert Lloyd | Virginia Ruzici | 6–0, 6–3 |
| 1981 | Hana Mandlikova | Sylvia Hanika | 6–2, 6–4 |
| 1982 | Martina Navratilova | Andrea Jaeger | 7–6, 6–1 |
| 1983 | Chris Evert Lloyd | Mima Jausovec | 6–1, 6–2 |
| 1984 | Martina Navratilova | Chris Evert Lloyd | 6–3, 6–1 |
| 1985 | Chris Evert Lloyd | Martina Navratilova | 6–3, 6–7, 7–5 |
| 1986 | Chris Evert Lloyd | Martina Navratilova | 2–6, 6–3, 6–3 |
| 1987 | Steffi Graf | Martina Navratilova | 6–4, 4–6, 8–6 |
| 1988 | Steffi Graf | Natalia Zvereva | 6–0, 6–0 |
| 1989 | Arantxa Sánchez Vicario | Steffi Graf | 7–6, 3–6, 7–5 |
| 1990 | Monica Seles | Steffi Graf | 7–6, 6–4 |
| 1991 | Monica Seles | Arantxa Sánchez Vicario | 6–3, 6–4 |
| 1992 | Monica Seles | Steffi Graf | 6–2, 3–6, 10–8 |
| 1993 | Steffi Graf | Mary Joe Fernandez | 4–6, 6–2, 6–4 |
| 1994 | Arantxa Sánchez Vicario | Mary Pierce | 6–4, 6–4 |
| 1995 | Steffi Graf | Arantxa Sánchez Vicario | 7–5, 4–6, 6–0 |
| 1996 | Steffi Graf | Arantxa Sánchez Vicario | 6–3, 6–7 (4–7), 10–8 |
| 1997 | Iva Majoli | Martina Hingis | 6–4, 6–2 |
| 1998 | Arantxa Sánchez Vicario | Monica Seles | 7–6 (7–5), 0–6, 6–2 |
| 1999 | Steffi Graf | Martina Hingis | 4–6, 7–5, 6–2 |
| 2000 | Mary Pierce | Conchita Martinez | 6–2, 7–5 |
| 2001 | Jennifer Capriati | Kim Clijsters | 1–6, 6–4, 12–10 |
| 2002 | Serena Williams | Venus Williams | 7–5, 6–3 |
| 2003 | Justine Henin-Hardenne | Kim Clijsters | 6–0, 6–4 |
| 2004 | Anastasia Myskina | Elena Dementieva | 6–1, 6–2 |
| 2005 | Justine Henin-Hardenne | Mary Pierce | 6–1, 6–1 |
| 2006 | Justine Henin-Hardenne | Svetlana Kuznetsova | 6–4, 6–4 |
| 2007 | Justine Henin | Ana Ivanovic | 6–1, 6–2 |
| 2008 | Ana Ivanovic | Dinara Safina | 6–4, 6–3 |
| 2009 | Svetlana Kuznetsova | Dinara Safina | 6–4, 6–2 |
| 2010 | Francesca Schiavone | Samantha Stosur | 6–4, 7–6 (7–2) |
| 2011 | Li Na | Francesca Schiavone | 6–4, 7–6 (7–0) |

## Wimbledon Championships

| Year | Winner | Finalist | Score |
|------|--------|----------|-------|
| 1884 | Maud Watson | Lilian Watson | 6–8, 6–3, 6–3 |
| 1885 | Maud Watson | Blanche Bingley | 6–1, 7–5 |
| 1886 | Blanche Bingley | Maud Watson | 6–3, 6–3 |
| 1887 | Charlotte Dod | Blanche Bingley | 6–2, 6–0 |
| 1888 | Charlotte Dod | Blanche Bingley Hillyard | 6–3, 6–3 |
| 1889 | Blanche Bingley Hillyard | n/a | n/a |
| 1890 | Lena Rice | n/a | n/a |
| 1891 | Charlotte Dod | n/a | n/a |
| 1892 | Charlotte Dod | Blanche Bingley Hillyard | 6–1, 6–1 |
| 1893 | Charlotte Dod | Blanche Bingley Hillyard | 6–8, 6–1, 6–4 |
| 1894 | Blanche Bingley Hillyard | n/a | n/a |
| 1895 | Charlotte Cooper | n/a | |
| 1896 | Charlotte Cooper | Mrs. W. H. Pickering | 6–2, 6–3 |
| 1897 | Blanche Bingley Hillyard | Charlotte Cooper | 5–7, 7–5, 6–2 |
| 1898 | Charlotte Cooper | n/a | n/a |
| 1899 | Blanche Bingley Hillyard | Charlotte Cooper | 6–2, 6–3 |
| 1900 | Blanche Bingley Hillyard | Charlotte Cooper | 4–6, 6–4, 6–4 |
| 1901 | Charlotte Cooper Sterry | Blanche Bingley Hillyard | 6–2, 6–2 |
| 1902 | Muriel Robb | Charlotte Cooper Sterry | 7–5, 6–1 |
| 1903 | Dorothea Douglass | n/a | n/a |

Note: Prior to 1922 the tournament was run on a challenge-round system. The previous year's winner "stood out" of an All-Comers event, which produced a challenger to play her for the title.

### WOMEN *(Cont.)*
### Wimbledon Championships *(Cont.)*

| Year | Winner | Finalist | Score |
|------|--------|----------|-------|
| 1904 | Dorothea Douglass | Charlotte Cooper Sterry | 6–0, 6–3 |
| 1905 | May Sutton | Dorothea Douglass | 6–3, 6–4 |
| 1906 | Dorothea Douglass | May Sutton | 6–3, 9–7 |
| 1907 | May Sutton | Dorothea Douglass Lambert Chambers | 6–1, 6–4 |
| 1908 | Charlotte Cooper Sterry | n/a | n/a |
| 1909 | Dora Boothby | n/a | n/a |
| 1910 | Dorothea Douglass Lambert Chambers | Dora Boothby | 6–2, 6–2 |
| 1911 | Dorothea Douglass Lambert Chambers | Dora Boothby | 6–0, 6–0 |
| 1912 | Ethel Larcombe | n/a | n/a |
| 1913 | Dorothea Douglass Lambert Chambers | | |
| 1914 | Dorothea Douglass Lambert Chambers | Ethel Larcombe | 7–5, 6–4 |
| 1915–18 | No tournament | | |
| 1919 | Suzanne Lenglen | Dorothea Douglass Lambert Chambers | 10–8, 4–6, 9–7 |
| 1920 | Suzanne Lenglen | Dorothea Douglass Lambert Chambers | 6–3, 6–0 |
| 1921 | Suzanne Lenglen | Elizabeth Ryan | 6–2, 6–0 |
| 1922 | Suzanne Lenglen | Molla Mallory | 6–2, 6–0 |
| 1923 | Suzanne Lenglen | Kathleen McKane | 6–2, 6–2 |
| 1924 | Kathleen McKane | Helen Wills | 4–6, 6–4, 6–2 |
| 1925 | Suzanne Lenglen | Joan Fry | 6–2, 6–0 |
| 1926 | Kathleen McKane Godfree | Lili de Alvarez | 6–2, 4–6, 6–3 |
| 1927 | Helen Wills | Lili de Alvarez | 6–2, 6–4 |
| 1928 | Helen Wills | Lili de Alvarez | 6–2, 6–3 |
| 1929 | Helen Wills | Helen Jacobs | 6–1, 6–2 |
| 1930 | Helen Wills Moody | Elizabeth Ryan | 6–2, 6–2 |
| 1931 | Cilly Aussem | Hilde Kranwinkel | 7–5, 7–5 |
| 1932 | Helen Wills Moody | Helen Jacobs | 6–3, 6–1 |
| 1933 | Helen Wills Moody | Dorothy Round | 6–4, 6–8, 6–3 |
| 1934 | Dorothy Round | Helen Jacobs | 6–2, 5–7, 6–3 |
| 1935 | Helen Wills Moody | Helen Jacobs | 6–3, 3–6, 7–5 |
| 1936 | Helen Jacobs | Hilde Kranwinkel Sperling | 6–2, 4–6, 7–5 |
| 1937 | Dorothy Round | Jadwiga Jedrzejowska | 6–2, 2–6, 7–5 |
| 1938 | Helen Wills Moody | Helen Jacobs | 6–4, 6–0 |
| 1939 | Alice Marble | Kay Stammers | 6–2, 6–0 |
| 1940–45 | No tournament | | |
| 1946 | Pauline Betz | Louise Brough | 6–2, 6–4 |
| 1947 | Margaret Osborne | Doris Hart | 6–2, 6–4 |
| 1948 | Louise Brough | Doris Hart | 6–3, 8–6 |
| 1949 | Louise Brough | Margaret Osborne duPont | 10–8, 1–6, 10–8 |
| 1950 | Louise Brough | Margaret Osborne duPont | 6–1, 3–6, 6–1 |
| 1951 | Doris Hart | Shirley Fry | 6–1, 6–0 |
| 1952 | Maureen Connolly | Louise Brough | 6–4, 6–3 |
| 1953 | Maureen Connolly | Doris Hart | 8–6, 7–5 |
| 1954 | Maureen Connolly | Louise Brough | 6–2, 7–5 |
| 1955 | Louise Brough | Beverly Fleitz | 7–5, 8–6 |
| 1956 | Shirley Fry | Angela Buxton | 6–3, 6–1 |
| 1957 | Althea Gibson | Darlene Hard | 6–3, 6–2 |
| 1958 | Althea Gibson | Angela Mortimer | 8–6, 6–2 |
| 1959 | Maria Bueno | Darlene Hard | 6–4, 6–3 |
| 1960 | Maria Bueno | Sandra Reynolds | 8–6, 6–0 |
| 1961 | Angela Mortimer | Christine Truman | 4–6, 6–4, 7–5 |
| 1962 | Karen Hantze Susman | Vera Sukova | 6–4, 6–4 |
| 1963 | Margaret Smith | Billie Jean Moffitt | 6–3, 6–4 |
| 1964 | Maria Bueno | Margaret Smith | 6–4, 7–9, 6–3 |
| 1965 | Margaret Smith | Maria Bueno | 6–4, 7–5 |
| 1966 | Billie Jean King | Maria Bueno | 6–3, 3–6, 6–1 |
| 1967 | Billie Jean King | Ann Haydon Jones | 6–3, 6–4 |
| 1968* | Billie Jean King | Judy Tegart | 9–7, 7–5 |

Note: Prior to 1922 the tournament was run on a challenge-round system. The previous year's winner "stood out" of an All-Comers event, which produced a challenger to play her for the title.

*Became Open (amateur and professional) in 1968, but restricted to only contract professionals in 1972.

## WOMEN (Cont.)
## Wimbledon Championships (Cont.)

| Year | Winner | Finalist | Score |
|------|--------|----------|-------|
| 1969 | Ann Haydon Jones | Billie Jean King | 3–6, 6–3, 6–2 |
| 1970 | Margaret Smith Court | Billie Jean King | 14–12, 11–9 |
| 1971 | Evonne Goolagong | Margaret Smith Court | 6–4, 6–1 |
| 1972 | Billie Jean King | Evonne Goolagong | 6–3, 6–3 |
| 1973 | Billie Jean King | Chris Evert | 6–0, 7–5 |
| 1974 | Chris Evert | Olga Morozova | 6–0, 6–4 |
| 1975 | Billie Jean King | Evonne Goolagong Cawley | 6–0, 6–1 |
| 1976 | Chris Evert | Evonne Goolagong Cawley | 6–3, 4–6, 8–6 |
| 1977 | Virginia Wade | Betty Stove | 4–6, 6–3, 6–1 |
| 1978 | Martina Navratilova | Chris Evert | 2–6, 6–4, 7–5 |
| 1979 | Martina Navratilova | Chris Evert Lloyd | 6–4, 6–4 |
| 1980 | Evonne Goolagong Cawley | Chris Evert Lloyd | 6–1, 7–6 |
| 1981 | Chris Evert Lloyd | Hana Mandlikova | 6–2, 6–2 |
| 1982 | Martina Navratilova | Chris Evert Lloyd | 6–1, 3–6, 6–2 |
| 1983 | Martina Navratilova | Andrea Jaeger | 6–0, 6–3 |
| 1984 | Martina Navratilova | Chris Evert Lloyd | 7–6, 6–2 |
| 1985 | Martina Navratilova | Chris Evert Lloyd | 4–6, 6–3, 6–2 |
| 1986 | Martina Navratilova | Hana Mandlikova | 7–6, 6–3 |
| 1987 | Martina Navratilova | Steffi Graf | 7–5, 6–3 |
| 1988 | Steffi Graf | Martina Navratilova | 5–7, 6–2, 6–1 |
| 1989 | Steffi Graf | Martina Navratilova | 6–2, 6–7, 6–1 |
| 1990 | Martina Navratilova | Zina Garrison | 6–4, 6–1 |
| 1991 | Steffi Graf | Gabriela Sabatini | 6–4, 3–6, 8–6 |
| 1992 | Steffi Graf | Monica Seles | 6–2, 6–1 |
| 1993 | Steffi Graf | Jana Novotna | 7–6, 1–6, 6–4 |
| 1994 | Conchita Martinez | Martina Navratilova | 6–4, 3–6, 6–3 |
| 1995 | Steffi Graf | Arantxa Sánchez Vicario | 4–6, 6–1, 7–5 |
| 1996 | Steffi Graf | Arantxa Sánchez Vicario | 6–3, 7–5 |
| 1997 | Martina Hingis | Jana Novotna | 2–6, 6–3, 6–3 |
| 1998 | Jana Novotna | Nathalie Tauziat | 6–4, 7–6 |
| 1999 | Lindsay Davenport | Steffi Graf | 6–4, 7–5 |
| 2000 | Venus Williams | Lindsay Davenport | 6–3, 7–6 |
| 2001 | Venus Williams | Justine Henin | 6–1, 3–6, 6–0 |
| 2002 | Serena Williams | Venus Williams | 7–6 (7–4), 6–3 |
| 2003 | Serena Williams | Venus Williams | 4–6, 6–4, 6–2 |
| 2004 | Maria Sharapova | Serena Williams | 6–1, 6–4 |
| 2005 | Venus Williams | Lindsay Davenport | 4–6, 7–6 (7–4), 9–7 |
| 2006 | Amelie Mauresmo | Justine Henin-Hardenne | 2–6, 6–3, 6–4 |
| 2007 | Venus Williams | Marion Bartoli | 6–4, 6–1 |
| 2008 | Venus Williams | Serena Williams | 7–5, 6–4 |
| 2009 | Serena Williams | Venus Williams | 7–6 (7–3), 6–2 |
| 2010 | Serena Williams | Vera Zvonareva | 6–3, 6–2 |
| 2011 | Petra Kvitova | Maria Sharapova | 6–3, 6–4 |

## United States Championships

| Year | Winner | Finalist | Score |
|------|--------|----------|-------|
| 1887 | Ellen Hansell | Laura Knight | 6–1, 6–0 |
| 1888 | Bertha L. Townsend | Ellen Hansell | 6–3, 6–5 |
| 1889 | Bertha L. Townsend | Louise Voorhes | 7–5, 6–2 |
| 1890 | Ellen C. Roosevelt | Bertha L. Townsend | 6–2, 6–2 |
| 1891 | Mabel Cahill | Ellen C. Roosevelt | 6–4, 6–1, 4–6, 6–3 |
| 1892 | Mabel Cahill | Elisabeth Moore | 5–7, 6–3, 6–4, 4–6, 6–2 |
| 1893 | Aline Terry | Alice Schultze | 6–1, 6–3 |
| 1894 | Helen Hellwig | Aline Terry | 7–5, 3–6, 6–0, 3–6, 6–3 |
| 1895 | Juliette Atkinson | Helen Hellwig | 6–4, 6–2, 6–1 |
| 1896 | Elisabeth Moore | Juliette Atkinson | 6–4, 4–6, 6–2, 6–2 |
| 1897 | Juliette Atkinson | Elisabeth Moore | 6–3, 6–3, 4–6, 6–3 |
| 1898 | Juliette Atkinson | Marion Jones | 6–3, 5–7, 6–4, 2–6, 7–5 |
| 1899 | Marion Jones | Maud Banks | 6–1, 6–1, 7–5 |
| 1900 | Myrtle McAteer | Edith Parker | 6–2, 6–2, 6–0 |
| 1901 | Elisabeth Moore | Myrtle McAteer | 6–4, 3–6, 7–5, 2–6, 6–2 |
| 1902* | Marion Jones | Elisabeth Moore | 6–1, 1–0, ret. |

*Five-set final abolished;

### WOMEN (Cont.)
### United States Championships (Cont.)

| Year | Winner | Finalist | Score |
|------|--------|----------|-------|
| 1903 | Elisabeth Moore | Marion Jones | 7–5, 8–6 |
| 1904 | May Sutton | Elisabeth Moore | 6–1, 6–2 |
| 1905 | Elisabeth Moore | Helen Homans | 6–4, 5–7, 6–1 |
| 1906 | Helen Homans | Maud Barger-Wallach | 6–4, 6–3 |
| 1907 | Evelyn Sears | Carrie Neely | 6–3, 6–2 |
| 1908 | Maud Barger–Wallach | Evelyn Sears | 6–3, 1–6, 6–3 |
| 1909 | Hazel Hotchkiss | Maud Barger–Wallach | 6–0, 6–1 |
| 1910 | Hazel Hotchkiss | Louise Hammond | 6–4, 6–2 |
| 1911 | Hazel Hotchkiss | Florence Sutton | 8–10, 6–1, 9–7 |
| 1912† | Mary K. Browne | Eleanora Sears | 6–4, 6–2 |
| 1913 | Mary K. Browne | Dorothy Green | 6–2, 7–5 |
| 1914 | Mary K. Browne | Marie Wagner | 6–2, 1–6, 6–1 |
| 1915 | Molla Bjurstedt | Hazel Hotchkiss Wightman | 4–6, 6–2, 6–0 |
| 1916 | Molla Bjurstedt | Louise Hammond Raymond | 6–0, 6–1 |
| 1917‡ | Molla Bjurstedt | Marion Vanderhoef | 4–6, 6–0, 6–2 |
| 1918 | Molla Bjurstedt | Eleanor Goss | 6–4, 6–3 |
| 1919 | Hazel Hotchkiss Wightman | Marion Zinderstein | 6–1, 6–2 |
| 1920 | Molla Bjurstedt Mallory | Marion Zinderstein | 6–3, 6–1 |
| 1921 | Molla Bjurstedt Mallory | Mary K. Browne | 4–6, 6–4, 6–2 |
| 1922 | Molla Bjurstedt Mallory | Helen Wills | 6–3, 6–1 |
| 1923 | Helen Wills | Molla Bjurstedt Mallory | 6–2, 6–1 |
| 1924 | Helen Wills | Molla Bjurstedt Mallory | 6–1, 6–3 |
| 1925 | Helen Wills | Kathleen McKane | 3–6, 6–0, 6–2 |
| 1926 | Molla Bjurstedt Mallory | Elizabeth Ryan | 4–6, 6–4, 9–7 |
| 1927 | Helen Wills | Betty Nuthall | 6–1, 6–4 |
| 1928 | Helen Wills | Helen Jacobs | 6–2, 6–1 |
| 1929 | Helen Wills | Phoebe Holcroft Watson | 6–4, 6–2 |
| 1930 | Betty Nuthall | Anna McCune Harper | 6–1, 6–4 |
| 1931 | Helen Wills Moody | Eileen Whitingstall | 6–4, 6–1 |
| 1932 | Helen Jacobs | Carolin Babcock | 6–2, 6–2 |
| 1933 | Helen Jacobs | Helen Wills Moody | 8–6, 3–6, 3–0, ret. |
| 1934 | Helen Jacobs | Sarah Palfrey | 6–1, 6–4 |
| 1935 | Helen Jacobs | Sarah Palfrey Fabyan | 6–2, 6–4 |
| 1936 | Alice Marble | Helen Jacobs | 4–6, 6–3, 6–2 |
| 1937 | Anita Lizane | Jadwiga Jedrzejowska | 6–4, 6–2 |
| 1938 | Alice Marble | Nancye Wynne | 6–0, 6–3 |
| 1939 | Alice Marble | Helen Jacobs | 6–0, 8–10, 6–4 |
| 1940 | Alice Marble | Helen Jacobs | 6–2, 6–3 |
| 1941 | Sarah Palfrey Cooke | Pauline Betz | 7–5, 6–2 |
| 1942 | Pauline Betz | Louise Brough | 4–6, 6–1, 6–4 |
| 1943 | Pauline Betz | Louise Brough | 6–3, 5–7, 6–3 |
| 1944 | Pauline Betz | Margaret Osborne | 6–3, 8–6 |
| 1945 | Sarah Palfrey Cooke | Pauline Betz | 3–6, 8–6, 6–4 |
| 1946 | Pauline Betz | Patricia Canning | 11–9, 6–3 |
| 1947 | Louise Brough | Margaret Osborne | 8–6, 4–6, 6–1 |
| 1948 | Margaret Osborne duPont | Louise Brough | 4–6, 6–4, 15–13 |
| 1949 | Margaret Osborne duPont | Doris Hart | 6–4, 6–1 |
| 1950 | Margaret Osborne duPont | Doris Hart | 6–4, 6–3 |
| 1951 | Maureen Connolly | Shirley Fry | 6–3, 1–6, 6–4 |
| 1952 | Maureen Connolly | Doris Hart | 6–3, 7–5 |
| 1953 | Maureen Connolly | Doris Hart | 6–2, 6–4 |
| 1954 | Doris Hart | Louise Brough | 6–8, 6–1, 8–6 |
| 1955 | Doris Hart | Patricia Ward | 6–4, 6–2 |
| 1956 | Shirley Fry | Althea Gibson | 6–3, 6–4 |
| 1957 | Althea Gibson | Louise Brough | 6–3, 6–2 |
| 1958 | Althea Gibson | Darlene Hard | 3–6, 6–1, 6–2 |
| 1959 | Maria Bueno | Christine Truman | 6–1, 6–4 |
| 1960 | Darlene Hard | Maria Bueno | 6–4, 10–12, 6–4 |
| 1961 | Darlene Hard | Ann Haydon | 6–3, 6–4 |
| 1962 | Margaret Smith | Darlene Hard | 9–7, 6–4 |
| 1963 | Maria Bueno | Margaret Smith | 7–5, 6–4 |
| 1964 | Maria Bueno | Carole Graebner | 6–1, 6–0 |
| 1965 | Margaret Smith | Billie Jean Moffitt | 8–6, 7–5 |
| 1966 | Maria Bueno | Nancy Richey | 6–3, 6–1 |
| 1967 | Billie Jean King | Ann Haydon Jones | 11–9, 6–4 |

†Challenge round abolished. ‡National Patriotic Tournament.

## WOMEN *(Cont.)*

### United States Championships *(Cont.)*

| Year | Winner | Finalist | Score |
|------|--------|----------|-------|
| 1968** | Virginia Wade | Billie Jean King | 6–4, 6–4 |
| 1968# | Margaret Smith Court | Maria Bueno | 6–2, 6–2 |
| 1969 | Margaret Smith Court | Nancy Richey | 6–2, 6–2 |
| 1969# | Margaret Smith Court | Virginia Wade | 4–6, 6–3, 6–0 |
| 1970 | Margaret Smith Court | Rosie Casals | 6–2, 2–6, 6–1 |
| 1971 | Billie Jean King | Rosie Casals | 6–4, 7–6 |
| 1972 | Billie Jean King | Kerry Melville | 6–3, 7–5 |
| 1973 | Margaret Smith Court | Evonne Goolagong | 7–6, 5–7, 6–2 |
| 1974 | Billie Jean King | Evonne Goolagong | 3–6, 6–3, 7–5 |
| 1975 | Chris Evert | Evonne Goolagong Cawley | 5–7, 6–4, 6–2 |
| 1976 | Chris Evert | Evonne Goolagong Cawley | 6–3, 6–0 |
| 1977 | Chris Evert | Wendy Turnbull | 7–6, 6–2 |
| 1978 | Chris Evert | Pam Shriver | 7–6, 6–4 |
| 1979 | Tracy Austin | Chris Evert Lloyd | 6–4, 6–3 |
| 1980 | Chris Evert Lloyd | Hana Mandlikova | 5–7, 6–1, 6–1 |
| 1981 | Tracy Austin | Martina Navratilova | 1–6, 7–6, 7–6 |
| 1982 | Chris Evert Lloyd | Hana Mandlikova | 6–3, 6–1 |
| 1983 | Martina Navratilova | Chris Evert Lloyd | 6–1, 6–3 |
| 1984 | Martina Navratilova | Chris Evert Lloyd | 4–6, 6–4, 6–4 |
| 1985 | Hana Mandlikova | Martina Navratilova | 7–6, 1–6, 7–6 |
| 1986 | Martina Navratilova | Helena Sukova | 6–3, 6–2 |
| 1987 | Martina Navratilova | Steffi Graf | 7–6, 6–1 |
| 1988 | Steffi Graf | Gabriela Sabatini | 6–3, 3–6, 6–1 |
| 1989 | Steffi Graf | Martina Navratilova | 3–6, 6–4, 6–2 |
| 1990 | Gabriela Sabatini | Steffi Graf | 6–2, 7–6 |
| 1991 | Monica Seles | Martina Navratilova | 7–6, 6–1 |
| 1992 | Monica Seles | Arantxa Sánchez Vicario | 6–3, 6–2 |
| 1993 | Steffi Graf | Helena Sukova | 6–3, 6–3 |
| 1994 | Arantxa Sánchez Vicario | Steffi Graf | 1–6, 7–6, 6–4 |
| 1995 | Steffi Graf | Monica Seles | 7–6, 0–6, 6–3 |
| 1996 | Steffi Graf | Monica Seles | 7–5, 7–4 |
| 1997 | Martina Hingis | Venus Williams | 6–0, 6–4 |
| 1998 | Lindsay Davenport | Martina Hingis | 6–3, 7–5 |
| 1999 | Serena Williams | Martina Hingis | 6–3, 7–6 |
| 2000 | Venus Williams | Lindsay Davenport | 6–4, 7–5 |
| 2001 | Venus Williams | Serena Williams | 6–2, 6–4 |
| 2002 | Serena Williams | Venus Williams | 6–4, 6–3 |
| 2003 | Justine Henin-Hardenne | Kim Clijsters | 7–5, 6–1 |
| 2004 | Svetlana Kuznetsova | Elena Dementieva | 6–3, 7–5 |
| 2005 | Kim Clijsters | Mary Pierce | 6–3, 6–1 |
| 2006 | Maria Sharapova | Justine Henin-Hardenne | 6–4, 6–4 |
| 2007 | Justine Henin | Svetlana Kuznetsova | 6–1, 6–3 |
| 2008 | Serena Williams | Jelena Jankovic | 6–4, 7–5 |
| 2009 | Kim Clijsters | Caroline Wozniacki | 7–5, 6–3 |
| 2010 | Kim Clijsters | Vera Zvonareva | 6–2, 6–1 |
| 2011 | Samantha Stosur | Serena Williams | 6–2, 6–3 |

**Became Open (amateur and professional) in 1968. #Amateur event held.

## Single-Year Grand Slam Winners

### Singles

Don Budge, 1938
Maureen Connolly, 1953
Rod Laver, 1962, 1969
Margaret Smith Court, 1970
Steffi Graf, 1988

### Doubles

Frank Sedgman and Ken McGregor, 1951
Martina Navratilova and Pam Shriver, 1984
Maria Bueno and two partners, 1960
   Christine Truman (Australian),
   Darlene Hard (French, Wimbledon and U.S.)
Martina Hingis and two partners, 1998
   Mirjana Lucic (Australian),
   Jana Novotna (French, Wimbledon and U.S.)

### Mixed Doubles

Margaret Smith and Ken Fletcher, 1963
Owen Davidson and two partners, 1967
   Lesley Turner (Australian),
   Billie Jean King (French, Wimbledon and U.S.)

## Alltime Grand Slam Champions (Singles, Doubles, and Mixed Doubles)

### MEN

| Player | Aus. S-D-M | French S-D-M | Wim. S-D-M | U.S. S-D-M | Total |
|---|---|---|---|---|---|
| Roy Emerson | 6-3-0 | 2-6-0 | 2-3-0 | 2-4-0 | 28 |
| John Newcombe | 2-5-0 | 0-3-0 | 3-6-0 | 2-3-1 | 25 |
| Frank Sedgman | 2-2-2 | 0-3-2 | 1-2-2 | 2-2-2 | 22 |
| Todd Woodbridge | 0-3-1 | 0-1-1 | 0-9-1 | 0-3-3 | 22 |
| Bill Tilden | † | 0-0-1 | 3-1-0 | 7-5-4 | 21 |
| Rod Laver | 3-4-0 | 2-1-1 | 4-1-2 | 2-0-0 | 20 |
| John Bromwich | 2-8-1 | 0-0-0 | 0-2-2 | 0-3-1 | 19 |
| Jean Borotra | 1-1-1 | 1-5-2 | 2-3-1 | 0-0-1 | 18 |
| Fred Stolle | 0-3-1 | 1-2-0 | 0-2-3 | 1-3-2 | 18 |
| Ken Rosewall | 4-3-0 | 2-2-0 | 0-2-0 | 2-2-1 | 18 |
| Neale Fraser | 0-3-1 | 0-3-0 | 1-2-0 | 2-3-3 | 18 |
| Adrian Quist | 3-10-0 | 0-1-0 | 0-2-0 | 0-1-0 | 17 |
| John McEnroe | 0-0-0 | 0-0-1 | 3-4-0 | 4-5-0 | 17 |
| Jack Crawford | 4-4-3 | 1-1-1 | 1-1-1 | 0-0-0 | 17 |
| Mark Woodforde | 0-2-2 | 0-1-1 | 0-6-1 | 0-3-1 | 17 |

†Did not compete.

### WOMEN

| Player | Aus. S-D-M | French S-D-M | Wim. S-D-M | U.S. S-D-M | Total |
|---|---|---|---|---|---|
| Margaret Smith Court | 11-8-2 | 5-4-4 | 3-2-5 | 5-5-8 | 62 |
| Martina Navratilova | 3-8-1 | 2-7-2 | 9-7-4 | 4-9-3 | 59 |
| Billie Jean King | 1-0-1 | 1-1-2 | 6-10-4 | 4-5-4 | 39 |
| Doris Hart | 1-1-2 | 2-5-3 | 1-4-5 | 2-4-5 | 35 |
| Helen Wills Moody | † | 4-2-0 | 8-3-1 | 7-4-2 | 31 |
| Louise Brough | 1-1-0 | 0-3-0 | 4-5-4 | 1-8-3 | 30** |
| Margaret Osborne duPont | † | 2-3-0 | 1-5-1 | 3-8-6 | 29** |
| *Serena Williams | 5-4-0 | 1-2-0 | 4-4-1 | 3-2-1 | 27 |
| Elizabeth Ryan | † | 0-4-0 | 0-12-7 | 0-1-2 | 26 |
| Steffi Graf | 4-0-0 | 6-0-0 | 7-1-0 | 5-0-0 | 23 |
| Pam Shriver | 0-7-0 | 0-4-1 | 0-5-0 | 0-5-0 | 22 |
| Chris Evert | 2-0-0 | 7-2-0 | 3-1-0 | 6-0-0 | 21 |
| Darlene Hard | † | 1-3-2 | 0-4-3 | 2-6-0 | 21 |
| Suzanne Lenglen | † | 2-2-2# | 6-6-3 | 0-0-0 | 21 |
| *Venus Williams | 0-4-1 | 0-2-1 | 5-4-0 | 2-2-0 | 21 |
| Nancye Wynne Bolton | 6-10-4 | 0-0-0 | 0-0-0 | 0-0-0 | 20 |
| Maria Bueno | 0-1-0 | 0-1-1 | 3-5-0 | 4-4-0 | 19 |
| Thelma Coyne Long | 2-12-4 | 0-0-1 | 0-0-0 | 0-0-0 | 19 |

*Active player in 2011. †Did not compete. **From 1940–45, with competition in the U.S. Championships thinned due to war, Louise Brough Clapp won four doubles titles (1942–45) and one mixed doubles title (1942); and Margaret Osborne duPont won five doubles titles (1941–45) and three mixed doubles titles (1943–45).

## Alltime Grand Slam Singles Champions

### MEN

| Player | Aus. | French | Wim. | U.S. | Total |
|---|---|---|---|---|---|
| *Roger Federer | 4 | 1 | 6 | 5 | 16 |
| Pete Sampras | 2 | 0 | 7 | 5 | 14 |
| Roy Emerson | 6 | 2 | 2 | 2 | 12 |
| Bjorn Borg | 0 | 6 | 5 | 0 | 11 |
| Rod Laver | 3 | 2 | 4 | 2 | 11 |
| *Rafael Nadal | 1 | 6 | 2 | 1 | 10 |
| Bill Tilden | † | 0 | 3 | 7 | 10 |
| Jimmy Connors | 1 | 0 | 2 | 5 | 8 |
| Ivan Lendl | 2 | 3 | 0 | 3 | 8 |
| Fred Perry | 1 | 1 | 3 | 3 | 8 |
| Ken Rosewall | 4 | 2 | 0 | 2 | 8 |
| Andre Agassi | 4 | 1 | 1 | 2 | 8 |
| Henri Cochet | † | 4 | 2 | 1 | 7 |
| Rene Lacoste | † | 3 | 2 | 2 | 7 |
| Bill Larned | † | † | 0 | 7 | 7 |
| John McEnroe | 0 | 0 | 3 | 4 | 7 |
| John Newcombe | 2 | 0 | 3 | 2 | 7 |
| Willie Renshaw | † | † | 7 | † | 7 |
| Dick Sears | † | † | 0 | 7 | 7 |

### WOMEN

| Player | Aus. | French | Wim. | U.S. | Total |
|---|---|---|---|---|---|
| Margaret Smith Court | 11 | 5 | 3 | 5 | 24 |
| Steffi Graf | 4 | 6 | 7 | 5 | 22 |
| Helen Wills Moody | † | 4 | 8 | 7 | 19 |
| Chris Evert | 2 | 7 | 3 | 6 | 18 |
| Martina Navratilova | 3 | 2 | 9 | 4 | 18 |
| *Serena Williams | 5 | 1 | 4 | 3 | 13 |
| Billie Jean King | 1 | 1 | 6 | 4 | 12 |
| Maureen Connolly | 1 | 2 | 3 | 3 | 9 |
| Monica Seles | 4 | 3 | 0 | 2 | 9 |
| Suzanne Lenglen | † | 2# | 6 | 0 | 8 |
| Molla Bjurstedt Mallory | † | † | 0 | 8 | 8 |
| Maria Bueno | 0 | 0 | 3 | 4 | 7 |
| Evonne Goolagong | 4 | 1 | 2 | 0 | 7 |
| Dorothea D.L. Chambers | † | † | 7 | 0 | 7 |
| Justine Henin | 1 | 4 | 0 | 2 | 7 |
| *Venus Williams | 0 | 0 | 5 | 2 | 7 |

*Active player in 2011. †Did not compete. #Suzanne Lenglen won four singles titles at the French Championships before competition was opened to entries from all nations in 1925.

# Golf

OPEN CHAMPIONSHIP

22-year-old Rory McIlroy shot a record-setting 16-under par to win the 2011 U.S. Open

## Men's Majors

### The Masters
**Augusta National GC (par 72; 7,435 yds);**
**Augusta, Ga., April 7–10, 2011**

| Player | Score | Earnings ($) |
|---|---|---|
| Charl Schwartzel | 69-71-68-66--274 | 1,440,000 |
| Jason Day | 72-64-72-68--276 | 704,000 |
| Adam Scott | 72-70-67-67--276 | 704,000 |
| Tiger Woods | 71-66-74-67--278 | 330,667 |
| Geoff Ogilvy | 69-69-73-67--278 | 330,667 |
| Luke Donald | 72-68-69-69--278 | 330,667 |
| Angel Cabrera | 71-70-67-71--279 | 251,250 |
| Bo Van Pelt | 73-69-68-70--280 | 240,000 |
| K.J. Choi | 67-70-71-72--280 | 240,000 |
| Ryan Palmer | 71-72-69-70--282 | 216,000 |
| Justin Rose | 73-71-71-68--283 | 176,000 |
| Steve Stricker | 72-70-71-70--283 | 176,000 |
| Lee Westwood | 72-67-74-70--283 | 176,000 |
| Edoardo Molinari | 74-70-69-70--283 | 176,000 |
| Trevor Immelman | 69-73-73-69--284 | 128,000 |
| Brandt Snedeker | 69-71-74-70--284 | 128,000 |
| Fred Couples | 71-68-72-73--284 | 128,000 |
| Ross Fisher | 69-71-71-73--284 | 128,000 |
| Rory McIlroy | 65-69-70-80--284 | 128,000 |
| Ryo Ishikawa | 71-71-73-70--285 | 93,200 |
| Ricky Barnes | 68-71-75-71--285 | 93,200 |
| Y.E. Yang | 67-72-73-73--285 | 93,200 |
| Martin Laird | 74-69-69-73--285 | 93,200 |
| Gary Woodland | 69-73-74-70--286 | 70,400 |
| Jim Furyk | 72-68-74-72--286 | 70,400 |
| David Toms | 72-69-73-70--286 | 70,400 |

### U.S. Open
**Congressional Country Club (par 71; 7,574 yds);**
**Bethesda, Md., June 16–19, 2011**

| Player | Score | Earnings ($) |
|---|---|---|
| Rory McIlroy | 65-66-68-69--268 | 1,440,000 |
| Jason Day | 71-72-65-68--276 | 865,000 |
| Kevin Chappell | 76-67-69-66--278 | 364,241 |
| Robert Garrigus | 70-70-68-70--278 | 364,241 |
| Lee Westwood | 75-68-65-70--278 | 364,241 |
| Y.E. Yang | 68-69-70-71--278 | 364,241 |
| Peter Hanson | 72-71-69-67--279 | 228,416 |
| Sergio Garcia | 69-71-69-70--279 | 228,416 |
| Charl Schwartzel | 68-74-72-66--280 | 192,962 |
| Louis Oosthuizen | 69-73-71-67--280 | 192,962 |
| Brandt Snedeker | 70-70-72-69--281 | 163,083 |
| Davis Love III | 70-71-70-70--281 | 163,083 |
| Heath Slocum | 71-70-70-70--282 | 129,517 |
| Graeme McDowell | 70-74-69-69--282 | 129,517 |
| Webb Simpson | 75-71-66-70--282 | 129,517 |
| Matt Kuchar | 72-68-69-73--282 | 129,517 |
| Fredrik Jacobson | 74-69-66-73--282 | 129,517 |
| Bo Van Pelt | 76-67-68-71--282 | 129,517 |
| Johan Edfors | 70-72-74-67--283 | 105,905 |
| Steve Stricker | 75-69-69-70--283 | 105,905 |
| Ryan Palmer | 69-72-73-70--284 | 97,242 |
| a-Patrick Cantlay | 75-67-70-72--284 | — |

a-Amateur.

### British Open
**Royal St. George's G.C. (par 70; 7,211 yds);**
**Sandwich, Kent, England, July 14–17, 2011**

| Player | Score | Earnings ($) |
|---|---|---|
| Darren Clarke | 65-67-69-71--275 | 1,452,078 |
| Phil Mickelson | 67-71-71-70--278 | 689,737 |
| Dustin Johnson | 69-69-67-75--278 | 689,737 |
| Thomas Bjorn | 63-80-69-68--279 | 419,489 |
| Chad Campbell | 68-74-67-71--280 | 293,105 |
| Anthony Kim | 69-70-72-70--280 | 293,105 |
| Rickie Fowler | 69-71-68-74--280 | 293,105 |
| Raphael Jacquelin | 67-72-72-71--281 | 209,745 |
| Simon Dyson | 68-78-67-69--282 | 168,333 |
| Sergio Garcia | 67-73-71-71--282 | 168,333 |
| Davis Love III | 73-72-69-69--282 | 168,333 |
| Steve Stricker | 73-69-72-69--283 | 126,384 |
| Lucas Glover | 72-70-74-67--283 | 126,384 |
| Martin Kaymer | 79-67-71-67--283 | 126,384 |
| George Coetzee | 71-71-70-72--283 | 109,713 |
| Charl Schwartzel | 69-71-73-71--285 | 90,352 |
| Y.E. Yang | 70-72-70-72--285 | 90,352 |
| Webb Simpson | 69-72-69-74--285 | 90,352 |
| Zach Johnson | 69-71-72-72--285 | 90,352 |
| Richard Green | 71-68-75-70--285 | 90,352 |
| Fredrik Jacobson | 71-75-68-70--285 | 90,352 |
| Tom Watson | 68-70-74-72--286 | 72,067 |
| Anders Hansen | 68-70-74-72--286 | 72,067 |
| Tom Lehman | 68-70-74-72--286 | 72,067 |

### PGA Championship
**Atlanta Athletic Club G.C. (par 70; 7,46 yds);**
**Johns Creek, Ga., August 11–14, 2011**

| Player | Score | Earnings ($) |
|---|---|---|
| *Keegan Bradley | 71-64-69-68--272 | 1,445,000 |
| Jason Dufner | 70-65-68-69--272 | 865,000 |
| Anders Hansen | 68-69-70-66--273 | 545,000 |
| Robert Karlsson | 70-71-67-67--275 | 331,000 |
| David Toms | 72-71-65-67--275 | 331,833 |
| Scott Verplank | 67-69-69-70--275 | 331,833 |
| Adam Scott | 69-69-70-68--276 | 259,833 |
| Lee Westwood | 71-68-70-68--277 | 224,500 |
| Luke Donald | 70-71-68-68--277 | 224,500 |
| Kevin Na | 72-69-70-67--278 | 188,800 |
| D.A. Points | 69-67-71-71--278 | 188,800 |
| Gary Woodland | 70-70-71-68--279 | 132,786 |
| Trevor Immelman | 69-71-71-68--279 | 132,786 |
| Sergio Garcia | 72-69-69-69--279 | 132,786 |
| Bill Haas | 68-73-69-69--279 | 132,786 |
| Nick Watney | 70-71-68-70--279 | 132,786 |
| Charl Schwartzel | 71-71-66-71--279 | 132,786 |
| Steve Stricker | 63-74-69-73--279 | 81,214 |
| Brian Davis | 69-73-69-69--280 | 81,214 |
| Phil Mickelson | 71-70-69-70--280 | 81,214 |
| Ryan Palmer | 71-70-69-70--280 | 81,214 |
| Matt Kuchar | 71-71-68-70--280 | 81,214 |
| Hunter Mahan | 72-72-66-70--280 | 81,214 |
| John Senden | 68-68-72-72--280 | 81,214 |
| Brendan Steele | 69-68-66-77--280 | 81,214 |

*won in playoff

## PGA Tour Results

### Late 2010 PGA Tour Events

| Tournament | Final Round | Winner | Score/ Under Par | Earnings ($) |
|---|---|---|---|---|
| Viking Classic | Oct 3 | Matt Kuchar | 271/-17 | 1,080,000 |
| McGladrey Classic | Oct 10 | Heath Slocum | 266/-14 | 720,000 |
| Frys.com Open | Oct 17 | Rocco Mediate | 269/-15 | 900,000 |
| *Shriners Hosptials for Children Open | Oct 24 | Jonathan Byrd | 263/-21 | 774,000 |
| Children's Miracle Network Classic | Nov 14 | Robert Garrigus | 267/-21 | 846,000 |

### 2011 PGA Tour Events

| Tournament | Final Round | Winner | Score/ Under Par | Earnings ($) |
|---|---|---|---|---|
| Hyundai Tournament of Champions | Jan 9 | Jonathan Byrd | 268/-24 | 1,120,000 |
| Sony Open in Hawaii | Jan 16 | Mark Wilson | 264/-16 | 990,000 |
| †Humana Challenge | Jan 23 | Jhonattan Vegas | 333/-27 | 900,000 |
| Farmers Insurance Open | Jan 30 | Bubba Watson | 272/-16 | 1,044,000 |
| Phoenix Open | Feb 6 | Mark Wilson | 266/-18 | 1,098,000 |
| AT&T Pebble Beach National Pro-Am | Feb 13 | D.A. Points | 271/-15 | 1,134,000 |
| Northern Trust Open | Feb 20 | Aaron Baddeley | 272/-12 | 1,170,000 |
| *Mayakoba Classic at Riviera Maya | Feb 27 | Johnson Wagner | 267/-17 | 666,000 |
| WGC Match Play Championship | Feb 27 | Luke Donald | 3 & 2 | 1,400,000 |
| Honda Classic | Mar 6 | Rory Sabbatini | 271/-9 | 1,026,000 |
| *Puerto Rico Open | Mar 13 | Michael Bradley | 272/-16 | 630,000 |
| WGC-Cadillac Championship | Mar 13 | Nick Watney | 272/-16 | 1,400,000 |
| Transitions Championship | Mar 20 | Gary Woodland | 269/-15 | 990,000 |
| Arnold Palmer Invitational | Mar 27 | Martin Laird | 280/-8 | 1,080,000 |
| Shell Houston Open | Apr 3 | Phil Mickelson | 268/-20 | 1,062,000 |
| The Masters | Apr 10 | Charl Schwartzel | 274/-14 | 1,440,000 |
| Valero Texas Open | Apr 17 | Brendan Steele | 280/-8 | 1,116,000 |
| *The Heritage | Apr 24 | Brandt Snedeker | 272/-12 | 1,026,000 |
| Zurich Classic | May 1 | Bubba Watson | 273/-15 | 1,152,000 |
| *Wells Fargo Championship | May 8 | Lucas Glover | 273/-15 | 1,170,000 |
| *The Players Championship | May 15 | K.J. Choi | 275/-13 | 1,710,000 |
| Crowne Plaza Invitational at Colonial | May 22 | David Toms | 265/-15 | 1,116,000 |
| *Byron Nelson Championship | May 29 | Keegan Bradley | 277/-3 | 1,170,000 |
| Memorial Tournament | June 5 | Steve Stricker | 272/-16 | 1,116,000 |
| *St. Jude Classic | June 12 | Harrison Frazar | 267/-13 | 1,008,000 |
| U.S. Open Championship | June 19 | Rory McIlroy | 268/-16 | 1,440,000 |
| *Travelers Championship | June 26 | Fredrik Jacobson | 260/-20 | 1,080,000 |
| AT&T National | July 3 | Nick Watney | 267/-13 | 1,116,000 |
| John Deere Classic | July 10 | Steve Stricker | 262/-22 | 792,000 |
| Viking Classic | July 17 | Chris Kirk | 266/-22 | 648,000 |
| The Open Championship (British Open) | July 17 | Darren Clarke | 275/-5 | 1,452,078 |
| *Canadian Open | July 24 | Sean O'Hair | 276/-4 | 936,000 |
| Greenbrier Classic | July 31 | Scott Stallings | 270/-10 | 1,080,000 |
| Reno-Tahoe Open | Aug 7 | Scott Piercy | 273/-15 | 540,000 |
| WGC-Bridgestone Invitational | Aug 7 | Adam Scott | 263/-17 | 1,400,000 |
| *PGA Championship | Aug 14 | Keegan Bradley | 272/-8 | 1,445,000 |
| *Wyndham Championship | Aug 21 | Webb Simpson | 262/-18 | 936,000 |
| **‡The Barclays | Aug 27 | Dustin Johnson | 194/-19 | 1,440,000 |
| *‡Deutsche Bank Championship | Sept 4 | Webb Simpson | 269/-15 | 1,440,000 |
| ‡BMW Championship | Sept 18 | Justin Rose | 271/-13 | 1,440,000 |
| *‡TOUR Championship | Sept 25 | Bill Haas | 272/-8 | 1,440,000 |

† Five-round tournament. * Won in playoff. **Hurricane Irene forced the cancellation of tournament's final round. ‡Events part of four-tournament FedEx Cup, the PGA Tour's 30-player playoff.

## 2011 FedEx Cup Playoff Results

| | Player | Points | Earnings ($) |
|---|---|---|---|
| 1. | Bill Haas | 2,760 | 10,000,000 |
| 2. | Webb Simpson | 2,745 | 3,000,000 |
| 3. | Luke Donald | 2,567 | 2,000,000 |
| 4. | Dustin Johnson | 2,488 | 1,500,000 |
| 5. | Justin Rose | 2,253 | 1,000,000 |
| 6. | Matt Kuchar | 1,853 | 800,000 |
| 7. | Hunter Mahan | 1,800 | 700,000 |
| 8. | Brandt Snedeker | 1,668 | 600,000 |
| 9. | Nick Watney | 1,420 | 550,000 |
| 10. | Chez Reavie | 1,220 | 500,000 |

## Kraft Nabisco Championship

**Mission Hills CC (par 72; 6,738 yds);
Rancho Mirage, Ca., March 31–April 3, 2011**

| Player | Score | Earnings ($) |
| --- | --- | --- |
| Stacy Lewis | 66-69-71-69--275 | 300,000 |
| Yani Tseng | 70-68-66-74--278 | 184,255 |
| Katie Futcher | 70-71-74-69--284 | 106,763 |
| Angela Stanford | 72-72-67-73--284 | 106,763 |
| Morgan Pressel | 70-69-69-76--284 | 106,763 |
| Michelle Wie | 74-67-69-75--285 | 68,093 |
| Julieta Granada | 72-70-75-69--286 | 50,608 |
| Chie Arimura | 68-73-71-74--286 | 50,608 |
| Mika Miyazato | 67-75-70-74--286 | 50,608 |
| I.K. Kim | 75-67-75-70--287 | 37,997 |
| Anna Nordqvist | 69-74-73-71--287 | 37,997 |
| Se Ri Pak | 73-71-71-72--287 | 37,997 |
| Karrie Webb | 69-74-74-71--288 | 32,079 |
| Brittany Lincicome | 66-72-74-76--288 | 32,079 |
| Christel Boeljon | 74-73-71-71--289 | 27,035 |
| Juli Inkster | 73-73-71-72--289 | 27,035 |
| Sandra Gal | 67-74-75-73--289 | 27,035 |
| Sophie Gustafson | 72-68-74-75--289 | 27,035 |
| Stacy Prammanasudh | 71-75-73-71--290 | 21,992 |
| Suzann Pettersen | 75-71-72-72--290 | 21,992 |
| Paula Creamer | 73-74-70-73--290 | 21,992 |
| Maria Hjorth | 75-70-72-73--290 | 21,992 |
| Amy Yang | 70-69-76-75--290 | 21,992 |
| Jimin Kang | 72-69-72-77--290 | 21,992 |
| Meaghan Francella | 75-71-73-72--291 | 18,562 |
| a-Ariya Jutanugarn | 74-73-71-73--291 | — |
| Alena Sharp | 71-73-73-74--291 | 18,562 |
| Eun-Hee Ji | 75-71-69-76--291 | 18,562 |

a-Amateur.

## U.S. Women's Open

**The Broadmoor, East Course (par 71; 7,047 yds);
Colorado Springs, Colo., July 7–10, 2011**

| Player | Score | Earnings ($) |
| --- | --- | --- |
| *So Yeon Ryu | 74-69-69-69--281 | 585,000 |
| Hee Kyung Seo | 72-73-68-68--281 | 350,000 |
| Cristie Kerr | 71-72-69-71--283 | 215,493 |
| Angela Stanford | 72-70-70-72--284 | 150,166 |
| Mika Miyazato | 70-67-76-72--285 | 121,591 |
| Karrie Webb | 70-73-72-71--286 | 98,128 |
| Ai Miyazato | 70-68-76-72--286 | 98,128 |
| Inbee Park | 71-73-70-72--286 | 98,128 |
| Ryann O'Toole | 69-72-75-71--287 | 81,915 |
| Jiyai Shin | 73-72-73-70--288 | 70,996 |
| Amy Yang | 75-69-73-71--288 | 70,996 |
| I.K. Kim | 70-69-76-73--288 | 70,996 |
| Chella Choi | 71-76-70-72--289 | 60,780 |
| Candie Kung | 76-69-71-73--289 | 60,780 |
| Karen Stupples | 72-77-73-68--290 | 48,658 |
| Suzann Pettersen | 71-75-72-72--290 | 48,658 |
| Junthima Gulyanamitta | 73-76-68-73--290 | 48,658 |
| Yani Tseng | 73-73-71-73--290 | 48,658 |
| Paula Creamer | 72-70-73-75--290 | 48,658 |
| Lizette Salas | 69-73-73-75--290 | 48,658 |
| Catriona Mathew | 76-70-74-71--291 | 36,374 |
| Meena Lee | 75-71-72-73--291 | 36,374 |
| Morgan Pressel | 75-72-71-73--291 | 36,374 |
| Leta Lindley | 73-71-72-75--291 | 36,374 |

*Won in playoff.

## LPGA Championship

**Locust Hill C.C. (par 72; 6,506 yds);
Rochester, N.Y., June 23–26, 2011**

| Player | Score | Earnings ($) |
| --- | --- | --- |
| Yani Tseng | 66-70-67-66--269 | 375,000 |
| Morgan Pressel | 69-69-70-71--279 | 228,695 |
| Suzann Pettersen | 72-72-69-67--280 | 132,512 |
| Paula Creamer | 67-72-72-69--280 | 132,512 |
| Crisite Kerr | 72-72-67-69--280 | 132,512 |
| Meena Lee | 68-73-70-71--282 | 77,630 |
| Stacy Lewis | 69-72-70-71--282 | 77,630 |
| Maria Hjorth | 71-71-70-71--283 | 53,840 |
| Pat Hurst | 70-67-75-71--283 | 53,840 |
| Mika Miyazato | 72-72-68-71--283 | 53,840 |
| Azahara Munoz | 70-71-71-71--283 | 53,840 |
| Amy Yang | 70-69-74-71--284 | 42,445 |
| I.K. Kim | 73-70-69-72--284 | 42,445 |
| Amy Hung | 69-73-73-70--285 | 33,765 |
| Heather Bowie Young | 72-70-73-70--285 | 33,765 |
| Inbee Park | 73-69-71-72--285 | 33,765 |
| Katie Futcher | 75-68-69-73--285 | 33,765 |
| Hee Young Park | 69-69-72-75--285 | 33,765 |
| Cindy LaCrosse | 70-69-69-77--285 | 33,765 |
| Brittany Lincicome | 74-72-71-69--286 | 26,795 |
| Sun Young Yoo | 73-72-72-69--286 | 26,795 |
| Paige Mackenzie | 72-73-70-71--286 | 26,795 |
| Karrie Webb | 74-69-71-72--286 | 26,795 |
| Candie Kung | 71-71-71-73--286 | 26,795 |
| Hee-Won Han | 71-72-74-70--287 | 22,162 |
| Anna Nordqvist | 73-70-74-70--287 | 22,162 |
| Jimin Kang | 71-70-73-73--287 | 22,162 |
| Pornanong Phatlum | 71-72-71-73--287 | 22,162 |
| Tiffany Joh | 71-70-72-74--287 | 22,162 |

## Women's British Open

**Carnoustie Golf Links (par 72; 6,490 yds);
Carnoustie, Scotland, July 28–31, 2011**

| Player | Score | Earnings ($) |
| --- | --- | --- |
| Yani Tseng | 68-68-68-73--272 | 392,133 |
| Brittany Lang | 68-74-66-70--276 | 231,065 |
| Sophie Gustafson | 74-70-69-68--277 | 161,746 |
| Amy Yang | 70-72-68-71--278 | 126,536 |
| Catriona Mathew | 69-71-74-68--279 | 96,828 |
| Caroline Masson | 73-67-72-70--279 | 96,828 |
| Anna Nordqvist | 73-69-70-70--280 | 70,695 |
| Sun Young Yoo | 77-71-65-71--280 | 70,695 |
| Na Yeon Choi | 72-71-77-66--280 | 70,695 |
| Inbee Park | 76-70-73-67--280 | 70,695 |
| Stacy Lewis | 74-68-70-74--281 | 52,815 |
| Dewi Claire Schreefel | 72-70-70-74--281 | 52,815 |
| Maria Hjorth | 69-71-71-75--282 | 46,213 |
| Katie Futcher | 73-70-73-71--283 | 35,132 |
| Cristie Kerr | 71-71-72-73--283 | 35,132 |
| Candie Kung | 73-68-71-75--283 | 35,132 |
| Sun-Ju Ahn | 71-75-72-70--283 | 35,132 |
| Song-Hee Kim | 70-76-71-71--283 | 35,132 |
| Mika Miyazato | 75-73-71-70--283 | 35,132 |
| Se Ri Pak | 74-71-72-72--283 | 35,132 |
| Jiyai Shin | 74-73-74-69--284 | 28,608 |

## Late 2010 LPGA Tour Events

| Tournament | Final Round | Winner | Score/ Under Par | Earnings ($) |
|---|---|---|---|---|
| Navistar Classic | Oct 10 | Katherine Hull | 269/-19 | 195,000 |
| CVS/pharmacy Challenge | Oct 17 | Beatriz Recari | 274/-14 | 165,000 |
| Sime Darby Malaysia | Oct 24 | Jimin Kang | 204/-9 | 270,000 |
| Hana Bank Championship | Oct 31 | Na Yeon Choi | 206/-10 | 270,000 |
| Mizuno Classic | Nov 7 | Jiyai Shin | 198/-18 | 180,000 |
| Lorena Ochoa Invitational | Nov 14 | I.K. Kim | 269/-19 | 220,000 |

## 2011 LPGA Tour Events

| Tournament | Final Round | Winner | Score/ Under Par | Earnings ($) |
|---|---|---|---|---|
| Honda Thailand | Feb 20 | Yani Tseng | 273/-15 | 217,500 |
| HSBC Champions | Feb 27 | Karrie Webb | 275/-13 | 210,000 |
| Founders Cup | Mar 20 | Karrie Webb | 204/-12 | 150,000 |
| KIA Classic | Mar 27 | Sandra Gal | 276/-16 | 255,000 |
| Kraft Nabisco Championship | Apr 3 | Stacy Lewis | 275/-13 | 300,000 |
| Avnet Classic | May 1 | Maria Hjorth | 278/-10 | 195,000 |
| Sybase Match Play Championship | May 22 | Suzann Pettersen | 1-up | 375,000 |
| Brazil Cup | May 29 | Mariajo Uribe | 135/-9 | 108,000 |
| ShopRite Classic | June 5 | Brittany Lincicome | 202/-11 | 225,000 |
| State Farm Classic | June 12 | Yani Tseng | 267/-21 | 255,000 |
| LPGA Championship | June 26 | Yani Tseng | 269/-19 | 375,000 |
| *U.S. Women's Open | July 10 | So Yeon Ryu | 281/-3 | 585,000 |
| Evian Masters | July 24 | Ai Miyazato | 273/-15 | 487,500 |
| Women's British Open | July 31 | Yani Tseng | 272/-16 | 392,133 |
| *Safeway Classic | Aug 21 | Suzann Pettersen | 207/-6 | 225,000 |
| Canadian Women's Open | Aug 28 | Brittany Lincicome | 275/-13 | 337,500 |
| NW Arkansas Championship | Sept 11 | Yani Tseng | 201/-12 | 300,000 |
| Navistar Classic | Sept 18 | Lexi Thompson | 271/-17 | 195,000 |

* Won in playoff.

# Champions Tour Results

## Late 2010 Champions Tour Events

| Tournament | Final Round | Winner | Score/ Under Par | Earnings ($) |
|---|---|---|---|---|
| *Senior Players Championship | Oct 10 | Mark O'Meara | 273/-7 | 405,000 |
| Administaff Small Business Classic | Oct 24 | Fred Couples | 199/-17 | 255,000 |
| *AT&T Championship | Oct 31 | Rod Spittle | 201/-12 | 262,500 |
| Charles Schwab Cup Championship | Nov 7 | John Cook | 267/-17 | 440,000 |

## 2011 Champions Tour Events

| Tournament | Final Round | Winner | Score/ Under Par | Earnings ($) |
|---|---|---|---|---|
| Mitsubishi Electric Championship | Jan 23 | John Cook | 194/-22 | 305,000 |
| Allianz Championship | Feb 13 | Tom Lehman | 203/-13 | 270,000 |
| ACE Group Classic | Feb 20 | Bernhard Langer | 196/-20 | 240,000 |
| Toshiba Senior Classic | Mar 13 | Nick Price | 196/-17 | 255,000 |
| Mississippi Gulf Resort Classic | Apr 3 | Tom Lehman | 200/-16 | 240,000 |
| *Outback Steakhouse Pro-Am | Apr 17 | John Cook | 204/-9 | 255,000 |
| Legends of Golf | Apr 24 | David Eger/Mark McNulty | 189/-27 | 230,000 each |
| *Regions Tradition | May 8 | Tom Lehman | 275/-13 | 330,000 |
| *Senior PGA Championship | May 29 | Tom Watson | 278/-10 | 360,000 |
| Principal Charity Classic | June 5 | Bob Gilder | 199/-14 | 258,750 |
| Greater Hickory Classic | June 12 | Mark Wiebe | 197/-19 | 262,500 |
| Dick's Sporting Goods Open | June 26 | John Huston | 200/-16 | 262,500 |
| Montreal Championship | July 3 | John Cook | 195/-21 | 270,000 |
| First Tee Open at Pebble Beach | July 10 | Jeff Sluman | 206/-10 | 240,000 |
| Senior Open Championship (British) | July 24 | Russ Cochran | 276/-12 | 315,600 |
| U.S. Senior Open Championship | July 31 | Olin Browne | 269/-15 | 500,000 |
| 3M Championship | Aug 7 | Jay Haas | 201/-15 | 262,500 |
| Senior Players Championship | Aug 21 | Fred Couples | 273/-11 | 405,000 |
| Boeing Classic | Aug 28 | Mark Calcavecchia | 202/-14 | 300,000 |
| *Songdo IBD Championship | Sept 18 | Jay Don Blake | 203/-13 | 456,000 |
| SAS Championship | Oct 2 | Kenny Perry | 205/-11 | 315,000 |

* Won in playoff.

## 2011 U.S. Amateur Championships Results

| Tournament | Final Round | Winner | Score | Runner-Up |
|---|---|---|---|---|
| Women's Amateur Public Links | July 2 | Brianna Do | 1-up | Marissa Dodd |
| Men's Amateur Public Links | July 2 | Corbin Mills | 37 holes | Derek Ernst |
| Girls' Junior Amateur | July 23 | Ariya Jutanugarn | 2 & 1 | Dottie Ardina |
| Boys' Junior Amateur | July 24 | Jordan Spieth | 6 & 5 | Chelso Barrett |
| Women's Amateur | Aug 14 | Danielle Kang | 6 & 5 | Moriya Jutanugarn |
| Men's Amateur | Aug 28 | Kelly Kraft | 2-up | Patrick Cantlay |
| Senior Amateur | Sept 15 | Philip Pleat | 1-up | Louis Lee |
| Senior Women's Amateur | Sept 15 | Terri Frohnmayer | 2 & 1 | Mina Hardin |
| Women's Mid-Amateur | Sept 22 | Ellen Port | 2 & 1 | Martha Leach |
| Men's Mid-Amateur | Sept 22 | Randal Lewis | 3 & 2 | Kenny Cook |

## 2011 International Results

| Tournament | Final Round | Winner | Score | Runner-Up |
|---|---|---|---|---|
| Walker Cup | Sept 11 | Great Britain & Ireland | 14–12 | United States |
| Solheim Cup | Sept 25 | Europe | 15–13 | United States |

## PGA Tour Final 2010 Money Leaders

| Name | Events | Best Finish | Scoring Average | Money ($) |
|---|---|---|---|---|
| Matt Kuchar | 26 | 1 (1) | 69.43 | 4,910,477 |
| Jim Furyk | 21 | 1 (3) | 70.23 | 4,809,622 |
| Ernie Els | 20 | 1 (2) | 70.37 | 4,558,861 |
| Dustin Johnson | 23 | 1 (2) | 70.46 | 4,473,122 |
| Steve Stricker | 19 | 1 (2) | 69.78 | 4,190,235 |
| Phil Mickelson | 20 | 1 (1) | 70.34 | 3,821,733 |
| Luke Donald | 20 | 2 (3) | 70.25 | 3,665,234 |
| Paul Casey | 17 | 2 (2) | 69.93 | 3,613,194 |
| Justin Rose | 22 | 1 (2) | 69.92 | 3,603,331 |
| Hunter Mahan | 25 | 1 (2) | 70.64 | 3,574,550 |

## LPGA Tour Final 2010 Money Leaders

| Name | Events | Best Finish | Scoring Average | Money ($) |
|---|---|---|---|---|
| Na Yeon Choi | 23 | 1 (2) | 69.87 | 1,871,166 |
| Jiyai Shin | 18 | 1 (2) | 70.25 | 1,783,127 |
| Cristie Kerr | 21 | 1 (2) | 69.95 | 1,601,552 |
| Yani Tseng | 19 | 1 (3) | 70.66 | 1,573,529 |
| Suzann Pettersen | 19 | 2 (6) | 70.09 | 1,557,175 |
| Ai Miyazato | 21 | 1 (5) | 70.65 | 1,457,384 |
| I.K. Kim | 21 | 1 (1) | 70.51 | 1,210,068 |
| Song-Hee Kim | 22 | 2 (2) | 70.21 | 1,208,698 |
| Michelle Wie | 19 | 1 (1) | 71.34 | 888,017 |
| Paula Creamer | 14 | 1 (1) | 71.00 | 883,870 |

## Champions Tour Final 2010 Money Leaders

| Name | Events | Best Finish | Scoring Average | Money ($) |
|---|---|---|---|---|
| Bernhard Langer | 23 | 1 (5) | 69.18 | 2,648,939 |
| Fred Couples | 17 | 1 (4) | 67.96 | 2,344,894 |
| John Cook | 25 | 1 (1) | 70.09 | 1,924,305 |
| Russ Cochran | 25 | 1 (2) | 69.96 | 1,754,003 |
| Nick Price | 18 | 1 (2) | 69.09 | 1,457,815 |
| Fred Funk | 23 | 1 (1) | 70.31 | 1,419,759 |
| Dan Forsman | 25 | 1 (1) | 70.14 | 1,243,781 |
| Mark O'Meara | 20 | 1 (2) | 70.30 | 1,210,430 |
| Michael Allen | 14 | 2 (1) | 71.22 | 1,196,770 |
| Loren Roberts | 21 | 1 (1) | 70.11 | 1,195,416 |

## Men's Golf

## THE MAJOR TOURNAMENTS
### The Masters

| Year | Winner | Score | Runner-Up | Year | Winner | Score | Runner-Up |
|---|---|---|---|---|---|---|---|
| 1934 | Horton Smith | 284 | Craig Wood | 1976 | Ray Floyd | 271 | Ben Crenshaw |
| 1935 | Gene Sarazen* (144) | 282 | Craig Wood (149) | 1977 | Tom Watson | 276 | Jack Nicklaus |
|  | (only 36-hole playoff) |  |  | 1978 | Gary Player | 277 | Hubert Green |
| 1936 | Horton Smith | 285 | Harry Cooper |  |  |  | Rod Funseth |
| 1937 | Byron Nelson | 283 | Ralph Guldahl |  |  |  | Tom Watson |
| 1938 | Henry Picard | 285 | Ralph Guldahl | 1979 | Fuzzy Zoeller* (4–3)† | 280 | Ed Sneed (4–4) |
|  |  |  | Harry Cooper |  |  |  | Tom Watson (4–4) |
| 1939 | Ralph Guldahl | 279 | Sam Snead | 1980 | Seve Ballesteros | 275 | Gibby Gilbert |
| 1940 | Jimmy Demaret | 280 | Lloyd Mangrum |  |  |  | Jack Newton |
| 1941 | Craig Wood | 280 | Byron Nelson | 1981 | Tom Watson | 280 | Johnny Miller |
| 1942 | Byron Nelson* (69) | 280 | Ben Hogan (70) |  |  |  | Jack Nicklaus |
| 1943–45 | No tournament |  |  | 1982 | Craig Stadler* (4) | 284 | Dan Pohl (5) |
| 1946 | Herman Keiser | 282 | Ben Hogan | 1983 | Seve Ballesteros | 280 | Ben Crenshaw |
| 1947 | Jimmy Demaret | 281 | Byron Nelson |  |  |  | Tom Kite |
|  |  |  | Frank Stranahan | 1984 | Ben Crenshaw | 277 | Tom Watson |
| 1948 | Claude Harmon | 279 | Cary Middlecoff | 1985 | Bernhard Langer | 282 | Curtis Strange |
| 1949 | Sam Snead | 282 | Johnny Bulla |  |  |  | Seve Ballesteros |
|  |  |  | Lloyd Mangrum |  |  |  | Ray Floyd |
| 1950 | Jimmy Demaret | 283 | Jim Ferrier | 1986 | Jack Nicklaus | 279 | Greg Norman |
| 1951 | Ben Hogan | 280 | Skee Riegel |  |  |  | Tom Kite |
| 1952 | Sam Snead | 286 | Jack Burke Jr.. | 1987 | Larry Mize* (4–3) | 285 | Seve Ballesteros (5) |
| 1953 | Ben Hogan | 274 | Ed Oliver Jr. |  |  |  | Greg Norman (4–4) |
| 1954 | Sam Snead* (70) | 289 | Ben Hogan (71) | 1988 | Sandy Lyle | 281 | Mark Calcavecchia |
| 1955 | Cary Middlecoff | 279 | Ben Hogan | 1989 | Nick Faldo* (5–3) | 283 | Scott Hoch (5–4) |
| 1956 | Jack Burke Jr. | 289 | Ken Venturi | 1990 | Nick Faldo* (4–4) | 278 | Ray Floyd (4–x) |
| 1957 | Doug Ford | 282 | Sam Snead | 1991 | Ian Woosnam | 277 | José María |
| 1958 | Arnold Palmer | 284 | Doug Ford |  |  |  | Olazábal |
|  |  |  | Fred Hawkins | 1992 | Fred Couples | 275 | Ray Floyd |
| 1959 | Art Wall Jr. | 284 | Cary Middlecoff | 1993 | Bernhard Langer | 277 | Chip Beck |
| 1960 | Arnold Palmer | 282 | Ken Venturi | 1994 | José María Olazábal | 279 | Tom Lehman |
| 1961 | Gary Player | 280 | Charles R. Coe | 1995 | Ben Crenshaw | 274 | Davis Love III |
|  |  |  | Arnold Palmer | 1996 | Nick Faldo | 276 | Greg Norman |
| 1962 | Arnold Palmer* (68) | 280 | Gary Player (71) | 1997 | Tiger Woods | 270 | Tom Kite |
|  |  |  | D. Finsterwald (77) | 1998 | Mark O'Meara | 279 | David Duval |
| 1963 | Jack Nicklaus | 286 | Tony Lema |  |  |  | Fred Couples |
| 1964 | Arnold Palmer | 276 | Dave Marr | 1999 | José María Olazábal | 280 | Davis Love III |
|  |  |  | Jack Nicklaus | 2000 | Vijay Singh | 278 | Ernie Els |
| 1965 | Jack Nicklaus | 271 | Arnold Palmer | 2001 | Tiger Woods | 272 | David Duval |
|  |  |  | Gary Player | 2002 | Tiger Woods | 276 | Retief Goosen |
| 1966 | Jack Nicklaus* (70) | 288 | Tommy Jacobs (72) | 2003 | Mike Weir | 281 | Len Mattiace |
|  |  |  | Gay Brewer Jr. (78) | 2004 | Phil Mickelson | 279 | Ernie Els |
| 1967 | Gay Brewer Jr. | 280 | Bobby Nichols | 2005 | Tiger Woods | 276 | Chris DiMarco |
| 1968 | Bob Goalby | 277 | Roberto DeVicenzo | 2006 | Phil Mickelson | 281 | Tim Clark |
| 1969 | George Archer | 281 | Billy Casper | 2007 | Zach Johnson | 289 | Tiger Woods |
|  |  |  | George Knudson |  |  |  | Retief Goosen |
|  |  |  | Tom Weiskopf |  |  |  | Rory Sabbatini |
| 1970 | Billy Casper* (69) | 279 | Gene Littler (74) | 2008 | Trevor Immelman | 280 | Tiger Woods |
| 1971 | Charles Coody | 279 | Johnny Miller | 2009 | Angel Cabrera | 276 | Chad Campbell |
|  |  |  | Jack Nicklaus |  |  |  | Kenny Perry |
| 1972 | Jack Nicklaus | 286 | Bruce Crampton | 2010 | Phil Mickelson | 272 | Lee Westwood |
|  |  |  | Bobby Mitchell | 2011 | Charl Schwartzel | 274 | Jason Day |
|  |  |  | Tom Weiskopf |  |  |  | Adam Scott |
| 1973 | Tommy Aaron | 283 | J.C. Snead |  |  |  |  |
| 1974 | Gary Player | 278 | Tom Weiskopf |  |  |  |  |
|  |  |  | Dave Stockton |  |  |  |  |
| 1975 | Jack Nicklaus | 276 | Johnny Miller |  |  |  |  |
|  |  |  | Tom Weiskopf |  |  |  |  |

*Winner in playoff. Playoff scores are in parentheses. †Playoff cut from 18 holes to sudden death.
Note: Played at Augusta National Golf Club, Augusta, GA.

## United States Open Championship

| Year | Winner | Score | Runner-Up | Site |
|------|--------|-------|-----------|------|
| 1895 | Horace Rawlins | †173 | Willie Dunn | Newport GC, Newport, RI |
| 1896 | James Foulis | †152 | Horace Rawlins | Shinnecock Hills GC, Southampton, NY |
| 1897 | Joe Lloyd | †162 | Willie Anderson | Chicago GC, Wheaton, IL |
| 1898 | Fred Herd | 328 | Alex Smith | Myopia Hunt Club, Hamilton, MA |
| 1899 | Willie Smith | 315 | George Low<br>Val Fitzjohn<br>W.H. Way | Baltimore CC, Baltimore, MD |
| 1900 | Harry Vardon | 313 | John H. Taylor | Chicago GC, Wheaton, IL |
| 1901 | Willie Anderson* (85) | 331 | Alex Smith (86) | Myopia Hunt Club, Hamilton, MA |
| 1902 | Laurie Auchterlonie | 307 | Stewart Gardner | Garden City GC, Garden City, NY |
| 1903 | Willie Anderson* (82) | 307 | David Brown (84) | Baltusrol GC, Springfield, NJ |
| 1904 | Willie Anderson | 303 | Gil Nicholls | Glen View Club, Golf, IL |
| 1905 | Willie Anderson | 314 | Alex Smith | Myopia Hunt Club, Hamilton, MA |
| 1906 | Alex Smith | 295 | Willie Smith | Onwentsia Club, Lake Forest, IL |
| 1907 | Alex Ross | 302 | Gil Nicholls | Philadelphia Cricket Club, Chestnut Hill, PA |
| 1908 | Fred McLeod* (77) | 322 | Willie Smith (83) | Myopia Hunt Club, Hamilton, MA |
| 1909 | George Sargent | 290 | Tom McNamara | Englewood GC, Englewood, NJ |
| 1910 | Alex Smith* (71) | 298 | John McDermott (75)<br>Macdonald Smith (77) | Philadelphia Cricket Club, Chestnut Hill, PA |
| 1911 | John McDermott* (80) | 307 | Mike Brady (82)<br>George Simpson (85) | Chicago GC, Wheaton, IL |
| 1912 | John McDermott | 294 | Tom McNamara | CC of Buffalo, Buffalo, NY |
| 1913 | Francis Ouimet* (72) | 304 | Harry Vardon (77)<br>Edward Ray (78) | The Country Club, Brookline, MA |
| 1914 | Walter Hagen | 290 | Chick Evans | Midlothian CC, Blue Island, IL |
| 1915 | Jerry Travers | 297 | Tom McNamara | Baltusrol GC, Springfield, NJ |
| 1916 | Chick Evans | 286 | Jock Hutchison | Minikahda Club, Minneapolis. MN |
| 1917–18 | No tournament | | | |
| 1919 | Walter Hagen* (77) | 301 | Mike Brady (78) | Brae Burn CC, West Newton, MA |
| 1920 | Edward Ray | 295 | Harry Vardon<br>Jack Burke<br>Leo Diegel<br>Jock Hutchison | Inverness CC, Toledo, OH |
| 1921 | Jim Barnes | 289 | Walter Hagen<br>Fred McLeod | Columbia CC, Chevy Chase, MD |
| 1922 | Gene Sarazen | 288 | John L. Black<br>Bobby Jones | Skokie CC, Glencoe, IL |
| 1923 | Bobby Jones* (76) | 296 | Bobby Cruickshank (78) | Inwood CC, Inwood, NY |
| 1924 | Cyril Walker | 297 | Bobby Jones | Oakland Hills CC, Birmingham, MI |
| 1925 | W. MacFarlane* (75–72) | 291 | Bobby Jones (75–73) | Worcester CC, Worcester, MA |
| 1926 | Bobby Jones | 293 | Joe Turnesa | Scioto CC, Columbus, OH |
| 1927 | Tommy Armour* (76) | 301 | Harry Cooper (79) | Oakmont CC, Oakmont, PA |
| 1928 | Johnny Farrell* (143) | 294 | Bobby Jones (144) | Olympia Fields CC, Matteson, IL |
| 1929 | Bobby Jones* (141) | 294 | Al Espinosa (164) | Winged Foot GC, Mamaroneck, NY |
| 1930 | Bobby Jones | 287 | Macdonald Smith | Interlachen CC, Hopkins, MN |
| 1931 | Billy Burke* (149–148) | 292 | George Von Elm (149–149) | Inverness Club, Toledo, OH |
| 1932 | Gene Sarazen | 286 | Phil Perkins<br>Bobby Cruickshank | Fresh Meadows CC, Flushing, NY |
| 1933 | Johnny Goodman | 287 | Ralph Guldahl | North Shore CC, Glenview, IL |
| 1934 | Olin Dutra | 293 | Gene Sarazen | Merion Cricket Club, Ardmore, PA |
| 1935 | Sam Parks Jr. | 299 | Jimmy Thompson | Oakmont CC, Oakmont, PA |
| 1936 | Tony Manero | 282 | Harry Cooper | Baltusrol GC (Upper Course), Springfield, NJ |
| 1937 | Ralph Guldahl | 281 | Sam Snead | Oakland Hills CC, Birmingham, MI |
| 1938 | Ralph Guldahl | 284 | Dick Metz | Cherry Hills CC, Denver, CO |
| 1939 | Byron Nelson* (68–70) | 284 | Craig Wood (68–73)<br>Denny Shute (76) | Philadelphia CC, Philadelphia, PA |
| 1940 | Lawson Little* (70) | 287 | Gene Sarazen (73) | Canterbury GC, Cleveland, OH |
| 1941 | Craig Wood | 284 | Denny Shute | Colonial Club, Fort Worth, TX |
| 1942–45 | No tournament | | | |
| 1946 | Lloyd Mangrum* (72–72) | 284 | Vic Ghezzi (72–73)<br>Byron Nelson (72–73) | Canterbury GC, Cleveland, OH |
| 1947 | Lew Worsham* (69) | 282 | Sam Snead (70) | St. Louis CC, Clayton, MO |
| 1948 | Ben Hogan | 276 | Jimmy Demaret | Riviera CC, Los Angeles, CA |
| 1949 | Cary Middlecoff | 286 | Sam Snead<br>Clayton Heafner | Medinah CC, Medinah, IL |
| 1950 | Ben Hogan* (69) | 287 | Lloyd Mangrum (73)<br>George Fazio (75) | Merion GC, Ardmore, PA |

## United States Open Championship *(Cont.)*

| Year | Winner | Score | Runner-Up | Site |
|------|--------|-------|-----------|------|
| 1951 | Ben Hogan | 287 | Clayton Heafner | Oakland Hills CC, Birmingham, MI |
| 1952 | Julius Boros | 281 | Ed Oliver | Northwood CC, Dallas, TX |
| 1953 | Ben Hogan | 283 | Sam Snead | Oakmont CC, Oakmont, PA |
| 1954 | Ed Furgol | 284 | Gene Littler | Baltusrol GC (Lower Course), Springfield, NJ |
| 1955 | Jack Fleck* (69) | 287 | Ben Hogan (72) | Olympic Club (Lake Course), San Fran., CA |
| 1956 | Cary Middlecoff | 281 | Ben Hogan | Oak Hill CC, Rochester, NY |
| | | | Julius Boros | |
| 1957 | Dick Mayer* (72) | 282 | Cary Middlecoff (79) | Inverness Club, Toledo, OH |
| 1958 | Tommy Bolt | 283 | Gary Player | Southern Hills CC, Tulsa, OK |
| 1959 | Billy Casper | 282 | Bob Rosburg | Winged Foot GC, Mamaroneck, NY |
| 1960 | Arnold Palmer | 280 | Jack Nicklaus | Cherry Hills CC, Denver, CO |
| 1961 | Gene Littler | 281 | Bob Goalby | Oakland Hills CC, Birmingham, MI |
| | | | Doug Sanders | |
| 1962 | Jack Nicklaus* (71) | 283 | Arnold Palmer (74) | Oakmont CC, Oakmont, PA |
| 1963 | Julius Boros* (70) | 293 | Jacky Cupit (73) | The Country Club, Brookline, MA |
| | | | Arnold Palmer (76) | |
| 1964 | Ken Venturi | 278 | Tommy Jacobs | Congressional CC, Bethesda, MD |
| 1965 | Gary Player* (71) | 282 | Kel Nagle (74) | Bellerive CC, St. Louis, MO |
| 1966 | Billy Casper* (69) | 278 | Arnold Palmer (73) | Olympic Club (Lake Course), San Fran., CA |
| 1967 | Jack Nicklaus | 275 | Arnold Palmer | Baltusrol GC (Lower Course), Springfield, NJ |
| 1968 | Lee Trevino | 275 | Jack Nicklaus | Oak Hill CC, Rochester, NY |
| 1969 | Orville Moody | 281 | Deane Beman | Champions GC (Cypress Creek Course), |
| | | | Al Geiberger | Houston, TX |
| | | | Bob Rosburg | |
| 1970 | Tony Jacklin | 281 | Dave Hill | Hazeltine GC, Chaska, MN |
| 1971 | Lee Trevino* (68) | 280 | Jack Nicklaus (71) | Merion GC (East Course), Ardmore, PA |
| 1972 | Jack Nicklaus | 290 | Bruce Crampton | Pebble Beach GL, Pebble Beach, CA |
| 1973 | Johnny Miller | 279 | John Schlee | Oakmont CC, Oakmont, PA |
| 1974 | Hale Irwin | 287 | Forrest Fezler | Winged Foot GC, Mamaroneck, NY |
| 1975 | Lou Graham* (71) | 287 | John Mahaffey (73) | Medinah CC, Medinah, IL |
| 1976 | Jerry Pate | 277 | Tom Weiskopf | Atlanta Athletic Club, Duluth, GA |
| | | | Al Geiberger | |
| 1977 | Hubert Green | 278 | Lou Graham | Southern Hills CC, Tulsa, OK |
| 1978 | Andy North | 285 | Dave Stockton | Cherry Hills CC, Denver, CO |
| | | | J.C. Snead | |
| 1979 | Hale Irwin | 284 | Gary Player | Inverness Club, Toledo, OH |
| | | | Jerry Pate | |
| 1980 | Jack Nicklaus | 272 | Isao Aoki | Baltusrol GC (Lower Course), Springfield, NJ |
| 1981 | David Graham | 273 | George Burns | Merion GC, Ardmore, PA |
| | | | Bill Rogers | |
| 1982 | Tom Watson | 282 | Jack Nicklaus | Pebble Beach GL, Pebble Beach, CA |
| 1983 | Larry Nelson | 280 | Tom Watson | Oakmont CC, Oakmont, PA |
| 1984 | Fuzzy Zoeller* (67) | 276 | Greg Norman (75) | Winged Foot GC, Mamaroneck, NY |
| 1985 | Andy North | 279 | Dave Barr | Oakland Hills CC, Birmingham, MI |
| | | | T.C. Chen | |
| | | | Denis Watson | |
| 1986 | Ray Floyd | 279 | Lanny Wadkins | Shinnecock Hills GC, Southampton, NY |
| | | | Chip Beck | |
| 1987 | Scott Simpson | 277 | Tom Watson | Olympic Club (Lake Course), San Fran., CA |
| 1988 | Curtis Strange* (71) | 278 | Nick Faldo (75) | The Country Club, Brookline, MA |
| 1989 | Curtis Strange | 278 | Chip Beck | Oak Hill CC, Rochester, NY |
| | | | Mark McCumber | |
| | | | Ian Woosnam | |
| 1990 | Hale Irwin* (74) (3) | 280 | Mike Donald (74) (4) | Medinah CC, Medinah, IL |
| 1991 | Payne Stewart* (75) | 282 | Scott Simpson (77) | Hazeltine GC, Chaska, MN |
| 1992 | Tom Kite | 285 | Jeff Sluman | Pebble Beach GL, Pebble Beach, CA |
| 1993 | Lee Janzen | 272 | Payne Stewart | Baltusrol GC, Springfield, NJ |
| 1994 | Ernie Els* | 279 | Loren Roberts | Oakmont CC, Oakmont, PA |
| | | | Colin Montgomerie | |
| 1995 | Corey Pavin | 280 | Greg Norman | Shinnecock Hills GC, Southampton, NY |
| 1996 | Steve Jones | 278 | Davis Love III | Oakland Hills CC, Birmingham, MI |
| | | | Tom Lehman | |
| 1997 | Ernie Els | 276 | Colin Montgomerie | Congressional CC, Bethesda, MD |
| 1998 | Lee Janzen | 280 | Payne Stewart | Olympic Club (Lake Course), San Fran., CA |
| 1999 | Payne Stewart | 279 | Phil Mickelson | Pinehurst Resort and CC, Pinehurst, NC |
| 2000 | Tiger Woods | 272 | Miguel Angel Jiménez | Pebble Beach GL, Pebble Beach, CA |
| | | | Ernie Els | |

## United States Open Championship (Cont.)

| Year | Winner | Score | Runner-Up | Site |
|---|---|---|---|---|
| 2001 | Retief Goosen* (70) | 276 | Mark Brooks (72) | Southern Hills CC, Tulsa, OK |
| 2002 | Tiger Woods | 277 | Phil Mickelson | Bethpage State Park (Black), Farmingdale, NY |
| 2003 | Jim Furyk | 272 | Stephen Leaney | Olympia Fields CC, Olympia Fields, IL |
| 2004 | Retief Goosen | 276 | Phil Mickelson | Shinnecock Hills GC, Southampton, NY |
| 2005 | Michael Campbell | 280 | Tiger Woods | Pinehurst Resort and CC, Pinehurst, NC |
| 2006 | Geoff Ogilvy | 285 | Jim Furyk | Winged Foot GC, Mamaroneck, NY |
| | | | Colin Montgomerie | |
| | | | Phil Mickelson | |
| 2007 | Angel Cabrera | 285 | Jim Furyk | Oakmont CC, Oakmont, PA |
| | | | Tiger Woods | |
| 2008 | Tiger Woods* (71) (4) | 283 | Rocco Mediate | Torrey Pines GC (South), San Diego, CA |
| 2009 | Lucas Glover | 276 | Phil Mickelson | Bethpage State Park (Black), Farmingdale, NY |
| | | | David Duval | |
| | | | Ricky Barnes | |
| 2010 | Graeme McDowell | 284 | Gregory Havret | Pebble Beach GL, Pebble Beach, CA |
| 2011 | Rory McIlroy | 268 | Jason Day | Congressional CC, Bethesda, MD |

*Winner in playoff. Playoff scores are in parentheses. The 1990 and 2008 playoffs went to one hole of sudden death after an 18-hole playoff. In the 1994 playoff, Montgomerie was eliminated after 18 playoff holes, and Els beat Roberts on the 20th.
†Before 1898, 36 holes. From 1898 on, 72 holes.

## The Open Championship (British Open)

| Year | Winner | Score | Runner-Up | Site |
|---|---|---|---|---|
| 1860† | Willie Park | 174 | Tom Morris Sr. | Prestwick, Scotland |
| 1861‡ | Tom Morris Sr. | 163 | Willie Park | Prestwick, Scotland |
| 1862 | Tom Morris Sr. | 163 | Willie Park | Prestwick, Scotland |
| 1863 | Willie Park | 168 | Tom Morris Sr. | Prestwick, Scotland |
| 1864 | Tom Morris, Sr. | 160 | Andrew Strath | Prestwick, Scotland |
| 1865 | Andrew Strath | 162 | Willie Park | Prestwick, Scotland |
| 1866 | Willie Park | 169 | David Park | Prestwick, Scotland |
| 1867 | Tom Morris Sr. | 170 | Willie Park | Prestwick, Scotland |
| 1868 | Tom Morris Jr. | 154 | Tom Morris Sr. | Prestwick, Scotland |
| 1869 | Tom Morris Jr. | 157 | Tom Morris Sr. | Prestwick, Scotland |
| 1870 | Tom Morris Jr. | 149 | David Strath | Prestwick, Scotland |
| | | | Bob Kirk | |
| 1871 | No tournament | | | |
| 1872 | Tom Morris Jr. | 166 | David Strath | Prestwick, Scotland |
| 1873 | Tom Kidd | 179 | Jamie Anderson | St. Andrews, Scotland |
| 1874 | Mungo Park | 159 | No record | Musselburgh, Scotland |
| 1875 | Willie Park | 166 | Bob Martin | Prestwick, Scotland |
| 1876 | Bob Martin# | 176 | David Strath | St. Andrews, Scotland |
| 1877 | Jamie Anderson | 160 | Bob Pringle | Musselburgh, Scotland |
| 1878 | Jamie Anderson | 157 | Robert Kirk | Prestwick, Scotland |
| 1879 | Jamie Anderson | 169 | Andrew Kirkaldy | St. Andrews, Scotland |
| | | | James Allan | |
| 1880 | Robert Ferguson | 162 | No record | Musselburgh, Scotland |
| 1881 | Robert Ferguson | 170 | Jamie Anderson | Prestwick, Scotland |
| 1882 | Robert Ferguson | 171 | Willie Fernie | St. Andrews, Scotland |
| 1883 | Willie Fernie* | 159 | Robert Ferguson | Musselburgh, Scotland |
| 1884 | Jack Simpson | 160 | Douglas Rolland | Prestwick, Scotland |
| | | | Willie Fernie | |
| 1885 | Bob Martin | 171 | Archie Simpson | St. Andrews, Scotland |
| 1886 | David Brown | 157 | Willie Campbell | Musselburgh, Scotland |
| 1887 | Willie Park Jr. | 161 | Bob Martin | Prestwick, Scotland |
| 1888 | Jack Burns | 171 | Bernard Sayers | St. Andrews, Scotland |
| | | | David Anderson | |
| 1889 | Willie Park Jr.* (158) | 155 | Andrew Kirkaldy (163) | Musselburgh, Scotland |
| 1890 | John Ball | 164 | Willie Fernie | Prestwick, Scotland |
| 1891 | Hugh Kirkaldy | 166 | Andrew Kirkaldy | St. Andrews, Scotland |
| | | | Willie Fernie | |
| 1892 | Harold Hilton | **305 | John Ball | Muirfield, Scotland |
| | | | Hugh Kirkaldy | |
| 1893 | William Auchterlonie | 322 | John E. Laidlay | Prestwick, Scotland |

## The Open Championship (British Open) (Cont.)

| Year | Winner | Score | Runner-Up | Site |
|------|--------|-------|-----------|------|
| 1894 | John H. Taylor | 326 | Douglas Rolland | Royal St. George's, England |
| 1895 | John H. Taylor | 322 | Alexander Herd | St. Andrews, Scotland |
| 1896 | Harry Vardon* (157) | 316 | John H. Taylor (161) | Muirfield, Scotland |
| 1897 | Harold Hilton | 314 | James Braid | Royal Liverpool (Hoylake), England |
| 1898 | Harry Vardon | 307 | Willie Park Jr. | Prestwick, Scotland |
| 1899 | Harry Vardon | 310 | Jack White | Royal St. George's, England |
| 1900 | John H. Taylor | 309 | Harry Vardon | St. Andrews, Scotland |
| 1901 | James Braid | 309 | Harry Vardon | Muirfield, Scotland |
| 1902 | Alexander Herd | 307 | Harry Vardon | Royal Liverpool (Hoylake), England |
| 1903 | Harry Vardon | 300 | Tom Vardon | Prestwick, Scotland |
| 1904 | Jack White | 296 | John H. Taylor | Royal St. George's, England |
| 1905 | James Braid | 318 | John H. Taylor | St. Andrews, Scotland |
|      |            |     | Rolland Jones | |
| 1906 | James Braid | 300 | John H. Taylor | Muirfield, Scotland |
| 1907 | Arnaud Massy | 312 | John H. Taylor | Royal Liverpool (Hoylake), England |
| 1908 | James Braid | 291 | Tom Ball | Prestwick, Scotland |
| 1909 | John H. Taylor | 295 | James Braid | Deal, England |
|      |            |     | Tom Ball | |
| 1910 | James Braid | 299 | Alexander Herd | St. Andrews, Scotland |
| 1911 | Harry Vardon | 303 | Arnaud Massy | Royal St. George's, England |
| 1912 | Ted Ray | 295 | Harry Vardon | Muirfield, Scotland |
| 1913 | John H. Taylor | 304 | Ted Ray | Royal Liverpool (Hoylake), England |
| 1914 | Harry Vardon | 306 | John H. Taylor | Prestwick, Scotland |
| 1915–19 | No tournament | | | |
| 1920 | George Duncan | 303 | Alexander Herd | Deal, England |
| 1921 | Jock Hutchison* (150) | 296 | Roger Wethered (159) | St. Andrews, Scotland |
| 1922 | Walter Hagen | 300 | George Duncan | Royal St. George's, England |
|      |            |     | Jim Barnes | |
| 1923 | Arthur G. Havers | 295 | Walter Hagen | Troon, Scotland |
| 1924 | Walter Hagen | 301 | Ernest Whitcombe | Royal Liverpool (Hoylake), England |
| 1925 | Jim Barnes | 300 | Archie Compston | Prestwick, Scotland |
|      |            |     | Ted Ray | |
| 1926 | Bobby Jones | 291 | Al Watrous | Royal Lytham & St. Annes, England |
| 1927 | Bobby Jones | 285 | Aubrey Boomer | St. Andrews, Scotland |
| 1928 | Walter Hagen | 292 | Gene Sarazen | Royal St. George's, England |
| 1929 | Walter Hagen | 292 | Johnny Farrell | Muirfield, Scotland |
| 1930 | Bobby Jones | 291 | Macdonald Smith | Royal Liverpool (Hoylake), England |
|      |            |     | Leo Diegel | |
| 1931 | Tommy Armour | 296 | Jose Jurado | Carnoustie, Scotland |
| 1932 | Gene Sarazen | 283 | Macdonald Smith | Prince's, England |
| 1933 | Denny Shute* (149) | 292 | Craig Wood (154) | St. Andrews, Scotland |
| 1934 | Henry Cotton | 283 | Sidney F. Brews | Royal St. George's, England |
| 1935 | Alfred Perry | 283 | Alfred Padgham | Muirfield, Scotland |
| 1936 | Alfred Padgham | 287 | James Adams | Royal Liverpool (Hoylake), England |
| 1937 | Henry Cotton | 290 | Reginald A. Whitcombe | Carnoustie, Scotland |
| 1938 | Reginald A. Whitcombe | 295 | James Adams | Royal St. George's, England |
| 1939 | Richard Burton | 290 | Johnny Bulla | St. Andrews, Scotland |
| 1940–45 | No tournament | | | |
| 1946 | Sam Snead | 290 | Bobby Locke | St. Andrews, Scotland |
|      |            |     | Johnny Bulla | |
| 1947 | Fred Daly | 293 | Reginald W. Horne | Royal Liverpool (Hoylake), England |
|      |            |     | Frank Stranahan | |
| 1948 | Henry Cotton | 294 | Fred Daly | Muirfield, Scotland |
| 1949 | Bobby Locke* (135) | 283 | Harry Bradshaw (147) | Royal St. George's, England |
| 1950 | Bobby Locke | 279 | Roberto DeVicenzo | Troon, Scotland |
| 1951 | Max Faulkner | 285 | Tony Cerda | Portrush, Ireland |
| 1952 | Bobby Locke | 287 | Peter Thomson | Royal Lytham & St. Annes, England |
| 1953 | Ben Hogan | 282 | Frank Stranahan | Carnoustie, Scotland |
|      |            |     | Dai Rees | |
|      |            |     | Peter Thomson | |
|      |            |     | Tony Cerda | |
| 1954 | Peter Thomson | 283 | Sidney S. Scott | Royal Birkdale, Southport, England |
|      |            |     | Dai Rees | |
|      |            |     | Bobby Locke | |
| 1955 | Peter Thomson | 281 | John Fallon | St. Andrews, Scotland |
| 1956 | Peter Thomson | 286 | Flory Van Donck | Royal Liverpool (Hoylake), England |
| 1957 | Bobby Locke | 279 | Peter Thomson | St. Andrews, Scotland |

## The Open Championship (British Open) (Cont.)

| Year | Winner | Score | Runner-Up | Site |
|------|--------|-------|-----------|------|
| 1958 | ...........Peter Thomson* (139) | 278 | Dave Thomas (143) | Royal Lytham & St. Annes, England |
| 1959 | ...........Gary Player | 284 | Fred Bullock | Muirfield, Scotland |
| | | | Flory Van Donck | |
| 1960 | ...........Kel Nagle | 278 | Arnold Palmer | St. Andrews, Scotland |
| 1961 | ...........Arnold Palmer | 284 | Dai Rees | Royal Birkdale, Southport, England |
| 1962 | ...........Arnold Palmer | 276 | Kel Nagle | Troon, Scotland |
| 1963 | ...........Bob Charles* (140) | 277 | Phil Rodgers (148) | Royal Lytham & St. Annes, England |
| 1964 | ...........Tony Lema | 279 | Jack Nicklaus | St. Andrews, Scotland |
| 1965 | ...........Peter Thomson | 285 | Brian Huggett | Royal Birkdale, Southport, England |
| | | | Christy O'Connor | |
| 1966 | ...........Jack Nicklaus | 282 | Doug Sanders | Muirfield, Scotland |
| | | | Dave Thomas | |
| 1967 | ...........Robert DeVicenzo | 278 | Jack Nicklaus | Royal Liverpool (Hoylake), England |
| 1968 | ...........Gary Player | 289 | Jack Nicklaus | Carnoustie, Scotland |
| | | | Bob Charles | |
| 1969 | ...........Tony Jacklin | 280 | Bob Charles | Royal Lytham & St. Annes, England |
| 1970 | ...........Jack Nicklaus* (72) | 283 | Doug Sanders (73) | St. Andrews, Scotland |
| 1971 | ...........Lee Trevino | 278 | Lu Liang Huan | Royal Birkdale, Southport, England |
| 1972 | ...........Lee Trevino | 278 | Jack Nicklaus | Muirfield, Scotland |
| 1973 | ...........Tom Weiskopf | 276 | Johnny Miller | Troon, Scotland |
| 1974 | ...........Gary Player | 282 | Peter Oosterhuis | Royal Lytham & St. Annes, England |
| 1975 | ...........Tom Watson* (71) | 279 | Jack Newton (72) | Carnoustie, Scotland |
| 1976 | ...........Johnny Miller | 279 | Jack Nicklaus | Royal Birkdale, Southport, England |
| | | | Seve Ballesteros | |
| 1977 | ...........Tom Watson | 268 | Jack Nicklaus | Turnberry, Scotland |
| 1978 | ...........Jack Nicklaus | 281 | Ben Crenshaw | St. Andrews, Scotland |
| | | | Tom Kite | |
| | | | Ray Floyd | |
| | | | Simon Owen | |
| 1979 | ...........Seve Ballesteros | 283 | Ben Crenshaw | Royal Lytham & St. Annes, England |
| | | | Jack Nicklaus | |
| 1980 | ...........Tom Watson | 271 | Lee Trevino | Muirfield, Scotland |
| 1981 | ...........Bill Rogers | 276 | Bernhard Langer | Royal St. George's, England |
| 1982 | ...........Tom Watson | 284 | Nick Price | Troon, Scotland |
| | | | Peter Oosterhuis | |
| 1983 | ...........Tom Watson | 275 | Andy Bean | Royal Birkdale, Southport, England |
| 1984 | ...........Seve Ballesteros | 276 | Tom Watson | St. Andrews, Scotland |
| | | | Bernhard Langer | |
| 1985 | ...........Sandy Lyle | 282 | Payne Stewart | Royal St. George's, England |
| 1986 | ...........Greg Norman | 280 | Gordon Brand | Turnberry, Scotland |
| 1987 | ...........Nick Faldo | 279 | Paul Azinger | Muirfield, Scotland |
| | | | Rodger Davis | |
| 1988 | ...........Seve Ballesteros | 273 | Nick Price | Royal Lytham & St. Annes, England |
| 1989†† | .......Mark Calcavecchia* | 275 | Wayne Grady (4-4-4-4) | Troon, Scotland |
| | (4-3-3-3) | | Greg Norman (3-3-4-x) | |
| 1990 | ...........Nick Faldo | 270 | Payne Stewart | St. Andrews, Scotland |
| | | | Mark McNulty | |
| 1991 | ...........Ian Baker-Finch | 272 | Mike Harwood | Royal Birkdale, Southport, England |
| 1992 | ...........Nick Faldo | 272 | John Cook | Muirfield, Scotland |
| 1993 | ...........Greg Norman | 267 | Nick Faldo | Royal St. George's, England |
| 1994 | ...........Nick Price | 268 | Jesper Parnevik | Turnberry, Scotland |
| 1995 | ...........John Daly* (4-3-4-4) | 282 | C. Rocca (5-4-7-3) | St. Andrews, Scotland |
| 1996 | ...........Tom Lehman | 271 | Mark McCumber | Royal Lytham & St. Annes, England |
| | | | Ernie Els | |
| 1997 | ...........Justin Leonard | 272 | Jesper Parnevik | Troon, Scotland |
| | | | Darren Clarke | |
| 1998 | ...........Mark O'Meara* (4-4-5-4) | 280 | Brian Watts (5-4-5-5) | Royal Birkdale, Southport, England |
| 1999 | ...........Paul Lawrie* (5-4-3-3) | 290 | Jean Van de Velde (6-4-3-5) | Carnoustie, Scotland |
| | | | Justin Leonard (5-4-4-5) | |
| 2000 | ...........Tiger Woods | 269 | Thomas Bjorn | St. Andrews, Scotland |
| | | | Ernie Els | |
| 2001 | ...........David Duval | 274 | Niclas Fasth | Royal Lytham & St. Annes, England |
| 2002 | ..............Ernie Els* | 278 | Stuart Appleby | Muirfield, Scotland |
| 2003 | ...........Ben Curtis | 283 | Vijay Singh | Royal St. George's, England |
| 2004 | ...........Todd Hamilton* | 274 | Ernie Els | Troon, Scotland |

## The Open Championship (British Open) *(Cont.)*

| Year | Winner | Score | Runner-Up | Site |
|------|--------|-------|-----------|------|
| 2005 | Tiger Woods | 274 | Colin Montgomerie | St. Andrews, Scotland |
| 2006 | Tiger Woods | 270 | Chris DiMarco | Royal Liverpool (Hoylake), England |
| 2007 | Padraig Harrington* | 277 | Sergio Garcia | Carnoustie, Scotland |
| 2008 | Padraig Harrington | 283 | Ian Poulter | Royal Birkdale, Southport, England |
| 2009 | Stewart Cink* | 278 | Tom Watson | Turnberry, Scotland |
| 2010 | Louis Oosthuizen | 272 | Lee Westwood | St. Andrews, Scotland |
| 2011 | Darren Clarke | 275 | Phil Mickelson | Royal St. George's, England |
| | | | Dustin Johnson | |

*Winner in playoff. †The first event was open only to professional golfers.
‡The second annual open was open to amateurs and pros. #Tied, but refused playoff.
**Championship extended from 36 to 72 holes. ††Playoff cut from 18 holes to 4 holes.

## PGA Championship

| Year | Winner | Score | Runner-Up | Site |
|------|--------|-------|-----------|------|
| 1916 | Jim Barnes | 1 up | Jock Hutchison | Siwanoy CC, Bronxville, NY |
| 1917–18 | No tournament | | | |
| 1919 | Jim Barnes | 6 & 5 | Fred McLeod | Engineers CC, Roslyn, NY |
| 1920 | Jock Hutchison | 1 up | J. Douglas Edgar | Flossmoor CC, Flossmoor, IL |
| 1921 | Walter Hagen | 3 & 2 | Jim Barnes | Inwood CC, Far Rockaway, NY |
| 1922 | Gene Sarazen | 4 & 3 | Emmet French | Oakmont CC, Oakmont, PA |
| 1923 | Gene Sarazen | 1 up 38 holes | Walter Hagen | Pelham CC, Pelham, NY |
| 1924 | Walter Hagen | 2 up | Jim Barnes | French Lick CC, French Lick, IN |
| 1925 | Walter Hagen | 6 & 5 | William Mehlhorn | Olympia Fields CC, Olympia Fields, IL |
| 1926 | Walter Hagen | 5 & 3 | Leo Diegel | Salisbury GC, Westbury, NY |
| 1927 | Walter Hagen | 1 up | Joe Turnesa | Cedar Crest CC, Dallas, TX |
| 1928 | Leo Diegel | 6 & 5 | Al Espinosa | Five Farms CC, Baltimore, MD |
| 1929 | Leo Diegel | 6 & 4 | Johnny Farrell | Hillcrest CC, Los Angeles, CA |
| 1930 | Tommy Armour | 1 up | Gene Sarazen | Fresh Meadow CC, Flushing, NY |
| 1931 | Tom Creavy | 2 & 1 | Denny Shute | Wannamoisett CC, Rumford, RI |
| 1932 | Olin Dutra | 4 & 3 | Frank Walsh | Keller GC, St. Paul, MN |
| 1933 | Gene Sarazen | 5 & 4 | Willie Goggin | Blue Mound CC, Milwaukee, WI |
| 1934 | Paul Runyan | 1 up | Craig Wood | Park CC, Williamsville, NY |
| 1935 | Johnny Revolta | 5 & 4 38 holes | Tommy Armour | Twin Hills CC, Oklahoma City, OK |
| 1936 | Denny Shute | 3 & 2 | Jimmy Thomson | Pinehurst CC, Pinehurst, NC |
| 1937 | Denny Shute | 1 up 37 holes | Harold McSpaden | Pittsburgh FC, Aspinwall, PA |
| 1938 | Paul Runyan | 8 & 7 | Sam Snead | Shawnee CC, Shawnee-on-Delaware, PA |
| 1939 | Henry Picard | 1 up 37 holes | Byron Nelson | Pomonok CC, Flushing, NY |
| 1940 | Byron Nelson | 1 up | Sam Snead | Hershey CC, Hershey, PA |
| 1941 | Vic Ghezzi | 1 up 38 holes | Byron Nelson | Cherry Hills CC, Denver, CO |
| 1942 | Sam Snead | 2 & 1 | Jim Turnesa | Seaview CC, Atlantic City, NJ |
| 1943 | No tournament | | | |
| 1944 | Bob Hamilton | 1 up | Byron Nelson | Manito G & CC, Spokane, WA |
| 1945 | Byron Nelson | 4 & 3 | Sam Byrd | Morraine CC, Dayton, OH |
| 1946 | Ben Hogan | 6 & 4 | Ed Oliver | Portland GC, Portland, OR |
| 1947 | Jim Ferrier | 2 & 1 | Chick Harbert | Plum Hollow CC, Detroit, MI |
| 1948 | Ben Hogan | 7 & 6 | Mike Turnesa | Norwood Hills CC, St. Louis, MO |
| 1949 | Sam Snead | 3 & 2 | Johnny Palmer | Hermitage CC, Richmond, VA |
| 1950 | Chandler Harper | 4 & 3 | Henry Williams Jr. | Scioto CC, Columbus, OH |
| 1951 | Sam Snead | 7 & 6 | Walter Burkemo | Oakmont CC, Oakmont, PA |
| 1952 | Jim Turnesa | 1 up | Chick Harbert | Big Spring CC, Louisville, KY |
| 1953 | Walter Burkemo | 2 & 1 | Felice Torza | Birmingham CC, Birmingham, MI |
| 1954 | Chick Harbert | 4 & 3 | Walter Burkemo | Keller CC, St. Paul, MN |
| 1955 | Doug Ford | 4 & 3 | Cary Middlecoff | Meadowbrook CC, Detroit, MI |
| 1956 | Jack Burke | 3 & 2 | Ted Kroll | Blue Hill CC, Boston, MA |
| 1957 | Lionel Hebert | 2 & 1 | Dow Finsterwald | Miami Valley CC, Dayton, OH |
| 1958 | Dow Finsterwald | 276 | Billy Casper | Llanerch CC, Havertown, PA |
| 1959 | Bob Rosburg | 277 | Jerry Barber | Minneapolis GC, St. Louis Park, MN |
| | | | Doug Sanders | |

## PGA Championship *(Cont.)*

| Year | Winner | Score | Runner-Up | Site |
|------|--------|-------|-----------|------|
| 1960 | Jay Hebert | 281 | Jim Ferrier | Firestone CC, Akron, OH |
| 1961 | Jerry Barber* (67) | 277 | Don January (68) | Olympia Fields CC, Olympia Fields, IL |
| 1962 | Gary Player | 278 | Bob Goalby | Aronimink GC, Newton Square, PA |
| 1963 | Jack Nicklaus | 279 | Dave Ragan Jr. | Dallas Athletic Club, Dallas, TX |
| 1964 | Bobby Nichols | 271 | Jack Nicklaus<br>Arnold Palmer | Columbus CC, Columbus, OH |
| 1965 | Dave Marr | 280 | Billy Casper<br>Jack Nicklaus | Laurel Valley CC, Ligonier, PA |
| 1966 | Al Geiberger | 280 | Dudley Wysong | Firestone CC, Akron, OH |
| 1967 | Don January* (69) | 281 | Don Massengale (71) | Columbine CC, Littleton, CO |
| 1968 | Julius Boros | 281 | Bob Charles<br>Arnold Palmer | Pecan Valley CC, San Antonio, TX |
| 1969 | Ray Floyd | 276 | Gary Player | NCR CC, Dayton, OH |
| 1970 | Dave Stockton | 279 | Arnold Palmer<br>Bob Murphy | Southern Hills CC, Tulsa, OK |
| 1971 | Jack Nicklaus | 281 | Billy Casper | PGA Nat'l GC, Palm Beach Gardens, FL |
| 1972 | Gary Player | 281 | Tommy Aaron<br>Jim Jamieson | Oakland Hills CC, Birmingham, MI |
| 1973 | Jack Nicklaus | 277 | Bruce Crampton | Canterbury GC, Cleveland, OH |
| 1974 | Lee Trevino | 276 | Jack Nicklaus | Tanglewood GC, Winston-Salem, NC |
| 1975 | Jack Nicklaus | 276 | Bruce Crampton | Firestone CC, Akron, OH |
| 1976 | Dave Stockton | 281 | Ray Floyd<br>Don January | Congressional CC, Bethesda, MD |
| 1977† | Lanny Wadkins* (4-4-4) | 282 | Gene Littler (4-4-5) | Pebble Beach GL, Pebble Beach, CA |
| 1978 | John Mahaffey* (4–3) | 276 | Jerry Pate (4–4)<br>Tom Watson (4–5) | Oakmont CC, Oakmont, PA |
| 1979 | David Graham* (4-4-2) | 272 | Ben Crenshaw (4-4-4) | Oakland Hills CC, Birmingham, MI |
| 1980 | Jack Nicklaus | 274 | Andy Bean | Oak Hill CC, Rochester, NY |
| 1981 | Larry Nelson | 273 | Fuzzy Zoeller | Atlanta Athletic Club, Duluth, GA |
| 1982 | Raymond Floyd | 272 | Lanny Wadkins | Southern Hills CC, Tulsa, OK |
| 1983 | Hal Sutton | 274 | Jack Nicklaus | Riviera CC, Pacific Palisades, CA |
| 1984 | Lee Trevino | 273 | Gary Player<br>Lanny Wadkins | Shoal Creek, Birmingham, AL |
| 1985 | Hubert Green | 278 | Lee Trevino | Cherry Hills CC, Denver, CO |
| 1986 | Bob Tway | 276 | Greg Norman | Inverness CC, Toledo, OH |
| 1987 | Larry Nelson* (4) | 287 | Lanny Wadkins (5) | PGA Natl GC, Palm Beach Gardens, FL |
| 1988 | Jeff Sluman | 272 | Paul Azinger | Oak Tree GC, Edmond, OK |
| 1989 | Payne Stewart | 276 | Mike Reid | Kemper Lakes GC, Hawthorn Woods, IL |
| 1990 | Wayne Grady | 282 | Fred Couples | Shoal Creek, Birmingham, AL |
| 1991 | John Daly | 276 | Bruce Lietzke | Crooked Stick GC, Carmel, IN |
| 1992 | Nick Price | 278 | Jim Gallagher Jr. | Bellerive CC, St. Louis, MO |
| 1993 | Paul Azinger* (4–4) | 272 | Greg Norman (4–5) | Inverness CC, Toledo, OH |
| 1994 | Nick Price | 269 | Corey Pavin | Southern Hills CC, Tulsa, OK |
| 1995 | Steve Elkington* (3) | 267 | Colin Montgomerie (4) | Riviera CC, Pacific Palisades, CA |
| 1996 | Mark Brooks* (3) | 277 | Kenny Perry (x) | Valhalla GC, Louisville, KY |
| 1997 | Davis Love III | 269 | Justin Leonard | Winged Foot GC, Mamaroneck, NY |
| 1998 | Vijay Singh | 271 | Steve Stricker | Sahalee CC, Redmond, WA |
| 1999 | Tiger Woods | 277 | Sergio Garcia | Medinah CC, Medinah, IL |
| 2000‡ | Tiger Woods* (3-4-5) | 270 | Bob May (4-4-x) | Valhalla GC, Louisville, KY |
| 2001 | David Toms | 265 | Phil Mickelson | Atlanta AC, Duluth, GA |
| 2002 | Rich Beem | 278 | Tiger Woods | Hazeltine National GC, Shaska, MN |
| 2003 | Shaun Micheel | 276 | Chad Campbell | Oak Hill CC, Rochester, NY |
| 2004 | Vijay Singh* | 280 | Chris DiMarco | Whistling Straits GC, Kohler, WI |
| 2005 | Phil Mickelson | 276 | Steve Elkington | Baltusrol GC, Springfield, NJ |
| 2006 | Tiger Woods | 270 | Shaun Micheel | Medinah CC, Medinah, IL |
| 2007 | Tiger Woods | 272 | Woody Austin | Southern Hills CC, Tulsa, OK |
| 2008 | Padraig Harrington | 277 | Sergio Garcia | Oakland Hills CC, Birmingham, MI |
| 2009 | Y.E. Yang | 280 | Tiger Woods | Hazeltine National GC, Chaska, MN |
| 2010 | Martin Kaymer* (4-2-5) | 277 | Bubba Watson (3-3-6) | Whistling Straits GC, Kohler, WI |
| 2011 | Keegan Bradley* (3-3-4) | 272 | Jason Dufner (4-4-3) | Atlanta Athletic Club, Johns Creek, GA |

*Winner in playoff. †Playoff changed from 18 holes to sudden death. ‡ Playoff changed from sudden death to three-hole playoff.

## THE PGA TOUR

### Most Career Wins†

| | Wins | | Wins | | Wins |
|---|---|---|---|---|---|
| Sam Snead | 82 | Billy Casper | 51 | Lloyd Mangrum | 36 |
| Jack Nicklaus | 73 | Walter Hagen | 44 | *Vijay Singh | 34 |
| *Tiger Woods | 71 | Cary Middlecoff | 40 | Horton Smith | 32 |
| Ben Hogan | 64 | Gene Sarazen | 39 | Harry Cooper | 31 |
| Arnold Palmer | 62 | Tom Watson | 39 | Jimmy Demaret | 31 |
| Byron Nelson | 52 | *Phil Mickelson | 39 | Leo Diegel | 30 |

† Through 10/03/11. * Active player.

### Alltime Major Championship Winners

| | Masters | U.S. Open | British Open | PGA Champ. | U.S. Amateur | British Amateur | Total |
|---|---|---|---|---|---|---|---|
| Jack Nicklaus | 6 | 4 | 3 | 5 | 2 | 0 | 20 |
| *Tiger Woods | 4 | 3 | 3 | 4 | 3 | 0 | 17 |
| Bobby Jones | 0 | 4 | 3 | 0 | 5 | 1 | 13 |
| Walter Hagen | 0 | 2 | 4 | 5 | 0 | 0 | 11 |
| Ben Hogan | 2 | 4 | 1 | 2 | 0 | 0 | 9 |
| Gary Player | 3 | 1 | 3 | 2 | 0 | 0 | 9 |
| John Ball | 0 | 0 | 1 | 0 | 0 | 8 | 9 |
| Arnold Palmer | 4 | 1 | 2 | 0 | 1 | 0 | 8 |
| Tom Watson | 2 | 1 | 5 | 0 | 0 | 0 | 8 |
| Harold Hilton | 0 | 0 | 2 | 0 | 1 | 4 | 7 |
| Gene Sarazen | 1 | 2 | 1 | 3 | 0 | 0 | 7 |
| Sam Snead | 3 | 0 | 1 | 3 | 0 | 0 | 7 |
| Harry Vardon | 0 | 1 | 6 | 0 | 0 | 0 | 7 |

*Active PGA Tour player.

### Alltime Multiple Professional Major Winners

| MASTERS | | U.S. OPEN | | BRITISH OPEN | | PGA CHAMPIONSHIP | |
|---|---|---|---|---|---|---|---|
| Jack Nicklaus | 6 | Willie Anderson | 4 | Harry Vardon | 6 | Walter Hagen | 5 |
| Arnold Palmer | 4 | Ben Hogan | 4 | James Braid | 5 | Jack Nicklaus | 5 |
| *Tiger Woods | 4 | Bobby Jones | 4 | J.H. Taylor | 5 | *Tiger Woods | 4 |
| Jimmy Demaret | 3 | Jack Nicklaus | 4 | Peter Thomson | 5 | Gene Sarazen | 3 |
| Nick Faldo | 3 | Hale Irwin | 3 | Tom Watson | 5 | Sam Snead | 3 |
| *Phil Mickelson | 3 | *Tiger Woods | 3 | Walter Hagen | 4 | Jim Barnes | 2 |
| Gary Player | 3 | Julius Boros | 2 | Bobby Locke | 4 | Leo Diegel | 2 |
| Sam Snead | 3 | Billy Casper | 2 | Tom Morris Sr. | 4 | Raymond Floyd | 2 |
| Seve Ballesteros | 2 | *Ernie Els | 2 | Tom Morris Jr. | 4 | Ben Hogan | 2 |
| Ben Crenshaw | 2 | *Retief Goosen | 2 | Willie Park | 4 | Byron Nelson | 2 |
| Ben Hogan | 2 | Ralph Guldahl | 2 | Jamie Anderson | 3 | Larry Nelson | 2 |
| *Bernhard Langer | 2 | Walter Hagen | 2 | Seve Ballesteros | 3 | Gary Player | 2 |
| Byron Nelson | 2 | *Lee Janzen | 2 | Henry Cotton | 3 | Paul Runyan | 2 |
| *José María Olazábal | 2 | John McDermott | 2 | Nick Faldo | 3 | Denny Shute | 2 |
| Horton Smith | 2 | Cary Middlecoff | 2 | Robert Ferguson | 3 | Dave Stockton | 2 |
| Tom Watson | 2 | Andy North | 2 | Bobby Jones | 3 | Lee Trevino | 2 |
| | | Gene Sarazen | 2 | Jack Nicklaus | 3 | *Vijay Singh | 2 |
| | | Alex Smith | 2 | Gary Player | 3 | | |
| | | Payne Stewart | 2 | *Tiger Woods | 3 | | |
| | | Curtis Strange | 2 | *Padraig Harrington | 2 | | |
| | | Lee Trevino | 2 | Harold Hilton | 2 | | |
| | | | | Bob Martin | 2 | | |
| | | | | *Greg Norman | 2 | | |
| | | | | Arnold Palmer | 2 | | |
| | | | | Willie Park Jr. | 2 | | |
| | | | | Lee Trevino | 2 | | |

*Active PGA Tour player.

## THE PGA TOUR (Cont.)
### Season Money Leaders

| Year | Player | Earnings ($) |
|---|---|---|
| 1934 | Paul Runyan | 6,767.00 |
| 1935 | Johnny Revolta | 9,543.00 |
| 1936 | Horton Smith | 7,682.00 |
| 1937 | Harry Cooper | 14,138.69 |
| 1938 | Sam Snead | 19,534.49 |
| 1939 | Henry Picard | 10,303.00 |
| 1940 | Ben Hogan | 10,655.00 |
| 1941 | Ben Hogan | 18,358.00 |
| 1942 | Ben Hogan | 13,143.00 |
| 1943 | No statistics compiled | |
| 1944 | Byron Nelson* | 37,967.69 |
| 1945 | Byron Nelson* | 63,335.66 |
| 1946 | Ben Hogan | 42,556.16 |
| 1947 | Jimmy Demaret | 27,936.83 |
| 1948 | Ben Hogan | 32,112.00 |
| 1949 | Sam Snead | 31,593.83 |
| 1950 | Sam Snead | 35,758.83 |
| 1951 | Lloyd Mangrum | 26,088.83 |
| 1952 | Julius Boros | 37,032.97 |
| 1953 | Lew Worsham | 34,002.00 |
| 1954 | Bob Toski | 65,819.81 |
| 1955 | Julius Boros | 63,121.55 |
| 1956 | Ted Kroll | 72,835.83 |
| 1957 | Dick Mayer | 65,835.00 |
| 1958 | Arnold Palmer | 42,607.50 |
| 1959 | Art Wall | 53,167.60 |
| 1960 | Arnold Palmer | 75,262.85 |
| 1961 | Gary Player | 64,540.45 |
| 1962 | Arnold Palmer | 81,448.33 |
| 1963 | Arnold Palmer | 128,230.00 |
| 1964 | Jack Nicklaus | 113,284.50 |
| 1965 | Jack Nicklaus | 140,752.14 |
| 1966 | Billy Casper | 121,944.92 |
| 1967 | Jack Nicklaus | 188,998.08 |
| 1968 | Billy Casper | 205,168.67 |
| 1969 | Frank Beard | 164,707.11 |
| 1970 | Lee Trevino | 157,037.63 |
| 1971 | Jack Nicklaus | 244,490.50 |
| 1972 | Jack Nicklaus | 320,542.26 |
| 1973 | Jack Nicklaus | 308,362.10 |
| 1974 | Johnny Miller | 353,021.59 |
| 1975 | Jack Nicklaus | 298,149.17 |
| 1976 | Jack Nicklaus | 266,438.57 |
| 1977 | Tom Watson | 310,653.16 |
| 1978 | Tom Watson | 362,428.93 |
| 1979 | Tom Watson | 462,636.00 |
| 1980 | Tom Watson | 530,808.33 |
| 1981 | Tom Kite | 375,698.84 |
| 1982 | Craig Stadler | 446,462.00 |
| 1983 | Hal Sutton | 426,668.00 |
| 1984 | Tom Kite | 476,260.00 |
| 1985 | Curtis Strange | 542,321.00 |
| 1986 | Greg Norman | 653,296.00 |
| 1987 | Curtis Strange | 925,941.00 |
| 1988 | Curtis Strange | 1,147,644.00 |
| 1989 | Tom Kite | 1,395,278.00 |
| 1990 | Greg Norman | 1,165,477.00 |
| 1991 | Corey Pavin | 979,430.00 |
| 1992 | Fred Couples | 1,344,188.00 |
| 1993 | Nick Price | 1,478,557.00 |
| 1994 | Nick Price | 1,499,927.00 |
| 1995 | Greg Norman | 1,654,959.00 |
| 1996 | Tom Lehman | 1,780,159.00 |
| 1997 | Tiger Woods | 2,066,833.00 |
| 1998 | David Duval | 2,591,031.00 |
| 1999 | Tiger Woods | 6,616,585.00 |
| 2000 | Tiger Woods | 9,188,321.00 |
| 2001 | Tiger Woods | 5,687,777.00 |
| 2002 | Tiger Woods | 6,912,625.00 |
| 2003 | Vijay Singh | 7,573,907.00 |
| 2004 | Vijay Singh | 10,905,166.00 |
| 2005 | Tiger Woods | 10,628,024.00 |
| 2006 | Tiger Woods | 9,941,563.00 |
| 2007 | Tiger Woods | 10,867,052.00 |
| 2008 | Vijay Singh | 6,601,094.00 |
| 2009 | Tiger Woods | 10,508,163.00 |
| 2010 | Matt Kuchar | 4,910,477.00 |

* War bonds. Note: Total money listed from 1968 through 1974. Official money listed from 1975 on.

### Year-by-Year Statistical Leaders

| | SCORING AVERAGE | | DRIVING DISTANCE | Yds | | DRIVING ACCURACY | |
|---|---|---|---|---|---|---|---|
| 1980 | Lee Trevino | 69.73 | Dan Pohl | 274.3 | Mike Reid | 79.5 |
| 1981 | Tom Kite | 69.80 | Dan Pohl | 280.1 | Calvin Peete | 81.9 |
| 1982 | Tom Kite | 70.21 | Bill Calfee | 275.3 | Calvin Peete | 84.6 |
| 1983 | Raymond Floyd | 70.61 | John McComish | 277.4 | Calvin Peete | 81.3 |
| 1984 | Calvin Peete | 70.56 | Bill Glasson | 276.5 | Calvin Peete | 77.5 |
| 1985 | Don Pooley | 70.36 | Andy Bean | 278.2 | Calvin Peete | 80.6 |
| 1986 | Scott Hoch | 70.08 | Davis Love III | 285.7 | Calvin Peete | 81.7 |
| 1987 | David Frost | 70.09 | John McComish | 283.9 | Calvin Peete | 83.0 |
| 1988 | Greg Norman | 69.38 | Steve Thomas | 284.6 | Calvin Peete | 82.5 |
| 1989 | Payne Stewart | 69.485† | Ed Humenik | 280.9 | Calvin Peete | 82.6 |
| 1990 | Greg Norman | 69.10 | Tom Purtzer | 279.6 | Calvin Peete | 83.7 |
| 1991 | Fred Couples | 69.59 | John Daly | 288.9 | Hale Irwin | 78.3 |
| 1992 | Fred Couples | 69.38 | John Daly | 283.4 | Doug Tewell | 82.3 |
| 1993 | Greg Norman | 68.90 | John Daly | 288.9 | Doug Tewell | 82.5 |
| 1994 | Greg Norman | 68.81 | Davis Love III | 283.8 | David Edwards | 81.6 |
| 1995 | Greg Norman | 69.06 | John Daly | 289.0 | Fred Funk | 81.3 |
| 1996 | Tom Lehman | 69.32 | John Daly | 288.8 | Fred Funk | 78.7 |
| 1997 | Nick Price | 68.98 | John Daly | 302.0 | Allen Doyle | 80.8 |
| 1998 | David Duval | 69.13 | John Daly | 299.4 | Bruce Fleisher | 81.4 |
| 1999 | Tiger Woods | 68.43 | John Daly | 305.6 | Fred Funk | 80.2 |
| 2000 | Tiger Woods | 67.79 | John Daly | 301.4 | Fred Funk | 79.7 |
| 2001 | Tiger Woods | 68.81 | John Daly | 306.7 | Joe Durant | 81.1 |
| 2002 | Tiger Woods | 68.13 | John Daly | 306.8 | Fred Funk | 81.2 |
| 2003 | Tiger Woods | 68.41 | Hank Kuehne | 321.4 | Fred Funk | 77.9 |
| 2004 | Vijay Singh | 69.19 | Hank Kuehne | 314.4 | Fred Funk | 77.2 |
| 2005 | Tiger Woods | 68.66 | Scott Hend | 318.9 | Jeff Hart | 76.0 |
| 2006 | Tiger Woods | 68.11 | Bubba Watson | 319.6 | Joe Durant | 78.4 |
| 2007 | Tiger Woods | 67.79 | Bubba Watson | 315.2 | Jose Coceres | 75.5 |
| 2008 | Sergio Garcia | 69.12 | Bubba Watson | 315.1 | Olin Browne | 80.4 |
| 2009 | Tiger Woods | 68.05 | Robert Garrigus | 312.3 | Joe Durant | 74.8 |
| 2010 | Matt Kuchar | 69.61 | Robert Garrigus | 315.5 | Omar Uresti | 76.1 |

Note: Scoring average per round, with adjustments made at each round for the field's course scoring average.

Note: Average uses distance of two tee shots on a predetermined par-four or par-five hole (front & back).

Note: Percentage of fairways hit on number of par-four and par-five holes played; par-three holes excluded.

# THE PGA TOUR (Cont.)

### Year by Year Statistical Leaders (Cont.)

## GREENS IN REGULATION

| | | |
|---|---|---|
| 1980 | Jack Nicklaus | 72.1 |
| 1981 | Calvin Peete | 73.1 |
| 1982 | Calvin Peete | 72.4 |
| 1983 | Calvin Peete | 71.4 |
| 1984 | Andy Bean | 72.1 |
| 1985 | John Mahaffey | 71.9 |
| 1986 | John Mahaffey | 72.0 |
| 1987 | Gil Morgan | 73.3 |
| 1988 | John Adams | 73.9 |
| 1989 | Bruce Lietzke | 72.6 |
| 1990 | Doug Tewell | 70.9 |
| 1991 | Bruce Lietzke | 73.3 |
| 1992 | Tim Simpson | 74.0 |
| 1993 | Fuzzy Zoeller | 73.6 |
| 1994 | Bill Glasson | 73.0 |
| 1995 | Lenny Clements | 72.3 |
| 1996 | Fred Couples | 71.8 |
| | Mark O'Meara | 71.8 |
| 1997 | Tom Lehman | 72.7 |
| 1998 | Hal Sutton | 71.3 |
| 1999 | Tiger Woods | 71.4 |
| 2000 | Tiger Woods | 75.2 |
| 2001 | Tom Lehman | 74.5 |
| 2002 | Tiger Woods | 74.0 |
| 2003 | Joe Durant | 72.9 |
| 2004 | Joe Durant | 73.3 |
| 2005 | Sergio Garcia | 71.8 |
| 2006 | Tiger Woods | 74.2 |
| 2007 | Tiger Woods | 71.0 |
| 2008 | Joe Durant | 71.1 |
| 2009 | John Senden | 70.9 |
| 2010 | John Senden | 72.5 |

Note: Average of greens reached in regulation out of total holes played; hole is considered hit in regulation if any part of the ball rests on the putting surface in two shots less than the hole's par—a par-5 hit in two shots is one green in regulation.

## PUTTING

| | | |
|---|---|---|
| 1980 | Jerry Pate | 28.81 |
| 1981 | Alan Tapie | 28.70 |
| 1982 | Ben Crenshaw | 28.65 |
| 1983 | Morris Hatalsky | 27.96 |
| 1984 | Gary McCord | 28.57 |
| 1985 | Craig Stadler | 28.627† |
| 1986 | Greg Norman | 1.736 |
| 1987 | Ben Crenshaw | 1.743 |
| 1988 | Don Pooley | 1.729 |
| 1989 | Steve Jones | 1.734 |
| 1990 | Larry Rinker | 1.7467† |
| 1991 | Jay Don Blake | 1.7326† |
| 1992 | Mark O'Meara | 1.731 |
| 1993 | David Frost | 1.739 |
| 1994 | Loren Roberts | 1.737 |
| 1995 | Jim Furyk | 1.708 |
| 1996 | Brad Faxon | 1.709 |
| 1997 | Don Pooley | 1.718 |
| 1998 | Rick Fehr | 1.722 |
| 1999 | Brad Faxon | 1.723 |
| 2000 | Brad Faxon | 1.704 |

## PUTTING (Cont.)

| | | |
|---|---|---|
| 2001 | David Frost | 1.708 |
| 2002 | Bob Heintz | 1.682 |
| 2003 | John Huston | 1.713 |
| 2004 | Stewart Clink | 1.723 |
| 2005 | Arjun Atwal | 1.710 |
| 2006 | Daniel Chopra | 1.712 |
| 2007 | Tim Clark | 1.727 |
| 2008 | Bob Tway | 1.718 |
| 2009 | Patrick Sheehan | 1.358 |
| 2010 | Jerod Turner | 1.372 |

Note: Average number of putts taken for all holes played; prior to 1986, based on average number of putts per 18 holes.

## SAND SAVES

| | | |
|---|---|---|
| 1980 | Bob Eastwood | 65.4 |
| 1981 | Tom Watson | 60.1 |
| 1982 | Isao Aoki | 60.2 |
| 1983 | Isao Aoki | 62.3 |
| 1984 | Peter Oosterhuis | 64.7 |
| 1985 | Tom Purtzer | 60.8 |
| 1986 | Paul Azinger | 63.8 |
| 1987 | Paul Azinger | 63.2 |
| 1988 | Greg Powers | 63.5 |
| 1989 | Mike Sullivan | 66.0 |
| 1990 | Paul Azinger | 67.2 |
| 1991 | Ben Crenshaw | 64.9 |
| 1992 | Mitch Adcock | 66.9 |
| 1993 | Ken Green | 64.4 |
| 1994 | Corey Pavin | 65.4 |
| 1995 | Billy Mayfair | 68.6 |
| 1996 | Gary Rusnak | 64.0 |
| 1997 | Bob Estes | 70.3 |
| 1998 | Keith Fergus | 71.0 |
| 1999 | Jeff Sluman | 67.3 |
| 2000 | Fred Couples | 67.0 |
| 2001 | Franklin Langham | 68.9 |
| 2002 | J. Olazabal | 64.9 |
| 2003 | Stuart Appleby | 62.1 |
| 2004 | Dan Forsman | 62.3 |
| 2005 | Pat Perez | 63.0 |
| 2006 | Luke Donald | 63.6 |
| 2007 | Tim Clark | 68.1 |
| 2008 | Dudley Hart | 63.7 |
| 2009 | Luke Donald | 64.4 |
| 2010 | Luke Donald | 66.4 |

Note: Percentage of up-and-down efforts from greenside sand traps only—fairway bunkers excluded.

## EAGLES

| | | |
|---|---|---|
| 1980 | Dave Eichelberger | 16 |
| 1981 | Bruce Lietzke | 12 |
| 1982 | Tom Weiskopf | 10 |
| | J.C. Snead | 10 |
| | Andy Bean | 10 |
| 1983 | Chip Beck | 15 |
| 1984 | Gary Hallberg | 15 |
| 1985 | Larry Rinker | 14 |
| 1986 | Joey Sindelar | 16 |
| 1987 | Phil Blackmar | 20 |
| 1988 | Ken Green | 21 |

## EAGLES (Cont.)

| | | |
|---|---|---|
| 1990 | Lon Hinkle | 14 |
| | Duffy Waldorf | 14 |
| 1990 | Paul Azinger | 14 |
| 1991 | Andy Bean | 15 |
| 1992 | Dan Forsman | 18 |
| 1993 | Davis Love III | 15 |
| 1994 | Davis Love III | 18 |
| 1995 | Kelly Gibson | 16 |
| 1996 | Tom Watson | 97.2 |
| 1997 | Tiger Woods | 104.1 |
| 1998 | Davis Love III | 83.3 |
| 1999 | Vijay Singh | 104.8 |
| 2000 | Tiger Woods | 72.0 |
| 2001 | Phil Mickelson | 73.8 |
| 2002 | John Daly | 78.4 |
| 2003 | Tiger Woods | 76.5 |
| 2004 | Nick Price | 90.0 |
| 2005 | Brenden Pappas | 70.6 |
| 2006 | J.B. Holmes | 72.9 |
| 2007 | Chris Tidland | 88.5 |
| 2008 | Chad Campbell | 105.8 |
| 2009 | Bubba Watson | 75.2 |
| 2010 | Dustin Johnson | 92.3 |

Note: Total of eagles scored 1980–1995. Since 1996 winner determined by number of holes played per eagle.

## BIRDIES

| | | |
|---|---|---|
| 1980 | Andy Bean | 388 |
| 1981 | Vance Heafner | 388 |
| 1982 | Andy Bean | 392 |
| 1983 | Hal Sutton | 399 |
| 1984 | Mark O'Meara | 419 |
| 1985 | Joey Sindelar | 411 |
| 1986 | Joey Sindelar | 415 |
| 1987 | Dan Forsman | 409 |
| 1988 | Dan Forsman | 465 |
| 1989 | Ted Schulz | 415 |
| 1990 | Mike Donald | 401 |
| 1991 | Scott Hoch | 446 |
| 1992 | Jeff Sluman | 417 |
| 1993 | John Huston | 426 |
| 1994 | Brad Bryant | 397 |
| 1995 | Steve Lowery | 410 |
| 1996 | Fred Couples | 4.20 |
| 1997 | Tiger Woods | 4.25 |
| 1998 | David Duval | 4.29 |
| 1999 | Tiger Woods | 4.46 |
| 2000 | Tiger Woods | 4.92 |
| 2001 | Phil Mickelson | 4.49 |
| 2002 | Tiger Woods | 4.47 |
| 2003 | Vijay Singh | 4.41 |
| 2004 | Vijay Singh | 4.40 |
| 2005 | Tiger Woods | 4.57 |
| 2006 | Tiger Woods | 4.65 |
| 2007 | Tiger Woods | 4.03 |
| 2008 | Ryan Palmer | 4.16 |
| 2009 | Tiger Woods | 4.15 |
| 2010 | Tom Gillis | 4.06 |

Note: Total of birdies scored 1980–95. Since 1996, winner determined by average number of birdies per round.

† Number had to be carried to extra decimal place to determine winner.

## THE PGA TOUR (Cont.)

### Year-by-Year Statistical Leaders (Cont.)

| ALL-AROUND | | ALL-AROUND (Cont.) | | ALL-AROUND (Cont.) | |
|---|---|---|---|---|---|
| 1987 | Dan Pohl 170 | 1997 | Bill Glasson 282 | 2007 | Tiger Woods 240 |
| 1988 | Payne Stewart 170 | 1998 | John Huston 151 | 2008 | Pat Perez 323 |
| 1989 | Paul Azinger 250 | 1999 | Tiger Woods 120 | 2009 | Tiger Woods 151 |
| 1990 | Paul Azinger 162 | 2000 | Tiger Woods 113 | 2010 | Matt Kuchar 270 |
| 1991 | Scott Hoch 283 | 2001 | Phil Mickelson 174 | | |
| 1992 | Fred Couples 256 | 2002 | Phil Mickelson 259 | | |
| 1993 | Gil Morgan 252 | 2003 | Tiger Woods 206 | | |
| 1994 | Bob Estes 227 | 2004 | Jeff Ogilvy 268 | | |
| 1995 | Justin Leonard 323 | 2005 | Tiger Woods 265 | | |
| 1996 | Fred Couples 214 | 2006 | Tiger Woods 216 | | |

Note: Sum of the places of standing from the other statistical categories; the player with the number closest to zero leads.

### PGA Player of the Year Award

| | | | | | |
|---|---|---|---|---|---|
| 1948 | Ben Hogan | 1969 | Orville Moody | 1990 | Wayne Levi |
| 1949 | Sam Snead | 1970 | Billy Casper | 1991 | Fred Couples |
| 1950 | Ben Hogan | 1971 | Lee Trevino | 1992 | Fred Couples |
| 1951 | Ben Hogan | 1972 | Jack Nicklaus | 1993 | Nick Price |
| 1952 | Julius Boros | 1973 | Jack Nicklaus | 1994 | Nick Price |
| 1953 | Ben Hogan | 1974 | Johnny Miller | 1995 | Greg Norman |
| 1954 | Ed Furgol | 1975 | Jack Nicklaus | 1996 | Tom Lehman |
| 1955 | Doug Ford | 1976 | Jack Nicklaus | 1997 | Tiger Woods |
| 1956 | Jack Burke | 1977 | Tom Watson | 1998 | David Duval |
| 1957 | Dick Mayer | 1978 | Tom Watson | 1999 | Tiger Woods |
| 1958 | Dow Finsterwald | 1979 | Tom Watson | 2000 | Tiger Woods |
| 1959 | Art Wall | 1980 | Tom Watson | 2001 | Tiger Woods |
| 1960 | Arnold Palmer | 1981 | Bill Rogers | 2002 | Tiger Woods |
| 1961 | Jerry Barber | 1982 | Tom Watson | 2003 | Tiger Woods |
| 1962 | Arnold Palmer | 1983 | Hal Sutton | 2004 | Vijay Singh |
| 1963 | Julius Boros | 1984 | Tom Watson | 2005 | Tiger Woods |
| 1964 | Ken Venturi | 1985 | Lanny Wadkins | 2006 | Tiger Woods |
| 1965 | Dave Marr | 1986 | Bob Tway | 2007 | Tiger Woods |
| 1966 | Billy Casper | 1987 | Paul Azinger | 2008 | Padraig Harrington |
| 1967 | Jack Nicklaus | 1988 | Curtis Strange | 2009 | Tiger Woods |
| 1968 | Not awarded | 1989 | Tom Kite | 2010 | Jim Furyk |

### Vardon Trophy: Scoring Average

| Year | Winner | Avg | Year | Winner | Avg | Year | Winner | Avg |
|---|---|---|---|---|---|---|---|---|
| 1937 | Harry Cooper | *500 | 1965 | Billy Casper | 70.85 | 1989 | Greg Norman | 69.49 |
| 1938 | Sam Snead | 520 | 1966 | Billy Casper | 70.27 | 1990 | Greg Norman | 69.10 |
| 1939 | Byron Nelson | 473 | 1967 | Arnold Palmer | 70.18 | 1991 | Fred Couples | 69.59 |
| 1940 | Ben Hogan | 423 | 1968 | Billy Casper | 69.82 | 1992 | Fred Couples | 69.38 |
| 1941 | Ben Hogan | 494 | 1969 | Dave Hill | 70.34 | 1993 | Nick Price | 69.11 |
| 1942–46 | No award | | 1970 | Lee Trevino | 70.64 | 1994 | Greg Norman | 68.81 |
| 1947 | Jimmy Demaret | 69.90 | 1971 | Lee Trevino | 70.27 | 1995 | Steve Elkington | 69.62 |
| 1948 | Ben Hogan | 69.30 | 1972 | Lee Trevino | 70.89 | 1996 | Tom Lehman | 69.32 |
| 1949 | Sam Snead | 69.37 | 1973 | Bruce Crampton | 70.57 | 1997 | Nick Price | 68.98 |
| 1950 | Sam Snead | 69.23 | 1974 | Lee Trevino | 70.53 | 1998 | David Duval | 69.13 |
| 1951 | Lloyd Mangrum | 70.05 | 1975 | Bruce Crampton | 70.51 | 1999 | Tiger Woods | 68.43 |
| 1952 | Jack Burke | 70.54 | 1976 | Don January | 70.56 | 2000 | Tiger Woods | 67.79 |
| 1953 | Lloyd Mangrum | 70.22 | 1977 | Tom Watson | 70.32 | 2001 | Tiger Woods | 68.81 |
| 1954 | E.J. Harrison | 70.41 | 1978 | Tom Watson | 70.16 | 2002 | Tiger Woods | 68.13 |
| 1955 | Sam Snead | 69.86 | 1979 | Tom Watson | 70.27 | 2003 | Tiger Woods | 68.41 |
| 1956 | Cary Middlecoff | 70.35 | 1980 | Lee Trevino | 69.73 | 2004 | Vijay Singh | 68.84 |
| 1957 | Dow Finsterwald | 70.30 | 1981 | Tom Kite | 69.80 | 2005 | Tiger Woods | 68.66 |
| 1958 | Bob Rosburg | 70.11 | 1982 | Tom Kite | 70.21 | 2006 | Jim Furyk | 68.86 |
| 1959 | Art Wall | 70.35 | 1983 | Raymond Floyd | 70.61 | 2007 | Tiger Woods | 67.79 |
| 1960 | Billy Casper | 69.95 | 1984 | Calvin Peete | 70.56 | 2008 | Sergio Garcia | 69.12 |
| 1961 | Arnold Palmer | 69.85 | 1985 | Don Pooley | 70.36 | 2009 | Tiger Woods | 68.05 |
| 1962 | Arnold Palmer | 70.27 | 1986 | Scott Hoch | 70.08 | 2010 | Matt Kuchar | 69.61 |
| 1963 | Billy Casper | 70.58 | 1987 | Don Pohl | 70.25 | | | |
| 1964 | Arnold Palmer | 70.01 | 1988 | Chip Beck | 69.46 | | | |

*Point system used, 1937–41. NOTE: As of 1988, based on minimum of 60 rounds per year. Adjusted for average score of field in tournaments entered.

# THE MAJOR TOURNAMENTS
## LPGA Championship

| Year | Winner | Score | Runner-Up | Site |
|------|--------|-------|-----------|------|
| 1955 | Beverly Hanson†(4 & 3) | 220 | Louise Suggs | Orchard Ridge CC, Ft Wayne, IN |
| 1956 | Marlene Hagge* | 291 | Patty Berg | Forest Lake CC, Detroit, MI |
| 1957 | Louise Suggs | 285 | Wiffi Smith | Churchill Valley CC, Pittsburgh, PA |
| 1958 | Mickey Wright | 288 | Fay Crocker | Churchill Valley CC, Pittsburgh, PA |
| 1959 | Betsy Rawls | 288 | Patty Berg | Sheraton Hotel CC, French Lick, IN |
| 1960 | Mickey Wright | 292 | Louise Suggs | Sheraton Hotel CC, French Lick, IN |
| 1961 | Mickey Wright | 287 | Louise Suggs | Stardust CC, Las Vegas, NV |
| 1962 | Judy Kimball | 282 | Shirley Spork | Stardust CC, Las Vegas, NV |
| 1963 | Mickey Wright | 294 | Mary Lena Faulk Mary Mills Louise Suggs | Stardust CC, Las Vegas, NV |
| 1964 | Mary Mills | 278 | Mickey Wright | Stardust CC, Las Vegas, NV |
| 1965 | Sandra Haynie | 279 | Clifford A. Creed | Stardust CC, Las Vegas, NV |
| 1966 | Gloria Ehret | 282 | Mickey Wright | Stardust CC, Las Vegas, NV |
| 1967 | Kathy Whitworth | 284 | Shirley Englehorn | Pleasant Valley CC, Sutton, MA |
| 1968 | Sandra Post* | 294 | Kathy Whitworth (75) | Pleasant Valley CC, Sutton, MA |
| 1969 | Betsy Rawls | 293 | Susie Berning Carol Mann | Concord GC, Kiameshia Lake, NY |
| 1970 | Shirley Englehorn* | 285 | Kathy Whitworth (78) | Pleasant Valley CC, Sutton, MA |
| 1971 | Kathy Whitworth | 288 | Kathy Ahern | Pleasant Valley CC, Sutton, MA |
| 1972 | Kathy Ahern | 293 | Jane Blalock | Pleasant Valley CC, Sutton, MA |
| 1973 | Mary Mills | 288 | Betty Burfeindt | Pleasant Valley CC, Sutton, MA |
| 1974 | Sandra Haynie | 288 | JoAnne Carner | Pleasant Valley CC, Sutton, MA |
| 1975 | Kathy Whitworth | 288 | Sandra Haynie | Pine Ridge GC, Baltimore, MD |
| 1976 | Betty Burfeindt | 287 | Judy Rankin | Pine Ridge GC, Baltimore, MD |
| 1977 | Chako Higuchi | 279 | Pat Bradley Sandra Post Judy Rankin | Bay Tree Golf Plantation, N Myrtle Beach, SC |
| 1978 | Nancy Lopez | 275 | Amy Alcott | Jack Nicklaus GC, Kings Island, OH |
| 1979 | Donna Caponi | 279 | Jerilyn Britz | Jack Nicklaus GC, Kings Island, OH |
| 1980 | Sally Little | 285 | Jane Blalock | Jack Nicklaus GC, Kings Island, OH |
| 1981 | Donna Caponi | 280 | Jerilyn Britz Pat Meyers | Jack Nicklaus GC, Kings Island, OH |
| 1982 | Jan Stephenson | 279 | JoAnne Carner | Jack Nicklaus GC, Kings Island, OH |
| 1983 | Patty Sheehan | 279 | Sandra Haynie | Jack Nicklaus GC, Kings Island, OH |
| 1984 | Patty Sheehan | 272 | Beth Daniel Pat Bradley | Jack Nicklaus GC, Kings Island, OH |
| 1985 | Nancy Lopez | 273 | Alice Miller | Jack Nicklaus GC, Kings Island, OH |
| 1986 | Pat Bradley | 277 | Patty Sheehan | Jack Nicklaus GC, Kings Island, OH |
| 1987 | Jane Geddes | 275 | Betsy King | Jack Nicklaus GC, Kings Island, OH |
| 1988 | Sherri Turner | 281 | Amy Alcott | Jack Nicklaus GC, Kings Island, OH |
| 1989 | Nancy Lopez | 274 | Ayako Okamoto | Jack Nicklaus GC, Kings Island, OH |
| 1990 | Beth Daniel | 280 | Rosie Jones | Bethesda CC, Bethesda, MD |
| 1991 | Meg Mallon | 274 | Pat Bradley Ayako Okamoto | Bethesda CC, Bethesda, MD |
| 1992 | Betsy King | 267 | Karen Noble | Bethesda CC, Bethesda, MD |
| 1993 | Patty Sheehan | 275 | Lauri Merten | Bethesda CC, Bethesda, MD |
| 1994 | Laura Davies | 279 | Alice Ritzman | DuPont CC, Wilmington, DE |
| 1995 | Kelly Robbins | 274 | Laura Davies | DuPont CC, Wilmington, DE |
| 1996 | Laura Davies | 213† | Julie Piers | DuPont CC, Wilmington, DE |
| 1997 | Chris Johnson* | 281 | Leta Lindley | DuPont CC, Wilmington, DE |
| 1998 | Se Ri Pak | 273 | Donna Andrews | DuPont CC, Wilmington, DE |
| 1999 | Juli Inkster | 268 | Liselotte Neumann | DuPont CC, Wilmington, DE |
| 2000 | Juli Inkster* | 281 | Stefania Croce | DuPont CC, Wilmington, DE |
| 2001 | Karrie Webb | 270 | Laura Diaz | DuPont CC, Wilmington, DE |
| 2002 | Se Ri Pak | 279 | Beth Daniel | DuPont CC, Wilmington, DE |
| 2003 | Annika Sorenstam* | 278 | Grace Park | DuPont CC, Wilmington, DE |
| 2004 | Annika Sorenstam | 271 | Shi Hyun Ahn | DuPont CC, Wilmington, DE |
| 2005 | Annika Sorenstam | 277 | Michelle Wie | Bulle Rock GC, Havre de Grace, MD |
| 2006 | Se Ri Pak* | 280 | Karrie Webb | Bulle Rock GC, Havre de Grace, MD |
| 2007 | Suzann Pettersen | 274 | Karrie Webb | Bulle Rock GC, Havre de Grace, MD |
| 2008 | Yani Tseng* | 276 | Maria Hjorth | Bulle Rock GC, Havre de Grace, MD |
| 2009 | Anna Nordqvist | 273 | Lindsey Wright | Bulle Rock GC, Havre de Grace, MD |
| 2010 | Cristie Kerr | 269 | Song-Hee Kim | Bulle Rock GC, Havre de Grace, MD |
| 2011 | Yani Tseng | 269 | Morgan Pressel | Locust Hill CC, Rochester, NY |

*Won playoff. †Won match-play final. #Shortened due to rain.

## U.S. Women's Open

| Year | Winner | Score | Runner-Up | Site |
|---|---|---|---|---|
| 1946 | Patty Berg | 5 & 4 | Betty Jameson | Spokane CC, Spokane, WA |
| 1947 | Betty Jameson | 295 | Sally Sessions | Starmount Forest CC, Greensboro, NC |
| | | | Polly Riley | |
| 1948 | Babe Zaharias | 300 | Betty Hicks | Atlantic City CC, Northfield, NJ |
| 1949 | Louise Suggs | 291 | Babe Zaharias | Prince George's G & CC, Landover, MD |
| 1950 | Babe Zaharias | 291 | Betsy Rawls | Rolling Hills CC, Wichita, KS |
| 1951 | Betsy Rawls | 293 | Louise Suggs | Druid Hills GC, Atlanta, GA |
| 1952 | Louise Suggs | 284 | Marlene Bauer | Bala GC, Philadelphia, PA |
| | | | Betty Jameson | |
| 1953 | Betsy Rawls* (71) | 302 | Jackie Pung (77) | CC of Rochester, Rochester, NY |
| 1954 | Babe Zaharias | 291 | Betty Hicks | Salem CC, Peabody, MA |
| 1955 | Fay Crocker | 299 | Mary Lena Faulk | Wichita CC, Wichita, KS |
| | | | Louise Suggs | |
| 1956 | Kathy Cornelius* (75) | 302 | Barbara McIntire (82) | Northland CC, Duluth, MN |
| 1957 | Betsy Rawls | 299 | Patty Berg | Winged Foot GC, Mamaroneck, NY |
| 1958 | Mickey Wright | 290 | Louise Suggs | Forest Lake CC, Detroit, MI |
| 1959 | Mickey Wright | 287 | Louise Suggs | Churchill Valley CC, Pittsburgh |
| 1960 | Betsy Rawls | 292 | Joyce Ziske | Worcester CC, Worcester, MA |
| 1961 | Mickey Wright | 293 | Betsy Rawls | Baltusrol GC (Lower Course), Springfield, NJ |
| 1962 | Murle Breer | 301 | Jo Ann Prentice | Dunes GC, Myrtle Beach, SC |
| | | | Ruth Jessen | |
| 1963 | Mary Mills | 289 | Sandra Haynie | Kenwood CC, Cincinnati,OH |
| | | | Louise Suggs | |
| 1964 | Mickey Wright* (70) | 290 | Ruth Jessen (72) | San Diego CC, Chula Vista, CA |
| 1965 | Carol Mann | 290 | Kathy Cornelius | Atlantic City CC, Northfield, NJ |
| 1966 | Sandra Spuzich | 297 | Carol Mann | Hazeltine Natl GC, Chaska, MN |
| 1967 | Catherine LaCoste | 294 | Susie Berning | Hot Springs GC (Cascades Course), |
| | | | Beth Stone | Hot Springs, VA |
| 1968 | Susie Berning | 289 | Mickey Wright | Moslem Springs GC, Fleetwood, PA |
| 1969 | Donna Caponi | 294 | Peggy Wilson | Scenic Hills CC, Pensacola, FL |
| 1970 | Donna Caponi | 287 | Sandra Haynie | Muskogee CC, Muskogee, OK |
| | | | Sandra Spuzich | |
| 1971 | JoAnne Carner | 288 | Kathy Whitworth | Kahkwa CC, Erie, PA |
| 1972 | Susie Berning | 299 | Kathy Ahern | Winged Foot GC, Mamaroneck, NY |
| | | | Pam Barnett | |
| | | | Judy Rankin | |
| 1973 | Susie Berning | 290 | Gloria Ehret | CC of Rochester, Rochester, NY |
| | | | Shelley Hamlin | |
| 1974 | Sandra Haynie | 295 | Carol Mann | La Grange CC, La Grange, IL |
| | | | Beth Stone | |
| 1975 | Sandra Palmer | 295 | JoAnne Carner | Atlantic City CC, Northfield, NJ |
| | | | Sandra Post | |
| | | | Nancy Lopez | |
| 1976 | JoAnne Carner* (76) | 292 | Sandra Palmer (78) | Rolling Green CC, Springfield, PA |
| 1977 | Hollis Stacy | 292 | Nancy Lopez | Hazeltine Natl GC, Chaska, MN |
| 1978 | Hollis Stacy | 289 | JoAnne Carner | CC of Indianapolis, Indianapolis, IN |
| | | | Sally Little | |
| 1979 | Jerilyn Britz | 284 | Debbie Massey | Brooklawn CC, Fairfield, CT |
| | | | Sandra Palmer | |
| 1980 | Amy Alcott | 280 | Hollis Stacy | Richland CC, Nashville, TN |
| 1981 | Pat Bradley | 279 | Beth Daniel | La Grange CC, La Grange, IL |
| 1982 | Janet Anderson | 283 | Beth Daniel | Del Paso CC, Sacramento,CA |
| | | | Sandra Haynie | |
| | | | Donna White | |
| | | | JoAnne Carner | |
| 1983 | Jan Stephenson | 290 | JoAnne Carner | Cedar Ridge CC, Tulsa, OK |
| | | | Patty Sheehan | |
| 1984 | Hollis Stacy | 290 | Rosie Jones | Salem CC, Peabody, MA |
| 1985 | Kathy Baker | 280 | Judy Dickinson | Baltusrol GC (Upper Course), Springfield, NJ |
| 1986 | Jane Geddes* (71) | 287 | Sally Little (73) | NCR GC, Dayton, OH |
| 1987 | Laura Davies* (71) | 285 | Ayako Okamoto (73) | Plainfield CC, Plainfield, NJ |
| | | | JoAnne Carner (74) | |
| 1988 | Liselotte Neumann | 277 | Patty Sheehan | Baltimore CC, Baltimore, MD |
| 1989 | Betsy King | 278 | Nancy Lopez | Indianwood G & CC, Lake Orion, MI |
| 1990 | Betsy King | 284 | Patty Sheehan | Atlanta Athletic Club, Duluth, GA |
| 1991 | Meg Mallon | 283 | Pat Bradley | Colonial Club, Fort Worth, TX |

### U.S. Women's Open *(Cont.)*

| Year | Winner | Score | Runner-Up | Site |
|------|--------|-------|-----------|------|
| 1992 | Patty Sheehan* (72) | 280 | Juli Inkster | Oakmont CC, Oakmont, PA |
| 1993 | Lauri Merten | 280 | Donna Andrew | Crooked Stick, Carmel, IN |
| | | | Helen Alfredsson | |
| 1994 | Patty Sheehan | 277 | Tammie Green | Indianwood G & CC, Lake Orion, MI |
| 1995 | Annika Sorenstam | 278 | Meg Mallon | The Broadmoor GC, Colorado Springs,CO |
| 1996 | Annika Sorenstam | 272 | Kris Tschetter | Pine Needles GC, Southern Pines, NC |
| 1997 | Alison Nicholas | 274 | Nancy Lopez | Pumpkin Ridge CC, North Plains, OR |
| 1998 | Se Ri Pak† | 290 | Jenny Chuasiriporn | Blackwolf Run Golf Resort, Kohler, WI |
| 1999 | Juli Inkster | 272 | Sherri Turner | Old Waverly GC, West Point, MS |
| 2000 | Karrie Webb | 282 | Cristie Kerr/ Meg Mallon | Merit GC, Libertyville, IL |
| 2001 | Karrie Webb | 273 | Se Ri Pak | Pine Needles GC, Southern Pines, NC |
| 2002 | Juli Inkster | 276 | Annika Sorenstam | Prairie Dunes CC, Hutchinson, KS |
| 2003 | Hilary Lunke* | 283 | Kelly Robbins | Pumpkin Ridge GC, North Plains, OR |
| 2004 | Meg Mallon | 274 | Annika Sorenstam | The Orchards GC, South Hadley, MA |
| 2005 | Birdie Kim | 287 | Brittany Lang | Cherry Hills CC, Cherry Hills Village, CO |
| | | | Morgan Pressel | |
| 2006 | Annika Sorenstam* | 284 | Pat Hurst | Newport CC, Newport, RI |
| 2007 | Cristie Kerr | 279 | Angela Park | Pine Needles GC, Southern Pines, NC |
| | | | Lorena Ochoa | |
| 2008 | Inbee Park | 283 | Helen Alfredsson | Interlachen CC, Edina, MN |
| 2009 | Eun-Hee Ji | 284 | Candie Kung | Saucon Valley CC-Old Course, Bethlehem, PA |
| 2010 | Paula Creamer | 281 | Na Yeon Choi | Oakmont CC, Oakmont, PA |
| 2011 | So Yeon Ryu* | 281 | Hee Kyung Seo | The Broadmoor GC, Colorado Springs,CO |

* Winner in playoff. † Winner on second hole of sudden death after 18-hole playoff ended in a tie.

### Kraft Nabisco Championship

| Year | Winner | Score | Runner-Up | Year | Winner | Score | Runner-Up |
|------|--------|-------|-----------|------|--------|-------|-----------|
| 1972 | Jane Blalock | 213 | Carol Mann | 1993 | Helen Alfredsson | 284 | Amy Benz |
| | | | Judy Rankin | | | | Tina Barrett |
| 1973 | Mickey Wright | 284 | Joyce Kazmierski | | | | Betsy King |
| 1974 | Jo Ann Prentice* | 289 | Jane Blalock | 1994 | Donna Andrews | 276 | Laura Davies |
| | | | Sandra Haynie | 1995 | Nanci Bowen | 285 | Susie Redman |
| 1975 | Sandra Palmer | 283 | Kathy McMullen | 1996 | Patti Sheehan | 281 | Kelly Robbins |
| 1976 | Judy Rankin | 285 | Betty Burfeindt | | | | Meg Mallon |
| 1977 | Kathy Whitworth | 289 | JoAnne Carner | | | | Annika Sorenstam |
| | | | Sally Little | 1997 | Betsy King | 276 | Kris Tschetter |
| 1978 | Sandra Post* | 283 | Penny Pulz | 1998 | Pat Hurst | 281 | Helen Dobson |
| 1979 | Sandra Post | 276 | Nancy Lopez | 1999 | Dottie Pepper | 269 | Meg Mallon |
| 1980 | Donna Caponi | 275 | Amy Alcott | 2000 | Karrie Webb | 274 | Dottie Pepper |
| 1981 | Nancy Lopez | 277 | Carolyn Hill | 2001 | Annika Sorenstam | 281 | five players |
| 1982 | Sally Little | 278 | Hollis Stacy | 2002 | Annika Sorenstam | 280 | Liselotte Neumann |
| | | | Sandra Haynie | 2003 | P. Meunier-Lebouc | 281 | Annika Sorenstam |
| 1983 | Amy Alcott | 282 | Beth Daniel | 2004 | Grace Park | 277 | Aree Song |
| | | | Kathy Whitworth | 2005 | Annika Sorenstam | 273 | Rosie Jones |
| 1984 | Juli Inkster* | 280 | Pat Bradley | 2006 | Karrie Webb* | 279 | Lorena Ochoa |
| 1985 | Alice Miller | 275 | Jan Stephenson | 2007 | Morgan Pressel | 285 | Catriona Matthew |
| 1986 | Pat Bradley | 280 | Val Skinner | | | | Brittany Lincicome |
| 1987 | Betsy King* | 283 | Patty Sheehan | | | | Suzann Pettersen |
| 1988 | Amy Alcott | 274 | Colleen Walker | 2008 | Lorena Ochoa | 277 | Annika Sorenstam |
| 1989 | Juli Inkster | 279 | Tammie Green | 2009 | Brittany Lincicome | 279 | Kristy McPherson |
| | | | JoAnne Carner | | | | Cristie Kerr |
| 1990 | Betsy King | 283 | Kathy Postlewait | 2010 | Yani Tseng | 275 | Suzann Pettersen |
| | | | Shirley Furlong | 2011 | Stacy Lewis | 275 | Yani Tseng |
| 1991 | Amy Alcott | 273 | Dottie Mochrie | | | | |
| 1992 | Dottie Mochrie* | 279 | Juli Inkster | | | | |

*Winner in sudden-death playoff. Note: Designated fourth major in 1983; played at Mission Hills CC, Rancho Mirage, CA.

### du Maurier Classic

| Year | Winner | Score | Runner-Up | Site |
|------|--------|-------|-----------|------|
| 1973 | Jocelyne Bourassa* | 214 | Sandra Haynie<br>Judy Rankin | Montreal GC, Montreal |
| 1974 | Carole Jo Callison | 208 | JoAnne Carner | Candiac GC, Montreal |
| 1975 | JoAnne Carner* | 214 | Carol Mann | St. George's CC, Toronto |
| 1976 | Donna Caponi* | 212 | Judy Rankin | Cedar Brae G & CC, Toronto |
| 1977 | Judy Rankin | 214 | Pat Meyers<br>Sandra Palmer | Lachute G & CC, Montreal |
| 1978 | JoAnne Carner | 278 | Hollis Stacy | St. George's CC, Toronto |
| 1979 | Amy Alcott | 285 | Nancy Lopez | Richelieu Valley CC, Montreal |
| 1980 | Pat Bradley | 277 | JoAnne Carner | St. George's CC, Toronto |
| 1981 | Jan Stephenson | 278 | Nancy Lopez<br>Pat Bradley | Summerlea CC, Dorion, Quebec |
| 1982 | Sandra Haynie | 280 | Beth Daniel | St. George's CC, Toronto |
| 1983 | Hollis Stacy | 277 | JoAnne Carner<br>Alice Miller | Beaconsfield GC, Montreal |
| 1984 | Juli Inkster | 279 | Ayako Okamoto | St. George's G & CC, Toronto |
| 1985 | Pat Bradley | 278 | Jane Geddes | Beaconsfield CC, Montreal |
| 1986 | Pat Bradley* | 276 | Ayako Okamoto | Board of Trade CC, Toronto |
| 1987 | Jody Rosenthal | 272 | Ayako Okamoto | Islesmere GC, Laval, Quebec |
| 1988 | Sally Little | 279 | Laura Davies | Vancouver GC, Coquitlam, British Columbia |
| 1989 | Tammie Green | 279 | Pat Bradley<br>Betsy King | Beaconsfield GC, Montreal |
| 1990 | Cathy Johnston | 276 | Patty Sheehan | Westmount G & CC, Kitchener, Ontario |
| 1991 | Nancy Scranton | 279 | Debbie Massey | Vancouver GC, Coquitlam, British Columbia |
| 1992 | Sherri Steinhauer | 277 | Judy Dickinson | St. Charles CC, Winnipeg, Manitoba |
| 1993 | Brandie Burton | 277 | Betsy King | London Hunt and CC, London, Ontario |
| 1994 | Martha Nause | 279 | Michelle McGann | Ottawa Hunt and GC, Ottawa, Ont. |
| 1995 | Jenny Lidback | 280 | Liselotte Neumann | Beaconsfield GC, Pointe-Claire, Quebec |
| 1996 | Laura Davies | 277 | Nancy Lopez<br>Karrie Webb | Edmonton CC, Edmonton, Alberta |
| 1997 | Colleen Walker | 278 | Liselotte Neumann | Glen Abbey GC, Oakville, Ontario |
| 1998 | Brandie Burton | 270 | Annika Sorenstam | Essex G & CC, Windsor, Ontario |
| 1999 | Karrie Webb | 277 | Laura Davies | Priddis Greens G & CC, Calgary, Alberta |
| 2000 | Meg Mallon | 282 | Rosie Jones | Royal Ottawa GC, Aylmer, Quebec |

*Winner in sudden-death playoff. Note: Designated third major in 1979. Tournament discontinued in 2001.

### Women's British Open

| Year | Winner | Score | Runner-Up | Site |
|------|--------|-------|-----------|------|
| 2001 | Se Ri Pak | 277 | Mi Hyun Kim | Sunningdale GC, Berkshire, England |
| 2002 | Karrie Webb | 273 | Michelle Ellis<br>Paula Marti | Turnberry GC, Ailsa, Scotland |
| 2003 | Annika Sorenstam | 278 | Se Ri Pak | Royal Lytham & St. Annes, England |
| 2004 | Karen Stupples | 269 | Rachel Teske | Sunningdale GC, Berklshire, England |
| 2005 | Jeong Jang | 272 | Sophie Gustafson | Royal Birkdale CC, Merseyside, England |
| 2006 | Sherri Steinhauer | 281 | Cristie Kerr | Royal Lytham & St. Anne's, England |
| 2007 | Lorena Ochoa | 287 | Jee Young Lee<br>Maria Hjorth | Old Course, St. Andrew's, Scotland |
| 2008 | Ji-Yai Shin | 270 | Yani Tseng | Sunningdale GC, Berkshire, England |
| 2009 | Catriona Matthew | 285 | Karrie Webb | Royal Lytham & St. Annes, England |
| 2010 | Yani Tseng | 277 | Katherine Hull | Royal Birkdale CC, Merseyside, England |
| 2011 | Yani Tseng | 272 | Brittany Lang | Carnousie GL, Carnoustie, Scotland |

Note: Designated fourth major in 2001.

# THE LPGA TOUR

## Most Career Wins†

| | Wins | | Wins | | Wins |
|---|---|---|---|---|---|
| Kathy Whitworth | 88 | Sandra Haynie | 42 | *Juli Inkster | 31 |
| Mickey Wright | 82 | Babe Zaharias | 41 | Amy Alcott | 29 |
| Annika Sorenstam | 72 | Carol Mann | 38 | Jane Blalock | 27 |
| Patty Berg | 60 | *Karrie Webb | 38 | Lorena Ochoa | 27 |
| Louise Suggs | 58 | Patty Sheehan | 35 | Marlene Hagge | 26 |
| Betsy Rawls | 55 | Betsy King | 34 | Judy Rankin | 26 |
| Nancy Lopez | 48 | Beth Daniel | 33 | *Se Ri Pak | 25 |
| JoAnne Carner | 43 | Pat Bradley | 31 | Donna Caponi | 24 |

†Through 10/03/11. *Active player.

## Alltime Major Championship Winners

| | LPGA | U.S. Open | Nabisco | Brit. Open | ‡du Maurier | #Titleholders | †Western | U.S. Am | Brit. Am | Total |
|---|---|---|---|---|---|---|---|---|---|---|
| Patty Berg | 0 | 1 | 0 | 0 | 0 | 7 | 7 | 1 | 0 | 16 |
| Mickey Wright | 4 | 4 | 0 | 0 | 0 | 2 | 3 | 0 | 0 | 13 |
| Louise Suggs | 1 | 2 | 0 | 0 | 0 | 4 | 4 | 1 | 1 | 13 |
| Babe Zaharias | 0 | 3 | 0 | 0 | 0 | 3 | 4 | 1 | 1 | 12 |
| *Juli Inkster | 2 | 2 | 2 | 0 | 1 | 0 | 0 | 3 | 0 | 10 |
| Annika Sorenstam | 3 | 3 | 3 | 1 | 0 | 0 | 0 | 0 | 0 | 10 |
| Betsy Rawls | 2 | 4 | 0 | 0 | 0 | 0 | 2 | 0 | 0 | 8 |
| JoAnne Carner | 0 | 2 | 0 | 0 | 0 | 0 | 0 | 5 | 0 | 7 |
| *Karrie Webb | 1 | 2 | 2 | 1 | 1 | 0 | 0 | 0 | 0 | 7 |
| Kathy Whitworth | 3 | 0 | 0 | 0 | 0 | 2 | 1 | 0 | 0 | 6 |
| Pat Bradley | 1 | 1 | 1 | 0 | 3 | 0 | 0 | 0 | 0 | 6 |
| Patty Sheehan | 3 | 2 | 1 | 0 | 0 | 0 | 0 | 0 | 0 | 6 |
| Glenna Vare | 0 | 0 | 0 | 0 | 0 | 0 | 0 | 6 | 0 | 6 |
| Betsy King | 1 | 2 | 3 | 0 | 0 | 0 | 0 | 0 | 0 | 6 |

*Active LPGA player.
#Major from 1937–1972. †Major from 1937–1967. ‡Major from 1979–2000.

## Alltime Multiple Professional Major Winners

### LPGA

| | |
|---|---|
| Mickey Wright | 4 |
| Nancy Lopez | 3 |
| Se Ri Pak | 3 |
| Patty Sheehan | 3 |
| Annika Sorenstam | 3 |
| Kathy Whitworth | 3 |
| Donna Caponi | 2 |
| Sandra Haynie | 2 |
| Mary Mills | 2 |
| Betsy Rawls | 2 |
| Laura Davies | 2 |
| *Juli Inkster | 2 |
| *Yani Tseng | 2 |

### BRITISH OPEN

| | |
|---|---|
| *Yani Tseng | 2 |

### U.S. OPEN

| | |
|---|---|
| Betsy Rawls | 4 |
| Mickey Wright | 4 |
| Susie Maxwell Berning | 3 |
| Hollis Stacy | 3 |
| Babe Zaharias | 3 |
| Annika Sorenstam | 3 |
| JoAnne Carner | 2 |
| Donna Caponi | 2 |
| Betsy King | 2 |
| Meg Mallon | 2 |
| Patty Sheehan | 2 |
| Louise Suggs | 2 |
| Karrie Webb | 2 |
| *Juli Inkster | 2 |

### NABISCO/DINAH SHORE

| | |
|---|---|
| Amy Alcott | 3 |
| Betsy King | 3 |
| Annika Sorenstam | 3 |
| *Juli Inkster | 2 |
| *Karrie Webb | 2 |

### TITLEHOLDERS

| | |
|---|---|
| Patty Berg | 7 |
| Louise Suggs | 4 |
| Babe Zaharias | 3 |
| Dorothy Kirby | 2 |
| Marilynn Smith | 2 |
| Kathy Whitworth | 2 |
| Mickey Wright | 2 |

### WESTERN OPEN

| | |
|---|---|
| Patty Berg | 7 |
| Louise Suggs | 4 |
| Babe Zaharias | 4 |
| Mickey Wright | 3 |
| June Beebe | 2 |
| Opal Hill | 2 |
| Betty Jameson | 2 |
| Betsy Rawls | 2 |

### DU MAURIER

| | |
|---|---|
| Pat Bradley | 3 |
| Brandie Burton | 2 |
| JoAnne Carner | 2 |

*Active player.

## THE LPGA TOUR *(Cont.)*

### Season Money Leaders

| | | Earnings ($) | | | Earnings ($) | | | Earnings ($) |
|---|---|---|---|---|---|---|---|---|
| 1950 | Babe Zaharias | 14,800 | 1971 | Kathy Whitworth | 41,181 | 1992 | Dottie Mochrie | 693,335 |
| 1951 | Babe Zaharias | 15,087 | 1972 | Kathy Whitworth | 65,063 | 1993 | Betsy King | 595,992 |
| 1952 | Betsy Rawls | 14,505 | 1973 | Kathy Whitworth | 82,864 | 1994 | Laura Davies | 687,201 |
| 1953 | Louise Suggs | 19,816 | 1974 | JoAnne Carner | 87,094 | 1995 | Annika Sorenstam | 666,533 |
| 1954 | Patty Berg | 16,011 | 1975 | Sandra Palmer | 76,374 | 1996 | Karrie Webb | 1,002,000 |
| 1955 | Patty Berg | 16,492 | 1976 | Judy Rankin | 150,734 | 1997 | Annika Sorenstam | 1,236,789 |
| 1956 | Marlene Hagge | 20,235 | 1977 | Judy Rankin | 122,890 | 1998 | Annika Sorenstam | 1,092,748 |
| 1957 | Patty Berg | 16,272 | 1978 | Nancy Lopez | 189,814 | 1999 | Karrie Webb | 1,591,959 |
| 1958 | Beverly Hanson | 12,639 | 1979 | Nancy Lopez | 197,489 | 2000 | Karrie Webb | 1,876,853 |
| 1959 | Betsy Rawls | 26,774 | 1980 | Beth Daniel | 231,000 | 2001 | Annika Sorenstam | 2,105,868 |
| 1960 | Louise Suggs | 16,892 | 1981 | Beth Daniel | 206,998 | 2002 | Annika Sorenstam | 2,863,904 |
| 1961 | Mickey Wright | 22,236 | 1982 | JoAnne Carner | 310,400 | 2003 | Annika Sorenstam | 2,029,506 |
| 1962 | Mickey Wright | 21,641 | 1983 | JoAnne Carner | 291,404 | 2004 | Annika Sorenstam | 2,544,707 |
| 1963 | Mickey Wright | 31,269 | 1984 | Betsy King | 266,771 | 2005 | Annika Sorenstam | 2,588,240 |
| 1964 | Mickey Wright | 29,800 | 1985 | Nancy Lopez | 416,472 | 2006 | Lorena Ochoa | 2,592,872 |
| 1965 | Kathy Whitworth | 28,658 | 1986 | Pat Bradley | 492,021 | 2007 | Lorena Ochoa | 4,364,994 |
| 1966 | Kathy Whitworth | 33,517 | 1987 | Ayako Okamoto | 466,034 | 2008 | Lorena Ochoa | 2,763,193 |
| 1967 | Kathy Whitworth | 32,937 | 1988 | Sherri Turner | 350,851 | 2009 | Jiyai Shin | 1,807,334 |
| 1968 | Kathy Whitworth | 48,379 | 1989 | Betsy King | 654,132 | 2010 | Na Yeon Choi | 1,871,166 |
| 1969 | Carol Mann | 49,152 | 1990 | Beth Daniel | 863,578 | | | |
| 1970 | Kathy Whitworth | 30,235 | 1991 | Pat Bradley | 763,118 | | | |

### LPGA Player of the Year

| | | | | | |
|---|---|---|---|---|---|
| 1966 | Kathy Whitworth | 1981 | JoAnne Carner | 1996 | Laura Davies |
| 1967 | Kathy Whitworth | 1982 | JoAnne Carner | 1997 | Annika Sorenstam |
| 1968 | Kathy Whitworth | 1983 | Patty Sheehan | 1998 | Annika Sorenstam |
| 1969 | Kathy Whitworth | 1984 | Betsy King | 1999 | Karrie Webb |
| 1970 | Sandra Haynie | 1985 | Nancy Lopez | 2000 | Karrie Webb |
| 1971 | Kathy Whitworth | 1986 | Pat Bradley | 2001 | Annika Sorenstam |
| 1972 | Kathy Whitworth | 1987 | Ayako Okamoto | 2002 | Annika Sorenstam |
| 1973 | Kathy Whitworth | 1988 | Nancy Lopez | 2003 | Annika Sorenstam |
| 1974 | JoAnne Carner | 1989 | Betsy King | 2004 | Annika Sorenstam |
| 1975 | Sandra Palmer | 1990 | Beth Daniel | 2005 | Annika Sorenstam |
| 1976 | Judy Rankin | 1991 | Pat Bradley | 2006 | Lorena Ochoa |
| 1977 | Judy Rankin | 1992 | Dottie Mochrie | 2007 | Lorena Ochoa |
| 1978 | Nancy Lopez | 1993 | Betsy King | 2008 | Lorena Ochoa |
| 1979 | Nancy Lopez | 1994 | Beth Daniel | 2009 | Lorena Ochoa |
| 1980 | Beth Daniel | 1995 | Annika Sorenstam | 2010 | Yani Tseng |

### Vare Trophy: Best Scoring Average*

| | | Avg | | | Avg | | | Avg |
|---|---|---|---|---|---|---|---|---|
| 1953 | Patty Berg | 75.00 | 1973 | Judy Rankin | 73.08 | 1993 | Nancy Lopez | 70.83 |
| 1954 | Babe Zaharias | 75.48 | 1974 | JoAnne Carner | 72.87 | 1994 | Beth Daniel | 70.90 |
| 1955 | Patty Berg | 74.47 | 1975 | JoAnne Carner | 72.40 | 1995 | Annika Sorenstam | 71.00 |
| 1956 | Patty Berg | 74.57 | 1976 | Judy Rankin | 72.25 | 1996 | Annika Sorenstam | 70.47 |
| 1957 | Louise Suggs | 74.64 | 1977 | Judy Rankin | 72.16 | 1997 | Karrie Webb | 70.00 |
| 1958 | Beverly Hanson | 74.92 | 1978 | Nancy Lopez | 71.76 | 1998 | Annika Sorenstam | 69.99 |
| 1959 | Betsy Rawls | 74.03 | 1979 | Nancy Lopez | 71.20 | 1999 | Karrie Webb | 69.43 |
| 1960 | Mickey Wright | 73.25 | 1980 | Amy Alcott | 71.51 | 2000 | Karrie Webb | 70.05 |
| 1961 | Mickey Wright | 73.55 | 1981 | JoAnne Carner | 71.75 | 2001 | Annika Sorenstam | 69.42 |
| 1962 | Mickey Wright | 73.67 | 1982 | JoAnne Carner | 71.49 | 2002 | Annika Sorenstam | 68.70 |
| 1963 | Mickey Wright | 72.81 | 1983 | JoAnne Carner | 71.41 | 2003 | Se Ri Pak | 70.03 |
| 1964 | Mickey Wright | 72.46 | 1984 | Patty Sheehan | 71.40 | 2004 | Grace Park | 69.99 |
| 1965 | Kathy Whitworth | 72.61 | 1985 | Nancy Lopez | 70.73 | 2005 | Annika Sorenstam | 69.33 |
| 1966 | Kathy Whitworth | 72.60 | 1986 | Pat Bradley | 71.10 | 2006 | Lorena Ochoa | 69.23 |
| 1967 | Kathy Whitworth | 72.74 | 1987 | Betsy King | 71.14 | 2007 | Lorena Ochoa | 69.69 |
| 1968 | Carol Mann | 72.04 | 1988 | Colleen Walker | 71.26 | 2008 | Lorena Ochoa | 69.70 |
| 1969 | Kathy Whitworth | 72.38 | 1989 | Beth Daniel | 70.38 | 2009 | Lorena Ochoa | 70.16 |
| 1970 | Kathy Whitworth | 72.26 | 1990 | Beth Daniel | 70.54 | 2010 | Na Yeon Choi | 69.87 |
| 1971 | Kathy Whitworth | 72.88 | 1991 | Pat Bradley | 70.76 | | | |
| 1972 | Kathy Whitworth | 72.38 | 1992 | Dottie Mochrie | 70.80 | | | |

*Must play 70 rounds or more to qualify; Annika Sorenstam compiled an average of 69.02 in 60 rounds in 2003.

## U.S. Senior Open

| Year | Winner | Score | Runner-Up | Site |
|------|--------|-------|-----------|------|
| 1980 | Roberto DeVicenzo | 285 | William C. Campbell | Winged Foot GC, Mamaroneck, NY |
| 1981 | Arnold Palmer* (70) | 289 | Bob Stone (74) Billy Casper (77) | Oakland Hills CC, Birmingham, MI |
| 1982 | Miller Barber | 282 | Gene Littler, Dan Sikes, Jr. | Portland GC, Portland, OR |
| 1983 | Billy Casper* (75) (3) | 288 | Rod Funseth (75) (4) | Hazeltine GC, Chaska, MN |
| 1984 | Miller Barber | 286 | Arnold Palmer | Oak Hill CC, Rochester, NY |
| 1985 | Miller Barber | 285 | Roberto DeVicenzo | Edgewood Tahoe GC, Stateline, NV |
| 1986 | Dale Douglass | 279 | Gary Player | Scioto CC, Columbus, OH |
| 1987 | Gary Player | 270 | Doug Sanders | Brooklawn CC, Fairfield, CT |
| 1988 | Gary Player* (68) | 288 | Bob Charles (70) | Medinah CC, Medinah, IL |
| 1989 | Orville Moody | 279 | Frank Beard | Laurel Valley GC, Ligonier, PA |
| 1990 | Lee Trevino | 275 | Jack Nicklaus | Ridgewood CC, Paramus, NJ |
| 1991 | Jack Nicklaus* (65) | 282 | Chi Chi Rodriguez (69) | Oakland Hills CC, Birmingham, MI |
| 1992 | Larry Laoretti | 275 | Jim Colbert | Saucon Valley CC, Bethlehem, PA |
| 1993 | Jack Nicklaus | 278 | Tom Weiskopf | Cherry Hills CC, Englewood, CO |
| 1994 | Simon Hobday | 274 | Jim Albus | Pinehurst Resort & CC, Pinehurst, NC |
| 1995 | Tom Weiskopf | 275 | Jack Nicklaus | Congressional CC, Bethesda, MD |
| 1996 | Dave Stockton | 277 | Hale Irwin | Canterbury GC, Beachwood, OH |
| 1997 | Graham Marsh | 280 | Hale Irwin | Olympia Fields CC, Olympia Fields, IL |
| 1998 | Hale Irwin | 285 | Vicente Fernandez | Riviera CC, Pacific Palisades, CA |
| 1999 | Dave Eichelberger | 281 | Ed Dougherty | Des Moines G & CC, Des Moines, IA |
| 2000 | Hale Irwin | 267 | Bruce Fleisher | Saucon Valley CC, Bethlehem, PA |
| 2001 | Bruce Fleisher | 280 | Isao Aoki, Gil Morgan | Salem CC, Peabody, MA |
| 2002 | Don Pooley* (19) (5) | 274 | Tom Watson (18) | Caves Valley GC, Owings Mill, MD |
| 2003 | Bruce Lietzke | 277 | Tom Watson | Inverness GC, Toledo, OH |
| 2004 | Peter Jacobsen | 272 | Hale Irwin | Bellerive CC, St. Louis, MO |
| 2005 | Allen Doyle | 274 | D.A. Weibring Loren Roberts | NCR GC, Kettering, OH |
| 2006 | Allen Doyle | 272 | Tom Watson | Prairie Dunes CC, Hutchinson, KS |
| 2007 | Brad Bryant | 282 | Ben Crenshaw | Whistling Straits GC, Kohler, WI |
| 2008 | Eduardo Romero | 274 | Fred Funk | Broadmoor GC, Colorado Springs, CO |
| 2009 | Fred Funk | 268 | Joey Sindelar | Crooked Stick GC, Carmel, IN |
| 2010 | Bernhard Langer | 272 | Fred Couples | Sahalee CC, Sammamish, WA |
| 2011 | Olin Browne | 269 | Mark O'Meara | Inverness GC, Toledo, OH |

*Winner in playoff. Playoff scores are in parentheses. The 1983 playoff went to one hole of sudden death after an 18-hole playoff.

## CHAMPIONS TOUR
### Season Money Leaders

| Year | Winner | Earnings ($) | Year | Winner | Earnings ($) | Year | Winner | Earnings ($) |
|------|--------|-------------|------|--------|-------------|------|--------|-------------|
| 1980 | Don January | 44,100 | 1990 | Lee Trevino | 1,190,518 | 2000 | Larry Nelson | 2,708,005 |
| 1981 | Miller Barber | 83,136 | 1991 | Mike Hill | 1,065,657 | 2001 | Allen Doyle | 2,553,582 |
| 1982 | Miller Barber | 106,890 | 1992 | Lee Trevino | 1,027,002 | 2002 | Hale Irwin | 3,028,304 |
| 1983 | Don January | 237,571 | 1993 | Dave Stockton | 1,175,944 | 2003 | Tom Watson | 1,853,108 |
| 1984 | Don January | 328,597 | 1994 | Dave Stockton | 1,402,519 | 2004 | Craig Stadler | 2,306,066 |
| 1985 | Peter Thomson | 386,724 | 1995 | Jim Colbert | 1,444,386 | 2005 | Dana Quigley | 2,170,258 |
| 1986 | Bruce Crampton | 454,299 | 1996 | Jim Colbert | 1,627,890 | 2006 | Jay Haas | 2,420,227 |
| 1987 | Chi Chi Rodriguez | 509,145 | 1997 | Hale Irwin | 2,449,420 | 2007 | Jay Haas | 2,581,001 |
| 1988 | Bob Charles | 533,929 | 1998 | Hale Irwin | 2,861,945 | 2008 | Bernhard Langer | 2,035,073 |
| 1989 | Bob Charles | 725,887 | 1999 | Bruce Fleisher | 2,515,705 | 2009 | Bernhard Langer | 2,164,451 |
| 1990 | Lee Trevino | 1,190,518 | 2000 | Larry Nelson | 2,708,005 | 2010 | Bernhard Langer | 2,648,939 |

### Most Career Wins†

| | Wins | | Wins |
|---|------|---|------|
| Hale Irwin | 45 | *Gary Player | 19 |
| Lee Trevino | 29 | Larry Nelson | 19 |
| Gil Morgan | 25 | George Archer | 19 |
| Miller Barber | 24 | Bruce Fleisher | 18 |
| Bob Charles | 23 | Mike Hill | 18 |
| Don January | 22 | *Jay Haas | 15 |
| Chi Chi Rodriguez | 22 | Raymond Floyd | 14 |
| Jim Colbert | 20 | *Dave Stockton | 14 |
| Bruce Crampton | 20 | *Tom Watson | 14 |
| | | *Bernhard Langer | 14 |

*Active player.
†Through 10/03/11.

## Ryder Cup Matches

| Year | Results | Site |
|------|---------|------|
| 1927 | United States 9½, Great Britain 2½ | Worcester CC, Worcester, MA |
| 1929 | Great Britain 7, United States 5 | Moortown GC, Leeds, England |
| 1931 | United States 9, Great Britain 3 | Scioto CC, Columbus, OH |
| 1933 | Great Britain 6½, United States 5½ | Southport and Ainsdale Courses, Southport, England |
| 1935 | United States 9, Great Britain 3 | Ridgewood CC, Ridgewood, NJ |
| 1937 | United States 8, Great Britain 4 | Southport and Ainsdale Courses, Southport, England |
| 1939–1945 | No tournament | |
| 1947 | United States 11, Great Britain 1 | Portland GC, Portland, OR |
| 1949 | United States 7, Great Britain 5 | Ganton GC, Scarborough, England |
| 1951 | United States 9½, Great Britain 2½ | Pinehurst CC, Pinehurst, NC |
| 1953 | United States 6½, Great Britain 5½ | Wentworth Club, Surrey, England |
| 1955 | United States 8, Great Britain 4 | Thunderbird Ranch & CC, Palm Springs, CA |
| 1957 | Great Britain 7½, United States 4½ | Lindrick GC, Yorkshire, England |
| 1959 | United States 8½, Great Britain 3½ | Eldorado CC, Palm Desert, CA |
| 1961 | United States 14½, Great Britain 9½ | Royal Lytham & St. Annes GC, St Anne's-on-the-Sea, England |
| 1963 | United States 23, Great Britain 9 | East Lake CC, Atlanta |
| 1965 | United States 19½, Great Britain 12½ | Royal Birkdale GC, Southport, England |
| 1967 | United States 23½, Great Britain 8½ | Champions GC, Houston |
| 1969 | United States 16, Great Britain 16 | Royal Birkdale GC, Southport, England |
| 1971 | United States 18½, Great Britain 13½ | Old Warson CC, St. Louis |
| 1973 | United States 19, Great Britain 13 | Hon Co of Edinburgh Golfers, Muirfield, Scotland |
| 1975 | United States 21, Great Britain 11 | Laurel Valley GC, Ligonier, PA |
| 1977 | United States 12½, Great Britain 7½ | Royal Lytham & St. Annes GC, St. Annes-on-the-Sea, Eng. |
| 1979 | United States 17, Europe 11 | Greenbrier, White Sulphur Springs, WV |
| 1981 | United States 18½, Europe 9½ | Walton Heath GC, Surrey, England |
| 1983 | United States 14½, Europe 13½ | PGA National GC, Palm Beach Gardens, FL |
| 1985 | Europe 16½, United States 11½ | Belfry GC, Sutton Coldfield, England |
| 1987 | Europe 15, United States 13 | Muirfield Village GC, Dublin, OH |
| 1989 | Europe 14, United States 14 | Belfry GC, Sutton Coldfield, England |
| 1991 | United States 14½, Europe 13½ | Ocean Course, Kiawah Island, SC |
| 1993 | United States 15, Europe 13 | Belfry GC, Sutton Coldfield, England |
| 1995 | Europe 14½, United States 13½ | Oak Hill CC, Rochester, NY |
| 1997 | Europe 14½, United States 13½ | Valderrama GC, Sotogrande, Spain |
| 1999 | United States 14½, Europe 13½ | The Country Club, Brookline, MA |
| 2002 | Europe 15½, Unites States 12½ | Belfry GC, Sutton Coldfield, England |
| 2004 | Europe 18½, United States 9½ | Oakland Hills CC, Bloomfield Hills, MI |
| 2006 | Europe 18½, United States 9½ | The K Club, County Kildare, Ireland |
| 2008 | United States 16½, Europe 11½ | Valhalla GC, Louisville, KY |
| 2010 | Europe 14½, United States 13½ | Celtic Manor GC, Newport, Wales |

Team matches held every odd year between U.S. professionals and those of Great Britain/Europe. Team members selected on basis of finishes in PGA and European tour events. Match in 2001 canceled due to 9/11 terrorist attacks.

## Presidents Cup Matches

| Year | Results | Site |
|------|---------|------|
| 1994 | United States 20, International 12 | Robert Trent Jones GC, Lake Manassas, VA |
| 1996 | United States 16½, International 15½ | Robert Trent Jones GC, Lake Manassas, VA |
| 1998 | International 20½ United States 11½ | Royal Melbourne GC, Melbourne, Australia |
| 2000 | United States 21½, International 10½ | Robert Trent Jones GC, Lake Manassas, VA |
| 2003 | International 17, United States 17 | Fan Court Hotel CC, George, South Africa |
| 2005 | United States 18½, International 15½ | Robert Trent Jones GC, Lake Manassas, VA |
| 2007 | United States 19½, International 14½ | Royal Montreal GC, Bizard, Quebec |
| 2009 | United States 19½, International 14½ | Harding Park GC, San Francisco, CA |

A biennial event played in non-Ryder Cup years designed to provide non-European players with international team and match play. 2011 event completed after publication, on Nov. 20.

## Curtis Cup Matches

| Year | Results | Site |
|---|---|---|
| 1932 | United States 5½, British Isles 3½ | Wentworth GC, Wentworth, England |
| 1934 | United States 6½, British Isles 2½ | Chevy Chase Club, Chevy Chase, MD |
| 1936 | United States 4½ British Isles 4½ | King's Course, Gleneagles, Scotland |
| 1938 | United States 5½, British Isles 3½ | Essex CC, Manchester, MA |
| 1940–46 | No tournament | |
| 1948 | United States 6½, British Isles 2½ | Birkdale GC, Southport, England |
| 1950 | United States 7½, British Isles 1½ | CC of Buffalo, Williamsville, NY |
| 1952 | British Isles 5, United States 4 | Muirfield, Scotland |
| 1954 | United States 6, British Isles 3 | Merion GC, Ardmore, PA |
| 1956 | British Isles 5, United States 4 | Prince's GC, Sandwich Bay, England |
| 1958 | British Isles 4½, United States 4½ | Brae Burn CC, West Newton, Mass. |
| 1960 | United States 6½, British Isles 2½ | Lindrick GC, Worksop, England |
| 1962 | United States 8, British Isles 1 | Broadmoor CG, Colorado Springs,CO |
| 1964 | United States 10½, British Isles 7½ | Royal Porthcawl GC, Porthcawl, South Wales |
| 1966 | United States 13, British Isles 5 | Va. Hot Springs G & TC, Hot Springs, VA |
| 1968 | United States 10½, British Isles 7½ | Royal County Down GC, Newcastle, N. Ire. |
| 1970 | United States 11½, British Isles 6½ | Brae Burn CC, West Newton, MA |
| 1972 | United States 10, British Isles 8 | Western Gailes, Ayrshire, Scotland |
| 1974 | United States 13, British Isles 5 | San Francisco GC, San Francisco |
| 1976 | United States 11½, British Isles 6½ | Royal Lytham & St. Annes GC, England |
| 1978 | United States 12, British Isles 6 | Apawamis Club, Rye, NY |
| 1980 | United States 13, British Isles 5 | St. Pierre G & CC, Chepstow, Wales |
| 1982 | United States 14½, British Isles 3½ | Denver CC, Denver |
| 1984 | United States 9½ British Isles 8½ | Muirfield, Scotland |
| 1986 | British Isles 13, United States 5 | Prairie Dunes CC, Hutchinson, KS |
| 1988 | British Isles 11, United States 7 | Royal St. George's GC, Sandwich, England |
| 1990 | United States 14, British Isles 4 | Somerset Hills CC, Bernardsville, NJ |
| 1992 | Great Britain/Ireland 10, United States 8 | Royal Liverpool GC, Hoylake, England |
| 1994 | Great Britain/Ireland 9, United States 9 | The Honors Course, Ooltewah, TN |
| 1996 | Great Britain/Ireland 11½, United States 6½ | Killarney Golf & Fishing Club, Killarney, Ireland |
| 1998 | United States 10, Great Britain/Ireland 8 | The Minikahda Club, Minneapolis |
| 2000 | United States 10, Great Britain/Ireland 8 | Ganton GC, North Yorkshire, England |
| 2002 | United States 11, Great Britain/Ireland 7 | Fox Chapel GC, Pittsburgh, PA |
| 2004 | United States 10, Great Britain/Ireland 8 | Formby GC, Merseyside, England |
| 2006 | United States 11½, Great Britain/Ireland 6½ | Bandon Dunes GC, Bandon, OR |
| 2008 | United States 13, Great Britain/Ireland 7 | Old Course, St. Andrews, Scotland |
| 2010 | United States 12½, Great Britain/Ireland 7½ | Essex County Club, Manchester, Mass. |

Women's amateur team competition every other year between the United States and Great Britain/Ireland. U.S. team members selected by USGA.

## Solheim Cup Matches

| Year | Results | Site |
|---|---|---|
| 1990 | United States 11½, Europe 4½ | Lake Nona GC, Orlando, FL |
| 1992 | Europe 11½, United States 6½ | Dalmahoy Hotel GC, Edinburgh |
| 1994 | United States 13, Europe 7 | The Greenbrier, White Sulphur Springs, WV |
| 1996 | United States 17, Europe 11 | Marriott St Pierre Hotel & CC, Chepstow, Wales |
| 1998 | United States 16, Europe 12 | Muirfield Village GC, Dublin, OH |
| 2000 | Europe 14½, United States, 11 ½ | Loch Lomond GC, Luss, Scotland |
| 2002 | United States 15½, Europe 12 ½ | Interlachen CC, Minneapolis, MN |
| 2003 | Europe 17½, United States 10 ½ | Barseback G&CC, Malmo, Sweden |
| 2005 | United States 15½, Europe 12 ½ | Crooked Stick GC, Carmel, IN |
| 2007 | United States 16, Europe 12 | Halmstad GC, Halmstad, Sweden |
| 2009 | United States 16, Europe 12 | Rich Harvest Farms GC, Sugar Grove, IL |
| 2011 | Europe 15, United States 13 | Killeen Castle GC, Ireland |

Women's team matches held every other year between U.S. professionals and those of Europe. Team members selected on the basis of finishes in LPGA and European tour events.

# Soccer

XU LIANG

Japan scored a stunning, final-match upset victory over the United States at the 2011 Women's World Cup

## 2010 Major League Soccer

### 2010 Final Standings

#### WESTERN CONFERENCE

| Team | GP | W | L | T | Pts | GF | GA |
|---|---|---|---|---|---|---|---|
| †Los Angeles...| 30 | 18 | 7 | 5 | 59 | 44 | 26 |
| *Real Salt Lake..| 30 | 15 | 4 | 11 | 56 | 45 | 20 |
| *FC Dallas........| 30 | 12 | 4 | 14 | 50 | 42 | 28 |
| *‡Seattle...........| 30 | 14 | 10 | 6 | 48 | 39 | 35 |
| *Colorado.........| 30 | 12 | 8 | 10 | 46 | 44 | 32 |
| *San Jose.........| 30 | 13 | 10 | 7 | 46 | 34 | 33 |
| Houston...........| 30 | 9 | 15 | 6 | 33 | 40 | 49 |
| Chivas USA......| 30 | 8 | 18 | 4 | 28 | 31 | 45 |

#### EASTERN CONFERENCE

| Team | GP | W | L | T | Pts | GF | GA |
|---|---|---|---|---|---|---|---|
| †New York........| 30 | 15 | 9 | 6 | 51 | 38 | 29 |
| *Columbus ........| 30 | 14 | 8 | 8 | 50 | 40 | 34 |
| Kansas City......| 30 | 11 | 13 | 6 | 39 | 36 | 35 |
| Chicago............| 30 | 9 | 12 | 9 | 36 | 37 | 38 |
| Toronto FC........| 30 | 9 | 13 | 8 | 35 | 33 | 41 |
| New England ....| 30 | 9 | 16 | 5 | 32 | 32 | 50 |
| Philadelphia ....| 30 | 8 | 15 | 7 | 31 | 35 | 49 |
| D.C. United ......| 30 | 6 | 20 | 4 | 22 | 21 | 47 |

Note: Three points for a win. One point for a tie. †Conference champion. *Qualified for playoffs. ‡U.S. Open cup winner.

### SCORING LEADERS

| Player, Team | GP | G | A | Pts |
|---|---|---|---|---|
| Sebastien Le Toux, PHI ........| 28 | 14 | 11 | 25 |
| Landon Donovan, LA ............| 24 | 7 | 16 | 23 |
| David Ferreira, DAL ..............| 30 | 8 | 13 | 21 |
| Fredy Montero, SEA..............| 29 | 10 | 10 | 20 |
| Edson Buddle, LA ................| 25 | 17 | 2 | 19 |
| Conor Casey, COL ................| 27 | 13 | 6 | 19 |
| Chris Wondolowski, SJ ........| 26 | 18 | 1 | 19 |
| Dwayne De Rosario, TOR ....| 27 | 15 | 3 | 18 |
| Guill. Barros Schelotto, CLB ..| 29 | 9 | 9 | 18 |

**MLS Regular Season MVP:** David Ferreira, DAL.

### GOALS LEADERS

| Player, Team | GP | G |
|---|---|---|
| Chris Wondolowski, SJ ....................| 28 | 18 |
| Edson Buddle, LA ...........................| 25 | 17 |
| Dwayne De Rosario, TOR..................| 27 | 15 |
| Omar Cummings, COL.......................| 29 | 14 |
| Sebastien Le Toux, PHI....................| 28 | 14 |
| Juan Pablo Angel, NY.......................| 30 | 13 |
| Conor Casey, COL............................| 27 | 13 |
| Alvaro Saborio, RSL..........................| 27 | 12 |
| Jeff Cunningham, DAL.......................| 27 | 11 |

### ASSISTS LEADERS

| Player, Team | GP | A |
|---|---|---|
| Landon Donovan, LA ..........................| 24 | 16 |
| David Ferreira, DAL ............................| 30 | 13 |
| Brad Davis, HOU ................................| 27 | 12 |
| Sebastien Le Toux, PHI ......................| 28 | 11 |
| Bobby Convey, SJ ..............................| 28 | 10 |
| Fredy Montero, SEA............................| 29 | 10 |
| Patrick Nyarko, CHI ............................| 27 | 10 |
| Freddie Ljungberg, CHI ......................| 30 | 10 |
| Guillermo Barros Schelotto, CLB........| 29 | 9 |
| Javier Morales, RSL............................| 29 | 9 |

### GOALS-AGAINST-AVERAGE LEADERS

| Player, Team | GAA |
|---|---|
| Kevin Hartman, DAL ...........................| 0.62 |
| Nick Rimando, RSL..............................| 0.67 |
| Donovan Ricketts, LA..........................| 0.90 |
| Bouna Coundoul, NY............................| 1.04 |
| Jon Busch, SJ .....................................| 1.06 |
| William Hesmer, CLB ..........................| 1.10 |
| Matt Pickens, COL...............................| 1.10 |
| Kasey Keller, SEA...............................| 1.15 |
| Jimmy Nielsen, KC.............................| 1.17 |
| Joe Cannon, SJ ..................................| 1.17 |

### 2010 MLS Playoffs

| 1ST ROUND (TWO LEGS) | | | CONF. FINALS | |
|---|---|---|---|---|
| Los Angeles...**1** | **2–3** | | Los Angeles......**0** | |
| Seattle...........**0** | **1–1** | | FC Dallas..........**3** | |
| | | | | |
| Real Salt Lake...**1** | **1–2** | | | |
| FC Dallas........**2** | **1–3** | | | |

| 1ST ROUND (TWO LEGS) | | | CONF. FINALS | |
|---|---|---|---|---|
| New York........**1** | **1–2** | | Colorado.............**1** | |
| San Jose.........**0** | **3–3** | | San Jose...........**0** | |
| | | | | |
| Columbus......**0** | **2–2** | | | |
| Colorado..........**1** | **1–2** | **(5-4, PSO)** | | |

### 2010 MLS CUP (November 21, 2010 in Toronto, Canada)

| | | | | |
|---|---|---|---|---|
| Colorado....................**0** | **1** | **0** | **1 — 2** | |
| FC Dallas...................**1** | **0** | **0** | **0 — 1** | |

**FIRST HALF:** Scoring: 1, DAL, Ferreira (John), 34th minute.

**SECOND HALF:** Scoring: 1, COL, Casey (Smith), 56th minute.

**FIRST OVERTIME:** Scoring: None

**SECOND OVERTIME:** Scoring: 1, COL, John (DAL), own goal (from Kandji, COL)

**Colorado:** Pickens, Moor, Wynne, Kimura, Wallace (Thompson 90), Smith (Baudet 90), Mullan, Mastroeni, Larentowicz, Cummings (Kandji 98), Casey.

**FC Dallas:** Hartman, Goncalves (Lloyd 34), John, Ihemelu, Benitez, Chavez (Avila), McCarty, Hernandez, Shea (Cunningham 64), Ferreira, Harris.

Attendance: 21,700. Referee: M. Morales. Asst. Referees: M. Torrentera, H. Delgadillo.

**MLS Cup MVP:** Conor Casey (forward), Colorado.

# 2011 Women's World Cup Results

## Group Stage

### GROUP A

| Country | MP | W | L | D | Pts |
|---|---|---|---|---|---|
| *Germany | 3 | 3 | 0 | 0 | 9 |
| *France | 3 | 2 | 1 | 0 | 6 |
| Nigeria | 3 | 1 | 2 | 0 | 3 |
| Canada | 3 | 0 | 3 | 0 | 0 |

### GROUP B

| Country | MP | W | L | D | Pts |
|---|---|---|---|---|---|
| *England | 3 | 2 | 0 | 1 | 7 |
| *Japan | 3 | 2 | 1 | 0 | 6 |
| Mexico | 3 | 0 | 1 | 2 | 2 |
| New Zealand | 3 | 0 | 2 | 1 | 1 |

### GROUP C

| Country | MP | W | L | D | Pts |
|---|---|---|---|---|---|
| *Sweden | 3 | 3 | 0 | 0 | 9 |
| *United States | 3 | 2 | 1 | 0 | 6 |
| North Korea | 3 | 0 | 2 | 1 | 1 |
| Colombia | 3 | 0 | 2 | 1 | 1 |

### GROUP D

| Country | MP | W | L | D | Pts |
|---|---|---|---|---|---|
| *Brazil | 3 | 3 | 0 | 0 | 9 |
| *Australia | 3 | 2 | 1 | 0 | 6 |
| Norway | 3 | 1 | 2 | 0 | 3 |
| Equa. Guinea | 3 | 0 | 3 | 0 | 0 |

*Moved on to quarterfinals.
Note: in group play, three points are awarded for a win, one for a tie.

## Quarterfinals

| | | | | |
|---|---|---|---|---|
| Germany | 0 0 0—0 | Sweden | 2 1—3 |
| Japan | 0 0 1—1 | Australia | 1 0—1 |
| a.e.t. | | | |

| | | | | |
|---|---|---|---|---|
| England | 0 1 0-1 (3) | Brazil | 0 1 1—2 (3) |
| France | 0 1 0-1 (4) | U.S. | 1 0 1—2 (5) |
| a.e.t. (PSO) | | a.e.t. (PSO) | |

## Semifinals

| | | | |
|---|---|---|---|
| Japan | 1 2—3 | France | 0 1—1 |
| Sweden | 1 0—1 | U.S. | 1 2—3 |

## Third-Place Consolation Match

| | |
|---|---|
| Sweden | 1 1—2 |
| France | 0 1—1 |

## 2011 Women's World Cup Final

### (July 17, 2011 in Frankfurt, Germany)

| | | | |
|---|---|---|---|
| Japan | 0 | 1 | 1 — — 2 (3) |
| United States | 0 | 1 | 1 — — 2 (1) |

**FIRST HALF:** Scoring: None.

**SECOND HALF:** Scoring: 1, United States, Morgan (Rapinoe), 69th minute; 1, Japan, Miyama, 81st minute.

**EXTRA TIME:** Scoring: 1, United States, Wambach (Morgan), 104th minute; 1, Japan, Sawa (Miyama), 117th minute.

**PENALTY SHOOT-OUT:** Scoring: 1, United States, Boxx (saved), Lloyd (missed), Heath (saved), Wambach (goal); 3, Japan: Miyama (goal), Nagasato (saved), Sakaguchi (goal), Kumagai (goal).

**Japan:** Kaihori, Kinga, Iwashimizu, Kumagai, Sakaguchi, Ando (Nagasato 66), Miyama, Kawasumi, Sawa, Ohno (Maruyama 66, Iwabuchi 119), Sameshima.

**United States:** Solo, Rampone, Le Peilbet, Boxx, O'Reilly, Lloyd, Krieger, Cheney (Morgan 46), Rapinoe (Heath 114), Buehler, Wambach.

Referee: Bibiana Steinhaus. Asst. Referees: Marina Wozniak, Katrin Rafalksi.

Final match attendance: 48,817.

**2011 World Cup Golden Boot & Golden Ball Winner:** Homare Sawa, Japan

## The World Cup

### Results—Men

| Year | Champion | Score | Runner-Up | Winning Coach |
|---|---|---|---|---|
| 1930 | Uruguay | 4–2 | Argentina | Alberto Supicci |
| 1934 | Italy | 2–1 | Czechoslovakia | Vittorio Pozzo |
| 1938 | Italy | 4–2 | Hungary | Vittorio Pozzo |
| 1950 | Uruguay | 2–1 | Brazil | Juan Lopez |
| 1954 | West Germany | 3–2 | Hungary | Sepp Herberger |
| 1958 | Brazil | 5–2 | Sweden | Vicente Feola |
| 1962 | Brazil | 3–1 | Czechoslovakia | Aymore Moreira |
| 1966 | England | 4–2 | West Germany | Alf Ramsey |
| 1970 | Brazil | 4–1 | Italy | Mario Zagalo |
| 1974 | West Germany | 2–1 | Netherlands | Helmut Schoen |
| 1978 | Argentina | 3–1 | Netherlands | César Menotti |
| 1982 | Italy | 3–1 | West Germany | Enzo Bearzot |
| 1986 | Argentina | 3–2 | West Germany | Carlos Bilardo |
| 1990 | West Germany | 1–0 | Argentina | Franz Beckenbauer |
| 1994 | Brazil | 0–0 (3–2) | Italy | Carlos Alberto Parreira |
| 1998 | France | 3–0 | Brazil | Aime Jacquet |
| 2002 | Brazil | 2–0 | Germany | Luis Felipe Scolari |
| 2006 | Italy | 1–1 (5–3) | France | Marcello Lippi |
| 2010 | Spain | 1–0 (2 OT) | Netherlands | Vicente Del Bosque |

### Alltime World Cup Participation

| Nation | Matches | W | T | L | Goals For | Goals Against |
|---|---|---|---|---|---|---|
| Brazil | 97 | 67 | 15 | 15 | 210 | 89 |
| *Germany | 99 | 60 | 19 | 20 | 206 | 119 |
| Italy | 80 | 44 | 21 | 15 | 126 | 78 |
| Argentina | 70 | 37 | 13 | 20 | 123 | 79 |
| Spain | 56 | 28 | 12 | 16 | 88 | 57 |
| England | 59 | 26 | 19 | 14 | 77 | 52 |
| France | 54 | 25 | 11 | 18 | 96 | 70 |
| Netherlands | 43 | 22 | 10 | 11 | 71 | 42 |
| Uruguay | 47 | 18 | 12 | 17 | 76 | 64 |
| †Russia | 37 | 17 | 6 | 14 | 64 | 44 |
| Yugoslavia | 37 | 17 | 6 | 14 | 60 | 46 |
| Sweden | 46 | 16 | 13 | 17 | 74 | 71 |
| Poland | 31 | 15 | 5 | 11 | 44 | 40 |
| Hungary | 32 | 15 | 3 | 14 | 87 | 58 |
| Portugal | 23 | 12 | 3 | 8 | 39 | 23 |
| Austria | 29 | 12 | 4 | 13 | 43 | 49 |
| Czech Republic | 33 | 12 | 5 | 16 | 47 | 48 |
| Mexico | 49 | 12 | 13 | 24 | 52 | 87 |
| Belgium | 36 | 10 | 9 | 17 | 46 | 64 |
| Switzerland | 29 | 9 | 6 | 14 | 38 | 51 |
| Chile | 29 | 9 | 6 | 14 | 34 | 45 |
| Denmark | 16 | 8 | 2 | 6 | 27 | 24 |
| Romania | 21 | 8 | 5 | 8 | 30 | 32 |
| Paraguay | 27 | 7 | 10 | 10 | 30 | 38 |
| United States | 29 | 7 | 5 | 17 | 32 | 57 |
| Croatia | 13 | 6 | 2 | 5 | 15 | 11 |
| Turkey | 10 | 5 | 1 | 4 | 20 | 17 |
| South Korea | 28 | 5 | 8 | 15 | 28 | 60 |
| Ghana | 9 | 4 | 2 | 3 | 9 | 10 |
| Japan | 14 | 4 | 3 | 7 | 12 | 16 |
| Nigeria | 14 | 4 | 2 | 8 | 17 | 21 |
| Peru | 15 | 4 | 3 | 8 | 19 | 31 |
| Cameroon | 20 | 4 | 7 | 9 | 17 | 34 |
| Scotland | 23 | 4 | 7 | 12 | 25 | 41 |
| Ecuador | 7 | 3 | 0 | 4 | 7 | 8 |
| Northern Ireland | 13 | 3 | 5 | 5 | 13 | 23 |
| Costa Rica | 10 | 3 | 1 | 6 | 12 | 21 |
| Colombia | 13 | 3 | 2 | 8 | 14 | 22 |
| Bulgaria | 26 | 3 | 8 | 15 | 22 | 52 |

| Nation | Matches | W | T | L | Goals For | Goals Against |
|---|---|---|---|---|---|---|
| Senegal | 5 | 2 | 2 | 1 | 7 | 6 |
| Ukraine | 5 | 2 | 1 | 2 | 5 | 7 |
| East Germany | 6 | 2 | 2 | 2 | 5 | 6 |
| Norway | 8 | 2 | 3 | 3 | 7 | 9 |
| Cote d'Ivoire | 6 | 2 | 1 | 3 | 9 | 9 |
| South Africa | 9 | 2 | 4 | 3 | 11 | 15 |
| Republic of Ireland | 13 | 2 | 8 | 3 | 10 | 10 |
| Algeria | 9 | 2 | 2 | 5 | 6 | 12 |
| Morocco | 13 | 2 | 4 | 7 | 12 | 17 |
| Saudi Arabia | 13 | 2 | 2 | 9 | 9 | 32 |
| Australia | 10 | 2 | 3 | 5 | 8 | 16 |
| Wales | 5 | 1 | 3 | 1 | 4 | 4 |
| Cuba | 3 | 1 | 1 | 1 | 5 | 12 |
| Slovakia | 3 | 1 | 1 | 1 | 5 | 5 |
| Jamaica | 3 | 1 | 0 | 2 | 3 | 9 |
| Slovenia | 6 | 1 | 1 | 4 | 5 | 10 |
| North Korea | 7 | 1 | 1 | 5 | 6 | 21 |
| Serbia | 6 | 1 | 0 | 5 | 4 | 13 |
| Greece | 6 | 1 | 0 | 5 | 2 | 15 |
| Iran | 9 | 1 | 2 | 6 | 6 | 17 |
| Tunisia | 12 | 1 | 4 | 7 | 8 | 17 |
| Angola | 3 | 0 | 2 | 1 | 1 | 2 |
| Israel | 3 | 0 | 2 | 1 | 1 | 3 |
| Indonesia | 1 | 0 | 0 | 1 | 0 | 6 |
| Egypt | 4 | 0 | 2 | 2 | 3 | 6 |
| Kuwait | 3 | 0 | 1 | 2 | 2 | 6 |
| Trinidad and Tobago | 3 | 0 | 1 | 2 | 0 | 4 |
| New Zealand | 6 | 0 | 3 | 3 | 4 | 14 |
| Honduras | 6 | 0 | 3 | 3 | 2 | 6 |
| United Arab Emirates | 3 | 0 | 0 | 3 | 2 | 11 |
| Haiti | 3 | 0 | 0 | 3 | 2 | 14 |
| Iraq | 3 | 0 | 0 | 3 | 1 | 4 |
| Togo | 3 | 0 | 0 | 3 | 1 | 6 |
| Canada | 3 | 0 | 0 | 3 | 0 | 5 |
| China | 3 | 0 | 0 | 3 | 0 | 9 |
| Dem. Rep. of Congo | 3 | 0 | 0 | 3 | 0 | 14 |
| Bolivia | 6 | 0 | 1 | 5 | 1 | 20 |
| El Salvador | 6 | 0 | 0 | 6 | 1 | 22 |

*Includes West Germany 1950–90. †Includes USSR 1930–1990.
Note: Matches decided by penalty kicks are shown as drawn games.

## World Cup Final Box Scores

### URUGUAY 1930

| | | | |
|---|---|---|---|
| **Uruguay** | 1 | 3 | —4 |
| **Argentina** | 2 | 0 | —2 |

**FIRST HALF:** Scoring: 1, Uruguay, Dorado (12); 2, Argentina, Peucelle (20); 3, Argentina, Stabile (37).

**SECOND HALF:** Scoring: 4, Uruguay, Cea (57); 5, Uruguay, Iriarte (68); 6, Uruguay, Castro (89).

**Argentina:** Botosso, Della Toree, Paternoster, J. Evaristo, Monti, Suarez, Peucelle, Varallo, Stabile, Ferreira, M. Evaristo.

**Uruguay:** Ballesteros, Nasazzi, Mascheroni, Andrade, Fernandez, Gestido, Dorado, Scarone, Castro, Cea, Iriarte.

Referee: Langenus (Belgium).

### ITALY 1934

| | | | |
|---|---|---|---|
| **Italy** | 0 | 1 | 1—2 |
| **Czechoslovakia** | 0 | 1 | 0—1 |

**SECOND HALF:** Scoring: 1, Czech., Puc (70); 2, Italy, Orsi (80).

**OVERTIME:** Scoring: 3, Italy, Schiavio (95).

**Italy:** Combi, Monzeglio, Allemandi, Ferraris Monti, Monti, Bertolini, Guaita, Meazza, Schiavio, Ferrari, Orsi.

**Czechoslovakia:** Planicka, Zenisek, Ctyroky, Kostalek, Cambal, Cambal, Krcil, Junek, Svoboda, Sobotka, Nejedly, Puc.

Referee: Eklind (Sweden).

### FRANCE 1938

| | | | |
|---|---|---|---|
| **Italy** | 3 | 1 | —4 |
| **Hungary** | 1 | 1 | —2 |

**FIRST HALF:** Scoring: 1, Italy, Colaussi (5); 2, Hungary, Titkos (7); 3, Italy, Piola (16); 4, Italy, Piola (35).

**SECOND HALF:** Scoring: 5, Hungary, Sarosi (70); 6, Italy, Colaussi (82).

**Italy:** Olivieri, Foni, Rava, Serantoni, Andreolo, Locatelli, Biavati, Meazza, Piola, Ferrari, Colaussi.

**Hungary:** Szabo, Polger, Biro, Szalay, Szucs, Lazar, Sas, Vincze, Sarosi, Zsengeller, Titkos.

Referee: Capdeville (France).

### BRAZIL 1950

| | | | |
|---|---|---|---|
| **Uruguay** | 0 | 2 | —2 |
| **Brazil** | 0 | 1 | —1 |

**SECOND HALF:** Scoring: 1, Brazil, Friaca (47); 2, Uruguay, Schiaffino (66); 3, Uruguay, Ghiggia (79).

**Uruguay:** Maspoli, Gonzales, Tejera, Gambretta, Varela, Andrade, Ghiggia, Perez, Miguez, Schiffiano, Moran.

**Brazil:** Barbosa, Augusto, Juvenal, Bauer, Banilo, Bigode, Friaca, Zizinho, Ademir, Jair, Chico.

Referee: Reader (England).

### SWITZERLAND 1954

| | | | |
|---|---|---|---|
| **West Germany** | 2 | 1 | —3 |
| **Hungary** | 2 | 0 | —2 |

**FIRST HALF:** Scoring: 1, Hungary, Puskas (6); 2, Hungary, Czibor (8); 3, W Germ., Morlock (10); 4, W Germ., Rahn (18).

**SECOND HALF:** Scoring: 5, W Germany, Rahn (84).

**West Germany:** Turek, Posipal, Kohlmeyer, Eckel, Liebrich, Mai, Rahn, Morlock, O.Walter, F. Walter, Schaefer.

**Hungary:** Grosics, Buzansky, Lantos, Bozsik, Lorant, Zakarias, Czibor, Kocsis, Hidegkuti, Puskas, Toth.

Referee: Ling (England).

### SWEDEN 1958

| | | | |
|---|---|---|---|
| **Brazil** | 2 | 3 | —5 |
| **Sweden** | 1 | 1 | —2 |

**FIRST HALF:** Scoring:1, Sweden, Liedholm (3); 2, Brazil, Vava (9); 3, Brazil, Vava (32).

**SECOND HALF:** Scoring: 4, Brazil, Pelé (55); 5, Brazil, Zagalo (68); 6, Sweden Simonsson (80); 7, Brazil, Pelé (90).

**Brazil:** Glymar, D. Santos, N. Santos, Zito, Bellini, Orlando, Garrincha, Didi, Vava, Pelé, Zagalo.

**Sweden:** Svensson, Bergmark, Axbom, Boerjesson, Gustavsson, Parling, Hamrin, Gren, Simonsson, Liedholm, Skoglund.

Referee: Guigue (France).

### CHILE 1962

| | | | |
|---|---|---|---|
| **Brazil** | 1 | 2 | —3 |
| **Czechoslovakia** | 1 | 0 | —1 |

**FIRST HALF:** Scoring: 1, Czech., Masopust (15); 2, Brazil, Amarildo (17).

**SECOND HALF:** Scoring: 3, Brazil, Zito (68); 4, Brazil, Vava (77).

**Brazil:** Glymar, D. Santos, N. Santos, Zito, Mauro, Zozimo, Garrincha, Didi, Vava, Amarildo, Zagalo.

**Czechoslovakia:** Schroiff, Tichy, Novak, Pluskal, Popluhar, Masopust, Pospichal, Scherer, Kvasnak, Kadraba, Jelinek.

Referee: Latychev (USSR).

### ENGLAND 1966

| | | | |
|---|---|---|---|
| **England** | 1 | 1 | 2—4 |
| **West Germany** | 1 | 1 | 0—2 |

**FIRST HALF:** Scoring: 1, W Germany, Haller (12); 2, England, Hurst (18).

**SECOND HALF:** Scoring: 3, England, Peters (78); 4, W. Germany, Weber (90).

**OVERTIME:** Scoring: 5, England, Hurst (101); 6, England, Hurst (120).

**England:** Banks, Cohen, Wilson, Stiles, J. Charlton, Moore, Ball, Hurst, Hunt, R. Charlton, Peters.

**West Germany:** Tilkowski, Hottges, Schmellinger, Beckenbauer, Schulz, Weber, Held, Haller, Seeler, Overath, Emmerich.

Referee: Dienst (Switzerland).

## World Cup Final Box Scores (*Cont.*)

### MEXICO 1970

| Brazil.................1 | 3 — 4 |
| Italy .................1 | 0 — 1 |

**FIRST HALF:** Scoring: 1, Brazil, Pelé (18); 2, Italy, Boninsegna (32).

**SECOND HALF:** Scoring: 3, Brazil, Gerson (65); 4, Brazil, Jairzinho (70); 5, Brazil, Alberto (86).

**Brazil:** Feliz, Alberto, Brito, Wilson, Piazza, Everaldo, Clodoaldo, Gerson, Jairzinho, Tostao, Pelé, Rivelino.

**Italy:** Albertosi, Burgnich, Cera, Rosato, Facchetti, Bertini (Juliano), Mazzola, De Sisti, Domenghini, Boninsegna (Rivera), Riva.

Referee: Glockner (E Germany).

### WEST GERMANY 1974

| West Germany......2 | 0 — 2 |
| Netherlands............1 | 0 — 1 |

**FIRST HALF:** Scoring: 1, Netherlands, Neeskens, PK (1); 2, W Germany, Breitner, PK (26); 3, W Germany, Müller (44).

**West Germany:** Maier, Vogts, Beckenbauer, Schwarzenbeck, Breitner, Hoeness, Bonhof, Overath, Grabowski, Müller, Holzenbein.

**Netherlands:** Jongbloed, Suurbier, Rijsbergen (de Jong), Haan, Krol, Jansen, Neeskens, van Hanagem, Cruyff, Rensenbrink (van der Kerkhof).

Referee: Taylor (England).

### ARGENTINA 1978

| Argentina ...............1 | 0 | 2 — 3 |
| Netherlands...........0 | 1 | 0 — 1 |

**FIRST HALF:** Scoring: 1, Argentina, Kempes (38).

**SECOND HALF:** Scoring: 2, Netherlands, Nanninga (81).

**OVERTIME:** Scoring: 3, Arg., Kempes (104); 4, Arg., Bertoni (114).

**Argentina:** Fillol, Olguin, Galvan, Passarella, Tarantini, Ardiles (Larrosa), Gallego, Kempes, Bertoni, Luque, Ortiz (Houseman).

**Netherlands:** Jongbloed, Jansen (Suurbier), Krol, Brandts, Poortvliet, Neeskens, Haan, W. van der Kerkhoff, R. van der Kerkhoff, Rep (Nanninga), Rensenbrink.

Referee: Gonella (Italy).

### ITALY 1982

| Italy ..................0 | 3 — 3 |
| West Germany......0 | 1 — 1 |

**SECOND HALF:** Scoring: 1, Italy, Rossi (57); 2, Italy, Tardelli (68); 3, Italy, Altobelli (81); 4, W Germany, Breitner (83).

**Italy:** Zoff, Bergomi, Scirea, Collovati, Cabrini, Oriali, Gentile, Tardelli, Conti, Rossi, Graziani (Altobelli, Causio).

**West Germany:** Schumacher, Kaltz, Stielike, K. Foerster, B. Foerster, Dremmler (Hrubesch), Breitner, Briegel, Rummenigge (Müller), Fishcher (Littbarski).

Referee: Coelho (Brazil).

### MEXICO 1986

| Argentina ...............1 | 2 — 3 |
| West Germany......0 | 2 — 2 |

**FIRST HALF:** Scoring: 1, Argentina, Brown (22).

**SECOND HALF:** Scoring: 2, Arg., Valdano (55); 3, W Germ., Rummenigge (73); 4, W Germ., Voller (81); 5, Arg., Burruchaga (83).

**Argentina:** Pumpido, Brown, Cuciuffo, Ruggeri, Olarticoecha, Bastista, Giusti, Burruchaga (Trobbiani 90), Enrique, Maradona, Valdona.

**West Germany:** Schumacher, Jakobs, Forster, Eder, Brehme, Matthaus, Berthold, Magath (Hoeness 62), Briegel, Rummenigge, Allofs (Voller 46).

Referee: Filho (Brazil).

### ITALY 1990

| West Germany .........0 | 1 — 1 |
| Argentina ...................0 | 0 — 0 |

**SECOND HALF:** Scoring: 1, W Germany, Brehme, PK (84).

**West Germany:** Illgner, Brehme, Kohler, Augenthaler, Buchwald, Berthold (Reuter), Littbarski, Haessler, Mattaeus, Voeller, Klinsmann.

**Argentina:** Goychoechea, Lorenzo, Serrizuela, Sensini, Ruggeri (Monzon), Simon, Basualdo, Burruchag (Calderon), Maradona, Troglio, Dezottir.

Referee: Coelho (Brazil).

### UNITED STATES 1994

| Italy .....................0 | 0 | 0 — 0 |
| Brazil.....................0 | 0 | 0 — 0 |

Scoring: None. Shootout goals: Italy—2: Albertini, Evani; Brazil—3: Romario, Branco, Dunga.

**Italy:** Pagliuca, Benarrivo, Maldini, Baresi, Mussi (Apolloni 35), Albertini, D. Baggio (Evani 95), Berti, Donadoni, Baggio, Massaro.

**Brazil:** Taffarel, Jorginho (Cafu 21), Branco, Aldair, Santos, Silva, Dunga, Zinho (Viola 106), Mazinho, Bebeto, Romario.

Referee: Puhl (Hungary).

### FRANCE 1998

| Brazil ..........................0 | 0 — 0 |
| France..........................2 | 1 — 3 |

**FIRST HALF:** Scoring: 1, France, Zidane (27); 2, France, Zidane (45).

**SECOND HALF:** Scoring: 3, France, Petit (90).

**Brazil:** Taffarel, Cafu, Aldair, Baiano, Carlos, Sampaio (Edmundo 74), Dunga, Rivaldo, Leonardo, (Denilson 46), Bebeto, Ronaldo.

**France:** Barthez, Lizarazu, Desailly, Thuram, Leboeuf, Djorkaeff (Vieira 75) Deschamps, Zidane, Petit, Karembeu (Boghossian 57), Guivarc'h (Dugarry 66).

Referee: Belqola (Morocco).

## World Cup Final Box Scores *(Cont.)*

### KOREA/JAPAN 2002

| | | |
|---|---|---|
| Brazil.....................0 | | 2——2 |
| Germany................0 | | 0——0 |

**SECOND HALF:** Scoring: 1, Brazil, Ronaldo (67); 2, Brazil, Ronaldo (79).

**Brazil:** Marcos, Cafu, Lucio, Roque Junior, Edmilson, Carlos, Silva, Ronaldo (Denilson, 90), Rivaldo, Ronaldinho (Juninho, 85), Kleberson.

**Germany:** Kahn, Linke, Ramelow, Neuville, Hamann, Klose (Bierhoff, 74), Jeremies (Asamoah, 77), Bode (Ziege, 84), Schneider, Metzelder, Frings.

Referee: Collina (Italy).

### GERMANY 2006

| | | |
|---|---|---|
| Italy.............l | 0 | 0 ——l |
| France........l | 0 | 0 ——l |

**Italy won on penalty kicks, 5–3.**

**FIRST HALF:** Scoring: 1, France, Zidane (7); 1, Italy, Materazzi (19).

SHOOTOUT GOALS: Italy—Pirlo, Materazzi, De Rossi, Del Piero, Grosso; France—Wiltord, Abidal, Sagnol.

**Italy:** Buffon, Zambrotta, Cannavaro, Materazzi, Grosso, Camoranesi (Del Piero 86), Pirlo, Gattuso, Perrotta (Iaquinta 61), Totti (De Rossi 61), Toni.

**France:** Barthez, Sagnol, Thuram, Gallas, Abidal, Ribery (Trezeguet 100), Vieira (Diarra 56), Makelele, Zidane, Malouda, Henry (Wiltord 107).

Referee: Elizondo (Argentina).

### SOUTH AFRICA 2010

| | | | | |
|---|---|---|---|---|
| Spain...................0 | 0 | 0 | l——l |
| Netherlands........0 | 0 | 0 | 0——0 |

**2ND EXTRA TIME:** Scoring: 1, Spain, Iniesta (Fabregas), 116.

**Spain:** Casillas, Pique, Puyol, Iniesta, Pedro (Navas 60), Xavi, Capdevila, Fabregas (Alonso 87), Ramos, Busquets, Villa (Torres 105).

**Netherlands:** Stekelenburg, Van der Wiel, Heitinga, Mathijsen, Van Brommel, Robben, Sneijder, Kuyt (Elia 71), De Jong (Van der Vaart 99), Van Bronckhorst (Braafheid 105), Van Persie.

Referee: Howard Webb (England).

## Alltime Leaders

### GOALS

| Player, Nation | Tournaments | Goals | Player, Nation | Tournaments | Goals |
|---|---|---|---|---|---|
| Ronaldo, Brazil | 1994, '98, 2002, '06 | 15 | Teofilo Cubillas, Peru | 1970, '78, '82 | 10 |
| Gerd Müller, West Germany | 1970, '74 | 14 | Grzegorz Lato, Poland | 1974, '78, '82 | 10 |
| Miroslav Klose, Germany | 2002, '06, '10 | 14 | Ademir, Brazil | 1950 | 9 |
| Just Fontaine, France | 1958 | 13 | Eusebio, Portugal | 1966 | 9 |
| Pelé, Brazil | 1958, '62, '66, '70 | 12 | Jairzinho, Brazil | 1970, '74 | 9 |
| Sandor Kocsis, Hungary | 1954 | 11 | Paolo Rossi, Italy | 1982, '86 | 9 |
| Jurgen Klinsmann, Germany | 1990, '94, '98 | 11 | K.H. Rummenigge, W. Germany | 1978, '82, '86 | 9 |
| Helmut Rahn, West Germany | 1954, '58 | 10 | Uwe Seeler, West Germany | 1958, '62, '66, '70 | 9 |
| Gary Lineker, England | 1986, '90 | 10 | Vava, Brazil | 1958, '62 | 9 |
| Gabriel Batistuta, Argentina | 1998, 2002 | 10 | Christian Vieri, Italy | 1998, 2002 | 9 |

### LEADING SCORER, CUP BY CUP

| Year | Player, Nation | Goals | Year | Player, Nation | Goals |
|---|---|---|---|---|---|
| 1930 | Guillermo Stabile, Argentina | 8 | 1978 | Mario Kempes, Argentina | 6 |
| 1934 | Oldrich Nejedly, Czechoslovakia | 5 | 1982 | Paolo Rossi, Italy | 6 |
| 1938 | Leonidas da Silva, Brazil | 8 | 1986 | Gary Lineker, England | 6 |
| 1950 | Ademir de Menenzes, Brazil | 9 | 1990 | Salvatore Schillaci, Italy | 6 |
| 1954 | Sandor Kocsis, Hungary | 11 | 1994 | Hristo Stoichkov, Bulgaria | 6 |
| 1958 | Just Fontaine, France | 13 | | Oleg Salenko, Russia | |
| 1962 | Florian Albert, Hungary | 4 | 1998 | Davor Suker, Croatia | 6 |
| | Valentin Ivanov, USSR, Garrincha, Brazil, | | 2002 | Ronaldo, Brazil | 8 |
| | Vava, Brazil, Drazan Jerkovic, Yugoslavia | | 2006 | Miroslav Klose, Germany | 5 |
| | Leonel Sanchez, Chile | | 2010 | Thomas Mueller, Germany | 5 |
| 1966 | Eusebio Ferreira, Portugal | 9 | | Diego Forlan, Uruguay | |
| 1970 | Gerd Müller, W Germany | 10 | | Wesley Sneijder, Netherlands | |
| 1974 | Gregorz Lato, Poland | 7 | | David Villa, Spain | |

## Most Goals, Individual, One Game

| Goals | Player, Nation | Score | Date |
|---|---|---|---|
| 5 | Oleg Salenko, Russia | Russia–Cameroon, 6–1 | 6-28-94 |
| 4 | Leonidas, Brazil | Brazil–Poland, 6–5 | 6-5-38 |
| 4 | Ernest Willimowski, Poland | Brazil–Poland, 6–5 | 6-5-38 |
| 4 | Gustav Wetterstrim, Sweden | Sweden–Cuba, 8–0 | 6-12-38 |
| 4 | Juan Alberto Schiaffino, Uruguay | Uruguay–Bolivia, 8–0 | 7-2-50 |
| 4 | Ademir, Brazil | Brazil–Sweden, 7–1 | 7-9-50 |
| 4 | Sandor Kocsis, Hungary | Hungary–W Germany, 8–3 | 6-20-54 |
| 4 | Just Fontaine, France | France–W Germany, 6–3 | 6-28-58 |
| 4 | Eusebio, Portugal | Portugal–N Korea, 5–3 | 7-23-66 |
| 4 | Emilio Butragueño, Spain | Spain–Denmark, 5–1 | 6-18-86 |

Note: 31 players have scored 32 World Cup hat tricks. Gerd Müller of West Germany is the only man to have two World Cup hat tricks, both in 1970. The last hat tricks were 6-1-02, Miroslav Klose (Ger) vs. Saudi Arabia; 6-21-98, Gabriel Batistuta (Arg) vs. Jamaica; 6-23-90, Tomas Skuhravy (Czech) vs. Costa Rica; and 6-17-90, Michel (Spain) vs. S Korea.

### Attendance and Goal Scoring, Year by Year

| Year | Site | No. of Games | Goals | Goals/Game | Attendance | Avg Att |
|------|------|--------------|-------|------------|------------|---------|
| 1930 | Uruguay | 18 | 70 | 3.89 | 434,500 | 24,139 |
| 1934 | Italy | 17 | 70 | 4.12 | 395,000 | 23,235 |
| 1938 | France | 18 | 84 | 4.67 | 483,000 | 26,833 |
| 1950 | Brazil | 22 | 88 | 4.00 | 1,337,000 | 60,773 |
| 1954 | Switzerland | 26 | 140 | 5.38 | 943,000 | 36,269 |
| 1958 | Sweden | 35 | 126 | 3.60 | 868,000 | 24,800 |
| 1962 | Chile | 32 | 89 | 2.78 | 776,000 | 24,250 |
| 1966 | England | 32 | 89 | 2.78 | 1,614,677 | 50,459 |
| 1970 | Mexico | 32 | 95 | 2.97 | 1,673,975 | 52,312 |
| 1974 | W Germany | 38 | 97 | 2.55 | 1,774,022 | 46,685 |
| 1978 | Argentina | 38 | 102 | 2.68 | 1,610,215 | 42,374 |
| 1982 | Spain | 52 | 146 | 2.80 | 1,856,277 | 35,698 |
| 1986 | Mexico | 52 | 132 | 2.54 | 2,441,731 | 46,956 |
| 1990 | Italy | 52 | 115 | 2.21 | 2,514,443 | 48,354 |
| 1994 | United States | 52 | 140 | 2.69 | 3,567,415 | 68,604 |
| 1998 | France | 64 | 171 | 2.67 | 2,775,400 | 43,366 |
| 2002 | Korea/Japan | 64 | 161 | 2.52 | 2,705,216 | 42,269 |
| 2006 | Germany | 64 | 147 | 2.23 | 3,353,655 | 52,400 |
| 2010 | South Africa | 64 | 145 | 2.27 | 3,178,856 | 49,670 |
| Totals | | 708 | 2,046 | 2.89 | 31,597,166 | 44,629 |

### Results—Women's World Cup

| Year | Champion | Score | Runner-Up | Third Place | Fourth Place |
|------|----------|-------|-----------|-------------|--------------|
| 1991 | United States | 2–1 | Norway | Sweden | Germany |
| 1995 | Norway | 2–0 | Germany | United States | China |
| 1999 | United States | 0–0 (5–4 PK) | China | Brazil | Norway |
| 2003 | Germany | 2–1 | Sweden | United States | Canada |
| 2007 | Germany | 2–0 | Brazil | United States | Norway |
| 2011 | Japan | 2–2 (3–1 PK) | United States | Sweden | France |

# Major League Soccer Finals

## MLS Cup Results

| Year | Champion | Score | Runner-up | Regular Season MVP |
|------|----------|-------|-----------|--------------------|
| 1996 | D.C. United | 3–2 (OT) | Los Angeles | Carlos Valderrama, TB |
| 1997 | D.C. United | 2–1 | Colorado | Preki, Kansas City |
| 1998 | Chicago | 2–0 | D.C. United | Marco Etcheverry, D.C. |
| 1999 | D.C. United | 2–0 | Los Angeles | Jason Kreis, Dallas |
| 2000 | Kansas City | 1–0 | Chicago | Tony Meola, Kansas City |
| 2001 | San Jose | 2–1 (OT) | Los Angeles | Alex Pineda Chacon, Miami |
| 2002 | Los Angeles | 1–0 (OT) | New England | Carlos Ruiz, Los Angeles |
| 2003 | San Jose | 4–2 | Chicago | Preki, Kansas City |
| 2004 | D.C. United | 3–2 | Kansas City | Amado Guevara, MetroStars |
| 2005 | Los Angeles | 1–0 (OT) | New England | Taylor Twellman, NE |
| 2006 | Houston | 1–1 (OT, 4-3 PKs) | New England | Christian Gomez, D.C. |
| 2007 | Houston | 2–1 | New England | Luciano Emilio, D.C. |
| 2008 | Columbus | 3–1 | New York | Guillermo Schelotto, Clb |
| 2009 | Real Salt Lake | 1–1 (OT, 5-4 PKs) | Los Angeles | Landon Donovan, LA |
| 2010 | Colorado | 2–1 (OT) | FC Dallas | David Ferreira, DAL |

# United Soccer League Finals

| Year | Champion | Score | Runner-Up | Regular Season MVP |
|------|----------|-------|-----------|--------------------|
| 1991 | San Francisco | 1–3, 2–0 (1–0 PKs) | Albany | Jean Harbor, Maryland |
| 1992 | Colorado | 1–0 | Tampa Bay | Taifour Diane, Colorado |
| 1993 | Colorado | 3–1 (OT) | Los Angeles | Taifour Diane, Colorado |
| 1994 | Montreal | 1–0 | Colorado | Paulinho, Los Angeles |
| 1995 | Seattle | 1–2 (SO), 3–0, 2–1 (SO) | Atlanta | Peter Hattrup, Seattle |
| 1996 | Seattle | 2–0 | Rochester | Wolde Harris, Colorado |
| 1997 | Milwaukee | 2–1 (SO) | Carolina | Doug Miller, Rochester |
| 1998 | Rochester | 3–1 | Minnesota | Mark Baena, Seattle |
| 1999 | Minnesota | 2–1 | Rochester | John Swallen, Minnesota |
| 2000 | Rochester | 3–1 | Minnesota | Vitalis Takawira, Mil |
| 2001 | Rochester | 2–0 | Vancouver | Paul Conway, Charleston |
| 2002 | Milwaukee | 2–1 (2 OT) | Richmond | Leighton O'Brien, Seattle |
| 2003 | Charleston | 3–0 | Minnesota | Thiago Martins, Pittsburgh |
| 2004 | Montreal | 2–0 | Seattle | Greg Sutton, Montreal |
| 2005 | Seattle | 1–1 (4–3 on PKs) | Richmond | Jason Jordan, Vancouver |
| 2006 | Vancouver | 3–0 | Rochester | Joey Gjertsen, Vancouver |
| 2007 | Seattle | 4–0 | Atlanta | Sebastien Le Toux, Seattle |
| 2008 | Vancouver | 2–1 | Puerto Rico | Jonathan Steele, Puerto Rico |
| 2009 | Montreal | 6–3 (two legs) | Vancouver | Cristian Arietta, Puerto Rico |
| 2010 | Puerto Rico | 3–1 (two legs) | Carolina | Ryan Pore, Portland |
| 2011 | Orlando City | 2–2 (3–2 PKs) | Harrisburg City | Yordany Alvarez, Orlando City |

# Motor Sports

20-year-old rookie Trevor Bayne earned his debut Sprint Cup victory at the 2011 Daytona 500

## Indy Racing League

### Indianapolis 500

Results of the 95th running of the Indianapolis 500 and fifth race of the 2011 Indy Racing League season. Held Sunday, May 29, 2011, at the 2.5-mile Indianapolis Motor Speedway in Indianapolis, Indiana. Distance, 500 miles; starters, 33; winning time of race, 2 hours, 56 minutes, 11.7267 seconds; average speed, 170.265 mph; margin of victory (under caution); caution flags, 21 for 26 laps; lead changes, 23 among 10 drivers.

#### TOP 10 FINISHERS

| Pos. | Driver (start pos.) | C/E/T | Qual. Speed | Laps | Status |
|------|---------------------|-------|-------------|------|--------|
| 1 | Dan Wheldon (6) | D/H/F | 226.490 | 200 | running |
| 2 | JR Hildebrand† (12) | D/H/F | 225.579 | 200 | running |
| 3 | Graham Rahal (29) | D/H/F | 224.380 | 200 | running |
| 4 | Tony Kanaan (22) | D/H/F | 224.417 | 200 | running |
| 5 | Scott Dixon (2) | D/H/F | 227.340 | 200 | running |
| 6 | Oriol Servia (3) | D/H/F | 227.168 | 200 | running |
| 7 | Bertrand Baguette (14) | D/H/F | 225.285 | 200 | running |
| 8 | Tomas Scheckter (21) | D/H/F | 224.433 | 200 | running |
| 9 | Marco Andretti (27) | D/H/F | 224.628 | 200 | running |
| 10 | Danica Patrick (25) | D/H/F | 224.861 | 200 | running |

† Rookie.

### 2011 Indy Racing League Results

| Date | Race | Winner (start pos.) | C/E/T | Winning Time |
|------|------|---------------------|-------|--------------|
| Mar 27 | Grand Prix of St. Petersburg | Dario Franchitti (2) | D/H/F | 2:00:59.6886 |
| Apr 10 | Grand Prix of Alabama | Will Power (1) | D/H/F | 2:14:42.9523 |
| Apr 17 | Grand Prix of Long Beach | Mike Conway (3) | D/H/F | 1:53:11.1000 |
| May 2 | Sao Paulo 300 | Will Power (1) | D/H/F | 2:04:05.2964 |
| May 29 | Indianapolis 500 | Dan Wheldon (6) | D/H/F | 2:56.11.7267 |
| June 11 | Texas 275 (race #1) | Dario Franchitti (2) | D/H/F | 54:47.2787 |
| June 11 | Texas 275 (race #2) | Will Power (3) | D/H/F | 48:08.9739 |
| June 19 | Milwaukee 225 | Dario Franchitti (1) | D/H/F | 1:56:43.5877 |
| June 25 | Iowa 250 | Marco Andretti (17) | D/H/F | 1:53:00.1074 |
| July 10 | Toronto 200 | Dario Franchitti (3) | D/H/F | 1:56:32.1501 |
| July 24 | Edmonton 95* | Will Power (2) | D/H/F | 1:57:22.5177 |
| Aug 7 | Mid-Ohio 200 | Scott Dixon (1) | D/H/F | 1:48:46.9509 |
| Aug 14 | New Hampshire 225 | Ryan Hunter-Reay (5) | D/H/F | 1:58.01.5843 |
| Aug 28 | Sonoma Grand Prix | Will Power (1) | D/H/F | 1:47:29.7619 |
| Sept 4 | Baltimore Grand Prix | Will Power (1) | D/H/F | 2:02:19.4998 |
| Sept 17 | Japan 300 | Scott Dixon (1) | D/H/F | 1:56:44.0107 |
| Oct 2 | Kentucky 300 | Ed Carpenter (4) | D/H/F | 1:42:02.7825 |

Note: Distances are in miles unless followed by * (laps).

### 2011 Final IRL Standings

| Driver | Pts |
|--------|-----|
| Dario Franchitti | 573 |
| Will Power | 555 |
| Scott Dixon | 518 |
| Oriol Servia | 425 |
| Tony Kanaan | 366 |
| Ryan Briscoe | 364 |
| Ryan Hunter-Reay | 347 |
| Marco Andretti | 337 |
| Graham Rahal | 320 |
| Danica Patrick | 314 |

### Daytona 500†

Results of the 53rd Daytona 500, the opening round of the 2011 Sprint Cup series. Held Sunday, February 20, 2011, at the 2.5-mile high-banked Daytona International Speedway. Distance, 500 miles; starters, 43; winning time of race, 3 hours, 59 minutes, 24 seconds; average speed, 130.326 mph; margin of victory 0.118 seconds; caution flags, 16 for 60 laps; lead changes, 74 among 22 drivers.

#### TOP 10 FINISHERS

| Pos. | Driver (start pos.) | Car | Laps | Winnings ($) |
|---|---|---|---|---|
| 1 | Trevor Bayne (32) | Ford | 208 | 1,463,810 |
| 2 | Carl Edwards (22) | Ford | 208 | 1,108,400 |
| 3 | David Gilliland (39) | Ford | 208 | 818,171 |
| 4 | Bobby Labonte (31) | Toyota | 208 | 654,233 |
| 5 | Kurt Busch (3) | Dodge | 208 | 573,576 |
| 6 | Juan Pablo Montoya (13) | Chevrolet | 208 | 443,271 |
| 7 | Regan Smith (5) | Chevrolet | 208 | 400,933 |
| 8 | Kyle Busch (10) | Toyota | 208 | 388,729 |
| 9 | Paul Menard (19) | Chevrolet | 208 | 327,913 |
| 10 | Mark Martin (17) | Chevrolet | 208 | 318,038 |

### 2010 Sprint Chase for the Cup* Final Season Standings

| Driver | Pts | Starts | Wins | Top 5 | Top 10 |
|---|---|---|---|---|---|
| Jimmie Johnson | 6622 | 36 | 6 | 17 | 23 |
| Denny Hamlin | 6583 | 36 | 8 | 14 | 18 |
| Kevin Harvick | 6581 | 36 | 3 | 16 | 26 |
| Carl Edwards | 6393 | 36 | 2 | 9 | 19 |
| Matt Kenseth | 6294 | 36 | 0 | 6 | 15 |
| Greg Biffle | 6247 | 36 | 2 | 9 | 19 |
| Tony Stewart | 6221 | 36 | 2 | 9 | 17 |
| Kyle Busch | 6182 | 36 | 3 | 10 | 18 |
| Jeff Gordon | 6176 | 36 | 0 | 11 | 17 |
| Clint Bowyer | 6155 | 36 | 2 | 7 | 18 |
| Kurt Busch | 6142 | 36 | 2 | 9 | 17 |
| Jeff Burton | 6033 | 36 | 0 | 6 | 15 |

### 2010 Sprint Cup* Final Season Driver Winnings

| Driver | Winnings ($) |
|---|---|
| Jimmie Johnson | 7,264,780 |
| Jamie McMurray | 6,858,690 |
| Kevin Harvick | 6,812,580 |
| Kurt Busch | 6,732,740 |
| Kyle Busch | 6,291,690 |
| Denny Hamlin | 5,856,550 |
| Carl Edwards | 5,716,360 |
| Jeff Gordon | 5,703,710 |
| Tony Stewart | 5,664,250 |
| Matt Kenseth | 5,621,480 |
| Kasey Kahne | 5,289,130 |
| Jeff Burton | 5,178,400 |

### 2011 Sprint Chase for the Cup Late-Season Standings†

| Driver | Pts | Starts | Wins | Top 5 | Top 10 |
|---|---|---|---|---|---|
| Carl Edwards | 2161 | 30 | 1 | 15 | 21 |
| Kevin Harvick | 2160 | 30 | 4 | 8 | 16 |
| Jimmie Johnson | 2157 | 30 | 2 | 13 | 20 |
| Brad Keselowski | 2150 | 30 | 3 | 9 | 13 |
| Matt Kenseth | 2149 | 30 | 2 | 9 | 17 |
| Kurt Busch | 2145 | 30 | 2 | 8 | 16 |
| Tony Stewart | 2142 | 30 | 2 | 5 | 13 |
| Kyle Busch | 2141 | 30 | 4 | 13 | 17 |
| Dale Earnhardt Jr. | 2118 | 30 | 0 | 4 | 10 |
| Jeff Gordon | 2114 | 30 | 3 | 11 | 15 |
| Ryan Newman | 2107 | 30 | 1 | 8 | 14 |
| Denny Hamlin | 2082 | 30 | 1 | 4 | 10 |

*Series name changed from Winston Cup to Nextel Cup after 2003 season, then to Sprint Cup beginning in 2008.
†2011 Sprint Chase for the Cup standings through October 10, 2010 (30 of 36 races).

### Late 2010 Sprint Cup Series Results

| Date | Track/Distance | Winner (start pos.) | Car | Laps | Winnings ($) |
|------|----------------|---------------------|-----|------|--------------|
| *Oct 10 | Fontana 400 | Tony Stewart (22) | Chevrolet | 200 | 262,598 |
| *Oct 16 | Charlotte 500 | Jamie McMurray (27) | Chevrolet | 334 | 266,129 |
| *Oct 24 | Martinsville 500 | Denny Hamlin (1) | Toyota | 500 | 177,375 |
| *Oct 31 | Talladega 500 | Clint Bowyer (2) | Chevrolet | 188 | 226,450 |
| *Nov 7 | Texas 500 | Denny Hamlin (30) | Toyota | 334 | 453,575 |
| *Nov 14 | Phoenix 500 | Carl Edwards (1) | Ford | 312 | 247,098 |
| *Nov 21 | Homestead/Miami 400 | Carl Edwards (2) | Ford | 267 | 356,823 |

### 2011 Sprint Cup Series Results†

| Date | Track/Distance | Winner (start pos.) | Car | Laps | Winnings ($) |
|------|----------------|---------------------|-----|------|--------------|
| Feb 20 | Daytona 500 | Trevor Bayne (32) | Ford | 208 | 1,463,810 |
| Feb 27 | Phoenix 500 | Jeff Gordon (20) | Chevrolet | 312 | 230,586 |
| Mar 6 | Las Vegas 400 | Carl Edwards (3) | Ford | 267 | 401,541 |
| Mar 20 | Bristol 500 | Kyle Busch (12) | Toyota | 500 | 192,416 |
| Mar 27 | Fontana 500 | Kevin Harvick (24) | Chevrolet | 200 | 331,961 |
| Apr 3 | Martinsville 500 | Kevin Harvick (9) | Chevrolet | 500 | 200,786 |
| Apr 9 | Texas 500 | Matt Kenseth (4) | Ford | 334 | 525,886 |
| Apr 17 | Talladega 499 | Jimmie Johnson (2) | Chevrolet | 188 | 329,386 |
| Apr 30 | Richmond 400 | Kyle Busch (20) | Toyota | 400 | 239,316 |
| May 7 | Darlington 500 | Regan Smith 23) | Chevrolet | 370 | 272,745 |
| May 15 | Dover 400 | Matt Kenseth (24) | Ford | 400 | 314,311 |
| May 21 | Showdown | David Ragan (1) | Ford | 40 | N/A |
| May 21 | All-Star Race | Carl Edwards (4) | Ford | 100 | N/A |
| May 29 | Charlotte 600 | Kevin Harvick (28) | Chevrolet | 402 | 406,786 |
| June 5 | Kansas 400 | Brad Keselowski (25) | Dodge | 267 | 216,633 |
| June 12 | Pocono 500 | Jeff Gordon (3) | Chevrolet | 200 | 223,836 |
| June 19 | Michigan 400 | Denny Hamlin (10) | Toyota | 200 | 202,200 |
| June 26 | Sonoma 350 | Kurt Busch (11) | Dodge | 110 | 293,300 |
| July 2 | Daytona 400 | David Ragan (5) | Ford | 170 | 302,425 |
| July 9 | Kentucky 400 | Kyle Busch (1) | Toyota | 267 | 213,316 |
| July 17 | Loudon 301 | Ryan Newman (1) | Chevrolet | 301 | 268,050 |
| July 31 | Brickyard 400 | Paul Menard (15) | Chevrolet | 160 | 373,575 |
| Aug 7 | Pocono 500 | Brad Keselowski (13) | Dodge | 200 | 201,408 |
| Aug 15 | Watkins Glen 220 | Marcos Ambrose (3) | Ford | 92 | 217,741 |
| Aug 21 | Michigan 400 | Kyle Busch (17) | Toyota | 203 | 204,941 |
| Aug 27 | Bristol 500 | Brad Keselowski (8) | Dodge | 500 | 291,883 |
| Sept 6 | Atlanta 500 | Jeff Gordon (5) | Chevrolet | 325 | 329,786 |
| Sept 10 | Richmond 400 | Kevin Harvick (7) | Chevrolet | 400 | 256,736 |
| *Sept 19 | Chicago 400 | Tony Stewart (26) | Chevrolet | 267 | 332,308 |
| *Sept 25 | Loudon 300 | Tony Stewart (20) | Chevrolet | 300 | 254,083 |
| *Oct 2 | Dover 400 | Kurt Busch (2) | Dodge | 400 | 223,625 |
| *Oct 9 | Kansas 400 | Jimmie Johnson (19) | Chevrolet | 272 | 331,336 |

† Through October 10, 2011.
* Part of 10-race Chase for the Cup.

# Formula One Grand Prix Racing

## 2011 Formula One Results†

| Grand Prix | Date | Winner | Car | Laps | Time |
|---|---|---|---|---|---|
| Australia | Mar 27 | Sebastian Vettel | RBR-Renault | 58 | 1:29:30.259 |
| Malaysia | Apr 10 | Sebastian Vettel | RBR-Renault | 56 | 1:37:39.832 |
| China | Apr 17 | Lewis Hamilton | McLaren-Mercedes | 56 | 1:36:58.226 |
| Turkey | May 8 | Sebastian Vettel | RBR-Renault | 58 | 1:30:17.558 |
| Spain | May 22 | Sebastian Vettel | RBR-Renault | 66 | 1:39:03.301 |
| Monaco | May 29 | Sebastian Vettel | RBR-Renault | 78 | 2:09:38.373 |
| Canada | June 12 | Jenson Button | McLaren-Mercedes | 70 | 4:04:39.537 |
| Europe | June 26 | Sebastian Vettel | RBR-Renault | 57 | 1:39:36.169 |
| Great Britain | July 10 | Fernando Alonso | Ferrari | 52 | 1:28:41.196 |
| Germany | July 24 | Lewis Hamilton | McLaren-Mercedes | 60 | 1:37:30.334 |
| Hungary | July 31 | Jenson Button | McLaren-Mercedes | 70 | 1:46:42.337 |
| Belgium | Aug 28 | Sebastian Vettel | RBR-Renault | 44 | 1:26:44.893 |
| Italy | Sept 11 | Sebastian Vettel | RBR-Renault | 53 | 1:20:46.172 |
| Singapore | Sept 25 | Sebastian Vettel | RBR-Renault | 61 | 1:59:06.757 |
| Japan | Oct 9 | Jenson Button | McLaren Mercedes | 53 | 1:30:53.427 |

† Through October 10, 2011.

## 2010 World Championship Final Standings

Drivers compete in Grand Prix races for the title of World Driving Champion. Below are the top 10 drivers from the 2010 season. Points are awarded for places 1–10 as follows: 25-18-15-12-10-8-6-4-2-1.

| Driver | Country | Team | Pts |
|---|---|---|---|
| Sebastian Vettel | Germany | RBR-Renault | 256 |
| Fernando Alonso | Spain | Ferrari | 252 |
| Mark Webber | Australia | RBR-Renault | 242 |
| Lewis Hamilton | Great Britain | McLaren-Mercedes | 240 |
| Jenson Button | Great Britain | McLaren-Mercedes | 214 |
| Felipe Massa | Brazil | Ferrari | 144 |
| Nico Rosberg | Germany | Mercedes GP | 142 |
| Robert Kubica | Poland | Renault | 136 |
| Michael Schumacher | Finland | Mercedes GP | 72 |
| Rubens Barrichello | Brazil | Williams-Cosworth | 47 |
| Adrian Sutil | Germany | Force India-Mercedes | 47 |

# Professional Sports Car Racing

## The 24 Hours of Daytona

Held at the Daytona International Speedway on Jan 29–30, 2011, the 24 Hours of Daytona serves as the opening round of the Grand American Road Racing Association's season.

| Place | Drivers | Car (Class) | Distance |
|---|---|---|---|
| 1 | J. Hand, S. Pruett, G. Rahal, M. Rojas | BMW Riley | 721 laps (106.877 mph) |
| 2 | S. Dixon, D. Franchitti, J. McMurray, J. Montoya | BMW Riley | 721 |
| 3 | J. Barbosa, T. Borcheller, C. Fittipaldi, J.C. France, M. Papis | Porsche Riley | 721 |
| 4 | M.Blundell, Z. Brown, M. Brundle, M. Patterson | Ford Riley | 721 |
| 5 | M. Angelelli, R. Briscoe, W. Taylor, R. Taylor | Chevrolet Dallara | 720 |

## 2011 American Le Mans Series—Prototype Class

| Date | Race | Winners | Car |
|---|---|---|---|
| Mar 19 | 12 Hours of Sebring | N, Lapierre, L. Duval, O. Panis | Peugeot 908 HDI |
| April 16 | Grand Prix of Long Beach | L. Luhr, K. Graf | Lola B08 Aston Martin |
| July 9 | Northeast Grand Prix | C. Dyson, G. Smith | Lola B09 86 Mazda |
| July 24 | Grand Prix of Mosport | L. Luhr, K. Graf | Lola B08 Aston Martin |
| Aug 6 | Mid-Ohio Challenge | L. Luhr, K. Graf | Lola B08 Aston Martin |
| Aug 20 | Road America 500 | L. Luhr, K. Graf | Lola B08 Aston Martin |
| Sept 3 | Baltimore Grand Prix | S. Kane, H. Al Masaood | Lola B08 Aston Martin |
| Sept 17 | Laguna Seca | S. Mucke, H. Primat | Lola B08 Aston Martin |
| Oct 1 | Petit Le Mans | S. Sarrazin, F. Montagny, A. Wurz | Peugeot 908 |

### 2011 American Le Mans Series—GT Class

| Date | Race | Winners | Car |
|---|---|---|---|
| Mar 19 | 12 Hours of Sebring | D. Mueller, J. Hand | BMW M3 GT |
| April 16 | Grand Prix of Long Beach | D. Mueller, J. Hand | BMW E92 M3 |
| July 9 | Northeast Grand Prix | D. Mueller, J. Hand | BMW E92 M3 |
| July 24 | Grand Prix of Mosport | O. Gavin, J. Magnussen | Chevy Corvette C6 ZR1 |
| Aug 6 | Mid-Ohio Challenge | B. Sellers, W. Henzler | Porsche 911 GT3 RSR |
| Aug 20 | Road America 500 | J. Melo, T. Vilander | Ferrari F458 Italia |
| Sept 3 | Baltimore Grand Prix | B. Sellers, W. Henzler | Porsche 911 GT3 RSR |
| Spet 17 | Laguna Seca | P. Long, J. Bergmeister | Porsche 911 GT3 RSR |
| Oct 2 | Petit Le Mans | G. Fisichella, G. Bruni, P. Kaffer | Ferrari F458 Italia |

### 2011 American Le Mans Series—GTC Class

| Date | Race | Winners | Car |
|---|---|---|---|
| Mar 19 | 12 Hours of Sebring | D. Faulkner, T. Pappas, S. Bleekemolen | Porsche 911 GT3 |
| April 16 | Grand Prix of Long Beach | T. Pappas, J. Bleekemolen | Porsche 911 GT3 |
| July 9 | Northeast Grand Prix | M. Piera, D. von Moltke | Porsche 911 GT3 |
| July 24 | Grand Prix of Mosport | D. Ende, S. Pumpelly | Porsche 911 GT3 |
| Aug 6 | Mid-Ohio Challenge | D. Ende, S. Pumpelly | Porsche 911 GT3 |
| Aug 20 | Road America 500 | T. Pappas, J. Bleekemolen | Porsche 911 GT3 |
| Sept 3 | Baltimore Grand Prix | T. Pappas, J. Bleekemolen | Porsche 911 GT3 |
| May 22 | Laguna Seca | D. Ende, S. Pumpelly | Porsche 911 GT3 |
| Oct 1 | Petit Le Mans | T. Pappas, J. Bleekemolen | Porsche 911 GT3 |

### 2011 American Le Mans Series Championship Final Standings

| PROTOTYPE CLASS | Pts | GTC CLASS | Pts | GT CLASS | Pts |
|---|---|---|---|---|---|
| Guy Smith | 186 | Timothy Pappas | 185 | Dirk Mueller | 159 |
| Chris Dyson | 186 | Duncan Ende | 157 | Joey Hand | 159 |
| Klaus Graf | 124 | Spencer Pumpelly | 157 | Oliver Gavin | 135 |
| Lucas Luhr | 114 | Jeroen Bleekemolen | 132 | Jan Magnussen | 135 |
| Chris McMurry | 85 | Bill Sweedler | 117 | Bill Auberlen | 129 |
| Tony Burgess | 85 | Dion von Moltke | 108 | Dirk Werner | 129 |

## 24 Hours of Le Mans

Held at Le Mans, France, on June 11–12, 2011, the 24 Hours of Le Mans is the most prestigious international event in endurance racing.

| Place | Drivers | Car | Laps |
|---|---|---|---|
| 1 | M. Fassler, A. Lotterer, B Treluyer | Audi R18 TDI | 355 (125.27 mph) |
| 2 | S. Bourdais, S. Pagenaud, P. Lamy | Peugeot 908 | 355 |
| 3 | S. Sarrazin, F. Montagny, N. Minassian | Peugeot 908 | 353 |
| 4 | A. Davidson, M. Gene, A. Wurz | Peugeot 908 | 351 |
| 5 | N. Lapierre, L. Duval, O. Panis | Peugeot 908 HDI-FAP | 339 |

## Indianapolis 500

First held in 1911, the Indianapolis 500—200 laps of the 2.5-mile Indianapolis Motor Speedway Track (called the Brickyard in honor of its original pavement)—grew to become the most famous auto race in the world. Though the Memorial Day weekend event lost participants and prestige in the mid-1990s due to feuding in the world of U.S. open-wheel racing, it annually attracts crowds of over 100,000.

| Year | Winner (start pos.) | Chassis-Engine | Avg Speed | Pole Winner | Speed |
|------|--------------------|-----------------|-----------|-------------|-------|
| 1911 | Ray Harroun (28) | Marmon-Marmon | 74.590 | Lewis Strang | First entered |
| 1912 | Joe Dawson (7) | National-National | 78.720 | Gil Anderson | First entered |
| 1913 | Jules Goux (7) | Peugeot-Peugeot | 75.930 | Caleb Bragg | Drew pole |
| 1914 | Rene Thomas (15) | Delage-Delage | 82.470 | Jean Chassagne | Drew pole |
| 1915 | Ralph DePalma (2) | Mercedes-Mercedes | 89.840 | Howard Wilcox | 98.90 |
| 1916 | Dario Resta (4) | Peugeot-Peugeot | 84.000 | John Aitken | 96.69 |
| 1917–18 | No race | | | | |
| 1919 | Howard Wilcox (2) | Peugeot-Peugeot | 88.050 | Rene Thomas | 104.78 |
| 1920 | Gaston Chevrolet (6) | Frontenac-Frontenac | 88.620 | Ralph DePalma | 99.15 |
| 1921 | Tommy Milton (20) | Frontenac-Frontenac | 89.620 | Ralph DePalma | 100.75 |
| 1922 | Jimmy Murphy (1) | Duesenberg-Miller | 94.480 | Jimmy Murphy | 100.50 |
| 1923 | Tommy Milton (1) | Miller-Miller | 90.950 | Tommy Milton | 108.17 |
| 1924 | L.L. Corum Joe Boyer (21) | Duesenberg-Duesenberg | 98.230 | Jimmy Murphy | 108.037 |
| 1925 | Peter DePaolo (2) | Duesenberg-Duesenberg | 101.130 | Leon Duray | 113.196 |
| 1926 | Frank Lockhart (20) | Miller-Miller | 95.904 | Earl Cooper | 111.735 |
| 1927 | George Souders (22) | Duesenberg-Duesenberg | 97.545 | Frank Lockhart | 120.100 |
| 1928 | Louis Meyer (13) | Miller-Miller | 99.482 | Leon Duray | 122.391 |
| 1929 | Ray Keech (6) | Miller-Miller | 97.585 | Cliff Woodbury | 120.599 |
| 1930 | Billy Arnold (1) | Summers-Miller | 100.448 | Billy Arnold | 113.268 |
| 1931 | Louis Schneider (13) | Stevens-Miller | 96.629 | Russ Snowberger | 112.796 |
| 1932 | Fred Frame (27) | Wetteroth-Miller | 104.144 | Lou Moore | 117.363 |
| 1933 | Louis Meyer (6) | Miller-Miller | 104.162 | Bill Cummings | 118.524 |
| 1934 | Bill Cummings (10) | Miller-Miller | 104.863 | Kelly Petillo | 119.329 |
| 1935 | Kelly Petillo (22) | Wetteroth-Offy | 106.240 | Rex Mays | 120.736 |
| 1936 | Louis Meyer (28) | Stevens-Miller | 109.069 | Rex Mays | 119.664 |
| 1937 | Wilbur Shaw (2) | Shaw-Offy | 113.580 | Bill Cummings | 123.343 |
| 1938 | Floyd Roberts (1) | Wetteroth-Miller | 117.200 | Floyd Roberts | 125.681 |
| 1939 | Wilbur Shaw (3) | Maserati-Maserati | 115.035 | Jimmy Snyder | 130.138 |
| 1940 | Wilbur Shaw (2) | Maserati-Maserati | 114.277 | Rex Mays | 127.850 |
| 1941 | Floyd Davis Mauri Rose (17) | Wetteroth-Offy | 115.117 | Mauri Rose | 128.691 |
| 1942–45 | No race | | | | |
| 1946 | George Robson (15) | Adams-Sparks | 114.820 | Cliff Bergere | 126.471 |
| 1947 | Mauri Rose (3) | Deidt-Offy | 116.338 | Ted Horn | 126.564 |
| 1948 | Mauri Rose (3) | Deidt-Offy | 119.814 | Rex Mays | 130.577 |
| 1949 | Bill Holland (4) | Deidt-Offy | 121.327 | Duke Nalon | 132.939 |
| 1950 | Johnnie Parsons (5) | Kurtis-Offy | 124.002 | Walt Faulkner | 134.343 |
| 1951 | Lee Wallard (2) | Kurtis-Offy | 126.244 | Duke Nalon | 136.498 |
| 1952 | Troy Ruttman (7) | Kuzma-Offy | 128.922 | Fred Agabashian | 138.010 |
| 1953 | Bill Vukovich (1) | KK500A-Offy | 128.740 | Bill Vukovich | 138.392 |
| 1954 | Bill Vukovich (19) | KK500A-Offy | 130.840 | Jack McGrath | 141.033 |
| 1955 | Bob Sweikert (14) | KK500C-Offy | 128.209 | Jerry Hoyt | 140.045 |
| 1956 | Pat Flaherty (1) | Watson-Offy | 128.490 | Pat Flaherty | 145.596 |
| 1957 | Sam Hanks (13) | Salih-Offy | 135.601 | Pat O'Connor | 143.948 |
| 1958 | Jim Bryan (7) | Salih-Offy | 133.791 | Dick Rathmann | 145.974 |
| 1959 | Rodger Ward (6) | Watson-Offy | 135.857 | Johnny Thomson | 145.908 |
| 1960 | Jim Rathmann (2) | Watson-Offy | 138.767 | Eddie Sachs | 146.592 |
| 1961 | A.J. Foyt (7) | Trevis-Offy | 139.130 | Eddie Sachs | 147.481 |
| 1962 | Rodger Ward (2) | Watson-Offy | 140.293 | Parnelli Jones | 150.370 |
| 1963 | Parnelli Jones (1) | Watson-Offy | 143.137 | Parnelli Jones | 151.153 |
| 1964 | A.J. Foyt (5) | Watson-Offy | 147.350 | Jim Clark | 158.828 |
| 1965 | Jim Clark (2) | Lotus-Ford | 150.686 | A.J. Foyt | 161.233 |
| 1966 | Graham Hill (15) | Lola-Ford | 144.317 | Mario Andretti | 165.899 |
| 1967 | A.J. Foyt (4) | Coyote-Ford | 151.207 | Mario Andretti | 168.982 |
| 1968 | Bobby Unser (3) | Eagle-Offy | 152.882 | Joe Leonard | 171.559 |
| 1969 | Mario Andretti (2) | Hawk-Ford | 156.867 | A.J. Foyt | 170.568 |
| 1970 | Al Unser (1) | PJ Colt-Ford | 155.749 | Al Unser | 170.221 |
| 1971 | Al Unser (5) | PJ Colt-Ford | 157.735 | Peter Revson | 178.696 |
| 1972 | Mark Donohue (3) | McLaren-Offy | 162.962 | Bobby Unser | 195.940 |

| Year | Winner (start pos.) | Chassis-Engine | Avg speed | Pole Winner | Speed |
|------|---------------------|----------------|-----------|-------------|-------|
| 1973 | Gordon Johncock (11) | Eagle-Offy | 159.036 | Johnny Rutherford | 198.413 |
| 1974 | Johnny Rutherford (25) | McLaren-Offy | 158.589 | A.J. Foyt | 191.632 |
| 1975 | Bobby Unser (3) | Racers Eagle-Offy | 149.213 | A.J. Foyt | 193.976 |
| 1976 | Johnny Rutherford (1) | McLaren-Offy | 148.725 | Johnny Rutherford | 188.957 |
| 1977 | A.J. Foyt (4) | Coyote-Ford | 161.331 | Tom Sneva | 198.884 |
| 1978 | Al Unser (5) | Lola-Cosworth | 161.361 | Tom Sneva | 202.156 |
| 1979 | Rick Mears (1) | Penske-Cosworth | 158.899 | Rick Mears | 193.736 |
| 1980 | Johnny Rutherford (1) | Chaparral-Cosworth | 142.862 | Johnny Rutherford | 192.256 |
| 1981 | Bobby Unser (1) | Penske-Cosworth | 139.084 | Bobby Unser | 200.546 |
| 1982 | Gordon Johncock (5) | Wildcat-Cosworth | 162.026 | Rick Mears | 207.004 |
| 1983 | Tom Sneva (4) | March-Cosworth | 162.117 | Teo Fabi | 207.395 |
| 1984 | Rick Mears (3) | March-Cosworth | 163.612 | Tom Sneva | 210.029 |
| 1985 | Danny Sullivan (8) | March-Cosworth | 152.982 | Pancho Carter | 212.583 |
| 1986 | Bobby Rahal (4) | March-Cosworth | 170.722 | Rick Mears | 216.828 |
| 1987 | Al Unser (20) | March-Cosworth | 162.175 | Mario Andretti | 215.390 |
| 1988 | Rick Mears (1) | Penske-Chevrolet | 144.809 | Rick Mears | 219.198 |
| 1989 | Emerson Fittipaldi (3) | Penske-Chevrolet | 167.581 | Rick Mears | 223.885 |
| 1990 | Arie Luyendyk (3) | Lola-Chevrolet | 185.981* | Emerson Fittipaldi | 225.301 |
| 1991 | Rick Mears (1) | Penske-Chevrolet | 176.457 | Rick Mears | 224.113 |
| 1992 | Al Unser Jr. (12) | Galmer-Chevrolet | 134.477 | Roberto Guerrero | 232.482 |
| 1993 | Emerson Fittipaldi (9) | Penske-Chevrolet | 157.207 | Arie Luyendyk | 223.967 |
| 1994 | Al Unser Jr. (1) | Penske-Mercedes | 160.872 | Al Unser Jr. | 228.011 |
| 1995 | Jacques Villeneuve (5) | Reynard-Ford | 153.616 | Scott Brayton | 231.616 |
| 1996 | Buddy Lazier (5) | Reynard-Ford | 147.956 | Tony Stewart | 233.100† |
| 1997 | Arie Luyendyk (1) | G Force-Oldsmobile | 145.827 | Arie Luyendyk | 231.468 |
| 1998 | Eddie Cheever (17) | Dallara-Oldsmobile | 145.155 | Billy Boat | 223.503 |
| 1999 | Kenny Brack (8) | Dallara-Oldsmobile | 153.176 | Arie Luyendyk | 225.179 |
| 2000 | Juan Montoya (2) | G Force-Oldsmobile | 167.607 | Greg Ray | 223.471 |
| 2001 | Helio Castroneves (11) | Dallara-Oldsmobile | 153.601 | Scott Sharp | 226.037 |
| 2002 | Helio Castroneves (13) | Dallara-Chevrolet | 166.499 | Bruno Junqueira | 231.342 |
| 2003 | Gil de Ferran | Panoz-Toyota | 156.291 | Helio Castroneves | 231.725 |
| 2004 | Buddy Rice (1) | G Force-Honda | 138.518 | Buddy Rice | 222.024 |
| 2005 | Dan Wheldon | Dallara-Honda | 157.603 | Tony Kanaan | 227.566 |
| 2006 | Sam Hornish Jr.(1) | Dallara-Honda | 157.085 | Sam Hornish Jr. | 228.985 |
| 2007 | Dario Franchitti (3) | Dallara-Honda | 151.744 | Helio Castroneves | 225.817 |
| 2008 | Scott Dixon (1) | Dallara-Honda | 143.567 | Scott Dixon | 226.366 |
| 2009 | Helio Castroneves (1) | Dallara-Honda | 150.138 | Helio Castroneves | 224.864 |
| 2010 | Dario Franchitti (3) | Dallara-Honda | 161.623 | Helio Castroneves | 227.970 |
| 2011 | Dan Wheldon (6) | Dallara-Honda | 170.265 | Alex Tagliani | 227.472 |

*Track record, winning speed. †Track record, qualifying speed.

## Indianapolis 500 Rookie of the Year Award

| | | |
|---|---|---|
| 1952 | Art Cross | 1974 | Pancho Carter | 1994 | Jacques Villeneuve* |
| 1953 | Jimmy Daywalt | 1975 | Bill Puterbaugh | 1995 | Gil de Ferran* |
| 1954 | Larry Crockett | 1976 | Vern Schuppan | 1996 | Tony Stewart |
| 1955 | Al Herman | 1977 | Jerry Sneva | 1997 | Jeff Ward |
| 1956 | Bob Veith | 1978 | Rick Mears* | 1998 | Steve Knapp |
| 1957 | Don Edmunds | | Larry Rice | 1999 | Robby McGehee |
| 1958 | George Amick | 1979 | Howdy Holmes | 2000 | Juan Montoya* |
| 1959 | Bobby Grim | 1980 | Tim Richmond | 2001 | Helio Castroneves* |
| 1960 | Jim Hurtubise | 1981 | Josele Garza | 2002 | Alex Barron |
| 1961 | Parnelli Jones* | 1982 | Jim Hickman | | Tomas Scheckter |
| | Bobby Marshman | 1983 | Teo Fabi | 2003 | Tora Tagaki |
| 1962 | Jimmy McElreath | 1984 | Michael Andretti | 2004 | Kosuke Matsuura |
| 1963 | Jim Clark* | | Roberto Guerrero | 2005 | Danica Patrick |
| 1964 | Johnny White | 1985 | Arie Luyendyk* | 2006 | Marco Andretti |
| 1965 | Mario Andretti* | 1986 | Randy Lanier | 2007 | Phil Giebler |
| 1966 | Jackie Stewart | 1987 | Fabrizio Barbazza | 2008 | Ryan Hunter-Reay |
| 1967 | Denis Hulme | 1988 | Billy Vukovich III | 2009 | Alex Tagliani |
| 1968 | Billy Vukovich | 1989 | Bernard Jourdain | 2010 | Simona De Silvestro |
| 1969 | Mark Donohue* | | Scott Pruett | 2011 | JR Hildebrand |
| 1970 | Donnie Allison | 1990 | Eddie Cheever* | | |
| 1971 | Denny Zimmerman | 1991 | Jeff Andretti | | |
| 1972 | Mike Hiss | 1992 | Lyn St. James | | |
| 1973 | Graham McRae | 1993 | Nigel Mansell | | |

*Future winner of Indy 500.

## Champ Car World Series Champions

From 1909 to 1955, this championship was awarded by the American Automobile Association (AAA), and from 1956 to 1979 by the United States Auto Club (USAC). During the 1979 season, Championship Auto Racing Teams (CART) split from the USAC and conducted the championship. Known as PPG CART World Series until 1998. Series name changed to Champ Car World Series for 2005 racing season. On Februray 22, 2008, the Champ Car World Series merged with the Indy Racing League.

| Year | Champion | Year | Champion | Year | Champion |
|---|---|---|---|---|---|
| 1909 | George Robertson | 1942–45 | No racing | 1978 | Tom Sneva |
| 1910 | Ray Harroun | 1946 | Ted Horn | 1979 | A.J. Foyt (USAC) |
| 1911 | Ralph Mulford | 1947 | Ted Horn | 1979 | Rick Mears (CART) |
| 1912 | Ralph DePalma | 1948 | Ted Horn | 1980 | Johnny Rutherford |
| 1913 | Earl Cooper | 1949 | Johnnie Parsons | 1981 | Rick Mears |
| 1914 | Ralph DePalma | 1950 | Henry Banks | 1982 | Rick Mears |
| 1915 | Earl Cooper | 1951 | Tony Bettenhausen | 1983 | Al Unser |
| 1916 | Dario Resta | 1952 | Chuck Stevenson | 1984 | Mario Andretti |
| 1917 | Earl Cooper | 1953 | Sam Hanks | 1985 | Al Unser |
| 1918 | Ralph Mulford | 1954 | Jimmy Bryan | 1986 | Bobby Rahal |
| 1919 | Howard Wilcox | 1955 | Bob Sweikert | 1987 | Bobby Rahal |
| 1920 | Tommy Milton | 1956 | Jimmy Bryan | 1988 | Danny Sullivan |
| 1921 | Tommy Milton | 1957 | Jimmy Bryan | 1989 | Emerson Fittipaldi |
| 1922 | Jimmy Murphy | 1958 | Tony Bettenhausen | 1990 | Al Unser Jr. |
| 1923 | Eddie Hearne | 1959 | Rodger Ward | 1991 | Michael Andretti |
| 1924 | Jimmy Murphy | 1960 | A.J. Foyt | 1992 | Bobby Rahal |
| 1925 | Peter DePaolo | 1961 | A.J. Foyt | 1993 | Nigel Mansell |
| 1926 | Harry Hartz | 1962 | Rodger Ward | 1994 | Al Unser Jr. |
| 1927 | Peter DePaolo | 1963 | A.J. Foyt | 1995 | Jacques Villeneuve |
| 1928 | Louis Meyer | 1964 | A.J. Foyt | 1996 | Jimmy Vasser |
| 1929 | Louis Meyer | 1965 | Mario Andretti | 1997 | Alex Zanardi |
| 1930 | Billy Arnold | 1966 | Mario Andretti | 1998 | Alex Zanardi |
| 1931 | Louis Schneider | 1967 | A.J. Foyt | 1999 | Juan Montoya |
| 1932 | Bob Carey | 1968 | Bobby Unser | 2000 | Gil de Ferran |
| 1933 | Louis Meyer | 1969 | Mario Andretti | 2001 | Gil de Ferran |
| 1934 | Bill Cummings | 1970 | Al Unser | 2002 | Cristiano da Matta |
| 1935 | Kelly Petillo | 1971 | Joe Leonard | 2003 | Paul Tracy |
| 1936 | Mauri Rose | 1972 | Joe Leonard | 2004 | Sebastian Bourdais |
| 1937 | Wilbur Shaw | 1973 | Roger McCluskey | 2005 | Sebastian Bourdais |
| 1938 | Floyd Roberts | 1974 | Bobby Unser | 2006 | Sebastian Bourdais |
| 1939 | Wilbur Shaw | 1975 | A.J. Foyt | 2007 | Sebastian Bourdais |
| 1940 | Rex Mays | 1976 | Gordon Johncock | | |
| 1941 | Rex Mays | 1977 | Tom Sneva | | |

## Alltime Champ Car* Leaders

| WINS | | POLE POSITIONS | |
|---|---|---|---|
| A.J. Foyt | 67 | Mario Andretti | 67 |
| Mario Andretti | 52 | A.J. Foyt | 53 |
| Michael Andretti | 42 | Bobby Unser | 49 |
| Al Unser | 39 | Rick Mears | 40 |
| Bobby Unser | 35 | Michael Andretti | 32 |
| Al Unser Jr | 31 | Sebastian Bourdais | 28 |
| Paul Tracy | 31 | Al Unser | 27 |
| Rick Mears | 29 | Paul Tracy | 25 |
| Sebastian Bourdais | 29 | Johnny Rutherford | 23 |
| Johnny Rutherford | 27 | Gordon Johncock | 20 |
| Rodger Ward | 26 | Rex Mays | 19 |
| Gordon Johncock | 25 | Danny Sullivan | 19 |
| Bobby Rahal | 24 | Bobby Rahal | 18 |
| Ralph DePalma | 24 | Emerson Fittipaldi | 17 |
| Tommy Milton | 23 | Gil de Ferran | 16 |
| Tony Bettenhausen | 22 | Tony Bettenhausen | 14 |
| Emerson Fittipaldi | 22 | Juan Montoya | 14 |
| Earl Cooper | 20 | Don Branson | 14 |
| Jimmy Bryan | 19 | Tom Sneva | 14 |
| Jimmy Murphy | 19 | Parnelli Jones | 12 |
| Danny Sullivan | 17 | | |
| Ralph Mulford | 17 | | |

*Series known as CART prior to 2003 season

## Stock Car Racing's Major Events

### Daytona 500

| Year | Winner (start pos.) | Chassis-Engine | Avg speed | Pole Winner | Qual. speed |
|------|---------------------|----------------|-----------|-------------|-------------|
| 1959 | Lee Petty | Oldsmobile | 135.520 | Cotton Owens | 143.198 |
| 1960 | Junior Johnson | Chevrolet | 124.740 | Fireball Roberts | 151.556 |
| 1961 | Marvin Panch | Pontiac | 149.601 | Fireball Roberts | 155.709 |
| 1962 | Fireball Roberts | Pontiac | 152.529 | Fireball Roberts | 156.995 |
| 1963 | Tiny Lund | Ford | 151.566 | Johnny Rutherford | 165.183 |
| 1964 | Richard Petty | Plymouth | 154.345 | Paul Goldsmith | 174.910 |
| 1965 | Fred Lorenzen | Ford | 141.539 | Darel Dieringer | 171.151 |
| 1966 | Richard Petty | Plymouth | 160.627 | Richard Petty | 175.165 |
| 1967 | Mario Andretti | Ford | 149.926 | Curtis Turner | 180.831 |
| 1968 | Cale Yarborough | Mercury | 143.251 | Cale Yarborough | 189.222 |
| 1969 | Lee Roy Yarbrough | Ford | 157.950 | David Pearson | 190.029 |
| 1970 | Pete Hamilton | Plymouth | 149.601 | Cale Yarborough | 194.015 |
| 1971 | Richard Petty | Plymouth | 144.462 | A.J. Foyt | 182.744 |
| 1972 | A.J. Foyt | Mercury | 161.550 | Bobby Isaac | 186.632 |
| 1973 | Richard Petty | Dodge | 157.205 | Buddy Baker | 185.662 |
| 1974 | Richard Petty | Dodge | 140.894 | David Pearson | 185.017 |
| 1975 | Benny Parsons | Chevrolet | 153.649 | Donnie Allison | 185.827 |
| 1976 | David Pearson | Mercury | 152.181 | A.J. Foyt | 185.943 |
| 1977 | Cale Yarborough | Chevrolet | 153.218 | Donnie Allison | 188.048 |
| 1978 | Bobby Allison | Ford | 159.730 | Cale Yarborough | 187.536 |
| 1979 | Richard Petty | Oldsmobile | 143.977 | Buddy Baker | 196.049 |
| 1980 | Buddy Baker | Oldsmobile | 177.602* | A.J. Foyt | 195.020 |
| 1981 | Richard Petty | Buick | 169.651 | Bobby Allison | 194.624 |
| 1982 | Bobby Allison | Buick | 153.991 | Benny Parsons | 196.317 |
| 1983 | Cale Yarborough | Pontiac | 155.979 | Ricky Rudd | 198.864 |
| 1984 | Cale Yarborough | Chevrolet | 150.994 | Cale Yarborough | 201.848 |
| 1985 | Bill Elliott | Ford | 172.265 | Bill Elliott | 205.114 |
| 1986 | Geoff Bodine | Chevrolet | 148.124 | Bill Elliott | 205.039 |
| 1987 | Bill Elliott | Ford | 176.263 | Bill Elliott | 210.364† |
| 1988 | Bobby Allison | Buick | 137.531 | Ken Schrader | 193.823 |
| 1989 | Darrell Waltrip | Chevrolet | 148.466 | Ken Schrader | 196.996 |
| 1990 | Derrike Cope | Chevrolet | 165.761 | Ken Schrader | 196.515 |
| 1991 | Ernie Irvan | Chevrolet | 148.148 | Davey Allison | 195.955 |
| 1992 | Davey Allison | Ford | 160.256 | Sterling Marlin | 192.213 |
| 1993 | Dale Jarrett | Chevrolet | 154.972 | Kyle Petty | 189.426 |
| 1994 | Sterling Marlin | Chevrolet | 156.931 | Loy Allen Jr | 190.158 |
| 1995 | Sterling Marlin | Chevrolet | 141.710 | Dale Jarrett | 193.498 |
| 1996 | Dale Jarrett | Ford | 154.308 | Dale Earnhardt | 189.510 |
| 1997 | Jeff Gordon | Chevrolet | 148.295 | Mike Skinner | 189.813 |
| 1998 | Dale Earnhardt | Chevrolet | 172.712 | Bobby Labonte | 192.415 |
| 1999 | Jeff Gordon | Chevrolet | 161.551 | Jeff Gordon | 195.067 |
| 2000 | Dale Jarrett | Ford | 155.669 | Dale Jarrett | 191.091 |
| 2001 | Michael Waltrip | Chevrolet | 161.783 | Bill Elliott | 183.570 |
| 2002 | Ward Burton | Dodge | 142.971 | Jimmie Johnson | 185.831 |
| 2003 | Michael Waltrip | Chevrolet | 133.870 | Jeff Green | 186.606 |
| 2004 | Dale Earnhardt Jr. | Chevrolet | 156.345 | Greg Biffle | 188.387 |
| 2005 | Jeff Gordon | Chevrolet | 135.173 | Dale Jarrett | 188.312 |
| 2006 | Jimmie Johnson | Chevrolet | 142.667 | Jeff Burton | 188.887 |
| 2007 | Kevin Harvick | Chevrolet | 149.335 | David Gilliland | 186.320 |
| 2008 | Ryan Newman | Dodge | 152.672 | Jimmie Johnson | 187.075 |
| 2009 | Matt Kenseth | Ford | 132.816 | Martin Truex Jr. | 188.001 |
| 2010 | Jamie McMurray | Chevrolet | 137.284 | Mark Martin | 191.188 |
| 2011 | Trevor Bayne | Ford | 130.326 | Dale Earnhardt Jr. | 186.089 |

Note: The Daytona 500, held annually in February, now opens the NASCAR season with 200 laps around the 2.5-mile high-banked Daytona International Speedway. Starting in 1988, cars racing at Daytona have used restrictor plates that curb power and acceleration.

*Track record, winning speed. †Track record, qualifying speed.

## Brickyard 400

| Year | Winner | Car | Avg Speed | Pole Winner | Qual. Speed |
|------|--------|-----|-----------|-------------|-------------|
| 1994 | Jeff Gordon | Chevrolet | 131.977 | Rick Mast | 172.414 |
| 1995 | Dale Earnhardt | Chevrolet | 155.206 | Jeff Gordon | 172.536 |
| 1996 | Dale Jarrett | Ford | 139.508 | Jeff Gordon | 176.419 |
| 1997 | Ricky Rudd | Ford | 130.814 | Ernie Irvan | 177.736 |
| 1998 | Jeff Gordon | Chevrolet | 126.772 | Ernie Irvan | 179.394 |
| 1999 | Dale Jarrett | Ford | 148.194 | Jeff Gordon | 179.612 |
| 2000 | Bobby Labonte | Pontiac | 155.912* | Ricky Rudd | 181.068 |
| 2001 | Jeff Gordon | Chevrolet | 130.790 | Jimmy Spencer | 179.666 |
| 2002 | Bill Elliott | Dodge | 125.033 | Tony Stewart | 182.960 |
| 2003 | Kevin Harvick | Chevrolet | 134.554 | Kevin Harvick | 184.343 |
| 2004 | Jeff Gordon | Chevrolet | 115.037 | Casey Mears | 186.293† |
| 2005 | Tony Stewart | Chevrolet | 148.782 | Elliott Sadler | 184.117 |
| 2006 | Jimmie Johnson | Chevrolet | 137.182 | Jeff Burton | 182.778 |
| 2007 | Tony Stewart | Chevrolet | 117.379 | Reed Sorenson | 184.207 |
| 2008 | Jimmie Johnson | Chevrolet | 115.117 | Jimmie Johnson | 181.763 |
| 2009 | Jimmie Johnson | Chevrolet | 145.882 | Mark Martin | 182.054 |
| 2010 | Jamie McMurray | Chevrolet | 136.054 | Juan Montoya | 182.278 |
| 2011 | Paul Menard | Chevrolet | 140.762 | David Ragan | 182.994 |

Note: Held at the 2.5-mile Indianapolis Motor Speedway.*Track record, winning speed. †Track record, qualifying speed.

## Talladega 500

| Year | Winner | Car | Avg Speed | Pole Winner | Qual Speed |
|------|--------|-----|-----------|-------------|------------|
| 1970 | Pete Hamilton | Plymouth | 152.321 | Bobby Isaac | 199.658 |
| 1971 | Donnie Allison | Mercury | 147.419 | Donnie Allison | 185.869 |
| 1972 | David Pearson | Mercury | 134.400 | Bobby Isaac | 192.428 |
| 1973 | David Pearson | Mercury | 131.956 | Buddy Baker | 193.435 |
| 1974 | David Pearson | Mercury | 130.220 | David Pearson | 186.086 |
| 1975 | Buddy Baker | Ford | 144.94 | Buddy Baker | 189.947 |
| 1976 | Buddy Baker | Ford | 169.887 | Dave Marcis | 189.197 |
| 1977 | Darrell Waltrip | Chevrolet | 164.887 | A.J. Foyt | 192.424 |
| 1978 | Cale Yarborough | Oldsmobile | 155.699 | Cale Yarborough | 191.904 |
| 1979 | Bobby Allison | Ford | 154.770 | Darrell Waltrip | 195.644 |
| 1980 | Buddy Baker | Oldsmobile | 170.481 | David Pearson | 197.704 |
| 1981 | Bobby Allison | Buick | 149.376 | Bobby Allison | 195.864 |
| 1982 | Darrell Waltrip | Buick | 156.697 | Benny Parsons | 200.176 |
| 1983 | Richard Petty | Pontiac | 135.936 | Cale Yarborough | 202.650 |
| 1984 | Cale Yarborough | Chevrolet | 172.988 | Cale Yarborough | 202.692 |
| 1985 | Bill Elliott | Ford | 186.288 | Bill Elliott | 209.398 |
| 1986 | Bobby Allison | Buick | 157.698 | Bill Elliott | 212.229 |
| 1987 | Davey Allison | Ford | 154.228 | Bill Elliott | 221.809† |
| 1988 | Phil Parsons | Oldsmobile | 156.547 | Davey Allison | 198.969 |
| 1989 | Davey Allison | Ford | 155.869 | Mark Martin | 193.061 |
| 1990 | Dale Earnhardt | Chevrolet | 159.571 | Bill Elliott | 199.388 |
| 1991 | Harry Gant | Oldsmobile | 165.620 | Ernie Irvan | 195.186 |
| 1992 | Davey Allison | Ford | 167.609 | Ernie Irvan | 192.831 |
| 1993 | Ernie Irvan | Chevrolet | 155.412 | Dale Earnhardt | 192.355 |
| 1994 | Dale Earnhardt | Chevrolet | 157.478 | Ernie Irvan | 193.298 |
| 1995 | Mark Martin | Ford | 178.902 | Terry Labonte | 196.532 |
| 1996 | Sterling Marlin | Chevrolet | 149.999 | Ernie Irvan | 192.855 |
| 1997 | Mark Martin | Ford | 188.354* | John Andretti | 193.627 |
| 1998 | Dale Jarrett | Ford | 159.318 | Ken Schrader | 196.153 |
| 1999 | Dale Earnhardt | Chevrolet | 166.632 | Joe Nemechek | 198.331 |
| 2000 | Dale Earnhardt | Chevrolet | 165.681 | Joe Nemechek | 190.279 |
| 2001 | Dale Earnhardt Jr. | Chevrolet | 164.185 | Stacy Compton | 185.240 |
| 2002 | Dale Earnhardt Jr. | Chevrolet | 183.665 | qualifying cancelled | — |
| 2003 | Michael Waltrip | Chevrolet | 156.045 | Elliott Sadler | 189.943 |
| 2004 | Jeff Gordon | Chevrolet | 129.396 | Ricky Rudd | 191.180 |
| 2005 | Dale Jarrett | Ford | 143.818 | Elliott Sadler | 189.260 |
| 2006 | Brian Vickers | Chevrolet | 157.602 | David Gilliland | 191.712 |
| 2007 | Jeff Gordon | Chevrolet | 143.438 | Michael Waltrip | 189.070 |
| 2008 | Kyle Busch | Toyota | 157.409 | Joe Nemechek | 187.396 |
| 2009 | Brad Keselowski | Chevrolet | 147.565 | Juan Pablo Montoya | 188.171 |
| 2010 | Kevin Harvick | Chevrolet | 150.590 | qualifying cancelled | — |
| 2011 | Jimmie Johnson | Chevrolet | 156.261 | Jeff Gordon | 178.248 |

*Track record, winning speed. †Track record, qualifying speed.

## Charlotte 600

| Year | Winner | Car | Avg Speed | Pole Winner |
|------|--------|-----|-----------|-------------|
| 1960 | Joe Lee Johnson | Chevrolet | 107.752 | Joe Lee Johnson |
| 1961 | David Pearson | Pontiac | 111.634 | Richard Petty |
| 1962 | Nelson Stacy | Ford | 125.552 | Fireball Roberts |
| 1963 | Fred Lorenzen | Ford | 132.418 | Junior Johnson |
| 1964 | Jim Paschal | Plymouth | 125.772 | Junior Johnson |
| 1965 | Fred Lorenzen | Ford | 121.772 | Fred Lorenzon |
| 1966 | Marvin Panch | Plymouth | 135.042 | Paul Goldsmith |
| 1967 | Jim Paschal | Plymouth | 135.832 | Cale Yarborough |
| 1968 | Buddy Baker | Dodge | 104.207 | Donnie Allison |
| 1969 | Lee Roy Yarbrough | Mercury | 134.631 | Donnie Allison |
| 1970 | Donnie Allison | Ford | 129.680 | Bobby Isaac |
| 1971 | Bobby Allison | Mercury | 140.442 | Charlie Glotzbach |
| 1972 | Buddy Baker | Dodge | 142.255 | Bobby Allison |
| 1973 | Buddy Baker | Dodge | 134.890 | Buddy Baker |
| 1974 | David Pearson | Mercury | 135.720 | David Pearson |
| 1975 | Richard Petty | Dodge | 145.327 | David Pearson |
| 1976 | David Pearson | Mercury | 137.352 | David Pearson |
| 1977 | Richard Petty | Dodge | 137.636 | David Pearson |
| 1978 | Darrell Waltrip | Chevrolet | 138.355 | David Pearson |
| 1979 | Darrell Waltrip | Chevrolet | 136.674 | Neil Bonnet |
| 1980 | Benny Parsons | Chevrolet | 119.265 | Cale Yarborough |
| 1981 | Bobby Allison | Buick | 129.326 | Neil Bonnett |
| 1982 | Neil Bonnett | Ford | 130.508 | David Pearson |
| 1983 | Neil Bonnett | Chevrolet | 140.406 | Buddy Baker |
| 1984 | Bobby Allison | Buick | 129.233 | Harry Gant |
| 1985 | Darrell Waltrip | Chevrolet | 141.807 | Bill Elliott |
| 1986 | Dale Earnhardt | Chevrolet | 140.406 | Geoff Bodine |
| 1987 | Kyle Petty | Ford | 131.483 | Bill Elliott |
| 1988 | Darrell Waltrip | Chevrolet | 124.460 | Davey Allison |
| 1989 | Darrell Waltrip | Chevrolet | 144.077 | Alan Kulwicki |
| 1990 | Rusty Wallace | Pontiac | 137.650 | Ken Schrader |
| 1991 | Davey Allison | Ford | 138.951 | Mark Martin |
| 1992 | Dale Earnhardt | Chevrolet | 132.980 | Bill Elliott |
| 1993 | Dale Earnhardt | Chevrolet | 145.504 | Ken Schrader |
| 1994 | Jeff Gordon | Chevrolet | 139.445 | Jeff Gordon |
| 1995 | Bobby Labonte | Chevrolet | 151.952* | Jeff Gordon |
| 1996 | Dale Jarrett | Ford | 147.581 | Jeff Gordon |
| 1997 | Jeff Gordon | Chevrolet | 136.745 | Jeff Gordon |
| 1998 | Jeff Gordon | Chevrolet | 136.424 | Jeff Gordon |
| 1999 | Jeff Burton | Ford | 151.367 | Bobby Labonte |
| 2000 | Matt Kenseth | Ford | 142.640 | Dale Earnhardt Jr |
| 2001 | Jeff Burton | Ford | 138.107 | Ryan Newman |
| 2002 | Mark Martin | Ford | 137.729 | Jimmie Johnson |
| 2003 | Jimmie Johnson | Chevrolet | 126.198 | Ryan Newman |
| 2004 | Jimmie Johnson | Chevrolet | 142.763 | Jimmie Johnson |
| 2005 | Jimmie Johnson | Chevrolet | 114.698 | Ryan Newman |
| 2006 | Kasey Kahne | Dodge | 128.840 | Scott Riggs |
| 2007 | Casey Mears | Chevrolet | 130.222 | Ryan Newman |
| 2008 | Kasey Kahne | Dodge | 135.772 | Kyle Busch |
| 2009 | David Reutimann | Toyota | 120.899 | Ryan Newman |
| 2010 | Kurt Busch | Dodge | 144.966 | Ryan Newman |
| 2011 | Kevin Harvick | Chevrolet | 132.414 | Brad Keselowski |

Note: Held at the 1.5 mile high-banked Lowe's Motor Speedway in Charlotte on Memorial Day weekend.
*Track record, winning speed.

## Darlington 500

| Year | Winner | Car | Avg Speed | Pole Winner |
|------|--------|-----|-----------|-------------|
| 1950 | Johnny Mantz | Plymouth | 76.260 | Wally Campbell |
| 1951 | Herb Thomas | Hudson | 76.900 | Marshall Teague |
| 1952 | Fonty Flock | Oldsmobile | 74.510 | Dick Rathman |
| 1953 | Buck Baker | Oldsmobile | 92.780 | Fonty Flock |
| 1954 | Herb Thomas | Hudson | 94.930 | Buck Baker |
| 1955 | Herb Thomas | Chevrolet | 92.281 | Tim Flock |
| 1956 | Curtis Turner | Ford | 95.067 | Buck Baker |
| 1957 | Speedy Thompson | Chevrolet | 100.100 | Paul Goldsmith |
| 1958 | Fireball Roberts | Chevrolet | 102.590 | Fireball Roberts |
| 1959 | Jim Reed | Chevrolet | 111.836 | Fireball Roberts |
| 1960 | Buck Baker | Pontiac | 105.901 | Cotton Owens |
| 1961 | Nelson Stacy | Ford | 117.880 | Fireball Roberts |
| 1962 | Larry Frank | Ford | 117.965 | Fireball Roberts |
| 1963 | Fireball Roberts | Ford | 129.784 | Fireball Roberts |
| 1964 | Buck Baker | Dodge | 117.757 | Richard Petty |
| 1965 | Ned Jarrett | Ford | 115.924 | Junior Johnson |
| 1966 | Darel Dieringer | Mercury | 114.830 | Lee Yarborough |
| 1967 | Richard Petty | Plymouth | 131.933 | David Pearson |
| 1968 | Cale Yarborough | Mercury | 126.132 | Charlie Glotzbach |
| 1969 | Lee Roy Yarbrough | Ford | 105.612 | Cale Yarborough |
| 1970 | Buddy Baker | Dodge | 128.817 | David Pearson |
| 1971 | Bobby Allison | Mercury | 131.398 | Bobby Allison |
| 1972 | Bobby Allison | Chevrolet | 128.124 | David Pearson |
| 1973 | Cale Yarborough | Chevrolet | 134.033 | David Pearson |
| 1974 | Cale Yarborough | Chevrolet | 111.075 | Richard Petty |
| 1975 | Bobby Allison | Matador | 116.825 | David Pearson |
| 1976 | David Pearson | Mercury | 120.534 | David Pearson |
| 1977 | David Pearson | Mercury | 106.797 | Darrell Waltrip |
| 1978 | Cale Yarborough | Oldsmobile | 116.828 | David Pearson |
| 1979 | David Pearson | Chevrolet | 126.259 | Bobby Allison |
| 1980 | Terry Labonte | Chevrolet | 115.210 | Darrell Waltrip |
| 1981 | Neil Bonnett | Ford | 126.410 | Harry Gant |
| 1982 | Cale Yarborough | Buick | 126.703 | David Pearson |
| 1983 | Bobby Allison | Buick | 123.343 | Neil Bonnett |
| 1984 | Harry Gant | Chevrolet | 128.270 | Harry Gant |
| 1985 | Bill Elliott | Ford | 121.254 | Bill Elliott |
| 1986 | Tim Richmond | Chevrolet | 121.068 | Tim Richmond |
| 1987 | Dale Earnhardt | Chevrolet | 115.520 | Davey Allison |
| 1988 | Bill Elliott | Ford | 128.297 | Bill Elliott |
| 1989 | Dale Earnhardt | Chevrolet | 135.462 | Alan Kulwicki |
| 1990 | Dale Earnhardt | Chevrolet | 123.141 | Dale Earnhardt |
| 1991 | Harry Gant | Oldsmobile | 133.508 | Davey Allison |
| 1992 | Darrell Waltrip | Chevrolet | 129.114 | Sterling Marlin |
| 1993 | Mark Martin | Ford | 137.932 | Ken Schrader |
| 1994 | Bill Elliott | Ford | 127.915 | Geoff Bodine |
| 1995 | Jeff Gordon | Chevrolet | 121.231 | John Andretti |
| 1996 | Jeff Gordon | Chevrolet | 135.757 | Dale Jarrett |
| 1997 | Jeff Gordon | Chevrolet | 121.149 | Bobby Labonte |
| 1998 | Jeff Gordon | Chevrolet | 139.031* | Dale Jarrett |
| 1999 | Jeff Burton | Ford | 100.816 | Kenny Irwin |
| 2000 | Bobby Labonte | Pontiac | 108.275 | Jeremy Mayfield |
| 2001 | Ward Burton | Dodge | 122.773 | Kurt Busch |
| 2002 | Jeff Gordon | Chevrolet | 118.617 | Sterling Marlin |
| 2003 | Terry Labonte | Chevrolet | 120.744 | Ryan Newman |
| 2004 | Jimmie Johnson | Chevrolet | 125.044 | Kurt Busch |
| 2005 | Greg Biffle | Ford | 135.127 | Kasey Kahne |
| 2006 | Greg Biffle | Ford | 123.031 | Kasey Kahne |
| 2007 | Jeff Gordon | Chevrolet | 124.372 | Clint Bowyer |
| 2008 | Kyle Busch | Toyota | 140.350 | Greg Biffle |
| 2009 | Mark Martin | Chevrolet | 119.687 | Matt Kenseth |
| 2010 | Denny Hamlin | Toyota | 126.605 | Jamie McMurray |
| 2011 | Regan Smith | Chevrolet | 129.678 | Kasey Kahne |

Note: Through 2004, results listed were for the Southern 500, traditionally the second race of the year at the 1.366-mile Darlington (S.C.) Raceway. Starting in 2005, Darlington only hosted one race a year, in May.

*Track record, winning speed.

## Sprint Cup* NASCAR Champions

| Year | Driver | Car | Wins | Poles | Winnings ($) |
|------|--------|-----|------|-------|--------------|
| 1949 | Red Byron | Oldsmobile | 2 | 1 | 5,800 |
| 1950 | Bill Rexford | Oldsmobile | 1 | 0 | 6,175 |
| 1951 | Herb Thomas | Hudson | 7 | 4 | 18,200 |
| 1952 | Tim Flock | Hudson | 8 | 4 | 20,210 |
| 1953 | Herb Thomas | Hudson | 11 | 10 | 27,300 |
| 1954 | Lee Petty | Dodge | 7 | 3 | 26,706 |
| 1955 | Tim Flock | Chrysler | 18 | 19 | 33,750 |
| 1956 | Buck Baker | Chrysler | 14 | 12 | 29,790 |
| 1957 | Buck Baker | Chevrolet | 10 | 5 | 24,712 |
| 1958 | Lee Petty | Oldsmobile | 7 | 4 | 20,600 |
| 1959 | Lee Petty | Plymouth | 10 | 2 | 45,570 |
| 1960 | Rex White | Chevrolet | 6 | 3 | 45,260 |
| 1961 | Ned Jarrett | Chevrolet | 1 | 4 | 27,285 |
| 1962 | Joe Weatherly | Pontiac | 9 | 6 | 56,110 |
| 1963 | Joe Weatherly | Mercury | 3 | 6 | 58,110 |
| 1964 | Richard Petty | Plymouth | 9 | 8 | 98,810 |
| 1965 | Ned Jarrett | Ford | 13 | 9 | 77,966 |
| 1966 | David Pearson | Dodge | 14 | 7 | 59,205 |
| 1967 | Richard Petty | Plymouth | 27 | 18 | 130,275 |
| 1968 | David Pearson | Ford | 16 | 12 | 118,824 |
| 1969 | David Pearson | Ford | 11 | 14 | 183,700 |
| 1970 | Bobby Isaac | Dodge | 11 | 13 | 121,470 |
| 1971 | Richard Petty | Plymouth | 21 | 9 | 309,225 |
| 1972 | Richard Petty | Plymouth | 8 | 3 | 227,015 |
| 1973 | Benny Parsons | Chevrolet | 1 | 0 | 114,345 |
| 1974 | Richard Petty | Dodge | 10 | 7 | 299,175 |
| 1975 | Richard Petty | Dodge | 13 | 3 | 378,865 |
| 1976 | Cale Yarborough | Chevrolet | 9 | 2 | 387,173 |
| 1977 | Cale Yarborough | Chevrolet | 9 | 3 | 477,499 |
| 1978 | Cale Yarborough | Oldsmobile | 10 | 8 | 530,751 |
| 1979 | Richard Petty | Chevrolet | 5 | 1 | 531,292 |
| 1980 | Dale Earnhardt | Chevrolet | 5 | 0 | 588,926 |
| 1981 | Darrell Waltrip | Buick | 12 | 11 | 693,342 |
| 1982 | Darrell Waltrip | Buick | 12 | 7 | 873,118 |
| 1983 | Bobby Allison | Buick | 6 | 0 | 828,355 |
| 1984 | Terry Labonte | Chevrolet | 2 | 2 | 713,010 |
| 1985 | Darrell Waltrip | Chevrolet | 3 | 4 | 1,318,735 |
| 1986 | Dale Earnhardt | Chevrolet | 5 | 1 | 1,783,880 |
| 1987 | Dale Earnhardt | Chevrolet | 11 | 1 | 2,099,243 |
| 1988 | Bill Elliott | Ford | 6 | 6 | 1,574,639 |
| 1989 | Rusty Wallace | Pontiac | 6 | 4 | 2,247,950 |
| 1990 | Dale Earnhardt | Chevrolet | 9 | 4 | 3,083,056 |
| 1991 | Dale Earnhardt | Chevrolet | 4 | 0 | 2,396,685 |
| 1992 | Alan Kulwicki | Ford | 2 | 6 | 2,322,561 |
| 1993 | Dale Earnhardt | Chevrolet | 6 | 2 | 3,353,789 |
| 1994 | Dale Earnhardt | Chevrolet | 4 | 2 | 3,400,733 |
| 1995 | Jeff Gordon | Chevrolet | 7 | 9 | 4,347,343 |
| 1996 | Terry Labonte | Chevrolet | 2 | 4 | 4,030,648 |
| 1997 | Jeff Gordon | Chevrolet | 10 | 1 | 4,201,227 |
| 1998 | Jeff Gordon | Chevrolet | 13 | 7 | 6,175,867 |
| 1999 | Dale Jarrett | Ford | 4 | 0 | 3,608,829 |
| 2000 | Bobby Labonte | Pontiac | 4 | 2 | 4,041,750 |
| 2001 | Jeff Gordon | Chevrolet | 6 | 8 | 6,649,076 |
| 2002 | Tony Stewart | Pontiac | 3 | 4 | 4,695,150 |
| 2003 | Matt Kenseth | Ford | 1 | 2 | 4,038,120 |
| 2004 | Kurt Busch | Ford | 3 | 1 | 4,200,330 |
| 2005 | Tony Stewart | Chevrolet | 5 | 3 | 6,987,530 |
| 2006 | Jimmie Johnson | Chevrolet | 5 | 1 | 8.909,140 |
| 2007 | Jimmie Johnson | Chevrolet | 10 | 4 | 7,646,420 |
| 2008 | Jimmie Johnson | Chevrolet | 7 | 6 | 7,354,860 |
| 2009 | Jimmie Johnson | Chevrolet | 7 | 4 | 7,339,630 |
| 2010 | Jimmie Johnson | Chevrolet | 6 | 2 | 7,264,780 |

*Series name changed from Winston Cup after 2003 season, then to Sprint Cup beginning in 2008.

### Alltime NASCAR Leaders

| | WINS | | WINS | POLE POSITIONS | | POLE POSITIONS | |
|---|---|---|---|---|---|---|---|
| Richard Petty | 200 | Rusty Wallace | 55 | Richard Petty | 126 | Bobby Isaac | 51 |
| David Pearson | 105 | Lee Petty | 54 | David Pearson | 113 | *Mark Martin | 50 |
| *Jeff Gordon | 85 | Ned Jarrett | 50 | *Jeff Gordon | 70 | *Ryan Newman | 49 |
| Bobby Allison | 84 | Junior Johnson | 50 | Cale Yarborough | 70 | Junior Johnson | 47 |
| Darrell Waltrip | 84 | Herb Thomas | 48 | Darrell Waltrip | 59 | Buck Baker | 44 |
| Cale Yarborough | 83 | Buck Baker | 46 | Bobby Allison | 57 | Buddy Baker | 40 |
| Dale Earnhardt | 76 | David Pearson | 45 | David Pearson | 55 | Tim Flock | 39 |
| *Jimmie Johnson | 55 | | | Bill Elliott | 54 | Herb Thomas | 39 |

*Active drivers. Note: NASCAR wins leaders and pole position leaders through Oct 10, 2011.

## Formula One Grand Prix Racing

### World Driving Champions

| Year | Winner | Car | Year | Winner | Car |
|---|---|---|---|---|---|
| 1950 | Guiseppe Farina, Italy | Alfa Romeo | 1978 | Mario Andretti, U.S. | Lotus-Ford |
| 1951 | Juan-Manuel Fangio, Argentina | Alfa Romeo | 1979 | Jody Scheckter, S. Africa | Ferrari |
| 1952 | Alberto Ascari, Italy | Ferrari | 1980 | Alan Jones, Australia | Williams-Ford |
| 1953 | Alberto Ascari, Italy | Ferrari | 1981 | Nelson Piquet, Brazil | Brabham-Ford |
| 1954 | Juan-Manuel Fangio, Argentina | Maserati-Mercedes | 1982 | Keke Rosberg, Finland | Williams-Ford |
| 1955 | Juan-Manuel Fangio, Argentina | Mercedes | 1983 | Nelson Piquet, Brazil | Brabham-BMW |
| | | | 1984 | Niki Lauda, Austria | McLaren-Porsche |
| 1956 | Juan-Manuel Fangio, Argentina | Ferrari | 1985 | Alain Prost, France | McLaren-Porsche |
| | | | 1986 | Alain Prost, France | McLaren-Porsche |
| 1957 | Juan-Manuel Fangio, Argentina | Maserati | 1987 | Nelson Piquet, Brazil | Williams-Honda |
| | | | 1988 | Ayrton Senna, Brazil | McLaren-Honda |
| 1958 | Mike Hawthorn, Grt. Britain | Ferrari | 1989 | Alain Prost, France | McLaren-Honda |
| 1959 | Jack Brabham, Australia | Cooper-Climax | 1990 | Ayrton Senna, Brazil | McLaren-Honda |
| 1960 | Jack Brabham, Australia | Cooper-Climax | 1991 | Ayrton Senna, Brazil | McLaren-Honda |
| 1961 | Phil Hill, U.S. | Ferrari | 1992 | Nigel Mansell, Great Britain | Williams-Renault |
| 1962 | Graham Hill, Great Britain | BRM | 1993 | Alain Prost, France | Williams-Renault |
| 1963 | Jim Clark, Scotland | Lotus-Climax | 1994 | Michael Schumacher, Ger. | Benetton-Ford |
| 1964 | John Surtees, Great Britain | Ferrari | 1995 | Michael Schumacher, Ger. | Benetton-Renault |
| 1965 | Jim Clark, Scotland | Lotus-Climax | 1996 | Damon Hill, Great Britain | Williams-Renault |
| 1966 | Jack Brabham, Australia | Brabham-Repco | 1997 | Jacques Villeneuve, Can. | Williams-Renault |
| 1967 | Denny Hulme, New Zealand | Brabham-Repco | 1998 | Mika Hakkinen, Finland | McLaren-Mercedes |
| 1968 | Graham Hill, Great Britain | Lotus-Ford | 1999 | Mika Hakkinen, Finland | McLaren-Mercedes |
| 1969 | Jackie Stewart, Scotland | Matra-Ford | 2000 | Michael Schumacher, Ger. | Ferrari |
| 1970 | Jochen Rindt, Austria* | Lotus-Ford | 2001 | Michael Schumacher, Ger. | Ferrari |
| 1971 | Jackie Stewart, Scotland | Tyrell-Ford | 2002 | Michael Schumacher, Ger. | Ferrari |
| 1972 | Emerson Fittipaldi, Brazil | Lotus-Ford | 2003 | Michael Schumacher, Ger. | Ferrari |
| 1973 | Jackie Stewart, Scotland | Tyrell-Ford | 2004 | Michael Schumacher, Ger. | Ferrari |
| 1974 | Emerson Fittipaldi, Brazil | McLaren-Ford | 2005 | Fernando Alonso, Spain | Renault |
| 1975 | Niki Lauda, Austria | Ferrari | 2006 | Fernando Alonso, Spain | Renault |
| 1976 | James Hunt, Great Britain | McLaren-Ford | 2007 | Kimi Raikkonen, Finland | Ferrari |
| 1977 | Niki Lauda, Austria | Ferrari | 2008 | Lewis Hamilton, Great Britain | McLaren-Mercedes |
| | | | 2009 | Jenson Button, Great Britain | Brawn-Mercedes |
| | | | 2010 | Sebastian Vettel, Germany | RBR-Renault |

*The championship was awarded posthumously, after Rindt was killed during practice for the Italian Grand Prix.

### Alltime F/1 Grand Prix Winners

| Driver | Wins | Driver | Wins |
|---|---|---|---|
| *Michael Schumacher, Germany | 91 | Jackie Stewart, Great Britain | 27 |
| Alain Prost, France | 51 | Jim Clark, Great Britain | 25 |
| Ayrton Senna, Brazil | 41 | Niki Lauda, Austria | 25 |
| Nigel Mansell, Great Britain | 31 | Juan Manuel Fangio, Argentina | 24 |
| *Fernando Alonso, Spain | 27 | Nelson Piquet, Brazil | 23 |

### Alltime F/1 Grand Prix Pole Winners

| Driver | Poles | Driver | Poles |
|---|---|---|---|
| *Michael Schumacher, Germany | 68 | *Sebastian Vettel, Germany | 27 |
| Ayrton Senna, Brazil | 65 | Mika Hakkinen, Finland | 26 |
| Alain Prost, France | 33 | Niki Lauda, Austria | 24 |
| Jim Clark, Great Britain | 33 | Nelson Piquet, Brazil | 24 |
| Nigel Mansell, Great Britain | 32 | Damon Hill, Great Britain | 20 |
| Juan Manuel Fangio, Argentina | 29 | *Fernando Alonso, Spain | 20 |

*Active driver in 2011. Note: Grand Prix winners and pole winners through Oct 10, 2011.

## The 24 Hours of Daytona

| Year | Winner | Car | Avg Speed | Distance |
|---|---|---|---|---|
| 1962 | Dan Gurney | Lotus 19-Class SP11 | 104.101 mph | 3 hrs (312.42 mi) |
| 1963 | Pedro Rodriguez | Ferrari-Class 12 | 102.074 mph | 3 hrs (308.61 mi) |
| 1964 | Pedro Rodriguez/Phil Hill | Ferrari 250 LM | 98.230 mph | 2,000 km |
| 1965 | Ken Miles/Lloyd Ruby | Ford | 99.944 mph | 2,000 km |
| 1966 | Ken Miles/Lloyd Ruby | Ford Mark II | 108.020 mph | 24 hrs (2,570.63 mi) |
| 1967 | Lorenzo Bandini/Chris Amon | Ferrari 330 P4 | 105.688 mph | 24 hrs (2,537.46 mi) |
| 1968 | Vic Elford/Jochen Neerpasch | Porsche 907 | 106.697 mph | 24 hrs (2,565.69 mi) |
| 1969 | Mark Donohue/Chuck Parsons | Chevy Lola | 99.268 mph | 24 hrs (2,383.75 mi) |
| 1970 | Pedro Rodriguez/Leo Kinnunen | Porsche 917 | 114.866 mph | 24 hrs (2,758.44 mi) |
| 1971 | Pedro Rodriguez/Jackie Oliver | Porsche 917K | 109.203 mph | 24 hrs (2,621.28 mi) |
| 1972* | Mario Andretti/Jacky Ickx | Ferrari 312/P | 122.573 mph | 6 hrs (738.24 mi) |
| 1973 | Peter Gregg/Hurley Haywood | Porsche Carrera | 106.225 mph | 24 hrs (2,552.7 mi) |
| 1974 | (No race) | | | |
| 1975 | Peter Gregg/Hurley Haywood | Porsche Carrera | 108.531 mph | 24 hrs (2,606.04 mi) |
| 1976† | Peter Gregg/Brian Redman/ John Fitzpatrick | BMW CSL | 104.040 mph | 24 hrs (2,092.8 mi) |
| 1977 | John Graves/Hurley Haywood/ Dave Helmick | Porsche Carrera | 108.801 mph | 24 hrs (2,615 mi) |
| 1978 | Rolf Stommelen/ Antoine Hezemans/Peter Gregg | Porsche Turbo | 108.743 mph | 24 hrs (2,611.2 mi) |
| 1979 | Ted Field/Danny Ongais/ Hurley Haywood | Porsche Turbo | 109.249 mph | 24 hrs (2,626.56 mi) |
| 1980 | Volkert Meri/Rolf Stommelen/ Reinhold Joest | Porsche Turbo | 114.303 mph | 24 hrs |
| 1981 | Bob Garretson/Bobby Rahal/ Brian Redman | Porsche Turbo | 113.153 mph | 24 hrs |
| 1982 | John Paul Jr/John Paul Sr/ Rolf Stommelen | Porsche Turbo | 114.794 mph | 24 hrs |
| 1983 | Preston Henn/Bob Wollek/ Claude Ballot-Lena/A.J. Foyt | Porsche Turbo | 98.781 mph | 24 hrs |
| 1984 | Sarel van der Merwe/ Graham Duxbury/Tony Martin | Porsche March | 103.119 mph | 24 hrs (2,476.8 mi) |
| 1985 | A.J. Foyt/Bob Wollek/ Al Unser/Thierry Boutsen | Porsche 962 | 104.162 mph | 24 hrs (2,502.68 mi) |
| 1986 | Al Holbert/Derek Bell/Al Unser Jr. | Porsche 962 | 105.484 mph | 24 hrs (2,534.72 mi) |
| 1987 | Chip Robinson/Derek Bell/ Al Holbert/Al Unser Jr. | Porsche 962 | 111.599 mph | 24 hrs (2,680.68 mi) |
| 1988 | Martin Brundle/John Nielsen/ Raul Boesel | Jaguar XJR-9 | 107.943 mph | 24 hrs (2,591.68 mi) |
| 1989 | John Andretti/Derek Bell/ Bob Wollek | Porsche 962 | 92.009 mph | 24 hrs (2,210.76 mi) |
| 1990 | Davy Jones/ Jan Lammers/ Andy Wallace | Jaguar XJR-12 | 112.857 mph | 24 hrs (2,709.16 mi) |
| 1991 | Hurley Haywood/ John Winter/ Frank Jelinski/ Henri Pescarolo/ Bob Wollek | Porsche 962C | 106.633 mph | 24 hrs (2,559.64 mi) |
| 1992 | Massahiro Hasemi/ Kazuoyshi Hoshino/ Toshio Suzuki/ Anders Olofsson | Nissan R91CP | 112.987 mph | 24 hrs (2,712.72 mi) |
| 1993 | P.J. Jones/Mark Dismore/ Rocky Moran | Toyota Eagle MK III | 103.537 mph | 24 hrs (2,484.88 mi) |
| 1994 | Paul Gentilozzi/ Scott Pruett/ Butch Leitzinger/ Steve Millen | Nissan 300 ZX | 104.80 mph | 24 hrs (2,693.67 mi) |
| 1995 | Jurgen Lassig/ Christophe Buochut/ Giovanni Lavaggi/ Marco Werner | Porsche Spyder K8 | 102.28 mph | 690 laps (2,456.4 mi) |
| 1996 | Wayne Taylor/ Scott Sharp/ Jim Pace | Oldsmobile Mark III | 103.32 mph | 697 laps (2,481.32 mi) |
| 1997 | Elliot Forbes-Robinson/ John Schneider/Rob Dyson/ John Paul Jr/Butch Leitzinger/James Weaver/Andy Wallace | Ford R & S MK III | 102.292 mph | 690 laps (2,456.4 mi) |
| 1998 | Arie Luyendyk/Didier Theys/ Mauro Baldi | Ferrari 333 SP | 105.565 mph | 711 laps (2,531.16 mi) |
| 1999 | Elliott Forbes-Robinson/ Butch Leitzinger/ Andy Wallace | Ford R & S MK III | 104.9 mph | 708 laps (2,520.48 mi) |
| 2000 | Olivier Beretta/Karl Wendlinger/ Dominique Dupuy | Dodge Viper | 107.207 mph | 723 laps (2,573.88 m) |

*Race shortened due to fuel crisis. †Course lengthened from 3.81 miles to 3.84 miles.

### The 24 Hours of Daytona *(Cont.)*

| Year | Winner | Car | Speed | Distance |
|---|---|---|---|---|
| 2001 | Ron Fellows/Chris Kneifel/Franck Freon/Johnny O'Connell | Corvette | 97.293 mph | 656 laps (2,335.360 mi) |
| 2002 | Didier Theys/Fredy Lienhard/Max Papis/Mauro Baldi | Dallara-Judd (SRP) | 106.143 mph | 716 laps (2,548.96 mi) |
| 2003 | Kevin Buckler/Michael Schrom Timo Bernhard/Jorg Bergmeister | Porsche GT3 RS | 114.068 mph (top speed) | 694 laps (2,470.64 mi) |
| 2004 | Forest Barber/Terry Borcheller Andy Pilgrim/Christian Fittipaldi | Pontiac Doran | 117.651 mph | 526 laps (1,872.56 mi) |
| 2005 | Wayne Taylor/Max Angelelli Emmanuel Collard | Pontiac Riley | 119.397 mph | 710 laps (2,527.60 mi) |
| 2006 | Scott Dixon/Dan Wheldon Casey Mears | Lexus Riley | 108.826 mph | 734 laps (2,613.04 mi) |
| 2007 | Scott Pruett/Salvador Duran Juan Montoya | Lexus Riley | 99.020 mph | 668 laps (2,378.08 mi) |
| 2008 | Scott Pruett/Memo Rojas Juan Montoya/Dario Franchitti | Lexus Riley | 103.057 mph | 695 laps (2,474.20 mi) |
| 2009 | Darren Law/David Donohue Buddy Rice/Antonio Garcia | Porsche Riley | 108.994 mph | 735 laps (2,616.60 mi.) |
| 2010 | Terry Borcheller/Joao Barbosa Ryan Dalziel/Mike Rockenfeller | Porsche Riley | 111.930 mph | 755 laps (2,687.77 mi.) |
| 2011 | Joey Hand/Scott Pruett Graham Rahal/Memo Rojas | BMW Riley | 106.877 mph | 721 laps (2,566.76 mi.) |

### World SportsCar Champions*

| Year | Winner | Car | Year | Winner | Car |
|---|---|---|---|---|---|
| 1978 | Peter Gregg | Porsche 935 | 1989 | Geoff Brabham | Nissan GTP |
| 1979 | Peter Gregg | Porsche 935 | 1990 | Geoff Brabham | Nissan GTP |
| 1980 | John Fitzpatrick | Porsche 935 | 1991 | Geoff Brabham | Nissan NPT |
| 1981 | Brian Redman | Chevy Lola | 1992 | Juan Fangio II | Toyota EGL MKIII |
| 1982 | John Paul Jr | Chevy Lola | 1993 | Juan Fangio II | Toyota EGL MKIII |
| 1983 | Al Holbert | Chevy March | 1994 | Wayne Taylor | Mazda Kudzu |
| 1984 | Randy Lanier | Chevy March | 1995 | Fermin Velez | Ferrari 333 SP |
| 1985 | Al Holbert | Porsche 962 | 1996 | Wayne Taylor | Mazda Kudzu |
| 1986 | Al Holbert | Porsche 962 | 1997 | Butch Leitzinger | Ford R&S MKIII |
| 1987 | Chip Robinson | Porsche 962 | 1998 | Butch Leitzinger | Ford R&S MKIII |
| 1988 | Geoff Brabham | Nissan GTP | | | |

| Year | Prototype | GTC | GT |
|---|---|---|---|
| 1999 | Elliott Forbes-Robinson | Olivier Beretta | Cort Wagner |
| 2000 | Allan McNish | Olivier Beretta | Sascha Maassen |
| 2001 | Emanuele Pirro | Terry Borcheller | Jörg Müller |
| 2002 | Tom Kristensen | Ron Fellows | Lucas Luhr |
| 2003 | Frank Biela/Marco Werner | Ron Fellows/John O'Connell | Sascha Maassen/L. Luhr |
| 2004 | Frank Biela/Emanuele Pirro | Olivier Gavin/Olivier Beretta | Patrick Long/Jorg Bergmeister |
| 2005 | Frank Biela/Emanuele Pirro | Olivier Gavin/Olivier Beretta | Patrick Long/Jorg Bergmeister |
| 2006 | R. Capello/A. McNish | Olivier Gavin/Olivier Beretta | Johannes van Overbeek |
| 2007 | R. Capello/A. McNish | Olivier Gavin/Olivier Beretta | Mika Salo/Jaime Melo |
| 2008 | Lucas Luhr/Marco Werner | Jan Magnussen/J. O'Connell | Jorg Bergmeister/Wolf Henzler |
| 2009 | David Brabham/Scott Sharp | Olivier Gavin/Olivier Beretta | Jorg Bergmeister/Patrick Long |
| 2010 | D. Brabham/Simon Pagenaud | Tim. Pappas/Jer. Bleekemolen | Jorg Bergmeister/Patrick Long |
| 2011 | Guy Smith/Chris Dyson | Timothy Pappas | Joey Hand/Dirk Mueller |

### Alltime SportsCar Leaders

| PROTOTYPE WINS | | GTC AND GT WINS | |
|---|---|---|---|
| Rinaldo Capello | 34 | Al Holbert | 49 |
| Allan McNish | 27 | *Olivier Beretta | 41 |
| Marco Werner | 25 | Peter Gregg | 41 |
| Frank Biela | 22 | Johnny O'Connell | 38 |
| J.J. Lehto | 19 | *Jorg Bergmeister | 34 |
| Emanuele Pirro | 19 | *Oliver Gavin | 34 |
| James Weaver | 16 | Hurley Haywood | 31 |

* Active driver in 2011.

| Year | Winning Drivers | Car |
|------|-----------------|-----|
| 1923 | André Lagache/René Léonard | Chenard & Walker |
| 1924 | John Duff/Francis Clement | Bentley |
| 1925 | Gérard de Courcelles/André Rossignol | La Lorraine |
| 1926 | Robert Bloch/André Rossignol | La Lorraine |
| 1927 | J. Dudley Benjafield/Sammy Davis | Bentley |
| 1928 | Woolf Barnato/Bernard Rubin | Bentley |
| 1929 | Woolf Barnato/Sir Henry Birkin | Bentley Speed 6 |
| 1930 | Woolf Barnato/Glen Kidston | Bentley Speed 6 |
| 1931 | Earl Howe/Sir Henry Birkin | Alfa Romeo 8C-2300 sc |
| 1932 | Raymond Sommer/Luigi Chinetti | Alfa Romeo 8C-2300 sc |
| 1933 | Raymond Sommer/Tazio Nuvolari | Alfa Romeo 8C-2300 sc |
| 1934 | Luigi Chinetti/Philippe Etancelin | Alfa Romeo 8C-2300 sc |
| 1935 | John Hindmarsh/Louis Fontés | Lagonda M45R |
| 1936 | RACE CANCELLED | |
| 1937 | Jean-Pierre Wimille/Robert Benoist | Bugatti 57G sc |
| 1938 | Eugene Chaboud/Jean Tremoulet | Delahaye 135M |
| 1939 | Jean-Pierre Wimille/Pierre Veyron | Bugatti 57G sc |
| 1940–48 | RACES CANCELLED | |
| 1949 | Luigi Chinetti/Lord Selsdon | Ferrari 166MM |
| 1950 | Louis Rosier/Jean-Louis Rosier | Talbot-Lago |
| 1951 | Peter Walker/Peter Whitehead | Jaguar C |
| 1952 | Hermann Lang/Fritz Reiss | Mercedes-Benz 300 SL |
| 1953 | Tony Rolt/Duncan Hamilton | Jaguar C |
| 1954 | Froilan Gonzales/Maurice Trintignant | Ferrari 375 |
| 1955 | Mike Hawthorn/Ivor Bueb | Jaguar D |
| 1956 | Ron Flockhart/Ninian Sanderson | Jaguar D |
| 1957 | Ron Flockhart/Ivor Bueb | Jaguar D |
| 1958 | Olivier Gendebien/Phil Hill | Ferrari 250 TR58 |
| 1959 | Carroll Shelby/Roy Salvadori | Aston Martin DBR1 |
| 1960 | Olivier Gendebien/Paul Frère | Ferrari 250 TR59/60 |
| 1961 | Olivier Gendebien/Phil Hill | Ferrari 250 TR61 |
| 1962 | Olivier Gendebien/Phil Hill | Ferrari 250P |
| 1963 | Lodovico Scarfiotti/Lorenzo Bandini | Ferrari 250P |
| 1964 | Jean Guichel/Nino Vaccarella | Ferrari 275P |
| 1965 | Jochen Rindt/Masten Gregory | Ferrari 250LM |
| 1966 | Chris Amon/Bruce McLaren | Ford Mk2 |
| 1967 | Dan Gurney/A.J. Foyt | Ford Mk4 |
| 1968 | Pedro Rodriguez/Lucien Bianchi | Ford GT40 |
| 1969 | Jacky Ickx/Jackie Oliver | Ford GT40 |
| 1970 | Hans Herrmann/Richard Attwood | Porsche 917 |
| 1971 | Helmut Marko/Gijs van Lennep | Porsche 917 |
| 1972 | Henri Pescarolo/Graham Hill | Matra-Simca MS670 |
| 1973 | Henri Pescarolo/Gérard Larrousse | Matra-Simca MS670B |
| 1974 | Henri Pescarolo/Gérard Larrousse | Matra-Simca MS670B |
| 1975 | Jacky Ickx/Derek Bell | Mirage-Ford MB |
| 1976 | Jacky Ickx/Gijs van Lennep | Porsche 936 |
| 1977 | Jacky Ickx/Jurgen Barth/Hurley Haywood | Porsche 936 |
| 1978 | Jean-Pierre Jaussaud/Didier Pironi | Renault-Alpine A442 |

| Year | Winning Drivers | Car |
|------|-----------------|-----|
| 1979 | Klaus Ludwig/Bill Whittington/Don Whittington | Porsche 935 |
| 1980 | Jean-Pierre Jaussaud/Jean Rondeau | Rondeau-Ford M379B |
| 1981 | Jacky Ickx/Derek Bell | Porsche 936-81 |
| 1982 | Jacky Ickx/Derek Bell | Porsche 956 |
| 1983 | Vern Schuppan/Hurley Haywood/Al Holbert | Porsche 956-83 |
| 1984 | Klaus Ludwig/Henri Pescarolo | Porsche 956B |
| 1985 | Klaus Ludwig/Paolo Barilla/John Winter | Porsche 956B |
| 1986 | Derek Bell/Hans-Joachim Stuck/Al Holbert | Porsche 962C |
| 1987 | Derek Bell/Hans-Joachim Stuck/Al Holbert | Porsche 962C |
| 1988 | Jan Lammers/Johnny Dumfries/Andy Wallace | Jaguar XJR9LM |
| 1989 | Jochen Mass/Manuel Reuter/Stanley Dickens | Sauber-Mercedes C9-88 |
| 1990 | John Nielsen/Price Cobb/Martin Brundle | TWR Jaguar XJR-12 |
| 1991 | Volker Weidler/Johnny Herbert/Bertrand Gachot | Mazda 787B |
| 1992 | Derek Warwick/Yannick Dalmas/Mark Blundell | Peugeot 905B |
| 1993 | Geoff Brabham/Christophe Bouchut/Eric Helary | Peugeot 905 |
| 1994 | Yannick Dalmas/Hurley Haywood/Mauro Baldi | Porsche 962 |
| 1995 | Yannick Dalmas/J.J. Lehto/Masanori Sekiya | McLaren BMW |
| 1996 | Manuel Reuter/Davy Jones/Alexander Wurz | TWR Porsche |
| 1997 | Michele Alboreto/Stefan Johansson/Tom Kristensen | TWR Porsche |
| 1998 | Allan McNish/Laurent Aiello/Stephane Ortelli | Porsche GT One |
| 1999 | Yannick Dalmas/Joachim Winkelhock/Pierluigi Martini | BMW V12 LMR |
| 2000 | Frank Biela/Tom Kristensen/Emanuele Pirro | Audi R8 |
| 2001 | Frank Biela/Tom Kristensen/Emanuele Pirro | Audi R8 |
| 2002 | Frank Biela/Tom Kristensen/Emanuele Pirro | Audi R8 |
| 2003 | Rinaldo Capello/Tom Kristensen/Guy Smith | Bentley EXP Speed 8 |
| 2004 | Rinaldo Capello/Seiji Ara/Tom Kristensen | Audi R8 |
| 2005 | J.J. Lehto/Marco Werner/Tom Kristensen | Audi R8 |
| 2006 | Frank Biela/Emanuele Pirro/Marco Werner | Audi R10 |
| 2007 | Frank Biela/Emanuele Pirro/Marco Werner | Audi R10 |
| 2008 | Rinaldo Capello/Tom Kristensen/Allan McNish | Audi R10 |
| 2009 | Marc Gene/Alexander Wurz/David Brabham | Peugeot 908 |
| 2010 | Timo Bernhard/Romain Dumas/Mike Rockenfeller | Audi R15 |
| 2011 | Marcel Fassler/Andre Lotterer/Benoit Treluyer | Audi R18 |

Jockey John Velazquez won his first Kentucky Derby in 13 tries on Animal Kingdom

BILL FRAKES

# Horse Racing

# FOR THE RECORD • 2010—2011

## The Triple Crown

### 137th Kentucky Derby

May 7, 2011. Grade I, 3-year-olds; 11th race, Churchill Downs, Louisville. All:126 lbs. Distance: 1¼ miles. Purse: $2,000,000 guaranteed. Track: fast. Off: 6:31 p.m. Winner: Animal Kingdom (By Leroidesanimaux, out of Dalicia by Acatenango) ; Times: 0:23.24, 0:48.63, 1:13.40, 1:37.49, 2:02.04. Won: Driving. Breeder: Team Valor (Kentucky). Scratched: Uncle Mo.

| Horse | Finish-PP | Margin | Jockey/Trainer |
|---|---|---|---|
| Animal Kingdom | 1–16 | 2¾ | John Velazquez/Graham H. Motion |
| Nehro | 2–18 | neck | Corey Nakatani/Steve Asmussen |
| Mucho Macho Man | 3–13 | ¾ | Rajiv Maragh/Katherine Ritvo |
| Shackleford | 4–14 | 1¾ | Jesus Castanon/Dale Romans |
| Master of Hounds | 5–11 | nose | Garrett Gomez/Aidan O'Brien |
| Santiva | 6–12 | nose | Shaun Bridgmohan/Eddie Kenneally |
| Brilliant Speed | 7–2 | 2 | Joel Rosario/Thomas Albertrani |
| Dialed In | 8–8 | neck | Julien Leparoux/Nick Zito |
| Pants On Fire | 9–7 | 2¾ | Rosie Napravnik/Kelly Breen |
| Twice the Appeal | 10–3 | neck | Calvin Borel/Jeff Bonde |
| Soldat | 11–17 | ½ | Alan Garcia/Kiaran McLaughlin |
| Stay Thirsty | 12–4 | 3¼ | Ramon Dominguez/Todd Pletcher |
| Derby Kitten | 13–9 | 1¼ | Javier Castellano/Mike Maker |
| Decisive Moment | 14–5 | 1 | Kerwin Clark/Juan Arias |
| Archarcharch | 15–1 | 1 | Jon Court/William Fires |
| Midnight Interlude | 16–15 | ½ | Victor Espinoza/Bob Baffert |
| Twinspired | 17–10 | 3¾ | Mike Smith/Mike Maker |
| Watch Me Go | 18–19 | ½ | Rafael Bejarano/Kathleen O'Connell |
| Comma to the Top | 19–6 | — | Patrick Valenzuela/Peter Miller |

### 136th Preakness Stakes

May 21, 2011. Grade I, 3-year-olds; 12th race, Pimlico Race Course, Baltimore. All: 126 lbs. Distance: 1³⁄₁₆ miles; Stakes value: $1,500,000. Track: fast. Off: 6:21 p.m. Winner: Shackleford (By Forestry out of Oatsee by Unbridled); Times: 0:22.69, 0:46.87, 1:12.01, 1:37.22, 1:56.47. Won: driving. Breeders: Mike Lauffer and Bill Cubbedge (Kentucky).

| Horse | Finish-PP | Margin | Jockey/Trainer |
|---|---|---|---|
| Shackleford | 1–5 | ½ | Jesus Castanon/Dale Romans |
| Animal Kingdom | 2–11 | 1¼ | John Velazquez/Graham H. Motion |
| Astrology | 3–1 | 2½ | Mike Smith/Steve Asmussen |
| Dialed In | 4–10 | 2 | Julien Leparoux/Nick Zito |
| Dance City | 5–8 | 1¼ | Ramon Dominguez/Todd Pletcher |
| Mucho Macho Man | 6–9 | 1½ | Rajiv Maragh/Katherine Ritvo |
| King Congie | 7–3 | ³⁄₄ | Robby Albarado/Thomas Albertrani |
| Mr. Commons | 8–14 | 1½ | Victor Espinoza/John Shirreffs |
| Isn't He Perfect | 9–12 | 1¼ | Edgar Prado/Doodnauth Shivmangal |
| Concealed Identity | 10–13 | neck | Sheldon Russell/Edmond Gaudet |
| Norman Asbjornson | 11–2 | 1¾ | Julian Pimentel/Christopher Grove |
| Sway Away | 12–6 | 7 | Garrett Gomez/Jeff Bonde |
| Mignight Interlude | 13–7 | neck | Martin Garcia/Bob Baffert |
| Flashpoint | 14–4 | — | Corenlio Velasquez/Wesley Ward |

### 143rd Belmont Stakes

June 11, 2011. Grade I, 3-year-olds; 11th race, Belmont Park, Elmont, NY. All: 126 lbs. Distance: 1½ miles. Stakes value: $1,000,000. Track: sloppy. Off: 6:39 p.m. Winner: Ruler On Ice (By Roman Ruler out of Champagne Glow by Saratoga Six); Times: 0:23.92, 0:49.08, 1:14.51, 1:39.95, 2:05.09, 2:30.88. Won: driving. Breeders: Liberation Farm and Brandywine Farm (Kentucky).

| Horse | Finish-PP | Margin | Jockey/Trainer |
|---|---|---|---|
| Ruler On Ice | 1–3 | ¾ | Jose Valdivia Jr./Kelly Breen |
| Stay Thirsty | 2–2 | 1½ | Javier Castellano/Todd Pletcher |
| Brilliant Speed | 3–5 | 5¼ | Joel Rosario/Thomas Albertrani |
| Nehro | 4–6 | neck | Corey Nakatani/Steve Asmussen |
| Shackleford | 5–12 | 1½ | Jesus Castanon/Dale Romans |
| Animal Kingdom | 6–9 | 15 | John Velazquez/Graham H. Motion |
| Mucho Macho Man | 7–10 | 3½ | Ramon Dominguez/Katherine Ritvo |
| Santiva | 8–4 | nose | Shaun Bridgmohan/Eddie Kenneally |
| Monzon | 9–7 | 1½ | Jose Lezcano/Ignacio Correas |
| Master of Hounds | 10–1 | 1 | Garrett Gomez/Aidan O'Brien |
| Prime Cut | 11–8 | 1 | Edgar Prado/Neil Howard |
| Isn't He Perfect | 12–11 | — | Rajiv Maragh/Doodnauth Shivmangal |

### Late 2010

| Date | Race | Track | Distance | Winner | Trainer/Jockey | Purse ($) |
|---|---|---|---|---|---|---|
| Oct 2 | Hirsch Turf Classic Invt'l | Belmont | 1½ miles | Winchester | C. Clement/ C. Velasquez | 500,000 |
| Oct 2 | Flower Bowl Invitational | Belmont | 1¼ miles | Ave | R. Attfield/ J. Castellano | 500,000 |
| Oct 2 | Indiana Derby | Hoosier | 1¹⁄₁₆ miles | Lookin at Lucky | B. Baffert/ M. Garcia | 510,900 |
| Oct 2 | Fitz Dixon Cotillion | Philadelphia | 1¹⁄₁₆ miles | Havre De Grace | A. Dutrow/ J. Rose | 750,000 |
| Oct 2 | Vosburgh Stakes | Belmont | 6 furlongs | Girolamo | S. bin Suroor/ A. Garcia | 350,000 |
| Oct 2 | Jockey Club Gold Cup | Belmont | 1¼ miles | Haynesfield | S. Asmussen/ R. Dominguez | 750,000 |
| Oct 8 | Darley Alcibiades Stakes | Keeneland | 1¹⁄₁₆ miles | Wickedly Perfect | D. O'Neill/ R. Bejarano | 400,000 |
| Oct 9 | First Lady Stakes | Keeneland | 1 mile | Proviso | W. Mott/ M. Smith | 400,000 |
| Oct 9 | Shadwell Turf Mile | Keeneland | 1 mile | Gio Ponti | C. Clement/ R. Dominguez | 600,000 |
| Oct 9 | Dixiana Breeders' Futurity | Keeneland | 1¹⁄₁₆ miles | J.B's Thunder | A. Stall/ S. Bridgmohan | 400,000 |
| Oct 9 | Champagne Stakes | Belmont | 1 mile | Uncle Mo | T. Pletcher/ J. Velazquez | 300,000 |
| Oct 9 | Frizette Stakes | Belmont | 1 mile | A Z Warrior | B. Baffert/ A. Garcia | 300,000 |
| Oct 10 | Oklahoma Derby | Remington Park | 1⅛ miles | Pleasant Prince | W. Ward/ J. Rosario | 400,000 |
| Oct 10 | Juddmonte Spinster Stakes | Keeneland | 1⅛ miles | Acoma | D. Carroll/ A. Garcia | 500,000 |
| Oct 16 | Queen Elizabeth II Challenge Cup | Keeneland | 1⅛ miles | Harmonious | J. Shirreffs/ J. Rosario | 400,000 |
| Oct 16 | Nearctic Stakes | Woodbine | 6 furlongs | Serious Attitude | R. Guest/ G. Gomez | 502,794 |
| Oct 16 | E.P. Taylor Stakes | Woodbine | 1¼ miles | Reggane | A. De Royer Dupre/ C. Soumillon | 990,175 |
| Oct 16 | Canadian Int'l Stakes | Woodbine | 1½ miles | Joshua Tree | A. O'Brien/ C. O'Donoghue | 1,989,838 |
| Nov 5 | Breeders Cup Juvenile Fillies | Churchill Downs | 1¹⁄₁₆ miles | Awesome Feather | S. Gold/ J. Sanchez | 1,818,000 |
| Nov 5 | Breeders Cup Juvenile Fillies Turf | Churchill Downs | 1 mile | More Than Real | T. Pletcher/ G. Gomez | 909,000 |
| Nov 5 | Breeders Cup F & M Turf | Churchill Downs | 1⅜ miles | Shared Account | G. Motion/ E. Prado | 1,818,000 |
| Nov 5 | Breeders Cup Ladies' Classic | Churchill Downs | 1⅛ miles | Unrivaled Belle | W. Mott/ K. Desormeaux | 1,818,000 |
| Nov 5 | Breeders Cup F & M Sprint | Churchill Downs | 7 furlongs | Dubai Majesty | B. Calhoun/ J. Theriot | 909,000 |
| Nov 5 | Breeders Cup Marathon | Churchill Downs | 1¾ miles | Eldaafer | D. Alvarado/ J. Velazquez | 454,500 |
| Nov 6 | Breeders Cup Classic | Churchill Downs | 1¼ miles | Blame | A. Stall Jr./ G. Gomez | 4,545,000 |
| Nov 6 | Breeders Cup Turf | Churchill Downs | 1½ miles | Dangerous Midge | B. Meehan/ L. Dettori | 2,727,000 |
| Nov 6 | Breeders Cup Turf Sprint | Churchill Downs | 5 furlongs | Chamberlain Bridge | B. Calhoun/ J. Theriot | 909,000 |
| Nov 6 | Breeders Cup Mile | Churchill Downs | 1 mile | Goldikova | F. Head/ O. Peslier | 1,818,000 |
| Nov 6 | Breeders Cup Juvenile | Churchill Downs | 1¹⁄₁₆ miles | Uncle Mo | T. Pletcher/ J. Velazquez | 1,818,000 |
| Nov 6 | Breeders Cup Sprint | Churchill Downs | 6 furlongs | Big Drama | D. Fawkes/ E. Coa | 1,818,000 |
| Nov 20 | Jackpot Stakes | Delta Downs | 1¹⁄₁₆ miles | Gourmet Dinner | S. Standridge/ S. Madrid | 1,000,000 |
| Nov 20 | Princess Stakes | Delta Downs | 1 mile | Bouquet Booth | S. Margolis/ S. Bridgmohan | 500,000 |

## 2011

| Date | Race | Track | Distance | Winner | Trainer/Jockey | Purse ($) |
|---|---|---|---|---|---|---|
| Jan 29 | Sunshine Millions Classic | Gulfstream | 1⅛ miles | Tackleberry | L. Olivares/ J. Santiago | 500,000 |
| Jan 29 | Sunshine Millions Turf | Santa Anita | 1⅛ miles | Caracortado | M. Machowsky/ J. Talamo | 300,000 |
| Jan 29 | Sunshine Millions Filly & Mare Stakes | Gulfstream | 1⅛ miles | Trip for A.J. | M. Wolfston/ J. Velazquez | 300,000 |
| Jan 29 | Sunshine Millions Distaff | Santa Anita | 1¹⁄₁₆ miles | Evening Jewel | J. Cassidy/ V. Espinoza | 300,000 |
| Jan 30 | Holy Bull Stakes | Gulfstream | 1 mile | Dialed In | N. Zito/ J. Leparoux | 400,000 |
| Feb 5 | Donn Handicap | Gulfstream | 1⅛ miles | Giant Oak | C. Block/ S. Bridgmohan | 500,000 |
| Feb 5 | Gulfstream Turf Handicap | Gulfstream | 1⅛ miles | Teaks North | J. Sallusto/ J. Valdivia | 300,000 |
| Feb 19 | Risen Star Stakes | La. Fair Grounds | 1¹⁄₁₆ miles | Mucho Macho Man | K. Ritvo/ R. Maragh | 300,000 |
| Feb 26 | Fountain of Youth Stakes | Gulfstream | 1⅛ miles | Soldat | K. McLaughlin/ A. Garcia | 400,000 |
| Mar 5 | Santa Anita Handicap | Santa Anita | 1¼ miles | Game on Dude | B. Baffert/ C. Sutherland | 750,000 |
| Mar 12 | Tampa Bay Derby | Tampa Bay Downs | 1¹⁄₁₆ miles | Watch Me Go | K. O'Connell/ L. Garcia | 350,000 |
| Mar 26 | Dubai World Cup | Meydan | 2000m | Victoire Pisa | K. Sumii/ M. Demuro | 10,000,000 |
| Mar 26 | Dubai Sheema Classic | Meydan | 2400m | Rewilding | M. Al Zarooni/ F. Dettori | 5,000,000 |
| Mar 26 | Dubai Duty Free Stakes | Meydan | 1800m | Presvis | L. Cumani/ R. Moore | 5,000,000 |
| Mar 26 | Dubai Golden Shaheen | Meydan | 1200m | Rocket Man | P. Shaw/ F. Coetzee | 2,000,000 |
| Mar 26 | UAE Derby | Meydan | 1900m | Kwahlah | S. bin Suroor/ M. Barzalona | 2,000,000 |
| Mar 26 | Godolphin Mile | Meydan | 1600m | Skysurfers | S. bin Suroor/ F. Dettori | 1,000,000 |
| Mar 26 | Louisiana Derby | La. Fair Grounds | 1⅛ miles | Pants on Fire | K. Breen/ A.R. Napravnik | 1,000,000 |
| Mar 26 | New Orleans Handicap | La. Fair Grounds | 1⅛ miles | Mission Impazible | T. Pletcher/ G. Gomez | 396,000 |
| Mar 26 | Fair Ground Oaks | La. Fair Grounds | 1¹⁄₁₆ miles | Daisy Devine | A. McKeever/ J. Graham | 500,000 |
| Mar 26 | Mervin Muniz Jr. Handicap | La. Fair Grounds | 1⅛ miles | Smart Bid | G. Motion/ E. Prado | 396,000 |
| Mar 26 | Vinery Racing Stakes | Turfway | 1⅛ miles | Animal Kingdom | G. Motion/ A. Garcia | 500,000 |
| Mar 27 | Sunland Derby | Sunland | 1⅛ miles | Twice the Appeal | J. Bonde/ C. Reyes | 800,000 |
| Apr 3 | Florida Derby | Gulfstream | 1⅛ miles | Dialed In | N. Zito/ J. Leparoux | 1,000,000 |
| Apr 10 | Wood Memorial Stakes | Aqueduct | 1⅛ miles | Toby's Corner | G. Motion/ E. Castro | 1,000,000 |
| Apr 10 | Santa Anita Derby | Santa Anita | 1⅛ miles | Midnight Interlude | B. Baffert/ V. Espinoza | 1,000,000 |
| Apr 10 | Ashland Stakes | Keeneland | 1¹⁄₁₆ miles | Lilacs and Lace | J. Castellano/ J. Teranova/ | 400,000 |
| Apr 10 | Oaklawn Handicap | Oaklawn | 1⅛ miles | Win Willy | M. Robertson/ M. Berry | 350,000 |
| Apr 16 | Blue Grass Stakes | Keeneland | 1⅛ miles | Brilliant Speed | T. Albertrani/ J. Rosario | 750,000 |
| Apr 16 | Arkansas Derby | Oaklawn | 1⅛ miles | Archarcharch | W. Fires/ J. Court | 1,000,000 |
| Apr 16 | Charles Town Classic | Charles Town | 1⅛ miles | Duke of Mischief | D. Fawkes/ J. Bravo | 1,000,000 |
| May 6 | Kentucky Oaks | Churchill Downs | 1⅛ miles | Plum Pretty | B. Baffert/ M. Garcia | 1,000,000 |
| May 6 | La Troienne Stakes | Churchill Downs | 1¹⁄₁₆ miles | Blind Luck | J. Hollendorfer/ G. Gomez | 333,900 |
| May 6 | Alysheba Stakes | Churchill Downs | 1¹⁄₁₆ miles | First Dude | B. Baffert/ M. Garcia | 358,500 |

## 2011 (through September 30) (Cont.)

| Date | Race | Track | Distance | Winner | Trainer/Jockey | Purse ($) |
|------|------|-------|----------|--------|----------------|-----------|
| May 7 | Kentucky Derby | Churchill Downs | 1¼ miles | Animal Kingdom | G. Motion/ J. Velazquez | 2,171,800 |
| May 7 | Woodford Reserve Turf Classic | Churchill Downs | 1⅛ miles | Get Stormy | T. Bush/ R. Dominguez | 576,000 |
| May 7 | Humana Distaff | Churchill Downs | 7 furlongs | Sassy Image | D. Romans/ R. Albarado | 345,600 |
| May 7 | Churchill Downs Stakes | Churchill Downs | 7 furlongs | Aikenite | T. Pletcher/ J. Velazquez | 348,900 |
| May 21 | Preakness Stakes | Pimlico | 1³⁄₁₆ miles | Shackleford | D. Romans/ J. Castanon | 1,500,000 |
| June 4 | Nassau Stakes | Woodbine | 1 mile | Bay To Bay | B. Lynch/ L. Contreras | 307,888 |
| June 11 | Belmont Stakes | Belmont | 1½ miles | Ruler On Ice | K. Breen/ J. Valdivia | 1,000,000 |
| June 11 | Just a Game Stakes | Belmont | 1 mile | C.S. Silk | D. Romans/ J. Castellano | 400,000 |
| June 11 | Manhattan Handicap Turf | Belmont | 1¼ miles | Mission Approved | N. Chatterpaul/ J. Espinoza | 400,000 |
| June 26 | Queen's Plate Stakes | Woodbine | 1¼ miles | Inglorious | J. Carroll/ L. Contreras | 1,015,445 |
| July 2 | United Nations Stakes | Monmouth | 1⅜ miles | Teaks North | J. Sallusto/ E. Castro | 765,000 |
| July 9 | Hollywood Gold Cup | Hollywood | 1¼ miles | First Dude | B. Baffert/ M. Garcia | 500,000 |
| July 9 | Princess Rooney Handicap | Calder | 6 furlongs | Sassy Image | D. Romans/ M. Smith | 350,000 |
| July 9 | Smile Sprint Handicap | Calder | 6 furlongs | Giant Ryan | B. Parboo/ C. Velasquez | 350,000 |
| July 9 | Man O'War Stakes Turf | Belmont | 1⅜ miles | Cape Blanco | A. O'Brien/ J. Spencer | 600,000 |
| July 16 | Virginia Derby | Colonial Downs | 1¼ miles | Air Support | C. McGaughey/ A. Solis | 600,000 |
| July 16 | Delaware Handicap | Delaware | 1¼ miles | Blind Luck | J. Hollendorfer/ G. Gomez | 765,000 |
| July 30 | Diana Stakes | Saratoga | 1⅛ miles | Zagora | C. Brown/ J. Castellano | 500,000 |
| July 30 | Jim Dandy Stakes | Saratoga | 1⅛ miles | Stay Thirsty | T. Pletcher/ J. Castellano | 500,000 |
| July 31 | Haskell Invitational | Monmouth | 1⅛ miles | Coil | B. Baffert/ M. Garcia | 1,020,000 |
| Aug 6 | Whitney Invitational | Saratoga | 1⅛ miles | Tizway | H. James Bond/ R. Maragh | 750,000 |
| Aug 6 | West Virginia Derby | Mountaineer | 1⅛ miles | Prayer for Relief | B. Baffert/ R. Bejarano | 750,000 |
| Aug 13 | Sword Dancer Invitational | Saratoga | 1½ miles | Winchester | C. Clement/ C. Velasquez | 500,000 |
| Aug 13 | Arlington Million Stakes | Arlington | 1¼ miles | Cape Blanco | A. O'Brien/ J. Spencer | 1,000,000 |
| Aug 13 | Beverly D. Stakes | Arlington | 1³⁄₁₆ miles | Stacelita | C. Brown/ R. Dominguez | 750,000 |
| Aug 13 | Secretariat Stakes | Arlington | 1¼ miles | Treasure Beach | A. O'Brien/ C. O'Donoghue | 400,000 |
| Aug 20 | Alabama Stakes | Saratoga | 1¼ miles | Royal Delta | W. Mott/ J. Lezcano | 500,000 |
| Aug 27 | Travers Stakes | Saratoga | 1¼ miles | Stay Thirsty | T. Pletcher/ J. Castellano | 1,000,000 |
| Aug 28 | Pacific Classic | Del Mar | 1¼ miles | Acclamation | D. Warren/ P. Valenzuela | 1,000,000 |
| Sept 3 | Woodward Stakes | Saratoga | 1⅛ miles | Havre de Grace | L. Jones/ R. Dominguez | 750,000 |
| Sept 18 | Woodbine Mile | Woodbine | 1 mile | Turallure | C. Lopresti/ J. Leparoux | 1,025,981 |
| Sept 18 | Northern Dancer Stakes Turf | Woodbine | 1½ miles | Wigmore Hall | M. Bell/ J. Spencer | 512,174 |
| Sept 24 | Pennsylvania Derby | Philadelphia | 1⅛ miles | To Honor and Serve | W. Mott/ J. Lezcano | 1,000,000 |

# FOR THE RECORD • Year by Year

## THOROUGHBRED RACING

### Kentucky Derby

Run at Churchill Downs, Louisville, KY, on the first Saturday in May.

| Year | Winner (Margin) | Jockey | Second | Third | Time |
|---|---|---|---|---|---|
| 1875 | Aristides (1) | Oliver Lewis | Volcano | Verdigris | 2:37¾ |
| 1876 | Vagrant (2) | Bobby Swim | Creedmoor | Harry Hill | 2:38¼ |
| 1877 | Baden-Baden (2) | William Walker | Leonard | King William | 2:38 |
| 1878 | Day Star (2) | Jimmie Carter | Himyar | Leveler | 2:37¼ |
| 1879 | Lord Murphy (1) | Charlie Shauer | Falsetto | Strathmore | 2:37 |
| 1880 | Fonso (1) | George Lewis | Kimball | Bancroft | 2:37½ |
| 1881 | Hindoo (4) | Jimmy McLaughin | Lelex | Alfambra | 2:40 |
| 1882 | Apollo (½) | Babe Hurd | Runnymede | Bengal | 2:40¼ |
| 1883 | Leonatus (3) | Billy Donohue | Drake Carter | Lord Raglan | 2:43 |
| 1884 | Buchanan (2) | Isaac Murphy | Loftin | Audrain | 2:40¼ |
| 1885 | Joe Cotton (Neck) | Erskine Henderson | Bersan | Ten Booker | 2:37¼ |
| 1886 | Ben Ali (½) | Paul Duffy | Blue Wing | Free Knight | 2:36½ |
| 1887 | Montrose (2) | Isaac Lewis | Jim Gore | Jacobin | 2:39¼ |
| 1888 | MacBeth II (1) | George Covington | Gallifet | White | 2:38¼ |
| 1889 | Spokane (Nose) | Thomas Kiley | Proctor Knott | Once Again | 2:34½ |
| 1890 | Riley (2) | Isaac Murphy | Bill Letcher | Robespierre | 2:45 |
| 1891 | Kingman (1) | Isaac Murphy | Balgowan | High Tariff | 2:52¼ |
| 1892 | Azra (Nose) | Alonzo Clayton | Huron | Phil Dwyer | 2:41½ |
| 1893 | Lookout (5) | Eddie Kunze | Plutus | Boundless | 2:39¼ |
| 1894 | Chant (2) | Frank Goodale | Pearl Song | Sigurd | 2:41 |
| 1895 | Halma (3) | Soup Perkins | Basso | Laureate | 2:37½ |
| 1896 | Ben Brush (Nose) | Willie Simms | Ben Eder | Semper Ego | 2:07¼ |
| 1897 | Typhoon II (Head) | Buttons Garner | Ornament | Dr. Catlett | 2:12½ |
| 1898 | Plaudit (Neck) | Willie Simms | Lieber Karl | Isabey | 2:09 |
| 1899 | Manuel (2) | Fred Taral | Corsini | Mazo | 2:12 |
| 1900 | Lieut. Gibson (4) | Jimmy Boland | Florizar | Thrive | 2:06¼ |
| 1901 | His Eminence (2) | Jimmy Winkfield | Sannazarro | Driscoll | 2:07¾ |
| 1902 | Alan-a-Dale (Nose) | Jimmy Winkfield | Inventor | The Rival | 2:08¾ |
| 1903 | Judge Himes (¾) | Hal Booker | Early | Bourbon | 2:09 |
| 1904 | Elwood (½) | Frankie Prior | Ed Tierney | Brancas | 2:08½ |
| 1905 | Agile (3) | Jack Martin | Ram's Horn | Layson | 2:10¾ |
| 1906 | Sir Huon (2) | Roscoe Troxler | Lady Navarre | James Reddick | 2:08⅕ |
| 1907 | Pink Star (2) | Andy Minder | Zal | Ovelando | 2:12⅗ |
| 1908 | Stone Street (1) | Arthur Pickens | Sir Cleges | Dunvegan | 2:15⅕ |
| 1909 | Wintergreen (4) | Vincent Powers | Miami | Dr. Barkley | 2:08⅕ |
| 1910 | Donau (½) | Fred Herbert | Joe Morris | Fighting Bob | 2:06⅖ |
| 1911 | Meridian (¾) | George Archibald | Governor Gray | Colston | 2:05 |
| 1912 | Worth (Neck) | Carroll H. Schilling | Duval | Flamma | 2:09⅖ |
| 1913 | Donerail (½) | Roscoe Goose | Ten Point | Gowell | 2:04⅘ |
| 1914 | Old Rosebud (8) | John McCabe | Hodge | Bronzewing | 2:03⅖ |
| 1915 | Regret (2) | Joe Notter | Pebbles | Sharpshooter | 2:05⅖ |
| 1916 | George Smith (Neck) | Johnny Loftus | Star Hawk | Franklin | 2:04 |
| 1917 | Omar Khayyam (2) | Charles Borel | Ticket | Midway | 2:04⅗ |
| 1918 | Exterminator (1) | William Knapp | Escoba | Viva America | 2:10⅘ |
| 1919 | Sir Barton (5) | Johnny Loftus | Billy Kelly | Under Fire | 2:09⅘ |
| 1920 | Paul Jones (Head) | Ted Rice | Upset | On Watch | 2:09 |
| 1921 | Behave Yourself (Head) | Charles Thompson | Black Servant | Prudery | 2:04⅕ |
| 1922 | Morvich (½) | Albert Johnson | Bet Mosie | John Finn | 2:04⅗ |
| 1923 | Zev (1½) | Earl Sande | Martingale | Vigil | 2:05⅖ |
| 1924 | Black Gold (½) | John Mooney | Chilhowee | Beau Butler | 2:05⅕ |
| 1925 | Flying Ebony (1½) | Earl Sande | Captain Hal | Son of John | 2:07⅗ |
| 1926 | Bubbling Over (5) | Albert Johnson | Bagenbaggage | Rock Man | 2:03⅗ |
| 1927 | Whiskery (Head) | Linus McAtee | Osmond | Jock | 2:06 |
| 1928 | Reigh Count (3) | Chick Lang | Misstep | Toro | 2:10⅖ |
| 1929 | Clyde Van Dusen (2) | Linus McAtee | Naishapur | Panchio | 2:10⅘ |
| 1930 | Gallant Fox (2) | Earl Sande | Gallant Knight | Ned O. | 2:07⅗ |
| 1931 | Twenty Grand (4) | Charles Kurtsinger | Sweep All | Mate | 2:01⅘ |
| 1932 | Burgoo King (5) | Eugene James | Economic | Stepenfetchit | 2:05⅕ |
| 1933 | Brokers Tip (Nose) | Don Meade | Head Play | Charley O. | 2:06⅘ |

## Kentucky Derby *(Cont.)*

| Year | Winner (Margin) | Jockey | Second | Third | Time |
|---|---|---|---|---|---|
| 1934 | Cavalcade (2½) | Mack Garner | Discovery | Agrarian | 2:04 |
| 1935 | Omaha (1½) | Willie Saunders | Roman Soldier | Whiskolo | 2:05 |
| 1936 | Bold Venture (Head) | Ira Hanford | Brevity | Indian Broom | 2:03⅗ |
| 1937 | War Admiral (1¾) | Charles Kurtsinger | Pompoon | Reaping Reward | 2:03⅕ |
| 1938 | Lawrin (1) | Eddie Arcaro | Dauber | Can't Wait | 2:04⅘ |
| 1939 | Johnstown (8) | James Stout | Challedon | Heather Broom | 2:03⅖ |
| 1940 | Gallahadion (1½) | Carroll Bierman | Bimelech | Dit | 2:05 |
| 1941 | Whirlaway (8) | Eddie Arcaro | Staretor | Market Wise | 2:01⅖ |
| 1942 | Shut Out (2½) | Wayne Wright | Alsab | Valdina Orphan | 2:04⅖ |
| 1943 | Count Fleet (3) | John Longden | Blue Swords | Slide Rule | 2:04 |
| 1944 | Pensive (4½) | Conn McCreary | Broadcloth | Stir Up | 2:04⅕ |
| 1945 | Hoop Jr. (6) | Eddie Arcaro | Pot o' Luck | Darby Dieppe | 2:07 |
| 1946 | Assault (8) | Warren Mehrtens | Spy Song | Hampden | 2:06⅗ |
| 1947 | Jet Pilot (Head) | Eric Guerin | Phalanx | Faultless | 2:06⅘ |
| 1948 | Citation (3½) | Eddie Arcaro | Coaltown | My Request | 2:05⅖ |
| 1949 | Ponder (3) | Steve Brooks | Capot | Palestinian | 2:04⅕ |
| 1950 | Middleground (1¼) | William Boland | Hill Prince | Mr. Trouble | 2:01⅗ |
| 1951 | Count Turf (4) | Conn McCreary | Royal Mustang | Ruhe | 2:02⅗ |
| 1952 | Hill Gail (2) | Eddie Arcaro | Sub Fleet | Blue Man | 2:01⅗ |
| 1953 | Dark Star (Head) | Hank Moreno | Native Dancer | Invigorator | 2:02 |
| 1954 | Determine (1½) | Ray York | Hasty Road | Hasseyampa | 2:03 |
| 1955 | Swaps (1½) | Bill Shoemaker | Nashua | Summer Tan | 2:01⅘ |
| 1956 | Needles (¾) | Dave Erb | Fabius | Come On Red | 2:03⅖ |
| 1957 | Iron Liege (Nose) | Bill Hartack | Gallant Man | Round Table | 2:02⅕ |
| 1958 | Tim Tam (½) | Ismael Valenzuela | Lincoln Road | Noureddin | 2:05 |
| 1959 | Tomy Lee (Nose) | Bill Shoemaker | Sword Dancer | First Landing | 2:02⅕ |
| 1960 | Venetian Way (3½) | Bill Hartack | Bally Ache | Victoria Park | 2:02⅖ |
| 1961 | Carry Back (¾) | John Sellers | Crozier | Bass Clef | 2:04 |
| 1962 | Decidedly (2¼) | Bill Hartack | Roman Line | Ridan | 2:00⅖ |
| 1963 | Chateaugay (1¼) | Braulio Baeza | Never Bend | Candy Spots | 2:01⅘ |
| 1964 | Northern Dancer (Neck) | Bill Hartack | Hill Rise | The Scoundrel | 2:00 |
| 1965 | Lucky Debonair (Neck) | Bill Shoemaker | Dapper Dan | Tom Rolfe | 2:01⅕ |
| 1966 | Kauai King (½) | Don Brumfield | Advocator | Blue Skyer | 2:02 |
| 1967 | Proud Clarion (1) | Bobby Ussery | Barbs Delight | Damascus | 2:00⅗ |
| 1968 | Forward Pass (Disq.) | Ismael Valenzuela | Francie's Hat | T.V. Commercial | 2:02⅕ |
| 1969 | Majestic Prince (Neck) | Bill Hartack | Arts and Letters | Dike | 2:01⅘ |
| 1970 | Dust Commander (5) | Mike Manganello | My Dad George | High Echelon | 2:03⅖ |
| 1971 | Canonero II (3¾) | Gustavo Avila | Jim French | Bold Reason | 2:03⅕ |
| 1972 | Riva Ridge (3¼) | Ron Turcotte | No Le Hace | Hold Your Peace | 2:01⅘ |
| 1973 | Secretariat (2½) | Ron Turcotte | Sham | Our Native | 1:59⅖ |
| 1974 | Cannonade (2¼) | Angel Cordero Jr. | Hudson County | Agitate | 2:04 |
| 1975 | Foolish Pleasure (1¾) | Jacinto Vasquez | Avatar | Diabolo | 2:02 |
| 1976 | Bold Forbes (1) | Angel Cordero Jr. | Honest Pleasure | Elocutionist | 2:01⅗ |
| 1977 | Seattle Slew (1¾) | Jean Cruguet | Run Dusty Run | Sanhedrin | 2:02⅕ |
| 1978 | Affirmed (1¼) | Steve Cauthen | Alydar | Believe It | 2:01⅕ |
| 1979 | Spectacular Bid (2¾) | Ronald J. Franklin | General Assembly | Golden Act | 2:02⅖ |
| 1980 | Genuine Risk (1) | Jacinto Vasquez | Rumbo | Jaklin Klugman | 2:02 |
| 1981 | Pleasant Colony (¾) | Jorge Velasquez | Woodchopper | Partez | 2:02 |
| 1982 | Gato Del Sol (2½) | Eddie Delahoussaye | Laser Light | Reinvested | 2:02⅕ |
| 1983 | Sunny's Halo (2) | Eddie Delahoussaye | Desert Wine | Caveat | 2:02⅕ |
| 1984 | Swale (3¼) | Laffit Pincay Jr. | Coax Me Chad | At the Threshold | 2:02⅖ |
| 1985 | Spend A Buck (5) | Angel Cordero Jr. | Stephan's Odyssey | Chief's Crown | 2:00⅕ |
| 1986 | Ferdinand (2¼) | Bill Shoemaker | Bold Arrangement | Broad Brush | 2:02⅘ |
| 1987 | Alysheba (¾) | Chris McCarron | Bet Twice | Avies Copy | 2:03⅖ |
| 1988 | Winning Colors (Neck) | Gary Stevens | Forty Niner | Risen Star | 2:02⅕ |
| 1989 | Sunday Silence (2½) | Pat Valenzuela | Easy Goer | Awe Inspiring | 2:05 |
| 1990 | Unbridled (3½) | Craig Perret | Summer Squall | Pleasant Tap | 2:02 |
| 1991 | Strike the Gold (1¾) | Chris Antley | Best Pal | Mane Minister | 2:03 |
| 1992 | Lil E. Tee (1) | Pat Day | Casual Lies | Dance Floor | 2:03 |
| 1993 | Sea Hero (2½) | Jerry Bailey | Prairie Bayou | Wild Gale | 2:02⅖ |
| 1994 | Go for Gin (2½) | Chris McCarron | Strodes Creek | Blumin Affair | 2:03⅗ |
| 1995 | Thunder Gulch (2¼) | Gary Stevens | Tejano Run | Timber Country | 2:01⅕ |
| 1996 | Grindstone (Nose) | Jerry Bailey | Cavonnier | Prince of Thieves | 2:01 |
| 1997 | Silver Charm (Head) | Gary Stevens | Captain Bodgit | Free House | 2:02⅖ |
| 1998 | Real Quiet (½) | Kent Desormeaux | Victory Gallop | Indian Charlie | 2:02⅒ |
| 1999 | Charismatic (Neck) | Chris Antley | Menifee | Cat Thief | 2:03⅕ |

## Kentucky Derby *(Cont.)*

| Year | Winner (Margin) | Jockey | Second | Third | Time |
|---|---|---|---|---|---|
| 2000 | Fusaichi Pegasus (1½) | Kent Desormeaux | Aptitude | Impeachment | 2:01.12 |
| 2001 | Monarchos (4¾) | Jorge Chavez | Invisible Ink | Congaree | 1:59.97 |
| 2002 | War Emblem (4) | Victor Espinoza | Proud Citizen | Perfect Drift | 2:01.13 |
| 2003 | Funny Cide (1¾) | Jose Santos | Empire Maker | Peace Rules | 2:01.19 |
| 2004 | Smarty Jones (2¾) | Stewart Elliott | Lion Heart | Imperialism | 2:04.06 |
| 2005 | Giacomo (½) | Mike Smith | Closing Argument | Afleet Alex | 2:02.75 |
| 2006 | Barbaro (1½) | Edgar Prado | Bluegrass Cat | Steppenwolfer | 2:01.36 |
| 2007 | Street Sense (2¼) | Calvin Borel | Hard Spun | Curlin | 2:02.17 |
| 2008 | Big Brown (4¾) | Kent Desormeaux | Eight Belles | Denis of Cork | 2:01.82 |
| 2009 | Mine That Bird (6¾) | Calvin Borel | Pioneerof the Nile | Musket Man | 2:02.66 |
| 2010 | Super Saver (2½) | Calvin Borel | Ice Box | Paddy O'Prado | 2:04.45 |
| 2011 | Animal Kingdom (2¾) | John Velazquez | Nehro | Mucho Macho Man | 2:02.04 |

Note: Distance: 1½ miles (1875–95), 1¼ miles (1896–present).

## Preakness

Run at Pimlico Race Course, Baltimore, Md., two weeks after the Kentucky Derby.

| Year | Winner (Margin) | Jockey | Second | Third | Time |
|---|---|---|---|---|---|
| 1873 | Survivor (10) | G. Barbee | John Boulger | Artist | 2:43 |
| 1874 | Culpepper (¾) | W. Donohue | King Amadeus | Scratch | 2:56½ |
| 1875 | Tom Ochiltree (2) | L. Hughes | Viator | Bay Final | 2:43½ |
| 1876 | Shirley (4) | G. Barbee | Rappahannock | Algerine | 2:44¾ |
| 1877 | Cloverbrook (4) | C. Holloway | Bombast | Lucifer | 2:45½ |
| 1878 | Duke of Magenta (6) | C. Holloway | Bayard | Albert | 2:41¾ |
| 1879 | Harold (3) | L. Hughes | Jericho | Rochester | 2:40½ |
| 1880 | Grenada (¾) | L. Hughes | Oden | Emily F. | 2:40½ |
| 1881 | Saunterer (½) | T. Costello | Compensation | Baltic | 2:40½ |
| 1882 | Vanguard (Neck) | T. Costello | Heck | Col Watson | 2:44½ |
| 1883* | Jacobus (4) | G. Barbee | Parnell | | 2:42½ |
| 1884* | Knight of Ellerslie (2) | S. Fisher | Welcher | | 2:39½ |
| 1885 | Tecumseh (2) | Jim McLaughlin | Wickham | John C. | 2:49 |
| 1886 | The Bard (3) | S. Fisher | Eurus | Elkwood | 2:45 |
| 1887 | Dunboyne (1) | W. Donohue | Mahoney | Raymond | 2:39½ |
| 1888 | Refund (3) | F. Littlefield | Judge Murray | Glendale | 2:49 |
| 1889* | Buddhist (8) | W. Anderson | Japhet | | 2:17½ |
| 1890 | Montague (3) | W. Martin | Philosophy | Barrister | 2:36¾ |
| 1894 | Assignee (3) | Fred Taral | Potentate | Ed Kearney | 1:49¼ |
| 1895 | Belmar (1) | Fred Taral | April Fool | Sue Kittie | 1:50½ |
| 1896 | Margrave (1) | H. Griffin | Hamilton II | Intermission | 1:51 |
| 1897 | Paul Kauvar (1½) | C. Thorpe | Elkins | On Deck | 1:51¼ |
| 1898 | Sly Fox (2) | C. W. Simms | The Huguenot | Nuto | 1:49⅗ |
| 1899 | Half Time (1) | R. Clawson | Filigrane | Lackland | 1:47 |
| 1900 | Hindus (Head) | H. Spencer | Sarmation | Ten Candles | 1:48⅖ |
| 1901 | The Parader (2) | F. Landry | Sadie S. | Dr. Barlow | 1:47⅕ |
| 1902 | Old England (Nose) | L. Jackson | Major Daingerfield | Namtor | 1:45⅘ |
| 1903 | Flocarline (½) | W. Gannon | Mackey Dwyer | Rightful | 1:44⅘ |
| 1904 | Bryn Mawr (1) | E. Hildebrand | Wotan | Dolly Spanker | 1:44⅕ |
| 1905 | Cairngorm (Head) | W. Davis | Kiamesha | Coy Maid | 1:45⅘ |
| 1906 | Whimsical (4) | Walter Miller | Content | Larabie | 1:45 |
| 1907 | Don Enrique (1) | G. Mountain | Ethon | Zambesi | 1:45⅖ |
| 1908 | Royal Tourist (4) | E. Dugan | Live Wire | Robert Cooper | 1:46⅖ |
| 1909 | Effendi (1) | Willie Doyle | Fashion Plate | Hilltop | 1:39⅘ |
| 1910 | Layminster (½) | R. Estep | Dalhousie | Sager | 1:40⅗ |
| 1911 | Watervale (1) | E. Dugan | Zeus | The Nigger | 1:51 |
| 1912 | Colonel Holloway (5) | C. Turner | Bwana Tumbo | Tipsand | 1:56⅗ |
| 1913 | Buskin (Neck) | J. Butwell | Kleburne | Barnegat | 1:53⅖ |
| 1914 | Holiday (¾) | A. Schuttinger | Brave Cunarder | Defendum | 1:53⅘ |
| 1915 | Rhine Maiden (1½) | Douglas Hoffman | Half Rock | Runes | 1:58 |
| 1916 | Damrosch (1½) | Linus McAtee | Greenwood | Achievement | 1:54⅘ |
| 1917 | Kalitan (2) | E. Haynes | Al M. Dick | Kentucky Boy | 1:54⅖ |
| 1918* | War Cloud (¾) | Johnny Loftus | Sunny Slope | Lanius | 1:53⅗ |
| 1918* | Jack Hare, Jr (2) | C. Peak | The Porter | Kate Bright | 1:53⅖ |
| 1919 | Sir Barton (4) | Johnny Loftus | Eternal | Sweep On | 1:53 |
| 1920 | Man o' War (1½) | Clarence Kummer | Upset | Wildair | 1:51⅗ |

## Preakness *(Cont.)*

| Year | Winner (Margin) | Jockey | Second | Third | Time |
|---|---|---|---|---|---|
| 1921 | Broomspun (¾) | F. Coltiletti | Polly Ann | Jeg | 1:54⅕ |
| 1922 | Pillory (Head) | L. Morris | Hea | June Grass | 1:51⅗ |
| 1923 | Vigil (1¼) | B. Marinelli | General Thatcher | Rialto | 1:53⅗ |
| 1924 | Nellie Morse (1½) | J. Merimee | Transmute | Mad Play | 1:57⅕ |
| 1925 | Coventry (4) | Clarence Kummer | Backbone | Almadel | 1:59 |
| 1926 | Display (Head) | J. Maiben | Blondin | Mars | 1:59⅘ |
| 1927 | Bostonian (½) | A. Abel | Sir Harry | Whiskery | 2:01⅗ |
| 1928 | Victorian (Nose) | Sonny Workman | Toro | Solace | 2:00⅕ |
| 1929 | Dr. Freeland (1) | Louis Schaefer | Minotaur | African | 2:01⅗ |
| 1930 | Gallant Fox (¾) | Earl Sande | Crack Brigade | Snowflake | 2:00⅗ |
| 1931 | Mate (1½) | G. Ellis | Twenty Grand | Ladder | 1:59 |
| 1932 | Burgoo King (Head) | E. James | Tick On | Boatswain | 1:59⅘ |
| 1933 | Head Play (4) | Charles Kurtsinger | Ladysman | Utopian | 2:02 |
| 1934 | High Quest (Nose) | R. Jones | Cavalcade | Discovery | 1:58⅕ |
| 1935 | Omaha (6) | Willie Saunders | Firethorn | Psychic Bid | 1:58⅖ |
| 1936 | Bold Venture (Nose) | George Woolf | Granville | Jean Bart | 1:59 |
| 1937 | War Admiral (Head) | Charles Kurtsinger | Pompoon | Flying Scot | 1:58⅖ |
| 1938 | Dauber (7) | M. Peters | Cravat | Menow | 1:59⅘ |
| 1939 | Challedon (1¼) | George Seabo | Gilded Knight | Volitant | 1:59⅘ |
| 1940 | Bimelech (3) | F. A. Smith | Mioland | Gallahadion | 1:58⅗ |
| 1941 | Whirlaway (5½) | Eddie Arcaro | King Cole | Our Boots | 1:58⅘ |
| 1942 | Alsab (1) | B. James | Requested<br>Sun Again | (dead heat<br>for second) | 1:57 |
| 1943 | Count Fleet (8) | Johnny Longden | Blue Swords | Vincentive | 1:57⅖ |
| 1944 | Pensive (¾) | Conn McCreary | Platter | Stir Up | 1:59⅕ |
| 1945 | Polynesian (2½) | W. D. Wright | Hoop Jr. | Darby Dieppe | 1:58⅘ |
| 1946 | Assault (Neck) | Warren Mehrtens | Lord Boswell | Hampden | 2:01⅖ |
| 1947 | Faultless (1¼) | Doug Dodson | On Trust | Phalanx | 1:59 |
| 1948 | Citation (5½) | Eddie Arcaro | Vulcan's Forge | Boyard | 2:02⅖ |
| 1949 | Capot (Head) | Ted Atkinson | Palestinian | Noble Impulse | 1:56 |
| 1950 | Hill Prince (5) | Eddie Arcaro | Middleground | Dooley | 1:59⅕ |
| 1951 | Bold (7) | Eddie Arcaro | Counterpoint | Alerted | 1:56⅖ |
| 1952 | Blue Man (3½) | Conn McCreary | Jampol | One Count | 1:57⅖ |
| 1953 | Native Dancer (Neck) | Eric Guerin | Jamie K. | Royal Bay Gem | 1:57⅘ |
| 1954 | Hasty Road (Neck) | Johnny Adams | Correlation | Hasseyampa | 1:57⅖ |
| 1955 | Nashua (1) | Eddie Arcaro | Saratoga | Traffic Judge | 1:54⅗ |
| 1956 | Fabius (¾) | Bill Hartack | Needles | No Regrets | 1:58⅖ |
| 1957 | Bold Ruler (2) | Eddie Arcaro | Iron Liege | Inside Tract | 1:56⅕ |
| 1958 | Tim Tam (1½) | I. Valenzuela | Lincoln Road | Gone Fishin' | 1:57⅕ |
| 1959 | Royal Orbit (4) | William Harmatz | Sword Dancer | Dunce | 1:57 |
| 1960 | Bally Ache (4) | Bobby Ussery | Victoria Park | Celtic Ash | 1:57⅗ |
| 1961 | Carry Back (¾) | Johnny Sellers | Globemaster | Crozier | 1:57⅗ |
| 1962 | Greek Money (Nose) | John Rotz | Ridan | Roman Line | 1:56⅕ |
| 1963 | Candy Spots (3½) | Bill Shoemaker | Chateaugay | Never Bend | 1:56⅕ |
| 1964 | Northern Dancer (2¼) | Bill Hartack | The Scoundrel | Hill Rise | 1:56⅘ |
| 1965 | Tom Rolfe (Neck) | Ron Turcotte | Dapper Dan | Hail to All | 1:56⅕ |
| 1966 | Kauai King (1¾) | Don Brumfield | Stupendous | Amberoid | 1:55⅖ |
| 1967 | Damascus (2¼) | Bill Shoemaker | In Reality | Proud Clarion | 1:55⅕ |
| 1968 | Forward Pass (6) | I. Valenzuela | Out of the Way | Nodouble | 1:56⅘ |
| 1969 | Majestic Prince (Head) | Bill Hartack | Arts and Letters | Jay Ray | 1:55⅗ |
| 1970 | Personality (Neck) | Eddie Belmonte | My Dad George | Silent Screen | 1:56⅕ |
| 1971 | Canonero II (1½) | Gustavo Avila | Eastern Fleet | Jim French | 1:54 |
| 1972 | Bee Bee Bee (1¼) | Eldon Nelson | No Le Hace | Key to the Mint | 1:55⅗ |
| 1973 | Secretariat (2½) | Ron Turcotte | Sham | Our Native | 1:54⅖ |
| 1974 | Little Current (7) | Miguel Rivera | Neapolitan Way | Cannonade | 1:54⅗ |
| 1975 | Master Derby (1) | Darrel McHargue | Foolish Pleasure | Diabolo | 1:56⅖ |
| 1976 | Elocutionist (3) | John Lively | Play the Red | Bold Forbes | 1:55 |
| 1977 | Seattle Slew (1½) | Jean Cruguet | Iron Constitution | Run Dusty Run | 1:54⅖ |
| 1978 | Affirmed (Neck) | Steve Cauthen | Alydar | Believe It | 1:54⅖ |
| 1979 | Spectacular Bid (5½) | Ron Franklin | Golden Act | Screen King | 1:54⅕ |
| 1980 | Codex (4¾) | Angel Cordero Jr. | Genuine Risk | Colonel Moran | 1:54⅕ |
| 1981 | Pleasant Colony (1) | Jorge Velasquez | Bold Ego | Paristo | 1:54⅗ |
| 1982 | Aloma's Ruler (½) | Jack Kaenel | Linkage | Cut Away | 1:55⅖ |
| 1983 | Deputed Testamony (2¾) | Donald Miller Jr. | Desert Wine | High Honors | 1:55⅖ |
| 1984 | Gate Dancer (1½) | Angel Cordero Jr. | Play On | Fight Over | 1:53⅗ |
| 1985 | Tank's Prospect (Head) | Pat Day | Chief's Crown | Eternal Prince | 1:53⅖ |
| 1986 | Snow Chief (4) | Alex Solis | Ferdinand | Broad Brush | 1:54⅘ |

## Preakness (*Cont.*)

| Year | Winner (Margin) | Jockey | Second | Third | Time |
|---|---|---|---|---|---|
| 1987 | Alysheba (½) | Chris McCarron | Bet Twice | Cryptoclearance | 1:55⅘ |
| 1988 | Risen Star (1¼) | E. Delahoussaye | Brian's Time | Winning Colors | 1:56⅕ |
| 1989 | Sunday Silence (Nose) | Pat Valenzuela | Easy Goer | Rock Point | 1:53⅘ |
| 1990 | Summer Squall (2¼) | Pat Day | Unbridled | Mister Frisky | 1:53⅗ |
| 1991 | Hansel (Head) | Jerry Bailey | Corporate Report | Mane Minister | 1:54 |
| 1992 | Pine Bluff (¾) | Chris McCarron | Alydeed | Casual Lies | 1:55⅗ |
| 1993 | Prairie Bayou (½) | Mike Smith | Cherokee Run | El Bakan | 1:56⅗ |
| 1994 | Tabasco Cat (¾) | Pat Day | Go For Gin | Concern | 1:56⅖ |
| 1995 | Timber Country (½) | Pat Day | Oliver's Twist | Thunder Gulch | 1:54⅖ |
| 1996 | Louis Quatorze (3¼) | Pat Day | Skip Away | Editor's Note | 1:53⅖ |
| 1997 | Silver Charm (Head) | Gary Stevens | Free House | Captain Bodgit | 1:54⅖ |
| 1998 | Real Quiet (2¼) | Kent Desormeaux | Victory Gallop | Classic Cat | 1:54⅗ |
| 1999 | Charismatic (1½) | Chris Antley | Menifee | Badge | 1:55⅕ |
| 2000 | Red Bullet (3¾) | Jerry Bailey | Fusaichi Pegasus | Impeachment | 1:56.04 |
| 2001 | Point Given (2¼) | Gary Stevens | A P Valentine | Congaree | 1:55.51 |
| 2002 | War Emblem (¾) | Victor Espinoza | Magic Weisner | Proud Citizen | 1:56.36 |
| 2003 | Funny Cide (9¾) | Jose Santos | Midway Road | Scrimshaw | 1:55.61 |
| 2004 | Smarty Jones (11½) | Stewart Elliott | Rock Hard Ten | Eddington | 1:55.59 |
| 2005 | Afleet Alex (7) | Jeremy Rose | Scrappy T | Giacomo | 1:55.04 |
| 2006 | Bernardini (5¼) | Javier Castellano | Sweetnorthernsaint | Hemingway's Key | 1:54.65 |
| 2007 | Curlin (Head) | Robby Albarado | Street Sense | Hard Spun | 1:53.46 |
| 2008 | Big Brown (5¼) | Kent Desormeaux | Macho Again | Icabad Crane | 1:54.80 |
| 2009 | Rachel Alexandra (1) | Calvin Borel | Mine That Bird | Musket Man | 1:55.08 |
| 2010 | Lookin at Lucky (1¾) | Martin Garcia | First Dude | Jackson Bend | 1:55.47 |
| 2011 | Shackleford (½) | Jesus Castanon | Animal Kingdom | Astrology | 1:56.47 |

*Preakness was a two-horse race in 1883, '84 and '89. It was not run 1891–1893; and in 1918, it was run in two divisions.
Note: Distance: 1½ miles (1873–88), 1¼ miles (1889), 1½ miles (1890), 1$\frac{1}{16}$ miles (1894–1900), 1 mile and 70 yards

## Belmont

Run at Belmont Park, Elmont, NY, three weeks after the Preakness Stakes. Held previously at two locations in the Bronx (NY): Jerome Park (1867–1889) and Morris Park (1890–1904).

| Year | Winner (Margin) | Jockey | Second | Third | Time |
|---|---|---|---|---|---|
| 1867 | Ruthless (Head) | J. Gilpatrick | De Courcy | Rivoli | 3:05 |
| 1868 | General Duke (2) | R. Swim | Northumberland | Fannie Ludlow | 3:02 |
| 1869 | Fenian (Unknown) | C. Miller | Glenelg | Invercauld | 3:04¼ |
| 1870 | Kingfisher (½) | E. Brown | Foster | Midday | 2:59½ |
| 1871 | Harry Bassett (3) | W. Miller | Stockwood | By-the-Sea | 2:56 |
| 1872 | Joe Daniels (¾) | James Rowe | Meteor | Shylock | 2:58¼ |
| 1873 | Springbok (4) | James Rowe | Count d'Orsay | Strachino | 3:01¾ |
| 1874 | Saxon (Neck) | G. Barbee | Grinstead | Aaron Pennington | 2:39½ |
| 1875 | Calvin (2) | R. Swim | Aristides | Milner | 2:40¼ |
| 1876 | Algerine (Head) | W. Donahue | Fiddlestick | Barricade | 2:40½ |
| 1877 | Cloverbrook (1) | C. Holloway | Loiterer | Baden-Baden | 2:46 |
| 1878 | Duke of Magenta (2) | L. Hughes | Bramble | Sparta | 2:43½ |
| 1879 | Spendthrift (5) | S. Evans | Monitor | Jericho | 2:42¾ |
| 1880 | Grenada (½) | L. Hughes | Ferncliffe | Turenne | 2:47 |
| 1881 | Saunterer (Neck) | T. Costello | Eole | Baltic | 2:47 |
| 1882 | Forester (5) | James McLaughlin | Babcock | Wyoming | 2:43 |
| 1883 | George Kinney (2) | James McLaughlin | Trombone | Renegade | 2:42½ |
| 1884 | Panique (½) | James McLaughlin | Knight of Ellerslie | Himalaya | 2:42 |
| 1885 | Tyrant (3½) | Paul Duffy | St. Augustine | Tecumseh | 2:43 |
| 1886 | Inspector B (1) | James McLaughlin | The Bard | Linden | 2:41 |
| 1887* | Hanover (28-32) | James McLaughlin | Oneko | | 2:43½ |
| 1888* | Sir Dixon (12) | James McLaughlin | Prince Royal | | 2:40¼ |
| 1889 | Eric (Head) | W. Hayward | Diable | Zephyrus | 2:47 |
| 1890 | Burlington (1) | S. Barnes | Devotee | Padishah | 2:07¾ |
| 1891 | Foxford (Neck) | E. Garrison | Montana | Laurestan | 2:08¾ |
| 1892* | Patron (Unknown) | W. Hayward | Shellbark | | 2:17 |
| 1893 | Comanche (Head) | Willie Simms | Dr. Rice | Rainbow | 1:53¼ |
| 1894 | Henry of Navarre (2-4) | Willie Simms | Prig | Assignee | 1:56½ |
| 1895 | Belmar (Head) | Fred Taral | Counter Tenor | Nanki Pooh | 2:11½ |
| 1896 | Hastings (Neck) | H. Griffin | Handspring | Hamilton II | 2:24½ |
| 1897 | Scottish Chieftain (1) | J. Scherrer | On Deck | Octagon | 2:23¼ |
| 1898 | Bowling Brook (8) | P. Littlefield | Previous | Hamburg | 2:32 |
| 1899 | Jean Bereaud (Head) | R. R. Clawson | Half Time | Glengar | 2:23 |

## Belmont *(Cont.)*

| Year | Winner (Margin) | Jockey | Second | Third | Time |
|---|---|---|---|---|---|
| 1900 | Ildrim (Head) | N. Turner | Petrucio | Missionary | 2:21½ |
| 1901 | Commando (½) | H. Spencer | The Parader | All Green | 2:21 |
| 1902 | Masterman (2) | John Bullmann | Ranald | King Hanover | 2:22½ |
| 1903 | Africander (2) | John Bullmann | Whorler | Red Knight | 2:23⅕ |
| 1904 | Delhi (3½) | George Odom | Graziallo | Rapid Water | 2:06⅗ |
| 1905 | Tanya (1/2) | E. Hildebrand | Blandy | Hot Shot | 2:08 |
| 1906 | Burgomaster (4) | L. Lyne | The Quail | Accountant | 2:20 |
| 1907 | Peter Pan (1) | G. Mountain | Superman | Frank Gill | Unknown |
| 1908 | Colin (Head) | Joe Notter | Fair Play | King James | Unknown |
| 1909 | Joe Madden (8) | E. Dugan | Wise Mason | Donald MacDonald | 2:21⅗ |
| 1910* | Sweep (6) | J. Butwell | Duke of Ormonde | | 2:22 |
| 1913 | Prince Eugene (½) | Roscoe Troxler | Rock View | Flying Fairy | 2:18 |
| 1914 | Luke McLuke (8) | M. Buxton | Gainer | Charlestonian | 2:20 |
| 1915 | The Finn (4) | G. Byrne | Half Rock | Pebbles | 2:18⅖ |
| 1916 | Friar Rock (3) | E. Haynes | Spur | Churchill | 2:22 |
| 1917 | Hourless (10) | J. Butwell | Skeptic | Wonderful | 2:17⅘ |
| 1918 | Johren (2) | Frank Robinson | War Cloud | Cum Sah | 2:20⅖ |
| 1919 | Sir Barton (5) | Johnny Loftus | Sweep On | Natural Bridge | 2:17⅖ |
| 1920* | Man o' War (20) | Clarence Kummer | Donnacona | | 2:14⅕ |
| 1921 | Grey Lag (3) | Earl Sande | Sporting Blood | Leonardo II | 2:16⅘ |
| 1922 | Pillory (2) | C. H. Miller | Snob II | Hea | 2:18⅘ |
| 1923 | Zev (1½) | Earl Sande | Chickvale | Rialto | 2:19 |
| 1924 | Mad Play (2) | Earl Sande | Mr. Mutt | Modest | 2:18⅘ |
| 1925 | American Flag (8) | Albert Johnson | Dangerous | Swope | 2:16⅘ |
| 1926 | Crusader (1) | Albert Johnson | Espino | Haste | 2:32⅕ |
| 1927 | Chance Shot (1½) | Earl Sande | Bois de Rose | Flambino | 2:32⅖ |
| 1928 | Vito (3) | Clarence Kummer | Genie | Diavolo | 2:33⅕ |
| 1929 | Blue Larkspur (¾) | Mack Garner | African | Jack High | 2:32⅘ |
| 1930 | Gallant Fox (3) | Earl Sande | Whichone | Questionnaire | 2:31⅗ |
| 1931 | Twenty Grand (10) | Charles Kurtsinger | Sun Meadow | Jamestown | 2:29⅗ |
| 1932 | Faireno (1½) | T. Malley | Osculator | Flag Pole | 2:32⅘ |
| 1933 | Hurryoff (1½) | Mack Garner | Nimbus | Union | 2:32⅗ |
| 1934 | Peace Chance (6) | W. D. Wright | High Quest | Good Goods | 2:29⅕ |
| 1935 | Omaha (1½) | Willie Saunders | Firethorn | Rosemont | 2:30⅗ |
| 1936 | Granville (Nose) | James Stout | Mr. Bones | Hollyrood | 2:30 |
| 1937 | War Admiral (3) | Charles Kurtsinger | Sceneshifter | Vamoose | 2:28⅗ |
| 1938 | Pasteurized (Neck) | James Stout | Dauber | Cravat | 2:29⅖ |
| 1939 | Johnstown (5) | James Stout | Belay | Gilded Knight | 2:29⅗ |
| 1940 | Bimelech (¾) | F. A. Smith | Your Chance | Andy K | 2:29⅗ |
| 1941 | Whirlaway (2½) | Eddie Arcaro | Robert Morris | Yankee Chance | 2:31 |
| 1942 | Shut Out (2) | Eddie Arcaro | Alsab | Lochinvar | 2:29⅕ |
| 1943 | Count Fleet (25) | Johnny Longden | Fairy Manhurst | Deseronto | 2:28⅕ |
| 1944 | Bounding Home (½) | G. L. Smith | Pensive | Bull Dandy | 2:32⅕ |
| 1945 | Pavot (5) | Eddie Arcaro | Wildlife | Jeep | 2:30⅕ |
| 1946 | Assault (3) | Warren Mehrtens | Natchez | Cable | 2:30⅘ |
| 1947 | Phalanx (5) | R. Donoso | Tide Rips | Tailspin | 2:29⅖ |
| 1948 | Citation (8) | Eddie Arcaro | Better Self | Escadru | 2:28⅕ |
| 1949 | Capot (½) | Ted Atkinson | Ponder | Palestinian | 2:30⅕ |
| 1950 | Middleground (1) | William Boland | Lights Up | Mr. Trouble | 2:28⅗ |
| 1951 | Counterpoint (4) | D. Gorman | Battlefield | Battle Morn | 2:29 |
| 1952 | One Count (2½) | Eddie Arcaro | Blue Man | Armageddon | 2:30⅕ |
| 1953 | Native Dancer (Neck) | Eric Guerin | Jamie K. | Royal Bay Gem | 2:38⅗ |
| 1954 | High Gun (Neck) | Eric Guerin | Fisherman | Limelight | 2:30⅘ |
| 1955 | Nashua (9) | Eddie Arcaro | Blazing Count | Portersville | 2:29 |
| 1956 | Needles (Neck) | David Erb | Career Boy | Fabius | 2:29⅘ |
| 1957 | Gallant Man (8) | Bill Shoemaker | Inside Tract | Bold Ruler | 2:26⅗ |
| 1958 | Cavan (6) | Pete Anderson | Tim Tam | Flamingo | 2:30⅕ |
| 1959 | Sword Dancer (¾) | Bill Shoemaker | Bagdad | Royal Orbit | 2:28⅖ |
| 1960 | Celtic Ash (5½) | Bill Hartack | Venetian Way | Disperse | 2:29⅗ |
| 1961 | Sherluck (2¼) | Braulio Baeza | Globemaster | Guadalcanal | 2:29⅕ |
| 1962 | Jaipur (Nose) | Bill Shoemaker | Admiral's Voyage | Crimson Satan | 2:28⅘ |
| 1963 | Chateaugay (2½) | Braulio Baeza | Candy Spots | Choker | 2:30⅕ |
| 1964 | Quadrangle (2) | Manuel Ycaza | Roman Brother | Northern Dancer | 2:28⅖ |
| 1965 | Hail to All (Neck) | John Sellers | Tom Rolfe | First Family | 2:28⅖ |
| 1966 | Amberold (2½) | William Boland | Buffle | Advocator | 2:29⅗ |
| 1967 | Damascus (2½) | Bill Shoemaker | Cool Reception | Gentleman James | 2:28⅘ |

## Belmont *(Cont.)*

| Year | Winner (Margin) | Jockey | Second | Third | Time |
|---|---|---|---|---|---|
| 1968 | Stage Door Johnny (1¼) | Hellodoro Gustines | Forward Pass | Call Me Prince | 2:27⅕ |
| 1969 | Arts and Letters (5½) | Braulio Baeza | Majestic Prince | Dike | 2:28⅘ |
| 1970 | High Echelon (¾) | John L. Rotz | Needles N Pins | Naskra | 2:34 |
| 1971 | Pass Catcher (¾) | Walter Blum | Jim French | Bold Reason | 2:30⅖ |
| 1972 | Riva Ridge (7) | Ron Turcotte | Ruritania | Cloudy Dawn | 2:28 |
| 1973 | Secretariat (31) | Ron Turcotte | Twice a Prince | My Gallant | 2:24 |
| 1974 | Little Current (7) | Miguel A. Rivera | Jolly Johu | Cannonade | 2:29⅕ |
| 1975 | Avatar (Neck) | Bill Shoemaker | Foolish Pleasure | Master Derby | 2:28⅕ |
| 1976 | Bold Forbes (Neck) | Angel Cordero Jr. | McKenzie Bridge | Great Contractor | 2:29 |
| 1977 | Seattle Slew (4) | Jean Cruguet | Run Dusty Run | Sanhedrin | 2:29⅗ |
| 1978 | Affirmed (Head) | Steve Cauthen | Alydar | Darby Creek Road | 2:26⅘ |
| 1979 | Coastal (3¼) | Ruben Hernandez | Golden Act | Spectacular Bid | 2:28⅗ |
| 1980 | Temperence Hill (2) | Eddie Maple | Genuine Risk | Rockhill Native | 2:29⅘ |
| 1981 | Summing (Neck) | George Martens | Highland Blade | Pleasant Colony | 2:29 |
| 1982 | Conquistador Cielo (14½) | Laffit Pincay, Jr. | Gato Del Sol | Illuminate | 2:28⅕ |
| 1983 | Caveat (3½) | Laffit Pincay Jr. | Slew o'Gold | Barberstown | 2:27⅘ |
| 1984 | Swale (4) | Laffit Pincay Jr. | Pine Circle | Morning Bob | 2:27⅕ |
| 1985 | Creme Fraiche (½) | Eddie Maple | Stephan's Odyssey | Chief's Crown | 2:27 |
| 1986 | Danzig Connection (1¼) | Chris McCarron | Johns Treasure | Ferdinand | 2:29⅘ |
| 1987 | Bet Twice (14) | Craig Perret | Cryptoclearance | Gulch | 2:28⅕ |
| 1988 | Risen Star (14¾) | Eddie Delahoussaye | Kingpost | Brian's Time | 2:26⅖ |
| 1989 | Easy Goer (8) | Pat Day | Sunday Silence | Le Voyageur | 2:26 |
| 1990 | Go and Go (8¼) | Michael Kinane | Thirty Six Red | Baron de Vaux | 2:27⅕ |
| 1991 | Hansel (Head) | Jerry Bailey | Strike the Gold | Mane Minister | 2:28 |
| 1992 | A.P. Indy (¾) | Eddie Delahoussaye | My Memoirs | Pine Bluff | 2:26 |
| 1993 | Colonial Affair (2¼) | Julie Krone | Kissin Kris | Wild Gale | 2:29⅘ |
| 1994 | Tabasco Cat (2) | Pat Day | Go For Gin | Strodes Creek | 2:26⅘ |
| 1995 | Thunder Gulch (2) | Gary Stevens | Star Standard | Citadeed | 2:32 |
| 1996 | Editor's Note (1) | Rene Douglas | Skip Away | My Flag | 2:28⅘ |
| 1997 | Touch Gold (¾) | Chris McCarron | Silver Charm | Free House | 2:28⅘ |
| 1998 | Victory Gallop (Nose) | Gary Stevens | Real Quiet | Thomas Jo | 2:28⅘ |
| 1999 | Lemon Drop Kid (Head) | Jose Santos | Vision and Verse | Charismatic | 2:27⅘ |
| 2000 | Commendable (1½) | Pat Day | Aptitude | Unshaded | 2:31.19 |
| 2001 | Point Given (12¼ ) | Gary Stevens | A P Valentine | Monarchos | 2:26.56 |
| 2002 | Sarava (½) | Edgar Prado | Medaglia d'Oro | Sunday Break | 2:29.71 |
| 2003 | Empire Maker (¾) | Jerry Bailey | Ten Most Wanted | Funny Cide | 2:28.26 |
| 2004 | Birdstone (1) | Edgar Prado | Smarty Jones | Royal Assault | 2:27.59 |
| 2005 | Afleet Alex(4¾) | Jeremy Rose | Andromeda's Hero | Nolan's Cat | 2:28.75 |
| 2006 | Jazil (1¼) | Fernando Jara | Bluegrass Cat | Sunriver | 2:27.86 |
| 2007 | Rags to Riches (Head) | John Velazquez | Curlin | Tiago | 2:28.74 |
| 2008 | Da' Tara (5¼) | Alan Garcia | Denis of Cork | Ready's Echo | 2:29.65 |
| 2009 | Summer Bird (2¾) | Kent Desormeaux | Dunkirk | Mine That Bird | 2:27.54 |
| 2010 | Drosselmeyer (1¾) | Mike Smith | Fly Down | First Dude | 2:31.57 |
| 2011 | Ruler On Ice (¾) | Jose Valdivia Jr. | Stay Thirsty | Brilliant Speed | 2:30.88 |

*Belmont was a two-horse race in 1887, '88, '92, 1910 and '20; and was not held in 1911–1912.

Note: Distance: 1 mile 5 furlongs (1867–89), 1¼ miles (1890–1905), 1⅜ miles (1906–25), 1½ miles (1926–present).

## Triple Crown Winners

| Year | Horse | Jockey | Owner | Trainer |
|---|---|---|---|---|
| 1919 | Sir Barton | John Loftus | J. K. L. Ross | H. G. Bedwell |
| 1930 | Gallant Fox | Earle Sande | Belair Stud | James Fitzsimmons |
| 1935 | Omaha | William Saunders | Belair Stud | James Fitzsimmons |
| 1937 | War Admiral | Charles Kurtsinger | Samuel D. Riddle | George Conway |
| 1941 | Whirlaway | Eddie Arcaro | Calumet Farm | Ben Jones |
| 1943 | Count Fleet | John Longden | Mrs J. D. Hertz | Don Cameron |
| 1946 | Assault | Warren Mehrtens | King Ranch | Max Hirsch |
| 1948 | Citation | Eddie Arcaro | Calumet Farm | Jimmy Jones |
| 1973 | Secretariat | Ron Turcotte | Meadow Stable | Lucien Laurin |
| 1977 | Seattle Slew | Jean Cruguet | Karen L. Taylor | William H. Turner Jr. |
| 1978 | Affirmed | Steve Cauthen | Harbor View Farm | Laz Barrera |

# Boxing

While the boxing world waited in vain for the Manny Pacquiao-Floyd Mayweather Jr. superbout in 2011, it had to settle for a spirited unanimous decision by Pacquiao over "Sugar" Shane Mosley

# FOR THE RECORD • 2010—2011

## Current World Champions

| Division | Weight Limit | WBA Champion | WBC Champion | IBF Champion |
|---|---|---|---|---|
| Heavyweight | None | Alexander Povetkin | Vitali Klitschko | Wladimir Klitschko |
| Cruiserweight | 200 | Guillermo Jones | Krzysztof Wlodarczyk | Yoan Pablo Hernande |
| Light Heavyweight | 175 | Beibut Shumenov | Bernard Hopkins | Tavoris Cloud |
| Super Middleweight | 168 | Karoly Balzsay | Carl Froch | Lucian Bute |
| Middleweight | 160 | Gennady Golovkin | Julio Cesar Chavez Jr. | Daniel Geale |
| Super Welterweight | 154 | Austin Trout | Saul Alvarez | Cornelius Bundrage |
| Welterweight | 147 | Vyacheslav Senchenko | Floyd Mayweather Jr. | Andre Berto |
| Super Lightweight | 140 | Amir Khan | Erik Morales | Amir Khan |
| Lightweight | 135 | Brandon Rios | Vacant | Miguel Vazquez |
| Super Featherweight | 130 | Takashi Uchiyama | Takahiro Aoh | Juan Carlos Salgado |
| Featherweight | 126 | Jonathan Barros | Jhonny Gonzalez | Billy Dib |
| Super Bantamweight | 122 | Rico Ramos | Toshiaki Nishioka | Takalani Ndlovu |
| Bantamweight | 118 | Koki Kameda | Nonito Donaire Vacant | Abner Mares |
| Super Flyweight | 115 | Tomonobu Shimizu | Suriyan Sor Rungvisai | Vacant |
| Flyweight | 112 | Hernan Marquez | Pongsaklek Wonjongkam | Moruti Mthalane |
| Light Flyweight | 108 | Roman Gonzalez | Adrian Hernandez | Ulises Solis |
| Strawweight | 105 | Porsawan Porpamook | Kazuto Ioka | Nkosinathi Joyi |

Note: WBA=World Boxing Association; WBC=World Boxing Council; IBF=International Boxing Federation. Champions as of October 1, 2011. *Denotes unified, mulit-title or super champion.

## Title and Major Boxing Matches of Late 2010 and 2011

Abbreviations: WBC=World Boxing Council; WBA= World Boxing Association; IBF=International Boxing Federation; KO=knockout; TKO=technical knockout; UD=unanimous decision; SD=split decision; MD=major decision; TD=technical decision; DQ=disqualification; NC=no contest. Bouts from Oct. 1, 2010 to Oct. 1, 2011.

| | Date | Winner | Loser | Result | Title/Org. | Site |
|---|---|---|---|---|---|---|
| **HEAVYWEIGHT** | Oct 16 | Vitali Klitschko | Shannon Briggs | UD | WBC | Hamburg, German |
| | Nov 13 | David Haye | Audley Harrison | TKO 3 | WBA | Manchester, Engla |
| | Mar 19 | Vitali Klitschko | Odlanier Solis | TKO 1 | WBC | Cologne, Germany |
| | July 2 | Wladimir Klitschko | David Haye | UD | WBA/IBF | Hamburg, German |
| | Aug 27 | Alexander Povetkin | Ruslan Chagaev | UD | WBA | Erfurt, Germany |
| | Sept 10 | Vitali Klitschko | Tomasz Adamek | TKO 10 | WBC | Wroclaw, Poland |
| **CRUISERWEIGHT** | Oct 1 | Yoan Pablo Hernandez | Steve Cunningham | TD 6 | IBF | Neubrandenburg, Ge |
| | Oct 2 | Guillermo Jones | Valery Brudov | TKO 11 | WBA | Panama City, Pana |
| | Feb 12 | Steve Cunningham | Enad Licina | UD | IBF | Muelheim, German |
| | Feb 12 | Yoan Pablo Hernandez | Steve Herelius | TKO 7 | WBA | Muelheim, German |
| | Apr 2 | Krzysztof Wlodarczyk | Francisco Palacios | SD | WBC | Bydgoszcz, Poland |
| **LIGHT HEAVYWEIGHT** | Dec 17 | Tavoris Cloud | Fulgencio Zuniga | UD | IBF | Miami, Florida |
| | Dec 18 | Jean Pascal | Bernard Hopkins | M. Draw | WBC | Quebec City, Quebe |
| | Jan 8 | Beibut Shumenov | William Joppy | KO 6 | WBA | Shymkent, Kazakhs |
| | May 21 | Bernard Hopkins | Jean Pascal | UD | WBC | Montreal, Canada |
| | June 25 | Tavoris Cloud | Yusaf Mack | TKO 8 | IBF | St. Charles, Missou |
| | July 29 | Beibut Shumenov | Danny Santiago | TKO 9 | WBA | Las Vegas, Nevada |
| **SUPER MIDDLEWEIGHT** | Oct 15 | Lucian Bute | Jesse Brinkley | KO 9 | IBF | Montreal, Canada |
| | Nov 27 | Andre Ward | Sakio Bika | UD | WBA | Oakland, California |
| | Nov 27 | Carl Froch | Arthur Abraham | UD | WBC | Helsinki, Finland |
| | Feb 19 | Felix Sturm | Ronald Hearns | TKO 7 | WBA | Stuttgart, Germany |
| | Mar 19 | Lucian Bute | Brian Magee | TKO 10 | IBF | Montreal, Canada |
| | May 14 | Andre Ward | Arthur Abraham | UD | WBA | Carson, California |
| | June 4 | Carl Froch | Glen Johnson | MD | WBC | Atlantic City, New J |
| | July 9 | Lucian Bute | Jean Paul Mendy | KO 4 | IBF | Bucharest, Romani |
| | July 30 | Brian Magee | Jaime Barboza | UD | WBA | San Jose, Costa Ri |
| | Aug 26 | Karoly Balzsay | Stanyslav Kashtanov | SD | WBA | Donetsk, Ukraine |

| | Date | Winner | Loser | Result | Title/Org. | Site |
|---|---|---|---|---|---|---|
| **DLEWEIGHT** | Oct 30 | Sebastian Sylvester | Mahir Oral | UD | IBF | Rostock, Germany |
| | Oct 30 | Hassan N'Dam N'Jikam | Avtandil Khurtsidze | UD | WBA | Paris, France |
| | Nov 20 | Sergio Martinez | Paul Williams | KO 2 | WBC | Atlantic City, New Jersey |
| | Dec 16 | Gennady Golovkin | Nilson Julio Tapia | KO 3 | WBA | Astana, Kazakhstan |
| | Feb 19 | Felix Sturm | Ronald Hearns | TKO 7 | WBA | Stuttgart, Germany |
| | Mar 12 | Sergio Martinez | Serhiy Dzinziruk | TKO 8 | WBC (Diam.) | Mashantucket, Conn. |
| | Apr 2 | Hassan N'Dam N'Jikam | Giovanni Lorenzo | UD | WBA | Le Cannet, France |
| | May 7 | Daniel Geale | Sebastian Sylvester | SD | IBF | Neubrandenburg, Germany |
| | Aug 31 | Daniel Geale | Eromosele Albert | UD | IBF | Hobart, Australia |
| | June 17 | Gennady Golovkin | Kassim Ouma | TKO 10 | WBA | Panama City, Panama |
| | June 25 | Felix Sturm | Matthew Macklin | SD | WBA | Cologne, Germany |
| | Oct 1 | Sergio Martinez | Darren Barker | KO 11 | WBC (Diam.) | Atlantic City, New Jersey |
| **MIDDLEWT.** **PER WELTERT.)** | Oct 9 | Rigoberto Alvarez | Nobuhiro Ishida | SD | WBA | Tepic, Mexico |
| | Nov 13 | Manny Pacquiao | Antonio Margarito | UD | WBC | Arlington, Texas |
| | Feb 5 | Austin Trout | Rigoberto Alvarez | UD | WBA | Guadalajara, Mexico |
| | Mar 5 | Saul Alvarez | Matthew Hatton | UD | WBC | Anaheim, California |
| | Mar 12 | Miguel Cotto | Ricardo Mayorga | TKO 12 | WBA | Las Vegas, Nevada |
| | June 11 | Austin Trout | David Lopez | UD | WBA | San Luis Potosi, Mex. |
| | June 25 | Cornelius Bundrage | Sechew Powell | UD | IBF | St. Charles, Missouri |
| | Sept 17 | Saul Alvarez | Alfonso Gomez | TKO 6 | WBC | Los Angeles, California |
| **TERWEIGHT** | Nov 27 | Andre Berto | Freddy Hernandez | TKO 1 | WBC | Las Vegas, Nevada |
| | Feb 18 | Jan Zaveck | Paul Delgado | TKO 5 | IBF | Ljubljana, Slovenia |
| | Apr 16 | Victor Ortiz | Andre Berto | UD | WBC | Mashantucket, Conn. |
| | May 7 | Manny Pacquiao | Shane Mosley | UD | WBO | Las Vegas, Nevada |
| | July 14 | Ismael El Massoudi | Souleymane M'Baye | TKO 12 | WBA | Marrakech, Morocco |
| | Aug 26 | Vyacheslav Senchenko | Marco Avendano | TKO 6 | WBA | Donetsk, Ukraine |
| | Sept 3 | Andre Berto | Jan Zaveck | TKO 5 | IBF | Biloxi, Mississippi |
| | Sept 17 | Floyd Mayweather Jr. | Victor Ortiz | KO 4 | WBC | Las Vegas, Nevada |
| **PER** **HTWEIGHT** **NIOR** **LTERWEIGHT)** | Dec 11 | Amir Khan | Marcos Maidana | UD | WBA | Las Vegas, Nevada |
| | Jan 29 | Timothy Bradley | Devon Alexander | TD 10 | WBC | Pontiac, Michigan |
| | Mar 5 | Zab Judah | Kaizer Mabuza | TKO 7 | IBF | Newark, New Jersey |
| | Apr 9 | Marcos Maidana | Erik Morales | MD | WBA | Las Vegas, Nevada |
| | Apr 16 | Amir Khan | Paul McCloskey | TD 6 | WBA | Manchester, England |
| | July 23 | Amir Khan | Zab Judah | KO 5 | WBA/IBF | Las Vegas, Nevada |
| | Sept 17 | Erik Morales | Pablo Cesar Cano | TKO 10 | WBC | Las Vegas, Nevada |
| | Sept 23 | Marcos Maidana | Petr Petrov | TKO 4 | WBA | Villa Ballester, Argentina |
| **HTWEIGHT** | Nov 27 | Juan Manuel Marquez | Michael Katsidis | TKO 9 | WBA | Las Vegas, Nevada |
| | Nov 27 | Miguel Vazquez | Ricardo Dominguez | UD | IBF | Tijuana, Mexico |
| | Dec 4 | Humberto Soto | Urbano Antillon | UD | WBC | Anaheim, California |
| | Feb 26 | Brandon Rios | Miguel Acosta | TKO 10 | WBA | Las Vegas, Nevada |
| | Mar 12 | Miguel Vazquez | Leonardo Zappavigna | UD | IBF | Las Vegas, Nevada |
| | Apr 9 | Robert Guerrero | Michael Katsidis | UD | WBA | Las Vegas, Nevada |
| | June 25 | Humberto Soto | Motoki Sasaki | TD 11 | WBC | Cozumel, Mexico |
| | July 9 | Brandon Rios | Urbano Antillon | TKO 3 | WBA | Carson, California |
| **PER** **THERWEIGHT** **NIOR** **HTWEIGHT)** | Nov 26 | Takahiro Aoh | Vitali Tajbert | UD | WBC | Nagoya, Japan |
| | Jan 31 | Takashi Uchiyama | Takashi Miura | TKO 8 | WBA | Tokyo, Japan |
| | Apr 8 | Takahiro Aoh | Humberto Gutierrez | KO 4 | WBC | Kobe, Japan |
| | Sept 10 | Juan Carlos Salgado | Argenis Mendez | UD | IBF | Zapopan, Mexico |
| **ATHERWEIGHT** | Nov 26 | Hozumi Hasegawa | Juan Burgos | UD | WBC | Nagoya, Japan |
| | Dec 4 | Jonathan Barros | Irving Berry | TKO 7 | WBA | Las Heras, Argentina |
| | Dec 5 | Chris John | Fernando Saucedo | UD | WBA | Jakarta, Indonesia |
| | Mar 12 | Jonathan Barros | Miguel Roman | UD | WBA | Junin, Argentina |
| | Mar 26 | Yuriokis Gamboa | Jorge Solis | TKO 4 | WBA/IBF | Atlantic City, New Jersey |
| | Apr 8 | Jhonny Gonzalez | Hozumi Hasegawa | TKO 4 | WBC | Kobe, Japan |
| | Apr 17 | Chris John | Daud Yordan | UD | WBA | Jakarta, Indonesia |
| | July 2 | Jonathan Barros | Celestino Caballero | SD | WBA | Junin, Argentina |
| | July 9 | Jhonny Gonzalez | Tomas Villa | TKO 4 | WBC | Atlantic City, New Jersey |
| | July 29 | Billy Dib | Jorge Lacierva | UD | IBF | Homebush, Australia |
| | Sept 15 | Jhonny Gonzalez | Rogers Mtagwa | TKO 2 | WBC | El Paso, Texas |

| | Date | Winner | Loser | Result | Title/Org. | Site |
|---|---|---|---|---|---|---|
| **SUPER BANTAMWEIGHT (JUNIOR FEATHERWEIGHT)** | Oct 2 | Lee Ryol-Li | P. Kratingdaenggym | UD | WBA | Tokyo, Japan |
| | Oct 24 | Toshiaki Nishioka | Rendall Munroe | UD | WBC | Tokyo, Japan |
| | Nov 13 | Guillermo Rigondeaux | Ricardo Cordoba | SD | WBA | Arlington, Texas |
| | Jan 31 | Akifumi Shimoda | Lee Ryol-Li | UD | WBA | Tokyo, Japan |
| | Mar 19 | Guillermo Rigondeaux | Willie Casey | TKO 1 | WBA | Dublin, Ireland |
| | Mar 26 | Takalani Ndlovu | Steve Molitor | UD | IBF | Johannesburg, Sou |
| | Apr 8 | Toshiaki Nishioka | Mauricio Munoz | KO 9 | WBC | Kobe, Japan |
| | July 9 | Rico Ramos | Akifumi Shimoda | KO 7 | WBA | Atlantic City, New J |
| | Oct 1 | Toshiaki Nishioka | Rafael Marquez | UD | WBC | Las Vegas, Nevada |
| **BANTAMWEIGHT** | Dec 11 | Joseph Agbeko | Yonnhy Perez | UD | IBF | Tacoma, Washington |
| | Dec 26 | Koki Kameda | Alexander Munoz | UD | WBA | Saitama, Japan |
| | Feb 19 | Nonito Donaire | Fernando Montiel | TKO 2 | WBC | Las Vegas, Nevada |
| | Jan 22 | Hugo Ruiz | Alvaro Perez | TD 9 | WBA | C. Nezahualcoytl, N |
| | May 7 | Koki Kameda | Daniel Diaz | TKO 11 | WBA | Osaka, Japan |
| | May 14 | Hugo Ruiz | Francisco Arce | UD | WBA | Los Mochis, Mexico |
| | June 17 | Anselmo Moreno | Lorenzo Parra | TKO 8 | WBA | Panama City, Panar |
| | Aug 13 | Abner Mares | Joseph Agbeko | MD | IBF | Las Vegas, Nevada |
| | Aug 31 | Koki Kameda | David de la Mora | UD | WBA | Tokyo, Japan |
| **SUPER FLYWEIGHT (JUNIOR BANTAMWEIGHT)** | Oct 9 | Hugo Cazares | Alberto Rossel | TKO 9 | WBA | Tlalnepantla, Mexic |
| | Nov 30 | Drian Francisco | Duan. Kokietgym | TKO 10 | WBA | Bueng Kan, Thailan |
| | Dec 11 | Cristian Mijares | Juan Alberto Rosas | UD | IBF | Torreon, Mexico |
| | Dec 23 | Hugo Cazares | Hiroyuki Hisataka | UD | WBA | Osaka, Japan |
| | Feb 5 | Tomas Rojas | Nobuo Nashiro | UD | WBC | Osaka, Japan |
| | May 1 | Tepp. Singwancha | Drian Francisco | UD | WBA | Petchaburi, Thailan |
| | May 14 | Cristian Mijares | Carlos Rueda | UD | IBF | Durango, Mexico |
| | May 21 | Tomas Rojas | Juan Jose Montes | TKO 11 | WBC | Tuxtla Gutierrez, Me |
| | July 9 | Hugo Cazares | Arturo Badillo | TKO 3 | WBA | Mazatlan, Mexico |
| | Aug 19 | Suri. Sor Rungvisai | Tomas Rojas | UD | WBC | Srisaket, Thailand |
| | Aug 31 | Tomonobu Shimizu | Hugo Cazares | SD | WBA | Tokyo, Japan |
| **FLYWEIGHT** | Oct 2 | Luis Concepcion | Denk. Kaovichit | TKO 1 | WBA | Panama City, Panar |
| | Oct 8 | Pong. Wonjongkam | Suri. Por Chokchai | UD | WBC | Nonghai, Thailand |
| | Dec 26 | Daiki Kameda | Silvio Olteanu | SD | WBA | Saitama, Japan |
| | Jan 29 | Jean Piero Perez | Jesus Jimenez | UD | WBA | Guadalajara, Mexic |
| | Mar 26 | Moruti Mthalane | Johnriel Casimero | TKO 5 | IBF | Johannesburg, South |
| | Apr 2 | Hernan Marquez | Luis Concepcion | TKO 10 | WBA | Panama City, Panar |
| | June 10 | Juan Reveco | Jean Piero Perez | KO 2 | WBA | Las Heras, Mexico |
| | July 1 | Pong. Wonjongkam | Takuya Kogawa | UD | WBC | Hat Yai, Thailand |
| | July 2 | Hernan Marquez | Edrin Dapudong | KO 3 | WBA | Hermosillo, Mexico |
| **LIGHT FLYWEIGHT (JUNIOR FLYWEIGHT)** | Oct 24 | Roman Gonzalez | Francisco Rosas | KO 2 | WBA | Tokyo, Japan |
| | Nov 6 | Gilberto Keb Baas | Omar Nino | MD | WBC | Merida, Mexico |
| | Dec 18 | Luis Lazarte | Ulises Solis | M. Draw | IBF | Mar del Plata, Argent |
| | Feb 26 | Gilberto Keb Baas | Jose Aguirre | TKO 8 | WBC | Merida, Mexico |
| | Mar 19 | Roman Gonzalez | Manuel Vargas | UD | WBA | San Pedro Cholula, |
| | Apr 30 | Adrian Hernandez | Gilberto Keb Baas | TKO 10 | WBC | Texcoco, Mexico |
| | Apr 30 | Ulises Solis | Luis Lazarte | SD | IBF | Mar del Plata, Argent |
| | July 16 | Roman Gonzalez | Omar Salado | TKO 7 | WBA | Cancun, Mexico |
| | Aug 27 | Ulises Solis | Jether Oliva | UD | IBF | Guadalajara, Mexic |
| | Sept 24 | Adrian Hernandez | Gideon Buthelezi | KO 2 | WBC | Mexico City, Mexico |
| | Oct 1 | Roman Gonzalez | Omar Soto | KO 2 | WBA | Las Vegas, Nevada |
| **STRAWWEIGHT (MINI FLYWT.) (MINIMUM WT.)** | Oct 23 | Sammy Gutierrez | Luis Carrillo | TKO 3 | WBA | San Martin Texmeluca |
| | Nov 5 | Kwanthai Sithmorseng | Pigmy Kokietgym | SD | WBA | Bangkok, Thailand |
| | Jan 29 | Nkosinathi Joyi | Katsunari Takayama | NC 3 | IBF | Brakpan, South Afri |
| | Feb 11 | Kazuto Ioka | Oley. Sithsamerchai | TKO 5 | WBC | Kobe, Japan |
| | Feb 12 | Sammy Gutierrez | Renan Trongco | TKO 6 | WBA | Monte Hermoso, Ar |
| | Apr 19 | Muhammad Rachman | Kwan. Sithmorseng | KO 9 | WBA | Bangkok, Thailand |
| | May 21 | Juan Palacios | Sammy Gutierrez | UD | WBA | San Martin Texmeluca |
| | July 30 | Porns. Porpramook | Muh. Rachman | MD | WBA | West Jakarta, Indon |
| | Aug 10 | Kazuto Ioka | Juan Hernandez | UD | WBC | Tokyo, Japan |
| | Aug 13 | Juan Palacios | Armando Torres | TKO 9 | WBA | Acapulco, Mexico |

## World Champions

Sanctioning bodies: the National Boxing Association (NBA), the New York State Athletic Commission (NY), the World Boxing Association (WBA), the World Boxing Council (WBC), and the International Boxing Federation (IBF).

### Heavyweights (Weight: Unlimited)

| Champion | Reign | Champion | Reign | Champion | Reign | Champion | Reign |
|---|---|---|---|---|---|---|---|
| John L. Sullivan* | 1885–92 | Muhammad Ali* | 1964–70† | Trevor Berbick WBC | 1986 | Hasim Rahman* WBC, | |
| James J. Corbett* | 1892–97 | Ernie Terrell WBA | 1965–67 | Mike Tyson WBC | 1986–87 | IBF | 2001–05 |
| Bob Fitzsimmons* | 1897–99 | Joe Frazier* NY | 1968–70 | James Smith WBA | 1986–87 | Chris Byrd IBF | 2002–06 |
| James J. Jeffries* | 1899–05† | Jimmy Ellis WBA | 1968–70 | Tony Tucker IBF | 1987 | Roy Jones Jr. WBA | 2003–05 |
| Marvin Hart* | 1905–06 | Joe Frazier* | 1970–73 | Mike Tyson* | 1987–90 | Lennox Lewis* WBC | 2001–04 |
| Tommy Burns* | 1906–08 | George Foreman* | 1973–74 | Buster Douglas* | 1990 | John Ruiz, WBA | 2003–05 |
| Jack Johnson* | 1908–15 | Muhammad Ali* | 1974–78 | Evander Holyfield* | 1990–92 | Vitali Klitschko WBC | 2004–05 |
| Jess Willard* | 1915–19 | Leon Spinks* | 1978 | Lennox Lewis WBC | 1993–95 | Hasim Rahman WBC | 2005–06 |
| Jack Dempsey* | 1919–26 | Ken Norton WBC | 1978 | Riddick Bowe* | 1992–93 | Nikolay Valuev WBA | 2005–07 |
| Gene Tunney* | 1926–28† | Larry Holmes WBC | 1978–80 | Evander Holyfield* | 1993–94 | Oleg Maskaev WBA | 2006–08 |
| Max Schmeling* | 1930–32 | Muhammad Ali* | 1978–79† | Michael Moorer* | 1994 | Wladimir Klitschko. | |
| Jack Sharkey* | 1932–33 | John Tate WBA | 1979–80 | George Foreman* | 1994–95 | IBF | 2006– |
| Primo Carnera* | 1933–34 | Mike Weaver WBA | 1980–82 | Oliver McCall WBC | 1995 | Ruslan Chagaev WBA | |
| Max Baer* | 1934–35 | Larry Holmes* | 1980–85 | Frank Bruno WBC | 1995–96 | 2007–08 | |
| James J. Braddock* | 1935–37 | Michael Dokes WBA | 1982–83 | Bruce Seldon WBA | 1995–96 | Samuel Peter WBC | 2008 |
| Joe Louis* | 1937–49† | Gerrie Coetzee WBA | 1983–84 | Mike Tyson WBA | 1996 | Nikolai Valuev WBA | 2008–09 |
| Ezzard Charles* | 1949–51 | Tim Witherspoon | | Michael Moorer IBF | 1996–97 | Vitali Klitschko WBC | 2008– |
| Jersey Joe Walcott* | 1951–52 | WBC | 1984 | Shannon Briggs* | 1997–98 | David Haye WBA | 2009–11 |
| Rocky Marciano* | 1952–56† | Pinklon Thomas WBC | 1984–86 | Lennox Lewis* WBC | 1997–01 | Alexander Povetkin | |
| Floyd Patterson* | 1956–59 | Greg Page WBC | 1984–85 | E. Holyfield WBA, IBF | 1996–99 | WBA | 2011– |
| Ingemar Johansson* | 1959–60 | Michael Spinks* | 1985–87 | Lennox Lewis | 1999–01 | | |
| Floyd Patterson* | 1960–62 | Tim Witherspoon | | E. Holyfield WBA | 2000–01 | | |
| Sonny Liston* | 1962–64 | WBA | 1986 | John Ruiz WBA | 2001–03 | | |

### Cruiserweights (Weight Limit: 200 pounds)

| Champion | Reign | Champion | Reign | Champion | Reign | Champion | Reign |
|---|---|---|---|---|---|---|---|
| Marvin Camel* WBC | 1980 | Evander Holyfield* | 1988† | Imamu Mayfield IBF | 1997–98 | David Haye WBC | 2007–08 |
| Carlos De Leon* WBC | | Toufik Belbouli WBA | 1989 | Fabrice Tiozzo WBA | 1997–00 | David Haye WBA | 2007–08† |
| 1980–82 | | Robert Daniels WBA | 1989–91 | J.C. Gomez* WBC | 1998–02† | Guillermo Jones | |
| Ossie Ocasio WBA | 1982–84 | Carlos De Leon* WBC | | Arthur Williams IBF | 1998–99 | WBA | 2009– |
| S.T. Gordon* WBC | 1982–83 | 1989–90 | | Vassiliy Girov* IBF | 1999–03 | Giacobbe Fragomeni | |
| Carlos De Leon* WBC | | Glenn McCrory IBF | 1989–90 | James Toney* IBF | 2003 | WBC | 2008–09 |
| 1983–85 | | Jeff Lampkin IBF | 1990 | Virgil Hill WBA | 2000–02 | Zsolt Erdei WBC | 2009–10 |
| Marvin Camel IBF | 1983–84 | M. Duran* WBC | 1990–91 | Wayne Braithwaite | | Tomasz Adamek IBF | 2008–09† |
| Lee Roy Murphy IBF | 1984–86 | Bobby Czyz WBA | 1991–92† | WBC | 2002–05 | Kryzysztof Wlodarczyk | |
| Piet Crous WBA | 1984–85 | Anaclet Wamba* WBC | 1991–95† | J.M. Mormeck WBA | 2002–06 | WBC | 2010– |
| Alfonso Ratliff* | | James Pritchard IBF | 1991 | J.M. Mormeck WBC | 2005–06 | Steve Cunningham, | |
| WBC | 1985 | James Warring IBF | 1991–92 | Melvin Davis IBF | 2004–05 | IBF | 2010–11 |
| Dwight Braxton WBA | 1985–86 | Alfred Cole IBF | 1992–96 | O'Neil Bell IBF | 2005–06 | Yoan Pablo Hernandez, | |
| Bernard Benton* WBC | 1985–86 | Orlin Norris WBA | 1993–95 | O'Neil Bell WBC/WBA | | IBF | 2011– |
| Carlos DeLeon* WBC | 1986–88 | Nate Miller WBA | 1995–97 | 2006–07 | | | |
| Evander Holyfield* | | M. Dominguez* | | Steve Cunningham | | | |
| WBA | 1986–87 | WBC | 1996–98 | IBF | 2006–08 | | |
| Ricky Parkey IBF | 1986–87 | A. Washington IBF | 1996–97 | J.M. Mormeck | | | |
| Evander Holyfield* | | Uriah Grant IBF | 1997 | WBC/WBA | 2007 | | |
| WBA, IBF | 1987–88 | | | | | | |

*Lineal champion.    †Champion relinquished title to retire or switch weight classes, or had title stripped by boxing organization.

### Light Heavyweights  (Weight Limit: 175 pounds)

| Champion | Reign | Champion | Reign | Champion | Reign | Champion | Reign |
|---|---|---|---|---|---|---|---|
| Jack Root* | 1903 | Jose Torres* | 1965–66 | Dennis Andries WBC | 1986–87 | Mehdi Sahnoune | |
| George Gardner* | 1903 | Dick Tiger* | 1966–68 | Bobby Czyz IBF | 1986–87 | WBA | 2003 |
| Bob Fitzsimmons* | 1903–05 | Bob Foster* | 1968–74† | Leslie Stewart WBA | 1987 | Silvio Branco WBA | 2003–04 |
| Jack O'Brien* | 1905–12† | Vicente Rondon WBA | 1971–72 | Virgil Hill* WBA | 1987–91 | Antonio Tarver | |
| Jack Dillon* | 1914–16 | John Conteh WBC | 1974–77 | Pr Charles Williams | | WBC, IBF | 2003 |
| Battling Levinsky* | 1916–20 | Victor Galindez* WBA | 1974–78 | IBF | 1987–93 | Roy Jones Jr. WBC | 2003 |
| Georges Carpentier* | 1920–22 | Miguel A. Cuello WBC | 1977–78 | Thomas Hearns WBC | 1987† | Glencoffe Johnson | |
| Battling Siki* | 1922–23 | Mate Parlov WBC | 1978 | Donny Lalonde WBC | 1987–88 | IBF | 2004–05 |
| Mike McTigue* | 1923–25 | Mike Rossman* | | Sugar Ray Leonard | | Fabrice Tiozzo WBA | 2004–5 |
| Paul Berlenbach* | 1925–26 | WBA | 1978–79 | WBC | 1988 | Antonio Tarver* WBC | 2004–05 |
| Jack Delaney* | 1926–27† | Victor Galindez* | | Dennis Andries WBC | 1989 | Silvio Branco WBA | 2005–07 |
| Jimmy Slattery NBA | 1927 | WBA | 1979 | Jeff Harding WBC | 1989–90 | Clinton Woods IBF | 2005–08 |
| Tommy Loughran* | 1927–29† | Marvin Johnson* | | Dennis Andries WBC | 1990–91 | Tomasz Adamek WBC | |
| Maxie Rosenbloom* | 1930–34 | WBC | 1978–79 | Thomas Hearns* WBA | 1991–92 | | 2005–07 |
| George Nichols NBA | 1932 | M.S. Muhammad* | | Jeff Harding WBC | 1991–94 | Stipe Drews WBA | 2007 |
| Bob Godwin NBA | 1933 | WBC | 1979–81 | Iran Barkley* WBA | 1992 | Chad Dawson WBC | 2007–08 |
| Bob Olin* | 1934–35 | Marvin Johnson | | Virgil Hill* WBA | 1992–97 | | 2008–09† |
| John Henry Lewis* | 1935–38† | WBA | 1979–80 | Henry Maske IBF | 1993–96 | Danny Green WBA | 2007–08 |
| Melio Bettina | 1939 | E.M. Muhammad* | | Mike McCallum WBC | 1994–95 | Hugo Garay WBA | 2008–09 |
| Billy Conn* | 1939–40† | WBA | 1980–81 | Fabrice Tiozzo WBC | 1995–96 | Antonio Tarver IBF | 2008 |
| Anton Christoforidis | 1941 | Michael Spinks* WBA | | D. Michalczewski* | | Adrian Diaconu WBC | 2008–09 |
| Gus Lesnevich* | 1941–48 | 1981–83 | | IBF | 1997† | Gabriel Campillo WBA | 2009–10 |
| Freddie Mills* | 1948–50 | Dwight Qawi WBC | 1981–83 | Roy Jones Jr. | | Jean Pascal WBC | 2009–11 |
| Joey Maxim* | 1950–52 | Michael Spinks* | 1983–85† | WBC, WBA | 1997–03 | Tavoris Cloud IBF | 2009– |
| Archie Moore* | 1952–62† | J. B. Williamson WBC | 1985–86 | William Guthrie IBF | 1997–98 | Beibut Shumenov, | |
| Harold Johnson NBA | 1961 | Slobodan Kacar IBF | 1985–86 | Reggie Johnson IBF | 1998–99 | WBA | 2010– |
| Harold Johnson* | 1962–63 | Marvin Johnson* | | Roy Jones Jr.* | 1999–03 | Bernard Hopkins, | |
| Willie Pastrano* | 1963–65 | WBA | 1986–87 | Bruno Girard WBA | 2001–03 | WBC | 2011– |

### Super Middleweights  (Weight Limit: 168 pounds)

| Champion | Reign | Champion | Reign | Champion | Reign | Champion | Reign |
|---|---|---|---|---|---|---|---|
| Murray Sutherland* | | Iran Barkley IBF | 1992 | Byron Mitchell* WBA | 1999–00 | Joe Calzaghe IBF | 2006–07 |
| IBF | 1984 | Nigel Benn WBC | 1992–96 | Markus Beyer WBC | 1999–00 | Mikkel Kessler WBC | 2006–07 |
| Chong-Pal Park* IBF | 1984–87 | James Toney IBF | 1992–94 | Bruno Girard* WBA | 2000–01† | Robert Stieglitz IBF | 2007 |
| Chong-Pal Park* WBA | | Michael Nunn* WBA | 1992–94 | Glenn Catley WBC | 2000–01 | Alejandro Berrio IBF | 2007 |
| 1987–88 | | Steve Little* WBA | 1994 | Eric Lucas WBC | 2000–03 | Joe Calzaghe, WBC | 2007–08 |
| G. Rocchigiani IBF | 1988–89 | Frank Liles* WBA | 1994–99 | Byron Mitchell WBA | 2000–03 | Lucian Bute IBF | 2007– |
| F. Obelmejias* WBA | 1988–89 | Roy Jones Jr. IBF | 1994–96 | Sven Ottke WBA | 2003† | Joe Calzaghe WBA | 2007–08 |
| Sugar Ray Leonard | | Thulane Malinga WBC | 1996 | Anthony Mundine WBA | 2003 | Carl Froch WBC | 2008–10 |
| WBC | 1988–90† | V. Nardiello WBC | 1996 | Markus Beyer WBC | 2003–04 | Mikkel Kessler WBA | 2008–09 |
| In-Chul Baek* WBA | 1989–90 | Robin Reid WBC | 1996–97 | Sven Ottke, IBF | 2003–05 | Andre Ward‡ WBA | 2009– |
| Lindell Holmes IBF | 1990–91 | Charles Brewer IBF | 1997–98 | Cristian Sanavia WBC | 2004 | Mikkel Kessler WBC | 2010† |
| Chris Tiozzo* WBA | 1990–91 | Thulane Malinga | | Manny Siaca, WBA | 2004 | Carl Froch WBC | 2011– |
| Mauro Galvano WBC | 1990–92 | WBC | 1997–98 | Mikel Kessler WBA | 2004–07 | Karoly Balzsay WBA | 2011– |
| Victor Cordova* WBA | 1991 | Richie Woodhall WBC | 1998–99 | Markus Beyer WBC | 2004–06 | | |
| Darrin Van Horn IBF | 1991–92 | Sven Ottke IBF | 1998–03 | Jeff Lacy IBF | 2005 | | |

*Lineal champion.  ‡ Super champion.  †Champion relinquished title to retire or switch weight classes, or had title stripped by boxing organization.

## Middleweights (Weight Limit: 160 pounds)

| Champion | Reign | Champion | Reign | Champion | Reign | Champion | Reign |
|---|---|---|---|---|---|---|---|
| Jack Dempsey* | 1884–91 | Marcel Cerdan* | 1948–49 | Alan Minter* | 1980 | William Joppy WBA | 1998–01 |
| Bob Fitzsimmons* | 1891–97† | Jake La Motta* | 1949–51 | Marvin Hagler* | 1980–87 | Hassine Cherifi WBC | 1998–99 |
| Kid McCoy | 1897–98 | Sugar Ray Robinson* | 1951 | Sugar Ray Leonard* | 1987† | Keith Holmes WBC | 1999–00 |
| Tommy Ryan* | 1898–07† | Randy Turpin* | 1951 | Frank Tate IBF | 1987–88 | Felix Trinidad WBA | 2001 |
| Stanley Ketchel* | 1908 | Sugar Ray Robinson* | 1951–52† | Sumbu Kalambay | | William Joppy WBA | 2001–03 |
| Billy Papke* | 1908 | Bobo Olson* | 1953–55 | WBA | 1987–89 | Bernard Hopkins* | |
| Stanley Ketchel* | 1908–10† | Sugar Ray Robinson* | 1955–57 | Thomas Hearns* | | WBC/IBF | 2001–05 |
| Frank Klaus* | 1913 | Gene Fullmer* | 1957 | WBC | 1987–88 | Bernard Hopkins WBA | |
| George Chip* | 1913–14 | Sugar Ray Robinson* | 1957 | Iran Barkley* WBC | 1988–89 | 2003–05 | |
| Al McCoy* | 1914–17 | Carmen Basilio* | 1957–58 | Michael Nunn IBF | 1988–91 | Jermain Taylor IBF | 2005 |
| Mike O'Dowd* | 1917–20 | Sugar Ray Robinson* | 1958–60 | Roberto Duran* WBC | 1989–90† | Jermain Taylor WBA | 2005–06 |
| Johnny Wilson* | 1920–23 | Gene Fullmer NBA | 1959–62 | Michael Nunn* IBF | 1991 | Jermain Taylor WBC | 2005–07 |
| Harry Greb* | 1923–26 | Paul Pender* | 1960–61 | Mike McCallum WBA | | Arthur Abraham IBF | 2005–09† |
| Tiger Flowers* | 1926 | Terry Downes* | 1961–62 | 1989–91 | | Felix Sturm WBA | 2006 |
| Mickey Walker* | 1926–31† | Paul Pender* | 1962–63† | Julian Jackson WBC | 1990–93 | Javier Castillejo WBA | |
| Gorilla Jones* | 1931–32 | Dick Tiger WBA | 1962–63 | James Toney* IBF | 1991–93† | 2006–07 | |
| Marcel Thil* | 1932–37 | Dick Tiger | 1963 | Reggie Johnson WBA | | Felix Sturm WBA‡ | 2007– |
| Fred Apostoli* | 1937–39 | Joey Giardello* | 1963–65 | 1992–94 | | Kelly Pavlik WBC | 2007–10 |
| Al Hostak NBA | 1938 | Dick Tiger* | 1965–66 | Roy Jones Jr.* IBF | 1993–95† | Sebastian Sylvester | |
| Solly Krieger NBA | 1938–39 | Emile Griffith* | 1966–67 | G. McClellan WBC | 1993–95† | IBF | 2009–11 |
| Al Hostak NBA | 1939–40 | Nino Benvenuti* | 1967 | Jorge Castro WBA | 1994–95 | Sergio Gabriel Martinez, | |
| Ceferino Garcia* | 1939–40 | Emile Griffith* | 1967–68 | Shinji Takehara WBA | 1995–96 | WBC | 2010–11† |
| Ken Overlin* | 1940–41 | Nino Benvenuti* | 1968–70 | Jullian Jackson WBC | 1995 | Sebastian Zbik WBC | 2011 |
| Tony Zale NBA | 1940–41 | Carlos Monzon* | 1970–77† | Quincy Taylor WBC | 1995–96 | Julio Cesar Chavez Jr., | |
| Billy Soose* | 1941 | Rodrigo Valdez WBC | 1974–76 | Bernard Hopkins* IBF | 1994– | WBC | 2011– |
| Tony Zale* | 1941–47 | Rodrigo Valdez* | 1977–78 | Keith Holmes WBC | 1996–98 | Gennady Golovkin, | |
| Rocky Graziano* | 1947–48 | Hugo Corro* | 1978–79 | William Joppy WBA | 1996–97 | WBA | 2011– |
| Tony Zale* | 1948 | Vito Antuofermo* | 1979–80 | J.C. Green WBA | 1997 | Daniel Geale IBF | 2011– |

## Junior Middleweights (Weight Limit: 154 pounds)

| Champion | Reign | Champion | Reign | Champion | Reign | Champion | Reign |
|---|---|---|---|---|---|---|---|
| Emile Griffith (EBU) | 1962–63 | WBC | 1982–84 | Paul Vaden IBF | 1995 | Roman Karmazin | |
| Dennis Moyer* | 1962–63 | Roberto Duran WBA | 1983–84 | Carl Daniels WBA | 1995 | IBF | 2005–06 |
| Ralph Dupas* | 1963 | Mark Medal IBF | 1984 | Terry Norris* WBC | 1995–97 | Jose A. Rivera WBA | 2006–07 |
| Sandro Mazzinghi* | 1963–65 | Thomas Hearns* | 1984–86† | Terry Norris* IBF | 1995–96† | Oscar De La Hoya | |
| Nino Benvenuti* | 1965–66 | Mike McCallum* | | L. Boudouani WBA | 1996–99 | WBC | 2006–07 |
| Ki-Soo Kim* | 1966–68 | WBA | 1984–87† | Raul Marquez IBF | 1997 | Cory Spinks IBF | 2006–08 |
| Sandro Mazzinghi* | 1968 | Carlos Santos IBF | 1984–86 | Keith Mullings* WBC | 1997–99 | | 2009– |
| Freddie Little* | 1969–70 | Buster Drayton IBF | 1986–87 | Yori Boy Campas IBF | 1997–98 | Travis Simms WBA | 2007 |
| Carmelo Bossi* | 1970–71 | Duane Thomas | | Fernando Vargas IBF | 1998–00 | Floyd Mayweather Jr. | |
| Koichi Wajima* | 1971–74 | WBC | 1986–87 | F. Javier Castillejo* | | WBC | 2007 |
| Oscar Albarado* | 1974–75 | Matthew Hilton IBF | 1987–88 | WBC | 1999–01 | Joachim Alcine WBA | 2007–08 |
| Koichi Wajima* | 1975 | Lupe Aquino WBC | 1987 | David Reid WBA | 1999–00 | Vernon Forrest WBC | 2007–08 |
| Miguel de Oliveira WBC | | Gianfranco Rosi | | Felix Trinidad WBA | 2000–01 | Sergio Mora WBC | 2008 |
| 1975–76 | | WBC | 1987–88 | Felix Trinidad | | Verno Phillips IBF | 2008† |
| Jae-Do Yuh* | 1975–76 | Julian Jackson WBA | 1987–90 | WBA, IBF | 2001† | Daniel Santos WBA | 2008–09 |
| Elisha Obed WBC | 1975–76 | Donald Curry WBC | 1988–89 | Oscar De La Hoya* | | Vernon Forrest | |
| Koichi Wajima* | 1976 | Robert Hines IBF | 1988–89 | WBC | 2001–03 | WBC | 2008–09 |
| Jose Duran* | 1976 | Darrin Van Horn IBF | 1989 | Fernando Vargas | | Cory Spinks IBF | 2009–10 |
| Eckhard Dagge WBC | 1976–77 | Rene Jacquot WBC | 1989 | WBA | 2001–02 | Sergio Gabriel Martinez | |
| Miguel Angel | | John Mugabi* WBC | 1989–90 | Ronald Wright IBF† | 2001–04 | WBC | 2009–10† |
| Castellini* | 1976–77 | Gianfranco Rosi IBF | 1989–94 | Oscar De La Hoya* | | Yuri Foreman WBA | 2009–10 |
| Eddie Gazo* | 1977–78 | Terry Norris* WBC | 1990–93 | WBC/WBA | 2002–03 | Miguel Cotto WBA‡ | 2010– |
| Rocky Mattioli WBC | 1977–79 | Gilbert Dele WBA | 1991 | Shane Mosley* WBC | 2003–04 | Manny Pacquiao WBC | 2010–11† |
| Masashi Kudo* | 1978–79 | Vinny Pazienza | | Alejandro Garcia WBA | | Saul Alvarez WBC | 2011– |
| Maurice Hope WBC | 1979–81 | WBA | 1991–92 | 2003–05 | | Austin Trout WBA | 2011– |
| Ayub Kalule* | 1979–81 | Julio C. Vasquez WBA | | Ronald Wright | | Cornelius Bundrage | |
| Wilfred Benitez WBC | 1981–82 | 1992–95 | | WBA/WBC | 2004–05 | IBF | 2011– |
| Sugar Ray Leonard* | 1981–82† | Simon Brown* WBC | 1993–94 | Verno Phillips IBF | 2004–05 | | |
| Tadashi Mihara WBA | 1981–82 | Terry Norris* WBC | 1994 | Ricardo Mayora | | | |
| Davey Moore WBA | 1982–83 | Luis Santana* WBC | 1995–95 | WBC | 2005–06 | | |
| Thomas Hearns* | | Vincent Pettway IBF | 1994–95 | Alex T. Garcia WBA | 2005–06 | | |

*Lineal champion. ‡Super champion. †Champion relinquished title to retire or switch weight classes, or had title stripped by boxing organization.

## Welterweights (Weight Limit: 147 pounds)

| Champion | Reign |
|---|---|
| Faddy Duffy* | 1888–90† |
| Mysterious Billy Smith* | 1892–94 |
| Tommy Ryan* | 1894–98† |
| Mysterious Billy Smith* | 1898–1900 |
| Rube Ferns* | 1900 |
| Matty Matthews* | 1900–01 |
| Rube Ferns* | 1901 |
| Joe Walcott* | 1901–04 |
| The Dixie Kid* | 1904–05† |
| Honey Mellody* | 1906–07 |
| Mike Sullivan* | 1907–08† |
| Jimmy Gardner* | 1908† |
| Jimmy Clabby* | 1910–1† |
| Waldemar Holberg* | 1914 |
| Tom McCormick* | 1914 |
| Matt Wells* | 1914–15 |
| Mike Glover* | 1915 |
| Jack Britton* | 1915 |
| Ted "Kid" Lewis* | 1915–16 |
| Jack Britton* | 1916–17 |
| Ted "Kid" Lewis* | 1917–19 |
| Jack Britton* | 1919–22 |
| Mickey Walker* | 1922–26 |
| Pete Latzo* | 1926–27 |
| Joe Dundee* | 1927–29 |
| Jackie Fields* | 1929–30 |
| Young Jack Thompson* | 1930 |
| Tommy Freeman* | 1930–31 |
| Young Jack Thompson* | 1931 |
| Lou Brouillard* | 1931–32 |
| Jackie Fields* | 1932–33 |
| Young Corbett III* | 1933 |
| Jimmy McLarnin* | 1933–34 |
| Barney Ross* | 1934 |
| Jimmy McLarnin* | 1934–35 |
| Barney Ross* | 1935–38 |
| Henry Armstrong* | 1938–40 |
| Fritzie Zivic* | 1940–41 |
| Red Cochrane* | 1941–46 |
| Marty Servo* | 1946 |
| Sugar Ray Robinson* | 1946–51† |
| Johnny Bratton* | 1951 |
| Kid Gavilan* | 1951–54 |
| Johnny Saxton* | 1954–55 |
| Tony DeMarco* | 1955 |
| Carmen Basilio* | 1955–56 |
| Johnny Saxton* | 1956 |
| Carmen Basilio* | 1956–57† |
| Virgil Akins* | 1958 |
| Don Jordan* | 1958–60 |
| Kid Paret* | 1960–61 |
| Emile Griffith* | 1961 |
| Kid Paret* | 1961–62 |
| Emile Griffith* | 1962–63 |
| Luis Rodriguez* | 1963 |
| Emile Griffith* | 1963–66† |
| Curtis Cokes* | 1966–69 |
| Jose Napoles* | 1969–70 |
| Billy Backus* | 1970–71 |
| Jose Napoles* | 1971–75 |
| Hedgemon Lewis NY | 1972–73 |
| Angel Espada WBA | 1975–76 |
| John H. Stracey* | 1975–76 |
| Carlos Palomino* | 1976–79 |
| Pipino Cuevas WBA | 1976–80 |
| Wilfredo Benitez* | 1979 |
| Sugar Ray Leonard* | 1979–80 |
| Roberto Duran* | 1980 |
| Thomas Hearns WBA | 1980–81 |
| Sugar Ray Leonard* | 1980–82† |
| Donald Curry* WBA | 1983–85 |
| Milton McCrory WBC | 1983–85 |
| Donald Curry* | 1985–86 |
| Lloyd Honeyghan* | 1986–87 |
| Jorge Vaca* WBC | 1987–88 |
| Lloyd Honeyghan* WBC | 1988–89 |
| Mark Breland WBA | 1987 |
| Marlon Starling WBA | 1987–88 |
| Tomas Molinares WBA | 1988–89 |
| Simon Brown IBF | 1988–91 |
| Mark Breland WBA | 1989–90 |
| Marlon Starling* WBC | 1989–90 |
| Aaron Davis WBA | 1990–91 |
| Maurice Blocker* WBC | 1990–91 |
| Meldrick Taylor WBA | 1991–92 |
| Simon Brown* WBC | 1991 |
| Buddy McGirt* WBC | 1991–93 |
| Felix Trinidad IBF | 1993–00 |
| Pernell Whitaker* WBC | 1993–97 |
| Crisanto Espana WBA | 1992–94 |
| Ike Quartey WBA | 1994–97† |
| Oscar De La Hoya* WBC | 1997–99 |
| James Page WBA | 1998–01 |
| Felix Trinidad* IBF, WBC | 1999–00† |
| Shane Mosley* WBC | 2000–02 |
| Andrew Lewis WBA | 2001–02 |
| Vernon Forrest IBF | 2001 |
| Vernon Forrest* WBC | 2001–03 |
| Ricardo Mayorga WBA | 2002 |
| Ricardo Mayorga* WBC | 2003–05 |
| Michele Piccirillo IBF | 2002–03 |
| Jose Rivera WBA | 2003 |
| Cory Spinks IBF, WBC, WBA | 2003–05 |
| Zab Judah WBA/WBC/IBF | 2005–06 |
| Luis Collazo WBA | 2006 |
| Ricky Hatton WBA | 2006 |
| Carlos Baldomir WBC | 2006 |
| F. Mayweather, Jr. IBF | 2006 |
| Miguel Cotto WBA | 2006–08 |
| F. Mayweather Jr. WBC | 2006–08 |
| Kermit Cintron IBF | 2006–08 |
| A. Margarito IBF | 2008 |
| Joshua Clottey IBF | 2008–09† |
| Ant. Margarito WBA | 2008–09 |
| Andre Berto WBC | 2008–11 |
| Shane Mosley WBA | 2009 |
| Isaac Hlatshwayo IBF | 2009 |
| Vyacheslav Senchenko WBA | 2009– |
| Dejan Zavec IBF | 2009–11 |
| Victor Ortz WBC | 2011 |
| F. Mayweather Jr., WBC | 2011– |
| Andre Berto IBF | 2011– |

## Super Lightweights (Weight Limit: 140 pounds)

| Champion | Reign |
|---|---|
| Pinkey Mitchell* | 1922–25 |
| Red Herring | 1925 |
| Mushy Callahan* | 1926–30 |
| Jack (Kid) Berg* | 1930–31 |
| Tony Canzoneri* | 1931–32 |
| Johnny Jadick* | 1932–33 |
| Sammy Fuller | 1932–33 |
| Battling Shaw* | 1933 |
| Tony Canzoneri* | 1933 |
| Barney Ross* | 1933–35† |
| Tippy Larkin* | 1946 |
| Carlos Ortiz* | 1959–60 |
| Duilio Loi* | 1960–62 |
| Eddie Perkins* | 1962 |
| Duilio Loi* | 1962–63† |
| Roberto Cruz WBA | 1963 |
| Eddie Perkins* | 1963–65 |
| Carlos Hernandez* | 1965–66 |
| Sandro Lopopolo* | 1966–67 |
| Paul Fujii* | 1967–68 |
| Nicolino Loche* | 1968–72 |
| Pedro Adigue WBC | 1968–70 |
| Bruno Arcari WBC | 1970–74 |
| Alfonso Frazer* | 1972 |
| Antonio Cervantes* | 1972–76 |
| Perico Fernandez WBC | 1974–75 |
| S. Muangsurin WBC | 1975–76 |
| Wilfred Benitez* | 1976–79† |
| M. Velasquez WBC | 1976 |
| S. Muangsurin WBC | 1976–78 |
| A. Cervantes WBA | 1977–80 |
| Sang-Hyun Kim WBC | 1978–80 |
| Saoul Mamby WBC | 1980–82 |
| Aaron Pryor* WBA | 1980–83 |
| Leroy Haley WBC | 1982–83 |
| Aaron Pryor* IBF | 1983–85† |
| Bruce Curry WBC | 1983–84 |
| Johnny Bumphus WBA | 1984 |
| Bill Costello WBC | 1984–85 |
| Gene Hatcher WBA | 1984–85 |
| Ubaldo Sacco WBA | 1985–86 |
| Lonnie Smith* WBC | 1985–86 |
| Patrizio Oliva WBA | 1986–87 |
| Gary Hinton IBF | 1986 |
| Rene Arredondo* WBC | 1986 |
| Tsuyoshi Hamada WBC | 1986–87 |
| Joe Louis Manley IBF | 1986–87 |
| Terry Marsh IBF | 1987 |
| Juan Coggi WBA | 1987–90 |
| Rene Arredondo WBC | 1987 |
| R. Mayweather* WBC | 1987–89 |
| James McGirt IBF | 1988 |
| Meldrick Taylor IBF | 1988–90 |
| Julio César Chávez* WBC | 1989–94 |
| Julio César Chávez* IBF | 1990–91 |
| Loreto Garza WBA | 1990–91 |
| Juan Coggi WBA | 1991 |
| Edwin Rosario WBA | 1991–92 |
| Rafael Pineda IBF | 1991–92 |
| Akinobu Hiranaka WBA | 1992 |
| Pernell Whitaker IBF | 1992–93† |
| Charles Murray IBF | 1993–94 |
| Jake Rodriguez IBF | 1994–95 |
| Juan Coggi WBA | 1993–94 |
| Frankie Randall* WBC | 1994 |
| Frankie Randall WBA | 1994–96 |
| Juan Coggi WBA | 1996 |
| Julio César Chávez* WBC | 1994–96 |
| Kostya Tszyu IBF | 1995–97 |
| Frankie Randall WBA | 1996–97 |
| Oscar De La Hoya* WBC | 1996–97† |
| Khalid Rahilou WBA | 1997–98 |
| Vincent Phillips* IBF | 1997–99 |
| Sharmba Mitchell WBA | 1998–01 |
| Kostya Tszyu WBC | 1998– |
| Terronn Millett* IBF | 1999–00 |
| Zab Judah* IBF | 2000–01 |
| Kostya Tszyu*† WBA/C | 2001–03 |
| Kostya Tszyu* IBF | 2003–05 |
| Vivian Harris WBA | 2003–05 |
| Arturo Gatti WBC | 2004–05 |
| F. Mayweather Jr. WBC | 2005–06 |
| Carlos Maussa WBA | 2005–06 |
| Ricky Hatton IBF | 2005–06 |
| Souleymane M'baye WBA | 2006–07 |
| Juan Urango IBF | 2006–07 |

*Lineal champion. †Champion relinquished title to retire or switch weight classes, or had title stripped by boxing organization.

### Super Lightweights (Cont.)

| Champion | Reign | Champion | Reign | Champion | Reign | Champion | Reign |
|---|---|---|---|---|---|---|---|
| Lovemore N'Dou | | WBC | .2008–09 | Amir Khan WBA‡ | .2009– | Zab Judah IBF | .2011 |
| IBF | .2007 | Andreas Kotelnik | | Juan Urango IBF | 2009–10 | Timothy Bradley | |
| Paul Malignaggi | | WBA | .2008–09 | Devon Alexander, | | WBC | .2011† |
| IBF | .2007–09† | Devon Alexander | | IBF | .2010† | Erik Morales WBC | .2011– |
| Timothy Bradley | | WBC | .2009–11 | Marcos Maidana WBA | .2010 | Amir Khan WBA/IBF | .2011– |

## Lightweights (Weight Limit: 135 pounds)

| Champion | Reign | Champion | Reign | Champion | Reign | Champion | Reign |
|---|---|---|---|---|---|---|---|
| Jack McAuliffe* | .1886–94† | Joe Brown* | .1956–62 | Julio César Chávez* | | Steve Johnston* | |
| Kid Lavigne* | .1896–99 | Carlos Ortiz* | .1962–65 | WBA | .1987–88 | WBC | .1999–00 |
| Frank Erne* | .1899–1902 | Ismael Laguna* | .1965 | Jose Luis Ramirez | | Julien Lorcy WBA | .1999 |
| Joe Gans* | .1902–04 | Carlos Ortiz* | .1965–68 | WBC | .1987–88 | Stefano Zoff WBA | .1999 |
| Jimmy Britt* | .1904–05 | Carlos Teo Cruz* | .1968–69 | Julio César Chávez* | .1988–89† | Paul Spadafora IBF | .1999–03 |
| Battling Nelson* | .1905–06 | Mando Ramos* | .1969–70 | Vinny Pazienza IBF | .1987–88 | Gilbert Serrano WBA | .1999–00 |
| Joe Gans* | .1906–08 | Ismael Laguna* | .1970 | Greg Haugen IBF | .1988–89 | T. Hatakeyama WBA | .2000–01 |
| Battling Nelson* | .1908–10 | Ken Buchanan* | .1970–72 | P. Whitaker* | | Jose Luis Castillo* | |
| Ad Wolgast* | .1910–12 | Roberto Duran* | .1972–79† | WBC, IBF | .1989–90 | WBC | .2000–02 |
| Willie Ritchie* | .1912–14 | Chango Carmona | | Edwin Rosario WBA | .1989–90 | Julien Lorcy WBA | .2001 |
| Freddie Welsh* | .1915–17 | WBC | .1972 | Juan Nazario WBA | .1990 | Raul Balbi WBA | .2001 |
| Benny Leonard* | .1917–25† | Rodolfo Gonzalez | | P. Whitaker* | | F. Mayweather* WBC | .2002–03 |
| Jimmy Goodrich* | .1925 | WBC | .1972–74 | WBA, WBC | .1990–92† | Leonard Dorin WBA | .2002–03 |
| Rocky Kansas* | .1925–26 | Ishimatsu Suzuki | | Pernell Whitaker* | | Javier Jauregui IBF | .2003–04 |
| Sammy Mandell* | .1926–30 | WBC | .1974–76 | IBF | .1991–92† | Julio Diaz IBF | .2004–05 |
| Al Singer* | .1930 | Esteban DeJesus | | Julio César Chávez | | Lakva Sim WBA | .2004 |
| Tony Canzoneri* | .1930–33 | WBC | .1976–78 | IBF | .1990–91 | Juan Diaz WBA | .2004–08 |
| Barney Ross* | .1933–35† | Jim Watt WBC* | .1979–81 | Edwin Rosario WBA | .1991–92 | Jose Luis Castillo | |
| Tony Canzoneri* | .1935–36 | Ernesto Espana | | Julio César Chávez | | WBC | .2004–05 |
| Lou Ambers* | .1936–38 | WBA | .1979–80 | WBC | .1990–92 | Diego Corrales WBC | .2005–06 |
| Henry Armstrong* | .1938–39 | Hilmer Kenty WBA | .1980–81 | Miguel Gonzalez | | Jesus Chavez IBF | .2005–07 |
| Lou Ambers* | .1939–40 | Sean O'Grady WBA | .1981 | WBC | .1992–95 | Joel Casamayor | |
| Sammy Angott NBA | .1940–41 | Claude Noel WBA | .1981 | Joey Gamache | | WBC | .2006–07 |
| Lew Jenkins* | .1940–41 | Alexis Arguello* | | WBA | .1992–93 | Julio Diaz IBF | .2007 |
| Sammy Angott* | .1941–42† | WBC | .1981–82† | Dingaan Thobela | | Juan Diaz | .2007–08 |
| Beau Jack* NY | .1942–43 | Arturo Frias WBA | .1981–82 | WBA | .1993 | David Diaz WBC | .2008 |
| Bob Montgomery* | | Ray Mancini* WBA | .1982–84 | Fred Pendleton* IBF | .1993–94 | Yusuke Kobori WBA | .2008–09 |
| NY | .1943 | Alexis Arguello | .1982–83 | Orzubek Nazarov | | Nate Campbell IBF | .2008–09† |
| Sammy Angott NBA | .1943–44 | Edwin Rosario WBC | .1983–84 | WBA | .1993–98 | Manny Pacquiao | |
| Beau Jack* NY | .1943–44 | Choo Choo Brown | | Rafael Ruelas* IBF | .1994–95 | WBC | .2008–09† |
| Bob Montgomery* | | IBF | .1984 | Oscar De La Hoya* | | Juan Manual Marquez‡ | |
| NY | .1944–47 | L. Bramble* WBA | .1984–86 | IBF | .1995† | WBA | .2009– |
| Juan Zurita NBA | .1944–45 | Jose Luis Ramirez | | Phillip Holiday IBF | .1995–97 | Edwin Valero WBC | .2009–10† |
| Ike Williams* | .1947–51 | WBC | .1984–85 | Jean B. Mendy* | | Miguel Vazquez IBF | .2010– |
| James Carter* | .1951–52 | Harry Arroyo IBF | .1984–85 | WBC | .1996–97 | Humberto Soto WBC | .2010– |
| Lauro Salas* | .1952 | Jimmy Paul IBF | .1985–86 | Steve Johnston* | | Miguel Acosta WBA | .2010–11 |
| James Carter* | .1952–54 | Hector Camacho | | WBC | .1997–98 | Brandon Rios WBA | .2011– |
| Paddy DeMarco* | .1954 | WBC | .1985–86 | Shane Mosley IBF | .1997–99† | | |
| James Carter* | .1954–55 | Greg Haugen IBF | .1986–87 | Jean B. Mendy WBA | .1998–99 | | |
| Wallace Smith* | .1955–56 | Edwin Rosario* WBA | .1986–87 | Cesar Bazan* WBC | .1998–99 | | |

*Lineal champion. †Champion relinquished title to retire or switch weight classes, or had title stripped by boxing organization.

### Super Featherweights (Weight Limit: 130 pounds)

| Champion | Reign | Champion | Reign | Champion | Reign |
|---|---|---|---|---|---|
| Johnny Dundee* | 1921–23 | Hector Camacho WBC | 1983–84 | Steve Forbes IBF | 2000–02† |
| Jack Bernstein* | 1923 | Rocky Lockridge* | 1984–85 | Acelino Freitas* WBA | 2002–04 |
| Johnny Dundee* | 1923–24 | Hwan-Kil Yuh IBF | 1984–85 | Y. Nantchachai WBA | 2002–05 |
| Steve (Kid) Sullivan* | 1924–25 | Julio César Chávez WBC | 1984–87 | S. Singmanassak WBC | 2002–03 |
| Mike Ballerino* | 1925 | Lester Ellis IBF | 1985 | Jesus Chavez WBC | 2003–04 |
| Tod Morgan* | 1925–29 | Wilfredo Gomez* | 1985–86 | Carlos Hernandez IBF | 2003–04 |
| Benny Bass* | 1929–31 | Barry Michael IBF | 1985–87 | Erik Morales WBC/IBF | 2004–05 |
| Kid Chocolate* | 1931–33 | Alfredo Layne* WBA | 1986 | Erik Morales IBF | 2004–05 |
| Frankie Klick* | 1933–34† | Brian Mitchell* WBA | 1986–91† | Marco A. Barrera WBC | 2005–07 |
| Sandy Saddler* | 1949–50† | Rocky Lockridge IBF | 1987–88 | Vicente Mosquera WBA | 2005–06 |
| Harold Gomes* | 1959–60 | Azumah Nelson* WBC | 1988–94 | Robbie Peden IBF | 2005 |
| Gabriel (Flash) Elorde* | 1960–67 | Tony Lopez IBF | 1988–89 | Marco A. Barrera, IBF | 2005–06 |
| Yoshiaki Numata* | 1967 | Juan Molina IBF | 1989–90 | Cassius Baloyi IBF | 2006 |
| Hiroshi Kobayashi* | 1967–71 | Tony Lopez IBF | 1990–91 | Edwin Valero WBA | 2006–08 |
| Rene Barrientos WBC | 1969–70 | Joey Gamache WBA | 1991 | Gairy St. Clair IBF | 2006 |
| Yoshiaki Numata WBC | 1970–71 | Brian Mitchell IBF | 1991 | Malcolm Klassen IBF | 2006–07 |
| Alfredo Marcano* | 1971–72 | Genaro Hernandez WBA | 1991–95 | Mzonke Fana IBF | 2007–08 |
| R. Arredondo WBC | 1971–74 | James Leija* WBC | 1994 | Juan Manuel Marquez WBC | 2007–08 |
| Ben Villaflor* | 1972–73 | Juan Molina IBF | 1991–95 | Manny Pacquiao WBC | 2008 |
| Kuniaki Shibata* | 1973 | Gabriel Ruelas* WBC | 1994–95 | Jorge Llnares WBA | 2008–09 |
| Ben Villaflor* | 1973–76 | Eddie Hopson IBF | 1995 | Cassius Baloyi IBF | 2008–09 |
| Kuniaki Shibata WBC | 1974–75 | Tracy Patterson IBF | 1995 | Humberto Soto WBC | 2008–10† |
| Alfredo Escalera WBC | 1975–78 | Azumah Nelson* WBC | 1995–97 | Malcom Klassen IBF | 2009 |
| Samuel Serrano* | 1976–80 | Choi Yong-Soo WBA | 1995–98 | Juan Carlos Salgado IBF | 2009 |
| Alexis Arguello WBC | 1978–80 | Arturo Gatti IBF | 1995–98† | Juan Carlos Salgado WBA | 2009–10 |
| Yasutsune Uehara* | 1980–81 | Genaro Hernandez* WBC | 1997–98 | Robert Guerrero IBF | 2009–10† |
| Rafael Limon WBC | 1980–81 | Roberto Garcia IBF | 1998–99 | Takashi Uchiyama WBA | 2010– |
| C. Boza-Edwards WBC | 1981 | Floyd Mayweather Jr.* WBC | 1998–01† | Vitaly Tajbert WBC | 2010 |
| Samuel Serrano* | 1981–83 | T. Hatakeyama WBA | 1998–99 | Takahiro Aoh WBC | 2010– |
| R. Navarrete WBC | 1981–82 | Lakva Sim WBA | 1999 | Mzonke Fana IBF | 2010–11† |
| Rafael Limon WBC | 1982 | Diego Corrales IBF | 1999–01 | Juan Carlos Salgado IBF | 2011– |
| Bobby Chacon WBC | 1982–83 | Jong Kwon Baek WBA | 1999–00 | | |
| Roger Mayweather* | 1983–84 | Joel Casamayor WBA | 2000–02 | | |

### Featherweights (Weight Limit: 126 pounds)

| Champion | Reign | Champion | Reign | Champion | Reign |
|---|---|---|---|---|---|
| Torpedo Billy Murphy* | 1890 | Joey Archibald* | 1941 | Poison Kotey WBC | 1975–76 |
| Young Griffo* | 1890–92† | Richie Lamos NBA | 1941 | Danny Lopez* WBC | 1976–80 |
| George Dixon* | 1892–97 | Chalky Wright* | 1941–42 | Rafael Ortega WBA | 1977 |
| Solly Smith* | 1897–98 | Jackie Wilson NBA | 1941–43 | Cecilio Lastra WBA | 1977–78 |
| Dave Sullivan* | 1898 | Willie Pep* | 1942–48 | Eusebio Pedroza* WBA | 1978–85 |
| George Dixon* | 1898–1900 | Jackie Callura NBA | 1943 | S. Sanchez* WBC | 1980–82† |
| Terry McGovern* | 1900–01 | Phil Terranova NBA | 1943–44 | Juan LaPorte WBC | 1982–84 |
| Young Corbett II* | 1901–03† | Sal Bartolo NBA | 1944–46 | Wilfredo Gomez WBC | 1984 |
| Abe Attell* | 1903–04 | Sandy Saddler* | 1948–49 | Min-Keun Oh IBF | 1984–85 |
| Tommy Sullivan* | 1904–05† | Willie Pep* | 1949–50 | Azumah Nelson WBC | 1984–88 |
| Abe Attell* | 1906–12 | Sandy Saddler* | 1950–57† | Barry McGuigan* WBA | 1985–86 |
| Johnny Kilbane* | 1912–23 | Kid Bassey* | 1957–59 | Ki Young Chung IBF | 1985–86 |
| Johnny Dundee* | 1923 | Davey Moore* | 1959–63 | Steve Cruz* WBA | 1986–87 |
| Johnny Dundee* | 1923–24† | Sugar Ramos* | 1963–64 | Antonio Rivera IBF | 1986–88 |
| "Kid" Kaplan* | 1925–26† | Vicente Saldivar* | 1964–67† | A. Esparragoza* WBA | 1987–91 |
| Tony Canzoneri* | 1927–28 | Paul Rojas WBA | 1968 | Calvin Grove IBF | 1988 |
| Andre Routis* | 1928–29 | Jose Legra WBA | 1968–69 | Jorge Paez IBF | 1988–91 |
| Battling Battalino* | 1929–32† | Shozo Saijyo WBA | 1968–71 | Jeff Fenech WBC | 1988–90† |
| Tommy Paul NBA | 1932–33 | J. Famechon* WBC | 1969–70 | Marcos Villasana WBC | 1990–91 |
| Kid Chocolate NY | 1932–33† | Vicente Saldivar* WBC | 1970 | Paul Hodkinson WBC | 1991–93 |
| Freddie Miller NBA | 1933–36 | Kuniaki Shibata* WBC | 1970–72 | Troy Dorsey IBF | 1991 |
| Mike Beloise NY | 1936–37 | Antonio Gomez WBA | 1971–72 | Manuel Medina IBF | 1991–93 |
| Petey Sarron NBA | 1936–37 | C. Sanchez* WBC | 1972 | Yung Kyun Park* WBA | 1991–93 |
| Maurice Holtzer | 1937–38 | Ernesto Marcel WBA | 1972–74 | Gregorio Vargas WBC | 1993 |
| Henry Armstrong* | 1937–38† | Jose Legra* WBC | 1972–73 | Tom Johnson IBF | 1993–97† |
| Joey Archibald* NY | 1938–39 | Eder Jofre* WBC | 1973–74† | Eloy Rojas* WBA | 1993–96 |
| Leo Rodak NBA | 1938–39 | Ruben Olivares WBA | 1974 | Kevin Kelley WBC | 1993–95 |
| Joey Archibald | 1939–40 | Bobby Chacon WBC | 1974–75 | A. Gonzalez WBC | 1995 |
| Petey Scalzo NBA | 1940–41 | Alexis Arguello* WBA | 1974–76† | Manuel Medina WBC | 1995–95 |
| Harry Jeffra* | 1940–41 | Ruben Olivares WBC | 1975 | Luisito Espinosa WBC | 1995–99 |

*Lineal champion. †Champion relinquished title to retire or switch weight classes, or had title stripped by boxing organization.

## Featherweights *(Cont.)*

| Champion | Reign |
|---|---|
| Wilfredo Vazquez* WBA | 1996–98 |
| Hector Lizarraga IBF | 1997–98 |
| Naseem Hamed* WBA | 1998† |
| Naseem Hamed* | 1998–01 |
| Freddy Norwood WBA | 1998 |
| Manuel Medina WBA | 1998–99 |
| Antonio Cermeno WBA | 1998–99 |
| Cesar Soto WBC | 1999 |
| Freddy Norwood WBA | 1999–00 |
| Naseem Hamed* WBC | 1999† |
| Paul Ingle IBF | 1999–00 |
| Guty Espadas WBC | 2000–01 |
| Erik Morales WBC | 2000–02 |
| Derrick Gainer WBA | 2000–03 |
| Mbulelo Botile IBF | 2001 |
| Frankie Toledo IBF | 2001 |
| Manuel Medina IBF | 2001–02 |

| Champion | Reign |
|---|---|
| Marco A. Barrera*WBA/WBC | 2001–03 |
| Johnny Tapia IBF | 2002 |
| Marco A. Barrera* WBC | 2002† |
| Erik Morales WBC | 2002–03 |
| Juan Marquez IBF | 2003–06 |
| Chris John WBA‡ | 2003– |
| In Jin Chi WBC | 2004–06 |
| Valdemir Pereira, IBF | 2006 |
| Eric Aiken IBF | 2006 |
| T. Koshimoto, WBC | 2006 |
| Rudolfo Lopez WBC | 2006 |
| Robert Guerrero IBF | 2006 |
| Orlando Salido IBF | 2006 |
| In Jin Chi WBC | 2006–07 |
| Robert Guerrero IBF | 2007–08† |
| Jorge Linares WBC | 2007–08 |
| Oscar Larios WBC | 2008–09 |

| Champion | Reign |
|---|---|
| Cristobal Cruz IBF | 2008–10 |
| Takahiro Aoh WBC | 2009 |
| Elio Rojas WBC | 2009–10† |
| Yuriorkis Gamboa WBA | 2009–11† |
| Hozumi Hasegawa WBC | 2010–11 |
| Orlando Salido IBF | 2010† |
| Yuriorkis Gamboa IBF | 2010–11 |
| Jhonny Gonzalez WBC | 2011– |
| Jonathan Barros WBA | 2011– |
| Billy Dib IBF | 2011– |

## Super Bantamweights (Weight Limit: 122 pounds)

| Champion | Reign |
|---|---|
| Jack (Kid) Wolfe* | 1922–23 |
| Carl Duane* | 1923–24 |
| Rigoberto Riasco* WBC | 1976 |
| R. Kobayashi* WBC | 1976 |
| Dong-Kyun Yum* WBC | 1976–77 |
| Wilfredo Gomez* WBC | 1977–83† |
| Soo-Hwan Hong WBA | 1977–78 |
| Ricardo Cardona WBA | 1978–80 |
| Leo Randolph WBA | 1980 |
| Sergio Palma WBA | 1980–82 |
| Leonardo Cruz WBA | 1982–84 |
| Jaime Garza* WBC | 1983 |
| Bobby Berna IBF | 1983–84 |
| Loris Stecca WBA | 1984 |
| Seung-Il Suh IBF | 1984–85 |
| Victor Callejas WBA | 1984–86 |
| Juan Meza* WBC | 1984–85 |
| Ji-Won Kim IBF | 1985–86 |
| Lupe Pintor* WBC | 1985–86 |
| S. Payakaroon* WBC | 1986–87 |
| Seung-Hoon Lee IBF | 1987–88 |
| Louie Espinoza WBA | 1987 |
| Jeff Fenech* WBC | 1987† |
| Julio Gervacio WBA | 1987–88 |
| Daniel Zaragoza* WBC | 1988–90 |
| Jose Sanabria IBF | 1988–89 |

| Champion | Reign |
|---|---|
| B. Pinango WBA | 1988 |
| J.J. Estrada WBA | 1988–89 |
| Fabrice Benichou IBF | 1989–90 |
| Jesus Salud WBA | 1989–90 |
| Welcome Ncita IBF | 1990–92 |
| Paul Banke* WBC | 1990 |
| Luis Mendoza WBA | 1990–91 |
| Raul Perez WBA | 1992 |
| Pedro Decima* WBC | 1990–91 |
| K. Hatanaka* WBC | 1991 |
| Daniel Zaragoza* WBC | 1991–92 |
| Thiery Jacob* WBC | 1992 |
| Tracy Patterson* WBC | 1992–94 |
| Kennedy McKinney IBF | 1993–94 |
| Wilfredo Vasquez WBA | 1992–95 |
| Vuyani Bungu IBF | 1994–99† |
| H. Acero* Sanchez WBC | 1994–95 |
| Antonio Cermeno WBA | 1995–98† |
| Daniel Zaragoza* WBC | 1995–97 |
| Erik Morales* WBC | 1997–00† |
| Enrique Sanchez WBA | 1998 |
| Nestor Garza WBA | 1998–00 |
| Benedict Ledwaba IBF | 1999–01 |
| Clarence Adams WBA | 2000–01† |
| Willie Jorrin WBC | 2000–02 |
| Manny Pacquiao IBF | 2001–04 |

| Champion | Reign |
|---|---|
| Yober Ortega WBA | 2001–02 |
| Y. Sithyodthong WBA | 2002 |
| Osamu Sato WBA | 2002 |
| Salim Medjkoune WBA | 2002–03 |
| Mahyar Monshipour WBA | 2003–06 |
| Oscar Larios WBC | 2002–05 |
| Israel Vazquez IBF | 2004–05 |
| S. Sithchatchawal WBA | 2006 |
| Israel Vazquez WBC | 2005–07 |
| C. Caballero WBA‡ | 2006–10† |
| IBF | 2008– |
| Michael Hunter IBF | 2006 |
| Steve Molitor IBF | 2006–08 |
| Rafael Marquez WBC | 2007 |
| Israel Vazquez WBC | 2007–08† |
| Ricardo Cordoba WBA | 2008–09 |
| Bernard Dunne WBA | 2009 |
| Toshiaki Nishioka WBC | 2008– |
| Poon. Kratingdaenggym WBA | 2009–10 |
| Steve Molitor IBF | 2010–11 |
| Ryol Li Lee WBA | 2010–11 |
| Akifumi Shimoda WBA | 2011 |
| Rico Ramos WBA | 2011– |
| Takalani Ndlovu IBF | 2011– |

## Bantamweights (Weight Limit: 118 pounds)

| Champion | Reign |
|---|---|
| Spider Kelly | 1887 |
| Hughey Boyle | 1887–88 |
| Spider Kelly | 1889 |
| Chappie Moran | 1889–90 |
| George Dixon | 1890–91 |
| Pedlar Palmer | 1895–99 |
| Terry McGovern* | 1899–00† |
| Harry Harris | 1901 |
| Harry Forbes* | 1901–03 |
| Frankie Neil* | 1903–04 |
| Joe Bowker* | 1904–05† |
| Jimmy Walsh* | 1905–06† |
| Owen Moran | 1907–08 |
| Monte Attell | 1909–10 |
| Frankie Conley | 1910–11 |
| Johnny Coulon* | 1910–14 |

| Champion | Reign |
|---|---|
| Kid Williams* | 1914–17 |
| Kewpie Ertle | 1915 |
| Pete Herman* | 1917–20 |
| Joe Lynch* | 1920–21 |
| Pete Herman* | 1921 |
| Johnny Buff* | 1921–22 |
| Joe Lynch* | 1922–24 |
| Abe Goldstein* | 1924 |
| Cannonball Martin* | 1924–25 |
| Phil Rosenberg* | 1925–27† |
| Bud Taylor NBA | 1927–28 |
| Bushy Graham NY | 1928–29 |
| Panama Al Brown* | 1929–35 |
| Sixto Escobar NBA | 1934–35 |
| Baltazar Sangchilli* | 1935–36 |
| Lou Salica NBA | 1935 |

| Champion | Reign |
|---|---|
| Sixto Escobar NBA | 1935–36 |
| Tony Marino* | 1936 |
| Sixto Escobar* | 1936–37 |
| Harry Jeffra* | 1937–38 |
| Sixto Escobar* | 1938–39† |
| Georgie Pace NBA | 1939–40 |
| Lou Salica* | 1940–42 |
| Manuel Ortiz* | 1942–47 |
| Harold Dade* | 1947 |
| Manuel Ortiz* | 1947–50 |
| Vic Toweel* | 1950–52 |
| Jimmy Carruthers* | 1952–54† |
| Robert Cohen* | 1954–56 |
| Paul Macias NBA | 1955–57 |
| Mario D'Agata* | 1956–57 |
| Alphonse Halimi* | 1957–59 |

| Champion | Reign |
|---|---|
| Joe Becerra* | 1959–60† |
| Eder Jofre* | 1961–65 |
| Fighting Harada* | 1965–68 |
| Lionel Rose* | 1968–69 |
| Ruben Olivares* | 1969–70 |
| Chucho Castillo* | 1970–71 |
| Ruben Olivares* | 1971–72 |
| Rafael Herrera* | 1972 |
| Enrique Pinder* | 1972–73 |
| Romeo Anaya* | 1973 |
| Arnold Taylor* | 1973–74 |
| Rafael Herrera WBC | 1973–74 |
| Soo-Hwan Hong* | 1974–75 |
| Rodolfo Martinez | |
| WBC | 1974–76 |
| Alfonso Zamora* | 1975–77 |

*Lineal champion. †Champion relinquished title to retire or switch weight classes, or had title stripped by boxing organization.

## Bantamweights *((Cont.)*

| Champion | Reign | Champion | Reign | Champion | Reign | Champion | Reign |
|---|---|---|---|---|---|---|---|
| Carlos Zarate* WBC | 1976–79 | Moon Sung-Kil WBA | 1988–89 | Yasuei Yakushiji WBC 1993–95 | | V. Sahaprom* WBC | 1998–05 |
| Jorge Lujan | 1977–80 | Kaokor Galaxy WBA | 1989 | Junior Jones WBA | 1994 | Paulie Ayala* WBA | 1999–01† |
| Lupe Pintor* WBC | 1979–83† | Raul Perez WBC | 1988–91 | John M. Johnson | | Eidy Moya WBA | 2001–02 |
| Julian Solis | 1980 | O. Canizales* IBF | 1988–95† | WBA | 1994 | Johnny Bredahl WBA | 2002–05 |
| Jeff Chandler* | 1980–84 | Luisito Espinosa WBA 1989–91 | | D. Chuvatana WBA | 1994–95 | Rafael Marquez IBF | 2003–07 |
| Albert Davila WBC | 1983–85 | Israel Contreras WBA 1991–92 | | V. Sahaprom* WBA | 1995–96 | W. Sidorenko WBA | 2005–08 |
| Richard Sandoval* | 1984–86 | Eddie Cook WBA | 1992–93 | W. McCullough WBC | 1995–96 | H. Hasegawa WBC | 2005–10 |
| Satoshi Shingaki IBF | 1984–85 | Greg Richardson | | Harold Mestre IBF | 1995 | Luis Perez IBF | 2007 |
| Jeff Fenech IBF | 1985 | WBC | 1991 | Mbuleto Botile IBF | 1995–97 | Joseph Agbeko IBF | 2007–09 |
| Daniel Zaragoza WBC | 1985 | J. Tatsuyoshi, WBC | 1991–92 | Nana Konadu* WBA | 1996–98 | Anselmo Moreno†WBA | 2008– |
| Miguel Lora WBC | 1985–88 | Victor Rabanales | | S. Singmanassak | | Yohnny Perez IBF | 2009–10 |
| Gaby Canizales* | 1986 | WBC | 1992–93 | WBC | 1996–97 | Fernando Montiel WBC | 2010–11 |
| Bernardo Pinango* | 1986–87† | Jung-Il Byun WBC | 1993 | Tim Austin IBF | 1997–03 | Joseph Agbeko IBF | 2010–11 |
| W. Vasquez WBA | 1987–88 | Jorge Julio WBA | 1993 | J.Tatsuyoshi WBC | 1997–98 | Koki Kameda WBA | 2010– |
| Kevin Seabrooks* IBF | 1987–88 | | | Johnny Tapia* WBA | 1998–99 | Nonito Donaire WBC | 2011– |
| Kaokor Galaxy WBA | 1988 | | | | | Abner Mares IBF | 2011– |

## Super Flyweights (Weight Limit: 115 pounds)

| Champion | Reign | Champion | Reign | Champion | Reign | Champion | Reign |
|---|---|---|---|---|---|---|---|
| Rafael Orono* WBC | 1980–81 | Giberto Roman* | | Harold Grey IBF | 1996 | M. Tokuyama WBC | 2005–06 |
| Chul-Ho Kim* WBC | 1981–82 | WBC | 1988–89 | Danny Romero IBF | 1996–97 | Jose M. Castillo WBA 2005–06 | |
| Gustavo Ballas WBA | 1981 | Juan Polo Perez IBF | 1989–90 | Gerry Penalosa* | | Nobuo Nashiro WBA | 2006–08 |
| Rafael Pedroza WBA | 1981–82 | Nana Konadu* WBC | 1989–90 | WBC | 1997–98 | Cristian Mijares WBC | 2006–08 |
| Jiro Watanabe WBA | 1982–84 | Sung-Kil Moon* | | Johnny Tapia IBF | 1997–99† | Dmitri Kirilov IBF | 2007–08 |
| Rafael Orono* WBC | 1982–83 | WBC | 1990–93 | Satoshi Iida WBA | 1997–98 | Vic Darchinyan | |
| Payao Poontarat* | | Robert Quiroga IBF | 1990–93 | In-Joo Cho* WBC | 1998–00 | WBC, WBA | 2008–10† |
| WBC | 1983–84 | Julio Borboa IBF | 1993–94 | Jesus Rojas WBA | 1998–99 | IBF | 2006–09† |
| Joo-Do Chun IBF | 1983–85 | Katsuya Onizuka | | Mark Johnson IBF | 1999–00 | Simphiwe Nongqayi | |
| Jiro Watanabe* | 1984–86 | WBA | 1993–94 | Hideki Todaka WBA | 1999–00 | IBF | 2009–10 |
| Kaosai Galaxy WBA | 1984 | Lee Hyung-Chul | | Felix Machado IBF | 2000–03 | Juan Alberto Rosas, | |
| Ellyas Pica IBF | 1985–86 | WBA | 1994–95 | M. Tokuyama* WBC | 2000–04 | IBF | 2010 |
| Cesar Polanco IBF | 1986 | Jose Luis Bueno* | | Leo Gamez WBA | 2000–01 | Cristian Mijares IBF | 2010–11† |
| Gilberto Roman* | | WBC | 1993–94 | Celes Kobayashi | | Hugo Cazares WBA | 2010–11 |
| WBC | 1986–87 | H. Kawashima* WBC | 1994–97 | WBA | 2001–02 | Tomas Rojas WBC | 2010–11 |
| Ellyas Pical IBF | 1986 | Harold Grey IBF | 1994–95 | Alexander Munoz | | Suriyan Sor Rungvisai, | |
| Santos Laciar* WBC | 1987 | Alimi Goitia WBA | 1995–96 | WBA | 2002–05 | WBC | 2011– |
| Tae-Il Chang IBF | 1987 | Yokthai Sith-Oar | | Luis Alberto Perez IBF | 2003–06 | Tomonobu Shimizu, | |
| Sugar Rojas* WBC | 1987–88 | WBA | 1996–97 | Katsushige Kawashima | | WBA | 2011– |
| Ellyas Pical IBF | 1987–89 | Carlos Salazar IBF | 1995–96 | WBC | 2004–05 | | |

## Flyweights (Weight Limit: 112 pounds)

| Champion | Reign | Champion | Reign | Champion | Reign | Champion | Reign |
|---|---|---|---|---|---|---|---|
| Sid Smith* | 1913 | Jackie Paterson* | 1943–48 | Masao Ohba WBA | 1970–73 | | 1980–81 |
| Bill Ladbury* | 1913–14 | Rinty Monaghan* | 1948–50† | Erbito Salavarria* | 1970–73† | Santos Laciar WBA | 1981 |
| Percy Jones* | 1914† | Terry Allen* | 1950 | B. Gonzalez WBA | 1972 | Antonio Avelar* WBC 1981–82 | |
| Joe Symonds* | 1914–16 | Dado Marino* | 1950–52 | V. Borkorsor WBC | 1972–73† | Luis Ibarra WBA | 1981 |
| Jimmy Wilde* | 1916–23 | Yoshio Shirai* | 1952–54 | Venice Borkorsor* | 1973† | Juan Herrera WBA | 1981–82 |
| Pancho Villa* | 1923–25† | Pascual Perez* | 1954–60 | Chartchai Chionoi WBA 1973–74 | | P. Cardona* WBC | 1982 |
| Fidel La Barba* | 1925–27† | Pone Kingpetch* | 1960–62 | B. Gonzalez* WBA | 1973–74 | Santos Laciar WBA | 1982–85 |
| Frenchy Belanger* | | Masahiko Harada* | 1962–63 | Shoji Oguma* WBC | 1974–75 | Freddie Castillo* WBC 1982 | |
| NBA | 1927–28 | Pone Kingpetch* | 1963 | S. Hanagata WBA | 1974–75 | E. Mercedes* WBC | 1982–83 |
| Izzy Schwartz NY | 1927–29 | Hiroyuki Ebihara* | 1963–64 | Miguel Canto* WBC | 1975–79 | Charlie Magri* WBC | 1983 |
| Frankie Genaro* | | Pone Kingpetch* | 1964–65 | Erbito Salavarria | | Frank Cedeno* WBC | 1983–84 |
| NBA | 1928–29 | Salvatore Burrini* | 1965–66 | WBA | 1975–76 | Soon-Chun Kwon IBF | 1983–85 |
| Spider Pladner* NBA | 1929 | H. Accavallo WBA | 1966–68 | Alfonso Lopez WBA | 1976 | Koji Kobayashi* | |
| Frankie Genaro* | | Walter McGowan* | 1966 | G. Espadas WBA | 1976–78 | WBC | 1984 |
| NBA | 1929–31 | Chartchai Chionoi* | 1966–69 | B. Gonzalez WBA | 1978–79 | Gabriel Bernal* | |
| Midget Wolgast NY | 1930–35 | Efren Torres* | 1969–70 | Chan-Hee Park* | | WBC | 1984 |
| Young Perez* NBA | 1931–32 | Hiroyuki Ebihara WBA 1969 | | WBC | 1979–80 | Sot Chitalada* WBC | 1984–88 |
| Jackie Brown* NBA | 1932–35 | B. Villacampo WBA | 1969–70 | Luis Ibarra WBA | 1979–80 | Hilario Zapate WBA | 1985–87 |
| Benny Lynch* | 1935–38† | Chartchai Chionoi* | 1970 | Tae-Shik Kim WBA | 1980 | Chong-Kwan Chung | |
| Small Montana NY | 1935–37 | B. Chartvanchai | | Shoji Oguma* WBC | 1980–81 | IBF | 1985–86 |
| Peter Kane* | 1938–43 | WBA | 1970 | Peter Mathebula WBA | | | |
| Little Dado NY | 1938–40 | | | | | | |

*Lineal champion. †Champion relinquished title to retire or switch weight classes, or had title stripped by boxing organization.

## Flyweights (Cont.)

| Champion | Reign | Champion | Reign | Champion | Reign | Champion | Reign |
|---|---|---|---|---|---|---|---|
| Bi-Won Chung IBF | 1986 | M. Kittikasem* WBC | 1991–92 | WBC | 1997–98 | Takefumi Sakata WBA | 2007–08 |
| Hi-Sup Shin IBF | 1986–87 | Yuri Arbachakov* | | Hugo Soto WBA | 1998–99 | Daisuke Naito WBC | 2007–09 |
| Dodie Penalosa IBF | 1987 | WBC | 1992–97 | Manny Pacquiao* WBC | | Nonito Donaire IBF | 2007–09† |
| Fidel Bassa WBA | 1987–89 | Yong Kang Kim WBA | 1991–92 | 1998–99 | | Denkaosan Kaovichit | |
| Choi-Chang Ho IBF | 1987–88 | Rodolfo Blanco IBF | 1992–93 | Leo Gamez WBA | 1999 | WBA | 2008–10 |
| Rolando Bohol IBF | 1988 | P. Sithbangprachan IBF | 1993–95 | Irene Pacheco IBF | 1999–05 | Koki Kameda WBC | 2009–10 |
| Yong-Kang Kim* WBC | 1988–89 | David Griman WBA | 1992–94 | S. Pisnurachan WBA | 1999–00 | Moruti Mthalane IBF | 2009– |
| Duke McKenzie IBF | 1988–89 | S.S. Ploenchit WBA | 1994–96 | M. Sinsurat* WBC | 1999–00 | Daiki Kameda WBA | 2010–11† |
| Sot Chitalada* WBC | 1989–91 | Francisco Tejedor IBF | 1995 | Malcolm Tunacao* WBC | 2000–01 | Pongsaklek Wonjongkam | |
| Dave McAuley IBF | 1989–92 | Danny Romero IBF | 1995–96 | Eric Morel WBA | 2000–03 | WBC | 2010– |
| Jesus Rojas WBA | 1989–90 | Mark Johnson IBF | 1996–99† | P. Wonjongkam* WBC | 2001–07 | Luis Concepcion WBA | 2011 |
| Yul-Woo Lee WBA | 1990 | Jose Bonilla WBA | 1996–98 | Lorenzo Parra WBA | 2003–07 | Hernan Marquez WBA | 2011– |
| L. Tamakuma WBA | 1990–91 | Chatchai Sasakul* | | Vic Darchinyan IBF | 2005–07 | | |

## Light Flyweights (Weight Limit: 108 pounds)

| Champion | Reign | Champion | Reign | Champion | Reign |
|---|---|---|---|---|---|
| Franco Udella WBC | 1975 | German Torres WBC | 1988–89 | Beibis Mendoza WBA | 2000–01 |
| Jaime Rios WBA | 1975–76 | Yul-Woo Lee WBC | 1989 | Rosendo Alvarez WBA | 2001–05 |
| Luis Estaba* WBC | 1975–78 | M. Kittikasem IBF | 1989–90 | Jorge Arce* WBC | 2002–05 |
| Juan Guzman WBA | 1976 | H. Gonzalez WBC | 1989–90 | Jose Burgos IBF | 2003–05 |
| Yoko Gushiken WBA | 1976–81 | Michael Carbajal IBF | 1990–94 | Brian Viloria WBC | 2005–06 |
| Freddy Castillo* WBC | 1978 | R. Pascua WBC | 1990 | R. Vasquez WBA | 2005–06 |
| Sor Vorasingh* WBC | 1978 | M. C. Castro WBC | 1991 | Will Grigsby IBF | 2005–06 |
| Sung-Jun Kim* WBC | 1978–80 | H. Gonzalez WBC | 1991–93 | Koki Kameda WBA | 2006–07 |
| Shigeo Nakajima* WBC | 1980 | Hirokia Ioka* WBA | 1991–92 | Omar Nino Rivero WBC | 2006–07 |
| Hilario Zapata* WBC | 1980–82 | Myung-Woo Yuh* WBA | 1993† | Ulises Solis IBF | 2006–09 |
| Pedro Flores WBA | 1981 | Michael Carbajal* WBC | 1993–94 | Juan Carlos Reveco WBA | 2007 |
| Hwan-Jin Kim WBA | 1981 | Leo Gamez WBA | 1993–95 | Edgar Sosa WBC | 2007–09 |
| Katsuo Tokashiki WBA | 1981–83 | H. Gonzalez* WBC, IBF | 1994–95 | Brahim Asloum WBA | 2007–09† |
| Amado Urzua* WBC | 1982 | Choi Hi-Yong WBA | 1995–96 | Giovanni Segura WBA‡ | 2009–10† |
| Tadashi Tomori* WBC | 1982 | S. Sor Jaturong WBC, IBF | 1995–96 | Brian Viloria IBF | 2009–10 |
| Hilario Zapata* WBC | 1982–83 | Carlos Murillo WBA | 1996 | Rodel Mayol WBC | 2009–10 |
| Jung-Koo Chang* WBC | 1983–88† | Keiji Yamaguchi WBA | 1996 | Omar Nino Romero WBC | 2010 |
| Lupe Madera WBA | 1983–84 | Michael Carbajal IBF | 1996–97 | Carlos Tamara IBF | 2010 |
| Dodie Penalosa IBF | 1983–86 | Saman Jaturong* WBC | 1995–99 | Juan Carlos Reveco WBA | 2010–1 |
| Francisco Quiroz WBA | 1984–85 | Phichitchor Siriwat WBA | 1996–00 | Luis Alberto Lazarte IBF | 2010–11 |
| Joey Olivo WBA | 1985 | Mauricio Pastrana IBF | 1997–98† | Gilberto Keb Bass WBC | 2010–11 |
| Myung-Woo Yuh* WBA | 1985–91 | Will Grigsby IBF | 1998–99 | Ulises Solis IBF | 2011– |
| Jum-Hwan Choi IBF | 1986–88 | Ricardo Lopez IBF | 1999–02 | Adrian Hernandez WBC | 2011– |
| Tacy Macalos IBF | 1988–89 | Yo-Sam Choi* WBC | 1999–02 | Roman Gonzalez WBA | 2011– |

## Strawweights (Weight Limit: 105 pounds)

| Champion | Reign | Champion | Reign | Champion | Reign |
|---|---|---|---|---|---|
| Kyung-Yun Lee* IBF | 1987 | R. Sor Vorapin IBF | 1996–97 | Yukata Niida WBA | 2004–08 |
| Hiroki Ioka* WBC | 1987–88 | Zolani Petelo* IBF | 1997–00† | K. Takayama WBC | 2005 |
| Leo Gamez WBA | 1988–89 | W. Chor Charoen WBC | 1998–00 | Eagle Junlaphan WBC | 2005–07 |
| S. Sithnaruepol IBF | 1988–89 | R. Lopez* WBA, WBC | 1998–99† | M. Rachman IBF | 2005–07 |
| N. Kiatwanchai* WBC | 1988–89 | Songkram Popaoin WBA | 1999 | Florante Condes IBF | 2007–08 |
| Bong-Jun Kim WBA | 1989–91 | Noel Arambulet WBA | 1999–00 | O. Sithsamerchai WBC | 2007–11 |
| Nico Thomas IBF | 1989 | Jose Aguirre* WBC | 2000–04 | Roman Gonzalez WBA | 2008–10† |
| Eric Chavez IBF | 1989–90 | Joma Gamboa WBA | 2000 | Raul Garcia IBF | 2008–10 |
| Jum-Hwan Choi* WBC | 1989–90 | Keitaro Hoshino WBA | 2000–01 | Kwanthai Sithmorseng WBA | 2010–11 |
| Hideyuki Ohashi* WBC | 1990 | Chana Porpaoin WBA | 2001 | Nkosinathi Joyi IBF | 2010– |
| F. Lookmingkwan IBF | 1990–92 | Roberto Leyva IBF | 2001–02 | Muhammad Rachman WBA | 2011 |
| Ricardo Lopez* WBC | 1990–98† | Yutaka Niida WBA | 2001† | Kazuto Ioka WBC | 2011– |
| Hi-Yong Choi WBA | 1991–92 | Miguel Barrera IBF | 2002–03 | Pornsawan Porpramook WBA | 2011– |
| Manny Melchor IBF | 1992 | Edgar Cardenas IBF | 2003 | | |
| Hideyuki Ohashi WBA | 1992–93 | Noel Arambulet WBA | 2002–04 | | |
| R.S. Voraphin IBF | 1992–96 | Daniel Reyes IBF | 2003–05 | | |
| Chana Porpaoin WBA | 1993–95 | Eagle Junlaphan WBC | 2004 | | |
| Rosendo Alvarez WBA | 1995–98 | Isaac Bustos WBC | 2004–05 | | |

*Lineal champion.  †Champion relinquished title to retire or switch weight classes, or had title stripped by boxing organization.

## Lineal Heavyweight Champions

| Champion | Reign | Age* | Career | W-L-D (KO) | SD |
|---|---|---|---|---|---|
| John L. Sullivan | 1885–92 | 26 | 1878–92 | 38-1-3 (33) | 0 |
| James J. Corbett | 1892–97 | 26 | 1884–03 | 11-4-2 (7) | 1 |
| Bob Fitzsimmons | 1897–99 | 33 | 1880–16 | 74-8-3 (67) | 0 |
| James J. Jeffries† | 1899–05 | 24 | 1896–10 | 18-1-2 (15) | 7 |
| Marvin Hart | 1905–06 | 28 | 1899–10 | 28–7–4 (19) | 0 |
| Tommy Burns | 1906–08 | 24 | 1900–20 | 46-5-8 (37) | 11 |
| Jack Johnson | 1908–15 | 30 | 1894–28 | 77-13-14 (48) | 9 |
| Jess Willard | 1915–19 | 33 | 1911–23 | 23-6-1 (20) | 1 |
| Jack Dempsey | 1919–26 | 24 | 1914–27 | 60-6-8 (50) | 5 |
| Gene Tunney† | 1926–28 | 29 | 1915–28 | 61-1-1 (45) | 2 |
| Max Schmeling | 1930–32 | 24 | 1924–48 | 56-10-4 (39) | 1 |
| Jack Sharkey | 1932–33 | 29 | 1924–36 | 38-13-3 (14) | 1 |
| Primo Carnera | 1933–34 | 26 | 1928–37 | 88-14-0 (69) | 2 |
| Max Baer | 1934–35 | 25 | 1929–41 | 72-12-0 (53) | 0 |
| James J. Braddock | 1935–37 | 29 | 1926–38 | 51-26-7 (26) | 0 |
| Joe Louis† | 1937–49 | 23 | 1934–51 | 68-3-0 (54) | 25 |
| Ezzard Charles | 1949–51 | 27 | 1940–59 | 96-25-1 (59) | 8 |
| Jersey Joe Walcott | 1951–52 | 37 | 1930–53 | 53-18-1 (33) | 1 |
| Rocky Marciano† | 1952–56 | 29 | 1947–56 | 49-0-0 (43) | 6 |
| Floyd Patterson | 1956–59 | 21 | 1952–72 | 55-8-1 (40) | 4 |
| Ingemar Johansson | 1959–60 | 26 | 1952–63 | 26-2-0 (17) | 0 |
| Floyd Patterson | 1960–62 | 25 | 1952–72 | 55-8-1 (40) | 2 |
| Sonny Liston | 1962–64 | 30 | 1953–70 | 50-4-0 (39) | 1 |
| Muhammad Ali | 1964–71 | 22 | 1960–81 | 56-5-0 (37) | 9 |
| Joe Frazier | 1971–73 | 27 | 1965–81 | 32-4-1 (27) | 2 |
| George Foreman | 1973–74 | 24 | 1969–97 | 76-5-0 (68) | 2 |
| Muhammad Ali | 1974–78 | 32 | 1960–81 | 56-5-0 (37) | 10 |
| Leon Spinks | 1978 | 24 | 1977–95 | 26-17-3 (14) | 0 |
| Muhammad Ali† | 1978–79 | 36 | 1960–81 | 56-5-0 (37) | 0 |
| Larry Holmes | 1980–85 | 29 | 1973–2002 | 69-6-0 (44) | 20 |
| Michael Spinks | 1985–88 | 29 | 1977–88 | 32-1-0 (21) | 3 |
| Mike Tyson | 1988–90 | 21 | 1985–2005 | 49-4-0 (43) | 2 |
| Buster Douglas | 1990 | 29 | 1981–99 | 38-6-1 (25) | 0 |
| Evander Holyfield | 1990–92 | 28 | 1984– | 38-5-2 (26) | 3 |
| Riddick Bowe | 1992–93 | 25 | 1989–96 | 40-1-0 (32) | 2 |
| Evander Holyfield | 1993–94 | 31 | 1984–94; 1995– | 44-10-2 (29) | 0 |
| Michael Moorer | 1994 | 26 | 1988–97 | 52-4-1 (40) | 0 |
| George Foreman | 1994–97 | 45 | 1969–97 | 76-5-0 (68) | 3 |
| Shannon Briggs | 1997–98 | 25 | 1992–00 | 32-3-1 (25) | 0 |
| Lennox Lewis | 1998–01 | 32 | 1989–2004 | 41-2-1 (32) | 5 |
| Hasim Rahman | 2001 | 28 | 1994– | 50-7-2 (41) | 0 |
| Lennox Lewis‡ | 2001–04 | 36 | 1989–2004 | 41-2-1 (32) | 2 |
| Chris Byrd | 2002–06 | 35 | 1993–2009 | 41-5-1 (20) | 3 |
| John Ruiz | 2001–03 | 31 | 1992–2010 | 44-9-1 (30) | 2 |
| Roy Jones, Jr. | 2003 | 34 | 1989– | 54-8-0 (40) | 0 |
| John Ruiz | 2003–05 | 33 | 1992–2010 | 41-6-1 (28) | 2 |
| Vitali Klitschko† | 2004–05 | 34 | 1996–2005; 2007– | 43-2-0 (40) | 1 |
| Hasim Rahman | 2005-06 | 33 | 1994– | 41-5-2 (33) | 1 |
| Oleg Maskaev | 2006–08 | 37 | 1993–2009 | 36-7-0 (27) | 0 |
| Wladimir Klitschko‡ | 2006– | 33 | 1996– | 56-3-0 (49) | 0 |
| Nikolay Valuev | 2005–07; 2008–09 | 32 | 1993– | 50-2-0 (34) | 1 |
| Ruslan Chagaev | 2007–08 | 28 | 2001– | 27-2-1 (17) | 1 |
| Samuel Peter | 2008 | 28 | 2004– | 34-5-0 (27) | 0 |
| Vitali Klitschko^ | 2008– | 38 | 1996–2005; 2007– | 43-2-0 (40) | 1 |
| Nikolay Valuev | 2008–09 | 36 | 1993– | 50-1-0 (34) | 0 |
| David Haye | 2009–11 | 30 | 2002– | 25-2-0 (23) | 0 |
| Alexander Povetkin | 2011– | 31 | 2005– | 22-0-0 (15) | 0 |

*Age when boxer won world championship.
† Boxer retired or relinquished world title.
‡ Maintains WBA Super Champion status
^ Boxer returned from retirement.

In 2011, South Carolina repeated asCollege World Series champions thanks to clutch hitting by CWS Most Outstanding Player 2B Scott Wingo

# NCAA Sports

# FOR THE RECORD • 2010—2011

## NCAA Team Champions

### Fall 2010

| | | | Champion | Runner-Up |
|---|---|---|---|---|
| **Cross-Country** | MEN | Division I: | Oklahoma St | Florida St |
| | | Division II: | Adams St | Western St |
| | | Division III: | Haverford | North Central (Ill.) |
| | WOMEN | Division I: | Villanova | Florida St |
| | | Division II: | Grand Valley St | Western St |
| | | Division III: | Middlebury | Washington-St. Louis |
| **Field Hockey** | WOMEN | Division I: | Maryland | North Carolina |
| | | Division II | UMass-Lowell | Shippensburg |
| | | Division III: | Bowdoin | Messiah |
| **Football** | MEN | FCS (I-AA): | Eastern Washington | Delaware |
| | | Division II: | Minnesota-Duluth | Delta St |
| | | Division III: | UW-Whitewater | Mount Union |
| **Soccer** | MEN | Division I: | Akron | Louisville |
| | | Division II: | Northern Kentucky | Rollins |
| | | Division III: | Messiah | Lynchburg (Va.) |
| | WOMEN | Division I: | Notre Dame | Stanford |
| | | Division II: | Grand Valley St | UC-San Diego |
| | | Division III: | Hardin-Simmons | Messiah |
| **Volleyball** | WOMEN | Division I: | Penn St | California |
| | | Division II: | Concordia-St. Paul | Tampa |
| | | Division III: | Calvin | Emory |
| **Water Polo** | MEN | | USC | California |

### Winter 2010–11

| | | | Champion | Runner-Up |
|---|---|---|---|---|
| **Bowling** | WOMEN | | Md.-Eastern Shore | Vanderbilt |
| **Basketball** | MEN | Division I: | Connecticut | Butler |
| | | Division II: | Bellarmine | BYU-Hawaii |
| | | Division III: | St. Thomas | Wooster |
| | WOMEN | Division I: | Texas A&M | Notre Dame |
| | | Division II: | Clayton St | Michigan Tech |
| | | Division III: | Amherst | Washington-St. Louis |
| **Fencing** | | | Notre Dame | Penn St |
| **Gymnastics** | MEN | | Stanford | Oklahoma |
| | WOMEN | | Alabama | UCLA |
| **Ice Hockey** | MEN | Division I: | Minnesota-Duluth | Michigan |
| | | Division III: | St. Norbert | Adrian |
| | WOMEN | Division I: | Wisconsin | Boston University |
| | | Division III: | Norwich | RIT |
| **Rifle** | | | Kentucky | West Virginia |
| **Skiing** | | | Colorado | Utah |
| **Swimming and Diving** | MEN | Division I: | California | Texas |
| | | Division II: | Drury | UC-San Diego |
| | | Division III: | Denison | Kenyon |
| | WOMEN | Division I: | California | Georgia |
| | | Division II: | Drury | Wayne St (Mich.) |
| | | Division III: | Emory | Denison |

## Winter 2010-2011 (Cont.)

| | | | Champion | Runner-Up |
|---|---|---|---|---|
| **Wrestling** | MEN | Division I: | Penn St | Cornell |
| | | Division II: | Neb.-Omaha | St. Cloud St |
| | | Division III: | Wartburg | Augsburg (Minn.) |
| **Indoor Track and Field** | MEN | Division I: | Florida | Texas A&M |
| | | Division II: | Abilene Christian | Ashland |
| | | Division III: | North Central (Ill.) | Central College |
| | WOMEN | Division I: | Oregon | Texas |
| | | Division II: | Grand Valley St | Lincoln (Mo.) |
| | | Division III: | UW-Oshkosh | Wartburg |

## Spring 2011

| | | | Champion | Runner-Up |
|---|---|---|---|---|
| **Baseball** | | Division I: | South Carolina | Florida |
| | | Division II: | West Florida | Winona St |
| | | Division III: | Marietta | Chapman |
| **Golf** | MEN | Division I: | Augusta St | Georgia |
| | | Division II: | CSU-Monterey Bay | Lynn |
| | | Division III: | Greensboro | Illinois Wesleyan |
| | WOMEN | Division I: | UCLA | Purdue |
| | | Division II: | Nova Southeastern | Rollins |
| | | Division III | Methodist | Gustavus Adophus |
| **Lacrosse** | MEN | Division I: | Virginia | Maryland |
| | | Division II: | Mercyhurst | Adelphi |
| | | Division III: | Salisbury | Tufts |
| | WOMEN | Division I: | Northwestern | Maryland |
| | | Division II | Adelphi | Limestone |
| | | Division III: | Gettysburg | Bowdoin |
| **Rowing** | WOMEN | Division I: | Brown | Princeton |
| | | Division II | Western Washington | Mercyhurst |
| | | Division III: | Williams | Bates |
| **Softball** | | Division I: | Arizona St | Florida |
| | | Division II: | UC-San Diego | Ala.-Huntsville |
| | | Division III: | Linfield | Chris. Newport |
| **Tennis** | MEN | Division I: | USC | Virginia |
| | | Division II: | Valdosta St | Barry |
| | | Division III: | Amherst | Emory |
| | WOMEN | Division I: | Florida | Stanford |
| | | Division II: | Barry | Lynn |
| | | Division III: | Williams | Amherst |
| **Outdoor Track and Field** | MEN | Division I: | Texas A&M | Florida St |
| | | Division II: | Abilene Christian | Adams St |
| | | Division III: | North Central (Ill.) | UW-LaCrosse |
| | WOMEN | Division I: | Texas A&M | Oregon |
| | | Division II: | Grand Valley St | Lincoln (Mo.) |
| | | Division III: | UW-Oshkosh | Wartburg |
| **Volleyball** | MEN | | Ohio St | UC-Santa Barbara |
| **Water Polo** | WOMEN | | Stanford | California |

# NCAA Division I Individual Champions

## Fall 2010 – Cross Country (Div. I)

| | | |
|---|---|---|
| MEN | **Champion** | **Runner-Up** |
| | Samuel Chelanga, Liberty | Stephen Sambu, Arizona |
| WOMEN | **Champion** | **Runner-Up** |
| | Sheila Reid, Villanova | Emily Infield, Georgetown |

## Winter 2010–11

### Gymnastics

| | Champion | Runner-Up |
|---|---|---|
| **MEN** | | |
| All-around | Sam Mikulak, Michigan | Tyler Mizoguchi, Illinois |
| Vault | Jacob Dalton, Oklahoma | Christian Monteclaro, California |
| Parallel bars | Tyler Mizoguchi, Illinois | Jacob Dalton, Oklahoma |
| Horizontal bar | Alex Buscaglia, Stanford | Ian Mackowske, Michigan |
| Floor exercise | Jacob Dalton, Oklahoma | Steven Legendre, Oklahoma |
| Pommel horse | Alex Naddour, Oklahoma | Daniel Ribeiro, Illinois |
| Rings | Brandon Wynn, Ohio St | Anthony Sacramento, Illinois |
| **WOMEN** | | |
| All-around | Kylee Botterman, Michigan | Kayla Hoffman, Alabama |
| Balance beam | Samantha Peszek, UCLA | Kayla Hoffman, Alabama/ Aisha Gerber, UCLA |
| Uneven bars | Kat Ding, Georgia | Jen Kessler, Oregon St |
| Floor exercise | Geralen Stack-Easton, Alabama | Kylee Botterman, Michigan Brittani McCollough, UCLA Maranda Smith, Florida |
| Vault | Marrisa King, Florida | Madison Mooring, Oklahoma |

### Skiing

| | Champion | Runner-Up |
|---|---|---|
| **MEN** | | |
| Slalom | Tim Kelley, Vermont | Gabriel Rivas, Colorado |
| Giant slalom | Seppi Stiegler, Denver | Kevin Drury, Vermont |
| 10-kilometer free | Sam Tarling, Dartmouth | Vegard Kjoelhamar, Colorado |
| 20-kilometer classic | Reid Pletcher, Colorado | Erik Bjornsen, Alaska-Anchorage |
| **WOMEN** | | |
| Slalom | Sterling Grant, Denver | Lindsay Cone, Denver |
| Giant slalom | Ida Dillingoen, Denver | Sara Hjertman, Colorado |
| 5-kilometer free | Maria Graefnings, Utah | Eliska Hajkova, Colorado |
| 15-kilometer classic | Eliska Hajkova, Colorado | Maria Graefnings, Utah |

### Wrestling

| | Champion | Runner-Up |
|---|---|---|
| 125 lb | Anthony Robles, Arizona St | Matt McDonough, Iowa |
| 133 lb | Jordan Oliver, Oklahoma St | Andrew Hochstrasser, Boise St |
| 141 lb | Kellen Russell, Michigan | Boris Novachkov, Cal Poly |
| 149 lb | Kyle Dake, Cornell | Frank Molinaro, Penn St |
| 157 lb | Bubba Jenkins, Arizona St | David Taylor, Penn St |
| 165 lb | Jordan Burroughs, Nebraska | Tyler Caldwell, Oklahoma |
| 174 lb | Jon Reader, Iowa St | Nick Amuchastegui, Stanford |
| 184 lb | Quentin Wright, Penn St | Robert Hamlin, Lehigh |
| 197 lb | Dustin Kilgore, Kent St | Clayton Foster, Oklahoma St |
| 285 lb | Zach Rey, Lehigh | Ryan Flores, American |

### Swimming and Diving — Men

| | Champion | Time | Runner-Up | Time |
|---|---|---|---|---|
| 50-yd freestyle | Nathan Adrian, California | 18.66a | Adam Brown, Auburn | 18.72 |
| 100-yd freestyle | Nathan Adrian, California | 41.10 | James Feigen, Texas | 41.66 |
| 200-yd freestyle | Brett Fraser, Florida | 1:32.21 | Dax Hill, Texas | 1:32.64 |
| 500-yd freestyle | Matt McLean, Virginia | 4:10.15 | Bobby Bollier, Stanford | 4:13.94 |
| 1650-yd freestyle | Michael McBroom, Texas | 14:32.86 | Martin Grodzki, Georgia | 14:34.80 |
| 100-yd backstroke | Tom Shields, California | 45.02 | Eric Ress, Indiana | 45.14 |
| 200-yd backstroke | Cory Chitwood, Arizona | 1:38.84 | Eric Ress, Indiana | 1:38.96 |
| 100-yd breaststroke | Damir Dugonjic, California | 50.94 | Nolan Koon, California | 51.63 |
| 200-yd breaststroke | Eric Friedland, Texas | 1:52.43 | Martti Aljand, California | 1:52.88 |
| 100-yd butterfly | Austin Staab, Stanford | 44.69 | Tom Shields, California | 44.91 |
| 200-yd butterfly | Mark Dylla, Georgia | 1:40.60 | Bobby Bollier, Stanford | 1:40.76 |
| 200-yd IM | Austin Staab, Stanford | 1:41.57 | Cory Chitwood, Arizona | 1:42.28 |
| 400-yd IM | Bill Cregar, Georgia | 3:40.97 | Kyle Whitaker, Michigan | 3:41.69 |
| 200-yd free relay | Stanford | 1:15.26a | California | 1:15.34 |
| 400-yd free relay | California | 2:47.39 | Auburn | 2:49.47 |
| 800-yd free relay | Florida | 6:14.88 | Virginia | 6:16.59 |
| 200-yd medley relay | California | 1:23.12 | Texas | 1:24.13 |
| 400-yd medley relay | California | 3:02.28 | Texas | 3:06.10 |
| 1-meter diving | David Boudia, Purdue | 461.00 | Grant Nel, Texas A&M | 425.85 |
| 3-meter diving | David Boudia, Purdue | 472.30 | Grant Nel, Texas A&M | 471.35 |
| Platform | Nick McCrory, Duke | 548.90 | David Boudia, Purdue | 479.10 |

a-American record.

## Winter 2010-11 (Cont.)
### Swimming and Diving — Women

| | Champion | Time/Pts | Runner-Up | Time/Pts |
|---|---|---|---|---|
| 50-yd freestyle | A. Vanderpool-Wallace, Auburn | 21.38 | Liv Jensen, California | 20.50 |
| 100-yd freestyle | A. Vanderpool-Wallace, Auburn | 47.07 | Kate Dwelley, Stanford | 47.78 |
| 200-yd freestyle | Allison Schmitt, Georgia | 1:42.08 | Laure Perdue, Virginia | 1:42.51 |
| 500-yd freestyle | Allison Schmitt, Georgia | 4:34.20 | Meredith Budner, Towson | 4:34.56 |
| 1650-yd freestyle | Wendy Trott, Georgia | 15:40.32 | Meredith Budner, Towson | 15:44.26 |
| 100-yd backstroke | Cindy Tran, California | 51.30 | Deborah Roth, California | 51.51 |
| 200-yd backstroke | Maggie Meyer, Wisconsin | 1:50.76 | Dominique Bouchard, Missouri | 1:51.54 |
| 100-yd breaststroke | Jillian Tyler, Minnesota | 58.39 | Breeja Larson, Texas A&M | 58.51 |
| 200-yd breaststroke | Haley Spencer, Minnesota | 2:06.12 | Breeja Larson, Texas A&M | 2:06.18 |
| 100-yd butterfly | Amanda Sims, California | 50.49 | Claire Donahue, Western Ky. | 51.68 |
| 200-yd butterfly | Katinka Hosszu, USC | 1:51.69 | Cammile Adams, Texas A&M | 1:52.93 |
| 200-yd IM | Katinka Hosszu, USC | 1:53.39 | Julia Wilkinson, Texas A&M | 1:54.45 |
| 400-yd IM | Katinka Hosszu, USC | 3:59.75 | Elizabeth Beisel, Florida | 4:00.87 |
| 200-yd free relay | California | 1:27.36 | Arizona | 1:28.02 |
| 400-yd free relay | Georgia | 3:11.30 | Auburn | 3:11.70 |
| 800-yd free relay | Georgia | 6:55.40 | California | 6:58.71 |
| 200-yd medley relay | California | 1:35.03 | Wisconsin | 1:35.71 |
| 400-yd medley relay | California | 3:28.53 | USC | 3:29.82 |
| 1-meter diving | Kelci Bryant, Minnesota | 349.65 | Lauren Figueroa, Missouri | 335.30 |
| 3-meter diving | Abby Johnston, Duke | 409.35 | Kelci Bryant, Minnesota | 395.85 |
| Platform | Brittany Viola, Miami (Fla.) | 354.25 | Elina Eggers, Arizona St | 345.60 |

*NCAA record.   #American reKatrin Smigun, Utah**Indoor Track and Field**

### Indoor Track and Field — Men

| | Champion | Time/Mark | Runner-Up | Time/Mark |
|---|---|---|---|---|
| 60-meter dash | Jeff Demps, Florida | 6.53 | Michael Granger, Mississippi | 6.55 |
| 60-meter hurdles | Andrew Riley, Illinois | 7.58 | Barrett Nugent, LSU | 7.61 |
| 200-meter dash | Rakieem Salaam, Oklahoma | 20.41 | Maurice Mitchell, Florida St | 20.41 |
| 400-meter dash | Demetrius Pinder, Texas A&M | 45.33 | Torrin Lawrence, Georgia | 45.96 |
| 800-meter run | Fred Samoei, Alabama | 1:48.33 | Michael Rutt, Connecticut | 1:48.37 |
| 4x400-meter relay | Texas A&M | 3:04.24 | Baylor | 3:05.42 |
| Mile run | Miles Batty, BYU | 3:59.49 | Chris O'Hare, Tulsa | 3:59.62 |
| 3,000-meter run | Elliott Heath, Stanford | 8:03.71 | Ben Blankenship, Minnesota | 8:04.65 |
| 5,000-meter run | Leonard Korir, Iona | 13:26.01 | Sam Chelanga, Liberty | 13:27.34 |
| Distance medley | BYU | 9:29.28 | Indiana | 9:29.65 |
| High jump | Derek Drouin, Indiana | 2.33m | Ricky Roberston, Mississippi | 2.23m |
| Pole Vault | Scott Roth, Washington | §5.50m | Ben Peterson, Minnesota | 5.50m |
| Long jump | Ngonidzashe Makusha, Florida St | 8.14m | Will Claye, Florida | 8.04m |
| Triple jump | Will Claye, Florida | 17.32m | Christian Taylor, Florida | 16.99m |
| Shot put | Leif Arrhenius, BYU | 19.92m | Mason Finley, Kansas | 19.75m |
| 35-pound wt throw | Walter Henning, LSU | 22.16m | Alexander Ziegler, Virginia Tech | 21.27m |
| Heptathlon | Miller Moss, Clemson | 5,986 pts | Lars Rice, Missouri | 5,902 pts |

### Indoor Track and Field — Women

| | Champion | Time/Mark | Runner-Up | Time/Mark |
|---|---|---|---|---|
| 60-meter dash | Lakya Brookins, South Carolina | 7.09 | Jessica Young, TCU | 7.17 |
| 60-meter hurdles | Brianna Rollins, Clemson | 7.96 | Tiffani Reynolds, Baylor | 8.03 |
| 200-meter dash | Kimberlyn Duncan, LSU | 22.85 | Jeneba Tarmoh, Texas A&M | 22.88 |
| 400-meter dash | Jessica Beard, Texas A&M | 50.79 | Regina George, Arkansas | 52.30 |
| 800-meter run | Lacey Bleazard, BYU | 2:04.09 | Jillian Smith, Michigan | 2:04.78 |
| 4x400-meter relay | Texas A&M | 3:29.72 | Arkansas | 3:30.08 |
| Mile run | Jordan Hasay, Oregon | 4:33.01 | Kate Van Buskirk, Duke | 4:33.71 |
| 3,000-meter run | Jordan Hasay, Oregon | 9:13.71 | Sheila Reid, Villanova | 9:13.86 |
| 5,000-meter run | Jackie Areson, Tennessee | 16:04.16 | Mia Behm, Texas | 16:08.56 |
| Distance medley | Villanova | 10:52.52 | Oregon | 10:52.90 |
| High jump | Brigetta Barrett, Arizona | 1.90m | Shannay Briscoe, Texas | 1.87m |
| Pole vault | Tina Sutej, Arkansas | 4.45m | Katerina Stefandi, Stanford | 4.40m |
| Long jump | Tori Bowie, Southern Mississippi | 6.52m | Kimberly Williams, Florida St | 6.40m |
| Triple jump | Kimberly Williams, Florida St | 13.96m | April Sinkler, Clemson | 13.46m |
| Shot Put | Julie Labonte, Arizona | 17.53m | Tia Brooks, Oklahoma | 17.40m |
| 20-pound wt throw | Felisha Johnson, Indiana St | 22.69m | Jeneva McCall, Southern Illinois | 22.46m |
| Pentathlon | Brianne Theisen, Oregon | 4,540 pts | Chantae McMillan, Nebraska | 4,396 pts |

### Rifle

| | Champion | Pts | Runner-Up | Pts |
|---|---|---|---|---|
| Smallbore | Ethan Settlemires, Kentucky | 691.0 | Nicco Campriani, West Virginia | 689.0 |
| Air rifle | Nicco Campriani, West Virginia | 701.0 | Petra Zublasing, West Virginia | 698.1 |

§-Final place determined by which athlete cleared height first.

## Spring 2011

### Golf

| | Champion | Score | Runners-Up | Score |
|---|---|---|---|---|
| MEN | John Peterson, LSU | 211 | Patrick Cantlay, UCLA | 212 |
| WOMEN | Austin Ernst, LSU | 281 | Kelli Shean, Arkansas | 284 |

### Outdoor Track and Field

#### MEN

| | Champion | Mark | Runner-Up | Mark |
|---|---|---|---|---|
| 100-meter dash | Ngonidzashe Makusha, Florida St | 9.89 | Rakieem Salaam, Oklahoma | 9.97 |
| 200-meter dash | Maurice Mitchell, Florida St | 19.99 | Marek Niit, Arkansas | 20.38 |
| 400-meter dash | Kirani James, Alabama | 45.10 | Tony McQuay, Florida | 45.14 |
| 4x100-meter relay | Florida St | 38.77 | Texas A&M | 38.91 |
| 800-meter run | Robby Andrews, Virginia | 1:44.71 | Charles Jock, UC-Irvine | 1:44.75 |
| 1,500-meter run | Matthew Centrowitz, Oregon | 3:42.54 | Dorian Ulrey, Arkansas | 3:43.06 |
| 4x400-meter relay | Texas A&M | 3:00.62 | LSU | 3:01.07 |
| 5,000-meter run | Sam Chelanga, Liberty | 13:29.30 | Lawi Lalang, Arizona | 13:31.69 |
| 10,000-meter run | Leonard Korir, Iona | 28:07.63 | Sam Chelanga, Liberty | 28:12.18 |
| 110-meter hurdles | Barrett Nugent, LSU | 13.28 | Andrew Riley, Illinois | 13.33 |
| 400-meter hurdles | Jeshua Anderson, Washington St | 48.56 | Amaechi Morton, Stanford | 49.08 |
| 3,000-meter steeple | Matt Hughes, Louisville | 8:24.87 | Donn Cabral, Princeton | 8:32.14 |
| High jump | Erik Kynard, Kansas St | 2.29m | Ricky Robertson, Mississippi | 2.26m |
| Pole vault | Scott Roth, Washington | 5.40m | Jack Whitt, Oral Roberts | 5.35m |
| Long jump | Damar Forbes, LSU | 8.23m | Tarik Batchelor, Arkansas | 7.94m |
| Triple jump | Christian Taylor, Florida | 17.80m | Hasheem Halim, Virginia Tech | 16.25m |
| Shot put | Jordan Clarke, Arizona St | 19.75m | Leif Arrhenius, BYU | 19.37m |
| Discus throw | Julian Wruck, Texas Tech | 61.81m | Mason Finley, Kansas | 60.16m |
| Hammer throw | Marcel Lomnicky, Virginia Tech | 72.35m | Walter Henning, LSU | 69.03m |
| Javelin throw | Tim Glover, Illinois St | 80.33m | Sam Humphreys, Texas A&M | 75.05m |
| Decathlon | Michael Morrison, California | 8,118 pts | Curtis Beach, Duke | 8,084 pts |

#### WOMEN

| | Champion | Mark | Runner-Up | Mark |
|---|---|---|---|---|
| 100-meter dash | Candyce McGrone, Oklahoma | 11.08 | Kimberlyn Duncan, LSU | 11.09 |
| 200-meter dash | Kimberlyn Duncan, LSU | 22.24 | Jeneba Tarmoh, Texas A&M | 22.34 |
| 400-meter dash | Jessica Beard, Texas A&M | 51.10 | Joanna Atkins, Auburn | 51.50 |
| 4x100-meter relay | LSU | 42.64 | Texas A&M | 42.93 |
| 800-meter run | Anne Kesselring, Oregon | 2:02.15 | Natalja Piliusina, Oklahoma St | 2:02.16 |
| 1,500-meter run | Sheila Reid, Villanova | 4:14.57 | Lucy Van Dalen, Stony Brook | 4:15.33 |
| 4x400-meter relay | Texas A&M | 3:26.31 | Auburn | 3:26.46 |
| 5,000-meter run | Sheila Reid, Villanova | 15:37.57 | Emily Infeld, Georgetown | 15:38.23 |
| 10,000-meter run | Juliet Bottorff, Duke | 34:25.86 | Kate Harrison, West Virginia | 34:30.35 |
| 100-meter hurdles | Nia Ali, USC | 12.63 | Christina Manning, Ohio St | 12.72 |
| 400-meter hurdles | Ti'erra Brown, Miami (Fla.) | 55.65 | Turquoise Thompson, UCLA | 55.65 |
| 3,000-meter steeple | Emma Coburn, Colorado | 9:41.14 | Stephanie Garcia, Virginia | 9:47.29 |
| High jump | Brigetta Barrett, Arizona | 1.86m | Victoria Lucas, Texas | §1.83m |
| Pole vault | Melissa Gergel, Oregon | §4.45m | Tina Sutej, Arkansas | 4.45m |
| Long jump | Jamesha Youngblood, Oregon | 6.59m | Whitney Gipson, TCU | 6.51m |
| Triple jump | Patricia Mamona, Clemson | 14.05m | Kimberly Williams, Florida St | 13.67m |
| Shot put | Tia Brooks, Oklahoma | 18.00m | Annie Alexander, Tennessee | 17.66m |
| Discus throw | Annie Alexander, Tennessee | 57.55m | Simone du Toit, SMU | 56.83m |
| Hammer throw | Jeneva McCall, Southern Illinois | 67.74m | Chelsea Cassulo, UNLV | 64.07m |
| Javelin throw | Brittany Borman, Oklahoma | 54.32m | Eda Karesin, Stanford | 52.33m |
| Heptathlon | Ryann Krais, Kansas St | 5,961 pts | Liane Weber, Clemson | 5,857 pts |

### Tennis

| | | Champion | Score | Runner-Up |
|---|---|---|---|---|
| MEN | Singles | Steve Johnson, USC | 4–6, 6–2, 6–1 | Rhyne Williams, Tennessee |
| | Doubles | J. Dadamo/A. Krajicek | 7–6 (4), 6–3 | B. Klahn/R. Thacher, Stanford |
| | | Texas A&M | | |
| WOMEN | Singles | Jana Juricova, California | 6–0, 7–6 (2) | Stacey Tan, Stanford |
| | Doubles | H. Barte/M. Burdette, Stanford | 7–6 (6), 6–0 | J. Bek/K. Wong, Clemson |

§—Final place determined by which athlete cleared height first.

# FOR THE RECORD • Year by Year
## CHAMPIONSHIP RESULTS
### Baseball

**DIVISION I**

| Year | Champion | Coach | Score | Runner-Up | Most Outstanding Player |
|------|----------|-------|-------|-----------|-------------------------|
| 1947 ....California* | Clint Evans | 8–7 | Yale | No award |
| 1948 ....USC | Sam Barry | 9–2 | Yale | No award |
| 1949 ....Texas* | Bibb Falk | 10–3 | Wake Forest | Charles Teague, Wake Forest, 2B |
| 1950 ....Texas | Bibb Falk | 3–0 | Washington St | Ray VanCleef, Rutgers, CF |
| 1951 ....Oklahoma* | Jack Baer | 3–2 | Tennnessee | Sidney Hatfield, Tennessee, P-1B |
| 1952 ....Holy Cross | Jack Barry | 8–4 | Missouri | James O'Neill, Holy Cross, P |
| 1953 ....Michigan | Ray Fisher | 7–5 | Texas | J.L. Smith, Texas, P |
| 1954 ....Missouri | John (Hi) Simmons | 4–1 | Rollins | Tom Yewcic, Michigan St, C |
| 1955 ....Wake Forest | Taylor Sanford | 7–6 | Western Michigan | Tom Borland, Oklahoma St, P |
| 1956 ....Minnesota | Dick Siebert | 12–1 | Arizona | Jerry Thomas, Minnesota, P |
| 1957 ....California* | George Wolfman | 1–0 | Penn St | Cal Emery, Penn St, P-1B |
| 1958 ....USC | Rod Dedeaux | 8–7† | Missouri | Bill Thom, USC, P |
| 1959 ....Oklahoma St | Toby Greene | 5–3 | Arizona | Jim Dobson, Oklahoma St, 3B |
| 1960 ....Minnesota | Dick Siebert | 2–1‡ | USC | John Erickson, Minnesota, 2B |
| 1961 ....USC* | Rod Dedeaux | 1–0 | Oklahoma St | Littleton Fowler, Oklahoma St, P |
| 1962 ....Michigan | Don Lund | 5–4 | Santa Clara | Bob Garibaldi, Santa Clara, P |
| 1963 ....USC | Rod Dedeaux | 5–2 | Arizona | Bud Hollowell, USC, C |
| 1964 ....Minnesota | Dick Siebert | 5–1 | Missouri | Joe Ferris, Maine, P |
| 1965 ....Arizona St | Bobby Winkles | 2–1# | Ohio St | Sal Bando, Arizona St, 3B |
| 1966 ....Ohio St | Marty Karow | 8–2 | Oklahoma St | Steve Arlin, Ohio St, P |
| 1967 ....Arizona St | Bobby Winkles | 11–2 | Houston | Ron Davini, Arizona St, C |
| 1968 ....USC* | Rod Dedeaux | 4–3 | Southern Illinois | Bill Seinsoth, USC, 1B |
| 1969 ....Arizona St | Bobby Winkles | 10–1 | Tulsa | John Dolinsek, Arizona St, LF |
| 1970 ....USC | Rod Dedeaux | 2–1 | Florida St | Gene Ammann, Florida St, P |
| 1971 ....USC | Rod Dedeaux | 7–2 | Southern Illinois | Jerry Tabb, Tulsa, 1B |
| 1972 ....USC | Rod Dedeaux | 1–0 | Arizona St | Russ McQueen, USC, P |
| 1973 ....USC* | Rod Dedeaux | 4–3 | Arizona St | Dave Winfield, Minnesota, P-OF |
| 1974 ....USC | Rod Dedeaux | 7–3 | Miami (Fla.) | George Milke, USC, P |
| 1975 ....Texas | Cliff Gustafson | 5–1 | S Carolina | Mickey Reichenbach, Texas, 1B |
| 1976 ....Arizona | Jerry Kindall | 7–1 | Eastern Michigan | Steve Powers, Arizona, P-DH |
| 1977 ....Arizona St | Jim Brock | 2–1 | S Carolina | Bob Horner, Arizona St, 3B |
| 1978 ....USC* | Rod Dedeaux | 10–3 | Arizona St | Rod Boxberger, USC, P |
| 1979 ....CSU–Fullerton | Augie Garrido | 2–1 | Arkansas | Tony Hudson, CSU–Fullerton, P |
| 1980 ....Arizona | Jerry Kindall | 5–3 | Hawaii | Terry Francona, Arizona, LF |
| 1981 ....Arizona St | Jim Brock | 7–4 | Oklahoma St | Stan Holmes, Arizona St, LF |
| 1982 ....Miami (Fla.)* | Ron Fraser | 9–3 | Wichita St | Dan Smith, Miami (Fla.), P |
| 1983 ....Texas* | Cliff Gustafson | 4–3 | Alabama | Calvin Schiraldi, Texas, P |
| 1984 ....CSU–Fullerton | Augie Garrido | 3–1 | Texas | John Fishel, CSU–Fullerton, LF |
| 1985 ....Miami (Fla.) | Ron Fraser | 10–6 | Texas | Greg Ellena, Miami (Fla.), DH |
| 1986 ....Arizona | Jerry Kindall | 10–2 | Florida St | Mike Senne, Arizona, LF |
| 1987 ....Stanford | Mark Marquess | 9–5 | Oklahoma St | Paul Carey, Stanford, RF |
| 1988 ....Stanford | Mark Marquess | 9–4 | Arizona St | Lee Plemel, Stanford, P |
| 1989 ....Wichita St | Gene Stephenson | 5–3 | Texas | Greg Brummett, Wichita St, P |
| 1990 ....Georgia | Steve Webber | 2–1 | Oklahoma St | Mike Rebhan, Georgia, P |
| 1991 ....LSU | Skip Bertman | 6–3 | Wichita St | Gary Hymel, LSU, C |
| 1992 ....Pepperdine | Andy Lopez | 3–2 | CSU–Fullerton | Phil Nevin, CSU–Fullerton, 3B |
| 1993 ....LSU | Skip Bertman | 8–0 | Wichita St | Todd Walker, LSU, 2B |
| 1994 ....Oklahoma | Larry Cochell | 13–5 | Georgia Tech | Chip Glass, Oklahoma, CF |
| 1995 ....CSU–Fullerton* | Augie Garrido | 11–5 | USC | Mark Kotsay, CSU–Fullerton, CF-P |
| 1996 ....LSU* | Skip Bertman | 9–8 | Miami (Fla.) | Pat Burrell, Miami (Fla.), 3B |
| 1997 ....LSU* | Skip Bertman | 13–6 | Alabama | Brandon Larson, LSU, SS |
| 1998 ....USC | Mike Gillespie | 21–14 | Arizona St | Wes Rachels, USC, 2B |
| 1999 ....Miami (Fla.) | Jim Morris | 6–5 | Florida St | Marshall McDougall, FSU 3B/2B |
| 2000 ....LSU* | Skip Bertman | 6–5 | Stanford | Trey Hodges, LSU, P |
| 2001.....Miami (Fla.)* | Jim Morris | 12–1 | Stanford | Charlton Jimerson, Miami (Fla.), OF |
| 2002 ....Texas | Augie Garrido | 12–6 | South Carolina | Huston Street, Texas, P |
| 2003 ....Rice | Wayne Graham | 14–2^ | Stanford | John Hudgins, Stanford, P |
| 2004 ....CSU–Fullerton | George Horton | 3–2^ | Texas | Jason Windsor, CSU–Fullerton |
| 2005 ....Texas | Augie Garrido | 6–2^ | Florida | David Maroul, Texas |

*Undefeated teams in College World Series play.
†12 innings.  ‡10 innings.  #15 innings.  ^Score of decisive game of best-of-three series.

## DIVISION I (CONT.)

| Year | Champion | Coach | Score | Runner-Up | Most Outstanding Player |
|------|----------|-------|-------|-----------|-------------------------|
| 2006 ....Oregon St | Pat Casey | 3–2^ | North Carolina | Jonah Nickerson, Oregon St, P |
| 2007 ....Oregon St | Pat Casey | 9–3^ | North Carolina | Jorge Reyes, Oregon St, P |
| 2008 ....Fresno St | Mike Batesole | 6–1^ | Georgia | Tommy Mendonca. Fresno St, 3B |
| 2009 ....LSU | Paul Mainieri | 11–4^ | Texas | Jared Mitchell, LSU, OF |
| 2010 ....South Carolina | Ray Tanner | 2–1^† | UCLA | Jackie Bradley Jr., South Carolina, OF |
| 2011 ....South Carolina | Ray Tanner | 5–2^ | Florida | Scott Wingo, South Carolina, 2B |

*Undefeated teams in College World Series play. †11 innings. ^Score of decisive game of best-of-three series.

## DIVISION II

| Year | Champion |
|------|----------|
| 1968 ...Chapman* |
| 1969 ...Illinois St* |
| 1970 ...CSU-Northridge |
| 1971 ...Florida Southern |
| 1972 ...Florida Southern |
| 1973 ...UC–Irvine* |
| 1974 ...UC–Irvine |
| 1975 ...Florida Southern |
| 1976 ...Cal Poly–Pomona |
| 1977 ...UC–Riverside |
| 1978 ...Florida Southern |
| 1979 ...Valdosta St |
| 1980 ...Cal Poly–Pomona* |
| 1981 ...Florida Southern* |

| Year | Champion |
|------|----------|
| 1982 ...UC–Riverside* |
| 1983 ...Cal Poly–Pomona* |
| 1984 ...CSU–Northridge |
| 1985 ...Florida Southern* |
| 1986 ...Troy St |
| 1987 ...Troy St* |
| 1988 ...Florida Southern* |
| 1989 ...Cal Poly–SLO |
| 1990 ...Jacksonville St |
| 1991 ...Jacksonville St |
| 1992 ...Tampa* |
| 1993 ...Tampa |
| 1994 ...Central Missouri St |
| 1995 ...Florida Southern* |
| 1996 ...Kennesaw St* |

| Year | Champion |
|------|----------|
| 1997 ...CSU–Chico* |
| 1998 ...Tampa* |
| 1999 ...CSU–Chico |
| 2000 ...SE Oklahoma St |
| 2001 ...St. Mary's (Tex.) |
| 2002 ...Columbus St |
| 2003 ...Central Missouri St |
| 2004 ...Kennesaw St |
| 2005 ...Florida Southern |
| 2006 ...Tampa |
| 2007 ...Tampa |
| 2008 ...Mount Olive |
| 2009 ...Lynn |
| 2010 ...Southern Indiana |
| 2011 ...West Florida |

## DIVISION III

| Year | Champion |
|------|----------|
| 1976 .........CSU-Stanislaus |
| 1977 .........CSU-Stanislaus |
| 1978 .........Glassboro St |
| 1979 .........Glassboro St |
| 1980 .........Ithaca |
| 1981 .........Marietta |
| 1982 .........Eastern Connecticut St |
| 1983 .........Marietta |
| 1984 .........Ramapo |
| 1985 .........UW-Oshkosh |
| 1986 .........Marietta |
| 1987 .........Montclair St |

| Year | Champion |
|------|----------|
| 1988 .........Ithaca |
| 1989 .........N. Carolina Wesleyan |
| 1990 .........Eastern Connecticut St |
| 1991 .........Southern Maine |
| 1992 .........William Paterson |
| 1993 .........Montclair St |
| 1994 .........UW-Oshkosh |
| 1995 .........La Verne |
| 1996 .........William Paterson |
| 1997 .........Southern Maine |
| 1998 .........Eastern Connecticut St |
| 1999 .........N.Carolina Wesleyan |

| Year | Champion |
|------|----------|
| 2000 .........Montclair St |
| 2001 .........St. Thomas (Minn.) |
| 2002 .........Eastern Connecticut St |
| 2003 .........Chapman |
| 2004 .........UW-Stevens Pt |
| 2005 .........Wisconsin |
| 2006 .........Marietta |
| 2007 .........Kean |
| 2008 .........Trinity (Conn.) |
| 2009 .........St. Thomas (Minn.) |
| 2010 .........Illinois Wesleyan |
| 2011 .........Marietta |

# Ice Hockey

## Men

### DIVISION I

| Year | Champion | Coach | Score | Runner-Up | Most Outstanding Player |
|------|----------|-------|-------|-----------|-------------------------|
| 1948 .....Michigan | Vic Heyliger | 8–4 | Dartmouth | Joe Riley, Dartmouth, F |
| 1949 .....Boston College | John Kelley | 4–3 | Dartmouth | Dick Desmond, Dartmouth, G |
| 1950 .....Colorado College | Cheddy Thompson | 13–4 | Boston University | Ralph Bevins, Boston University, G |
| 1951 .....Michigan | Vic Heyliger | 7–1 | Brown | Ed Whiston, Brown, G |
| 1952 .....Michigan | Vic Heyliger | 4–1 | Colorado College | Kenneth Kinsley, Colorado Coll, G |
| 1953 .....Michigan | Vic Heyliger | 7–3 | Minnesota | John Matchefts, Michigan, F |
| 1954 .....Rensselaer | Ned Harkness | 5–4 (OT) | Minnesota | Abbie Moore, Rensselaer, F |
| 1955 .....Michigan | Vic Heyliger | 5–3 | Colorado College | Philip Hilton, Colorado College, D |
| 1956 .....Michigan | Vic Heyliger | 7–5 | Michigan Tech | Lorne Howes, Michigan, G |
| 1957 .....Colorado College | Thomas Bedecki | 13–6 | Michigan | Bob McCusker, Colorado Coll, F |
| 1958 .....Denver | Murray Armstrong | 6–2 | North Dakota | Murray Massier, Denver, F |
| 1959 .....North Dakota | Bob May | 4–3 (OT) | Michigan St | Reg Morelli, North Dakota, F |
| 1960 .....Denver | Murray Armstrong | 5–3 | Michigan Tech | Bob Marquis, Boston University, F |
| 1961 .....Denver | Murray Armstrong | 12–2 | St. Lawrence | Barry Urbanski, Boston Univ, G |
| 1962 .....Michigan Tech | John MacInnes | 7–1 | Clarkson | Louis Angotti, Michigan Tech, F |
| 1963 .....North Dakota | Barney Thorndycraft | 6–5 | Denver | Al McLean, North Dakota, F |
| 1964 .....Michigan | Allen Renfrew | 6–3 | Denver | Bob Gray, Michigan, G |
| 1965 .....Michigan Tech | John MacInnes | 8–2 | Boston College | Gary Milroy, Michigan Tech, F |
| 1966 .....Michigan St | Amo Bessone | 6–1 | Clarkson | Gaye Cooley, Michigan St, G |
| 1967 .....Cornell | Ned Harkness | 4–1 | Boston University | Walt Stanowski, Cornell, D |

## Men (Cont.)

### DIVISION I (CONT.)

| Year | Champion | Coach | Score | Runner-Up | Most Outstanding Player |
|------|----------|-------|-------|-----------|-------------------------|
| 1968 | Denver | Murray Armstrong | 4–0 | North Dakota | Gerry Powers, Denver, G |
| 1969 | Denver | Murray Armstrong | 4–3 | Cornell | Keith Magnuson, Denver, D |
| 1970 | Cornell | Ned Harkness | 6–4 | Clarkson | Daniel Lodboa, Cornell, D |
| 1971 | Boston University | Jack Kelley | 4–2 | Minnesota | Dan Brady, Boston University, G |
| 1972 | Boston University | Jack Kelley | 4–0 | Cornell | Tim Regan, Boston University, G |
| 1973 | Wisconsin | Bob Johnson | 4–2 | Vacated | Dean Talafous, Wisconsin, F |
| 1974 | Minnesota | Herb Brooks | 4–2 | Michigan Tech | Brad Shelstad, Minnesota, G |
| 1975 | Michigan Tech | John MacInnes | 6–1 | Minnesota | Jim Warden, Michigan Tech, G |
| 1976 | Minnesota | Herb Brooks | 6–4 | Michigan Tech | Tom Vanelli, Minnesota, F |
| 1977 | Wisconsin | Bob Johnson | 6–5 (OT) | Michigan | Julian Baretta, Wisconsin, G |
| 1978 | Boston University | Jack Parker | 5–3 | Boston College | Jack O'Callahan, Boston Univ, D |
| 1979 | Minnesota | Herb Brooks | 4–3 | North Dakota | Steve Janaszak, Minnesota, G |
| 1980 | North Dakota | John Gasparini | 5–2 | Northern Michigan | Doug Smail, North Dakota, F |
| 1981 | Wisconsin | Bob Johnson | 6–3 | Minnesota | Marc Behrend, Wisconsin, G |
| 1982 | North Dakota | John Gasparini | 5–2 | Wisconsin | Phil Sykes, North Dakota, F |
| 1983 | Wisconsin | Jeff Sauer | 6–2 | Harvard | Marc Behrend, Wisconsin, G |
| 1984 | Bowling Green | Jerry York | 5–4 (OT) | Minn.–Duluth | Gary Kruzich, Bowling Green, G |
| 1985 | Rensselaer | Mike Addesa | 2–1 | Providence | Chris Terreri, Providence, G |
| 1986 | Michigan St | Ron Mason | 6–5 | Harvard | Mike Donnelly, Michigan St, F |
| 1987 | North Dakota | John Gasparini | 5–3 | Michigan St | Tony Hrkac, North Dakota, F |
| 1988 | Lake Superior St | Frank Anzalone | 4–3 (OT) | St. Lawrence | Bruce Hoffort, Lake Superior St, G |
| 1989 | Harvard | Bill Cleary | 4–3 (OT) | Minnesota | Ted Donato, Harvard, F |
| 1990 | Wisconsin | Jeff Sauer | 7–3 | Colgate | Chris Tancill, Wisconsin, F |
| 1991 | Northern Michigan | Rick Comley | 8–7 (3OT) | Boston University | Scott Beattie, Northern Michigan, F |
| 1992 | Lake Superior St | Jeff Jackson | 4–2 | Wisconsin | Paul Constantin, Lake Superior St, F |
| 1993 | Maine | Shawn Walsh | 5–4 | Lake Superior St | Jim Montgomery, Maine, F |
| 1994 | Lake Superior St | Jeff Jackson | 9–1 | Boston University | Sean Tallaire, Lake Superior St, F |
| 1995 | Boston University | Jack Parker | 6–2 | Maine | Chris O'Sullivan, Boston Univ, F |
| 1996 | Michigan | Red Berenson | 3–2 (OT) | Colorado College | Brendan Morrison, Michigan, F |
| 1997 | North Dakota | Dean Blais | 6–4 | Boston University | Matt Henderson, North Dakota, F |
| 1998 | Michigan | Red Berenson | 3–2 (OT) | Boston College | Marty Turco, Michigan, G |
| 1999 | Maine | Shawn Walsh | 3–2 (OT) | New Hampshire | Alfie Michaud, Maine, G |
| 2000 | North Dakota | Dean Blais | 4–2 | Boston College | Lee Goren, North Dakota, F |
| 2001 | Boston College | Jerry York | 3–2 (OT) | North Dakota | Chuck Kobasew, Boston Coll, F |
| 2002 | Minnesota | Don Lucia | 4–3 (OT) | Maine | Grant Potulny, Minnesota, F |
| 2003 | Minnesota | Don Lucia | 5–1 | New Hampshire | Thomas Vanek, Minnesota, F |
| 2004 | Denver | George Gwozdecky | 1–0 | Maine | Adam Berkhoel, Denver, G |
| 2005 | Denver | George Gwozdecky | 4–1 | North Dakota | Peter Mannino, Denver |
| 2006 | Wisconsin | Mike Eaves | 2–1 | Boston College | Robbie Earl, Wisconsin, F |
| 2007 | Michigan St | Rick Comley | 3–1 | Boston College | Justin Abdelkader, Michigan St, F |
| 2008 | Boston College | Jerry York | 4–1 | Notre Dame | Nathan Gerbe, Boston Coll, F |
| 2009 | Boston University | Jack Parker | 4–3 (OT) | Miami (Ohio) | Colby Cohen, Boston University, D |
| 2010 | Boston College | Jerry York | 5–0 | Wisconsin | Ben Smith, Boston College, F |
| 2011 | Minn.–Duluth | Scott Sandelin | 3–2 (OT) | Michigan | J.T. Brown, Minn.-Dultuth, F |

### DIVISION II (Discontinued)

| Year | Champion | Coach | Score | Runner-Up |
|------|----------|-------|-------|-----------|
| 1978 | Merrimack | Thom Lawler | 12–2 | Lake Forest |
| 1979 | Lowell | Bill Riley Jr | 6–4 | Mankato St |
| 1980 | Mankato St | Don Brose | 5–2 | Elmira |
| 1981 | Lowell | Bill Riley Jr | 5–4 | Plattsburgh St |
| 1982 | Lowell | Bill Riley Jr | 6–1 | Plattsburgh St |
| 1983 | RIT | Brian Mason | 4–2 | Bemidji St |
| 1984 | Bemidji St | R.H. (Bob) Peters | 14–4* | Merrimack |
| 1993 | Bemidji St | R.H. (Bob) Peters | 15–6* | Mercyhurst |
| 1994 | Bemidji St | R.H. (Bob) Peters | 7–6* | Ala.–Huntsville |
| 1995 | Bemidji St | R.H. (Bob) Peters | 11–6* | Mercyhurst |
| 1996 | Ala.–Huntsville | Doug Ross | 10–1* | Bemidji St |
| 1997 | Bemidji St | R.H. (Bob) Peters | 7–4* | Ala.–Huntsville |
| 1998 | Ala.–Huntsville | Doug Ross | 11–4* | Bemidji St |
| 1999 | St. Michael's (Vt.) | Lou DiMasi | 12–9* | New Hamp. Coll |

*Two-game, total-goal series.

## Men *(Cont.)*
### DIVISION III

| Year | Champion | Coach | Score | Runner-Up |
|------|----------|-------|-------|-----------|
| 1984 | Babson | Bob Riley | 8–0 | Union (N.Y.) |
| 1985 | RIT | Bruce Delventhal | 5–1 | Bemidji St |
| 1986 | Bemidji St | R.H. (Bob) Peters | 8–5 | Vacated |
| 1987 | Vacated | | | Oswego St |
| 1988 | UW-River Falls | Rick Kozuback | 7–1, 3–5, 3–0 | Elmira |
| 1989 | UW-Stevens Point | Mark Mazzoleni | 3–3, 3–2 | RIT |
| 1990 | UW-Stevens Point | Mark Mazzoleni | 10–1, 3–6, 1–0 | Plattsburgh St |
| 1991 | UW-Stevens Point | Mark Mazzoleni | 6–2 | Mankato St |
| 1992 | Plattsburgh St | Bob Emery | 7–3 | UW-Stevens Point |
| 1993 | UW-Stevens Point | Joe Baldarotta | 4–3 | UW-River Falls |
| 1994 | UW-River Falls | Dean Talafous | 6–4 | UW-Superior |
| 1995 | Middlebury | Bill Beaney | 1–0 | Fredonia St |
| 1996 | Middlebury | Bill Beaney | 3–2 | RIT |
| 1997 | Middlebury | Bill Beaney | 3–2 | UW-Superior |
| 1998 | Middlebury | Bill Beaney | 2–1 | UW-Stevens Point |
| 1999 | Middlebury | Bill Beaney | 5–0 | UW-Superior |
| 2000 | Norwich | Michael McShane | 2–1 | St. Thomas (Minn.) |
| 2001 | Plattsburgh | Bob Emery | 6–2 | RIT |
| 2002 | UW-Superior | Dan Stauber | 3–2 | Norwich |
| 2003 | Norwich | Michael McShane | 2–1 | Oswego St |
| 2004 | Middlebury | Bill Beaney | 1–0 | St. Norbert |
| 2005 | Middlebury | Bill Beaney | 5–0 | St. Thomas (Minn.) |
| 2006 | Middlebury | Bill Beaney | 3–0 | St. Norbert |
| 2007 | Oswego | Ed Gosek | 4–3 | Middlebury |
| 2008 | St. Norbert | Tim Coghlin | 2–0 | Plattsburgh St |
| 2009 | Neumann | Dominick Dawes | 4–1 | Gustavus Adolphus |
| 2010 | Norwich | Michael McShane | 2–1 | St. Norbert |
| 2011 | St. Norbert | Tim Coghlin | 4–3 | Adrian |

## Women – DIVISION I

| Year | Champion | Coach | Score | Runner-Up |
|------|----------|-------|-------|-----------|
| 2001 | Minn.-Duluth | Shannon Miller | 4–2 | St. Lawrence |
| 2002 | Minn.-Duluth | Shannon Miller | 3–2 | Brown |
| 2003 | Minn.-Duluth | Shannon Miller | 4–3 (2 OT) | Harvard |
| 2004 | Minnesota | Laura Halldorson | 6–2 | Harvard |
| 2005 | Minnesota | Laura Halldorson | 4–3 | Harvard |
| 2006 | Wisconsin | Mark Johnson | 3–0 | Minnesota |
| 2007 | Wisconsin | Mark Johnson | 4–1 | Minnesota |
| 2008 | Minn.-Duluth | Shannon Miller | 4–0 | Wisconsin |
| 2009 | Wisconsin | Mark Johnson | 5–0 | Mercyhurst |
| 2010 | Minn.-Duluth | Shannon Miller | 3–2 (3 OT) | Cornell |

# Soccer
## Men – DIVISION I

| Year | Champion | Coach | Score | Runner-Up |
|------|----------|-------|-------|-----------|
| 1959 | St. Louis | Bob Guelker | 5–2 | Bridgeport |
| 1960 | St. Louis | Bob Guelker | 3–2 | Maryland |
| 1961 | West Chester | Mel Lorback | 2–0 | St. Louis |
| 1962 | St. Louis | Bob Guelker | 4–3 | Maryland |
| 1963 | St. Louis | Bob Guelker | 3–0 | Navy |
| 1964 | Navy | F.H. Warner | 1–0 | Michigan St |
| 1965 | St. Louis | Bob Guelker | 1–0 | Michigan St |
| 1966 | San Francisco | Steve Negoesco | 5–2 | LIU–Brooklyn |
| 1967 | Michigan St | Gene Kenney | 0–0 | Game called due to |
| | St. Louis | Harry Keough | | inclement weather |
| 1968 | Maryland | Doyle Royal | 2–2 (2 OT) | |
| | Michigan St | Gene Kenney | | |
| 1969 | St. Louis | Harry Keough | 4–0 | San Francisco |
| 1970 | St. Louis | Harry Keough | 1–0 | UCLA |
| 1971 | Vacated | | 3–2 | St. Louis |
| 1972 | St. Louis | Harry Keough | 4–2 | UCLA |
| 1973 | St. Louis | Harry Keough | 2–1 (OT) | UCLA |
| 1974 | Howard | Lincoln Phillips | 2–1 (4 OT) | St. Louis |
| 1975 | San Francisco | Steve Negoesco | 4–0 | SIU–Edwardsville |
| 1976 | San Francisco | Steve Negoesco | 1–0 | Indiana |
| 1977 | Hartwick | Jim Lennox | 2–1 | San Francisco |

### Men - DIVISION I (CONT.)

| | Champion | Coach | Score | Runner-Up |
|---|---|---|---|---|
| 8 | Vacated | | 2–0 | Indiana |
| 9 | SIU–Edwardsville | Bob Guelker | 3–2 | Clemson |
| 0 | San Francisco | Steve Negoesco | 4–3 (OT) | Indiana |
| 1 | Connecticut | Joe Morrone | 2–1 (OT) | Alabama A&M |
| 2 | Indiana | Jerry Yeagley | 2–1 (8 OT) | Duke |
| 3 | Indiana | Jerry Yeagley | 1–0 (2 OT) | Columbia |
| 4 | Clemson | I.M. Ibrahim | 2–1 | Indiana |
| 5 | UCLA | Sigi Schmid | 1–0 (8 OT) | American |
| 6 | Duke | John Rennie | 1–0 | Akron |
| 7 | Clemson | I.M. Ibrahim | 2–0 | San Diego St |
| 8 | Indiana | Jerry Yeagley | 1–0 | Howard |
| 9 | Santa Clara | Steve Sampson | 1–1 (2 OT) | |
| | Virginia | Bruce Arena | | |
| 0 | UCLA | Sigi Schmid | 1–0 (OT) | Rutgers |
| 1 | Virginia | Bruce Arena | 0–0* | Santa Clara |
| 2 | Virginia | Bruce Arena | 2–0 | San Diego |
| 3 | Virginia | Bruce Arena | 2–0 | South Carolina |
| 4 | Virginia | Bruce Arena | 1–0 | Indiana |
| 5 | Wisconsin | Jim Launder | 2–0 | Duke |
| 6 | St. John's (N.Y.) | Dave Masur | 4–1 | Florida International |
| 7 | UCLA | Sigi Schmid | 2–1 | Virginia |
| 8 | Indiana | Jerry Yeagley | 3–1 | Stanford |
| 9 | Indiana | Jerry Yeagley | 1–0 | Santa Clara |
| 0 | Connecticut | Ray Reid | 2–0 | Creighton |
| 1 | N.Carolina | Elmar Bolowich | 2–0 | Indiana |
| 2 | UCLA | Tom Fitzgerald | 1–0 | Stanford |
| 3 | Indiana | Jerry Yeagley | 2–1 | St. John's (N.Y.) |
| 4 | Indiana | Jerry Yeagley | 1–1 (2 OT 3-2) | UC–Santa Barbara |
| 5 | Maryland | Sasho Cirovski | 1–0 | New Mexico |
| 6 | UC-Santa Barbara | Tim Vom Steeg | 2–1 | UCLA |
| 7 | Wake Forest | Tony da Luz | 2–0 | Ohio St |
| 8 | Maryland | Sasha Cirovski | 1–0 | North Carolina |
| 9 | Virginia | George Gelnovatch | 0–0 (3–2 PKs) | Akron |
| 0 | Akron | Caleb Porter | 1–0 | Louisville |

der a rule passed in 1991, the NCAA determined that when a score is tied after regulation and overtime, and the npionship is determined by penalty kicks, the official score will be 0–0.

### Men - DIVISION II

| | Champion | Year | Champion | Year | Champion |
|---|---|---|---|---|---|
| 2 | SIU–Edwardsville | 1985 | Seattle Pacific | 1998 | Southern Conn St |
| 3 | Missouri–St. Louis | 1986 | Seattle Pacific | 1999 | Southern Conn St |
| 4 | Adelphi | 1987 | Southern Conn St | 2000 | CSU–Dominguez Hills |
| 5 | Baltimore | 1988 | Florida Tech | 2001 | Tampa |
| 6 | Loyola (Md.) | 1989 | New Hampshire College | 2002 | Sonoma St |
| 7 | Alabama A&M | 1990 | Southern Conn St | 2003 | Lynn |
| 8 | Seattle Pacific | 1991 | Florida Tech | 2004 | Seattle |
| 9 | Alabama A&M | 1992 | Southern Conn St | 2005 | Fort Lewis |
| 0 | Lock Haven | 1993 | Seattle Pacific | 2006 | Dowling (N.Y.) |
| 1 | Tampa | 1994 | Tampa | 2007 | Franklin Pierce |
| 2 | Florida International | 1995 | Southern Conn St | 2008 | Cal St.-Dominguez Hills |
| 3 | Seattle Pacific | 1996 | Grand Canyon | 2009 | Fort Lewis |
| 4 | Florida International | 1997 | CSU-Bakersfield | 2010 | Northern Kentucky |

### Men - DIVISION III

| | Champion | Year | Champion | Year | Champion |
|---|---|---|---|---|---|
| 4 | Brockport St | 1987 | N.C.–Greensboro | 2000 | Messiah |
| 5 | Babson | 1988 | UC–San Diego | 2001 | Richard Stockton |
| 6 | Brandeis | 1989 | Elizabethtown | 2002 | Messiah |
| 7 | Lock Haven | 1990 | Glassboro St | 2003 | Trinity (Tex.) |
| 8 | Lock Haven | 1991 | UC–San Diego | 2004 | Messiah |
| 9 | Babson | 1992 | Kean | 2005 | Messiah |
| 0 | Babson | 1993 | UC–San Diego | 2006 | Messiah |
| 1 | Glassboro St | 1994 | Bethany (W.V.) | 2007 | Middlebury |
| 2 | N.C.–Greensboro | 1995 | Williams | 2008 | Messiah |
| 3 | N.C.–Greensboro | 1996 | The College of New Jersey* | 2009 | Messiah |
| 4 | Wheaton (Ill.) | 1997 | Wheaton (Ill.) | 2010 | Messiah |
| 5 | N.C.–Greensboro | 1998 | Ohio Wesleyan | | |
| 6 | N.C.–Greensboro | 1999 | St. Lawrence | | |

*Formerly Trenton St

## Women - DIVISION I

| Year | Champion | Coach | Score | Runner-Up |
|------|----------|-------|-------|-----------|
| 1982 | North Carolina | Anson Dorrance | 2–0 | Central Florida |
| 1983 | North Carolina | Anson Dorrance | 4–0 | George Mason |
| 1984 | North Carolina | Anson Dorrance | 2–0 | Connecticut |
| 1985 | George Mason | Hank Leung | 2–0 | North Carolina |
| 1986 | North Carolina | Anson Dorrance | 2–0 | Colorado College |
| 1987 | North Carolina | Anson Dorrance | 1–0 | Massachusetts |
| 1988 | North Carolina | Anson Dorrance | 4–1 | North Carolina St |
| 1989 | North Carolina | Anson Dorrance | 2–0 | Colorado College |
| 1990 | North Carolina | Anson Dorrance | 6–0 | Connecticut |
| 1991 | North Carolina | Anson Dorrance | 3–1 | Wisconsin |
| 1992 | North Carolina | Anson Dorrance | 9–1 | Duke |
| 1993 | North Carolina | Anson Dorrance | 6–0 | George Mason |
| 1994 | North Carolina | Anson Dorrance | 5–0 | Notre Dame |
| 1995 | Notre Dame | Chris Petrucelli | 1–0 | Portland |
| 1996 | North Carolina | Anson Dorrance | 1–0 | Notre Dame |
| 1997 | North Carolina | Anson Dorrance | 2–0 | Connecticut |
| 1998 | Florida | Becky Burleigh | 1–0 | North Carolina |
| 1999 | North Carolina | Anson Dorrance | 2–0 | Notre Dame |
| 2000 | North Carolina | Anson Dorrance | 2–1 | UCLA |
| 2001 | Santa Clara | Jerry Smith | 1–0 | North Carolina |
| 2002 | Portland | Clive Charles | 2–1 | Santa Clara |
| 2003 | North Carolina | Anson Dorrance | 6–0 | Connecticut |
| 2004 | Norte Dame | Randy Waldrum | 1–1 (OT 4–3) | UCLA |
| 2005 | Portland | Garrett Smith | 4–0 | UCLA |
| 2006 | North Carolina | Anson Dorrance | 2–1 | Notre Dame |
| 2007 | USC | Ali Khosroshahin | 2–0 | Florida St |
| 2008 | North Carolina | Anson Dorrance | 2–1 | Notre Dame |
| 2009 | North Carolina | Anson Dorrance | 1–0 | Stanford |
| 2010 | Notre Dame | Randy Waldrum | 1–0 | Stanford |

## Women - DIVISION II

| Year | Champion | Year | Champion | Year | Champion |
|------|----------|------|----------|------|----------|
| 1988 | CSU–Hayward | 1996 | Franklin Pierce | 2004 | Metro St |
| 1989 | Barry | 1997 | Franklin Pierce | 2005 | Nebraska-Omaha |
| 1990 | Sonoma St | 1998 | Lynn | 2006 | Metro St |
| 1991 | CSU–Dominguez Hills | 1999 | Franklin Pierce | 2007 | Tampa |
| 1992 | Barry | 2000 | UC-San Diego | 2008 | Seattle Pacific |
| 1993 | Barry | 2001 | UC-San Diego | 2009 | Grand Valley St |
| 1994 | Franklin Pierce | 2002 | Christian Brothers | 2010 | Grand Valley St |
| 1995 | Franklin Pierce | 2003 | Kennesaw St | | |

## Women - DIVISION III

| Year | Champion | Year | Champion | Year | Champion |
|------|----------|------|----------|------|----------|
| 1986 | Rochester | 1995 | UC–San Diego | 2004 | Wheaton College |
| 1987 | Rochester | 1996 | UC–San Diego | 2005 | Messiah |
| 1988 | William Smith | 1997 | UC–San Diego | 2006 | Wheaton (Ill.) |
| 1989 | UC–San Diego | 1998 | Macalester | 2007 | Wheaton (Ill.) |
| 1990 | Ithaca | 1999 | UC–San Diego | 2008 | Messiah |
| 1991 | Ithaca | 2000 | The College of New Jersey* | 2009 | Messiah |
| 1992 | Cortland St | 2001 | Ohio Wesleyan | 2010 | Hardin-Simmons |
| 1993 | Trenton St | 2002 | Ohio Wesleyan | | |
| 1994 | Trenton St | 2003 | Oneonta St | | |

*formerly Trenton St

Though he didn't dominate the Worlds in 2011 like he did two years ago, Jamaican sprinter Usain Bolt still helped set a new world record in the 4 x 100 relay

# Track & Field

## 2011 IAAF World Championships

### Daegu, South Korea, August 27–September 4, 2011

### Men

**100 METERS**
1. ....Yohan Blake, Jamaica — 9.92
2. ....Walter Dix, United States — 10.08
3. ....Kim Collins, St. Kitts & Nevis — 10.09

**200 METERS**
1. ....Usain Bolt, Jamaica — 19.40
2. ....Walter Dix, United States — 19.70
3. ....Christophe Lemaitre, France — 19.80

**400 METERS**
1. ....Kirani James, Grenada — 44.60
2. ....LaShawn Merritt, United States — 44.63
3. ....Kevin Borlee, Belguim — 44.90

**800 METERS**
1. ....David Lekuta Rudisha, Kenya — 1:43.91*
2. ....Abubaker Kaki, Sudan — 1:44.41
3. ....Yuriy Borzakovskiy, Russia — 1:44.49

**1,500 METERS**
1. ....Asbel Kiprop, Kenya — 3:35.69
2. ....Silas Kiplagat, Kenya — 3:35.92
3. ....Matthew Centrowitz, U.S. — 3:36.08

**3,000-METER STEEPLECHASE**
1. ....Ezekiel Kemboi, Kenya — 8:14.85
2. ....Brimin Kiprop Kipruto, Kenya — 8:16.05
3. ....M. Mekhissi-Benabbad, France — 8:16.09

**5,000 METERS**
1. ....Mohamed Farah, U.K. — 13:23.36
2. ....Bernard Lagat, United States — 13:23.64
3. ....Dejen Gebremeskel, Ethiopia — 13:23.92

**10,000 METERS**
1. ....Ibrahim Jeilan, Ethiopia — 27:13.81
2. ....Mohamed Farah, U.K. — 27:14.07
3. ....Imane Merga, Ethiopia — 27:19.14

**110-METER HURDLES**
1. ....Jason Richardson, United States — 13.16
2. ....Xiang Liu, China — 13.27
3. ....Andrew Turner, United Kingdom — 13.44

**400-METER HURDLES**
1. ....David Greene, United Kingdom — 48.26
2. ....Javier Culson, Puerto Rico — 48.44
3. ....L.J. van Zyl, South Africa — 48.80

**4 x 100-METER RELAY**
1. ....Jamaica — 37.04WR
(Carter, Frater, Blake, Bolt)
2. ....France — 38.20
(Tinmar, Lemaitre, Lesourd, Vicaut)
3. ....St. Kitts & Nevis — 38.49
(Rogers, Collins, Adams, Lawrence)

**4 x 400-METER RELAY**
1. ....United States — 2:59.31
(Nixon, Jackson, Taylor, Merritt)
2. ....South Africa — 2:59.87
(Victor, Mogawane, de Beer, van Zyl)
3. ....Jamaica — 3:00.10
(Fothergill, Gonzales, Hylton, Green)

**20-KILOMETER RACE WALK**
1. ....Valeriy Borchin, Russia — 1:19:56
2. ....Vladimir Kanaykin, Russia — 1:20:27
3. ....Luis Fernando Lopez, Colombia — 1:20:38

**50-KILOMETER RACE WALK**
1. ....Sergey Bakulin, Russia — 3:41:24
2. ....Denis Nizhegorodov, Russia — 3:42:45
3. ....Jared Tallent, Australia — 3:43:36

**MARATHON**
1. ....Abel Kirui, Kenya — 2:07:38
2. ....Vincent Kipruto, Kenya — 2:10:06
3. ....Feyisa Lilesa, Ethiopia — 2:10:32

**POLE VAULT**
1. ....Pawel Wojciechowski, Poland — §5.90m
2. ....Lazaro Borges, Cuba — 5.90m
3. ....Renaud Lavillenie, France — §5.85m

**LONG JUMP**
1. ....Dwight Phillips, United States — 8.
2. ....Mitchell Watt, Australia — 8.
3. ....Ngonidzashe Makusha, Zimbabwe — 8.

**TRIPLE JUMP**
1. ....Christian Taylor, United States — 17.
2. ....Phillips Idowu, United Kingdom — 17.
3. ....Will Claye, United States — 17.

**HIGH JUMP**
1. ....Jesse Williams, United States — §2.
2. ....Aleksey Dmitrik, Russia — 2.
3. ....Trevor Barry, Bahamas — §2.

**SHOT PUT**
1. ....David Storl, Germany — 21.
2. ....Dylan Armstrong, Canada — 21.
3. ....Andrei Mikhenevich, Belarus — 21.

**DISCUS THROW**
1. ....Robert Harting, Germany — 68.
2. ....Gerd Kanter, Estonia — 66.
3. ....Ehsan Hadadi, Iran — 66.

**HAMMER THROW**
1. ....Koji Murofushi, Japan — 81.
2. ....Krisztian Pars, Hungary — 81.
3. ....Primoz Kozmus, Slovenia — 79.

**JAVELIN THROW**
1. ....Andreas Thorkildsen, Norway — 89.
2. ....Guillermo Martinez, Cuba — 86.
3. ....Yukifumi Murakami, Japan — 82.

**DECATHLON**
1. ....Trey Hardee, United States — 860
2. ....Ashton Eaton, United States — 850
3. ....Leonel Suarez, Cuba — 850

### Women

**100 METERS**
1. ....Carmelita Jeter, United States — 10.90
2. ....Veronica Campbell-Brown, Jamaica — 10.97
3. ....Kelly-Ann Baptiste, Trin. & Tob. — 10.98

**200 METERS**
1. ....Veronica Campbell-Brown, Jamaica — 22.22
2. ....Carmelita Jeter, United States — 22.37
3. ....Allyson Felix, United States — 22.42

**400 METERS**
1. ....Amantie Montsho, Botswana — 49.56
2. ....Allyson Felix, United States — 49.59
3. ....Anastasiya Kapachinskaya, Russia — 50.24

**800 METERS**
1. ....Mariya Savinova, Russia — 1:55.87
2. ....Caster Semenya, South Africa — 1:56.35
3. ....Janeth Busienei, Kenya — 1:57.42

**1,500 METERS**
1. ....Jennifer Simpson, United States — 4:05.40
2. ....Hannah England, U.K. — 4:05.68
3. ....Natalia Rodriguez, Spain — 4:05.87

**3,000-METER STEEPLECHASE**
1. ....Yuliya Zaripova, Russia — 9:07.03
2. ....Habiba Ghribi, Tunisia — 9:11.97
3. ....Milcah Chemos Cheywa, Kenya — 9:17.16

**5,000 METERS**
1. ....Vivian Cheruiyot, Kenya — 14:55.36
2. ....Sylvia Jebiwott Kibet, Kenya — 14:56.21
3. ....Meseret Defar, Ethiopia — 14:56.94

**10,000 METERS**
1. ....Vivian Cheruiyot, Kenya — 30:48.98
2. ....Sally Kipyego, Kenya — 30:50.04
3. ....Linet Masai, Kenya — 30:53.59

**100-METER HURDLES**
1. ....Sally Pearson, Australia — 12.
2. ....Danielle Carruthers, United States — 12.
3. ....Dawn Harper, United States — 12.

**400-METER HURDLES**
1. ....Lashinda Demus, United States — 52.
2. ....Melaine Walker, Jamaica — 52.
3. ....Natalya Antyukh, Russia — 52.

**4 x 100-METER RELAY**
1. ....United States — 4
(Knight, Felix, Myers, Jeter)
2. ....Jamaica — 4
(Fraser-Pryce, Stewart, Simpson, Campbell-Brown)
3. ....Ukraine — 4.
(Povh, Pohrebnyak, Ryemyen, Stuy)

WR–World record. *Athletes tied after clearing same height same number of times. §Place decided by which athlete cleared height first.

## Daegu, South Korea, August 27–September 4, 2011
### Women (*Cont.*)

**4 x 400-METER RELAY**
1. ....United States .................. 3:18.09
(Richards-Ross, Felix, Beard, McCrory)
2. ....Jamaica ......................... 3:18.71
(Whyte, Prendergast, Williams-Mills, Williams)
3. ....Russia ........................... 3:19.36
(Krizoshatka, Antyukh, Litvinova, Kapachinskaya)

**20-KILOMETER RACE WALK**
1. ....Olga Kaniskina, Russia ..... 1:29:42
2. ....Hong Liu, China .............. 1:30:00
3. ....Anisya Kirdyapkina, Russia . 1:30:13

**MARATHON**
1. ....Edna Kiplagat, Kenya ....... 2:28:43
2. ....Priscah Jeptoo, Kenya ...... 2:29:00
3. ....Sharon Cherop, Kenya ...... 2:29:14

**HIGH JUMP**
1. ....Anna Chicherova, Russia ... §2.03m
2. ....Blanka Vlasic, Croatia ...... 2.03m
3. ....Antonietta Di Martino, Italy . 2.00m

**POLE VAULT**
1. ....Fabiana Murer, Brazil ........ 4.85m
2. ....Martina Strutz, Germany .... 4.80m
3. ....Svetlana Feofanova, Russia . 4.75m

**LONG JUMP**
1. ....Brittney Reese, United States . 6.82m
2. ....Olga Kucherenko, Russia ... 6.77m
3. ....Ineta Radevica, Latvia ....... 6.76m

**TRIPLE JUMP**
1. ....Olha Saladuha, Ukraine ..... 14.94m
2. ....Olga Rypakova, Kazakhstan . 14.89m
3. ....Caterine Ibarguen, Colombia . 14.84m

**SHOT PUT**
1. ....Valerie Adams, New Zealand . 21.24m
2. ....Nadzeya Ostapchuk, Belarus . 20.05m
3. ....Jill. Camarena-Williams, U.S. . 20.02m

**DISCUS THROW**
1. ....Yanfeng Li, China ............. 66.52m
2. ....Nadine Muller, Germany ..... 65.97m
3. ....Yarelis Barrios, Cuba ......... 65.73m

**HAMMER THROW**
1. ....Tatyana Lysenko, Russia .... 77.13m
2. ....Betty Heidler, Germany ...... 76.06m
3. ....Wenxiu Zhang, China ........ 75.03m

**JAVELIN THROW**
1. ....Maria Abakumova, Russia ... 71.99m
2. ....Barbora Spotakova, Czech Rep. 71.58m
3. ....Sunette Viljoen, South Africa . 68.38m

**HEPTATHLON**
1. ....Tatyana Chernova, Russia ... 6880pts
2. ....Jessica Ennis, United Kingdom 6751pts
3. ....Jennifer Oeser, Germany .... 6572pts

WR–World record. *Athletes tied after clearing same height same number of times. § Final place decided by which athlete cleared height first.

# World and American Outdoor Records

As of October 1, 2011. World outdoor records are recognized by the International Amateur Athletics Federation (IAAF). American records recognized by U.S.A. Track & Field.

## Men

| Event | Mark | Record Holder | Date | Site |
|---|---|---|---|---|
| 100 meters | 9.58 | Usain Bolt, Jamaica (W) | 8-16-09 | Berlin |
| | 9.69 | Tyson Gay (A) | 9-20-09 | Shanghai |
| 200 meters | 19.19 | Usain Bolt, Jamaica (W) | 8-20-09 | Berlin |
| | 19.32 | Michael Johnson (A) | 8-01-96 | Atlanta |
| 400 meters | 43.18 | Michael Johnson, U.S. (W,A) | 8-26-99 | Seville, Spain |
| 800 meters | 1:41.01 | David Lekuta Rudisha, Kenya (W) | 8-29-10 | Rieti, Italy |
| | 1:42.60 | Johnny Gray (A) | 8-28-85 | Koblenz, Germany |
| 1,000 meters | 2:11.96 | Noah Ngeny, Kenya (W) | 9-05-99 | Rieti, Italy |
| | 2:13.90 | Rick Wohlhuter (A) | 8-31-03 | Oslo |
| 1,500 meters | 3:26.00 | Hicham El Guerrouj, Morocco (W) | 7-14-98 | Rome |
| | 3:29.30 | Bernard Lagat (A) | 8-28-05 | Rieti, Italy |
| Mile | 3:43.13 | Hicham El Guerrouj, Morocco (W) | 7-07-99 | Rome |
| | 3:46.91 | Alan Webb (A) | 7-21-07 | Brasschaat, Belguim |
| 2,000 meters | 4:44.79 | Hicham El Guerrouj, Morocco (W) | 9-07-99 | Berlin |
| | 4:52.44 | Jim Spivey (A) | 9-15-87 | Lausanne, Switzerland |
| 3,000 meters | 7:20.67 | Daniel Komen, Kenya (W) | 9-01-96 | Rieti, Italy |
| | 7:29.00 | Bernard Lagat (A) | 8-29-10 | Rieti, Italy |
| 3,000-m Steeplechase | 7:53.63 | Saif Saaeed Shaheen, Qatar (W) | 9-03-04 | Brussels |
| | 8:08.82 | Daniel Lincoln (A) | 7-14-06 | Rome |
| 5,000 meters | 12:52.79 | Kenenisa Bekele, Ethiopia (W) | 5-31-04 | Hengelo, Netherlands |
| | 12:53.60 | Bernard Lagat (A) | 7-22-11 | Fontvielle, Monaco |
| 10,000 meters | 26:17.53 | Kenenisa Bekele, Ehtiopia (W) | 8-26-05 | Brussels |
| | 26:48.00 | Galen Rupp (A) | 9-16-11 | Brussels |
| Marathon | 2:03:59 | Haile Gebrselassie, Ethiopia (W) | 9-28-08 | Berlin |
| | 2:05.38 | Khalid Khannouchi (A) | 4-14-02 | London |
| 110-meter hurdles | 12.87 | Dayron Robles, Cuba (W) | 6-12-08 | Ostrava, Czech Republic |
| | 12.89 | David Oliver (A) | 7-16-10 | St. Denis, France |
| 400-meter hurdles | 46.78 | Kevin Young, United States (W,A) | 8-6-92 | Barcelona |
| 20-kilometer walk | 1:17.16 | Vladimir Kanaykin, Russia (W) | 9-29-07 | Saransk, Russia |
| | 1:23:40 | Tim Seaman (A) | 3-07-99 | Chula Vista, Calif. |
| 50-kilometer walk | 3:34:14 | Denis Nizhegorodov, Russia (W) | 5-11-08 | Cheboksary, Russia |
| 4 x 100-meter relay | 37.04 | Jamaica (Nesta Carter, (W) Michael Prater, Yohan Blake, Usain Bolt) | 9-04-11 | Daegu, South Korea |

## Men (*Cont.*)

| Event | Mark | Record Holder | Date | Site |
|---|---|---|---|---|
| 4 x 100-meter relay | 37.40 | Mike Marsh, Leroy Burrell, (A) Dennis Mitchell, Carl Lewis | 8-08-92 | Barcelona |
| | 37.40 | Jon Drummond, Andrew Canson, (A) Dennis Mitchell, Leroy Burrell | 8-21-93 | Stuttgart, Germany |
| 4 x 200-meter relay | 1:18.68 | U.S. (Mike Marsh, Leroy Burrell, (W,A) Floyd Heard, Carl Lewis) | 4-17-94 | Walnut, Calif. |
| 4 x 400-meter relay | 2:54.29 | United States (Andrew Valmon, (W,A) Quincy Watts, Harry Reynolds, Michael Johnson) | 7-22-93 | Stuttgart, Germany |
| 4 x 800-meter relay | 7:02.43 | Kenya (Wilfred Bungei, (W) William Yiampoy, Joseph Mutua, Ismael Kombich) | 8-25-06 | Brussels |
| | 7:02.82 | Jebreh Harris, Khadevis Robinson, (A) Sam Burley, David Krummenacker | 8-25-06 | Brussels |
| 4 x 1,500-meter relay | 14:36.28 | Kenya (W) (Willaim Biwoot Tanui, Gideon Gathimba, Geoffrey Kipkoech Rono, Augustine Kiprono Choge) | 9-04-09 | Brussels |
| | 14:46.30 | Dan Aldridge, Andy Clifford, (A) Todd Harbour, Tom Dults | 6-24-79 | Bourges, France |
| High jump | 2.45m | Javier Sotomayor, Cuba (W) | 7-27-93 | Salamanca, Spain |
| | 2.40m | Charles Austin (A) | 8-07-91 | Zurich |
| Pole vault | 6.14m | Sergei Bubka, Ukraine (W) | 7-31-94 | Sestriere, Italy |
| | 6.04m | Brad Walker (A) | 6-08-08 | Eugene, Oregon |
| Long jump | 8.95m | Mike Powell, United States (W,A) | 8-30-91 | Tokyo |
| Triple jump | 18.29m | Jonathan Edwards, U.K. (W) | 8-07-95 | Göteborg, Sweden |
| | 18.09m | Kenny Harrison (A) | 7-27-96 | Atlanta |
| Shot put | 23.12m | Randy Barnes, United States (W,A) | 5-20-90 | Westwood, Calif. |
| Discus throw | 74.08m | Jürgen Schult, East Germany (W) | 6-06-86 | Neubrandenburg, Germ. |
| | 72.34m | Ben Plucknett (A) | 7-07-81 | Stockholm |
| Hammer throw | 86.74m | Yuriy Sedykh, USSR (W) | 8-30-86 | Stuttgart, Germany |
| | 82.52m | Lance Deal (A) | 9-17-96 | Milan |
| Javelin throw | 98.48m | Jan Zelezny, Czech Republic (W) | 5-25-96 | Jena, Germany |
| | 91.29m | Breaux Greer (A) | 6-21-07 | Indianapolis |
| Decathlon | 9026 pts | Roman Sebrle, Czech Rep. (W) | 5-27-01 | Goetzis, Austria |
| | 8891 pts | Dan O'Brien (A) | 9-04-92 | Talence, France |

Note: The decathlon consists of 10 events: the 100 meters, long jump, shot put, high jump and 400 meters on the first day; the 110-meter hurdles, discus, pole vault, javelin and 1,500 meters on the second.

## Women

| Event | Mark | Record Holder | Date | Site |
|---|---|---|---|---|
| 100 meters | 10.49 | Florence Griffith Joyner, U.S. (W,A) | 7-16-88 | Indianapolis |
| 200 meters | 21.34 | Florence Griffith Joyner, U.S. (W,A) | 9-29-88 | Seoul |
| 400 meters | 47.60 | Marita Koch, E Germany (W) | 10-6-85 | Canberra, Australia |
| | 48.70 | Sanya Richards (A) | 9-17-06 | Athens |
| 800 meters | 1:53.28 | Jarmila Kratochvílová, Czech. (W) | 7-26-83 | Munich |
| | 1:56.40 | Jearl Miles-Clark (A) | 8-11-99 | Zurich |
| 1,000 meters | 2:28.98 | Svetlana Masterkova, Russia (W) | 8-23-96 | Brussels |
| | 2:31.80 | Regina Jacobs (A) | 7-02-99 | Brunswick, Maine |
| 1,500 meters | 3:50.46 | Yunxia Qu, China (W) | 9-11-93 | Beijing |
| | 3:57.12 | Mary Slaney (A) | 7-26-83 | Stockholm |
| Mile | 4:12.56 | Svetlana Masterkova, Russia (W) | 8-14-96 | Zurich |
| | 4:16.71 | Mary Slaney (A) | 8-21-85 | Zurich |
| 2,000 meters | 5:25.36 | Sonia O'Sullivan, Ireland (W) | 7-08-94 | Edinburgh |
| | 5:32.70 | Mary Slaney (A) | 8-03-84 | Eugene, Oregon |
| 3,000 meters | 8:06.11 | Junxia Wang, China (W) | 9-13-93 | Beijing |
| | 8:25.83 | Mary Slaney (A) | 9-07-85 | Rome |
| 3,000-m Steeplechase | 8:58.81 | Gulnara Samitova-Galkina, Russia (W) | 8-17-08 | Beijing |
| | 9:12.50 | Jenny Barringer (A) | 8-17-09 | Berlin |
| 5,000 meters | 14:11.15 | Tirunesh Dibaba, Ethiopia (W) | 6-06-08 | Oslo |
| | 14:44.76 | Molly Huddle (A) | 8-27-10 | Brussels |
| 10,000 meters | 29:31.78 | Junxia Wang, China (W) | 9-08-93 | Beijing |
| | 30:22.22 | Shalane Flanagan (A) | 8-15-08 | Beijing |
| Marathon | 2:15:25 | Paula Radcliffe, Great Britain (W) | 4-13-03 | London |
| | 2:19:36 | Deena Kastor (A) | 4-23-06 | London |

### Women (Cont.)

| | | | |
|---|---|---|---|
| 100-meter hurdles | 12.21 | Yordanka Donkova, Bulgaria (W) | 8-20-88 | Stara Zagora, Bulgaria |
| | 12.33 | Gail Devers (A) | 7-23-00 | Sacramento, Calif.. |
| 400-meter hurdles | 52.34 | Yuliya Pechenkina, Russia (W) | 8-08-03 | Tula, Russia |
| | 52.61 | Kim Batten (A) | 8-11-95 | Gothenburg, Sweden |
| 20-kilometer walk | 1:25:08 | Vera Sokolova, Russia (W) | 2-26-11 | Sochi, Russia |
| | 1:33:28.15 | Teresa Vaill (A) | 6-25-05 | Carson, Calif. |
| 4 x 100-meter relay | 41.37 | East Germany (Silke Gladisch, (W) 10-6-85 Sabine Reiger, Ingrid Auerswald, Marlies Göhr) | | Canberra, Australia |
| | 42.36 | Khrystal Carter, Porscha Lucas, (A) 6-12-09 Dominique Duncan, Gabby Mayo | | Fayetteville, Ark. |
| 4 x 200-meter relay | 1:27.46 | United States (LaTasha Jenkins, (W,A) 4-29-00 LaTasha Colander-Richardson, Nanceen Perry, Marion Jones) | | Philadelphia |
| 4 x 400-meter relay | 3:15.17 | USSR (Tatyana Ledovskaya, (W) 10-01-88 Olga Nazarova, Maria Pinigina, Olga Bryzgina) | | Seoul |
| | 3:15.51 | Denean Howard, Diane Dixon (A) 10-01-88 Valerie Brisco, Florence Griffith-Joyner | | Seoul |
| 4 x 800-meter relay | 7:50.17 | USSR (Nadezhda Olizarenko, 8-05-84 Lyubov Gurina, Lyudmila Borisova, Irina Podyalovskaya) | | Moscow |
| | 8:17.91 | Chanelle Price, Phoebe Wright (A) 4-24-09 Rolanda Bell, Sarah Bowman | | Philadelphia |
| High jump | 2.09m | Stefka Kostadinova, Bulgaria (W) | 8-30-87 | Rome |
| | 2.05m | Chaunte Howard-Lowe (A) | 8-26-10 | Des Moines, Iowa |
| Pole vault | 5.06m | Yelena Isinbayeva, Russia (W) | 8-28-09 | Zurich |
| | 4.92m | Jenn Stuczynski (A) | 7-06-08 | Eugene, Ore. |
| Long jump | 7.52m | Galina Chistyakova, USSR (W) | 6-11-88 | Leningrad |
| | 7.49m | Jackie Joyner-Kersee (A) | 7-31-94 | Sestriere, Italy |
| Triple jump | 15.50m | Inessa Kravets, Ukraine (W) | 8-10-95 | Gothenburg, Sweden |
| | 14.45m | Tiombe Hurd (A) | 7-11-04 | Sacramento, Calif.. |
| Shot put | 22.63m | Natalya Lisovskaya, USSR (W) | 6-07-87 | Moscow |
| | 20.18m | Ramona Pagel (A) | 6-25-88 | San Diego, Calif. |
| Discus throw | 76.80m | Gabriele Reinsch, East Germany (W) | 7-09-88 | Neubrandenburg, Germ. |
| | 67.67m | Suzy Powell-Roos (A) | 4-14-07 | Wailuku, Haw. |
| Hammer throw | 79.42m | Betty Heidler, Germany (W) | 5-21-11 | Halle, Germany |
| | 73.87m | Erin Gilreath (A) | 6-25-05 | Carson, Calif. |
| Javelin throw | 72.28m | Barbora Spotakova, Czech Rep. (W) | 9-13-08 | Stuttgart |
| | 66.679m | Kara Patterson (A) | 6-25-10 | Des Moines, Iowa |
| Heptathlon | 7291 pts | Jackie Joyner-Kersee, U.S. (W,A) | 9-24-88 | Seoul |

Note: The heptathlon consists of 7 events: the 100-meter hurdles, high jump, shot put and 200 meters on the first day; the long jump, javelin and 800 meters on the second.

## World and American Indoor Records

As of October 1, 2011. American indoor records are recognized by USA Track and Field. World Indoor records are recognized by the International Amateur Athletics Federation (IAAF). (A) represents an American record, (W) represents a World record.

### Men

| Event | Mark | Record Holder | Date | Site |
|---|---|---|---|---|
| 50 meters | 5.56 | Donovan Bailey, Canada (W) | 2-09-96 | Reno, Nev. |
| | 5.56 | Maurice Greene (A) | 2-12-99 | Los Angeles |
| 55 meters* | 6.00 | Lee McRae (A) | 3-14-86 | Oklahoma City |
| 60 meters | 6.39 | Maurice Greene (W, A) | 2-03-98 | Madrid |
| | 6.39 | Maurice Greene (W, A) | 3-03-01 | Atlanta |
| 200 meters | 19.92 | Frankie Fredericks, Namibia (W) | 2-18-96 | Liévin, France |
| | 20.10 | Wallace Spearmon (A) | 3-11-05 | Fayetteville, Ark. |
| 400 meters | 44.57 | Kerron Clement (W, A) | 3-12-05 | Fayetteville, Ark. |
| 800 meters | 1:42.67 | Wilson Kipketer, Denmark (W) | 3-09-97 | Paris |
| | 1:45.00 | Johnny Gray (A) | 3-08-92 | Sindelfingen, Germany |
| 1,000 meters | 2:14.96 | Wilson Kipketer, Denmark (W) | 2-20-00 | Birmingham, England |
| | 2:17.86 | David Krummenacker (A) | 1-27-02 | Boston |
| 1,500 meters | 3:31.18 | Hicham El Guerrouj, Morocco (W) | 2-02-97 | Stuttgart, Germany |
| | 3:33.34 | Bernard Lagat (A) | 2-11-05 | Fayetteville, Ark. |
| Mile | 3:48.45 | Hicham El Guerrouj, Morocco (W) | 2-12-97 | Ghent, Belgium |
| | 3:49.89 | Bernard Lagat (A) | 2-11-05 | Fayetteville, Ark. |

## Men *(Cont.)*

| Event | Mark | Record Holder | Date | Site |
|---|---|---|---|---|
| 3,000 meters | 7:24.90 | Daniel Komen, Kenya (W) | 2-06-98 | Budapest, Hungary |
| | 7:32.43 | Bernard Lagat (A) | 2-17-07 | Birmingham, England |
| 5,000 meters | 12:49.60 | Kenenisa Bekele, Ethiopia (W) | 2-20-04 | Birmingham, England |
| | 13:18.22 | Galen Rupp (A) | 2-13-09 | Fayetteville, Ark. |
| 50-meter hurdles | 6.25 | Mark McKoy, Canada (W) | 3-05-86 | Kobe, Japan |
| | 6.35 | Greg Foster (A) | 1-31-87 | Ottawa |
| | 6.35 | Greg Foster (A) | 1-27-85 | Rosemont, Illinois |
| 55-meter hurdles* | 6.89 | Renaldo Nehemiah (A) | 1-20-79 | New York City |
| 60-meter hurdles | 7.30 | Colin Jackson, Great Britain (W) | 3-6-94 | Sindelfingen, Germany |
| | 7.36 | Greg Foster (A) | 1-16-87 | Los Angeles |
| | 7.36 | Allen Johnson (A) | 3-06-04 | Budapest, Hungary |
| 5,000-meter walk | 18:07.08 | Mikhail Shchennikov, Russia (W) | 2-14-95 | Moscow |
| | 19:15.88 | Tim Seaman (A) | 3-07-87 | Indianapolis |
| 4 x 200-meter relay | 1:22.11 | United Kingdom (Linford Christie, (W) Darren Braithwaite, Ade Mafe, John Regis) | 3-03-91 | Glasgow |
| | 1:22.71 | National Team (A) (Thomas Jefferson, Raymond Pierre, Antonio McKay Kevin Little) | 3-03-91 | Glasgow |
| 4 x 400-meter relay | 3:02.83 | United States (W, A) (Milton Campbell, Deon Minor Dameon Johnson, Andre Morris) | 3-07-99 | Maebashi, Japan. |
| 4 x 800-meter relay | 7:13.94 | United States (W, A) (Joey Woody, Karl Paranya, Rich Kenah, David Krummenacker) | 2-06-00 | Boston |
| High jump | 2.43m | Javier Sotomayor, Cuba (W) | 3-4-89 | Budapest, Hungary |
| | 2.40m | Hollis Conway (A) | 3-10-91 | Seville |
| Pole vault | 6.15m | Sergei Bubka, Ukraine (W) | 2-21-93 | Donetsk, Ukraine |
| | 6.02m | Jeff Hartwig (A) | 3-10-02 | Sindelfingen, Germany |
| Long jump | 8.79m | Carl Lewis (W, A) | 1-27-84 | New York City |
| Triple jump | 17.90m | Teddy Tamgho, France (W) | 3-14-10 | Doha, Qatar |
| | 17.76m | Mike Conley (A) | 2-27-87 | New York City |
| Shot put | 22.66m | Randy Barnes (W, A) | 1-20-89 | Los Angeles |
| Weight throw* | 25.86m | Lance Deal (A) | 3-04-95 | Atlanta |
| Pentathlon* | 4478 pts | Steve Fritz, (A) | 1-14-95 | Lawrence, Kan. |
| Heptathlon | 6499 pts | Ashton Eaton (W, A) | 3-12-10 | Fayetteville, Ark. |

*No recognized world record.

## Women

| Event | Mark | Record Holder | Date | Site |
|---|---|---|---|---|
| 50 meters | 5.96 | Irina Privolova, Russia (W) | 2-09-95 | Madrid |
| | 6.02 | Gail Devers (A) | 2-22-99 | Liévin, France |
| 55 meters* | 6.56 | Gwen Torrence (A) | 3-14-87 | Oklahoma City, Okla. |
| 60 meters | 6.92 | Irina Privalova, Russia (W) | 2-11-93 | Madrid |
| | 6.92 | Irina Privalova, Russia (W) | 2-09-95 | Madrid |
| | 6.95 | Gail Devers (A) | 3-12-93 | Toronto |
| | 6.95 | Marion Jones (A) | 3-07-98 | Maebashi, Japan |
| 200 meters | 21.87 | Merlene Ottey, Jamaica (W) | 2-13-93 | Liévin, France |
| | 22.33 | Gwen Torrence (A) | 3-02-66 | Atlanta |
| 400 meters | 49.59 | Jarmila Kratochvílová, Czecho. (W) | 3-07-82 | Milan |
| | 50.54 | Francena McCorory (A) | 3-13-10 | Fayetteville, Ark. |
| 800 meters | 1:55.82 | Jolanda Batageli, Slovenia (W) | 3-03-02 | Vienna |
| | 1:58.71 | Nicole Teter (A) | 3-02-02 | New York City |
| 1,000 meters | 2:30.94 | Maria Mutola, Mozambique (W) | 2-25-99 | Stockholm |
| | 2:34.19 | Jennifer Toomey (A) | 2-20-04 | Birmingham, England |
| 1,500 meters | 3:58.28 | Yelena Soboleva, Russia (W) | 2-18-06 | Moscow |
| | 3:59.98 | Regina Jacobs, United States ( A) | 2-01-03 | Boston |
| Mile | 4:17.14 | Doina Melinte, Romania (W) | 2-09-90 | East Rutherford, N.J. |
| | 4:20.50 | Mary Slaney (A) | 2-19-82 | San Diego |
| 3,000 meters | 8:23.72 | Meseret Defar, Ethiopia (W) | 2-03-07 | Stuttgart |
| | 8:33.25 | Shalane Flanagan (A) | 1-27-07 | Boston |
| 5,000 meters | 14:24.37 | Meseret Defar, Ethiopia (W) | 2-18-09 | Stockholm |
| | 14:47.62 | Shalane Flanagan (A) | 2-07-09 | Boston |
| 50-meter hurdles | 6.58 | Cornelia Oschkenat, E Germany (W) | 2-20-88 | Berlin |
| | 6.67 | Jackie Joyner-Kersee (A) | 2-10-95 | Reno, Nev. |
| 55-meter hurdles* | 7.37 | Jackie Joyner-Kersee (A) | 2-03-89 | New York City |
| 60-meter hurdles | 7.68 | Susanna Kallur, Sweden (W) | 2-20-08 | Berlin |
| | 7.72 | Lolo Jones (A) | 3-13-10 | Doha, Qatar |

## Women (Cont.)

| Event | Mark | Record Holder | Date | Site |
|---|---|---|---|---|
| 3,000-meter walk | 11:40.33 | Claudia Stef, Romania | 1-30-99 | Bucharest, Romania |
|  | 12:20.79 | Debbi Lawrence (A) | 3-12-93 | Toronto |
| 4 x 200-meter relay | 1:32.41 | Russia (Y, Kondratyeva, (W) | 1-29-05 | Glasgow |
|  |  | I. Khabarova, Y.Pechonkina, Y. Gushchina) | | |
|  | 1:33.24 | Flirtisha Harris, Chryste Gaines, (A) | 2-12-94 | Glasgow |
|  |  | Terri Dendy, Michele Collins | | |
| 4 x 400-meter relay | 3:23.37 | Russia (Y. Gushchina, (W) | 1-28-06 | Glasgow |
|  |  | O. Kotlyarova, O. Zaytseva, O. Krasnomovets) | | |
|  | 3:27.34 | Debbie Dunn, DeeDee Trotter (A) | 3-14-10 | Doha, Qatar |
|  |  | Natasha Hastings, Allyson Felix | | |
| 4 x 800-meter relay | 8:12.41 | Russia, (T. Andrianova, E. Kofanova (W) | 2-28-10 | Moscow, Russia |
|  |  | O. Sukhachova-Spasovkhodskaya, Y. Zinurova) | | |
|  | 8:28.41 | Univ. of Wisconsin (Sarah Renk, (A) | 3-14-92 | Indianapolis |
|  |  | Kim Sherman, Sue Gentes, Amy Wickus) | | |
| High jump | 2.08m | Kajsa Bergqvist, Sweden (W) | 2-4-06 | Arnstadt, Germany |
|  | 2.01m | Tisha Waller (A) | 2-28-98 | Atlanta |
| Pole vault | 5.00m | Yelena Isinbaeva, Russia (W) | 2-15-09 | Donetsk, Ukraine |
|  | 4.83m | Jenn Stuczynski (A) | 3-01-09 | Boston |
| Long jump | 7.37m | Heike Drechsler, East Germany (W) | 2-13-88 | Vienna |
|  | 7.13m | Jackie Joyner-Kersee (A) | 3-5-94 | Atlanta |
| Triple jump | 15.36m | Tatyana Lebedeva, Russia (W) | 3-6-04 | Budapest, Hungary |
|  | 14.23m | Sheila Hudson-Strudwick (A) | 3-4-95 | Atlanta |
| Shot put | 22.50m | Helena Fibingerová, Czecho. (W) | 2-19-77 | Jablonec, Czecho. |
|  | 19.83m | Ramona Pagel (A) | 2-20-87 | Inglewood, Calif. |
| Weight throw* | 25.56m | Brittany Riley (A) | 3-10-07 | Fayetteville, Ark. |
| Pentathlon | 4991 pts | Irina Belova, Russia (W) | 2-15-92 | Berlin |
|  | 4753 pts | DeDee Nathan (A) | 3-4/5-99 | Maebashi, Japan |
|  | 4753 pts | Hyleas Fountain (A) | 3-12/13-10 | Doha, Qatar |

*No recognized world record.

# World Track and Field Championships

## Men

### 100 METERS

| | | |
|---|---|---|
| 1983 | Carl Lewis, United States | 10.07 |
| 1987* | Carl Lewis, United States | 9.93 WR |
| 1991 | Carl Lewis, United States | 9.86 WR |
| 1993 | Linford Christie, Great Britain | 9.87 |
| 1995 | Donovan Bailey, Canada | 9.97 |
| 1997 | Maurice Greene, United States | 9.86 |
| 1999 | Maurice Greene, United States | 9.80 |
| 2001 | Maurice Greene, United States | 9.82 |
| 2003 | Kim Collins, St. Kitts & Nevis | 10.07 |
| 2005 | Justin Gatlin, United States | 9.88 |
| 2007 | Tyson Gay, United States | 9.85 |
| 2009 | Usain Bolt, Jamaica | 9.58WR |
| 2011 | Yohan Blake, Jamaica | 9.92 |

### 200 METERS

| | | |
|---|---|---|
| 1983 | Calvin Smith, United States | 20.14 |
| 1987 | Calvin Smith, United States | 20.16 |
| 1991 | Michael Johnson, United States | 20.01 |
| 1993 | Frank Fredericks, Namibia | 19.85 |
| 1995 | Michael Johnson, United States | 19.79 |
| 1997 | Ato Boldon, Trinidad and Tobago | 20.04 |
| 1999 | Maurice Greene, United States | 19.90 |
| 2001 | Konstadínos Kedéris, Greece | 20.04 |
| 2003 | John Capel, United States | 20.30 |
| 2005 | Justin Gatlin, United States | 20.04 |
| 2007 | Tyson Gay, United States | 19.76 |
| 2009 | Usain Bolt, Jamaica | 19.19WR |
| 2011 | Usain Bolt, Jamaica | 19.40 |

### 400 METERS

| | | |
|---|---|---|
| 1983 | Bert Cameron, Jamaica | 45.05 |
| 1987 | Thomas Schoenlebe, E Germany | 44.33 |
| 1991 | Antonio Pettigrew, United States | 44.57 |
| 1993 | Michael Johnson, United States | 43.65 |
| 1995 | Michael Johnson, United States | 43.39 |
| 1997 | Michael Johnson, United States | 44.12 |
| 1999 | Michael Johnson, United States | 43.18 WR |
| 2001 | Avard Moncur, Bahamas | 44.64 |
| 2003 | Jerome Young, United States | 44.50 |
| 2005 | Jeremy Wariner, United States | 43.93 |
| 2007 | Jeremy Wariner, United States | 43.45 |
| 2009 | LaShawn Merritt, United States | 44.06 |
| 2011 | Kirani James, Grenada | 44.60 |

### 800 METERS

| | | |
|---|---|---|
| 1983 | Willi Wulbeck, W Germany | 1:43.65 |
| 1987 | Billy Konchellah, Kenya | 1:43.06 |
| 1991 | Billy Konchellah, Kenya | 1:43.99 |
| 1993 | Paul Ruto, Kenya | 1:44.71 |
| 1995 | Wilson Kipketer, Denmark | 1:45.08 |
| 1997 | Wilson Kipketer, Denmark | 1:43.38 |
| 1999 | Wilson Kipketer, Denmark | 1:43.30 |
| 2001 | André Bucher, Switzerland | 1:43.70 |
| 2003 | Djabir Saïd-Guerni, Algeria | 1:44.81 |
| 2005 | Rashid Ramzi, Brunei | 1:44.24 |
| 2007 | Alfred Kirwa Yego | 1:47.09 |
| 2009 | Mbulaeni Mulaudzi, South Africa | 1:45.29 |
| 2011 | David Lekuta Rudisha, Kenya | 1:43.91 |

WR=World record. *Ben Johnson, Canada, disqualified.

## Men (Cont.)

### 1,500 METERS

| | | |
|---|---|---|
| 1983 | Steve Cram, Great Britain | 3:41.59 |
| 1987 | Abdi Bile, Somalia | 3:36.80 |
| 1991 | Noureddine Morceli, Algeria | 3:32.84 |
| 1993 | Noureddine Morceli, Algeria | 3:34.24 |
| 1995 | Noureddine Morceli, Algeria | 3:33.73 |
| 1997 | Hicham El Guerrouj, Morocco | 3:35.83 |
| 1999 | Hicham El Guerrouj, Morocco | 3:27.65 |
| 2001 | Hicham El Guerrouj, Morocco | 3:30.68 |
| 2003 | Hicham El Guerrouj, Morocco | 3:31.77 |
| 2005 | Rashid Ramzi, Brunei | 3:37.88 |
| 2007 | Bernard Lagat, United States | 3:34.77 |
| 2009 | Yusuf Kamel, Bahrain | 3:35.93 |
| 2011 | Asbel Kiprop, Kenya | 3:35.69 |

### 3,000-METER STEEPLECHASE

| | | |
|---|---|---|
| 1983 | Patriz Ilg, W Germany | 8:15.06 |
| 1987 | Francesco Panetta, Italy | 8:08.57 |
| 1991 | Moses Kiptanui, Kenya | 8:12.59 |
| 1993 | Moses Kiptanui, Kenya | 8:06.36 |
| 1995 | Moses Kiptanui, Kenya | 8:04.16 |
| 1997 | Wilson Boit Kipketer, Kenya | 8:05.84 |
| 1999 | Christopher Koskei, Kenya | 8:11.76 |
| 2001 | Reuben Kosgei, Kenya | 8:15.16 |
| 2003 | Saif Saaeed Shaheen, Qatar | 8:04.39 |
| 2005 | Saif Saaeed Shaheen, Qatar | 8:13.31 |
| 2007 | Brimin Kipruto, Kenya | 8:13.82 |
| 2009 | Ezekiel Kemboi, Kenya | 8:00.43 |
| 2011 | Ezekiel Kemboi, Kenya | 8:14.85 |

### 5,000 METERS

| | | |
|---|---|---|
| 1983 | Eamonn Coghlan, Ireland | 13:28.53 |
| 1987 | Said Aouita, Morocco | 13:26.44 |
| 1991 | Yobes Ondieki, Kenya | 13:14.45 |
| 1993 | Ismael Kirui, Kenya | 13:02.75 |
| 1995 | Ismael Kirui, Kenya | 13:16.77 |
| 1997 | Daniel Komen, Kenya | 13:07.38 |
| 1999 | Salah Hissou, Morocco | 12:58.13 |
| 2001 | Richard Limo, Kenya | 13:00.77 |
| 2003 | Eliud Kipchoge, Kenya | 12:52.79 |
| 2005 | Benjamin Limo, Kenya | 13:32.55 |
| 2007 | Bernard Lagat, United States | 13:45.87 |
| 2009 | Kenenisa Bekele, Ethiopia | 13:17.09 |
| 2011 | Mohamed Farah, U.K. | 13:23.36 |

### 10,000 METERS

| | | |
|---|---|---|
| 1983 | Alberto Cova, Italy | 28:01.04 |
| 1987 | Paul Kipkoech, Kenya | 27:38.63 |
| 1991 | Moses Tanui, Kenya | 27:38.74 |
| 1993 | Haile Gebrselassie, Ethiopia | 27:46.02 |
| 1995 | Haile Gebrselassie, Ethiopia | 27:12.95 |
| 1997 | Haile Gebrselassie, Ethiopia | 27:24.58 |
| 1999 | Haile Gebrselassie, Ethiopia | 27:57.27 |
| 2001 | Charles Kamathi, Kenya | 27:53.25 |
| 2003 | Kenenisa Bekele, Ethiopia | 26:49.57 |
| 2005 | Kenenisa Bekele, Ethiopia | 27:08.33 |
| 2007 | Kenenisa Bekele, Ethiopia | 27:05.90 |
| 2009 | Kenenisa Bekele, Ethiopia | 26:46.31 |
| 2011 | Ibrahim Jeilan, Ethiopia | 27:13.81 |

### MARATHON

| | | |
|---|---|---|
| 1983 | Rob de Castella, Australia | 2:10:03 |
| 1987 | Douglas Wakiihuri, Kenya | 2:11:48 |
| 1991 | Hiromi Taniguchi, Japan | 2:14:57 |
| 1993 | Mark Plaatjes, United States | 2:13:57 |
| 1995 | Martín Fiz, Spain | 2:11:41 |
| 1997 | Abel Anton, Spain | 2:13:16 |
| 1999 | Abel Anton, Spain | 2:13:36 |

### MARATHON (Cont.)

| | | |
|---|---|---|
| 2001 | Gezahegne Abera, Ethiopia | 2:12:42 |
| 2003 | Jaouad Gharib, Morocco | 2:08.31 |
| 2005 | Jaouad Gharib, Morocco | 2:10:10 |
| 2007 | Luke Kibet, Kenya | 2:15:59 |
| 2009 | Abel Kirui, Kenya | 2:06.54 |
| 2011 | Abel Kirui, Kenya | 2:07:38 |

### 110-METER HURDLES

| | | |
|---|---|---|
| 1983 | Greg Foster, United States | 13.42 |
| 1987 | Greg Foster, United States | 13.21 |
| 1991 | Greg Foster, United States | 13.06 |
| 1993 | Colin Jackson, Great Britain | 12.91 WR |
| 1995 | Allen Johnson, United States | 13.00 |
| 1997 | Allen Johnson, United States | 12.93 |
| 1999 | Colin Jackson, Great Britain | 13.04 |
| 2001 | Allen Johnson, United States | 13.04 |
| 2003 | Allen Johnson, United States | 13.12 |
| 2005 | Ladji Doucoure, France | 13:07 |
| 2007 | Liu Xiang, China | 12.95 |
| 2009 | Ryan Brathwaite, Barbados | 13.14 |
| 2011 | Jason Richardson, United States | 13.16 |

### 400-METER HURDLES

| | | |
|---|---|---|
| 1983 | Edwin Moses, United States | 47.50 |
| 1987 | Edwin Moses, United States | 47.46 |
| 1991 | Samuel Matete, Zambia | 47.64 |
| 1993 | Kevin Young, United States | 47.18 |
| 1995 | Derrick Adkins, United States | 47.98 |
| 1997 | Stéphane Diagana, France | 47.70 |
| 1999 | Fabrizio Mori, Italy | 47.72 |
| 2001 | Felix Sánchez, Dominican Rep. | 47.49 |
| 2003 | Felix Sánchez, Dominican Rep. | 47.25 |
| 2005 | Bershawn Jackson, United States | 47.30 |
| 2007 | Kerron Clement, United States | 47.61 |
| 2009 | Kerron Clement, United States | 47.91 |
| 2011 | David Greene, United Kingdom | 48.26 |

### 20-KILOMETER WALK

| | | |
|---|---|---|
| 1983 | Ernesto Canto, Mexico | 1:20:49 |
| 1987 | Maurizio Damilano, Italy | 1:20:45 |
| 1991 | Maurizio Damilano, Italy | 1:19:37 |
| 1993 | Valentin Massana, Spain | 1:22:31 |
| 1995 | Michele Didoni, Italy | 1:19:59 |
| 1997 | Daniel Garcia, Mexico | 1:21:43 |
| 1999 | Ilya Markov, Russia | 1:23:34 |
| 2001 | Roman Rasskazov, Russia | 1:20:31 |
| 2003 | Jefferson Pérez, Ecuador | 1:17.21 WR |
| 2005 | Jefferson Pérez, Ecuador | 1:18:35 |
| 2007 | Jefferson Pérez, Ecuador | 1:22:20 |
| 2009 | Valeriy Borchin, Russia | 1:18.41 |
| 2011 | Valeriy Borchin, Russia | 1:19.56 |

### 50-KILOMETER WALK

| | | |
|---|---|---|
| 1983 | Ronald Weigel, East Germany | 3:43:08 |
| 1987 | Hartwig Gauder, East Germany | 3:40:53 |
| 1991 | Aleksandr Potashov, USSR | 3:53:09 |
| 1993 | Jesus Angel Garcia, Spain | 3:41:41 |
| 1995 | Valentin Kononen, Finland | 3:43:42 |
| 1997 | Robert Korzeniowski, Poland | 3:44:46 |
| 1999 | German Skurygin, Russia | 3:44:23 |
| 2001 | Robert Korzeniowski, Poland | 3:42:08 |
| 2003 | R. Korzeniowski, Poland | 3:36:03 WR |
| 2005 | S. Kirdyapkin, Russia | 3:38:08 |
| 2007 | Nathan Deakes, Australia | 3:43:53 |
| 2009 | Sergey Kirdyapkin, Russia | 3:38.35 |
| 2011 | Sergey Bakulin, Russia | 3:41.24 |

WR=World record.

## Men *(Cont.)*

### 4 X 100-METER RELAY

| | | |
|---|---|---|
| 1983 | United States (Emmit King, Willie Gault, Calvin Smith, Carl Lewis) | 37.86 |
| 1987 | United States (Lee McRae, Lee McNeil, Harvey Glance, Carl Lewis) | 37.90 |
| 1991 | United States (A. Cason L. Burrell, D. Mitchell, C. Lewis) | 37.50 WR |
| 1993 | United States (J. Drummond, A. Cason, D. Mitchell, L. Burrell) | 37.48 |
| 1995 | Canada (Robert Esmie, Glenroy Gilbert, Bruny Surin, Donovan Bailey) | 38.31 |
| 1997 | Canada (Robert Esmie, Glenroy Gilbert, Bruny Surin, Donovan Bailey) | 37.86 |
| 1999 | United States (Jon Drummond, Tim Montgomery, Brian Lewis, Maurice Greene) | 37.59 |
| 2001 | United States (Mickey Grimes, Bernard Williams, Dennis Mitchell, Tim Montgomery) | 37.96 |
| 2003 | United States (J. Capel, B. Williams D.Patton, J. Johnson) | 38.06 |
| 2005 | Trinidad and Tobago (L. Doucoure, R. Pognon, E. De Lepine, Dovy Lueyi) | 38.08 |
| 2007 | United States (D. Patton, W. Spearmon, T. Gay, L. Dixon) | 37.78 |
| 2009 | Jamaica (Steve Mullings, Michael Frater, Usain Bolt, Asafa Powell) | 37.31 |
| 2011 | Jamaica (Nesta Carter, Michael Frater, Yohan Blake, Usain Bolt) | 37.04WR |

### 4 X 400-METER RELAY

| | | |
|---|---|---|
| 1983 | USSR (S. Lovachev,A. Troschilo, N. Chernyetski, V. Markin) | 3:00.79 |
| 1987 | United States (Danny Everett Rod Haley, Antonio McKay, Butch Reynolds) | 2:57.29 |
| 1991 | Great Britain (Roger Black Derek Redmond, John Regis, Kriss Akabusi) | 2:57.53 |
| 1993 | United States (Andrew Valmon, Quincy Watts, Butch Reynolds, Michael Johnson) | 2:54.29 WR |
| 1995 | United States (Marlon Ramsey, Derek Mills, Butch Reynolds, Michael Johnson) | 2:57.32 |
| 1997 | United States (J. Young, A. Pettigrew, C. Jones, T. Washington) | 2:56.47 |
| 1999 | United States (Jerome Davis, Antonio Pettigrew, Angelo Taylor, Michael Johnson) | 2:56.45 |
| 2001 | United States (L. Byrd, A. Pettigrew, D. Brew, A. Taylor) | 2:57.54 |
| 2003 | United States (C. Harrison, T. Washington, D. Brew, J. Young) | 2:58.88 |
| 2005 | United States (D. Brew, R. Andrew, D. Williamson, B. Wariner) | 2:56.91 |
| 2007 | United States (LaShawn Merritt, Angelo Taylor, Darold Williamson, Jeremy Wariner) | 2:55.56 |
| 2009 | United States (Angelo Taylor, Jeremy Wariner, Kerron Clement, LaShawn Merritt) | 2:57.86 |
| 2011 | United States (Greg Nixon, Bershawn Jackson, Angelo Taylor, LaShawn Merritt) | 2:59.31 |

### HIGH JUMP

| | | |
|---|---|---|
| 1983 | Gennadi Avdeyenko, USSR | 2.32m |
| 1987 | Patrik Sjoberg, Sweden | 2.38m |
| 1991 | Charles Austin, United States | 2.38m |
| 1993 | Javier Sotomayor, Cuba | 2.40mWR |
| 1995 | Troy Kemp, Bahamas | 2.37m |
| 1997 | Javier Sotomayor, Cuba | 2.37m |
| 1999 | Vyacheslav Voronin, Russia | 2.37m |
| 2001 | Martin Buss, Germany | 2.36m |
| 2003 | Jacques Freitag, South Africa | 2.35m |
| 2005 | Yuriy Krymarenko,Ukraine | 2.32m |
| 2007 | Donald Thoma, Bahamas | 2.35m |
| 2009 | Yaroslav Rybakov, Russia | 2.32m |
| 2011 | Jesse Williams, United States | 2.35m |

### POLE VAULT

| | | |
|---|---|---|
| 1983 | Sergei Bubka, USSR | 5.70m |
| 1987 | Sergei Bubka, USSR | 5.85m |
| 1991 | Sergei Bubka, USSR | 5.95m |
| 1993 | Sergei Bubka, Ukraine | 6.00m |
| 1995 | Sergei Bubka, Ukraine | 5.92m |
| 1997 | Sergei Bubka, Ukraine | 6.01m |
| 1999 | Maksim Tarasov, Russia | 6.02m |
| 2001 | Dmitri Markov, Australia | 6.05mWR |
| 2003 | Guisepe Gibilisco, Italy | 5.90m |
| 2005 | Rens Blom, Netherlands | 5.80m |
| 2007 | Brad Walker, United States | 5.86m |
| 2009 | Steven Hooker, Australia | 5.90m |
| 2011 | Pawel Wojciechowski, Poland | 5.90m |

### LONG JUMP

| | | |
|---|---|---|
| 1983 | Carl Lewis, United States | 8.55m |
| 1987 | Carl Lewis, United States | 8.67m |
| 1991 | Mike Powell, United States | 8.95mWR |
| 1993 | Mike Powell, United States | 8.59m |
| 1995 | Iván Pedroso, Cuba | 8.71m |
| 1997 | Iván Pedroso, Cuba | 8.51m |
| 1999 | Iván Pedroso, Cuba | 8.62m |
| 2001 | Iván Pedroso, Cuba | 8.43m |
| 2003 | Dwight Phillips, United States | 8.29m |
| 2005 | Dwight Phillips, United States | 8.60m |
| 2007 | Irving Saladino, Panama | 8.57m |
| 2009 | Dwight Phillips, United States | 8.54m |
| 2011 | Dwight Phillips, United States | 8.45m |

### TRIPLE JUMP

| | | |
|---|---|---|
| 1983 | Zdzislaw Hoffmann, Poland | 17.42m |
| 1987 | Hristo Markov, Bulgaria | 17.92m |
| 1991 | Kenny Harrison, United States | 17.78m |
| 1993 | Mike Conley, United States | 17.86m |
| 1995 | Jonathan Edwards, G.B. | 18.29m WR |
| 1997 | Yoelvis Quesada, Cuba | 17.85m |
| 1999 | Charles Friedek, Germany | 17.59m |
| 2001 | Jonathan Edwards, G. Britain | 17.92m |
| 2003 | Christian Olsson, Sweden | 17.72m |
| 2005 | Walter Davis, United States | 17.57m |
| 2007 | Nelson Evora, Portugal | 17.74m |
| 2009 | Phillips Idowu, United Kingdom | 17.73m |
| 2011 | Christian Taylor, United States | 17.96m |

### SHOT PUT

| | | |
|---|---|---|
| 1983 | Edward Sarul, Poland | 21.39m |
| 1987 | Werner Günthör, Switz. | 22.23mWR |
| 1991 | Werner Günthör, Switz. | 21.67m |
| 1993 | Werner Günthör, Switz. | 21.97m |
| 1995 | John Godina, United States | 21.47m |
| 1997 | John Godina, United States | 21.44m |
| 1999 | C.J. Hunter, United States | 21.79m |
| 2001 | John Godina, United States | 21.87m |

## Men *(Cont.)*

### SHOT PUT *(Cont.)*

| | | |
|---|---|---|
| 2003 | Andrei Mikahnevic, Bulgaria | 21.69m |
| 2005 | Adam Nelson, United States | 21.73m |
| 2007 | Reese Hoffa, United States | 22.04m |
| 2009 | Christian Cantwell, United States | 22.03m |
| 2011 | David Storl, Germany | 21.78m |

### DISCUS THROW

| | | |
|---|---|---|
| 1983 | Imrich Bugar, Czechoslovakia | 67.72m |
| 1987 | Juergen Schult, E Germany | 68.74m |
| 1991 | Lars Riedel, Germany | 66.20m |
| 1993 | Lars Riedel, Germany | 67.72m |
| 1995 | Lars Riedel, Germany | 68.76m |
| 1997 | Lars Riedel, Germany | 68.54m |
| 1999 | Anthony Washington, U.S. | 69.08m |
| 2001 | Lars Riedel, Germany | 69.72m |
| 2003 | Virgilijus Alekna, Lithuania | 69.69m |
| 2005 | Virgilijus Alekna, Lithuania | 70.17mWR |
| 2007 | Gerd Kanter, Estonia | 68.94m |
| 2009 | Robert Harting, Germany | 69.43m |
| 2011 | Robert Harting, Germany | 68.97m |

### HAMMER THROW

| | | |
|---|---|---|
| 1983 | Sergei Litvinov, USSR | 82.68m |
| 1987 | Sergei Litvinov, USSR | 83.06m |
| 1991 | Yuriy Sedykh, USSR | 81.70m |
| 1993 | Andrey Abduvaliyev, Tajikistan | 81.64m |
| 1995 | Andrey Abduvaliyev, Tajikistan | 81.56m |
| 1997 | Heinz Weis, Germany | 81.78m |
| 1999 | Karsten Kobs, Germany | 80.24m |
| 2001 | Szymon Ziolkowski, Poland | 83.38m |
| 2003 | Ivan Tikhon, Belarus | 83.05m |
| 2005 | Ivan Tikhon, Belarus | 83.89mWR |
| 2007 | Ivan Tsikhan, Belarus | 83.63m |

### HAMMER THROW *(Cont.)*

| | | |
|---|---|---|
| 2009 | Primoz Kozmus, Slovenia | 80.84m |
| 2011 | Koji Murofushi, Japan | 81.24m |

### JAVELIN

| | | |
|---|---|---|
| 1983 | Detlef Michel, East Germany | 89.48m |
| 1987 | Seppo Räty, Finland | 83.54m |
| 1991 | Kimmo Kinnunen, Finland | 90.82m |
| 1993 | Jan Zelezny, Czech Rep. | 85.98m |
| 1995 | Jan Zelezny, Czech Rep. | 89.58m |
| 1997 | Marius Corbett, South Africa | 88.40m |
| 1999 | Aki Parviainen, Finland | 89.52m |
| 2001 | Jan Zelezny, Czech Rep. | 92.80mWR |
| 2003 | Sergey Makarov, Russia | 85.44m |
| 2005 | Andrus Varnik, Estonia | 87.17m |
| 2007 | Tero Pitkämäki, Finland | 90.33m |
| 2009 | Andreas Thorkildsen, Norway | 89.59m |
| 2011 | Matthias de Zordo, Germany | 86.27m |

### DECATHLON

| | | |
|---|---|---|
| 1983 | Daley Thompson, Great Britain | 8666 pts |
| 1987 | Torsten Voss, East Germany | 8680 pts |
| 1991 | Dan O'Brien, United States | 8812 pts |
| 1993 | Dan O'Brien, United States | 8817 pts |
| 1995 | Dan O'Brien, United States | 8695 pts |
| 1997 | Tomás Dvorák, Czech Rep. | 8837 pts |
| 1999 | Tomás Dvorák, Czech Rep. | 8744 pts |
| 2001 | Tomás Dvorák, Czech Rep. | 8902 ptsWR |
| 2003 | Tom Pappas, United States | 8750 pts |
| 2005 | Bryan Clay, United States | 8732 pts |
| 2007 | Roman Sebrle, Czech Rep. | 8676 pts |
| 2009 | Trey Hardee, United States | 8790 pts |
| 2011 | Trey Hardee, United States | 8607 pts |

## Women

### 100 METERS

| | | |
|---|---|---|
| 1983 | Marlies Gohr, East Germany | 10.97 |
| 1987 | Silke Gladisch, East Germany | 10.90 |
| 1991 | Katrin Krabbe, Germany | 10.99 |
| 1993 | Gail Devers, United States | 10.82 |
| 1995 | Gwen Torrence, United States | 10.85 |
| 1997 | Marion Jones, United States | 10.83 |
| 1999 | Marion Jones, United States | 10.70 |
| 2001 | Zhanna Pintusevich-Block, Ukraine | 10.82 |
| 2003 | Kelli White, United States | 10.85 |
| 2005 | Lauryn Williams, United States | 10.93 |
| 2007 | Veronica Campbell, Jamaica | 11.01 |
| 2009 | Shelly-Ann Fraser, Jamaica | 10.73 |
| 2011 | Carmelita Jeter, United States | 10.90 |

### 200 METERS

| | | |
|---|---|---|
| 1983 | Marita Koch, East Germany | 22.13 |
| 1987 | Silke Gladisch, East Germany | 21.74 |
| 1991 | Katrin Krabbe, Germany | 22.09 |
| 1993 | Merlene Ottey, Jamaica | 21.98 |
| 1995 | Merlene Ottey, Jamaica | 22.12 |
| 1997 | Zhanna Pintusevich, Ukraine | 22.32 |
| 1999 | Inger Miller, United States | 21.77 |
| 2001 | Marion Jones, United States | 22.39 |
| 2003 | Kelli White, United States | 22.05 |
| 2005 | Allyson Felix, United States | 22.16 |
| 2007 | Allyson Felix, United States | 21.81 |
| 2009 | Allyson Felix, United States | 22.02 |
| 2011 | Veronica Campell-Brown, Jamaica | 22.22 |

### 400 METERS

| | | |
|---|---|---|
| 1983 | Jarmila Kratochvilova, Czech. | 47.99 |
| 1987 | Olga Bryzgina, USSR | 49.38 |
| 1991 | Marie-José Pérec, France | 49.13 |

### 400 METERS *(Cont.)*

| | | |
|---|---|---|
| 1993 | Jearl Miles, United States | 49.82 |
| 1995 | Marie-José Pérec, France | 49.28 |
| 1997 | Cathy Freeman, Australia | 49.77 |
| 1999 | Cathy Freeman, Australia | 49.67 |
| 2001 | Amy Mbacke Thiam, Senegal | 49.86 |
| 2003 | Ana Guevara, Mexico | 48.89 |
| 2005 | Darling Williams, Bahamas | 49.55 |
| 2007 | Christine Ohuruogu, Great Britain | 49.61 |
| 2009 | Sanya Richards, United States | 49.00 |
| 2011 | Amantle Montsho, Botswana | 49.56 |

### 800 METERS

| | | |
|---|---|---|
| 1983 | Jarmila Kratochvilova, Czech. | 1:54.68 |
| 1987 | Sigrun Wodars, East Germany | 1:55.26 |
| 1991 | Lilia Nurutdinova, USSR | 1:57.50 |
| 1993 | Maria Mutola, Mozambique | 1:55.43 |
| 1995 | Ana Quirot, Cuba | 1:56.11 |
| 1997 | Ana Quirot, Cuba | 1:57.14 |
| 1999 | Ludmila Formanová, Czech Rep. | 1:56.68 |
| 2001 | Maria Mutola, Mozambique | 1:57.17 |
| 2003 | Maria Mutola, Mozambique | 1:59.89 |
| 2005 | Zulia Calatayud, Cuba | 1:58.82 |
| 2007 | Janeth Jepkosgei, Kenya | 1:56.04 |
| 2009 | Caster Semenya, South Africa | 1:55.45 |
| 2011 | Mariya Savinova, Russia | 1:55.87 |

### 1,500 METERS

| | | |
|---|---|---|
| 1983 | Mary Slaney, United States | 4:00.90 |
| 1987 | Tatyana Samolenko, USSR | 3:58.56 |
| 1991 | Hassiba Boulmerka, Algeria | 4:02.21 |
| 1993 | Dong Liu, China | 4:00.50 |
| 1995 | Hassiba Boulmerka, Algeria | 4:02.42 |
| 1997 | Carla Sacramento, Portugal | 4:04.24 |

WR=World record.

## Women *(Cont.)*

### 1,500 METERS *(Cont.)*

| | | |
|---|---|---|
| 1999 | Svetlana Masterkova, Russia | 3:59.53 |
| 2001 | Gabriela Szabo, Romania | 4:00.57 |
| 2003 | Tatyana Tomashova, Russia | 3:58.52 |
| 2005 | Tatyana Tomashova, Russia | 4:00.35 |
| 2007 | Maryam Yusuf Jamal, Bahrain | 3:58.75 |
| 2009 | Maryam Yusuf Jamal, Bahrain | 4:03.74 |
| 2011 | Jennifer Simpson, United States | 4:05.40 |

### 3,000 METERS

| | | |
|---|---|---|
| 1983 | Mary Slaney, United States | 8:34.62 |
| 1987 | Tatyana Samolenko, USSR | 8:38.73 |
| 1991 | Tatyana Dorovskikh, USSR | 8:35.82 |
| 1993 | Qu Yunxia, China | 8:28.71 |

### 3,000 METER STEEPLECHASE

| | | |
|---|---|---|
| 2005 | Docus Inzikuru, Uganda | 9:18.24 |
| 2007 | Yekaterina Volkova, Russia | 9:06.57 |
| 2009 | Marta Dominguez, Spain | 9:07.32 |
| 2011 | Yuliya Zaripova, Russia | 9:07.03 |

### 5,000 METERS

| | | |
|---|---|---|
| 1995 | Sonia O'Sullivan, Ireland | 14:46.47 |
| 1997 | Gabriela Szabo, Romania | 14:57.68 |
| 1999 | Gabriela Szabo, Romania | 14:41.82 |
| 2001 | Olga Yegorova, Russia | 15:03.39 |
| 2003 | Tirunesh Dibaba, Ethiopia | 14:51.72 |
| 2005 | Tirunesh Dibaba, Ethiopia | 14:38.59 |
| 2007 | Meseret Defar, Ethiopia | 14:57.91 |
| 2009 | Vivian Cheruiyot, Kenya | 14:57.97 |
| 2011 | Vivian Cheruiyot, Kenua | 14:55.36 |

### 10,000 METERS

| | | |
|---|---|---|
| 1987 | Ingrid Kristiansen, Norway | 31:05.85 |
| 1991 | Liz McColgan, Great Britain | 31:14.31 |
| 1993 | Wang Junxia, China | 30:49:30 |
| 1995 | Fernanda Ribeiro, Portugal | 31:04.99 |
| 1997 | Sally Barsosio, Kenya | 31:32.92 |
| 1999 | Gete Wami, Ethiopia | 30:24.56 |
| 2001 | Derartu Tulu, Ethiopia | 31:48.81 |
| 2003 | Berhane Adere, Ethiopia | 30:04.18 |
| 2005 | Tirunesh Dibaba, Ethiopia | 30:24.02 |
| 2007 | Tirunesh Dibaba, Ethiopia | 31:55.41 |
| 2009 | Linet Masai, Kenya | 30:51.24 |
| 2011 | Vivian Cheruiyot, Kenya | 30:48.98 |

### MARATHON

| | | |
|---|---|---|
| 1983 | Grete Waitz, Norway | 2:28:09 |
| 1987 | Rosa Mota, Portugal | 2:25:17 |
| 1991 | Wanda Panfil, Poland | 2:29:53 |
| 1993 | Junko Asari, Japan | 2:30:03 |
| 1995 | Manuela Machado, Portugal | 2:25:39* |
| 1997 | Hiromi Suzuki, Japan | 2:29:48 |
| 1999 | Jong Song-Ok, North Korea | 2:26:59 |
| 2001 | Lidia Simon, Romania | 2:26:01 |
| 2003 | Catherine Ndereba, Kenya | 2:23:55 |
| 2005 | Paula Radcliffe, Great Britain | 2:20:57 |
| 2007 | Catherine Ndereba, Kenya | 2:30:37 |
| 2009 | Xue Bai, China | 2:25.15 |
| 2011 | Edna Kiplagat, Kenya | 2:28.43 |

### 100-METER HURDLES

| | | |
|---|---|---|
| 1983 | Bettine Jahn, East Germany | 12.35 |
| 1987 | Ginka Zagorcheva, Bulgaria | 12.34 |
| 1991 | Lyudmila Narozhilenko, USSR | 12.59 |
| 1993 | Gail Devers, United States | 12.46 |
| 1995 | Gail Devers, United States | 12.68 |
| 1997 | Ludmila Engquist, Sweden | 12.50 |
| 1999 | Gail Devers, United States | 12.37 |
| 2001 | Anjanette Kirkland, United States | 12.42 |
| 2003 | Perdita Felicien, Canada | 12.53 |

*400 meters short. WR=World Record.

### 100-METER HURDLES *(Cont.)*

| | | |
|---|---|---|
| 2005 | Michelle Perry, United States | 12:66 |
| 2007 | Michelle Perry, United States | 12:46 |
| 2009 | Brigitte Foster-Hylton, Jamaica | 12.51 |
| 2011 | Sally Pearson, Australia | 12.28 |

### 400-METER HURDLES

| | | |
|---|---|---|
| 1983 | Yekaterina Fesenko, USSR | 54.14 |
| 1987 | Sabine Busch, East Germany | 53.62 |
| 1991 | Tatyana Ledovskaya, USSR | 53.11 |
| 1993 | Sally Gunnell, Great Britain | 52.74WR |
| 1995 | Kim Batten, United States | 52.61 |
| 1997 | Nezha Bidouane, Morocco | 52.97 |
| 1999 | Daimi Pernia, Cuba | 52.89 |
| 2001 | Nezha Bidouane, Morocco | 53.34 |
| 2003 | Jana Pittman, Australia | 53.22 |
| 2005 | Yuliya Pechonkina, Russia | 52.90 |
| 2007 | Jana Rawlinson, Australia | 53.31 |
| 2009 | Melaine Walker, Jamaica | 52.42 |
| 2011 | Lashinda Demus, United States | 52.47 |

### 20-KILOMETER WALK

| | | |
|---|---|---|
| 1999 | Hongyu Liu, China | 1:30:50 |
| 2001 | Olimpiada Ivanova, Russia | 1:27:48 |
| 2003 | Yelena Nikolayeva, Russia | 1:26:52 |
| 2005 | Olimpiada Ivanova, Russia | 1:25:41 |
| 2007 | Olga Kaniskina, Russia | 1:30:09 |
| 2009 | Olga Kaniskina, Russia | 1:28.09 |
| 2011 | Olga Kaniskina, Russia | 1:29.42 |

### 4 X 100-METER RELAY

| | | |
|---|---|---|
| 1983 | E Germany (S. Gladisch, M. Koch, I. Auerswald, M. Gohr) | 41.76 |
| 1987 | United States (A. Brown, D. Williams, F. Griffith, P. Marshall) | 41.58 |
| 1991 | Jamaica (Dalia Duhaney, Juliet Cuthbert, Beverley McDonald, Merlene Ottey) | 41.94 |
| 1993 | Russia (Olga Bogoslovskaya, Galina Malchugina, Natalya Voronova, Irina Privalova) | 41.49 |
| 1995 | United States (Celena Mondie-Milner, Carlette Guidry, Chryste Gaines, Gwen Torrence) | 42.12 |
| 1997 | United States (C. Gaines, M. Jones, I. Miller, G.Devers) | 41.47 |
| 1999 | Bahamas (S. Fynes, C. Sturrup, P. Davis-Thompson, D. Ferguson) | 41.92 |
| 2001 | United States (Kelli White, Chryste Gaines, Inger Miller, Marion Jones) | 41.71 |
| 2003 | France (P. Girard, M. Hurtis S. Félix, C. Arron) | 41.78 |
| 2005 | Jamaica, (A. Daigie, M. Lee, M. Billiams | 41.78 |
| 2007 | United States (Lauryn Williams, Allyson Felix, Mikele Barber, Torri Edwards) | 41.98 |
| 2009 | Jamaica (Simone Facey, S. Fraser, Aleen Bailey, Kerron Stewart) | 42.06 |
| 2011 | United States (Bianca Knight, Allyson Felix, Marshevet Myers, Carmelita Jeter) | 41.56 |

### 4 X 400-METER RELAY

| | | |
|---|---|---|
| 1983 | East Germany (Kerstin Walther, Sabine Busch, Marita Koch, Dagmar Rubsam) | 3:19.73 |
| 1987 | East Germany (Dagmar Neubauer, Kirsten Emmelmann, Petra Müller, Sabine Busch) | 3:18.63 |
| 1991 | USSR (Tatyana Ledovskaya, Lyudmila Dzhigalova, Olga Nazarova, Olga Bryzgina) | 3:18.43 |

## Women *(Cont.)*

### 4 X 400-METER RELAY *(Cont.)*

| | | |
|---|---|---|
| 1993 | United States (Gwen Torrence, Maicel Malone, Natasha Kaiser-Brown, Jearl Miles) | 3:16.71 |
| 1995 | United States (Kim Graham, Rochelle Stevens, Camara Jones, Jearl Miles) | 3:22.39 |
| 1997 | Germany (A. Feller, U. Rohlander, A. Rucker, G. Breuer) | 3:20.92 |
| 1999 | Russia (Tatyana Chebykina, Svetlana Goncharenko, Olga Kotylarova, Natalya Nazarova) | 3:21.98 |
| 2001 | Jamaica (Sandie Richards, Catherine Scott, Debbie Ann Parris, Lorraine Fenton) | 3:20.65 |
| 2003 | United States (M. Barber, D. Washington, Miles-Clark, S. Richards) | 3:22.63 |
| 2005 | Russia (Y. Pechonkina, O. Krasnomovets, N. Antyukh, S. Pospelova) | 3:20.95 |
| 2007 | United States (D. Trotter, A. Felix, M. Wineberg, S.Richards) | 3:18.55 |
| 2009 | United States (Debbie Dunn, A. Felix Lashinda Demus, Sanya Richards) | 3:17.83 |
| 2011 | United States (Sanya Richards-Ross, A. Felix, Jessica Beard, Francena McCrory) | 3:18.09 |

### HIGH JUMP

| | | |
|---|---|---|
| 1983 | Tamara Bykova, USSR | 2.01m |
| 1987 | Stefka Kostadinova, Bulgaria | 2.09mWR |
| 1991 | Heike Henkel, Germany | 2.05m |
| 1993 | Ioamnet Quintero, Cuba | 1.99m |
| 1995 | Stefka Kostadinova, Bulgaria | 2.01m |
| 1997 | Hanne Haugland, Norway | 1.99m |
| 1999 | Inga Babakova, Ukraine | 1.99m |
| 2001 | Hestrie Cloete, South Africa | 2.00m |
| 2003 | Hestrie Cloete, South Africa | 2.06m |
| 2005 | Kajsa Bergvist, Sweden | 2.02m |
| 2007 | Blanka Vlasic, Croatia | 2.05m |
| 2009 | Blanka Vlasic, Croatia | 2.04m |
| 2011 | Anna Chicerova, Russia | 2.03m |

### POLE VAULT

| | | |
|---|---|---|
| 1999 | Stacy Dragila, United States | 4.06mEWR |
| 2001 | Stacy Dragila, United States | 4.75m |
| 2003 | Svetlana Feofanova, Russia | 4.75m |
| 2005 | Yelena Isinbayeva, Russia | 5.01mWR |
| 2007 | Yelena Isinbayeva, Russia | 4.80m |
| 2009 | Anna Rogowska, Poland | 4.75m |
| 2011 | Fabiana Murer, Brazil | 4.85m |

### LONG JUMP

| | | |
|---|---|---|
| 1983 | Heike Daute, E Germany | 7.27m |
| 1987 | Jackie Joyner-Kersee, U.S. | 7.36mWR |
| 1991 | Jackie Joyner-Kersee, United States | 7.32m |
| 1993 | Heike Drechsler, Germany | 7.11m |
| 1995 | Fiona May, Italy | 6.98m |
| 1997 | Lyudmila Galkina, Russia | 7.05m |
| 1999 | Niurka Montalvo, Spain | 7.06m |
| 2001 | Fiona May, Italy | 6.87m |
| 2003 | Eunice Barber, France | 6.99m |
| 2005 | Tianna Madison, United States | 6.89m |
| 2007 | Tatyana Lebedeva, Russia | 7.03m |
| 2009 | Brittney Reese, United States | 7.10m |
| 2011 | Brittney Reese, United States | 6.82m |

### TRIPLE JUMP

| | | |
|---|---|---|
| 1993 | Ana Biryukova, Russia | 15.09m |
| 1995 | Inessa Kravets, Ukraine | 15.50mWR |
| 1997 | S. Kasparkova, Czech Rep. | 15.20m |
| 1999 | Paraskevi Tsiamita, Greece | 14.88m |
| 2001 | Tatyana Lebedeva, Russia | 15.25m |
| 2003 | Tatyana Lebedeva, Russia | 15.18m |
| 2005 | Trecia Smith, Jamaica | 15.11m |

### TRIPLE JUMP *(Cont.)*

| | | |
|---|---|---|
| 2007 | Yargeris Savigne, Cuba | 15.28m |
| 2009 | Yargeris Savigne, Cuba | 14.95m |
| 2011 | Olha Saladuha, Ukraine | 14.94m |

### SHOT PUT

| | | |
|---|---|---|
| 1983 | Helena Fibingerova, Czech. | 21.05m |
| 1987 | Natalya Lisovskaya, USSR | 21.24mWR |
| 1991 | Zhihong Huang, China | 20.83m |
| 1993 | Zhihong Huang, China | 20.57m |
| 1995 | Astrid Kumbernuss, Germany | 21.22m |
| 1997 | Astrid Kumbernuss, Germany | 20.71m |
| 1999 | Astrid Kumbernuss, Germany | 19.85m |
| 2001 | Yanina Korolchik, Belarus | 20.61m |
| 2003 | Svetlana Krivelyova, Russia | 20.63m |
| 2005 | Nadezhda Ostapchuk, Russia | 20.51m |
| 2007 | Valerie Vili, New Zealand | 20.54m |
| 2009 | Valerie Vili, New Zealand | 20.44m |
| 2011 | Valerie Adams, New Zealand | 21.24m |

### HAMMER THROW

| | | |
|---|---|---|
| 1999 | Mihaéla Melinte, Romania | 75.20mWR |
| 2001 | Yipsi Moreno, Cuba | 70.65m |
| 2003 | Yipsi Moreno, Cuba | 70.30m |
| 2005 | Olga Kuzenkova, Russia | 75.10m |
| 2007 | Betty Heidler, Germany | 74.76m |
| 2009 | Anita Wlodarczyk, Poland | 77.96mWR |
| 2011 | Tatyana Lysenko, Russia | 77.13 |

### JAVELIN

| | | |
|---|---|---|
| 1983 | Tiina Lillak, Finland | 70.82m |
| 1987 | Fatima Whitbread, United Kingdom | 76.64m |
| 1991 | Xu Demei, China | 68.78m |
| 1993 | Trine Solberg-Hattestad, Norway | 69.18m |
| 1995 | Natalya Shikolenko, Belarus | 67.56m |
| 1997 | Trine Hattestad, Norway | 68.78m |
| 1999 | Mirela Manjani-Tzelili, Greece | 67.09m |
| 2001 | Osleidys Menendez, Cuba | 69.53m |
| 2003 | Mirela Manjani, Greece | 66.52m |
| 2005 | Osleidys Menendez, Cuba | 71.70m |
| 2007 | Barbora Spotakova, Czech Rep. | 67.07m |
| 2009 | Steffi Nerius, Germany | 67.30m |
| 2011 | Maria Abakumova, Russia | 71.99m |

### DISCUS THROW

| | | |
|---|---|---|
| 1983 | Martina Opitz, E Germany | 68.94m |
| 1987 | Martina Hellmann, East Germ. | 71.62mWR |
| 1991 | Tsvetanka Khristova, Bulgaria | 71.02m |
| 1993 | Olga Burova, Russia | 67.40m |
| 1995 | Ellina Zvereva, Belarus | 68.64m |
| 1997 | Beatrice Faumuina, New Zeal. | 66.82m |
| 1999 | Franka Dietzsch, Germany | 68.14m |
| 2001 | Ellina Zvereva,, Belarus | 67.10m |
| 2003 | Irina Yatchenko, Belarus | 67.32m |
| 2005 | Franka Dietzsch, Germany | 66.56m |
| 2007 | Franka Dietzsch, Germany | 66.61m |
| 2009 | Dani Samuels, Australia | 65.44m |
| 2011 | Yanfeng Li, China | 66.52m |

### HEPTATHLON

| | | |
|---|---|---|
| 1983 | Ramona Neubert, E. Germany | 6714 pts |
| 1987 | Jackie Joyner-Kersee, U.S. | 7128 pts |
| 1991 | Sabine Braun, Germany | 6672 pts |
| 1993 | Jackie Joyner-Kersee, U.S. | 6831 pts |
| 1995 | Ghada Shouaa, Syria | 6651 pts |
| 1997 | Sabine Braun, Germany | 6739 pts |
| 1999 | Eunice Barber, France | 6861 pts |
| 2001 | Yelena Prokhorova, Russia | 6694 pts |
| 2003 | Carolina Kluft, Sweden | 7001 pts |
| 2005 | Carolina Kluft, Sweden | 6887 pts |
| 2007 | Carolina Kluft, Sweden | 7032 pts |
| 2009 | Jessica Ennis, United Kingdom | 6731 pts |
| 2011 | Tatyana Chernova, Russia | 6880 pts |

WR=World Record. EWR=Equals world record.

# Swimming

**U.S. swimmers
Ryan Lochte (r.) and Michael Phelps
dominated the 2011 Worlds,
winning 13 medals—nine gold—
between them**

HEINZ KLUETMEYER

## World and American Records

### Men

| Freestyle | Time | Record Holder | Date | Site |
|---|---|---|---|---|
| 50 meters | 20.91 | Cesar Cielo Filho, Brazil (W) | 12-18-09 | Sao Paulo |
| | 21.40 | Cullen Jones (A) | 8-01-09 | Rome |
| 100 meters | 46.91 | Cesar Cielo Filho, Brazil (W) | 7-30-09 | Rome |
| | 47.33 | David Walters (A) | 7-30-09 | Rome |
| 200 meters | 1:42.00 | Paul Biedermann, Germany (W) | 7-28-09 | Rome |
| | 1:42.96 | Michael Phelps (A) | 8-12-08 | Beijing |
| 400 meters | 3:40.07 | Paul Biedermann, Germany (W) | 7-26-09 | Rome |
| | 3:42.78 | Larsen Jensen (A) | 8-10-08 | Beijing |
| 800 meters | 7:32.12 | Lin Zhang, China (W) | 7-29-09 | Rome |
| | 7:45.63 | Larsen Jensen (A) | 7-27-05 | Montreal |
| 1,500 meters | 14:34.14 | Sun Yang (W) | 7-31-11 | Shanghai |
| | 14:45.29 | Larsen Jensen (A) | 8-21-04 | Athens |

| Backstroke | Time | Record Holder | Date | Site |
|---|---|---|---|---|
| 50 meters | 24.04 | Liam Tancock, United Kingdom (W) | 8-02-09 | Rome |
| | 24.33 | Randall Bal (A) | 12-05-08 | Eindhoven, Neth. |
| 100 meters | 51.94 | Aaron Peirsol (W,A) | 7-08-09 | Indianapolis |
| 200 meters | 1:51.92 | Aaron Peirsol (W,A) | 7-31-09 | Rome |

| Breaststroke | Time | Record Holder | Date | Site |
|---|---|---|---|---|
| 50 meters | 26.67 | Cameron Van Der Burgh, South Africa (W) | 7-29-09 | Rome |
| | 26.86 | Mark Gangloff (A) | 7-29-09 | Rome |
| 100 meters | 58.58 | Brenton Rickard, Australia (W) | 7-27-09 | Rome |
| | 58.96 | Eric Shanteau (A) | 7-26-09 | Rome |
| 200 meters | 2:07.31 | Christian Sprenger, Australia (W) | 7-30-09 | Rome |
| | 2:07.42 | Eric Shanteau (A) | 7-11-09 | Indianapolis |

| Butterfly | Time | Record Holder | Date | Site |
|---|---|---|---|---|
| 50 meters | 22.43 | Rafael Munoz, Spain (W) | 4-05-09 | Malaga, Spain |
| | 22.91 | Bryan Lundqvist (A) | 7-18-09 | Knoxville, Tenn. |
| 100 meters | 49.82 | Michael Phelps (W,A) | 8-01-09 | Rome |
| 200 meters | 1:51.51 | Michael Phelps (W,A) | 7-29-09 | Rome |

| Individual Medley | Time | Record Holder | Date | Site |
|---|---|---|---|---|
| 200 meters | 1:54.00 | Ryan Lochte (W,A) | 7-28-11 | Shanghai |
| 400 meters | 4:03.84 | Michael Phelps (W,A) | 8-10-08 | Beijing |

| Relays | Time | Record Holder | Date | Site |
|---|---|---|---|---|
| 4 x100-meter medley | 3:27.28 | United States (W,A) | 8-02-09 | Rome |
| | | (Aaron Peirsol, Eric Shanteau, Michael Phelps, and David Walters) | | |
| 4 x100-meter freestyle | 3:08.24 | United States (W,A) | 8-11-08 | Beijing |
| | | (Michael Phelps, Garrett Weber-Gale, Cullen Jones and Jason Lezak) | | |
| 4 x 200-meter freestyle | 6:58.55 | United States (W,A) | 7-31-09 | Rome |
| | | (Michael Phelps, Ricky Berens, David Walters and Ryan Lochte) | | |

Note: Records through Oct 1, 2011.

### Women

| Freestyle | Time | Record Holder | Date | Site |
|---|---|---|---|---|
| 50 meters | 23.73 | Britta Steffen, Germany (W) | 8-02-09 | Rome |
| | 24.07 | Dara Torres (A) | 8-17-08 | Beijing |
| 100 meters | 52.07 | Britta Steffen, Germany (W) | 7-31-09 | Rome |
| | 53.02 | Amanda Weir (A) | 7-30-09 | Rome |
| 200 meters | 1:52.98 | Federica Pellegrini, Italy (W) | 7-29-09 | Rome |
| | 1:54.96 | Allison Schmitt (A) | 7-29-09 | Rome |
| 400 meters | 3:59.15 | Federica Pellegrini, Italy (W) | 7-26-09 | Rome |
| | 4:02.20 | Katie Hoff (A) | 2-16-08 | Columbia, Mo. |
| 800 meters | 8:14.10 | Rebecca Adlington, Great Britain (W) | 8-16-08 | Beijing |
| | 8:16.22 | Janet Evans (A) | 8-20-89 | Tokyo |
| 1,500 meters | 15:42.54 | Kate Ziegler (W,A) | 6-17-07 | Mission Viejo, Calif. |

| Backstroke | Time | Record Holder | Date | Site |
|---|---|---|---|---|
| 50 meters | 27.06 | Jing Zhao, China (W) | 7-30-09 | Rome |
| | 27.80 | Hayley McGregory (A) | 6-07-08 | Austin, Tex. |
| 100 meters | 58.12 | Gemma Spofforth, United Kingdom (W) | 7-28-09 | Rome |
| | 58.94* | Natalie Coughlin (A) | 8-17-08 | Beijing |
| 200 meters | 2:04.81 | Kirsty Coventry, Zimbabwe (W) | 8-01-09 | Rome |
| | 2:05.10 | Melissa Franklin (A) | 7-30-11 | Shanghai |

| Breaststroke | Time | Record Holder | Date | Site |
|---|---|---|---|---|
| 50 meters | 29.80 | Jessica Hardy (W,A) | 8-07-09 | Federal Way, Wash. |
| 100 meters | 1:04.45 | Jessica Hardy (W,A) | 8-07-09 | Federal Way, Wash. |
| 200 meters | 2:20.12 | Annamay Pierse, Canada (W) | 7-30-09 | Rome |
| | 2:20.22 | Rebecca Soni (A) | 8-15-08 | Beijing |

| Butterfly | Time | Record Holder | Date | Site |
|---|---|---|---|---|
| 50 meters | 25.07 | Therese Alshammar, Sweden (W) | 7-31-09 | Rome |
| | 25.50 | Dara Torres (A) | 7-11-09 | Indianapolis |
| 100 meters | 56.06 | Sarah Sjostrom, Sweden (W) | 7-27-09 | Rome |
| | 56.47 | Dana Vollmer (A) | 7-24-11 | Shanghai |
| 200 meters | 2:01.81 | Zige Liu, China (W) | 10-21-09 | Jinan, China |
| | 2:04.14 | Mary DeScenza (A) | 7-30-09 | Rome |

| Individual Medley | Time | Record Holder | Date | Site |
|---|---|---|---|---|
| 200 meters | 2:06.15 | Ariana Kukors (W,A) | 7-27-09 | Rome |
| 400 meters | 4:29.45 | Stephanie Rice, Australia (W) | 8-10-08 | Beijing |
| | 4:31.12 | Katie Hoff (A) | 6-29-08 | Omaha, Neb. |

| Relays | Time | Record Holder | Date | Site |
|---|---|---|---|---|
| 4 x100-meter medley | 3:52.19 | China (W) | 8-01-09 | Rome |
| | | (Jing Zhao, Huijia Chen, Liuyang Jiao and Zhesi Li ) | | |
| | 3:52.36 | United States (A) | 7-30-11 | Shanghai |
| | | (Natalie Coughlin, Rebecca Soni, Dana Vollmer and Melissa Franklin) | | |
| 4 x100-meter freestyle | 3:31.72 | Netherlands (W) | 7-26-09 | Rome |
| | | (Inge Dekker, Ranomi Kromowidjojo, Frederike Heemskerk and Magdalena Veldhuis) | | |
| | 3:34.33 | United States (A) | 8-10-08 | Beijing |
| | | (Natalie Coughlin, Lacey Nymeyer, Kara Lynn Joyce and Dara Torres) | | |
| 4 x 200-meter freestyle | 7:42.08 | China (W) | 7-30-09 | Rome |
| | | (Yu Yang, Qian Wei Zhu, Jing Liu, Jiaying Pang) | | |
| | 7:42.56 | United States (A) | 7-30-09 | Rome |
| | | (Dana Vollmer, Lacey Nymeyer, Ariana Kukors and Allison Schmitt) | | |

Note: Records through Oct 1, 2011. *relay lead-off split.

## World Championships History

### Men

#### 50-METER FREESTYLE

| | | |
|---|---|---|
| 1986 | Tom Jager, United States | 22.49‡ |
| 1991 | Tom Jager, United States | 22.16‡ |
| 1994 | Alexander Popov, Russia | 22.17 |
| 1998 | Bill Pilczuk, United States | 22.29 |
| 2001 | Anthony Ervin, United States | 22.09 |
| 2003 | Alexander Popov, Russia | 21.92‡ |
| 2005 | Roland Schoeman, Russia | 21.69 |
| 2007 | Benjamin Wildman-Tobriner, U.S. | 21.88 |
| 2009 | Cesar Cielo Filho, Brazil | 21.08‡ |
| 2011 | Cesar Cielo Filho, Brazil | 21.52 |

#### 100-METER FREESTYLE

| | | |
|---|---|---|
| 1973 | Jim Montgomery, United States | 51.70 |
| 1975 | Andy Coan, United States | 51.25 |
| 1978 | David McCagg, United States | 50.24 |
| 1982 | Jorg Woithe, E. Germany | 50.18 |
| 1986 | Matt Biondi, United States | 48.94 |
| 1991 | Matt Biondi, United States | 49.18 |
| 1994 | Alexander Popov, Russia | 49.12 |
| 1998 | Alexander Popov, Russia | 48.93‡ |
| 2001 | Anthony Ervin, United States | 48.33‡ |
| 2003 | Alexander Popov, Russia | 48.42 |
| 2005 | Filippo Magnini, Italy | 48:12 |
| 2007 | Filippo Magnini, Italy | 48.43 |
| 2009 | Cesar Cielo Filho, Brazil | 46.91* |
| 2011 | James Magnussen, Australia | 47.63 |

#### 200-METER FREESTYLE

| | | |
|---|---|---|
| 1973 | Jim Montgomery, United States | 1:53.02 |
| 1975 | Tim Shaw, United States | 1:52.04‡ |
| 1978 | Billy Forrester, United States | 1:51.02‡ |
| 1982 | Michael Gross, W Germany | 1:49.84 |
| 1986 | Michael Gross, W Germany | 1:47.92 |
| 1991 | Giorgio Lamberti, Italy | 1:47.27‡ |
| 1994 | Antti Kasvio, Finland | 1:47.32 |
| 1998 | Michael Klim, Australia | 1:47.41 |
| 2001 | Ian Thorpe, Australia | 1:44.06* |
| 2003 | Ian Thorpe, Australia | 1:45.14 |
| 2005 | Michael Phelps, United States | 1:45.20 |
| 2007 | Michael Phelps, United States | 1:43.86* |
| 2009 | Paul Biedermann, Germany | 1:42.00* |
| 2011 | Ryan Lochte, United States | 1:44.44 |

#### 400-METER FREESTYLE

| | | |
|---|---|---|
| 1973 | Rick DeMont, United States | 3:58.18‡ |
| 1975 | Tim Shaw, United States | 3:54.88‡ |
| 1978 | Vladimir Salnikov, U.S.S.R. | 3:51.94‡ |
| 1982 | Vladimir Salnikov, U.S.S.R. | 3:51.30‡ |
| 1986 | Rainer Henkel, W Germany | 3:50.05 |
| 1991 | Joerg Hoffman, Germany | 3:48.04‡ |
| 1994 | Kieran Perkins, Australia | 3:43.80* |
| 1998 | Ian Thorpe, Australia | 3:46.29 |
| 2001 | Ian Thorpe, Australia | 3:40.17* |
| 2003 | Ian Thorpe, Australia | 3:42.58 |
| 2005 | Grant Hackett, Australia | 3:42.91 |
| 2007 | Tae Hwan Park, South Korea | 3:44.30 |
| 2009 | Paul Biedermann, Germany | 3:40.07* |
| 2011 | Tae Hwan Park, South Korea | 3:42.04 |

#### 800-METER FREESTYLE

| | | |
|---|---|---|
| 2001 | Ian Thorpe, Australia | 7:39.16* |
| 2003 | Grant Hackett, Australia | 7:43.82 |
| 2005 | Grant Hackett, Australia | 7:38.65* |
| 2007 | Przemyslav Stanczyk, Poland | 7:47.91† |
| 2009 | Lin Zhag, China | 7:32.12* |
| 2011 | Sun Yang, China | 7:38.57 |

#### 1,500-METER FREESTYLE

| | | |
|---|---|---|
| 1973 | Stephen Holland, Australia | 15:31.85 |
| 1975 | Tim Shaw, United States | 15:28.92‡ |
| 1978 | Vladimir Salnikov, U.S.S.R. | 15:03.99‡ |
| 1982 | Vladimir Salnikov, U.S.S.R. | 15:01.77‡ |
| 1986 | Rainer Henkel, W Germany | 15:05.31 |
| 1991 | Joerg Hoffman, Germany | 14:50.36* |
| 1994 | Kieran Perkins, Australia | 14:50.52 |
| 1998 | Grant Hackett, Australia | 14:51.70 |
| 2001 | Grant Hackett, Australia | 14:34.56* |
| 2003 | Grant Hackett, Australia | 14:43.14 |
| 2005 | Grant Hackett, Australia | 14:42.58 |
| 2007 | Mateusz Sawrymowicz, Poland | 14:45.94 |
| 2009 | Oussama Mellouli, Tunisia | 14:37.28 |
| 2011 | Sun Yang, China | 14:34.14* |

#### 50-METER BACKSTROKE

| | | |
|---|---|---|
| 2001 | Randall Bal, United States | 25.34 |
| 2003 | Thomas Rupprath, Germany | 24.80* |
| 2005 | Aristeidis Grigoriadis, Greece | 24.95 |
| 2007 | Gerhard Zandberg, South Africa | 24.98 |
| 2009 | Liam Tancock, United Kingdom | 24.04* |
| 2011 | Liam Tancock, United Kingdom | 24.50 |

#### 100-METER BACKSTROKE

| | | |
|---|---|---|
| 1973 | Roland Matthes, E. Germany | 57.47 |
| 1973 | Roland Matthes, E. Germany | 58.15 |
| 1978 | Bob Jackson, United States | 56.36‡ |
| 1982 | Dirk Richter, E. Germany | 55.95 |
| 1986 | Igor Polianski, U.S.S.R. | 55.58‡ |
| 1991 | Jeff Rouse, United States | 55.23‡ |
| 1994 | Martin Lopez Zubero, Spain | 55.17‡ |
| 1998 | Lenny Krayzelburg, United States | 55.00‡ |
| 2001 | Matt Welsh, Australia | 54.31‡ |
| 2003 | Aaron Peirsol, United States | 53.61‡ |
| 2005 | Aaron Peirsol, United States | 53:62 |
| 2007 | Aaron Peirsol, United States | 52.98* |
| 2009 | Junya Koga, Japan | 52.26‡ |
| 2011 | Camille Lacourt, France | 52.76 |

#### 200-METER BACKSTROKE

| | | |
|---|---|---|
| 1973 | Roland Matthes, E. Germany | 2:01.87‡ |
| 1975 | Zoltan Varraszto, Hungary | 2:05.05 |
| 1978 | Jesse Vassallo, United States | 2:02.16 |
| 1982 | Rick Carey, United States | 2:00.82‡ |
| 1986 | Igor Polianski, U.S.S.R. | 1:58.78‡ |
| 1991 | Martin Zubero, Spain | 1:59.52 |
| 1994 | Vladimir Selkov, Russia | 1:57.42‡ |
| 1998 | Lenny Krayzelburg, United States | 1:58.84 |
| 2001 | Aaron Peirsol, United States | 1:57.13‡ |
| 2003 | Aaron Peirsol, United States | 1:55.92 |
| 2005 | Aaron Peirsol, United States | 1:54.66* |
| 2007 | Ryan Lochte, United States | 1:54.32* |
| 2009 | Aaron Peirsol, United States | 1:51.92* |
| 2011 | Ryan Lochte, United States | 1:52.96 |

* World Record. ‡ Meet Record. †After cancellation of Oussam Mellouli's results.

## Men (*Cont.*)

### 50-METER BREASTSTROKE

| | | |
|---|---|---|
| 2001 | Oleg Lisogor, Ukraine | 27.52 |
| 2003 | James Gibson, United Kingdom | 27.56 |
| 2005 | Mark Warnecke, Germany | 27.63 |
| 2007 | Oleg Lisogor, Ukraine | 27.66 |
| 2009 | Cameron Van Der Burgh, S. Africa | 26.67* |
| 2011 | Felipe Alves Franca Da Silva, Brazil | 27.01 |

### 100-METER BREASTSTROKE

| | | |
|---|---|---|
| 1973 | Roland Matthes, E. Germany | 2:01.87‡ |
| 1973 | John Hencken, United States | 1:04.02‡ |
| 1975 | David Wilkie, Great Britain | 1:04.26‡ |
| 1978 | Walter Kusch, W Germany | 1:03.56‡ |
| 1982 | Steve Lundquist, United States | 1:02.75‡ |
| 1986 | Victor Davis, Canada | 1:02.71 |
| 1991 | Norbert Rozsa, Hungary | 1:01.45* |
| 1994 | Norbert Rozsa, Hungary | 1:01.24‡ |
| 1998 | Frederik Deburghgraeve, Belgium | 1:01.34 |
| 2001 | Roman Sloudnov, Russia | 1:00.16 |
| 2003 | Kosuke Kitajima, Japan | 59.78* |
| 2005 | Brendan Hansen, United States | 59:13* |
| 2007 | Brendan Hansen, United States | 59.80 |
| 2009 | Brenton Rickard, Australia | 58.58* |
| 2011 | Alexander Dale Oen, Norway | 58.71 |

### 200-METER BREASTSTROKE

| | | |
|---|---|---|
| 1973 | David Wilkie, Great Britain | 2:19.28‡ |
| 1975 | David Wilkie, Great Britain | 2:18.23‡ |
| 1978 | Nick Nevid, United States | 2:18.37 |
| 1982 | Victor Davis, Canada | 2:14.77* |
| 1986 | Jozsef Szabo, Hungary | 2:14.27‡ |
| 1991 | Mike Barrowman, United States | 2:11.23* |
| 1994 | Norbert Rozsa, Hungary | 2:12.81 |
| 1998 | Kurt Grote, United States | 2:13.40 |
| 2001 | Brendan Hansen, United States | 2:10.69‡ |
| 2003 | Kosuke Kitajima, Japan | 2:09.42* |
| 2005 | Brendan Hansen, United States | 2:08.74* |
| 2007 | Kosuke Kitajima, Japan | 2:09.80 |
| 2009 | Daniel Gyurta, Hungary | 2:07.64 |
| 2011 | Daniel Gyurta, Hungary | 2:08.41 |

### 50-METER BUTTERFLY

| | | |
|---|---|---|
| 2001 | Geoff Huegill, Australia | 23.50 |
| 2003 | Matt Welsh, Australia | 23.43* |
| 2005 | Roland Schoeman, South Africa | 22.96* |
| 2007 | Roland Schoeman, South Africa | 23.18 |
| 2009 | Milorad Cavic, Serbia | 22.67‡ |
| 2011 | Cesar Cielo Filho, Brazil | 23.10 |

### 100-METER BUTTERFLY

| | | |
|---|---|---|
| 1973 | Bruce Robertson, Canada | 55.69 |
| 1975 | Greg Jagenburg, United States | 55.63 |
| 1978 | Joe Bottom, United States | 54.30 |
| 1982 | Matt Gribble, United States | 53.88‡ |
| 1986 | Pablo Morales, United States | 53.54‡ |
| 1991 | Anthony Nesty, Suriname | 53.29‡ |
| 1994 | Rafal Szukala, Poland | 53.51 |
| 1998 | Michael Klim, Australia | 52.25‡ |
| 2001 | Lars Frolander, Sweden | 52.10‡ |
| 2003 | Ian Crocker, United States | 50.98* |

### 100-METER BUTTERFLY (*Cont.*)

| | | |
|---|---|---|
| 2005 | Ian Crocker, United States | 50:40* |
| 2007 | Michael Phelps, United States | 50.77 |
| 2009 | Michael Phelps, United States | 49.82* |
| 2011 | Michael Phelps, United States | 50.71 |

### 200-METER BUTTERFLY

| | | |
|---|---|---|
| 1973 | Robin Backhaus, United States | 2:03.32 |
| 1975 | Bill Forrester, United States | 2:01.95‡ |
| 1978 | Mike Bruner, United States | 1:59.38‡ |
| 1982 | Michael Gross, E. Germany | 1:58.85‡ |
| 1986 | Michael Gross, E. Germany | 1:56.53‡ |
| 1991 | Melvin Stewart, United States | 1:55.69* |
| 1994 | Denis Pankratov, Russia | 1:56.54 |
| 1998 | Denys Sylantyev, Ukraine | 1:56.61 |
| 2001 | Michael Phelps, United States | 1:54.58* |
| 2003 | Michael Phelps, United States | 1:54.35 |
| 2005 | Pawel Korzeniowski, Poland | 1:55.02 |
| 2007 | Michael Phelps, United States | 1:52.09* |
| 2009 | Michael Phelps, United States | 1:51.51* |
| 2011 | Michael Phelps, United States | 1:53.34 |

### 200-METER INDIVIDUAL MEDLEY

| | | |
|---|---|---|
| 1973 | Gunnar Larsson, Sweden | 2:08.36 |
| 1975 | Andras Hargitay, Hungary | 2:07.72 |
| 1978 | Graham Smith, Canada | 2:03.65* |
| 1982 | Aleksandr Sidorenko, U.S.S.R. | 2:03.30‡ |
| 1986 | Tamás Darnyi, Hungary | 2:01.57‡ |
| 1991 | Tamás Darnyi, Hungary | 1:59.36* |
| 1994 | Jani Sievin, Finland | 1:58.16* |
| 1998 | Marcel Wouda, Netherlands | 2:01.18 |
| 2001 | Massimiliano Rosolino, Italy | 1:59.71 |
| 2003 | Michael Phelps, United States | 1:56.04* |
| 2005 | Ryan Lochte, United States | 1:58.06 |
| 2007 | Michael Phelps, United States | 1:54.98* |
| 2009 | Ryan Lochte, United States | 1:54.10* |
| 2011 | Ryan Lochte, United States | 1:54.00* |

### 400-METER INDIVIDUAL MEDLEY

| | | |
|---|---|---|
| 1975 | Andras Hargitay, Hungary | 4:32.57 |
| 1978 | Jesse Vassallo, United States | 4:20.05* |
| 1982 | Ricardo Prado, Brazil | 4:19.78* |
| 1986 | Tamás Darnyi, Hungary | 4:18.98‡ |
| 1991 | Tamás Darnyi, Hungary | 4:12.36* |
| 1994 | Tom Dolan, United States | 4:12.30* |
| 1998 | Tom Dolan, United States | 4:14.95 |
| 2001 | Alessio Boggiatto, Italy | 4:13.15 |
| 2003 | Michael Phelps, United States | 4:09.09* |
| 2005 | Laszlo Cseh, Hungary | 4:09.63 |
| 2007 | Michael Phelps, United States | 4:06.22* |
| 2009 | Ryan Lochte, United States | 4:07.01 |
| 2011 | Ryan Lochte, United States | 4:07.13 |

* World Record; ‡ Meet Record.

### Men (Cont.)

#### 4 x 100-METER MEDLEY RELAY

1973.....United States (Mike Stamm, John Hencken, Joe Bottom, Jim Montgomery) — 3:49.49

1975.....United States (John Murphy, Rick Colella, Greg Jagenburg, Andy Coan) — 3:49.00

1978.....United States (Robert Jackson, Nick Nevid, Joe Bottom, David McCagg) — 3:44.63

1982.....United States (Rick Carey, Steve Lundquist, Matt Gribble, Rowdy Gaines) — 3:40.84*

1986.....United States (Dan Veatch, David Lundberg, Pablo Morales, Matt Biondi) — 3:41.25

1991.....United States (Jeff Rouse, Eric Wunderlich, Mark Henderson, Matt Biondi) — 3:39.66‡

1994.....United States (Jeff Rouse, Eric Wunderlich, Mark Henderson, Gary Hall Jr.) — 3:37.74‡

1998 — Australia (Matt Welsh, Phil Rogers, Robin Backhaus, Rick Klatt, Jim Montgomery) — 3:37.98

2001.....Australia (Matt Welsh, Ian Thorpe, Geoff Huegill, Regan Harrison) — 3:35.35

2003.....United States (Aaron Peirsol, Brendan Hansen, Ian Crocker, Jason Lezak) — 3:31.54*

2005.....United States (Aaron Peirsol, Brendan Hansen, Ian Crocker, Jason Lezak) — 3:31.85

2007.....Australia (Matt Welsh, Brenton Rickard, Andrew Lauterstein, Eamon Sullivan) — 3:34.93

2009.....United States (Aaron Peirsol, Eric Shanteau, Michael Phelps, David Walters) — 3:27.28*

2011.....United States (Nicholas Thoman, Mark Gangloff, Michael Phelps, Nathan Adrian) — 3:32.06

#### 4 x 100-METER FREESTYLE RELAY

1973.....United States (Mel Nash, Joe Bottom, Jim Montgomery, John Murphy) — 3:27.18

1975 ....United States (Bruce Furniss, Jim Montgomery, Andy Coan, John Murphy) — 3:24.85

1978 ....United States (Jack Babashoff, Rowdy Gaines, Jim Montgomery, David McCagg) — 3:19.74

1982 ....United States (Chris Cavanaugh, Robin Leamy, David McCagg, Rowdy Gaines) — 3:19.26*

1986 ....United States (Tom Jager, Mike Heath, Paul Wallace, Matt Biondi) — 3:19.89

1991 ....United States (Tom Jager, Brent Lang, Doug Gjertsen, Matt Biondi) — 3:17.15‡

1994 ....United States (Jon Olsen, Josh Davis, Ugur Taner, Gary Hall Jr.) — 3:16.90‡

1998 ....United States (Bryan Jones, Jon Olsen, Bradley Schumacher, Gary Hall Jr.) — 3:16.69‡

2001 ....Australia (Michael Klim, Ian Thorpe, Todd Pearson, Ashley Callus) — 3:14.10‡

2003 ....Russia (Andrei Kapralov, Ivan Usov, Denis Pimankov, Alexander Popov) — 3:14.06‡

2005 ....United States (Michael Phelps, Neil Walker, Nate Dusing, Jason Lezak) — 3:13.77

2007 ....United States (Michael Phelps, Neil Walker, Cullen Jones, Jason Lezak) — 3:12.72

2009 ....United States (Michael Phelps, Ryan Lochte, Mattew Grevers, Nathan Adrian) — 3:09.21‡

2011 ....Australia (James Magnussen, Matthew Targett, Matthew Abood, Eamon Sullivan) — 3:11.00

#### 4 x 200-METER FREESTYLE RELAY

1973.....United States (Kurt Krumpholz, Robin Backhaus, Rick Klatt, Jim Montgomery) — 7:33.22*

1975.....W Germany (Klaus Steinbach, Werner Lampe, Hans Joachim Geisler, Peter Nocke) — 7:39.44

1978.....United States (Bruce Furniss, Billy Forrester, Bobby Hackett, Rowdy Gaines) — 7:20.82

1982.....United States (Rich Saeger, Jeff Float, Kyle Miller, Rowdy Gaines) — 7:21.09

1986.....E. Germany (Lars Hinneburg, Thomas Flemming, Dirk Richter, Sven Lodziewski) — 7:15.91‡

1991.....Germany (Peter Sitt, Steffan Zesner, Stefan Pfeiffer, Michael Gross) — 7:13.50‡

1994.....Sweden (Christer Waller, Tommy Werner, Lars Frolander, Anders Holmertz) — 7:17.34

1998 — Australia (Daniel Kowalski, Grant Hackett, Ian Thorpe, Anthony Rogis) — 7:12.48‡

2001.....Australia (Michael Klim, Ian Thorpe, William Kirby, Grant Hackett) — 7:04.66*

2003.....Australia (Grant Hackett, Craig Stevens, Nicholas Springer, Ian Thorpe) — 7:08.58

2005.....United States (Michael Phelps, Ryan Lochte, Peter Vanderkaay, Klete Keller) — 7:06.58

2007.....United States (Michael Phelps, Ryan Lochte, Peter Vanderkaay, Klete Keller) — 7:03.24*

2009.....United States (Michael Phelps, Ricky Berens, David Walters, Ryan Lochte) — 6:58.55*

2011.....United States (Michael Phelps, Peter Vanderkaay, Richard Berens, Ryan Lochte) — 7:02.67

Note: Records through Oct 1, 2010.  * World record; ‡ Meet record

# Women

### 50-METER FREESTYLE

| | | |
|---|---|---|
| 1986 | Tamara Costache, Romania | 25.28* |
| 1991 | Zhuang Yong, China | 25.47 |
| 1994 | Le Jingyi, China | 24.51* |
| 1998 | Amy Van Dyken, United States | 25.15 |
| 2001 | Inge de Bruijn, Netherlands | 24.47 |
| 2003 | Inge de Bruijn, Netherlands | 24.47 |
| 2005 | Lisbeth Lenton, Australia | 24.59 |
| 2007 | Lisbeth Lenton, Australia | 24.53 |
| 2009 | Britta Steffen, Germany | 23.73* |
| 2011 | Therese Alshammar, Sweden | 24.14 |

### 100-METER FREESTYLE

| | | |
|---|---|---|
| 1973 | Kornelia Ender, E. Germany | 57.54 |
| 1975 | Kornelia Ender, E. Germany | 56.50 |
| 1978 | Barbara Krause, E. Germany | 55.68‡ |
| 1982 | Birgit Meineke, E. Germany | 55.79 |
| 1986 | Kristin Otto, E. Germany | 55.05‡ |
| 1991 | Nicole Haislett, United States | 55.17 |
| 1994 | Le Jingyi, China | 54.01* |
| 1998 | Jenny Thompson, United States | 54.95 |
| 2001 | Inge de Bruijn, Netherlands | 54.18 |
| 2003 | Hanna-Maria Seppälä, Finland | 54.37 |
| 2005 | Britta Steffen, Germany | 53.30* |
| 2007 | Lisbeth Lenton, Australia | 53.40 |
| 2009 | Britta Steffen, Germany | 52.07* |
| 2011 | Jeanette Ottesen, Denmark | 53.45 |

### 200-METER FREESTYLE

| | | |
|---|---|---|
| 1973 | Keena Rothhammer, United States | 2:04.99 |
| 1975 | Shirley Babashoff, United States | 2:02.50 |
| 1978 | Cynthia Woodhead, United States | 1:58.53* |
| 1982 | Annemarie Verstappen, Netherlands | 1:59.53‡ |
| 1986 | Heike Friedrich, E. Germany | 1:58.26‡ |
| 1991 | Hayley Lewis, Australia | 2:00.48 |
| 1994 | Franziska Van Almsick, Germany | 1:56.78* |
| 1998 | Claudia Poll, Costa Rica | 1:58.90 |
| 2001 | Giaan Rooney, Australia | 1:58.57 |
| 2003 | Alena Popchanka, Bulgaria | 1:58.32 |
| 2005 | Solenne Figues, France | 1:58.60 |
| 2007 | Laure Manaudou, France | 1:55.52* |
| 2009 | Federica Pellegrini, Italy | 1:52.98* |
| 2011 | Federica Pellegrini, Italy | 1:55.58 |

### 400-METER FREESTYLE

| | | |
|---|---|---|
| 1973 | Heather Greenwood, United States | 4:20.28 |
| 1975 | Shirley Babashoff, United States | 4:22.70 |
| 1978 | Tracey Wickham, Australia | 4:06.28* |
| 1982 | Carmela Schmidt, E. Germany | 4:08.98 |
| 1986 | Heike Friedrich, E. Germany | 4:07.45 |
| 1991 | Janet Evans, United States | 4:08.63 |
| 1994 | Yang Aihua, China | 4:09.64 |
| 1998 | Chen Yan, China | 4:06.72 |
| 2001 | Yana Klochkova, Ukraine | 4:07.30 |
| 2003 | Hannah Stockbauer, Germany | 4:06.75 |
| 2005 | Laure Manaudou, France | 4:02.13* |
| 2007 | Laure Manaudou, France | 4:02.61 |
| 2009 | Federica Pellegrini, Italy | 3:59.15* |
| 2011 | Federica Pellegrini, Italy | 4:01.97 |

### 800-METER FREESTYLE

| | | |
|---|---|---|
| 1973 | Novella Calligaris, Italy | 8:52.97 |
| 1975 | Jenny Turrall, Australia | 8:44.75‡ |
| 1978 | Tracey Wickham, Australia | 8:24.94‡ |
| 1982 | Kim Linehan, United States | 8:27.48 |
| 1986 | Astrid Strauss, E. Germany | 8:28.24 |
| 1991 | Janet Evans, United States | 8:24.05‡ |
| 1994 | Janet Evans, United States | 8:29.85 |
| 1998 | Brooke Bennett, United States | 8:28.71 |
| 2001 | Hannah Stockbauer, Germany | 8:24.66 |
| 2003 | Hannah Stockbauer, Germany | 8:23.66‡ |
| 2005 | Kate Ziegler, United States | 8:25.31 |
| 2007 | Kate Ziegler, United States | 8:18.62 |
| 2009 | Lotte Friis, Denmark | 8:15.92‡ |
| 2011 | Rebecca Adlington, United Kingdom | 8:17.51 |

### 1,500-METER FREESTYLE

| | | |
|---|---|---|
| 2001 | Hannah Stockbauer, Germany | 16:01.02 |
| 2003 | Hannah Stockbauer, Germany | 16:00.108 |
| 2005 | Kate Ziegler, United States | 16:00.41 |
| 2007 | Kate Ziegler, United States | 15:53.05 |
| 2009 | Alessia Filippi, Italy | 15:44.93‡ |
| 2011 | Lotte Friis, Denmark | 15:49.59 |

---

* World record; ‡ Meet record.

## Women (Cont.)

### 50-METER BACKSTROKE

| | | |
|---|---|---|
| 2001 | Haley Cope, United States | 28.51 |
| 2003 | Nina Zhivanevskaya, Spain | 28.48 |
| 2005 | Giaan Rooney, Australia | 28.63 |
| 2007 | Leila Vaziri, United States | 28.16e |
| 2009 | Jiing Zhao, China | 27.06* |
| 2011 | Anastasia Zueva, Russia | 27.79 |

### 50-METER BREASTSTROKE

| | | |
|---|---|---|
| 2001 | Xuejuan Luo, China | 30.84 |
| 2003 | Xuejuan Luo, China | 30.67 |
| 2005 | Jade Edmistone, Australia | 30.45* |
| 2007 | Jessica Hardy, United States | 30.63 |
| 2009 | Yuliya Efimova, Russia | 30.09* |
| 2011 | Jessica Hardy, United States | 30.19 |

### 100-METER BACKSTROKE

| | | |
|---|---|---|
| 1973 | Ulrike Richter, E. Germany | 1:05.42 |
| 1975 | Ulrike Richter, E. Germany | 1:03.30‡ |
| 1978 | Linda Jezek, United States | 1:02.55‡ |
| 1982 | Kristin Otto, E. Germany | 1:01.30‡ |
| 1986 | Betsy Mitchell, United States | 1:01.74 |
| 1991 | Krisztina Egerszegi, Hungary | 1:01.78 |
| 1994 | He Cihong, China | 1:00.57 |
| 1998 | Lea Maurer, United States | 1:01.16 |
| 2001 | Natalie Coughlin, United States | 1:00.37 |
| 2003 | Antje Buschschulte, Germany | 1:00.50 |
| 2005 | Kirsty Coventry, Zimbabwe | 1:00.24 |
| 2007 | Natalie Coughlin, United States | 59.44* |
| 2009 | Gemma Spofforth, United Kingdom | 58.12* |
| 2011 | Jing Zhao, China | 59.05 |

### 100-METER BREASTSTROKE

| | | |
|---|---|---|
| 1973 | Renate Vogel, E. Germany | 1:13.74 |
| 1975 | Hannalore Anke, E. Germany | 1:12.72 |
| 1978 | Julia Bogdanova, U.S.S.R. | 1:10.31* |
| 1982 | Ute Geweniger, E. Germany | 1:09.14‡ |
| 1986 | Sylvia Gerasch, E. Germany | 1:08.11* |
| 1991 | Linley Frame, Australia | 1:08.81 |
| 1994 | Samantha Riley, Australia | 1:07.96* |
| 1998 | Kristy Kowal, United States | 1:08.42 |
| 2001 | Xuejuan Luo, China | 1:07.18‡ |
| 2003 | Xuejuan Luo, China | 1:06.80 |
| 2005 | Leisel Jones, Australia | 1:05.09* |
| 2007 | Leisel Jones, Australia | 1:05.72 |
| 2009 | Rebecca Soni, United States | 1:04.93 |
| 2011 | Rebecca Soni, United States | 1:05.05 |

### 200-METER BACKSTROKE

| | | |
|---|---|---|
| 1973 | Melissa Belote, United States | 2:20.52 |
| 1975 | Birgit Treiber, E. Germany | 2:15.46* |
| 1978 | Linda Jezek, United States | 2:11.93* |
| 1982 | Cornelia Sirch, E. Germany | 2:09.91* |
| 1986 | Cornelia Sirch, E. Germany | 2:11.37 |
| 1991 | Krisztina Egerszegi, Hungary | 2:09.15‡ |
| 1994 | He Cihong, China | 2:07.40 |
| 1998 | Roxanna Maracineanu, France | 2:11.26 |
| 2001 | Diana Mocanu, Romania | 2:09.94 |
| 2003 | Katy Sexton, Great Britain | 2:08.74 |
| 2005 | Kirsty Coventry, Zimbabwe | 2:08.52 |
| 2007 | Margaret Hoelzer, United States | 2:07.16 |
| 2009 | Kirsty Coventry, Zimbabwe | 2:04.81* |
| 2011 | Melissa Franklin, United States | 2:05.10 |

### 200-METER BREASTSTROKE

| | | |
|---|---|---|
| 1973 | Renate Vogel, E. Germany | 2:40.01 |
| 1975 | Hannalore Anke, E. Germany | 2:37.25‡ |
| 1978 | Lina Kachushite, U.S.S.R. | 2:31.42* |
| 1982 | Svetlana Varganova, U.S.S.R. | 2:28.82‡ |
| 1986 | Silke Hoerner, E. Germany | 2:27.40* |
| 1991 | Elena Volkova, U.S.S.R. | 2:29.53 |
| 1994 | Samantha Riley, Australia | 2:26.87‡ |
| 1998 | Agnes Kovacs, Hungary | 2:25.45‡ |
| 2001 | Agnes Kovacs, Hungary | 2:24.90 |
| 2003 | Amanda Beard, United States | 2:22.99* |
| 2005 | Leisel Jones, Australia | 2:20.54* |
| 2007 | Leisel Jones, Australia | 2:21.84 |
| 2009 | Nadja Higl, Serbia | 2:21.62 |
| 2011 | Rebecca Soni, United States | 2:21.47 |

Note: Records through Oct 1, 2011. * World record; ‡Meet record

## Women (Cont.)

### 50-METER BUTTERFLY

| | | |
|---|---|---|
| 2001 | Inge De Bruijn, Netherlands | 25.90 |
| 2003 | Inge De Bruijn, Netherlands | 25.84 |
| 2005 | Danni Miatke, Australia | 26.11 |
| 2007 | Therese Alshammar, Sweden | 25.91 |
| 2009 | Marieke Guehrer, Australia | 25.48 |
| 2011 | Inge Dekker, Netherlands | 25.71 |

### 100-METER BUTTERFLY

| | | |
|---|---|---|
| 1973 | Kornelia Ender, E. Germany | 1:02.53 |
| 1975 | Kornelia Ender, E. Germany | 1:01.24* |
| 1978 | Joan Pennington, United States | 1:00.20‡ |
| 1982 | Mary T. Meagher, United States | 59.41‡ |
| 1986 | Kornelia Gressler, E. Germany | 59.51 |
| 1991 | Qian Hong, China | 59.68 |
| 1994 | Liu Limin, China | 58.98‡ |
| 1998 | Jenny Thompson, United States | 58.46‡ |
| 2001 | Petria Thomas, Australia | 58:27 |
| 2003 | Jenny Thompson, United States | 57.96‡ |
| 2005 | Jessicah Schipper, Australia | 57.23‡ |
| 2007 | Lisbeth Lenton, Australia | 57.15 |
| 2009 | Sarah Sjostrom, Sweden | 56.06* |
| 2011 | Dana Vollmer, United States | 56.87 |

### 200-METER BUTTERFLY

| | | |
|---|---|---|
| 1973 | Rosemarie Kother, E. Germany | 2:13.76‡ |
| 1975 | Rosemarie Kother, E. Germany | 2:15.92 |
| 1978 | Tracy Caulkins, United States | 2:09.87* |
| 1982 | Ines Geissler, E. Germany | 2:08.66‡ |
| 1986 | Mary T. Meagher, United States | 2:08.41‡ |
| 1991 | Summer Sanders, United States | 2:09.24 |
| 1994 | Liu Limin, China | 2:07.25‡ |
| 1998 | Susie O'Neill, Australia | 2:07.93‡ |
| 2001 | Petria Thomas, Australia | 2:06.73‡ |
| 2003 | Otylia Jedrzejczak, Poland | 2:07.56 |
| 2005 | Otylia Jedrzejczak, Poland | 2:05.61* |
| 2007 | Jessicah Schipper, Australia | 2:06.39 |
| 2009 | Jessicah Schipper, Australia | 2:03.41* |
| 2011 | Liuyang Jiao, China | 2:05.55 |

### 200-METER INDIVIDUAL MEDLEY

| | | |
|---|---|---|
| 1973 | Andrea Huebner, E. Germany | 2:20.51 |
| 1975 | Kathy Heddy, United States | 2:19.80 |
| 1978 | Tracy Caulkins, United States | 2:14.07* |
| 1982 | Petra Schneider, E. Germany | 2:11.79 |
| 1986 | Kristin Otto, E. Germany | 2:15.56 |
| 1991 | Li Lin, China | 2:13.40 |
| 1994 | Lu Bin, China | 2:12.34‡ |
| 1998 | Wu Yanyan, China | 2:10.88 |
| 2001 | Martha Bowen, United States | 2:11.93 |
| 2003 | Yana Klochkova, Ukraine | 2:10.75‡ |
| 2005 | Katie Hoff, United States | 2:10.41‡ |
| 2007 | Katie Hoff, United States | 2:10.13 |
| 2009 | Ariana Kukors, United States | 2:06.15* |
| 2011 | Shiwen Yen, China | 2:08.90 |

### 400-METER INDIVIDUAL MEDLEY

| | | |
|---|---|---|
| 1973 | Gudrun Wegner, E. Germany | 4:57.71 |
| 1975 | Ulrike Tauber, E. Germany | 4:52.76‡ |
| 1978 | Tracy Caulkins, United States | 4:40.83* |
| 1982 | Petra Schneider, E. Germany | 4:36.10* |
| 1986 | Kathleen Nord, E. Germany | 4:43.75 |
| 1991 | Lin Li, China | 4:41.45 |
| 1994 | Dai Guohong, China | 4:39.14 |
| 1998 | Chen Yan, China | 4:36.66 |
| 2001 | Yana Klochkova, Ukraine | 4:36.98 |
| 2003 | Yana Klochkova, Ukraine | 4:36.74 |
| 2005 | Katie Hoff, United States | 4:36.07‡ |
| 2007 | Katie Hoff, United States | 4:32.89* |
| 2009 | Katinka Hosszu, Hungary | 4:30.31‡ |
| 2011 | Elizabeth Beisel, United States | 4:31.78 |

* World record; ‡ Meet record.

### Women *(Cont.)*

#### 4 x 100-METER MEDLEY RELAY

1973 ....E. Germany (Ulrike Richter,     4:16.84
Renate Vogel, Rosemarie Kother, Kornelia Ender)

1975 ....E. Germany (Ulrike Richter,     4:14.74
Hannelore Anke, Rosemarie Kother,
Kornelia Ender)

1978 ....United States (Linda Jezek,     4:08.21‡
Tracy Caulkins, Joan Pennington,
Cynthia Woodhead)

1982 ....E. Germany (K. Otto, U. Gewinger,     4:05.8*
I. Geissler, B. Meineke)

1986 ....E. Germany (K. Zimmermann, S. Gerasch,     4:04.82
K. Gressler, K. Otto)

1991 ....United States (Janie Wagstaff,     4:06.51
Tracey McFarlane, Crissy
Ahmann-Leighton, Nicole Haislett)

1994 ....China (He Cihong, Dai Guohong,     4:01.67*
Liu Limin, Lu Bin)

1998 ....United States (K. Kowal, L. Maurer,     4:01.93
J.Thompson, A. Van Dyken)

2001 ....Australia (Dyana Calub, Sarah     4:07.30
Ryan, Petria Thomas, Leisel Jones)

2003 ....China (Shu Xhan, Xuejuan Luo,     3:59.89‡
Yafei Zhou, Yu Yang)

2005 ....Australia (S. Edington, L. Jones,     3:56.30*
J. Schipper, L. Lenton)

2007 ....Australia (E. Seebohm, L. Jones,     3:55.74*
J. Schipper, L. Lenton)

2009 ....China (Jing Zhao, Huijia Chen,     3:52.19*
Liuyang Jiao, Zhesi Li)

2011 ....United States (Natalie Coughlin,     3:52.36
Rebecca Soni, Dana Vollmer, Melissa Franklin)

#### 4 x 100-METER FREESTYLE RELAY

1973 ....E. Germany (K. Ender, A. Eife,     3:52.45
A. Huebner, S. Eichner)

1975 ....E. Germany (K. Ender, B. Krause,     3:49.37
C. Hempel, U. Bruckner)

1978 ....United States (T. Caulkins,     3:43.43*
S. Elkins, J. Pennington, C. Woodhead)

1982 ....E. Germany (B. Meineke, S. Link,     3:43.97
K. Otto, C. Metschuk)

1986 ....E. Germany (K. Otto, M. Stellmach,     3:40.57*
S. Schulze, H. Friedrich)

1991 ....United States (N. Haislett,     3:43.26
J.Cooper, W. Hedgepeth, J. Thompson)

1994 ....China (Le Jingyi, Ying Shan,     3:37.91*
Le Ying, Lu Bin)

1998 ....United States (C. Fox, L. Farella,     3:42.11
M. Valerio, B.J. Bedford)

2001 ....Germany (P. Dallman,     3:39.58
A. Buschschulte, K. Meissner, S. Volkner)

2003 ....United States (N. Coughlin,     3:38.09
L. Benko, R. Jeffrey, J. Thompson)

2005 ....Germany (P. Dallman,     3:35.22*
D. Goetz, B. Steffen, A. Liebs)

2007 ....Netherlands (I. Dekker,     3:35.48
R. Kromowidjojo, F. Heemskerk, M. Veldhuis)

2009 ....Netherlands (I. Dekker,     3:31.72*
R. Kromowidjojo, F. Heemskerk, M. Veldhuis)

2011 ....Netherlands (I. Dekker,     3:33.96
R. Kromowidjojo, M. Veldhuis, F. Heemskerk)

#### 4 x 200-METER FREESTYLE RELAY

1986 ....E. Germany (Manuela     7:59.33*
Stellmach, Astrid Strauss,
Nadja Bergknecht, Heike Friedrich)

1991 ....Germany (Kerstin Kielgass, Manuela 8:02.56
Stellmach, Dagmar Hase, Stephanie
Ortwig)

1994     China (Le Ying, Yang Alhua,     7:57.96
Zhou Guabin, Lu Bin)

1998 ....Germany (Silvia Szalai, Antje     8:02.56
Buschschulte, Janina Goetz,
Franziska Van Almsick)

2001 ....Great Britain (Nicola Jackson, Janine 7:58.69
Belton, Karen Legg, Karen Pickering)

2003 ....United States (L. Benko, R. Komisarz 7:55.70‡
R. Jeffrey, D. Munz)

2005 ....Germany (Petra Dallman, Daniela     7:50.82*
Samulski, Britta Steffen, Annika Liebs)

2007 ....United States (Natalie Coughlin,     7:50.09*
Dana Vollmer, Lacey Nymeyer, Katie Hoff)

2009 ....China (Yu Yang, Qian Wei Zhu,     7:42.08*
Jing Liu, Jiaying Pang)

2011 ....United States (Melissa Franklin,     7:46.14
Dagny Knutson, Katie Hoff, Allison Schmitt)

* World record; ‡Meet record.

# Miscellaneous Sports

**Ice dancing partners
Charlie White and Meryl Davis
won gold at the 2011 World
Figure Skating Championships**

# FOR THE RECORD • 2010—2011

## Miscellaneous Sport Champions

| Archery | 2011 U.S. National Field Championships | Winner (Recurve) | Winner (Compound) |
|---|---|---|---|
| | MEN | Brady Ellison | Jesse Broadwater |
| | WOMEN | Jennifer Nichols | Jamie Van Natta |

| Bowling | 2010–11 PBA Tour | Money Winner ($) | Highest Average (pts.) |
|---|---|---|---|
| | TOUR LEADERS | Mika Koivuniemi | Mika Koivuniemi |
| | | ($333,040) | (222.50) |
| | 2010–11 PBA Senior Tour | Money Winner ($) | Highest Average (pts.) |
| | TOUR LEADERS | Ron Mohr | Walter Ray Williams Jr. |
| | | ($56,100) | (229.56) |

| Curling | 2011 World Championships | Winner | Runner-up |
|---|---|---|---|
| | MEN | Canada (6–5) | Scotland |
| | WOMEN | Sweden (7–5) | Canada |
| | 2011 U.S. Club National Championships | Winner | Runner-up |
| | MEN | Minnesota | Illinois |
| | WOMEN | New Jersey | Washington |

| Cycling | | Winner | Time |
|---|---|---|---|
| | 2011 ROAD RACE WORLD CHAMPIONSHIP | Mark Cavendish, U.K. | 5:40:27 |
| | 2011 TOUR DE FRANCE | Cadel Evans, Australia | 86:12:22 |

| Sled Dog Racing | | Winner | Time |
|---|---|---|---|
| | 2011 IDITAROD | John Baker | 8 days, 18:46:39 |

| Figure Skating | 2011 ISU World Championships | Winner | Country |
|---|---|---|---|
| | MEN | Patrick Chan | Canada |
| | WOMEN | Miki Ando | Japan |
| | PAIRS | Aliona Savchenko/ | Germany |
| | | Robin Szolkowy | |
| | ICE DANCING | Meryl Davis/ | United States |
| | | Charlie White | |
| | 2011 U.S. Figure Skating Nat'l Championships | Winner | Club |
| | MEN | Ryan Bradley | Broadmoor SC |
| | WOMEN | Alissa Czisny | Detroit SC |
| | PAIRS | Caitlin Yankowskas/ | Broadmoor SC/ |
| | | John Coughlin | Kansas City FSC |
| | ICE DANCING | Meryl Davis/ | Arctic FSC/ |
| | | Charlie White | Detroit SC |

| Handball | 2011 U.S.One-Wall Nat'l Championships | Winner | Runner-up |
|---|---|---|---|
| | MEN | Yuber Castro | Tyree Bastidas |
| | WOMEN | Sandy Ng | Theresa Haley |
| | 2011 U.S.Three-Wall Nat'l Championships | Winner | Runner-up |
| | MEN | Sean Lenning | Nikolai Nihorniak |
| | WOMEN | Megan Mehilos | Tracy Davis |

| Lacrosse | League | Winner (Score) | Runner-up |
|---|---|---|---|
| | AMERICAN LACROSSE LEAGUE | New York A.C. (15–12) | Magerks |
| | NATIONAL LACROSSE LEAGUE | Toronto Rock (8–7) | Washington Stealth |
| | MAJOR LEAGUE LACROSSE | Boston Cannons (10–9) | Hamilton Nationals |

| Little League Baseball | | Winner | Runner-up | Score |
|---|---|---|---|---|
| | WORLD SERIES CHAMPION | Huntington Beach, Calif. | Hamamatsu, Japan | 2–1 |

| Motor Boat Racing | American Power Boat Association | Winning Boat | Winning Driver |
|---|---|---|---|
| | GOLD CUP CHAMPION (UNLIMITED) | U-96 Spirit of Qatar | Dave Villwock |

| Polo | 2011 U.S. Open | Winner | Runner-up |
|---|---|---|---|
| | U.S. POLO ASSOCIATION | Lechuza (8–6) | Audi |

## Miscellaneous Sport Champions

**Rodeo**

| 2010 PRCA World Champions | Winner(s) |
|---|---|
| ALL-AROUND | Trevor Brazile |
| SADDLE BRONC RIDING | Cody Wright |
| BAREBACK RIDING | Bobby Mote |
| BULL RIDING | J.W. Harris |
| STEER WRESTLING | Dean Gorsuch |
| STEER ROPING | Cody Scheck |
| CALF TIE-DOWN ROPING | Trevor Brazile |
| TEAM ROPING (Header, Heeler) | Trevor Brazile, Patrick Smith |

**Rowing**

| 2011 Intercollegiate Rowing Association | Winner | Runner-Up |
|---|---|---|
| MEN (VARSITY EIGHTS) | Washington | Harvard |

**Rugby**

| 2011 Rugby World Cup | Winner | Runner-Up |
|---|---|---|
| MEN | New Zealand | France |
| 2011 Rugby Union | | |
| COLLEGE PREMIER DIVISION | California | BYU |
| 2011 USA Rugby League | Winner | Runner-Up |
| U.S. CHAMPION | Philadelphia Fight | New Haven Axemen |

**Skiing**

| FIS World Cup Season Points Champion | Men's Winner (Season) | Women's Winner (Season) |
|---|---|---|
| OVERALL | Ivica Kostelic (CRO) | Maria Hoefl-Riesch (GER) |
| DOWNHILL | Didier Cuche (SUI) | Lindsey Vonn (USA) |
| SLALOM | Ivica Kostelic (CRO) | Marlies Schild (AUT) |
| GIANT SLALOM | Ted Ligety (USA) | Viktoria Rebensburg, (GER) |
| SUPER G | Didier Cuche (SUI) | Lindsey Vonn (USA) |
| COMBINED | Ivica Kostelic (CRO) | Lindsey Vonn (USA) |

**Softball**

| 2011 U.S. ASA Championship | Major Fast Pitch Winner | Slow Pitch Winner |
|---|---|---|
| MEN | Jarvis Travelers/ New York Gremlins(tie) | Tides |
| WOMEN | Tournament cancelled | Enough Said |

**Speed Skating**

| 2011 ISU All-Around World Champion | Winner |
|---|---|
| MEN | Ivan Skobrev (RUS) |
| WOMEN | Ireen Wust (NET) |

**Squash**

| 2011 U.S. Open Championships | Winner |
|---|---|
| MEN | Amr Shabana |
| WOMEN | Laura Massaro |

**Triathlon**

| 2011 Ironman World Championship | Winner | Time |
|---|---|---|
| MEN | Craig Alexander | 8:03:56 |
| WOMEN | Chrissie Wellington | 8:55:08 |
| 2011 U.S. Elite Triathlon Championship | Winner | Time |
| MEN | Hunter Kemper | 1:48:24 |
| WOMEN | Laura Bennett | 1:59:37 |

**Volleyball**

| 2011 U.S. Adult Championship (Open Div.) | Winner | Runner-Up |
|---|---|---|
| MEN | Creole | Team GoNation |
| WOMEN | USA Blue | USA Red |

**Wrestling**

| 2011 U.S. Championship | Freestyle | Greco-Roman |
|---|---|---|
| 121 LBS. | Sam Hazewinkel | Spenser Mango* |
| 132 LBS. | Reece Humphrey | Joe Betterman |
| 145.5 LBS. | Teyon Ware* | Justin Lester |
| 163 LBS. | Jordan Burroughs | Ben Provisor |
| 185 LBS. | Jake Herbert | Jordan Holm |
| 211.5 LBS. | Jake Varner | Justin Ruiz |
| 264.5 LBS. | Tervel Dlagnev | Dremiel Byers |
| TEAM | New York AC | U.S. Army (Div. I) Sunkist Kids (Div. II) |

*Most Outstanding Wrestler

# FOR THE RECORD • Year by Year

## Bowling

### 2010-11 PBA TOUR RESULTS

| Date | Event | Winner/s | Earnings ($) | Runner/s-Up |
|------|-------|----------|-------------|-------------|
| Oct 25 & Nov 5 | Cheetah Championship | Eugene McCune | 15,200 | Norm Duke |
| Oct 26 & Nov 5 | Viper Championship | Bill O'Neill | 15,100 | Andres Gomez |
| Oct 27 & Nov 5 | Chameleon Championship | Scott Norton | 15,000 | Sean Rash |
| Oct 28 & Nov 6 | Scorpion Championship | Yong-Jin Gu | 15,000 | Jun-Yung Kim |
| Oct 29 & Nov 6 | Shark Championship | Osku Palermaa | 15,000 | Dan MacLelland |
| Dec 13–14 | Chris Paul Celebrity Invitational | Jason Belmonte/ | — | Norm Duke/ |
| | | Chris Paul | | Lil Wayne |
| Jan 14–16 | WSOB World Championship | Chris Barnes | 50,000 | Bill O'Neill |
| Jan 15–22 | PBA Tournament of Champions | Mika Koivuniemi | 25,000 | Tom Smallwood |
| Jan 26–30 | Earl Anthony Memorial Classic | Ryan Ciminelli | 20,000 | Patrick Allen |
| Feb 6–13 | USBC Masters | Tom Hess | 50,000 | Jack Jurek |
| Feb 21–27 | 68th U.S. Open | Norm Duke | 80,000 | Mika Koivuniemi |
| Mar 2–6 | Plastic Ball Championship | Jason Couch | 20,000 | Parker Bohn III |
| Mar 8–Apr 17 | Dick Weber Playoffs | Dick Allen | 50,000 | Chris Barnes |

### 2011 SENIOR PBA TOUR RESULTS

| Date | Event | Winner | Earnings ($) | Runner-Up |
|------|-------|--------|-------------|-----------|
| Apr 17–21 | Don Carter Open | Mike Dias | 7,500 | Tom Howison |
| Apr 23–26 | Senior Sun Bowl | Harry Sullins | 7,550 | Walter Ray Williams Jr. |
| May 1–4 | Miller High Life Classic | Ron Mohr | 8,050 | Timothy Kauble |
| May 21–24 | Mark Roth Allentown Open | Walter Ray Williams Jr. | 7,550 | Ron Mohr |
| June 12–17 | Senior U.S. Open | Ron Mohr | 15,100 | Walter Ray Williams Jr. |
| June 19–22 | Northern California Classic | Ron Mohr | 8,050 | Hugh Miller |
| July 31–Aug 5 | USBC Senior Masters | Dale Traber | 14,000 | Walter Ray Williams Jr. |
| Aug 8–11 | Lake County Open | Harry Sullins | 7,500 | Ron Mohr |
| Aug 13–16 | Senior Decatur Open | Dale Eagle | 7,500 | Kent Wagner |
| Aug 22–25 | Senior Jackson Open | Ron Mohr | 7,500 | Rick Vittone |
| Aug 27–30 | Senior Dayton Classic | Hugh Miller | 8,050 | Tom Baker |

### TOUR LEADERS - PBA: 2010-11

| MONEY LEADERS | Events | Earnings ($) | AVERAGE | Events | Average |
|---------------|--------|-------------|---------|--------|---------|
| Mika Koivuniemi | 12 | 333,040 | Mika Koivuniemi | 12 | 222.50 |
| Chris Barnes | 12 | 133,260 | Osku Palermaa | 7 | 221.91 |
| Tom Smallwood | 12 | 127,200 | Dick Allen | 10 | 220.96 |
| Norm Duke | 11 | 113,900 | Bill O'Neill | 12 | 220.24 |
| Bill O'Neill | 12 | 97,290 | Tom Smallwood | 12 | 220.03 |

### TOUR LEADERS - SENIOR PBA: 2010-11

| MONEY LEADERS | Events | Earnings ($) | AVERAGE | Events | Average |
|---------------|--------|-------------|---------|--------|---------|
| Ron Mohr | 10 | 56,100 | Walter Ray Williams Jr. | 11 | 229.56 |
| Walter Ray Williams Jr. | 11 | 37,400 | Ron Mohr | 10 | 225.98 |
| Harry Sullins | 11 | 33,650 | Hugh Miller | 6 | 224.23 |
| Dale Traber | 11 | 23,625 | Tom Baker | 10 | 223.84 |
| Tom Baker | 10 | 22,050 | Harry Sullins | 11 | 221.16 |

### PBA Career Statistics

| CAREER EARNINGS | | CAREER TITLES | |
|-----------------|--|---------------|--|
| *Walter Ray Williams Jr. | $4,312,541 | *Walter Ray Williams Jr. | 47 |
| *Pete Weber | $3,433,407 | Earl Anthony | 43 |
| *Norm Duke | $2,982,019 | *Pete Weber | 35 |
| *Parker Bohn III | $2,789,447 | Mark Roth | 34 |
| *Brian Voss | $2,474,038 | *Norm Duke | 34 |
| *Amleto Monacelli | $2,150,124 | *Parker Bohn III | 32 |
| Mike Aulby | $2,097,520 | Dick Weber | 30 |
| *Chris Barnes | $1,947,827 | Mike Aulby | 29 |
| Tom Baker | $1,897,879 | Don Johnson | 26 |
| *Jason Couch | $1,745,517 | *Brian Voss | 25 |

Note: Career leaders through Sept. 1, 2011. *Active in 2010–11 season.

# Cycling

## Tour de France Winners

| Year | Winner | Time | Year | Winner | Time |
|------|--------|------|------|--------|------|
| 1903 | Maurice Garin, France | 94 hrs, 33 min | 1962 | Jacques Anquetil, France | 114 hrs, 31 min, 54 sec |
| 1904 | Henry Cornet, France | 96 hrs, 5 min, 56 sec | 1963 | Jacques Anquetil, France | 113 hrs, 30 min, 5 sec |
| 1905 | Louis Trousselier, France | 110 hrs, 26 min, 58 sec | 1964 | Jacques Anquetil, France | 127 hrs, 9 min, 44 sec |
| 1906 | Rene Pottier, France | Not available | 1965 | Felice Gimondi, Italy | 116 hrs, 42 min, 6 sec |
| 1907 | Lucien Petit-Breton, France | 158 hrs, 54 min, 5 sec | 1966 | Lucien Aimar, France | 117 hrs, 34 min, 21 sec |
| 1908 | Lucien Petit-Breton, France | Not available | 1967 | Roger Pingeon, France | 136 hrs, 53 min, 50 sec |
| 1909 | Francois Faber, Luxembourg | 157 hrs, 1 min, 22 sec | 1968 | Jan Janssen, Netherlands | 133 hrs, 49 min, 32 sec |
| 1910 | Octave Lapize, France | 162 hrs, 41 min, 30 sec | 1969 | Eddy Merckx, Belgium | 116 hrs, 16 min, 2 sec |
| 1911 | Gustave Garrigou, France | 195 hrs, 37 min | 1970 | Eddy Merckx, Belgium | 119 hrs, 31 min, 49 sec |
| 1912 | Odile Defraye, Belgium | 190 hrs, 30 min, 28 sec | 1971 | Eddy Merckx, Belgium | 96 hrs, 45 min, 14 sec |
| 1913 | Philippe Thys, Belgium | 197 hrs, 54 min | 1972 | Eddy Merckx, Belgium | 108 hrs, 17 min, 18 sec |
| 1914 | Philippe Thys, Belgium | 200 hrs, 28 min, 48 sec | 1973 | Luis Ocana, Spain | 122 hrs, 25 min, 34 sec |
| 1915–18 | NO RACE | | 1974 | Eddy Merckx, Belgium | 116 hrs, 16 min, 58 sec |
| 1919 | Firmin Lambot, Belgium | 231 hrs, 7 min, 15 sec | 1975 | Bernard Thevenet, France | 114 hrs, 35 min, 31 sec |
| 1920 | Philippe Thys, Belgium | 228 hrs, 36 min, 13 sec | 1976 | Lucien Van Impe, Belgium | 116 hrs, 22 min, 23 sec |
| 1921 | Leon Scieur, Belgium | 221 hrs, 50 min, 26 sec | 1977 | Bernard Thevenet, France | 115 hrs, 38 min, 30 sec |
| 1922 | Firmin Lambot, Belgium | 222 hrs, 8 min, 6 sec | 1978 | Bernard Hinault, France | 108 hrs, 18 min |
| 1923 | Henri Pelissier, France | 222 hrs, 15 min, 30 sec | 1979 | Bernard Hinault, France | 103 hrs, 6 min, 50 sec |
| 1924 | Ottavio Bottechia, Italy | 226 hrs, 18 min, 21 sec | 1980 | Joop Zoetemelk, Netherlands | 109 hrs, 19 min, 14 sec |
| 1925 | Ottavio Bottechia, Italy | 219 hrs, 10 min, 18 sec | 1981 | Bernard Hinault, France | 96 hrs, 19 min, 38 sec |
| 1926 | Lucien Buysse, Belgium | 238 hrs, 44 min, 25 sec | 1982 | Bernard Hinault, France | 92 hrs, 8 min, 46 sec |
| 1927 | Nicolas Frantz, Luxembourg | 198 hrs, 16 min, 42 sec | 1983 | Laurent Fignon, France | 105 hrs, 7 min, 52 sec |
| 1928 | Nicolas Frantz, Luxembourg | 192 hrs, 48 min, 58 sec | 1984 | Laurent Fignon, France | 112 hrs, 3 min, 40 sec |
| 1929 | Maurice Dewaele, Belgium | 186 hrs, 39 min, 16 sec | 1985 | Bernard Hinault, France | 113 hrs, 24 min, 23 sec |
| 1930 | Andre Leducq, France | 172 hrs, 12 min, 16 sec | 1986 | Greg LeMond, United States | 110 hrs, 35 min, 19 sec |
| 1931 | Antonin Magne, France | 177 hrs, 10 min, 3 sec | 1987 | Stephen Roche, Ireland | 115 hrs, 27 min, 42 sec |
| 1932 | Andre Leducq, France | 154 hrs, 12 min, 49 sec | 1988 | Pedro Delgado, Spain | 84 hrs, 27 min, 53 sec |
| 1933 | Georges Speicher, France | 147 hrs, 51 min, 37 sec | 1989 | Greg LeMond, United States | 87 hrs, 38 min, 35 sec |
| 1934 | Antonin Magne, France | 147 hrs, 13 min, 58 sec | 1990 | Greg LeMond, United States | 90 hrs, 43 min, 20 sec |
| 1935 | Romain Maes, Belgium | 141 hrs, 32 min | 1991 | Miguel Induráin, Spain | 101 hrs, 1 min, 20 sec |
| 1936 | Sylvere Maes, Belgium | 142 hrs, 47 min, 32 sec | 1992 | Miguel Induráin, Spain | 100 hrs, 49 min, 30 sec |
| 1937 | Roger Lapebie, France | 138 hrs, 58 min, 31 sec | 1993 | Miguel Induráin, Spain | 95 hrs, 57 min, 9 sec |
| 1938 | Gino Bartali, Italy | 148 hrs, 29 min, 12 sec | 1994 | Miguel Induráin, Spain | 103 hrs, 38 min, 38 sec |
| 1939 | Sylvere Maes, Belgium | 132 hrs, 3 min, 17 sec | 1995 | Miguel Induráin, Spain | 92 hrs, 44 min, 59 sec |
| 1940–46 | NO RACE | | 1996 | Bjarne Riis, Denmark | 95 hrs, 57 min, 16 sec |
| 1947 | Jean Robic, France | 148 hrs, 11 min, 25 sec | 1997 | Jan Ullrich, Germany | 100 hrs, 30 min, 35 sec |
| 1948 | Gino Bartali, Italy | 147 hrs, 10 min, 36 sec | 1998 | Marco Pantani, Italy | 92 hrs, 49 min, 46 sec |
| 1949 | Fausto Coppi, Italy | 149 hrs, 40 min, 49 sec | 1999 | Lance Armstrong, United States | 91 hrs, 32 min, 16 sec |
| 1950 | Ferdi Kubler, Switzerland | 145 hrs, 36 min, 56 sec | 2000 | Lance Armstrong, United States | 92 hrs, 33 min, 8 sec |
| 1951 | Hugo Koblet, Switzerland | 142 hrs, 20 min, 14 sec | 2001 | Lance Armstrong, United States | 86 hrs, 17 min, 28 sec |
| 1952 | Fausto Coppi, Italy | 151 hrs, 57 min, 20 sec | 2002 | Lance Armstrong, United States | 82 hrs, 5 min, 12 sec |
| 1953 | Louison Bobet, France | 129 hrs, 23 min, 25 sec | 2003 | Lance Armstrong, United States | 83 hrs, 41 min, 12 sec |
| 1954 | Louison Bobet, France | 140 hrs, 6 min, 5 sec | 2004 | Lance Armstrong, United States | 83 hrs, 36 min, 2 sec |
| 1955 | Louison Bobet, France | 130 hrs, 29 min, 26 sec | 2005 | Lance Armstrong, United States | 82 hrs, 34 min, 5 sec |
| 1956 | Roger Walkowiak, France | 124 hrs, 1 min, 16 sec | †2006 | Oscar Pereiro, Spain | 82 hrs, 48 min, 30 sec |
| 1957 | Jacques Anquetil, France | 129 hrs, 46 min, 11 sec | 2007 | Alberto Contador, Spain | 91 hrs, 26 sec |
| 1958 | Charly Gaul, Luxembourg | 116 hrs, 59 min, 5 sec | 2008 | Carlos Sastre, Spain | 87 hrs, 52 min, 52 sec |
| 1959 | Federico Bahamontes, Spain | 123 hrs, 46 min, 45 sec | 2009 | Alberto Contador, Spain | 85 hrs, 48 min, 35 sec |
| 1960 | Gastone Nencini, Italy | 112 hrs, 8 min, 42 sec | *2010 | Alberto Contador, Spain | 91 hrs, 58 min, 48 sec |
| 1961 | Jacques Anquetil, France | 122 hrs, 1 min, 33 sec | 2011 | Cadel Evans, Australia | 86 hrs, 12 min, 22 sec |

†Floyd Landis, the initial winner, was officially stripped of his title on Sept. 20, 2007 by the ICU after a hearing affirmed that he had tested positive for using banned substances during Stage 17 of the 2006 Tour.

*Alberto Contador's 2010 Tour de France title is under review due to a test sample that showed trace amounts of a performance-enhancing stimulant in one of that race's final stages.

## WORLD CHAMPIONS

### Women

| | | |
|---|---|---|
| 1906.....Madge Sayers-Cave, Great Britain | 1951.....Jeannette Altwegg, Great Britain | 1984.....Katarina Witt, E. Germany |
| 1907.....Madge Sayers-Cave, Great Britain | 1952.....Jacqueline duBief, France | 1985.....Katarina Witt, E. Germany |
| 1908.....Lily Kronberger, Hungary | 1953.....Tenley Albright, United States | 1986.....Debi Thomas, United States |
| 1909.....Lily Kronberger, Hungary | 1954.....Gundi Busch, W. Germany | 1987.....Katarina Witt, E. Germany |
| 1910.....Lily Kronberger, Hungary | 1955.....Tenley Albright, United States | 1988.....Katarina Witt, E. Germany |
| 1911.....Lily Kronberger, Hungary | 1956.....Carol Heiss, United States | 1989.....Midori Ito, Japan |
| 1912.....Opika von Meray Horvath, Hungary | 1957.....Carol Heiss, United States | 1990.....Jill Trenary, United States |
| 1913.....Opika von Meray Horvath, Hungary | 1958.....Carol Heiss, United States | 1991.....Kristi Yamaguchi, United States |
| 1914.....Opika von Meray Horvath, Hungary | 1959.....Carol Heiss, United States | 1992.....Kristi Yamaguchi, United States |
| 1915–21    NO COMPETITION | 1960.....Carol Heiss, United States | 1993.....Oksana Baiul, Ukraine |
| 1922.....Herma Plank-Szabo, Austria | 1961    NO COMPETITION | 1994.....Yuka Sato, Japan |
| 1923.....Herma Plank-Szabo, Austria | 1962.....Sjoukje Dijkstra, Netherlands | 1995.....Chen Lu, China |
| 1924.....Herma Plank-Szabo, Austria | 1963.....Sjoukje Dijkstra, Netherlands | 1996.....Michelle Kwan, United States |
| 1925.....Herma Jaross-Szabo, Austria | 1964.....Sjoukje Dijkstra, Netherlands | 1997.....Tara Lipinski, United States |
| 1926.....Herma Jaross-Szabo, Austria | 1965.....Petra Burka, Canada | 1998.....Michelle Kwan, United States |
| 1927.....Sonja Henie, Norway | 1966.....Peggy Fleming, United States | 1999.....Maria Butyrskaya, Russia |
| 1928.....Sonja Henie, Norway | 1967.....Peggy Fleming, United States | 2000.....Michelle Kwan, United States |
| 1929.....Sonja Henie, Norway | 1968.....Peggy Fleming, United States | 2001.....Michelle Kwan, United States |
| 1930.....Sonja Henie, Norway | 1969.....Gabriele Seyfert, E. Germany | 2002.....Irina Slutskaya, Russia |
| 1931.....Sonja Henie, Norway | 1970.....Gabriele Seyfert, E. Germany | 2003.....Michelle Kwan, United States |
| 1932.....Sonja Henie, Norway | 1971.....Beatrix Schuba, Austria | 2004.....Shizuka Arakawa, Japan |
| 1933.....Sonja Henie, Norway | 1972.....Beatrix Schuba, Austria | 2005.....Irina Slutskaya, Russia |
| 1934.....Sonja Henie, Norway | 1973.....Karen Magnussen, Canada | 2006.....Kimmie Meissner, United States |
| 1935.....Sonja Henie, Norway | 1974.....Christine Errath, E. Germany | 2007.....Miki Ando, Japan |
| 1936.....Sonja Henie, Norway | 1975.....Dianne DeLeeuw, Netherlands | 2008.....Mao Asada, Japan |
| 1937.....Cecilia Colledge, Great Britain | 1976.....Dorothy Hamill, United States | 2009.....Yu-Na Kim, South Korea |
| 1938.....Megan Taylor, Great Britain | 1977.....Linda Fratianne, United States | 2010.....Mao Asada, Japan |
| 1939.....Megan Taylor, Great Britain | 1978.....Annett Poetzsch, E. Germany | 2011.....Miki Ando, Japan |
| 1940–46    NO COMPETITION | 1979.....Linda Fratianne, United States | |
| 1947.....Barbara Ann Scott, Canada | 1980.....Annett Poetzsch, E. Germany | |
| 1948.....Barbara Ann Scott, Canada | 1981.....Denise Biellmann, Switzerland | |
| 1949.....Alena Vrzanova, Czechoslovakia | 1982.....Elaine Zayak, United States | |
| 1950.....Alena Vrzanova, Czechoslovakia | 1983.....Rosalynn Sumners, United States | |

### Men

| | | |
|---|---|---|
| 1896.....Gilbert Fuchs, Germany | 1928.....Willy Bockl, Austria | 1960.....Alan Giletti, France |
| 1897.....Gustav Hugel, Austria | 1929.....Gillis Grafstrom, Sweden | 1961.....No competition |
| 1898.....Henning Grenander, Sweden | 1930.....Karl Schafer, Austria | 1962.....Donald Jackson, Canada |
| 1899.....Gustav Hugel, Austria | 1931.....Karl Schafer, Austria | 1963.....Donald McPherson, Canada |
| 1900.....Gustav Hugel, Austria | 1932.....Karl Schafer, Austria | 1964.....Manfred Schneldorfer, W. Germany |
| 1901.....Ulrich Salchow, Sweden | 1933.....Karl Schafer, Austria | 1965.....Alain Calmat, France |
| 1902.....Ulrich Salchow, Sweden | 1934.....Karl Schafer, Austria | 1966.....Emmerich Danzer, Austria |
| 1903.....Ulrich Salchow, Sweden | 1935.....Karl Schafer, Austria | 1967.....Emmerich Danzer, Austria |
| 1904.....Ulrich Salchow, Sweden | 1936.....Karl Schafer, Austria | 1968.....Emmerich Danzer, Austria |
| 1905.....Ulrich Salchow, Sweden | 1937.....Felix Kaspar, Austria | 1969.....Tim Wood, United States |
| 1906.....Gilbert Fuchs, Germany | 1938.....Felix Kaspar, Austria | 1970.....Tim Wood, United States |
| 1907.....Ulrich Salchow, Sweden | 1939.....Graham Sharp, Great Britain | 1971.....Andrej Nepela, Czechoslovakia |
| 1908.....Ulrich Salchow, Sweden | 1940–46    NO COMPETITION | 1972.....Andrej Nepela, Czechoslovakia |
| 1909.....Ulrich Salchow, Sweden | 1947.....Hans Gerschwiler, Switzerland | 1973.....Andrej Nepela, Czechoslovakia |
| 1910.....Ulrich Salchow, Sweden | 1948.....Dick Button, United States | 1974.....Jan Hoffmann, E. Germany |
| 1911.....Ulrich Salchow, Sweden | 1949.....Dick Button, United States | 1975.....Sergei Volkov, USSR |
| 1912.....Fritz Kachler, Austria | 1950.....Dick Button, United States | 1976.....John Curry, Great Britain |
| 1913.....Fritz Kachler, Austria | 1951.....Dick Button, United States | 1977.....Vladimir Kovalev, USSR |
| 1914.....Gosta Sandhal, Sweden | 1952.....Dick Button, United States | 1978.....Charles Tickner, United States |
| 1915–21    NO COMPETITION | 1953.....Hayes Alan Jenkins, United States | 1979.....Vladimir Kovalev, USSR |
| 1922.....Gillis Grafstrom, Sweden | 1954.....Hayes Alan Jenkins, United States | 1980.....Jan Hoffmann, E. Germany |
| 1923.....Fritz Kachler, Austria | 1955.....Hayes Alan Jenkins, United States | 1981.....Scott Hamilton, United States |
| 1924.....Gillis Grafstrom, Sweden | 1956.....Hayes Alan Jenkins, United States | 1982.....Scott Hamilton, United States |
| 1925.....Willy Bockl, Austria | 1957.....David W. Jenkins, United States | 1983.....Scott Hamilton, United States |
| 1926.....Willy Bockl, Austria | 1958.....David W. Jenkins, United States | 1984.....Scott Hamilton, United States |
| 1927.....Willy Bockl, Austria | 1959.....David W. Jenkins, United States | 1985.....Aleksandr Fadeev, USSR |

## WORLD CHAMPIONS (Cont.)
### Men (Cont.)

1986.....Brian Boitano, United States
1987.....Brian Orser, Canada
1988.....Brian Boitano, United States
1989.....Kurt Browning, Canada
1990.....Kurt Browning, Canada
1991.....Kurt Browning, Canada
1992.....Viktor Petrenko, CIS
1993.....Kurt Browning, Canada
1994.....Elvis Stojko, Canada

1995.....Elvis Stojko, Canada
1996.....Todd Eldredge, United States
1997.....Elvis Stojko, Canada
1998.....Alexei Yagudin, Russia
1999.....Alexei Yagudin, Russia
2000.....Alexei Yagudin, Russia
2001.....Evgeni Plushenko, Russia
2002.....Alexei Yagudin, Russia
2003.....Evgeni Plushenko, Russia

2004.....Evgeni Plushenko, Russia
2005.....Stephane Lambiel, Switzerland
2006.....Stephane Lambiel, Switzerland
2007.....Brian Joubert, France
2008.....Jeffrey Buttle, Canada
2009.....Evan Lysacek, United States
2010.....Daisuke Takahaski, Japan
2011.....Patrick Chan, Canada

## Pairs

1908.....Anna Hubler, Heinrich Burger, Germany
1909.....Phyllis Johnson, James H. Johnson, Great Britain
1910.....Anna Hubler, Heinrich Burger, Germany
1911.....Ludowika Eilers, Walter Jakobsson, Germany/Finland
1912.....Phyllis Johnson, James H. Johnson, Great Britain
1913.....Helene Engelmann, Karl Majstrik, Germany
1914.....Ludowika Jakobsson-Eilers, Walter Jakobsson-Eilers, Finland
1915–21     NO COMPETITION
1922.....Helene Engelmann, Alfred Berger, Germany
1923.....Ludowika Jakobsson-Eilers, Walter Jakobsson-Eilers, Finland
1924.....Helene Engelmann, Alfred Berger, Germany
1925.....Herma Jaross-Szabo, Ludwig Wrede, Austria
1926.....Andree Joly, Pierre Brunet, France
1927.....Herma Jaross-Szabo, Ludwig Wrede, Austria
1928.....Andree Joly, Pierre Brunet, France
1929.....Lilly Scholz, Otto Kaiser, Austria
1930.....Andree Brunet-Joly, Pierre Brunet-Joly, France
1931.....Emilie Rotter, Laszlo Szollas, Hungary
1932.....Andree Brunet-Joly, Pierre Brunet-Joly, France
1933.....Emilie Rotter, Laszlo Szollas, Hungary
1934.....Emilie Rotter, Laszlo Szollas, Hungary
1935.....Emilie Rotter, Laszlo Szollas, Hungary
1936.....Maxi Herber, Ernst Bajer, Germany
1937.....Maxi Herber, Ernst Bajer, Germany
1938.....Maxi Herber, Ernst Bajer, Germany
1939.....Maxi Herber, Ernst Bajer, Germany
1940–46     NO COMPETITION
1947.....Micheline Lannoy, Pierre Baugniet, Belgium
1948.....Micheline Lannoy, Pierre Baugniet, Belgium
1949.....Andrea Kekessy, Ede Kiraly, Hungary
1950.....Karol Kennedy, Peter Kennedy, United States
1951.....Ria Baran, Paul Falk, W. Germany
1952.....Ria Baran Falk, Paul Falk, W. Germany
1953.....Jennifer Nicks, John Nicks, Great Britain
1954.....Frances Dafoe, Norris Bowden, Canada
1955.....Frances Dafoe, Norris Bowden, Canada
1956.....Sissy Schwarz, Kurt Oppelt, Austria
1957.....Barbara Wagner, Robert Paul, Canada
1958.....Barbara Wagner, Robert Paul, Canada
1959.....Barbara Wagner, Robert Paul, Canada
1960.....Barbara Wagner, Robert Paul, Canada
1961.....NO COMPETITION
1962.....Maria Jelinek, Otto Jelinek, Canada
1963.....Marika Kilius, Hans-Jurgen Baumler, W Germany
1964.....Marika Kilius, Hans-Jurgen Baumler, W Germany

1965.....Ljudmila Protopopov, Oleg Protopopov, USSR
1966.....Ljudmila Protopopov, Oleg Protopopov, USSR
1967.....Ljudmila Protopopov, Oleg Protopopov, USSR
1968.....Ljudmila Protopopov, Oleg Protopopov, USSR
1969.....Irina Rodnina, Aleksey Ulanov, USSR
1970.....Irina Rodnina, Aleksey Ulanov, USSR
1971.....Irina Rodnina, Aleksey Ulanov, USSR
1972.....Irina Rodnina, Aleksey Ulanov, USSR
1973.....Irina Rodnina, Aleksandr Zaytsev, USSR
1974.....Irina Rodnina, Aleksandr Zaytsev, USSR
1975.....Irina Rodnina, Aleksandr Zaytsev, USSR
1976.....Irina Rodnina, Aleksandr Zaytsev, USSR
1977.....Irina Rodnina, Aleksandr Zaytsev, USSR
1978.....Irina Rodnina, Aleksandr Zaytsev, USSR
1979.....Tai Babilonia, Randy Gardner, United States
1980.....Maria Cherkasova, Sergei Shakhrai, USSR
1981.....Irina Vorobieva, Igor Lisovsky, USSR
1982.....Sabine Baess, Tassilio Thierbach, E. Germany
1983.....Elena Valova, Oleg Vasiliev, USSR
1984.....Barbara Underhill, Paul Martini, Canada
1985.....Elena Valova, Oleg Vasiliev, USSR
1986.....Ekaterina Gordeeva, Sergei Grinkov, USSR
1987.....Ekaterina Gordeeva, Sergei Grinkov, USSR
1988.....Elena Valova, Oleg Vasiliev, USSR
1989.....Ekaterina Gordeeva, Sergei Grinkov, USSR
1990.....Ekaterina Gordeeva, Sergei Grinkov, USSR
1991.....Natalia Mishkutienok, Artur Dmitriev, USSR
1992.....Natalia Mishkutienok, Artur Dmitriev, CIS
1993.....Isabelle Brasseur, Lloyd Eisler, Canada
1994.....Evgenia Shishkova, Vadim Naumov, Russia
1995.....Radka Kovarikova, Rene Novotny, Czech Republic
1996.....Marina Eltsova, Andrey Buskhov, Russia
1997.....Mandy Wötzel, Ingo Steuer, Germany
1998.....Jenni Meno, Todd Sand, United States
1999.....Elena Berezhnaya, Anton Sikharulidze, Russia
2000.....Maria Petrova, Aleksei Tikhonov, Russia
2001.....Jamie Salé, David Pelletier, Canada
2002.....Xue Shen, Hongbo Zhao, China
2003.....Xue Shen, Hongbo Zhao, China
2004.....Tatiana Totmianina, Maxim Marinin, Russia
2005.....Tatiana Totmianina, Maxim Marinin, Russia
2006.....Qing Pang, Jian Tong, China
2007.....Shen Xue, Zhao Hongbo, China
2008.....Aliona Savchenko, Robin Szolkowy, Germany
2009.....Aliona Savchenko, Robin Szolkowy, Germany
2010.....Qin Pang, Jian Tong, China
2011.....Aliona Savchenko, Robin Szolkowy, Germany

## WORLD CHAMPIONS *(Cont.)*
### Dance

| | |
|---|---|
| 1950 ....Lois Waring, Michael McGean, United States | 1981 ....Jayne Torvill, Christopher Dean, Great Britain |
| 1951 ....Jean Westwood, Lawrence Demmy, Great Britain | 1982 ....Jayne Torvill, Christopher Dean, Great Britain |
| 1952 ....Jean Westwood, Lawrence Demmy, Great Britain | 1983 ....Jayne Torvill, Christopher Dean, Great Britain |
| 1953 ....Jean Westwood, Lawrence Demmy, Great Britain | 1984 ....Jayne Torvill, Christopher Dean, Great Britain |
| 1954 ....Jean Westwood, Lawrence Demmy, Great Britain | 1985 ....Natalia Bestemianova, Andrei Bukin, USSR |
| 1955 ....Jean Westwood, Lawrence Demmy, Great Britain | 1986 ....Natalia Bestemianova, Andrei Bukin, USSR |
| 1956 ....Pamela Wieght, Paul Thomas, Great Britain | 1987 ....Natalia Bestemianova, Andrei Bukin, USSR |
| 1957 ....June Markham, Courtney Jones, Great Britain | 1988 ....Natalia Bestemianova, Andrei Bukin, USSR |
| 1958 ....June Markham, Courtney Jones, Doreen D. Denny, Courtney Jones, Great Britain | 1989 ....Marina Klimova, Sergei Ponomarenko, USSR |
| | 1990 ....Marina Klimova, Sergei Ponomarenko, USSR |
| 1960 ....Doreen D. Denny, Courtney Jones, Great Britain | 1991 ....Isabelle Duchesnay, Paul Duchesnay, France |
| 1961 ....NO COMPETITION | 1992 ....Marina Klimova, Sergei Ponomarenko, CIS |
| 1962 ....Eva Romanova, Pavel Roman, Czechoslovakia | 1993 ....Renee Roca, Gorsha Sur, United States |
| 1963 ....Eva Romanova, Pavel Roman, Czechoslovakia | 1994 ....Oksana Grishuk, Evgeny Platov, Russia |
| 1964 ....Eva Romanova, Pavel Roman, Czechoslovakia | 1995 ....Oksana Grishuk, Evgeny Platov, Russia |
| 1965 ....Eva Romanova, Pavel Roman, Czechoslovakia | 1996 ....Oksana Grishuk, Evgeny Platov, Russia |
| 1966 ....Diane Towler, Bernard Ford, Great Britain | 1997 ....Oksana Grishuk, Evgeny Platov, Russia |
| 1967 ....Diane Towler, Bernard Ford, Great Britain | 1998 ....Anjelika Krylova, Oleg Ovsyannikov, Russia |
| 1968 ....Diane Towler, Bernard Ford, Great Britain | 1999 ....Anjelika Krylova, Oleg Ovsyannikov, Russia |
| 1969 ....Diane Towler, Bernard Ford, Great Britain | 2000 ....Marina Anissina, Gwendal Peizerat, France |
| 1970 ....Ljudmila Pakhomova, Aleksandr Gorshkov, USSR | 2001 ....Barbara Fusar Poli, Maurizio Margaglio, Italy |
| 1971 ....Ljudmila Pakhomova, Aleksandr Gorshkov USSR | 2002 ....Irina Lobacheva, Ilia Averbukh, Russia |
| 1972 ....Ljudmila Pakhomova, Aleksandr Gorshkov, USSR | 2003 ....Shae-Lynn Bourne, Victor Kraatz, Canada |
| 1973 ....Ljudmila Pakhomova, Aleksandr Gorshkov, USSR | 2004 ....Tatiana Navka, Roman Kostomarov, Russia |
| 1974 ....Ljudmila Pakhomova, Aleksandr Gorshkov, USSR | 2005 ....Tatiana Navka, Roman Kostomarov, Russia |
| 1975 ....Irina Moiseeva, Andreij Minenkov, USSR | 2006 ....Albena Denkova, Maxim Staviski, Bulgaria |
| 1976 ....Ljudmila Pakhomova, Aleksandr Gorshkov USSR | 2007 ....Albena Denkova ,Maxim Staviski, Bulgaria |
| 1977 ....Irina Moiseeva, Andreij Minenkov, USSR | 2008 ....Isabelle Delobel, Olivier Schoenfelder, France |
| 1978 ....Natalia Linichuk, Gennadi Karponosov, USSR | 2009 ....Oksana Domnina, Maxim Shabalin, Russia |
| 1979 ....Natalia Linichuk, Gennadi Karponosov, USSR | 2010 ....Tessa Virtue, Scott Moir, Canada |
| 1980 ....Krisztina Regoeczy, Andras Sallai, Hungary | 2011 ....Meryl Davis, Charlie White, United States |

## CHAMPIONS OF THE UNITED STATES
### Women

The championships held in 1914, 1918, 1920 and 1921 under the auspices of the International Skating Union of America were open to Canadians, although the competitions were considered to be United States championships. Beginning in 1922, the championships have been held under the auspices of the United States Figure Skating Association.

| | | |
|---|---|---|
| 1914 ....Theresa Weld, SC of Boston | 1932 ....Maribel Y. Vinson, SC of Boston | 1947 ....Gretchen Van Zandt Merrill, SC of Boston |
| 1915–17    NO COMPETITION | 1933 ....Maribel Y. Vinson, SC of Boston | |
| 1918 ....Rosemary S. Beresford, New York SC | 1934 ....Suzanne Davis, SC of Boston | 1948 ....Gretchen Van Zandt Merrill, SC of Boston |
| | 1935 ....Maribel Y. Vinson, SC of Boston | |
| 1919    NO COMPETITION | 1936 ....Maribel Y. Vinson, SC of Boston | 1949 ....Yvonne Claire Sherman, SC of New York |
| 1920 ....Theresa Weld, SC of Boston | 1937 ....Maribel Y. Vinson, SC of Boston | |
| 1921 ....Theresa Weld Blanchard, SC of Boston | 1938 ....Joan Tozzer, SC of Boston | 1950 ....Yvonne Claire Sherman, SC of New York |
| | 1939 ....Joan Tozzer, SC of Boston | |
| 1922 ....Theresa Weld Blanchard, SC of Boston | 1940 ....Joan Tozzer, SC of Boston | 1951 ....Sonya Klopfer, Junior SC of New York |
| 1923 ....Theresa Weld Blanchard, SC of Boston | 1941 ....Jane Vaughn, Philadelphia SC & HS | 1952 ....Tenley E. Albright, SC of Boston |
| | | 1953 ....Tenley E. Albright, SC of Boston |
| 1924 ....Theresa Weld Blanchard, SC of Boston | 1942 ....Jane Vaughn Sullivan, Philadelphia SC & HS | 1954 ....Tenley E. Albright, SC of Boston |
| | | 1955 ....Tenley E. Albright, SC of Boston |
| 1925 ....Beatrix Loughran, New York SC | 1943 ....Gretchen Van Zandt Merrill, SC of Boston | 1956 ....Tenley E. Albright, SC of Boston |
| 1926 ....Beatrix Loughran, New York SC | 1944 ....Gretchen Van Zandt Merrill, SC of Boston | 1957 ....Carol E. Heiss, SC of New York |
| 1927 ....Beatrix Loughran, New York SC | | 1958 ....Carol E. Heiss, SC of New York |
| 1928 ....Maribel Y. Vinson, SC of Boston | 1945 ....Gretchen Van Zandt Merrill, SC of Boston | 1959 ....Carol E. Heiss, SC of New York |
| 1929 ....Maribel Y. Vinson, SC of Boston | | 1960 ....Carol E. Heiss, SC of New York |
| 1930 ....Maribel Y. Vinson, SC of Boston | 1946 ....Gretchen Van Zandt Merrill, SC of Boston | 1961 ....Laurence R. Owen, SC of Boston |
| 1931 ....Maribel Y. Vinson, SC of Boston | | |

## CHAMPIONS OF THE UNITED STATES (Cont.)

### Women (Cont.)

1962 ....Barbara Roles Pursley, Arctic Blades FSC
1963 ....Lorraine G. Hanlon, SC of Boston
1964 ....Peggy Fleming, Arctic Blades FSC
1965 ....Peggy Fleming, Arctic Blades FSC
1966 ....Peggy Fleming, City of Colorado Springs
1967 ....Peggy Fleming, Broadmoor SC
1968 ....Peggy Fleming, Broadmoor SC
1969 ....Janet Lynn, Wagon Wheel FSC
1970 ....Janet Lynn, Wagon Wheel FSC
1971 ....Janet Lynn, Wagon Wheel FSC
1972 ....Janet Lynn, Wagon Wheel FSC
1973 ....Janet Lynn, Wagon Wheel FSC
1974 ....Dorothy Hamill, SC of New York
1975 ....Dorothy Hamill, SC of New York

1976 ....Dorothy Hamill, SC of New York
1977 ....Linda Fratianne, Los Angeles FSC
1978 ....Linda Fratianne, Los Angeles FSC
1979 ....Linda Fratianne, Los Angeles FSC
1980 ....Linda Fratianne, Los Angeles FSC
1981 ....Elaine Zayak, SC of New York
1982 ....Rosalynn Sumners, Seattle SC
1983 ....Rosalynn Sumners, Seattle SC
1984 ....Rosalynn Sumners, Seattle SC
1985 ....Tiffany Chin, San Diego FSC
1986 ....Debi Thomas, Los Angeles FSC
1987 ....Jill Trenary, Broadmoor SC
1988 ....Debi Thomas, Los Angeles FSC
1989 ....Jill Trenary, Broadmoor SC
1990 ....Jill Trenary, Broadmoor SC
1991 ....Tonya Harding, Carousel FSC
1992 ....Kristi Yamaguchi, St Moritz ISC
1993 ....Nancy Kerrigan, Colonial FSC
1994 ....Tonya Harding, Portland FSC

1995 ....Nicole Bobek, Los Angeles FSC
1996 ....Michelle Kwan, Los Angeles FSC
1997 ....Tara Lipinski, Detroit SC
1998 ....Michelle Kwan, Los Angeles FSC
1999 ....Michelle Kwan, Los Angeles FSC
2000 ....Michelle Kwan, Los Angeles FSC
2001 ....Michelle Kwan, Los Angeles FSC
2002 ....Michelle Kwan, Los Angeles FSC
2003 ....Michelle Kwan, Los Angeles FSC
2004 ....Michelle Kwan, Los Angeles FSC
2005 ....Michelle Kwan, Los Angeles FSC
2006 ....Sasha Cohen, Orange County FSC
2007 ....Kimmie Meissner, Univ. of Delaware FSC
2008 ....Mirai Nagasu, Pasadena FSC
2009 ....Alissa Czisny, Detroit SC
2010 ....Rachael Flatt, Broadmoor SC
2011 ....Alissa Czisny, Detroit SC

### Men

1914    Norman M. Scott, WC of Montreal
1915–17    NO COMPETITION
1918 ....Nathaniel W. Niles, SC of Boston
1919    NO COMPETITION
1920 ....Sherwin C. Badger, SC of Boston
1921 ....Sherwin C. Badger, SC of Boston
1922 ....Sherwin C. Badger, SC of Boston
1923 ....Sherwin C. Badger, SC of Boston
1924 ....Sherwin C. Badger, SC of Boston
1925 ....Nathaniel W. Niles, SC of Boston
1926    Chris I. Christenson, Twin City FSC
1927 ....Nathaniel W. Niles, SC of Boston
1928 ....Roger F. Turner, SC of Boston
1929 ....Roger F. Turner, SC of Boston
1930 ....Roger F. Turner, SC of Boston
1931 ....Roger F. Turner, SC of Boston
1932 ....Roger F. Turner, SC of Boston
1933 ....Roger F. Turner, SC of Boston
1934 ....Roger F. Turner, SC of Boston
1935 ....Robin H. Lee, SC of New York
1936 ....Robin H. Lee, SC of New York
1937 ....Robin H. Lee, SC of New York
1938 ....Robin H. Lee, Chicago FSC
1939 ....Robin H. Lee, St Paul FSC
1940 ....Eugene Turner, Los Angeles FSC
1941 ....Eugene Turner, Los Angeles FSC
1942 ....Robert Specht, Chicago FSC
1943    Arthur R. Vaughn Jr., Phila. SC & HS
1944–45    NO COMPETITION
1946    Dick Button, Philadelphia SC & HS
1947 ....Dick Button, Philadelphia SC & HS
1948 ....Dick Button, Philadelphia SC & HS
1949 ....Dick Button, Philadelphia SC & HS

1950 ....Dick Button, SC of Boston
1951 ....Dick Button, SC of Boston
1952 ....Dick Button, SC of Boston
1953 ....Hayes Alan Jenkins, Cleveland SC
1954 ....Hayes Alan Jenkins, Broadmoor SC
1955 ....Hayes Alan Jenkins, Broadmoor SC
1956 ....Hayes Alan Jenkins, Broadmoor SC
1957 ....David Jenkins, Broadmoor SC
1958 ....David Jenkins, Broadmoor SC
1959 ....David Jenkins, Broadmoor SC
1960 ....David Jenkins, Broadmoor SC
1961 ....Bradley R. Lord, SC of Boston
1962 ....Monty Hoyt, Broadmoor SC
1963 ....Thomas Litz, Hershey FSC
1964 ....Scott Ethan Allen, SC of New York
1965 ....Gary C. Visconti, Detroit SC
1966 ....Scott Ethan Allen, SC of New York
1967 ....Gary C. Visconti, Detroit SC
1968 ....Tim Wood, Detroit SC
1969 ....Tim Wood, Detroit SC
1970 ....Tim Wood, City of Colorado Springs
1971 ....John Misha Petkevich, Great Falls FSC
1972 ....Kenneth Shelley, Arctic Blades FSC
1973 ....Gordon McKellen Jr., SC of Lake Placid
1974 ....Gordon McKellen Jr., SC of Lake Placid
1975 ....Gordon McKellen Jr., SC of Lake Placid
1976 ....Terry Kubicka, Arctic Blades FSC
1977 ....Charles Tickner, Denver FSC
1978 ....Charles Tickner, Denver FSC

1979 ....Charles Tickner, Denver FSC
1980 ....Charles Tickner, Denver FSC
1981 ....Scott Hamilton, Philadelphia SC & HS
1982 ....Scott Hamilton, Philadelphia SC & HS
1983 ....Scott Hamilton, Philadelphia SC & HS
1984 ....Scott Hamilton, Philadelphia SC & HS
1985 ....Brian Boitano, Peninsula FSC
1986 ....Brian Boitano, Peninsula FSC
1987 ....Brian Boitano, Peninsula FSC
1988 ....Brian Boitano, Peninsula FSC
1989 ....Christopher Bowman, Los Angeles FSC
1990 ....Todd Eldredge, Los Angeles FSC
1991 ....Todd Eldredge, Los Angeles FSC
1992 ....Christopher Bowman, Los Angeles FSC
1993 ....Scott Davis, Broadmoor SC
1994 ....Scott Davis, Broadmoor SC
1995 ....Todd Eldredge, Detroit SC
1996 ....Rudy Galindo, St Moritz ISC
1997 ....Todd Eldredge, Detroit SC
1998 ....Todd Eldredge, Detroit SC
1999 ....Michael Weiss, Washington FSC
2000 ....Michael Weiss, Washington FSC
2001 ....Timothy Goebel, Winterhurst FSC
2002 ....Todd Eldredge, Los Angeles FSC
2003 ....Michael Weiss, Washington FSC
2004 ....Johnny Weir, SC of New York
2005 ....Johnny Weir, SC of New York
2006 ....Johnny Weir, SC of New York
2007 ....Evan Lysacek, DuPage FSC
2008 ....Evan Lysacek, DuPage FSC
2009 ....Jeremy Abbott, Broadmoor SC
2010 ....Jeremy Abbott, Detroit SC
2011 ....Ryan Bradley, Broadmoor SC

## CHAMPIONS OF THE UNITED STATES *(Cont.)*
### Pairs

1914 Jeanne Chevalier, Norman M. Scott, WC of Montreal
1915–17 NO COMPETITION
1918 Theresa Weld, Nathaniel W. Niles, SC of Boston
1919 No competition
1920 Theresa Weld, Nathaniel W. Niles, SC of Boston
1921 Theresa Weld Blanchard, Nathaniel W. Niles, SC of Boston
1922 Theresa Weld Blanchard, Nathaniel W. Niles, SC of Boston
1923 Theresa Weld Blanchard, Nathaniel W. Niles, SC of Boston
1924 Theresa Weld Blanchard, Nathaniel W. Niles, SC of Boston
1925 Theresa Weld Blanchard, Nathaniel W. Niles, SC of Boston
1926 Theresa Weld Blanchard, Nathaniel W. Niles, SC of Boston
1927 Theresa Weld Blanchard, Nathaniel W. Niles, SC of Boston
1928 Maribel Y. Vinson, Thornton L. Coolidge, SC of Boston
1929 Maribel Y. Vinson, Thornton L. Coolidge, SC of Boston
1930 Beatrix Loughran, Sherwin C. Badger, SC of New York
1931 Beatrix Loughran, Sherwin C. Badger, SC of New York
1932 Beatrix Loughran, Sherwin C. Badger, SC of New York
1933 Maribel Y. Vinson, George E. B. Hill, SC of SC of Boston
1936 Maribel Y. Vinson, George E. B. Hill, SC of Boston
1937 Maribel Y. Vinson, George E. B. Hill, SC of Boston
1938 Joan Tozzer, M. Bernard Fox, SC of Boston
1939 Joan Tozzer, M. Bernard Fox, SC of Boston
1940 Joan Tozzer, M. Bernard Fox, SC of Boston
1941 Donna Atwood, Eugene Turner, Mercury FSC/Los Angeles FSC
1942 Doris Schubach, Walter Noffke, Springfield Ice Birds
1943 Doris Schubach, Walter Noffke, Springfield Ice Birds
1944 Doris Schubach, Walter Noffke, Springfield Ice Birds
1945 Donna Jeanne Pospisil, Jean-Pierre Brunet, SC of New York
1946 Donna Jeanne Pospisil, Jean-Pierre Brunet, SC of New York
1947 Yvonne Claire Sherman, Robert J. Swenning, SC of New York
1948 Karol Kennedy, Peter Kennedy, Seattle SC
1949 Karol Kennedy, Peter Kennedy, Seattle SC
1950 Karol Kennedy, Peter Kennedy, Broadmoor SC
1951 Karol Kennedy, Peter Kennedy, Broadmoor SC
1952 Karol Kennedy, Peter Kennedy, Broadmoor SC

1953 Carole Ann Ormaca, Robin Greiner, SC of Fresno
1954 Carole Ann Ormaca, Robin Greiner, SC of Fresno
1955 Carole Ann Ormaca, Robin Greiner, St Moritz ISC
1956 Carole Ann Ormaca, Robin Greiner, St Moritz ISC
1957 Nancy Rouillard Ludington, Ronald Ludington, Commonwealth FSC/SC of Boston
1958 Nancy Rouillard Ludington, Ronald Ludington, Commonwealth FSC/SC of Boston
1959 Nancy Rouillard Ludington, Ronald Ludington, Commonwealth FSC
1960 Nancy Rouillard Ludington, Ronald Ludington, Commonwealth FSC
1961 Maribel Y. Owen, Dudley S. Richards, SC of Boston
1962 Dorothyann Nelson, Pieter Kollen, Village of Lake Placid
1963 Judianne Fotheringill, Jerry J. Fotheringill, Broadmoor SC
1964 Judianne Fotheringill, Jerry J. Fotheringill, Broadmoor SC
1965 Vivian Joseph, Ronald Joseph, Chicago FSC
1966 Cynthia Kauffman, Ronald Kauffman, Seattle SC
1967 Cynthia Kauffman, Ronald Kauffman, Seattle SC
1968 Cynthia Kauffman, Ronald Kauffman, Seattle SC
1969 Cynthia Kauffman, Ronald Kauffman, Seattle SC
1970 Jo Jo Starbuck, Kenneth Shelley, Arctic Blades FSC
1971 Jo Jo Starbuck, Kenneth Shelley, Arctic Blades FSC
1972 Jo Jo Starbuck, Kenneth Shelley, Arctic Blades FSC
1973 Melissa Militano, Mark Militano, SC of New York
1974 Melissa Militano, Johnny Johns, SC of New York/Detroit SC
1975 Melissa Militano, Johnny Johns, SC of New York/Detroit SC
1976 Tai Babilonia, Randy Gardner, LA FSC
1977 Tai Babilonia, Randy Gardner, LA FSC
1978 Tai Babilonia, Randy Gardner, Los Angeles FSC/Santa Monica FSC
1979 Tai Babilonia, Randy Gardner, Los Angeles FSC/Santa Monica FSC
1980 Tai Babilonia, Randy Gardner, Los Angeles FSC/Santa Monica FSC
1981 Caitlin/Peter Carruthers, SC of Wilmington
1982 Caitlin/Peter Carruthers, SC of Wilmington

1983 Caitlin/Peter Carruthers, SC of Wilmington
1984 Caitlin/Peter Carruthers, SC of Wilmington
1985 Jill Watson, Peter Oppegard, LA FSC
1986 Gillian Wachsman, Todd Waggoner, SC of Wilmington
1987 Jill Watson, Peter Oppegard, LA FSC
1988 Jill Watson, Peter Oppegard, LA FSC
1989 Kristi Yamaguchi, Rudy Galindo, St Mortiz ISC
1990 Kristi Yamaguchi, Rudy Galindo, St Mortiz ISC
1991 Natasha Kuchiki, Todd Sand, LA FSC
1992 Calla Urbanski, Rocky Marval, U of Delaware FSC/SC of New York
1993 Calla Urbanski, Rocky Marval, U of Delaware FSC/SC of New York
1994 Jenni Meno, Todd Sand, Winterhurst FSC/Los Angeles FSC
1995 Jenni Meno, Todd Sand, Winterhurst FSC/Los Angeles FSC
1996 Jenni Meno, Todd Sand, Winterhurst FSC/Los Angeles FSC
1997 Kyoko Ina, Jason Dungjen, SC of New York
1998 Kyoko Ina, Jason Dungjen, SC of New York
1999 Danielle Hartsell, Steve Hartsell, Detroit SC
2000 Kyoko Ina, John Zimmerman, SC of New York/Birmingham FSC
2001 Kyoko Ina, John Zimmerman, SC of New York/Birmingham FSC
2002 Kyoko Ina, John Zimmerman, SC of New York/Birmingham FSC
2003 Tiffany Scott, Philip Dulebohn, Colonial FSC/Univ of Delaware FSC
2004 Rena Inoue, John Baldwin, All Year FSC
2005 Kathryn Orscher, Garrett Lucash, Charter Oak FSC
2006 Rena Inoue, John Baldwin, All Year FSC
2007 Brooke Castile, Benjamin Okolski, Arctic FSC
2008 Keauna McLaughlin, Los Angeles FSC/Rockne Brubaker, Broadmoor SC
2009 Keauna McLaughlin, Los Angeles FSC/Rockne Brubaker, Broadmoor SC
2010 Caydee Denney, SW Florida FSC/Jeremy Barrett, SW Florida FSC
2011 Caitlin Yankowskas, Broadmoor SC/John Coughlin, Kansas City FSC

## CHAMPIONS OF THE UNITED STATES (Cont.)

### Dance

| | | |
|---|---|---|
| 1914 | Waltz: Theresa Weld, Nathaniel W. Niles, SC of Boston | |
| 1915–19 | NO COMPETITION | |
| 1920 | Waltz: Theresa Weld, Nathaniel W. Niles, SC of Boston | |
| | Fourteenstep: Gertrude Cheever Porter, Irving Brokaw, New York SC | |
| 1921 | Waltz and Fourteenstep: Theresa Weld Blanchard, Nathaniel W. Niles, SC of Boston | |
| 1922 | Waltz: Beatrix Loughran, Edward M. Howland, New York SC/ SC of Boston | |
| | Fourteenstep: Theresa Weld Blanchard, Nathaniel W. Niles, SC of Boston | |
| 1923 | Waltz: Mr. & Mrs. Henry W. Howe, New York SC | |
| | Fourteenstep: Sydney Goode, James B. Greene, New York SC | |
| 1924 | Waltz: Rosaline Dunn, Frederick Gabel, New York SC | |
| | Fourteenstep: Sydney Goode, James B. Greene, New York SC | |
| 1925 | Waltz and Fourteenstep: Virginia Slattery, Ferrier T. Martin, New York SC | |
| 1926 | Waltz: Rosaline Dunn, Joseph K. Savage, New York SC | |
| | Fourteenstep: Sydney Goode, James B.Greene, New York SC | |
| 1927 | Waltz and Fourteenstep: Rosaline Dunn, Joseph K. Savage, New York SC | |
| 1928 | Waltz: Rosaline Dunn, Joseph K. Savage, New York SC | |
| | Fourteenstep: Ada Bauman Kelly, George T. Braakman, New York SC | |
| 1929 | Waltz and Original Dance combined: Edith C. Secord, Joseph K. Savage, SC of New York | |
| 1930 | Waltz: Edith C. Secord, Joseph K. Savage, SC of New York | |
| | Original: Clara Rotch Frothingham, George E. B. Hill, SC of Boston | |
| 1931 | Waltz: Edith C. Secord, Ferrier T. Martin, SC of New York | |
| | Original: Theresa Weld Blanchard, Nathaniel W. Niles, SC of Boston | |
| 1932 | Waltz: Edith C. Secord, Joseph K. Savage, SC of New York | |
| | Original: Clara Rotch Frothingham, George E. B. Hill, SC of Boston | |
| 1933 | Waltz: Ilse Twaroschk, Frederick F. Fleishmann, Brooklyn FSC | |
| | Original: Suzanne Davis, Frederick Goodridge, SC of Boston | |
| 1934 | Waltz: Nettie C. Prantel, Roy Hunt, SC of New York | |
| | Original: Suzanne Davis, Frederick Goodridge, SC of Boston | |
| 1935 | Waltz: Nettie C. Prantel, Roy Hunt, SC of New York | |
| 1936 | Marjorie Parker, Joseph K. Savage, SC of New York | |
| 1937 | Nettie C. Prantel, Harold Hartshorne, SC of New York | |
| 1938 | Nettie C. Prantel, Harold Hartshorne, SC of New York | |
| 1939 | Sandy Macdonald, Harold Hartshorne,SC of New York | |
| 1940 | Sandy Macdonald, Harold Hartshorne, SC of New York | |
| 1941 | Sandy Macdonald, Harold Hartshorne, SCNY | |
| 1942 | Edith B. Whetstone, Alfred N. Richards, Jr, Philadelphia SC & HS | |
| 1943 | Marcella May, James Lochead Jr., Skate & Ski Club | |
| 1944 | Marcella May, James Lochead Jr., Skate & Ski Club | |
| 1945 | Kathe Mehl Williams, Robert J. Swenning,SC of New York | |
| 1946 | Anne Davies, Carleton C. Hoffner Jr., Washington FSC | |
| 1947 | Lois Waring, Walter H. Bainbridge Jr., Baltimore FSC/Washigton FSC | |
| 1948 | Lois Waring, Walter H. Bainbridge Jr.,Baltimore FSC/Washington FSC | |
| 1949 | Lois Waring, Walter H. Bainbridge Jr.,Baltimore FSC/Washington FSC | |
| 1950 | Lois Waring, Michael McGean, Baltimore FSC | |
| 1951 | Carmel Bodel, Edward L. Bodel, St. Moritz ISC | |
| 1952 | Lois Waring, Michael McGean, Baltimore FSC | |
| 1953 | Carol Ann Peters, Daniel C. Ryan, Washington FSC | |
| 1954 | Carmel Bodel, Edward L. Bodel, St Moritz ISC | |
| 1955 | Carmel Bodel, Edward L. Bodel, St Moritz ISC | |
| 1956 | Joan Zamboni, Roland Junso, Arctic Blades FSC | |
| 1957 | Sharon McKenzie, Bert Wright, Los Angeles FSC | |
| 1958 | Andree Anderson, Donald Jacoby, Buffalo SC | |
| 1959 | Andree Anderson Jacoby, Donald Jacoby, Buffalo SC | |
| 1960 | Margie Ackles, Charles W. Phillips Jr., Los Angeles FSC/Arctic Blades FSC | |
| 1961 | Diane C. Sherbloom, Larry Pierce, Los Angeles FSC/ WC of Indianapolis | |
| 1962 | Yvonne N. Littlefield, Peter F. Betts, Arctic Blades FSC/ Paramount, CA | |
| 1963 | Sally Schantz, Stanley Urban, SC of Boston/Buffalo SC | |
| 1964 | Darlene Streich, Charles D. Fetter Jr., WC of Indianapolis | |
| 1965 | Kristin Fortune, Dennis Sveum, Los Angeles FSC | |
| 1966 | Kristin Fortune, Dennis Sveum, Los Angeles FSC | |
| 1967 | Lorna Dyer, John Carrell, Broadmoor SC | |
| 1968 | Judy Schwomeyer, James Sladky, WC of Indianapolis/Genesee FSC | |
| 1969 | Judy Schwomeyer, James Sladky, WC of Indianapolis/Genesee FSC | |
| 1970 | Judy Schwomeyer, James Sladky, WC of Indianapolis/Genesee FSC | |
| 1971 | Judy Schwomeyer, James Sladky, WC of Indianapolis/Genesee FSC | |
| 1972 | Judy Schwomeyer, James Sladky, WC of Indianapolis/Genesee FSC | |
| 1973 | Mary Karen Campbell, Johnny Johns, Lansing SC/Detroit SC | |
| 1974 | Colleen O'Connor, Jim Millns, Broadmoor SC/ City of Colorado Springs | |
| 1975 | Colleen O'Connor, Jim Millns, Broadmoor SC | |
| 1976 | Colleen O'Connor, Jim Millns, Broadmoor SC | |
| 1977 | Judy Genovesi, Kent Weigle, SC of Hartford/Charter Oak FSC | |
| 1978 | Stacey Smith, John Summers, SC of Wilmington | |
| 1979 | Stacey Smith, John Summers, SC of Wilmington | |
| 1980 | Stacey Smith, John Summers, SC of Wilmington | |
| 1981 | Judy Blumberg, Michael Seibert, Broadmoor SC/ISC of Indianapolis | |
| 1982 | Judy Blumberg, Michael Seibert, Broadmoor SC/ISC of Indianapolis | |
| 1983 | Judy Blumberg, Michael Seibert, Pittsburgh FSC | |
| 1984 | Judy Blumberg, Michael Seibert, Pittsburgh FSC | |
| 1985 | Judy Blumberg, Michael Seibert, Pittsburgh FSC | |
| 1986 | Renee Roca, Donald Adair, Genesee FSC/Academy FSC | |
| 1987 | Suzanne Semanick, Scott Gregory, U of Delaware SC | |
| 1988 | Suzanne Semanick, Scott Gregory, U of Delaware SC | |
| 1989 | Susan Wynne, Joseph Druar, Broadmoor SC/Seattle SC | |
| 1990 | Susan Wynne, Joseph Druar, Broadmoor SC/Seattle SC | |
| 1991 | Elizabeth Punsalan, Jerod Swallow, Broadmoor SC | |
| 1992 | April Sargent, Russ Witherby, Ogdensburg FSC/ U of Delaware FSC | |
| 1993 | Renee Roca, Gorsha Sur, Broadmoor SC | |
| 1994 | Elizabeth Punsalan, Jerod Swallow, Broadmoor SC/Detroit SC | |
| 1995 | Renee Roca, Gorsha Sur, Broadmoor SC | |
| 1996 | Elizabeth Punsalan, Jerod Swallow, Detroit SC | |
| 1997 | Elizabeth Punsalan, Jerod Swallow, Detroit SC | |

## CHAMPIONS OF THE UNITED STATES *(CONT.)*

### Dance *(Cont.)*

| | | | | | |
|---|---|---|---|---|---|
| 1998 | Elizabeth Punsalan, Jerod Swallow, Detroit SC | 2003 | Naomi Lang, Peter Tchernyshev, American Academy FSC | 2008 | Tanith Belbin, Ben Agosto, Arctic FSC |
| 1999 | Naomi Lang, Peter Tchernyshev, Detroit SC | 2004 | Tanith Belbin, Ben Agosto, Detroit SC | 2009 | Meryl Davis, Arctic FSC/ Charlie White, Detroit SC |
| 2000 | Naomi Lang, Peter Tchernyshev, Detroit SC | 2005 | Tanith Belbin, Ben Agosto, Detroit SC | 2010 | Meryl Davis, Arctic FSC/ Charlie White, Detroit SC |
| 2001 | Naomi Lang, Peter Tchernyshev, Detroit SC | 2006 | Tanith Belbin, Ben Agosto, Arctic FSC | 2011 | Meryl Davis, Arctic FSC/ Charlie White, Detroit SC |
| 2002 | Naomi Lang, Peter Tchernyshev, American Academy FSC | 2007 | Tanith Belbin, Ben Agosto, Arctic FSC | | |

# Gymnastics

## WORLD CHAMPIONS — Men

### All-Around

| Year | Champion, Nation |
|---|---|
| 1903 | Joseph Martinez, France |
| 1905 | Marcel Lalue, France |
| 1907 | Joseph Czada, Czechoslovakia |
| 1909 | Marcos Torres, France |
| 1911 | Ferdinand Steiner, Czechoslovakia |
| 1913 | Marcos Torres, France |
| 1922 | Peter Sumi, Yugoslavia |
| | F. Pechacek, Czechoslovakia |
| 1926 | Peter Sumi, Yugoslavia |
| 1930 | Josip Primozic, Yugoslavia |
| 1934 | Eugene Mack, Switzerland |
| 1938 | Jan Gajdos, Czechoslovakia |
| 1950 | Walter Lehmann, Switzerland |
| 1954 | Valentin Mouratov, USSR |
| | Victor Chukarin, USSR |
| 1958 | Boris Shaklin, USSR |
| 1962 | Yuri Titov, USSR |
| 1966 | Mikhail Voronin, USSR |
| 1970 | Eizo Kenmotsu, Japan |
| 1974 | Shigeru Kasamatsu, Japan |
| 1978 | Nikolai Andrianov, USSR |
| 1979 | Alexander Ditiatin, USSR |
| 1981 | Yuri Korolev, USSR |
| 1983 | Dimitri Bilozertchev, USSR |
| 1985 | Yuri Korolev, USSR |
| 1987 | Dimitri Bilozertchev, USSR |
| 1989 | Igor Korobchinsky, USSR |
| 1991 | Grigori Misutin, CIS |
| 1993 | Vitaly Scherbo, Belarus |
| 1994 | Ivan Ivankov, Belarus |
| 1995 | Li Xiaoshuang, China |
| 1997 | Ivan Ivankov, Belarus |
| 1999 | Nicolae Krukov, Russia |
| 2001 | Feng Jing, China |
| 2003 | Paul Hamm, United States |
| 2005 | Hiroyuki Tomita, Japan |
| 2007 | Yang Wei, China |
| 2009 | Kohei Uchimura, Japan |
| 2011 | Kohei Uchimura, Japan |

### Pommel Horse

| Year | Champion, Nation |
|---|---|
| 1930 | Josip Primozic, Yugoslavia |
| 1934 | Eugene Mack, Switzerland |
| 1938 | Michael Reusch, Switzerland |
| 1950 | Josef Stalder, Switzerland |
| 1954 | Grant Chaguinjan, USSR |
| 1958 | Boris Shaklin, USSR |
| 1962 | Miroslav Cerar, Yugoslavia |
| 1966 | Miroslav Cerar, Yugoslavia |
| 1970 | Miroslav Cerar, Yugoslavia |
| 1974 | Zoltan Magyar, Hungary |
| 1978 | Zoltan Magyar, Hungary |
| 1979 | Zoltan Magyar, Hungary |
| 1981 | Michael Mikolai, East Germany |
| 1983 | Dmitri Bilozertchev, USSR |
| 1985 | Valentin Moguilny, USSR |
| 1987 | Zsolt Borkai, Hungary |
| | Dmitri Bilozertchev, USSR |
| 1989 | Valentin Moguilny, USSR |
| 1991 | Valeri Belenki, USSR |
| 1992 | Pae Gil Su, North Korea |
| | Vitaly Scherbo, CIS |
| | Li Jing, China |
| 1993 | Pae Gil Su, North Korea |
| 1994 | Marius Urzica, Romania |
| 1995 | Li Donghua, Switzerland |
| 1996 | Pae Gil Su, North Korea |
| 1997 | Valeri Belenki, Germany |
| 1999 | Alexei Nemov, Russia |
| 2001 | Marius Urzica, Romania |
| 2003 | Teng Haibin, China |
| | Takehiro Kashima, Japan |
| 2005 | Qin Xiao, China |
| 2007 | Qin Xiao, China |
| 2009 | Hongtao Zhang, China |
| 2011 | Krisztian Berki, Hungary |

### Floor Exercise

| Year | Champion, Nation |
|---|---|
| 1930 | Josip Primozic, Yugoslavia |
| 1934 | Georges Miesz, Switzerland |
| 1938 | Jan Gajdos, Czechoslovakia |
| 1950 | Josef Stalder, Switzerland |
| 1954 | Valentin Mouratov, USSR |
| | Masao Takemoto, Japan |
| 1958 | Masao Takemoto, Japan |
| 1962 | Nobuyuki Aihara, Japan |
| | Yukio Endo, Japan |
| 1966 | Akinori Nakayama, Japan |
| 1970 | Akinori Nakayama, Japan |
| 1974 | Shigeru Kasamatsu, Japan |
| 1978 | Kurt Thomas, United States |
| 1979 | Kurt Thomas, United States |
| | Roland Brucker, East Germ. |
| 1981 | Yuri Korolev, USSR, |
| | Li Yuejui, China |
| 1983 | Tong Fei, China |
| 1985 | Tong Fei, China |
| 1987 | Lou Yun, China |
| 1989 | Igor Korobchinsky, USSR |
| 1991 | Igor Korobchinsky, USSR |
| 1993 | Grigori Misutin, Ukraine |
| 1994 | Vitaly Scherbo, Belarus |
| 1995 | Vitaly Scherbo, Belarus |
| 1996 | Vitaly Scherbo, Belarus |
| 1997 | Alexei Nemov, Russia |
| 1999 | Alexei Nemov, Russia |
| 2001 | Marian Dragulescu, Romania |
| 2003 | Paul Hamm, United States |
| | Jordan Jovtchev, Bulgaria |
| 2005 | Diego Hypolito, Brazil |
| 2007 | Zou Kai, China |
| 2009 | Marian Dragulescu, Romania |
| 2011 | Kohei Uchimura, Japan |

## WORLD CHAMPIONS — Men

### Rings

| Year | Champion, Nation |
|------|------------------|
| 1930 | Emanuel Loffler, Czechoslovakia |
| 1934 | Alois Hudec, Czechoslovakia |
| 1938 | Alois Hudec, Czechoslovakia |
| 1950 | Walter Lehmann, Switzerland |
| 1954 | Albert Azarian, USSR |
| 1958 | Albert Azarian, USSR |
| 1962 | Yuri Titov, USSR |
| 1966 | Mikhail Voronin, USSR |
| 1970 | Akinori Nakayama, Japan |
| 1974 | N. Andrianov, USSR D. Grecu, Rom. |
| 1978 | Nikolai Andrianov, USSR |
| 1979 | Alexander Ditiatin, USSR |
| 1981 | Alexander Ditiatin, USSR |
| 1983 | Dimitri Bilozertchev, USSR |
| 1985 | Li Ning, China, Yuri Korolev, USSR |
| 1987 | Yuri Korolev, USSR |
| 1989 | Andreas Aguilar, West Germ. |
| 1991 | Grigory Misutin, USSR |
| 1992 | Vitaly Scherbo, CIS |
| 1993 | Yuri Chechi, Italy |
| 1994 | Yuri Chechi, Italy |
| 1995 | Yuri Chechi, Italy |
| 1996 | Yuri Chechi, Italy |
| 1997 | Yuri Chechi, Italy |
| 1999 | Zhen Dong, China |
| 2001 | Jordan Jovtchev, Bulgaria |
| 2003 | Jordan Jovtchev, Bulgaria Dimosthenis Tampakos, Greece |
| 2005 | Yuri Van Gelder, Netherlands |
| 2007 | Diego Hypolito, Brazil |
| 2009 | Mingyong Yan, China |
| 2011 | Yibing Chen, China |

### Parallel Bars

| Year | Champion, Nation |
|------|------------------|
| 1930 | Josip Primozic, Yugoslavia |
| 1934 | Eugene Mack, Switzerland |
| 1938 | Michael Reusch, Switzerland |
| 1950 | Hans Eugster, Switzerland |
| 1954 | Victor Chukarin, USSR |
| 1958 | Boris Shaklin, USSR |
| 1962 | Miroslav Cerar, Yugoslavia |
| 1966 | Sergei Diamidov, USSR |
| 1970 | Akinori Nakayama, Japan |
| 1974 | Eizo Kenmotsu, Japan |
| 1978 | Eizo Kenmotsu, Japan |
| 1979 | Bart Conner, United States |
| 1981 | Koji Gushiken, Japan Alexandr Ditiatin, USSR |
| 1983 | Vladimir Artemov, USSR Lou Yun, China |
| 1985 | Sylvio Kroll, East Germany Valentin Moguilny, USSR |
| 1987 | Vladimir Artemov, USSR |
| 1989 | Li Jing, China Vladimir Artemov, USSR |
| 1991 | Li Jing, China |
| 1992 | Li Jin, China, Alexei Voropaev, CIS |
| 1993 | Vitaly Scherbo, Belarus |
| 1994 | Huang Liping, China |
| 1995 | Vitaly Scherbo, Belarus |
| 1996 | Rustam Sharipov, Ukraine |
| 1997 | Zhang Jinjing, China |

### Parallel Bar *(Cont.)*

| Year | Champion, Nation |
|------|------------------|
| 1999 | Joo-Hyung Lee, South Korea |
| 2001 | Sean Townsend, U.S. |
| 2003 | Li Xiao-Peng, China |
| 2005 | Mitja Petkovsek, Slovenia |
| 2007 | Mitja Petkovsek, Slovenia |
| 2009 | Guanyin Yang, China |
| 2011 | Danell Leyva, United States |

### Horizontal Bar

| Year | Champion, Nation |
|------|------------------|
| 1930 | Istvan Pelle, Hungary |
| 1934 | Ernst Winter, Germany |
| 1938 | Michael Reusch, Switzerland |
| 1950 | Paavo Aaltonen, Finland |
| 1954 | Valentin Mouratov, USSR |
| 1958 | Boris Shaklin, USSR |
| 1962 | Takashi Ono, Japan |
| 1966 | Akinori Nakayama, Japan |
| 1970 | Eizo Kenmotsu, Japan |
| 1974 | Eberhard Gienger, W Germany |
| 1978 | Shigeru Kasamatsu, Japan |
| 1979 | Kurt Thomas, United States |
| 1981 | Alexander Takchev, USSR |
| 1983 | Dimitri Bilozertchev, USSR |
| 1985 | Tong Fei, China |
| 1987 | Dimitri Bilozertchev, USSR |
| 1989 | Li Chunyang, China |
| 1991 | Li Chunyang, China R. Buechner, Germ |
| 1992 | Grigori Misutin, CIS |
| 1993 | Sergei Kharkov, Russia |
| 1994 | Vitaly Scherbo, Belarus |
| 1995 | Andreas Wecker, Germany |
| 1996 | Jesús Carballo, Spain |
| 1997 | Jani Tanskanen, Finland |
| 1999 | Jesus Carballo, Spain |
| 2001 | Vlasios Maras, Greece |
| 2003 | Takehiro Kashima, Japan |
| 2005 | Vlasios Maras, Greece |
| 2007 | Fabian Hambuechen, Germ. |
| 2009 | Kai Zou, China |
| 2011 | Kai Zou, China |

### Vault

| Year | Champion, Nation |
|------|------------------|
| 1934 | Eugene Mack, Switzerland |
| 1938 | Eugene Mack, Switzerland |
| 1950 | Ernst Gebendinger, Switzerland |
| 1954 | Leo Sotornik, Czechoslovakia |
| 1958 | Yuri Titov, USSR |
| 1962 | Premysel Krbec, Czechoslovakia |
| 1966 | Haruhiro Yamashita, Japan |
| 1970 | Mitsuo Tsukahara, Japan |
| 1974 | Shigeru Kasamatsu, Japan |
| 1978 | Junichi Shimizu, Japan |
| 1979 | Alexander Ditiatin, USSR |
| 1981 | Ralf-Peter Hemmann, East Germany |
| 1983 | Arthur Akopian, USSR |
| 1985 | Yuri Korolev, USSR |
| 1987 | Lou Yun, China Sylvio Kroll, East Germany |

### Vault *(Cont.)*

| Year | Champion, Nation |
|------|------------------|
| 1989 | Joreg Behrend, East Germany |
| 1991 | Yoo Ok Youl, South Korea |
| 1992 | Yoo Ok Youl, South Korea |
| 1993 | Vitaly Scherbo, Belarus |
| 1994 | Vitaly Scherbo, Belarus |
| 1995 | G. Misutin, Ukraine A. Nemov, Russia |
| 1996 | Alexei Nemov, Russia |
| 1997 | Sergei Fedorchenko, Kazakhstan |
| 1999 | Li Xiao-Peng, China |
| 2001 | Marian Dragulescu, Romania |
| 2003 | Li Xiao-Peng, China |
| 2005 | Eichi Sekiguchi, Japan |
| 2007 | Leszek Blanik, Poland |
| 2009 | Marian Dragulescu, Romania |
| 2011 | Hak-seon Yang , South Korea |

## WORLD CHAMPIONS — Women

### All-Around

| Year | Champion, Nation |
|------|------------------|
| 1934 | Vlasta Dekanova, Czechoslovakia |
| 1938 | Vlasta Dekanova, Czechoslovakia |
| 1950 | Helena Rakoczy, Poland |
| 1954 | Galina Roudiko, USSR |
| 1958 | Larissa Latynina, USSR |
| 1962 | Larissa Latynina, USSR |
| 1966 | Vera Caslavska, Czechoslovakia |
| 1970 | Ludmilla Tourischeva, USSR |
| 1974 | Ludmilla Tourischeva, USSR |
| 1978 | Elena Mukhina, USSR |
| 1979 | Nelli Kim, USSR |
| 1981 | Olga Bicherova, USSR |
| 1983 | Natalia Yurchenko, USSR |
| 1985 | Elena Shoushounova, USSR |
|      | Oksana Omeliantchik, USSR |
| 1987 | Aurelia Dobre, Romania |
| 1989 | Svetlana Bouguinskaia, USSR |
| 1991 | Kim Zmeskal, United States |
| 1993 | Shannon Miller, United States |
| 1994 | Shannon Miller, United States |
| 1995 | Lilia Podkopayeva, Ukraine |
| 1997 | Svetlana Khorkina, Russia |
| 1999 | Maria Olaru, Romania |
| 2001 | Svetlana Khorkina, Russia |
| 2003 | Svetlana Khorkina, Russia |
| 2005 | Chellsie Memmel, United States |
| 2007 | Shawn Johnson, United States |
| 2009 | Bridget Sloan, United States |
| 2011 | Jordyn Wieber, United States |

### Floor Exercise

| Year | Champion, Nation |
|------|------------------|
| 1950 | Helena Rakoczy, Poland |
| 1954 | Tamara Manina, USSR |
| 1958 | Eva Bosakava, Czechoslovakia |
| 1962 | Larissa Latynina, USSR |
| 1966 | Natalia Kuchinskaya, USSR |
| 1970 | Ludmilla Tourischeva, USSR |
| 1974 | Ludmilla Tourischeva, USSR |
| 1978 | Nelli Kim, USSR |
|      | Elena Mukhina, USSR |
| 1979 | Emilia Eberle, Romania |
| 1981 | Natalia Ilenko, USSR |
| 1983 | Ecaterina Szabo, Romania |
| 1985 | Oksana Omeliantchik, USSR |
| 1987 | Elena Shoushounova, USSR |
|      | Daniela Silivas, Romania |
| 1989 | Svetlana Bouguinskaia, USSR |
|      | Daniela Silivas, Romania |
| 1991 | Cristina Bontas, Romania |
|      | Oksana Tchusovitina, USSR |
| 1992 | Kim Zmeskal, United States |
| 1993 | Shannon Miller, United States |
| 1994 | Dina Kochetkova, Russia |
| 1995 | Gina Gogean, Romania |
| 1996 | Gina Gogean, Romania |
| 1997 | Gina Gogean, Romania |
| 1999 | Andreea Raducan, Romania |
| 2001 | Andreea Raducan, Romania |
| 2003 | Daiane Dos Santos, Brazil |
| 2005 | Nastia Liukin, United States |
| 2007 | Shawn Johnson, United States |
| 2009 | Elizabeth Tweddle, United Kingdom |
| 2011 | Kseniia Afanaseva, Russia |

### Uneven Bars

| Year | Champion, Nation |
|------|------------------|
| 1950 | Gertchen Kolar, Austria |
|      | Anna Pettersson, Sweden |
| 1954 | Agnes Keleti, Hungary |
| 1958 | Larissa Latynina, USSR |
| 1962 | Irina Pervuschina, USSR |
| 1966 | Natalia Kuchinskaya, USSR |
| 1970 | Karin Janz, East Germany |
| 1974 | Annelore Zinke, East Germany |
| 1978 | Marcia Frederick, United States |
| 1979 | Ma Yanhong, China |
|      | Maxi Gnauck, East Germany |
| 1981 | Maxi Gnauck, East Germany |
| 1983 | Maxi Gnauck, East Germany |
| 1985 | Gabriele Fahnrich, East Germany |
| 1987 | Daniela Silivas, Romania |
|      | Doerte Thuemmler, East Germany |
| 1989 | Fan Di, China |
|      | Daniela Silivas, Romania |
| 1991 | Gwang Suk Kim, North Korea |
| 1992 | Lavinia Milosivici, Romania |
| 1993 | Shannon Miller, United States |
| 1994 | Luo Li, China |
| 1995 | Svetlana Khorkina, Russia |
| 1996 | Svetlana Khorkina, Russia |
| 1997 | Svetlana Khorkina, Russia |
| 1999 | Svetlana Khorkina, Russia |
| 2001 | Svetlana Khorkina, Russia |
| 2003 | Chellsie Memmel, U.S. |
|      | Hollie Vise, United States |
| 2005 | Nastia Liukin, United States |
| 2007 | Ksenia Semenov, Russia |
| 2009 | Kexin He, China |
| 2011 | Viktoria Komova, Russia |

### Balance Beam

| Year | Champion, Nation |
|------|------------------|
| 1950 | Helena Rakoczy, Poland |
| 1954 | Keiko Tanaka, Japan |
| 1958 | Larissa Latynina, USSR |
| 1962 | Eva Bosakova, Czech. |
| 1966 | Natalia Kuchinskaya, USSR |
| 1970 | Erika Zuchold, East Germany |
| 1974 | Ludmilla Tourischeva, USSR |
| 1978 | Nadia Comaneci, Romania |
| 1979 | Vera Cerna, Czechoslovakia |
| 1981 | Maxi Gnauck, East Germany |
| 1983 | Olga Mostepanova, USSR |
| 1985 | Daniela Silivas, Romania |
| 1987 | Aurelia Dobre, Romania |
| 1989 | Daniela Silivas, Romania |
| 1991 | Svetlana Boguinskaia, USSR |
| 1992 | Kim Zmeskal, United States |
| 1993 | Lavinia Milosivici, Romania |
| 1994 | Shannon Miller, United States |
| 1995 | Mo Huilan, China |
| 1996 | Dina Kochetkova, Russia |
| 1997 | Gina Gogean, Romania |
| 1999 | E. Zamolodchikova, Russia |
| 2001 | Andreea Raducan, Romania |
| 2003 | Fan Ye, China |
| 2005 | Nan Zhang, China |
| 2007 | Nastia Liukin, United States |
| 2009 | Linlin Deng, China |
| 2011 | Lu Sui, China |

### Vault

| Year | Champion, Nation |
|------|------------------|
| 1950 | Helena Rakoczy, Poland |
| 1954 | T. Manina, USSR |
|      | Anna Pettersson, Sweden |
| 1958 | Larissa Latynina, USSR |
| 1962 | Vera Caslavska, Czech. |
| 1966 | Vera Caslavska, Czech. |
| 1970 | Erika Zuchold, East Germany |
| 1974 | Olga Korbut, USSR |
| 1978 | Nelli Kim, USSR |
| 1979 | Dumitrita Turner, Romania |
| 1981 | Maxi Gnauck, East Germany |
| 1983 | Boriana Stoyanova, Bulgaria |
| 1985 | Elena Shoushounova, USSR |
| 1987 | Elena Shoushounova, USSR |
| 1989 | Olesia Durnik, USSR |
| 1991 | Lavinia Milosovici, Romania |
| 1992 | Henrietta Onodi, Hungary |
| 1993 | Elena Piskun, Belarus |
| 1994 | Gina Gogean, Romania |
| 1995 | L. Podkopayeva, Ukraine |
|      | Simona Amanar, Rom. |
| 1996 | Gina Gogean, Romania |
| 1997 | Simona Amanar, Romania |
| 1999 | Jie Ling, China |
| 2001 | Svetlana Khorkina, Russia |
| 2003 | Oksana Chusovitina, Uzbekistan |
| 2005 | Fei Cheng, China |
| 2007 | Fei Cheng, China |
| 2009 | Kayla Williams, United States |
| 2011 | McKayla Maroney, United States |

## CHAMPIONS OF THE UNITED STATES — Men

### All-Around

| Year | Champion |
|---|---|
| 1963 | Art Shurlock |
| 1964 | Rusty Mitchell |
| 1965 | Rusty Mitchell |
| 1966 | Rusty Mitchell |
| 1967 | Katsuzoki Kanzaki |
| 1968 | Yoshi Hayasaki |
| 1969 | Steve Hug |
| 1970 | Makoto Sakamoto, Mas Watanabe |
| 1971 | Yoshi Takei |
| 1972 | Yoshi Takei |
| 1973 | Marshall Avener |
| 1974 | John Crosby |
| 1975 | Tom Beach, Bart Conner |
| 1976 | Kurt Thomas |
| 1977 | Kurt Thomas |
| 1978 | Kurt Thomas |
| 1979 | Bart Conner |
| 1980 | Peter Vidmar |
| 1981 | Jim Hartung |
| 1982 | Peter Vidmar |
| 1983 | Mitch Gaylord |
| 1984 | Mitch Gaylord |
| 1985 | Brian Babcock |
| 1986 | Tim Daggett |
| 1987 | Scott Johnson |
| 1988 | Dan Hayden |
| 1989 | Tim Ryan |
| 1990 | John Roethlisberger |
| 1991 | Chris Waller |
| 1992 | John Roethlisberger |
| 1993 | John Roethlisberger |
| 1994 | Scott Keswick |
| 1995 | John Roethlisberger |
| 1996 | Blaine Wilson |
| 1997 | Blaine Wilson |
| 1998 | Blaine Wilson |
| 1999 | Blaine Wilson |
| 2000 | Blaine Wilson |
| 2001 | Sean Townsend |
| 2002 | Paul Hamm |
| 2003 | Paul Hamm |
| 2004 | Paul Hamm |
| 2005 | Todd Thornton |
| 2006 | Alexander Artemev |
| 2007 | David Durante |
| 2008 | David Sender |
| 2009 | Jonathan Horton |
| 2010 | Jonathan Horton |
| 2011 | Danell Leyva |

### Floor Exercise

| Year | Champion |
|---|---|
| 1963 | Tom Seward |
| 1964 | Rusty Mitchell |
| 1965 | Rusty Mitchell |
| 1966 | Dan Millman |
| 1967 | Katsuzoki Kanzaki, Ron Aure |
| 1968 | Katsuzoki Kanzaki |
| 1969 | Steve Hug, Dave Thor |
| 1970 | Makoto Sakamoto |
| 1971 | John Crosby |
| 1972 | Yoshi Takei |

### Floor Exercise *(Cont.)*

| Year | Champion |
|---|---|
| 1973 | John Crosby |
| 1974 | John Crosby |
| 1975 | Peter Korman |
| 1977 | Ron Galimore |
| 1978 | Kurt Thomas |
| 1979 | Ron Galimore |
| 1980 | Ron Galimore |
| 1981 | Jim Hartung |
| 1982 | Jim Hartung |
| 1983 | Mitch Gaylord |
| 1984 | Peter Vidmar |
| 1985 | Mark Oates |
| 1986 | Robert Sundstrom |
| 1987 | John Sweeney |
| 1988 | Mark Oates, Charles Lakes |
| 1989 | Mike Racanelli |
| 1990 | Bob Stelter |
| 1991 | Mike Racanelli |
| 1992 | Gregg Curtis |
| 1993 | Kerry Huston |
| 1994 | Jeremy Killen |
| 1995 | Daniel Stover |
| 1996 | Jay Thornton |
| 1997 | Jason Gatson |
| 1998 | Jason Gatson |
| 1999 | Jason Gatson |
| 2000 | Blaine Wilson |
| 2001 | Sean Townsend |
| 2002 | Morgan Hamm |
| 2003 | Morgan Hamm |
| 2004 | Paul Hamm |
| 2005 | Guillermo Alvarez |
| 2006 | Jonathan Horton |
| 2007 | Paul Hamm |
| 2008 | Morgan Hamm |
| 2009 | Steven Legendre |
| 2010 | Joshua Dixon |
| 2011 | Jacob Dalton |

### Pommel Horse

| Year | Champion |
|---|---|
| 1963 | Larry Spiegel |
| 1964 | Sam Bailie |
| 1965 | Jack Ryan |
| 1966 | Jack Ryan |
| 1967 | Paul Mayer/Dave Doty |
| 1968 | Katsuoki Kanzaki |
| 1969 | Dave Thor |
| 1970 | Mas Watanabe |
| 1971 | Leonard Caling |
| 1972 | Sadao Hamada |
| 1973 | Marshall Avener |
| 1974 | Marshall Avener |
| 1975 | Bart Conner |
| 1977 | Gene Whelan |
| 1978 | Jim Hartung |
| 1979 | Bart Conner |
| 1980 | Jim Hartung |
| 1981 | Jim Hartung |
| 1982 | Jim Hartung |
| 1983 | Bart Conner |
| 1984 | Tim Daggett |
| 1985 | Phil Cahoy |

### Pommel Horse *(Cont.)*

| Year | Champion |
|---|---|
| 1986 | Phil Cahoy |
| 1987 | Tim Daggett |
| 1988 | Kevin Davis |
| 1989 | Kevin Davis |
| 1990 | Patrick Kirksey |
| 1991 | Chris Waller |
| 1992 | Chris Waller |
| 1993 | Chris Waller |
| 1994 | Mihai Begiu |
| 1995 | Mark Sohn |
| 1996 | Josh Stein |
| 1997 | John Roethlisberger |
| 1998 | John Roethlisberger |
| 1999 | John Roethlisberger |
| 2000 | John Roethlisberger |
| 2001 | Brett McClure |
| 2002 | Paul Hamm |
| 2003 | Paul Hamm |
| 2004 | Brett McClure |
| 2005 | Yewki Tomita |
| 2006 | Alexander Artemev |
| 2007 | Alexander Artemev |
| 2008 | Yewki Tomita |
| 2009 | Luke Stannard |
| 2010 | Daniel Ribiero |
| 2011 | Alexander Naddour |

### Rings

| Year | Champion |
|---|---|
| 1963 | Art Shurlock |
| 1964 | Glen Gailis |
| 1965 | Glen Gailis |
| 1966 | Glen Gailis |
| 1967 | Fred Dennis, Don Hatch |
| 1968 | Yoshi Hayasaki |
| 1969 | Fred Dennis, Bob Emery |
| 1970 | Makoto Sakamoto |
| 1971 | Yoshi Takei |
| 1972 | Yoshi Takei |
| 1973 | Jim Ivicek |
| 1974 | Tom Weeder |
| 1975 | Tom Beach |
| 1977 | Kurt Thomas |
| 1978 | Mike Silverstein |
| 1979 | Bart Conner |
| 1980 | Jim Hartung |
| 1981 | Jim Hartung |
| 1982 | Jim Hartung, Peter Vidmar |
| 1983 | Mitch Gaylord |
| 1984 | Jim Hartung |
| 1985 | Dan Hayden |
| 1986 | Dan Hayden |
| 1987 | Scott Johnson |
| 1988 | Dan Hayden |
| 1989 | Scott Keswick |
| 1990 | Scott Keswick |
| 1991 | Scott Keswick |
| 1992 | Tim Ryan |
| 1993 | John Roethlisberger |
| 1994 | Scott Keswick |
| 1995 | Paul O'Neill |
| 1996 | Kip Simons |
| 1997 | Blaine Wilson |

### Rings *(Cont.)*

| Year | Champio |
|---|---|
| 1998 | Jeff Johnson |
| 1999 | Blaine Wilson |
| 2000 | Blaine Wilson |
| 2001 | Sean Townsend |
| 2002 | Blaine Wilson |
| 2003 | Blaine Wilson |
| 2004 | Raj Bhavsar |
| 2005 | Sean Golden |
| 2006 | Kevin Tan |
| 2007 | Kevin Tan |
| 2008 | Kevin Tan |
| 2009 | Jonathan Horton |
| 2010 | Brandon Wynn |
| 2011 | Brandon Wynn |

### Vault

| Year | Champion |
|---|---|
| 1963 | Art Shurlock |
| 1964 | Gary Hery |
| 1965 | Brent Williams |
| 1966 | Dan Millman |
| 1967 | Jack Kenan, Sid Jensen |
| 1968 | Rich Scorza |
| 1969 | Dave Butzman |
| 1970 | Makoto Sakamoto |
| 1971 | Gary Morava |
| 1972 | Mike Kelley |
| 1973 | Gary Morava |
| 1974 | John Crosby |
| 1975 | Tom Beach |
| 1977 | Ron Galimore |
| 1978 | Jim Hartung |
| 1979 | Ron Galimore |
| 1980 | Ron Galimore |
| 1981 | Ron Galimore |
| 1982 | Jim Hartung/Jim Mikus |
| 1983 | Chris Reigel |
| 1984 | Chris Reigel |
| 1985 | Scott Johnson, Mark Oates |
| 1986 | Scott Wilbanks |
| 1987 | John Sweeney |
| 1988 | John Sweeney/Bill Paul |
| 1989 | Bill Roth |
| 1990 | Lance Ringnald |
| 1991 | Scott Keswick |
| 1992 | Trent Dimas |
| 1993 | Bill Roth |
| 1994 | Keith Wiley |
| 1995 | David St. Pierre |
| 1996 | Blaine Wilson |
| 1997 | Blaine Wilson |
| 1998 | Brent Klaus |
| 1999 | Guard Young |
| 2000 | Blaine Wilson |
| 2001 | Jason Furr |
| 2002 | Paul Hamm |
| 2003 | Raj Bhavsar |
| 2004 | David Sender |
| 2005 | Sean Golden |
| 2006 | David Sender |
| 2007 | Sean Golden |
| 2008 | David Sender |
| 2009 | Jake Dalton |
| 2010 | Steven Legendre |
| 2011 | Jacob Dalton |

## CHAMPIONS OF THE UNITED STATES - Men *(Cont.)*

### Parallel Bars

| Year | Champion |
|------|----------|
| 1963 | Tom Seward |
| 1964 | Rusty Mitchell |
| 1965 | Glen Gailis |
| 1966 | Ray Hadley |
| 1967 | Katsuzoki Kanzaki Tom Goldsborough |
| 1968 | Yoshi Hayasaki |
| 1969 | Steve Hug |
| 1970 | Makoto Sakamoto |
| 1971 | Brent Simmons |
| 1972 | Yoshi Takei |
| 1973 | Marshall Avener |
| 1974 | Jim Ivicek |
| 1975 | Bart Conner |
| 1977 | Kurt Thomas |
| 1978 | Bart Conner |
| 1979 | Bart Conner |
| 1980 | Phil Cahoy/Larry Gerard |
| 1981 | Bart Conner |
| 1982 | Peter Vidmar |
| 1983 | Mitch Gaylord |
| 1984 | Peter Vidmar, Mitch Gaylord, Tim Daggett |
| 1985 | Tim Daggett |
| 1986 | Tim Daggett |
| 1987 | Scott Johnson |
| 1988 | D. Hayden/K. Davis |
| 1989 | Conrad Voorsanger |
| 1990 | Trent Dimas |

### Parallel Bars *(Cont.)*

| Year | Champion |
|------|----------|
| 1991 | Scott Keswick |
| 1992 | Jair Lynch |
| 1993 | Chainey Umphrey |
| 1994 | Steve McCain |
| 1995 | John Roethlisberger |
| 1996 | Jair Lynch |
| 1997 | Blaine Wilson |
| 1998 | Blaine Wilson |
| 1999 | Jason Gatson |
| 2000 | Trent Wells |
| 2001 | Sean Townsend |
| 2002 | Sean Townsend |
| 2003 | Jason Gatson |
| 2004 | Alexander Artemev |
| 2005 | D.J. Bucher |
| 2006 | Alexander Artemev |
| 2007 | David Durante |
| 2008 | Justin Spring |
| 2009 | Tim McNeill |
| 2010 | Danell Leyva |
| 2011 | Danell Leyva |

### Horizontal Bar

| Year | Champion |
|------|----------|
| 1963 | Art Shurlock |
| 1964 | Glen Gailis |
| 1965 | Rusty Mitchell |
| 1966 | Katsuzoki Kanzaki |
| 1967 | Katsuzoki Kanzaki Jerry Fontana |
| 1968 | Yoshi Hayasaki |
| 1969 | Rich Grisby |
| 1970 | Makoto Sakamoto |
| 1971 | Yoshi Takei |
| 1972 | Tom Lindner |
| 1973 | John Crosby |
| 1974 | Brent Simmons |
| 1975 | Tom Beach |
| 1977 | Kurt Thomas |
| 1978 | Kurt Thomas |
| 1979 | Yoichi Tomita |
| 1980 | Jim Hartung |
| 1981 | Bart Conner |
| 1982 | Mitch Gaylord |
| 1983 | Mario McCutcheon |
| 1983 | Mario McCutcheon |
| 1984 | Peter Vidmar Tim Daggett Mitch Gaylord |
| 1985 | Dan Hayden |
| 1986 | D. Hayden/D. Moriel |
| 1987 | David Moriel |

### Horiz. Bar *(Cont.)*

| Year | Champion |
|------|----------|
| 1988 | Dan Hayden |
| 1989 | Tim Ryan |
| 1990 | Trent Dimas Lance Ringnald |
| 1991 | Lance Ringnald |
| 1992 | Jair Lynch |
| 1993 | Steve McCain |
| 1994 | Scott Keswick |
| 1995 | John Roethlisberger |
| 1996 | Bill Roth |
| 1997 | Douglas Stibel |
| 1998 | Jason Gatson |
| 1999 | Jamie Natalie |
| 2000 | Trent Wells Jamie Natalie |
| 2001 | Daniel Diaz-Luong |
| 2002 | Blaine Wilson |
| 2003 | Paul Hamm |
| 2004 | Paul Hamm |
| 2005 | D.J. Bucher |
| 2006 | Chris Brooks |
| 2007 | Justin Spring |
| 2008 | Joseph Hagerty |
| 2009 | Jonathan Horton |
| 2010 | Chris Brooks |
| 2011 | Danell Leyva |

## CHAMPIONS OF THE UNITED STATES — Women

### All-Around

| Year | Champion |
|------|----------|
| 1963 | Donna Schanezer |
| 1965 | Gail Daley |
| 1966 | Donna Schanezer |
| 1968 | Linda Scott |
| 1969 | Joyce Tanac Schroeder |
| 1970 | Cathy Rigby |
| 1971 | Joan Moore Gnat Linda Metheny Mulvihill |
| 1972 | Joan Moore Gnat Cathy Rigby |
| 1973 | Joan Moore Gnat |
| 1974 | Joan Moore Gnat |
| 1975 | Tammy Manville |
| 1976 | Denise Cheshire |
| 1977 | Donna Turnbow |
| 1978 | Kathy Johnson |
| 1979 | Leslie Pyfer |
| 1980 | Julianne McNamara |
| 1981 | Tracee Talavera |
| 1982 | Tracee Talavera |
| 1983 | Dianne Durham |
| 1984 | Mary Lou Retton |
| 1985 | Sabrina Mar |
| 1986 | Jennifer Sey |
| 1987 | Kristie Phillips |
| 1988 | Phoebe Mills |
| 1989 | Brandy Johnson |
| 1990 | Kim Zmeskal |
| 1991 | Kim Zmeskal |

### All-Around *(Cont.)*

| Year | Champion |
|------|----------|
| 1992 | Kim Zmeskal |
| 1993 | Shannon Miller |
| 1994 | Dominique Dawes |
| 1995 | Dominique Moceanu |
| 1996 | Shannon Miller |
| 1997 | V. Adler/ K. Powell |
| 1998 | Kristen Maloney |
| 1999 | Kristen Maloney |
| 2000 | Elise Ray |
| 2001 | Tasha Schwikert |
| 2002 | Tasha Schwikert |
| 2003 | Courtney Kupets |
| 2004 | Courtney Kupets/Carly Patterson |
| 2005 | Nastia Liukin |
| 2006 | Nastia Liukin |
| 2007 | Shawn Johnson |
| 2008 | Shawn Johnson |
| 2009 | Bridget Sloan |
| 2010 | Rebecca Bross |
| 2011 | Jordyn Wieber |

### Vault

| Year | Champion |
|------|----------|
| 1963 | Donna Schanezer |
| 1965 | Gail Daley |
| 1966 | Donna Schanezer |
| 1968 | Terry Spencer |
| 1969 | Joyce Tanac Schroeder Cleo Carver |
| 1970 | Cathy Rigby |

### Vault *(Cont.)*

| Year | Champion |
|------|----------|
| 1971 | Joan Moore Gnat/Adele Gleaves |
| 1972 | Cindy Eastwood |
| 1973 | Roxanne Pierce Mancha |
| 1974 | Dianne Dunbar |
| 1975 | Kolleen Casey |
| 1976 | Debbie Wilcox |
| 1977 | Lisa Cawthron |
| 1978 | Rhonda Schwandt/Sharon Shapiro |
| 1979 | Christa Canary |
| 1980 | J. McNamara/B. Kline |
| 1981 | Kim Neal |
| 1982 | Yumi Mordre |
| 1983 | Dianne Durham |
| 1984 | Mary Lou Retton |
| 1985 | Yolanda Mavity |
| 1986 | Joyce Wilborn |
| 1987 | Rhonda Faehn |
| 1988 | Rhonda Faehn |
| 1989 | Brandy Johnson |
| 1990 | Brandy Johnson |
| 1991 | Kerri Strug |
| 1992 | Kerri Strug |
| 1993 | Dominique Dawes |
| 1994 | Dominique Dawes |
| 1995 | Shannon Miller |
| 1996 | Dominique Dawes |
| 1997 | Vanessa Atler |
| 1998 | Dominique Moceanu |
| 1999 | Vanessa Atler |
| 2000 | Kristen Maloney |
| 2001 | Mohini Bhardwaj |

### CHAMPIONS OF THE UNITED STATES— Women *(Cont.)*

#### Vault *(Cont.)*

| Year | Champion |
|------|----------|
| 2002 | Elizabeth Tricase |
| 2003 | Annia Hatch |
| 2004 | Liz Tricase |
| 2005 | Alicia Sacramone |
| 2006 | Alicia Sacramone |
| 2007 | Alicia Sacramone |
| 2008 | Alicia Sacramone |
| 2009 | Kayla Williams |
| 2010 | Alicia Sacramone |
| 2011 | McKayla Maroney |

#### Uneven Bars

| Year | Champion |
|------|----------|
| 1963 | Donna Schanezer |
| 1965 | Irene Haworth |
| 1966 | Donna Schanezer |
| 1968 | Linda Scott |
| 1969 | Joyce Tanac Schroeder |
|      | Lisa Nelson |
| 1970 | Roxanne Pierce Mancha |
| 1971 | Joan Moore Gnat |
| 1972 | Cathy Rigby |
| 1973 | Roxanne Pierce Mancha |
| 1974 | Diane Dunbar |
| 1975 | Leslie Wolfsberger |
| 1976 | Leslie Wolfsberger |
| 1977 | Donna Turnbow |
| 1978 | Marcia Frederick |
| 1979 | Marcia Frederick |
| 1980 | Marcia Frederick |
| 1981 | Julianne McNamara |
| 1982 | Marie Roethlisberger |
| 1983 | Julianne McNamara |
| 1984 | Julianne McNamara |
| 1985 | Sabrina Mar |
| 1986 | Marie Roethlisberger |
| 1987 | Melissa Marlowe |
| 1988 | Chelle Stack |
| 1989 | Chelle Stack |
| 1990 | Sandy Woolsey |
| 1991 | Elisabeth Crandall |
| 1992 | Dominique Dawes |
| 1993 | Shannon Miller |
| 1994 | Dominique Dawes |
| 1995 | Dominique Dawes |
| 1996 | Dominique Dawes |
| 1997 | Kristy Powell |
| 1998 | Elise Ray |
| 1999 | Jamie Dantzscher |
|      | Jennie Thompson |
| 2000 | Elise Ray |
| 2001 | Katie Heenan |
| 2002 | Tasha Schwikert |
| 2003 | Katie Heenan |
| 2004 | Courtney Kupets |
| 2005 | Nastia Liukin |
| 2006 | Nastia Liukin |
| 2007 | Nastia Liukin |
| 2008 | Nastia Liukin |
| 2009 | Bridget Sloan |
| 2010 | Rebecca Bross |
| 2011 | Jordyn Wieber |

#### Balance Beam

| Year | Champion |
|------|----------|
| 1963 | Leissa Krol |
| 1965 | Gail Daley |
| 1966 | Irene Haworth |
|      | Linda Scott |
| 1968 | Linda Scott |
| 1969 | Lonna Woodward |
| 1970 | Joyce Tanac Schroeder |
| 1971 | Linda Metheny Mulvihill |
| 1972 | Kim Chace |
| 1973 | Nancy Thies Marshall |
| 1974 | Joan Moore Gnat |
| 1975 | Kyle Gayner |
| 1976 | Carrie Englert |
| 1977 | Donna Turnbow |
| 1978 | Christa Canary |
| 1979 | Heidi Anderson |
| 1980 | Kelly Garrison-Steves |
| 1981 | Tracee Talavera |
| 1982 | Julianne McNamara |
| 1983 | Dianne Durham |
| 1984 | Pam Bileck |
|      | Tracee Talavera |
| 1986 | Angie Denkins |
| 1987 | Kristie Phillips |
| 1985 | Kelly Garrison-Steves |
| 1988 | Kelly Garrison-Steves |
| 1989 | Brandy Johnson |
| 1990 | Betty Okino |
| 1991 | Shannon Miller |
| 1992 | Kerri Strug |
|      | Kim Zmeskal |
| 1993 | Dominique Dawes |
| 1994 | Dominique Dawes |
| 1995 | Doni Thompson |
|      | Monica Flammer |
| 1996 | Dominique Dawes |
| 1997 | Kendall Beck |
| 1998 | Dominique Moceanu |
| 1999 | Vanessa Atler |
| 2000 | Alyssa Beckerman |
|      | Amy Chow |
| 2001 | Tasha Schwikert |
| 2002 | Tasha Schwikert |
| 2003 | Hollie Vise |
| 2004 | Courtney Kupets |
| 2005 | Nastia Liukin |
| 2006 | Nastia Liukin |
| 2007 | Shawn Johnson |
| 2008 | Nastia Liukin |
| 2009 | Ivana Hong |
| 2010 | Rebecca Bross |
| 2011 | Alicia Sacramone |

#### Floor Exercise

| Year | Champion |
|------|----------|
| 1963 | Donna Schanezer |
| 1965 | Gail Daley |
| 1966 | Donna Schanezer |
| 1968 | Linda Scott |
| 1970 | Cathy Rigby |
| 1971 | Joan Moore Gnat |
|      | Linda Metheny Mulvihill |
| 1972 | Joan Moore Gnat |
| 1973 | Joan Moore Gnat |
| 1974 | Joan Moore Gnat |
| 1975 | Kathy Howard |
| 1976 | Carrie Englert |
| 1977 | Kathy Johnson |
| 1978 | Kathy Johnson |
| 1979 | Heidi Anderson |
| 1980 | Beth Kline |
| 1981 | Michelle Goodwin |
| 1982 | Amy Koopman |
| 1983 | Dianne Durham |
| 1984 | Mary Lou Retton |
| 1985 | Sabrina Mar |
| 1986 | Yolanda Mavity |
| 1987 | Kristie Phillips |
| 1988 | Phoebe Mills |
| 1989 | Brandy Johnson |
| 1990 | Brandy Johnson |
| 1991 | Kim Zmeskal |
|      | Dominique Dawes |
| 1992 | Kim Zmeskal |
| 1993 | Shannon Miller |
| 1994 | Dominique Dawes |
| 1995 | Dominique Dawes |
| 1996 | Dominique Dawes |
| 1997 | Lindsay Wing |
| 1998 | Vanessa Atler |
| 1999 | Elise Ray |
| 2000 | Kristen Maloney |
| 2001 | Tabitha Yim |
| 2002 | Tasha Schwikert |
| 2003 | Ashley Postell |
| 2004 | Carly Patterson |
| 2005 | Alicia Sacramone |
| 2006 | Alicia Sacramone |
|      | Randi Stageberg |
| 2007 | Shawn Johnson |
| 2008 | Shawn Johnson |
| 2009 | Bridget Sloan |
| 2010 | Mattie Larson |
| 2011 | Jordyn Wieber |

# Skiing World Cup Season Title Holders

## Men – OVERALL

| | |
|---|---|
| 1967 | Jean-Claude Killy, France |
| 1968 | Jean-Claude Killy, France |
| 1969 | Karl Schranz, Austria |
| 1970 | Karl Schranz, Austria |
| 1971 | Gustavo Thoeni, Italy |
| 1972 | Gustavo Thoeni, Italy |
| 1973 | Gustavo Thoeni, Italy |
| 1974 | Piero Gros, Italy |
| 1975 | Gustavo Thoeni, Italy |
| 1976 | Ingemar Stenmark, Sweden |
| 1977 | Ingemar Stenmark, Sweden |
| 1978 | Ingemar Stenmark, Sweden |
| 1979 | Peter Lüscher, Switzerland |
| 1980 | Andreas Wenzel, Liechtenstein |
| 1981 | Phil Mahre, United States |
| 1982 | Phil Mahre, United States |
| 1983 | Phil Mahre, United States |
| 1984 | Pirmin Zurbriggen, Switzerland |
| 1985 | Marc Girardelli, Luxembourg |
| 1986 | Marc Girardelli, Luxembourg |
| 1987 | Pirmin Zurbriggen, Switzerland |
| 1988 | Pirmin Zurbriggen, Switzerland |
| 1989 | Marc Girardelli, Luxembourg |
| 1990 | Pirmin Zurbriggen, Switzerland |
| 1991 | Marc Girardelli, Luxembourg |
| 1992 | Paul Accola, Switzerland |
| 1993 | Marc Girardelli, Luxembourg |
| 1994 | Kjetil André Aamodt, Norway |
| 1995 | Alberto Tomba, Italy |
| 1996 | Lasse Kjus, Norway |
| 1997 | Luc Alphand, France |
| 1998 | Hermann Maier, Austria |
| 1999 | Lasse Kjus, Norway |
| 2000 | Hermann Maier, Austria |
| 2001 | Hermann Maier, Austria |
| 2002 | Stephan Eberharter, Austria |
| 2003 | Stephan Eberharter, Austria |
| 2004 | Hermann Maier, Austria |
| 2005 | Bode Miller, United States |
| 2006 | Benjamin Raich, Austria |
| 2007 | Aksel Lund Svindal, Norway |
| 2008 | Bode Miller, United States |
| 2009 | Aksel Lund Svindal, Norway |
| 2010 | Carlo Janka, Switzerland |
| 2011 | Ivica Kostelic, Croatia |

## Women – OVERALL

| | |
|---|---|
| 1967 | Nancy Greene, Canada |
| 1968 | Nancy Greene, Canada |
| 1969 | Gertrud Gabl, Austria |
| 1970 | Michèle Jacot, France |
| 1971 | Annemarie Pröll, Austria |
| 1972 | Annemarie Pröll, Austria |
| 1973 | Annemarie Pröll, Austria |
| 1974 | Annemarie Moser-Proell, Austria |
| 1975 | Annemarie Moser-Proell, Austria |
| 1976 | Rosi Mitermaier, W Germany |
| 1977 | Lise-Marie Morerod, Switzerland |
| 1978 | Hanni Wenzel, Liechtenstein |
| 1979 | Annemarie Moser-Proell, Austria |
| 1980 | Hanni Wenzel, Liechtenstein |
| 1981 | Marie-Thérèse Nadig, Switzerland |
| 1982 | Erika Hess, Switzerland |
| 1983 | Tamara McKinney, United States |
| 1984 | Erika Hess, Switzerland |
| 1985 | Michela Figini, Switzerland |
| 1986 | Maria Walliser, Switzerland |
| 1987 | Maria Walliser, Switzerland |
| 1988 | Michela Figini, Switzerland |
| 1989 | Vreni Schneider, Switzerland |
| 1990 | Petra Kronberger, Austria |
| 1991 | Petra Kronberger, Austria |
| 1992 | Petra Kronberger, Austria |
| 1993 | Anita Wachter, Austria |
| 1994 | Vreni Schneider, Switzerland |
| 1995 | Vreni Schneider, Switzerland |
| 1996 | Katja Seizinger, Germany |
| 1997 | Pernilla Wiberg, Sweden |
| 1998 | Katja Seizinger, Germany |
| 1999 | Alexandra Meissnitzer, Austria |
| 2000 | Renate Goetschl, Austria |
| 2001 | Janica Kostelic, Croatia |
| 2002 | Michaela Dorfmeister, Austria |
| 2003 | Janica Kostelic, Austria |
| 2004 | Anja Paerson, Sweden |
| 2005 | Anja Paerson, Sweden |
| 2006 | Janica Kostelic, Croatia |
| 2007 | Nicole Hosp, Austria |
| 2008 | Lindsey Vonn, United States |
| 2009 | Lindsey Vonn, United States |
| 2010 | Lindsey Vonn, United States |
| 2011 | Maria Hoefl-Riesch, Germany |

## United States National Champions

### 1983
#### FREESTYLE
105.5 ......Rich Salamone
114.5 ......Joe Gonzales
125.5 ......Joe Corso
136.5 ......Rich Dellagatta*
149.5 ......Bill Hugent
163 ..........Lee Kemp
180.5 ......Chris Campbell
198 ..........Pete Bush
220 ..........Greg Gibson
Hvy ........Bruce Baumgartner
Team .......Sunkist Kids

#### GRECO-ROMAN
105.5 ......T.J. Jones
114.5 ......Mark Fuller
125.5 ......Rob Hermann
136.5 ......Dan Mello
149.5 ......Jim Martinez
163 ..........James Andre
180.5 ......Steve Goss
198 ..........Steve Fraser*
220 ..........Dennis Koslowski
Hvy ........No champion
Team ........Minn. Wrestling Club

### 1984
#### FREESTYLE
105.5 ......Rich Salamone
114.5 ......Charlie Heard
125.5 ......Joe Corso
136.5 ......Rich Dellagatta*
149.5 ......Andre Metzger
163 ..........Dave Schultz*
180.5 ......Mark Schultz
198 ..........Steve Fraser
220 ..........Harold Smith
Hvy .........Bruce Baumgartner
Team .......Sunkist Kids

#### GRECO-ROMAN
105.5 ......T.J. Jones
114.5 ......Mark Fuller
136.5 ......Dan Mello
149.5 ......Jim Martinez*
163 ..........John Matthews
180.5 ......Tom Press
198 ..........Mike Houck
220 ..........No champion
Hvy ..........No champion
Team ........Adirondack 3-Style, Wash.

### 1985
#### FREESTYLE
105.5 ......Tim Vanni
114.5 ......Jim Martin
125.5 ......Charlie Heard
136.5 ......Darryl Burley
149.5 ......Bill Nugent*
163 ..........Kenny Monday
180.5 ......Mike Sheets
198 ..........Mark Schultz
220 ..........Greg Gibson
286 ..........Bruce Baumgartner
Team ........Sunkist Kids

### 1985 (Cont.)
#### GRECO-ROMAN
105.5 ......T.J. Jones
114.5 ......Mark Fuller
125.5 ......Eric Seward*
136.5 ......Buddy Lee
149.5 ......Jim Martinez
163 ..........David Butler
180.5 ......Chris Catallo
198 ..........Mike Houck
220 ..........Greg Gibson
286 ..........Dennis Koslowski
Team ........U.S. Marine Corps

### 1986
#### FREESTYLE
105.5 ......Rich Salamone
114.5 ......Joe Gonzales
125.5 ......Kevin Darkus
136.5 ......John Smith
149.5 ......Andre Metzger*
163 ..........Dave Schultz
180.5 ......Mark Schultz
198 ..........Jim Scherr
220 ..........Dan Severn
286 ..........Bruce Baumgartner
Team ........Sunkist Kids (Div. I)
Hawkeye Wrestling
Club (Div. II)

#### GRECO-ROMAN
105.5 ......Eric Wetzel
114.5 ......Shawn Sheldon
125.5 ......Anthony Amado
136.5 ......Frank Famiano
149.5 ......Jim Martinez
163 ..........David Butler*
180.5 ......Darryl Gholar
198 ..........Derrick Waldroup
220 ..........Dennis Koslowski
286 ..........Duane Koslowski
Team ........U.S. Marine Corps (Div. I)
U.S. Navy (Div. II)

### 1987
#### FREESTYLE
105.5 ......Takashi Irie
114.5 ......Mitsuru Sato
125.5 ......Barry Davis
136.5 ......Takumi Adachi
149.5 ......Andre Metzger
163 ..........Dave Schultz*
180.5 ......Mark Schultz
198 ..........Jim Scherr
220 ..........Bill Scherr
286 ..........Bruce Baumgartner
Team ........Sunkist Kids (Div. I)
Team Foxcatcher (Div. II)

### 1987 (Cont.)
#### GRECO-ROMAN
105.5 ......Eric Wetzel
114.5 ......Shawn Sheldon
125.5 ......Eric Seward
136.5 ......Frank Famiano
149.5 ......Jim Martinez
163 ..........David Butler
180.5 ......Chris Catallo
198 ..........Derrick Waldroup*
220 ..........Dennis Koslowski
286 ..........Duane Koslowski
Team ......U.S. Marine Corp (Div. I)
U.S. Army (Div. II)

### 1988
#### FREESTYLE
105.5 ......Tim Vanni
114.5 ......Joe Gonzales
125.5 ......Kevin Darkus
136.5 ......John Smith*
149.5 ......Nate Carr
163 ..........Kenny Monday
180.5 ......Dave Schultz
198 ..........Melvin Douglas III
220 ..........Bill Scherr
286 ..........Bruce Baumgartner
Team ........Sunkist Kids (Div. I)
Team Foxcatcher (Div. II)

#### GRECO-ROMAN
105.5 ......T.J. Jones
114.5 ......Shawn Sheldon
125.5 ......Gogi Parseghian*
136.5 ......Dalen Wasmund
149.5 ......Craig Pollard
163 ..........Tony Thomas
180.5 ......Darryl Gholar
198 ..........Mike Carolan
220 ..........Dennis Koslowski
286 ..........Duane Koslowski
Team ........U.S. Marine Corps (Div. I)
Sunkist Kids (Div. II)

### 1989
#### FREESTYLE
105.5 ......Tim Vanni
114.5 ......Zeke Jones
125.5 ......Brad Penrith
136.5 ......John Smith
149.5 ......Nate Carr
163 ..........Rob Koll
180.5 ......Rico Chiapparelli
198 ..........Jim Scherr*
220 ..........Bill Scherr
286 ..........Bruce Baumgartner
Team ........Sunkist Kids (Div. I)
Team Foxcatcher (Div. II)

*Outstanding wrestler.

## United States National Champions

### 1989 *(Cont.)*
#### GRECO-ROMAN
105.5 ......Lew Dorrance
114.5 ......Mark Fuller
125.5 ......Gogi Parseghian
136.5 ......Isaac Anderson
149.5 ......Andy Seras*
163 ..........David Butler
180.5 ......John Morgan
198 ..........Michial Foy
220 ..........Steve Lawson
286 ..........Craig Pittman
Team.......USMC (Div. I)
      Jets USA (Div. II)

### 1990
#### FREESTYLE
105.5 ......Rob Eiter
114.5 ......Zeke Jones
125.5 ......Joe Melchiore
136.5 ......John Smith
149.5 ......Nate Carr
163 ..........Rob Koll
180.5 ......Royce Alger
198 ..........Chris Campbell*
220 ..........Bill Scherr
286 ..........Bruce Baumgartner
Team.......Sunkist Kids (Div. I)
      Team Foxcatcher (Div. II)

#### GRECO-ROMAN
105.5 ......Lew Dorrance
114.5 ......Sam Henson
125.5 ......Mark Pustelnik
136.5 ......Isaac Anderson
149.5 ......Andy Seras
163 ..........David Butler
180.5 ......Derrick Waldroup
198 ..........Randy Couture*
220 ..........Chris Tironi
286 ..........Matt Ghaffari
Team.......Jets USA (Div. I)
      California Jets (Div. II)

### 1991
#### FREESTYLE
105.5 ......Tim Vanni
114.5 ......Zeke Jones
125.5 ......Brad Penrith
136.5 ......John Smith*
149.5 ......Townsend Saunders
163 ..........Kenny Monday
180.5 ......Kevin Jackson
198 ..........Chris Campbell
220 ..........Mark Coleman
286 ..........Bruce Baumgartner
Team.......Sunkist Kids (Div. I)
      Jets USA (Div. II)

### 1991 *(Cont.)*
#### GRECO-ROMAN
105.5 ......Eric Wetzel
114.5 ......Shawn Sheldon
125.5 ......Frank Famiano
136.5 ......Buddy Lee
149.5 ......Andy Seras
163 ..........Gordy Morgan
180.5 ......John Morgan*
198 ..........Michial Foy
220 ..........Dennis Koslowski
286 ..........Craig Pittman
Team.......Jets USA (Div. I)
      Sunkist Kids (Div. II)

### 1992
#### FREESTYLE
105.5 ......Rob Eiter
114.5 ......Jack Griffin
125.5 ......Kendall Cross*
136.5 ......John Fisher
149.5 ......Matt Demaray
163 ..........Greg Elinsky
180.5 ......Royce Alger
198 ..........Dan Chaid
220 ..........Bill Scherr
286 ..........Bruce Baumgartner
Team.......Sunkist Kids (Div. I)
      Team Foxcatcher (Div. II)

#### GRECO-ROMAN
105.5 ......Eric Wetzel
114.5 ......Mark Fuller
125.5 ......Dennis Hall
136.5 ......Buddy Lee*
149.5 ......Rodney Smith
163 ..........Travis West
180.5 ......John Morgan
198 ..........Michial Foy
220 ..........Dennis Koslowski
286 ..........Matt Ghaffari
Team.......N.Y. Athletic Club (Div. I)
      Sunkist Kids (Div. II)

### 1993
#### FREESTYLE
105.5 ......Rob Eiter
114.5 ......Zeke Jones
125.5 ......Brad Penrith
136.5 ......Tom Brands
149.5 ......Matt Demaray
163 ..........Dave Schultz*
180.5 ......Kevin Jackson
198 ..........Melvin Douglas
220 ..........Kirk Trost
286 ..........Bruce Baumgartner
Team.......Sunkist Kids (Div. I)
      Team Foxcatcher (Div. II)

### 1993 *(Cont.)*
#### GRECO-ROMAN
105.5 ......Eric Wetzel
114.5 ......Shawn Sheldon
125.5 ......Dennis Hall*
136.5 ......Shon Lewis
149.5 ......Andy Seras
163 ..........Gordy Morgan
180.5 ......Dan Henderson
198 ..........Randy Couture
220 ..........James Johnson
286 ..........Matt Ghaffari
Team.......N.Y. Athletic Club (Div. I)
      Sunkist Kids (Div. II)

### 1994
#### FREESTYLE
105.5 ......Tim Vanni
114.5 ......Zeke Jones
125.5 ......Terry Brands
136.5 ......Tom Brands
149.5 ......Matt Demaray
163 ..........Dave Schultz
180.5 ......Royce Alger
198 ..........Melvin Douglas
220 ..........Mark Kerr
286 ..........Bruce Baumgartner*
Team.......Sunkist Kids (Div. I)
      Team Foxcatcher (Div. II)

#### GRECO-ROMAN
105.5 ......Isaac Ramaswamy
114.5 ......Shawn Sheldon
125.5 ......Dennis Hall
136.5 ......Shon Lewis
149.5 ......Andy Seras*
163 ..........Gordy Morgan
180.5 ......Dan Henderson
198 ..........Derrick Waldroup
220 ..........James Johnson
286 ..........Matt Ghaffari
Team.......Armed Forces (Div. I)
      N.Y. Athletic Club (Div. II)

### 1995
#### FREESTYLE
105.5 ......Tim Vanni
114.5 ......Zeke Jones
125.5 ......Terry Brands
136.5 ......Tom Brands
149.5 ......Matt Demaray
163 ..........Dave Schultz
180.5 ......Royce Alger
198 ..........Melvin Douglas
220 ..........Mark Kerr
286 ..........Bruce Baumgartner*
Team.......Sunkist Kids (Div. I)
      Team Foxcatcher (Div. II)

*Outstanding wrestler.

## United States National Champions *(Cont.)*

### 1995 *(Cont.)*
#### GRECO-ROMAN
105.5 ......Isaac Ramaswamy
114.5 ......Shawn Sheldon
125.5 ......Dennis Hall
136.5 ......Shon Lewis
149.5 ......Andy Seras*
163 .........Gordy Morgan
180.5 ......Dan Henderson
198 .........Derrick Waldroup
220 .........James Johnson
286 .........Matt Ghaffari
Team........Armed Forces (Div. I)
　　　　　　N.Y. Athletic Club (Div. II)

### 1996
#### FREESTYLE
105.5 ......Rob Eiter
114.5 ......Lou Rosselli
125.5 ......Kendall Cross*
136.5 ......Tom Brands
149.5 ......Matt Demaray
163 .........Dave Schultz
180.5 ......Kevin Jackson
198 .........Melvin Douglas
220 .........Kurt Angle
286 .........Bruce Baumgartner
Team........Sunkist Kids (Div. I)
　　　　　　Team Foxcatcher (Div. II)

#### GRECO-ROMAN
105.5 ......Isaac Ramaswamy
114.5 ......Shawn Sheldon
125.5 ......Dennis Hall*
136.5 ......Van Fronhofer
149.5 ......Heath Sims
163 .........Matt Lindland
180.5 ......Marty Morgan
198 .........Michial Foy
220 .........James Johnson
286 .........Rulon Gardner
Team........Armed Forces (Div. I)
　　　　　　Sunkist Kids (Div. II)

### 1997
#### FREESTYLE
110 .........Kanamti Soloman
119 .........Zeke Jones
127.75 .....Terry Brands
138.75 .....Carl Kolat
152 .........Lincoln McIlravy*
167.5 ......Dan St. John
187.25 .....Les Gutches
213.75 .....Melvin Douglas
275.5 ......Tom Erikson
Team........Sunkist Kids (Div. I)
　　　　　　N.Y. Athletic Club (Div. II)

#### GRECO-ROMAN
110 .........Mark Yanagihara
119 .........Broderick Lee
127.75 .....Dennis Hall
138.75 .....Kevin Bracken
152 .........Chris Saba
167.5 ......Miguel Spencer
187.25 .....Dan Henderson
213.75 .....Randy Couture*
275.5 ......Rulon Gardner
Team........Armed Forces (Div. I)
　　　　　　N.Y. Athletic Club (Div. II)

### 1998
#### FREESTYLE
119 .........Sam Henson
127.75 .....Tony Purler
138.75 .....Shawn Charles
152 .........Lincoln McIlravy
167.5 ......Steve Marianetti
187.25 .....Les Gutches*
213.75 .....Melvin Douglas
286 .........Tolly Thompson
Team........Sunkist Kids (Div. I)
　　　　　　N.Y. Athletic Club (Div. II)

#### GRECO-ROMAN
119 .........Shawn Sheldon
127.75 .....Dennis Hall
138.75 .....Shon Lewis
152 .........Chris Saba
167.5 ......Matt Lindland
187.25 .....Dan Niebuhr*
213.75 .....Jason Klohs
286 .........Matt Ghaffari
Team........Armed Forces (Div. I)
　　　　　　Sunkist Kids (Div. II)

### 1999
#### FREESTYLE
119 .........Lou Rosselli
127.75 .....Terry Brands
138.75 .....Cary Kolat
152 .........Lincoln McIlravy
167.5 ......Joe Williams
187.25 .....Les Gutches
213.75 .....Dominic Black
286 .........Stephen Neal*
Team........Sunkist Kids (Div. I)
　　　　　　N.Y. Athletic Club (Div. II)

#### GRECO-ROMAN
119 .........Steven Mays
127.75 .....Dennis Hall
138.75 .....Glen Nieradka
152 .........David Zuniga
167.5 ......Matt Lindland
187.25 .....Quincey Clark
213.75 .....Randy Couture
286 .........Dremiel Byers*
Team........Minnesota Storm (Div. I)
　　　　　　Sunkist Kids (Div. II)

### 2000
#### FREESTYLE
119 .........Sammie Henson
127.75 .....Keyy Boumans
138.75 .....Cary Kolat
152 .........Lincoln McIlravy
167.5 ......Brandon Slay*
187.25 .....Les Gutches
213.75 .....Melvin Douglas
286 .........Kerry McCoy
Team........Sunkist Kids (Div. I)
　　　　　　N.Y. Athletic Club (Div. II)

### 2000 *(Cont.)*
#### GRECO-ROMAN
119 .........Brandon Paulson
127.75 .....Dennis Hall
138.75 .....Kevin Bracken
152 .........Heath Sims
167.5 ......Matt Lindland
187.25 .....Quincey Clark*
213.75 .....Jason Gleasman
286 .........Rulon Gardner
Team........Armed Forces (Div. I)
　　　　　　Sunkist Kids (Div. II)

### 2001
#### FREESTYLE
119 .........Eric Akin
127.75 .....Eric Guerrero
138.75 .....Bill Zadick
152 .........Ramico Blackmon
167.5 ......Joe Williams
187.25 .....Cael Sanderson*
213.75 .....Dominic Black
286 .........Kerry McCoy
Team........Sunkist Kids (Div. I)
　　　　　　New York A.C. (Div. II)

#### GRECO-ROMAN
119 .........Jeff Cervone
127.75 .....Dennis Hall
138.75 .....Kevin Bracken
152 .........Marcel Cooper
167.5 ......Keith Sieracki
187.25 .....Matt Lindland*
213.75 .....Garrett Lowney
286 .........Rulon Gardner
Team........U.S. Army (Div. I)
　　　　　　Sunkist Kids (Div. II)

### 2002
#### FREESTYLE
121 .........Teague Moore
132 .........Eric Guerrero
145.5 ......Bill Zadick
163 .........Joe Williams*
185 .........Cael Sanderson
211.5 ......Tim Hartung
264.5 ......Kerry McCoy
Team........Sunkist Kids (Div. I)
　　　　　　New York A.C. (Div. II)

#### GRECO-ROMAN
121 .........Brandon Paulson
132 .........Glenn Nieradka*
145.5 ......Kevin Bracken
163 .........Keith Sieracki
185 .........Ethan Bosch
211.75 .....Garrett Lowney
264.5 ......Dremiel Byers
Team........U.S. Army (Div. I)
　　　　　　New York A.C. (Div. II)

*Outstanding wrestler.

## United States National Champions

### 2003
#### FREESTYLE
121 .........Stephen Abas
132 .........Eric Guerrero*
145.5 ......Chris Bono
163 .........Joe Williams
185 .........Cael Sanderson
211.5 ......Daniel Cormier
264.5 ......Kerry McCoy
Team........Sunkist Kids (Div. I)
........Gator WC (Div. II)

#### GRECO-ROMAN
121 .........Brandon Paulson
132 .........James Gruenwald*
145.5 ......Kevin Bracken
163 .........Keith Sieracki
185 .........Brad Vering
211.5 ......Garrett Lowney
264.5 ......Dremiel Byers
Team........U.S. Army (Div. I)
........Air Force (Div. II)

### 2004
#### FREESTYLE
121 .........Stephen Abbas
132 .........Eric Guerrero
145.5 ......Jamill Kelly
163 .........Joe Williams
185 .........Lee Fullhart*
211.5 ......Daniel Cormier
264.5 ......Kerry McCoy
Team........Sunkist Kids (Div. I)
........Gator WC (Div. II)

#### GRECO-ROMAN
121 .........Brandon Paulson
132 .........James Gruenwald
145.5 ......Faruk Sahin
163 .........Darryl Christian
185 .........Brad Vering
211.5 ......Justin Ruiz
264.5 ......Dremiel Byers*
Team........New York A.C. (Div. I)
........Air Force (Div. II)

### 2005
#### FREESTYLE
121 .........Sam Henson
132 .........Michael Lightner*
145.5 ......Chris Bono
163 .........Joe Williams
185 .........Mo Lawal
211.5 ......Daniel Cormier
264.5 ......Tolly Thompson
Team........Sunkist Kids (Div. I)
........Gator WC (Div. II)

#### GRECO-ROMAN
121 .........Sam Hazewinkel
132 .........Joseph Warren
145.5 ......Harry Lester
163 .........Darryl Christian
185 .........Brad Vering
211.5 ......Justin Ruiz
264.5 ......Dremiel Byers*
Team........New York A.C. (Div.I)
........Air Force (Div. II)

### 2006
#### FREESTYLE
121 .........Henry Cejudo
132 .........Zach Roberson
145.5 ......Chris Bono
163 .........Donny Pritzlaff*
185 .........Mo Lawal
211.5 ......Daniel Cormier
264.5 ......Tolly Thompson
Team........Sunkist Kids (Div. I)
........Gator WC (Div. II)

#### GRECO-ROMAN
121 .........Lindsey Durlacher
132 .........Joseph Warren
145.5 ......Marcel Cooper
163 .........T.C. Dantzler
185 .........Jacob Clark*
211.5 ......Justin Ruiz
264.5 ......Dremiel Byers
Team........U.S. Army (Div. I)
........New York A.C. (Div. II)

### 2007
#### FREESTYLE
121 .........Henry Cejudo
132 .........Nate Gallick*
145.5 ......Chris Bono
163 .........Joe Heskett
185 .........Joe Williams
211.5 ......Daniel Cormier
264.5 ......Tommy Rowlands
Team........Sunkist Kids (Div. I)
........Gator WC (Div. II)

#### GRECO-ROMAN
121 .........Sam Hazewinkel*
132 .........Joseph Warren
145.5 ......Glenn Garrison
163 .........T.C. Dantzler
185 .........Brad Vering
211.5 ......Justin Ruiz
264.5 ......Russ Davie
Team........U.S. Army (Div. I)
........New York A.C. (Div. II)

### 2008
#### FREESTYLE
121 .........Matt Azevedo*
132 .........Shawn Bunch
145.5 ......Doug Schwab
163 .........Ben Askren
185 .........Mo Lawal
211.5 ......Daniel Cormier
264.5 ......Tommy Rowlands
Team........Sunkist Kids (Div. I)
........New York A.C. (Div. II)

#### GRECO-ROMAN
121 .........Spencer Mango*
132 .........Jim Gruenwald
145.5 ......Mark Rial
163 .........T.C. Dantzler
185 .........Brad Ahearn
211.5 ......Justin Ruiz
264.5 ......Dremiel Byers
Team........U.S. Army (Div. I)
........New York A.C. (Div. II)

### 2009
#### FREESTYLE
121 .........Nick Simmons
132 .........Mike Zadick
145.5 ......Trent Paulson
163 .........Travis Paulson
185 .........Jake Herbert*
211.5 ......Jake Varner
264.5 ......Steve Mocco
Team........Sunkist Kids (Div. I)
........Gator WC (Div. II)

#### GRECO-ROMAN
121 .........Jermaine Hodge
132 .........Joe Betterman
145.5 ......Faruk Sahin
163 .........Harry Lester*
185 .........T.C. Dantzler
211.5 ......Brad Ahearn
264.5 ......Dremiel Byers
Team........U.S. Army (Div. I)
........Sunkist Kids (Div. II)

### 2010
#### FREESTYLE
121 .........Obe Blanc
132 .........Shawn Bunch
145.5 ......Jared Frayer
163 .........Andrew Howe*
185 .........Jake Herbert
211.5 ......J.D. Bergman
264.5 ......Les Sigman
Team........New York AC (Div. I)
........Gator WC (Div. II)

#### GRECO-ROMAN
121 .........Spenser Mango
132 .........Nathan Piasecki
145.5 ......Glenn Garrison
163 .........Jake Fisher
185 .........Cheney Haight*
211.5 ......Justin Ruiz
264.5 ......Brandon Rupp
Team........U.S. Army (Div. I)
........Sunkist Kids (Div. II)

### 2011
#### FREESTYLE
121 .........Sam Hazewinkel
132 .........Reece Humphrey
145.5 ......Teyon Ware*
163 .........Jordan Burroughs
185 .........Jake Herbert
211.5 ......Jake Varner
264.5 ......Tervel Dlagnev
Team........New York AC

#### GRECO-ROMAN
121 .........Spenser Mango*
132 .........Joe Betterman
145.5 ......Justin Lester
163 .........Ben Provisor
185 .........Jordan Holm
211.5 ......Justin Ruiz
264.5 ......Dremiel Byers
Team........U.S. Army (Div. I)
........Sunkist Kids (Div. II)

*Outstanding wrestler.

# Awards

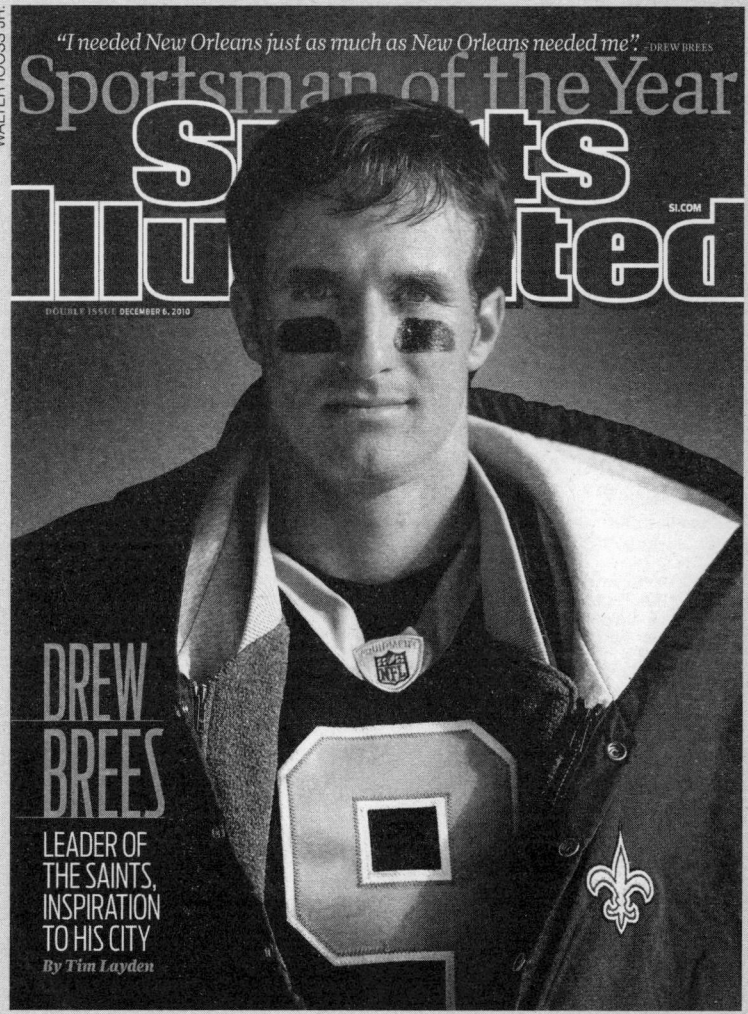

"I needed New Orleans just as much as New Orleans needed me." -DREW BREES

Sportsman of the Year

Sports Illustrated

SI.COM

DOUBLE ISSUE DECEMBER 6, 2010

DREW
BREES

LEADER OF
THE SAINTS,
INSPIRATION
TO HIS CITY
By Tim Layden

**SPORTS ILLUSTRATED'S
2010 Sportsman of the Year
Drew Brees**

## Athlete Awards

### *Sports Illustrated* Sportsman of the Year

| | | |
|---|---|---|
| 1954..........Roger Bannister, Track and Field | 1979..............Terry Bradshaw, Pro Football | 1994 ..............Bonnie Blair, Speed Skating |
| 1955....................Johnny Podres, Baseball | Willie Stargell, Baseball | Johann Olav Koss, Speed Skating |
| 1956..........Bobby Morrow, Track and Field | 1980 ................U.S. Olympic Hockey Team | 1995....................Cal Ripken Jr, Baseball |
| 1957....................Stan Musial, Baseball | 1981..........Sugar Ray Leonard, Boxing | 1996..........................Tiger Woods, Golf |
| 1958..........Rafer Johnson, Track and Field | 1982......................Wayne Gretzky, Hockey | 1997..........Dean Smith, College Basketball |
| 1959............Ingemar Johansson, Boxing | 1983..........Mary Decker, Track and Field | 1998..............Mark McGwire, Sammy Sosa, |
| 1960..........................Arnold Palmer, Golf | 1984 ......Mary Lou Retton, Gymnastics | Baseball |
| 1961......................Jerry Lucas, Basketball | Edwin Moses, Track and Field | 1999..........U.S. Women's Soccer Team |
| 1962......................Terry Baker, Football | 1985 ......Kareem Abdul-Jabbar, Pro Basketball | 2000..........................Tiger Woods, Golf |
| 1963............Pete Rozelle, Pro Football | 1986......................Joe Paterno, Football | 2001....C. Schilling/ R. Johnson, Baseball |
| 1964 ..............................Ken Venturi, Golf | 1987 ............................Athletes Who Care: | 2002..............Lance Armstrong, Cycling |
| 1965....................Sandy Koufax, Baseball | Bob Bourne, Hockey | 2003....Tim Duncan/David Robinson, |
| 1966..........Jim Ryun, Track and Field | Kip Keino, Track and Field | Basketball |
| 1967............Carl Yastrzemski, Baseball | Judi Brown King, Track and Field | 2004..............Boston Red Sox, Baseball |
| 1968..........Bill Russell, Pro Basketball | Dale Murphy, Baseball | 2005................Tom Brady, Pro Football |
| 1969....................Tom Seaver, Baseball | Chip Rives, Football | 2006....Dwyane Wade, Pro Basketball |
| 1970................................Bobby Orr, Hockey | Patty Sheehan, Golf | 2007..............Brett Favre, Pro Football |
| 1971..............................Lee Trevino, Golf | Rory Sparrow, Pro Basketball | 2008..........Michael Phelps, Swimming |
| 1972....B.J. King, Tennis/ J. Wooden, Bask | Reggie Williams, Pro Football | 2009..........................Derek Jeter, Baseball |
| 1973..........Jackie Stewart, Auto Racing | 1988......................Orel Hershiser, Baseball | 2010..................Drew Brees, Pro Football |
| 1974..........Muhammad Ali, Boxing | 1989....................Greg LeMond, Cycling | |
| 1975..............................Pete Rose, Baseball | 1990................Joe Montana, Pro Football | |
| 1976..............................Chris Evert, Tennis | 1991 ..........Michael Jordan, Pro Basketball | |
| 1977........Steve Cauthen, Horse Racing | 1992..............................Arthur Ashe, Tennis | |
| 1978..............................Jack Nicklaus, Golf | 1993....................Don Shula, Pro Football | |

### Associated Press Athletes of the Year

| MEN | WOMEN | MEN | WOMEN |
|---|---|---|---|
| 1931..........Pepper Martin, Baseball | .....Helene Madison, Swimming | 1955......Hopalong Cassidy, Football | ......................Patty Berg, Golf |
| 1932..................Gene Sarazen, Golf | ..................Babe Didrikson, Track and Field | 1956..........Mickey Mantle, Baseball | ..........Pat McCormick, Diving |
| 1933..............Carl Hubbell, Baseball | ..............Helen Jacobs, Tennis | 1957..........Ted Williams, Baseball | ..............Althea Gibson, Tennis |
| 1934..............Dizzy Dean, Baseball | ........Virginia Van Wie, Golf | 1958......Herb Elliott, Track and Field | ..............Althea Gibson, Tennis |
| 1935..............Joe Louis, Boxing | ........Helen Wills Moody, Tennis | 1959......Ingemar Johansson, Boxing | ................Maria Bueno, Tennis |
| 1936 .Jesse Owens, Track and Field | ..................Helen Stephens, Track and Field | 1960......................Rafer Johnson, Track and Field | ....................Wilma Rudolph, Track and Field |
| 1937....................Don Budge, Tennis | ....................Katherine Rawls, Swimming | 1961..................Roger Maris, Baseball | ....................Wilma Rudolph, Track and Field |
| 1938....................Don Budge, Tennis | ....................Patty Berg, Golf | 1962............Maury Wills, Baseball | ..........Dawn Fraser, Swimming |
| 1939..........Nile Kinnick, Football | ................Alice Marble, Tennis | 1963..........Sandy Koufax, Baseball | ................Mickey Wright, Golf |
| 1940..............Tom Harmon, Football | ................Alice Marble, Tennis | 1964 ....Don Schollander, Swimming | ..................Mickey Wright, Golf |
| 1941..........Joe DiMaggio, Baseball | ........Betty Hicks Newell, Golf | 1965..........Sandy Koufax, Baseball | ..............Kathy Whitworth, Golf |
| 1942..........Frank Sinkwich, Football | ..........Gloria Callen, Swimming | 1966..........Frank Robinson, Baseball | ..............Kathy Whitworth, Golf |
| 1943......................Gunder Haegg, Track and Field | ....................Patty Berg, Golf | 1967..........Carl Yastrzemski, Baseball | ..........Billie Jean King, Tennis |
| 1944..................Byron Nelson, Golf | ..............Ann Curtis, Swimming | 1968..........Denny McLain, Baseball | ..........Peggy Fleming, Skating |
| 1945..................Bryon Nelson, Golf | ........Babe Didrikson Zaharias, Golf | 1969..................Tom Seaver, Baseball | ........Debbie Meyer, Swimming |
| 1946 ..............Glenn Davis, Football | ........Babe Didrikson Zaharias, Golf | 1970 ....George Blanda, Pro Football | ....Chi Cheng, Track and Field |
| 1947..........Johnny Lujack, Football | ........Babe Didrikson Zaharias, Golf | 1971......................Lee Trevino, Golf | ......Evonne Goolagong, Tennis |
| 1948..........Lou Boudreau, Baseball | ............Fanny Blankers-Koen, Track and Field | 1972..........Mark Spitz, Swimming | ......Olga Korbut, Gymnastics |
| 1949..................Leon Hart, Football | ..............Marlene Bauer, Golf | 1973....O.J. Simpson, Pro Football | ..........Billie Jean King, Tennis |
| 1950..................Jim Konstanty, Baseball | ........Babe Didrikson Zaharias, Golf | 1974..................Muhammad Ali, Boxing | ..................Chris Evert, Tennis |
| 1951..........Dick Kazmaier, Football | ..........Maureen Connolly, Tennis | 1975..............Fred Lynn, Baseball | ..................Chris Evert, Tennis |
| 1952..Bob Mathias, Track and Field | ........Maureen Connolly, Tennis | 1976....................Bruce Jenner, Track and Field | ..................Nadia Comaneci, Gymnastics |
| 1953..................Ben Hogan, Golf | ........Maureen Connolly, Tennis | 1977....................Steve Cauthen, Horse Racing | ..................Chris Evert, Tennis |
| 1954..................Willie Mays, Baseball | ........Babe Didrikson Zaharias, Golf | 1978..................Ron Guidry, Baseball | ..................Nancy Lopez, Golf |
| | | 1979......Willie Stargell, Baseball | ................Tracy Austin, Tennis |
| | | 1980....U.S. Olympic Hockey Team | ......Chris Evert Lloyd, Tennis |
| | | 1981..............John McEnroe, Tennis | ................Tracy Austin, Tennis |
| | | 1982..........Wayne Gretzky, Hockey | ..........................Mary Decker, Track and Field |
| | | 1983......Carl Lewis, Track and Field | ....Martina Navratilova, Tennis |

## Associated Press Athletes of the Year (Cont.)

| MEN | WOMEN | | MEN | WOMEN |
|---|---|---|---|---|
| 1984......Carl Lewis, Track and Field | Mary Lou Retton, Gymnastics | | 1997 ..................Tiger Woods, Golf | Martina Hingis, Tennis |
| 1985 ........Dwight Gooden, Baseball | Nancy Lopez, Golf | | 1998 ........Mark McGwire, Baseball | Se Ri Pak, Golf |
| 1986......Larry Bird, Pro Basketball | Martina Navratilova, Tennis | | 1999 ..................Tiger Woods, Golf | U.S. Women's Soccer Team |
| 1987 ......................Ben Johnson, Track and Field | Jackie Joyner-Kersee, Track and Field | | 2000 ..................Tiger Woods, Golf | Marion Jones, Track and Field |
| 1988 ..........Orel Hershiser, Baseball | Florence Griffith Joyner, Track and Field | | 2001......Barry Bonds, Baseball | Jennifer Capriati, Tennis |
| 1989......Joe Montana, Pro Football | Steffi Graf, Tennis | | 2002.......Lance Armstrong, Cycling | Serena Williams, Tennis |
| 1990......Joe Montana, Pro Football | Beth Daniel, Golf | | 2003......Lance Armstrong, Cycling | Annika Sorenstam, Golf |
| 1991......................Michael Jordan, Pro Basketball | Monica Seles, Tennis | | 2004.......Lance Armstrong, Cycling | Annika Sorenstam, Golf |
| 1992......................Michael Jordan, Pro Basketball | Monica Seles, Tennis | | 2005.......Lance Armstrong, Cycling | Annika Sorenstam, Golf |
| 1993......................Michael Jordan, Pro Basketball | Sheryl Swoopes, Basketball | | 2006 ..................Tiger Woods, Golf | Lorena Ochoa, Golf |
| 1994........George Foreman, Boxing | Bonnie Blair, Speed Skating | | 2007........Tom Brady, Pro Football | Lorena Ochoa, Golf |
| 1995............Cal Ripken Jr, Baseball | Rebecca Lobo, Basketball | | 2008......Michael Phelps, Swimming | Candace Parker, Basketball |
| 1996..................Michael Johnson, Track and Field | Amy Van Dyken, Swimming | | 2009...Jimmie Johnson, Auto Racing | Serena Williams, Tennis |
| | | | 2010........Drew Brees, Pro Football | Lindsey Vonn, Skiing |

## James E. Sullivan Award

Presented annually by the AAU to the athlete who "by his or her performance, example and influence as an amateur, has done the most during the year to advance the cause of sportsmanship."

| | | |
|---|---|---|
| 1930 .............................Bobby Jones, Golf | 1959............Parry O'Brien, Track and Field | 1988 ............Florence Griffith Joyner, Track |
| 1931 ........Barney Berlinger, Track and Field | 1960 ..........Rafer Johnson, Track and Field | 1989.....................Janet Evans, Swimming |
| 1932 ........Jim Bausch, Track and Field | 1961 ..........Wilma Rudolph, Track and Field | 1990.....................John Smith, Wrestling |
| 1933 ....Glenn Cunningham, Track and Field | 1962 ...............Jim Beatty, Track and Field | 1991...........Mike Powell, Track and Field |
| 1934..............Bill Bonthron, Track and Field | 1963 ...............John Pennel, Track and Field | 1992 ...............Bonnie Blair, Speed Skating |
| 1935..............................Lawson Little, Golf | 1964................Don Schollander, Swimming | 1993 ......Charlie Ward, Football, Basketball |
| 1936......Glenn Morris, Track and Field | 1965..........................Bill Bradley, Basketball | 1994..............Dan Jansen, Speed Skating |
| 1937 .........................Don Budge, Tennis | 1966....................Jim Ryun, Track and Field | 1995...........Bruce Baumgartner, Wrestling |
| 1938 ........Don Lash, Track and Field | 1967..........Randy Matson, Track and Field | 1996......Michael Johnson, Track and Field |
| 1939 .............................Joe Burk, Rowing | 1968 ..................Debbie Meyer, Swimming | 1997..................Peyton Manning, Football |
| 1940 ...........Greg Rice, Track and Field | 1969 ..........Bill Toomey, Track and Field | 1998.........Chamique Holdsclaw, Basketball |
| 1941 ....Leslie MacMitchell, Track and Field | 1970.....................John Kinsella, Swimming | 1999........Kelly and Coco Miller, Basketball |
| 1942 ...........Cornelius Warmerdam, Track | 1971......................Mark Spitz, Swimming | 2000..........................Rulon Gardner, Wrestling |
| 1943..............Gilbert Dodds, Track and Field | 1972..............Frank Shorter, Track and Field | 2001............Michelle Kwan, Figure Skating |
| 1944 ......................Ann Curtis, Swimming | 1973.........................Bill Walton, Basketball | 2002............Sarah Hughes, Figure Skating |
| 1945..........................Doc Blanchard, Football | 1974..........Rich Wohlhuter, Track and Field | 2003.................Michael Phelps, Swimming |
| 1946......................Arnold Tucker, Football | 1975 ......................Tim Shaw, Swimming | 2004.......................Paul Hamm, Gymnastics |
| 1947.....................John B. Kelly Jr, Rowing | 1976.............Bruce Jenner, Track and Field | 2005............J. J. Redick, College Basketball |
| 1948 ..............Bob Mathias, Track and Field | 1977......................John Naber, Swimming | 2006 ....Jessica Long, Paralympic Swimmer |
| 1949..........................Dick Button, Skating | 1978 ...............Tracy Caulkins, Swimming | 2007............Tim Tebow, College Football |
| 1950.....................Fred Wilt, Track and Field | 1979 ............Kurt Thomas, Gymnastics | 2008.................Shawn Johnson, Gymnastics |
| 1951 ............Bob Richards, Track and Field | 1980.................Eric Heiden, Speed Skating | 2009...Amy Palmiero-Winters, Ultra Marathon |
| 1952 ....Horace Ashenfelter, Track and Field | 1981.............Carl Lewis, Track and Field | 2010.................Evan Lysacek, Figure Skating |
| 1953 ..............................Sammy Lee, Diving | 1982.........Mary Decker, Track and Field | |
| 1954.................Mal Whitfield, Track and Field | 1983............Edwin Moses, Track and Field | |
| 1955.........Harrison Dillard, Track and Field | 1984.........................Greg Louganis, Diving | |
| 1956 ......................Pat McCormick, Diving | 1985 ..................Joan B.-Samuelson, T & F | |
| 1957..........Bobby Morrow, Track and Field | 1986 .........Jackie Joyner-Kersee, T & F | |
| 1958 ..............Glenn Davis, Track and Field | 1987.............................Jim Abbott, Baseball | |

## *The Sporting News* Sportsman of the Year

| | | |
|---|---|---|
| 1968 ..................Denny McLain, Baseball | 1984 ............Peter Ueberroth, LA Olympics | 2000..............Kurt Warner/Marshall Faulk, Pro Football |
| 1969...........................Tom Seaver, Baseball | 1985.............................Pete Rose, Baseball | 2001 .....................Curt Schilling, Baseball |
| 1970..........John Wooden, Basketball | 1986 .........Larry Bird, Pro Basketball | 2002................Tyrone Willingham, Football |
| 1971 ................................Lee Trevino, Golf | 1987..................................No award | 2003....................Jack McKeon, Baseball |
| 1972..........Charles O. Finley, Baseball | 1988 ............Jackie Joyner-Kersee, T & F | Dick Vermeil, Pro Football |
| 1973.................O.J. Simpson, Pro Football | 1989 ................Joe Montana, Pro Football | 2004 ...................Tom Brady, Pro Football |
| 1974............................Lou Brock, Baseball | 1990.......................Nolan Ryan, Baseball | 2005............Matt Leinart, College Football |
| 1975...................Archie Griffin, Football | 1991 .........Michael Jordan, Pro Basketball | 2006......LaDainian Tomlinson, Pro Football |
| 1976 ............Larry O'Brien, Pro Basketball | 1992...........Mike Krzyzewski, Basketball | 2007 ...................Tom Brady, Pro Football |
| 1977.........Steve Cauthen, Horse Racing | 1993........Pat Gillick/Cito Gaston, Baseball | 2008................Eli Manning, Pro Football* |
| 1978 ........................Ron Guidry, Baseball | 1994.................Emmitt Smith, Pro Football | 2009 .................Mariano Rivera, Baseball* |
| 1979.................Willie Stargell, Baseball | 1995.....................Cal Ripken Jr, Baseball | 2011 .....................Roy Halladay, Baseball* |
| 1980.......................George Brett, Baseball | 1996 ..............................Joe Torre, Baseball | *named Pro Athlete of the Year |
| 1981......................Wayne Gretzky, Hockey | 1997 ................Michael Jordan, Basketball | |
| 1982......................Whitey Herzog, Baseball | 1998 ....................Mark McGwire, Baseball | |
| 1983.......................Bowie Kuhn, Baseball | 1999...............New York Yankees, Baseball | |

## United Press International Male and Female Athlete of the Year

| MEN | WOMEN |
|---|---|
| 1974...............................Muhammad Ali, Boxing | Irena Szewinska, Track and Field |
| 1975...............................Joao Oliveira, Track and Field | Nadia Comaneci, Gymnastics |
| 1976...............................Alberto Juantorena, Track and Field | Nadia Comaneci, Gymnastics |
| 1977...............................Alberto Juantorena, Track and Field | Rosie Ackermann, Track and Field |
| 1978...............................Henry Rono, Track and Field | Tracy Caulkins, Swimming |
| 1979...............................Sebastian Coe, Track and Field | Marita Koch, Track and Field |
| 1980...............................Eric Heiden, Speed Skating | Hanni Wenzel, Alpine Skiing |
| 1981........................Sebastian Coe, Track and Field | Chris Evert Lloyd, Tennis |
| 1982...............................Daley Thompson, Track and Field | Marita Koch, Track and Field |
| 1983...............................Carl Lewis, Track and Field | Jarmila Kratochvilova, Track and Field |
| 1984...............................Carl Lewis, Track and Field | Martina Navratilova, Tennis |
| 1985...............................Steve Cram, Track and Field | Mary Decker Slaney, Track and Field |
| 1986...............................Diego Maradona, Soccer | Heike Drechsler, Track and Field |
| 1987...............................Ben Johnson, Track and Field | Steffi Graf, Tennis |
| 1988...............................Matt Biondi, Swimming | Florence Griffith Joyner, Track and Field |
| 1989...............................Boris Becker, Tennis | Steffi Graf, Tennis |
| 1990...............................Stefan Edberg, Tennis | Merlene Ottey, Track and Field |
| 1991...............................Michael Jordan, Pro Basketball | Monica Seles, Tennis |
| 1992...............................Mario Lemieux, Hockey | Monica Seles, Tennis |
| 1993...............................Michael Jordan, Pro Basketball | Steffi Graf, Tennis |
| 1994...............................Nick Price, Golf | Bonnie Blair, Speed Skating |
| 1995...............................Cal Ripken Jr, Baseball | Steffi Graf, Tennis |

Note: Award not given since 1995.

## Dial Award

Presented by the Dial Corporation to the male and female national high school athlete/scholar of the year.

| BOYS | GIRLS |
|---|---|
| 1979...............................Herschel Walker, Football | No award |
| 1980...............................Bill Fralic, Football | Carol Lewis, Track and Field |
| 1981...............................Kevin Willhite, Football | Cheryl Miller, Basketball |
| 1982...............................Mike Smith, Basketball | Elaine Zayak, Skating |
| 1983...............................Chris Spielman, Football | Melanie Buddemeyer, Swimming |
| 1984...............................Hart Lee Dykes, Football | Nora Lewis, Basketball |
| 1985...............................Jeff George, Football | Gea Johnson, Track and Field |
| 1986...............................Scott Schaffner, Football | Mya Johnson, Track and Field |
| 1987...............................Todd Marinovich, Football | Kristi Overton, Water Skiing |
| 1988...............................Carlton Gray, Football | Courtney Cox, Basketball |
| 1989...............................Robert Smith, Football | Lisa Leslie, Basketball |
| 1990...............................Derrick Brooks, Football | Vicki Goetze, Golf |
| 1991...............................Jeff Buckey, Football, Track and Field | Katie Smith, Basketball, Volleyball, Track |
| 1992...............................Jacque Vaughn, Basketball | Amanda White, Track and Field, Swimming |
| 1993...............................Tiger Woods, Golf | Kristin Folkl, Basketball |
| 1994...............................Taymon Domzalski, Basketball | Shannon Miller, Gymnastics |
| 1995...............................Brent Abernathy, Baseball | Shea Ralph, Basketball |
| 1996...............................Grant Irons, Football | Grace Park, Golf |
| 1997...............................Ronald Curry, Football | Michelle Kwan, Figure Skating |

Note: Award not given since 1997.

# Obituaries

**Al Davis**
**1929–2011**

**Dan Wheldon, 33, racecar driver.** *Two-time Indy 500 champion.*

(AP) Dan Wheldon, who moved to the United States from his native England with hopes of winning the Indianapolis 500 and went on to twice prevail at his sport's most famed race, died after a massive, fiery wreck at the Las Vegas Indy 300.

He called the Indy 500 "the biggest sporting event in the world," and his second and final win there in 2011 came in a most unexpected fashion. Trailing rookie JR Hildebrand with only one turn remaining, Wheldon was resigned to finishing second for the third straight year. Then Hildebrand brushed the wall just seconds away from what seemed like certain victory, giving Wheldon one of the luckiest breaks ever at the Brickyard. He crossed the line in front, making the final lap the only one he led in the entire race.

Wheldon began driving go-karts as a 4-year-old, and racing was a constant in his life as he attended school in England as a child, winning eight British national titles along the way. He moved to the U.S. in 1999, trying to find sponsor money to fund his dream, and by 2002—after stints in some lower-profile open-wheel series—he was on the IndyCar grid for the first time.

In Las Vegas, Nev., from injuries sustained during a race crash, on October 16, 2011.

**Al Davis, 82, football owner.** *Longtime owner of the Oakland Raiders and former American Football League commissioner.*

(AP) Al Davis was one of the most important figures in NFL history. That was most evident during the 1980s when he fought in court—and won—for the right to move his team from Oakland to Los Angeles. Even after he moved them back to the Bay Area in 1995, he went to court, suing for $1.2 billion to establish that he still owned the rights to the L.A. market.

Until the decline of the Raiders into a perennial loser in the first decade of the 21st century he was a winner, the man who as a coach, then owner-general manager-de facto coach, established what he called "the team of the decades" based on another slogan: "commitment to excellence." And the Raiders were excellent, winning three Super Bowls during the 1970s and 1980s and contending almost every other season—an organization filled with castoffs and troublemakers who turned into trouble for opponents.

Davis, elected in 1992 to the Pro Football Hall of Fame, also was a trailblazer. He hired the first black head coach of the modern era—Art Shell in 1988. He hired the first Latino coach, Tom Flores; and the first woman CEO, Amy Trask. And he was infallibly loyal to his players and officials: to be a Raider was to be a Raider for life.

But it was his rebellious spirit, that willingness to buck the establishment, that helped turn the NFL into THE establishment in sports — the most successful sports league in American history. He was the last commissioner of the American Football league and led it on personnel forays that helped force a merger that turned the expanded NFL into the colossus it remains.

In Oakland, Calif., of natural causes, on October 8, 2011.

**Peter Gent, 69, football player.** *Former Dallas Cowboys receiver famous for writing the wry, behind-the-scenes football book "North Dallas Forty."*

(AP) A star basketball player at Michigan State University in the 1960s, Gent didn't play college football but got an NFL tryout with the Dallas Cowboys in 1964 and played five seasons with the team. His 1973 novel "North Dallas Forty" offered a rare look at the inside world of professional football and it dealt with drugs, sex, greed and self-preservation. It was made into a movie six years later, starring Nick Nolte as an aging player and Mac Davis as a quarterback. Gent wrote a sequel, "North Dallas After Forty," as well as other books, including a memoir about coaching his son's baseball team, "The Last Magic Summer: A Season With My Son."

In Bangor, Mich., of complications from pulmonary disease, on September 30, 2011.

**Dorothy Harrell, 87, baseball player.** *Former AAGPBL shortstop.*

A slick-fielding shortstop for the All-American Girls Professional Baseball League, Harrell led the Rockford Peaches to four titles during her career, including three straight between 1947 and 1950. Known by her nickname "Snookie," Harrell was a popular AAGPBL personality who was named an All-Star five times during her career (1947-50; '52). Her 306 career RBIs rank as 13th best in the league's 12-year span. In 1988, the National Baseball Hall of Fame opened a display "Women in Baseball" that features Harrell as well as other notable stars from the AAGPBL.

In Cathedral City Calif., after a brief illness, on September 15, 2011.

**Lokomotiv Yaroslavl, hockey team.** *Russian hockey team killed after team charter crashed.*

A Russian jet carrying the popular Lokomotiv Yaroslavl hockey team crashed into a river bank while taking off in western Russia, killing 43 people and all but one member of the team. Two people survived the crash. The Yak-42 plane was carrying the Lokomotiv team to Minsk where it was to play the opening game of the 2011–12 season of the Kontinental Hockey League.

Lokomotiv Yaroslavl is a leading force in Russian hockey and came third in the KHL in the 2010–11 season. The Russian team featured several top European players and former NHL stars, including Slovakian forward and national team captain Pavol Demitra, who played in the NHL for the St. Louis Blues and Vancouver Canucks. Other top names include forward Josef Vasicek of the Czech Republic, Czech defenseman Karel Rachunek, Russian defensemen Ruslan Salei and Karlis Skrastins, and Swedish goalie Stefan Liv.

In Yaroslavl, Russia,. from plane crash, on September 7, 2011.

**Lee Roy Selmon, 56, football player.** *Hall of Fame defensive end.*

(AP) Lee Roy Selmon and his brother, Dewey, were both chosen as All-America defensive players in 1975 when the Sooners won their second straight championship under Barry Switzer. Selmon followed his Hall of Fame college career, during which he won the 1975 Lombardi Award and Outland Trophy, with an equally impressive run in the NFL. He was the No. 1 pick in the 1976 draft—the first ever selection by the expansion Tampa Bay Buccaneers—but suffered through a winless inaugural season before achieving success. In 1979, he won the NFL Defensive Player of the Year award when he helped Tampa Bay make it to the NFC championship game. Selmon was inducted into the Pro Football Hall of Fame in 1995.

In Tampa, Fla., of complications from a stroke, on September 4, 2011.

**Wade Belak, 35, hockey player.** *Longtime NHL enforcer.*

(AP) Belak, a 6' 5", 233-pound forward, played for Colorado, Calgary, Toronto, Florida and finished his career with Nashville, playing in 549 career NHL games with eight goals, 25 assists and 1,263 penalty minutes. He was scheduled to work as a sideline reporter on Nashville television broadcasts this season.

His was the third death of so-called NHL enforcers since May of this year. Winnipeg's Rick Rypien was found dead at the age of 27 in early August at his home in Alberta. Former Rangers enforcer Derek Boogaard died in May at 28 due to an accidental mix of alcohol and the painkiller oxycodone.

In Toronto, Canada, of suicide by hanging, on August 31, 2011.

**Bubba Smith, 66, football player.** *All-Pro Baltimore Colts defensive end.*

(AP) The top overall pick in the 1967 draft after a sensational career at Michigan State, the 6' 7" Smith spent five seasons with the Baltimore Colts and two seasons each with Oakland and Houston. He won the 1971 Super Bowl with the Colts. One of the best pass rushers in the game, Smith often drew two blockers, yet was effective enough to make two Pro Bowls and one All-Pro team. Smith was enshrined in the College Football Hall of Fame in 1988.

After retiring from football, Smith went on to enjoy a successful career as an actor, where his most memorable role was playing Moses Hightower, the soft-spoken officer in the "Police Academy" series. He also appeared in such television series as "Good Times," "Charlie's Angels," and "Half Nelson," and was a regular in the ground-breaking Miller Lite commercials featuring retired players.

In Baldwin Hills, Calif., of natural causes, on August 3, 2011.

**Hideki Irabu, 42, baseball player.** *Former New York Yankees pitcher.*

(AP) Irabu joined the New York Yankees in 1997 in a swell of international excitement. The quirky, flame-throwing Japanese right-hander seemed destined to become a pioneering star for American baseball's marquee franchise.

Before going to the major leagues, Irabu was one of the most dominant pitchers in Nippon Professional Baseball. He led the Pacific League in wins in 1994 with 15 and ERA in 1995 and 1996 (2.53, 2.40) when he played for the Chiba Lotte Marines. In a country where finesse pitchers are prevalent, Irabu's power stood out. In 1993, he threw a 158 kph (98 mph) fastball, which still stands as the fastest pitch thrown in the Pacific League.

But Irabu never reached those enormous expectations, and his career spiraled. He finished 34–35 with a 5.15 ERA in his tenure with the Yankees, two years in Montreal and a final season in the Texas bullpen in 2002. He was a member of two Yankees teams that won the World Series, but his only postseason action was a single relief appearance in the 1999 AL Championship Series when Boston tagged him for 13 hits.

"He was a world-class pitcher," said former major league manager Bobby Valentine, who managed Irabu in Japan in 1995. "When Nolan Ryan saw him, he said he had never seen anything like it. There were just some days when he was as good a pitcher as I had ever seen. A fabulous arm."

In Rancho Palos Verdes, Calif., of suicide by hanging on July 27, 2011.

**John Mackey, 69, football player.** *Hall of Fame Baltimore Colts tight end.*

(AP) Mackey played for the Baltimore Colts from 1963-71 and, perhaps most famously, helped the team beat the Dallas Cowboys in the 1971 Super Bowl by catching a pass from Johnny Unitas after it deflected off two other players for a 75-yard touchdown. As a rookie out of Syracuse in 1963, he caught 35 passes for 726 yards and was selected to the first of five Pro Bowls. He also was voted first-team All-Pro by the Associated Press in 1966, '67 and '68. He finished his 10-year career with 331 catches for 5,236 yards and 38 touchdowns.

After he retired, Mackey joined Mike Ditka as the first tight ends selected to the Pro Football Hall of Fame. His efforts after his playing days were just as important as his performance on the field. An NFL labor agreement ratified in 2006 includes the "88 Plan," named for Mackey's number, 88. It provides up to $88,000 a year for nursing care or day care for ex-players with dementia or Alzheimer's disease, or $50,000 for home care. Prior to his death, Mackey arranged to donate his brain for research into brain trauma on athletes.

In Baltimore, Md., of complications from dementia, on July 6, 2011.

**Margo Dydek, 37, basketball player and coach.** *Tallest female professional basketball player in the world.*

(AP) Born in Poland, the 7' 2" Dydek was once said to be the tallest active professional female basketball player in the world. She was the No. 1 pick in the 1998 WNBA draft by the Utah Starzz. She also played for San Antonio, Connecticut and Los Angeles. Dydek held the record for most blocks in a WNBA career, with 877 in 323 games, and led the league in blocks nine times, from 1998 to 2003 and again from 2005–07.

In Brisbane, Australia, of a heart attack, on May 27, 2011.

**Randall Poffo, 58, professional wrestler.** *Longtime WWF and WCW wrestler whose ring name was Randy "Macho Man" Savage.*

(AP) Known for his raspy voice, the sunglasses and bandanas he wore in the ring, Poffo was a charismatic wrestler made famous for his "Macho Man" nickname and his "Oooh Yeah!" catchphrase. He was a champion in Vince McMahon's World Wrestling Federation, and later Ted Turner's now-defunct World Championship Wrestling.

Poffo was under contract with the WWF (now WWE) from 1985 to 1993. His outlandish behavior defined the larger-than-life personalities of the era and made him both at times the most popular and most hated wrestler in entertainment. His flying elbow off the top rope was mimicked by basement and backyard wrestlers everywhere. He's most known for his legendary rivalries with Hulk Hogan, Ricky Steamboat and Ric Flair.

Later, Poffo made good use of his deep, raspy voice as a corporate pitchman, for years ordering Slim Jim fans to "Snap into it!"

In Seminole, Fla., of a heart attack, on May 20, 2011.

**Samuel Wanjiru, 24, distance runner.** *2008 Olympic gold medalist in the marathon.*

Wanjiru burst onto the running world at age 18, when he broke the world record for the half marathon. Then, in 2008, he became the first Kenyan to win a gold medal in the marathon when he set a new Olympic record at the 2008 Beijing Summer Games. In 2009, he won both the London and Chicago marathons and defended his Chicago victory a year later.

His death was reportedly the result of a domestic dispute with his wife, who locked him in the bedroom of their apartment after catching him with another woman. Though investigated as a possible suicide, Wanjiru's subsequent fall from the bedroom's second story balcony was explained by his lover as an accident

In Nyahururu, Kenya. of injuries sustained from a fall off a balcony, on May 15, 2011.

**Robert Traylor, 34, basketball player.** *NBA power forward.*

(AP) A McDonald's All America player in high school, Traylor, affectionately nicknamed "Tractor" due to his 6' 8", 300-pound frame, became a standout power forward at the University of Michigan in the late 1990s. But Traylor's ties to Michigan booster Ed Martin later resulted in the school vacating its 1997 NIT title and the NCAA instituting sanctions against the basketball program.

Traylor was drafted by the Dallas Mavericks as the sixth pick overall in 1998 but played for the Milwaukee Bucks his first two seasons. He spent seven years in the NBA and also played for Cleveland, Charlotte and New Orleans. He was playing for the Puerto Rican basketball team Bayamon Cowboys at the time of his death.

In Isla Verde, Puerto Rico, of a heart attack, on May 11, 2011.

**Seve Ballesteros, 54, golfer.** *Five-time major winner.*

(AP) Born in Spain, Ballesteros was a five-time major champion whose incomparable imagination and fiery passion made him one of the most significant figures in modern golf. He was as inspirational in Europe as Arnold Palmer was in America, a handsome figure who feared no shot and often played from where no golfer had ever been.

During his career, Ballesteros won a record 50 times on the European tour, his first victory coming as a 19-year-old in the Dutch Open, his last when he was 38 at the Spanish Open in 1995. He won the Masters at 23, leading by 10 shots at one point in the final round. He was a three-time winner of the British Open, with no moment greater than his 1984 victory at St. Andrews.

"He was a man who got into trouble. Only for Seve, there was no such thing as trouble," Gary Player, his longtime friend, has said.

In a long list of spectacular shots, the most memorable came from a parking lot next to the 16th fairway at Royal Lytham & St. Anne's in the 1979 British Open. Leading by two shots in the final round, he drove his ball into the lot, had a car removed to get his free drop, then fired his second shot to 15 feet and made birdie on his way to his first major.

Despite his five majors and 87 titles around the world, Ballesteros forever will be linked to the Ryder Cup since he was the reason the Ryder Cup was expanded in 1979 to include continental Europe. While others have played in more matches and won more points, no player better represents the spirit and desire of Europe than Ballesteros.He developed an "us against them" attitude that became infectious with what had been an inferior European team.

"His desire to beat the Americans was paramount, and probably the reason they beat us," Tom Watson said. "The Ryder Cup became the focus of world golf, and Seve was right there."

He was inducted into the World Golf Hall of Fame in 1999.

In Pedrena, Spain, from brain cancer, on May 5, 2011.

**Grete Waitz, 57, distance runner.** *World champion marathoner.*

A former schoolteacher from Olso, Norway, Waitz won her first New York City Marathon in 1978, setting a world best in 2 hours, 32 minutes, 30 seconds in her first attempt at running the distance. She went on to win eight more times—more than any other runner, male or female—with her last victory coming in 1988. She also won the 1983 World Championship marathon and the silver medal at the 1984 Los Angeles Summer Olympics.

In Oslo, Norway, of complications from cancer, on April 19, 2011.

**Duke Snider, 84, baseball player.** *Centerfielder on the legendary Brooklyn Dodgers teams of the 1950s.*

(AP) Snider was the Hall of Fame centerfielder for the charmed "Boys of Summer" who helped the Dodgers bring their elusive and only World Series crown to Brooklyn.

"The Duke of Flatbush," as Snider was known, hit .295 with 407 career home runs, played in the World Series six times and won two titles. Snider hit at least 40 home runs in five straight seasons and led the NL in total bases three times. He never won an MVP award, although a voting error may have cost him the prize in 1955, when he hit .309 with 42 homers and a career-high 136 RBIs. He lost to teammate Roy Campanella by a very narrow margin.

But the eight-time All-Star was defined by much more than his stats—he was, after all, part of the love affair between the borough of Brooklyn and "Dem Bums" who lived in the local neighborhoods. Ebbets Field was filled with stars such as Pee Wee Reese, Roy Campanella and Gil Hodges during that 1955 championship season. Snider wore No. 4 in Dodger blue and was often regarded as the third-best center fielder in New York at that time—behind Willie Mays of the Giants and Mickey Mantle of the Yankees—during what many fans considered the city's golden era of baseball.

Born Edwin Donald Snider, he got his nickname at an early age. Noticing his son return home from a game with somewhat of a strut, Snider's dad said, "Here comes the Duke." The name stuck. So did Snider, once he played his first game in the majors in 1947, two days after Jackie Robinson's historic debut.

Snider was elected to the Hall of Fame in 1980 on his 11th try.

In Escondido, Calif., of natural causes, on February 27, 2011.

**Dave Duerson, 50, football player.** *Former All-Pro safety.*

(AP) A native of Muncie, Indiana, and an All-America safety at Notre Dame, Duerson was a third-round draft pick by the Chicago Bears in 1983 and became a key figure on one of the greatest defenses ever assembled. After winning Super Bowl XX with the Bears, Duerson moved on to the New York Giants where he won a second championship in Super Bowl XXV. He was named to four straight Pro Bowls from 1986–89 and set a then NFL single-season record for most sacks by a defensive back with seven.

After Duerson's suicide, researchers studying his brain tissue found that he had suffered from a degenerative disease linked to repetitive head trauma, like concussions.

In Sunny Isles Beach, Fla., of self-inflicted gunshot wound to the chest, on February 17, 2011.

**Jack LaLanne, 96, fitness advocate.** *Workout studio pioneer.*

(AP) LaLanne credited a sudden interest in fitness with transforming his life as a teen, and he worked tirelessly over the next eight decades to transform others' lives, too. His workout show was a television staple from the 1950s to the '70s and he developed exercises that used no special equipment, just a chair and a towel.

When he turned 43 in 1957, he performed more than 1,000 push-ups in 23 minutes on the "You Asked For It" television show. At 60, he swam from Alcatraz Island to Fisherman's Wharf in San Francisco—handcuffed, shackled and towing a boat.

He also founded a chain of fitness studios that bore his name and in recent years touted the value of raw fruit and vegetables as he helped market a machine called Jack LaLanne's Power Juicer. He ate healthy and exercised every day of his life up until the end, joking in 2006 that "I can't afford to die. It would wreck my image."

In Morro Bay, Calif., of respiratory failure due to pneumonia, on January 23, 2011.

**Bob Feller, 92, baseball player.** *Hall of Fame Cleveland Indians pitcher.*

(AP) Blessed with a right arm that earned the Iowa farmboy the nickname "Rapid Robert" and made him one of the greatest pitchers in baseball history, Feller was part of a vaunted Indians' rotation in the 1940s and '50s with fellow Hall of Famers Bob Lemon and Early Wynn. Feller, in fact, was part of the rotation the last time the Indians won the World Series—in 1948.

He finished with 266 wins and 2,581 career strikeouts in 18 seasons, led the American League in strikeouts seven times, pitched three no-hitters—including the only one on opening day—and recorded a jaw-dropping 12 one-hitters.

Fiercely proud and patriotic, Feller's life was much like one of his overpowering fastballs. He seemed unstoppable, whether on the mound or in conversation. Feller, who broke into the majors at the tender age of 17, could always bring the heat. But stirred by Japan's bombing of Pearl Harbor on Dec. 7, 1941, Feller left baseball in the prime of his career to enlist in the Navy the following day—the first major league player to do so. He served as a gun captain on the USS Alabama, earning several battle commendations and medals.

The first pitcher to win 20 games before he turned 21, Feller was enshrined in Cooperstown in 1962, his first year of eligibility. The Indians retired his No. 19 jersey in 1957 and immortalized the greatest player in franchise history with a statue when they opened their downtown stadium in 1994. The sculpture is vintage Feller, captured forever in the middle of his patented windmill windup, rearing back to fire another pitch.

In Cleveland, Ohio, of leukemia, on December 15, 2010.

**Don Meredith, 72, football player.** *Former Dallas Cowboys QB and Monday Night Football analyst.*

(AP) While "Dandy Don," as he was known, never took the Cowboys to the Super Bowl, Meredith was one of the franchise's first stars. He led the Cowboys to three straight division titles and to consecutive NFL Championship games in 1966 and 1967, where they lost both times to eventual champion Green Bay.

Over his nine-year career, Meredith threw for 17,199 yards and 111 touchdowns. He retired unexpectedly before the 1969 season and just two years later joined Keith Jackson and Howard Cosell in the broadcast booth as part of the "Monday Night Football" crew.

He quickly became one of the most popular broadcasters in sports with a homespun humor that played off Cosell in particular. Meredith's signature call was singing the famous Willie Nelson song "Turn Out the Lights" when it appeared a game's outcome had been determined.

In Santa Fe, N.M., of a brain hemorrhage, on December 5, 2010.

**Jim Kelley, 61, sportswriter.** *Longtime SI columnist and Hall of Fame hockey writer for the Buffalo News. SI writes:*

"He was a superb hockey writer. The Professional Hockey Writers Association honored him with the Elmer Ferguson Award in 2004 and if you enter the Great Hall of the Hockey Hall of Fame in Toronto and look to your right, Kelley's name is there among the media honorees. He wrote eloquently and passionately, with fewer misses than the rest of us. He was principled, which is more than a polite word for stubborn in his case, although he could be stubborn, too. He held Commissioner Gary Bettman's feet to the fire more diligently than the rest of us. He never became inured to the inanities of the grand sport that he covered like the rest of us.

"If you find another hockey writer of comparable style and substance in the coming decades, treasure him the way most of us around hockey regarded Kelley's words."

In Buffalo, N.Y., of pancreatic cancer, on November 30, 2010.

**Sparky Anderson, 76, baseball manager.** *Hall of Fame manager of the Cincinnati Reds and Detroit Tigers.*

(AP) George "Sparky" Anderson got his nickname in the minor leagues because of his spirited play. He made it to the majors for only one season, batting .218 for the Phillies in 1959.

Anderson learned to control a temper that nearly scuttled his fledgling career as a manager in the minors, and went on to become one of baseball's best at running a team. The white-haired skipper directed Cincinnati's Big Red Machine to back-to-back World Series championships in 1975 and 1976. After leaving Cincinnati, Anderson won another title with the Detroit Tigers in 1984, making him the first manager to win World Series titles in both leagues and the only manager to lead two franchises in career wins.

His total of 2,194 wins as a manager were the third highest when he retired after the 1995 season, trailing only Connie Mack and John McGraw. Anderson currently ranks sixth all-time, also trailing Tony La Russa, Bobby Cox and Joe Torre.

"I got good players, stayed out of their way, let them win a lot and then just hung around for 26 years," he said during his Hall of Fame acceptance speech in 2000.

In Thousand Oaks, Calif., of complications from dementia, on November 4, 2010.

# 2012 MAJOR EVENTS

## JANUARY

| | |
|---|---|
| NHL Winter Classic | Jan 2 |
| Major College BCS Bowl Games | Jan 2–4 |
| NFL Wild-Card Playoffs | Jan 7–8 |
| BCS Championship Game | Jan 9 |
| NFL Divisional Playoffs | Jan 14–15 |
| Australian Open | Jan 16–29 |
| NFL Conference Championships | Jan 22 |
| NFL Pro Bowl | Jan 29 |

## FEBRUARY

| | |
|---|---|
| Super Bowl XLVI | Feb 5 |
| Millrose Games | Feb 11 |
| *MLB Spring Training begins (voluntary)* | *Feb 12* |
| NBA All-Star Game | Feb 26 |
| Daytona 500 | Feb 26 |
| *MLB Spring Training begins (mandatory)* | *Feb 28* |

## MARCH

| | |
|---|---|
| March Madness Begins | Mar 15 |
| NCAA Women's Hockey Frozen Four | Mar 16 & 18 |
| Major League Soccer season begins | Mar 17 |
| World Figure Skating Championships | Mar 25–Apr 1 |
| Kraft Nabisco Championship (Golf) | Mar 29–Apr 1 |
| NCAA Men's Basketball Final Four Games | Mar 31 |

## APRIL

| | |
|---|---|
| NCAA Women's B-ball Final Four & Champ. Games | Apr 1 & 3 |
| NCAA Men's Basketball Championship Game | Apr 2 |
| Major League Baseball Opening Day | Apr 4 |
| NCAA Men's Hockey Frozen Four & Champ. Games | Apr 5 & 7 |
| The Masters | Apr 5–8 |
| NHL Playoffs begin | Apr 11 |
| NBA Playoffs begin | Apr 20 |
| Boston Marathon | Apr 16 |
| NFL Draft | Apr 26–28 |

## MAY

| | |
|---|---|
| Kentucky Derby | May 5 |
| *WNBA Season Begins* | *May 6* |
| The Players Championship (Golf) | May 10–13 |
| NBA Draft Lottery | May 15 |
| Preakness Stakes | May 19 |
| NASCAR Sprint Cup All-Star Race | May 19 |
| *NHL Stanley Cup Final begins* | *May 24* |
| Indianapolis 500 | May 27 |
| French Open | May 27–June 9 |
| *NBA Finals Begin* | *May 31* |

## JUNE

| | |
|---|---|
| MLB Entry Draft | June 4–6 |
| UEFA Cup (Soccer) | June 8–July 1 |
| Belmont Stakes | June 9 |
| U.S. Men's Open (Golf) | June 14–17 |
| College World Series | June 16–27 |
| NBA Draft | June 21 |
| LPGA Championship | June 21–24 |
| US Olympic Team Trials (Track & Field) | June 22–July 1 |
| NHL Entry Draft | June 24–25 |

*Approximate date.*

## JULY

| | |
|---|---|
| Wimbledon | June 25–July 8 |
| Tour de France | June 30–July 22 |
| U.S. Women's Open (Golf) | July 7–10 |
| MLB All-Star Game | July 10 |
| Men's British Open | July 19–22 |
| Summer Olympics | July 27–Aug 12 |
| Brickyard 400 | July 29 |

## AUGUST

| | |
|---|---|
| NFL Hall of Fame Induction | Aug 4 |
| PGA Championship | Aug 9–12 |
| PGA Championship | Aug 16 |
| Little League World Series | Aug 17–26 |
| U.S. Open (Tennis) | Aug 20–Sept 2 |
| College Football Season Begins | Aug 30 |

## SEPTEMBER

| | |
|---|---|
| NFL Season Begins | Sept 6 |
| *NASCAR Chase for the Cup Begins* | *Sept 9* |
| Women's British Open (Golf) | Sept 13–16 |
| PGA TOUR Championship | Sept 20–23 |
| *WNBA Finals Begin* | *Sept 25* |
| Ryder Cup (Men's Golf) | Sept 27–30 |
| *MLB Divisional Series Begin* | *Sept 29* |

## OCTOBER

| | |
|---|---|
| *NHL Season Begins* | *Oct 4\** |
| *MLB League Championship Series Begin* | *Oct 7\** |
| World Series Begins | Oct 17 |
| *NBA Regular Season Begins* | *Oct 23* |
| Women's World Tour Championships (Tennis) | Oct 23–28 |

## NOVEMBER

| | |
|---|---|
| Breeders' Cup | Nov 2–3 |
| New York Marathon | Nov 4 |
| *NASCAR Chase for the Cup Ends* | *Nov 11* |
| Davis Cup Final (Tennis) | Nov 16–18 |
| MLS Cup | Nov 18 |
| Men's World Tour Finals (Tennis) | Nov 18–25 |

## DECEMBER

| | |
|---|---|
| Major Conf. Championships (Coll. Football) | Dec 1 |
| Heisman Trophy Presentation | Dec 15 |
| *College Football Bowl Games Begin* | *Dec 20* |

HORSE RACING

BOXING

NCAA SPORTS

TRACK & FIELD

SWIMMING

MISCELLANEOUS
SPORTS

AWARDS

OBITUARIES &
MAJOR EVENTS